EVIDENCE

ASPEN PUBLISHERS

EVIDENCE

FOURTH EDITION

Christopher B. Mueller

Henry S. Lindsley Professor of Law
University of Colorado
School of Law

Laird C. Kirkpatrick

Louis Harkey Mayo Research Professor of Law
George Washington University
School of Law

Wolters Kluwer
Law & Business

AUSTIN   BOSTON   CHICAGO   NEW YORK   THE NETHERLANDS

Aspen Publishers
Attn: Permissions Department
76 Ninth Avenue, 7th Floor
New York, NY 10011-5201

To contact Customer Care, e-mail customer.care@aspenpublishers.com,
call 1-800-234-1660, fax 1-800-901-9075, or mail correspondence to:

Aspen Publishers
Attn: Order Department
PO Box 990
Frederick, MD 21705

Printed in the United States of America.

1 2 3 4 5 6 7 8 9 0

ISBN 978-0-73557968-2 (CB)

ISBN 978-0-7355-7967-5 (PB)

Library of Congress Cataloging-in-Publication Data

Mueller, Christopher B.
  Evidence / Christopher B. Mueller, Laird C. Kirkpatrick.—4th ed.
    p. cm.
  Includes bibliographical references and index.
  ISBN 978-0-7355-7968-2 (casebound)—ISBN 978-0-7355-7967-5 (pbk.)
  1. Evidence (Law)—United States. I. Kirkpatrick, Laird C. II. Title.

KF8935.M836 2009
347.73'6—dc22   2009003428

About Wolters Kluwer Law & Business

Wolters Kluwer Law & Business is a leading provider of research information and workflow solutions in key specialty areas. The strengths of the individual brands of Aspen Publishers, CCH, Kluwer Law International and Loislaw are aligned within Wolters Kluwer Law & Business to provide comprehensive, in-depth solutions and expert-authored content for the legal, professional and education markets.

CCH was founded in 1913 and has served more than four generations of business professionals and their clients. The CCH products in the Wolters Kluwer Law & Business group are highly regarded electronic and print resources for legal, securities, antitrust and trade regulation, government contracting, banking, pension, payroll, employment and labor, and healthcare reimbursement and compliance professionals.

Aspen Publishers is a leading information provider for attorneys, business professionals and law students. Written by preeminent authorities, Aspen products offer analytical and practical information in a range of specialty practice areas from securities law and intellectual property to mergers and acquisitions and pension/benefits. Aspen's trusted legal education resources provide professors and students with high-quality, up-to-date and effective resources for successful instruction and study in all areas of the law.

Kluwer Law International supplies the global business community with comprehensive English-language international legal information. Legal practitioners, corporate counsel and business executives around the world rely on the Kluwer Law International journals, loose-leafs, books and electronic products for authoritative information in many areas of international legal practice.

Loislaw is a premier provider of digitized legal content to small law firm practitioners of various specializations. Loislaw provides attorneys with the ability to quickly and efficiently find the necessary legal information they need, when and where they need it, by facilitating access to primary law as well as state-specific law, records, forms and treatises.

Wolters Kluwer Law & Business, a unit of Wolters Kluwer, is headquartered in New York and Riverwoods, Illinois. Wolters Kluwer is a leading multinational publisher and information services company.

To Martha, Gretchen, and David
CBM

To Lind, Ryan, and Morgan
LCK

SUMMARY OF CONTENTS

CONTENTS

—— CHAPTER 1 ——
Preliminary Matters

—— *CHAPTER 2* ——

Judicial Notice

Contents

Contents

Contents

_____ CHAPTER 5 _____

Privileges

CHAPTER 6

Witnesses

Contents

—— *Chapter 7* ——

Opinions and Expert Testimony; Scientific Evidence

Contents

—————— CHAPTER 8 ——————

Hearsay

Contents

Contents

Contents

_____ CHAPTER 9 _____

Foundational Evidence, Authentication

Contents

───── *Chapter 10* ─────

The Best Evidence Doctrine

Contents

PREFACE

In the first edition of this book, we said our aim was to provide for students an account that is readable and detailed enough to paint a true picture of evidence law in its most important applications. We have been pleased to discover that the book has proved useful to judges and scholars too, and it has been cited in scholarly articles and judicial opinions across the country, including the Supreme Court. In preparing this fourth edition, our aim is to provide a source that is clear and concise enough for students in their first encounter with evidence law, yet comprehensive enough to be a book that they can carry forward into the profession. We have been rewarded and gratified in learning that this book continues to find many uses, and we hope this fourth edition succeeds in those ways too. This time our major task has involved adding new content where developments warrant, expanding coverage in some areas, and adding references to (and sometimes discussions of) new cases by cutting back where necessary to keep the book compact.

In this fourth edition, appearing as it does six years after the prior edition, the biggest change was produced by the revolution in confrontation jurisprudence that came with the Supreme Court's decisions in *Crawford, Davis,* and *Giles. Crawford* shifted the focus of confrontation jurisprudence, which applies in criminal cases to hearsay offered against defendants, from the reliability of the statement and the availability of the speaker to the character of the statement: Is it "testimonial" (which usually means "given to police investigating crimes" or given in proceedings under oath), or is it something else (which usually means private communications)? *Davis* created an apparent "exception" to the *Crawford* rule, so statements made for the purpose of dealing with an emergency can be admitted after all if they fit some hearsay exception. And the decision in *Giles* decided that the "forfeiture doctrine," as it relates to the right to exclude "testimonial" hearsay, is available only if the defendant engaged in wrongful conduct with the *intent of making the declarant unavailable* to testify. These developments led to a complete rewriting of §§8.78 and 8.83-8.91 in this fourth edition.

Other developments in evidence law are recounted in this work. Especially important are many changes in the Rules themselves. We find new language in four of the 63 Rules. These include FRE 404 (admissibility of character evidence), 408 (admissibility offers of compromise in civil cases), 606 (juror testimony offered to impeach a verdict), and 609 (admissibility of prior convictions to impeach). The present edition reflects other changes and developments as well. Thus we have new material on the problems of authenticating emails and web pages (§9.15) and an expanded discussion of the admissibility of forensic lab reports and related materials (§8.51). We have also gone through every page and footnote and have updated citations and made other modifications. This book cites many cases decided in the last two or three years, and many fewer cases decided in the twentieth century.

At this writing, the Rules have been in effect in the federal system for more than 33 years. Their influence on state law is manifest, as 42 states have codes based on them (the list is set out in §1.2, footnote 2). Moreover, state variations and experimentation with versions of the Rules are paying off in yielding new approaches to persistent problems (one of the benefits of federalism). Hence it makes good sense for books about American evidence law to follow the organization of the Rules. That is our approach here. Again in this edition, we include the text of each Rule prior to the discussion that goes with it, and we employ marginal tags on each page ("ears" as they are known among printers), which cite the Rule being discussed.

This book tries both to raise and to answer questions. When we think the answer is clear, we say so. When we think the answer is elusive, troublesome, or unsatisfying, we say that too. In these areas of uncertainty, we provide the best guidance that we can, based on policy and our own assessment of the approach that is most appropriate in light of the suggestion in FRE 102 that the Rules should be construed, *inter alia,* to "secure fairness" and to promote "growth and development" of the law.

There are many places where the Rules provide little or nothing of a prescriptive nature, and places where the Rules don't even provide broad standards. In areas like these—and they include privileges, criminal presumptions, and much of the topic of impeachment of witnesses—the whole focus is on caselaw, on policy, and on the wisdom or folklore of the common law, which survived enactment of the Rules for just such uses.

As before, we have not ignored constitutional values lurking behind evidence issues. Thus we include consideration of the confrontation clause as it relates to hearsay evidence offered against defendants in criminal cases, and also discussions of the *Bruton* problem (using admissions by co-offenders), the *Doyle* problem (using silence by the accused), the doctrines developed in *Havens, Harris,* and *Harvey* (using evidence barred by the fourth, fifth, or sixth amendments to impeach), and the *Giles* doctrine, which affects application of the hearsay forfeiture exception. Also, much of the discussion of criminal presumptions is in fact a discussion of constitutional principles.

As teachers for many years, we know that evidence law is both vivid and engaging, and that it captures the interest of almost everyone. The hearsay doctrine has to do with language and meaning, with courtroom testing and fears over untested evidence from human sources. And when students struggle with the basic concept, and eventually the light goes on, we know they have changed their understanding of the world in a way that will last them a lifetime. The law relating to proving prior bad acts has to do with human character, and with concerns over prejudice to defendants and to victims, and looking at the Rules that govern this material is another eye-opening experience.

Mastering evidence law is a crucial part of the professional education of lawyers. When students learn something about hearsay, relevancy and its limits, impeaching witnesses, and authenticating exhibits, they have taken huge steps toward becoming competent trial lawyers, and have achieved a level of understanding that will help them in many other aspects of their professional lives, whether the problem at hand involves contract negotiation, initiating or resisting government enforcement actions, dealing with workplace injuries and grievances, or drafting wills. In short, understanding evidence law is part of the background knowledge that every lawyer needs.

We hope our commitment and interest in the subject comes across in these pages, and that what we have set out in this book is of use to students, judges, and practitioners alike.

We owe debts of gratitude to our schools for supporting this project. At Colorado, Dean David Getches supported Christopher Mueller's work. At George Washington, Dean Frederick Lawrence supported Laird Kirkpatrick's efforts. Students and former students have also helped. In particular, the authors wish to thank Melissa Aubin and Danielle Rosche, and wish as well to express their appreciation to their evidence students, whose questions and suggestions over the last six year have led us to consider and discuss many of the issues raised in these pages.

Any author quickly learns the importance of administrative assistants. At Colorado we thank Barb Cooper and Cynthia Carter, and at George Washington we thank Kierre Hannon.

This edition owes much as well to the support and efforts of people at Aspen Publishers. We wish to thank Dana Wilson and Anne Sloniker for work on the manuscript, and also our friends Carol McGeehan and Melody Davies for their support on this project.

Finally, every author knows how important is the understanding and support of family. Laird Kirkpatrick dedicates his work on this revision to his wife Lind, to his sons Ryan and Morgan, and to his sister Meredith, with love and appreciation. Christopher Mueller owes much to his wife Martha Whittaker, and to his children Gretchen and David (now very much grown and independent, but still important in the author's life), and to his late mother Henrietta Mueller, to whom he dedicates this edition with his thanks and appreciation for their love, support, and understanding.

Laird C. Kirkpatrick
Washington, DC

Christopher B. Mueller
Boulder, Colorado

April 2009

Christopher Mueller is the Henry S. Lindsley Professor of Procedure and Trial Advocacy at the University of Colorado Law School, where he has been teaching since 1985. Concentrating on Evidence, Civil Procedure, and Complex Civil Litigation, Professor Mueller's area of scholarly research has been Evidence. Professor Mueller has written widely throughout the last 35 years in articles dealing with privileges, hearsay, character evidence, cross-examination, presumptions, and impeachment of jury verdicts. Professor Mueller has given many presentations to state and federal judges and practitioners in Colorado and elsewhere.

Serving on the Colorado Civil Rules Committee and the Colorado Evidence Rules Committee, Professor Mueller is also an elected member of the American Law Institute. He has served on the faculty of the National Judicial College, teaching advanced Evidence courses to judges. Professor Mueller has also taught in the law schools of the University of Wyoming (1972-1981), Emory University (1981-1982), and the University of Illinois (1982-1985). Immediately following law school, he practiced law for Pillsbury, Madison & Sutro in San Francisco from 1969 to 1973.

Laird Kirkpatrick is the Louis Harkey Mayo Research Professor of Law at the George Washington University Law School. Previously the Philip H. Knight Dean and Hershner Professor of Jurisprudence at the University of Oregon Law School, Professor Kirkpatrick is a former trial lawyer and federal prosecutor who has taught Evidence and related courses for more than 25 years.

Professor Kirkpatrick has served as counsel to the head of the Criminal Division, U.S. Department of Justice, and was a member of the United States Sentencing Commission. The former chair of the Evidence Section of the American Association of Law Schools, Professor Kirkpatrick is also an elected member of the American Law Institute, a life fellow of the American Bar Foundation, and a former member of the American Bar Association House of Delegates. He also has served on the Advisory Committee on Evidence and the

Advisory Committee on Criminal Rules for the United States Judicial Conference.

In addition to this book, Professors Mueller and Kirkpatrick have co-authored several authoritative volumes on Evidence, including *Evidence Under the Rules, Sixth Edition,* with Aspen Publishers.

Table of Abbreviations

ACN	Advisory Committees Notes on the Federal Rules of Evidence
Conference Report	House of Representatives Conference Report No. 94-414, 94th Cong. 1st Sess. (1975)
FRCP	Federal Rules of Civil Procedure
FRCrimP	Federal Rules of Criminal Procedure
FRE	Federal Rules of Evidence
House Report	House of Representatives Report No. 93-650, 93d Cong., 1st Sess. (1973)
Senate Report	Senate Report No. 93-1277, 93d Cong., 2d Sess. (1974)
URE	Uniform Rules of Evidence

EVIDENCE

CHAPTER 1

Preliminary Matters

A. INTRODUCTION
B. ADMITTING AND EXCLUDING EVIDENCE
C. PRELIMINARY ISSUES IN EVIDENCE RULINGS
D. LIMITED ADMISSIBILITY
E. RULE OF COMPLETENESS

A. INTRODUCTION

FRE 101

These rules govern proceedings in the courts of the United States and before the United States bankruptcy judges and United States magistrate judges, to the extent and with the exceptions stated in rule 1101.

FRE 102

These rules shall be construed to secure fairness in administration, elimination of unjustifiable expense and delay, and promotion of growth and development of the law of evidence to the end that the truth may be ascertained and proceedings justly determined.

---

§1.1 Purposes of Evidence Law

Evidence law governs the process of proof at trial, in effect taking up where rules governing civil and criminal procedure leave off.

For the most part, evidence law puts in place a set of restraints that courts enforce against lawyers in an attempt to manage the various risks and opportunities that the trial process presents in an adversary setting. There are many reasons for evidence law, but five stand out.

Mistrust of juries

The first is mistrust of juries (a point that seems strange in a country that puts such faith in the jury system), and this point goes far to prove that faith in juries is limited. The hearsay doctrine exists, for example, largely because we think lay jurors cannot properly evaluate statements made outside their presence, and the rules governing character evidence assume that juries place too much weight on such proof or employ it improperly for punitive purposes.

Related substantive policies

A second reason for evidence law is to serve substantive policies relating to matter being litigated. Rules that set and allocate burdens of persuasion are examples. They amount to substantive evidence law, existing in the hope and belief that they affect outcome (recovery or exoneration from liability in civil suits, conviction or acquittal in criminal cases), and these rules are nearly as important as purely substantive principles. For example, the prospect for recovery in negligence is enhanced or inhibited by adjusting substantive law to allow or preclude recovery where plaintiff is partly to blame. Similar results may be achieved by setting and allocating burden of persuasion: Plaintiff has a better chance if he only needs to prove his case by a "preponderance" (lowest known standard of proof) as opposed to "clear and convincing" evidence; his prospects also improve if defendant bears the burden of showing plaintiff's negligence and diminish if plaintiff must prove due care.

Unrelated substantive policies

A third reason is to further substantive policies unrelated to the matter in suit (extrinsic substantive policies). Typically rules in this category seek to affect behavior or quality of life outside the courtroom, and privileges are the prime example. The two spousal privileges (one covering marital confidences, the other covering testimony by one spouse against another) aim to protect marriage, thus protecting marital privacy and removing (or limiting) the specter of pitting spouse against spouse in court.

Accurate factfinding

A fourth reason for the law of evidence is to insure accurate factfinding. Thus the rules on authenticating documents and things ("laying the foundation") and the Best Evidence doctrine (requiring content of a writing to be proved by the writing itself) exist largely to insure accuracy—to force litigants and courts to be careful.

Control scope, duration

The fifth reason for evidence law is pragmatic—to control the scope and duration of trials. Lawsuits must be resolved with reasonable dispatch, and finality is valuable even if the outcome is imperfect. Hence the rules authorize the trial judge to confine and organize the dispute. The judge can control the sequence of proof and manner of examining witnesses (FRE 611) and can exclude evidence because it would take more time than it is worth and might confuse the jury (FRE 403).

This account of reasons for evidence law echoes analyses by classical scholars in the field.[1] Some modern scholars have made different arguments. One has argued that the overarching reason for evidence law is to secure the best available proof.[2] Others have emphasized different functional concerns served by evidence law. From one perspective, what counts most is the process of trial and appearance of fairness, and evidence laws serve those ends more surely than they serve the interests of truth-gathering.[3] From another perspective, what counts is verdicts that are seen as projections of legal norms. Evidence law helps in this way by setting up a system in which verdicts cannot be easily attacked or falsified or read merely as decisions about the evidence itself.[4] Whether these accounts are more accurate than the classical account is open to debate. Whether they provide a normative basis to reform evidence law is similarly open to debate.

Other rationales

§1.2 Rules Supplant Common Law

Making evidence law accessible is the main reason for the code that has become the most influential body of American evidence law—the Federal Rules of Evidence. The Rules set forth the bulk of the law of evidence in 68 short provisions in language easily read and largely free from technicality and cross-referencing. The text of the Rules may be printed in a small book easily carried to court, quickly perused, and readily understandable.

Accessible

It is in part because of their brevity and simplicity that the Federal Rules have become so influential. Their quality and widespread success make them a logical focal point for a book on American evidence law. They apply in federal courts across the land in both criminal and civil cases, and generally they apply regardless whether federal or state law

Rules are influential

§1.1   1. *See* Thayer, Preliminary Treatise on the Law of Evidence (1898); Wigmore, Science of Judicial Proof (1937); McCormick, Tomorrow's Law of Evidence, 24 A.B.A. L.J. 507 (1938).

2. *See* Nance, The Best Evidence Principle, 73 Iowa L. Rev. 227, 229 (1988) (apart from rules like privileges that serve extrinsic policies, evidence law serves "epistemic concerns" more than "concerns about the irrational behavior of weak-minded lay jurors"). *But see* Imwinkelried, The Worst Evidence Principle: The Best Hypothesis as to the Logical Structure of Evidence Law, 46 U. Miami L. Rev. 1069 (1992) (evidence rules seek primarily to detect and prevent deliberate perjury).

3. *See* Leonard, The Use of Character to Prove Conduct: Rationality and Catharsis in the Law of Evidence, 58 U. Colo. L. Rev. 1, 3 (1987) (despite lack of scientific basis, rules of character evidence are "intuitively sound" and help insure that trials serve "cathartic function"). *See also* Walker, Lind & Thibaut, The Relation Between Procedural and Distributive Justice, 65 Va. L. Rev. 1401 (1979) (outcome matters less to litigants than fair process).

4. *See* Nesson, The Evidence of the Event? On Judicial Proof and the Acceptability of Verdicts, 98 Harv. L. Rev. 1357 (1985). *But see* Park, The Hearsay Rule and the Stability of Verdicts: A Response to Professor Nesson, 70 Minn. L. Rev. 1057 (1986).

supplies the rule of decision.[1] Within the first 25 years after the Rules were adopted in the federal system in 1975, more than four-fifths of the states adopted codes that closely track them.[2] Even in states that have not adopted the Rules, appellate opinions cite them and sometimes adopt their underlying principles.

Common law tradition

It was not always this way. Before 1975, evidence law was mostly a creature of common law tradition. To be sure, in most jurisdictions there were statutes addressing such matters as physician-patient privilege, admissibility of business and public records, and some aspects of impeaching witnesses. But comprehensive codes were longer in coming and slower to gain acceptance.

Other codes

Numerous efforts to codify evidence law preceded the Federal Rules, and four of these are noteworthy.[3] First, Dean Wigmore wrote an early code in 1909 when he was a young man. It was a cumbersome and lengthy document that achieved no success in practice, except perhaps in proving that evidence law could be codified.[4] Second, in 1945 the American Law Institute proposed the Model Code of Evidence. Professor Edmund Morgan drafted and later defended it, and he vigorously disagreed with Wigmore on important points. But the Model Code was radical and highly technical. It would have largely discarded the hearsay doctrine, and its cross-referencing and precise terminology put it on a par with the modern Commercial Code in complexity.[5] Third, in 1953 the first (or original) Uniform Rules of Evidence appeared, proposed by the National Commissioners on Uniform State Laws. It drew from the Model Code but was shorter, less technical, simpler in design, and not so radical. In 1974, the Uniform Rules were amended to track the Federal Rules in large measure, but with some variation, and in 1999 the Uniform Rules were extensively revised and updated.[6] In 1965 came the California Evidence Code, a comprehensive statutory scheme put together by a public commission and enacted by the legislature. It proved highly successful and made important modifications in common law tradition.

---

§1.2   1. In diversity cases where federal courts apply state substantive law, the Rules make state evidence law applicable in the limited areas of presumptions, competency of witnesses, and privileges. *See* FRE 302, 501, and 601.

2. As of 2009, 42 states had adopted codes based on the federal model: Alabama, Alaska, Arizona, Arkansas, Colorado, Connecticut, Delaware, Florida, Hawaii, Idaho, Indiana, Iowa, Kentucky, Louisiana, Maine, Maryland, Michigan, Minnesota, Mississippi, Montana, Nebraska, Nevada, New Hampshire, New Jersey, New Mexico, North Carolina, North Dakota, Ohio, Oklahoma, Oregon, Pennsylvania, Rhode Island, South Carolina, South Dakota, Tennessee, Texas, Utah, Vermont, Washington, West Virginia, Wisconsin, and Wyoming.

3. On early reform efforts and New York's modern experience in considering evidence codes, *see* Salken, To Codify or Not to Codify—That Is the Question: A Study of New York's Efforts to Enact an Evidence Code, 58 Brook. L. Rev. 641 (1992).

4. *See* Wigmore, Code of Evidence (1909).

5. *See* Model Code of Evidence (ALI 1945) (adopted in no jurisdiction).

6. *See* original Uniform Rules of Evidence (National Conference of Commissioners on Uniform State Laws 1953), which were the basis of codes adopted in New Jersey, Kansas, Utah, the Canal Zone, and Virgin Islands. The current text of the Uniform Rules (referred to in this book as URE) may be found at *www.nccusl.org.*

The Federal Rules of Evidence are by far the most successful codification. They were proposed by a distinguished Advisory Committee comprised of practitioners, judges, and law professors appointed by the United States Supreme Court. The Committee was chaired by Albert Jenner (a prominent Chicago trial attorney), and the principal task of drafting the rules fell to the late Professor Edward Cleary (then of the University of Illinois). The Committee labored for more than eight years, producing two published drafts that were publicized among bench and bar and a would-be final version that the Supreme Court accepted and transmitted to Congress pursuant to the enabling act.[7]

By accident of history, the Rules arrived at Congress as the Watergate scandal was erupting. Amidst claims of executive privilege by President Nixon stirring impassioned resentment in Congress, the privilege provisions in the Rules attracted immediate attention. Acutely sensitive on the matter of legislative prerogative as against presidential power, members of Congress saw the Rules as an encroachment by the other branch—an infringement of legislative prerogative by the judiciary. Hence the Rules were not destined to pass quietly into law. Instead Congress held hearings[8] and prepared committee reports, scrutinized the Rules, changed them substantially, and finally enacted the changed version in statutory form.[9]

Congressional role

Most significant among congressional changes was the deletion of the privilege rules and the adoption in their place of a single provision (FRE 501) leaving privilege to common law evolution. Also significant was congressional rejection of a proposal to admit prior inconsistent statements by testifying witnesses as "substantive" (and not merely "impeaching") evidence, by defining them as "not hearsay." Congress would not go along with this proposal even though years earlier the Supreme Court had implied that such a provision would pass constitutional muster.[10]

For many years, the United States Judicial Conference had no committee with responsibility for the Rules of Evidence, and occasional changes in the Rules came either from other committees (such as the Criminal Rules Advisory Committee) or from Congress. In 1993, however, the Court appointed an Advisory Committee on Evidence Rules, which undertook the process of review and revision, proposing amendments to many Rules that were in fact adopted (approved by the

7. *See* Proposed Federal Rules of Evidence, Preliminary Draft of March 1969, 46 F.R.D. 161 (1969) (cited in this book as Preliminary Draft); Proposed Federal Rules of Evidence, Revised Draft of March 1971, 51 F.R.D. 315 (1971) (the Revised Draft); Proposed Federal Rules of Evidence, Revised Definitive Draft of 1972, 56 F.R.D. 183 (1972) (the Revised Definitive Draft). *See* 28 U.S.C. §2076 (enabling act as amended after adoption of the Rules to provide for future amendment).

8. *See* Hearings on Proposed Rules of Evidence Before the Special Subcommittee on the Reform of Federal Criminal Laws of the House Committee on the Judiciary, 93d Cong., 1st Sess., ser. 2 (1973) (House Hearings); Hearings on H.R. 5463 Before the Senate Committee on the Judiciary, 93d Cong., 2d Sess. (1974) (Senate Hearings).

9. *See* H.R. No. 93-650, 93d Cong., 1st Sess. (1973) (House Report); Sen. Rep. 93-1277, 93d Cong., 2d Sess. (1974) (Senate Report); H.R. Conf. Rep. No. 94-414, 94th Cong., 1st Sess. (1975) (Conference Report).

10. *See* California v. Green, 399 U.S. 149 (1970) (approving substantive use of prior inconsistent statements where speaker was cross-examinable at trial, and use of prior testimony from preliminary hearing where speaker could be cross-examined).

Judicial Conference and the Court, submitted to Congress, and allowed to take effect), and of course these changes are reflected in the present work. In 2007, the Judicial Conference (on the recommendation of the Committee) approved and forwarded to Congress new Rule 502 on waiver of the attorney-client privilege, and this provision was enacted in statutory form in 2008 (unlike other evidence rules, privilege rules become law only upon congressional approval).[11]

B. ADMITTING AND EXCLUDING EVIDENCE

FRE 103 (as amended December 1, 2000)

(a) **Effect of erroneous ruling.** Error may not be predicated upon a ruling which admits or excludes evidence unless a substantial right of the party is affected, and

(1) **Objection.** In case the ruling is one admitting evidence, a timely objection or motion to strike appears of record stating the specific ground of objection, if the specific ground was not apparent from the context; or

(2) **Offer of proof.** In case the ruling is one excluding evidence, the substance of the evidence was made known to the court by offer or was apparent from the context within which questions were asked.

Once the court makes a definitive ruling on the record admitting or excluding evidence, either at or before trial, a party need not renew an objection or offer of proof to preserve a claim of error for appeal.

(b) **Record of offer and ruling.** The court may add any other or further statement which shows the character of the evidence, the form in which it was offered, the objection made, and the ruling thereon. It may direct the making of an offer in question and answer form.

(c) **Hearing of jury.** In jury cases, proceedings shall be conducted, to the extent practicable, so as to prevent inadmissible evidence from being suggested to the jury by any means, such as making statements or offers of proof or asking questions in the hearing of the jury.

(d) **Plain error.** Nothing in this rule precludes taking notice of plain errors affecting substantial rights although they were not brought to the attention of the court.

---

11. Perhaps the most important changes adopted to date are 1997 adoption of the hearsay forfeiture exception in FRE 804(b)(5), which is discussed in §8.78, *infra*, and the 2000 revision to FRE 702 on the admissibility of expert scientific testimony, which is discussed in §7.17, *infra*. The work of the Committee, and other committees of the Judicial Conference, may be tracked online by going to *www.uscourts.gov*.

§1.3   Objections

To preserve arguments that the court erred in admitting evidence at trial, FRE 103 requires a timely objection or motion to strike. There are three reasons: First, objections help the trial court avoid error by reconsidering its ruling and taking corrective measures if necessary. Second, objections give the proponent a chance to avoid problems in proof. Third, requiring parties to object serves the broader interest of providing a fair but not endless chance to litigate, in effect burdening them with the job of being watchful and alert to prevent infractions of the rules.

Reasons for objections

In appropriate cases a motion to strike is also essential in preserving rights to argue error in admitting evidence. A party must make such a motion if the judge admits evidence conditionally and later on it becomes clear that the condition failed. In substance, a motion to strike is a delayed objection. A party must also move to strike if the judge admits evidence and it later appears that the evidence should not have come in, or if the evidence comes in so quickly that there was not time to object in advance.

Motion to strike

Failing to object or move to strike is described as a kind of waiver. Lawyers know instinctively that if they do not comply with this requirement, the result is to put many evidence errors effectively beyond reach of review. But despite failing to object or move to strike, the door is not closed completely on the aggrieved litigant, who may still obtain relief if she can persuade a reviewing court that the mistake was very serious, obvious, and essentially devastating.[1]

Waiver

Absent an appropriate objection or motion to strike, evidence that the trial court admits may be considered (to the extent it is relevant) by the trier of fact and by the trial judge (in deciding the facts in cases tried to a bench or deciding posttrial motions or other questions) and by reviewing courts.[2]

Where one of several parties raises a timely and sufficient objection that the judge overrules, the better rule is that the ground for review is preserved as much for a party who did not object as for one who did.[3] If the ground applies as much to a silent party, who is in that sense aligned with the objector, clearly inaction does not diminish the informative quality of the objection, nor deprive the proponent of the chance to correct any problem in his proof. Hence two of the three purposes for the objection requirement are served despite inaction of the silent party. The other purpose of requiring objections—to provide fair but

Objection by one of several parties

---

§1.3   1. *See* the discussion of plain error in §1.8, *infra*.

2. Dixon v. International Harvester Co., 754 F.2d 573, 580 (5th Cir. 1985) (in ruling on J.N.O.V. motion, court "may not exclude or disregard evidence admitted at trial" on ground that it was admitted in error and must "take the record as presented to the jury"); United States v. Johnson, 577 F.2d 1304, 1312 (5th Cir. 1978) (absent objection, evidence could be considered for whatever value it might have, even if hearsay).

3. U.S. v. Baker, 458 F.3d 513, 518 (6th Cir. 2006) (where court was made aware of objection and basis by codefendant, fact that defendant did not join in objection did not matter); United States v. Hardy, 279 F.3d 856, 860 n.1 (9th Cir. 2002) (codefendant's objection "preserved the issue for both defendants").

not endless procedural opportunities and bring litigation to an end—is more troublesome. On balance, it seems that this aim is not disserved by permitting the nonobjecting party to urge on appeal the ground advanced by her colleague. Inaction cannot be called deliberate or negligent "waiver" of rights since the nonobjecting party might reasonably conclude that joining an objection already made would not significantly affect the ruling. It seems, then, that the nonobjecting party should be allowed to advance on appeal the ground urged in an objection by a coparty.

Prompt; grounds stated

In order to avoid error and let the proponent obviate problems of proof while the trial is in progress, an objection must be promptly made and accompanied by a statement of grounds. An objection is timely if stated when the grounds first become apparent. Usually that means an objection to testimony must be made after the question is put and before it is answered (courts sometimes say counsel may not wait for the answer to see whether it helps or hurts). It follows that usually a motion to strike not preceded by an objection to a prior answer is too late.[4]

Such promptness is not required when the witness jumps the gun and answers before an objection can be raised, gives an unresponsive answer so the question did not forewarn opposing counsel,[5] or gives testimony that seems proper at the time but later becomes objectionable because necessary conditions are not met or counsel later learns crucial facts or points of which he lacked knowledge or notice.[6]

If an objection is to help the court avoid mistakes and help the proponent cure problems in proof, the objecting party must usually state reason or ground for excluding evidence.[7] Sometimes it is even necessary for the objecting lawyer to cite a specific provision, although courts do not require "chapter and verse" in a stand-up objection, and asking lawyers to perform with such precision makes no sense unless the court allows at least a moment to consult the Rules or time to search for pertinent case authority.[8]

4. Hutchinson v. Groskin, 927 F.2d 722, 725 (2d Cir. 1991) (objection should be made after question and before answer, but rule "is not inflexible") (objection just after response was adequate); Terrell v. Poland, 744 F.2d 637, 638-639 (8th Cir. 1984) (motion at close of evidence to strike hearsay from written document was untimely).

5. United States v. Lewis, 651 F.2d 1163, 1166-1167 (6th Cir. 1981) (failing to object did not waive error where defense did not know witness was reading from excludable memorandum; also answer was "unresponsive").

6. Benjamin v. Peter's Farm Condominium Owners Assn., 820 F.2d 640, 642 n.5 (3d Cir. 1987) (motion to strike direct after cross was timely; objection may come when its "applicability is known or could reasonably have been known"); Gerald v. Caterers, Inc., 382 S.W.2d 740, 743 (Mo. App. 1964) (if questions or answers do not show evidence was hearsay, motion to strike promptly made on discovery should be granted).

7. Noonan v. Caledonia Mining Co., 121 U.S. 393 (1887) (objection that is so general that it fails to indicate specific grounds is unavailing on appeal); United States v. Carrillo-Figueroa, 34 F.3d 33, 39-40 (1st Cir. 1994) (objection without stated basis not specific enough).

8. Kowalski v. Gagne, 914 F.2d 299, 306-307 (1st Cir. 1990) (objection was inadequate in failing to cite Dead Man's Statute); American Fidelity & Casualty Co. v. Drexler, 220 F.2d 930, 934 (5th Cir. 1955) (counsel must state ground and sometimes "authority which supports his position").

Thus a so-called general objection is inadequate to preserve claims of error, and this broad term reaches vague complaints like "that's unfair," "she can't do that," "I object to that," and the hackneyed alliterative phrase "incompetent, irrelevant and immaterial."[9] Of course lawyers object for reasons other than preserving claims of error (a general objection can interrupt damaging testimony, disrupt the adversary's rhythm, convey an impression of outrage, and help counsel gather his wits and come up with something better), and sometimes a general objection actually does preserve arguments for review: It has this effect when the reviewing court concludes that there is no ground on which the evidence could be admitted (a notion akin to plain error).[10] Most importantly, a general objection sustained can accomplish exactly what the objecting party desires. If the trial judge excludes evidence under a general objection, even on a mistaken theory, the ruling is usually upheld if excluding the evidence was right for any reason at all.[11]

A statement of ground is not necessary if (in the words of FRE 103) it is "apparent from the context." Ordinarily the ground is apparent if the parties have previously argued the point, as happens if one or the other made a motion in limine leading to exploration of the issues, or a previous question to a witness raised the same or a substantially similar point that the objector obviously means to raise again. And sometimes the ground is apparent from the nature of the questions to which objection is raised or because the underlying principle raised by the objector is elementary and obvious in the context. In these and similar settings, a simple objection without reference to underlying reasons is sufficient.[12]

Litigants need not repeat objections every time testimony similar to that previously challenged is offered.[13] Repetition not only casts the

9. *See* Noonan v. Caledonia Mining Co., 121 U.S. 393 (1887); Bandera v. City of Quincy, 344 F.3d 47, 54–55 (1st Cir. 2003) (if basis is not obvious, must state ground; counsel said "objection," but testimony might have been excluded if explanation had been given); Owen v. Patton, 925 F.2d 1111, 1114 (8th Cir. 1991) ("I'm going to object to that, judge" was too general and insufficient to preserve error).

10. *See* United States v. Klein, 488 F.2d 481, 482 (2d Cir. 1973) (general objection preserves claim of error if evidence cannot properly be admitted for any purpose), *cert. denied*, 419 U.S. 1091.

11. *See* Hamling v. United States, 418 U.S. 87 (1974) (if sustained, a specific objection is sufficient even if it rests on the wrong ground, if a tenable one exists); Los Angeles Trust Deed & Mortgage Exchange v. SEC, 285 F.2d 162, 178 (9th Cir. 1960) (excluding evidence that is clearly inadmissible on any ground, whether urged or not, is not error), *cert. denied*, 366 U.S. 919.

12. United States v. Musacchia, 900 F.2d 493, 496-497 (2d Cir. 1990) (objection to questions asking witnesses on direct about truth-telling promises in plea agreements preserved claim of error; ground was improper bolstering, which was apparent from context); Werner v. Upjohn Co., 628 F.2d 848, 853 (4th Cir. 1980) (drugmaker made pretrial motion to exclude evidence of change in warning label and objected at trial; ground was clear to everyone).

13. Douglas v. Alabama, 380 U.S. 415 (1965); United States v. Peterson, 808 F.2d 969, 973 (2d Cir. 1987) (defendant did not state ground each time he objected to other acts, but objections told court he objected to other acts for any purpose). *But see* Peteet v.

objecting party in a bad light, but distracts and interrupts and wastes time.[14]

Motion in limine   Where a party makes a motion in limine to exclude evidence, courts used to be split on the question whether the movant must restate the objection during trial if the proponent actually offers the evidence. As amended in 2000, FRE 103 provides that an objection need not be raised again if the court has already made "a definitive ruling on the record," either "at or before trial." This seems the preferable approach, since it is usually futile and distracting (hence wasteful of time and effort) to insist on renewing an objection once the court has ruled against it.[15] Prior to this change, decisions requiring renewal of objections stressed that motions in limine presented issues in a somewhat removed or hypothetical setting, that trial courts do not always give such motions serious consideration, and that courts may change their minds at trial, either because things do not go as anticipated or just because the court decides that its earlier ruling was wrong. Decisions favoring the view that an objection need *not* be renewed stressed that often the disposition of such motions materially affects the course of trial, that the parties often brief fully and argue carefully the relevant points, and that trial judges often make definitive rulings in this setting.[16] In the federal system, in states that have adopted similar changes to their rules, and in some other states as well (since no formal rule *expressly* required litigants to renew objections), it is now clear that there is no requirement to renew the objection after a definitive pretrial ruling rejecting the objection.[17] Obviously, however, lawyers acting prudently will renew objections, particularly if there is any room to doubt that prior action by the trial court was "definitive."[18]

Dow Chem. Co., 868 F.2d 1428, 1432 n.4 (5th Cir. 1989) (in toxic tort suit, company argued in motion for summary judgment that doctor's testimony lacked basis but failed to renew objection during trial, waiving claim of error).

14. *See* Ladd, Common Errors in Trial Technique, 22 Iowa L. Rev. 609, 612-614 (1937) *and* Federal Jury Practice and Instructions (2001) §11.3 (lawyers have a duty to object, and rulings on objections do not reflect judge's view of the case); Keen v. Overseas Tankship Corp., 194 F.2d 515, 519 (2d Cir. 1952) ("reiterated insistence" on proposition that judge has considered and decided is disruptive; litigant need not "reassert what has been overruled every time the occasion comes up"), *cert. denied,* 343 U.S. 966.

15. As of spring 2009, fourteen states had adopted the federal change in their Rules (Colorado, Delaware, Florida, Hawaii, Michigan, Minnesota, New Mexico, North Carolina, Pennsylvania, South Dakota, Tennessee, Utah, Vermont, and West Virginia).

16. Among decisions holding that objection need not be renewed after a motion in limine to exclude evidence has been rejected, *see* Wells, 629 N.W.2d 346, (Iowa 2001) (where court ruled on admissibility in definitive manner, defendant was not required to object at trial). Among contrary decisions, *see* Oesby v. State, 788 A.2d 662, 671 n.1 (Md. App. 2002) (after making motion in limine to exclude evidence, defendant failed inexplicably to renew objection at trial, as required in order to preserve the issue).

17. Wipf v. Kowalski, 519 F.3d 380, 385 (7th Cir. 2008) (plaintiff made motion in limine objecting to use of article by nontestifying expert, but court denied motion and admitted the evidence; because court made "a definitive ruling," plaintiff preserved objection regardless whether she renewed it at trial).

18. *See* ADP Marshall, Inc. v. Brown University, 784 A.2d 309 (R.I. 2001) (where judge "specifically told" parties that he would reconsider question of admissibility at trial, it

Some modern authority, following the lead of a 1984 Supreme Court decision that refused to permit defendant to appeal from an adverse ruling on a motion in limine to exclude evidence of prior convictions if he declined to testify at trial, has extended this principle to other cases in which a party unsuccessfully seeks to exclude evidence by means of a motion in limine. The notion is that a party who seeks but fails to obtain such a ruling waives the right to urge error in that ruling if he then declines to pursue the matter at trial, either by testifying or by offering the proof that can be challenged or refuted by the evidence that the party unsuccessfully sought to exclude.[19]

§1.4 Waiving Objections—Invited Error, Opening the Door

Affirmative trial strategies, like introducing or relying on evidence, raising points in argument, or questioning witnesses, bear importantly on evidence issues. In effect, a litigant is limited in the objections he can make by these and similar strategies he pursues, and the result is hardly surprising in an adversary system stressing party responsibility. Thus he may lose the right to exclude evidence by introducing or eliciting, using, or relying on it. And since affirmative strategies bear on what evidence another party can introduce (and what questions she may ask and arguments she may advance), a litigant may lose the right to object to strategies pursued by other parties by way of countermoves.

These consequences come from notions of waiver and are similar to what happens when parties fail to object or make offers of proof, so the subject at hand connects with FRE 103. In describing the consequences of affirmative strategies, courts speak of "invited error" and "opening the door."

Typically "invited error" describes what happens when a party puts a question to a witness and gets a fair and responsive answer: If it injects something that the questioner might otherwise exclude, perhaps reporting hearsay or mentioning unrelated criminal acts, the questioner is usually saddled with the response. Often the situation suggests accident or miscalculation. The questioner was expecting or looking

Invited error

---

was up to defendant "to reassert its objection at the appropriate time," and failing to do so was "fatal"); Doty v. Sewall, 908 F.2d 1053, 1056 (1st Cir. 1990) (if court declines to rule until evidence is offered, objection must be restated at trial).

19. *See* Luce v. United States, 469 U.S. 38 (1984), discussed in §6.35, *infra. And see* U.S. v. Wilson, 307 F.3d 596, 599 (7th Cir. 2002) (defendant made pretrial motion to exclude his "post-arrest selective silence" in mentioning associate but refusing to name him; judge ruled that government could not prove this point in case-in-chief; at trial, defendant proposed to offer part of his statement but still sought to block government from proving that he refused to name associate; court held that if he proved statement about associate, government could prove that defendant did not name him, so defense did not proceed; hence government proof never came in; impossible to decide whether it would have impermissible effect).

for some other kind of response but is stuck with the answer because he "invited" it by the question he asked, and the answer is allowed to stand.

Opening the door

Typically "opening the door" describes what happens when one party introduces evidence and another introduces counterproof to refute or contradict the initial evidence. Usually it really is a matter of strategy—the first party *chooses* to go down a particular avenue in proving her case, and there is nothing accidental about it. Doing so, however, provokes a response that might not have been expected or that proves more threatening or successful than anticipated. If the first party objects to the counterproof, or loses the case and claims error in admitting it, usually the objection or claim of error is rejected because she "opened the door" to the countermoves by the opposing party.

In these door-opening cases, usually the counterproof would be excludable if it were not for the opening gambit. Often the counterproof violates a doctrine relating to character evidence by showing an act by a party, or would be excluded as prejudicial or irrelevant but for the fact that it refutes the initial evidence. And sometimes the initial evidence was excludable too, and it got in simply because no objection was raised. Hence it is sometimes tempting to see the open door doctrine as a kind of tit-for-tat rule: The first party broke a rule, so others can too. But this account smacks of the gaming table, and courts that consider the propriety of admitting counterproof seldom address the question whether the initial evidence was excludable. The real concern of the open door doctrine is that evidence that might affect outcome should not be immune from rebuttal. If counterproof is available, the fact that the initial proof was admitted counts in favor of allowing some reply.

Strategic choices

In practice, the doctrines of invited error and opening the door are even broader than these descriptions suggest. At the heart of each is the notion that a party who broaches a subject in almost any way—by argument, by relying on evidence, by putting questions to witnesses called by others, by calling witnesses and adducing their testimony—is limited by these strategic choices. She can neither object to her own folly nor complain about reasonable countermoves by others. In practice, the two doctrines overlap and converge and even the terms themselves are sometimes used interchangeably.

Affirmative trial strategies also raise questions of relevancy, trial sequence, and scope of cross.[1] And questioning and argument that come as countermoves—responses by one party to another's affirmative strategies—are also viewed in terms of impeachment by contradiction. That mechanism raises many concerns at once, including the purpose and proper scope of rules of exclusion, the impact of party strategy, the balance between probative worth and risk of prejudice (or confusion and waste of time), and what is usually termed the "collateral matter" bar.[2]

Immediate: "Invited error"

One effect of introducing evidence is immediate and obvious. By doing so, a party loses any right to exclude it or claim that admitting

---

§1.4 1. *See* §§6.54 (sequence) and 6.63 (scope of cross), *infra*.
2. On contradiction and the "collateral matter" limit, *see* §§6.43-6.48, *infra*.

12

it was error. In a sense, this immediate consequence is but another way of saying that ours is an adversary system. Letting parties introduce evidence and examine witnesses while relieving them from the consequences of their strategic choices would be wasteful and even worse if continuous litigation proved more attractive to a resourceful party than reaching a final judgment. Hence courts are on solid ground in refusing to let parties complain about evidence they themselves introduce.[3]

The more far-reaching effect of introducing evidence is to pave the way for other parties to introduce evidence, question witnesses, and offer argument on the subject in attempts to rebut or confine the initial evidence. In the customary phrase, the party who offers evidence on a point is said to have "opened the door," meaning that the other side may now make countermoves to answer or rebut the initial evidence, "fighting fire with fire" (to use the phrase coined by McCormick).

Further: "Opening the door"

Suppose a party deliberately introduces evidence that advances his case, undercuts his opponent's, appeals to sympathy, or arouses prejudice. Suppose further that another party offers counterproof tending squarely to contradict or undercut the initial evidence without injecting new elements of sympathy or prejudice or aggravating whatever might be objectionable in the initial evidence. In short, there is a good "fit" between initial proof and rebuttal evidence. In such settings the open door doctrine is useful and routinely invoked, letting parties rebut whatever might be false in the initial evidence, provide perspective, and increase understanding.[4] In offering this chance, the open door doctrine confers significant benefits (Wigmore's term "curative admissibility" seems apt). Admitting evidence under it can cure any error that might be predicated on the initial proof, which means a court can preserve ongoing litigation against the infection of reversible error.

Unfortunately the "fit" between initial proof and later response is not always there. Unfortunately too, the open door doctrine is so vague that it often sheds little real light on what should happen. Suppose, for instance, the rebuttal evidence is covered by some exclusionary principle. Or the initial proof is itself objectionable under such a principle. Or the initial proof is marginal or bland but the counterproof is dramatic or explosive. Or the counterproof does not squarely meet the initial evidence but tends only in some indirect or incomplete way to shed light on the subject. In such settings, admitting rebuttal evidence may diminish or undercut the purposes of exclusionary

---

3. A.A.B. Joint Venture v. United States, 77 Fed. Cl. 702, 704 (Fed. Cl. 2007) (by offering evidence, a party "opens the door" and "waives its right to object," and immediate effect is "loss of the right to exclude the evidence or to claim that admitting the evidence was other than harmless error," and courts are "generally on solid ground" in "refusing to let parties complain about evidence they themselves introduce") (citing authors of this Treatise).

4. State v. Carvalho, 892 A.2d 140, 145 (R.I. 2006) (in trial for assaulting officer, defendant won motion in limine to exclude evidence of intoxication, but then testified that he walked the streets for three hours, so jury was entitled to hear that he "exhibited clear signs of intoxication").

doctrines or inject prejudice or confusion. The question whether to admit turns not only on the strategies of the parties but on the nature of the evidence and counterproof, the terms and purposes of relevant exclusionary doctrines, the degree of "fit" between initial proof and counterproof, the importance of the issue at stake, and the balance of probative worth and prejudicial effect.[5] More generally, the effect of an affirmative strategy in justifying countermeasures is a matter of degree and proportion, and concerns of prejudice, distraction, and confusion of issues justify careful limits on countermoves. Context is important, and many decisions have only the most general bearing on other cases. The open door doctrine is supposed to prevent prejudice (not introduce or exacerbate it), and it is often wise to limit or block attempts to offer rebuttal evidence.[6]

Surprise, nonresponsive answers
Putting a question does not always mean a party opens the door to whatever subject the answer touches. Unresponsive answers, or those that are responsive but broader than the question, should not be viewed as the responsibility of the questioner. He should not be viewed as having waived objections to counterstrategies suggested by such answers. Answers of this sort are most likely to crop up during cross-examination or direct questioning of hostile witnesses. In such settings, carelessly applying the open door doctrine would unfairly saddle a party with responsibility for what happens.[7] It is one thing to hold the examiner to the intended and foreseeable consequences of his strategy, quite another to make him responsible for whatever his questions produce.

Sometimes it is appropriate to let a party who elicits a surprise or unresponsive answer introduce rebuttal evidence, although it may be hard to sort things out if such evidence would otherwise be excluded. Obviously a party should not be allowed to get around an exclusionary rule by deliberately (even carelessly) asking questions that produce predictable responses, then claiming that the rule should not apply because rebuttal is appropriate. Suppose, for example, prosecutor questions defendant in a way that invites (or tends to force) a broad claim of innocence, then offers proof of specific instances to contradict

---

5. *See* the discussion in §§6.43-6.48, *infra.*

6. United States v. Sine, 493 F.3d 1021, 1028 (9th Cir. 2007) (defendant made "passing reference" to finding in which judge "wrote up some bad things about me," which was "insufficient to open the door" to government's otherwise impermissible references to finding; defendant "did not introduce an inaccurate portrait" or use finding to "create an appeal to the professional authority of the judge") (error was harmless); United States v. Martinez, 988 F.2d 685, 702 (7th Cir. 1993) (open door doctrine "does not give opponent unbridled license to introduce otherwise inadmissible evidence," which may be admitted only to extent necessary to remove unfair prejudice).

7. United States v. Taylor, 508 F.2d 761, 763-764 (5th Cir. 1975) (in bank robbery trial of *H* and *T*, government agreed not to introduce *H*'s pretrial statement incriminating *T*, but his lawyer brought out part of statement while cross-examining government witness; invited error doctrine did not apply because he "had no way to know" question would disclose statement).

this response. If the instances would not otherwise be provable, rewarding the prosecutor for this strategy invites abuse. A party should not be allowed to bootstrap himself into an advantageous position in this way.[8]

A party who makes and loses a pretrial motion to exclude or suppress evidence faces a serious strategic dilemma. On the one hand, she can object again at trial and hope the court changes its mind and excludes. Its refusal to grant the motion might, after all, reflect only a preference to rule when the issue is most clearly presented at trial, so a timely objection might still succeed. On the other hand, she might "bite the bullet" by going into the subject herself. Doing so gives her the advantage of choosing time and manner and she may be able to minimize damage in this way, and drain out the rhetorical advantage the opposition would otherwise have.

Anticipatory damage control

Obviously, renewing the objection preserves claims of error. The question is whether the other strategy loses those claims. To mix metaphors for a moment, one might ask whether biting the bullet also opens the door. Occasionally courts have said no, at least where the court's ruling on the pretrial motion clearly indicates that the evidence is admissible, on the theory that making the motion demonstrates a determination to keep it out. Therefore the objecting party should be allowed to rely on what the court did and minimize damage without waiving the claim that the evidence should have been excluded.[9]

Arguably, however, the better answer is yes: Trying but failing to exclude evidence does not absolve a party of responsibility for introducing it. After all, the party who bites the bullet in anticipation of damage deprives the opponent of the choice whether to go into the matter, and there is usually no way to know whether the evidence would have been offered at all. The usual rule is that a court has no obligation to rule in advance, nor to stick with whatever pretrial ruling it makes, so the outcome of a pretrial motion does not _necessarily_ determine what will happen at trial. In the _Ohler_ case, which involved a defendant who lost a pretrial motion to exclude prior convictions and who "preemptively" introduced those convictions at trial, the Court held that his strategy foreclosed any claim of error in the original ruling. _Ohler_ points toward the conclusion that the bite-the-bullet plan described here should be viewed as a strategic choice that is to be treated in the same way as door-opening strategies.[10]

8. _See_ Walder v. United States, 347 U.S. 62 (1954) (prosecutor may rebut overbroad claim by defendant on direct that he never sold or possessed drugs; this situation should be "sharply contrasted" with case where government tries "to smuggle it in" on cross by asking whether defendant ever saw drugs).

9. Moorhead v. Mitsubishi Aircraft Intl., Inc., 828 F.2d 278, 287 (5th Cir. 1987); Reyes v. Missouri Pac. R. Co., 589 F.2d 791, 793 n.2 (5th Cir. 1979).

10. _See_ Ohler v. United States, 529 U.S. 753 (2000) (forcing defendant to wait, if he wants to preserve claim of error, until prosecutor raises prior convictions, is _not_ unfair and does _not_ violate defense right to testify). _See generally_ the discussion in §1.6, _infra_.

§1.5 Offers of Proof

In order to preserve for appeal arguments that the trial court erred in excluding evidence, it is necessary under FRE 103 to make an adequate offer of proof unless one of several exceptions applies. Excluding evidence where no offer of proof was made is unlikely to be plain error because the absence of the offer usually produces a record that does not disclose the error.

Reasons to require offers The reasons to require offers of proof are to let the trial judge "reevaluate his decision in light of the actual evidence to be offered" and help the reviewing court decide whether "exclusion affected the substantial rights" of the offering party.[1] Reviewing courts often comment that without an offer of proof they cannot evaluate claims of error, that the mere possibility of error in excluding evidence is not ground for reversal, and that assessing error in such cases is difficult or impossible. Clearly the burden rests with the appellant to show that excluding evidence affected a substantial right (meaning it likely affected the judgment), and this burden cannot easily be carried if no offer of proof was made.[2]

Offer by one of several parties Just as one party should be allowed to seek relief on the basis of an objection to evidence made by another where the objection applies similarly to both, so too it seems that one party should be permitted to argue for relief on the basis of an offer of proof by another if the evidence applies similarly to his case or claim.[3] The purpose of requiring offers of proof, which include providing a chance for the trial judge to reevaluate his decision and permitting the reviewing court to determine whether exclusion affects substantial rights, is adequately served even if the party seeking relief did not join in the proffer.

Substance apparent An offer of proof is not required if the substance of the evidence is apparent from the context. This condition is satisfied if questions, in light of any answers given and the setting and other evidence in the case, make clear not only the general subject of the expected response, but its tenor or substance.[4] In this situation the purposes normally served by the offer of proof have been achieved without one. But open-ended questions, and others to which the witness might

---

§1.5 1. The quoted phrases are from Fortunato v. Ford Motor Co., 464 F.2d 962, 967 (2d Cir. 1972), *cert. denied*, 409 U.S. 1038. *See also* Kasper v. Saint Mary of Nazareth Hosp., 135 F.3d 1170, 1176 (7th Cir. 1998) (give trial judge a fair chance to avoid error); Christinson v. Big Stone County Co-Op, 13 F.3d 1178, 1180-1181 (8th Cir. 1994) (inform court and counsel so they can take action; make record).

2. Palmer v. Hoffman, 318 U.S. 109 (1943) (witness statement was not marked or made part of record, so court could not decide whether it might impeach or was prejudicial; appellant did not carry burden of showing prejudice).

3. *See* Rockwood Ins. Co. v. Clark Equip. Co., 713 F.2d 577, 578-579 (10th Cir. 1983).

4. Beech Aircraft Corp. v. Rainey, 488 U.S. 153 (1988) (in wrongful death suit against maker of Air Force plane, defense cross-examined plaintiff on passages in his letter on cause of accident; on redirect, court erred in preventing counsel from asking about additional passages; nature of testimony was "apparent from the very question" and issue was preserved).

reasonably reply in any of several different ways, do not fit this exception, and here an offer remains necessary.[5]

The offer-of-proof requirement is not so strictly enforced when a party who wants to develop a point is cross-examining a witness. Since cross-examination usually proceeds by leading questions, the substance of the expected testimony is often apparent and the requirement is excused for that reason. There are other reasons to be generous with the litigant in this setting. For one thing, cross often seeks to test, probe, and limit the effect of the direct, and this process is ill-suited to the kind of explaining that an offer of proof typically involves. And while the essence of cross from the lawyer's perspective is to control the witness and ask questions he can answer in only one (anticipated) way, still the cross-examiner cannot always know how the witness will answer and cannot always control him. Hence questioning during cross is legitimately exploratory, and the cross-examiner should have leeway to persist in some blind questioning without being able to say what will develop. Finally, the right to cross-examine is fundamental to a fair trial, and insisting on offers of proof in this setting would pose a serious threat to this ideal.[6] It is clear, however, that the court can require an offer of proof during direct examination of adverse witnesses, and on cross-examination of the opponent's witnesses where counsel apparently has a good idea of the substance of the testimony he seeks to elicit.[7]

To serve its intended purposes, an offer of proof should indicate the nature or content of the evidence and describe its purpose and why it is relevant (at least if there is room for doubt).[8] If the evidence is the only proof on point, the proponent may have to show (argue persuasively) that it is sufficient to prove that point, either alone or with other proof the proponent expects later in the case.[9] Finally, the proponent should show the evidence is competent, at least if there is room for doubt.[10]

Indicate nature, relevance

---

5. United States v. Jadusingh, 12 F.3d 1162, 1166 (1st Cir. 1994) (court sustained objection to question asking government witness whether she had arrest warrants; defense failed to make known the substance of the evidence sought) (no plain error).

6. Alford v. United States, 282 U.S. 687 (1931) (often counsel cannot know what facts will come out on cross, which is "necessarily exploratory," and rule requiring examiner to indicate purpose does not generally apply; cross-examiner must have "reasonable latitude" even if he cannot say what might develop; requiring proffer would deny substantial right and withdraw safeguard essential to fair trial).

7. FRE 103 does not create an exception to the offer-of-proof requirement during cross. *See* United States v. Lopez, 944 F.2d 33, 41 (1st Cir. 1991) (offer on cross).

8. United States v. Thompson, 279 F.3d 1043, 1047-1048 (D.C. Cir. 2002) (must alert court to substance; defense did not indicate expected response from witness or describe evidence or purpose for which it was offered); Porter-Cooper v. Dalkon Shield Claimants Trust, 49 F.3d 1285, 1287 (8th Cir. 1995) (proffer must state substance of testimony, and show it is not cumulative); United States v. Willie, 941 F.2d 1384, 1392-1393 (10th Cir. 1991) (excluding where defense did not indicate purpose of documents).

9. Idaho & Oregon Land Improv. Co. v. Bradbury, 132 U.S. 509 (1889) (proponent offered to show plaintiffs were told *C* lacked authority to change contract terms, not that he actually lacked such authority).

10. Phillips v. Hillcrest Medical Center, 244 F.3d 790, 802 (10th Cir. 2001) (proponent must explain what he expects evidence to show and ground on which it is admissible); United States v. Burnett, 890 F.2d 1233, 1240-1241 (D.C. Cir. 1989) (sustaining objection where witness said he lacked knowledge).

An offer is insufficient if it is too vague or general to enable the court to understand or evaluate it.[11] Thus, for example, offers to prove a statement or conversation without stating its substance and offers couched in conclusory terms are likely to be insufficient.[12]

On appeal, if it is urged that the trial judge erred in refusing an offer of proof, the sufficiency of the offer is judged only in the light of the ground of admissibility and the purpose stated at trial, and not by reference to a ground or purpose advanced for the first time on appeal.[13] If the offer is accepted and the evidence comes in, however, and the objecting party urges that the theory on which the court relied does not support the result, the court may still be sustained if the evidence was admissible on some other theory.[14]

Methods of making offer   For testimony, the most thorough method of making the offer is to put the witness on the stand, ask questions, and put his answers in the record.[15] But this approach is cumbersome and time-consuming, and the court typically lets counsel offer testimony without calling the witness to the stand[16] unless the judge doubts the good faith of the offer.[17] Where a proffer is a physical object of a common sort like a document, the proponent should mark it as an exhibit and lodge it with the clerk to make it part of the record, in addition to making clear to the judge that he is seeking to offer the document or thing in evidence.[18] The proffer should be made on the record, and the judge may augment the offer by making a further statement on the form or character of the evidence, the objection, and ruling.

---

11. United States v. Kelly, 510 F.3d 433, 438-439 (4th Cir. 2007) (defense did not explain that prior conviction, offered to impeach under FRE 609(a)(2), required proof that witness knew she had insufficient funds when she wrote check; defense proffered no evidence and "simply cited the Florida statute" without disclosing text or making "textual" argument he now makes) (claim of error waived); Polys v. Trans-Colorado Airlines, Inc., 941 F.2d 1404, 1409 (10th Cir. 1991) (proffer of expert testimony was inadequate where counsel did not explain "substance or purpose").

12. United States v. West, 898 F.2d 1493, 1498 (11th Cir. 1990); United States v. Winkle, 587 F.2d 705, 710 (5th Cir. 1979).

13. United States v. Powell, 894 F.2d 895, 901 n.5 (7th Cir. 1990); United States v. Cruz, 894 F.2d 41, 43-44 (2d Cir. 1990).

14. U.S. v. Brothers Const. Co. of Ohio, 219 F.3d 300, 310 (4th Cir. 2000); United States v. Cruz, 797 F.2d 90, 97 n.2 (2d Cir. 1986).

15. *See* FRE 103(b) (court "may direct the making of an offer in question and answer form"); United States v. Adams, 271 F.3d 1236, 1241 (10th Cir. 2001) (most desirable, from all standpoints except cost, is proffer that includes examining witness on record, which necessitates excusing jury unless done in pretrial hearing; other side may also cross-examine on matters relating to proffer) (other methods include oral or written statements by counsel and written summaries prepared by witness).

16. United States v. Smith, 940 F.2d 710, 713 (1st Cir. 1991); Fox v. Dannenberg, 906 F.2d 1253, 1255 (8th Cir. 1990).

17. Scotland County v. Hill, 112 U.S. 183 (1884) (can require production of witness if court doubts good faith); United States v. Kartman, 417 F.2d 893, 896 n.7 (9th Cir. 1969) (record suggests offer may not have been well-founded, so proponent may be required to call and question witness).

18. Palmer v. Hoffman, 318 U.S. 109 (1943) (since document was not marked for identification or included in record, court did not know contents and defense did not show prejudice).

Where one party offers an out-of-court statement and another raises a hearsay objection (showing the statement is offered to prove what it asserts), the proponent bears the burden of showing it fits an exception.[19] The proponent should identify the exception so the trial judge can apply it.[20]

Outside jury's hearing

Proffers should be made out of the hearing of the jury whenever doing so may be important to prevent exposing the jury to inadmissible evidence.[21] The importance of shielding the jury in this way varies widely with the situation and nature of the proof.

Holding hearings on proffers outside the jury's hearing has other benefits. It gives the judge a chance to assess the evidence in relatively relaxed circumstances and it helps her to exercise her option to reserve ruling on the evidence until more of the case has unfolded—in other words to require the proponent to put on other proof first. When conducted outside the jury's presence, a hearing on a proffer can be far less formal than a trial. The factfinder is not affected and the court may resolve issues of admissibility without worrying about being bound by the Rules of Evidence.[22] Both sides may call and examine witnesses, if necessary, and it might well be necessary to do so in order to resolve factual issues that arise in applying the Rules: The business records exception, for instance, applies only if the record is routinely kept, and the proponent and the objecting party should be allowed to explore and develop this point if any serious question is raised. But an elaborate proceeding is often unnecessary, and either side might prefer not to make serious contest on the preliminary points, accepting whatever ruling the trial judge makes on the evidence issues and reserving any response and rebuttal for trial.

Repeating offer unnecessary

Where repeating an offer of proof would be a useless gesture because the trial judge has said the evidence would not be admitted, no further offers are necessary,[23] at least so long as the proponent adheres to his position that the evidence should be admitted and does not expressly acquiesce in the court's ruling.[24] An offer is similarly unnecessary as a useless gesture where the trial court excludes in advance a whole class of evidence, or accomplishes the same end by narrowing the issues to be tried.[25]

---

19. *See* §1.12, *infra.*

20. Maddox v. Patterson, 905 F.2d 1178, 1181 nn.2 & 3 (8th Cir. 1990) (plaintiff did not offer medical history as business record or adoptive admission, so these points were not preserved).

21. *See* §1.12, *infra.*

22. *See* FRE 104(a) (court not bound by Rules apart from privileges in deciding preliminary matters); *also* §1.12, *infra.*

23. *See* FRE 103(a), as amended in December, 2001 (after "definitive" ruling excluding evidence, proponent need not "renew" proffer); Heyne v. Caruso, 69 F.3d 1475, 1481-1482 (9th Cir. 1995) (reversible error to exclude other instances despite failure to offer proof; in pretrial ruling, court "excluded all evidence of sexual harassment" not directly related to claim).

24. United States v. Weiss, 930 F.2d 185, 198-199 (2d Cir. 1991); United States v. Rogers, 918 F.2d 207, 211-212 (D.C. Cir. 1990).

25. Garner v. Santoro, 865 F.2d 629, 636 (5th Cir. 1989) (court barred government contractor defense, so defendant needed not make offer of proof on this defense);

Underlying the idea that there are limits in the persistence required of the offering party is the reality that offers of proof may disrupt the trial and lead to friction and tension between counsel and judge, and the notion that a trial judge who rules on an offer should not have to reconsider the question time and again. Litigants also stand to gain because counsel cannot be expected to focus continually on past strategic gambits and should be allowed to readjust thinking and strategies to the realities of an ongoing trial. (These notions and others underlie the "law of the case" doctrine.) It is also noteworthy that renewed offers of proof, if made after a ruling and in the presence of the jury, can be viewed as improper attempts to influence the jury, which is itself potentially a form of misconduct and ground for new trial or reversal.[26] If the trial judge postpones ruling on a question, or otherwise indicates that an offer of proof may later be accepted, the proponent must renew the offer at an appropriate time.[27]

§1.6 Pretrial Rulings (Motions in Limine)

Courts routinely rule in advance on evidence objections when requested by a party in a pretrial "motion in limine" (the Latin phrase means "at the threshold").[1] Generally speaking, this practice is optional for all concerned. Litigants are not required to seek advance rulings, and courts are not required to make such rulings when asked. For the most part, both court and counsel may wait until the issue arises at trial—then counsel must object and the court must rule.

Virtues and difficulties The virtue in pretrial rulings is that the court can settle evidentiary disputes without interrupting an ongoing trial to entertain arguments (even briefs) on complicated points, and without the risk that objecting and deciding evidence questions will themselves convey to the jury the substance of the matter, or subject the parties to risks of adverse jury reaction because of the contentious nature of the arguments. Not incidentally too, lawyerly arguments on evidence matters can focus more effectively on the issues if they are made to a judge alone, with no jury listening in. The difficulty is that this practice asks a court to rule on an evidence point without benefit of the larger factual

---

Greatreaks v. United States, 211 F.2d 674, 676 (9th Cir. 1954) (specific offer not needed where "entire class of evidence" is declared inadmissible in advance; ruling relates forward to other offers of such evidence).

26. Greatreaks v. United States, 211 F.2d 674, 676 (9th Cir. 1954) (after ruling excludes class of evidence, persistence repeating offers may be improper attempts to get effect of evidence to jury).

27. Tennison v. Circus Circus Enterprises, Inc., 244 F.3d 684, 688-689 (9th Cir. 2001) (defense moved in limine to exclude evidence of sexual harassment before 1994, and judge granted motion but said plaintiffs could renew request, outside presence of jury; failure to make later proffer mean plaintiffs cannot challenge exclusion of evidence on appeal).

§1.6 1. Luce v. United States, 469 U.S. 38 (1984) (court has inherent authority to make rulings in limine).

picture that develops during trial—out of context, so to speak. Trial judges are often unreceptive to motions in limine because they seem to ask for "advisory opinions" on matters that do not yet actually have to be decided.

It is because of the power in the latter argument that the practice is usually optional. There are only a few instances in which litigants must raise objections by pretrial motion (and of course in these cases courts are expected to rule).[2] For the most part too, courts need not make definitive pretrial evidentiary rulings, and have broad discretion to do so or not as they may choose.[3] In the common setting of pretrial motions by defendants to limit or block use of prior convictions for impeachment purposes, some cases say the trial judge should address and resolve the issue before trial (and courts often do so), but the bulk of authority stops short of requiring definitive rulings.[4]

Pretrial ruling is optional

When a court grants a pretrial motion to exclude evidence, it can surely refuse at trial to entertain renewed argument on the point, and in this sense the ruling takes on the aspect of the "law of the case." Yet a pretrial ruling is usually considered only tentative, and this fact has important consequences: First and most obviously, usually no appeal can be had, although the government may obtain immediate review from certain kinds of pretrial rulings excluding evidence.[5] Second, the party who lost the motion can put the issue again by offering the evidence at the appropriate time at trial, although renewing the offer is not essential (at least if the trial judge, under FRE 103 as amended in 2000, has made a "definitive" ruling that excludes the evidence). At least as important, the party who lost the motion should not be allowed to expose sensitive points to the jury by renewing the offer, or the purpose of the prior ruling excluding the evidence would be defeated. Third, the party who obtains a pretrial ruling that excludes evidence probably should renew the objection at trial if the other side offers the evidence, although FRE 103 (as amended in 2000) means that the objection need not be renewed if the court has made a "definitive" ruling that the evidence is admissible.[6] Fourth, it seems that the judge may change his ruling during trial.[7] There is no doubt on this point if the testimony or other relevant developments turn out differently from

Pretrial ruling is tentative

---

2. A few objections are waived unless raised before trial. *See* FRCrimP 12(b)(3) (motions to suppress evidence must be made before trial); FRCP 32(d)(3)(B) (errors in "form of the questions or answers" and others that "might be obviated, removed, or cured if promptly presented" are waived unless raised in deposition).

3. United States v. Layton, 767 F.2d 549, 554 (9th Cir. 1985); United States v. Dahlin, 734 F.2d 393, 395-396 (8th Cir. 1984).

4. *See* discussion of FRE 609 in §6.35, *infra.*

5. United States v. Williams, 900 F.2d 823, 825 (5th Cir. 1990) (government appeals from pretrial ruling granting defense motion to exclude prior crimes). *See also* 18 U.S.C. §3731 (addressing government appeals).

6. *See* §1.3, *supra.*

7. *See* Luce v. United States, 469 U.S. 38 (1984) ("even if nothing unexpected happens," court may "alter a previous in limine ruling"); United States v. Nivica, 887 F.2d 1110, 1116 (1st Cir. 1989) (judge "may always alter" rulings on motions in limine as case unfolds).

what was expected at the time of the pretrial ruling, and probably the judge may simply change the ruling because, in the actual context of trial, the issues and merits seem different and the ruling made before seems wrong.

Finally, a party who fails in the attempt to obtain a favorable pretrial ruling that would exclude evidence probably cannot test the ruling after judgment unless the issue was actually put at trial. If a party elects not to call a witness, for example, because the pretrial ruling indicated that certain impeaching attacks would (or might be) allowed, and the result is that the impeachment never goes forward, there is no trial ruling to test on appeal, and it is usually said that no review may be had. In *Luce v. United States,* the Supreme Court resolved this issue in the setting of pretrial rulings permitting impeachment by prior convictions,[8] and it seems probable that the *Luce* doctrine has far wider application.[9]

§1.7 Evidence Errors—Harmless

The harmless error principle holds that on appellate review (and posttrial motions to set aside a verdict or judgment), the critical point is not the mere occurrence of error, but the effect of error on substantial rights.[1] Long ago a distinguished commentator characterized the problem of harmless error as one of "professional psychology,"[2] and this observation seems true in two respects. First, the profession must be aware that its tools (including evidence rules) are not perfect enough to make perfect trials a reasonable goal. Second, the profession must bear in mind that the process of review is imperfect, particularly in jury-tried cases, since a reviewing court has no sure way to assess the actual effect of error on the mind or minds of jurors and their collective judgment.

Kotteakos
guidelines
A good starting point for looking at harmless error is the opinion by Justice Rutledge in *Kotteakos v. United States,* which discussed the matter at length and adopted five guidelines: First, "technicality" should be avoided unless it affects the rights of the parties, meaning the

---

8. Luce v. United States, 469 U.S. 38 (1984).

9. United States v. Sanderson, 966 F.2d 184, 189-190 (6th Cir. 1992) (court said government could not prove prior thefts by defendant, but could raise point on cross if he testified; he could not claim error because he did not take stand).

§1.7 1. *See* FRE 103(a) (error "may not be predicated" on ruling admitting or excluding evidence "unless a substantial right of the party is affected"); 28 U.S.C. §2111 (reviewing court to ignore "errors or defects which do not affect the substantial rights of the parties").

2. Sunderland, The Problem of Appellate Review, 5 Tex. L. Rev. 126, 146-148 (1927). *See also* Kotteakos v. United States, 328 U.S. 750 (1946) (judging error involves "the play of impression and conviction along with intelligence" and "varies with judges and also with circumstance").

outcome of the trial. The message is not to insist on applying rules for their own sake, but to see them as tools that can help achieve a fair and just result. Second, the reviewing court should appraise error by examining the proceedings in their entirety. Mistakes should be viewed in the context of the whole trial. Third (perhaps most important), the problem is not to assess the sufficiency of evidence to support the result reached, but to decide whether error affected outcome.[3] Fourth, precedent is not very helpful, and the judgment of the court should be "tempered but not governed in any rigid sense" by what has been done in similar situations. Fifth, the task of review is not to decide what the outcome should be or speculate on the outcome of a new trial, but to decide whether the error affected the judgment.[4]

In cases where an error might have affected the judgment, the process of describing reasons to reverse or affirm is likely to generate language implying a standard of some sort. Three have some current support: One is a likelihood standard similar to the one usually applied in civil trials. Under it, error generates reversal or correction unless it "probably" did not affect the judgment.[5] Another involves a "high probability" standard proposed by a distinguished jurist under which a judgment is reversed unless the court "believes it highly probable that the error" had no effect. This standard seems to fall midway between the standards of proof applied in civil and criminal trials, and some modern decisions endorse this view.[6] Finally, it has been suggested that an error hurting the defense in criminal cases should lead to reversal of convictions unless it appears beyond a reasonable doubt that it did not affect the judgment, and some modern authority endorses this approach.[7]

Competing standards

Appellants bear the burden of showing that error was committed, in civil and criminal cases alike. Inevitably the task connects closely with

---

3. Kotteakos v. United States, 328 U.S. 750, 764-765 (1946) (if "the conviction is sure that the error did not influence the jury, or had but very slight effect," verdict and judgment should stand, but "if one cannot say, with fair assurance" that the judgment was not substantially swayed by the error, one cannot conclude that substantial rights were not affected; question is not "merely whether there was enough to support the result," but whether the error had substantial influence).

4. Kotteakos v. United States, 328 U.S. 750, 764 (1946) (while question is not how next trial will come out or court's opinion on the merits, "the outcome does count" and the error must be appraised "against the entire setting of the record").

5. *See* United States v. Crosby, 75 F.3d 1343, 1349 (9th Cir. 1996).

6. Traynor, The Riddle of Harmless Error 35 (1970) (anything more lenient "entails too great a risk of affirming a judgment that was influenced by an error" and would fail to deter appellate judges from focusing improperly on correctness of result, and anything more stringent risks returning to the automatic reversal practice, which the harmless error doctrine was designed to avoid). *See* United States v. Madden, 38 F.3d 747, 753 (4th Cir. 1994), *cert. denied,* 519 U.S. 898; United States v. Casoni, 950 F.2d 893, 917-918 (3d Cir. 1991).

7. *See* Saltzburg, The Harm of Harmless Error, 59 Va. L. Rev. 988, 991-997 (1973). *See also* Haddad v. Lockheed California Corp., 720 F.2d 1454, 1458-1459 (9th Cir. 1983) (standard should "reflect the burden of proof" at trial).

arguments that error affected the judgment, and both sides have substantially similar burdens in briefing and arguing this point. While all three standards indicate that uncertainty over effect leads to reversal, appellants can take little comfort. They do and must approach an appeal as if they bear the burden of establishing the effect of error.[8]

Assessing error   Reviewing courts follow certain strategies for assessing errors in admitting or excluding evidence. In two polar circumstances, the question whether error was harmless and the question of sufficiency intersect. An error in admitting an item of evidence is not harmless if all the evidence is sufficient only when that item is counted. An error in excluding an item is not harmless if what is left is insufficient and the item would have made it sufficient.[9] In two other situations, other evidence has great impact in assessing error. Sometimes other evidence strongly favors one side or the other, or is barely adequate. If the evidence favoring the prevailing party seems overwhelming, even a serious mistake usually seems harmless.[10] If evidence favoring the prevailing party seems barely adequate or closely balanced, even a small mistake might have affected outcome and is not harmless.[11]

Cumulative evidence   Appellate courts routinely describe cases as falling into an intermediate and less clearcut category where other evidence seems more closely in balance. Here the presence of other evidence is harder to assess, but reviewing courts routinely conclude that errors were harmless because the proof affected by them was or would have been "cumulative." This idea is helpful if it is understood to mean that other evidence on the issue affected by the error is really quite strong, so it is hard to imagine that proof erroneously admitted or excluded made or could have made a difference in outcome. Here it is often plausible to conclude that an error in admitting evidence was harmless because it was merely "cumulative" of abundant other evidence properly admitted,[12] and that an error in excluding evidence was likewise harmless because it would have been merely cumulative of other evidence admitted on the point.[13]

---

8. *See* Satcher v. Honda Motor Co., 52 F.3d 1311, 1317 (5th Cir. 1995), *cert. denied*, 516 U.S. 1045; K-B Trucking Co. v. Riss Intl. Corp., 763 F.2d 1148, 1155-1156 (10th Cir. 1985).

9. Kotteakos v. United States, 328 U.S. 750 (1946); United States v. Peak, 856 F.2d 825, 834-835 (7th Cir. 1988), *cert. denied*, 488 U.S. 969.

10. *See* Lutwak v. United States, 344 U.S. 604 (1953) (error in admitting hearsay was not prejudicial since record "fairly shrieks the guilt of the parties"); United States v. Robinson, 8 F.3d 398, 411 (7th Cir. 1993) (error in asking defendant about prior conviction was harmless, since evidence of guilt was "simply overwhelming").

11. Traynor, The Riddle of Harmless Error 70-71 (1970) (when proof "is closely balanced or affords minimal support for judgment," error in admitting cannot be harmless).

12. *See* Doty v. Sewall, 908 F.2d 1053, 1057 (1st Cir. 1990) (since testimony was cumulative, court needed not decide whether admitting it was error).

13. City of Long Beach v. Standard Oil of Cal., 46 F.3d 929, 937 (9th Cir. 1995) (error in excluding handwritten notes was harmless; little probative value, cumulative); Agristor Leasing v. Meuli, 865 F.2d 1150, 1153 (10th Cir. 1988) (in light of other evidence, rulings excluding evidence did not affect substantial right).

One difficulty in predicating a claim of error on rulings admitting or excluding evidence lies in the fact that the trial judge has broad discretion. In the first instance, she decides whether probative worth is outweighed by the dangers and considerations described in FRE 403 (unfair prejudice, confusion of issues, waste of time), and she has considerable discretion to strike the balance. She has less discretion where specific rules come into play, such as the hearsay doctrine and the principles in FRE 404-412. But applying these specific rules often requires the judge to make preliminary findings of fact under FRE 104(a), and here too she has leeway, since these are normally reviewed under the "clear error" doctrine.

Judicial discretion

Often prejudice from error in admitting evidence can be cured at trial, and sometimes error in excluding evidence. One common curative step is to instruct the jury by limiting the purposes for which evidence may be considered, directing that it be disregarded, or explaining it in other ways. Usually reviewing courts conclude that such instructions make any error in admitting evidence harmless.

Curing error at trial

The first of these (limiting instruction) prevents or discourages improper use, reducing the likelihood of prejudice or jury confusion.[14] The second (instruction to disregard) helps prevent mistakes in admitting evidence from affecting outcome, or at least improves the chance for an untainted verdict.[15] Sometimes such instructions are described in terms of "striking the evidence," and an after-stated objection is described as a "motion to strike," these terms being dramatic ways of describing the intended effect of this curative measure. The third (explanatory instruction) is similar to the limiting instruction, but its purpose is to add context or perspective, so the jury can reach a true understanding.[16]

Cure by instruction

In oft-quoted and forceful language, Justice Jackson railed against this instructions to disregard, bemoaning the "naive assumption that prejudicial effects can be overcome by instructions to the jury" as one that "all practicing lawyers know to be unmitigated fiction," and in some settings this point has carried the day: For instance, the *Bruton* doctrine holds that error in admitting a statement by one of several codefendants implicating another by name cannot be cured, as a matter of constitutional principle, by telling the jury to consider the statement as evidence only against the declarant.[17] And sometimes instructions do not succeed in neutralizing error: Evidence erroneously admitted may be too explosive, or its effect may be made indelible by

---

14. Paoletto v. Beech Aircraft Corp., 464 F.2d 976, 982 (3d Cir. 1972). Ordinarily courts only give such instructions on request. *See* §1.16, *infra*.

15. *See* United States v. Steele, 727 F.2d 580, 588 (6th Cir. 1984), *cert. denied,* 467 U.S. 1209; Worcester v. Pure Torpedo Co., 127 F.2d 945, 947 (7th Cir. 1942).

16. United States v. Corey, 566 F.2d 429, 433 (2d Cir. 1977); Duff v. Page, 249 F.2d 137, 141 (9th Cir. 1957).

17. *See* Krulewitch v. United States, 336 U.S. 440 (1949) (Jackson concurring); *see also* Bruton v. United States, 391 U.S. 123 (1968) (discussed in §8.28, *infra*).

repetition, or curative instructions may come too late or fail to convey the necessary message.[18]

Cure by verdict

A second kind of cure occurs when a verdict shows the jury ruled in favor of appellant on the only claims or charges affected by any error. "Saved-by-the-outcome" cures can neutralize errors in both admitting and excluding evidence.[19]

Cure by other evidence

A third kind of cure involves admitting other evidence that has the effect of rebutting or explaining evidence erroneously admitted, thus keeping it from having unwanted effect.[20] It is of course the theory of the doctrine letting parties "fight fire with fire" that the effect of evidence improperly admitted can be neutralized in this way, and this doctrine has proved a reliable workhorse that often satisfies reviewing courts.[21]

Cure by mistrial

Finally, granting a mistrial can usually cure errors in admitting evidence. In criminal cases, the constitutional right against double jeopardy would foreclose a second prosecution unless defendant consents on the understanding that he will be tried again. For this reason alone, it is understandable that defense refusal of an offer of mistrial waives the right to seek reversal on account of error generating such an offer.[22]

Invited error

Error is usually considered harmless if it was invited by a party in eliciting a response from a witness[23] or exploring a particular subject, thereby opening the door for the other side to introduce rebuttal evidence.[24] But this doctrine may be applied unwisely, and a false step should not open the gate to evidence that is inappropriate in tenor or disproportionate in impact.[25]

§1.8 —Reversible and Plain

Reversible error

"Reversible error" means a mistake that affected substantial rights in a way that seems serious enough to warrant relief from a judgment.

---

18. Tipton v. Socony Mobile Oil Co., 375 U.S. 34 (1963); Aetna Casualty & Sur. Co. v. Gosdin, 803 F.2d 1153, 1159-1160 (11th Cir. 1986).

19. United States v. Cammisano, 917 F.2d 1057, 1060 (8th Cir. 1990); Schneider v. Revici, 817 F.2d 987, 991-992 (2d Cir. 1987).

20. United States v. Hefler, 159 F.2d 831, 834 (2d Cir. 1947), *cert. denied,* 331 U.S. 811.

21. *See* the discussion in §1.4, *supra.*

22. Ladakis v. United States, 283 F.2d 141, 143 (10th Cir. 1960) (court offered to strike testimony or declare mistrial; in choosing to proceed, defendant waived right to claim harm was not cured by instruction).

23. *See* United States v. Schaff, 948 F.2d 501, 505-506 (9th Cir. 1991); United States v. Gonzales, 606 F.2d 70, 76-77 (5th Cir. 1979); Horibe v. Continental Baking Co., 298 F.2d 43, 45-46 (7th Cir. 1962).

24. Neu v. Grant, 548 F.2d 281, 287 (10th Cir. 1977) (appellant may not complain of errors he induced or invited); United States v. Benson, 495 F.2d 475, 478-479 (5th Cir. 1974) (defense may not create error by forcing the government to introduce evidence and then claim on appeal that evidence was prejudicial), *cert. denied,* 419 U.S. 1035.

25. United States v. Marrero, 486 F.2d 622, 626 (7th Cir. 1973) (attacking identification testimony did not justify proof that defendant's name was in file of major violators).

A mistake qualifies as reversible error if it probably affected the result reached below. In practice, courts often describe reversible error by explaining why it was not harmless. "Plain error" means about the same thing, but with the additional point that the error was somehow obvious or especially egregious or serious, so any shortcoming by the parties in failing to object or call the point to the attention of the trial court may be excused.

Descriptions of error are usually cast both in terms of seriousness and procedural context: Did the error affect a substantial right? Did the complaining party make a timely and appropriate objection or offer of proof? If the answer to either question is "no," the error is usually harmless. If the error was obvious and especially serious, it may be termed plain and the judgment may be reversed even if the error passed unnoticed, sometimes even if no party raised it on appeal. Between the extremes of harmless and plain error lies the category of reversible error. If the party made timely and appropriate offer of proof or objection, and error in admitting or excluding the evidence affected the judgment, then the error is reversible error and corrective measures are taken.

The plain error principle is best understood as a device for mitigating the harshness of the adversary system, serving as a safety valve or an anchor to windward.[1] Under it, trial courts may note and correct errors on their own, either during trial or posttrial motion, and courts directly reviewing a judgment may also note and correct errors not raised below or even on appeal.

Plain error

Courts describe plain error in different ways, almost always in broad and general terms. The most common phrases focus on the seriousness of the mistake. It is commonly said that plain error means only those mistakes that are serious or egregious, substantial, manifest, highly prejudicial, or grave,[2] and that plain error can be found only if failure to correct would be a miscarriage of justice.[3] Also visible in common descriptions is the notion that plain error can be found only in a mistake that was obvious. It is often said that plain error is the sort of mistake that calls into question the integrity or fairness of judicial proceedings, so failing to correct it might threaten the system or the

---

§1.8   1. *See* United States v. Young, 470 U.S. 1 (1984) (plain error doctrine tempers contemporaneous objection requirement); Herzog v. United States, 235 F.2d 664, 666 (9th Cir. 1956) (plain error rule is anchor to windward and safety provision, precise scope of which is undefined); ACN to FRE 103 (mentioning judicial unwillingness to be constricted by mechanical breakdowns).

2. United States v. Simpson, 992 F.2d 1224, 1228-1229 (D.C. Cir. 1993) (obvious and substantially undermines fairness), *cert. denied*, 510 U.S. 906; United States v. Young, 470 U.S. 1 (1984) (particularly egregious).

3. United States v. Young, 470 U.S. 1 (1984) (expanding plain error would skew balance between encouraging careful lawyering and correcting injustice); U.S. v. Shwayder, 312 F.3d 1109, 1120 (9th Cir. 2002) (relief is warranted for plain error only if it was clear or obvious, affected substantial rights, and seriously affected fairness, integrity or public reputation of proceedings) (refusing relief here).

administration of criminal justice. The party seeking relief bears the burden of showing that the mistake qualifies for plain error treatment.[4]

In the end, precision seems beyond reach. Verbal formulae do little to help distinguish between ordinary and plain error in degree of seriousness or obviousness, nor to explain just when errors adversely affect the integrity of the system or the administration of criminal law. Decisions finding plain error or rejecting claims of such error reflect little more than the conclusions reached, and the descriptive phrases are best viewed as general indicators of the nature of the inquiry.

Cannot look beyond record

The plain error principle does not authorize reviewing courts to look beyond the record. Hence rulings that exclude evidence are unlikely to merit plain error treatment simply because the required offer is missing. The absence of such offer usually forecloses plain error treatment because the record does not reflect the nature of the excluded evidence,[5] although refusing to allow a party to make an appropriate offer invites reversal on this ground.[6]

Plain error is only sparingly invoked as grounds for reversal, and only in "extraordinary circumstances."[7] Where the record reflects or even smacks of a lawyer's strategic decision not to object, reversal for plain error is unlikely.[8]

§1.9 —Constitutional

When an evidence ruling errs by infringing a constitutional right, almost always a protection accorded to the accused in a criminal case, usually the question whether reversal is required turns on applying a special harmless error standard. That standard requires reversal unless the court believes beyond reasonable doubt that the error did not affect the verdict.

Harmless constitutional error

With good reason, it was once thought that constitutional errors stood on different footing from others because they required automatic

4. United States v. McKinney, 954 F.2d 471, 476 (7th Cir. 1992) (putting burden on defendant encourages litigants to seek fair trial the first time).

5. *See* ACN for FRE 103(d) (plain error treatment is more likely for errors in admitting evidence than for errors in excluding it because failing to comply with requirement to offer proof is likely to produce a record that does not disclose the error); Sullivan v. Rowan Cos., 952 F.2d 141, 146-147 (5th Cir. 1991) (in product liability suit, granting defense motion to exclude testimony on warnings; others did not object and failed to make offer of proof, which precludes review).

6. Williams v. Wal-Mart Stores, Inc., 922 F.2d 1357, 1362 (8th Cir. 1990) (plaintiff made no offer, but court refused to let him ask experts their opinion on causation, refused to let him rephrase, and responded harshly to questioning).

7. United States v. King, 505 F.2d 602, 605 (5th Cir. 1974); Walker v. Continental Life & Acc. Co., 445 F.2d 1072, 1074 (9th Cir. 1971).

8. United States v. McGill, 951 F.2d 16, 19-20 (1st Cir. 1991); Marshall v. United States, 409 F.2d 925, 927 (9th Cir. 1969).

reversal.[1] The Supreme Court put that view to rest in *Chapman v. California,* which considered and rejected an automatic reversal rule for all constitutional errors, concluding that "some constitutional errors" may be "so unimportant and insignificant" in the setting of the case that they may be "deemed harmless."[2] Despite its modest tone and its finding that the error was *not* harmless, *Chapman* had great impact in expanding the concept of harmless constitutional error. Later decisions leave no doubt that most constitutional errors involving evidence issues are judged under a harmless error standard. *Chapman* and other cases give meaning to the view that no trial can be "perfect" or "error-free," given the "myriad safeguards" provided by the Constitution and the "human fallibility" of judges and lawyers, that many if not most constitutional violations are harmless, and that larger interests in efficiency and avoiding needless retrials require a harmless error doctrine, even for constitutional violations.[3]

Prominent among the kinds of constitutional mistakes subject to *Chapman* are errors in (a) denying the right of cross-examination in violation of the confrontation clause, whether the aim is to show bias, influence, or motive,[4] or to attack testimony by prosecution witnesses in other ways;[5] (b) admitting hearsay in violation of the confrontation clause as interpreted in the *Crawford* case;[6] (c) admitting a statement by one defendant identifying and incriminating another in violation of the *Bruton* doctrine;[7] (d) commenting on the failure of the accused to testify in violation of the *Griffin* doctrine (the very setting in which *Chapman* was decided);[8] (e) admitting statements taken in violation of defendant's Fifth Amendment *Miranda* rights;[9] (f) admitting evidence of

---

§1.9 1. *See* Mause, Harmless Constitutional Error: The Implications of Chapman v. California, 53 Minn. L. Rev. 519, 520-521 (1969); Gibbs, Prejudicial Error: Admissions and Exclusions of Evidence in the Federal Courts, 3 Vill. L. Rev. 48 (1957).

2. Chapman v. California, 386 U.S. 18, 22 (1967).

3. *See also* Rose v. Clark, 478 U.S. 570, 579 (1986) (if defendant had counsel and impartial adjudicator, there is strong presumption that other errors are subject to harmless error analysis); United States v. Hasting, 461 U.S. 498 (1983) (given myriad safeguards that assure fair trial and considering human fallibility of participants, there can be no error-free trial, and Constitution does not guarantee one).

4. Delaware v. Van Arsdall, 475 U.S. 673, 681 (1985); United States v. Gambler, 662 F.2d 834, 840-841 (D.C. Cir. 1981).

5. United States v. Begay, 937 F.2d 515, 524-525 (10th Cir. 1991); United States ex rel. Scarpelli v. George, 687 F.2d 1012, 1013-1015 (7th Cir. 1982).

6. United States v. Alvarado-Valdez, 521 F.3d 337, 341-342 (5th Cir. 2008) (violations of *Crawford* doctrine are subject to harmless error analysis) (see §§8.84-8.90, *infra*).

7. The reference is to Bruton v. United States, 391 U.S. 123 (1968) (discussed in §8.28, *infra*). For the proposition that *Bruton* errors can be harmless, *see* Brown v. United States, 411 U.S. 223 (1973); Schneble v. Florida, 405 U.S. 427 (1972); Harrington v. California, 395 U.S. 250 (1969).

8. The reference is to Griffin v. California, 380 U.S. 609 (1965). For the proposition that *Griffin* errors can be harmless, *see* United States v. Hasting, 461 U.S. 498 (1983); Chapman v. California, 386 U.S. 18 (1967).

9. Campaneria v. Reid, 891 F.2d 1014, 1022 (2d Cir. 1989); United States v. Wilson, 690 F.2d 1267, 1273-1275 (9th Cir. 1982).

defendant's post-warning silence in violation of the *Doyle* doctrine;[10] (g) admitting statements taken in violation of defendant's Sixth Amendment right to counsel;[11] (h) admitting evidence seized in violation of the Fourth Amendment and the *Mapp* doctrine;[12] (i) admitting out-of-court statements of identification taken in violation of the Sixth Amendment right to counsel and the *Wade-Gilbert* doctrine;[13] (j) admitting psychiatric testimony obtained in violation of the Sixth Amendment right to counsel;[14] and (k) admitting involuntary confessions.[15]

Automatic reversal standard survives

Neither *Chapman* nor ensuing cases hold that all constitutional errors are subject to a harmless error standard. *Chapman* itself acknowledged that some rights are "so basic to a fair trial" that constitutional violations "can never be treated as harmless," and on other occasions the Court referred to rights that remain subject to an automatic reversal standard.[16]

Few constitutional issues likely to connect with evidence issues remain subject to an automatic reversal standard, but some do.[17] They include (a) giving an erroneous instruction on intent couched in language suggesting a conclusive presumption that a person intends the natural and necessary consequences of his acts[18] although the strength of this doctrine is open to some doubt;[19] and (b) admitting an uncounseled guilty plea.[20] Using convictions obtained in violation of the constitutional right of counsel to enhance punishment in a later case may qualify for

---

10. The reference is to Doyle v. Ohio, 426 U.S. 610 (1976) (discussed in §8.30, *infra*). For the proposition that *Doyle* errors can be harmless, *see* United States v. Gonzalez, 921 F.2d 1530, 1550 (11th Cir. 1991); Leecan v. Lopes, 893 F.2d 1434 (2d Cir. 1990).

11. Milton v. Wainwright, 407 U.S. 371, 372-373 (1972).

12. The reference is to Mapp v. Ohio, 367 U.S. 643 (1961). For the proposition that *Mapp* errors can be harmless, *see* Chambers v. Maroney, 399 U.S. 42, 53 (1970); Whitely v. Warden, Wyoming State Penitentiary, 401 U.S. 560, 569 n.13 (1971).

13. The reference is to United States v. Wade, 388 U.S. 218 (1967) and Gilbert v. California, 388 U.S. 263 (1967). Both *Wade* and *Gilbert* say *Chapman* applies, which the Court confirmed later. *See* Moore v. Illinois, 434 U.S. 220 (1977).

14. Satterwhite v. Texas, 486 U.S. 251, 258-260 (1986).

15. *See* Arizona v. Fulminante, 499 U.S. 279, 310 (1991) (harmless error standard applies to evidence of involuntary confessions). *See also* Crane v. Kentucky, 476 U.S. 688 (1986) (error in excluding evidence on voluntariness may be harmless).

16. *See* Rose v. Clark, 478 U.S. 570, 577-578 (1986) (citing coerced confessions, denial of right to trial counsel, biased judge, directing verdict against accused); Delaware v. Van Arsdall, 475 U.S. 673, 681 (1985) (citing denial of trial counsel, use of trier of fact with financial stake in outcome).

17. *See* Comment, Principles for Application of the Harmless Error Standard, 41 U. Chi. L. Rev. 616 (1974) (considering factors that might indicate choice of automatic reversal or application of *Chapman* standard).

18. Connecticut v. Johnson, 460 U.S. 73 (1983) (instruction authorized jury to ignore evidence on intent; such error cannot be harmless, but in rare situations it might not affect verdict, as where defendant concedes intent or is acquitted on charge to which instruction relates) (four-member plurality opinion by Blackmun). *See also* Sandstrom v. Montana, 442 U.S. 510 (1979) (such instruction violates due process).

19. *See* Estelle v. McGuire, 502 U.S. 62, 73 n.4 (1991) (*Boyde, infra*, sets standard for ambiguous instructions); Boyde v. California, 494 U.S. 370, 380 (1990) (question is whether there is "reasonable likelihood" that jury applied ambiguous instruction in way that "prevents the consideration of constitutionally relevant evidence").

20. White v. Maryland, 373 U.S. 59 (1963).

automatic reversal—at least error of this sort is judged by a very strict standard that approaches automatic reversal.[21]

For years, modern authority suggested that rulings denying the right secured by the confrontation clause to cross-examine witnesses required automatic reversal, but it is now clear that such rulings too are subject to the *Chapman* test.[22]

While *Chapman* adopts a harmless error standard, constitutional errors do not get the same treatment as ordinary evidence errors. In two respects, appraising constitutional error differs from appraising ordinary error. First, in criminal cases *Chapman* permits affirmance of a conviction only if it is clear beyond a reasonable doubt that the error did not affect the judgment.[23] This standard seems more stringent than the one that applies in cases of nonconstitutional error, and probably the government bears the burden if defendants appeal from criminal convictions.[24] Second, constitutional errors are somewhat more likely than ordinary errors to call for reversal under the plain error doctrine.

C. PRELIMINARY ISSUES IN EVIDENCE RULINGS

FRE 104

　　(a) Questions of admissibility generally. Preliminary questions concerning the qualification of a person to be a witness, the existence of a privilege, or the admissibility of evidence shall be determined by the court, subject to the provisions of subdivision (b). In making its determination it is not bound by the rules of evidence except those with respect to privileges.

　　(b) Relevancy conditioned on fact. When the relevancy of evidence depends upon the fulfillment of a condition of fact, the court shall admit it upon, or subject to, the introduction of evidence sufficient to support a finding of the fulfillment of the condition.

　　(c) Hearing of jury. Hearings on the admissibility of confessions shall in all cases be conducted out of the hearing of the jury. Hearings on other preliminary matters shall be so conducted when the interests of justice require, or when an accused is a witness and so requests.

21. Burgett v. Texas, 389 U.S. 109 (1967); United States v. Tucker, 404 U.S. 443 (1972).

22. *See* Brookhart v. Janis, 384 U.S. 1 (1966) (denying cross without waiver "would be constitutional error of the first magnitude and no amount of showing of want of prejudice would cure it"); Davis v. Alaska, 415 U.S. 308 (1974) (quoting and relying on *Brookhart*). *Brookhart* was limited, if not overruled, and the broadest implications of *Davis* were trimmed in Delaware v. Van Arsdall, 475 U.S. 673 (1986).

23. *See* Chapman v. California, 386 U.S. 18, 24 (1967); Schneble v. Florida, 405 U.S. 427 (1972); Harrington v. California, 395 U.S. 250 (1969).

24. United States v. McKinney, 954 F.2d 471, 475 (7th Cir. 1992).

> **(d) Testimony by accused.** The accused does not, by testifying upon a preliminary matter, become subject to cross-examination as to other issues in the case.
>
> **(e) Weight and credibility.** This rule does not limit the right of a party to introduce before the jury evidence relevant to weight or credibility.

§1.10   Court-Determined Issues (Admissibility, Witness Qualifications, Privileges)

The trial judge (not the jury) determines most issues relating to admissibility, witness qualification, and privileges. FRE 104(a) says as much, and the result is unsurprising insofar as those issues are "legal." Everybody understands, for example, that the trial judge decides whether the spousal testimony privilege can be invoked by the defendant or only by the testifying witness, which is as pure a legal question as one can imagine.

Judge decides fact questions   Slightly more surprising is the fact that the trial judge also decides factual questions in ruling on such issues: He decides, for example, whether someone who made an out-of-court statement was "excited" for purposes of applying the excited utterance exception to the hearsay doctrine. The issue is one of "admissibility," and being excited or not is factual. The judge also decides whether someone called to testify qualifies as an expert. That is an issue of "witness qualification," and it presents a mix of factual and legal conclusions that can be summed up this way: What background (training or experience) does she have, and is it enough to make her an expert? And if a witness invokes the spousal testimony privilege, the judge decides whether she and the defendant are married (a "privilege" issue presenting mixed questions of law and fact).

In short, some fact questions are resolved by judges even in jury cases. To make the point dramatically, the factfinding mission can involve judges in taking testimony, resolving conflicts, and assessing credibility.[1] It is sometimes preferable to hold what amounts to a "mini-hearing" outside the presence of the jury, particularly if resolving the preliminary questions will expose the jury to the evidence whose admissibility is in issue or might otherwise inject prejudice or confusion.[2]

Admissibility questions   Questions of admissibility arise in applying rules on relevancy and its limits, impeachment of witnesses, hearsay, and Best Evidence. In all

---

§1.10   1. In these cases, the court was deciding whether the coconspirator exception applies: U.S. v. Freeman, 208 F.3d 332, 342 (1st Cir. 2000) (judge "can make credibility assessments and draw inferences from the facts"); Precision Piping v. E. I. du Pont de Nemours, 951 F.2d 613, 621 (4th Cir. 1991) (court may "weigh the credibility and reliability of evidence").

2. *See* the discussion in §1.12, *infra.*

these settings, preliminary questions may be mostly legal or mostly factual, but the court decides them under FRE 104(a).

The basic question of relevance is for the judge to decide.[3] Invariably the question arises with "circumstantial" as opposed to "direct" evidence, and the judge has to decide whether the evidence makes a consequential fact more or less likely than it would be without the evidence.[4] To answer this question the judge must consider evidence in very much the same spirit as the jury. The judge thinks about what facts make a difference, whether the proffered evidence bears on them (making them more or less probable), and he appraises the evidence in light of reason and his own experience in life. Later the jury does much the same thing if the evidence is admitted, but there is one difference. Unlike the jury, the judge tries to imagine what maximum effect a reasonable person could give the evidence with respect to the issues if such person fully credited the testimony or otherwise gave as much credit to the proof as a reasonable person might. In other words, what matters to the judge is not whether he is personally persuaded on such points but whether he thinks a reasonable juror could be.

As nearly everyone discovers sooner or later, much of what goes into this process has to do with intuition and hunches and cannot be easily put into words or distinguished from feelings or impressions. What we expect from judges is intelligence, competence, even wisdom and shrewdness, and a certain mature detachment. The latter quality puts them in a better position than the parties or their lawyers to decide such things, and in a better position than most lay juries, which are comprised of people lacking experience in deciding contested facts on the basis of conflicting evidence, particularly when matters of great moment hang in the balance (usually transfers of money or incarceration). To take a single example, suppose a negligence suit in which a point of interest is the speed of one car at its point of collision with another. Testimony of an eyewitness that the car was going faster than the speed limit ten blocks before the impact would raise a question of relevancy for the judge to resolve under FRE 104(a): Could a reasonable juror who credits such testimony infer that the car was going faster than the speed limit at the point of impact?[5]

---

3. In contrast, questions of "conditional relevancy" are for the jury under FRE 104(b). The distinction between relevancy and conditional relevancy blurs at the edges: The concern of relevancy is the nature and soundness of the inferences connecting evidence with conclusion, while the concern of conditional relevancy is the various points that must be proved before the inferences may be drawn. In the end, these are closely related elements. *See* §1.13, *infra*.

4. *See* the discussion of FRE 401 in §4.2, *infra*.

5. *See* Fleming v. Lawson, 240 F.2d 119, 121 (10th Cir. 1956) (admitting evidence that defendant's car was seen 33 miles before accident traveling 90 miles per hour; question whether to admit is for judge to decide). *See also* Comins v. Scrivener, 214 F.2d 810 (10th Cir. 1954); MacCurdy v. United States, 143 F. Supp. 60, 64 (D. Fla. 1956), *aff'd*, 246 F.2d 67 (5th Cir.), *cert. denied*, 355 U.S. 933. *Compare* Jamison v. Kline, 319 F. Supp. 951, 952 (D. Pa. 1970) (excluding as too remote testimony by officer that defendant's car passed him three miles before accident going faster than other cars), *aff'd*, 454 F.2d 1256 (3d Cir.).

In this same setting courts might also find questions of conditional relevancy that juries decide under FRE 104(b). Suppose the car is a green sedan but the testifying witness offers little assurance that the car he saw is the one that crashed ten blocks later. Even if the relevancy question is answered in the affirmative (proof of speeding ten blocks before the crash does suggest speeding at the time of the crash), gaps in the data may make it plausible to allow the overall inference only if the sighting is "connected up" with the crash by proof that the car the witness observed is the green sedan that crashed.[6] This conditional relevancy issue could lead the court in several different directions: It might exclude proof of the sighting if the proponent could not promise to offer further proof connecting it to the car that crashed, or require such proof first (before testimony as to the speed of the car at the sighting), or instruct the jury to consider the testimony on speed only if it found that the witness saw the car that crashed.

Judge decides pragmatic relevancy

Judges also make what might be called "pragmatic relevancy" decisions, meaning that they decide whether probative worth is outweighed by risks of prejudice or confusion under FRE 403.[7] These decisions represent continuous efforts to keep trials in hand, exclude evidence that contributes less in the way of understanding and more in the way of emotionalism, potential misuse, confusion, and waste of time.

Judge decides impeachment issues

In a related vein, judges decide many issues relating to impeachment of witnesses, which are also questions of "admissibility." Judges, for example, decide simple relevance issues like whether prior acts of theft bear on veracity. And they decide pragmatic relevance issues like whether a defendant who testifies in his own car theft trial can be asked whether he was once convicted of bank robbery.

Judge decides hearsay issues

Most preliminary questions that arise when an out-of-court statement is offered over a hearsay objection are for judges to decide under FRE 104(a). Thus judges decide whether proffered statements fit standard hearsay exceptions or the catchall,[8] and in doing so they may have to decide factual questions.[9] Judges also decide whether various conditions are satisfied, such as the declarant being unavailable to testify

---

6. *See* State v. Freeman, 71 P.2d 196, 202-203 (Utah 1937) (admitting testimony that car was seen going 60 miles per hour two blocks from scene; testimony did not describe color, make, or driver, so it was not connected with defendant or accident, except that no other cars met or passed witness while he was traveling to the scene) (defendant could move to strike, if not connected up).

7. *See* the discussion of FRE 403 in §§4.9-4.10, *infra*.

8. Re Korean Air Lines Disaster, 932 F.2d 1475, 1483 (D.C. Cir. 1991); Wallace Motor Sales, Inc. v. American Motor Sales Corp., 780 F.2d 1049, 1060-1061 (1st Cir. 1985).

9. United States v. Toney, 161 F.3d 404, 407-408 (6th Cir. 1998) (in applying FRE 801(d)(1)(B), judge determines when alleged motive to lie arose; findings are reviewed under clear error standard), *cert. denied,* 526 U.S. 1045 (1999); Miller v. Keating, 754 F.2d 507, 510-512 (3d Cir. 1985) (judge makes findings necessary for excited utterance exception, including knowledge and excitement).

or the existence of corroboration.[10] And judges decide whether a statement or other conduct should even be considered hearsay, which is important if it appears the actor or speaker lacked assertive purpose or that what he said or did is to be used to prove something other than what was asserted.[11]

It is clearly right to assign these preliminary questions to judges. Hearsay is generally excluded because remote statements may be untrustworthy, and they are neither tested by cross-examination nor illuminated by demeanor evidence, which leaves the jury without enough for a good appraisal. By experience and education, judges are better situated to decide whether an out-of-court statement comes with enough assurance of trustworthiness to be admitted, and only judges can competently decide whether the statement is in fact hearsay or whether an exception applies.

When a party wants to prove the contents of a writing, recording, or photograph, the Best Evidence doctrine requires production of the document, or an acceptable excuse for not doing so, in which case other evidence of content may be admitted. At common law, producing the document normally meant producing the original. Now duplicates (machine-made copies) are just as good unless there is a "genuine question" about authenticity of the original or admitting the copy would be unfair.[12] Most issues affecting admissibility of other evidence of contents are for the court to resolve under FRE 104(a), and this point is confirmed by FRE 1008.[13] Before admitting other evidence (like testimony by someone who saw the original), the court decides whether the original was lost or destroyed or is unavailable, or is in the possession of the opponent who objects to the other proof.[14] Under FRE 1003 the judge also decides whether it would be unfair to admit a duplicate offered in lieu of the original, and the judge plays at least a gatekeeping role under FRE 1003 in deciding whether a "genuine question" has been raised on authenticity of the original.[15] Not all questions affecting

Judge decides Best Evidence issues

---

10. United States v. Alvarez, 584 F.2d 694, 701 (5th Cir. 1978) (corroboration requirement for against-interest statements implicating defendant is question for judge); United States v. Bell, 500 F.2d 1287, 1290 (2d Cir. 1974) (whether witness suffering temporary illness is unavailable is for court to decide).

11. *See* Finman, Implied Assertions as Hearsay: Some Criticisms of the Uniform Rules of Evidence, 14 Stan. L. Rev. 682, 696-697 (1962) (on question whether conduct was intended as assertion, court can often decide either way; hearsay doctrine should be broadened to reach conduct).

12. The basic principle is set out in FRE 1002, the exceptions in FRE 1004, and the provision on duplicates in FRE 1003. *See* §§10.6-10.13, *infra*.

13. *See* FRE 1008 (when admissibility of other evidence "depends upon the fulfillment of a condition of fact, the question whether the condition has been fulfilled is ordinarily for the court to determine" under FRE 104).

14. Seiler v. Lucasfilm, Ltd., 797 F.2d 1504, 1507 (9th Cir. 1986); United States v. Gerhart, 538 F.2d 807, 809 (8th Cir. 1976); Sylvania Elec. Prod., Inc. v. Flanagan, 352 F.2d 1005, 1008 (1st Cir. 1965).

15. It is hard to reconcile the "genuine question" standard with FRE 1008, which says the jury decides whether "the asserted writing ever existed" and whether "other evidence" correctly reflects the original. Proof by the objecting party that there never was an original, or the duplicate does not reproduce it, raises issues covered by both

application of the Best Evidence doctrine are for the judge, however, for invariably proving the content of writings, photographs, or recorded statements brings issues of authenticity, where the jury has a role to play.[16]

Judge decides witness qualification

The judge determines issues of witness qualification,[17] but such issues are few and far between. The one related question that arises every time a witness takes the stand is largely for the jury to decide, and that is whether the witness has personal knowledge. Here the court plays only a screening role, passing to the jury the question of knowledge if a reasonable juror could decide the witness knows what he is talking about.[18]

Since most restrictions on witness competency were abolished long ago, there are only four areas where competency issues still matter. The first and perhaps most important area relates to expert testimony. Courts decide under FRE 104(a) whether a witness qualifies as an expert under FRE 702, so his opinion may be admitted on a technical matter, and whether the testimony of the expert satisfies the criterion of scientific validity or reliability.[19] In addition to questions of the latter sort, the court may have to consider, for example, whether academic degrees qualify a witness to give an expert opinion, and whether training or job experience is adequate. And the court decides related questions—whether expert opinion can help the factfinder, whether an expert has an adequate basis to testify, and whether proposed testimony presents valid science.[20]

A second area where courts decide witness qualification, or something close to that, involves children who give evidence in abuse cases. Here the question is not so much whether the child satisfies some formal standard (neither youth nor immaturity are disqualifying facts), but whether she is able to testify: Can she face the ordeal of taking the stand, understand and commit herself to the truth, and express herself

---

FRE 1003 and 1008. If the judge excludes the duplicate (finding a "genuine question" under FRE 1003), there is no way to let the jury decide whether the duplicate accurately reflects the original (as FRE 1008 requires). *See* §§10.8 and 10.18, *infra.*

16. *See* §10.17, *infra.*

17. Kingsley Assoc., Inc. v. Del-Met, Inc., 918 F.2d 1277, 1286 (6th Cir. 1990) (qualification of expert "unquestionably" raises preliminary question for court); Alfonso v. Lund, 783 F.2d 958, 962 (10th Cir. 1986) (court decides competency subject to clear error standard) (no error to let doctor testify).

18. As the ACN to FRE 602 makes clear, the issue of personal knowledge is an example of conditional relevancy governed by FRE 104(b). The trial judge only decides whether the proponent has offered sufficient evidence to support a finding of personal knowledge, and the jury actually decides the point. *See* §6.5, *infra.*

19. *See* Stillwell and Bierce Mfg. Co. v. Phelps, 130 U.S. 520 (1889); United States v. Mitchell, 954 F.2d 663, 666-667 (11th Cir. 1992). *See also* Goebel v. Denver and Rio Grande Western R.R. Co., 215 F.3d 1083, 1086-1089 (10th Cir. 2000) (*Daubert* allows trial judges great discretion in the manner of assessing reliability, but there is no discretion "regarding the actual *performance* of the gatekeeping function," and trial judge should make specific findings); In re Paoli R.R. Yard PCB Litigation, 35 F.3d 717, 743-745 (3d Cir. 1994) (under *Daubert* standard and FRE 104(a), court must conduct preliminary factfinding on question of scientific reliability). The *Daubert* standard is considered in §7.7, *infra.*

20. *See* discussion of expert qualifications and helpfulness standard in §§7.5 and 7.6, *infra,* and the discussion of the scientific validity standard in §7.7, *infra.*

in useful ways? Typically there are other mechanisms that could be used (videotaped depositions or remote testimony by television monitor), and the question whether to resort to these are for the trial judge under FRE 104(a).[21] Where a child cannot speak intelligibly or apparently does not recognize any obligation to speak the truth, a qualification decision might lead to excluding her testimony in any form.[22]

There is a third rather amorphous area of competency issues. When a witness may be insane or delusional, or addicted to drugs or under the influence, questions relating to capacity to receive and recount just impressions arise. But again these facts seldom disqualify a witness from testifying, and these matters are likely to be explored on cross or proved by extrinsic evidence as points that impeach credibility.[23]

Finally, judges decide issues arising under Dead Man's Statutes.[24] Often, in order to prevent fraud and preserve estates, these provisions disqualify living parties from giving testimony when they sue estates claiming tort or contract liability—the notion being that this bar makes a more level playing field since the decedent cannot tell his side of the story. Sometimes they take the opposite tack, allowing the survivor to testify but also paving the way to admit hearsay by decedents.

The court decides under FRE 104(a) whether privileges apply. In connection with the attorney-client privilege, for example, the judge decides whether the appropriate relationship existed, whether the communication was confidential, and whether the crime-or-fraud exception applies.[25] In applying either of the spousal privileges (spousal testimony and spousal confidences), the court decides whether the two people are married to each other.[26] The judge similarly decides questions relating to claims of many other privileges, such as doctor-patient, psychotherapist-patient, and penitential, and newer, less-settled privileges, such as journalist-source. In making these preliminary decisions, the judge puts the burden of persuasion on the claimant to show that a privilege applies, but puts the burden on the party seeking information or offering evidence to prove an exception applies.[27]

Judge decides privilege issues

§1.11   Preliminary Questions on Confessions

Inquiry into the admissibility of confessions must be "conducted out of the hearing of the jury" under FRE 104(c). This provision complies with

---

21. On psychological unavailability of children, *see* §8.67, *infra*. On depositions and remote testimony by child victims, *see* §§8.70 and 8.91, *infra*.

22. Usually competency concerns do not block out-of-court statements that fit exceptions to the hearsay doctrine. *See* §8.42, *infra* (medical statements exception applies regardless of competency of young speaker).

23. *See* impeachment by showing lack of mental capacity §§6.21-6.22, *infra*.

24. Hoyt v. Clancey, 180 F.2d 152, 157 (8th Cir. 1950).

25. Robinson v. United States, 144 F.2d 392, 405 (6th Cir. 1944), *aff'd* 324 U.S. 282; Steiner v. United States, 134 F.2d 931, 935 (5th Cir. 1943), *cert. denied*, 319 U.S. 774.

26. United States v. Barnes, 368 F.2d 567, 568 (4th Cir. 1966).

27. *See* §1.12, *infra*.

the constitutional requirement announced in the Supreme Court's 1964 decision in *Jackson v. Denno* and accords with federal statute.[1] Defense requests to exclude confessions as involuntary and motions to suppress evidence on other constitutional grounds are typically made before trial and resolved before a jury is impaneled. But such issues are not always resolved before trial, and they raise not only the question whether the jury should be excluded but also other procedural issues.

New York procedure rejected
Jackson rejected as inadequate the New York procedure of submitting the confession to the jury along with all the evidence, including evidence on voluntariness. *Jackson* said the risks of giving everything to the jury at once are serious because a jury is likely to give effect to confessions thought reliable, and that this procedure makes appellate review impossible. The constitutional principle excluding involuntary confessions is not premised on trustworthiness alone, but on the notion that the state should not wring a confession out of someone against his will, and that allowing this practice would pose larger dangers to society.

Orthodox and Massachusetts rules
Jackson requires either a procedure where the judge "solely and finally determines" voluntariness (the "orthodox rule") or one where the jury "passes on voluntariness only after the judge has fully and independently resolved the issue against the accused" (the "Massachusetts rule").[2] In the wake of *Jackson,* some states follow the orthodox rule, and some follow the Massachusetts rule.[3]

In providing that hearings on admissibility of confessions must be held out of the hearing of the jury, FRE 104(c) complies with *Jackson* but allows either the orthodox or Massachusetts approach. The Court has come close to holding that voluntariness must be determined in proceedings conducted outside the hearing of the jury, which is *Jackson*'s obvious implication,[4] but this precaution is necessary only if the defendant raises the point.[5] In these proceedings, the burden of proving a confession voluntary rests on the prosecutor, but the point need not be proved beyond reasonable doubt because the preponderance standard applies.[6]

Federal practice
In federal courts, reading FRE 104(c) with the federal statute makes it clear that defendants may present evidence on voluntariness to the jury after the judge resolves the same issue in favor of admissibility

---

§1.11 1. *See* Jackson v. Denno, 378 U.S. 368 (1964); 18 U.S.C. §3501.

2. Jackson v. Denno, 378 U.S. 368 (1964) (under New York procedure, reviewing court cannot tell whether jury "found the confession voluntary and relied upon it, or involuntary and supposedly ignored it").

3. *See* Deeds v. People, 747 P.2d 1266 (Colo. 1987) (doubting juries disregard confessions they find involuntary; judge decides; jury gets credibility instruction). *But see* State v. Ferola, 518 A.2d 1339 (R.I. 1986); Laursen v. State, 634 P.2d 1230, 1231 (Nev. 1981) (following Massachusetts rule).

4. Pinto v. Pierce, 389 U.S. 31 (1967) (since jury that decides guilt or innocence is not to hear involuntary confession, "it would seem prudent to hold voluntariness hearings outside the presence of the jury"); Sims v. Georgia, 385 U.S. 538 (1967) (jury is not to hear confession unless and until judge determines it was voluntary).

5. Wainwright v. Sykes, 433 U.S. 72 (1977); United States v. Espinoza-Seanez, 862 F.2d 526, 535-536 (5th Cir. 1988).

6. Lego v. Twomey, 404 U.S. 477 (1972).

(federal courts follow the Massachusetts rule giving defendant a second bite).[7] Even following the orthodox rule does not mean a court may exclude evidence bearing on voluntariness, since defendants have a constitutional right to offer evidence of this sort when it bears on whether the confession should be believed.[8]

There is some risk that the Massachusetts approach may provide inadequate protection. The combination of the lenient preponderance standard and the fact that a court knows that the jury also can consider voluntariness may lead courts to admit confessions too freely. And of course the Massachusetts approach can introduce the difficulty that confronted *Jackson*, which is that jurors are exposed to, and might consider on the issue of guilt or innocence, a confession they consider involuntary. This possibility can be lost in a general verdict, hence avoiding appellate review. The short answer to these objections is that the Court has held that the preponderance standard suffices, and there is no reason to suppose courts cannot appreciate the risk that juries exposed to confessions might consider them as evidence regardless what they think about voluntariness.

§1.12 Procedure for Determining Preliminary Matters

Regardless whether the judge actually decides preliminary questions or plays a more limited screening role leaving the final decision to the jury,[1] resolving such questions raises four basic procedural issues.[2] Should the jury observe the proceedings? Which party bears the burden of proof? What standard of proof applies? Do the Rules apply on these preliminary questions? FRE 104 addresses the first and the last of these issues. When the accused testifies on preliminary points, the additional question arises whether what he says can be used later.

FRE 104(c) requires hearings outside the jury's presence on the admissibility of confessions and when the accused is a witness (if he requests), and when "the interests of justice require." The language was left vague in the belief that detailed treatment is not feasible and that practical concerns may militate against excluding the jury, particularly if evidence on preliminary matters is likely to be introduced on the merits.

Jury presence

---

7. *See* 18 U.S.C. §3501(a) (confession shall be admitted if judge decides it was "voluntarily made," and court shall "permit the jury to hear relevant evidence on the issue of voluntariness" and instruct it "to give such weight to the confession as the jury feels it deserves under all the circumstances").

8. Crane v. Kentucky, 476 U.S. 683 (1986) ("physical and psychological environment" of confession can be relevant to guilt or innocence, and confessions found voluntary "are not conclusive and may indeed be unworthy of belief").

§1.12 1. The judge alone decides issues of witness qualification, application of hearsay doctrine, and many Best Evidence questions. The judge plays a limited role in authentication, "conditional relevancy," and personal knowledge of witnesses.

2. Some procedural issues relating to the process of admitting or excluding are resolved by reference to particular lines of authority, and are considered elsewhere. On use of prior acts to prove points like intent, *see* §4.15, *infra*. On coconspirator statements, *see* §8.34, *infra*.

FRE 104(c) should be read in connection with FRE 103(c), which tells courts to conduct proceedings to the extent practicable to "prevent inadmissible evidence from being suggested to the jury" by offers of proof or otherwise. In practice, offers and objections tend to merge with the determination of preliminary matters, particularly if the judge asks for something beyond a short statement by the proponent and the adversary in resolving evidence issues. It is sometimes appropriate to exclude juries when parties explain or expand on objections or offers of proof.[3]

There are two obvious reasons to hold hearings on admissibility outside the jury's presence: One is to keep from exposing the jury to evidence that might ultimately be excluded, which would undercut the purposes of excluding it. The other is to keep the objecting party from having to incur additional risks (beyond those that come with objecting) by making arguments needed to support objections. These concerns often call for excluding the jury from hearings on the admissibility of hearsay where the judge normally considers the statement itself in deciding whether it fits an exception. For similar reasons, preliminary questions on privilege claims should often be resolved outside the hearing of the jury.[4]

On the other hand, preliminary questions on matters like personal knowledge of a witness or authentication of physical evidence are less likely to require this precaution.[5] For one thing, the judge plays simply a screening role on these matters because they raise issues of "conditional relevancy" under FRE 104(b). In practice, that means the judge only decides whether there is enough evidence to support a jury finding, and generally that standard is easily met. Moreover, exposing the jury to the foundation facts and surrounding arguments on such points is not likely to be risky. Finally, much of the evidence and argument on these points relate to weight and credibility as well, and of course such matters are for juries to assess.

Allocation of burdens   The burden of proof on preliminary matters relating to admissibility of evidence generally rests on the proponent. Apart from tradition and ease in application, there seem to be three reasons for this allocation. First, usually the offering party is best situated to explain and justify the evidence that it chooses to present and can best aid the court in applying the rule in question. Second, the standard allocation is simply an outgrowth or particular application of the broader idea that a party who asks a court to do anything usually bears the burden of explaining and justifying the request. Third, this allocation is an aspect of the adversary

---

3. Williams v. Board of Regents, 629 F.2d 993, 999-1000 (5th Cir. 1980) (conducting hearing on relevancy outside hearing of jury); United States v. Fosher, 568 F.2d 207, 216 (1st Cir. 1978) (offer of mug shot should be made outside hearing of jury).

4. Courtney v. United States, 390 F.2d 521, 528-529 (9th Cir. 1968) (reversing where prosecutor examined witness on defendant's motivation in marrying, suggesting that purpose was to keep her from testifying), *cert. denied,* 393 U.S. 857.

5. United States v. Peele, 574 F.2d 489, 491 (9th Cir. 1978) (identifying witness who said she was helped by photo testified without hearing outside jury's presence; hearings are needed on competency questions only where "grave doubt" appears).

system in which parties gather and present evidence, and part of the necessary burden is explaining and justifying consideration of the evidence.

In the area of hearsay, the party who offers out-of-court statement against a hearsay objection bears the burden of showing the statement fits an exception.[6] On the other hand, the hearsay doctrine applies only to assertions (mostly verbal statements and assertive conduct), and where a proponent offers evidence of behavior that seems nonassertive, a party objecting on the basis of hearsay bears the burden of showing the actor intended to assert something.[7] The proponent also bears the burden of showing a witness or declarant has the requisite personal knowledge.[8] For witnesses presented as experts, the calling party also bears the burden of showing the necessary qualifications, meaning that the witness has the experience, education, or training necessary to give opinion testimony on a technical matter, although cases applying the *Daubert* standard differ on the question whether this burden should be termed a "burden of proof" as opposed to "satisfying a standard."[9]

Privilege issues represent a departure from the usual pattern. Here the burden is on the one who would exclude, for he must show that a privilege applies.[10] If he carries that burden, the party seeking to overcome the privilege bears the burden of showing some exception applies.[11] Sometimes the privilege claimant has the benefit of presumptions that help carry the burden. For example, the authority of a lawyer to assert the attorney-client privilege on behalf of his client is presumed, and private spousal conversations are presumed to be confidential.[12]

The preponderance standard applies to most court-determined preliminary questions (those relating to admissibility, witness

Standard of proof

---

6. United States v. Lowe, 65 F.3d 1137, 1145 (4th Cir. 1995) (offering party bears burden of satisfying against-interest exception, which includes showing corroborating circumstances), *cert. denied,* 519 U.S. 807.

7. United States v. Hensel, 699 F.2d 18, 30-31 (1st Cir. 1983) (burden of proving assertive intent rests on one who claims such intent; drinking glass with label was not shown to be hearsay), *cert. denied,* 464 U.S. 824.

8. *See* Meder v. Everest & Jennings, Inc., 637 F.2d 1182, 1186-1187 (8th Cir. 1981); Wilcox v. Herbst, 295 P.2d 755, 760 (Wyo. 1956).

9. Arnold v. Loose, 352 F.2d 959, 962 (3d Cir. 1965) (attorney who calls medical expert has burden on qualifications). On the *Daubert* question, compare Meister v. Medical Engineering Corp., 267 F.3d 1123, 1127 n.9 (D.C. Cir. 2001) (proponent had burden of establishing that *Daubert* standard was satisfied by a "preponderance of proof") with Maryland Casualty Co. v. Therm-O-Disc, Inc., 137 F.3d 780, 784 (4th Cir. 1998) (*Daubert* makes no mention of burden of proof, but requires proponent to satisfy "burden of coming forward with evidence" from which trial court can determine that *Daubert* is satisfied) and Cavallo v. Star Enterprise, 100 F.3d 1150, 1157 (4th Cir. 1996) (standard for admitting testimony, including *Daubert*, is not a burden of proof because it "governs whether evidence is admitted, not how persuasive it must be to the factfinder").

10. *See* United States v. Hamilton, 19 F.3d 350, 354 (7th Cir. 1994), *cert. denied,* 513 U.S. 986; Re Grand Jury etc., 603 F.2d 469, 474 (3d Cir. 1979).

11. Pfizer, Inc. v. Lord, 456 F.2d 545, 549 (8th Cir. 1972).

12. Blau v. United States, 340 U.S. 332 (1951) (spousal talks presumptively confidential); United States v. Long, 468 F.2d 755, 757 (8th Cir. 1972) (similar).

competency, and privileges). This standard applies to preliminary questions in civil cases[13] and to preliminary questions affecting evidence offered by both the prosecutor and the defendant in criminal cases.[14] The sources for this broad conclusion are a series of decisions by the Supreme Court. In the setting of coconspirator hearsay, the Court adopted the preponderance standard in *Bourjaily v. United States,* holding that the government bears the burden of establishing the predicate facts for the exception by a preponderance.[15] And in *Huddleston v. United States* the Court brushed off any suggestion that the government needed to satisfy a higher standard when offering prior crimes evidence under FRE 404(b).[16] Also the Court has repeatedly adopted this standard for important constitutional issues relating to evidence.[17]

Where proffered evidence is relevant only if a condition of fact is satisfied, the proponent must offer enough proof of the fact to allow a reasonable jury to find it. There are many difficulties in knowing when this "conditional relevancy" principle applies, but when it does, that is the standard. Trying to quantify the standard is harder because conditional relevancy issues seldom generate formal jury instructions. Probably the preponderance standard applies, and in connection with authentication (the clearest instance of conditional relevancy in operation) juries are expected to resolve them by a preponderance of the evidence.[18]

Evidence rules inapplicable Under FRE 104(a) the judge is not bound by evidence rules in making preliminary decisions,[19] except for privileges.[20] When privilege claims are made, and the purpose of the hearing is to determine the validity of these claims, the court may require disclosure of the material

---

13. *See* Daubert v. Merrell Dow Pharmaceuticals, Inc., 509 U.S. 579 (1993) (preliminary matters under FRE 104 are established by a preponderance); Miller v. Keating, 754 F.2d 507, 511 (3d Cir. 1985) (preponderance standard applies to excited utterance).

14. United States v. Harvey, 117 F.3d 1044, 1049-1050 (7th Cir. 1997) (determining that statement fits admissions doctrine requires proof by preponderance); United States v. Rembert, 863 F.2d 1023, 1028 (D.C. Cir. 1988) (refusing "heightened burden" in authenticating photographic evidence offered by prosecutor; beyond reasonable doubt standard does not apply to admissibility issues).

15. Bourjaily v. United States, 483 U.S. 171 (1987), discussed in §8.34, *infra.*

16. Huddleston v. United States, 485 U.S. 681 (1988), discussed in §4.15, *infra.*

17. Colorado v. Connelly, 479 U.S. 157 (1986) (waiver of *Miranda* rights); United States v. Matlock, 415 U.S. 164 (1974) (suppression motions raising Fourth Amendment); Lego v. Twomey, 404 U.S. 477 (1972) (voluntariness of confessions).

18. *See* Huddleston v. United States, 485 U.S. 681 (1988) (prior act is relevant only if jury "can reasonably conclude" it occurred and defendant did it; court examines all the evidence, decides whether jury could make finding by preponderance).

19. Bourjaily v. United States, 483 U.S. 171 (1987) (courts may consider hearsay in making factual decisions necessary in applying evidence rules); United States v. Matlock, 415 U.S. 164 (1974) (evidence rules do not operate with full force at hearings to determine admissibility of evidence); United States v. Mangual-Garcia, 505 F.3d 1, 8 (1st Cir. 2007) (in ruling on admissibility of coconspirator statements, court may consider any evidence it wishes, regardless of admissibility under the Rules).

20. *See* FRE 104(a) (apart from privileges, rules of evidence do not apply to preliminary questions of admissibility, qualifications, and privileges); FRE 1101(c) (privilege rules apply "at all stages of all actions, cases, and proceedings").

in order to rule except when the claim asserts the privilege against self-incrimination.[21]

While the judge is not bound by most evidence rules in deciding preliminary questions, courts have traditionally been reluctant to let the judge decide whether a hearsay exception applies by relying on the very statement being offered. The possibility of "bootstrapping" (or circularity) arises in four common situations involving both exceptions for statements by agents, the coconspirator exception, and the excited utterance exception. Statements offered under these provisions often assert a fact that is central in applying the exceptions: For example, many coconspirator statements directly assert or imply in the strong sense (intentionally expressing) that there is a conspiracy and defendant is involved. If such a statement can itself be offered to prove these very facts, it seems to bootstrap itself into admissibility and the judge's decision on admissibility seems circular.

By conventional wisdom, if not settled practice, courts deciding admissibility of statements offered under these exceptions once required "independent evidence" of the predicate facts. Sometimes the cases even said the judge had to decide the predicate facts entirely on the basis of independent evidence. There is some force to this view because the fact that the various exceptions impose these conditions implies that statements are not to be trusted to prove what they say unless they survive scrutiny, and taking them as proof of their own provenance conflicts with the skepticism giving rise to the condition.

FRE 104(a), which says the judge "is not bound by the rules of evidence" (other than privileges) in deciding questions of admissibility, changed traditional practice. Obviously this language can be read to mean that judges can find preliminary facts like conspiracy and agency by relying on the statement. In the setting of coconspirator statements the Supreme Court decided in the *Bourjaily* case that the judge may indeed look at the statements in determining the issue of conspiracy, reasoning that out-of-court statements are not necessarily unreliable (they are only "presumed unreliable") and that the "sum" of all the relevant pieces of evidence (including the statement being offered) "may well be greater than its constituent parts." In 1998, the coconspirator exception was amended to adopt the *Bourjaily* holding, including the hint in *Bourjaily* that at least *some* independent evidence should still be required.[22] At the same time, the exceptions for authorized admissions and for admissions by agents were amended to adopt the *Bourjaily* approach, meaning that the statement counts deciding

---

21. United States v. Zolin, 491 U.S. 554 (1989) (no per se rule bars disclosure in applying crime-fraud exception to attorney-client privilege, but court should require factual showing supporting good-faith belief that exception applies).

22. *See* Bourjaily v. United States, 483 U.S. 171 (1987). *See also* FRE 801(d)(2)(E) and discussion of this point in §8.34, *infra*.

whether the necessary conditions are satisfied, but independent evidence is also required.[23]

Excited utterances pose essentially the same challenge since they almost always assert the happening of the event on which admissibility depends. As in the coconspirator cases, there is usually independent evidence of the exciting event, but problems arise when the declarant fell or suffered sudden severe pain (like a heart attack) while by himself: Even here, typically the declarant behaves in some way that strongly confirms the sudden onset of pain or exhibits physical symptoms of pain (sweating, elevated heart rate), and these points are themselves "independent" evidence of the exciting events, and should suffice under FRE 104(a) to prove this point. When literally nothing but the statement tends to prove the event, here arguably the statement should be admitted as proof of the event because there are many additional reasons to suppose the declarant will speak accurately, including his need for medical help and the absence of motive to falsify.[24]

Protecting criminal defendants FRE 104 places no direct limit on the use at trial of testimony taken in hearings on preliminary questions. If the jury is present, it is exposed to such testimony. Even if it is excluded, testimony in such hearings is sometimes later offered under a variety of theories, most notably as admissions and for impeachment. Mainly to permit criminal defendants to invoke protective doctrines without giving up their Fifth Amendment right not to testify, FRE 104 imposes one limit: In testifying on a preliminary matter a criminal defendant does not subject himself to cross-examination on "other issues in the case," and this minimal protection seems essential if defendants are to have any real opportunity to invoke the various exclusionary doctrines. Without it the accused would face a risk of being subjected to broad questioning, and there is only a narrow constitutional doctrine (explored below) that bars some testimony on preliminary matters from later use at trial. While FRE 104(d) entitles the accused to testify in preliminary hearings without opening himself to cross on "other issues," it does not follow that he is immune from questioning then on the matters to which he testifies.[25]

The narrow constitutional doctrine is a product of standing rules and the *Simmons* rule in Fourth Amendment suppression cases. The Court once endorsed a doctrine of "automatic" standing that let a defendant suppress an item seized by police if it was claimed that he possessed the item (which was often true). However, in *United States v. Salvucci* the Court held that defendants may invoke the Fourth Amendment only if "their own" rights were violated, adding later that ownership does not confer standing unless defendant has "a legitimate expectation of

---

23. *See* the discussion of FRE 801(d)(2)(C) in §8.31, and the discussion of FRE 801(d)(2)(D) in §8.32, *infra*.

24. *See* the discussion of FRE 803(2) in §8.36, *infra*.

25. *See* United States v. Jaswal, 47 F.3d 539, 543 (2d Cir. 1995) (on direct in suppression hearing, defendant went beyond saying he had not been advised of his rights, claiming that agents fabricated his confession; government properly cross-examined about accuracy, for purposes of rebuttal and impeachment).

privacy."[26] *Salvucci* rested largely on the fact that the *Simmons* rule bars the government from offering during its case-in-chief testimony given by the accused in a suppression hearing. That led the majority in *Salvucci* to say that the premise underlying automatic standing was gone: Requiring defendant to concede an interest in or connection to the matter to be suppressed cannot under *Simmons* convict him thereafter. *Simmons* was a bank robbery case where defendant tried to suppress a suitcase containing a sack and holster, and the Court broadly held that when defendant testifies in a suppression motion under the Fourth Amendment, the government may not use his testimony "on the issue of guilt" at trial.[27]

Simmons means that testimony by the accused attempting to suppress evidence allegedly seized in violation of the Fourth Amendment cannot be used as substantive evidence, thus being excludable from the prosecutor's case-in-chief.[28] The same is true of testimony by defendants seeking to exclude evidence for violations of the Fifth and Sixth Amendments, for here too defendants cannot make much headway without giving testimony that could hurt them at trial.[29] There is, however, no general bar independent of *Simmons* that prevents use of defendant's testimony in hearings on preliminary matters. Thus if defendants testify in hearings on ordinary evidence issues, prosecutors should be able to offer their testimony later if it is relevant and not subject to some other exclusionary rule.[30] And *Simmons* does not block use of testimony by the accused in suppression motions when it is later offered to impeach his trial testimony. Illegally obtained evidence can itself be offered at trial to impeach the accused if he testifies even if taken in violation of the Fourth, Fifth, or Sixth Amendments,[31] and testimony in support of efforts to invoke those protections is also usable to impeach.[32]

26. *See* Rawlings v. Kentucky, 448 U.S. 98 (1980) (ownership not enough); United States v. Salvucci, 448 U.S. 83 (1980) (abolishing automatic standing); Rakas v. Illinois, 439 U.S. 128 (1978) (expectation-of-privacy); Brown v. United States, 411 U.S. 223 (1973) (automatic standing might be unnecessary); Jones v. United States, 362 U.S. 257 (1960) (automatic standing).

27. Simmons v. United States, 390 U.S. 377 (1968) (defendant would be deterred if he could only prove standing with words that "may later be used to incriminate him").

28. *See* United States v. Williams, 754 F.2d 672, 676 (6th Cir. 1985); United States v. Gomez-Diaz, 712 F.2d 949, 950-952 & n.1 (5th Cir. 1983), *cert. denied,* 464 U.S. 1051.

29. United States v. Charles, 738 F.2d 686, 698 (5th Cir. 1984) (testimony in *Miranda* suppression motion could not be used at trial except to impeach).

30. *See* United States v. Benson, 640 F.2d 136, 138-139 (8th Cir. 1981) (statements in hearing leading to unwithdrawn guilty plea not excludable). *But see* Gordon v. United States, 383 F.2d 936, 941 (D.C. Cir. 1967) (testimony by defendant in hearing to decide whether convictions can be used to impeach would be admissible only to impeach), *cert. denied,* 390 U.S. 1029.

31. *See* §6.46, *infra.*

32. *See* United States v. Jaswal, 47 F.3d 539, 543 (2d Cir. 1995); United States v. Beltran-Guttierrez, 19 F.3d 1287, 1289-1290 (9th Cir. 1994) (both approving use of suppression hearing testimony to impeach).

§1.13   Jury-Determined Issues (Conditional Relevancy, Authenticity, Personal Knowledge)

FRE 104(b) says the jury decides whether a condition of fact has been fulfilled if the relevancy of evidence depends on it. Juries do the work of sorting out various pieces of fragmented evidence and deciding whether the resulting picture supports conviction or acquittal or recovery or rejection of claims. FRE 104(b) is useful in codifying the point that separate items of evidence may be interdependent, so accepting or rejecting one item can make others rise in importance or fall away altogether. And FRE 104(b) confirms that juries play a vital role in assessing such matters.

"Connecting up" evidence   When coordinate facts supporting a proposition can be proved only through testimony by two or more witnesses or testimony tending to establish several related points, courts speak of the need of "connecting up" initial proof with other proof.[1] Assuming enough evidence is offered to permit a finding of both, it is generally constructive to let the jury decide whether both are proved. If things were otherwise—if the judge decided whether such factual conditions were proved—the job of factfinding could become largely a shared responsibility and the trial judge would often decide critical points that juries could well decide.

One illustrative example of conditional relevancy might be proving notice or warning to X by means of an oral statement, where the statement is arguably irrelevant without some indication that X heard it. Arguably proof of the statement should be admitted only if there is also enough evidence that X heard it to enable a jury to find that he did.[2] Arguably if reasonable people could not conclude from the evidence that X heard the statement, proof that it was spoken should be excluded.[3] Of course a single witness in one breath might well provide ample evidence of both speaking and hearing: If he describes the scene and what was said, the witness is likely to have given enough evidence to support a conclusion that X heard the warning, even if the witness never expressly addresses that point. The example makes sense in implicitly recognizing that sometimes proof is fragmented among several or many witnesses. If a barrier separated speaker W from listener X, conceivably W (or a witness standing close to her) would doubt whether the warning was heard, and conceivably X (or a witness standing close to him) would be in a good position to say that it was (or was not) heard.

---

§1.13   1. *See* §1.3, *supra* (motion to strike evidence).

2. *See* ACN to FRE 104(b) (suggesting this example).

3. *See* Gila Valley, G.&N.&R. Co. v. Hall, 232 U.S. 94 (1914) (excluding evidence that someone 20 yards away said wheel was defective, since court was not convinced plaintiff heard); Alvarado v. Anderson, 346 P.2d 73 (Cal. App. 1959) (excluding evidence that someone shouted to plaintiff not to dive from handrail of high platform from which diving board was removed; judge could decide foundation evidence was not enough to support finding that warning was heard in midst of crowd).

There are several ways to handle this situation. A court might admit proof that the warning was spoken, subject to a motion to strike if the proponent does not offer enough evidence to support a finding that it was heard. Or the court might ask for assurance from the proponent that further proof will be forthcoming and exclude evidence of what was said if the assurance is not provided: FRE 104(b) says the court may admit evidence "subject to" introduction of enough evidence to support a finding that the condition is satisfied. Or the court might insist that the first witness testify that the warning was heard, and presumably he could also prove its substance or tenor: FRE 104(b) says the court may admit evidence "upon" introduction of enough other evidence to support a finding that the condition is satisfied.[4] Finally, assuming enough evidence is offered to support all the necessary facts, the court might instruct the jury that it should pay attention to proof of one fact (warning was spoken) only if it concludes that the other necessary fact is proved (warning was heard), although ordinarily such instructions are given only if requested. In deciding whether there is enough evidence to prove the necessary points, the court should consider all the proof presented to the jury.[5]

Unfortunately the notion of conditional relevancy is deeply problematic. In even the simplest trials, much evidence makes sense only in conjunction with other evidence, and at almost every step of the way it would be plausible, in an arid and coldly logical sense, to say that the proof at hand can only make a difference if some other point is proved or accepted on the basis of common experience in the world. Yet stopping a trial to entertain such arguments, decide which point should be proved first, obtain a commitment to prove some other point, assess the sufficiency of proof, and even instruct the jury—doing all that would confound trials, confuse everyone, and hamstring lawyers and judges.

Beyond this practical point lie further difficulties:

First, it is often a close question whether proof of one point also tends to prove another point when the two seem separate but dependent. In conspiracy cases, defendants often complain that proof of apparently coordinated acts by one or more people does not prove conspiracy. Hence, the argument runs, evidence of acts by one is not relevant against others, or is at best only conditionally relevant, and such evidence should be admitted only on proof of agreement or tacit understanding among members to act in concert for a criminal purpose when the acts show the operation of the venture. The objection appeals to the commonsense notion that waiting in a car outside a bank does not prove a connection with the gunman inside demanding money from the teller. In reality, typically other proof does tend to tie

Often a close question

4. Huddleston v. United States, 485 U.S. 681 (1988) (court exercises "the broadest sort of discretion in controlling the order of proof") (court may let proponent prove similar act and later assess whether there is enough evidence to support jury finding that defendant did it).
5. Huddleston v. United States, 485 U.S. 681 (1988) (in assessing sufficiency under FRE 104(b), court "must consider all the evidence presented to the jury").

one conspirator to another but may be circumstantial—the two are shown to be friends, to have engaged in other ventures or attended meetings together or talked to one another, and so forth. In the end, much proof of what one or another of them did increases the likelihood that the two were cooperating but leaves room for doubt. In this setting, courts overwhelmingly reject objections couched in terms of relevancy, although spectacular gaps sometimes produce other results.[6]

Logically false

Second, the concept of conditional relevancy seems to assume a proposition that is intuitively true but logically false. The proposition is that if two independent points must be proved to make a difference, evidence raising the probability of one does not raise the probability of both. But raising the probability of one of two independent points also raises the probability of both being true.[7] In the setting of a spoken warning, proving the warning was spoken raises the probability that the warning was both spoken and heard even without proof of the latter point, and even in circumstances in which proving what was said does not itself seem to show what was heard.

Could have paralyzing effect

Third, focusing too much on conditional relevancy could have paralyzing effect and might undercut jury factfinding. Suppose the question is what speed a car was going at the time of a highway accident, and the proffered evidence is a sighting of a car exceeding the speed limit 30 miles before the accident. In common experience, drivers on an open highway cruise for long periods at about the same speed, but they change speed if weather or road conditions change, and sometimes when distractions arise in the car, or traffic conditions change, and for many other reasons. There is no rule or tradition that answers the question whether these points should be viewed as conditions affecting the admissibility of testimony describing the speeding car, but any of them might be. A court is unlikely to think all these conditions should be addressed in instructions or by way of regulating or excluding the sighting evidence, but the reason is probably that judges are generally reluctant and have too much common sense to intervene in these ways—nothing in the concept itself or the apparent meaning of FRE 104(b) saves courts from this course. Dividing elements of proof too finely and treating each as a condition indispensable to a conclusion may make the factfinder less likely to draw the conclusion.[8]

---

6. *Compare* United States v. Cote, 744 F.2d 913, 916 (2d Cir. 1984) (reversible error to admit other acts) *with* United States v. Ortiz-Rengifo, 832 F.2d 722, 724-725 (2d Cir. 1987); *and* United States v. Penney, 416 F.2d 850, 852 (6th Cir. 1969), *cert. denied*, 398 U.S. 932 (rejecting such objection).

7. *See* Ball, The Myth of Conditional Relevancy, 14 Ga. L. Rev. 435 (1980) (demonstrating this point and arguing that FRE 104(b) should be repealed).

8. Suppose speed at the time of sighting, similarity of traffic conditions and absence of distraction in the car must all be shown before speed at sighting may be considered proof of speed at impact. If these points are independent, a rational factfinder would have to think each reaches a probability of close to 80 percent to draw the required conclusion (since multiplying that number by itself three times produces a probability of 51.2 percent), but might well credit the sighting testimony as proof of speed at impact if no conditions were imposed even if it thought the witness was just slightly

For anyone who thinks jury factfinding is too casual and outcomes are too much affected by sympathies unrelated to the merits, such precautions might seem commendable. It is even arguable that mechanisms designed to address this general issue are inadequate (motions for summary judgment, new trial, and judgment as a matter of law) or would benefit from additional support. But there is no sign, either in the history of FRE 104 or in tradition, that the conditional relevancy notion was intended to enable courts to do on a "micro" level what they do on a "macro" level by these other procedural mechanisms. Outside the area of authentication, few cases actually consider conditional relevancy issues.[9]

Authentication problems are generally allocated to the jury under FRE 104(b). The framers made it clear that questions on authenticity of documentary evidence[10] and identification of other kinds of real evidence[11] are examples of conditional relevancy for the jury to resolve under FRE 104(b).

Jury decides authentication

In applying the Best Evidence doctrine, courts turn over to the jury some issues relating to authenticity. That doctrine requires a party who would prove the content of writings (also recordings or photographs) to produce those very items or offer a reasonable excuse for not doing so. When a party offers other evidence of contents, like testimony describing what a document said, the opponent might raise questions such as whether the writing "ever existed," whether "another" produced at trial "is the original," and whether the other evidence "correctly reflects the contents" of the original, and these questions are "for the trier of fact to determine as in the case of other issues of fact."[12]

---

more likely to be right than wrong in saying the vehicle was speeding. *See generally* Nesson, The Evidence or the Event? On Judicial Proof and the Acceptability of Verdicts, 98 Harv L. Rev. 1357, 1388 (1985) (conjunctions of probability matter for various items of evidence, so multiplied probabilities should be more than 50 percent to make finding on single point; conjunctions do not matter for elements in claims or defenses; plaintiff can win if probability is 60 percent that defendant was negligent and 60 percent that negligence caused injury, although conjoint probability is less than 50 percent).

9. Huddleston v. United States, 485 U.S. 681 (1988) (proving other acts to show intent raises questions of conditional relevancy) (other acts are relevant only on condition that jury decide defendant committed them); United States v. Costa, 947 F.2d 919, 923-924 (11th Cir. 1991) (testimony that defendant was known as drug importer but not smuggler raised conditional relevancy issue if there was enough to interpret testimony as tending to clear defendant of charged crime).

10. *See* ACN to FRE 901 (showing authenticity or identity "falls in the category of relevancy dependent upon fulfillment of a condition of fact"); United States v. Carriger, 592 F.2d 312, 316 (6th Cir. 1979); Re James E. Long Constr. Co., 557 F.2d 1039, 1040-1041 (4th Cir. 1977).

11. United States v. Chaplinski, 579 F.2d 373, 374-375 (5th Cir. 1978) (admitting envelopes of cocaine; adequacy of chain of custody was for jury to decide); United States v. Weiner, 578 F.2d 757, 772-773 (9th Cir. 1978) (in securities fraud trial, admitting 1968 workpapers despite claim that chain of custody was incomplete; jury is free to evaluate authenticity).

12. United States v. Gerhart, 538 F.2d 807, 809 (8th Cir. 1976) (when proponent proves contents of writing by secondary evidence, opposing party may attack, which goes to weight and not admissibility).

Jury decides personal knowledge

It is ultimately for the jury to determine under FRE 104(b) whether a witness satisfies the personal knowledge requirement of FRE 602. Under standard practice, the proponent establishes in the initial phase of the direct that the witness personally observed the acts or occurrences about which he is to testify. If objection is raised on this score, the question is for the jury to decide and the judge plays only the screening role envisioned by FRE 104(b): The witness may testify if enough evidence of knowledge is offered to enable a reasonable jury to conclude that he had it. The opportunity threshold is not high, and even a brief chance to observe suffices.[13] When the objection is raised, it is usually better not to allow questioning to proceed until the calling party makes a sufficient showing to support the necessary jury finding.[14]

D. LIMITED ADMISSIBILITY

FRE 105

When evidence which is admissible as to one party or for one purpose but not admissible as to another party or for another purpose is admitted, the court, upon request, shall restrict the evidence to its proper scope and instruct the jury accordingly.

§1.14 Evidence Admissible on One Issue But Not Others

Inevitably much evidence can be used for only limited purposes, for three reasons. One is that there are many restrictions on the use of evidence found in such doctrines as those governing hearsay, impeachment, and various aspects of relevancy. These restrictions bar some but not all uses. Another reason is that there are some restrictions on the forms or mechanisms by which various points may be proved, and these restrictions apply to certain strategies but not others. Third, modern trials may involve multiple claims, charges, and defenses, each resting on its own substantive principles that in turn make different kinds of evidence relevant or irrelevant,

---

13. Folio Impressions, Inc. v. Byer California, 937 F.2d 759, 763-764 (2d Cir. 1991) (test is whether "reasonable trier of fact could believe" witness had knowledge); United States v. Mooney, 417 F.2d 936, 939 (8th Cir. 1969) (identification testimony based on 15-second view on closed-circuit TV), *cert. denied,* 397 U.S. 1029.

14. United States v. Davis, 792 F.2d 1299, 1303-1305 (5th Cir. 1986) (proponent bears "initial burden" to show knowledge; witness was asked whether he knew "of his own knowledge" when guns were released from property room and he said yes after saying he put them there himself), *cert. denied,* 479 U.S. 964. *See* FRE 602 (wording suggests that calling party shows knowledge before proceeding further).

important or unimportant. Hence if there were no rule of limited admissibility of the sort embodied in FRE 105, it would pretty much have to be invented.[1]

Out-of-court statements may be admitted for many limited purposes even if the hearsay doctrine would block their use to prove what they assert. Common limited uses include impeachment (considered further below), showing verbal acts that constitute crimes or civil transactions, and showing what information was conveyed to one who heard or read the statement. More challenging limited uses involve statements offered to prove the speaker's state of mind either on the theory that they are nonhearsay circumstantial evidence or on the theory that they are hearsay that fit the state-of-mind exception.[2] Out-of-court statements are often admitted to show the basis for expert testimony even when they cannot be used to prove what they assert, although some such statements may be used for all purposes under FRE 803(18), which creates an exception for learned treatises to the extent "called to the attention" of an expert witness on cross or relied upon during direct.[3]

Out-of-court statements

Many relevancy provisions in Article IV block or restrict broad uses of various kinds of circumstantial evidence but allow narrower specific uses. In practice, sometimes the issues in a case are such that the only possible use of certain evidence is the broad use that is forbidden, so the effect is to exclude the evidence. But sometimes the issues invite a narrower permissible use, and the evidence is admitted for that limited purpose. For example, FRE 407 bars proof of subsequent remedial measures as evidence of negligence but allows such proof to show ownership or control of the premises. Thus evidence that defendant fixed the stairs after plaintiff fell would not be admissible to prove defendant was negligent in maintaining the stairs but might be admissible to show he was in charge of the stairs.[4] In this example and countless others, the proof covered by the restrictive rule could be admitted for a narrow purpose (such as showing control) but not for a broad purpose (such as showing negligence).

Relevancy limits

In any such case, admitting such evidence involves taking advantage of the principle in FRE 105. Of course the mere fact that the principle of limited admissibility could apply does not mean it should. If there is little or no doubt, for example, that defendant controls the stairs where plaintiff fell, either because the point is admitted by the pleadings or because it is directly shown by other evidence that defendant does not seriously

---

§1.14 1. *See* United States v. Abel, 469 U.S. 45 (1984) (no rule excludes evidence admissible for one purpose but not another; it would be "strange" to exclude competent evidence of bias merely because it also depicted the witness as a liar).

2. *See* Syracuse Broadcasting Corp. v. Newhouse, 295 F.2d 269, 276 (2d Cir. 1961) (false articles about plaintiff in defendant newspapers were hearsay but would be admissible to show state of mind of advertisers). *See also* §8.20, *infra.*

3. *See* discussion of FRE 703 in §7.10, the discussion of FRE 705 in §7.14, and the discussion of FRE 803(18) in §8.60, all *infra.*

4. Woolard v. Mobil Pipe Line Co., 479 F.2d 557, 563 (5th Cir. 1973) (subsequent measures may be shown under limiting instruction on question whether defendant controlled premises), *cert. denied,* 414 U.S. 1025.

contest, there may be little need for additional circumstantial evidence of defendant's control. Admitting proof of the repair would invite jury misuse of the evidence as proof that defendant had been negligent, and a court might well exclude the evidence under FRE 403 rather than admit the evidence under FRE 105 and the exemption in FRE 407. The short of it is that whenever there is a possibility of admitting evidence for a limited purpose, there is also the possibility of excluding evidence as bringing unnecessary risk of prejudice or confusion of issues.

Impeachment   Among the five methods of impeachment, three of them usually bring serious problems of limiting use of the evidence to its proper purpose.[5] Prior inconsistent statements are typically admissible to show vacillation but not to prove what they assert. Prior bad acts or convictions are often usable to suggest that the witness is untruthful, but often when the witness is a party the bad acts and convictions cannot be used to show he committed the charged crime or committed the tort or other act underlying a civil claim or defense. Impeachment by contradiction often involves evidence that would otherwise be excluded under some Rule or constitutional restriction. It is admissible only to refute something the witness has said (and suggest more generally that he should not be believed) and not to prove other points that it might naturally tend to prove.

Character evidence   Finally, it is worth taking note of the rules governing character evidence. These rules are too complicated to recite or even sum up here, but they block some mechanisms and some forms of proof for some purposes, but leave those same mechanisms and forms available for other purposes. Often, for example, specific acts by a person may not be offered to show his character, but may be shown when they are relevant in other ways. And often specific acts by a party or witness may not be proved through testimony by others if the purpose is to show the character of the party or witness, but such acts may be proved through testimony by others if the purpose is to show something else (like bias or intent). In these instances, the restrictions that the Rules impose on the form and mechanisms of proof when the purpose is to show character do not block resort to those forms or mechanisms when the purpose is to show something else.[6]

§1.15 Evidence Admissible Against One Party But Not Others

Evidence is routinely admissible against one defendant but not another in a criminal case, and courts routinely admit such evidence with

---

5. The other two methods (showing bias or lack of capacity) can raise issues of limited admissibility too. *See* Sprinkle v. Davis, 111 F.2d 925, 931-932 (4th Cir. 1940) (proof of collateral source payments to plaintiff bore slightly on bias, and excluding would not have been reversible error).

6. United States v. Abel, 469 U.S. 45 (1984) (if purpose were to suggest *M*'s lack of veracity, fact that he and defendant belonged to secret club requiring members to lie to protect others could only be explored on cross, but *E* could testify to this point since point was to show *M* was biased).

limiting instructions. Long ago the Supreme Court praised this approach as necessary to the jury system and criticized "unfounded speculation" that jurors might disregard limiting instructions.[1] Routinely courts in criminal trials admit prior convictions of one of several codefendants and real evidence like guns or demonstrative evidence like photographs that are linked only to one defendant. Here courts rely on instructions to guide the jury, and only occasionally do the unwanted "spillover effects" require such evidence to be excluded altogether.[2]

Where the government offers an admission or confession by one defendant that implicates another by name or reference ("Bob and I robbed the bank" or "he and I robbed the bank"), there is an important constitutional limit on the doctrine of limited admissibility. In _Bruton v. United States_, the Supreme Court discarded the qualified endorsement it had earlier given to the practice of admitting a statement by one defendant and relying on limiting instructions to protect the rights of the other defendant named or mentioned in the statement.[3] In _Bruton_, the Court concluded that the "basic premise" that a jury could disregard such a confession in assessing the guilt of the other person had been "repudiated" by the decision holding that the judge must determine whether a confession was voluntary before submitting it to the jury, and by the amendment to the Criminal Rules authorizing severance where a defendant might be prejudiced by a joint trial.[4] While there are ways to avoid or accommodate _Bruton_, the case continues to mean it is constitutional error, in trials of more than one defendant, to use the admissions doctrine to admit statements by one that incriminate others by name or obvious reference.[5] Of course _Bruton_ does not require exclusion of statements by co-offenders that fit exceptions to the hearsay doctrine apart from the admissions doctrine, where such other exceptions would make the statements generally admissible against persons other than the declarant.[6]

> **Criminal cases:** _Bruton_ issues

In civil litigation, it seldom happens that evidence is excluded altogether because it is incompetent as against one or more parties, where it is competent as against one or more other parties. FRE 105 clearly contemplates that in such situations the evidence will be routinely received, subject only to the right of objecting parties to

> **Civil cases**

---

§1.15 1. Delli Paoli v. United States, 352 U.S. 232 (1957) (jury system assumes jury can follow clear instructions); Opper v. United States, 348 U.S. 84 (1954) (dismissing as "unfounded speculation" the idea that jurors disregarded clear instructions).

2. _See_ United States v. Figueroa, 618 F.2d 934, 946-948 (2d Cir. 1980); Castro v. United States, 296 F.2d 540, 543 (5th Cir. 1961).

3. Bruton v. United States, 391 U.S. 123 (1968) (jury system not threatened by withholding evidence that is devastating to codefendant, and unreliable because untested by cross since speaker cannot be called; severance can protect defendant).

4. _See_ Jackson v. Denno, 378 U.S. 368 (1964). _See also_ FRCrimP 14 (amended in 1966), and United States v. Johnson, 478 F.2d 1129, 1133 (5th Cir. 1973) (error to deny severance motion where confession by one directly implicates movant).

5. _See_ generally the discussion in §8.28, _infra_.

6. United States v. Saks, 964 F.2d 1514, 1525 (5th Cir. 1992); United States v. Vazquez, 857 F.2d 857, 864 (1st Cir. 1988).

appropriate limiting instructions. It is in criminal cases, particularly in respect of admissions by one defendant incriminating himself and another, that complete exclusion is likely to be required. But there is no doubt that even in civil cases the trial judge may altogether exclude evidence on account of its incompetence as to one party where the danger of jury misuse of the evidence as proof against that party is too high to ignore.[7] FRE 403 is clearly broad enough to justify this result.

§1.16   Limiting Instructions

When evidence is admissible against one party but not others, or for some purpose but not others, FRE 105 requires the court on request to restrict the evidence to its proper scope by instructing the jury.[1] It is incumbent on trial counsel to request limiting instructions where desired, and ordinarily it is not reversible error to admit evidence without them when no request is made.[2] Occasionally, however, the evidence is so obviously admissible only for a limited purpose and so clearly threatens serious prejudice to the opponent that there are reversals on the basis of the plain error doctrine even in the absence of a request for instructions.[3]

Instructions must be requested   There are sound reasons for leaving it up to the opponent to ask for a limiting instruction. In the first place, the requirement serves much the same purposes as the requirement for timely and sufficient objections—it helps the court avoid error, allows the proponent to remedy any problems in his proof, and brings an end to litigation after each side has had a fair procedural opportunity to present his case. In the second place, this manner of proceeding is wise in leaving to the opposing trial counsel the option of concluding that he is better off without an instruction than with one since an instruction would remind the jury

---

7. Re Beverly Hills Fire Litig., 695 F.2d 207, 217-218 (6th Cir. 1982) (in class action against makers of aluminum wiring arising out of night club fire killing 165 people, excluding documents that were admissions by some defendants but inadmissible hearsay against others) (but "dilemma caused by these exhibits" argues against bifurcation of liability and causation since documents might be admitted under FRE 105 with limiting instructions if both issues are tried).

§1.16   1. Frederick v. Kirby Tankships, Inc., 205 F.3d 1277 (11th Cir. 2000), *cert. denied*, 531 U.S. 813; United States v. Werme, 939 F.2d 108, 113-115 (3d Cir. 1991) (government brought out that witness pled guilty; error to refuse defense request for limiting instruction).

2. United States v. Rhodes, 63 F.3d 1449, 1453-1454 (D.C. Cir. 1995) (no error to fail to give limiting instruction on use of statement to impeach; defense may have chosen to forgo instruction "to avoid highlighting the evidence"); United States v. Jefferson, 925 F.2d 1242, 1258 (10th Cir. 1991) (defense did not request limiting instruction for prior crimes; no error in not giving one).

3. United States v. Copelin, 996 F.2d 379, 381-382 (D.C. Cir. 1993) (reversing for failure to give limiting instruction even though defendant asked for none). *But see* United States v. Lewis, 693 F.2d 189, 196-197 (D.C. Cir. 1982) (court must instruct sua sponte only if evidence has potential for substantial prejudice; court must offer chance to waive instruction, and failing to do so is reversible error).

of what it has heard, re-emphasize the evidence, and perhaps suggest a use that is best left unmentioned. The necessity of requesting limiting instructions creates strategy problems of its own. If the request is to serve purposes similar to those served by objections, it must be specific. Hence trial counsel has two options—either requesting an instruction that the evidence be considered only for particular purposes, in which case there is a double problem of anticipating all limited purposes and tipping counsel's hand to the adversary, or requesting an instruction that the evidence not be considered for a particular purpose, in which case the risk of emphasizing dangerous and forbidden purposes increases.

The notion that instructions do more to sensitize the jury to evidence than to dispel the risk that the jury will misuse it appears to rest more on common sense than empirical data. But this idea has been recognized by decisions and commentators,[4] and there is some empirical support for it.[5] Even if jurors could follow limiting instructions and were willing to do so, there remains doubt on their capacity to remember them. This latter difficulty may be alleviated if instructions are given in writing to take to deliberations, a practice that the judge may (but need not) follow.

Instruction may sensitize jury

The timing of limiting instructions may be critical. The bulk of authorities hold that the judge has discretion either immediately to instruct or to include limiting instructions with the general charge at the end of the case.[6] Occasionally, however, courts require immediate instructions on the ground that the passage of time and accumulation of other evidence make it hard to accomplish the intended purpose at the end of the case.[7]

Timing of instruction

Ordinarily judges should not give limiting instructions without any request and should not insist on giving instructions if the intended beneficiary objects. Still, the area of discretion is broad, and sometimes instructions may be given over objection.[8] The court should, however, solicit and respect the views of trial counsel on the desirability of

---

4. United States v. Bobbitt, 450 F.2d 685, 689, 693 (D.C. Cir. 1971) (defense "may have rejoiced" that court did not instruct). *See also* Broeder, The University of Chicago Jury Project, 38 Neb. L. Rev. 744, 754 (1959); 5 Busch, Law Tactics in Jury Trials §706; Keeton, Trial Tactics and Methods §4.18 (2d ed. 1973).

5. Letters to Yale Law Journal quoted in Comment, "Other Crimes Evidence at Trial: Of Balancing and Other Matters," 70 Yale L.J. 763, 777 (1961) (participant in jury project reported inability or unwillingness to understand or follow instruction on use of criminal record to impeach; jurors used record to conclude defendant was bad, hence probably guilty).

6. United States v. Misle Bus & Equip. Co., 967 F.2d 1227, 1234 (8th Cir. 1992); United States v. Sliker, 751 F.2d 477, 487 (2d Cir. 1984), *cert. denied,* 471 U.S. 1137.

7. United States v. Bobbitt, 450 F.2d 685, 691 (D.C. Cir. 1971) (when other crimes are introduced to impeach, court "should give an appropriate instruction immediately before or after"). *See also* Jones v. United States, 385 F.2d 296 (D.C. Cir. 1967); Menendez v. United States, 393 F.2d 312, 315 (5th Cir. 1968), *cert. denied,* 393 U.S. 1029.

8. *See* Lakeside v. Oregon, 435 U.S. 333 (1978) (instructing jury to draw no inference from fact that defendant did not testify despite defense request not to instruct); United States v. McGann, 431 F.2d 1104, 1109 (5th Cir. 1970) (similar), *cert. denied,* 401 U.S. 919.

instructions, to protect the role of counsel in assessing the risk of jury misuse of the evidence.[9]

E. RULE OF COMPLETENESS

> **FRE 106**
>
> When a writing or recorded statement or part thereof is introduced by a party, an adverse party may require the introduction at that time of any other part or any other writing or recorded statement which ought in fairness to be considered contemporaneously with it.

§1.17 Getting Related Material In—When and How, Limits

When parts of a written or recorded statement are offered, FRE 106 entitles opposing parties to introduce other parts that shed light on the parts already introduced. The opportunity may come almost immediately after the proponent first mentions the statement (during cross-examination of a testifying witness or at the time part of the writing or recording is offered) or later when other parties call witnesses and present evidence. FRE 106 actually goes further because it entitles other parties to require the proponent, as part of the original presentation, to include other parts of the writing or recorded statement that ought in fairness to be considered with the parts that the proponent wants to use.[1] The notion is that sometimes waiting until later is just not good enough, and contextual data is more easily understood if it is provided in the first instance. In effect, FRE 106 lets the court interrupt a party's presentation to permit the other side to insist that other relevant parts of a statement be offered, and in effect to offer them.

Good reasons to offer only part   There are many good reasons for the proponent to offer only part of a writing. One may be that only part is relevant, other parts being irrelevant or prejudicial. Another is that the proponent wants to use a writing to prove a particular point (perhaps the speed of a car at the time of impact, and not the identity of the driver or whether he was intoxicated). A third good reason is that part of the writing may be admissible and part may not, as might be true if a court decides to admit a medical

---

9. Delgado v. State, 235 S.W.3d 244, 250 nn.24 & 25 (Tex. Crim. App. 2007) (whether to request limiting instruction relating to extraneous offenses is matter of trial strategy) (quoting authors of this Treatise on reasons to leave it to objecting party).

§1.17 1. Beech Aircraft Corp. v. Rainey, 488 U.S. 153 (1988) (out-of-context statement "may create such prejudice that it is impossible to repair by a subsequent presentation"); United States v. Sutton, 801 F.2d 1346, 1369 (D.C. Cir. 1986) (best to let prosecutor introduce inculpatory parts of coconspirator statements, then let defense argue they are misleading, then admit other parts to remove distortion).

record to prove a doctor's diagnosis but not to prove matters said during an examination. For any of these reasons the proponent might properly offer only part of a writing, which means other parties have no right under FRE 106 to offer other parts. The point of FRE 106 is not to insist on completeness as an end in itself, but to allow others to insist on admitting enough to put a statement in context.[2]

Sometimes parties who could claim the protection of FRE 106 choose instead to attack a statement by arguing that the selection made by the proponent distorts meaning. When an adverse party takes this tack, the proponent should be able to show that in fact the part of the statement he presented does not distort meaning, and the best way to do that may be to admit additional parts of the statement.[3]

FRE 106 does not say whether additional statements (or parts) may be admitted when necessary to provide context if they are excludable under other rules. Nor does FRE 106 say whether additional statements (or parts) are to be admitted for all purposes when needed for context or whether use of such material can or should be limited in some way.

It seems that hearsay objections should *not* block use of a related statement (part of the original or some additional statement) when it is needed to provide context for statements already admitted.[4] If a statement by a witness is used to impeach him, this nonhearsay use justifies admitting other parts of the statement if necessary for context even if the hearsay doctrine would bar their use as substantive evidence.[5] Suppose the proponent offers a statement to prove what it asserts, and the other side wants to introduce a related statement. If the initial proffer satisfies an exception but the related statement does not, this fact should not require exclusion of the latter. There are several reasons: First, the related statement can provide context even if it is not taken as proof of what it asserts, and it could be admitted with limiting instruction (if requested).[6] Second, if the initial statement fits an exception and the related statement would fit if the proponent offered it originally, the fact that the same exception would not be available to adverse parties should matter much less (or not at all) since the original proponent should not

Hearsay objection should fail

---

2. United States v. Wright, 826 F.2d 938, 946 (10th Cir. 1987) (no right for defense to introduce other parts of diary that were not demonstrably relevant).

3. Haddigan v. Harkins, 441 F.2d 844, 849 (3d Cir. 1970) (after plaintiff complained that defense presented distorted picture of deposition, offering to allow omitted portions with explanation that defense did nothing wrong).

4. Engebretsen v. Fairchild Aircraft Corp., 21 F.3d 721, 729-730 (6th Cir. 1994) (after defense introduced expert report, adverse cross entitled defense to introduce other parts to rebut charge of inconsistency and bias). *See generally* Dale Nance, Verbal Completeness and Exclusionary Rules under the Federal Rules of Evidence, 75 Tex. L. Rev. 521 (1996).

5. *See* Short v. United States, 271 F.2d 73, 78 (9th Cir. 1959), *cert. denied*, 361 U.S. 948; United States v. Apuzzo, 245 F.2d 416, 421-422 (2d Cir. 1957), *cert. denied*, 355 U.S. 831.

6. United States v. Bohle, 445 F.2d 54, 66 (7th Cir. 1971) (court should tell jury "other parts are admissible only as background").

be able to misuse an exception in a misleading way.[7] In this respect the rule of completeness connects with the "open door" doctrine.[8] Some decisions reject this conclusion, holding that excludable evidence cannot be offered under FRE 106 because it only governs order of proof.[9]

Not written or recorded

FRE 106 does not itself apply to statements that are not memorialized in permanent form (not written or recorded).[10] Still, fairness in presenting evidence of other statements may require courts to observe the same principle, and courts sometimes invoke it in this setting.[11] The result can be justified by resort to ordinary notions of relevancy under FRE 401-403.

§1.18 Coverage and Application—Documents and Letters; Confessions and Recordings; Other

The completeness rule applies to letters and records, recordings, and documents of all sorts. The rule is useful with medical records in civil cases offered to prove diagnosis, treatment, or condition, or used as the basis for expert testimony. In either case selectively using some passages while ignoring others may be misleading.[1] The same is true of investigative reports, which are sometimes offered for their truth under the public records exception or used as the basis for cross-examining a police officer or preparer.[2]

Depositions

The rule of completeness applies to depositions and other prior testimony offered at trial. Depositions present a particularly vivid instance of the use of remote statements since they are elicited with an eye toward trial. In a leading case requiring introduction at one time of relevant portions of a deposition, the Supreme Court pointedly commented that the rule of completeness seeks to avoid "misimpressions from selective use of deposition testimony," adding that the opposing party is entitled to show "the context of any statement, or any qualifications made as a part of the deponent's testimony," and at a minimum the opposing party may require introduction of additional relevant

7. Short v. United States, 271 F.2d 73, 78 (9th Cir. 1959) (for limited purpose of showing credibility, admitting parts of police reports after other parts were used on cross), *cert. denied,* 361 U.S. 948.

8. *See* the discussion in §1.4, *supra.*

9. United States v. Terry, 702 F.2d 299, 314 (2d Cir. 1983) (FRE 106 "does not render admissible evidence that is otherwise inadmissible"), *cert. denied,* 461 U.S. 931; United States v. Costner, 684 F.2d 370, 372-373 (6th Cir. 1982) (FRE 106 covers order of proof and "is not designed to make something admissible that should be excluded").

10. United States v. Harvey, 959 F.2d 1371, 1376 (7th Cir. 1992); United States v. Bigelow, 914 F.2d 966, 972 (7th Cir. 1990).

11. *See* United States v. Haddad, 10 F.3d 1252, 1258-1259 (7th Cir. 1994) (court has same authority over oral statements as it has over written ones under FRE 106); Iowa Rules of Evidence, Rule 106 (completeness principle applies to evidence problems across the board).

§1.18 1. United States v. Bohle, 445 F.2d 54, 66 (7th Cir. 1971); Rivers v. Union Carbide Corp., 426 F.2d 633, 639 (3d Cir. 1970).

2. Short v. United States, 271 F.2d 73, 78 (9th Cir. 1959) (daily police reports), *cert. denied,* 361 U.S. 948; Affronti v. United States, 145 F.2d 3, 7-8 (8th Cir. 1944) (official investigative reports).

passages "at the conclusion of the reading of the deposition."[3] Because of the nature of depositions, trial counsel is likely to know (or can easily figure out) what additional passages need to be considered, and the court can expect help from counsel in designating material that can easily be presented at the same time.

The completeness question often arises when a party attacks the credibility of a witness by means of her prior statement, arguing essentially that it is inconsistent with her present testimony. On the one hand, the attacking party should not be allowed to isolate a small piece of a prior statement and argue that it demonstrates a change of position when compared with the trial testimony of the speaker if other parts of the statement suggest that nothing of the kind has happened.[4] On the other hand, the completeness doctrine does not suggest that the whole statement should be admitted just because the attacking party showed that part of it was inconsistent with part of the testimony,[5] nor does the doctrine justify admitting other parts that are consistent with other parts of the testimony.[6]

Prior statements by witness

When impeachment by prior statements is undertaken on cross, usually the other side has a chance on redirect to repair the damage, so there is no compelling need to force the attacking party to offer additional parts of a statement. And interrupting the attack to force the lawyer to read or ask about additional parts is particularly unattractive, given the nature of cross and the need to press the witness. On a related point, the general rule is that impeachment by showing a prior inconsistency on some point does not pave the way for repair by showing a prior consistent statement on the same point (the inconsistency remains),[7] and the completeness doctrine has a role to play only if the inconsistent statement was isolated from a larger statement in such way that its use is misleading.[8] It can even be argued that FRE 106 is inapplicable to impeachment by cross-examination on prior statements since the cross-examiner need not formally introduce any part of the statement (he just asks about it).[9] But this somewhat

---

3. Westinghouse Elec. Corp. v. Wray Equip. Corp., 286 F.2d 491, 494 (1st Cir. 1961) (supplementary testimony was separated by more than 1,000 transcript pages from part originally offered, unduly impeding orderly consideration) (nonjury case).

4. Beech Aircraft Corp. v. Rainey, 488 U.S. 153 (1988) (defendant cross-examined plaintiff about letter to commanding officer, reading passages suggesting he did not believe power failure caused crash; thrust of letter was to argue power failure; court should have let plaintiff bring out other statements).

5. United States v. Pendas-Martinez, 845 F.2d 938, 943-945 (11th Cir. 1988); United States v. Costner, 684 F.2d 370, 372-373 (6th Cir. 1982).

6. *See* United States v. Cochran, 499 F.2d 380, 386 (5th Cir. 1974), *cert. denied*, 419 U.S. 1124.

7. *See* §6.52, *infra.*

8. United States v. Greene, 497 F.2d 1068, 1082 (7th Cir. 1974), *cert. denied*, 420 U.S. 909; United States v. Smith, 328 F.2d 848, 850 (6th Cir. 1964), *cert. denied*, 379 U.S. 936.

9. *See* United States v. Greene, 497 F.2d 1068, 1082 (7th Cir. 1974) (on redirect, refusing to let defendant bring out other parts of letter raised on cross; completeness rule applies to "documents partially admitted" and letter was not evidence), *cert. denied*, 420 U.S. 909.

mechanical point has little force if a statement used on cross to impeach is effectively before the trier of fact.

Recorded statements   Where a recording is offered to prove a statement or conversation, completeness problems arise if the recording is partially destroyed or inaudible. The judge has broad discretion to decide whether to admit the recording anyway, and the question is whether the inaudible or unavailable parts are so important to the point to be proved that the recording should be excluded altogether as too misleading.[10] Sometimes such difficulties lead to exclusion.[11] The purpose for which the recording is offered counts, and the presence of long inaudible passages may be of little importance if the tape is used to show only that a conversation occurred, but more important if words and demeanor of the speakers are important.[12]

Admissions and confessions   On request by the accused, the court should require the prosecutor who wants to offer parts of his admission or confession to introduce at the same time not only the incriminating parts but also self-serving or exculpatory parts that should in fairness be heard and considered at the same time. If for any reason the prosecutor introduces less than all, in the process deleting self-serving or exculpatory remarks that the accused wishes to have heard by the trier of fact, the rule of completeness requires the court to receive the latter. FRE 106 applies if the statement is written or recorded, regardless whether it admits all necessary elements of guilt (a confession in the fullest sense) or only states some relevant fact (an ordinary admission).

Government can be required   For admissions and confessions, FRE 106 often works by allowing the defendant to repair whatever damage might have been done because the government offered part of what he said.[13] But the Rule also means the defense can require the government to offer additional parts of the statement at the outset, and this approach seems especially appropriate in this setting.[14] Proceeding this way serves several useful purposes: It reduces distortion at the outset, prevents the government from putting the accused on the defensive unfairly by forcing him to offer material that was part and parcel of the government's own proof, and it keeps the government from putting what amounts to unfair pressure on the accused to take the witness stand.[15]

---

10. United States v. Abroms, 947 F.2d 1241, 1250 (5th Cir. 1991); United States v. Devous, 764 F.2d 1349, 1353 (10th Cir. 1985).

11. Bryan v. John Bean Div. of FMC Corp., 566 F.2d 541, 550 (5th Cir. 1978) (excluding recording because inaudible).

12. *See* United States v. Frazier, 479 F.2d 983, 985 (2d Cir. 1973); United States v. Skillman, 442 F.2d 542, 552 (8th Cir. 1971), *cert. denied*, 404 U.S. 833.

13. United States v. Le Fevour, 798 F.2d 977, 980-981 (7th Cir. 1986) (taped conversation).

14. United States v. Walker, 652 F.2d 708, 712-714 (7th Cir. 1981) (government introduced 14 pages of testimony by defendant in first trial; court should have made government offer 14 more pages).

15. United States v. Walker, 652 F.2d 708, 713-714 (7th Cir. 1981) (prevent misleading impression, recognize inadequacy of repair when delayed; incomplete presentation of former testimony may have "painted a distorted picture" defendant could only remedy by taking stand, which penalizes him for not testifying).

If a statement by the accused is written or recorded, the risk in letting the government introduce less than all is that the impression of first hearing may be hard to overcome later during defendant's case-in-chief by introducing self-serving and exculpatory portions, especially if the latter are viewed in the context of an otherwise weak defense when it may be easy to forget that the statements were not in fact afterthoughts and were instead part of his earlier assessment. If a statement by the accused is neither written nor recorded, the risk in beginning with less than all may be lessened by the fact that the witness who testifies to it may be immediately cross-examined and self-serving or exculpatory parts can be brought out. If the prosecutor can get away with introducing only fragments, there is some risk that the accused can only prove the rest by testifying. When probative evidence properly admitted presses the accused to testify, it seems there should be no concern, but it is troublesome if the pressure comes from tactics that are misleading and unfair.[16]

FRE 106 leaves room for the court to allow the prosecution to introduce less than all of a written or recorded statement by the accused if doing so does not unfairly distort presentation of the statement. The accused still has a right then to introduce self-serving or exculpatory portions[17] but not to introduce other parts irrelevant to the charges.[18]

Occasionally there are powerful reasons to admit less than all of a confession or admission by the accused. When such reasons appear, exclusions raise issues under the rule of completeness. Omissions sometimes lead to the conclusion that defendant should be allowed to exclude the balance of an admission or confession because it is misleading or distorted,[19] or because it was taken in a setting in which defendant was not given a chance to explain or justify acts that he admits doing.[20] Sometimes the problem is that the whole statement is not written or recorded, or part of a writing is lost, or part of a recording is lost or inaudible. Sometimes the problem is that defendant has a right to exclude references in his own statement to other crimes

Admit less than all

16. *See* United States v. Marin, 669 F.2d 73, 83-85 & n.6 (2d Cir. 1982) (if oral statement by defendant is admitted, Fifth Amendment might require court to take whole statement to avoid distortion that defendant cannot prevent without testifying).

17. United States v. Kershner, 432 F.2d 1066, 1072 (5th Cir. 1970) (admitting entire confession may be required so "exculpatory and mitigating parts will be included"); Government of Virgin Islands v. Lovell, 378 F.2d 799, 806 (if statement is comprised of exculpatory and inculpatory remarks, all of it is admissible), *later app.*, 410 F.2d 307 (3d Cir.), *cert. denied*, 396 U.S. 964.

18. United States v. Myers, 972 F.2d 1566, 1575-1576 (11th Cir. 1992) (where government used defendant's written statement to impeach his testimony on one point, no error to block defense from using unrelated parts).

19. United States v. Le Fevour, 798 F.2d 977, 980-981 (7th Cir. 1986) (if evidence needed to correct misleading impression is excludable, "maybe because of privilege," misleading evidence must be excluded too).

20. United States v. Wenzel, 311 F.2d 164, 168-169 (4th Cir. 1962) (cannot admit confession of crime if process is interrupted to keep defendant "from adding anything which might explain the reason" or otherwise justify conduct).

that would not be admissible against him,[21] but it does not follow that the whole confession or admission should be excluded under the rule of completeness.[22] Sometimes the problem is that the *Bruton* doctrine requires that references to codefendants be deleted ("redacted") from a written or recorded confession or admission,[23] and such redactions might distort what remains, although they do not require exclusion of the balance to the extent that it stands independent of what was removed and its use would not be misleading.[24]

Different statements   FRE 106 expressly reaches not only different parts of the same statement, but different statements, implicitly recognizing that mechanical notions of what makes a statement or what must be shown to reach an adequate understanding of a statement are not helpful. Hence FRE 106 authorizes the court at the behest of an adverse party to require the proponent to introduce not only the recorded statement he wants to introduce, but other written or recorded statements that ought in fairness to be considered at the same time. (And implicitly FRE 106 provides that the court should let other parties introduce the other writing if the proponent does not.)

This application of the completeness rule has been important when a letter is introduced and it can best be understood in the context of earlier or later letters or enclosures. Where one letter makes a proposal or inquiry and another replies to the first, it is likely that neither can be adequately understood without the other, so admitting one should lead to admitting both.[25] Neither physical proximity of writings nor contemporaneous preparation or execution means that a document, attachment, or cover letter should be admitted if another writing is admitted,[26] but other circumstances may combine with these to indicate the contrary.[27]

21. United States v. Wiggins, 509 F.2d 454, 462 (D.C. Cir. 1975) (error to admit defendant's confession, including statement that he killed before, where other crime was not admissible).

22. Marcus v. United States, 86 F.2d 854, 858 (D.C. Cir. 1936) (rejecting claim that whole confession should have been excluded, where defense conceded that court could not admit parts describing former holdups and other unconnected crimes).

23. Bruton v. United States, 391 U.S. 123 (1968), discussed in §8.28, *infra.*

24. Howard v. Moore, 131 F.3d 399, 421-422 (4th Cir. 1997) (in murder trial of H and W, redacted confession did not distort what H said because redacted portions would have invited jury to infer that W killed victim, which "requires a tortured and speculative interpretation of two phrases").

25. United States v. Morello, 250 F.2d 631, 634 (2d Cir. 1957) (in drug trial, admitting letter because government introduced reply); Flint v. Youngstown Sheet & Tube Co., 143 F.2d 923, 925 (2d Cir. 1944) (admitting prior correspondence because plaintiff introduced letter referring to it).

26. United States v. Boyland, 898 F.2d 230, 256-257 (1st Cir. 1990) (in trial for police shakedown of bar owners, admitting personnel orders indicating job assignments of defendants but excluding other items in files on commendations, suspensions, punishments, outside studies).

27. Brown v. Financial Serv. Corp., Intl., 489 F.2d 144, 149-150 (5th Cir. 1974) (in suit by former employee, error to exclude cover letter to plaintiff summarizing phone conversation on stock purchase agreement and enclosing agreement itself; cover letter may be part of agreement).

CHAPTER 2

Judicial Notice

A. SCOPE OF FRE 201
B. PROCESS OF TAKING NOTICE
C. INSTRUCTING THE JURY

A. SCOPE OF FRE 201

§2.1 Introduction

Judicial notice is a process by which an adjudicative fact can be established without formal evidentiary proof.[1] Judicial notice is thus a substitute for evidence.[2] When judicial notice is taken, the requesting party is relieved of the burden he would otherwise have to produce evidence on the point.

Common law judges developed the concept of judicial notice to avoid the expense and delay of proving facts that are essentially incontestable.[3] By furthering trial efficiency, the doctrine benefits both courts and litigants. At least in civil cases, where juries may not make findings contrary to matters established by judicial notice, the doctrine

---

§2.1 1. *See* 9 Wigmore, Wigmore on Evidence §2567(a) (3d ed. 1940) ("That a matter is judicially noticed means merely that it is taken as true without the offering of evidence by the party who should ordinarily have done so.").

2. *See* Varcoe v. Lee, 180 Cal. 338, 344, 181 P. 223, 226 (1919) (judicial notice is "a judicial short cut," dispensing with "the formal necessity for evidence").

3. The history is recounted in Thayer, A Preliminary Treatise on Evidence at the Common Law 281-298 (1898). Starkie was one of first commentators to discuss judicial notice as a subcategory of evidence law. *See* Starkie, Law of Evidence 735-739 (4th ed. 1853). *See also* Bentham, A Treatise on Judicial Evidence 46 (M. Dumont ed. 1987) (judge may pronounce decision on a question of fact "when the facts in question are too notorious to require a special proof").

provides a measure of control over juries and helps insure the rationality of jury deliberations.

FRE 201 addresses the scope and procedures for taking judicial notice in federal courts, and numerous states have adopted similar provisions based on either FRE 201 or URE 201.[4] FRE 201(a) makes clear that the rule governs judicial notice only of adjudicative facts. Judicial notice of basic facts, legislative facts, and law are not regulated by the Federal Rules of Evidence.[5] These related but distinct doctrines are discussed in later sections.[6]

It can sometimes be difficult to classify the type of notice being taken—whether of adjudicative, legislative, or basic facts.[7] Classification is essential not only in determining the applicability of FRE 201 but also in making proper use of precedent. An appellate decision taking judicial notice of a legislative fact provides no precedent for noticing the same fact as an adjudicative fact because the requirements for noticing adjudicative facts are so much more stringent.[8] The bulk of appellate decisions involve judicial notice of legislative facts, but courts frequently fail to identify the fact as such.[9]

FRE 201(b) allows a court to take judicial notice of an adjudicative fact only where it is "not subject to reasonable dispute" either because it is "generally known"[10] (for example, New York City is located in the state of New York) or readily verifiable by reliable sources (August 8, 1993, was a Sunday).[11] FRE 201(c) makes clear that a court is allowed to take judicial notice on its own initiative,[12] and FRE 201(d) requires a

---

4. The primary difference between the two provisions is that FRE 201(g) makes judicial notice binding on the jury only in civil cases, whereas URE 201(g) makes judicial notice binding in both civil and criminal cases. *See* §§2.11-2.12, *infra*.

5. FRE 201 thus regulates only a small fraction of the total instances where the courts take some form of judicial notice during the course of litigation. *See* Thayer, A Preliminary Treatise on Evidence at the Common Law 279 (1898) ("The careful observer will notice that a very great proportion of the cases involving judicial notice raise no question at all in that part of the law [relating to proof of facts]; they relate to pleading, to the construction of the record or of other writings, the legal definition of words, the interpretation of conduct, the process of reasoning, and the regulation of trials.").

6. *See* §§2.3, 2.4, 2.13, *infra*.

7. *See, e.g.,* Goodman v. Stalfort, Inc., 411 F. Supp. 889, 894 (D.N.J. 1976) (confessing to uncertainty whether noticed fact should be viewed as "adjudicative" or "legislative" under FRE 201), *aff'd in part, rev'd in part*, 564 F.2d 89 (3d Cir. 1977).

8. *See* Chartrand v. Coos Bay Tavern, Inc., 298 Or. 689, 694, 696 P.2d 513, 517 (1985) ("In determining the appropriateness of a court's action in taking judicial notice, it must constantly be borne in mind that judicial notice may be employed for a wide variety of purposes. A failure to distinguish between the purposes for which courts take judicial notice of fact creates the danger that someone will assume that once an appellate court has at one time or another taken judicial notice of a fact for one purpose it is a proper subject for notice for a completely different purpose.").

9. *See* Turner, Judicial Notice and Federal Rule of Evidence 201—A Rule Ready for Change, 45 U. Pitt. L. Rev. 181, 185 (1983) (out of the thousands of cases decided since the adoption of FRE 201, in only a "few dozen" of those cases did the court indicate the type of fact noticed, thus suggesting "that the heart of F.R.E. 201 has not been well-received by the judges who actually have to work with it").

10. *See* §2.6, *infra*.

11. *See* §2.7, *infra*.

12. *See* §2.8, *infra*.

court to take judicial notice when requested by a party and supplied with the necessary information.[13] FRE 201(e) guarantees the parties an opportunity to be heard on the propriety of taking judicial notice.[14]

Under FRE 201(f), judicial notice is authorized at any stage of the proceeding. Thus a judge can take notice of adjudicative facts not only during trial, but also during pretrial and posttrial proceedings as well as on appeal.[15] In a jury trial, the judge must inform the jury by instruction of the fact to be noticed in order for notice to be effective. FRE 201(g) governs the form of instruction and provides that notice is binding on the jury in civil cases and permissive in criminal cases.[16] When the judge serves as trier of fact, of course no instruction is given. A party can effect notice merely by obtaining the acknowledgment of the court that notice will be taken.

FRE 201 does not directly apply to the determination of preliminary questions of fact affecting the admissibility of evidence[17] although its provisions are appropriately followed as guidelines.[18] It also does not apply in various proceedings such as preliminary examinations in criminal cases, probation revocations, or sentencing hearings, which are exempted from application of the Federal Rules of Evidence by FRE 1101(d).

FRE 201(a)

Scope of Rule. This rule governs only judicial notice of adjudicative facts.

---

§2.2   Adjudicative Facts

"Adjudicative facts" are not defined in FRE 201, which seems an unfortunate omission given that the scope of the rule is demarcated by this term. The Advisory Committee's Note cites a useful definition by Professor Davis, which provides in relevant part: "[A]djudicative facts are those to which the law is applied in the process of adjudication. They are the facts that normally go to the jury in a jury case."[1] Other helpful definitions have also been offered.[2]

Professor Davis goes on to describe adjudicative facts as those facts "concerning the immediate parties—who did what, where, when, how

---

13. *See* §2.8, *infra.*

14. *See* §2.9, *infra.*

15. *See* §2.10, *infra.*

16. *See* §§2.11-2.12, *infra.*

17. FRE 104(a) (rules of evidence do not apply to such determinations, except for rules of privilege).

18. *Cf.* Marshall v. Bramer, 828 F.2d 355, 358 (6th Cir. 1987) (applying FRE 201 as a "guideline" in affirming taking of judicial notice by trial court in ruling on pretrial discovery motion).

§2.2   1. ACN, FRE 201, quoting 2 Davis, Administrative Law Treatise §15.03, at 353 (1958).

2. *See* The Evidence Project, 171 F.R.D. 330, 392 (1997) (recommending amendment of FRE 201(a) to define adjudicative facts as "those facts that gave rise to and must be proved to resolve the action").

and with what motive or intent" and generally relate to "their activities, their properties, their businesses." This aspect of the description is less useful and potentially misleading. Courts have frequently found facts to be "adjudicative" (and hence subject to FRE 201) even though they have no unique or special relationship to either the litigants or the dispute. Facts relating to dates, tide tables, phases of the moon, geographical boundaries, and world history are frequent subjects of judicial notice, yet can hardly be said to relate to the immediate litigants more than to anyone else.[3]

Perhaps the best way to view the matter is to consider adjudicative facts as *those facts that are necessary to prove or are used to prove a question of fact as distinguished from a question of law.* Noticed facts are adjudicative if evidence of such facts would be required if judicial notice were not taken.[4] Whether proof of a particular fact is required, hence making the fact adjudicative, is often determined by law external to the Federal Rules of Evidence.[5]

§2.3 Legislative Facts Distinguished

The Federal Rules of Evidence do not regulate the process of noticing legislative facts.[1] The Advisory Committee's Note to FRE 201(a) explains:

> The omission of any treatment of legislative facts results from fundamental differences between adjudicative facts and legislative facts. Adjudicative facts are simply the facts of the particular case. Legislative facts, on the other hand, are those which have relevance to legal reasoning and the law making process, whether in the formulation of a legal principle or ruling by a judge or court or in the enactment of a legislative body.

In the course of litigation, at both the trial and appellate levels, it is often necessary for courts to interpret constitutions, statutes, or regulations or to create or modify rules of common law. In order to discharge this most basic judicial function, courts often must consider facts other

3. *See* §2.7, *infra.*

4. *See* Davis, Judicial Notice, 55 Colum. L. Rev. 945, 952 (1955) ("Judicial notice means use by a court of extra record facts at any stage of any proceeding in which, apart from judicial notice, a finding of adjudicative facts is required to be based on evidence in the record.").

5. Such external law includes the substantive law defining the charge, claim or defense, rules allocating burdens of proof, and federal and state constitutional law governing the scope of a jury trial.

§2.3 1. *See* ACN, FRE 201(a) (legislative facts are not covered by "any limitation in the form of indisputability, any formal requirements of notice other than those already inherent in affording opportunity to hear and be heard and exchanging briefs, and any requirement of formal findings at any level."). *See also* Cleary, Foreword to Symposium on Proposed Federal Rules of Evidence, 1969 Law & Soc. Order 509, 510 ("The absence of provision for judicial notice of facts other than adjudicative does not mean that judicial notice cannot be taken of them; it simply means that no attempt is made to regulate them.").

than the adjudicative facts proved at trial. The facts considered by a court in the course of making legal interpretations and rulings are known as legislative facts.[2] In the historic case of *Brown v. Board of Education,* the Court relied on social science research on the psychological effects of segregation in reaching its *legal* conclusion that segregated schools are inherently unequal and violate the Equal Protection Clause. These studies, which were cited by the Court in a famous footnote, represent a classic example of legislative facts.[3]

In most cases, legislative facts are outside the record of the case, although occasionally parties bring them to the attention of the court as part of the trial or appellate record, for example by submission of a "Brandeis" brief.[4]

Types of facts noticed

If the ruling creates or modifies rule of case law, a court may notice as legislative facts a limitless array of factual matters that bear upon the appropriate legal decision.[5] If the ruling requires the court to interpret a statute, constitution, or administrative regulation, courts may notice a wide range of facts bearing on the question, including legislative history,[6] empirical research,[7] medical literature,[8] current social

---

2. Professor Kenneth Davis appears to have contributed the term "legislative facts" to the professional vocabulary. *See* 2 Davis, Administrative Law Treatise §15.03 (1958) ("When a court or an agency develops law or policy, it is acting legislatively; the courts have created the common law through judicial legislation, and the facts which inform the tribunal's legislative judgment are called legislative facts.").

3. Brown v. Board of Education, 347 U.S. 483, 494 n.11 (1954) (Court noticed social science studies showing that segregation creates a feeling of inferiority among people in the excluded group). The *Brown* decision's reliance on legislative facts sparked some controversy. *See* Clark, The Desegregation Cases: Criticism of the Social Scientist's Role, 5 Vill. L. Rev. 224 (1960); Van den Haag, Social Science Testimony in the Desegregation Cases—A Reply to Professor Kenneth Clark, 6 Vill. L. Rev. 69 (1960).

4. *See* Muller v. Oregon, 208 U.S. 412, 419-421 n.1 (1908) (Court upheld constitutionality of Oregon statute limiting maximum hours women can work in laundries and factories; Louis D. Brandeis, as counsel for respondent, submitted a brief compiling not only similar legislation in other states and foreign countries but also "extracts from over ninety reports of committees, bureaus of statistics, commissioners of hygiene, inspectors of factories, both in this country and in Europe, to the effect that long hours of labor are dangerous for women, primarily because of their special physical organization"; material in the brief is another classic example of legislative facts).

5. Javins v. First Natl. Realty Corp., 428 F.2d 1071, 1079-1080 (D.C. Cir. 1970) (in finding implied warranty of habitability in residential housing, court noticed "findings by various studies of the social impact of bad housing has led to the realization that poor housing is detrimental to the whole society, not merely to the unlucky ones who must suffer the daily indignity of living in a slum"), *cert. denied,* 400 U.S. 925; People v. Collins, 68 Cal. 2d 319, 438 P.2d 33, 66 Cal. Rptr. 497 (1968) (taking notice of statistical principles in assessing dangers of mathematical proof).

6. Green v. Bock Laundry Mach. Co., 490 U.S. 504 (1989) (noticing legislative history in interpreting FRE 609(a)).

7. Ballew v. Georgia, 435 U.S. 223 (1978) (noticing empirical studies on question whether a state may use juries of less than six in criminal case).

8. Roe v. Wade, 410 U.S. 113, 149 n.44 (1973) (summarizing data indicating that mortality rates for early abortions are as low or lower than those for childbirth); Powell v. Texas, 392 U.S. 514 (1968) (noticing medical literature viewing alcoholism as a

conditions,[9] the dangerousness of certain activities,[10] aspects of human nature,[11] factors affecting the maintenance of marital harmony,[12] language and word usage,[13] and miscellaneous other matters.[14]

Sometimes when a court notices legislative facts in constitutional litigation, the purpose is not to establish the truth of the noticed facts but only to find that a legislature or administrative body had a "rational basis" for adopting the challenged statute or regulation.[15] Some commentators have suggested that the extent to which a court is willing to consider legislative facts in deciding constitutional questions depends on the court's judicial philosophy and its receptivity to policy arguments.[16]

The process of taking judicial notice of legislative facts, although pervasive, is largely invisible. Only rarely do trial courts reveal the

---

disease). *But see* Fingarette, The Perils of *Powell*: In Search of a Factual Foundation for the "Disease Concept of Alcoholism," 83 Harv. L. Rev. 793, 798 (1970) (challenging Court's use of judicial notice in *Powell*).

9. Frontiero v. Richardson, 411 U.S. 677, 684-688 (1973) ("[W]omen still face pervasive, although at times more subtle, discrimination in our educational institutions, in the job market and, perhaps most conspicuously, in the political arena.").

10. Neeld v. National Hockey League, 594 F.2d 1297, 1300 (9th Cir. 1979) (rejecting challenge by one-eyed hockey player to league by-law that prevented him from playing; court takes judicial notice that "ice hockey is a very rough physical contact sport, and that there is bound to be danger to players who happen to be on [plaintiff's] blind side, no matter how well his mask may protect his one good eye").

11. Paris Adult Theater I v. Slaton, 413 U.S. 49, 63 (1973) ("[A] sensitive, key relationship of human existence, central to family life, community welfare, and the development of the human personality, can be debased and distorted by the crass commercial exploitation of sex."); Snell v. Suffolk County, 782 F.2d 1094, 1105-1106 (2d Cir. 1986) (in suit by black and Hispanic corrections officers alleging racial discrimination in employment, court approves judicial notice of "the social consequences of ethnic humor").

12. Hawkins v. United States, 358 U.S. 74, 78 (1958) (justifying rule making both spouses holders of the spousal testimonial privilege by stating that "[a]dverse testimony given in criminal proceedings would, we think, be likely to destroy almost any marriage"). *But see* United States v. Trammel, 445 U.S. 40 (1980) (modifying rule by eliminating right of the defendant spouse to assert privilege; concluding that if one spouse is willing to testify against the other, the relationship "is almost certainly in disrepair" and there is "little in the way of marital harmony" left to preserve).

13. United States v. Dorfman, 542 F. Supp. 345, 370 n.23 (N.D. Ill. 1982) ("The meaning of the term 'organized crime' is a legislative fact which may properly be subject to judicial notice."), *aff'd*, 737 F.2d 594 (7th Cir. 1984), *cert. denied*, 470 U.S. 1003.

14. *See, e.g.*, Turner v. United States, 396 U.S. 398, 417 (1970) (heroin and cocaine are imported so statutory presumptions to this effect are constitutionally valid); Bykofsky v. Borough of Middletown, 401 F. Supp. 1242, 1255 (M.D. Pa. 1975) (in a challenge to a municipal curfew law for juveniles, court notices as a basis for upholding the law "the rapidly increasing crime rate among juveniles" and the "high percentage of all serious crime" that teenagers commit), *aff'd*, 535 F.2d 1245 (3d Cir.), *cert. denied*, 429 U.S. 964.

15. *See, e.g.*, Metromedia, Inc. v. City of San Diego, 453 U.S. 490, 509 (1981) (in upholding municipal ordinance prohibiting billboards, the Court "agreed with many other courts that a legislative judgment that billboards are traffic hazards is not manifestly unreasonable and should not be set aside"; similarly, the Court refused to reject "the accumulated, common-sense judgments of local lawmakers and of the many reviewing courts that billboards are real and substantial hazards to traffic safety").

16. *See generally* Alfange, The Relevance of Legislative Facts in Constitutional Law, 114 U. Pa. L. Rev. 637 (1966); Karst, Legislative Facts in Constitutional Litigation, 1960

legislative facts considered in reaching a legal decision.[17] At the appellate level, the process is somewhat more apparent, and the vast majority of appellate decisions where the taking of judicial notice is acknowledged involve legislative rather than adjudicative facts.[18]

There is continuing debate about whether formal regulations should govern the process of judicial notice of legislative facts.[19] Some have urged that such regulation be included in the Federal Rules of Evidence.[20] Whatever the merits of those suggestions, applying the existing FRE 201(b) to legislative facts would be unduly restrictive[21] and constitutionally questionable[22] because the only facts authorized for notice are those "not subject to reasonable dispute." Many sources of factual information on which courts need to rely in making legal rulings could not meet this "indisputability" standard. A leading commentator has stated:

Process unregulated

> My opinion is that judge-made law would stop growing if judges, in thinking about questions of law and policy, were forbidden to take into account the facts they believe, as distinguished from facts which are "clearly . . . within the domain of the indisputable." Facts most needed

Sup. Ct. Rev. 75. *See also* J. Johnson, The Dimensions of Non-Legal Evidence in the American Legal Process: The Supreme Court's Use of Extra-Legal Materials in the Twentieth Century (1990).

17. If the legislative facts noticed by the trial court are stated, they are not entitled to special deference by appellate courts, unlike findings of adjudicative facts. See Keeton, Legislative Facts and Similar Things: Deciding Disputed Premise Facts, 73 Minn. L. Rev. 1, 41 (1988).

18. 21 Wright & K. Graham, Federal Practice and Procedure §5102 at 464 (1977) (criticizing FRE 201 as being "severed" from decisional law since "hundreds of appellate decisions each year" deal with judicial notice "but only a handful of them deal with judicial notice of adjudicative fact").

19. *See, e.g.,* Keeton, Legislative Facts and Similar Things: Deciding Disputed Premise Facts, 73 Minn. L. Rev. 1, 45-46 (1988) (finding a need for a "set of procedural and evidentiary rules for deciding premise-fact disputes, analogous to the rules of procedure and rules of evidence for adjudicative fact-finding"; suggesting that courts should (1) place their tentative findings before the advocates, inviting comment and suggested modifications; (2) invite amicus submissions when the decision may set a precedent affecting parties with interests significantly different from those of the litigants; and (3) develop efficient procedures for resolving premise fact disputes); Davis, Facts in Lawmaking, 80 Colum. L. Rev. 931 (1980) (advocating system of advance notice and comment when Supreme Court relies upon judicially noticed legislative facts to make broad policy decisions).

20. *See* Davis, Judicial Notice, 1969 Law & Soc. Order 513 (advocating regulation of judicial notice of legislative facts as part of FRE 201). Neither the Model Code of Evidence (1942) nor the Uniform Rules of Evidence (1953) attempted to regulate judicial notice of legislative facts.

21. *See* Houser v. State, 85 Wash. 2d 803, 540 P.2d 412, 414 (1975) ("The restrictive rules governing judicial notice are not applicable to factual findings that simply supply premises in the process of legal reasoning. In interpreting and developing the constitution and laws, courts cannot operate in a vacuum."), *overruled on other grounds,* State v. Smith, 93 Wash. 2d 329, 610 P.2d 869 (1980).

22. A separation-of-powers issue would arise if Congress attempted to prevent or unduly restrict federal courts from considering legislative facts in carrying out their judicial decisionmaking responsibilities.

in thinking about difficult problems of law and policy have a way of being outside the domain of the clearly indisputable. . . .

. . . What the law needs at its growing points is more, not less judicial thinking about the factual ingredients of problems of what the law ought to be, and the needed facts are seldom "clearly" indisputable.[23]

Any attempt to confine consideration of legislative facts to matters in the record would also unduly restrict judicial decisionmaking. Courts often need to notice legislative facts outside the record because they cannot expect parties to anticipate and supply all the factual information that a court might find relevant in making a particular legal ruling. Legal decisions, particularly at the appellate level, often have ramifications that transcend the immediate controversy and require judges to consider factual matters beyond the concerns of the litigants. Moreover, a rule that required formal proof of legislative facts would consume undue time and expense.

It would be difficult, if not futile, to restrict notice of legislative facts in cases where the court has preexisting knowledge of the facts in question. There is no appropriate or decorous way to probe the knowledge base that a judge brings to the legal task at hand, and even the most conscientious judge is often unable to identify the influence of previously acquired factual information upon her legal rulings.

In most cases, the integrity of the litigation process can be adequately protected if parties are allowed an opportunity to present factual information bearing on any legal issues to be decided without requiring the court to notify the parties of particular legislative facts that it may consider. However, when a court conducts an independent factual investigation, it should inform the parties and allow them an opportunity to challenge or supplement the proposed legislative facts, at least if there is any possibility of reasonable dispute about those facts.[24] The greater the potential for dispute, the more cautious courts should be about noticing legislative facts and the more opportunity they should provide for party input.

23. Davis, A System of Judicial Notice Based on Fairness and Convenience, in Perspectives on Law at 82-83 (1964). *See also id.* at 87 (most social science data cannot be called "indisputable"; practically speaking, the choice in lawmaking "is often between proceeding in ignorance and following the uncertain, tentative, and far from indisputable teachings of social science such as they are, for the simple reason that clearly indisputable facts are unavailable"). Although Professor Davis favored regulation of judicial notice of legislative facts, he would not have imposed a standard of indisputability for such notice. Davis, Judicial Notice, 1969 Law & Soc. Order 513.

24. *See* Karst, Legislative Facts in Constitutional Litigation, 1960 Sup. Ct. Rev. 75, 108-109 ("Wholly apart from the court's legislative functions, there are sufficient reasons for allowing the litigants to present their arguments as to the legal standards which should govern their case. Some such reasons relate to the quality of the decision: the parties may, by their partisan presentations, help the judge to reach a decision which gives the optimum protection to their contesting interests. Other reasons are mainly political: a loser is less likely to take his grievance into the streets if he feels his case has been given proper attention by the tribunal.").

Independent factgathering by a court without providing parties an opportunity to be heard can create a perception of unfairness, particularly if the information is obtained from private sources.[25] Courts occasionally give parties advance notice of the legislative facts they tentatively plan to consider[26] although more commonly they simply invite the litigants to assist them in establishing legislative facts.[27] Some writers have suggested that machinery be provided, such as special masters or an independent research agency, to assist courts in determining legislative facts.[28]

Classification of a noticed fact as adjudicative or legislative requires distinguishing questions of fact from questions of law. If a particular fact tends to answer a question within the province of the jury, the fact is adjudicative and notice is governed by FRE 201. But if the fact is used as a basis for a decision of the court, it is legislative and outside the parameters of FRE 201. Whether a matter is a question of fact for the jury or a question of law for the court is determined by the substantive law defining the charge, claim or defense.[29]

Sometimes courts are able to avoid reversal for violation of FRE 201 by determining that the noticed fact was legislative rather than adjudicative and hence that FRE 201 does not apply. For example, in *United States v. Gould,* the trial judge took notice that cocaine hydrochloride was a derivative of coca leaves, hence a Schedule II controlled substance, and instructed the jury to so find. On appeal, the defendant argued that this binding instruction violated FRE 201(g), but the Eighth Circuit found no error, holding that the fact noticed was legislative rather than adjudicative and that FRE 201 did not apply.[30]

Distinguishing legislative from adjudicative facts

25. *See* United States v. Roth, 237 F.2d 796, 814 (2d Cir. 1956) (obscenity prosecution; concurring appellate judge relied in part on letter from a sociologist sent in response to his own inquiry), *aff'd,* 354 U.S. 476 (1957); Triangle Publications v. Rohrlich, 167 F.2d 969, 976 (2d Cir. 1948) (plaintiff claimed that its magazine trademark "Seventeen" was infringed by defendant's use of "Miss Seventeen" for its teenage underwear; dissenting appellate judge conducted a limited, random, and unscientific survey of teenagers and concluded that "no one could reasonably believe that any relationship existed between plaintiff's magazine and defendant's girdles").

26. *See, e.g.,* Bulova Watch Co. v. K. Hattori & Co., 508 F. Supp. 1322, 1328 (E.D.N.Y. 1981) (court provided advance notice and invited input of parties about facts court intended to notice concerning history and development of multinational corporations for purposes of deciding jurisdictional question).

27. *See* Borden's Farm Products Co. v. Baldwin, 293 U.S. 194 (1934) (case remanded to take evidence concerning economic conditions and trade practices underlying the New York Milk Control Law); Durham v. United States, 214 F.2d 862 (D.C. Cir. 1954) (parties invited to brief and argue adequacy of traditional test for insanity).

28. *See* Davis, Judicial, Legislative and Administrative Lawmaking: A Proposed Research Service for the Supreme Court, 71 Minn. L. Rev. 1 (1986). *But see* Woolhandler, Rethinking the Judicial Reception of Legislative Facts, 41 Vand. L. Rev. 111, 120-121 (1988) (opposing formalized mechanisms for reception of legislative facts).

29. *Compare* Green v. United States, 405 F.2d 1368, 1369 (D.C. Cir. 1968) (whether gun is a deadly weapon is question of law for court) *with* Greenfield v. United States, 341 F.2d 411, 412 (D.C. Cir. 1964) (whether soda pop bottle is dangerous weapon is question of fact for jury).

30. 536 F.2d 216 (8th Cir. 1976).

Similarly, courts may take judicial notice of—and give binding instructions concerning—geographical facts that determine such legal issues as venue and jurisdiction. If, for example, the defendant is accused of committing a crime on federal property, the jury must find the location where the crime was committed (for example, Fort Benning, Georgia). It is, however, proper for the court to instruct the jury that Fort Benning is property within the jurisdiction of the United States.[31]

§2.4 Basic Facts Distinguished

It is sometimes said that the mind of the trier of fact should be a tabula rasa at the beginning of trial. Jurors are to have no preexisting knowledge of the matter in litigation, and the same is true of judges in bench-tried cases. The trier of fact is to render a verdict solely on the evidence formally admitted at trial. To a significant degree, of course, this notion of a clean slate is a fiction. The minds of jurors and judges in the courtroom are not vacant, and we would not want them to be. They need to know certain basic facts in order to understand and appraise the adjudicative facts of the case. Such basic facts are referred to by the Advisory Committee as "non-evidence facts."[1]

Whatever the descriptive term, it is important to note that FRE 201 has nothing to say on this matter, and indeed the whole area is largely unregulated.[2] Commentators have long understood that background information is indispensable to the factfinding process and that it appears "inconspicuously and interstitially in [the] elementary processes of understanding and reasoning."[3] Thayer put it this way: "In conducting a process of judicial reasoning, as of other reasoning, not a step can be taken without assuming something which has not been proved; and the capacity to do this with competent judgment and efficiency, is imputed to judge and juries as part of their necessary mental outfit."[4] Obviously the main useful functions of background

---

31. United States v. Bowers, 660 F.2d 527, 530-531 (5th Cir. 1981) (fact that Fort Benning is within territorial jurisdiction of the United States is a legislative fact). *See also* United States v. Hernandez-Fundora, 58 F.3d 802, 808-812 (2d Cir. 1995) (district court entitled to determine that Raybrook penitentiary falls within territorial jurisdiction of United States and to remove that issue from consideration by jury because such geographical/jurisdictional issues are legislative rather than adjudicative facts).

§2.4 1. ACN, FRE 201(a).

2. *See* ACN, FRE 201(a) (finding that use of non-evidence facts to evaluate adjudicative facts in case "is not an appropriate subject for a formalized judicial notice treatment").

3. McNaughton, Judicial Notice—Excerpts Relating to the Morgan-Wigmore Controversy, 14 Vand. L. Rev. 779, 789 (1961).

4. Thayer, Preliminary Treatise on Evidence 279-280 (1898). *See also* ACN, FRE 201(a) ("When a witness in an automobile accident case says 'car,' everyone, judge and jury included, furnishes, from non-evidence sources within himself, the supplementing information that the 'car' is an automobile, not a railroad car, that it is self-propelled, probably by an internal combustion engine, that it may be assumed to have four wheels with pneumatic rubber tires, and so on. The judicial process cannot

information are to enable the trier of fact (judge or jury) to understand and evaluate the evidence and to reach what we hope is a wise result.

Focusing for the moment on jurors, where most of the points of difficulty have arisen in this area, the system depends on their having at least two kinds of background knowledge:

First, in order to function effectively jurors must know a subspecies of basic facts, which might be called "communicative facts." They must know enough of the English language and have a sufficient vocabulary to understand at least lay testimony in the case. Trials would be interminable if they had to be stopped to define the meaning of every term used by a witness such as "fire truck," "red light," or "freeway."[5] Jurors should understand not only the ordinary meaning of common words but also idioms, common shorthand and slang expressions, and the usual meaning of nonverbal cues (like shrugging and pointing).

Communicative facts

Second, jurors should understand what we might call general background facts necessary to evaluate or appraise the evidence in the case (sometimes therefore called "evaluative facts"). Such facts are matters of essentially universal knowledge in human experience everywhere or at least throughout our national life and culture—that fire burns, for example, that freeways can be crowded with fast-moving cars, that deprivation of oxygen causes death, that gravity causes things to fall, that sexual intercourse can cause pregnancy, that threats can induce fear, that love or hate or jealousy can influence the behavior of one person toward another.[6] At least in general terms, courts routinely instruct juries to take such information into account in deciding the case,[7] and lawyers are permitted to refer to such information in their arguments to the jury.[8]

Evaluative facts

Practically speaking, both kinds of background information are indispensable to the factfinding process for it is just such knowledge that enables jurors to comprehend and evaluate the evidence formally adduced in the case.[9] Because such information enters the case without

---

construct every case from scratch, like Descartes creating a world based on the postulate Cogito, ergo sum. These items could not possibly be introduced into evidence, and no one suggests that they be.").

5. *See* Mansfield, Jury Notice, 74 Geo. L.J. 395 (1985) (presupposing no juror knowledge "would place an intolerable burden on the adjudicatory process").

6. *See* United States v. McAfee, 8 F.3d 1010, 1014 (5th Cir. 1993) (juries are free to "apply common knowledge, observation, and experience gained in the ordinary affairs of life when giving effect to inferences that may reasonably be drawn from the evidence").

7. *See, e.g.,* Devitt & Blackmar, Federal Jury Practice and Instructions 15.01 (6th ed. 2006) ("You are expected to use your good sense, consider the evidence in the case for only those purposes for which it has been admitted, and give it a reasonable and fair construction, in the light of your common knowledge of the natural tendencies and inclinations of human beings.").

8. *See* Commonwealth v. Brown, 309 Pa. 515, 522-523, 164 A. 726, 728-729 (1933) ("[C]ounsel in their argument have the right to use illustrations from history or literature or any other stock of common knowledge."). *See generally* Levin & Levy, Persuading the Jury with Facts Not in Evidence: The Fiction-Science Spectrum, 105 U. Pa. L. Rev. 139 (1956).

9. *See* Kalven & Zeisel, The American Jury 132 (1966) ("Bringing knowledge such as this to bear on its deliberations is, of course, one of the jury's most engaging and flavorsome characteristics.").

formal proof, the term "judicial notice" comes naturally to mind. Indeed this is the term often used to explain the behavior of judges. After all, they too need such information in order to act effectively as factfinders and wisely in making legal rulings such as ruling on questions of admissibility (especially questions of relevance) and motions for summary judgment, directed verdict (or J.N.O.V.) and new trial, as well as evaluating the sufficiency of evidence on appeal.[10] When juries take into account such information, the process is often referred to as "jury notice."

Although there are no regulating rules, it is commonly understood that there are limits to the kinds of knowledge that judges and jurors may properly bring to bear in performing their factfinding tasks. Usually it is said that they should take into account that common body of knowledge that informed people in the community would be expected to have.[11] And it is understood that a juror should not bring into play some unique knowledge relating to the case, especially if that knowledge is particular to the parties or transactions in issue. If a juror has such knowledge, his participation in the case amounts to misconduct that may warrant a new trial, especially if he shares his knowledge with other jurors (which is likely to be the only situation in which the effect of such knowledge becomes detectable afterwards).[12] One of the intended functions of voir dire is to detect the presence of such knowledge. If the topic is raised at this time and a juror falsely denies his special knowledge, this fact provides an additional basis for finding misconduct and awarding a new trial[13] although sometimes the failure of a party to ask questions reasonably calculated

10. *See, e.g.,* United States v. Murray, 492 F.2d 178, 195 (9th Cir. 1973) (trial judge properly refused to allow defendant to talk to government witnesses until just prior to trial; judge "could, and apparently did, take judicial notice of the personal danger a narcotics conspirator risks when he becomes a turncoat and Government informer"), *cert. denied,* 419 U.S. 854 and 419 U.S. 942.

11. *See* Mansfield, Jury Notice, 74 Geo. L.J. 395, 407 (1985) (standard for permissible jury notice should be whether "a substantial number of people in the community have the information or hold the belief in question."). Some cases take a narrow view of the scope of jury notice allowed. *See, e.g.,* United States v. Dior, 671 F.2d 351, 358 n.11 (9th Cir. 1982) (jury not allowed to find without evidence or a notice instruction that $13,690 in Canadian currency was equivalent to at least $5,000 of United States currency); United States v. Jones, 580 F.2d 219 (6th Cir. 1978) (jury not allowed to find without evidence or a notice instruction that Southern Central Bell Telephone Company was a common carrier). *But see* United States v. Thomas, 610 F.2d 1166, 1171-1172 (3d Cir. 1979) (from testimony that bank was a "National" bank, jury allowed to find that it was federally chartered, an essential element of federal jurisdiction).

12. *See, e.g.,* United States v. Howard, 506 F.2d 865 (5th Cir. 1975) (error for one juror to inform others that defendant had previously been in trouble with the law); State v. Larue, 68 Haw. 575, 722 P.2d 1039, 1041 (1986) (child molestation prosecution; defendant denied right to impartial jury where jury foreperson told other jurors: "Well, I know for a fact that [children] do remember because when I was a little girl, about three years old, my uncle molested me."). However, an attempt to establish that a juror improperly disclosed information outside the scope of jury notice to other jurors is often blocked by FRE 606(b). *See* §6.11, *infra.*

13. *See* Crump, Peremptory Challenges After *McDonough Power Equipment, Inc. v. Greenwood:* A Problem of Fairness, Finality and Falsehood, 69 Or. L. Rev. 741, 762 (1990) (addressing issue of false statements by jurors during voir dire).

to elicit such knowledge is thought to waive a claim of misconduct. It is also improper for judges to rely on personal or specialized knowledge in evaluating the evidence in the case.[14]

The line between basic facts and adjudicative facts "generally known within the territorial jurisdiction of the trial court" is particularly fine. If a party is unwilling to rely on the preexisting knowledge of the jury and seeks to inform the jury by means of a notice instruction, then FRE 201 applies, just as the other evidentiary rules would apply if the party offered evidence to prove the point. For example, in an extortion prosecution for alleged threats made in a letter, the prosecutor might be content to rely on the jury's own knowledge of language to persuade them that the words used in the letter were threatening.[15] However, if the prosecutor requests judicial notice that the words used were threatening, the facts would become adjudicative rather than basic and FRE 201 would control.[16] The distinction between basic facts and adjudicative facts "capable of accurate and ready determination" by unchallengeable authorities is sharper. Most facts in the latter category (for example, high tide was at 4:07 A.M. on January 17) are clearly beyond the realm of common knowledge or jury notice.

Basic facts v. adjudicative facts

For the most part, background knowledge must be preexisting. After trial begins, attempts by jurors to mount an investigation, gather facts, or conduct experiments on particular points in controversy are impermissible,[17] and similar limits apply to judges. Although in evaluating evidence judges sometimes utilize external sources that are beyond common knowledge, such as tables of stopping distances,[18] they should

14. *See* United States v. Lewis, 833 F.2d 1380, 1385 (9th Cir. 1987) (improper for trial judge to rule confession by defendant coming out of surgery to be involuntary on basis of the trial judge's personal experience and reaction to anesthetic when he underwent surgery); United States v. Sorrells, 714 F.2d 1522, 1527 n.6 (11th Cir. 1983) (in ruling on challenge to sufficiency of search warrant, improper for trial judge to rely upon his personal knowledge of informant's reliability because he had been before the court on other occasions). *But see* Hersch v. United States, 719 F.2d 873, 878 (6th Cir. 1983) (not improper for trial judge to bring his military and sailing experience to bear in assessing evidence).

15. *Cf.* United States v. Prochaska, 222 F.2d 1, 3 (7th Cir. 1955) (court rejects defense challenge to extortion conviction based on insufficiency of evidence, stating "We note judicially that the slang expressions employed are part of the stereotyped vocabulary of the Hollywoodesque underworld and are essentially synonymous with a promise of a 'one-way ride.'"), *cert. denied*, 350 U.S. 836.

16. Similarly, in a court trial if a party is not willing to assume preexisting knowledge and formally requests the judge to take judicial notice of a fact as an element of the party's proof, then the requirements of FRE 201 must be satisfied.

17. *See, e.g.,* United States v. Posner, 644 F. Supp. 885, 889 (S.D. Fla. 1986) (unauthorized jury view), *aff'd sub nom.* United States v. Scharrer, 828 F.2d 773 (11th Cir. 1987); Thomas v. Kansas Power & Light Co., 185 Kan. 6, 340 P.2d 379 (1959) (new trial granted where juror borrowed book on electricity and shared information he learned about arcing characteristics of electricity with other jurors).

18. *See, e.g.,* Ennis v. Dupree, 262 N.C. 224, 136 S.E.2d 702 (1964) (affirming judgment of nonsuit against plaintiff citing table of stopping distances indicating defendant could not have stopped in time to avoid hitting eight-year-old boy on bike).

not do so if there is any question about the accuracy of such sources without notifying the attorneys.

While background information is mostly unregulated and invisible, occasionally it enters a case by means of jury instructions or facts cited in opinions or decisions in explanation of a judgment.[19] Here the term "judicial notice" seems appropriate to describe what is happening although it remains true that FRE 201 does not apply.

FRE 201(b)

Kinds of Facts. A judicially noticed fact must be one not subject to reasonable dispute in that it is either (1) generally known within the territorial jurisdiction of the trial court or (2) capable of accurate and ready determination by resort to sources whose accuracy cannot reasonably be questioned.

---

§2.5　Indisputability Requirement

Judicial notice under FRE 201(b) may be taken only of adjudicative facts that are "not subject to reasonable dispute,"[1] a stringent standard that significantly limits the facts subject to notice.[2] This high standard is made necessary by the fact that FRE 201(g) makes notice binding on the jury, at least in civil cases. Binding notice of disputable facts would undermine the adversary process and infringe on the right to jury trial.[3]

Prior to the adoption of FRE 201, some writers had urged a broader approach that would allow judicial notice of both indisputable facts and facts unlikely to be disputed.[4] Coupled with this broader approach was the suggestion that judicial notice should function like a rebuttable presumption and a noticed fact should be treated as established unless

---

19. *See, e.g.,* State v. Dunn, 221 Mo. 530, 120 S.W. 1179, 1182 (1909) (trial judge instructed jury that one who "uses upon another at some vital part a deadly weapon, as a heavy wooden club" must be presumed to intend death; reviewing court approved assumption that club was a deadly weapon, stating that "[n]o one of ordinary intelligence would hesitate for a moment in concluding that the club in question" was a dangerous weapon; "such things as all persons of ordinary intelligence are presumed to know are not required to be proven").

§2.5　1. *See* ACN, FRE 201(b) (referring to a tradition of "caution" and "circumspection" limiting notice to facts lying "beyond reasonable controversy").

2. *See* Hardy v. Johns-Manville Sales Corp., 681 F.2d 334, 347 (5th Cir. 1982) (under FRE 201 judicial notice applies only to "self-evident truths that no reasonable person could question, truisms that approach platitudes or banalities").

3. *See* Davis, A System of Judicial Notice Based on Fairness and Convenience, in Perspectives of Law 69, 93 (R. Pound ed. 1964) (taking evidence "is the best way to resolve controversies involving disputes of adjudicative facts" and fair procedure "calls for giving each party a chance to meet in the appropriate fashion the facts that come to the tribunal's attention, and the appropriate fashion for meeting disputed facts includes rebuttal evidence, cross-examination, usually confrontation, and argument").

4. *See* Davis, Judicial Notice, 1969 Law and the Social Order 513, 515-516 ("[T]he practical course is to take notice and allow challenge later whenever the court believes

challenged.[5] But the drafters of FRE 201 rejected these suggestions and instead adopted a narrow form of notice with binding effect.[6]

The party requesting notice has the burden of proving that the standard of FRE 201(b) is satisfied, and the opponent may offer counterproof to persuade the court that the matter is subject to reasonable dispute.[7] Notice may be taken upon a finding of indisputability[8] and refused where a reasonable dispute exists.[9]

The Advisory Committee took the view that judicial notice should not extend to "propositions of generalized knowledge."[10] The apparent concern was that FRE 201 should not permit courts to notice generalized statements in medical or scientific treatises and similar works. Treatises often contain statements that are broad, abstract, or theoretical, hence more likely to be subject to reasonable dispute. No clear line, however, distinguishes "generalized" knowledge from "specific" knowledge. The real inquiry, and the one sanctioned by FRE 201(b), focuses upon the certainty of the proposition, not its specificity. General propositions of knowledge that are reasonably indisputable, for example, the movement of planets in the solar system, are appropriate subjects of notice under FRE 201. Such knowledge may be found in encyclopedias or treatises as well as in almanacs, atlases, and other similar sources.

---

that challenge is unlikely"); Thayer, A Preliminary Treatise on Evidence 308 (1898) ("Taking notice does not import that the matter is indisputable"); 9 Wigmore, Evidence §2567a, at 716-718 (Chadbourn rev. 1981).

5. Various writers favored this approach, most notably Professor Edmund Morgan of Harvard. *See* Morgan, The Law of Evidence, 1941-1945, 59 Harv. L. Rev. 481, 482-487 (1946) *and* Morgan, Judicial Notice, 57 Harv. L. Rev. 269 (1944). *See also* Maguire, Evidence—Common Sense and Common Law 174 (1947); McNaughton, Judicial Notice—Excerpts Relating to the Morgan-Wigmore Controversy, 14 Vand. L. Rev. 779, 787-788 (1961); McCormick, Judicial Notice, 5 Vand. L. Rev. 296, 321-322 (1952).

6. The Preliminary Draft of FRE 201(g) limited binding judicial notice to civil cases, but the Rule promulgated by the Supreme Court made notice binding in both civil and criminal cases. Congress restored the position taken in the Preliminary Draft. URE 201(g) (1974) follows the Supreme Court version and makes judicial notice binding in both civil and criminal cases. *See* discussion of the effect of judicial notice in §2.11, *infra,* and special problems in criminal cases in §2.12, *infra.*

7. *See* Ohio River Co. v. Peavey Co., 731 F.2d 547, 550 (8th Cir. 1984) ("Nor could the district court take judicial notice that a 10 percent [prejudgment interest] rate was appropriate when evidence was offered to the contrary"); Hardy v. Johns-Manville Sales Corp., 681 F.2d 334, 347-348 (5th Cir. 1982) (refusing to take judicial notice that asbestos causes cancer in face of rebutting evidence offered by defendant).

8. *See, e.g.,* O'Toole v. Northrop Grumman Corp., 499 F.3d 1218, 1224 (10th Cir. 2007) (error to refuse notice of historical retirement fund earnings posted on defendant employer's website for purposes of determining damages when employer did not dispute its own information).

9. *See, e.g.,* Jespersen v. Harrah's Operating Co., Inc., 444 F.3d 1104, 1110-1111 (9th Cir. 2006) (refusing to take judicial notice that it is more costly and time-consuming for women to comply with employer's grooming policy than for men; not beyond dispute).

10. ACN, FRE 201(b) ("It is not believed that judges now instruct juries as to 'propositions of generalized knowledge' derived from encyclopedias or other sources, or that they are likely to do so, or, indeed, that it is desirable that they do so.").

§2.6   Generally Known Facts

FRE 201(b)(1) provides that judicial notice may be taken of adjudicative facts "generally known" within the territorial jurisdiction of the trial court. "General" knowledge does not mean universal knowledge nor does it necessarily require knowledge by a majority of citizens. It should suffice that the fact is generally known by well-informed persons within the district or even within the geographical subdivision of the district where the case is being tried. The personal experience or private knowledge of the judge is not a proper foundation for judicial notice[1] although trial judges occasionally overlook this well-established rule.[2]

The "generally known" standard covers a "breathtaking variety"[3] of facts, including matters of geography,[4] current events,[5] language and word usage,[6] history and politics,[7] economic conditions,[8] and similar facts[9] although courts sometimes cite FRE 201 even when noticing facts that are not clearly adjudicative.[10] Courts have denied notice of other

---

§2.6   1. *See* United States v. Berber-Tinoco, 510 F.3d 1083, 1091 (9th Cir. 2007) (improper for trial judge to notice traffic conditions on certain route based on personal knowledge); United States v. Hoyts Cinemas Corp., 380 F.3d 558, 570-71 (1st Cir. 2004) (trial judge should not have taken notice that moviegoers prefer to sit in middle or back rows based on judge's own experience).

2. *See, e.g.*, SEC v. Musella, 578 F. Supp. 425, 439 (S.D.N.Y. 1984) (noticing that law firms train employees to respect client confidentiality; "I have not been so long removed from the world inhabited by firms like Sullivan [& Cromwell] to have forgotten what life is like there.").

3. Dippin' Dots, Inc. v. Frosty Bites Distrib., LLC, 369 F3d 1197, 1204 (11th Cir. 2004) (taking notice that color indicates flavor of ice cream).

4. *See, e.g.*, United States v. Southard, 700 F.2d 1, 25-26 (1st Cir. 1983) (driving time from New Haven to Rhode Island is more than 15 minutes), *cert. denied sub nom.* Ferris v. United States, 464 U.S. 823; United States v. Blunt, 558 F.2d 1245, 1247 (6th Cir. 1977) (Federal Correctional Institution at Lexington, Kentucky is within territorial jurisdiction of United States).

5. *See, e.g.*, Nationalist Movement v. City of Cumming, 913 F.2d 885, 893 (11th Cir. 1990) (notice that "plaintiff's rallies and marches are often loud and attract boisterous and sometimes violent counter-demonstrators," based upon local and national media accounts as well as public records), *cert. denied*, 498 U.S. 1053; Ritter v. Hughes Aircraft Co., 58 F.3d 454, 458 (9th Cir. 1995) (taking judicial notice that there had been widespread layoffs at defendant's plant because it was fact generally known).

6. *See, e.g.*, B.V.D. Licensing Corp. v. Body Action Design, Inc., 846 F.2d 727, 728 (Fed. Cir. 1988) ("the B.V.D. trademark is at least widely, if not universally, known"); United States v. Dolan, 544 F.2d 1219, 1223 n.8 (4th Cir. 1976) (PCP is another name for phencyclidine).

7. *See, e.g.*, United Klans of America v. McGovern, 453 F. Supp. 836, 838-839 (N.D. Ala. 1978) ("The United Klans has been and continues to be a 'white supremacy' organization whose purposes and policies are implemented by acts of terror and intimidation."), *aff'd*, 621 F.2d 152 (5th Cir. 1980).

8. *See* Rutherford v. Sea-Land Service, Inc., 575 F. Supp. 1365, 1370 (N.D. Cal. 1983) (eight dollars per day is an unreasonably low maintenance sum for obtaining lodging and three meals a day in San Francisco Bay area).

9. *See, e.g.*, Sullivan v. City of Augusta, 511 F.2d 16, 36 (1st Cir. 2007) (traffic control is a major responsibility of police departments around the nation); Goldberg v. Cablevision Sys. Corp., 261 F.3d 318 (2d Cir. 2001) (taking judicial notice that educational programs aired on television and radio commonly conclude with directions for obtaining a transcript or duplicate tape).

10. *See* §2.4, *supra*.

matters that fall short of the "generally known" standard.[11] Courts have been particularly unwilling to take judicial notice of the knowledge or mental state of an individual on the ground that such a "fact" is neither generally known nor verifiable.[12]

§2.7   Verifiable Facts

FRE 201(b)(2) authorizes judicial notice of facts that are beyond reasonable dispute because they are subject to accurate and ready verification by resort to sources whose accuracy cannot reasonably be questioned. This provision authorizes notice of those innumerable facts that can be determined from unimpeachable sources, even if not generally known.[1]

Courts take notice of a wide variety of verifiable facts, including matters of geography,[2] history,[3] science,[4] economics,[5] politics,[6] government records and regulations,[7] calendars,[8] language,[9] learned

11. *See, e.g.,* United States v. Bramble, 641 F.2d 681, 683 (9th Cir. 1981) (on issue of whether defendant was cultivating marijuana for purposes of commercial sale, court refuses to take judicial notice of amount of usable marijuana from 21 plants, stating: "To some segments of the population these facts might be said to be common knowledge. They are not to the members of this panel."), *cert. denied,* 459 U.S. 1072; Eain v. Wilkes, 641 F.2d 504, 512 n.9 (7th Cir. 1981) (refusing to take judicial notice that Israel routinely tortures political prisoners), *cert. denied,* 454 U.S. 894.

12. *See* United States v. Southard, 700 F.2d 1, 26 (1st Cir. 1983) ("Although we hesitate to lay down a hard and fast rule, we are hard put to think of a situation in which a judicially-noticed fact could be used as the basis for proving knowledge of that fact by the defendant."), *cert. denied sub nom.* Ferris v. United States, 464 U.S. 823; United States v. Wilson, 631 F.2d 118, 120 (9th Cir. 1980) (improper to take judicial notice of defendant's willfulness in prosecution for bail jumping).

§2.7   1. *See, e.g.,* Davis v. Freels, 583 F.2d 337, 339 n.2 (7th Cir. 1978) (exact time of sunrise on a specific date).

2. *See, e.g.,* United States v. Coutchavlis, 260 F.3d 1149, 1153 (9th Cir. 2001) (court may take judicial notice of a map in determining whether a defendant known to have driven from one location to another passed through a particular jurisdiction).

3. *See, e.g.,* Smith v. Pro Football, Inc., 593 F.2d 1173, 1213 n.71 (D.C. Cir. 1978) (Jack Snow was drafted in the first round by Minnesota Vikings, relying upon the Encyclopedia of Pro Football).

4. Miller Brewing Co. v. G. Heileman Brewing Co., 561 F.2d 75, 81 n.11 (7th Cir. 1977) (alcoholic and caloric content go hand in hand), *cert. denied,* 434 U.S. 1025.

5. Greenhouse v. MCG Capital Corp., 392 F.3d 650, 655 (4th Cir. 2004) (taking judicial notice of published stock prices); Transorient Navigators Co., S.A. v. M/S Southwind, 788 F.2d 288, 293 (5th Cir. 1986) (prevailing interest rates).

6. *See, e.g.,* Schaffer v. Clinton, 240 F.3d 878 (10th Cir. 2001) (taking judicial notice of percentage of vote Congressman received in successive elections).

7. *See, e.g.,* Oran v. Stafford, 226 F.3d 275, 289 (3d Cir. 2000) (SEC filings); Driebel v. City of Milwaukee, 298 F.3d 622, 630 n.2 (7th Cir. 2002) (police department manual containing rules and regulations).

8. United States v. Warneke, 199 F.3d 906, 909 n.1 (7th Cir. 1999) (district court set case on trial calendar for March 8, 2000); Allen v. Allen, 518 F. Supp. 1234, 1235 n.2 (E.D. Pa. 1981) (Father's Day occurred on June 17 in 1979).

9. Nestle Co. v. Chester's Market, Inc., 571 F. Supp. 763, 775 n.9 (D. Conn. 1983) (notice of dictionary and cookbook excerpts).

treatises,[10] and other matters[11] although courts sometimes rely upon FRE 201(b)(2) even when noticing facts that are not clearly adjudicative.[12]

Judges may notice court records and material in court files under FRE 201(b)(2), including indictments,[13] transcripts,[14] convictions,[15] settlements,[16] judgments,[17] and affirmances and reversals on appeal.[18] Courts may also notice administrative proceedings,[19] agency records,[20] and court records in related proceedings[21] or previous proceedings involving one or more of the same parties.[22] In addition, courts sometimes take notice based upon matters adjudicated in earlier proceedings.[23]

10. United States v. Norman, 415 F.3d 466, 473 (5th cir. 2005) (noticing learned treatise). *But see* Baker v. Barnhart, 457 F.3d 882, 890-891 (8th Cir. 2006) (error to notice article discrediting agency's capacity; article was not learned treatise that is authoritative and presumptively trustworthy, but rather was commercial and not peer reviewed).

11. *See, e.g.,* Crane v. Crest Tankers, Inc., 47 F.3d 292 (8th Cir. 1995) (notice of plaintiff's life expectancy); Blake v. United States, 841 F.2d 203, 206 n.2 (7th Cir. 1988) (kilogram of cocaine weighs approximately 2.2 pounds).

12. *See, e.g.,* United States v. Holmes, 414 F. Supp. 831, 834 n.3 (D. Md. 1976) (notice of an Army regulation). But occasionally a rule of law is submitted to the jury as an adjudicative fact. *See* Smith v. United States, 431 U.S. 291, 309 (1977) (Iowa law on obscenity introduced into evidence and "jurors were told that they could consider it as evidence of the community standard").

13. Ives Laboratories, Inc. v. Darby Drug Co., 638 F.2d 538, 544 n.8 (2d Cir. 1981), *rev'd on other grounds sub nom.* Inwood Laboratories, Inc. v. Ives Laboratories, Inc., 456 U.S. 844 (1981).

14. United States v. Rey, 811 F.2d 1453, 1457 n.5 (11th Cir. 1987) (notice of transcript from previous trial), *cert. denied,* 484 U.S. 830.

15. Kowalski v. Gagne, 914 F.2d 299 (1st Cir. 1990) (approving judicial notice of defendant's prior conviction).

16. ITT Rayonier, Inc. v. United States, 651 F.2d 343, 345 n.2 (5th Cir. 1981) (notice of settlement in related proceeding).

17. Stutzka v. McCarville, 420 F.3d 757, 760 n.2 (8th Cir. 2005) (noticing bankruptcy judgment).

18. Miles v. State of California, 320 F.3d 986, 987 n.1 (9th Cir. 2003) (notice of appeal).

19. Kavowras v. New York Times Co., 328 F.3d 50, 57 (2d Cir. 2003) (taking judicial notice of public filing of an unfair labor practice charge with the NLRB).

20. City of Sausalito v. O'Neill, 386 F.3d 1186, 1224 n.2 (9th Cir. 2004) (federal courts may take judicial notice of agency records not reasonably in dispute); Mack v. South Bay Beer Distribs., Inc., 798 F.2d 1279, 1282 (9th Cir. 1986) (notice of "records and reports of administrative bodies").

21. Bias v. Moynihan, 508 F.3d 1212, 1225 (9th Cir. 2007) (taking notice of five prior cases that plaintiff litigated pro se to evaluate argument that she was prejudiced by pro se status); Patterson v. Mobil Oil Corp., 335 F.3d 476, 481 n.1 (5th Cir. 2003) (related state court proceedings).

22. Biomedical Patent Management Corp. v Calif. Dept. of Health Services, 505 F.3d 1328, 1331 n.1 (Fed Cir. 2007) (taking judicial notice of court filings in previous litigation between parties).

23. United States v. Salinas, 611 F.2d 128, 130 (5th Cir. 1980) (notice taken of facts adjudicated in a previous criminal proceeding regarding the location and physical aspects of a border checkpoint).

Although courts sometimes express reluctance to notice records of court proceedings not involving the same parties,[24] the same litigation,[25] or the same court,[26] no such restrictions are contained in FRE 201(b)(2). Records of any court can properly be noticed, provided that a "ready" determination can be made from sources whose accuracy cannot reasonably be questioned.[27] If notice of facts in another court's records will cause undue delay or difficulty, or the authenticity or current status of those records remains uncertain, proof by the parties is required.[28]

When a judge notices a court record, a distinction must be drawn between noticing its existence and noticing the truth of matters stated therein.[29] A judge can properly notice that a pleading was filed on a particular day and contained specific allegations, but generally cannot notice the truth of those allegations, because they are usually disputable and often, in fact, disputed.[30] Similarly, notice may be taken that various findings of fact were made by another court, but not the truth of those findings, unless they otherwise satisfy the indisputability requirement of FRE 201(b).[31] However, courts are more willing to

---

24. Ives Laboratories, Inc. v. Darby Drug Co., 638 F.2d 538, 544 n.8 (2d Cir. 1981) (noticing indictments of other defendants for similar offense, court states that it is "somewhat unusual to take judicial notice of proceedings not directly involving the parties to an action"), *rev'd on other grounds sub nom.* Inwood Laboratories, Inc. v. Ives Laboratories, Inc., 456 U.S. 844 (1981).

25. *See, e.g.,* Wilson v. Volkswagen of America, Inc., 561 F.2d 494, 510 n.38 (4th Cir. 1977) (refusing to notice other proceedings against defendant and approving principle that court will not notice even its own records of other litigation between the same parties), *cert. denied,* 434 U.S. 1020.

26. *See, e.g.,* United States v. Rey, 811 F.2d 1453, 1457 n.5 (11th Cir. 1987) (noticing transcript from previous trial in Fifth Circuit only because Fifth Circuit is a predecessor of Eleventh Circuit and its records are records of Eleventh Circuit for judicial notice purposes), *cert. denied,* 484 U.S. 830.

27. *See* Opoka v. I.N.S., 94 F.3d 392, 394 (7th Cir. 1996) (courts may take judicial notice of decisions of courts and administrative agencies "both within and outside the federal judicial system"); Kowalski v. Gagne, 914 F.2d 299, 305 (1st Cir. 1990) (federal courts may take judicial notice of proceedings in other courts if those proceedings have relevance to the matters at hand).

28. When a party has obtained properly certified copies of court records, they will generally be admissible under FRE 803(8), FRE 902(4), and FRE 1005, making reliance on judicial notice unnecessary.

29. *See* Colonial Leasing Co. v. Logistics Control Group Intl., 762 F.2d 454, 459-460 (5th Cir. 1985) (court should take care "to identify the fact it is noticing, and its justification for doing so," particularly where "a document, such as a court judgment, from which any number of distinct facts might be drawn, is the object of the notice"), *modified,* 770 F.2d 479 (5th Cir. 1985).

30. Nolte v. Capital One Fin. Corp., 390 F.3d 311, 317 (4th Cir. 2004) (facts alleged in SEC complaint not subject to judicial notice, but fact that complaint was filed is indisputable and subject to notice).

31. Gray ex rel. Rudd v. Beverly Enters, Mississippi, Inc. 390 F.3d 400, 407 (5th Cir. 2004) (findings of other courts not subject to judicial notice); Capital v. Lease Resolution, 128 F.3d 1074, 1082 (7th Cir. 1997) (generally courts will only notice existence of findings in court records but not truth of those findings because these findings are usually both disputable and disputed; however, it is conceivable that some findings of fact may satisfy indisputability requirement).

accept judgments as at least prima facie evidence of facts essential to sustain such a judgment.[32]

Courts also often take judicial notice of general principles underlying well-recognized scientific instruments, tests or procedures, or the acceptance of such tests or procedures in the scientific community.[33] However, when the court notices such facts for the purpose of deciding the admissibility of scientific evidence, the process is not governed by FRE 201 because it relates to a preliminary question.[34] Today the admissibility of many forms of scientific evidence no longer depends on judicial notice because it has been made admissible by statute.[35] Courts generally do not take judicial notice of the qualifications of the person conducting the test, the reliability of any individual instrument, or the manner in which a test or procedure was conducted on a specific occasion.[36]

In a number of cases, courts have refused requests for judicial notice under FRE 201(b)(2).[37] The Advisory Committee cautioned against noticing tables of reaction time of drivers and stopping distances of automobiles as adjudicative facts[38] although notice of such tables is often taken in evaluating evidence.[39]

The party requesting notice has the burden not only to provide a source on which notice can be based but also to establish that it is a source "whose accuracy cannot reasonably be questioned."[40] Courts

32. Mike's Train House, Inc. v. Lionel, L.L.C., 472 F.3d 398 (6th Cir. 2006) (foreign criminal and civil judgments are admissible as proof that they were rendered, and it is common for courts to use them as "prima facie evidence" of facts stated).

33. See, e.g., United States v. Janis, 387 F.3d 682, 690 (8th Cir. 2004) (notice of principles underlying fingerprint identification); United States v. Martinez, 3 F.3d 1191, 1197 (8th Cir. 1993) (taking judicial notice of reliability of DNA profiling).

34. See FRE 104(a) (rules of evidence other than privilege do not apply to preliminary questions concerning the admissibility of evidence).

35. See, e.g., Uniform Act on Paternity §7, 9B U.L.A. 359 (1987) (blood tests); Fla. Stat. Ann. §§316.1905-316.1906 (radar speed tests).

36. See, e.g., United States v. Dreos, 156 F. Supp. 200, 208 (D. Md. 1957) (although court noticed principles underlying radar, prosecution still must "show that the equipment has been properly tested and checked, that it was manned by a competent operator, that proper operative procedures were followed, and that proper records were kept").

37. See, e.g., Berte v. Ashcroft, 396 F.3d 993, 997 (8th Cir. 2005) (improper to take judicial notice of human rights situation in Ivory Coast); Kushner v. Beverly Enters., Inc., 317 F.3d 820, 829-830 (8th Cir. 2003) (refusing judicial notice of government's sentencing memorandum because facts contained therein were disputed).

38. See ACN, FRE 201(a) (citing Hughes v. Vestal, 264 N.C. 500, 142 S.E.2d 361 (1965), which disallowed notice of such tables as an adjudicative fact to establish the precise reaction time or stopping distance). The Committee's apparent concern was that a fact not be noticed with more precision than the underlying data permits. The Committee may also have wanted to avoid an inference that drivers falling below the average in reaction time or stopping distance are presumptively negligent.

39. See ACN, FRE 201(a) (approving use of a table of stopping distances of automobiles for judicial evaluation of testimony, citing Ennis v. Dupree, 262 N.C. 224, 136 S.E.2d 702 (1964)). See also Wise v. George C. Rothwell, Inc., 382 F. Supp. 563, 568 (D. Del. 1974) (court notices table of National Conference on Uniform Stopping Distance Charts in evaluating record), aff'd without opinion, 513 F.2d 627 (3d Cir. 1975).

40. FRE 201(b).

are reluctant to treat newspapers as such a source,[41] and decisions conflict on when websites qualify.[42]

It should be noted that the source itself need not qualify for admission under the rules of evidence because the purpose of judicial notice is to provide a substitute for formal proof. The determination of the propriety of judicial notice is analogous to the resolution of a question preliminary to the admissibility of evidence under FRE 104(a). Therefore, as under FRE 104(a), parties can offer their proof and counterproof on the propriety of taking notice without being constrained by the rules of evidence, except the rules of privilege. The court may consult any additional sources it finds reliable in deciding whether the proof satisfies the requirements of FRE 201(b). To facilitate appellate review, the source relied upon for notice, as well as other references consulted in establishing the authoritativeness of the primary source, should be set forth in the record.

B.   PROCESS OF TAKING NOTICE

FRE 201(c)

When discretionary. A court may take judicial notice whether requested or not.

FRE 201(d)

When mandatory. A court shall take judicial notice if requested by a party and supplied with the necessary information.

---

§2.8   Initiation of Judicial Notice

A trial judge has discretion to take judicial notice under FRE 201(c) whether or not the parties request it.[1] Courts occasionally take notice

---

41. *See, e.g.,* Shahar v. Bowers, 120 F.3d 211, 214 (11th Cir. 1997) (refusing to take notice that Attorney-General of Georgia had engaged in adultery with a member of his staff based only on newspaper reports).

42. *Compare* Victaulic Co. v. Tieman, 499 F.3d 227, 236 (3d Cir. 2007) (trial court erred in taking judicial notice of facts about plaintiff company based on its website, as private corporate websites, "particularly when describing their own business, generally are not the sort of sources" whose accuracy is beyond question) *with* O'Toole v. Northrop Grumman Corp., 499 F.3d 1218, 1224 (10th Cir. 2007) (error to refuse notice of historical earnings on retirement fund posted on defendant employer's website when offered against defendant, and defendant did not dispute its own information). *See also* Laborer's Pension Fund v. Blackmore Sewer Constr., Inc., 298 F.3d 600, 607 (7th Cir. 2002) (notice that one bank was branch of second bank proper because issue could be resolved with quick internet inquiry).

§2.8   1. ACN, FRE 201(c) (authorizing courts to take notice sua sponte avoids "troublesome distinctions in the many situations in which the process of taking judicial notice is not recognized as such").

of adjudicative facts without being asked to do so (and sometimes without realizing it), and the rule is drafted to accommodate such an exercise of judicial prerogative. Courts generally do not take judicial notice when a party indicates a preference for offering evidence on the point.

FRE 201(d) requires that judicial notice be taken when a party requests it and supplies the court with the necessary information. The mandatory feature enables parties to rely on judicial notice as a method of establishing reasonably indisputable facts at trial, thereby assisting them in their trial planning and preparation.[2] The rule does not eliminate all uncertainty about whether notice will be taken, however, because counsel must reasonably anticipate what information will be found "necessary" to support the taking of notice.[3]

The type and extent of necessary information depends on the nature of the fact to be noticed. For notice of a "generally known" fact under FRE 201(b)(1), it usually suffices to bring the fact to the court's attention and no supporting sources are needed. For notice of points established by indisputable sources under FRE 201(b)(2), the requesting party generally must produce those sources. But judicial notice operates as a shortcut that obviates the need for formal proof, and neither the source itself nor secondary evidence used to verify its accuracy is required to meet admissibility standards (such as satisfying an exception to the hearsay rule).

FRE 201 does not specify a deadline for requesting judicial notice. FRE 201(f) allows the court to take notice at any stage of the proceeding. But a court need not take notice on request by a party if it would be hard or impossible to permit adverse parties to take issue with the propriety of judicial notice as they are entitled to do under FRE 201(e), nor does FRE 201(f) oblige a court to take judicial notice at an awkward or difficult moment when the party requesting notice could easily have acted earlier and avoided the problem. The request should be made early enough to allow the adverse party an adequate opportunity to be heard in opposition. The opponent may need time to gather information to show that the fact in question is reasonably disputable or that the underlying source supporting notice is of questionable accuracy. FRE 201(f) was not intended to rescue parties from every failure of proof, and an appellate court may decline to take notice where a point has not been timely raised in the trial court.[4]

---

2. As an alternative to judicial notice, parties in civil cases also have available a request for admission under FRCP 36, which provides that if a requested admission of fact is not disputed it is deemed admitted at trial. In contrast to judicial notice, requests for admission are not limited to reasonably indisputable facts.

3. *See, e.g.,* Clark v. Southern Cent. Bell Tel. Co., 419 F. Supp. 697, 703-704 (W.D. La. 1976) (court refused to take judicial notice of the black population in Caddo Parish because court was not presented with reliable sources such as recent United States census data).

4. *See* §2.10, *infra.*

FRE 201(e)

Opportunity to be heard. A party is entitled upon timely request to an opportunity to be heard as to the propriety of taking judicial notice and the tenor of the matter noticed. In the absence of prior notification, the request may be made after judicial notice has been taken.

§2.9   Opportunity for Party Input

FRE 201(e) provides that upon timely request parties are entitled to an opportunity to be heard concerning the propriety of judicial notice and the tenor of the matter noticed.[1] Unlike some earlier codifications, the Rule does not require advance notice to the parties that judicial notice is being taken.[2] However, to insure procedural fairness, the court should inform the parties in advance whenever it proposes to notice an adjudicative fact, at least if there is any possibility that a party may reasonably dispute its accuracy.[3]

The drafters omitted a rigid advance notice requirement to avoid creating automatic error whenever the judge fails to provide notice. The Advisory Committee observed that courts sometimes fail to inform parties that notice is being taken because of "frequent failure to recognize judicial notice as such."[4] In such cases, allowing an opportunity for party input after notice has been taken, with rescission of the notice if it is found improper, seems preferable to a rule that would result in error whenever the parties were not informed in advance.

Nonetheless, courts should inform the parties before giving a notice instruction to the jury. In a jury trial, it is harder to remedy the error if notice is later found to be improper, and failure to inform the parties in advance creates an unnecessary risk of a mistrial.

A court can take judicial notice either on a party's request or on its own initiative.[5] If a party requests notice, the request itself constitutes

---

§2.9   1. Rose v. Hartford Underwriters Ins. Co., 203 F.3d 417, 421 (6th Cir. 2000) (in suit against insurance company for denying fire coverage for plaintiff's house, court abused its discretion in refusing to allow plaintiff an opportunity to be heard on propriety of taking judicial notice of plaintiff's arson indictment, which led to acquittal).

2. Rule 804 of the Model Code of Evidence (1942) requires the judge to "inform the parties" of matters to be judicially noticed and allow them "reasonable opportunity" to present information concerning the proposed notice. Some state provisions similarly require notice to parties. *See* Cal. Evid. Code §455 (West 1990); N.J. Evid. R. 10; Kan. R. of Civ. P. §60-410.

3. *See* Cooperativa De Ahorro Y Credito Aguada v. Kidder, 993 F.2d 269, 273 (1st Cir. 1993) (ordinarily before taking notice court should notify parties and allow them opportunity to be heard); United States v. Garcia, 672 F.2d 1349, 1356 n.9 (11th Cir. 1982) (in criminal trial failure to give notice and allow parties an opportunity to be heard may deprive an accused of Due Process).

4. ACN, FRE 201(c).

5. *See* FRE 201(c) and (d), discussed in §2.8, *supra*.

notice to the adverse party.[6] Therefore, failure to inform the parties is most likely to occur where the court takes judicial notice sua sponte. In such cases, the parties may learn that an adjudicative fact was noticed only after the court renders its findings or opinion.[7] A party's right to a hearing under FRE 201(e) applies regardless whether the court uses the term "judicial notice" to describe its extrarecord consideration of an adjudicative fact. The court must rescind the taking of judicial notice, and if necessary modify the decision, if the taking of notice is shown to be improper.[8]

Timely request   A request to be heard under FRE 201(e) must be made in a "timely" manner and can be either oral or written. In the case of a party opposing notice, timeliness is measured from the date the party is informed that notice is being requested or considered. Although the Rule specifies no time period, timeliness should be construed to mean as soon as is reasonable, considering the stage and schedule of the proceedings.[9] In most cases the tenor of any requested notice is uncontroversial and so clearly within the scope of FRE 201 that the adverse party does not request a hearing. Failure to request a hearing, however, usually renders the court's decision to take judicial notice nonappealable.[10]

Whenever a party requests an opportunity to be heard under FRE 201(e), the hearing addresses two points—the propriety of notice and the tenor of the matter to be noticed. The first requires a determination whether the general requirements of FRE 201(b) are satisfied. The second refers to the specific nature or precise scope of the notice with particular attention to the phrasing of any jury instruction.[11]

The hearing under FRE 201(e) is analogous to a hearing under FRE 104(a) on a preliminary question as to the admissibility of evidence. Hence the parties can offer proof and counterproof on whether the indisputability requirement of FRE 201(b) is satisfied, including treatises and affidavits, and such presentations need not comply with the

6. If a party requests judicial notice outside a trial or hearing, it must serve a copy of the request upon the opposing party. *See* FRCP 5(a).

7. *See* United States v. Doss, 563 F.2d 265, 269 n.2 (6th Cir. 1977) (court takes judicial notice of its own records without notifying parties or giving them an opportunity to be heard).

8. If the trial court refuses to honor a party's right to be heard under FRE 201(e), the reviewing court must consider whether this violates a "substantial right" of the party under FRE 103(a) and hence constitutes reversible error. FRE 103(a) sets the general standard of review for any ruling which "admits or excludes evidence" and should be interpreted to govern review of claimed error in taking judicial notice under FRE 201.

9. During trial, a party may need to make a request to be heard immediately after the court indicates that judicial notice is being considered. If a party does not learn that notice was taken until after a hearing or appeal, the time to request a FRE 201(e) hearing should be comparable to the time allowed under the applicable rule for motions for rehearing or similar motions.

10. Nationalist Movement v. City of Cumming, 913 F.2d 885, 893 (11th Cir. 1990), *cert. denied*, 498 U.S. 1053 (1991); Carter v. State, 173 Md. App. 128, 917 A.2d 1195, 1199 (2007).

11. The drafters apparently adopted the reference to "tenor" of the fact noticed from earlier codifications. *See* Model Code of Evidence, Rule 804 (1942); Uniform Rules of Evidence, Rule 10 (1953).

Rules of Evidence.[12] These presentations should be part of the record, thus available for review on appeal. FRE 103(c) normally requires such hearings to be conducted outside the presence of the jury. The court need not invite an oral statement and can limit the parties to a written presentation.

Apart from FRE 201(e), constitutional principles of due process may require the tribunal to give the litigants notice and an opportunity to be heard on the propriety of judicial notice. In *Ohio Bell Telephone Co. v. Public Utilities Commission*,[13] the Supreme Court found a due process violation in an administrative proceeding where the Commission took judicial notice of extrarecord facts and rested its decision in part upon them. The Commission, however, failed to specify precisely what those facts were and denied the opposing party an opportunity to challenge the propriety of noticing them.[14] Although *Ohio Bell* was an administrative proceeding, it applies with equal force to judicial proceedings and to criminal as well as civil cases. At least that is the indication of a later opinion where the Court concluded that judicial notice could not fill a gap in prosecutorial proof that a sit-in at a segregated lunch counter would "foreseeably disturb or alarm the public." In this setting, the Court concluded that failure to notify the defendant deprived him of due process:

> [U]nless an accused is informed at the trial of the facts of which the court is taking judicial notice, not only does he not know upon what evidence he is being convicted, but, in addition, he is deprived of any opportunity to challenge the deductions drawn from such notice or to dispute the notoriety or truth of the facts allegedly relied upon. Moreover, there is no way by which an appellate court may review the facts and law of a case and intelligently decide whether the findings of the lower court are supported by the evidence where that evidence is unknown. Such assumption would be a denial of due process.[15]

The right of jury trial might also be infringed if the lack of a hearing were to cause a court to notice a fact in a jury trial that was subject to reasonable dispute, at least in civil cases where judicial notice is conclusive upon the jury.

Due process requirements

FRE 201(f)

Time of taking notice. Judicial notice may be taken at any stage of the proceeding.

---

12. *See* discussion in §2.5, *supra*.
13. 301 U.S. 292 (1937).
14. *Id.* at 302-303 ("[E]ven now we do not know the particular or evidential facts of which the Commission took judicial notice and on which it rested its conclusion. Not only are the facts unknown; there is no way to find them out. . . . This will never do if hearings and appeals are to be more than empty forms.").
15. Garner v. Louisiana, 368 U.S. 157, 173-174 (1961).

§2.10   Notice at Any Stage

Judicial notice of adjudicative facts is most commonly taken during trial. However, FRE 201(f) makes clear that a court can take notice of adjudicative facts at any stage of the proceedings, including during pretrial and posttrial hearings as well as on appeal. Notice of legislative facts and evaluative facts—applications of judicial notice unregulated by FRE 201—can also be taken at all stages of the proceeding.

Courts sometimes take judicial notice in ruling on pretrial motions,[1] particularly those raising questions of jurisdiction or venue.[2] Occasionally courts take notice to reject the truth of facts alleged in a party's pleading.[3] Courts may also notice adjudicative facts in ruling on a motion for summary judgment.[4]

A party may request judicial notice well in advance of the time that the jury instruction on notice is to be given. Sometimes the request is made before trial so that the party can find out whether evidence will be necessary on the point. If the court grants the request for notice, it normally instructs the jury about the effect of such notice during the presentation of the requesting party's case. The instruction may also be given at the conclusion of the trial, and sometimes it is given on both occasions.

If a party neglects to request notice or offer evidence of an adjudicative fact during her case-in-chief, the party may request notice later in the trial. Often parties make such requests in response to a motion challenging the sufficiency of the evidence such as a motion for a directed verdict or nonsuit. Courts generally entertain such requests without insisting that the requesting party first move to reopen its case, and FRE 201(f) encourages this practice. Giving a judicial notice instruction on behalf of a party who has rested does not pose the same threat to the orderliness of the trial process as allowing the party to call a parade of new witnesses. On the other hand, one court held it improper to instruct a jury to take notice of additional adjudicative facts once deliberations have begun[5] although the dangers to the deliberative process seem insufficient to justify a rigid rule on this point.

§2.10   1. Dippin' Dots, Inc. v. Frosty Bites Distrib., LLC, 369 F.3d 1197, 1204 (11th Cir. 2004) (court may take judicial notice "at any stage in a proceeding, including at the summary judgment stage"). But see Victaulic Co. v. Tieman, 499 F.3d 227, 236-237 (3d Cir. 2007) (notice should be taken "sparingly at the pleading stages").

2. *See, e.g.,* Lang v. American Motors Corp., 254 F. Supp. 892, 894 (E.D. Wis. 1966) (motion to remand cause to state court; court took notice for purpose of finding federal jurisdiction that defendant was involved in an "industry affecting commerce").

3. *See* Powers v. United States, 996 F.2d 1121, 1125 (11th Cir. 1993) (in reviewing dismissal on the pleadings, court is "not constrained to accept allegations clearly refuted by that which we can judicially notice"). But see Victaulic Co. v. Tieman, 499 F.3d 227, 236-237 (3d Cir. 2007) (notice should be taken "sparingly at the pleading stages").

4. St. Louis Baptist Temple v. F.D.I.C., 605 F.2d 1169, 1171-1172 (10th Cir. 1979) ("[A] district court may utilize the doctrines underlying judicial notice in hearing a motion for summary judgment substantially as they would be used at trial").

5. Creasy v. Hogan, 292 Or. 154, 171, 637 P.2d 114, 124 (1981) (error to instruct jury on medical dictionary definition of word "transverse" after jury had retired to deliberate; request for notice is normally made during presentation of party's evidence and "at all events prior to the commencement of jury deliberations").

Judicial notice can be taken to challenge as well as to support a party's case. When a court rules on a motion for a directed verdict, it traditionally considers all facts in a light most favorable to the party against whom the motion is made, except that it disregards any evidence contradicted by facts of which judicial notice may be taken.[6]

The primary use of judicial notice of adjudicative facts after the conclusion of the trial is to remedy gaps in proof.[7] Subject to FRE 201, courts may take judicial notice of any essential adjudicative facts that a party failed to prove at trial. Often courts take such notice in ruling on posttrial challenges to the sufficiency of a party's evidence. Courts may also take posttrial judicial notice of adjudicative facts that rebut proof that was offered, thereby establishing a basis for setting aside the jury's verdict.[8]

Posttrial notice

In criminal jury trials, posttrial judicial notice against a criminal defendant is generally prohibited because under FRE 201(g) the jury must be given an opportunity to reject the noticed fact.[9] Even in civil cases, courts have sometimes found posttrial notice improper where one party adversely relied on the other's failure to prove the subsequently noticed fact at trial.[10]

Subject to the general limits on posttrial notice already discussed, courts may take judicial notice of adjudicative facts for the first time on appeal.[11] Appellate notice of adjudicative facts occurs relatively infrequently because appellate courts have a limited original factfinding role and are reluctant to expand the evidentiary record on appeal.[12] By far

6. *See, e.g.,* Kansas City Pub. Serv. Co. v. Shephard, 184 F.2d 945, 947 (10th Cir. 1950) (verdict should be directed for defendant where "natural laws of physics or uncontroverted physical facts speak with such commanding force that they completely overcome and reduce to sheer absurdity the evidence offered by plaintiff to the contrary").

7. *See, e.g.,* Dionne v. Shalala, 209 F.3d 705, 708 (8th Cir. 2000) (where district court erred in considering wrong agency employment policy, taking judicial notice of appropriate policy).

8. *See* James & Hazard, Civil Procedure §7.13 at 355 (3d ed. 1985) (courts do not allow verdicts to rest on "testimony which is flatly contradicted by indisputable physical facts or laws of nature").

9. *See* §2.12, *infra.*

10. Colonial Leasing Co. v. Logistics Control Group Intl., 762 F.2d 454, 461 (5th Cir.), *modified,* 770 F.2d 479 (5th Cir. 1985) (plaintiff sued a transferee of assets alleging that the transfer defrauded creditors; at trial plaintiff failed to prove it was a creditor and hence had standing; more than a month after winning a verdict, plaintiff requested the trial court to take judicial notice of its creditor status; the court did so by noticing a prior judgment for plaintiff against the transferor, but the appellate court reversed, finding that defendant "relied on [plaintiff's] failure to establish its prima facie case" in declining to produce its own evidence challenging the validity of the judgment and was thus "deprived of the opportunity to adduce evidence on a critical fact placed in issue by the court's action taking place as it did after the jury was discharged.").

11. United States v. Esquivel, 88 F.3d 722, 726-727 (9th Cir. 1996) (in reviewing challenge to jury selection procedure, proper for appellate court to take judicial notice of Government's census data where offered to rebut similar data offered by defendant); Clemmons v. Bohannon, 918 F.2d 858, 865 n.5 (10th Cir. 1990) ("appellate courts may notice facts not noticed below").

12. United States v. Bonds, 12 F.3d 540, 553 (6th Cir. 1993) (in ruling on admissibility of DNA evidence, declining to take judicial notice on appeal of National Research Committee Report; taking notice would bypass trial court factfinding where report presented new data not available to trial court).

the most common type of notice taken in appellate decisions is notice of legislative facts, which aids reviewing courts to carry out their responsibilities for legal interpretation and case law development.

An appellate court is not required to take judicial notice when it is requested for the first time on appeal. Otherwise, judicial notice would become an escape mechanism whereby parties could avoid their usual responsibility to raise points of importance in the first instance at trial.[13] The timeliness requirement set forth in FRE 201(e) should be construed to apply to the request for notice, and an appellate court can find a request made for the first time on appeal to be untimely. An appellate court should take notice, however, where judicial efficiency or the interests of justice would be served or where judicial notice was requested at the trial level but was erroneously denied.

If an appellate court contemplates taking notice of an adjudicative fact, it should notify the parties so they can be heard on the propriety of notice, at least if there is any possibility of reasonable dispute about the fact to be noticed.[14] They should have an opportunity to assert their position in the appellate briefs, in supplemental briefs, or at oral argument. If the parties are not informed that notice is being taken until the appellate opinion is issued, the opportunity to petition for a rehearing should normally be sufficient to satisfy FRE 201(e), which states that "[i]n the absence of prior notification, the request [to be heard] may be made after judicial notice has been taken."

C. INSTRUCTING THE JURY

FRE 201(g)

Instructing Jury. In a civil action or proceeding, the court shall instruct the jury to accept as conclusive any fact judicially noticed. In a criminal case, the court shall instruct the jury that it may, but is not required to, accept as conclusive any fact judicially noticed.

§2.11 Instructing the Jury

When a court takes judicial notice of adjudicative facts in civil cases, it instructs the jury to accept as conclusive the fact judicially noticed. However, in criminal cases the fact judicially noticed does not bind

---

13. *See* City of New Brunswick v. Borough of Milltown, 686 F.2d 120, 131 n.3 (3d Cir. 1982) ("The doctrines of 'legislative facts' and 'judicial notice' are not talismans by which gaps in a litigant's evidentiary presentation before the district court may be repaired on appeal."), *cert. denied,* 459 U.S. 1201.

14. *See* Massachusetts v. Westcott, 431 U.S. 322, 323 n.2 (1977) ("The parties were given an opportunity to comment on the propriety of our taking notice of the license, and both sides agreed that we could properly do so.").

the jury but rather functions as a permissible inference or comment on the evidence.[1] The jury is allowed, but not required, to accept as conclusive any fact judicially noticed. Thus FRE 201(g) is one of the few provisions in the Federal Rules of Evidence that draws a significant distinction between civil and criminal proceedings.[2]

Because judicial notice of adjudicative facts is conclusive in civil cases, it follows that the party opposing notice is not permitted to present evidence rebutting the fact noticed.[3] To allow rebutting evidence would undermine the purpose of judicial notice, countermand the court's instructions, and permit irrational results that judicial notice rules should help prevent. A party who wishes to submit proof challenging the fact noticed should present it to the court at the hearing allowed by FRE 201(e). If the court concludes that the fact qualifies for notice under FRE 201(b), a civil litigant cannot challenge the court's decision by presenting contrary evidence to the jury and cannot urge the jury to disregard a judicially noticed fact.

Under FRE 201(g), judicial notice is not conclusive in criminal cases and functions as a permissive inference.[4] The Rule does not explicitly bar the opposing party from offering evidence rebutting the fact noticed,[5] although it is clearly preferable for the party to present any rebutting evidence to the court at a hearing under FRE 201(e) so the court can make an informed decision whether to take notice.[6] If the opposing party is allowed to present counterproof to the jury, the party seeking to establish the noticed fact should be allowed to offer evidence supporting the noticed fact and, if necessary, to reopen its case in order to do so.

FRE 201(g) does not address the effect of judicial notice in non-jury trials and specifies only the form of instruction to be given to a jury. However, similar procedures should apply in a bench trial. In a nonjury civil trial, the party opposing judicial notice should offer its counterproof in a hearing under FRE 201(e). The court should require the objecting party to present all of its counterproof at such a hearing, and it is to the party's advantage to do so, because the rules of evidence

---

§2.11   1. *See* §3.14, *infra,* on inferences in criminal cases. A permissive notice instruction in a criminal case violates neither due process nor the right to jury trial because under FRE 201(b) the fact noticed must be beyond reasonable dispute and under FRE 201(g) the instruction does not bind the jury.

2. *See also* FRE 404(a)(1) & (2); FRE 609(a).

3. *See* ACN, FRE 201(g) (subject to the hearing provision in FRE 201(e), "there is to be no evidence before the jury in disproof" of judicially noticed adjudicative facts).

4. *See, e.g.,* United States v. Chapel, 41 F.3d 1338, 1342 (9th Cir. 1994) (in bank robbery trial court took judicial notice on basis of FDIC certificate that bank was federally insured; jury told it could accept court's declaration and accept point as proved but was not required to since it was sole judge of facts).

5. *See* United States v. Garland, 991 F.2d 328, 333 (6th Cir. 1993) (in criminal cases "parties may contest facts judicially noticed"; dictum).

6. The purpose of FRE 201(g), which is to preserve the jury's fact-determining role, can be adequately accomplished by prohibiting binding judicial notice without also allowing rebutting evidence about a fact that the court has found to be beyond reasonable dispute.

do not restrict the evidence that may be received. If after the hearing the court decides that the fact is properly subject to notice, it should normally permit no further rebutting evidence.

In a nonjury criminal trial, the issue is more complicated. Because judicial notice does not bind the jury in a criminal case, one might assume it also does not bind the court. However, such an analogy ignores the fact that in a nonjury trial the trier of fact is the very judge who already ruled the fact to be beyond reasonable dispute. Moreover, the purpose of FRE 201(g) is to protect the right to jury trial, a right the defendant waived by consenting to have the case tried to the court. Therefore, once a court decides to take notice in a criminal bench trial (after a FRE 201(e) hearing where the party opposing notice has been given an opportunity to present its counterproof), its decision normally should be final. However, the spirit of FRE 201(g) suggests that the court should be willing to reconsider its decision if the defendant subsequently offers evidence indicating that the fact noticed is reasonably disputable.

§2.12   Special Problems in Criminal Cases

The version of FRE 201(g) originally promulgated by the Supreme Court provided for binding notice in both civil and criminal cases,[1] and URE 201(g) and a number of states adopt this approach.[2] However, Congress amended the rule to make notice nonbinding in criminal cases,[3] concluding that conclusive notice in criminal cases would be "contrary to the spirit of the Sixth Amendment right to a jury trial."[4]

FRE 201(g) as finally enacted is consistent with the established principles that courts cannot direct a verdict of guilty against a criminal defendant no matter how conclusive the evidence of guilt[5] nor are they allowed to make an order partially directing a verdict on an

---

§2.12   1. *See* proposed FRE 201(g), 65 F.R.D. 131 (1974) ("The judge shall instruct the jury to accept as established any facts judicially noticed.").

2. *See* 13A Unif. Laws Ann. 61-62.

3. *See generally* Turner, Judicial Notice and Federal Rule of Evidence 201—A Rule Ready for Change, 45 U. Pitt. L. Rev. 181 (1983).

4. *See* House Report, at 6. *But see* 10 Moore's Federal Practice §201.70 (2d ed. 1985) ("Under the Congressional Rule, in the morning when the judge tries a civil case the world is round. That afternoon when he tries a criminal case the world is flat."); Advisor's Notes to Maine Rule of Evidence 201(g) (it is "as absurd in a criminal case as in a civil action to allow jurors to question the accuracy of the court's instruction as to what day of the week December 4, 1972, actually was.").

5. Sparf v. United States, 156 U.S. 51, 105 (1895) (improper for court in a criminal case "to instruct the jury peremptorily to find the accused guilty of the offense charged or of any criminal offense less than that charged"); United States v. Garaway, 425 F.2d 185 (9th Cir. 1970) (trial court instruction was "contrary to the well-settled rule that a trial judge may not direct a verdict of guilty in a criminal case").

element of the charge.[6] The inability of courts to direct a verdict against a defendant in effect gives juries the power of "nullification" and allows them to acquit a defendant despite overwhelming or indisputable evidence of guilt.[7] By adopting a nonbinding form of judicial notice in criminal cases, FRE 201(g) preserves the power of juries to reject noticed facts.

The Advisory Committee, however, took the position that there is no constitutional impediment to conclusive judicial notice in criminal cases, reasoning that "the right of a jury trial does not extend to matters which are beyond reasonable dispute."[8] This issue remains unsettled as a matter of federal constitutional law, and regardless how it is ultimately resolved under the Sixth Amendment, state rules authorizing conclusive judicial notice against criminal defendants are potentially subject to state constitutional attack.[9]

To take conclusive judicial notice against a criminal defendant would both violate FRE 201(g) and raise constitutional concerns.[10] However, nothing in the Constitution bars conclusive notice in a defendant's favor. By prohibiting conclusive notice in criminal cases, even on behalf of a criminal defendant, the language of FRE 201(g) exceeds its underlying policy.[11]

Most courts bar posttrial notice of adjudicative facts in criminal cases tried to a jury, holding that judicial notice after trial would conflict with FRE 201(g) and undermine a defendant's right to a jury trial.[12] The leading case is *United States v. Jones*, where defendant was convicted of unlawful interception of interstate telephonic communications. After the jury found defendant guilty on three counts, the district court

Posttrial notice

---

6. United States v. Lee, 483 F.2d 959, 960 (5th Cir. 1973) (jury instructions "deciding a material fact issue as a matter of law are erroneous because they amount to a partial directed verdict of guilty").

7. *See, e.g.,* United States v. Moylan, 417 F.2d 1002, 1006 (4th Cir. 1969) (recognizing "undisputed power of the jury to acquit, even if its verdict is contrary to the law as given by the judge and contrary to the evidence," which is "a power that must exist as long as we adhere to the general verdict in criminal cases, for the courts cannot search the minds of the jurors to find the basis upon which they judge"), *cert. denied,* 397 U.S. 910; United States v. Spock, 416 F.2d 165, 180-182 (1st Cir. 1969). *Cf.* United States v. Dougherty, 473 F.2d 1113, 1130-1137 (D.C. Cir. 1972) (improper to instruct jury about power of jury nullification).

8. ACN, FRE 201(g).

9. *See* State v. Lawrence, 120 Utah 323, 234 P.2d 600, 603 (1951) (violation of state constitutional guarantee of a jury trial for judge to take conclusive judicial notice, instructing jury to find that car allegedly stolen by defendant had a value of over $50; "If a court can take one important element of an offense from the jury and determine the facts for them because such fact seems plain enough to him, then which element cannot be similarly taken away, and where would the process stop?").

10. *See* United States v. Mentz, 840 F.2d 315, 322-323 (6th Cir. 1988) (constitutional error to notice "facts constituting an essential element of the crime" without giving instruction in permissive form as required by FRE 201(g)).

11. Some states have adopted a narrower version of FRE 201(g). *See* Or. Rule of Evidence 201(g)(2) ("In a criminal case, the court shall instruct the jury that it may, but is not required to, accept as conclusive any fact judicially noticed *in favor of the prosecution*") (emphasis added).

12. *See* cases cited in note 14, *infra*.

granted defendant's motion for judgment of acquittal on the ground that the government failed to prove that Southern Bell Telephone Company was a common carrier of interstate telephonic communications, an essential element for federal jurisdiction. The government appealed the ruling of the trial court and urged that judicial notice be taken of Southern Bell's status as a common carrier. The Sixth Circuit refused to do so, holding that posttrial notice against a criminal defendant would violate FRE 201(g) by preventing the jury from considering the issue.[13]

Most courts follow *Jones* and hold posttrial judicial notice to be unavailable in criminal cases tried to a jury[14] even though failure of proof on the part of the prosecution generally bars retrial of the defendant.[15] Other courts have allowed posttrial judicial notice in favor of the prosecution, at least for the purposes of establishing jurisdiction or venue.[16] Some courts take a harmless error approach focusing on whether the defendant was prejudiced by the fact that notice was taken after trial rather than during trial.[17]

13. United States v. Jones, 580 F.2d 219, 223-229 (6th Cir. 1978). The issue of posttrial judicial notice must be distinguished from the question whether the jury was properly instructed to find all elements of the crime, including the element that the court is subsequently requested to notice. For example, if in *Jones* the court had failed to instruct the jury that it must find Southern Bell to be a common carrier, the error clearly could not be remedied by taking judicial notice after trial because the jury would never have passed on the question.

14. *See, e.g.,* United States v. Dior, 671 F.2d 351, 357-358 (9th Cir. 1982) (refusing to take judicial notice for first time on appeal that $13,690 in Canadian currency had a value of $5,000 or more in United States currency; judicial notice of an adjudicative fact after a jury's discharge in a criminal case "would cast the court in the role of a factfinder and violate defendant's Sixth Amendment right to trial by jury"); United States v. Bliss, 642 F.2d 390, 392 n.2 (10th Cir. 1981) (affirming acquittal of defendant on charges of falsifying federal bank records where there was no evidence that bank was member of federal reserve system; no judicial notice requested on appeal, but court citing *Jones* expresses doubt that it could properly be taken).

15. *See* Burks v. United States, 437 U.S. 1 (1978) (Double Jeopardy Clause bars retrial after reversal of conviction for lack of sufficient evidence to sustain jury's verdict).

16. *See, e.g.,* United States v. Marks, 209 F.3d 577, 583 (6th Cir. 2000) (proper to instruct jury that Louisville is located in Western District of Kentucky). United States v. Hernandez-Fundora, 58 F.3d 802, 808-812 (2d Cir. 1995) (proper for issue of whether Raybrook Prison is within federal jurisdiction to be removed from jury leaving jury to decide only whether assault occurred at Raybrook; determination of "geographical/ jurisdictional" issues involves judicial notice of legislative facts rather than adjudicative facts making FRE 201 inapplicable).

17. *See, e.g.,* United States v. Bartole, 16 M.J. 534 (A.C.M.R. 1983) (error in failing to take judicial notice that military base where kidnapping occurred was within the territorial jurisdiction of the United States was not prejudicial, where it was unlikely that members of trial court would have acquitted the accused if they had been instructed that they were not bound by the taking of notice and there was overwhelming evidence of the accused's guilt; notice taken by appellate court), *aff'd,* 21 M.J. 234 (C.M.A. 1986). *Cf.* United States v. Piggie, 622 F.2d 486, 488 (10th Cir. 1980) (failure of court to give permissive notice instruction "did not create prejudice"), *cert. denied,* 449 U.S. 863. Certainly in a case such as *Jones,* where the jury was willing to find Southern Bell to be a common carrier without a nonbinding judicial notice instruction on the point, it is difficult to believe that the result would have been different with such an

Occasionally courts avoid the need for posttrial judicial notice by adopting an expansive view of facts that the jury may infer from the evidence adduced at trial.[18] Sometimes courts find the noticed fact to be legislative rather than adjudicative, hence outside the requirements of FRE 201(g).[19] In criminal cases tried to a court, posttrial notice of adjudicative facts is generally allowed on the theory that FRE 201(g) does not apply because the defendant has waived the right to a jury trial.[20]

§2.13 "Judicial Notice" of Law

Another process sometimes called "judicial notice" is the determination of the law applicable to the case. The determination of controlling law is a classic judicial function that must be undertaken in order for the court to make proper legal rulings and instruct the jury at the conclusion of the trial. The Advisory Committee proposed no rule on this point:

> [T]he . . . manner in which the law is fed into the judicial process is never a proper concern of the rules of evidence but rather of the rules of procedure. The Advisory Committee . . . proposes no evidence rule with respect to judicial notice of law, and suggests that those matters of law which, in addition to foreign-country law, have traditionally been treated as requiring pleading and proof and more recently as subjects of judicial notice be left to the Rules of Civil and Criminal Procedure.[1]

At common law, finding the content of foreign law was considered a question of "fact" that was to be pleaded and proved by the parties.[2]

---

instruction. Although the harmless error approach might seem to violate the fundamental rule that a conviction cannot stand where there is a failure of proof with respect to an element of the offense, FRE 201 dispenses with the requirement of evidentiary proof, even in criminal cases, for matters that are "not subject to reasonable dispute."

18. *See* United States v. Thomas, 610 F.2d 1166, 1171-1172 (3d Cir. 1979) (bank embezzlement prosecution; jury allowed to find that bank was federally chartered, an essential element for federal jurisdiction, on basis of trial testimony referring to bank as "First National Bank" since use of word "National" in title "is virtually conclusive that the bank is federally chartered").

19. *See* United States v. Bowers, 660 F.2d 527, 530-531 (5th Cir. 1981) (fact that Fort Benning is within territorial jurisdiction of United States is a legislative fact); United States v. Gould, 536 F.2d 216, 219-221 (8th Cir. 1976) (trial court took conclusive notice that cocaine hydrochloride is a Schedule II controlled substance, and defendant claimed instruction violated FRE 201(g); court found no error on ground that noticed fact was legislative rather than adjudicative).

20. Government of Canal Zone v. Burjan, 596 F.2d 690, 694 (5th Cir. 1979) (*Jones* not applicable to bench trial).

§2.13   1. ACN on Judicial Notice of Law, 56 F.R.D. 183, 207 (1973) (citing FRCP 44.1 and FRCrimP 26.1).

2. Miller, Federal Rule 44.1 and the "Fact" Approach to Determining Foreign Law: Death Knell for a Die-Hard Doctrine, 65 Mich. L. Rev. 613, 624 (1967) ("[T]he common law constructed a procedural microcosm based on an equation between

The term "judicial notice" was used to distinguish between law that was deemed to be known by the court and law that the parties had to prove. A court would take "judicial notice" of domestic law, thereby relieving the parties of the burden of offering formal proof. But for foreign law, formal proof was generally required, usually in the form of authenticated copies of cases and statutes, affidavits, and testimony of expert witnesses. Sometimes, because a question of "fact" was thought to be involved, the proof was made to the jury although the inappropriateness of having juries make determinations of law is now generally recognized.[3]

Under the modern view, when parties must establish applicable law, the court normally makes the determination rather than the jury, and informal proof not subject to the rules of evidence is allowed. If a statute or rule authorizes judicial notice of a particular law, the parties are generally relieved of the burden of formally proving such law. In practice, however, (depending on the difficulty of finding or interpreting the applicable law), the trial judge may request or require counsel to assist in making the determination, either by argument or by submitting memoranda or briefs.[4]

Scope of notice   In federal courts, the scope of judicial notice of law and the procedures for taking such notice are regulated by case law, statutes, and the Federal Rules of Civil and Criminal Procedure. Federal courts take judicial notice of the United States Constitution, federal statutes, and federal case law, as well as the constitutions, statutes, and case law of every state of the union.[5] Federal courts may also take notice of federal and state administrative regulations.[6] There is a greater reluctance on the part of federal courts to notice municipal ordinances[7] although

---

'foreign law' and 'fact.' Over the years, the resulting pastiche became so entangled in detail and so fertile a field for adversarial machinations that it actually exacerbated the difficulties inherent in proving foreign law.").

3. *See* Keeffe, Landis & Shaad, Sense and Nonsense About Judicial Notice, 2 Stan. L. Rev. 664, 675 (1950).

4. Uniform Interstate and International Procedure Act §4.02, 13 U.L.A. 396 Comment (1986) (if court "cannot or does not wish to engage in its own research," it may "insist on a complete presentation of the issues of foreign law by counsel"). Watts v. State, 99 S.W.3d 604 (Tex. Crim. App. 2003) (counsel may be required to assist in determining applicable law).

5. *See, e.g.,* Lamar v. Micou, 114 U.S. 218, 223 (1885) ("The law of any State of the Union, whether depending upon statutes or upon judicial opinions, is a matter of which the courts of the United States are bound to take judicial notice, without plea or proof.").

6. City of Wichita, Kan. v. U.S. Gypsum Co., 72 F.3d 1491, 1496 (10th Cir. 1996) (OSHA regulations subject to judicial notice); In re Madeline Marie Nursing Homes, 694 F.2d 433, 446 (6th Cir. 1982) (although "exact parameters of judicial notice of state laws and regulations are rarely tested," ordinarily "recourse may be had to published and easily available documents evidencing them").

7. *See* Getty Petroleum Mktg., Inc. v. Capital Terminal Co., 391 F.3d 312, 326-332 (1st Cir. 2004) (courts may refuse notice of municipal ordinances or private codes, particularly when they are neither readily available nor submitted to court); Bryant v. Liberty Mut. Ins. Co., 407 F.2d 576, 579-580 n.2 (4th Cir. 1969) (collecting cases for and against taking judicial notice of ordinances).

notice generally is taken when the ordinance is readily accessible in compiled form.[8] The Code of Federal Regulations is subject to judicial notice under the Federal Register Act,[9] and other federal statutes authorize judicial notice of particular types of law.[10]

Proof of the law of foreign nations is regulated by FRCP 44.1 and FRCrimP 26.1. The civil rule requires a party who intends to rely on the law of another country to give written notice, in the pleadings or otherwise, and the court "may consider any relevant material or source, including testimony, whether or not submitted by a party or admissible under the Federal Rules of Evidence" in determining the content of such law. The criminal rule contains virtually identical provisions (but omits any reference to pleadings), and both rules provide that determining the content of foreign law is itself a matter of "law" rather than "fact," meaning that the judge alone decides the point, and that her decision is fully reviewable and not immunized by any deferential (or "clear error") standard.[11]

In diversity and other cases where federal courts are required to follow state substantive law under the doctrine of *Erie v. Tompkins*,[12] the question arises whether a federal court must defer to state provisions regarding judicial notice of law. Whether or not to take judicial notice is not itself a substantive matter for it merely affects the manner and extent to which parties will be required to prove that law and the procedures for doing so. Hence *Erie* does not require federal courts to defer to state judicial notice provisions.[13]

Federal courts appear more inclined to follow state provisions that expressly authorize judicial notice[14] than those that restrict such notice, for example, by requiring pleading of foreign law or establishing a presumption that foreign law is the same as that of the forum.[15]

---

8. Tollis, Inc. v. County of San Diego, 505 F.3d 935, 938 n.1 (9th Cir. 2007) (municipal ordinances are proper subjects for judicial notice); Zimora v. Alamo Rent-A-Car, Inc., 111 F.3d 1495, 1503 (10th Cir. 1997) (same).

9. 44 U.S.C. §1507 (1988).

10. *See, e.g.,* Extortionate Credit Transactions Act, 18 U.S.C. §891(9) (1988) (federal courts shall notice state law "governing the enforceability through civil judicial processes of repayment of any extension of credit or the performance of any promise given in consideration thereof").

11. *See* FRCP 44.1 *and* FRCrimP 26.1 (both containing the phrases quoted in the text). *See also* Abdille v. Ashcroft, 242 F.3d 477 (3d Cir. 2001) (refusing to take judicial notice of South African law where procedures of FRCP 44.1 were not followed).

12. 304 U.S. 64 (1938).

13. *Accord* 1A Moore, Taggart, & Wicker, Moore's Federal Practice; ¶ 0.316[4] (3d ed. 1997); Miller, Federal Rule 44.1 and the "Fact" Approach to Determining Foreign Law: Death Knell for a Die-Hard Doctrine, 65 Mich. L. Rev. 613, 716-717 (1965).

14. *See* Case v. Kelly, 133 U.S. 21, 27 (1890) (state statute requiring notice of private law should be followed by federal courts in the same state).

15. Reeves v. Schulmeier, 303 F.2d 802, 807 (5th Cir. 1962) (finding no need to allege or prove state law in federal courts "notwithstanding state law which requires special pleading and proof"); Tarbert v. Ingraham Co., 190 F. Supp. 402, 406-407 (D. Conn. 1960) (refusing to follow state presumption that sister-state law is same as that of forum; to carry *Erie* to this area of judicial notice is an "unwarranted extension of the doctrine").

Despite great variation in state provisions,[16] most states authorize judicial notice of both federal and state case law, statutes, and constitutional provisions. Many states also authorize notice of federal and state administrative regulations.[17] State courts, however, often do not take judicial notice of municipal ordinances or private laws simply because they are less accessible than state statutes and case law.[18] Many states now have statutes that authorize notice of foreign law or at least simplify the procedures for its proof.[19]

Expansion of noticed law

During the twentieth century, there has been a steady trend toward expansion of the categories of law subject to "judicial notice." Nonetheless, the rules governing judicial notice of law remain an incomplete patchwork in most jurisdictions. Reformers have focused on expanding the categories of law noticed, and sometimes it remains unclear what procedures govern the determination of extraforum law when notice is not taken. State statutes are sometimes silent on such issues as whether the law must be pleaded, whether notice is mandatory or discretionary, whether courts should notice out-of-state law sua sponte or await the request of a party, whether parties must be informed before notice is taken, whether they are obliged to assist the court in establishing the applicable law, and what evidentiary standards govern proof of law offered by the parties.

At the federal level, no single statute or rule governs the determination of law. A more comprehensive approach is needed, and such a goal is likely to be the focus of continuing reform efforts over the coming years.[20]

Needed reform

The direction of reform should proceed along the following lines: First, determining law should be a function for judges not juries. When the content of law is open to question, that question almost never raises issues of historical fact of the sort that juries should determine, and instead the subject almost begs for the expertise of a law-trained person. And of course any decision on such points should be subject to the same standard of review that applies to questions of law generally, meaning

---

16. The greatest number of state judicial notice statutes are based on the Uniform Judicial Notice of Foreign Law Act. *See* Handbook, National Conference of Commissioners on Uniform State Laws 355-359 (1936) (authorizing judicial notice of the statutes and common law of sister states although not entirely on a par with notice of domestic law because notification to adverse parties is required). For a listing of adopting states, *see* 13 Uniform Laws Ann. §403 Comment (1986). A handful of states follow FRCP 44.1, and others have enacted a variety of provisions of their own.

17. *See, e.g.,* Mont. Code Ann. §26-10, R. Evid. 202(b)(3) (1985); Haw. Rev. Stat. §626-1, R. Evid. 202 (1976).

18. *See, e.g.,* Summit Realty, Inc. v. Gipe, 315 A.2d 428 (Me. 1974).

19. *See generally* Saltzburg, Discovering and Applying Foreign and International Law in Domestic Tribunals: An Introduction to the Second Annual Sokol Colloquium, 18 Va. J. Intl. L. 609 (1978); Baade, Proving Foreign and International Law in Domestic Tribunals, *id.* at 619; Schmertz, The Establishment of Foreign and International Law in American Courts: A Procedural Overview, *id.* at 697; Yates, Foreign Law Before Domestic Tribunals, *id.* at 725.

20. For example, FRCP 44.1 and FRCrimP 26.1 are currently limited to proof of the law of foreign nations and should be expanded to cover a broader range of law.

that a reviewing court is entirely free to make its own decision on the content of the law in question.[21]

Second, the manner of proving the content of extrajurisdictional law should be free of formal regulation. Like decisions on the admissibility of evidence, which FRE 104(a) authorizes courts to make without applying the Rules of Evidence (apart from privileges), any proof of the content of law provided to a court should be free of formal evidentiary restrictions.[22]

Third, courts should accord reasonable opportunity for party input and participation when questions of the content of extraforum law arise. While judges are far better able than juries to make such decisions, it does not follow that judges can be counted on to make the right decisions unaided, or aided by only one of the parties, and here is an area in which more rather than less party participation is desirable.

Fourth, although participation by the parties should be invited, the court should not be limited to sources provided by the parties in determining the content of extrajurisdictional law. The court may consider any relevant matter or authority in making its determination, whether or not provided or cited by a party.

Finally, parties wishing to raise issues of foreign nation law should be required to provide reasonable notice to the court and adversary. Determining the content of such law is sometimes nearly as easy as it is for a state court to determine the content of sister-state law, but often language and cultural barriers and the difficulty of access to source material make this task very difficult indeed. Not only is party assistance needed but also reasonable warning that the task is likely to arise in the case.

As noted earlier, the Advisory Committee took the view that the determination of controlling law should be treated solely as an aspect of procedure rather than evidence.[23] A number of states have rejected this view and adopted rules governing determination of law as part of their state evidence codes.[24] Nonetheless, there is a growing consensus that the term "judicial notice" of law should be abandoned[25] because it has uncertain meaning and invites unnecessary confusion with other forms of judicial notice.[26]

---

21. _Cf._ Salve Regina College v. Russell, 499 U.S. 225, 1221 (1991) (appellate courts must review de novo district court's determinations of state law).

22. _See_ ACN, FRCP 44.1 (commenting that the rules of evidence "are often inapposite to the problem of determining foreign law and have in the past prevented examination of material which could have provided a proper basis for the determination").

23. _See_ note 1, _supra._

24. _See, e.g.,_ Okla. R. Evid. 2201; Or. R. Evid. 202.

25. The term "judicial notice" does not appear in either FRCP 44.1 or FRCrimP 26.1. The Advisory Committee's Note to the former provision explains that it avoids the term "because of the uncertain meaning of that concept as applied to foreign law."

26. At one time, the distinction between law that could be judicially noticed and law that could not be was relatively sharp. If notice was taken, no proof was necessary; if not, formal proof was required. But this distinction has almost disappeared. Modern statutes often make judicial notice of law "conditional" upon help by the parties in supplying

Whether the rule is part of a state's procedure code or evidence code is less important than that it provide a workable mechanism for feeding law into the trial process. Rather than simply continuing to expand the categories of law noticed, future legislation should focus on the appropriate allocation of responsibility between court and litigants with respect to all determinations of out-of-forum law and the procedures that govern the process.

necessary information by informal proof. At the same time, the rules for proving law when notice is not taken have been relaxed, so that a party's burden may also be satisfied by informal proof.

CHAPTER 3

Burdens and Presumptions

A. CIVIL CASES

1. Burdens

§3.1 Burdens of Pleading, Production, and Persuasion

Courts normally act only when parties ask them to do so and provide a solid basis for action. Hence it is customary to say litigants must carry certain burdens in order to obtain a court judgment or order. Unfortunately the subject of burdens is among the most slippery in the larger areas of procedure and evidence, and the devices that define and impose burdens are easily misunderstood and misapplied. Sometimes they disguise what is happening and gloss over real problems.

In some ways, the burden of pleading is neither important nor troublesome. There is a trend toward reducing the impact of pleadings. Parties set out claims and defenses in a short and plain manner, and amendments are allowed as of course; motions to dismiss for failure to state a claim or for judgment on the pleadings seldom succeed. Pleadings no longer have much impact on the shape of trial, which is more a function of discovery and pretrial. And many pleading conventions are clear and settled, sometimes by express provision in Rules or statute and sometimes by a

Pretrial burdens

101

monotony of judicial holdings. Typically this body of custom can be located easily in apt descriptions in standard civil practice texts.

Despite the trend toward simplification, and counter to the prevailing pattern of reduced emphasis on pleadings, modern courts sometimes revive traditions of using pleading rules to achieve faster resolution of lawsuits. Thus we find pleading burdens sometimes set or allocated in conscious response to difficulties posed by litigation in an era of expanded statutory schemes and rights. Courts have experimented with what might be called "heightened pleading" requirements as a way of implementing substantive policies behind such doctrines as qualified public immunity (the idea being that higher levels of specificity bring more clearly into focus issues that may quickly dispose of a case). Courts have also recognized that relaxed pleading rules can prolong litigation and force settlements based on pressures generated simply by the litigation process itself.[1] The Supreme Court has spoken to these matters several times, but has sent mixed signals, sometimes disapproving efforts to impose heightened pleading standards and sometimes demanding such standards out of concern for costs and in the belief that other pretrial regulating mechanisms are insufficient,[2] and the Court's work in this area has renewed a longstanding debate over the proper role of pleadings in regulating and resolving civil suits.[3] In 1995, Congress jumped in with both feet, enacting the Private Securities Litigation Reform Act that imposes special requirements on claimants bringing class suits in this area, and part of the aim is to force more detailed disclosures in the beginning of lawsuits and to discourage "professional plaintiffs."[4]

§3.1 1. *See* Richard L. Marcus, The Revival of Fact Pleading Under the Federal Rules of Civil Procedure, 86 Colum. L. Rev. 433, 454-458 (1986) (contrasting "public interest" and "dispute resolution" models; heightened pleading standards implement the latter by helping litigants resolve their differences); Richard L. Marcus, Puzzling Persistence of Pleading Practice, 76 Texas L. Rev. 1749, 1752 (1998) (describing persistence of detailed pleading requirements in civil rights and securities fraud cases).

2. *Compare* Bell Atlantic Corp. v. Twombly, 550 U.S. 544 (2007) (in class suit alleging antitrust conspiracy, approving dismissal for failure to state claim; complaint must state "more than labels and conclusions," and must include "enough factual matter" to suggest "plausible grounds to infer an agreement," and "bare allegation of conspiracy" is not enough; it is not enough that a claim might be "weeded out early" in discovery, since the success of judicial supervision of discovery has been "modest") *with* Swierkiewicz v. Sorema, 534 U.S. 506 (2002) (in employment discrimination cases, plaintiff need not plead elements required by *McDonnell Douglas* framework for prima facie case, which sets evidentiary standard, not pleading standard).

3. *Compare* A. Benjamin Spencer, Plausibility Pleading, 49 Boston C. L. Rev. 31 (2008) (attacking *Twombly* for raising pleading bar "to a point where it will inevitably screen out claims that could have been proven if given the chance") *with* Richard A. Epstein, *Bell Atlantic v. Twombly*: How Motions to Dismiss Become (Disguised) Summary Judgments, 25 Was. U. J.L. & Policy 61 (2007) (defending *Twombly* for recognizing that litigation "has real costs that should be justified only if there is some confidence that the investment in process improves the overall decision-making procedures").

4. See 15 U.S.C. §§77z-1 and 78u-4(b)(2) (plaintiff to supply "sworn certification" stating that he reviewed complaint and authorized its filing, that he did not purchase the security "at the direction of plaintiff's counsel," and setting forth "all of the

Consider now the simple example of a contract suits. Here plaintiff must usually plead agreement and consideration, his own performance, breach by the defendant, and resultant damages. Agreement and consideration can be pleaded by attaching to the complaint a copy of the contract showing mutual promises. Plaintiff's performance may be averred generally, and damage allegations need to be particular only if plaintiff seeks remote or "consequential" damages that are not apparent from looking at the agreement and the allegations of breach. Obviously these are not all the points that might affect the right to recover (others include capacity to contract, legality, modification, and accord and satisfaction), but ordinarily they suffice in a complaint.[5]

Sometimes pleading burdens are allocated out of concerns peculiar to the process of pleading. The purpose may be to help the pleadings make sense: In a suit on a promissory note, usually plaintiff must plead nonpayment; in a defamation action, plaintiff should plead untruth (such complaints would seem odd if these allegations were missing). In these instances the burden of pleading does not match later trial burdens. Usually at trial a defendant sued on a promissory note must prove payment and a defendant sued for defamation must prove truth.[6] Another purpose peculiar to pleading is simply to provide certainty so litigators know what to do at the beginning of the lawsuit.[7]

Trial burdens

The term "burden of proof" embraces two related but different concepts that come into play at trial. One is the burden of producing evidence. The other is the burden of persuasion.

Burden of production

To say a party bears the burden of producing evidence is to say she runs the risk of losing automatically (on motion to dismiss or for judgment as a matter of law) if she does not offer sufficient evidence to enable a reasonable person to find in her favor.[8] At the outset, the party who bears the burden of persuasion usually bears the burden of production as well. In a suit for personal injuries arising from a car accident, for example, plaintiff usually bears the burden of producing evidence of defendant's negligence. By carrying that burden, plaintiff earns the right to have the trier of fact consider and weigh her evidence, a benefit that is most visible in jury-tried cases.

---

transactions" of plaintiff in security during class period; complaint "shall, with respect to each act or omission alleged to violate this chapter, state with particularity facts giving rise to a strong inference that the defendant acted with the required state of mind").

5. *See* FRCP 9(c) (conditions precedent may be alleged generally; denial to be specific).

6. *See* James, Hazard & Leubsdorf, Civil Procedure §3.20 (5th ed. 2001) (usually burden of proving payment is on defendant; usually plaintiff is required to plead nonpayment); 5 Wright & Miller, Federal Practice and Procedure §1245 (1990) ("at least one court" in federal system says plaintiff must plead falsity in libel case); FRCP 8(e) (defendant must plead truth as defense).

7. *See* Palmer v. Hoffman, 318 U.S. 109 (1943) (FRCP 8 requires defendant to plead contributory negligence in diversity case, although state law puts burden of persuasion on plaintiff).

8. Martini ex rel. Dussault v. State, 89 P.3d 250, 256 n.28 (Wash. App. 2004) (quoting this Treatise), *rev. denied*, 108 P.3d 133 (Wash. 2005).

Burden of persuasion

To say a party bears the burden of persuasion (or risk of nonpersuasion) is to say she can win only if the evidence persuades the trier of the existence of the facts that she needs in order to prevail. Ordinarily that means that she wins only if, on the basis of the evidence, the facts seem more likely true than not. Perhaps because this burden operates at the end of trial, courts often say it never "shifts."[9] Usually it is actually mentioned only in jury trials, in argument and instructions.

Elements in burdens

Parties need not produce evidence on every point in a claim or defense any more than they must plead them. The best reason to ignore many points is that ordinarily they do not affect outcome. As one scholar remarked, requiring plaintiff in a contract suit to establish the existence or nonexistence of "every concept treated in Corbin and Williston" would be burdensome and would force the lawsuit to cover "unnecessary territory."[10]

Thus evidence sufficient to enable the trier to find agreement, consideration, performance, breach, and damages normally satisfies the burden of production in a contract suit. Absent defense evidence, plaintiff prevails if the trier is persuaded on these points. Yet the right to recover might turn on points like the fulfillment of conditions, legality of agreement or performance, modification of terms, waiver, estoppel, or accord and satisfaction. If such issues are raised (normally defendant must do so), the outcome might turn on how they are resolved.[11]

Allocating burdens

On any particular point, ordinarily burdens of pleading, producing evidence, and persuading the trier of fact are all cast on the same party. Hence the pleadings provide a reasonable guide to the way trial burdens are allocated.[12]

As with pleading burdens, trial burdens are often allocated by specific custom. In the typical contract suit, plaintiff bears the burdens of production and persuasion on the elements of agreement, consideration, performance, breach, and damages. If nonfulfillment of a condition is an issue, plaintiff bears the burdens on this point too. If failure of consideration is an issue, the burdens of production

---

9. *See* FRE 301 (presumption affects burden of producing evidence but not burden of persuasion, "which remains throughout the trial on the party on whom it was originally cast").

10. Cleary, Presuming and Pleading: An Essay on Juristic Immaturity, 12 Stan. L. Rev. 5, 7 (1959).

11. *See* Kevin F. O'Malley, Jay E. Grenig & Hon. William C. Lee, Federal Jury Practice and Instructions §126.12 (5th ed. 2000) (may waive right to performance; defendant has burden of proof on question whether plaintiff "intended to give up its rights under the contract" while knowing relevant facts).

12. It is not clear that pleading burdens set trial burdens, and the contrary seems more likely. Text writers sometimes give confusing signals, implying that one leads the other but disagreeing about which one is in the driver's seat. *Compare* 2 McCormick, Evidence §337 (6th ed. 2006) (usually "party who has the burden of pleading a fact will have the burdens of producing evidence and of persuading the jury of its existence") *with* Friedenthal, Miller, Sexton and Hershkoff, Civil Procedure Cases and Materials 542 (2008 Revised Ninth Edition) (burden of pleading "usually is assigned to the party who has the burden of producing evidence on that issue at trial"). For the most part, we think burden of pleading should follow burden of persuasion.

and persuasion usually fall on defendant.[13] Beyond these customs, there are some broad notions that account for the allocation of trial burdens. Perhaps the broadest and most accepted idea is that the person who seeks court action should justify the request, which means plaintiffs bear the burdens on the elements in their claims. An idea of trial convenience is sometimes visible too: Defendants bear the burden of proving payment partly because they present their case after plaintiffs have rested, and payment is a fact that would naturally be explored at this stage. Courts sometimes grasp at thin and insufficient notions that do not explain much and can do some mischief.[14]

Four other concerns of broad application help explain the allocation of trial burdens:

First and perhaps most important, burdens are allocated to serve substantive policy, making it easier or harder for plaintiffs to recover or defendants to avoid liability. In negligence cases, plaintiffs are more likely to recover if defendants bear the burdens on the issue of contributory negligence, which is the conventional modern allocation. In a suit against an insurance carrier on a double indemnity life insurance policy, the beneficiary, seeking recovery for alleged accidental death, will more likely recover the full sum if the carrier bears the burdens on the question whether suicide was the cause of death.[15] Sometimes the policy is more negative than positive, as is true of some disfavored or handicapped claims (like fraud) or defenses (like statute of limitations), which are not only allocated as burdens on the party who claims them but sometimes subject to heavier pleading and persuasion

Substantive policy

13. Normally failure of condition becomes an issue only if defendant pleads it specifically under FRCP 9(c). Normally failure of consideration is an affirmative defense under FRCP 8(c), which is another way of saying defendant bears all the burdens—pleading, production, persuasion.

14. There is a standard notion that parties need not "prove a negative," which is misleading because most positive propositions can be reframed as negatives (proof of performance of a contract could be recast as proof of lack of breach). More importantly, it is better to approach the question who has to prove performance of a contract by thinking about substantive issues, access to proof, probability, and trial sequence. There is a standard notion that each party must prove the facts essential to his case, but this idea begs the question, which is "whose case is it?"

15. Usually the carrier pays the face amount of the policy if the insured dies of natural causes (illness or old age) but double if he dies by accident. The underlying logic is that accidental death is sudden and unexpected, and policyholders pay more for greater protection against this eventuality. If the insured commits suicide, the carrier might pay nothing if the policy is less than two years old, but face amount if the policy is older. (Statutes or regulations often address this point. The idea is to keep someone from buying insurance, then killing himself to help his family. If suicide comes much later, the inference of fraud is far weaker and recovery is allowed.) In policies that insure only against accidental death, usually the carrier is liable if the insured dies accidentally but not if he dies of suicide or natural causes. In this setting, ordinarily claimant bears the burden of proving accident. *See* Schleunes v. American Casualty Co., 528 F.2d 634 (5th Cir. 1976). In all these cases the carrier is often exempt from liability if the insured dies in committing a criminal act. *See* 10 Couch on Insurance 3d §139:63 (Lee. R. Russ and Thomas F. Segella, 2000); 17 *id.* §254:46; 21A Appleman, Insurance Law and Practice §12571 (rev. ed. 1981).

burdens.[16] Often the important policies are contained in elaborate statutory and regulatory schemes, and at least some statutes and regulations drafted by modern lawmakers and agencies are carefully phrased to give clear guidance on underlying burdens,[17] although some statutory language may be accidental or perhaps the product of mere ease in expression.[18]

Sometimes presumptions are used to express substantive policies by allocating burdens, and ensuing sections examine the operation of presumptions in detail.

Access to proof   Second, burdens are allocated to put them on the party most likely to be able to carry them, meaning the party most likely to have access to the proof.[19] For example, it is easier for a debtor to prove payment of an obligation than for the creditor to prove nonpayment, and for this reason usually the burden of proving payment is allocated to the defendant.[20] But this relative convenience criterion is often departed from because policy reasons override it: In an ordinary negligence case, for example, plaintiff must prove defendant's negligence and defendant must prove plaintiff's. The explanation is that the party seeking relief must support the request (so plaintiff has a central burden), but we prefer to provide full recovery if negligence is shown unless defendant provides good reasons by showing that plaintiff is all or partly at fault.

Probable truth   Third, burdens are allocated to recognize what is probably true. In a contract suit, it is likely that most conditions precedent to defendant's obligations have occurred because few plaintiffs (or lawyers) would waste time and money bringing suit if many important conditions have not occurred. In light of this reality, the Rules put on defendant the burden of specifically alleging that any necessary conditions have not occurred. In a similar vein, a properly posted letter is almost always delivered to the addressee in due course, and a presumption helps on

---

16. *See* James, Hazard & Leubsdorf, Civil Procedure §§3.9 & 3.10 (5th ed. 2001) (discussing policies relating to specificity in pleading), 7.14 (preponderance standard prevails; occasionally "clear and convincing" standard applies); FRE 9(c) (fraud pleaded with particularity). *And see* Bruce Hay, Allocating the Burden of Proof, 72 Ind. L.J. 651 (1997) (suggesting cost-benefit model for allocating burdens).

17. *Compare* Usery v. Turner Elkhorn Mining Co., 428 U.S. 1 (1976) (construing statute creating black lung presumptions) *with* American Coal Co. v. Benefits Review Bd., 738 F.2d 387, 390 (10th Cir. 1984) (construing regulations creating other black lung presumptions).

18. Cleary, Presuming and Pleading: An Essay on Juristic Immaturity, 12 Stan. L. Rev. 5 (1959) (examining apparent accidental phrasing in statutes construed as allocating burdens).

19. *See* Gomez v. Toledo, 446 U.S. 635 (1980) (in civil rights suit, defendant bears burden of pleading qualified immunity; defense "depends on facts peculiarly within the knowledge and control of the defendant" and subjective belief that defendant must prove "will frequently turn on factors which a plaintiff cannot reasonably be expected to know").

20. *See* Clark, Code Pleading 610 (2d ed. 1947); James, Hazard & Leubsdorf, Civil Procedure §3.11 (5th ed. 2001); Reppy, The Anomaly of Payment as an Affirmative Defense, 10 Cornell L.Q. 269 (1925).

this point.[21] More generally, the litigant claiming that something unusual happened that relates directly to a claim or defense—some departure from the ordinary course of events or human affairs—usually has the burden of pleading the point.[22]

Fourth, burdens are allocated to help resolve cases where definitive proof is unavailable. Thus, absence for seven years without tidings raises a presumption of death unless someone offers proof that the person in question is still alive, and a presumption of due care is sometimes applied with respect to behavior by people killed in accidents when suits are brought by or against their estates.[23]

Proof unavailable

§3.2 Carrying the Burden of Production (Sufficiency Standard)

A party carries the burden of production by introducing evidence sufficient to support the findings of fact that are necessary if she is to prevail. At the beginning of trial, both the burden of production and the burden of persuasion usually rest on the plaintiff. Success in carrying the burden of production assures her that the case is strong enough to be considered on the merits by the trier of fact (jury if there is one; otherwise judge), and it is often said that she has made out a "prima facie case."[1] Failing to carry the production burden means essentially the opposite, and she may lose summarily. On motion by an adverse party, the court may enter judgment as a matter of law and the trier of fact does not decide the case on the merits.[2] Whether the production

21. *See* United States v. Perry, 496 F.2d 429 (10th Cir. 1974); Employers' Liability Assur. Corp. v. Maes, 235 F.2d 918 (10th Cir. 1956); Atlantic Dredging & Constr. Co. v. Nashville Bridge Co., 57 F.2d 519 (5th Cir. 1932).

22. *See* James, Hazard & Leubsdorf, Civil Procedure §3.11 (5th ed. 2001) (citing example of someone who hires a lawyer, where "there is usually a mutual expectation that the lawyer will be paid," but noting that "the usual expectation is the opposite" if a family member asks the lawyer's advice, and observing that the one who claims "the unusual occurrence can be required to plead it affirmatively").

23. *See* Re Chicago & NW Railroad Co., 138 F.2d 753, 755 (7th Cir. 1943) (state presumption of death at end of seven-year absence), *cert. denied*, 321 U.S. 789; Monger v. Cessna Aircraft Co., 812 F.2d 402, 404-405 (8th Cir. 1987) (state presumption that decedents exercised due care).

§3.2 1. Martini ex rel. Dussault v. State, 89 P.3d 250, 256 n.28 (Wash. App. 2004) (quoting this Treatise). Whether she has also succeeded in carrying the burden of persuasion can be known only when the jury returns its verdict or the judge announces his decision. *See* §3.3, *infra*.

2. In a bench trial, the judge throws out the case without finding facts, although the court might retire to ponder the question whether there is enough evidence. As noted at the end of this section, judgment as a matter of law has dramatic effect in jury-tried cases. Either judgment is entered for the moving party and the case does not go to the jury at all, or the judge lets the jury retire and return a verdict, but in the latter event the judge still enters judgment for the moving party (throwing out any verdict favoring the party who failed to carry the production burden). *See* FRCP 50. *And see generally* McNauthton, Burden of Production of Evidence: A Function of a Burden of Persuasion, 68 Harv. L. Rev. 1382 (1955) (classic exposition of production burden with diagrams).

burden has been satisfied is for the judge to decide as a matter of law. The question is one of sufficiency of the evidence.

Success takes case to factfinder

Success for the party with the burden of production does not necessarily shift this burden to the adversary. Suppose plaintiff Agnes offers enough evidence to support a finding that defendant Burt was negligent. Ordinarily the trier of fact remains free to accept or reject her proof. Her success takes her case to the factfinder to decide on the merits, but the burden of production does not pass to Burt and he might win without producing evidence in his favor (counterproof). Resting in the face of evidence that might be believed is risky, however, and usually a party in his position does offer counterproof.

Production burden may shift

If the party with the production burden carries it very well, it does shift to her opponent. That means that the opponent loses summarily if he does not offer counterproof. Jurisdictions vary in defining the quantum or quality of evidence that shifts the burden of production in this way. The term "cogent and compelling" can serve as a convenient shorthand, but the concept is not uniform.[3] Agnes might shift the burden to Burt if she offers unequivocal testimony by neutral observers reflecting simple observations that leave little room for differences in judgment, such as testimony that Burt rear-ended her car while she was stopped at an intersection for a red light, especially if Burt fails to make any headway in discrediting the witnesses by cross-examination. In effect at this juncture Burt must produce some counterproof, such as evidence that he did not run into Agnes or did so only because he was struck by another car from his rear. Failing to produce counterproof puts him at risk of a partial judgment as a matter of law on negligence even though plaintiff Agnes bears the burden of persuasion on that issue.[4]

The example is a vivid illustration of what happens if a party carries the burden of production so well that it shifts to the other side. It is rare, however, for courts to enter judgment as matter of law in favor of the party who bears both the burdens of production and persuasion, and rare for courts to take control over issues like negligence. The cases are more common in which defending parties, meaning

---

3. Most jurisdictions agree that testimonial proof cannot have burden-shifting effect if a reasonable person could disbelieve the witnesses. Jurisdictions vary on the question whether all the evidence may be considered or only that offered by the opponent. *See* Friedenthal, Kane & Miller, Civil Procedure §12.3 (3d ed. 1999) (describing competing standards framed in terms of "scintilla" and "substantial evidence"); James, Hazard & Leubsdorf, Civil Procedure §7.19 (5th ed. 2001) (describing concepts of sufficiency).

4. The jury would still have to determine damages. *See* James, Hazard & Leubsdorf, Civil Procedure §7.19 (5th ed. 2001) (some courts say juries could disbelieve testimony and refuse to find for plaintiff, so a verdict may never be directed in favor of party with burden of persuasion; prevailing view is that "clear, uncontradicted, unimpeached testimony of even interested witnesses" suffices to direct a verdict "in favor of the party having both the burden of persuasion and the initial burden of production"); Prosser and Keeton on Torts §40 (5th ed. 1984) (unanswered proof that defendant struck plaintiff's stationary vehicle from the rear might generate judgment as matter of law even though plaintiff bears burden of persuasion).

those who bear neither the burden of production nor the burden of persuasion, produce cogent and compelling evidence that leads courts to conclude that no reasonable person could find in favor of the claimant. And often courts still let the jury deliberate, reserving power to intervene after the verdict is returned by granting a posttrial motion, again seeking judgment as a matter of law (or judgment notwithstanding the verdict, to use the older terminology), for this deferred intervention allows the court to restore a verdict already given in case a reviewing court thinks the evidence was sufficient after all.[5]

§3.3 Carrying the Burden of Persuasion (Preponderance and Other Standards)

A party carries the burden of persuasion, as the term itself suggests, by introducing evidence that persuades the judge or jury to find the facts she must have to prevail. On most issues in the typical civil trial, the burden of persuasion rests on the plaintiff, who must prove the elements of her case, although the defendant bears the burden of persuasion on affirmative defenses. Ordinarily a party must first carry the burden of production on claims or defenses on which she bears the burden of persuasion. Whether she has done so is a question of law for the judge to decide, as a matter of sufficiency of the evidence. Whether she has carried the burden of persuasion, on the other hand, is a question of fact for trier to decide (jury if there is one; judge in a bench trial), as a matter of the weight of the evidence.

The burden of persuasion becomes most important and most visible when the proof is in and the parties rest their cases. Normally the burden of persuasion in civil cases is defined in terms of a preponderance of the evidence. This standard applies unless there is some special reason to prefer a higher one.[1] If the plaintiff is to win (to take the most common situation), she must carry the burden by proving the elements in her case by a preponderance. By the prevailing view, this standard means the jury is persuaded that the points to be proved are more probably so than not.[2]

Preponderance standard

Understood this way, the preponderance standard is the most generous or lenient standard possible. At least in theory it is satisfied if the factfinder believes by the thinnest conceivable margin that the points

Most lenient or generous

5. *See* Friedenthal, Kane & Miller, Civil Procedure §12.3 (3d ed. 1999) (discussing motions for judgment under FRCP 50).

§3.3 1. *See* Grogan v. Garner, 498 U.S. 279 (1991) (preponderance standard applies in civil actions between private litigants unless especially important individual interests or rights are at stake).

2. *See* Kevin F. O'Malley, Jay E. Grenig & Hon. William C. Lee, Federal Jury Practice and Instructions §104.01 (5th ed. 2000) (preponderance means proving "something is more likely so than not," producing in jurors "belief that what is sought to be proved is more likely true than not").

to be proved are so, and anything less would not be a standard of proof at all.[3] What counts is not volume of evidence but quality—not how many witnesses or how long they testify but how persuasive their testimony. Preponderance is usually said to describe a state of proof in which the "weight of the evidence" favors (or does not favor) a particular conclusion. And preponderance is often said to describe a state of proof that persuades the factfinders that the points in question are "more probably so than not." Yet jurors are to determine what actually happened and reveal truth in the verdict, so the language of probability is not entirely congenial to the aims of the system.[4] Preponderance is not a comparative standard: The question is not whether plaintiff's case is better than defendant's but whether the evidence makes the points that the plaintiff must prove more probably true than not.

Clear and convincing standard

While the preponderance standard applies across the board in civil cases, sometimes a higher standard of "clear and convincing evidence" applies. This higher standard applies in civil commitment cases, termination of parental rights, and deportation and denaturalization cases, where the Court has found that due process requires more persuasive proof.[5] Beyond these examples, strong and enduring common law tradition typically requires proof to satisfy a similar high standard in cases claiming fraud or undue influence, suits to set aside or reform a contract for fraud or mistake, suits on oral contracts to make a will or seeking to establish the terms of a lost will, suits for specific performance of an oral contract, and in other special situations involving disfavored claims or defenses.[6]

3. It is almost irresistible to draw an analogy to likelihood or comparative probability: 51:49 (or for that matter 50.0001:49.9999) is enough. *See also* Grogan v. Garner, 498 U.S. 279 (1991) (preponderance standard "results in a roughly equal allocation of the risk of error between litigants").

4. Ortiz v. Principi, 274 F.3d 1361, 1365 (Fed. Cir. 2001) (preponderance describes state of proof that persuades factfinder that points in question are more probably so than not) (quoting this Treatise). *See generally* Ball, The Moment of Truth: Probability Theory and Standards of Proof, 14 Vand. L. Rev. 807 (1961); Nesson, The Evidence or the Event? On Judicial Proof and the Acceptability of Verdicts, 98 Harv. L. Rev. 1357 (1985). *See also* Sargent v. Massachusetts Accident Co., 29 N.E.2d 825, 827 (Mass. 1940) (it is "not enough that mathematically the chances somewhat favor a proposition to be proved"); Lampe v. Franklin American Trust Co., 96 S.W.2d 710, 723 (Mo. 1936) (refusing instruction in terms of what is "more probable," since verdict must rest on "what the jury finds to be facts").

5. *See* Addington v. Texas, 441 U.S. 418 (1979) (civil commitment proceedings; due process requires clear and convincing standard); Santosky v. Kramer, 455 U.S. 745 (1982) (same for termination of parental rights); Schneiderman v. United States, 320 U.S. 118 (1943) (denaturalization); Woodby v. INS, 385 U.S. 276 (1966) (deportation).

6. *See* cases collected in 2 McCormick on Evidence §340 (6th ed. 2006).

2.   *Presumptions*

> **FRE 301**
>
> In all civil actions and proceedings not otherwise provided for by Act of Congress or by these rules, a presumption imposes on the party against whom it is directed the burden of going forward with evidence to rebut or meet the presumption, but does not shift to such party the burden of proof in the sense of the risk of non-persuasion, which remains throughout the trial upon the party on whom it was originally cast.

§3.4   Presumptions—What They Are, How They Work

The term "presumption" describes a device that sometimes requires the trier to draw a particular conclusion on the basis of certain facts. If the "basic facts" are established, the trier must find the "presumed fact," at least in the absence of evidence tending to disprove it ("counterproof"). In effect, presumptions have at least the effect of shifting the burden of production to the party who would be disadvantaged by a finding of the presumed fact, as FRE 301 confirms as a general rule in federal courts.[1] When enough counterproof is offered, the conclusion is no longer required.

Assume a bailor sues for damages to bailed goods. A presumption often operates in his favor. If he shows the goods were turned over to the bailee in good condition and returned in damaged condition (the basic facts), it is presumed that the bailee's negligence caused the damage (the presumed fact). If there is no counterproof that the damage was caused by something else (earthquake, crime, fire from nearby property), the trier of fact must find the bailee's negligence caused the damage. If there is enough counterproof suggesting another cause, the trier is no longer required to find the presumed fact.

The essence of the device is that if the basic facts of a presumption are established, the presumption controls decision on the presumed fact unless there is counterproof that the presumed fact is not so. In jury-tried cases the judge gives an appropriate instruction. In bench-tried cases the judge must find the presumed fact. **Unanswered presumption controls**

Things can be more complicated, and details are worked out in later sections. Sometimes the basic facts are not "established" in the sense of being proved by evidence that every reasonable person would credit (whether a bailed item was originally in good shape may be disputed). Here the effect of the presumption is contingent on a finding of the **Contingent cases**

---

§3.4   1. FRE 301 says a presumption "imposes on the party against whom it is directed the burden of going forward with evidence to rebut or meet" it. Many state counterparts say the same thing. Questions arise whether civil presumptions should have more effect, but most agree that they have at least this effect.

basic facts, and in jury cases the jury must determine the basic facts, and instructions to this effect are needed.[2]

Easy cases   Sometimes the presumed fact is met by counterproof (like evidence that the goods were damaged or destroyed by fire from nearby property). In cases that are easily dealt with, the counterproof is either insufficient or cogent and compelling. If insufficient, the presumption still controls (bailee's negligence caused the damage). If cogent and compelling, the presumption vanishes and the presumed fact is rejected (bailee's negligence did not cause the damage).[3]

Harder "in-between" cases   In cases that are harder to deal with, the counterproof falls somewhere in between: It is sufficient but not conclusive, strong enough to support a finding against the presumed fact but not so cogent and compelling as to require that finding. The bailee might offer evidence that there was a fire, but the question of his negligence might turn on whether the fire started on the premises or elsewhere, and the proof might leave room for either conclusion. Here the trier need not draw an inference of negligence (presumption no longer controls). Whether the trier may still draw the inference depends on two things: One is the doctrinal content of the presumption, and the other is the natural probative force of the basic facts.

Doctrinal content is set by a statute, formal rule, and common law tradition. These sources produce many doctrines and a range of possibilities. Under the reformist approach championed by Morgan, presumptions are strong. They affect not only the burden of production but also the burden of persuasion. In the bailed goods case, this approach means the presumption insures that the trier may still find fault by the bailee since the counterproof does not compel a finding against fault and the bailee bears the burden of persuasion. Under the traditional approach, presumptions are fragile. They affect only the burden of production. In the bailed goods case, this approach means the question whether the trier can still find negligence by the bailee depends heavily on the natural probative force of the basic facts as shown by the particular evidence. Sometimes the traditional approach splits into several different approaches. These range from a minimalist or "bursting bubble" approach (presumption vanishes completely when sufficient counterproof is offered) to intermediate approaches (like one that says the presumption protects the possibility of inferring the presumed fact unless counterproof is "substantial and uncontradicted").

Federal Rule   The general rule in the federal system is that presumptions do not affect the burden of persuasion (only the burden of production). Thus FRE 301 says a presumption "does not shift" to the other side "the burden of proof in the sense of the risk of nonpersuasion." It is possible, even likely, that this language enshrines the minimalist ("bursting

---

2. _See_ §3.6, _infra._ In addition, sometimes there is counterproof that the presumed fact is not so, which has the effect of combining the contingent and the hard situations described later in the text of this section.

3. _See_ §3.7, _infra._

bubble") theory, but many federal presumptions are created by statute, and FRE 301 applies only in cases "not otherwise provided for by Act of Congress." In effect, this language exempts federal statutory presumptions, and courts may give such presumptions greater effect than FRE 301 would allow. Many states adopted FRE 301 as part of their own Rules, but others adopted language that says presumptions affect the burden of persuasion.[4]

Many terms are used to describe presumptions, and some are redundant or conflicting or have shifting meanings. Here are the more common terms: **Terminology**

Conclusive or irrebuttable presumption. Substantive law sometimes borrows the language of presumptions. Under the Coal Mine Health and Safety Act of 1969, for example, a miner shown by X-ray or other clinical evidence to have pneumoconiosis (black lung disease) is "irrebuttably presumed" to be totally disabled, and the presumption "operates conclusively to establish entitlement to benefits." Under a California statute, it was irrebuttably presumed that a husband was the father of a child born to his wife during marriage (absent proof that they did not cohabit or that he was impotent), and the presumption still cannot be rebutted by ordinary evidence (testimony denying intercourse or evidence that the wife had intercourse with another).[5] These rules are not really presumptions but substantive principles expressed in the language of presumptions.

Mandatory presumption or presumption of law. Generally these terms refer to the true presumption (the device that is the main focus of this and the next six sections), of which the bailed goods presumption is one example. A presumption controls decision if unopposed, so in jury-tried cases an instruction is in order and in bench trials the judge has no option but to find the presumed fact. "Mandatory" is redundant, and "presumption" by itself conveys the intended meaning.

Permissive presumption, inference, presumption of fact. These terms usually refer to conclusions that are permitted but not required. "Inference" is a better word to describe what is happening here, and using the term "presumption" clouds the message because inference doctrines seldom generate mandatory instructions like the ones given for presumptions. Of course jurors draw inferences on their own from the evidence, viewed in the light of their own lifetime experiences, and in this sense inferences are just conclusions drawn by reasonable persons on the basis of information provided to them.

There is another kind of inference. It is the kind that the judge mentions to the jury in formal instructions—a conclusion that is permissible on the basis of evidence to which the judge openly draws the jury's attention. Probably the best known inference is the "res ipsa loquitur" device, which is usually conveyed by an instruction that if

---

4. *See* the discussion in §3.8, *infra.*
5. *See* 30 U.S.C. §921 (black lung presumptions). *See* also Cal. Evid. Code §621 (paternity presumption; statute now requires finding of nonpaternity if blood tests so indicate).

the jury finds that defendant was in control of the instrument that caused injury, and that such injury would not likely have occurred if defendant had exercised due care, then it may find that defendant was negligent.[6] Inference instructions amount to judicial comment on the evidence, almost nudging or inviting the jury to draw a conclusion. Sometimes inference instructions are given when a presumption is met by counterproof, if the court thinks the basic facts are established or might be found on the basis of the evidence, and if those basic facts have enough logical force to support an inference. In effect, this kind of inference is the residue of a presumption, and the instruction allows the jury to draw the conclusion that the presumption would otherwise require.[7]

Prima facie case. This common but ambiguous term is used in two different ways. Usually it describes evidence that allows a particular conclusion in the setting of particular claims, so the party who introduces such evidence carries his burden of production and the case goes to the jury (judge in a bench trial) for decision on the merits. By this interpretation, a prima facie case is similar to an inference because the proof supports but does not require the conclusion in question.

Sometimes prima facie case is used in another sense: Certain evidence *requires* a particular conclusion, at least if it is not met by counterproof. When used this way, the party who makes out a prima facie case carries the burden of production so well that it shifts to the other side. In this meaning, a prima facie case is the functional equivalent of cogent and compelling evidence that leads to judgment as a matter of law. And it is substantially similar to a presumption that requires a conclusion unless the other side offers counterproof. Often the term prima facie case appears in statutes, and often courts construe it to mean essentially "presumption."[8]

§3.5 —Underlying Reasons and Examples

Civil presumptions have much in common with burdens of production and persuasion. Like the latter burdens, presumptions help (a) implement substantive policies by making claims or defenses easier or harder to maintain, (b) insure that parties with better access to proof will produce it (penalizing them for not doing so), providing relief to parties less able to obtain evidence, (c) establish what is most likely

---

6. *See* discussion of FRE 302 in §3.10, *infra.*

7. Inference instructions are discouraged in many states, used sparingly in others, and sometimes disallowed altogether. Even federal judges may be reluctant to give them, but they have more latitude to comment on evidence.

8. *See* St. Mary's Honor Center v. Hicks, 509 U.S. 502 (1993) (construing "prima facie case" in Title VII of Civil Rights Act of 1964); Texas Dept. of Community Affairs v. Burdine, 450 U.S. 248 (1981) (similar); ITC LTD. v. Punchgini, Inc., 482 F.3d 135, 148 (2nd Cir. 2007) (in Lanham Act, "prima facie case" means rebuttable presumption of abandonment, shifting to owner of trademark the burden to come forward with proof that it intended to resume use in foreseeable future).

to be true anyway, and (d) resolve cases where definitive proof is unavailable.

In addition to their common origins, presumptions and burdens are similar in what they do. Unanswered presumptions require a finding of the presumed fact, which means they affect at least the burden of production (FRE 301 confirms this point as a general rule in federal courts). Some states give presumptions the additional effect of shifting the burden of persuasion, and there are some intermediate possibilities.[1]

In important ways, presumptions also differ from burdens of production and persuasion.

First, the burden of persuasion and initial burden of production are set in advance, depending largely on issues framed in pleadings and pretrial orders. In addition, it is usually said that the burden of persuasion does not shift after trial begins, but the burden of production can (if the party on whom it is initially cast introduces cogent and compelling evidence). In contrast to these burdens, presumptions appear as the trial unfolds and depend on proof of the basic facts that bring them into play (proof of proper posting brings into play a presumption of delivery in due course of the mails).

Appear as trial unfolds

Second, presumptions are important only when they operate in favor of the party who would otherwise bear the burden of production and persuasion on the presumed fact. Presumptions operating against the party who bears this burden fade into the larger landscape and play essentially no role. In a suit on an accidental death policy, a presumption of accident (arising on proof that death was sudden and violent) may be important because it helps the claimant who would otherwise bear the burdens of production and persuasion on the question of accident. The same presumption is not important in a suit on a life insurance policy where suicide is an affirmative defense (death coming soon after the policy was purchased) because the insurer already bears the burdens of production and persuasion on the issue.[2]

Favor burdened party; presumption of accident, not suicide

There are so many presumptions that collecting them in one place would serve no useful purpose. Some regularly apply in specific settings and implement policies closely related to substantive rules. For example, there is a presumption, arising on proof that someone suffering black lung disease worked at least ten years in a coal mine, that the disease came from mining. On one level this presumption simply helps deal with a hard problem of proof (thus serves an

Examples: Black lung disease

§3.5 1. *See* the discussion in §3.8, *infra.*

2. *See* §3.1, *supra. See also* Horton v. Reliance Standard Life Insurance Co., 141 F.3d 1038, 1041 (11th Cir. 2004) (presumption that death was accidental rather than suicide applies in widow's ERISA suit; presumption never drops out "until the factfinder becomes convinced, given all the evidence, that it is more likely than not" that decedent committed suicide); O'Brien v. Equitable Life Assur. Soc., 212 F.2d 383, 388-389 (8th Cir. 1954) (presumption of accidental death destroyed by evidence that decedent was perpetrating crime), *cert. denied,* 348 U.S. 835; Zanca v. Life Ins. Co., 770 So. 2d 1, 4 (La. App. 2000) (in suit on accident policy, presumption that accident rather than suicide was cause; burden rests on carrier to establish suicide).

evidentiary or procedural purpose). On another level, the presumption is part of a substantive judgment that claimants who suffer a disease associated with mining should recover even if there is room to doubt cause in particular cases.[3]

Mailed letter   Others are more or less unattached and can crop up in many settings. The mailed letter presumption is of this kind: Proof of proper posting gives rise to a presumption that a letter was delivered in due course. Here is a presumption of obvious utility since those who mail letters are seldom in a position to show that what they sent was delivered at the distant end, and the presumption arises in many different settings. It can be useful in suits on insurance claims, for instance, where it can help a claimant prove renewal of a policy or help the carrier prove cancellation; it can be useful in an infringement action to prove the date or fact of patent registration, and in other settings too.[4]

Some presumptions grew out of common law and seem to express judgments on recurrent evidential or procedural issues. A list of these would be long and would of course include the mailed letter presumption.[5] Other presumptions are aspects of basic reasoning and express commonsense notions that are essential in thinking about any problem,[6] such as the presumption that a status or condition, once shown to exist, continues to exist.[7] Of course these notions cannot be as general as they seem: It makes sense to presume that a road, shown to be stripped to the base for resurfacing on Monday, remains under construction on Tuesday, but no sense to presume that a street in Denver, shown to be covered by glare ice at midnight on Wednesday, remains slick on Thursday at noon.

Other presumptions embody a mix of substantive and evidential judgments, although they do not seem to connect with any particular substantive doctrine. Many jurisdictions recognize, for example, presumptions that official duties are faithfully and properly discharged and that formal processes or procedures achieved proper outcomes, and these have substantive content insofar as they set a beginning

3. *See* Usery v. Turner Elkhorn Mining Co., 428 U.S. 1 (1976) (construing black lung presumption in 30 U.S.C. §921). *See also* City of Frederick v. Shankle, 765 A.2d 1008 (Ct. App. Md. 1999) (statutory presumption reflects legislative social policy and shifts burden of persuasion).

4. Busquets-Ivars v. Ashcroft, 333 F.3d 1008, 1010 (9th Cir. 2003) (recognizing presumption on basis of 19th century holding; failing to include zip code means mailing was not "properly directed"); McCray v. State Farm Fire and Casualty Ins. Co., 892 So. 2d 363 (Ala. 2004) (recognizing presumption; counterproof of nonreceipt left question for jury to resolve).

5. Dobson v. Harris, 530 S.E.2d 829 (N.C. 2000) (in suit alleging mental distress, applying presumption that store employee acted in good faith in reporting that plaintiff abused her child); Valance v. Wisel, 110 F.3d 1269, 1279 (7th Cir. 1997) (in civil rights suit, presumption of unreasonableness attaches to warrantless search).

6. *See* United States v. One 1971 Ford Truck, 346 F. Supp. 613, 620 (9th Cir. 1972) (describing presumption that private transactions are fair, things happen according to ordinary habits of life, and law has been obeyed).

7. Jund v. Town of Hempstead, 941 F.2d 1271, 1288 (2d Cir. 1991) (presumption that status or condition continues, once shown to exist).

point for any inquiry into what happened and tell courts what to think about central facts in issue in widely differing situations.[8]

Since so much law is now codified (both state and federal), it is not surprising that many presumptions are statutory or closely associated with statutory policies. FRE 301 exempts some statutory presumptions from coverage (it applies except when "otherwise provided" by act of Congress), so courts give such presumptions the effect suggested by statute or associated substantive principles. As a practical matter, usually that means courts give more effect to those statutory presumptions than FRE 301 would otherwise allow. And courts have broad interpretive leeway in deciding whether statutory presumptions are independent of FRE 301 or not.[9]

Other presumptions are typically recognized as a matter of state law and often applied in federal court as well, including the following common ones:

(a) In accident suits, on proof of ownership of a car or truck, several **Loaned auto** common presumptions help claimants show that the owner (or his insurance carrier) is liable for the driver's tort. There is a simple presumption, arising on proof of ownership, that the person at the wheel had permission to drive.[10] In practical effect, this presumption brings into play the omnibus clause in car insurance policies and makes the owner's insurer liable for damages caused by the negligence of the driver. To hold the owner personally liable, it is typically necessary to show that the driver was acting on the owner's behalf, and a somewhat larger presumption may come into play: On proof of ownership, it is often presumed that the driver not only had permission but was on an errand or mission for the owner.[11]

(b) There are numerous presumptions relating to injuries suffered **Scope of** in the workplace and injuries caused by employees generating suits **employment** against their employers. There is, for example, a broad presumption, arising on proof of employment, that an employee was acting within the scope of his duties, and a presumption, arising on proof of an injury or ailment, that it was work-related.[12] Obviously the first of these helps

8. Carrion v. Linzey, 675 A.2d 527, 536 (Ct. App. Md. 1996) (presumption of correct outcome in arbitration carried out under statute in medical malpractice cases); Parsons v. United States, 670 F.2d 164, 166 (Ct. Cl. 1982) (presumption that public officers perform duties correctly, lawfully, fairly, in good faith).

9. *See* Texas Dept. of Community Affairs v. Burdine, 450 U.S. 248 (1981) (presumption of discrimination in Title VII gender discrimination suit); Usery v. Turner Elkhorn Mining Co., 428 U.S. 1 (1976) (statutory black lung presumptions for coal miners); United States v. Jessup, 757 F.2d 378, 380-384 (1st Cir. 1985) (statutory presumption in bail reform act that person charged with serious crime will flee). For an example from a state system, *see* Frederick v. Shankle, 765 A.2d 1008 (Md. 2001) (presumption that police officer suffering coronary artery disease incurred ailment at work).

10. *See* Smith v. Savannah Homes, Inc., 389 F. Supp. 384, 386 (D. Tenn. 1974); Royal Indem. Co. v. Wingate, 353 F. Supp. 1002, 1004 (D. Md. 1973), *aff'd without op.*, 487 F.2d 1398 (4th Cir.).

11. Newell v. Harold Shaffer Leasing Co., 489 F.2d 103, 106, 109 (5th Cir. 1974).

12. Cohen v. Wal-Mart, 93 P.3d 420 (Alaska 2004) (link between employment and injury raises statutory presumption that injury is work-related; burden of production on employer); Nakamura v. State, 47 P.3d 730, 734 (Hawaii 2002) (injury presumed

third parties hold employers responsible for the torts of their employees, and the second tends to insure compensation in workers compensation and similar statutory schemes. There is also a narrower presumption, arising on proof of employment, that an employee remained the responsibility of his employer for purposes of respondeat superior even while on loan to another employer for a special project.[13]

Decedent exercising care

(c) There is a presumption often applied in wrongful death suits that decedent was exercising due care at the time of the accident.[14] In many settings this presumption may simply be another way of reaching the result that ordinary rules allocating burdens of persuasion would also reach: Plaintiffs in suits against estates bear the burden of proving decedent's negligence, and defendants in suits for wrongful death bear the burden of showing that plaintiff's decedent was careless.

Missing for seven years

(d) In suits for wrongful death, or for death benefits, pensions or annuities payable during life, on proof that the person has been missing without tidings for some fixed period of years (typically five or seven), there is a presumption that she is dead.[15] The underlying policy concern is to help claimants recover where they lack positive proof of death, and the logic is that most people who disappear without tidings for so long probably are dead.

The presumption can only be invoked if the requisite period has elapsed since the person was heard from. It is another question whether the presumption points toward finding that she died at the end or beginning of the period: Choosing the end of the period could maximize recovery for people seeking annuities or pensions payable for life, and block defenses based on statutes of limitations or notification requirements. Choosing the beginning might support claims for prejudgment interest on sums payable at death.[16] Both choices are supportable: One reason the passage of years without tidings suggests death is that we suppose the person would have made contact during the period, so silence suggests that he died early. But disappearance without explanation usually suggests that there is no particular reason to suppose the person died when he was first missed, which suggests that he died much later in the period. Perhaps the wiser choice is to use

---

work-related; employer bears burden of persuasion); Kas v. Gilkerson, 199 F.2d 398, 399 (D.C. Cir. 1952) (driver of employer's vehicle presumed to be acting within scope of duties).

13. Dornan v. United States, 460 F.2d 425, 428 (9th Cir. 1972); Kiff v. Travelers Ins. Co., 402 F.2d 129, 131 (5th Cir. 1968).

14. Monger v. Cessna Aircraft Co., 812 F.2d 402, 404-405 (8th Cir. 1987); Eldred v. Barton, 505 F.2d 186 (2d Cir. 1974). *But see* McQuay v. Schertle, 730 A.2d 714 (Ct. App. Md. 1998) (jury need not be instructed if eyewitnesses testify that decedent exercised due care).

15. Ahn v. Kim, 678 A.2d 1073 (N.J. 1996) (in suit against psychiatric hospital, claimant could rely on presumption of death after decedent was missing five years; death is presumed to occur at the end of the period unless the contrary is shown); Mutual Life Ins. Co. v. Blodgett, 126 F.2d 273, 275, 278-279 (4th Cir. 1942) (suit on life insurance policy; widow could rely on presumption of death after seven years).

16. Re Chicago & NW Railroad Co., 138 F.2d 753, 755 (7th Cir. 1943), *cert. denied*, 321 U.S. 789.

the presumption to help claimants, which justifies applying the presumption sometimes to mean that death came at the beginning and sometimes to mean that death came at the end.

(e) Most states recognize a strong presumption, arising on proof of a **Valid marriage** marriage ceremony or a showing that the man and woman lived as spouses and considered themselves to be married, that there is a valid marriage that continues in force. This presumption rests on the great likelihood that marriage ceremonies in fact create valid marriages and the similar likelihood that couples who consider themselves married probably are married. The presumption rests as well on a strong policy of preferring to uphold marital arrangements to vindicate important expectations and reliance interests, insure legitimacy of children and responsibility for their welfare, and provide appropriately for one person in the couple when the other dies.[17]

§3.6 Operation of Presumptions—Contingent Case Where Basic Facts Are Disputed

Sometimes there is enough proof of the basic facts to support a finding **Contingent** that they exist but not enough to require such a finding. Hence the trier **instruction** might find against the basic facts, disbelieving witnesses or resolving a conflict of proof by concluding that the basic facts are just not so. Here the presumption can affect the decision only if the trier finds the basic facts to be so. Assuming there is no counterproof tending to disprove the presumed fact, the court tells the jury that if it finds the basic facts, then it must find the presumed fact.

Normally the bailor bears the burdens of production and persuasion on the basic facts (delivery of undamaged goods and return of damaged goods). If he succeeds on the basic facts, he gets the benefit of the presumption. Success on the basic facts might mean demonstrating them by proof that no reasonable juror could disregard (cogent and compelling) or by sufficient proof to allow (but not require) a jury to find them. The level of success determines what the jury can be told about the presumption. In addition, the operation of the presumption is affected by the evidence introduced by the bailee to refute the presumed fact of his negligence.

Language originally proposed by the Advisory Committee would have told courts and lawyers how to handle the contingent situation.[1] Unfortunately it is too complicated to be described in a short

---

17. *See* 1 Clark, Law of Domestic Relations in the United States §2.7 (2d ed. 1987) (presumptions validating marriages rest on strong policy favoring morality of parties and legitimacy of children; they serve "the need to vindicate expectations on which the parties have arranged their lives," rest on likelihood, and serve important interest of helping parties establish what might otherwise be hard or impossible to prove) ("a substantial amount of evidence is needed to overthrow" these presumptions).

§3.6 1. *See* Preliminary Draft, Rule 3-03(2), 46 F.R.D. 161, 212-213 (1969) (if there is no counterproof against presumed fact, then (a) if reasonable minds would agree that basic facts are probably so, then judge "shall direct the jury to find" presumed fact,

expression, and the proposal assumed that the success or failure of proof of the basic facts necessarily determined the existence of the presumed facts (if unopposed). But there might be other evidence that would support a finding of the presumed fact even if proof of the basic facts fell short, and the proposal did not take this possibility into account. The proposal anticipated that the factfinder passes on the preliminary facts, and that point seems settled, although one commentator has argued for a different approach.[2]

Few cases consider the contingent situation, perhaps because proof of basic facts is likely to be strong and unopposed, and the battle usually concentrates on the presumed fact or on the question whether the presumption applies and what effect it should have.[3]

§3.7 —Easy Cases Where Counterproof Is Either Insufficient or Conclusive

Assuming the basic facts are established, there are two easy situations. One arises when there is essentially no counterproof against the presumed fact, and the other arises when there is cogent and compelling counterproof.

No counterproof   In the first situation, if the other side offers no evidence contesting the presumed fact (or evidence that is insufficient to support a finding against it), the presumption controls and the trier must find the presumed fact. In jury cases the court should instruct that the fact must be taken as established. On these points there is virtual unanimity, whether the effect of the presumption is set by FRE 301 or by some other standard.[1]

---

and (b) if reasonable minds would agree that basic facts are probably not so, the judge "shall direct the jury to find against" presumed fact, and (c) if reasonable minds could find either way on basic facts, then judge "shall submit the matter to the jury with an instruction to find" presumed fact if it finds basic facts are probably so, but "otherwise to find against" presumed fact).

2. *See, e.g.,* 2 McCormick, Evidence §344 (6th ed. 2006); 3 Colorado Jury Instructions 3d (Civil) §3:5 (1988). *But see* Allen, Presumptions in Civil Actions Reconsidered, 66 Iowa L. Rev. 843, 852 (1981) (for purpose of allocating burden of persuasion, basic facts underlying presumptions are preliminary facts court should decide) (article suggests abandoning presumption device).

3. *See* St. Mary's Honor Center v. Hicks, 509 U.S. 502, 509 n.3 (1993) (if adverse party fails to offer sufficient counterproof against basic facts but reasonable minds could disagree on whether they are established by a preponderance, then if trier finds those facts it must find presumed fact); Flemming v. Hall, 132 N.W.2d 35, 45-46 (Mich. 1965).

§3.7   1. St. Mary's Honor Center v. Hicks, 509 U.S. 502 (1993) (presumption means that finding predicate facts requires conclusion in absence of explanation); Apex Inc. v. Raritan Computer, Inc., 325 F.3d 1364, 1372 (Fed. Cir. 2003) (if one who "must bring forth evidence" in face of presumption "fails to proffer sufficient evidence to meet its burden," presumption prevails); Brown v. Roadway Express, Inc., 740 A.2d 352, 354 (Vt. 1999) (presumption arising on breach of road safety statute establishes negligence "as a matter of law," and court must charge jury accordingly) (applying rule similar to FRE 301).

This mandatory effect distinguishes presumptions from permissive inferences. Presumptions belong in the category of legal conclusions that are sometimes required. Functionally, proving the basic facts is equivalent to carrying the burden of production on the presumed fact with such great success that this burden shifts to the other side. Presumptions express the conclusion that the basic facts are "cogent and compelling" evidence of the presumed fact. When the natural probative worth of categorical proof of those basic facts would require reasonable minds to find the presumed fact, a presumption is little more than a standardized determination that those facts are cogent and compelling evidence of the presumed fact. When the natural probative force of the basic facts would not require a finding of the presumed fact, a presumption must be justified on other grounds. Essentially the justification expresses a policy determination that the party benefited by the presumption should win if the basic facts are shown.

In the other easy situation, the presumption is vanquished and completely put to flight if there is cogent and compelling evidence that the presumed fact is not so. In this situation, in effect the counterproof offered by the adverse party is considered so powerful that no reasonable person could reject it, and the presumption is completely overcome.

Cogent and compelling counterproof

§3.8 —Hard Cases Where Counterproof Is Sufficient But Inconclusive

If the basic facts are established, the hard case is the one where counterproof is offered, and it is sufficient to support a finding against the presumed fact but not so cogent and compelling that such a finding is required. In this in-between case, a presumption does not control in the sense of requiring a finding of the presumed fact. Thus sufficient evidence that goods were carefully handled or stored means the bailed goods presumption no longer requires a finding that bailee's negligence caused the damage.

Sufficient counterproof

The in-between case raises three questions: Does the presumption disappear completely? Can the factfinder still find the presumed fact? Does the presumption protect this possibility? On these points, practice varies widely among jurisdictions, and because of the difficulties presented by the in-between cases, states adopting their own versions of the Rules did not as faithfully follow the federal model as they did in other areas.[1] The two main lines of doctrine and some intermediate lines are explored below.

---

§3.8 1. Among 42 states that have adopted the Rules, 20 states have provisions that give at least some presumptions more effect than the "bursting bubble" approach. Among these, 12 states provide that civil presumptions shift the burden of persuasion (Arkansas, Delaware, Louisiana, Maine, Montana, Nebraska, Nevada, North Dakota, Oregon, Utah, Wisconsin, and Wyoming). At the opposite end of the spectrum, 17 states adopted provisions similar to FRE 301, under which presumptions affect only the

Under the reformist approach followed by about a dozen states and federal courts in some settings not governed by FRE 301, presumptions are strong and affect the burden of persuasion. Under this approach, a presumption does not disappear when sufficient counterproof is offered. The trier may still find the presumed fact, and the presumption protects this possibility. Under the traditional approach taken in FRE 301, presumptions are fragile and affect only the burden of production. A common minimalist interpretation of this approach, known as the "bursting bubble" theory, holds that a presumption disappears when sufficient counterproof is offered. In some cases the trier may still find the presumed fact, but only if the natural probative force of the basic facts that brought the presumption into play is sufficient to support such a finding (or the evidence as a whole supports it). Otherwise the presumed fact may not be found, and the presumption does not protect this possibility. The intermediate approaches are harder to sum up, but they can be viewed as compromises between reform and tradition or as variations of the traditional approach.

Reformist approach   Long ago evidence scholars led by Edmund Morgan argued that presumptions should affect the burden of persuasion, and the framers of the Rules tried to adopt this approach.[2] Congress rejected the attempt, but this reformist approach applies in many settings. Some states follow it, and FRE 301 exempts cases "otherwise provided for" by federal statute. Many federal presumptions are created by or connected with federal statutes, so the exemption gives considerable leeway to apply the reformist or other approaches. Various versions of the bailed goods presumption are codified in both state and federal law, and they are often construed as affecting the burden of persuasion.[3]

As noted, the reformist approach protects the possibility of finding the presumed fact despite the presence of sufficient counterproof to support a finding that the fact is not so. The reason is that the

---

burden of production (Alaska, Colorado, Idaho, Indiana, Kentucky, Maryland, Michigan, Minnesota, New Hampshire, New Jersey, New Mexico, North Carolina, Ohio, South Carolina, South Dakota, Vermont, and West Virginia). Eight other states do not prescribe by rule the effect of presumptions in civil cases (Arizona, Connecticut, Iowa, Louisiana, Pennsylvania, Tennessee, Texas, and Washington). The other five provide that some presumptions shift the burden of persuasion, while others shift only the burden of production (Alabama, Florida, Hawaii, Oklahoma, and Rhode Island).

2. *See* Morgan, Some Problems of Proof 81 (1956) (usually presumptions should fix burden of persuasion); Morgan, Basic Problems of Evidence 31-44 (1963); Morgan, Foreword to Model Code of Evidence, at 52-69 (1942); Morgan, Instructing the Jury Upon Presumptions and Burdens of Proof, 47 Harv. L. Rev. 59 (1933); Morgan, Some Observations Concerning Presumptions, 44 Harv. L. Rev. 906 (1931). *See also* McCormick, Evidence §317 (1954); Gausewitz, Presumptions in a One-Rule World, 5 Vand. L. Rev. 324 (1952). *But see* Bohlen, The Effect of Rebuttable Presumptions of Law Upon the Burden of Proof, 68 U. Pa. L. Rev. 307 (1920) (finding both views of presumptions proper). *And see* the proposed draft of FRE 301, at 56 FRE 208 (1972).

3. Plough, Inc. v. Mason & Dixon Lines, 630 F.2d 468, 470-472 (6th Cir. 1980) (under Interstate Commerce Act, shipper makes prima facie case by showing delivery in good condition and arrival damaged; carrier bears burden of persuasion on negligence and cause); Knowles v. Gilchrist Co., 289 N.E.2d 879 (Mass. 1972) (bailed goods presumption shifts persuasion burden on due care).

presumption affects (or shifts) the burden of persuasion: Typically the bailor as plaintiff in a suit against the bailee has the burdens of production and persuasion on negligence and causation, but if the basic facts are established (items delivered in good condition, damaged on return), the burden of persuasion on care or external cause is on the bailee. Even if his counterproof is sufficient, the claimant can still prevail.

Substantial common law tradition, once accepted by Wigmore and Thayer, holds that presumptions should affect only the burden of production. Congress agreed, and FRE 301 says a presumption "imposes on the party against whom it is directed the burden of going forward with evidence to rebut or meet the presumption, but does not shift" the burden of persuasion. A majority of states take this approach (including most that adopted FRE 301).

Traditional approach

As noted, a common minimalist interpretation holds that a presumption does not insure that the factfinder may find the presumed fact if sufficient counterproof is offered to support a finding against it. The "bursting bubble" theory says a presumption disappears when sufficient counterproof is introduced. A presumption, it is said, "smokes out" the opponent, making him produce counterproof, but it is "put to flight" when he produces enough.[4] Some modern decisions hold that FRE 301 adopts the bursting bubble approach and some modern commentators support this outcome.[5]

Bursting bubble

The bursting bubble approach does not always mean a claim or defense that depends on the presumed fact must fail. Sometimes the natural probative force of the basic facts is sufficient to support a finding of the presumed fact (or the evidence as a whole suffices),[6] and the

---

4. E. L. Cheeney Co. v. Gates, 346 F.2d 197, 202 (5th Cir. 1965) ("smoke out"); Cleary, Presuming and Pleading: An Essay in Juristic Immaturity, 12 Stan. L. Rev. 5, 16-17 (1959) ("bursting bubble"). Hence presumptions are like "bats of the law, flitting in the twilight, but disappearing in the sunshine of actual facts," *see* Mackowik v. Kansas City, St. J. & C.B. R.R., 94 S.W. 256, 262 (Mo. 1906). They are also like "Maeterlinck's male bee" ("having functioned they disappear"), *see* Bohlen, The Effect of Rebuttable Presumptions of Law Upon the Burden of Proof, 68 U. Pa. L. Rev. 307, 314 (1920). *And see* accounts of the bursting bubble theory in Thayer, Preliminary Treatise on Evidence, ch. 8 (1898); 9 Wigmore, Evidence §§2491(2) and 2498a (21) (3d ed. 1940).

5. Rentschler v. Lewis, 33 S.W.3d 518, 520 (Ky. 2000) (when party opposing presumption introduces sufficient evidence, presumption "disappears and plays no further role"); Cooper v. Burnor, 750 A.2d 974, 976 (Vt. 1999) (presumption of negligence from violation of statute "disappears" when defense "produces evidence that fairly and reasonably tends to support" finding of due care); A. C. Aukerman Co. v. R. L. Chaides Const. Co., 960 F.2d 1020, 1037-1038 (Fed. Cir. 1992) (FRE 301 embodies bursting bubble theory; presumption "completely vanishes upon the introduction of evidence sufficient to support a finding of the nonexistence of the presumed fact"). See also Lansing, Enough Is Enough: A Critique of the Morgan View of Rebuttable Presumptions in Civil Cases, 62 Or. L. Rev. 485 (1983).

6. *See* America Online, Inc. v. AT&T Corp., 243 F.3d 812, 818 (4th Cir. 2000) (evidence rebutting presumed fact may "neutralize" presumption, but "does not eliminate" evidence that "gave rise to the presumption"); Sorrentino v. United States, 198 F. Supp. 2d 1068, 1076 n.4 (D. Colo. 2002) (even after bubble has burst, factual question of receipt of letter in due course remains open; factfinder may find receipt by drawing inference from proof of mailing).

judge may give an inference instruction that allows or invites a jury to make this finding. Sometimes, however, the natural probative force of the basic facts is not sufficient to permit a finding of the presumed fact.[7] Absent other evidence, the party who must prove the fact loses the case.

Consider the case where a claimant shows that 400 factory-packaged televisions were turned over to a trucking company for shipment but were water-damaged on arrival. The proof supports an inference of negligence by the trucking company even if it shows that the trucks and storage facilities did not leak. The initial proof does more than establish the basic facts. It shows the goods were properly packaged for transit and that the damage would not likely happen without the bailee's negligence. Even without the presumption, the trier could decide in favor of the claimant, and a jury should get the case. But suppose the initial proof shows a shipment of china plates was packed in boxes with thin pads between them and that half the plates were broken on arrival. The counterproof might indicate that the trucking company carefully handled the boxes and nothing untoward happened in transit. The initial proof brought the presumption into play. Under the bursting bubble theory, it disappeared in the face of the counterproof. Here and the natural probative force of the initial proof does not support finding negligence by the bailee. If the presumption is gone, the case is gone too, unless there is other proof of negligence.

Intermediate approaches

Under the intermediate approaches, the presumed fact may still be found, and the presumption protects the possibility. These approaches are rooted in tradition. They avoid the "bursting bubble" effect but do not violate the terms of FRE 301 because they do not shift the burden of persuasion.

Substantial and uncontradicted

Perhaps the most promising alternative holds that a presumption has continuing effect unless the counterproof is "substantial and uncontradicted."[8] By this approach, the bailed goods presumption takes the case to the trier of fact despite counterproof of careful handling and uneventful trip. The case goes to the jury not only in the first situation sketched above (factory-packaged televisions arriving with water damage) but in the second (breakage of china packed with thin pads), and the presumption insures this possibility unless and until the court decides the counterproof is substantial and uncontradicted. An instruction conveys the message that a jury may still find the presumed fact.[9] A problem with the approach is that it requires courts to

---

7. *See* Fisher v. Vassar College, 114 F.3d 1332 (2d Cir. 1997), *cert. denied,* 522 U.S. 1075 (1998); A. C. Aukerman Co. v. R. L. Chaides Const. Co., 960 F.2d 1020, 1038 (Fed. Cir. 1992).

8. *See* United States v. Jessup, 757 F.2d 378, 380-384 (1st Cir. 1985); NLRB v. Tahoe Nugget, Inc., 584 F.2d 293, 297 (9th Cir. 1978); E. L. Cheeney v. Gates, 346 F.2d 197, 201, 204 (5th Cir. 1965).

9. Here is one way to put it: "There is evidence that the china was turned over to the bailee in good condition but half of it was broken on delivery, and evidence that the china was carefully handled and the trip was uneventful. Based on this evidence, you may find that there was or was not negligence by the bailee and, if there was, that it was or was not the cause of the damage."

draw yet another distinction relating to the probative force of evidence. To the three recognized categories (insufficient, sufficient, cogent and compelling) we add a fourth (substantial and uncontradicted), making something that is already complicated even more so.

Another alternative holds that presumptions remain alive unless the factfinder believes the counterproof.[10] The bailed goods presumption would take the broken china case to the trier of fact, and an instruction would let a jury find for the claimant unless it "believed" the proof of careful handling and uneventful journey.[11] This approach comes perilously close to shifting the burden of persuasion (which would violate FRE 301) because it seems to say the factfinder should decide for the claimant unless it thinks the counterproof preponderates.[12]

Believe the counterproof

The "equipoise" alternative presents a third possibility. Here the presumption requires a finding of the presumed fact unless the factfinder thinks the counterproof makes nonexistence of that fact at least as likely as its existence.[13] The bailed goods presumption would take the broken china case to the trier of fact, and it would find for the claimant unless the counterproof makes due care or external cause at least as likely as negligence by the bailee causing the damage. This approach gives a presumption the greatest possible effect short of shifting the burden of persuasion. The drawback is that it has a self-defeating quality: An instruction would tell a jury to find the presumed fact unless the evidence makes it seem as likely to be untrue as true, which seems to convey what McCormick aptly called an "impression of futility" that could "mystify rather than help."[14]

Equipoise

There are other ways of trying to give presumptions more effect. Some have thought it would help to tell the jury a presumption is "evidence" that should be considered unless refuted. In enacting FRE 301, Congress considered and rejected a proposal to take this

Presumptions as evidence

10. Progressive Northern Ins. Co. v. Flores, 2004 WL 944904 (Conn. Super. Ct. 2004), following Sutphen v. Hagelin, 344 A.2d 270 (Conn. 1975) (should tell jury presumption applies if it disbelieves counterproof).

11. Here is one way to put it: "There is evidence that the china was turned over to the bailee in good condition but half of it was broken on delivery, and evidence that the bailee carefully handled the china and that the trip was uneventful. If you believe the evidence that the bailee carefully handled the china and that the trip was uneventful, you should find that there was no negligence. Otherwise, you should find that there was negligence and that the bailee was the cause of the damage."

12. If "believe the counterproof" does not shift the burden of persuasion, then it is hard to interpret. Perhaps proof of careful handling and uneventful journey is only circumstantial evidence of due care, so it could be believed and yet the trier might think due care was not shown.

13. *See* Hinds v. John Hancock Mut. Life Ins. Co., 155 A.2d 721 (Me. 1959) (leading case adopting equipoise approach) (later Maine adopted rule in which presumption shifts burden of persuasion); Speck v. Sarver, 128 P.2d 16, 20 (Cal. 1942) (presumption should persist until there is evidence that "persuades the jury that the non-existence of the facts presumed is as probable as their existence") (Traynor dissent).

14. "You should find for the claimant on the issues of negligence and causation," the instruction could say, "unless you find that proof of due care or other cause makes it at least equally likely that the bailee was not negligent or did not cause the breakage." The critical comments quoted above are in 2 McCormick on Evidence §344 (6th ed. 2006).

approach. The problem is that a presumption is not evidence but a way of looking at or dealing with evidence, so the instruction seems incoherent and false. Another possibility is an instruction telling the jury about a presumption and explaining it, or an instruction simply telling the jury that it may still find the presumed fact, or taking the course of *allowing* the jury to do so.[15] Unfortunately the word "presumption" has the oddness of suggesting both too much and too little. The term itself seems to invite action without factual basis, and it fails to convey any sense of underlying policies, and these defects warrant rejecting this approach.[16]

Critique of traditional approach

Allowing presumptions to affect one burden but not another (production but not persuasion) is open to criticism on three grounds. First, as a matter of doctrinal coherence, it is hard to say why a presumption controls decision in the absence of counterproof but does not suffice to take the case to the factfinder if the counterproof is merely sufficient. Second, presumptions may embody strong policy preferences that are inadequately served if only the burden of production is affected. Third, these realities have led to attempts to find intermediate approaches. One result is added complication in what is already a complicated area, and another is that courts may be trying to avoid FRE 301.

Two modern examples shed light on these criticisms:

First, consider the employment discrimination presumption construed in *Texas Department of Community Affairs v. Burdine* and other cases. If plaintiff shows that she applied for an open job for which she qualified and that she was not hired, it is presumed that the reason was discrimination. The Court has said the presumption requires a finding for plaintiff if defendant offers no counterproof, but it drops from the case if defendant offers proof of nondiscriminatory reasons. Still, the trier may infer discrimination from proof of the basic facts if it concludes that the reasons are "pretextual."[17] Under a bursting bubble theory, the woman in *Burdine* would lose because the probative force of

---

15. *See* Alaska Rule 301 (if opponent meets burden of producing evidence, court "must instruct the jury that it may, but is not required to, infer the existence of the presumed fact from the proved fact," without mentioning the term "presumption"); Indiana Rule 301 (presumption "shall have continuing effect" even when met by counterproof); Maryland Rule 5-301 (when opponent offers counterproof, "the presumption will retain the effect of creating a question to be decided by the trier of fact" unless the counterproof is "conclusive"); North Carolina Rule 301 (similar to Alaska wording). *See also* United States Natl. Bank v. Underwriters at Lloyd's, London, 396 P.2d 765, 775 (Or. 1964) (jury should be told basis of presumption against suicide, resting on "normal human revulsion against taking one's own life," and jury may be told it "may infer that because people normally do not take their own lives"); Grier v. Rosenberg, 248, 131 A.2d 737 (Md. 1957) (should mention presumption, so jury "may appreciate the legal recognition of a slant of policy or probability").

16. *See* Alaska Rule 301(a) (when other side satisfies burden of production, court may not mention "presumption" to jury); Vermont Rule 301(c)(2) (similar).

17. *See* St. Mary's Honor Center v. Hicks, 509 U.S. 502 (1993); Texas Dept. of Community Affairs v. Burdine, 450 U.S. 248 (1981) (both citing FRE 301 without actually applying it; both saying presumption drops away, but protects possibility of pro-plaintiff finding). *But see* Fisher v. Vassar College, 114 F.3d 1332 (2d Cir. 1997) (after employer shows legitimate reasons, presumption of sex discrimination falls away and plaintiff

the basic facts does not suffice to prove discrimination.[18] It is hard to imagine that the policies apparently underlying the presumptions are well served by such results.

Second, consider the black lung presumption construed in *American Coal Co. v. Benefits Review Board*, a case involving a claim for permanent disability under the Black Lung Benefits Act. The coal miner invoked a presumption established by regulation, arising on proof of being in the mines for ten years plus certain medical test results, that he was permanently disabled from the disease. The mining company met the presumption by medical testimony based on other tests indicating heart problems, not black lung disease. In *Usery v. Turner Elkhorn Mining Co.*, the Supreme Court had applied FRE 301 to related presumptions (suggesting they affected only the burden of production) and the company in *American* claimed the presumption was rebutted and *Turner Elkhorn* meant claimant must lose. The Tenth Circuit disagreed, concluding that this presumption shifted the burden of persuasion to the defendant.[19] The coal miner in *American* would lose if FRE 301 applied and the conflicting medical evidence produced a toss-up in the mind of the trier of fact. It is hard to imagine that this result adequately serves the underlying policies.

§3.9 Conflicting Presumptions

The Rules do not say what to do when presumptions conflict. Assuming that presumptions governed by FRE 301 all have the same "bursting bubble" effect (calling for them to disappear when met with sufficient evidence to find against the presumed fact), it appears that a conflict between two presumptions means that both vanish.[1] But in the common situation in which presumptions relating to marriage come into conflict, going forward without any presumption or equivalent device is unattractive.

Even where FRE 301 applies, it seems better to recognize that presumptions do not all express policies of equal importance and that one may prove more significant than others. There are three and perhaps

Not equally important

---

must offer more evidence; rejecting defense explanation does not necessarily add to probative force of basic facts; presumption does not then suffice as basis for decision for plaintiff) (split en banc opinion), *cert. denied,* 522 U.S. 1075 (1998).

18. *See* Reeves v. General Foods Corp., 682 F.2d 515, 520-526 & nn.9-10 (5th Cir. 1982) (proof of basic facts of discrimination presumption may not support finding of discrimination if presumption drops away) (in this case, age discrimination was shown by additional evidence).

19. American Coal Co. v. Benefits Review Bd., 738 F.2d 387, 390 (10th Cir. 1984) (FRE 301 does not apply since Congress has "otherwise provided" by delegating authority to Labor Secretary who promulgated presumption). *See also* Usery v. Turner Elkhorn Mining Co., 428 U.S. 1 (1976) (construing other black lung presumptions and citing FRE 301).

§3.9 1. *See* Legille v. Dann, 544 F.2d 1, 10 (D.C. Cir. 1976) ("presumptions are incapable of waging war among themselves"); Thayer, A Preliminary Treatise on Evidence 343-351 (1898); 9 Wigmore, Evidence §2493 (3d ed. 1940); Morgan, Some Observations Concerning Presumptions, 44 Harv. L. Rev. 906, 916-917 (1931).

more possible approaches: One is to invoke a third presumption that in effect resolves or avoids the conflict produced by the other two presumptions. A second approach is to give effect to the presumption that expresses weightier considerations of policy or logic, and this approach enjoys considerable support.[2] A third approach is simply to sidestep the presumption device and allocate the burdens of production and persuasion in light of the situation. In what might be a fourth approach, one modern court faced with an apparent conflict in presumptions concluded that the proof giving rise to one of the two presumptions was persuasive evidence whose effect should not be cabined by the presumption device, and that it overcame the other presumption and controlled the case.[3] In the end, it seems essential by some means to allocate the burden of production to one party or another rather than trying to decide the case without any way to implement the various policies underlying the presumptions.[4]

Validity of later marriage

The most common example of conflicting presumptions involves death benefits or life insurance where the claimant is the spouse of the decedent, but it is shown that either she or the decedent was involved in a prior marriage. There is a presumption, arising on proof of a marriage ceremony or an ongoing relationship that purports to be a marriage, that the people involved are validly married to each other, and an additional presumption that a marriage once shown to exist continues in force. Where a surviving spouse seeks death benefits or life insurance, but she or the decedent had been married before, these marital presumptions can conflict: The prior marriage is presumed valid and continuing and the later marriage is presumed valid and continuing, but if the prior marriage is valid then the later one is not. Usually courts find a way of preferring the validity of the later marriage by means of presumptions, and usually the outcome favors recovery of benefits.[5]

2. *Compare* Charlson Realty Co. v. United States, 384 F.2d 434, 444 (Ct. Cl. 1967) (treating presumption of delivery in due course as stronger than presumption of office regularity) *with* Legille v. Dann, 544 F.2d 1, 9 (D.C. Cir. 1976) (doing the opposite). *See* URE 301(b) (1974) (if presumptions are inconsistent, "the presumption applies that is founded upon weightier considerations of policy," but neither applies if considerations of policy are of "equal weight"); Rule 15, Uniform Rules of Evidence (1953) (apply presumption "founded on the weightier considerations of policy and logic," but if neither qualifies then both are disregarded). Although language varies, some states follow essentially this approach. *See* counterparts to FRE 301-302 in Alaska, Delaware, Hawaii, Maine, Montana, North Dakota, Oregon, Utah, and Wyoming.

3. Legille v. Dann, 544 F.2d 1, 10 (D.C. Cir. 1976) (should not treat proof of office routine as raising mere presumption that official duties were performed, which might be too weak to destroy mailed letter presumption, where patent office routine suggested that patent application was not timely delivered).

4. *See* Allen, Presumptions in Civil Actions Reconsidered, 66 Iowa L. Rev. 843, 853-854 (1981) (instead of conflicting presumptions, court should treat problem of sufficiency of evidence; assuming first marriage was long before second, proving the former is not enough to show invalidity of the latter).

5. *See* 1 Clark, Law of Domestic Relations in the United States §2.7 (2d ed. 1987) (presumed validity of latest of successive marriages "is the stronger one and will prevail").

One route to preferring the validity of the later marriage is to invoke a third presumption that displaces the others: On proof that a person was twice married, it is presumed that the first marriage was validly terminated and that the second marriage was valid and continuing.[6] Another is to hold that the presumed validity of a marriage expresses the more weighty policy when applied to the second of two marriages or that it embodies a more weighty policy than the presumed continuance of an earlier marriage.[7] By either approach, the end result seems right. It is at least highly probable that people who enter successive marriages do so because they are free to do so (or think they are) and when people arrange their lives on the supposition that what they have done is proper, that arrangement should be honored unless there is clearly something wrong. The presumed validity of the later marriage is especially strong and it applies in other settings: Most state decisions hold that it can be overcome only by strong or cogent evidence, and the presumption also applies in divorce and annulment proceedings and suits to determine legitimacy of children.[8]

FRE 302

In civil actions and proceedings, the effect of a presumption respecting a fact which is an element of a claim or defense as to which State law supplies the rule of decision is determined in accordance with state law.

---

§3.10 State Versus Federal Law

FRE 302 accepts the view that state presumptions are matters of substance rather than procedure for *Erie* purposes when they bear on elements of claims or defenses that are governed by state law.[1] In such cases, FRE 302 requires federal courts to give state presumptions the same effect state law would give them. This provision virtually assumes (if it does not quite require) that federal courts under *Erie* recognize and apply state presumptions because they are substantive law.

Presumptions are substantive

Many common presumptions clearly bear on elements of claims or defenses and fit the terms of FRE 302. Examples include the presumption that sudden violent death was accident rather than suicide, the presumption that an employee was acting within the scope of his duties, and the presumption that the driver of a loaned car had the owner's permission.[2] It seems settled as well that res ipsa loquitur is

Bear on elements

---

6. *See* Steele v. Richardson, 472 F.2d 49, 51 (2d Cir. 1972); John Hancock Mut. Life Ins. Co. v. Willis, 438 F.2d 1207, 1209 (6th Cir. 1971).

7. Gainey v. Flemming, 279 F.2d 56, 59 (10th Cir. 1960).

8. *See* 1 Clark, Law of Domestic Relations in the United States §2.7 (2d ed. 1987).

§3.10 1. *See* Erie Railroad v. Tompkins, 304 U.S. 64 (1938) (in diversity cases federal courts apply state substantive law).

2. *See* the discussion in §3.5, *supra.*

substantive under *Erie,* and there is no room to doubt that this presumption bears on an element of a claim (conceivably even a defense), so state versions of this doctrine apply in suits in federal court governed by state law.[3]

Tactical presumptions

According to the ACN, FRE 302 does not require federal courts to apply state "tactical" presumptions that operate on "lesser aspects" than "substantive" elements of claims or defenses. The principal architect of the Rules thought that in a suit to collect an account the common mailed letter presumption was only tactical if it was deployed to show that defendant received a statement because "the presumed fact of delivery is much smaller than an element in the case."[4] It is true that neither defendant's receipt of an account nor his silent acquiescence or admission of liability is an element in the claim in the usual sense of the term (plaintiff need not plead these matters and may prevail without proving them). Apparently the idea is that such a presumption only affects details of proof, so state substantive policies are not implicated.[5]

Problematic idea

This idea of tactical presumptions is problematic. It invites a distinction between situations where the presumed fact coincides exactly with an element in a case and situations where it does not. And it is not clear that exempting tactical presumptions from the directive in FRE 302 is sound. Pre-Rules decisions did not distinguish between tactical and other presumptions, and the language (if not holdings) in the decisions indicate that presumptions are generic examples of matters that are substantive under *Erie.* Nor can it be said with certainty that Congress adopted what the Committee proposed even though Congress did not change the Rule.[6]

Perhaps more important, the suggested distinction sometimes accords less recognition to state presumptions than *Erie* seems to require. A state presumption may embody and implement state substantive policy even if it does not bear on a fact amounting to an element of a claim or defense. For example, a presumption of a valid and existing marriage, arising on proof that a marriage ceremony was performed, may well bear on the propriety of invoking the spousal

---

3. *See* Koppinger v. Cullen-Schiltz & Assocs., 513 F.2d 901, 906 (8th Cir. 1975) (applying state res ipsa doctrine); Kelly v. American Airlines, Inc., 508 F.2d 1379, 1380 (5th Cir. 1975) (applying Texas version of res ipsa).

4. *See* ACN to FRE 302. *See also* Cleary, Presuming and Pleading: An Essay on Juristic Immaturity, 12 Stan. L. Rev. 5, 26 (1959).

5. *See* Herbert v. Wal-Mart Stores, Inc., 911 F.2d 1044, 1047-1048 (5th Cir. 1990) (in bench-tried slip-and-fall suit leading to judgment for defendant, court did not err in failing to draw adverse inference from defense failure to call available witness; FRE 302 did not require federal court to apply state "uncalled-witness rule" because it does not create true presumption and "merely permits an inference").

6. While the ACN to FRE 302 uses the term "tactical" to describe presumptions playing a "lesser" role in the case, it provides no examples and the only likely source is a 1959 article by the Reporter for the Committee. One commentator flatly rejects the approach of exempting some presumptions from the mandate of FRE 302. *See* 21 Wright & Graham, Federal Practice and Procedure (Evidence) §5134 (1977).

testimony privilege. In a case where FRE 501 requires application of state law to resolve the privilege issue, there is no apparent reason to ignore a state presumption merely because it does not bear on an element of a claim or defense. There is reason to doubt an interpretation of *Erie* that, in the course of dismissing this presumption as tactical, would overlook the strength of underlying state policies and the obvious fact that they would be served by applying the state presumption.

Distinguishing tactical presumptions from others might even accord more recognition to state presumptions than seems warranted under *Erie*. It is at least possible for a state presumption to embody no substantive policy, and instead to rest only on the same kind of logic and experience that underlie relevancy rules.

The phrase "element of a claim or defense" in FRE 302 should be construed sensibly to encompass any fact that provides direct support of elements even if the fact itself is not co-extensive with the element.[7] In the area of real property, for example, many common state presumptions bear on facts like authenticity and delivery of a deed.[8] Such facts may be a step removed from the actual elements of many claims and defenses, yet critical in establishing such elements. In a quiet title action usually plaintiff must prove he holds title, and in trespass suits commonly plaintiff must prove he holds a possessory interest. In neither case is it necessary to show plaintiff holds a valid deed. But if plaintiff seeks to prove he took delivery of a valid deed to establish title or a possessory interest, state-created presumptions bearing on these facts should be applied. These presumptions should not be dismissed as merely "tactical" because it would lead to confusion and futile semantic distinctions.

Construed sensibly

More faithful to *Erie* would be a determination whether a state presumption embodies substantive policy and whether applying the presumption would serve the policy in the case. If so, the state presumption should be applied. It is sometimes hard to know whether state presumptions express substantive policies, but that point is true across the whole range of *Erie* issues, and giving *Erie* its due requires that the task be undertaken.

---

7. *See* Dodson v. Imperial Motors, Inc., 295 F.2d 609 (6th Cir. 1961) (applying state presumption on truth of notarial certificate that determined crucial issue of car title).

8. One such presumption is that a document at least 30 years old (sometimes 20 years) is genuine if found where a genuine document of the sort might naturally be found, and not suspicious on its face. At least it is admissible, and the question of authenticity is submitted to the jury. *See* 7 Wigmore, Evidence §§2138-2146 (3d ed. 1940); FRE 901(8) (20-year provision). Another is a presumption, arising from an acknowledgment by notary, that a document was duly executed and that the facts recited in the acknowledgement are true. *See* 5 Wigmore, Evidence §167a (3d ed. 1940) (collecting state statutes). Commonly possession of a deed by the grantee, or the fact that a deed is recorded, gives rise to a presumption of delivery of the deed to the grantee. 9 Wigmore, Evidence §2520 (Chadbourn rev. 1981).

B. CRIMINAL CASES

§3.11 Standard of Proof (Beyond a Reasonable Doubt)

It has long been Anglo-American practice to require a higher standard of proof in criminal cases because of the more serious consequences of an erroneous verdict, which include loss of liberty and even life itself. A fundamental value inherent in our legal system is that criminal trials must safeguard against the wrongful conviction of the innocent even at the price of sometimes allowing the guilty to go free.[1]

As a reflection of this judgment, the standard was developed at early common law that the state must prove an accused guilty "beyond a reasonable doubt."[2] Because this standard was so widely accepted by case law, statutes, and state constitutions, the issue seldom arose whether it was required as a component of due process guaranteed by the federal constitution. In the *Winship* case, the Supreme Court finally addressed the question and held that "the Due Process Clause protects the accused against conviction except upon proof beyond a reasonable doubt of every fact necessary to constitute the crime with which he is charged."[3]

There are divergent views on exactly what "beyond a reasonable doubt" means,[4] and some authorities take the view that no elaboration or explanation is needed.[5] A variety of definitions have been submitted to juries,[6] and some have been found to be in error.[7] In one case, the Supreme Court held that an instruction allowing acquittal only for "grave uncertainty" or "actual substantial doubt" and equating beyond

---

§3.11   1. In re Winship, 397 U.S. 358, 372 (1970) (Harlan, J., concurring) (it is "a fundamental value determination of our society that it is far worse to convict an innocent man than to let a guilty man go free").

2. *See* Morano, A Reexamination of the Development of the Reasonable Doubt Rule, 55 B.U. L. Rev. 507, 512-520 (1975). *See generally* Shapiro, "Beyond Reasonable Doubt" and "Probable Cause": Historical Perspectives on the Law of Anglo-American Evidence (1991); Thayer, Preliminary Treatise on Evidence at the Common Law 558, 559 (1898) (tracing historical development of "beyond reasonable doubt" standard).

3. In re Winship, 397 U.S. 358, 359 (1970) (construing Fourteenth Amendment on review of state juvenile adjudication).

4. Victor v. Nebraska, 511 U.S. 1, 5, 14 (1994) (approving instruction requiring jury to have an "abiding conviction as to guilt"); Holland v. United States, 348 U.S. 121, 140 (1954) (approving definition of reasonable doubt as "a doubt that would cause a reasonable person to hesitate to act"). *But see* Newman, Beyond "Reasonable Doubt," 68 N.Y.U. L. Rev. 979 (1993) (questioning "hesitate to act" definition).

5. United States v. Adkins, 937 F.2d 947, 950 (4th Cir. 1991) (warning against defining reasonable doubt unless jury requests it); United States v. Glass, 846 F.2d 386, 387 (7th Cir. 1988) (instruction given illustrates "all too well" that attempts to explain term reasonable doubt do not usually make it clearer).

6. For a commonly used definition, *see* 1 Devitt & Blackmar, Federal Jury Practice and Instructions 11.14 (3d ed. 1977) (reasonable doubt is one that is "based upon reason and common sense—the kind of doubt that would make a reasonable person hesitate to act," so proof beyond reasonable doubt must be so convincing that "a reasonable person would not hesitate to rely and act upon it in the most important of his own affairs").

7. *See, e.g.*, McCullough v. State, 657 P.2d 1157, 1158 (Nev. 1983) (error to instruct jury that beyond reasonable doubt means a 75 percent probability of guilt).

reasonable doubt with "moral certainty" overstated the degree of doubt that would justify acquittal.[8] In another case, a federal court held that requiring only that the jury have a "strong belief" in the defendant's guilt understated the requirement of proof beyond a reasonable doubt.[9]

It is generally agreed that the beyond reasonable doubt standard applies to each element of the crime but not to each piece of evidence offered to prove an element. Thus evidence may be admitted to prove an element even where authenticity has not been established beyond a reasonable doubt.[10] And of course this standard also does not apply to preliminary questions that the trial judge decides under FRE 104(a), such as whether a witness qualifies as an expert, or an out-of-court statement fits a hearsay exception, or a confession was voluntary.

Meaning of term

Winship applies only to criminal proceedings. For purposes of applying *Winship,* the issue whether a state proceeding is civil or criminal is a federal question, and the state's designation of the proceeding as "civil" is not dispositive if the penalties are inherently criminal.[11]

Applies to elements

In criminal proceedings a "presumption of innocence" operates in favor of the accused,[12] which has been described as the "golden thread" that runs throughout the criminal law.[13] In some cases failure to instruct the jury on this presumption amounts to constitutional error.[14] However, the presumption of innocence is not a true presumption at all. Rather it is a way of forcefully emphasizing to the jury that the

Presumption of innocence

---

8. Cage v. Louisiana, 498 U.S. 39, 41 (1990). *See also* Victor v. Nebraska, 511 U.S. 1 (1994) (disapproving use of "to a moral certainty" in defining beyond reasonable doubt, but finding no error in light of instructions as a whole).

9. United States v. Merlos, 984 F.2d 1239, 1240-1242 (D.C. Cir. 1993) (error to give instruction that "[p]roof beyond reasonable doubt is proof that leaves you with a strong belief in defendant's guilt").

10. An exhibit requires only a foundation "sufficient to support a finding that the matter in question is what its proponent claims." FRE 901(a). And a witness may testify on the basis of evidence "sufficient to support a finding" that she has personal knowledge. FRE 602. Neither rule requires foundation facts to be established beyond a reasonable doubt. *See generally* §1.12, *supra.* But the prosecutor must produce an aggregate of evidence sufficient for a reasonable jury to find each element of the offense beyond a reasonable doubt.

11. Hicks v. Feiock, 485 U.S. 624, 630 (1988) (a state's classification of a proceeding as "civil" or "criminal" is "not determinative of the issue" for purposes of federal constitutional law).

12. Estelle v. Williams, 425 U.S. 501, 503 (1976) ("although not articulated in the Constitution," presumption of innocence "is a basic component of a fair trial").

13. Cross, The Golden Thread of the English Criminal Law 2 (1976). *See also* Abraham, The Judicial Process 96 (6th ed. 1993) (describing presumption of innocence as the "cornerstone of Anglo-Saxon justice"); Fox, The "Presumption of Innocence" as Constitutional Doctrine, 28 Cath. U.L. Rev. 253 (1979).

14. Kentucky v. Whorton, 441 U.S. 786, 789 (1979) (holding that "the failure to give a requested instruction on the presumption of innocence does not in and of itself violate the Constitution" but must be evaluated "in light of the totality of the circumstances"); Taylor v. Kentucky, 436 U.S. 478, 486 (1978) (where jury was exposed to facts outside trial record, failure to give "presumption of innocence" instruction upon request was constitutional error; this presumption is "one means of protecting the accused's constitutional right to be judged solely on the basis of proof adduced at trial").

prosecutor has the obligation to prove each element of the offense beyond a reasonable doubt, that the accused bears no proof burden whatsoever with respect to any element of the crime, and that no adverse inference should be drawn against him from the fact of his arrest, indictment, or presence in court.[15]

§3.12   Affirmative Defenses

There are basically two types of defenses in criminal cases. The first serves to negate an element of the offense charged. Examples include alibi in a robbery case and consent in a rape prosecution. The second goes beyond negating an element of the crime and instead proves additional facts that exculpate or excuse the defendant or mitigate the severity of the punishment. Usually the defenses of duress, necessity, self-defense, and entrapment fall into this latter category. Such defenses are commonly described as "affirmative" defenses (which for purposes of this discussion mean defenses that go beyond negating an element in the charge).

For both types of defenses, the accused normally has at least the burden of going forward with evidence.[1] If the defendant does not produce sufficient evidence to enable a reasonable jury to find the facts constituting the defense, it is not submitted to the jury, and it effectively drops out of the case.[2]

Allocations of burdens   The burden of persuasion on affirmative defenses may also be allocated to the defendant. Whether that burden goes to him is determined by the substantive law of the jurisdiction and depends on the particular defense. If the burden of persuasion is on the prosecution, it must disprove the defense beyond a reasonable doubt after the defendant satisfies his burden of production on the matter.[3] If the burden is on the defendant (as is typically true for the defense of insanity), usually he

---

15. *See* LaFave, Criminal Law §1.8 at 55 (4th ed. 2003).

§3.12   1. Simopoulous v. Virginia, 462 U.S. 506 (1983) (medical necessity defense); United States v. Bailey, 444 U.S. 394, 425-426 (1980) (duress and necessity); Holloway v. McElroy, 632 F.2d 605, 635 (5th Cir. 1980) (self-defense), *cert. denied*, 451 U.S. 1028. *See also* Model Penal Code, §1.13, Comment, p.110 (Tent. Draft No. 4, 1955) (may shift to the defendant the burden of going forward with sufficient evidence in support of a defense "to justify [a reasonable] doubt upon the issue").

2. Leach v. Kolb, 911 F.2d 1249, 1256-1257 (7th Cir. 1990) (may direct verdict on insanity where defendant failed to introduce supporting evidence), *cert. denied*, 498 U.S. 972. *See also* Model Penal Code §1.12(2)(a) (Code does not "require the disproof of an affirmative defense unless and until there is evidence supporting such defense").

3. United States v. Smith, 981 F.2d 887, 892 (6th Cir. 1992) (where "statutory exception" creates affirmative defense, "ultimate burden of persuasion" remains with prosecution, although defendant has "burden of going forward with sufficient evidence to raise the exception as an issue").

must prove the defense by a preponderance of the evidence,[4] although occasionally a higher standard is imposed.[5]

Mullaney:
Elements

The *Winship* doctrine that the prosecutor is constitutionally required to prove every element of the crime beyond a reasonable doubt has important but uncertain implications for affirmative defenses. In the *Mullaney* case,[6] decided five years after *Winship,* the Court reviewed a murder conviction from Maine, where mens rea (the crucial mental element) was "malice aforethought." The defendant claimed that he had acted in the heat of passion, which would (if established) reduce murder to manslaughter. Applying Maine law, the trial judge instructed the jury that malice aforethought and heat of passion were "two inconsistent things," and this statement seemed to mean that "by proving the latter the defendant would negate the former." Yet the trial judge instructed the jury that malice aforethought is established by a showing of "any deliberate cruel act" unless defendant proved he acted in "heat of passion, on sudden provocation." In this setting, a unanimous Supreme Court found constitutional error in placing the burden of persuasion on the defendant.

On a narrow view, *Mullaney* is completely unsurprising because it means only that the state cannot constitutionally shift the burden of persuasion to the defendant to disprove an element of the charged offense like mens rea.[7] On a broader view, *Mullaney* could be read to mean the prosecutor must not only bear the burden on central elements like mens rea but on every factor that makes a difference in punishment or stigma, including defenses raising new matter. After all, heat of passion does not seem to be only the absence of malice (or only the negation of mens rea) since it carries as well a broad idea of being excusably out of control. And not everyone would agree that heat of passion necessarily disproves the requisite intent, although the Maine criminal code apparently adopted that theory. Hence a holding that the defense cannot be burdened with proving heat of passion might also mean the defense cannot be burdened with proving any new matter that serves as a defense or lessens the seriousness of the offense, whether or not such matter is broader than an

---

4. United States v. Brown, 367 F.3d 549, 556 (6th Cir. 2004) (where affirmative defense bears necessary relationship to element of charged offense, burden does not shift to defendant; where affirmative defense does not negate an element of charged offense, defendant must prove it by a preponderance of evidence; here defendant had burden of proving defense of necessity to charge of being a felon in possession of a firearm).

5. 18 U.S.C. §17(b) (requiring insanity defense in federal prosecutions to be established by defendant by "clear and convincing" evidence); Leland v. Oregon, 343 U.S. 790, 798 (1952) (upholding constitutionality of state statute requiring accused to prove defense of insanity beyond a reasonable doubt).

6. Mullaney v. Wilbur, 421 U.S. 684, 686-687 (1975).

7. Indeed, *Mullaney* might have been decided on a narrower ground, since Maine employed a presumption of malice aforethought arising from "any deliberate cruel act" committed "suddenly" against another without "considerable provocation." Four years after *Mullaney,* the Court disapproved a similar presumption. *See* the discussion in §3.13, *infra.*

element in the charged crime or necessarily tends to refute such an element.

Patterson:
**Affirmative
defense**

Two years later in the _Patterson_ case, the Court confirmed that the narrow reading of _Mullaney_ is right.[8] _Patterson_ was brought under a trim and modern statute requiring the state to prove "intent to cause the death of another person" and "caus[ing] the death." The New York scheme let defendant raise the affirmative defense of being "under the influence of extreme emotional disturbance," which would (like "heat of passion" in Maine) reduce the offense to manslaughter. _Patterson_ approved allocating to the defense the burden of persuasion on this point, because under the New York statute the defense did not negate any element of the crime. The Court noted that the New York judge (unlike his Maine counterpart) told the jury that intent to cause death could coexist with extreme emotional disturbance.

Taken together, _Mullaney_ and _Patterson_ are tantalizing but unsatisfying decisions. _Mullaney_ held the promise of a protective jurisprudence that might restrain legislatures and courts in allocating to the accused the burden of proving elements bearing on culpability but adopted no principle or standard to define those limits. _Patterson_ drew back from this enterprise in favor of legislative (and judicial) flexibility, expressing concern that if the prosecution had to bear the burden to disprove every factor that might mitigate or diminish the offense, the legislature might be reluctant to recognize such factors at all.[9]

**Legislature may
reallocate**

Patterson raises the danger that a legislature could circumvent _Winship_ by rewriting its criminal code to transform elements of an offense into affirmative defenses and shifting the burden of persuasion to the defendant. Thus a criminal statute with elements _A_, _B_, and _C_ could be redrafted so the state had to prove only _A_ and _B_ with _C_ being converted into an affirmative defense. For example, larceny could conceivably be redefined as merely the act of taking another's property, with absence of mens rea being allocated as a defense for the accused to prove. The _Patterson_ majority did say "there are obviously constitutional limits beyond which the States may not go in this regard," but did not explain further.[10]

**Constitutional
restraints**

The Eighth Amendment prohibition against "cruel and unusual punishment" is one source of constitutional limitation on the ways that

8. Patterson v. New York, 432 U.S. 197, 200 (1977).

9. _See_ Patterson v. New York, 432 U.S. at 207-208 (1977) (state criminal code has 25 affirmative defenses "which must be established by the defendant to be operative" and Due Process Clause should not put state "to the choice of abandoning those defenses or undertaking to disprove their existence in order to convict of a crime which otherwise is within its constitutional powers to sanction").

10. Patterson v. New York, 432 U.S. at 210 and 223 (Powell, J., dissenting) (criticizing majority for ignoring "the constitutional values for which _Winship_ stands" because it "allows a legislature to shift, virtually at will, the burden of persuasion with respect to any factor in a criminal case, so long as it is careful not to mention the nonexistence of that factor in the statutory language that defines the crime").

legislatures (and courts) can define crimes.[11] If a legislature were to eliminate traditional elements of culpability from a penal statute, it would be criminalizing conduct that was previously innocent, and the "new" crime might be vulnerable to constitutional challenge. The Eighth Amendment embodies the principle that crimes normally require an act, blameworthy mental attitude, and proportionality in punishment, and these notions necessarily limit the permissible definitions of crimes and defenses.[12] But Eighth Amendment jurisprudence is not well developed, and it has little "bite" in limiting legislative prerogative.[13] The dissenters in *Patterson* argued for the view that defendants cannot constitutionally be given the burden of persuasion on factors that make a "substantial difference in punishment and stigma" if these have historically "held that level of importance" in Anglo-American legal tradition.[14]

Some writers have criticized the *Mullaney-Patterson* doctrine as being overly formalistic because it does not bar a state from shifting the burden of persuasion to the defendant, but only requires the proper means of doing so (by redefining the crime and recognizing an affirmative defense). So long as a matter is included as an element of a crime, the burden of persuasion cannot be shifted to the defendant directly or by means of a presumption (see discussion in next section). Under the "greater includes the lesser" theory, it is argued that a state should be prohibited from shifting the burden of persuasion on an element to a defendant only where it would be unconstitutional to eliminate such an element from the definition of the offense.[15]

11. Jeffries & Stephan, Defenses, Presumptions, and Burden of Proof in the Criminal Law, 88 Yale L.J. 1325, 1370-1379 (1979) (Eighth Amendment bar against cruel and unusual punishment limits legislative capacity to define criminality by requiring an act, a blameworthy mental attitude, and proportionality in punishment).

12. *See* Moran v. Ohio, 469 U.S. 948, 955 (1984) (Brennan and Marshall dissenting from denial of certiorari) (arguing that a state could not repudiate the defense of self-defense because "both the Due Process Clause and the Eighth Amendment may restrict the State's ability to so punish a defendant whose 'crime,' for example, consisted in an immediate response to a murderous attack upon him").

13. Harmelin v. Michigan, 501 U.S. 957 (1991) (upholding against Eighth Amendment challenge a mandatory life sentence without possibility of parole for first-time offender who possessed more than 650 grams of cocaine); Rummel v. Estelle, 445 U.S. 263 (1980) (upholding imposition of life sentence under Texas habitual offender statute, where defendant had been convicted on three occasions for fraudulently obtaining money and goods worth a total of $229.11).

14. Patterson v. New York, 432 U.S. at 228-229 (Powell, Brennan, and Marshall dissenting). Under the approach of the dissenters, traditional defenses and mitigating factors could be eliminated but not shifted to the defendant. *See* Jeffries & Stephan, Defenses, Presumptions and Burdens of Proof in the Criminal Law, 88 Yale L.J. 1325, 1362 (1979) (describing this approach as "conceptually schizophrenic" because it would "disallow shifting the burden of proof even as it recognizes legislative authority to redefine the substance of the law").

15. *See* Allen, The Restoration of In re Winship: A Comment on Burdens of Persuasion in Criminal Cases After Patterson v. New York, 76 Mich. L. Rev. 30, 42-46 (1977) (arguing that if a state can constitutionally eliminate an element from definition of a crime, it should be able to keep it but shift the burden of proof to the defendant because the "greater power should include the lesser"). *But see* Saltzburg, Burdens of Persuasion in Criminal Cases: Harmonizing the Views of the Justices, 20 Am.

But this view ignores the important policy advantages of requiring legislatures to address directly what factors should be included as elements
of crimes[16] and the burden and inappropriateness of requiring courts
to play a vastly expanded role as constitutional referees deciding the
permissible boundaries of the criminal law.[17]

Deference to statute Courts applying the *Mullaney-Patterson* doctrine clearly must give great
deference to statutory definitions of claims and defenses.[18] If the factor
in question is an element in the offense, the prosecutor must bear the
burden of persuasion beyond a reasonable doubt. If it is a "new matter"
affirmative defense that can coexist with all the elements of the offense
(as in *Patterson*, where a defendant was thought to be capable of having
the requisite intent to kill while laboring under extreme emotional
distress), then the burden of persuasion can be put on the defendant.
Thus the burden of persuasion on a defense like "alibi" that necessarily
negates completely the central element of "identity" in any charged
crime cannot be allocated to the defense (even though the prosecutor's
burden in proving identity is not specifically to refute the alibi but
rather to prove defendant's presence at the crime scene).[19] But the
accused usually can be burdened with proving duress,[20] entrapment,[21]
self-defense,[22] and other defenses that do more than negate a statutory
element.[23] Where statutes are ambiguous or uncertain in defining the

---

Crim. L. Rev. 393, 407 (1983) (greater-includes-lesser theory "must be rejected because
it permits the imposition of stigma without requiring the government to prove that
there is a difference between greater and lesser offenders").

16. *See* Underwood, The Thumb on the Scales of Justice: Burdens of Persuasion in
Criminal Cases, 86 Yale L.J. 1299 (1977) (criticizing the "greater includes the lesser"
argument because it encourages legislative avoidance of policy issues that should be
faced directly; also noting that selected, unpopular defendants may be denied the
benefits of a defense if they have to bear the burden of persuasion).

17. *See, e.g.,* Sundby, The Reasonable Doubt Rule and the Meaning of Innocence, 40
Hastings L.J. 457 (1989) (criticizing as impractical and undemocratic the view that the
Supreme Court should be required to develop detailed constitutional standards governing minimum elements of crimes and limits of punishment; generally favoring view
of dissenters in *Patterson*).

18. Hicks v. Feiock, 485 U.S. 624, 629 (1988) (in challenge to state presumption that
person is able to make child support payments, first step is to determine whether ability
to comply with order is an element of the offense or whether inability to comply is an
affirmative defense; federal courts defer to state interpretation of its own statutes on
this issue); McMillan v. Pennsylvania, 477 U.S. 79, 85 (1986) (in determining elements
of offense, "state legislature's definition" is usually dispositive).

19. Stump v. Bennett, 398 F.2d 111, 113, 116 (8th Cir. 1968) (improper to shift
burden of persuasion to defendant to establish alibi defense because such a defense
merely negates elements of the crime that must be proven by the government), *cert.
denied*, 393 U.S. 1001.

20. Rodriguez v. Scully, 788 F.2d 62, 65 (2d Cir. 1986) (no "constitutional infirmity"
in requiring defendant to establish duress defense).

21. *See* LaFave & Scott, Criminal Law 430 (2d ed. 1986).

22. Smart v. Leeke, 873 F.2d 1558 (4th Cir. 1989) (defense must establish self-
defense by a preponderance of the evidence), *cert. denied*, 493 U.S. 867.

23. Farrell v. Czartnetzky, 566 F.2d 381, 382 (2d Cir. 1977) (where statute defined
first degree robbery as a robbery with what appears to be a firearm, proper for state to
create affirmative defense that gun was not loaded and allocate burden of proving that
defense to the accused), *cert. denied*, 434 U.S. 1077.

elements essential for conviction, there is resulting confusion as to how proof burdens should be allocated.[24] Sometimes the inquiry becomes entirely formalistic and ends in judicial hair-splitting,[25] although clues to policy and purpose can often be found in the statutory scheme or drawn from judicial supervisory authority. Some courts resist application of the *Patterson-Mullaney* doctrine to certain defenses.[26]

The most challenging constitutional questions arise where a defense tends both to negate an element of the offense and to raise new mitigating matter. Thus it is not surprising that constitutional challenges to proof allocation first surfaced in cases like *Mullaney* and *Patterson* because the relationship between criminal intent and emotional disturbance (and between intent and insanity)[27] is extraordinarily problematic. The extent to which such a defense negates intent or raises new matter depends on specific circumstances and on the ways that we define criminal intent and emotional disturbance, and modern authorities take different views. Some jurisdictions follow New York in *Patterson* and treat emotional disturbance as a factor independent of intent on which defendant bears the burden,[28] but under other murder statutes defendants cannot be burdened with proving heat of passion because it negates the requisite intent.[29]

The Supreme Court faced an "overlapping" defense in *Martin v. Ohio*, where defendant, despite a self-defense claim, was convicted of

Defense that negates element

24. *See* United States v. Smith, 981 F.2d 887, 891-892 (6th Cir. 1992) (issue whether gun was "antique," hence within exception to statutory definition of "firearm," was an affirmative defense on which defendant had burden of production but government bore burden of persuasion).

25. *Compare* Wynn v. Mahoney, 600 F.2d 448, 451 (4th Cir. 1979) (unconstitutional to place burden of proving self-defense on defendant because in North Carolina "unlawfulness" is an element of murder and self-defense negates unlawfulness), *cert. denied*, 444 U.S. 950, *with* Williams v. Mohn, 462 F. Supp. 756, 759 (N.D. W. Va. 1978) (constitutional to place burden of proving self-defense on defendant because in West Virginia "unlawfulness" is not an element of murder).

26. For example, some courts hold that a defendant can be required to bear the burden of persuasion with respect to intoxication even though evidence of intoxication is offered to negate intent. *See, e.g.,* Long v. Brewer, 667 F.2d 742 (8th Cir. 1982) (upholding state conviction where defendant was required to prove intoxication by a preponderance, although court admits difficulty with distinction that prohibits defendant from being required to disprove an element of a crime but requires him to prove a defense—here intoxication—that may negative an element of the crime), *cert. denied*, 459 U.S. 883. *But see* Montana v. Egelhof, 518 U.S. 37 (1996) (approving state homicide conviction despite rule barring defendant from raising intoxication as defense). Arguably *Egelhof* means defendant may be burdened with proving intoxication, since the defense need not be recognized at all.

27. See *Mullaney*, 421 U.S. at 706 (Rehnquist, J., concurring) (existence or not of legal insanity "bears no necessary relationship to the existence or nonexistence of the required mental elements").

28. Krzeminski v. Perini, 614 F.2d 121, 123 (6th Cir. 1980) (state can properly place on defendant the burden of proving self-defense, extreme emotional disturbance or insanity), *cert. denied*, 449 U.S. 866.

29. United States v. Lesina, 833 F.2d 156, 160 (9th Cir. 1987) (under federal murder statute, burden of proving heat of passion cannot constitutionally be shifted to defendant); United States v. Lofton, 776 F.2d 918, 920 (10th Cir. 1985) (same).

aggravated murder (defined under Ohio law as killing "purposely" with "prior calculation and design"). Defendant argued that it was constitutional error to assign to her the burden of persuasion on the self-defense claim, since such a defense tended to negate the element of purposeful killing by "prior calculation and design." Because the jury had been told that the prosecutor must prove every element beyond a reasonable doubt, including "prior calculation and design," the Court found no constitutional error in requiring the defendant to prove self-defense. The decision in *Martin* adds two important points to the puzzle presented by *Mullaney-Patterson*. First, where an affirmative defense raising new matter does overlap (hence tends to undercut) an element in the charged offense, the jury must still be instructed that the prosecution has the burden of proving all elements of the offense beyond a reasonable doubt. Second, the jury should be told that it may consider defense evidence not merely insofar as it tends to establish the defense itself but also on the question whether the state has proven each element of the crime beyond a reasonable doubt.[30]

The *Martin* approach to "overlapping" defenses has been followed in other contexts. For example, even though proof of the insanity defense may constitutionally be allocated to the accused,[31] generally the jury must be instructed that the prosecution has the burden of proving every element, including mens rea, beyond a reasonable doubt,[32] and the defendant's evidence relating to his mental state should be considered in determining whether the government has carried this burden.[33]

§3.13 "Presumptions" in Criminal Cases

To help the prosecutor carry the heavy burden imposed on the state in criminal cases, courts and legislatures have created what are often called "presumptions," but which, because of constitutional constraints, can only operate as inferences. Consider, for example, the critical element of mens rea (criminal intent). Often it is hard to prove because there is no direct evidence, and yet intent may be strongly suggested by what the defendant apparently did—shooting someone at close range is likely to suggest intent to kill. Hence many jurisdictions have recognized a "presumption" inviting an inference of

30. Martin v. Ohio, 480 U.S. 228, 233 (1987) (indicating result might have been different if jury had been instructed that evidence of self-defense could not be considered in deciding whether there was reasonable doubt on any element of state's case).

31. *See* Leland v. Oregon, 343 U.S. 790 (1953). *See also* Patterson v. New York, 432 U.S. 197 (1977) (Court "unwilling to reconsider" *Leland* holding that burden of persuasion on insanity can be put on defendant); Rivera v. Delaware, 429 U.S. 877 (1976) (dismissing challenge to Leland for want of substantial federal question).

32. Leland v. Oregon, 343 U.S. 790, 794 (1952) (noting that jury was instructed that prosecutor had "to prove beyond a reasonable doubt every element of the crime charged").

33. Humanik v. Beyer, 871 F.2d 432, 442-443 (3d Cir. 1989) (error to refuse to allow jury to consider defense evidence of insanity and diminished capacity to negate intent), *cert. denied*, 493 U.S. 812.

intent on the basis of proved behavior. After the government offers evidence indicating that the defendant committed the charged criminal act, it may be entitled to an instruction at the end of the case suggesting to the jury that one usually "intends the natural and probable consequences of his voluntary acts."[1]

Properly framing such an instruction is hard since a presumption operating against the accused cannot properly be a substitute for evidence that is not there, and should not enhance or supplement the evidence offered beyond its natural probative force in the eyes of the jury. Yet even the mildest language that urges or reassures the jury may have such effects. Hence presumption instructions raise multiple concerns: They might dilute or undercut the requirement of proof beyond a reasonable doubt; they might amount to an adverse comment on the fact that the accused has not testified, or they might deprive him of the right to a jury trial on important factual issues. When such instructions are required or invited by statutory enactment, they raise questions about legislative determination (or predetermination) of points that courts rightly think they should decide, such as the sufficiency of evidence.[2]

Presumption instruction

The term "presumption" is a misnomer in criminal cases. Certainly the notorious "conclusive presumption," which purports to require the jury to find a particular point no matter what the evidence shows to be true, has no proper place in criminal trials.[3]

"Presumption" is misnomer

Criminal presumptions relating to elements of a charged offense are best understood—and explained to the jury—not as presumptions at all, but as permissive inferences that the trier may draw or not as it

---

§3.13 1. *See, e.g.,* Agnew v. United States, 165 U.S. 36, 53 (1896) (recognizing common law presumption that one intends the natural and probable consequences of voluntary acts). Often it is said that "general intent" crimes are those from which it is possible to infer the necessary mens rea from the act itself and that "specific intent" crimes are those in which additional evidence is required to prove intent. *See generally* 1 LaFave & Scott, Substantive Criminal Law §§3.5-3.6 (1986).

2. Carella v. California, 491 U.S. 263, 266 (1989) (mandatory instructions "directly foreclosed independent jury consideration" of intent and improperly relieved state of burden of persuasion); County Court of Ulster v. Allen, 442 U.S. 140, 156 (1979) (ultimate test of constitutional validity is that the device "must not undermine the factfinder's responsibility at trial, based on evidence adduced by the State, to find the ultimate facts beyond a reasonable doubt"); Leary v. United States, 395 U.S. 6, 55 (1969) (Black, J., concurring) (Congress has "no more constitutional power to tell a jury it can convict" upon "false and baseless evidence" than it has to tell juries they can convict "without any evidence at all"); United States v. Gainey, 380 U.S. 63, 87 (1965) (Black, J., dissenting) (founders designed federal government so that assessment of facts in lawsuits, and instructions given to juries, were matters within exclusive judicial competence). *See generally* Ashford & Risinger, Presumptions, Assumptions and Due Process in Criminal Cases: A Theoretical Overview, 79 Yale L.J. 165, 203-205 (1969).

3. *See* Carella v. California, 491 U.S. 263, 266 (1989) (disapproving "mandatory directions" as foreclosing independent jury consideration and relieving prosecution of burden of persuasion); Morissette v. United States, 342 U.S. 246, 275 (1952) (disapproving a conclusive presumption because it would "effectively eliminate intent as an ingredient of the offense" and conflict with presumption of innocence).

chooses. In civil cases "presumption" means a finding that must be made in the absence of counterproof challenging the basic or presumed facts. But in criminal cases the trier of fact must be left free to draw or reject the conclusion suggested by presumption instructions. Hence the very term "presumption" should be avoided altogether in criminal jury instructions, at least when used against the defendant.[4]

Procedural function of presumptions

In civil cases presumptions have a powerful effect, often implementing important substantive policies by helping take cases to the jury that might otherwise fail and by sometimes imposing mandatory findings. A hallmark of civil presumptions is that they shift to the party against whom they operate the burden of production (sometimes even the burden of persuasion), and it is this aspect of their nature that makes them so powerful. Criminal presumptions cannot operate in these ways for at least two reasons.

Cannot have mandatory effect

First, a criminal presumption cannot have mandatory effect on an element of a charged offense. As the Supreme Court has held, "verdicts may not be directed against [criminal] defendants" in whole or in part.[5] It logically follows that a criminal presumption cannot shift the burden of production to the defendant on an element in the offense[6] because failing to meet that burden would logically generate an instruction directing the jury to find the presumed fact.[7]

Cannot shift burden of proof on element

Second, *Winship* held that the prosecution has the burden of proving every element of the crime beyond a reasonable doubt. To the extent a presumption shifts or dilutes this burden, it violates due process. But the constitutional limits imposed by *Winship* are developed further in *Mullaney* and *Patterson*, which address the allocation of burdens in connection with criminal defenses,[8] and it is unclear how far *Mullaney* and *Patterson* restrict legislatures in defining the elements of crimes and defenses, hence not entirely certain how

---

4. A presumption in favor of an accused does not raise the same constitutional concerns. The jury is normally instructed on the presumption of innocence, which is simply a way to emphasize that the burden of proof rests entirely on the government, which must establish the defendant's guilt beyond a reasonable doubt. *See* §3.11, *supra.*

5. Sandstrom v. Montana, 442 U.S. 510, 516 n.5 (1979). *See also* United States v. Piche, 981 F.2d 706, 716 (4th Cir. 1992) (judge "may not direct a verdict, even a partial verdict, for the government" in criminal case).

6. Whether a finding can be directed with respect to a fact that is not an element, but tends to prove an element, is similarly questionable. Such direction may infringe on the right to a jury trial. This issue is intertwined with the constitutionality of binding judicial notice in criminal proceedings. *See* §2.12, *supra.* Proposed-but-rejected FRE 303 would not have allowed mandatory presumptions even for lesser facts. *See* ACN (although arguably judge could direct jury to find against accused on fact that is not an element, "tradition is against it").

7. It is true that an inference instruction may also shift the burden of production because the defendant takes the risk of an adverse jury finding if rebutting evidence is not produced. But this is different from a mandatory instruction directing the jury to find the inferred fact in absence of counterproof.

8. *See* §§3.11-3.12, *supra.*

far the Constitution restricts use of statutory presumptions to allocate burdens.[9]

Ambiguity pitfall

The leading case addressing these issues is *Sandstrom v. Montana,* where the trial court told the jury that the law "presumes that a person intends the ordinary consequences of his voluntary acts." Defendant was convicted of murder on facts indicating a brutal attack with a knife and shovel, but the Supreme Court reversed because it found that the quoted phrase was ambiguous and could have been interpreted in four different ways, at least two of which violated defendant's due process rights. First, the jury could have thought it had no choice on the issue of intent—that the presumption was conclusive. Second, it could have thought the presumption shifted to defendant the burden of persuasion—that it was to find intent unless defendant proved lack of intent. Third, the jury could have thought the presumption shifted to the defendant the burden of production—that it was to find intent unless defendant offered evidence that he lacked intent. And fourth, the jury could have thought the instruction invited an inference of intent—that it was being told it could find intent on the basis of defendant's behavior. When viewed in either of the first two ways, the presumption instruction violated the *Winship* requirement of proof beyond reasonable doubt of every element in the offense, so the Court in *Sandstrom* reversed the conviction.[10]

Sandstrom sends a clear warning that ambiguities in presumption instructions can be costly and may violate a defendant's due process rights when they bear on elements in the offense and seem either to be conclusive or to shift the burden of persuasion to the defendant. Several years later in *Francis v. Franklin,* the Court reached the same result in another murder prosecution that generated a similar instruction, even though the trial judge emphasized that the presumption may be rebutted and that the prosecutor bore the burden of proving intent beyond a reasonable doubt.[11] And the Supreme Court and many lower courts have often found constitutional error in similar ambiguities in presumption instructions.[12]

---

9. One type of criminal presumption that seems likely to survive constitutional challenge is one that merely requires the defendant to produce evidence in support of a defense before it will be submitted to the jury. For example, the "presumption of sanity" means that insanity does not become an issue in the case (and no insanity instruction is given) unless the defendant comes forward with evidence sufficient to support the defense of insanity. *See* Leach v. Kolb, 911 F.2d 1249, 1256 (7th Cir. 1990) (no constitutional violation to dismiss insanity defense where defendant fails to introduce sufficient evidence), *cert. denied,* 498 U.S. 972. *See also* Model Penal Code §1.12(2)(a) (1962) (Code does not "require the disproof of an affirmative defense unless and until there is evidence supporting such defense").

10. Sandstrom v. Montana, 442 U.S. 510, 520-524 (1979). *See also* Patterson v. New York, 432 U.S. 197, 215 1977) (a state "must prove every ingredient of an offense beyond a reasonable doubt" and "may not shift the burden of proof to the defendant by presuming that ingredient upon proof of the other elements").

11. Francis v. Franklin, 471 U.S. 307, 311-312 (1985).

12. Yates v. Evatt, 500 U.S. 391, 397 (1991) (cannot instruct that malice is "implied or presumed by the law from the willful, deliberate, and intentional doing of an unlawful act without any just cause or excuse"); Carella v. California, 491 U.S. 263, 264-266

Neither *Sandstrom* nor *Francis* condemned a presumption instruction that clearly conveys either the third or the fourth message—shifting burden of production or inviting an inference.[13] Inference instructions do not violate *Sandstrom*,[14] although to satisfy due process the inference must follow rationally from proven basic facts (see next section). But it is doubtful that a presumption can be used to shift the burden of production with respect to an element of the crime. In response to the state's argument in *Sandstrom* that shifting the burden of production meant only that defendant had to "produce some evidence," the Court commented with obvious skepticism that this burden "is often described quite differently" when it rests on the prosecution. The Court also observed that a prosecutor who fails to carry the burden suffers "a directed verdict in favor of the defense," but such direction "is not possible" when defendants fail to carry the burden.[15] Some states have been more emphatic yet, simply prohibiting the use of presumptions to shift the burden of production regarding an element to defendants in criminal cases,[16] a result generally supported by cases and commentators.[17]

(1989) (constitutional error to use presumption terminology even though taken directly from statute); Medley v. Runnels, 506 F.3d 857 (9th Cir. 2007) (courts may not create mandatory presumptions that relieve prosecutor of burden to prove facts to jury beyond reasonable doubt; presumption that flare gun qualified as firearm under state law violated due process).

13. *See* Francis v. Franklin, 471 U.S. 307, 314 n.3 (1985) (not deciding "whether a mandatory presumption that shifts only a burden of production to the defendant" is consistent with due process); Sandstrom v. Montana, 442 U.S. 510, 527 (1979) (Rehnquist, J., concurring) (if charge had "merely described a permissive inference," it would not offend constitutional jurisprudence). See also Dupuy v. Cain, 201 F.3d 582, 587 (5th Cir. 2000) (instruction that jury may conclude that one intends the natural and probable consequences of his actions unless "evidence in this cases leads the jury to a different or contrary conclusion" did not create a presumption of intent).

14. United States v. Vreeken, 803 F.2d 1085, 1092 (D.C. Cir. 1986) (upholding instruction that "[y]ou may consider it reasonable to draw the inference and find that a person intends the natural and probable consequences of acts knowingly done"), *cert. denied*, 484 U.S. 963; United States v. Silva, 745 F.2d 840, 850-852 (4th Cir. 1984) (upholding instruction that "it is reasonable to infer that a person ordinarily intends the natural and probable consequences of acts"), *cert. denied*, 470 U.S. 1031.

15. Sandstrom v. Montana, 442 U.S. 510, 516 n.5 (1979) (comment seems implicitly to acknowledge that carrying the burden of production means not just offering "some evidence," but offering enough to support a jury finding in light of the burden of persuasion; for points prosecutors must prove, that would mean evidence to support a finding beyond reasonable doubt; on points in affirmative defenses, that would mean enough evidence to support a finding by a preponderance).

16. *See, e.g.,* Alaska R. Evid. 303(a)(1) & (d); Vermont R. Evid. 303(d).

17. *See, e.g.,* United States v. Silva, 745 F.2d 840, 851-852 (4th Cir. 1984) (disapproving instruction that inference may be drawn "unless the contrary appears from the evidence" because it might suggest defendant has a proof burden), *cert. denied*, 470 U.S. 1031; United States v. Garrett, 574 F.2d 778, 780-783 (3d Cir. 1978) (condemning introductory phrase "unless the evidence of a case leads you to a contrary conclusion"), *cert. denied*, 436 U.S. 919. *And see generally* Burke, The Tension Between In re Winship and the Use of Presumptions in Jury Instructions After Sandstrom, Allen and Clark, 17 N.M.L. Rev. 55, 68-71 (1987); M. Graham, Presumptions—More Than You Wanted to Know and Yet Were Too Disinterested to Ask, 17 Crim. L. Bull. 431, 441 (1981); Note, After Sandstrom: The Constitutionality of Presumptions That Shift the Burden of Production, 1981 Wis. L. Rev. 519, 549-554.

Clearly the greatest constitutional concerns relate to presumptions that bear on elements of charged offenses and are the basis for jury instructions, as in *Sandstrom* itself. Courts often use presumptions in resolving preliminary issues such as the propriety of a search or the competency of the accused to stand trial, and *Sandstrom* has no application in these peripheral settings.[18]

Peripheral presumptions

§3.14 Inferences in Criminal Cases

For reasons examined in the previous section, presumptions relating to elements of the charged offense create constitutional error if they are deployed against criminal defendants in conclusive terms or use language that has burden-shifting effect. However, these problems are largely avoided if presumptions are conveyed by way of inference instructions that invite the jury to consider evidence on one or more points (the basic facts) as it may bear on another point at issue in the case (the inferred or presumed fact). In *United States v. Gainey*, for example, the Supreme Court upheld a statutory inference that presence at a still is "sufficient evidence to authorize conviction" for the crime of operating a still, which was conveyed by instructions emphasizing that the jury "may, if it sees fit," convict on such evidence but that it should also "analyze the evidence pro and con" and consider other "facts and circumstances."[1]

These instructions serve an important purpose. In effect, they urge the jury to consider the implications of circumstantial evidence and assure the jury that it may draw important conclusions from such evidence. An inference may also help establish the sufficiency of evidence on a particular point justifying submission of that issue to the jury. But even inference instructions raise some of the concerns mentioned in the prior section, and careless wording can improperly shift burdens to the accused. And instructions that avoid this problem face an additional constitutional hurdle: They must satisfy a rationality requirement imposed by the Due Process Clause, which requires that the fact to be inferred must follow more likely than not from the basic facts giving rise to the inference.

Urge, reassure

It has long been understood that presumptions or inferences operating against defendants in criminal cases must satisfy a "rational connection" test.[2] For many years it was unclear exactly how this standard operated or what it meant. In *Gainey* the Court concluded

Rationality standard

18. Medina v. California, 505 U.S. 437, 449-452 (1992) (although criminal trial of an incompetent defendant violates due process, state may create a presumption of competency or put burden of proving incompetency on defendant); United States v. Nunez, 877 F.2d 1470, 1472-1473 (10th Cir. 1989) (wiretap authorization order is presumptively valid; defendants failed to prove the contrary).

§3.14 1. United States v. Gainey, 380 U.S. 63, 69-70 (1965).

2. Leary v. United States, 395 U.S. 6, 36-37 (1969) (striking down as irrational and arbitrary a presumption that person possessing marijuana knows it is imported); Tot v. United States, 319 U.S. 463, 467 (1943) (invalidating presumption that possession is

that the standard was satisfied without really saying what it meant. Some presumptions and inferences were approved when the basic facts made the invited conclusion true beyond a reasonable doubt, and others were disapproved because the basic facts did not even make the invited conclusion more probably true than not.[3] The test case, where the basic facts make the fact to be inferred more probably true than not but fail to prove it beyond a reasonable doubt, never arose. Observers were left wondering whether "rational connection" required the latter or could be satisfied by the former.

New look: *Allen* case

In 1979 the Supreme Court took a new look at its prior decisions and found a new and unexpected pattern. In *County Court of Ulster v. Allen*, it decided that there are actually two devices commonly described as "presumptions" and two standards of rational connection. One device is the "permissive presumption" or inference that "allows" ("but does not require") the jury to reach the suggested conclusion. Such an inference is generally valid if the inferred fact follows from the basic facts more likely than not, because there is no more reason to impose a beyond reasonable doubt requirement for an inference that is merely part of the proof than there is "to require that degree of probative force for any other relevant evidence before it may be admitted."[4]

True presumption: Beyond reasonable doubt

The other device is what might be called a true presumption (described in *Allen* by the redundant term "mandatory presumption"), which is valid only if the basic facts make the presumed fact true beyond reasonable doubt.[5] According to *Allen*, the main distinguishing feature of these devices is that the former is conveyed to the jury in highly

---

presumptive evidence that firearm was received in interstate commerce; statutory presumption is invalid "if there be no rational connection between the fact proved and the ultimate fact presumed").

3. *Compare* Turner v. United States, 396 U.S. 398, 405-419 (1970) (approving presumption, arising on proof of possession of heroin, that defendant knew it was imported, which satisfied beyond reasonable doubt standard; disapproving same presumption as to cocaine, which did not satisfy even more-likely-than-not standard) *with* Leary v. United States, 395 U.S. 6, 36-37 (1969) (disapproving presumption, arising on proof of possession of marijuana, that defendant knew it was imported, which did not satisfy preponderance standard).

4. County Court of Ulster v. Allen, 442 U.S. 140, 167 (1979) (beyond reasonable doubt standard required where inference is "the sole and sufficient basis for a finding of guilt," but such cases are exceedingly rare). *See also* United States v. Warren, 25 F.3d 890, 898-900 (9th Cir. 1994) (approving inference instruction relating to intent in murder case; question is whether inference is justified by reason and common sense in light of proved facts).

5. In its long footnote 16, the Court in *Allen* made confusing comments: It said usually mandatory presumptions "merely shift the burden of production to the defendant," then referred to presumptions that "entirely shift the burden of proof" (citing no cases) and then remarked that "almost uniformly" the cases involve presumptions of the former kind. We know of no presumption establishing an element of a charged offense that allocates either the burden of production or the burden of persuasion to the defendant. Finally, the Court said a presumption that "imposes an extremely low burden of production" might well be analyzed as a permissive inference, a comment that is perhaps best understood to mean that virtually any inference puts some incremental pressure on the defense to explain or rebut the suggested conclusion, and the Court is willing to tolerate such effect.

contextual instructions worded permissively while the latter is conveyed to the jury in stand-alone isolation stating that proof of the basic facts is deemed sufficient as a matter of law to establish the indicated conclusion.[6]

It follows, said the Court in *Allen*, that validity of the permissive inference is to be determined by reference to the evidence in the case and not by scrutinizing the presumption on its face, and it generally passes constitutional muster if it supports the invited conclusion more likely than not.[7] (Of course a guilty verdict in a case in which such an inference plays a role must be supported by a totality of evidence that persuades the jury of guilt beyond a reasonable doubt.) The validity of a mandatory presumption must be assessed "on its face" and not in the context of proof actually adduced at trial, and it passes muster only if it supports the invited conclusion beyond a reasonable doubt.[8]

Inference: Preponderance

In *Allen*, a bare 5-4 majority held that the inference in question met the rationality standard. *Allen* involved four persons traveling by car (three adult men and a 16-year-old girl) who were arrested and charged with possessing two guns found on the front seat or floor in a handbag apparently belonging to the girl, who was sitting in the front passenger seat. The Court approved inference instructions based on a statutory presumption arising on proof that the guns were in the car, that all four possessed the guns. The Court thought the instructions were contextual and fit the permissive inference category. And the Court commented that the invited inference seemed reasonable: It was "highly improbable" that the girl alone had the guns—they were too big to fit the handbag; as a juvenile in the company of three adult men, she was "least likely" to be carrying two heavy handguns, and it was "far more probable" that she relied for protection on the knife in her brassiere.[9]

---

6. *Allen* cites three decisions exemplifying mandatory presumptions. They are Turner v. United States, 396 U.S. 398, 408 (1970) (approving presumption, arising on proof that defendant possessed heroin, that he knew it was imported, since all heroin is imported); Leary v. United States, 395 U.S. 6, 30, 37 (1969) (striking down similar presumption, arising on proof that defendant possessed marijuana, since marijuana is grown domestically); United States v. Romano, 382 U.S. 136, 138 (1965) (striking down presumption that presence at still suffices to convict for controlling the still, as opposed to participating in its operation).

7. United States v. Verduzco, 373 F.3d 1022, 1032 n.5 (9th Cir. 2004) (inference instruction is constitutionally valid only if its suggested conclusion is justified by reason and common sense in light of proven facts).

8. The basic facts that give rise to inferences and presumptions (such as being present at a still or possessing drugs) might be shown by evidence that is itself contested or less than conclusive. Here it seems that evidence of such facts must satisfy the standard that applies to the inference or presumption itself. Hence evidence of the basic facts of a contextual inference must satisfy the preponderance standard, and evidence of the basic facts of a stand-alone mandatory presumption must satisfy the beyond reasonable doubt standard.

9. County Court of Ulster v. Allen, 442 U.S. 140, 163-164 (1979) (the presumption included an exception making it inapplicable if weapons were found "upon the person" of one occupant of the car).

Allen holds that a contextual inference instruction is proper if the conclusion suggested by the instruction, from the trained perspective of the trial judge and reviewing court in light of the evidence presented, follows more likely than not.[10] If this standard is not satisfied, the instruction should not be given. If the men in the backseat had been hitchhikers picked up shortly before the car was stopped, it could not have been said that the guns in the handbag in front probably belonged to them, and the *Allen* instruction would not have been proper with respect to them.

Form of instruction

Although *Allen* approved an instruction using the phrase "presumptive evidence," it is risky, undesirable, and unnecessary to use the term "presume" in jury instructions in this setting. That message was confirmed a few weeks later in *Sandstrom*[11] and driven home further in a case that condemned use of the term even though it appeared in the underlying statute (as indeed it did in *Allen*).[12] The problems with the term are that it is ambiguous and overdoes the message—wrongly suggesting that the presumption is conclusive or requires defendant to shoulder the burden of persuasion. Almost as bad are other strong linking terms like "require"[13] or legalistic phrases such as "the law implies"[14] or "prima facie evidence,"[15] which suggest that some high authority has already made the decision and that it is cloaked in special dignity meriting great respect.

It is also dangerous to use phrases that invite the jury to draw a conclusion unless it is persuaded to the contrary, or the suggested conclusion is outweighed by other evidence, or the defendant offers another explanation. Such words tend to shift the burden of persuasion to the defendant[16] and can sometimes be construed as an improper comment on his failure to testify.[17] However, some language in *Allen*

---

10. *See* Hanna v. Riveland, 87 F.3d 1034, 1036-1037 (9th Cir. 1996) (permissive inference instructing inviting jury to infer recklessness from speeding failed to satisfy *Ulster County*'s "more likely than not standard," hence violated due process).

11. Sandstrom v. Montana, 442 U.S. 510 (1979) (invalidating instruction stating "the law presumes that a person intends the ordinary consequences of his voluntary acts").

12. Carella v. California, 491 U.S. 263, 266 (1989) (constitutional error to use presumption terminology even though taken directly from statute).

13. *See* State v. Short, 88 Or. App. 567, 746 P.2d 742 (1987) (error to tell jury that it was "not required to draw this inference" unless it found all the facts giving rise to it have been proved beyond reasonable doubt).

14. Hill v. Maloney, 927 F.2d 646, 649-650 (1st Cir. 1990) (error to instruct that "malice is implied from any deliberate or cruel act against another" because wording is not permissive in form).

15. State v. Jasper, 467 N.W.2d 855, 858-859 (Neb. 1991) (constitutional error to tell jury that prima facie evidence means "evidence sufficient in law to raise a presumption of fact or establish the fact in question unless rebutted," which shifts burden of persuasion to defendant; the term does not belong in jury instruction).

16. *See, e.g.,* United States v. Silva, 745 F.2d 840, 851-852 (4th Cir. 1984) (disapproving instruction that inference may be found "unless the contrary appears from the evidence"), *cert. denied,* 470 U.S. 1031; United States v. Garrett, 574 F.2d 778, 780-783 (3d Cir. 1978) (condemning introductory phrase "unless the evidence of a case leads you to a contrary conclusion"), *cert. denied,* 436 U.S. 919.

17. *See* Griffin v. California, 380 U.S. 609, 615 (1965) (commenting on defendant's failure to testify violates privilege against self-incrimination).

seems to approve instructions that invite inferences in the absence of explanation even though such language seems to shift to the defendant the burden of producing at least "some evidence" in refutation of an inference that applies to an element in the charged offense.[18] Of course it is not necessarily error to indicate that other evidence may undermine or explain away the suggested inference and that the jury need not draw the inference if such is the case.

Advising the jury that it "may infer" the suggested conclusion from the basic facts is preferable,[19] although it is doubtful that lay jurors who are not conversant in the ideas and concerns described here would be so attuned to semantic nuance that this milder term by itself would achieve the intended purpose (infer is obscure to many people who confuse it with imply).[20] Far more promising are instructions that highlight the basic facts while referring to all the evidence in the case and gently invite the jury to accord them their probative worth. At the very least, the instruction should stress that the suggested conclusion is not binding,[21] and perhaps the best approach is to tell the jury essentially that it is often possible to draw the indicated conclusion from the basic facts, while emphasizing the context of the case, the beyond reasonable doubt standard, and the jury's role as ultimate factfinder.[22]

"May infer" is preferable

18. *See also* Barnes v. United States, 412 U.S. 837, 844-846 (1972) (approving instruction that possessing recently stolen property, "if not satisfactorily explained," is a circumstance from which jury may reasonably infer knowledge that it was stolen, which in light of all the evidence sufficed to indicate guilt beyond reasonable doubt of knowing possession of stolen Treasury check). *See generally* Nesson, Rationality, Presumptions, and Judicial Comment: A Response to Professor Allen, 94 Harv. L. Rev. 1574, 1586 (1981) (arguing that an inference that comes into play due to absence of "explanation" by the defense is unconstitutional where there is insufficient other evidence to justify submitting case to jury).

19. United States v. Nelson, 277 F.3d 164, 197 (2d Cir. 2002) (instruction that jury "may infer and find that defendants intended all consequences that a person, standing in circumstances and possessing like knowledge, should have expected to result from acts he knowingly committed" does not violate *Sandstrom* as it merely let jury infer that accused intends consequences of actions).

20. *See* Harris, Constitutional Limits on Criminal Presumptions as an Expression of Changing Concepts of Fundamental Fairness, 77 J. Crim. Law & Criminology 308, 356 (1986) (whether jury would understand "you may infer" as being "substantially less coercive" than "the law presumes" seems doubtful).

21. *See* URE 303 and proposed FRE 303 (requiring instruction that would tell jury that it "may" but is "not required" to find the suggested conclusion). *See also* United States v. Warren, 25 F.3d 890, 898-900 (9th Cir. 1994) (in murder case, approving instruction stressing that jury "may find" malice from use of deadly weapon, absent explanatory or mitigating circumstances, that jury was "not obliged" to find intent and "may not find" guilt unless satisfied that each element is proved beyond reasonable doubt; also stressing that jury should consider all the evidence).

22. *See* Nesson, Rationality, Presumptions, and Judicial Comment: A Response to Professor Allen, 94 Harv. L. Rev. 1574, 1589 (1981) (suggesting for the *Allen* case an instruction that "it is often possible to infer from the presence of loaded firearms in an automobile that the occupants" possessed the weapons, but that jury "must decide whether, in the context of this case, such a conclusion is justified" by considering "all the facts," including location of guns, whether they were in plain sight, and how easy they were to reach, and that in the end jury "must decide whether the prosecution has proved beyond reasonable doubt that each defendant is guilty").

Form of judicial comment

An inference instruction is a form of judicial comment on the evidence because it tells jurors what conclusion might be drawn from particular evidence.[23] Traditionally, state judges have less freedom to comment on evidence than their federal counterparts, and in keeping with this tradition some states do not permit even mild inference instructions of the sort considered here.[24]

Scrutiny on review

Since FRE 606(b) blocks attempts to learn how jurors actually interpret presumption or inference instructions, review proceeds on the basis of reasonable meaning and probable interpretation. How the state classifies the presumption does not matter,[25] and the question is what a reasonable juror would likely have thought the instruction meant[26] when considered in the context of the instructions as a whole.[27] Errors under *Sandstrom* can be harmless,[28] but a conviction that follows flawed presumption instructions is subject to a special form of the closer scrutiny that comes with the constitutional error standard, meaning that reversal is warranted if "there is a reasonable likelihood that the jury has applied the challenged instruction in a way" that violates the Constitution.[29]

---

23. Erickson v. Municipality of Anchorage, 662 P.2d 963, 966 (Alaska App. 1983) (presumptions in criminal cases have the same effect as a comment on the evidence).

24. *See, e.g.,* State v. Rainey, 693 P.2d 635, 640 (Or. 1985) (inference instruction ought not to be used against a defendant on an element of a crime; it is "the task of the advocate, not the judge," to comment on inferences).

25. Francis v. Franklin, 471 U.S. 307, 315-316 (1985) (Georgia interpreted instruction as raising only a permissive inference, but Court is not bound; critical issue for constitutional purposes is "what a reasonable juror could have understood the charge as meaning").

26. Sandstrom v. Montana, 442 U.S. 510, at 514 (1979) (focus must be on "the words actually spoken to the jury" and "the way in which a reasonable juror could have interpreted the instruction").

27. Francis v. Franklin, 471 U.S. 307, 315 (1985) (challenged instruction must be considered in context of charges as a whole because other instructions might explain the "particular infirm language" so that "a reasonable juror could not have considered the charge to have created an unconstitutional presumption").

28. Rose v. Clark, 478 U.S. 570, 580-581 (1986) (in some cases "the predicate facts conclusively establish intent, so no rational jury could find that the defendant committed the relevant criminal act but did not intend to cause injury").

29. Estelle v. McGuire, 502 U.S. 62, 73 n.4 (1991) (adopting "reasonable likelihood" standard as single standard of review for jury instructions challenged as unconstitutional). *See also* Yates v. Evatt, 500 U.S. 391, 403-405 (1991) (test for harmless error for *Sandstrom* violation is "whether the force of the evidence presumably considered by the jury in accordance with the instructions is so overwhelming as to leave it beyond a reasonable doubt that the verdict resting on that evidence would have been the same in the absence of the presumption").

CHAPTER 4

Relevancy and Its Limits

A. LOGICAL RELEVANCE
B. PRAGMATIC RELEVANCE
C. CHARACTER EVIDENCE
D. HABIT AND ROUTINE PRACTICE
E. SUBSEQUENT REMEDIAL MEASURES
F. SETTLEMENTS AND MEDICAL PAYMENTS
G. PLEA BARGAINS
H. LIABILITY INSURANCE
I. SEXUAL BEHAVIOR OF COMPLAINING WITNESS
J. SIMILAR CRIMES BY DEFENDANT IN SEXUAL ASSAULT AND MOLESTATION CASES

§4.1 Introduction

The most fundamental evidentiary principle is the requirement of relevancy. If evidence is not relevant, it is not admissible.[1] Relevancy is thus the primary threshold determination that must be made for each item of proffered evidence.[2]

FRE 401 establishes a low threshold of relevance requiring only that evidence have any tendency to make the existence of a fact that is of consequence to the determination or the action more probable or less probable than it would be without the evidence.[3] However, evidence having only the slightest probative force is more likely to be excluded under FRE 403 on grounds of unfair prejudice, confusion of the issues,

---

§4.1 1. FRE 402. *See also* Thayer, A Preliminary Treatise on Evidence at the Common Law 264-265 (1898) (exclusion of irrelevant evidence is "a presupposition involved in the very conception of a rational system of evidence").

2. *See* Nance, Conditional Relevance Reinterpreted, 70 B.U. L. Rev. 447 (1990) (describing relevance as a "cornerstone of modern evidence law").

3. *See* ACN, FRE 401 (concluding that a more stringent relevancy requirement would be "unworkable and unrealistic").

misleading the jury, undue delay, waste of time, or needless presentation of cumulative evidence.[4]

Relevancy must be distinguished from the related issues of weight and sufficiency. While relevancy is primarily a question of admissibility, "weight" describes the persuasive force assigned to the evidence by the trier of fact once it has been admitted.[5] "Sufficiency" refers to the quantum and persuasive force of evidence necessary to take an issue to the jury. A party must produce evidence sufficient to support a finding in its favor in order to avoid a directed verdict, dismissal, or similar adverse order. Article IV does not address questions of weight or sufficiency of evidence.[6]

FRE 401 sets forth only a general standard and makes no attempt to resolve all questions of relevance arising in individual cases.[7] FRE 404 to 415, however, address the admissibility of specific categories of evidence, balancing as a matter of law the general standard of relevancy against the grounds of exclusion listed in FRE 403 as well as external policy considerations.[8]

The most complex set of relevancy rules pertains to proof of character. FRE 404(a) sets forth the general rule that evidence of a person's character traits cannot be used to prove that the person acted in accordance with that character on a particular occasion, subject to exceptions for criminal defendants,[9] crime victims,[10] and witnesses.[11] FRE 404(b) reaffirms that general rule, but allows evidence of other crimes, wrongs or acts by a person to prove more narrow points, such as intent, motive, opportunity, plan, or identity.[12]

While FRE 404 defines when character evidence is admissible, FRE 405 addresses the form of proof that may be used to prove character when it is admissible. If character is being admitted under one of the

---

4. *See* §§4.9, 4.10, *infra.*

5. Relevancy and weight are closely interrelated, and we sometimes speak of jurors making their own assessment of the "relevance" of the evidence. But there is a significant chronological difference. Relevance for purposes of FRE 401 must be determined by the court at the time the evidence is offered. Weight is decided by the jury during its deliberations. Thus the testimony of an eyewitness may be clearly "relevant" under FRE 401, but if the witness is disbelieved the testimony may be given no "weight" by the jury. Where evidence is only "conditionally" relevant under FRE 104(b), the respective roles of the judge and the jury are somewhat more complicated. *See* §4.3, *infra.*

6. ACN, FRE 401 ("Dealing with probability in the language of the rule has the added virtue of avoiding confusion between questions of admissibility and questions of the sufficiency of the evidence.").

7. *See* ACN, FRE 401 (noting that the "variety of relevancy problems is coextensive with the ingenuity of counsel in using circumstantial evidence as a means of proof" and that an "enormous number of cases fall in no set pattern" and therefore FRE 401 is intended only "as a guide for handling them").

8. ACN, FRE 401 (noting that some situations "recur with sufficient frequency to create patterns susceptible of treatment by specific rules" and FRE 404-412 "are of that variety," serving "as illustrations of the application of [FRE 401] as limited by the exclusionary principles of Rule 403").

9. *See* §4.12, *infra.*

10. *See* §4.13, *infra.*

11. *See* §4.14, *infra.*

12. *See* §§4.15-4.18, *infra.*

exceptions to FRE 404(a), it may be proved only by reputation or opinion evidence, except that inquiry into specific instances of conduct is allowed on cross-examination.[13] In those rare cases where character is an element of a charge, claim or defense, then FRE 405(b) allows it also to be proved by evidence of specific instances of conduct.[14]

The framework for admitting and excluding character evidence adopted by FRE 404 and 405 generally mirrors common law doctrine. However, since the Rules became effective in 1975, Congress has enacted four additional character evidence rules that significantly modify traditional doctrine in certain categories of cases. FRE 412, the federal "rape shield" statute, generally bars evidence of the past sexual behavior or predisposition of a sex crime victim. A 1994 amendment extended FRE 412 to civil cases, thereby limiting sexual history evidence pertaining to an alleged victim in any civil proceeding involving alleged sexual misconduct.[15]

FRE 413, 414, and 415 were enacted by Congress as part of the Violent Crime Control and Law Enforcement Act of 1994. FRE 413 applies in sexual assault prosecutions and provides that evidence that defendant committed a prior sexual assault is admissible.[16] FRE 414 adopts a similar rule in child molestation prosecutions.[17] FRE 415 provides that in civil cases where a claim for damages or other relief rest on claims that a party committed acts constituting an offense of sexual assault or child molestation, evidence that the party committed another offense of sexual assault or child molestation is admissible.[18]

A.   LOGICAL RELEVANCE

> **FRE 401**
>
>   "Relevant evidence" means evidence having any tendency to make the existence of any fact that is of consequence to the determination of the action more probable or less probable than it would be without the evidence.

§4.2   Defining Relevance

FRE 401 defines "relevant evidence" as evidence that has any tendency to make the existence of a fact that is of consequence to the determination of the action more probable or less probable than it would be

---

13. *See* §4.19, *infra.*
14. *See* §4.20, *infra.*
15. *See* §§4.32-4.34, *infra.*
16. *See* §4.35, *infra.*
17. *Id.*
18. *See* §4.36, *infra.*

without the evidence.[1] Evidence having any probative value whatsoever can satisfy the definition. There is no requirement that the evidence make the existence of the fact to be proved more probable than not or that it provide a sufficient basis for sending the issue to the jury.[2]

Courts have characterized FRE 401 as embodying a "liberal standard"[3] favoring a policy of "broad admissibility."[4] The drafters adopted the Thayerian view requiring only logical relevance[5] and rejected Wigmore's standard of legal relevance, which would require each item of proof to carry a "plus value."[6] However, the liberal definition of relevance adopted by FRE 401 is tempered by the discretion given to judges by FRE 403 to exclude evidence on grounds of unfair prejudice, confusion of the issues, misleading the jury, undue delay, waste of time, or needless presentation of cumulative evidence.[7]

Relational concept Relevance is a relational concept and carries meaning only in context. Relevance is determined by the issues raised by the parties, the other evidence introduced, and the applicable substantive law. A determination of relevancy may depend on the content of pleadings, indictments, pretrial orders, and pleas, as well as the testimony of other witnesses and the opening statements and arguments of counsel.

Relevance requires a "relation between an item of evidence and a matter properly provable in the case," and the existence of such a relationship is to be determined by "principles evolved by experience or science, applied logically to the situation at hand."[8] In ruling upon

§4.2 1. Strictly speaking no piece of evidence can make the actual existence of a fact more probable or less probable. Either the fact exists or it does not. Evidence can serve only to make the trier more or less likely to find such a fact. Thus FRE 401 should be interpreted to require only that the proffered evidence have some tendency to make the *apparent* existence of a consequential fact more or less probable. *See* Brain & Broderick, The Derivative Relevance of Demonstrative Evidence: Charting Its Proper Evidentiary Status, 25 U.C. Davis L. Rev. 957, 976 n.64, 1023 (1992) (proposing that FRE 401 be amended to add "apparent" before existence).

2. ACN, FRE 401 (noting that fact to be proved "may be ultimate, intermediate, or evidentiary" and quoting observations of Professor McCormick that "A brick is not a wall" and Professor McBaine that "[I]t is not to be supposed that every witness can make a home run"). *See also* United States v. Marks, 816 F.2d 1207, 1212 (7th Cir. 1987) (probative value of evidence "often depends upon its being part of a mosaic").

3. International Merger & Acquisition Consultants v. Armac Enters., Inc., 531 F.2d 821, 823 (7th Cir. 1976).

4. Conway v. Chemical Leaman Tank Lines, Inc., 525 F.2d 927, 930, *rev'd on reh'g on other grounds*, 540 F.2d 837 (5th Cir. 1976). *See generally* Crump, On the Uses of Irrelevant Evidence, 34 Hous. L. Rev. 1 (1997) (analyzing breadth of FRE 401 standard); Friedman, Irrelevance, Minimal Relevance, and Meta-Relevance, 34 Hous. L. Rev. 55 (1997).

5. *See* Thayer, A Preliminary Treatise on Evidence at the Common Law 530 (1898). The drafters did not use "logical" in the rule, however, so as not to ignore "the need to draw upon experience or science to validate the general principle upon which relevancy in the particular situation depends." ACN, FRE 401.

6. 1A Wigmore, Evidence 28, at 969 (Tillers rev. 1983) ("legal relevancy" denotes evidence having "more than a minimum of probative value" and instead having "a plus value"). *See* ACN, FRE 401 (concluding that a more stringent relevancy requirement would be "unworkable and unrealistic").

7. *See* §§4.9-4.10, *infra.*

8. ACN, FRE 401.

relevancy, the court must draw on its own experience, knowledge, and common sense in assessing whether a logical relationship exists between proffered evidence and the fact to be proven.[9]

It is sometimes appropriate for counsel to submit additional information to assist the court in making this determination.[10] Scientific research has disproved many linkages thought to exist and has identified other connections and correlations that are not commonly known.[11] Thus in some cases counsel would be wise not to rely solely on the personal knowledge that the judge brings to the ruling at hand.

Evidence may be found so "remote" as a matter of chronology, geography, or circumstances that it lacks probative value under FRE 401 or at least has such marginal persuasive force that exclusion is justified under FRE 403.[12] Similarly "speculative" evidence is sometimes condemned as failing to meet minimum requirements of relevancy.[13] Evidence that a third person may have committed the crime for which a defendant is charged is sometimes excluded on relevancy grounds when it is weak or conjectural, but a sounder basis for exclusion in those cases where such evidence should be excluded at all is FRE 403.[14]

Evidence is commonly classified as either direct or circumstantial. Direct evidence asserts the existence of the fact to be proven or, in the case of "real evidence," embodies or represents that fact. Circumstantial evidence is proof that does not actually assert or represent the fact to be proven but from which a factfinder can infer an increased probability that the fact exists. However, there is no legal distinction between the two forms of proof. Courts generally hold that circumstantial

Circumstantial proof

---

9. *See* Thayer, A Preliminary Treatise on Evidence at the Common Law 265 (1898) ("The law furnishes no test of relevancy.").

10. Evidence offered to assist the court in making a relevancy determination, such as scientific studies or treatises, is not limited by the rules of evidence, other than the rules of privilege. *See* FRE 104(a).

11. *See* Strong, Questions Affecting the Admissibility of Scientific Evidence, 1970 U. Ill. L. Forum 1.

12. *See, e.g.,* Kelsay v. Consolidated Rail Corp., 749 F.2d 437, 441-445 (7th Cir. 1984) (evidence of two similar accidents at same railroad crossing in previous decades held irrelevant).

13. An objection that evidence is "speculative" may be made where a lay witness offers an opinion not based on personal perception (*see* FRE 701) or an expert offers an opinion not based on an adequate foundation (*see* FRE 703). But damage calculations often unavoidably involve an element of speculation that is permissible, provided there is a sufficient basis in the record for any assumptions made. *See* Croce v. Bromley Corp., 623 F.2d 1084, 1094 (5th Cir. 1980) ("speculative nature" of evidence about decedent's likely professional advancement "affects only the weight of the evidence"), *cert. denied,* 450 U.S. 981.

14. Everhart, Putting a Burden of Production on the Defendant Before Admitting Evidence That Someone Else Committed the Crime Charged: Is It Constitutional?, 76 Neb. L. Rev. 272 (1997) (arguing that since evidence of third-party guilt is not an affirmative defense but directly rebuts the charges, burden must be on government to show why it should be excluded); McCord, "But Perry Mason Made It Look *So Easy*!": The Admissibility of Evidence Offered by a Criminal Defendant to Suggest That Someone Else Is Guilty, 63 Tenn. L. Rev. 917 (1996).

evidence should not be viewed as an "inferior" form of proof,[15] and circumstantial evidence is entirely sufficient to support a criminal conviction.[16]

Virtually all questions of relevance relate to circumstantial proof rather than direct proof because by definition direct evidence is probative on the point for which it is offered.[17] However, the question whether an inference of one fact may properly be drawn from proof of another can lead to substantial dispute.

Inductive approach   In assessing the relevancy of circumstantial proof, Wigmore favored reliance on inductive reasoning.[18] Under an inductive approach, if experience shows that persons with a motive to kill another are more likely to do so than persons without a motive, evidence that a particular defendant had a motive to kill the victim would be relevant.

Deductive approach   Other commentators have favored transmuting the inferential argument into a deductive form in order to highlight the major premise.[19] Under the deductive approach, a syllogism such as the following might be constructed: Persons with a motive to kill have a tendency to act on that motive; defendant had a motive to kill the victim; therefore it is more likely that defendant killed the victim. Once such a syllogism has been constructed, its major premise can be more easily analyzed and tested. How often do persons with a motive to kill actually act on that motive? Most of the time? Sometimes? Rarely?

Whether the inferential argument is made in inductive or deductive form, the critical question is the validity of the "evidential hypothesis."[20] If the court is persuaded that persons with a motive to kill have some heightened probability of killing as compared to persons without a motive, then the relevance standard of FRE 401 is satisfied and the evidence is admissible (unless there are grounds for exclusion under FRE 403 or another rule). But the strength of the evidential hypothesis (that is, the probability that a person with a motive as compared to one without a motive would actually kill) may be a subject of continuing debate and bears directly on the weight that should be assigned such evidence by the trier of fact.

15. *See, e.g.,* United States v. Andrino, 501 F.2d 1373, 1378 (9th Cir. 1974) ("Circumstantial evidence is not less probative than direct evidence, and, in some instances, is even more reliable.").

16. *See* United States v. Young, 568 F.2d 588, 589 (8th Cir. 1978) ("A conviction can rest solely on circumstantial evidence, which is intrinsically as probative as direct evidence.").

17. Some qualification is necessary because even with direct evidence there may be dispute whether the fact proved is "of consequence" to the proceeding.

18. 1 Wigmore, Evidence 30 (3d ed. 1940).

19. James, Relevancy, Probability and the Law, 29 Cal. L. Rev. 689, 699 (1941) ("The advantage of the transmutation into deductive (though not strictly syllogistic) form is that we know to what degree of proof we have attained, and do not overstate our results.").

20. Michael & Adler, The Trial of an Issue of Fact (pt. I), 34 Colum. L. Rev. 1224, 1298 (1934) ("What is traditionally treated as a question of relevancy can now be seen . . . to focus on the probabilities of the general propositions which must serve as the evidential hypotheses.").

At common law a distinction was drawn between relevancy and materiality. "Relevancy" meant that evidence had probative value in establishing a particular point, and "materiality" meant the point had legal significance in the case. For example, in a products liability action for injuries caused by a power mower, evidence that plaintiff was mowing wet grass in bare feet would be relevant on the issue of whether plaintiff was negligent, but such issue would be immaterial if the actual cause of the injuries was the blade flying off the mower.

Under FRE 401, "materiality" is merged into the definition of relevancy by the requirement that the fact proved must be "of consequence to the determination of the action."[21] Therefore an objection on grounds of irrelevancy now encompasses an objection on grounds of immateriality, and a separate immateriality objection is no longer required or appropriate.[22] Determining whether evidence is "consequential" depends on the applicable substantive law.[23]

Evidence is "of consequence to the determination of the action" even if it is introduced to impeach the credibility of a witness rather than to establish a substantive element of a party's claim or defense.[24] Therefore evidence that supports a permissible impeaching attack satisfies the relevance standard of FRE 401.

According to the Advisory Committee, "[t]he fact to which the evidence is directed need not be in dispute."[25] Thus evidence tending to prove an uncontested but otherwise material point satisfies the FRE 401 standard of relevancy[26] and can be admitted even in the face of an opponent's offer to stipulate to or admit that point.[27] However,

---

21. United States v. Carriger, 592 F.2d 312, 315 (6th Cir. 1979) ("The word 'material' does not appear in the federal rules and appears to be subsumed into the language of Rule 401.").

22. Schmertz, Relevancy Under Rule 401: A Dual Concept, 14 Litig., Spring 1988, at 12 (a relevancy objection under FRE 401 can convey three distinct messages: (1) that the evidence lacks probative value, (2) that it has probative value but not on an issue provable in the litigation, or (3) that the evidence lacks both qualities).

23. Phillips v. Western Co. of N. Am., 953 F.2d 923, 930 (5th Cir. 1992) (error to allow defendant to introduce evidence of disability benefits received by injured plaintiff on issue of damages because "collateral source" rule of substantive tort law disallows a setoff from liability of tortfeasor for benefits received by plaintiff from other sources).

24. United States v. Abel, 469 U.S. 45, 52 (1984) (approving as relevant evidence that defense witness and defendant were members of prison gang that required members to commit perjury for one another "because the jury, as finder of fact and weigher of credibility, has historically been entitled to assess all evidence which might bear on the accuracy and truth of a witness's testimony").

25. ACN, FRE 401 ("While situations will arise which call for the exclusion of evidence offered to prove a point conceded by the opponent, the ruling should be made on the basis of such considerations as waste of time and undue prejudice, rather than under any general requirement that evidence is admissible only if directed to matters in dispute."). Some state Codes take a contrary approach. *See, e.g.,* Cal. Evid. Code 210 (defining relevant evidence as tending to prove a disputed fact).

26. Old Chief v. United States, 117 S. Ct. 644, 649 (1997) (availability of alternative proof, while it may affect probative worth of evidence in balancing under FRE 403, does not alter relevance under FRE 401).

27. *See, e.g.,* United States v. Grassi, 602 F.2d 1192, 1197 (5th Cir. 1979) (in prosecution for sending five obscene films in interstate commerce, no error to allow jury to

evidence offered on an issue not in dispute has greater likelihood of exclusion under FRE 403,[28] and the availability of alternative, less prejudicial evidence (including an offer to stipulate or admit) is a factor that must be considered in FRE 403 balancing.[29]

Evidence that is essentially "background" in nature is admissible where it serves as an aid to understanding other evidence or the overall issues in the case[30] although the trial court retains discretion to limit the extent of background evidence.[31] Demonstrative evidence is also routinely received subject to the discretion of the court.[32]

Opening the door   Where one party "opens the door" by introducing certain evidence, the opposing party is generally entitled to rebut it. Where the initial evidence is both relevant and admissible, or for that matter relevant but inadmissible for some reason, rebuttal evidence is relevant too, even if its only probative value lies in the fact that it refutes prior relevant evidence. Where the initial evidence is irrelevant (and presumably excludable on proper objection for that reason and perhaps others),

---

view three of films even though defense offered to stipulate that films were obscene; an offer to stipulate cannot be used to deprive a party "of the legitimate moral force of his evidence"), *vacated on other grounds,* 448 U.S. 902 (1980).

28. United States v. Yeagin, 927 F.2d 798, 801-803 (5th Cir. 1991) (in prosecution for narcotics offenses and possessing firearm, defendant offered to stipulate to intent if the government proved possession, and on firearm charge offered to stipulate that he was a convicted felon; in light of these offers it was reversible error to admit five prior drug felonies; prosecutor's need was negligible compared with "extremely prejudicial effect" of prior convictions).

29. Old Chief v. United States, 519 U.S. 172 (1997) (in prosecution for assault with a dangerous weapon and possession by convicted felon of a firearm, defendant offered to stipulate that he was a convicted felon and to have jury instructed that this element of charge was satisfied without informing them of nature of prior offense, which was a conviction for felony assault causing bodily injury; it was an abuse of discretion under FRE 403 for trial judge to refuse this stipulation because of danger of unnecessary and unfair prejudice to defendant; availability of alternative and less prejudicial forms of proof such as stipulation offered here must be considered when court undertakes FRE 403 balancing).

30. ACN, FRE 401 ("Evidence which is essentially background in nature can scarcely be said to involve disputed matter, yet it is universally offered and admitted as an aid to understanding.").

31. United States v. Solomon, 686 F.2d 863, 873-874 (11th Cir. 1982) (court may prohibit inquiry into witness's family history and military service).

32. *See* ACN, FRE 401 (noting routine judicial allowance of "[c]harts, photographs, views of real estate"). *See generally* §9.31. It has been questioned whether demonstrative evidence technically satisfies the definition of relevance in FRE 401. *See* Brain & Broderick, The Derivative Relevance of Demonstrative Evidence: Charting Its Proper Evidentiary Status, 25 U.C. Davis L. Rev. 957, 975-976, 1023 (1992) (demonstrative evidence does not satisfy FRE 401 because it does not tend to prove a consequential fact but only illustrates and explains other relevant evidence; proposing amendment of FRE 401 to admit "evidence that fairly and accurately explains, illustrates, or clarifies other admissible evidence"). Although such an amendment might provide clarification, demonstrative evidence has probative value under FRE 401 as written. By giving other evidence greater impact, it has some tendency "to make the existence of any fact that is of consequence to the determination of the action more probable or less probable than it would be without the evidence." Demonstrative evidence thus operates similarly to impeachment and rehabilitation evidence (which is clearly admissible under FRE 401) by assisting the trier of fact to understand and evaluate other evidence.

rebuttal evidence is still often admitted if the initial evidence might make a difference by swaying the factfinder toward one result or another by appealing to prejudice or sympathy.

This doctrine, which is sometimes described as "curative admissibility" or more colloquially as "fighting fire with fire," creates the danger of injecting highly prejudicial evidence into the trial.[33] Hence evidence that is offered only to contradict earlier evidence is typically subject to careful scrutiny to insure that it tends fairly to meet the earlier proof. Where the rebuttal evidence is unfairly prejudicial or too confusing or distracting under FRE 403, courts typically exclude it. These subjects are explored elsewhere.[34]

§4.3   Roles of Judge and Jury

In most cases, the determination of relevancy is a matter for the court.[1] In assessing whether the proffered evidence supports the inference claimed by its proponent, the court may draw upon its own knowledge, experience, and judgment. Counsel may present the court with additional information, including scientific studies, publications, and even expert testimony,[2] to establish inferential linkages that might not otherwise be apparent or to disprove relationships that might otherwise be erroneously presumed. In furnishing information to assist the court in making a relevancy determination, parties are not restricted by the rules of evidence other than rules of privilege.[3]

Occasionally appellate precedents are available to assist a court in making a FRE 401 ruling. However, the relevancy determination depends so much on the facts and issues of each case that precedents generally have limited utility.

33. United States v. Winston, 447 F.2d 1236, 1240 (D.C. Cir. 1971) (doctrine of curative admissibility is "dangerously prone to overuse" and should be relied on only "to prevent prejudice" and not to inject prejudice; introduction of otherwise inadmissible evidence under this doctrine is permitted "only to the extent necessary to remove any unfair prejudice which might otherwise have ensued from the original evidence").

34. *See* §§1.4, 4.10, 6.47, and 6.48.

§4.3   1. Whether relevancy is to be determined from the viewpoint of the judge or jury is a subject of academic comment. Some scholars advocate a standard more deferential to juries. *See* Allen, The Myth of Conditional Relevancy, 25 Loy. L.A. L. Rev. 871 (1992) (recommending amendment of FRE 104(a) to require a court to admit evidence "over a relevancy objection upon, or subject to, a finding that the evidence could rationally influence a reasonable person's assessment of any fact that is of consequence to the determination of the action"); Nance, Conditional Probative Value and the Reconstruction of the Federal Rules of Evidence, 94 Mich. L. Rev. 419, 421 (1995) (recommending amendment of FRE 402 to provide "[a]ll evidence that a reasonable person could consider relevant is admissible"); Friedman, Conditional Probative Value: Neoclassicism Without Myth, 93 Mich. L. Rev. 439 (1994) (endorsing more deferential standard).

2. *See* Strong, Questions Affecting the Admissibility of Scientific Evidence, 1970 U. Ill. L. Forum 1, 2-3.

3. FRE 104(a).

Conditional relevancy   Sometimes the relevancy of an item of evidence depends upon proof of a preliminary question of fact. In such cases where evidence is conditionally relevant, FRE 104(b) allocates to the jury the ultimate responsibility of deciding whether the preliminary question of fact has been proven.

To use the example of conditional relevancy cited by the ACN to FRE 104(b), if a party offers evidence of a spoken statement to prove notice, the relevancy of the oral statement depends on proof of the preliminary fact that the party sought to be charged with notice in fact heard the statement. The jury, not the court, ultimately decides whether the statement was heard. Only after the jury determines the statement was heard can its content properly be considered on the question whether proper notice was given.

The purpose of FRE 104(b) is to prevent the judge from intruding on the province of the jury by excluding evidence where she is not persuaded that the preliminary fact has been proven.[4] For example, in the above hypothetical, the judge cannot bar evidence of the oral statement merely because she is not personally convinced that it was heard.[5] Exclusion of the evidence is proper only where no reasonable jury could find that it was heard.[6]

Role of judge   However, FRE 104(b) does not wholly exclude the court from a fact assessment role with respect to conditionally relevant evidence. First, the court must decide whether the evidence (the oral statement) would be relevant assuming the preliminary fact (that it was heard) were proven. If the content of the oral statement could not reasonably be construed as giving notice, then it should be excluded as irrelevant quite apart from whether it was heard. Second, even with respect to

4. ACN, FRE 104(b) ("If preliminary questions of conditional relevancy were determined solely by the judge, as provided in subdivision (a), the functioning of the jury as a trier of fact would be greatly restricted and in some cases virtually destroyed.").

5. For an argument that the conditional relevancy doctrine can nonetheless lead to the exclusion of relevant evidence, *see* 1A Wigmore, Evidence 14.1 (Tillers rev. 1983).

6. The authentication requirement of FRE 901(a) is also described as an application of the conditional relevancy doctrine (*see* ACN, FRE 901(a)) because it requires "evidence sufficient to support a finding that the matter in question is what its proponent claims" before the proffered evidence may be admitted. *See also* ACN, FRE 104(b) ("[I]f a letter purporting to be from Y is relied upon to establish an admission by him, it has no probative value unless Y wrote or authorized it"). This view has been challenged on the ground that an item of evidence may in fact be relevant under the liberal standard of FRE 401 even where it has not been authenticated. Nance, Conditional Relevance Reinterpreted, 70 B.U. L. Rev. 447, 484 (1990) (finding error in the Advisory Committee's example, "for the document is relevant (provided of course the admission therein is itself relevant) unless one knows for certain that Y did not write or authorize it"). Similarly, the personal knowledge requirement of FRE 602, which requires "evidence sufficient to support a finding that the witness has personal knowledge of the matter" before a witness may testify to a matter, is described as "a specialized application of . . . conditional relevancy." ACN, FRE 602. Yet unless it is certain that the witness did not observe the event, the witness's claim of knowledge makes it somewhat more likely the witness perceived the event and hence is relevant under FRE 401. Nance, *supra,* at 489. The authentication and personal knowledge requirements should be viewed as trial safeguards that go beyond merely assuring relevancy.

the preliminary fact, the court plays a screening function. Although the court need not be personally persuaded that the statement was heard before submitting evidence of it to the jury, FRE 104(b) requires the court to find evidence sufficient to support a jury finding that the statement was heard. In absence of such evidence, the statement must be excluded.[7]

FRE 104(b) has been subject to cogent scholarly criticism,[8] and the very concept of conditional relevancy as a category distinct from general relevancy has been characterized as a "myth."[9] Certainly there is no bright line between the two concepts. All relevancy determinations rest on factual premises. If those factual premises can reasonably be assumed to be known by the trier of fact, the question is appropriately treated as one of "pure" relevancy to be determined by the court without requiring proof of the underlying factual premises. However, if the factual premises are not reasonably known, the proponent is properly required to produce evidence of them as a condition of admissibility so the trier of fact can understand and determine those underlying facts that make the proffered evidence relevant.[10]

Although normally the court requires that sufficient evidence of the preliminary fact be produced before it allows the primary evidence to go to the jury, FRE 104(b) authorizes the judge to admit the primary evidence "subject to" later introduction of evidence of the preliminary fact (often referred to as "connecting up"). If such evidence is not subsequently introduced, the conditionally relevant evidence may be stricken. A mistrial may be required if exposure of the jury to the improper evidence caused irreparable prejudice.

Connecting up

A trial court's rulings under FRE 401 are subject to appellate review, provided a proper record is made. The purpose for which evidence is claimed to be relevant generally must be explained to the trial judge in

Appellate review

7. Sometimes facts described as being conditionally relevant are not. *See* Nance, *supra* note 6, at 453 (criticizing frequently cited example of a suit between *P* and *D* on a contract, where verbal agreements allegedly made by *A* on *D*'s behalf are said to be conditionally relevant on a showing that *A* is in fact *D*'s agent; the agreements and the issue of authority are both elements of the claim and neither is conditionally relevant on the other). *See also* Allen, The Myth of Conditional Relevancy, 25 Loy. L.A. L. Rev. 871, 873 (1992) (noting that in any case involving more than one element, "evidence of one element is relevant so long as the probability of no other element is 0.0"; only if one element were clearly disproven would evidence of another element be irrelevant, or at least pointless, because an adverse verdict would be directed for insufficiency of proof).

8. 1A Wigmore, Evidence 14.1 (Tillers rev. 1983); Nance, *supra* note 6; Allen, The Explanatory Value of Analyzing Codifications by Reference to Organizing Principles Other Than Those Employed in the Codification, 79 Nw. U. L. Rev. 1080 (1984).

9. Allen, The Myth of Conditional Relevancy, 25 Loy. L.A. L. Rev. 871, 879 (1992) ("All cases of conditional relevancy are cases of relevancy, and all cases of relevancy are cases of conditional relevancy."); Ball, The Myth of Conditional Relevancy, 14 Ga. L. Rev. 435, 456 (1980) ("It seems to me safe to say that instead of some, virtually all offers of evidence can raise problems of conditional relevancy, the chief question being whether they raise one only, or two or more such problems.").

10. Allen, *supra*, at 880 (arguing that "'conditional relevancy' is simply the label applied to a case that the judge finds insufficient to go to the jury and 'relevancy' is the label applied to a case that the judge finds sufficient to go to the jury").

order to preserve any error in the exclusion of such evidence. Although appellate opinions often suggest that the trial judge has broad discretion to decide whether evidence is relevant under FRE 401,[11] such statements are more appropriate to FRE 403 where the trial judge must balance probative worth against other dangers.[12] A question of pure relevancy is more a matter of logic and experience, and on this point there is less reason for deference to the trial judge.[13]

At the same time, rulings erroneously excluding evidence under FRE 401 often involve evidence that has only marginal relevance. Rulings erroneously admitting evidence under FRE 401 necessarily involve evidence lacking probative force or pertaining to an inconsequential issue. Therefore, even if an appellate court finds a trial court's ruling under FRE 401 to be error, it is often found to be harmless.

§4.4 Circumstantial Proof—Indications of a Guilty Mind

Courts generally admit evidence of behavior indicating consciousness of guilt to establish that the actor was involved in wrongful conduct. Behavior thought to indicate a "guilty mind" includes flight,[1] resisting arrest,[2] escape,[3] use of aliases,[4] wearing a disguise or otherwise concealing or altering appearance,[5] fabricating evidence,[6] destroying or concealing evidence,[7] lying,[8] subornation of perjury,[9]

11. *See, e.g.,* Perkins v. Volkswagen of America, Inc., 596 F.2d 681, 682 (5th Cir. 1979) (trial judge has broad discretion in determining whether evidence is "relevant and admissible").

12. *See* §4.9, *infra. See generally* Leonard, Appellate Review of Evidentiary Rulings, 70 N.C.L. Rev. 1155 (1992).

13. United States v. Donley, 878 F.2d 735, 737 & n.4 (3d Cir. 1989) (applicable "standard for review for relevancy rulings is plenary" rather than abuse of discretion), *cert. denied,* 494 U.S. 1058.

§4.4 1. United States v. Levy-Cordero, 67 F.3d 1002, 1011 (1st Cir. 1995) (admitting evidence that upon being told police were coming to arrest him defendant fled apartment with false passport, social security card, a pager and $1,200 cash).

2. United States v. De Parias, 805 F.2d 1447, 1454 (11th Cir. 1986) (evidence of resisting arrest "is admissible to demonstrate consciousness of guilt").

3. United States v. Hankins, 931 F.2d 1256, 1261 (8th Cir. 1991) ("Flight or escape from custody is generally considered 'admission by conduct.'").

4. United States v. Levy, 865 F.2d 551, 558 (3d Cir. 1989) (use of false identities and passports); United States v. Boyle, 675 F.2d 430, 432 (1st Cir. 1982) (use of false name after commission of a crime is "commonly accepted as being relevant on the issue of consciousness of guilt").

5. United States v. Jackson, 476 F.2d 249, 253 (7th Cir. 1973) (prior to lineup accused altered his appearance).

6. United States v. Abney, 508 F.2d 1285, 1286 (4th Cir. 1975) (attempted fabrication of an alibi), *cert. denied,* 420 U.S. 1007.

7. Marcoux v. United States, 405 F.2d 719, 721 (9th Cir. 1968) (concealment). *But see* Stanojev v. Ebasco Servs., Inc., 643 F.2d 914, 923-924 (2d Cir. 1981) (no adverse inference should be drawn where disposal of records done in good faith).

8. United States v. Johnson, 46 F.3d 1166, 1171 (D.C. Cir. 1995) (upon arrest defendant made false statement that he worked as clerk at sporting goods store).

9. McQueeney v. Wilmington Trust Co., 779 F.2d 916, 921 (3d Cir. 1985).

bribing,[10] threatening[11] or attempting to kill[12] a witness, bribing a law enforcement officer to obtain release,[13] making false exculpatory statements,[14] failing to raise defense of alibi at an earlier date,[15] refusing to comply with a lawful order to furnish fingerprints or similar identifying data,[16] attempting suicide,[17] and similar behavior.[18]

However, courts generally hold that evidence indicating consciousness of guilt is entitled to little weight[19] and find it insufficient, standing alone, to support a conviction.[20] The Supreme Court has recognized that there may be innocent explanations for the party's conduct,[21] and a criminal defendant is generally entitled to an instruction calling the jury's attention to such possibilities.[22]

Little weight

10. United States v. Mendez-Ortiz, 810 F.2d 76, 78-79 (6th Cir. 1986) ("[S]poliation evidence, including evidence that defendant attempted to bribe and threatened a witness, is admissible to show consciousness of guilt."), *cert. denied,* 480 U.S. 922.

11. United States v. Ramirez-Lopez, 315 F.3d 1143, 1154 (9th Cir. 2003) (in trial for alien smuggling, admitting proof that defendant threatened government witness "by moving his finger in a back and forth direction" just before witness took stand, telling him "not to say anything").

12. United States v. Richardson, 338 F.3d 653, 661-62 (7th Cir. 2003) (admitting evidence that defendant planned "to murder state prosecutor, intimidate a juror, and bribe a judge").

13. United States v. Posey, 611 F.2d 1389, 1391 (5th Cir. 1980).

14. United States v. Kemp, 500 F.3d 257, 296-97 (3d Cir. 2007) (false testimony to grand jury).

15. United States v. Johns, 734 F.2d 657, 664 (11th Cir. 1984).

16. United States v. Jackson, 886 F.2d 838, 845-848 (7th Cir. 1989) (refusal to give handwriting exemplars); United States v. Terry, 702 F.2d 299, 313-314 (2d Cir. 1983) (refusal to furnish palm prints), *cert. denied,* 464 U.S. 992.

17. Annot., 22 A.L.R. 3d 840 (1968).

18. On the related issue of whether an adverse inference can be drawn against a party from his failure to call a witness within his control, *see* Graves v. United States, 150 U.S. 118, 121 (1893) ("[I]f a party has it peculiarly within his power to produce witnesses whose testimony would elucidate the transaction, the fact that he does not do it creates the presumption that the testimony, if produced, would be unfavorable."). *But see* Herbert v. Wal-Mart Stores, Inc., 911 F.2d 1044, 1048-1049 (1990) (missing witness inference should be rejected under Federal Rules of Evidence).

19. Wong Sun v. United States, 371 U.S. 471, 483 n.10 (1963) ("[W]e have consistently doubted the probative value in criminal trials of evidence that the accused fled the scene of an actual or supposed crime.").

20. *See, e.g.,* Alberty v. United States, 162 U.S. 499, 511 (1896) (finding flight instruction to be error because it laid "too much stress on the fact of flight" and allowed the jury "to infer that this fact alone is sufficient to create a presumption of guilt").

21. Alberty v. United States, 162 U.S. 499, 511 (1896) ("[I]t is a matter of common knowledge that men who are entirely innocent do sometimes fly from the scene of a crime through fear of being apprehended as the guilty parties, or from an unwillingness to appear as witnesses. Nor is it true as an accepted axiom of criminal law that 'the wicked flee when no man pursueth, but the righteous are bold as a lion.' Innocent men sometimes hesitate to confront a jury; not necessarily because they fear that the jury will not protect them, but because they do not wish their names to appear in connection with criminal acts, are humiliated at being obliged to incur the popular odium of an arrest and trial, or because they do not wish to be put to the annoyance or expense of defending themselves.").

22. *See* United States v. Stewart, 579 F.2d 356, 359 n.3 (5th Cir. 1978) (approving instruction warning jury that flight might result from "fear of being apprehended, unwillingness to confront the police, or reluctance to confront the witness"), *cert. denied,* 439 U.S. 936.

Was it flight?   It is sometimes questionable whether the defendant's conduct amounted to "flight,"[23] and four inferences are generally required: (1) the behavior must indicate flight; (2) the flight must indicate consciousness of guilt; (3) the consciousness of guilt must be for the crime charged; (4) the consciousness of guilt must support an inference of actual guilt.[24] It has been held error to admit flight evidence if one or more of these links is missing.[25] Even where the defendant's conduct can reasonably be interpreted as "flight," it may be better practice to forgo any jury instruction on the point and to allow the jury to decide what inferences should be drawn from such evidence.

§4.5   —Other Accidents or Claims

The general rule is that evidence of prior accidents or mishaps is not admissible to prove negligence or contributory negligence in the accident giving rise to the lawsuit.[1] This rule is misleading, however, because such evidence is often admitted to prove one or more elements of a negligence claim, such as (1) existence of a particular condition;[2] (2) dangerousness of the condition;[3] (3) the possibility that the condition might cause an accident or injury of the type alleged;[4] (4) cause in fact (it did cause the accident or injury at issue);[5] or (5) knowledge or notice of the condition and its dangerousness.[6]

Substantial similarity requirement   To be admissible for even these narrower purposes, the other accidents or events must normally be "substantially similar" to the one at

---

23. United States v. Beahm, 664 F.2d 414, 419-420 (4th Cir. 1981) (evidence that, on receipt of note from FBI requesting interview three weeks after the crime, defendant went from Virginia to Florida could not be viewed as flight indicating consciousness of guilt).

24. United States v. Levine, 5 F.3d 1100, 1107 (7th Cir. 1993) (detailing these four inferences).

25. United States v. Sanchez, 790 F.2d 245, 252-253 (2d Cir. 1986) (flight instruction error where only evidence was that defendant failed to appear).

§4.5   1. *See, e.g.,* Nelson v. Brunswick Corp., 503 F.2d 376, 380 (9th Cir. 1974) (evidence of other explosions during resurfacing of bowling alleys was "inadmissible to show that Brunswick was negligent in the performance of this particular work").

2. Four Corners Helicopters, Inc. v. Turbomeca, S.A., 979 F.2d 1434, 1439-1442 (10th Cir. 1992) (in products liability action, proper to admit evidence of other incidents of loose labyrinth screws in helicopter engines).

3. Exum v. General Elec. Co., 819 F.2d 1158, 1162-1163 (D.C. Cir. 1987) (abuse of discretion not to admit evidence of other similar accidents offered to prove dangerousness).

4. Rimer v. Rockwell Intl. Corp., 641 F.2d 450, 456 (6th Cir. 1981) (error to exclude evidence of 24 other airplane accidents allegedly caused by same design defect in fuel intake system); Wojciechowski v. Long-Airdox Div. of Marmon Group, Inc., 488 F.2d 1111, 1116 n.7 (3d Cir. 1973) (evidence of prior similar event admissible to rebut manufacturer's claim that accident "couldn't have happened" in the manner claimed by plaintiff).

5. Gulf States Utils. Co. v. Ecodyne Corp., 635 F.2d 517, 519 (5th Cir. 1981) (error to exclude evidence of earlier structural failure of similar towers built by defendant).

6. Smith v. Ingersoll-Rand Co., 214 F.3d 1235, 1246-50 (10th Cir. 2000) (admitting evidence of other accidents to show notice of dangerous condition).

issue, a matter to be determined in the sound exercise of discretion by the trial judge.[7] The similarity requirement is enforced somewhat less strictly where the evidence is offered to prove notice rather than dangerousness or causation,[8] and in design defect cases where offered to prove the existence of a defect rather than any single way it could cause injury.[9] There may be dissimilarities as well, provided the differences can easily be brought out on cross-examination and understood by the jury.[10] Such differences are said to affect the "weight" of the evidence but not necessarily its admissibility. Even accidents occurring after the event in question can be admissible[11] except where offered to prove knowledge.[12]

Mishaps, defects, or mechanical failures occurring under different conditions or at remote times in the past are excluded as irrelevant under FRE 402.[13] Even where the relevancy standard is satisfied, prior event evidence can be excluded under FRE 403 as unfairly prejudicial, misleading, confusing, cumulative, or wasteful of time.

The party defending against a claim may show the absence of other accidents involving the same or like place or instrumentality as counterproof on the issues of dangerousness, causation, or knowledge.[14] This type of evidence is also subject to the "substantial similarity" requirement[15] and the possibility of exclusion under FRE 403. The defending

Absence of other accidents

---

7. Ross v. Black & Decker, Inc., 977 F.2d 1178 (7th Cir. 1992) (approving admission of two other accidents involving saw manufactured by defendant because circumstances were substantially similar to plaintiff's accident); Brooks v. Chrysler Corp., 786 F.2d 1191, 1195 (D.C. Cir. 1986) (evidence of other accidents not admissible because not sufficiently similar), *cert. denied,* 479 U.S. 853. *See generally* Sachs, "Other Accident" Evidence in Product Liability Actions: Highly Probative or an Accident Waiting to Happen? 49 Okla. L. Rev. 257 (1996).

8. Four Corners Helicopters, Inc. v. Turbomeca, 979 F.2d 1434, 1440 (10th Cir. 1992) (requirement of substantial similarity is "relaxed" when evidence of other incidents is used "to demonstrate notice or awareness of a potential defect").

9. Ballweg v. City of Springfield, 114 Ill.2d 107, 499 N.E.2d 1373, 1376 (1986) (prior accidents involving sailboat mast manufactured by defendant sufficiently similar to show notice when they resulted in electrocution even though they did not occur in exactly same manner as plaintiff's accident).

10. Joy v. Bell Helicopter Textron, Inc., 999 F.2d 549, 555 (D.C. Cir. 1993) (admitting evidence of other accidents despite dissimilarities).

11. Ross v. Black & Decker, Inc., 977 F.2d 1178, 1185 (7th Cir. 1992) (approving admission of evidence of two other accidents subsequent to one in litigation; fact that other accidents occurred after plaintiff's injury does not make them "any less probative of the unreasonably dangerous design and condition of the saw or of the cause of the accident").

12. Magayanes v. Terrance, 739 F.2d 1131, 1136 (7th Cir. 1983) (subsequent accident not admissible as evidence of notice to city regarding defective design of police transport vehicle).

13. Kelsay v. Consolidated Rail Corp., 749 F.2d 437, 441-445 (7th Cir. 1984) (evidence of two other accidents at same railroad crossing in previous decades found irrelevant).

14. Pandit v. American Honda Motor Co., Inc., 82 F.3d 376, 379-380 (10th Cir. 1996) (allowing evidence of absence of prior similar claims to show absence of defect, lack of cause, and nonexistence of dangerous condition).

15. Walker v. Trico Mfg. Co., 487 F.2d 595, 599-600 (7th Cir. 1973) (error to admit evidence of absence of prior accidents where there was no foundation "that the

party may also sometimes introduce evidence of prior accidents to establish an alternative theory of causation.[16]

Prior lawsuits   Courts are reluctant to admit evidence of prior lawsuits by the plaintiff offered to establish that the plaintiff is a chronic litigator[17] except where such prior claims establish a pattern of fraud.[18] Such evidence tends not only to be unfairly prejudicial under FRE 403 but generally runs afoul of FRE 404's prohibition on the use of character evidence to prove conduct in accordance with that character on a particular occasion.[19] Absent a showing of fraud, such evidence is not a permissible mode of impeachment under FRE 608(b) because it does not show dishonesty but perhaps just bad luck.[20] In rare circumstances, evidence of a pattern of prior claims by the plaintiff against the same defendant may be admissible to show bias. Courts are more receptive to evidence of prior claims against the defendant or an employee of the defendant where offered to establish notice or supervisory liability.[21]

§4.6   —Other Contracts or Transactions

Evidence of other contracts or business transactions is sometimes admitted to prove the existence of a contract in litigation, its terms or their intended meaning. For example, where the terms of an oral contract are disputed, a prior written contract between the parties

---

absence of prior accidents took place with respect to machines substantially identical to the one at issue and used in settings and circumstances sufficiently similar to those surrounding the machine at the time of the accident"), *cert. denied,* 415 U.S. 978.

16. Glover v. BIC Corp., 987 F.2d 1410, 1421 (9th Cir. 1993) (in product liability suit alleging that defect in lighter resulted in house fire and death, error to exclude evidence of other fires in home of decedent; given claim that he was intoxicated and caught himself on fire while bending over stove, excluded evidence was relevant to central issue, which was whether fire was started by lighter or by careless use of stove).

17. Outley v. City of New York, 837 F.2d 587, 592-593 (2d Cir. 1988) (error to admit evidence that plaintiff had filed several other lawsuits against the city and police officials where evidence tended to portray plaintiff as a chronic litigant); Smith v. State Farm Fire & Casualty Co., 633 F.2d 401, 402-404 (5th Cir. 1980) (no error to refuse to admit evidence that plaintiff had owned five insured buildings destroyed by fire; evidence irrelevant to present claim). *Cf.* Hemphill v. Washington Metro. Area Transit Auth., 982 F.2d 572, 573 (D.C. Cir. 1993) (finding reversible error where trial court instructed jury to consider whether plaintiff "was merely unlucky" or whether she was "claims minded," and that it is unusual for "a person not engaged in a hazardous activity to suffer negligent injuries repeatedly within a short period of time and at the hands of different persons").

18. Outley v. New York, 837 F.2d 587, 591-595 (2d Cir. 1988) (while prior claims might be admissible under FRE 404(b) as proof of a "fraudulent pattern," evidence of such pattern was "lacking" in this case).

19. *See* §4.15, *infra.*

20. For a discussion of FRE 608(b), *see* §§6.25-6.28.

21. *See, e.g.,* Gutierrez-Rodriguez v. Cartagena, 882 F.2d 553, 572-574 (1st Cir. 1989) (in action alleging police misconduct, proper to admit evidence of 13 prior complaints against officer in charge to establish "supervisory liability" and the "effectiveness of the police disciplinary mechanisms"); Soden v. Freightliner Corp., 714 F.2d 498, 507-510 (5th Cir. 1983) (other lawsuits arising from same alleged defect admissible to show notice).

involving the same matters may be relevant circumstantial evidence of the nature of the agreement.[1] Also prior agreements may shed light on the scope or meaning of particular provisions in the contract at issue.[2]

Other contracts are most likely to be admitted where they are between the same parties to the litigation and involve the same or similar subject matter. Contracts with third persons are often deemed irrelevant under the doctrine of "res inter alios acta" (transactions involving others).[3] However, sometimes evidence of contracts between one of the parties and third persons is admissible to show the usual practice of the party regarding the inclusion or exclusion of a particular provision in such contracts.[4] For example, in a case where a discharged employee sued for violation of an alleged oral contract of employment for a fixed term, the employer was permitted to introduce evidence of its contracts with other employees "as tending to prove a practice of the defendant company not to make . . . contracts for definite periods of time."[5]

Evidence of prior agreements between the parties may be barred by the parol evidence rule if offered to contradict or vary provisions of a final integrated written contract.[6] However, the Uniform Commercial Code recognizes the relevance of "course of dealing" and "usage of trade" in interpreting and supplementing the terms of a contract.[7]

§4.7 —Industry Safety Standards

In negligence cases, industry standards are sometimes admitted as a basis for assessing a party's conduct. Where the evidence shows that a defendant conformed to industry standards, it is said to have threefold relevancy. It warns the trier of fact that liability will have potentially far-reaching effects; it focuses attention on the practicability and feasibility of exercising greater care than the defendant did and discouraging unfounded speculation on this point; and it shows that the defendant

§4.6 1. Hyde v. Lane-Of-Sky Regional Council, 572 F.2d 988, 990 n.4 (4th Cir. 1978) (prior written employment contract admissible to prove terms of oral contract for continued employment).

2. Hartford Steam Boiler Inspection & Ins. Co. v. Schwartzman Packing Co., 423 F.2d 1170, 1173-1174 (10th Cir. 1970) (prior insurance agreements admitted "to show the pattern of how the parties had used more general definitions and specific exclusions in connection with boilers and the piping apparatus").

3. Herlihy Mid-Continent Co. v. Northern Indiana Pub. Serv. Co., 245 F.2d 440, 444 (7th Cir. 1957) (error to receive evidence of contracts between plaintiff and a third person for these were "res inter alios," and plaintiff might have made different kinds of agreements with different persons), *cert. denied,* 355 U.S. 894.

4. *See* ACN, FRE 406 (noting "trend towards admitting evidence of business transactions between one of the parties and a third person as tending to prove that he made the same bargain or proposal in the litigated situation").

5. Joseph v. Krull Wholesale Drug Co., 147 F. Supp. 250, 258 (E.D. Pa. 1956), *aff'd,* 245 F.2d 231 (3d Cir. 1957).

6. UCC 2-202; Restatement of Contracts §240 (1942).

7. UCC 2-202 and 1-205(2)-(6). *See also* Posttape Assocs. v. Eastman Kodak Co., 537 F.2d 751, 757-758 (3d Cir. 1976) (proper to admit evidence of custom of film manufacturers to limit liability to replacement of defective film).

should not be charged with failure to learn from the experience of others with respect to similar problems.[1]

Proof that defendant's methods did not conform to industry standards tends to prove the converse of these three points: Liability will not have far-reaching effect, safer methods are feasible, and defendant either did not learn or did not implement what could be garnered from the experience of others.

To prove negligence

Evidence of conformity[2] or nonconformity[3] to industry standards is often admitted as bearing circumstantially on the issue of negligence. However, the standard "must be so general or well known that the actor may be charged with knowledge of it or with negligence in not knowing of it."[4]

The weight to be given to industry standards is for the jury. Evidence of conformity to custom is not enough to establish due care,[5] and evidence of nonconformity does not by itself prove negligence.[6]

Governmental safety standards

Safety standards promulgated by governmental agencies,[7] including OSHA regulations,[8] are sometimes admitted to assist the trier of fact in determining the question of negligence or, in a products

---

§4.7 1. Morris, Custom and Negligence, 42 Colum. L. Rev. 1147 (1942).

2. Touch v. Master Unit Die Prods., Inc., 43 F.3d 754, 757 (1st Cir. 1995) (evidence that defendant designer or manufacturer met pertinent industry safety standards prevailing at time of manufacture is material, albeit nondispositive, evidence that defendant was not negligent).

3. Anderson v. Malloy, 700 F.2d 1208, 1211-1212 (8th Cir. 1983) (in action against motel for failure to provide proper security, evidence of security measures taken by other motels in the area was properly received); Muncie Aviation Corp. v. Party Doll Fleet, Inc., 519 F.2d 1178, 1181 (5th Cir. 1975) (FAA advisory materials concerning aircraft landing procedures, coupled with proof that they were generally followed in the industry, properly admitted as evidence in determining whether due care exercised).

4. Doss v. Apache Powder Co., 430 F.2d 1317, 1322-1323 (5th Cir. 1970) (error to receive evidence of Canadian industry standards).

5. M/V American Queen v. San Diego Marine Constr. Corp., 708 F.2d 1483, 1491 (9th Cir. 1983) (refusing to "condone use of industry custom and practice as fixing the legal standard for reasonableness in marine repair contracts" and disapproving "use of industry custom by a party to a contract containing unreasonable terms to justify those terms simply by showing that others in the industry use similar terms"); B & B Insulation, Inc. v. Occupational Safety & Health Review Com., 583 F.2d 1364, 1370 (5th Cir. 1978) (evidence of industry custom is probative but not dispositive on the question of negligence because benchmark is reasonable prudence standard not conduct of others).

6. Muncie Aviation Corp. v. Party Doll Fleet, Inc., 519 F.2d 1178, 1181 (5th Cir. 1975) (failure to follow customary aircraft landing procedures was not conclusive on issue of negligence but tended to show that pilot fell below the standard of care ordinarily exercised in such cases).

7. Campbell v. Keystone Aerial Surveys, Inc., 138 F.3d 996, 1003 (5th Cir. 1998) ("Even if violation of a regulation does not constitute negligence per se, failure to comply with a regulation may still provide evidence that the defendant deviated from the applicable standard of care.").

8. Robertson v. Burlington Northern R.R., 32 F.3d 408, 410 (9th Cir. 1994) (OSHA regulations may be admitted in FELA case as some evidence of applicable standard of care but violation does not establish negligence per se). See Siris, OSHA Compliance or Non-Compliance: Admissible in Federal Products Liability Actions to Prove a Machine's Safety or Defect?, 25 Ariz. St. L.J. 659 (1993) (noting division among federal courts on question).

liability action, whether a product was unreasonably dangerous. Standards of independent safety or testing agencies are also admissible for similar purposes.[9]

FRE 402

All relevant evidence is admissible, except as otherwise provided by the Constitution of the United States, by Act of Congress, by these rules, or by other rules prescribed by the Supreme Court pursuant to statutory authority. Evidence which is not relevant is not admissible.

---

§4.8 Relevant Evidence Generally Admissible

FRE 402 provides that all relevant evidence is admissible except as otherwise provided by the Constitution of the United States, federal statutes, other provisions of the Federal Rules of Evidence, or other rules prescribed by the Supreme Court, such as the Federal Rules of Civil Procedure and Federal Rules of Criminal Procedure.

The reference to the Constitution recognizes that evidence obtained in violation of constitutional guarantees may be excluded even though relevant.[1] The Federal Rules of Evidence contain numerous exclusionary provisions,[2] and various federal statutes prohibit disclosure of certain types of evidence.[3] The Federal Rules of Civil Procedure contain several evidentiary provisions,[4] as do the Federal Rules of Criminal Procedure.[5]

---

9. Miller v. Yazoo Mfg. Co., 26 F.3d 81, 82-83 (8th Cir. 1994) (in suit arising out of lawnmower accident, admitting safety standard published by American National Standards Institute; ANSI standard reflects national consensus among manufacturers, consumers, scientific and professional organizations, which would help jury understand condition of mower and determine whether it was unreasonably dangerous); Ross v. Black & Decker, Inc., 977 F.2d 1178, 1184 (7th Cir. 1992) (approving admission of safety standards of Underwriters Laboratory, an independent testing agency, in determining whether a product was unreasonably dangerous; fact that standard was promulgated subsequent to manufacture "goes to the weight and not admissibility").

§4.8 1. *See, e.g.,* Miranda v. Arizona, 384 U.S. 436 (1966) (excluding confessions obtained in police custody without required warnings); Mapp v. Ohio, 367 U.S. 643 (1961) (excluding evidence seized in violation of Fourth Amendment).

2. *See, e.g.,* FRE 404, 407-412, 501, 602, 605, 606, 610, 701, 702, 802, 901, 1002.

3. *See, e.g.,* 18 U.S.C. 2510-2520 (excluding unlawfully obtained wiretap evidence); 47 U.S.C. 605 (prohibiting persons involved in the transmission of messages by telegraph and telephone from divulging contents). To the extent a federal statute creates a privilege, exclusion is mandated under FRE 501 as well as FRE 402.

4. *See, e.g.,* FRCP 26(b)(3) (creating qualified immunity for work product); FRCP 36(b) (admissions not usable in other proceedings); FRCP 37(b)(2) (exclusion for failure to comply with discovery rules); FRCP 68 (evidence of unaccepted offer of judgment inadmissible).

5. *See, e.g.,* FRCrimP 6(e) (grand jury proceedings secret); FRCrimP 11(e)(6) (statements made in plea agreements inadmissible); FRCrimP 12.1(d) and 12.2(d) (exclusion of evidence for failure to give notice of alibi defense or insanity defense); FRCrimP 16(d)(2) (exclusion for failure to comply with discovery order).

It is important to note the exclusionary doctrines that are not recognized as an exception to admissibility by FRE 402. First, FRE 402 does not recognize preexisting common law grounds for evidentiary exclusion.[6] Second, FRE 402 does not recognize state exclusionary rules whether based upon state statutes, common law, or constitutional provisions.[7] Thus, in a federal proceeding, evidence is generally not excluded even if it was obtained in violation of state law.[8]

The issue of relevance is traditionally thought to be procedural rather than substantive, and even in proceedings where state law supplies the rule of decision, FRE 402, unlike some other evidence rules,[9] does not defer to state law. Therefore, federal standards of relevancy generally control.[10] However, in diversity cases where the relevancy ruling implicates a significant state substantive policy, courts occasionally enforce a state exclusionary provision.[11]

Although not recognized as a basis for exclusion by FRE 402, some courts exclude evidence to sanction an attorney or witness for misconduct,[12] to enforce ethical strictures such as the rule prohibiting an attorney representing a party from testifying on a substantive matter,[13] or to uphold the dignity or impartiality of the proceeding.[14]

6. United States v. Abel, 469 U.S. 45, 51 (1984) ("In principle, under the Federal Rules no common law of evidence remains," quoting Cleary, Preliminary Notes on Reading the Rules of Evidence, 57 Neb. L. Rev. 908, 915 (1978)). *See generally* Imwinkelried, The Meaning of Probative Value and Prejudice in Federal Rule of Evidence 403: Can Rule 403 Be Used to Resurrect the Common Law of Evidence?, 41 Vand. L. Rev. 879, 882 (1988) (omission of case law from FRE 402 "suggests that rule 402 deprives the judiciary of the common-law power to prescribe exclusionary rules of evidence, and the legislative history of rule 402 confirms that suggestion").

7. United States v. Jacobs, 547 F.2d 772, 777 (2d Cir. 1976) ("The obvious purpose of the catchall clause [in FRE 402] was to bar common law rules of evidence or state rules of evidence, if inconsistent."), *cert. dismissed,* 429 U.S. 909.

8. Leitman v. McAusland, 934 F.2d 46, 50 (4th Cir. 1991) (refusing to apply state exclusionary rule pertaining to taping of conversation); United States v. Chavez-Vernaza, 844 F.2d 1368, 1371 (9th Cir. 1987) (refusing to consider claim that records were seized in violation of state law because a violation of state law "is irrelevant to the admissibility of evidence in a federal criminal prosecution"). *See generally* Melilli, Exclusion of Evidence in Federal Prosecutions on the Basis of State Law, 22 Ga. L. Rev. 667 (1988).

9. *See* FRE 302 (presumptions); FRE 501 (privileges); FRE 601 (competency of witness).

10. *See* McInnis v. A.M.F., Inc., 765 F.2d 240, 245 (1st Cir. 1985) (federal standard of relevance applies even in diversity proceedings). *See generally* Wellborn, The Federal Rules of Evidence and the Application of State Law in the Federal Courts, 55 Tex. L. Rev. 371 (1977).

11. *See* Hottle v. Beech Aircraft Corp., 47 F.3d 106, 108-110 (4th Cir. 1995) (deferring to Virginia rule of evidence excluding evidence of private internal rules of party when offered to prove negligence even though such evidence was assumed to be admissible under FRE 402).

12. *See, e.g.,* United States v. Thomas, 474 F.2d 110, 112 (10th Cir. 1973) (excluding evidence obtained from interviews of defendant by prosecutor where defendant's counsel was not informed of the interviews), *cert. denied,* 412 U.S. 932.

13. *See, e.g.,* United States v. Brown, 417 F.2d 1068 (5th Cir. 1969), *cert. denied,* 397 U.S. 998. *See also* §6.9, *infra.*

14. *See* Kennedy v. Great Atl. & Pac. Tea Co., 551 F.2d 593 (5th Cir. 1977) (error to admit testimony by law clerk of judge presiding at trial).

B. PRAGMATIC RELEVANCE

FRE 403

Although relevant, evidence may be excluded if its probative value is substantially outweighed by the danger of unfair prejudice, confusion of the issues, or misleading the jury, or by considerations of undue delay, waste of time, or needless presentation of cumulative evidence.

§4.9 Discretionary Exclusion

As a counterpoise to the liberal definition of relevancy contained in FRE 401, FRE 403 grants the trial judge discretion to exclude evidence of unquestioned relevance where its probative value is substantially outweighed by the possibility of unfair prejudice, confusion of the issues, misleading the jury, undue delay, waste of time, or needless presentation of cumulative evidence.

By authorizing exclusion only where the probative value is "substantially" outweighed by the listed competing considerations, the Rule is designed to favor admissibility. Where probative value is equally balanced against a ground of exclusion, the evidence is to be admitted,[1] in contrast to balancing tests found elsewhere in the Rules.[2]

In undertaking the required balancing, the trial judge may consider **Balancing** additional factors such as the centrality of the point to be proved,[3] the need for the particular evidence,[4] the availability of alternative sources of proof,[5] and the likelihood that the jury will understand and follow a limiting instruction under FRE 105.[6]

---

§4.9 1. Blancha v. Raymark Indus., 972 F.2d 507, 516 (3d Cir. 1992) (balance "should be struck in favor of admissibility"). The FRE 403 balancing test is occasionally misstated by courts. *See, e.g.,* United States v. Cordell, 912 F.2d 769, 775 (5th Cir. 1990) (describing test as involving determination whether "the probative value of the evidence outweighs the prejudice that might result from its introduction").

2. *See* FRE 609(a); FRE 412(b)(2).

3. United States v. Herman, 589 F.2d 1191, 1198 (3d Cir. 1978) (in balancing under FRE 403 court should consider extent to which proposition is directly at issue in case), *cert. denied,* 441 U.S. 913.

4. United States v. Cook, 538 F.2d 1000, 1004 (3d Cir. 1976) (trial court must consider the government's "actual need for that evidence").

5. ACN, FRE 403 ("The availability of other means of proof may also be an appropriate factor."). *See also* Gross v. Black & Decker (US), Inc., 695 F.2d 858, 863 (5th Cir. 1983) (a factor to be considered in balancing under FRE 403 "is whether the same facts could have been proved by other evidence").

6. United States v. Figueroa, 618 F.2d 934, 943-944 (2d Cir. 1980) (in balancing under FRE 403 trial judge "should carefully consider the likely effectiveness of a cautionary instruction that tries to limit the jury's consideration of the evidence to the purpose for which it is admissible"). *See also* ACN, FRE 403 ("In reaching a decision whether to exclude on grounds of unfair prejudice, consideration should be given to the probable effectiveness or lack of effectiveness of a limiting instruction."); ACN, FRE 105

Stipulations or admissions

One alternative source of proof is a stipulation or admission by the objecting party, and an offer to stipulate or admit must be considered by the court in making a FRE 403 ruling.[7] The trial judge has discretion to exclude the evidence where the opposing party is willing to stipulate to the point,[8] and an unequivocal stipulation accepted by the court should be viewed as removing the issue from the jury.[9] A party is not necessarily required to accept an opponent's offer to stipulate,[10] however, and courts reject stipulations where they are incomplete[11] or would unfairly deny a party the full force of its proof.[12] The Supreme Court has approved the general principle that the prosecution "is entitled to prove its case by evidence of its own choice" and a defendant cannot "force the substitution of an admission for evidence" where it would prevent the prosecutor from creating a coherent narrative with sufficient descriptive richness.[13]

("The availability and effectiveness of this practice [of giving limiting instructions] must be taken into consideration in reaching a decision whether to exclude for unfair prejudice under Rule 403.").

7. Old Chief v. United States, 117 S. Ct. 644, 651 (1997) (in prosecution for assault with dangerous weapon and possession by convicted felon of a firearm, defendant offered to stipulate that he was a convicted felon and to have jury instructed that this element of charge was satisfied without informing them of nature of prior offense, which was a conviction for felony assault; it was an abuse of discretion under FRE 403 for trial judge to refuse this stipulation because of danger of unnecessary and unfair prejudice to defendant; availability of alternative and less prejudicial forms of proof such as stipulation offered here must be considered and should cause trial court to "discount" probative value of evidence when it undertakes FRE 403 balancing). For further discussion of *Old Chief, see* §4.16, *infra.*

8. United States v. Schwartz, 790 F.2d 1059, 1060-1062 (3d Cir. 1986) (reversible error to admit other crimes where defendant offered sweeping stipulations).

9. Courts are divided on this point. *Compare* United States v. Mason, 85 F.3d 471 (10th Cir. 1996) (stipulation amounts to waiver of right to jury trial on matter stipulated) *with* United States v. Muse, 83 F.3d 672, 677-681 (4th Cir. 1996) (jurors should only be told that they "may" or "should" regard a stipulated matter as having been proved, not that they "must").

10. United States v. Ellison, 793 F.2d 942, 949 (8th Cir. 1986) (generally government "is not bound by a defendant's offer to stipulate to an element of a crime"), *cert. denied,* 479 U.S. 937.

11. United States v. Vretta, 790 F.2d 651, 656 (7th Cir. 1986) (defense counsel's proposed stipulation "would have left a 'sanitized' version of the crime with too many gaps and questions left dangling concerning the crime scenario, thus forcing the jury to speculate"), *cert. denied,* 479 U.S. 851.

12. United States v. Davis, 792 F.2d 1299, 1305-1306 (5th Cir. 1986) (offer to stipulate bears on FRE 403 determination, but court refuses to adopt "an inflexible rule that allows a party by stipulation to prevent his adversary's case from being presented in its appropriately full and real life context"), *cert. denied,* 479 U.S. 964; United States v. Thevis, 665 F.2d 616, 635-636 (5th Cir. 1982) (no error to reject stipulation where "stipulation could not have carried the same force in proving motive"), *cert. denied,* 456 U.S. 1008.

13. Old Chief v. United States, 117 S. Ct. 644, 654-656 (1997) (recognizing need of prosecutor not merely to prove discrete elements of offense but "to convince the jurors that a guilty verdict would be morally reasonable"). *But see* Duane, "Screw Your Courage to the Sticking Place": The Roles of Evidence, Stipulations, and Jury Instructions in Criminal Verdicts, 49 Hastings L.J. — (1998) (arguing that if collateral facts of crime are admitted to make jurors more likely to convict should not defendants be allowed as a counterbalance to put on evidence showing personal consequences of conviction on

Unlike some earlier codifications,[14] FRE 403 does not recognize surprise as an independent ground for exclusion. According to the Advisory Committee, "the granting of a continuance is a more appropriate remedy [for surprise] than exclusion of the evidence."[15] However, surprise may sometimes be a factor in a finding that evidence will result in unfair prejudice, confusion of the issues, and undue delay.[16]

Surprise

Evidence may not be excluded under FRE 403 merely because the trial judge does not find the evidence to be credible although the court may consider the probative value of the evidence in undertaking the required balancing. Nothing in FRE 403 alters the fundamental principle that questions of credibility are for the jury.[17]

Credibility questions for jury

Evidence may generally be excluded under FRE 403 even though it otherwise qualifies for admission under the Rules of Evidence.[18] FRE 609(a)(1), which authorizes impeachment by evidence of prior convictions, expressly incorporates FRE 403 as a limit on impeachment of witnesses other than the accused.[19] FRE 403 is also frequently used as a limit on evidence otherwise admissible under FRE 404(b).[20] It also serves to restrict the use of specific instances of conduct during the cross-examination of a character witness under FRE 405(a)[21] and

---

themselves and their families). *See also* Risinger, John Henry Wigmore, Johnny Lynn Old Chief and "Legitimate Moral Force": Keeping the World Safe for Heartstrings and Gore, 49 Hastings L.J. — (1998) (proof of "bloody photos and weeping widows" ought to be more readily excludable than prior convictions but courts often take opposite position). For further discussion *see* §4.16, *infra*.

14. *See* URE, Rule 45 (1953).

15. ACN, FRE 403. *See also* Le Maire v. United States, 826 F.2d 949, 951-952 (10th Cir. 1987) (no error where plaintiff claimed surprise but failed to request a continuance).

16. *See, e.g.*, Smith v. Ford Motor Co., 626 F.2d 784 (10th Cir. 1980) (judgment for plaintiff reversed where court finds plaintiff materially misled defendant about nature of expert testimony to be offered at trial; pretrial submission indicated that physician would testify to medical treatment and prognosis and made no reference to causation; because defendant did not have opportunity to conduct discovery on this point it was prejudiced in presenting its defense); Lease America Corp. v. Insurance Co. of North America, 88 Wis. 2d 395, 276 N.W.2d 767, 769 (1979) ("[T]estimony which results in surprise may be excluded if the surprise would require a continuance causing undue delay or if surprise is coupled with the danger of prejudice or confusion of issues.").

17. United States v. Thompson, 615 F.2d 329, 332-333 (5th Cir. 1980) ("Rule 403 does not permit exclusion of evidence because the judge does not find it credible."). *See generally* Imwinkelried, The Meaning of Probative Value and Prejudice in Federal Rule of Evidence 403: Can Rule 403 Be Used to Resurrect the Common Law of Evidence?, 41 Vand. L. Rev. 879, 884-888 (1988) (FRE 403 "does not authorize the trial judge to exclude evidence because of doubts about the credibility of the source of the evidence").

18. The only apparent exception is evidence of criminal convictions involving false statement or dishonesty offered to impeach a witness under FRE 609(a)(2). Because a balancing test is expressly incorporated in FRE 609(a)(1) and omitted in 609(a)(2), courts probably lack authority to exclude convictions offered pursuant to the latter rule. *See* §6.32.

19. *See* §§6.30, 6.31. When the accused is a witness, FRE 609(a) contains its own more restrictive balancing test that governs prior crime impeachment.

20. *See* §4.16, *infra*.

21. *See* §4.19, *infra*.

during inquiry into prior acts bearing on truthfulness or untruthfulness under FRE 608(b).[22]

Broad discretion   Trial judges are given broad discretion in applying FRE 403.[23] It is generally held that their rulings are entitled to "substantial deference" on appeal and are reversed only for "clear abuse" of discretion.[24] Significant leeway is given for two reasons. First, the dangers and considerations listed in FRE 403 are impossible to define with particularity. Despite the frequency with which FRE 403 objections are made, there is rarely controlling appellate precedent because the required balancing depends so much on the facts of each case. Second, the trial judge is in a far better position than an appellate court to weigh the probative value of the evidence in the context of the case and to assess its potential impact on the jury.[25] Nonetheless, FRE 403 rulings may involve significant (although usually implicit) moral and political judgments, and commentators have urged appellate courts not to abdicate totally their supervisory responsibilities over how the Rule is applied.[26]

Although appellate courts are hesitant to reverse trial courts for error in applying FRE 403,[27] they do so when the trial judge's ruling was outside the range of permissible discretion.[28] Appellate courts encourage but generally do not require trial judges to make formal findings for

22. *See* §6.26, *infra.*

23. *See* Mengler, The Theory of Discretion in the Federal Rules of Evidence, 74 Iowa L.J. 413 (1989).

24. Veranda Beach Club Ltd. Partnership v. Western Sur. Co., 936 F.2d 1364, 1372 (1st Cir. 1991) ("[T]he trial court's construction of the probative value/unfair prejudice balance, hammered out during the rough and tumble of the trial itself, is subject to substantial deference on appeal.").

25. Olson v. Ford Motor Co., 481 F.3d 619, 623-24 (8th Cir. 2007) (FRE 403 balancing "depends on what trial judge sees and hears" which can include factors "almost invisible to an appellate judge").

26. Leonard, Power and Responsibility in Evidence Law, 63 S. Cal. L. Rev. 937 (1990) (trial courts do not have "true discretion" in sense of a right to be wrong or to disregard standards); Tanford, A Political-Choice Approach to Limiting Prejudicial Evidence, 64 Ind. L.J. 831 (1989) (appellate courts should make more of the value choices involved in FRE 403 rulings to reduce disparity); Gold, Limiting Judicial Discretion to Exclude Prejudicial Evidence, 18 U.C. Davis L. Rev. 59 (1984).

27. Freeman v. Package Mach. Co., 865 F.2d 1331, 1340 (1st Cir. 1988) (only "rarely" and in "extraordinarily compelling circumstances" will court "from the vista of a cold appellate record, reverse a district court's on-the-spot judgment concerning the relative weighing of probative value and unfair effect"); Adams v. Providence and Worcester Co., 721 F.2d 870, 872 (1st Cir. 1983) ("[A]lthough appellate courts do not often second-guess trial courts in balancing relevance against prejudice, in this case we are willing to do so."), *cert. denied,* 466 U.S. 973 (1984).

28. *See, e.g.,* Old Chief v. United States, 519 U.S. 172 (1997) (in prosecution for being ex-felon in possession of firearm, abuse of discretion under FRE 403 to allow prosecution to prove nature of prior felony rather than accepting defense stipulation); Llaguno v. Mingey, 763 F.2d 1560, 1569 (7th Cir. 1985) (in civil rights action against police arising out of warrantless search of a home, error to permit defense to bring out gruesome details of crimes police were investigating).

the record of factors considered in FRE 403 balancing,[29] although an explanation greatly assists the process of appellate review.

It has been questioned whether it is meaningful to exclude evidence on grounds of unfair prejudice in a bench trial where the trier of fact must hear the evidence in order to rule on the objection.[30] Nonetheless, exclusion seems justified to insure the integrity of the factfinding process and to make clear for the parties and the appellate court the basis for the trial court's decision. Exclusion is also warranted where the evidence is cumulative or wasteful of time because trial efficiency is as important in bench trials as jury trials.

§4.10 Unfair Prejudice, Confusion, Delay, Collateral

The first and most frequently asserted ground of exclusion in FRE 403 is "unfair prejudice." The qualification "unfair" was included out of recognition that relevant evidence is by nature prejudicial to the opposing party.[1] The Rule expects courts to distinguish between prejudice resulting from the reasonable persuasive force of evidence and prejudice resulting from excessive emotional or irrational effects that could distort the accuracy and integrity of the factfinding process.[2]

FRE 403 encompasses two analytically distinct but frequently overlapping forms of unfair prejudice. The first is the injection of undue emotionalism into the proceeding arousing hostility, anger, or sympathy on the part of the jury.[3] The second is the likelihood that the jury will misuse the evidence in some way or give it undue weight.[4]

Because most human assessments rest at least in part on emotion, no attempt is made to exclude emotion from the trial or even all evidence likely to evoke an emotional response. Rather FRE 403 provides a trial

29. United States v. Long, 574 F.2d 761, 766-767 (3d Cir. 1978) (while an explanation of trial court's analysis is helpful on appeal, "to require a detailed balancing statement in each and every case is unrealistic"), *cert. denied*, 439 U.S. 985.

30. Gulf States Utils. Co. v. Ecodyne Corp., 635 F.2d 517, 519 (5th Cir. 1981) (questioning whether exclusion of evidence as unfairly prejudicial has any "logical application to bench trials," but approving exclusion on other grounds set forth in FRE 403).

§4.10 1. Mullen v. Princess Anne Volunteer Fire Co., 853 F.2d 1130, 1134 (4th Cir. 1988) (all relevant evidence is "prejudicial" in that it "may prejudice the party against whom it is admitted").

2. Westfield Insurance Co. v. Harris, 134 F.3d 608, 613 (4th Cir. 1998) ("prejudice" means "a genuine risk that the emotions of the jury will be excited to irrational behavior"). *But see* Teitelbaum, Sutton-Barbere & Johnson, Evaluating the Prejudicial Effect of Evidence: Can Judges Identify the Impact of Improper Evidence on Juries?, 1983 Wis. L. Rev. 1147 (questioning ability of courts to assess prejudicial effect of evidence).

3. United States v. Pintado-Isiordia, 448 F.3d 1155, 1158 (9th Cir. 2006) (in trial for illegal reentry after deportation, excluding photo of defendant in military uniform; his service was shown by other evidence, and only purpose of photograph was "to elicit the jury's sympathy and patriotism").

4. *See* ACN, FRE 403 (unfair prejudice is "an undue tendency to suggest decision on an improper basis, commonly, though not necessarily, an emotional one"). *See* United States v. Looking Cloud, 419 F.3d 781, 785 (8th Cir. 2005) evidence is unfairly prejudicial if it encourages jury to find guilt on basis of "improper reasoning."

judge with the ability to regulate the nature and extent of emotional appeals during trial.

Appeal to emotion
Thus courts may exclude evidence that is found to be "inflammatory," "shocking," or "sensational."[5] Evidence may also be excluded where it evokes the anger or punitive impulses of the jury,[6] unfairly puts a party or witness in a negative light,[7] appeals to the jury's prejudices,[8] or gives rise to overly strong sympathetic reactions.[9] But sometimes evidence that is "egregious" is admitted on the theory that it has even greater probative value, such as where evidence of vicious prior beatings by police officers is offered to show a municipality's tolerance of the practice.[10] Various forms of demonstrative evidence often have strong emotional impact justifying careful regulation under FRE 403.[11]

The fact that certain evidence may be emotionally discomforting to the jury does not mean it should be excluded.[12] Thus gory photographs depicting injuries of the plaintiff are often received in personal injury or wrongful death cases on the issue of damages.[13] Photographs of dead bodies or injured victims are also often admitted in criminal cases,[14]

5. Carter v. District of Columbia, 795 F.2d 116, 128-132 (D.C. Cir. 1986) (abuse of discretion for trial judge to admit "highly inflammatory" information from defendants' personnel files).

6. Douglass v. Hustler Magazine, Inc., 769 F.2d 1128, 1142 (7th Cir. 1985) (in suit for invasion of privacy by woman pictured in Hustler magazine, trial court erred under FRE 403 in admitting slide show of 128 of magazine's "worst pictures").

7. Old Chief v. United States, 117 S. Ct. 644 (1997) (in prosecution for assault with dangerous weapon and possession by convicted felon of firearm, error to admit copy of defendant's prior conviction for felony assault causing bodily injury when defendant was willing to stipulate that he was a convicted felon and to have jury instructed that this element of offense was proven); United States v. Simpson, 910 F.2d 154, 156-158 (4th Cir. 1990) (in prosecution for trying to board plane with a firearm, reversible error to introduce evidence that defendant fit drug courier profile).

8. In re Air Crash Disaster Near New Orleans, Louisiana, on July 9, 1982, 767 F.2d 1151, 1154 (5th Cir. 1985) (where plaintiff sought damages for death of wife in airline crash, proper to exclude evidence that plaintiff had venereal disease; because plaintiff admitted he had once been unfaithful to wife, evidence "would have proved nothing more").

9. United States v. Paccione, 949 F.2d 1183 (2d Cir. 1991) (no error to exclude evidence that defendant's son had cerebral palsy and that defendant had devoted life to son's care), *cert. denied*, 505 U.S. 1220.

10. Foley v. City of Lowell, Mass., 948 F.2d 10, 15 (1st Cir. 1991) (where a plaintiff attempts to show similar prior acts of a municipality tolerating police misconduct, "egregiousness is a hallmark of probative value").

11. *See* §9.31.

12. Allen v. Seacoast Prods., Inc., 623 F.2d 355, 365 (5th Cir. 1980) (no unfair prejudice in allowing plaintiff to demonstrate procedure for removing and replacing artificial eye).

13. Walker v. Norris, 917 F.2d 1449, 1453 n.9 (6th Cir. 1990) (in civil rights action against prison guards arising out of death of inmate, no error to admit photographs of decedent's body).

14. United States v. Sides, 944 F.2d 1554, 1562-1563 (10th Cir. 1991) (photographs of murder victims properly admitted where one supported government claim that victim was killed during struggle and others showed relative locations of victims, method of murder, and crime scene).

although exclusion is more likely when the nature or extent of injuries is not an element of the prosecution's case.[15]

The court has authority under FRE 403 and 611(a) to minimize the emotional impact of such evidence, for example, by limiting the number of photographs introduced, requiring that they be in black and white rather than color, or requiring that a drawing or diagram be offered in lieu of a photograph. In order to make exclusion more likely, the objecting party can offer to stipulate to all matters properly provable by such evidence, although the court is not bound to accept such a stipulation.[16]

Limiting emotional impact

The danger of jury misuse of evidence arises most often with evidence admitted for a limited purpose under FRE 105. The jury may be instructed to consider it only on a particular issue or only against a particular party. However, sometimes the evidence has such powerful or dramatic impact that it is unrealistic to expect the jury to comply with a limiting instruction.[17] In such situations, the court has discretion to exclude the evidence under FRE 403.[18]

Limited purpose

Evidence bringing out the criminal background of a defendant[19] or why he was being investigated[20] is often found unfairly prejudicial under FRE 403. Evidence of other crimes or wrongs committed by a party may be excluded under FRE 403 even where such evidence otherwise qualifies for admission under FRE 404(b).[21]

Evidence of a gun or other weapon seized from the accused at the time of arrest may be admitted where the weapon is an element of the charged crime or was allegedly used during commission of the charged

---

15. *Compare* United States v. Lopez, 271 F.3d 472, 482 (3d Cir. 2001) (admitting photograph's of victim's mutilated hand which "related to the charge of mayhem") *with* State v. Wilson, 310 S.E.2d 486, 487-488 (W. Va. 1983) (gruesome photographs are not per se excludable but are presumptively prejudicial and state must show that they have "essential value" to the case; reversible error to admit such photographs here).

16. State v. Chapple, 135 Ariz. 281, 660 P.2d 1208, 1217 (1983) (exhibits that have the tendency to cause prejudice "may often be admissible despite offers to stipulate" because testimony "may be difficult to comprehend without photographs, or exhibits may corroborate or illustrate controverted testimony"). For a discussion of offers to stipulate, *see* §4.9, *supra*.

17. *Cf.* Shepard v. United States, 290 U.S. 96, 103-104 (1933) (Cardozo, J.) (rejecting use of deceased wife's statement "Dr. Shepard has poisoned me" for limited purpose of showing her will to live and unlikelihood of her committing suicide; "Discrimination so subtle is a feat beyond the compass of ordinary minds. The reverberating clang of those accusatory words would drown all weaker sounds. It is for ordinary minds, and not for psychoanalysts, that the rules of evidence are framed.").

18. *See* ACN, FRE 105 ("availability and effectiveness" of giving a limiting instruction "must be taken into consideration in reaching a decision whether to exclude for unfair prejudice under Rule 403").

19. United States v. Bland, 908 F.2d 471, 473 (9th Cir. 1990) (in prosecution for being an ex-felon in possession of a firearm, it was error to admit evidence that basis of arrest warrant was the torture murder of a seven-year-old girl, because it might suggest that acquittal meant "releasing an exceedingly dangerous child molester and killer").

20. United States v. Lamberty, 778 F.2d 59, 60-61 (1st Cir. 1985) (in prosecution against postmaster for improperly opening package, reversible error to admit "highly prejudicial" testimony of postal inspector that defendant was being investigated because of "information" that defendant was "taking out packages which had been missent").

21. *See* §4.16, *infra*.

offense.[22] Otherwise such evidence is generally excluded as unfairly prejudicial,[23] although some decisions admit weapons found in a defendant's possession to support charges of organized criminal activity such as drug trafficking.[24]

Confusing and misleading

Evidence may be excluded where it is likely to confuse or mislead the jury, such as by distracting them with immaterial or side issues.[25] There is considerable overlap between the dangers of confusing the issues and misleading the jury, and courts often cite both dangers without attempting to distinguish between them.

Examples of evidence found confusing and misleading include evidence about developments in related legal proceedings,[26] the failure to prosecute other parties,[27] reports containing ambiguous legal terminology,[28] and private agreements between defendants purporting to apportion any liability imposed.[29]

Inculpating third party

An important and controversial application of this ground of exclusion is to prevent defendants from attempting to show that a third person committed the crime for which they are charged unless the court finds the proffered evidence sufficiently probative.[30] Although courts understandably seek to prevent improper attempts to divert the

22. United States v. Eatherton, 519 F.2d 603, 611 (1st Cir. 1975) (upon proof that a weapon was used during bank robbery, court may permit introduction of that weapon or a weapon of a similar kind to show identity), *cert. denied,* 423 U.S. 987.

23. United States v. Warledo, 557 F.2d 721, 725 (10th Cir. 1977) ("The courts have quite uniformly condemned the introduction in evidence of testimony concerning dangerous weapons, even though found in the possession of a defendant, which have nothing to do with the crime charged.").

24. United States v. Green, 887 F.2d 25, 27 (1st Cir. 1989) (no error to admit proof of firearms, which are "tools of the trade" in drug trafficking).

25. *See, e.g.,* Blancha v. Raymark Indus., 972 F.2d 507, 516 (3d Cir. 1992) (evidence may be excluded under FRE 403 "when its admission would lead to litigation of collateral issues, thereby creating a side issue which might distract the jury from the main issues").

26. Rozier v. Ford Motor Co., 573 F.2d 1332, 1346-1348 (5th Cir. 1978) (in products liability action where decedent was killed when gas tank exploded after car rear-ended by another driver, error to allow manufacturer to introduce guilty plea of other driver to involuntary manslaughter because such evidence was likely to be "confusing" and "potentially misleading" to jury).

27. United States v. Steffen, 641 F.2d 591, 596 (8th Cir. 1981) (excluding evidence offered by defendant that other persons alleged to be involved were not prosecuted), *cert. denied,* 452 U.S. 943.

28. Pucalik v. Holiday Inns, 777 F.2d 359, 363 (7th Cir. 1985) (in wrongful death action arising out of killing of security guard, no error to exclude government document finding that guard died "in the line of duty" and therefore was acting as "a licensee, not an invitee"; document was "conclusory and not based on findings under Indiana law" and its probative value was "clearly outweighed by the potential for confusing and misleading the jury").

29. In re Air Crash Disaster at John F. Kennedy Intl. Airport on June 24, 1975, 635 F.2d 67, 73 (2d Cir. 1980) (in litigation arising out of air crash, no error to exclude evidence that United States and airline had agreed to a 40-60 split of any damages awarded; court finds that such evidence "would have only served to mislead the jurors and confuse the issues").

30. *See, e.g.,* United States v. Perkins, 937 F.2d 1397 (9th Cir. 1990) (excluding evidence of insufficiently similar crimes by third person as likely to confuse and mislead

attention of the jury and put a nonparty on trial on the basis of spec-ulative evidence,[31] judicial caution is warranted because of the due process dangers of excluding evidence of third party culpability that is sufficient to raise a reasonable doubt in the minds of the jury about defendant's own guilt.[32]

FRE 403 permits exclusion based on considerations of "undue delay, waste of time or needless presentation of cumulative evidence." Such grounds for exclusion can be viewed as a "concession to the shortness of life"[33] as well as an acknowledgment of the limited resources of the judicial system. Pretrial conferences under FRCP 16 share the same goal of avoiding unnecessary proof at trial.[34]

Waste of time, delay, cumulative

It is sometimes difficult to decide whether evidence is "needlessly" cumulative because it is hard to know how much evidence on a particular issue is required to convince the jury. Litigants are generally allowed to call more than one witness on a point and to introduce corroborative or duplicative evidence. But under FRE 403 courts clearly have discretion to limit the number of witnesses called,[35] the number of examples on the same point,[36] and generally to prevent unnecessary repetition.[37]

"Needlessly" cumulative

Courts may exclude documentary evidence offered on a point that has already been established by testimony[38] and similarly may refuse to require the playing of a tape recording on matters already adequately

---

jury). *See generally* McCord, "But Perry Mason Made It Look *So Easy!*": The Admissibility of Evidence Offered by a Criminal Defendant to Suggest That Someone Else Is Guilty, 63 Tenn. L. Rev. 917 (1996).

31. United States v. Jordan, 485 F.3d 1214, 1222 (10th Cir. 2007) (no abuse of discretion to exclude evidence of possible third party guilt because it was speculative); Perry v. Rushen, 713 F.2d 1447 (9th Cir. 1983) (court must balance legitimate interests of defendant to present a defense against interests of state in fair and reliable trial; where state interest is strong, "only the exclusion of critical, reliable and highly pro-bative evidence will violate due process").

32. Holmes v. South Carolina, 547 U.S. 319 (2006) (constitutional error to exclude evidence of third party guilt merely because prosecution's case against defendant seemed strong). *See also* Everhart, Putting a Burden of Production on the Defendant Before Admitting Evidence That Someone Else Committed the Crime Charged: Is It Constitutional? 76 Neb. L. Rev. 272 (1997). On the constitutional right to produce evidence, *see* §5.5, *infra.*

33. Reeve v. Dennett, 145 Mass. 23, 28, 11 N.E. 938, 944 (1887) (Holmes, J.).

34. FRCP 16(c)(4) and (15) (subjects for consideration at pretrial conferences include "avoidance of unnecessary proof and of cumulative evidence" and "an order establishing a reasonable limit on the time allowed for presenting evidence").

35. United States v. Garrett, 716 F.2d 257, 272 (5th Cir. 1983) (after eight character witnesses had already testified, trial judge did not abuse his discretion by excluding similar testimony from ten additional proposed witnesses), *cert. denied,* 466 U.S. 937.

36. United States v. Gleason, 616 F.2d 2, 22 (2d Cir. 1979) (limiting evidence to two out of eight examples of defendant's alleged cohort acting unlawfully on his own), *cert. denied,* 444 U.S. 1082.

37. Melton v. Deere & Co., 887 F.2d 1241, 1245 (5th Cir. 1989) (in personal injury suit against manufacturer of farm combine, no error for trial court to admit evidence of three similar accidents and exclude six others because court has discretion to exclude "unnecessarily cumulative" evidence).

38. United States v. Lomax, 598 F.2d 582, 584-585 (10th Cir. 1979) (proper to refuse to receive stolen check as an exhibit to impeach prosecution witness where witness already admitted stealing the check).

established by other evidence.[39] However, the trial judge should not become so concerned about keeping up the pace of the trial that a litigant is prevented from presenting evidence critical to his claim or defense.[40]

Collateral   Although not listed as a ground for exclusion in FRE 403, evidence can be excluded if it is "collateral," which may encompass several grounds listed in the Rule including unfairly prejudicial, confusing, misleading, waste of time and undue delay. "Collateral" is a durable term carried forward from common-law tradition. In a general sense, the term describes testimony and other evidence far removed from what is important or central in a case. Such proof is usually seen as tangential, unimportant, or trivial, hence distracting or time-consuming, and often prejudicial. In practice, the term "collateral" appears in several specific settings where it describes important limits on various evidential doctrines.

First, it is often said that impeachment on collateral points is improper. The central idea is that evidence should not be admitted if it tends only to contradict or refute other evidence that is unimportant in a case. Contradiction is one of the recognized methods of impeachment, and in this setting the term "collateral" has developed into a hard-edged limit with well-defined meaning. Putting aside details, the idea is that counterproof may be admitted to contradict only testimony or other evidence that really counts.[41] If a witness says he was wearing a coat when he saw the accident, proof that he was in his shirtsleeves might well be excluded as impeachment on a collateral point.

Another recognized method of impeachment involves the use of prior statements by a witness that conflict with his testimony. Here too it is sometimes said that impeachment on collateral points is improper although the limit is not so carefully observed in this setting.[42]

In connection with impeaching attacks that seek to show bias or defects in mental or sensory capacity, extrinsic evidence is generally admissible. Essentially that means that one witness may be called to testify on such facts as they relate to another witness, and this outcome is often explained by the comment that such issues and such evidence are not collateral.[43]

Second, it is often said that the "open door" doctrine does not pave the way for evidence on collateral points. Essentially, the idea of the open door doctrine is that affirmative party strategies in offering evidence or questioning witnesses bear importantly on what other

39. United States v. Hearst, 563 F.2d 1331, 1348 (9th Cir. 1977) (court refused to allow playing of one hour and forty-five-minute tape of psychiatric interview of defendant; tape found needlessly cumulative), *cert. denied*, 435 U.S. 1000.

40. Bower v. O'Hara, 759 F.2d 1117, 1123-1124 (3d Cir. 1985) (error to exclude evidence "plainly relevant to the issue of damages" where the trial court ruling "seemed to have been prompted chiefly if not solely by the court's impatience about the length of trial").

41. *See* the discussion in §6.47, *infra.* In connection with attempts to show a witness is untruthful, extrinsic evidence of acts by the witness is excludable (testimony by another witness), and courts sometimes explain the point by saying extrinsic evidence is inadmissible on such collateral points. *See* FRE 608(b) *and* the discussion in §6.27, *infra.*

42. *See* the discussion in §6.40, *infra.*

43. *See* the discussion of bias in §6.19 *and* the discussion of capacity in §6.21, *infra.*

parties may do by way of reply or counterproof. But when such strategies result in introducing evidence that is unimportant and likely to have little effect, or when counterproof that might refute such evidence would introduce risks of prejudice that are out of all proportion to the original proof, the counterproof may properly be excluded, and often it is labeled as collateral.[44]

Underlying these uses of the term "collateral" are the concerns embodied in FRE 403. Far preferable to quick and careless use of the term is a more direct explanation of underlying concerns. If the concern is that probative worth is slight when compared to the complexity of the argument or issue, or the time required to explore the matter, it helps to say that. If the concern is that the evidence, while relevant on the point in question, has an unintentional spillover effect posing a risk of serious prejudice to the parties or humiliation or harassment for the witness, it helps to say that as well. Occasionally courts exhibit impatience with use of the label alone.[45]

C. CHARACTER EVIDENCE

FRE 404

   (a) **Character evidence generally.** Evidence of a person's character or a trait of character is not admissible for the purpose of proving action in conformity therewith on a particular occasion, except:

   (1) **Character of accused.** In a criminal case, evidence of a pertinent trait of character offered by an accused, or by the prosecution to rebut the same; or if evidence of a trait of character of the alleged victim of the crime is offered by an accused and admitted under subdivision (a)(2), evidence of the same trait of character of the accused offered by the prosecution;

   (2) **Character of alleged victim.** In a criminal case, and subject to the limitations imposed by Rule 412, evidence of a pertinent trait of character of the alleged victim of the crime offered by an accused, or by the prosecution to rebut the same, or evidence of a character trait of peacefulness of the alleged victim offered by the prosecution in a homicide case to rebut evidence that the alleged victim was the first aggressor;

   (3) **Character of witness.** Evidence of the character of a witness, as provided in rules 607, 608, and 609.

---

44. *See generally* the discussion of the open door doctrine in §1.4 and §4.2, *supra.*
45. United States v. Robinson, 530 F.2d 1076, 1081 (D.C. Cir. 1976) (analysis is cursory when judge comments that evidence is only collateral in impeaching character; preferable to confront problem by "acknowledging and weighing" prejudice and probative worth).

§4.11 Character Evidence—Generally

Evidence bearing on the character of a party or witness sometimes has significant probative value but also brings substantial dangers of unfair prejudice, confusion, and waste of time. For this reason, the Federal Rules impose a complicated scheme that limits the situations in which character may be proved and the form of proof permitted.

Definition As used in the Rules, "character" means a person's disposition or propensity to engage or not engage in various forms of conduct.[1] Viewed from this perspective, character is not a unitary concept. Everyone has multiple traits of character that may include a propensity to be truthful (or dishonest), drive safely (or recklessly), drink temperately (or excessively or not at all), or act peaceably (or violently).

Uses Character evidence may be offered for several different purposes. Proof of character is obviously important if character itself is an element of a particular charge, claim, or defense.[2] And narrow aspects of character are often proved by evidence of prior crimes or wrongs by a person in order to show such specific points as motive, intent, knowledge, or plan and sometimes to show modus operandi or identity.[3] Perhaps the most commonly attempted and heavily regulated use of character evidence is to prove that a person acted in accordance with his character or propensities on a particular occasion. This usage is known as "circumstantial" use of character evidence and is subject to a general prohibition in FRE 404(a) with broad exceptions set forth in FRE 404(a)(1)-(3) as well as FRE 413-415.

Thus a plaintiff in an automobile accident case may not offer evidence that defendant had a propensity toward negligence (such as a record of repeated traffic citations or accidents) to prove he was driving recklessly at the time of the accident.[4] Nor may the defendant offer evidence of his flawless driving record to prove absence of negligence or other culpable conduct at the time in question.[5] And in the criminal setting a prosecutor generally may not be the first to offer proof of a defendant's criminal propensities or prior criminal history

---

§4.11 1. Generally "character" refers to demonstrated inclinations toward particular conduct. It does not include one's innate abilities. *See* United States v. West, 670 F.2d 675, 682 (7th Cir. 1982) ("[I]ntelligence is [not] a character trait within the meaning of [FRE 404(a)(1)]."), *cert. denied,* 457 U.S. 1124. While the term includes one's proclivities, it is uncertain whether it includes personal attitudes or values not yet translated into conduct.

2. *See* §4.20, *infra.*

3. *See* §§4.15-4.18, *infra.*

4. Sparks v. Gilley Trucking Co., Inc., 992 F.2d 50, 53 (4th Cir. 1993) (error to admit prior speeding tickets of plaintiff to prove plaintiff was speeding at time of accident; this inference "is the one specifically prohibited by Rule 404"); Bonilla v. Yamaha Motors Corp., 955 F.2d 150, 154 (1st Cir. 1992) (same).

5. Gates v. Rivera, 993 F.2d 697, 700 (9th Cir. 1993) (in civil rights action where defendant police officer shot and killed burglary suspect, error to receive evidence that defendant in 16 years as a police officer had never shot anyone before).

to show that he committed the charged crime.[6] Nor may the prosecutor interject such evidence indirectly.[7]

Such evidence is not necessarily irrelevant under FRE 401, and often it has strong probative force. But as a matter of both law and policy,[8] its probative value is viewed as generally outweighed by competing dangers.[9] The rationale underlying FRE 404(a) was perhaps most lucidly expounded by Justice Jackson in the famous decision of *Michelson v. United States:*

> The state may not show defendant's prior trouble with the law, specific criminal acts, or ill name among his neighbors, even though such facts might logically be persuasive that he is by propensity a probable perpetrator of the crime. The inquiry is not rejected because character is irrelevant; on the contrary, it is said to weigh too much with the jury and to so overpersuade them as to prejudge one with a bad general record and deny him a fair opportunity to defend against a particular charge. The overriding policy of excluding such evidence, despite its admitted probative value, is the practical experience that its disallowance tends to prevent confusion of issues, unfair surprise and undue prejudice.[10]

FRE 404(a) might seem to establish a rule of exclusion that is not only counterintuitive but also contrary to the usual practice in social and business relationships of judging persons by their past behavior.[11] Past conduct or performance is usually thought to be one of the best predictors of future behavior. But while a person's propensities are a useful gauge of likely behavior patterns over a period of time, they are less accurate when used to decide what happened on one particular occasion because people do not always act in accordance with their propensities.[12]

(margin note: Not necessarily irrelevant)

---

6. United States v. Mothershed, 859 F.2d 585, 589-590 (8th Cir. 1988) ("We do not convict people of crimes simply because of their propensities; we do so because of what they have actually done."). The prosecutor may offer evidence about the accused's character to rebut character evidence offered by the accused or to impeach the defendant's credibility if he takes the stand. *See* §4.12 *and* §§6.29-6.39, *infra.*

7. United States v. Shelton, 628 F.2d 54, 56-57 (D.C. Cir. 1980) (error to insinuate on cross-examination that defendant and defense witnesses "were members of the drug underworld involved in all sorts of skulduggery").

8. FRE 404 and the succeeding rules in Article IV, can be viewed as balancing the relevancy of evidence under FRE 401 against the competing dangers listed in FRE 403 as a matter of law. Such an approach avoids the inconsistency and unpredictability that would result if such balancing were undertaken on a case-by-case basis.

9. United States v. Daniels, 770 F.2d 1111, 1116 (D.C. Cir. 1985) (exclusion of other act evidence "is founded not on a belief that the evidence is irrelevant, but rather on a fear that juries will tend to give it excessive weight").

10. 335 U.S. 469, 475-476 (1948).

11. The evaluation of job applicants, political candidates, applicants to universities, athletes, and candidates for admission to professional organizations is commonly based on their past conduct and performance.

12. Campbell v. Greer, 831 F.2d 700, 707 (7th Cir. 1987) ("[M]oral conduct in one situation is not highly correlated with moral conduct in another," citing psychological studies). *See also* Mendez, California's New Law on Character Evidence:

Freely admitting evidence of past conduct would also divert the jury's attention from the issue of what he did on the occasion in dispute to what he did at other times in the past.[13] A defendant would be forced not only to answer the allegations in the indictment or complaint but to defend his entire personal history. Proof and counterproof of a person's character could waste time as well, and a litigant with a less than sterling character could be denied a fair trial despite the justness of his cause.[14]

Absent FRE 404(a), courts would be required to balance the relevance of character evidence under FRE 401 against the competing dangers listed in FRE 403 on a case-by-case basis. By establishing a general rule of exclusion, FRE 404(a) enhances predictability and ensures uniformity.

Exception for criminal defendants

FRE 404(a) contains three specific and important exceptions that allow use of character evidence to prove conduct on a particular occasion. First, FRE 404(a)(1) allows a criminal defendant to put on evidence of a "pertinent" trait of character, such as his disposition to be honest or peaceable, as proof that he was unlikely to have committed the crime charged. If he introduces such evidence, the prosecutor may call character witnesses in rebuttal or bring out relevant specific instances of defendant's prior behavior during cross-examination of defendant's character witnesses.[15]

Exception for crime victims

FRE 404(a)(2) authorizes a criminal defendant to introduce evidence of a "pertinent" character trait of a crime victim, such as evidence that an alleged assault victim was inclined toward violence, as proof that in fact he was the first aggressor. If the accused introduces evidence of the victim's character, the prosecutor may call character witnesses to give rebuttal testimony that the victim was inclined toward nonviolence. In a homicide prosecution, even if the defendant does not offer evidence of the character of the victim, the prosecutor may introduce evidence of the victim's peaceable character if the defendant introduces evidence that the victim was the first aggressor.[16] In prosecutions

---

Evidence Code Section 352 and the Impact of Recent Psychological Studies, 31 UCLA L. Rev. 1003, 1050-1059 (1984) (discussing psychological studies showing limited probative value of character evidence). If a person's response is invariable, it may amount to evidence of habit rather than character and be admissible under FRE 406. *See* §4.21, *infra.*

13. United States v. Lewis, 787 F.2d 1318, 1332 (9th Cir. 1986) (government may not introduce "evidence of a defendant's prior crimes to show that the defendant has a bad character and is therefore likely to have committed the crime with which he is charged"), *cert. denied*, 489 U.S. 1032.

14. United States v. McCourt, 925 F.2d 1229, 1235-1236 & n.2 (9th Cir. 1991) (rule reflects "deep seated notion that our system of justice should not permit the trier of fact to infer that because someone was a bad guy once, he is likely to be a bad guy again"), *cert. denied*, 502 U.S. 837; United States v. Hodges, 770 F.2d 1475, 1479 (9th Cir. 1985) ("Defendant must be tried for what he did, not for who he is."). *See also* Kalven & Zeisel, The American Jury 160 (1966) (in simulated criminal trial, defendant's chance of acquittal dropped from 65 percent to 38 percent when his criminal record was made known to jurors).

15. *See* §4.12, *infra.*

16. *See* §4.13, *infra.*

for sexual offenses, the right of the accused to offer character evidence of past sexual behavior by the complaining witness is expressly limited by FRE 412.[17] If an accused attacks the character of the victim, the door is opened to evidence of the same trait of character of the accused offered by the prosecutor.

Finally, FRE 404(a)(3) authorizes any party in either a civil or criminal proceeding to introduce character evidence (to the extent provided by FRE 607, 608, and 609) to impeach or rehabilitate the credibility of a witness.[18] Because evidence bearing on the untruthful or truthful disposition of a witness is being offered to show conduct consistent with that character at trial (giving untruthful or truthful testimony), an exception to FRE 404(a) is required to make such evidence admissible. Each of these exceptions is discussed in more detail in the sections that follow.

Exception for witnesses

Although not listed as exceptions to FRE 404(a), FRE 413-415 have that effect because they allow evidence of a defendant's prior acts of sexual assault or child molestation to show the defendant's propensity to commit such crimes.[19]

§4.12   —Criminal Defendant

A historic exception to the Rule prohibiting character evidence to prove conduct in conformity therewith on a particular occasion is that an accused may offer evidence of a pertinent trait of his character to support an inference that he was unlikely to have committed the charged offense. For example, an accused may offer evidence of his peaceable disposition when charged with a crime of violence or his honest tendencies when charged with a crime of larceny.

Along with the presumption of innocence and requirement of proof beyond reasonable doubt, this exception (sometimes called the "mercy rule") gives a criminal defendant some counterweight against the strong investigative and prosecutorial resources of the government. As the Advisory Committee put it, this exception is "so deeply imbedded in our jurisprudence as to assume almost constitutional proportions and to override doubts of the basic relevancy of the evidence."[1]

Although some courts applied this exception in civil cases where the defendant was sued for conduct that was criminal in nature,[2] a 2006 amendment to the rule added the language "[i]n a criminal case" to

An accused

---

17. *See* §§4.32-4.34, *infra.*
18. *See* §4.14, *infra.*
19. *See* §§4.35, 4.36.

§4.12   1. ACN, FRE 404(a). *See also* United States v. Daniels, 770 F.2d 1111, 1118 (D.C. Cir. 1985) (allowing such evidence "gives meaning to a central precept of our system of criminal justice, the presumption of innocence").

2. Perrin v. Anderson, 784 F.2d 1040, 1043-1045 (10th Cir. 1986) (despite "the literal language of the exceptions to Rule 404(a)," defendant in a civil case may invoke those exceptions when the central issue "is in nature criminal"). *See generally* Leonard, The

make clear that this exception is limited to criminal proceedings. Some states have broader language in their counterparts of FRE 404(a) that allows character evidence in certain civil proceedings.[3]

Defendant must initiate   Under FRE 404(a)(1), any evidence of defendant's character must first be offered by the defense, except in cases where the defendant has attacked the victim's character.[4] Only then may the prosecutor respond with counterproof. By offering evidence of his character, the defendant is sometimes said to place his character "at issue,"[5] but this expression is misleading and should be avoided because only his conduct (not his character) is truly at issue. The character evidence merely supports an inference as to his likely conduct. Moreover, by offering evidence of a pertinent trait of his character the defendant does not open the door to rebuttal evidence of his entire character. This circumstantial use of character evidence should not be confused with cases where character itself is an element of a charge, claim, or defense.[6]

An accused clearly invokes this exception, and invites prosecutorial counterproof, by calling a character witness to give reputation or opinion testimony on a pertinent trait of his character or by asking a government witness on cross-examination to give an opinion or describe his reputation with respect to a particular character trait.[7] If an accused is successful in introducing evidence of a victim's pertinent trait of character under FRE 404(a)(2), the door is opened to "evidence of the same trait of character of the accused offered by the prosecution."

An accused does not raise the issue of his character (apart from veracity) merely by taking the stand,[8] providing general background

---

Use of Character to Prove Conduct: Rationality and Catharsis in the Law of Evidence, 58 U. Colo. L. Rev. 1, 56-57 (1987) (arguing that FRE 404(a) should be amended to permit use of character evidence in civil cases).

3. *See, e.g.,* Or. Rev. Stat. 40.170(2)(d) (allowing "[e]vidence of the character of a party for violent behavior offered in a civil assault and battery case when self-defense is pleaded and there is evidence to support such defense").

4. The prosecutor may be able to raise issues reflecting on the defendant's character under other provisions, however, such as FRE 404(b), or, if the defendant testifies, under FRE 608(b) and FRE 609. Where the case presents the issue whether the victim was placed in fear of the defendant, the prosecutor may be able to prove such fear by presenting evidence of the defendant's history of violence, or reputation therefore, provided such information was known to the victim. *See* United States v. Zannino, 895 F.2d 1, 11-12 (1st Cir. 1990) (victim's testimony admitted that "he feared the use of force if he did not make his scheduled payments" as he knew of defendant's "reputation for violence"), *cert. denied,* 494 U.S. 1082.

5. *See, e.g.,* United States v. Mills, 704 F.2d 1553, 1563 (11th Cir. 1983), *cert. denied,* 467 U.S. 1243 (1984).

6. *See* §4.20, *infra.*

7. United States v. Mills, 704 F.2d 1553, 1562-1563 (11th Cir. 1983) (in cross-examination of prosecution witness, defendant elicited personal opinion of witness that defendant never presented himself "as a madman" who would "just run around wanting to kill everybody" and that in general defendant presented himself "as being basically fair and just towards everyone in a general way"; such cross-examination amounted to presentation of defense character evidence thereby allowing the government to rebut with evidence of his bad character).

8. In this setting, defendant's veracity may be attacked by character evidence offered under FRE 608 or 609.

information,[9] or claiming self-defense.[10] However, if he gives an opinion on his own character or tries to present a portrait of himself as an honest or law-abiding or peaceful person, most courts properly admit rebuttal evidence offered by the prosecution.[11] The prosecutor cannot "open his own door" to such damaging evidence by asking defendant or a defense witness about defendant's character and then offering rebutting evidence.[12]

The trait of character shown by defense evidence must be "pertinent" to the crime charged.[13] Evidence of the defendant's veracity has been properly excluded in a prosecution for a crime of violence[14] and a narcotics prosecution,[15] and evidence of defendant's peaceful disposition should not be admitted in a prosecution for a nonviolent crime. But evidence that defendant has a law-abiding character is admissible in any criminal prosecution.[16] If he testifies and his character for truthfulness is attacked by the government, he may offer evidence of his veracity under FRE 608(a) for purposes of rehabilitation even though the crime charged does not involve dishonesty.[17]

Trait must be pertinent

---

9. United States v. Gillespie, 852 F.2d 475, 479-481 (9th Cir. 1988) (by testifying about his childhood and general background defendant did not open door allowing prosecutor to offer counterproof by clinical psychologist that he had "characteristics common to child molesters").

10. United States v. Fountain, 768 F.2d 790, 795 (7th Cir. 1985) (by claiming self-defense defendant does not open his character to attack; such a rule "would make mincemeat of the limitations in Rule 404(a) on the use of character evidence"), *cert. denied,* 475 U.S. 1124.

11. United States v. Gaertner, 705 F.2d 210, 216 (7th Cir. 1983) (testimony by defendant that "I'm not into the cocaine thing, the drug thing" found to be character evidence allowing prosecutor to introduce evidence of a seven-year-old conviction for possessing marijuana), *cert. denied,* 464 U.S. 1071.

12. United States v. Gilliland, 586 F.2d 1384, 1386-1389 (10th Cir. 1978) (error for prosecutor to ask defense witness whether he believed defendant was kind of person who would not commit the charged offense and, after obtaining an affirmative answer, ask witness questions about defendant's prior criminal record).

13. United States v. Nazzaro, 889 F.2d 1158, 1168 (1st Cir. 1989) (evidence of prior commendations for bravery and attention to duty were not pertinent to charged crimes of mail fraud and perjury).

14. Darland v. United States, 626 F.2d 1235, 1237 (5th Cir. 1980) (in robbery prosecution, proper to exclude evidence of defendant's "reputation for truth and veracity"), *cert. denied,* 454 U.S. 1157.

15. United States v. Jackson, 588 F.2d 1046, 1055 (5th Cir.), *cert. denied,* 442 U.S. 941 (in narcotics prosecution, evidence of defendant's reputation for truth and veracity not admissible).

16. United States v. Angelini, 678 F.2d 380, 381 (1st Cir. 1982) (reversible error to exclude evidence that defendant was "a law-abiding person"); United States v. Hewitt, 634 F.2d 277, 278-280 (5th Cir. 1981) (reversible error to exclude defense testimony as to defendant's "character for veracity and lawfulness"; court states that a general trait of character is "no less pertinent for being general").

17. *See* §6.50, *infra. Cf.* United States v. Lechoco, 542 F.2d 84, 86-88 (D.C. Cir. 1976) (where defendant asserted an insanity defense and prosecutor suggested that defendant lied to the psychiatrist, defendant entitled to offer evidence of his reputation for truthfulness and honesty).

Character bears on reasonable doubt

Some courts, relying on an early Supreme Court precedent,[18] have held that a criminal defendant is entitled to a jury instruction that character evidence "standing alone" may create a reasonable doubt on the question of guilt.[19] However, such an instruction invites the jury to consider character evidence without reference to the prosecution's evidence and may distract it from assessing the weight or persuasive force of such evidence.[20] It might even create the impression that defendant bears some burden of proof.[21] Today most courts hold that a defendant is entitled only to an instruction that character evidence should be considered along with all the other evidence in deciding whether the prosecution has proven guilt beyond reasonable doubt.[22]

Reputation or opinion evidence

If character evidence is offered pursuant to FRE 404(a)(1), it must be in the form of reputation or opinion evidence rather than specific instances of conduct.[23] However, some courts allow criminal defendants to go beyond reputation or opinion evidence in presenting "background" evidence about themselves.[24]

18. Edgington v. United States, 164 U.S. 361, 366 (1896) ("The circumstances may be such that an established reputation for good character, if it is relevant to the issue, would alone create a reasonable doubt, although, without it, the other evidence would be convincing.").

19. United States v. Hewitt, 634 F.2d 277, 278-279 (5th Cir. 1981) (jury should be told that good character evidence alone may create a reasonable doubt as to guilt); United States v. Lewis, 482 F.2d 632, 637 (D.C. Cir. 1973) (defendant entitled to "standing alone" instruction).

20. Smith v. United States, 305 F.2d 197, 206 (9th Cir. 1962) ("The danger in using the word alone when not required to meet a special trial problem, is that the jury may mistakenly take it as an invitation to consider good character evidence to the exclusion of all other evidence."), *cert. denied,* 371 U.S. 890.

21. United States v. Burke, 781 F.2d 1234, 1238-1242 & n.5 (7th Cir. 1985) (noting that a "stand alone" instruction might have the "unintended and pernicious effect" of suggesting that defendant "bears some burden of establishing his innocence").

22. United States v. Winter, 663 F.2d 1120, 1146-1148 (1st Cir. 1981) (rejecting "character alone" instruction but approving instruction that jury may consider character evidence along with all the other evidence, and that character evidence may cause jury to have reasonable doubt as to guilt), *cert. denied,* 460 U.S. 1011. *Cf.* United States v. Burke, 781 F.2d 1234, 1242 n.5 (7th Cir. 1985) (stronger instruction may be appropriate in cases where defendant has offered only character evidence).

23. *See* FRE 405(a), discussed in §4.19, *infra. See also* United States v. Hill, 40 F.3d 164, 169 (7th Cir. 1994) (in trial of postal employee for stealing check, excluding proof that he did not later steal test letters; proper way to prove law-abidingness is reputation or opinion testimony).

24. United States v. Blackwell, 853 F.2d 86 (2d Cir. 1988) (error, but harmless, to exclude testimony by defendant that he had never been arrested before this incident; court viewed this testimony as permissible background information rather than prohibited character evidence). *But see* Government of Virgin Islands v. Petersen, 553 F.2d 324, 328-329 (3d Cir. 1977) (proper to exclude evidence of defendant's religious beliefs as proof of his character; "A person may or may not act in accordance with a professed belief; it is the observation of the defendant's behavior over a length of time which is the recognized basis for both reputation and opinion testimony.").

Once the accused presents character evidence, the prosecutor may call rebuttal character witnesses.[25] Such witnesses are limited to reputation or opinion testimony and cannot testify to specific instances of conduct.[26] Occasionally, rebuttal evidence consists of the defendant's own earlier characterization of himself that conflicts with the character evidence defendant offered at trial.[27]

The defendant does not open the door to an attack on his entire character by presenting evidence on only one aspect of character. If his character witnesses testify to his peaceable nature, the prosecutor cannot call rebuttal witnesses to testify to his dishonesty.

Rather than by calling rebuttal witnesses, the prosecutor usually elects to challenge the defense character evidence by cross-examining the character witnesses on specific instances of defendant's past conduct.[28] By offering character evidence, the accused opens the door to inquiry on events from his past that the prosecutor would otherwise be barred from mentioning.[29] As the Supreme Court has noted, "[t]he price a defendant must pay for attempting to prove his good name is to throw open the entire subject which the law has kept closed for his benefit and to make himself vulnerable where the law otherwise shields him."[30]

Because such cross-examination can be devastating, defendants seldom raise the issue of character unless full investigation of the likely counterproof persuades defense counsel that there is little in defendant's past that could be damaging or, if there is, character evidence is nonetheless critical to the defense.

On cross-examination, the prosecutor can inquire only about prior conduct of the defendant that is relevant to the trait of character about

---

25. United States v. Murphy, 768 F.2d 1518, 1535 (7th Cir. 1985) (in bribery prosecution where defendant put on a parade of character witnesses to establish his good character for honesty, proper for government witnesses to testify that he "had a reputation for dishonesty").

26. *See* FRE 405(a) discussed in §4.19, *infra*. *See also* United States v. Pantone, 609 F.2d 675, 680 (3d Cir. 1979) (in prosecution for kickback scheme, government could not rebut defense evidence of good character with proof that defendants took kickbacks other than those mentioned in the indictment because FRE 405 bars proof of "specific instances" except where character is an element).

27. United States v. Rising, 867 F.2d 1255, 1258 (10th Cir. 1989) (in prosecution for killing in prison where defendant presented evidence that he was "a peaceful, nonviolent person," proper for prosecutor to offer testimony that defendant had admitted that he "reacted violently" to homosexuals and to false charges that he was a homosexual).

28. Michelson v. United States, 335 U.S. 469, 479 (1948) (cross-examination is allowed to provide "tests of credibility" and to prevent accused "from profiting by a mere parade of partisans").

29. United States v. Alvarez, 860 F.2d 801, 826 (7th Cir. 1988) (after defendant presented character testimony on her "peacefulness and law abidance," proper to inquire of character witnesses whether they had heard that defendant (1) acquired resident status on the basis of a bogus marriage; (2) entered the country and remained as an illegal alien; (3) knew that her second husband was dealing in cocaine; and (4) was convicted of drug trafficking and helped her husband escape from prison), *cert. denied,* 493 U.S. 829.

30. Michelson v. United States, 335 U.S. 469, 479 (1948).

which the witness testified on direct.[31] The prosecutor must have a good-faith basis for each question asked, and the court may require disclosure of such foundation before permitting the question to be posed. A good-faith basis should be based on information from a person having first-hand knowledge, not merely on rumor or speculation.[32] The cross-examination of defense character witnesses must be regulated with care because merely by posing a question the prosecutor may "waft an unwarranted innuendo into the jury box."[33] The defendant is entitled to a jury instruction explaining the limited purpose for such inquiry.[34]

Discretion to disallow
The trial judge has discretion under FRE 403 and 611(a) to disallow questions that are unfairly prejudicial or otherwise improper.[35] The clear weight of authority disapproves questioning by the prosecutor designed to suggest that the opinion of the witness or his assessment of reputation would change if the defendant were in fact guilty of the charged crime.[36] Questions on incidents from the remote past may also be excluded.[37] Although *Michelson* allowed inquiry on defendant's prior arrests,[38] the better view is to permit such questioning only where there are additional facts demonstrating defendant's involvement in the underlying conduct.[39]

---

31. Aaron v. United States, 397 F.2d 584, 585 (5th Cir. 1968) (in embezzlement prosecution where accused introduced evidence that he had a reputation for "honesty and fair dealing," improper for prosecutor to ask on cross-examination whether witness had heard that defendant was dismissed from his bank job because of an affair with a woman).

32. See further discussion in §4.19, infra.

33. Michelson v. United States, 335 U.S. 469, 481 (1948).

34. Mullins v. United States, 487 F.2d 581 (8th Cir. 1973) (trial judge has "function of carefully instructing the jury as to the limited purpose of this type of evidence, which bears only on the impeachment of the character witness's testimony and is not to be taken and considered for any other purpose"). *Cf.* Michelson v. United States, 335 U.S. 469, 484-485 (1948) (recognizing importance of limiting instruction and danger that jury might misuse evidence).

35. United States v. Monteleone, 7 F.3d 1086, 1089-1091 (8th Cir. 1996) (reversible error to let government cross about instances in early 1970s when defendant allegedly perjured himself before grand jury, which was not likely to be known in the community).

36. United States v. Shwayder, 312 F.3d 1109, 1120-1121 (9th Cir. 2002) ("use of guilt assuming hypotheticals" in cross-examining defense character witnesses "undermines the presumption of innocence and thus violates the defendant's right to due process"); United States v. Williams, 738 F.2d 172, 177 (7th Cir. 1984) (such questions found objectionable because they "allowed the prosecution to foist its theory of the case repeatedly on the jury" and forced the character witnesses to speculate about a possible conviction).

37. Ewing v. Winans, 749 F.2d 607 (10th Cir. 1984) (proper to bar questioning about two earlier convictions of victim that were more than 30 years old, where defendant sought to suggest victim was aggressor).

38. Michelson v. United States, 335 U.S. 469, 481 (1948) (permitting inquiry about an arrest "whether or not it culminated in a conviction").

39. United States v. McCollom, 664 F.2d 56, 58 (5th Cir. 1981) (allowing inquiry of witness about prior arrest only because additional evidence indicated defendant's involvement in the underlying misconduct), *cert. denied*, 456 U.S. 934; State v. Kramp, 200 Mont. 383, 651 P.2d 614, 618 (1982) (in theft case, improper to cross-examine defense character witnesses about defendant's prior arrests because "an arrest record has no substance of itself to establish character"). *See generally* C. Mueller, *Of*

§4.13 —Crime Victim

As a second exception to the general rule against circumstantial use of character evidence to prove conduct on a particular occasion, FRE 404(a)(2) permits an accused to introduce evidence of a pertinent trait of character of a crime victim. For example, in an assault prosecution the accused may introduce evidence of the victim's propensity toward violence to prove that the victim was the aggressor.

If the accused introduces evidence of the character of the victim, the prosecutor may offer character evidence in rebuttal. In addition, if the defendant attacks the character of the alleged victim, the door is opened for the prosecutor to offer evidence bearing on the same trait of character of the defendant.[1]

The prosecutor may not be the first party to introduce character evidence pertaining to the victim except in one circumstance. In a homicide prosecution where the accused offers evidence that the victim was the first aggressor, the prosecutor may introduce evidence of the victim's peaceable character. The obvious reason for this narrow exception is that in a homicide case the victim is not available to rebut the defense claim that he was the first aggressor.

Although FRE 404(a)(2) as originally worded would permit evidence of the character of a rape victim on the issue of consent,[2] FRE 412 (which was enacted subsequently) largely closes off this possibility by narrowly restricting evidence of the prior sexual behavior of a sex crime victim.[3]

The character of the victim must be proved by reputation or opinion testimony rather than specific instances of conduct.[4] But independently of FRE 404(a)(2) an accused may be entitled to introduce evidence bearing on the victim's character (such as evidence of past threats or acts of violence by the victim known to the accused) on the issue of defendant's fear of the victim, which is in turn relevant in assessing a claim that defendant acted in reasonable self-defense.[5] Such evidence is not restricted by FRE 404(a)(2) because it is not offered to prove that the victim acted in accordance with his character,

No specific acts

Misshapen Stones and Compromises: Michelson and the Modern Law of Character Evidence, published in R. Lempert, Evidence Stories 75, 87 (2006) (criticizing practice of allowing cross-examination about arrests).

§4.13 1. The last sentence of FRE 404(a)(1) was added by an amendment effective December 1, 2000. Under the amended rule, if the defendant offers evidence of the alleged victim's character for violence (e.g., to support a self-defense claim), the prosecution may now offer evidence of the defendant's character for violence.

2. *See* ACN, FRE 404(a) (noting that FRE 404(a)(2) would permit "evidence of the character of the victim" offered to prove "consent in a case of rape").

3. *See* §4.32, *infra.*

4. *See* FRE 405(a) discussed in §4.19, *infra. See also* United States v. Talamante, 981 F.2d 1153, 1155 (10th Cir. 1992) (evidence of specific acts by victim not admissible to prove he was first aggressor).

5. United States v. Burks, 470 F.2d 432, 434-435 (D.C. Cir. 1972) (evidence of specific instances of victim's violent character known to the defendant may be admissible "on the issue of whether or not the defendant reasonably feared he was in danger of imminent great bodily injury").

but to prove the state of mind of the accused.[6] The admissibility of such evidence is governed by general principles of relevancy under FRE 401 and by FRE 403 and 404(b).[7]

§4.14 —Witness

FRE 404(a)(3) establishes a third exception to the general rule prohibiting evidence of character used to prove action in conformity with that character on a particular occasion. Such evidence may be received where admissible to impeach or rehabilitate the credibility of a witness under FRE 607, 608, or 609. Unlike the first two exceptions (which are limited to the character of the accused and of a crime victim in criminal proceedings), this exception applies to all party and nonparty witnesses in both civil and criminal cases.

Where evidence of the witness's character for honesty or dishonesty is admitted for impeachment or rehabilitation, it is being offered to prove that the witness is acting in conformity with that character at the time of giving testimony (by testifying truthfully or falsely). Because such circumstantial use of character evidence would otherwise be prohibited by FRE 404(a), the exception in FRE 404(a)(3) is needed to allow the Rules governing impeachment and rehabilitation to operate.

These Rules are discussed in more detail in a later chapter. They include FRE 608(a), which allows impeachment or rehabilitation by reputation or opinion evidence referring to the witness's character for truthfulness or untruthfulness;[1] FRE 608(b), which allows inquiry on cross-examination about prior specific instances of conduct of the witness if probative of truthfulness or untruthfulness;[2] FRE 609(a)(1), which authorizes impeachment of a witness by evidence of prior felony convictions subject to a balancing test;[3] and FRE 609(a)(2), which authorizes impeachment of a witness by evidence of prior convictions of felonies or misdemeanors involving dishonesty or false statement without a balancing test.[4]

---

6. An accused may also offer evidence of prior threats by the victim against the accused, whether or not such threats were communicated to the accused, as evidence that the victim may have acted on such threats. Under the *Hillmon* doctrine, a declarant's statement of intent is admissible to prove future conduct in accordance with such intent. *See* §8.39.

7. Government of Virgin Islands v. Carino, 631 F.2d 226, 229-230 (3d Cir. 1980) (in assault prosecution where defendant claimed self-defense, error to exclude evidence that alleged victim had previously been convicted of manslaughter and that this fact was known by defendant; defendant's knowledge of victim's conviction "was admissible under Rule 404(b) to show fear or state of mind").

§4.14 1. *See* §6.23 *and* §6.50, *infra.*

2. *See* §§6.25-6.28, *infra.*

3. *See* §6.29, *infra.*

4. *See* §6.32, *infra.*

FRE 404(b)

Other crimes, wrongs, or acts. Evidence of other crimes, wrongs, or acts is not admissible to prove the character of a person in order to show action in conformity therewith. It may, however, be admissible for other purposes, such as proof of motive, opportunity, intent, preparation, plan, knowledge, identity, or absence of mistake or accident, provided that upon request by the accused, the prosecution in a criminal case shall provide reasonable notice in advance of trial, or during trial if the court excuses pretrial notice on good cause shown, of the general nature of any such evidence it intends to introduce at trial.

§4.15   Prior Wrongs to Prove Specific Points

FRE 404(b) restates the exclusionary principle of FRE 404(a) that evidence of other crimes, wrongs, or acts is inadmissible to prove the character of a person in order to show conduct in conformity therewith on a particular occasion. However, FRE 404(b) expressly permits evidence of prior crimes, wrongs, or acts to be introduced for other diverse purposes, including proof of "motive, opportunity, intent, preparation, plan, knowledge, identity, or absence of mistake or accident."[1]

The Rule adopts an inclusionary rather than exclusionary approach making evidence of prior crimes, wrongs, or acts potentially admissible, subject to FRE 403, where offered for any relevant purpose that does not require an inference from character to conduct.[2] Thus FRE 404(b) does not require the proponent to force the evidence into a particular listed pigeonhole but only to show a relevant purpose other than proving conduct by means of the general propensity inference ("he's a drug dealer, so he probably sold drugs this time"). However, the specific purpose must be identified and the jury instructed to limit its consideration of the evidence to this purpose.[3] Appellate courts have held that it is not sufficient for the proponent merely to cite the litany of possible uses listed in FRE 404(b).[4]

Nonexclusive listing

---

§4.15   1. For cases admitting evidence for these limited purposes, *see* §4.17, *infra.*

2. United States v. Watford, 894 F.2d 665, 671 (4th Cir. 1990) (FRE 404(b) is a rule of inclusion that "allows admission of evidence of other acts relevant to an issue at trial except that which proves only criminal disposition").

3. United States v. Tai, 994 F.2d 1204, 1211 (7th Cir. 1993) (trial judge instructed jury about all listed uses of FRE 404(b) evidence; instructions were in error "to the extent they informed the jury that the extrinsic act evidence could be considered for purposes other than the proper purposes for which it was admitted").

4. United States v. Sampson, 980 F.2d 883, 888 (3d Cir. 1992) (record must clearly show purpose for which prior act evidence admitted; "a mere listing of the purposes found in FRE 404(b) is insufficient"); United States v. Mehrmanesh, 689 F.2d 822, 830 (9th Cir. 1982) (government "must articulate precisely the evidential hypothesis by which a fact of consequence may be inferred from the other acts evidence").

FRE 404(b) determinations are among the most frequently appealed of all evidentiary rulings, and erroneous admission of other acts evidence is one of the most frequent grounds for reversal of criminal convictions.[5] The proliferation of appeals is attributable to the highly prejudicial nature of evidence offered under FRE 404(b), particularly where it involves prior crimes or wrongs of a criminally accused.[6] Where the trial court erroneously admits evidence under FRE 404(b), such error is more likely to be prejudicial than other types of evidentiary error.[7]

"Reverse" FRE 404(b) evidence

In criminal cases, FRE 404(b) evidence is usually offered by the prosecutor. However, defendants are also entitled to introduce what is sometimes called "reverse" 404(b) evidence,[8] particularly where misconduct by a third person tends to show that he, and not the defendant, was the perpetrator of the crime.[9] Although defense evidence offered under FRE 404(b) is also subject to FRE 403, the risk of prejudice is significantly less than when such evidence is offered by the prosecution because the third person is not a party and cannot be the object of an angry or vengeful verdict.[10]

Application in civil cases

Although FRE 404(b) is most frequently invoked in criminal prosecutions, it also applies in civil cases.[11] For example, evidence of prior misconduct has been admitted in civil cases to prove improper motive,[12]

---

5. *See* Imwinkelried, Uncharged Misconduct Evidence 1:04, at 8 (1984); Patterson, Evidence of Prior Bad Acts: Admissibility Under the Federal Rules, 38 Baylor L. Rev. 331 (1986); Weissenberger, Making Sense of Extrinsic Act Evidence: Federal Rule of Evidence 404(b), 70 Iowa L. Rev. 579 (1985).

6. *See* DiBiagio, Intrinsic and Extrinsic Evidence in Federal Criminal Trials: Is the Admission of Collateral Other-Crimes Evidence Disconnected to the Fundamental Right to a Fair Trial? 47 Syr. L. Rev. 1229 (1997).

7. United States v. Sanders, 964 F.2d 295, 298-299 (4th Cir. 1992) (in assault prosecution involving directly conflicting evidence, reversible error to allow evidence of prior assault conviction, which could only show defendant's "propensity to commit assaults on other prisoners or his general propensity to commit violent crimes" and "obviously has the capacity to tip the balance" in the jury's deliberations); Government of Virgin Islands v. Toto, 529 F.2d 278, 283 (3d Cir. 1976) (reversing for erroneous admission of prior act evidence; "A drop of ink cannot be removed from a glass of milk.").

8. United States v. Herrera, 600 F.2d 502, 505 (5th Cir. 1979) (evidence of a "systematic campaign of threats and intimidation" by third person may be admissible under FRE 404(b) "to support a defendant's defense of duress").

9. United States v. Stevens, 935 F.2d 1380, 1401-1406 (3d Cir. 1991) (where defendant charged with aggravated sexual assault and robbery on a military base claimed mistaken identity, reversible error to exclude testimony that a different man who resembled defendant committed a similar crime on the same base under very similar circumstances).

10. United States v. Cohen, 888 F.2d 770, 777 (11th Cir. 1989) ("normal risk of prejudice" is absent when defendant offers evidence of third-party misconduct).

11. *See, e.g.,* Bonilla v. Yamaha Motors Corp., 955 F.2d 150, 154 (1st Cir. 1992) (recognizing applicability of FRE 404(b) in civil context, although here court excludes evidence).

12. Roshan v. Fard, 705 F.2d 102, 104-106 (4th Cir. 1983) (civil action arising out of altercation in a bar; error to exclude defense evidence that plaintiff had been convicted of a crime where defendant had acted as an informant because such evidence tended to demonstrate plaintiff's motive to initiate assault).

notice,[13] a wrongful "pattern or practice,"[14] and discriminatory[15] or fraudulent[16] intent.

Prior conduct may be proved under FRE 404(b) even where it is not a crime and even where it is not wrongful.[17] But courts tend to analyze the admissibility of prior conduct that is not wrongful under the more general standards of FRE 401 and 403 rather than FRE 404(b).

Nature and timing of prior act

FRE 404(b) requires only that the prior act have logical relevancy, not that it necessarily be similar in nature to the charged crime.[18] For some uses of prior act evidence, such as showing motive, similarity is not required. For other uses, such as proving intent or knowledge similarity is generally necessary to establish probative value. When offered to prove modus operandi, the prior act must have a high degree of distinctive similarity in order to show that the charged offense bears the "trademark" or "signature" of the accused.[19]

The "other" crimes, wrongs, or acts admissible under FRE 404(b) need not have occurred prior to the time of the crime or other event at issue in the trial. Conduct occurring after the charged offense is sometimes relevant to prove points such as knowledge or intent.[20]

Often the charged crime is connected with other criminal acts. Where it is hard or impossible to prove one without proving or at least exposing the other, courts aptly say the various acts are "inextricably intertwined." For example, proof that a defendant sold contraband usually requires proof that he possessed it.

"Inextricably intertwined" acts

Where crimes truly are inextricably intertwined, courts generally hold that FRE 404(b) does not apply, on the theory that the uncharged crime is not an extrinsic offense or "other" crime[21] but is instead simply

---

13. Fiacco v. City of Rensselaer, 783 F.2d 319, 328 (2d Cir. 1986) (in negligence action against city, proper to admit evidence of prior complaints of police brutality because "such claims put City on notice that there was a possibility that its police officers had used excessive force"), *cert. denied,* 480 U.S. 922.

14. Dosier v. Miami Valley Broadcasting Corp., 656 F.2d 1295, 1300-1301 (9th Cir. 1981) (instances of alleged racial discrimination may be used "to establish the existence of a pattern or scheme" under FRE 404(b)).

15. Miller v. Poretsky, 595 F.2d 780, 784 (D.C. Cir. 1978) (prior acts of alleged racial discrimination relevant to prove "landlord's motive").

16. Edgar v. Fred Jones Lincoln-Mercury, Inc., 524 F.2d 162, 164-167 (10th Cir. 1975) (in fraud action alleging an odometer rollback on car, error to exclude evidence of prior similar acts to show "knowledge or intent").

17. United States v. Rubio-Gonzalez, 674 F.2d 1067, 1075 (5th Cir. 1982) (fact that records did not show appellant's prior conduct to be criminal "is immaterial").

18. *See* United States v. Vest, 842 F.2d 1319, 1327 n.6 (1st Cir. 1988) (" '[S]imilarity' is not a general requirement for admissibility under Rule 404(b)."), *cert. denied,* 488 U.S. 965.

19. *See* §4.17, *infra.*

20. United States v. Brugman, 364 F.3d 613, 619-620 (5th Cir. 2004) (in trial of border patrol agent for deprivation of rights under color of law, admitting evidence of later instance in which defendant beat a person who was not resisting apprehension as proof of intent).

21. United States v. Dula, 989 F.2d 772, 777 (5th Cir. 1993) (evidence of an uncharged offense "arising out of the same transaction or series of transactions as the charged offense" is not an "extrinsic offense" within the meaning of Rule 404(b) and "is therefore not barred by the rule").

part of the proof of the charged offense.[22] There is some confusion and imprecision on this point, however. Courts sometimes erroneously use the "inextricably intertwined" label to describe prior crimes that are separate in place and time and should more properly be categorized as extrinsic.[23] While FRE 404(b) is inapplicable to acts necessarily included in the charged offense, its standards and safeguards do apply to crimes more loosely connected to the charged offense and offered to provide background and context.[24]

Proving prior crimes or wrongs

The most certain way of proving a prior crime under FRE 404(b) is by evidence of a criminal conviction, whether based on a verdict or guilty plea. Convictions have been held admissible under FRE 404(b) even where based on a plea of nolo contendere, although the better practice in such cases is to prove the underlying acts.[25] Juvenile adjudications may be admitted[26] as well as convictions in courts of foreign nations, provided the defendant was granted procedural protections essential to fundamental fairness.[27]

Prior crimes may be proved under FRE 404(b) even where there has been no conviction and where prosecution would be barred by a grant of immunity or the running of the statute of limitations.[28] The government may prove a defendant's involvement in a prior crime even in cases where the defendant has been acquitted because an acquittal establishes only the presence of reasonable doubt rather than a specific

22. United States v. Williams, 291 F.3d 1180, 1189 (9th Cir. 2002) (in trial for inducing women to travel interstate for prostitution, admitting proof of violent assaults; these were not elements in the crime, but were the "means by which Defendant maintained the necessary control," so they were "necessarily part of the transactions and therefore were inextricably intertwined"); United States v. Bettelyoun, 892 F.2d 744, 746-747 (8th Cir. 1989) (evidence that defendant assaulted mother of his child one hour before killing his current lover admissible as an "integral part of the operative facts of the crime charged and as such is not governed by Rule 404(b)").

23. *See, e.g.,* United States v. Strong, 485 F.3d 985, 990 (7th Cir. 2007) (in felon-in-possession of firearm prosecution, finding evidence of "contemporaneous uncharged drug trafficking" admissible under "inextricably intertwined doctrine").

24. United States v. Bowie, 232 F.3d 923, 927-929 (D.C. Cir. 2000) (caution warranted, because bifurcating universe into "intrinsic" and "extrinsic" evidence is difficult, and "bypasses Rule 404(b) and its attendant notice requirement" while carrying "implicit finding that the evidence is admissible for all purposes, notwithstanding its bearing on character"). *See also* §4.18, *infra.*

25. United States v. Frederickson, 601 F.2d 1358, 1368 n.10 (8th Cir. 1979) (in applying FRE 404(b) court finds "no reason to distinguish between a judgment of conviction based on a plea of nolo contendere and a judgment of conviction obtained in any other manner"), *cert. denied,* 444 U.S. 934. *Contra* United States v. Wyatt, 762 F.2d 908, 911 (11th Cir. 1985).

26. United States v. Rogers, 918 F.2d 207, 210-211 (D.C. Cir. 1990) (FRE 609(d) does not bar juvenile adjudications from being introduced under FRE 404(b)).

27. United States v. Rodarte, 596 F.2d 141, 146 (5th Cir. 1979) (proper to admit prior Mexican drug conviction because "foreign convictions stand on the same footing as domestic proceedings" provided that foreign jurisdiction observes necessary procedural protections). *See generally* Comment, The Collateral Use of Foreign Convictions in American Criminal Trials, 47 U. Chi. L. Rev. 82 (1979).

28. *See, e.g.,* United States v. DeFiore, 720 F.2d 757, 764 (2d Cir. 1983) (no error to admit evidence of prior tax frauds even though prosecution barred by statute of limitations), *cert. denied,* 467 U.S. 1241.

determination that the defendant was not involved in the earlier crime.[29] Evidence of a prior crime resulting in an acquittal has considerable probative value in cases where a defendant claims lack of knowledge of the unlawful nature of his conduct, and the prior unsuccessful prosecution tends to rebut such a claim.[30] Nonetheless, the fact of acquittal is a factor properly considered in deciding whether prior acts evidence should be excluded under FRE 403.[31]

Evidence of arrests or charges is generally not admissible to prove crimes or misconduct under FRE 404(b) because such evidence by itself is insufficient to establish that the underlying conduct occurred.[32] Also, evidence of charges raises hearsay concerns if offered to prove the underlying conduct, and evidence of arrests as such usually carries hidden hearsay if such arrests amount to official action based on reports by others.[33]

At one time, many federal courts required proof by clear and convincing evidence that a defendant committed the prior crime, wrong, or act before evidence thereof could be presented to the jury.[34] However, in *Huddleston v. United States*,[35] the Supreme Court approved a significantly lower standard requiring only evidence sufficient to support a jury finding by a preponderance of the evidence that the wrongful conduct occurred.[36] Under *Huddleston*, the question whether the prior misconduct occurred is ultimately resolved by the jury under FRE 104(b), with the trial court retaining discretion to exclude evidence of the

Standard of proof

---

29. United States v. Dowling, 493 U.S. 342, 347-354 (1990) (neither Double Jeopardy nor Due Process Clause prevents prosecutor from offering evidence of prior misconduct by accused even though he has been tried and acquitted of such misconduct; receipt of such evidence does not violate notion of "fundamental fairness" because jury remains free to weigh probative value of evidence and defendant to refute it). However, a number of states bar proof of crimes of which defendant was acquitted under their counterparts of FRE 404(b). *See, e.g.*, State v. Wakefield, 278 N.W.2d 307, 308-309 (Minn. 1979) (admission of crimes of which defendant has been acquitted "prejudices and burdens" defendant and is "fundamentally unfair"); State v. Perkins, 349 So. 2d 161, 163 (Fla. 1977) (finding it "fundamentally unfair to a defendant to admit evidence of acquitted crimes").

30. *See, e.g.*, United States v. Rocha, 553 F.2d 615, 616 (9th Cir. 1977) (in prosecution for illegally transporting marijuana in furniture, defendant claimed lack of knowledge; court approves admission of earlier incident where defendant was prosecuted for transporting marijuana in furniture, even though he was acquitted based on his asserted lack of knowledge).

31. United States v. Day, 591 F.2d 861, 869 n.19 (D.C. Cir. 1978) (fact of acquittal is one factor to be considered in applying FRE 403 to prior act evidence).

32. F.D.I.C. v. Bakkebo, 506 F.3d 286, 296 (4th Cir. 2007) (indictment is not admissible to prove prior wrong under FRE 404(b)).

33. Butler v. Oak Creek-Franklin Sch. Dist., 172 F. Supp. 2d 1102, 1124 (7th Cir. 2001) (neither arrest nor charges may be used to prove prior acts under FRE 404(b), because neither suffices to prove that defendant committed the acts).

34. *See, e.g.*, United States v. Weber, 818 F.2d 14, 14 (8th Cir. 1987); United States v. Vaccaro, 816 F.2d 443, 452 (9th Cir. 1987), *cert. denied*, 484 U.S. 914.

35. 485 U.S. 681 (1988).

36. 485 U.S. at 685. The lower standard had been previously recognized by some courts. *See, e.g.*, United States v. Beechum, 582 F.2d 898 (5th Cir. 1978), *cert. denied*, 440 U.S. 920.

prior act if the evidence falls short of establishing this fact by a preponderance.[37]

Huddleston seems wrong to view prior acts evidence as raising fact questions for a jury to decide under FRE 104(b) and to ignore the danger of allowing highly prejudicial evidence of defendant's alleged misconduct to come before the jury when the prosecutor has not even persuaded the trial court that such misconduct occurred.[38] The concerns raised by the *Huddleston* standard can be mitigated in part by careful application of FRE 403. The less certainty there is that the prior misconduct occurred, or that defendant was the actor, the greater the justification for exclusion under FRE 403. States remain free to determine the required evidentiary threshold under their counterparts of FRE 404(b), and many have refused to adopt the lenient *Huddleston* standard.[39]

Notice requirement
FRE 404(b) requires that the prosecution, on request by an accused,[40] provide pretrial notice of any evidence it intends to introduce under FRE 404(b). The notice requirement "does not extend to evidence of acts which are 'intrinsic' to the charged offense."[41] The time and form of notice are left undefined but must be reasonable under the circumstances of the case.[42] If the prosecutor fails to comply

---

37. *See* 485 U.S. *supra*, at 689-690. In cases where the issue is contested, the court should inform the jury that it should not consider the prior crime or act unless it finds by a preponderance of the evidence that defendant in fact committed it.

38. In January 1989, the American Bar Association passed a resolution disapproving the result in *Huddleston*. *See* 3 BNA Criminal Practice Manual 75 (Feb. 22, 1989) (recommending that "1. Questions of preliminary fact regarding the admissibility of evidence of extrinsic act will be determined by the court; and 2. The existence of any preliminary fact required as a precondition to the admission of evidence of the extrinsic act must be demonstrated by the proponent by clear and convincing evidence."). *See also* Ordover, Balancing the Presumptions of Guilt and Innocence: Rules 404(b), 608(b) and 609(a), 38 Emory L.J. 135 (1989) (calling for legislative amendment to overturn result in *Huddleston*).

39. *See, e.g.,* State v. Cofield, 127 N.J. 328, 605 A.2d 230, 234-235 (1992) (evidence of other crimes "must be clear and convincing"); Daniels v. United States, 613 A.2d 342, 347 (D.C. 1992); Phillips v. State, 591 So. 2d 987, 989 (Fla. 1991); People v. Garner, 806 P.2d 366, 370-374 (Colo. 1991) (rejecting *Huddleston* analysis and adopting preponderance standard; whether prior crime occurred is question for court under Rule 104(a)); Pena v. State, 780 P.2d 316 (Wyo. 1989) (one factor for determining admissibility is whether "[t]he proof of the other similar crimes is plain, clear and convincing"). *But see* State v. Wheel, 587 A.2d 933, 943 (Vt. 1990) (adopting *Huddleston* analysis).

40. United States v. Tuesta-Toro, 29 F.3d 771, 774 (1st Cir. 1994) (defense request must be "sufficiently clearly and particular" to alert prosecution that defense is invoking right to pretrial notification under FRE 404(b)).

41. ACN to 1991 amendment. *See also* United States v. Severe, 29 F.3d 444, 447 (8th Cir. 1994) (admitting testimony describing earlier drug deliveries by defendants; acts were inextricably intertwined with charged conspiracy so notice requirement of FRE 404(b) did not apply).

42. ACN to 1991 amendment (counsel are expected "to submit the necessary request and information in a reasonable and timely fashion," which will "depend largely on the circumstances of each case"). *See also* United States v. Perez-Tosta, 36 F.3d 1552, 1560-1562 (11th Cir. 1994) (notice immediately before trial sufficed, where government only recently learned of potential evidence, evidence was significant, and no prejudice to defendant shown).

with the notice requirement, the offered evidence is to be excluded.[43] The notice requirement is a continuing one that extends to newly discovered evidence.[44]

Particularly in criminal cases, an instruction should normally be given informing the jury of the limited purpose for which evidence has been admitted under FRE 404(b),[45] and in some circumstances failure to give such a limiting instruction may amount to plain error. It is not proper for the instruction merely to cite the litany of permissible purposes listed in FRE 404(b).[46]

Instructing jury

FRE 404(b) must be distinguished from FRE 608(b), which permits, in the discretion of the court, impeachment or rehabilitation of a witness by inquiry into prior instances of conduct bearing on the "truthfulness" of the witness. FRE 608(b) is limited to impeachment or rehabilitation of witnesses. It cannot be used against a party who does not take the stand, and it paves the way only for questions about conduct that bears on veracity (such as prior false statements). Finally, FRE 608(b) authorizes only questions to the witness whose veracity is in issue, and it expressly prohibits extrinsic evidence of conduct (such as testimony by another witness). FRE 404(b) contains no such limitations.

Comparison with FRE 608(b)

§4.16 Discretion to Exclude Prior Wrongs

The proponent of evidence under FRE 404(b) has the burden of identifying a relevant purpose that does not involve the prohibited inference from character to conduct.[1] Adversarial incentives predictably generate pretextual purposes that courts reject,[2] and proponents must be ready to show that the probative force of the evidence on the specific point for which it is offered is sufficient to offset the danger of illegitimate use by the trier of fact as mere propensity evidence. In addition, the proponent has the burden of producing evidence

43. United States v. Carrasco, 381 F.3d 1237, 1241 (11th Cir. 2004) (reversible error to admit prior convictions on issue of intent when government failed to give proper notice and matter of intent "went to heart" of the defense).

44. United States v. Barnes, 49 F.3d 1144, 1148 (6th Cir. 1995) (government has continuing obligation to disclose evidence discovered after previous request was answered).

45. United States v. Nabors, 761 F.2d 465, 470-471 (8th Cir. 1985) (when admitting prior acts evidence, a "cautionary instruction" to the jury should be given), *cert. denied*, 474 U.S. 851.

46. United States v. Sampson, 980 F.2d 883, 889 (3d Cir. 1992) (error found where jury instruction simply recited FRE 404(b) and failed to limit government to specific theories offered in support of admission of prior acts evidence).

§4.16 1. United States v. Birch, 39 F.3d 1089, 1093-1094 (10th Cir. 1994) (in prosecution for assaulting federal officer, error to admit two prior convictions for battery on law enforcement officers since government failed to provide specific articulation of proper purpose for such evidence).

2. Kunz v. DeFelice, 2008 WL 3483442 (7th Cir. 2008) (in §1983 action against police, proper to exclude prior theft conviction of plaintiff offered to prove a consistent pattern of criminality; court finds this is simply "propensity by another name").

sufficient to support a finding by a preponderance that the defendant (or other alleged actor) did the prior act.[3]

Even where the proponent satisfies all the requirements of FRE 404(b), however, the evidence is still subject to exclusion under FRE 403.[4] The net effect of FRE 404(b) is to invite the careful exercise of judicial discretion when evidence of prior acts is offered,[5] and the objecting party should cite both FRE 404(b) and FRE 403 to be certain of preserving any claim of error.[6]

Nine factors

There are at least nine factors to be considered by the court in undertaking the required FRE 403 balancing:

(1) *Extent to which point to be proved is disputed.* Courts often limit FRE 404(b) evidence to issues on which the evidence actually conflicts.[7] The more strongly an issue is contested, the greater the justification for admitting other act evidence bearing on the point.[8] Sometimes notice of contest is provided by a defendant's opening statement, thereby opening the door to proof of prior acts during the government's case-in-chief.[9] Courts may require the government to delay introduction of prior crimes evidence until the end of its case when it is clearer

---

3. *See* §4.15, *supra. See also* United States v. Wright, 943 F.2d 748, 751-752 (7th Cir. 1991) (adopting four-part test requiring trial judge to determine whether the evidence (1) relates to a matter in issue other than general propensity; (2) proves an act that is similar enough and close enough in time to be relevant; (3) suffices to support a jury finding that the act happened and that defendant committed it; and (4) possesses probative value that is not outweighed by the risk of unfair prejudice).

4. *See, e.g.,* United States v. Harvey, 845 F.2d 760, 762-763 (8th Cir. 1988) (in tax fraud prosecution, reversible error to admit defendant's statement that he had imported drugs ten years earlier and invested the profits in the Cayman Islands; such conduct was "both dissimilar and remote from the charged offense" and the evidence was "highly prejudicial and could have been offered in reality only to prove [defendant] had a criminal past"). For a discussion of FRE 403, *see* §§4.9-4.10, *supra.*

5. Weissenberger, Making Sense of Extrinsic Act Evidence: Federal Rule of Evidence 404(b), 70 Iowa L. Rev. 579, 607-611 (1985) (propensity inference arising from specific act evidence is difficult to rebut even though inaccurate; therefore, specific acts from which propensity might be inferred should be scrutinized with special attention to avoid unfairness); Teitelbaum & Hertz, Evidence II: Evidence of Other Crimes as Proof of Intent, 13 N.M.L. Rev. 423 (1983); Imwinkelried, The Need to Amend Federal Rule of Evidence 404(b): The Threat to the Future of the Federal Rules of Evidence, 30 Vill. L. Rev. 1465, 1497 (1985) (FRE 404(b) raises such dangers of prejudice that it should be amended to shift the burden to the prosecutor to show that the probative value of the evidence outweighs its prejudice).

6. United States v. Acosta-Cazares, 878 F.2d 945, 950 n.3 (6th Cir. 1989) (objection citing only FRE 404(b) held insufficient to preserve error under FRE 403), *cert. denied,* 493 U.S. 899.

7. United States v. Sumner, 119 F.3d 658, 662 (8th Cir. 1997) (in sex abuse prosecution, error to admit evidence of prior sex abuse conviction to prove "intent" when defendant did not dispute intent but relied solely on defense that alleged criminal act did not occur and made no denial or arguments concerning his mental state).

8. United States v. Mills, 895 F.2d 897, 907 (2d Cir. 1990) (in prosecution for counterfeiting conspiracy, evidence that defendant previously had "intentionally engaged in counterfeiting activity" was properly admitted where defendant raised issue of intent in his opening statement to the jury), *cert. denied,* 495 U.S. 951.

9. United States v. Estabrook, 774 F.2d 284, 289 (8th Cir. 1985) (where it is "made clear at the outset" that lack of knowledge is principal defense, government "may take the defendant at his word and introduce the evidence in its case-in-chief").

what issues are actually contested.[10] Defendants sometimes can eliminate any contest by admitting or stipulating to the point the prosecutor seeks to prove,[11] a subject discussed further below.

(2) *The adequacy of proof of the prior misconduct.* The strongest form of proof that a prior crime occurred is a properly certified conviction. Although other forms of proof are permissible, they require closer scrutiny. Despite the lenient standard established in *Huddleston* requiring only evidence sufficient to support a finding of prior misconduct,[12] there is increased justification for exclusion under FRE 403 where the government's proof is weak. The inevitable risk of prejudice to the accused merits greater weight if there is substantial doubt that such misconduct occurred.

(3) *Probative force of the evidence.* Some prior acts have only marginal relevance on the point to be proved, while others have strong probative force. The strength of the evidence in establishing the point it is offered to prove is properly considered by courts in undertaking FRE 403 balancing. Courts have discretion to exclude prior acts where their remoteness in time diminishes probative force.[13]

(4) *Proponent's need for the evidence.* The proponent's need for the evidence is an important factor considered by courts in deciding the admissibility of FRE 404(b) evidence.[14] If the evidence is offered on a minor point or is cumulative of evidence already introduced, exclusion is more likely.[15]

(5) *Availability of less prejudicial proof.* Even if evidence is needed on the point to be proved, the court must consider the availability of alternative forms of proof less prejudicial to the accused.[16]

(6) *Inflammatory or prejudicial effect.* Clearly the most important factor is the risk of unfair prejudice, and this risk is most acute in criminal

10. United States v. Hadaway, 681 F.2d 214, 218-219 (4th Cir. 1982) (reasonable for trial court to require government "to delay presentation of the other crimes evidence until the end of its case" because evidence coming in earlier "might be followed by additional evidence which would establish intent beyond a reasonable doubt" and therefore prove "not only quite unnecessary but highly prejudicial as well").

11. United States v. Schwartz, 790 F.2d 1059, 1061-1062 (3d Cir. 1986) (error to admit evidence of other crimes where defendant had offered a "sweeping stipulation"; "absence of a genuine need for the questioned evidence is a legitimate part of the balancing analysis required by [FRE] 403").

12. Huddleston v. United States, 485 U.S. 681 (1988), discussed in §4.15, *supra.*

13. United States v. Fields, 871 F.2d 188, 198 (1st Cir. 1989) (where acts offered under FRE 404(b) are remote in time, this "substantially weakens their probative value" and "weighs in favor of exclusion," especially in cases where the evidence is offered to prove intent), *cert. denied,* 493 U.S. 955.

14. United States v. Vance, 871 F.2d 572, 576 (6th Cir. 1989) ("An important indication of probative value of evidence is the prosecution's need for the evidence in proving its case."), *cert. denied,* 493 U.S. 933.

15. United States v. Dolliole, 597 F.2d 102, 106 (7th Cir. 1979) ("When the government has ample evidence to establish an element of the crime, the probative value of the prior crime evidence is greatly reduced, and the risk of prejudice which accompanies the admission of such evidence will not be justified."), *cert. denied,* 422 U.S. 946.

16. Old Chief v. United States, 117 S. Ct. 644, 652 (1997) (availability of alternative forms of proof lowers "probative value" of proffered evidence and must be considered in FRE 403 balancing).

cases where the government offers proof of prior misconduct by the defendant. Sometimes the risk comes from the shocking, heinous, or morally repugnant nature of prior acts (like killings or violence, sexual assaults or abuse of children or defenseless people), and the fear is that juries may be so angered that they ignore doubts or are so distracted that they become careless in appraising other evidence that is more important on the question of guilt or innocence.[17] Sometimes the risk comes from the fact that the evidence shows the defendant to be a frequent offender or a bad person,[18] and the fear is that juries may misuse the evidence by deciding to convict despite doubts believing he should be penalized or removed from society regardless whether he committed the charged offense.

Courts have discretion to admit prior acts evidence only in part, barring the most prejudicial aspects and striking sordid or inflammatory details.[19] When multiple counts are charged or several defendants are joined, the prejudice of prior bad act evidence can sometimes be avoided by granting a severance.[20]

(7) *Similarity to charged crime.* Ironically, the risk of unfair prejudice sometimes increases even as probative worth increases. For at least some legitimate evidential uses, prior acts that closely resemble the charged offense may have greater relevance than prior acts that are different in important ways. But the very resemblance to the charged offense also increases the risk that juries may misuse evidence of prior acts by convicting the defendant as a bad person or deciding that the prior acts prove the charged offense simply because they support the one inference that FRE 404 forbids: He did it before, so he probably did it this time, too.[21]

(8) *Effectiveness of limiting instructions.* In deciding whether to admit proof of other offenses, courts also consider whether a limiting instruction is likely to be effective in mitigating the prejudicial effect

---

17. United States v. Harvey, 991 F.2d 981, 996 (2d Cir. 1993) (in trial for receiving child pornography, reversible error to admit X-rated material involving adults and bestiality, sadomasochism, and gross acts with human waste; government did not need to introduce other types of pornography for which defendant was not charged, and such material was highly likely to inflame jury).

18. United States v. Hodges, 770 F.2d 1475, 1479 (9th Cir. 1985) (other acts evidence "creates a significant danger that the jury will draw the impermissible inference that because [defendant] acted ruthlessly and with greed on a much later occasion, he must have knowingly committed the earlier [charged] fraudulent acts").

19. United States v. Green, 648 F.2d 587 (9th Cir. 1981) (proper to admit evidence of defendant's prior drug dealing, but not evidence that he was known as the "Acid King" of California").

20. *See* United States v. Lewis, 787 F.2d 1318, 1323 (9th Cir. 1986) (in trial where defendant charged with killing to obtain a getaway vehicle but where evidence against him was "weak," failure to sever charge of being a felon in possession of a firearm "manifestly prejudiced [defendant's] chance for acquittal on the killing charge"), *amended,* 798 F.2d 1250 (9th Cir. 1986).

21. Government of Virgin Islands v. Pinney, 967 F.2d 912 (3d Cir. 1992) (in prosecution for rape of seven-year-old girl, error to admit testimony by her thirteen-year-old sister that defendant also raped sister when she was six).

of such evidence.[22] The greater the likelihood of jury confusion between the permissible and impermissible uses of FRE 404(b) evidence, the stronger the argument for exclusion under FRE 403.[23]

(9) *Extent to which prior act evidence prolongs proceedings.* In undertaking the FRE 403 balancing, courts properly consider the extent to which other acts evidence will consume time or prolong the proceedings. Obviously more trial time is required if the other acts have to be proved by extrinsic evidence than if they are conceded by the party against whom they are offered. Extrinsic proof, if required, can range from the simple introduction of a prior conviction to eliciting extensive testimony from multiple witnesses.

Findings

Appellate courts have encouraged trial judges to make express findings in performing the required balancing of probative worth against unfair prejudice under FRE 404(b) and 403.[24] Most reviewing courts, however, stop short of formally requiring such findings[25] although some require trial judges to make findings if requested by defendants in criminal cases.[26]

Stipulations or admissions

In some cases, defendants may admit or offer to stipulate to certain points in order to avoid the prejudice that would result from the prosecutor introducing evidence of defendant's prior wrongs to prove such points. In one type of case, prosecution for illegal possession of a firearm by a convicted felon, the Supreme Court in *Old Chief v. United States* found error where the trial judge refused to accept the defendant's offer to stipulate to his status as a convicted felon and instead allowed the government to prove the nature of the prior conviction.[27]

Although the Court made clear that its holding was confined to this particular type of prosecution,[28] the opinion included as dictum a generalized discussion of the use of stipulations and the application of

---

22. Government of Virgin Islands v. Pinney, 967 F.2d 912, 918 (3d Cir. 1992) (error to admit evidence of prior crime despite limiting instructions because "risk that jurors will not follow the court's instructions is unacceptably high").

23. *See generally* Ordover, Balancing the Presumptions of Guilt and Innocence: Rules 404(b), 608(b) and 609(a), 38 Emory L.J. 135, 152-153 (1989).

24. Government of Virgin Islands v. Pinney, 967 F.2d 912, 918 (3d Cir. 1992) (conviction reversed because trial court "did not explain why it was denying defendant's motion under Rule 403 and the reason for doing so is not otherwise apparent from the record").

25. United States v. De La Cruz, 902 F.2d 121, 123 (1st Cir. 1990) ("[E]xplicit findings need not always be made.").

26. United States v. Ridlehuber, 11 F.3d 516, 521 (5th Cir. 1993) (if defendant requests on-the-record findings, failing to make them requires remand unless factors on which probative value and prejudice depend are readily apparent and there is no uncertainty about correctness of ruling).

27. 117 S. Ct. 644 (1997) (in prosecution for assault with dangerous weapon and possession by convicted felon of a firearm, defendant offered to stipulate that he was a convicted felon and to have jury instructed that this element of charge was satisfied without informing them of nature of prior offense, which was a conviction for felony assault causing bodily injury; it was an abuse of discretion under FRE 403 for trial judge to refuse this stipulation because of danger of unnecessary and unfair prejudice to defendant; availability of alternative and less prejudicial forms of proof such as stipulation offered here must be considered in FRE 403 balancing).

28. *Id.* at 651 n.7 ("[O]ur holding is limited to cases involving proof of felon status").

FRE 403 in criminal prosecutions.[29] The Court noted the "general presumption that the prosecution may choose its evidence"[30] and announced the unexceptionable proposition that "the prosecutor's choice will generally survive a Rule 403 analysis when a defendant seeks to force the substitution of an admission for evidence creating a coherent narrative of his thought and actions in perpetrating the offense for which he is being tried."[31] Certainly a defendant cannot prevent a jury from hearing a rape victim's testimony by stipulating that she was raped by someone or block introduction of the physical and testimonial evidence typically used to prove a bank robbery by stipulating that the bank was in fact robbed. And it has long been the rule that stipulations are inappropriate where they would leave chronological or contextual gaps in a party's proof or deny a party the legitimate moral force of its evidence.[32]

Application of FRE 403

But nothing in *Old Chief* limits application of FRE 403 to FRE 404(b) evidence.[33] The opinion quoted with approval the Advisory Committee's Note to FRE 404(b), which states that prior acts evidence is subject to FRE 403 balancing[34] and holds that one factor that must be considered in such balancing is the availability of alternative proofs, including admissions and stipulations.[35] The Court also demonstrated sensitivity to the dangers of propensity evidence[36] and the risk of juries deciding guilt on the basis of defendant's past conduct rather than the evidence supporting the current charge.[37] Moreover, exclusion of prior acts evidence, unlike evidence relating to the immediate circumstances of the charged offense, is much less likely to affect the prosecutor's ability to tell a convincing and continuous story, which was a central concern of the Court in *Old Chief*.[38]

29. It may have been unwise for the Court to engage in such an abstract discussion about the application of FRE 403 to stipulated evidence in criminal cases not before the Court. Even the drafters of FRE 403 abjured specific guidelines as to its application. More than any other rule, FRE 403 is intended to rely on the sound judgment of the trial judge within the varying factual and legal context of each case.

30. *Id.* at 655.

31. *Id.* at 656.

32. United States v. Vretta, 790 F.2d 651, 656 (7th Cir. 1986) (defense counsel's proposed stipulation "would have left a 'sanitized' version of the crime with too many gaps and questions left dangling concerning the crime scenario, thus forcing the jury to speculate"), *cert. denied,* 479 U.S. 851.

33. *See generally* Jacobs, Evidence Rule 403 After *United States v. Old Chief,* 20 Am. J. Trial Advoc. 563 (1997).

34. 117 S. Ct. at 652.

35. *Id.*

36. *Id.* at 654 ("There is . . . no question that propensity would be an 'improper basis' for conviction and that evidence of a prior conviction is subject to analysis under Rule 403 for relative probative value and for prejudicial risk of misuse as propensity evidence.").

37. *Id.* at 650 (unfair prejudice "speaks to the capacity of some concededly relevant evidence to lure the factfinder into declaring guilt on a ground different from proof specific to the offense charged").

38. *Id.* at 655 ("Proving status without telling exactly why that status was imposed leaves no gap in the story of a defendant's subsequent criminality, and its demonstration by stipulation or admission neither displaces a chapter from a continuous sequence of conventional evidence nor comes across as an officious substitution to confuse or offend or provoke reproach.").

To have the greatest likelihood of acceptance the admission or stipulation must be complete and unequivocal.[39] Moreover, the defendant must be willing to accept a binding instruction telling the jury to find the point.[40] A mere failure of a defendant to contest an issue is not the same as making a formal admission or stipulation.[41]

Stipulation must be unequivocal

§4.17   Motive, Intent, Identity, and Similar Points

FRE 404(b) invites so many uses of prior acts to prove specific points that any listing is bound to be incomplete. Still it is useful to look at the more common categories expressly mentioned in FRE 404(b) itself.

Motive is normally not an element of a crime but may be relevant in proving an actor's intent or identifying the defendant as the one who committed the crime.[1] Possible motives include financial pressures,[2] personal animosity,[3] political opposition,[4] drug habits,[5] sexual desire,[6] and fear of prosecution.[7] While proof of some common motives (desire for money, or drugs, or sex) may do little to distinguish a particular defendant from the populace at large, such proof may shed important

Motive

---

39. United States v. Crowder, 141 F.3d 1202, 1210 (D.C. Cir. 1998) (rejecting proposed stipulation that was "ambiguous, conditional and tentative"; court also noted that defendant had not proposed a jury instruction requiring jury to find "the conceded element of intent").

40. Duane, Stipulations, Judicial Notice, and a Prosecutor's Supposed "Right" to Prove Undisputed Facts: Oral Argument from an Amicus Curiae in Old Chief v. United States, 168 F.R.D. 405, 420 (1996) (if government is to be precluded from proving details of prior conviction, defendant "must consent to having the jury told they *must* accept the fact judicially noticed"; noting long-standing presumption that juries will follow court's instructions, a presumption that generally favors government).

41. United States v. Roberts, 619 F.2d 379, 383 (5th Cir. 1980) (statement by defense counsel that "he would not actively contest the issue" of intent insufficient to remove issue from case).

§4.17   1. United States v. Bradshaw, 690 F.2d 704, 708 (9th Cir. 1982) (even though motive need not be proven in a criminal prosecution, it is "far from irrelevant"; motive is "evidence of the commission of any crime"), *cert. denied*, 463 U.S. 1210.

2. United States v. Kuzlik, 468 F.3d 972, 974 (7th Cir. 2006) (in embezzlement trial, admitting proof of "sorry state" of defendant's finances, including "debts, default judgments, and bank overdrafts" as evidence of motive).

3. United States v. Garcia-Meza, 403 F.3d 364, 368 (6th Cir. 2005) (in trial of man for murdering wife, admitting proof of prior assault against her, which helped show motive of apparent jealousy over boyfriend).

4. Hitt v. Connell, 301 F.3d 240, 249-50 (5th Cir. 2002) (in suit alleging that constable fired plaintiff for engaging in pro-union activity, admitting proof that he fired others or discriminated against them for similar reasons, to show motive).

5. United States v. Miranda, 986 F.2d 1283, 1285 (9th Cir. 1993) (no abuse of discretion to admit "evidence of a drug habit to demonstrate motive to commit a bank robbery").

6. United States v. Bradshaw, 690 F.2d 704, 708-709 (9th Cir. 1982) (alleged kidnaping of nine-year-old boy; evidence properly admitted that defendant had homosexual relationship with boy after kidnaping to prove motive), *cert. denied*, 463 U.S. 1210.

7. United States v. Vance, 871 F.2d 572, 576 (6th Cir. 1989) (in prosecution of legislative aide for his alleged role in murder of state attorney general, proper to admit evidence of prior crimes that tended to show motive for defendant to participate in the conspiracy), *cert. denied*, 493 U.S. 933.

light on his behavior and give meaning to other evidence connecting him to the crime. Where prior crimes are offered to prove motive, they need not be similar in nature to the charged offense.[8]

Opportunity

Prior crime evidence is likely to be admitted to show opportunity where a prosecutor seeks to place the defendant in the geographical vicinity of the crime at the time it was committed[9] or to show that he had access to some crucial place or instrumentality.[10] Such evidence may also be admitted to prove that he had some necessary knowledge, familiarity, capability, or expertise.[11]

Intent

Intent is the broadest category for evidence of prior crimes, mostly because intent in some form is almost always an element in the charged offense, and almost always the prosecutor must prove it by circumstantial evidence. Prior conduct by the defendant often sheds light on his state of mind at the time of the event in question.[12]

The distinction between using prior acts for the prohibited purpose of proving conduct on a specific occasion and the permissible purpose of proving intent on that occasion is subtle, however, and some commentators even call it "illusory."[13] Admitting prior criminal acts whenever they shed light on defendant's intent would mean admitting such proof very often indeed, and little would be left of the rule that generally character evidence cannot be used to convict.[14] Hence courts

---

8. United States v. Shriver, 842 F.2d 968, 974 (7th Cir. 1988) (in cases where prior bad acts evidence is introduced to show motive, "similarity is not an appropriate requirement").

9. United States v. Stover, 565 F.2d 1010, 1013-1014 (8th Cir. 1977) (fact that defendant had escaped from prison admissible to establish his presence in vicinity where car stolen as well as his motive for theft).

10. United States v. DeJohn, 638 F.2d 1048, 1052-1053 (7th Cir. 1981) (in prosecution for alleged theft of U.S. Treasury checks, no error to admit evidence that defendant was earlier seen behind reception desk at YMCA where he lived because it "was highly probative of the defendant's ability to obtain checks from the mailboxes" behind desk).

11. United States v. Maravilla, 907 F.2d 216, 222 (1st Cir. 1990) (evidence of a customs officer "surreptitiously whisking" a person through customs on previous occasion admissible "to show that he had the ability to have done the same with the victim" in the instant case), *cert. denied,* 504 U.S. 917.

12. United States v. Hurn, 496 F.3d 784, 787 (7th Cir. 2007) (in drug trial, admitting proof of 1995 drug dealing conviction as proof that defendant intended to distribute the drugs he possessed).

13. Uviller, Evidence of Character to Prove Conduct: Illusion, Illogic, and Injustice in the Courtroom, 130 U. Pa. L. Rev. 845, 879 (1982) (noting "inexplicable paradox" that an element of a crime "may be proved by evidence of prior misconduct" even though "the crime itself may not be"). *See also* Imwinkelried, The Use of Evidence of an Accused's Uncharged Misconduct to Prove Mens Rea: The Doctrines Which Threaten to Engulf the Character Evidence Prohibition, 51 Ohio St. L.J. 575, 583 (1990) (describing the two theories of admissibility as "indistinguishable in terms of the pertinent policy considerations" because "the prosecutor must assume the accused's propensity to entertain the same intent in similar situations.").

14. Thompson v. United States, 546 A.2d 414, 421 (D.C. Cir. 1988) (because intent "is an element of virtually every crime," if "intent exception" allowed evidence of similar crimes "simply to prove the intent element of the offense on trial, the exception would swallow the rule").

have properly drawn limits on the extent to which evidence of prior acts may be admitted to show intent.

The most generally accepted limitation is that intent must be a genuine issue in the case before prior acts may be proved.[15] Intent is clearly in issue if defendant expressly disputes it at trial, as happens if he testifies that the charged event was merely an accident or that he was only joking or acting under a mistake of fact.[16] Intent may be found not in issue where defendant stipulates that the perpetrator acted with the requisite mental state but denies that he was the perpetrator.[17]

When offered to prove intent, the prior acts generally must involve similar conduct committed under similar circumstances.[18] Evidence of prior acts is more likely to be admitted to prove intent where the defendant is charged with a crime involving planning or premeditation[19] than a crime where the defendant acted on sudden impulse.[20] Where a defendant is charged with drug trafficking, courts are particularly likely to admit evidence of prior drug manufacture or distribution to prove intent to sell,[21] although not necessarily prior convictions for mere use or possession.[22]

Prior act evidence is also admissible in civil cases on related issues such as showing fraudulent or discriminatory intent.[23]

---

15. For a discussion of the requirement that intent be a disputed issue, *see* §4.16, *supra. See also* United States v. Dudley, 562 F.2d 965, 966 (5th Cir. 1977) (in prosecution for car theft, defense claim that defendant "borrowed the automobile" made his intent a "very material" issue; thus evidence of prior conviction for same offense properly admitted).

16. United States v. Naranjo, 710 F.2d 1465, 1467-1468 (10th Cir. 1983) (in murder prosecution of husband for shooting of wife, proper to admit evidence that on prior occasions defendant beat her to rebut defendant's testimony that the shooting was "accidental and thus done without the requisite criminal intent").

17. United States v. Colon, 880 F.2d 650, 657 (2d Cir. 1989) (drawing distinction "between defense theories that claim that the defendant did not do the charged act at all, and those that claim that the defendant did the act innocently or mistakenly, with only the latter truly raising a disputed issue of intent").

18. United States v. Sanders, 951 F.2d 34, 37 (4th Cir. 1991) (in assault prosecution where defendant admitted the stabbing but claimed self-defense, error to admit evidence of a prior assault on another prisoner because it "had nothing to do with" his reason for stabbing victim here; evidence impermissibly tended only to show propensity to commit assaults).

19. United States v. Hearst, 563 F.2d 1331, 1335-1337 (9th Cir. 1977) (evidence of subsequent crimes committed by accused properly admitted to prove voluntary participation in bank robbery and negate anticipated defense of duress), *cert. denied*, 435 U.S. 100.

20. United States v. Bettencourt, 614 F.2d 214, 217 & n.6 (9th Cir. 1980) (cases "in which this court has approved the admission of evidence of prior similar acts to prove state of mind have concerned offenses involving nonspontaneous intent").

21. United States v. Logan, 949 F.2d 1370, 1379-1380 (5th Cir. 1991) (conviction for growing marijuana admissible to show intent, knowledge, and absence of mistake in prosecution for drug conspiracy), *cert. denied*, 504 U.S. 925.

22. United States v. Hill, 936 F.2d 450, 454-457 (9th Cir. 1991) (evidence of prior drug use not admissible to prove defendant was involved in drug distribution).

23. Goldsmith v. Bagby Elevator Co., Inc., 513 F.3d 1261, 1286 (11th Cir. 2008) (admitting on issue of intent evidence of four other instances where employees were

Preparation, plan   Evidence of prior acts may be admitted to show preparation[24] or a plan, pattern, scheme, or design.[25] Such evidence is not admissible where the prior conduct was too remote in time or circumstances to shed light on a current plan.[26] Similarity of incidents or even repetitive activity does not necessarily establish that conduct was part of a plan.[27] There must be a showing of an overarching design or purpose on the part of the defendant, not mere commonality of features between the charged and uncharged misconduct, in order for a plan properly to be established under FRE 404(b).[28]

Knowledge   Sometimes evidence of prior crimes, wrongs, or acts is relevant to prove knowledge as happens when defendant is charged with knowing possession of stolen property,[29] counterfeit currency,[30] drugs,[31] pornography,[32] firearms,[33] or transportation of illegal aliens.[34] Evidence of

---

retaliated against for complaining about racial discrimination); Jannotta v. Subway Sandwich Shops, Inc., 125 F.3d 503 (7th Cir. 1997) (prior similar deceptions by defendant admissible on issue of fraudulent intent).

24. United States v. Carroll, 510 F.2d 507, 509 (2d Cir. 1975) (evidence properly admitted of other crimes committed as a "try out" for the charged crime), *cert. denied*, 426 U.S. 923.

25. United States v. Ausmus, 774 F.2d 722, 727-728 (6th Cir. 1985) (in prosecution for nonpayment of taxes, evidence that defendant failed to pay taxes both prior to and following the years charged was admissible under FRE 404(b) as proof of "pattern, plan or scheme").

26. Government of Virgin Islands v. Pinney, 967 F.2d 912, 916-917 (3d Cir. 1992) (in prosecution for rape of seven-year-old girl in his apartment, error to admit evidence that seven years earlier defendant had raped victim's older sister in the same apartment; insufficient temporal connection to establish "common plan").

27. United States v. LeCompte, 99 F.3d 274 (8th Cir. 1996) (where defendant was charged with sexual abuse of niece, error to admit evidence of his sexual abuse of another niece; such acts did not tend to prove a "common plan or scheme").

28. *Cf.* Mendez & Imwinkelried, *People v. Ewoldt*: The California Supreme Court's About-Face on the Plan Theory for Admitting Evidence of an Accused's Uncharged Misconduct, 28 Loy. L.A. L. Rev. 473 (1995) (criticizing view allowing "unlinked" acts as a plan).

29. Huddleston v. United States, 485 U.S. 681, 691 (1988) (to prove defendant's knowledge that goods were stolen, proper to admit evidence of other sales by defendant of stolen property obtained from same source).

30. United States v. Beaver, 524 F.2d 963, 966 (5th Cir. 1975) (in prosecution for passing a counterfeit $20 bill, proper to receive evidence that defendant had previously sold counterfeit notes to show knowledge that bill he passed was counterfeit), *cert. denied*, 425 U.S. 905.

31. United States v. Smith, 995 F.2d 662, 672-673 (7th Cir. 1993) (admitting evidence that defendant previously hauled truckload of marijuana to rebut his claim that he did not know it was marijuana he was carrying in his truck).

32. United States v. Garot, 801 F.2d 1241, 1246-1247 (10th Cir. 1986) (in prosecution for alleged mailing of obscene matter, evidence that defendant possessed other items of hard-core child pornography admissible as proof of defendant's "knowledge of the contents of the package").

33. United States v. Uzenski, 434 F.3d 690, 710 (4th Cir. 2006) (admitting proof that defendant tried as teenager to make pipe bombs, to show knowledge of such matters).

34. United States v. Eufracio-Torres, 890 F.2d 266, 271-272 (10th Cir. 1989) (in prosecution for illegal transportation of aliens, prior convictions for illegal entry were properly admitted as proof of knowledge that aliens were here illegally).

knowledge may also tend to prove other mental states such as malice or recklessness.[35]

Evidence of acts after the charged crime usually fails to prove knowledge at the time of the offense,[36] but sometimes subsequent conduct does bear on earlier knowledge and is admitted for this purpose.[37]

Identity overlaps with several other categories. Proof of defendant's **Identity** motive, knowledge, opportunity, intent, plan, and preparation may all tend to identify defendant as the perpetrator.[38]

Usually, however, prior acts show identity by establishing a distinctive modus operandi. If the defendant is shown to have committed prior crimes in a distinctive way, sometimes referred to as "signature" crimes,[39] and the charged crime is identical or similar in these distinctive ways, evidence of what defendant did before tends to identify him as the culprit.[40]

Quite rightly, most courts require a high degree of similarity before admitting evidence of prior crimes to establish modus operandi,[41] even more than for intent,[42] although the prior crimes need not be identical in every detail.[43] The identity category of course does not include evidence offered on the theory that it tends to identify defendant as the perpetrator by showing the crime is consistent with his general propensities.[44]

35. United States v. New, 491 F.3d 369, 375 (8th Cir. 2007) (in trial for involuntary manslaughter arising out of single car accident killing two people, admitting proof of defendant's prior DUI convictions to show that defendant "knew, or could reasonably foresee, that his conduct was a threat to the lives of others").

36. United States v. Garcia-Rosa, 876 F.2d 209, 221-222 (1st Cir. 1989) (in drug prosecution, reversible error to admit evidence of later possession of cocaine; later possession tends to prove knowledge of or familiarity with cocaine only if earlier episode is taken as proof of defendant's character, which is inference barred by FRE 404(b)).

37. *See, e.g.,* United States v. Rutkoske, 505 F.3d 170, 177 (2d Cir. 2007) (admitting facts occurring almost four years after charged offense to show knowledge).

38. *See, e.g.,* United States v. Walters, 351 F.3d 159, 166-167 (5th Cir. 2003) (fact that defendant had access to particular book on bombmaking admissible to establish his identity as person who made bomb in question).

39. United States v. Price, 516 F.3d 597 (7th Cir. 2008) (in bank robbery trial, admitting evidence that defendant committed a later robbery to show modus operandi, where banks were robbed under similar circumstances).

40. United States v. Howe, 538 F.3d 842, 849-850 (8th Cir. 2008) (evidence admissible of prior similar crime where robbery victims were made to strip naked, because "unusual and distinctive enough to be like a signature").

41. United States v. Anifowoshe, 307 F.3d 643, 646 (7th Cir. 2002) (in bank fraud trial, admitting defendant's prior state conviction, citing "numerous and striking similarities between the crimes").

42. United States v. Fields, 871 F.2d 188, 197 (1st Cir. 1989) (proof of identity by modus operandi evidence requires greater degree of similarity).

43. United States v. Hamilton, 684 F.2d 380, 384 (6th Cir. 1982) (although crimes must be so similar "as to be a 'signature' of the defendant," it is not necessary that they "be identical in every detail"), *cert. denied,* 459 U.S. 976.

44. United States v. DeVillio, 983 F.2d 1185, 1194-1195 (2d Cir. 1993) (in prosecution for transportation of stolen goods, error to introduce evidence of burglars' tools found in defendant's residence after his arrest; evidence did not show modus operandi but rather that appellants were "professional burglars," a crime not charged).

Absence of mistake or accident

Evidence of prior acts may be offered to negate a claim of accident or mistake with respect to the charged conduct.[45] If the same type of incident has occurred several times previously, under the doctrine of chances it is less likely that the conduct giving rise to the current charge was an accident or mistake.[46]

In a prosecution of a parent or guardian for abuse or murder of a child, evidence of prior abuse or injuries to the child may be admitted as proof that the current injuries were not the result of an accident.[47] Generally such evidence is properly admissible only where it supports the inference that defendant, rather than some other party, was the actor causing the earlier injuries.[48]

§4.18 Unlisted Uses for Evidence of Prior Wrongs

In addition to the purposes expressly listed in FRE 404(b) which are discussed in the preceding section, there are other proper uses for evidence of prior crimes, wrongs, or acts. The following are some of the more important unlisted uses:

Providing context

Sometimes in the course of proving the charged crime it is necessary for the prosecutor to present proof of other crimes to provide background or context critical to an understanding of the facts surrounding the charged offense.[1] For example, proving a bank robber stole a car

---

45. United States v. Vieth, 397 F.3d 615, 618 (8th Cir. 2005) (admitting proof that defendant previously possessed equipment used to make methamphetamine, to refute arguments that he "was merely present" in car in which similar equipment was found, and was not part of charged conspiracy).

46. Westfield Ins. Co. v. Harris, 134 F.3d 608, 615 (4th Cir. 1998) (seven prior suspicious fire claims admissible on issue of whether fire caused by arson; doctrine of chances means that "the more often an accidental or infrequent incident occurs, the more likely it is that its subsequent reoccurrence is not accidental or fortuitous"; repeated reoccurrence of an act takes on "increasing relevance to support the proposition that there is absence of accident").

47. United States v. Boise, 916 F.2d 497, 501-502 (9th Cir. 1990) (in prosecution of father for murder of six-week-old son, proper to admit evidence of prior injuries to child to prove malice and absence of accident), *cert. denied,* 111 S. Ct. 2057. *See generally* Cammack, Using the Doctrine of Chances to Prove Actus Reus in Child Abuse and Acquaintance Rape, 29 U.C. Davis L. Rev. 355 (1996); Myers, Uncharged Misconduct Evidence in Child Abuse Litigation, 1988 Utah L. Rev. 479.

48. United States v. Brown, 608 F.2d 551, 554-555 (5th Cir. 1979) (in prosecution of mother for allegedly injuring two-year-old son of her husband, reversible error to show that child had been previously injured and hospitalized where government did not show that previous injuries resulted from offense committed by defendant). *But see* Estelle v. McGuire, 502 U.S. 62, 67-69 (1991) (in state prosecution of father for murdering six-month-old daughter, no federal constitutional violation for prosecutor to introduce evidence of earlier injuries to child, even though state lacked proof that defendant caused these injuries; evidence could properly be taken as proof that child died at hands of another, and not by accident, and that whoever inflicted the injuries did so intentionally).

§4.18 1. United States v. Wilson, 481 F.3d 475, 483 (7th Cir. 2007) (admitting proof that defendant ordered beating of a "wayward gang member," which was "part of the conspiracy" showing defendant's "leadership role and shedding light on how the [gang] enforced their drug sale policies").

after leaving the scene would be useful if it helped explain pursuit, capture, planning, or preparation. Evidence necessary for a full understanding[2] or to bridge a chronological gap in the government's proof is properly admissible under FRE 404(b).[3] However, other crimes or acts are not admissible merely because they are temporally related.[4]

Sometimes several crimes are "inextricably intertwined" so that one simply cannot be proven without proof of the other. For example, proof that a defendant sold contraband requires proof of possession, and proof that defendant murdered a man in an apartment might require proof that he was burglarizing the place when the man returned and was killed. The murder might make no sense without any indication of the burglary, and practically speaking the prosecutor must allude to the burglary in proving the murder. Courts generally take the view that the intertwined crime is not an extrinsic or "other" crime and therefore may be proven without justifying its admission under FRE 404(b).[5] But relatively few "other crimes" are inextricably intertwined with the charged offense in the ways illustrated above. Usually they are more loosely linked with the charged offense and are offered to provide background and a fuller picture of what happened.[6] Here FRE 404(b) applies, which means that the evidence merits a close look to see whether it really does tend to shed useful light on points such as intent, motive, or plan, and that the court should consider the problems of probative worth versus prejudice under FRE 403.

Where an entrapment defense is asserted, evidence of prior acts is generally admissible on the issue of a defendant's predisposition to

Rebutting entrapment defense

---

2. United States v. Powers, 59 F.3d 1460, 1465-1467 (4th Cir. 1995) (in trial of father for molesting seven-year-old daughter, admitting proof of prior acts of violence against her and her family, which showed their inability to resist or report his violent acts; seeing "entire context of the crime" would help jury understand the victim's inability to reject defendant's advances).

3. United States v. Hattaway, 740 F.2d 1419, 1424-1425 (7th Cir. 1984) (in kidnapping prosecution, no error to admit evidence that during abduction of man and woman, defendants killed the man by shoving him down a mineshaft; this evidence "helped the jury understand" the events and "excluding this evidence would have left a 'chronological and conceptual void' in the story of [the woman's] ordeal"), *cert. denied*, 469 U.S. 1028.

4. United States v. Childs, 598 F.2d 169, 173 (D.C. Cir. 1979) (court does not "subscribe to the broad proposition that evidence of other offenses may be introduced simply because it recounts events temporally related to the commission of a crime for which the accused is on trial").

5. United States v. Price, 877 F.2d 334, 337 (5th Cir. 1989) (in prosecution for possession of unregistered firearms, tape recording of defendant's plans to sell them properly admitted as evidence "inextricably intertwined" with the charged offense; therefore, unnecessary to consider its admissibility under FRE 404(b)).

6. *See, e.g.,* United States v. Treff, 942 F.2d 975, 980-981 (10th Cir. 1991) (in prosecution for firebombing his former supervisor's home, defendant's killing of wife a short time earlier presented a "close question" as to whether killing "was extrinsic to the firebombing"; court would "prefer to turn this case on the basis that Rule 404(b) has application").

commit the crime,[7] at least in jurisdictions where the entrapment defense puts predisposition at issue.[8] Such evidence is most commonly offered by the prosecutor to rebut an entrapment defense by showing that the defendant was already predisposed to commit the crime.[9] Under the better view, the prosecutor is not allowed to rely on prior arrests or rumors about the defendant but must prove actual prior misconduct to establish the defendant's predisposition.[10] Entrapment can also be viewed as a defense where defendant's character is an element, thereby making admissible evidence bearing on the defendant's pertinent criminal propensities.[11]

Rebutting insanity defense

Where an insanity defense is asserted, evidence of prior acts is sometimes admitted on the question whether the defendant had cognitive ability or volitional control.[12] Where an expert relies on evidence of prior acts as a basis for an opinion about the defendant's sanity, such underlying information is sometimes admitted to allow the trier of fact to better understand and assess the expert's testimony.[13]

Prior conduct of victim

As discussed in a prior section, evidence of the character of the victim of an alleged assault or murder is sometimes admissible under FRE 404(a)(2) to show his behavior on the occasion of the crime.[14]

---

7. United States v. Simtob, 901 F.2d 799, 807 (9th Cir. 1990) (where entrapment is an issue, evidence of other crimes is admissible under FRE 404(b) to prove "predisposition"). *See also* Sorrells v. United States, 287 U.S. 435, 451-452 (1932) ("[I]f the defendant seeks acquittal by reason of entrapment he cannot complain of an appropriate and searching inquiry into his own conduct and predisposition as bearing upon that issue.").

8. The federal courts and a majority of states adopt a subjective standard making the test of entrapment whether the defendant was predisposed to commit the crime charged. *See, e.g.,* Jacobson v. United States, 503 U.S. 540 (1992) (prosecution must prove beyond reasonable doubt "that the defendant was predisposed to commit the criminal act prior to first being approached by government agents"). Under the objective standard followed by some states, the entrapment defense focuses on whether the conduct of law enforcement agents would induce a normally law-abiding person to commit the offense, and the predisposition or character of the individual defendant is not at issue. *See, e.g.,* State v. Nakamura, 65 Haw. 74, 648 P.2d 183, 186 (1982); People v. Barraza, 23 Cal. 3d 675, 153 Cal. Rptr. 459, 591 P.2d 947, 956 (1979); Model Penal Code, T.D. No. 9 pp.19-20.

9. United States v. Mack, 643 F.2d 1119, 1121-1122 (5th Cir. 1981) (other incidents of drug dealing by defendant admissible to rebut defense of entrapment by showing a specific propensity to deal in drugs).

10. *Cf.* United States v. Miller, 799 F.2d 985, 991 (5th Cir. 1986) (extrajudicial statements "otherwise admissible" under hearsay rules "may be admitted as evidence of predisposition").

11. *See* §4.20, *infra.*

12. United States v. Johnson, 14 F.3d 766, 772 (2d Cir. 1994) (prior crimes evidence tended to establish that defendant "appreciated the wrongfulness of his conduct" and was not "merely responding to auditory hallucinations").

13. United States v. Emery, 682 F.2d 493, 497-499 (5th Cir. 1982) (in prosecution for bank robbery, evidence of prior similar robbery properly admitted where psychiatrist witnesses relied upon this evidence to determine defendant's ability to conform to law; evidence tends "to help the trier of fact choose among expert explanations" of defendant's conduct), *cert. denied,* 459 U.S. 1044.

14. *See* §4.13, *supra.*

For example, it might show that the victim was by character or disposition violent or aggressive, hence he probably acted accordingly at the time of the crime. FRE 405(a) requires this type of evidence to be cast in the form of opinion or reputation testimony, not specific instances.[15]

Sometimes, however, prior specific acts by the victim, such as making threats or other hostile behavior, may be introduced under FRE 404(b) to prove a plan or intent to harm the defendant, thereby supporting a self-defense claim. Threats serve as direct evidence of the victim's intention to attack the defendant, which under the *Hillmon* doctrine makes it more likely that he did so.[16]

There is yet another theory under which some kinds of prior acts by the victim may be proved. Defendant sometimes may prove prior violent behavior by the victim coupled with evidence that defendant knew about such incidents, which together bear on defendant's fear of the victim and belief in the need to use self-defense.[17] When offered for this purpose, such evidence does not involve the propensity argument prohibited by FRE 404.[18] Instead, such evidence is relevant in explaining what the defendant would have supposed or understood at the time of the crime when he and the victim confronted each other and resorted to violence.[19]

Extortion prosecutions

In extortion cases, evidence of defendant's reputation as a ruthless, powerful, or violent person is often admitted to prove fear on the part of the victim, which is itself an element in the charged offense.[20] In this setting, evidence of specific acts by the defendant may be admitted where it is shown (or is reasonable to suppose) that the victim knew about them, and the legitimate purpose of such evidence is to prove fear. In other situations, fear by the victim may bear on his likely behavior at the time of the crime, and again that fear is sometimes properly provable by means of evidence of defendant's reputation or acts known to the victim.[21]

Rebutting sweeping claims

If a party makes sweeping claims of an innocent or unblemished past, evidence of prior crimes may be admissible to impeach by

---

15. *See* §4.19, *infra.*

16. *See* §8.39, *infra.*

17. Government of Virgin Islands v. Carino, 631 F.2d 226, 229-230 (3d Cir. 1980) (victim's prior manslaughter conviction known to defendant admissible to show defendant's fear and state of mind at time of incident).

18. *See* United States v. Talamante, 981 F.2d 1153, 1157 (10th Cir. 1992) (evidence of victim's past conduct offered to demonstrate defendant's reasonable fear).

19. *See, e.g.,* Crawford v. Edmonson, 764 F.2d 479, 484-485 (7th Cir. 1985) (in civil rights action, defendant police officer allowed to introduce evidence of prior misconduct of plaintiffs involving guns, incidents known to defendant, to show reasonableness of his belief that fleeing suspects would fire at him), *cert. denied,* 474 U.S. 905.

20. United States v. Zannino, 895 F.2d 1, 11-12 (1st Cir. 1990) (debtor's testimony that "he feared the use of force if he did not make his scheduled payments" as he knew of defendant's "reputation for violence" helped provide evidence sufficient to support loansharking conviction), *cert. denied,* 494 U.S. 1082.

21. United States v. Stubbs, 476 F.2d 626, 627 (6th Cir. 1973) (in Hobbs Act prosecution, proper to receive victim's testimony regarding defendant's reputation for violence).

contradiction,[22] subject to the limitations governing this form of impeachment.[23]

FRE 405(a)

Reputation or opinion. In all cases in which evidence of character or a trait of character of a person is admissible, proof may be made by testimony as to reputation or by testimony in the form of an opinion. On cross-examination, inquiry is allowable into relevant specific instances of conduct.

---

§4.19 Methods of Proving Character

While FRE 404 both authorizes and limits the use of character evidence to prove conduct, FRE 405 regulates the methods of proof. The three possible methods of proving character are by evidence of reputation, opinion, or specific instances of conduct.[1] Which form is allowed depends on the purpose for which the character evidence is offered.

If the evidence is offered to prove conduct on a specific occasion under one of the three exceptions in FRE 404(a), the proof must be in the form of reputation or opinion, not specific instances of conduct.[2] On cross-examination of a witness who has given opinion or reputation evidence, however, inquiry is allowed into relevant specific instances of conduct. (In sexual assault prosecutions, FRE 412 puts in place a different regulating mechanism when it comes to proof of the prior sexual behavior of the complaining witness: Here, proof is limited to specific instances, and then only in special situations, and reputation or opinion evidence is not allowed.[3])

FRE 404(b) expressly allows evidence of specific instances of conduct to prove matters like knowledge or intent even though proof of such instances might otherwise be excluded as character evidence. If character is an essential element of a charge, claim, or defense,

---

22. United States v. Martinez, 979 F.2d 1424, 1433 (10th Cir. 1992) (in prosecution for distribution of cocaine where defendant claimed never to have personally used cocaine, proper to admit small amount of cocaine found on his person at arrest), *cert. denied,* 507 U.S. 1022.

23. *See* §§6.43-6.48, *infra.*

§4.19 1. There are some types of proof that do not fit easily into these three categories, for example, evidence relating to conditions such as pregnancy, virginity, or drug addiction. Often such proof is offered merely as an indirect means of proving specific instances of conduct.

2. *See, e.g.,* United States v. Gravely, 840 F.2d 1156, 1164 (4th Cir. 1988) (testimony of specific activities with March of Dimes inadmissible to show good character). *See generally* Leonard, The Use of Character to Prove Conduct: Rationality and Catharsis in the Law of Evidence, 58 U. Colo. L. Rev. 1 (1986) (urging greater flexibility in methods of proving character); Crump, How Should We Treat Character Evidence Offered to Prove Conduct?, 58 U. Colo. L. Rev. 279 (1987).

3. *See* §4.33, *infra.*

FRE 405(b) authorizes any of the three forms of proof—reputation, opinion, or specific instances.

Although reputation is the most well-established method for proving **Reputation** character, it is also generally regarded as the least reliable.[4] Reputation testimony has nonetheless been favored by courts because of its efficiency. It takes little time to present[5] and (in contrast to specific instances) is unlikely to divert the trial to disputes over collateral matters.

Before a witness may testify to a person's reputation for a particular **Relevant** trait of character, it must be shown that the witness is familiar with that **community** reputation in a relevant community. At one time the "community" was the geographical area where the person resided. Today as our society has become more mobile and impersonal, courts focus less on neighborhood acquaintance and allow character witnesses to testify to a person's reputation among colleagues or associates in the workplace, school, church, and other organizational settings.[6] The witness's knowledge of reputation must be drawn during a period reasonably close to the time of the conduct at issue and before the charge against him became publicized.[7]

While the reputation witness must be shown to have heard discussion of the person's character within the relevant community, it is not essential that the witness be personally acquainted with the person about whose reputation she is testifying. It is generally permissible for her to testify that she has heard nothing bad about the person, or at least nothing of a negative nature relating to the trait at issue.[8]

Whether a witness knows enough to give reputation testimony raises **Personal** an issue of personal knowledge under FRE 602, and the judge plays a **knowledge** screening role under FRE 104(b) in this setting. The witness should be allowed to testify if there is a foundation sufficient to support a reasonable jury decision that she has enough knowledge of reputation to be worth listening to, but otherwise the testimony should be excluded.

---

4. Uviller, Evidence of Character to Prove Conduct: Illusion, Illogic, and Injustice in the Courtroom, 130 U. Pa. L. Rev. 845, 885 (1982) (reputation evidence should be disallowed because it is the least trustworthy and least testable form of character evidence).

5. The trial court has discretion to limit the number of character witnesses called. *See* United States v. Henry, 560 F.2d 963, 965 (9th Cir. 1977) (no error to limit number of defense character witnesses).

6. United States v. Oliver, 492 F.2d 943, 948 (8th Cir. 1974) (college roommate may testify), *cert. denied*, 424 U.S. 973; United States v. White, 225 F. Supp. 514 (D.D.C. 1963) (community "is not necessarily a geographical unit, but is rather composed of the relationships with others which arise where a man works, worships, shops, relaxes and lives").

7. United States v. Lewis, 482 F.2d 632, 641 (D.C. Cir. 1973) (character witness should be allowed to testify to reputation existent "during a period prior to and not remote from the offense date" but not to subsequent reputation because "his reputation in the community after the charge became publicized might not be a trustworthy index to his actual character").

8. Michelson v. United States, 335 U.S. 469, 478 (1948) (approving testimony that witness had heard nothing ill of defendant to support inference that his reputation "must be good").

Courts are sometimes reluctant to admit reputation testimony from a witness hired specifically to determine a person's reputation such as a private investigator.[9]

Reputation evidence is hearsay because it is a distilled version of statements by persons in the community about an individual offered to prove the truth of those statements. However, FRE 803(21) establishes an exception to the hearsay rule for "[r]eputation of a person's character among associates or in the community."[10]

Opinion

FRE 405(a) makes a significant break from common law tradition by allowing character to be proved by the opinion of a witness.[11] The drafters authorized this form of proof in recognition that reputation evidence is often nothing more than "opinion in disguise."[12] The trier is less likely to be misled when an opinion on a person's character is labeled as such rather than masqueraded as reputation.

A character witness seeking to offer an opinion on a pertinent trait of a person's character must be shown to have sufficient knowledge to support such an opinion.[13] This determination requires the court to play a screening role under FRE 602 and 104(b), allowing the witness to testify if enough evidence of knowledge is presented to enable a reasonable jury to find her opinion worth listening to.

It is uncertain how far FRE 405(a) opens the door to expert testimony on a person's character.[14] Such testimony often may advance the search for truth without presenting significant dangers of prejudice,[15] and some decisions approve expert opinion testimony on character.[16] But sometimes witnesses lack sufficient expertise to render such an opinion, and courts exclude this type of evidence where it is unhelpful.[17]

---

9. United States v. Perry, 643 F.2d 38, 52 (2d Cir. 1980), *cert. denied,* 454 U.S. 835.

10. *See* §8.61, *infra.*

11. 7 Wigmore, Evidence 1986, at 244 (3d ed. 1940) ("The Anglo-American rules of evidence have . . . never done anything so curious in the way of shutting out evidential light as when they decided to exclude the person who knows as much as humanly can be known about the character of another, and have still admitted the secondhand, irresponsible product of multiplied guesses and gossip which we term 'reputation' ").

12. ACN, FRE 405.

13. United States v. Salazar, 425 F.2d 1284, 1286 (9th Cir. 1970) (insufficient foundation where character witnesses had only casual business dealings with defendant over two-month period).

14. The Advisory Committee appeared to contemplate use of expert opinions concerning a person's character. *See* ACN, FRE 405 (citing as permissible opinion evidence "the opinion of the psychiatrist based upon examination and testing").

15. *See* Taslitz, Myself Alone: Individualizing Justice Through Psychological Character Evidence, 52 Md. L. Rev. 1 (1993) (urging greater use of expert testimony on issues of individual character).

16. United States v. Roberts, 887 F.2d 534, 536 (5th Cir. 1989) (in drug prosecution, error to exclude expert testimony concerning defendant's "naive and autocratic" personality traits that supported his claim to have been acting as a self-appointed undercover operative).

17. United States v. MacDonald, 688 F.2d 224, 227-228 (4th Cir. 1982) (in prosecution for murdering wife and children no error to exclude testimony by a forensic psychiatrist that defendant possessed "a personality configuration inconsistent with the outrageous and senseless murders of [his] family"), *cert. denied,* 459 U.S. 1103.

Arguably, specific instances of conduct are the most reliable indica- **Specific instances**
tors of a pertinent trait of character because they are more objective **of conduct**
and fact-oriented than reputation or opinion. Evidence in this form
also leaves to the trier of fact the question of what inferences should
be drawn from a person's past behavior. But even testimony describing
specific instances carries risks of subjective distortion by the witness,
and such instances may themselves be aberrational or misleading, particularly if taken in isolation or in unrepresentative samples. While the
drafters thought specific instances had the greatest reliability,[18] they
nonetheless excluded such proof under FRE 405(a) because it has "the
greatest capacity to arouse prejudice, to confuse, to surprise, and to
consume time."[19] For example, if a defendant charged with a barroom
assault were permitted to prove the victim's violent character by
reference to other fights involving the victim, the attention of the
jury could be diverted from the crime charged to a detailed review of
past altercations having marginal probative value, all at the cost of a
greatly lengthened trial.

The prohibition against proof by specific instances of conduct is
difficult for many character witnesses, who may be naturally inclined
to explain the basis for their reputation or opinion testimony by citing
such specific instances. The witnesses should be briefed on the limitations on character evidence imposed by FRE 405(a) before they testify.

Many courts enforce the rule prohibiting specific instances of con- **Testimony by**
duct even when it comes to evidence offered by the defendant in a **defendant**
criminal case to prove his good character, hence his likely innocence.[20]
But courts properly let defendants testify in various ways that they "have
never been in trouble before" or "have never done drugs" because
such testimony is closer in form to opinion than specific instances
and is realistically viewed as a natural self-endorsement.[21] The biggest
problem with such self-endorsements is that they "open the door" to
counterproof in the form of cross-examination on specific instances
that prove the falsity or exaggeration of the initial assertion, and
even to other evidence of specific instances.[22]

Even though a character witness normally cannot testify about **Cross-**
specific instances of conduct on direct examination, cross-examination **examination**
on relevant prior specific instances of conduct is expressly allowed.[23]
Such cross-examination is not permitted as actual proof of character

---

18. ACN, FRE 405 ("Of the three methods of proving character provided by the rule,
evidence of specific instances of conduct is the most convincing.").

19. *Id.*

20. United States v. Solomon, 686 F.2d 863, 873-874 (11th Cir. 1982) (no error to
disallow defense evidence about his background, family, service in armed forces, and
acquisition of a business; if offered as proof of good character such evidence must be in
the form of opinion or reputation).

21. *See* United States v. Blackwell, 853 F.2d 86, 87-88 (2d Cir. 1988) (error but
harmless for court to strike testimony by defendant that he had never been arrested
before; such information "is something that the trier of fact has a right to know in
gauging the credibility of a witness").

22. *See* §1.4, *supra,* and §6.48, *infra.*

23. FRE 405(a).

but only for the more narrow purpose of testing the knowledge and credibility of the character witness,[24] or sometimes to prove falsity or exaggeration in self-endorsements by criminal defendants or civil litigants.[25]

In one sense, questioning a character witness about specific conduct by the person in question is a no-lose strategy. If the witness has not heard of the prior conduct, her qualifications to be a character witness or the sufficiency of her knowledge become suspect.[26] If she has heard of the prior conduct, the soundness of her judgment in reaching a contrary conclusion about character is called into question.[27] In either case, such cross-examination bears on the weight that should be given to the witness's testimony by the trier of fact.

Thus the witness may be asked on cross-examination about prior convictions, uncharged misconduct, and other conduct that is relevant to the character testimony given.[28] But such questioning brings risks as well if it seems unfair or fails to shake a firm and convincing presentation by a strong witness.

Because the proper function of cross-examination about specific instances is not to prove character but only to test the credibility of the character witness, the questioner is not allowed to prove that the conduct inquired about actually occurred where the witness denies knowledge of it. And proof that the conduct did not occur is also normally excluded, except where fundamental fairness compels its admission to correct a groundless insinuation on a critical point.

Cross-examination on prior conduct obviously has enormous potential for injecting unfair prejudice into the trial. Even though the affected party is entitled to a limiting instruction that such inquiry is being allowed only to assess the credibility of the character witness

---

24. United States v. Finley, 934 F.2d 837 (7th Cir. 1991) (where defendant elicited favorable character evidence from coworker of defendant, no error for prosecutor to ask witness if he had heard about an extortion incident involving defendant).

25. *See, e.g.,* United States v. Gaertner, 705 F.2d 210, 216 (7th Cir. 1983) (testimony by defendant that "I'm not into the cocaine thing, the drug thing" found to be character evidence allowing prosecutor to introduce evidence of a prior conviction for possessing marijuana).

26. United States v. Hewitt, 663 F.2d 1381, 1390-1391 (11th Cir. 1981) ("If the reputation witness has not heard of a fact that is likely to have caused a negative community impression of the defendant, the government has shown that the witness' knowledge of the defendant's reputation is shallow and unreliable.").

27. *Id.* ("If the reputation witness has heard of this fact but nevertheless testifies that the defendant's reputation is good, then the government has shown that the witness is either lying or is applying a lowered standard by which he assesses the defendant's good reputation.").

28. United States v. Watson, 587 F.2d 365, 369 (7th Cir. 1978), *cert. denied,* 439 U.S. 1132 (arrests); United States v. Reese, 568 F.2d 1246, 1251 (6th Cir. 1977) (other misconduct). But courts have discretion to exclude inquiry about prior arrests where there is insufficient evidence of the defendant's participation in the underlying conduct. *See, e.g.,* United States v. McCollom, 664 F.2d 56, 58 (5th Cir. 1981) (allowing inquiry of witness about prior arrest only because additional evidence indicated defendant's involvement in the underlying misconduct), *cert. denied,* 456 U.S. 934.

and not as proof of character,[29] there is great danger that the jury will fail to understand or disregard such an instruction. The potential for unfair prejudice is aggravated by the fact that actual proof of the conduct is generally prohibited.

Several safeguards exist as a check against abuses in the cross-examination of character witnesses. First, the cross-examiner must have a good-faith basis for any question asked on cross-examination.[30] The fact that a rumor exists or an unsubstantiated allegation of prior misconduct has been made is not sufficient. The good-faith basis must go to whether the misconduct actually occurred. Such a foundation might consist of an official record indicating that the conduct occurred or reliance on provable information from persons with firsthand knowledge who are reasonably believed to be credible. Asking a question without a good-faith basis may constitute grounds for a mistrial as well as a disciplinary proceeding against the attorney.[31]

Safeguards against abuse

Second, judges generally require an in camera showing of the underlying basis before permitting the question to be put to the witness, or at least the formal assurance of the attorney that such a basis exists.[32]

Third, the incidents inquired about must be relevant under FRE 401. Thus cross-examination is limited to conduct pertinent to the trait of character about which the witness testified on direct.[33]

Fourth, courts retain discretion under FRE 403 to exclude questions regarding matters that are insignificant, remote, conjectural, or otherwise unfair.[34] For example, courts almost uniformly prohibit a prosecutor from asking defense character witnesses whether their opinion of the defendant's character would change if he were in fact guilty of the charged offense.[35] Most courts also prohibit questioning about the effect of defendant's arrest for the charged offense on his

---

29. United States v. Tempesta, 587 F.2d 931, 936 (8th Cir. 1978) ("better practice" is for court to instruct jury "as to the limited purpose of the conviction even without a motion by the defendant"), *cert. denied*, 441 U.S. 910.

30. United States v. Adair, 951 F.2d 316, 319 (11th Cir. 1992) (government must have "a good faith factual basis for the incidents raised during the cross-examination of the witness").

31. *See* In re Conduct of Tichenor, 340 Or. 108, 129 P3d 690 (2006) (State Bar disciplinary proceeding against prosecutor for cross-examining defense character witnesses about defendant allegedly having a relationship with a 14-year-old girl without a good faith basis for posing such questions).

32. Michelson v. United States, 335 U.S. 469, 481 (1948) (noting that trial judge "took pains to ascertain, out of presence of the jury . . . that counsel was not merely taking a random shot at a reputation imprudently exposed or asking a groundless question to waft an unwarranted innuendo into the jury box").

33. United States v. Adair, 951 F.2d 316, 319 (11th Cir. 1992) (incidents inquired about must be relevant to character trait at issue in case).

34. United States v. Curtis, 644 F.2d 263, 269 (3d Cir. 1981) (reputation witness can only be examined on "matters reasonably proximate to the time of the alleged offense and likely to have been known to the relevant community at that time").

35. United States v. Shwayder, 312 F.3d 1109, 1120-21 (9th Cir. 2002) ("use of guilt assuming hypotheticals" in cross-examining defense character witnesses "undermines the presumption of innocence and thus violates a defendant's right to due process"). *See also* cases cited in §4.12, *supra*.

reputation on the ground that any evidence of reputation subsequent to the time of the crime is irrelevant.[36]

It is generally improper to ask a character witness about prior misconduct that occurred in private and has not become publicly known.[37] Asking reputation witnesses about such incidents seems inappropriate because they have reported only the information circulating in the community. Asking opinion witnesses about such matters seems unfair if intended to undermine their credibility by suggesting they should have known. But where such questions are asked only to test the effect of the incidents on their opinion, some courts allow them.[38]

Form of question   On cross-examination, the traditional practice has been to ask a reputation witness whether he "has heard" of certain specific instances of conduct of the person about whom he testifies because such inquiry tests the extent of his knowledge about the person's reputation.[39] If the witness has testified to an opinion, a cross-examination question about prior acts is commonly prefaced by "do you know" or "are you aware," although "have you heard" is also permissible.[40] The Advisory Committee found such distinctions in phraseology to be "of slight if any practical significance" and stated that FRE 405(a) "eliminates them as a factor in formulating questions."[41] Although the Committee was surely right to downplay the importance of such semantic distinctions, there is likely to be less jury confusion if cross-examination of reputation witnesses about specific instances is prefaced with "have you heard." Such phraseology tends to focus the jury's attention on the only legitimate use of such evidence—to test the witness's knowledge—and away from concern about whether the incident actually occurred.[42]

---

36. United States v. Curtis, 644 F.2d 263, 268-269 (3d Cir. 1981), *cert. denied*, 459 U.S. 1018.

37. United States v. Monteleone, 77 F.3d 1086, 1090 (8th Cir. 1996) (character witness can only be cross-examined about prior bad acts likely to be known in community; here alleged lying before grand jury many years earlier was unlikely to be known and was therefore improper).

38. United States v. Reich, 479 F.3d 179, 190-91 (2d Cir. 2007) (while reputation witnesses cannot be asked about acts unlikely to be known, opinion witnesses may be asked about such acts).

39. Michelson v. United States, 335 U.S. 469, 482 (1948) ("Since the whole inquiry . . . is calculated to ascertain the general talk of people about defendant, rather than the witness' own knowledge of him, the form of inquiry, Have you heard? has general approval, and Do you know? is not allowed.").

40. United States v. Collins, 779 F.2d 1520, 1532 (11th Cir. 1986) (no error for prosecutor to pose "have you heard" questions to defense character witness who gave opinion testimony).

41. ACN, FRE 405(a).

42. United States v. Curtis, 644 F.2d 263, 268-269 (3d Cir. 1981) (FRE 405(a) "has not effected a merger between reputation and opinion evidence" and cross-examination of reputation witness should focus on conduct and charges "which may have come to the attention of the relevant community"; but for opinion evidence "relevant cross-examination is only that which bears on the fact or factual basis for formulation of the opinion"), *cert. denied*, 459 U.S. 1018.

> **FRE 405(b)**
>
> **Specific instances of conduct.** In cases in which character or a trait of character of a person is an essential element of a charge, claim, or defense, proof may also be made of specific instances of that person's conduct.

§4.20   Character as Element of Charge, Claim, or Defense

Although the most common use of character evidence is to prove conduct in accordance with that character on a particular occasion, such evidence also has a very different use. In a few relatively rare instances, a person's character constitutes an element of a charge, claim, or defense. In such instances, evidence of that person's character is admissible without restriction, and in all forms, including opinion, reputation, and specific instances.

The rule allowing character evidence where character is an element of a charge, claim, or defense is unfortunately not codified in the Federal Rules. The Advisory Committee's Note, however, makes clear that character evidence offered for this purpose is admissible.[1] The forms of proof allowed for this use of character evidence are addressed by FRE 405(b).[2]

Evidence of character as an element of a charge, claim, or defense must be distinguished from cases where reputation, not character, is at issue.[3] Sometimes reputation has independent relevance and is admissible regardless whether it accurately reflects a person's character. For example, in a defamation action, the plaintiff's reputation, not his character, is the benchmark from which to assess injury and compute damages.[4] FRE 405(b) is inapplicable to such cases, although courts are occasionally confused on this point.[5] In an extortion prosecution,

Reputation at issue

---

§4.20   1. ACN, FRE 404(a) (one permissible use of character evidence is where character is an element of a crime, claim, or defense; for such use "[n]o problem of the general relevancy of [such] character evidence is involved" and therefore the present rule "has no provision on the subject").

2. FRE 405(a) allows proof by reputation or opinion "in all cases in which evidence of character" is admissible, and FRE 405(b) provides that "proof may also be made of specific instances of that person's conduct" whenever character "is an essential element of a charge, claim, or defense."

3. "Character" means a person's propensity to engage or not engage in certain forms of behavior, while "reputation" is one means of proving character. *See* §4.11, *supra*.

4. Braun v. Flynt, 726 F.2d 245, 250 (5th Cir. 1984) (principal element of injury in a defamation action "is impairment of reputation"); Restatement (Second) of Torts 621 ("One who is liable for a defamatory communication is liable for the proved, actual harm caused to the reputation of the person defamed.").

5. *See* Schafer v. Time, Inc., 142 F.3d 1361 (11th Cir. 1998) (in defamation action court mistakenly holds that FRE 405(b) applies and that defendant's character is essential element of proving damages).

evidence of a defendant's reputation for violence, as well as specific instances of violent conduct, may be admissible to establish coercion, provided such reputation was known to the victim.[6]

Criminal cases The cases where character is an element of a criminal charge or defense are exceedingly rare. The elements of a crime virtually always relate to the accused's conduct on a particular occasion, not to his general character or propensities.[7] The Advisory Committee cites a seduction prosecution where the "chastity of the victim" may be a statutory element of the offense,[8] but the example is so obsolete that resorting to it helps prove the rarity of such cases.

Possibly "habitual offender" statutes provide an example where the person's "character" for committing crimes is an element of the charge, but it is probably more accurate to regard such statutes as merely requiring proof of a requisite number of prior convictions rather than proof of the defendant's character. Statutes prohibiting ex-felons from possessing firearms allow proof of the prior felony conviction as an element of the charge,[9] but again the defendant's "character" is not really at issue in such prosecutions.

Insanity defense It is uncertain whether the accused's character can properly be viewed as an element of an insanity defense. Arguably the issue depends on the nature of the mental condition alleged. If the defendant claims cognitive impairment, character is not implicated. If the defendant claims lack of volitional control as a result of a mental disease or defect, such a condition does bear on the defendant's proclivities or character.[10] In any case, prior acts supporting or rebutting an insanity defense are generally admissible under FRE 404(b).[11]

Entrapment Despite occasional decisions to the contrary,[12] it seems clear that the defendant's character is an element of an entrapment defense,[13] at least where the substantive law adopts a subjective test of entrapment focusing on whether the defendant was "predisposed" to commit such a crime rather than an objective standard focusing on the extent of

---

6. United States v. DeVincent, 546 F.2d 452, 456-457 (1st Cir. 1976) (defendant's criminal record known to victim), *cert. denied,* 431 U.S. 903.

7. In fact, criminal statutes punishing a person on the basis of personal proclivities such as drug addiction have been held unconstitutional. *See* Robinson v. California, 370 U.S. 660 (1962).

8. ACN, FRE 404(a).

9. United States v. Blackburn, 592 F.2d 300, 301 (6th Cir. 1979) (in prosecution for possession of firearms by one previously convicted of a felony, prosecution allowed to prove prior felonies despite defense offer to stipulate).

10. Although some states recognize lack of volitional control as an aspect of the insanity defense, it is no longer recognized under federal law. *See* 18 U.S.C. 20(a).

11. *See* §4.18, *supra.*

12. United States v. Richardson, 764 F.2d 1514, 1522 n.2 (11th Cir. 1985) (entrapment defense does not put character at issue), *cert. denied,* 474 U.S. 952.

13. United States v. Thomas, 134 F.3d 975, 978 (9th Cir. 1998) (defendant's predisposition or character is an essential element of an entrapment defense, and both favorable and unfavorable character evidence, including specific acts, is admissible under FRE 405(b)).

government misconduct.[14] Proof of his predisposition or lack of it amounts to proof of his propensities or character. Evidence of prior crimes, wrongs, or acts is also generally admissible to rebut an entrapment defense under FRE 404(b).[15]

There are only a handful of civil cases where character constitutes an element of the claim or defense. For example, almost all tort claims focus only on the defendant's conduct on a particular occasion rather than on his character or general propensities. | **Civil cases**

One exception is tort claims where the defendant is alleged to have been negligent in entrusting a particular instrumentality to a third person[16] or in hiring or failing to supervise or control a person having dangerous propensities.[17] The untrustworthy character of that third person is an element of the claim and must be proven in order to establish that the defendant's conduct was negligent. | **Negligent entrustment**

In defamation cases where truth is asserted as a defense, the plaintiff's character may be an element of that defense. A defendant is entitled to prove the truth of an allegedly defamatory statement and in doing so may necessarily offer evidence bearing on plaintiff's character. However, character evidence of a general nature, such as proof of plaintiff's reputation for corruption, is generally insufficient to establish the truth of a defamatory statement that is specific in nature, such as that plaintiff took a bribe on a particular occasion. | **Defamation**

In defamation cases, damages are measured by the harm to plaintiff's reputation. However, just as reputation evidence is admissible to prove character, some courts with less legitimacy have allowed character evidence as circumstantial evidence of reputation.[18] The better-reasoned cases exclude such evidence on the theory that it shows "not that the plaintiff's reputation is bad, but that it ought to be bad."[19]

---

14. Under the subjective test, a claim of entrapment is measured by whether the defendant was induced by the government to commit a crime he was not predisposed to commit. *See* Jacobson v. United States, 503 U.S. 540 (1992) (prosecution must prove beyond reasonable doubt "that the defendant was predisposed to commit the criminal act prior to first being approached by government agents"). Under the objective test, the entrapment defense focuses on whether the conduct of law enforcement agents would induce a normally law-abiding person to commit the offense, and the predisposition or character of the individual defendant is not at issue. *See, e.g.,* Model Penal Code, T.D. No. 9 pp.19-20; State v. Nakamura, 65 Haw. 74, 648 P.2d 183, 186 (1982); People v. Barraza, 23 Cal. 3d 675, 153 Cal. Rptr. 459, 591 P.2d 947, 956 (1979).

15. *See* §4.18, *supra.*

16. In re Aircrash in Bali, Indonesia, 684 F.2d 1301, 1315 (9th Cir. 1982) (in wrongful death action against airline, records indicating pilot "had made similar mistakes on prior occasions" admissible on negligent entrustment theory to show that airline had notice of pilot's alleged incompetence).

17. Hirst v. Gertzen, 676 F.2d 1252, 1263 (9th Cir. 1982) (prior acts of prisoner abuse by sheriff admissible to show government negligence in supervising sheriff).

18. Meiners v. Moriarity, 563 F.2d 343, 351 (7th Cir. 1977) (trial court should have permitted party charged with libel to cross-examine claimant concerning "relevant specific instances of conduct" that might have "resulted in publicity adverse to defendants," including events other than incident mentioned in the allegedly defamatory statement).

19. Sun Printing & Pub. Assn. v. Schenck, 98 F. 925, 929 (2d Cir. 1900). *See also* Shirley v. Freunscht, 303 Or. 234, 735 P.2d 600, 603 (1987) (in defamation suit, error to receive

Element of
damages

In wrongful death cases, the character of the decedent is often viewed as an element of damages.[20] Thus evidence of the decedent's work habits, criminal record, drunkenness, adultery, gambling, and similar forms of behavior is generally received, subject to relevancy standards, on the issue of likely future earnings and the emotional loss to his survivors.[21]

The most common example where character is at issue is in child custody disputes. The fitness or character of each parent for good parenting is a central issue and is often viewed as an element of each party's claim.[22] Thus evidence of reputation, opinion, and specific instances of conduct are all admissible on the point.[23]

D.   HABIT AND ROUTINE PRACTICE

FRE 406

Evidence of the habit of a person or of the routine practice of an organization, whether corroborated or not and regardless of the presence of eyewitnesses, is relevant to prove that the conduct of the person or organization on a particular occasion was in conformity with the habit or routine practice.

§4.21   Habit Evidence

While evidence of character is generally inadmissible to prove conduct under FRE 404, evidence of habit is generally admissible for this

---

evidence of specific instances of "business misconduct" by the plaintiff because such instances "have no relevance unless they were generally known in the business community" and here the witnesses did not so testify).

20. It is questionable whether the character of the decedent is actually an "element" of damages. It is instead a method of proving damages by showing the type of life the decedent would likely have led, based on his propensities, if he had not been killed. In a sense, the evidence is being used circumstantially to prove likely future behavior. However, this use is not prohibited by FRE 404(a) because the evidence is not being offered to prove conduct on a particular past occasion.

21. Gates v. Rivera, 993 F.2d 697, 700 (9th Cir. 1993) (in civil rights action for death of plaintiff's son, proper to receive evidence that he had "history of drug use" on issue of damages); St. Clair v. Eastern Air Lines, Inc., 279 F.2d 119, 121 (2d Cir. 1960) (personal habits and qualities are "relevant considerations in determining an individual's earning ability and the support that his family would have received from him but for his death"), *cert. denied,* 364 U.S. 882.

22. An alternate view is that the character of the parents is not an "element," but rather their propensities are being used to predict their likely future parenting behavior. *Cf.* Care and Protection of Martha, 407 Mass. 319, 553 N.E.2d 902 (1990) (in proceeding to place children for adoption and terminate parental rights, proper for judge to consider mother's fitness as parent on basis of her prior convictions for sexually abusing her children).

23. Berryhill v. Berryhill, 410 So. 2d 416, 418-419 (Ala. 1982) (proper to admit reputation evidence and specific acts bearing on parenting in a child custody dispute).

purpose under FRE 406.[1] Why is such a sharp distinction drawn between character evidence, which is generally excluded, and habit evidence, which is generally admitted? The primary reason is that habit describes particular behavior in a specific setting, and it is by nature at least regular if not invariable, so it has greater probative value in proving conduct on a particular occasion than does evidence of more general propensities. Also habit evidence is less likely to carry moral overtones or to present serious dangers of unfair prejudice or confusion.[2]

Unfortunately "habit" is not defined by FRE 406, and the distinction between character and habit is hard to draw in practice. Character and habit occupy different areas on the same continuum, and reasonable minds can differ on where the line should be drawn between them.[3] The three criteria that courts find useful in distinguishing habit from character relate to the specificity and regularity of the behavior and the degree to which it is automatic or unreflective.

The more specific the behavior, the better its chance of being habit.[4] **Specific behavior** A driver's tendency to be accident-prone (or routinely careful) is too general to qualify, but a driver's practice of always honking at a particular blind intersection or taking a particular route to the office is specific enough to be a habit.

Perhaps the most important criterion is regularity. Evidence that a **Regularity** person engages in specific conduct (like fastening a seat belt) some of the time has little probative value in proving conduct on a particular occasion. It is surely not habit and is likely to be excluded.[5] Repetition may indicate habit even if the actor does not invariably conform to pattern, but regularity of response raises probative value, makes the "habit" designation more compelling, and raises the likelihood that

---

§4.21 1. By common law tradition, habit evidence required corroboration and was generally admitted only if there were no eyewitnesses, but FRE 406 expressly rejects these two restrictions. *See* ACN, FRE 406.

2. *See, e.g.,* Weissenberger v. Senger, 381 N.W.2d 187, 191 (N.D. 1986) (proper to exclude habit evidence under Rule 403 as cumulative).

3. *See* ACN, FRE 406 (noting that there has long been disagreement "upon the question what constitutes habit," particularly regarding the "extent to which instances must be multiplied" and the "consistency of behavior maintained in order to rise to the status of habit"). *See also* Mengler, The Theory of Discretion in the Federal Rules of Evidence, 74 Iowa L.J. 413, 416 (1989) (citing FRE 406 as an example of broad discretion allowed under Federal Rules).

4. Camfield v. City of Oklahoma City, 248 F.3d 1214, 1232 (10th Cir. 2001) (habit is "a regular practice of meeting a particular situation with a specific type of conduct," like going down a particular stairway two steps at a time, or giving a hand signal for a left turn, and habitual acts may become semiautomatic) (announcing seizure of child pornography upon walking into video rental store "is not a semi-automatic act and could not serve as the basis for habit evidence"); Frase v. Henry, 444 F.2d 1228, 1232 (10th Cir. 1971) ("habit" is "more specific" than character and "designates a regular practice of meeting a particular kind of situation with a certain type of conduct, or a reflex behavior in a specific set of circumstances").

5. United States v. Serrata, 425 F.3d 886, 906 (10th Cir. 2005) (proof that inmate twice previously resisted arrest did not qualify as habit).

the evidence qualifies under FRE 406.[6] Thus testimony by a close family member that somebody buckles up "all the time" or even "almost always" is likely to show habit.[7] An obvious line of attack when conduct is offered as "habit" involves exploring how often the actor deviates from the pattern.

Automatic Conduct is more likely to indicate habit where it represents semiautomatic or unreflective behavior.[8] The most indisputable habits tend to be those involving conduct requiring no conscious thought or purpose, like going down the stairs in repeated double-step rhythms or signaling lane changes and turns. The greater the extent of reflection or volition in a particular behavior, the less likely it is to be habit.[9]

The Advisory Committee took the position that a pattern of intemperate drinking cannot be used to prove drunkenness on a specific occasion.[10] The cases generally endorse this view,[11] but the answer should turn on the regularity and specificity of the behavior. Distinctive drinking practices that are routinely followed may qualify as habit under FRE 406[12] although evidence that a party is a heavy drinker may sometimes raise sufficient concerns about unfair prejudice or confusion of the issues to justify exclusion under FRE 403.[13] Evidence of habitual moderation or abstinence involves invariable behavior with less danger of prejudice, thereby justifying a more receptive attitude toward its admission.

6. United States v. Arrendondo, 349 F.3d 310, 315 (6th Cir. 2003) (to rebut convicted defendant's claim of incompetent counsel, admitting lawyer's testimony that "he always passed on plea offers to clients," which was "habit testimony" admissible under FRE 406 to prove that he did so in this case).

7. Babcock v. General Motors, 299 F.3d 60, 66 (1st Cir. 2002) (admitting proof that decedent habitually wore seat belt after three witnesses who rode with him many times testified that decedent "always wore his seat belt," regardless of length of trip).

8. Weil v. Seltzer, 873 F.2d 1453, 1460 (D.C. Cir. 1989) ("It is the non-volitional character of habit evidence that makes it probative.").

9. United States v. Troutman, 814 F.2d 1428, 1455 (10th Cir. 1987) (refraining from extortion is not a semiautomatic act and does not constitute habit); Levin v. United States, 338 F.2d 265 (1964) (excluding as support for defendant's alibi defense his alleged "habit" of staying home on Sabbath because volitional basis of the activity "raises serious questions as to its invariable nature, and hence its probative value"), *cert. denied*, 379 U.S. 999.

10. ACN, FRE 406 (noting that "evidence of intemperate 'habits' " is generally excluded "when offered as proof of drunkenness in accident cases").

11. Reyes v. Missouri Pac. R.R., 589 F.2d 791, 795 (5th Cir. 1979) (evidence that plaintiff had been convicted of public intoxication four times over a three-and-one-half-year period was "of insufficient regularity to rise to the level of 'habit' evidence").

12. Loughan v. Firestone Tire & Rubber Co., 749 F.2d 1519, 1523-1524 (11th Cir. 1985) (admitting as habit evidence testimony that a certain employee "routinely carried a cooler of beer on his truck," was "in the habit of drinking on the job," and "normally had something to drink in the early morning hours"); Keltner v. Ford Motor Co., 748 F.2d 1265, 1268-1269 (8th Cir. 1984) (admitting evidence of habit of drinking a six-pack of beer four nights a week).

13. *See* Mydlarz v. Palmer/Duncan Constr. Co., 682 P.2d 695, 704 (Mont. 1984) (improper to receive "evidence of a general drinking problem" to prove why painter fell off ladder).

The Advisory Committee also disapproved evidence of a civil defendant's prior assaults to prove that he was the assailant on a particular occasion.[14] Surely the Committee was on firm ground here, and the point should apply equally in criminal cases. Violent behavior, even when it reflects anger or happens repeatedly in relationships, cannot be called unreflective or nonvolitional and should not be viewed as habit.[15] Sometimes, however, violent behavior directed toward a particular person or group might be provable under FRE 404(b) to show hostility, which bears on intent and may tend to prove plan or scheme.

Under FRE 406 or its state counterparts, courts have admitted evidence of a person's habit or distinctive manner of conducting interviews,[16] filling out insurance medical forms,[17] fraudulent tax planning,[18] crossing a street,[19] passing out in a chair from drinking while holding a lighted cigarette,[20] keeping of a regular schedule,[21] always arranging for child care when going out at night,[22] informing patients of medical

---

14. ACN, FRE 406 (evidence of other assaults is "inadmissible to prove the instant one in a civil assault action").

15. Thompson v. Boggs, 33 F.3d 847, 854-855 (7th Cir. 1994) (in police brutality suit, excluding proof of other violent episodes; plaintiff failed to show defendant regularly responded with excessive force in semiautomatic way so failed to show habit). *But see* Perrin v. Anderson, 784 F.2d 1040, 1043-1045 (10th Cir. 1986) (testimonial accounts of four officers adequate to establish that plaintiff "invariably reacted with extreme violence to any contact with a uniformed police officer").

16. Boswell v. Phoenix Newspapers, Inc., 730 P.2d 178, 181 (Ariz. 1985) (admitting as habit testimony of reporter that she began every interview by obtaining correct spelling of names).

17. Lee v. National Life Assurance Co., 632 F.2d 524, 528-529 (5th Cir. 1980) (statement of medical examiner that she "did not usually record the answers" to health history questions in same way applicant "verbally answered them" should have been considered in deciding whether applicant intended to make misrepresentations on his life insurance application).

18. Karme v. Commissioner, 673 F.2d 1062, 1064 (9th Cir. 1982) (admitting under FRE 406 evidence that taxpayer's attorney had a "pattern or practice of tax planning" by taking fraudulent interest deductions).

19. Charmley v. Lewis, 729 P.2d 567, 573 (Or. 1986) (proper to admit testimony by five witnesses that they "frequently had observed" plaintiff go straight across street within unmarked crosswalk to show that plaintiff was in that crosswalk when struck by defendant's car).

20. Sams v. Gay, 288 S.E.2d 822, 823-824 (Ga. App. 1982) (admitting testimony that "it was the decedent's custom and habit to chain-smoke while drinking and that 'many times' he had passed out under such circumstances while holding a lighted cigarette and had burned holes in the furniture").

21. Derring v. State, 619 S.W.2d 644, 646-647 (Ark. 1981) (where body of murder victim was never found, admitting evidence that he was "very dependable in his routine, kept a fairly rigid schedule, always had breakfast with the same person each day, attended school regularly, had no bad habits, and returned home to his apartment at the same time each evening," to show that he "did not disappear on his own volition").

22. State v. Hedger, 768 P.2d 1331, 1335 (Idaho 1989) (admitting testimony describing kidnap victim's "way of dealing with her children in a particular situation, which may be considered as habit").

risks,[23] and approaching railroad crossings with caution.[24] Evidence that a person did not engage in a certain type of behavior is also admissible as "negative" habit evidence under FRE 406.[25]

Proving habit

Habit is usually proved by witnesses testifying to prior specific instances of conduct. There must be a large enough sample to determine whether a pattern of behavior exists.[26] If a person has responded to a particular situation only twice, even if the response was the same both times, a court is unlikely to find the response to be a habit.[27]

Assuming a large enough sample of observations, the proponent of the evidence must also establish a sufficient uniformity of response.[28] The Advisory Committee made no attempt to specify how regular the response must be to qualify as a habit and deliberately left this issue to the courts to determine on a case-by-case basis.[29] The determination should be made by the court under FRE 104(a) to avoid exposing the jury to evidence of past conduct that has not been determined to be habit.

Opinion testimony

As originally drafted, FRE 406 would have authorized proof of habit by opinion testimony as well as by specific instances of conduct.[30] Although Congress deleted this provision,[31] use of opinion evidence to prove habit or routine practice seems entirely proper.[32] The congressional change does not indicate that lay opinion evidence on such

23. Meyer v. United States, 464 F. Supp. 317, 321 (D. Colo. 1979) (habit of dentist to inform his patients of the risks of a particular surgical procedure), *aff'd*, 638 F.2d 155 (10th Cir. 1980).

24. Kovacs v. Chesapeake & Ohio Ry., 351 N.W.2d 581, 594 (Mich. App. 1984) (approving testimony that decedent had "habit of approaching railroad crossings in a prudent and careful manner").

25. State v. Libby, 546 A.2d 444, 449 (Me. 1988) (evidence that decedent "never went into the water" and took only sponge baths because of a skin condition admissible as habit evidence to prove murder where he was found drowned in a bathtub).

26. Charmley v. Lewis, 729 P.2d 567, 570 (Or. 1986) (frequency requirement satisfied by testimony that plaintiff crossed intersection in unmarked crosswalk nearly every day).

27. United States Football League v. National Football League, 842 F.2d 1335, 1373 (2d Cir. 1988) (testimony as to "three or four episodes over a 20-year period" insufficient to support finding of habit).

28. United States v. Newman, 982 F.2d 665, 669 (1st Cir. 1992) (excluding evidence of particular handcuffing practice offered as habit; witness had observed this practice on 75-100 occasions, but no evidence was offered of total number of times prisoners were handcuffed; so it was impossible to determine regularity of response).

29. ACN, FRE 406 (while "adequacy of sampling" and "uniformity of response" are "key factors," no precise standards for measuring their sufficiency can be formulated).

30. *See* proposed FRE 406(b) (habit may be proved by "opinion and specific instances sufficient in number to warrant a finding that the habit or routine practice in fact existed").

31. House Report, at 5 (Committee deleted this subdivision "believing that the method of proof of habit and routine practice should be left to the courts to deal with on a case-by-case basis" but did not intend generally to authorize opinion evidence).

32. Maynard v. Sayles, 817 F.2d 50, 52 (8th Cir. 1987) (foundation for habit evidence "can be established by a lay opinion"; affirming judgment by evenly divided court), *vacated*, 831 F.2d 173.

subjects is improper, and testimony in that form by witnesses with knowledge should readily satisfy the standards in FRE 701.

§4.22 Evidence of Routine Practice

FRE 406 paves the way to prove the routine practice of an organization in order to show that it acted in accordance with that practice on a particular occasion.[1] Courts tend to be even more receptive to evidence of organizational routine than to evidence of personal habit, probably because the impersonal and often professional or bureaucratic nature of the former puts it far out of the realm of moral judgments and provides ample insurance that factfinders will not be invited to draw the improper inference from "character" to conduct.

Courts admit evidence of a wide range of routine practices under FRE 406 or its state counterparts, including proof of deportation practices of the Immigration and Naturalization Service,[2] disciplinary practices of an employer,[3] obtaining consent of subjects for a research study,[4] an insurance company's practice in waiving policy requirements,[5] customary mailing practices,[6] a tavern's practice of serving drinks to intoxicated persons,[7] racially discriminatory practices,[8] the

Examples

§4.22 1. Reliance on FRE 406 is necessary only where a litigant seeks to prove conduct on a specific occasion by evidence of routine practice. Where a litigant seeks to prove a pattern or practice that has independent relevance, such evidence is admissible under FRE 401. *See* Pennsylvania v. Porter, 659 F.2d 306, 320 (3d Cir. 1981) (in litigation seeking equitable relief, evidence of pattern of constitutional violations by police is admissible; court erroneously cites FRE 406), *cert. denied*, 458 U.S. 1121.

2. United States v. Quezada, 754 F.2d 1190, 1195 (5th Cir. 1985) (proper for INS agent to describe "the normal procedure followed in executing a warrant of deportation" by his agency to establish conformity with those procedures in instant case).

3. Holley v. Seminole Cty. Sch. Dist., 755 F.2d 1492, 1505 (11th Cir. 1985) (evidence that school board had not punished others who engaged in similar conduct should have been admitted).

4. Wetherill v. University of Chicago, 570 F. Supp. 1124 (N.D. Ill. 1983) (in battery action against university hospitals, proper to receive evidence that defendant's physicians followed the "routine practice" of "asking patients to participate in the study after discussing its experimental nature").

5. Rosenburg v. Lincoln Am. Life Ins. Co., 883 F.2d 1328, 1336 (7th Cir. 1989) (evidence that defendant insurance company had a practice of waiving written policy conditions admissible as routine business practice).

6. Wells Fargo Business Credit v. Ben Kozloff, Inc., 695 F.2d 940, 944 (5th Cir. 1983) (placing letters in mail "may be proved by circumstantial evidence, including customary mailing practices used in the sender's business"), *cert. denied*, 464 U.S. 818.

7. Tommy's Elbow Room, Inc. v. Kavorkian, 727 P.2d 1038, 1049 (Alaska 1986) (proper to admit evidence that tavern's "routine practice was to serve drunks" to refute defendant's claim to the contrary).

8. Williams v. Anderson, 562 F.2d 1081, 1086 & n.7 (8th Cir. 1977) (evidence of prior racially discriminatory practices admissible to support inference that discrimination continued).

practice of making certain representations as to the effective date of insurance policies,[9] and similar practices.[10]

Occasionally cases approve evidence of organizational routine in preparing documents or contracts, to prove that certain terms were included in a particular document or contract, or that the document or contract was prepared in a certain way.[11] Some courts admit evidence of the routine practice of an organization as proof of a member's own practice or intent,[12] but others exclude such evidence on the ground that it is improper to draw inferences about individual behavior from the routine practices of a group.[13] Such use of routine practice evidence should be distinguished from admitting evidence of industry custom or practice to help the jury assess whether a defendant's conduct was negligent or otherwise in violation of applicable legal standards.[14]

Required familiarity Routine practice can be proved by a witness who does not personally engage in that practice on behalf of the organization, provided that he is familiar with it.[15] Courts exclude evidence of routine practice where there is insufficient evidence of the existence of the practice or its routine nature.[16]

9. Rosenburg v. Lincoln Am. Life Ins. Co., 883 F.2d 1328, 1336 (7th Cir. 1989) (evidence admissible to establish a routine practice that defendant's agents regularly gave or were trained to "give oral assurances that insurance coverage was effective immediately despite written conditions to the contrary").

10. *See* Morris v. Travelers Indem. Co. of America, 518 F.3d 755 (10th Cir. 2008) (routine practice of informing insurance customers about certain policy provisions). *But see* Leonard v. Nationwide Mut. Ins. Co., 499 F.3d 419, 442 (5th Cir. 2007) (proof that insurance agent told five customers in a decade about the need for additional flood coverage did not "remotely qualify or quantify" as habit under FRE 406).

11. Gillingham Constr., Inc. v. Newby-Wiggins Constr., Inc., 42 P.3d 680, 685 (Idaho 2002) (admitting proof that, in preparing bid, contractor always uses spot elevations to calculate the quantity of dirt to be moved); Amoco Prod. Co. v. United States, 619 F.2d 1383, 1389-1390 (10th Cir. 1980) (under FRE 406, admitting proof of routine practice of the Federal Farm Mortgage Company "to reserve a one-half mineral interest in all property transferred during the relevant period" to prove that such a provision was contained in the deed in question).

12. Wetherill v. University of Chicago, 570 F. Supp. 1124, 1128 (N.D. Ill. 1983) (practice of two doctors could be proved by evidence of routine practice of an informal organization of physicians to which they belonged).

13. United States v. Angelilli, 660 F.2d 23, 40 (2d Cir. 1981) ("[I]t would defy the principle of the individuality of guilt to hold that a defendant's mere membership in an organization practicing a particular type of crime could be used to show that the defendant himself committed such a crime."), *cert. denied*, 455 U.S. 910.

14. *See* §4.7, *supra*.

15. United States v. Quezada, 754 F.2d 1190, 1195, 1196 n.14 (5th Cir. 1985) (agent with requisite familiarity with office procedure could testify to routine practice of INS in executing warrant of deportation despite the fact that "he had never personally observed the execution of the warrant"; all that is necessary "is some competent evidence as to the routine practice followed by the organization, given by someone familiar with these procedures").

16. Simplex, Inc. v. Diversified Energy Sys., 847 F.2d 1290, 1293 (7th Cir. 1988) (in suit for breach of contract, proper to exclude evidence of "routine practices of late deliveries and defective performance" under other contracts because defendant failed to show "any specific, repetitive conduct that might approach evidence of habit").

E.   SUBSEQUENT REMEDIAL MEASURES

> **FRE 407**
>
> When, after an injury or harm allegedly caused by an event, measures are taken that, if taken previously, would have made the injury or harm less likely to occur, evidence of the subsequent measures is not admissible to prove negligence, culpable conduct, a defect in the product, a defect in the product's design, or a need for a warning or instruction. This rule does not require the exclusion of evidence of subsequent measures when offered for another purpose, such as proving ownership, control, or feasibility of precautionary measures, if controverted, or impeachment.

§4.23   Subsequent Remedial Measures Generally Excluded

FRE 407 bars evidence of subsequent remedial measures to prove negligence, culpable conduct, product or design defects, or the need for a warning or instruction. For example, evidence that defendant made repairs at a place where plaintiff had sustained injuries in an accident cannot be proved in a later lawsuit to prove that defendant was negligent in maintaining the place at the time of the accident.

Such evidence is excluded for three reasons. First, the fact that a party made repairs after an accident may not indicate negligence or fault. Often premises or instrumentalities that are safe can be made safer, and a party undertaking repairs may be employing a higher standard of safety than due care requires. Second, even if subsequent repair tends to show negligence, there is a strong social policy to encourage people and companies to make such repairs to enhance the safety of others. Parties might be deterred from undertaking them if their efforts could be used against them in a later suit arising out of an accident.[1] Finally, regardless whether FRE 407 encourages parties to undertake subsequent remedial measures, it seems unfair to penalize them for socially responsible conduct.

Reasons to exclude

What seems the most important rationale (encouraging subsequent repairs) is open to considerable doubt. Most ordinary citizens are unaware of FRE 407 and do not consult a lawyer in deciding whether to undertake repairs. And it is doubtful that large manufacturers, even if well-advised and familiar with litigation, need the incentive of

---

§4.23   1. Werner v. Upjohn Co., 628 F.2d 848, 857 (4th Cir. 1980) (rationale behind FRE 407 is that "people in general would be less likely to take subsequent remedial measures if their repairs or improvements would be used against them in a lawsuit arising out of a prior accident"), *cert. denied,* 449 U.S. 1080. *See also* ACN, FRE 407 (most important ground for exclusion is "social policy of encouraging people to take, or at least not discouraging them from taking, steps in furtherance of added safety").

FRE 407 to make their products safer. They are likely to do so regardless of evidentiary consequences in order to prevent further injuries and lawsuits and avoid the possibility that inaction in the face of repeated accidents or injuries will itself be taken as proof of negligence, or even as the basis for the award of punitive damages. Evidence of subsequent remedial measures satisfies the liberal relevancy standard of FRE 401 and at least sometimes does tend to prove negligence or culpable conduct, and therefore some state counterparts of FRE 407 take precisely the opposite approach.[2]

Remedial measures

The term "remedial measures" in FRE 407 and its state counterparts is interpreted broadly to include changes in design,[3] installation of protective devices,[4] new warnings,[5] removal of dangerous conditions,[6] revision of contracts,[7] changes in policies[8] or regulations[9] or procedures or protocol,[10] and discipline[11] or dismissal of employees.[12] It also includes instructions to take remedial measures,[13] but post-event investigations, tests, or reports are not themselves subsequent remedial

2. *See* Rhode Island Rule 407 ("When, after an event, measures are taken which, if taken previously, would have made the event less likely to occur, evidence of the subsequent measures is admissible.").

3. Hardy v. Chemetron Corp., 870 F.2d 1007, 1010 (5th Cir. 1989) (wiring change on bacon slicer); Cann v. Ford Motor Co., 658 F.2d 54, 59 (2d Cir. 1981) (modification of transmission), *cert. denied,* 456 U.S. 960.

4. Reddin v. Robinson Property Group Ltd. Partnership, 239 F.3d 756, 760 (5th Cir. 2001) (area of fall on gambling barge taped off afterwards).

5. Chlopek v. Federal Ins. Co., 499 F.3d 692, 700 (7th Cir. 2007) (modified warning label).

6. Rush v. Troutman Investment Co., 121 Or. App. 355, 854 P.2d 968 (1993) (manager ordered clothing rack removed that had injured plaintiff).

7. R. M. Perlman v. N.Y. Coat, Suit, Union Local 89-22-1, 33 F.3d 145, 156 (2d Cir. 1994) (letter from union suggesting changes in contract clause could not be used to prove clause was unlawful; recommendation in letter was subsequent remedial measure); Noble v. McClatchy Newspapers, 533 F.2d 1081, 1090 (9th Cir. 1975) (deletion of anticompetitive provision from distributor contracts after they were challenged), *cert. denied,* 433 U.S. 908.

8. Pastor v. State Farm Mutual Auto Insurance Co., 487 F.3d 1042, 1045 (7th Cir. 2007) (change in language of insurance policy stating that "day" meant 24 hours could not be used to prove that "day" in earlier version of contract meant "any part of a day"; such use would violate FRE 407 by "discouraging efforts to clarify contractual obligations" and "perpetuating any confusion caused by unclarified language").

9. Ford v. Schmidt, 577 F.2d 408, 410-411 (7th Cir. 1978) (change in prison regulations after incident giving rise to suit), *cert. denied,* 439 U.S. 870; SEC v. Geon Indus., Inc., 531 F.2d 39, 52 (2d Cir. 1976) (new company regulation concerning brokerage practices).

10. Tuer v. McDonald, 701 A.2d 1101 (Md. 1997) (change in preoperative procedure, after death of heart surgery patient).

11. Specht v. Jensen, 863 F.2d 700, 701-702 (10th Cir. 1988) (in civil rights action, evidence excluded that city had stated that "appropriate disciplinary action would be taken" against officers); Maddox v. City of Los Angeles, 792 F.2d 1408, 1417-1418 (9th Cir. 1986) (excluding evidence of disciplinary proceeding against police officer because it was a remedial measure).

12. Hull v. Chevron U.S.A., Inc., 812 F.2d 584, 586-587 (10th Cir. 1987) (after a forklift accident defendant employer fired the forklift driver).

13. Rush v. Troutman Inv. Co., 121 Or. App. 355, 854 P.2d 968 (1993) ("Instructions to take remedial measures are themselves remedial measures.").

measures excluded by the Rule,[14] even where they lead to later adoption of such measures.[15]

Despite the broad language of FRE 407, the prevailing view is that third-party remedial measures or repairs are not covered by the exclusionary principle, which means (for example) that plaintiffs suing manufacturers may prove remedial measures undertaken by employers or owners of the equipment or processes that caused the injury, who are not themselves being sued.[16] Some courts recognize an even broader exemption, holding that only "voluntary" remedial measures are covered by FRE 407,[17] with the result that measures mandated by governmental or regulatory authority (such as many product recalls) are not covered because they do not represent self-motivated socially responsible behavior of the sort that FRE 407 seeks to encourage.[18] Arguably, however, voluntary product recalls undertaken by manufacturers on their own are and should be covered by the principle, even though undertaken under the pressure of a legal regime that might impose liability if the defect goes uncorrected. In any event, proof of recalls is sometimes excluded under FRE 403, and findings and communications mandating recalls raise hearsay issues.[19]

Third-party and mandated measures

As originally enacted, FRE 407 left room to argue that a "subsequent" measure reaches steps taken after the date of the manufacture of the product or the creation of the condition that

Subsequent measures

14. Rocky Mountain Helicopters, Inc. v. Bell Helicopters Textron, Div. of Textron, Inc., 805 F.2d 907, 918-919 (10th Cir. 1986) (it "would strain the spirit of the remedial measure prohibition in Rule 407 to extend its shield to evidence contained in post-event tests or reports" as distinguished from actual remedial measures). Mere tests or reports do not fit FRE 407 because they do not make the event giving rise to the claim "less likely to occur."

15. Prentiss & Carlisle v. Koehring-Waterous, 972 F.2d 6, 10 (1st Cir. 1992) (FRE 407 does not bar evidence of a party's postaccident analysis of its products, even though "the analysis may often result in remedial measures being taken").

16. Diehl v. Blaw-Knox, 360 F.3d 426, 429-30 (3d Cir. 2004) (error to exclude evidence that owner of machine, who was not a party, made post-accident modifications to prevent similar accidents in future; FRE 407 does not apply to evidence of remedial measures taken by a nonparty); Buchanna v. Diehl Machine, Inc., 98 F.3d 366, 369 (8th Cir. 1996) (in suit against maker of saw, proof that plaintiff's employer installed T-guard after accident supported finding of liability and was not excludable under FRE 407).

17. Millennium Partners, L.P. v. Colmar Storage, LLC, 494 F.3d 1293 (11th Cir. 2007) (FRE 407 does not apply to remedial measures "taken without the voluntary participation of the defendant").

18. O'Dell v. Hercules, Inc., 904 F.2d 1194, 1204 (8th Cir. 1990) (recognizing exception "for evidence of remedial action mandated by superior government authority"); In re Aircrash in Bali, Indonesia, 871 F.2d 812, 817 (9th Cir. 1989) (purpose of FRE 407 "is not implicated in cases involving subsequent measures in which the defendant did not voluntarily participate"), *cert. denied,* 493 U.S. 1017. *See generally* Note, The "Superior Authority Exception" to Federal Rule of Evidence 407: The "Remedial Measure" Required to Clarify a Confused State of Evidence, 1991 U. Ill. L. Forum 843.

19. *Compare* Lindsay v. Ortho Pharmaceutical Corp., 637 F.2d 87, 94 (2d Cir. 1980) (drug label changes made in response to FDA pressure excludable under FRE 403) *with* Chase v. General Motors Corp., 856 F.2d 17, 21-22 (4th Cir. 1988) (recall of automobiles was covered by FRE 407). Official findings underlying government-required remedial measures are hearsay, but they may fit FRE 803(8)(C). *See* §8.50, *infra.*

caused the injury, rather than after the accident.[20] This argument was eliminated by a 1997 amendment defining subsequent to mean "after an injury or harm allegedly caused by an event." Hence a remedial measure taken after manufacture of a product but before plaintiff's injury is not covered,[21] although proof of such a measure is sometimes excludable under FRE 403.[22] Some courts admit evidence of a modification planned before plaintiff's accident even though implemented afterwards.[23]

The policy of FRE 407 arguably applies only to remedial measures taken in response to an accident, and some authority holds that measures taken after plaintiff's accident are not excludable if defendant was unaware of it and no claim had yet been made.[24]

Measures after similar accident

FRE 407 does *not* bar evidence of remedial measures taken after an accident similar to the one giving rise to plaintiff's claim but before plaintiff's own accident (a point that is clear under the 1997 amendment, even if it was uncertain under the prior language).[25] Arguably, however, a defendant who takes responsible steps after one accident to prevent a later accident should be protected against adverse use of the remedial measure by the later plaintiff.[26] Sometimes, of course, accidents or repairs prior to the event in suit may themselves be proved to show that defendant had knowledge or notice of a dangerous situation, which may bear on negligence in design, manufacture, or maintenance or may be relevant to claims of failure to warn or even recall a product.

20. *Compare* Huffman v. Caterpillar Tractor Co., 908 F.2d 1470, 1481 (10th Cir. 1990) ("wording and history of Rule 407" make it clear that "event" refers to "the time of the accident or injury to the plaintiff, not to the time of manufacture of the product or creation of the hazard") *with* Petree v. Victor Fluid Power, Inc., 831 F.2d 1191, 1197-1198 (3d Cir. 1987) (no abuse of discretion to exclude warning decals that were added subsequent to manufacture but prior to accident because offered on issue of foreseeability, and danger "must be foreseeable at the time of sale").

21. Cates v. Sears, Roebuck & Co., 928 F.2d 679, 686 (5th Cir. 1991) (error to exclude changes to warning placard and instruction manual made after sale but prior to accident); Roberts v. Harnischfeger Corp., 901 F.2d 42, 44 n.1 (5th Cir. 1989) (proper to admit evidence of change implemented in January 1984 where accident did not occur until February 1984).

22. Bogosian v. Mercedes-Benz of North America, Inc., 104 F.3d 472, 481 (1st Cir. 1997) (trial judge may exclude evidence of post-manufacture, pre-accident design modifications if its probative value is substantially outweighed by its prejudicial effects).

23. Raymond v. Raymond Corp., 938 F.2d 1518, 1523 (1st Cir. 1991) (FRE 407 does not exclude evidence of design modifications used on later model when these "were on the drawing board" before machine involved in accident was made, but evidence properly excluded as more prejudicial than probative).

24. Van Gordon v. Portland Gen. Elec. Co., 693 P.2d 1285, 1289-1290 (Or. 1985) (evidence of new signs posted after accident were not "subsequent repairs" where defendant did not know of injury to plaintiff at time they were posted).

25. Trull v. Volkswagen of Am., Inc., 187 F.3d 88, 96 (1st Cir. 1999) ("measures that take place *before* the accident at issue do not fall within the prohibition") (but excluding under FRE 403).

26. *See* Kelly v. Crown Equip. Co., 970 F.2d 1273, 1277 (3d Cir. 1992) (policy of FRE 407 supports "exclusion of evidence of safety measures taken before someone is injured by a newly manufactured product, even if those measures are taken in response to experience with an older product of the same or similar design").

Originally FRE 407 barred evidence of subsequent remedial measures only when offered to prove "negligence or culpable conduct," inviting arguments that the Rule did not apply to strict liability claims. Most federal circuits, however, applied FRE 407 in strict liability actions,[27] and this approach was codified by a 1997 amendment to the Rule specifying that "evidence of subsequent remedial measures is not admissible to prove negligence, culpable conduct, a defect in a product, a defect in a product's design, or a need for a warning or instruction."

By way of contrast, many state courts interpreting their state counterpart of original FRE 407 have taken the opposing view that evidence of subsequent remedial measures is admissible in strict liability actions.[28] In some states, legislative commentary resolves the issue.[29]

The argument for applying FRE 407 to strict liability claims is that they raise many of the same issues as a negligence claim.[30] Plaintiffs often assert both, and instructions could not be effective in limiting juries to considering proof of subsequent remedial measures on the strict liability claim but not the negligence claim. Moreover, the policies of FRE 407 are said to apply with full force to strict liability claims in order to encourage manufacturers to make their products safer, or at least to avoid deterring them from doing so.[31]

Courts refusing to apply Rule 407 to strict liability claims take the view that manufacturers are likely to make their product safer without the incentive provided by Rule 407. Remedial measures are implemented regardless of whether they are later provable, simply to prevent future claims and the possibility of punitive damage awards for failure to correct a known defect.[32] And in strict liability cases, subsequent

---

27. Among pre-amendment federal cases taking the view that FRE 407 applies in strict liability cases, *see* Raymond v. Raymond Corp., 938 F.2d 1518 (1st Cir. 1991); Cann v. Ford Motor Co., 658 F.2d 54, 60 (2d Cir. 1981), *cert. denied,* 456 U.S. 960.

28. *See, e.g.,* Forma Scientific, Inc. v. Biosera, Inc., 960 P.2d 908 (Colo. 1998); Dura Corp. v. Harned, 703 P.2d 396, 411 (Alaska 1985); Chart v. General Motors Corp., 258 N.W.2d 680, 684 (Wis. 1977). *But see* Krause v. American Aerolights, 762 P.2d 1011, 1015 n.6 (Or. 1988) (state counterpart of FRE 407 applies in products liability actions; listing split of federal and state authorities on question).

29. *Compare* Commentary, N.C. R. Ev. 407 ("It is the intent of the Committee that the rule should apply to all types of actions.") *with* Committee Comment, Colo. R. Ev. 407 ("The phrase 'culpable conduct' is not deemed to include proof of liability in a 'strict liability' case based on defect, where the subsequent measures are properly admitted as evidence of the original defect.").

30. Flaminio v. Honda Motor Co., 733 F.2d 463, 467 (7th Cir. 1984) (strict liability is "something of a misnomer in products cases" for liability exists only "if a product is defective or unreasonably dangerous," which "bring[s] into play factors of cost and risk similar to those that determine negligence").

31. Grenada Steel Indus. v. Alabama Oxygen Co., 695 F.2d 883, 886-889 (5th Cir. 1983) (assumption that admitting design changes evidence would deter "is not demonstrably inapplicable to manufacturers").

32. Ault v. International Harvester Co., 13 Cal. 3d 113, 117 Cal. Rptr. 812, 528 P.2d 1148 (1974) ("manifestly unrealistic" to suggest that a manufacturer "will forego making improvements in its product, and risk innumerable additional lawsuits and the attendant adverse effect upon its public image" because evidence of such improvement may be admitted in suit).

remedial measures often have particularly high probative value on the question whether a product was designed defectively. Even if Rule 407 were applicable, evidence of subsequent remedial measures is often admissible on the issue of feasibility. Rather than confuse the jury with a limiting instruction directing them to distinguish between feasibility and liability, arguably it is preferable to make the evidence generally admissible.

Erie issue Since many states refuse to apply their own Rule 407 to strict liability claims, the issue arises whether federal courts must defer to state law in diversity cases. Most federal courts hold that FRE 407 controls in diversity cases, and the 1997 amendment at least *assumes* that this view is correct.[33] A significant minority of pre-1997 decisions reached the opposite conclusion, insisting that *state* counterparts should be honored.[34]

The best argument for applying state law is that the issue is substantive and there is no federal intent to legislate on substantive points relating to product liability, hence FRE 407 should not apply even though no express language points toward this result. (It is not possible to argue that this substantive area is beyond *federal power* to regulate, since Congress obviously could enter the field of product liability. There is only an argument that Congress did not intend, when the Rules were enacted and when FRE 407 was amended, to regulate this area.) The best argument *for* applying federal law on this point is that there is no *textual* basis for refusing to apply FRE 407, and the provision has a procedural component in preventing jury confusion and furthering the cause of efficient and accurate fact ascertainment.[35]

§4.24 Admissible for Limited Purposes

By express terms, FRE 407 does not bar evidence of subsequent remedial measures when offered to prove "ownership, control, or feasibility of precautionary measures, if controverted" or for impeachment. Although these uses are sometimes described as "exceptions" to

---

33. *See, e.g.,* Flaminio v. Honda Motor Co., 733 F.2d 463, 470 (7th Cir. 1984) (excluding subsequent remedial measure under FRE 407 and rejecting claim that *Erie* requires application of identical state rule interpreted by state courts as being inapplicable in product cases); 1997 ACN to FRE 407 (speaking of a "uniform federal rule" applicable in product cases, most of which are brought under state law).

34. *See* Wheeler v. John Deere Co., 862 F.2d 1404, 1410 (10th Cir. 1988) (whether to admit evidence of subsequent remedial measures is based on policy considerations, so "it is governed by state law in diversity actions"). *See also* Donahue v. Phillips Petroleum Co., 866 F.2d 1008, 1013 & n.10 (8th Cir. 1989) ("not clear whether federal or state law" applies). *See generally* Note, Design Defects in the Rules Enabling Act: The Misapplication of Federal Rule of Evidence 407 to Strict Liability, 65 N.Y.U. L. Rev. 736 (1990) (endorsing minority view).

35. Flaminio v. Honda Motor Co., 733 F.2d 463, 470 (7th Cir. 1984) (no deference to state law required in diversity case because "substantive judgment that underlies Rule 407 is entwined with procedural considerations" and so occupies "that borderland where procedure and substance are interwoven" that it passes muster under Hanna v. Plumer).

FRE 407, they are more accurately viewed as lying beyond the reach of the exclusionary principle.

Evidence of subsequent remedial measures may be introduced to establish the defendant's ownership or control of the premises or instrumentality causing the injury. Relevance here is plain, for it is unlikely that a party would repair or take other remedial measures respecting property that he did not own or control.

Ownership or control

While the wording of FRE 407 leaves it unclear whether the phrase "if controverted" in the last sentence relates to evidence offered to prove ownership and control or only to evidence offered to prove feasibility, it should be construed as applying to all three uses,[1] as the Advisory Committee apparently intended.[2] Whether or not the "if controverted" proviso applies, evidence of subsequent remedial measures offered to prove ownership or control is excludable under FRE 403 if these issues are not in dispute.[3]

An important permissible use of subsequent remedial measures is to prove the feasibility of preventive measures.[4] If a defendant manufacturer claims that no safer product design was feasible, evidence that later a safer design was implemented is admissible to prove feasibility.[5] Such evidence also impeaches the defendant's claim that nothing better could be done, illustrating the common overlap between feasibility and impeachment under FRE 407. The remedial measure must be one that could feasibly have been implemented earlier. Evidence of a subsequent remedial measure is irrelevant if it was the result of technology that was not available at the time the plaintiff's claim arose.[6]

Feasibility of preventative measures

Evidence of subsequent remedial measures is admissible to prove feasibility only "if controverted." Clearly feasibility is controverted if defendant disputes it by evidence or argument, but not if defendant stipulates to it.[7] Stipulations are specifically endorsed by the Advisory

"If controverted"

§4.24   1. Hull v. Chevron U.S.A., Inc., 812 F.2d 584, 587 (10th Cir. 1987) (evidence of repairs offered to show control properly excluded where defendant admitted control at trial).

2. ACN, FRE 407 (after citing a case where evidence of remedial measures was offered to show control, stating that "[t]he requirement that the other purpose be controverted calls for automatic exclusion unless a genuine issue be present and allows the opposing party to lay the groundwork for exclusion by making an admission").

3. ACN, FRE 407 (noting that "the factors of undue prejudice, confusion of issues, misleading the jury, and waste of time remain for consideration under FRE 403").

4. Donahue v. Phillips Petroleum Co., 866 F.2d 1008, 1013 (8th Cir. 1989) (where defendant claimed it was not feasible for seller of propane gas to give warnings to ultimate consumer, proper to introduce brochure for consumers prepared by defendant after accident to rebut this claim).

5. Dixon v. International Harvester Co., 754 F.2d 573, 584 (5th Cir. 1985) (where defendant claimed the addition of protective metal screening was not feasible because it would interfere with vision of driver of logging vehicle, proper to admit evidence that defendant later installed such screening on similar vehicles).

6. Meller v. Heil Co., 745 F.2d 1297, 1301-1302 (10th Cir. 1984) (design changes or subsequent warnings are "simply not relevant" if "not scientifically known at the time of the sale"), *cert. denied,* 467 U.S. 1206.

7. Kerr-McGee Corp. v. Ma-Ju Marine Services, Inc., 830 F.2d 1332, 1344 (5th Cir. 1987) (no dispute regarding feasibility where defendant stipulated to it).

Committee as a ground for excluding evidence of subsequent remedial measures on the issue of feasibility.[8] The stipulation need not concede fault in the failure to use a particular safety measure, but only that such a measure was feasible.[9]

Some courts hold that only an express stipulation is effective to bar evidence of subsequent measures,[10] but others say it suffices that defendant refrains from offering evidence or argument on the point.[11] A defendant does not controvert feasibility merely by arguing or introducing evidence that a device, process, or design is reasonably safe,[12] but claiming that all precautions were taken or that no safer design was possible clearly does put feasibility in issue.[13]

The obvious purpose of the phrase "if controverted" is to protect defending parties against evidence of subsequent measures unless their litigation strategy in effect "opens the door" to such proof. This limit invites attempts at manipulation, and there is considerable risk that claimants cross-examining defense witnesses may try to push them into making statements that sound like claims that greater safety could not have been achieved. Some courts do not allow feasibility to be raised for the first time by the cross-examiner.[14] Nonetheless, defending parties have reason to take care lest their witnesses slip into overstated, exaggerated claims that no improvement in safety was possible.

The feasibility exception to FRE 407 normally does not apply where the jury has been sufficiently informed by other evidence of the

---

8. *See* ACN, FRE 407 ("The requirement that the other purpose be controverted calls for automatic exclusion unless a genuine issue be present and allows the opposing party to lay the groundwork for exclusion by making an admission.").

9. Fish v. Georgia-Pacific Corp. 779 F.2d 836, 839-840 (2d Cir. 1985) (feasibility not disputed where defendant was willing to concede that it could have given a warning but was under no legal duty to do so).

10. Herndon v. Seven Bar Flying Service, Inc., 716 F.2d 1322, 1329 (10th Cir. 1983) (in absence off an express concession by the manufacturer that it would have been possible to make a safer product, "the manufacturer should be deemed to dispute that fact and plaintiff should be able to present evidence of later remedial measures to show their feasibility prior to the accident"), *cert. denied*, 466 U.S. 958.

11. Gauthier v. AMF, Inc., 788 F.2d 634, 636-638 (9th Cir. 1986) (reversible error to admit evidence of the subsequent measure because even though defendant refused formal stipulation it did not argue or introduce evidence of nonfeasibility); Flaminio v. Honda Motor Co., 733 F.2d 463, 468 (7th Cir. 1984) (evidence of subsequent remedial measure not admissible where defendant "did not deny the feasibility of precautionary measures").

12. Grenada Steel Indus., Inc. v. Alabama Oxygen Co., 695 F.2d 883, 888 (5th Cir. 1983) (evidence of remedial measure properly excluded where "defense was only that the design it used was not defective").

13. *See, e.g.,* Anderson v. Malloy, 700 F.2d 1208, 1214 (8th Cir. 1983) (motel owners testified "that they had done everything necessary for a secure motel, and that chain locks and peep holes would not be successful"; rape victim plaintiff was "entitled to show affirmatively that these devices were feasible").

14. *See* Albrecht v. Baltimore & O. R. Co., 808 F.2d 329, 331 (4th Cir. 1987) (error to admit evidence of subsequent remedial measures where feasibility "was not in issue until the plaintiff began questioning the witness explicitly on these measures" because "it is not for the plaintiff to put feasibility in issue").

availability of alternative designs or processes.[15] In such cases, evidence of subsequent remedial measures may be excluded as cumulative under FRE 403.[16]

FRE 407 also does not block proof of subsequent remedial measures when offered for impeachment.[17] As noted above, often the claim being impeached is that no better protective measures were feasible, and the use of evidence of subsequent measures for impeachment overlaps with its use to prove feasibility.[18]

Evidence of subsequent remedial measures cannot be used to impeach a witness who testifies merely that a product, design, or process is reasonably safe because evidence of subsequent measures is "no more admissible to rebut a claim of non-negligence than it is to prove negligence directly."[19] Impeachment may be allowed if the witness denies the existence of a particular hazard,[20] testifies that the product was as safe as it could be,[21] or characterizes an alternative design or protective measure subsequently adopted as unnecessary,[22]

---

15. Knight v. Otis Elevator Co., 596 F.2d 84, 91 (3d Cir. 1979) (feasibility not controverted where at time evidence of remedial measure offered there was already evidence that design change could have been made easily and inexpensively).

16. Foster v. Ford Motor Co., 621 F.2d 715, 721 (5th Cir. 1980) (where defense engineer conceded that an alternative design was feasible, trial court could exclude evidence of subsequent design change as cumulative under FRE 403).

17. *See, e.g.,* Kenny v. Southeastern Pa. Transp. Auth., 581 F.2d 351, 356 (3d Cir. 1978) (in action against railroad to recover damages for rape where plaintiff claimed defendant did not maintain adequate lighting on platform where attack occurred, proper to receive evidence that railroad installed new lighting after the attack to impeach testimony by railroad employee that all reasonable care was being exercised at the time), *cert. denied,* 439 U.S. 1073.

18. *See, e.g.,* Anderson v. Malloy, 700 F.2d 1208, 1212-1214 (8th Cir. 1983) (suit against motel for failing to take security precautions that could have prevented plaintiff's rape; after defense evidence suggesting that nothing more could have been done, it was proper to bring out subsequent measures taken by defendant of installing chain locks and peepholes).

19. Hardy v. Chemetron Corp., 870 F.2d 1007, 1010-1011 (5th Cir. 1989). *See also* Flaminio v. Honda Motor Co., Ltd., 733 F.2d 463, 468 (7th Cir. 1984) (impeachment exception must be applied with care since "any evidence of subsequent remedial measures might be thought to contradict and so in a sense impeach a defendant's testimony that he was using due care at the time of the accident" and "if this counted as 'impeachment' the exception would swallow the rule").

20. Petree v. Victor Fluid Power, Inc., 887 F.2d 34, 38-41 (3d Cir. 1989) (where defense engineer testified that danger of metal spacers being ejected from press had been "designed out of the equipment" so there was no need to warn of projectile hazard, error to refuse evidence that defendant had added a warning decal to impeach this testimony).

21. Muzyka v. Remington Arms Co., 774 F.2d 1309, 1313-1314 (5th Cir. 1985) (where defense witnesses appeared to characterize rifle causing injury as "the ultimate in gun safety," plaintiff should have been allowed to impeach such testimony by showing that safety had been redesigned three weeks after accident).

22. Rimkus v. Northwest Colo. Ski Corp., 706 F.2d 1060, 1065-1066 (10th Cir. 1983) (where plaintiff sued defendant for negligence in failing to mark a rock outcropping on one of its ski slopes, defendant presented evidence that the outcropping was clearly visible on the day in question; because evidence that the hazard was obvious raised the inference that no warning was necessary, plaintiff was properly permitted to rebut that inference by showing the subsequent placing of warning signs).

ineffectual,[23] or unsafe.[24] Generally testimony describing a remedial measure merely as inadvisable is not enough to remove evidence of its implementation from the exclusionary policy of FRE 407.[25] In this area trial judges must balance impeachment value against risks of prejudice and confusion and may exclude under FRE 403 if warranted.[26]

Trial testimony may be impeached by evidence of inconsistent conduct by the witness.[27] Thus a defense witness who expresses an opinion that the product is safe may be impeached by evidence that he sent a warning letter to dealers informing them of the hazard.[28] Similarly, where a manufacturer claims that only dealers could properly instruct consumers, the court may properly admit evidence of warnings subsequently given by the manufacturer to consumers.[29]

Other purposes   Evidence of subsequent remedial measures is sometimes admitted for other relevant purposes that do not require an inference of negligence or culpable conduct on the part of the person implementing the measures. For example, evidence of subsequent remedial measures may be used to rebut a defense of contributory negligence based on the theory that any danger in the premises or instrumentality causing

23. Anderson v. Malloy, 700 F.2d 1208, 1214 (8th Cir. 1983) (where defendant testified that installation of peepholes and chain locks on doors of a motel room where plaintiff had been raped would provide only a false sense of security, it was proper to receive evidence that such remedial measures had been subsequently installed).

24. Tuer v. McDonald, 701 A.2d 1101 (Md. Ct. App. 1997) (although statement that remedial measure was "unsafe" would normally open door to proof that measure had in fact been implemented, here court construes testimony as saying only that measure would have been "inadvisable," which does not waive protection of Rule 407).

25. Gauthier v. AMF, Inc., 788 F.2d 634, 638 (9th Cir. 1986), *opinion amended* 805 F.2d 337 (9th Cir. 1986) (subsequent measures inadmissible where defendant conceded feasibility and argued only "that the safety problem was not great enough to warrant the trade-off of consumer frustration, increased complexity of the product, and risk of consumer efforts to disconnect the safety device"). *But see* Bickerstaff v. South Cent. Bell Tel. Co., 676 F.2d 163, 167-169 (5th Cir. 1982) (where one defense expert testified that while a warning was feasible it was not advisable or appropriate where risks were minimal, and another testified that all customers could be expected to know of the particular danger that caused the injury, trial judge should have allowed evidence of subsequent warnings given by phone company for impeachment purposes).

26. Petree v. Victor Fluid Power, Inc., 887 F.2d 34, 40-41 (3d Cir. 1989) (trial court has discretion under FRE 403 to exclude evidence offered for impeachment under FRE 407 although court abused discretion in excluding evidence on facts of this case).

27. Bickerstaff v. South Cent. Bell Tel. Co., 676 F.2d 163, 168 (5th Cir. 1982) (trial court should have allowed defense experts "to be impeached by the telephone company's subsequent conduct that tended to contradict their opinions").

28. Dollar v. Long Mfg., N.C., Inc., 561 F.2d 613, 618 (5th Cir. 1977) (in wrongful death action where defense engineer testified that in his opinion the backhoe was safe to operate while affixed to a roll-bar-equipped tractor, trial judge should have allowed for impeachment evidence that this same engineer sent a letter to backhoe dealers "warning them about the death dealing propensities of the Long backhoe when used in the fashion employed here"), *cert. denied*, 435 U.S. 996.

29. Reese v. Mercury Marine Div. of Brunswick Corp., 793 F.2d 1416, 1428-1429 (5th Cir. 1986) (where defendant suggested during trial "that only the retailer could properly instruct the ultimate consumer" about proper use of the kill switch, it was proper to introduce evidence of subsequent manufacturer warnings for purposes of impeachment).

injury should have been obvious to the plaintiff.[30] Also where a photograph of the accident scene has been introduced or a jury view taken, evidence of subsequent remedial measures is occasionally admitted to explain the changed conditions, although courts prohibit such use where it would undermine the policy of FRE 407.[31]

F.   SETTLEMENTS AND MEDICAL PAYMENTS

FRE 408

(a) **Prohibited Uses.** Evidence of the following is not admissible on behalf of any party, when offered to prove liability for, invalidity of, or amount of a claim that was disputed as to validity or amount, or to impeach through a prior inconsistent statement or contradiction:

(1) furnishing or offering or promising to furnish—or accepting or offering or promising to accept—a valuable consideration in compromising or attempting to compromise the claim, and

(2) conduct or statements made in compromise negotiations regarding the claim, except when offered in a criminal case and the negotiations related to a claim by a public office or agency in the exercise of regulatory, investigative or enforcement authority.

(b) **Permitted uses.** This rule does not require exclusion if the evidence is offered for purposes not prohibited by subdivision (a). Examples of permissible purposes included proving a witness's bias or prejudice, negating a contention of undue delay, and proving an effort to obstruct a criminal investigation or prosecution.

§4.25   Civil Settlement Offers Generally Excluded

Settlement negotiations play a vital role in the American litigation process. They enable parties to resolve lawsuits themselves and thereby

---

30. Pitasi v. Stratton Corp., 968 F.2d 1558, 1560-1561 (2d Cir. 1992) (evidence of postaccident posting of warnings at entrances to ski slope admissible to rebut claim that dangerous conditions were so obvious that warning signs were unnecessary); Rimkus v. Northwest Colorado Ski Corp., 706 F.2d 1060, 1065-1066 (10th Cir. 1983) (similar).

31. Johnson v. William C. Ellis & Sons Iron Works, Inc., 604 F.2d 950, 958 (5th Cir. 1979) (no error to exclude motion picture of machinery which "showed the guards that had been installed on the press after the accident" where such evidence was "cumulative" and created a risk of undue prejudice; also no error in refusing to allow a jury view of the machinery in its redesigned condition), *opinion amended on other grounds*, 609 F.2d 820 (5th Cir. 1980).

reduce unnecessary court congestion, delay, and costs. The overwhelming majority of lawsuits filed are settled rather than tried.[1] FRE 408 furthers the strong social policy in favor of private resolution of disputes by making settlements or offers of compromise generally inadmissible on the issues of liability or damages.[2] If a case does not settle, litigants are protected from having their settlement efforts used against them at trial.[3]

Offers of settlement sometimes also lack relevancy under FRE 401.[4] An offer to pay very low or nominal damages may demonstrate only the defendant's desire to avoid the nuisance costs of defending against a meritless claim rather than consciousness of fault.[5] Similarly, where a plaintiff offers to accept a sum only slightly below the amount claimed, such an offer has little tendency to prove invalidity of the claim. Admitting such offers could result in unfair prejudice, confusion of issues, and misleading of the jury, thus justifying exclusion under FRE 403.

Defining a claim FRE 408 applies only to offers made in an attempt to compromise a disputed "claim," but the Rule does not define a "claim." Clearly the filing of a lawsuit is the assertion of a claim, but FRE 408 also applies to settlement offers made in response to oral or written claims made before suit is filed.[6]

Properly understood, FRE 408 does not apply to offers made before a claim is asserted.[7] Even if it is obvious that one party has caused injury to another under circumstances that might result in liability, the "implicit" or potential claim does not mean that all offers of aid or compensation are necessarily covered by FRE 408.[8]

---

§4.25 1. *See* McMunigal, The Costs of Settlement: The Impact of Scarcity of Adjudication on Litigating Lawyers, 37 UCLA L. Rev. 833, 838 (1990).

2. FRE 408 is consistent with FRCP 68, which generally prohibits introduction into evidence of offers of judgment which are not accepted.

3. Cheyenne River Sioux Tribe v. United States, 806 F.2d 1046, 1050 (Fed. Cir. 1986) (error for court to base judgment on unaccepted settlement agreement negotiated between attorneys), *cert. denied,* 482 U.S. 913.

4. United States v. Contra Costa Water Dist., 678 F.2d 90, 92 (9th Cir. 1982) (evidence of settlement may be "irrelevant as being motivated by a desire for peace rather than from a concession of the merits of the claim").

5. ACN, FRE 408 (a settlement offer does not necessarily reflect "weakness of position").

6. Pierce v. F. R. Tripler & Co., 955 F.2d 820, 827 (2d Cir. 1992) (where a party threatens litigation and has initiated the first steps, "any offer made between attorneys will be presumed to be an offer within the scope of Rule 408").

7. Rodriguez-Garcia v. Municipality of Caguas, 495 F.3d 1, 11-12 (1st Cir.2007) (error to apply FRE 408 to precontroversy correspondence).

8. Cassino v. Reichhold Chems., Inc., 817 F.2d 1338, 1342-1343 (9th Cir. 1987) (FRE 408 does not bar evidence of termination package where employer offers to give severance pay in exchange for release of potential age discrimination claim because plaintiff "had not asserted any claim at the time [defendant] asked for the release"), *cert. denied,* 484 U.S. 1047; Deere & Co. v. International Harvester Co., 710 F.2d 1551, 1556-1557 (Fed. Cir. 1983) (FRE 408 not applicable to offer to license patent because no dispute existed, despite "probability" of eventual dispute).

FRE 408 applies only to offers to settle claims "disputed as to validity or amount."[9] Thus if a debtor concedes the amount of debt but offers to pay a lesser sum, evidence of such an offer is not barred by FRE 408.[10] Similarly, if a tortfeasor concedes liability and offers to pay damages in full, evidence of such an offer is not barred by FRE 408.[11] Where no dispute between the parties has emerged, their ongoing discussions may be viewed as "business communications" rather than settlement negotiations.[12] Still, it is not necessary for a discussion to reach the point of threatened litigation before a dispute may be found.[13]

> **Claim must be disputed**

The underlying policy of FRE 408 is to encourage parties to make concessions in order to settle the dispute and to protect them as they do so, including making an internal assessment of a disputed claim.[14] If the offeror is not making a concession or attempting to compromise but merely stating his position, FRE 408 is inapplicable.[15] FRE 408 should apply only where one party makes some movement away from the original boundaries of the dispute and toward the other's position.

> **Intent to compromise required**

9. Schlossman & Gunkelman, Inc. v. Tallman, 593 N.W.2d 374, 378 (N.D. 1999) (whether dispute exists depends on party intent and whether there is "a difference in interests or views" that parties seek to resolve); S. A. Healy Co. v. Milwauke Metro. Sewerage Dist., 50 F.3d 476, 480 (7th Cir. 1995) (dispute arises only when claim is rejected "at the initial or some subsequent level"; no dispute would have arisen if defendant had accepted claim).

10. In re B. D. International Discount Corp., 701 F.2d 1071, 1074 (2d Cir. 1983) (in bankruptcy proceeding, admitting statement by president of bankrupt corporation acknowledging accuracy of claims and seeking more time for payment because corporation did not dispute the claim), *cert. denied,* 464 U.S. 830. *See also* ACN, FRE 408 (policies behind encouraging settlements "do not come into play when the effort is to induce a creditor to settle an admittedly due amount for a lesser sum").

11. Greenstreet v. Brown, 623 A.2d 1270, 1272 (Me. 1993) (attorney's admission of malpractice and promise to compensate client admissible under state counterpart to FRE 408; "there is no evidence that a dispute existed about the validity of a claim or the amount claimed").

12. Big O Tire Dealers, Inc. v. Goodyear Tire & Rubber Co., 561 F.2d 1365, 1372-1373 (10th Cir. 1977) (statements were part of "business communications" rather than compromise negotiations because "discussions had not crystalized to the point of threatened litigation, a clear cutoff point"), *cert. dismissed,* 434 U.S. 1052 (1978). *But see* Olin Corp. v. Insurance Co. of North America, 603 F. Supp. 445, 450 (S.D.N.Y. 1985) (FRE 408 applied because plaintiff reasonably "contemplated that litigation might be necessary").

13. Affiliated Mfrs., Inc. v. Aluminum Co. of America, 56 F.3d 521, 527 (3d Cir. 1995) (FRE 408 "applies where an actual dispute or a difference of opinion exists, rather than when discussions crystallize to the point of threatened litigation"); Winchester Packaging, Inc. v. Mobil Chem. Co., 14 F.3d 316, 320 (7th Cir. 1994) (involvement of lawyers counts but does not itself determine existence of dispute). *Cf.* Bradbury v. Phillips Petroleum Co., 815 F.2d 1356, 1364 (10th Cir. 1987) (if application of FRE 408 is uncertain, better practice is to exclude evidence of compromise negotiations).

14. Affiliated Mfrs., Inc. v. Aluminum Co. of America, 56 F.3d 521, 529 (3d Cir. 1995) (FRE 408 reaches internal memoranda evaluating claims). *See also* Blu-J Inc. v. Kemper C.P.A. Group, 916 F.2d 637, 642 (11th Cir. 1990) (excluding accountant's evaluation "prepared by mutual agreement [of parties] as part of their settlement negotiations").

15. United States v. Hooper, 596 F.2d 219, 225 (7th Cir. 1979) (because check was intended as payment in full and not as offer of compromise, it was properly received as an admission).

First offers

FRE 408 should not be so rigidly applied, however, that a party's first offer is always found to be a position statement rather than an offer to compromise. Often the true positions of the parties are not fully developed or expressed because they recognize that concessions are necessary for settlement. Thus a party's first offer may indeed represent an attempt to compromise.[16]

Party's own offer

The rule generally precludes a party from introducing evidence of its own settlement offer on the theory that "this could itself reveal the fact that the adversary entered into settlement discussions."[17] Moreover, proof of such offers would often require calling counsel as witnesses, thereby inviting motions for disqualification.[18] A party may be allowed to offer evidence of its own settlement initiatives for a purpose other than proving validity or invalidity of a claim or its amount.[19]

Sometimes in employment cases where a claim of discrimination or wrongful discharge has been made, the employer offers to reinstate the plaintiff or place her in another position. Here it is often the employer who seeks to prove the offer at trial to demonstrate good faith and, where the offer is refused, failure of the plaintiff to mitigate damages. Courts are divided on whether evidence offered on the issue of mitigation should be excluded as bearing on the "amount" of a disputed claim or admitted for a permissible "other purpose."[20] FRE 408 applies only where the offer was made to settle the pending claim, and therefore courts look to whether the employer sought a release as a condition of the offer.[21]

16. Winchester Packaging, Inc. v. Mobil Chem. Co., 14 F.3d 316, 320 (7th Cir. 1994) (reasonable to interpret a bill submitted "in an atmosphere in which the threat of a lawsuit was looming" as a compromise offer intended to head off litigation rather than a true statement of full amount claimed, so it was properly excluded). *See generally* Brazil, Protecting the Confidentiality of Settlement Negotiations, 39 Hastings L.J. 955, 973 (1988) (opening offers "are often in fact 'compromise' proposals, made in an environment in which everyone knows that parties do not see eye-to-eye about how a particular matter should be resolved").

17. ACN to FRE 408. See also Bridgeport Music, Inc. v. Justin Combs Publg., 507 F.3d 470 (6th Cir. 2007) (no error in barring defendant from introducing its own settlement offer to prove lack of a "malicious" state of mind in copyright infringement case; evidence not relevant to issue of whether defendants infringed willfully).

18. Pierce v. F. R. Tripler & Co., 955 F.2d 820, 827 (2d Cir. 1992) (allowing offeror to introduce its own settlement offers "could inhibit settlement discussions and interfere with the effective administration of justice" because attorneys for both sides might be required to testify on such offers, thereby disqualifying them as trial counsel).

19. Kennon v. Slipstreamer, Inc., 794 F.2d 1067, 1069 (5th Cir. 1986) (FRE 408 bars even evidence that "favors the settling party," unless it is relevant for purpose other than proving "liability for or invalidity of the claim or its amount").

20. *Compare* Stockman v. Oakcrest Dental Center PC, 480 F3d 791 (6th Cir. 2007) (trial court erred in admitting plaintiff's acceptance of offer of reinstatement with conditions; defendant did not open door to such evidence by raising issue of plaintiff's failure to mitigate damages) *with* Bhandari v. First Nat'l Bank of Commerce, 808 F.2d 1082, 1103 (5th Cir. 1987), *cert. denied,* 494 U.S. 1061 (evidence offered on issue of mitigation is for a permissible "other purpose").

21. Thomas v. Resort Health Related Facility, 539 F. Supp. 630 (E.D.N.Y. 1982) (employer's offer of reinstatement was unconditional and did not require release of pending claim, so it was admissible to show that any lost pay subsequent to time of offer of reinstatement was not attributable to defendant).

FRE 408 excludes evidence that a party or witness settled or offered to settle a claim with a third person if offered to prove the validity or invalidity of the claim or its amount in the instant case.[22] Thus in an action against driver *D*, passenger *A* cannot introduce evidence that *D* settled with passenger *B* as evidence of *D*'s liability to passenger *A*. Similarly, *D* cannot introduce evidence that passenger *A* settled a claim against another driver involved in the same collision as evidence of the invalidity of passenger *A*'s claim against *D*.[23] And of course statements made in the course of such negotiations with third parties are normally not admissible on the issue of liability or damages in the instant case.[24]

Settlements with third parties

Evidence of settlements with third parties may, however, be admissible to show bias or prejudice of a witness or party,[25] to demonstrate the existence of a nonadversarial relationship between certain parties,[26] or to explain why certain defendants are not in court.[27] Not surprisingly, FRE 408 applies not only to testimony and other evidence of settlement, but also when information about settlement is conveyed by jury instructions.[28]

As noted above, FRE 408 excludes evidence of conduct or statements made during the course of "compromise negotiations,"[29] and clearly the rule of exclusion applies to statements made during settlement negotiations in other lawsuits.[30] FRE 408 allows lawyers and parties to

Settlement discussions

22. Kennon v. Slipstreamer, Inc., 794 F.2d 1067, 1069 (5th Cir. 1986) (judge erred, in product liability suit, in telling jury that plaintiff settled with wholesaler, retailer, and material supplier for $10 apiece, because this low amount tended to point finger at manufacturer). *See also* ACN, FRE 408 (specifically contemplating application of Rule in situations where "a party to the present litigation has compromised with a third person").

23. McInnis v. A.M.F., Inc., 765 F.2d 240, 247-251 (1st Cir. 1985) (settlement with third party inadmissible to show invalidity of plaintiff's claim against defendant).

24. Missouri Pacific Ry. v. Arkansas Sheriff Boy's Ranch, 655 S.W.2d 389, 394-395 (Ark. 1983) (statements by agent of defendant in settling similar claim of third party inadmissible under Rule 408).

25. *See* §4.26, *infra.*

26. Brocklesby v. United States, 767 F.2d 1288, 1292-1293 (9th Cir. 1985) (plaintiff could prove indemnity agreement between two defendants to show lack of adverse relationship between them and also to attack credibility of their witnesses), *cert. denied,* 474 U.S. 1101. *Cf.* Reichenbach v. Smith, 528 F.2d 1072, 1073 n.7 (5th Cir. 1976) (no abuse of discretion to reject evidence of a "Mary Carter" agreement, defined as "a contract by which one co-defendant secretly agrees with the plaintiff that, if such defendant will proceed to defend himself in court, his own maximum liability will be diminished proportionally by increasing the liability of the other co-defendants") (but better practice is to admit such agreements).

27. Kennon v. Slipstreamer, Inc., 794 F.2d 1067, 1070 (5th Cir. 1986) (trial court could disclose fact of settlement, but not its amount, to avoid jury confusion about absence of defendants previously in court).

28. Kennon v. Slipstreamer, Inc., 794 F.2d 1067, 1069-1071 (5th Cir. 1986) (FRE 408 applies to bar trial judge from telling jury amount of plaintiff's settlements with third parties).

29. Ramada Dev. Co. v. Rauch, 644 F.2d 1097, 1107 (5th Cir. 1981) (FRE 408 applies to report specifically prepared for settlement negotiations to help parties evaluate claim).

30. Fiberglass Insulators, Inc. v. Dupuy, 856 F.2d 652, 654-655 (4th Cir. 1988) (proper to exclude statements made in settlement negotiations in earlier litigation).

negotiate freely, without concern that what they say can be introduced against them as admissions, and the language is broad enough to cover background memoranda and studies prepared by a party in order to present or assess settlement proposals.[31]

FRE 408 is intended to apply to settlement negotiations in civil cases, as indicated by the reference to compromising a "claim" rather than a "charge." Plea bargaining in criminal cases is addressed by FRE 410. The language of FRE 410, however, refers only to plea bargaining statements by the accused, not those by the prosecutor. Hence some courts cite the policy of FRE 408 as justification for excluding plea bargain offers or statements by the prosecutor, such as a proposal to drop certain charges in exchange for a plea to other charges.[32]

Application to criminal cases Subject to one important qualification, the rule provides that statements made during compromise negotiations in a civil case are not admissible against a party in a later criminal prosecution, at least when offered for the purposes prohibited by FRE 408(a). If the rule permitted use of compromise statements in subsequent criminal prosecutions, it would undoubtedly chill civil settlement discussions.[33] The exception to this protection arises in negotiations with a public office or agency acting "in the exercise of its regulatory, investigative, or enforcement authority." Here a party's statements made in the course of civil settlement negotiations (although not settlement offers themselves) are admissible in a later criminal prosecution to prove liability for or the validity or invalidity of a disputed claim or its amount, and also may be admitted to impeach a party.[34] Thus caution is warranted in civil settlement negotiations with a government agency, and a party would be wise to seek an agreement protecting against subsequent disclosure before beginning negotiations. In certain situations, such as where an individual negotiated with a government agency without counsel or under other circumstances suggesting unfairness, the court has discretion to exclude the statements under FRE 403.[35]

---

31. Affiliated Mfrs., Inc. v. Aluminum Co. of America, 56 F.3d 521, 529 (3d Cir. 1995) (FRE 408 covers internal memoranda).

32. United States v. Verdoorn, 528 F.2d 103, 107 (8th Cir. 1976) (under rationale of FRE 408 government proposals concerning pleas should be excluded). *But see* United States v. Baker, 926 F.2d 179 (2d Cir. 1991).

33. United States v. Arias, 431 F.3d 1327, 1336-1337 (11th Cir. 2005) (in criminal trial, error to admit statement by defendant seeking to compromise civil claim; application in criminal cases "furthers the policy interests" of the Rule); United States v. Bailey, 327 F.3d 1131, 1144-1146 (10th Cir. 2003) (evidence of civil settlement efforts "can be more devastating to a criminal defendant than to a civil litigant").

34. United States v. Logan, 250 F.3d 350, 366-367 (6th Cir. 2001) (in trial of mortgage lenders for fraud, admitting evidence of settlement negotiations between defendants and HUD); United States v. Prewitt, 34 F.3d 436, 439 (7th Cir. 1994) (in mail fraud prosecution, admitting civil compromise negotiations with SEC).

35. *See* ACN to FRE 408 ("[I]f an individual was unrepresented at the time the statement was made . . . its probative value in a subsequent criminal case may be minimal. But there is no absolute exclusion imposed by Rule 408.").

§4.26 Admissible for Limited Purposes

FRE 408 does not require exclusion of offers of settlement where offered for purposes other than proving liability or damages, such as "proving a witness's bias or prejudice; negating a contention of undue delay; and proving an effort to obstruct a criminal investigation or prosecution."

Subject to FRE 403, evidence of prior settlements or offers to compromise is admissible to show that a witness was biased or prejudiced, as might happen if a witness has settled her own claim against one of the parties and thus may be disposed (or perhaps feel obliged as a matter of human impulse or feeling) to testify favorably for that party. Sometimes nearly the opposite situation arises: A witness who tried unsuccessfully to settle might be inclined to slant her testimony against the party who rejected her overtures. Some settlement agreements formally obligate a person to testify in a case, although it is illegal to seek to bind a person to a particular version of events.[1]

Bias or prejudice

Evidence of prior settlements or offers to compromise may be relevant in challenging a contention of undue delay. The party denying the allegation may show that good-faith negotiations were being conducted in an effort to resolve the suit.[2]

Rebut claim of undue delay

A settlement or offer to compromise may be proved where it is evidence of an effort to obstruct a criminal investigation or prosecution.[3] As stated in the ACN to FRE 408, an effort to "buy off" the prosecutor or a prosecuting witness "is not within the policy of the rule of exclusion." Even an offer that does not amount to illegal inducement or outright bribery, such as an offer to return missing property, may be admissible under FRE 408.[4] It goes almost without saying that unlawful threats made during compromise negotiations are not excludable under FRE 408.[5]

Obstructing criminal investigation

Many states now authorize civil compromise of certain minor criminal charges, on the theory that it is better to allow individuals to resolve such matters than to insist on the state's traditional prerogatives (often the statutes carve out exceptions for crimes committed "riotously" or with intent to commit a felony, or for crimes within a family,

Civil compromise of criminal charges

---

§4.26 1. *See* Hudspeth v. Commissioner of IRS, 914 F.2d 1207, 1213-1214 (9th Cir. 1990) (error to exclude settlement with Commissioner that was relevant to show bias or prejudice of testifying valuation expert).

2. Californian & Hawaiian Sugar Co. v. Kansas City Terminal Warehouse Co., 602 F. Supp. 183, 188 (W.D. Mo. 1985) (where defendant claimed plaintiffs delayed selling damaged sugar until market price fell significantly, settlement negotiations between parties admissible to explain why plaintiffs delayed in disposing of sugar).

3. United States v. Technic Servs., Inc., 314 F.3d 1031, 1045 (9th Cir. 2002) (evidence offered to prove obstruction of EPA investigation is outside protection of FRE 407).

4. United States v. Peed, 714 F.2d 7, 9-10 (4th Cir. 1983) (admitting defendant's offer to return missing property because it appeared motivated by purpose of persuading victim to drop criminal charges rather than to compromise civil claim).

5. Uforma/Shelby Business Forms, Inc. v. NLRB, 111 F.3d 1284, 1294 (6th Cir. 1997) (FRE 408 does not cover "evidence of alleged threats to retaliate for protected activity," and the threats may be shown in proving liability for the threats themselves or for acting upon them).

where private compromise remains illegal).[6] Where an offer of civil compromise is proper under the law of the jurisdiction where the alleged crime occurred, it should not be admissible under the "obstruction" provision of FRE 408. And when the victim of a criminal act brings a civil suit, FRE 408 does indeed apply, and requires exclusion of evidence of the compromise negotiations, whether offered in the civil case or in the criminal prosecution.[7]

Other purposes
The list of permissible purposes in FRE 408 is not exclusive. Evidence of settlements or offers to compromise may be admissible for many relevant purposes, subject to FRE 403, provided they are not offered to prove liability or damages.[8] Such evidence is admissible to prove the good faith or bad faith of a party conducting settlement negotiations,[9] a party's intent with respect to the scope of a release,[10] a party's knowledge of its agent's prior wrongs or dangerous propensities,[11] or notice to a party of the unlawfulness of certain conduct.[12]

Breach of agreement
If one party breaches a settlement agreement and the other party sues to enforce it, FRE 408 does not bar proof of the settlement because it is offered to prove the contractual obligation, not the validity of the underlying claim.[13] But if the aggrieved party sues on the claim rather than the agreement, it seems that FRE 408 applies, although it is at least arguable that a party who repudiates a valid settlement agreement should lose the protection of FRE 408.[14]

---

6. *See, e.g.,* Ariz. Rev. Stat. Ann. 13-3981 (authorizing compromise of certain misdemeanors and petty offenses); Cal. Penal Code 1377-1379 (authorizing compromises of certain misdemeanors); Or. Rev. Stat. 135.703-.709 (similar).

7. United States v. Meadows, 598 F.2d 984, 988-989 (5th Cir. 1979) (FRE 408 governs "the admission of related civil settlement negotiations in a criminal trial"). *But see* Manko v. United States, 87 F.3d 50 (2d Cir. 1996) (FRE 408 does not necessarily bar civil settlements from criminal trials, although they may be excluded under FRE 403).

8. Sometimes evidence offered for "another" purpose nonetheless violates the policy of FRE 408. *See, e.g.,* McInnis v. A.M.F., Inc., 765 F.2d 240, 248-249 (1st Cir. 1985) (evidence of settlement offered to prove "causation" was a "camouflaged" way of proving liability, hence barred by FRE 408).

9. Athey v. Farmers Ins. Exchange, 234 F.3d 357 (8th Cir. 2000) (bad faith); Weir v. Federal Ins. Co., 811 F.2d 1387, 1395 (10th Cir. 1987) (good faith). But see Pierce v. F. R. Tripler & Co., 955 F.2d 820, 826-827 (2d Cir. 1992) (FRE 408 excludes defense evidence of offer to obtain other position for plaintiff to show defendant's "state of mind" at time plaintiff was denied promotion, which was not an "other purpose" but involved an attempt to show invalidity of claim).

10. Coakley & Williams v. Structural Concrete Equip., 973 F.2d 349, 353-354 (4th Cir. 1992).

11. Gagliardi v. Flint, 564 F.2d 112, 116 (3d Cir. 1977) (settlement agreement negotiations with third party beaten by same police officer admissible to prove city's knowledge of police officer's dangerous propensities; relevant to issue of punitive damages), *cert. denied,* 438 U.S. 904.

12. United States v. Austin, 54 F.3d 394 (7th Cir. 1995) (evidence of defendant's prior settlement with FTC admitted to prove defendant was on notice that his conduct was wrongful).

13. Cates v. Morgan Portable Bldg. Corp., 780 F.2d 683, 691 (7th Cir. 1985) (FRE 408 does not bar evidence of settlement offered to prove breach of settlement agreement).

14. Ball, Admissions Arising Out of Compromise—Are They Irrelevant?, 31 Tex. L. Rev. 239, 258-259 (1953) (arguing that protection for offers to settle should continue even where settlement is breached).

Under the original version of the rule, there was uncertainty whether statements made by a party during settlement negotiations were admissible to impeach that party or his witnesses by contradicting their testimony at trial.[15] Under an amendment adopted in 2006, the rule now expressly bars use of offers or statements made in compromise negotiations "to impeach through a prior inconsistent statement or contradiction." Permitting the use of statements made during settlement negotiations for purposes of impeachment could significantly undermine the policies and protections of FRE 408 and inhibit the willingness of parties to talk freely.

> **FRE 409**
>
> Evidence of furnishing or offering or promising to pay medical, hospital, or similar expenses occasioned by an injury is not admissible to prove liability for the injury.

§4.27   Payment of Medical Expenses

FRE 409 excludes evidence of offers to pay or payment of medical, hospital, or similar expenses occasioned by an injury to prove liability for the injury. The Rule thus shields the "advance payment" programs currently implemented by many insurance companies from evidentiary use against the insured on the issue of liability.[1]

FRE 409 also protects the "good Samaritan" who offers to pay an injured person's medical bills out of compassion. For example, a pedestrian who is struck by a car may refuse to seek medical attention if he lacks medical insurance. If the driver offers to take the pedestrian to a doctor and pay for the medical expenses, FRE 409 prevents the offer from being introduced to prove the driver's liability.

The evidence is excluded in part because of its questionable relevance on the issue of fault. Such an offer may be motivated entirely by the compassion of the driver rather than any sense of legal responsibility for the injuries. Such evidence is also excluded on grounds of social policy. By barring adverse evidentiary use, FRE 409 encourages citizens to act on their humane impulses, or at least avoids penalizing those who do.

---

15. In many cases, practical or ethical considerations bar the presentation of such evidence. Proof of one lawyer's earlier statements often requires testimony by the other lawyer, and a lawyer is generally prohibited from being a witness and an advocate in the same case. *See* §6.9, *infra.*

§4.27   1. Under an "advance payment" program, an insurance carrier agrees to pay medical bills and related expenses prior to settlement or trial of any damage claim. Such programs are thought to further good will between the carrier and the injured victim and to enhance the likelihood of an amicable settlement. Advance payment programs are sometimes mandated by statute.

Unlike FRE 408 (the provision barring proof of settlement offers), FRE 409 does not exclude collateral admissions of liability by the offeror.[2] The settlement provision has a broader exclusionary scope because it is intended to facilitate and protect the entire settlement negotiation process.[3] In another respect, however, FRE 409 is the broader rule because unlike FRE 408 it does not require that there be a disputed claim or that the offer be an attempt to compromise such a claim.

FRE 409 applies not only to medical and hospital expenses but also to other "similar expenses" occasioned by an injury. "Similar expenses" should be construed broadly to cover expenses related to treatment or rehabilitation from the injury or personal care necessitated by the injury.

Although evidence of an offer to pay or payment of medical expenses is prohibited to prove liability for the injury, it may be admissible, subject to FRE 403, for other purposes such as to prove the existence of the injury, mitigation of damages, or the existence of an employment relationship.[4]

G. PLEA BARGAINS

FRE 410

Except as otherwise provided in this rule, evidence of the following is not, in any civil or criminal proceeding, admissible against the defendant who made the plea or was a participant in the plea discussions:

(1) a plea of guilty which was later withdrawn;

(2) a plea of nolo contendere;

(3) any statement made in the course of any proceedings under Rule 11 of the Federal Rules of Criminal Procedure or comparable state procedure regarding either of the foregoing pleas; or

(4) any statement made in the course of plea discussions with an attorney for the prosecuting authority which do not result in a plea of guilty or which result in a plea of guilty later withdrawn.

2. *Cf.* Port Neches Indep. Sch. Dist. v. Soignier, 702 S.W.2d 756, 757 (Tex. App. 1986) (portion of letter stating that all bills should be sent to employer's insurer and acknowledging that injury was covered by worker's compensation properly received as an admission).

3. ACN, FRE 409 (broad protection of statements is needed "if compromises are to be effected," but not in cases of payments or offers to pay medical expenses, "where factual statements may be expected to be incidental in nature").

4. *See, e.g.,* Savoie v. Otto Candies, Inc., 692 F.2d 363, 370 n.7 (5th Cir. 1982) ("maintenance payment" admissible to show recipient was employee).

However, such a statement is admissible (i) in any proceeding wherein another statement made in the course of the same plea or plea discussions has been introduced and the statement ought in fairness be considered contemporaneously with it, or (ii) in a criminal proceeding for perjury or false statement if the statement was made by the defendant under oath, on the record and in the presence of counsel.

§4.28   Withdrawn Guilty Pleas; Nolo Contendere Pleas

A withdrawn guilty plea or plea of nolo contendere (whether accepted or withdrawn) may not be admitted against the defendant who made the plea in any civil or criminal proceeding.[1] Any statements made in the course of the court proceedings where such a plea is entered or withdrawn are similarly inadmissible.[2]

A guilty plea may be withdrawn for many reasons, including incompetency of counsel, misunderstanding of the possible penalties, and newly discovered evidence. A withdrawn guilty plea is excluded because evidence that the defendant once pled guilty would undermine the purpose of allowing the plea to be withdrawn.

A nolo contendere plea is excluded for two reasons. First, a defendant who enters such a plea is not admitting guilt but simply refusing to contest the charges. Therefore, such a plea has less probative value on the question whether defendant actually committed the crime than a guilty plea. Second, granting immunity against subsequent adverse use is central to the purpose and function of pleas of nolo contendere. It allows defendants to accept criminal consequences for their conduct without increasing their exposure to civil liability, thereby encouraging compromise dispositions of criminal cases.

Nolo pleas

Often criminal defendants know that civil liability is likely to ensue from their criminal conduct. Subsequent civil litigation is particularly probable against criminal defendants charged with white collar crimes such as antitrust or securities law violations, but it is becoming increasingly common for crimes of violence such as rape and assault. A criminal defendant who is reluctant to plead guilty out of concern for civil consequences may be willing to plead nolo contendere,

§4.28   1. FRE 410 should be construed to apply to nolo pleas and withdrawn guilty pleas in state as well as federal prosecutions. It should also apply to nolo pleas and guilty pleas that are tendered but not accepted and to nolo pleas and guilty pleas that are set aside by appeal or collateral attack. FRCrimP 11(e)(6) is virtually identical to FRE 410.

2. FRE 410(3) (excluding any statement made "in the course of any proceedings under Rule 11 of the Federal Rules of Criminal Procedure or comparable state procedure" concerning a plea of guilty later withdrawn or a nolo contendere plea). *See also* ACN, FRCrimP 11(e)(6) (statements need not be made in court and Rule may exclude statements that are part of a probation officer's presentence report).

thereby saving the government the often substantial cost of proving its case.[3]

A conviction based on a nolo contendere plea is also generally inadmissible against a defendant in any subsequent civil or criminal proceedings.[4] However, judgments entered on nolo contendere pleas are usually admitted for limited evidentiary purposes, such as to impeach a witness under FRE 609,[5] to prove "prior crimes" under FRE 404(b),[6] or to establish a prior conviction where it is an element of a charge.[7]

Unwithdrawn guilty pleas

FRE 410 does not bar proof of guilty pleas that are accepted and not withdrawn. If the guilty plea is accepted, there is no need for a trial, and the most likely evidential use of the plea is in later civil or criminal proceedings.[8] In later litigation, an accepted guilty plea is generally admissible against the defendant as an admission[9] and may be admissible against other parties as a statement against interest.[10] It can be used either as substantive evidence or for impeachment as a prior inconsistent statement. A conviction based on a guilty plea is also admissible both as substantive evidence[11] and for impeachment.[12]

---

3. A nolo contendere plea denies later civil litigants the "piggyback" effect they otherwise would receive from a guilty plea or a conviction. Trial judges have discretion to refuse a defendant's offer to plead nolo contendere and sometimes reject the plea where there is significant public interest in a definitive resolution of the charge.

4. See FRE 803(22) (creating a hearsay exception for felony convictions, but excluding felony convictions based on nolo pleas).

5. United States v. Lipscomb, 702 F.2d 1049, 1070 (D.C. Cir. 1983) (conviction based on nolo plea can be used for impeachment under FRE 609).

6. United States v. Frederickson, 601 F.2d 1358, 1365 n.10 (8th Cir. 1979) (convictions based on nolo pleas admissible as "other crimes" evidence under FRE 404(b), and there is "no reason to distinguish between a judgment of conviction based on a plea of *nolo contendere* and a judgment of conviction obtained in any other manner"), *cert. denied*, 444 U.S. 934.

7. Pearce v. United States Dept. of Justice, DEA, 836 F.2d 1028, 1029 (6th Cir. 1988) (in doctor's license revocation proceeding, using conviction for distributing controlled substances, even though based on nolo plea).

8. FRE 410 does not address the admissibility of guilty pleas or nolo contendere pleas by co-offenders. Such pleas are generally considered irrelevant in proving the guilt of the defendant. Bisaccia v. Attorney General of State of New Jersey, 623 F.2d 307, 312 (3d Cir. 1980) (allowing guilty plea of co-offender as substantive evidence of defendant's guilt was error serious enough to raise "specter of unconstitutionality"), *cert. denied*, 449 U.S. 1042. If the co-offender appears as a witness, however, the plea is sometimes admitted with an instruction limiting its use to matters of credibility. United States v. Werme, 939 F.2d 108, 113-114 (3d Cir. 1991) (proof that witness pled guilty or agreed to plead guilty is "highly relevant" to show bias), *cert. denied*, 502 U.S. 1092.

9. *See* FRE 801(d)(2) (admissions of a party-opponent), discussed in §8.27, *infra*. Sometimes guilty pleas to petty crimes or traffic offenses are excludable by statute, apparently in order to encourage expeditious resolution of such matters or because such pleas are entered simply as a convenience and are not very reliable, when the stakes are raised in civil damage suits, as proof of liability.

10. *See* FRE 804(b)(3) (statements against interest), discussed in §§8.72-8.76, *infra*.

11. *See* FRE 803(22) (conviction of felony admissible to prove any fact essential to sustain the judgment).

12. *See* FRE 609(a).

§4.29   Plea Bargaining Statements

One of the most important uses of FRE 410 is to protect plea negotiations, which are a vital aspect of the criminal justice process.[1] FRE 410(4) renders any statement made in the course of plea discussions with the prosecutor inadmissible against the defendant in any civil or criminal proceeding, at least where those discussions fail to produce agreement or lead to pleas later withdrawn. Thus defense attorneys and defendants can negotiate freely with the government without concern that if the case ultimately goes to trial their factual statements will be received as admissions against the defendant.

FRE 410(4) requires courts to define "plea discussion."[2] Where the defendant or his lawyer and the prosecutor or her agent expressly agree to try to negotiate a plea, ensuing discussions clearly qualify. FRE 410 also applies where both parties engage in discussions with the objective of negotiating a plea even though the purpose goes unspoken.[3] In some circumstances, the Rule protects a defendant's attempt to open plea negotiations even though his effort is ultimately rebuffed by the prosecutor,[4] but informing a defendant of the effect of his cooperation under Federal Sentencing Guidelines does not convert an interrogation session into plea bargaining.[5]

Defining "plea discussion"

Ordinarily the presence of defense counsel and prosecutor in a meeting also attended by the defendant means that the purpose on all sides is to engage in plea bargaining, and in this situation FRE 410 applies unless something is said or done to indicate that the purpose is something else.[6] Usually in such cases the parties (or one of them)

---

§4.29   1. *See* Blackledge v. Allison, 431 U.S. 63, 71 (1977) (guilty plea and plea bargain are "important components of this country's criminal justice system").

2. United States v. Brooks, 670 F.2d 625, 626-628 (5th Cir. 1982) (statements properly admitted where "volunteered" immediately upon arrest; defense position "would permit every defendant, leaping from his automobile at the first sign of a uniform and confessing his guilt, to exclude any such testimony as a part of a plea bargain").

3. United States v. Martin, 431 F.3d 846, 851-852 (5th Cir. 2005) (letters from defendant to U.S. Attorney's office admitting involvement in robberies and indicating wish to plead guilty were excludable plea bargaining statements); United States v. Herman, 544 F.2d 791, 797 (5th Cir. 1977) (defendant's statements need not be "accompanied by a preamble explicitly demarcating the beginning of plea discussions" because such a requirement invites use of the Rule as "a sword rather than a shield").

4. United States v. Robertson, 582 F.2d 1356, 1367 (5th Cir. 1978) (even if "nascent overtures" are ignored by the government, "express unilateral offers" to plead ought to be held inadmissible if reasonable in context). *See also* ACN, FRCrimP 11(e)(6) (referring to "plea discussions" rather than "an offer to plead," ensures that "even an attempt to open plea bargaining" is covered by the Rule) (citing United States v. Brooks, 536 F.2d 1137 (6th Cir. 1976)).

5. United States v. Hare, 49 F.3d 447, 450-451 (8th Cir. 1995) (after being told about benefits of cooperation under Sentencing Guidelines, defendant may have been "hopeful of improving his situation," but no plea bargain was offered or discussed, so FRE 410 did not apply).

6. United States v. Wood, 879 F.2d 927, 935-936 (D.C. Cir. 1989) (meetings attended by defendant, her lawyer, the prosecutor, and government investigators were "plea bargaining sessions" and defendant's statements therein should have been excluded).

give additional indications of their purpose to discuss a plea, in effect confirming what is otherwise implicit.

Reasonable belief   If a prosecutor participates in what she views as mere police interrogation, but defendant or defense counsel reasonably believes the purpose on both sides is to discuss a plea, FRE 410 can apply. If a prosecutor attends police interrogation sessions without giving appropriate disclaimers, otherwise-admissible statements by the defendant may be excluded under FRE 410.[7] On the other hand, if a prosecutor repudiates any interest in pursuing a deal and makes clear that her purpose is to gather evidence (as by giving *Miranda* warnings or just telling the defendant that what he says may be used against him), the resulting discussions do not qualify as plea bargaining.[8] In the latter situation, where normal understandings about purpose to bargain are dislodged, defendant's unspoken hope for leniency is not enough to trigger application of FRE 410 because a silent or uncommunicated expectation gives the prosecutor "no chance to reject a confession" she did not seek.[9]

The reference in FRE 410 to "plea discussions" has sometimes prompted courts to require an expressed willingness on the part of the defendant to plead guilty to some charge in exchange for prosecutorial concessions.[10] However, the policy underlying the Rule also applies where the defendant seeks to provide information in exchange for total dismissal of the charges or a grant of immunity. Moreover, even where defendant's express purpose is to obtain a dismissal of all charges, arguably the situation should be treated as one in which some sort of plea bargain was also on the table.

Negotiations to be with "Attorney for Prosecuting Authority"   By virtue of an amendment adopted in 1980, FRE 410 covers only statements made in plea discussions with "an attorney for the prosecuting authority." This limitation is intended to prevent defendants from claiming that incriminating statements made to law enforcement officers during police interrogation or on other occasions were part of "plea discussions," when in fact law enforcement personnel generally lack authority to negotiate pleas.[11] Thus

7. People v. Manges, 350 N.W.2d 829, 834 (Mich. App. 1984) (barring defendant's statements, where prosecutor said he could not deal because he did not know enough about the case but encouraged defendant to talk and never warned him that his attempts to bargain could be used against him).

8. *See* Rachlin v. United States, 723 F.2d 1373, 1376-1377 (8th Cir. 1983) (U.S. Attorney indicated that she was not ready to bargain a plea; later discussions with agents were not plea bargaining).

9. United States v. Levy, 578 F.2d 896, 900-901 (2d Cir. 1978).

10. United States v. Sitton, 968 F.2d 947 (9th Cir. 1992) (FRE 410 inapplicable because defendant may have been negotiating for leniency but "gave no indication that he was offering to enter a plea" and in fact expressed confidence that he could "beat" the charges in court), *cert. denied*, 506 U.S. 979.

11. *See* ACN, FRCrimP 11(e)(6) (reference to "an attorney for the prosecuting authority" was added by amendment in 1980 in order to negate any suggestion "that an otherwise voluntary admission to law enforcement officials is rendered inadmissible merely because it was made in the hope of obtaining leniency by a plea"). *See* United States v. Olson, 450 F.3d 655, 681 (7th Cir. 2006) (defendant's statements to FBI agent were not excludable under FRE 410, because agent was not an attorney for the

statements made to police officers,[12] probation officers,[13] or others[14] are usually not subject to exclusion under FRE 410,[15] even where such persons promise to report defendant's cooperation to the prosecutor or judge.[16]

A sound approach to the problem of direct talks between defendants and law enforcement personnel employs a "two-tiered" standard in which statements by the accused are excludable if he exhibits "an actual subjective expectation to negotiate a plea" and that expectation was "reasonable given the totality of the objective circumstances."[17] Reasonableness is a function of the behavior of law enforcement officials. To the extent a prosecutor, either directly or through police officers acting as agents, makes it reasonable for defendants to think plea bargaining is going forward, and if they think so in fact, then FRE 410 should apply.

Two-tier standard

Although FRE 410 requires the statements to have been made "in the course of plea discussions with an attorney with the prosecuting authority," it does not require that they be made to or even in the presence of the prosecutor.[18] If the prosecutor undertakes plea discussions with the defendant or his attorney, and is absent during followup sessions, statements made during those ensuing discussions normally involve continued bargaining and are subject to exclusion under FRE 410.[19]

---

prosecuting authority; agent said that all he could do was recommend a plea, and that cooperation would likely lead to a better outcome, which could not lead defendant to think he was plea bargaining).

12. United States v. Mangine, 302 F.3d 819, 822 (8th Cir. 2002) (statements made by defendant to police officer were not excluded by FRE 410, because there was no evidence that officer represented himself to be an attorney for the government or implied that he had authority to bargain).

13. United States v. Perez-Franco, 873 F.2d 455, 461 (1st Cir. 1989) (defendant's comments to probation officer for his presentence report are admissible in subsequent proceedings).

14. United States v. Castillo, 615 F.2d 878, 885 (9th Cir. 1980) (defendant had no reasonable belief that he was plea bargaining when making statements to prison counselor).

15. United States v. Karr, 742 F.2d 493, 496 (9th Cir. 1984) (admitting post-arrest statement to officers where defendant "never offered to plead guilty" and "never inquired into the authority" of officers to negotiate).

16. Rachlin v. United States, 723 F.2d 1373, 1377 n.7 (8th Cir. 1983) (even though agents may have told the defendant that his cooperation would be made known to the prosecutor, defendant "could not reasonably view this as a plea offer").

17. United States v. Robertson, 582 F.2d 1356, 1366 (5th Cir. 1978) (source of language quoted above). *See also* United States v. Sitton, 968 F.2d 947, 957 (9th Cir. 1992) (conversations with government agents are not plea discussions unless defendant "exhibits a subjective belief that he is negotiating a plea, and that belief is reasonable under the circumstances").

18. United States v. Serna, 799 F.2d 842, 849 (2d Cir. 1986) (fairly read, FRE 410 requires "participation" of government attorney, but "not necessarily his physical presence" when defendant makes a statement to agents who are authorized to engage in plea discussions), *cert. denied,* 481 U.S. 1013.

19. United States v. Grant, 622 F.2d 308, 313-315 (8th Cir. 1980) (FRE 410 applies where Secret Service agents stated at a subsequent meeting at which prosecutor was not present that prosecutor would go for a plea to a one-count indictment).

Sometimes a prosecutor expressly authorizes law enforcement officers to initiate or continue plea negotiations with a defendant or his attorney. Statements made to an officer acting as an authorized agent of the prosecutor are clearly subject to exclusion under FRE 410.[20] A more difficult question arises where the law enforcement officer has only ostensible but not actual authority to engage in plea bargaining. If the prosecutor had any role in creating the impression that the officer was acting on behalf of the prosecutor, FRE 410 is fully applicable. If it is the officer's words and conduct alone that created the impression of ostensible authority, arguably the policy of FRE 410 still justifies exclusion, but in any case the statements are excludable on other grounds as a remedy for such police misconduct.[21]

Concessions to a third party

The framers of FRE 410 seem to have given no thought to the question whether attempts to strike a bargain on behalf of third persons should be protected or not, and the text of the Rule leaves the matter much in doubt. There seem to be three possible approaches. One holds that such bargaining is protected on the same terms that apply when a person bargains for himself.[22] Another construes such attempts as lying beyond reach of the Rule, since typically the defendant offers in effect to "take the blame" if charges can be dropped against others, and statements of this sort are not necessarily offers to plead guilty to anything.[23] A third and preferred approach holds that statements made conditionally to gain liberty or leniency for another should be excluded if release or leniency is not granted, but admitted against the defendant if the other party is given the requested concession. The reason is that, if the defendant intends to "take the blame" for the sake of another, he necessarily assumes that the offered evidence will be used against himself if the other party is not charged or is otherwise granted leniency.[24]

20. United States v. Lawrence, 952 F.2d 1034, 1037 (8th Cir. 1992) (FRE 410 applies "where law-enforcement officials enter into negotiations with express authority from a government attorney").

21. *See* ACN of Criminal Rules Advisory Committee to amended FRCrimP 11(e)(6) (noting that when "agents purport to have authority to bargain" exclusion can be based on "that body of law dealing with police interrogations"). *See also* State v. Aguilar, 891 P.2d 668 (Or. App. 1995) (error to admit defendant's confession to two robberies where officer falsely claimed authority to plea bargain and told defendant that if he confessed to both robberies he would only be charged with one).

22. United States v. Ross, 493 F.2d 771, 775 (5th Cir. 1974) (reversible error to admit statement by defendant to federal narcotics agent en route from place of arrest to jail, in which defendant asked whether his wife could be released if he took the blame; since prosecutor had been consulted, and wife was in fact later released, defendant's statement was "an effort to bargain a plea").

23. United States v. Doe, 655 F.2d 920, 924-925 & n.8 (9th Cir. 1980) (in trial of *D* and *R*, admitting *D*'s statements seeking a reduced sentence and asking that charges be dropped against *R*; *D* never "pled or offered to plead," so he was not plea bargaining, but was simply trying to exonerate *R* by implicating himself, "making the best of a bad situation by cooperating").

24. The earlier panel opinion in the *Robertson* case took this approach. *See* United States v. Robertson, 560 F.2d 647, 651 (5th Cir. 1977) ("[I]f a bargain is consummated

By its terms, FRE 410 excludes plea bargaining statements only when offered against the defendant. When a plea bargaining statement is offered against the government (such as an offer by the prosecutor to allow the defendant to plead to a lesser charge), it is also properly subject to exclusion in order to carry out the underlying policy of FRE 410.[25] Some courts cite FRE 408 in rejecting such evidence even though the language of this Rule suggests it was intended to apply only in civil proceedings.[26] FRE 403 also sometimes provides a proper basis for excluding prosecution plea bargaining offers or related statements.

Plea bargaining statements offered against prosecutor

It seems clear that FRE 410(3) and 410(4) do not exclude statements accompanying unwithdrawn guilty pleas.[27] But the purpose of encouraging plea negotiations is undercut if the cost to the defendant in reaching a plea agreement (at least an agreement that sticks) is that everything he says during negotiations becomes usable against him. Presumably there is no trial on the charges to which the plea is entered, but there may be other trials on other charges and there might be civil suits. The better outcome, and one that is at least consistent with the purpose of the doctrine, is to exclude plea bargaining statements of all sorts, regardless whether the parties reach or perform their agreement and regardless whether the agreement involves a nolo plea or a guilty plea.

Subsequent use of statements when guilty plea not withdrawn

FRE 410 provides that a statement made during plea proceedings or discussion is admissible in two situations. First, where one such statement has been introduced, another made in the course of the same plea or plea discussions may be introduced if it "ought in fairness be considered contemporaneously" with the other. This exception implements the policy of FRE 106 by making plea bargaining statements subject to the rule of completeness. If a defendant introduces a plea bargaining statement in his favor, the prosecutor may introduce another that is needed to put the first in appropriate context.[28]

Permissible uses

Second, a statement made during plea proceedings or discussions is admissible in a prosecution for perjury or false statement, provided that it was made by the defendant under oath, on the record, and in the

---

and leniency is obtained for a third party, admissions made pursuant to that bargain are not privileged"). But on this point the later en banc opinion displaced the panel opinion. *See* 582 F.2d 1356 (5th Cir. 1978).

25. *See* ACN, FRCrimP 11(e)(6) (exclusionary principle applies only to statements offered "against" defendant, but there is no intent to suggest that statements by government agents are "inevitably" admissible on defendant's behalf; Committee intends "no disapproval" of cases like *Verdoorn* that approve the exclusion of proof that prosecutor sought to a plea bargain; meaningful dialogue is impossible if either party must assume that offers will be admissible in evidence).

26. United States v. Verdoorn, 528 F.2d 103, 107 (8th Cir. 1976) (holding that "government proposals concerning pleas should be excludable" under FRE 408 rather than FRE 410).

27. United States v. Paden, 908 F.2d 1229, 1235 (5th Cir. 1990) (FRE 410(4) and FRCrimP 11(e)(6)(D) "do not prohibit statements made during plea negotiations that lead to a plea of guilty"), *cert. denied*, 498 U.S. 1039.

28. *See* ACN, FRCrimP 11(e)(6) (if defense, in motion to dismiss, offers in his favor statements made in aborted plea discussions, "then other relevant statements made in the same plea discussions" should be admissible against the defendant in the interest of determining the truth).

presence of counsel.[29] This second exception allows the prosecution of defendants who give false testimony at plea proceedings. In most jurisdictions defendants are not placed under oath during plea proceedings, hence are not subject to a perjury prosecution for statements made therein. Moreover, perjury prosecutions are unlikely to arise out of a proceeding where the defendant gives predominantly inculpatory rather than exculpatory testimony. However, this exception also covers cases where a defendant gives perjured testimony at a later trial and statements otherwise within the scope of FRE 410 are needed to prove the perjury.

Impeachment   With the major exception created by the waiver doctrine described below, it seems that plea bargaining statements by the defendant, whether made in court when a plea is entered or during plea negotiations with the prosecutor, are not admissible to impeach him by contradiction if he takes the stand at trial and testifies inconsistently with his earlier statements. The categorical language of FRE 410 supports this conclusion by saying expressly that plea bargaining statements are not "admissible against the defendant," except as otherwise provided in the Rule, and there is no language creating an exception for impeachment. The subject was also discussed on the floor of the House, where a member of the Judiciary Committee said that plea bargaining statements could not be used this way,[30] and modern authority agrees.[31]

Waiver   The real situation is quite different from that described above, however, because the Supreme Court held, in its decision in *Mezzanatto* in 1995, that defendants may waive their protection against the use of their plea bargaining statements to impeach, and waivers are routinely obtained at the outset of the bargaining process.[32] Seven Justices in *Mezzanatto* wrote that the case did not mean that a defense waiver could pave the way to the use of plea bargaining statements during the government's case in chief, but some lower courts have extended the effect of waiver to include situations in which the statements

---

29. United States v. Gleason, 766 F.2d 1239, 1245-1246 (8th Cir. 1985) (FRCrimP 11(c)(6)(D)(ii) contemplates use of plea bargaining statements in later perjury trials), *cert. denied*, 474 U.S. 1058.

30. *See* the remarks by Representative Wiggins of California (member of Judiciary Committee) set forth in 121 Cong. Rec. 17492-93 (daily ed. June 6, 1975) (with reference to statements by defendant in court admitting guilt in connection with a plea later withdrawn, suggesting that FRE 410 "will preclude the prosecutor from impeaching the credibility of the defendant by his prior inconsistent statements, and literally his confession in open court," for the "sole remedy" is to bring perjury charges, even though defendant "may escape punishment" for the charged offense).

31. United States v. Lawson, 683 F.2d 688, 690-693 (2d Cir. 1982) (legislative history demonstrates congressional intent "to preclude use of statements made in plea negotiations for impeachment purposes").

32. United States v. Mezzanatto, 513 U.S. 196, 202 (1995) (protections of FRE 410 may be waived; indeed, "evidentiary stipulations are a valuable and integral part of everyday trial practice," and they routinely lead to the use of evidence that would otherwise be excluded). State courts applying counterparts to FRE 410 are, of course, free to go in other directions. *But see* People v. Stevens, 610 N.W.2d 881 (Mich. 2000) (following *Mezzanatto*).

contradict other evidence offered by the defense in its case (which involves not merely an impeaching use, but substantive use, of statements by the defendant),[33] and a few have even approved use during the government's case-in-chief.[34] Clearly the waiver doctrine puts added pressure on defendants who enter into plea bargaining to avoid taking the stand in the event of trial. The waiver-of-rights regime makes lawyers reluctant to allow clients to speak during plea bargaining, and may well complicate or chill the bargaining process. Arguably any impeachment allowed under *Mezzanatto* should not lead to informing the jury that the statements were made during plea bargaining.

H. LIABILITY INSURANCE

> **FRE 411**
>
> Evidence that a person was or was not insured against liability is not admissible upon the issue whether the person acted negligently or otherwise wrongfully. This rule does not require the exclusion of evidence of insurance against liability when offered for another purpose, such as proof of agency, ownership, or control, or bias or prejudice of a witness.

§4.30   Evidence of Insurance Generally Excluded

Evidence that a person carried liability insurance, or did not carry it, is inadmissible on the issue whether the person "acted negligently or otherwise wrongfully."[1] The Advisory Committee concluded "the inference of fault from the fact of insurance coverage is a tenuous one, as is its converse."[2] In the modern world, this laconic comment seems almost an understatement, and in most settings it is utterly implausible to argue that personal behavior is affected by the existence or absence of insurance coverage.

---

33. United States v. Rebbe, 314 F.3d 402, 406-408 (9th Cir. 2002) (court properly admitted defendant's plea bargaining statements to rebut testimony of defense witnesses).

34. United States v. Burch, 156 F.3d 1315, 1319-1321 (D.C. Cir. 1998) (where defendant did not cooperate as contemplated in plea bargain, enforcing requirement imposed by court as condition for permitting withdrawal of plea, that defendant waive all protection of FRE 410, and admitting, during government's case in chief, defendant's plea bargaining statements); United States v. Young, 223 F.3d 905, 909-911 (8th Cir. 2000).

§4.30   1. FRE 411 blocks not only evidence that defendant was insured, but also evidence that plaintiff was insured, even if defendant pleads contributory negligence or asserts a counterclaim. *See* ACN, FRE 411 (the Rule is drafted "in broad terms" so as to include "contributory negligence or other fault of a plaintiff as well as fault of a defendant").

2. ACN, FRE 411.

Misuse by jury   Adding to concerns over relevancy is the conviction that evidence of insurance (or lack of it) would be misused by the jury. Knowledge of insurance might cause the jury to find liability where it otherwise would not or to increase the damage award.[3] Conversely, knowing there is no coverage or not enough[4] might arouse sympathy and lead the jury to find for the defendant where it otherwise would not or to give an unjustifiably low damage award.[5]

Unfortunately, the result of FRE 411 and related doctrines is that in many cases the jury resolves a dispute that is largely staged. Under the "collateral source" rule, the jury usually does not hear about replacement costs or medical benefits that a claimant has already collected, nor does it typically learn that subrogation rules may result in transferring damage recoveries to an insurance carrier. FRE 411's cure may be as bad as the disease since, perhaps worst of all, juries may well make their own guesses about insurance coverage,[6] and mistaken suppositions may themselves raise or depress damage awards.

FRE 411 complements other procedural and substantive rules that require litigation to be maintained against the insured even though an insurance carrier is managing the defense (including hiring the defense attorney) and is obligated to pay any judgment awarded. Even in states having "direct action" statutes that allow the claim to be brought directly against the insurance carrier, the policy of FRE 411 should bar any argument to the jury that fault can be inferred from the existence of insurance. Although FRE 411 does not apply to voir dire, its underlying policy prohibits injection of insurance at that early stage of the proceeding.[7]

Ambiguities in Rule   The phrasing of FRE 411 contains several ambiguities. First, it expressly refers only to evidence that "a person" was or was not insured against liability, which invites argument that the provision does not

---

3. Ouachita Natl. Bank v. Tosco Corp., 686 F.2d 1291, 1301 (8th Cir. 1982) (FRE 411 is designed "to avoid the possibility of prejudice to the insured party"; knowledge that defendant carries liability insurance might increase amount of damages awarded by jury).

4. Reed v. General Motors Corp., 773 F.2d 660, 663-664 (5th Cir. 1985) (reversible error to admit evidence in personal injury action that defendants had coverage in amount of only $5,000 per person and $10,000 per accident). *Compare* Perrin v. Anderson, 784 F.2d 1040, 1047-1048 (10th Cir. 1986) (in civil rights suit, defense counsel could properly argue that judgment against defendants would be "paid by them and no one else," since punitive damages were sought and "ultimate source of payment is therefore relevant").

5. ACN, FRE 411 (primary justification for excluding evidence of insurance is "the feeling that knowledge of the presence or absence of liability insurance would induce juries to decide cases on improper grounds").

6. *See, e.g.,* Shingleton v. Bussey, 223 So. 2d 713, 718 (Fla. 1969) (excluding evidence of insurance "may mislead jurors often to think insurance coverage is greater than it is").

7. *See* Lowe v. Steele Const. Co., 368 N.W.2d 610 (S.D. 1985) (voir dire questions "asked to prejudice the jury concerning defendant's liability insurance coverage" allowed trial court to exercise its discretion to grant a mistrial). *See generally* Calnan, The Admissibility of Insurance Questions During Voir Dire: A Critical Survey of Federal Approaches and Proposals for Change, 44 Rutgers L. Rev. 241 (1992).

apply to liability coverage carried by entities such as hospitals or corporations. But there is no indication that the framers intended to apply the principle only to individual actors, and the underlying policies and concerns apply as well to corporate and other entities.[8] Second, the Rule by its terms bars use of insurance to prove that someone "acted negligently or otherwise wrongfully." Similar phrasing in the original version of FRE 407 governing subsequent measures left room for some courts to conclude that it did not apply in strict liability cases, and a similar argument could be mounted in connection with FRE 411.[9] But the best argument for admitting subsequent measures in the setting of product liability litigation turns on public policy, not on any semantic point, and FRE 411 should be fully applicable in strict liability cases.

Not surprisingly, FRE 411 does not say whether a mistrial should be   **Mistrials** granted where insurance is erroneously raised during the proceeding. Some jurisdictions follow a strict rule under which improper mention of insurance is ground for an automatic mistrial.[10] Today with widespread insurance coverage and mandatory insurance laws in many states,[11] most courts are reluctant to grant a mistrial or reverse a verdict merely because the issue of insurance was inadvertently raised in ways that are likely to be harmless.[12] It is virtually never an accident, however, when lawyers "let slip" a reference to insurance, and courts have discretion to grant a mistrial for harmful references to insurance. The very fact that a lawyer deliberately injects insurance into the proceeding may be some indication that it is not harmless.

§4.31   Exceptions Where Admissible

Evidence of liability insurance may be admitted for a variety of relevant purposes.[1] Often the question is whether defendant owned or controlled the premises or instrumentality giving rise to the claim, and FRE 411 specifically authorizes evidence of liability insurance on the

8. Posttape Assoc. v. Eastman Kodak Co., 537 F.2d 751, 758 (3d Cir. 1976) (FRE 411 bars evidence of liability insurance where "a party is accused of acting wrongfully," even if such parties are "commercial entities").

9. *See* §4.23, *supra.*

10. Neibauer v. Well, 319 N.W.2d 143 (N.D. 1982) (despite state's compulsory auto liability insurance statute, court finds inadvertent reference to insurance requires automatic reversal).

11. *See* B-Amused Co., Inc. v. Millrose Sporting Club, Inc., 168 F. Supp. 709, 710 (E.D.N.Y. 1958) ("nearly every juryman knows that the average negligence case is being defended by an insurance company").

12. Koppinger v. Cullen-Schiltz & Assocs., 513 F.2d 901, 910 (8th Cir. 1975) (absent showing of prejudice, no error to deny motion for mistrial after marshal told juror that a person in the courtroom was connected with insurance company). *Cf.* Varlack v. SWC Caribbean, Inc., 550 F.2d 171, 176-177 (3d Cir. 1977) (reference to insurance does not require mistrial in bench trial).

§4.31   1. *See, e.g.,* Varlack v. SWC Caribbean, Inc., 550 F.2d 171, 176-177 (3d Cir. 1977) (to show defendant had actual knowledge of lawsuit, permissible to prove he gave statement to investigator for insurance carrier).

issue of "ownership or control."[2] It is highly unlikely that anyone would have liability insurance for property over which he had no control. Courts retain discretion under FRE 403 to allow such proof only where less prejudicial evidence of ownership or control is unavailable. Similarly, FRE 411 makes evidence of liability insurance admissible on the issue of agency. Evidence that the defendant carried liability insurance covering the conduct of the person who caused the injury suggests an agency relationship.[3]

Bias or prejudice
Probably the most important permissible use of liability insurance is to show the bias or prejudice of a witness. A plaintiff is generally allowed to impeach a witness called by the defendant by showing that the witness is employed by the defendant's insurance carrier[4] although sometimes courts allow disclosure only that the witness was hired by the "defense" without mention of insurance.[5] The party calling the witness is allowed to bring out the witness's affiliation with an insurance company on direct examination to avoid an inference that this fact was being hidden from the jury.[6]

Where a defendant offers a witness's earlier statement, either for impeachment or as substantive evidence, the plaintiff may be allowed to prove that the statement was taken by an agent of the defendant's insurance carrier, at least where there is a claim that the statement was coerced, fabricated, or inaccurately recorded.[7]

Intertwined with admission
Sometimes the admission of a party is intertwined with a reference to insurance as happens when a defendant states at the accident scene, "I'm sure my insurance will cover the damage to your car." Courts may require that the reference to insurance be excised from the statement if possible.[8] If doing so would make the statement unintelligible or change its meaning, courts should admit the whole statement subject to a limiting instruction.[9]

2. Newell v. Harold Shaffer Leasing Co., 489 F.2d 103, 110 (5th Cir. 1974) (where defendant denied ownership of truck, admitting evidence that it carried liability insurance on the truck).

3. Hunziker v. Scheidemantle, 543 F.2d 489, 495 n.10 (3d Cir. 1976) (evidence of liability insurance admissible to show agency).

4. *See, e.g.,* Charter v. Chleborad, 551 F.2d 246, 248-249 (8th Cir. 1977) (reversible error to refuse to allow plaintiff to impeach by evidence that witness was employed by defendant's liability carrier), *cert. denied,* 434 U.S. 856.

5. Foulk v. Kotz, 673 P.2d 799, 801 (Ariz. 1983) (defendants could show that witness was acting as "representative" of defense when he interviewed plaintiff, but evidence that he worked for an insurance company was properly excluded under Rule 403).

6. Ouachita Natl. Bank v. Tosco Corp., 686 F.2d 1291, 1301 (8th Cir. 1982).

7. Heisler v. Boule, 226 Mont. 332, 735 P.2d 516, 520 (1987) (reversible error to admit tape-recorded statement of party taken by that party's insurance adjuster without allowing other party to show bias in questions and answers).

8. Cameron v. Columbia Builders, Inc., 212 Or. 388, 320 P.2d 251, 254 (1958) (reference to insurance should be severed from admission wherever possible).

9. Reid v. Owens, 93 P.2d 680, 685 (Utah 1939) (reference to insurance admissible because "freighted with admission").

I. SEXUAL BEHAVIOR OF COMPLAINING WITNESS

FRE 412

(a) Evidence generally inadmissible. The following evidence is not admissible in any civil or criminal proceeding involving alleged sexual misconduct except as provided in subdivisions (b) and (c):

(1) Evidence offered to prove that any alleged victim engaged in other sexual behavior.

(2) Evidence offered to prove any alleged victim's sexual predisposition.

(b) Exceptions.

(1) In a criminal case, the following evidence is admissible, if otherwise admissible under these rules:

(A) evidence of specific instances of sexual behavior by the alleged victim offered to prove that a person other than the accused was the source of semen, injury or other physical evidence;

(B) evidence of specific instances of sexual behavior by the alleged victim with respect to the person accused of the sexual misconduct offered by the accused to prove consent or by the prosecution; and

(C) evidence the exclusion of which would violate the constitutional rights of the defendant.

(2) In a civil case, evidence offered to prove the sexual behavior or sexual predisposition of any alleged victim is admissible if it is otherwise admissible under these rules and its probative value substantially outweighs the danger of harm to any victim and of unfair prejudice to any party. Evidence of an alleged victim's reputation is admissible only if it has been placed in controversy by the alleged victim.

(c) Procedure to determine admissibility.

(1) A party intending to offer evidence under subdivision (b) must—

(A) file a written motion at least 14 days before trial specifically describing the evidence and stating the purpose for which it is offered unless the court, for good cause requires a different time for filing or permits filing during trial; and

(B) serve the motion on all parties and notify the alleged victim or, when appropriate, the alleged victim's guardian or representative.

(2) Before admitting evidence under this rule the court must conduct a hearing in camera and afford the victim and parties a right to attend and be heard. The motion, related papers, and the record of the hearing must be sealed and remain under seal unless the court orders otherwise.

§4.32 Sexual History of Complainant Generally Excluded

FRE 412, the federal "rape shield" statute, was enacted by Congress three years after the Federal Rules went into effect.[1] Originally the Rule applied only in criminal prosecutions for specified sex offenses. A 1994 amendment extended it to all criminal and civil proceedings involving alleged sexual misconduct.[2] It now applies to all criminal proceedings involving sexual misconduct even where a sex crime is not charged, such as a kidnapping prosecution where the prosecutor seeks to prove that the victim was sexually assaulted. It also covers civil proceedings involving alleged sexual misconduct, including actions for sexual battery or sexual harassment.[3] The Rule applies regardless whether the alleged victim or the person accused is a party to the litigation. Thus the Rule applies to litigation over discharge of an employee for sexual harassment even though the alleged victim is not a party and to litigation against an employer by the alleged victim even though the person accused is not a party.

Rationale   FRE 412 represents a significant qualification on FRE 404(a)(2), which might otherwise allow evidence of an alleged victim's sexual history on the issue of consent.[4] The Rule is based on the same policy concerns that led to the enactment of state "rape shield" statutes. Evidence of the sexual history of a rape victim often has little if any probative value in proving consent on the occasion in question.[5] In most cases, it is a collateral issue having the potential to divert the jury's attention from the facts of the charged incident.[6] Evidence of sexual history can be used to harass and embarrass victims of sexual misconduct, making them less likely to report or prosecute sexual

---

§4.32 1. Pub. L. No. 95-540 [H.R. 4727], 92 Stat. 2046 (1978) (entitled "Privacy Protection for Rape Victims Act of 1978").

2. Pub. L. No. 103-22, Title IV, §40141(b), 108 Stat. 1919, Sept. 13, 1994. Although the Judicial Conference had recommended the extension to civil cases, the Supreme Court approved only the extension in criminal cases. *See* statement of Chief Justice Rehnquist, 154 F.R.D. 510 (1994). But Congress overrode the Supreme Court in the Violent Crime Control and Enforcement Act of 1994 and adopted the extension to civil cases.

3. Despite the significant expansion in scope, the Rule is still limited to civil cases involving "sexual misconduct." Thus it does not affect tort cases where a plaintiff's sexual history is relevant to show an alternative explanation for an injury such as infection or sterility nor does it apply to defamation cases involving statements concerning sexual misconduct offered to show the alleged defamatory statements were true or did not damage plaintiff's reputation. *See* ACN to amended FRE 412.

4. *See* §4.13, *supra.*

5. Sandoval v. Acevedo, 996 F.2d 145, 149 (7th Cir. 1993) (Posner, J.) ("The essential insight behind the rape shield statute is that in an age of post-Victorian sexual practice, in which most unmarried young women are sexually active, the fact that the woman has voluntarily engaged in a particular sexual activity on previous occasions does not provide appreciable support for an inference that she *consented* to engage in this activity with the defendant on the occasion on which she claims that she was raped.").

6. McLean v. United States, 377 A.2d 74, 77-79 (D.C. 1977) (evidence of a complainant's prior sexual acts "diverts the jury's attention to collateral matters" and results in prejudice to the victim, which "greatly outweighs its extremely limited probative value").

offenses. The humiliation that rape victims suffered under prior law was thought to be a major factor causing rape to be an underreported crime.[7] According to the ACN, FRE 412 "encourages victims of sexual misconduct to institute and participate in legal proceedings against alleged offenders" and safeguards against "sexual stereotyping that is associated with public disclosure of intimate sexual details."[8]

FRE 412(a) imposes a general prohibition against evidence of an alleged victim's "other sexual behavior" or "sexual predisposition."[9] It bars such evidence whether offered as substantive evidence or for impeachment, subject to four exceptions (discussed in the next section) where the probative value of the evidence is viewed as significantly outweighing potential harm to the alleged victim.

The ACN states that "sexual behavior" includes not only actual physical conduct, but also evidence that implies sexual intercourse or sexual contact, including the use of contraceptives or evidence of pregnancy[10] or venereal disease.[11] The ACN also makes the more questionable suggestion that "behavior" be construed to include "activities of the mind," such as fantasies and dreams,[12] a view properly rejected by some courts under the prior version of the Rule.[13] An alleged victim's statements about her earlier sexual activities are generally covered by the Rule,[14] but courts have differed on whether activities such as posing

Other sexual behavior

---

7. *See* Remarks of Rep. Elizabeth Holtzman, 124 Cong. Rec. H11945 (daily ed. Oct. 10, 1978) ("Too often in this country victims of rape are humiliated and harassed when they report and prosecute the rape. Bullied and cross-examined about their prior sexual experiences, many find the trial almost as degrading as the rape itself. Since rape trials become inquisitions into the victim's morality, not trials of the defendant's innocence or guilt, it is not surprising that it is the least reported crime.").

8. Because FRE 412 is designed to further social policy by protecting rape victims and encouraging the reporting of sex crimes, some commentators have characterized it as a rule of privilege. *See* Tuerkheimer, A Reassessment and Redefinition of Rape Shield Laws, 50 Ohio St. L.J. 1245, 1272-1273 (1989). The prevailing view, however, is that the Rule is predominantly concerned with relevance and countervailing prejudice, a view consistent with its legislative placement in Article IV of the Federal Rules of Evidence. *See* Althouse, Thelma and Louise and the Law: Do Rape Shield Rules Matter?, 25 Loy. L.A. L. Rev. 757, 764 n.34 (1992).

9. The term "sexual predisposition" presumably includes sexual orientation, sexual preferences, and a person's propensity to engage or not to engage in sexual activity of various types.

10. *But see* State v. DeLawder, 28 Md. App. 212, 344 A.2d 446, 454-455 (1975) (defendant constitutionally entitled to offer evidence that complainant thought she was made pregnant by someone else and falsely accused defendant because she was afraid to tell her mother of her sexual activity with others).

11. *See* Cruz-Sanchez v. Rivera-Cordero, 835 F.2d 947, 948-949 (1st Cir. 1987) (FRE 412 would not allow evidence that alleged rape victim was pregnant at time of trial).

12. Even if this interpretation were adopted by courts, fantasies involving the defendant would nonetheless be potentially admissible under FRE 412(b)(1)(B).

13. Jeffries v. Nix, 912 F.2d 982, 988 (8th Cir. 1990) (holding that "delusions about sexual abuse are not 'past sexual behavior' as defined in Rule 412(d)").

14. Wood v. State, 736 P.2d 363, 364-365 (Alaska Ct. App. 1987) (state statute barred victim's statement to defendant that she had posed and acted in pornographic movies); Velos v. State, 752 P.2d 411, 414 (Wyo. 1988) (victim's statement to defendant that she had performed fellatio on a third person barred by state statute).

in the nude amount to sexual behavior.[15] Evidence of *absence* of sexual activity, such as virginity, should qualify as sexual behavior or as evidence of sexual predisposition generally excluded by the Rule.[16] However, statements made by the victim to the accused at the time of the alleged attack about her virginity or lack of sexual experience may sometimes be relevant to rebut a claim of consent.[17]

The Rule uses the term "other" sexual behavior rather than "past" sexual behavior to make clear that behavior subsequent to the incident in question is covered by the Rule. But the Rule does not exclude evidence of sexual activity that is intrinsic to the charged incident, such as sexual foreplay or closely related sexual acts, nor does it exclude evidence that someone else was the perpetrator of the charged crime.[18] The Rule speaks of sexual behavior in which one "engaged," and therefore could be interpreted as meaning conduct that was voluntary. Under this interpretation, evidence of prior nonconsensual sexual behavior would not necessarily be excluded by the Rule (although it also would rarely be relevant).[19] However, many courts view proof that the complainant had been raped or molested before as prior sexual behavior.[20]

Going beyond the original rule, FRE 412 now bars evidence of the alleged victim's "sexual predisposition," which the ACN describes as evidence that "may have a sexual connotation for the factfinder," such as evidence relating to dress, speech, or lifestyle.[21]

Victim's sexual "predisposition"   The Advisory Committee's interpretation of the Rule seems overbroad in some circumstances. It could result in excluding nearly every prior act by the complaining witness that could be relevant to the more common issues in trials for sex crimes. For example, an alleged victim's

---

15. State v. Zaehringer, 280 N.W.2d 416 (Iowa 1979) (evidence that complainant told defendant she had posed in the nude was admissible; posing nude is not prior sexual conduct excluded by rape shield statute).

16. State v. Penigar, 139 Wis. 2d 569, 408 N.W.2d 28, 36 (1987) (prosecution evidence that rape victim was a virgin should generally be excluded under rape shield statute). *But see* People v. Johnson, 671 P.2d 1017, 1020 (Co. Ct. App. 1983) (statute does not bar testimony of "*lack* of prior sexual activity").

17. State v. Gavigan, 111 Wis. 2d 150, 330 N.W.2d 571, 577-578 (1983) (statement by victim concerning lack of sexual experience demonstrated her unwillingness to engage in sexual act; not barred by state rape shield statute).

18. United States v. Yazzie, 59 F.3d 807, 814-815 (9th Cir. 1995) (in sexual abuse trial, error to exclude defense testimony describing very behavior at issue in case, apparently indicating that alleged victim was actually the perpetrator; FRE 412 only applies to sexual conduct other than conduct at issue in case).

19. Lemacks v. State, 207 Ga. App. 160, 427 S.E.2d 536, 537 (1993) (sexual behavior does not include proof of victim's prior rape).

20. *See, e.g.,* United States v. Nez, 661 F.2d 1203, 1205-06 (10th Cir. 1981) (blocking cross-examination of complainant on statement she made to investigator that she had been raped twice before); State v. Muyingo, 171 Or. App. 218, 15 P.3d 83, 87 (2000) (past sexual behavior includes proof that victim had been raped before).

21. *See* Williams v. State, 263 Ga. App. 597, 588 S.E.2d 790, 792 (2003) (excluding mode of dress and marital history); State v. Hill, 309 Minn. 206, 244 N.W.2d 728, 730 (1976) (excluding evidence of cohabitation with another); B.K.B. v. Maui Police Dept., 276 F.3d 1091, 1105 (9th Cir. 2002) (excluding evidence of fantasies and autoerotic sexual practices).

"speech" (i.e., the actual words spoken to the defendant and perhaps to others) will sometimes be highly relevant on the issue of consent. If the defendant offers credible evidence that the alleged rape was actually an act of prostitution, FRE 412 should not be construed as automatically excluding evidence that the complainant's "lifestyle" included being a prostitute. Moreover, courts need to assess carefully whether the activity was sexual behavior or merely related to sex.[22] What a person says, reads, watches or thinks, even if of a sexual nature, does not necessarily qualify as sexual behavior.[23] If FRE 412(a)(2) is construed too expansively, it will increase the number of cases where the excluded evidence will be found to be constitutionally required and hence admissible under FRE 412(b)(1)(C).

As the ACN acknowledges, the making of prior false charges of sexual misconduct is not "sexual behavior" and is not excluded by the Rule.[24] Most courts had reached the same conclusion under the previous version of the Rule.[25]

Prior false charges

If there is insufficient evidence that the complainant victim fabricated the previous charges, courts generally exclude the evidence on the ground that it is irrelevant under FRE 401, substantially outweighed by the considerations set forth in FRE 403, or involves sexual behavior excluded by FRE 412.[26] The mere fact that prosecution was declined or charges dismissed does not establish the falsity of the charges and may reflect more on law enforcement priorities or resources than the

---

22. *Compare* State v. Currier, 148 N.H. 203, 808 A.2d 527, 531 (2002) (viewing pornographic video was not covered by rape shield law) *with* Sweeney v. State, 233 Ga. App. 862, 506 S.E.2d 150 (1998) (making phone-sex audio tape was sexual behavior). *See also* Bobo v. State, 267 Ark. 1, 589 S.W.2d 5, 8 (1979) (posing nude in magazine was not sexual conduct).

23. *See* Jeffries v. Nix, 912 F.2d 982, 988 (8th Cir. 1990) ("delusions about sexual abuse" are not "past sexual behavior" under FRE 412); State v. Thompson, 139 N.C. App. 299, 533 S.E.2d 834, 841 (2000) (sexual behavior does not include "language or conversations whose topic might be sexual behavior"); State v. Wright, 97 Or. App. 401, 776 P.2d 1294, 1297-1298 (1989) ("past sexual behavior" does not include evidence that complaining witness "wrote sexually explicit notes" to a schoolmate, "received sex counseling" or described oral copulation to a counselor, or "watched pornographic films" or "spoke freely about sex" or was "preoccupied" with sex).

24. United States v. No Neck, 472 F.3d 1048, 1054 (8th Cir. 2007) (error to block defense effort to cross-examine complainant on prior accusations; defense had right to ask whether she falsely accused brother of similar offense).

25. Clinebell v. Commonwealth, 368 S.E.2d 263, 266 (Va. 1988) (error to exclude evidence of child's prior false accusations; such statements are not "conduct" under rape shield statute, and defendant has constitutional right to present evidence if "reasonable probability of falsity exists"); State v. LeClair, 83 Or. App. 121, 730 P.2d 609, 613 (1986) (evidence of "previous false *accusations* by an alleged victim is not evidence *of past sexual behavior* within the meaning of the Rape Shield Law and, therefore, is not inadmissible" under that law), *rev. denied*, 303 Or. 74, 734 P.2d 354 (1987).

26. United States v. Kenyon, 481 F.3d 1054, 1063-1064 (8th Cir. 2007) (in child sex abuse prosecution, no error to block defense cross-examination of child about claimed false allegations against another, because accusations were "never made to an authority figure" and amounted to "childish gossip" rather than "actual accusations," and evidence of falsity was weak).

credibility of the complainant.[27] Even an acquittal proves only the existence of reasonable doubt as to whether the offense was committed, not that the charge was fabricated.[28] But recantation of the charges by the complainant is usually sufficient.[29]

Evidence of prior sexual offense charges that are demonstrably false or threats to file false charges should normally be admissible to impeach the veracity of the complainant whenever she testifies as a witness because evidence bearing on animus and motivation has special relevance in a sexual assault prosecution.[30] FRE 608(b) sometimes presents an independent obstacle to proof of such matters. Although FRE 608(b) allows inquiry upon cross-examination into prior conduct bearing on truthfulness or untruthfulness (which certainly encompasses the making of false sexual assault charges), the Rule *bars* extrinsic evidence of such conduct. Nonetheless, FRE 608(b) does not restrict extrinsic proof offered under other theories of impeachment, such as to show bias, and in some circumstances a defendant is constitutionally entitled to offer such proof.[31] Evidence of a "plan" or "scheme" to file false charges may also be admissible under FRE 404(b).[32]

While proving that prior *claims* of sexual misconduct are false is generally beyond the scope of FRE 412, proving that an alleged victim's *denials* of sexual activity are false does trigger application of the Rule.[33]

---

27. Hughes v. Raines, 641 F.2d 790, 792 (9th Cir. 1981) (failure of district attorney to prosecute does not prove falsity of allegations); State v. Anderson, 686 P.2d 193, 201 (Mont. 1984) (dismissal of charges does not establish falsity; mother did not want victim to go through trial).

28. State v. Schwartzmiller, 107 Idaho 89, 685 P.2d 830, 833 (1984) (acquittal "can never be taken to establish that the charges brought were based on false accusations"); People v. Alexander, 116 Ill. App. 3d 855, 452 N.E.2d 591 (1983) (hung jury does not prove falsity).

29. State v. Boggs, 588 N.E.2d 813 (Ohio 1992); People v. Burrell-Hart, 237 Cal. Rptr. 654, 657 (Cal. Ct. App. 1987); Smith v. State, 377 S.E.2d 158 (Ga. 1989).

30. This remains true even where proving the falsity of the earlier charges requires proving prior consensual sexual relations (which the complainant later claimed falsely to be nonconsensual). *See* State v. Caswell, 320 N.W.2d 417, 419 (Minn. 1982) (evidence that complainant made a false rape accusation against former boyfriend should have been admitted; "[W]e question whether one who has falsely accused another of rape has standing to claim she is harassed by evidence of that false accusation.").

31. United States v. Bartlett, 856 F.2d 1071, 1088 (8th Cir. 1988) (defendant has qualified constitutional right to offer evidence of prior false accusations by rape victim to show bias, prejudice, or ulterior motive but not to attack general credibility of victim), *cert. denied*, 479 U.S. 934.

32. United States v. Stamper, 766 F. Supp. 1396, 1405-1406 (W.D.N.C. 1991) (evidence that child sexual abuse victim had made prior false accusations against three other persons admissible under FRE 404(b) as demonstrating the "complainant's scheme of fabricating sexual abuse allegations"), *aff'd*, 959 F.2d 231 (4th Cir. 1992).

33. United States v. White Buffalo, 84 F.3d 1052 (8th Cir. 1996) (FRE 412 prevents defendant from introducing laboratory tests to prove complainant falsely told doctor at hospital that she had not had consensual sexual intercourse with anyone other than defendant in last 72 hours; even if this statement were false, FRE 412 precludes evidence of victim's sexual activities with others).

§4.33 Exceptions Where Admissible

FRE 412 establishes three exceptions in criminal cases and one exception in civil cases where evidence of the prior sexual conduct of a sex crime victim may be admitted, provided that it satisfies other requirements of admissibility under the Rules including FRE 401 and FRE 403. The criminal exceptions allow proof only of specific instances of conduct and do not permit reputation or opinion evidence, unless such evidence is constitutionally required to be admitted. The criminal exceptions also do not extend to evidence of the alleged victim's "sexual predisposition," unless its admission is constitutionally required. In a civil case, evidence of reputation may be received only if the alleged victim has put her reputation in controversy.

First exception. Evidence of the complainant's past sexual behavior with persons other than the accused may be allowed when offered "to prove that a person other than the accused was the source of semen, injury or other physical evidence."[1] Thus where the prosecutor introduces evidence of semen to prove sexual intercourse but defendant denies sexual involvement, he may be entitled to prove complainant's sexual activity with a third person to establish the source of the semen.[2] This exception is normally not available, however, where the defendant admits intercourse but claims consent, because the actual source of the semen is generally irrelevant.[3]

To prove source of semen or injury

Similarly, if the prosecutor introduces evidence of injury to the complainant to prove that sexual activity occurred, or that such activity was nonconsensual, this exception is available to allow the accused to prove that the injury resulted from sexual activity between the complainant and a third person.[4] The language "other physical evidence," which was not in the original rule, allows the defendant a fair response to any physical evidence introduced by the prosecutor indicating sexual activity on the occasion in question, including stretching of the hymen, contracting venereal disease, or becoming pregnant. Since the purpose of this exception is to allow rebuttal of prosecution evidence, courts have been generally unwilling to allow defendants to offer evidence

---

§4.33   1. FRE 412(b)(1)(A).

2. Evidence of sexual activity with a third person must be more than speculative, however. *See, e.g.,* State v. Cervantes, 130 Or. App. 147, 881 P.2d 151 (1994) (where prosecutor offered evidence that semen was found in cervix of complainant, excluding testimony by friend that she had been "hanging all over" another man shortly before the alleged rape and admitted having sexual relations with that person on a past occasion; evidence insufficient to establish third person was possible alternative source of the semen at time of alleged rape).

3. *Cf.* United States v. White Buffalo, 84 F.3d 1052, 1053-1054 (8th Cir. 1996) (defense evidence of semen from third party inadmissible under FRE 412 where prosecutor did not present evidence of semen in vagina of complainant).

4. *See, e.g.,* United States v. Begay, 937 F.2d 515, 523-524 (10th Cir. 1991) (because prosecutor emphasized victim's physical condition as proof of assault and penetration, reversible constitutional error to exclude proof of earlier assaults by another person against the girl offered to explain her unusually enlarged hymenal opening and abrasions).

**Prior behavior
with accused**

under this exception where the prosecution made no claim that defendant was the source of the semen or injury.[5]

Second exception. A second exception to FRE 412 covers evidence of prior sexual behavior between the complainant and the accused "offered by the accused to prove consent or by the prosecution."[6] Such evidence should be admitted only where consent appears to be a genuine issue.[7] Where the prior sexual activity between the complainant and the accused occurred in the distant past, the evidence has less probative value on the issue of consent on the occasion in question. However, there is no bright line establishing how close in time the prior consent must be to the charged offense. Relevancy depends not only on the elapsed time but also on the nature and circumstances of the prior activity. FRE 403 balancing is required.

According to the ACN, prior sexual behavior with the accused includes statements in which the alleged victim "expressed an intent to engage in sexual intercourse with the accused or voiced sexual fantasies involving the accused."[8] Such evidence is clearly relevant on the issue of consent.

The rule also allows the prosecutor to offer evidence under this exception to cover those situations where evidence of prior sexual behavior between the accused and the alleged victim is admissible under some other rule, such as when offered under FRE 404(b) to prove motive, pattern, plan, intent, or absence of mistake.

**Constitutionally
required**

Third exception. The third and most indeterminate exception to FRE 412 is for evidence of the alleged complainant's past sexual behavior or predisposition "the exclusion of which would violate the constitutional rights of the defendant."[9] Such an exception is arguably unnecessary because FRE 412 is of course subordinate to the Constitution. But its inclusion obviates the possibility of constitutional conflict and demonstrates the awareness of the drafters that sometimes a criminal defendant has a constitutional right to produce evidence that is paramount to the general rule of exclusion.

Criminal defendants have a qualified right to present evidence in their defense that is derived from three separate constitutional provisions—those guaranteeing confrontation, compulsory process, and due process.[10] However, the scope of this constitutional right is

5. United States v. Richards, 118 F.3d 622, 624 (8th Cir. 1997) (excluding evidence that victim had intercourse with others to prove semen in victim was not his, when it was defendant who introduced semen evidence and prosecutor did not claim semen was defendant's).

6. FRE 412(b)(1)(B). *See* United States v. Kasto, 584 F.2d 268, 271 (8th Cir. 1978) (fact that complainant engaged in consensual relations with defendant in past bears on consent).

7. FRE 412(b)(1) says such evidence is admissible "if otherwise admissible" under the Rules, which clearly includes FRE 401's requirement of relevancy.

8. ACN to amended FRE 412.

9. FRE 412(b)(1)(C). *See generally* Imwinkelried, Exculpatory Evidence: The Accused's Constitutional Right to Introduce Favorable Evidence §9-4 (1990).

10. Holmes v. South Carolina, 547 U.S. 319 (2006) (whether "rooted directly in the Due Process Clause of the Fourteenth Amendment or in the Compulsory Process or

ill-defined, making it hard to determine the breadth of the exception it creates to FRE 412.[11] Certainly it does not apply to evidence of complainant's prior sexual behavior that lacks a demonstrable relationship to the issues in the case for there is no constitutional right to introduce irrelevant evidence.[12]

Sexual history evidence that is admissible under FRE 412(b)(2)(A) and (B) may also be constitutionally required to be admitted under FRE 412(b)(1). There is no indication that Congress intended these exceptions to be mutually exclusive. Courts have held that evidence of prior sexual activity between the complainant and the accused and evidence of an alternative source for the semen or injury is sometimes constitutionally required to be admitted.[13]

A defendant may be constitutionally entitled to offer sexual history evidence for either substantive purposes or impeachment. Perhaps the most common impeachment use is to show bias on the part of the complainant or a motive to fabricate the charges.[14] The Sixth Amendment right of confrontation guarantees criminal defendants the right to challenge the credibility of prosecution witnesses and to expose their possible motives to fabricate testimony[15] even where such inquiry leads to revelations regarding the complainant's past sexual behavior.[16] However, courts exclude sexual history evidence where the bias of

Motive or bias

Confrontation clauses of the Sixth Amendment, the Constitution guarantees criminal defendants a meaningful opportunity to present a complete defense"). For further discussion of the constitutional right to produce evidence, *see* §5.5, *infra*.

11. For an excellent review of the caselaw, *see* Fishman, Consent, Credibility and the Constitution: Evidence Relating to a Sex Offense Complainant's Past Sexual Behavior, 44 Cath. U.L. Rev. 709 (1995). *See also* Galvin, Shielding Rape Victims in the State and Federal Courts: A Proposal for the Second Decade, 70 Minn. L. Rev. 763, 893, 903-905 (1986) (criticizing "constitutionally required" exception of FRE 412 because of its uncertain scope; proposing list of more specific exceptions where sexual history evidence would be allowed).

12. Jeffries v. Nix, 912 F.2d 982, 986 (8th Cir. 1990) (a defendant "has no constitutional right to introduce irrelevant evidence of [a victim's] past sexual behavior"), *cert. denied*, 499 U.S. 927.

13. United States v. Bear Stops, 997 F.2d 451, 455 (8th Cir. 1993) (constitutional error to exclude evidence that other boys abused victim at about same time, where important to rebut inference that defendant must have caused victim's symptoms of being sexually abused child).

14. Olden v. Kentucky, 488 U.S. 227 (1988) (reversible error to refuse to allow defendant to ask complainant whether she claimed rape in order to preserve her relationship with boyfriend with whom she was cohabiting); Commonwealth v. Black, 337 Pa. Super. 548, 487 A.2d 396 (1985) (unconstitutional to preclude sexual history evidence of victim's incestuous relationship with brother "which may logically demonstrate" complainant's "bias, interest or prejudice" against defendant father for stopping relationship); State v. Jalo, 27 Or. App. 845, 557 P.2d 1359 (1976) (state rape shield statute unconstitutional to the extent it would prevent defendant from introducing "evidence of the complainant's ulterior motive for making a false charge").

15. Davis v. Alaska, 415 U.S. 308 (1974).

16. United States v. Platero, 72 F.3d 806, 814-816 (10th Cir. 1995) (defendant constitutionally entitled to prove a sexual relationship between complainant and her male companion in order to establish that complainant had a motive to fabricate rape charge against defendant; such a false charge would cover for fact that she actually consented and thus preserve her relationship with her companion).

the complainant can be adequately established without it.[17] Sometimes a balance is struck between the rights of the defendant and the privacy of the victim by admitting allegations about the victim's prior sexual behavior that could give rise to bias but excluding evidence of whether those allegations are true.[18]

An accused may also have a constitutional right to introduce evidence bearing on the complainant's sexual history where necessary to correct misrepresentations or impeach the complainant with prior inconsistent statements.[19] For example, defense evidence has been admitted to challenge prosecution evidence concerning the complainant's innocent sexual past,[20] her virginity,[21] or the nature of her relationship with the accused.[22]

To explain precocious sexual knowledge   Another use of sexual history evidence occurs where a child complainant has unusually precocious sexual knowledge and evidence of such knowledge is offered to prove that improper sexual activity occurred. In such cases, the accused should be allowed to show that such knowledge may have been acquired from sexual activity with others,[23] at least where the prosecutor is unwilling to stipulate to the existence of such alternative sources of knowledge. Here, in effect, the prosecutor has "opened the door" to such evidence by suggesting that sexual involvement with the defendant explains the knowledge of the complainant. Therefore, counterproof of other sexual experience is directly relevant in rebuttal, and some courts understandably conclude

17. *See, e.g.,* Marr v. State, 470 So. 2d 703, 706 (Fla. Dist. Ct. App. 1985) ("proper balance" was struck by "allowing evidence as to the bias of the prosecutrix, without permitting specific references to sexual intimacies").

18. State v. Rogers, 642 A.2d 932, 934-935 (N.H. 1994) (allowing cross-examination of complainant about whether defendant had told her he had observed her having sex with other men and threatened to report this to her mother, but precluding cross-examination about truth of alleged other episodes).

19. *See also* State v. Carver, 37 Wash. App. 122, 678 P.2d 842 (1984) (where child testified that her stepfather had abused her, earlier statement to police that only her grandfather abused her should have been admitted as a prior inconsistent statement under state statute).

20. *See, e.g.,* Cox v. State, 102 Nev. 253, 721 P.2d 358, 360 (1986) (where prosecutor introduced evidence that complainant was a born-again Christian who worked as a secretary at a local high school, defendant had a right to offer evidence that she had applied for an "escort's license"); State v. Lantz, 44 Or. App. 695, 607 P.2d 197 (1980) (defendant allowed to introduce evidence that complainant used to be a prostitute to contradict her testimony that she waited three days to report the anal rape because of embarrassment).

21. State v. LaClair, 121 N.H. 743, 433 A.2d 1326, 1329 (1981) (victim told investigating officer she was previously a virgin but later in her deposition testified to the contrary; her inconsistency on this point cast "at least some doubt on her credibility" and due process compelled admission of the testimony).

22. State v. Reiter, 65 Or. App. 304, 672 P.2d 56 (1983) (where rape victim described her relationship with defendant "as a friend," defendant was entitled to cross-examine victim to show victim and defendant had consensual sexual intercourse one week prior to alleged rape).

23. Commonwealth v. Wall, 606 A.2d 449, 458 (Pa. Super. 1992) (refusal to allow defendant's offer of evidence concerning prior abuse of complainant violated rights of confrontation and cross-examination; defendant entitled to introduce evidence to show complainant had knowledge and motive to fabricate allegation).

that defendant has a constitutional right to offer such counterproof.[24] But merely because a victim could have acquired sexual knowledge from others does not give defendant a right to prove such relationships in absence of an attempt by the prosecutor to draw adverse inferences against the defendant from the victim's sexual sophistication.[25]

A defendant may also have a constitutional right to prove a *pattern* of distinctive, consensual sexual behavior by the alleged victim that is highly similar to the facts of the incident being charged.[26] For example, if the defendant claims that the alleged conduct was a consensual act of prostitution, evidence that the prosecutrix was a prostitute may be constitutionally required.[27] However, evidence that the complainant was a prostitute cannot be offered merely to impugn her character[28] or in cases where there is no indication that the charged offense was an act of prostitution.[29] Very few cases find the prior sexual conduct to be sufficiently distinctive or regular to establish a pattern,[30] and evidence offered under this theory is properly rejected where the circumstances were dissimilar.[31]

Distinctive pattern

24. State v. Jacques, 558 A.2d 706, 708 (Me. 1989) (as a matter of constitutional law a defendant "must be permitted to rebut the inference a jury might otherwise draw that the victim was so naive sexually that she could not have fabricated the charge").

25. United States v. Johns, 15 F.3d 740, 744 (8th Cir. 1994) (evidence that victim had consensual sex with others properly excluded).

26. State v. Johnson, 632 A.2d 152 (Md. 1993) (error to preclude defendant from cross-examining victim about recent practice of trading sex for drugs under circumstances highly similar to alleged rape); State v. Colbath, 540 A.2d 1212, 1217 (N.H. 1988) (Souter, J.) (defendant constitutionally entitled to introduce evidence of closely related pattern of sexually provocative behavior by complainant on issue of consent). *See* Galvin, Shielding Rape Victims in the State and Federal Courts: A Proposal for the Second Decade, 70 Minn. L. Rev. 763, 834-835 (1986) (conduct that is distinctive and similar to the circumstances of the alleged rape evidence may be received to establish "pattern" or "plan" where probative value "is so high that fairness mandates its admission"); Berger, Man's Trial, Woman's Tribulation: Rape Cases in the Courtroom, 77 Colum. L. Rev. 1, 59-60 (1977).

27. Connecticut v. DeJusus, 270 Conn. 825, 856 A.2d 345 (2004) (excluding evidence of complainant's involvement in prostitution violated defendant's Sixth Amendment rights because it was critical to defense). *See generally* Bryden & Lengnick, 87 J. Crim. L. & Criminology 1194, 1365 (1997).

28. United States v. Saunders, 943 F.2d 388, 392 (4th Cir. 1991) (it is "intolerable" to suggest that because victim is a prostitute "she automatically is assumed to have consented with anyone at any time").

29. Jeffries v. Nix, 912 F.2d 982, 987 (8th Cir. 1990) (evidence of prostitution inadmissible because "even if [victim] did exchange sex for money on previous occasions, there is no evidence that she offered to do so in this situation").

30. *See, e.g.,* State v. Vaughn, 448 So. 2d 1260 (La. 1983) (evidence of consensual sexual activity by a young female runaway five days earlier was admissible where court found a "pattern of actual consent"); State v. Shoffner, 62 N.C. App. 245, 302 S.E.2d 830 (1983) (pattern of making public sexual advances). *See generally* Kessler, Pattern of Sexual Conduct Evidence and Present Consent: Limiting the Admissibility of Sexual History Evidence in Rape Prosecutions, 14 Women's Rts. L. Rep. 79 (1992).

31. State v. Rhinehart, 68 N.C. App. 615, 316 S.E.2d 118 (1984) (sexual relations with boyfriend dissimilar to alleged assault later in same evening by a stranger); State v. Hudlow, 99 Wash. 2d 1, 659 P.2d 514, 523 (1983) (finding insufficient similarity between past and present incidents of group sex where there was no common male participant); State v. Patnaude, 140 Vt. 361, 438 A.2d 402, 410 (1981) (past group sex and sex for consideration not similar to alleged sexual assault by five strangers).

Courts generally exclude evidence of statements by the complainant to the defendant recounting her sexual experiences[32] although sometimes a defendant is constitutionally entitled to introduce such statements where they bear on defendant's reasonable perception that the complainant was consenting to sexual acts.[33] But it is generally unreasonable for a defendant to base a belief that he had consent on the complainant's prior conduct with third persons,[34] although a statement by an alleged victim indicating indiscriminate interest in having sex with anyone on a given occasion may be constitutionally required to be admitted.[35] Evidence of the complainant's sexual orientation is rarely appropriate because the underlying policies of FRE 412 apply as well in the case of homosexual assaults.[36]

Fourth exception. In civil cases the amended Rule adopts a balancing test that allows evidence to prove the alleged victim's sexual behavior or predisposition if it is otherwise admissible and its probative value "substantially outweighs the danger of harm to any victim and of unfair prejudice to any party."[37] Such evidence may be admissible on the issue of liability[38] and may also bear on the extent of damages.[39] In Title VII litigation where sexual harassment or similar misconduct in the workplace is alleged, a plaintiff's sexual behavior or predisposition may have considerable bearing on whether the alleged misconduct was unwelcomed and on whether plaintiff was forced to work in a "hostile environment."[40]

32. Velos v. State, 752 P.2d 411, 414 (Wyo. 1988) (victim's statement to defendant that she had performed fellatio on a third person barred by state statute).

33. State v. Calbero, 71 Haw. 115, 785 P.2d 157, 162 (1989) (victim's recounting her prior sexual experiences to defendant held relevant to issue of consent). *Cf.* Bobo v. State, 267 Ark. 1, 589 S.W.2d 5 (1979) (on issue of reasonable belief in consent, defendant allowed to introduce evidence that complainant engaged in sexual relations with third person in defendant's presence).

34. United States v. Saunders, 943 F.2d 388, 392 (4th Cir. 1991) (victim's statements to third party that she had posed in nude were irrelevant and properly excluded; policy of the Rule generally bars defendant from relying on complainant's sexual behavior with others in assuming he had consent), *cert. denied*, 502 U.S. 1105.

35. The ACN cites the example of an alleged victim who "has expressed an intent to have sex with the first person encountered on a particular occasion."

36. Commonwealth v. Quartman, 312 Pa. Super. 349, 458 A.2d 994 (1983) (no constitutional error to exclude evidence of complainant's prior homosexual encounters when sole purpose is to imply consent; this is precise use that rape shield statutes seek to preclude); Kvasnikoff v. State, 674 P.2d 302, 306 (Alaska 1983) (evidence precluded by rape shield statute should not be admitted "only because the sexual preference of the victim changes").

37. FRE 412(b)(2).

38. Rodriguez-Hernandez v. Miranda-Velez, 132 F.3d 848, 856 (1st Cir. 1998) (admitting evidence that plaintiff flirted with man she accused to determine whether advances were unwanted).

39. Berry v. Deloney, 28 F.3d 604, 408 (7th Cir. 1994) (in civil suit for emotional and physical injuries caused by sexual abuse, evidence of relationships with others relevant on issue of damages); Giron v. Corrections Corp. of America, 981 F. Supp. 1406, 1408 (D.N.M. 1997) (same).

40. Meritor Savings Bank, FSB v. Vinson, 477 U.S. 57, 67-69, 106 S. Ct. 2399, 91 L.Ed.2d 49 (1986) (harassment suits raise question whether claimant "by her conduct indicated that the alleged sexual advances were unwelcome," and matters such as

As a general matter, evidence of the plaintiff's sexual conduct outside her place of employment[41] is less likely to survive the balancing test than evidence of her workplace conduct.[42] However, even evidence of sexual activity outside the workplace may be admissible when it bears on how plaintiff was likely to perceive the alleged workplace misconduct[43] or on the damages suffered by the plaintiff.[44]

The balancing test of FRE 412(b)(2) differs in three ways from the balancing test of FRE 403. First, it shifts the burden to the proponent to establish admissibility rather than making the opponent justify exclusion. Second, it is slanted against admissibility by requiring a showing that the probative value of the evidence *substantially* outweighs the specified dangers. Third, it requires that "harm to the victim" be considered as well as prejudice to the parties.

The Rule provides that evidence of the alleged victim's reputation is admissible only if it has been placed in controversy by the alleged victim, but it does not place restrictions on opinion evidence beyond those already established.[45] Although FRE 412 is a Rule governing only admissibility, courts regularly rely on its civil case balancing provision to inform the proper scope of pretrial discovery.[46]

"sexually provocative speech or dress" are "obviously relevant"); Rodriguez-Hernandez v. Miranda-Velez, 132 F.3d 848, 856 (1st Cir. 1988) (admitting evidence that plaintiff flirted with man she accused of harassment),

41. Wolak v. Spucci, 217 F.3d 157, 160 (2d Cir. 2000) (in hostile work environment claim, excluding non-work sexual experiences, including watching pornographic videos and attending parties where sexual activity occurred; question whether one perceives work environment as offensive does not turn on private sexual behavior, because expectations about working conditions are not a function of sexual disposition).

42. *See, e.g.,* Beard v. Flying J., Inc., 266 F.3d 792, 800-801 (8th Cir. 2001) (employee's workplace behavior "is highly relevant to the question of whether the alleged harassment was welcome"). But not all workplace-related sexual activity by a plaintiff is necessarily admissible. *See* Howard v. Historic Tours of America, 177 F.R.D. 48 (D.D.C. 1997) (barring asking plaintiffs whether they had sexual relationship with employees not named as harassers).

43. *Cf.* Judd v. Rodman, 109 F.3d 1339 (11th Cir. 1997) (no error to admit evidence that plaintiff previously worked as nude dancer because it bore on her claim of mental distress).

44. Alberts v. Wickes Lumber Co., 1995 WL 117886 (N.D. Ill. 1995) (admitting evidence of plaintiff's sexual relationships after alleged assault where effect on such relationships was part of plaintiff's damage claim).

45. *See* FRE 701-703. It should be noted that FRE 412(b)(2) allows evidence only to the extent "it is otherwise admissible under these rules." If evidence is offered for a FRE 404(b) purpose, arguably it must be in the form of specific instances rather than opinion. *See* §4.19, *supra.*

46. Herchenroeder v. John Hopkins Univ., 171 F.R.D. 179, 182 (D. Md. 1997) (in sexual harassment case court must consider both FRCP 26 and FRE 412 in determining scope of discovery).

§4.34 Procedures for Applying Rule and Exceptions

Before evidence of an alleged victim's prior sexual behavior or predisposition may be introduced under FRE 412, certain procedural requirements must be satisfied. First, the party seeking to offer evidence normally must file a written motion at least 14 days before trial describing the evidence and stating the purpose for which it is offered. If the moving party fails to comply with this requirement, the evidence is excludable,[1] and exclusion as a sanction for noncompliance is not a per se violation of a defendant's constitutional rights.[2] The court has discretion to allow the motion to be filed later, including during trial, upon a showing of good cause. "Good cause" is likely to be found where the evidence in question was not known earlier or its use at trial was occasioned by prosecution evidence or strategy of which defendant was not given advance notice.[3] The motion must be served on all other parties, and notice must also be given to the alleged victim, or where appropriate, to the victim's guardian or representative.

Hearing   Second, the court must conduct a hearing in camera on the motion. All parties as well as the alleged victim must be afforded a right to attend and be heard. The phrase "in camera" carries its usual meaning of a proceeding "in the judge's chambers out of the presence of the jury and the general public."[4] Thus the Rule appears to require the judge to exclude observers and seal the record of the proceeding. It is possible that in rare cases closing the hearing could violate the defendant's Sixth Amendment right to a public trial[5] or the public right of access to judicial proceedings rooted in the First Amendment.[6] However open hearings would undermine the very purpose of FRE 412.

---

§4.34   1. United States v. Seymour, 468 F.3d 378, 386 (6th Cir. 2006) (excluding proof of "friendly" or "sexual" behavior of alleged assault victim with defendant two years after alleged crime; defense failed to follow notice requirement of FRE 412).

2. Michigan v. Lucas, 500 U.S. 145 (1991) (no per se constitutional violation where defense evidence of victim's sexual history excluded because defendant failed to give notice within ten days after arraignment; whether exclusion is a constitutionally permissible sanction must be determined on a case-by-case basis; Court declines to express an opinion "as to whether or not preclusion was justified in this case"). *But see* State v. Calbero, 71 Haw. 115, 785 P.2d 157, 161 (1989) (defendant had right under state constitution to cross-examine victim concerning sexual conduct to impeach her testimony even where introduction of such evidence would otherwise be barred by rape shield statute for failure to give required notice).

3. United States v. Rouse, 100 F.3d 560 (8th Cir. 1996) (trial judge must consider allowing filing for good cause where defendant did not learn of information earlier).

4. 124 Cong. Rec. H11944 (daily ed. Oct. 10, 1978).

5. Waller v. Georgia, 467 U.S. 39 (1984) (closure orders may violate defendant's Sixth Amendment right to a public trial).

6. Globe Newspaper Co. v. Superior Court for the County of Norfolk, 457 U.S. 596 (1982) (holding unconstitutional state rule requiring mandatory exclusion of the public from trial of sex offense cases involving minor victims); Richmond Newspapers, Inc. v. Virginia, 448 U.S. 555 (1980) (First Amendment implies a right of access by the press and public to criminal proceedings). *See generally* Note, The Constitutionality of Statutorily Restricting Public Access to Judicial Proceedings: The Case of the Rape Shield Mandatory Closure Provision, 66 B.U. L. Rev. 271 (1986) (arguing that statutory closure of rape shield hearings does not violate First Amendment).

A closed hearing is particularly likely to be approved where it is based on case-specific findings.[7]

> **Remain under seal**

The motion, related papers, and the record of the hearing must be sealed and remain under seal until the court orders otherwise in order to protect the privacy of the alleged victim in cases where the court ultimately rules the evidence inadmissible. A party who fails to seal the motion and supporting documents takes the risk of having the evidence excluded as a sanction for noncompliance.[8]

> **Balancing test**

Evidence satisfying FRE 412(b)(1)(A) or (B) is subject to the balancing test of FRE 403.[9] Evidence that is constitutionally required to be admitted is not subject to balancing. The exception for civil cases set forth in FRE 412(b)(1)(C) contains its own balancing test.

Amended FRE 412 also eliminates the provision of the former Rule authorizing the court to determine preliminary questions of fact.[10] Preliminary questions such as whether the alleged victim and the accused actually had a prior sexual relationship are FRE 104(b) questions for the jury rather than FRE 104(a) questions for the judge.[11]

Appellate courts have occasionally allowed interlocutory review of pretrial rulings under FRE 412, including appeals by the alleged victim seeking to exclude the evidence.[12]

---

7. Press-Enterprise Co. v. Superior Court of California, 464 U.S. 501 (1984) (trial court failed to make findings necessary to justify closure of proceedings); Globe Newspaper Co. v. Superior Court for County of Norfolk, 457 U.S. 596 (1982) (balancing on a case-by-case basis is required).

8. Sheffield v. Hilltop Sand & Gravel Co., 895 F. Supp. 105, 109 (E.D. Va. 1995) (in sexual harassment case, plaintiff filed in limine motion to bar evidence pertaining to her sexual history other than with defendant; defendant responded with compendium of statements from several coworkers about her sexual behavior with others and moved for admission of such evidence under FRE 412; because defendant failed to submit such motion and statement under seal, court sanctioned defendant by having all such evidence excluded except for testimony by alleged harasser; court criticized defendant for allowing this sensitive material to become part of public record and invade plaintiff's privacy before court had opportunity to rule on its admissibility).

9. FRE 403 favors admissibility because it allows exclusion only where probative value is substantially outweighed by the danger of unfair prejudice, confusion, or similar factors. Although "harm to the victim" is listed only in connection with the balancing test in civil cases, the primary purpose of FRE 412 is to protect complaining witnesses, and this consideration is equally applicable in criminal cases.

10. *See* former FRE 412(c)(2) ("Notwithstanding subdivision (b) of rule 104, if the relevancy of the evidence which the accused seeks to offer in the trial depends upon the fulfillment of a condition of fact, the court, at the hearing in chambers or at a subsequent hearing in chambers scheduled for such purpose, shall accept evidence on the issue of whether such condition of fact is fulfilled and shall determine the issue.").

11. United States v. Platero, 72 F.3d 806 (10th Cir. 1995) (in rape trial defendant claimed victim consented and falsely accused him to protect her relationship with male companion with whom she was having a sexual relationship; trial court erred in disallowing evidence on finding there was no sexual relationship between victim and companion; jury should have been allowed to hear evidence and to decide question of a prior relationship for itself under FRE 104(b)).

12. Doe v. United States, 666 F.2d 43, 46 (4th Cir. 1981) (complainant in rape case allowed to appeal from ruling in pretrial hearing that evidence concerning the complainant's sexual history would be admitted at trial). *Cf.* Commonwealth v. Yelle, 390

FRE 412 does not directly apply to discovery, which continues to be regulated by the Federal Rules of Civil Procedure. The discovery process allows a party to seek information that would not be admissible at trial provided that it is "reasonably calculated to lead to the discovery of admissible evidence."[13] However, since FRE 412 narrows the scope of admissibility it necessarily has an impact on the discovery process. Courts have authority under FRCP 26(c) to enter orders limiting the scope of discovery or requiring that certain information be kept confidential. Such protective orders give courts a tool for enforcing the policy of FRE 412 and protecting victims from unnecessarily intrusive inquiries and unwarranted invasion of their privacy.[14]

J. SIMILAR CRIMES BY DEFENDANT IN SEXUAL ASSAULT AND MOLESTATION CASES

FRE 413

(a) In a criminal case in which the defendant is accused of an offense of sexual assault, evidence of the defendant's commission of another offense or offenses of sexual assault is admissible, and may be considered for its bearing on any matter to which it is relevant.

(b) In a case in which the Government intends to offer evidence under this rule, the attorney for the Government shall disclose the evidence to the defendant, including statements of witnesses or a summary of the substance of any testimony that is expected to be offered, at least fifteen days before the scheduled date of trial or at such later time as the court may allow for good cause.

(c) This rule shall not be construed to limit the admission or consideration of evidence under any other rule.

(d) For purposes of this rule and Rule 415, "offense of sexual assault" means a crime under Federal law or the law of a State (as defined in section 513 of title 18, United States Code) that involved—

(1) any conduct proscribed by chapter 109A of title 18, United States Code;

Mass. 678, 459 N.E.2d 461, 467 (1984) (denying interlocutory appeal by prosecutor; to allow appeal would "create a potential for disruption of every criminal trial where a disgruntled prosecutor could cause the stay of the proceeding").

13. FRCP 26(b)(1).

14. Sanchez v. Zabihi, 166 F.R.D. 500 (D.N.M. 1996) (in order not to undermine policy of FRE 412, courts should enter appropriate orders pursuant to FRCP 26(c) to protect the victim against unwarranted inquiries).

(2) contact, without consent, between any part of the defendant's body or an object and the genitals or anus of another person;

(3) contact, without consent, between the genitals or anus of the defendant and any part of another person's body;

(4) deriving sexual pleasure or gratification from the infliction of death, bodily injury, or physical pain on another person; or

(5) an attempt or conspiracy to engage in conduct described in paragraphs (1)-(4).

FRE 414

(a) In a criminal case in which the defendant is accused of an offense of child molestation, evidence of the defendant's commission of another offense or offenses of child molestation is admissible, and may be considered for its bearing on any matter to which it is relevant.

(b) In a case in which the Government intends to offer evidence under this rule, the attorney for the government shall disclose the evidence to the defendant, including statements of witnesses or a summary of the substance of any testimony that is expected to be offered, at least fifteen days before the scheduled date of trial or at such later time as the court may allow or good cause.

(c) This rule shall not be construed to limit the admission or consideration of evidence under any other rule.

(d) For purposes of this rule and Rule 415, "child" means a person below the age of fourteen, and "offense of child molestation" means a crime under Federal law or the law of a State (as defined in section 513 of title 18, United States Code) that involved—

(1) any conduct proscribed by chapter 109A of title 18, United States Code, that was committed in relation to a child;

(2) any conduct proscribed by chapter 110 of title 18, United States Code;

(3) contact between any part of the defendant's body or an object and the genitals or anus of a child;

(4) contact between the genitals or anus of the defendant and any part of the body of a child;

(5) deriving sexual pleasure or gratification from the infliction of death, bodily injury, or physical pain on a child; or

(6) an attempt or conspiracy to engage in conduct described in paragraphs (1)-(5).

§4.35 Evidence of Similar Offenses in Sexual Assault and Child Molestation Cases

New rules enacted by Congress in 1994 mark a significant erosion in the long-established doctrine prohibiting the use of character evidence against a defendant in a criminal case.[1] Under FRE 413, evidence of the defendant's commission of another offense of sexual assault is now admissible in a criminal case where the defendant is accused of sexual assault. FRE 414 similarly allows evidence of the defendant's commission of a prior offense of child molestation in a case where the defendant is accused of child molestation.[2] FRE 415, which is discussed in the following section, provides that such evidence is also admissible in civil cases "for damages or other relief" predicated on a party's commission of an offense of sexual assault or child molestation.

Any relevant purpose These rules provide that evidence of the earlier offense may be considered "for its bearing on any matter to which it is relevant." Thus evidence may be admitted under these Rules to show the defendant's propensity toward committing such offenses. Such use of character evidence conflicts with the policy of FRE 404, which generally prohibits the use of character evidence "to prove action in conformity therewith on a particular occasion."[3] Such use also extends beyond FRE 404(b), which permits evidence of prior offenses only to prove narrow points such as the actor's motive, intent, or plan but not to prove his character in order to show action in conformity therewith. FRE 413-415 thus amount to an implicit amendment of FRE 404.[4]

Strong opposition FRE 413-415 provoked strong opposition from the Judicial Conference,[5] the organized bar,[6] and the academic community,[7] although

---

§4.35 1. FRE 413-415 were enacted as part of the Violent Crime Control and Law Enforcement Act of 1994.

2. It was probably unnecessary to enact FRE 413 and FRE 414 as separate rules, given that they accomplish essentially the same purpose. Moreover, there is overlap between them with respect to the offenses covered. Some acts of sexual assault as defined under FRE 413(d) qualify as acts of child molestation under FRE 414(d) if committed against a child under the age of fourteen.

3. See United States v. Tail, 459 F.3d 854, 858 (8th Cir. 2006) (policy behind FRE 413 is unique to cases involving sexual assaults and "renders the general prohibition on propensity evidence in Rule 404(b) inapposite").

4. This point was clearly recognized by the Judicial Conference, which in submitting an alternative version of FRE 413-415 to Congress drafted it as a new exception to FRE 404(a). See 159 F.R.D. 51 (1995).

5. Pursuant to a unique proviso sending FRE 413-415 to the Judicial Conference for review prior to its effective date, the Judicial Conference proposed an alternative rule (which Congress did not adopt) and urged Congress to reconsider FRE 413-415, noting the "highly unusual unanimity of the members of the Standing and Advisory Committees, composed of over 40 judges, practicing lawyers and academicians" in opposing the proposed rules. Id.

6. In February 1995 the ABA House of Delegates adopted a resolution opposing FRE 413-415.

7. See, e.g., Duane, The New Federal Rules of Evidence on Prior Acts of Accused Sex Offenders: A Poorly Drafted Version of a Very Bad Idea, 157 F.R.D. 95 (1994); Sheft, Federal Rule of Evidence 413: A Dangerous New Frontier, 33 Am. Crim. L. Rev. 57 (1995).

there has also been approving commentary.[8] A primary concern is that the new Rules may encourage juries to judge a defendant on the basis of his past behavior rather than the evidence against him in the current case, thereby undermining the presumption of innocence and depriving him of a fair trial.[9] Although such prosecutions understandably draw public compassion and concern, critics of the new rules contend that Congress acted without a sufficient showing of empirical evidence that a defendant's past conduct has higher probative value in these types of prosecutions than in other prosecutions where such evidence is not allowed.[10] Many also contend that FRE 404(b) already provides an adequate basis for admitting prior crimes evidence in those cases where it is most needed, such as to establish motive, intent, preparation, plan, absence of mistake, and similar points.[11] Certainly it cannot be argued that evidence that a defendant has committed prior sexual assaults or child molestations has *less* prejudicial effect than evidence of other misconduct. It is likely to provoke substantially *more* jury antipathy against the defendant than other types of misbehavior. Some critics have objected that it is unfair to open the door to evidence bearing on the past sexual behavior of the defendant when the complainant's sexual history is shielded by FRE 412.[12] To date, only a few states have enacted provisions similar to FRE 413-415.

One point of initial uncertainty was whether evidence admissible **Application of** under FRE 413-415 could be excluded under FRE 403 in cases where its **FRE 403** probative value was substantially outweighed by the dangers of unfair prejudice, jury confusion, or undue consumption of time. FRE 413-415 provide that evidence of prior specified offenses "is admissible," but also state that the new rules are not to be construed to limit consideration of evidence under any other rule, which presumably includes FRE 403. The legislative history makes clear that FRE 403 was intended to

---

8. Park, The Crime Bill of 1994 and the Law of Character Evidence: Congress Was Right About Consent Defense Cases, 22 Fordham Urb. L.J. 271 (1994) (supporting FRE 413-415 in sex crime prosecutions where a consent defense is asserted); Danna, The New Federal Rules of Evidence 413-415: The Prejudice of Politics or Just Plain Common Sense?, 41 St. Louis U.L.J. 277 (1996). *See also* Karp, Evidence of Propensity and Probability in Sex Offense Cases and Other Cases, 70 Chi.-Kent L. Rev. 15 (1994) (statement by principal draftsman of FRE 413-415 that has been incorporated as part of legislative history of Rules—*see* 140 Cong. Rec. H8991-92 (Aug. 21, 1994)).

9. Sheft, Federal Rule of Evidence 413: A Dangerous New Frontier, 33 Am. Crim. L. Rev. 57, 74 (1995) (evidence of prior offenses may dilute "beyond reasonable doubt" standard by lowering jurors' regret threshold about a wrongful conviction).

10. Recidivism rates vary greatly depending on the type of sexual crime, and many crimes of a nonsexual nature have even higher recidivism rates. *See* E. Imwinkelried, Uncharged Misconduct Evidence §4.16 (2002 cumulative supplement).

11. *See* §§4.15-4.18, *supra*.

12. *But see* Bryden & Park, "Other Crimes" Evidence in Sex Offense Cases, 78 Minn. L. Rev. 529 (1994) (supporting FRE 413-415 in "date rape" prosecutions and rejecting argument that FRE 413 and FRE 412 are in conflict because commission of prior sexual crimes by a defendant generally has more probative value than evidence that an alleged victim has previously consented to sexual relations with others).

apply,[13] and courts construing FRE 413-415 have uniformly held that their authority to exclude under FRE 403 has not been preempted.[14] Some courts have gone so far as to hold that if FRE 403 did not apply they would be required to declare the new rules unconstitutional.[15]

In conducting the balancing required by FRE 403, courts should consider the following factors:

(1) *Similarity to charged offense.* A salient factor in assessing probative worth is the extent to which prior incidents are similar to the charged offense. What counts is not only the physical nature of the offense, but any relationship between the victims and the defendant and the strategy followed by the defendant in committing the offenses. The greater the similarity, the stronger the claim of relevance.[16]

(2) *Specificity of the inference.* If the prior offense tends to support a specific inference, such as knowledge, plan, modus operandi, or absence of accident, it may be admissible under FRE 404(b). When evidence of a prior offense satisfies FRE 404(b), it is likely to be admissible under the more generalized requirements of FRE 413-415 as well.[17]

(3) *Wrongfulness and emotional impact of the act.* The most important single factor bearing on prejudice is the degree to which evidence of the prior offense is likely to have an unfair emotional impact on the jury.[18] Sexual offenses vary in the degree to which they trigger emotional responses and the degree to which they distract juries from more particular evidence or tempt juries to punish the defendant for the past

---

13. *See, e.g.,* 140 Cong. Rec. H5438 (June 29, 1994) (remarks of Representative Kyl (Ariz.) that courts retain "total discretion to exclude the evidence if its probative value is substantially outweighed by the danger of unfair prejudice"); 140 Cong. Rec. H8991-92 (Aug. 21, 1994) (FRE 403 "will continue to apply").

14. Johnson v. Elk Lake School Dist., 283 F.3d 138, 152-153 (3d Cir. 2002) (evidence satisfying FRE 413 or 415 may still be excluded under FRE 403 if probative value is substantially outweighed by danger of unfair prejudice); United States v. Velarde, 214 F.3d 1204, 1212 (10th Cir. 2000) (error not to balance under FRE 403).

15. United States v. Enjady, 134 F.3d 1427, 1433 (10th Cir. 1998) ("without the safeguards embodied in Rule 403 we would hold the rule [FRE 413] unconstitutional"); United States v. Castillo, 140 F.3d 874, 882 (10th Cir. 1998) ("most significant factor favoring Rule 414's constitutionality" is procedural protections of Rule 403).

16. United States v. Hawpetoss, 478 F.3d 820, 824-826 (7th Cir. 2007) (in child abuse trial, admitting proof of other similar acts involving two other children with whom defendant "had a familial or quasi-familial relationship"); United States v. Crawford, 413 F.3d 873, 874 (8th Cir. 2005) (in trial for abusive sexual conduct with eight-year-old girl, admitting conviction for abusive contact with another eight-year-old girl; conviction involved a "similar crime").

17. United States v. Roberts, 185 F.3d 1125, 1140-1142 (10th Cir. 1999) (in trial of chief for sexually abusing women working in tribal office, allowing testimony by six women other than victims of charged offenses about similar misconduct; evidence was admissible under FRE 404(b) to show common scheme and also admissible under FRE 413).

18. However, the sole fact that the evidence will be considered for a propensity purpose is not necessarily "unfair" prejudice because that is the purpose of the rule. *See* United States v. Benais, 460 F.3d 1059, 1063 (8th Cir. 2006) (FRE 403 must be applied in a manner that permits FRE 413 and 414 to have their "intended effect," which is to let jury "consider a defendant's prior bad acts" on issue of propensity).

conduct or for simply being a bad person. When the prior offense was particularly egregious, such as where it involved violence, humiliation, or serious physical or psychological injuries, the incident is more likely to be shocking and explosive, and these factors weigh more heavily in the calculus.[19] Such evidence may make it hard for the jury to maintain its commitment to the presumption of innocence and the requirement of proof beyond a reasonable doubt.

(4) *Proximity in time and intervening circumstances.* Although FRE 413-415 do not contain any particular time limitations,[20] the time elapsed between the prior conduct and the charged offense bears on its probative worth.[21] Probative value is less if the earlier incident appears to be a remote and isolated event. On the other hand, intervening circumstances, such as commission by the defendant of additional offenses of the same nature, may increase the probative value of an earlier crime. Offenses committed *subsequent* to the charged crime are admissible under these rules,[22] just as they are under FRE 404(b).[23]

(5) *Certainty that prior offense occurred.* FRE 413-415 do not require that the prior offense have resulted in a conviction.[24] Nonetheless, a judgment of conviction has higher probative value and can be more efficiently proven at trial. Proving prior offenses not resulting in a conviction can lead to trials within trials that are peculiarly distracting. Proving the prior offense may take as much time as proving the charged offense itself, at least where defendant contests the issue. It can be unfairly burdensome to a defendant to defend against the charged crime and at the same time against allegations of past offenses that have never been prosecuted and perhaps never even previously reported. Jurors may be distracted and confused about the basis upon which they are to judge the defendant. If the jury concludes that he committed a prior uncharged offense, this fact may actually be more prejudicial than evidence of a prior conviction, which at

19. United States v. Peters, 133 F.3d 933 (10th Cir. 1998) (evidence excluded of victim's physical injuries); People v. Harris, 60 Cal. App. 4th 727, 70 Cal. Rptr.2d 689, 697 (3d Dist. 1998) (error to admit evidence of prior rape; graphic evidence was inflammatory and circumstances differed from charged offense; applying state statute similar to FRE 413).

20. United States v. Velarde, 214 F.3d 1204, 1212 (10th Cir. 2000) (admitting evidence of child molestation 20 years earlier); United States v. Larson, 112 F.3d 600, 605 (2d Cir. 1997) (admitting prior sexual molestation of others 16-20 years earlier since they were committed under similar circumstances).

21. United States v. Julian, 427 F.3d 471 (7th Cir. 2005) (date of prior offense is a proper factor for court to consider); Doe ex rel. Rudy-Glanzer, 232 F.3d 1258 (9th Cir. 2000) (no error in excluding evidence of prior sexual misconduct when there was significant time lapse between that event and charged offense and no evidence of sexual misconduct in the interim, and circumstances were not similar; applying FRE 415).

22. United States v. Sioux, 362 F.3d 1241, 1244-1247 (9th Cir. 2004) (FRE 413 "unambiguously allows for the admission of subsequent acts" as well as prior acts).

23. See §4.15, *supra.*

24. United States v. Guidry, 456 F.3d 493, 502-503 n.4 (5th Cir. 2006) (prior sexual misconduct need not have led to conviction because "crime" and "offense" in FRE 413 merely describe "harm that may be punishable by law").

least suggests he has paid his debt to society. If the defendant was not convicted of his earlier offense, the jury may be more inclined to punish him for the prior acts regardless of what it thinks about the charged offense.

(6) *Possibility of minimizing prejudice.* The decision whether to admit proof of prior sexual assaults should take into account the possibility of controlling and minimizing the risk of prejudice. It is appropriate to limit the number of offenses than can be proved, and particularly to limit the details that can be proved, particularly where shocking or heinous elements are not themselves important and can safely be omitted from accounts of prior offenses without undermining probative worth.[25] Courts sometimes require prior offenses to be proved without inviting emotionally charged testimony by victims.[26] It may also be possible to accept defense stipulations that the prior offenses occurred, although courts are not required to do so.

(7) *Other factors.* Other factors that count are the degree to which the point to be proved is important, whether it is contested, and the availability of other less prejudicial forms of proof.[27]

Balancing factors

While courts should not give FRE 413-415 an overly narrow construction, one court has observed that there is no language in the rules "that supports an especially lenient application of FRE 403."[28]

Other rules apply

Other evidentiary rules, such as the restrictions of the hearsay doctrine, privileges, authentication and best evidence requirements, as well as the opinion and expert testimony rules, continue to apply to proof of prior offenses under the new Rules.[29]

Roles of judge and jury

The evidence must be sufficient to support a finding by a preponderance of the commission of a qualifying criminal offense under the law of the jurisdiction where the prior conduct occurred, and a preliminary hearing on this matter may be required.[30] Whether such

25. United States v. Peters, 133 F.3d 933 (10th Cir. 1998) (noting that potential prejudice was reduced by "excluding details that would most likely inflame a jury, such as information about a victim's physical injuries"); United States v. McHorse, 179 F.3d 889, 894-899 (10th Cir. 1999) (excluding evidence relating to abuse of half-sister of accused on ground that it was too dissimilar, remote, and potentially confusing).

26. United States v. Granbois, 119 Fed. Appx. 35, 38 (9th Cir. 2004) (noting that prior acts were not proved by "emotional and highly charged testimony" of victim or her relative, but by testimony of criminal investigator).

27. United States v. Enjady, 134 F.3d 1427, 1433 (10th Cir. 1998).

28. United States v. Guardia, 135 F.3d 1326, 1331 (10th Cir. 1998) (trial court "should not alter its normal process of weighing the probative value of the evidence against the danger of unfair prejudice"; in applying FRE 403 to FRE 413 evidence, it is particularly important that the court "make a clear record of the reasoning behind its findings").

29. *See* 140 Cong. Rec. H8991-92 (Aug. 21, 1994) (general standards of rules of evidence, including hearsay doctrine, continue to apply to FRE 413-415).

30. United States v. Enjady, 134 F.3d 1427, 1434 (10th Cir. 1998) (trial court should ensure "that jury does not hear evidence of similar acts that likely did not occur"; district court failed to hold hearing on whether prior rape occurred and this could be abuse of discretion in some cases, but not here where alleged victim had filed a contemporaneous police report).

a criminal offense exists in that jurisdiction and whether the proffered evidence, if believed, would satisfy the elements of such an offense are questions for the court. As under FRE 404(b), courts generally assign to the jury under FRE 104(b) the ultimate question of whether the prior offense was in fact committed and require only evidence sufficient to support a jury finding by a preponderance.[31] But since evidence under FRE 413-415 is admitted to show a defendant's propensity (which FRE 404(b) expressly forbids), more safeguards are arguably needed and the determination should be one for the court under FRE 104(a).

Notice must be given to the defendant at least fifteen days prior to trial (unless a later time is allowed for good cause) of evidence that is expected to be offered under these Rules, including witness statements or a summary of the substance of any testimony.[32]

Notice Requirement

FRE 415

     (a) In a civil case in which a claim for damages or other relief is predicated on a party's alleged commission of conduct constituting an offense of sexual assault or child molestation, evidence of that party's commission of another offense or offenses of sexual assault or child molestation is admissible and may be considered as provided in Rule 413 and Rule 414 of these rules.

     (b) A party who intends to offer evidence under this Rule shall disclose the evidence to the party against whom it will be offered, including statements of witnesses or a summary of the substance of any testimony that is expected to be offered, at least fifteen days before the scheduled date of trial or at such later time as the court may allow for good cause.

     (c) This rule shall not be construed to limit the admission or consideration of evidence under any other rule.

---

31. *See, e.g.,* United States v. Norris, 428 F.3d 907, 913-914 (9th Cir. 2005) (under FRE 413-415, trial court need not make preliminary determination that defendant committed prior act, but instead examines all the evidence and decides whether jury could reasonably find that fact by a preponderance). *See also* Huddleston v. United States, 485 U.S. 681 (1988) (under FRE 404(b), whether prior crime committed is FRE 104(b) question for jury), discussed in §4.15, *supra.*

32. United States v. Guidry, 456 F.3d 493, 504 (5th Cir. 2006) (good cause shown where evidence of prior sexual assault not discovered until after trial began and defendant was given time to challenge it). *Cf.* Johnson v. Elk Lake School Dist., 283 F.3d 138, 152-153 (3d Cir. 2002) (under FRE 415, plaintiff did not need to provide notice of intent to offer evidence of similar sexual assaults where defense counsel was present at deposition of witness who was proffered to testify about alleged prior assault).

§4.36   Civil Cases Involving Sexual Assault or Child Molestation

FRE 415 allows the same types of evidence in civil cases seeking damages or other relief for a party's alleged act of sexual assault or child molestation that FRE 413 and 414 permit in criminal prosecutions.[1] Thus the Rule incorporates by reference the definitions of "sexual assault" and "child molestation" set forth in these prior rules. Even though FRE 415 provides that such prior act evidence "is admissible," the introduction of such evidence remains subject to general evidentiary requirements, including the hearsay rule and perhaps most importantly FRE 403.[2] In undertaking FRE 403 balancing, courts tend to give careful attention to the similarity of the prior conduct, its remoteness in time, and the availability of other evidence.[3]

FRE 415 is most likely to come into play in cases where a plaintiff is suing for sexual harassment or similar sexual misconduct, at least if it was serious enough to amount to a sexual assault as defined by criminal law.[4] It also will play a role in the increasing number of cases where a victim of a violent sexual crime brings a civil suit for damages in addition to filing criminal charges.

Because individuals sued for sexual assault often lack financial resources and their insurance, if any, generally will not cover such claims, it is likely that civil actions by alleged victims will sometimes be brought against the defendant's corporate employer. In such cases, it is unlikely, although not implausible, that a plaintiff will seek to offer evidence of prior sexual offenses by the corporation itself.[5] It is more probable that a plaintiff will seek to introduce evidence of prior

§4.36   1. *See generally* Aiken, Sexual Character Evidence in Civil Actions: Refining the Propensity Rule, 1997 Wis. L. Rev. 1221 (1997); Note, Federal Rule of Evidence 415: Making It Work, 36 Washburn L.J. 89 (1996).

2. Jones v. Clinton, 993 F. Supp. 1217, 1221 (E.D. Ark. 1998) (general evidentiary standards apply to FRE 415 evidence, including restrictions on hearsay and discretion to exclude under FRE 403).

3. Frank v. County of Hudson, 924 F. Supp. 620, 625 (D.N.J. 1996) (in sexual harassment suit excluding evidence of alleged incidents of child abuse by defendant in past on grounds of unfair prejudice; a primary purpose of FRE 415 was to help resolve swearing contests between defendant and alleged victim and there is lessened need for FRE 415 evidence in cases with numerous witnesses to alleged harassment).

4. Frank v. County of Hudson, 924 F. Supp. 620, 625 (D.N.J. 1996) (although ordinary sexual harassment or discrimination cases will not trigger FRE 415, those that involve assaultive behavior may fall within purview of FRE 415).

5. Under the Model Penal Code, corporations can be held liable for crimes by corporate agents that are authorized or recklessly tolerated by corporate management. *See* Model Penal Code §2.07. In addition, even where a corporation is unable to commit an offense itself, it may be guilty of conspiring to commit such an offense. Under FRE 415, the "commission" of a prior sexual offense includes a conspiracy to engage in the proscribed conduct.

sexual offenses by a corporate agent despite the fact that FRE 415 speaks only of admitting prior sexual offenses committed by a "party." Although the issue is not free of doubt, some courts have been willing to allow evidence of prior sexual offenses by a corporate agent under FRE 415 in circumstances where the corporation is vicariously liable for the acts of such agent.[6]

6. Cleveland v. KFC Natl. Management Co., 948 F. Supp. 62, 65 (N.D. Ga. 1996).

CHAPTER 5
Privileges

A. GENERAL POLICIES

§5.1 Introduction

Privileges are a unique aspect of evidence law because they rest upon a different rationale than most other rules of evidence and sweep more broadly. They are not designed to enhance the reliability of the factfinding process. On the contrary, they impede the search for truth by excluding evidence that may be highly probative. They exempt certain testimony, and sometimes certain witnesses, from the scope of compulsory process.[1] They are not designed to further litigation efficiency. Instead they may cause delay and consume judicial resources in resolving claims of privilege both at trial and during discovery. They are the only rules of evidence that are largely beyond the control of the litigants. Only the holder of the privilege, who may or may not be a party, has the power to assert or waive the privilege.[2]

---

§5.1 1. Branzburg v. Hayes, 408 U.S. 665, 688 (1972) (public has a right "to every man's evidence except for those persons protected by a constitutional, common-law or statutory privilege"). Thus, in the absence of recognized privilege, the court has the authority to use civil contempt powers to compel a witness to testify, 28 U.S.C. §1826, or to punish a witness who refuses to testify, 18 U.S.C. §401.

2. See §5.3, infra.

Moreover, privileges, unlike other rules of evidence, apply at all stages of the proceeding.[3]

Justifications for privileges

Privileges are justified because they encourage the free flow of information in certain relationships and protect privacy in those relationships.[4] Some privileges serve other objectives, such as furthering the effective functioning of government by protecting state secrets or the confidentiality of agency deliberations. The privilege against self-incrimination implements the societal belief that an individual should not be compelled by the government to be his own accuser. By protecting relationships and values outside the courtroom, privileges show that even though searching for truth is of critical importance in litigation, it does not necessarily trump all other interests of society.[5]

Instrumental grounds

Many privileges, particularly those covering professional relationships, rest mostly on instrumental grounds. Without a privilege, clients or patients might not communicate freely and would withhold information needed for professionals effectively to provide their services. For every instance where a privilege serves as an obstacle to the discovery of truth at a trial, there may be many more occasions where the existence of the privilege serves to solidify a professional relationship or enhance the quality of professional services.

The instrumental justification has been questioned on the ground that laypersons are generally unaware of the existence or nonexistence of evidentiary privileges, from which it is argued that the candor of their communications in protected relationships is not influenced by the protection accorded by privileges.[6] Empirical studies suggest, however,

---

3. FRE 1101(c). Privileges apply even in determining preliminary questions concerning the admissibility of evidence. *See* FRE 104(a) (in making its preliminary determination, court "is not bound by the rules of evidence except those with respect to privileges").

4. United States v. Philip Morris Inc., 314 F.3d 612, 618 (D.C. Cir. 2003) (attorney-client privilege promotes "sound legal advocacy" by ensuring that lawyer knows all that is necessary to represent client).

5. *See* Louisell, Confidentiality, Conformity and Confusion: Privileges in Federal Court Today, 31 Tulane L. Rev. 101, 110 (1956) (it is "historic judgment of the common law" that "whatever handicapping of the adjudicatory process is caused by recognition of the privileges, it is not too great a price to pay for secrecy in certain communicative relations"); Pearse v. Pearse, 63 Eng. Rep. 950, 957 (1846) ("Truth, like all other good things, may be loved unwisely—may be pursued too keenly—may cost too much," and "the general evil of infusing reserve and dissimulation, uneasiness, and suspicion and fear, into those communications which must take place" is "too great a price to pay for truth itself").

6. *See, e.g.,* Hutchins & Slesinger, Some Observations on the Law of Evidence: Family Relations, 13 Minn. L. Rev. 675, 682 (1929) ("practically no one outside the legal profession knows anything about the rules regarding privileged communications between spouses" and as far as writers are aware "marital harmony among lawyers who know about privileged communications is not vastly superior to that of other professional groups"). *But see* Krattenmaker, Testimonial Privileges in Federal Courts: An Alternative to the Proposed Federal Rules of Evidence, 62 Geo. L.J. 61, 92 (1973) (even though individuals may communicate in certain relationships without awareness of the privilege, "[t]his proves little without the further assumption that subconscious, unarticulated knowledge never can influence human conduct"). *Cf.* Zacharias, Rethinking Confidentiality, 74 Iowa L. Rev. 351 (1989) (survey of lawyers and laypeople about effect of confidentiality duty on lawyer-client communications).

that users of professional services are more likely than the general public to be aware of evidentiary privileges, and professional persons often advise their clients or patients at the commencement of the relationship about the existence (and limits) of a privilege.[7]

It is also sometimes argued that the openness of communication in personal and professional relationships depends more on the level of trust between the parties than on the existence or nonexistence of a privilege. Certainly disclosure of private and even incriminating information occurs in relationships that are known not to be protected by a privilege, such as close friendships. But the fact that other circumstances bear on one's willingness to confide does not negate the premise that the flow of information in particular relationships may be influenced significantly by the existence or nonexistence of a privilege.[8]

In addition to the instrumental rationale, privileges are also justified as necessary to safeguard the values of privacy, freedom, trust, and honor in important personal and professional relationships. Some relationships are considered too sacred to allow the government to invade.[9] In an increasingly intrusive society, privileges provide a means to maintain zones of privacy.[10] If the state were able to compel a breach of loyalty in a confidential relationship, there would be a sense of betrayal that would adversely affect both the communicator and the recipient of confidences. An ethical conflict would be created for professional persons such as lawyers and psychotherapists, who would know that in seeking information necessary to the delivery of their professional services they would be placing their clients or patients at risk of future liability or embarrassment. If there were no privilege, such professional persons would likely feel obliged to relate this fact to patients or clients, which clearly would chill their ensuing conversations. Thus privileges manifest and preserve basic ethical and societal values.[11]

Protecting privacy

The extent to which privileges interfere with the factfinding process is sometimes exaggerated. If a communication would not have been made in the absence of a privilege, the privilege can scarcely be said to have

Interference with factfinding process

7. *See* Shuman & Weiner, The Privilege Study: An Empirical Examination of the Psychotherapist-Patient Privilege, 60 N.C.L. Rev. 893 (1982).

8. In re Grand Jury Investigation (Sun Co.), 599 F.2d 1224, 1235 (3d Cir. 1979) (incentive to confide "is at least partially dependent" on client's "ability to predict" that communication will kept confidential).

9. *See* Louisell, Confidentiality, Conformity and Confusion: Privileges in Federal Court Today, 31 Tulane L. Rev. 101, 113 (1956) (marriage without right of complete privacy of communication "would necessarily be an imperfect union," and freedom of marital communication "from all government supervision, constraint, control or observation, save only when the communications are for an illegal purpose, is a psychological necessity for the perfect fulfillment of marriage" and "promotes the public policy of furthering and safeguarding the objective of marriage just as other institutions in the area of domestic relations or family law promote it").

10. S. Bok, Secrets 282 (Oxford, 1984) (with "no capacity for keeping secrets" or "choosing when to reveal them," humans "would lose their sense of identity and every shred of autonomy").

11. *See* Levinson, Testimonial Privileges and the Preferences of Friendship, 1984 Duke L.J. 631, 662 (privileges raise issues at the center of contemporary debate about "foundations of liberal society").

caused a loss of evidence. Moreover, the alternative to recognizing certain privileges is not necessarily disclosure of the truth, but perhaps perjury.[12] Most privileges shield only the holder's communications, not the holder's underlying knowledge of facts. The attorney-client privilege, for example, does not bar the adverse party from fully exploring the client's knowledge of facts through discovery, or by calling the client as a witness. She may be asked what she knows, even if she may not be asked what she discussed with her attorney.[13] Particularly in civil cases, then, the attorney-client privilege does not keep others from getting at client knowledge, although perhaps the privilege does prevent others from verifying the accuracy of what the client says by comparing that with what she said before to her attorney. (In criminal cases, often the privilege against self-incrimination blocks or limits what adversaries can ask the accused.)

Still, the loss of evidence caused by privileges should not be minimized. In criminal cases, where the defendant cannot be called as a witness, the attorney-client privilege plays a crucial role in blocking what might be the next-best strategy, which is to go after the lawyer for information about what the client has said. Here the privilege effectively blocks access to the underlying facts. Some privileges, such as the spousal testimonial privilege and the privilege against self-incrimination, exclude broad categories of evidence, not just communications. It must be recognized that the price paid for the existence of any privilege may be that a litigant is deprived of evidence needed to prove a charge, claim, or defense. For this reason, a privilege should be construed to exclude no more evidence than is necessary to accomplish the purposes for which it was created.[14]

Wide variation in privilege law   There is continuing controversy over what privileges should be recognized, and there is wide variation in the scope of privilege law from jurisdiction to jurisdiction. Some commentators maintain that the number of privileges is already excessive.[15] Others take the view that privilege law may be both overinclusive and underinclusive, being skewed to favor groups with political power at the expense of more fundamental personal relationships and values.[16]

---

12. *See* Louisell, Confidentiality, Conformity and Confusion: Privileges in Federal Court Today, 31 Tulane L. Rev. 101 (1956) (privileges, by avoiding conflicts of conscience that could lead to perjury, may ultimately promote truth ascertainment).

13. *See* United States v. Cunningham, 672 F.2d 1064, 1073 n.8 (2d Cir. 1982) (privilege attaches not to information known to client, but to "communication of the information"), *cert. denied,* 466 U.S. 951.

14. University of Pennsylvania v. EEOC, 493 U.S. 182, 189 (1990) (privileges contravene principle that public "has a right to every man's evidence," so any such privilege "must be strictly construed"); United States v. Nixon, 418 U.S. 683, 710 (1974) ("Whatever their origins, these exceptions to the demand for every man's evidence are not lightly created nor expansively construed, for they are in derogation of the search for truth.").

15. *See, e.g.,* Krattenmaker, Testimonial Privileges in Federal Courts: An Alternative to the Proposed Federal Rules of Evidence, 62 Geo. L.J. 60, 85 (1973).

16. *See, e.g.,* Developments in the Law—Privileged Communications, 98 Harv. L. Rev. 1450, 1493-1498 (1985) (discussing the power theory, which "explains privilege law not as an effort to encourage communications or to protect privacy, but as special treatment won by the power of those privileged," noting that those enjoying privileges today "constitute some of the most politically powerful professions and institutions in America: lawyers, doctors, the Church, the news media, and the government").

There are ongoing efforts, particularly at the state level, to obtain recognition of new privileges. As courts have become increasingly reluctant to recognize additional privileges, the forum for such efforts has largely shifted to state legislatures. It is necessary to scrutinize requests for the creation of new privileges carefully because their ultimate costs (potentially erroneous verdicts in future civil and criminal cases) may seem remote, hence be undervalued. Caution is also warranted because a request for a new privilege may be motivated by professional rivalry or a desire for enhanced professional status, rather than genuine need for confidentiality in the relationship.[17]

Requests for new privileges should be evaluated by considering (1) the importance to the community of the relationship sought to be protected; (2) whether community values would be offended by governmental intrusion into the privacy of the relationship; (3) the extent to which societal traditions and professional standards create a reasonable expectation of confidentiality in such a relationship; (4) whether the purpose of the relationship depends on full and open communication; (5) the extent to which communication would be impeded by not recognizing a privilege; (6) the direct and indirect benefits to the public from encouraging the communication and protecting privacy in the relationship, when compared to the cost to the litigation process resulting from loss of evidence.[18]

Criteria for recognizing new privileges

§5.2 Duty of Confidentiality Distinguished

Many professions have a code of ethics imposing a duty on members to protect confidences of a client or patient, regardless whether the law of the jurisdiction recognizes an evidentiary privilege.[1] Such ethical duties are enforced independently of the law of evidentiary privilege.

---

17. *See* ABA Committee on Improvements in the Law of Evidence (J. Wigmore, Chairman), 63 ABA Report 570, 595 (1938) (in recent years, several legislatures have adopted "certain novel privileges of secrecy" which "bear the marks of having been enacted at the instances of certain occupational organizations of semi-national scope" and demand for these privileges seems to have been due "in part to a pride in their organization and a desire to give it some mark of professional status, and in part to the invocation of a false analogy to the long established privileges for certain professional communications").

18. *Compare* the classic four-part test set forth in 8 Wigmore, Evidence §2285 (McNaughton rev. 1961) ("(1) The communications must originate in a confidence that they will not be disclosed; (2) This element of confidentiality must be essential to the full and satisfactory maintenance of the relation between the parties; (3) The relation must be one which in the opinion of the community ought to be sedulously fostered; and (4) The injury that would inure to the relation by the disclosure of the communications must be greater than the benefit thereby gained for the correct disposal of the litigation."). *See also* University of Pennsylvania v. EEOC, 493 U.S. 182, 189 (1990) ("We do not create and apply an evidentiary privilege unless it 'promotes sufficiently important interests to outweigh the need for probative evidence' ") (quoting Trammel v. United States, 445 U.S. 40, 51 (1980)).

§5.2 1. *See, e.g.*, ABA Model Code of Professional Responsibility DR 4-101 (B) (a lawyer shall not knowingly "[r]eveal a confidence or secret of his client"); ABA Model

Sanctions for violating ethical requirements of confidentiality include professional censure, expulsion from professional organizations, and (in the case of regulated professions) possible suspension or loss of certification or license. Apart from duties imposed by the standards of a profession, individual members may observe an ethic of confidentiality as a matter of personal conscience or may obligate themselves to safeguard confidences by express or implied contract.[2] Sometimes a duty of confidentiality is created by statute independent of privilege law.[3]

Broader protection   In some respects, the duty of confidentiality provides greater protection for privacy than an evidentiary privilege.[4] A privilege applies only when testimony is sought in a legal proceeding,[5] whereas the duty of confidentiality applies to prevent disclosure of secrets in extrajudicial settings as well. Moreover, the ethical obligation of nondisclosure extends to matters that would not be within an evidentiary privilege such as secrets that are not communications and communications that are not confidential.[6] For example, what a client tells an attorney in the

---

Rules of Professional Conduct Rule 1.6(a) (a lawyer "shall not reveal information relating to representation of a client unless the client gives informed consent,[or] the disclosure is impliedly authorized in order to carry out the representation"); American Medical Association Principles of Medical Ethics 5.05 (information disclosed to a physician during the course of the relationship between physician and patient "is confidential to the greatest possible degree" and "physician should not reveal confidential communications or information without the express consent of the patient, unless required to do so by law"); American Nurses Association, Code for Nurses 2 ("The nurse safeguards the client's right to privacy by judiciously protecting information of a confidential nature"); American Psychological Association, Ethical Principles of Psychologists 5 ("Psychologists have a primary obligation to respect the confidentiality of information obtained from persons in the course of their work as psychologists."). The ethical codes of various professions are collected in Codes of Professional Responsibility, 2d ed. (R. Gorlin ed. BNA 1990).

2. *See, e.g.,* Mull v. String, 448 So. 2d 952, 955 (Ala. 1984) (upholding cause of action against physician for breach of implied contract not to disclose confidential patient information).

3. *See, e.g.,* State v. Keenan, 307 Or. 515, 771 P.2d 244, 246 (1989) (apart from privilege rule, statute regulating legal profession required attorneys to "[m]aintain inviolate the confidence, and at every peril to the attorney, preserve the secrets of the clients of the attorney").

4. *See* ABA Code of Professional Responsibility EC 4-4 (attorney-client privilege "is more limited than the ethical obligation of a lawyer to guard the confidence and secrets of his client").

5. *But see* Mosteller, Child Abuse Reporting Laws and Attorney-Client Confidences: The Reality and the Specter of Lawyer as Informant, 42 Duke L.J. 203, 230 (1992) (arguing that attorney-client privilege should apply under child abuse reporting laws). *See generally* Subin, The Lawyer as Superego: Disclosure of Client Confidences to Prevent Harm, 70 Iowa L. Rev. 1091, 1106 (1985) (although "[s]trictly speaking the privilege is not relevant to the attorney's out-of-court treatment of client confidences," if "attorneys were free to divulge confidences out of court that were protected by the privilege in court, the privilege would be of limited value, if not useless").

6. *See* ABA Model Code of Professional Responsibility DR 4-101(A) (" 'Confidence' refers to information protected by the attorney-client privilege under applicable law, and 'secret' refers to other information gained in the professional relationship that the client has requested be held inviolate or the disclosure of which would be embarrassing or would be likely to be detrimental to the client.").

presence of an unprivileged third person is outside the attorney-client privilege, but the ethical duty of confidentiality bars the attorney from disclosing the communication publicly.

Nonetheless, complete confidentiality can generally be guaranteed only if an evidentiary privilege also applies. In the absence of a privilege, a person called as a witness can normally be compelled to disclose confidential communications, regardless whether a professional standard of confidentiality applies and regardless what personal assurances or contractual commitments were given to the communicant. Hence practitioners are generally careful not to make a commitment to confidentiality beyond what is allowed by privilege law, and most ethical standards of confidentiality contain a qualification that permits disclosure when required by law or compelled by court order.[7] A professional person who seeks to maintain a higher standard of confidentiality than is recognized by evidence law may do so only at the risk of being held in contempt of court.

§5.3 General Principles—Assertion; Waiver; Interception

A distinctive attribute of a privilege is that it has a holder, who may not be a party to the litigation. Only the holder has the ultimate power to assert or waive the privilege, although other persons may be expressly or impliedly authorized to take such action on behalf of the holder.[1]

With respect to professional privileges, the holder is usually the recipient of the professional services rather than the provider. It is the client (not the lawyer) and it is the patient (not the psychotherapist) who decides whether to assert or waive the privilege.[2] The professional person lacks authority to waive a privilege that the holder wishes to maintain, or to assert a privilege that the holder wishes to waive.[3] Still, the professional person generally has an ethical obligation to assert the privilege on the holder's behalf unless the holder has indicated an intention that to waive it.

If the holder or his attorney is present, the privilege must be asserted at any point in the proceedings where someone makes an

Holder

Invoking privilege

7. See, e.g., ABA, Model Code of Professional Responsibility DR 4-101(C)(2); American Medical Association, Principles of Medical Ethics 5.05. But see American Newspaper Guild Code of Ethics, Canon 5 ("[N]ewspapermen shall refuse to reveal confidences or disclose sources of confidential information in court or before judicial or investigating bodies. . . .") (Proceedings of First Annual Convention, American Newspaper Guild, 1934).

§5.3 1. See §5.27, infra.

2. See Hunt v. Blackburn, 128 U.S. 464, 470 (1888) (privilege is that "of the client alone" and "if the client has voluntarily waived the privilege, it cannot be insisted on to close the mouth of the attorney"); Timken Roller Bearing Co. v. United States, 38 F.R.D. 57, 64 (N.D. Ohio 1964) ("[O]nly the client can unseal his attorney's lips; only the patient can authorize disclosure of sickbed confidences.").

3. See United States v. Frazier, 580 F.2d 229, 230 (6th Cir. 1978) ("[T]he attorney has no right to waive the privilege and only the client can waive it."), cert. denied, 439 U.S. 930.

attempt to inquire into matters covered by the privilege, or it is waived. If the holder or his attorney is not present, the parties or others who are there may call a matter of privilege to the attention of the court, which may then delay disclosure until it ascertains the holder's wishes.[4]

The holder must assert the privilege not only when privileged information is sought directly from her, but also when it is sought from the other party to the communication, or from third parties who come into possession of the privileged information.[5] The holder must claim the privilege at all stages of the proceeding, including discovery.[6]

Waiver   A privilege is waived if its holder voluntarily discloses or consents to disclosure of any significant part of the privileged matter unless the disclosure is itself privileged.[7] By disclosing in an unprivileged setting, the holder shows a lack of concern for confidentiality.[8] The privilege is waived even if the holder makes only selective disclosure to some selected person or persons, while seeking to maintain confidentiality as against the rest of the world.[9] In other words, intentional unprivileged disclosure to one person waives the privilege as against everyone else, with some qualifications.[10]

For waiver to occur, the disclosure must be voluntary. Testimony that is erroneously compelled by a court does not foreclose a claim of privilege in later proceedings,[11] provided that the claim was properly asserted in the court that compelled disclosure.[12] Thus the holder can

---

4. *See* Restatement (Third) of Law Governing Lawyers (Proposed Final Draft No. 1, 1996) §135(1)(C) (in absence of objection by person with standing, "presiding officer may order that a communication not be disclosed if it is privileged").

5. Morganroth & Morganroth v. DeLorean, 123 F.3d 374, 383 (6th Cir. 1997) (marital communication privilege waived by failure to properly assert it when wife testified earlier at deposition).

6. Perrignon v. Bergen Brunswig Corp., 77 F.R.D. 455, 459-461 (N.D. Cal. 1978) (privilege waived when disclosure made without objection during deposition).

7. *See* proposed-but-rejected FRE 511.

8. *See* United States v. Lilley, 581 F.2d 182, 189 (8th Cir. 1978) ("The [spousal] confidential communications privilege is waived, by definition, when the allegedly confidential communication is disclosed by the spouse claiming the privilege because the communications are no longer confidential.").

9. *See* In re Qwest Communications International, Inc., 450 F.3d 1179 (10th Cir. 2006) (rejecting selective waiver theory); In re John Doe Corp., 675 F.2d 482, 488-489 (2d Cir. 1982) (disclosure to accountants conducting annual audit held to waive attorney-client privilege).

10. FRE 502, enacted in 2008, recognizes some limits on waiver. See discussion in §5.28, *infra*.

11. *See* proposed-but-rejected FRE 512 (evidence of a statement or other disclosure of privileged matter "is not admissible against the holder of the privilege if the disclosure was . . . compelled erroneously").

12. *See* ACN, proposed-but-rejected FRE 512 (holder is not required to "stand his ground, refuse to answer, perhaps incur a judgment of contempt, and exhaust all legal recourse, in order to sustain his privilege" because "this exacts of the holder greater fortitude in the face of authority than ordinary individuals are likely to possess, and assumes unrealistically that a judicial remedy is always available").

sometimes relitigate the privilege claim in a later proceeding, at least where the original ruling was not appealed.[13]

Under the modern view, a privilege is not lost because an eavesdropper overhears a privileged communication, or because a thief stole a privileged document, or because someone intercepted a communication in some other manner, provided that the privilege holder took reasonable precautions to prevent such mishaps.[14]

Interception

The same principles apply to protect the holder in the rare situation where an attorney, psychotherapist, or other professional person breaches professional ethics and reveals secrets of the client or patient without authorization in a setting where the holder lacked opportunity to claim the privilege. Even though confidences become known to others because of such an ethical breach, the holder can nonetheless prevent their later use in a legal proceeding.[15]

Unauthorized
disclosure

§5.4   Adverse Comment or Inference

Under the Fifth Amendment, it is established that a defendant in a criminal case cannot be called to the stand and compelled to assert the privilege against self-incrimination in front of the jury.[1] If he does take the stand, and at some point claims the privilege, neither the court nor counsel on the other side can comment on the privilege claim.[2] If defendant does not take the stand, he is entitled to an instruction advising the jury not to draw an adverse inference from his failure to testify.[3] The direction of modern cases and statutes is toward

13. *See* ACN, proposed-but-rejected FRE 512 ("modest departure" from principles of *res judicata* occurring when judicial compulsion forces disclosure is justified by "the advantage of having one simple rule, assuring at least one opportunity for judicial supervision"). An appeal may not have been available in the original case, as happens if the holder prevailed despite compelled disclosure.

14. Gray v. Bicknell, 86 F.3d 1472, 1484 (8th Cir. 1996) (adopting reasonable precautions standard); Kenyatta v. Kelly, 375 F. Supp. 1175, 1177-1179 (E.D. Pa. 1974) (official information privilege not lost with respect to documents that were stolen from government). This view has now been adopted for the attorney-client privilege by recently-enacted FRE 502, discussed in §5.28, *infra*.

15. Bryson v. Tillinghast, 749 P.2d 110, 112 (Okla. 1988) (can use privileged information disclosed to police by doctor as basis for arrest, but privilege can still block testimony by doctor at trial). *See* proposed-but-rejected FRE 512(b) (no waiver where disclosure happened "without opportunity to claim privilege").

§5.4   1. *See* United States v. Echeles, 352 F.2d 892, 897 (7th Cir. 1965) ("universally held" interpretation of Fifth Amendment is that it prohibits "any person who is on trial for a crime from being called to the witness stand" by either prosecutor or codefendant). It is also generally improper to question defense witnesses about prior claims of privilege against self-incrimination before the grand jury.

2. Griffin v. California, 380 U.S. 609, 614 (1965) (comment on refusal to testify is remnant of "inquisitorial system," which Fifth Amendment outlaws; it is "a penalty imposed by courts" for exercising a constitutional privilege and it "cuts down on the privilege by making its assertion costly").

3. Carter v. Kentucky, 450 U.S. 288, 300 (1981). *Cf.* Lakeside v. Oregon, 435 U.S. 333, 340 (1978) (defendant failed to testify, failing to give no-inference instruction was not constitutional error).

extending these procedural protections to statutory and common law privileges as well,[4] even though such protection is not constitutionally mandated.[5]

No adverse comment

The framers of proposed-but-rejected FRE 513 thought courts and counsel should not comment adversely on a claim of privilege. The rule provides for claims of privilege to be made outside the presence of the jury, and entitles parties to an instruction that no adverse inference is to be drawn.[6] This rule has been adopted as URE 512 and is in the evidence code of numerous states.[7] In proceedings where state law supplies the rule of decision, federal courts must defer to state statutes restricting comment or argument about privilege claims.[8]

At least one state has construed its counterpart to proposed-but-rejected FRE 513 as applying to all privileges, thus prohibiting adverse inference from claims of the privilege against self-incrimination in a civil case,[9] even though such inference is constitutionally permissible.[10] A few states specifically allow adverse inference from assertion of the privilege against self-incrimination in civil proceedings.[11]

Prevent jury misunderstanding

In jurisdictions that have not adopted proposed-but-rejected FRE 513, privilege issues should generally be resolved outside the presence

4. *See, e.g.*, United States v. Chapman, 866 F.2d 1326 (11th Cir. 1989) (error for prosecutor to call accused's wife to witness stand for purpose of making her invoke privilege in front of jury).

5. Labbe v. Berman, 621 F.2d 26, 27-28 (1st Cir. 1980) (it is not *constitutional* error to call defendant's wife as adverse witness and requiring her to claim testimonial privilege even though defendant had told prosecutor that she would). *Cf.* American Bar Association Standards Relating to the Administration of Justice, Standard 3-5.7(c) (prosecutor "should not call a witness" knowing she will "claim a valid privilege" merely for purpose of "impressing upon the jury" the claim of privilege).

6. *See* proposed-but-rejected FRE 513 (claim of privilege, whether in present proceeding or on prior occasion, is not "proper subject of comment by judge or counsel," and "no inference" may be drawn; in jury cases, "proceedings shall be conducted, to the extent practicable, so as to facilitate the making of claims of privilege without the knowledge of the jury," and on request "any party against whom the jury might draw an adverse inference" from privilege claim is entitled to instruction not to draw inference).

7. *See* 13A U.L.A. 326 (listing states adopting URE 512). *Cf.* Me. R. Evid. 512, 513 (adopting no adverse inference rule for criminal cases but not civil cases).

8. Home Indem. Co. v. Lane Powell Moss & Miller, 43 F.3d 1322, 1328 (9th Cir. 1995) (in suit against insurance carrier seeking damages beyond policy limit for bad-faith refusal to settle, rejecting argument that defense could force plaintiffs to claim attorney-client privilege in front of jury; FRE 501 required application of Alaska Rule 512 barring comment and inference on privilege claim).

9. *See* John Deere Co. v. Epstein, 307 Or. 348, 354, 769 P.2d 766, 769 (1989) (state counterpart of proposed-but-rejected FRE 513 applies to assertion of Fifth Amendment privilege in civil cases; "privilege" in Rule 513 "must be interpreted to encompass all privileges, including privileges not enumerated within the code").

10. *See* Baxter v. Palmigiano, 425 U.S. 308, 318 (1976) (in civil prison disciplinary proceeding, adverse inference could be drawn against an inmate who declined to testify; "prevailing rule" is that Fifth Amendment "does not forbid adverse inferences against parties to civil actions when they refuse to testify in response to probative evidence offered against them"). *See generally* Heidt, The Conjurer's Circle—The Fifth Amendment Privilege in Civil Cases, 91 Yale L.J. 1062 (1982).

11. *See, e.g.*, Alaska R. Evid. 512(d); Tex. R. Evid. 513(c); Wis. R. Evid. §905.13(4). *See also* Asplin v. Mueller, 687 P.2d 1329, 1332 (Colo. App. 1984).

of the jury, to avoid exposing it to extraneous information or inviting speculation about the nature of privileged matter. Such an approach is consistent with the general policy of FRE 103(c) and FRE 104(c). The rule against adverse comment prevents potential misunderstanding by the jury about the reasons behind claiming a privilege. A party should not be expected to explain such a decision, or to be penalized for asserting a legal right. If no adverse inference is permitted, the court should be willing to instruct the jury to this effect, although the privilege claimant may choose to forgo such an instruction to avoid highlighting the unwanted inference. In the end, parties should anticipate and litigate issues of privilege in a manner that does not alert the jury.[12]

§5.5   Constitutional Right to Produce Evidence

There is some conflict between evidentiary privileges and the constitutional right of criminal defendants to present exculpatory evidence. It is established that criminal defendants, and perhaps even civil litigants,[1] have a constitutional right to introduce relevant evidence that occasionally overrides evidentiary rules of exclusion, including privilege rules.[2]

Although the right to present evidence is guaranteed by some state constitutions,[3] it is not expressly set out in the federal Constitution. Still, three lines of federal authority—and these rest on constitutional guarantees of compulsory process, confrontation, and due process—have converged to establish such a right. First, the Court in *Washington v. Texas*[4] struck down a state statute that rendered an accomplice incompetent to testify on behalf of a criminal defendant on the ground that it violated the defendant's right of compulsory process.[5] Second,

Three lines of authority

---

12. *See* ACN, proposed-but-rejected FRE 513 (calling witness in presence of jury, then excusing him after sidebar conference "may effectively convey to the jury" that privilege has been claimed; should avoid destruction of privilege "by innuendo").

§5.5   1. *See* Imwinkelried, The Case for Recognizing a New Constitutional Entitlement: The Right to Present Favorable Evidence in Civil Cases, 1990 Utah L. Rev. 1, 7-18 (arguing for recognition of constitutional right of civil litigants to introduce evidence in certain circumstances, even where it would be excluded under applicable evidentiary rules including rules of privilege).

2. Holmes v. South Carolina, 547 U.S. 319 (2006) (whether "rooted directly in the Due Process Clause of the Fourteenth Amendment or in the Compulsory Process or Confrontation clauses of the Sixth Amendment, the Constitution guarantees criminal defendants 'a meaningful opportunity to present a complete defense'") (error to exclude evidence of possible third party guilt).

3. *See, e.g.,* Mass. Const. pt. 1, art. XII; New Hampshire Const. pt. 1, art. 15. *See generally* Westen, The Compulsory Process Clause, 73 Mich. L. Rev. 71, 94 (1974). In states lacking an express guarantee, such a right may be derived from other constitutional provisions.

4. 388 U.S. 14, 18 (1967).

5. *See also* Rock v. Arkansas, 483 U.S. 44, 52 (1987) (holding on ground of compulsory process that state statute barring testimony by witness whose memory had been hypnotically refreshed could not be used to prevent criminal defendant from testifying on own behalf).

the Court held in *Davis v. Alaska*[6] that a state statute protecting the confidentiality of juvenile proceedings must yield to the defendant's right of confrontation, hence that the defendant must be allowed to impeach a state witness for bias by showing that he was on probation from a juvenile court adjudication.[7] Third, the Court in the *Chambers* case[8] found a violation of due process where state evidence law barred the defendant from introducing evidence that a third party had confessed to the murder for which he was being prosecuted and further prohibited impeaching the third party with his earlier confession.

The Court in the *Nixon* case[9] explicitly recognized the right to present evidence, in these words:

> The right to the production of all evidence at a criminal trial similarly has constitutional dimensions. The Sixth Amendment explicitly confers upon every defendant in a criminal trial the right "to be confronted with the witnesses against him" and "to have compulsory process for obtaining witnesses in his favor." Moreover, the Fifth Amendment also guarantees that no person shall be deprived of liberty without due process of law. It is the manifest duty of the courts to vindicate those guarantees, and to accomplish that it is essential that all relevant and admissible evidence be produced.[10]

Despite this broad statement, the Court has also made it clear that the constitutional right to present evidence does not necessarily supersede evidentiary privileges[11] or other evidentiary rules.[12] In *Rock v. Arkansas*, the Court noted:

> [T]he right to present relevant testimony is not without limitation. The right "may, in appropriate cases, bow to accommodate other legitimate interests in the criminal trial process." . . . In applying its evidentiary

---

6. 415 U.S. 308, 319-320 (1974).

7. *See also* Olden v. Kentucky, 488 U.S. 227, 232-233 (1988) (error to prevent defendant from asking complainant whether she claimed rape in order to preserve an ongoing extramarital affair with another).

8. Chambers v. Mississippi, 410 U.S. 284 (1973) (discussed in §8.92, *infra*).

9. United States v. Nixon, 418 U.S. 683, 713 (1974) (upholding subpoena by special prosecutor for confidential presidential communications; claim of absolute executive privilege would not prevail "over the fundamental demands of due process of law in the fair administration of criminal justice").

10. United States v. Nixon, 418 U.S. at 711 (1974).

11. *See* United States v. Nixon, 418 U.S. 683, 709-710 (1974) (privileges "are designed to protect weighty and legitimate competing interests" to a party's constitutional right to offer evidence); Chambers v. Mississippi, 410 U.S. 284, 302 (1973) (in exercise of right to offer evidence, accused "must comply with established rules of procedure and evidence designed to assure both fairness and reliability").

12. *See* United States v. Scheffer, 118 S. Ct. 1261 (1998) (evidentiary exclusionary rules abridge right to present defense only where "arbitrary" or "disproportionate to the purposes they are designed to serve") (approving exclusion of polygraph evidence offered by defendant); Michigan v. Lucas, 500 U.S. 145 (1991) (upholding state rape shield statute excluding evidence of past consensual sexual relations between defendant and victim; defendant failed to comply with notice and offer of proof requirements of statute).

rules a State must evaluate whether the interests served by a rule justify the limitation imposed on the defendant's constitutional right to testify.[13]

Although courts have not settled on a formula to resolve conflicts between a criminal defendant's constitutional right to present evidence and evidentiary privileges, they tend to favor a balancing approach.[14] Under this approach, the court assesses the importance and necessity of the privileged evidence to a fair defense, including legitimate impeachment of prosecution witnesses.[15] To make such an assessment, the court can require *in camera* disclosure of privileged material.[16] Then the court balances defendant's need for the material against the policies and interests underlying the privilege. If defendant's right to present evidence outweighs the interests protected by the privilege, the court decides whether the appropriate remedy is to compel disclosure or impose some other sanction, such as refusing to let a prosecution witness testify unless the privilege is waived, or striking testimony that was given, or dismissing the charges.

Balancing approach

A factor that counts in weighing the interests underlying a privilege is its source—whether deriving from the Constitution, from statute, or from common law. Thus a defendant's constitutional right to present evidence is unlikely to prevail over a privilege that is itself constitutionally guaranteed.[17] For example, it is established that the right to present evidence does not generally override the claim by a witness of his Fifth Amendment privilege against self-incrimination.[18] In extraordinary circumstances, courts sometimes resolve this tension by requiring the witness to disclose, while granting him immunity for disclosure.[19]

Constitutional or statutory privileges

Another factor that counts is the holder of the privilege—whether government or witness. Courts are more likely to allow defendant's constitutional right to present evidence to prevail over a privilege if it is held by the prosecuting entity.[20] Thus a state cannot simultaneously

Governmental privileges

---

13. Rock v. Arkansas, 483 U.S., at 55-56 (1987) (quoting *Chambers* case).

14. *See, e.g.,* Imwinkelried, Exculpatory Evidence 1-1b (2004).

15. *See generally* Note, Defendant v. Witness: Measuring Confrontation and Compulsory Process Rights Against Statutory Communications Privileges, 30 Stan. L. Rev. 935, 989 (1978).

16. White, Evidentiary Privileges and the Defendant's Constitutional Right to Introduce Evidence, 80 J. Crim. L. & Criminology 377, 398 n.81 (1989) (*in camera* inspection of evidence protected by privilege proper on showing "reasonable basis for believing that the evidence may be sufficiently material").

17. *But see* United States v. Criden, 633 F.2d 346, 356 (3d Cir. 1980) (even though reporter's privilege is "deeply rooted in the first amendment" it can be overcome by defendant's need for exculpatory evidence), *cert. denied,* 449 U.S. 1113.

18. *See* United States v. Khan, 728 F.2d 676, 678 (5th Cir. 1984) (right to compulsory process "must give way to the witness' Fifth Amendment privilege not to give testimony" that would incriminate him).

19. United States v. Bahadar, 954 F.2d 821, 826 (2d Cir. 1992) (may require immunity or dismissal where government engages in "discriminatory use of immunity to gain a tactical advantage," if testimony is "material, exculpatory, and not cumulative" and unobtainable elsewhere), *cert. denied,* 506 U.S. 850.

20. Pennsylvania v. Ritchie, 480 U.S. 39, 57-58 (1987) (prosecution's obligation to give defendant exculpatory evidence in its possession applies even to evidence protected by qualified statutory privilege).

prosecute a defendant and deny her access to exculpatory evidence by asserting a privilege.[21] For example, the prosecutor cannot shield the identity of a confidential informant where doing so significantly interferes with defendant's ability to prepare and present a defense.[22]

Privileges overridden

Although most decisions—by far the greater number in fact—uphold nongovernmental privileges against constitutional attack,[23] some strike the balance the other way—in favor of defendant's constitutional right to present evidence.[24] Many evidentiary privileges, in a wide range of situations, have had to give way in particular circumstances, including the privileges for confidential communications to marital partners,[25] physicians,[26] psychotherapists,[27] marriage

---

21. *See, e.g.,* United States v. Coplon, 185 F.2d 629, 638 (2d Cir. 1950) (because government chose to prosecute defendant, "it was not free to deny him the right to meet the case made against him by introducing relevant documents, otherwise privileged"), *cert. denied,* 342 U.S. 920.

22. *See* Roviaro v. United States, 353 U.S. 53 (1957). *See also* proposed-but-rejected FRE 510(c)(2) (qualifying government's privilege to refuse to disclose informer's identity where informer "may be able to give testimony necessary to a fair determination of the issue of guilt or innocence in a criminal case or of a material issue on the merits in a civil case to which the government is a party").

23. *See* United States v. Turkish, 623 F.2d 769, 773-774 (2d Cir. 1980) (traditionally Compulsory Process Clause gives defendant "the right to bring his witness to court and have [his] nonprivileged testimony heard," but not right to "displace a proper claim of privilege"), *cert. denied,* 449 U.S. 1077.

24. *See, e.g.,* United States v. Lindstrom, 698 F.2d 1154, 1167 (11th Cir. 1983) (certain privileges must "yield to the paramount right of the defense to cross-examine effectively the witness in a criminal case"); United States v. Brown, 634 F.2d 819, 824 (5th Cir. 1981) (in some cases a privilege or rule of evidence "must give way to the defendant's Sixth Amendment rights"). *See generally* Westen, The Compulsory Process Clause, 73 Mich. L. Rev. 71, 172 (1974) ("private privileges are unconstitutional as applied whenever the additional benefit derived from extending them to exculpatory information in criminal cases is insufficient to justify their burden on the defendant's right to present a defense").

25. People v. Foskey, 529 N.E.2d 1158, 1163 (Ill. App. 1988) (acknowledging state's interest in "protecting confidential communications between spouses," but defendant's rights to effective cross-examination and due process of law "must prevail"), *aff'd,* 544 N.E.2d 192; Salazar v. State, 559 P.2d 66, 79 (Alaska 1976) (although protected by marital communications privilege, husband's confession to wife that he committed murder for which defendant was on trial should have been admitted; he was denied his "day in court" and "opportunity to present his story"). Some jurisdictions recognize an exception to the privilege where the communication is offered by the spouse accused of a crime. *See* §5.32, *infra.* In such jurisdictions, defendant can introduce the privileged evidence without relying on constitutional argument.

26. *See* State v. Trammell, 435 N.W.2d 197, 201 (Neb. 1989) (defendant entitled to victim's medical records for cross-examination and impeachment); State v. Hembd, 232 N.W.2d 872, 874 (Minn. 1975) (defendant entitled to privileged medical records of alleged kidnapping victim that showed she previously tried to commit suicide, to support claim that defendant detained her only to keep her from doing that).

27. In re John Doe, 964 F.2d 1325, 1329 (2d Cir. 1992) (overriding psychotherapist-patient privilege, in part because of confrontation concerns); United States v. Lindstrom, 698 F.2d 1154, 1167 (11th Cir. 1983) (defense right to cross-examine and impeach key government witness outweighed claim for privacy of her records of psychotherapy).

counselors,[28] rape counselors,[29] and journalists.[30] The spousal testimonial privilege has given way in some cases,[31] as have the doctrines protecting secrecy of both grand juries[32] and trial juries.[33]

Almost all decisions have struck the balance in favor of attorney-client privilege,[34] perhaps in part because it has constitutional underpinnings.[35] Yet circumstances can be imagined where even this privilege should yield,[36] as in a case where a privileged attorney-client communication could exonerate someone who is mistakenly charged with a serious crime apparently committed by a client who has told his lawyer that he is the guilty party, in which case a court would probably have to compel disclosure by the attorney while immunizing the client against use of what he told his lawyer. One commentator has said that English law lets the attorney disclose client confidences in this situation.[37] Compelling disclosure is especially appropriate if the client is now deceased, so that other proof of his guilt (hence the innocence of the party charged with the crime) is hard to come by.[38]

28. *See* M. v. K., 452 A.2d 704, 709 (N.J. 1982) (child's due process rights in custody proceeding infringed by statutory privilege for communications between marriage counselor and counselees).

29. *See* People v. Caruso, 521 N.W.2d 557 (Mich. 1994) (privilege for private counseling records of victim of sexual offense may be overridden where defendant shows reasonable probability that records contain information necessary to his defense). *See generally* Note, The Constitutionality of an Absolute Privilege for Rape Crisis Counseling: A Criminal Defendant's Sixth Amendment Rights Versus a Rape Victim's Right to Confidential Therapeutic Counseling, 30 B.C. L. Rev. 411 (1989).

30. *See* In re Farber, 394 A.2d 330, 351-352 (N.J. 1978) (compulsory process provision of state constitution held to prevail over state journalist shield law), *cert. denied*, 439 U.S. 997.

31. State v. Quintero, 823 P.2d 981 (Or. App. 1991) (trial court ordered wife of one defendant to testify despite her claim of spousal testimonial privilege; confrontation rights of other defendants were superior to her statutory privilege), *rev. denied*, 840 P.2d 710.

32. Chesney v. Robinson, 403 F. Supp. 306, 310 (D.C. Conn. 1975) (state privilege for grand jury proceedings must yield to defendant's Sixth Amendment right to cross-examine prosecution witness about inconsistent grand jury testimony), *cert. denied*, 429 U.S. 867.

33. Durr v. Cook, 589 F.2d 891, 893 (5th Cir. 1979) (defendant had constitutional right to present evidence of juror misconduct to impeach verdict despite state statute restricting such testimony).

34. *See, e.g.,* Jenkins v. Wainwright, 763 F.2d 1390 (11th Cir. 1985), *cert. denied*, 476 U.S. 1164; Valdez v. Winans, 738 F.2d 1087, 1090 (10th Cir. 1984); United States ex rel. Blackwell v. Franzen, 688 F.2d 496, 501-502 (7th Cir. 1982) (approving a balancing test), *cert. denied*, 460 U.S. 1072.

35. *See* §5.8, *infra*.

36. Vela v. Superior Court, 255 Cal. Rptr. 921 (Cal. App. 1989) (statutory attorney-client privilege gives way when it deprives defendant of "constitutional rights of confrontation and cross-examination").

37. Cross on Evidence 399-400 (6th ed. 1985).

38. In re Death of Eric Miller, 584 S.E.2d 772 (N.C. 2003) (recognizing qualified exception to privilege allowing court to compel disclosure of communications about murder investigation when client took his own life on discovering he would be arrested for the murder). *See also* Restatement (Third) of the Law Governing Lawyers (Proposed Final Draft No. 1, 1996) §127 cmt. d ("Permitting disclosure of a decedent's confidential communication in such an exceptional case would do little to

Remedies   Where a conflict is found between the constitutional right to present evidence and a nonconstitutional privilege held by a private party, there is uncertainty about the appropriate remedy. The answer depends in part on whether the defendant seeks to use the privileged evidence for impeachment or as substantive evidence. In the former case, the defendant's claim rests on the right of confrontation; in the latter, on the right of compulsory process or due process. The traditional remedy where a defendant is denied the right to confront is to strike the direct testimony of the witness or preclude the witness from testifying.[39] Also courts assess whether there are other adequate means available to challenge the credibility of the prosecution witness.[40] In most cases the right of confrontation can be vindicated without breaching the privilege.

Where the defendant is found to have a constitutional right to offer privileged matter substantively in his own defense as a matter of compulsory process or due process, a more difficult conflict arises. The conflict can be avoided if the holder is willing to waive the privilege. If not, a more stark choice may be presented between compelled disclosure or dismissal of the prosecution.

Where the prosecuting authority holds or controls a privilege that would keep from the defendant evidence that is important in mounting a defense, the prosecuting authority must choose between waiving the privilege and bringing the charges, or preserving the privilege and dismissing the charges.[41] Where a private party holds the privilege, the court determines whether the privilege must yield to defendant's constitutional right to present evidence.

---

inhibit clients from confiding in their lawyers. Assuring litigants a just outcome in their disputes in some cases would be a superior interest."). *But see* Swidler & Berlin v. United States, 524 U.S. 399, 409-410 (1998) (federal privilege survives death of client); In re John Doe Grand Jury Investigation, 562 N.E.2d 69 (Mass. 1990) (upholding absolute privilege for deceased client who may have made admissions to his attorney about murder of his wife). *See* further discussion of this issue in §5.26, *infra*.

39. *See, e.g.,* Fountain v. United States, 384 F.2d 624, 628 (5th Cir. 1967) (ultimate inquiry is whether defendant "has been deprived of his right to test the truth of the direct testimony," and if he has, "so much of the direct testimony as cannot be subjected to sufficient inquiry must be struck"), *cert. denied*, 390 U.S. 1005; State v. Trammell, 435 N.W.2d 197, 201 (Neb. 1989) (if complaining witness refused to waive privilege for medical records her testimony should be stricken).

40. United States v. Brown, 634 F.2d 819, 825 (5th Cir. 1981) (whether Sixth Amendment rights are violated depends on "alternative means open to the defendant to impeach the credibility of the witness").

41. *Cf.* Classified Information Procedures Act (CIPA), 18 U.S.C. App. 1-16 (allowing dismissal where use of government secrets is essential to fair defense but government refuses to relinquish privilege). *See generally* Westen, The Compulsory Process Clause, 73 Mich. L. Rev. 71, 162 (1974) (where conflict is unavoidable, government must choose between prosecuting and preserving the privilege).

B. SCOPE OF FRE 501

FRE 501

Except as otherwise required by the Constitution of the United States or provided by Act of Congress or in rules prescribed by the Supreme Court pursuant to statutory authority, the privilege of a witness, person, government, State, or political subdivision thereof shall be governed by the principles of the common law as they may be interpreted by the courts of the United States in the light of reason and experience. However, in civil actions and proceedings, with respect to an element of a claim or defense as to which State law supplies the rule of decision, the privilege of a witness, person, government, State, or political subdivision thereof shall be determined in accordance with State law.

§5.6 Preserving Federal Common Law of Privileges

As originally proposed, Article V of the Federal Rules of Evidence would have codified the law of privileges into 13 rules. Nine of those rules would have defined specific privileges covering required reports, lawyer-client and psychotherapist-patient communications, spousal testimony, communications to clergymen, political vote, trade secrets, secrets of state, and informant's identity.[1] Another rule would have provided that only the privileges set forth in Article V or other act of Congress would be recognized in federal courts, thereby superseding the common law of privileges, and ignoring state privilege law.[2] The three remaining rules would have addressed procedural incidents privileges, such as waiver by voluntary disclosure, protection of privileged matter disclosed under court order, and the propriety of making adverse comments or suggesting adverse inferences based on a party's claim of privilege.[3]

When Congress considered the proposed rules, Article V turned out to be particularly controversial for a number of reasons. First, it did not include some privileges, such as those covering communications between physician and patient, between spouses, and between journalists and sources, thereby arousing the opposition of many who supported those privileges.[4] Second, proposed FRE 509 redefined the

Proposed Article V controversial

---

§5.6   1. *See* proposed-but-rejected FRE 502-510.

2. *See* proposed-but-rejected FRE 501.

3. *See* proposed-but-rejected FRE 511-513.

4. A prescient observer foresaw the controversy that ultimately ensued. *See* Weinstein, The Uniformity-Conformity Dilemma Facing Draftsmen of Federal Rules of Evidence, 69 Colum. L. Rev. 353, 373 (1969) (proposed privilege rules "will excite many who will fight to the death to save the privacy of the bedroom and the doctor's office," and "[n]o one who has not been in a state capitol when the press sought a reporter's privilege can appreciate how heavy the pressures of the press can be").

scope of the privileges covering state secrets official information, and the latter was an exceedingly sensitive issue for Congress because the rules were being considered at the time of the Watergate affair, in which an embattled President Nixon claimed a privilege with respect to conversations with his advisors relating to that affair. Third, the proposed privilege rules would have applied even in diversity cases and other cases where state law supplied the rule of decision, thereby overriding state privilege law.[5]

Congress refused to codify privileges

Unable to resolve the controversies surrounding proposed Article V, Congress ultimately rejected the attempt to codify the federal law of privileges. Instead Congress enacted a new FRE 501 providing that privileges "shall be governed by the principles of the common law" as interpreted "in the light of reason and experience." Rule FRE 501, however, specifically provides for continuing recognition of privileges, immunities, or nondisclosure provisions established by federal statute or other rules promulgated pursuant to statutory authority.[6] Moreover, FRE 501 applies only to judicial proceedings[7] although the privileges developed in that setting are often recognized in legislative and administrative proceedings as well.[8]

The legislative history makes clear that congressional rejection of proposed Article V was not to be construed as disapproval of the specific privileges contained therein.[9] Congress intended to leave privilege law where it was, and not to freeze the evolution of the federal common law with respect to creation, modification, or repeal of specific privileges.[10] Congress did, however, remove privileges from the general rulemaking power of the Supreme Court and adopted legislation providing that no formal rules of privilege promulgated by the Court could become effective until approved by Act of Congress.[11]

Common law of privilege

The reference to "principles of the common law" in FRE 501 appears to contemplate that federal courts applying federal privilege law in federal criminal cases and federal question litigation may look to all useful sources for guidance, beginning with existing federal precedent

---

5. *See* §5.7, *infra.*

6. The reference to other rules prescribed by the Supreme Court refers to the Federal Rules of Civil Procedure and Federal Rules of Criminal Procedure. *See, e.g.,* FRCP 26(b)(3) (qualified immunity for work product); FRCP 26(b)(4) (restricting discovery of experts); FRCrimP 6(e)(2) (secrecy of grand jury proceedings); FRCrimP 16(a)(2) and (b)(2) (work product limitation on discovery in criminal cases).

7. *See* FRE 1101.

8. *See* Millet, The Applicability of Evidentiary Privileges for Confidential Communications Before Congress, 21 J. Marshall L. Rev. 309 (1988); Note, The Attorney-Client Privilege in Congressional Investigations, 88 Colum. L. Rev. 145 (1988).

9. *See* Senate Report, at 13 (action of Congress "should not be understood as disapproving any recognition of a psychiatrist-patient, or husband-wife, or any other of the enumerated privileges contained in the Supreme Court rules" but rather as reflecting view that recognition of privileges "should be determined on a case-by-case basis").

10. *See* University of Pennsylvania v. EEOC, 493 U.S. 182, 189 (1990) (although FRE 501 "provide[s] the courts with flexibility to develop rules of privilege on a case-by-case basis, we are disinclined to exercise this authority expansively").

11. 28 U.S.C. 2074(b) (1988) ("Any such rule creating, abolishing, or modifying an evidentiary privilege shall have no force or effect unless approved by Act of Congress.").

and consulting state precedent for whatever light it might shed on sound principles.[12] Any doubt about the authority of federal courts to consider state law is removed by the charge to interpret the common law principles "in the light of reason and experience." In developing the federal common law of privilege, federal courts consider state judicial opinions as well as state statutes.[13]

Courts and commentators have differing views on the force that should be given to the proposed federal rules of privilege that were rejected by Congress.[14] Some have urged that they be viewed as "standards,"[15] but others have been reluctant to give them such force.[16] Because the proposed rules were drafted by a distinguished Advisory Committee and were ultimately approved and promulgated by the Supreme Court, they are certainly entitled to respect. They provide a starting point in the development of the federal common law of privilege under FRE 501.[17] In some instances they represent an unexceptionable statement of prevailing doctrine (to a large extent this is true for the attorney-client privilege), but other rules (such as the spousal privileges) differ markedly from current federal common law. Because of their rejection by Congress, the proposed federal rules cannot be thought authoritative on the substance of the federal common law of privileges. They have had considerable influence at the state level, however, where they have often served as a model for codified state rules of privilege.[18]

Effect of proposed rules

---

12. *See* United States v. Crain, 589 F.2d 996, 999 (9th Cir. 1979) (federal courts may draw on "any and all traditional sources" in developing federal common law; often state law is "an appropriate source").

13. *See, e.g.,* Trammel v. United States, 445 U.S. 40, 49-50 (1980) (federal spousal testimonial privilege belongs to witness spouse and not defendant spouse; substantial weight given to trend in state legislation and judicial decisions toward such a rule).

14. Even the Supreme Court has vacillated on the deference due to the proposed-but-rejected rules in developing privilege law under FRE 501. *Compare* United States v. Gillock, 445 U.S. 360, 367-368 (1980) (refusing to create federal privilege for state legislators; neither Evidence Rules Advisory Committee nor Judicial Conference nor Court saw fit to provide such privilege) *with* Trammel v. United States, 445 U.S. 40, 52-53 (1980) (defendant spouse no longer holds spousal testimonial privilege, even though recognized as holder in proposed-but-rejected FRE 505(a)).

15. *See* 2 Weinstein & Berger, Weinstein's Evidence ¶501[03] at 501-32-34 (1989). *See also* In re Grand Jury Proceedings, 434 F. Supp. 648, 650 n.1 (E.D. Mich. 1977) ("What more accurate expression of the principles of the common law and of the application of reason and experience could exist than a draft that was developed by a representative committee of the bench, bar and scholars, twice published and commented on by the bench and bar, adopted by the Judicial Conference and finally forwarded by the Supreme Court to Congress for promulgation."), *aff'd,* 570 F.2d 562 (6th Cir. 1978).

16. 23 Wright & Graham, Federal Practice and Procedure 5422 at 691-693 (1980); Krattenmaker, Interpersonal Testimonial Privileges Under the Federal Rules of Evidence: A Suggested Approach, 64 Georgetown L.J. 613, 666 (1976) (proposed-but-rejected rules are not product of "reason and experience" under FRE 501).

17. *See* United States v. BDO Seidman, LLP, 492 F.3d 806, 815 (7th Cir. 2007), cert. denied, 128 S.Ct. 1471 (2008) (proposed-but-rejected FRE 503 is "source of general guidance" on federal common law).

18. The proposed-but-rejected Rules served as the basis for the 1974 revision of the Uniform Rules of Evidence, which in turn were adopted by a number of states.

§5.7 When State Privilege Law Applies

As originally promulgated, proposed FRE 501 contained no deference to state law and would have required that federal privilege law control even in diversity cases and other cases where state law supplied the rule of decision. Although the proposal was criticized as violating the *Erie* doctrine and the Rules Enabling Act,[1] the Advisory Committee believed that such an approach could be taken as a matter of judicial rulemaking under the authority of *Hanna v. Plumer*.[2] The Committee took the view that application of federal privilege law in all federal proceedings would not significantly interfere with state policy.[3] The Advisory Committee's proposal provoked considerable scholarly debate.[4]

Defer where state law controls
Congress ultimately rejected proposed FRE 501, concluding that the approach taken by the Advisory Committee would violate the principle of comity,[5] if not the *Erie* doctrine itself,[6] and would encourage forum shopping.[7] Instead, Congress added a proviso to the final version of FRE 501 requiring that federal courts defer to state privilege law in all civil cases "with respect to an element of a claim or defense as to which

§5.7 1. *See* Erie R. Co. v. Tompkins, 304 U.S. 64 (1938); 28 U.S.C. 2072 (court-promulgated rules shall not "abridge, enlarge or modify any substantive right"). *See also* House Hearings, at 142-148 (statement of Arthur Goldberg).

2. Hanna v. Plumer, 380 U.S. 460 (1965). *See* ACN to proposed-but-rejected FRE 501 (regardless what "might once have been thought" to be the command of *Erie* on applying state privileges in diversity cases, *Hanna* "is believed to locate the problem in the area of choice rather than necessity").

3. *See* ACN to proposed-but-rejected FRE 501 (state privileges "traditionally have given way in federal criminal prosecutions" and if a privilege "is denied in the area of greater sensitivity, it tends to become illusory as a significant aspect" of relationship that it covers; in state with accountant's privilege, "only the most imperceptible added force" would accrue by putting the accountant in position "to assure his client that, while he could not block disclosure in a federal criminal prosecution, he could do so in diversity cases" as well as state proceedings). *See also* Ladd, Privileges, 1969 Law & Soc. Ord. 555, 571 (practical effect on freedom of communication by holders of state privileges would be "but very little different" whether federal rules applied in all federal trials or "only those involving a federal question").

4. *See* Kaminsky, State Evidentiary Privileges in Federal Civil Litigation, 43 Fordham L. Rev. 923, 953 (1975) (finding Advisory Committee's position unpersuasive); Ely, The Irrepressible Myth of *Erie,* 87 Harv. L. Rev. 693, 740 (1974) (criticizing Advisory Committee view, but stating that Congress would have authority to mandate federal rules of privilege in diversity cases by legislation); Ladd, Privileges, 1969 Law & Soc. Ord. 555, 559-574 (defending Advisory Committee position); Wright, Procedural Reform: Its Limitations and Its Future, 1 Ga. L. Rev. 563, 573 (1967) (federal rule could deny privilege where state would grant one, and *Hanna* means federal rule "could be applied in any kind of case").

5. House Report, at 9 (federal law "should not supersede that of the States in substantive areas such as privilege absent a compelling reason," and in diversity cases "there is no federal interest strong enough to justify departure from State policy").

6. House Report, at 9 (applying state privilege law in civil actions and proceedings governed by *Erie* is "a result in accord with current federal court decisions").

7. House Report, at 9 (proposed rules would have "promoted forum shopping in some civil actions," depending on differences in privilege among state and federal courts; requiring federal courts to apply state privilege law in diversity suits "removes the incentive to 'shop'").

state law supplies the rule of decision."[8] Thus federal privilege law controls in federal criminal trials,[9] and in civil cases litigated in federal court not based on diversity jurisdiction.[10] On the other hand, state privilege law governs in diversity cases,[11] and in some other situations when claims or defenses based on state law are advanced, subject to limited exceptions.[12] When more than one state's privilege law is involved, federal courts generally apply the doctrine of the *Klaxon* case,[13] under which the forum state's choice-of-law rules control.[14]

Federal privilege law controls even where a federal statute incorporates state law by reference "to fill interstices or gaps in federal statutory phrases."[15] However, difficulties are presented when federal and state claims are joined in the same proceeding for it is generally not practical to instruct the jury to consider the privileged evidence on one claim but not the other.[16]

Federal and state claims joined

8. The ambiguous reference to an "element of a claim or defense" is clarified by legislative history, which indicates that state privilege law governs all evidence relevant to a state claim or defense, even if it is not sufficient by itself to constitute an "element." *See* Conference Report, at 7 ("If an item of proof tends to support or defeat a claim or defense, or an element of a claim or defense, and if state law supplies the rule of decision for that claim or defense, then state privilege law applies to that item of proof.").

9. *See, e.g.,* United States v. Schoenheinz, 548 F.2d 1389, 1390 (9th Cir. 1977) (state employer-stenographer privilege cannot be asserted in federal criminal proceeding).

10. *See, e.g.,* Babasa v. LensCrafters, Inc., 498 F.3d 972, 974 (9th Cir. 2007) (state privilege law applies in civil actions only "with respect to an element of a claim or defense as to which State law supplies the rule of decision," so state mediation privilege could not preclude determination that letter constituted notice under §1446(b) for purpose of removal to federal court); Hollins v. Powell, 773 F.2d 191, 196 (8th Cir. 1985) (in federal civil rights action, federal law of privilege controls), *cert. denied,* 475 U.S. 1119.

11. *See, e.g.,* DiBella v. Hopkins, 403 F.3d 102, 120 (2d Cir. 2005) (state privilege law applies in defamation suit based on diversity jurisdiction); Pamida, Inc. v. E.S. Originals, Inc., 281 F.3d 726, 731 (8th Cir. 2002) (in diversity actions, state law supplies rule of decision).

12. *See* Conference Report, at 7 (in diversity cases, there may be some claims or defenses based on federal law, in which "federal privilege law will apply to evidence relevant to the federal claim or defense"). *See generally* Dudley, Federalism and Federal Rule of Evidence 501: Privilege and Vertical Choice of Law, 82 Geo. L.J. 1781 (1994).

13. Klaxon v. Stentor Electric Mfg. Co., 313 U.S. 487, 435-436 (1941).

14. *See, e.g.,* Pritchard-Keang Nam Corp. v. Jaworski, 751 F.2d 277, 281 n.4 (8th Cir. 1984), *cert. dismissed,* 472 U.S. 1022; Samuelson v. Susen, 576 F.2d 546, 550-551 (3d Cir. 1978) (where Pennsylvania was forum state, looking to its choice-of-law rules, under which Ohio law satisfies significant relationship standard) (so Ohio privilege law controls). *See generally* Sterk, Testimonial Privileges: An Analysis of Horizontal Choice of Law Problems, 61 Minn. L. Rev. 461 (1977); Seidelson, The Federal Rules of Evidence: Rule 501, Klaxon and the Constitution, 5 Hofstra L. Rev. 21 (1976).

15. Conference Report, at 7-8 (when federal court "chooses to absorb state law," it applies that law "as a matter of federal common law," and state law "does not supply the rule of decision (even though the federal court may apply a rule derived from state decisions)," so state privilege law would not apply).

16. The Senate Judiciary Committee suggested that in case of conflict between state and federal privilege law, "the rule favoring reception of the evidence should be applied." *See* Senate Report at 12, n.17. Under this approach any federal privilege not also recognized by state law would be lost, and, similarly, state privilege claims would be limited by the boundaries of federal privilege law.

When state and federal claims are joined, most federal courts apply federal privilege law to both claims,[17] although some make accommodation to state law when possible.[18] Sometimes there are sufficiently strong state interests to justify application of state privilege law apply to the adjudication of the state claims, and severance of those claims becomes appropriate,[19] particularly if a federal privilege that applies to federal claims joined in the suit would keep a litigant from establishing state law claims or defenses.

"Reason and experience" Even where federal law supplies the rule of decision, a federal court, applying "reason and experience," may incorporate state privilege law as part of the developing federal common law of privilege under FRE 501.[20] Moreover, sometimes federal courts defer to a state privilege as a matter of comity even where the claim is based on federal rather than state law,[21] although such an approach can cause uncertainty and undermine the uniformity of federal privilege law. Where federal interests are strong, as in federal criminal prosecutions, considerations of comity should yield to federal privilege law.[22]

The proviso to FRE 501 requires deference to state privileges when state law supplies the rule of decision, but the Rule does not define a "privilege." Thus it is sometimes necessary for federal courts to

---

17. *See, e.g.,* Pearson v. Miller, 211 F.3d 57, 65 (3d Cir. 2000) (in case raising both federal and state claims, federal preference for disclosure controls despite state law requiring confidentiality for facts pertaining to mental health) (state statutes speak of "confidentiality," not "privilege"); Hancock v. Hobbs, 967 F.2d 462, 466 (11th Cir. 1992) (federal privilege law governs even where evidence is relevant to pendent state claim; it would be "impractical to apply two different rules of privilege to the same evidence before a single jury").

18. Sprague v. Thorn Americas, Inc., 129 F.3d 1355, 1368-1369 (10th Cir. 1997) (state privilege law should be applied to state claims joined with federal claims to extent possible).

19. *See* Research Inst. for Med. & Chem., Inc. v. Wisconsin Alumni Res. Found., 114 F.R.D. 672, 675 n2 (W.D. Wis. 1987) (separate trial of state and federal claims may be necessary to maintain integrity of privilege rules).

20. *See* Wm. T. Thompson Co. v. General Nutrition Corp., 671 F.2d 100, 103-104 (3d Cir. 1982) (federal courts may "resort to state law analogies for the development of a federal common law of privileges" where federal rule is unsettled); Riley v. City of Chester, 612 F.2d 708, 715 (3d Cir. 1979) (in recognizing federal privilege for journalists, court considers state law establishing privilege).

21. Socialist Workers Party v. Grubisic, 619 F.2d 641, 643-644 (7th Cir. 1980) (in civil rights action, recognizing qualified privilege for secrecy of state grand jury minutes, in part because "principles of comity dictate that we carefully consider the integral role secrecy plays in the Illinois grand jury system, which is in turn crucial to the operation of the criminal justice system of that state"); Burke v. New York City Police Dept., 115 F.R.D. 220, 225 (S.D.N.Y. 1987) (courts should give weight to state statutes requiring confidentiality even in actions based on federal claims); In re Cruz, 561 F. Supp. 1042, 1046 (D. Conn. 1983) (deferring to state privilege for state tax records as basis for quashing federal grand jury subpoena); United States v. King, 73 F.R.D. 103, 105 (E.D.N.Y. 1976) (strong policy of comity between state and federal sovereignties "impels federal courts to recognize state privileges where this can be accomplished at no substantial cost to federal substantive and procedural policy").

22. United States v. Gillock, 445 U.S. 360, 373 (1980) (comity yields where "important federal interests are at stake, as in the enforcement of federal criminal statutes").

determine whether a state rule of nondisclosure or confidentiality constitutes a "privilege" within the meaning of FRE 501.[23]

If a confidentiality statute contains an express or implied exception for cases where the information is sought by subpoena, the statute does not create a privilege because the essence of a privilege is protection against compelled revelation of protected information. Even if the state statute does not create a privilege, the matter it protects may be within federal privilege, such as the one covering government reports or official information.

FRE 501's directive to apply state privilege law includes not only rules that create and define privileges, but also related rules restricting comment or argument about assertion of privileges.[24]

C. ATTORNEY-CLIENT PRIVILEGE

§5.8 Attorney-Client Privilege: Rationale

The oldest of all evidentiary privileges is the privilege for confidential communications between attorney and client,[1] and this privilege had its origins in Roman and canon law.[2] The privilege developed contemporaneously with the right of compulsory process and as an exception to it.[3] From its earliest days, the privilege has played the important role of protecting the private bond of trust between attorney and client[4] and upholding the honor and dignity of the lawyer.[5] To compel disclosure

---

23. *See* Montone v. Radio Shack, 698 F. Supp. 92, 94-95 (E.D. Pa. 1988) (federal court refused to exclude evidence taken in violation of state anti-wiretap law; "because the Pennsylvania wiretap statute focuses on the manner in which a conversation is heard rather than the nature of the parties to the conversation, it does not create a privilege within the meaning of Rule 501"); Railroad Salvage v. Japan Freight Consolidators, 97 F.R.D. 37, 40 (E.D.N.Y. 1983) (state work product rule is not a privilege and therefore need not be applied by the court under FRE 501).

24. Home Indem. Co. v. Lane Powell Moss & Miller, 43 F.3d 1322, 1328 (9th Cir. 1995) (rejecting argument that defense should have been allowed to force plaintiffs to claim attorney-client privilege in front of jury; FRE 501 requires application of Alaska Rule 512, which bars comment and inference based on privilege claim, and which requires courts to avoid informing jury of privilege claims; state rule was part and parcel of its body of privilege law).

§5.8 1. The privilege was recognized in English cases as early as 1577. *See* Berd v. Lovelace, 21 Eng. Rep. 33 (1577); Dennis v. Codrington, 21 Eng. Rep. 53 (1580).

2. Radin, The Privilege of Confidential Communication Between Lawyer and Client, 16 Calif. L. Rev. 487 (1928).

3. Gardner, A Re-Evaluation of the Attorney-Client Privilege, 8 Vill. L. Rev. 279, 288-289 (1963).

4. *See* Bacon's Essays, XX, Of Counsel 51 (MacMillan & Co., 1892) ("The greatest trust between man and man, is the trust of giving counsel. For in other confidences, men commit the parts of life; their lands, their goods, their children, their credit, some particular affair; but to such, as they make their counselors, they commit the whole: by how much the more they are obliged to all faith and integrity.").

5. *See* 8 Wigmore, Evidence, §2286 at 530-531 (McNaughton rev. 1961) (in seventeenth century trials, obligations of "honor among gentlemen," which expressed the dominant standard, were considered "sufficient ground for maintaining silence").

of client secrets would force an act of betrayal and violate the attorney's assurance of loyalty, undermining the very essence of professionalism.[6] Few lawyers in such a regime would fail to warn clients that the law provided no protection for what they were about to say, and lawyers would be cast in the beginning as potential adversaries to their own clients. The privilege thus manifests societal respect for the importance of confidentiality and trust in the attorney-client relationship.[7]

Instrumental justifications

While these humanistic justifications for the privilege continue to have force,[8] the prevailing modern rationale for the privilege is instrumental or utilitarian.[9] Without the privilege, any client would be deterred from seeking legal assistance in the first instance, or at least inhibited from making full and candid disclosure of relevant facts bearing on her case.[10] Thus attorneys would be deprived of the factual information necessary to provide effective legal representation.[11] Some valid claims or defenses would be lost,[12] and attorneys would be ambushed at trial by evidence that they would be unprepared to rebut. By encouraging more open communication, the privilege helps lawyers provide the legal advice, and render legal services, that are needed if

---

Hence the attorney, not the client, was viewed as holder of the privilege. *See id.,* §2321 at 629 (under "original theory of the privilege," it belonged to attorney, not client).

6. Hazard, An Historical Perspective on the Attorney-Client Privilege, 66 Calif. L. Rev. 1061 (1978). *See also* 8 Wigmore on Evidence §2291, at 553 (J. McNaughton rev. 1961) (it is "repugnant to any honorable man to feel that the confidences which his relation naturally invites are liable at the opponent's behest to be laid open through his own testimony," and lawyer "cannot but feel the disagreeable inconsistency of being at the same time the solicitor and the revealer of the secrets of the cause," which "double-minded attitude" would create "an unhealthy moral state").

7. 1 Livingston, Works 461 (1873) ("Every feeling of justice, honour and humanity, would be shocked" by attorney's breach of client confidences). *See generally* Fried, The Lawyer as Friend: The Moral Foundations of the Lawyer-Client Relation, 85 Yale L.J. 1060 (1976).

8. *See* Luban, Lawyers and Justice: An Ethical Study 192-197 (1988).

9. In re Colton, 201 F. Supp. 13, 15 (S.D.N.Y. 1961) (in eighteenth century, when desire for truth "overcame the wish to protect the honor of witnesses," several privileges disappeared, but attorney-client privilege was kept, on "new theory that it was necessary to encourage clients to make the fullest disclosures to their attorneys, to enable the latter properly to advise the clients," which is today's basis for the privilege), *aff'd,* 306 F.2d 633 (2d Cir. 1962), *cert. denied,* 371 U.S. 951.

10. In re Grand Jury Proceeding, Cherney, 898 F.2d 565, 569 (7th Cir. 1990) (invading privilege "will have a grave effect on our justice system as clients, knowing that their confidential communications may be subject to disclosure, will eventually be less than candid with their attorneys or will consider foregoing legal advice altogether"). *But see* Developments in the Law—Privileged Communications, 98 Harv. L. Rev. 1450, 1474 (1985) (noting that "no solid empirical data exists" to support estimates regarding the extent to which the privilege facilitates client communications or other benefits or costs of privileges).

11. *See* Upjohn Co. v. United States, 449 U.S. 383, 389 (1981) (privilege recognizes "that sound legal advice or advocacy serves public ends and that such advice or advocacy depends upon the lawyer's being fully informed by the client"); United States v. Buckley, 586 F.2d 498, 502-503 (5th Cir. 1978) (policy behind privileges is "to encourage the free-flowing communication and candid disclosure so vitally necessary to effective representation by counsel"), *cert. denied,* 440 U.S. 982.

12. Allen, Grady, Polsby & Yashko, A Positive Theory of the Attorney-Client Privilege and the Work Product Doctrine, 19 J. Legal Studies 359, 374-383 (1990) (privilege is necessary to allow clients to assert "contingent claims," i.e., claims whose existence is contingent on disclosure of unfavorable information about the client).

clients are to assert their rights effectively,[13] to defend themselves, and to avoid litigation and other difficulties in an increasingly complex and regulated society.[14]

Despite its various theoretical justifications, the attorney-client privilege continues to draw detractors.[15] It has been criticized as creating an obstacle to truth, and it has even been labeled a shelter for the guilty.[16] Some commentators argue that the privilege should be qualified rather than absolute so that disclosure could be required when necessary in the interests of justice.[17] Such an approach, however, would undermine the certainty that confidences are protected, and would inhibit attorney-client communications.[18]

Critics of privilege

13. Strauss, Toward a Revised Model of Attorney-Client Relationship: The Argument for Autonomy, 65 N.C. L. Rev. 315, 336-349 (1987) (candid communication promotes client autonomy, allowing clients to become better informed and more capable of participating in decisions affecting their futures); Fried, Correspondence, 86 Yale L.J. 573, 586 (1977) (attorney-client privilege is rooted in personal autonomy; it is "immoral for society to constrain anyone from discovering what the limits of its power over him are").

14. *See* ALI Model Code of Evidence Rule 210, cmt. a at 147 (1942): "In a society as complicated in structure as ours and governed by laws as complex and detailed as those imposed upon us, expert legal advice is essential. To the furnishing of such advice the fullest freedom and honesty of communication of pertinent facts is a prerequisite. To induce clients to make such communications, the privilege to prevent their later disclosure is said by courts and commentators to be a necessity. The social good derived from the proper performance of the functions of lawyers acting for their clients is believed to outweigh the harm that may come from the suppression of the evidence in specific cases." *See also* Saltzburg, Privileges and Professionals: Lawyers and Psychiatrists, 66 Va. L. Rev. 597, 605 (1980) (attorney-client privilege helps laymen protect their rights and understand complex laws); Miller, The Challenges to the Attorney-Client Privilege, 49 Va. L. Rev. 262, 268-269 (1963) (privilege promotes obedience to law by allowing attorneys to dissuade clients from unlawful conduct).

15. *See, e.g.,* Kaplow & Shavell, Legal Advice About Information to Present in Litigation: Its Effects and Social Desirability, 102 Harv. L. Rev. 565 (1989) (questioning benefits of attorney-client privilege).

16. *See* 5 Bentham, Rationale of Judicial Evidence 301-304 (J. S. Mill ed. 1827) (attorney-client privilege protects only the guilty; disclosure of communications by an innocent client would not be damaging; although absence of a privilege would deter disclosure by guilty clients, the only consequence would be "[t]hat a guilty person will not in general be able to derive quite so much assistance from his law adviser, in the way of concerting a false defence, as he may do at present"). Bentham's argument assumes clients are either entirely innocent or guilty and ignores the possibility of clients who are victims of incriminating circumstances they reasonably would not want disclosed.

17. McCormick, Evidence 206 (3d ed. E. Cleary) (1984) (suggesting balancing approach under which "the lawyer's duty as an officer of the court to lend his aid in the last resort to prevent a miscarriage of justice" would be given "primacy"); Frankel, The Search for Truth Continued: More Disclosure, Less Privilege, 54 U. Colo. L. Rev. 51 (1982).

18. Alschuler, The Search for Truth Continued, The Privilege Retained: A Response to Judge Frankel, 54 U. Colo. L. Rev. 67 (1982); Alschuler, The Preservation of a Client's Confidences: One Value Among Many or a Categorical Imperative?, 52 U. Colo. L. Rev. 349 (1981) (both articles criticizing balancing approach that would allow attorney-client privilege to be overridden). *Cf.* Upjohn Co. v. United States, 449 U.S. 383, 393 (1981) (if purpose of privilege is to be served, attorney and client "must be able to predict with some degree of certainty whether particular discussions will be protected," because an "uncertain privilege, or one which purports to be certain but results in widely varying applications by the courts, is little better than no privilege at all").

Wigmore made the easy comment that the privilege should be narrowly construed,[19] and courts often endorse this suggestion.[20] The privilege protects crucial values and interests, but at some cost to the truthfinding process,[21] and courts and legislators naturally try to avoid extravagant applications of the privilege that would block access to information while contributing little to the values and interests at stake.[22]

Constitutional underpinnings

The attorney-client privilege has constitutional underpinnings.[23] The defendant's right to counsel in criminal cases, guaranteed by the Sixth Amendment and most state constitutions, require some degree of confidentiality.[24] It is doubtful that constitutional standards for adequate legal representation could be satisfied if prosecutors could demand access to a defendant's candid statements to his attorney.

The privilege has also been viewed as a necessary adjunct to the privilege against self-incrimination.[25] If incriminating admissions by a defendant to his attorney could be extracted from the attorney, a defendant could be convicted on the basis of his own confidential statements, rather than on evidence independently adduced by the

---

19. 8 Wigmore on Evidence §2291, at 554 (J. McNaughton rev. 1961) (claiming that benefits of privilege "are all indirect and speculative," while obstruction is "plain and concrete," and concluding that it is worth preserving for policy reasons, but that it is "an obstacle to the investigation of the truth" that should be "strictly confined within the narrowest possible limits" consistent with the underlying logic).

20. *See, e.g.,* Fisher v. United States, 425 U.S. 391, 403 (1976) (because privilege withholds relevant information, it applies "only where necessary to achieve its purpose" and "protects only those disclosures necessary to obtain informed legal advice which might not have been made absent the privilege").

21. *See generally* Luban, Lawyers and Justice: An Ethical Study 177-205 (1988); Gardner, A Re-Evaluation of the Attorney-Client Privilege, 8 Vill. L. Rev. 279 (1963).

22. *See* Goode, Identity, Fees, and the Attorney-Client Privilege, 59 Geo. Wash. L. Rev. 307, 360 (1991).

23. *See* Martin v. Lauer, 686 F.2d 24, 32-33 (D.C. Cir. 1982) (protection for attorney-client communications is interwoven with right to effective assistance of counsel and access to courts), *aff'd in part, rev'd in part on other grounds,* 740 F.2d 36 (D.C. Cir. 1984); People v. Swearingen, 649 P.2d 1102, 1104 (Colo. 1982) (privilege in criminal trials is interrelated with right against self-incrimination and right to effective counsel). *See generally* Subin, The Lawyer as Superego: Disclosure of Client Confidences to Prevent Harm, 70 Iowa L. Rev. 1091, 1119-1134 (1985); Seidelson, The Attorney-Client Privilege and Client's Constitutional Rights, 6 Hofstra L. Rev. 693 (1978).

24. United States v. Blasco, 702 F.2d 1315, 1329 (11th Cir. 1983) (communication that is protected by attorney-client privilege is also "protected from government intrusion by the sixth amendment"), *cert. denied,* 464 U.S. 914. *See also* United States v. Henry, 447 U.S. 264, 295 (1980) (Rehnquist, J., dissenting) (Sixth Amendment "protects the confidentiality of communications between the accused and his attorney").

25. The attorney-client privilege cannot rest directly on the privilege against self-incrimination, however, because incriminating disclosures to a lawyer are not compelled by the government, which is essential to a Fifth Amendment claim. *See* Fisher v. United States, 425 U.S. 391, 410 n.11 (1976) (writings given to lawyer not subject to Fifth Amendment where preparation was not compelled by government).

prosecution.[26] Absent a privilege, defense counsel could be forced into the appalling role of agent and informer for the government.[27]

§5.9   Client or Representative of Client

A "client" is a person, organization, or entity that receives professional legal services from a lawyer or consults a lawyer for the purpose of obtaining such services.[1] Although originally the privilege applied only where the attorney represented the client in litigation, the modern privilege applies whenever the lawyer renders professional legal services, whether in preparing contracts or wills, in negotiating with government regulators, or in advising clients on the requirements of regulations.[2]

The client may be a private entity, such as a corporation,[3] partnership, or unincorporated association, or the client may be a public entity, such as a federal, state, or municipal government, or an agency, executive department, or other governmental unit.[4]

The attorney-client relationship springs into being when a person **Reasonable belief** consulting a lawyer reasonably believes that the lawyer is willing to undertake, or consider undertaking, professional legal services on behalf of the client.[5] The privilege applies to preliminary discussions about representation, even if the lawyer ultimately declines to provide representation or the client decides not to retain the lawyer.[6] The

---

26. 3 Blackstone, Commentaries 370 (1765) ("[N]o man is to be examined to prove his own infamy. And no counsel, attorney, or other person, intrusted with the secrets of the cause by the party himself, shall be compelled, or perhaps allowed, to give evidence of such conversation or matters of privacy, as came to his knowledge by virtue of such trust and confidence.").

27. *See* Bentham, A Treatise on Judicial Evidence 247 (M. Dumont ed.) (footnote by Dumont as editor responding to Bentham argues that abolishing privilege would mean that the accused "have no longer counsel," but would be "surrounded by agents of justice and the police, against whom they ought to be so much the more upon their guard," and pointing out that "no man of a noble or elevated mind would stoop" to employment as lawyer, so lawyers would be "spies and informers placed round the accused").

§5.9   1. In re Grand Jury Subpoena: Under Seal, 415 F.3d 333, 339 (4th Cir. 2005) (one claiming privilege must prove that he is client or "affirmatively sought to become client" in order to show reasonable subjective belief that professional relationship existed; former employees interviewed in internal investigation prior to SEC probe could not have thought they were represented by in-house counsel, hence could not assert privilege). *See* proposed-but-rejected FRE 503(a)(1) (client is "a person, public officer, or corporation, association, or other organization or entity, either public or private," who receives professional legal services from lawyer, or who consults lawyer "with a view to obtaining professional legal services").

2. *See* ACN, proposed-but-rejected FRE 503(a)(1) (client "need not be involved in litigation" and "rendition of legal services or advice under any circumstances suffices").

3. *See* §5.16, *infra.*

4. *See* §5.18, *infra.*

5. United States v. Costanzo, 625 F.2d 465, 468 (3d Cir. 1980), *cert. denied*, 472 U.S. 1017; Hughes v. Paine, Webber, Jackson & Curtis, Inc., 565 F. Supp. 663, 669 (N.D. Ill. 1983).

6. *See* In re Auclair, 961 F.2d 65, 69 (5th Cir. 1992) (no person "could ever safely consult an attorney for the first time" if privilege "depended on the chance of whether the attorney after hearing the statement of facts decided to accept employment or decline it").

privilege does not apply to communications that occur after it becomes clear that representation will not be provided.[7] There is no requirement that fees be paid or promised for the lawyer's services, and the privilege extends to legal consultation or representation that is supplied without charge[8] or that is paid for by a third person.[9] No express contract is required to establish an attorney-client relationship.[10] Once an attorney-client relationship has been established, the privilege can apply even to "self-initiated" advice given by the lawyer to inform the client of pertinent legal developments.[11]

Corporate clients   Where a corporation is the client, the entity itself is the client, not the board of directors, officers, employees, or individual shareholders.[12] A lawyer for a corporation may also represent agents or employees of the corporation when they are parties to a suit because of what they did while acting for the corporation,[13] but the lawyer can undertake such dual representation only if there is no conflict of interest.[14] Corporate management controls the corporation's privilege on behalf of the corporation,[15] but in shareholder derivative actions, management's power to assert the corporation's privilege against shareholders is qualified.[16]

Partnerships   Where a partnership is the client, the attorney-client privilege usually covers communications from any partner to the attorney, provided that they are made in furtherance of obtaining professional legal

7. United States v. Dennis, 843 F.2d 652, 656-657 (2d Cir. 1988) (no privilege for communications made after lawyer expressly declined representation).

8. United States v. Costanzo, 625 F.2d 465, 468 (3d Cir. 1980) (attorney-client relationship is not dependent on payment of a fee), *cert. denied,* 472 U.S. 1017. *See generally* Friedman, The Creation of the Attorney-Client Relationship: An Emerging View, 22 Cal. W. L. Rev. 209, 212-213 (1986).

9. Dole v. Milonas, 889 F.2d 885, 888 n.5 (9th Cir. 1989) (attorney-client relationship and privilege may exist even where attorney's fees are paid by a third person).

10. Westinghouse Elec. Corp. v. Kerr-McGee Corp., 580 F.2d 1311, 1317 n.7 (7th Cir. 1978), *cert. denied,* 439 U.S. 955.

11. *See* Jack Winter, Inc. v. Koratron Co., 54 F.R.D. 44, 46 (N.D. Cal. 1971) (privilege applies to documents where client made "implied request for legal advice" and also to "self-initiated attorney communications" intended to keep client posted on legal developments and implications).

12. United States v. Munoz, 233 F.3d 1117, 1128 (9th Cir. 2000) (company's sales representative was not client of company's attorney; no express or implied contract between attorney and representative). See ABA Model Code of Professional Responsibility EC 5-18 (lawyer retained by corporation or similar entity "owes his allegiance to the entity and not to a stockholder, director, officer, employee, representative, or other person connected with the entity").

13. *See, e.g.,* Continental Oil Co. v. United States, 330 F.2d 347, 349 (9th Cir. 1964) (corporate counsel represented corporate officers at grand jury proceeding). *See* §5.16, *infra.*

14. ABA Model Code of Professional Conduct EC 5-18 (occasionally lawyer for entity is "requested by a stockholder, director, officer, employee, representative, or other person connected with the entity to represent him in an individual capacity," in which case lawyer "may serve the individual only if the lawyer is convinced that differing interests are not present.").

15. *See* §5.16, *infra.*

16. *See* §5.17, *infra.*

services for the partnership. An individual partner may be viewed as a representative of the partnership entity or as a joint client.[17]

Where the client is some other kind of unincorporated association, some decisions hold that each member is a client, and that communications by any member to the lawyer are within the privilege.[18] Such a rule seems appropriate where the association is limited in size, and where members play an active role in its activities. Where the association is large and has many passive members, the privilege should not reach quite that far, and should be limited as it is when applied to corporate clients, where the privilege applies either to those in the "control group" (to cite the standard observed for corporate clients in many states) or to those who speak to lawyers about matters within the scope of their responsibilities (to cite the modern federal standard for corporate clients).[19]

Unincorporated association

If the client is a trustee, it is generally held that the actual clients are the trust beneficiaries, and the attorney-client privilege cannot be asserted to shield from them communications between the trustee and the attorney.[20]

A minor or other legal incompetent can be a client, but such a client should have a guardian appointed to protect her interests in dealing with the lawyer,[21] in which case communications between guardian and lawyer and communications between minor (or incompetent) and lawyer are equally within the privilege.[22]

Usually a person who hires an attorney to provide legal services to another is not himself the client. Instead, the client is the person to whom the legal services are actually rendered.[23] If the person who pays the lawyer's fee is already the lawyer's client, however, he continues to

---

17. *See* §5.14, *infra. See* Pucci v. Santi, 711 F. Supp. 916, 927 n.4 (N.D. Ill. 1989) ("general view" is that "where an entity is by law an aggregate of individuals, the lawyer has an attorney-client relationship with each of those individuals").

18. *See, e.g.,* Philadelphia Hous. Auth. v. American Radiator & Standard Sanitary Corp., 294 F. Supp. 1148, 1150 (E.D. Pa. 1969) (finding each association member to be a client).

19. *See* §5.16, *infra.*

20. United States v. Mett, 178 F.3d 1058, 1062-1066 (9th Cir. 1999) (employer acting as ERISA fiduciary cannot assert attorney-client privilege against plan beneficiaries on matters of plan administration where advice does not implicate trustee in personal capacity; attorney-client privilege reasserts itself as to advice that fiduciary obtains to protect herself from criminal liability); Wildbur v. Arco Chemical Co., 974 F.2d 631, 645 (5th Cir. 1992) (when attorney advises pension plan administrators on plan administration, attorney's clients "are the plan beneficiaries for whom the fiduciary acts, not the plan administrators").

21. On representing a client under a disability, *see* Restatement (Third) of the Law Governing Lawyers (Proposed Final Draft. No.1, 1996) §35.

22. Grubbs v. K-Mart Corp., 161 Mich. App. 584, 411 N.W.2d 477, 480 (1987) (communications between parents of minor plaintiff and her attorney were privileged; parents acted as her agents in seeking legal advice). *See* Fickett v. Superior Court of Pima County, 558 P.2d 988, 990 (Ariz. App. 1976) (attorney who represents guardian of incompetent assumes relationship not only with guardian but with ward).

23. In re Grand Jury Subpoenas, 906 F.2d 1485, 1489 (10th Cir. 1990) (mere payment of attorney's fees for another held not to make payer a client). *See generally* §5.19, *infra.*

**Representative of
the client**

be the lawyer's client, and the person whose fees are thus paid is also a client.[24]

Clients sometimes act through representatives in communicating with their attorney, and of course entities that are clients (such as corporations and government agencies) can only communicate through representatives. Many states observe a definition of "representative of the client" that is modeled after URE 502(a)(4).[25] Whatever definition is chosen by a particular jurisdiction is of critical importance, because it generally determines the scope of the privilege for corporations and governmental entities.[26]

A representative can be appointed by the client to obtain or act on legal advice, or to talk to the lawyer, and the privilege covers what such intermediaries say to the lawyer (and what he says to them). A representative of the client need not be an employee of the client, and may be an independent contractor.[27] A client representative may include an expert, such as an accountant, whose knowledge and expertise is needed to help translate or explain the legal problem to the lawyer.[28] The privilege extends to such a representative, however, only for communications intended to help in obtaining professional legal services for the client. It does not cover client communications with the representative prior to or independent of such professional consultations with the lawyer.[29]

§5.10 Lawyer or Representative of Lawyer

For purposes of the privilege, a "lawyer" is someone who is authorized to practice law in any jurisdiction, domestic or foreign, as well as someone whom the client reasonably thinks to be authorized to practice

---

24. In re Grand Jury Subpoena for Attorney Representing Criminal Defendant Reyes-Requena, 926 F.2d 1423 (5th Cir. 1991).

25. URE 502(a)(4) (1999) ("representative of the client" means someone "having authority to obtain professional legal services, or to act on advice thereby rendered on behalf of the client," and "any other person who, for the purpose of effectuating legal representation for the client, makes or receives a confidential communication while acting in the scope of employment for the client").

26. See §5.16, §5.18, *infra.*

27. In re Bieter Co., 16 F.3d 929 (8th Cir. 1994) (independent real estate consultant who assisted client in real estate project and in dealing with client's lawyers held to be representative of client).

28. *See* United States v. Kovel, 296 F.2d 918, 922 (2d Cir. 1961) (presence of accountant, whether hired by lawyer or by client, while client is relating "complicated tax story" to lawyer, ought not destroy the privilege "any more than would that of the linguist" used to translate). *See generally* Restatement (Third) of the Law Governing Lawyers (Proposed Final Draft No. 1, 1996) §120 cmt. g (business person "may be accompanied by a business associate who has special knowledge of the situation and who can both facilitate communication from the client and translate to the client the lawyer's questions and advice").

29. In re Grand Jury Proceedings Under Seal v. United States, 947 F.2d 1188, 1191 (4th Cir. 1991) (where client hired lawyer on advice of accountant and used accountant to explain facts to lawyer, privilege protected only communications at meeting with attorney and those which occurred immediately prior thereto in preparing for meeting; earlier accountant-client communications outside privilege).

law.[1] Statutes and decisions sometimes refer to "attorneys" rather than "lawyers" in connection with the privilege, and sometimes the terms do differ in meaning, but usually they are viewed as synonymous, and we use them interchangeably in this book.[2]

A communication to a lawyer authorized to practice in any state or nation may be privileged even though she is not authorized to practice in the jurisdiction where the communication occurs.[3] The privilege applies even to a communication that would not be privileged where the lawyer has her license.[4]

Nonlawyer

Even communications with a nonlawyer are privileged if the client has a reasonable basis to believe that he is talking to a lawyer.[5] But communications are not privileged merely because someone provides law-related services if the client should know the person is not authorized to practice law.[6] In rare cases, courts extend the privilege to non-attorneys who lawfully perform the functions of an attorney, like representing a client in administrative proceedings.[7]

Multiple lawyers

A client may have more than one lawyer. In such cases, the privilege reaches confidential communications between the client and any of the lawyers, as well as communications among the lawyers, if made in the course of rendering professional legal services to the client.[8]

House counsel

It is established that house counsel to a corporation are entitled to the privilege on the same basis as outside counsel.[9] They are within the privilege, however, only when providing legal services, and not when

§5.10   1. *See* proposed-but-rejected FRE 503(a)(2); URE 502(a)(3) (1999).

2. Binkley v. People, 716 P.2d 1111, 1114 (Colo. 1986) (lawyer is "synonymous with an attorney at law"). "Attorney" can have broader meaning, referring to anyone who is appointed or acts as an agent or substitute for another, but in legal proceedings "attorney" is presumed to mean "attorney-at-law" unless something else is clearly indicated. In re Morse, 126 A. 550, 551-552 (Vt. 1924). *See generally* Black's Law Dictionary 128 (6th ed. 1990).

3. *See* Renfield Corp. v. E. Remy Martin & Co., S.A., 98 F.R.D. 442, 444-445 (D. Del. 1982) (communications between French in-house attorneys and corporate employees held within attorney-client privilege because attorneys were authorized to give legal advice under French law).

4. *See* ACN, proposed-but-rejected FRE 503(a)(2) ("no requirement that the licensing state or nation recognize the attorney-client privilege, thus avoiding excursions into conflict of laws questions").

5. United States v. Boffa, 513 F. Supp. 517, 523 (D. Del. 1981) (privilege extends to person who makes confidential communications to a person "in the mistaken, but genuine belief that he is an attorney," but "such belief should be reasonable"), *modified on other grounds*, 688 F.2d 919 (3d Cir. 1982).

6. Dabney v. Investment Corp. of America, 82 F.R.D. 464, 465 (E.D. Pa. 1979) (communications with law student not acting as attorney's representative, nor thought to be such by client, are not privileged).

7. In re Ampicillin Antitrust Litig., 81 F.R.D. 377, 392-394 (D.D.C. 1978) (registered patent agent "stands on the same footing" as attorney in proceedings before the Patent Office); Welfare Rights Org. v. Crisan, 33 Cal. 3d 766, 190 Cal. Rptr. 919, 923, 661 P.2d 1073 (1983) (interpreting statute authorizing lay representation in administrative proceedings to extend attorney-client privilege to lay representatives).

8. *See* proposed-but-rejected FRE 503(b); URE 502(b) (1999). *See also* Stix Prods., Inc. v. United Merchants & Mfrs., Inc., 47 F.R.D. 334, 339 (S.D.N.Y. 1969) (privilege applies to communications between co-counsel containing legal advice).

9. Upjohn Co. v. United States, 449 U.S. 383, 394-397 (1981) (attorney-client privilege applied; Court draws no distinction between house and outside counsel, and both participated in internal investigation).

acting managers of the corporate entity.[10] When house counsel serve as officers or directors, privilege claims merit special scrutiny, to ensure that the privilege applies only when counsel renders legal services, and not when acting in managerial capacity.[11]

Representative of the lawyer

The privilege covers not only lawyers but also persons employed to assist a lawyer in providing legal services.[12] Such persons include law clerks, paralegals, investigators, and similar agents[13] as well as members of the office staff who assist in transmitting messages back and forth between lawyer and client, such as secretaries, receptionists, messengers, and other office personnel.[14]

Consultants

The privilege also reaches outside experts employed to help the attorney provide legal services to the client,[15] such as an accountant,[16] physician,[17] psychotherapist,[18] appraiser,[19] patent agent,[20] interpreter,[21]

---

10. In re Grand Jury Subpoena, 599 F.2d 504, 511 (2d Cir. 1979) (participation by general counsel "does not automatically cloak the investigation with legal garb"); Valente v. Pepsico, Inc., 68 F.R.D. 361, 367 (D. Del. 1975) (house counsel are "to be treated in the same fashion as outside counsel with respect to activities in which they are engaged as attorneys," and where house counsel "is engaged in giving business advice or mere technical information, no privilege attaches").

11. *See* §5.11, *infra.*

12. *See* Restatement (Third) of the Law Governing Lawyers (Proposed Final Draft No. 1, 1996) §120 (for purposes of attorney-client privilege, "privileged persons" include "communicating" and "representing" agents of lawyer).

13. United States v. Davis, 131 F.R.D. 391, 397-398 (S.D.N.Y. 1990) (privilege applies to interview of federal Maritime Administration officials by an FBI agent acting as a representative of Justice Department attorneys). *But see* United States v. Hayes, 216 F.3d 789, 798 (9th Cir. 2000) (conversations about marijuana growing with investigator retained by attorney were not privileged; investigator was told *not* to relay conversations to attorney).

14. *See* United States v. Kovel, 296 F.2d 918, 921 (2d Cir. 1961) ("complexities of modern existence prevent attorneys from effectively handling clients' affairs without the help of others; few lawyers could now practice without the assistance of secretaries, file clerks, telephone operators, messengers, clerks not yet admitted to the bar, and aides of other sorts").

15. United States v. BDO Seidman, LLP, 492 F.3d 806, 827 (7th Cir. 2007), cert. denied, 128 S. Ct. 1471 (2008) (privilege maintained despite disclosure of confidential communications by attorney to expert retained for purpose of rendering legal services). *Cf.* ACN, proposed-but-rejected FRE 503(a) (whether compensation of the lawyer's representative "is derived immediately from the lawyer or the client is not material").

16. In the matter of Grand Jury Proceedings, 220 F.3d 568, 571 (7th Cir. 2000) (documents prepared by accountant as agent of attorney may be covered by privilege if purpose is to render legal advice).

17. San Francisco v. Superior Court of San Francisco, 37 Cal. 2d 227, 231 P.2d 26, 29-31 (1951) (privilege applies where assistance of physician is needed to interpret client's condition to attorney).

18. Ursry v. State, 428 So. 2d 713, 714-715 (Fla. App. 1983) (error to allow state to introduce testimony of psychiatrist "employed by counsel for a defendant to assist him in preparing a defense"), *rev. denied*, 438 So. 2d 834.

19. Brink v. Multnomah County, 356 P.2d 536 (Or. 1960).

20. Golden Trade v. Lee Apparel Co., 143 F.R.D. 514, 518 (S.D.N.Y. 1992) (communications between patent agent and attorney or client should be privileged if "patent agent is acting to assist an attorney to provide legal services").

21. United States v. Kovel, 296 F.2d 918, 921 (2d Cir. 1961) (dictum).

polygraph examiner,[22] or similar consultant. Courts have begun to grapple with the question whether communications with public relations consultants can be privileged, and the better answer is that they should be within the privilege when the attorney hires such consultants, and when the purpose of doing so is to help the lawyer formulate legal strategy in connection with the matter on which he has been retained.[23] The privilege does not apply where a client retains a consultant independently of legal representation[24] or is referred to an expert for purposes other than assisting the attorney rendering professional legal services to the client.[25]

A retained expert is within the privilege when he transmits or interprets client communications to the lawyer or relies on them in formulating opinions that the expert reports (or will report) to the lawyer.[26] Under the better view, the privilege does not shield expert opinions or communications with the lawyer that are derived independently of communications from client or lawyer,[27] although such opinions or communications constitute work product of the attorney, and are protected as such, when prepared in anticipation of litigation.

22. State v. Rickabaugh, 361 N.W.2d 623, 625 (S.D. 1985) (independent polygraph examiner hired by defense lawyer is representative of attorney; defendant's communications with him are privileged).

23. *Compare* In re Grand Jury Subpoenas Dated March 24, 2003, 265 F. Supp. 2d 321, 330-331 (S.D.N.Y. 2003) (confidential communications between client, under investigation by grand jury, and attorney's public relations firm were privileged when made at behest of lawyers or aimed at helping them formulate strategy, whether or not communications took place in presence of lawyers) *with* Calvin Klein Trademark Trust v. Wachner, 198 F.R.D. 53, 48 Fed. R. Serv. 3d 1055 (S.D.N.Y. 2000) (fact that communications between law firm and public relations consultant "may help" lawyer formulate legal advice was not sufficient to bring privilege to bear). *See also* Ann M. Murphy, Spin Control and the High-Profile Client—Should the Attorney-Client Privilege Extend to Communications with Public Relations Consultants? 55 Syracuse L. Rev 545 (2005) (PR firms are retained to transmit information to the public and do not provide legal advice; information from clients to consultants will be accurate whether privilege exists or not; hence communications should not be privileged).

24. *See, e.g.,* Roach v. Keane, 243 N.W.2d 508, 513 (Wis. 1976) (privilege inapplicable to reports of detective agency hired by wife to investigate husband; they had been requested by and delivered to her personally, even though she turned them over to divorce lawyer).

25. *See* State v. Copeland, 448 N.W.2d 611, 615-616 (N.D. 1989) (attorney referred client in divorce action to county social worker for "evaluation and treatment"; privilege inapplicable because purpose was not to assist providing legal services).

26. *See, e.g.,* United States v. Alvarez, 519 F.2d 1036, 1045-1046 (3d Cir. 1975) (attorney-client privilege applies to client communications to psychotherapist retained by defense attorney to examine client for possible insanity defense).

27. *See, e.g.,* Knoff v. American Crystal Sugar Co., 380 N.W.2d 313, 320-321 (N.D. 1986) (appraiser's opinion on value of farm land was "a matter of subjective knowledge" not protected by attorney-client privilege, even though appraiser had been hired by one of the attorneys). *See generally* Imwinkelried, The Applicability of the Attorney-Client Privilege to Non-Testifying Experts: Reestablishing the Boundaries Between the Attorney-Client Privilege and the Work Product Protection, 68 Wash. U. L.Q. 19, 30 (1990) (no justification for "cloaking expert information" with attorney-client privilege when expert "acquires the information from other sources").

While experts hired to testify are generally not viewed as representatives of the lawyer for purposes of the privilege[28] (their statements and reports to the lawyer are often discoverable, and to that extent they are not confidential),[29] their opinions and reports constitute work product which is subject to disclosure in accord with the principles set out in FRCP 26(b)(4), which basically require disclosure of underlying reports by experts who are to testify at trial.

Communications with insurer

There is no independent privilege for communications between an insured and his insurer, and such communications are generally outside the attorney-client privilege.[30] An insurance agent, however, sometimes acts as a lawyer's representative by helping prepare for litigation, providing investigative services, and relaying communications between client and lawyer. Where the insured's communications are made in confidence to the insurance agent at the request of the lawyer, or with the intention that they be conveyed to the lawyer to be used in the insured's defense, they are within the attorney-client privilege.[31] No privilege normally exists, however, where the communications are offered in a later dispute between the insured and the insurance company.[32]

§5.11 Professional Legal Services

The attorney-client privilege applies only where the lawyer provides legal services, and those services need not involve litigation. The privilege does not attach if the attorney acts in some other capacity, such as business advisor,[1] business agent,[2] investment partner,[3]

---

28. *See* ACN, proposed-but-rejected FRE 503(a) ("representative of the lawyer" includes "an expert employed to assist in the planning and conduct of litigation, though not one employed to testify as a witness").

29. *See* §5.13, *infra.*

30. Pasteris v. Robillard, 121 F.R.D. 18, 21-22 (D. Mass. 1988) (fact that statements to insurance agent may be used by lawyer in future did not create privilege when agent was not acting as or on behalf of attorney).

31. Asbury v. Beerbower, 589 S.W.2d 216 (Ky. 1979) (when after accident insured "would normally confide in counsel" he "should not be penalized for his prudence" in communicating with insurer). *See generally* Comment, The Attorney-Client Privilege and Its Availability to Insured Persons, 36 UCLA L. Rev. 977 (1989).

32. *See, e.g.,* Independent Petrochemical Corp. v. Aetna Casualty & Surety Co., 654 F. Supp. 1334, 1365 (D.D.C. 1986).

§5.11 1. United States v. Davis, 636 F.2d 1028, 1044 (5th Cir. 1981) (attorney who acts as client's business advisor "is not acting in a legal capacity" so records of such transactions are not privileged), *cert. denied,* 454 U.S. 862.

2. United States v. Huberts, 637 F.2d 630, 640 (9th Cir. 1980) (no privilege where attorney acted as "business agent" in supervising consignment sale of printing press), *cert. denied,* 451 U.S. 975.

3. Federal Sav. & Loan Ins. Corp. v. Fielding, 343 F. Supp. 537, 546 (D. Nev. 1972) (where attorney and client act as investment partners "their relationship is a business relationship not a professional one, and their confidences are business confidences unprotected by a professional privilege").

investment counselor,[4] accountant,[5] corporate director,[6] claims adjuster,[7] nonlegal investigator,[8] coconspirator,[9] shipping agent,[10] negotiator of nonlegal matters,[11] lobbyist,[12] government policy advisor,[13] messenger,[14] delivery agent,[15] scrivener,[16] attesting witness,[17] prosecutor,[18] or judge.[19] The client must be seeking legal advice,[20]

4. Liew v. Breen, 640 F.2d 1046, 1050 (9th Cir. 1981) (where clients consult attorney "with the aim of finding meritorious litigation to finance" privilege does not apply).

5. In re Grand Jury Investigation, 842 F.2d 1223, 1224 (11th Cir. 1987) (no privilege for communications to taxpayer's accountant, who was also an attorney; communications were for accounting purposes rather than legal advice).

6. In re Grand Jury Proceedings of Browning Arms Co., 528 F.2d 1301, 1303 (8th Cir. 1976) (privilege inapplicable to communications between lawyer and corporation; lawyer served as member of board of directors; relationship was not "attorney and client," but rather "director and corporation").

7. Mission Natl. Ins. Co. v. Lilly, 112 F.R.D. 160, 163-165 (D. Minn. 1986).

8. Diamond v. City of Mobile, 86 F.R.D. 324, 328-329 (S.D. Ala. 1978) (in civil rights action against city, interviews between city attorney and members of police force were not within privilege, since purpose "was not to provide legal advice" but to provide city " with information relating to alleged indiscretions" in the police department). Courts sometimes hold investigations to be within the privilege where legal issues are involved or lawyer's skills are necessary to a proper and effective investigation. *See* Dunn v. State Farm & Cas. Co., 927 F.2d 869, 875 (5th Cir. 1991) (privilege applies to attorney's investigation of cause of fire because investigation involved "rendition of legal services").

9. United States v. Harrelson, 754 F.2d 1153, 1166-1167 (5th Cir. 1985) (no privilege where "substantial and convincing evidence" showed the relationship "to have been that of conspirators rather than attorney and client"), *cert. denied*, 474 U.S. 908.

10. United States v. Palmer, 536 F.2d 1278 (9th Cir. 1976) (privilege not applicable because attorney acted as transfer-shipping agent, not as a legal advisor).

11. J. P. Foley & Co., Inc. v. Vanderbilt, 65 F.R.D. 523, 526 (S.D.N.Y. 1974).

12. North Carolina Elec. Membership Corp. v. Carolina Power & Light Co., 110 F.R.D. 511, 517 (M.D.N.C. 1986) (communications to and from corporation's house counsel regarding lobbying efforts were not privileged when communications did not relate to legal problems).

13. Coastal Corp. v. Duncan, 86 F.R.D. 514, 521 (D. Del. 1980) (government has burden of showing attorneys were acting as legal advisors rather than policymakers).

14. United States v. Wilson, 798 F.2d 509, 513 (1st Cir. 1986) (privilege denied where attorney characterized his role as that of "messenger").

15. State v. Carter, 578 P.2d 1275, 1277 (Utah 1978) (no privilege where attorney hired as middleman in extortion scheme); Hughes v. Meade, 453 S.W.2d 538, 542 (Ky. 1970) (no privilege where lawyer hired to return stolen property).

16. Canaday v. United States, 354 F.2d 849, 857 (8th Cir. 1966) (no privilege where attorney "acted not as a lawyer, but merely as a scrivener"). The scrivener exclusion applies where the lawyer acts solely as an amanuensis. The privilege applies to any legal advice given in connection with preparation of the document.

17. Jones v. Smith, 206 Ga. 162, 56 S.E.2d 462, 465 (1949). *See also* §5.25, *infra*.

18. Clavir v. United States, 84 F.R.D. 612, 614 (S.D.N.Y. 1979) (privilege did not apply to interview of FBI agent by Justice Department lawyer regarding surreptitious break-ins, because relationship was not that of attorney and client but of prosecutor and potential grand jury witness).

19. Lindsey v. People ex rel. Rush, 66 Col. 343, 181 P. 531, 535-536 (1919) (privilege inapplicable to communications to a juvenile court judge).

20. In re County of Erie, 473 F.3d 413, 422-423 (2d Cir. 2007) (e-mails between county attorney and corrections officers proposing changes in strip search policy were privileged; each was sent for predominant purpose of asking or providing legal advice, in order to comply with constitutional standards); Barton v. United States Dist. Court, 410 F.3d 1104, 1111-1112 (9th Cir. 2005) (applying California law, holding that on-line

and the privilege does not apply where the client acts with some other motive.[21]

Communications to an attorney as family member or friend rather than as professional legal advisor are not privileged.[22] Investigative factfinding for the purpose of giving legal advice is often within the privilege, but not if the client was merely seeking to purchase a privilege, and only if the nature of the investigation requires the capabilities of a lawyer.[23]

Primarily legal   The party claiming the privilege has the burden of proving that the purpose of the communications was to obtain professional legal services.[24] Where a lawyer acts in more than one capacity, as may happen when she provides both business and legal advice, courts generally hold that the work must be "predominantly" or "primarily" legal in order to fall within the privilege,[25] although occasionally courts extend the privilege a little further in these mixed situations.[26] The mere fact that an attorney was involved in the communication, however, does not bring it within the privilege.

Tax advice   Giving tax advice is clearly a professional legal service for purposes of the privilege.[27] Some courts hold, however, that the actual preparation of returns is not a professional legal service, apparently because it is too

---

questionnaires to law firm on antidepressant were submitted in course of attorney-client relationship and were privileged; responses were made for purpose of obtaining legal representation).

21. *See, e.g.,* United States v. Alexander, 287 F.3d 811, 816 (9th Cir. 2002) (attorney testified that client made threats; threats were not protected by privilege; not communications to obtain legal advice).

22. United States v. Tedder, 801 F.2d 1437, 1441-1443 (4th Cir. 1986) (defendant spoke to attorney "as a friend personally involved" in case, not as "professional legal advisor"), *cert. denied,* 480 U.S. 938.

23. Better Gov. Bureau, Inc. v. McGraw, 106 F.3d 582, 602 (4th Cir. 1997) (outside counsel was hired to conduct investigation of document mismanagement in attorney general's office; confidential communications to attorney "hired to investigate through trained eyes" of attorney are privileged).

24. *See, e.g.,* United States v. Abrahams, 905 F.2d 1276, 1283 (9th Cir. 1990) (attorney claiming privilege on behalf of clients regarding tax records must show that privilege applies). *See* §5.27, *infra.*

25. In re Spalding Sports Worldwide, Inc., 203 F.3d 800, 805 (Fed. Cir. 2000) (invention record including prior work on project forwarded to patent office of company for determination of patentability was within attorney-client privilege because patentability determinations are primarily legal); Sedco Intl., S.A. v. Cory, 683 F.2d 1201, 1205-1206 (8th Cir. 1982) (test is whether communications "primarily legal" in nature), *cert. denied,* 459 U.S. 1017. See also ACN to proposed-but-rejected FRE 503(b) (communications "must be specifically for the purpose of obtaining legal services for the client," or privilege "does not attach"). *See generally* Corby Brooks, A Double-Edged Sword Cuts Both Ways: How Clients of Dual Capacity Legal Practitioners Often Lose Their Evidentiary Privileges, 35 Texas Tech L. Rev. 1069 (2004) (when attorney's advice is delivered along with advice on nonlegal matters, entire communication may not be privileged).

26. *See, e.g.,* In re Arthur Treacher's Franchisee Litig., 92 F.R.D. 429, 435-436 (E.D. Pa. 1981) ("discussions of a purely financial or business nature are not privileged"); United States v. Chen, 99 F.3d 1495, 1500-1501 (9th Cir. 1996) (privilege applies even where lawyer is involved in "business decision-making" by providing legal advice about what decision should be made).

27. Colton v. United States, 306 F.2d 633, 637 (2d Cir. 1962) (no question that giving tax advice is "prima facie subject to the attorney-client privilege"), *cert. denied,* 371 U.S. 951.

mechanical and too similar to the function that accountants normally perform (for which there is no privilege).[28] Whether tax assistance is privileged should depend on the extent of legal expertise required, and also the extent to which the client relies on the attorney's legal advice and judgment, as opposed to merely using the attorney as a scrivener.[29] Courts generally hold that information from the client that is intended to be disclosed on the return is not privileged because the requirement of confidentiality is not satisfied when future disclosure is anticipated.[30] There is a division of authority, however, on the question whether disclosure beyond the information on the tax return can be required.[31]

Services by an attorney that are clerical or ministerial in nature are not professional legal services.[32] Some courts extend this idea beyond reasonable boundaries, holding that even preparation of some legal documents does not involve professional legal services, apparently on the theory that at least some such documents are routine and simple in nature.[33]

In cases where the attorney serves merely as a conduit for transmitting information, courts generally deny the privilege.[34] The issue sometimes arises where the client is prosecuted for "bail jumping," and the government seeks to determine whether the attorney notified the client of the hearing date. Most courts hold that the attorney can be required to say whether they gave such notice, finding that giving notice is not a professional legal service, or alternatively that information on the date of a trial or hearing is not a confidential legal communication.[35]

Attorney acting as conduit

28. *See* In re Grand Jury Investigation, 842 F.2d 1223, 1222-1225 (11th Cir. 1987) (collecting cases); United States v. Davis, 636 F.2d 1028, 1043 (5th Cir. 1981) (accountants do not have a privilege in preparing tax returns, so it would "make little sense to permit a taxpayer to invoke a privilege merely because he hires an attorney to perform the same task"), *cert. denied,* 454 U.S. 862.

29. *See* United States v. Schmidt, 360 F. Supp. 339, 347 (M.D. Pa. 1973) (upholding privilege "to the extent that preparation of a return requires the exercise of legal judgment").

30. *See* Re Grand Jury Subpoena Duces Tecum, 697 F.2d 277, 280 (10th Cir. 1983) (privilege does not apply to "documents given by a client to an attorney for inclusion in the client's income tax return, because such information is obviously not intended to remain confidential").

31. *Compare* United States v. Cote, 456 F.2d 142, 144 (8th Cir. 1972) (requiring disclosure of underlying data for each item on tax return) *with* United States v. Schlegel, 313 F. Supp. 177, 179 (D. Neb. 1970) ("more realistic rule" would be that client intends that "only as much of the information will be conveyed to the government as the attorney concludes should be, and ultimately is," sent to government).

32. United States v. Bartone, 400 F.2d 459, 461 (6th Cir. 1968) (ministerial or clerical services not within privilege), *cert. denied,* 393 U.S. 1027.

33. *See, e.g.,* United States v. Davis, 636 F.2d 1028, 1044 n.19 (5th Cir. 1981) (drafting trust instrument was not professional legal service), *cert. denied,* 454 U.S. 862.

34. United States v. Defazio, 899 F.2d 626, 635 (7th Cir. 1990) (testimony by attorney on what IRS agent said to him and stating that he relayed statements to defendant did not violate privilege "because it did not reveal, either directly or implicitly," any legal advice or client confidences).

35. *See* United States v. Gray, 876 F.2d 1411, 1415-1416 (9th Cir. 1989) (attorney's notification to client of sentencing hearing date not privileged because not confidential in nature), *cert. denied,* 495 U.S. 930; United States v. Woodruff, 383 F. Supp. 696, 698 (E.D. Pa. 1974) (communications between counsel and defendant on trial date "do not involve the subject matter of defendant's legal problem" and are "nonlegal in nature," and counsel was "simply performing a notice function").

§5.12   Communication

The attorney-client privilege applies only to confidential communications. "Communications" are usually made orally or in writing[1] although expressive nonverbal conduct such as nodding, pointing, reenactment of a past event, or similar behavior intended as a substitute for words can also be a communication.[2] Conduct by the client that is not communicative is outside the privilege.[3] Silence or nondisclosure by the client is privileged only if it constitutes a statement or tends to reveal the scope of a protected communication.[4]

Observations by attorney
One cannot invoke the privilege to keep the attorney from testifying to observations about the client's appearance, dress, physical condition, demeanor, or conduct, at least where such matters would be generally observable by others.[5] Courts often require lawyers to testify about the client's mental condition or competency, however, at least to the extent that it does not reveal the client's confidential communications.[6]

The identification of a client's photograph or handwriting is not privileged[7] nor is identification of a client's clothing, jewelry, briefcase, or other physical items in the possession of the client, except where such items were an integral part of a confidential communication to the attorney.[8] The privilege generally does apply to observations made by the attorney as a result of confidential client communications.[9]

---

§5.12   1. United States v. Spector, 793 F.2d 932, 938 (8th Cir. 1986) (defendant's recorded statements, made at lawyer's direction to assist in defense, were privileged), *cert. denied,* 479 U.S. 1031.

2. Restatement (Third) of the Law Governing Lawyers (Proposed Final Draft No. 1, 1996) §119 (privileged communication is "any expression" through which privileged person "undertakes to convey information to another privileged person and any document or other record that embodies such expression"). *See generally* Saltzburg, Communications Falling Within the Attorney-Client Privilege, 66 Iowa L. Rev. 811 (1981).

3. In re Grand Jury Proceedings, 13 F.3d 1293, 1296 (9th Cir. 1994) (privilege does not apply to attorney's observation of client's expenditures on European trip; such information does not involve confidential communications made for purpose of rendering legal services).

4. United States v. White, 950 F.2d 426, 430 n.2 (7th Cir. 1991) (nondisclosure of assets by bankruptcy client to attorney was not privileged; nondisclosure was not communication but "lack" thereof); United States v. Andrus, 775 F.2d 825, 852 (7th Cir. 1985). *But see* United States v. Marable, 574 F.2d 224, 231 (5th Cir. 1978).

5. *See* In re Walsh, 623 F.2d 489, 494 (7th Cir. 1980) (lawyer's observations of client's appearance, including complexion, demeanor, and dress, were not privileged), *cert. denied,* 449 U.S. 994.

6. *See* §5.20, *infra.*

7. In re Grand Jury Proceedings, 791 F.2d 663, 665 (8th Cir. 1986) (attorney compelled to authenticate signatures and photographs of client before grand jury; appearance and handwriting are not confidential communications; they were not exposed on "assumption that others would not learn of them").

8. *See, e.g.,* In re January 1976 Grand Jury (Gensen), 534 F.2d 719, 728-729 (7th Cir. 1976) (privilege inapplicable to money that client transfers to attorney) (suspected proceeds of bank robbery).

9. Clutchette v. Rushen, 770 F.2d 1469, 1472 (9th Cir. 1985) (privilege applies to location of incriminating receipts examined by attorney, but it was lost when attorney removed receipts), *cert. denied,* 475 U.S. 1088. See also §5.21, *infra,* discussing privilege in connection with objects that client delivers to lawyer.

The only communications protected by the privilege are those made by the client, the client's representative, the lawyer, or the lawyer's representative.[10] Communications from third parties to the lawyer are not within the attorney-client privilege even if they are later transmitted to the client.[11]

The attorney-client privilege does not prevent compelled disclosure either during discovery or at trial of relevant facts known to the client. Only the communications to the attorney are privileged, not the facts as the client knows them.[12] Similarly the privilege does not protect facts as known by the lawyer, when that knowledge does not rest on confidential communications from the client, although such independent knowledge is often within work product protection. Courts are understandably cautious about ordering a lawyer to testify, however, not only because doing so would have a disruptive effect on the work of the lawyer and his relationship with the client, but because of the likelihood that any information he could provide is within either privilege or work product protection.[13]

Confidential written communications by the client to the attorney for the purpose of obtaining legal advice are privileged, as are drawings, sketches, or diagrams made by the client to elucidate the legal problem for the attorney. A client cannot, however, cloak preexisting documents with immunity by turning them over to her attorney.[14] If the documents were prepared for business or other purposes, and not a confidential communication to the attorney, they are not privileged.[15] Thus, for example, a client's personal diary is normally not privileged even if turned over to the attorney to inform him about relevant events, although entries making specific

Writings or other recorded statements

---

10. *See* proposed-but-rejected FRE 503(b); URE 502(b) (1999)

11. *See, e.g.,* In re Sealed Case, 737 F.2d 94, 99 (D.C. Cir. 1984) (privilege does not apply "when an attorney conveys to his client facts acquired from other persons or sources").

12. *See* Upjohn Co. v. United States, 449 U.S. 383, 395 (1981) (privilege "only protects disclosure of communications," not "disclosure of the underlying facts" by those who communicated with attorney).

13. *See* Southern Film Extruders, Inc. v. Coca-Cola Co., 117 F.R.D. 559, 561 (M.D.N.C. 1987) (client entitled to protective order against attempt to take deposition of lawyer, absent showing by discovery seeker showing propriety of inquiry and need for deposition). *But see* United States v. Bollin, 264 F.3d 391, 412 (4th Cir. 2001) (privilege does not prevent keep from taking stand, provided that his testimony is limited to nonconfidential matters).

14. United States v. Robinson, 121 F.3d 971, 975 (5th Cir. 1997) (privilege does not attach to preexisting document transferred to lawyer if it could have been obtained by process from client when he was in possession).

15. *See, e.g.,* Simon v. G. D. Searle & Co., 816 F.2d 397, 402-404 (8th Cir. 1987) (risk management documents prepared for business planning purposes in connection with product liability suit not privileged), *cert. denied,* 484 U.S. 917; Radiant Burners, Inc. v. American Gas Assn., 320 F.2d 314, 324 (7th Cir. 1963) (privilege "would never be available to allow a corporation to funnel its papers and documents into the hands of its lawyers for custodial purposes and thereby avoid disclosure"), *cert. denied,* 375 U.S. 929.

reference to attorney-client communications may be within the privilege.[16]

Normally the writing must have been created for the primary purpose of communicating with the attorney. Sometimes, however, the client has more than one purpose, and sends an original letter or message to a lawyer and also a copy to someone else, or sends the original to someone else with a copy to the lawyer. In this situation, if the other person is not within the privilege, there is also no protection for whatever went to the lawyer. Conceivably, however, what the lawyer received may be within the attorney-client privilege if what was sent to the other fits some other privilege (such as the privilege for spousal confidences), and if the purpose of sending the matter to the lawyer was to obtain legal services.

If a writing is subject to subpoena, discovery, or search warrant when in the possession of the client, it remains so after transfer to the lawyer.[17] But if the document is privileged in the hands of the client, the attorney-client privilege applies if the client turns it over to the lawyer in confidence in the course of seeking legal advice.[18]

When an attorney prepares a document in a professional capacity on the client's behalf, courts generally hold that the content of the document is privileged to the extent it reflects confidential client communications.[19] Information on the existence, execution, or delivery of such a document is, however, normally not privileged.[20]

Similarly the privilege is not applicable to the attorney's work product except where it records or otherwise reveals confidential client communications.[21] Thus witness lists, time sheets, appointment diaries, phone logs, and accounting records of the attorney are normally outside the privilege, even though they may merit work product protection if prepared in preparation for litigation.[22]

---

16. Moore v. Tri-City Hosp. Auth., 118 F.R.D. 646, 650 (N.D. Ga. 1988) (privilege applies to diary entries that describe communications from attorneys or are based on such communications).

17. *See* Fisher v. United States, 425 U.S. 391, 403-404 (1976) (courts uniformly hold that "pre-existing documents which could have been obtained by court process from the client" may also be obtained from the attorney "following transfer by the client in order to obtain more informed legal advice").

18. Fisher v. United States, 425 U.S. 391, 403-404 (1976) (client would be reluctant to transfer privileged documents to lawyer unless they "are also privileged in the latter's hands" and purposes of privilege "would be defeated" unless it applies).

19. *See* United States v. Davis, 636 F.2d 1028, 1044 (5th Cir. 1981) (client's will in custody of attorney was privileged and beyond the reach of an IRS subpoena), *cert. denied,* 454 U.S. 862.

20. United States v. Robinson, 121 F.3d 971, 975 (5th Cir. 1997) (fact that client transferred document to attorney not privileged; fact of delivery was not communication).

21. *See* United States v. Willis, 565 F. Supp. 1186, 1194 (S.D. Iowa 1983) (privilege protects attorney's notes and research materials to extent they reflect confidential communications).

22. *See, e.g.,* United States v. Amerada Hess Corp., 619 F.2d 980, 986-987 (3d Cir. 1980) (list of persons interviewed not privileged); Gannet v. First Natl. State Bank of New Jersey, 546 F.2d 1072, 1076 (3d Cir. 1976) (privilege does not attach to attorney's bank records), *cert. denied,* 431 U.S. 954.

Although the privilege was developed to protect confidential disclo- **Communications**
sures by the client to the attorney, it applies as well to communications **from the attorney**
from the attorney to the client, at least to the extent that such communications would tend to reveal confidences of the client.[23] Indeed, most
courts go further than that, and hold that the privilege extends to legal
advice given by the attorney, regardless whether it would reveal a
confidential client communication.[24]

The trend of modern authority is toward recognition of a two-way
privilege covering all confidential communications between the attorney and the client in the course of legal representation.[25] Both proposed FRE 503(b) and URE 502(b) adopt the broader view and make
the lawyer's communications to the client privileged as well as the client's communications to the lawyer.

The broader rule is justified on grounds of both pragmatism and
policy. Because most communications by the attorney are likely to
reflect client communications, a two-way privilege furthers judicial efficiency by eliminating the need for case-by-case examination. Also,
under the broader rule, attorneys can speak more freely with their
clients without concern that their statements might later be subject
to compelled disclosure. However, even under the broader view, conduct by the attorney is not privileged except where it would reveal a
confidential communication.[26]

§5.13 Confidentiality

The attorney-client privilege applies only to communications that are
confidential. Communications made by the client to the lawyer publicly, in the presence of outsiders, or with the intent that they be disclosed later in a nonprivileged setting are not confidential.[1] The lawyer

---

23. *See, e.g.,* Wells v. Rushing, 755 F.2d 376, 379 n.2 (5th Cir. 1985) (communications
from lawyer to client are privileged to extent necessary to avoid revealing "confidential
information provided by the client" or "advice or opinions of the attorney").

24. United States v. Defazio, 899 F.2d 626, 635 (7th Cir. 1990) (communications
from attorney to client are privileged if they constitute legal advice).

25. Sprague v. Thorn Americas, Inc., 129 F.3d 1355, 1370-1372 (10th Cir. 1997)
(privilege protects communications from attorney to client as well as client to attorney);
United States v. Ramirez, 608 F.2d 1261, 1268 n.12 (9th Cir. 1979) (states are "divided"
on whether communications from attorney to client are privileged, but federal courts
generally hold that "communications in both directions" are covered). *Cf.* Upjohn
Co. v. United States, 449 U.S. 383, 389 (1981) (purpose of privilege is "to encourage
full and frank communications *between* attorneys and their clients") (emphasis added).

26. *See* United States v. Brickey, 426 F.2d 680, 685 (8th Cir. 1970) (privilege does not
cover act of mailing check on behalf of client), *cert. denied,* 400 U.S. 828.

§5.13 1. Bogle v. McClure, 332 F.3d 1347, 1358 (11th Cir. 2003) (in §1983 suit
alleging discrimination, privilege did not protect memoranda from county counsel to
library board on personnel reorganization, absent showing that memo was to remain
confidential, or that it was reasonable to expect confidentiality). *See* proposed-but-
rejected FRE 503(a)(4) (communication is confidential if "not intended to be disclosed to third persons other than those to whom disclosure is in furtherance of the
rendition of professional legal services to the client or those reasonably necessary for
the transmission of the communication"); URE 502(b) (1999).

has an ethical responsibility to safeguard the confidences and secrets of the client and to take all precautions reasonably necessary to prevent their disclosure to unauthorized persons.[2]

Intent Confidentiality is defined in terms of intent. When making a communication to a lawyer, the client must intend that there be neither contemporaneous nor subsequent disclosure to unprivileged third persons.[3]

Intent is inferable from the circumstances, including statements or behavior by the client bearing on the desire for confidentiality, the nature of the communications, and the precautions taken, that would lead a reasonable person to conclude that confidentiality was intended.[4] In most circumstances it is reasonable to presume that lawyer-client communications were intended to be confidential in absence of a contrary indication from the client.[5]

However, even a stated desire for confidentiality will not guarantee confidentiality if the client's actions are inconsistent with such a request; for example, by failing to take reasonable steps to safeguard the privacy of the communications.[6]

Certain communications by their nature are deemed not confidential. For example, courts generally hold that notification by the attorney to the client regarding the date of trial or other hearing is not a confidential communication.[7]

Presence of others The presence of others during talks between the lawyer and the client, or disclosure to others of the substance of such talks, does not remove the element of confidentiality or defeat a claim of privilege if the others were agents of the attorney used in providing legal service.[8] The same is true if the others were communicative intermediaries for

---

2. *See* ABA Model Code of Professional Responsibility DR 4-101; ABA Model Rules of Professional Conduct Rule 1.6(a).

3. *See* United States v. Noriega, 917 F.2d 1543, 1551 (11th Cir. 1990) (remanding to decide whether client could reasonably expect confidentiality for telephone communications with attorney when he had signed release acknowledging that calls would be recorded by government), *cert. denied*, 498 U.S. 976.

4. United States v. Hatcher, 323 F.3d 666, 674 (8th Cir. 2003) (when inmates and lawyers knew conversations are recorded by prison surveillance equipment, no reasonable expectation of privacy; recording device was "functional equivalent" of third party, and taped conversations were not privileged).

5. In re Sealed Case, 737 F.2d 94, 102 (D.C. Cir. 1984) (conversations on airplane between corporate counsel and company's president were privileged even though president did not state that communications were to be confidential). *But see* State of Maine v. United States Dept. of Interior, 298 F.3d 60, 71 (1st Cir. 2002) (privilege is not satisfied merely by establishing that documents are communications between attorney and client; documents must be *confidentially* communicated).

6. *See* Leathers v. United States, 250 F.2d 159, 166 (9th Cir. 1957) (client-attorney communication in presence of IRS agents were not privileged).

7. *See* United States v. Gray, 876 F.2d 1411, 1415-1416 (9th Cir. 1989) (information on client's obligation to appear for sentencing is not confidential and privileged), *cert. denied*, 495 U.S. 930.

8. Jenkins v. Bartlett, 487 F.3d 482, 490-491 (7th Cir. 2007) (presence of union representative at conversation between client and attorney did not destroy privilege; he was there "solely to assist the attorney in rendering legal services to the client").

the client aiding from his side in obtaining or acting on legal advice, or in transmitting information back and forth. But if outsiders who do not fit these descriptions are present, or if the client intends the substance of the communication to be communicated to outsiders, or if the lawyer on the client's behalf makes such disclosure, the privilege normally does not apply.[9] However, if the disclosure is to another privileged person, such as a spouse or joint client, then the privilege is preserved.

A nurse, relative, or aide may attend the meeting if necessary to provide support to the client or otherwise facilitate the communication with the attorney.[10] But if insufficient justification is shown for their presence, such persons may be viewed as outsiders and destroy confidentiality.[11]

Representatives of lawyers

The lawyer may also have representatives in attendance, such as associates, law clerks, paralegals, investigators, litigation consultants, and retained experts, provided they are present to assist in the rendition of professional legal services to the client.[12]

Disclosure may also be made to persons employed by either the client or the lawyer who are reasonably necessary to facilitate the communications, such as secretaries, receptionists, and fax or photocopy machine operators. Such individuals need not be regular employees of either the client or lawyer.

Subsequent disclosure intended

Even if the initial communication was made in private, it is not considered confidential if the client intended that the communication be later disclosed either publicly or to particular outsiders.[13] Confidentiality is preserved only if the subsequent disclosure is limited to other persons within the circle of privilege. Courts generally reject the concept of "limited waiver" or "selective disclosure."[14]

9. United States v. Evans, 113 F.3d 1457 (7th Cir. 1997) (no privilege arises where attorney-client communication was made in presence of defendant's family attorney, who was present as friend and potential character witness, not as attorney).

10. Kevlik v. Goldstein, 724 F.2d 844, 849 (1st Cir. 1984) (confidentiality not destroyed by presence of father acting in "normal and supportive parental fashion"); Hoffman v. Conder, 712 P.2d 216, 217 (Utah 1985) (presence of nurse of client did not destroy confidentiality; her presence was reasonably necessary to assist client in communicating with lawyer; trial court was too strict in requiring that her presence be necessary for urgent or lifesaving procedures).

11. Cafritz v. Koslow, 167 F.2d 749, 751-752 (D.C. Cir. 1948) (privilege lost when client was accompanied by sister at time of communication to attorney; no sufficient reason for her presence).

12. *See* §5.10, *supra.*

13. United States v. (Under Seal), 748 F.2d 871, 875 (4th Cir. 1984) (if client communicates information to attorney with understanding that it "will be revealed to others," information and details underlying the data are not privileged).

14. In re Columbia/HCA Healthcare Corp. Billing Practices Litig., 293 F.3d 289, 302 (6th Cir. 2002) (client cannot waive privilege by releasing otherwise privileged documents to government agencies during investigation while continuing privilege against other parties). *But see* Diversified Indus., Inc. v. Meredith, 572 F.2d 596, 611 (8th Cir. 1977) (surrender of documents under agency subpoena in connection with "separate and nonpublic SEC investigation" resulted in "only a limited waiver"). On selective disclosure, see §5.28, *infra.*

Client communications given to the attorney for subsequent disclosure, by inclusion in tax returns,[15] bankruptcy petitions,[16] pleadings, prospectuses,[17] citizenship applications,[18] or reports to be filed with a private auditor or government agency,[19] are generally held to be outside the privilege, but related communications bearing on preparation of the documents may be privileged.[20] Similarly, information that the client intends the attorney to disclose in unprivileged correspondence or in court is not privileged.[21] However, because wills can be modified, they are generally held to be privileged during the client's lifetime.[22]

Public disclosure not made

If the client intended subsequent disclosure at the time the communication was made to the attorney, confidentiality generally does not attach even if the subsequent disclosure is never made.[23] But this rule applies only if the client's intent to disclose is certain. Communications intended only for possible disclosure to third parties remain privileged until actual disclosure is made.[24] Thus a communication made while seeking legal advice about the possibility of filing public papers is privileged if the client, after receiving the legal advice, decides against disclosure.[25] And preliminary drafts of documents intended for subsequent filing or disclosure have also been held privileged on the

15. United States v. Lawless, 709 F.2d 485, 487 (7th Cir. 1983) (where client transmits information to attorney so that it might be used on tax return "such a transmission destroys any expectation of confidentiality which might have otherwise existed").

16. United States v. White, 970 F.2d 328, 334 (7th Cir. 1992); United States v. White, 950 F.2d 426, 430 (7th Cir. 1991).

17. In re Grand Jury Proceedings, 727 F.2d 1352, 1356-1358 (4th Cir. 1984) (statements to attorney conveying information to be included in prospectus were not within attorney-client privilege "because confidentiality was not intended").

18. United States v. Oloyede, 982 F.2d 133, 141 (4th Cir. 1992) (information communicated by clients "was specifically intended to be used to file their citizenship applications with the INS").

19. United States v. El Paso Co., 682 F.2d 530, 538-541 (5th Cir. 1982) (no privilege when tax pool analysis intentionally disclosed to outside auditors), *cert. denied,* 466 U.S. 944.

20. In re Grand Jury Subpoena, 341 F.3d 331, 335-336 (4th Cir. 2003) (attorney-client communications about immigration petition are privileged, regardless whether immigration form became public document).

21. *See* United States v. Tellier, 255 F.2d 441, 447 (2d Cir. 1958) (client's communication to be incorporated in a letter to others), *cert. denied,* 358 U.S. 821.

22. In re Guardianship of York, 723 P.2d 448, 452-453 (Wash. App. 1986) (while client is alive, "his or her communications with an attorney concerning preparation of a will remain privileged.").

23. In re Grand Jury Proceedings, 727 F.2d 1352, 1356-1358 (4th Cir. 1984) (information for inclusion in a prospectus not privileged even though prospectus was never issued).

24. *See* Schenet v. Anderson, 678 F. Supp. 1280, 1283 (E.D. Mich. 1988) (privilege "applies to all information conveyed by clients to their attorneys for the purpose of drafting documents to be disclosed to third persons and all documents reflecting such information, to the extent that such information is not contained in the document published and is not otherwise disclosed to third persons").

25. *See* United States v. (Under Seal), 748 F.2d 871, 875-876 (4th Cir. 1984) (privilege applies to communications regarding possible public disclosure where "client was able to conclude, presumably through full and frank discussions with his attorney, [that the matter] should remain private" and "tells his attorney before the release").

theory that they do not manifest the client's final decision on the scope of disclosure.[26]

If the communication, or any significant part of it, is voluntarily disclosed by the client in a nonprivileged setting, the privilege is waived.[27] But if the communication was obtained by theft, fraud, or in a manner that could not be reasonably anticipated or guarded against, the disclosure is usually considered involuntary, and the privilege may be asserted to block introduction of the communication in a later legal proceeding.[28] Thus the privilege can continue to be claimed even when the communication has in fact become known to others, including the opposing party.[29]

Voluntary disclosure

When disclosure is accidental or involuntary, the situation raises questions of intent and due care on the part of the privilege holder, and there is some confusion in the cases about whether disclosure of this sort should be viewed as waiving protection or causing loss of the required confidentiality. If the communication was intended to remain confidential when made, and reasonable precautions were taken at that time to assure confidentiality, any later disclosure should normally be viewed as presenting purely a question of waiver.[30]

Inadvertent disclosure

Older authorities generally held that if a confidential communication between an attorney and client was overheard by an eavesdropper the eavesdropper could testify. In the face of increasingly sophisticated and intrusive forms of electronic surveillance, modern authority has abandoned the earlier rule. Today most jurisdictions allow the client to assert the privilege against an eavesdropper provided the client took reasonable precautions to safeguard the confidentiality of the communication.[31] Both proposed-but-rejected Federal Rule 503 and Uniform Rule 503, which have been adopted by many states, define "confidential" as "not intended to be disclosed to third persons" (with

Eavesdroppers

---

26. In re Grand Jury Subpoena Duces Tecum Dated Sept. 15, 1983, 731 F.2d 1032, 1037 (2d Cir. 1984) (privilege applies to drafts of documents even though final versions were to be sent to others).

27. See §5.28, *infra.*

28. See §5.29, *infra.*

29. *See, e.g.,* Haines v. Liggett Group, Inc., 975 F.2d 81, 97 (3d Cir. 1992) (upholding privilege claim with respect to certain matters that had been erroneously disclosed publicly in trial court's opinion); In re Dayco Corp. Derivative Sec. Litig., 102 F.R.D. 468, 470 (S.D. Ohio 1984) (upholding attorney-client privilege claim even where privileged matter had been published in newspaper).

30. *See* §5.29, *infra.* But some cases view later disclosure as bearing on whether the communications were ever intended to be confidential. *See, e.g.,* United States v. Kelsey-Hayes Wheel Co., 15 F.R.D. 461, 465 (E.D. Mich. 1954) (finding it "difficult to be persuaded that these documents were intended to remain confidential in the light of the fact that they were indiscriminately mingled" with routine documents of corporation and there was no special effort to preserve them in segregated files with special protections).

31. Lively v. Washington County Dist. Court, 747 P.2d 320, 321 (Okla. Crim. App. 1987) (no loss of privilege for telephone conversation between defendant and his attorney that was videotaped by hidden camera, where defendant had no knowledge the conversation was being taped).

limited exceptions)[32] and allow the client to prevent "any other person" from disclosing confidential communications, which would include an eavesdropper.[33]

If the client speaks to the lawyer in a place where the conversation is likely to be overheard,[34] or sends a written communication to the attorney in a manner such that it is likely to be seen by others,[35] it will be assumed that the client did not intend the communication to be confidential. However, full use of all available technology to prevent interception is not required, and courts require only those steps reasonable under the circumstances.

Although case law is not entirely settled on the point, otherwise private attorney-client communications by facsimile, cellular telephone, or e-mail (even if unencrypted) should qualify as confidential for purposes of the privilege,[36] but the parties should be aware of the increased dangers of interception when these modes of communication are utilized. There are both federal and state statutory prohibitions against wiretapping and electronic surveillance, and evidence obtained in violation of such statutes is subject to exclusion.[37] Moreover, in criminal cases interception of privileged communications may violate the defendant's Fourth Amendment rights as well as the Sixth Amendment right to effective assistance of counsel.[38]

32. Proposed-but-rejected FRE 503(a)(4); URE 502(a)(2) (1999).

33. Proposed-but-rejected FRE 503(b); URE 502(b) (1999).

34. *See* United States v. Gann, 732 F.2d 714, 723 (9th Cir. 1984) (no privilege where defendant made statements to attorney on phone within earshot of law enforcement agents; defendant "surrounded by officers searching his residence"), *cert. denied,* 469 U.S. 1034; United States v. Blasco, 702 F.2d 1315, 1329 (11th Cir. 1983) (privilege denied when consultation took place in corridor outside courtroom in voices loud enough to be overheard by passersby), *cert. denied,* 464 U.S. 914.

35. United States v. Waller, 581 F.2d 585, 586-587 (6th Cir. 1978) (after defendant absconded in midtrial, judge ordered seizure of notepad on which he had been writing at counsel table for purposes of making handwriting comparisons; no violation privilege; leaving notepad "in a prominent place in a public courtroom" was not consistent with claim of privacy), *cert. denied,* 439 U.S. 1051.

36. *Cf.* United States v. Maxwell, 45 M.J. 406 (U.S. Ct. App. Armed Servs. 1996) (America On Line protects privacy of e-mail messages, so using that service on personal and private computer has expectation of privacy). An early decision held that communications by cordless phone do not qualify for privilege, apparently on the theory that cordless phones are less secure than cellular, but this distinction seems insufficient, and conversations by both media should be eligible for privilege protection. *See* McKamey v. Roach, 55 F.3d 1236 (6th Cir. 1995) (no reasonable expectation of privacy).

37. *See, e.g.,* Federal Wiretap Act, 18 U.S.C. 2510 et seq. and particularly 18 U.S.C. 2517(4) ("otherwise privileged wire, oral or electronic" communication, when intercepted, "shall lose its privileged character"). *Cf.* United States v. Carrazana, 921 F.2d 1557 (1991) (cellular telephonic communications given same protection under Act as "wire" communications).

38. *See, e.g.,* United States v. Valencia, 541 F.2d 618, 621-623 (6th Cir. 1976) (Sixth Amendment right of counsel violated where secretary for defense counsel was actually a government informer).

§5.14 Joint Clients

If two or more clients retain or consult the same attorney with respect to a matter of common interest, the communications made between the joint clients and the attorney are privileged with respect to outsiders.[1] Thus joint clients are within the class of persons to whom otherwise confidential communications can be disclosed without destroying confidentiality.[2] However, if the joint clients have a falling out, the communications are not privileged in subsequent litigation between themselves[3] unless they have expressly agreed otherwise.[4] Attorneys may have an ethical obligation to advise joint clients of this exception to the privilege.[5]

The traditional rationale for recognizing this exception is that joint clients do not intend their communications to be confidential from each other, and typically their communications are made in each other's presence. At the time the communications are made, joint clients generally are not in a position to know whether subsequent disclosure in litigation between themselves would be to their benefit or detriment. Moreover, there is no basis for favoring a joint client who seeks to assert the privilege as against a joint client who seeks to waive it in subsequent litigation between themselves. Therefore, agreeing to joint representation means that each joint client accepts the risk that another joint client may later use what she has said to the lawyer.

Rationale for exception

A common example of joint representation is the typical insurance defense case, where the attorney retained by an insurance carrier represents both the insurer and the insured.[6] Statements made by the insured to the attorney retained by the carrier are privileged in

---

§5.14 1. Ohio-Sealy Mattress Mfg. Co. v. Kaplan, 90 F.R.D. 21, 29 (N.D. Ill. 1980) (confidential communications by joint clients with common attorney, "although known to each other, will of course be privileged in a controversy of either or both of the clients with the outside world").

2. In re Auclair, 961 F.2d 65, 69 (5th Cir. 1992) (privilege not waived when communication is shared with third person who has common legal interest with respect to subject matter of communication).

3. *See* Garner v. Wolfinbarger, 430 F.2d 1093, 1103 (5th Cir. 1970) (where attorney acts for two or more persons having common interest, neither may claim privilege in subsequent controversy with the other), *cert. denied*, 401 U.S. 974. *See also* proposed-but-rejected FRE 503(d)(5) (no privilege for "communication relevant to a matter of common interest between two or more clients" if it was made "by any of them to a lawyer retained or consulted in common, when offered in an action between any of the clients").

4. Restatement (Third) of the Law Governing Lawyers (Proposed Final Draft No. 1, 1997) §125 (unless co-clients "have explicitly agreed otherwise" their communications with lawyer or other privileged person "are not privileged as between the co-clients in subsequent litigation between them").

5. *See* ABA Model Rules of Professional Conduct Rule 1.7(b)(2) (requiring "informed consent, confirmed in writing"); ABA Model Code of Professional Responsibility EC 5-16 (before representing multiple clients, lawyer "should explain fully to each" the implications of common representation).

6. Reavis v. Metropolitan Property & Liab. Ins. Co., 117 F.R.D. 160, 165 (S.D. Cal. 1987) (insurer and insured are "joint clients of the attorney appointed to defend a liability suit against the insured").

litigation with third parties but not in subsequent litigation between the insured and the insurer.[7]

The joint client or common interest doctrine does not apply unless both clients are seeking and are entitled to legal advice or representation with respect to the same matter.[8] It also does not apply if their interests with respect to a matter of common concern are conflicting or adverse.[9]

Assert against outsiders

Each joint client may assert the privilege with respect to outsiders.[10] One cannot waive the privilege of another,[11] but, absent an agreement to the contrary, each may disclose his own statements provided such disclosure does not reveal protected communications by another.[12] Where two clients who received joint legal advice are being jointly tried, and one of them waives the privilege at trial with respect to such advice, the other may sometimes be allowed a separate trial to protect his claim of attorney-client privilege.[13]

§5.15 Joint Defense; Pooled Information

Even where clients are not jointly represented, communications from a client (or his lawyer) to a lawyer (or a representative of the lawyer) representing another in a matter of common interest are generally within the privilege.[1] This application of the privilege originated in

---

7. Simpson v. Motorist Mut. Ins. Co., 494 F.2d 850, 855 (7th Cir. 1974) (no privilege where insured files suit against insurer for bad-faith refusal to settle claim against insured), *cert. denied,* 419 U.S. 901.

8. Reed v. Baxter, 34 F.3d 351, 355-357 (6th Cir. 1998) (communications between city attorney and members of city council were not privileged when subject was matter within jurisdiction of city manager and fire chief rather than council; council members were not clients for purposes of this communication).

9. Opus Corp. v. IBM, 956 F. Supp. 1503, 1506-1507 (D. Minn. 1996) (common interest doctrine does not apply where interests of clients adverse).

10. Restatement (Third) of the Law Governing Lawyers (Proposed Final Draft No. 1, 1997) §125 cmt. f (each co-client has "standing to assert the privilege," regardless which client was source of communication and regardless whether co-client asserting privilege knew of communication when made, or learned later, or never knew of it).

11. State v. Maxwell, 691 P.2d 1316, 1320 (Kan. Ct. App. 1984) (even majority of co-clients cannot waive privilege of nonconsenting co-client).

12. In re Teleglobe Communications Corp., 493 F.3d 345, 365 (3d Cir. 2007) (joint client may unilaterally waive privilege covering his own communications with attorney, but may not waive privilege as to communications by any other joint client).

13. United States v. Walters, 913 F.2d 388, 393 (7th Cir. 1990) (first client waived privilege by asserting defense of reliance on advice of counsel; where attorney-client privilege "is compromised by joint trials, we must rule on the side of severance").

§5.15 1. *See* Restatement (Third) of the Law Governing Lawyers (Proposed Final Draft No. 1, 1996) §126 (covering communications between "a client, the client's communicating agents, the client's lawyer, the lawyer's representing agent" with those of another client sharing a "common interest" in a matter); United States v. Austin, 416 F.3d 1016, 1021 (9th Cir. 2005) (joint defense privilege "protects not only the confidentiality of communications passing from a party to his or her attorney but also from one party to the attorney for another party where a joint defense effort or strategy has been decided upon and undertaken by the parties and their respective counsel").

criminal cases,[2] where attorneys for different defendants often pool information or mount a joint defense.[3] Without such protection, attorneys representing clients on matters of common interest would be reluctant to collaborate out of concern that the information shared could someday be used against their clients.[4]

Protecting collaborative efforts by parties with common interests is said to encourage better case preparation and reduce time and expense.[5] The litigation process is generally not deprived of evidence that would otherwise be available because the collaborative communications are unlikely to be made in absence of the privilege. The crime-fraud exception to the privilege serves as a check against the use of pooling arrangements for illegitimate purposes.[6] **Rationale**

Although this application of the privilege is occasionally referred to as the "pooled defense" doctrine, it has broader dimensions.[7] It applies in civil as well as criminal cases,[8] and to clients who are plaintiffs as well as defendants.[9] Normally protection under this doctrine requires that the parties be involved in litigation or facing an imminent threat of litigation,[10] although sometimes courts recognize the doctrine where only one party is so threatened.[11]

2. *See* Chahoon v. Commonwealth, 62 Va. (21 Gratt.) 822, 836-839 (1871) (one of earliest cases recognizing the doctrine).

3. *See, e.g.,* Hunydee v. United States, 355 F.2d 183, 185 (9th Cir. 1965) (privilege applies to statement made by defendant husband in presence of his own counsel and his wife's separate counsel regarding their joint defense in a tax fraud prosecution).

4. United States v. McPartlin, 595 F.2d 1321, 1335-1337 (7th Cir. 1979) (uninhibited communication among joint parties and counsel on matters of common concern is "often important to the protection of their interests" and in criminal cases "can be necessary"), *cert. denied,* 444 U.S. 833.

5. *See* In re LTV Sec. Litig., 89 F.R.D. 595, 604 (N.D. Tex. 1981) (no policy "is disserved by recognition of the joint defense privilege" and "its recognition makes savings in expense and effort likely").

6. *See* §5.22, *infra.*

7. *See* United States v. Schwimmer, 892 F.2d 237, 243-244 (2d Cir. 1989) (need to protect free flow of information from client to attorney "logically exists whenever multiple clients share a common interest about a legal matter"), *cert. denied,* 502 U.S. 810.

8. *See, e.g.,* Western Fuels Assn., Inc. v. Burlington N. R.R., 102 F.R.D. 201, 203 (D. Wyo. 1984) (civil codefendants); In re LTV Securities Litig., 89 F.R.D. 595 (N.D. Tex. 1981) (prospective administrative proceedings).

9. *See, e.g.,* Miller, Anderson, Nash, Yerke & Wiener v. United States Dept. of Energy, 499 F. Supp. 767, 771 (D. Or. 1980) (privilege applicable to disclosure by civil plaintiff to prospective coplaintiff).

10. United States v. Newell, 315 F.3d 510, 526 (5th Cir. 2002) (common legal interest theory shields communications between potential codefendants and their counsel if there is threat of litigation; mere awareness that litigation might come some day does not suffice; defendant sought counsel to guard against possible, not imminent, criminal action, so common legal interest exception did not apply); In re Santa Fe Intl. Corp., 272 F.3d 705, 709-712 (5th Cir. 2001) (a "palpable" threat of litigation is required rather than "a mere awareness that one's questionable conduct might some day result in litigation").

11. United States v. BDO Seidman, LLP, 492 F.3d 806, 816 (7th Cir. 2007) (in IRS action to enforce administrative summonses against accounting firm, common interest doctrine applied to memorandum written by accounting firm's attorney and sent to attorney at law firm, even though accounting firms' common interest was not shared under threat of litigation; memorandum requested legal advice on pending IRS regulations and firms jointly served other clients).

Against outsiders   Each participant may assert the privilege against outsiders,[12] and all participants must consent to a general waiver of the privilege.[13] A client may waive the privilege for his own statements[14] although in doing so he should not be permitted to reveal indirectly the privileged communications of other participants.[15]

Later litigation between clients   It is not yet settled whether the privilege may be asserted in subsequent litigation between the formerly allied parties,[16] although the policy of the privilege generally supports its recognition in this context.[17] Clients who are allied, but not jointly represented (often because they have some conflicting interests), may be inhibited from collaborating if they fear their statements will be used against them in subsequent litigation with the other. A careful attorney will negotiate an agreement barring such use before disclosure is made.

Confidentiality required   The privilege only applies in the pooled defense setting if the communications are confidential, and the presence of an outsider vitiates the privilege.[18] The privilege normally does not apply to communications between the individual clients outside the presence of counsel or a representative of a lawyer,[19] although the attending counsel need not represent the communicating party.[20] If an attorney for at least one of the parties is present, the privilege should be recognized for client-to-client communications made in furtherance of the common legal interest.

12. _See_ Restatement (Third) of the Law Governing Lawyers (Proposed Final Draft No. 1, 1996) §126.

13. _See_ United States v. BDO Seidman, LLP, 492 F.3d 806, 817 (7th Cir. 2007) (waiver of joint defense privilege requires consent of all parties).

14. _See_ ACN, proposed-but-rejected FRE 503(b) ("[E]ach client [is allowed] a privilege as to his own statements. Thus if all resist disclosure, none will occur. But, if for reasons of his own, a client wishes to disclose his own statements made at the joint conference, he should be permitted to do so, and the rule is to that effect.").

15. Ohio-Sealy Mattress Mfg. Co. v. Kaplan, 90 F.R.D. 21, 29 (N.D. Ill. 1980) (disclosure not allowed where communications contained in document reflecting communications of other nonwaiving participants).

16. _See_ Welles, A Survey of Attorney-Client Privilege in Joint Defense, 35 U. Miami L. Rev. 321, 337 (1981) ("[I]f former clients disagree among themselves and subsequently become opposing parties in a lawsuit the privilege is inapplicable.").

17. _See generally_ Note, Separating the Joint-Defense Doctrine from the Attorney-Client Privilege, 68 Tex. L. Rev. 1273, 1301-1302 (1990) (policy underlying joint-defense privilege "requires that the privilege remain intact even when parties to the privileged communications later become adversaries"). _But see_ Restatement (Third) of the Law Governing Lawyers (Proposed Final Draft No. 1, 1996) §126(2) (requiring express agreement to prevent use of communications between allied parties in subsequent litigation).

18. United States v. Keplinger, 776 F.2d 678, 701 (7th Cir. 1985) (pooled defense privilege does not apply where communication between attorneys is made in presence of third parties), _cert. denied,_ 476 U.S. 1183.

19. Schachar v. American Academy of Ophthalmology, Inc., 106 F.R.D. 187, 192 (N.D. Ill. 1985) (communications among clients in absence of attorney not privileged even though statements reiterated matters confided to their attorneys).

20. United States v. McPartlin, 595 F.2d 1321, 1335-1337 (7th Cir. 1979) (privilege applied to communications by client to an investigator acting on behalf of the attorney for a codefendant; interview was conducted in absence of client's attorney but with his consent), _cert. denied,_ 444 U.S. 833.

The pooled defense privilege is only available when the clients have a sufficient common interest.[21] The privilege does not apply if clients meet or discuss in purely adversarial or arm's-length situations.[22] The privilege does not apply to a communication requesting a party to participate in a joint defense where no commonality of interest has yet been established[23] or to a communication seeking to persuade the other client to take responsibility for the offense.[24] Sufficient commonality has been found where the parties had a similar interest in impeaching a particular witness.[25] The burden is on the party claiming the privilege to establish that the communication was made in pursuance of a common interest.[26]

Commonality of interest

Generally there will be conflicting interests as well as common interests,[27] and the privilege is not denied merely because the clients' interests are not identical.[28] The privilege applies only to communications that relate to the matters of common interest.[29]

Parties who are pooling information or planning strategy on a matter of common interest would be wise to memorialize their understandings in a written agreement.[30] Here the parties may specify the conditions under which the information will be disclosed, require notice to other

Joint defense agreement

21. In re Grand Jury Subpoena: Under Seal, 415 F.3d 333, 341 (4th Cir. 2005) (privilege claimant must show that parties had common interest about legal matter, and "cooperation in internal investigation" is not itself sufficient; joint strategy is necessary); In re Grand Jury Subpoena Duces Tecum, 112 F.3d 910 (8th Cir. 1997) (insufficient commonality of interest to justify joint defense privilege for discussions between Hillary Rodham Clinton and her private lawyers in presence of White House counsel).

22. *See* ACN, proposed-but-rejected FRE 503(b) (privilege inapplicable where parties meet "on a purely adversary basis"); Government of Virgin Islands v. Joseph, 685 F.2d 857, 861-862 (3d Cir. 1982) (no privilege where defendants' interests were antagonistic).

23. *See, e.g.,* Strong v. State, 773 S.W.2d 543, 549-552 (Tex. Crim. App. 1989) (common defense rule does not apply to letter client wrote to an accomplice's lawyer urging a joint defense; communication was not made as part of a joint defense).

24. Government of Virgin Islands v. Joseph, 685 F.2d 857, 861-862 (3d Cir. 1982) (no privilege where attorney for one codefendant attempted to obtain a confession from other codefendant).

25. United States v. McPartlin, 595 F.2d 1321, 1335-1337 (7th Cir. 1979), *cert. denied,* 444 U.S. 833.

26. In re Bevill, Bresler & Schulman Asset Mgmt. Corp., 805 F.2d 120, 126 (3d Cir. 1986) (party asserting privilege bears burden of proving applicability of privilege).

27. *See* ACN, proposed-but-rejected FRE 503(b) (frequent reason for retaining different attorneys by various clients is presence of "actually or potentially conflicting interests in addition to the common interest which brings them together").

28. *See* Eisenberg v. Gagnon, 766 F.2d 770, 787-788 (3d Cir. 1985) ("Communications to an attorney to establish a common defense strategy are privileged even though the attorney represents another client with some adverse interests."), *cert. denied,* 474 U.S. 946.

29. United States v. Cariello, 536 F. Supp. 698, 702 (D.N.J. 1982) ("Communications among attorneys and codefendants are privileged only if the communications are designed to further a joint or common defense.").

30. *See* John Morrell & Co. v. Local Union 304A, United Food and Commercial Workers, 913 F.2d 544, 555 (8th Cir. 1990) (company and employee class entered into "joint defense agreement" concerning sharing of documents in prior litigation), *cert. denied,* 111 S. Ct. 1683.

parties of discovery requests or proposed settlements, and prohibit disclosure of shared information by the recipient in any subsequent controversy between the parties.[31] Parties may also seek a court order protecting communications on matters of pooled defense or other common interest and barring adverse use by members of the group.[32]

§5.16 Corporate Clients

The proper scope of the attorney-client privilege for corporate clients has long been a matter of uncertainty and controversy. One early decision (later reversed) denied the privilege to corporations[1] and another extended the privilege to all corporate officers or employees.[2]

An overly broad privilege could unfairly impede discovery in litigation against corporate opponents. Large modern corporations have many agents and employees, and an expansive privilege could cast a cloak of secrecy around corporate communications that are otherwise relevant and potentially discoverable.[3] Since corporations act only through human agents, the key to finding a middle ground between no privilege and one that reaches everyone is to extend privilege protection to a group comprised of some but not all agents or employees, and find a way of defining this group.

Control group test One approach that began to gain acceptance prior to the adoption of the Federal Rules was to limit the privilege to members of the "control group" of the corporation, which was defined as those persons authorized to seek and act upon advice received from corporate counsel.[4] In the Preliminary Draft of proposed FRE 503, the Advisory Committee

---

31. *See* Waller v. Financial Corp. of America, 828 F.2d 579, 583-584 (9th Cir. 1987) (joint defense agreement required party to protect confidentiality even if no longer a part of joint defense).

32. Waller v. Financial Corp. of America, 828 F.2d 579, 583-584 (9th Cir. 1987) (court may "frame a protective order which will assure against any improper disclosure" of terms of joint defense agreement).

§5.16 1. Radiant Burners v. American Gas Assoc., 207 F. Supp. 771, 773 (N.D. Ill. 1962) (corporate clients have no attorney-client privilege, which is "historically and fundamentally personal in nature" and confidentiality could not apply in corporate setting; corporations cannot assert privilege against self-incrimination either), *rev'd*, 320 F.2d 314 (7th Cir. 1963), *cert. denied*, 375 U.S. 929.

2. United States v. United Shoe Machinery, 89 F. Supp. 357, 359 (D. Mass. 1950).

3. *See* Jarvis, Inc. v. AT&T, 84 F.R.D. 286, 292 (D. Colo. 1979) (under broad view of attorney-corporate client privilege, "communications from all 40,000 Mountain Bell employees could qualify for the attorney-client privilege"; court refuses to "legitimize such an impediment to reasonable and necessary discovery"). *See also* Simon, The Attorney-Client Privilege as Applied to Corporations, 65 Yale L.J. 953, 955 (1956) ("Where corporations are involved, with their large number of agents, masses of documents, and frequent dealings with lawyers, the zone of silence grows large.").

4. *See* Philadelphia v. Westinghouse Elec. Corp., 210 F. Supp. 483, 485 (E.D. Pa. 1962) (control group consists of those people "of whatever rank" who are "in a position to control or even to take a substantial part in a decision about any action which the corporation may take upon the advice of the attorney"), *cert. denied*, 372 U.S. 943.

included a definition of "representative of the client" which would have codified the "control group" standard.[5]

However, at about the same time, a competing approach called the "subject matter" test was announced in the decision of *Harper & Row Publishers, Inc. v. Decker:*

> [A]n employee of a corporation, though not a member of its control group, is sufficiently identified with the corporation so that his communication to the corporation's attorney is privileged where the employee makes the communication at the direction of his superiors in the corporation and where the subject matter upon which the attorney's advice is sought by the corporation and dealt with in the communication is the performance by the employee of the duties of his employment.[6]

After *Harper & Row* was affirmed by an equally divided Supreme Court, the Advisory Committee deleted the "control group" test from proposed FRE 503 and left the issue to case law development.[7]

In 1981 the Supreme Court directly addressed the scope of the attorney-corporate client privilege in the *Upjohn* case.[8] Although the Court disclaimed any intention to formulate a new rule applicable to all cases, it rejected the control group test, concluding that it should not govern the development of the federal law in this area.

The Court articulated three criticisms of the "control group" standard. First, it was said to be inconsistent with the realities of the modern corporation, in which middle management personnel often possess and are best able to communicate information needed by the attorney in order to give sound legal advice to the corporation. Second, by not protecting the conveyance of important information to the corporation's attorney, it impeded the attorney's ability to help the corporation comply with legal requirements. Finally, the test was viewed as difficult and unpredictable in application, although this criticism seems disingenuous in light of the fact that *Upjohn* failed to establish a more certain standard.

The Court concluded that granting a broader privilege to corporate clients would not undercut the discovery process; adversaries could still obtain information known by corporate employees and would be

5. Revised Draft, Rule 5-03(a)(3), 51 F.R.D. 315, 361 (1971) (defining "representative of a client" to mean "one having authority to obtain professional legal services, and to act on advice rendered pursuant thereto, on behalf of the client").

6. 423 F.2d 487, 491-492 (7th Cir. 1970), *aff'd by equally divided court*, 400 U.S. 348 (1971).

7. *See* ACN, proposed-but-rejected FRE 503(a) ("The rule contains no definition of 'representative of the client.' In the opinion of the Advisory Committee, the matter is best left to resolution by decision on a case-by-case basis."). In the House Hearings, Professor Cleary testified that the Committee had "never receded" from its view that the control group test was the proper one, but stated that the issue had become "too hot to handle." *See* House Hearings, at 524.

8. Upjohn Co. v. United States, 449 U.S. 383 (1981).

foreclosed only from discovering what communications were made of the information to corporate counsel.[9]

**The *Upjohn*
criteria**

In *Upjohn*, the IRS sought to enforce a summons to obtain employee responses to a questionnaire prepared by the corporation's counsel as part of an internal investigation, as well as notes and memoranda of counsel based on oral interviews with employees.[10] The investigation concerned possible improper payments by the corporation to foreign government officials. Even though many of the employees questioned were outside the "control group," the Court found their responses to be within the corporation's attorney-client privilege.

Upjohn has a modest tone and expressly disclaimed any broad prescriptive purpose, but the Court stressed four factors that seem to set a federal standard. First, the communications were made by corporate employees to corporate counsel for the purpose of enabling counsel to provide legal advice to the corporation, and the employees were aware that this was the purpose of the communications. Second, the communications were made at the request of the employee's corporate superiors. Third, the communications concerned matters within the scope of the employees' corporate duties.[11] Fourth, the communications were treated as confidential from beginning to end, having been gathered in private interviews and memorialized in notes and memoranda that were not generally circulated within the corporation and were not shown to outsiders.[12]

Upjohn did not say all four factors had to appear, but the first and fourth (requiring legal as opposed to other services and confidentiality) are essential for all applications of the privilege. The second factor (communications made at request of superiors) seems convenient but not essential. Corporate agents often consult with counsel on legal questions affecting matters within the scope of their responsibilities without first being asked by superiors to do so. While such directive sheds some light on purpose, its presence or absence hardly tells the

9. *Id.* at 390-396 (noting that middle-level and even lower-level employees can "embroil the corporation in serious legal difficulties" and often these employees have "the relevant information needed by corporate counsel"; application of attorney-client privilege to communications such as those involved here "puts the adversary in no worse position than if the communications had never taken place" because privilege "only protects disclosure of communications; it does not protect disclosure of the underlying facts by those who have communicated with the attorney").

10. Confidential disclosures were made to both house counsel and outside counsel, and the Court drew no distinctions based on the status of the attorney. *See* 449 U.S. at 387.

11. 449 U.S. at 394. The Court noted that the information provided by the employees was not available from top management. While some observers have viewed this factor as an additional criterion for the privilege, it seems unlikely to have such significance. Information available to any corporate employees could presumably be obtained by the control group and then communicated to the corporate attorney. Recognition of the privilege is unlikely to depend on whether management takes this step or allows the information to be communicated directly to counsel by lower-echelon employees.

12. 449 U.S. at 394-395. On the issue of whether the privilege is waived by subsequent disclosure to outsiders, see discussion in §5.28, *infra*.

whole story and hardly seems indispensable.[13] The real heart of the *Upjohn* standard is the third factor (statement must relate to matter within scope of duties of agent who talks to lawyer).

This third factor is important to provide a reasonable limit on the scope of the privilege for corporate employees, and it is consistent with the holding in *Hickman* that agents who are mere eyewitnesses to events do not come within the charmed circle of privilege when they speak to counsel.[14] This subject matter requirement is clearly satisfied when the communication concerns the employee's area of responsibility.[15] It should also be satisfied when the communication relates to the conduct of subordinates for whom the employee is responsible.[16] It should not be satisfied, however, if the employee is speaking merely as a witness to the events that are the subject of the communication unless those events have a direct connection with the employee's own corporate duties.[17]

One of the most difficult issues in applying the attorney-client privilege in the corporate context is determining whether the communication was made to secure legal advice or for business purposes. Corporate lawyers are often involved in business decisions, and as information moves through the decisionmaking process it can be

Legal or business purpose

---

13. *See* Restatement (Third) of the Law Governing Lawyers (Proposed Final Draft No. 1, 1996) §123 cmt. h (rejecting requirement that corporate employee communicate at the direction of superiors).

14. Hickman v. Taylor, 329 U.S. 495 (1947). This aspect of *Upjohn* incorporates the "subject matter" test of *Harper & Row, see* text at note 6, *supra,* and excludes from the privilege statements by employees who were merely witnesses to events unrelated to their own responsibilities. If an employee is directed to give a statement to corporate counsel regarding an event the employee witnessed, it might be argued that the giving of the statement is a matter of corporate duty. In *Upjohn,* "corporate duty" appears to refer to the employee's regular work assignment rather than acts of reporting undertaken in response to an ad hoc corporate directive.

15. One post-*Upjohn* decision applied the privilege to communications by a current corporate employee about matters occurring prior to his employment. *See* Baxter Travenol Laboratories, Inc. v. Lemay, 89 F.R.D. 410, 414 (S.D. Ohio 1981) (privilege's protection "should not be made to depend upon the content of the communication, or the context in which (or status of the person by whom) such content was originally developed"). *But see* Alexander, The Corporate Attorney-Client Privilege: A Study of the Participants, 63 St. Johns L. Rev. 191 (1989) ("Such a bootstrap approach would enable corporations to convert mere witnesses into sources of privileged information simply by designating them litigation consultants.").

16. United States v. AT&T, 86 F.R.D. 603, 618 (D.D.C. 1979) (privilege covers matters directly related to employee's own corporate activities or those of employee's subordinates).

17. *See* Hickman v. Taylor, 329 U.S. 495 (1947) (statements to company lawyer by employee witnesses to accident held outside attorney-client privilege); Leer v. Chicago, M., St. P. & P. Ry., 308 N.W.2d 305, 309 (Minn. 1981) (witnessing of an accident by employee not within scope of employee's duties), *cert. denied,* 455 U.S. 939. *See generally* Alexander, The Corporate Attorney-Client Privilege: A Study of the Participants, 63 St. Johns L. Rev. 191, 321 (1989) ("Limiting eligible communications to those that deal closely with the employee's particular corporate duties maintains the integrity of the principle that the privilege encompasses only communications with the client, not with bystander witnesses, and thus preserves a degree of symmetry with the scope of the privilege as it applies to individuals.").

difficult to determine the motives underlying particular communications. A corporation has greater potential than an individual client to manipulate the privilege to conceal information that is nonlegal in nature.[18]

Distinguishing business communications from legal communications can be particularly difficult when they involve counsel who serve as corporate officers or otherwise participate in the management of the corporation. A writing made in the ordinary course of business does not become privileged by being channeled to corporate counsel nor are oral communications automatically privileged because counsel attended the meeting where the communications were made. However, *Upjohn* expressly approves extending the privilege to attorneys undertaking internal investigations on behalf of a corporation, at least where there is a significant legal component to such investigations.

Confidentiality   Assuming the other elements in the *Upjohn* standard are satisfied, the privilege also requires confidentiality, which means at least that the communications cannot be made in the presence of outsiders and that documents containing or reflecting the substance of the communication cannot be circulated generally within the corporation.[19] Probably file copies of privileged communications cannot be commingled with other broadly available corporate records, and access must be restricted to those personnel whose responsibilities require knowledge of the communications.[20] In ruling on a claim of privilege, the court should have discretion to require the corporation to reveal the persons to whom the privileged material was disclosed.

The steps taken to preserve confidentiality are measured against the usual recordkeeping practices of the corporation and the techniques used to safeguard other types of confidential material.[21] In *Upjohn* the Court noted that the employees responding to the questionnaire had been told that the investigation was confidential and instructed not to discuss it with outsiders. The absence of such formal directives should not be fatal when other circumstances indicate confidentiality was

---

18. *See* Waldman, Beyond *Upjohn:* The Attorney-Client Privilege in the Corporate Context, 28 Wm. & Mary L. Rev. 473, 493 n.104 (1987) (characteristics of corporations "create an enormous potential for abuse of the privilege"); Nath, *Upjohn:* A New Prescription for the Attorney-Client Privilege and Work Product Defenses in Administrative Investigations, 30 Buffalo L. Rev. 11, 93 (1981) (criticizing *Upjohn* as drawing up a "blueprint" for fabrication of spurious corporate privilege claims).

19. *See* Diversified Indus., Inc. v. Meredith, 572 F.2d 596, 609 (8th Cir. 1977) (establishing as one criterion for recognition of the privilege that "the communication is not disseminated beyond those persons who, because of the corporate structure, need to know its contents.").

20. *See* James Julian, Inc. v. Raytheon Co., 93 F.R.D. 138, 142 (D. Del. 1982) (documents in question were not broadly circulated or used as training materials; they were simply indexed and placed in the appropriate file where they would be available to those corporate employees who needed them; confidentiality is destroyed "only when the facts have been made known to persons other than those who need to know them").

21. *See* Simon, The Attorney-Client Privilege as Applied to Corporations, 65 Yale L.J. 953, 985 (1956) (corporation's own internal security practices "should ordinarily be indicative of its desire for secrecy").

intended by those who directed others to speak with counsel or by those who took it upon themselves to seek legal advice.[22]

If a protected communication is later spread widely throughout the corporation or disclosed to outsiders at the direction or with the acquiescence of those responsible to decide whether to disclose, the privilege is waived.[23] Privileged corporate communications generally cannot be disclosed selectively, even to a governmental agency such as the SEC.[24] However, disclosure may be made to an attorney for a party sharing a common legal interest without destroying confidentiality.[25]

The scholarly commentary on the *Upjohn* decision has been mixed although much of it is critical.[26] Commentators generally agree that *Upjohn* provides increased incentive for corporate management to undertake internal investigations into matters involving potential civil or criminal liability on the part of the corporation. In absence of a privilege for communications to corporate counsel by lower-echelon employees, such investigations might be deterred because their results could be used against the corporation. To the extent such internal investigations increase corporate compliance with the law, the public interest is served.

Scholarly Criticism of Upjohn

Commentators have questioned, however, whether the broader scope of privilege developed in *Upjohn* is necessary to provide an incentive for corporate employees to speak candidly with corporate counsel because agents can be required to cooperate with lawyers as part of their job. Because the corporation rather than the agent owns the corporate privilege and can claim or waive it, the argument runs, the privilege does not provide assurance encouraging agents to talk to counsel.[27] However, corporations often make common cause with their agents and do not waive or relinquish the privilege so its existence

---

22. *See* Leucadia, Inc. v. Reliance Ins. Co., 101 F.R.D. 674, 678 (S.D.N.Y. 1983) (privilege applies to corporate internal investigation even though employees were not specifically told that their communications to corporate lawyer would be held in confidence).

23. *See* §5.28, *infra. See also* United States v. Jones, 696 F.2d 1069, 1072-1073 (4th Cir. 1982) (appellants waived the protection for records relating to legal opinions when they "publicized portions of the legal opinions in brochures and other printed material").

24. *See generally* §5.13, *supra,* and §5.28, *infra.*

25. *See* §5.15, *supra.*

26. For the differing views of commentators, *see* Waldman, Beyond *Upjohn*: The Attorney-Client Privilege in the Corporate Context, 28 Wm. & Mary L. Rev. 473, 493-497 (1987) (*Upjohn* Court ignored special difficulties of discovery against a corporate opponent and high social cost of an expansive corporate client privilege: "Today's corporate misdeeds—financial institutions laundering money for organized crime, fraudulent securities schemes on a huge scale, massive overcharges by defense contractors, and illegal handling and dumping of toxic material—inflict a much higher cost on society"); Saltzburg, Corporate and Related Attorney-Client Privilege Claims: A Suggested Approach, 12 Hofstra L. Rev. 279, 304-306 (1984) (criticizing *Upjohn* as going beyond rationale of the privilege; suggesting that privilege be recognized only for corporate employees "who have the authority to control the subsequent use and distribution of the communications").

27. Diversified Indus., Inc. v. Meredith, 572 F.2d 596, 611 n.5 (8th Cir. 1977) ("Ordinarily, the privilege belongs to the corporation and an employee cannot himself claim the attorney-client privilege and prevent disclosure of communications between himself and the corporation's counsel if the corporation has waived the privilege.").

contributes to the willingness of corporations to ask their agents to talk to lawyers, and as a practical matter it often does assure agents that what they say is protected. In the common situation where an agent is at risk of personal liability for what he has done, often the corporate lawyer represents both the entity and the agent, which means that the agent has a personal privilege and does have power to block disclosure of what he tells counsel.[28]

Since internal corporate investigations enjoy work product protection if undertaken in anticipation of litigation, as *Upjohn* itself recognized,[29] some have argued that recognition of an attorney-client privilege is unnecessary in this setting.[30] But sometimes internal studies and investigations on regulatory matters are undertaken long before enforcement is threatened in settings where work product protection would not apply. Work product protection can be overcome by an ordinary showing of need when it comes to statements by corporate agents (or by any ordinary witness), so a privilege provides stronger assurance of confidentiality. Others have argued that the privilege should be narrowed or limited in other ways. It has been suggested that the privilege should be qualified rather than absolute for agents outside the control group,[31] that it should apply to lower-echelon employees only after litigation begins,[32] or that it should be reduced to a "self-evaluative" privilege that is more focused on internal review and reform efforts.[33]

Upjohn and state law

Because *Upjohn* was decided as a matter of federal common law, it is not binding on the states. Some states have rejected *Upjohn* and continue to apply the "control group" test.[34] Others have adopted *Upjohn*

---

28. In this setting, the entity and the agent may be joint clients, allowing each to claim the privilege against outsiders but not in subsequent litigation between themselves. *See* the discussion in §5.14, *supra.*

29. Upjohn Co. v. United States, 449 U.S. 383, 401-402 (1981) (giving work product protection to notes and memoranda of witness interviews).

30. *See* Saltzburg, Corporate and Related Attorney-Client Privilege Claims: A Suggested Approach, 12 Hofstra L. Rev. 279, 294 n.81 (1984) (arguing that work product protection "would have justified the same result").

31. Alexander, The Corporate Attorney-Client Privilege: A Study of the Participants, 63 St. Johns L. Rev. 191, 381-389 (1989).

32. *See* Waldman, Beyond *Upjohn*: The Attorney-Client Privilege in the Corporate Context, 28 Wm. & Mary L. Rev. 473, 503-505 (1987) (corporation is "less likely to manipulate privilege if the communications protected are generated in response to an existing lawsuit").

33. *See, e.g.,* Leonard, Codifying a Privilege for Self-Critical Analysis, 25 Harv. J. on Legis. 113 (1988); Crissman & Mathews, Limited Waiver of Attorney-Client Privilege and Work Product in Internal Corporate Investigations: An Emerging Corporate "Self-Evaluative" Privilege, 21 Am. Crim. L. Rev. 123, 176 (1983).

34. *See, e.g.,* Consolidation Coal Co. v. Bucyrus-Erie Co., 89 Ill. 2d 103, 106, 432 N.E.2d 250, 256-257 (1982) (privilege poses "an absolute bar to the discovery of relevant and material evidentiary facts," and given the large number of corporate employees, frequent dealings with lawyers and masses of documents, that result "is fundamentally incompatible" with State's broad discovery policies; control-group test appears to "strike a reasonable balance by protecting consultations with counsel by those who are the decisionmakers or who substantially influence corporate decisions and by minimizing the amount of relevant factual material which is immune from discovery").

by judicial decision or statute,[35] and URE 502 was amended in 1986 to incorporate a standard similar to *Upjohn*.[36]

The corporation's attorney-client privilege is held by management.[37] **Holder**
The "control group" concept, even though it no longer defines the boundary of the federal privilege, has continuing vitality in determining who may assert or waive the privilege on behalf of the corporation.

Corporate managers are required to "exercise the privilege in a manner consistent with their fiduciary duty to act in the best interests of the corporation and not of themselves as individuals."[38] In shareholder derivative litigation, management's right to assert the privilege is qualified and may be overcome upon a showing of good cause.[39]

The position of current management concerning assertion or waiver controls. Former managers cannot prevent waiver, even for confidential communications made to counsel by the former managers.[40] In the case of insolvent corporations, the power to assert or waive the privilege is transferred to the trustee in bankruptcy.[41] Parent and subsidiary corporations are both considered to be clients for purposes of the attorney-client privilege.[42]

A privileged statement given by a current employee does not lose **Former** its privileged status merely because the employee subsequently ter- **employees** minates employment.[43] However, the status of statements made by

---

35. *See, e.g.,* National Farmers Union Prop. & Cas. Co. v. District Court, 718 P.2d 1044, 1048-1050 (Colo. 1986) (applying *Upjohn* criteria to reject claim of privilege); Or. Rev. Stat. 40.225(1)(d) (1991) (adopting *Upjohn* standard by redefining "representative of the client").

36. URE 502(a)(4) (1999) (amending definition of "representative of the client" to include "a person who, for the purpose of effectuating legal representation for the client, makes or receives a confidential communication while acting in the scope of employment for the client"). *See also* Restatement (Third) of the Law Governing Lawyers (Proposed Final Draft No. 1, 1996) §123 (attorney-organizational client privilege applies where the communication to the organization's lawyer is from "a person communicating pursuant to an agency relationship with the organization").

37. Commodity Futures Trading Commn. v. Weintraub, 471 U.S. 343, 348 (1985) ("[F]or solvent corporations, the power to waive the corporate attorney-client privilege rests with the corporation's management and is normally exercised by its officers and directors.").

38. Commodity Futures Trading Commn., 471 U.S. at 349.

39. *See* §5.17, *infra.*

40. Commodity Futures Trading Commn., 471 U.S. at 349 (when control of corporation passes to new management, "authority to assert and waive the corporation's attorney-client privilege passes as well"; new managers may waive attorney-client privilege with respect to communications made by former officers and directors but displaced managers "may not assert the privilege over the wishes of current managers, even as to statements that the former might have made to counsel concerning matters within the scope of their corporate duties").

41. *Id.* at 354.

42. Glidden Co. v. Jandernoa, 173 F.R.D. 459, 472 (W.D. Mich. 1997) (parent and subsidiary corporations share a community of interest such that parent as well as subsidiary is client for purposes of attorney-client privilege).

43. *See* In re Coordinated Pretrial Proceedings in Petroleum Prods. Antitrust Litig., 658 F.2d 1355, 1361 n.7 (9th Cir. 1981) (attorney-client privilege is served by "certainty that conversations between the attorney and client will remain privileged after the employee leaves"), *cert. denied sub nom.,* California v. Standard Oil of Calif., 455 U.S. 990.

former employees is less certain. The majority opinion in *Upjohn* did not say whether communications from former employees about matters relating to their prior corporate duties are within the attorney-corporate client privilege.[44] The concurring opinion of Chief Justice Burger took the position that the privilege should apply to statements by former employees,[45] and a number of subsequent decisions accept this view.[46] These decisions rest on the rationale that expanded sources of information enhance the quality of legal advice for the corporate client, but such a rationale confuses the lawyer work product immunity with the attorney-client privilege. The privilege should not apply to communications from former employees except where they have a continuing agency relationship sufficient to justify treating their communications as those of the corporate client.[47]

Representing corporate officers or employees individually

Often the interests of the corporate entity and its agents mesh closely enough to enable corporate counsel effectively to represent both. In the common situation where acts by corporate agents are at the heart of a litigated dispute, the agents themselves may be personally named as defendants (as is commonly done in tort litigation) or plaintiffs (especially if the corporate plaintiff is a closely held entity and the agent is a major owner), and it is commonplace for both to be represented by the corporate lawyer.[48] Here both entity and agent may hold the privilege, although a court may require evidence that individual representation is

---

44. In *Upjohn*, seven of the 86 persons interviewed had terminated their employment with the company by the time of the interview. The lower courts did not consider this issue, and the Supreme Court "decline[d] to decide it without the benefit of treatment below." 449 U.S. at 394 n.3.

45. *Id.* at 403 (Burger, C.J., concurring) (privilege applies where either "an employee or former employee speaks at the direction of the management with an attorney regarding conduct or proposed conduct within the scope of employment").

46. *See* In re Richard Roe, 168 F.3d 69, 72 (2nd Cir. 1999) (document written by former attorney for corporation, which reflected knowledge obtained while attorney was acting as corporate counsel, was subject to attorney-client privilege, regardless whether attorney still worked for corporation; privilege belonged to corporation, not attorney); Better Government Bureau v. McGraw, 106 F.3d 582, 605-606 (4th Cir. 1997) (*Upjohn* analysis of which employees fall within privilege applies equally to former employees).

47. Alexander, The Corporate Attorney-Client Privilege: A Study of the Participants, 63 St. Johns L. Rev. 191 (1989) ("Once the agency relationship has come to an end, there is no longer any conceptual basis for treating the former agent as a spokesperson for the principal."). *See also* Restatement (Third) of the Law Governing Lawyers (Proposed Final Draft No. 1, 1996) §123 cmt. e (statements by a former agent to corporate counsel are privileged only where there is "a continuing legal obligation to furnish to the organization as principal the information that the former agent communicated to the lawyer for the organization"; scope of such obligation "is determined by the law of agency and the terms of the employment contract").

48. Diversified Indus., Inc. v. Meredith, 572 F.2d 596, 611 n.5 (sometimes circumstances may reveal that employee "sought legal advice from the corporation's counsel for himself or that counsel acted as a joint attorney," in which case the individual "may have a privilege.").

also being undertaken.[49] If the corporate employee neither sought nor received legal representation from corporate counsel on individual matters the privilege does not apply.[50]

In other situations, officers or employees may reasonably believe the lawyer represents them. Here the privilege should apply,[51] at least if the belief is shown to be reasonable,[52] but not all courts recognize the "reasonable belief" test.[53] A corporate lawyer cannot represent both the entity and the agent where there is a conflict of interest,[54] and even in cases where joint representation is proper, explanation to the clients of the implications of common representation is generally required.[55] If the lawyer represents only the corporation, clearly the employee must be informed.[56] It is misleading and contrary to standards of professional responsibility to describe the communication as privileged without making clear that the holder of the privilege is the corporation, not the employee.[57]

§5.17 Shareholder Litigation

Although corporate management holds the attorney-client privilege on behalf of the corporation, the privilege may be overcome by a showing

49. United States v. Munoz, 233 F.3d 1117 (9th Cir. 2000) (evidence insufficient to support claim that corporate attorney also represented defendant individually); In re Grand Jury Subpoena, 274 F.3d 563 (1st Cir. 2001) (an individual privilege may exist only to extent that communications made in a corporate officer's personal capacity are separable from those made in his corporate capacity, which is not case here; it is a "default assumption" that a corporate attorney represents only the corporate entity, and it is "the individual's burden to dispel that presumption").

50. United States v. Munoz, 233 F.3d 1117 (9th Cir. 2000) (evidence insufficient to support claim that corporate attorney also represented defendant individually).

51. Wylie v. Marley Co., 891 F.2d 1463, 1471 (10th Cir. 1989) (privilege applies where employee had reasonable belief that corporation's general counsel was giving him personal legal advice).

52. United States v. Aramony, 88 F.3d 1369, 1389 (4th Cir. 1996) (defendant had no basis for believing he was receiving personal representation from corporate counsel).

53. United States v. International Bhd. of Teamsters, 119 F.3d 210, 217 (2d Cir. 1997) (declining invitation to adopt "reasonable belief" test, and also suggesting belief in individual representation may have been unreasonable).

54. *See* Model Code of Professional Responsibility EC 5-18 (1986) ("A lawyer employed or retained by a corporation or similar entity owes his allegiance to the entity and not to a stockholder, director, officer, employee, representative, or other person connected with the entity."). *See generally* Leary, Is There a Conflict in Representing a Corporation and Its Individual Employees?, 36 Bus. Law. 591 (1981).

55. *See* §5.14, *supra*.

56. *See* ABA Model Rules of Professional Conduct Rule 1.13, Official Comment ("Care must be taken to assure that the individual understands that, when there is such adversity of interest, the lawyer for the organization cannot provide legal representation for that constituent individual, and that discussions between the lawyer for the organization and the individual may not be privileged.").

57. United States v. International Bhd. of Teamsters, 119 F.3d 210, 217 (2d Cir. 1997) ("[W]e join the district court in reiterating that attorneys in all cases are required to clarify exactly whom they represent"; district court found that law firm violated spirit if not letter of Code of Professional Responsibility by repeatedly describing communication with officer as "privileged" without informing him that they represented only entity, which meant officer did not have any privilege).

of good cause when shareholders bring derivative or other suits alleging corporate mismanagement.[1] The privilege is qualified in this situation because corporate management has a potential conflict of interest when its own conduct is challenged. The assertion of the corporation's privilege could be an attempt by management to hide its own malfeasance rather than to protect the corporation's interests.

The landmark case of *Garner v. Wolfinbarger*[2] held that:

> The corporation is not barred from asserting the [attorney-client] privilege merely because those demanding information enjoy the status of stockholders. But where the corporation is in suit against its stockholders on charges of acting inimically to stockholder interests, protection of those interests as well as those of the corporation and of the public require that the availability of the privilege be subject to the right of the stockholders to show cause why it should not be invoked in the particular instance.

Nine factors   The court listed nine factors to be considered in determining whether good cause exists to override the assertion of privilege.[3] In making the determination, trial judges may examine the privileged matter in camera.[4]

Although some commentators have criticized the *Garner* rule as one that inhibits corporate management from seeking legal advice,[5] other commentators have defended the rule as a necessary compromise in order to check corporate mismanagement and protect the

---

§5.17   1. *See* Restatement (Third) of the Law Governing Lawyers (Proposed Final Draft, No. 1, 1996) §34 (in proceeding involving dispute between organizational client and constituents of organization to whom officers or directors of organization bear fiduciary responsibilities, attorney-client privilege of the organization does not apply where (1) directors or officers are charged with breach of their obligations to organization or constituents; (2) communication in question occurred prior to suit and relates directly to charges; and (3) tribunal concludes that need to discover communication is sufficiently compelling and threat to confidentiality sufficiently confined to justify setting privilege aside).

2. 430 F.2d 1093, 1103-1104 (5th Cir. 1970), *cert. denied sub nom.* Garner v. First American Life Ins. Co., 401 U.S. 974.

3. *Id.* at 1104 ((1) "the number of shareholders and the percentage of stock they represent"; (2) "the bona fides of the shareholders"; (3) "the nature of the shareholders' claim and whether it is obviously colorable"; (4) "the apparent necessity or desirability of the shareholders having the information and the availability of it from other sources"; (5) "whether, if the shareholders' claim is of wrongful action by the corporation, it is of action criminal, or illegal but not criminal, or of doubtful legality"; (6) "whether the communication related to past or to prospective actions"; (7) "whether the communication is of advice concerning the litigation itself"; (8) "the extent to which the communication is identified versus the extent to which the shareholders are blindly fishing"; (9) "the risk of revelation of trade secrets or other information in whose confidentiality the corporation has an interest for independent reasons").

4. *Id.*

5. *See generally* Saltzburg, Corporate Attorney-Client Privilege in Shareholder Litigation and Similar Cases: *Garner* Revisited, 12 Hofstra L. Rev. 817 (1984) (criticizing *Garner* as creating uncertainty regarding when privilege will be overridden and thereby deterring corporate management from seeking legal advice).

interests of shareholders.[6] *Garner* has been widely followed by federal courts.[7]

Shareholders have a particularly strong claim to information about advice given by counsel prior to management's allegedly wrongful conduct.[8] More protection is properly granted to communications made after the claim by shareholders has arisen or after the alleged offense has occurred.[9]

In many cases it is unnecessary to rely on the *Garner* rule because the crime-fraud exception serves as an independent ground for denying the privilege claim. If shareholders can make a sufficient preliminary showing of crime or fraud by corporate management, the privilege may be overcome.[10] At present the crime-fraud exception is not broad enough to cover cases where the claim against corporate management is based on mere negligence or dereliction of duty, although some commentators have urged that the crime-fraud exception be expanded as an alternative to the *Garner* rule.[11]

Crime-fraud exception

The *Garner* doctrine has been extended to suits involving fiduciary or quasi-fiduciary relationships like those between pension fund beneficiaries and trustees,[12] a limited partner and a general partner,[13] union officers and union members,[14] and a creditor's committee and creditors in a bankruptcy proceeding.[15] *Garner* has even been applied to

Extensions of *Garner*

6. Nill, *Garner* Is Good: A Re-examination of Assumptions Underlying Application of the Attorney-Client Privilege in Shareholder Suits, 15 Ohio N.U. L. Rev. 641, 652-653 (1988) (noting economic power of modern corporations and social cost of corporate mismanagement; concluding that corporate managers are professionals who "concede a certain amount of privacy to shareholders when they elect to run a corporation" and that public interest is not served by allowing corporate managers "to predict confidently that they will be able to cloak misconduct from the eyes of their shareholder-owners").

7. Sandberg v. Virginia Bankshares, Inc., 979 F.2d 332, 352 (4th Cir. 1992) (adopting "holding and rationale" of *Garner*); Fausek v. White, 965 F.2d 126, 130 (6th Cir. 1992) (adopting *Garner*).

8. Sandberg v. Virginia Bankshares, Inc., 979 F.2d 332, 354 (4th Cir. 1992) (fact that communication occurred prior to shareholders' meeting where action could still have been taken to protect minority shareholders' interests supports finding of good cause to override privilege).

9. *See* In re LTV Sec. Litig., 89 F.R.D. 595, 607-608 (N.D. Tex. 1981) (drawing a distinction between "after-the-fact communications concerning offenses already completed," which retain the privilege, and communications made in connection with management's allegedly wrongful acts, for which the privilege may be overridden; "Forced disclosure of counsel's remedial advice would do great injury to the corporation's interest in self-investigation and preparation for litigation.").

10. For a discussion of the crime-fraud exception, *see* §5.22, *infra*.

11. *See* Note, The Shareholders' Derivative-Claim Exception to the Attorney-Client Privilege, 48 Law & Contemp. Probs. 199, 214 (1985).

12. Helt v. Metropolitan Dist. Commn., 113 F.R.D. 7, 9-11 (D. Conn. 1986) (applying *Garner* rule to claim by retirement plan beneficiary to recover benefits denied by an alleged violation of Title VII).

13. *See* Quintel Corp. v. Citibank, 567 F. Supp. 1357, 1363 (S.D.N.Y. 1983).

14. Aguinaga v. John Morrell & Co., 112 F.R.D. 671, 680-682 (D. Kan. 1986); *but see* Cox v. Administrator, U.S. Steel & Carnegie, 17 F.3d 1386, 1415 (11th Cir. 1994) (refusing to decide whether *Garner* applies "to disputes between a union and its members").

15. In re Christian Life Center, First Assembly of God, 16 Bankr. 35, 37-40 (Bankr. N.D. Cal. 1981).

actions by minority shareholders for their own benefit rather than on behalf of the corporation.[16] However, it does not extend to actions by investors where no breach of fiduciary duty is alleged.[17] The *Garner* rule qualifies only the attorney-client privilege and does not establish an exception to the work product doctrine.[18]

§5.18   Government Clients

A governmental entity can generally claim the attorney-client privilege for confidential communications to its lawyers for purposes of legal advice or representation.[1] Moreover, government documents protected by the attorney-client privilege are generally exempt from production under the Freedom of Information Act.[2]

Proposed-but-rejected FRE 503 expressly includes governmental entities within the definition of "clients" entitled to assert the privilege and would extend the privilege to all types of governmental legal consultation.[3] In contrast, URE 502 limits the attorney-client privilege for

16. Fausek v. White, 965 F.2d 126, 133 (6th Cir. 1992) (action by former minority shareholders against defendant who became sole owner of all shares; under state law a controlling stockholder owes a fiduciary duty to other stockholders), *cert. denied sub nom.* Selox, Inc. v. Fausek, 113 S. Ct. 814 (1992). *See* Summerhays, The Problematic Expansion of *Garner v. Wolfinbarger* Exception to the Corporate Attorney-Client Privilege, 31 Tulsa L.J. 275 (1995) (criticizing extension of *Garner* to nonderivative suits).

17. *See* Weil v. Investment/Indicators, Research & Mgmt., Inc., 647 F.2d 18, 23 (9th Cir. 1981) ("*Garner*'s holding and policy rationale simply do not apply.").

18. In re International Sys. & Controls Corp. Sec. Litig., 693 F.2d 1235, 1239 (5th Cir. 1982) (refusing to apply *Garner* rule to material protected by work product because work product doctrine "is based on the existence of an adversarial relationship, not the quasi-fiduciary relationship analogized to in *Garner*").

§5.18   1. Ross v. City of Memphis, 423 F.3d 596, 601-602 (6th Cir. 2005) (government entity can assert privilege in civil context; governments must follow law, and are under additional constitutional and ethical obligations; privilege insures that conversations between officials and attorneys can be honest and complete, thus "encourages and facilitates the fulfillment of those obligations"); In re County of Erie, 473 F.3d 413, 417-422 (2d Cir. 2007) (privilege protects communications between government lawyer and public official, where primary purpose of was to assess legality of a policy and propose alternatives in light of legal considerations). *But see* Nancy Leong, Attorney-Client Privilege in the Public Sector: Survey of Government Attorneys, 20 Georgetown J. Legal Ethics, 163 (2007) (absolute privilege does not necessarily enhance effective communication between government officials and attorneys).

2. *See, e.g.,* NLRB v. Sears, Roebuck & Co., 421 U.S. 132, 154 (1975) (FOIA Exemption 5 includes "documents which would come within the attorney-client privilege if applied to private parties").

3. See proposed-but-rejected FRE 503(a)(1) (defining "client" as "a person, public officer, or corporation, association, or other organization or entity, either public or private"). *See also* Restatement (Third) of the Law Governing Lawyers (Proposed Final Draft No. 1, 1997) §124 (generally recognizing attorney-client privilege for governmental clients).

governmental entities and officers to a qualified privilege covering only litigation, claims, and investigations.[4]

The attorney-client privilege does not apply to purely intragovernmental communications made for purposes other than to facilitate the rendition of legal services to the government client,[5] although sometimes such communications are protected by the official information privilege.[6] Nor does the privilege cover documents that have independent legal effect in setting forth governmental policy[7] or communications from third parties that are relayed to counsel by a public official.[8] The privilege is recognized only for communications that are made and kept in confidence by the governmental entity.[9]

Nonprotected communications

When a lawyer represents a governmental entity or officer, difficulties sometimes arise in determining who is the client.[10] The named client may actually be a department or sub-unit of a larger governmental entity which should itself be viewed as the client.[11] If the named client is a public officer sued only in an official capacity, the actual client is usually considered to be the public entity employing the officer.[12]

Who is client

Governments, like corporations, can act only through their agents or representatives. As in the corporate setting, the scope of the privilege

Upjohn **criteria**

4. URE 502(d)(7) (1999) (no privilege recognized for "a communication between a public officer or agency and its lawyers unless the communication concerns a pending investigation, claim, or action and the court determines that disclosure will seriously impair the ability of the public officer or agency to process the claim or conduct a pending investigation, litigation, or proceeding in the public interest").

5. *See, e.g.,* Spell v. McDaniel, 591 F. Supp. 1090, 1120 (E.D.N.C. 1984) (privilege does not apply to police internal investigative reports even if later communicated to attorney).

6. *See also* Note, Attorney-Client Privilege for the Government Entity, 97 Yale L.J. 1725, 1742-1744 (1988) (availability of governmental privileges should be considered when courts define contours of attorney-client privilege for governmental entities).

7. Falcone v. IRS, 479 F. Supp. 985, 989-990 (E.D. Mich. 1979) (official statements of policy and interpretation are outside attorney-client privilege).

8. Schlefer v. United States, 702 F.2d 233, 245 (D.C. Cir. 1983) (privilege does not apply where factual information provided not by client but by outsider seeking ruling from agency).

9. Coastal States Gas Corp. v. Department of Energy, 617 F.2d 854, 863 (D.C. Cir. 1980) (test is whether documents were circulated no further than among those members "of the organization who are authorized to speak or act for the organization in relation to the subject matter of the communication," quoting Mead Data Cent., Inc. v. United States Dept. of Air Force, 566 F.2d 242, 253 n.24 (D.C. Cir. 1977)).

10. *See generally* Josephson & Pearce, To Whom Does the Government Lawyer Owe the Duty of Loyalty When Clients Are in Conflict?, 29 How. L.J. 539 (1986); Lawry, Who *Is* the Client of the Federal Government Lawyer? An Analysis of the Wrong Question, 37 Fed. B.J. 61 (1978).

11. Model Rules of Professional Conduct Rule 1.13, Official Comment (defining precisely the identity of the client is "more difficult" in government context; although sometimes client may be specific agency, "it is generally the government as a whole"). *See also* Restatement (Third) of the Law Governing Lawyers (Proposed Final Draft No. 1, 1997) §124 cmt. e ("As a general proposition, the officer or body who is empowered to assert or forego a claim or defense is entitled to assert or forego the privilege for communications relating to the claim or defense.").

12. Will v. Michigan Dept. of State Police, 491 U.S. 58, 71 (1989) (suit against state officer in official capacity "is not a suit against the official but rather is a suit against the official's office" and is "no different from a suit against the State itself").

for governmental entities depends on defining a group of people whose communications with counsel merit protection, and courts often draw upon the corporate analogy in establishing the boundaries of the privilege for governmental clients.[13] In *Upjohn Co. v. United States*,[14] the Supreme Court held that the representatives need not be members of the corporate "control group" and that the privilege extends to confidential communications by lower-level corporate employees, provided that they relate to the employee's duties and are made for purposes of securing legal advice for the corporation.[15] Many courts have held that the *Upjohn* standard applies as well to governmental entities.[16]

Rationale   Recognition of the attorney-client privilege for governmental entities encourages more open communication between governmental officials and their lawyers, thereby enhancing the quality of governmental decisionmaking.[17] Denial of a privilege would put public entities at an unfair disadvantage in both criminal prosecutions and civil litigation. Claimants against the government are often asserting private rather than public interests, and the government is entitled to contest such claims in good faith and defend the public treasury. Even where a private litigant asserts a public legal right, the scope of such right may be subject to legitimate factual or legal dispute.

More narrow privilege   However, there are significant distinctions between public and private entities that may warrant a more narrow scope of privilege for governmental clients.[18] Governmental operations are subject to greater public scrutiny and are regulated by "sunshine laws," open meetings requirements, and public records laws. Governments have duties to the public and responsibilities to advance the cause of justice that are significantly different from those of a private litigant.[19] A lawyer for a

---

13. United States v. AT&T Co., 86 F.R.D. 603, 619-621 (D.D.C. 1979) (drawing parallel with corporate privilege).

14. 449 U.S. 383 (1981).

15. For a discussion of the privilege for corporate clients, *see* §5.16, *supra*.

16. *See, e.g.,* Deuterium Corp. v. United States, 19 Cl. Ct. 697, 699 (1990) (applying "same reasoning" as in *Upjohn* to "Government employees at all levels").

17. Murphy v. TVA, 571 F. Supp. 502, 506 (D.D.C. 1983) (attorney-client privilege helps improve quality of agency decisionmaking "by safeguarding the free flow of information").

18. In re Witness Before Special Grand Jury 2000-2, 288 F.3d 289, 293 (7th Cir. 2002) (in federal criminal investigation into corruption of state officeholder, no attorney-client privilege existed between state officeholder and state government lawyer; government lawyers have different responsibilities and obligations to state and public than do members of private bar). *See also* ABA Model Rules of Professional Conduct Rule 1.13, Official Comment (1983) ("[W]hen the client is a governmental organization, a different balance may be appropriate between maintaining confidentiality and assuring that the wrongful official act is prevented or rectified, for public business is involved.").

19. *See* Berger v. United States, 295 U.S. 78, 88 (1935) (United States Attorney is representative "not of an ordinary party to a controversy, but of a sovereignty" and interest of prosecution "is not that it shall win a case, but that justice shall be done"); Model Code of Professional Responsibility EC 7-13 (1980) (duty of public prosecutor is to "seek justice, not merely to convict"); Model Code of Professional Responsibility EC 7-14 (1980) (duty of government in civil case is to "seek justice" and avoid unfair settlements or results).

public entity has ethical responsibilities to disclose evidence and report wrongdoing that go beyond the obligations of attorneys for private parties.[20] In other contexts, courts have held that the interests of the public should be considered in deciding the proper scope of an evidentiary privilege.[21]

Partly for the above reasons, some recent decisions have denied the governmental attorney-client privilege entirely where the communication was deemed relevant to an investigation by a federal grand jury.[22] However, courts should not narrow the privilege so severely that public officials are deterred from seeking guidance from government lawyers when facing legitimate legal uncertainties or force them necessarily to retain private counsel in order to obtain confidential advice.[23]

§5.19   Client Identity; Fee Arrangements

The general rule is that the attorney-client privilege does not shield the identity of the client.[1] Under the traditional view, a client's identity is not covered by the privilege because it is not a confidential communication made to facilitate the rendition of legal services, but rather a preliminary matter bearing on the formation and existence of the attorney-client relationship. Knowledge of the client's identity is more a matter of interpersonal and business necessity than a fact critical to the giving of legal advice.

In most instances the client does not intend her identity to be confidential. A lawyer commonly acts as the client's spokesperson, and visits to a lawyer's office are usually not made surreptitiously. Moreover, many types of legal representation require disclosure of the client's

---

20. *See, e.g.,* Brady v. Maryland, 373 U.S. 83, 87 (1963) (prosecutor has constitutional obligation to disclose exculpatory evidence to defendant).

21. United States v. Arthur Young & Co., 465 U.S. 805, 817 (1984) (refusing to extend work product privilege to public accountants, because they have "a public responsibility transcending any employment relationship with the client").

22. In re A Witness Before Special Grand Jury, 288 F.3d 289 (2002) (declining to recognize governmental attorney-client privilege in grand jury proceedings); In re Lindsey, 148 F.3d 1100 (D.C. Cir. 1998) (when government attorneys learn of information related to criminal misconduct even from their clients, they may not rely on the governmental attorney-client privilege to shield such information from disclosure to a grand jury); In re Grand Jury Subpoena Duces Tecum, 112 F.3d 910 (8th Cir. 1997) (White House counsel not entitled to assert governmental attorney-client privilege as basis for withholding documents from a federal grand jury; government's need for confidentiality is subordinate to needs of criminal justice process).

23. In re Grand Jury Investigation, 399 F.3d 527 (2d Cir. 2005) (in investigation of state executive officials, federal grand jury subpoenaed testimony by chief legal counsel in governor's office; privilege applies in grand jury proceeding; government attorney need not disclose confidential communication unless agency representative consents to waiver; protections provided by privilege ultimately promote public interest, even when they "impede the search for truth in a particular criminal investigation").

§5.19   1. In re Shargel, 742 F.2d 61, 62-64 (2d Cir. 1984) (disclosure of identity of client stands "on a footing different from communications intended by the client to explain a problem to a lawyer in order to obtain legal advice").

identity. In litigation, for example, parties are entitled to know their opponents, and the client's identity normally must be stated in the pleadings.[2]

Client's intent   There are cases, however, where a client wants to have her identity kept confidential and reasonably claims that the identifying information she gave to her lawyer is itself a confidential communication made to help obtain legal services.[3] The client's interests or wishes cannot be controlling, and the privilege should be recognized only where justified by its underlying policies.[4] Courts are understandably suspicious of the motives of a client who retains a lawyer to act on her behalf under a cloak of anonymity, and in some cases a claim of privilege for a client's identity can be defeated by showing that the attorney's services were employed to assist the client in committing a crime or fraud.[5]

Three lines of cases   Courts have recognized three exceptions to the general rule that a client's identity is not within the attorney-client privilege—the legal advice exception, the last link exception, and the confidential communications exception, although the modern trend is toward recognition only of the third.

All of these exceptions are derived from the seminal decision of the Ninth Circuit in *Baird v. Koerner.*[6] Baird, a tax attorney, was retained to give advice to accountants and attorneys representing unidentified taxpayers who had probable tax liabilities. To put the taxpayers in a more favorable position, Baird transmitted to the IRS a cashier's check for a substantial amount on the taxpayers' behalf. In a summons enforcement proceeding, the IRS sought to compel Baird to reveal the "identity and addresses of each and every person" who employed Baird in connection with his transmittal of the check to the IRS. The court held the identity of such persons to be within the attorney-client privilege.

Three lines of cases have evolved from *Baird,* each relying on different language of the opinion. Since *Baird* says identity is privileged if the circumstances are such that the name of the client is important to show "an acknowledgment of guilt" of the offenses "on account of which the attorney was employed," some courts read the opinion to establish a legal advice exception whereby identity is privileged if there

---

2. *But see* Southern Methodist Univ. Assn. of Women Law Students v. Wynne & Jaffe, 599 F.2d 707, 712-713 (5th Cir. 1979) (under special circumstances "where the issues involved are matters of sensitive and highly personal nature," courts allow parties to use fictitious names).

3. *See* Goode, Identity, Fees, and the Attorney-Client Privilege, 59 Geo. Wash. L. Rev. 307, 334 (1991) ("If a client reasonably believes that he must identify himself to a lawyer when he initiates the relationship, it is difficult to see how this would not be a communication made for the purpose of facilitating the rendition of legal services.").

4. *See generally* Glanzer & Taskier, Attorneys Before the Grand Jury: Assertion of the Attorney-Client Privilege to Protect a Client's Identity, 75 J. Crim. L. & Criminology 1070, 1071-1074 (1984).

5. *See* §5.22, *infra.*

6. 279 F.2d 623, 632-633 (9th Cir. 1960) (ensuing paragraphs of text quote these pages).

is a strong probability that disclosure would implicate the client in the very matter about which he consulted the lawyer.[7]

Other courts have interpreted *Baird* as establishing a last link exception, building on language in the case indicating that the government wanted to learn the identity of the client there as a "link that could form the chain of testimony" needed to convict for a federal crime.[8] Finally, virtually all courts read *Baird* as establishing a confidential communications exception, building on language in the case indicating that identity is protected if disclosure "conveys information" that would normally be confidential, in substance revealing the true confidences that the client shared with counsel.[9]

The trend of recent decisions is away from recognizing the first two exceptions, and several circuits have expressly rejected the last link exception,[10] noting that the fact that a client's identity may be incriminating is not a sufficient justification for making it privileged.[11] There is an emerging consensus that the "confidential communications" exception is the only exception consistent with the policies and purposes underlying the attorney-client privilege.[12]

The Ninth Circuit has explicitly held that the confidential communications exception is the only legitimate progeny of *Baird*, stating that "[a] careful reading of *Baird*, and close examination of subsequent cases, indicates that *Baird* applies only when it is shown that, because of exceptional circumstances, disclosure of the client's identity or the existence of a fee arrangement would reveal information that is tantamount to a confidential professional communication."[13] Those courts

Confidential communications exception

7. *See, e.g.,* In re Grand Jury Investigation No. 83-2-35 (Durant), 723 F.2d 447, 452-454 (6th Cir. 1983), *cert. denied,* 467 U.S. 1246.

8. *See e.g.,* In re Grand Jury Proceedings (Twist), 689 F.2d 1351, 1352-1353 (11th Cir. 1982) (recognizing narrow exception where "disclosure of the client's identity by his attorney would supply the last link in an existing chain of incriminating evidence likely to lead to the client's indictment").

9. *See, e.g.,* In re Grand Jury Matter No. 91-01386, 969 F.2d 995, 998 n.2 (11th Cir. 1992) (*Baird* based on fact that attorney "had already disclosed the motive for his client's retaining his legal services and the substance of his legal advice to him" and therefore disclosing the client's name would reveal "those confidential communications pertaining to the matter of representation").

10. *See, e.g.,* In re Grand Jury Investigation No. 83-2-35 (Durant), 723 F.2d 447, 453-454 (6th Cir. 1983) (although last link exception "may promote concepts of fundamental fairness against self-incrimination, these concepts are not proper considerations to invoke the attorney-client privilege"; focus of inquiry "is whether disclosure of the identity would adversely implicate the confidentiality of communications" and therefore court "rejects the last link exception"), *cert. denied,* 467 U.S. 1246.

11. In re Grand Jury Matter No. 91-01386, 969 F.2d 995, 998 (11th Cir. 1992) (merely because matter disclosed "may incriminate the client" does not make it privileged).

12. *See, e.g.,* Vingelli v. U.S. Drug Enforcement Agency, 992 F.2d 449, 453 (2d Cir. 1993) (noting agreement of circuits on "confidential communications" exception). *But see* In re Grand Jury Subpoena, 204 F.3d 516 (4th Cir. 2000) (Court "does not recognize an exception that protects the client's identity because the client has authorized the disclosure of information that he could have kept confidential").

13. Tornay v. United States, 840 F.2d 1424, 1428 (9th Cir. 1988). *See also* In re Osterhoudt, 722 F.2d 591, 593 (9th Cir. 1983) (privilege recognized in *Baird* only because "disclosure of the identity of the client was in substance a disclosure of the confidential communication in the professional relationship between the client and the attorney").

that continue to recognize the "legal advice" and "last link" exceptions have generally reformulated them to apply only where revelation of the client's identity or related information would result in disclosure of a confidential communication.[14]

Five recurring patterns   There are five recurring situations where lawyers have claimed the identity of their client is protected: (1) The attorney was hired to make restitution or other payment for the client; (2) the attorney was hired as an intermediary to report illegal or improper conduct by a third person; (3) the attorney was hired by an undisclosed person to represent another in a criminal case; (4) the government seeks to learn the identity of clients paying more than $10,000 cash for legal services, by use of a cash reporting form; (5) the attorney is asked to name clients to whom he gave particular legal advice.

In the first two situations, the critical question is whether an attorney hired to transmit payment or report information on behalf of an anonymous client is providing professional legal services.[15] If the attorney is acting merely as a messenger or transmitting agent, no privilege arises.[16] In *Baird*, the court relied on the fact that Baird was a tax lawyer who was consulted regarding "defenses and steps to be taken to place the undisclosed taxpayers in the most favorable position in the event criminal charges were to be brought against them by the Internal Revenue Service."[17] Nonetheless, commentators have questioned whether mailing a check on behalf of a client constitutes professional legal services or the lease of a privilege.[18] If the transmitting of restitution or information on behalf of a client is found to qualify as professional legal services, the privilege should apply if disclosure of the client's identity would reveal the confidential lawyer-client communications.[19]

Identity of fee payer   In the third situation, where the prosecutor seeks to learn the identity of the person paying the defendant's legal fees, it must first be

---

14. *See, e.g.,* In re Grand Jury Subpoenas, 906 F.2d 1485, 1492 (10th Cir. 1990) (applying legal advice exception, but requiring that advice sought "must have concerned the case then under investigation and disclosure of the client's identity would now be, in substance, the disclosure of a confidential communication by the client, such as establishing the identity of the client as the perpetrator of the alleged crime at issue").

15. *See generally* §5.11, *supra.*

16. *See* Vingelli v. United States Drug Enforcement Agency, 992 F.2d 449, 454 (2d Cir. 1993) (it is "not fitting for lawyers to serve as conduits of information or money essential to the success of a criminal scheme" and "proper administration of criminal justice will be advanced by the bar becoming aware that its members may not provide clients with a safe haven from disclosure of such service"); Hughes v. Meade, 453 S.W.2d 538, 542 (Ky. Ct. App. 1970) (attorney-client privilege inapplicable to identity of client who hired attorney to return a stolen typewriter).

17. *Baird,* 279 F.2d at 626.

18. *See* Goode, *supra* note 3, at 339 (Baird was not "exercising any legal skills when he procured a cashier's check for them and mailed it to the IRS"; knowing that "friends, bankers, or other agents could be forced to disclose their identity," the taxpayers "chose to employ a lawyer instead").

19. *See* In re Kozlov, 79 N.J. 232, 398 A.2d 882, 887 (1979) (privilege applies where lawyer reports misconduct on behalf of anonymous client); In re Kaplan, 8 N.Y.2d 214, 168 N.E.2d 660, 661 (1960) (privilege held to protect identity of client who confided in his lawyer to have lawyer disclose certain wrongdoings to public officials).

determined whether the fee payer is also a client of the attorney. If the fee payer is not a client, most courts hold that no privileged relationship exists, and therefore disclosure of his identity can be compelled.[20] A fee payer does not become a client merely by paying the legal fees of another.[21] Even where the fee payer is a current or former client, most courts hold that the privilege does not shield his identity as the fee payer[22] except where disclosure would reveal confidential communications made for the purpose of facilitating legal services to the fee payer.[23] Where payment of legal fees is shown to be an element of a criminal conspiracy, some courts have required disclosure of the identity of the fee payer on the theory that such payment falls within the ongoing or future crime-fraud exception to the attorney-client privilege.[24]

In the fourth situation, where the government seeks to learn the identity of clients paying more than $10,000 cash for legal services, the privilege claim is weak and has been rejected. Congress enacted 26 U.S.C. §6050I, which requires disclosure to the IRS of the identity of persons paying more than $10,000 in cash for goods or services. Congress rejected lobbying efforts to exempt the legal profession from the reporting requirement.[25] The courts have upheld this disclosure obligation against claims that it invades the attorney-client privilege.[26]

---

20. In re Grand Jury Subpoena for Attorney Representing Criminal Defendant Reyes-Requena, 913 F.2d 1118, 1123 (5th Cir. 1990) (privilege denied where no contention made that fee payer was a current or former client), *cert. denied,* 111 S. Ct. 1581.

21. *See* §5.9, *supra.*

22. Vingelli v. United States Drug Enforcement Agency, 992 F.2d 449, 453 (2d Cir. 1993) (where unidentified client hired Arizona attorney to transmit fee to Vermont attorney representing a drug defendant, identity of client not privileged because it would reveal neither a confidential communication nor client's motive for paying fee; client's concern that he will be "tarnished by guilt by association" insufficient to prevent disclosure); In re Grand Jury Subpoenas, 803 F.2d 493, 498 (9th Cir. 1986) (privilege denied even though fee payer was a "long-time client," because he was not seeking legal representation in the instant case).

23. In re Subpoenaed Grand Jury Witness, 171 F.3d 511, 514, (7th Cir. 1999) (identity of person who paid attorney's legal fees to represent certain clients was privileged; information would identify client as potentially involved in targeted criminal activity giving rise to motive to pay legal bills for some other clients); Ralls v. United States, 52 F.3d 223, 226 (9th Cir. 1995) (fee payer was previous client in same matter and his identity and fee arrangements were "intertwined" with confidential communications made for purpose of obtaining legal advice for fee payer himself).

24. In re Grand Jury Proceedings (Pavlick), 680 F.2d 1026, 1029 (5th Cir. 1982) (where government makes prima facie showing that agreement to furnish legal assistance was part of a conspiracy, crime-fraud exception applies "to deny a privilege to the identity of him who foots the bill—and this even though he be a client of the attorney and the attorney unaware of the improper arrangement").

25. *See* United States v. Goldberger & Dubin, P.C., 935 F.2d 501, 506 (2d Cir. 1991).

26. United States v. Blackman, 72 F.3d 1418, 1424-1426 (9th Cir. 1995) (absent extraordinary circumstances, §6050I reporting requirement does not violate attorney-client privilege; "there is no reason to grant law firms a potential monopoly on money laundering simply because their services are personal and confidential"). *But see* United States v. Sindel, 53 F.3d 874, 876 (8th Cir. 1995) (privilege prevails over reporting requirement where disclosure of client identity would reveal substance of confidential communication).

To whom advice given

In the fifth situation, where the lawyer is asked to identify a client to whom he gave certain advice, it seems clear that giving the name would in substance uncover a confidence thereby violating the *Baird* doctrine. Thus where the government sought the identity of clients investing in a tax shelter after learning that a law firm advised such clients that legal fees for the arrangement were deductible, the court held that their identities were privileged because disclosure "would provide all there is to know about a confidential communication between the taxpayer-client and the attorney."[27] And in a case where the NLRB learned that a law firm hired a detective to investigate a union organizer, the court held that the client's identity was protected (assuming the lawyer was providing professional legal services) since so much of the communication had been learned that disclosing the name would amount to disclosure of a confidential communication.[28]

Fee arrangements

The fee arrangements between the client and attorney are also generally outside the attorney-client privilege.[29] Courts have ordered attorneys to divulge the fee agreement,[30] the identity of the fee payer,[31] the amounts billed to the client,[32] the dates or duration of consultation,[33] records of money received from the client,[34] and the form or manner of payment,[35] even where such information is incriminating to the client.[36] The bank records or other financial records of the attorney are also subject to disclosure.[37]

27. United States v. Liebman, 742 F.2d 807, 809-810 (3d Cir. 1984).

28. NLRB v. Harvey, 349 F.2d 900, 905 (4th Cir. 1965) (remanding for further evidence on the nature of attorney's services). *Cf.* Note, Public Assault on the Attorney-Client Privilege: Ramifications of Baltes v. Does, 3 Geo. J. Legal Ethics 351 (1989) (approving Florida trial court ruling that attorney-client privilege prevented disclosure of identity of client who admitted to attorney that he was involved in hit-and-run auto accident and asked attorney to negotiate plea bargain with prosecutor).

29. In re Grand Jury Subpoenas, 906 F.2d 1485, 1492 (10th Cir. 1990) (privilege does not apply to "the amount of the fees, the manner of payment, the date of payment, the name of any others partially responsible for payment of the fee, and whether any part of the fee came from the client or his family").

30. In re Shargel, 742 F.2d 61, 65 (2d Cir. 1984).

31. Vingelli v. United States Drug Enforcement Agency, 992 F.2d 449, 453 (2d Cir. 1993) (even where fee transmitted by an out-of-state lawyer acting on behalf of fee-payer client, identity of fee payer required to be disclosed).

32. Clarke v. American Commerce Natl. Bank, 974 F.2d 127, 130 (9th Cir. 1992) (attorney billing statement which identified client and the general nature of services performed held not to be privileged).

33. Condon v. Petacque, 90 F.R.D. 53, 54 (N.D. Ill. 1981) (dates on which services performed are not privileged).

34. In re Witnesses Before the Special March 1980 Grand Jury, 729 F.2d 489, 494-495 (7th Cir. 1984).

35. In re Two Grand Jury Subpoenas Duces Tecum Dated August 21, 1985, 793 F.2d 69, 71-72 (2d Cir. 1986).

36. In re Grand Jury Matter No. 91-01386, 969 F.2d 995, 999 (11th Cir. 1992) (privilege does not prevent disclosure of identity of client who paid fee with counterfeit currency); In re Grand Jury Investigation No. 83-2-35 (Durant), 723 F.2d 447, 453-454 (6th Cir. 1983) (no privilege as to identity of client who paid fee with stolen check), *cert. denied*, 467 U.S. 1246.

37. Gannet v. First Natl. State Bank, 546 F.2d 1072, 1076 (3d Cir. 1976) (attorney-client privilege does not apply to bank records "merely because they derive from

The general rule that fee arrangements are outside the privilege is subject to the same exceptions applicable to client identity. Thus fee information is protected where disclosure of retainer agreements, time records, billing documents, and similar matters would reveal confidential attorney-client communications.[38] Courts may require fee documents to be produced for in camera inspection before ordering disclosure to assure that no privileged material is contained therein.[39]

Fact of consultation

The fact that the client consulted an attorney, and the identity of the attorney, are matters generally outside the privilege[40] although the jury is not permitted to draw an adverse inference of guilt from the fact of consultation.[41] While inquiry is usually allowed into the general nature of the attorney's employment,[42] any details on the nature of the services provided or the client's specific motive for seeking legal advice are privileged, at least if they would tend to reveal client confidences.[43]

Client's whereabouts

Most decisions hold that the privilege does not protect the attorney's knowledge of the whereabouts of the client[44] except where such information is closely intertwined with the purpose of the client in seeking legal assistance[45] or where nondisclosure is necessary to protect the safety or other legitimate interests of the client or a third

---

transactions involving an attorney's trust account"; otherwise attorneys would have "discretion to insulate certain transactions from investigation by employing their trust accounts"), *cert. denied*, 431 U.S. 954.

38. *See, e.g.,* In re Grand Jury Subpoenas, 906 F.2d 1485, 1492 (10th Cir. 1990) (no disclosure required where revealing "the actual fee contracts has the potential for revealing confidential information along with unprotected fee information").

39. Clarke v. American Commerce Natl. Bank, 974 F.2d 127, 129 (9th Cir. 1992) (district court may conduct line-by-line in camera inspection of billing statement to determine whether privilege applies).

40. Howell v. Jones, 516 F.2d 53, 58 (5th Cir. 1975) (client can be required to identify attorney he consulted; fact of consultation not privileged), *cert. denied*, 424 U.S. 916.

41. *See* United States v. Liddy, 509 F.2d 428, 442-445 (D.C. Cir. 1974) (error to instruct jury that an inference could be drawn regarding defendant's guilty knowledge from the fact that he sought legal counsel soon after the crime for which he was later charged), *cert. denied*, 420 U.S. 911.

42. Clarke v. American Commerce Natl. Bank, 974 F.2d 127, 130 (9th Cir. 1992) (attorney billing statement that identified client and the general nature of services performed but did not reveal specific research or litigation strategy held not to be privileged).

43. *See* In re Grand Jury Witness, 695 F.2d 359, 361-362 (9th Cir. 1982) (correspondence revealing the client's "motivation" or "litigation strategy" ought to be protected, as should "bills, ledgers, statements, time records and the like which also reveal the nature of the services provided, such as researching particular areas of law").

44. Litton Indus. v. Lehman Bros. Kuhn Loeb, 130 F.R.D. 25, 26 (S.D.N.Y. 1990) (no privilege where client's address not related to legal advice requested); Burden v. Church of Scientology, 526 F. Supp. 44, 45-46 (M.D. Fla. 1981) (requiring lawyer to disclose client's whereabouts so that service of process could be made; applying Florida law); Dike v. Dike, 75 Wash. 2d 1, 448 P.2d 490, 497-498 (1968) (disclosure required when client disappeared with children in alleged violation of custody decree). *See generally* Przypyszny, Asserting the Attorney-Client Privilege: Client Identity, Fee Information, Whereabouts, and Documents, 3 Geo. J. Legal Ethics 113, 120-121 (1989).

45. *See* In re Grand Jury Subpoena (Stolar), 397 F. Supp. 520, 523-524 (S.D.N.Y. 1975) (where client sought legal advice regarding his obligation to be interviewed by FBI, attorney not required to disclose client's address and phone number).

person.[46] Occasionally the crime-fraud exception is held applicable to communications from a fugitive client as to his whereabouts.[47]

§5.20   Lawyer's Impressions About Client

Occasionally a lawyer is called to testify on the mental competency of his client, and the question is whether the lawyer may invoke his client's privilege to avoid answering questions on this general subject since the answers necessarily convey impressions the attorney gleans from the demeanor and statements of the client. Usually the underlying issue is competency to stand trial on criminal charges, and the matter is typically raised before trial begins, but it can arise afterwards on post-verdict challenge.

It is generally agreed that the privilege does not cover observations made by the lawyer, as distinguished from confidential statements by the client.[1] Unfortunately, however, this insight does not resolve the problem because the attorney's impressions of the competency of the client are usually very much tied up in his impressions of what the client has said.[2]

Client competency   Courts generally allow a lawyer to testify on client competency to the extent that such testimony can be given without revealing the actual substance of what the client has said.[3] Thus attorneys have been allowed to give testimony on such matters as the client's responsiveness, cooperativeness, and reasoning ability, which have been aptly called "objectively observable particularizations of the client's demeanor and attitude."[4]

Some courts, however, disallow attorney testimony on client competency on the theory that such observations and conclusions are necessarily derived from privileged communications.[5] It is questionable whether a lawyer could give a full or understandable account of client

46. Taylor v. Taylor, 45 Ill. App. 3d 352, 359 N.E.2d 820, 824 (1977) (attorney need not disclose whereabouts of wife who feared injury from husband).

47. In re Grand Jury Proceedings (Doe), 602 F. Supp. 603, 608-609 (D.R.I. 1985) (lawyer's services were in furtherance of a criminal conspiracy).

§5.20   1. See §5.12, supra. See also United States v. Kendrick, 331 F.2d 110, 114 (4th Cir. 1964) ("physical characteristics of the client, such as his complexion, his demeanor, his bearing, his sobriety and his dress," are not privileged, for such matters "are observable by anyone who talked with the client").

2. See generally Cohen, The Attorney-Client Privilege, Ethical Rules and the Impaired Criminal Defendant, 52 U. Miami L. Rev. 529 (1998); Pizzi, Competency to Stand Trial in Federal Courts: Conceptual and Constitutional Problems, 45 U. Chi. L. Rev. 21, 57-64 (1977).

3. See, e.g., Darrow v. Gunn, 594 F.2d 767, 774 (9th Cir. 1979) (in habeas corpus proceeding, no error found in allowing petitioner's former attorney to testify to observations bearing on client's competency), cert. denied, 444 U.S. 849.

4. United States v. Kendrick, 331 F.2d 110, 114 (4th Cir. 1964) (in proceeding on motion to vacate sentence because of incompetency, attorney permitted to testify that client "was responsive, readily supplied the attorney with his version of the facts and the names of other people involved, was logical in his conversation and his reasoning, and appeared to know and understand everything that went on before and during the trial").

5. Gunther v. United States, 230 F.2d 222, 223-224 (D.C. Cir. 1956) (lawyer should not have been allowed to testify that client was competent to stand trial, for necessarily

competency without disclosing at least part of what the client has said, and doubtful that any party who wants to challenge such an account could do so effectively without asking the lawyer to disclose at least some matters of substance.[6]

In cases where a client attacks a conviction claiming he was not competent to stand trial, testimony by the lawyer on the competency of the client should be permitted. Such a claim by the client necessarily challenges the adequacy of his legal representation, and an exception to the attorney-client privilege is recognized for a communication relevant to a claim of breach of duty by the lawyer to his client.[7]

§5.21   Evidence Delivered to Lawyer

An attorney may not receive physical evidence from a client or a third party for the purpose of unlawfully concealing or destroying it.[1] Moreover, the attorney cannot advise the client or another to destroy evidence without risking criminal liability as an accessory.[2]

---

he may "also be asked for the factual data upon which he premised his opinion," which would open up "the entire relationship between the accused and his counsel," violating both the privilege and defendant's right to counsel).

6. *See* Bishop v. Superior Court, 150 Ariz. 404, 724 P.2d 23, 29 (1986) (allowing attorney to testify at competency hearing; still, "it defies reality to pretend that the lawyer has formed opinions on competency without relying upon discussions" with client; disclosure of privileged matter on cross raises concern). *See generally* Pizzi, Competency to Stand Trial in Federal Courts: Conceptual and Constitutional Problems, 45 U. Chi. L. Rev. 21, 60 (1977) (if attorney's opinion is sought because he is "in the best position to judge," whether client's mental disabilities present problem in formulating defense, still it is "inescapable" that these opinions rest on conversations that fall within the privilege).

7. *See* §5.23, *infra.*

§5.21   1. ABA Model Rules of Professional Conduct Rule 3.4 (lawyer shall not "unlawfully obstruct another party's access to evidence or unlawfully alter, destroy or conceal a document or other material having potential evidentiary value," and lawyer "shall not counsel or assist another person to do any such act"). *See* United States v. Kellington, 139 F.3d 909 (9th Cir. 1998) (affirming felony conviction of lawyer for burning envelope at request of client; "burning envelopes with contents unknown is not taught in American law schools."); In re Ryder, 263 F. Supp. 360, 369-370 (E.D. Va. 1967) (lawyer suspended from law practice for 18 months for transferring a sawed-off shotgun and proceeds of a bank robbery to his own safe deposit box; court held such conduct not to be within the privilege and found that the lawyer "allowed the office of attorney to be used in violation of law"), *aff'd*, 381 F.2d 713, 777 (4th Cir. 1967). *See generally* Note, Legal Ethics and the Destruction of Evidence, 88 Yale L.J. 1665, 1669-1673 (1979) (most jurisdictions have laws prohibiting the destruction of evidence if done with intent to prevent its production in legal proceeding).

2. Clark v. State, 159 Tex. Crim. 187, 261 S.W.2d 339, 346-347 (1953) (client confessed to murder in telephone conversation with attorney; attorney advised client to "get rid of the weapon"; court holds such advice was unprivileged because it was unlawful, noting that "[o]ne who knowing that an offense has been committed conceals the offender or aids him to evade arrest or trial becomes an accessory"; fact "that the aider may be a member of the bar and the attorney for the offender will not prevent his becoming an accessory"), *cert. denied*, 346 U.S. 855. *Cf.* United States v. Brashier, 548 F.2d 1315, 1325 (9th Cir. 1976) (evidence of document destruction admissible to show consciousness of guilt or liability), *cert. denied*, 429 U.S. 1111.

If an attorney does receive physical evidence from a client or a third party that is either contraband or an instrumentality or fruit of a crime, the prevailing view is that the attorney has an ethical obligation to turn it over to the prosecution in an unaltered form, although he may retain it for a reasonable period of time for purposes of examination and testing.[3] Many courts go further and require a defense attorney to turn over other physical evidence as well,[4] although generally not documentary evidence such as incriminating financial records.[5] If the attorney does not voluntarily transfer the evidence to the prosecutor, its production can be compelled.[6]

Disclosing source of evidence

If the evidence is received from a third person, the attorney is required to disclose the source.[7] However, if the evidence is received from the client, it is generally held that the source of the evidence is protected by the attorney-client privilege.[8] The prosecutor can introduce the evidence at trial if it can be independently authenticated or linked to the defendant, but authenticating testimony cannot be

3. The leading case is State ex rel. Sowers v. Olwell, 394 P.2d 681, 684-685 (Wash. 1964) (defense attorney after examining physical evidence received from client should deliver it to the prosecution).

4. State v. Carlin, 7 Kan. App. 2d 219, 640 P.2d 324 (1982) (tape recordings of defendant's threats); Morrell v. State, 575 P.2d 1200, 1209 (Alaska 1978) (lawyer had duty to turn over "kidnapping plan" written by defendant and given to attorney by third party; court refused to draw distinction between physical evidence which is "mere evidence" of a client's crime and "a fruit or instrumentality of the crime").

5. See generally Reitz, Clients, Lawyers and the Fifth Amendment: The Need for a Protected Privilege, 41 Duke L.J. 572, 605-608 (1991) (acknowledging that courts generally do not apply *Olwell* doctrine to documentary evidence but criticizing that result as well as underlying theory of *Olwell*); Lefstein, Incriminating Physical Evidence, the Defense Attorney's Dilemma, and the Need for Rules, 64 N.C. L. Rev. 897, 916-918 (1986). Judicial reluctance to extend the *Olwell* doctrine to documentary evidence of the client is presumably based on the fact that documentary evidence usually demonstrates on its face the linkage with the client, whereas *Olwell* forbids disclosure that the physical evidence came from the client. Also documentary evidence is usually much more closely related to the giving of legal advice than is physical evidence.

6. See In re January 1976 Grand Jury, 534 F.2d 719, 728, 731 (7th Cir. 1976) (Tone, J., concurring) (money turned over to attorney by clients suspected of bank robbery may be subpoenaed from attorney; finding no reason "for shielding from judicial inquiry either the fruits of the robbery or the fact of the later criminal act of turning over the money to appellant").

7. Morrell v. State, 575 P.2d 1200, 1210 (Alaska 1978) (where evidence is received from a third person, attorney can be required to reveal the source).

8. State v. Olwell, 64 Wash. 2d 828, 394 P.2d 681, 685 (1964) (defense counsel, after examining physical evidence, should deliver it to the prosecution but should not reveal source of the evidence; by allowing prosecution to recover such evidence, "the public interest is served, and by refusing the prosecution an opportunity to disclose the source of the evidence, the client's privilege is preserved and a balance is reached between these conflicting interests"); State v. Green, 493 So. 2d 1178, 1182-1183 (La. 1986) (error to require attorney to disclose to jury that gun he turned over to prosecutor had come from his client). *But see* Hughes v. Meade, 453 S.W.2d 538, 541-542 (Ky. 1970) (lawyer was not performing professional legal services when hired to turn stolen property over to police; therefore attorney-client privilege did not protect identity of client).

compelled from the client or attorney.[9] Although this approach seems the fairest accommodation of the conflicting interests, it has been criticized as providing an improper means for the client to sever his connection with contraband or other incriminating evidence.[10]

If the attorney removes, conceals, or alters evidence after its location has been disclosed by the client, law enforcement efforts may be impeded because the evidence might eventually have been discovered if left undisturbed in its original location. Therefore, in such cases courts have held that the attorney can be required to disclose the location from which the evidence was taken even though this information may be incriminating to the client.[11]

Removing, concealing, altering evidence

In the leading case of *People v. Meredith,* the client told the attorney that a wallet seized from the murder victim could be found in an incinerator in the client's backyard. The attorney sent an investigator to retrieve the wallet and, after inspecting it, turned it over to the prosecutor. The California Supreme Court ruled that because the wallet had been removed from its original location the investigator could be required to disclose that it was found in the defendant's backyard despite the damaging nature of such testimony.[12]

In cases where evidence is merely observed by the attorney, courts generally hold that no disclosure is required.[13] The nature of the observations, the location of the observations, and the fact that the evidence was found through information supplied by the client are normally

Mere observations

---

9. United States v. Authement, 607 F.2d 1129, 1131-1132 (5th Cir. 1979) (attorney-client privilege not violated where prosecutor introduced brass knuckles, which defendant had turned over to his attorney and which were obtained from defendant's attorney by subpoena; jury was never told how the brass knuckles were obtained and they were authenticated by another police officer).

10. 2 Weinstein & Berger, Weinstein's Evidence ¶503(b)[03] at 503-554.

11. Clutchette v. Rushen, 770 F.2d 1469, 1472 (9th Cir. 1985) (fact that client disclosed location of incriminating receipts to attorney was privileged; however, once attorney retrieved them he was obligated to turn them over to the prosecution; applying California law), *cert. denied,* 475 U.S. 1088.

12. People v. Meredith, 175 Cal. Rptr. 612, 29 Cal. 3d 682, 631 P.2d 46, 54 (1981) (concluding that whenever defense counsel "removes or alters evidence," even to "examine or test it" privilege does not bar "revelation of the original location or condition of the evidence in question," but if defense counsel leaves evidence where he found it, "his observations derived from privileged communications are insulated from revelation").

13. *See* People v. Belge, 83 Misc. 2d 186, 372 N.Y.S.2d 798, 803 (1975) (attorney-client privilege applied to prevent disclosure of locations where bodies of two young women were buried because attorney found bodies only because of confidential communications from client who admitted murdering them; attorney indicted for violating public health law by failing to report bodies; privilege held to shield him from prosecution), *aff'd,* 50 A.D.2d 1088, 376 N.Y.S.2d 771. The entire case is recounted in Alibrandi & Armani, Privileged Information (1984). *See generally* Freedman, Where the Bodies Are Buried: The Adversary System and the Obligation of Confidentiality, 10 Crim. L. Bull. 979 (1974); Edwards, Hard Answers for Hard Questions: Dissenting in Part from Dean Freedman's Views on the Attorney-Client Privilege, 11 Crim. L. Bull. 478 (1975).

within the privilege, provided that the attorney does not move, conceal, or alter the evidence.[14]

§5.22 Crime-Fraud Exception

Although the attorney-client privilege shields a client's confidential statements to an attorney relating to past misconduct, statements seeking the services of the attorney with respect to ongoing or future crimes or frauds are not privileged.[1] The exception extends even to crimes of a relatively minor nature.[2] Substantial authority favors an even broader exception encompassing communications about ongoing or future conduct that is tortious, whether or not involving crime or fraud.[3]

Rationale   The rationale for this exception is that clients are not entitled to use lawyers to help them in pursuing unlawful or fraudulent objectives.[4] If the privilege were to cloak such activity, the result would be loss of public confidence and corruption of the profession. Moreover, when an attorney's services are knowingly used to further a crime or fraud, such activity hardly qualifies as "professional legal services," an essential element of the privilege.[5] If a client intends to use the attorney's services to violate legal obligations rather than comply with the law or vindicate legally arguable positions, there is no social interest in protecting confidentiality. The future crime-fraud exception thus marks the boundaries of proper advocacy and insures an appropriate

14. People v. Meredith, *supra,* at 53-54; State v. Douglass, 20 W. Va. 770, 783 (1882) (trial court erred in admitting an attorney's testimony as to the location of a pistol he had discovered as a result of privileged communication from client; "All that the said attorney knew about the pistol, or where it was to be found, he knew only from the communications which had been made to him by his client confidentially and professionally, as counsel in this case.").

§5.22   1. In re Antitrust Grand Jury, 805 F.2d 155, 162 (6th Cir. 1986) (reasons for privilege are "completely eviscerated when a client consults an attorney not for advice on past misconduct, but for legal assistance in carrying out a contemplated or ongoing crime or fraud"). *See also* Restatement (Third) of the Law Governing Lawyers (Proposed Final Draft, No. 1, 1996) §132 (privilege "does not apply to a communication occurring when a client consults a lawyer for the purpose of obtaining assistance in engaging in conduct or aiding a third person in engaging in conduct if the client, at the time of the communication, knows or reasonably should know that the conduct is a crime or fraud").

2. United States v. Friedman, 445 F.2d 1076, 1085-1086 (9th Cir. 1971) (crime-fraud exception applies to unlawful possession of grand jury transcript), *cert. denied sub nom.* Jacobs v. United States, 404 U.S. 958.

3. *See* Commodity Futures Trading Commn. v. Weintraub, 471 U.S. 343, 354 (1985) (citing authorities holding that privilege "does not shield the disclosure of communications relating to the planning or commission of ongoing fraud, crimes, and ordinary torts"); In re Sealed Case, 754 F.2d 395, 399 (D.C. Cir. 1985) (describing exception as applicable to "crime, fraud, or other misconduct").

4. *See* Clark v. United States, 289 U.S. 1, 15 (1933) (privilege "takes flight if the relation is abused," and client who consults attorney for advice that "will serve him in the commission of a fraud" has no protection and "must let the truth be told").

5. *See* §5.11, *supra.*

balance between the duty to a client and the broader interests of society.[6]

The determination whether the crime-fraud exception applies has been held to involve a two-part test:

> First, there must be a prima facie showing that the client was engaged in criminal or fraudulent conduct when he sought the advice of counsel, that he was planning such conduct when he sought the advice of counsel, or that he committed a crime or fraud subsequent to receiving the benefit of counsel's advice. Second, there must be a showing that the attorney's assistance was obtained in furtherance of the criminal or fraudulent activity or was closely related to it.[7]

Two-part test

The client must know or reasonably be expected to know that the conduct would be criminal or fraudulent,[8] although the attorney need not be aware of the client's unlawful purpose.[9] Nor is it necessary that the attorney actually assist the illegality in any way.[10] The exception does not apply if the client innocently inquires about a course of conduct she had no reason to know was unlawful.[11] Nor does it apply even if the client later engages in such conduct pursuant to counsel's

6. *See generally* Fried, Too High a Price for Truth: The Exception to the Attorney-Client Privilege for Contemplated Crimes and Frauds, 64 N.C. L. Rev. 443 (1986); Silbert, The Crime-Fraud Exception to the Attorney-Client Privilege and Work Product Doctrine, the Lawyer's Obligations of Disclosure, and the Lawyer's Response to Accusation of Wrongful Conduct, 23 Am. Crim. L. Rev. 351 (1986).

7. In re Grand Jury Investigation (Schroeder), 842 F.2d 1223, 1226 (11th Cir. 1987). *See also* United States v. Roe, 68 F.3d 38, 39 (2d Cir. 1995) (not sufficient that communication may be "relevant evidence" of a crime but must actually be "in furtherance" of it).

8. *See* Chaudhry v. Gallerizzo, 174 F.3d 394, 403404 (4th Cir. 1999) (party asserting the crime-fraud exception must make a prima facie showing that (1) client was engaged in or planning criminal or fraudulent scheme when he sought advice of counsel to further the scheme and (2) documents containing privileged materials bear close relationship to client's existing or future scheme to commit crime or fraud), *cert. denied*, 120 S. Ct. 215 (1999); Unlimited, Inc. v. Video Shack, Inc., 661 F. Supp. 1482, 1487 (N.D. Ill. 1987) (no privilege where there was sufficient evidence to support conclusion that client "either knew or recklessly disregarded that his wiretapping activities were illegal").

9. In re Grand Jury Investigation, 445 F.3d 266, 275-276 (3d Cir. 2006) (exception applied to conversations between attorney and client where client could have been engaged in obstruction of justice, and attorney discussed material subject to government subpoena, which let client destroy evidence; did not matter whether attorney knew client's intent); United States v. Chen, 99 F.3d 1495, 1503-1504 (9th Cir. 1996) (exception applies even where lawyer "in the dark" about client's illegal purpose).

10. In re Grand Jury Proceedings, 87 F.3d 377, 381 (9th Cir. 1996) (exception applies even if attorney takes no affirmative step that furthers crime; communication can be "in furtherance" even if it turns out not to help or even hinders client's completion of a crime).

11. United States v. Doe, 429 F.3d 450, 453, 454 (3d Cir. 2005) (privilege is not lost if client innocently proposes course of conduct and is advised by counsel that it is illegal); In re Grand Jury Proceedings, 87 F.3d 377, 381 (9th Cir. 1996) (not enough for government to show "sneaking suspicion" that client was intending to engage in crime when consulting attorney, because such a low threshold could discourage would-be clients from consulting attorney about legitimate legal dilemmas).

erroneous advice that it was lawful.[12] While some courts require that the unlawful intent be formulated at the time the client solicits the lawyer's advice,[13] other courts focus on the client's intent when consultation is concluded.[14]

Under the better view, the exception applies to communications about a future crime or fraud that never occurs, provided the client knew of the illegality and intended to use the attorney's advice or services in connection with the crime or fraud.[15] The crime or fraud need not be one committed by the client to be within the exception.[16] The exception applies even in a proceeding other than one arising out of the particular crime or fraud that was the subject of the communication.[17]

Examples   The future crime-fraud exception applies to plans to assert a false claim,[18] commit fraud against a public agency,[19] kill a witness,[20] bribe a juror,[21] fabricate evidence or commit perjury,[22] conceal or destroy evidence,[23] or file fraudulent documents.[24]

12. *See* ACN, proposed-but-rejected FRE 503(d)(1) (requiring that client "knew or reasonably should have known of the criminal or fraudulent nature of the act is designed to protect the client who is erroneously advised" that proposed action is legal).

13. *See, e.g.,* In re Sealed Case, 754 F.2d 395, 399 (D.C. Cir. 1985) (crime-fraud exception applies if client "was engaged in or planning a criminal or fraudulent scheme when it sought the advice of counsel to further the scheme").

14. United States v. Ballard, 779 F.2d 287, 292 (5th Cir. 1986) (client filed fraudulent bankruptcy petition through services of second attorney after first attorney told him to list recently sold real property; communications between client and first attorney were not privileged), *cert. denied,* 475 U.S. 1109.

15. In re Grand Jury Proceedings, 87 F.3d 377, 381 (9th Cir. 1996) (crime-fraud exception does not require completed crime). *Contra* In re Sealed Case, 107 F.3d 46, 49 (D.C. Cir. 1997) (client must have carried out crime or fraud).

16. *See* Matter of Doe, 551 F.2d 899, 900-902 (2d Cir. 1977) (client informed attorney of scheme by others to bribe a juror; attorney advised client to have nothing to do with it; communications held not privileged because future crime potentially benefiting client and to which he might be a participant falls within the crime-fraud exception). *See also* proposed-but-rejected FRE 503(d)(1) (exception applies where services of lawyer were "sought or obtained to enable or aid *anyone* to commit" a crime or fraud) (emphasis added).

17. In re Berkley & Co., Inc., 629 F.2d 548, 554-555 (8th Cir. 1980) (exception also applies where communication is sought in proceeding unrelated to subject of crime or fraud).

18. Whetstone v. Olson, 46 Wash. App. 308, 732 P.2d 159, 162 (1986) (fabrication of sexual harassment claim).

19. Natta v. Zletz, 418 F.2d 633, 636 (7th Cir. 1969) (fraud on patent office).

20. United States v. Lentz, 524 F.3d 501, 518-519 (4th Cir. 2008) (defendant's communications in phone call to attorney from prison were not privileged; they sought advice about murder-for-hire scheme to kill witnesses, hence fit crime/fraud exception).

21. Matter of Doe, 551 F.2d 899, 902 (2d Cir. 1977).

22. United States v. Gordon-Nikkar, 518 F.2d 972, 975 (5th Cir. 1975) (plan to commit perjury).

23. *See* United States v. Davis, 1 F.3d 606, 609 (7th Cir. 1993) (fraudulent noncompliance with grand jury subpoena); United States v. Sutton, 732 F.2d 1483, 1494 (10th Cir. 1984) (privilege does not apply to client's statement that he intended to destroy records sought by government), *cert. denied,* 469 U.S. 1157.

24. United States v. Ballard, 779 F.2d 287, 291-293 (5th Cir. 1986) (defendant was advised by his first attorney of need to disclose certain transfers in bankruptcy proceeding; defendant then sought services of a second lawyer who filed petition without making required disclosures), *cert. denied,* 475 U.S. 1109.

The line between past and future (or ongoing) criminal conduct is often hard to draw.[25] Deciding which communication is protected and which is part of an ongoing fraud is particularly hard in organized economic ventures regulated by complex criminal statutes where a client's conduct may be a mix of legitimate and criminal behavior. The most that can be expected of linedrawing in these areas is that courts will somehow be able to decide that one element "outweighs" the other and allow protection or require disclosure accordingly, and there is little doubt that courts will tend to err in requiring disclosure rather than protecting confidences.

Ongoing criminal conduct

Clearly the future crime-fraud exception applies even if disclosure is sought after the contemplated conduct has occurred, so long as the communication itself looked to future acts.[26] The exception removes from the privilege only communications that relate to the crime or fraud, not all prior communications between the lawyer and client.[27]

The exception applies even where the plan for the future crime or fraud originated with the attorney,[28] although under the better view the client must ultimately know and share the purpose of the wrongful conduct.[29] Contemporaneous illegal conduct involving the client and attorney such as joint use of drugs does not by itself establish that the attorney-client communications were for the purposes of committing an ongoing crime or fraud.[30]

25. *See, e.g.,* In re Grand Jury Proceedings (Pavlick), 680 F.2d 1026, 1028-1029 (5th Cir. 1982) (identity of client paying legal fees of another falls within the crime-fraud exception where such payment is being made under agreement that is part of ongoing criminal conspiracy). *See generally* Stuart, Child Abuse Reporting: A Challenge to Attorney-Client Confidentiality, 1 Geo. J. Legal Ethics 243, 253 (1987) ("The crime of child abuse is both a continuing and a future crime, as well as a past crime").

26. State v. Phelps, 24 Or. App. 329, 545 P.2d 901, 903 (1976) (future crime exception applicable where defendant told first attorney he intended to call witnesses to fabricate defense claiming that someone else was driving; on receiving assurances that perjured testimony would not be used, attorney withdrew; defendant retained another attorney who successfully defended by using false testimony; client was subsequently prosecuted for perjury; held, testimony of the first attorney is admissible at the perjury trial).

27. Ohio-Sealy Mattress Mfg. Co. v. Kaplan, 90 F.R.D. 21, 30 (N.D. Ill. 1980) ("the ongoing fraud exception lifts the attorney-client privilege only with respect to documents relevant to the fraudulent conduct").

28. *See* White v. American Airlines, Inc., 915 F.2d 1414, 1423-1424 (10th Cir. 1990) (in preparing employee for deposition, corporate attorney advised him to "forget" certain information; such advice is within exception); In re A. H. Robins Co., Inc., 107 F.R.D. 2, 9-15 (D. Kan. 1985) (corporation and counsel allegedly conspired to conceal dangerous defects in IUD manufactured by client).

29. Some courts apply what might be more aptly viewed as an "attorney misconduct" exception, where the privilege is vitiated even where the unlawful intent is solely that of the attorney. *See, e.g.,* In re Impounded Case (Law Firm), 879 F.2d 1211, 1213-1214 (3d Cir. 1989) (exception applies to defeat privilege, even where "pertinent alleged criminality is solely that of the law firm"; court finds no interest served by permitting attorney to assert "an innocent client's privilege with respect to documents tending to show criminal activity by the lawyer").

30. United States v. Fortna, 796 F.2d 724, 729-731 (5th Cir. 1986) (use of cocaine by attorney with client does not establish that communications were in furtherance of illegal activities), *cert. denied,* 479 U.S. 950.

Establishing the crime-fraud exception

The party seeking production of the allegedly privileged material has the burden of proving that the exception applies. Although some courts once required the exception to be proved by "independent evidence,"[31] the Supreme Court held in *United States v. Zolin* that the allegedly privileged material can be examined and considered by the trial judge in camera.[32] Thus a communication can be found within the exception based on the content of the communication itself.[33]

Factual basis

Review of the allegedly privileged material is available only where the party seeking the evidence has shown a factual basis "'adequate to support a good faith belief by a reasonable person' that in camera review of the materials may reveal evidence to establish the claim that the crime-fraud exception applies."[34] In making the threshold showing necessary for in camera review, a party may offer any relevant evidence that has been "lawfully obtained" and that has not already been adjudicated to be privileged.[35]

The necessary threshold showing for in camera review may be made ex parte.[36] The court may defer in camera review until additional evidence in support of the crime-fraud exception is produced, and the decision whether to undertake in camera review is discretionary with the trial court.[37]

A judicial decision to engage in camera review is less of an intrusion on the attorney-client privilege than ultimate recognition of the crime-fraud exception. For this reason, courts sometimes allow ex parte determination of the crime-fraud exception in grand jury proceedings.[38] However, prior to trial or other public disclosure of privileged material

---

31. *See, e.g.,* United States v. Shewfelt, 455 F.2d 836, 840 (9th Cir. 1972), *cert. denied,* 406 U.S. 944.

32. United States v. Zolin, 491 U.S. 554, 566-568 (1989) (FRE 104(a), which generally bars consideration of privileged evidence when court makes preliminary findings, does not prevent in camera review; until applicability of crime-fraud exception is resolved, there is "no basis" for regarding the contested evidence as privileged).

33. Although *Zolin* clearly approves in camera review of documents, it is less clear whether the trial judge may require the attorney or client to testify on the record to the substance of communications between them in this context, even during in camera proceedings. Doing so would create evidence of the substance of the communication that did not exist before although the difficulty might be handled by sealing the record in the event the privilege claim is ultimately sustained and barring use of what is disclosed.

34. *Zolin, supra* note 32, at 572 (quoting Caldwell v. District Court, 644 P.2d 26, 33 (Colo. 1982)).

35. *Id.* at 575.

36. Haines v. Liggett Group, Inc., 975 F.2d 81, 96-97 (3d Cir. 1992) (for in camera inspection, trial court has discretion "to consider only the presentation made by the party challenging the privilege").

37. *Zolin, supra* note 32, at 572 (court should consider facts and circumstances, including volume of materials to be reviewed, the relative importance of the alleged privileged information, and "the likelihood that the evidence produced through in camera review, together with other available evidence then before the court, will establish that the crime-fraud exception does apply").

38. *See, e.g.,* In re Grand Jury Subpoenas, 144 F.3d 653, 660-661 (10th Cir. 1998) (showing of foundation for crime-fraud exception can be made ex parte and court is not required to conduct "minihearing" or allow rebuttal evidence).

based on recognition of the crime-fraud exception, the party invoking the privilege should normally be allowed to be heard.[39] Moreover, steps should be taken to preserve the confidentiality of the material until all avenues of appeal are exhausted.[40]

A question not answered by *Zolin* is the quantum of evidence ultimately required to vitiate the privilege on grounds of crime or fraud.[41] The traditional rule is that the party seeking the evidence must make only a prima facie showing of the applicability of the exception.[42] Courts have generally held the required showing to be satisfied by evidence sufficient to support a finding of wrongdoing[43] although other formulations have also been articulated.[44] The prima facie standard originated in cases where the exception was established by independent evidence without in camera inspection of the contested material. In cases where that material has been examined in camera by the trial judge, a preponderance standard should normally be imposed, at least in cases where the crime or fraud, if any exists, is likely to be revealed by the documents or communications themselves.[45] Courts are increasingly recognizing, at least in civil cases, that the party seeking to preserve the privilege should be allowed to respond.[46]

Quantum of evidence

39. Haines v. Liggett Group, Inc., 975 F.2d 81, 96-97 (3d Cir. 1992) (due process requires that party asserting privilege "be given the opportunity to be heard, by evidence and argument, at the hearing seeking an exception to the privilege," although court notes that a different rule may be appropriate in the grand jury context); Matter of Feldberg, 862 F.2d 622, 626 (7th Cir. 1988) (party asserting privilege should be allowed to rebut evidence of crime or fraud).

40. Haines v. Liggett Group, Inc., 975 F.2d 81, 97 (3d Cir. 1992) (after crime-fraud exception is found to apply, allegedly privileged matter should "be kept under seal or appropriate court-imposed privacy procedures until all avenues of appeal are exhausted").

41. 491 U.S. at 563 ("[W]e need not decide the quantum of proof necessary ultimately to establish the applicability of the crime-fraud exception.").

42. *See* Clark v. United States, 289 U.S. 1, 14 (1933); In re Grand Jury Subpoena Duces Tecum Dated September 15, 1983, 731 F.2d 1032, 1039 (2d Cir. 1984) (requiring prima facie showing or probable cause to believe a fraud or crime committed and communications were in furtherance thereof).

43. In re Grand Jury Subpoena, 419 F.3d 329, 336-337 (5th Cir. 2005) (for prima facie showing, party invoking exception must produce evidence that "will suffice until contradicted and overcome by other evidence," meaning enough to support a finding if contrary evidence is disregarded; allegations in pleading insufficient); Kilpatrick v. King, 499 F.3d 759, 766 (8th Cir. 2007) (questioner must present facts warranting reasonable belief that privilege holder obtained legal advice to further crime or fraud).

44. United States v. Davis, 1 F.3d 606, 610 (7th Cir. 1993) (all that is needed is something "to give color to the charge" of crime or fraud, and "[w]hether pale or rich or vivid, there is indubitably color here"); In re Grand Jury Subpoena Duces Tecum, 731 F.2d 1032, 1039 (2d Cir. 1984) (applying standard that "a prudent person have a reasonable basis to suspect the perpetration or attempted perpetration of a crime or fraud, and that the communications were in furtherance thereof").

45. In re Napster, Inc. Copyright Litigation, 479 F.3d 1078 (9th Cir. 2007) (where court has examined allegedly privileged documents, information seeker has burden of establishing crime-fraud exception by preponderance of evidence, not merely by prima facie standard; privilege holder has right to introduce countervailing evidence).

46. United States v. BDO Seidman, LLP, 492 F.3d 806, 818 (7th Cir. 2007) (information seeker has initial burden of production to show that exception has foundation in fact; burden then shifts to privilege claimant to provide explanation).

The crime-fraud exception to the attorney-client privilege has a complex relationship with other legal doctrines. There is also an exception to the attorney's ethical duty of confidentiality that covers at least some future crimes or frauds.[47] Each exception has an independent sphere of operation.[48] If the client's communication fits the exception to the privilege, the attorney can be compelled to make judicial disclosure of the communication, but the ethical duty may continue to forbid disclosure to others.[49]

Helping a client in an unlawful scheme may make the attorney liable as an accessory.[50] The lawyer may also have civil liability for providing legal assistance to client conduct that is fraudulent or otherwise unlawful.[51] An attorney could also face civil liability for failure to disclose certain types of unlawful conduct by a client to regulatory authorities.[52] She might conceivably face liability for failing to warn prospective victims if the client makes credible threats of assault or destruction, although the only prominent authority that points in this direction is a famous California case imposing liability in the very different setting of psychiatric counseling.[53]

47. *See* ABA Model Rule of Professional Conduct 1.6(b) (lawyer may reveal confidential information "to the extent the lawyer reasonably believes necessary" (1) "prevent reasonably certain death or substantial bodily harm" (2) "to prevent the client from committing a crime or fraud that is reasonably certain to result in substantial injury to the financial interests or property of another. . . ."). *Compare* ABA Model Code of Professional Responsibility DR 4-101(C) (lawyer may reveal "intention of his client to commit a crime and the information necessary to prevent the crime").

48. *See generally* Fried, Too High a Price for Truth: The Exception to the Attorney-Client Privilege for Contemplated Crimes and Frauds, 64 N.C. L. Rev. 443, 490 (1986) (finding "a profound theoretical tension between the view of the attorney-client relationship implicit in the modern law of privilege and the view of the relationship that underlies the ethical duty of confidentiality").

49. *See* Subin, The Lawyer as Superego: Disclosure of Client Confidences to Prevent Harm, 70 Iowa L. Rev. 1091 (1985); Callan & David, Professional Responsibility and the Duty of Confidentiality: Disclosure of Client Misconduct in an Adversary System, 29 Rutgers L. Rev. 332, 362-365 (1976).

50. Matter of Aloi, 141 A.D.2d 270, 534 N.Y.S.2d 49 (1988) (attorney convicted of being an accessory after the fact for knowingly assisting client to avoid apprehension); State ex rel. Oklahoma Bar Assn. v. Harlton, 669 P.2d 774, 777 (Okla. 1983) (attorney convicted as accessory and suspended from bar for concealing gun on behalf of client).

51. *See, e.g.,* Meyerhofer v. Empire Fire & Marine Ins. Co., 497 F.2d 1190, 1192-1193 (2d Cir. 1974) (attorney sued along with client for securities violations), *cert. denied,* 419 U.S. 998.

52. *See generally* Myers, The Attorney-Client Relationship and the Code of Professional Responsibility: Suggested Attorney Liability for Breach of Duty to Disclose Fraud to the Securities and Exchange Commission, 44 Fordham L. Rev. 1113, 1138-1142 (1976).

53. Tarasoff v. Regents of Univ. of California, 131 Cal. Rptr. 14, 17 Cal. 3d 425, 450, 551 P.2d 334, 353 (1976) (upholding cause of action against psychotherapists who failed to warn potential murder victim of threats made by a patient). *But see* Restatement (Third) of the Law Governing Lawyers (Proposed Final Draft No. 2, 1998) §117A (lawyer who fails to warn third person is not liable for damages "solely by reason of such inaction").

§5.23 Breach of Duty by Lawyer or Client

Another exception to the attorney-client privilege covers communications relevant to an alleged breach of duty by lawyer to client or client to lawyer,[1] and a similar exception is recognized to the ethical duty of confidentiality.[2] Under both, disclosure is permitted only to the extent reasonably necessary to defend against or otherwise litigate the charge.[3]

Breach of duty by the attorney usually involves professional malpractice, incompetence, or ethical violations, while a breach by a client usually means not paying a fee. Allegations of breach of duty are most commonly made in criminal proceedings where a client seeks to withdraw a guilty plea[4] or asks for other forms of post-conviction relief on ground of incompetency or inadequacy of counsel.[5] The exception is also invoked when a lawyer defends against a complaint of professional malpractice, unlawful conduct, or ethical impropriety.[6]

§5.23 1. Johnson v. Alabama, 256 F.3d 1156, 1178 (11th Cir. 2001) (by alleging his attorneys provided ineffective assistance of counsel in their choice of a defense strategy, defendant waived any privilege as to contents of conversations with those attorneys bearing on trial strategy). *See also* proposed-but-rejected FRE 503(d)(3) and URE 502(d)(3) (1999) (no privilege for "communication relevant to an issue of breach of duty by the lawyer to his client or by the client to his lawyer").

2. *See* ABA Model Rules of Professional Conduct Rule 1.6(b)(5) (lawyer may disclose information about client "to establish a claim or defense on behalf of the lawyer in a controversy between the lawyer and the client, to establish a defense to a criminal charge or civil claim against the lawyer based upon conduct in which the client was involved, or to respond to allegations in any proceeding concerning the lawyer's representation of the client"); ABA Model Code of Professional Responsibility DR 4-101(C) (lawyer may reveal confidences or secrets "necessary to establish or collect his fee or to defend himself or his employees or associates against an accusation of wrongful conduct")

3. Bittaker v. Woodford, 331 F.3d 715, 719-721 (9th Cir. 2003) (habeas petitioner asserting claim of ineffective assistance of counsel waives privilege for all communications, but waiver must be "no broader than needed to ensure the fairness of the proceedings," and privilege holder may preserve confidentiality "by choosing to abandon the claim," and one who complies and turns over privileged materials is "entitled to rely on the contours of the waiver the court imposes"). *See also* ABA Model Rules of Professional Conduct Rule 1.6, Comment 10 (disclosure should be "no greater than the lawyer reasonably believes is necessary to vindicate innocence" and should be made so as to limit access to the information to the court or others with "a need to know it," and lawyer should seek protective orders or other arrangements "to the fullest extent practicable").

4. *See, e.g.,* United States v. Glass, 761 F.2d 479 (8th Cir. 1985) (where client claimed inadequate advice from attorney on consequences of guilty plea, attorney properly testified about advice given), *cert. denied,* 474 U.S. 856.

5. Tasby v. United States, 504 F.2d 332, 336 (8th Cir. 1974) (claim of ineffective assistance of counsel waived attorney-client privilege by putting advice in issue), *cert. denied,* 419 U.S. 1125.

6. *See, e.g.,* Kalyawongsa v. Moffett, 105 F.3d 283 (6th Cir. 1997) (privilege waived where client filed disciplinary charges against former attorney); Meyerhofer v. Empire Fire & Marine Ins. Co., 497 F.2d 1190, 1194-1195 (2d Cir. 1974) (attorney charged with securities law violations allowed to reveal privileged information necessary to defend his reputation and conduct), *cert. denied,* 419 U.S. 998.

It is not necessary for the client to bring formal charges or proceedings against the attorney.[7] Publication of allegations seriously reflecting on the attorney's professional competence or character may occasionally be a sufficient basis for invoking this exception,[8] but an attorney cannot use the exception offensively simply to retaliate against a client for criticism that the attorney considers unjustified.[9]

Defending charges by third party

The "self-defense" exception is sometimes justified on the theory that the client impliedly "waives" the privilege by making allegations of breach of duty against the attorney.[10] The waiver theory does not apply, however, where charges against the attorney are made by someone other than the client. Nonetheless, many courts allow an attorney a qualified right to use privileged material in defending against charges brought by a third party.[11] The attorney should generally notify the client before making such disclosure and, where feasible, obtain advance judicial approval.[12] When a lawyer discloses client confidences in order to defend against outside charges, obviously the interests of the client are taking second place to the professional concerns of the lawyer, and especially in this setting some sense of proportion is in order. The lawyer may be able to mount an adequate defense without disclosing everything, and a minor and inconsequential charge against the lawyer does not justify disclosure of communications that may be very damaging to the client while only marginally useful to the lawyer.[13]

---

7. Pruitt v. Peyton, 243 F. Supp. 907, 909 (E.D. Va. 1965) (claim that petitioner did not pursue state remedies because of dissatisfaction with state counsel constituted implied attack on attorney; privilege waived).

8. SEC v. Forma, 117 F.R.D. 516, 524 (S.D.N.Y. 1987) (attorney can reveal client communications when accused of wrongdoing by SEC; he need not be formally charged or threatened with prosecution).

9. Siedle v. Putnam Inves., Inc., 147 F.3d 7, 11 (1st Cir. 1998) (exception is shield, not sword; lawyer cannot use confidential information offensively even he chafed at client's and viewed it as defamatory).

10. *See* §5.30, *infra*.

11. *See* In re National Mortg. Equity Corp. Mtg. Pool Certificates Sec. Litig., 120 F.R.D. 687, 690-692 (C.D. Cal. 1988) (in action for securities fraud against law firm and client, latter could not prevent former from disclosing privileged documents under self-defense exception).

12. *See* ABA Model Rules of Professional Conduct Rule 1.6, Comment 10 (where "practical and not prejudicial" to lawyer's defense, lawyer "should advise the client of the third party's assertion and request that the client respond appropriately"); Application of Friend, 411 F. Supp. 776 (S.D.N.Y. 1975) (corporate client allowed an opportunity to be heard on motion of corporate attorney seeking court permission to disclose privileged communications in self-defense). *See generally* Levine, Self-Interest or Self-Defense: Lawyer Disregard of the Attorney-Client Privilege for Profit and Protection, 5 Hofstra L. Rev. 783, 819-826 (1977); McMonigle & Mallen, The Attorney's Dilemma in Defending Third Party Lawsuits: Disclosure of the Client's Confidences or Personal Liability?, 14 Willamette L.J. 355 (1978) (both articles recommending that judicial approval be obtained before disclosure of privileged matter in self-defense).

13. *See* Note, Eliminating "Backdoor" Access to Client Confidences: Restricting the Self-Defense Exception to the Attorney-Client Privilege, 65 N.Y.U. L. Rev. 992 (1990).

The fact that a client has instituted a malpractice action against the attorney does not constitute a waiver of all confidential communications, thereby making them available to a third party.[14] However, if the complaint or evidence against the attorney reveals confidential matter, then the privilege is waived as to the subject of the disclosed communications.[15]

§5.24 Claimants Through a Deceased Client

Even though the attorney-client privilege survives the death of a client and can be asserted by the personal representative,[1] an exception is recognized for communications by a deceased client relevant to litigation between parties who both claim through that very client.[2] The rationale is that in will contests and similar litigation it is not known who stands in the shoes of the deceased client.[3] His communications may be essential to accurate resolution of competing claims of succession, and the testator would presumably favor disclosure of the communications in order to dispose of his estate in accord with his intentions.[4]

The exception applies only between parties who claim "through" the same deceased client.[5] Generally it continues as against "strangers" or "outsiders" making claims against the estate,[6] and those claiming

Privilege continues against outsiders

---

14. Industrial Clearinghouse v. Browning Mfg., 953 F.2d 1004, 1007 (5th Cir. 1992) ("mere institution of suit" against a lawyer "is insufficient to waive the attorney-client privilege as to third parties in a separate action that concerns the same subject matter as the attorney malpractice action").

15. Industrial Clearinghouse v. Browning Mfg., 953 F.2d 1004, 1007 (5th Cir. 1992) (it is revelation of confidential communications, "not the institution of suit" that determines whether party waives the attorney-client privilege "as to the subject matter of the disclosed communications").

§5.24 1. *See* §5.26, *infra*.

2. *See* proposed-but-rejected FRE 503(d)(2) and URE 502(d)(2) (1999) (no privilege for communication "relevant to an issue between parties who claim through the same deceased client," whether claims are by testate or intestate succession or inter vivos transaction). *See also* United States v. Osborn, 561 F.2d 1334, 1340 (9th Cir. 1977) (general rule is that confidential communications between attorney and client for the purpose of preparing client's will are privileged during the testator's lifetime and after his death "unless sought to be disclosed in litigation between the testator's heirs, legatees, devisees, or other parties, all of whom claim under the deceased client").

3. *See* ACN, proposed-but-rejected FRE 503(d)(2) (where identity of the person who "steps into the client's shoes" is in issue, as in a will contest, the identity of the person holding the privilege "remains undetermined until the conclusion of litigation" and choice is between allowing "both sides or neither" to assert the privilege; authority and reason favor the latter view).

4. 8 Wigmore, Evidence 2314 (McNaughton rev. 1961) (a testator is likely to intend only "temporary confidentiality" during his lifetime for communications on making of a will).

5. Note, Wills and the Attorney-Client Privilege, 14 Ga. L. Rev. 325, 332-337 (1980).

6. *See* Glover v. Patten, 165 U.S. 394, 406 (1897) (communications regarding execution of a will might be privileged "if offered by third persons to establish claims against an estate").

through the decedent normally retain the same right to assert the privilege against outsiders as the decedent would have. The notion here is that those claiming through the estate are in effect transferees or successors in interest of the decedent, while outsiders claim not a right of title or inheritance, but an unsatisfied obligation owed by the decedent. In the tragic and common circumstance in which the "outsider" is someone who cared for the decedent during a final decline or terminal illness and claims the decedent promised to make just provision in a will, the claim is still one that is "against" the estate and the privilege applies.

§5.25 Lawyer as Attesting Witness

The privilege does not apply to communications relevant to an issue concerning an attested document where the lawyer served as an attesting witness.[1] Although this qualification is often categorized as an "exception" to the privilege, it is more accurate to say that the privilege never arises because a lawyer who acts as an attesting witness is not providing professional legal services.[2]

Additionally, communications relevant to the lawyer's role as attesting witness cannot be viewed as confidential because it is understood that attesting witnesses are to testify to relevant facts surrounding the signing of the document if it is offered in evidence. Thus the client's consent to the lawyer acting as an attesting witness can be viewed as a waiver of the privilege for communications relevant to the execution and validity of the document.[3]

§5.26 Duration of the Privilege

Although the attorney-client privilege applies only to communications occurring during the existence of the professional relationship, the privilege continues to protect those communications after its termination.[1] The attorney's ethical duty of confidentiality also continues.[2]

---

§5.25 1. *See* proposed-but-rejected FRE 503(d)(4).

2. *See* §5.11, *supra.*

3. *See* ACN, proposed-but-rejected FRE 503(d)(4) (when lawyer acts as attesting witness, "approval of the client to his so doing may safely be assumed, and waiver of the privilege as to any relevant lawyer-client communications is a proper result").

§5.26 1. United States v. White, 970 F.2d 328, 334 (7th Cir. 1992) (once the attorney-client privilege attaches, "the communication retains the protection of the privilege even after the termination of the attorney-client relationship"). *See also* Restatement (Third) of the Law Governing Lawyers (Proposed Final Draft No. 1, 1996) §127 (unless waived or subject to an exception, privilege may be invoked "at any time during and after the termination of the client-lawyer relationship").

2. ABA Model Code of Professional Responsibility EC 4-6 (lawyer's obligation to preserve confidences and secrets of client "continues after the termination of his employment").

The prevailing common law view, which has been announced as federal law by a Supreme Court decision, is that the privilege is not terminated even by the death of the client.[3] However, this view has its critics[4] and is not adopted by all courts.[5] Where the client is deceased, the privilege may be asserted (or waived) by the client's attorney[6] or personal representative.[7] Some authorities take the position that the privilege of a deceased client continues only through administration of the estate.[8] According to modern codes, the privilege of a corporation does not terminate upon dissolution but may be asserted by a successor,[9] although earlier authorities had taken a contrary position.[10]

Privilege survives death of client

The rule allowing the privilege to be asserted after the death of the client is significantly qualified by the exception for communications concerning a dispute between parties claiming through the same deceased client.[11] This exception makes the privilege generally inapplicable in cases where the confidential communications between the

3. Swidler & Berlin v. United States, 118 S. Ct. 2081, 2086-2088 (1998) (privilege survives death of client, thereby protecting attorney's notes of conversation with a White House lawyer who committed suicide from discovery by Independent Counsel).

4. *Id.* at 2089 (O'Connor, J., dissenting) (paramount value of protecting an innocent defendant "should outweigh a deceased client's interest in preserving confidences"). *See also* 2 C. Wright & K. Graham, Federal Practice & Procedure 5498 (1986) (opposing continuation of privilege after the death of the client).

5. *See* In re Death of Eric Miller, 357 N.C. 316, 584 S.E.2d 772 (2003) (recognizing exception to privilege allowing trial court to compel disclosure of communications about murder investigation when client took his own life on discovering that he would be arrested for the murder; during *in camera* review, court should consider whether disclosure would harm client's rights, as by exposing client to civil or criminal liability or harm to reputation; if not, and if disclosure would assist in determining rights of third party, "the underlying justification for the privilege should cease to apply"); Cohen v. Jenkintown Cab Co., 238 Pa. Super. 456, 357 A.2d 689, 693 (1976) (adopting balancing approach to override attorney-client privilege; court compelled disclosure of privileged communications of deceased cab driver that he was driver of cab that struck plaintiff pedestrian; action was against cab company and not his estate). *Contra* In re John Doe Grand Jury Investigation, 408 Mass. 480, 562 N.E.2d 69 (1990) (upholding absolute privilege for deceased client who may have made admissions to his attorney about murder of his wife).

6. Cooper v. State, 661 P.2d 905, 907 (Okla. Crim. App. 1983) (attorney allowed to claim privilege of deceased client, even where deceased client allegedly made incriminating statements regarding a murder for which another person was being prosecuted); State v. Macumber, 112 Ariz. 569, 544 P.2d 1084, 1086-1087 (1976) (same), *cert. denied*, 439 U.S. 1006. *But see* §5.5, *supra*.

7. *See* proposed-but-rejected FRE 503(c) (allowing privilege to be asserted by "the personal representative of a deceased client").

8. *See* Comment, Cal. Evid. Code 954 (West 1966) (privilege "ceases to exist when the client's estate is finally distributed and his personal representative is discharged").

9. *See* proposed-but-rejected FRE 503(c) and URE 502(c) (1999) (privilege may be claimed by "successor, trustee, or similar representative of a corporation, association, or other organization, whether or not in existence").

10. *See* URE 26(1) (1954) (privilege of "corporation or association terminates upon dissolution").

11. *See* §5.24, *supra*.

deceased client and his attorney are most likely to be sought, such as will contests and similar litigation involving competing claimants to the decedent's estate.

Qualification of privilege suggested   Arguably the privilege of a deceased client should be qualified in cases where extreme injustice would be done to a party deprived of critical evidence.[12] For example, if a deceased client has confessed to criminal acts that are later charged to another, surely the latter's need for evidence sometimes outweighs the interest in preserving the confidences. A rule requiring occasional disclosure in this setting would not seriously undercut the utilitarian basis of the privilege, which emphasizes the importance of candor between client and lawyer in securing adequate legal representation.[13] Few clients are focused on what will happen sometime after the death that everyone expects but few anticipate in an immediate or definite sense. Limited disclosure of confessions after death of a client would, of course, threaten the humanistic basis of the privilege because it would invade privacy in potentially serious ways. Clearly a client is concerned not only about himself but about his larger human situation that includes spouses, parents, children, siblings, and extended family and friends and business associates.

A rule allowing qualified disclosure of statements by a deceased client that bear directly on the guilt of a third person charged with a crime would further justice, although disclosure should be limited in an effective way. The issue could be resolved by the court that tries a third-party defendant, and it should be testable by an immediate appeal if the lawyer or family of the client decides to do so. The court resolving the privilege issue could also consider the question of admissibility under a hearsay exception such as the one for statements against interest and override a privilege claim only for statements that would actually be usable.

§5.27 Claiming the Privilege

The attorney-client privilege is not self-enforcing. It must be asserted at each stage of a proceeding where privileged evidence is sought or it is waived.[1] The making of a privilege objection is not by itself sufficient to preserve the privilege. The holder normally must refrain from disclosing the privileged matter until the court has ruled on the privilege

---

12. *See* Restatement (Third) of the Law Governing Lawyers (Proposed Final Draft No. 1, 1996) §127 cmt. d ("The tribunal could balance the confidentiality of privileged communications against any demonstrated exceptional need to reveal the communication in the litigation. . . . Permitting disclosure of a decedent's confidential communication in such an exceptional case would do little to inhibit clients from confiding in their lawyers. Assuring litigants a just outcome in their disputes in some cases would be a superior interest.").

13. *See* §5.8, *supra.*

§5.27   1. United States v. Gurtner, 474 F.2d 297, 299 (9th Cir. 1973) (failure to assert the privilege when evidence was first presented "constituted a voluntary waiver").

claim.[2] The lawyer has an ethical obligation to advise the client of the existence of the privilege and to claim it when necessary to protect the interests of the client.[3] The lawyer's authority to claim the privilege is presumed in the absence of evidence to the contrary.[4]

Corporate management has the authority to assert the privilege on behalf of a corporate client. If a corporation is insolvent, the privilege may be asserted by the bankruptcy trustee,[5] and if dissolved, by a successor corporation.[6] The privilege may be claimed by a guardian or conservator on behalf of an incapacitated client, and by a personal representative on behalf of a deceased client.[7]

If the client or a representative of the client is not present at the proceeding, the privilege may be called to the court's attention by anyone present, and the court may raise the issue of privilege sua sponte.[8] Where privileged matter has already been obtained by an adversary, such as by interception or seizure, a privilege claim is usually asserted by appropriate motion seeking suppression or return of the material.[9]

The burden of establishing the existence of the privilege rests on the claimant.[10] The claimant must show that an attorney-client relationship existed between the communicants, the communication was made for the purpose of obtaining professional legal services, and the communication was made and kept in confidence.[11]

Establishing the privilege

2. Perrignon v. Bergen Brunswig Corp., 77 F.R.D. 455, 460 (N.D. Cal. 1978) (privilege waived where witness, a former officer of the corporate holder, disclosed privileged information at a deposition; raising privilege objection was insufficient to prevent waiver; further steps should have been taken, such as seeking a protective order or terminating deposition to obtain court ruling).

3. ABA Model Code of Professional Responsibility EC 4-4 (lawyer obligated "to advise the client of the attorney-client privilege and timely to assert the privilege unless it is waived by the client").

4. Fisher v. United States, 425 U.S. 391, 402 n.8 (1976) (it is "universally accepted" that attorney-client privilege "may be raised by the attorney").

5. Commodity Futures Trading Commn. v. Weintraub, 471 U.S. 343, 357-358 (1985).

6. *See* proposed-but-rejected FRE 503(c); URE 502(c) (1999).

7. *Id.*

8. *See* People v. Flores, 139 Cal. Rptr. 546, 548, 71 Cal. App. 3d 559 (1977) (requiring trial judge to assert privilege on behalf of an absent holder and advise unrepresented holder of availability of privilege); Restatement (Third) of the Law Governing Lawyers (Proposed Final Draft, No. 1, 1996) §135(1)(C) (even in absence of objection by person with standing, "presiding officer may order that a communication not be disclosed if it is privileged").

9. In re Impounded Case (Law Firm), 879 F.2d 1211, 1213-1214 (3d Cir. 1989) (motion to prevent government from inspecting and to have sealed allegedly privileged documents seized from law office pursuant to search warrant).

10. United States v. Abrahams, 905 F.2d 1276, 1283 (9th Cir. 1990) (privilege denied where claimant's showing of elements was "meager, amorphous, and ultimately inadequate"). *See also* Restatement (Third) of the Law Governing Lawyers (Proposed Final Draft, No. 1, 1996) §135(2) (one entitled to assert privilege "must ordinarily object contemporaneously" and "if the objection is contested, demonstrate each element of the privilege").

11. In re Excel Innovations, Inc., 502 F.3d 1086, 1099 (9th Cir. 2007) (party asserting privilege bears burden of establishing all its elements).

Courts do not honor "blanket" claims of privilege[12] and generally require that the privilege be invoked on a "document-by-document" basis supported by specific facts.[13] If a privilege claim is overbroad, its denial may be affirmed on appeal, even where a more narrow privilege claim could have been validly asserted.[14]

The attorney-client privilege does not automatically disqualify an attorney from being called by the opposing party as a witness at a deposition or trial. The attorney may be required to appear and assert the privilege in response to specific inquiries,[15] although before allowing an attorney to be deposed courts may require a preliminary showing that the information sought is relevant, nonprivileged, unavailable by other means, and crucial to the case.[16]

If a party seeking to offer otherwise privileged evidence claims it falls within an exception to the privilege, that party has the burden of showing that the exception applies.[17] The existence of a privilege is a preliminary question for the court under FRE 104(a), and its findings on the elements of the privilege, the applicability of an exception, or the occurrence of waiver are generally sustained on appeal unless they are clearly erroneous or indicate an abuse of discretion.[18] Privilege issues sometimes present mixed questions of law and fact that are reviewed de novo.[19]

In order to rule on a claim of privilege, the trial court may require production of the allegedly privileged material for in camera inspection.[20] Because the task can require detailed scrutiny of numerous

12. In re Grand Jury Subpoena, 831 F.2d 225, 226-227 (11th Cir. 1987) (error for trial judge to permit "blanket" assertion of privilege for all subpoenaed documents).

13. United States v. Legal Servs. for New York City, 249 F.3d 1077 (D.C. Cir. 2001) (rejecting blanket claim of attorney-client privilege for names of clients represented by Legal Services organization during a particular year; more particularized claim of privilege is required).

14. In re Grand Jury Witness, 695 F.2d 359 (9th Cir. 1982) (noting court's authority to affirm denial of overbroad privilege claim, but here allowing privilege claim to be more narrowly asserted on remand).

15. *See* In re Walsh, 623 F.2d 489, 493 (7th Cir. 1980) (reversing order quashing grand jury subpoenas directing attorney to testify about disappearance of former client; privilege must be asserted in response to each question rather than as bar to all testimony by attorney), *cert. denied*, 449 U.S. 994.

16. *See, e.g.,* Shelton v. American Motors Corp., 805 F.2d 1323, 1327 (8th Cir. 1986).

17. *See* In re Grand Jury Subpoena, 884 F.2d 124, 127 (4th Cir. 1989); Pfizer, Inc. v. Lord, 456 F.2d 545, 549 (8th Cir. 1972). *See also* Restatement (Third) of the Law Governing Lawyers (Proposed Final Draft, No. 1, 1996) §35(3) (burden of proof on party seeking to establish waiver or exception).

18. United States v. Wilson, 798 F.2d 509, 512 (1st Cir. 1986) (trial court determines preliminary facts supporting claim of privilege, and its findings of fact can be overturned only if clearly erroneous); In re Berkley & Co., 629 F.2d 548, 553 (8th Cir. 1980) (applying abuse of discretion standard).

19. Sandberg v. Virginia Bankshares, Inc., 979 F.2d 332, 350 (4th Cir. 1992) (applicability of privilege presents "mixed question of law and fact that should be reviewed de novo").

20. Schwimmer v. United States, 232 F.2d 855, 864 (8th Cir. 1956) (attorney-client privilege "is not self-operative against a judicially required production," since court is entitled to a chance to inspect any such documents "to satisfy itself that they are in fact privileged"), *cert. denied,* 352 U.S. 833.

documents,[21] it is sometimes delegated to a special master.[22] Submission of privileged material to a court for in camera examination does not waive the privilege.[23]

If a privilege claim is erroneously sustained, generally no interlocutory appeal of the trial court's order is available. The party who was barred from introducing evidence on grounds of privilege must raise the issue on appeal from an adverse final judgment.[24] If the privilege claim is erroneously denied and disclosure is ordered, the remedy depends on whether the party opposing introduction of the evidence is the client. If the party is not the client and the evidence is otherwise admissible, there is no ground for appeal because denial of a privilege belonging to another is not an error that a party has standing to assert.[25] If the party is the client, the party's rights are of course adversely affected. The party can comply with the order to disclose the material and challenge the denial of the privilege claim on appeal.[26] If the client is a nonparty, an interlocutory appeal will generally be allowed.[27]

Interlocutory appellate review

What if the client is unwilling to disclose without first obtaining interlocutory review of the trial court's order compelling disclosure? Although the order itself is generally not subject to interlocutory appeal,[28] the traditional method for obtaining appellate review is for the client to refuse to comply, be held in contempt, and seek review of the merits of the privilege claim by appealing the contempt

21. *See, e.g.,* Mead Data Cent., Inc. v. United States Dept. of Air Force, 566 F.2d 242, 250 n.10 (D.C. Cir. 1977) (in camera inspection of disputed documents places "burdensome demands" on courts, and it is unreasonable to expect courts "to do as thorough an investigation as would a party interested in forcing disclosure," particularly where documents run to hundreds or thousands of pages).

22. Collins & Aikman Corp. v. J. P. Stevens & Co., 51 F.R.D. 219, 221 (D.S.C. 1971) (delegation to special master if in camera inspection necessary).

23. United States v. Zolin, 491 U.S. 554, 568-569 (1989) (disclosing allegedly privileged materials to the court for purposes of determining merits of a privilege claim "does not have the legal effect of terminating the privilege").

24. *See, e.g.,* Johnston v. Baker, 445 F.2d 424, 428 (3d Cir. 1971). *But see* 18 U.S.C. 3731 (entitling government to appeal, under certain circumstances, from an order "suppressing or excluding evidence").

25. *See* Restatement (Third) of the Law Governing Lawyers (Proposed Final Draft, No. 1, 1996) §135 cmt. i (appealing party who is not the client may not claim that judgment should be set aside because of error in admitting privileged evidence). *See generally* 8 Wigmore, Evidence §2321 (3d ed. 1940) ("[W]hen the client is not a party, then on general principles . . . the party cannot invoke the privilege, and, if the privilege is erroneously refused, the party cannot appeal on the ground of this error.").

26. In re Grand Jury Proceedings (Vargas), 723 F.2d 1461, 1464 (10th Cir. 1983) (ordinarily "only a party" aggrieved by order or judgment "may appeal that decision"), *cert. denied,* 469 U.S. 819.

27. Dellwood Farm, Inc. v. Cargill, Inc., 128 F.3d 1122, 1125 (7th Cir. 1997) (discovery order denying a privilege is not subject to interlocutory appeal by a party but can be immediately appealed when holder is a nonparty).

28. Alexander v. United States, 201 U.S. 117, 122 (1906). *But see* Interlocutory Appeals Act, 28 U.S.C. 1292(b) (1988) (reviewing court may hear an interlocutory appeal from order certified by a trial court to involve "controlling question of law as to which there is substantial ground for difference of opinion" where interlocutory review "may materially advance the ultimate determination of the litigation").

citation.[29] If the citation is for criminal contempt, it is a final judgment, and appellate review can be obtained of the merits of the privilege claim whether or not the client is a party.[30] If the citation is for civil contempt and is rendered against a client who is not a party, it is also subject to immediate review because the client has no other recourse and the appeal "does not interfere with the orderly progress of the main case."[31] However, prevailing doctrine holds that a client who is a party cannot obtain interlocutory review of a privilege ruling if the citation is only for civil contempt,[32] although some decisions depart from this tradition.[33]

Rationale   There are several justifications for the established rule. First, interlocutory appeals disrupt and delay the proceeding. Second, when the citation is civil, the client "holds the key" to his discharge and can be purged of contempt by making the required disclosure. Finally, if the client is a party she can raise the privilege issue on appeal of the final judgment, although penalties imposed for noncompliance cannot be recouped unless the order is reversed. However, the traditional rule has been criticized as allowing trial judges to control the appealability of their own privilege rulings by their selection between civil and criminal contempt. Moreover, the distinction between civil and criminal sanctions is merely formal, as civil sanctions include both deprivation of liberty and substantial fines. Thus a party can be unfairly "put to a choice between his privileges and his liberty (or purse)."[34]

There are several limited circumstances where a party client is allowed to appeal a civil contempt citation, such as where the adjudication is a "collateral order,"[35] where it is adjoined to an appealable

29. *See* Olson v. United States, 872 F.2d 820, 821 (8th Cir. 1989) (privilege claimant must "complete the contempt proceedings and suffer some sanction" for failure to comply with order before being allowed to appeal).

30. *See* Powers v. Chicago Transit Auth., 846 F.2d 1139, 1141 (7th Cir. 1988) (criminal contempt is appealable "on the theory that it is the terminating order of a separate proceeding, the criminal prosecution").

31. International Business Mach. Corp. v. United States, 493 F.2d 112, 115 n.1 (2d Cir. 1973) (civil contempts against nonparties are immediately appealable), *cert. denied*, 416 U.S. 995.

32. *See* Fox v. Capital Co., 299 U.S. 105, 107 (1936) (no interlocutory appeal because civil contempt is not a "final judgment"); Powers v. Chicago Transit Auth., 846 F.2d 1139, 1140 (7th Cir. 1988) (upholding $150 per day fine for failure to turn over material petitioner contended was privileged; refusing review on merits because an adjudication of contempt "is no more final than the discovery order it enforces").

33. *See, e.g.,* Southern Methodist Univ. Assn. v. Wynne & Jaffe, 599 F.2d 707, 711-712 (5th Cir. 1979) (allowing appeal of privilege ruling enforced by civil contempt citation against privilege holder).

34. Powers v. Chicago Transit Auth., 846 F.2d 1139, 1140 (7th Cir. 1988) (noting arguments for revision of rule, but finding it "too well established to be changed by us"). *See generally* Andre, The Final Judgment Rule and Party Appeals of Civil Contempt Orders: Time for a Change, 55 N.Y.U. L. Rev. 1041, 1108 (1980) (party appeal of civil contempt orders should be allowed from orders "that are injurious in themselves," or that "operate to discourage a party from asserting important rights, or when compliance with the underlying order might result in the irrevocable loss of such rights").

35. Gulfstream Aerospace Corp. v. Mayacamas Corp., 485 U.S. 271, 276-277 (1988) (to be subject to interlocutory review, collateral order must be a "final decision" separate from the merits and unreviewable on appeal).

order such as a preliminary injunction,[36] or where the contempt proceeding is otherwise sufficiently separate from the main proceeding.[37]

A special problem is presented if the witness ordered to disclose is the attorney or a party to the privileged communication other than the client. Such persons may be unwilling to suffer a judgment of contempt merely to facilitate appellate review of the client's privilege claim.[38] Usually such cases involve attorneys, and attorneys normally have no obligation to their client to defy a court order to disclose. The ethical duty of confidentiality ends once the privilege claim has been properly asserted and overruled.[39]

For this reason, most courts recognize the *Perlman* doctrine[40] under which the client is allowed to intervene and seek interlocutory review of an order directing an attorney or other third person to disclose allegedly privileged material,[41] although there is contrary authority.[42] The doctrine rests on the theory that "[f]or all practical purposes, the discovery order is final as to the person otherwise powerless to prevent compliance."[43] Some courts require a clear showing that the witness will choose disclosure rather than risk contempt,[44] and others refuse to recognize the doctrine where the witness is closely affiliated with the client.[45] The *Perlman* doctrine is perhaps most commonly applied in grand jury proceedings where the client's lawyer has been ordered to

Perlman doctrine

36. State of New York v. Shore Realty Corp., 763 F.2d 49, 51-52 (2d Cir. 1985).

37. Sanders v. Monsanto Co., 574 F.2d 198, 199 (5th Cir. 1978) (contempt motions that are not "part and parcel of a continuing litigation" are final and subject to review).

38. In re Grand Jury Proceedings (Fine), 641 F.2d 199, 202 (5th Cir. 1981) (willingness of lawyer to protect client's privilege in face of contempt citation "will vary greatly, and have a direct relationship to the value of the client's business and the power of the client in relation to the attorney"; court was reluctant to pin the appealability on such "precarious considerations").

39. *See* ABA Model Code of Professional Responsibility DR 4-101(C) (lawyer may reveal confidences or secrets when "required by law or court order"). *Cf.* proposed-but-rejected FRE 512 (privilege claim is not lost where disclosure is erroneously compelled).

40. *See* Perlman v. United States, 247 U.S. 7, 10-13 (1918) (client allowed to intervene in a grand jury proceeding to challenge order directing court clerk to produce documents retained from previous case on ground that disclosure would violate his rights under Fourth and Fifth Amendments).

41. *See, e.g.,* In re Grand Jury Subpoenas, 123 F.3d 695, 689-699 (1st Cir. 1997) (where allegedly privileged documents are in possession of attorney, client can appeal order requiring attorney to disclose even though attorney has not been cited for contempt; client should not be at mercy of attorney's willingness to face contempt citation and lawyer should not be required to choose between own interests and those of client); United States v. Davis, 1 F.3d 606, 607 (7th Cir. 1993).

42. *See* In re Sealed Case, 655 F.2d 1298, 1301 (D.C. Cir. 1981) (there is no "general third party exception to the finality rule" permitting privilege holder to appeal order directing another to produce allegedly privileged material).

43. Conkling v. Turner, 883 F.2d 431, 433 (5th Cir. 1989).

44. *See, e.g.,* In re Sealed Case, 737 F.2d 94, 98 (D.C. Cir. 1984) (immediate appeal allowed where former attorney in possession of documents filed affidavit swearing he would turn them over if ordered to do so by court rather than risking contempt).

45. In re Grand Jury Subpoena Served Upon Niren, 784 F.2d 939, 941-942 (9th Cir. 1986) (no immediate appeal where grand jury subpoena directed to in-house counsel).

testify or produce documents after unsuccessfully asserting a claim of privilege on behalf of the client.[46]

Mandamus Mandamus may be used as a vehicle for appellate review of privilege rulings in extraordinary circumstances,[47] such as where there has been a clear abuse of judicial power or there are important unresolved issues of broad legal significance.[48]

FRE 502

The following provisions apply, in the circumstances set out, to disclosure of a communication or information covered by the attorney-client privilege or work-product protection.

(a) **Disclosure made in a federal proceeding or to a federal office or agency; scope of a waiver.**—When the disclosure is made in a federal proceeding or to a federal office or agency and waives the attorney-client privilege or work-product protection, the waiver extends to an undisclosed communication or information in a federal or state proceeding only if:

(1) the waiver is intentional;

(2) the disclosed and undisclosed communications or information concern the same subject matter; and

(3) they ought in fairness to be considered together.

(b) **Inadvertent disclosure.**—When made in a federal proceeding or to a federal office or agency, the disclosure does not operate as a waiver in a federal or state proceeding if:

(1) the disclosure is inadvertent;

(2) the holder of the privilege or protection took reasonable steps to prevent disclosure; and

(3) the holder promptly took reasonable steps to rectify the error, including (if applicable) following Fed. R. Civ. P. 26(b)(5)(B).

(c) **Disclosure made in a state proceeding.**—When the disclosure is made in a state proceeding and is not the subject of a state-court order concerning waiver, the disclosure does not operate as a waiver in a federal proceeding if the disclosure:

(1) would not be a waiver under this rule if it had been made in a federal proceeding; or

---

46. *See, e.g.,* In re Grand Jury Proceedings (Gordon), 722 F.2d 303, 306 (6th Cir. 1983), *cert. denied sub nom.* Doe v. United States, 467 U.S. 1246 (1984) (client permitted to intervene in grand jury proceeding where lawyer ordered to disclose).

47. Kerr v. United States Dist. Court, 426 U.S. 394, 402 (1976) (only most extraordinary circumstances permit use of mandamus to regulate discovery); Powers v. Chicago Transit Auth., 846 F.2d 1139, 1143 (7th Cir. 1988) (although criticizing trial court disclosure order, an error "is not usurpation of power").

48. In re Perrigo Co., 128 F.3d 430, 433-434 (6th Cir. 1997) (mandamus proper to review privilege ruling because of lack of other means to obtain relief, potential for irreparable harm, and novel issues presented); Rhone-Poulenc Rorer, Inc. v. Home Indem. Co., 32 F.2d 851 (3d Cir. 1994) (mandamus proper where court committed clear errors of law and right to writ is clear and indisputable).

(2) is not a waiver under the law of the state where the disclosure occurred.

(d) Controlling effect of a court order.—A federal court may order that the privilege or protection is not waived by disclosure connected with the litigation pending before the court—in which event the disclosure is also not a waiver in any other federal or state proceeding.

(e) Controlling effect of a party agreement.—An agreement on the effect of disclosure in a federal proceeding is binding only on the parties to the agreement, unless it is incorporated into a court order.

(f) Controlling effect of this rule.—Notwithstanding Rules 101 and 1101, this rule applies to state proceedings and to federal court-annexed and federal court-mandated arbitration proceedings, in the circumstances set out in the rule. And notwithstanding Rule 501, this rule applies even if state law provides the rule of decision.

(g) Definitions.—In this rule:

(1) "attorney-client privilege" means the protection that applicable law provides for confidential attorney-client communications; and

(2) "work-product protection" means the protection that applicable law provides for tangible material (or its intangible equivalent) prepared in anticipation of litigation or for trial.

§5.28   Waiver by Voluntary Disclosure

Unless protected by a judicial non-waiver order under FRE 502(d), the attorney-client privilege is waived by the client's voluntary disclosure or consent to disclosure of any significant part of the privileged communication or matter in a nonprivileged setting. Waiver by disclosure can occur at any stage of a proceeding,[1] including discovery,[2] or in settings far removed from court proceedings.[3]

Disclosure that waives the privilege can be made by the client personally or by an attorney or other agent acting on the client's behalf.[4] Disclosure that waives the privilege can also be made by a third party

---

§5.28   1. Velsicol Chem. Corp. v. Parsons, 561 F.2d 671, 674-675 (7th Cir. 1977) (grand jury testimony by house counsel waived corporation's privilege), *cert. denied*, 435 U.S. 942.

2. *See, e.g.,* Weil v. Investors/Indicators, Research & Mgmt., Inc., 647 F.2d 18, 23-25 (9th Cir. 1981) (disclosure by officer-director on deposition waived privilege). On asserting the privilege during discovery, *see* §5.27, *supra.*

3. United States v. Mendelsohn, 896 F.2d 1183 (9th Cir. 1990) (privilege waived where defendant told detective about legal advice received from attorney).

4. United States v. Bump, 605 F.2d 548, 551 (10th Cir. 1979) (attorney-client privilege waived when attorney disclosed information to government and client had no proof disclosure was without his consent).

who has knowledge of the privileged matter, and waiver results if the client or his lawyer makes no objection at the time.[5]

Because the client holds the privilege, the attorney cannot waive it over the client's objection. The attorney has, however, some degree of implied authority to assert or waive the privilege on the client's behalf in the course of legal representation,[6] and the scope of such authority is determined by the law of agency.[7] If the client fails to object to disclosure of privileged information by the attorney, the client impliedly consents.[8] If the attorney testifies on behalf of the client, the privilege is waived for communications that bear on the attorney's testimony.[9] The client may not assert the privilege to block discovery with respect to matters that she plans to disclose at trial.[10]

Disclosure of significant part

For waiver to occur, the disclosure must reveal a significant part of the privileged communication.[11] Waiver does not occur merely because a client discusses with others the same facts that she earlier discussed with the attorney[12] but only where she reveals the substance of the attorney-client communications,[13] whether accurately or inaccurately.[14] A client's statement that she discussed the subject with her

5. Hollins v. Powell, 773 F.2d 191, 197 (8th Cir. 1985) (city waived claim of attorney-client privilege when mayor voluntarily testified about privileged communications and city's attorney did not object), *cert. denied,* 475 U.S. 1119.

6. *See* ABA Model Rules of Professional Conduct Rule 1.6(a) (lawyer has authority to reveal confidential information when the disclosure is "impliedly authorized in order to carry out the representation").

7. Restatement (Third) of the Law Governing Lawyers (Proposed Final Draft, No. 1, 1996) §128, cmt. c ("The power of an agent to waive the privilege is determined under the customary rules of the law of agency.").

8. *See* von Bulow v. von Bulow, 114 F.R.D. 71, 76 (S.D.N.Y. 1987) (privilege waived in part where client encouraged lawyer to write a book about legal representation and reveal other confidences on television program), *modified,* 828 F.2d 94 (2d Cir. 1987).

9. In re Pioneer Hi-Bred Int'l, Inc., 238 F.3d 1370, 1376 (Fed. Cir. 2001) (counsel for party may be deposed by opposing party as fact witness without waiving attorney-client privilege, but privilege is waived if counsel discloses privileged matters); Leybold-Heraeus Technologies, Inc. v. Midwest Instrument Co., Inc., 118 F.R.D. 609, 614 (E.D. Wis. 1987) (where attorney took stand, privilege waived for information necessary to cross-examine attorney).

10. Clark v. City of Munster, 115 F.R.D. 609, 615 (N.D. Ind. 1987) (if client plans to waive privilege at trial but refuses to allow discovery on privileged matter, court has discretion to exclude privileged matter if offered at trial).

11. Proposed-but-rejected FRE 511; URE 510 (1999). *See also* Dayco Corp. Derivative Sec. Litig., 99 F.R.D. 616, 619 (S.D. Ohio 1983) (no waiver where press release summarizing findings of internal investigation did not disclose "significant part" of report).

12. United States v. O'Malley, 786 F.2d 786, 794 (7th Cir. 1986) (in order to waive privilege, client "must disclose the communication with the attorney itself"). *See also* ACN, proposed-but-rejected FRE 511 (client does not waive attorney-client privilege "merely by disclosing a subject which he had discussed with his attorney").

13. United States v. Bernard, 877 F.2d 1463, 1465 (10th Cir. 1989) (defendant waived privilege on whether he verified the legality of loans with his attorney when he told third party prior to trial that such communication had occurred).

14. United States v. Jacobs, 117 F.3d 82, 87-89 (2d Cir. 1997) (privilege waived where client gave inaccurate extrajudicial summary of letters from attorney, claiming he approved scheme when actually he disapproved it; disclosure of content waives privilege and so does inaccurate statement of privileged communication).

attorney does not waive the privilege for the contents or substance of what she told her lawyer.[15]

A promise to waive the privilege in the future is not itself a waiver if the privileged communications are never actually disclosed.[16] But communications *made with the intent* that they eventually be disclosed are usually not confidential, and no privilege arises in the first instance.[17]

The party asserting waiver has the burden of proving that waiver occurred.[18] If the material claimed to be privileged is in the possession of a third party, however, the holder is expected to bear the burden of showing that the privilege was not waived because, under the circumstances, sharing with the third party was itself privileged.[19]

The standard for evidentiary waiver is less strict than for constitutional waiver. While waiver of constitutional guarantees affecting the fairness of a trial requires the "intentional relinquishment or abandonment of a known right,"[20] an evidentiary privilege can be waived by voluntary disclosure even if the holder did not intend to relinquish the privilege.[21]

"Voluntary" disclosure

Disclosure is generally involuntary if privileged matter was procured by fraud, deception, or theft, which means that waiver does not occur.[22] Disclosure is also involuntary if it is compelled by court order after a privilege claim is overruled, and again waiver does not occur,[23] which

15. Mitchell v. Superior Court, 37 Cal. 3d 591, 603, 691 P.2d 642, 648, 208 Cal. Rptr. 886, 892 (1984) (plaintiff did not waive privilege "through her mere acknowledgment" that she discussed certain matters with attorney).

16. Tennenbaum v. Deloitte & Touche, 77 F.3d 337, 339-341 (9th Cir. 1996).

17. *See* §5.13, *supra.*

18. Restatement (Third) of the Law Governing Lawyers (Proposed Final Draft, No. 1, 1996) §135(3) (one seeking to establish waiver or exception "must assert the waiver or exception and, if the assertion is contested, demonstrate each of its elements").

19. Status Time Corp. v. Sharp Elecs. Corp., 95 F.R.D. 27, 34 (S.D.N.Y. 1982) (where third party was in possession of privileged letter, burden on claimant to establish that privilege was not waived).

20. Johnson v. Zerbst, 304 U.S. 458, 464 (1938). *But see* Schneckloth v. Bustamonte, 412 U.S. 218, 235-237, 248 (1973) ("knowing and intelligent" standard applies to constitutional guarantees necessary for fair trial; knowledge of right to refuse a search is only one factor in determining whether consent to search is valid under Fourth Amendment).

21. In re Grand Jury Investigation of Ocean Transp., 604 F.2d 672, 675 (D.C. Cir. 1979) (intent to waive privilege "is not necessary for such waiver to occur"), *cert. denied sub nom.* Sea Land Serv., Inc. v. United States, 444 U.S. 915.

22. *See, e.g.,* In re Grand Jury Proceedings Involving Berkley & Co., Inc., 466 F. Supp. 863, 869 (D. Minn. 1979) (upholding privilege claim for stolen documents), *aff'd,* 629 F.2d 548 (8th Cir. 1980). *See also* proposed-but-rejected FRE 512 (no waiver where disclosure occurred "without opportunity to claim the privilege"). *Compare* Suburban Sew 'N Sweep v. Swiss-Bernina, 91 F.R.D. 254, 260 (N.D. Ill. 1981) (privilege lost where opponent found privileged correspondence in client's dumpster).

23. *See* Hollins v. Powell, 773 F.2d 191, 196 (8th Cir. 1985) (no waiver where privileged matter disclosed at deposition, because privilege objection had previously been asserted to entire line of questioning and court had overruled objection), *cert. denied,* 475 U.S. 1119; Transamerica Computer v. International Business Machs., 573 F.2d 646, 651 (9th Cir. 1978) (party does not waive privilege "for documents which he is compelled to produce"). *See also* proposed-but-rejected FRE 512 and URE 510 (1999) (even though privileged matter has already been disclosed, privilege not lost if disclosure was "compelled erroneously").

means that the holder of the privilege (or the person in possession of the privileged material) may disclose it, and the holder can challenge the order later. If the order was erroneous, the privilege can be reasserted in subsequent proceedings.[24]

Disclosure is voluntary when made as a result of economic pressure rather than legal compulsion.[25] Disclosure in response to a subpoena is considered voluntary if the privilege holder produces the sought-after material without objecting.[26] If that material is obtained without the holder's consent during a government search, the privilege is not lost,[27] but the holder may lose the privilege if he does not reclaim it or file a suppression motion, or take other reasonable steps to preserve its confidentiality.[28]

If a client discloses privileged matter without objection on direct or cross-examination, doing so is a voluntary waiver unless the client was misled or confused by the question to such a degree that that it would be unfair to find waiver.[29]

Most authorities hold that waiver need not be "knowing" in the sense of awareness by the client that disclosure would result in loss of the privilege.[30] Still, the disclosure itself must be "knowing" or it does not amount to waiver,[31] except that even accidental disclosure amounts to

24. *See* ACN, proposed-but-rejected FRE 512 (even where holder does not "exhaust all legal recourse" in contesting order to disclose, holder may later challenge order as "erroneously compelled," and this "modest departure from usual principles of res judicata" is justified by fact that appeal is not always available and the advantage of having "one simple rule, assuring at least one opportunity for judicial supervision in every case").

25. *See* In re John Doe Corp., 675 F.2d 482, 489 (2d Cir. 1982) (privilege held waived even though client claimed disclosure to underwriter was involuntary "because it was coerced by the legal duty of due diligence and the millions of dollars riding on the public offering"; once disclosure is made "no matter what the economic imperatives" privilege is lost).

26. Westinghouse v. Republic of the Philippines, 951 F.2d 1414, 1427 n.14 (3d Cir. 1991) (finding disclosure in response to subpoena voluntary, where client withdrew motion to quash subpoena and produced documents; had client "continued to object to the subpoena and produced the documents only after being ordered to do so, we would not consider its disclosure of those documents to be voluntary").

27. United States v. De La Jara, 973 F.2d 746, 749 (9th Cir. 1992) (privilege can still be asserted where government discovered letter in course of executing search warrant).

28. *See, e.g.,* United States v. De La Jara, 973 F.2d 746 (9th Cir. 1992) (privilege waived where holder "did nothing to recover the letter or protect its confidentiality during the six month interlude between its seizure and introduction into evidence").

29. *See, e.g.,* Hoyas v. State, 456 So. 2d 1225, 1229 (Fla. App. 1984) (privilege waived where court found appellant was not surprised or misled on direct examination and disclosed communication made to attorney).

30. *See, e.g.,* Miller v. Continental Ins. Co., 392 N.W.2d 500, 505 (Iowa 1986) (waiver found when clients disclosed privileged communications in sworn affidavits, although they did not know such disclosure would waive privilege). *See generally* 8 Wigmore, Evidence §2327 at 636 (McNaughton rev. 1961) (privilege would seldom be found waived if holder's "intention not to abandon could alone control").

31. *See, e.g.,* In re Grand Jury Proceedings Involving Berkley & Co., Inc., 466 F. Supp. 863, 869 (D. Minn. 1979) (privilege not waived when documents were stolen by former employee and given to government), *aff'd,* 629 F.2d 548 (8th Cir. 1980). *See also* proposed-but-rejected FRE 512 and URE 511 (1999) (no waiver where disclosure made "without opportunity to claim the privilege").

waiver if the client (or his lawyer) did not take reasonable care to avoid it.[32]

Privileged disclosure

The privilege is not waived if disclosure is made to a person who is within the attorney-client privilege, such as a representative of the attorney[33] or a joint client[34] or someone who asserts a common defense.[35] Nor is the privilege lost if disclosure is made to a person having an independent privilege, such as a spouse, physician, or psychotherapist (provided that such disclosure meets the requirements of the independent privilege).[36]

Although disclosure in a prior court hearing normally waives the privilege,[37] obviously this principle does not mean that waiver occurs when the client or lawyer discloses privileged matter to the court during an *in camera* proceeding where the whole purpose is to determine whether the privilege applies, and the court needs assistance in ruling on the privilege claim.[38]

Selective or limited disclosure

A client generally cannot make "selective" or "limited" disclosure of privileged matter to unprivileged third persons without waiving the privilege.[39] Most authorities find waiver even when disclosure is made to government agencies in connection with an official investigation,[40] although some courts have recognized a limited waiver doctrine in this context.[41] Under FRE 502, which governs disclosures in a federal proceeding or to a federal office or agency, any waiver as a result of selective disclosure is limited to the material actually disclosed, and does not extend to additional privileged communications unless "they ought in fairness" be considered with the disclosed material.[42]

---

32. *See generally* §5.29, *infra.*

33. *See* §5.10, *supra.*

34. *See* §5.14, *supra.*

35. *See* §5.15, *supra.*

36. *See* proposed-but-rejected FRE 511 (rule of waiver by voluntary disclosure does not apply "if the disclosure is itself a privileged communication"); URE 510 (1999) (no waiver if "disclosure itself is privileged").

37. United States v. Suarez, 820 F.2d 1158, 1159-1160 (11th Cir. 1987) (privilege waived where defendant permitted attorney to testify at hearing on motion to withdraw guilty plea and could not be reasserted at trial to bar attorney from testifying to same subject matter), *cert. denied,* 484 U.S. 987.

38. United States v. Zolin, 491 U.S. 554, 568 (1989) (disclosing allegedly privileged materials to court for purposes of determining merits of claim "does not have the legal effect of terminating the privilege").

39. In re Qwest Communications International, Inc., 450 F.3d 1179 (10th Cir. 2006) (rejecting selective waiver theory); Permian Corp. v. United States, 665 F.2d 1214, 1221 (D.C. Cir. 1981) (client cannot "pick and choose among his opponents, waiving the privilege for some and resurrecting the claim of confidentiality to obstruct others," nor invoke privilege for communications if he has already "compromised" confidentiality for his own benefit).

40. Westinghouse v. Republic of the Philippines, 951 F.2d 1414, 1425-1427 (3d Cir. 1991) (rejecting selective waiver doctrine; privilege is not necessary "to encourage voluntary cooperation with government investigations").

41. United States v. Shyres, 898 F.2d 647, 657 (8th Cir. 1990) (privilege not waived by voluntary disclosure to the government in connection with grand jury investigation), *cert. denied,* 498 U.S. 821.

42. *See* FRE 502(a). Even prior to the adoption of FRE 502, most courts followed a similar standard. *See, e.g.,* Gray v. Bicknell, 86 F.3d 1472, 1484 (8th Cir. 1996).

The privilege is waived by disclosure to an adversary,[43] and by disclosure to outside auditors,[44] and even by disclosure to a person paying the client's legal fees (except where the payer is also a client of the lawyer).[45] If disclosure to an unprivileged person was anticipated at the time of the communication, no privilege arises because the client did not intend the communication to be confidential.[46]

Although the holder cannot preserve his privilege by a unilateral statement of nonwaiver at the time of disclosing to another,[47] the holder may enter into a nondisclosure or nonwaiver agreement with the party to whom disclosure is made.[48] Such agreements typically allow the holder to reclaim any documents inadvertently produced and to assert the privilege later. Such private agreements are enforceable between the parties,[49] and FRE 502 specifically recognizes this point.[50] The difficulty, however, is that private agreements do not bind outsiders who later seek the disclosed material, and these outsiders can argue that disclosure waived the privilege.[51]

The most significant impact of FRE 502 is that it authorizes courts to enter protective orders that prevent waiver of privilege even where disclosure to an unprivileged third party is made intentionally or without taking "reasonable steps" to prevent disclosure. As the ACN states, a court order may provide for "return of documents without waiver irrespective of the care taken by the disclosing party" and contemplates use

43. Smith v. Alyeska Pipeline Serv. Co., 538 F. Supp. 977, 980-982 (D. Del. 1982) (sending opposing party a copy of letter from attorney to client waived privilege with respect to letter and related communications), *aff'd without opinion,* 758 F.2d 668 (1st Cir. 1984), *cert. denied,* 471 U.S. 1066.

44. United States v. M.I.T., 129 F.3d 681, 684-688 (1st Cir. 1997) (university waived attorney-client privilege by disclosing privileged documents to government audit agency); United States v. Textron Inc., 507 F. Supp. 2d 138 (D.R.I. 2007) (disclosure to outside auditor waives attorney-client privilege).

45. Grand Jury Subpoena (Wine), 841 F.2d 230, 234 (8th Cir. 1988) (privilege waived when client disclosed confidential attorney-client communications to fee payer).

46. *See* §5.13, *supra. See also* United States v. Jones, 696 F.2d 1069, 1072-1073 (4th Cir. 1982) (privilege as to legal opinions waived when clients publicized portions in brochures; court questions whether privilege ever attached, given intent for future disclosure).

47. In re Subpoena Duces Tecum, 99 F.R.D. 582, 584-586 (D.D.C. 1983) (disclosing party waived privilege even though it stated in transmittal letter to SEC that it did not waive privilege by submission of information), *aff'd,* 738 F.2d 1367, 1370 (D.C. Cir. 1984).

48. In re Sealed Case, 676 F.2d 793, 824 (D.C. Cir. 1982) (SEC or other government agency "could expressly agree to any limit on disclosure to other agencies consistent with their responsibilities under law").

49. Chubb Integrated Sys. Ltd. v. National Bank, 103 F.R.D. 52, 67-68 (D.D.C. 1984) (agreement is contract between parties "to refrain from raising the issue of waiver" or "otherwise utilizing" information).

50. *See* FRE 502(e).

51. *See* FRE 502(d) (agreement on effect of disclosure in federal proceeding is "binding only on the parties to the agreement, unless it is incorporated into a court order"). *See also* United States v. M.I.T., 129 F.3d 681, 684-688 (1st Cir. 1997) (nondisclosure agreement with government audit agency not binding on nonparties such as IRS).

of "claw-back" and "quick peek" arrangements "as a way to avoid the excessive costs of pre-production review."[52]

Such a "nonwaiver" order of the court is binding not only in the proceeding where it was entered, but in "any other federal or state proceeding." Thus this federal limitation on privilege waiver prevails over any state law to the contrary, which is one reason why it was necessary for this provision to be enacted by Congress.[53] With respect to disclosure of privileged material in a state proceeding, Rule 502 adopts the position that whichever waiver provision—state or federal—is most protective of the privilege should control.[54]

Effect of agreements and pretrial orders

Difficult waiver questions arise when privileged documents are used to refresh the recollection of a witness for the purpose of testifying. FRE 612 provides that writings so used by a witness at trial are required to be produced at the request of an adverse party, and if the writings are used to refresh recollection before trial the court has discretion to order production. If the witness is outside the circle of persons who may receive the communication without destroying confidentiality,[55] it is unnecessary to consider the effect of FRE 612, because the privilege is lost under traditional principles of waiver. But if she is within the circle (perhaps a client or representative of a client or expert assisting counsel in trial preparation), the question arises whether FRE 612 overrides the privilege so production of the writing may be ordered.[56]

Writings used to refresh recollection

Courts are divided on the question whether (or the degree to which) an attorney's use of work product or privileged material in preparing experts to testify has the effect of waiving protections of the work product doctrine or attorney-client privilege. Some courts hold that FRE 612, which says a court may order disclosure of written material reviewed by a witness before testifying, includes authority to overrule

52. ACN to FRE 502.

53. FRE 502 was enacted by Congress in 2008 as Senate Bill 2450 and signed by the president on September 19, 2008. It applies "in all proceedings commenced after the date of enactment of this Act and, insofar as is just and practicable, in all proceedings pending on such date of enactment." (Pub. L. No. 110-322, 122 Stat. 3537).

54. *See* FRE 502(c): "When the disclosure is made in a state proceeding and is not the subject of a state-court order concerning waiver, the disclosure does not operate as a waiver in a federal proceeding if the disclosure: (1) would not be a waiver under this rule if it had been made in a federal proceeding; or (2) is not a waiver under the law of the state where the disclosure occurred."

55. *See* §5.13, *supra*.

56. Although the House Judiciary Committee stated its intent "that nothing in the Rule be construed as barring the assertion of a privilege with respect to writings used by a witness to refresh his memory," the Committee also viewed FRE 612 as consistent with "existing federal law." House Report, at 13. Under preexisting federal law, a privileged document used to refresh a witness's recollection during his testimony was subject to production. *See, e.g.,* Bailey v. Meister Brau, Inc., 57 F.R.D. 11, 13 (N.D. Ill. 1972). There is no indication that the Committee intended a different rule to apply to writings used to refresh prior to testifying. *See* Wheeling-Pittsburg Steel Corp. v. Underwriters Laboratories, Inc., 81 F.R.D. 8, 10 (N.D. Ill. 1978) ("If the paramount purpose of federal discovery rules is the ascertainment of the truth, the fact that a document was used to refresh one's recollection prior to his testimony instead of during his testimony is of little significance.").

claims of privilege or work product,[57] and the underlying policy behind these holdings is that is unfair to let a witness rely on writings or conversations with counsel that are beyond reach of discovery or protected from inquiry on cross-examination of the expert.[58] Some courts have concluded that FRE 612 allows them even to require pretrial production of privileged writings reviewed by the witness before testifying.[59]

Other courts are more cautious, and the underlying policy is that opening up conversations with the lawyer for the calling party, and exposing materials covered by work product or attorney-client privilege, drive lawyers away from using written material and toward reliance on oral briefings, force lawyers to hire experts who never testify, and lead to disclosure going beyond the actual basis of any testimony ultimately offered. Courts taking this view ask whether production is "necessary in the interests of justice"[60] or require the other side to show that the witness actually did rely on a particular writing in refreshing his memory or in formulating his testimony.[61] Of course showing reliance can be hard if a witness is uncooperative or untruthful, and it seems that a witness should not be able to block production simply by denying that he relied on something, particularly if he spent a lot of time reviewing it or if his testimony reflects detailed information that he could not readily have memorized or gotten somewhere else. Before ordering production, some courts undertake *in camera* review to determine the extent of reliance, if any, on documents and conversations with counsel.[62] If privilege

57. *See, e.g.,* Marshall v. United States Postal Serv., 88 F.R.D. 348, 350 (D.D.C. 1980) (FRE 612 authorizes a finding of waiver when privileged documents are used to refresh witness's recollection).

58. *See* Bailey v. Meister Brau, Inc., 57 F.R.D. 11, 13 (N.D. Ill. 1972) (accepting plaintiff's claim would ignore "unfair disadvantage" that could be placed on the cross-examiner "by the simple expedient of using only privileged writings to refresh recollection"). *But see* Davidson & Voth, Waiver of the Attorney-Client Privilege, 64 Or. L. Rev. 637, 666 (1986) (criticizing cases requiring production of privileged writings used to refresh, because allowing witnesses to review prior statements "is hardly a means to influence testimony improperly"; moreover, production can be easily evaded by briefing witnesses orally, a method that may have a greater danger of improperly influencing the witness's testimony).

59. James Julian, Inc. v. Raytheon Co., 93 F.R.D. 138, 144-146 (D. Del. 1982) (when counsel made decision to "educate" witness with protected work product, opponent is entitled "to know the content of that education"); Wheeling-Pittsburg Steel Corp. v. Underwriters Laboratories, Inc., 81 F.R.D. 8, 9 (N.D. Ill. 1978) (use of documents to refresh memory prior to deposition effectively waived attorney-client privilege).

60. *See, e.g.,* Baker v. CNA Ins. Co., 123 F.R.D. 322, 327 (D. Mont. 1988) (no waiver from disclosure for purposes of refreshment unless testimony discloses significant portion of privileged material). *See generally* Floyd, A "Delicate and Difficult Task": Balancing the Competing Interests of Federal Rule of Evidence 612, the Work Product Doctrine, and the Attorney-Client Privilege, 44 Buffalo L. Rev. 101 (1996).

61. Sporck v. Peil, 759 F.2d 312, 318 (3d Cir. 1985) (party cannot seek production of refreshment material without first asking questions at deposition and showing that testimony related to documents used to refresh), *cert. denied,* 474 U.S. 903.

62. Barrer v. Women's Natl. Bank, 96 F.R.D. 202, 205 (D.D.C. 1982) (court resolved conflict between FRE 612 and attorney-client privilege by undertaking *in camera* review of documents to determine whether there was discrepancy between testimony and documents used to refresh).

or work product protection is lost, any waiver applies only to documents and other material actually considered, not to other things.[63]

If a client discloses or consents to disclosure of any significant part of a communication, the traditional rule has been that the privilege is waived not only for the matter disclosed but for all other related communications.[64] The rationale for this "part-whole" rule of waiver is that a litigant should not be allowed to make partial disclosure of a privileged communication[65] because the part disclosed might be unrepresentative, misleading to the opponent or trier of fact, or unduly favorable to the disclosing party.[66]

Scope of waiver

The trend of modern cases, however, has been toward limiting general subject matter waiver to situations where fairness requires disclosure of underlying or related documents,[67] and this is the position adopted in FRE 502(a), which provides that waiver extends to undisclosed communications relating to the same subject matter only where "they ought in fairness to be considered together." Courts are most likely to rule that partial disclosure results in broad waiver when it is made to a trier of fact who could be misled by a privileged communication taken out of context[68] or when a party tries to gain some advantage by partial disclosure.[69] If a party makes partial disclosure of privileged matter prior to trial, this tactic could be unfair if it interferes with the opponent's ability to prepare for trial or distorts settlement expectations.[70]

---

63. Marshall v. United States Postal Serv., 88 F.R.D. 348, 351 (D.D.C. 1980) (using a document to aid recollection "requires only the disclosure of the document to opposing counsel" and disclosure does not "constitute any further waiver of the attorney-client privilege").

64. *See, e.g.,* In re Sealed Case, 676 F.2d 793, 809 (D.C. Cir. 1982) (voluntary disclosure of privileged document to third party waives the privilege not only for document but "all the communications relating to the same subject matter").

65. 8 Wigmore, Evidence §2327, at 638 (attorney-client privilege is "intended only as an incidental means of defense, and not as an independent means of attack").

66. International Paper Co. v. Fiberboard Corp., 63 F.R.D. 88, 92 (D. Del. 1974) (it would be "manifestly unfair" to allow one party to make factual assertions and then deny the other party "the foundation for those assertions in order to contradict them"). A factor to be considered is how intertwined the disclosed communication is with other communications necessary to present a balanced account. *Cf.* FRE 106, discussed in §§1.17-1.18, *supra.*

67. Hercules, Inc. v. Exxon Corp., 434 F. Supp. 136, 156 (D. Del. 1977) (privilege or immunity is waived only if factors relevant to particular and narrow subject have been disclosed "in circumstances in which it would be unfair to deny the other party an opportunity to discover other relevant facts with respect to that subject matter").

68. *See, e.g.,* ITT Corp. v. United Tel. Co., 60 F.R.D. 177, 185-186 (M.D. Fla. 1973) (once litigant introduces part of correspondence with attorney, production of all related correspondence may be required).

69. In re Sealed Case, 676 F.2d 793, 809 n.54 (D.C. Cir. 1982) (courts retain discretion not to impose full waiver for all communications on same subject "where the client has merely disclosed a communication to a third party, as opposed to making some use of it").

70. *See generally* Marcus, The Perils of Privilege: Waiver and the Litigator, 84 Mich. L. Rev. 1605, 1633-1637 (1986).

Once the attorney-client privilege is waived, it generally cannot be reasserted.[71] If disclosure occurs without waiver, however, as happens when a court compels disclosure erroneously, the holder can assert the privilege to bar introduction of the evidence against in a later proceeding.[72]

Even though theft, interception, or breach of confidentiality by the attorney can destroy the secrecy of the communication, the privilege itself is not lost.[73]

§5.29   Inadvertent Disclosure

Prior to the enactment of FRE 502 by Congress in 2008, federal courts had been divided on the question whether the attorney-client privilege was lost by accidental or inadvertent disclosure, as happens when a privileged document is released during discovery. One minority view held that the privilege was waived by any unprivileged disclosure that was voluntary, even though made inadvertently and without intent to waive.[1] A second minority view held that the privilege was waived only when the disclosing party actually intended to waive it.[2]

Intermediate approach   The prevailing intermediate view was that the question whether disclosure during discovery results in loss of privilege protection depended very much on the circumstances,[3] and the issue should be resolved by looking at the degree of care apparently exercised by the claimant[4] and her behavior in taking remedial steps after disclosing

---

71. United States v. Suarez, 820 F.2d 1158, 1160 (11th Cir. 1987) (attorney-client privilege waived when defendant's attorney testified at pretrial hearing to withdraw guilty plea; once attorney testified at hearing to withdraw guilty plea, privilege "could not bar his testimony on the same subject at trial"), *cert. denied*, 484 U.S. 987.

72. *See* proposed-but-rejected FRE 512; URE 510 (1999).

73. United States v. Sindona, 636 F.2d 792, 804-805 (2d Cir. 1980) (allowing assertion of privilege with respect to evidence improperly divulged by lawyer in breach of duty of confidentiality), *cert. denied*, 451 U.S. 912; In re Dayco Corp. Derivative Sec. Litig., 102 F.R.D. 468, 470 (S.D. Ohio 1984) (upholding privilege to prevent introduction of privileged matter at trial, despite fact that it had already been published in newspaper).

§5.29   1. *See, e.g.*, In re Sealed Case, 877 F.2d 976, 980 (D.C. Cir. 1989) (refusing to "distinguish between various degrees of 'voluntariness' in waivers of the attorney-client privilege" or to "grant greater protection to those who assert the privilege than their own precautions warrant"; court requires that parties "treat the confidentiality of attorney-client communications like jewels—if not crown jewels").

2. Eisenberg v. Gagnon, 766 F.2d 770, 788 (3d Cir. 1985) (no waiver where defense counsel discussing privileged correspondence at side bar assumed discussion was off the record since the "waiver must be knowing" by any standard), *cert. denied*, 474 U.S. 946.

3. *See, e.g.*, Gray v. Bicknell, 86 F.3d 1472, 1484 (8th Cir. 1996) (intermediate approach considering precautions taken to preserve privilege is "best suited to achieving a fair result").

4. In re Grand Jury Investigation of Ocean Transp., 604 F.2d 672, 674-675 (D.C. Cir. 1979) (after producing documents for the government, counsel was asked whether documents marked "P" were privileged, and then failed to assert privilege), *cert. denied*, 444 U.S. 915; Eigenheim Bank v. Halpern, 598 F. Supp. 988, 991 (S.D.N.Y. 1984) (waiver by inadvertence found where procedures used to maintain confidentiality were "lax, careless, inadequate or indifferent to consequences").

privileged material.[5] Promptness in discovering the fact of disclosure and seeking return or suppression of material was thought to support the notion that disclosure was truly accidental and it lessened the likelihood that other parties would rely on the disclosed material.[6]

FRE 502(b) codifies the intermediate view for inadvertent disclosures made in a federal proceeding or to a federal officer or agency. The rule provides that such disclosures do not operate as a waiver if the holder of the privilege took reasonable steps to prevent disclosure and also took reasonable steps to rectify the error, which often includes complying with the requirement stated in Civil Rule 26 to give notice and try to retrieve materials that were mistakenly disclosed.[7]

Under FRE 502, as under prior decisions, courts must decide whether a party took "reasonable steps" to preserve the privilege. Factors that are relevant in determining whether inadvertent disclosure is a waiver include the volume of discovery, the time taken to rectify the error, the scope of discovery, the extent of disclosure, and considerations of fairness.[8] The ACN to FRE 502 comments that a party using "advanced analytical software applications and linguistic tools in screening privilege" may have taken "reasonable steps" to prevent inadvertent disclosure, and notes that implementation of "an efficient system of records management" by the privilege holder may be relevant.

5. *See, e.g.,* United States v. De La Jara, 973 F.2d 746, 749-750 (9th Cir. 1992) (privilege waived where holder failed to reclaim privileged letter seized during government search); In re Grand Jury Investigation of Ocean Transp., 604 F.2d 672, 675 (D.C. Cir. 1979) (privilege waived where attorney allowed disclosure of certain documents that appeared to be privileged but a year later sought return on ground that they were privileged and disclosure was inadvertent), *cert. denied,* 444 U.S. 915.

6. United States v. Ary, 518 F.3d 775, 785 (10th Cir. 2008) (defendant waited six weeks after Rule 16 discovery meeting to claim privilege for documents seized on execution of search warrant at his home; privilege waived). *See generally* Davidson and Voth, Waiver of the Attorney-Client Privilege, 64 Or. L. Rev. 637, 644-645 (1986) (courts should uphold privilege where attorney who inadvertently releases document takes prompt steps to recover it before reliance by opposing side).

7. FRCivP 26(b)(5)(B) provides that if information produced in discovery is subject to a claim of privilege or work product, "the party making the claim may notify any party that received the information of the claim and the basis for it," after which the latter "must promptly return, sequester, or destroy the specified information and any copies it has" and cannot "use or disclose the information until the claim is resolved." Indeed, the latter must take "reasonable steps to retrieve the information" if disclosure has already occurred. The information can be promptly presented in court under seal "for a determination of the claim," and the party who produced the information "must preserve" it until the claim is resolved.

8. Judson Atkinson Candies v. Latini-Hohberger, 529 F.3d 371, 388-389 (7th Cir. 2008) (on issue of reasonable care when privileged document is disclosed in discovery, court considers volume of documents and precautions taken to safeguard privilege; there was nothing "clearly inadequate" here; no waiver); Lois Sportswear, U.S.A., Inc. v. Levi Strauss & Co., 104 F.R.D. 103, 105 (S.D.N.Y. 1985); Hartford Fire Ins. Co. v. Garvey, 109 F.R.D. 323, 332 (N.D. Cal. 1985). *See generally* Marcus, The Perils of Privilege: Waiver and the Litigator, 84 Mich. L. Rev. 1605, 1654-1655 (1986) (waivers "should be based on fairness, which is the emerging trend," and main concern is that litigant "may affirmatively use privileged material to garble the truth, while invoking the privilege to deny his opponent access to related privileged material that would put the proffered evidence in perspective").

Other factors   Also important are extenuating circumstances, the most obvious being the press of massive discovery going forward under tight deadlines, where even caution in producing documents may fail to prevent all mistakes.[9] Other factors bear on the calculus as well, including the number of disclosures, the volume, nature, and importance of disclosed material, the obviousness of privilege issues, and whether the interests of justice would be served by relieving the party of its error.[10] With greater volume, disclosure is more likely to seem careless and perhaps even purposeful. In such cases, the notion of waiver more clearly applies, and loss of protection seems justified.[11] Much the same applies if the material is central to issues that are well defined, if the privilege claim seems obvious, and if the claimant grants wide access or discloses more than once.[12] Finally, it should count in the calculus that the receiving party has relied or has not relied on the disclosed material in developing litigation strategy.[13]

Inadvertent or accidental disclosure may happen for reasons having little to do with the discovery process. The age of express delivery, fax machines, and e-mail has brought new opportunities for putting material into the wrong hands through misaddress and misadventure. If materials are misdelivered or mistransmitted through simple accident (misdialing a fax number or misaddressing an e-mail), or through misadventure (a delivery service leaves material at the wrong address), surely privilege protection should not be lost. Outsiders are likely sometimes to gain a windfall from unanticipated material that goes astray by accident or misadventure. But the privilege itself should survive these common pitfalls in an age that offers so many opportunities for mistake.[14]

9. Transamerica Computer Co. v. International Business Mach. Corp., 573 F.2d 646, 648 (9th Cir. 1978) (no waiver where IBM had been ordered to produce 17 million pages of material in 90 days; court found that IBM had made a "herculean effort" to cull out privileged items).

10. Gray v. Bicknell, 86 F.3d 1472, 1481-1482 (8th Cir. 1996); Parkway Gallery Furniture, Inc. v. Kittinger/Pennsylvania House Group, 116 F.R.D. 46, 50 (M.D.N.C. 1987) (in determining whether there has been waiver by inadvertent disclosure, court should consider "(1) The reasonableness of the precautions taken to prevent inadvertent disclosure in view of the extent of the document production; (2) the number of inadvertent disclosures; (3) the extent of the disclosure; (4) any delay and measures taken to rectify the disclosures; (5) whether the overriding interests of justice would or would not be served by relieving a party of its error.").

11. *See, e.g.,* Lois Sportswear, U.S.A., Inc. v. Levi Strauss & Co., 104 F.R.D. 103, 105 (S.D.N.Y. 1985) (listing "extent of disclosure" as factor in determining whether waiver occurred).

12. Eigenheim Bank v. Halpern, 598 F. Supp. 988, 991-992 (S.D.N.Y. 1984) (waiver found where inadvertent disclosure made for a second time after documents were returned after a first inadvertent disclosure).

13. *See, e.g.,* Weil v. Investment/Indicators, Research & Mgmt., Inc., 647 F.2d 18, 25 (9th Cir. 1981) (court considers fact that disclosure was made to opposing counsel rather than to court, came early in the case, and no prejudice resulted).

14. *Cf.* ABA Model Rule of Professional Conduct 4.4(b): "A lawyer who receives a document [including e-mails] relating to the representation of the lawyer's client and knows or reasonably should know that the document was inadvertently sent shall promptly notify the sender." The accompanying Comment says that lawyers "may choose to return" an inadvertently sent document "unread" as "a matter of professional judgment."

Inadvertent or accidental disclosure brings two additional issues: **Authority to waive**
First, how far should the actions of the attorney bind the client, considering that the client owns the privilege and ultimately has authority to claim or waive it? Most courts hold that retaining a lawyer to represent the client means that the client is in effect charged with the lawyer's mistakes in disclosure during the course of legal representation,[15] although some courts have said the client should not be bound by counsel's mistakes in disclosing or failing to protect the confidentiality of privileged materials, particularly if such conduct seems negligent.[16]

Second, does waiver (if it happened at all) apply only to the matter **Scope of waiver** disclosed, or does it reach other related communications that are also privileged? Rule 502 answers this question for inadvertent disclosures made in a federal proceeding or to a federal office or agency. The answer is that there is no subject matter waiver at all, except where the disclosure was "intentional" and the related undisclosed matter "ought in fairness" be considered with the privileged material already disclosed.

For inadvertent disclosures in circumstances not covered by FRE 502, a similar policy should apply. The purpose of the rule of waiver by partial disclosure is to prevent a party from obtaining unfair advantage by disclosing a portion of privileged matter that may be unrepresentative or misleading. This danger is generally nonexistent in cases where the disclosure was inadvertent.[17] Therefore, the better approach is to limit the scope of waiver by inadvertent disclosure to the material already disclosed, and this view is adopted by most courts.[18] A broader scope of waiver is justified in cases where the disclosing party has obtained unfair advantage by the disclosure or refuses to stipulate that the disclosed material will not be used at trial, thereby creating a need for the opposing party to discover related communications on the same subject.[19]

15. Weil v. Investment/Indicators, Research & Mgmt., Inc., 647 F.2d 18, 25 n.13 (9th Cir. 1981) (waiver found where privileged communications voluntarily disclosed without objection by asserting party's counsel); In re Grand Jury Investigation of Ocean Transp., 604 F.2d 672, 675 (D.C. Cir. 1979) (where "counsel acted within the scope of authority conferred upon it," client "may not now be heard to complain about how that authority was exercised"), *cert. denied,* 444 U.S. 915.

16. *See, e.g.,* KL Group v. Case, Kay & Lynch, 829 F.2d 909, 918-919 (9th Cir. 1987) (inadvertent waiver by lawyer not charged to client when client did not disclose or consent to disclosure); Mendenhall v. Barber-Greene Co., 531 F. Supp. 951, 955 (N.D. Ill. 1982) ("[I]f we are serious about the attorney-client privilege and its relation to the client's welfare, we should require more than such negligence by counsel before the client can be deemed to have given up the privilege.").

17. First Wis. Mortgage Trust v. First Wis. Corp., 86 F.R.D. 160, 173-174 (E.D. Wis. 1980) (where inadvertent disclosure is not advantageous to disclosing party, privilege is not waived for related documents).

18. Gray v. Bicknell, 86 F.3d 1472, 1481-1482 (8th Cir. 1996) (where privilege waived inadvertently by mistaken disclosure of privileged letters during discovery, waiver is limited to two letters actually disclosed; privilege continues to protect related documents).

19. Hercules, Inc. v. Exxon Corp., 434 F. Supp. 136, 156 (D. Del. 1977) (broad waiver occurs only where "facts relevant to a particular, narrow subject matter have been disclosed in circumstances in which it would be unfair to deny the other party an opportunity to discover other relevant facts with respect to that subject matter").

There has been confusion in the cases on the question whether inadvertent disclosure should be addressed as a problem of failed confidentiality or as a matter of waiver.[20] The two issues are analytically distinct. The confidentiality requirement generally focuses on the intent of the communicator at the time the communication was made not to disclose the communication to persons who are outside the privilege.[21] The client's subsequent conduct bears on confidentiality only to the extent that it provides circumstantial evidence of the client's intent at the time the communication was made.

Waiver focuses on whether the holder "voluntarily" disclosed or consented to disclosure of the privileged matter.[22] Waiver occurs only after the making of a confidential communication—the privilege does not attach if the communication was not confidential. As a practical matter, similar standards have tended to evolve under both lines of analysis. If the holder did not take reasonable steps to protect against interception at the time of the communication, the privilege is denied because of lack of confidentiality. If the holder (or the attorney acting as his agent) did not take reasonable steps to protect against later disclosure, the privilege is lost on grounds of waiver.

Stolen or intercepted communications

If confidences are seized or stolen by private parties, such as employees or outsiders who trespass, eavesdrop, intercept mails or deliveries, or rummage through dumpsters (which sometimes does and sometimes does not involve trespass or any invasion of property rights), the client should have an opportunity later to claim the protection of the privilege.[23] Some modern authority holds otherwise, however, apparently under the influence of Wigmore's overstrict opinion that essentially any disclosure causes loss of protection.[24]

With respect to these private initiatives, the wiser rule is that a claim of privilege survives, at least where the lawyer and client have taken reasonable care to keep privileged material confidential.[25] The privilege should not be lost if unseen eavesdroppers tap the line or listen at the door, or outsiders succeed in pilfering, spying, or rummaging through garbage. Reasonable care surely does not require lawyers or parties to have soundproofed offices or to hire security guards or

---

20. *See, e.g.,* Weil v. Investment/Indicators Research & Mgmt., Inc., 647 F.2d 18, 24 n.11 (9th Cir. 1981) (finding waiver by inadvertent disclosure but noting that other courts have reached the same result by finding that disclosure has extinguished confidentiality).

21. *See* proposed-but-rejected FRE 503(a)(4), discussed in §5.13, *supra.*

22. Proposed-but-rejected FRE 511. *See generally* §5.28, *supra.*

23. *See* proposed-but-rejected FRE 512 and URE 510 (1999) (privilege not lost where disclosure occurred "without opportunity to claim the privilege").

24. *See* Suburban Sew 'N Sweep, Inc. v. Swiss-Bernina, Inc., 91 F.R.D. 254, 260 (N.D. Ill. 1981) (court finds loss of privilege with respect to copies of letters from defendant to defendant's attorney obtained by plaintiff from defendant's trash dumpster). *But see* Mendenhall v. Barber-Greene Co., 531 F. Supp. 951, 955 n.8 (N.D. Ill. 1982) (criticizing Sew 'N Sweep approach).

25. In re Victor, 422 F. Supp. 475, 476 (S.D.N.Y. 1976) (privilege waived where client left papers in public hallway outside the office of his attorney: "[I]t certainly could not be said that the client expected these papers to be kept from the eyes of third parties.").

experts to check for bugs or wiretaps. The privilege requires ordinary care, not elaborate counteroffenses.[26]

§5.30 Implied Waiver by Claim Assertion

When a client advances a claim or defense that put in issue the nature of a communication with his lawyer, substantial authority agrees that this action impliedly waives any claim of privilege for that communication.[1] For example, if the client asserts that he acted under advice of counsel, he waives a claim of privilege with respect to specific advice given,[2] and the same thing happens when a client claims she did not understand a lawyer's advice.[3] She also waives a claim of privilege by alleging malpractice, incompetence, or breach of ethics by the attorney, paving the way to use any privileged matter that is necessary to defend against such charges.[4] It is generally agreed, however, that a client does not waive the privilege merely by denying the allegations of an indictment or complaint.[5]

A variety of justifications support the doctrine of waiver by claim assertion. Sometimes the allegation itself is viewed as partial disclosure

Rationale

26. This view found its way into proposed-but-rejected FRE 503, which was adopted by many states. Clause (a)(4) defines a confidential communication as one that is not intended for further disclosure to unprivileged third persons, thereby preserving confidentiality despite interception that could not reasonably be anticipated. Under proposed-but-rejected FRE 503(b), the holder has power "to refuse to disclose *and to prevent any other person from disclosing*" confidential communications, which would include eavesdroppers or thieves. Finally, clause (b) provides that there is no waiver where disclosure occurred "without opportunity to claim the privilege," which covers intercepted communications.

§5.30 1. Courts use the term "implied" waiver to distinguish this doctrine from traditional principles of waiver by voluntary disclosure. *See generally* Thornburg, Attorney-Client Privilege: Issue-Related Waivers, 50 J. Air. L. & Com. 1039 (1985).

2. *See, e.g.,* Glenmede Trust Co. v. Thompson, 56 F.3d 476, 486 (3d Cir. 1995) (where party claimed reliance on advice of counsel, proper to allow discovery of documents bearing on such advice in order to "test" what information had actually been conveyed by client to counsel and "vice versa"). *See also* Restatement (Third) of the Law Governing Lawyers (Proposed Final Draft No. 1, 1996) §130(1)(a) (attorney-client privilege waived if client asserts as to a material issue that he "acted upon the advice of a lawyer or that the advice was otherwise relevant to the legal significance of the client's conduct").

3. Livingston v. North Belle Vernon Borough, 91 F.3d 515, 536-537 (3d Cir. 1996) (where civil rights claimant claimed she did not understand legal impact of a release agreement with defendant that she had previously signed, she waived the attorney-client privilege as to legal advice given by prior attorney who represented her in negotiating agreement).

4. *See, e.g.,* United States v. Moody, 923 F.2d 341, 352-353 (5th Cir. 1991) (privilege may be waived concerning discussions with bankruptcy attorney when during opening statement defendant blamed attorney for improperly listing assets in bankruptcy petition), *cert. denied,* 112 S. Ct. 80. *See also* Restatement (Third) of the Law Governing Lawyers (Proposed Final Draft No. 1, 1996) §130(1)(b) (attorney-client privilege waived if client asserts as to a material issue that "lawyer's assistance was ineffective, negligent, or for some other reason wrongful"). *Compare* proposed-but-rejected FRE 503(d)(3), discussed in §5.23, *supra,* which creates an exception to privilege for communications "relevant to an issue of breach of duty by the lawyer," thereby allowing attorney to disclose privileged matter in self-defense.

5. Lorenz v. Valley Forge Ins. Co., 815 F.2d 1095, 1098 (7th Cir. 1987) (denial of allegations in complaint is not same as affirmatively injecting issues into litigation).

of a privileged communication.[6] A finding of waiver may be necessary in order to let the adversary verify or explore the actual advice given.[7] Sometimes the assertion of a claim or defense is viewed as an "anticipatory waiver," at least where it is clear that privileged evidence will be needed to support the claim or defense.[8] Finally, courts sometimes find implied waiver when the holder asserts a claim that can only be rebutted if privileged matter is disclosed.[9] Under this latter view, even if the claim asserted by the holder does not entail disclosure of privileged communications, the privilege is waived to the extent that the opposing party needs to draw on privileged matter to make a fair response.[10]

Courts taking a broad view of waiver by claim assertion hold that the privilege is waived in a wide variety of circumstances where access to privileged evidence is considered critical to the opposing party in responding to a contention made by the holder.[11] For example, some courts find waiver when a client places his mental state at issue by

6. United States v. Jacobs, 117 F.3d 82, 87-89 (2d Cir. 1997) (privilege waived because client gave inaccurate extrajudicial summary of letters from attorney, claiming he approved scheme when actually he disapproved it; disclosure of content waives privilege and so does inaccurate statement of privileged communication). But see In re Seagate Technology, LLC, 497 F.3d 1360, 1073-1076 (Fed. Cir. 2007) (in patent case, claiming defense based on advice of counsel and disclosing counsel's opinions do not waive privilege for communications with trial counsel; roles of the two lawyers differ significantly; opinion counsel provides objective assessment for making business decisions, but trial counsel focuses on litigation strategy; court has discretion "in unique circumstances" to extend waiver to trial counsel, as might happen if party or lawyer "engages in chicanery").

7. *See* Chevron Corp. v. Pennzoil Co., 974 F.2d 1156, 1162-1163 (9th Cir. 1992) (where defendant claimed reliance on advice of counsel, privilege waived as to specific advice given, because it is improper to use the privilege as both "sword" and "shield" and once defendant put the advice at issue it would be unfair to deny opponent "access to the very information [it] must refute"). *Cf.* Columbia Pictures TV v. Krypton Broad., 259 F.3d 1186, 1196 (9th Cir. 2001) (district court within its discretion in precluding party from invoking "advice of counsel" defense where party had refused to answer questions regarding relevant communications with counsel).

8. *See* Developments in the Law—Privileged Communications, 98 Harv. L. Rev. 1450, 1643 (1985) (anticipatory waiver applies where holder intends to prove issue asserted by use of privileged evidence).

9. *See, e.g.,* United States v. Bilzerian, 926 F.2d 1285, 1292 (2d Cir. 1991) (privilege may "implicitly be waived when defendant asserts a claim that in fairness requires examination of protected communications"), *cert. denied,* 112 S. Ct. 63; Byers v. Burleson, 100 F.R.D. 436, 440 (D.D.C. 1983) (by claiming that statute of limitations was tolled by his lack of knowledge that he had a cause of action, plaintiff waived attorney-client privilege with respect to communications bearing on such knowledge).

10. Greater Newburyport Clamshell Alliance v. Public Serv. Co., 838 F.2d 13, 20 (1st Cir. 1988) (privilege ends at the point "where the defendant can show that the plaintiff's civil claim, and the probable defenses thereto, are enmeshed in important evidence that will be unavailable to the defendant if the privilege prevails"); Webster v. Ornoski, 2007 WL 1521048 (E.D. Cal. 2007) (waiver should be "no broader than needed to ensure the fairness of the proceedings," and waiver must be "closely tailored" so scope is determined by "needs of the opposing party in litigating the claims").

11. *See, e.g.,* Ideal Electronics Sec. Co. v. International Fidelity Ins., 129 F.3d 143, 151 (D.C. Cir. 1997) (by claiming indemnification for attorney's fees and offering billing statements as evidence, client waived privilege with respect to redacted portions of billing statements and other communications going to reasonableness of fee award).

asserting good faith based on advice of counsel,[12] or by asserting justifiable reliance on statements claimed to be fraudulent (where claimant may have relied on counsel instead),[13] by claiming lack of knowledge,[14] by claiming lack of criminal intent,[15] or by claiming a certain contractual intent where advice of counsel might shed light on this position.[16]

Jurisdictions are divided on the question whether asserting an insanity defense waives a criminal defendant's attorney-client privilege with respect to communications to a psychotherapist employed by defense counsel.[17] If the defendant calls the psychotherapist to testify, virtually all jurisdictions hold the privilege is waived as to underlying communications between the defendant and the psychotherapist where these are necessary for a fair evaluation of the testimony.[18] The more difficult question is whether calling one psychotherapist waives the privilege with respect to other psychotherapists who previously examined the defendant on his mental condition, but were not called as defense witnesses.

Many courts do not allow a psychotherapist originally retained by defense counsel to be called as a prosecution witness.[19] Some

Waiver when insanity defense asserted

12. In re County of Erie, 2008 WL 4554920 (2d Cir. 2008) (only claimed *reliance* on advice of counsel waives privilege, not mere claim that action was legal, criticizing *Rhay* standard, *infra* this note, as too broad); Cox v. Administrator, U.S. Steel & Carnegie, 17 F.3d 1386, 1419 (11th Cir. 1994) (going beyond denial of intent by claiming good-faith belief in legality of conduct waives attorney-client privilege, which is lost when one injects "an issue that in fairness requires an examination of otherwise protected communications"). See also Hearn v. Rhay, 68 F.R.D. 574, 580-582 (E.D. Wash. 1975) (claiming good faith in civil rights suit against prison officials waived privilege for legal advice on their conduct).

13. Sedco Intl. S.A. v. Cory, 683 F.2d 1201, 1206 (8th Cir. 1982) (asserting fraud defense waived privilege for conversations with lawyer that might rebut this claim), *cert. denied*, 459 U.S. 1017.

14. Conkling v. Turner, 883 F.2d 431, 434 (5th Cir. 1989) (claimed tolling of statute of limitations waived privilege for communications with lawyer bearing on when claimant learned of claim).

15. United States v. Bilzerian, 926 F.2d 1285, 1292 (2d Cir. 1991) (defendant's testimony that he thought his actions were legal "put his knowledge of the law and the basis for his understanding of what the law required in issue," thus waived privilege), *cert. denied*, 112 S. Ct. 63. *But see* United States v. White, 887 F.2d 267, 270 (D.C. Cir. 1989) ("forfeiting the privilege upon denial of mens rea would deter individuals from consulting with their lawyers to ascertain the legality of contemplated actions").

16. Pitney-Bowes, Inc. v. Mestre, 86 F.R.D. 444, 447 (S.D. Fla. 1980) (attorney-client privilege waived where plaintiff placed in issue its intent underlying certain agreements).

17. A few jurisdictions hold the privilege to be waived merely upon assertion of a mental status defense. *See, e.g.,* State v. Pawlyk, 800 P.2d 338, 340 (Wash. 1990). This approach is said to represent the "clear minority view" and is "sharply criticized." Miller v. District Ct., City & Cty. of Denver, 737 P.2d 834, 838 (Colo. 1987). *See generally* Saltzburg, Privileges and Professionals: Lawyers and Psychiatrists, 66 Va. L. Rev. 597, 635-642 (1980).

18. *See, e.g.,* Tucker v. State, 484 So. 2d 1299, 1301-1302 (Fla. App. 1986) (privilege waived when defense used psychiatrist as witness at trial), *rev. denied*, 484 So. 2d 1153.

19. United States v. Alvarez, 519 F.2d 1036, 1041-1042 (3d Cir. 1975) (where defense counsel retained psychiatrist to examine client, attorney-client privilege as to consultation not waived by subsequent assertion of insanity defense; error to allow doctor to be called as a prosecution witness). *See generally* Imwinkelried, The Applicability of the Attorney-Client Privilege to Non-Testifying Experts: Reestablishing the Boundaries Between the Attorney-Client Privilege and the Work Product Protection, 68 Wash. U. L.Q. 19, 21-22 (1990).

jurisdictions allow the prosecutor to call a defense-retained expert over a privilege objection but limit the testimony to opinions of sanity and nonincriminating statements made by the defendant.[20] State provisions allowing the prosecutor to call a defense psychotherapist have been held not to violate the Sixth Amendment.[21]

In all these settings, the attorney-client privilege should not be overridden merely because access to privileged evidence would be useful to an adverse party in responding to a claim or assertion made by a client.[22] The purpose of the privilege is to preserve values external to the litigation process even at the cost of excluding probative evidence. Therefore, in applying the doctrine of implied waiver by claim assertion, courts must be careful to target only the "type of unfairness that is distinguishable from the unavoidable unfairness generated by every assertion of privilege."[23]

D. MARITAL PRIVILEGES

§5.31 Spousal Testimonial Privilege

There are two commonly recognized marital privileges. One is the spousal testimonial privilege, and the other is the marital confidences privilege.[1] The testimonial privilege gives witnesses the right to refuse to testify against their spouse in criminal proceedings, and, in some jurisdictions, gives criminal defendants the power to prevent their spouses from testifying against them. The confidences privilege allows witnesses to refuse to reveal their own confidential marital communications and to prevent their spouse from doing so.

The testimonial privilege is the broader of the two in that it precludes all adverse testimony by the spouse, not merely disclosure of confidential communications. The testimonial privilege normally extends even to matters occurring prior to the marriage,[2] while the communications

---

20. Haynes v. State, 739 P.2d 497, 503 (Nev. 1987) (defense psychiatrist called as prosecution witness allowed to give only his opinions on defendant's mental condition and not to reveal specific communications with defendant or defense counsel).

21. Lange v. Young, 869 F.2d 1008, 1013 (7th Cir. 1989) (no violation of Sixth Amendment where Wisconsin law allowed psychiatrist originally retained by defense counsel to be called as a prosecution witness, but prosecutor cannot disclose that expert was originally employed by the defendant), *cert. denied,* 490 U.S. 1094 (1989).

22. In re County of Erie, 2008 WL 4554920 (2d Cir. 2008) (claimed reliance on advice of counsel waives privilege, not mere claim that action was legal, criticizing decision favoring broader waiver); Baker v. General Motors Corp., 209 F.3d 1051, 1054 (8th Cir. 2000) (no waiver by claim assertion "where a party has used witness testimony and made factual representations that were allegedly contrary to what the privileged documents will reveal").

23. Developments in the Law—Privileged Communications, 98 Harv. L. Rev. 1450, 1642 (1985).

§5.31 1. The marital confidences privilege is discussed in §5.32, *infra.*

2. *See* URE 504(b) (1999). *But see* proposed-but-rejected FRE 505(c)(2) (containing an exception for "matters occurring prior to the marriage").

privilege covers only those confidential communications made during the course of the marriage.

The testimonial privilege is the narrower of the two, in that it applies only in criminal prosecutions where one spouse is a defendant.[3] In contrast, the communications privilege applies in both criminal and civil cases and does not require either spouse to be a party. Also the testimonial privilege lasts only as long as the marriage relationship, while the communications privilege provides ongoing protection for confidential communications uttered during the marriage. Thus former spouses may not assert a privilege to refuse to testify against one another, but they cannot testify to matters covered by the marital communications privilege.

Doctrine of spousal incompetency

The testimonial privilege evolved from the common law doctrine rendering a spouse incompetent to testify for or against the other. This incompetency resulted from the rule that a party was ineligible to testify on his own behalf, combined with the legal fiction that husband and wife were but one person.[4]

In the 1933 decision of *Funk v. United States*,[5] the Supreme Court abolished the doctrine of spousal incompetency so as to permit a defendant's spouse to testify in the defendant's behalf. However, *Funk* left unaltered the rule that either spouse could prevent the other from presenting adverse testimony. The rule thus evolved from a ground of incompetency to a spousal privilege.

Rationale for privilege

The rationale for the testimonial privilege is to protect the harmony and sanctity of the marital relationship.[6] Testimony by one spouse against the other in a criminal prosecution would likely be an "unforgivable act" sealing the fate of any marriage.[7] Also, letting the state pit spouse against spouse without the consent of either would offend fundamental societal values. It is repellant to force husband or wife to breach the trust of marriage by becoming the instrument of the other's criminal conviction.[8]

---

3. *See* United States v. Burks, 470 F.2d 432, 435-436 (D.C. Cir. 1972) (where husband was murder victim rather than defendant, wife had no privilege to refuse to testify about his violent character when called as a witness by defendant in support of his self-defense claim).

4. *See* Blackstone, Commentaries on the Law of England, Bk. 1 at 441 (1768) ("By marriage, the husband and wife are one person in law.").

5. 290 U.S. 371 (1933).

6. Hawkins v. United States, 358 U.S. 74, 77 (1958) (basic reason for refusing "to pit wife against husband or husband against wife in a trial where life or liberty is at stake was a belief that such a policy was necessary to foster family peace, not only for the benefit of husband, wife and children, but for the benefit of the public as well").

7. *Id.* at 78-79 (law should not "force or encourage testimony which might alienate husband and wife, or further inflame existing domestic differences").

8. *See* 8 Wigmore, Evidence §2228 at 217 (McNaughton rev. 1961). *But see* 5 Bentham, Rationale of Judicial Evidence 340 (1827) (spousal testimonial privilege goes far beyond making "every man's house his castle" and permits a person to convert his house into "a den of thieves"; it "secures, to every man, one safe and unquestionable and ever ready accomplice for every imagineable crime"); Medine, The Adverse Testimony Privilege: Time to Dispose of a "Sentimental Relic," 67 Or. L. Rev. 519 (1988). Both the Model Code of Evidence Rule 215 (1942) and the Uniform Rules of Evidence Rule 28 (1953) omitted the spousal testimonial privilege but included a spousal confidences privilege.

Who holds
privilege

In *Hawkins v. United States,*[9] the Court held that both spouses were holders of the privilege, and that each could prevent adverse testimony by the other. Most often a defendant in a criminal case claimed the privilege to keep the prosecutor from calling defendant's spouse as a witness.[10] Twenty-two years after *Hawkins,* however, the Court in *Trammel v. United States*[11] reconsidered the issue, and decided that only the witness spouse holds the privilege. Under *Trammel,* the witness spouse may testify against the defendant spouse voluntarily, regardless of the wishes of the defendant, but cannot be compelled to do so against her own wishes.

The *Trammel* Court noted the trend in state statutes away from vesting the privilege in the defendant spouse and concluded that modification of the federal rule was appropriate because "[w]hen one spouse is willing to testify against the other in a criminal proceeding—whatever the motivation—their relationship is almost certainly in disrepair; there is probably little in the way of marital harmony for the privilege to preserve."[12] When both spouses are potentially subject to prosecution, however, *Trammel* makes it more likely that they will be pitted against each other in negotiating with the prosecutor for favorable individual treatment. It is at least doubtful that testimony given by a spouse in exchange for leniency is voluntary in any realistic sense of that term, or that caving in to pressure from the prosecutor indicates a breakdown of the marriage,[13] and *Trammel's* views on this subject seem shortsighted.[14]

The *Trammel* holding is binding only on federal courts, although URE 504 was amended in 1986 to conform with the holding.[15] Since *Trammel,* some states have amended their testimonial privilege statutes to make the witness spouse the sole holder of the privilege.[16]

The testimonial privilege only allows the witness spouse to refuse to give adverse testimony, and does not entitle the witness spouse to refuse to give testimony that would be helpful to the defendant spouse.[17] According to the clear weight of authority, the spousal testimonial privilege applies only in criminal cases,[18] including grand jury

---

9. 358 U.S. 74, 77-79 (1958).

10. *See* proposed-but-rejected FRE 505(a) (making defendant spouse the sole holder of privilege).

11. 445 U.S. 40, 53 (1980).

12. *Id.* at 52. *Compare* Hawkins v. United States, 358 U.S. 74, 77 (1958) ("[N]ot all marital flare-ups in which one spouse wants to hurt the other are permanent.").

13. *See* Lempert, A Right to Every Woman's Evidence, 66 Iowa L. Rev. 725, 733-737 (1981).

14. *Cf.* United States v. Bad Wound, 203 F.3d 1072, 1075 (8th Cir. 2000) (spouse's plea agreement promise to provide "complete and truthful testimony before grand juries, at trial, and at other proceedings as required" was sufficient to waive spousal testimonial privilege).

15. *See* URE 504(b) (1999) (spouse of an accused "has a privilege to refuse to testify against the accused spouse").

16. *See, e.g.,* Or. Rev. Stat. 40.255.

17. Trammel v. United States, 445 U.S. 40, 51 (1980) (privilege applies only to "adverse spousal testimony").

18. *See* proposed-but-rejected FRE 505(a); URE 504(c) (1999). *Cf.* Ryan v. Commissioner, 568 F.2d 531 (7th Cir. 1977) (leaving open question whether spousal testimonial privilege can ever apply in civil cases), *cert. denied,* 439 U.S. 820.

proceedings and criminal forfeiture proceedings.[19] The privilege extends only to couples who are lawfully married,[20] although some states now extend the privilege to partners in civil unions.[21]

Common law marriages are covered too, but only if they are recognized as valid by the jurisdiction where the couple resides.[22] Courts have not extended the privilege to other intimate relationships,[23] even where the parties are living together and are "for all practical purposes husband and wife."[24]

The privilege does not apply to "sham" marriages, where the parties do not intend to live or remain as husband and wife but are using their temporary marital status for a fraudulent purpose such as to violate immigration laws.[25] The fact that the parties married shortly before trial of one spouse on criminal charges, thereby preventing the other spouse from being a witness, does not necessarily prove that the marriage is a sham.[26] Proposed-but-rejected Rule 505(c)(2) would have created an exception for "matters occurring prior to the marriage," thereby preventing a defendant from "suppressing testimony by marrying the witness," but of course this provision was not enacted, and in fact the privilege applies not only to testimony on acts, events, or conditions occurring during marriage, but to acts, events, or conditions occurring prior to the marriage.[27]

Scope of privilege

Sham marriages

19. *See* United States v. Yerardi, 192 F.3d 14 (1st Cir. 1999) (adverse spousal testimony privilege applicable in criminal forfeiture proceeding); In re Grand Jury Matter, 673 F.2d 688, 692-694 (3d Cir. 1982) (if integrity of privilege is to be maintained, "a wife who asserts the privilege should not be compelled to testify before a grand jury when her spouse is a target of the same underlying investigation as the party against whom she is called to testify and her testimony is sought with the expectation that it may lead to his indictment by a subsequent grand jury"), *cert. denied*, 459 U.S. 1015.

20. United States v. Snyder, 707 F.2d 139, 147 (5th Cir. 1983) (privilege requires "a valid marital relationship").

21. See, e.g., N.H. Rev. Stat. Ann. §457-A:6 (2008); N.J. Stat. Ann. §37:1-32(o) (2008); Vt. Stat. Ann. Tit. 15, §1204(e)(15) (2008).

22. *See* United States v. Lustig, 555 F.2d 737, 747-748 (9th Cir. 1977) (privilege depends upon "existence of a valid marriage, as determined by state law"), *cert. denied*, 434 U.S. 926.

23. *See* United States v. Acker, 52 F.3d 509, 514 (4th Cir. 1995) (court refuses to recognize marital communications privilege or spousal testimonial privilege for couple who had lived together for 25 years but had not gotten married and states in which they had lived did not recognize common law marriage; court rejects Equal Protection challenge to rule limiting privilege to married couples).

24. United States v. Snyder, 707 F.2d 139, 147 (5th Cir. 1983).

25. Lutwak v. United States, 344 U.S. 604, 614-615 (1953) (war brides case where defendants and aliens had apparently married abroad without intending to live together as spouses; such "sham, phony, empty ceremony" rendered testimonial privilege unavailable).

26. In re Grand Jury Proceedings No. 84-5, 777 F.2d 508 (9th Cir. 1985) (privilege upheld where parties lived together two years and got married after partner was served with subpoena).

27. ACN, proposed-but-rejected FRE 505. Such an exception seems overly broad, because it allows compulsion of one spouse to incriminate the other on premarital matters even where the privilege was not a motive for the marriage.

Moribund marriages   Some courts have held that the privilege is inapplicable to marriages that are moribund,[28] although most courts are justifiably reluctant to undertake a detailed inquiry into the health of a marriage.[29] The privilege has also been held inapplicable where the government grants immunity against use of a spouse's testimony or any fruits thereof against the other spouse.[30]

Extrajudicial statements   Most courts hold that the privilege applies only to testimony by the spouse and does not block admission of extrajudicial statements of one spouse offered against the other, where such statements are admissible under the hearsay doctrine.[31] However, some authorities view the privilege as barring introduction of extrajudicial disclosures of a spouse,[32] and such extrajudicial statements are of course often excludable on hearsay grounds.[33]

Exceptions   There are several generally recognized exceptions to the privilege. The privilege is inapplicable in proceedings where one spouse is charged with a crime or tort against the person or property of the other or a minor child of either.[34] URE 504 recognizes an exception where a spouse is charged with a crime or tort against the person or property of "an individual residing in the household of either" and also where the victim is a third person "if the crime or tort is committed in

---

28. In re Witness Before the Grand Jury (Carter), 791 F.2d 234 (2d Cir. 1986) (witness spouse and defendant had been married 23 years but had lived apart for last 11 years; court held they "did not have the kind of vital marriage for which the privilege was created").

29. Appeal of Malfitano, 633 F.2d 276, 279 (3d Cir. 1980) (doubting that courts "can assess the social worthiness of particular marriages" or their need for protection of privilege); States v. Lilley, 581 F.2d 182, 189 (8th Cir. 1978) (refusing to condition privilege "on a judicial determination that the marriage is a happy or successful one"). *See generally* Note, "Honey, the Judge Says We're History": Abrogating the Marital Privileges via Modern Doctrines of Marital Worthiness, 77 Cornell L. Rev. 843 (1992).

30. In re Grand Jury, 111 F.3d 1083 (3d Cir. 1997) (privilege against being compelled to testify against spouse defeated where government grants use and derivative use immunity thereby promising wife that neither her testimony or any fruits thereof will be used against her husband).

31. *See, e.g.,* United States v. Chapman, 866 F.2d 1326, 1333 (11th Cir. 1989) (extrajudicial statements "are not excludable on the basis of the spousal privilege"), *cert. denied,* 493 U.S. 932; United States v. Tsinnijinnie, 601 F.2d 1035, 1037-1039 (9th Cir. 1979), *cert. denied,* 445 U.S. 966 (marital privilege "should not be extended to bar a witness from relating an excited utterance by a spouse").

32. *See* 8 Wigmore, Evidence 225-226 (McNaughton rev. 1961) (it can be argued that privilege extends to "testimonial utterance in any form" and therefore hearsay statements "are equally privileged with testimony on the stand").

33. United States v. Hall, 989 F.2d 711, 715 (4th Cir. 1993) (where wife asserted privilege to refuse to testify against defendant, error for prosecutor to cross-examine defendant about "statement" wife allegedly gave to prosecutor because such statement was inadmissible hearsay).

34. Trammel v. United States, 445 U.S. 40, 46 n.7 (1980) (recognizing exceptions to testimonial privilege where "one spouse commits a crime against the other" or "crimes against the spouse's property" or "crimes against children of either spouse"). *But see* United States v. Jarvison, 409 F.3d 1221, 1231 (10th Cir. 2005) (declining to recognize exception allowing court to compel adverse spousal testimony relating to child abuse within household).

the course of committing a crime or tort" against the spouse, a minor child of either, or an individual residing in the household of either.[35]

Some courts recognize an exception for situations in which spouses were joint participants in the crime about which testimony is sought,[36] but most hold that the privilege continues even if both spouses were involved in criminal activity.[37] In any case, recognition of a joint participants exception to the testimonial privilege would not necessarily make a spouse's testimony available, because the spouse could assert the Fifth Amendment privilege to block inquiries that would be personally incriminating.

Joint participants

§5.32 Marital Confidences Privilege

The marital confidences privilege prevents compelled disclosure of confidential communications made between spouses during the course of their marriage. The marital confidences privilege is narrower than the spousal testimonial privilege in that it applies only to confidential communications, while the testimonial privilege bars all testimony.[1] The confidences privilege is broader than the testimonial privilege, however, in that it applies in civil as well as criminal proceedings and can be asserted after the termination of the marriage.

The rationale of the privilege is to protect the privacy and trust of the marital relationship, and to enable spouses freely to communicate and confide in one another.[2] The privilege is intended to preserve and strengthen the institution of marriage.[3] Without the privilege, a witness could be compelled by the state to breach the bonds of trust

Rationale

35. URE 504(d)(3) (1999). *See also* proposed-but-rejected FRE 505(c)(1).

36. *See, e.g.*, United States v. Clark, 712 F.2d 299, 300-301 (7th Cir. 1983) (recognizing joint participant exception; "rehabilitative effect of a marriage, which in part justifies the privilege, is diminished when both spouses are participants in the crime").

37. *See* In re Grand Jury Subpoena (Koecher), 755 F.2d 1022, 1026-1027 (2d Cir. 1985) (court "unable to accept the proposition that a marriage cannot be a devoted one simply because at some time the partners have decided to engage in a criminal activity"), *vacated as moot*, 475 U.S. 133; In re Malfitano, 633 F.2d 276, 278 (3d Cir. 1980) (court aware "of no public policy requiring that a marriage be dissolved when the partners engage in crime"); United States v. Ramos-Oseguera, 120 F.3d 1028, 1041 (9th Cir. 1997) (rejecting exception). *See generally* Note, Partners in Crime: The Joint Participants Exception to the Privilege Against Adverse Spousal Testimony, 53 Fordham L. Rev. 1019 (1985).

§5.32 1. *See* United States v. Davis, 714 F. Supp. 853, 870 (S.D. Ohio 1988) (communications privilege cannot be used to preclude all testimony by former wife out of concern that she might "blurt out" privileged communications; defendant must object at trial to any testimony about confidential marital communications). The spousal testimonial privilege is discussed in §5.31, *supra*.

2. United States v. Neal, 532 F. Supp. 942, 946 (D. Colo. 1982) (courts have endeavored "to preserve inviolable some island of privacy as a refuge for the human spirit where government may not intrude").

3. Wolfle v. United States, 291 U.S. 7, 14 (1934) (marital confidences are regarded "as so essential to the preservation of the marriage relationship as to outweigh the disadvantages to the administration of justice which the privilege entails"); Stein v.

between husband and wife and reveal the intimacies and secrets of their relationship.[4]

The marital confidences privilege is well established as a matter of federal common law[5] and is recognized by virtually all states.[6] The proposed Federal Rules would have codified only a spousal testimonial privilege, omitting a spousal confidences privilege.[7] The Advisory Committee viewed the privilege as ineffectual because married persons are generally unaware of it.[8] The decision of the drafters to abrogate the marital confidences privilege prompted public outcry and contributed to the ultimate defeat of the proposed privilege rules.[9]

Holder　　Under the prevailing view, both spouses hold the confidences privilege—that is to say, both the spouse who says something and the spouse who listens to what is being said—and either can refuse to disclose and prevent the other from disclosing confidential marital communications.[10] Some authorities favor a narrower approach, vesting each spouse with a privilege covering only what he or she has said to

---

Bowman, 38 U.S. 209, 223 (1839) (privilege "is founded upon the deepest and soundest principles of our nature" and helps preserve the marriage relationship, which Court described as "the best solace of human existence").

4. *See* Note, Pillow Talk, Grimbribbers and Connubial Bliss: The Marital Communication Privilege, 56 Ind. L.J. 121, 139-142 (1980) (suggesting privilege may have constitutional underpinning stemming from right of privacy). *Cf.* In re Grand Jury Investigation (Hipes) v. United States, 603 F.2d 786, 788-789 (9th Cir. 1979) (privilege protects privacy of communications, not merely their incriminatory use; privilege can be asserted even where other spouse has been granted immunity so that there is no risk of criminal liability).

5. *See* Trammel v. United States, 445 U.S. 40, 45 n.5 (1980); Blau v. United States, 340 U.S. 332 (1951); Wolfle v. United States, 291 U.S. 7 (1934).

6. 8 Wigmore, Evidence §2336 at 250 n.1 (McNaughton rev. 1961).

7. *See* proposed-but-rejected FRE 505.

8. *See* ACN, proposed-but-rejected FRE 505 (unlikely that "marital conduct will be affected by a privilege for confidential communications of whose existence the parties in all likelihood are unaware" whereas "other communications privileges, by way of contrast, have as one party a professional person who can be expected to inform the other of the existence of the privilege").

9. *See, e.g.,* Black, Marital and Physician Privileges—A Reprint of a Letter to a Congressman, 1975 Duke L.J. 45, 48 (by failing to include communications privilege, proposed-but-rejected FRE 505 means "that, however intimate, however private, however embarrassing may be a disclosure by one spouse to another, or some fact discovered, within the privacies of marriage, by one spouse about another, that disclosure or fact can be wrung from the spouse under penalty of being held in contempt of court, if it is thought barely relevant to the issues in anybody's lawsuit for breach of a contract to sell a carload of apples. It ought to be enough to say of such a rule that it could easily—even often—force any decent person—anybody any of us would want to associate with—either to lie or to go to jail. No rule can be good that has that consequence—that compels the decent and honorable to evade or to disobey it.").

10. *See, e.g.,* United States v. Montgomery, 384 F.3d 1050 (9th Cir. 2004) (adopting position of majority of states that either spouse may invoke marital confidence privilege; restricting privilege to communicating spouse "invites attempts to prove circumstantially the statements of one spouse by proof of what the other has said") (quoting authors of this Treatise).

the other, and not vesting the listening spouse with the privilege.[11] Such a limitation appears in URE 504,[12] but it seems a wholly artificial distinction that invites attempts to prove circumstantially the statements of one spouse by proof of what the other says, which should no more be allowed in this context than it would be in the context of attorney and client.[13]

If one spouse discloses confidential marital communications of the other without consent, the privilege can still be asserted by the nondisclosing spouse to block their subsequent use in a legal proceeding.[14] Thus the privilege can be asserted to prevent introduction of an incriminating letter from a husband to his wife where the wife had turned the letter over to the prosecutor.[15]

A number of jurisdictions provide by statute that in criminal cases the privilege belongs to the defendant spouse, thereby allowing the defendant spouse to introduce confidential marital communications that are exculpatory.[16] A similar result has been reached by some court decisions.[17] The privilege applies only to parties who are legally married,[18] although some states now extend the privilege to partners in civil unions.[19]

The privilege covers common law marriages to the extent they are recognized by the law of the state where the couple resides.[20] The privilege has sometimes been held inapplicable to spouses who are

Valid marriage required

---

11. United States v. Figueroa-Paz, 468 F.2d 1055, 1057 (9th Cir. 1972); United States v. Neal, 532 F. Supp. 942, 944-947 (D. Colo. 1982).

12. *See* URE 504(a) (1999) (individual has a privilege "to refuse to testify or to prevent his or her spouse or former spouse from testifying as to any confidential communications made by the individual to the spouse during their marriage").

13. *See* §5.12, *supra.*

14. *See, e.g.,* State v. Compton, 104 N.M. 683, 726 P.2d 837, 841 (1986) (wife disclosed confidential marital communication to police; defendant allowed to assert privilege to prevent introduction of communication at trial), *cert. denied,* 479 U.S. 890.

15. United States v. Wood, 924 F.2d 399, 401-402 (1st Cir. 1991) (wife could not waive husband's marital communications privilege with respect to an incriminating letter sent from husband to wife while both were in jail). *Cf.* Annot., Applicability of Marital Privilege to Written Communications Between Spouses Inadvertently Obtained by Third Person, 32 A.L.R.4th 1177, 1180-1184 (1984).

16. *See, e.g.,* Ark. Stat. Ann. 16-41-101, R. Evid. 504(b) (1987); Okla. Stat. Ann. tit. 12, 2504(B) (West 1983); S.D. Codified Laws Ann. 19-13-13 (1987).

17. *See, e.g.,* United States v. Ammar, 714 F.2d 238, 257 (3d Cir. 1983) (testimony essential to spouse's defense admissible even if it requires revelation of marital confidences), *cert. denied,* 464 U.S. 936. *See generally* 8 Wigmore §2338(4) (McNaughton rev. 1961) (where an accused spouse needs evidence of marital communications, "the privilege should cease or a cruel injustice may be done").

18. U.S. v. Rivera, 527 F.3d 891, 906 n.4 (9th Cir. 2008) (marital communications privilege recognized by federal common law does not cover conversations between unmarried individuals even though they have children in common); United States v. Knox, 124 F.3d 1360, 1365 (10th Cir. 1997) (federal courts routinely apply state law to determine whether couples are spouses for purposes of privilege).

19. See, e.g., N.H. Rev. Stat. Ann. §457-A:6 (2008); N.J. Stat. Ann. §37:1-32(o) (2008); Vt. Stat. Ann. Tit. 15, §1204(e)(15) (2008).

20. United States v. Lustig, 555 F.2d 737, 747 (9th Cir. 1977) (privilege inapplicable because Alaska recognizes no common law marriage), *cert. denied,* 434 U.S. 926.

permanently separated[21] or to moribund marriages[22] although other courts properly refuse to condition the privilege on the health of the marriage.[23]

Communications during course of marriage

The privilege applies only to communications made during the course of the marriage. Premarital or postmarital communications are excluded.[24] However, if the confidential communication was made while the parties were married, the privilege may be asserted even after the marriage is terminated.[25] The privilege survives the death of a spouse and may be asserted by the spouse's personal representative.[26]

Protects communications only

Most modern authorities and particularly federal decisions limit the privilege to confidential spousal communications.[27] Assertive or expressive conduct that is intended to convey a meaning or message to another is within the privilege,[28] but not mere observations of a spouse's noncommunicative behavior, appearance, physical or emotional condition, and similar facts,[29] even where such observations

---

21. United States v. Singleton, 260 F.3d 1295 (11th Cir. 2001) (defendant wife convicted in part on basis of taped inculpatory statements she made to husband whom she was in process of divorcing; court rejects claim of marital communications privilege because spouses were permanently separated with no prospect of reconciliation; proof of permanently separated status at time of communication renders privilege inapplicable).

22. United States v. Roberson, 859 F.2d 1376, 1380-1382 (9th Cir. 1988) (husband's admission to estranged wife that he had raped someone was admissible; couple had been separated for two months, wife had obtained a restraining order against husband, and there had been no discussion of reconciliation; trial court finding that marriage was "defunct" was not clearly erroneous).

23. *See, e.g.,* In re Grand Jury Investigation of Hugle, 754 F.2d 863, 865 (9th Cir. 1985) (privilege available "to a partner in an existing, albeit disharmonious, marriage").

24. United States v. Termini, 267 F.2d 18, 19-20 (2d Cir. 1959), *cert. denied,* 361 U.S. 822 (postmarital communication excluded); State v. Dikstaal, 320 N.W.2d 164, 166 (S.D. 1982) (premarital communication excluded).

25. Pereira v. United States, 347 U.S. 1, 5 (1954) (divorce does not terminate privilege for confidential marital communications made during marriage).

26. United States v. Burks, 470 F.2d 432, 436 (D.C. Cir. 1972) (privilege survives death of spouse).

27. United States v. Bolzer, 556 F.2d 948, 951 (9th Cir. 1977) (marital communications privilege did not bar testimony of a former wife of the defendant identifying pants as belonging to the defendant because this testimony pertained to an observation, not a communication).

28. United States v. Bahe, 128 F.3d 1440, 1441-1443 (10th Cir. 1997) (physical manner in which husband initiated sex with wife was confidential marital communication, because it was way of signaling his desire); United States v. Estes, 793 F.2d 465, 467 (2d Cir. 1986) (testimony concerning a spouse's conduct is precluded "only in the rare instances where the conduct was intended to convey a confidential message from the actor to the observer").

29. United States v. Hook, 781 F.2d 1166, n.11 (6th Cir. 1986) (giving money to wife to pay bills was not a communicative act), *cert. denied,* 479 U.S. 882; United States v. Ferris, 719 F.2d 1405, 1408 (9th Cir. 1983) (wife's observation of LSD in trunk of husband's vehicle was not a privileged communication); United States v. Smith, 533 F.2d 1077, 1079 (8th Cir. 1976) (wife may testify about defendant's conduct of hiding and transporting heroin by taping it to her body). *But see* Rubio v. Superior Court, 202 Cal. App. 3d 1343, 249 Cal. Rptr. 419, 421 (1988) (videotape of husband and wife engaging in sexual activity is a confidential communication subject to the privilege).

might not have occurred but for the marital relationship.[30] Thus the definition of privileged marital conduct parallels the definition of non-verbal conduct qualifying as a "statement" for purposes of the hearsay doctrine.[31] A minority of courts take a broader view and extend the privilege to confidential disclosures and observations that occurred only because of the privacy and trust of the marriage relationship.[32] But even under the broader view a spouse's conduct should not be privileged where the spouse was unaware that he was being observed or was attempting to hide or conceal his conduct from the witness spouse.[33]

Information known to a spouse that is derived from confidential spousal communications is privileged.[34] Even verbal expressions by a spouse, however, are sometimes outside the privilege when they amount to verbal acts, such as threats of bodily harm, rather than communications of the more usual sort.[35]

The privilege applies only to communications that are confidential. **Confidentiality** Communications made in the presence of third persons,[36] or intended **requirement** to be disclosed to others,[37] are outside the privilege. The presence of children of tender years does not destroy the privilege,[38] but communications made in the presence of older children, friends, relatives,

---

30. United States v. Espino, 317 F.3d 788, 795-796 (8th Cir. 2003) (wife's testimony describing defendant's drug trading activities before and during marriage was not protected by confidential communications privilege; testimony did not describe communicative gesture); United States v. Estes, 793 F.2d 465, 467 (2d Cir. 1986) (acts do not become privileged "simply because they are performed in the presence of the actor's spouse").

31. *See* FRE 801(a)(2) (a statement is "nonverbal conduct of a person, if it is intended by the person as an assertion").

32. People v. Daghita, 299 N.Y. 194, 86 N.E.2d 172, 174 (1949) (privilege applies to "knowledge derived from the observance of disclosive acts done in the presence of view of one spouse by the other because of the confidence existing between them by reason of the marital relation and which would not have been performed except for the confidence so existing").

33. United States v. Lewis, 433 F.2d 1146, 1151 (D.C. Cir. 1970) (clandestine conduct by husband is not privileged).

34. *See* Blau v. United States, 340 U.S. 332 (1951) (testimony by husband about whereabouts of wife is presumptively within confidential communications privilege, unless it can be shown such knowledge was not based upon a communication); Hipes v. United States, 603 F.2d 786, 788 n.1 (9th Cir. 1979) (wife could not testify about nature of husband's job responsibilities because presumably her knowledge came from privileged communications).

35. Chaney v. State, 42 Md. App. 563, 402 A.2d 86, 93 (1979) (wife testified she did not report husband to police because he had threatened her; privilege held not to apply because husband's words was verbal act and not substantive communication).

36. *See, e.g.,* United States v. Marashi, 913 F.2d 724, 730 (9th Cir. 1990) (presence of a third person destroyed privilege).

37. United States v. Strobehn, 421 F.3d 1017, 1021 (9th Cir. 2005) (in bank robbery trial, defendant's letter to wife and 24 others was not shielded by marital communications privilege regardless whether defendant assumed wife would not pass message to others if he survived robbery; letter indicated communication was intended for others besides wife).

38. Hicks v. Hicks, 271 N.C. 204, 155 S.E.2d 799, 802 (1967) (presence of eight-year-old child did not destroy confidentiality).

or other persons are generally not privileged.[39] Courts generally recognize a presumption that communications between a husband and wife are confidential, and the party seeking disclosure has the burden of overcoming the presumption.[40]

The privilege does not apply where a third person assists in preparing the communication, as happened in one case in which a husband dictated a letter to his wife using a stenographer.[41] Nor does the privilege apply to communications that are relayed to the recipient spouse through third persons.[42]

A marital confidence is outside the privilege if the communicating party did not take reasonable precautions to keep it from being heard by outsiders or intercepted by a third party.[43] A spouse cannot, however, destroy the privilege through connivance by arranging to have a third person overhear the communication without the knowledge of the communicating spouse.[44] There is a well-recognized exception to the privilege in proceedings in which one spouse is charged with a crime or tort against the person or property of the other spouse or a child of either.[45] Similarly, an exception is traditionally recognized in any civil action, such as a divorce proceeding, where the spouses are adverse parties.[46]

Exceptions
Virtually all circuits recognize an exception for marital confidences that relate to ongoing or future crimes in which the spouses were joint participants at the time of the communication,[47] although some limit

---

39. State v. Muenick, 26 Ohio App. 3d 3, 498 N.E.2d 171, 173 (1985) (marital communications privilege inapplicable to communications made in presence of two sons who were 10 and 11 at the time).

40. Pereira v. United States, 347 U.S. 1, 6 (1954); United States v. Marashi, 913 F.2d 724, 730 (9th Cir. 1990) (marital communications are "presumptively confidential" and government has burden of "demonstrating they are not").

41. Wolfle v. United States, 291 U.S. 7, 15-17 (1934) (communications made in presence of third party "usually regarded as not privileged").

42. Gutridge v. State, 236 Md. 514, 204 A.2d 557, 559 (1964) (husband's message conveyed by third party telling wife to retrieve contents from a locker held not privileged).

43. SEC v. Lavin, 111 F.3d 921 (D.C. Cir. 1997) (remanding for further evidence on whether husband should have known that telephone conversations with his wife were being recorded and hence were not confidential).

44. United States v. Neal, 532 F. Supp. 942, 947 (D. Colo. 1982), *aff'd*, 743 F.2d 1441 (10th Cir. 1984) (privilege claim upheld where wife allowed federal agents to eavesdrop on telephone conversation without husband's knowledge), *cert. denied*, 470 U.S. 1086. *See also* Annot., Spouse's Betrayal or Connivances as Extending Marital Communications Privilege to Testimony of Third Person, 3 A.L.R.4th 1104 (1981).

45. United States v. White, 974 F.2d 1135, 1138 (9th Cir. 1992) (privilege does not apply to "statements relating to a crime where a spouse or a spouse's children are the victims"). See also URE 504 (1999) (recognizing an exception to the marital privilege "in any proceeding in which one spouse is charged with a crime or tort against the person or property of (i) the other, (ii) a minor child of either, (iii) an individual residing in the household of either, or (iv) a third person if the crime or tort is committed in the course of committing a crime or tort against any of the individuals previously named in this sentence.").

46. *See* URE 504(d)(1)(1999).

47. *See, e.g.,* United States v. Darif, 446 F.3d 701, 706 (7th Cir. 2006) (husband and putative wife were indicted as conspirators in marriage fraud; his letter urging her to change testimony to avoid charge if marriage fraud charge was admissible against

the exception to "patently illegal activity."[48] The exception is justified on the theory that the need for effective law enforcement must prevail when two spouses engage in joint criminal activity, and the interest in protecting marital privacy is diminished in this setting.[49]

The joint participants exception applies even where only one of the spouses is prosecuted for their joint crimes.[50] The exception does not apply to communications made before both spouses have become involved in the criminal activity[51] or after the conspiracy has been terminated by arrest or otherwise.[52]

§5.33 Other Familial Privileges

There is no broadly recognized testimonial or communications privilege for family members other than spouses.[1] Thus a parent can usually be ordered to testify against a child and a child against a parent,[2] even in cases where such testimony will reveal confidential communications made by either.[3] Similarly courts have rejected privilege claims by other family members such as siblings and in-laws.[4]

---

husband under joint crime exception to communications privilege even if they were married; they were participants in underlying offense); United States v. Westmoreland, 312 F.3d 302, 309 (7th Cir. 2002) (initial disclosure of crime to spouse is covered by marital communications privilege; if the spouse later joins in conspiracy, communications from that point are not protected).

48. United States v. Evans, 966 F.2d 398, 401 (8th Cir. 1992), *cert. denied*, 113 S. Ct. 502.

49. United States v. Marashi, 913 F.2d 724, 731 (9th Cir. 1990) (policies underlying marital communications privilege "pale in the face of public concerns about bringing criminals to justice").

50. United States v. Marashi, 913 F.2d 724, 731 (9th Cir. 1990) (exception applies even where government decides "to forego prosecution of one spouse in order to secure her testimony against the other").

51. United States v. Estes, 793 F.2d 465, 467-468 (2d Cir. 1986) (privilege applies to incriminating communications of husband made to wife before she became involved in crime but not to those made subsequently).

52. United States v. Wood, 924 F.2d 399, 401-402 (1st Cir. 1991) (privilege applies to incriminating letter sent by husband to wife after both had been arrested and were in jail; court finds letter was written "after the conclusion of the alleged conspiracy between them").

§5.33 1. In re Grand Jury—Impounded, 103 F.3d 1140 (3d Cir. 1997) (refusing to recognize parent-child communications privilege).

2. Port v. Heard, 764 F.2d 423, 428-432 (5th Cir. 1985) (refusing privilege claim of parents seeking to avoid testifying against their child who was charged with murder); In re Grand Jury Proceedings (Starr), 647 F.2d 511, 513 (5th Cir. 1981) (child could be questioned about her mother and stepfather's involvement in a homicide).

3. Grand Jury Proceedings of John Doe v. United States, 842 F.2d 244, 245-248 (10th Cir. 1988) (affirming civil contempt order against 15-year-old who refused to testify before grand jury on basis of claimed parent-child privilege and family privilege), *cert. denied*, 488 U.S. 894.

4. In re Grand Jury Subpoena (Matthews), 714 F.2d 223, 224 (2d Cir. 1983) (refusing to recognize a privilege not to testify against one's in-laws). *But see* In re Ryan, 123 Misc. 2d 854, 855, 474 N.Y.S.2d 931, 932 (N.Y. Fam. Ct. 1984) (recognizing privilege for communications to grandmother with whom child lived for almost 15 years).

Family privileges have been widely discussed in the legal literature,[5] with powerful arguments being made that the justifications for a parent-child privilege are at least as compelling as those supporting other types of privileges.[6] In contrast to Anglo-American common law, family privileges are well established in many European countries whose legal systems descend from Roman law.[7]

Little authority

To date only a few decisions have recognized a parent-child privilege,[8] although occasional intimations in modern authority suggest that some kind of limited protection for familial confidences may be available in some circumstances.[9]

A number of courts have taken the position that creation of a parent-child privilege is a matter for the legislature.[10] At least two states have enacted a statutory privilege protecting confidential communications by minor children to their parents.[11] In Massachusetts, minor children

---

5. *See, e.g.,* Kraft, The Parent-Child Testimonial Privilege: Who's Minding the Kids?, 18 Fam. L.Q. 505 (1985); Kandoian, The Parent-Child Privilege and Parent-Child Crime: Observations on *State v. DeLong* and *In re Agosto,* 36 Me. L. Rev. 59 (1984); Stanton, Child-Parent Privilege for Confidential Communications: An Examination and Proposal, 16 Fam. L.Q. 1 (1982); Note, Parent-Child Loyalty and Testimonial Privilege, 100 Harv. L. Rev. 910 (1987).

6. *See, e.g.,* Watts, The Parent-Child Privileges: Hardly a New or Revolutionary Concept, 28 Wm. & Mary L. Rev. 583, 619 (1987) (containing proposed parent-child privilege statute drafted by an ABA committee); Bauer, Recognition of a Parent-Child Testimonial Privilege, 23 St. Louis U. L.J. 676 (1979). *But see* Schlueter, The Parent-Child Privilege: A Response to Calls for Adoption, 19 St. Mary's L.J. 35 (1987) (arguing against privilege).

7. *See, e.g.,* Kunert, Some Observations on the Origin and Structure of Evidence Rules under the Common Law System and the Civil Law System of "Free Proof" in the German Code of Civil Procedure, 16 Buffalo L. Rev. 122, 149 (1966) (stating that under German Code of Criminal Procedure, following persons are exempt from giving testimony: "the person engaged to marry the accused; the spouse of the accused, even if the marriage no longer exists; whoever is related directly by blood, marriage or adoption, or collaterally related by blood to the third degree or by marriage to the second degree to the accused, even if the marriage upon which the relationship is based on longer exists"). *See also* In re Erato, 2 F.3d 11, 15 (2d Cir. 1993) (discussing Dutch parent-child privilege but denying its recognition in federal criminal proceeding).

8. In re Grand Jury Proceedings (Agosto), 553 F. Supp. 1298, 1325-1326 (D. Nev. 1983) (recognizing both testimonial and communications privilege; associating privilege with constitutional right to privacy); In re Grand Jury Proceedings (Greenberg), 11 Fed. R. Evid. Serv. 579 (D. Conn. 1982) (recognizing privilege based on religious beliefs of defendant and mother); People v. Harrell, 87 A.D.2d 21, 26, 450 N.Y.S.2d 501, 504 (1982), *aff'd,* 59 N.Y.2d 620, 449 N.E.2d 1263, 463 N.Y.S.2d 185 (1983).

9. In re Erato, 2 F.3d 11, 15 (2d Cir. 1993) (refusing to recognize privilege claim to prevent mother from testifying against adult son, but stating that a more sympathetic claim would be presented if the child were a minor; court notes that "compelling a parent to inculpate a minor child risks a strain on the family relationship that might impair the mother's ability to provide parental guidance during the child's formative years"); Port v. Heard, 764 F.2d 423, 430 (5th Cir. 1985) (finding no parent-child privilege under state law, but holding might be different under FRE 501 because "case presents a compelling argument in favor of recognition").

10. *See, e.g.,* United States ex rel. Riley v. Franzen, 653 F.2d 1153, 1160 (7th Cir. 1981), *cert. denied,* 454 U.S. 1067.

11. *See* Idaho Code 9-203(7) (1990); Minn. Stat. 595.02(1)(j) (1988).

who live at home are disqualified from testifying against their parents in criminal proceedings.[12]

E.   PHYSICIANS AND PSYCHOTHERAPISTS

§5.34   Physician-Patient Privilege

Although a physician-patient privilege was not recognized at common law, the vast majority of states have adopted a physician-patient privilege by statute.[1] The drafters of the Federal Rules found the commonly recognized exceptions to the privilege so numerous "as to leave little if any basis for the privilege."[2] Therefore the Advisory Committee omitted a physician-patient privilege and instead proposed a privilege for psychotherapists.[3] Federal courts have declined to create a physician-patient privilege as a matter of federal common law,[4] although they recognize state law creating such a privilege in cases in which state law supplies the rule of decision.[5] Despite the absence of a federal physician-patient privilege, various federal statutes protect the confidentiality of particular types of medical information.[6]

The rationale for a physician-patient privilege is to encourage full and open disclosure on the part of patients to facilitate proper medical treatment.[7] Given a patient's natural incentive to disclose when seeking medical treatment, some commentators have questioned whether the additional inducement to communicate provided by an evidentiary privilege is necessary.[8] Protection of patient privacy provides an

Rationale for privilege

---

12. Mass. Ann. Laws, ch. 233, §20 (1987).

§5.34   1. Many state statutes are modeled after URE 503 (1974), which at the option of the adopting jurisdiction, extends a privilege to physicians as well as psychotherapists. For a listing of state provisions, *see* 1 Joseph & Saltzburg, Evidence in America: The Federal Rules in the States §25.4 (1987).

2. ACN, proposed-but-rejected FRE 504 (enumerating commonly recognized exceptions and concluding that they leave "virtually nothing covered by the privilege").

3. *See* §5.35, *infra.*

4. *See,* e.g., United States v. Bek, 493 F.3d 790, 802 (7th Cir.), cert. den., 128 S.Ct. 549 (2007) (declining to recognize doctor-patient privilege under power of federal courts to define new privileges).

5. *See* §5.7, *supra.*

6. *See, e.g.,* 42 U.S.C. §290dd-2(a) (protection for confidential information obtained in drug abuse prevention program); 42 U.S.C. 242a(b) (protecting privacy of persons participating in mental health research).

7. *See* Trammel v. United States, 445 U.S. 40, 51 (1980) (in discussing justification for privileges, Court noted that physician-patient privilege is based on policy that "the physician must know all that a patient can articulate in order to identify and to treat disease.").

8. Morgan, Foreword to ALI Model Code of Evidence 28-29 (1942) (ordinary citizen "has no idea whether a communication to a physician is or is not privileged" and "will have no hesitation about permitting the disclosure of his ailments except in case of a disease which he considers disgraceful"). *But see* Whalen v. Roe, 429 U.S. 589, 595 n.16 (1977) (noting that when New York required doctors to report to a state agency the names of all patients who were prescribed certain narcotic medications, some patients discontinued use of the medication or obtained it from another state).

additional rationale for the privilege,[9] one that is necessary to justify its recognition in circumstances where the doctor's knowledge of intimate or potentially embarrassing information was acquired by means other than voluntary patient communications.[10]

Scope of privilege   Some states limit the privilege to confidential "communications" made in the course of professional medical treatment.[11] Other states have a broader privilege protecting information acquired by observation, testing, or examination,[12] although only to the extent such matters are not generally observable by others.[13]

Where recognized the privilege generally applies to medical records of a physician or hospital that would reveal matters protected by the privilege.[14] Incidental information, such as fee arrangements or the date, time, or place of consultation is not within the privilege.[15] The identity of the patient is privileged only where its disclosure would reveal a privileged communication or matter.[16]

To be privileged, the communications or disclosures to a physician must be made for the purpose of medical diagnosis or treatment.[17] Thus statements by the patient about the cause of an accident or injury

9. *See* Shuman, The Origins of the Physician-Patient Privilege and Professional Secret, 39 Sw. L.J. 661 (1985); Krattenmaker, Testimonial Privileges in Federal Courts: An Alternative to the Proposed Federal Rules of Evidence, 62 Geo. L.J. 61, 92 (1973) (discussing privacy rationale for privilege).

10. The privacy rationale is necessary to support a privilege for an unconscious, incompetent or deceased patient. *See* Meyer v. Supreme Lodge, Knights of Pythias, 178 N.Y. 63, 70 N.E. 111, 115 (1904) (privilege applies to involuntary patients).

11. *See, e.g.,* Oxford v. Hamilton, 297 Ark. 512, 763 S.W.2d 83, 84 (1989) (admission of results of blood alcohol tests held not to violate privilege between defendant and hospital doctor; physician-patient privilege applies only to communications, not to observations); Bussard v. State, 295 Ark. 72, 747 S.W.2d 71, 73 (1988) (testimony about bullet removal from defendant's chest did not violate physician-patient privilege because evidence did not concern any communication made for purposes of diagnosis or treatment). *See* URE 503(b) (1974) (privilege limited to communications). *But see* Cal. Evid. Code 992 (West Supp. 1992) (defining "communications" expansively to include information derived during course of examination or treatment).

12. *See, e.g.,* State v. More, 382 N.W.2d 718, 721 (Iowa App. 1985) (privilege applies to all knowledge "gained by the physician in the observation and personal examination of the patient").

13. *See* In re Albert Lindley Lee Memorial Hosp., 115 F. Supp. 643, 645 (N.D.N.Y. 1953), *aff'd,* 209 F.2d 122 (2d Cir. 1953) (facts "which are plain to the observation of anyone" are not within New York privilege), *cert. denied,* 347 U.S. 960.

14. Hall v. Spencer, 472 So. 2d 1205, 1206 (Fla. App. 1985) (privilege applies to hospital records), *rev. denied,* 479 So. 2d 118 (Fla. 1985).

15. *See, e.g.,* People v. Doe, 107 Misc. 2d 605, 607, 435 N.Y.S.2d 656, 658 (Sup. Ct. 1981) (patient had no reasonable expectation of privacy about date, time, and place of treatment by physician).

16. In re Grand Jury Investigation, 59 N.Y.2d 130, 135, 450 N.E.2d 678, 680, 463 N.Y.S.2d 758, 760 (1983) (quashing subpoena seeking names and addresses of patients treated for knife wounds because that information concerned diagnosis and treatment); Smith v. Superior Court, 118 Cal. App. 3d 136, 173 Cal. Rptr. 145, 147 (1981) (finding it "well-settled that the disclosure of the identity of the patient violates the physician-patient privilege where such disclosure reveals the patient's ailment").

17. URE 503(b) (1999).

are privileged only to the extent that such information is relevant to medical treatment.[18]

Although it is generally required that the communication or disclosure be confidential, the privilege is not destroyed by the presence of family members or others who communicate on behalf of the patient or help him to obtain treatment.[19] Similarly, the presence of nurses, medical assistants, and other employees who assist the physician in providing medical services does not vitiate confidentiality.[20]

Confidentiality required

The privilege does not apply where disclosure to an unprivileged third party is contemplated, as in court-ordered examinations,[21] or tests conducted for law enforcement purposes,[22] or medical examinations undertaken for the benefit of another such as a life insurance company, employer, or opposing litigant.[23]

Exceptions

Most states recognize numerous exceptions to the physician-patient privilege that significantly limit its scope. For example, the privilege is often made inapplicable in criminal cases, commitment proceedings, will contests, malpractice cases, and disciplinary proceedings.[24]

Modern statutes often recognize a patient-litigant exception to the privilege,[25] which is intended to prevent the privilege from being used as a shield for fraud.[26] This exception applies in any proceeding where the patient relies on a physical condition as an element of his claim or defense.[27] In some jurisdictions, this qualification is viewed as an aspect of the waiver doctrine.[28]

18. Van Wie v. United States, 77 F. Supp. 22, 46 (N.D. Iowa 1948) (physician-patient privilege inapplicable to description of accident).

19. *See* URE 503(a)(4) (1986) (confidentiality requires an intention not to disclose to third persons other than those "present to further the interest of the patient in the consultation, examination, or interview, persons reasonably necessary for the transmission of the communication, or persons who are participating in the diagnosis and treatment under the direction of the [physician or] psychotherapist, including members of the patient's family").

20. Ramon v. State, 387 So. 2d 745, 750 (Miss. 1980) (communications to nurse privileged where nurse acts as agent of physician).

21. *See* URE 503(d)(2) (1986).

22. *See, e.g.,* State v. Santeyan, 136 Ariz. 108, 110, 664 P.2d 652, 654 (1983) (test results not privileged if taken at direction of law enforcement officer or prosecutor).

23. *See, e.g.,* FRCP 35(b)(2) (governing physical or mental examinations of parties or witnesses).

24. *See, e.g.,* Cal. Evid. Code §§990-1007 (West 1966 & Supp. 1991); Blunt v. State, 724 S.W.2d 79, 81 (Tex. Crim. App. 1987) (physician-patient privilege inapplicable in any criminal case where the patient is "a victim, witness, or defendant").

25. *See* URE 503(d)(3) (1986).

26. Degnan, The Law of Federal Evidence Reform, 76 Harv. L. Rev. 275, 300 (1962) (discussing danger of privilege being used to block disclosures that could "defeat dishonest claims or defenses").

27. *See* State v. Doughty, 554 A.2d 1189, 1191 (Me. 1989) (in DWI prosecution defendant placed her "physical condition" in issue as an element of her defense by testifying that she had only two drinks; prosecution allowed to introduce privileged statement to her treating physician that she had four drinks).

28. *See, e.g.,* Lee v. Calhoun, 948 F.2d 1162, 1166-1167 (10th Cir. 1991) (placing physical condition "in issue" waives physician-patient privilege under Oklahoma law), *cert. denied,* 112 S. Ct. 2940.

Statutes requiring reporting of certain types of illnesses or injuries, such as gunshot and knife wounds, venereal diseases, and child abuse, often operate as a qualification upon the privilege,[29] although their precise effect can be determined only by careful examination of the statutory language.[30]

§5.35 Psychotherapist-Patient Privilege

Although the psychotherapist-patient privilege evolved from the physician-patient privilege,[1] it has now achieved an independent status and a degree of acceptance exceeding that of its progenitor.[2] The justifications for a psychotherapist-patient privilege are viewed as stronger than those underlying the physician-patient privilege.[3] A psychotherapist relies almost entirely on disclosures from the client, whereas the physician often treats injuries or illnesses that can be observed, diagnosed, and treated by procedures not dependent on patient communications.[4] Matters disclosed in psychotherapy are often more personal and more likely to cause embarrassment (or potential civil or criminal liability) than matters disclosed to a physician,[5] leading some to conclude that the privilege has a constitutional basis in the right to privacy.[6]

---

29. *See, e.g.,* Cal. Evid. Code §1006 (West 1966) (excluding from privilege "information that the physician or the patient is required to report to a public employee").

30. A mandatory reporting statute may create an exception only to the physician's duty of confidentiality but not the privilege. Thus it may require a particular fact to be reported to authorities without overriding the patient's privilege to prevent the physician from testifying about the fact in a legal proceeding.

§5.35 1. Slovenko, Psychiatry and A Second Look at the Medical Privilege, 6 Wayne L. Rev. 175 (1960) (recounting history of privilege).

2. The drafters of the Federal Rules of Evidence proposed a psychotherapist-patient privilege but not a physician-patient privilege. *See* proposed-but-rejected FRE 504. *See also* URE 503 (1974) (psychotherapist-patient privilege modeled after proposed-but-rejected FRE 504 with state option to extend privilege to physicians).

3. *See* Louisell, The Psychologist in Today's Legal World: Part II, 41 Minn. L. Rev. 731, 745 (1957) (because there is "hardly any situation in the gamut of human relations where one human being is so much subject to the scrutiny and mercy of another human being as in the psychodiagnostic and psychotherapeutic relationships" it is hard to see how such functions "adequately can be carried on in the absence of a pervading attitude of privacy and confidentiality").

4. *See* Report No. 45, Group for the Advancement of Psychiatry 92 (1960), quoted in ACN, proposed-but-rejected FRE 504 (psychiatrist has a "special need" to maintain confidentiality because his capacity to help his patients "is completely dependent upon their willingness and ability to talk freely").

5. *See* Guttmacher & Weihofen, Psychiatry and the Law 272 (1952) ("The psychiatric patient confides more utterly than anyone else in the world. He exposes to the therapist not only what his words directly express; he lays bare his entire self, his dreams, his fantasies, his sins, and his shame. Most patients who undergo psychotherapy know that this is what will be expected of them, and that they cannot get help except on that condition. . . . It would be too much to expect them to do so if they know that all they say—and all that the psychotherapist learns from what they say—may be revealed to the whole world from the witness stand.").

6. *See, e.g.,* Parle v. Runnels, 505 F.3d 922 (9th Cir. 2007) (defendant's right to privacy in communications with psychotherapist are grounded in federal and state constitutions; admitting such communications violated due process); In re Zuniga,

Society has an interest in successful treatment of persons who might pose a danger to the community because of their mental illness. Persons in need of psychotherapy generally require greater incentive to disclose than persons seeking medical attention for an injury or illness,[7] and the privilege is intended to serve this instrumental function.[8]

All 50 states recognize some form of psychotherapist-patient privilege,[9] often based on proposed-but-rejected FRE 504 or URE 503.[10] In the landmark decision of *Jaffe v. Redmond*,[11] the Supreme Court held that confidential communications between a licensed psychotherapist and her patients in the course of diagnosis or treatment are protected from compelled disclosure under FRE 501. The Court concluded on the basis of "reason and experience" that such a privilege "promotes sufficiently important interests to outweigh the need for probative evidence."[12] The Court was persuaded that if the privilege were rejected, confidential conversations between psychotherapists and clients "would surely be chilled," particularly where it was foreseeable that such statements might be used in litigation.[13] Because the types of statements most useful in litigation, such as incriminating admissions by a patient, would probably not be made in absence of a

Federal privilege recently recognized

---

714 F.2d 632, 641 (6th Cir. 1983) (noting that "inability to obtain effective psychiatric treatment may preclude the enjoyment and exercise of many fundamental freedoms"), *cert. denied,* 464 U.S. 983.

7. *See* Taylor v. United States, 222 F.2d 398, 401 (D.C. Cir. 1955) (while physical ailments "might be treated with some degree of effectiveness by a doctor whom the patient did not trust," a psychiatrist "must have his patient's confidence or he cannot help him").

8. The available data on the extent to which the privilege facilitates psychotherapist-patient communications is based only upon surveys, and rigorous empirical research has yet to be conducted. *See* Comment, Functional Overlap Between the Lawyer and Other Professionals: Its Implications for the Privileged Communications Doctrine, 71 Yale L.J. 1226, 1255 (1962) (73 percent of laypersons surveyed believed their communications with a therapist would be inhibited by absence of a privilege); Corcoran, et al., Absence of Privileged Communications and Its Impact on Air Force Officers, 19 A.F. L. Rev. 51, 56 (1977) (survey showed most Air Force officers preferred civilian to military psychiatrists, primarily for the reason that there is no privilege under military law). *But see* Shuman & Weiner, The Privilege Study: An Empirical Examination of the Psychotherapist-Patient Privilege, 60 N.C. L. Rev. 893, 924-925 (1982) (concluding from a research study that patients rely primarily on medical Code of Ethics to protect confidentiality and that "patients are probably not deterred from seeking psychiatric help to any significant degree" by absence of the privilege); Imwinkelried, The Rivalry Between Truth and Privilege: The Weakness of the Supreme Court's Instrumental Reasoning in *Jaffee v. Redmond,* 49 Hastings L.J. 969 (1998) (arguing that instrumentalist justification for privilege has not been made and privilege should rest on right of privacy).

9. Jaffee v. Redmond, 116 S. Ct. 1923, 1929 n.11 (1996) (listing state provisions). Such state provisions must be followed in federal proceedings where state law supplies the rule of decision. *See* Haney v. Mizell Memorial Hosp., 744 F.2d 1467 (11th Cir. 1984). *See generally* §5.7, *supra.*

10. *See* 13A U.L.A. 1 (listing states adopting URE 503).

11. 116 S. Ct. 1923, 1931 (1996).

12. *Id.* at 1928.

13. *Id.* at 1929.

privilege, it was thought unlikely that recognition of the privilege would cause a significant loss of evidence.[14]

The *Jaffee* decision goes beyond proposed-but-rejected FRE 504 and the law in a number of states by extending the psychotherapist-patient privilege to licensed social workers as well as licensed psychiatrists and psychologists.[15] The Court found that the reasons for recognizing the privilege apply with equal force to social workers, at least when they are engaged in psychotherapy rather than other types of social services.[16] However, given the wide variation in state licensing standards for social workers, the persons protected by this new privilege may differ significantly in education, training and qualifications.

The privilege applies only to communications, although some state courts have defined "communications" broadly.[17] The communications must be made for the purpose of diagnosis or treatment of the patient's mental or emotional condition.[18] The communications must be made in confidence, which means that unprivileged third parties cannot be present, although the presence of others who are participating in the diagnosis or treatment under the direction of the psychotherapist does not destroy confidentiality.[19] The privilege does not attach to communications by a patient, such as threats of violence, where the psychotherapist has informed the patient in advance that such communications will be reported to proper authorities.[20]

Marital counseling normally involves a significant emotional component making it subject to the privilege, but vocational and

14. *Id. See generally* Mueller, The Federal Psychotheapist-Patient Privilege After *Jaffe: Truth and Other Values in a Therapeutic Age*, 49 Hastings L.J. 947, 955-957 (1998) (although *Jaffe* may be criticized as overbroad or too narrow, decision merits respect as "a compromise between functionality and precision").

15. *See, e.g.*, proposed-but-rejected FRE 504(a)(2) (limiting definition of "psychotherapist" to persons "authorized to practice medicine" and licensed or certified psychologists).

16. The Court noted that social workers provide a significant amount of mental health treatment to poor clients or clients of modest means and found no public purpose to be served by drawing a distinction "between the counseling provided by costly psychotherapists and the counseling provided by more readily accessible social workers." 116 S. Ct. at 1929.

17. *See* In re Doe, 98 N.M. 442, 649 P.2d 510, 514-515 (1982) (protected communications to psychotherapists include not only verbal communications, but information derived from observation and personal examination of patient and inferences and conclusions drawn therefrom).

18. *See* proposed-but-rejected FRE 504(b).

19. Doe v. Oberweis Dairy, 456 F.3d 704, 718 (7th Cir. 2006) (relatives of plaintiff in sexual harassment suit, who were present and involved in her psychological evaluation, may intervene to ask court to exclude records pertaining to them). *See also* proposed-but-rejected FRE 504(a)(3); Cross, Privileged Communications between Participants in Group Psychotherapy, 1970 L. & Soc. Order 191.

20. United States v. Auster, 517 F.3d 312, 316-317 (5th Cir., 2008) (application of psychotherapist-patient privilege requires reasonable expectation of confidentiality; privilege was unavailable to defendant where defendant had been informed that therapist had duty under state law to disclose defendant's report that he would seek "violent retribution" against those whom he believed withheld his workers' compensation benefits and nonetheless chose to inform therapist of his plan).

educational counseling generally do not. Although some courts have held that the privilege does not protect the identity of the client or the fact of consultation,[21] the privacy interests of the client would seem to justify such protection.[22]

The privilege extends to preliminary communications made for the purpose of establishing a psychotherapist-patient relationship, even where no such relationship is actually formed, provided the psychotherapist has indicated an apparent willingness to enter such a relationship.[23] At least one court has held that the privilege applies when the patient reasonably but mistakenly believes that she was being counseled by a licensed psychotherapist.[24]

The privilege normally covers persons either assisting the psychotherapist or reasonably necessary for the transmission of communications between the patient and psychotherapist.[25] In addition, the privilege applies to persons who are present to further the interests of the patient, such as family members participating in the treatment under the direction of the psychotherapist.[26]

The *Jaffee* decision rejected the argument that the privilege should have a balancing component, because making the promise of confidentiality contingent on a later evaluation by the trial judge of the relative importance of patient privacy against a party's need for the evidence "would eviscerate the effectiveness of the privilege."[27] Nonetheless, the Court

Exceptions

21. *See* In re Zuniga, 714 F.2d 632, 640 (6th Cir. 1983) (as general rule, "identity of a patient or the fact and time of his treatment does not fall within the scope of the psychotherapist-patient privilege"), *cert. denied*, 464 U.S. 983.

22. *See* Lora v. Board of Educ., 74 F.R.D. 565, 586-587 (E.D.N.Y. 1977) (often it is identity "that patients generally wish to have shielded from exposure"). *See generally* Slovenko, Psychiatry and a Second Look at the Medical Privilege, 6 Wayne L. Rev. 175, 188 (1960) (it is "vital to maintain confidentiality as to the fact of treatment" or a person "may hesitate to visit a psychiatrist out of fear that he will be set apart from his fellow men"); Note, The Case for a Federal Psychotherapist-Patient Privilege That Protects Patient Identity, 1985 Duke L.J. 1217.

23. State v. Miller, 300 Or. 203, 709 P.2d 225, 234-236 (1985) (inculpatory statements made by defendant on telephone to receptionist and psychiatrist at state hospital were privileged even though psychiatrist testified that she was not intending to provide psychotherapy and was interrogating defendant to hold him until police could arrive at pay phone where he placed the call), cert. denied, 475 U.S. 1141.

24. Speaker v. County of San Bernardino, 82 F.Supp.2d 1105, 1112 (C.D. Cal. 2000) (privilege applies even though mental health therapist was not licensed to give the type of care involved here, where client reasonably believed that therapist had the necessary license).

25. *See* State v. Miller, 300 Or. 203, 709 P.2d 225, 235-236 (1985) (privilege applied to defendant's murder confession made to receptionist over telephone while seeking to talk with a psychiatrist at state mental hospital; receptionist asked defendant to describe his problem before she would refer him to a psychiatrist), *cert. denied*, 475 U.S. 1141. *But see* Commonwealth v. Mandeville, 386 Mass. 393, 436 N.E.2d 912, 923 (1982) (where patient never spoke with a psychotherapist, health center staff member was held not to be an "agent" of psychotherapist).

26. *See* proposed-but-rejected FRE 504(a)(3).

27. 116 S. Ct. at 1932 (quoting an earlier statement in Upjohn Co. v. United States, 449 U.S. 383, 393 (1981) that "[a]n uncertain privilege, or one which purports to be certain but results in widely varying applications by the courts, is little better than no

indicated that there should be some exceptions to the privilege,[28] citing specifically the situation where "a serious threat of harm to the patient or to others can be averted only by means of a disclosure by the therapist."[29] Interestingly, proposed-but-rejected FRE 504 does not contain a future crime or tort exception, seemingly adopting the view that there is less danger of such threats being carried out if patients are allowed the freedom to vent their angers and discuss their criminal intentions with a psychotherapist. The courts are divided on whether a future crime exception should be recognized as a matter of federal common law.[30] Some courts hold that even if a psychotherapist has a duty to warn a potential victim,[31] it does not follow that the threatening statement by the patient is admissible in a later criminal prosecution (in effect, the privilege may still apply in this setting).[32] Some courts focus on whether the patient was told that threatening statements would be outside the privilege,[33] while others focus on whether the threats are sufficiently serious.[34]

An exception to the privilege is generally recognized for court-ordered examinations, although the judge has discretion to limit disclosure and maintain the privilege.[35] Generally such examinations would not be subject to the privilege in any case because their results are to be

---

privilege at all."). *See* In re Sealed Case (Medical Records), 381 F.3d 1205, 1213-1214 (D.C. Cir. 2004) (federal psychotherapist-patient privilege is absolute and not subject to balancing).

28. *Id.* at n.19 (although it is unnecessary and premature to delineate the full contours of the privilege, "we do not doubt that there are situations in which the privilege must give way").

29. *Id.*

30. *Compare* United States v. Chase, 340 F.3d 978, 992 (9th Cir. 2003) (declining to recognize "dangerous patient" exception in federal law because it would "significantly injure" interests justifying privilege, have "little practical advantage" and "encroach significantly" on policy prerogatives of states, and would "go against the experience of all but one state in Ninth Circuit, as well as the Proposed Rules) *with* In re Grand Jury Proceedings, 183 F.3d 71, 74-78 (1st Cir. 1999) (crime-fraud exception applies to psychotherapist-patient privilege). *See generally* Daniel M. Buroker, The Psychotherapist-Patient Exception and Post-Jaffee Confusion, 89 Iowa L. Rev. 1373 (2004).

31. *See* Tarasoff v. Regents of Univ. of Cal., 17 Cal. 3d 425, 131 Cal. Rptr. 14, 551 P.2d 334, 340 (1976) (psychotherapist may be subject to tort liability for failure to warn potential victims of such threats). *See generally* Stone, The *Tarasoff* Decisions: Suing Psychotherapists to Safeguard Society, 90 Harv. L. Rev. 358 (1976).

32. United States v. Hayes, 227 F.3d 578 (6th Cir. 2000) (exception to confidentiality and privilege are not co-extensive; psychotherapist who complies with duty to warn is still entitled to invoke testimonial privilege in later criminal proceeding against patient).

33. United States v. Auster, 517 F.3d 312, 315-320 (5th Cir. 2008) (patient had no reasonable expectation of confidentiality where psychotherapist had informed patient repeatedly that any violent threats would be communicated to potential victims).

34. *See* United States v. Glass, 133 F.3d 1356 (10th Cir. 1998) (defendant convicted for making threats against President which were reported to Secret Service by his psychiatrist; trial judge rejected psychotherapist-patient privilege claim relying on future crimes exception; appellate court remands for determination of whether threat sufficiently serious to vitiate privilege and whether its disclosure "was the only means of averting harm to the President").

35. Proposed-but-rejected FRE 504(d)(2) ("If the judge orders an examination of the mental or emotional condition of the patient, communications made in the course thereof are not privileged under this rule with respect to the particular purpose for

reported to the court and parties, thereby negating the requirement of confidentiality. An exception is also usually recognized in proceedings to hospitalize the patient for mental illness.[36]

The privilege does not apply where the patient or someone acting on his behalf relies upon her mental or emotional condition as an element of a claim or defense.[37] However, the privilege is lost only with respect to communications bearing on the particular mental condition at issue.[38]

There is a division of authority on the question whether parties place their mental condition at issue in proceedings to determine child custody, with some courts upholding the privilege[39] but others taking the position that the privilege must yield in order to determine the "best interests" of the child,[40] at least where the mental health of a party is clearly in controversy[41] or circumstances indicate abuse or neglect.[42] Some courts hold that a patient's mental condition is placed at issue

Placing mental condition at issue

---

which the examination is ordered unless the judge orders otherwise."). The use of statements made by a defendant in the course of a court-ordered examination is often restricted by statute or rule. *See, e.g.,* FRCrimP 12.2(c) ("No statement made by the defendant in the course of any examination provided for by this rule, whether the examination be with or without the consent of the defendant, no testimony by the expert based upon such statement, and no other fruits of the statement shall be admitted in evidence against the defendant in any criminal proceeding except on an issue respecting mental condition on which the defendant has introduced testimony."). *Cf.* Estelle v. Smith, 451 U.S. 454, 462-463 (1981) (criminal defendant has constitutional right not to answer questions at court ordered examination where answers may be used against defendant at sentencing hearing).

36. Proposed-but-rejected FRE 504(d)(1).

37. Doe v. Oberweis Dairy, 456 F.3d 704, 718 (7th Cir. 2006) (privilege waived when litigant places psychological state at issue, as in this sexual harassment suit claiming emotional damage; defendant may demand evaluation; plaintiff may move to seal records and limit use to extent "interest in privacy" outweighs probative value); Schoffstall v. Henderson, 223 F.3d 818, 823 (8th Cir. 2000) (in suit claiming mental and emotional damages from sex discrimination and harassment, plaintiff put psychological condition in issue, hence waived privilege). But see In re Sims, 534 F.3d 117, 134 (2d Cir. 2008) (plaintiff does not forfeit privilege by asserting claim for injuries that do not include emotional damage, nor by stating that he suffers condition such as depression for which he does not seek damages; plaintiff may withdraw or formally abandon claims for emotional distress to avoid forfeiting privilege).

38. Britt v. Superior Court, 20 Cal. 3d 844, 862-864, 574 P.2d 766, 777-779, 143 Cal. Rptr. 695, 706-708 (1978).

39. Navarre v. Navarre, 191 Mich. App. 395, 479 N.W.2d 357, 358-359 (1991) (legislature did not intend to suspend medical privilege in custody disputes); Peisach v. Antuna, 539 So. 2d 544, 546 (Fla. App. 1989) (wife's denials of husband's allegations that she was mentally unfit to be custodial parent did not place her mental health in issue or "eviscerate" privilege).

40. In re M.M., 569 A.2d 463, 465 (Vt. 1989) (one who "seeks to resist action by the State to terminate his or her parental rights over a child places his or her mental health in issue"), *cert. denied,* 494 U.S. 1059.

41. Matter of Von Goyt, 461 So. 2d 821, 823 (Ala. 1984) (where mental state of party in a custody suit "is clearly in controversy" and a proper resolution of custody issue requires disclosure of privileged medical records, "psychologist-patient privilege must yield.").

42. *See generally* Slovenko, Child Custody and the Psychotherapist-Patient Privilege, 19 J. Psych. & Law 163 (Spring-Summer 1991).

when evidence about such condition is necessary for a fair response to an issue raised by the patient.[43]

When a defendant in a criminal case enters an insanity plea or advances some other defense based on mental condition, many courts conclude that doing so waives a claim privilege for communications to all psychotherapists consulted on the condition,[44] although some authorities hold that that waiver occurs only when defendant introduces testimony on the mental condition.[45]

Child abuse reporting laws

Today many states have laws requiring psychotherapists and other professionals to report child abuse. Although generally these reporting requirements override the psychotherapist-patient privilege,[46] careful examination of the statutory scheme is necessary because a reporting law occasionally may require disclosure to a public official without abrogating the privilege of the patient to prevent the psychotherapist from testifying in a judicial proceeding.[47]

Like other privileges, the psychotherapist-patient privilege can be overridden where necessary to protect a defendant's right of confrontation, as happens where psychiatric history tends directly to impeach a prosecution witness.[48]

43. *See, e.g.,* Flora v. Hamilton, 81 F.R.D. 576, 579-580 (M.D.N.C. 1978) (by challenging discharge from employment, plaintiff waived psychotherapist-privilege on issue of "ability to work in a structured institution"). But see In re Sims, 534 F.3d 117, 134 (2d Cir. 2008) (party's privilege is not overcome when other party puts his mental state in issue).

44. *See, e.g.,* United States v. Meagher, 531 F.2d 752, 753 (5th Cir. 1976) (claim of psychotherapist-patient privilege cannot be asserted "when the defendant in a criminal trial claims insanity as a defense"), *cert. denied,* 429 U.S. 853. But a psychotherapist who was retained by the defense attorney to examine the client may also be covered by the attorney-client privilege as a "representative of the lawyer." *See* §5.10, *supra.* On whether such a psychotherapist can be called as a prosecution witness, *see* §5.30, *supra.*

45. *See, e.g.,* Or. Rev. Stat. 40.280 (1991).

46. *See, e.g.,* Del. R. Evid. 503(d)(4) (1991); Wis. Stat. Annot. 905.04(4)(e) (1993). *See generally* Smith, Medical and Psychotherapy Privileges and Confidentiality: On Giving With One Hand and Removing With the Other, 75 Ky. L.J. 473 (1987).

47. *Cf.* United States v. Hayes, 227 F.3d 578, 579 (6th Cir. 2000) (suggesting similar result under federal case law). Mosteller, Child Abuse Reporting Laws and Attorney-Client Confidences: The Reality and Specter of Lawyer as Informant, 42 Duke L.J. 203, 230 (1992).

48. In re Doe, 964 F.2d 1325, 1328 (2d Cir. 1992) (precluding inquiry into psychiatric history of prosecution witness would violate defendant's constitutional right to cross-examine witnesses). *See generally* §5.5, *supra.*

CHAPTER 6

Witnesses

§6.1 Introduction

Most of the law of witnesses addresses four questions: Who may testify? What initial conditions must be satisfied before one may testify? How is testimony to be adduced? How may witnesses be attacked and supported? Missing from this summary is the law relating to opinion and expert testimony, which in the Federal Rules is found in Article VII. This subject is taken up in Chapter 7, *infra*.

Who may testify?   On the question who may testify, the modern answer is "essentially everyone." Under FRE 601, age and mental capacity are essentially irrelevant, and the same is true of past criminal convictions and relationship to the parties. Under FRE 606(a), the judge who presides may not testify, and ethical rules discourage the lawyer who tries a case from testifying (although no formal rule of law secures this result). Many states have statutes barring testimony by a party against the estate of a deceased person (so-called Dead Man's Statutes), and these statutes are honored in federal court under FRE 601. These and the requirements that expert witnesses qualify by training or experience (FRE 702) are the main "competency rules" that courts apply. When competency issues arise, they are resolved by the judge as matters relating to the "qualification of witnesses" under FRE 104(a), which means that the judge decides any factual and legal issues that arise in applying Dead Man's Statutes and the qualifications of experts.

Initial conditions   Initial conditions include the requirement that the witness commit herself to the truth, typically by oath or affirmation (*see* FRE 603). And as a preliminary matter, the witness must have personal knowledge on the matters about which she is to testify, which ordinarily means that she must have personally seen or heard what she is to describe (firsthand knowledge). This point is addressed at the outset, as part of "laying the foundation," and the question whether one has the requisite knowledge is considered an issue of conditional relevancy under FRE 104(b), which means that the jury determines the point (the judge can block a witness from testifying for lack of knowledge only if there is insufficient evidence of knowledge to support a reasonable conclusion that there is such knowledge). Normally the witness herself provides the information required to determine the issue of personal knowledge, and normally testimony placing her at the scene and stating that she heard or saw what happened is enough to resolve the point.

How testimony is adduced   Testimony is normally adduced in question-and-answer format, meaning that the lawyer for the calling party puts particular questions to the witness: "Were you at the intersection of Fourth and Green on Wednesday January 28th of last year?" "Did you see a collision involving two cars at that time?" "What kind of cars were involved?"—and so forth. Under FRE 611(c), the calling party must normally ask nonleading questions (meaning essentially questions that do not suggest the desired answer), but exceptions sometimes allow even the calling party to ask leading questions (usually questions that push the witness toward an answer suggested by the phrasing): "Isn't it true that the truck that you saw ran a red light?" Where a witness falters because of faded memory, it is permissible under FRE 613 to try to refresh recollection by showing the witness a document (or other object), and when this tactic is successful the witness may provide the information she now recalls.

To help protect the trial process, the "witness rule" in FRE 615 requires the trial judge (on request by a party) to exclude from the courtroom those people who are to testify later on, so they cannot hear the testimony of others before taking the stand themselves. There are exceptions that allow case agents, experts, and parties to remain in court even if they are to testify later, but this "sequestration" provision represents an important safeguard.

Attacking and supporting witnesses

After their direct testimony, witnesses are tested by cross-examination, where leading questions are normal. Cross-examination can test the witness, delving into matters relating to perception, memory, honesty or bias, and verbal meaning. Often cross-examination leads to impeachment, which is a large subject regulated in whole or in part by many provisions in the Rules. When impeachment occurs, the calling party sometimes chooses to support the witness, and this subject too is regulated at least in part. (See the discussion of these aspects of the witness rules in §6.18 and ensuing sections, *infra.*)

Protect verdicts

One aspect of the law of witnesses is quite different, and that is the exclusionary principle in FRE 606(b). Framed as a competency restriction, this provision actually protects verdicts against attack by means of testimony or affidavits by jurors. The purposes are to protect privacy of deliberations, to minimize the temptation to harass jurors afterwards in hope of attacking the verdict, to avoid temptations on the part of unhappy jurors to undercut verdicts they supported only reluctantly, and to preserve finality.

A. WITNESS COMPETENCY

FRE 601

Every person is competent to be a witness except as otherwise provided in these rules. However, in civil actions and proceedings, with respect to an element of a claim or defense as to which State law supplies the rule of decision, the competency of a witness shall be determined in accordance with State law.

§6.2 Ordinary Witnesses

FRE 601 serves two essential purposes. First, it abolishes virtually all common law grounds for disqualifying witnesses, affirming that unless otherwise provided in the Rules "[e]very person is competent to be a witness." Second, it provides that federal rather than state law governs witness competency, except for witnesses whose testimony bears upon claims or defenses as to which state law supplies the rule of decision, in which case state law also governs competency.

Common law
grounds of
incompetency

Early common law recognized numerous disabilities that made many potential witnesses incompetent to testify. Parties, spouses of parties, accomplices, persons with an interest in the litigation, convicted felons, children, and atheists were all at one time viewed as incompetent.[1] This overdrawn concern about perjury meant that the persons having the greatest knowledge of the facts often could not relate that information to the trier of fact.[2] Because such sweeping rules of incompetency could cause significant injustice, they were targeted by early reformers, most notably Jeremy Bentham.[3]

Nineteenth-
century reforms

By the end of the nineteenth century, most common law grounds of incompetency had been abolished and converted into grounds for impeachment,[4] and this approach is followed by the Federal Rules. Thus interest (as an aspect of bias) is now a basis for impeachment,[5] and convicted felons may testify, but their records may be used to impeach them, and spouses too may testify for or against each other, subject to the rules of privilege.[6]

Witnesses deemed
competent

FRE 601 says all witnesses are competent "except as otherwise provided." The only Rules rendering specific persons incompetent to testify are FRE 605, barring judges from testifying in cases in which they are presiding, and FRE 606(a), barring jurors from testifying before fellow jury members in the case in which they are sitting. But FRE 601 is subject to the provisions requiring witnesses to have personal knowledge and memory (FRE 602) and take an oath or make an affirmation of truth before testifying (FRE 603). Arguably FRE 604 (endorsing use of interpreters where needed) imposes a third requirement, which is that the witness be capable of making himself understood.

The judge decides whether the witness has made an adequate oath or affirmation and can communicate with the jury, for these are issues of "competency" under FRE 104(a). But the jury decides whether the witness has adequate perception and memory, for these matters are issues of conditional relevancy under FRE 104(b). Here the judge plays only a screening role, barring a witness from testifying only if

---

§6.2 1. *See* Greenleaf, Evidence §29 (parties), §30 (accomplices), §34 (spouses), §35 (interested persons), §67 (children), §68 (atheists), and §72 (convicted criminals) (1972).

2. *See* Imwinkelried, The Worst Evidence Principle: The Best Hypothesis as to the Logical Structure of Evidence Law, 46 U. Miami L. Rev. 1069, 1071-1072 (1992) (concern of common law courts in "preventing, deterring, and exposing perjury" is "best explanatory hypothesis" for evidence law).

3. *See* Bentham, Rationale of Judicial Evidence, bk. 9, parts III-V, III at 388 (Bowring 1843) (opposing most grounds of incompetency; if jurors cannot be trusted to assess credibility, "what is it that they are fit to be trusted with?").

4. Thayer, Preliminary Treatise on Evidence 526 (1898) (exclusion of witnesses has nearly ended).

5. United States v. Zeiler, 470 F.2d 717, 720 (3d Cir. 1972) (courts "long ago abandoned" practice of disqualifying witnesses because of presumed bias, which can be examined on cross).

6. *See* discussion of spousal testimony privilege in §5.31, *supra*.

there is not enough evidence of perception and memory to enable a reasonable jury to rely on the witness.[7]

Mental disabilities

Even a witness who has severe mental disabilities resulting from mental illness or retardation is competent to testify under FRE 601.[8] In our adversary system, it is unlikely that a party would call a witness whose testimony is utterly valueless, and an active role by the judiciary in evaluating witness competency might simply encourage unfounded challenges. Nonetheless, in extreme circumstances the testimony of a raving or incoherent witness could be excluded as irrelevant under FRE 401 and 402, as unfairly prejudicial, misleading, or confusing under FRE 403, as lacking in perception or memory under FRE 602, as lacking in understanding of the duty to tell the truth under FRE 603, or as needlessly consuming time or embarrassing the witness under FRE 611(a).[9]

Voir dire examination of competency

Courts sometimes order a preliminary hearing or voir dire examination to determine the competency of a witness.[10] In doing so, courts are acting pursuant to their inherent authority, because the Rules themselves do not provide for such a procedure.[11] It is at least doubtful that courts have inherent authority to compel witnesses or parties to undergo a mental examination, other than criminal defendants who plead insanity or raise issues of competency.[12] But where truly alarming questions of mental competency are raised, courts probably can exclude testimony unless the witness is examined to see whether he has the requisite capacity to perceive and remember.[13] Witnesses are

7. *See* McCrary-El v. Shaw, 992 F.2d 809, 810-811 (8th Cir. 1993) (excluding testimony by fellow inmate; court reasonably concluded that he could not have seen event from adjacent cell).

8. *See* United States v. Allen J., 127 F.3d 1292, 1295-1296 & n.3 (10th Cir. 1997) (in abuse trial, letting 12-year-old victim testify despite developmental delay and mild retardation; competency exam not required; not shown that she did not understand truth and falsehood), *cert. denied*, 523 U.S. 1013.

9. *See* United States v. Lightly, 677 F.2d 1027, 1028 (4th Cir. 1982) (witness is presumed competent unless he "does not have personal knowledge" or lacks capacity to recall or does not understand duty to be truthful); Huff v. White Motor Co., 609 F.2d 286, 294 n.12 (7th Cir. 1979) (in extreme case where incompetence is clear, judge could "exercise his balancing authority under Rule 403" to exclude testimony).

10. United States v. Gutman, 725 F.2d 417, 420 (7th Cir. 1984) (insanity is no longer ground of disqualification, but judge has "power, and in an appropriate case the duty," to hold hearing to determine whether witness should not be allowed to testify because of insanity), *cert. denied*, 469 U.S. 880.

11. United States v. Roach, 590 F.2d 181, 185-186 (5th Cir. 1979) (if views of ACN to FRE 601 are "rigorously adhered to," no longer any basis for competency hearings).

12. *See* Government of Virgin Islands v. Leonard, 922 F.2d 1141, 1144 (3d Cir. 1991) (denying psychiatric examination of 10-year-old and 13-year-old rape victims; must have "persuasive evidential showing" of substantial need for hearing); United States v. Benn, 476 F.2d 1127, 1131 (D.C. Cir. 1972) (psychiatric examination "may seriously impinge" on right to privacy and examination "could serve as a tool of harassment" and deter victim from lodging complaint).

13. United States v. Ramirez, 871 F.2d 582, 584 (6th Cir. 1989) (court cannot order nonparty witness to be examined by psychiatrist; most it can do is condition testimony on prior examination), *cert. denied*, 493 U.S. 841; United States v. Martino, 648 F.2d 367, 384-385 (5th Cir. 1981) (court appointed psychiatrist to examine key government witness to help determine competency), *cert. denied*, 456 U.S. 943.

subject to cross-examination on their ability to observe, recollect, and narrate as well as their ability to understand the duty to testify truthfully, and extrinsic evidence may be introduced on these points.

Drug, alcohol use Drug or alcohol use by a witness, whether at the time of events[14] or of testifying,[15] does not make a witness incompetent unless no reasonable jury could find that she had the ability to perceive and recall such events. Testimony by a witness who is under the influence of drugs or alcohol when called may also be delayed until a later time.[16] Addiction to drugs or alcohol is also not a ground of incompetency,[17] but use of alcohol or drugs at the time of the events (and perhaps even habitually) may be raised by way of impeachment.[18]

Dead Man's statutes Although they vary widely, state Dead Man's Statutes generally make claimants against estates incompetent to testify about conversations or transactions with the decedent. They survive as a historical remnant of the common law disqualification based on interest. Their purpose is to prevent the fabrication of claims that neither the deceased nor the executor of the estate is in a position to rebut[19] and to preserve estates for the benefit of heirs of the decedent whenever there is any room to doubt the merits of the claims being brought. Dead Man's Statutes have long been criticized by scholars, because they bar legitimate claims as well fraudulent ones.[20] Also their effectiveness is questionable because a claimant bent on fraud may be able to fabricate some other form of evidence or suborn perjury by a third person whose testimony is not barred. Nonetheless, while acknowledging "substantial disagreement as to the merit of Dead Man's Statutes," the House Judiciary Committee concluded that they represent important state policy.[21]

Although it is clear that federal courts are required to apply state Dead Man's Statutes in proceedings where state law supplies the rule of

14. United States v. Sinclair, 109 F.3d 1527, 1536-1537 (10th Cir. 1997) (being "very strung out" on Dilaudid on morning of events, coupled with proof that witness abused Xanax, did not disqualify her, but raised questions of credibility); United States v. Strahl, 590 F.2d 10, 12 (1st Cir. 1978) (fact that witness had drunk heavily at time of events goes to credibility rather than competency), *cert. denied*, 440 U.S. 918.

15. *See* State v. Cruz, 181 P.3d 196, 213 (Ariz. 2008) (admitting testimony by visibly intoxicated state witness, which was "rambling" but "coherent") (not shown to be so intoxicated as to be incompetent).

16. *See* United States v. Hyson, 721 F.2d 856 (1st Cir. 1985).

17. United States v. Harris, 542 F.2d 1283, 1303 (7th Cir. 1976) (admitting testimony by witness who had taken dose of Demerol; condition was matter of credibility for jury), *cert. denied*, 430 U.S. 934.

18. *See* discussion of impeachment by showing lack of capacity in §6.21, *infra*.

19. *See* In re Estate of Hall, 535 A.2d 47, 53 (Pa. 1987) (purpose is to "prevent the injustice that would result from permitting a surviving party to a transaction to testify favorably to himself and adversely to the interest of a decedent," whose death hampers representative in responding).

20. *See generally* Ladd, The Dead Man's Statute: Some Further Observations and a Legislative Proposal, 26 Iowa L. Rev. 207 (1941); Ray, Dead Man's Statutes, 24 Ohio St. L.J. 89 (1963).

21. House Report, at 9 (policy "should not be overturned" in absence of compelling federal interest).

decision,[22] it is uncertain to what extent federal courts are required to defer to other state competency provisions. Congress appeared to contemplate that the second sentence of FRE 601 might apply to at least some other state competency provisions.[23]

Probably the best approach is for courts to interpret the second sentence of FRE 601 as applying only to state competency rules based on substantive policy considerations.[24] Also the second sentence of FRE 601 should not be construed as applying to state rules governing expert witnesses, because the general issue of competency is limited to the qualifications of witnesses to testify at all, and not whether they are qualified as experts on particular subjects.[25] However, the "location rule," which requires doctors and similar professional people who testify on local standards of professional services to be familiar with those standards, is so closely connected to the substantive standard of proper care in professional services that federal courts should apply it.[26]

§6.3 Children

Difficult questions of competency are sometimes presented by child witnesses.[1] Very young children may lack the mental development and verbal skills to present coherent testimony or understand and respond to questions (particularly on cross-examination). Even older children, particularly if they are victims of sexual or physical abuse, may have difficulty testifying in open court in the presence of their abuser. In recent years a variety of procedures and devices have been adopted to facilitate testimony by children, including the use of anatomical dolls to help overcome verbal inhibitions in describing sexual activity and liberalized rules allowing the child's parent or other trusted person to sit near the child and provide support while she is testifying.[2]

---

22. *See* Lovejoy Electronics, Inc. v. O'Berto, 873 F.2d 1001, 1005 (7th Cir. 1989); Brand v. Brand, 811 F.2d 74, 79 (2d Cir. 1987).

23. House Report, at 9 (implying awareness of other state competency provisions).

24. *See, e.g.,* Waltzer v. Transidyne Gen. Corp., 697 F.2d 130, 134 (6th Cir. 1983) (in diversity action, state law controls admissibility of testimony by defendant's attorney).

25. Garbincius v. Boston Edison Co., 621 F.2d 1171, 1174 (1st Cir. 1980) (in diversity action, FRE govern admissibility of expert testimony). *But see* Bearce v. United States, 433 F. Supp. 549 (N.D. Ill. 1977) (deferring to Illinois statute that witness not competent to testify on blood/urine analysis).

26. Legg v. Chopra, 286, F.3d 286, 289-292 (6th Cir. 2002) (in medical malpractice suit, federal court applies state law requiring expert testimony; FRE 601 recognizes that some state evidence rules have substantive impact, including statutes requiring expert testimony on standard of care).

§6.3 1. *See generally* Myers, The Testimonial Competence of Children, 25 J. Fam. L. 287 (1986-1987); Goodman & Helgeson, Child Sexual Assault: Children's Memory and the Law, 40 U. Miami L. Rev. 181 (1985).

2. *See* Bulkley, Background and Overview of Child Sexual Abuse: Law Reforms in the Mid-1980s, 40 U. Miami L. Rev. 5, 9 (1985); Perry & Teply, Interviewing, Counseling, and in Court Examination of Children: Practical Approaches for Attorneys, 18 Creighton L. Rev. 1369 (1984).

Many statutes enacted in the closing decades of the twentieth century authorize children to testify by closed-circuit television or use of one-way screens to shield them from the defendant while testifying, and every state adopted new hearsay exceptions as a substitute for live testimony by child victims of abuse.[3] Yet serious constitutional questions arise whenever an accused is denied a full opportunity to confront and cross-examine a child witness called by the prosecutor.[4]

Expanded testimony by children

Many states once had statutes regulating child competency by specific age and using presumptions to attain some flexibility. Typically they made children incompetent below a certain age (usually around seven), presumptively incompetent below some other age, and presumptively competent above that age (usually twelve). In the crucial area of child abuse prosecutions, however, every state enacted reforms in the 1980s that swept away most objections to testimony by even the youngest children, making essentially anyone who can talk at least presumptively competent.[5] And it is now common practice in these cases to hold a voir dire examination to determine the competency of a children before allowing them to take the stand. Even though FRE 601 does not limit child testimony in this way, this practice seems consistent with the Rule, because it helps assure that children understand their duty to speak truthfully.[6] It also might alert the court and the parties to risks that are so serious that precautions are necessary, and in rare cases it might lead to exclusion of testimony under FRE 403 and 611.

Federal statute governs

In federal court, a statute enacted quietly in 1990 regulates the subject of child testimony in abuse cases in elaborate detail.[7] Under the federal constitution, a criminal defendant does not have an absolute right to be personally present at a competency hearing for a child witness, at least in cases where defense counsel is present and all

---

3. Maryland v. Craig, 497 U.S. 836, 855 (1990) (approving one-way closed-circuit television procedure where other aspects of confrontation rights were preserved and state made adequate showing of necessity on basis of case-specific findings). *See generally* M. Graham, Indicia for Reliability and Face to Face Confrontation: Emerging Issues in Child Sex Abuse Prosecutions, 40 U. Miami L. Rev. 19 (1985); Barry, Witness Shield Laws and Child Sexual Abuse Prosecutions: A Presumption of Guilt, 15 S. Ill. U. L.J. 99 (1990). *But see* Coy v. Iowa, 487 U.S. 1012, 1020 (1988) (condemning use of screens to shield children in absence of "individualized findings that these particular witnesses needed special protection").

4. *See* the discussion of constitutional issues surrounding protected witness testimony in §8.92, *infra.*

5. *See* 18 U.S.C. §3509(c)(2) (children are "presumed competent"); Colo. Rev. Stat. §13-090-106 (children under ten are incompetent if they "appear incapable of receiving just impressions" or "relating them truly," but this limit does not apply to victims testifying in abuse cases who can describe facts in age-appropriate language).

6. *See* State v. G.C., 902 A.2d 1174, 1181 (N.J. 2006) (5-year-old girl told judge on voir dire it was "good" to speak the truth and "bad" to lie, and she would "tell the truth") (judge could find her competent).

7. 18 U.S.C. §3509(c) (creating presumption that children are competent, authorizing examinations to determine competency only on showing of compelling reason other than age).

questions put to the child could be asked again at trial in the defendant's presence.[8]

It is commonplace in child abuse prosecutions to offer the deposition testimony of children or let them testify from another room using video technology. In these cases the prosecutor must first show that the child is "unavailable" in the special sense that she could not give live testimony or would suffer serious trauma if required to do so. Hence it is often necessary to hold a special hearing that considers a range of issues from general competency to psychological trauma and capacity to face up to giving courtroom testimony. A finding of "psychological unavailability" may pave the way not only for depositions and remote testimony, but for other hearsay statements.[9]

[margin: Unavailability of child]

§6.4 Hypnotically Refreshed Testimony

Hypnosis is sometimes used as a law enforcement tool to enhance the recollection of witnesses.[1] While hypnosis may help some witnesses recall details they have forgotten or bring subconscious perceptions and memories into their consciousness, it also presents significant dangers. Hypnotized subjects may "confabulate" facts that never occurred, as creative imagination displaces memory and witnesses lose, for the moment and perhaps forever, their capacity to sort out what really happened at a particular time from what they feared or wanted or otherwise imagined.[2] As the Supreme Court observed in a leading case, perhaps the most common response to hypnosis is "an increase in both correct and incorrect recollections."[3] Persons under hypnosis are also highly suggestible and may be led into making unfounded statements or providing answers that they think the hypnotist wants to hear. They also may become "hardened" in their memories, having greater confidence in both true and false memories.[4]

[margin: Hypnotized witnesses]

Aware of these dangers, courts have developed at least four different approaches to hypnotically refreshed testimony. The trend among states is toward a per se rule barring such testimony.[5] Some states

---

8. Kentucky v. Stincer, 482 U.S. 730, 745-747 (1987) (suggesting possibility of limited circumstances where defendant would be entitled to be present).

9. *See* discussion of psychological unavailability in §8.67, *infra*.

§6.4 1. *See generally* Mickenberg, Mesmerizing Justice: The Use of Hypnotically Induced Testimony in Criminal Trials, 34 Syracuse L. Rev. 927 (1983).

2. *See generally* Beaver, Memory Restored or Confabulated by Hypnosis: Is It Competent?, 6 U. Puget Sound L. Rev. 155 (1983); Orne, The Use and Misuse of Hypnosis in Court, 27 Intl. J. Clinical & Experimental Hypnosis 311, 317-318 (1979).

3. Rock v. Arkansas, 483 U.S. 44, 59 (1987).

4. Diamond, Inherent Problems in the Use of Pretrial Hypnosis on a Prospective Witness, 68 Cal. L. Rev. 313 (1980).

5. State v. Fertig, 688 A.2d 1076, 1081 (N.J. 1996) (reporting that 26 states now exclude hypnotically refeshed testimony under a per se rule.). See Beaudine, Growing Disenchantment with Hypnotic Means of Refreshing Witness Recall, 41 Vand. L. Rev. 379 (1988).

take the view that hypnosis fails to satisfy the standard for scientific evidence because the use of hypnosis to enhance memory is not generally accepted as reliable by the scientific community.[6] Other states take the opposite view, adopting a per se rule of admissibility, holding that hypnosis affects credibility, not admissibility.[7] In these states, parties are often allowed to offer expert testimony on the reliability of hypnotically refreshed testimony and to request cautionary instructions that will enable the jury to determine the proper weight to be given to the evidence. A third view, endorsed by many federal courts, is the "totality-of-the-circumstances" approach, under which the probative value of the evidence is balanced against its prejudicial effect on a case-by-case basis.[8] Finally, some courts impose procedural safeguards, conditioning admissibility on observing the safeguards.[9]

The last two approaches have the greatest potential for minimizing the dangers of hypnotically refreshed testimony in cases where it is admitted. Commonly suggested guidelines include requiring that the hypnosis be conducted only by a psychologist or psychiatrist who has special training in its use. The hypnotist should be independent of the investigation and should conduct the hypnosis in a neutral setting without the presence of other persons. It is extremely helpful if the hypnosis session is recorded by videotape so that the trier of fact can later be assured that no improperly suggestive interrogation was used. It is important to establish carefully the extent of the subject's memory prior to hypnosis so that the degree of any "enhancement" can be precisely identified. This latter protection makes it likely that even if the hypnotically refreshed memory is disallowed the witness will still be able to testify to matters known prior to hypnosis.[10] A cautionary

---

6. State v. Martin, 684 P.2d 651, 654 (Wash. 1984) ("absent general scientific acceptance of hypnosis as a reliable means of refreshing recollection, the dangers and possibility of prejudice should preclude admission"). *See also* Shaw, Trances, Trials and Tribulations, 11 Touro L. Rev. 145, 157 (1994) (under *Daubert* hypnotically enhanced testimony should clearly be inadmissible).

7. *See, e.g.,* Kater v. Maloney, 459 F.3d 56 (1st Cir. 2006) (rejecting constitutional challenge to state conviction resting in part on post-hypnotic testimony; witness testified to "facts that were documented" before hypnosis); United States v. Awkard, 597 F.2d 667, 668-669 (9th Cir 1979) (fact of hypnosis "may affect the credibility of the evidence, but not its admissibility"), *cert. denied,* 444 U.S. 885.

8. Borawick v. Shay, 68 F.3d 597 (2d Cir. 1995) (court should consider, *inter alia,* purpose of hypnosis, whether subject received suggestions from hypnotist or others, whether record of session made, qualifications of hypnotist, existence of corroborating evidence, "hypnotizability" of subject, and expert evidence on reliability of procedures used).

9. *See, e.g.,* Beck v. Norris, 801 F.2d 242, 244-245 (6th Cir. 1986) (procedures used safeguard right to fair trial); State v. Hurd, 432 A.2d 86, 95-97 (N.J. 1981) (seminal case).

10. *See* Sprynczynatyk v. General Motors, 771 F.2d 1112, 1123 n.14 (8th Cir. 1985) (in pretrial hearing, judges must consider following procedural safeguards: (1) hypnotic session should be conducted by impartial, properly trained, licensed psychiatrist or psychologist; (2) information given to hypnotist concerning case is to be noted, preferably in written form, so that extent of new information from hypnotist may be

instruction should always be given informing the jury of the effect hypnosis could have on a witness's testimony.[11]

There are constitutional limits on how far a state can go in excluding hypnotically refreshed testimony. In its 1987 decision in the *Rock* case,[12] the Supreme Court considered the constitutionality of a state rule that barred testimony by a defendant in a murder prosecution as to her hypnotically refreshed version of the shooting incident. The Court held that a per se rule excluding all post-hypnosis testimony impermissibly infringes on the right of a criminal defendant to testify on her own behalf. The Court did not address the constitutionality of a per se bar to hypnotically refreshed testimony by other witnesses, and such issues would seem primarily a matter of evidentiary policy rather than constitutional law.[13]

B. PERSONAL KNOWLEDGE

> **FRE 602**
>
> A witness may not testify to a matter unless evidence is introduced sufficient to support a finding that the witness has personal knowledge of the matter. Evidence to prove personal knowledge may, but need not, consist of the witness' own testimony. This rule is subject to the provisions of Rule 703, relating to opinion testimony by expert witnesses.

§6.5 Personal Knowledge

FRE 602 provides that before a witness can testify evidence must be introduced sufficient to support a finding that she has personal knowledge of the subject matter, and she cannot simply testify to knowledge based on what others have told her.[1] "Personal knowledge" means

---

determined; (3) subject should provide detailed description of facts before hypnosis; (4) session should be recorded, preferably on videotape, so permanent record is available to ensure against suggestive procedures; (5) only hypnotist and subject should be present during hypnotic session), *cert. denied*, 475 U.S. 1046. Cf. Or. Rev. Stat. 136.675-136.695 (1991) (example of safeguards required by state statute).

11. State v. Fertig, 668 A.2d 1076, 1082 (N.J. 1996) (requiring cautionary jury instruction in cases where hypnotically refreshed testimony admitted).

12. Rock v. Arkansas, 483 U.S. 44, 59 (1987).

13. *See* United States v. Scheffer, 523 U.S. 303 (1998) (upholding rules excluding evidence that could reasonably be found unreliable, such as polygraph results). *See also* Note, Between a *Rock* and *Hurd* Place: Protecting the Criminal Defendant's Right to Testify After Her Testimony Has Been Hypnotically Refreshed, 65 Fordham L. Rev. 2151 (1997) (hypnotically refreshed testimony should be per se inadmissible; except that it should be considered on case-by-case basis when the accused testifies).

§6.5 1. State v. Frazier, 592 S.E.2d 621 (S.C. 2004) (error to let witness testify to statement; he did not know who defendant was talking to and could not recall statement) ("too speculative").

firsthand knowledge that comes to the witness though her own senses and includes two components—perception and memory. A witness cannot testify to perceptions that she cannot remember, nor to memories that are not based on her own perceptions. FRE 701 reaffirms that opinion testimony by lay witnesses must rest on personal knowledge, although FRE 703 exempts expert opinions from this requirement (they cannot parrot what others say but can rely on secondhand information, so long as a reasonable expert in the field would do so).

Firsthand knowledge often (perhaps always) includes some inferences or opinions gleaned from experience.[2] Equally important, the difference between firsthand knowledge and secondhand knowledge, which is central to FRE 602, can be overstated: Knowledge is framed, expressed, and organized in light of remembered experiences, and affected by information gleaned in school or simply in living, and most memories produced by direct sensory experience are infused with some mixture of hearsay information, and it can still satisfy FRE 602 as long as it is largely based on firsthand observation.[3]

Showing of personal knowledge

The witness herself may supply the necessary foundation showing personal knowledge.[4] Customary trial procedures call for the witness to be asked, before she relates factual information, preliminary questions asking whether she personally perceived the facts she is about to relate. Thus in an automobile accident case a witness is typically asked questions designed to bring out that she was at the scene and saw the accident before she describes what she saw. Personal knowledge can also be shown by testimony of other witnesses or other evidence.

The position held by a person, or her job responsibilities, or the general experience of a person, or his particular living situation or routines, such as the manner in which he gets to work or the routes he follows to work or to common destinations, or his experience in traveling by airline or bus or train, may well show—without further proof—that one has enough experience-based knowledge to give certain kinds of testimony. In short, for purposes of satisfying FRE 602, knowledge can be shown by circumstantial proof.[5]

Mixed question for judge and jury

The requirement of personal knowledge is an element of competency.[6] However, the Rules draw a distinction between personal knowledge and other components of competency. The "qualification

---

2. U.S. v. Santos, 201 F.3d 953, 963 (7th Cir. 1999) (FRE 701 does not block inferences by lay witnesses; "even testimony as to what one has seen, is inferential in the sense that a reasoning process, however rudimentary, is being applied to the raw sense data").

3. Agfa-Gevaert, A.G. v. A.B. Dick Company, 879 F.2d 1518 (7th cir. 1989) (perception is "inferential," and most knowledge is "social," so knowledge "acquired through others may still be personal knowledge" under FRE 602 and not hearsay).

4. United States v. Cantu, 167 F.34d 198, 204 (5th Cir. 1999).

5. Sheek v. Asia Badger, Inc., 325 F.3d 687, 694-695 (1st Cir. 2000) ("experience and observations" as employee for oil company provided basis to testify on workplace and design hazards); State v. Enderson, 804 A.2d 448, 453 (N.H. 2002) (as sole employee of defendant for seven years, witness who answered phones and accepted bets had knowledge to testify that defendant took bets from a certain person).

6. *See generally* Raitt, Personal Knowledge Under the Federal Rules of Evidence: A Three Legged Stool, 18 Rutgers L.J. 591 (1988).

of a person to be a witness" is a matter for the court under FRE 104(a), but personal knowledge is a "mixed question" for the judge and jury under FRE 104(b). The only responsibility of the judge, before letting a witness testify, is to insure that enough evidence has been offered to support a decision by the jury that the witness has personal knowledge, and a judge bars testimony under FRE 602 only where the proponent fails to satisfy this standard.[7] Even if a witness saw the event only for a split second, or from a great distance, or in darkness, normally such factors go only to credibility rather than admissibility, provided that a jury could find that the witness did in fact perceive the event. The jury, rather than the court, makes the ultimate determination whether the witness has personal knowledge, and the jury may disregard the testimony if it is not persuaded on this point.[8] If cross-examination or other evidence shows that the witness lacked knowledge so a reasonable jury could not find that she had knowledge, then the court may strike the testimony and tell the jury to disregard it.

An objection based on lack of personal knowledge sometimes overlaps with an objection that the testimony is hearsay.[9] The right objection depends mainly on the form of the testimony. If the witness repeats on the stand the out-of-court statement of another and the purpose is to prove what the statement asserts, the better objection is hearsay. If the witness simply describes some act, event, or condition in the world, and later it appears that the witness was simply reciting what he had been told, the better objection is lack of personal knowledge, and of course a motion to strike is appropriate.[10] In cases where there is overlap or doubt as to the proper objection, it is wise to object on both grounds, although an objection on either ground should be sufficient to preserve the error.[11]

Overlap with hearsay objection

Where the very purpose of testimony is to prove an out-of-court statement, as happens, for example, when such a statement is offered under a hearsay exception to prove whatever it asserts, the personal knowledge requirement means only that the witness must actually have heard or (less often) read the statement itself. In other words, the witness need not have personal knowledge of the acts, events, or conditions that the

---

7. State v. Bryant, 888 A.2d 965, 971 (R.I. 2006) (refusing to strike testimony by 13-year-old describing domestic assault; whether she had adequate knowledge is for jury to decide)United States v. Hickey, 917 F.2d 901, 904 (6th Cir. 1990) (testimony should be allowed "unless no reasonable juror could believe that the witness had the ability and opportunity to perceive the event").

8. United States v. Villata, 662 F.2d 1205 (5th Cir. 1981) (uncertainty went to weight), *cert. denied,* 456 U.S. 916.

9. *See* United States v. Mandel, 591 F.2d 1347, 1369 (4th Cir. 1979) (referring to "sometimes formal" distinction, which is "blurred in practice"), *cert. denied,* 445 U.S. 961.

10. *See* United States v. Becerril-Lopez, 528 F.3d 1133, 1139-1140 (9th Cir. 2008) (agent relied not on what he saw, but on what he read in report; defense moved to strike for lack of knowledge) (error to allow testimony, but harmless); Kaczmarek v. Allied Chem. Corp., 836 F.2d 1055, 1060 (7th Cir. 1987).

11. Elizarraras v. Bank of El Paso, 631 F.2d 366, 373-374 (5th Cir. 1980) (finding error under FRE 602 even though appellant objected only on basis of hearsay).

statement is offered to prove.[12] Normally the person who made such a statement must have had personal knowledge of the acts, events, or conditions or the statement will not fit one of the exceptions,[13] although admissions by party opponents do not require personal knowledge.[14]

Categorical certainty not required

The personal knowledge requirement does not require categorical certainty or mathematical precision (unless exactness is important to the point to be proved),[15] and a witness can give his "impression," or testify to what he "thinks," or "believes" he saw, provided that he perceived the event with his own senses.[16] If the witness engages in speculation or conjecture, or bases his conclusions on inadmissible statements by other people, the testimony should be excluded.[17]

C.   OATH OR AFFIRMATION REQUIREMENT

> **FRE 603**
>
> Before testifying, every witness shall be required to declare that the witness will testify truthfully, by oath or affirmation administered in a form calculated to awaken the witness' conscience and impress the witness' mind with the duty to do so.

§6.6   Oath or Affirmation

FRE 603 requires that before testifying a witness must swear or affirm to testify truthfully.[1] The purpose is to impress on the witness the duty to

---

12. *See* ACN, FRE 602 (Rule "does not govern" witness who testifies to hearsay statement if he has personal knowledge of making of statement).

13. *See* ACN, FRE 803 (neither FRE 803 nor FRE 804 "dispenses with the requirement of first-hand knowledge"). *But see* FRE 804(b)(4)(A) (creating exception for statement of personal or family history "even though the declarant had no means of acquiring personal knowledge").

14. *See* discussion of FRE 801(d)(2) in §§8.27-8.34, *infra*.

15. United States v. Castro, 89 F.3d 1443, 1454-1455 (11th Cir. 1996) (witness testified that federal grants exceeded 90 million, even though witness could not "recall the specific number"), *cert. denied*, 519 U.S. 1118; United States v. Rodriguez, 968 F.2d 130, 143 (2d Cir. 1992) (observations need not be "positive or absolutely certain"), *cert. denied*, 506 U.S. 487.

16. M.B.A.F.B. Federal Credit Union v. Cumis Ins. Socy., 681 F.2d 930, 932 (4th Cir. 1982) (FRE 602 does not require that knowledge be positive or rise to level of absolute certainty).

17. State v. Frazier, 592 S.E.2d 621 (S.C. 2004) (witness "guessed" defendant was speaking to R and thought statement was serious, but could not recall content, making testimony "too speculative") (reversing); Palucki v. Sears, Roebuck & Co., 879 F.2d 1568, 1572 (7th Cir. 1989) (awarding summary judgment where critical witness for opponent had only a "gut feeling" that defendant discriminated).

§6.6   1. The very term "testimony" connotes oral statements under oath or affirmation. Even where the Rules do not apply, courts require an oath or affirmation when witnesses give evidence.

speak the truth[2] and pave the way for a perjury prosecution for deliberately false testimony.[3] The oath or affirmation requirement is one element of competency. A witness who refuses to swear or affirm an obligation to testify truthfully, including a criminal defendant, may be barred from testifying.[4] Refusal to testify may be punished as contempt, and probably refusal to swear or affirm may be treated the same way.

There is no legal distinction between an oath (where traditionally the witness "swears" to be truthful, and concludes with the phrase "so help me God") and an affirmation (a solemn declaration to tell the truth).[5] Allowing the witness to affirm rather than swear amounts to a concession to the strong national tradition of religious freedom. It has long been settled that a witness who does not believe in God or hold any particular religious belief is not for that reason incompetent.[6]

Oath, affirmation are the same

The words to be used in administering an oath or affirmation are not specified by FRE 603 or by most state rules on the subject. Standard forms are in common use, but the trial court may fashion an oath or affirmation that is suitable for a witness who objects to the usual wording, and state statutory and constitutional provisions prohibiting religious tests are mandates for flexibility.[7] Use of words such as "solemnly" or "swear" or "affirm" is not required.[8] Courts sometimes cave in perhaps too far to uncooperative witnesses who insist on committing themselves no further than saying they are aware of their duty to tell the

Verbal formulation may vary

2. United States v. Turner, 558 F.2d 46, 50 (2d Cir. 1977) ("those who have been impressed with the moral, religious or legal significance of formally undertaking to tell the truth are more likely to do so").

3. *Compare* United States v. Mandujano, 425 U.S. 564 (1976) (no requirement to warn witnesses that they are subject to penalty for perjury) *with* United States v. Vosper, 493 F.2d 433, 436 (5th Cir. 1974) (cautioning witness about consequences of oath must "be done with care" so it cannot be interpreted as "prejudgment" or attempt to pressure him into rescinding).

4. United States v. Fowler, 605 F.2d 181, 185 (4th Cir. 1979) (refusing to let defendant testify after he would neither swear nor affirm that he would tell truth), *cert. denied*, 445 U.S. 950.

5. *See* United States v. Saget, 991 F.2d 702, 710 (11th Cir. 1993) (refusing to strike testimony by government witness who took oath even though he was an atheist; he testified that he respected oath and was telling truth "to the best of my ability").

6. At common law, witnesses had to believe in a divine being who would punish false swearing. Most states have abandoned this competency restriction. *See, e.g.*, California Constitution 1879, art. I, §4 (nobody incompetent to testify on account of "opinions on matters of religious belief").

7. United States v. Ward, 989 F.2d 1015, 1019-1020 (9th Cir. 1992) (reversible error to refuse to allow defendant to take both standard oath and his own variant); Spigarolo v. Meachun, 934 F.2d 19, 24 (2d Cir. 1991) (oath for child witnesses).

8. Moore v. United States, 348 U.S. 966 (1955) (error to exclude testimony by witnesses who declined on religious ground to say "solemnly" in affirming to tell truth) (reversing).

truth.[9] FRE 603 should be interpreted to require an actual commitment on the part of witnesses to tell the truth.[10]

Form of ceremony

FRE 603 also does not address the form of ceremony to be followed in taking the oath or affirmation. Courts have held that raising of a hand by the witness is not required.[11] A leading pre-Rules case commented that English courts "have permitted Chinese to break a saucer, a Mohammedan to bow before the Koran and touch it to his head, and a Parsee to tie a rope around his waist" as satisfying the oath requirement, and a similar spirit of accommodation to differing religious beliefs and moral philosophies is required by FRE 603.[12]

Possibility of prejudice

Courts should recognize the risk of prejudice and intrusion into personal beliefs that might come from unusual approaches to this matter. Probably any colloquy between the witness and the judge should be heard outside the presence of the jury,[13] and a witness should not be questioned on his reasons to affirm rather than swear, nor can any adverse inference be drawn from it.[14]

The formality of the occasion and personal involvement of the judge may have more effect in impressing on a witness the duty to tell the truth than the wording of the oath or affirmation. It seems preferable for the judge to administer the oath personally, that witnesses be sworn individually rather than in groups, and for witnesses to say something like "I swear to tell the truth" (or "affirm that I will tell the truth"),[15] although in the press of business clerks routinely administer the oath and witnesses are routinely required to say no more than "I do" or "I will."

9. *See* Gordon v. Idaho, 778 F.2d 1397, 1401 (9th Cir. 1985) (upholding this statement as sufficient: "I understand that I must tell the truth. I agree to testify under penalty of perjury. I understand that if I testify falsely I may be subject to criminal prosecution.").

10. *See* United States v. Allen J., 127 F.3d 1292, 1295-1296 & n.3 (10th Cir. 1997) (12-year-old child said she "understood she had promised to tell the truth," knew difference between truth and lie and knew she was to tell the truth and would be punished if she lied).

11. Gordon v. Idaho, 778 F.2d 1397 (9th Cir. 1985) (witness in deposition need not raise right hand when making oath or affirmation).

12. United States v. Looper, 419 F.2d 1405, 1407 n.4 (4th Cir. 1969). See also State v. G.C., 902 A.2d 1174, 1181 (N.J. 2006) (letting 5-year-old testify; forcing oath might mean losing testimony; in voir dire, judge focused on "duty to tell the truth," which implicates consequences from failure to comply, and decided that she understood) (she said would "tell the truth" and that was enough).

13. *See* United States v. Rabb, 394 F.2d 230, 233 (3d Cir. 1968) (where defendant is follower of minority religion, particularly one that may be unpopular, better "to permit him to affirm"). *See also* FRE 103(c) and FRE 104(c).

14. *See* FRE 610 (barring evidence of religious beliefs for purpose of impeaching or enhancing credibility of witness). *See also* United States v. Kalaydjian, 784 F.2d 53, 57 (2d Cir. 1986) (right to affirm rather than swear would be "meaningless" if witness could be cross-examined on reasons).

15. *See* 63 Reports of the American Bar Association 586 (1938) (judge should administer oath; witness should repeat it word for word; oath should be taken individually rather than by groups; everyone in court should stand).

D.   INTERPRETERS

FRE 604

An interpreter is subject to the provisions of these rules relating to qualification as an expert and the administration of an oath or affirmation to make a true translation.

§6.7   Interpreters

FRE 604 subjects interpreters to the requirements of the Rules on qualification of experts and administration of the oath or affirmation. It requires interpreters to be experts by knowledge, skill, experience, training, or education under FRE 702 and to swear or affirm in conformance with FRE 603 that they will make a true translation of the proceedings. The Rule does not address the procedures for appointment of an interpreter nor the question of compensation, and these matters are instead covered by the Civil and Criminal Rules and by federal statute.[1]

Interpreters may be appointed where the witness speaks only a foreign language or has a hearing or speech impairment.[2] The court has broad discretion in deciding whether to appoint interpreters and determining their qualifications.[3]

An interpreter can play several different roles at trial. First, an interpreter may be needed to translate testimony so that it can be comprehended by the trier of fact. Second, an interpreter may translate the entire proceedings, including testimony of witnesses, questions of counsel, and statements by the court, so that they are comprehensible to a party who speaks a different language or has a hearing impairment. Finally, an interpreter may serve as an intermediary who translates communications between a party and his counsel. A single interpreter may fill all of these roles.

Interpreter can play several roles

It might be argued that FRE 604 covers only interpreters performing the first role. Interpreters who translate testimony by witnesses are conveying information to the trier of fact, which is the primary concern of Article VI. Thus it is not surprising that interpreters performing such a function should be required to meet the same qualifications as other experts and to take an oath to make a true translation.[4] It is less clear

§6.7   1. *See* FRCP 43(F); FRCrimP 28; 28 U.S.C. §1827 (certification of interpreters by Director of Administrative Office of United States Courts).

2. *See* 28 U.S.C. §1827(d) (on interpreter where witness speaks something other than English "only or primarily" or suffers "hearing impairment").

3. United States v. Ball, 988 F.2d 7, 9 (5th Cir. 1993) (appointing wife of witness as interpreter).

4. *Cf.* United States v. Taren-Palma, 997 F.2d 525 (9th Cir. 1993) (government expert who translated recorded conversations in foreign language and testified about content took standard oath; FRE 604 applies only to interpreters who translate testimony).

that the drafters intended FRE 604 to regulate interpreters who are merely translating the proceedings for a party or serving as an intermediary between a party and his attorney. Such matters are normally beyond the concern of the law of evidence. Moreover, parties should arguably be allowed freedom to select their own interpreters, particularly for translating confidential attorney-client communications, without scrutiny of qualifications or other intrusion by the court.[5]

Right to interpreter

On the other hand, there is a strong public interest in ensuring that interpreters performing the latter two roles are properly qualified and are sworn to translate correctly, particularly in criminal cases where the defendant does not speak English or is hearing-impaired. A trial would be a sham if language barriers prevented a criminal defendant from communicating effectively with his counsel or comprehending what was said in the courtroom. The ACN to FRE 604 could be read to suggest that its coverage extends beyond interpreters who translate testimony.[6]

In any case, it is well recognized that when either the accused or a witness on his behalf can neither speak nor understand English, the accused has a right to an interpreter, at public expense if necessary, and this right is of constitutional dimension.[7] The trial judge should advise a defendant of this right as soon as language difficulties become evident.[8] When a party or witness has some comprehension of English, but less than full ability to speak or understand, the judge has a measure of discretion on the question whether an interpreter should be appointed.[9] An interpreter should be appointed, however, whenever there is doubt about the defendant's ability to understand, even though he has partial comprehension. Some cases hold that a defendant must demand an interpreter or waive his right to one,[10] although in egregious cases failure to provide an interpreter may be plain error.[11]

---

5. *See* 28 U.S.C. §1827(f) (allowing party to waive right to court-certified interpreter and to select noncertified interpreter of party's choice).

6. The ACN says FRE 604 "implements" FRCP 43(f) and FRCrimP 28(b). The ACN to FRCrimP 28 says interpreters "may be needed to interpret the testimony of non-English speaking witnesses or to assist non-English speaking defendants" understand the proceedings and communicate with assigned counsel.

7. State v. Calderon, 13 P.3d 871 (Kan. 2000) (error to refuse to appoint interpreter, during closing argument in murder trial, which violated confrontation rights) (reversing conviction).

8. United States ex rel. Negron v. New York, 434 F.2d 386 (2d Cir. 1970) (knowing about severe language difficulty, court should tell defendant he has right to translator, at state expense if need be).

9. United States v. Martinez, 616 F.2d 185 (5th Cir. 1980) (interpreter not required where bilingual counsel assured court he could translate for defendant), *cert. denied*, 450 U.S. 994.

10. *See, e.g.*, United States v. Barrios, 457 F.2d 680, 682 (9th Cir. 1972).

11. United States ex rel. Negron v. New York, 434 F.2d 386, 390 (2d Cir. 1970).

E.   COMPETENCY OF JUDGES AND LAWYERS AS WITNESSES

> **FRE 605**
>
> The judge presiding at the trial may not testify in that trial as a witness. No objection need be made in order to preserve the point.

§6.8   Judges as Witnesses

FRE 605 provides that a judge is absolutely disqualified from testifying in a trial at which she presides. The Rule is necessary for at least four reasons. First, testifying would cast her in an unavoidably conflicted role. She would have to pass on the competency of her own testimony and weigh evidence she herself produced. Difficult questions would arise as to who should rule on objections or compel answers. Second, testimony by a presiding judge would destroy the appearance of judicial impartiality and undermine the dignity of the court. In criminal trials, testimony by the judge would probably deprive the accused of his constitutional right to have guilt determined by an impartial tribunal.[1] Third, it would inevitably inject an unwarranted risk of unfair prejudice for the judge to take the stand. The jury would likely give her testimony considerable (perhaps overwhelming) weight and would have difficulty separating the impartial instructions at the conclusion of the trial from the judge's earlier partisan testimony. Perhaps in some cases the jury might go in the other direction and react with sympathy for the party against whom the judge's testimony is directed. Finally, if the presiding judge were to testify, the litigants would be placed in an awkward position. By cross-examining the judge, objecting to her testimony, or utilizing normal modes of impeachment, a party would risk antagonizing the very judicial officer who is presiding over the trial.

Presiding judge disqualified to testify

Invocation of FRE 605 is seldom necessary to prevent a presiding judge from taking the witness stand, because a judge having any personal knowledge concerning the matter in litigation is required to disqualify herself prior to trial.[2] When a trial judge does violate FRE 605, a party need make no objection to preserve the error for appeal. The Rule secures to each party an "automatic" objection, thus creating an exception to the usual requirements of FRE 103. The reason is that a spoken objection is likely to call into question

Federal statute requires disqualification

§6.8   1. Gonzales v. Beto, 405 U.S. 1052, 1055-1056 (1972) (constitutional violation to call bailiff as prosecution witness; adversary system requires that roles of prosecution, defense, and court be "separate and distinct," and system of justice is "perverted" where officer of court testifies for prosecution) (Stewart, J., concurring).

2. 28 U.S.C. §455 (judge must disqualify herself when, inter alia, she has "personal knowledge of disputed evidentiary facts concerning the proceeding"). This provision is self-executing in the sense that it obligates the judge to act sua sponte to recuse herself, although the parties may raise the matter too.

the integrity of the trial judge, and a party should not be forced to preserve appeal rights at the cost of continuing a trial before a judge who feels she has been personally attacked.

Nothing in the Rule keeps a judge from testifying in a trial where she is not presiding.[3] A judge is not privileged to refuse to testify about matters she observed, even in the course of judicial duties,[4] although she cannot be compelled to testify about her mental processes in reaching a judicial decision.[5]

Functional equivalent of testimony by judge

Clearly FRE 605 reaches the case in which the trial judge leaves the bench, takes the witness stand, and formally testifies. But FRE 605 should be interpreted as also barring testimony by the judge's law clerk[6] or any functional equivalent of testimony by the judge.[7] One example is questioning by the judge that improperly imparts factual data. Although FRE 614(b) authorizes the court to interrogate witnesses, FRE 605 should be viewed as barring any questioning by the trial judge that conveys to the jury factual information not previously put in evidence, except insofar as such information might be judicially noticeable.[8] A judge who takes judicial notice on the basis of personal experience violates FRE 201(b) and the policy if not the letter of FRE 605 as well.[9] FRE 605 also is implicated if a judge, while serving as trier of fact, takes an unauthorized view[10] or has his law clerk take a view and report his findings to the court.[11]

3. *See* United States v. Frankenthal, 582 F.2d 1102, 1108 (7th Cir. 1978) (calling federal judge as witness in trial in which he had been originally assigned but from which he had disqualified himself).

4. United States v. Dowdy, 440 F. Supp. 894, 896 (W.D. Va. 1977) (judge "enjoys no special privilege from being subpoenaed as a witness").

5. Washington v. Strickland, 693 F.2d 1243, 1263 (5th Cir. 1982) (judge may not be asked "about his mental processes in reaching a judicial decision"), *rev'd on other grounds*, 466 U.S. 668.

6. *See* Kennedy v. Great Atl. & Pac. Tea Co., 551 F.2d 593, 598-599 (5th Cir. 1977) (error to deny defendant's motion disqualifying law clerk of judge from testifying or in alternative disqualifying judge from continuing to try case).

7. *See* Jones v. Benefit Trust Life Ins. Co., 800 F.2d 1397, 1400 (5th Cir. 1986) (excluding evidence that judge had denied plaintiff's motion for summary judgment on allegations that insurance carrier wrongfully reduced monthly payments; admitting such evidence "would seem at odds" with FRE 605).

8. *See* United States v. Nickl, 427 F.3d 1286, 1292-1295 (10th Cir. 2005) (judge "reshaped" equivocal testimony into "definitive answer" on ultimate issue, amounting to testimony) (reversing); United States v. Paiva, 892 F.2d 148, 158-159 (1st Cir. 1989) (judge's explanation of drug identification field test improper; it amounted to testimony rather than comment on evidence).

9. United States v. Lewis, 833 F.2d 1380, 1385 (9th Cir. 1987) (error to rule confession involuntary; judge found on basis of personal experience that as you emerge from anesthesia "you are not accountable for what you do"; judge not competent witness). *See also* discussion of judicial notice in §2.6, *supra*.

10. Lillie v. United States, 953 F.2d 1188, 1191 (10th Cir. 1992) (in bench trial, error for court to view accident scene without notice to parties; judge engaging in "off-the-record factgathering" is witness).

11. Price Bros. Co. v. Philadelphia Gear Corp., 629 F.2d 444, 447 (6th Cir. 1980) (law clerk visited plaintiff's plant and viewed malfunctioning pipewrapping machine; judge "may not direct his law clerk to do that which is prohibited to the judge"), *cert. denied*, 454 U.S. 1099.

§6.9 Lawyers as Witnesses

The Rules do not make lawyers incompetent as witnesses in cases they are trying, and a number of courts hold that they are competent.[1] Nonetheless, the Code of Professional Responsibility[2] and the Model Rules of Professional Conduct[3] generally prohibit lawyers from serving as both witness and advocate in the same case unless the testimony falls into one of several narrow exceptions.[4] The ethical proscription is based on the inherent conflict between the roles of witness and advocate and the diminished effectiveness likely to result when a lawyer serves in both capacities.[5] The ethical rules do not, however, bar testimony by employees of a lawyer, such as a law clerk or investigator.[6]

Judges probably have inherent authority to refuse to allow an attorney to testify where doing so would violate ethical rules.[7] Some authorities, however, hold that the judge must allow the lawyer to testify subject to later disciplinary sanctions.[8] Other courts allow testimony by the lawyer, provided that he has withdrawn or agrees to withdraw from the case.[9] Occasionally parties are able to stipulate to the matter about

Lawyer testimony may be barred

---

§6.9   1. United States v. Marshall, 75 F.3d 1097, 1106 (7th Cir. 1996) (where attorney appears as advocate and witness, mistrial or reversal may be warranted); United States v. Birdman, 602 F.2d 547, 556 (3d Cir. 1979) (admission of such testimony is a matter of discretion), *cert. denied*, 444 U.S. 1032.

2. ABA Code of Professional Responsibility DR 5-101(b) (lawyer should not accept employment in contemplated or pending litigation "if he knows or it is obvious that he or a lawyer in his firm ought to be called as a witness"); DR 5-102(a) (requiring lawyer to withdraw as counsel when "it is obvious that he or a lawyer in his firm ought to be called as a witness on behalf of his client").

3. Model Rule 3.7(a) (lawyer not to try case where he "is likely to be a necessary witness").

4. ABA Code of Professional Responsibility DR 5-101(b) (trial counsel may testify on matters that are "uncontested" or related only to "a matter of formality" where opposing evidence is not expected, on nature and value of legal services rendered in case, or on other matters if withdrawing would work "substantial hardship"); ABA Rules of Professional Conduct, Rule 3.7 (similar). *See generally* Wydick, Trial Counsel as Witness, The Code and Model Rules, 15 U.C. Davis L. Rev. 651 (1982).

5. Gusman v. Unisys Corp., 986 F.2d 1146, 1148 (7th Cir. 1993) (witness is "supposed to present the facts without a slant" while attorney "is to advocate a partisan view of the significance of the facts" and one person trying to do both "is apt to be a poor witness, a poor advocate, or both").

6. United States v. Nyman, 649 F.2d 208, 210-211 (4th Cir. 1980) (error to exclude testimony by defense counsel's "law clerk/investigator," which would have impeached government witnesses).

7. United States v. Roberson, 897 F.2d 1092, 1098 (11th Cir. 1990) (one can call attorney for opposing party as witness only on showing "compelling need"); United States v. Johnston, 664 F.2d 152, 156-157 (7th Cir. 1981) (prosecutor could not testify in suppression hearing on question whether defendant's statements were induced by promise not to prosecute).

8. Universal Athletic Sales Co. v. American Gym Recreational & Athletic Equip. Corp., 546 F.2d 530 (3d Cir. 1976) (attorney competent even if testifying violates disciplinary rules), *cert. denied*, 430 U.S. 984.

9. Will v. Comprehensive Accounting Corp., 776 F.2d 665, 676 (7th Cir. 1985) (admitting testimony by attorney for defendant who "withdrew as counsel well before he testified"), *cert. denied*, 475 U.S. 1129.

which the lawyer's testimony is sought, thereby avoiding the need for disqualification.

There is a difference between a lawyer who calls himself as a witness and one who is called by the opposing party.[10] In the latter situation, courts need to consider whether the party calling the lawyer is motivated by a desire to embarrass or disqualify the opposing lawyer rather than to obtain testimony.[11]

A recurring ethical issue arises when a lawyer tries to impeach a witness with an inconsistent statement made to the lawyer himself. Suppose, for instance, the lawyer asks the witness "You just testified to *X*, but didn't you tell me *Y* two days ago?" Many courts view such a question as improper unless the lawyer is prepared to prove the statement if the witness denies it. Because the lawyer normally cannot testify, he must have proof of the statement in the form of testimony by another. Sound practice suggests arranging to have third parties attend crucial pretrial interviews, who can be called to testify if needed.

F. JUROR COMPETENCY: IMPEACHMENT OF VERDICTS

FRE 606

(a) At the trial. A member of the jury may not testify as a witness before that jury in the trial of the case in which the juror is sitting. If the juror is called so to testify, the opposing party shall be afforded an opportunity to object out of the presence of the jury.

(b) Inquiry into validity of verdict or indictment. Upon an inquiry into the validity of a verdict or indictment, a juror may not testify as to any matter or statement occurring during the course of the jury's deliberations or the effect of anything upon that or any other juror's mind or emotions as influencing the juror to assent to or dissent from the verdict or indictment or concerning the juror's mental processes in connection therewith. But a juror may testify about (1) whether extraneous prejudicial information was improperly brought to the jury's attention, (2) whether any outside influence was improperly brought to bear upon any juror, or (3) whether there was a mistake in entering the verdict onto the verdict form. A juror's affidavit or evidence of any statement by the juror may not be received on a matter about which the juror would be precluded from testifying.

---

10. *See* ABA Model Code of Professional Responsibility DR 5-102(b) (counsel who learns he is to be called by another may continue "until it is apparent that his testimony is or may be prejudicial" to client).

11. United States v. Dupuy, 760 F.2d 1492, 1497-1500 (9th Cir. 1985) (court may refuse to let defense call prosecutor cross-examine about notes of witness interviews; no "compelling need" shown, and counsel examined on notes and did not call agents present at interviews). *See generally* Lewis, The Ethical Dilemma of the Testifying Advocate: Fact or Fancy?, 19 Hous. L. Rev. 75, 88-89 (1981).

§6.10 Reasons to Limit Impeachment of Verdicts

FRE 606(b) bars testimony or statements by jurors (whether proved by affidavit or in any other way) offered to prove virtually anything about deliberations—any matter occurring or statement made, or the effect of anything on the mind or emotions of any juror, or the mental processes of the juror whose testimony or statement is offered.

There are valid and powerful reasons behind the exclusionary rule.[1] First, it is needed to keep jurors from being harassed by the losing party in efforts to snatch victory from the jaws of defeat by turning up facts that might show misconduct serious enough to set aside the verdict. Second, it is needed to guard the privacy of deliberations in the interest of encouraging full and frank discussions, which surely would not go forward if jurors knew they would have to account later for what they said in deliberations. Third, letting jurors attack verdicts would undermine their finality. As one jurist put it, judges "would become Penelopes, forever engaged in unraveling the webs they wove."[2] Review on the basis of a trial record is one thing, but it would add a frightening new dimension to scrutinize the deliberative process itself. Fourth, allowing juror attacks would invite tampering with the process. A juror who reluctantly joined a verdict is likely to be sympathetic to overtures by the loser and persuadable to the view that his own consent rested on false or impermissible considerations, and the truth will be hard to know. The triers themselves would be tried at the behest of the verdict loser, who would have much to gain in the attempt and little to lose.

Powerful reasons

Clearly the Rule is convenient as well. By sharply restricting the kinds of argument that can be made in motions for a new trial or relief from a judgment, and in appeals and collateral attacks on judgments, the Rule offers "an easy escape from embarrassing choices."[3] It helps courts avoid deciding what irregularities in a jury's deliberative process can upset a verdict and submerges ultimate questions on the value of the jury system by keeping its imperfections out of sight. And in shielding verdicts from scrutiny it also forestalls questions that might be raised about how judges decide cases.

The best justification of the Rule, however, is not that it protects a process that is somehow irrational, erratic, or shameful, but that it protects a good system that cannot be made perfect. The jury's deliberative processes cannot be insulated from all irrational or unwanted

Protects imperfect system

---

§6.10 1. Tanner v. United States, 483 U.S. 107 (1987) (preserves full and frank discussion, willingness to return unpopular verdict, and public trust); McDonald v. Pless, 238 U.S. 264 (1915) (prevents jurors from being "harassed and beset by the defeated party," keeps what was intended as private from becoming subject to public scrutiny, which would destroy "frankness and freedom of discussion"); Walsh v. State, 166 S.W.3d 641 (Tenn. 2005) (promotes full and frank discussion, protects privacy of deliberations, prevents harassment of jurors).

2. Jorgensen v. York Ice Mach. Corp., 160 F.2d 432, 435 (2d Cir. 1947) (Learned Hand), *cert. denied*, 332 U.S. 764.

3. Jorgensen v. York Ice Mach. Corp., 160 F.2d 432, 435 (2d Cir. 1947) (Learned Hand), *cert. denied*, 332 U.S. 764.

preconceptions, ideas, and considerations. In the end, we must make do with the best we can hope to attain.[4]

Two major exceptions

There are two major exceptions to the Rule: First, juror testimony or statements can prove "extraneous prejudicial information" improperly brought to the jury's attention. Second, such testimony or statements may be used to prove any "outside influence" improperly brought to bear on any juror. These exceptions allow proof in some of the normally out-of-bounds areas (matters occurring and statements made), but others remain off limits, for even the exceptions do not allow proof relating to the effect of anything on the minds or emotions of jurors or the mental processes of the juror whose testimony or statement is offered.

Manner versus grounds

In its common law antecedents and in FRE 606(b), the exclusionary rule regulates the manner of proof, not the grounds on which verdicts may be impeached. In keeping with this notion, some cases interpreting the common law rule allowed other kinds of proof (eavesdropper testimony or physical evidence from the jury room) where juror testimony would be barred.[5] But as a practical matter the Rule does effectively limit the grounds of permissible impeachment of verdicts because it so thoroughly limits use of the only sure source of information. In rare instances where someone other than a juror observes deliberations or where some physical or other evidence could prove what occurred during deliberations, the Rule should bar such testimony and evidence to the same extent it would bar similar evidence from a juror.[6] And the Rule should bar proof of statements made by jurors during deliberations, when accidentally discovered by (or inadvertently made to) court or counsel.[7]

Problems on face of verdict

Even interpreting the Rule as barring other kinds of proof would not keep courts from awarding relief where serious problems reflecting juror misconduct appear on the face of the verdict or in the record of trial. Thus courts may set aside verdicts that cannot be supported by the evidence offered at trial, or where mistakes in admitting or excluding evidence apparently affected the outcome.

American compromise

The exclusionary rule traces its origin to an opinion by Lord Mansfield in *Vaise v. Delaval* that announced a blanket rule framed as a moral principle captured in the shorthand expression that "jurors may not

---

4. *See* State v. Boyles, 567 N.W.2d 856, 860 (S.D. 1997) (endorsing this position).

5. *See* Consolidated Rendering Co. v. New Haven Hotel Co., 300 F. 627, 629 (D.C. Conn. 1924) (implying that bailiff could testify); Reich v. Thompson, 142 S.W.2d 486 (Mo. 1940) (eavesdropping court clerk); Central of G. R. v. Holmes, 134 S. 875 (Ala. 1931) (papers in jury room examined).

6. *See* United States v. Dempsey, 830 F.2d 1084, 1088-1090 (10th Cir. 1987) (interpreter serving as deaf juror's ears could not testify to what happened in deliberations).

7. *See* United States v. Bowling, 900 F.2d 926, 935 (6th Cir. 1990) (refusing to take testimony to determine whether comments by juror referred to defendant), *cert. denied*, 498 U.S. 837; Domeracki v. Humble Oil & Ref. Co., 443 F.2d 1245, 1247 (3d Cir. 1971) (refusing to consider scratch paper accidentally discovered attached to verdict), *cert. denied*, 404 U.S. 883.

impeach their verdict."[8] This doctrine found widespread acceptance in the United States, sometimes in its (blanket) form,[9] but more often in modified forms. One such form was the Iowa Rule, which distinguished between matters that "inhere in the verdict" and "independent facts," excluding juror statements or testimony on the former but allowing them on the latter.[10] Another was the federal rule, which distinguished between the "actual effect" of anything on jurors and "extraneous matter" that might cause unwanted effect, excluding proof of the former but admitting proof of the latter.[11] In either form, the American compromise would seemingly allow jurors to testify to improper contact with outsiders during deliberations (such as the bailiff or parties) when such conduct conveyed pressures or threats or information relating to the case, and to describe any improper evidence introduced into the jury room during deliberations (like evidence gathered by a juror who did original research or had prior knowledge of the case).[12]

FRE 606(b) echoes this tradition by paving the way to show "improper influence" or "extraneous prejudicial information." But other arguably improper or dysfunctional elements are off limits, including proof of jury decisions to abide a majority vote (instead of requiring unanimity), misinterpretation of instructions, or misuse of evidence.[13] Far more difficult is the question whether to allow proof of quotient verdicts, or coin flips (chance verdicts), belligerent behavior, or blatant prejudice in the jury room. Pretty clearly FRE 606(b) bars proof of quotient verdicts, which is arguably correct insofar as such verdicts might approximate the process of compromise that might be expected from extended discussion and thought. As indicated in the

8. Vaise v. Delaval, 1 Term. Rep. 11, 99 Eng. Rep. 944 (K.B. 1785) ("no one should be allowed to allege his own turpitude," from Latin phrase that also prevented married men from testifying to nonaccess in cases involving legitimacy, and prevented drawers of commercial paper from alleging usury as defense). *See* 8 Wigmore, Evidence §2352 (McNaughton rev. 1961).

9. Until adopting the Rules in 1976, Arkansas barred examination of jurors except to determine whether verdict was reached by lot. *See* former Ark. Stat. Ann. §43-2204 (1964); Brock v. State, 371 S.W.2d 539 (Ark. 1963).

10. In the former category was evidence that a juror did not assent to the verdict, misunderstood pleadings, testimony, or instructions, or was unduly influenced by statements of fellow jurors, or mistaken in calculations or judgment. In the latter was evidence that a juror was improperly approached by a party, that witnesses communicated with jurors on the merits out of court, and that the verdict was reached by quotient or chance. *See* Wright v. Illinois & Miss. Tel. Co., 20 Iowa 195, 210-212 (1866) (leading case); Perry v. Bailey (1874) 12 Kan. 539, 544-545 (jurors may testify to "overt acts," meaning objective misconduct that another juror could verify).

11. *See* Mattox v. United States, 146 U.S. 140 (1892) (juror may testify to facts bearing on "existence of any extraneous influence" but not "how far that influence operated upon his mind" and may not testify to "motives and influences").

12. Parker v. Gladden, 385 U.S. 363 (1966) (contact with bailiff); Washington Gas Light Co. v. Connolly, 214 F.2d 254, 257 (D.C. Cir. 1954) (contact with parties); Stiles v. Lawrie, 211 F.2d 188, 190 (6th Cir. 1954) (unauthorized evidence).

13. McDonald v. Pless, 238 U.S. 264 (1915) (quotient verdicts); Bryson v. United States, 238 F.2d 657, 665 (9th Cir. 1956) (not following instructions), *cert. denied*, 355 U.S. 817 (1957); Jorgensen v. York Ice Mach. Corp., 160 F.2d 432, 435 (2d Cir. 1947) (decision to abide majority vote), *cert. denied*, 332 U.S. 764.

next section, apparently FRE 606(b) also bars proof of these other points as well, which seems more troubling.

§6.11 Juror Testimony and Affidavits Barred

FRE 606(b) bars juror testimony or statements to prove any matter occurring or statement made during deliberations unless it fits either of two exceptions (discussed in ensuing sections). It bars such testimony or statements to prove the effect of anything on the mind or emotions of a juror or to prove the mental processes of the juror whose testimony or statement is offered. Obviously the categories overlap: A juror could hardly describe his mental processes without revealing the effect of something on his mind or emotions, and proof of a statement during deliberations would inevitably tell something about mental processes or the effect of something on the mind or emotions of jurors. The important point is that it would be hard to paint with a broader brush, and the Rule reaches everything relating to deliberations unless an exception applies.

Evidence or reasons   So often do unhappy litigants attack verdicts by juror testimony or statements (typically proved by affidavit) that many decided cases provide authoritative guidance, and the cases fall into patterns that are easy to describe. In what follows, it should be assumed that the evidence is offered in an attempt to set aside a verdict. To begin at an obvious point, the exclusionary principle bars use of juror testimony or statements as proof of the evidence that counted most or the reasons behind the verdict[1] or to show that certain instructions counted or would have counted if they had been given.[2]

Errors, misunderstandings   The exclusionary principle applies to juror testimony or statements describing even serious errors or misunderstandings on points of law or the proper basis of decision. Thus FRE 606(b) bars such testimony or statements indicating that one or more jurors ignored or misunderstood instructions[3] or interrogatories,[4] or ignored or misunderstood applicable legal principles[5] or the requirement of a unanimous

---

§6.11 1. Rushen v. Spain, 464 U.S. 114 (1983) (cannot generally testify about "mental processes by which" verdict was reached); United States v. Maree, 934 F.2d 196, 201 (9th Cir. 1991) (affidavit inadmissible insofar as it said friends with whom juror discussed case influenced her vote for conviction).

2. Capps v. Sullivan, 921 F.2d 260, 263 (10th Cir. 1990) (affidavits saying jurors would have voted to acquit if given entrapment instruction).

3. Marsingill v. O'Malley, 58 P.3d 495, 505 n.27 (Alaska 2002) (jurors misunderstood instructions); United States v. Febus, 218 F.3d 784, 794 (7th Cir. 2000) (instructions confused juror); United States v. Jones, 132 F.3d 232, 245 (5th Cir. 1998) (confusion on unanimity requirement).

4. Robles v. Exxon Corp., 862 F.2d 1201, 1206-1209 (5th Cir. 1989) (some jurors thought interrogatories meant court would award damages if plaintiff was more than 51 percent at fault), *cert. denied*, 490 U.S. 1051.

5. Peveto v. Sears, Roebuck & Co., 807 F.2d 486, 488-489 (5th Cir. 1987) ("always some danger that jurors will misunderstand the law or consider improper factors").

decision,[6] or misused evidence.[7] The Rule also bars proof that one or more jurors improperly speculated on extrarecord matters,[8] such as the impact of insurance on a judgment or the impact of a judgment on insurance rates,[9] or the impact of contingent fees[10] or taxes.[11] The Rule also bars proof that one or more jurors held it against the accused that he failed to take the stand,[12] or speculated that the court would be lenient or that defendant would be released on probation or quickly paroled,[13] or even that an insane defendant should be found guilty or would be released to commit more crimes,[14] or that jurors took into account the presence or absence of other co-offenders in deciding defendant's guilt.[15]

Usually the Rule bars proof of prejudicial attitudes toward the parties or the kinds of positions being taken in suit,[16] as well as proof of inappropriate or scornful or mocking comments about parties, lawyers, evidence, or theories presented.[17]

Prejudice

Somewhat surprisingly, the Rule also bars proof by juror testimony or affidavit that jurors consumed alcohol and indulged in substance abuse during trial. In 1987 this question reached the Supreme Court in

Using alcohol, drugs

---

6. United States v. Homer, 411 F. Supp. 972, 978 (W.D. Pa. 1976) (not hearing instruction that verdict had to be unanimous), *aff'd*, 545 F.2d 864 (3d Cir. 1976), *cert. denied*, 431 U.S. 954.

7. United States v. Stewart, 433 F.3d 273, 307-308 (2d Cir. 2006) (cannot show that jurors considered as proof against one defendant evidence they were instructed to consider only against another).

8. Morgan v. Woessner, 975 F.2d 629 (9th Cir. 1992) (jurors "wanted to send a message to City" on police misconduct); Dobbs v. Zant, 963 F.2d 1403, 1411 (11th Cir. 1991) (jury thought defendant would not be executed because Supreme Court had forbidden executions).

9. *See* Holden v. Porter, 405 F.2d 878, 879 (10th Cir. 1969); Farmers Co-operative Elevator Assoc. v. Strand, 382 F.2d 224, 230 (8th Cir. 1967), *cert. denied*, 389 U.S. 1014.

10. Gault v. Poor Sisters of St. Frances, 375 F.2d 539, 548-550 (6th Cir. 1967) (discussing amount of recovery that would go to plaintiff's attorney).

11. *Id.* 548-551 (6th Cir. 1967) (discussing income tax plaintiff might pay out of recovery).

12. United States v. Rutherford, 371 F.3d 634, 640 (9th Cir. 2004) (cannot prove that jury discussed failure of one codefendant to testify).

13. United States v. Gonzales, 227 F.3d 520, 526-527 (6th Cir. 2000) (statements that defendant would only get slap on wrist if convicted because he was charged with white collar crime).

14. Fulghum v. Ford, 850 F.2d 1529, 1535 (11th Cir. 1988) (jurors thought defendant was insane but feared that not guilty by reason of insanity would be "less effective" in removing from society), *cert. denied*, 488 U.S. 1013.

15. United States v. Falsia, 724 F.2d 1339, 1343 (9th Cir. 1983) (jurors affected by co-offender's absence from trial).

16. Carson v. Polley, 689 F.2d 562, 579-582 (5th Cir. 1982) (foreman's letter to judge said plaintiff had no case, legal fees were paid from public fund, and lawyers were making money while disserving plaintiff); Martinez v. Food City, Inc., 658 F.2d 369, 372-373 (5th Cir. 1981) (in suit for overtime wages, juror said defendant should be "taught a lesson").

17. United States v. Bowling, 900 F.2d 926, 935 (6th Cir. 1990) ("negative and inappropriate comments" by juror), *cert. denied*, 498 U.S. 837; United States v. Chiantese, 582 F.2d 974, 978-979 (5th Cir. 1978) (juror remark that defense cross was stupid and counsel was a "pain").

Tanner v. United States, where the evidence suggested that several jurors fell asleep during proceedings and were adversely affected in their reasoning abilities. *Tanner* concluded that allegations of alcohol and substance abuse during trial do *not* raise provable issues of "outside influence," and do *not* show that the jury was incompetent, accepting for the sake of argument that such a showing may be made.[18] One surprising point about *Tanner* is its implicit holding that the Rule governs proof of predeliberative jury misconduct,[19] but perhaps its greatest significance is in construing the term "outside influence" narrowly.

Shortcuts   The Rule also bars juror testimony or statements that tend to show improper decisional shortcuts that juries sometimes take during deliberations. Thus the Rule applies to proof that the jury agreed on a time limit for deliberations,[20] or that one or more jurors had prior knowledge about a party,[21] or entertained preconceptions about the case,[22] or began deliberations early before being formally charged or sent out to do so.[23] The Rule also applies to proof that one or more jurors compromised principles out of concern over personal matters in order to end deliberations quickly,[24] or engaged in vote trading, giving ground on one issue or party in exchange for concessions by other jurors on other issues or parties.[25] The Rule applies as well to evidence that one or more jurors agreed to abide the vote of a majority, or a number less than that necessary for a proper verdict,[26] or arrived at the sum to be awarded by adding the amounts each juror thought appropriate and dividing by the number of jurors (the classic "quotient verdict").[27] And the Rule bars juror testimony or statements indicating that one or more jurors gave in to pressure

18. Tanner v. United States, 483 U.S. 107 (1987) (regardless how "severe their effect and improper their use," drugs or alcohol voluntarily consumed by juror are no more an outside influence "than a virus, poorly prepared food, or a lack of sleep") (jurors drank beer, mixed drinks, and wine, and indulged in marijuana and cocaine).

19. *See* further discussion in §6.14, *infra.*

20. Capella v. Baumgartner, 59 F.R.D. 312, 314-315 (S.D. Fla. 1973) (jury agreed to give in by certain time or hour in reaching verdict).

21. United States v. Eagle, 539 F.2d 1166, 1170 (8th Cir. 1976) (juror realized during trial that defendant was wanted for shooting FBI agents in unrelated incident) (did not relay point to others), *cert. denied,* 429 U.S. 1110. But prior knowledge about the case can be proved as extrarecord information. *See* §6.12, *infra.*

22. Brofford v. Marshall, 751 F.2d 845, 852-853 (6th Cir. 1985), *cert. denied,* 474 U.S. 872.

23. Manley v. Ambase Corp., 337 F.3d 237, 250 (2d Cir. 2003) (jurors remarked at start that they had "made up their minds" against defendant).

24. United States v. Fozo, 904 F.2d 1166, 1171 (7th Cir. 1990) (impending Christmas holiday may have caused jury to rush deliberations); McElroy v. Firestone Tire & Rubber Co., 894 F.2d 1504, 1510-1511 & n.11 (11th Cir. 1990) (juror seen "crying and expressing a desire to be with her family").

25. Stein v. New York, 346 U.S. 156 (1953) (jurors exchanged convictions on one issue in return for concessions on another issue); Hyde & Schneider v. United States, 225 U.S. 347 (1912) (trading conviction of one for acquittal of another).

26. United States v. Marrero, 904 F.2d 251, 261 (5th Cir. 1990) (juror said majority rule controlled), *cert. denied,* 498 U.S. 1000; United States v. Howard, 507 F.2d 559, 561 n.3 (8th Cir. 1974) (foreman said jury was not unanimous).

27. *See* Stein v. New York, 346 U.S. 156 (1953); McDonald v. Pless, 238 U.S. 264 (1915).

from other jurors by casting votes against better judgment or conscience without being truly persuaded,[28] or gave in to pressures from the court in setting long hours for deliberations[29] or urging the jury to reach a verdict,[30] or reminding it that unanimity is required.[31]

Nor can jury testimony or statements be admitted to interpret the verdict or prove that mistakes were made. The Rule bars proof in the form of statements explaining or qualifying the verdict after it was taken,[32] or showing that one or more jurors did not agree with or believe in the verdict,[33] or erred in calculating the award,[34] or miscast his vote in a tenor opposite to what he intended[35] although an error in entering the verdict onto the form may be proved,[36] or that the verdict was the result of mistake[37] or prejudice.[38] And the Rule bars proof that one or more jurors was inattentive during trial or deliberations, sleeping or thinking about other matters,[39] or even drugged or intoxicated.[40]

Interpretation of verdict

In three difficult areas the mandate of FRE 606(b) remains uncertain. One is chance verdicts; another is verdicts tainted by racial bias; the third is violent intimidation in the jury room. Probably the Rule bars juror testimony or statements that a verdict was reached by chance or lot, although some states made special provision allowing such

Chance and quotient verdicts

---

28. United States v. Briggs, 291 F.3d 958, 963 (7th Cir. 2002) (juror said she had been "intimidated" by others into voting in favor of guilt); United States v. Tallman, 951 F.2d 164, 166-167 (8th Cir. 1991) (reported "harassment and insults" in jury room).

29. United States v. Marques, 600 F.2d 742, 746-748 (9th Cir. 1979) (reports of compromise because court kept jury deliberating until 11 P.M. Friday and 10 P.M. the following Monday), *cert. denied*, 444 U.S. 858.

30. United States v. Vincent, 648 F.2d 1046, 1049-1050 (5th Cir. 1981) (reports of pressure and weeping after court gave *Allen* charge).

31. Watson v. Alabama, 841 F.2d 1074, 1075-1076 (11th Cir. 1988) (reporting "distraught and upset" jurors; all twelve raised hands "but two women jurors were shaking their heads"; refusing to consider juror testimony on effect of instruction requiring unanimity when jury polled), *cert. denied*, 488 U.S. 864.

32. Sims' Crane Serv., Inc. v. Ideal Steel Prod., Inc., 800 F.2d 1553, 1555-1557 (11th Cir. 1986); Michaels v. Michaels, 767 F.2d 1185, 1204-1205 (7th Cir. 1985), *cert. denied*, 474 U.S. 1057.

33. Hall v. Levine, 104 P.2d 222 (Colo. 2005) (that verdict was not unanimous, where all signed verdict form and jury was polled); United States v. Miller, 806 F.2d 223, 225 (10th Cir. 1986) (juror having second thoughts, unsure of guilt).

34. Stewart v. Rice, 47 P.3d 316, 326 (Colo. 2002) (jurors may not have intended to award damages for physical impairment or may have forgotten to make award for physical impairment or may have confused interrogatory as asking for total award or may have disregarded its plain language).

35. York Chrysler-Plymouth, Inc. v. Chrysler Credit Corp., 447 F.2d 786, 794 (5th Cir. 1971) (foreman's affidavit said jury intended verdict to run against dealership as well as individuals).

36. *See* the discussion in §6.14, *infra*.

37. United States v. Sjeklocha, 843 F.2d 485, 488 (11th Cir. 1988); United States v. Schwartz, 787 F.2d 257, 261 (7th Cir. 1986).

38. Poches v. J. J. Newberry Co., 549 F.2d 1166, 1169 (8th Cir. 1977) (cannot impeach by showing prejudiced verdict).

39. *See* Government of Virgin Islands v. Nicholas, 759 F.2d 1073, 1079-1081 (3d Cir. 1985) (juror hearing impairment).

40. Tanner v. United States, 483 U.S. 107 (1987) (alcohol and drug abuse).

proof.[41] Reaching a verdict by chance or lot seems to be a matter occurring during deliberations (so the Rule applies), and the two exceptions do not seem to apply (flipping a coin is not extraneous prejudicial information or outside influence in the most obvious sense of those terms). But verdicts resting on chance or lot do more violence to the ideal of a consensus decision reflecting the wisdom and attitude of the community than does a quotient verdict: The latter contains elements of thought and may approximate what the bargaining process would otherwise produce, but decisions by chance or lot are essentially the negation of thought and give-and-take. Arguably a coin flip or its equivalent is outside influence: It introduces a decisive force that is outside the evidence and mental processes of the jury. However, the Court's insistence in *Tanner* that drug consumption is not outside influence makes this argument more difficult.

Racial, gender bias Verdicts tainted by serious prejudices along racial, ethnic, or gender lines are problematic for purposes of the Rule.[42] Arguably it bars juror testimony or statements on such points: Such evidence would either try to describe the effect of such prejudice on the minds or emotions of jurors, or (less probably) describe the thought processes of the juror whose statement or testimony is offered, or conceivably describe statements made by others during deliberations. Proof on all such points is covered by the Rule. Conceivably such prejudices could be called outside influence: Like a coin flip, such prejudices might be characterized as a force having decisive impact while being completely independent of the evidence or statements made during deliberations. But again *Tanner* makes such arguments problematic.

41. *See* Senate Hearings, at 50 (1974) (rule insulates verdicts from attack on ground that they were reached by chance). *See also* the counterparts in Idaho, Montana, and North Dakota (all allowing proof that verdict was reached by "chance"). *See also* Tennessee Rule 606 (allowing proof that jurors "agreed in advance to be bound by a quotient or gambling verdict").

42. *See* State v. Hidanovic, 747 N.W.2d 463, 472-473 (N.D. 2008) (in trial for riot of defendant of Bosnian extraction, affidavit said juror told others that Bosnians "stole from my business" and "lied to me"; strong public policy precludes "examination of the internal discussions and mental processes" of jurors, and use of affidavits to prove racial or ethnic bias presents "difficulties," but judge did not abuse discretion in deciding that statements would not affect verdict of "hypothetical average jury") (citing authors of this Treatise); Williams v. Price, 343 F.3d 223, 237-238 (3d Cir. 2003) (noting argument that showing racial bias should allowed; refusing to recognize such exception does not violate Constitution; remanding to determine whether juror lied about prejudice on voir dire) (quoting authors of this Treatise); United States v. Henley, 238 F.3d 1111, 1119-1122 (9th Cir. 2000) ("powerful case can be made" that FRE 606(b) is inapplicable to proof of juror bias; Court has said juror may testify to bias in matters unrelated to issues) (remanding to consider whether juror lied in voir dire on racial bias); Shillcutt v. Gagnon, 827 F.2d 1155, 1158-1160 (7th Cir. 1987) (rule excludes evidence of racial comments, but "cannot be applied in such an unfair manner as to deny due process").

Probably the Rule bars proof of physical intimidation or violence by one or more jurors against others during deliberations.[43] The system would likely be badly hobbled if charges of overbearing or challenging or argumentative behavior could upset a verdict, but arguably it is another matter if jurors resort to fistfights or kicking or throwing chairs to coerce a particular verdict, and some have suggested that the Rule should be amended to allow proof along these lines.[44]

Physical intimidation

§6.12 Exception for Proving Extrarecord Information

The first exception in FRE 606(b) allows verdicts to be attacked by proof that the jury improperly received "extraneous prejudicial information" during deliberations. This exception paves the way for evidence of any sort of information that might have affected the verdict if it was conveyed to the jury through extrarecord sources unless the information amounted to "common" or "regional" knowledge. A fact that falls in either of these categories may be judicially noticed, and the jury may take it into account in reaching a verdict.

It makes no difference that the extraneous matter could have been proved by evidence formally introduced. In the first place, juries should not decide on the basis of evidence that was never admitted even if it might have been. In the second place, the parties should have a chance to meet or rebut evidence, and they are deprived of that chance if juries get information from extrarecord sources. Hence something may be "prejudicial" for purposes of attacking a verdict even if evidence going to the same point would not be excluded for "unfair prejudice" under FRE 403 if it had been offered at trial.

The exception allows proof that one or more members of the jury brought to trial specific personal knowledge about the controversy,[1] or acquired such knowledge from sources outside the courtroom during

Personal knowledge

---

43. United States v. McGhee, 532 F.3d 733, 740-741 (8th Cir. 2008) (not ordering hearing when jurors alleged intimidation by others; FRE 606(b) bars testimony as to "how the jury reached its verdict" and jurors "were not competent to testify about alleged intimidation"); State v. Kim, 81 P.3d 1200, 1206 (Hawaii 2003) (juror "intimidated and harassed" another by saying "What the fuck are we doing this for? I want to know who voted for the Manslaughter. I want to know who the fuck said manslaughter?") (affirming murder conviction). *But see* Minnesota Rule 606(b) (allowing proof of "threats of violence or violent acts" against jurors, "from whatever source"); Ohio Rule 606(b) (authorizing juror testimony on "any threat, any bribe, any attempted threat or bribe, or any improprieties of any officer of the court").

44. Carlson & Sumberg, Attacking Jury Verdicts: Paradigms for Rule Revision, 1977 Ariz. State L.J. 247, 274 (should allow affidavit that "threat or act of violence was brought to bear" on juror to reach verdict). *And see* Robinson & Reed, A Review of the Proposed Michigan Rules of Evidence, 56 Mich. St. B.J. 21, 29 (1977).

§6.12 1. Rushen v. Spain, 464 U.S. 114 (1983) (juror learned defense witness was in custody for murdering someone she knew); Sassounian v. Roe, 230 F.3d 1097, 1108-1112 (9th Cir. 2000) (proof that one juror told others about phone call to consulate claiming credit for murder).

trial or deliberations,[2] often by way of media sources (newspaper, radio, television).[3] The exception also allows proof that one or more jurors conducted an unauthorized experiment in the jury room[4] or even outside it,[5] although it is proper for the jury to examine or scrutinize physical exhibits that the court lets it take to deliberations, and tinkering with such proof does not necessarily amount to improper experimentation.[6] The exception paves the way for proof that one or more jurors conducted a private investigation into the parties or controversy during trial or deliberations,[7] or accidentally saw the defendant in prison garb or manacles,[8] or got an unauthorized view of the premises involved in the controversy.[9] Also the exception paves the way for proof that the jury took to deliberations unauthorized objects like books or papers[10] or accidentally discovered such things in the jury room.[11]

It is not necessary for a party who attacks a verdict to show that extraneous information was communicated to other jurors. The likelihood of a tainted verdict rises, however, if the information is especially relevant to central issues or inflammatory, and risks associated with such information rise if it is communicated to more than one and conceivably to everyone on the panel. In short, general dissemination among jurors raises the likelihood that a new trial should be had, but this point relates to the sufficiency of the attack and not the admissibility of the proof.[12]

While juror testimony or statements are admissible to show that extraneous information came into the jury room, they are not admissible to

2. Pratt v. St. Christopher's Hospital, 866 A.2d 313, 320 (Pa. 2005) (in malpractice suit, jurors could testify to substance of contacts with outside professionals about medical standard of care).

3. United States v. Reid, 53 U.S. 361, 366 (1852) (newspaper); United States v. Brown, 108 F.3d 863, 867 (8th Cir. 1997) (news accounts).

4. Miller v. Harvey, 566 F.2d 879, 881 (4th Cir. 1977) (juror bit foreman's arm to compare results with photograph of defendant's arm taken hours after crime) (considering evidence, denying relief), *cert. denied*, 439 U.S. 838; United States v. Beach, 296 F.2d 153 (4th Cir. 1961) (prejudicial error to send drop cord to jury to test noise of adding machines).

5. Re Beverly Hills Fire Litig., 695 F.2d 207, 213-215 (6th Cir. 1982) (in class action against makers of wiring, ordering new trial; juror checked wiring in home and told jury binding screws were still tight).

6. United States v. Hawkins, 595 F.2d 751, 753-754 (D.C. Cir. 1978) (no error to let jury test binoculars), *cert. denied*, 441 U.S. 910; Taylor v. Reo Motors, Inc., 275 F.2d 699, 705 (10th Cir. 1960) (dismantling heat exchanger was not improper).

7. Isaacs v. Kemp, 778 F.2d 1482, 1484 n.6 (11th Cir. 1985), *cert. denied*, 476 U.S. 1164; Re Beverly Hills Fire Litig., 695 F.2d 207, 213-215 (6th Cir. 1982).

8. United States v. Simpson, 949 F.2d 1519, 1521-1522 (10th Cir. 1991) (accidental sighting of codefendant in handcuffs was prejudicial information).

9. United States ex rel. De Lucia v. McMann, 373 F.2d 759 (2d Cir. 1967), *later opinion*, People v. De Lucia, 229 N.E.2d 211 (N.Y. 1967).

10. Bates v. Preble, 151 U.S. 149, 158 (1894); United States v. Herrero, 893 F.2d 1512, 1538-1541 (7th Cir. 1990), *cert. denied*, 496 U.S. 927.

11. Government of Virgin Islands v. Joseph, 685 F.2d 857, 862-864 (3d Cir. 1982) (new trial because two written statements were "inadvertently" sent to deliberations).

12. United States v. Eagle, 539 F.2d 1166, 1170 (8th Cir. 1976), *cert. denied*, 429 U.S. 1110.

show what effect such information had on any juror or on the jury as a whole.[13] On this point, reviewing courts and trial judges are on their own, and they are supposed to act much in the way that courts act in considering the impact of errors in admitting evidence, which is to say that they try to decide whether the information likely affected the verdict.

It is impossible to make the jury room into "a laboratory, completely sterilized and freed from any external factors," partly because allowing verdicts to be set aside "merely for casual jury-room references on the basis of matters not in evidence" would make it too hard to get durable verdicts, and partly because there are places where it "might be impossible to find twelve jurors who were totally ignorant about a defendant."[14]

Jury room cannot be sterile

There is an even more important reason not to try to seal the jury room from external information: It is that juries do not think in purely mechanical ways that could be likened to computer programs, nor do we want them to do so. Beyond ineffable qualities relating to social and human values (senses or attitudes ranging from compassion and empathy to duty and dignity), we want good judgment—a capacity to evaluate a situation on the basis of maturity and experience and common sense that come from living and learning and understanding the community and the world at large. As the Supreme Court once commented, if the question is how much to award for a broken leg, of course the beginning point is that jurors should be "governed by the evidence" (not special facts "resting in their private knowledge"), but they should not be "controlled by the testimony of the surgeons." Instead they "may, and to act intelligently they must" evaluate the evidence by reference to "their own general knowledge of the subject," paying attention to their "knowledge and experience of the value of a sound limb."[15]

Knowledge, good judgment

Modern opinions conflict on the question whether using the Bible during deliberations constitutes improper resort to extra-record information. Not surprisingly, this question often arises in capital cases where universally known passages like "an eye for an eye" or "turn the other cheek" become points of argument in deliberations.[16]

Referring to Bible

---

13. United States v. Green, 523 F.2d 229, 235 (2d Cir. 1975), *cert. denied*, 423 U.S. 1074.

14. Rideau v. Louisiana, 373 U.S. 723, 733 (1963) (comment about laboratory) (Justice Clark in dissent); United States ex rel. Owen v. McMann, 435 F.2d 813, 817 (2d Cir. 1970) (mentioning ignorant jurors and casual comments, but referring to "fragile state of criminal convictions" rather than judgments generally), *cert. denied*, 402 U.S. 906.

15. Head v. Hargrave, 105 U.S. 45, 49-50 (1882) (jury weighs testimony of attorneys on value of services "by reference to their nature, the time occupied in their performance, and other attending circumstances, and by applying to it their own experience and knowledge of the character of such services").

16. Leviticus 21:23-27 ("an eye for an eye, a tooth for a tooth"), known as lex talionis (essentially "retaliation," or "let the punishment fit the crime"), can be a coded argument that one who kills should suffer a similar fate as punishment. Famously, this idea was revised in the Sermon on the Mount. *See* Matthew 5:38-42; Luke 6:28-31. In Mathew's version, Jesus replies to Leviticus: "I tell you, do not resist an evil person. If someone strikes you on the right cheek, turn to him the other also."

Judicial reaction to use of such material may reflect the discomfort felt in the profession over capital punishment, perhaps even more than concern over jury behavior. It is hard to conceive jurors in such life-and-death circumstance *not* resorting to moral codes that carry meaning in their lives, whether drawn from the Bible, from Kant or Shakespeare, or from other sources in philosophy or literature, or for that matter film and television and popular culture, and hard to imagine jurors who are in sympathy with the values they glean from such sources ignoring them when they reach the jury room. It is hard as well to imagine jurors who are not in sympathy with such sources being suddenly won over. Several courts have rejected challenges based on consultation of Biblical sources,[17] although one found such a challenge persuasive.[18]

The major problem that emerges in most cases in which juries refer to outside sources is that general knowledge (which we expect of jurors) merges into particular knowledge (which we expect jurors not to have) along a boundary that is blurred and vague. Reportedly in one suit, for example, jurors took into account that trucks "barrel through" town on Sunday morning, which bore on whether plaintiff was negligent in stepping into the street, and in another they took into account that a bar was two blocks from defendant's house (a point that a juror verified by investigation during trial), and this information may have been the basis for doubt when defendant testified that he'd never heard of the bar.[19]

Such points are hard to characterize as either general or particular knowledge, and it is hard to say whether verdicts affected by them merit respect or call for another trial. We might easily conclude that the juror described in the last example should not have done research, but much harder to say whether his information should be considered a taint (would we say the same thing if jurors already knew it?) and hard to say whether it is serious enough to justify retrial.

§6.13 Exception for Proving Outside Influence

The second exception in FRE 606(b) permits impeachment of verdicts by evidence of an "outside influence" improperly brought to bear on a juror.

17. Robinson v. Polk, 438 F.3d 350, 357-360 (4th Cir. 2006) (rejecting claim that reading "eye for an eye" passage from Bible supplied by clerk was extraneous prejudicial information; Bible is "not analogous to a private conversation, contact, or tampering with a juror"); Fields v. Brown, 431 F.3d 1186, 1206-1207 (9th Cir. 2005) (excluding evidence that jury leader made notes after checking Bible and other references, summing up reasons for and against death penalty; Bible verses are "common knowledge" and sharing notes "is not constitutionally infirm if sharing memory isn't").

18. People v. Harlan, 109 P.3d 616, 624 (Colo. 2005) (Bible was extraneous prejudicial information, much like dictionary meaning of "burglary" or internet description of drug) (vacating death sentence).

19. Broeder, The Impact of the Vicinage Requirement: An Empirical Look, 45 Neb. L. Rev. 99 (1966).

The exception paves the way for juror testimony or statements that show efforts by outsiders to interfere with deliberations. Attempts to bribe jurors[1] or threaten them or their families[2] are obvious examples, and nobody doubts that such attempts may be shown by juror testimony or statements. Far more common are contacts with outsiders that seem ambiguous and are not part of a plot to determine outcome. Many such contacts are inevitable, since courts are not well equipped to separate the jury from outsiders. Still, assessing an outside contact presupposes some account of the contact itself, and the exception paves the way to prove many contacts that might prove harmless. It is settled that juror testimony or statements are admissible to prove contact between jurors and the court itself,[3] the bailiff or other court functionary,[4] the parties[5] and people aligned with parties such as attorneys, officers, and employees.[6] Such proof may also be admitted to show juror contact with witnesses, who are often associated with one party or another, or any other outsider who might influence deliberations.[7] Such proof can also show the presence of outsiders in the jury room, including alternate jurors and court personnel.[8]

Bribes, threats, contracts

One might suppose the system would not uphold a verdict by jurors who abuse alcohol or drugs during trial or deliberations, or one by a panel containing a seriously incompetent (insane or radically

Use of alcohol, drugs

---

§6.13   1. Remmer v. United States, 347 U.S. 227 (1954) (proof of bribe offer), *later app.* 350 U.S. 377 (1956) (denying new trial); United States v. Henley, 238 F.3d 1111, 1114-1119 (9th Cir. 2001) (rebuttable presumption of prejudice; remanding for hearing).

2. *See* Gold v. United States, 352 U.S. 985 (1957) (FBI agents contacted families of jurors); Krause v. Rhodes, 570 F.2d 563, 566-570 (6th Cir. 1977) (juror and family had been threatened and juror had been assaulted), *cert. denied*, 435 U.S. 924.

3. *See* Rushen v. Spain, 464 U.S. 114, 117-120 (1983) (ex parte contacts between juror and judge raise concern, but are common and can be harmless); United States v. United States Gypsum Co., 438 U.S. 422, 462 (1978) (court might reverse "solely because of the risk that the foreman believed that the court was insisting on a dispositive verdict," which he probably conveyed to others).

4. Parker v. Gladden, 385 U.S. 363, 364-365 (1966) (bailiff told juror in presence of others that defendant was wicked and guilty, and Supreme Court would correct mistake); Turner v. Louisiana, 379 U.S. 466 (1965) (continuous contact during deliberations between jury and deputy sheriffs who were principal prosecution witnesses); Walsh v. State, 166 S.W.3d 641 (Tenn. 2005) (deputy sheriff as court officer told jury it had to reach verdict on battery count).

5. Washington Gas Light Co. v. Connolly, 214 F.2d 254, 257 (D.C. Cir. 1954) (company affidavit said juror contacted it during deliberations, perhaps to get information) (hearing required).

6. United States v. Rutherford, 371 F.3d 634, 640-644 (9th Cir. 2004) (contact between IRS officials and jurors; even innocuous contact with agents for prosecutor raise presumption of prejudice).

7. Jenkins v. State, 825 A.2d 1008 (Md. 2003) (midtrial contact between police officer testifying for state and juror in religious retreat raised presumption of prejudice) (reversing conviction).

8. United States v. Allison, 481 F.2d 468, 472 (5th Cir. 1973) (presence of alternate juror in jury room by stipulation), *later opinion,* 487 F.2d 339 (5th Cir. 1973) (no effect found), *cert. denied*, 416 U.S. 982; Little v. United States, 73 F.2d 861, 865 (10th Cir. 1934) (new trial required where court stenographer went to jury room and read court's instructions).

dysfunctional) person, at least where unanimity is required (criminal convictions and some civil cases). But it is not clear that such flaws in the decisionmaking process may be proved by juror testimony or statements. The salient modern authority is the Court's 1987 decision in the *Tanner* case, which held that the Rule bars proof that jurors imbibed alcohol and took drugs during trial, rejecting the argument that alcohol or drugs could be viewed as outside influence.[9] In likening intoxication and ingesting drugs to stomachaches, the Court essentially decided that the mind-dulling effects of liquor and drugs could not be distinguished from common human dysfunctions, apparently in fear of slippery slopes and perhaps in despair of policing or evaluating such conduct. Before *Tanner*, one might have said juror testimony or statements could prove someone on the panel became ill during trial or deliberations or suffered some serious impairment that prevented the person from serving effectively,[10] but *Tanner* cast doubt on this point too.

Whether juror testimony or statements can prove a juror was insane or mentally afflicted during deliberations is also hard to say. *Tanner* mentions this situation in passing and implies that extremely serious instances of mental difficulties might be provable,[11] and other courts have considered juror statements and affidavits describing such things,[12] but only rarely have claims of this sort generated any kind of relief from a conviction.[13]

§6.14   Exception for Proving Mistake on Verdict Form; Other Matters Beyond Reach of Rule

The third exception in FRE 606(b) invites juror testimony or affidavits on the question whether there was a "mistake in entering the verdict onto the verdict form." If the jury leader puts too many or too few zeros on the reported damage figure or says "guilty" when "not guilty" was intended (or the opposite), juror affidavits and testimony may be admitted to prove such points and make the necessary correction.

9. Tanner v. United States, 483 U.S. 107 (1987) (however "severe their effect and improper their use," drugs or alcohol voluntarily ingested is not outside influence any more than "virus, poorly prepared food, or a lack of sleep"). *See also* Bell v. Ozmint, 332 F.3d 229, 235-236 (4th Cir. 2003) (allegations of excessive alcohol consumption during sequestration were not ground for relief).

10. *See* Weaver v. Puckett, 896 F.2d 126, 127-128 (5th Cir. 1990) (can admit juror testimony if there is substantial evidence of incompetency; must be proof from nonjuror source), *cert. denied*, 498 U.S. 966.

11. *See* Tanner v. United States, 483 U.S. 107 (1987) (even if rule allows inquiry into juror incompetence in cases of substantial or conclusive evidence, showing here "falls far short").

12. United States v. Perry, 643 F.2d 38, 51-52 (2d Cir. 1981) (considering but rejecting claim that lack of mental stability in juror required reversal), *cert. denied*, 454 U.S. 835.

13. Sullivan v. Fogg, 613 F.2d 465 (2d Cir. 1980) (granting relief from state murder conviction).

Before 2006, the phrase quoted above did not appear in FRE 606(b), but courts nevertheless allowed juror testimony and affidavits on such points, perhaps because the exclusionary principle has always covered only behavior during deliberations, and entering or returning a verdict could be considered post-deliberative behavior. In any event, decisions handed down prior to 2006 went much *further* in allowing use of juror testimony or affidavits: In the *Eastridge* and *Attridge* cases, for example, courts admitted such evidence to correct apparent errors resulting from misunderstanding the effect of contributory negligence, and the framers of the 2006 amendment disapproved these decisions.[1] On the other hand, the framers endorsed a decision in the *Plummer* case approving the use of such evidence to correct an error in announcing the verdict in court, and a decision in the *Teevee Tunes* case allowing use of juror statements about the accuracy of a verdict.[2] The framers also endorsed a decision in the *Karl* case that juror affidavits *cannot* be used to show that figures on a verdict form *did* reflect a reduction needed on account of contributory negligence, where the form itself told the jury *not* to consider this point (allowing court to make reduction later), and a similar decision in the *Robles* case.[3]

In short, amended Rule 606(b) covers what might be called mechanical or clerical errors in filling out the form, or errors in *transmitting or announcing* the verdict, and *not* errors more deeply rooted in jury misunderstandings of the evidence, the instructions, or the meaning of the verdict forms.[4]

The usual precaution of polling the jury normally detects clerical errors in transmitting the verdict to court, and of course FRE 606(b) does not make this practice improper. Errors that come to light in this way may be corrected on the spot, or the jury may be sent out to continue deliberations, or, if necessary, a new trial may be ordered.[5] With respect to errors that would be obvious in a verbal report in court by the jury leader, a poll showing unanimous support for the verdict as thus

Effect of polling jury

§6.14   1. Eastridge Development Co. v. Halpert Associates, Inc., 853 F.2d 772, 783 (10th Cir. 1988) (jury returned verdict for $208,000, exactly 80% of what plaintiff sought; judge questioned jurors and found that they "mistakenly deducted" 20%, which court corrected); Attridge v. Cencorp Div. of Dover Technologies Intern., Inc., 836 F.2d 113, 115 (2d Cir. 1987) (special verdict awarded $100,000 to man and $50,000 to wife; form said plaintiff was 80 percent responsible, which yields recovery of $20,000 and $10,000; jurors said intent was to award $100,000 and $50,000 after reductions).

2. Plummer v. Springfield Terminal Railway Co., 5 F.3d 1, 3 (1st Cir. 1993) (approving juror testimony on "clerical error, such as announcing a verdict different than that agreed upon"); Teevee Tunes, Inc. v. MP3 Com., Inc., 148 F. Supp. 2d 276, 278 (S.D. N.Y. 2001) (can admit juror testimony that reported verdict is the one reached; can also testify that reported amount is *not* the one agreed to) (case to be retried).

3. Karl v. Burlington Northern R. Co., 880 F.2d 68, 73(8th Cir. 1989); Robles v. Exxon Corp., 862 F.2d 1201, 1208 (5th Cir. 1989).

4. Craig Outdoor Advertising v. Viacom Outdoor, Inc., 528 F.3d 1001, 1022 (8th Cir. 2008) ("mistake or ambiguity in the verdict form" is not "clerical error," and affidavits cannot "explain what the jury meant by its verdict and how the jury determined what numbers to transcribe onto the verdict form").

5. *See* ACN to 2006 amendment (quoting authors of this treatise).

reported should foreclose later attempts to "correct" it. The assent given in court makes any later affidavit or testimony hard or impossible to credit. In such situations, later affidavits and testimony look less like evidence of error in the original report of the verdict and more like an indication that jurors have had afterthoughts and want to change their minds,[6] and they are not allowed to do so.[7]

Examining jurors during trial
Rule 606(b) does not prevent a judge from examining jurors before or during trial on questions such as whether they have been exposed to pretrial publicity that might be damaging to a party.[8] Nor does it keep the judge from examining the jury to learn whether any of them saw or heard anything during trial that was accidental or inadvertent or not proper to consider.[9]

Nor does the Rule keep a judge from questioning jurors during deliberations on such matters as whether they talked to outsiders about the case or conducted experiments or examined material not admitted, since inquiry along these lines may proceed even after a verdict has been returned. Arguably pre-verdict questioning may also pursue the effect of any such exposure on the present thinking or deliberations of the jury (if the Rule itself does not apply, neither does the restriction against this form of inquiry), although this point is less clear because the reason to bar questioning on the effects of outside influence or extraneous information is to protect privacy of deliberations to insure that they remain free and frank.[10]

There is a broad range of situations where no juror testimony or statement is needed. The Rule does not affect the grant of a new trial for improper appeals to passion or prejudice in arguments by lawyers, or prejudice manifested in the verdict itself (as by excessive or inadequate awards), or failing to follow instructions (as by excessive or inconsistent verdicts), or returning what is self-evidently a compromise verdict.[11] And verdicts may be set aside for errors in admitting or excluding evidence, where one salient question is whether any error affected the verdict.

Predeliberative misconduct
Because FRE 606(b) limits only proof of matters occurring "during the course of the jury's deliberations," it seems inapplicable to jury

6. United States v. Weiner, 578 F.2d 757, 764 (9th Cir. 1978); Castleberry v. NRM Corp., 470 F.2d 1113, 1116-1117 (10th Cir. 1972).

7. United States v. Ortiz, 942 F.2d 903, 913 (5th Cir. 1991) (may testify to clerical error or that no verdict was reached, but may not "contradict four earlier statements" when judge polled each on her vote), *cert. denied*, 504 U.S. 985.

8. United States v. Awan, 966 F.2d 1415, 1431-1432 (11th Cir. 1992); United States v. Rowe, 906 F.2d 654, 656 n.3 (11th Cir. 1990).

9. United States v. Robinson, 645 F.2d 616, 617-618 (8th Cir. 1981).

10. State v. Robb, 723 N.E.2d 1019 (Ohio 2000) (court received report during deliberations that juror refused to consider death penalty; jurors can report such points before verdict is rendered).

11. On improper argument, *see* Leathers v. General Motors Corp., 546 F.2d 1083, 1086 (4th Cir. 1976) ("Golden Rule" argument). On prejudice in verdict, *see* Ajax Hardware Mfg. v. Industrial Plants Corp., 569 F.2d 181, 184 (2d Cir. 1977). On compromise verdicts, *see* Hatfield v. Seaboard A.L.R. Co., 396 F.2d 721, 724 (5th Cir. 1968).

misconduct occurring prior to deliberations. In its most common pre-deliberative misconduct involves false answers on voir dire.[12] Attacks based on this ground seldom succeed, probably because jurors seldom give false answers on important points, and mistakes or falsehoods are more likely to relate to peripheral matters. Sometimes false answers on voir dire suggest outside influence or extraneous prejudicial information that is independently provable by juror testimony or affidavit, which means such points may be shown even if the Rule applies to matters that occur after the jury is impaneled but before it retires. This point holds more than academic interest, since the Court decided in the *Tanner* case in 1987 that the Rule does apply to predeliberative jury misconduct despite a vigorous dissent arguing that the Rule "does not exclude juror testimony as to matters occurring before or after deliberations."[13]

Mysteriously the *Tanner* majority only *assumed* that the Rule applies (the opinion does not say so or reply to the dissent). *Tanner* provides two interpretive clues: First, the Court said the Rule reaches proof of objective misconduct, like physical behavior that can be seen by the naked eye and described without referring to mental processes. Thus the Rule reaches juror testimony or statements describing acts like consuming alcohol or drugs and resultant behavioral changes. Second, the Court rejected a distinction based on physical location (whether "inside or outside the jury room"), saying it would make no sense to bar proof that a juror read a newspaper in the jury room during deliberations but admit proof that he read one outside the jury room during the same period. *Tanner* is right on both points, but they do not answer the question whether the exclusionary rule reaches objective misconduct occurring before the jury retires. *Tanner* apparently means that the Rule reaches misconduct after empanelment but before the jury begins to deliberate. Perhaps the most obvious effect, in addition to barring juror testimony and statements to prove alcohol and drug use during trial, is that it extends the exclusionary rule to proof that jurors discussed the case among themselves before getting final instructions and being dismissed to deliberate.[14]

§6.15   Procedural Concerns

Some important procedural conventions have grown up around the use of juror testimony or statements to attack verdicts. Usually these attacks are made by motion for a new trial, and indeed the matter probably must first be raised in the trial court.

---

12. Williams v. Price, 343 F.3d 223, 233-234 (3d Cir. 2003) (should consider proof that juror made racial slur after trial ended, on question whether he lied during voir dire) (quoting authors of this Treatise).

13. Tanner v. United States, 483 U.S. 107 (1987) (Marshall and three others dissent).

14. United States v. Cuthel, 903 F.2d 1381, 1383 (11th Cir. 1990) (refusing to investigate allegations that jurors considered merits before told to begin).

Interviewing jurors

Neither professional ethics nor Rule 606(b) prevents counsel for the losing party from interviewing jurors afterwards.[1] The Code of Professional Responsibility imposes minimal protections against approaches of this sort by lawyers connected with the case, and some local rules also impose limits.[2] Also courts exercise supervisory control over such inquiries or order counsel not to approach jurors.[3]

A party seeking a new trial for jury misconduct is expected to make a preliminary showing by affidavit that something of sufficient seriousness may have occurred and the movant has good reason to think so.[4] A party who makes such a showing should not be blocked from interviewing jurors afterwards and should have an evidentiary hearing if necessary.[5]

The moving party has the burden of proving misconduct and that it likely affected the verdict.[6] In cases involving external contacts between jurors and court personnel, lawyers, parties, witnesses, or others the question is whether "actual prejudice" resulted, which means the standard for the party challenging the verdict is strict.[7] In cases involving extraneous factual information, the question is whether there is a reasonable possibility that it affected the verdict, which means the standard for the party challenging the verdict is more lenient.[8] The inquiry is similar to the one pursued on claims that errors in admitting or excluding evidence warrant relief from a judgment on appeal or posttrial motion.

Can show overt acts

Juror affidavits or testimony can only show overt acts and who learned or knew or participated. Whether prejudice resulted from

§6.15   1. Hanes v. State, 912 So.2d 940, 953 (Miss. 2005) (nothing in cases or Rule prohibits lawyer from asking jurors whether they acquired extraneous information; error to block lawyer here) (reversing).

2. *See* Code of Professional Responsibility DR 7-108 (after discharge, lawyer shall not ask questions or make comments "calculated merely to harass or embarrass" juror or influence future service); ABA Opinions of the Committee on Professional Ethics, Opinion 319 (1967) (lawyer may talk to and question jurors, but must not "harass, entice, induce or exert influence" on juror to obtain testimony, nor flatter or fawn over juror); Court Rules, W.D. Tex. R. 500-2 (interviews only by leave of court on good cause).

3. Big John, B.V. v. Indian Head Grain Co., 718 F.2d 143, 149-150 (5th Cir. 1983); Wilkerson v. Amco Corp., 703 F.2d 184, 185-186 (5th Cir. 1983).

4. *See* United States v. Sherrill, 388 F.3d 535, 537 (6th Cir. 2004) (defense offered "vague assertion" without supplying evidence that juror slept during trial or that behavior had prejudicial effect) (no new trial); United States v. Davis, 15 F.3d 1393, 1412 (7th Cir. 1994) (no obligation to inquire into influence until defendant makes colorable allegation), *cert. denied*, 513 U.S. 896.

5. Smith v. Phillips, 455 U.S. 209 (1982); Remmer v. United States, 350 U.S. 377, 378-379 (1956), *prior appeal*, 347 U.S. 227 (1954).

6. United States v. Winkle, 587 F.2d 587 F.2 705, 714-715 (5th Cir. 1979), *cert. denied*, 444 U.S. 827; Government of Virgin Islands v. Gereau, 523 F.2d 140, 148, 153 (3d Cir. 1975), *cert. denied*, 424 U.S. 917.

7. *See* Rushen v. Spain, 464 U.S. 114, 117-120 (1983); Smith v. Phillips, 455 U.S. 209, 217 (1982).

8. United States v. Mares, 934 F.2d 196, 201 (9th Cir. 1991) (new trial on "reasonable possibility" that extraneous material affected verdict); United States v. Rowe, 906 F.2d 654, 656 (11th Cir. 1990) ("reasonable possibility of prejudice").

outside influence must be resolved by drawing inferences, and the same is true of the question whether extraneous information raises a reasonable possibility that the verdict was affected. On these points a court lacking "even the insight of a psychiatrist" must evaluate "the subjective effects of objective facts without benefit of couch-interview introspections" and draw its conclusions without direct aid from jurors on the crucial point.[9]

Not surprisingly in this setting, courts usually say that a rebuttable presumption comes to the aid of the moving party,[10] but the presumption device does not solve everything. It cannot reasonably apply to every improper contact with witnesses, counsel, court personnel, or parties because incidental contact is inevitable and often trivial, nor even to all extrarecord information that comes to the attention of jurors because some seepage is inevitable—even sequestering does not shield jurors from glimpses of headlines or televised news, from hearing snippets of radio or television comments, and from accidentally hearing such matters in conversations with family. And much extrarecord information is trivial and unlikely to affect even jurors highly prone to suggestion.

Rebuttable presumption

Hence the presumption applies only if, on initial evaluation, the contact or information rises to a level of sufficient seriousness to justify a supposition that an ordinary juror might be affected.[11] While the presumption is rebuttable, the most direct kind of proof cannot be used for this purpose, since asking about the effect of anything on the minds of jurors is forbidden. In the end, the presumption is rebutted if a look at the whole picture indicates that the contact or information probably did not affect the jury.[12] Citing these problems with the presumption mechanism, some modern decisions express impatience with it,[13] and descriptions of the information or influence in the context of the case may be more helpful in explaining the result reached. Still, the presumption device is probably useful in suggesting

9. *See* United States v. Elder, 90 F.3d 1110, 1130-1131 (6th Cir. 1996) (refusing to consider juror notebooks), *cert. denied*, 117 S. Ct. 529, 993; United States v. Berry, 92 F.3d 597, 601 (7th Cir. 1996) (question of influence must be resolved without reference to juror comments); United States v. Howard, 506 F.2d 865, 869 (5th Cir. 1975) (source of phrase quoted in text above).

10. Remmer v. United States, 347 U.S. 227 (1954) (private communication, contact, or tampering presumptively prejudicial), *later appeal*, 350 U.S. 377 (1956) (quoting language from earlier opinion on presumptive prejudice); United States v. Cheek, 94 F.3d 136, 140-142 (4th Cir. 1996) (error to overrule magistrate's order for new trial on basis of interview with juror), *cert. denied*, 476 U.S. 1182.

11. United States v. Lloyd, 269 F.3d 228, 237-239 (3d Cir. 2001); United States v. Rowe, 906 F.2d 654, 656 (11th Cir. 1990).

12. United States v. Ruggiero, 56 F.3d 647, 652-653 (5th Cir. 1995) (presumption of prejudice rebutted), *cert. denied*, 516 U.S. 951. *But see* United States v. Greer, 620 F.2d 1383, 1385 (10th Cir. 1980) (presumption of prejudice "cannot be overcome" once jury reaches verdict).

13. United States v. Armstrong, 654 F.2d 1328, 1332 (9th Cir. 1981) (line drawing creates "artificial, discrete units where in reality a continuum exists," and it is "more judicially honest to acknowledge the continuum" and look less to nature of incidents and more to effect), *cert. denied*, 454 U.S. 1157.

that the losing party can prevail in a new trial bid even without actually showing that the unwanted contact or information affected the jury and in suggesting that some showings of contact or extrarecord information require the court to look more closely at what occurred.

G. VOUCHER RULE ABOLISHED

> **FRE 607**
>
>   The credibility of a witness may be attacked by any party, including the party calling the witness.

§6.16   Any Party May Impeach

A long-reviled rule of the common law had it that a party could not impeach his own witness. The rule was justified by arguments that seem wholly inadequate to the modern ear: Calling a witness implies endorsing or vouching for what she says, which suggests that the calling party is morally bound. Also letting the calling party impeach would lead to coercive tactics because he could force favorable testimony from a witness under the implied threat of blasting her character if she didn't deliver.[1]

These justifications have come to seem quaint. While calling a witness is surely a sign that the party thinks she will do more good than harm, it does not imply endorsement of everything she says. In many cases, the calling party has little or no choice and must call whoever knows the facts, so selecting witnesses has little tendency to suggest belief in their honesty or accuracy. While ethical rules bar lawyers from knowingly offering false testimony, they stop well short of forcing lawyers or litigants to offer only evidence or testimony known to be true. Treating the calling party as guarantor of veracity or correctness, or preventing him from attacking anything he offers would make litigating even more perilous and has simply stopped making sense.

While the fear of coerced testimony has substance, the reality is that the courtroom setting generates pressures on witnesses that the voucher rule did little to alleviate. Witnesses always face pressures from parties, brought to bear at trial through cross-examination and impeachment. But immunizing a witness from challenge by the calling party is not likely to right any imbalance in the process or encourage more truthfulness in court.[2] Even the voucher rule did not provide

---

§6.16   1. *See* Lipinski v. New York, 557 F.2d 289, 293-294 (2d Cir. 1977), *cert. denied*, 434 U.S. 1074; 1 McCormick, Evidence §38 (6th ed. 2006).

2. *See* 1 McCormick, Evidence §38 (6th ed. 2006) (if truth is on calling party's side but witness is untruthful, voucher rule invites attack if she tells truth; if she lies, "the adversary will not attack, and, under the rule, the calling party cannot").

anything resembling blanket protection for witnesses, nor block manipulative behavior by calling parties: It did not keep a party from later offering evidence or testimony that conflicted with what the party offered earlier, and often allowed the calling party to offer inconsistent statements by its own witnesses.

Abolishing the voucher rule means essentially three things:

First, a party is not "bound" by testimony or other evidence she introduces or sponsors.[3] That means she remains free to contradict or explain such evidence if it seems damaging to her case, and she may prevail even if crediting certain testimony or evidence she introduces would otherwise make her lose.

Party not bound

Of course testimony or other evidence that a party offers may (like testimony or evidence offered by others) damage or destroy her case if it is believed and goes unexplained or unrebutted. Hence even without a voucher rule a party may lose a case on motion on the basis of the evidence she offers if it disposes of the case. The reason is not that offering the evidence binds the calling party or gives testimony or other evidence artificial force, but that all evidence in the case may be given its natural probative force under the circumstances, and sometimes that force is so high that it cannot be ignored in the absence of countervailing proof.

Second, abolishing the voucher rule gives the calling party more freedom to offer prior statements by its own witnesses. "More freedom" is the right term because there is an important qualification, and the change from tradition is not quite as stark as it seems at first. The rule used to be that the calling party could impeach by prior inconsistent statements only if the witness gave testimony that affirmatively damaged his case (failing to live up to expectations was not enough) and the calling party was surprised by the testimony. Under FRE 607, these formal requirements no longer play a central role. The calling party need not show surprise before offering prior statements to impeach witnesses,[4] which seems sensible for much the same reasons expressed in criticism of the voucher rule itself— parties have little choice in witnesses and requiring surprise would penalize them for taking necessary risks. Probably the affirmative damage requirement is gone too, although courts may block or limit impeaching attacks on inconsequential witnesses.[5]

May offer prior statements

3. United States v. Rosa, 11 F.3d 315, 335-336 (2d Cir. 1993) (calling detective did not mean defense was bound by what he said), *cert. denied*, 511 U.S. 1042.

4. *See* United States v. Frappier, 807 F.2d 257, 259 (1st Cir. 1986), *cert. denied*, 481 U.S. 1006; United States v. Dennis, 625 F.2d 782, 795 n.6 (8th Cir. 1980).

5. Some decisions brush off suggestions that the damage requirement survives, *see* United States v. Webster, 734 F.2d 1191, 1192 (7th Cir. 1984) ("mistake to graft" requirement of harm to FRE 607), and some focus on the purpose of the calling party and whether the witness was essential, implicitly assuming the requirement did not survive. *See* §6.17, *infra*. Some state enactments retain the requirement. *See* Fla. Stat. Ann. §90.608; Michigan Rule 607; Ohio Rule 607. *See also* M. Graham, Employing Inconsistent Statements for Impeachment and as Substantive Evidence: A Critical Review and Proposed Amendments of Federal Rules of Evidence 801(d)(1)(A), 613, and 607, 75 Mich. L. Rev. 1565, 1610-1619 (1977) (FRE 607 should be amended to reinstate both requirements).

The important qualification in this development is that the more open practice gives way when a party abuses or manipulates it. Suppose a party calls a witness knowing the likely tenor of his testimony. Suppose too that the calling party adduces the testimony and later attacks the witness by offering his prior statements that can properly be used only to impeach but are likely to be misused as substantive evidence. Here courts sometimes conclude that the calling party is being unfair to the other side and putting the trial at risk, and the attempted impeachment is disallowed. Obviously this calculus is affected by what the calling party expected (should have expected) and what damage was done, so notions of "surprise" and "affirmative damage" creep back in and still bear on the matter (the subject is taken up in the next section).

All may impeach   Third, all parties may impeach witnesses they call by using other standard impeaching mechanisms. They include showing bias, problems in mental or sensory capacity, untruthful disposition, and contradiction. With one qualification, these other mechanisms are as available to the calling party as to others. Thus the government may impeach its own witnesses in criminal prosecutions, and defendants may call and impeach their own witnesses too. And clearly all parties in civil suits may attack the credibility of the witnesses they call. The one qualification involves impeachment by contradiction, which again brings serious dangers from manipulative practices. It is often possible to overcome or avoid a rule that normally excludes evidence that is useful or necessary to rebut or refute other evidence. But if the party who first offers evidence or testimony tries to contradict it by offering otherwise-excludable counterproof, the result may be intolerable because it amounts to abuse or evasion of important rules of exclusion. Hence calling parties face limits in contradicting witnesses that other parties would not face.[6]

Voucher rule and due process   In its 1973 decision in *Chambers v. Mississippi*, the Supreme Court held that limiting defense impeachment of prosecution witnesses can violate due process. The case was a state prosecution for murder of a police officer in Woodville, Mississippi, and Leon Chambers was convicted on testimony by several officers (one of whom said he saw Chambers fire the fatal shot) despite contrary testimony by another eyewitness and despite the fact that Gable McDonald repeatedly confessed to firing the fatal shot. The defense called McDonald, laid the foundation for his written confession, and read it to the jury. On cross, the state brought out that McDonald retracted his confession, and he said he confessed because he was promised a share in a tort recovery Chambers would win from Woodville. The trial court denied the defense request to treat McDonald as a hostile witness and excluded testimony describing his oral confessions. In *Chambers*, the Court decided the trial was unfair because "the combination" of Mississippi's voucher and hearsay rules kept defendant from cross-examining or

---

6. *See* §6.48, *infra*.

offering testimony that "would have discredited McDonald's repudiation" of his confession and "demonstrated his complicity."

Chambers is a decision with broad promise but narrow limits. On the one hand, it includes sweeping criticism of the voucher rule and round condemnation of its effect. The rule bears "little present relationship to the realities" of modern prosecutions where defendants can rarely select their witnesses and "must take them where they find them," and it was "doubly harmful" to Chambers because it restricted his direct examination (he was "bound by anything" McDonald might say) and prevented cross altogether.[7] On the other hand, *Chambers* went far to avoid condemning the voucher rule alone—it was the voucher rule in "combination" and "conjunction" with the hearsay doctrine that brought Chambers to grief. Moreover, the excluded confessions were reliable, and the Court was establishing "no new principles of constitutional law."[8]

In the end, *Chambers* disapproves the voucher rule in some circumstances but stops short of condemning it per se even in criminal cases when applied to limit defense impeachment. Some post-*Chambers* decisions find particular applications unconstitutional, but others find no violation.[9]

§6.17 Preventing Abuse by Calling Party

Although FRE 607 eased the old limits that sometimes kept the calling party from impeaching his own witness by prior statements, the new regime does not make it open season. Under the old limits, the calling party could use statements to attack the witness only if his testimony came as a surprise and caused affirmative damage. These restrictions no longer play pivotal roles. But an anything-goes approach would let parties call witnesses, adduce unfavorable testimony, then attack with favorable statements that cannot properly be used as substantive evidence but are likely to be misused in exactly that way. When this tactic seems abusive, courts refuse to allow it under their general authority to prevent unfair prejudice (FRE 403) and control the presentation of evidence (FRE 611).

The very idea of abuse hinges on continuing professional reluctance to put prior statements on a parity with live testimony. The framers of the Rules thought all prior inconsistent statements should be admissible as substantive evidence, which would have aligned the process of

Prior statements not like testimony

---

7. Chambers v. Mississippi, 410 U.S. 284, 294-297 (1973) (defendant proved written confession "countered by an arguably acceptable renunciation," but could not explore oral confessions or challenge renunciation of written confession).

8. Chambers v. Mississippi, 410 U.S. 284, 297, 302, 310 (1973).

9. *Compare* Welcome v. Vincent, 549 F.2d 853 (2d Cir. 1977) (barring defense cross on confession and excluding independent evidence violated right to fair trial), *cert. denied*, 432 U.S. 911, *with* Lipinski v. New York, 557 F.2d 289, 294 (2d Cir. 1977) (can apply voucher rule to disallow defendant from impeaching *B* by prior statements that would not have proved defense), *cert. denied*, 434 U.S. 1074.

impeaching witnesses with the process of proving facts. Had that been the outcome, probably there could be no such thing as abuse of FRE 607, for the calling party could use both live testimony and inconsistent statements as substantive evidence. But lawyers are not persuaded that all such statements should be usable in this way, and Congress enacted a narrower provision allowing substantive use of only a small subset of inconsistent statements—those given in proceedings under oath subject to penalty of perjury, which fit FRE 801(d)(1)(A) if the witness is cross-examinable about them at trial (as is normally true). The bottom line is that most prior statements—that is to say, all those that were *not* given in proceedings under oath subject to penalty of perjury, and those on which the declarant is for some reason *not* presently cross-examinable—are only admissible to impeach, and not as proof of what they assert.

In typical cases, the government has a statement by a witness describing critical aspects of a crime, given to a law enforcement official or someone else who is willing to testify (often under pressure because he too could be charged). Typically the statement does not fit any hearsay exception or qualify under FRE 801(d)(1)(A) because it was not given in proceedings under oath. The witness waffles at trial: He testifies to a different version of facts or is uncooperative and evasive, or omits details from the earlier statement or claims uncertainty or lack of memory. Typically these changes or contrasts are enough to justify use of the prior statement to impeach, for they support the conclusion that the prior statement is inconsistent with present testimony. Can the prosecutor offer testimony by the official or another describing what the witness said?

Primary purpose rule

If the "primary purpose" is to use the statement to prove what it says, many modern decisions refuse to let the prosecutor use it to impeach this turncoat or uncooperative witness. The origin of the primary purpose rule is the Fourth Circuit decision in *United States v. Morlang*, where the government tried to prove Morlang's complicity in profiteering and bribery on a public housing project. A man named Crist testified that while he and another named Wilmoth were in prison together, Wilmoth implicated Morlang: "One of us had to take the rap," Wilmoth reportedly told Crist, "so the other one could stay out and take care of the business" (the "other one" referred to Morlang). Taken as proof of Morlang's involvement, Wilmoth's statement was hearsay, and the government had already called Wilmoth and gotten his testimony blaming other defendants but exonerating Morlang. The Fourth Circuit thought the court should not have let Crist describe Wilmoth's statement. Apparently the government knew what Wilmoth would say, and its "real purpose" in calling him was to elicit his denial that he "ever had any conversation" implicating Morlang. Crist's testimony then came in only "for the purpose of attacking the credibility" of Wilmoth. While calling a witness does not mean vouching for his credibility and the new practice endorsed by FRE 607 lets the calling party impeach his own witnesses, still one may not call someone whose testimony is expected to be adverse "for the purpose of impeaching him."

Doing so would let the government "in the name of impeachment" present otherwise inadmissible testimony "by indirection." Impeachment by inconsistent statements cannot be allowed "as a mere subterfuge to get before the jury evidence not otherwise admissible."[1]

Morlang was decided the same year the Rules took effect (the trial preceded them and they did not apply in the case), and it became influential. Although "primary purpose" does not appear in the decision, the focus of the Fourth Circuit was on the prosecutor's purpose and the phrase has caught on. Under the primary purpose test, the government may not impeach its own witness with a prior inconsistent statement if it is inadmissible as substantive evidence and the prosecutor is more intent on using it to prove what it says than to impeach. Of course the hearsay doctrine applies in civil cases too, and limits defense evidence in criminal cases, so there is some justification for applying the primary purpose rule across the board.[2]

The primary purpose rule has the strength of recognizing that the strategy of the offering party bears on the degree of acceptable risk. It is one thing to let a party refute evidence it could not keep out initially, quite another to let one create her own opportunities to put the opponent at risk by introducing dangerous evidence. The same idea is found in doctrines governing impeachment by contradiction, which keep the calling party from eliciting testimony and then refuting it by evidence that would otherwise be excluded for reasons having nothing to do with hearsay. And the primary purpose test may be effective in that the strategy and arguments of the calling party are the most visible indication of what the factfinder will actually do with the combination of testimony and prior statement.

Still, the primary purpose test is inadequate because the central underlying concern is to limit or prevent damaging misuse of prior statements offered under the guise of impeachment. Looking to purpose helps appraise this risk, but other things affect risk too. Appraising risk requires consideration of the larger setting of the case, the importance of calling the witness to get his story, the importance of the story itself, the nature of his testimony and prior statement, and the nature and degree of conflict between them.[3]

---

§6.17 1. United States v. Morlang, 531 F.2d 183, 188-190 & n.11 (4th Cir. 1975) (people should not be "convicted on the basis of unsworn testimony").

2. United States v. Ince, 21 F.3d 576, 579-582 (4th Cir. 1994) (reversing under primary purpose test where government had no need to use prior statement to impeach its witness). *See also* State v. Benthall, 865 A.2d 693 (N.J. 2005) (can only use contradictory statement that is otherwise inadmissible if attacking party had "no prior knowledge" that witness would give harmful conflicting testimony). For a civil case applying *Morlang, see* Balogh's of Coral Gables, Inc. v. Getz, 798 F.2d 1356, 1358 n.2 (11th Cir. 1986).

3. United States v. Buffalo, 358 F.3d 519, 525-527 (8th Cir. 2004) (error to block defense attempt to impeach H by testimony of W and R that H admitted crime; his statements impeached testimony denying crime and denying that he told W and R otherwise; whether to let calling party impeach by inconsistent statements turns not on "primary purpose," but on FRE 403; defendant had to call H so jury could *see* "striking physical similarities" between defendant and H).

Beginning with a Second Circuit decision in *United States v. DeLillo*, modern cases have refined or qualified the primary purpose test. *DeLillo* resembles *Morlang* in that both involve a waffling government witness who gave incriminating statements but denied the central points at trial. But *DeLillo* found that the witness was essential to the government's case and approved use of his prior statements to impeach. In *DeLillo*, the government tried to prove Vincent DeLillo and others installed substandard concrete pipes and conspired to hide leaks and bribe inspectors. A schemer named Gorman testified that Vincent told him how much to pay inspectors and told subordinates to hide the leaks. The government called Monahan (another schemer), who corroborated Gorman's testimony on aspects of the bribery issue but said he heard what Vincent told subordinates, and that Vincent did *not* tell them to hide the leaks. The government introduced a taped statement in which Monahan said Vincent did give directions to hide the leaks after all, and the Second Circuit rejected a *Morlang* challenge to use of this statement:

> Beyond doubt, Monahan was not called to the stand by the government as a subterfuge with the primary aim of getting to the jury a statement impeaching him. Monahan's corroborating testimony was essential in many areas of the government's case. Once there, the government had the right to question him about those aspects of his testimony which conflicted with Gorman's account of the same events. *Morlang* itself explicitly recognizes the propriety of impeachment where it is "necessary to alleviate the harshness of subjecting a party to the mercy of a witness who is recalcitrant or may have been unscrupulously tampered with." To the extent that defendants rely on *Morlang* for the principle that a witness cannot be put on the stand if the side calling him knows that he will give testimony that it will have to impeach, it seems clear to us that the effect of FRE 607 . . . is to nullify the plausibility of such a reading. The *Morlang* opinion itself recognizes that enactment of FRE 607 might have such an effect.[4]

The opinion in *DeLillo* went far to establish that the government may call an essential witness and remain free to impeach him on some points by use of prior inconsistent statements even if they are inadmissible as substantive evidence and there is a risk of jury misuse.[5] In these circumstances impeachment has a purpose apart from putting in front of the jury evidence that it may misuse and cannot be labeled as mere "subterfuge." One way of describing the situation is to say the primary purpose in such cases is not to use the statements themselves. Indeed the primary purpose standard may be reframed as requiring "good

---

4. United States v. DeLillo, 620 F.2d 939, 946-947 (2d Cir. 1980) (citation omitted), *cert. denied*, 449 U.S. 835.

5. State v. Beltran, 904 A.3d 709, 716 (N.H. 2006) (prosecutor called G, who denied saying he talked to defendant about "someone coming out from Nevada to 'take care of' the situation" with victim; G's girlfriend testified that G did say that; where witness gives instrumental testimony, state can question and impeach part of account that conflicts with state's account); Walker v. State, 818 A.2d 1078, 1094 (Md. 2003) (similar).

faith" by the prosecutor in calling witnesses from whom useful evidence is expected and using prior statements to impeach only when the witness gives damaging testimony.[6]

Where a statement by a testifying witness is admissible as substantive evidence because it fits FRE 801(d)(1) or satisfies a hearsay exception, the calling party should be able to introduce it by way of impeachment of its witness under FRE 607 without being considered guilty of abuse of the Rule.[7] By definition, after all, statements that are admissible substantively need not be admitted only for their impeachment value, although of course other grounds of exclusion, such as unfair prejudice under FRE 403, might still apply.

In connection with impeachment by the calling party, the Rules might seem to illustrate the maxim that the more things change the more they stay the same. The voucher rule reduced occasions for impeachment by the calling party in pre-Rules practice, somewhat like the "primary purpose" test. Allowing the calling party to offer prior statements in cases of surprise and affirmative damage served a function somewhat like the essential witness exception. Indeed some modern critics have argued that the common law survived enactment of the Rules because it shows the way to apply FRE 607 in a regime making many prior statements inadmissible as substantive evidence, or that the common law standard should be reinstated by formal amendment to FRE 607.[8]

Despite the continuing inadmissibility of many statements as substantive evidence, and despite the resemblance between the old and new restrictions, the new regime is different in important ways from the old one. The human reality is that a person may be right on some points and wrong on others, and FRE 607 represents an advance in enabling parties to call witnesses whose testimony is a mixed blessing, and to use and support part of what they say while attacking other parts.

H. IMPEACHMENT OF WITNESSES

§6.18 Impeachment and Support

There are five recognized methods to impeach witnesses. Three involve casting doubt on his word in general, and two others focus on particular errors or falsehoods in his testimony.

---

6. United States v. Webster, 734 F.2d 1191, 1192 (7th Cir. 1984) (reading *Morlang* as setting good-faith standard).

7. United States v. O'Malley, 796 F.2d 891, 898-899 (7th Cir. 1986) (cases barring government from calling witness to impeach are inapposite; identification was "independently admissible substantive evidence").

8. *See* M. Graham, Examination of a Party's Own Witness Under the Federal Rules of Evidence: A Promise Unfulfilled, 54 Tex. L. Rev. 917 (1976); Employing Inconsistent Statements for Impeachment and as Substantive Evidence: A Critical Review and Proposed Amendments of Federal Rules of Evidence 801(d)(1)(A), and 607, 75 Mich. L. Rev. 1565, 1610-1619 (1977); The Relationship Among Federal Rules of Evidence 607, 801(d)(1)(A), and 403: A Reply to Weinstein's Evidence, 55 Tex. L. Rev. 573, 578 (1977).

General attacks In the category of casting doubt on the word of the witness in general, there are the following three mechanisms: One involves showing that the witness is affected by some bias or motivation that may tempt him to falsify or shade his testimony in one direction or another. See the discussion in §§6.19-6.20, *infra*. The second involves showing a defect in mental or sensory capacity, such as failed memory or poor eyesight, that undercuts what he says. See the discussion in §§6.21-6.22, *infra*. The third involves showing that the witness is by character or disposition untruthful. See the discussion in §§6.23-6.39, *infra*. This last mechanism, which is often described as attacking "truth and veracity," is usually subdivided into three different kinds of attack: One is cross-examination about particular instances of nonconviction misconduct, such as lying on an employment application, which is permissible under FRE 608(b). Another is cross-examining him about prior convictions, and these may also be proved by extrinsic evidence, as FRE 609 provides. The third is testimony by a character witness, who is allowed to give opinion or reputation testimony indicating that the target witness is untruthful, as FRE 608(a) provides. All three of these mechanisms are definite in the sense of suggesting theories or reasons that account for inaccuracies in testimony, but nonspecific in the sense that they fail to isolate particular errors or falsehoods.

Focused attacks The other category, which involves more focused attacks on particular testimony, includes two mechanisms: One is showing that the witness has made a prior inconsistent statement (one that conflicts with his testimony). See the discussion in §§6.40-6.42, *infra*. The other involves contradicting his testimony by showing on cross-examination or by extrinsic evidence (typically another witness) that something he said was wrong. See the discussion of this topic in §§6.43-6.48, *infra*. Some aspects of impeachment by prior inconsistent statement are regulated by FRE 613. No formal rule addresses impeachment by contradiction, and the process is regulated under the broad mandates of FRE 403 (which allows exclusion of evidence that is prejudicial, misleading, confusing, or wasteful of time) and 611 (which gives trial judges broad discretion to control the examination of witnesses).

It should be noted that *any* party may impeach a witness under FRE 607, including the calling party. Essentially FRE 607 means that the old voucher rule, under which the calling party could not mount such attacks, has been discarded. See the discussion of this subject in §§6.16-6.17, *supra*.

Repair and support The topic of repair and support of witnesses involves three strategies, and some important regulating principles. See generally the discussion in §§6.49-6.52, *infra*. At the outset it should be noted that generally a party may not *support* a witness who has not yet been attacked, which means especially that proof of good character may not be presented along with the initial testimony of a witness, and that prior *consistent* statements by the witness may not be offered along with his initial testimony.

That said, here are the three supporting strategies: First, the supporting party may seek to disarm expected attacks in advance (by bringing out impeaching facts as part of the direct testimony) and may seek to refute any impeaching attacks later by showing that the supposed impeaching facts are not true. Second, a witness whose "truth and veracity" has been attacked in one of the three ways described above may be rehabilitated by proof that he is in fact truthful. The cost of rehabilitating in this way, however, is to give the other side a chance to cross-examine the favorable character witness about unfavorable instances of conduct by the witness whose credibility is in issue. See FRE 608(a) and (b). Third, under some circumstances the supporting party may bring out prior consistent statements by the witness. In general, however, impeachment by prior *inconsistent* statements does not itself pave the way for prior consistent ones, and proving the latter is permitted only if the impeaching attack has charged the witness with fabricating his testimony or with improper motive, in which case consistent statements that were made *before* this motive came into play may be proved. This subject, however, is complicated, and the matter is taken up in detail in §6.52, *infra*.

1. Showing Bias

§6.19 Mechanics and Entitlement

"Bias" is a catchall term describing attitudes, feelings, or emotions of a witness that might affect her testimony, leading her to be more or less favorable to the position of a party for reasons other than the merits. The "fudge factors" that constitute bias may be conscious or unconscious or something in between. Sometimes bias relates to the parties or issues, as is true if a witness likes or dislikes, identifies with or fears a party, or holds strong general views about the behavior or issues in suit. Sometimes they relate to self-interest, as is true if the witness thinks she has something to gain or lose by the tenor of her testimony—financial or proprietary stake, career or social advantage, or government action (like decisions about prosecution, regulatory enforcement, or tax treatment). In a broad sense, bias embraces what we usually call "motive" or "interest" (and in their extreme form "corruption").[1]

As a matter of human nature, most people consider themselves fair-minded, and this view is honestly held when bias operates unconsciously. Hence proving it almost always means bringing out more-or-less objective facts that suggest bias whether or not the witness sees it that way, then pursuing the issue by argument and leaving it to the factfinder to decide in assessing credibility.

---

§6.19   1. State v. Greer, 635 N.W.2d 82, 88 (Minn. 2001) (bias is "catchall term describing attitudes, feelings, or emotions of a witness" that might affect testimony, leading her "to be more or less favorable to the position of a party for reasons other than the merits") (quoting authors of this Treatise).

Bias always relevant   Bias is always relevant and never collateral,[2] and the parties are entitled to reasonable latitude in cross-examining the target witness and offering extrinsic evidence (typically documents or testimony by other witnesses).[3] While the Rules do not expressly provide for impeachment by showing bias, the Supreme Court has held that such attacks are proper.[4] FRE 608(b) bars "extrinsic evidence" of acts by a witness, and courts occasionally make the mistake of thinking this provision applies to *all* attacks on veracity or credibility. But FRE 608(b) does not apply to proof of bias and speaks only to impeaching attacks aimed at undercutting the "character for truthfulness" of the witness (as the amendment adopted in 2002 was designed to make clear). In criminal cases, the accused is constitutionally entitled to a reasonable chance to show bias, which means developing the relevant points sufficiently to let the factfinder make an informed evaluation of credibility.[5] Rulings denying or too narrowly restricting such efforts (especially during cross-examination) infringe confrontation and due process rights,[6] although such errors are subject to the *Chapman* harmless error standard.[7]

The judge has discretion to limit such attacks, as a matter of both common and constitutional law. In civil and criminal cases alike, the court can act to prevent harassment of witnesses, confusion of issues, waste of time, and prejudice to parties. And the court may cut off attempts to show bias where the attacking party takes too much time "fishing" or "beating around the bush" by asking tangential questions, perhaps fearing that drawing too close to the critical point may produce a convincing denial, but hoping the innuendo of more distant questions will poison the well (sometimes the cases suggest the attacking party simply failed "to lay the foundation"). The cross-examiner is entitled to leeway until he has had a reasonable chance to develop the point, and then may be asked to move along.

Prior statements show bias   Of course bias may be shown by prior statements of the witness, and the hearsay doctrine poses no obstacle (statements of the witness fit the state-of-mind exception in FRE 803(3) when offered for this purpose or might qualify as nonhearsay circumstantial evidence of state of mind). The cases split on the question whether the attacking party must raise prior statements indicating bias during cross, or must otherwise accord

---

2. United States v. Abel, 469 U.S. 45 (1984) (bias "almost always relevant"); Davis v. Alaska, 415 U.S. 308, 316 (1974) (similar).

3. United States v. Abel, 469 U.S. 45 (1984) (common law allowed extrinsic evidence of bias, was not displaced by Rules).

4. United States v. Abel, 469 U.S. 45 (1984) (bias is "permissible and established basis of impeachment" under Rules).

5. Alford v. United States, 282 U.S. 687, 693-694 (1931); United States v. Hall, 653 F.2d 1002, 1007-1008 (5th Cir. 1981); United States v. Williams, 592 F.2d 1277, 1281 (5th Cir. 1979).

6. Olden v. Kentucky, 488 U.S. 227 (1988); Davis v. Alaska, 415 U.S. 308, 316-317 (1974); White v. Coplan, 399 F.3d 18, 23 (1st Cir. 2005).

7. Delaware v. Van Arsdall, 475 U.S. 673 (1986) (error disallowing defense cross for bias is subject to *Chapman* harmless error analysis). *See* §1.9, *supra*.

the witness some opportunity to explain. FRE 613 requires such an opportunity when a witness is impeached by "prior inconsistent statements." The language seems only to reach the quite different impeaching method of contradicting the witness by his prior statements,[8] but courts apply the same requirement to statements showing bias (only a few cases holding that statements offered to show bias merit different treatment).[9]

No similar foundation requirement reaches other kinds of proof, such as testimony by another witness describing behavior by the target witness or other circumstances indicating bias. FRE 613 clearly does not apply, and some commentators agree and others disagree with this result.[10] Surely it is good to give the witness a chance to answer suggestions of bias, and time is saved if the attacking party inquires about the relevant facts on cross, obviating the need to call another witness. But the need for explanation by the witness may be less acute where the evidence does not involve his own words, and there is more to be said for letting the attacking party select the weapon, means, and time. A strict rule seems worse than none at all (here as in the setting of impeachment by prior inconsistent statements, where FRE 613 rejects rigidity and permits flexibility).

On direct, the proponent may bring out facts his adversary might later explore as indications of bias on the part of the witness.[11] Otherwise the later attack takes on artificial meaning because it suggests not only that the witness is biased but that the proponent tried to hide it. Letting the proponent anticipate the attack does not conflict with the principle in FRE 608 that credibility may not be repaired until it is damaged.

Proponent may bring out

Where credibility has been attacked by evidence of bias, the proponent may introduce rebuttal evidence showing lack of bias, although usually such counterproof tends not so much to refute the initial suggestion as to explain or put it in perspective. Also the calling party may seek to show, typically by putting questions to the witness but also by extrinsic evidence, that he has risen above whatever bias might appear, being truthful and accurate in his testimony despite bias. Clearly such refutation and repair are appropriate, subject to reasonable limits

---

8. *See* §§640-641, *infra*.

9. United States v. Betts, 16 F.3d 748, 764 (7th Cir. 1994) (before proving statement, must give witness chance to explain or deny). *But see* Comer v. Pennsylvania R., 323 F.2d 863, 864 (2d Cir. 1963) (admitting record of railroad employee indicating possible hostility; unlike prior inconsistent statements, such evidence "requires no foundation" by questions on cross).

10. The ACN says FRE 613(b) does not apply where the attacking party proves conduct that is inconsistent with testimony. Wigmore thought no foundation should be required for proving bias by means of conduct, *see* 3A Wigmore, Evidence §955 (Chadbourn rev. 1970), but McCormick thought a flexible rule should apply to conduct and statements alike, whether offered to prove bias or to contradict, *see* 1 McCormick, Evidence §39 (6th ed. 2006). *See also* United States v. Betts, 16 F.3d 748, 764 (7th Cir. 1994) (in using statement to prove bias, must first give witness chance to explain).

11. United States v. Mealy, 851 F.2d 890, 898-899 (7th Cir. 1988); United States v. Cosentino, 844 F.2d 30, 33 (2d Cir. 1988), *cert. denied*, 488 U.S. 923.

under FRE 403 and 611—subject, in other words, to limits when the effort consumes more time than it is worth or injects untoward risks of unfair prejudice or confusion of the issues.[12] Some care is also warranted if the repair amounts to evidence of misconduct by the calling party that might readily be misused by the jury to infer that he is a person of bad character, hence likely to have acted in the manner alleged in the case.[13] When the attack amounts to a suggestion that testimony is fabricated, prior statements by the witness, consistent with his testimony and made before the motive to fabricate arose, are admissible to rebut this suggestion and as substantive evidence.[14]

§6.20 Varieties of Bias

There seems no end to the facts that may indicate bias. Generally the parties should be given considerable leeway to pursue wide-ranging inquiry on cross and to offer extrinsic proof.

Varieties of bias

Proof of bias may properly show (1) a personal relationship between the witness and a party based on friendship,[1] family ties,[2] sexual involvement,[3] or common membership in clubs or organizations;[4] (2) an employment or other business relationship between the witness and a party;[5] (3) a financial stake in the outcome of the suit;[6] (4) hatred

12. Penalver v. State, 926 So.2d 1118, 1135 (Fla. 2006) (questioning suggested that witness S wanted leniency for boyfriend; state could show that negotiations only affected S's information on another case).

13. United States v. Pintar, 630 F.2d 1270, 1283-1284 & nn.17-19 (8th Cir. 1980); Coleman Motor Co. v. Chrysler Corp., 525 F.2d 1338, 1350-1351 (3d Cir. 1975) (plaintiff's redirect went further than rebutting bias and injected prejudice).

14. *See* discussion in §§6.52 and 8.25, *infra*.

§6.20 1. United States v. Kerr, 464 F.2d 1367, 1372 (6th Cir. 1972) (asking defendant whether witness paid light and grocery bills for his wife during his incarceration).

2. State v. Campbell, 714 N.W.2d 622, 630 (Iowa 2006) (should have let defendant ask girlfriend about their argument over her nephews' involvement in charged crime; she sought to "protect her nephews") (reversing).

3. Olden v. Kentucky, 488 U.S. 227 (1988) (in trial for kidnapping and rape, blocking effort to ask *R* whether he and alleged victim *M* were having extramarital relationship violated confrontation rights; defense argued that *M* made up rape-kidnap story to protect relationship with *R*); State v. Cortes, 885 A.2d 153, 159 (Conn. 2005) (sexual relationship bore on bias of witness).

4. United States v. Abel, 469 U.S. 45 (1984) (membership of defendant and defense witness in Aryan Brotherhood, and tenets of group including willingness to lie to protect each other).

5. United States v. Coviello, 225 F.3d 54, 68 (1st Cir. 2000) (asking defense witness whether defendant was paying lawyer for witness), *cert. denied*, 531 U.S. 1102; United States v. Robinson, 530 F.2d 1076, 1079-1081 (D.C. Cir. 1976) (defendant and witness were in business together selling drugs).

6. Baker v. Kammerer, 187 S.W.3d 292, 294 (Ky. 2006) (witness was investigator employed by driver's insurer, which bore on bias); United States v. Dees, 34 F.3d 838, 844 (9th Cir. 1994) (witness sold movie rights to her story; value of story ending in acquittal is less).

or enmity between a witness and a party;[7] (5) fear by the witness for his personal safety or the safety of friends or family, relating to the parties or issues in suit;[8] (6) settlement or attempts to settle a claim between a witness and a party to the suit, especially if connected with the present suit;[9] (7) that the witness has been "coached" by trial counsel,[10] or has been influenced by conversations with or hearing the testimony of other witnesses;[11] (8) that the witness might be subject to criticism, embarrassment, or civil or criminal liability (apart from perjury) for testifying in a certain way;[12] (9) that the witness has taken or offered to take bribes in connection with the case, or has threatened a party, or has been threatened by or on behalf of a party.[13]

Many other facts or relationships may tend to prove bias too, and are proper grist for the mill of cross-examination and proper subjects for extrinsic evidence. Still, not everything tends to show bias, and courts may exclude evidence that is only marginally useful on this score, either because relevance is so low or because pushing the matter would waste time, engender confusion, or inject unnecessary prejudice.[14]

Fee arrangements

It is entirely proper to pay witnesses for aid in preparing the case and giving testimony at trial, although ethical rules bar compensating witnesses for testifying in a certain way and do not allow arrangements for payment contingent on outcome.[15] Typically, free arrangements are made for experts, and in criminal cases the government often compensates informers for continued services, usually because there is no other practical way to gain their cooperation and because the informers need compensation to help get them out of a life of crime. All such arrangements are suitable subjects for cross-examination, and the calling party commonly brings out in advance the fact and basic outlines of such arrangements.

7. United States v. Abel, 469 U.S. 45 (1984) (bias may come from "like, dislike, or fear of a party" or self-interest); United States v. Hatchett, 918 F.2d 631, 640-641 (6th Cir. 1990) (in tax trial, whether partner of defendant filed tax returns).

8. United States v. Abel, 469 U.S. 45 (1984) ("fear of a party").

9. *See* the discussion of FRE 408 in §§4.25-4.26, *supra*.

10. Geders v. United States, 425 U.S. 80, 89 (1976) (prosecutor may question defendant on coaching during recess).

11. United States ex rel. Clark v. Fike, 538 F.2d 750, 758 (7th Cir. 1976) (witnesses discussed testimony before trial; proper subject for impeachment and comment), *cert. denied*, 429 U.S. 1064. *See* discussion of FRE 615 in §§6.71-6.72, *infra*.

12. Atlantic C.L. R. Co. v. Dixon, 207 F.2d 899, 904 (5th Cir. 1953) (asking witness whether he would be in trouble and subject to criticism from superiors if there had not been plenty of lights under shed where accident occurred).

13. State v. Vance, 714 N.W.2d 428 (Minn. 2006) (threats); United States v. Manske, 186 F.3d 770, 777 (7th Cir. 1999) (threats); United States v. Honneus, 508 F.2d 566, 572 (1st Cir. 1974) (intermediary solicited bribe from defendant on behalf of witness), *cert. denied*, 421 U.S. 948.

14. State v. Cram, 718 N.W.2d 898 (Minn. 2006) (in murder trial, blocking defense questions aiming to show that brother of victim abused her 35 years earlier; not everything shows bias).

15. *See* DR 7-109(C) (lawyer shall not offer to pay witness "contingent upon the content of his testimony or the outcome of the case" but may pay expenses and compensation for attending or testifying and professional services of expert).

Informants and experts may be asked on cross to reveal the terms of their financial arrangements with the calling party for testifying in the case at hand.[16] Arguably the range of permissible questioning should extend much further: The cross-examiner might reasonably argue that the witness should have to answer questions on what other financial arrangements he has made with the calling party or the lawyer for that party, since these other arrangements may be part of a larger picture of cooperation and mutual financial interest. The witness should also have to answer questions about other cases in which he may have provided testimony that is similar to what is expected in the case at hand, and even to say what portion of his total income derives from such testimony.[17] Such broader questioning may be proper,[18] especially in the case of "professional witnesses" who regularly testify at trial, but sometimes courts decide that broader questioning is too far removed from the issues at hand and disallow it as collateral.[19]

Plea bargains Government witnesses in criminal trials have serious problems of their own because of their involvement in crime, and this subject too is commonly raised on defense cross. In perhaps the typical case, a government witness is persuaded to take the stand as part of a deal that lets him enter a plea bargain to avoid prosecution or incarceration, or to obtain leniency in sentencing. Often he is involved in the very crimes charged to the defendant, and sometimes he was originally charged along with the defendant. As a means of showing bias, defense questioning may properly delve into plea bargains[20] and the pendency of other charges.[21] Mere vulnerability to charges may put a witness under the thumb of the government, and the same is true if a witness

---

16. United States v. Lindemann, 85 F.3d 1232, 1242-1243 (7th Cir. 1996), *cert. denied*, 519 U.S. 966; United States v. Leja, 568 F.2d 493, 495-499 (6th Cir. 1977).

17. *See* M. Graham, Impeaching the Professional Expert Witness by a Showing of Financial Interest, 53 Ind. L.J. 35, 50 (1977-1978) (courts admit evidence of (a) financial interest in case by reason of remuneration for services, (b) continued employment by party, (c) prior testimony for same party or attorney; courts disagree about showing (d) amount of prior compensation from same party, (e) proportion of total income from testifying for party or type of party, and (f) fact that expert testifies more frequently for certain type of party) (evidence along all these lines ought to be permitted).

18. Cooper v. Schoffstall, 905 A.2d 482, 494-495 (Pa. 2006) (on showing of reasonable ground to think expert is professional witness, opponent may inquire into pattern of compensation that supports inference that expert "might color, shade, or slant" testimony in light of "financial incentives").

19. United States v. Gray, 626 F.2d 494, 499-500 (5th Cir. 1980) (defense not entitled to cross-examine informant on total compensation from other cases), *cert. denied*, 450 U.S. 919; United States v. 412.93 Acres of Land, 455 F.2d 1242, 1247 (3d Cir. 1972) (property owner could not question appraiser called by government on compensation for "entire project").

20. United States v. Roberts, 618 F.2d 530, 535 (9th Cir. 1980).

21. Davis v. Alaska, 415 U.S. 308 (1974) (probationer status of juvenile perhaps suspected of crime charged to defendant); Alford v. United States, 282 U.S. 687, 693 (1931) (witness charged with other offenses was affected by "fear or favor"); State v. Drummond, 854 N.E.2d 1038, 1060 (Ohio 2006) (pendency of charges against state witnesses is appropriate subject for defense cross, to show bias).

faces possible loss of probation or parole, and these subjects too may be explored.[22]

Not surprisingly, prosecutors respond to these tactics by trying to avoid damage and to repair whatever damage is inflicted. The government may bring out on direct that its witness is subject to pressures that may come from plea bargains and vulnerability to charges.[23] Most decisions approve use of the plea agreement itself,[24] although others would bar use of the agreement unless defense tactics require rebuttal (see below), and some older decisions criticize or condemn this practice.[25] Clearly such questions disarm the expected attack and avoid any suggestion that the government is concealing relevant information. This tactic does not amount to improper bolstering or violate the usual rule that credibility may not be repaired before the attack. Exploring the subject on direct also helps qualify the witness as someone with firsthand knowledge and experience, and thus plays a valuable role in assessing his testimony. But the government should not exploit the plea agreement by arguing in effect guilt by association (witness has pled guilty, so defendant is guilty) or using by standard truth clauses to suggest that the witness should be believed or that the government has outside information that he is right, although some case approve putting in front of juries that such a witness can be prosecuted or face additional charges for lying.[26] And cautionary instructions are essential.[27]

The defense in a criminal case may also bring out that a government witness has received assistance, financial and otherwise, by participating in the statutory Witness Protection Program.[28] This involvement

Witness protection program

22. Baltazar-Monterrosa v. State, 137 P.3d 1137, 1145 (Nev. 2006) (error to stop defense from asking whether witness had been threatened with deportation if he did not testify); State v. Patterson, 86 A.2d 777, 786 (Conn. 2005) (should have told jury to consider carefully the credibility of jailhouse informant testifying in hope of reduction in sentence) (reversing). *But see* State v. Robinson, 715 N.W.2d 531 (Neb. 2006) (excluding proof that witness faced charges; expectation of leniency, absent agreement, expressed or implied, need not be revealed) (witness said he was promised nothing).

23. United States v. Dworken, 855 F.2d 12, 30 (1st Cir. 1988) (government may elicit plea and agreement "to dampen the effect of anticipated attack").

24. United States v. Gaev, 24 F.3d 473, 478-479 (3d Cir. 1994), *cert. denied*, 513 U.S. 1015; United States v. Lord, 907 F.2d 1028, 1030-1031 (10th Cir. 1990).

25. United States v. Handly, 591 F.2d 1125, 1128-1130 & n.1 (5th Cir. 1979) (related pleas introduce obvious prejudice); Loraine v. United States, 396 F.2d 335, 339 (9th Cir. 1968), *cert. denied*, 393 U.S. 933.

26. United States v. Roundtree, 534 F.3d 876, 880-881 (8th Cir. 2008) (prosecutor brought out that witnesses pled guilty and were testifying in exchange for reduced sentences; one testified that lying would lead to a "slew of charges" in addition to what he was facing; another that consequences include contempt and loss of reduction in sentence) (no plain error). United States v. Musacchia, 900 F.2d 493, 496-498 (2d Cir. 1990) (error to question witnesses on direct about truth-telling promises before defense challenge).

27. United States v. Halbert, 640 F.2d 1000, 1004-1007 (9th Cir. 1981); United States v. Whitehead, 618 F.2d 523, 529-530 (4th Cir. 1980).

28. *See* 18 U.S.C. §§3521-3528 (part of Organized Crime Control Act of 1970 provides for relocation and protection of witnesses).

suggests too that the witness is beholden to the government and has at least one reason that others would not have to help the prosecutor.[29] But such an attack may backfire, since witnesses join the program to protect themselves and their families from harm. This fact is not likely to be lost on the jury, which might infer that conduct by the defendant or others associated with him is what brought the need for protection.

Anticipating the attack, the government may bring out on direct that the witness is in the program.[30] Again the rationale is that this approach prevents the defendant from distorting the impeaching effect of the underlying facts by suggesting that the government was trying to hide something. Some cases say the court may instruct the jury on direct examination that evidence of self-interest may be taken into account in evaluating witness credibility (with reference to financial benefits and protection), and that there is a program authorized by law to protect witnesses and families from physical and economic harm.[31]

The matter of being in the protection program must be handled delicately, and the prosecutor should not exploit it by raising the matter, for example, where the defense agrees in advance not to go into the subject.[32] To minimize this risk, it should be permissible to ask the defense whether it plans to impeach the witness by raising the fact of payments and other benefits during cross, and to give an instruction of the sort described in the previous paragraph if the answer is yes. The instruction seems dangerous and unnecessary if the answer is no, and if the defense later raises the issue anyway, instruction and even argument on the point are warranted, and it should be proper to interrupt defense cross-examination to give the instruction.

2. Showing Problems in Capacity

§6.21 Cross-Examination and Extrinsic Evidence

Limits or defects in sensory or mental capacities bear on both the likelihood that a witness accurately perceived events or occurrences and the accuracy or completeness of his testimony. In lawsuits, sensory capacity is often a matter of sight or hearing, and mental capacity is a matter of memory. But subjective factors also appear, like ability to make judgments or estimates, and mental capacity includes emotional

29. United States v. Partin, 601 F.2d 1000, 1009-1010 (9th Cir. 1979) (defense may show witness received substantial benefits in program).

30. United States v. Frankenberry, 696 F.2d 239, 242-243 (3d Cir. 1982), *cert. denied,* 463 U.S. 1210; United States v. Partin, 552 F.2d 621, 643-644 (5th Cir. 1977), *cert. denied,* 434 U.S. 903.

31. United States v. Partin, 601 F.2d 1000, 1009-1010 (9th Cir. 1979) (on government request, court could tell jury about program; instruction refers to possible threat, not that there was one or who made it).

32. United States v. Melia, 691 F.2d 672, 675-676 (4th Cir. 1982) (error to let government show witnesses received death threats and were in protection program; it became "positive evidence" of bad character and guilt, might suggest defendant was source of threats).

and psychological conditions that can introduce subjective distortions. Shortcomings in capacity are not a mark of incompetency but are appropriate subjects for questioning and proof, bearing on the weight or credit to be given to testimony.

It is said that proof of sensory or mental incapacity is always relevant and never collateral, which means that cross-examination is appropriate and extrinsic evidence is also admissible.[1] The court may block a line of questioning, however, if the attacking party lacks a reasonable basis and the questions are intrusive or embarrassing, confusing or prejudicial,[2] or if the attacking party skirts the edges of the issue for too long without putting the telling question.

Incapacity always relevant

When the attacking party proceeds by cross, he may hope not only to get information but in effect to demonstrate sensory or mental incapacity. He may probe matters such as sight or hearing by appropriate questions and may in effect test in a rough way the ability of the witness to see or hear. And the attacking party may put memory to the test, even by general questions somewhat collateral to the issues, in an effort to show circumstantially that seeming certainty is something less.

Both memory and perception may be affected by the use of drugs or alcohol. Hence the attacking party may go into the matter of intoxication[3] or influence of drugs at the time of events[4] and may similarly pursue intoxication or drug influence at time of trial.[5] Fortunately witnesses are seldom seriously under the influence at trial. Usually a day's delay can remove any problem, and the trier is likely to see such problems without formal proof.

Alcohol, drugs

Alcoholism or drug addiction is another story. Such conditions are not character traits that bear on truthfulness under FRE 608, but they lead to cumulative impairment of sensory and mental faculties that bears on credibility. Nevertheless evidence of alcoholism and addiction is usually excluded to protect witnesses from harassment and parties from unfair prejudice, and juries need not be warned to doubt the testimony of addicts.[6] Occasionally, however, courts admit such proof

---

§6.21   1. State v. Robinson, 817 So.2d 1131, 1135 (La. 2002) (defense can cross-examine witness on mental defect or treatment at time of incident or time of testifying; denying this right was constitutional error) (reversing); Behler v. Hanlon, 199 F.R.D. 553, 558 (D. Md. 2001) (quoting this Treatise).

2. United States v. Honneus, 508 F.2d 566, 573 (1st Cir. 1974), *cert. denied*, 421 U.S. 948.

3. Rheaume v. Patterson, 289 F.2d 611, 614 (2d Cir. 1961) (testimony that driver was drinking could show capacity to observe was impaired).

4. *See* Roberts v. Hollocher, 664 F.2d 200, 203 (8th Cir. 1981) (questions on plaintiff's drug use were relevant to ability to recall and physical state at time of incidents); United States v. Hickey, 596 F.2d 1082, 1090 (1st Cir. 1979) (allowing cross on drug use in period beginning one week before robbery and ending at trial), *cert. denied*, 444 U.S. 853.

5. Wilson v. United States, 232 U.S. 563, 568 (1914) (can ask defendant whether she was addicted to morphine and used it before coming to court).

6. United States v. Di Paolo, 804 F.2d 225, 229-230 (2d Cir. 1986) (refusing to let defense cross-examine victim on drinking problem); United States v. Kinnard, 465 F.2d 566, 571-572 (D.C. Cir. 1972) (need not warn jury that addiction discredits testimony).

on issues of capacity and when facts relating to drug use show bias or influence.[7]

Mental illness   The attacking party may show the witness suffers (or once did) from mental illness and may cross-examine on present or past problems and treatment.[8] Medical records indicating treatment for mental problems provide a proper basis for cross-examination, although the records themselves are usually excluded as primary evidence.[9] Such impeachment raises serious concerns over the personal privacy of the witness. The attack may be demeaning and unfair and should be blocked if psychiatric problems do not relate in important ways to capacity to observe or communicate, a point that is compounded when the inquiry leads to collateral issues, confusion, and counterproof.[10] Where the adverse party attacks a witness by questions or extrinsic evidence suggesting mental illness or incapacity, the calling party may offer counterproof in the form of expert testimony that the witness has the mental capacity to distinguish truth from fantasy or falsehood.[11]

Many kinds of data about a person, who would be considered in all respects normal, may bear on the accuracy of perception, memory, or narration. Such might be said, for example, about training or schooling, intelligence, interests or personality traits, and so forth. Information along such lines may come out in the course of routine background questions. It may also come out by accident, through skillful questioning, or in the form of demeanor evidence. Extrinsic proof along such lines is seldom offered and seldom necessary. Here certainly the court may impose limits pursuant to FRE 403 and 611 and should take steps to protect the witness from harassment or embarrassment.

May bring out on direct   The calling party may bring out on direct information that bears on sensory limits or defects, memory loss or impairment, or mental affliction.[12] This tactic does not run afoul of the doctrine that prohibits support of witnesses before attacks are made, since it is best understood

---

7. United States v. Arnold, 890 F.2d 825, 828 (6th Cir. 1989) (government could ask alibi witness about minor marijuana transaction with defendant 18 years ago, to show bias); United States v. Van Meerbeke, 548 F.2d 415, 419 (2d Cir. 1976) (extensive cross on addiction of prosecution witness), *cert. denied*, 430 U.S. 974.

8. United States v. Lindstrom, 698 F.2d 1154, 1159-1164 (11th Cir. 1983); United States v. Pacelli, 521 F.2d 135, 140-141 (2d Cir. 1975) (allowing cross on eccentric behavior indicating to psychiatrist that witness was "incapable of telling the truth"), *cert. denied*, 424 U.S. 911.

9. United States v. Butt, 955 F.2d 77, 81-82 (1st Cir. 1992); United States v. Moore, 786 F.2d 1308, 1314-1315 (5th Cir. 1986).

10. State v. Fichera, 903 A.2d 1030 (N.H. 2006) (defense must show that mental impairment affects perception of events, cannot impeach by "suggestion or innuendo" without foundation); Thomas v. State, 812 A.2d 1050, 358 (Md. 2002) (denying access to psychiatric records and blocking cross; defense failed to show likelihood that records contained relevant information, or that problems affect ability to perceive); United States v. Lopez, 611 F.2d 44, 45-46 (4th Cir. 1979) (raising privacy issue; blocking defense cross on court-ordered examination determining that witness was competent to be tried on unrelated charges).

11. United States v. A&S Council Oil Co., 947 F.2d 1128, 1132 (4th Cir. 1991).

12. *See* United States v. Gerry, 515 F.2d 130, 137 (2d Cir. 1975) (mental competency of prosecution witness explored on direct), *cert. denied*, 423 U.S. 832.

as disarming an expected attack and preventing adverse parties from claiming that the calling party was trying to hide something important.

§6.22   Expert Testimony

Expert testimony by a psychiatrist or psychologist on the mental condition of a witness has tough sledding. Such testimony might relate to capacity or to what we usually call truthful disposition (character for truth and veracity).[1] When expert opinion seems to relate to capacity, courts sometimes admit it, but often exclude.[2]

Many decisions say courts have inherent authority to order witnesses to undergo physical or mental examinations to help assess capacity (distinguishing truth from falsehood) and even general veracity (ability to be truthful). As a practical matter, there is more bark than bite in these claims, and courts routinely deny requests to order witnesses to be examined, citing concerns over privacy, failure to show need, and procedural reasons,[3] and often conclude that the necessary information on credibility can be developed other ways.[4]

Courts can in effect force parties to undergo examinations by demanding them as a condition of offering certain lines of evidence or advancing certain claims or defenses. Courts lack authority to *compel* nonparty witnesses to submit to such examinations but can *ask* them to do so,[5] and in extreme cases courts can exclude testimony by witnesses who refuse to undergo examinations, although this power too is seldom actually exercised.[6]

§6.22   1. *See* §6.50, *infra.*

2. *See* United States v. Gonzalez-Maldonado, 115 F.3d 9, 15-16 (1st Cir. 1997) (psychiatric testimony about verbosity, "grandeza" and "exaggeration," to explain taped statements); United States v. Shay, 57 F.3d 126, 132-134 (1st Cir. 1995) (error to exclude testimony that defendant suffered from "pseudologia fantastica" characterized by pathological lying). *But see* United States v. Butt, 955 F.2d 77, 85 (1st Cir. 1992) (excluding expert testimony explaining "hysteroid dysphoria" and "splitting" and "borderline personality disorder"). *And see* §7.22, *infra* (expert testimony on social frameworks and syndromes).

3. United States v. Rouse, 111 F.3d 561, 570 (8th Cir. 1997) (excluding testimony on implanted memory; expert may appraise dangers and suggestive practices but not credibility), *cert. denied*, 522 U.S. 905; United States v. Raineri, 670 F.2d 702, 709 (7th Cir. 1982) (privacy).

4. United States v. Brown, 770 F.2d 768, 770 (9th Cir. 1985) (extensive cross; jury instructed), *cert. denied*, 476 U.S. 1172; United States v. Riley, 657 F.2d 1377, 1387 (8th Cir. 1981) (cross); United States v. Benn, 476 F.2d 1127, 1130-1131 (D.C. Cir. 1972) (mentally retarded 18-year-old victim provided "comprehensible narrative" that was substantially corroborated).

5. United States v. Ramirez, 871 F.2d 582, 584 (6th Cir. 1989) (cannot order nonparty witness to be examined by psychiatrist), *cert. denied*, 493 U.S. 841. But see Hamill v. Powers, 164 P.3d 1083 (Okla. 2007) (in rape trial, state planned to use expert to prove that adult victim lacked capacity to consent; defense entitled to order requiring psychological or psychiatric examination) ("admittedly rare").

6. United States v. Ramirez, 871 F.2d 582, 584 (6th Cir. 1989) (condition testimony on psychiatric exam), *cert. denied*, 493 U.S. 841; United States v. Gutman, 725 F.2d 417, 420 (7th Cir. 1984) (similar), *cert. denied*, 469 U.S. 880.

3. Showing Untruthfulness

> **FRE 608**
>
> (a) **Opinion and reputation evidence of character.** The credibility of a witness may be attacked or supported by evidence in the form of opinion or reputation, but subject to these limitations:
>
> (1) the evidence may refer only to character for truthfulness or untruthfulness, and
>
> (2) evidence of truthful character is admissible only after the character of the witness for truthfulness has been attacked by opinion or reputation evidence or otherwise.
>
> (b) **Specific instances of conduct.** Specific instances of the conduct of a witness, for the purpose of attacking or supporting the witness' character for truthfulness, other than conviction of crime as provided in Rule 609, may not be proved by extrinsic evidence. They may, however, in the discretion of the court, if probative of truthfulness or untruthfulness, be inquired into on cross-examination of the witness
>
> (1) concerning the witness' character for truthfulness or untruthfulness, or
>
> (2) concerning the character for truthfulness or untruthfulness of another witness as to which character the witness being cross-examined has testified.
>
> The giving of testimony, whether by an accused or by any other witness, does not operate as a waiver of the accused's or the witness' privilege against self-incrimination when examined with respect to matters which relate only to credibility.

§6.23 Opinion and Reputation Testimony—In General

FRE 608(a) provides that a witness may be impeached by proof that he is by disposition untruthful. Untruthfulness on the part of a witness, who may be called for convenience the "principal" or "target" witness, may be shown in three different ways. One is testimony by a second (or "character") witness. The other two ways involve cross-examining the target witness about her own bad acts shedding light on veracity or on her own convictions shedding light on veracity.[1]

Reputation   Under FRE 608, a character witness may give either opinion or reputation testimony indicating that the principal witness is untruthful, although a handful of states retain the traditional rule allowing only

---

§6.23 1. On cross-examining the target witness about prior bad acts under FRE 608(b), *see* §6.25, *infra*. On cross-examining about convictions under FRE 609, *see* §§6.29-6.39, *infra*.

reputation,[2] which has long been a standard feature of trial practice. The litany of question and response is simple. Customarily it begins with foundation questions bringing out familiarity with reputation in the community, going to the obvious confirming question ("do you know *X*'s reputation in the community for truth and veracity?"), then getting to the point ("what is that reputation?") and eliciting the expected response ("it is bad"). Such testimony was proper by tradition and remains proper under FRE 608(a).[3] Common law tradition tolerated little departure from this pattern, and a character witness could not give her opinion on untruthfulness (the question "do you consider him a truthful person?" was improper). The litany could be safely expanded by asking whether the character witness would believe the target witness if he testified under oath, which remains proper under FRE 608(a).[4]

Rule 608(a) expresses the view that the distinction between reputation and opinion is artificial, as it has been long suspected that witnesses describing untruthful reputation were really giving disguised opinion testimony. The Rule endorses a new form of words and removes what seems a minor obstacle. But the change has real importance because a personal endorsement, particularly if the witness is appealing enough to be liked or respected, is more convincing than an endorsement purporting to convey what nameless others think.[5] **Opinion**

Whether directed at reputation or opinion, testimony by a character witness should shed light on truthfulness. The question is not whether a particular statement is true, but whether the principal witness is a truthful person, and the Rule does not contemplate testimony by a character witness indicating that she has listened to the principal witness and does not believe what he said.[6] Unlike character evidence offered to prove behavior at the time of the events, the purpose of testimony relating to truthfulness is to help assess behavior at trial (whether the principal witness is being truthful), so opinion or reputation testimony should shed light on truthfulness at the time of trial. If the principal witness is a party, especially if he is the defendant in a criminal case, impeaching testimony by a character witness should be excluded if it rests on (or has been affected by) impressions relating to defendant's guilt of the charged offense.[7]

---

2. States allowing only reputation evidence include Florida, Georgia, Illinois, Louisiana, Maine, Massachusetts, Missouri, New York, Pennsylvania, and Washington.

3. Fitzgerald v. Stanley Roberts, 895 A.2d 405, 421 (N.J. 2006) ("opinion and reputation" on untruthfulness); Deary v. City of Gloucester, 9 F.3d 191, 196 (1st Cir. 1993) (reputation for truthfulness).

4. United States v. McMurray, 20 F.3d 831, 834 (8th Cir. 1994) (can ask whether witness would believe defendant under oath); United States v. Davis, 787 F.2d 1501, 1504 (11th Cir. 1986) (witnesses "would not believe Davis under oath"), *cert. denied*, 479 U.S. 852.

5. Wilson v. City of Chicago, 6 F.3d 1233, 1239 (7th Cir. 1993) (opinion on untruthfulness), *cert. denied*, 114 S. Ct. 1844; United States v. Lashmett, 965 F.2d 179, 183 (7th Cir. 1992) (error to exclude opinion).

6. Liggett v. People, 135 P.3d 725, 731 (Colo. 2006) (cannot use character evidence to show whether witness was truthful on stand or on any particular occasion).

7. United States v. Null, 415 F.2d 1178, 1180 (4th Cir. 1969); Frith v. Commonwealth, 155 S.W.2d 851 (Ky. 1941).

Character testimony requires a foundation. For reputation testimony, the character witness must be acquainted with the community where the principal witness lives, works, or goes to school.[8] In twenty-first century America, relatively few people live in small and easily defined communities, and most of us seem to belong to many communities, sometimes defined in the old-fashioned geographical sense (neighborhoods, apartment complexes) but often defined more functionally in terms of common working or professional involvements or common educational, recreational, political, or religious pursuits. Perhaps reputation was a more real aspect of living in earlier days when more people lived in small communities and moved less often. Still it seems that most people, even in the twenty-first century, become well enough known on a day-to-day basis among neighbors and acquaintances at work, school, and elsewhere to provide funds of usable information in the form of the collective judgment that we call "reputation." The witness testifying to reputation need not reside, work, or study in the pertinent community, but must know the widespread feelings or views of the community, not just what one learn by talking to a handful of people.[9]

The foundation requirement for a character witness who is to give her opinion of the principal witness is simply that the former knew the latter for some period of time on some personal, business, or professional basis.[10] Where it is the defendant whose credibility as a witness is in issue, it is at least doubtful that the prosecutor should be permitted to attack by use of agents who became acquainted with the accused while performing investigative functions.[11] Real questions arise here on adequacy of basis for an opinion on credibility. There is a great risk that the opinion of the agent on credibility is dominated by (or subsumed in) the agent's belief in the guilt of the accused, and it is very likely that the agent's testimony will convey to the jury the impression

8. Fitzgerald v. Stanley Roberts, Inc., 895 A.2d 405, 420 n.13 (N.J. 2006) (foundation for reputation involves showing that witness is in same residential or social community, that subject resides there or has been associated with community for substantial period, that subject has reputation for truthfulness, and that witness knows it); State v. Kalex, 789 A.2d 1286 (Me. 2002) (can have one reputation in home neighborhood, another at work; knowledge from 50-person sample suffices, but not knowledge from 4-person sample; community must be "sufficiently large and diverse" to make reputation evidence reliable).

9. State v. Berry, 803 A.2d 593, 597 (N.H. 2002) (excluding testimony on reputation of victim that rested on "opinions of a small circle" of children and parents, which was not "of significant size"); United States v. Lewin, 467 F.2d 1132, 1139-1140 (7th Cir. 1972) (witness need not live in same community).

10. United States v. Turning Bear, 357 F.3d 730, 733-734 (8th Cir. 2004) (foster care parent had "daily contact" with child for four to six months and knew him well enough to testify that he was untruthful); United States v. McMurray, 20 F.3d 831, 834 (8th Cir. 1994) (witness whom *M* persuaded to apply for credit card, leading to improper charges, had rational basis for opinion on *M*'s truthfulness).

11. United States v. Dotson, 799 F.2d 189, 192-194 (5th Cir. 1986) (agents who knew accused only through criminal investigations did not have adequate basis).

that it ought to convict the accused for the crime charged because he is an unsavory character.

One party may not introduce evidence of the untruthful character of another until the latter has testified.[12] When a party has testified, however, others may introduce such proof, and the prosecutor is not limited by the bar in FRE 404 against proving the character of the accused to establish conduct unless the accused has introduced proof of good character. Usually attacking the truthfulness of the accused involves cross-examining on prior convictions and bad acts, but calling character witnesses to give opinion or reputation testimony is equally proper.

Generally a character witness cannot show a witness is untruthful by testifying to specific acts. The Rule contemplates reputation and opinion testimony, and expressly forecloses "extrinsic evidence" of prior acts by the principal witness. But a character witness can testify to such acts (even on direct examination) if they have some other impeaching purpose, such as showing bias or contradicting the target witness.[13]

§6.24 —Cross- and Redirect Examination of Adverse Character Witness

Not surprisingly, an adverse character witness who is called to attack the credibility of another witness is herself subject to cross. The cross-examiner may travel all the roads of impeachment that are normally open, since a character witness is as subject to impeachment as any other. As a practical matter, probably the most effective questioning aims ostensibly at testing her knowledge or judgment by suggesting limitations in what she knows, or showing that her judgment is poor or that the negative impression created by her direct has been overplayed.

When the character witness testifies that a principal witness is an untruthful person, the one who cross-examines the character witness is usually the one who called the principal witness and is in any event someone who wants to support him. Here cross-examination of the adverse character witness may delve into specific conduct by the principal witness. The syntax of FRE 608(b)(2) is awkward, but in substance it says that "in the discretion of the court, cross-examination of a character witness who testified to the untruthful character of the principal witness may include inquiry into specific instances of conduct by the principal witness if probative of his truthfulness or untruthfulness."

Cross on specific conduct

The indicated conclusion is that the party challenging the adverse character witness (and trying to aid the target witness) may ask the character witness about instances of good conduct by the target witness

12. *See* United States v. Nace, 561 F.2d 763, 771 (9th Cir. 1977).
13. One witness may testify to acts by another if they shed light on the latter's bias or contradict something the latter has said in his testimony. *See* discussion of bias in §§6.19-6.20, *supra*, and discussion of contradiction in §§6.43-6.48, *infra*.

if they reflect favorably on his veracity. Theoretically the purpose is to test the knowledge and judgment of the character witness (or, in the case of a character witness who has conveyed the collective judgment of a community in the form of reputation testimony, the judgment of the community). As a practical matter, cross-examiners do not often pursue this course. One good reason is that testimony by a character witness who says "I think that fellow is not worthy of belief" (or "by reputation he is untruthful") probably cannot effectively be countered by cross-questions asking about honest things the other fellow did (or reputedly did). Another good reason is that taking this course might open up a broader area of inquiry on prior bad conduct by the target witness.

On this last point, there is some room for doubt. FRE 608(b) says such instances may be explored "on cross-examination" and does not say anything about redirect. Insofar as the purpose of the Rule is to avoid specifics, arguably that purpose is best served by letting the specifics come out only insofar as may be necessary to challenge the adverse character witness (which explains why the Rule allows inquiry into specifics only "on cross-examination"). But arguably it is unfair to leave the attacking party with a character witness whose own judgment or knowledge has been undercut by questions that portray the target witness in a favorable light, which would justify letting the attacking party who called the adverse character witness go into other bad conduct by the principal witness during redirect examination of the character witness. Probably redirect should not be permitted to go in this direction if the party who cross-examined the adverse character witness did not go into any instances of good conduct by the target witness.[1]

Not an independent way   One point should be made with emphasis: FRE 608 does not imply that cross-examining an adverse character witness is an independent way to establish the truthful disposition of the principal witness.[2] Apparently cross may delve into good acts by the principal witness, but any response by the character witness is "extrinsic evidence" of such conduct, which is not supposed to be evidence of truthfulness of the principal witness under FRE 608(b). The only legitimate purpose of the cross is to undercut the testimony already given by the adverse character witness.[3]

§6.24   1. The Rules envision two ways to repel an attack that suggests untruthfulness—favorable testimony by a character witness, and questioning the principal witness on instances of conduct that support veracity. *See* United States v. McNatt, 931 F.2d 251, 255 (4th Cir. 1991) (after defendant brought out that *P* thought detective *C* was untruthful and government showed on cross that *P* previously thought *C* truthful; defense could not then bring out, on redirect, "what had changed [*P*'s] mind" about *C*; cross-examiner may ask character witness about specific conduct by the target, but one who calls character witness may not).

2. United States v. Edwards, 549 F.2d 362, 367-368 (5th Cir. 1977) (where defense called witnesses to testify to bad character of government witnesses, defendant could not inquire on direct and redirect on specific acts by government witnesses), *cert. denied*, 434 U.S. 828.

3. The most useful and influential opinion on cross-examining character witnesses remains Michelson v. United States, 335 U.S. 469 (1948). But *Michelson* involved a favorable character witness rather than one who was adverse. *See* §6.51, *infra. And see*

§6.25   Asking About Nonconviction Misconduct— In General

The second way to show that a witness is by character or disposition untruthful is to ask him about prior acts that bear on the point. Simply testifying puts veracity in issue, thus paving the way for questions on behavior shedding light on truthfulness. Usually cross-examination is the means (extrinsic evidence is barred), and leading, pointed, accusatory questions are proper.

At the heart of this kind of impeachment is an almost imponderable question. What kinds of acts bear on truthfulness? Not surprisingly, it seems possible to describe wide and more focused views and even to define a kind of middle view. The broad view is that virtually any conduct indicating bad character also indicates untruthfulness, including (for instance) robbery and assault. The more focused view is that behavior bears on veracity only if it actually involves falsehood or deception, so forgery or perjury count but not other behavior such as robbery and assault. The middle view is that behavior seeking personal advantage by taking from others in violation of their rights reflects on veracity (along with falsehood and deception), so theft in many forms qualifies but not "personal" crimes involving, for instance, violence or drugs. The central difficulties in the broad view are that it opens up the whole life of the witness to probing, that no witness would be immune from embarrassment and abuse, and that the indirect inferences on which the veracity argument depends are too weak to justify this approach. Both the middle view and the more focused view take these difficulties seriously. Clearly the middle and the more focused views insist on closer links between conduct and veracity.

Acts bearing on truthfulness

Three points are clear: First, FRE 608 and modern cases reject the broad view. Second, the cases approve questioning on falsehood and deception that satisfy the more focused view. Third, there is some support for the middle ground—for the view that the cross-examiner should be able to ask not only questions about misdeeds involving actual falsehood and deception, but also questions about acts in which the witness seeks to obtain personal advantage by depriving others of their rights. Of course the language of FRE 608 can be read to support the more focused view (it refers only to behavior bearing on "untruthfulness"), but this reading seems uncertain because everyone agrees that truthfulness is the issue and the question is whether conduct embraced by the middle and broader views bears on truthfulness.[1] The ACN rejects the broad view (purpose of FRE 608 was to focus on "veracity" rather than "character generally"),

Trend toward middle view

United States v. Whiting, 28 F.3d 1296, 1301 (1st Cir. 1994) (cross-examination of adverse character witness on instances of good conduct by target witness; proper to test character witness), *cert. denied*, 513 U.S. 956, 994, 1009.

§6.25   1. It would be easy to endorse the middle view by including a reference to "honesty," as some other codes do. *See* Uniform Rules of Evidence, Rules 20-22 (1953); Cal. Ev. Code §§780-788.

but has nothing to say about the middle view. Using convictions to prove untruthfulness presents a parallel issue (what kinds of convictions bear on veracity?), but FRE 609 provides almost no help.[2]

A few decisions address the larger issue,[3] but most confine analysis to the specific conduct raised by questioning in the case. Modern decisions approve questions that satisfy the focused view, including inquiry into nonfrivolous falsehoods[4] such as using false identification[5] and making false statements on affidavits, applications,[6] or government forms[7] like tax returns.[8] They also approve questions about giving false testimony,[9] engaging in corrupt or exploitive behavior involving concealment or deception,[10] cheating other people,[11] and deceiving or defrauding others.[12] Under some circumstances it seems wise to allow questions that would not be embraced by the more focused view but would pass

2. That Rule straddles all three views by allowing questions on serious crimes. Yet it seems closer to the middle view because (for minor offenses) it limits questioning to crimes involving "false statement" or "dishonesty." But modern decisions generally exclude theft convictions from the latter category and come close to reading dishonesty out of the Rule. *See* §§632-633, *infra*.

3. United States v. Miles, 207 F.3d 988, 993 (7th Cir. 2000) (behavior seeking personal advantage by taking from others in violation of rights reflects on veracity); United States v. Manske, 186 F.3d 770, 774-775 (7th Cir. 1999) ("our approach has been closer to the middle view" described in text; defense could ask whether witness threatened violence against witnesses in unrelated case to dissuade them from testifying truthfully); Varhol v. National R. Passenger Corp., 909 F.2d 1537, 1566-1567 (7th Cir. 1990) (stealing and receiving stolen goods reflect adversely on honesty; connection with credibility is close enough).

4. United States v. Sherlin, 67 F.3d 1208, 1214-1215 (6th Cir. 1995) (false statements to investigators denying knowledge of fires), *cert. denied*, 516 U.S. 1082, 1158; United States v. Farias-Farias, 925 F.2d 805, 809-810 (5th Cir. 1991) (not telling whole truth at border station).

5. United States v. Mansaw, 714 F.2d 785, 789 (8th Cir. 1983) (use of false names or false identities), *cert. denied*, 464 U.S. 986; United States v. Reid, 634 F.2d 469, 473-474 (9th Cir. 1980) (falsifying name, occupation, name of business, and purpose in letter seeking information from government), *cert. denied*, 454 U.S. 829.

6. United States v. Redditt, 381 F.3d 597, 602 (7th Cir. 2004) (employment application on which defendant omitted 1992 conviction for stealing electricity); Walters v. Monarch Life Ins. Co., 57 F.3d 899, 904-905 (10th Cir. 1995) (false statement on verified petition on income).

7. United States v. Whitmore, 359 F.3d 609, 619-620 (D.C. Cir. 2004) (police officer's failure to report suspension of drivers license) (reversing); United States v. Thiongo, 344 F.3d 55, 60 (1st Cir. 2003) (signing legal document attesting marriage entered for purpose of evading immigration laws).

8. *See* United States v. Jensen, 41 F.3d 946, 957 (5th Cir. 1994).

9. United States v. Bagaric, 706 F.2d 42, 64-65 (2d Cir. 1990), *cert. denied*, 464 U.S. 840; United States v. Terry, 702 F.2d 299, 316 (2d Cir. 1983), *cert. denied*, 461 U.S. 931.

10. United States v. Tomblin, 46 F.3d 1369, 1389 (5th Cir. 1995) (bribery); United States v. Girdner, 773 F.2d 257, 260-261 (10th Cir. 1985) (ballot fraud).

11. Navarro de Cosme v. Hospital Pavia, 922 F.2d 926, 932-933 (1st Cir. 1991) (inflated invoice for expert witness fees); Varhol v. National R. Passenger Corp., 909 F.2d 1537, 1566-1567 (7th Cir. 1990) (being suspended for purchase and use of stolen commuter tickets).

12. United States v. Simonelli, 237 F.3d 19, 23 (1st Cir. 2001) (altering time cards, inflating bills, stealing records); United States v. Gay, 967 F.2d 322, 327-328 (9th Cir. 1992) (fraudulent marketing).

muster under the middle view, and there appears to be a trend in this direction—toward approving questions on acts better described as dishonest than false. When the query is specific and well-founded, the cross-examiner should be allowed to ask about theft accomplished by stealth[13] as well as failing to make required disclosures or reports,[14] concealing or frightening off witnesses or suborning perjury (even in unrelated cases),[15] and other behavior amounting to a sharp and dishonest practice (unlawful or close to the line).[16]

Theft in all its forms is not always an appropriate subject for inquiry. It is doubtful, for instance, that involvement in robbery (where forced taking is the main fact) has much bearing on veracity, and questioning on such a matter seems improper.[17] For a somewhat different reason, questioning about minor pilfering or stealing should be carefully watched. It is probably true that virtually everyone has done something of this sort in a lifetime, and tarring every witness with broadbrush questions on such points would be intrusive, demeaning, distracting, and more likely to produce heat and resentment than probative facts. (Ironically, such questioning may generate more honest responses among witnesses who feel duty-bound by the oath to own up to some failings.) Hence dragnet questions on theft (did you ever steal anything at work?) should not be allowed. But specific and well-founded questions on nontrivial thefts involving stealth should be allowed. The cases give mixed signals.[18]

If all that can be said about behavior is that it might be called improper, immoral, or unlawful (qualities that bring it within the broader view), asking about it cannot be justified under FRE 608.[19]

---

13. Varhol v. National R. Passenger Corp., 909 F.2d 1537, 1566-1567 (7th Cir. 1990) (buying and using stolen commuter tickets); United States v. Girdner, 773 F.2d 257, 260-261 (10th Cir. 1985) (stealing voter registration forms).

14. Navarro de Cosme v. Hospital Pavia, 922 F.2d 926, 932-933 (1st Cir. 1991) (failing to submit required reports); United States v. O'Malley, 707 F.2d 1240, 1249 (11th Cir. 1983) (failing to report contributions).

15. United States v. Dawson, 434 F.3d 956, 957-959 (7th Cir. 2006) (lying in hearings); United States v. Zidell, 323 F.3d 412, 426 (6th Cir. 2003) (attempting to secure perjured testimony).

16. *See* United States v. Irizarry, 341 F.3d 273, 311-312 (3d Cir. 2003) (why defendant had driver's license and social security card in name of another, why he had "blank social security cards"); United States v. Sanders, 343 F.3d 511, 518-519 (5th Cir. 2003) (reneging on agreement with real estate agent, by obtaining partial refund of commission but never buying property, which indicated fraud and cheating).

17. Ellison v. State, 123 S.W.3d 874, 875 (Ark. 2003) (cannot ask about burglary not resulting in conviction); State v. Quiroz, 757 A.2d 464, 468 (Vt. 2000) (theft not probative of truthfulness, but lying about it is). *But see* Shumpert v. State, 935 So.2d 962, 971 (Miss. 2006) (allowing questions on theft).

18. *Compare* State v. Bashaw, 785 A.2d 897, 899 (N.H. 2001) (defense could not ask assault victim if he stole police badge; unrelated to veracity) *with* United States v. Smith, 80 F.3d 1188, 1193 (7th Cir. 1996) (allowing questions about theft and receiving stolen property).

19. Examples of questions found to be improper: State v. Drummond, 854 N.E.2d 1038, 1060 (Ohio 2006) (trafficking in marijuana); State v. Mayhorn, 720 N.W.2d 776, 789 (Minn. 2006) (adultery; involvement in more than one romantic relationship);

The cases seem entirely right to condemn questioning on use of drugs or alcohol, trafficking in drugs, violence against others, connections to vice or criminal enterprises, consumer, commercial or financial defaults, and less-than-honorable discharges from the armed services. They are also on strong ground when they disapprove questions about sexual relationships or inclinations, prostitution, and bearing illegitimate children. On such subjects the result indicated generally by FRE 608 is sometimes also required in sexual assault prosecutions by FRE 412, which bars most evidence of past sexual behavior of complainants in that setting.

Failure to register, obtain permit

Whether to allow questioning on the failure of a witness to comply with a legal requirement to register, file, or obtain a permit is truly hard to answer. If, for instance, one fails to get a building or a gun permit or driver's license but still engages in the activity covered by such requirements, is such behavior "dishonest" or "false" for purposes of appraising truthfulness? Surely such misconduct reflects on veracity in this sense *only* if the person knew of the requirement and knowingly ignored it, but even then an adverse inference on veracity is less than compelling. Arguably the inference becomes stronger if, for example, a person complies with such a requirement over some period but then selectively avoids compliance, as might happen if a builder routinely builds the cost of permits into his bids, but then selectively omits this element in certain bids in order to reduce the price, or if a taxpayer files state and federal returns over some period but then stops filing one or the other in order to reduce costs or liability. Perhaps the most that can be said is that usually inferences relating to veracity are speculative so questioning on such points should be disallowed, but under special circumstances an inference on veracity may become plausible and such questioning could be proper.[20]

Arrests, charges

Questions about being arrested, charged, or indicted are improper for the obvious reason that such facts are poor and unreliable proxies for the important point, which is behavior by the witness that bears on truthfulness,[21] and it is both easy and proper for the questioner to ask directly about the behavior itself.[22] Probably the mere fact of arrest

---

United States v. Novaton, 271 F.3d 968, 1006-1007 (11th Cir. 2001) (whether detective was involved in scandal leading to reprimand for failing to document conversation); United States v. Meserve, 271 F.3d 314, 322-323, 327-329 (1st Cir. 2001) (whether defense witness was a "tough guy" who got into "lots of fights"); Bonilla v. Yamaha Motors Corp., 955 F.2d 150, 154-155 (1st Cir. 1992) (getting fined for speeding).

20. United States v. Miles, 207 F.3d 933, 988 (7th Cir. 2000) (blocking questions on failing to register gun pursuant to local ordinance, which did not necessarily involve deceit, dishonesty, or deceptive intent) (witness carried valid state registration; failing to register with city may have been oversight).

21. Michelson v. United States, 335 U.S. 469, 482 (1948) (arrest without more "does not, in law any more than in reason," impeach integrity or impair credibility because it happens to "the innocent as well as the guilty"); Commonwealth v. Chmiel, 889 A.2d 501, 534 (Pa. 2005) (veracity may not be impeached by arrests not leading to conviction). Such questions can sometimes contradict testimony by one who claims not to have been arrested. *See* §6.44, *infra.*

22. United States v. Amahia, 825 F.2d 177, 180-181 (8th Cir. 1987) (can ask about acts leading to arrest for crimes of falsehood).

provides a reasonable basis to ask whether the witness did the deed, at least in the absence of some further indication that the arrest was a mistake or abuse of some kind.

§6.26   —Limits and Safeguards

In an important case the Supreme Court recognized that character may be impugned simply by putting questions on specific behavior, since a string of denials may leave a witness effectively impeached.[1] Particularly if he is a party, and perhaps especially if he is a criminal defendant, asking about misconduct for purposes of suggesting untruthful disposition is proper only if the questioner has a reasonable basis for the inquiry. On request by a party interested in protecting the witness (and probably on its own initiative if no request is forthcoming), the court should ask the questioner outside the jury's hearing to explain, requiring a reasonable or good-faith basis to think the conduct occurred (a notion very close to probable cause).[2]

Questions must have basis

Parties may make motions in limine requesting a decision to prevent (or allow) questioning on particular conduct under FRE 608(b), and this mechanism represents the most promising means for resolving the common question whether probative value of the impeaching attack is substantially outweighed by the danger of unfair prejudice or the risks of confusing the issues or misleading the jury. The trial court, however, may decline to rule in advance and may prefer to leave the matter to resolution when and if the issue arises at trial.[3] The disposition of such motions may be critically important to parties, but judges are reluctant to decide them in advance because they have not seen the trial unfold and do not have a full context in which to weigh probative worth against prejudice. In federal courts, a party who does not testify probably cannot claim error in a pretrial ruling that would allow such questioning.[4] The Supreme Court took this view in the related setting of pretrial motions seeking to exclude convictions under FRE 609.[5] States remain free to reject this approach in their own courts.

---

§6.26   1. Michelson v. United States, 335 U.S. 469, 481 (1948) (judge ascertains that arrests really happened before defense character witness is asked about them, so groundless question will not "waft an unwarranted innuendo into the jury box").

2. United States v. Whitmore, 359 F.3d 609, 619-620 (D.C. Cir. 2004) (reasonable basis required); State v. Fallin, 540 N.W.2d 518, 521 (Minn. 1995) (must back up questions about bad acts with admissible evidence); United States v. Schwab, 886 F.2d 509, 513-514 (2d Cir. 1989) (questions on criminal acts should go forward outside jury's hearing first), *cert. denied*, 493 U.S. 1080.

3. United States v. Daniele, 886 F.2d 1046, 1054 (8th Cir. 1989) (can delay ruling on government motion seeking permission to ask defendant about lies to IRS).

4. *See* United States v. Sanderson, 966 F.2d 184, 189-190 (6th Cir. 1992).

5. *See* Luce v. United States, 469 U.S. 38 (1984) (after rulings in limine paving the way for impeachment by convictions under FRE 609 if the accused testifies, he has no ground for appeal if he does not testify and the evidence is never admitted). For a critique of the *Luce* doctrine, *see* the discussion of FRE 609 in §6.35, *infra*. *See also* the discussion of FRE 103 in §1.6, *supra*.

Thoughtful state authority holds that a prosecutor may not cross-examine criminal defendants on nonconviction misconduct unless the prosecutor provides notice to the defense.[6] Taking this step makes sense because nonconviction misconduct is less likely to be known or anticipated when defendant must decide whether to take the stand. If the notice is given by pretrial motion, the court can take the necessary precautions to insure that questions have an adequate basis in fact. And a pretrial motion would also help the court assess prejudice and probative worth, although the pretrial setting is sometimes not ideally suited to this purpose.

In any attempt to show untruthfulness by questioning a witness on conduct, relevancy is affected by remoteness. In a related context, the Court once approved questions on conduct 27 years before trial, but this example is extreme. Court can and should disallow questions for remoteness when events occurred more recently. Passage of time quickly erodes relevancy and increases relative risk of prejudice, which trial judges may consider under FRE 403 and 611.[7]

Courts have discretion

More generally, courts have discretion under FRE 403 to allow or block questioning on behavior relating to veracity (FRE 608(b) puts the matter in "the discretion of the court"). The need for care in appraising probative worth against prejudice seems acute because there is seldom much certainty that nonconviction misconduct actually occurred. The major concerns are to protect parties from prejudice, witnesses from harassment and undue embarrassment, juries from being confused and misled, and all concerned (court, jury, parties) from trials unnecessarily prolonged.[8]

The risk to a testifying party is obvious, for behavior suggesting untruthfulness presents an unfavorable picture likely to incline a jury against that party. And if the behavior is similar to whatever acts are alleged, it invites the unattractive and disapproved propensity inference and may lead to convicting defendant as a bad person. Here especially, courts have good reason to bar questioning on acts having little probative worth on veracity but high potential for misuse,[9] although acts resembling the charged crime may be provable under

6. State v. Fallin, 540 N.W.2d 518, 521 (Minn. 1995) (may not cross-examine defendant or defense witness about misconduct without pretrial notice, providing evidentiary basis for questions and showing probative worth outweighs prejudice).

7. Michelson v. United States, 335 U.S. 469, 484 (1948) (examining character witness who said defendant was honest; purpose was to test knowledge and judgment). But see United States v. Stoecker, 215 F.3d 788, 790 (7th Cir. 2000) (improper to question realtor about facts leading to loss of license 15 years previously) ("far too remote" to be probative); Itin v. Ungar, 17 P.3d 129, 136 (Colo. 2000) (blocking questions on 30-year-old sanction, in part because it was "too remote").

8. Coverdale v. State, 844 A.2d 979, 980 (Del. 2004) (consider whether testimony of witness being attacked is crucial, logical relevance of conduct in question, danger of prejudice and confusion of issues).

9. United States v. Pintar, 630 F.2d 1270, 1285-1286 (8th Cir. 1980) (error to let government ask defendant about possible kickback payments; probative value questionable; tactic subverted FRE 404).

FRE 404(b) to show intent and similar points even if they have little bearing on veracity.[10]

While witnesses enjoy no privilege to be shielded from questions that harass or embarrass, common decency suggests they should have some protection against outrageous or embarrassing forays into their past behavior, and FRE 611 directs courts to consider those concerns.[11] Modern rape shield statutes address this problem in a narrow setting, and withholding protection in other settings would add to public cynicism about the legal process, discourage cooperation on which fact-finding depends, and cast courts in a bad light.

§6.27 —Extrinsic Evidence Excluded

Extrinsic evidence of acts by a witness that did not result in conviction is not admissible under FRE 608(b) as a way of showing untruthful disposition, or "character for truthfulness" (to use the words of the Rule itself).[1] In this way, the Rule gives meaning to the old maxim that the cross-examiner must "take the answer of the witness" when it comes to nonconviction misconduct.

This principle serves several useful purposes. It helps maintain the focus on substance and matters bearing immediately on credibility by keeping trials from being sidetracked. It reduces surprise that might unfairly confront the calling party if he were faced with unexpected proof requiring rebuttal witnesses, as would happen if evidence beyond the answer of the witness were allowed. And it reduces the prejudice that comes with opening the subject of behavior bearing on truthfulness, since it is likely to be comprised of acts that are bad or unattractive, and juries are likely to misuse the evidence, especially if the witness is a party. Limiting the inquiry also protects witnesses, since their conduct is only open to inquiry while they testify, which benefits parties who testify as well as nonparty witnesses. In addition, the limit finds practical justification in the fact that merely putting questions about misconduct may effectively warn the jury (rightly or wrongly) to entertain doubt on veracity, and the rhetorical impact can be countered or dealt with by lawyerly argumentation at close of trial.

---

10. United States v. Williams, 684 F.2d 296, 300-301 (4th Cir. 1982) (asking defendant whether he was involved in sexual assault was proper under FRE 404(b) even if not under FRE 608).

11. United States v. Bright, 630 F.2d 765, 766-767 (5th Cir. 1980) (cutting off questioning designed to suggest witness had affair with FBI agent); United States v. Kizer, 569 F.2d 504, 505 (9th Cir. 1978) (may limit cross where Sixth Amendment interest outweighed by danger of harassing witnesses or prejudicing jury), *cert. denied*, 435 U.S. 976.

§6.27 1. Prior to amendment in 2002, FRE 608(b) barred extrinsic evidence of specific instances to attack or support "credibility." The amendment substituted "character for truthfulness" in place of "credibility," making the original intent clearer: The bar on extrinsic evidence applies only to efforts to show untruthful disposition, not to other impeaching efforts, like contradicting the witness or showing bias. *See* discussion in §6.28, *infra*.

Testimony barred

In its main and most obvious application, this principle bars testimony by one witness describing behavior by another when the claim to relevance is that it shows the latter's untruthfulness.[2] Using a term surviving from common law tradition, it is often said that extrinsic evidence of conduct showing untruthfulness is merely collateral. It is of course true that the cross-examiner need not take the first answer given. The very idea of cross implies testing and probing, and the questioner is entitled to a chance to expose weakness or falsehood in testimony and awaken the conscience of the witness, perhaps in the end getting at truth that a witness seeks to avoid in the beginning. In short, the cross-examiner should have some chance to overcome an initial denial, and only after trying must he take the answer he gets.[3]

Physical evidence barred

Properly understood, FRE 608(b) also bars physical evidence offered to show a witness is untruthful.[4] But questioning that suggests untruthfulness often focuses on statements in documents relating to or describing conduct by the witness, and some decisions allow use of such documents that seems to violate the bar, approving or finding no error in reading from and even formally admitting them if the witness admits the relevant connection,[5] although some courts go the other way.[6] Letting the attacking party offer documents is likely to sidetrack proceedings and invite further examination and explanation. When the witness denies the connection, admitting the documents violates the Rule and invites reversal if the error is serious.[7]

Where the witness did something dishonest by way of a false written or oral statement, the cross-examiner may use and refer to the statement or writing in putting questions.[8] Referring to its substance during questioning, and even indicating that the questioner has a writing that

---

2. United States v. Abel, 469 U.S. 45 (1984) (cross-examiner may ask about conduct, but inquiry is limited to cross; no extrinsic evidence); Ellsworth v. Warden, 333 F.3d 1, 8 (1st Cir. 2003) (excluding testimony that complaining witness falsely accused boys of peeking at him in shower and toilet and stealing toys, as "classic" collateral evidence barred by FRE 608).

3. *See* Carter v. Hewitt, 617 F.2d 961, 969-973 (3d Cir. 1980) (need not take first answer); United States v. Ling, 581 F.2d 1118, 1121 (4th Cir. 1978) (may "continue to press" for an admission).

4. United States v. Pope, 132 F.3d 684, 688 (11th Cir. 1998) (excluding warrants; specific instances may not be shown by extrinsic evidence); United States v. Aponte, 31 F.3d 86, 87-88 (2d Cir. 1994) (documents are barred as extrinsic evidence).

5. *See* United States v. Drake, 932 F.2d 861, 866-867 (10th Cir. 1991) (defendant said he had psychology degree; questions referring to school record were not extrinsic evidence); United States v. Archer, 733 F.2d 354, 361 (5th Cir. 1984) (approving use of bank statement reflecting involvement of witness in check kiting; bar applies only when she "denies" misconduct), *cert. denied*, 469 U.S. 862.

6. United States v. Whitehead, 618 F.2d 523, 528-529 (4th Cir. 1980) (can impeach defendant by questions on suspension from law practice; error to rule that if he testified on suspension, document could be introduced).

7. United States v. Martz, 964 F.2d 787, 789 (8th Cir. 1992) (rejecting defense claim of entitlement to introduce document during cross).

8. United States v. Jackson, 882 F.2d 1444, 1448-1449 (9th Cir. 1989); United States v. Cole, 617 F.2d 151, 154 n.3 (5th Cir. 1980); Lewis v. Baker, 526 F.2d 470, 475 (2d Cir. 1975).

embodies the statement (or could produce a witness) should not run afoul of the restriction. The purpose, after all, is not to confine the questioner to a query that leaves the trier with no sense for the reason or basis. Rather, the purpose is to cut out collateral issues and prevent waste of time, and this purpose can be served by preventing the attacking party from calling additional witnesses or offering additional evidence.

§6.28   —Extrinsic Evidence Admitted for Some Purposes

Extrinsic evidence of nonconviction misconduct by a witness that may reflect untruthful disposition is not invariably excludable, even when offered solely on credibility issues. The reason is that nonconviction misconduct may tend to impeach in ways that do not require or invite any inference about the truthful or untruthful disposition.[1] Of course FRE 608(b) says it is alright to ask about such misconduct (the answer is not extrinsic evidence), and in three common situations this provision does not bar other evidence—extrinsic proof in the form of testimony by others or documents or physical exhibits—that shows nonconviction misconduct:

First, extrinsic evidence of misconduct is often admitted to show bias, interest, or influence,[2] or sometimes hostility or animus toward a party.[3] Sometimes such evidence even tends to show absence of bias or corruption.[4] And evidence of conduct by a witness may be admitted if it tends to show mental or sensory incapacity,[5] or shows a prior statement inconsistent with trial testimony.[6] These uses do not offend

Showing bias

---

§6.28   1. As amended in 2002, FRE 608(b) bars extrinsic proof of specific acts when offered to attack or support "character for truthfulness," displacing the broader term "credibility." The intent of the amendment was to make clear the original intent that the bar applies *only* to impeaching attacks that go to character, and not to the other impeaching attacks described above.

2. United States v. Abel, 469 U.S. 45 (1984) (testimony by one witness describing another's membership in secret prison group requiring members to commit perjury was not barred by FRE 608; it showed bias); Hall v. State, 109 P.3d 499 (Wyo. 2005) (extrinsic evidence of misconduct can impeach in ways described in text above) (quoting authors of this Treatise); Baumann v. State, 891 A.2d 146, 148 (Del. 2005) (extrinsic evidence of acts can show bias or motive; Rule 608 governs only character).

3. Lewy v. Southern Pac. Transp. Co., 799 F.2d 1281, 1298-1299 (9th Cir. 1986) (showing plaintiff and witness Brown had hostile relationship and she might therefore slant testimony).

4. United States v. Brown, 547 F.2d 438, 445 (8th Cir. 1997) (evidence that defendant policeman did not report data in arrest of prosecution witness was admissible to disprove claim that witness was hostile because of arrest), *cert. denied*, 430 U.S. 937.

5. United States v. Lindstrom, 698 F.2d 1154, 1159-1164 & n.6 (11th Cir. 1983) (FRE 608(b) did not control because impeachment went to mental capacity rather than moral qualities).

6. Kaasuri v. St. Elizabeth Hosp. Medical Ctr., 897 F.2d 845, 854 (6th Cir. 1990) (FRE 608(b) relates to acts undercutting credibility; deposition did not prove acts, but showed inconsistent statement).

FRE 608(b) because the purpose is not to show untruthful disposition but to show a motive or reason to slant testimony, or mental or sensory defect, or change in story. When arguments of these sorts are so attenuated as to be unconvincing and the impeaching evidence amounts to misconduct that undermines character, courts sometimes cite FRE 608 as a reason to exclude the evidence.

Testing character witness   Second, when a character witness repairs credibility by testifying that the principal witness is generally truthful, questioning on cross (and perhaps even redirect) may touch on conduct by the principal witness. For the cross-examiner, the purpose is to suggest that the character witness lacks knowledge or judgment: If he does not know about misconduct by the person whose veracity he attests, he lacks knowledge; if he does know about it and maintains a good opinion of veracity anyway, his judgment is suspect.[7]

Contradict   Third, past misconduct may often be used to contradict testimony by a witness describing a blameless life or claiming innocence of particular misdeeds. Contradiction may proceed by cross-examination or extrinsic evidence, and FRE 608(b) has no general application (it regulates only impeachment by showing untruthful disposition) although the Rule does have some limited effect: It forces the cross-examiner to "take the answer of the witness" after asking about behavior bearing on credibility only by suggesting untruthful disposition, so the questioner who gets a denial in this situation cannot contradict the denial by extrinsic evidence. And it does embody a preference against being sidetracked on elaborate collateral inquiries into behavior by witnesses, thus indicating low tolerance for thin excuses for evidence of behavior that contradicts only by elaborate and attenuated inference. But these points apart, FRE 608(b) simply does not regulate contradiction.[8] Losing sight of the focus of FRE 608(b), some courts mistakenly assume or imply that it imposes a more general restriction on impeachment by contradiction, and in this respect these decisions are unsound.

FRE 609(a)

(a) **General rule.** For the purpose of attacking the credibility of a witness, (1) evidence that a witness other than an accused has been convicted of a crime shall be admitted, subject to Rule 403, if the crime was punishable by death or imprisonment in excess of one year under the law under which the witness was convicted, and evidence that an accused has been convicted of such a crime shall be admitted if the court determines that the probative value of

---

7. For the party who calls the supporting character witness, questioning on redirect might raise good conduct by the principal witness, but it is not so clear that this avenue is open. *See* §6.51, *infra*.

8. United States v. Hinkson, 526 F.3d 1262, 1282-1283 (9th Cir. 2008) (FRE 608 does not bar "evidence contradicting a witness's statement"); Sweet v. Pace Membership Warehouse, Inc., 795 A.2d 524, 528 (R.I. 2002) (videotape showing plaintiff engaging in strenuous activity was admissible to contradict testimony on disability; FRE 608 did not bar this evidence).

admitting this evidence outweighs its prejudicial effect to the accused; and (2) evidence that any witness has been convicted of a crime shall be admitted regardless of the punishment, if it readily can be determined that establishing the elements of the crime required proof of or an admission of an act involved dishonesty or false statement by the witness.

§6.29 Showing Convictions—In General

Another way to show that a witness is by disposition untruthful is to ask about his record. Typically this form of attack proceeds on cross-examination, but the attacking party is not limited to this approach. If the calling party thinks another will ask about prior convictions, it is proper to blunt or deflate the expected impact by bringing out the pertinent facts immediately (typically on direct).[1] It is *not* alright, however, for the calling party to bring out the absence of convictions on direct, which amounts to supporting a witness before he has been attacked, nor should prosecutors ask their own witnesses about convictions relating to present charges as a way of suggesting that defendant must be guilty too.[2]

Clearly the questioner needs a basis for asking about convictions. The ready availability of public records reflecting convictions coupled with the substantial risk of misstep if a lawyer "wings it" by relying on memory in putting questions about convictions lend strong support to the practice of requiring the questioner to have a reliable record at hand.[3] The fact that the accused has not "put his character in issue" by introducing evidence of his own good character does not prevent questions on convictions if he testifies.[4]

It seems that a defendant should not be impeached by a conviction for acts that are part of the same transaction as the offense generating present charges, but courts are split on this point.[5] Admittedly the text of the Rule does not appear to impose this limit, but the underlying

§6.29 1. *See* United States v. Handly, 591 F.2d 1125, 1128 n.1 (5th Cir. 1979); United States v. Medical Therapy Sciences, Inc., 583 F.2d 36, 39 (2d Cir. 1978). *See also* ACN to 1990 amendment of FRE 609 (endorsing this practice).

2. *See* United States v. Hicks, 748 F.2d 854, 859 (4th Cir. 1984) (error to let government show on direct that witness had no record); United States v. Dougherty, 810 F.2d 763, 767-768 (8th Cir. 1987) (error for prosecutor to mention in opening that government witness had been convicted of related offense).

3. Wilson v. Attaway, 757 F.2d 1227, 1244 (11th Cir. 1985) (certified copy of conviction not required); United States v. Georgalis, 631 F.2d 1199, 1203 n.3 (5th Cir. 1980) (rap sheet).

4. United States v. Blackshear, 568 F.2d 1120, 1121 (5th Cir. 1978).

5. *Compare* United States v. Breckenridge, 782 F.2d 1317, 1323 (5th Cir. 1986) (conviction may have arisen "out of the same facts," but court kept government from saying so), *cert. denied*, 479 U.S. 837, *with* United States v. Burkhead, 646 F.2d 1283, 1285-1286 (8th Cir. 1981) (court should have excluded convictions arising on substantive counts underlying present conspiracy trial), *cert. denied*, 454 U.S. 898.

assumption of the framers was that defendants would be impeached by prior misconduct. At the very least a factual overlap between prior and present charges suggests that the risk of prejudice is vastly increased, which is a relevant and important fact for ordinary felony convictions offered under the first prong. It is clearly permissible to impeach a defendant by convictions occurring after the charged offense (even if the underlying acts occurred after the acts leading to present charges).[6]

Problems of relevancy Few areas have proved more difficult than impeachment by convictions, particularly for criminal defendants who testify.[7] There are problems of relevancy because there are widely disparate views on the kinds of convictions that bear on truthfulness. Common sense suggests that convictions for crimes involving deliberate false statement are most probative (perjury, fraud, forgery, and embezzlement), and the view that these crimes are relevant finds expression in Rule 609(a)(2). A broader notion of relevancy embraces crimes suggesting dishonesty, such as various kinds of theft. An even broader view holds that all crimes imply disregard for social obligations, hence a willingness or propensity to lie, or at least that serious crimes do so, like crimes of "moral turpitude," felonies, or crimes that are "infamous."

Humiliation, prejudice Assuming agreement on relevancy, the question of admissibility raises additional concerns: For a nonparty witness, convictions might be excluded to spare him from embarrassment or humiliation. Where the witness is the complainant in a criminal case, excluding convictions would forestall acquittal of the defendant on the improper ground that the victim "had it coming." For a witness who is a party, convictions might be excluded to prevent the jury from being disaffected from his cause. Where the party is the accused, jury disaffection might lead to conviction because the accused is a "bad person" or his convictions demonstrate criminal propensity, leading to the conclusion that he committed the crime charged. Such prejudicial inferences are of course wholly improper.

Whether to testify Any decision by an accused with past convictions to testify or not is very much affected by the risks that come with questioning on convictions, and the risks are real: Empirical evidence suggests that juries do not follow instructions to confine consideration of convictions to veracity.[8] But the need to take the stand is real too: Empirical evidence also

---

6. United States v. Bogers, 635 F.2d 749, 750 (8th Cir. 1980); United States v. Bennett, 539 F.2d 45, 54-55 (10th Cir. 1976), *cert. denied*, 429 U.S. 925.

7. *See* Spector, Impeachment Through Past Convictions: A Time for Reform, 18 De Paul L. Rev. 1, 3-8 (1968), and Impeaching the Defendant by His Prior Convictions and the Proposed Federal Rule of Evidence: A Half Step Forward and Three Steps Backward, 1 Loyola U. L.J. 247, 249-251 (1970).

8. *See* Spector, Commentary Rule 609: A Last Plea for Its Withdrawal, 32 Okla. L. Rev. 334, 351-353 (1979) (limiting instructions fail; psychological studies and theories indicate that one who gets specific information about another "will tend to draw a complete picture" of the other); Note, To Take the Stand or Not to Take the Stand: The Dilemma of the Defendant with a Criminal Record, 4 Colum. J. L. & Soc. Prob. 215, 218 (1968) (98 percent of attorneys and 43 percent of judges thought juries could not follow

suggests that juries more often convict those who do not testify than those who do, and the decision is made more difficult by the fact that courts are not always willing to rule in advance, and there is no way to test the point except by testifying and risking conviction. In the end, the accused makes a Hobson's choice in partial ignorance—testify and risk an adverse ruling that allows prior convictions or not testify and risk conviction because the testimony is not heard, and maybe because the jury infers guilt from silence.[9]

Similar risks intrude on the decision of the accused to call or not to call character witnesses. Under standard practice, witnesses who attest the good character of the accused under FRE 404 and 405 (some evidence of innocence) or FRE 608 (some evidence of truthfulness) may be cross-examined on specific misconduct by the accused, including that shown by convictions, for the purpose of assessing the knowledge and judgment of the character witness.[10] Here too the risk is real that the jury will consider prior convictions mentioned in questions for other impermissible purposes.

In the case of the accused as a witness, convictions should not be admissible to impeach, for the reason put forth by many writers, including Professor Friedman in an important article: Most people would at least stretch the truth, if not lie, to avoid going to jail, and juries are likely to understand this point. Hence proving convictions adds little or nothing to any their assessment of the veracity of a defendant on the stand. Juries are prepared to discount self-serving testimony, and by comparison the prejudicial effect of learning that the accused has been convicted before is trivial.[11] Against this major reality, the single reason to admit prior convictions of a criminal defendant (the veracity of all witnesses should be subject to scrutiny) seems puny, especially in view of the lingering suspicion that particular acts of untruthfulness have but modest bearing on the question of truthfulness on other occasions.[12]

Veracity important

These considerations suggest five different approaches, most of which find at least some support in various state codes or rules: One would admit all convictions to impeach, which is an easy rule to apply but cannot be squared with FRE 609. Another would separate convictions that bear on veracity from those that do not, on the basis of the

---

limiting instruction). *See also* Kalven & Zeisel, The American Jury 160 (1966) (suggesting disparity between acquittal rate for defendants with and without prior records of between 2 percent and 27 percent, but acknowledging methodological difficulties).

9. Sometimes courts rule before trial, on a motion in limine brought by prosecution or defense, either that convictions may be used to impeach if the defendant testifies or that they may not, which provides some certainty for defendants who are in a quandary about testifying. *See* the discussion in §6.35, *infra*.

10. *See* §§4.12, *supra*, and 6.51, *infra*.

11. *See* Richard D. Friedman, Character Impeachment Evidence: Psycho-Bayesian [!?] Analysis and a Proposed Overhaul, 38 U.C.L.A. L. Rev. 637, 638 (1991).

12. State v. Duke, 123 A.2d 745, 746 (N.H. 1956) (jury should know "what sort of person is asking them to take his word," and in everyday life "this is probably the first thing that they would wish to know").

gravity of the offense or its quality. A third approach would restrict use of convictions by provisions designed to protect the criminal defendant, perhaps barring convictions or admitting them only if he both testifies and introduces evidence of truthfulness, or restricting the kinds of convictions that may be used against him. A fourth approach would give the judge discretion, perhaps limited in various ways, to guard against prejudice and abuse, and this discretion might be allowed with respect to all convictions or only some, and to all witnesses or only some, and the discretion could be cast in terms favoring either admitting or excluding convictions. A fifth approach would prohibit all impeachment by convictions. Congress compromised between the extremes, combining aspects of the intermediate approaches described, and this compromise is examined in ensuing sections.

§6.30 —Felonies

FRE 609(a)(1) adopts the view that convictions for serious crimes bear on credibility. They are to be admitted unless other considerations warrant exclusion, and for defendants in criminal cases such convictions are admissible if the court decides probative value outweighs prejudicial effect. For other witnesses, they are admissible "subject to Rule 403," meaning admissible unless probative value is outweighed by risk of unfair prejudice or any of the other concerns specified there (waste of time, confusion of issues, and so forth).

Connection with untruthfulness It is not hard to understand the logic that connects crimes of falsehood like perjury to untruthfulness, but the connection between many felonies and untruthfulness is less obvious. An opinion by Judge Doyle in the Tenth Circuit explained the logic of admitting felonies in these terms:

> Truthfulness is unlikely to exist by itself and in a vacuum. It is a quality which a generally upstanding person is likely to have. It is improbable that one who undertakes to rob a bank with a gun will prove to be a person of high character who is devoted to the truth.[1]

This view implies that any kind of serious conviction bears on credibility, and FRE 609(a)(1) embodies this philosophy.[2] Hence it seems that courts cannot automatically block use of felonies like robbery and drug trafficking that do not seem directly to reflect untruthfulness, although the discretionary clauses send a clear message that caution should be exercised.

§6.30 1. United States v. Halbert, 668 F.2d 489, 495 (10th Cir. 1982) (admitting convictions for mail fraud, false pretenses, aggravated robbery), *cert. denied*, 456 U.S. 934.

2. United States v. Lipscomb, 702 F.2d 1049, 1059 (D.C. Cir. 1983) (Congress thought "all felonies are probative of credibility to some degree," but also though some "have little relationship to credibility").

The category of serious crimes described in FRE 609(a)(1) is felonies—crimes "punishable by death or imprisonment in excess of one year" by the law under which the witness was convicted. The definition tracks the federal definition of felonies and is congruent with the category of crimes defined as felonies by most states.[3] The phrase leaves no room to doubt that it is the possible nature and extent of punishment rather than punishment actually imposed that counts.[4] The quality of criminal acts included in the category is unlimited. It includes arson, assault, battery, breaking and entering, bribery, burglary, conspiracy,[5] dealing in controlled substances like drugs, escape from confinement, extortion, firearms offenses, forgery, fraud and false pretenses,[6] homicide of any sort, kidnapping, larceny, rape and sexual assault, receiving or possessing stolen property, robbery, theft,[7] and other crimes too numerous to be worth separate mention.[8]

§6.31   —Excluding Felonies for Unfair Prejudice

Briefly put, courts may block impeachment by felony convictions on account of the risk of prejudice, and in this sensitive area FRE 609(a)(1) provides what might be called strong protection for criminal

---

3. *See* 18 U.S.C. §1 (offense "punishable by death or imprisonment for a term exceeding one year" is a felony). In most states, a felony is punishable by death or imprisonment in the state penitentiary, and most crimes that fit this definition carry a possible term of imprisonment that exceeds a year. *See* 1 Wayne LaFave, Substantive Criminal Law §1.6 (2d ed. 2003).

4. 1 Wayne LaFave, Substantive Criminal Law §1.6 (2d ed. 2003) (defining phrases using "punishable," refer to possible sentence, not sentence actually imposed); United States v. Hall, 588 F.2d 613, 615 n.4 (8th Cir. 1978) (convictions resulting in suspended sentences may be used to impeach).

5. Green v. Bock Laundry Mach. Co., 490 U.S. 504 (1989) (burglary and conspiracy to commit burglary); United States v, Toney, 27 F.3d 1245, 1253-1254 (7th Cir. 1994) (burglary, aggravated battery); United States v. Walker, 817 F.2d 461, 464 (9th Cir. 1987) (arson), *cert. denied,* 484 U.S. 863; United States v. Givens, 767 F.2d 574, 579-580 (9th Cir. 1985) (assault with deadly weapon), *cert. denied,* 474 U.S. 953; United States v. Rosales, 680 F.2d 1304, 1306 (10th Cir. 1981) (conspiracy).

6. United States v. Rein, 848 F.2d 777, 781-783 (7th Cir. 1988) (delivery of controlled substance); United States v. Charmley, 764 F.2d 675, 677 (9th Cir. 1984) (forgery); United States v. Key, 717 F.2d 1206, 1208 (8th Cir. 1983) (escape); United States v. Booker, 706 F.2d 860, 862 (8th Cir. 1983) (possession of firearm), *cert. denied,* 464 U.S. 917; United States v. Provenzano, 620 F.2d 985, 1002-1003 (3d Cir. 1980) (extortion and kickback conspiracy), *cert. denied,* 449 U.S. 899.

7. United States v. Caudle, 48 F.3d 433, 435 (9th Cir. 1995) (theft); United States v. Morrow, 977 F.2d 222, 228 (6th Cir. 1992) (armed robbery); Petty v. Ideco, Div. of Dresser Indus., Inc., 761 F.2d 1146, 1152 (5th Cir. 1985) (kidnapping); United States v. Shaw, 701 F.2d 367, 385 (5th Cir. 1983) (rape); United States v. Fay, 642 F.2d 1083, 1091-1092 (7th Cir. 1981) (premeditated murder), *cert. denied,* 451 U.S. 993.

8. United States v. Blankenship, 870 F.2d 326, 329 (6th Cir. 1988) (sodomy); Lewis v. Sheriffs Dept. for St. Louis, 817 F.2d 465, 467 (8th Cir. 1987) (driving car without owner's permission; possession of burglary tools), *cert. denied,* 484 U.S. 929; United States v. Hayes, 553 F.2d 824, 828 (2d Cir. 1977) (smuggling), *cert. denied,* 434 U.S. 897.

defendants and standard protection for other witnesses. The discretionary power to exclude felony convictions applies only to those that fit FRE 609(a)(1) alone. If they also fit FRE 609(b)(2) because they involve "dishonesty or false statement," there is no discretion to exclude.

When accused testifies Overwhelmingly the question whether to exclude felony convictions as prejudicial is a problem in criminal rather than civil cases, and almost always the issue arises when defendant testifies. The framers of FRE 609(a)(1) made the judgment that prior convictions are especially risky for criminal defendants and the language of FRE 609(a)(1) is cast in favor of caution: The court is to allow impeachment by these first-prong felony convictions on determining that probative value outweighs prejudicial effect to the defendant. The strongly protective cast of the language favors excluding rather than admitting. It reverses the balance in FRE 403 (which generally favors admissibility), and such convictions should be excluded if probative worth and prejudicial effect seem equally balanced.[1] For other witnesses, FRE 609(a)(1) is cast in favor of admissibility, simply referring to FRE 403, which tells judges to admit unless probative value is "substantially outweighed" by unfair prejudice (or other dangers or concerns). Hence felony convictions are more likely to be admissible to impeach witnesses other than criminal defendants.[2]

Part of the problem for the accused is that using prior convictions to impeach him is likely to have a spillover effect, suggesting to factfinders that he likely committed the charged crime or is a bad person unworthy of sympathy, which raises the possibility of angry or emotional reaction or misuse of the conviction as evidence of guilt. Faced with such risks, defendants may elect not to testify, but staying off the stand is risky too: The rate of conviction is much higher for defendants who do not testify,[3] and staying off the stand may result in keeping from the jury persuasive proof that the facts differ in important ways from what other evidence suggests.

Gordon factors In deciding whether to admit felony convictions, courts consider the circumstances of the trial, what the record discloses about convictions offered to impeach, and sometimes individual factors not disclosed on the face of a conviction or "rap sheet" or "case jacket." Two pathbreaking decisions in the District of Columbia circuit provide invaluable guidance for courts facing these issues. One is the decision in *Gordon v. United States*, which preceded the Rules but is highly respected in its outline of factors bearing on the exercise of discretion. The second is

§6.31 1. *See* Christmas v. Sanders, 759 F.2d 1284, 1292 (7th Cir. 1985); United States v. Fountain, 642 F.2d 1083, 1092 (7th Cir. 1981), *cert. denied*, 451 U.S. 993.

2. Before the 1990 amendment, FRE 609(a)(1) only authorized exclusion of felony convictions on account of prejudice "to the defendant," which was interpreted to mean courts lacked authority to exclude first-prong convictions in civil cases. *See* Green v. Bock Laundry Mach. Co., 490 U.S. 504 (1989).

3. Self-selection probably skews the statistics, since a guilty defendant who cannot persuade factfinders of innocence is probably better off not testifying, and those who do testify may be "less guilty" than those who do not. *See also* §6.35, *infra*.

the en banc decision in *United States v. Lipscomb,* which acknowledges the *Gordon* factors and endorses a closer look at the individual facts that surround prior convictions.[4] It is useful to look first to the *Gordon* factors and a few others that are important, then to consider the closer individual look suggested by *Lipscomb.*

Many felonies (from drug use to bank robbery) bear only generally on credibility, and FRE 609(a)(1) invites courts to consider gradations in probative worth. The nature of the prior crime is perhaps the salient point. *Gordon* suggested that "deceit, fraud, cheating, or stealing" reflect adversely on honesty and integrity, but that crimes of "violence" may reflect such qualities as "short temper, a combative nature, extreme provocation, or other causes" and generally have "little or no direct bearing" on veracity.

(1) Nature of prior crime

Some felonies are directly related to veracity in the sense of exemplifying untruthful behavior. But most such crimes also fit FRE 609(a)(2), where courts have no discretion to exclude (felony convictions for fraud, embezzlement, false statement or pretense, perjury or suborning perjury are usually admissible automatically). Even so, some crimes that do not fit FRE 609(a)(2) fall relatively high on the scale of probative worth on veracity, including especially crimes of theft and receiving stolen property. Similarly high on the scale are crimes that involve evasions of responsibility or abuse of trust, a category that includes smuggling or failure to register or report when required, and at least sometimes drug importation and even sexual abuse of children in defendant's care.[5] Others fall lower on the scale, including especially crimes in which violence is the central feature, which in turn embraces many sex offenses.[6] Also low on the scale are many drug crimes, and crimes against public morality, such as prostitution.[7]

---

4. *See* United States v. Lipscomb, 702 F.2d 1049, 1062-1071 (D.C. Cir. 1983) (quoted in this section by reference to case name) (opinion by Judge Wald); Gordon v. United States, 383 F.2d 936, 940-941 (D.C. Cir. 1967) (quoted in this section by reference to case name) (opinion by Judge, later Chief Justice, Burger), *cert. denied,* 390 U.S. 1029. *See also* United States v. Montgomery, 390 F.3d 1013, 1015 (7th Cir. 2004) (citing *Gordon* factors), *cert. denied,* 544 U.S. 968.

5. United States v. Estrada, 430 F.3d 606, 616 (2d Cir. 2005) (crimes like smuggling or failure to register and report, and other involving "evasions of responsibility or abuse of trust" are relatively high in probativity) (quoting this Treatise), *cert. denied,* 547 U.S. 1048; United States v. Alexander, 48 F.3d 1477, 1488 (9th Cir. 1995) (robbery is probative of veracity), *cert. denied,* 516 U.S. 878; United States v. Halbert, 668 F.2d 489, 495 (10th Cir. 1982) (mail fraud, false pretenses, aggravated robbery were "not unrelated" to truthfulness; fraud and false pretenses were directly relevant), *cert. denied,* 456 U.S. 1038.

6. Foulk v. Charrier, 262 F.3d 687, 699 (8th Cir. 2001) (admitting convictions for rape and sodomy but barring mention of nature of crimes); United States v. Jackson, 627 F.2d 1198, 1208-1210 (D.C. Cir. 1980) (manslaughter ranks "comparatively low"); Christmas v. Sanders, 759 F.2d 1284, 1292 (7th Cir. 1985) (rape "not highly probative of credibility").

7. United States v. Martinez, 555 F.2d 1273, 1276 (5th Cir. 1977) (aiding and abetting drug crime had "slight" probative value); United States v. Cox, 536 F.2d 65, 71 (5th Cir. 1976) (prostitution conviction was immaterial).

Arguably, however, crimes requiring planning or preparation bear more strongly on veracity than violence alone suggests because planning indicates deliberate and injurious violation of basic standards rather than impulse or anger, and usually it involves some element of deceiving the victim.[8] The logic that underlies FRE 609(a) implies that the gravity of an offense bears on truthfulness on the theory that more serious offenses suggest stronger willingness to ignore legal obligations.

(2) Recency or remoteness

Even a conviction for a crime that has high probative worth on veracity should be excluded, the court in *Gordon* said, "if it occurred long before and has been followed by a legally blameless life." FRE 609(b) creates in effect a presumption that a conviction more than ten years old should be excluded, but even the age of a more recent conviction may tip the balance in favor of exclusion.[9] As *Gordon* suggests, the remoteness factor is affected by the presence or absence of more recent convictions, in part because a more recent conviction suggests that defendant has not changed his ways and in part because later convictions strengthen the inference that defendant is willing to violate the law.[10]

(3) Similarity to charged crime

When the accused is a witness, the closer the resemblance between the charged crime and the crime leading to the prior conviction offered, the greater the potential prejudice. In *Gordon*, the court said that prior convictions for the same crime "should be admitted sparingly," suggesting that the court might limit the impeachment by similar crimes to a "single conviction." Of course some resemblances between the prior and the charged offense justify admitting evidence of the former on such points as knowledge, motive, intent, and so forth under FRE 404(b).[11] But a crime may easily lead to conviction for the same offense without being sufficiently relevant on some particular point to be admissible under FRE 404(b), and then use of the conviction to impeach the defendant introduces the risk of prejudice that is the concern of FRE 609(a)(1), and for that matter the concerns of FRE 403 and 404.[12]

8. United States v. Fountain, 642 F.2d 1083, 1091-1092 (7th Cir. 1981) (premeditated murder "involves deliberation," meaning one is likely "willing to lie" on stand), *cert. denied*, 451 U.S. 993.

9. United States v. Beahm, 664 F.2d 414, 419 (4th Cir. 1981) (reversible error to admit nine-year-old conviction, partly because it was so remote); United States v. Shapiro, 565 F.2d 479, 481 (7th Cir. 1977) (reversing conviction mainly because of remoteness of convictions used to impeach).

10. United States v. Lipscomb, 702 F.2d 1049, 1071 (D.C. Cir. 1983) (defendant could be impeached by eight-year-old robbery conviction; he was repeat offender with more recent conviction, which enhances probativity of robbery conviction by showing it "was not merely an isolated criminal episode").

11. *See generally* §§4.15-4.18, *supra*.

12. United States v. Jiminez, 214 F.3d 1095, 1098 (9th Cir. 2000) (in felon-in-possession trial, should not have admitted conviction for assault with deadly weapon); United States v. Sanders, 964 F.2d 295, 297-298 (4th Cir. 1992) (error to let prosecutor ask defendant about conviction for crime involving "exact type of conduct" for which defendant was being tried here).

As *Gordon* and *Lipscomb* recognize, probative value may be affected by defendant's whole criminal record. All other things being equal, an isolated conviction by one who otherwise leads a "blameless life" carries less probative worth on credibility than a conviction that fits a pattern of criminal behavior.[13] Other convictions need not necessarily be mentioned in questioning, but appropriately bear in the court's balance of the risks of prejudice against probative value of convictions that are mentioned.

(4) Extent and nature of record

For a defendant with a criminal record, the question whether to take the stand is very much affected by the prospect of impeachment by convictions. *Gordon* noted that the judge may decide it is more important for the jury to have the benefit of the defendant's testimony than to have him remain silent out of fear of impeachment.[14]

(5) Importance of defendant's testimony

The court in *Gordon* approved use of prior convictions in part because the trial "had narrowed to the credibility" of defendant and his accuser so there was more reason "to shed light on which of the two witnesses was to be believed" (the accuser himself had been impeached by convictions, seemingly enhancing the need to reveal similar shortcomings in defendant's veracity), and the importance of credibility issues counts in the balance.[15]

(6) Importance of credibility issues

Other factors bear on the problem. Courts may consider the larger picture of criminal behavior in which a conviction is an element and take into account the role of the witness and the general nature of the criminal enterprise.[16] And the court may take into account any overlap between the criminal behavior underlying a conviction and the behavior leading to present charges, which raises special concerns by making it harder to avoid misusing the conviction as proof of present guilt.[17] Arguably a conviction after a plea of not guilty has more probative worth than one based on a guilty plea because the former

(7) Other factors

---

13. United States v. Lipscomb, 702 F.2d 1049, 1071 (D.C. Cir. 1983) (defendant was repeat offender with more recent conviction, which enhanced probativity of earlier conviction for robbery by showing that it was not "isolated criminal episode").

14. Gordon v. United States, 383 F.2d 936, 940-941 & n.11 (D.C. Cir. 1967) (where intent or knowledge is proved circumstantially, as from "unexplained possession of recently stolen property," importance of getting defendant's testimony is greater), *cert. denied*, 390 U.S. 1029. *See also* United States v. Browne, 829 F.2d 760, 763-764 (9th Cir. 1987); United States v. Oakes, 565 F.2d 170, 173 (1st Cir. 1977) (justice may be advanced if defendant is not "demoralized from taking the stand by fear that a prior conviction would overshadow" positive aspects of his testimony).

15. United States v. Johnson, 302 F.3d 139, 152 (3d Cir. 2002) (approving questions on felony convictions; credibility was "major issue" because defense depended on jury "believing his story"); United States v. Perkins, 937 F.2d 1397, 1407 (9th Cir. 1991) (admitting bank robbery conviction since defendant's credibility and testimony were central).

16. United States v. Ortiz, 553 F.2d 782, 784 (2d Cir. 1977) (drug trafficker lives life of "secrecy and dissembling" probative of credibility), *cert. denied*, 434 U.S. 897.

17. *Compare* United States v. Martinez, 555 F.2d 1273, 1276 (5th Cir. 1977) (in drug trial, reversible error to let prosecutor ask about defendant's conviction for aiding and abetting in offense being tried) *with* United States v. De La Torre, 639 F.2d 245, 248-249 (5th Cir. 1981) (approving questions to defendant on perjury conviction stemming from testimony he gave at first trial on same charges).

suggests that defendant took a position (or gave testimony) that the factfinder found to be false.[18]

No thoughtful person is likely to be satisfied with any list of factors. In the setting of FRE 609(a)(1), dishonesty and untruthfulness are not likely to be elements in the offense, and crimes are defined for the purpose of determining criminal responsibility rather than measuring veracity. Hence it is not surprising that courts exercising discretion under FRE 609 look behind those elements to particular facts and circumstances and to the more general picture of criminality that convictions suggest. In *Lipscomb*, the court provided useful guidance on the procedure and mechanics of taking a closer look. There the government argued that the court should decide without inquiring into underlying facts, relying on the name of the offense, underlying elements, and date of conviction (the judge also knew defendant was only 16 years old when convicted). The defense argued that the court erred in failing to conduct a fuller inquiry, and that in all but the simplest cases such inquiry is essential. *Lipscomb* staked out a middle ground. It held that a court may inquire into the underlying facts and ask the government to produce the necessary data, but it declined to set up "general guidelines" to decide when "inquiry beyond the name and date" of conviction is necessary and left the matter to the judge's discretion. The court commented that often a judge "may be satisfied" with readily available information such as a "case jacket or presentence report" and that in deciding whether to pursue additional facts the judge could consider the burden or delay that would be entailed.

Still, *Lipscomb* encouraged trial courts to engage in a factual inquiry. Invoking legislative history and the "plain meaning" of FRE 609, *Lipscomb* said this approach is the wisest one and that factual data is often useful. In an important clue acknowledging the worth of such inquiry, the court commented that with felony convictions the question of prejudice "is not if, but how much." Finally, the court noted that the prosecutor should routinely have "at least some details of the defendant's own past convictions" because the government is expected to consider such details before deciding whether to seek an indictment, which charges to bring, and what sort of plea bargain to offer. Assuming additional inquiry is pursued, *Lipscomb* cited examples to suggest facts that bear on admissibility—a manslaughter conviction arising from an incident where a man shot his wife and her lover, a case where defense witnesses were serving substantial prison terms and would have a motivation to testify falsely in a dispute with prison guards, a case where the crime was committed when defendant was only 20 years old, and finally a case in which defendant had been convicted after testifying in his own defense.

---

18. Gordon v. United States, 383 F.2d 936, 940 n.8 (D.C. Cir. 1967) (probative value varies between convictions based on guilty pleas and those following trial in which defendant testifies, where verdict amounts to finding that defendant "did not tell the truth when sworn to do so"), *cert. denied*, 390 U.S. 1029.

For witnesses other than defendants in criminal trials, FRE 609(a)(1) incorporates the balancing standard of FRE 403, so in these other settings felony convictions are admissible unless probative worth is substantially outweighed by the risk of prejudice or any of the dangers and concerns listed there. Use of convictions to impeach defense witnesses in criminal cases could have a spillover effect, causing prejudice to defendants by association, but such convictions are less dangerous to defendants than their own. Judging the prejudice issue by a standard cast more in favor of admissibility seems justified. Under FRE 609, the government also can seek to block defense impeachment of its witnesses under FRE 403, but such objections seldom succeed.[19]

Perhaps it is in the nature of things that witnesses called in civil cases are seldom impeached by prior convictions. In the case of impeaching the litigants themselves, many of the factors discussed above apply in this setting too—the question whether to admit or exclude felony convictions in civil actions is affected by the nature of the conviction, its similarity (if any) to the conduct in issue in the suit, and the importance of credibility issues.[20]

§6.32 —Crimes of Dishonesty or False Statement

FRE 609(a)(2) expresses the judgment that crimes of dishonesty or false statement have special probative worth on veracity. These second-prong convictions are automatically admissible to impeach unless one of the express exceptions applies—the ten-year rule, the limits on juvenile adjudications, or the bar against convictions that have led to official acknowledgment of rehabilitation, or to pardons or annulments based on innocence. Such convictions are not excludable on account of unfair prejudice under Rule 403.[1]

19. Green v. Bock Laundry Mach. Co., 490 U.S. 504 (1989) (FRE 609 "limits impeachment of not only a criminal defendant, but also any witness offered on the defendant's behalf") (before 1990 amendment). *Compare* State v. Randall, 639 N.W.2d 439, 447-448 (N.D. 2002) (in trial for attempted murder, error to exclude felony convictions of alleged victim; courts rarely exclude convictions impeaching prosecution witnesses; prosecutor bears burden of showing that unfair prejudice outweighs probative worth; error harmless) (quoting authors of this Treatise) *with* United States v. Galati, 230 F.3d 254, 261-262 (7th Cir. 2000) (blocking defense effort to impeach government witness; applying FRE 403).

20. Wierstak v. Heffernan, 789 F.2d 968, 972 (1st Cir. 1986) (nature); Murr v. Stinson, 752 F.2d 233, 234-235 (6th Cir. 1985) (recency and nature).

§6.32 1. FRE 609(a) uses a strong verb ("shall be admitted"), and there is no qualifying language in FRE 609(a)(2). *See* Green v. Bock Laundry Mach. Co., 490 U.S. 504 (1989) (general rule does not control when more specific rule applies; first-prong reference to excluding felonies for prejudice "to the defendant" means they cannot be excluded for prejudice to civil litigants). After *Green*, FRE 609(a) was amended to adjust the test for first-prong convictions, but no change was made for second-prong convictions. Hence there is no discretion to exclude second prong convictions. See United States v. Collier, 527 F.3d 695, 699 (8th Cir. 2008) ("automatically admissible and not subject to Rule 403").

Obviously a conviction may qualify under the second prong regardless whether the offense is a felony or misdemeanor, since the category reaches convictions "regardless of the punishment." And a conviction that qualifies under both prongs of FRE 609(a)—a felony of dishonesty or false statement such as perjury—is automatically admissible under FRE 609(a)(2).

For purposes of FRE 609(a)(2), crimes of "dishonesty or false statement" comprise what an authoritative decision in the *Smith* case termed a "fairly narrow subset of criminal activity," and legislative history supports this conclusion, as does modern interpretive tradition.[2] There is a core group of second-prong crimes, which includes the ones mentioned in the Reports (perjury or subornation of perjury, false statement, criminal fraud in many different forms, embezzlement, and false pretense).[3]

Narrow subset: Crimes that fit   The list in the Report is exemplary, not exhaustive, and the category also includes forgery and counterfeiting, along with a few other crimes of deceit, untruthfulness, or falsehood.[4] Most courts considering the matter hold that failing to file tax returns indicates dishonesty or false statement, although there is some disagreement.[5]

Crimes that don't fit   It is equally clear that some crimes *usually* do not fit FRE 609(a)(2), such as ordinary assault, rape or sexual assault, battery and other violent offenses, drunk or disorderly conduct, drug offenses, prostitution, and some other crimes.[6]

Category expands   In the previous paragraph, the qualifier "usually" is needed because the category of second-prong convictions expands if courts look to the particular facts underlying a conviction offered under the Rule. In this way, convictions for some other crimes can wind up being second-prong

2. *See* United States v. Smith, 551 F.2d 348, 362 (D.C. Cir. 1976) (extensive scholarly opinion). See also Conference Report, at 9 (perjury, false statement, criminal fraud, embezzlement, false pretense, and like crimes involving "deceit, untruthfulness, or falsification").

3. *See* United States v. Collier, 527 F.3d 695, 699 (8th Cir. 2008) (sale or receipt of access card to defraud); United States v. Caudle, 48 F.3d 433, 435 (9th Cir. 1995) (perjury; filing false claims); United States v. Lester, 749 F.2d 1288, 1300 (9th Cir. 1984) (filing false police report).

4. United States v. Harper, 527 F.3d 396, 408 (5th Cir. 2008) (theft by check); Wal-Mart Stores, Inc. v. Regions Bank Trust Dept., 69 S.W.2d 20, 28 (Ark. 2002) (check kiting) (quoting this Treatise); State v. Cheeseboro, 552 S.E.2d 300, 310 (S.C. 2002) (criminal impersonation); Elcock v. KMart Corp., 233 F.3d 734, 752 (3d Cir. 2000) (embezzlement); S.E.C. v. Sargent, 229 F.3d 68, 80 (1st Cir. 2000) (materially false statements); United States v. Morrow, 977 F.2d 222, 228 (6th Cir. 1992) (counterfeiting); United States v. Kane, 944 F.2d 1406, 1412 (7th Cir. 1991) (delivering check knowing it will not be honored).

5. *Compare* Dean v. Trans World Airlines, Inc., 924 F.2d 805, 811-812 (9th Cir. 1991) (qualifies) *with* Cree v. Hatcher, 969 F.2d 34, 36-37 (3d Cir. 1992) (does not qualify).

6. Coverdale v. State, 844 A.2d 979, 981 (Del. 2004) (drug offenses); Morris v. State, 795 A.2d 653, 655 (Del. 2002) (kidnapping); United States v. Meserve, 271 F.3d 314, 328 (1st Cir. 2001) (disorderly conduct; assault); United States v. Colbert, 116 F.3d 395, 396 (9th Cir. 1997) (lewd conduct), *cert. denied*, 522 U.S. 920; United States v. Wiman, 77 F.3d 981, 986 (7th Cir. 1996) (driving under influence); Czajka v. Hickman, 703 F.2d 317, 319 n1 (8th Cir. 1983) (rape); Gordon v. United States, 383 F.2d 936, 940 (D.C. Cir. 1967) (violent crimes have "little or no direct bearing" on veracity), *cert. denied*, 390 U.S. 1029.

convictions. In 2006, however, FRE 609(a)(2) was amended, and the language was tightened up with the stated purpose of making such arguments less often available. Yet state counterparts have not followed this federal change, so arguments based on underlying facts are often available in state systems, and the matter is taken up in detail in the next section.

There is an even simpler way in which convictions for theft find their way into FRE 609(a)(2): Simply put, crimes of theft are sometimes viewed as crimes of "dishonesty" that fit comfortably within the literal terms of the language in the second prong. This position is certainly plausible. After all, theft is not merely a "wrongful" act (like assault or selling illegal drugs), but an act that involves purposefully taking property belonging to another,[7] which is dishonest in the sense of showing a lack of integrity or principle. The principal architect of the Rules thought dishonesty included theft—he said the author of *Alice in Wonderland* "would have been pleased" with decisions that thought otherwise ("few would not agree that robbery or any other form of theft is dishonest").[8] There is also the fact that many forms of theft (like larceny and burglary) involve stealth and depend on the ability of the thief to avoid acknowledgment or discovery in his later possession of what he took, which seems dishonest in the sense of being deceitful. To these points, one might add that the term "dishonesty" in FRE 609(a)(2) must mean *something* beyond "false statement" (which accounts for most crimes in the "core group" described above), or else the term is a mere redundancy in the Rule, and theft is the most obvious way to give separate meaning to the term.

In the end, however, Congress probably did not think that FRE 609(a)(2) included theft convictions: The Committee Reports indicate as much, although admittedly this conclusion is less than certain, and floor debates revealed disagreement. Not surprisingly, the decisions conflict. Some modern authority says that "dishonesty" really means "deceit," not simply lack of integrity or principle,[9] which means that the term actually is redundant and has little or no independent meaning, and a strong majority of modern decisions *exclude* theft convictions from FRE 609(a)(2), at least in the absence of special facts showing deceit (a point explored further in the next section). A minority of decisions take the opposite tack.[10]

Theft and "dishonesty"

---

7. See LaFave, Substantive Criminal Law §19.5 (2d ed. 2007) (larceny requires intent "to deprive the owner of the possession of his property," which is missing if one thinks it is his own or nobody owns it).

8. Cleary, Preliminary Notes on Reading the Rules of Evidence, 57 Neb. L. Rev. 908, 919 (1978).

9. U.S. v. Brackeen, 969 F.2d 827, 829 (9th Cir. 1992) (dishonesty has more than one plain meaning; it connotes breach of trust or lack of integrity or principle, and also deceit; Congress used "dishonesty" in narrower sense, to mean only crimes that involve deceit) (not bank robbery); Altobello v. Borden Confectionery Prods., Inc., 872 F.2d 215, 216 (7th Cir. 1989) ("acquisitive crimes" are dishonest, but courts distinguish between crimes that do not involve deception and crimes that do).

10. Cases holding that theft crimes do not fit FRE 609(a)(2) include Walker v. Horn, 385 F.3d 321, 332-334 (3d Cir. 2004) (robbery), *cert. denied*, 544 U.S. 1021;

§6.33 —Looking to Underlying Facts

When dishonesty or falsehood lies at the heart of a crime (perjury and forgery, for instance), the questioner can proceed under the second prong on the basis of the record alone (rap sheet, case jacket, or copy of conviction). Short of showing that such a conviction runs afoul of one of the hard-edged restrictions in FRE 609, it qualifies for automatic admissibility, and there is no room to argue otherwise.

When falsity is *not* an element in the offense, the question arises whether a conviction can satisfy FRE 609(a)(2) anyway, because underlying facts show that the crime involved falsity. A shoplifter might get away with theft by telling the sales clerk that he'd "decided not to buy the watch," while paying for a small item, deceiving the clerk, or a drug seller might misrepresent the nature or quality of what he's providing. Does a theft or drug conviction fit FRE 609(a)(2) when the perpetrator has committed the crime by being dishonest or false in such ways?

2006 amendment   For the first thirty years, second-prong convictions were those "involving" dishonesty or false statement, and many courts thought crimes *committed by such means* did indeed "involve" dishonesty or false statements. In the federal system, the Evidence Committee amended Federal Rule 609(a)(2) in 2006, removing the term "involving" and substituting a more complicated phrase—"if it readily can be determined that establishing the elements of the crime required proof of or admission of an act of dishonesty or false statement."

Simply looking at the new language, one might read it in different ways. We can eliminate the extremes: The new wording did not leave things as they were, with the second prong embracing a conviction of any crime *committed by means of* dishonesty or false statement, because the ACN says the change in language was "meant to give effect to the [original] legislative intent," strongly implying that the approach taken hitherto was wrong. Nor does the new language mean that the second prong reaches only crimes whose *elements* require proof of dishonest or false statement, as the ACN makes clear (more on this point below). In other words, FRE 609(a)(2) is neither as broad as it once was nor as narrow as it could easily be made.

That leaves two possible interpretations: First, the new language could mean that convictions fit the second prong if, *as a practical matter,* the prosecutor had to prove acts of "false statement or dishonesty" in order to prevail. By this reading, the amendment would make only a modest change. The theft conviction for shoplifting described above would likely qualify, and most modern opinions that examine the

---

United States v. Galati, 230 F.3d 254, 261 (7th Cir. 2000) (shoplifting); United States v. Wiman, 77 F.3d 981, 986 (7th Cir. 1996) (theft); United States v. Foster, 227 F.3d 1096, 1099 (9th Cir. 2000) (receiving stolen property; shoplifting, burglary, grand theft, bank robbery); United States v. Scisney, 885 F.2d 325, 326 (6th Cir. 1989) (shoplifting). The following cases, however, hold that theft crimes *do* fit FRE 609(a)(2): Morris v. State, 795 A.2d 653, 665 (Del. 2002) (robbery, burglary, theft); McHenry v. Chadwick, 896 F.2d 184, 188-189 (6th Cir. 1990) (shoplifting, concealing stolen property).

underlying facts in admitting convictions under the second prong would be consistent with this approach. In the shoplifting case, the prosecutor *needs to prove* the statement ("I decided not to buy the watch") because it adds strength to the case and because it is part of what happened, and in this sense it is *necessary* to prove such facts. Yet the words were not absolutely essential to the case—taking goods from the store without paying completes the offense, and the words are not strictly necessary. Second, the new language could mean that convictions fit the second prong only if the prosecutor *absolutely must* prove an act of dishonesty or false statement in order to prevail, as would be true, for example, if a person were charged with theft by rigging a utility meter to avoid paying for gas or electricity: Here the act of theft *is* an act of deception, even though the charged crime does not require proof of dishonesty or false statement. The statement (rigging the meter) is not merely the ruse employed in order to accomplish the taking, but is the act itself. By this reading, the amendment makes a more significant change. The shoplifting conviction would not qualify, and the category is narrowed considerably.

Probably this second reading is the one intended, and FRE 609(a)(2) reaches convictions for crimes in which the prosecutor *must prove* an act of dishonesty or false statement because it is integral to the very act constituting the crime. The ACN cites the example of obstructing justice, commenting that a crime can fit FRE 609(a)(2) even if the statutory definition does not "expressly reference[ ] deceit," meaning "dishonesty or false statement."[1] This example is closer to the crime of theft in rigging a utility meter than to the example of shoplifting accomplished by lying. Hence a conviction for obstructing justice by making false statements to police fits FRE 609(a)(2) in its amended form, and the same is true of a theft conviction for stealing from the utility company by rigging the meter, but a theft conviction for shoplifting does not fit, even if the perpetrator lied to the clerk in leaving the store.[2]

Must prove (integral to the criminal act)

In state systems that retain the old language (a conviction fits the second prong if the crime "involved" dishonesty or false statement), it seems that both the shoplifting conviction and the one for stealing from the utility company can fit FRE 609(a)(2), as do other crimes accomplished by similar means.[3] In short, the original language

Original language broader

---

§6.33   1. See ACN to 2006 amendment to FRE 609, citing 18 U.S.C. §1001 (criminalizing act that knowingly or willfully "falsifies, conceals, or covers up by any trick, scheme, or device a material fact" or "makes any materially false, fictitious, or fraudulent" statement, or "makes or uses any false writing or document" on matters within federal jurisdiction).

2. See Altobello v. Borden Confectionery Prods., Inc., 872 F.2d 215, 216-217 (7th Cir. 1989) (conviction for tampering with electric meters involved dishonesty).

3. State v. Bryant, 633 S.E.2d 152 (S.C. 2006) (shoplifting and bad checks); Taylor v. State, 849 A.2d 405, 408 (Del. 2004) (shoplifting); State v. Hoverson, 710 N.W.2d 890, 896 (N.D. 2006) (theft is crime of dishonesty or false statement if underlying facts involve dishonesty or false statement).

covering convictions for crimes "involving" dishonesty or false statement has broader coverage, reaching any conviction in which the underlying crime was committed by means of dishonesty or false statement.

"Ready proof" requirement

Under the 2006 amendment, FRE 609(a)(2) applies only where "it readily can be determined" that a conviction fits the category. The purpose of this "ready proof" requirement, not yet found in state counterparts, is to avoid protracted disputes. Of course the proponent bears the burden, and must be prepared to offer the ready proof. If the question whether the conviction fits FRE 609(a)(2) cannot be resolved expeditiously, the court should bar its use, or shift the inquiry to FRE 609(a)(1) if the crime is a felony, in which case the court moves to comparing probative value against the risk of unfair prejudice. In the words of the ACN, a court applying FRE 609(a)(2) should not conduct a "mini-trial" that "plumbs the record" of the prior proceedings in figuring out whether the conviction really fits.[4]

The necessary showing can be made (according to the ACN) by resort to "information such as" the indictment or the jury instructions or "a statement of admitted facts." This listing describes obvious sources, without purporting to exhaust the possibilities. Courts can consider the transcript from the trial reflecting testimony, arguments of counsel, and jury instructions, and may consider extrinsic evidence, including testimony or representations by a judge or court reporter or lawyer involved in the prior proceedings. These are the kinds of things that courts consider in applying doctrines of collateral estoppel and *res judicata*.[5] Of course extended resort to extrinsic sources enmeshes the court in details, and the message of the amended language is that courts should avoid such inquiry. It is worth noting that some inquiry into underlying facts is usually necessary in applying FRE 609. The landmark decision in the *Lipscomb* case allows (even encourages) courts to inquire into facts in applying FRE 609(a)(1) because they count heavily in comparing probative worth against unfair prejudice. *Lipscomb* approves consideration of such things as "case jackets" (records maintained by prosecutors) in making such decisions.[6]

---

4. *See* U.S. v. Lipscomb, 702 F.2d 1049, 1067 (D.C. Cir. 1983) (court can take "burden or delay" into account in deciding how much information it needs in balancing probative worth against unfair prejudice in case of felony convictions offered under first prong of FRE 609).

5. See Restatement of Judgments Second §27, comment f (1982) (for issue preclusion, if pleadings and "other materials of record" do not show what was determined, "extrinsic evidence is admissible").

6. U.S. v. Lipscomb, 702 F.2d 1049, 1064-1071 (D.C. Cir. 1983) (judge may inquire into "background facts and circumstances," and consider whether witnesses testified in prior trial; if government "had shown" that they did, conviction would show that they did not tell truth; can also consider later record; can consider "case jacket or presentence report" if available). *Lipscomb* is discussed further in §6.31, *supra*.

§6.34   —Permitted Detail; Coordinating FRE 608 and 609; Letting Witness Explain

Because convictions can have explosive impact when used to impeach—and again the concern is especially parties, mostly criminal defendants—questioning should be narrowly focused. The attacking party should not go into details of the underlying acts or insinuate them by embellishment or argument. When the witness is a party (especially the accused), bringing out details injects unfair prejudice that courts should prevent under FRE 403. For nonparty witnesses, subjecting them to inquiry on details is harassment with little prospect of assisting the factfinder on credibility issues, and the court should protect against it.

Generally the questioner may ask about the date and nature of the conviction (name and elements of offense) and the punishment imposed.[1] It seems natural to ask about the place of conviction too, for otherwise such questions take on an unreal and unconnected quality. However, the few cases that note this matter are split and such questions have been criticized if the prior crime happened in the same community as the present trial because this point might raise jury fears and increases the chance of prejudicial misuse of the convictions.[2] Questioning that goes much beyond these basic points is usually condemned[3] although a few opinions insist that judges may properly allow wider inquiry,[4] especially if the witness (usually the accused) offers some reply, justification, rejoinder, or criticism of the prior proceedings.[5]

> **Permitted questions**

Coordinating the mandates of FRE 608 and 609 is harder than it looks. Suppose the purpose of the attacking party is to suggest that the witness is by disposition untruthful, and he has been convicted of tax evasion because of deliberate falsehoods he personally put in his return. Suppose too that asking about the conviction would violate the

> **Relation with FRE 608**

---

§6.34   1. United States v. Estrada, 430 F.3d 606, 616 (2d Cir. 2005) (nature or name of conviction, date, sentence imposed) (citing this Treatise); State v. LaMar, 767 N.E.2d 166, 205 (Ohio 2002) (can block questioning beyond name, date, and place of conviction, and punishment imposed) (more allowed here).

2. *Compare* Radtke v. Cessna Aircraft Co., 707 F.2d 999, 1001 (8th Cir. 1983) (may mention place) *with* Campbell v. Greer, 831 F.2d 700, 707 (7th Cir. 1987) (no reason to ask where rape occurred unless purpose was to place it in community where case was being tried and from which jurors probably came).

3. State v. Bryan, 804 N.E.2d 433, 457 (Ohio 2004) (details like victim's name and aggravating circumstances are inadmissible; questioning exceeded permissible limits) (harmless); United States v. Albers, 93 F.3d 1469, 1479-1481 (10th Cir. 1996) (improper to go into detail).

4. United States v. Wesley, 990 F.2d 360, 366 (8th Cir. 1993) (asking defendant about robbery conviction and use of gun) (relevant to show ownership of gun here); United States v. Brown, 794 F.2d 365, 366 (8th Cir. 1986) (questions about date of release).

5. United States v. Valencia, 61 F.3d 616, 619 (8th Cir. 1995) (defendant testified that cocaine belonged to someone else; since defendant opened door, government could clarify); United States v. Wolf, 561 F.2d 1376, 1381 (10th Cir. 1977) (defendant seeking to minimize guilt may be asked relevant facts).

ten-year limit and that questions about underlying acts (like falsely claiming large charitable contributions) would exceed the conventions described above. Can the questioner avoid these limits and conventions by invoking FRE 608 instead?

On behalf of the attacking party, it could be argued that FRE 609 governs only questions about convictions, hence that FRE 609 does not apply to questioning about the underlying acts. Asking about the acts under FRE 608(b) provides the questioner with a more favorable standard in assessing prejudice.[6] More importantly, pursuing this strategy could avoid the ten-year rule in FRE 609(b), the bar in FRE 609(c) against questions on convictions that have generated pardon or annulment or a certificate of rehabilitation, and the restriction against questions on juvenile adjudications contained in FRE 609(d). And questions on underlying acts might be more probative on credibility than questions on the convictions themselves.

Give attacking party a choice

One approach would give the attacking party a choice—either proceed under FRE 608(b) by asking about the underlying acts without mentioning the conviction or proceed under FRE 609 by asking about the conviction and accepting the various limits. In favor of this approach, it might be said that usually the attacking party may select any appropriate method, and the limits applicable to one do not affect another. Arguably too, the restrictions in FRE 609 are designed to limit and control the explosive impact of convictions as such, and the questioner who agrees not to mention a conviction can reasonably say those restrictions should not apply. Finally, it is the acts themselves that reflect on veracity, not the convictions as such.[7]

FRE 609 provides standard

Another approach would hold that FRE 609 provides the governing standard whenever acts lead to conviction and that the cross-examiner must proceed under that provision or not at all. In favor of this construction, it might be argued that questioning about criminal acts without mentioning a conviction would generate a distorted and incomplete picture, inviting the factfinder to believe, for instance, that the witness not only misbehaved but "got away with it." And arguably the purpose of the various specific restrictions in FRE 609, including the ten-year rule and the provision on juvenile adjudications, is not only to bar questions on convictions but to limit all reference to the whole subject and to put certain aspects of it out of bounds. Hence allowing resort to FRE 608 would essentially evade the restrictions.

It seems wise to remember that the subject at hand is a single theory of impeachment (prior behavior bears on disposition toward truthfulness). While FRE 608(b) lacks the detailed interpretive tradition on

---

6. Under FRE 609(a)(1), questioning the accused on felony convictions is proper only if probative worth exceeds prejudice (exclude if balance is equal), but the FRE 403 standard applies to FRE 608 (allow if balance is equal).

7. State v. Hoverson, 710 N.W. 890, 897 (N.D. 2006) (where court looks to underlying acts and determines that conviction fits Rule 609, court may allow questions about the acts under Rule 608); State v. Martisko, 566 S.E.2d 274, 279 (W. Va. 2002) (instead of using Rule 609, defense could invoke Rule 608 for documents showing that witness "made, and then recanted," similar accusations against boyfriend).

scope of questioning that has grown up around convictions under FRE 609, the important point is to permit reasonable inquiry while minimizing distraction, prejudice to parties, and abuse of witnesses. Clearly the mere fact that charges have been brought (or an indictment returned) does not bring into play the full regulatory impact of FRE 609: Neither FRE 608 nor 609 allows questions on arrest or charges or indictment, but these first steps on the road to prosecution, conviction, and punishment do not themselves block the attacking party from asking about underlying acts under FRE 608. More generally, however, when acts have led to conviction, the discretion clause in FRE 608(b) can and should usually be read consistently with the specific restrictions in FRE 609.

Finally, it should be noted that questions about underlying acts may be proper if the attacking party seeks to contradict the witness rather than show untruthful character as such, or to show such things as motive or intent under FRE 404(b) because FRE 609 does not regulate impeachment by contradiction at all, and the restrictions in FRE 609 simply do not apply to contradiction.[8]

When the attacking party asks a witness about convictions under FRE 609, ordinary notions of respect and fairness suggest that he should be allowed to make some reply, whether by way of suggesting that despite the conviction he is generally honest or being truthful now, or by way of explaining what happened before, or suggesting that the proceedings were unfair, or that he is innocent in fact. At least that much should be conceded to human dignity and the instinct for self-defense and personal justification. Hence courts generally permit such response by witnesses.[9] When the witness takes advantage of this possibility, however, he may be in for more than he anticipates and often will surely come out the worse for it. After such response, the attacking party can forcefully argue for bringing out some further detail revealed by the record of conviction or asking about further facts that bear on whatever explanation the witness offers.[10] Such sparring quickly leads to matters that are justifiably viewed as distracting and collateral, and the court has authority to limit these efforts under FRE 403 and 611.

Allowing reply

---

8. *See* §6.39, *infra.*

9. *See* United States v. Jackson, 627 F.2d 1198, 1208-1210 (D.C. Cir. 1980) (defendant can bring out underlying facts on redirect to mitigate "bad man" image) (he had shot wife and male companion); United States v. Bray, 445 F.2d 178, 182 (5th Cir. 1971) (witness should not be "cut off from explaining or extenuating the conviction or denying his guilt"), *cert. denied,* 404 U.S. 1002.

10. United States v. Jackson, 310 F.3d 1053, 1053 (8th Cir. 2002) (defendant brought out his own conviction, saying he received minimum penalty because there is "no self-defense law" in Arkansas; prosecutor could cross-examine about evidence that was inconsistent with his implication of self-defense); United States v. Williams, 272 F.3d 845, 860-861 (7th Cir. 2001) (defendant offered explanations on direct, opening door to government cross; ordinarily details are not to be exposed; the contrary is true when defense opens the matter).

§6.35   —Procedure, Pretrial Motions, Preserving Error

The process of deciding whether to allow or prohibit questioning on convictions has drawn considerable attention, mostly because convictions are potentially valuable for each side and potentially explosive too. Often the decision to admit or exclude is made on pretrial motion, and this point too has led to complications.

In the setting of felony convictions offered to impeach defendants in criminal cases, FRE 609(a)(1) admonishes courts to be careful. Such convictions are not automatically admissible, and the court should assess probative worth against prejudice for each conviction. The prosecutor who wants to attack the defendant with a felony conviction bears the burden of persuading the court not only that the conviction is a felony but that probative worth exceeds prejudicial effect.[1] Other attacking parties (defendants in criminal cases and civil litigants) face a standard that is more lenient (probative worth need only equal or exceed prejudicial impact), but they too bear the burden of showing that a conviction offered under the first prong is a felony and that the standard is satisfied.[2]

Better to make findings   Surely it is better for courts to make on-the-record findings that expressly consider probative value and prejudice and resolve the tension. Such findings aid reviewing courts and provide assurance that the trial court came to grips with the underlying problem. Some reviewing courts come close to telling judges they must make such findings,[3] but it is not so clear that insisting on this point would achieve much: Courts can recite the factors without much thought and are almost always affirmed when they perform the balancing task, and it is hard to imagine reversing convictions whenever the trial court fails to do the litany. Far more likely is a remand instructing the court to consider probative worth against prejudicial impact—a process that surely does not lead to many new trials. Still, a recitation of issues and reasoning is some indication of care, and reviewing courts have good reason to urge judges to perform the task in explicit detail and to give closer scrutiny to convictions after trials where impeachment went forward without express rulings. Most appellate cases continue to urge judges to be careful and methodical even though the cases stop just short of an iron rule.[4]

---

§6.35   1. United States v. Meserve, 271 F.3d 314, 327 (1st Cir. 2001) (government must do research, determine that offenses are admissible; should produce "concrete proof" of felony conviction); United States v. Lipscomb, 702 F.2d 1049, 1063 (D.C. Cir. 1983) (similar).

2. United States v. Tse, 375 F.3d 148, 164 (1st Cir. 2004) (difference in standards recognizes that prejudice to defendant "is simply not the same" as prejudice to government witness, where prior convictions are "unlikely to inflame the jury or invite a propensity inference").

3. United States v. Preston, 608 F.2d 626, 639 (5th Cir. 1979) (must make on-the-record finding that probative worth outweighs prejudicial effect).

4. See United States v. Martinez-Martinez, 369 F.3d 1076, 1088 (9th Cir. 2004) (judge need not analyze factors under FRE 609(a)(1); judge was aware of factors);

For a conviction offered under FRE 609(a)(2), the attacking party bears the burden of proving that it involves "dishonesty or false statement." Failing to satisfy this requirement means the attack may be disallowed.[5]

In criminal cases, defendants who want to testify often seek advance rulings on the admissibility of their convictions to impeach. Courts cannot block impeachment by second-prong convictions (crimes of dishonesty or false statement), but have discretion to block use of first-prong convictions (felonies). Also, issues arise that leave the defendant in doubt on the extent or nature of his exposure to impeachment if he testifies, including questions as to whether a conviction qualifies for automatic admissibility or could be excluded. **Advance rulings**

Whether to provide the desired assistance is up to the trial court in the exercise of sound discretion.[6] For a defendant, the stake in getting a preliminary ruling may be high because the decision whether to take the stand may turn on it. For the court, the difficulty is that pretrial rulings are made without the benefit of context. Lingering in the minds of some judges and courts is the suspicion that a defense motion may be essentially a strategy to inject issues for appeal.

If defendant makes a pretrial motion to exclude convictions, but the court declines to rule or decides that they may be used if he testifies, defendant may lose his right to urge error if he does not take the stand. For federal courts, this point was settled in the Supreme court's 1984 decision in the *Luce* case,[7] which announced three reasons: First, if the accused does not testify the process of review is "handicapped" because balancing requires knowledge of the "precise nature" of his testimony, which is by definition unavailable. Second, harm from a preliminary ruling is "wholly speculative." It is speculative because the ruling remains "subject to change" as the case unfolds (the judge remains "free, in the exercise of sound discretion, to alter a previous in limine ruling"), particularly if defendant's testimony differs from his proffer. And the ruling is speculative because the reviewing court "has no way of knowing" whether the government would have used the conviction if defendant had testified. Third, allowing review would mean "almost any error" in the pretrial ruling would produce "the windfall of automatic reversal" because the court could not say an error that "presumptively" kept defendant from testifying was harmless. *Luce* **doctrine**

Luce settles the matter in the federal system, but for five years federal courts almost unanimously went the opposite direction. Led by a 1979 en banc decision by the Ninth Circuit in *United States v. Cook*, many

---

United States v. De La Cruz, 902 F.2d 121, 123-124 (1st Cir. 1990) (good practice to make on-the-record findings); United States v. Wallace, 848 F.2d 1464, 1472-1473 (9th Cir. 1988) (need not analyze factors, but record should reflect awareness).

5. United States v. Motley, 940 F.2d 1079, 1083-1084 (7th Cir. 1991) (must show conviction involved dishonesty or false statement).

6. *See* United States v. Hood, 748 F.2d 439, 441 (8th Cir. 1984); United States v. York, 722 F.2d 714, 716 (11th Cir. 1984); United States v. Del Toro Soto, 676 F.2d 13, 18 (1st Cir. 1982).

7. Luce v. United States, 469 U.S. 38 (1984) (opinion by Chief Justice Burger).

opinions held that defendant could get review even without testifying.[8] The aim of the *Cook* doctrine was to protect defendant's right to testify against the terribly chilling effect of rulings that allow impeachment, which are unfortunate and costly to defendants if wrong. Just as clearly, the purpose of *Luce* is to guard against the risk of automatic reversal if the accused stays off the stand after error in a preliminary ruling. In effect, *Luce* says automatic reversal is too high a price to pay for protecting the accused against the chilling effect of error in applying FRE 609.

Yet the discarded *Cook* doctrine was sound, its summary rejection in *Luce* mistaken. From the perspective of the trial court, a commitment to testify and proffer of expected testimony should be adequate protection against requests for hypothetical or advisory opinions. From the perspective of a reviewing court, a proffer suffices as a basis for the required assessment. Rejecting a proffer as the basis for review (since actual testimony might "differ") is misguided simply because courts remain free (as *Luce* emphasized) to reconsider initial rulings. The point that harm is "speculative" is unpersuasive: Few doubt the importance of testimony by the accused or the effect on defendants of a ruling that permits use of convictions to impeach, and there is little reason to suppose prosecutors will refrain from using them if given the opportunity. Nor is there reason to think a proffer is insufficient to enable reviewing courts to assess the harm of error—a task they routinely perform now. Of course harm is always to some extent uncertain, but a proffer provides basis enough to assess the need for using convictions to impeach as well as their probative worth and potential for prejudice, just as a proffer suffices when the question is whether exclusion of testimony or other proof (which itself is usually made known by proffer) is error that warrants reversal. The states remain free to reject *Luce*, as some do.[9]

One-upping *Luce*, the Supreme Court held in its decision in the *Ohler* case in 2000, that the accused waives review of an unfavorable preliminary ruling if he testifies and brings out prior convictions himself in an attempt to undercut in advance an expected attack.[10] It is hard to see what else a defendant can do. The *Ohler* approach puts defendants in such a difficult position, and stretches so far the

---

8. United States v. Cook, 608 F.2d 1175 (9th Cir. 1979).

9. Decisions in New Jersey, New York, Oregon, and Pennsylvania reject *Luce*. *See* People v. Moore, 156 A.2d 344, 346 (N.Y. 1989); Commonwealth v. Jackson, 561 A.2d 335, 338 (Pa. Super. 1988); State v. Whitehead, 517 A.2d 373 (N.J. 1986); State v. McClure, 692 P.2d 579, 583-584 & n4 (Or. 1984). And see Tennessee Rule 609(a)(3) (if court determines that conviction is admissible, "the accused need not actually testify at trial to later challenge" the ruling). On the other hand, decisions in Alaska, Arkansas, Arizona, California, Delaware, Florida, Idaho, Michigan, Rhode Island, South Carolina, South Dakota, Utah, Washington, and Wyoming follow *Luce*. See, e.g., State v. Silva, 898 A.2d 707, 718 (R.I. 2006).

10. Ohler v. United States, 529 U.S. 753 (2000) (one who introduces evidence "cannot complain" of error; both government and defense "must make choices" during trial; allowing defense appeal would deny government its right to decide whether to use convictions).

notion of waiver, that some state courts have wisely declined to go along.[11]

FRE 609(b)-(c)

(b) Time limit. Evidence of a conviction under this rule is not admissible if a period of more than ten years has elapsed since the date of the conviction or of the release of the witness from the confinement imposed for that conviction, whichever is the later date, unless the court determines, in the interests of justice, that the probative value of the conviction supported by specific facts and circumstances substantially outweighs its prejudicial effect. However, evidence of a conviction more than 10 years old as calculated herein, is not admissible unless the proponent gives to the adverse party sufficient advance written notice of intent to use such evidence to provide the adverse party with a fair opportunity to contest the use of such evidence.

(c) Effect of pardon, annulment, or certificate of rehabilitation. Evidence of a conviction is not admissible under this rule if (1) the conviction has been the subject of a pardon, annulment, certificate of rehabilitation, or other equivalent procedure based on a finding of the rehabilitation of the person convicted, and that person has not been convicted of a subsequent crime which was punishable by death or imprisonment in excess of one year, or (2) the conviction has been the subject of a pardon, annulment or other equivalent procedure based on a finding of innocence.

---

§6.36 —Ten-Year Limit, Pardons, Rehabilitation, and Annulments

FRE 609 draws some hard-edged lines that block or discourage use of some convictions. Under FRE 609(b), asking a witness about convictions more than ten years old is usually improper. And under FRE 609(c) a conviction may not be used to show untruthful disposition if the witness has been rehabilitated in various ways and there is no later conviction that is admissible for this purpose.

The ten-year limit applies to all convictions, whether offered under the first prong of FRE 609(a) (felonies) or the second (crimes of dishonesty or false statement). Happily, a conviction is usually either more or less than ten years old by any reasonable reading of FRE 609(b). But close cases arise. Like most time limits, this one has no magical properties and serves mostly the need for a reasonable cutoff, so a simple interpretation of the beginning and end points is needed.

---

11. Decisions in Iowa, Vermont, Nebraska, and Washington decline to follow *Ohler. See* State v. Keiser, 807 A.2d 378 (Vt. 2002); State v. Daly, 623 N.W.2d 799 (Iowa 2001); State v. Trotter, 632 N.W.2d 325 (Neb. 2001); State v. Thang, 41 P.3d 1159, 1167-1168 (Wash. 2002).

Beginning point   The beginning point is the time of release of the witness from confinement or the time of conviction, whichever comes later.[1] Release is usually later, and a natural reading suggests that release means not only discharge after completing a full sentence, but release from custody on parole or terms that allow the person, by fulfilling the conditions set, to make the release final. Sometimes conviction occurs later, as happens when one is sentenced to time served. Here it seems that "conviction" should be construed to mean the date judgment is entered, regardless whether posttrial motions are made or appeals taken.

Determining the beginning point of the ten-year period is made harder if the witness was (a) originally released without imprisonment but later confined for violating substantive conditions of probation or (b) originally confined and then released before the end of his term but reconfined for violating substantive conditions of parole. The approach some courts have taken to these situations seems commendably simple and realistic. The beginning point is the still-later date of final release, which has the effect of counting (as part of the "confinement imposed") periods of confinement occasioned by probation violations and reconfinement occasioned by parole violations.[2] This view is realistic in the sense that confinement and reconfinement represent punishment for the original crime rather than penalties for violating terms of probation or parole.

End point   The end point of the ten-year period could be the date of indictment, the date trial begins, or the date the witness testifies. The date of indictment seems preferable.[3] There is little chance the government will rush an indictment to beat the ten-year period, and any incentive to act quickly seems good rather than bad. Defining the date of trial or testimony by the witness as the end point would add to defense incentives to delay, which seems undesirable.

The ten-year limit may be overcome if the attacking party gives advance written notice sufficient to provide a fair opportunity to object and the court decides probative worth substantially outweighs prejudicial impact. In deciding whether to admit convictions more than ten years old, the court exercises discretion that is in some ways like what FRE 609(a)(1) provides for felonies. Here too the record should reflect the considerations that led to admitting or excluding the conviction.[4] Here

§6.36   1. Lee v. State, 3 P.3d 517 (Wyo. 2000); United States v. Daniel, 957 F.2d 162, 168 & n.4 (5th Cir. 1992).

2. United States v. McClintock, 748 F.2d 1278, 1288 (9th Cir. 1984) (beginning point is date of release from confinement after violation of substantive terms of probation); United States v. Gray, 852 F.2d 136, 139 (4th Cir. 1988) (similar, when defendant reconfined for parole violation).

3. United States v. Jefferson, 925 F.2d 1242, 1256 (10th Cir. 1991) (noting but avoiding question); United States v. Ras, 713 F.2d 311, 317-318 (7th Cir. 1983) (citing date of indictment on current charges). *But see* U.S. v. Griffin, 437 F.3d 767, 769 (8th Cir. 2006) (trial court said end point is date of trial, not indictment; reviewing court does not reach issue).

4. United States v. Portillo, 699 F.2d 461, 463-464 (9th Cir. 1982); United States v. Beahm, 664 F.2d 414, 418 (4th Cir. 1981).

too there should be nothing automatic about a decision to admit, and FRE 609(b) establishes in effect a presumption against admitting convictions more than ten years old.[5] And the factors that guide the exercise of discretion bear close resemblance to those found useful under FRE 609(a)(1)—nature of the crime, remoteness, similarity to the charged crime (for convictions of defendant or defense witnesses), and importance of credibility issues.[6] For second-prong convictions involving "dishonesty or false statement," the ten-year limit provides the only clear basis for exclusion (assuming no pardon or juvenile adjudication).

The "thumb on the scales" in the exercise of discretion under FRE 609(b) strongly favors exclusion. In contrast to the felony provision that favors admission in the case of ordinary witnesses and exclusion for defendants, FRE 609(b) provides that convictions over ten years old are admissible only if probative worth "substantially outweighs" prejudicial effect. In short, barriers to admissibility are higher for old convictions. Still the ten-year rule is not absolute, and old convictions may be admitted to impeach[7] or excluded on ground of age.[8] The ten-year limit does not apply to using convictions to impeach defendant by contradicting his direct testimony that he has never been convicted before,[9] nor to other uses of convictions.[10]

Rehabilitation

Under FRE 609(c), a conviction may not be used to show untruthful disposition if the witness has been rehabilitated and there is no later conviction that is admissible to show untruthfulness. Rehabilitation may be shown by a pardon or annulment based on a finding of rehabilitation, or by certificate of rehabilitation or "other equivalent procedure."[11] Merely being released or successfully completing probation or parole does not show rehabilitation,[12] nor do judicial grants of

---

5. United States v. Pope, 132 F.3d 684, 687 (11th Cir. 1998); United States v. Hamilton, 48 F.3d 149, 154 (5th Cir. 1995); United States v. Pritchard, 973 F.2d 905, 908 (11th Cir. 1992).

6. U.S. v. Redditt, 381 F.3d 597, 601 (7th Cir. 2004) (admitting conviction more than ten years old; defendant's credibility was "critical factor") (citing contradiction in testimony on both sides).

7. United States v. Pritchard, 973 F.2d 905, 908 (11th Cir. 1992) (1978 conviction in 1991 trial); United States v. Brown, 956 F.2d 782, 787 (8th Cir. 1992) (1969 burglary conviction); United States v. Thomas, 914 F.2d 139, 142-143 (3d Cir. 1990) (1972 drug conviction).

8. American Home Assurance Co. v. American President Lines, 44 F.3d 774, 778 (9th Cir. 1994); United States v. Williams, 892 F.2d 296, 301 (3rd Cir. 1989), *cert. denied*, 496 U.S. 939; United States v. Lochmondy, 890 F.2d 817, 824 (6th Cir. 1989).

9. *See* §6.39, *infra.*

10. United States v. Hudson, 53 F.3d 744, 747 (6th Cir. 1995) (in felon-in-possession trial, admitting old convictions; firearm statute has no age limit), *cert. denied*, 516 U.S. 890, 952; United States v. Rubio-Gonzalez, 674 F.2d 1067, 1075 (5th Cir. 1982) (evidence admitted under FRE 404(b) is not controlled by ten-year limit).

11. Brown v. Frey, 889 F.2d 159, 171 (8th Cir. 1989) (amended pardon days before trial indicating rehabilitation blocks use of conviction), *cert. denied*, 493 U.S. 1088.

12. U.S. Xpress Enterprises, Inc. v. J.B. Hunt Transport, Inc., 320 F.3d 809, 816 (8th Cir. 2003) (fact that conviction was "absolved" under Canadian law did not make it inadmissible; absolution required defendant to pay $5,000 and comply with six-month probation).

pardon resting on some basis other than a finding of rehabilitation,[13] judicial relief from civil disabilities,[14] or community service.[15]

A pardon, annulment, or other equivalent procedure resting on a determination that a convicted person is innocent makes the conviction inadmissible to impeach under FRE 609(c).[16]

FRE 609(d)

(d) Juvenile adjudications. Evidence of juvenile adjudications is generally not admissible under this rule. The court may, however, in a criminal case allow evidence of a juvenile adjudication of a witness other than the accused if conviction of the offense would be admissible to attack the credibility of an adult and the court is satisfied that admission in evidence is necessary for a fair determination of the issue of guilt or innocence.

---

§6.37 —Juvenile Adjudications

Under FRE 609(d), "generally" evidence of juvenile adjudications is not admissible to show that the witness is untruthful. But in criminal cases witnesses other than defendants may be impeached in this way if a conviction for the underlying offense would be admissible to attack the credibility of an adult and the court decides that impeachment is "necessary for a fair determination" of guilt or innocence.

This provision governs use of juvenile adjudications to suggest untruthful disposition (only reaching use of adjudications "under this rule"). It applies to cross-examination of both prosecution and defense witnesses, and to both sides in civil suits.[1] The purpose is to implement the theory underlying special statutes for juveniles, which

13. United States v. Wood, 943 F.2d 1048, 1055-1056 (9th Cir. 1991) (court order letting defendant withdraw guilty plea did not show rehabilitation); Smith v. Tidewater Marine Towing, Inc., 927 F.2d 838, 840 (5th Cir. 1991) (automatic first offender pardon required completion of sentence, not showing rehabilitation; pardon based on good behavior does not show rehabilitation).

14. See ACN to FRE 609 (pardon or equivalent "granted solely for the purpose of restoring civil rights lost by virtue of a conviction has no relevance"); United States v. Felix, 867 F.2d 1068, 1074 n.9 (8th Cir. 1989) (expungement precludes use of conviction only if it rests on rehabilitation or innocence). *Contra*, United States v. Ferguson, 776 F.2d 217, 222-223 (8th Cir. 1985) (denying cross on fraud conviction that was subject of expungement certificate) (state statute entitles one not to mention conviction in applications or "appearance as a witness").

15. Zinman v. Black & Decker, Inc., 983 F.2d 431, 435 (2d Cir. 1993) (community service is not "express finding" of rehabilitation).

16. Weihofen, The Effect of a Pardon, 88 U. Pa. L. Rev. 177, 182-183 (1939) (pardon for political reasons or good behavior should not affect use of conviction; pardon based on innocence destroys presumption that conviction shows untrustworthiness).

§6.37 1. United States v. Ciro, 753 F.2d 248, 249-250 (2d Cir. 1985) (defense witness), *cert. denied*, 471 U.S. 1057; United States v. Hines, 398 F.3d 713, 716 (6th Cir. 2005) (government witness), *cert. denied*, 545 U.S. 1134.

holds that they should be treated differently from adults (juvenile adjudications are frequently considered not to be "convictions" at all) in the hope that rehabilitation may be more surely accomplished and the belief that youthful offenses do not reflect as seriously on character.

Commitment for delinquency under the Federal Juvenile Delinquency Act is a juvenile adjudication under FRE 609(d) and not a conviction.[2] But the fact that a witness was a minor when he was convicted (or at the time of the offense) does not bring FRE 609(d) into play. On request, for example, a person eligible for treatment under the Delinquency Act must be proceeded against "as an adult," which suggests that any resultant conviction is not a juvenile adjudication.[3]

For a witness other than the accused, FRE 609(d) is not categorical. **Other than defendants** Such a witness may be impeached by a juvenile adjudication if an adult conviction for the same offense would be admissible and the court considers the evidence "necessary for a fair determination" of guilt or innocence. A concurring opinion in an old-but-important decision said there is a need to allow impeachment of uncorroborated testimony by a young person thought to be the victim, in a trial for contributing to the delinquency of a minor, and saw a similar need in connection with delinquency charges brought by one juvenile against another.[4] Whatever the context, the argument for allowing impeachment becomes stronger when vital testimony is uncorroborated and other means of impeachment are lacking.[5]

Although FRE 609(d) does not allow impeachment by use of juvenile **Civil suits** adjudications in civil litigation, arguably it does not impose a categorical bar. The language does not limit exceptions to those specified in the second sentence, and the word "generally" in the first suggests that a court may make exceptions in civil cases too.[6] But the intent of the second sentence is to disallow use of juvenile adjudications relating to the accused when offered to show untruthful disposition.

2. *See* 18 U.S.C. §§5031-5042. *See* United States v. Canniff, 521 F.2d 565, 569 (2d Cir. 1975) (federal adjudication as juvenile delinquent may not be used), *cert. denied*, 423 U.S. 1059; Cotton v. United States, 355 F.2d 480, 482 (10th Cir. 1966) (adjudication determines status and is not conviction).

3. *See* 18 U.S.C. §5032 (juvenile "shall not be proceeded against" in federal court unless certain conditions obtain or he requests in writing on advice of counsel to be treated as adult); Luck v. United States, 348 F.2d 763, 766-767 (D.C. Cir. 1965) (defendant was sentenced as adult after being "waived out" of Juvenile Court, so juvenile statute did not bar use of conviction to impeach), *cert. denied*, 429 U.S. 982.

4. Thomas v. United States, 121 F.2d 905, 911 (D.C. Cir. 1941) (Stephens, J., concurring). *See* United States v. Iron Shell, 633 F.2d 77, 92 (8th Cir. 1980) (prosecutor asked witness whether she had ever been convicted of felony and elicited reply "when I was 14 years old"), *cert. denied*, 450 U.S. 1001.

5. *See* Giles v. Maryland, 386 U.S. 66 (1967) (remanding rape case to consider whether juvenile records of complaining witness should have been disclosed and whether prosecutor let false evidence go uncorrected); United States v. Jones, 557 F.2d 1237, 1238-1239 (8th Cir. 1977) (defense showed witness was adjudicated as delinquent, sent to reformatory, and crime was felony).

6. *See* Samples v. Atlanta, 916 F.2d 1548, 1552 (11th Cir. 1990) (in wrongful death suit alleging excessive force in arrest and shooting death of plaintiff's son, admitting son's juvenile record).

FRE 609(d) bars only the use of juvenile adjudications to impeach "under this rule," which means that it only applies to juvenile adjudications offered to show untruthful disposition. It does not speak to the use of adjudications to impeach a witness who testifies that he has never been in trouble, where an adjudication impeaches by contradiction and may be admitted for this purpose.[7] Nor does FRE 609(d) bar the use of juvenile adjudications to prove prior conduct for substantive purposes, such as proving intent or knowledge under FRE 404(b).[8]

Showing bias   FRE 609(d) does not speak to cases where juvenile adjudications show bias. In the *Davis* case, a probationer named Green gave critical testimony connecting defendant to a burglary. Defendant suggested through questions that Green himself might be under suspicion and asked whether he had "ever been questioned like that before," but Green falsely said no and the court blocked questions about his probation or juvenile adjudication. Sympathizing with the concerns on both sides, the Supreme Court drew a line. On the one side are attempts to show untruthful disposition. On the other is the "more particular attack" showing "biases, prejudices, or ulterior motives" that might "relate directly" to issues or personalities. Here the defense was engaging in efforts of the latter sort, and confronting the witness to bring out bias or prejudice was more important than protecting juvenile offenders.[9] FRE 609(d) is in harmony with *Davis* and does not bar use of juvenile adjudications indicating bias, but courts following *Davis* properly disallow questions to defendants about juvenile adjudications that raise only questions about truthful disposition.[10]

FRE 609(e)

(e) **Pendency of appeal.** The pendency of an appeal therefrom does not render evidence of a conviction inadmissible. Evidence of the pendency of an appeal is admissible.

---

§6.38   —Meaning of Conviction; Appeal and Finality

The central element in the method of attack governed by FRE 609 is "conviction," and the term connotes an unequivocal judicial pronouncement of guilt in a criminal proceeding. A judgment of conviction formally entered by the court most clearly satisfies the Rule, although a judgment need not be "final" in the sense of being beyond

---

7. *See* §6.39, *infra.*

8. United States v. Rogers, 918 F.2d 207, 210-211 (D.C. Cir. 1990) (asking defendant about distributing crack, which led to juvenile adjudication and commitment to group home, refuting claim of mistake and lack of intent).

9. Davis v. Alaska, 415 U.S. 308, at 316-319 (1974).

10. United States v. Williams, 963 F.2d 1337, 1340 (10th Cir. 1992); United States v. Jones, 557 F.2d 1237, 1238-1239 (8th Cir. 1977).

reach of ordinary appeal or challenge by posttrial motion. Probably a guilty verdict satisfies FRE 609, and perhaps pleas of guilty.

At a minimum, what FRE 609 means by "conviction" is not satisfied by indictments or arrests, nor civil judgments or administrative findings, nor acts that may be crimes.[1] On the other hand, "conviction" does not require a contested trial on a plea of innocent leading to a verdict of guilty, and a conviction under FRE 609 may rest on a *plea* of guilty or nolo contendere or an *Alford* plea (where defendant in effect claims to be innocent while consenting to judgment of conviction).[2] Nor does it matter that conviction leads to a suspended sentence.[3] Clearly FRE 609 contemplates state as well as federal convictions, and foreign nation judgments of conviction too.[4]

Under FRE 609(e), the pendency of an appeal does not make a conviction inadmissible,[5] and pendency of posttrial motions should not count either.[6] This practice rests on the sensible premise that a conviction is likely to be affirmed on appeal, and on the faith that the system usually reaches the right answer at trial. Doing otherwise would encourage jockeying for position—defendants facing other charges might take shallow appeals, and prosecutors might delay bringing other charges to trial.[7]

Under the second sentence of FRE 609(e), use of a conviction being appealed opens the door to the other side to bring out the fact of appeal, and the same applies to posttrial motions.[8] Admitting these facts in mitigation finds an analogue in the practice of allowing the witness to offer a word of explanation when impeached by a conviction.

FRE 609 does not by its terms say whether a guilty plea may be used, or a verdict of guilty. Some risks come with using pleas and verdicts, since a plea may be withdrawn even after sentencing, and FRE 410 bars proof of withdrawn guilty pleas even when offered to impeach, and a

§6.38 1. United States v. Spencer, 25 F.3d 1105, 1109 (D.C. Cir. 1994) (indictment or arrest is not conviction); United States v. McDonald, 905 F.2d 871, 875 (5th Cir. 1990) (drug use did not fit FRE 609; no conviction); *cert denied*, 498 U.S. 1002.

2. Specht v. State, 734 N.E.2d 239, 240 (Ind. 2000) (guilty plea); United States v. Sonny Mitchell Center, 934 F.2d 77, 79 (5th Cir. 1991) (nolo plea); United States v. Lipscomb, 702 F.2d 1049, 1070 (D.C. Cir 1983) (*Alford* plea).

3. Wilson v. Attaway, 757 F.2d 1227, 1244-1245 (11th Cir. 1985). *Contra*, United States v. Amaechi, 991 F.2d 374, 378 (7th Cir. 1993) (sentence of supervision is not conviction).

4. United States v. Manafzadeh, 592 F.2d 81, 90-91 (2d Cir. 1979) (Iranian conviction; defendant had to show unfairness); United States v. Wilson, 556 F.2d 1177, 1178 (4th Cir. 1977) (German rape conviction, without right to jury trial), *cert. denied*, 434 U.S. 986.

5. United States v. Klayer, 707 F.2d 892, 895 (6th Cir. 1983), *cert. denied*, 464 U.S. 858; United States v. De La Torre, 639 F.2d 245, 248-249 (5th Cir. 1981).

6. United States v. Vanderbosch, 610 F.2d 95, 96-97 (2d Cir. 1979); United States v. Rose, 526 F.2d 745, 747 (8th Cir. 1975), *cert. denied*, 425 U.S. 905.

7. United States v. Soles, 482 F.2d 105, 107-108 (2d Cir. 1973), *cert. denied*, 414 U.S. 1027.

8. United States v. Klayer, 707 F.2d 892, 895 (6th Cir. 1983) (proof of appeal), *cert. denied*, 464 U.S. 858; United States v. Smith, 623 F.2d 627, 631 (9th Cir. 1980) (posttrial motion for judgment of acquittal).

verdict may be set aside on motion.[9] There is also an obvious formal objection to using pleas and verdicts (a conviction is a conviction). FRE 609 seems to regulate the whole topic by authorizing some inquiries and forbidding others, so its silence about pleas and verdicts could mean they are beyond range of allowable inquiry. This conclusion finds support in policy, inasmuch as verdicts are more likely to be thrown out than convictions, and pleas rest on factfinding that is not as painstaking or thorough as convictions and are even less final than verdicts. But a conclusion that "conviction" under FRE 609(a) does not reach verdicts or pleas could support the argument that verdicts and pleas simply lie beyond reach of FRE 609, which suggests that asking about the underlying acts remains proper under FRE 608(b) if they reflect untruthful disposition.[10]

On balance, it seems wise to allow use of verdicts and pleas, and the critical point is that FRE 609(e) allows use of convictions that have been appealed. The key to FRE 609 is not so much finality as the existence of a reliable judicial act that signifies guilt on the underlying charges, and verdicts and pleas provide this element. This point underlies the willingness of courts to apply FRE 609 to convictions leading to suspended sentences. Applying FRE 609 brings into play the guidelines in the Rule (the crime must be a felony or one involving dishonesty or false statement, not more than ten years old, and so forth) and the interpretive conventions that limit the questions that may be asked, and the situation of a verdict or plea is so close to the intended scope of FRE 609 that applying these guidelines seems a good thing. Finally, both verdicts and pleas are reliable indicators of actual guilt. Verdicts present the strongest claim for use in questioning, since they reflect jury findings after trial and are less easily set aside,[11] but pleas too seem reliable enough.[12] On the latter point, there are some indications of disagreement in the cases.[13]

While the fact of appeal does not make a conviction inadmissible to impeach, a conviction that is already reversed or set aside is not a proper subject for questioning under FRE 609.[14] It seems that reversal of such a

9. *See* FRCrimP 32(d) (motion to withdraw plea of guilty or nolo contendere); FRCrimP 29 (motion for judgment of acquittal).

10. United States v. Bentley, 706 F.2d 1498, 1509-1510 (8th Cir. 1983) (FRE 609 does not authorize defense questions to witness indicted on drug charges because no conviction resulted; inquiry into underlying acts is allowed under FRE 608 if they relate to veracity), *cert. denied*, 467 U.S. 1209.

11. United States v. Mitchell, 886 F.2d 667, 670-671 (4th Cir. 1989) (approving questions on convictions for obstructing congressional inquiry and wire fraud); United States v. Smith, 623 F.2d 627, 630-631 (9th Cir. 1980) (felony guilty verdict was just as relevant as conviction).

12. *See* United States v. Chilcote, 724 F.2d 1498, 1502-1504 (11th Cir. 1984), *cert. denied*, 467 U.S. 1218; United States v. Leslie, 542 F.2d 285, 291-292 (5th Cir. 1976); United States v. Turner, 497 F.2d 406, 407 (10th Cir. 1974), *cert. denied*, 423 U.S. 848.

13. United States v. Klein, 560 F.2d 1236, 1241 (5th Cir. 1977) (distinguishing pleas from verdicts), *cert. denied*, 434 U.S. 1073.

14. United States v. Russell, 221 F.3d 615, 620 n.6 (4th Cir. 2000) (once reversed, conviction cannot be used under FRE 609); United States v. Van Dorn, 925 F.2d 1331, 1337 (11th Cir. 1991) (conviction had been reversed; defense could not offer).

conviction may have some impact in a trial where it was used. At the very least, reference to such a conviction should be stricken on request if the reversal comes while the trial is in progress, and a later reversal of the conviction should probably be treated as new evidence that can be offered in support of a motion for a new trial.[15]

§6.39   —Uses of Convictions Unregulated by FRE 609

FRE 609 regulates only the use of convictions to impeach by suggesting that a witness is by character or disposition untruthful. Like FRE 608, FRE 609 does not apply to the quite different device of impeachment by contradiction. Thus FRE 609 does not apply to convictions offered to contradict one who denies the underlying misconduct or to prove circumstantially such things as knowledge, intent, or identity under FRE 404(b).

Contradiction is an impeachment method that is not formally regulated by rules, and the underlying doctrine is discussed elsewhere.[1] To take the most common setting (and at some risk of oversimplifying), if the accused testifies on direct that he has not been involved before in the kind of behavior he is charged with or broadly claims never to have been involved in crime, he invites impeachment by contradiction. Testimony of the former description paves the way to prove convictions for misconduct of the sort he denies, and testimony of the latter description paves the way to prove any kind of conviction.[2] The same thing can happen in other settings where parties testify and make similar statements.[3] Here courts need not apply the balancing standards in FRE 609(a), although impeachment by contradiction often raises issues under FRE 403, nor are they bound by the hard-edged restriction on use of convictions more than ten years old or use of juvenile adjudications.

FRE 404(b) often paves the way to prove specific instances of misconduct to show knowledge, intent, identity, and so forth. Convictions are admissible in this context, and FRE 609 does not regulate these uses.[4]

---

15. *See* Note, Impeachment of Witnesses by Prior Convictions Pending Appeal, 46 U. Chi. L. Rev. 499, 520-524 (1979) (new trial as remedy); United States v. Fisher, 106 F.3d 622, 629 (5th Cir. 1997).

§6.39   1. *See* §§6.43-6.48, *infra.*

2. *See* United States v. Denetclaw, 96 F.3d 454, 458 (10th Cir. 1996) (admitting tribal court convictions as inconsistent with defendant's testimony), *cert. denied,* 519 U.S. 1141; United States v. Norton, 26 F.3d 240, 243 (1st Cir. 1994) (29-year-old conviction contradicts defendant's direct testimony).

3. United States v. Bender, 265 F.3d 464, 471 (6th Cir. 2001) (defendant's direct testimony that she "never sold drugs and did not begin using them until 1992," opened door to 1987 conviction for distributing cocaine); Gora v. Costa, 971 F.2d 1325, 1330-1331 (7th Cir. 1992) (using conviction and current incarceration to contradict direct testimony by civil rights plaintiff).

4. United States v. Wellington, 754 F.2d 1457, 1464 (9th Cir. 1985) (impeachment rules inapplicable because convictions were admitted to prove one co-offender knew

4. *Showing Prior Inconsistent Statements*

FRE 613

(a) **Examining witness concerning prior statement.** In examining a witness concerning a prior statement made by the witness, whether written or not, the statement need not be shown nor its contents disclosed to the witness at that time, but on request the same shall be shown or disclosed to opposing counsel.

(b) **Extrinsic evidence of prior inconsistent statement of witness.** Extrinsic evidence of a prior inconsistent statement by a witness is not admissible unless the witness is afforded an opportunity to explain or deny the same and the opposite party is afforded an opportunity to interrogate the witness thereon, or the interests of justice otherwise require. This provision does not apply to admissions of a party opponent as defined in Rule 801(d)(2).

---

§6.40 Cross-Examination and Extrinsic Evidence

Impeachment by showing that a witness made statements inconsistent with his testimony, "blowing hot and cold" in McCormick's apt metaphor,[1] undercuts credibility by raising doubts about both statements. This kind of attack has both specific and general effects, suggesting that a witness may have lied or erred on the very point of inconsistency, hence may have lied or erred on other points. Often, however, the attack has the weakness of being indefinite, suggesting error or falsity but not which or why. Is the witness biased? Generally untruthful? Is there some defect in perception, memory, or narrative ability? Or is it just human error?

It is settled that a party may impeach a witness by prior inconsistent statements.[2] Usually the attack proceeds by cross-examination, but as FRE 613(b) acknowledges, the attack may also be mounted by means of extrinsic evidence—usually calling another witness to testify to statements made by the witness being attacked, although such proof is admissible, according to that provision, only if the witness being attacked has a chance to explain (this point is examined in the next section). This kind of attack can go forward even if the hearsay doctrine blocks use of such statements as substantive evidence (proof of what they assert). The court on request should give a limiting instruction if using an inconsistent statement as substantive evidence would be

---

another's criminal past), *cert. denied*, 474 U.S. 1032; Roshan v. Fard, 705 F.2d 102, 104 (4th Cir. 1983) (error to exclude plaintiff's conviction where defendant acted as informant, to show motive; FRE 609 is inapplicable).

§6.40 1. 1 McCormick, Evidence §34 (6th ed. 2006).

2. United States v. Hale, 422 U.S. 171, 176 (1975).

improper, but not if the statement is generally admissible.[3] Even prior statements by the accused taken in violation of *Miranda* or related constitutional doctrines may be used to impeach his testimony, although some exclusionary rules bar use of some statements for impeachment.[4]

To be admissible as impeaching evidence, the prior statement must be inconsistent with present testimony.[5] This requirement is satisfied if the statement diametrically opposes or directly contradicts trial testimony. Far less suffices, however, and there is inconsistency enough if the thrust of a statement differs significantly from the thrust of trial testimony, or if comparing the statement with the trial testimony suggests that the witness has changed his view or made a mistake that matters.[6] If a prior statement omits a material detail, which under the circumstances would likely be included if true, the statement is inconsistent with testimony that includes this detail.[7] And if an observer ventures an opinion or conclusion on fault or responsibility, such a comment may be admitted as inconsistent if he later testifies to facts that are at odds with his earlier appraisal.[8]

Must be inconsistent

When a witness testifies that he lacks memory or knowledge, is an earlier positive assertion inconsistent? This question is especially important for "turncoat" government witnesses who give incriminating statements beforehand but "waffle" at trial. The stakes are magnified if the statement was given during grand jury proceedings or a preliminary hearing because such a statement is often admissible not only to impeach but as substantive evidence.[9] At least in theory, both a claimed lack of memory and a prior positive statement might be true and correct—what once was known may be forgotten, and the difference need not suggest that the witness lied or erred either time. But common

Testifies to lack of memory or knowledge

---

3. The framers tried to take *all* inconsistent statements out of the hearsay category: FRE 801(d)(1)(A) would have defined *all* of them as "not hearsay," provided that declarant testifies and can be cross-examined about what he said before. *See* Preliminary Draft, Rule 8-01. But Congress would not go along, and FRE 801(d)(1)(A) *as enacted* only takes prior inconsistent statements *given under oath in a proceeding* out of the hearsay category (and only if the witness can now be cross-examined). *See* §8.24, *infra.*

4. *See* Harris v. New York, 401 U.S. 222 (1971) (failure to warn bars substantive use of custodial statements; impeaching use is proper if defendant testifies). *But see* §4.29, supra (FRE 410 bars impeaching use of plea bargaining statements, although right to exclude is waivable). *And see generally* the discussion of the effect of exclusionary doctrines on impeachment by contradiction in §§6.45-6.46, *infra.*

5. United States v. Hale, 422 U.S. 171, 176 (1975) (prior statements should be inconsistent); United States v. Trzaska, 111 F.3d 1019, 1024-1025 (2d Cir. 1997) (reversible error to admit statement that was not inconsistent).

6. United States v. Strother, 49 F.3d 869, 874-875 (2d Cir. 1995) (statement need not be diametrically opposed); United States v. Agajanian, 852 F.2d 56, 58 (2d Cir. 1988) (court has discretion to determine whether statements inconsistent; need not be diametrically opposed).

7. Moylan v. Meadow Club, Inc., 979 F.2d 1246, 1249 (7th Cir. 1992) (statement omitting point that would naturally be mentioned is inconsistent enough to impeach).

8. Winans v. Rockwell Intl. Corp., 705 F.2d 1449, 1457 (5th Cir. 1983); Atlantic Greyhound Corp. v. Eddins, 177 F.2d 954, 958 (4th Cir. 1949).

9. *See* FRE 801(d)(1)(A), discussed in §8.24, *infra.*

sense rebels at the thought that such changes in knowledge or memory reflect only the vagaries of human understanding, and experience suggests that such changes may reflect a change of view, or uncertainty, mistake, or a determination to avoid telling the truth. After all, claiming not to know is a familiar way to keep distance and avoid involvement or controversy, or to mask confusion or insecurity or uncertainty.

In such cases, it seems easiest to conclude that a prior positive statement satisfies the inconsistency requirement if the claimed lack of memory or knowledge is false or feigned.[10] Here at least the inference is strong that it is not just the vagaries of human understanding that are at work, but something that really should cast doubt on trial testimony. But to require a false or feigned lack of memory seems unworkable: If the judge must assess credibility in deciding whether to admit a prior positive statement, he is playing a role normally reserved to the jury, and the question is one that often cannot be answered with confidence. It seems better not to impose this condition, and courts often do not mention it.[11]

In this setting, impeachment poses two problems:

First, if a witness gives no positive testimony and his prior statement is not admissible as substantive evidence, allowing impeachment promises little gain and considerable danger. The reason is that the impeaching effect of a prior positive statement cannot support a positive inference on the matters asserted in it. To put it another way, the prior statement can properly persuade the jury to disbelieve the witness when he testifies that he lacks knowledge or memory, but this disbelief is not an adequate basis for an inference that the prior statement is true.[12] Not surprisingly, in such cases the attacking party is often the calling party, and the substance of the prior statement is what that party hoped would emerge in testimony. Here tradition once barred use of prior statements to impeach unless the testimony came as a surprise and caused affirmative damage, and the old voucher rule supported this result. Although FRE 607 abolished the voucher rule, modern practice is in fact little changed.[13]

Second, it may be hard or impossible to cross-examine a witness who claims at trial to lack knowledge or memory about underlying events. The witness who replies to every question about those events by saying "I don't know" has not given much depth or context that might be useful in assessing what he said earlier. The same is true of the witness who gives that response when asked about his own prior statement. If the attacking party wants to use the prior statement as substantive evidence under FRE 801(d)(1)(A), the speaker must be "subject to cross-examination" on the statement. If the statement is offered against

---

10. United States v. Thompson, 708 F.2d 1294, 1299-1302 & n.2 (8th Cir. 1983) (judge may disbelieve claimed inability to recall); United States v. Rogers, 549 F.2d 490, 495-496 (8th Cir. 1976) (when "disbelieved" by judge, claimed inability to recall may be viewed as inconsistent with prior statement), *cert. denied*, 431 U.S. 918.

11. United States v. Tory, 52 F.3d 207, 210 (9th Cir. 1995).

12. *See* United States v. Crouch, 731 F.2d 621, 623 (9th Cir. 1984) (maximum legitimate effect of impeaching testimony can never be more than cancellation of adverse answer by which party is surprised), *cert. denied*, 469 U.S. 1105.

13. *See* §6.17, *supra*.

a criminal defendant, there are also confrontation concerns, although
modern decisions indicate that these have little effect in this setting.[14]

The opposite case, where someone says he does not know or recall
something but later gives positive testimony, seems to happen less
often. Here too, both statements might be correct, although it seems
improbable that one might honestly come to a *later* understanding of
events or conditions that one could not recall or put into words at an
earlier time. What sometimes happens, however, is that a witness gives
more detail in testimony than she provided in earlier statements. And
sometimes mere silence on a prior occasion is inconsistent with positive
assertions made later on. If a witness says nothing when circumstances
make it likely that he would state a fact if it were so, later testimony asserting it seems inconsistent and the earlier silence may be shown.[15]

Using prior inconsistent statements to impeach is subject to the rule
against impeachment on collateral matters. This limit, however, is not
enforced with much rigor, because inconsistent statements indicate
self-contradiction, which seems a more serious matter (one that merits
explanation) than counterproof from other sources, and courts allow
considerable leeway for prior statements by the witness.[16] Still, if a prior
statement tends *neither* to undermine his testimony on some point that
counts *nor* to demonstrate or refute bias, capacity, or truthful disposition on his part, *then* the statement relates only to a collateral matter
and may be excluded.[17]

> **Prior statement indicates lack of knowledge or memory**

FRE 613(a) provides that in cross-examining a witness about her
inconsistent statement, a party need not then show it to her or disclose
its contents, but that opposing counsel is entitled on request to see the
statement or learn its contents. The purpose is to abolish a principle
that emerged from *Queen Caroline's Case* in 1820, which required the
cross-examiner in effect to "telegraph his punch" to the witness.[18] The
lawyer was expected to display the statement to the witness if it was
written or to recall its substance and the time and surrounding

> **Need not show statement**

---

14. *See* §§8.24 and 8.88, *infra. See also* United States v. Owens, 484 U.S. 554 (1988);
United States v. Kelly, 436 F.3d 992, 995-996 (8th Cir. 2006) (where seven-year-old was
uncooperative, admitting his recorded testimony to impeach and rejecting claim that
he could not be cross-examined; FRE 613(b) requires opportunity to explain, not
actual explanation or denial).

15. United States v. Carr, 584 F.2d 612, 618 (2d Cir. 1978), *cert. denied*, 440 U.S. 935;
United States v. Rogers, 549 F.2d 490, 496 (8th Cir. 1976), *cert. denied*, 431 U.S. 918.

16. On the collateral matter limit, *see* §6.47, *infra*.

17. United States v. Roulette, 75 F.3d 418, 422-423 (8th Cir. 1996) (describing
collateral matter bar in context of prior inconsistent statements), *cert. denied*, 519
U.S. 853; United States v. Grooms, 978 F.2d 425, 428-429 (8th Cir. 1992) (mother
denied on cross that she told friend the girls were "coached by their father" in alleging
abuse; can exclude testimony describing statement; can't use extrinsic evidence to
impeach on collateral matter).

18. *See* Queen Caroline's Case, 2 Brod. & Bing. 284, 129 Eng. Rep. 976, 977 (1820)
(one may not ask about contents of letter without first showing it to witness and asking
whether he wrote it). But *see* Stat. 17 & 18 Vict. c. 125, §24 (witness may be cross-
examined on written statements "without such writing being shown to him") (essentially abolishing rule in *Queen Caroline's Case*).

circumstances if it was oral. The principle seems to have rested largely on the thought that it is somehow unfair to "spring" a prior inconsistent statement on an unsuspecting witness.

But the cure was worse than the disease: The required procedure increased the difficulties of the cross-examiner by forewarning the witness, who got a chance to explain the statement away even before its contents were made known to the trier of fact, depriving the questioner of the chance to make a convincing display of vacillation. In jurisdictions following FRE 613(a), the principle is a dead letter. The cross-examiner need not display the statement or disclose its substance to the witness when he inquires about it.[19]

It is true that innocent explanations may underlie a seeming inconsistency, and that a cross-examiner might ask a groundless question that implies an inconsistent statement the witness never made. FRE 613(a) reduces these risks to an acceptable minimum by providing that the cross-examiner must on request show the statement to opposing counsel or disclose its contents to her. That way opposing counsel may pursue the matter on redirect, refute false implications about statements that were never made, and bring to light any explanation that the witness may have.

§6.41 The Chance to Explain

FRE 613(b) provides that, with two exceptions, a prior inconsistent statement may not be proved by extrinsic evidence unless the witness has an opportunity to explain or deny and the opposite party has an opportunity to question the witness. One exception says that the described conditions do not apply to admissions by a party opponent; the other says the judge need not enforce the conditions if the interests of justice otherwise require.

Relax the rigor   The purpose of FRE 613(b) is to relax the rigor in *Queen Caroline's Case,* which held that *before* the attacking party may offer extrinsic evidence of an inconsistent statement the witness must have a chance to explain or deny.[1] The substance of the principle is retained because the witness must still have this chance, but FRE 613 does not specify time or sequence, so the chance for explanation or denial (and for additional questioning by parties defending or repairing credibility) may be provided either before or after the statement is proved by extrinsic evidence.[2] Occasionally, however, courts still insist on a foundation

---

19. NLRB v. Bakers of Paris, Inc., 929 F.2d 1427, 1436 (9th Cir. 1991) (no requirement that statement be presented to or authenticated by witness before it is used).

§6.41   1. Queen Caroline's Case, 2 Brod. & Bing. 284, 313, 129 Eng. Rep. 976 (1820) (before proving statement, witness must be asked whether he made it; if he admits it, proof becomes unnecessary and witness has chance to explain; if he denies it, attacking party can "contradict and falsify" by extrinsic evidence).

2. United States v. Della Rose, 403 F.3d 891 (7th Cir. 2005) (defense did not ask B about statement, which "did not necessarily preclude" eliciting D's testimony about it; government could recall B case and ask about statement then) (quoting authors of this Treatise).

first, as they can do under FRE 611. The cost of providing the chance to explain or deny after the statement has been proved is that sometimes the witness must be recalled, and preserving the intended flexibility requires courts to be open to this possibility. If the cost or difficulty in taking this course is considerable, however, this fact alone weighs against taking full advantage of the intended flexibility and extrinsic evidence is sometimes excluded.[3] A notion of fairness to the witness, and to her sponsoring or supporting parties, underlies the requirement that she have an opportunity to explain or deny. If her credibility is called into question, she should have a chance to reply. If her direct testimony is undermined, the calling party should have a chance to explain any vacillation or show that it has an innocent explanation or does not really cast doubt on her testimony. The purpose in relaxing the principle in *Queen Caroline's Case* is simply to remove a trap for unwary counsel.

The conditions set by FRE 613(b) are two: The witness must have a chance to explain or deny the statement,[4] and parties who would support or repair her credibility must have a chance to question her about it.[5] Where these requirements are not satisfied, extrinsic evidence should be excluded, but satisfying them gives the attacking party a strong argument that such evidence should be admitted.[6]

Explain, ask questions

FRE 613(b) does not require the attacking party to provide the chance to explain. The other side may be burdened with the task of pursuing whatever explanation there might be, by questioning the witness and even recalling her if she has already left the stand. Still, it seems that the attacking party should bear the risk that a witness may become unavailable after testifying: In other words, if the attacking party does not raise the inconsistency on cross, and if the witness then leaves the stand and becomes unavailable, or if the task of finding her and bringing her back would be a considerable burden to the supporting party, the court should ordinarily exclude extrinsic evidence of her prior statements, offered by the attacking party belatedly after the witness has left the courtroom.[7]

---

3. Jones v. Collier, 762 F.2d 71, 72 (8th Cir. 1985) (refusing to let plaintiff recall witness incarcerated 300 miles away); United States v. Di Napoli, 557 F.2d 962, 965 (2d Cir. 1977) (no error to refuse to recall witness so foundation could be laid), *cert. denied*, 434 U.S. 858.

4. United States v. Bonnett, 877 F.2d 1450, 1462-1463 (10th Cir. 1989); United States v. McLaughlin, 663 F.2d 949, 953-954 (9th Cir. 1981).

5. Barton v. Columbia Mut. Cas. Ins. Co., 930 F.2d 1337 (8th Cir. 1991); United States v. Elliott, 771 F.2d 1046, 1051 (7th Cir. 1985); Re Corrugated Container Antitrust Litig., 756 F.2d 411, 415 (5th Cir. 1985).

6. United States v. Allen, 540 F.3d 821, 825 (8th Cir. 2008) (H said he put gun in car "a few weeks" after purchase; detective could testify that H said he did it "four or five days" after purchase; prosecutor identified statement, gave H a chance to address inconsistency) (FRE 613 satisfied).

7. *See* Garcia v. Lee, 976 F.2d 1344, 1345 (10th Cir. 1992) (blocking use of deposition that plaintiff could have presented earlier to impeach); Gong v. Hirsch, 913 F.2d 1269, 1275 (7th Cir. 1990) ("curt use" of letter did not convey intent to impeach; not in interests of justice to burden to pursue matter).

In practice, the conditions set by FRE 613(b) are often satisfied before extrinsic evidence of a statement is introduced, for three reasons: First, the party who wants to prove a statement before satisfying the conditions should bear the risk of motions to strike or for a mistrial if the witness becomes unavailable after the statement is proved. Second, the court has authority under FRE 611 to require the attacking party to prove a statement immediately after the witness has testified and might well do so in the interest of minimizing inconvenience to the witness. Third, the Best Evidence doctrine sometimes requires use of the writing itself, and the need to authenticate it may force the attacking party to take care of this detail by means of testimony by the very witness he seeks to impeach.[8]

Admissions excepted from precautionary conditions

The conditions in FRE 613(b) do not apply to statements by a party when offered by the other side as admissions.[9] The reason is that the operation of the adversary system makes the conditions unnecessary. Usually a party has every opportunity to explain or deny a statement, either because his case-in-chief follows the impeaching effort or because he can testify in rebuttal.

Interests of justice

Under the final clause of the first sentence in FRE 613(b), a court may admit extrinsic evidence of an inconsistent statement even if the witness does not have a chance to explain and the other side does not have a chance to question him about the statement if "the interests of justice" would thus be served. Suppose, for example, someone testifies and later makes a statement that conflicts with her testimony: Here it seems that the attacking party should be allowed to prove the statement even if the witness has no chance to explain or deny it. Obviously the attacker cannot be faulted for failing to raise the point while the witness was on the stand, and the burden of recalling her can be put on parties who support her testimony, along with the risk that she cannot be recalled.[10]

FRE 613(b) does not apply to impeachment by prior conduct that is inconsistent with trial testimony,[11] nor does it cover extrinsic evidence of bias revealed in prior statements, although courts sometimes impose a similar foundation requirement in this situation.[12]

If a witness denies or fails to recall an inconsistent statement when confronted with it, such a response provides a good reason to admit

8. United States v. Saget, 991 F.2d 702, 710 (11th Cir. 1993) (blocking defense attempt to impeach *M* by statements in agent's summary; no showing that *M* adopted statements as his own; foundation lacking).

9. Lexington Ins. Co. v. Cooke's Seafood, 835 F.2d 1364, 1368-1369 (11th Cir. 1988); United States v. Cline, 570 F.2d 731, 735 (8th Cir. 1978).

10. United States v. Bibbs, 564 F.2d 1165, 1169 (5th Cir. 1977) (admitting rebuttal proof that witness made statement inconsistent with her testimony after her appearance), *cert. denied*, 435 U.S. 1007.

11. *See* ACN to FRE 613. *But see* United States v. Smith, 605 F.2d 839, 846-847 (5th Cir. 1979) (invoking FRE 613 in excluding evidence of conduct conflicting with testimony); United States v. Cutler, 676 F.2d 1245, 1249 (9th Cir. 1982) (similar, stressing failure to lay foundation).

12. *See* §6.19, *supra*.

extrinsic evidence of the statement. But some federal cases hold that if the witness admits making the statement, extrinsic evidence should be excluded.[13] This mechanical rule makes little sense: A party should be allowed to make a case by the most convincing evidence he has, and extrinsic proof of a prior statement may be far more convincing than the acknowledgment of the declarant. The court may block needless introduction of cumulative evidence, but it seems unwise to impose this mechanical rule, and the better cases have abandoned it.[14]

§6.42 Constitutional Limits on Impeachment by Prior Silence

It is settled that the prosecutor may not impeach by showing that defendant stood silent in the presence of law enforcement officers after being arrested and getting *Miranda* warnings. The Court so held in *Doyle v. Ohio*, concluding that the tactic violated due process. In *Doyle*, defendant was convicted in state court of selling marijuana after a trial in which he testified that he was not the seller in the transaction, but the buyer (thus innocent of the charged offense). On cross, the prosecutor put questions designed to show he never gave this version of events to arresting officers after receiving *Miranda* warnings.

Although the warnings do not say silence carries no penalty (only that what defendant *says* may be used against him), the Court thought this assurance was "implicit." Hence it is "fundamentally unfair" to use post-warning silence to impeach an explanation offered at trial, and *Miranda* warnings make later silence "insolubly ambiguous."[1] *Doyle* generally bars proof, questioning, and comment or argument on post-warning silence,[2] along with proof that defendant said he wished to remain silent or retain counsel.[3]

The limits of this doctrine seem as important as the doctrine itself. In followup decisions the Court held that *Doyle* does not apply in four common situations:

First, *Doyle* does not bar use of gaps in positive statements, where the argument is that defendant spoke of matters covered in his testimony

Gaps in positive statements

---

13. *See* United States v. Daniele, 886 F.2d 1046, 1052-1053 (8th Cir. 1989); United States v. Soundingsides, 820 F.2d 1232, 1240-1041 (10th Cir. 1987); United States v. McCrady, 774 F.2d 868, 872-874 (8th Cir. 1985).

14. *See* Gordon v. United States, 344 U.S. 414, 420-421 (1952) (admitting that writing contains contradiction should not bar use of writing itself); United States v. Young, 86 F.3d 944, 949 (9th Cir. 1996) (extrinsic evidence admissible even if witness admits statement).

§6.42   1. Doyle v. Ohio, 426 U.S. 610, 619 (1976). *See also* United States v. Hale, 422 U.S. 171 (1975) (arrested people "may find the situation so intimidating that they may choose to stand mute").

2. *See* United States v. Whitehead, 200 F.3d 634, 638-639 (9th Cir. 2000); United States v. Shue, 746 F.2d 1280, 1285-1288 (7th Cir. 1984); United States v. Lewis, 651 F.2d 1163, 1165-1170 (6th Cir. 1981).

3. United States v. Kallin, 50 F.3d 689, 693-695 (9th Cir. 1995) (retain counsel); United States v. Szymaniak, 934 F.2d 434, 439 (2d Cir. 1991) (remain silent).

but omitted points he now includes. The Court so held in the *Charles* case, which was a murder prosecution in which defendant had been arrested driving the victim's car. He testified that he did not do the killing, but found the car with keys in a parking lot next to the jail. On cross, the prosecutor asked why he did not mention the parking lot at the time of arrest, bringing out that he told a detective he stole the car somewhere else. The Court found no violation of *Doyle*.[4] Hence the prosecutor may prove (and ask about) gaps in statements given in custody after being warned.[5]

Charles surely does not mean silence is fair game simply because defendant said *something*. Narrow comments or general questions should still be viewed as part of a larger exercise of protected silence, not as opening the door to arguments or questions suggesting that defendant could have said what he now says at that earlier time.[6]

Pre-arrest silence

Second, *Doyle* does not reach pre-arrest silence. In the *Jenkins* case, the Court held that the prosecutor may show that defendant had a chance to report his story to police or a parole officer and would likely have done so if the story were true.[7] Clearly failing to do so may not be persuasive and may be excluded as irrelevant or only marginally so, but the Constitution does not require exclusion.[8]

Post-arrest pre-warning silence

Third, the Court held in the *Weir* case that *Doyle* does not apply to post-arrest pre-warning silence.[9] The obligation to warn is triggered by questioning rather than arrest, so no warning is necessary if no questions are asked. Courts may bar inquiry into pre-arrest silence if it seems irrelevant or only marginally so, but the Constitution does not require exclusion.[10]

---

4. Anderson v. Charles, 447 U.S. 404, 408 (1980) (where defendant talks after being arrested and warned, government may show he did not give explanation to which he later testifies even if conflict turns on points omitted earlier).

5. United States v. Moreno, 933 F.2d 362, 372 (6th Cir. 1991) (after defendant testified that J was his supplier, proving he said he did not know his supplier); United States v. Samples, 713 F.2d 298, 303-304 (7th Cir. 1983) (after defendant testified that he knew about stolen beef but did not help dispose of it, proving he had denied all knowledge).

6. United States v. Curtis, 644 F.2d 263, 270-271 n.4 (3d Cir. 1981); United States ex rel. Allen v. Rowe, 591 F.2d 391, 397-398 (7th Cir. 1979); Morgan v. Hill, 569 F.2d 1161, 1166-1167 (1st Cir. 1978).

7. Jenkins v. Anderson, 447 U.S. 231 (1980) (defendant cannot prevent cross and comment about failing to come forward and tell police what he says at trial).

8. United States v. Davenport, 929 F.2d 1169, 1174-1175 (7th Cir. 1991) (no Doyle violation to use noncustodial statements to IRS agents, including refusal to give information); Lebowitz v. Wainwright, 670 F.2d 974, 979-780 (11th Cir. 1982) (using silence during search).

9. Fletcher v. Weir, 455 U.S. 603 (1982) (defendant testified that killing was self-defense or accidental, and prosecutor brought out on cross that he did not say this to arresting officers; since he did not get *Miranda* warnings during period of silence after arrest, no due process violation) (per curiam).

10. United States v. Rivera, 926 F.2d 1564, 1568-1569 (11th Cir. 1991) (testimony on behavior of people undergoing customs search; government may comment on silence after arrest but before warnings).

Fourth, the Court in *Doyle* took pains to distinguish the situation where defendant testifies to an exculpatory version of events and also "claims to have told the police" the same thing on arrest, where the purpose of proving that he did not tell the story earlier is not to contradict his version of events, but to challenge what he says about how he behaved after arrest.[11] This important qualification surely does not invite questioning on every point defendant might conceivably have raised at the time of arrest and is properly confined to questioning that seeks to answer a claim that he helped in some particular way.[12]

5. Contradiction—FRE 403 and 611

§6.43 The Process

Contradicting a witness is a recognized method of impeachment. It is much at home in an adversary system, being essential to fairness and balance in presenting and appraising testimony and other evidence.

Impeaching a witness by contradiction means showing that something he said is not so. Although the following terms are inexact, it is convenient to describe what is to be contradicted as "initial testimony" and to use "counterproof" to describe testimony or other evidence having this impeaching effect.[1] Suppose a witness testifies that a crop was healthy and growing on June 1 when it was sprayed with an herbicide, and then it became stunted and started to die. Other testimony that the crop was stunted and dying before June 1 qualifies as counterproof that tends to contradict, both by suggesting that the earlier testimony was mistaken on the date when damage first appeared and by tending to refute the inference that spraying caused the damage (or might have). If either point matters, such counterproof will likely be admitted.

The impeaching effects of contradiction are both specific and general. If believed, counterproof may persuade the trier to think

11. Doyle v. Ohio, 426 U.S. 610, 619 n.11 (1976) (post-arrest silence may be used if defendant testifies to exculpatory version of events "and claims to have told the police the same version"). *See also* United States v. Laughlin, 772 F.2d 1382, 1386-1391 (7th Cir. 1985); United States v. Shaw, 701 F.2d 367, 384 (5th Cir. 1983); United States v. Allston, 613 F.2d 609 (5th Cir. 1980).

12. United States v. Shue, 746 F.2d 1280, 1285-1288 (7th Cir. 1984); Alo v. Olim, 639 F.2d 466, 467-469 (9th Cir. 1980) (cross "strayed far afield from the narrow confines" of refuting claim that defendant gave police the story he advanced at trial, placing "impermissible burden" on exercise of rights).

§6.43 1. Using "initial testimony" to describe what is to be contradicted is inexact because sometimes the target is a writing or a *suggested interpretation* of testimony or other evidence. But usually the focus of contradiction is indeed testimony. "Counterproof" also is inexact because contradiction can be accomplished by mere questioning and argument. The term "counterproof" should be understood as describing such questioning and argument as well as formal proof.

the witness lied or erred on the specific point contradicted.[2] More generally, crediting the counterproof may persuade the trier to think the witness lied or erred on other points, perhaps raising doubts on everything he said. Impeachment by contradiction also has an indefinite quality because it may fail to explain the cause of the lies or errors it exposes. Is there a problem of character (untruthful disposition)? Bias or influence? Defect in mental or sensory capacity affecting perception, memory, narrative ability? Or was the witness simply, humanly, mistaken?[3] Clues are likely to be found in the context, usually augmented by broader questioning and argument.

There are many ways[4] to contradict a witness:

(1) By close questioning, the attacking party may get the witness to concede he was wrong in what he said before. But dramatic turn-arounds are more the stuff of fiction than courtroom life, and "testimonial self-contradiction" usually involves backing off or qualifying a point, or admitting to other possibilities or uncertainty. Pretrial preparation weeds out many waffling witnesses, and cases that depend on thin testimony easily confounded are likely to settle, but cross-examiners often succeed in weakening or limiting testimony by getting the witness himself to rephrase and qualify what he said before.

(2) The attacking party may put to a witness the substance or implications of other evidence already introduced, using questions to suggest tensions or conflicts and inviting the inference that the witness lied or erred in something he said. (If a question assumes unproved facts, it is objectionable on that ground. While the attacking party can usually reframe such a question, doing so takes out the "bite," which is likely to have been the objector's main purpose.)

(3) The attacking party may ask a witness about his own prior statement that conflicts with his testimony. Typically the statement has not been introduced, and the first mention comes in a leading question asking, "Didn't you tell X something very different from what you've said here today?" If the witness indeed made a conflicting statement, impeachment again takes the form of self-contradiction. So common and useful is this kind of attack that impeachment by prior inconsistent statement is recognized as a separate mechanism, regulated in part by FRE 613.[5]

(4) The attacking party may introduce testimony by another witness that (if credited) rebuts or undercuts or limits, or raises doubts about or suggests tensions with, testimony by an earlier witness. It is proper for

2. In this respect, impeachment by contradiction is similar to impeachment by inconsistent statement. Most other kinds of impeachment, such as proving untruthful disposition, bias, or incapacity have only nonspecific effect.

3. A jury may believe the counterproof and accord the contradiction its full specific effect but still think the witness was not lying or laboring under shortcomings in abilities to perceive, recollect, or narrate. The jury might conclude that mistakes happen to everybody, and the error does not undermine the balance of his testimony.

4. Behler v. Hanlon, 199 F.R.D. 553, 557 (D. Md. 2001) (tracking this analysis, quoting this Treatise).

5. See §§6.40-6.42, supra.

counterproof to take this form even though it amounts to "extrinsic evidence." It is this form of contradiction that seems most often to generate argument over the appropriateness of the impeaching effort.

Attempts at contradiction are usually limited in the interests of fairness and preventing excursions into "collateral" matters. Subject to such limits, it is worth noting that impeachment by contradiction may properly attack any testimony, whether given on direct or on cross, and indeed all evidence and inferences or conclusions suggested by it.[6]

Collateral matter limit

FRE 608(b) does not regulate contradiction as such. It bars "extrinsic evidence" of misconduct by a witness, but only sometimes, for the subject of FRE 608(b) is impeachment by showing untruthful disposition, not impeachment by contradiction, and the reference to "extrinsic evidence" does not generally apply to counterproof in the form of testimony by one witness that contradicts testimony by another.

Effect of FRE 608

Still, FRE 608 does have one narrow impact on contradiction. It limits the attacking party to asking about prior misdeeds by a witness that bear on the case by indicating untruthful disposition. The attacking party must "take her answer" and cannot offer extrinsic evidence to contradict her denial, such as documents showing she made a false statement or testimony by another witness describing it.[7] And FRE 608(b) counsels against expansive arguments for extrinsic evidence of bad acts that impeach in some marginal fashion, since the purpose is to minimize prejudice and avoid collateral inquiries. But where contradiction is proper because it shows error or mistake in testimony, FRE 608(b) has no application.[8]

Important as contradiction is in its own right, it has two side effects that merit special mention: First, the role of counterproof in impeaching a witness may justify admitting it out of order,[9] even if doing so requires going to a new stage in the proceedings.[10] Suppose, for example, a product liability suit against an herbicide maker in which the question when the crop damage appeared is first raised during the defense case. If defense testimony indicates that the damage appeared before the herbicide was applied, the court would likely let plaintiff

Admitting proof out of order

---

6. McDougal v. McCammon, 455 S.E.2d 788, 795 (W.Va. 1995) (quoting authors of this Treatise).

7. *See* the discussion of FRE 608(b) in §6.27, *supra*.

8. *See* the discussion in §6.28, *supra*.

9. Each party is expected to present the evidence important to her case during her case-in-chief, and courts disallow attempts to "reopen" after other side presents its case. But if one party has evidence that rebuts proof offered by the other, and there was no reason to offer the rebutting evidence earlier, courts usually let the rebutting party reopen. *See* §6.54, *infra*.

10. United States v. Calvert, 523 F.2d 895, 911-912 (8th Cir. 1975) (courts disfavor "lying in the weeds" in ambush, and may exclude rebuttal if prosecutor acts unfairly), *cert. denied*, 424 U.S. 911; People v. Jeffrey, 43 Cal. Rptr. 524, 525 (Cal. Dist. Ct. App. 1965) (defendant testified that he was in alley behind store; officer testified that he was closer to the scene when officer entered after burglary; prosecutor cannot withhold evidence that is properly part of case-in-chief, but court properly admitted testimony to impeach).

open a case-in-rebuttal and call witnesses who testify that the crop was healthy before the spraying, and that the damage only appeared thereafter.

Overriding exclusionary rules

Second, the contradicting function of counterproof may justify overriding specific exclusionary principles embodied in Rules, statutes, and even the Constitution.[11] Typically such principles bar substantive use of particular evidence, or some specific use, but when it is valuable in contradicting other evidence (hence impeaching some witness or source) it is often admitted for this limited purpose. Codified statements of exclusionary principles are often silent or vague on the question whether evidence may be admitted to impeach, and court-made doctrines may leave the matter in doubt as well.

Collateral points

Since not all testimony is equally important, courts limit the points on which contradiction is allowed. Often the limit is phrased in terms of excluding counterproof that contradicts on "collateral" points, meaning that the attacking party may not refute testimony that does not itself bear independently on the merits or other credibility issues (like bias). More broadly, courts limit or curtail contradiction in the interests of preventing prejudice to parties, confusion, waste of time, and protecting witnesses against abuse. In short, courts have authority under FRE 403 and 611 to limit contradiction.[12]

Fairness

Notions of fairness also bear on the subject because some kinds of evidence offered to contradict would ordinarily be excluded. When counterproof is subject to objection under the Rules or Constitution or some other protective doctrine, the question whether to overrule the objection and permit contradiction turns partly on appraising the strategic behavior of the parties. In what might be termed the ordinary case, the initial testimony is proper but the attacking party has otherwise-excludable counterproof that tends squarely to refute it without risking much in terms of prejudice, abuse, or confusion. Here the attacker is entitled to some leeway, even if some rule would otherwise exclude the counterproof.

But not all cases are ordinary, and parties sometimes try to manipulate the rules. Sometimes the manipulator is the attacking party, who moves to "set up" the attack by offering testimony (or drawing it out from an adverse witness on cross) for the purpose of knocking it down later by offering more explosive and otherwise excludable counterproof. Here the attack itself may be unfair. Other times the manipulator is the calling party, who moves to take advantage of an exclusionary doctrine to prevent the factfinder from hearing counterproof that may be essential in getting at the truth. Here shielding the initial testimony is unfair. Often, then, courts must appraise party strategy in deciding whether contradiction amounts to abuse or a necessary corrective measure.[13]

11. *See* §§6.45-6.46, *infra.*
12. *See* §6.47, *infra.*
13. *See* §6.48, *infra.*

§6.44 Typical Instances

In civil and criminal cases alike, much testimony and other evidence is routinely exposed as false or mistaken, or undercut or cast in doubt by other testimony or evidence. Most cases involve attempts to contradict actual testimony given by parties, but impeachment by contradiction can properly target nonparty testimony, other forms of evidence, and inferences suggested by evidence.[1]

Not surprisingly, the contradicting effect of counterproof varies in degree. Sometimes initial testimony and counterproof conflict directly, and the one tends fully to refute the other. Perhaps more often the counterproof is more modest in its impact. The initial testimony, for example, may advance a broad claim ("I'm a careful driver"), while the counterproof merely presents a counterexample ("you drove too fast that time") that does not formally refute what came before. After all, broad propositions are understood as generalities that contain unmentioned exceptions. In such situations, even fully credited counterproof may only slightly lessen the force of the initial testimony. Still, a particularly vivid counterexample ("you drove recklessly and caused an accident killing three people") may destroy the broad claim altogether.

Degrees of contradiction

Yet other times the initial testimony and counterproof conflict in more subtle ways, as happens when the former provides details that support a general inference ("he was just doing business") while the latter adds further and very different details ("several times he ran drugs") that suggest a very different inference ("he was engaged in a criminal venture"). Not surprisingly too, the relevancy of counterproof is very much affected by the strategies of the parties in advancing claims or charges and defenses.

In civil suits, a common kind of contradiction involves counterproof tending to refute initial testimony suggesting that a party was generally careful or responsible. Often (perhaps most of the time) proof of the latter sort could be excluded on objection.[2] But often it comes in, sometimes because the party alludes to such points while talking about something else, sometimes because the other party does not object (which might seem churlish) and may even be glad to see the initial proof because it "opens the door" to specific counterproof that would be excluded otherwise. Thus in negligence litigation, evidence that a party generally exercises due care paves the way for cross-examination and extrinsic evidence bringing out examples of lack of care, and claims of an accident-free past supporting an inference of

Careful, responsible

---

§6.44   1. United States v. Rhodes, 779 F.2d 1019, 1031 (4th Cir. 1985) (defendant separated himself from drugs by asking what witnesses knew about his involvement with cocaine; that made his cocaine convictions admissible), *cert. denied*, 476 U.S. 1182; United States v. Spetz, 721 F.2d 1457, 1476-1477 (9th Cir. 1983) (contradicting testimony given on cross).

2. General carefulness is considered character, and proof of this sort cannot be used to prove due care or responsible behavior at the time. *See* FRE 404. General carefulness ("always drive carefully") usually does not qualify as habit or practice under FRE 407.

general carefulness pave the way for cross and counterproof about other accidents.[3]

Where initial testimony sticks to the facts, however, evidence of unrelated acts should not be viewed as counterproof. For example, if a civil litigant testifies to what he did on the occasion (even if he adds that he was "careful"), proof that he was careless other times should not be admitted on the theory that it contradicts by showing general carelessness, hence carelessness this time. Fairness concerns arise because a civil litigant cannot normally offer proof of other accidents to show negligence and should not be allowed to avoid rules barring such proof by attenuated arguments of inferential contradiction.[4]

Crime-free past In criminal cases, testimony by a defendant that he has a crime-free past paves the way for counterproof indicating the contrary. The conflict is literal and inescapable if he testifies that he never commits crimes and the counterproof shows criminal acts or convictions,[5] and the same is true if he claims he has not been arrested or charged before and the counterproof shows arrests or charges.[6] The conflict is attenuated, and counterproof is often admitted but sometimes excluded, when initial testimony (a) advances a broad claim of good behavior or character ("I don't do drugs") and counterproof presents a counterexample ("he did in one instance"),[7] (b) describes specific instances of good behavior (defendant "was honest in certain transactions") and counterproof presents other instances of contrasting behavior ("he was dishonest on

3. Croce v. Bromley Corp., 623 F.2d 1084, 1091-1093 & n.24 (5th Cir. 1980) (defense suggested that pilot was capable and experienced; court properly admitted rebuttal evidence of past conduct); Atkinson v. Atchison, T. & S.F.R., 197 F.2d 244, 245-246 (10th Cir. 1952) (plaintiff testified on direct that "she usually drives at a low rate of speed" and looks ahead, and on cross reiterated that she is a careful driver; railroad brought out on cross that she was in two-car accident where she was in wrong lane).

4. Neuren v. Adduci, Mastriani, Meeks & Schill, 43 F.3d 1507, 1511-1512 (D.C. Cir. 1995) (defense claimed plaintiff did not get along with staff; she said she left firm because she was not getting enough international work; proof of problems with people at earlier post did not impeach). If a civil litigant pushes a witness into an overbroad claim on cross, counterproof of specific instances should not be admitted to reward such manipulative behavior. *See* §6.48, *infra.*

5. United States v. Antonakeas, 255 F.3d 714, 724 (9th Cir. 2001) (on direct, defendant *A* made "sweeping denials" of involvement in drugs; government could contradict through *P*'s testimony that *A* twice sold *P* cocaine); United States v. Schenk, 983 F.2d 876, 880 (8th Cir. 1993) (defendant said on cross that he knew what LSD looked like but never had or sold it; can ask about prior sales of LSD).

6. United States v. Garcia, 900 F.2d 571, 575-576 (2d Cir. 1990) (defendant said he had never been accused of selling drugs and that arrest did not involve drugs; can show he was arrested for possession); United States v. Babbitt, 683 F.2d 21, 25 (1st Cir. 1982) (defendant said he had no record; can prove he was arrested twice).

7. United States v. Uzenski, 434 F.3d 690, 711 (4th Cir. 2006) (by asking whether defendant "was a good officer" before present charges and getting positive answer, defendant paved way to prove incidents when he made false radio report and shot at his own police car); United States v. Riggio, 70 F.3d 336, 339 (5th Cir. 1995) (in arson trial defendant testified that he never burned anything and was never involved in crime; cross inquired into other fires for which no charges were brought), *cert. denied,* 517 U.S. 1126.

these other occasions"),[8] (c) implies something generally positive while counterproof undercuts the inference,[9] or (d) suggests an innocent or innocuous explanation for some item of proof or obvious inference from evidence already admitted, but counterproof tends to refute the explanation.[10] And claims of a troublefree past (making no reference to arrests) should not be contradicted by proof of arrests, although proof that defendant did the deed may be proper.[11]

Once again when initial testimony sticks to the facts, evidence of unrelated acts should not be viewed as counterproof that contradicts. For example, if defendant describes what happened (saying he is "innocent" or "didn't do it"), proof that he committed other similar crimes should *not* be admitted on the theory that it contradicts. Again fairness concerns arise, since the prosecutor cannot normally prove other crimes in order to show criminal disposition (hence guilt) and should not be allowed to avoid rules barring this line of proof by attenuated arguments of inferential contradiction.[12]

§6.45 Effect of Rules of Exclusion

The importance of contradicting other testimony or evidence often justifies admitting counterproof for its impeaching value even though some exclusionary principle otherwise bars its use. This situation raises four general issues. First is coverage: Does the exclusionary doctrine address impeachment? Second is the fairness: Did the attacking party engage in a tactical maneuver to avoid or get around the doctrine? Third is prejudice: Does the risk of prejudice from misuse of the

---

8. United States v. Walsh, 928 F.2d 7, 10 (1st Cir. 1991) (union official testified that he put back all money he got from labor movement; can ask about uncharged incidents of submitting questionable claims for reimbursement and getting a car from the local cheap; these transactions tended to undercut his claim).

9. United States v. Rackley, 986 F.2d 1357, 1362-1363 (10th Cir 1993) (defendants painted picture of care and expertise in banking procedures; proper to show that they entered into consent decree imposing lifetime bar on banking), *cert. denied*, 510 U.S. 860; United States v. Walsh, 928 F.2d 7, 10 (1st Cir. 1991) (union official testified that he put back money he got from labor movement; can then ask about questionable claims for reimbursement and getting cheap car from local).

10. United States v. Cerno, 529 F.3d 926 (10th Cir. 2008) (defendant said he was alcoholic, hence easy mark for abuse charges; he said no when asked if drinking impaired judgment; government proved that he once passed out on couch with penis exposed, watching pornographic movie, which was relevant; jury could infer that it "showed poor judgment," refuting claim that alcoholism didn't affect judgment); United States v. Giese, 597 F.2d 1170, 1190-1191 (9th Cir. 1979) (defendant depicted himself as nonviolent activist, expounding content of radical book; can then ask about book and recite passages), *cert. denied*, 444 U.S. 979.

11. United States v. Labarbera, 581 F.2d 107, 109 (5th Cir. 1978) (defendant said he did not drink and had gun permits; should not then ask about arrest for drunk driving and carrying concealed weapon).

12. United States v. Tory, 52 F.3d 207, 210 (9th Cir. 1995) (suppressing holster and gunbelt found in garage; defendant did not open door by asking agent on cross whether he found gun, which was not a claim that defendant did not own gun). *See generally* §6.48, *infra.*

counterproof justify excluding it? Fourth is effect: If counterproof is admissible only to contradict, can it be counted as evidence supporting a positive inference of whatever point it tends to prove?

When an exclusionary principle is codified, sometimes the Rule deals expressly with the question whether evidence covered by the principle can be used to contradict testimony given at trial, and sometimes the Rule comes with open-ended exceptions that say or imply (or leave room to argue) that impeachment by contradiction is allowed. For example, FRE 408 (which covers settlement offers and statements) expressly deals with impeachment. It says such offers and statements cannot be used to "impeach through a prior inconsistent statement or contradiction" (with some exceptions). In contrast, FRE 407 (which covers subsequent remedial measures) takes the opposite approach by means of an open-ended exception: The Rule excludes subsequent measures when offered to prove negligence or culpable conduct, but allows their use to show "feasibility of precautionary measures if controverted, or impeachment," so subsequent measures can be used to contradict.[1]

Coverage issue

Often, however, the Rule or statute is silent on impeachment. In some such cases, the principle is stated in broad terms: For example, FRE 410 bars plea bargaining statements by the defendant (they are not "admissible"), and FRE 412 bars evidence of prior sexual conduct by complainants in sexual assault cases (most such evidence is "not admissible"). Both provisions contain exceptions, some of which contemplate the need to admit otherwise excludable evidence to rebut other evidence, but both provisions are silent on the use of the covered evidence to contradict other proof. Legislative history of FRE 410 answers the question whether plea bargaining statements may be admitted to contradict the defendant (the answer is no), but legislative history of FRE 412 offers no similar clue, and the question must be answered by resort to arguments about policy, purpose, and context.[2]

Other exclusionary principles are stated in narrower terms, and they almost invite the conclusion that the evidence is admissible to contradict. For example, FRE 404(a) bars character evidence to prove "action in conformity therewith" (stating numerous exceptions), but FRE 404(b) paves the way to use evidence of "other crimes, wrongs, or acts" for "other purposes" (providing a nonexclusive list).[3]

Fairness issue

Exclusionary rules deal with recurrent situations. The bar in FRE 407 against proving negligence or culpable conduct by proving subsequent

---

§6.45 1. *See* §§4.23-4.24 (subsequent measures) and §§4.25-4.26 (settlement offers), *supra*.

2. *See* United States v. Mezzanetto, 513 U.S. 196 (1995) (FRE 410 entitles defendants to block use of plea bargaining statements to impeach, but they can waive right by voluntary pretrial agreement).

3. *See* United States v. Powell, 50 F.2d 94, 101 (1st Cir. 1995) (testimony that defendant did not possess firearms made proof of constructive possession admissible despite FRE 404); United States v. Castenada, 555 F.2d 605, 608-609 (7th Cir. 1977) (psychiatrist examined defendant to determine sanity and competency; can then ask about his statements; statute bars use "on the issue of guilt," not to impeach psychiatrist), *cert. denied*, 434 U.S. 847.

measures, for example, seeks to limit evidentiary options for claimants and protect defending parties. The purpose is to encourage (or not discourage) socially responsible behavior after accidents, prevent unfairness (proving responsible post-accident behavior over objection), and keep factfinders from wrongly interpreting such measures as proof of misconduct. Assuming the soundness of these notions, claimants should not be allowed to get around FRE 407 unilaterally, and defending parties should not be allowed to use FRE 407 as a shield to present a false picture, both of which would be unfair.

Suppose plaintiff claims a step in a hotel lobby was dangerous, and that its condition caused his slip-and-fall. If he sues the hotel, FRE 407 stands in the way of proving liability by evidence that after the accident defendant added stripes as a visual cue to warn patrons. Suppose he calls the manager and asks her, "don't you think it was hard for anybody to see that step?" Suppose she answers "no, I think the step was obvious and visible." Still plaintiff should not be allowed to prove that the hotel marked the step after the accident. It is true that evidence of the new stripes is counterproof tending to contradict an obvious inference from her response ("nothing further was needed"), but the counterproof should not be admitted because it makes no sense for the exclusionary principle to operate at the sufferance of parties against whom it is aimed.

On the other hand, the hotel should not be permitted to exploit the exclusionary rule either. If it offers testimony that "nothing could be done to make the step safer" or that adding stripes "would make the situation more dangerous," plaintiff should be allowed to prove the postaccident addition of stripes in refutation of such claims. In a variety of settings, courts admit otherwise excludable counterproof to prevent similar exploitation.[4]

Prejudice issue

Courts have flexible authority under FRE 403 to exclude counterproof offered to contradict. When the proof is otherwise excludable, a court should exclude it if the factfinder seems likely to misuse it for a forbidden purpose, with the result that risk of prejudice outweighs probative worth.[5]

Effect issue

It is a familiar idea that evidence is sometimes admissible to prove one thing but not another even if it logically tends to prove both. This notion is formally enshrined in the Rules and deeply embedded in practice. It is obviously exemplified in the principle that allows use of inconsistent statements to impeach but not as proof of what they assert

---

4. *See* United States v. Porter, 842 F.2d 1021, 1025 (8th Cir. 1988) (defense asked about defendant's ability to distinguish right from wrong; government could question psychiatric witness on point even though her opinion might violate rule against describing mental conditions that are elements of defense); CCMS Publishing Co. v. Dooley-Maloof, Inc., 645 F.2d 33, 37-38 (10th Cir. 1981) (defense showed that plaintiff offered to pay; despite FRE 408, plaintiff could prove that defendant was later willing to accept, but that plaintiff declined on learning of defendant's misconduct).

5. *See* Barrera v. E. I. Du Pont de Nemours & Co., 653 F.2d 915, 920-921 (5th Cir. 1981) (error to block contradiction by evidence covered by collateral source doctrine, but balancing under FRE 403 would be proper).

(absent a hearsay exception).[6] When a court admits otherwise excludable evidence as counterproof tending to contradict initial testimony, the interplay between the exclusionary and the impeachment rules suggests, by a kind of arid doctrinal logic, that the counterproof may have impeaching effect but cannot be taken as positive proof of whatever point it might logically tend to prove.

Suppose, for example, a defendant charged with auto theft testifies on direct that he has never committed a crime. The rules on character evidence would normally exclude proof that he stole cars four other times, but such proof would likely be admitted to contradict his overbroad claim.[7] Doctrinal logic suggests that it cannot be taken as evidence of guilt (even though it tends logically to indicate propensity and therefore logically bears on guilt), hence that defendant is entitled to a limiting instruction. This doctrinal consequence does not often make a practical difference, but sometimes courts recognize the point.[8]

In a related vein, an old tradition born in another context holds that evidence contradicting initial testimony cannot support an inference that the opposite of what the testimony asserts is true. Suppose defendant testifies that he did not take his gun along but is met by counterproof in the form of his *Miranda*-barred statement admitting that he did take his gun. In accord with doctrinal logic, the statement cannot be used as proof that he took his gun (it is admissible only to impeach). The old tradition indicates that disbelieving defendant's testimony cannot support the conclusion that he took his gun, even in a clearcut either/or situation in which the logical consequence of rejecting a proposition is to accept its opposite. If the government has no other proof that defendant took his gun along, the government must lose on this issue.[9]

---

6. *See* FRE 105. On impeachment by inconsistent statements, *see* §§6.40-6.42, *supra*.

7. In substance, defendant says he is a law-abiding citizen, which is evidence of good character. It is not quite what FRE 404-405 envision, because it is neither reputation nor third-party opinion and because reporting an absence of bad acts is a somewhat lame endorsement. But such testimony has probative force, especially if unchallenged, and seems proper. When the accused offers good character evidence, FRE 404(a)(1) says the prosecutor may rebut, but FRE 405(a) says rebuttal should be by "opinion" or "reputation." The last sentence allows inquiry into specific instances on cross, which envisions testing third-party character witnesses, and that is not what is going on.

8. *See* United States v. Crouch, 731 F.2d 621, 623 (9th Cir. 1984) (maximum legitimate effect of impeaching testimony can never be more than canceling adverse answer by which party is surprised), *cert. denied*, 469 U.S. 1105; United States v. Whitson, 587 F.2d 948, 953 (9th Cir. 1978) (impermissible for jury to use impeaching evidence to decide guilt or innocence).

9. *See* Taylor v. Baltimore & O.R. Co., 344 F.2d 281, 284 (2d Cir. 1965), *cert. denied*, 382 U.S. 831; Kuhn v. United States, 24 F.2d 910, 913 (9th Cir. 1928), *cert. denied*, 278 U.S. 605; Dyer v. McDougal, 201 F.2d 265, 268-269 (2d Cir. 1952). The next section examines use of *Miranda*-barred statements.

§6.46 Effect of Constitutional Restrictions

In criminal cases, defense strategy or miscalculation can pave the way for evidence or questioning that the Constitution would otherwise prevent. Suppose, for example, that defendant testifies on direct that he did not commit the charged drug offense or has never possessed drugs. Suppose the government has evidence that he confessed (contradicting his testimony), but the confession was obtained in violation of *Miranda*. Or suppose the government could prove he possessed drugs in the past (again contradicting his testimony), but the proof is physical evidence seized in violation of the Fourth Amendment. These constitutional violations normally entitle the accused to exclude the evidence, but the Supreme Court has held that such proof may be admitted to impeach the accused by contradiction.[1]

The *Harris* case is the landmark decision approving use of *Miranda*-barred admissions to impeach in this way. *Harris* held that *Miranda* cannot be "perverted into a license to use perjury by way of a defense, free from the risk of confrontation with prior inconsistent utterances."[2] In *Harris*, no warning was given (defendant was arrested before *Miranda* was decided, which was not the basis of the decision because *Miranda* applied retroactively). In its later decision in the *Hass* case, the Court approved impeaching use of a statement that violated *Miranda* in a different way—police gave appropriate warnings but wrongfully kept on asking questions after the accused invoked his right of counsel (under *Miranda*, that means questioning must cease).[3] *Harris* probably applies to the impeaching use of statements taken in violation of other aspects of *Miranda*.[4]

> **Excludable admissions: *Miranda* and *Harris***

The logic of *Harris* was extended in the *Harvey* case, where the Court approved the impeaching use of a statement taken in violation of defendant's Sixth Amendment right of counsel under the *Massiah* doctrine.[5]

> **Excludable admissions: *Harvey* and *Massiah***

---

§6.46   1. By happy accident, the cases involve "H's" modifying "M's," which help in remembering salient points: *Harris* modifies *Miranda*, *Harvey* modifies *Massiah*, and *Havens* modifies *Mapp*.

2. Harris v. New York, 401 U.S. 222 (1971); Miranda v. Arizona, 384 U.S. 436 (1966) (police must give warnings before questioning suspect in custody; not doing so requires exclusion of his answers).

3. Oregon v. Hass, 420 U.S. 714 (1975) (post-warning statements after accused asks to see lawyer are usable to impeach). *See* Edwards v. Arizona, 451 U.S. 477 (1981); Oregon v. Bradshaw, 462 U.S. 1039 (1983) (invoking right of counsel means questioning must cease); Michigan v. Mosley, 423 U.S. 96 (1975) (decision not to talk after warning must be "scrupulously honored").

4. *Compare* Estelle v. Smith, 451 U.S. 454, 466-467 (1981) (use of statements to psychiatrist during court-ordered examination violated *Miranda*) *with* Booker v. Wainright, 703 F.2d 1251, 1257-1259 (11th Cir. 1983) (approving impeaching use of statements taken in violation of *Smith*).

5. Michigan v. Harvey, 494 U.S. 344 (1990) (post-indictment statement taken after defendant invoked right of counsel, after presumptively invalid waiver, usable to impeach). *See* Massiah v. United States, 377 U.S. 201 (1980) (post-indictment statements excludable under Sixth Amendment right to counsel).

Neither *Harris* nor *Harvey* paves the way for impeaching use of statements taken in violation of other aspects of the protections afforded by the Fifth and Sixth Amendments. In *Harris*, the Court took pains to say that there was no indication of coercion apart from failure to warn and strongly implied that "true" coercion would raise reliability concerns and preclude even impeaching use of statements. Similar language appears in *Harvey*.[6] Such concerns apply to statements that are involuntary in the broad constitutional sense because they are products of physical or psychological coercion.[7] Also *Harris* does not apply to statements obtained in connection with a grant of use immunity, where the defendant has no real choice (talk or face contempt), although trustworthiness is not the major concern in this setting.[8]

Harris is subject to criticism as a formalistic opinion that uses authority selectively, gives short shrift to a statement in *Miranda* that seemed to resolve the issue in favor of exclusion, and hardly mentions real policy questions.[9] Despite its shortcomings, however, *Harris* seems right for two reasons.

First, *Harris* probably does *not* undermine *Miranda*, which altered the stationhouse dynamic but did not change its basic nature. Police still seek and get admissions, and prosecutors still need to make full use of them. Hence there still is a "percentage" in getting statements, even if they cannot be used to prove guilt at trial—they are still helpful in investigation, making decisions about whether and whom to prosecute, in plea bargaining, in hearings on competency to stand trial, in probation or parole revocation proceedings.[10] Yet even after *Harris*, it is still much better to get statements in the right way, so they can be freely

---

6. In *Harris*, the Court said "no claim" had been made that the statements were "coerced or involuntary," and that *Miranda* does not bar all uses of trustworthy statements. And the Court in *Harvey* declined to consider impeaching use of a voluntary *Massiah*-barred statement made after a waiver that not only violates the bright-line "prophylactic rule" (waivers given in police-initiated discussions are invalid even if voluntary) but is *actually* involuntary.

7. Mincey v. Arizona, 437 U.S. 385 (1978) (cannot make impeaching use of involuntary statement taken from "seriously wounded" defendant in hospital); Rogers v. Richmond, 365 U.S. 534 (1961) (confession obtained by threat to take wife into custody is not voluntary); Bram v. United States, 168 U.S. 532 (1897) (confession obtained by direct or implied promises is not voluntary).

8. New Jersey v. Portash, 440 U.S. 450, 459 (1979) (testimony given under use immunity may not be used to impeach when witness testifies in his own case).

9. *Harris* relies on Walder v. United States, 347 U.S. 62 (1954), which approved use of illegally seized evidence to impeach, but *Walder* involved impeachment on a collateral point, and it said defendant "must be free to deny" elements in the case without opening himself to impeachment by illegally seized evidence. *Harris* ignored this limit. *Miranda* says prosecutors often use exculpatory statements to impeach and that they are "incriminating in any meaningful sense." Miranda v. Arizona, 384 U.S. 436, 477 (1966). *Harris* dismisses those comments as unnecessary to the holding.

10. *See* Oregon v. Elstad, 470 U.S. 298 (1985) (rejecting application of fruits doctrine to second confession obtained after initial confession taken in violation of *Miranda*); LaFave, Israel, King and Kerr, Criminal Procedure §6.10 & 9.5 (3d ed. 2007) (*Miranda* does not apply in hearings on competency to stand trial, or parole or probation revocation hearings; under *Elstad*, fruits doctrine does not apply to evidence uncovered as result of *Miranda* violations).

used at trial. Probably *no* police officer (whether conscientious or conniving) could figure out a way to adjust his behavior to take advantage of the opening given by *Harris*, so it is doubtful that disallowing the impeaching use of *Miranda*-barred confessions would better achieve *Miranda*'s regulatory purpose.

Second (as the majority *Harris* may have meant to say), a regime that keeps prosecutors from proving their cases by means of probative statements gotten illegally places high value on regulating police. To exclude such statements when the accused gives testimony conflicting with what he said before is to say that regulating police is more important than enforcing the duty of a defendant, if he testifies, to be truthful. Casting the balance this way is dubious if admitting *Miranda*-barred statements to impeach has little or no effect on police behavior.

Before *Harris*, the Court upheld use of evidence seized in violation of the Fourth Amendment to refute overbroad testimony by the defendant claiming an innocent (or drug-free) past. Such evidence is ordinarily excludable from federal and state trials under the *Weeks* and *Mapp* doctrines.[11] An early decision in the *Agnello* case implied that illegally seized drugs could be admitted to impeach an overbroad claim of an innocent past advanced by the accused on direct,[12] and later in *Walder* the Court approved this use of illegally seized drugs.[13]

> **Illegally seized evidence: *Havens* and *Mapp***

In a garbled 1980 decision in the *Havens* case, the Court again upheld use of illegally seized evidence to impeach testimony by the accused (evidence that would otherwise be excludable under the *Mapp* doctrine).[14] *Havens* too was a drug trial, but this time defendant did not claim an innocent past, but instead denied certain acts, saying he "did not ever engage in" sewing cloth swatches on a T-shirt worn by his friend (the swatches formed crude pockets containing cocaine). He reiterated these points on cross, and the prosecutor then asked about a suitcase illegally seized from him that contained the shirt from which the swatches were cut, later introducing the shirt itself and testimony that it was found in defendant's luggage. The Court in *Havens* approved, stressing defendant's "obligation to speak the truth in response to proper questions" and commenting that the government had not "smuggled in" the fruit of the illegal search.

Before *Havens*, it seemed clear that constitutionally excludable evidence could be used to refute testimony only if it was deliberately offered as part of the defense strategy to win acquittal (usually testimony by the accused on direct). If the initial testimony comes in as a result of government strategy, it is far more troublesome to admit otherwise excludable counterproof. Doing so raises the prospect that

---

11. Mapp v. Ohio, 367 U.S. 643 (1961) (14th Amendment excludes illegally seized evidence in state trials); Weeks v. United States, 232 U.S. 383 (1914) (similar rule in federal courts) (supervisory authority).

12. Agnello v. United States, 269 U.S. 20, 35 (1925).

13. Walder v. United States, 347 U.S. 62, 64-65 (1954) (defendant made "sweeping claim" on direct that he never possessed or dealt drugs; can ask about heroin illegally seized earlier, to impeach).

14. United States v. Havens, 446 U.S. 620 (1980) (6-3 opinion).

the party against whom an exclusionary rule operates can control and avoid its effect. Suppose, for instance, defendant in a drug case testifies that he did not possess the drugs. The prosecutor then asks on cross whether he "ever possessed drugs" and he says "No." Can the prosecutor then introduce drugs illegally seized on an earlier occasion? Here as in other areas of impeachment by contradiction, some notion of fairness should prevent manipulative behavior from being used to evade constitutional exclusionary rules.

Havens clouds the question whether such a limit applies to the use of constitutionally excludable evidence. In *Havens*, the Court went out of its way to approve use of illegally seized evidence to contradict "false testimony first given on cross-examination," pointedly remarking that the obligation to testify truthfully is "fully binding" during cross. Four dissenters bitterly complained that the majority "passes control" to the prosecutor, who "can lay the predicate for admitting otherwise suppressible evidence with his own questioning," with the result that defendants "will be compelled to forgo testifying" at all.

Whether *Havens* leads to this result is hard to say. The illegally seized suitcase contradicted the direct testimony every bit as much as it contradicted what defendant repeated on cross, so *Havens* on its facts does not involve the kind of unfairness described above. Also *Havens* stressed that it was approving the tactic only when cross was "reasonably suggested" by direct testimony. And *Havens* commented that in such cases one could not say that excludable counterproof was "smuggled in," which nods in the direction of the fairness issue.

Still *Havens* is troublesome. In cases where a defendant testifies that he did not possess the drugs that he is charged with having, only to be asked on cross whether he "ever possessed" drugs, arguably the latter question *is* "reasonably related" to the direct—it raises the character issue and casts doubt on the prior specific denial. If defendant says "no" (he "never possessed" drugs) and the prosecutor offers counterproof of prior possession that would otherwise be constitutionally excludable, the result seems unfair for the reasons voiced by the *Havens* dissenters, and the counterproof does seem to be "smuggled in."

In many modern cases, the otherwise excludable counterproof seems to contradict what the witness said on direct as much as what he said on cross, so (lie Havens itself) they do not raise fairness issues. In a few cases that do raise the fairness question, courts have excluded the counterproof, rightly realizing that applying Havens in such settings would work an injustice.[15] In such cases, as in *Havens*, the result seems fair. Occasionally, however, *Havens* seems to have opened possibilities

15. For decisions excluding counterproof on fairness grounds, *see* People v. Lawson, 762 N.E.2d 633 (Ill. App. 2001) (on direct, defendant said he was going from pool hall to store at time of robbery; error to let prosecutor ask on cross whether he told detective, in suppressed statement, that he "had witnesses" who saw him at pool hall but "couldn't name them," since question was "not related to any specific statements that defendant made on direct") (reversing), app. denied, 770 N.E.2d 222 (2002); People v. Williams, 564 N.E.2d 168 (Ill. App. 1990) (on direct, defendant described military service; on cross, prosecutor asked whether he had "ever" seen a .38 caliber

for using otherwise excludable counterproof in cases that reward prosecutorial manipulation, as the *Havens* dissenters feared.[16] There is little doubt that the *Havens* standard applies not only to counterproof seized in violation of the Fourth Amendment, but to counterproof that violates *Miranda*,[17] but probably *Havens* does not affect the standard for overcoming other exclusionary doctrines based on the Rules or common law tradition,[18] and some states offer more protection than *Havens* provides as a matter of state constitutional law.[19]

§6.47 Prejudice, Confusion, and "Collateral Matter" Bar

One hard-edged limit is captured in the notion that contradiction on "collateral matters" is improper. Courts also recognize a soft-edged limit based on balancing relevancy against considerations of prejudice and confusion under FRE 403.

The reason for the hard-edged limit is that the effects of contradiction have little value for unimportant testimony. Suppose a witness says he inspected a crop on June 5, but counterproof shows it was May 30. The discrepancy is exposed, but if six days make no difference, then the specific effect of showing he got the wrong day is not useful. Of course the more general effect remains: If he erred or lied on the date, did he do the same on points that count for more? But broader inferences of this sort are implausible without something more—additional clues that he is biased or untruthful or careless. The short of it is that contradiction on collateral matters is especially likely to waste time, create confusion, abuse witnesses, and inject prejudice, which FRE 403 and 611 allow courts to prevent.

Here is an easy way to describe this hard-edged limit: Counterproof is admissible if it contradicts on a matter that counts, but not otherwise. This condition is satisfied if the counterproof tends to prove or disprove

Contradicts something that counts

---

weapon or bullet, and he said no; prosecutor should not then have introduced such bullet illegally seized on arrest) (reversing), app. denied, 567 N.E.2d 341 (1991). For a decision applying *Havens* where counterproof contradicts defendant's direct testimony, *see* United States v. Atherton, 936 F.2d 728, 734 (2d Cir. 1991) (on direct defendant said government entered office and "never found anything," paving way for evidence seized in search; court rejects claim that subject was "broached only on cross").

16. United States v. Hernandez, 646 F.2d 970, 977-978 (5th Cir. 1981) (after saying he delivered gift-wrapped packages for friend thinking they were statues, defendant was asked on cross whether he would recognize quaaludes; he said no, so government introduced illegally seized briefcase containing quaaludes).

17. United States v. Miller, 676 F.2d 359, 363-364 (9th Cir. 1982) (invoking *Havens* for *Miranda*-barred statements), *cert. denied*, 459 U.S. 866.

18. United States v. Lawson, 683 F.2d 688, 692 (2d Cir. 1982) (error to admit plea bargaining statement conceding guilt; FRE 410 bars even use of statement to impeach, and *Havens* does not apply).

19. *See* State v. Brunelle, 534 A.2d 198 (Vt. 1987) (rejecting both *Havens* and *Harris* in holding that prosecutor cannot use suppressed evidence to impeach; even if defendant did not testify because court ruled that evidence could be used to impeach, he could still raise point on appeal).

something that bears on substantive issues, or to prove or disprove a point that bears on credibility. Suppose plaintiff brings a claim for crop damage against a pesticide maker. If initial testimony suggests the crop first showed damage after spraying, then counterproof that the crop was already dying when the spray was applied would be admitted because it contradicts testimony going to causation. Or suppose an accident case where a witness testifies that he has no connection with the party who called him. Counterproof that he is a longtime friend of the calling party would be admitted because it contradicts testimony going to credibility.

Must have dual relevancy Here is another way of describing the collateral matter limit: Counterproof always bears on a case for one reason, and sometimes for one or more of three additional reasons (total of four). First and always, it conflicts with initial testimony, thus undermining credibility by suggesting the witness erred or lied on some point, so he may have lied or erred on other points. Second, counterproof may tend to establish or refute a point with substantive importance (the crop was in trouble before it was sprayed). Third, counterproof may indicate bias or motive (witness is a friend of the calling party, or being paid by him), defect in capacity (witness has weak vision), or untruthful disposition (witness has untruthful character). Fourth, counterproof may tend to refute a point that a witness simply could not be mistaken about if he is truthful, revealing a "telltale" deception that more broadly undercuts what he said. When counterproof bears on the case *only* for the first reason, it is collateral. To be admissible, it must have at least *dual relevancy* in that it bears on the case for the second, third, or fourth reason too.

"Independently" relevant There is a more problematic approach to describing the collateral matter bar: It is sometimes said that counterproof is admissible (not collateral) if it is independently relevant, or that counterproof is admissible if it could be offered independent of the testimony it contradicts.[1] There is some truth in this account. Counterproof that is independent in these ways does escape the collateral category as the cited examples illustrate: Proof that crop damage appeared before spraying is independently relevant and could be offered even without testimony that damage first appeared afterwards, and the same applies to proof that the witness was a longtime friend of the calling party.

Unfortunately the "independence" idea is misleading unless it is understood in a narrow and special way. The problem is that counterproof may be admitted even if there would be little or no reason for it without the testimony it contradicts and its sole function is to refute that testimony. To take a common example, suppose defendant in a drug

---

§6.47 1. *See* Law v. State, 98 P.3d 181 (Wyo. 2004) (defendant told officer he carried knife in car for self-protection, which was not relevant; admitting testimony that he did *not* regularly carry knife was error, but harmless) (quoting authors of this Treatise); State v. Martinez, 824 A.2d 443, 448 (R.I. 2003) (whether something is collateral depends on whether point could be shown for a purpose independent of contradiction); United States v. Scott, 243 F.3d 1103, 1106 (8th Cir. 2001) (counterproof that contradicts is excluded unless independently admissible) (citing this Treatise).

trial testifies that he "has never committed a crime" or suppose defendant in a collision case testifies that he "never had an accident before." In the drug case, the prosecutor is usually allowed to introduce evidence (or show by cross) that defendant did commit a crime before—even a bank robbery completely unrelated to the pending drug charges. In the collision case, plaintiff would likely be allowed to introduce evidence (or show by cross) that defendant had another accident—even if it bore no resemblance to the one in suit. Such counterproof would probably not get in if it were not for the previous testimony, and it would be barred by the character rule and would not be admitted under FRE 404(b) to prove specific points like intent. Interpreting "independence" in the most obvious way, the counterproof in these cases does not seem independently relevant or independently admissible.

In a narrow and special sense, such counterproof is independently relevant. If credited, it contradicts what was said before and knocks out proof that might affect outcome. This thought can be expressed in the language of independence: The counterproof is relevant to contradict, hence raising specific and general doubts about credibility, and independently relevant in rebutting points that might matter. In the end, however, the idea of independence seems more misleading than helpful.

Generally speaking, collateral counterproof is excluded.[2] Of course errors in admitting counterproof on collateral matters seldom generate reversals unless something else appears, such as unfair prejudice or confusion of issues, since it would make no sense to hold a second trial simply to keep out unwanted counterproof. But some reversals emphasize this ground.[3]

Collateral counterproof excluded

The rule against contradiction on collateral matters has less bite when it proceeds by cross-examination of the target witness.[4] Indeed, "collateral matter" is sometimes thought to be almost synonymous with marginal points that may be probed on cross but not proved by other witnesses. Normally the scope-of-direct rule governs cross-examination, subject to the court's discretion to put an end to questioning that has gone far enough, and subject to limits on other kinds of impeachment.[5] The collateral matter bar should not be applied with rigor because

---

2. United States v. Williamson, 202 F.3d 974, 979-980 (7th Cir. 2000) (excluding testimony contradicting police officer because it was collateral); United States v. Phillips, 888 F.2d 38, 40-41 (6th Cir. 1989) (excluding proof that witnesses used drugs after they testified to not doing so).

3. State v. Oswalt, 381 P.2d 617, 618-619 (Wash. 1963) (in trial for July 14 Seattle robbery, proprietor of Oregon restaurant testified that defendant was a regular patron and was there at times that made it "impossible, as a practical matter" to commit offense; after he said on cross that defendant was there every day for months, detective should not have testified that he saw defendant in Seattle on June 12 and he said he'd been there a few days, which was "irrelevant and collateral") (reversing).

4. United States v. Ayotte, 741 F.2d 865, 870-871 (6th Cir. 1984) (latitude normally permitted in cross-examining prosecution witnesses), *cert. denied*, 469 U.S. 1076.

5. On the scope-of-direct rule, *see* §6.63, *infra*.

cross-questions are normally unrehearsed and exploratory, the questioner needs latitude, and it is impossible to draw a bright line between the process of clarifying, limiting, and exploring the substance of direct and the process of refuting it through careful probing on cross. And contradictory points can often be brought out much faster this way than by independent or extrinsic proof.

Still the bar against contradiction on collateral matters has some role, even in this setting. Suppose a witness to an accident says on direct he was carrying a grocery sack at the time but the cross-examiner presses him to admit he was carrying a package from the post office. Unless the collateral matter bar applies, only the court's general discretion to limit questioning supports a decision to cut off questions of this sort. The hard-edged rule serves well here, and the court need not extend the kind of patience that comes with the looser discretionary standard.

As suggested above, courts generally admit counterproof showing facts that bear on substantive issues, tend to impeach in some additional way besides contradiction, or undercut the witness on some telltale point:

Facts bearing on substantive issue

The first category is easy to recognize. In a suit to recover insurance on a warehouse destroyed by fire, the insurer claimed plaintiff burned the building. At trial he portrayed himself as "a well-to-do and successful businessman," so the court admitted counterproof that he wrote bad checks before the blaze, had outstanding judgments and liens against him, missed payments on the warehouse, and faced foreclosure. This counterproof tended to establish motive and undercut his account of his situation.[6] And in a trial for sexual assault where a 15-year-old complainant testified on direct that the encounter with defendant was her first sexual experience, the defense was entitled to prove her prior statements saying she'd had sex before with six boyfriends. The counterproof tended to refute direct testimony that bore on the crime by making it seem "even more offensive."[7]

Facts that impeach a witness

The category of facts tending to impeach a witness *in some additional way, beyond contradicting* him is also easily recognized. Where a codefendant who pled guilty before trial testified for the defense, for example, "and assumed full responsibility for the crimes," it was right for the prosecutor to be able to ask on cross whether he was taking the blame because of his fear of another defendant, then introduced extrinsic evidence of fear when he denied it. The counterproof not only contradicted the witness in his denial, but also showed a bias or motive indicating that he might be lying or stretching a point.[8]

---

6. Elgi Holding, Inc. v. Insurance Co. of North America, 511 F.2d 957, 959 (2d Cir. 1975) (counterproof properly admitted).

7. State v. Ritrovato, 905 A.2d 1079, 1091 (Conn. 2006) (state's rape shield statute makes exception to prove conduct bearing on victim's credibility if she testifies on direct to sexual conduct) (reversing).

8. United States v. Schennault, 429 F.2d 852, 855 (7th Cir. 1970) (rejecting claim that rebuttal was improper impeachment on collateral matter first raised on cross). *See also* United States v. Opager, 589 F.2d 799, 801-803 (5th Cir. 1979); Arpan v. United States, 260 F.2d 649, 658-659 (8th Cir. 1958).

What is important to a lawsuit and what is important in the life of a witness may be very different things. For this reason, a point in a story that is important in the story itself or in the way that it is experienced by the speaker may be far removed from issues in the case. Hence counterproof indicating falsehood or mistake on such a "telltale" point may be probative on credibility, and if so it should not be excluded merely because it is "collateral." Counterproof of points that a witness "would not be mistaken" about if he were there and telling the truth have special relevance,[9] and at least occasional decisions endorse contradiction on just such points, or indicate that the judge has discretion.[10]

Putting aside the case where the counterproof contradicts on a telltale point, faithful observance of the collateral matter limit produces the result that admissible counterproof has at least dual relevancy. It suggests that a witness lied or erred on some point (hence might have lied or erred on others) and it tends to prove or refute either a point of substance or a point relating to witness credibility in some other way (bias or motive, lack of capacity, untruthfulness). Since relevance in these latter senses may overshadow relevance in the first sense, the contradicting effect of counterproof may draw little or no attention. Where counterproof is relevant only in the first sense, where its only or most obvious effect is to refute something a witness said, the attacking party is likely to emphasize the contradiction (there is no other excuse to admit it), and it is exactly here that the counterproof is normally excluded as collateral.

Even if counterproof is not excludable as collateral, it may be excluded under the softer-edged restrictions in FRE 403 as unduly prejudicial or confusing, which calls for an appraisal of relative probative worth.[11] Clearly striking the proper balance involves looking at whether the counterproof is otherwise excludable under some specific exclusionary doctrine found in the Rules, statute, or Constitution.

Telltale facts

Collateral matter limit summarized

Exclude under FRE 403

§6.48   Matters of Fairness and "Open Door" Doctrine

Notions of fairness bear on impeachment by contradiction. The reason is that initial proof and counterproof are both sometimes objectionable, and parties sometimes engage in manipulative tactics seeking to avoid or exploit such principles unfairly.

For the attacking party, manipulation is possible because no general principle blocks calling a witness, adducing testimony and then

Attacking party

9. McCormick, Evidence §49 (6th ed. 2006).

10. *See* United States v. Hykel, 461 F.2d 721, 729 (3d Cir. 1972); United States v. Cuadrado, 413 F.2d 633, 635-636 (2d Cir. 1969), *cert. denied*, 397 U.S. 980.

11. United States v. Beverly, 5 F.3d 633, 640-641 (2d Cir. 1993) (after defendant said he never had gun in Albany, proving his involvement in shooting incidents there went too far and was prejudicial).

refuting it.[1] Hence introducing initial testimony can make an opening for otherwise excludable counterproof that may be dramatic and powerful. If a litigant could count on success, he could target a witness and force either of two bad outcomes: On the initial question the witness would concede the point, putting the excludable evidence before the factfinder, or deny it and the attacking party then would offer the excludable evidence to contradict her. Proceeding this way seems unfair.

The attacking party can sometimes gain an advantage without even refuting a denial. Suppose a collision case, where a party confines her direct to the pertinent facts. On cross, the attacking party shifts the inquiry: "Do you consider yourself a good driver?" or "Haven't you been in accidents before?" These questions are objectionable: Neither carefulness nor other accidents can be shown to prove care or negligence on the occasion. But forcing another to object would itself raise a red flag (she must be a bad driver; she must have been in accidents). The questions themselves are improper, but if they get by without objection or generate quick answers, the attacking party should not be allowed to contradict the reply ("yes, I'm a good driver" or "no, I haven't been in any accident").[2] The attack is manipulative, and success in contradicting the reply would let the questioner evade principles protecting the other side.

Suppose a criminal case, where defendant confines his direct testimony to the facts, but on cross he is asked more broadly whether he engages in criminal acts and he says no. Again the question is probably objectionable: Prosecutors cannot open the subject of character to prove guilt; self-endorsement ("I'm a law-abiding man") might be character evidence, but it is not the kind of opinion or reputation testimony that the Rules envision, and the same is true of a disclaimer of bad conduct ("I've never broken the law"). Forcing defendant to object would once again raise a red flag (he must be a crook), and if the question gets by without objection or he answers quickly, probably the prosecutor should not be allowed to contradict whatever he says ("no, I'm not involved in crime").[3]

---

§6.48 1. FRE 607 abolished the rule that a party vouches for witnesses it calls, and even common law tradition did not usually apply the voucher rule to contradiction. *See* §§6.16-6.17, *supra*.

2. Jones v. Southern Pac. R.R., 962 F.2d 447, 450 (5th Cir. 1992) (where plaintiff in grade crossing suit asked engineer whether he had been ticketed for speeding and he denied it, excluding evidence that he was ticketed; one cannot "delve into collateral matters" on one's own, then claim right to impeach); Bonilla v. Yamaha Motors Corp., 955 F.2d 150, 154-155 (1st Cir. 1992) (in suit against motorcycle maker, defense asked plaintiff about speeding incidents and he denied them; error to let defendant prove them by driving record; defendant cannot put improper questions, then contradict response).

3. United States v. Clemons, 32 F.3d 1504, 1511 (11th Cir. 1994) (in trial for murder of drug agent, defendant never denied using or selling drugs; codefendant could not raise issue on cross), *cert. denied*, 514 U.S. 1086; United States v. Jenkins, 7 F.3d 803, 806-808 (8th Cir. 1993) (defendant said he did not commit charged drug offense; on cross he said no when asked whether he ever sold drugs; error to admit proof of other transactions) (reversing).

Sometimes the shoe is on the other foot, and the manipulator is the calling party. Manipulation is possible because much testimony casting a party in a favorable light cannot be excluded as a practical matter. Sometimes objecting would seem churlish or produce a sympathetic response to a question that signals the answer; sometimes the evidence is arguably excludable, but there is no clear rule. Exploiting uncertainties and strategic awkwardness becomes possible, the "open door" doctrine applies to good purpose, and contradiction serves a laudable function.

Suppose a collision case, where a party testifies he is a careful driver or has never had an accident. This testimony is probably objectionable, but an objection would cast the other side in a bad light and might fail if the testimony is viewed as mere background. Here the other side is normally allowed to counter the initial suggestion by questioning and evidence indicating bad driving or other accidents (especially if the party claiming not to have had them was at fault). Or suppose a criminal case, where defendant paints himself as a law-abiding citizen, perhaps saying he has "never been in trouble before" or "doesn't traffic in drugs." Or he paints himself more generally as a good man, perhaps a hardworking family man, churchgoer, or war veteran, or one who began with little and achieved success. Here the initial testimony may or may not be objectionable: Arguably it is evidence of good character that defendants are entitled to offer. Yet it is not the usual kind of opinion or reputation testimony because it reports self-endorsement rather than views of others and comes close to the line between allowable opinion or reputation and excludable specific acts, and perhaps crosses the line.[4] Whatever the right answer, objecting would be strategically unwise. Certainly when defendant says he is law-abiding or does not traffic in drugs, prosecutors should be able to contradict by asking about criminal acts and even proving them.

It goes almost without saying that if a party confines his testimony to a brief and routine description of background (address, family, job) and then addresses the acts in issue, asking about or proving misconduct at other times does not contradict his position at trial.[5] Particularly in criminal cases, such misconduct sometimes can show points like intent under FRE 404(b), and questioning about misconduct may be proper under FRE 608(b) if it reflects ill on veracity.[6] But these provisions only sometimes pave the way; if they do not, evidence of misdeeds should be excluded and questions disallowed.

4. *See* Government of Virgin Islands v. Grant, 755 F.2d 508, 511-512 (3d Cir. 1985) (courts routinely admit testimony describing defendant's background, including education and employment and proof that he has never been arrested; line between background and character is "blurred").

5. United States v. Nichols, 808 F.2d 660, 663 (8th Cir. 1987) (after defendant denied selling drugs to C, error to prove prior transactions; he did not imply selling cocaine to C unknowingly, but denied any sale; nothing in earlier sales contradicted him), *cert. denied*, 481 U.S. 1038.

6. United States v. Pitman, 475 F.2d 1335, 1338 (9th Cir. 1973), *cert. denied*, 414 U.S. 873.

If the calling party elicits from the witness either a general claim of truthfulness or a claim that she was truthful in some instance, FRE 608(b) does not bar attempts to contradict by extrinsic evidence. Suppose she testifies "I believe in telling the truth," which is in substance a claim that she is generally truthful. Or suppose she says, "I told my employer about my back injury when I applied for the job," which is in substance a claim that she truthfully disclosed this point. In the first situation, the attacking party should be allowed not only to bring out instances of untruthfulness on cross (which would be proper even if she had not made the broad claim), but also to offer testimony describing such instances (which would not normally be proper) because they contradict the claim. In the second situation, the attacking party may press the witness on whether she really did disclose the injury, and offer extrinsic evidence that she did not. Here the avenue of impeachment is contradiction rather than proving untruthfulness, so FRE 608(b) is not an obstacle.[7]

Ambiguous strategies

Sometimes the strategies of the parties are hard to interpret and the notion of fairness is hard to apply. For instance, a party might open up a subject on which contradiction is expected by going into the matter on direct in order to be (and seem to be) forthcoming and disarm the expected attack. This strategy can be useful but should not block the other party from exploring the matter further on cross. There are likely to be points of embarrassment in the underlying facts that the first party did not fully explore, so cross to "make the record clear" (and incidentally "contradict" the witness on points of detail) is proper.[8] And the cross-examiner can usually say, with some credibility, that the other side "opened the matter up," so the court should permit the usual leeway to explore the subject.

Sometimes the cross-examiner asks a proper and specific question and the witness replies in an expansive vein. In this circumstance, at least when the witness is a party to the suit who has been prepared by counsel on how to reply on cross, it is often fair to treat the answer as purposefully injecting the broader point into the trial. That means that it is fair, after all, for the cross-examiner to try to contradict the answer through further questioning or other evidence.[9]

Considerations of fairness and the open door doctrine are sometimes expressed in procedural terms. Thus it is often said that offering initial testimony amounts to a "waiver of objection" against counterproof. It is also said that "any error" in admitting counterproof was "invited" by the party who offered the initial testimony, for that was the move that provided the occasion for the counterproof. Often these

---

7. United States v. Beverly, 5 F.3d 633, 639 (2d Cir. 1993); United States v. Farias-Farias, 925 F.2d 805, 810-811 (5th Cir. 1991).

8. United States v. Lopez, 979 F.2d 1024, 1032 (5th Cir. 1992); United States v. Vigliatura, 878 F.2d 1346, 1350-1351 (11th Cir. 1989).

9. _See_ United States v. Pantone, 609 F.2d 675, 683-684 (3d Cir. 1979) (otherwise excludable evidence admissible to contradict matters volunteered on cross).

ideas are variants of the fairness and "open door" doctrines, but sometimes they introduce new elements.[10]

I. REPAIR AND SUPPORT OF WITNESSES

§6.49 General Principles of Repair; Answering and Disarming

Not surprisingly, impeaching attacks may be answered. A party who would support a witness may try to rebut or explain away the impeaching facts and may anticipate the attack and bring out damaging facts at the outset to disarm the attack and minimize the damage.

The processes of repair and support are limited by two general principles: One is that litigants may not repair or support before an attack has been made. The other is that the repair or support must respond to the attack. When it comes to evidence bearing on truthfulness (character for truth and veracity), FRE 608 embodies both principles. The first means evidence of good character may not be offered before impeachment has occurred. The reason is that admitting character testimony would waste time if the need has not appeared and would invite parties to engage in fruitless "swearing matches."[1] The second principle means that such evidence may not be offered unless the impeachment takes the form of an attack on character.[2]

> **Principles: (1) May not repair before attack; (2) Must respond to attack**

The same principles apply as a matter of relevancy and tradition to evidence of prior statements by a witness. Hence prior consistent statements may not be proved before the witness is attacked. After an attack they are provable only if relevant, which means usually that they must tend to refute suggestions that a prior inconsistent statement shows that the testimony is the product of improper influence or motive, or amounts to fabrication.

In several respects, however, the two principles described above are misleading.

First is the point noted above: The calling party may anticipate an attack and bring out impeaching facts at the outset.[3] If the rule were otherwise, the attack would cast the calling party in a bad light. It would seem that this party was hiding the truth and asking the factfinder to

> **May anticipate attack**

---

10. *See* the discussion in §1.4, supra.

§6.49 1. United States v. McCulley, 178 F.3d 872, 876-877 (7th Cir. 1999); United States v. Dring, 930 F.2d 687, 690-691 (9th Cir. 1991); United States v. Taylor, 900 F.2d 779, 781 (4th Cir. 1990).

2. United States v. Candoli, 870 F.2d 496, 506 (9th Cir. 1989) (error to admit reputation testimony; cross-examiner did not attack truthfulness).

3. United States v. Montague, 958 F.2d 1094, 1096 (D.C. Cir. 1992) (government may anticipate that defense will impugn motive and put questions on direct that "defuse that impugning"); United States v. Schatzle, 901 F.2d 252, 256 (2d Cir. 1990) (court said defense could ask witness about failure to list arrest on bar application, so government brought it out on direct to present incident in "least damaging light").

accept the word of a witness when it is in fact open to doubt. But the calling party need not accept this role and may show at the outset, for example, prior convictions, connections between the witness and the calling party (facts indicating bias), or the fact that the witness is an expert who is being paid.[4]

If the adversary ignores impeaching facts brought out by the calling party, or goes no further than to revisit those matters briefly on cross, arguably the calling party should not be allowed to respond by proving truthful character. The situation smacks of bootstrapping and sandbagging: The proponent is not supposed to bolster an unattacked witness and should not be able to accomplish the same end by raising credibility points and then refuting them. On the other hand, impeachment has seemingly occurred, and sometimes repair is allowed.[5]

Framework evidence — The principles set out above are misleading in a second sense: Courts often admit what is aptly called "framework" or "syndrome" evidence by expert witnesses that is designed to support testimony. Such evidence is not viewed as "character" evidence, so it does not offend the principle that the calling party may not bolster credibility before an attack has been made, but framework or syndrome evidence has a bolstering effect that is similar to character evidence, and probably may be admitted before any attack has been made.[6]

Rebuttal — It goes almost without saying that most impeaching attacks may be specifically rebutted. If one party offers evidence or suggests by cross that a witness is biased or has been corrupted or influenced, others may refute or explain such implications by further examination or by offering counterproof that rebuts the initial proof. Similarly, if one party offers evidence or suggests by cross that the witness lacks capacity, other parties may seek to refute or explain away such suggestions by further questioning or by counterproof rebutting the original proof.

Attacks that suggest untruthful disposition may be rebutted too: If one party asks a witness about nonconviction conduct, the witness may deny the conduct or offer an explanation on redirect. Questions about convictions may elicit denials, explanations, or even proof that there was no conviction. And opinion or reputation testimony suggesting untruthfulness may be met by positive assessments of veracity and by cross-examination of the character witness to show misinformation, mistaken judgment, or failure to consider other points that bear on the veracity of the target witness. Supporting parties also may refute

---

4. Thus on direct the calling party may bring out facts showing bias (see §6.19, *supra*), nonconviction misconduct indicating untruthfulness (see §6.25, *supra*), or prior convictions, although it is another matter to show on direct that a witness has a clean record, which is improper bolstering (see §6.29, *supra*).

5. United States v. Montague, 958 F.2d 1094, 1097-1098 (D.C. Cir. 1992) (in bringing out impeaching facts, government did not surrender right to rebut charge of fabrication by offering consistent statements after defense attack); United States v. Medical Therapy Sciences, Inc., 583 F.2d 36, 39-40 (2d Cir. 1978) (allowing character evidence after defense questioned government witness on convictions first raised during direct), *cert. denied*, 439 U.S. 1130.

6. *See* the discussion in §7.22, *infra*.

evidence that contradicts the witness and may show that prior inconsistent statements were not made or that they mean something different from what the attacking party suggests.[7]

§6.50   Showing Truthful Character After Attack

In repairing damage left by an attack on the veracity of a witness, the most promising avenue may be further examination of the damaged witness, or sometimes a counterattack on the adverse character witness who did the damage. But the Rules authorize another approach, involving extrinsic evidence of good character in the form of positive testimony by a supporting witness who says that the principal witness is truthful.

Under FRE 608, a supporting character witness may testify in the form of opinion or reputation that the principal witness has a truthful disposition.[1] The heart of *opinion* testimony is an endorsement that is personal, resting on the firsthand knowledge of the supporting witness on the veracity of the attacked witness. The heart of *reputation* testimony is the community judgment on veracity. Much of the force of such testimony, whether opinion or reputation, comes from the appeal of the supporting witness. Her impact increases if she has an engaging personality, or can endorse veracity in the personal way that opinion testimony makes possible.

Supporting character testimony

The question for the character witness is not whether particular testimony is true, but whether the principal witness is truthful, and FRE 608 does not contemplate testimony by a character witness indicating that she has listened to the principal witness and believes what he said.[2] Of course a foundation is needed to show that the character witness knows the principal witness or is acquainted with his reputation in the community for truthfulness.[3] The difficulty with such supporting testimony is that the character witness must submit to cross-examination that may touch on particular instances of conduct by the witness being supported. In any case in which character has been attacked, such instances likely exist and can be uncovered, which may explain why this kind of support is often left out.

To know whether evidence of truthful disposition may be admitted, it is necessary to know whether untruthful disposition has been suggested. There is no question on this score when the attacking party

Has untruthful disposition been suggested?

---

7. On proving lack of bias, *see* §6.19, *supra*. On allowing explanation on prior convictions, *see* §6.34, *supra*. On explaining prior inconsistent statements, *see* §6.41, *supra*. Proving good character for veracity is discussed in the next section.

§6.50   1. United States v. Crippin, 570 F.2d 535, 538 (5th Cir. 1978) (mixture of reputation and opinion); United States v. Lechoco, 542 F.2d 84, 87-89 (D.C. Cir. 1976) (reputation).

2. United States v. Marshall, 173 F.3d 1312, 1315 (11th Cir. 1999).

3. United States v. Cortez, 935 F.2d 135, 139-140 (8th Cir. 1991) (rejecting testimony by officer and agent who did not investigate witness or know him well); Alverez v. United States, 282 F.2d 435, 438 (9th Cir. 1960) (rejecting testimony by witness who did not know anyone who knew accused).

directly assails character, and it makes no difference whether the attack takes the form of opinion or reputation testimony by a character witness or cross-examination of the principal witness on nonconviction misconduct or convictions. Other forms of attack can be harder to interpret. For example, attacks by inconsistent statements are often ambiguous. Viewed as an indication that the witness erred in his statement or testimony, they do not so much suggest untruthfulness as forgetfulness or lack of perception or judgment. But sometimes inconsistent statements suggest deliberate falsehood and can indeed impugn character.[4] Also, attacks indicating bias do not necessarily imply untruthfulness. The mere fact that a witness is shown to be a party or aligned with one (close family member, employee, or friend) does not mean the calling party can support credibility by evidence of truthful disposition.[5] But where more than simple interest in the outcome is shown, and facts showing corruption come to light, the appropriate response is counterproof showing the witness is not biased or corrupt or that the impeaching evidence is overstated or distorted. But impeachment of this sort may reflect adversely on character, and in such cases counterproof of good character should no doubt be admitted.[6]

Sharp suggestive cross-examination

When cross-examination is unusually sharp and suggestive, and succeeds in catching the witness in embarrassing inconsistencies or suggests by tone or innuendo that he is lying or corrupt, the court should admit counterproof indicating good character.[7] Occasionally untruthful disposition of a party may be implied by the adversary's cross-examination of the party's witnesses, and it seems that he should be able to prove his own truthful character, at least where his testimony or statements have been introduced.[8] In sum, character is sometimes assailed in the eyes of the trier of fact even though nothing is said about misconduct or general untruthfulness.

Contradiction does not impugn character

Usually impeachment by contradiction does not impugn character. When one witness testifies to one version of the facts and another presents a conflicting version, neither's character is assailed, and proof of

---

4. *Compare* Stokes v. Delcambre, 710 F.2d 1120, 1129 (5th Cir. 1983) (prior statement did not suggest bad character or pave way to show good character) *with* Beard v. Mitchell, 604 F.2d 485, 503 (7th Cir. 1979) (prior statements attacked character, paving way to prove reputation for truthfulness).

5. Renda v. King, 347 F.3d 550, 554 (3d Cir. 2003) (proof of bias does not open door to good character evidence) (citing authors of this Treatise).

6. United States v. Bonner, 302 F.3d 776, 780 (7th Cir. 2002) (defense suggested in opening statement that *A* would not confirm defendant's story because "she had recently been cleared" and cross-examined *A* on receiving money from VA for testifying, which invited rehabilitation) (admitting character testimony).

7. United States v. Dring, 930 F.2d 687, 692 (9th Cir. 1991) (where slashing cross suggests misconduct and bad character that denial will not remove, judge may admit proof of good character); United States v. Scholle, 553 F.2d 1109, 1123 (8th Cir. 1977) (similar), *cert. denied*, 434 U.S. 940.

8. United States v. Lechoco, 542 F.2d 84, 88-89 (D.C. Cir. 1976) (psychiatrists testified on insanity based on interviews; cross suggested that diagnoses depended on truthfulness, opening door to reputation testimony).

good character is ordinarily excluded.[9] If such proof gets in, however, any error is likely to be harmless, and sometimes even contradiction has been thought to impugn character.[10]

During redirect questioning of the principal witness, a party seeking to repair damage to her veracity (typically the party who called her) may seek to show that any misconduct she was asked about did not occur or that other circumstances are important in evaluating the conduct.[11] Although the language in the second sentence of FRE 608(b) is hard to read, the intent was apparently to recognize that specific instances of conduct may bear on "truthfulness" as well as "untruthfulness," and the modest redirect described here is permissible. The first sentence of FRE 608(b) leaves no doubt, however, that the truthfulness of the principal witness cannot be shown by extrinsic evidence, such as testimony by others, on specific instances of her conduct.[12] To reiterate, the supporting party may seek to show, on redirect examination of the principal witness, that she did not commit misconduct that may have been suggested on cross, but may not call others to testify that she did good deeds reflecting favorably on her character for truthfulness.

Generally experts are not allowed to testify that witnesses are truthful. Although FRE 608 removes one barrier to such proof by authorizing opinion testimony, there are many other reasons to be wary of expert testimony.[13] In the first place, FRE 608 envisions an appraisal of character or disposition, not an analysis of a particular story or recitation. In the second place, FRE 608 does not authorize expert supporting testimony unless character for veracity has been attacked. In the third place, even education and experience do not equip experts to appraise

Redirect questioning on misconduct; proof of good deeds is barred

Expert testimony

---

9. United States v. Thomas, 768 F.2d 611, 618 (5th Cir. 1985) (contradiction by other evidence does not constitute attack on character); United States v. Danehy, 680 F.2d 1311, 1314 (11th Cir. 1982) (similar); United States v. Angelini, 678 F.2d 380, 382 n.1 (1st Cir. 1982) (similar).

10. United States v. Medical Therapy Sciences, Inc., 583 F.2d 36, 41 n.6 (2d Cir. 1978) (contradiction suggested that prosecution witness stole from defendant and filed false claims to disguise her embezzlement; here contradiction impugned character), *cert. denied*, 439 U.S. 1130; Franklin Sugar Ref. Co. v. Luray Supply Co., 6 F.2d 218, 219-220 (4th Cir. 1925) (where witness is contradicted on point about which he could not innocently be mistaken, veracity is in issue).

11. *See* United States v. Lawton, 366 F.3d 550, 552-553 (7th Cir. 2004) (in trial for false statement in purchase of firearm, prosecutor asked defendant on cross about bad checks; he could testify that "he was not aware that the account was closed," suggesting "mistake" rather than "deceitfulness").

12. United States v. Murray, 103 F.3d 310, 32 (3d Cir. 1997) (error to let lieutenant testify that as result of information from informant *B*, who testified, police "made" more than 65 cases, which was "extrinsic evidence" of *B*'s truthfulness amounting to particular instances).

13. United States v. Brodie, 858 F.2d 492, 496 (9th Cir. 1988) (expert testimony "may not appropriately be used to buttress credibility"); United States v. Azure, 801 F.2d 336, 339-342 (8th Cir. 1986) (expert stamp of truthfulness goes "beyond the limitation" in FRE 608 of attesting truthfulness). *See also* State v. Rimmasch, 775 P.2d 388, 391-393 (Utah 1989) (expert testimony that child abuse victim was telling truth violated state rule 608); People v. Snook, 745 P.2d 647 (Colo. 1987) (state rule 608 barred testimony that abuse victim was telling truth because denying offense did not attack veracity).

character or disposition in ways that are useful in assessing veracity, so in the end expertise simply does not reach this subject. Finally, courts that exclude such testimony also stress that juries are to judge veracity issues. Beginning in the 1980s, however, the subject became more complicated with the arrival of expert testimony on social frameworks and syndromes, particularly in sexual assault and child abuse cases, and this subject is explored in sections dealing with expert testimony.[14]

§6.51 Cross-Examining the Supporting Character Witness

As is true of character witnesses used to attack the veracity of other witnesses, one who repairs or supports veracity is subject to cross-examination. Here too all impeaching mechanisms are available, but the most common response is one that aims ostensibly to test the knowledge and judgment of the supporting witness.

Testing the supporting witness

Here is the scene: On direct, the witness testifies, "I consider *X* to be a truthful person" (opinion) or "*X* has a reputation of being truthful" (reputation). On cross, the party who would attack this view may inquire into matters that would raise doubt whether the supporting witness really knows *X* or (in the case of reputation) whether the community knows her, or whether he has made a wise assessment of *X*'s veracity or (in the case of reputation) whether the community judgment is sound. The propriety of such probing is settled.[1] And perhaps the most telling (strategically attractive) questions ask the character witness whether he "knows" or "has heard"[2] about particular conduct of *X* that bears on her truthfulness.[3] The proper purpose is to test the knowledge and judgment of the character witness or the community: If he does *not* know, or if or the community has *not* heard, then arguably there is a lack of necessary *knowledge* about the principal witness. If he *does* know, or the community *has* heard, and still thinks the principal witness is truthful, then arguably the underlying *judgment* of the witness or the community is undercut.

Only misconduct that suggests untruthfulness

It is arguable that any misconduct by the principal witness, whether reflecting untruthfulness or not, may be made the subject of inquiry, because ignorance on any point might indicate lack of knowledge. The wiser approach, however, is more cautious in recognizing that lack of

---

14. *See* the discussion of FRE 702 in §7.22, *infra.*

§6.51 1. *See* Michelson v. United States, 335 U.S. 469 (1948) (classic opinion on cross-examining character witness, who testified to honesty of defendant in situation perhaps governed today by FRE 404-405, but principles apply also in situation governed by FRE 608).

2. Under FRE 608, a court might insist that cross follow the form of the direct—the question should be "did you know" if the character witness gave opinion on veracity, and "have you heard" if he testified to reputation. But argument over form of cross seems mostly pointless and trivial.

3. United States v. Jackson, 696 F.2d 578, 594 (8th Cir. 1982), *cert. denied*, 460 U.S. 1073; United States v. Bright, 588 F.2d 504, 511-512 (5th Cir. 1979), *cert. denied*, 440 U.S. 972.

information about misconduct by the principal witness that does not seriously undercut character testimony. Hence cross-examination of the character witness should be confined to misconduct by the principal witness that does suggest the latter's untruthfulness.[4] When the principal witness is also a party, particularly when she is a criminal defendant, there is a compelling additional reason for caution. The risk is great that the jury will misuse information about misconduct by the accused that enters the case through questions put on cross, giving rise to a special risk of prejudice that FRE 403 allows courts to prevent.[5]

Questions put to character witnesses about misconduct by the principal witness should have firm factual foundation (at least a good-faith belief that the misconduct occurred). If the risk of jury misuse is going to be run, at least the implications of the questions should reflect fact and not fiction.[6]

Factual foundation

Under the *Michelson* case, which involved questioning a character witness whose testimony would today proceed under FRE 405 rather than 608 (the testimony of the character in that case was offered to prove innocence of the defendant rather than his truthfulness), the cross-examiner may ask about charges against or arrests of the principal witness.[7] But we think *Michelson* went too far on this point, and the case is not necessarily authoritative as a guide to the meaning of FRE 608, which was adopted more than thirty years later and governs character evidence offered to impeach or support veracity rather than character offered to prove or disprove guilt.[8] Also an arrest is a poor proxy for the underlying deed, and in today's world one cannot realistically expect that an arrest will be common knowledge among character witnesses or relevant communities. Still, most modern decisions follow the lead of *Michelson* on this point, although a few bar questions on arrests.[9]

Prior charges, arrests

4. *See* United States v. Westbrook, 896 F.2d 330, 335 (8th Cir. 1990) (after brother testified that defendant was an honest man, court struck question asking whether he knew defendant was convicted of possessing drugs); United States v. Crippen, 570 F.2d 535, 538-539 (5th Cir. 1978) (may ask questions relevant to trait; turning back odometers is relevant to veracity).

5. *See* United States v. Lewis, 482 F.2d 632, 639 (D.C. Cir. 1973) (court has discretion to disallow questions that are more prejudicial to defendant than probative); Shimon v. United States, 352 F.2d 449, 453-454 (D.C. Cir. 1965) (similar).

6. Michelson v. United States, 335 U.S. 469, 481 n.18 (1948) (before inquiring, counsel must demonstrate privately to court "an irrelevant and possibly unprovable fact" such as arrest; since jury is likely to draw conclusions, inquiries must rest on legally irrelevant facts so "legally irrelevant conclusion" that jury may draw "will not be based on unsupported or untrue innuendo"); United States v. Bright, 588 F.2d 504, 511-512 (5th Cir. 1979) (questioner must have good-faith basis; letter of reprimand sufficed for question about professional discipline), *cert. denied*, 440 U.S. 972.

7. Michelson v. United States, 335 U.S. 469, 483 (1948); Harbin v. Interlake S.S. Co., 570 F.2d 99, 106 (6th Cir. 1978).

8. See generally Mueller, Of Misshapen Stones and Compromises: Michelson and the Modern Law of Character Evidence, in Evidence Stories 75 (Richard Lempert, ed. 2006).

9. *Compare* State v. Kramp, 651 P.2d 614, 617 (Mont. 1982) (cannot ask character witness testifying under state Rule 404 on truthfulness and veracity, among other things, about DUI arrest, because arrest "has no substance of itself to establish

Remote misconduct

While the Supreme Court once refused to overturn a conviction in which defense character witnesses described their acquaintance with the accused as one of 30 years duration and were asked on cross about an arrest 27 years before trial, it still seems that remote misconduct so far in the past is seldom important enough to justify the time or risk.[10] In the setting of asking witnesses about their own convictions, FRE 609(b) sets a ten-year remoteness standard that sheds some light on what remoteness should mean here. Just as old convictions are minimally probative on veracity, so events long past in the life of the target witness have little bearing on the assessment of veracity given by a character witness. For a character witness who gives opinion testimony, behavior by the principal witness before the character witness became acquainted with him would likely have less (and perhaps no) value in testing the latter's knowledge or judgment. For a character witness who describes community reputation, presumably behavior of the principal witness before the character witness became acquainted with that reputation might still bear on the knowledge of the character witness or the soundness of his report.

For all character witnesses, even behavior during the period of acquaintance is not automatically fit for questioning. It makes little sense in effect to penalize a principal witness for the fact that those who testify on his behalf are friends of long standing, and silly to suppose youthful indiscretions or isolated instances of conduct in the distant past bear importantly on today's assessment of veracity. Even assuming that particular misconduct by the principal witness bears on his veracity, the court has discretion to limit the extent to which cross-examination of a character witness may delve into it.

Redirect examination of character witness

On redirect examination of a character witness who has repaired the credibility of a principal witness and has then been cross-examined, it should be permissible to put into proper perspective any misconduct by the principal witness that the adversary raised on cross-examination.[11] Whether the character witness may then be asked on redirect about additional conduct, presumably of the sort that reflects favorably on the truthfulness of the principal witness, is open to question. Good acts may not be proved by testimony from a character witness in order to demonstrate truthfulness, but arguably they may be explored on redirect to bring out the foundation for the original testimony.

---

character") *with* Harbin v. Interlake S.S. Co., 570 F.2d 99, 106 (6th Cir. 1978) (if plaintiff offered evidence of good character, crimes and even arrests would be admissible).

10. *See* Michelson v. United States, 335 U.S. 469 (1948); Deary v. City of Gloucester, 9 F.3d 191, 196 (1st Cir. 1993) (incident ten years old); Harbin v. Interlake S.S. Co., 570 F.2d 99, 106 (6th Cir. 1978) (convictions 13 and 15 years old).

11. Shimon v. United States, 352 F.2d 449, 453-455 (D.C. Cir. 1965) (witness attested defendant's truthfulness and prosecutor asked about charges; he may say he understood defendant had been cleared).

§6.52   Showing Prior Consistent Statements

When the credibility of a witness is attacked by a prior inconsistent statement, the attack may be answered by efforts at refutation or repair.

Perhaps the most effective answer involves proof that the witness never made the supposed inconsistent statement. The supporting party may introduce testimony to this effect, not only by the witness under attack but by others who were present when the statement was supposedly made, who can testify that the statement was different was not made at all.[1] Potentially equal in effectiveness is an explanation of reasons for the inconsistency. FRE 613(b) assures an opportunity for such explanation, and the sponsoring party may call other witnesses to shed light on the true significance of the prior statement.

Showing inconsistent statement never made

Short of proving an inconsistent statement was never made, the best way to repair credibility may involve proving a *consistent* statement. But this approach is not always allowed: The simple fact is that no matter how persuasive the evidence of a prior *consistent* statement, and no matter how many such statements there are, an *inconsistency* remains.[2] Hence the conventional rule is that impeachment by a prior inconsistent statement does not necessarily pave the way to prove a consistent statement.[3]

Proving consistent statement

If a single ingredient is added, however, proof of consistent statements is admissible. If the attacking party suggests that the testimony is a recent fabrication or is explainable by improper motive or undue influence, then counterproof that the witness made a consistent statement may be admitted.[4] The conventional rule is that the consistent statement must have come before the supposed motive arose or influence was brought to bear, which means before any inconsistent statement that is offered to show motive or influence. This restriction is hard to apply, and its status as law had begun to slip, but the Supreme Court's 1995 decision in *Tome* (discussed below) breathed new life into it.

Fabrication, influence

Many other impeaching attacks can indicate improper motive or fabrication. Attacks suggesting bias commonly do (often bias is shown by means other than statements by the witness), and sometimes contradiction suggests improper motive or influence, as do some

---

§6.52   1. United States v. Laughlin, 772 F.2d 1382, 1394-1395 (7th Cir. 1985); Tri-State Transfer Co. v. Nowotny, 270 N.W. 684 (Minn. 1936).

2. Lilly, Introduction to the Law of Evidence 432 (4th ed. 2006) (if witness made inconsistent statement, consistent statement "adds very little," as trier already has "two conflicting accounts").

3. Ellicott v. Pearl, 35 U.S. 412 (1836) (admit consistent statements only if testimony is "assailed as a fabrication of a recent date, or a complaint recently made"); Conrad v. Griffey, 52 U.S. 480 (1851); United States v. Quinto, 582 F.2d 224, 232-234 (2d Cir. 1978).

4. United States v. Stuart, 718 F.2d 931, 934 (9th Cir. 1983) (cross about plea agreement called motive into question, so FBI agent properly testified that witness made consistent statements before plea); United States v. Feldman, 711 F.2d 758, 766-767 (7th Cir. 1983) (similar), *cert. denied*, 464 U.S. 939.

attacks indicating untruthful disposition. The suggestion of improper motive or bias can be express or implied.[5]

The reason to admit consistent statements is that they show that improper influence or motive does not explain the testimony—whatever the reason for the testimony, it is not recent fabrication. After all, the prior consistent statement shows that the witness said before the same thing he says now: If the consistent statement was not produced by the influence or motive suggested by the attack, then the trial testimony is also free of the taint and may be true after all.

Broader relevance Consistent statements actually have broader relevance for rehabilitation. If made close in time to a supposed inconsistent statement, consistent ones may tend to show the inconsistent statement was never made, or that it was not inconsistent with testimony (or not as inconsistent as appears). Commentators support these uses, as do modern decisions.[6] And consistent statements, made when the event was fresh in memory, should also be admitted to rebut claims of failed or faulty memory that are raised by use of prior inconsistent statements.[7]

Modern doctrine is in disarray on two points. One involves sorting out the interplay between hearsay doctrine and the rules on repairing credibility. The second involves the question whether prior consistencies are admissible only if they came before the alleged improper motive appeared, which is partly a matter of doctrine and partly a matter of application.

Hearsay question On the hearsay question, it seems indisputable as a matter of arid logic that when a consistent statement is offered to repair credibility, its relevance does not require taking it as proof of what it asserts. The statement repairs credibility because of its performative aspect: It is an instance of consistent behavior, and using it to prove this point does not depend on the assertive quality of the statement, so it need not be considered hearsay.[8] Yet there are obvious hearsay risks in this

---

5. *See* M. Graham, Prior Consistent Statements: Rule 801(d)(1)(B) of the Federal Rules of Evidence, Critique and Proposal, 30 Hastings L.J. 575, 586, 607 (1979) (as example of implied charge of motive or partiality, prosecutor asks defense witness whether she is defendant's mother; as example of express charge, followup question asks whether she would do anything she could to help son; as example of implied charge of fabrication, defendant asks whether witness talked with plaintiff's lawyer before testifying; as example of express charge, asking when witness first decided to change her testimony).

6. *See* United States v. Tome, 513 U.S. 150 (1995) (statements not covered by FRE 801(d)(2)(B) might have rehabilitative effect; Breyer dissent says such statements may rehabilitate by placing inconsistent statement "in context," by showing that inconsistent statement was not made, and by showing that memory is not faulty); United States v. Kenyon, 397 F.3d 1071, 1080 (8th Cir. 2005) (consistent statements may rehabilitate if they "clarify or amplify" inconsistent statement or bear on question whether there really was an inconsistency).

7. U.S. v. Coleman, 631 F.2d 908, 913 (D.C. Cir. 1980) (where contradiction only suggests "inaccurate memory," consistent statement is admissible to rebut inference).

8. *See* Beech Aircraft Corp. v. Rainey, 488 U.S. 153, 173 n.18 (1988) (plaintiff's letter about plane accident was not hearsay; defense had questioned plaintiff about passages; court erred in excluding other passages to contribute to understanding); United States v. Demarrias, 876 F.2d 674, 678 (8th Cir. 1989).

use of consistent statements, both because they may be taken as additional proof of what they (and the testimony) assert and because a statement might be considered consistent even if it covers some point not proved by live testimony.

FRE 801(d)(1)(B) allows unrestricted use of prior consistent statements offered to rebut an express or implied charge of "recent fabrication or improper influence or motive." This provision brings new problems: Read literally, it regulates only substantive use of prior consistencies, but the purpose was to pave the way for unrestricted use of all consistent statements that are admissible to repair credibility, thus avoiding the need for limiting instructions. Yet the provision does not cover quite all rehabilitative uses, and courts occasionally react to this gap in coverage by distinguishing between rehabilitative and substantive purposes, concluding that consistent statements may be admissible for the former but not the latter purpose. Alternatively, courts assume FRE 801(d)(1)(B) occupies the whole field of prior consistent statements, hence that every use of such statements raises issues under FRE 801(d)(1)(B).

On the question whether prior consistent statements are admissible *only if made before the supposed motive came into play*, the traditional and logically unimpeachable answer is an emphatic *YES*. And in its 1995 opinion in the *Tome* case, the Supreme Court concluded that FRE 801(d)(1)(B) embodies this principle.[9] There is room to debate *Tome*'s effect on the use of prior consistent statements, but probably the opinion means that such statements are only admissible, when offered to refute claims improper motive or recent fabrication, if made before the motive came into play, and if that condition is satisfied the statements may be used as substantive evidence too. Hence the premotive requirement, as developed in *Tome*, expresses both a condition of substantive use and a limit on the relevancy of statements offered to rehabilitate.

> **Statement precedes motive**

Suppose Witness says on Day 1 that the blue car had the light in its favor at the time of the accident. Suppose on Day 2 he meets and discusses the matter with Driver (operating blue car), on Day 3 Witness repeats the observation, and at trial he testifies the same way. If Witness is impeached by suggestions that he testified as he did because Driver bribed or threatened him, the consistent statement on Day 1 tends to rebut this attack by suggesting that Witness did not shape his testimony because of his later talk with Driver (because he held the same view *before* that). But the consistent statement on Day 3 does not have similar effect: It was made *after* the suggested motive or influence took hold and does not tend to refute the attack. Indeed, it tends to confirm the inference of motive or influence (Witness met Driver, and *then* said he had the light). No matter how compelling the logic of the premotive requirement, the unfortunate reality is that the requirement is hard to administer, since it is often impossible to know when a motive or

> **Explanatory example**

9. Tome v. United States, 513 U.S. 150 (1995) (consistent statements fit FRE 801(d)(1)(B) only if uttered before motive to fabricate arose).

influence made itself felt. Real-world facts, unlike the Witness-Driver example, are likely to be blurred.[10]

Why restrict use of prior consistencies? For reasons similar to those advanced in support of allowing free use of prior *inconsistent* statements, arguably prior *consistent* statements should be freely admissible both to bolster credibility and to prove the matters asserted. After all, the witness is present and can be questioned about what he said before. If his consistent behavior lends credibility to his trial testimony, why shouldn't the jury hear it?

There are two answers to these claims:

One is that restricting use of prior consistencies reduces or limits incentives that would otherwise encourage parties actively to collect statements prior to trial, and reduces or limits incentives to rely more and more on out-of-court statements and less and less on live testimony.[11] There is an abiding conviction, seemingly shared in a most heartfelt way among judges and practicing lawyers, that live testimony is far preferable to out-of-court statements, and that free use of statements should be discouraged.

Second, the conventional rule limits use of consistent statements to situations where they have greatest probative worth. If the witness is not impeached, the fact that he said before what he says now should be assumed (even jurors know that lawyers more or less expect their own witnesses to say what they say) and is not terribly persuasive. And some forms of impeachment do not make prior statements especially useful: Evidence of bad character for veracity might well undermine not only what the witness says at trial, but what he said before as well. Excluding evidence of prior consistent statements in these circumstances simply tends to enforce the rule that efforts to repair credibility must be directed to the very damage left by the attack.

But these arguments can be overstated. Since consistent statements are admissible to repair credibility after an attack that suggests bias or improper motive (by direct evidence or less definite implications emanating from evidence of prior inconsistent statements), pressure to produce prior consistencies already exists. And the unbridled use of them might not only be nonproductive but counterproductive from the standpoint of the supporting party, suggesting that self-interest will lead toward moderation.[12] Also the vagueness of the conventional rule leaves it uncertain whether repair by consistent statements is allowed,

---

10. *See* discussion of FRE 801(d)(1)(B) in §8.25, *infra*.

11. Dow, KLM v. Tuller: A New Approach to Admissibility of Prior Statements of a Witness, 41 Neb. L. Rev. 578, 607 (1962) (if prior statements are regularly admissible, pressure to secure them will increase, and trials will be "cluttered with" prior statements, "written and oral, drawn not with a view to preserving the memory of the witness or the lawyer but with a view to making the best case").

12. Maguire, Evidence: Common Sense and Common Law 62-63 (1947) (describing feared prospect of suit where main object of litigants is to obtain latest pretrial statement, but this tactic "could be made by forensic skill to recoil dreadfully upon the litigant whose lawyers had carried out the practice").

which makes it hard for the attacking party to know whether his strategy will or will not pave the way for use of prior consistencies.[13]

J. RELIGIOUS BELIEFS

> **FRE 610**
>
> Evidence of the beliefs or opinions of a witness on matters of religion is not admissible for the purpose of showing that by reason of their nature the witness' credibility is impaired or enhanced.

§6.53 Questioning on Religious Beliefs

FRE 610 bars inquiry into or extrinsic evidence of the religious belief or opinions of a witness where the purpose is only to shed light on his general truthfulness or untruthfulness, hence on the likelihood that his testimony is true or not.[1] In effect FRE 610 simply forecloses such inquiry or evidence as a means to establish the character or disposition of a witness toward truthfulness or untruthfulness.

Where religious affiliation bears on motive or bias of a witness, however, nothing in FRE 610 bars inquiry or evidence along this line.[2]   **Bias**

FRE 610 was not intended completely to insulate the trier of fact from all information about the religious affiliation of a witness that might come into the case incidentally. There is nothing improper about foundation questions that disclose that a witness is a minister, priest, or other religious functionary, and generally either the calling party or an adverse party may ask a witness about his calling or occupation. And in the case of character witnesses, being a parish priest or minister may bear on personal knowledge about the person whose character he attests. Of course the proponent may hope that the fact also bears on general veracity and judgment of the character witness, and FRE 610 does not seek to block whatever gain the proponent might   **Not insulate completely**

---

13. *See* Travers, Prior Consistent Statements, 57 Neb. L. Rev. 974, 991-995 (1978) (insightful discussion of impeaching and hearsay aspects of consistent statements).

§6.53   1. State v. Bolen, 632 S.E.2d 922, 927 (W. Va. 2006) (error to let prosecutor bring out that complainant went to member of her church to describe sexual assault, to explain why she waited eight years; prosecutor used point to bolster credibility) (reversing); Commonwealth v. Rodriguez, 782 N.E.2d 1129 (Mass. App. 2003) (defense should not suggest, based on fact that that victim had Bibles in house, that she would not make up testimony) (citing authors of this Treatise).

2. *See* ACN to FRE 610 (can inquire on "interest or bias"); North Carolina Rule 610 (can show bias). *And see* Fireman's Fund Ins. Co. v. Thien, 63 F.3d 754, 760-761 (8th Cir. 1995) (membership in religious group can show bias); State v. Cordeiro, 56 P.3d 692, 725 (Hawaii 2002) (can show that witness had undergone life change and walks "straight and narrow" and would not commit murder).

make in this way. Nor does FRE 610 prevent a witness from wearing any particular garb or emblem that he would normally wear without regard to the fact of the trial.[3]

FRE 610 implies a mandate to courts applying the oath or affirmation requirement of FRE 603 to be sensitive to the possibility that a particular religion may approve a particular way of committing a witness to the truth, and disapprove others. In such cases, courts should allow a determined witness to take such form of oath or affirmation as his religion may dictate. And preliminary questioning to establish the appropriate form of oath or affirmation, and perhaps even the ritual of swearing or affirming itself should take place outside the presence of the jury if prejudice to a party or embarrassment to a witness appears as a real possibility.

Clearly FRE 610 does not block inquiry into nonreligious ideological commitments that might cause a witness deliberately to give false testimony.

K. PRESENTING TESTIMONY

FRE 611

(a) **Control by court.** The Court shall exercise reasonable control over the mode and order of interrogating witnesses and presenting evidence so as to (1) make the interrogation and presentation effective for the ascertainment of the truth, (2) avoid needless consumption of time and, (3) protect witnesses from harassment or undue embarrassment.

(b) **Scope of cross examination.** Cross examination should be limited to the subject matter of the direct examination and matters affecting the credibility of the witness. The court may, in the exercise of discretion, permit inquiry into additional matters as if on direct examination.

(c) **Leading questions.** Leading questions should not be used on the direct examination of a witness except as may be necessary to develop the witness' testimony. Ordinarily leading questions should be permitted on cross-examination. When a party calls a hostile witness, an adverse party, or a witness identified with an adverse party, interrogation may be by leading questions.

---

3. *Compare* Commonwealth v. Trinkle, 124 A. 191, 193 (Pa. 1924) (in murder trial, removing proceedings to home of witness too ill to attend trial even though she was surrounded by images, pictures, and fixtures indicating Roman Catholic faith; same problem would arise if aged nun or priest testified) *with* La Rocca v. Lane, 338 N.E.2d 606 (N.Y. 1975) (prohibiting priest who was also lawyer acting as defense counsel in criminal jury trial from wearing clerical garb), *cert. denied,* 424 U.S. 968.

1.   *Sequence and Safeguards*

§6.54   Order of Proof; Reopening, Rebutting, Recalling

By long custom and universal practice, the civil plaintiff having the **Civil: Plaintiff** burden of persuasion on his claim goes first at trial, which means **goes first** that he calls all the witnesses and presents all his evidence first. He introduces the initial testimony of each witness, usually by question and answer on direct examination, and he offers tangible evidence or exhibits. After the direct for each witness ends, other parties have the chance to put questions in cross-examination. Generally plaintiff sets the agenda and controls the course of proof during this phase in what is called his case-in-chief. Part of this control comes from the fact that he selects witnesses and decides the sequence of presentation; part of it comes from the fact that ordinarily cross by other parties is confined to the scope of direct and impeachment.

When the plaintiff rests, the defense has a turn. The defendant calls **Defendant goes** the shots during what is usually called the "defense case-in-chief" or her **next** "case-in-defense." This time plaintiff must be content to sit at the sidelines, playing only the role of cross-examining each witness after the defense finishes the direct.

Criminal cases follow a similar pattern. First the prosecutor goes **Criminal: First** forward, then the defense. And in both civil and criminal cases the **prosecutor, then** party who goes first with proof usually goes first as well when it **defense** comes to opening statements and closing summation. However, in summation usually the party who goes first also has a last chance (after the other side has presented its close) to have a final word.

After plaintiff and defendant (or prosecution and defense) have **New phases** rested, the trial can move to new phases in which plaintiff or prosecutor may go forward with a case-in-rebuttal followed by a defense case-in-rejoinder, and the process sometimes goes to additional phases, with surrebuttal and further rejoinder. Each phase after the cases-in-chief, however, should be narrower in focus and content and should respond to whatever has gone immediately before.

The pattern of examining witnesses can similarly go through not just **Examining** two phases, but multiple phases: First comes direct, then cross, then **witnesses** sometimes redirect and recross, and occasionally further redirect and further recross. Again the phases are to be progressively narrower, and in each the presentation is to develop or reply to what came immediately before.

In sum, the phases of a case are normally these:

(1) plaintiff (or prosecutor) presents his case-in-chief, then rests;
(2) defendant presents her case-in-chief or case-in-defense, then rests;
(3) plaintiff (or prosecutor) presents his case-in-rebuttal;
(4) defendant presents her case-in-rejoinder (sometimes called defense case-in-rebuttal);
(5) each side may present further cases-in-rebuttal or rejoinder.

And the phases of examination are as follows:

(1) direct examination by the calling party
(2) cross-examination by adverse parties
(3) redirect examination by the calling party
(4) recross by adverse parties
(5) further redirect and recross as necessary.

No codified rule sets out the sequences of proof and examination described above, and FRE 611(a) confers broad discretion on the trial judges to depart from the pattern, although in fact departures are rare. Courts have this authority because some flexibility is essential and because someone must take charge to make an adversary system work. FRE 611 is broad and general for many reasons: Perhaps most importantly, judges generally have enough practical sense and skill to exercise power in this area so the facts and contentions can be presented with reasonable clarity and dispatch, and inconvenience to witnesses may be at least controlled if not minimized.

Particularized rules in areas like relevancy, impeachment, and hearsay do not themselves resolve such matters, and the circumstances of trial are too numerous and varied for specific regulation. And like much else that happens at trial, the real meaning of the way witnesses are questioned and evidence is presented cannot be ascertained from a transcript of proceedings, and reviewing courts cannot usefully second-guess much that happens.

By long custom and professional instinct, litigants normally follow the sequence of presenting evidence and calling and examining witnesses described above, and the court need not map out the course of trial or even pass specifically on the choices made by counsel as they select witnesses and call them. But FRE 611 confers broad discretion in trial judges, subject to review only for abuse, to affect all these points and to make appropriate rulings in many important areas.

The judge may decide the order in which evidence or testimony is admitted, and the sequence or schedule of the appearance of witnesses,[1] but sometimes there are such strong reasons to depart from the normal sequence or to refuse to allow departure from it that reversals may be had.[2] Sometimes setting the order of proof affects the way decisions on admissibility are made, or the way issues of conditional relevancy are presented, and sometimes it helps avoid prejudice or unnecessary presentations of evidence. But perhaps most often courts control the order of proof and depart from ordinary sequences in

§6.54 1. *See* Morales Feliciano v. Rullan, 378 F.3d 42, 57 (1st Cir. 2004) (in suit challenging prison conditions, can require official to testify first), *cert. denied*, 543 U.S. 1054; United States v. Puckett, 147 F.3d 765, 770 (8th Cir. 1998) (letting government recall law enforcement witnesses so the proof "could be presented in chronological order").

2. Loinaz v. EG&G, Inc., 910 F.2d 1 (1st Cir. 1990) (error to refuse request to present testimony of main witness out of order, interrupting plaintiff's case; defense was forced to use deposition) (reversing).

efforts to accommodate witnesses or see to it that the stories of the various litigants are presented in an understandable way.

With respect to questioning of witnesses, the judge decides whether (and the extent to which) redirect and recross is allowed[3] and whether witnesses should be recalled.[4] In these areas, too, reversal may sometimes be had.[5]

At least with evidence that could properly be introduced during the offering party's case-in-chief, the court has discretion to decide whether to allow it in rebuttal.[6] Where the evidence really would not have been useful (even proper) during the case-in-chief, but tends to rebut evidence later admitted, no doubt the trial judge still has discretion, but not so much, and rebuttal should usually be allowed.[7]

Setting up time limits, at least if done in a reasonable manner in light **Time limits** of the issues and the nature of the proof, and if the parties are consulted in a realistic fashion, can be a useful means of insuring efficiency. Trials consume limited judicial resources and can be costly to parties and to witnesses, not to mention the costs that trials bring for jurors who must serve with only nominal pay, and who sometimes complain about lengthy and repetitive presentations of evidence.[8] The main objection to time limits is that they can bring too much rigidity to the trial process, and focusing on the clock can distract the lawyers and judge from the issues that should be the center of attention.[9] It may be hard to avoid such rigidity while at the same time avoiding charges of unfairness if a judge allows parties to go beyond the period allotted. Still, if they can be administered judiciously, time limits can be helpful, particularly in civil cases. Courts can also insist that various kinds of evidence be presented

---

3. United States v. Allen, 930 F.2d 1270, 1272-1273 (7th Cir. 1991) (redirect); Nickerson v. G. D. Searle & Co., 900 F.2d 412, 419 (1st Cir. 1990) (recross).

4. *See* United States v. Rivera, 971 F.2d 876, 886 (2d Cir. 1992); United States v. Brown, 954 F.2d 1563, 1572 (11th Cir. 1991).

5. *See* Patrick v. Detroit, 906 F.2d 1108, 1113-1114 (6th Cir. 1990) (error to block defense cross of plaintiff, recalled after bifurcated presentations on liability and damages).

6. United States v. O'Brien, 119 F.3d 523, 531 (7th Cir. 1997) (judge has discretion to determine whether to permit surrebuttal testimony); United States v. Mitan, 966 F.2d 1165, 1176 (7th Cir. 1992) (excluding surrebuttal testimony).

7. Weiss v. Chrysler Motors Corp., 515 F.2d 449, 457-489 (2d Cir. 1975) (court may reject rebuttal evidence admissible in case-in-chief; if plaintiff has prima facie case without it, probative worth is high and it is not cumulative, it should come in).

8. ABA American Jury Project, *Principles for Juries and Jury Trials*, Principle 12 & comment (2004) (recommending that courts, after conferring with parties, impose and enforce reasonable time limits on trials or portions thereof to avoid unnecessary burdens on jurors). *See also* M. T. Bonk Co. v. Milton Bradley Co., 945 F.2d 1404, 1408-1409 (7th Cir. 1991); MCI Communications Corp. v. AT&T Co., 708 F.2d 1081 (7th Cir. 1983), *cert. denied*, 464 U.S. 891.

9. Flaminio v. Honda Motor Co., Ltd., 733 F.2d 463, 473 (7th Cir. 1984) (disapproving rigid hour limits on trial, as likely to engender "unhealthy preoccupation" with clock and complicated methods).

by use of scripts or written summaries, although such measures are controversial.[10]

Whether party may reopen

The judge has discretion to decide whether a party may reopen.[11] No doubt some allowance should be made if a party mistakenly and understandably forgets some formal point or element that is far from the main controversy,[12] and some requests to reopen are too obviously justified and important to deny.[13] When the party seeking to reopen has substantial evidence that for some understandable reason he did not introduce in his case-in-chief, the question whether he should be allowed to reopen turns on such factors as whether the adversary is unfairly surprised, or has a reasonable opportunity to rebut, or whether the adversary would be placed at a tactical disadvantage by the new proof.[14]

§6.55 Questioning Versus Narrative Testimony

Narrative

The trial judge may let a witness testify in narrative form or insist on the conventional question-and-answer approach. One leading case allowed a railroader suing his employer for workplace injuries to tell the jury his "complete story" in narrative form. After he described "the particulars of his employment, the use of a hand car, the method of stopping it, and the breaking of one of its wheels," the railroad objected that plaintiff was saying immaterial things and introducing hearsay, and that proceeding this way blocked objections. The trial court rejected this concern on the ground that narrative testimony was "the best way of getting at what he knew or could state," and the Eighth Circuit agreed, noting that the railroad still had the right to object and move to strike.[1]

Question and answer

Undoubtedly the usual question-and-answer approach presents fewer risks: The questions themselves provide signals if something

---

10. United States v. Petty, 132 F.3d 373, 378-379 (7th Cir. 1997) (requiring presentation of voluminous records by summary testimony); Chapman v. PT&T, 613 F.2d 193 (9th Cir. 1979) (contempt judgment against lawyer for refusing to prepare written narrative to be presented in lieu of live testimony, witnesses to be present and subject to cross). *And see* Richey, A Modern Management Technique for Trial Courts to Improve the Quality of Justice: Requiring Direct Testimony to Be Submitted in Written Form Prior to Trial, 72 Geo. L.J. 73 (1983) (advocating written summaries in lieu of oral direct testimony); Pratt, A Judicial Perspective on Opinion Evidence Under the Federal Rules, 39 Wash. & Lee L. Rev. 313, 322 (1982) (judge requires expert testimony to be written out in full in advance).

11. Blinzler v. Marriott Intl., Inc., 81 F.3d 1148, 1160 (1st Cir. 1996); Skehan v. Board of Trustees, 590 F.2d 470, 480 (3d Cir. 1978), *cert. denied*, 442 U.S. 832.

12. United States v. Alderete, 614 F.2d 726, 727 (10th Cir. 1980) (prosecutor reopened to show offense took place in New Mexico, which was necessary for jurisdiction).

13. United States v. Larson, 596 F.2d 759, 777-780 (8th Cir. 1979) (error to deny defense request to reopen; court should consider timeliness, character of testimony, effect of granting request) (reversing).

14. *See* United States v. Dossey, 558 F.2d 1336, 1339 (8th Cir. 1977).

§6.55 1. Northern P.R. v. Charless, 51 F. 562, 570 (9th Cir. 1892) (noting that plaintiff "proceeded to relate the facts in the case as requested"), *rev'd on other grounds*, 162 U.S. 359.

inadmissible is coming, and to a degree the professionalism of lawyers is likely to avoid obvious missteps. And lawyers are doubtless reluctant to interrupt witnesses with objections, lest their conduct seem arrogant or disrespectful. But a witness may be cautioned to "tell us what you know, not what others have told you," and often such an instruction is enough. In the end, if a witness is more at ease giving narrative testimony, and if it seems that he can do so without putting before the trier of fact too much material that is inadmissible or saying things that are seriously prejudicial, it is desirable to allow him to proceed this way.

Clearly trial courts have discretion to require testimony to be developed by question-and-answer or to let the witness tell his story in narrative form.[2]

§6.56   Formal Flaws in Questions to Witnesses

The court has discretion to control the mode of questioning witnesses under FRE 611, so it can bar questions that are unfair or misleading.[1] Objections on such grounds are usually "formal" in the sense that the questioner can solve the problem by rephrasing. They are also formal in the sense that typically the problem is not that the questioner is trying to violate some exclusionary rule such as the hearsay doctrine or the rule against proving settlement offers, but rather that he is deliberately abusing or accidentally misusing the questioning process. Of course the questioner's real purpose may be to impose a particular view on the witness or argue the case to the trier of fact, and the question may score rhetorical points even when the objection is sustained.

Obviously there are other kinds of objections. Many are "substantive" in that they rely on particular rules that exclude evidence, like the hearsay doctrine and restrictions framed as limits on relevancy (like those dealing with character and remedial measures). Sometimes the questioner can obviate those objections too, often by "laying a foundation" (proving authenticity or showing that a hearsay exception applies).[2]

Substantive objections

Putting aside substantive objections, here are common formal objections:

Formal objections

1. Asked and answered. Sometimes the questioner drums away too hard, putting a question time and again in hope of forcing the desired response. He must be allowed to press (especially on cross) and need

---

2. United States v. Silva, 748 F.2d 262, 264 (5th Cir. 1984) (background information in narrative form); United States v. Young, 745 F.2d 733, 761 (2d Cir. 1984) (broad discretion to allow narrative testimony; properly allowed in drug trial to accompany and explain videotape); Hutter N. Trust v. Door County Chamber of Commerce, 467 F.2d 1075, 1078 (7th Cir. 1972) (pro se plaintiff asked permission to testify in narrative form; hard to see "how a question propounded by a witness who is examining himself can rationally be objected to as leading").

§6.56   1. *See generally* 1 McCormick, Evidence §7 (6th ed. 2006); Dombroff, Trial Objections §§410-429 (1991); 3 Wigmore, Evidence §§780, 782 (Chadbourn rev. 1970).

2. *See* discussion of authentication issues in Chapter 9.

not take the first answer, for the witness would soon catch on that she can get out of the hot seat by denials or standard evasions ("I don't know" or "I don't remember"). But when the questioner has gotten an answer and has had a chance to test it and expose falsehood, the examination should move along, and objecting can force the point.

2. Assumes facts not in evidence. If a question embodies information that might count in some way, it should be supported by proof already admitted. If the support is not there, the question is objectionable as assuming too much. Asking "Where was *X* when he signed the agreement?" would be objectionable on this ground if there is no evidence that *X* did sign the agreement.

3. Argumentative. Sometimes the questioner tries to contradict the witness or confront her with disbelief rather than get an honest answer. Questioning in this vein, often sarcastic or contemptuous or patronizing, is grandstanding that may be permissible in closing argument but need not be tolerated during presentation of proof. Questions like "How can you seriously expect us to believe what you just said?" need not be taken seriously and can be viewed as argument thinly disguised. The difference between argumentative and leading questions can be a matter of degree, but questions that are too close to argument can be rejected.

4. Compound. Sometimes a question apparently seeks more than one answer or suggests alternative responses, while being framed in a way that invites a yes or no response. The problem is that a witness might fairly respond by saying yes or a no, and her meaning will then be obscure. For example, "Did you read the directions and use the drill properly?" If the witness says yes, a strict grammatical reading leads to the conclusion that she meant to say that she both read the directions and used the drill properly. But in relaxed everyday conversation, the witness or the jury might think yes means only that she used the drill properly (that being the latter and apparently more important part of the question). If the answer is no, the witness might mean (or the jury might think she meant) that she neither read the directions nor used the drill properly, or did one of the two but not both, but it is at least as likely that she meant only that she didn't use the drill properly (the latter and apparently more important part of the question).

5. Misleading. Here the question misstates the evidence or misquotes another witness. If there is evidence that the witness took an hour to drive someplace, and that the trip was ten miles (and no evidence that the trip was five miles), it is misleading to ask "Why did it take you an hour to drive five miles?" The question may properly be disallowed.

6. Speculation or conjecture. A witness is usually supposed to say what he knows, and not what he would guess or suppose or expect. Like hearsay objections, this one may have substantive content, and it may be impossible to fix the query because a lay witness cannot provide what is wanted. Asking a witness "what he would have done" if he knew something then that he knows now, or what someone else "was thinking when he did that" is typically objectionable on this ground. Sometimes the objection is more a matter of form, and the questioner who wants to know what the witness "would have done" with other information may get just about what she wants by asking "what made you do what you did?"

7. *Uncertain, ambiguous, and unintelligible.* This three-part protest (usually a single objection) is as customary as the alliterative general objection ("incompetent, irrelevant, and immaterial"). Essentially the claim is that the question has many meanings, or none at all, or its meaning is nonliteral and can only be understood figuratively. Sometimes the questioner has simply garbled her words and needs to begin again, but often the question is argumentative and there is no expectation of a serious response. In a challenge to the way a police officer put together a lineup, for example, this question illustrates the objection: "In arranging the lineup, you tried to pick seven men who weighed the same and didn't weigh the same, and who looked alike and didn't look alike, didn't you?"

8. *Nonresponsive to the question.* When lawyers ask proper questions on specific points, they are entitled to responsive answers. If counsel for plaintiff in an accident case asked defendant whether he "was driving faster than the posted limit" and he replies "maybe so, but your client darted out in front of me and I couldn't have stopped even if I'd been going slower," the questioner can ask the court to "strike the answer as nonresponsive and instruct the witness to answer the question." On request, the judge should do so and on request, or even without it, tell the jury to disregard the answer. The questioner must act quickly, however, or lose the objection, and sometimes the opposing party can object too, although the latter must usually provide some additional reason for the objection.[3]

Questioners and witnesses often have conflicting agendas and work at cross-purposes, and it may be hard to know who's manipulating whom. In trials, the court can provide guidance, and usually gives the lawyer leeway to decide what points to make and when to make them, and the witness is asked to cooperate. Since parties are pretty much stuck with answers their lawyers adduce, striking a nonresponsive answer may be important. Of course a fair response to an open-ended question is not nonresponsive: If the lawyer says "tell us what happened" and the witness says "your client darted out in front of me," the answer is responsive and the questioner is stuck with it.

This list does not exhaust the possibilities. Objections to "leading questions" or "going beyond the scope of direct" are in a sense formal too, since the claim is not that the evidence should be excluded, but that it should not be gotten in that way or at that time.[4] And there are others. "Calls for a conclusion" or "calls for an opinion" are common complaints. Here the objecting party claims that the witness does not have enough knowledge or that the question invites him to reply too

---

3. *See* discussion of making objections and motions to strike under FRE 103 in §1.3, *supra.*

4. *See* discussion of leading and nonleading questions in §§6.60 and 6.64, *supra.*

generally.[5] "Calls for narrative" is another. Here the complaint is that the witness should be asked particular questions rather than given freedom to recite at length. Often narrative responses are perfectly proper, but the more usual approach is by question and answer and the trial court may require the latter.

§6.57 Preventing Abuse of Witnesses

Sparing the witness from harassment or undue embarrassment is important mainly in three contexts:

First, impeachment by cross-examination on prior acts may be limited to protect the privacy of witnesses. Broad provisions in FRE 608 also serve this purpose, as do narrower focused limits in FRE 412 that protect complaining witnesses in sexual assault trials. Where prior acts have little or no bearing on veracity, questions about them should be disallowed under FRE 608, and inquiry into past sexual behavior is almost completely blocked by FRE 412.[1] In these and similar settings, FRE 611 supports the proposition that questions designed to embarrass or humiliate a witness should be disallowed.[2]

Second, conduct by trial counsel that seems designed to browbeat or bully the witness should be corrected by court admonition or penalty.[3] The court may disallow obvious and unnecessary efforts at physical or psychological intimidation: Standing or leaning too close may make the witness uncomfortable or put him off guard, or confuse him, and the same may happen with shouts or threats, or words or gestures that seem to ridicule, belittle, humiliate, or poke fun at the witness. Particularly when the result is serious pain or discomfort, or intimidation that might make the witness cave in to suggestion just to put an end to the ordeal, the court may act.

Something close to intimidation may of course be necessary on cross or its functional equivalents (questioning hostile witnesses). Here the essential and legitimate purpose of the questioner is to exercise a large measure of effective control over the witness by making him answer the questions that counsel chooses to ask, and necessarily there is an element of coercion. Questions that expose falsehood or mistake,

5. *See* discussion of FRE 602 (requiring personal knowledge) in §6.5, *supra*, and discussion of FRE 701 (limiting opinions to those that are rationally based) in §7.2, *infra*.

§6.57 1. *See* discussion of FRE 608 in §6.25, *supra*, and discussion of FRE 412 in §4.32, *supra*.

2. Smith v. Illinois, 390 U.S. 129, 132-133 (1968) (quoting *Alford* case, *infra*); Alford v. United States, 282 U.S. 687, 694 (1931) (court has duty "to protect a witness from questions which go beyond the bounds of proper cross-examination merely to harass, annoy or humiliate").

3. *See* Berger v. United States, 295 U.S. 78, 84-85 (1935) (judge should not allow prosecutor to bully and argue with witness); State v. Briggs, 886 A.2d 735, 747 (R.I. 2005) (can limit defense questions that border on harassment); 3 Wigmore, Evidence §781 (Chadbourn rev. 1970) (quoting Dickens, Trollope, Bentham, on browbeating witnesses; judge can prevent abuse).

uncertainty or bias, or for that matter a lying disposition, cannot be pleasant to experience and are destined to cause discomfort. The court's task is to prevent the excesses, but not to make testifying pleasant.

Third, questions on sensitive subjects that are necessarily hard to talk about (like some injuries or disabilities, or abuse, or sexual offenses) require special care, even more so when the witness is very young. Often gentle handling serves the interests of both sides, and counsel may be counted on to proceed with great care: One side probably hopes to get useful evidence, and the other cannot afford to be seen as abusing or unnecessarily embarrassing the witness. But sometimes courts must act to protect witnesses because the interests of the parties do not always insure respectful treatment, and sometimes guardians or companions are used to help support the witness.[4]

2.   *Foundational Matters*

§6.58   Context and Background

Generally the first questions to a witness are designed to show context and reveal something about the background of the witness, including name and address, and often occupation or business and name or address of place of work. Usually ensuing questions connect the witness to the parties or dispute in some way, often by putting them at the scene of important events.

In its decisions in the *Alford* and *Smith* cases, both reversing convictions because the court blocked defense inquiry, the Supreme Court recognized that preliminary information is relevant in two senses.[1] First, placing the witness in his setting helps the jury evaluate his testimony.[2] Second, disclosing basic data helps parties bring out facts that might impeach or support, as by showing bias or its absence, or characteristic truthfulness or untruthfulness.[3] As the Court recognized in *Alford*, asking where the witness lives is appropriate even without showing it will lead to something. As it recognized in *Smith*, the starting point in exposing falsehood is to ask the witness who he is and where he lives because these points open avenues of inquiry both in and out of court. Both cases also recognize that if the calling

Evaluation; impeach or support

---

4. *See generally* discussion of protected-witness testimony in connection with hearsay in §8.91, *infra*, and the discussion of child witnesses in §6.3, *supra*.

§6.58   1. Smith v. Illinois, 390 U.S. 129, 131 (1968) (name and address); Alford v. United States, 282 U.S. 687, 691-692 (1931) (where witness lives); Government of Virgin Islands v. Grant, 775 F.2d 508, 511-513 (3d Cir. 1985); United States v. Marti, 421 F.2d 1263, 1266 (2d Cir. 1970).

2. United States v. Blackwell, 853 F.2d 86, 87-88 (2d Cir. 1988) (service in Marine Corps and two years of college told jury something about witness as a person).

3. Alford v. United States, 282 U.S. 687 (1931) (question could show possible bias or prejudice).

party fails to bring out the preliminary information, the adversary is entitled to do so on cross.[4]

In a separate concurring opinion in *Smith*, Justice White said a trial court may cut off cross out of concern for the personal safety of a witness (he apparently concurred only because the state gave no reasons to block the inquiry),[5] and this principle has taken firm root. It seems settled that if the government shows that revealing address or place of business of the witness will endanger his safety, defense questioning on these points may be disallowed.[6] Sometimes such questioning is curtailed where it would undermine or impede ongoing investigations.[7] Where disclosing identifying information will subject the witness to personal danger, protective measures may be taken, such as blocking disclosure of such information in court while allowing the lawyer for the other side access to relevant data but keeping it from his client.[8]

§6.59   Voir Dire of Witnesses

Developing preliminary information is usually followed by questions that establish or test the personal knowledge of the witness and often bring to light his relation to events or occurrences and to the parties, thus "laying the foundation" for his testimony. For ordinary witnesses, usually this matter is quickly and readily handled on direct, and little or no question is raised. But other parties may object if they think the necessary foundation was not laid, and the objection should be raised before the witness gives any substantive testimony.

If the problem is that the calling party neglected this matter, further direct can quickly take care of it. If the calling party thinks the foundation was laid but an adversary thinks otherwise, the latter may ask for a chance to "voir dire" the witness. If the court thinks the foundation is adequate, the adverse party is usually told to "wait until your cross-examination," but if the court doubts the foundation laid on direct, it may ask the calling party to go further into it, or interrupt the calling party's case so the other side can go into preliminaries on voir dire.

---

4. *See* United States v. Opager, 589 F.2d 799, 804-806 (5th Cir. 1979) (address of government witness must be disclosed; burden falls on government to show why disclosure should not be made); United States v. Harris, 501 F.2d 1, 7-9 (9th Cir. 1974) (error to block question about residence of informant).

5. Smith v. Illinois, 390 U.S. 129, 133-134 (1968) (concurring opinion says inquiries that endanger personal safety belong in same category as questions that harass, annoy, or humiliate).

6. United States v. Varella, 692 F.2d 1352, 1355-1356 (11th Cir. 1982), *cert. denied*, 464 U.S. 838; United States v. Mesa, 660 F.2d 1070, 1075-1076 (5th Cir. 1981).

7. United States v. Gray, 626 F.2d 494, 499-500 (5th Cir. 1980), *cert. denied*, 449 U.S. 1091.

8. Withers v. Levine, 615 F.2d 158, 163 (4th Cir. 1980) (adopting this approach in civil rights action alleging sexual assaults in prison), *cert. denied*, 449 U.S. 849.

In the case of an expert, the inquiry is usually more elaborate because **Experts** it is designed to establish expertise as well as personal knowledge or some other basis for testifying. Here laying a foundation is important for other reasons: It expands the admissibility of opinion testimony and the bases on which it may rest, and lets the calling party question the witness more freely with less concern about leading. Unlike the practice in many states, establishing a witness as an expert in federal court does not entitle the prevailing party to win higher costs at the end.[1]

As in the case of lay witnesses, opposing parties may be dissatisfied with the foundation for expert testimony laid by the calling party. Here such issues are often serious and the proponent's foundation may even fail, though it seems enough on first glance, so opposing parties are usually allowed, on request and before the expert testifies on substantive points, to probe and test the foundation. One legitimate purpose is to show that he does not qualify as an expert. Another is to show that he lacks an adequate foundation.[2]

On the latter point, FRE 705 says in effect that usually an expert may **Conclusions may** state his conclusions before the bases are brought out, suggesting that **come first** only in unusual cases should the court let an opponent voir dire the expert before he states his conclusions. If the court does allow voir dire, the opponent should not be allowed to take advantage of this interruption in the calling party's case to develop substantive evidence or launch an attack that goes only to credibility before the witness has given substantive evidence, since impeachment and cross-examination normally follow the direct, and should not delay it in the beginning. But drawing a line between voir dire that tests the qualifications and foundation and voir dire that develops substantive points and undercuts credibility is a hard thing to do, and probably no entirely satisfactory line can be drawn.

Expert testimony must normally clear a "reliability standard" as well, **Reliability** meaning that the principles and methods applied by the expert must be **standard** valid science, the application of those principles and methods must be sound, and there must be an adequate basis. This hurdle, associated in federal courts with the *Daubert* standard and in states with cases adopting *Daubert* or taking similar approaches, has increased the use of pretrial hearings in which both sides develop the underlying issues, in what amounts to precautionary advance voir dire.[3] The result of voir dire may be to qualify the witness fully, to limit the areas and types of testimony he may give, and even to bar his testimony altogether.[4]

---

§6.59   1. *See* 28 U.S.C. §1821 (setting fee for lay and expert witnesses at $30 per day); Crawford Fitting Co. v. J. T. Gibbons, Inc., 482 U.S. 437 (1987) (expert fees taxed to losing party may not exceed statutory rate of $30 per day).

2. The court decides whether an expert is qualified, *see* §1.10, *supra*, and whether he expert has an adequate basis for his testimony, *see* §7.15, *infra*.

3. *See* Daubert v. Merrell Dow Pharmaceuticals, 509 U.S. 579 (1993), discussed in §7.7, *infra*.

4. *See* Vallot v. Central Gulf Lines, Inc., 641 F.2d 347, 350-351 (5th Cir. 1981) (excluding expert testimony where voir dire demolished prospective testimony). *See also* §7.15, *infra*.

3. Direct Examination

§6.60 Nonleading Questions

Developing the story is the great challenge for litigating lawyers, and direct examination is the usual mechanism. Meeting the challenge is largely a matter of rhetoric and style, but partly the challenge is practical, as there are many constraints that complicate the task of presentation: Recall that evidence rules limit or block the use of hearsay and proof of "other acts," both of which might come out in a natural telling. Recall too that the other side may interrupt with objections, and that normally a story must be told piece by piece, witness by witness, in segments separated by breaks, and that direct questioning is immediately followed by cross.

Focus on witness and story There is an important rule against leading questions on direct examination, and there are other formal issues and broad discretionary authority in the judge to control questioning and presentation.[1] Most of what makes for good direct, however, has nothing to do with rules, and everything to do with strategy, skill, and psychology. Without doing more than touch the subject, it seems worthwhile to note central points good practitioners know by instinct: In the usual case where witnesses are friendly (at least not hostile), the purpose of the direct is to get out what the witness has to say in a manner that is relaxed, natural, clear, and understandable. Good direct guides the witness and focuses everyone's attention on the unfolding story and on the witness, and the questions should be relatively open-ended, so she can say what she knows and can be the center of attention. Organization counts (the lawyer must know the way). So does simple but careful language (to set the tone, present the story in positive terms). So does pacing.[2]

The central rule that applies to direct examination is that usually the calling party must proceed by question and answer rather than narrative recitation, and the questions must be nonleading.[3] Generally the same holds true at later stages of questioning by the calling party (redirect), except that leading is allowed in exceptional situations where the usual assumptions about the nature of the situation do not apply (as discussed in the next section).

Usually a witness is reasonably friendly to the cause of the calling party, and the calling party's lawyer has gone over the subject with the witness, and a certain understanding has grown up between them.

---

§6.60 1. On formal objections, *see* §6.56, *supra*. On narrative testimony, *see* §6.55, *supra*. On judicial power to control order and sequence, *see* §6.54, *supra*.

2. *See* Mauet, Fundamentals of Trial Techniques §5.1 (6th ed. 2002) (direct examination should "let the witness be the center of attention"); Tanford, The Trial Process 224 (2d ed. 1993) (most important things are to "prepare your witness in advance to give direct and descriptive testimony" and "let the witness dominate the direct").

3. *See* Commonwealth v. Baker, 800 N.E.2d 267, 279 n.16 (Mass. 2003); Ellis v. Chicago, 667 F.2d 606, 613 (7th Cir. 1981); United States v. Orand, 491 F.2d 1173, 1176 (9th Cir. 1973), *cert. denied*, 414 U.S. 1006; United States v. Lewis, 406 F.2d 486, 493 (7th Cir. 1969), *cert. denied*, 394 U.S. 1013.

That means at least that she is attuned to the lawyer's needs and may even be sympathetic and helpful, so suggestive questions are both unnecessary and likely to influence her testimony.

In this setting leading questions pose three risks.[4] First, they may invoke a false memory of events, so testimony less accurately reflects what the witness actually saw or knew. Second, they may push her into ready acquiescence in suggestions. She is ill at ease (courtrooms are unfamiliar, formal, public, and intimidating); she is likely accustomed to the conventions of casual conversation where mistakes are often inconsequential and go unchallenged and uncorrected; she may not understand the issues and may hope to speed the process along; she knows what the lawyer wants and may already be inclined to help. Third, leading questions may distract the witness from important detail by directing her attention only to aspects of her story that the questioner considers favorable.

Just asking a leading question may cause damage, since an objection or motion to strike is not likely to erase the impression already made on the witness. But ordinarily the questioner is allowed to proceed, and all he has to do is rephrase the question.[5] Taking this step at least removes the sting, and helps the witness reply as she prefers.

Partly because objections to leading questions can be so readily cured, any objection to the form of questioning should be promptly stated. In depositions, objections to "the form of the questions" are lost if not stated at the time. The reason is that the objection can be dealt with by rephrasing the question without the need for a judicial ruling. Even at trial, objections on this ground should be stated immediately so they can be cured, or they are lost.[6]

Unlike objections that seem to keep information from the jury, a "leading question" objection is likely to evoke a positive reaction from jurors. Their natural sympathies rest with the witness, and the objecting lawyer is likely to be seen as helping the witness by keeping the questioner from pushing him around too much.

As the term "nonleading" implies, proper direct questions are usually described in terms of what to avoid (a nonleading question does not lead). A question is leading if it suggests the answer sought by the questioner. Many factors can make a question leading. Sometimes it is phrasing: Even in cold print, a question that begins "Isn't it a fact that" or "Did you not" suggests a response and is leading. So is one that

---

4. Bailey v. United States, 831 A.2d 973, 983 (D.C. Ct. App. 2003) (bar leading questions on direct to avoid supplying false memory for the witness); Williams v. State, 733 N.E.2d 919, 922 (Ind. 2000) (leading questions substitute "the language of the attorney for the thoughts of the witness").

5. Allen v. Hartford Life Ins. Co., 45 A. 955, 956 (Conn. 1900) (letting counsel substitute another question; perhaps harm was already done, but justice would often fail "if formal defects in the offer or introduction of testimony could not be corrected").

6. For depositions, *see* FRCP 32(d)(3)(B) and FRCrimP 15(f). *See also* Oberlin v. Marlin Am. Corp., 596 F.2d 1322, 1328 (7th Cir. 1979) (admitting deposition of plaintiff taken by his attorney through leading questions; no objection at the time).

is phrased in the alternative to highlight the desired answer in careful detail while diminishing the other choice in vagueness: "Did you understand that you were to meet him at your home at ten o'clock, or what?" But a question that frames the only likely alternatives in an evenhanded way is not leading: "Did you call him, or did he call you?"

Sometimes phrasing tells little and context is more important. In a trial for battery where defendant claims he struck no blow, the defense might ask an eyewitness "Did you see the defendant beat the victim?" and it would hardly be considered leading, but the question would be leading if put by the prosecutor. Sometimes inflection, facial expression, voice dynamics, or gestures tell the story. It is easy enough to imagine asking the question "Did he seem really angry to you?" in a leading manner that conveys that either a yes or a no is the sought-after answer, but also easy to imagine the question put in a neutral and nonleading way.

That a query is put in such way as to confine the witness to a yes or no answer is not necessarily the sign of a leading question. It is easy enough to see how the question "Did he say that the saw could be safely used for masonry?" could be leading, but the question "Did you see what happened?" is hardly ever leading. Both call for a yes or a no.

§6.61   Leading Adverse Parties, Hostile Witness, Others

While the usual rule is that leading questions are not allowed on direct examination, the first sentence of FRE 611(c) makes it clear that the trial judge has discretion to allow leading questions to be put to a witness whenever these may be "necessary to develop his testimony."

Young; timid; ignorant; infirm   Usually the questioner is allowed to put leading questions where the witness is (a) very young, and for that reason apprehensive, uncomprehending, or confused,[1] (b) unusually timid, reticent, or frightened,[2] (c) ignorant, uncomprehending, or unresponsive,[3] or (d) infirm on account of sickness or age.[4]

Of course witnesses who fit any of these descriptions seem more likely than others to be swayed by the suggestive influence of leading questions, and in that sense leading is even more dangerous in these settings. But the answer to this objection is that it is better to ask leading questions and have some hope of getting useful information than to go

---

§6.61   1. United States v. Lewis, 519 F.3d 816, 822 (8th Cir. 2008) (in trial for sexual abuse, prosecutor could lead child victim who was seven at time of trial).

2. United States v. Grey Bear, 883 F.2d 1382, 1393 (8th Cir. 1989) (government led "to develop testimony given by an unusually softspoken and frightened witness"), *cert. denied,* 493 U.S. 1047.

3. Jordan v. Hurley, 397 F.3d 360, 363 (6th Cir. 2005) (prosecutor could lead victim who had Down syndrome and difficulty responding); United States v. Ajmal, 67 F.3d 12, 16 (2d Cir. 1995) (government led witness who testified in Urdu with translator).

4. Preston v. Denkins, 382 P.2d 686, 692-693 (Ariz. 1963) (leading proper where witness was 78 years old and in poor health and seemed to have "difficulty in independently recalling events").

without it altogether. And juries have enough common sense to see at least some difference between the witness who plays along with suggestion and the one who answers from within, to know when they are hearing the witness and when they hear only an echo of the questioner, and to consider the impact of the questions in assessing what the witness says.

The third sentence of FRE 611(c) says leading questions are proper in other circumstances: Thus the questioner may lead a witness who is hostile,[5] or an adverse party or one who is identified with an adverse party.[6] Sometimes a witness employed by a party is hostile to that party,[7] and sometimes a witness is hostile to both parties (or more than one) and may be led by more than one side.[8] In these situations, the problem for the lawyer is that the witness is uncooperative, and more pointed questioning is a measured response, even on direct.

Hostile witnesses; adverse parties

The third sentence of FRE 611(c) also suggests that leading hostile witnesses is a matter over which the court has discretion (the verb form "may be" suggests as much). With respect to adverse parties and people identified with them, it would be a rare case where leading would be objectionable. But a measure of discretion is essential in determining whether a witness is "hostile," and sometimes in determining whether a person is "identified with an adverse party."[9] Former Civil Rule 43(b) said a party could cross-examine and lead a witness who was "an officer, director, or managing agent of a public or private corporation or of a partnership or association which is an adverse party," and some state counterparts include similar language.[10] The phrase "identified with an adverse party" is of course broader still.

Leading questions are commonly allowed in three other settings:

First, on preliminary or uncontested matters leading questions are allowed simply to save time.[11] Thus they are commonly used to show the name, address, and occupation of the witness, and often his relation to the parties, or the events in issue, or his qualifications as an expert.

Preliminaries

5. State v. Young, 87 P.3d 308, 317 (Kan. 2004) (once witness is declared hostile, he may be subjected to leading questions on direct).

6. United States v. Hicks, 748 F.2d 854, 859 (4th Cir. 1984) (government led defendant's girlfriend); Haney v. Mizell Memorial Hosp., 744 F.2d 1467, 1477-1478 (11th Cir. 1984) (court should have let plaintiff lead nurse employed by defendants).

7. Morvant v. Construction Aggregates Corp., 570 F.2d 626, 635 (6th Cir. 1978) (defendant asked leading questions when cross-examining its own employees, called by plaintiff).

8. Stine v. Marathon Oil Co., 976 F.2d 254, 266 (5th Cir. 1992) (both sides led to speed examination) (should limit to noncontroversial or background areas).

9. Winant v. Bostic, 5 F.3d 767, 773 (4th Cir. 1993); Chonich v. Wayne County Community College, 874 F.2d 359, 368 (6th Cir. 1989).

10. Arizona and Maine have counterparts to FRE 611 that contain such language.

11. Stine v. Marathon Oil Co., 976 F.2d 254, 266 (5th Cir. 1992) (noncontroversial or background areas); Shultz v. Rice, 809 F.2d 643, 654-655 (10th Cir. 1986) (preliminary questions related to undisputed facts).

Experts   Second, when the witness is testifying in the case as an expert, he is likely to be resistant to leading, and an objection to questioning in this mode usually fails.[12]

Refreshing memory   Third, leading questions are allowed as a means to refresh memory if the witness seems to have forgotten something he may once have known.[13] Some caution is necessary if the matter used to refresh recollection is a statement relating to the issues because it may not be admissible as proof of what it asserts, and asking about it puts the statement in front of the jury. If memory is not refreshed (the questioner fails in his ostensible purpose), there is a risk that the jury will consider what it learns from the questioning as proof. This risk would be a form of prejudice under FRE 403 (misuse of "evidence"), and the authority to control the "mode and order" of questioning under FRE 611 means the court may insist on suitable precautions and may cut short or curtail efforts to refresh recollection if the risk of such prejudice is serious or it seems that the questioner's main purpose is really to get the statement before the jury by hook or crook.[14]

When the calling party seeks to refresh memory by using prior statements by the witness himself, which is probably the most common way of proceeding, the process is subject to limits and safeguards set out in FRE 612.[15] In addition, the court may regulate the questioning under FRE 611 by (a) requiring the questioner to show the factual basis of the questions he intends to ask and disallow them if the foundation is too thin, (b) requiring the questioner to allude to the statement in a way that is specific enough to jog the memory of the witness but not so detailed that it exposes the substance of the statement at the outset, (c) putting a stop to the inquiry after the questioner has had a chance to prod the witness (when he should say what he remembers or the questioning should move along if he remembers no more now than before), and (d) even requiring questions designed to refresh recollection to be asked outside the presence of the jury in the first instance, permitting further questioning or a repeat performance before the jury only if the effort has been productive.[16] Refreshing recollection by prior statements tends to shade imperceptibly into other tactics, including impeachment by

---

12. Dees v. Louisiana Oil Ref. Corp., 162 S. 597, 600 (La. Ct. App. 1935).

13. United States v. McGovern, 499 F.2d 1140, 1142 (1st Cir. 1974); Feutralle v. United States, 209 F.2d 159, 162 (5th Cir. 1954).

14. United States v. Socony-Vacuum Oil Co., 310 U.S. 150, 234 (1940) (warning against misuse of refreshing matter and use of prior statements as evidence under pretext of refreshing recollection); United States v. Davis, 551 F.2d 233, 235 (8th Cir. 1977), *cert. denied*, 431 U.S. 923. *See generally* FRE 612, discussed in §§6.66-6.69, *infra*.

15. *See* the discussion of FRE 612 in §6.67, *infra*.

16. United States v. Shoupe, 548 F.2d 636, 641 (6th Cir. 1977) (can do limited incorporation of sworn statement of witness into questions to refresh recollection, but not "recitation in the presence of the jury of extended unsworn remarks" implicating defendant).

prior inconsistent statements and use of prior statements as substantive evidence (especially past recollection recorded).[17]

4. Cross-Examination

§6.62   Importance of Right; Remedies for Denial

Cross-examination is so highly regarded as a mechanism for testing the meaning and limits of testimony, along with the knowledge, capacity and truthfulness of witnesses, that it is considered a fundamental right. This view prevails in criminal cases where the right of the defendant to cross-examine witnesses against him is secured by the Confrontation Clause of the Sixth Amendment, and where defendant and other defense witnesses are also subject to cross,[1] and in civil cases too.[2]

If the calling party's opponent cannot subject a witness to cross-examination for reasons that are not his fault, some remedy is necessary. The problem can arise if the witness dies or becomes ill after his direct testimony, or disappears or makes a successful privilege claim or simply refuses to testify. If cross-examination is permanently blocked, the direct testimony usually should be stricken in both civil and criminal cases,[3] or a mistrial declared if the direct testimony is critical and striking it would not be effective. Even direct testimony by a defendant in a criminal case may be stricken if he refuses to submit to cross, and probably a mistrial may be declared without fear that reprosecution would be double jeopardy.[4]

Sometimes lesser remedies are possible. If the problem is temporary, a continuance may solve it (or declaring a mistrial and beginning again).[5] An order striking only a part of the testimony is appropriate if other parts were adequately tested on cross, and striking the direct is unnecessary if the purpose of the cross-examiner was substantially

17. On impeachment by inconsistent statements, _see_ discussion of FRE 613 in §6.40, and discussion of FRE 607 in §6.16, _supra._ On using sworn inconsistent statements in proceedings as substantive evidence, _see_ discussion of FRE 801(d)(1)(A) in §8.24, _infra._ On using prior statements as recorded recollection, _see_ discussion of FRE 803(5) in §8.43, _infra._

§6.62   1. Brown v. United States, 356 U.S. 148, 154-155 (1957) (defendant); United States v. Pardo, 636 F.2d 535, 542-547 (D.C. Cir. 1980) (defense witness).

2. Glass v. Philadelphia Elec. Co., 34 F.3d 188, 192-194 (3d Cir. 1994) (error to refuse to let plaintiff cross-examine defense witnesses); Degelos v. Fidelity & Casualty Co., 313 F.2d 809, 814 (5th Cir. 1963) (in action against insurer for death of husband in car driven by son, court should have let widow should cross-examine son; inclination to help was counterbalanced by wish to avoid conceding he killed father).

3. United States v. Rosario Fuentez, 231 F.3d 700, 706-707 (10th Cir. 2000); United States v. Deeds, 954 F.2d 1501 (9th Cir. 1996).

4. United States v. Panza, 612 F.2d 432, 436-439 (9th Cir. 1979). Double jeopardy does not bar reprosecution when defense misconduct leads to mistrial. _See_ Arizona v. Washington, 434 U.S. 497 (1978).

5. Gale v. State, 69 S.E. 537 (Ga. 1910) (witness collapsed before recross; can go forward without striking direct when defendant refused mistrial).

accomplished. Striking the testimony may also be unnecessary if it was only cumulative or related to collateral matters or issues affecting only veracity.[6] A court can also take other corrective steps, such as letting the prosecutor comment on defendant's unprivileged refusal to answer, or continuing to elicit unprivileged refusals as a means of impeachment, or telling the jury that it may consider the unprivileged refusal to answer in reaching a verdict, or instituting contempt proceedings.[7]

§6.63 Scope of Cross

The first sentence in FRE 611(b) says cross should be limited to the scope of the direct and matters affecting credibility; the second says the court may allow additional inquiry, to be pursued in the manner of direct examination. This ambivalence reflects a close division among the framers and within the profession between those who favor the traditional limit and those who favor broad cross. The same division is reflected in state adoptions of FRE 611, where a clear majority follows the scope-of-direct limit, but a significant minority prefers a wide-open rule.[1]

Limit is liberal The scope-of-direct limit seems liberal in any event. It is understood to authorize routine cross-examination on inferences, implications, and explanations suggested by or arising from the direct questioning.[2] And the same sentence that endorses the scope-of-direct limit also makes it clear that the scope-of-direct limit does not apply to questions

6. United States v. Cardillo, 316 F.2d 606, 613 (2d Cir. 1963) (partial striking), *cert. denied*, 375 U.S. 822. *See also* United States v. Williams, 461 F.3d 441 (4th Cir. 2006) (defendant demonstrated that fanny pack didn't fit; that was not testimony giving rise to right to cross-examine).

7. United States v. Rackstraw, 7 F.3d 1476, 1480-1481 (10th Cir. 1993) (defendant claimed not to know cooler contained crack, was not entitled to invoke Fifth Amendment when asked about crack in unrelated transactions, could be forced to claim privilege in front of jury).

§6.63 1. In a 2007 survey, we found that 27 states observe the scope-of-direct rule, and 17 states follow the wide-open rule. These 27 states favor the scope-of-direct rule: Alaska, Arkansas, California, Colorado, Connecticut, Delaware, Florida, Hawaii, Idaho, Indiana, Iowa, Kansas, Maryland, Minnesota, Montana, Nebraska, New Jersey, New Mexico, New York, North Dakota, Oklahoma, Oregon, Rhode Island, South Dakota, Utah, Washington, and Wyoming. These 17 states have the wide-open rule: Alabama, Arizona, Georgia, Kentucky, Louisiana, Maine, Massachusetts, Michigan, Mississippi, Missouri, New Hampshire, North Carolina, Ohio, South Carolina, Tennessee, Texas, and Wisconsin. The other six states fall out this way: Vermont and West Virginia allow wide open cross for witnesses who are parties. Pennsylvania allows wide open cross for parties in civil cases. Illinois, Nevada, and Virginia leave the matter to the discretion of the judge.

2. United States v. Arnott, 704 F.2d 322, 324 (6th Cir. 1983) (subject matter of direct is "liberally construed to include all inferences and implications"), *cert. denied*, 464 U.S. 948; Roberts v. Hollocher, 664 F.2d 200, 203 (8th Cir. 1981) (cross may embrace "any matter germane to direct examination, qualifying or destroying it, or tending to elucidate, modify, explain, contradict").

that test credibility.[3] While FRE 611(b) lets courts take either a restricted or open-ended approach to the scope of cross, the "default rule" is the scope-of-direct limit, and courts are to allow broader cross only in exceptional cases.[4]

Usually the scope-of-direct limit is not applied as stringently when the witness is a party, and here courts often exercise discretion to permit broader questioning.[5] For defendants who testify in criminal cases, however, the constitutional right against self-incrimination goes far to reinforce the scope-of-direct limit.[6]

Almost always cross-examination is an exploratory process. That is **Promotes order** especially so in criminal cases where discovery is limited, but it is true in civil cases too, as discovery is costly and does not always bring the questioner face-to-face with the witness. Hence the charge of "fishing expedition" should not curtail preliminary inquiry even if the questioner cannot define a specific purpose, and he should be allowed some latitude even if he can indicate only a general direction or purpose. The strong argument for the scope-of-direct limit is that it promotes order in presenting evidence. Each party can ensure that during its own case the main focus is on evidence that supports its side, and other parties cannot use cross to take the trial into other areas or develop other sides of the case. In this sense, the Rule helps assure an orderly presentation of proof in an adversary system.

Three other arguments for the scope-of-direct limit are less persuasive. One is that the purpose of cross is exhausted by questions that delve into the subject matter of the direct, which begs the question. A second is that broad cross would let the opponent make his case by leading questions. There is something to this point, since a cross-examiner who attacks the direct by leading questions establishes an element of control over the witness that makes a shift back to non-leading questions (as the questioning broaches new areas) less likely, and probably less effective. But regulating the scope of direct is not the same as regulating the manner of questioning, and to some extent it is possible to force the questioner to shift gears when he goes beyond the scope of the original testimony. The third argument rests on the old voucher rule: The calling party vouches for a witness only to the extent of the direct and should not be bound by or prevented from impeaching a witness who assists his adversary; conversely, the adversary should not make his case by a witness for whom

---

3. United States v. Moore, 917 F.2d 215, 222 (6th Cir. 1990); United States v. Sullivan, 803 F.2d 87, 90-91 (3d Cir. 1986), *cert. denied,* 479 U.S. 1036.

4. *See* Lis v. Robert Packer Hosp., 579 F.2d 819, 822-823 (3d Cir. 1978) (error to rule that cross could range beyond scope of direct throughout trial; court may not allow broad cross in every case; general prescription in FRE 611 is "precisely the opposite").

5. *See* Rivers v. Union Carbide Corp., 426 F.2d 633, 639 (3d Cir. 1970); Mahon v. Reading Co., 367 F.2d 25, 27 (3d Cir. 1966); Sleek v. J. C. Penney Co., 324 F.2d 467, 473-474 (3d Cir. 1963).

6. *See* §6.65, *infra.*

Wide-open rule

he does not vouch. Here too is a kernel of truth, but FRE 607 abolishes the whole idea of vouching.[7]

Two credible arguments support the wide-open rule, which permits cross on any relevant matter, and of course these arguments also expose the major drawbacks of the scope-of-direct rule: First, the wide-open rule encourages the search for truth by letting the parties bring to light at the outset all the witness knows, while the scope-of-direct rule encourages the proponent to control the witness to reveal only part of the truth and prevents the adversary from setting things right. Both Wigmore and McCormick found this argument persuasive because (in McCormick's words) the cross-examiner will be "unwilling to run the risk of calling the adversary's witness at a later stage" and will often "abandon the inquiry" rather than put questions that he might ask on cross.[8]

Second, the wide-open rule is easy to administer while the scope-of-direct rule is troublesome because of its imprecision. One astute observer thought the scope-of-direct rule could be interpreted in at least six different ways, and this vagueness encourages what one court called "pettifogging objections" on this score.[9] Wigmore concluded that the scope-of-direct rule was more trouble than it was worth, and that it brought a risk of reversal for trivial reasons.[10]

There is force in the suggestion that the scope-of-direct rule is an imperfect tool for promoting orderly presentation. Sometimes it stands in the way of cross that should be allowed: If, for example, plaintiff's first witness testifies that the light was red for the defendant and his second testifies that defendant was not keeping an adequate lookout, allowing the defense to cross-examine the second witness on the color of the light would not disrupt the order of proof. Yet it seems that this cross would lie beyond the scope of direct. Other times the limit fails to block cross that should be disallowed in the interests of orderly presentation: If a witness mentions a point on direct that has little importance to the calling party's case but great importance to the other side, the scope-of-direct limit would let the other side explore the point at length on cross.[11]

---

7. A party who rises to cross-examine a witness called by another puts less at risk if he tries to make headway but fails, and more at risk if he calls the witness. But the judgment underlying FRE 607 is that the Rules should not reinforce rhetorical or tactical risks inherent in calling witnesses. *See* §§6.16-6.17, *supra*.

8. *See* 1 McCormick, Evidence §23 (6th ed. 2006) (it is a "much chancier and less attractive option" to call an "unfriendly witness later when his first testimony is stale").

9. *See* Degnan, Non-Rules Evidence Law: Cross-Examination, 6 Utah L. Rev. 323, 330-331 (1959) (scope-of-direct rule might require answer to relate to (1) any issue in calling party's case, but not in cross-examiner's case, or (2) any issue in calling party's case-in-chief, or (3) any issue or inference raised by testimony already given, or (4) any issue or inference raised in testimony by witness, or (5) any transaction or occurrence mentioned by witness, (6) precise points mentioned on direct); Boller v. Cofrances, 166 N.W.2d 129, 134 (Wis. 1969) (decrying "pettifogging objections," adopting wide-open cross).

10. 6 Wigmore, Evidence §1888 (Chadbourn rev. 1976).

11. *See* Urling v. Fink, 141 F.2d 58, 60 (3d Cir. 1944) (it is not the purpose of questioner that counts, but the "character of the matter inquired into" that determines scope of cross).

Probably, however, FRE 611(b) is a good compromise. Courts may make allowance for broader (and sometimes narrower) cross where needed for orderly presentation. The discretion it confers in the trial judge goes far to ensure that losing parties cannot win unnecessary new trials, and the scope-of-direct limit is seldom more than a makeweight on review. The same point saps much of the force from the argument that the scope-of-direct limit is hard to administer.

Common pronouncements that the court has discretion to regulate the scope of direct does not mean that it may curtail cross before the questioner has had a reasonable chance to pursue the matters raised on direct, but rather that the judge has discretion to determine whether broader cross-examination is to be allowed. A ruling that too narrowly restricts the defense cross in a criminal case violates confrontation rights.[12]

§6.64 Leading Questions

Usually cross-examination proceeds by leading questions, and the term itself is almost synonymous with leading questions. Here, after all, the dynamic contrasts sharply with direct examination. Usually the witness is called by the cross-examiner's adversary, and often he has proved friendly to the adversary's cause. And usually the cross-examiner and the witness have not gone over the expected testimony and have only dealt with each other (if at all) at arm's length in a deposition.

In cross-examination, then, the qualities that were drawbacks if leading questions were asked on direct are now advantages. Here leading questions (a) appeal to the conscience and waken the memory of the witness in a way that is well calculated to get him past any falsehood or inaccuracy in what he said before and help him give an account that he himself considers more accurate or complete, (b) expose limits or inaccuracies in his memory or story that he may have overlooked or considered unimportant, and (c) focus his attention on details in what he knows that may be important.

There are three main exceptions where the questioner cannot properly lead on cross: First, the questioner should proceed "as if on direct" under FRE 611(b) when he goes beyond the scope of direct during cross, and here he should not lead.[1] But if the witness is an adversary, or the questioner shows by examining him that some other exception applies in which direct may proceed by leading questions, then the questioner should be allowed to lead on cross that proceeds beyond

12. Davis v. Alaska, 415 U.S. 308, 316 (1974) (constitutional error to block defense cross-examination of state witness on status as probationer).

§6.64 1. *See* MDU Resources Group v. W. R. Grace & Co., 14 F.3d 1274, 1282 (8th Cir. 1994) (cross beyond scope of direct seeking to prove affirmative defense should be nonleading), *cert. denied*, 513 U.S. 824; Lis v. Robert Packer Hosp., 579 F.2d 819, 823 (3d Cir. 1978) (after qualifying doctor called by plaintiff as defense witness, defendants were "limited to direct questions" and plaintiffs could cross).

the scope of direct. Suppose, for instance, plaintiff testifies during his own case-in-chief and the court lets the defense cross go beyond the scope of direct. Here the defense may properly lead because plaintiff is an adverse party.

Hostile—modes reversed

Second, when a party in a civil action calls an adverse party as a witness, or an agent or employee closely aligned with an adverse party, the usual modes of questioning are reversed. The direct proceeds by leading questions (the questioner being counsel for an adversary) and cross proceeds by nonleading questions (the questioner being counsel for the witness or a party aligned with the witness).[2]

Hostile to calling party

Third, if the calling party is allowed for some other reason to lead on direct, as happens if the witness proves hostile to the calling party under FRE 611(c), it is often appropriate to confine the cross-examiner to nonleading questions.[3] But sometimes a witness is hostile to both parties, or unable to testify helpfully without being led, in which case it is appropriate to allow both the calling party on direct and the adversary on cross to put leading questions.[4]

§6.65   Privilege Against Self-Incrimination

A criminal defendant who testifies at trial loses some constitutional protection that the privilege against self-incrimination otherwise provides. He loses protection for his own direct testimony, and he is also open to cross. As the Supreme Court said in the *Brown* case, defendant must weigh "the advantage of the privilege" against "the advantage of putting forward his version of the facts" and take his choice. If he decides to testify, he cannot claim "immunity from cross-examination on the matters he has himself put in dispute" because this approach would make the Fifth Amendment "a positive invitation to mutilate the truth."[1]

Matters related to the direct

It is customary to describe the reduction in Fifth Amendment protection that comes from testifying in terms of waiver, although it is not clear that there is any intentionality component. With that caveat, the prevailing and most useful formulation is that the waiver reaches matters related to the direct testimony, but not all matters that may be relevant, on either substantive issues or credibility. This approach enjoys support in the language of Supreme Court decisions including

2. Shultz v. Rice, 809 F.2d 643, 654-655 (10th Cir. 1986) (in malpractice suit, plaintiff called defendant physician as adverse witness and put leading questions; error to let defense lead).

3. Morvant v. Construction Aggregates Corp., 570 F.2d 626, 635 n.12 (6th Cir. 1978) (where witness is friendly to examiner, court may forbid leading on cross); United States v. Bensinger Co., 430 F.2d 584, 591-592 (8th Cir. 1970).

4. Ardoin v. J. Ray McDermott & Co., 684 F.2d 335, 336 (5th Cir. 1982) (in Jones Act suit, defendant properly led its own employees on cross after plaintiff called them); Morvant v. Construction Aggregates Corp., 570 F.2d 626, 635 (6th Cir. 1978).

§6.65   1. Brown v. United States, 356 U.S. 148 (1958). *See also* Raffel v. United States, 271 U.S. 494 (1926).

Brown, where the Court said a party who takes the stand "determines the area of disclosure and therefore of inquiry," and that "the breadth of his waiver is determined by the scope of relevant cross-examination."[2]

The main strength in this approach is that it recognizes that the privilege entitles the defendant not to testify or be called as a witness. By deciding to testify, a defendant brings into play rules that implement the truthfinding process, but the values underlying the privilege continue to be important. Those values relate to human dignity and freedom from compulsion, and these should not be sacrificed merely because defendant testifies.[3] The right accommodation provides continued protection against compulsion and self-accusation while allowing the prosecutor reasonable latitude to test the direct. This accommodation adequately ensures that the defendant cannot distort the factfinding process by telling only one side of the story, for he may be thoroughly cross-examined on matters reasonably related to what he says. If he chooses to remain silent on other aspects of the case, any tendency in this tactic to distort the truth is offset by the common sense and unavoidable likelihood that the jury will assume his silence on those matters indicates that he has something to hide.

The main difficulty with this accommodation is its vagueness and elasticity, which is compounded by the fact that the stakes on each side are high: In other contexts, restricting cross postpones disclosure but does not necessarily put evidence forever beyond reach, because the cross-examiner can recall the witness. Here waiver that is too narrow restricts cross and makes altogether unavailable whatever might have turned up in broader questioning. But waiver that is too broad trenches on an important right and might not make more information available because defendants may be less willing to testify.

Vague compromise

Where a defendant who testifies on his own behalf refuses to submit to cross under an unjustified claim of the privilege, the court may impose sanctions, including as a last resort striking the direct.[4] When a civil litigant invokes the privilege to avoid giving evidence, appropriate sanctions include dismissal of claims or defenses.[5]

When a defendant faces several charges of criminal misconduct, he must come to terms with the troublesome reality that testimony on one

Faces several charges

---

2. *See* Brown v. United States, 356 U.S. 148 (1958) (cannot claim privilege against cross "on matters reasonably related to the subject matter of his direct"); Harrison v. United States, 392 U.S. 219 (1968) (waives privilege "with respect to the testimony he gives"). *See* Carlson, Cross-Examination of the Accused, 52 Cornell L.Q. 705 (1967), *and* Scope of Cross-Examination and the Proposed Federal Rules, 32 Fed. B.J. 244 (1973); 1 McCormick, Evidence §129 (6th ed. 2006) (prosecutor must have "reasonable opportunity to test the defendant's assertions on direct").

3. *See* Tucker v. United States, 5 F.2d 818, 822 (8th Cir. 1925).

4. *See* §6.62, *supra*.

5. Bramble v. Kleindienst, 357 F. Supp. 1028, 1036 (D.C. Colo. 1973) (can dismiss where plaintiff invoked 5th Amendment in discovery), *aff'd*, 498 F.2d 968 (10th Cir.), *cert. denied*, 419 U.S. 1069.

charge might be used against him on another, or that his silence on one charge, made conspicuous by testifying on another, may count against him. In a related context the Supreme Court indicated little sympathy,[6] but sound authority suggests that defendant is entitled to a severance of separate and distinct charges where he shows *both* a serious risk of prejudice if the jury considers his testimony on other counts *and* a desire to testify on one count coupled with a reason not to testify on others.[7]

Prosecution witness
Where a prosecution witness claims a privilege (usually his Fifth Amendment privilege) during defense cross, defendant's Sixth Amendment confrontation right may be infringed if the privilege claim is sustained or the witness refuses to answer.[8] If defendant cannot probe the testimony on cross, he is entitled to have it stricken, and to a mistrial if striking the testimony is not likely to be effective.[9]

A prosecution witness may decline to answer questions about his own criminal acts by invoking the Fifth Amendment if they are relevant only on veracity. Here courts do not require the testimony to be stricken, often saying the curtailed inquiry pursued a collateral matter.[10] As a practical matter, claiming the privilege may have impeaching effect, and probably the court should let defendant ask a prosecution witness questions that elicit the claim, which goes far to satisfy the defense need to attack credibility.[11] While the privilege entitles defendant not to take the stand, and certainly not to be forced to claim the privilege in front of the jury (unless the court has overruled his claim), other witnesses have no such entitlement and are not injured by any inference the jury might draw.

Generally, testifying in one proceeding does not deprive the witness of his privilege against self-incrimination in a later proceeding.[12] In its most frequent application, this principle enables a witness who has testified before a grand jury to decline to testify at trial under a claim

6. McGautha v. California, 402 U.S. 183 (1971) (right against self-incrimination does not require bifurcation of capital case to let defendant testify on punishment without risking use of testimony on guilt).

7. *See* Baker v. United States, 401 F.2d 958, 976-977 (D.C. Cir. 1968), *later appeal*, 430 F.2d 499, *cert. denied*, 400 U.S. 965.

8. Douglas v. Alabama, 380 U.S. 415 (1965); Klein v. Harris, 667 F.2d 274, 289 (2d Cir. 1981).

9. Klein v. Harris, 667 F.2d 274, 289 (2d Cir. 1981); United States v. Newman, 490 F.2d 139, 145-146 (3d Cir. 1974); United States v. Cardillo, 316 F.2d 606, 613 (2d Cir. 1963), *cert. denied*, 375 U.S. 822.

10. United States v. Beale, 921 F.2d 1412, 1423-1424 (11th Cir. 1991); United States v. Lester, 749 F.2d 1288, 1301 (9th Cir. 1984).

11. United States v. Kaplan, 832 F.2d 676, 684 (1st Cir. 1987), *cert. denied*, 485 U.S. 907; United States v. Smith, 342 F.2d 525, 527 (4th Cir. 1965), *cert. denied*, 381 U.S. 913.

12. Re Beery, 680 F.2d 705, 720 n.17 (10th Cir. 1982) (testifying in earlier deposition in state receivership proceedings did not waive privilege), *cert. denied*, 459 U.S. 1037; United States v. Bush, 680 F.2d 468 (6th Cir. 1982) (in new trial, witness could claim privilege on questions she answered at first trial), *cert. denied*, 499 U.S. 922.

of the privilege.[13] Taking seriously the notion (discussed further below) that the privilege is unavailable once the cat is out of the bag, so to speak, it is hard to see why the mere fact of a later proceeding should make a difference. Some authority takes the view that a witness who testified before a grand jury cannot refrain from repeating the testimony at trial.[14] This result finds strong support in the argument that the other approach burdens the prosecution without according a corresponding benefit to the witness, whose earlier grand jury testimony has already incriminated him.

For witnesses other than criminal defendants who testify, claims of the privilege against self-incrimination differ in ways that bear on applying it: Only criminal defendants enjoy the right not even to be called (civil litigants and nonparties may be called regardless what they want). Only criminal defendants risk imprisonment or other penalty as the direct outcome of trial (nonparties have no direct stake, and civil litigants face risks that differ in important ways). Criminal defendants have some control over what they say (nonparty witnesses lack control, and civil litigants often lack it, especially if called by the other side). Nonparty witnesses usually provide crucial evidence against criminal defendants and often have important privilege claims themselves, which introduce tension between the rights of the accused and those of the prosecuting authority and nonparty witnesses.

Witnesses other than defendants

Because of the first of these differences (only criminal defendants are immune from being called), conventional doctrine rooted in the *Rogers* case holds that only they waive Fifth Amendment protection when they elect to testify, and that waiver does not apply where a witness other than the accused testifies freely but later invokes the privilege. If exempting all other witnesses from notions of waiver meant they could claim the privilege at any time, however, they could provide incomplete information and avoid being tested on cross. This problem appeared in *Rogers* itself. There a grand jury witness admitted she was a communist but declined on a claim of privilege to identify the person to whom she turned over books and records of the party. Confronted with the problem of the incomplete story, the Court adopted a narrow cat-out-of-the-bag reading of the privilege, holding that a witness who "freely testifies" to an incriminating point does not have a privilege from making "full disclosure of details," since the privilege does not apply to details that would not "further incriminate" the witness.[15]

---

13. *See* United States v. Licavoli, 604 F.2d 613, 623 (9th Cir. 1979); United States v. Housand, 550 F.2d 818, 821 n.3 (2d Cir. 1977), *cert. denied*, 431 U.S. 970. *See* 1 McCormick, Evidence §140 (6th ed. 2006) (most courts hold that testifying in earlier stage of "a single unit of litigation" does not preclude witness from invoking privilege at trial).

14. Ellis v. United States, 416 F.2d 791, 800-805 (D.C. Cir. 1969) (reiteration does not further incriminate; allowing privilege impedes enforcement) (rule inapplicable to defendants).

15. Rogers v. United States, 340 U.S. 367 (1951) (contempt remedy).

L. REFRESHING MEMORY

FRE 612

Except as otherwise provided in criminal proceedings by section 3500 of title 18, United States Code, if a witness uses a writing to refresh memory for the purpose of testifying, either

(1) while testifying, or
(2) before testifying, if the court in its discretion determines it is necessary in the interests of justice,

an adverse party is entitled to have the writing produced at the hearing, to inspect it, to cross-examine the witness thereon, and to introduce in evidence those portions which relate to the testimony of the witness. If it is claimed that the writing contains matters not related to the subject matter of the testimony the court shall examine the writing in camera, excise any portions not so related, and order delivery of the remainder to the party entitled thereto. Any portion withheld over objections shall be preserved and made available to the appellate court in the event of an appeal. If a writing is not produced or delivered pursuant to order under this rule, the court shall make any order justice requires, except that in criminal cases when the prosecution elects not to comply, the order shall be one striking the testimony or, if the court in its discretion determines that the interests of justice so require, declaring a mistrial.

§6.66 The Basic Process

Nowhere do the Rules regulate in detail the trial technique of refreshing the memory of a witness. Two provisions do touch separate aspects of the technique: One is FRE 611(c), which lets judges regulate use of leading questions (the usual mechanism by which the questioner refreshes memory). The other is FRE 612, which governs the right of the questioner's adversary to inspect a writing used to refresh memory, and to offer the writing itself. This right is perhaps the major safeguard against abuse of the technique of refreshing memory.

Anything may be used Refreshing memory is a last-ditch means to secure information known to the witness but apparently lost to conscious mind, hence lying beyond reach of ordinary direct. When memory seems exhausted, the questioner may try to refresh it by questions suggesting matters that may help. Anything may be used—an object, a sound, a gesture, "a song, a scent, a photograph, an allusion, even a past statement known to be false."[1] Prior testimony by the witness may be used, and a writing prepared by another person, or a copy of a writing, and it should make no difference when the writing was prepared.[2] Whatever is used to refresh memory need not be admissible initially[3] and does not become admissible at the behest of the questioner merely because it is used in this manner, although adverse parties are usually entitled to introduce such material.[4]

If memory is refreshed, so the witness affirms or adopts the matter suggested by the questioner, the fact that the questioner could not introduce the matter itself becomes inconsequential. The result is different, however, if the witness does not affirm or adopt the matter, particularly if it is a statement that relates to the issues but is inadmissible for its truth because of the hearsay doctrine or for some other reason. Merely questioning the witness may put such a statement before the trier of fact so graphically as to give rise to a serious risk that it will be considered for its truth, which amounts to "prejudice" within the meaning of FRE 403—a kind of misuse of evidence—and the trial judge should disallow the effort to refresh recollection when the risk of this kind of prejudice becomes serious.

Because of the problem described above, four limits on refreshing memory are commonly recognized: First, memory must be or seem to be exhausted after ordinary direct or cross before the questioner may try to refresh it.[5] Second, the judge may control the manner of broaching the prior statement (by requiring factual basis and an inquiry specific enough to jog memory without exposing the substance of the statement at the outset; also cutting off the effort after the questioner has had a chance to prod the witness; even requiring questions to refresh recollection to be asked outside the jury's presence in the first instance). Third, the witness should not testify to the matter suggested over objection by the questioner's adversary unless he first says his memory is indeed refreshed, so his testimony now represents

Limits

---

§6.66 1. *See* United States v. Rappy, 157 F.2d 964, 967 (2d Cir. 1946) (source of quoted phrase), *cert. denied*, 329 U.S. 806. *See also* United States v. Socony-Vacuum Oil Co., 310 U.S. 150, 231-237 (1940) (grand jury testimony); United States v. Muhammad, 120 F.3d 688, 699 (7th Cir. 1997) (FBI 302 report). *And see* Kline v. Ford Motor Co., 523 F.2d 1067, 1069-1070 (9th Cir. 1975); Wyller v. Fairchild Hiller Corp., 503 F.2d 506, 509-510 (9th Cir. 1974) (hypnosis to refresh memory of accident victim).

2. State v. Pritchett, 69 P.3d 1278, 1283 (Utah 2003) (in child abuse trial, using nine-year-old victim's preliminary hearing testimony to refresh her memory); United States v. Darden, 70 F.3d 1507, 1540-1541 (8th Cir. 1995) (DEA debriefing reports), *cert. denied*, 517 U.S. 1149; United States v. Church, 970 F.2d 401, 409 (7th Cir. 1992) (agent's notes).

3. 20th Century Wear, Inc. v. Sanmark-Stardust Inc., 747 F.2d 81, 93 n.17 (2d Cir. 1984) (evidence taken in violation of *Miranda* rights); United States v. Scott, 701 F.2d 1340, 1346 (11th Cir. 1983) (credit card applications that were inadmissible because government had not disclosed them to defense), *cert. denied*, 464 U.S. 856.

4. Rush v. Illinois Cent. R. Co., 399 F.3d 705, 719 (6th Cir. 2005) (in rail yard accident suit, error to let witness read aloud from interview transcript; FRE 612 requires refreshed memory and testifying from present recollection, not merely restating contents of writing), *cert. denied*, 546 U.S. 1172. On use by adverse parties, *see* §6.68, *infra*.

5. Hall v. American Bakeries Co., 873 F.2d 1133, 1136 (8th Cir. 1989).

independent recollection and not a mere reiteration of whatever was used to refresh.[6] Fourth, the questioner's adversary is entitled to inspect the matter used to refresh memory and to introduce it in evidence (a point taken up in the next section).

Despite the obvious danger that a witness who testifies, notes in hand, may simply be saying what he sees that the notes indicate, rather than providing what he now remembers about the events or facts reflected in the notes, some authority approves the practice of letting the witness hold and read the notes as he testifies.[7] Perhaps such latitude is warranted where precise numbers or dates are critical, but unless great care is taken, this use of the device is a shallow pretense. A better approach would require the proponent to resort to FRE 803(5) (past recollection recorded) or some other exception that justifies use of the document itself.

Sometimes a fifth safeguard is mentioned. It is said that the questioner must show that any statement used to refresh memory was made at or about the time of the events. This safeguard may be rationalized as a means of providing some circumstantial indication of accuracy, which arguably is needed because an inaccurate writing may have enough power of suggestion to lead witness and trier astray.[8] But this requirement seems to come from confusing refreshed memory with recorded recollection, which is different, and most courts wisely do not impose this requirement for writings used to refresh. The other safeguards provide protection enough.[9]

Different from recollection recorded

Refreshed recollection differs from the hearsay exception for past recollection recorded in FRE 803(5): Although the two are "clearest in their extremes" and in practice represent "converging rather than parallel lines," refreshed recollection emphasizes present testing of the witness and relies on what he says he recalls, while recorded recollection tests what he wrote against standards designed to ensure reliability, and depends on the prior writing itself.[10]

Using inconsistent statements to impeach involves contrasting what the witness said before against her present position, and arguing that

6. 20th Century Wear, Inc. v. Sanmark-Stardust Inc., 747 F.2d 81, 93 n.17 (2d Cir. 1984) (court must ensure that witness "actually has a present recollection").

7. United States v. Rinke, 778 F.2d 581, 587 (10th Cir. 1985); Chalmers v. Los Angeles, 762 F.2d 753, 761 (9th Cir. 1985).

8. Putnam v. United States, 162 U.S. 687, 695 (1896) (confusing refreshed memory with recorded recollection); NLRB v. Hudson Pulp & Paper Corp., 273 F.2d 660, 665 (5th Cir. 1960) (relying on *Putnam*). *See* Hutchins & Slesinger, Some Observations on the Law of Evidence—Memory, 41 Harv. L. Rev. 860, 868-869 (1928).

9. United States v. Riccardi, 174 F.2d 883, 889 (3d Cir. 1949) (writing used to refresh is likely to influence memory strongly, so "the nearer the writing to the truth, the lesser the deviation" of memory from truth, but this is not reason enough to insist on reliability of writing), *cert. denied*, 337 U.S. 941.

10. United States v. Riccardi, 174 F.2d 883, 886-889 (3d Cir. 1949) (with recollection refreshed, "the witness, by hypothesis, relates his present recollection, and under oath and subject to cross-examination asserts that it is true" so memory and perception can be attacked and tested, and claims of lack of memory undermine probative worth; past recollection recorded involves accepting writing for truth, so it "assumes a distinct significance as an independent probative force"), *cert. denied*, 337 U.S. 941.

she cannot be trusted on the point in question. If the witness claims to have forgotten what she once knew, impeachment and refreshing memory may overlap, especially if the prior statement favors the position of the questioner at trial. If that statement is not admissible as substantive evidence or the questioner hopes the witness will affirm it on the stand, the better strategy may be to try to refresh memory. But if the statement does not help the examining party much or if there is no real hope that the witness will affirm it, the questioner may be better off to spring it on her as inconsistent in an attempt to persuade the trier to reject what she says. Either way, the statement brings a risk of jury misuse, and the court should guard against this possibility, particularly where the examiner is the calling party.[11]

§6.67 Adversary's Right to Inspect and Question

Under FRE 612, a party adverse to one who uses a writing to refresh the memory of a witness *as she testifies* is entitled to see and ask questions about the writing. When the witness has used a writing to refresh *before she testifies*, FRE 612 allows the adverse party to inspect if the court decides it is necessary.

There are no qualifications to the right to inspect writing used on the stand to refresh. It would seem not only unfair but also bizarre in an adversary system to let a witness consult a document on the stand while keeping other parties from seeing it.[1] It is hard to say whether this unqualified right to inspect reaches the situation where the witness reviews documents after she has begun to testify but during breaks when she is off the stand. The time-honored practice of strolling down the hall to find a nook or room off the beaten path to go over documents one last time and get last-minute reminders might be treated as refreshing memory "while testifying." But there is a difference between the dependence on documents that is indicated if the witness must refresh memory on the stand and the capacity to recall well enough to leave the document at counsel's table or home or office. And in long or complicated trials where a witness testifies in separate sessions on different subjects, reviewing documents between sessions closely resembles pretrial preparation, where the right to inspect documents is discretionary. In short, it is also plausible to interpret "while testifying" as a reference to the time that the witness actually spends on the stand. The most that can be said is that if the witness has begun testifying and reviews documents during a short recess, disclosure should be ordered, but the mere fact that a witness reviews

---

11. On impeachment by inconsistent statements, *see* discussion of FRE 613 in §§6.40-6.42, *supra*. On preventing the calling party from misusing this mechanism, *see* discussion of FRE 607 in §6.17, *supra*. On substantive use of prior inconsistent statements, *see* discussion of FRE 801 in §8.24, *infra*.

§6.67 1. Spivey v. Zant, 683 F.2d 881, 885 n.5 (5th Cir. 1982); Marcus v. United States, 422 F.2d 752, 754 (5th Cir. 1970).

documents off the stand after she has once given testimony does not mean disclosure is automatic.[2]

Disclosure at the outset The purpose of requiring disclosure is to give other parties a chance to see the writing (or a copy) while the witness is still at hand, and in many instances it should be possible to require disclosure at the outset during the calling party's exploration of the matter with the witness on direct. The very fact that the witness has and consults the document is usually an indication that it is needed for her expected testimony. Unlike pretrial preparation, where a witness is likely to consult documents on matters her later testimony does not reach, a witness who uses documents on the stand is likely to hold only ones that are important to what she is saying. Hence there is usually no reason to defer disclosure until after the direct. Delay hampers efforts by other parties to understand how the testimony relates to the writing.

Disclosure deferred Occasionally the situation is more complicated, and it may be necessary to defer disclosure until after the direct. One reason is that sometimes a writing used to refresh memory is part of a larger array or contains severable parts, and the right of inspection reaches only those documents or parts that "relate to the testimony," not other parts or writings. The court decides what parts or documents satisfy the standard and may inspect the material in chambers if necessary and excise unrelated parts. In this situation it may be necessary to defer disclosure until the direct testimony is completed and the court can determine which parts or documents relate to the testimony. Trying to limit inspection to a few words, sentences, or paragraphs in a short document quickly reaches a point of diminishing returns, and the adversary should be able to inspect and use any parts or documents consulted by a witness that are relevant to her testimony.[3]

Writings consulted in advance Unlike material consulted by the witness on the stand, a writing consulted in advance is not automatically turned over to an adverse party for inspection and questioning on request. The cast of FRE 612 (referring to "discretion" and "the interests of justice") indicates that disclosure is not routine but unusual, and many cases approve denial of disclosure.[4] Whether disclosure should be required depends, of course, on whether the witness actually did examine or review a writing, since FRE 612 covers only writings that a witness "uses" before testifying "to refresh memory for the purpose of testifying." Under a broad reading, this "use" criterion is satisfied if the witness looked at

2. *But see* Johnson v. State, 388 S.E.2d 118 (Ga. 1989) (if documents are used to refresh "after the inception of a hearing or trial," questioner is entitled to examine).

3. Pollard v. Commissioner of IRS, 786 F.2d 1063, 1067 (11th Cir. 1986) (refusing to allow access to administrative file to which agent referred; court let counsel review "those writings that the agent actually used," but not "the full three boxes of documents"); United States v. Costner, 684 F.2d 370, 372-373 (6th Cir. 1982) (no right to see parts of documents witness consulted that were unrelated to testimony).

4. United States v. Blas, 947 F.2d 1320, 1326-1328 (7th Cir. 1991) (police and investigative reports reviewed by DEA agent before testifying); United States v. Williams, 875 F.2d 846, 854 (11th Cir. 1989); United States v. Sai Keung Wong, 886 F.2d 252, 257 (9th Cir. 1989).

a writing with this idea in mind (so long as her testimony then deals with the same subjects). Under a narrower reading, FRE 612 only covers writings reviewed before testifying if they actually refreshed memory in ways reflected in testimony. The latter construction seems too narrow, for it would empower the witness to turn aside attempts to look at a writing by claiming she did not rely on it, which under the circumstances would be impossible to check. Clearly, however, FRE 612 applies only if the witness did in fact examine or review a writing, and production of a writing used before testifying is ordered only in exceptional cases.[5]

In authorizing only discretionary disclosure of writings used prior to testifying, Congress rejected the automatic entitlement endorsed by the Advisory Committee and commentators, who argue that the risk of imposition is as great with writings reviewed before trial as it is with those used at trial.[6] The main clue behind the congressional purpose is a comment that requiring a party to turn over material reviewed by a witness before testifying would invite "fishing expeditions among a multitude of papers" in the files of the questioner.[7] The perceived risk is harassment and waste of time, overbroad disclosure, and perhaps infringement on work product protection and attorney-client privilege. Automatic disclosure would likely produce extensive demands for production and disrupt trials: Inspection could not easily be arranged during routine discovery because witnesses have not yet begun the preparation that brings the disclosure requirement into play. It seems as well that letting the calling party keep under wraps documents reviewed before trial does not present the risk of unfairness that would come if documents consulted on the stand were immune from inspection.

Usually disclosure of material reviewed by a witness before testifying should follow her testimony.[8] If disclosure were required before a witness testified, courts and parties would have to make predictions about subject, substance, and likely areas of reliance, and the probable outcome would be very broad disclosure, which is what Congress wanted to prevent. Moreover, the purpose of disclosure is to provide access to material that affects the testimony and to let adverse parties introduce related material, and these aims cannot be readily achieved before testimony is given. And certainly it would be hard for a court to exercise the discretion contemplated by FRE 612 without comparing the substance of the testimony with the documents.

---

5. United States v. Sheffield, 55 F.3d 341, 343-344 (8th Cir. 1995) (detective returned file to office because he "had trouble keeping up with it on breaks and did not want to carry it with him to the stand," and did not need it to refresh memory; defense not entitled to examine file).

6. *See* 13 Wigmore, Evidence §762 (J. Chadbourn rev. 1970).

7. House Report, at 13 (1973). *See also* Goldman v. United States, 316 U.S. 129, 132 (1942) (where witness does not use notes or memoranda in court, there is "no absolute right" to production or inspection).

8. Sporck v. Peil, 759 F.2d 312, 317-319 (3d Cir. 1985) (after eliciting testimony, counsel may then ask "which, if any, documents informed that testimony"), *cert. denied*, 474 U.S. 903.

§6.68 Introducing Material Used to Refresh

The fact that a writing was used to refresh the memory of a witness, whether before or during his testimony, does not make it admissible at the behest of the questioner. But FRE 612 makes it admissible at the behest of the questioner's adversaries, who may cross-examine the witness on the writing and "introduce in evidence those portions which relate to the testimony" already given.[1] It does not follow that a writing used to refresh memory and offered by the adversary is admissible for all purposes, for that depends on whether there is some other basis to admit the writing (whether, for instance, it fits a hearsay exception). Although FRE 612 covers only writings (the most common material used to refresh memories), adverse parties should have similar rights to ask about and use other material used on the stand to refresh memory, and counterparts in many states cover both writings and other materials.[2]

§6.69 Effects of Privilege, Work Product, and Discovery Limits

At least for documents reviewed *before* a witness takes the stand, the right to inspect and ask questions under FRE 612 is subject not only to judicial discretion, but to the uncertain effect of privilege rules and work product doctrine, and special limits on discovery in criminal cases originally codified in the Jencks Act and now found also in the Criminal Rules.

Waiver issue   There is little doubt that using documents to refresh memory *on the stand* waives or defeats claims of attorney-client privilege by the calling party or work product protection by the lawyer. In pre-Rules tradition, however, using documents to prepare witnesses *beforehand* did not have this effect. There are indications in legislative history that FRE 612 does not modify this bright-line distinction between such pretrial and courtroom use of documents. The House Report says FRE 612 has no effect on privilege claims (implying that tradition continues unmodified) and a long colloquy on the floor of the House seemed to reach the same conclusion.[1] A strong case can be made for this result: A doctrine that

---

§6.68   1. Borel v. Fibreboard Paper Prods. Corp., 493 F.2d 1076, 1102-1103 (5th Cir. 1973) (court may let jury inspect writing; opponent may offer it, and court may let jury inspect writing on its own), *cert. denied*, 419 U.S. 869. *See also* United States v. Smith, 521 F.2d 957, 969 (D.C. Cir. 1975).

2. *See* URE 612 (covering "writing or object" used to refresh memory). Counterparts with this broader language are found in Arkansas, Delaware, Idaho, Indiana, Louisiana, Maine, Maryland, Michigan, Mississippi, New Hampshire, North Carolina, North Dakota, Pennsylvania, South Dakota, Vermont, West Virginia, and Wyoming.

§6.69   1. *See* House Report, at 13 (nothing in FRE 613 should be construed "as barring the assertion of a privilege with respect to writings used by a witness to refresh his memory"). *See also* the colloquy between Representatives White (Texas) and Hungate (Missouri) in 120 Cong. Rec. 2381-2382 (1974).

pretrial use causes loss of privilege and work product protections would create huge opportunities to invade client confidences and lawyer files and would likely force lawyers to rely on oral briefings to avoid this outcome. And practically speaking, broad loss of protections would cause trial delays since witness preparation goes forward just before trial, and routine discovery cannot effectively unearth documents that witnesses will use in preparation.

The view that pretrial use does not relinquish attorney-client privilege or work product protection does not mean that all or even most of what witnesses consult before testifying is beyond reach. Otherwise-discoverable documents are not immune from disclosure because they find their way into lawyer's files. Correspondence, notes, or memoranda prepared for personal or business purposes are subject to disclosure and, at least in civil cases, are likely already to have been disclosed when witnesses come to review them in preparation for trial.

It is, however, plausible to reach the opposite conclusion. That is to say, it is possible, even plausible, that the traditional bright-line distinction did not survive. After all, FRE 612 changed pre-Rules practice by letting courts require production of documents reviewed before testifying, since the cross-examiner may need to see such documents for the same reason he needs to see documents used on the stand. Disclosure is not automatic for documents used before testifying, but the purpose is to prevent fishing expeditions into files and papers of the calling party, not to preserve privilege and work product protection as such.

Not surprisingly, the decisions are mixed and often qualified. Some point toward the conclusion that attorney-client privilege and work product protection survive pretrial use of documents to prepare witnesses,[2] but others say privilege and work product protection are lost.[3] On balance, it seems wiser to say that pretrial use does not automatically waive or defeat privilege claims and work product protection, but leaves room to order disclosure if egregious cases appear, particularly if testimony seems dependent on materials not already disclosed.

The adoption of automatic discovery in the federal system in 1995 brought additional pressure to disclose material considered by experts in formulating opinions that they are expected to give in trial

---

2. EEOC v. Continental Airlines, 395 F. Supp. 2d 738, 744 (N.D. Ill. 2005) (consulting document before testifying does not waive deliberative process privilege); Suss v. MXS International Engineering Services, Inc., 212 F.R.D. 159, 162 (S.D.N.Y. 2002) (reviewing documents before testifying does not waive attorney-client privilege); Sporck v. Peil, 759 F.2d 312, 317-319 (3d Cir. 1985) (documents reviewed before deposition privileged), *cert. denied*, 474 U.S. 903; Joseph Schlitz Brewing Co. v. Muller & Phipps, 85 F.R.D. 118, 119-120 (W.D. Mo. 1980) (documents reviewed before deposition privileged); Berkey Photo, Inc. v. Eastman Kodak Co., 74 F.R.D. 613, 615-617 (S.D.N.Y. 1977) (documents reviewed before deposition protected by work product).

3. James Julian, Inc. v. Raytheon Co., 93 F.R.D. 138, 144-146 (D. Del. 1982) (use of binder to refresh before deposition waived work product protection); Wheeling-Pittsburgh Steel v. Underwriters Labs., 81 F.R.D. 8, 9-11 (N.D. Ill. 1978) (similar; privilege and work product protection waived).

testimony. FRCP 26(a)(2) requires *automatic* disclosure of a great deal of material, including expert reports and "the data or other information considered by the [expert] in forming the opinions," and a comment in the ACN implies that this passage resolves privilege issues in favor of disclosure.[4] The passage seems excessive in its breadth, however, and the plain language of revised FRCP 26(a)(2) does not appear to cover privileged material on which the expert does not rely, nor the situation in which an expert reviews materials later assembled by the lawyer in preparing the expert to testify, after the report has been disclosed as required by the discovery rules.

Criminal discovery is hampered by the notion that discovery should be a two-way street but that it cannot operate this way in criminal cases because the Fifth Amendment blocks or impedes prosecutorial discovery from the defense. It is also hampered by the real fear that defense discovery brings risk of intimidation or harm to government witnesses. But criminal discovery has grown, partly because breakthrough decisions approve prosecutorial discovery and thus pave the way for expansion on both sides.[5] Under FRCrimP 16 and FRCrimP 26.2, limited discovery is available for both the defense and the prosecution. But FRCrimP 26.2 and 17(h) impose serious limits that were first codified in the Jencks Act, a statute named for the case it overruled.[6]

Jencks Act   These criminal discovery provisions bear on the application of FRE 612, which defers expressly to the Jencks Act. In federal practice, three central points seem important. First, each side is entitled to obtain from the other certain written or transcribed statements by witnesses (including grand jury testimony). Second, both parties may be compelled to produce such statements only after witnesses testify on direct at trial.[7] Third, it is not clear whether other materials that might be described as

---

4. *See* ACN to FRCP 26(a)(2): "Given this obligation of disclosure" set out in the amended Rule, "litigants should no longer be able to argue that materials furnished to their experts to be used in forming their opinions—whether or not ultimately relied upon by the expert—are privileged or otherwise protected from disclosure when such persons are testifying or being deposed."

5. *See* 4 Wayne R. LaFave, Jerold H. Israel, Nancy J. King, Criminal Procedure §20.1 (1999) (describing developments in criminal discovery, leading to new and expanded defense discovery, so defendants may obtain their own written, recorded, or oral statements, reports of physical and medical examinations, along with relevant documents and tangible objects).

6. *See* Jencks v. United States, 353 U.S. 657 (1957) (defense has right to reports by prosecution witnesses to FBI; right does not turn on proof that they were inconsistent with testimony, and government cannot claim they are privileged if it prosecutes; defense has right to everything relevant). The heart of the Jencks Act is a provision barring defense discovery of statements by prosecution witnesses before they testify. *See* 18 U.S.C. §3500(a). As amended in 1980, a provision in the Criminal Rules imposes the same limit on both defense and prosecutor. *See* FRCrimP 17(h) (statements by witnesses "may not be subpoenaed" from government or defendant under this rule, but "shall be subject to production only" in accord with Rule 26.2).

7. The Jencks Act begins by stating a limit that is broadly applicable to defense discovery: Subsection (a) says "no statement or report" by a government witness in the possession of the government can be discovered by the defense until the witness "has testified on direct" at trial. The Act then sets out a positive right of defense

statements by witnesses, such as written summaries of their statements prepared by investigators, must be turned over either before or during trial, and on these points state practice varies widely.[8]

The effect of FRE 612's deference to the Jencks Act (and probably the reference should be construed to reach the successor provisions that now appear in FRCrimP 17 and 26.2) remains uncertain because it has been worked out only in a few settings and not in a comprehensive body of caselaw. Still it is possible to describe some of the effects:

First, it seems that FRE 612 does not limit the rights of disclosure secured for the defense and the government by the discovery rules. FRE 612 provides only for discretionary disclosure of material that a witness consulted in pretrial preparation, meaning that a court may sometimes deny disclosure of such material. Under the discovery rules, however, the prosecutor and the defendant can discover certain statements by witnesses who testify regardless whether such statements were examined during trial preparation.[9]

Does not limit discovery

Second, FRE 612 probably does not entitle parties in criminal cases to get pretrial statements by testifying witnesses until after they give their direct testimony. For materials that a witness reviewed before testifying, delaying disclosure until after the direct seems necessary in order to apply FRE 612 sensibly. But necessary or not, the discovery rules (and the Jencks Act) reflect a policy decision to let the proponent block access to such statements before the direct testimony is given. This delay is actually inconvenient because it requires a halt in the trial to give the adverse party a chance to read the material. Insisting on going forward without delay would impede cross and make it muddled and inefficient, and prosecutors (the ones most often protected by this limit) may voluntarily turn over statements before the witness testifies. Arguably the calling party in a criminal case may also delay production

Only after testifying

---

discovery in subsection (b), but it can be exercised only after the witness testifies, and the right is framed in narrower terms to reach the kinds of statements described in text above. *See also* 18 U.S.C. §3500(e)(1)-(3) (defining statements defendants may obtain). As revised in 1980, the Criminal Rules faithfully carry forward the scheme of the Jencks Act, but make it applicable to both defense and government discovery. FRCrimP 17(h) largely reproduces subsection (a) of the Jencks Act, and FRCrimP 26.2 largely tracks the rest of the Jencks Act.

8. Unlike civil discovery rules, the Criminal Rules authorize discovery of specific material, and generally the parties may not discover material that is not listed. *See* Palermo v. United States, 360 U.S. 343, 351 (1959) (statement by government witness to government agent that is not covered by Jencks Act "cannot be produced at all"). *But see* United States v. Nobles, 422 U.S. 225 (1975). On state practice, *see* 4 Wayne R. LaFave, Jerold H. Israel, Nancy J. King, Criminal Procedure §20.2 (1999) (states independently expanded defense discovery; now state rules fall into "three basic coverage patterns," including (a) narrow rules following the federal model, (b) broad provisions based on an ABA recommendation, and (c) other rules falling between these; prosecutorial discovery, although narrower, also expanded, and again three groupings are visible, from the narrowest approach adopted in the federal system and some states to a broad approach similar to the ABA recommendation for defense discovery, and various in-between positions).

9. United States v. Jiminez, 613 F.2d 1373, 1377-1378 (5th Cir. 1980).

of a statement by a witness that he consults on the stand, but this conclusion is less certain.[10]

Materials consulted before testifying

Third, it seems probable that FRE 612 authorizes courts to order the calling party to turn over written materials consulted by witnesses before trial even if such documents do not fit the narrow definition of statements by witnesses found in the Jencks Act and discovery rules. FRE 612 defers to the Jencks Act, but the Supreme Court held in 1975 that the discovery rules do not limit the power of a court to order production once trial has begun.[11] Still the conclusion that courts may order disclosure of such materials is less than certain, and it is at least plausible to read reference to the Jencks Act in FRE 612 as meaning that courts cannot exercise the discretion that FRE 612 otherwise confers by ordering parties to turn over materials that are not within the scope of ordinary discovery.[12] Under this reading, a court could not order production of a statement by one witness that another witness reviewed before testifying if the person who made the statement never testified, although presumably it would have to be produced if the person who made it testified eventually.

M.   CALLING AND INTERROGATION BY COURT

> **FRE 614**
>
> **(a) Calling by court.** The court may, on its own motion or at the suggestion of a party, call witnesses, and all parties are entitled to cross-examine witnesses thus called.
>
> **(b) Interrogation by court.** The court may interrogate witnesses, whether called by itself or by a party.
>
> **(c) Objections.** Objections to the calling of witnesses by the court or to interrogation by it may be made at the time or at the next available opportunity when the jury is not present.

---

10. United States v. Jiminez, 613 F.2d 1373, 1377-1378 (5th Cir. 1980) (even where witness refreshed memory on stand, Jencks Act entitles government to defer disclosure). An earlier edition of McCormick disagreed, *see* McCormick, Evidence §9 n.60 (2d ed. 1972) (Jencks Act "is not related to production for inspection when the reports are used to refresh memory"), and the current edition calls for further work, *see* 1 McCormick, Evidence §97 (6th ed. 2006) (legislation required).

11. United States v. Nobles, 422 U.S. 225 (1975) (ordering defendant to disclose report by its investigator describing eyewitness statements; Criminal Rules do not limit "power to order production once trial has begun").

12. *See* United States v. Blas, 947 F.2d 1320, 1326-1328 (7th Cir. 1991) (before testifying, DEA agent reviewed reports; no error to refuse defense request for production; Jencks Act did not require production because reports were not statements by witness, nor did FRE 612 require production). *See also* United States v. Williams, 875 F.2d 846, 854 (11th Cir. 1989); United States v. Soto, 711 F.2d 1558, 1560-1561 (11th Cir. 1983).

§6.70 Judge May Question (and Call) Witnesses

Under FRE 614(b), a court may question a witness on its own and may even call witnesses, although judges do the latter far less often. A tradition of active judicial involvement in trial has long been part of the federal system,[1] although state practice is vastly different in that state judges are usually cautious and far less likely either to question or call witnesses.

Questioning by the trial judge seems appropriate when it helps clarify testimony by removing ambiguity or confusion,[2] or simply brings out the truth or helps understand the evidence or transactions in issue, or when the witness seems confused because of inadequate examination by counsel.[3] The judge may frame his own questions and elicit details on matters already explored or pursue new matters.[4] The judge should tell the jury that his questioning is not intended to intimate any view on the merits, and that the jury is responsible to decide the facts and should not draw an inference from the questions that the judge puts.[5]

Clarify testimony

Questioning by the trial judge should be undertaken with more than a little care. He should avoid introducing inadmissible evidence[6] and should not use questions to suggest that he does not believe a witness.[7]

Questioning conducted by trial judges brings other serious risks. His stature and assumed impartiality lend weight to his questions that does not come with similar questions by litigating attorneys; his questions are likely to impart a point of view and appraisal of evidence; his reactions

Serious risks

---

§6.70   1. United States v. Liddy, 509 F.2d 428, 438 (D.C. Cir. 1974) (concepts of fair trial and objectivity do not require judge to be "inert," and he need not act "as if he were merely presiding at a sporting match"; federal judge has inherent authority to call and question witnesses, but may not "tilt" or "oversteer" jury) (affirming conviction in *Watergate* case), *cert. denied*, 420 U.S. 911.

2. *See* State v. Gonzalez, 864 A.2d 847, 861 (Conn. 2005) (judge can question witnesses where testimony is confusing or unclear); Kapelanski v. Johnson, 390 F.3d 525, 534-535 (7th Cir. 2004) (approving questions "making the testimony clear for the jury," where judge only asked things that witness did not answer, and helped guide testimony); Logue v. Dore, 103 F.3d 1040, 1045-1047 (1st Cir. 1997) (judge tried to clarify testimony, expedite trial, maintain decorum); United States v. Gonzalez-Torres, 980 F.2d 788, 792 (1st Cir. 1992) (judge's 39-question series was designed to clarify confusing events).

3. People v. Guerra, 129 P.3d 321 (Cal. 2006) (court may question witnesses when it appears that counsel will not elicit material testimony) (but it is better to let counsel develop case); Sauerwein v. State, 629 S.E.2d 235, 237 (Ga. 2006) (trial judge can ask questions for purpose of developing fully the truth).

4. Stevenson v. D.C. Metropolitan Police Dept., 248 F.3d 1187, 1189-1190 (D.C. Cir. 2001) (approving hypothetical questions even though judge was using defense version of facts), *cert. denied*, 122 S. Ct. 459; Moore v. United States, 598 F.2d 439, 442-443 (5th Cir. 1979).

5. *See* United States v. Nickl, 427 F.3d 1286, 1292-1295 (10th Cir. 2005) (judge "reshaped" equivocal testimony into "definitive answer" addressing ultimate issue, amounting to testimony) (reversing).

6. *See* Amatucci v. Delaware & Hudson Ry., 745 F.2d 180, 182-184 (2d Cir. 1984); United States v. Auten, 570 F.2d 1284, 1286 (5th Cir. 1978).

7. United States v. Fernandez, 480 F.2d 726, 737-738 (2d Cir. 1973); Kowalsky v. United States, 290 F.2d 161, 164 (5th Cir. 1961), *cert. denied*, 368 U.S. 875.

may themselves become evidence, along with the answers. Yet these effects are precisely what the trial judge should try to avoid. In questioning witnesses, he should preserve impartiality and the appearance of it and should not become an advocate. Above all, the judge should not take over the functions of the lawyers or undermine their trial tactics or strategies, which means that he should avoid too many interruptions and overuse of leading questions. The adversary system rests on the notion that truth is more likely to come out when responsibility to develop facts rests mainly on interested parties. This point is an animating principle of the system, which operates in ways that tend to ensure that lawyers know more than the judge about the facts and issues and the strategic pitfalls of various strategies and lines of questioning.[8]

Judge may not testify

It should be noted that FRE 605 makes the presiding judge incompetent to testify as a witness, and the spirit if not the letter of that provision is violated if she questions witnesses in a way that imparts factual information known to her from extrarecord sources. Also judges should not utilize their authority to question witnesses as a mechanism for commenting on evidence or credibility, and some state counterparts to FRE 614 contain express language to this effect.[9]

Judge may call witnesses

Under FRE 614(a) a judge may also call witnesses, on her own initiative or on request by a party, and all parties may cross-examine.[10] There are several reasons to let judges call witnesses: One is that a party may be reluctant to call a witness who is for some reason unattractive or unsavory, in fear that the jury may hold against the calling party whatever it does not like.[11] When the court calls such a witness, the parties can keep a certain distance, and all may cross-examine in order to impeach or expand the testimony. Another reason is that the judge is entitled to see that the truth comes out, and is not confined to the facts that the parties choose to present. Calling witnesses is one way to break free of party presentations.[12]

---

8. United States v. Sanchez, 325 F.3d 600, 607-608 (5th Cir. 2003) (questions and comments "clearly helped the prosecution," gave appearance that court was partial, were unwise); Rodriguez v. Riddel Sports, Inc., 242 F.3d 567, 580 (5th Cir. 2001) (judge "should not comment on trial strategy"); United States v. Reyes, 227 F.3d 263, 266-267 (5th Cir. 2000) (judge appeared to endorse prosecution theory and expressed incredulity at possibility of innocent explanation).

9. In Montana, New Mexico, and Washington, for example, the state counterparts to FRE 614 bar judicial comment on the evidence.

10. United States v. Agajanian, 852 F.2d 56, 58 (2d Cir. 1988) (court called witness; full cross permitted); Holland v. Commissioner, 835 F.2d 675, 676 (6th Cir. 1987).

11. United States v. Leslie, 542 F.2d 285, 288-289 (5th Cir. 1976) (court called three accomplices who told government they would testify differently from statements they gave FBI; court "could properly protect" prosecution from tendency to associate witnesses with calling party).

12. Cunningham v. Housing Auth. of Opelousas, 764 F.2d 1097, 1100-1101 (5th Cir. 1985) (court may call witnesses, partly to avoid being imprisoned in case made by parties), *cert. denied*, 474 U.S. 1007.

N. SEQUESTERING WITNESSES

> **FRE 615**
>
> At the request of a party the court shall order witnesses excluded so that they cannot hear the testimony of other witnesses, and it may make the order of its own motion. This rule does not authorize exclusion of (1) a party who is a natural person, or (2) an officer or employee of a party which is not a natural person designated as its representative by its attorney, (3) a person whose presence is shown by a party to be essential to the presentation of the party's cause, or (4) a person authorized by statute to be present.

§6.71 Excluding or Sequestering Witnesses

Under FRE 615, the parties are entitled on request to a court order excluding witnesses so they cannot hear testimony by others. The court may also order exclusion on its own. In courtroom parlance, excluding or sequestering witnesses is known as invoking "the rule on witnesses." The purpose is to encourage truthful and independent testimony by lessening the chance that a witness will be subconsciously influenced by listening to what others say, and removing temptations or opportunities for witnesses deliberately to shape their testimony in light of what others say.

Exclusion on request is a matter of right, but FRE 615 is not self-executing and a party must ask for exclusion in order to claim any protection.[1] FRE 615 may be invoked any time, and a party does not waive her rights simply by letting the witness hear some testimony even though it may appear to the court that the damage has already been done. And FRE 615 applies to any witness whose testimony is to be offered later, including those who have testified and are likely to be recalled. — *Party must ask*

While FRE 615 does not mention instructions to the witness being excluded, an order removing him from court during testimony by others is largely ineffective unless he is also sequestered (separated from other witnesses outside the courtroom), and an appropriate directive should accompany orders of exclusion.[2] Probably the court should also tell witnesses not to confer with parties or their agents (at — *Court should instruct*

---

§6.71   1. United States v. Casas, 356 F.3d 104, 127 (1st Cir. 2004) (absent objection to presence of agent at beginning, judge has discretion); Hollman v. Dale Elec., Inc., 752 F.2d 311, 313 (8th Cir. 1985) (exclusion required on request).

2. *See* Williams v. United States, 859 A.2d 130, 138 (D.C. App. 2004) (common to instruct witness not to discuss testimony with third parties until trial is completed); Puckett v. State, 879 So.2d 920, 956 (Miss. 2004) (similar); Wis. Stat. Ann. §906.15 (1975) (court may direct that excluded witnesses be "kept separate until called" to keep them from communicating with one another).

least in the usual case where the witness is not a spouse or close family relative of a party).

Courts should not, however, try to block lawyers from conferring with the witnesses they call prior to their testimony, and FRE 615 says nothing on this point. Attempts to isolate a defendant from his lawyer in a criminal trial may violate the right to effective assistance of counsel,[3] and to a lesser extent contact between counsel and third-party witnesses seems essential to proper representation. Still, counsel should not defeat the purpose of an order excluding witnesses, and a lawyer who conveys to witnesses the substance of the testimony of others or who reads or shows daily trial transcripts to excluded witnesses has undercut the order of exclusion and thwarted its purpose.[4] Explicit directions to counsel should not be necessary, since lawyers fully understand the purpose of orders of exclusion.

FRE 615 applies during pretrial hearings on evidential issues where expected trial testimony may be discussed or previewed, and the principle should apply during opening statements because they almost always describe the testimony to come.[5] Occasionally the Rule is even applied during closing arguments, inasmuch as a new trial is always a possibility.[6]

There is no wholly satisfactory remedy where a witness violates an order excluding witnesses. Typical violations include staying in or returning to the courtroom, conferring with other witnesses, and reviewing transcripts, and remedies have a distinctly second-best flavor because courts are rightly reluctant to take the step of barring testimony

3. Perry v. Leeke, 488 U.S. 272, 281 (1989) (defendant has "absolute right" to consult lawyer before he testifies, but not to interrupt testimony to confer; alright to bar consultation in 15-minute interval between direct and cross); Geders v. United States, 425 U.S. 80 (1976) (cannot prohibit defendant from conferring with counsel during 17-hour overnight recess between direct and cross); United States v. Calderin-Rodriguez, 244 F.3d 977, 984-985 (8th Cir. 2001) (rejecting claim that contact between prosecutor and government witness violated sequestration order; FRE 615 "does not by its terms forbid an attorney from conferring with witnesses during trial"); United States v. Santos, 201 F.3d 953, 965-966 (7th Cir. 2000) (error to direct defense counsel not to confer with defendant after his direct testimony).

4. United States v. Friedman, 854 F.2d 535, 568 (2d Cir. 1988) (reading testimony may violate order excluding witnesses); Miller v. Universal City Studios, Inc., 650 F.2d 1365, 1372-1374 (5th Cir. 1981) (expert's receipt of daily trial transcripts violated order).

5. State v. Francis, 145 P.3d 48, 67 (Kan. 2006) (under state statute, sequestration is required during preliminary hearings); United States v. Brewer, 947 F.2d 404, 409-410 (9th Cir. 1991) (pretrial suppression hearing). *See also* Idaho Rule 615 (on request in preliminary hearing, magistrate must exclude nonparty witnesses who have not been examined); South Dakota Comp. Laws Ann. §19-24-29 (applies to "hearing or deposition" as well as trial). *And see* Hampton v. Kroger Co., 618 F.2d 498, 499 (8th Cir. 1980) (excluding expert during opening remarks).

6. *See* United States v. Juarez, 573 F.2d 267, 281 (5th Cir. 1978) (no violation of right to public trial where judge refused to admit defense witnesses for closing arguments and charge). *But see* United States v. Alvarez, 755 F.2d 830, 860-861 (11th Cir. 1985) (FRE 615 is inapplicable "after all witness testimony has been concluded"), *cert. denied*, 482 U.S. 908; Oregon Rule 615 (court may order exclusion "until the time of final argument").

by violators. Three partial remedies are available, and the judge has discretion to select among them. One is to hold the witness in contempt, which unfortunately does little or nothing for a party potentially hurt by the violation.[7] A second remedy is to let counsel question the witness about violations of the order, and comment and make arguments about his behavior.[8] This approach holds some promise, for questioning may bring to light actual efforts to tailor or change testimony as well as motives and even unconscious changes in testimony. And comment and argument on such points may be useful. These tactics, however, may not succeed in repairing the damage, and pursuing them may be counterproductive. The third remedy, which is to disallow the testimony of the disobedient witness, is draconian and seldom invoked. Many cases hold that violations of orders of exclusion or instructions not to confer do not disqualify a witness, but courts sometimes do exclude testimony completely.[9] Since this measure penalizes one or more parties for the act of the witness and deprives the court of evidence, it seems an appropriate response only in extreme cases, such as those where the very party seeking the testimony deliberately contrived to violate the order or instruction.

§6.72   Exemptions from Exclusion or Sequestration

Four categories of witnesses are exempted from orders of exclusion under FRE 615, including parties who are natural persons, representatives of other parties, persons necessary to the presentation of a case, and certain others. It is useful to take up the four exemptions in order:

Under exemption 1, the court should not exclude "a party who is a natural person" because doing so would raise questions of fundamental fairness and in criminal cases constitutional issues relating to confrontation and effective assistance of counsel.[1] In any event, the trier of fact is likely to be more skeptical of testimony by witnesses who are parties than testimony by other witnesses and less likely to be taken in by tailored testimony of parties.

Natural persons who are parties

---

7. Holder v. United States, 150 U.S. 91, 92-93 (1893) (witness who disobeys order "may be proceeded against for contempt"); United States v. McMahon, 104 F.3d 638, 642-644 (4th Cir. 1997) (holding criminal defendant in contempt for violating sequestration order by having his secretary attend trial and make notes).

8. United States ex rel. Clark v. Fike, 538 F.2d 750, 758 (7th Cir. 1976) (fact that government witnesses discussed their testimony in advance was "proper subject for impeachment on cross-examination and for comment during closing argument"), *cert. denied*, 429 U.S. 1064.

9. Holder v. United States, 150 U.S. 91, 92-93 (1893) (witness who disobeys order is not disqualified from testifying, but "right to exclude under particular circumstances may be supported"); United States v. Kindle, 925 F.2d 272, 276 (8th Cir. 1991); United States v. Wylie, 919 F.2d 969, 975-977 (5th Cir. 1990).

§6.72   1. Johnson v. United States, 780 F.2d 902, 909 (11th Cir. 1986) (in malpractice suit for death of infant, parents joined as parties were not excluded); Varlack v. SWC Carribean, Inc., 550 F.2d 171, 175-176 (3d Cir. 1977) (error to exclude restaurant manager named as defendant).

Officers and employees

Under exemption 2, the court cannot exclude "an officer or employee" of any other party who is designated as its representative by its attorney. This exemption extends parity of treatment to parties who are not natural persons. In criminal cases government investigative agents fit this exemption,[2] which also reaches officers or employees of corporations, partnerships, government entities, or associations of any sort that may sue or be sued.[3]

Essential people

Exemption 3 is open-ended. Under it, a court cannot exclude a person whose presence is shown "to be essential to the presentation" of a case. Experts are the most likely candidates, since FRE 703 lets experts testify to opinions or inferences based on facts or data made known at the hearing.[4] Moreover, it is just such a witness who is most likely to be needed as a coach to help counsel understand and cross-examine experts called by the adversary. Even experts do not automatically fit exemption 3,[5] however, nor is it limited to experts. Others may be essential to the presentation of a case, such as the agent of a party who handled the transaction or one who committed the act causing injury for which recovery is sought.[6] Some witnesses called for impeachment or rebuttal need to hear other testimony, although the argument for exempting such witnesses is not generally compelling. Sometimes the best reason to exempt them is that the parties do not anticipate calling them, so they are not apparently covered by exclusion orders.[7]

Authorized by statute

Exemption 4 (covering any person "authorized by statute to be present") was added to FRE 615 late in 1998, apparently to accommodate newly enacted crime victim legislation (discussed below).

How many are exempt?

All four exemptions speak in singular terms (exemption 1 refers to "a party"; exemption 2 speaks of "an officer or employee"; exemptions 3 and 4 refer to "a person"). Presumably the exemptions are cumulative, so potentially a litigant could exempt someone in each of the first three categories from an exclusion order. It is plausible to suppose the singular language in exemption 2 means that only one "officer or

---

2. *See* ACN on FRE 615 (referring to "police officer who has been in charge of an investigation") and Senate Report at 26 (investigative agent may be "extremely important" to government counsel and help meet surprise where even well-prepared lawyer "would otherwise have difficulty").

3. Nanoski v. General Motors Acceptance Corp., 874 F.2d 529, 531 (8th Cir. 1989) (in employment discrimination suit, defendant's corporate representative).

4. Nesvig v. Nesvig, 712 N.W.2d 299, 304 (N.D. 2006) (in suit for breach of fiduciary duty by lawyer, refusing to sequester defendant's expert); State v. Perez, 882 A.2d 574, 582 (R.I. 2005) (refusing to sequester prosecutor's psychiatric witness).

5. *See* U.S. v. Seschillie, 310 F.3d 1208, 1212 (9th Cir. 2002) (experts do not always satisfy Exemption 3; party requesting exemption must make fair showing that expert is essential to presentation).

6. *See* ACN to FRE 615 (exemption 3 contemplates "agent who handled the transaction being litigated"); Trans World Metals, Inc. v. Southwire Co., 769 F.2d 902, 910-911 (2d Cir. 1985) (in contract suit, defendant's managing director).

7. United States v. Hargrove, 929 F.2d 316, 320-321 (7th Cir. 1991) (unexpected rebuttal witness not covered by sequestration order); United States v. Bramlet, 820 F.2d 851, 855 (7th Cir. 1987) (rebuttal witness presented to refute medical findings needs to understand and address relevant prior evidence), *cert. denied*, 484 U.S. 861.

employee" of a party may be designated as "representative" of the party, although such an argument does not seem plausible in the case of exemptions 1 and 3.[8] Some decisions applying exemption 2 hold that it reaches only one person per party, but others note the question without resolving it.[9] Reading the singular term in exemption 2 as a limitation seems wrong in light of the looser meaning of the singular terms in exemptions 1 and 3, but the purpose of exclusion orders and the repeated use of the singular in the three exemptions provide a caution that exemptions are not to be freely given and witnesses should be exempt only when there is a clear need.

Victims in criminal cases present a special problem. On the one hand, they do not readily fit any exemption, which suggests that they may be excluded like other witnesses. To be sure, assault victims (and perhaps some others) may fit exemption 3 as persons essential to the prosecution, but many others (such as surviving spouses, children and relatives in homicide cases) probably do not fit.[10]

Victims, complaining witnesses

The victim rights movement has spurred both Congress and the states to take steps to ensure (among other things) that victims may be present at the trials of people accused of crimes against them, and exemption 4 in FRE 615 accommodates these statutes. One modern federal statute provides that a crime victim has a right to attend trial unless the court determines his testimony would be "materially affected" by exposure to other testimony, and another (enacted during the Oklahoma City Bombing trial in 1996) creates an entitlement to be present in federal trials even though victims are expected to testify during sentencing.[11]

Some state versions of Rule 615 exempt victims, either absolutely or with qualifications (similar to the federal provision allowing exclusion if hearing other testimony would likely affect testimony expected from

8. Exemption 1 reaches every natural person who is a party, so in any given suit many people may fit. The singular term in exemption 3 ("a person") cannot plausibly limit each party to one exempt person since the main purpose was to reach experts, and it is commonplace for parties to use more than one expert.

9. United States v. Pulley, 922 F.2d 1283, 1285-1286 (6th Cir. 1991) ("singular phrasing" means government may designate one agent; it may try to show second agent is essential and fits exemption 3); United States v. Farnham, 791 F.2d 331, 335 & n.5 (4th Cir. 1986) (error in refusing defense request to exclude one of two FBI agents).

10. *See* Government of Virgin Islands v. Edinborough, 625 F.2d 472, 475 (3d Cir. 1980) (mother of 13-year-old rape victim might fit exemption 3, which authorizes court in its discretion "to permit the presence of the parent of a young witness").

11. *See* 42 U.S.C. §10606(b) (crime victim has right "to be present at all public court proceedings related to the offense," unless court determines his testimony would be "materially affected" if he heard other testimony); 18 U.S.C. §3510 (in noncapital cases, federal courts shall exclude "any victim of an offense" from trial because she might later "make a statement or present any information" in sentencing; in capital cases, federal courts shall not exclude victims because they may testify during sentencing on "the effect of the offense" on victim and her family or on "any other factor for which notice is required"); U.S. v. Visinaiz, 428 F.3d 1300, 1314 (10th Cir. 2005) (under §3510(a), victim is one who "suffered direct physical, emotional, or pecuniary harm," which includes son of murder victim), *cert. denied*, 546 U.S. 1123.

the victim),[12] and victim rights legislation adopted in many states may also create absolute or qualified rights to be present during trial.[13]

In light of their special concerns and relationship to criminal proceedings, victims surely are entitled to special consideration when it comes to FRE 615. But a blanket rule exempting them from exclusion is not without problems: Ironically, continual presence throughout trial may taint victim testimony and might even lead to acquittal. More importantly, the concerns over tailored testimony sometimes do apply to victims in compelling ways. One solution, short of exclusion, may be to take victim testimony first or early, but even this attempt to accommodate the relative concerns over victims and defendants may not always work, and some residual power to exclude victims seems essential.[14]

12. *See* La. Code of Evidence, Art. 615 (exempting from sequestration orders the victim and "the family of the victim"); Or. Rule 615 (including exemption for "victim in a criminal case"); Tex. Evidence Rule 614 (victim is exempt unless he is to testify and court determines that testimony would be "materially affected" by hearing other testimony).

13. *See* Colo. Const. Art. 2 §16(a) (every crime victim, "or such person's designee, legal guardian, or surviving immediate family members if such person is deceased," has right to be present "at all critical stages"); Colo. Rev. Stat. §16-10-401 (victim's advocate may be allowed to remain even if members of general public are excluded).

14. *See generally* Robert P. Mosteller, Victim's Rights and the United States Constitution: An Effort to Recast the Battle in Criminal Litigation, 1997 Geo. L. J. 1691, 1698 (1997) (victim rights issues may be solved without constitutional amendment; armed robbery and similar cases with multiple victims bring danger that testimony would be "influenced" by victims' presence in court during testimony by others); Paul G. Cassell, Balancing the Scales of Justice: The Case for and the Effects of Utah's Victims' Rights Amendment, 1994 Utah L. Rev. 1373, 1390-1391 (1994) (defending victim rights measures; in cases raising genuine concern over altered testimony, courts can take victim testimony first; violation of defense rights is "unlikely in all but the most extreme circumstances"); United States v. Edwards, 526 F.3d 747, 757-758 (11th Cir. 2008) (exempting victim witnesses from sequestration; rejecting claim of constitutional entitlement to exclude).

CHAPTER 7

Opinions and Expert Testimony; Scientific Evidence

A. LAY TESTIMONY

FRE 701

If the witness is not testifying as an expert, the witness' testimony in the form of opinions or inferences is limited to those opinions or inferences which are (a) rationally based on the perception of the witness, (b) helpful to a clear understanding of the witness' testimony or the determination of a fact in issue, and (c) not based on scientific, technical, or other specialized knowledge within the scope of Rule 702.

§7.1 The Preference for Facts

FRE 701 invites lay opinion and inference testimony only under certain conditions (it must be rationally based and helpful), stating a mild rule of preference. Usually lay witnesses should testify in a specific vein (giving "facts") and not in generalities (giving "opinions" or "inferences"). A lay witness who saw an accident might say "the driver ran a red light" or "the driver shouldn't have entered the intersection," but the former is preferred as more factual and less inferential.

Provide details

The main reason to prefer the specific over the general is to provide details that help the factfinder make the necessary evaluative decisions and keep that function from being taken over by witnesses coached by counsel. In effect, more information is better.

Expertise required

Several lesser reasons support the mild preference for factual testimony. One is a reluctance to let lay witnesses give testimony on which expertise is required, for generalities typically have strong evaluative elements that are the stock in trade of experts. FRE 701 does not authorize lay opinion testimony on subjects outside the realm of common experience that require special skill or knowledge. For evaluative generalities that fall somewhere between everyday opinion and technical appraisals, it seems right to prefer the more specific and to let witnesses go further toward the general if they have special knowledge and understanding.[1]

Avoid guesswork

There is also a concern that generalities mask guesswork and lack of knowledge, so lay testimony cast in general terms may disguise a lack of adequate factual predicate. Far from doing away with the personal knowledge requirement, FRE 701 reinforces the basic message also contained in FRE 602.

Sometimes "opinion" connotes less than categorical certainty, and is used to describe ideas that are somewhat vague (an "impression" of something) or uncertain (what someone "thinks" or "believes"). Testimony cast in such terms should be acceptable so long as the personal knowledge requirement is met, as it well may be, and neither FRE 602 nor FRE 701 forecloses opinion testimony of this sort.[2]

In practice, the degree of generality permitted and the degree of specificity required are very much matters for the discretion of the trial judge.[3] And while FRE 701 does not expressly say the judge may require a statement of particulars before admitting more general descriptions, there is no doubt that the judge may do so, since the

---

§7.1 1. White v. Walker, 932 F.2d 1136, 1141 (5th Cir. 1991) (opinion of police chief on child psychology went "so clearly and obviously beyond the pale of lay opinion testimony as to render their proffer frivolous"); Randolph v. Collectramatic, Inc., 590 F.2d 844, 846-848 (10th Cir. 1979) (excluding restaurant owner's testimony that safety devices should have been built into pressure cooker).

2. United States v. Freeman, 619 F.2d 1112, 1120 (5th Cir. 1980).

3. United States v. Skeet, 665 F.2d 983, 985-986 (9th Cir. 1982) (excluding defense eyewitness testimony on question whether shooting was accidental; whether to allow such opinion is discretionary); Hansard v. Pepsi-Cola Metro. Bottling Co., 865 F.2d 1461, 1467 (5th Cir. 1989), *cert. denied*, 493 U.S. 842.

task of administering FRE 701 implies as much and FRE 611 invites courts to regulate the order of presentation.[4]

§7.2 Lay Opinions—Rational Basis

The mild preference stated in FRE 701 for specific or factual testimony is tempered by language approving lay inferences and opinions on three conditions. One is that the inference or opinion should be rationally based on the perception of the witness. The second and third are that that the inference or opinion should be helpful in understanding his testimony or determining facts in issue, and that it be of a nonscientific and nontechnical later. The first of these is discussed here, the second and third in the next section.

The first condition restates the personal knowledge requirement set by FRE 602 for all lay testimony, no matter how general.[1] In this setting, the idea is that the witness must know enough from firsthand observation about the underlying events or acts to support the inference or opinion that is to be given. Embedded in this standard is a notion that a reasonable person who knows what the witness knows might reach the conclusion he has reached.[2] Experts may properly rely on remote statements by others (hearsay) in the opinions they convey, but not lay witnesses, although some knowledge can *only* be had by relying on input from outside sources, and some such reliance is allowed in such cases, and even firsthand observations often impart *some* similar information.[3]

Personal knowledge

The standard is not rigorous: A person may have enough knowledge even though he doesn't know enough to be absolutely certain. The point is not that the witness must know every fact that would make the inference compelling: Like juries, witnesses may employ inductive logic, which by its nature involves drawing on experience and common sense to reach conclusions that the underlying facts do not categorically

---

4. United States v. Milne, 487 F.2d 1232, 1235 (5th Cir. 1973) (lay opinion testimony on defendant's insanity is admissible, although witness should first testify to unusual, abnormal, or bizarre conduct), *cert. denied*, 419 U.S. 1123.

§7.2 1. *See* ACN to FRE 701 (describing first limit as "the familiar requirement of firsthand knowledge or observation"); JGR, Inc. v. Thomasville Furniture Industries, Inc., 370 F.3d 519, 524 (6th Cir. 2004) (accountant should give lay testimony on business losses; he lacked knowledge and had not been owner, officer, or director; cannot evade reliability required by FRE 702 by calling expert as lay witness).

2. Staley v. Bridgestone/Firestone, Inc., 106 F.3d 1504, 1513 (10th Cir. 1997) (game wardens could describe "likely position" of worker mounting tire on grader before tire exploded, although "speculative").

3. Mississippi Chemical Corporation v. Dresser-Rand Company, 287 F.3d 359 (5th Cir. 2002) (director of risk management and property taxation could testify to lost profits; direct knowledge of business accounts was basis enough); Agfa-Gevaert, A.G. v. A. B. Dick Co., 879 F.2d 1518, 1523 (7th Cir. 1989) (board members could testify on quality of copiers, relying on what they heard from customers and engineers; all perception is inferential, most knowledge social, and "since Kant we have known that there is no unmediated contact between nature and thought").

demonstrate.[4] Thus a witness may testify that she watched and did not see something happen, hence that it probably did not happen.[5] And a witness should be allowed to identify a narcotic drug that he has ingested by comparing its effect with the effects he previously experienced from taking the drug,[6] and to identify a person on the basis of the briefest encounter.[7] Still, inferences and opinions should be excluded as not rationally based if the witness has little or no firsthand knowledge of pertinent facts or data.[8]

Counterfactual assumptions

Special pitfalls come with questions that ask lay witnesses to make counterfactual assumptions and testify to what would have happened or what they would have done if the facts had been other than what they are. Inevitably the question asks the witness to estimate or speculate, and there is an unreality about the process if the witness knows the facts to be otherwise: His answer does not have a rational basis in the usual sense, and such questions may be barred as speculative if the answer seems too much like a guess.[9] The questioner can sometimes get at the real point by asking a witness what facts are most critical in support of the conclusion he has reached. But there is no absolute rule against "what if" (or hypothetical) questions. Their rhetorical force is sometimes irresistible to lawyers, and courts sometimes conclude that the answers can satisfy the rational basis standard.[10]

Rational basis

The question whether such testimony is rationally based is in substance the same as the question whether the witness has the requisite personal knowledge under FRE 602, where the judge plays the lesser screening role contemplated by FRE 104(b), leaving the final decision

4. United States v. Burnette, 698 F.2d 1038, 1051 (9th Cir. 1983) (police sergeant saw defendant holding what seemed to be screwdriver and noticed that rear license was attached but missing shortly thereafter when no one else approached; his opinion that defendant was removing rear plate was rationally based), *cert. denied*, 461 U.S. 936.

5. United States v. Oaxaca, 569 F.2d 518, 525-526 (9th Cir. 1978) (in bank robbery trial, rational basis standard satisfied by testimony that witness would have seen anybody fleeing through rear of residence he was watching).

6. United States v. Sweeney, 688 F.2d 1131, 1145-1146 (7th Cir. 1982).

7. United States v. Jackson, 688 F.2d 1121, 1123-1126 (7th Cir. 1982).

8. Walton v. Nalco Chemical Co., 272 F.3d 13, 25 (1st Cir. 2001) (excluding sales manager's lay opinion on lost profits, resting on reports reflecting gross profits for part of period; no independent knowledge; witness did not know how reports were compiled); Gardner By and Through Gardner v. Chrysler Corp., 89 F.3d 729, 737 (10th Cir. 1996) (excluding testimony on effect of rear-end crash on seat in minivan, based on *60 Minutes* tape and contact with automaker's employees; witness lacked knowledge of recliner mechanism and did not see crash); Gorby v. Schneider Tank Lines, Inc., 741 F.2d 1015, 1021-1022 (7th Cir. 1984) (in suit arising out of collision between pickup and semi-tanker, excluding lay testimony that tanker driver did all he could and pickup driver could have avoided accident).

9. Washington v. Department of Transp., 8 F.3d 296, 298 (5th Cir. 1993) (in suit arising out of accident when spark from Shop Vac ignited acetone vapors in tank of ship, not letting operator say "what he would have done had he seen the warning label," which would be self-serving speculation).

10. Schwan's Sales Enterprises, Inc. v. Idaho Transportation Department, 136 P.3d 297, 301 (Idaho 2006) (driver would have been prepared to stop if there had been a "stop-ahead sign," which was not "some far-fetched possibility," but conveyed that he "knew what a stop-ahead sign looked like and what it meant").

to the jury where reasonable people could decide either way. It seems, however, that judges have independent responsibility in applying the rational basis requirement.[11] Clearly, for example, a judge may decide that a witness has enough knowledge to describe behavioral patterns of another but not enough knowledge to venture an opinion as to her purpose or mental condition: If so, the judge can insist that the witness confine his testimony to a description of observed behavior even if a reasonable person might conclude that he had sufficient basis to talk about the purpose or mental condition.

§7.3 —Helpful to Understanding or Deciding; Not Scientific or Technical

Rule 701 states two additional requirements. One is that any inference or opinion delivered by a lay witness must be helpful to a clear understanding of his testimony or determining a fact in issue. The other requirement is that the opinion or inference cannot rest on "scientific, technical or other specialized knowledge" that requires a qualified expert.

The helpfulness requirement lets courts exclude statements that simply take sides,[1] like claims that conduct is wrongful or justified.[2] Where a witness has the necessary particulars, however, he should usually be allowed to add his overall impression, since doing so brings the particulars into focus and adds dimension.[3] For example, if a witness describes the conditions of an accident and has enough knowledge and experience to draw inferences on what conditions likely caused it, letting him express the conclusion he has already reached that is implicit in the particulars he gave is likely to be helpful.[4] Also a witness who sees

Overall impressions

11. _See_ United States v. Rea, 958 F.2d 1206, 1216-1217 (11th Cir. 1992) (some preconditions are "principally factual" and judge admits under FRE 104(b) subject to introducing enough evidence to support necessary finding; whether lay opinion has rational basis could be treated this way, but judge determines helpfulness, and same evidence relates to rational basis) (rare to admit lay opinion subject to connection).

§7.3 1. _See_ ACN to FRE 701 (court may exclude "meaningless assertions that do little more than choosing up sides"); United States v. Phillips, 600 F.2d 535, 538-539 (5th Cir. 1979) (quoting ACN).

2. United States v. Garcia, 413 F.3d 201, 213-214 (2d Cir. 2005) (agent cannot testify that defendant was "culpable member of conspiracy" based on "total investigation" of charged crime; not helpful); Kostelecky v. NL Acme Tool/NL Indus., Inc., 837 F.2d 828, 830 (8th Cir. 1988) (error to admit report quoting coworker as saying plaintiff caused accident).

3. Gossett v. Board of Regents for Langston University, 245 F.3d 1172, 1178-1180 (10th Cir. 2001) (woman on admissions committee in nursing school opines that plaintiff suffered discrimination because of his gender; she provided basis for knowledge, and conclusion conveyed "impression based on what she had herself perceived" and was "predicated on concrete facts" she had seen); Soden v. Freightliner Corp., 714 F.2d 498, 510-512 (5th Cir. 1983) (service manager testifies that he saw puncture holes in tanks at step brackets, that these caused fires, and design was dangerous).

4. Lang v. Texas & P.R., 624 F.2d 1275, 1277 & 1280 n.10 (5th Cir. 1980) (in suit for death of railroader struck by cars coasting down switching track, yard was poorly lit, cars had no lights, and area was slick with oil; foreman could testify that possible causes were "slippage of oil and poor lighting").

an apparent robbery in the street can characterize it as such if he has enough particulars, and one who describes a sack containing "darkish-green, leafy plant material" can say it was marijuana if he has enough experience.[5]

Convenience and necessity

Considerations of convenience and necessity bear on applying the helpfulness requirement. Factors peculiar to the witness and the moment may make it easier in the long run to let a witness proceed in his own way rather than to force him to state the particulars first or exclusively. If the choice lies between halting and confused testimony by a witness confounded by admonitions to be "specific" or to "stick to the facts" and a more relaxed general narrative, or between doing without and getting something that is on the conclusory side, the helpfulness requirement often points to the latter choice.[6] The price may be too high, however, if the witness insists on using conclusory terms that are damaging and hotly contested, particularly if he cannot support his view convincingly and is perhaps simply opinionated.[7] Opinions and inferences may be excluded if they do not help understand testimony or determine facts, as is often true if they are too general or too closely identified with ultimate issues or represent too long an inferential leap.[8]

Not scientific or technical

The requirement that lay testimony *not* impart inferences or opinions that are scientific or technical represents an attempt to keep parties from doing an "end around" the requirements and special rules that apply to experts. One such requirement, embodied in federal courts and many states as the *Daubert* standard, requires a showing that expert testimony be reliable, and specifically under FRE 702 a showing

---

5. State v. Higgins, 898 So.2d 1219, 1233 (La. 2005) (witness four to six feet away saw defendant and another in "heated discussion, and exchanging hand gestures," and could say she thought robbery was taking place on basis of "interaction" between them); United States v. Honneus, 508 F.2d 566, 576 (1st Cir. 1974) (material "appeared similar to marijuana"), *cert. denied*, 421 U.S. 948.

6. Government of Virgin Islands v. Knight, 989 F.2d 619, 629-630 (3d Cir. 1993) (letting witnesses give opinions instead of describing all their observations leaves them "free to speak in ordinary language") (error to exclude lay testimony that defendant accidentally fired gun); United States v. Yazzie, 976 F.2d 1252, 1255 (9th Cir. 1992) (defendant claimed consent and said he thought 15-year-old girl was more than 16; reversible error to keep defense lay witnesses from saying they thought she was 16-20 years old); Stone v. United States, 385 F.2d 713, 716 (10th Cir. 1967) (government witness could describe car as "stolen," for lay witnesses often use shorthand descriptions or opinions, leaving them "free to speak in ordinary language unbewildered by admonition from the judge to testify to the facts"), *cert. denied*, 391 U.S. 966.

7. United States v. Ness, 665 F.2d 248, 249-250 (8th Cir. 1981) (colleagues cannot testify that defendant did not intend to hurt bank) (citing emotionalism in one "coming to the rescue of an embattled co-worker").

8. Hester v. BIC Corp., 225 F.3d 178, 180-185 (2d Cir. 2000) (co-workers could not opine that supervisor was racially motivated; they lacked knowledge, were not involved in decisionmaking, and focused on "subjective impressions" that "condescension" turned on race); United States v. Cox, 633 F.2d 871, 875-876 (9th Cir. 1980) (witness should not have testified that she understood from something defendant said that he was involved in bombing; her impression did not help jury understand what appellant "had said and done").

that it rests on an adequate basis, on reliable principles and methods, and on a showing that these have been appropriately brought to bear on the facts of the case.[9] Another requires proof that the expert is actually qualified, by training or experience, as an expert, and special rules flow from qualifying a witness as an expert—particularly the rule allowing experts to rely on hearsay if it is the sort of thing that similar experts rely on.[10] Finally, in both civil and criminal cases there are pretrial disclosure requirements and special aspects of discovery that apply to experts.[11] All these considerations led to the adoption of the third criterion in FRE 701, which aims to prevent parties from unfairly presenting what amounts to expert testimony in the guise of lay opinion.[12]

The question whether lay opinion testimony can be helpful to the factfinder is resolved by the judge under FRE 104(a).[13]

§7.4 Opinions on Standard Points

The nature or subject of proposed testimony bears importantly on the application of the helpfulness requirement. Sometimes a lay witness can be most helpful by giving opinions rather than facts. One reason is that a catalogue of particulars may be inadequate to convey important ideas that lay witnesses are competent to express. Another reason is that requiring too much particularity might take more time than it is worth, and it becomes expedient to leave any necessary testing to the cross-examiner. Hence lay witnesses may be allowed to convey some ideas generally, using common descriptive terms. These may sum up and give the full flavor of the particulars (to which the witness also testifies) or substitute for a catalogue that the witness may be unable to provide.

The collective facts doctrine recognizes this reality.[1] One common example is lay testimony that someone was intoxicated, and here the **Collective facts**

9. *See* Daubert v. Merrell Dow Pharmaceuticals, Inc., 509 U.S. 579 (1993), discussed in §7.7, *infra*.

10. On expert qualifications, *see* discussion of FRE 702 in §7.5, *infra*. On the nature of evidence that experts can rely on, *see* discussion of FRE 703 in §§7.8-7.11, *infra*.

11. *See* FRCivP 26(b)(2)-(3) (disclosure, discovery of experts); FRCrimP 16(a)(1)(G) (government disclosure of expert testimony on defendant's mental opinion); FRCrimP 16(b)(1)(C) (defense disclosure).

12. *See* Compania Administradora de Recuperacion v. Titan, 533 F.3d 555, 559-561 (7th Cir. 2008) (excluding T's affidavit in summary judgment motion, on value of collateral; T was not disclosed as expert; lay witnesses may testify to value of their property, but T relied on "generalized knowledge" of worldwide tire market) (purpose of FRE 701 is to block expert testimony in clothing of lay testimony).

13. United States v. Rea, 958 F.2d 1206, 1216-1217 (11th Cir. 1992) (whether lay opinion satisfies helpfulness requirement is for judge to decide).

§7.4 1. United States v. Thompson, 708 F.2d 1294, 1297-1299 (8th Cir. 1983) (approving testimony that *T* "was involved" in transporting stolen equipment, as shorthand rendition of what witness knew, resting on solid facts); United States v. McClintic, 570 F.2d 685, 689-690 (8th Cir. 1978) (approving testimony that defendant knew merchandise had been fraudulently obtained, as shorthand rendition).

witness is not confined to descriptions of glazed eyes, problems in speech or motor coordination, changes in behavior or mood or affect, but may say directly (assuming adequate observation and common experience) that the person seemed drunk or under the influence.[2] Another example is lay testimony that describes the scene of an accident and conveys overall conditions (there was not enough light, or the road was too torn up for travel at ordinary speed)[3] or fleeting events (he didn't have time to stop).[4] If a party takes issue with such testimony or thinks it unfounded, cross-examination should suffice to expose any deficiency in underlying data or overall judgment.

How generously to interpret the helpfulness requirement is affected by the setting in which testimony is offered. If it goes to the heart of contested issues, the court may properly insist on the greatest possible particularity that the witness can attain. On points lying at the outer edge of relevancy, more general testimony should be readily admitted.

Emotions, physical condition, speed, size, color, shape

Lay witnesses provide opinion or inference testimony on a wide range of standard points, where it is more or less obvious that an adequate account involves characterizing, synthesizing, estimating, or exercising judgment.[5] Thus a lay witness may describe the apparent emotional or psychological state of another, whether angry, nervous, frightened, upset, amused, or shocked,[6] and may provide conventional physical descriptions of another, whether tall or short, old or young, dark or fair, apparently healthy or sick, strong or weak, and so forth.[7] And lay witnesses may describe the speed of a car or similar moving object, ordinary distances, the overall appearance of objects (size, color, shape, texture, resemblance to other objects), the quality and

2. *See* State v. Sweet, 949 A.2d 809, 813 (N.J. 2008) (lay opinion on drunkenness); Singletary v. Secretary of HEW, 623 F.2d 217, 219 (2d Cir. 1980) (same). *But see* State v. Bealor, 902 A.2d 226, 233-234 (N.J. 2006) (lay witness cannot opine on marijuana intoxication; not the same as alcohol).

3. Mattison v. Dallas Carrier Corp., 947 F.2d 95, 110-111 (4th Cir. 1991) (eyewitness to accident in downpour testified that truck's emergency flashers did not provide adequate warning under weather conditions); Young v. Illinois C.G. R., 618 F.2d 332, 337 (5th Cir. 1980) (error to exclude lay opinion on "poor condition" of grade crossing).

4. Government of Virgin Islands v. Knight, 989 F.2d 619, 629-630 (3d Cir. 1993) (in trial for beating victim with pistol that discharged and killed him, error to exclude lay testimony that defendant "accidentally" fired); Robinson v. Bump, 894 F.2d 758, 762-763 (5th Cir. 1990) (driver of car following truck testified that truckdriver was "in total control" until collision), *cert. denied*, 498 U.S. 823.

5. Getter v. Wal-Mart Stores, Inc., 66 F.3d 1119, 1124 (10th Cir. 1995) (in slip-and-fall suit, admitting lay testimony that floor in vestibule was safe), *cert. denied*, 516 U.S. 1146; United States v. Skeet, 665 F.2d 983, 985 (9th Cir. 1982) (admit lay opinion where facts "could not otherwise be adequately presented" to help jury; may opine on matters of common observation, like "size, heights, odors, flavors, color, heat").

6. *See* Farfaras v. Citizens Bank and Trust of Chicago, 433 F.3d 558, 565-566 (7th Cir. 2006) (plaintiff was depressed); United States v. Santos, 201 F.3d 953, 963 (7th Cir. 2000) (treasurer's management style was "intrusive and dictatorial"); United States v. Meling, 47 F.3d 1546, 1556-1557 (9th Cir. 1995) (defendant feigning grief after poisonings), *cert. denied*, 516 U.S. 843; United States v. Mastberg, 503 F.2d 465, 469-470 (9th Cir. 1974) (defendant seemed nervous).

7. United States v. Yazzie, 976 F.2d 1252, 1255 (9th Cir. 1992) (error to exclude lay opinion that statutory rape victim looked 16 to 20 in appearance and behavior).

apparent source of sound, light, or odor, and many similar things,[8] and may draw ordinary inferences on the basis of incomplete data where common sense and factual context supports them.[9]

It seems settled that lay witnesses may give opinion testimony that a person is sane[10] or insane.[11] This general issue is so complicated, however, and behavior that seems strange or erratic is so commonplace and sometimes meaningless that it seems right to require an enhanced foundation in the form of acquaintance with the subject on an extended basis. Otherwise lay opinion testimony on this subject has little value, and witnesses who have little acquaintance should confine themselves to behavioral descriptions.[12]

Sanity or insanity

Lay witnesses who know a person, and usually that person is now the defendant in a criminal case, may testify that he is the one shown in pictures and videotape made by surveillance cameras at banks and elsewhere.[13] Such testimony is often useful in identifying robbers, burglars or assailants. Extrinsic factors sometimes make defense cross-examination hard, since lay witnesses may be probation officers or police, and

Persons shown in pictures, video-tapes

---

8. United States v. Barker, 735 F.2d 1280, 1283-1284 (11th Cir. 1984) (lay testimony identifying defendant's handwriting on traveler's checks), *cert. denied,* 469 U.S. 933; Singletary v. Secretary of HEW, 623 F.2d 217, 219 (2d Cir. 1980) (son could testify on father's alcoholism and inability to work); Altvater v. Battocletti, 300 F.2d 156, 159 (4th Cir. 1962) (that substantial object like a car could be seen for only 300 feet even though witness mistaken in thinking there was no street light).

9. United States v. Valdez, 880 F.2d 1230, 1234-1235 (11th Cir. 1989) (agent saw legs and feet of defendant and another "through the underside of the trailer," and testified that he thought both entered trailer because they did not appear around either side); United States v. McCullah, 745 F.2d 350, 352 (6th Cir. 1984) (lay opinion that tractor was hidden under trees); United States v. Darland, 659 F.2d 70, 72 (5th Cir. 1981) (after admitting on cross that no fingerprints were found in car used in bank robbery, sheriff explained why; after eliciting testimony about fingerprints, defendant cannot object to some retort).

10. United States v. Mota, 598 F.2d 995, 998-1000 (5th Cir. 1979); United States v. Hall, 583 F.2d 1288, 1293-1294 (5th Cir. 1978); United States v. Greene, 497 F.2d 1068, 1084 (7th Cir. 1974), *cert. denied,* 420 U.S. 909; Mims v. United States, 375 F.2d 135 (5th Cir. 1967); Kaufman v. United States, 350 F.2d 408, 414-415 (8th Cir. 1965), *cert. denied,* 383 U.S. 951.

11. State v. Fichera, 903 A.2d 1030, 1035 (N.H. 2006); United States v. Milne, 487 F.2d 1232, 1235 (5th Cir. 1973), *cert. denied,* 419 U.S. 1123; United States v. Alden, 476 F.2d 378, 385-386 (7th Cir. 1973).

12. White v. Commonwealth, 636 S.E.2d 353, 359 (Va. 2006) (lay witness can testify to facts, not mental disease); Diestel v. Hines, 506 F.3d 1249, 1271 (10th Cir. 2006) (lay witnesses provided "observations from which others," including experts and jury, could draw inferences); United States v. Anthony, 944 F.2d 780, 782 (10th Cir. 1991) (must have acquaintance of intimacy and duration); Mason v. United States, 402 F.2d 732, 738 (8th Cir. 1968) (did not say defendant was sane; brevity of observation affected weight rather of testimony on appearance and behavior), *cert. denied,* 394 U.S. 950.

13. United States v. Beck, 418 F.3d 1008, 1013-1014 (9th Cir. 2005) (probation officer had met defendant four times, for total of 70 minutes); United States v. Holmes, 229 F.3d 782, 789 (9th Cir. 2000) (had met defendant six times before), *cert. denied,* 531 U.S. 1175; United States v. Jackman, 48 F.3d 1, 4-6 (1st Cir. 1995) (ex-wife and two friends); United States v. Towns, 913 F.2d 434, 445 (7th Cir. 1990) (former girlfriend) (changed appearance case).

cross exposes other criminality, but this difficulty has not carried much weight.[14]

Interpreting mental state   It is hard to say how far a court should let a lay witness go in describing or interpreting the mental state of another—her knowledge, intent, understanding, emotions or feelings, or what she meant by what she said. On the one hand, such testimony is indeed interpretive, often subjective, affected by extraneous relational factors, and in common experience people are often mistaken on such points. And it is easy to get too much interpretive gloss and not enough specific underpinning, and to wind up with speculation and guesswork. Here obviously the testimony is not helpful and not rationally based, and it should be excluded.[15]

But such testimony can be useful too because firsthand observers often understand the mental state of another in ways not captured in the literal meaning of words spoken by the other nor readily conveyed in close analytical accounts of what exactly transpired. The old adage that "you had to be there" makes this point, and witnesses asked to give "factual" accounts of what another said or did may be confounded by their knowledge that doing so would be misleading, and that the surface of the words carries little of their real meaning. In everyday life, personal interaction is nuanced and nonliteral, and expressions and tone of voice, posture, and glance are crucial. Knowledgeable witnesses can easily satisfy the rational basis and helpfulness criteria in providing interpretive opinions on the mental states of others.[16]

B. EXPERT TESTIMONY: FOUNDATION AND RELIABILITY (*DAUBERT* AND FRE 702)

FRE 702

If scientific, technical, or other specialized knowledge will assist the trier of fact to understand the evidence or to determine a fact in issue, a witness qualified as an expert by knowledge, skill, experience, training, or education, may testify thereto in the

---

14. United States v. Allen, 787 F.2d 933, 935-936 (4th Cir. 1986) (probation officer and police detective; occupation not divulged). *But see* United States v. Calhoun, 544 F.2d 291, 295-296 (6th Cir. 1976) (court should have excluded testimony by parole officer; defendant could not freely cross-examine).

15. State v. Lorenzo, 891 A.2d 864, 872 (R.I. 2006) (defense could not ask victim why defendant would have stabbed her; describing motive would be "mere speculation or conjecture"); United States v. Henke, 222 F.3d 633, 639-640 (9th Cir. 2000) (error to admit lay testimony that defendants knew about revenue reporting scheme; jury had "all the information" underlying opinion); United States v. Anderskow, 88 F.3d 245, 250 (3d Cir. 1996) (testimony that defendant was not deceived by certain information was not helpful; reasons were before jury; opinion turned witness into thirteenth juror), *cert. denied*, 519 U.S. 1042.

16. United States v. Estrada, 39 F.3d 772 (7th Cir. 1994) (letting informant interpret conversations with defendant); United States v. Simas, 937 F.2d 459, 464-465 (9th Cir. 1991) (undercover agents interpreted defendant's statements; lay opinion on meaning of vague statements may help).

> form of an opinion or otherwise, if (1) the testimony is based upon sufficient facts or data, (2) the testimony is the product of reliable principles and methods, and (3) the witness has applied the principles and methods reliably to the facts of the case.

1. Requisites, Foundation, Reliability Standard

§7.5 Qualified Expert

Under FRE 702, a witness must qualify as an expert to testify on matters that are scientific, technical, or specialized in nature. The description of the kinds of testimony requiring expertise is broad, and so are the means to qualify a witness as an expert: What is required is "knowledge, skill, experience, training, or education."

Normally the calling party must qualify the witness to testify as an expert first, before any substantive testimony is given. Usually the calling party takes this step as a matter of course because qualifying the expert lends credibility to his testimony and insures that he can give opinion testimony that lay witnesses could not give. Also courts usually permit greater latitude in questioning experts and are less concerned to prevent leading questions. If the proponent does not qualify the witness, usually the opponent can force the issue by raising an appropriate objection. In either case, usually the proponent first explores and seeks to establish the qualifications of the witness and the adverse parties then have a chance immediately to question the witness on "voir dire" to test the qualifications.[1]

On the matter of what qualifies a witness as an expert, it is clear that formal education ordinarily suffices.[2] One who holds a graduate degree ordinarily qualifies as an expert in his field, and undergraduate education with suitable emphasis or major in the field may suffice as well despite any lack of experience.[3] But neither a degree nor a title is essential, and a person with knowledge or skill born of experience may qualify, unless the experience is too far removed from the subject at hand.[4]

Education, experience

§7.5 1. *See* the discussion of FRE 611 in §6.59, *supra.*

2. Garnac Grain Co. v. Blackley, 932 F.2d 1563, 1567 (8th Cir. 1991) (retired business professor who taught auditing 40 years qualified despite lack of experience in grain operations); Lavespere v. Niagara Mach. & Tool Works, Inc., 910 F.2d 167, 175-177 (5th Cir. 1990) (expert with PhD in mechanical engineering and master's in production engineering qualified although he never designed press brake).

3. Stagl v. Delta Air Lines, Inc., 117 F.3d 76, 81 (2d Cir. 1997) (error to reject licensed engineer whose specialty was interaction between machines and people; should not require specific expertise in terminal design or baggage handling); Friendship Heights Assocs. v. Vlastimil Koubek, A.I.A., 785 F.2d 1154, 1159-1160 (4th Cir. 1986) (witness with degrees in chemical and ceramic engineering and silicate sciences can testify on reasons paint might peel off concrete even if he lacked experience).

4. Tuf Racing Products, Inc. v. American Suzuki Motor Corp., 223 F.3d 585, 591 (7th Cir. 2000) (rules do not require experts to be academics or PhDs; accountant could testify to damages on basis of financial information supplied by plaintiff); Fox v.

A party to a suit, if otherwise qualified as an expert, may testify as such in the case, and neither FRE 702 nor concerns over the fact that such a person is self-interested prevents one from qualifying as an expert in her own cause.[5] Nor is a person disqualified from testifying as an expert by the fact that she also testifies as a "fact witness," so it is proper for investigative agents (among others) to give expert opinions and also testify to the underlying events.[6]

Skilled witnesses   Obviously in FRE 702 "expert" is not a term of art: The Rule "is not limited to experts in the strictest sense of the word."[7] In addition to those set apart by education or experience, "skilled" witnesses—the ACN cites "bankers or landowners testifying to land values"—also qualify as experts.[8] Thus a person who owns a business or property should be allowed to testify to its value,[9] and a person in business should be able to testify to the profits of the enterprise.[10]

Regardless how impressive the background of a witness, his area of expertise should match fairly closely the subject matter of his testimony. If it does not or his background fails to equip him to testify, he does not qualify as an expert.[11] Thus a clinical psychologist may generally testify

---

Dannenberg, 906 F.2d 1253, 1255 (8th Cir. 1990) (more than 20 years practical experience in accident reconstruction qualified engineers who investigated wreckage of single-car accident to say survivor was driving).

5. *See* Scheidt v. Klein, 956 F.2d 963, 968 n.4 (10th Cir. 1992); Tagatz v. Marquette Univ., 861 F.2d 1040, 1042 (7th Cir. 1988) (professor who sued for discrimination gave expert statistical testimony).

6. United States v. Penny, 60 F.3d 1257, 1265 (7th Cir. 1995) (deputy marshal testifies as both fact and expert opinion witness); United States v. Rivera, 971 F.2d 876, 888 (2d Cir. 1992) (expert who described drug trade could testify as fact witness; such dual testimony is not improper). *But see* United States v. Foster, 939 F.2d 445, 452 (7th Cir. 1991) (agent described drug courier profile; caution required where eyewitness testifies as expert, so jury is not confused by dual role).

7. In re Paoli R. Yard PCB Litig., 35 F.3d 717, 741 (3d Cir. 1994) (liberal policy of admissibility extends to formal qualifications); Fox v. Dannenberg, 906 F.2d 1253, 1255 (8th Cir. 1990) (FRE 702 reflects "attempt to liberalize" rules).

8. Western Indus., Inc. v. Newcor Canada, Ltd., 739 F.2d 1198, 1203 (7th Cir. 1984) (executives experienced in trade qualified as experts on trade custom; all were "skilled" witnesses); United States v. Thomas, 676 F.2d 239, 245 (7th Cir. 1980) (witness who worked in auto repair shop to finance college education and rebuilt cars in shops as hobby could testify that defendants were not operating such a shop since equipment was for taking apart cars, not assembling or repairing), *cert. denied*, 450 U.S. 931.

9. United States v. 68.94 Acres of Land, Kent County, 918 F.2d 389, 397-399 (3d Cir. 1990) (landowners have "special knowledge" that qualifies them to testify on value); Re Merritt Logan, Inc., 901 F.2d 349, 361-362 (3d Cir. 1990) (owner of grocery properly testified about lost profits and how to calculate them).

10. *See* Mississippi Chemical Corp. v. Dresser-Rand Co., 287 F.3d 359 (5th Cir. 2002) (director of risk management, with direct knowledge of accounts, may testify to lost profits); Greenwood Ranches, Inc. v. Skie Constr. Co., 629 F.2d 518, 522-523 (8th Cir. 1980) (rancher testified on value at maturity that crop would have if water transfer system had not failed).

11. Ralston v. Smith & Nephew Richards, Inc., 275 F.3d 965, 969-970 (10th Cir. 2001) (excluding testimony by orthopedic surgeon with expertise in oncology who had no experience in "intramedullary nailing" and had never researched bone-repairing nail giving rise to suit); McCullock v. H. B. Fuller Co., 981 F.2d 656, 657 (2d Cir. 1992) (in suit alleging injuries from breathing vapors, electrical and industrial engineer could testify on need for ventilation system, but not adequacy of warning).

to the sanity or insanity of a criminal defendant, but generally an experimental psychologist may not.[12]

A witness need not be renowned in any particular field to qualify as an expert,[13] nor need he be a specialist simply because his field contains recognized specialties.[14] On the other hand, preparation or experience that is minimal in nature should not be viewed as sufficient qualification under the Rule.[15] It is difficult to attain greater precision: Of course the question of qualification is for the trial judge to resolve pursuant to FRE 104(a), and he has broad discretion.

Need not be renowned

§7.6 Helpfulness Standard

Assuming the witness is qualified, the question whether he may testify as an expert turns mostly on whether his testimony will help the trier understand the evidence or determine a fact in issue. Expert testimony on matters of science must also satisfy a validity standard, however, and this subject is taken up in the next section.

Necessarily the helpfulness standard calls for decisions that are very much ad hoc, for the question is always whether a particular expert can help resolve the particular issue in the case at hand.[1] The standard works well if the subject is technical and lies beyond common experience.[2] Usually such a subject is connected with science or a professional discipline, with the conduct of a business or occupation, or with some recognized and special skill or pool of information.

Ad hoc decisions

---

12. *See* United States v. Lopez, 543 F.2d 1156, 1158 (5th Cir. 1977), *cert. denied,* 429 U.S. 1111; United States v. Portis, 542 F.2d 414, 420 (7th Cir. 1976); Jenkins v. United States, 307 F.2d 637, 644-646 (D.C. Cir. 1962) (leading case finding error in excluding defense testimony on insanity by psychologists lacking medical training; clinical psychologists treat mental disorders, but many psychologists may not qualify to testify on mental disease or defect).

13. San Francisco v. Wendy's International, Inc., 656 S.E.2d 485, 497 (W.Va. 2007) (need not be specialist); United States v. Rose, 731 F.2d 1337, 1346 (8th Cir. 1984) (need not be "outstanding practitioner"), *cert. denied,* 469 U.S. 931.

14. Holbrook v. Lykes Bros. S.S. Co., 80 F.3d 777, 783-784 (3d Cir. 1996) (treating physician could testify that decedent suffered from mesothelioma; doctor certified in internal and pulmonary medicine could testify on causes of disease); Peteet v. Dow Chem. Co., 868 F.2d 1428, 1431 (5th Cir. 1989) (doctor certified in toxicology testified that exposure to dioxin was contributing cause of Hodgkin's disease; objection that he was not specialist went to weight), *cert. denied,* 493 U.S. 935.

15. Doddy v. Oxy USA, Inc., 101 F.3d 448, 459-460 (5th Cir. 1996) (in contamination suit, excluding testimony by witness experienced in treating oil wells for corrosion, but not in chemical content, toxicity, or migration of chemicals); LuMetta v. United States Robotics, Inc., 824 F.2d 768, 771 (9th Cir. 1987) (excluding testimony on finder's fees; experience of one witness came after contract in issue and he paid fee only once; another had no experience with small computer companies; third knew of only one finder fee).

§7.6 1. Bridger v. Union R. Co., 355 F.2d 382, 388 (6th Cir. 1966) (calling for "ad hoc determination" predicated on probable value of testimony in relation to intricacies of suit).

2. United States v. Morales, 108 F.3d 1031, 1039 (9th Cir. 1997) (bookkeeping principles); Busby v. Orlando, 931 F.2d 764, 783-784 (11th Cir. 1991) (interpreting termination logs bearing on race bias claim).

In these settings, the helpfulness standard points toward admitting expert testimony on many subjects.

Civil cases   In civil cases, experts help by interpreting business practices and transactions that are complicated and beyond lay familiarity[3] and by explaining trade and business usages.[4] Experts help by analyzing dangerous conditions at accident scenes[5] and by suggesting the cause[6] or nature of accidents,[7] although the helpfulness standard is not satisfied (and testimony may be excluded) if the dangerous condition or causal factors are utterly commonplace.[8] Experts can also help show a product is or is not dangerous,[9] or that safety features would or would not improve the situation.[10] Experts can help by saying whether fire was the product of arson[11] and by describing the level of force appropriate to making an arrest in particular circumstances.[12] And economists can help by estimating the earnings a decedent probably would have had and calculating present discounted value, considering such factors as expected inflation and taxes,[13] although specific predictions on

---

3. TCBY Sys. v. RSP Co., 33 F.3d 925, 929 (8th Cir. 1994) (testimony that claimant did not meet standard of fast-food industry in assisting franchisees); Shad v. Dean Witter Reynolds, Inc., 799 F.2d 525, 527-530 (9th Cir. 1986) (testimony by broker on churning).

4. Phillips Oil Co. v. OKC Corp., 812 F.2d 265, 280 (5th Cir. 1987) (accountant on technical terms in net profit provisions), *cert. denied*, 484 U.S. 851; Huddleston v. Herman & MacLean, 640 F.2d 534, 552 (5th Cir. 1981) (lawyer on "prospectus boilerplate language" in securities industry).

5. Young v. Illinois C.G.R. Co., 618 F.2d 332, 337-338 (5th Cir. 1980) (experiment designed to show car might be deflected onto tracks at grade crossing); Frazier v. Continental Oil Co., 568 F.2d 378, 383 (5th Cir. 1978) (poor venting system for underground gas tanks increases risk of explosion).

6. Werth v. Makita Elec. Works, Ltd., 950 F.2d 643, 650-653 (10th Cir. 1991) (kickback in power saw); Kelsay v. Consolidated Rail Corp., 749 F.2d 437, 448-449 (7th Cir. 1984) (driver inattention caused grade crossing accident).

7. Sparks v. Gilley Trucking Co., 992 F.2d 50, 53-54 (4th Cir. 1993) (trooper's estimate that claimant was going 70 mph); Barron v. Ford Motor Co. of Canada, Ltd., 965 F.2d 195, 202 (7th Cir. 1992) (trooper's testimony that plaintiff was thrown through sunroof).

8. Evans v. Mathis Funeral Home, 996 F.2d 266, 268 (11th Cir. 1993) (excluding expert testimony on dangers of staircase); Andrews v. Metro N.C.R. Co., 882 F.2d 705, 707-709 (2d Cir. 1989) (forensic engineer should not have testified that trash, ice, and lighting conditions made train platform unsafe).

9. Compton v. Subaru of America, Inc., 82 F.3d 1513, 1516-1518 (10th Cir. 1996) (vehicle defectively designed in permitting too much roof crush), *cert. denied*, 519 U.S. 1042; Wheeler v. John Deere Co., 935 F.2d 1090, 1100-1101 (10th Cir. 1991) (combine "more dangerous than anticipated by ordinary consumers").

10. Exum v. General Elec. Co., 819 F.2d 1158, 1163-1164 (D.C. Cir. 1987) (expense and effectiveness of installing manual siphon in fryer).

11. United States v. Lundy, 809 F.2d 392, 394-395 (7th Cir. 1987) (fire was incendiary); American Home Assur. Co. v. Sunshine Supermarket, Inc., 753 F.2d 321, 325 (3d Cir. 1985) (fire was arson).

12. Kopf v. Skyrm, 993 F.2d 374, 378-380 (5th Cir. 1996) (appropriate force, use of dogs and slapjacks), *cert. denied*, 502 U.S. 1098; Kladis v. Brezek, 823 F.2d 1014, 1019 (7th Cir. 1987) ("proper level of force to be used by police in various situations").

13. Norfolk & W. Ry. v. Liepelt, 444 U.S. 490, 494 (1980) (taxes coming out of future earnings); Salas v. Wang, 846 F.2d 897, 903-906 (3d Cir. 1988) (aggregate economic damage; present value).

inflationary trends are too speculative to be useful.[14] Economists also help by estimating the economic value of uncompensated household services.[15]

In criminal cases experts can help by describing typical organizational and operational patterns in criminal activities ranging from drug trafficking, counterfeiting, and gambling to other forms of organized crime.[16] Here expert testimony can help by suggesting possible meaning and significance of activities that are likely to seem innocent or carry no particular meaning when seen in isolation or by an inexperienced observer.[17] And expert testimony can help by providing background information useful in understanding customs, conversations, transactions, or human relationships[18] and by describing and interpreting coded language in intercepted conversations, street transactions, and records.[19] Experts in photographic comparison can also help by testifying that someone in a bank surveillance film either can or cannot be identified as the defendant.[20]

Criminal cases

Arguably the helpfulness standard works best as one of inclusion (less well as one of exclusion). Hence the mere fact that a subject is within common knowledge and experience does not mean expert testimony cannot help, and special knowledge or skill may add precision or depth that is useful to the trier of fact.[21] Indeed, it is hard to imagine

14. Johnson v. Serra, 521 F.2d 1289, 1292-1296 (8th Cir. 1975); Johnson v. Penrod Drilling Co., 510 F.2d 234 (5th Cir. 1975), *cert. denied*, 423 U.S. 839.

15. *See* Haddigan v. Harkins, 441 F.2d 844, 851-852 (3d Cir. 1970); Har-Pen Truck Lines, Inc. v. Mills, 378 F.2d 705, 710-712 (5th Cir. 1967) (economic value of services of hypothetical housewife).

16. United States v. Lopez-Lopez, 282 F.3d 1, 13-14 (1st Cir. 2002) (how drug importing schemes use global positioning systems to facilitate air drops and boat-to-boat transfers, and cellular telephones for boat-to-ground communication), *cert. denied*, 536 U.S. 949; United States v. Mulder, 273 F.3d 91, 100-102 (2d Cir. 2001) (operations and effects of labor coalitions on hiring minority laborers), *cert. denied*, 535 U.S. 949; United States v. Murillo, 255 F.3d 1169, 1176-1178 (9th Cir. 2001) ("typical travel itineraries of drug curriers, why drug curriers use rental cars, and how drug traffickers do not entrust large quantities of drugs to people who are unaware that they are transporting them"), *cert. denied*, 535 U.S. 948.

17. United States v. Parra, 402 F.3d 752, 758 (7th Cir. 2005) (countersurveillance techniques in drug transactions); United States v. Davis, 397 F.3d 173, 179 (3d Cir. 2005) (methods of drug traffickers in South Philadelphia; *Daubert* standard satisfied); United States v. Hernandez-Vega, 235 F.3d 705, 710-711 (1st Cir. 2000) (describing as drug transactions scenes captured on videotapes in housing project), *cert. denied*, 532 U.S. 1032.

18. United States v. Pungitore, 910 F.2d 1084, 1148-1149 (3d Cir. 1990) (structure of crime families).

19. United States v. Villarman-Oviedo, 325 F.3d 1, 12-13 (1st Cir. 2003) (coded terms); United States v. Parker, 32 F.3d 395, 400 (8th Cir. 1994) (notebook entries).

20. United States v. Alexander, 816 F.2d 164, 169 (5th Cir. 1987) (photographic comparison expert and orthodontist testify); United States v. Sellers, 566 F.2d 884, 886 (4th Cir. 1977) (expert testimony that defendant was not person in bank surveillance photo).

21. Carroll v. Otis Elevator Co., 896 F.2d 210, 212 (7th Cir. 1990) (admitting expert testimony even though "one needn't be B. F. Skinner to know that brightly colored objects are attractive to small children"); United States v. Pino, 606 F.2d 908, 919 (10th Cir. 1979) (psychiatric testimony that one in shock would look drunk).

a serious question arising in a suit that some kind of expert could not illuminate in ways that might be useful to lay factfinders.

The experience of more than 30 years in applying FRE 702 suggests, however, that the helpfulness standard should also be understood to mean that sometimes expert testimony is inappropriate. Not surprisingly, appellate decisions approving the exclusion of expert testimony also comment, in passing or by way of trying to state limits, that the subject at hand is too commonplace to benefit from expert insights. And where the issue and subject are ones that lay jurors can appreciate and evaluate by applying common knowledge and good sense, admitting expert testimony seems the wrong thing to do and may warrant reversal if it is likely to dissuade the jury from exercising independent judgment or to take over the jury's traditional function of appraising the credibility of witnesses.[22]

Standards, descriptions, facts

Often the best thing an expert can do is to provide standards or criteria,[23] estimates of feasibility or likelihood,[24] or descriptions of social frameworks[25] that juries can then constructively use in resolving more particular issues relating to such things as due care, intent or purpose, and who likely did what and why. Here the helpfulness standard suggests that experts should provide those standards or criteria or frameworks, but should stop short of drawing conclusions because the jury is at least equally capable of taking this step.[26] Indeed, experts are sometimes most useful in providing "scientific facts" that the trier can consider, for there is no rule that experts can only give opinion testimony.

There are two other situations where expert testimony usually fails the helpfulness standard. One arises where experts are asked essentially to speculate, either because the question inevitably involves imponderables that no experience or field of knowledge can overcome[27] or because the expert is asked to apply knowledge that can only be connected to the case at hand by an improbable inferential leap.[28]

---

22. Saldana v. KMart Corp., 260 F.3d 228, 233 (3d Cir. 2001) (excluding expert opinion that spilled wax in store constituted failure to meet worker safety requirements, which would not help factfinder determine critical issue of responsibility).

23. United States v. Chappell, 6 F.3d 1095, 1100 (5th Cir. 1993) (methods for detecting counterfeit checks), *cert. denied*, 510 U.S. 1183, 1184; Harris v. Pacific Floor Mach. Mfg. Co., 856 F.2d 64, 67-68 (8th Cir. 1988) (criteria to judge adequacy of warnings).

24. United States v. Diallo, 40 F.3d 32, 34-35 (2d Cir. 1994) (smuggling gold more profitable than legal compliance); United States v. Onumonu, 967 F.2d 782, 787-788 (2d Cir. 1992) (feasibility of smuggling diamonds by balloon in alimentary canal).

25. *See* the discussion of framework and syndrome testimony in §7.22, *infra.*

26. United States v. Brown, 776 F.2d 397, 400-401 & n.6 (2d Cir. 1985) (officer should not have testified that defendant acted as steerer).

27. Navarro de Cosme v. Hospital Pavia, 922 F.2d 926, 931-932 (1st Cir. 1991) (excluding testimony by nun appraising grief); United States v. West, 670 F.2d 675, 682-683 (7th Cir. 1982) (warden could not estimate likelihood that inmate could have sex with wife or take drugs without other inmates knowing), *cert. denied*, 457 U.S. 1139; Scheib v. Williams-McWilliams Co., 628 F.2d 509, 511 (5th Cir. 1980) (cannot testify that wages would increase faster than inflation).

28. Air Disaster at Lockerbie, Scotland, 37 F.3d 804, 824-825 (2d Cir. 1994) (excluding testimony on alternatives to theory that bombing was work of terrorists), *cert. denied*, 513 U.S. 1126.

On such grounds it seems that experts should not be allowed to testify, for example, to the value of living.[29] The other arises where the expert proposes to testify on the basis of demonstrably false premises, or obviously faulty logic or principles,[30] or where the expert really has essentially no basis better than a hunch,[31] and here the objection comes close to raising the reasonable basis requirement of FRE 703. In such cases it seems that expert testimony would be superfluous and a waste of time, which means not only that it fails the helpfulness standard but also that it becomes excludable under Rule 403.

The fact that an expert cannot be categorical, and admits some uncertainty, does not mean his testimony fails the helpfulness requirement. Lay witnesses routinely testify to their recollection while admitting uncertainty, and at least as much latitude extends to experts. Where reasons for reservations can be made intelligible to a lay jury, it is entirely appropriate to let the expert lay them out so the jury may better evaluate his testimony and reach its own conclusions on its worth. On the other hand, uncertainty that is so acute that the testimony would amount to little more than a guess or a shrug does implicate the helpfulness criterion, and such testimony may properly be excluded as unhelpful.[32]

Effect of uncertainty

Expert testimony that would be helpful might also be prejudicial in the sense of inviting misuse or injecting too much risk of angry or emotional reaction, in which case it is excludable for unfair prejudice under FRE 403.[33] And expert testimony that seems helpful may be excluded on account of other concerns embodied in FRE 403, such as confusion of issues or misleading the jury.[34]

Trial courts decide whether expert testimony is helpful, and the decision is for the judge alone to make under FRE 703 and 104(a). It is not surprising that trial courts have broad discretion on this

29. Mercado v. Ahmed, 974 F.2d 863, 869-871 (7th Cir. 1992) (excluding testimony on value of living).

30. Re Air Crash Disaster at New Orleans, 795 F.2d 1230, 1233-1234 (5th Cir. 1986) (economist made false and unsupported assumptions, should not have calculated future income and assets).

31. Lang v. Kohl's Food Stores, Inc., 217 F.3d 919, 923-924 (7th Cir. 2000) (excluding testimony by self-employed consultant with PhD in labor relations whose report consisted of "unreasoned assertions"), *cert denied*, 531 U.S. 1076; United States v. Sorrentino, 726 F.2d 876, 885 (1st Cir. 1984) (striking "top-of-the-hat appraisal" where witness never made real appraisal).

32. *Compare* United States v. Allen, 390 F.3d 944, 949 (7th Cir. 2004) (testimony on shoe prints, which could assist jury even though "inconclusive" in saying only that shoes "could have made" impression in cement dust) *with* United States v. Brewer, 783 F.2d 841, 842 (9th Cir. 1986) (forensic anthropologist could not say defendant was not in photos; unhelpful), *cert. denied*, 479 U.S. 831.

33. United States v. Long, 917 F.2d 691, 702 (2d Cir. 1990) (expert testimony on "sweetheart contracts" was highly prejudicial).

34. Rogers v. Raymark Indus., Inc., 922 F.2d 1426, 1429-1432 (9th Cir. 1991) (testimony on asbestos insulation had minimal probative value and considerable potential to confuse); United States v. Rouco, 765 F.2d 983, 995-996 (11th Cir. 1985) (testimony on arrest procedure would mislead by creating impression that criminal responsibility depends on conformity to standards).

point, although misstating the applicable standard involves an error of law on which review is plenary.[35]

§7.7 Reliability Standard (*Daubert*, *Frye*)

The closing decade of the twentieth century brought a sea change in the approach to scientific evidence. In its 1993 opinion in the *Daubert* case, the Court decided (oversimplifying for a moment) that scientific evidence must satisfy a "reliability" standard in order to be admissible. In the *Kumho Tire* case in 1999, the Court held that *Daubert* applies to *all* expert testimony, not just to testimony that can be called scientific.[1] Capping off these developments, Rule 702 was amended in 2000 by the addition of three numbered clauses directing courts to consider whether the expert (1) has "sufficient facts or data" underlying the testimony, (2) applied "reliable principles and methods," and (3) "applied the principles and methods reliably to the facts" of the case.

Outline of discussion   The ensuing discussion begins with *Daubert*, focusing on the message and approach, and then on specific points that constitute the *Daubert* standard. Then we turn to the requirements set out in the amended Rule. Then this section discusses the problem of applying *Daubert* to experiential expertise and other forms of expert testimony that do not seem scientific in the usual sense. Next this section takes up procedural issues, focusing first on how courts resolve *Daubert* issues and on burdens, and then on scope of review. Finally, this section considers problems of integrating scientific and technical proof into the legal system. This section does not discuss the myriad issues specific to the common forms of scientific and technical evidence. These matters have generated full treatises devoted specifically to that subject.[2] As befits an epic case, *Daubert* has inspired a vast scholarly output, as well as newsletters and databanks devoted specifically to the problems of applying the case in specific situations.[3]

---

35. DeLuca v. Merrell Dow Pharmaceuticals, Inc., 911 F.2d 941, 944 (3d Cir. 1990) (review is plenary to extent ruling turns on interpretation of Rule; court misapplied FRE 703 in saying pediatric pharmacologist could not rely on published data to conclude Bendectin is teratogenic).

§7.7 1. Daubert v. Merrell Dow Pharmaceuticals, Inc., 509 U.S. 579 (1993) (scientific evidence must be reliable and must fit case, but can be excluded under FRE 403); Kumho Tire Co. v. Carmichael, 526 U.S. 137, 147 (1999) (in referring to "scientific" and to "technical" and "other specialized" knowledge, FRE 702 draws no distinctions; *Daubert* applies equally to all three, and to "experiential" expertise).

2. This work cannot cover scientific evidence in detail. Modern treatises provide admirable accounts. See Faigman, Kaye, Saks and Sanders, Modern Scientific Evidence (2d ed. 2002) (4 vols); Imwinkelried and Giannelli, Scientific Evidence (3d ed. 1999) (3 vols); Moenssens, Starrs, Henderson, and Inbau, Scientific Evidence in Civil and Criminal Cases (4th ed. 1995) (forensic science).

3. Here are a few of the many useful discussions: G. Michael Fenner, The *Daubert* Handbook: The Case, Its Essential Dilemma, and its Progeny, 29 Creighton L. Rev. 939 (1996); Michael H. Graham, Expert Witness Predicament: Determining "Reliable" Under the Gatekeeping Test of Daubert, Kumho, and Proposed Amended Rule 702 of the Federal Rules of Evidence, 54 U. Minn. L. Rev. 317 (2000); Imwinkelried,

Before *Daubert*, most courts followed the *Frye* standard, under which scientific evidence could be admitted only if it had attained "general acceptance" in the relevant scientific community.[4] In contrast, *Daubert* held that federal courts applying FRE 702 should consider multiple factors (including error rates and existence of standards) in assessing reliability. In net effect, *Daubert* tells courts to look closely and directly at the evidence and to consider a wide range of factors bearing on reliability, and in these ways *Daubert* rejects *Frye*. The crux of it is that courts act as gatekeepers when it comes to scientific (and now technical) evidence.[5] Yet *Daubert* includes, in its list of relevant considerations, the one factor that *Frye* deemed all-important (general acceptance), and the *Frye* standard also lives on in a more than a dozen states.

Daubert actually takes a three-pronged approach: Courts are to consider the "validity" or "reliability" of the evidence in question, its degree of "fit" with the facts and issues in the case, and the risks or dangers that the evidence will confuse the issues or mislead the jury (the concerns embodied in FRE 403). All three of these factors are important, and each can prove critical in any given case, but it is the reliability standard that presents by far the greatest challenge.

Three additional points merit stress at the outset.

First, *Daubert* does not let courts admit or exclude scientific evidence on the basis of simple tests. On the one hand, *Daubert* commissions courts to confront the reliability of science directly, and rejects the notion that merely qualifying an expert paves the way for whatever he might want to contribute.[6] On the other hand, *Daubert* also rejects the notion that scientific or technical evidence may be excluded simply because it represents a new approach that has not yet been subject to

---

Evaluating the Reliability of Nonscientific Expert Testimony: A Partial Answer to the Questions Left Unresolved by Kumho Tire Co. v. Carmichael, 52 Maine L. Rev. 19 (2000); Imwinkelried, The Taxonomy of Testimony Post-Kumho: Refocusing on the Bottomlines of Reliability and Necessity, 30 Cumberland L. Rev. 185 (2000); Risinger, Preliminary Thoughts on a Functional Taxonomy of Expertise for the Post-Kumho World, in 1 Modern Scientific Evidence (Faigman, Kaye, Saks and Sanders, eds. 2002); Risinger, Navigating Expert Reliability: Are Criminal Standards of Certainty Being Left on the Dock? 64 Albany L. Rev. 99 (2000); Slobogin, Psychiatric Evidence in Criminal Trials: To Junk or Not To Junk, 40 William and Mary L. Rev. 1 (1998); Slobogin, Doubts about Daubert: Psychiatric Anecdata as a Case Study, 57 Wash. and Lee L. Rev. 919 (2000).

4. Frye v. United States, 293 F. 1013 (D.C. Cir. 1923) (excluding polygraph because it had not attained "general acceptance" in its field).

5. Dodge v. Cotter Corp., 328 F.3d 1212, 1222 (10th Cir. 2003) (in suit claiming that uranium mill caused environmental contamination, court erred in admitting testimony on causation, by geologist and two physicians; *Daubert* requires courts to exercise gate-keeping responsibility; court faced "exceedingly difficult, complex case" and did not make "adequate findings" on record to assure that testimony was reliable and opinions were "based on valid reasoning and reliable methodology") (reversing); Daubert v. Merrell Dow Pharmaceuticals, Inc., 43 F.3d 1311, 1315 (9th Cir. 1995) (judges face "far more complex and daunting task in a post-*Daubert* world").

6. Valentine v. Conrad, 850 N.E.2d 683, 687 (Ohio 2006) (experience of "highly qualified" experts does not show legal reliability of opinions); Fuesting v. Zimmer, Inc., 421 F.3d 528, 535-536 (7th Cir. 2005) (cannot rely on credentials alone).

the discipline of professional scrutiny. Hence peer review and publication are not absolutely essential, and evidence developed for purposes of suit, or to analyze some issue or problem, may be admissible. Indeed, *Daubert* means that proponents may sometimes present new conclusions based on old data that have led others to contrary conclusions.[7] Nevertheless, it does count in the decision on reliability that the expert has reached conclusions that are consonant with those reached by others: If an expert has reached conclusions that are sharply discordant when compared to those reached by similar experts applying similar methods to similar facts, the disparity is a red flag suggesting that something about the method or the manner of application has gone wrong and that the reliability standard has not been satisfied.[8]

(2) Right or wrong is not the question

Second, the *Daubert* standard, buttressed and reinforced by amended FRE 702, does not invite courts to decide that the testimony is right or wrong or to displace the adversary system.[9] That system depends on cross-examination and allowing the other side to offer its own counterproof, and these mechanisms put before the trier of fact the necessary information to make a considered judgment, to decide which side should carry the day.[10]

(3) Conflicting opinions can pass muster

Third, and correlated with these points, sharply conflicting expert opinions can all pass muster under *Daubert* and amended FRE 702. Accepting the expertise of one witness does not entail rejecting the expertise of another witness who has come to the opposite conclusion.[11]

First factor: Reliability

The first *Daubert* requirement is that the science be reliable or valid, and courts usually speak of "reliability." *Daubert* expects judges to decide the question whether the theories, techniques, and data as applied can be trusted. Scientists commonly use this term to describe

7. Daubert v. Merrell Dow Pharmaceuticals, Inc., 509 U.S. 579 (1993) (publication is not sine qua non, nor "necessarily correlate" with reliability; new propositions may be "too particular, too new, or of too limited interest to be published").

8. General Electric Co. v. Joiner, 522 U.S. 136, 146 (1997) ("conclusions and methodology are not entirely distinct," and experts "commonly extrapolate from existing data," but court need not admit opinion that is "connected to existing data only by the ipse dixit of the expert," and "may conclude that there is simply too great an analytical gap" between data and opinion).

9. Daubert v. Merrell Dow Pharmaceuticals, Inc., 509 U.S. 579, 590 n.9 & 595 (1993) (should focus "solely on principles and methodology," not conclusions; the concern is scientific validity, and "evidentiary reliability" rests on "scientific validity"); Deputy v. Lehman Bros., Inc., 345 F.3d 494, 506, 62 Fed. R. Evid. Serv. 965 (7th Cir. 2003) (error to reject testimony on handwriting for reasons of "credibility and persuasiveness," which are "relevant only in valuing the testimony, not in determining its admissibility").

10. United States v. 14.38 Acres of land Situated in Leflore County, Mississippi, 80 F.3d 1074, 1078 (5th Cir. 1996) (gatekeeping role does not "serve as a replacement for the adversary system").

11. See ACN to FRE 702 (ruling that expert testimony is reliable "does not necessarily mean that contradictory expert testimony is unreliable"); State v. Farner, 66 S.W.3d 188, 207 (Tenn. 2002) (court "need not weigh or choose between two legitimate but conflicting scientific views"); Ruiz-Troche v. Pepsi Cola, 1 F.3d 77, 85 (1st Cir. 1998) (*Daubert* "neither requires nor empowers" courts to decide "which of several competing scientific theories has the best provenance").

consistent outcomes, but the concern of lawyers and the system as expressed in *Daubert* is practical and concrete, and what *Daubert* seeks is the best available assurance of reliability in the sense of accurate and correct outcomes.[12]

It bears emphasis that the focus is "the case at hand" (as the Court emphasized in *Kumho Tire*), not the type or form of analysis being offered, and it does not matter whether such analysis can be correct in other settings.[13]

Many lines of inquiry are pertinent in applying the reliability standard. *Daubert* provides suggestions for guidance, while stressing (as the Court repeated in *Kumho Tire*) that the inquiry is "flexible" and is shaped by the context of the particular case. Courts should consider (1) whether the theory or technique can be and has been tested, (2) whether it has been subjected to peer review and publication, (3) error rates, (4) the existence of standards governing the operation of the technique, and (5) degree of acceptance in the scientific community, since widespread acceptance is a positive sign and minimal support is a negative sign for a widely known technique. The Court in *Daubert* cited these factors.[14]

Daubert made it clear that the factors that it cited are exemplary rather than exhaustive. Hence many other factors count as well. The Third Circuit in the *Downing* case, which anticipated *Daubert*, cited additional factors that count, including (6) nonjudicial uses and experience with the process or technique, (7) its novelty and relationship to other methods of analysis, (8) the qualifications and professional stature of the expert witness, (9) the types of error experienced, whether likely to favor the offering party or understate what he seeks to prove, and (10) the existence of a body of professional literature appraising the process or technique, which tends to insure widespread attention and critical scrutiny.[15]

In addition to these factors, the ACN accompanying the amendment to FRE 702 in 2000 cited still more factors. Thus courts may consider

12. State v. O'Key, 899 P.2d 663, 678 n.19 (Or. 1995) (validity describes how well scientific method "reasons to its conclusions," while reliability describes ability of method "to produce consistent results when replicated"). See Faigman, To Have and Have Not: Assessing the Value of Social Science to the Law as Science and as Policy, 38 Emory L. J. 1005, n.16 (1989) (in standard usage, validity "refers to the ability of a scientific test to measure what it purports to measure" while reliability refers to ability of test "to obtain consistent results"); Black, A Unified Theory of Scientific Evidence, 56 Fordham L. Rev. 595, 599-600 (1988) (reliability means consistency; validity means "based on sound reasoning").

13. Kumho Tire Co. v. Carmichael, 526 U.S. 137, 153-154 (1999) (look at "case at hand," ask not whether it is reasonable for expert to rely on "visual and tactile inspection" of tire, but whether it was reasonable to take this approach in reaching "conclusion regarding *the particular matter to which the expert testimony was directly relevant*") (original emphasis).

14. Daubert v. Merrell Dow Pharmaceuticals, 509 U.S. 579, 595 (1993) ("flexible" inquiry); Kumho Tire Co. v. Carmichael, 526 U.S. 137, 146 (1999) (*Daubert* "should be applied flexibility" and *Daubert* factors are "simply illustrative") (others count too).

15. United States v. Downing, 753 F.2d 1224, 1237-1242 (3d Cir. 1985).

(11) whether the opinion grows from independent research or was developed for purposes of litigation, (12) whether the expert has unjustifiably extrapolated from an accepted premise to an unfounded conclusion, (13) whether the expert has adequately accounted for alternative explanations, (14) whether the expert has exercised the care appropriate to professional work, and (15) whether the field is known to reach reliable results in the area of the proposed testimony.

It is unnecessary for proffered scientific or technical evidence to satisfy the standards or tests suggested by *all fifteen* factors listed above. Trial courts have leeway in deciding which factors bear saliently on the proffered evidence, and leeway as well to decide whether those standards or tests are satisfied by the proffered evidence. Where proffered evidence does not satisfy any of these standards, its validity or reliability is not shown and it should be excluded.[16]

Second factor: Fit   The degree of "fit" between the proffered testimony and the facts and issues in the case is an aspect of relevancy. Expert testimony usually reflects, and brings to bear on the case, theories, tests, and experience generated in situations unrelated to the events in litigation. Hence its utility turns partly on the degree of resemblance between the transactions in suit and the situations in which the science or expertise was generated. Expert testimony also extrapolates or draws conclusions resting on theories, tests and experience, and its utility turns in part on how closely the conclusion is connected to the underlying data—whether it is but a short step from data to conclusion or a long inferential leap. The closer the connection, the better the fit, although this criterion does not demand that there be a perfect congruence between proffered testimony and facts or issues in the case.[17]

Sometimes the question of fit turns on outright conflicts between the facts or assumptions in a theoretical model and the facts of the case. In a product liability suit against the maker of a "dock lift" with a handrail, whose vertical path took it by a stationery catwalk with its own handrail, for example, a modern decision excluded testimony that a human hand holding an object two inches in diameter requires more than four inches of clearance, offered in support of plaintiff's claim that the lift was defective because a "pinch point" between the two handrails was too narrow. This testimony did not fit because plaintiff was not holding anything when the accident occurred.[18] Other times the question of "fit" turns on more subtle differences between models and the facts of the case, and the question is whether the science is

16. Cabrera v. Cordis Corp., 134 F.3d 1418, 1422-1423 (9th Cir. 1998) (excluding testimony by immunologist who could not say how he reached conclusions or explain test, or show that it had been peer-reviewed; excluding testimony by internist for "lack of supporting research," peer-reviewed articles, and failure to show he followed method embraced by other experts).

17. Daubert v. Merrell Dow Pharmaceuticals, Inc., 509 U.S. 579 (1993) (evidence must be "sufficiently tied to the facts" to aid jury, aptly described as "fit"); Guillory v. Domtar Industries Inc., 95 F.3d 1320, 1330 (5th Cir. 1996) (excluding testimony by engineer and accident reconstruction expert based "on altered facts and speculation").

18. Cipollone v. Yale Industrial Products, Inc., 202 F.3d 376, 379 (1st Cir. 2000).

close enough to reality to make it useful, as often happens in the area of expert testimony on eyewitness identification.[19]

The third element in *Daubert* is not so much a requirement as a reference to other considerations affecting admissibility: Most importantly, the technicality and complexity of modern science and technological learning bring concerns that such proof may be more confusing, time-consuming, or misleading than it is worth. For such reasons, proof of this sort may be excluded under FRE 403 even if it would otherwise qualify, as *Daubert* makes clear and as the Rules mandate more generally.[20]

The amendment to FRE 702 adopted in 2000 did not "codify" *Daubert*, but was proffered "in response to" *Daubert*, by which the ACN seems to mean that the point was *not* to put the substance of the case into a rule. Instead, the amended language gives direct expression to critical ideas that were almost invisible before, but were part of the mandate that *Daubert* brought forward. Instead of looking only at relevancy, qualifications of the expert, and helpfulness of testimony, *Daubert* said the trial judge is to decide whether the evidence is "reliable" enough to be considered. In performing this function, *Daubert* did *not* want the judge to take either the word of the expert or the representations of the proponent as definitive.

The idea behind the amendment, and this same idea is central to *Daubert*—and indeed central to any notion of gatekeeping—was to put into words three categories of inquiry by which judges can perform the gatekeeping function. In effect amended FRE 702 states three broad conditions of admissibility by sketching out three broad areas of inquiry. As a result of the amendment, the responsibility of judges in this department is grounded in clear language in the Rule itself. The amendment requires inquiry to determine whether the expert (1) has "sufficient facts or data," (2) applied "reliable principles and methods," and (3) applied those principles and methods "reliably to the facts" of the case.

Although the amended language does not say it in so many words, it seems that all three of the new conditions are matters for the judge to determine, as the ACN to the amended provision suggests.[21] All three affect "admissibility" of evidence, and not merely weight. In effect, they

19. United States v. Langan, 263 F.3d 613, 620-625 (6th Cir. 2001) (excluding testimony on "transference theory" producing memory of previous exposure to innocent person in lineup, which did not "fit" because expert lacked knowledge about eyewitness).

20. Daubert v. Merrell Dow Pharmaceuticals, 509 U.S. 579 (1993) (FRE 403 gives courts more authority to control experts than lay witnesses); Nimely v. City of New York, 414 F.3d 381, 398 (2d Cir. 2005) (in police shooting suit, error to let forensic pathologist attest truthfulness of police accounts, which was prejudicial, confusing, misleading) (reversing).

21. See ACN (amended FRE 702 affirms "court's role as gatekeeper," providing standards to use in assessing "reliability and helpfulness," and admissibility of expert testimony is governed by FRE 104(a), under which proponent has burden of establishing that "pertinent reliability requirements are met").

raise "preliminary questions" relating to "the admissibility of evidence" under FRE 104(a).

(1) Sufficient data

The first condition is that there be sufficient facts or data underlying the proffered expert testimony. This standard reflects prior law, at least in the broad sense that courts always had the power to reject expert opinion testimony that lacked a sufficient factual basis. Courts could reject lay testimony that was "speculative," and could block lay opinions that were unhelpful or did not reflect personal knowledge. The addition of the sufficiency standard in FRE 702 is important in providing express and visible authority to courts to screen out expert testimony that is not adequately supported. This standard underscores the authority of courts to examine expert testimony in the manner contemplated in *Daubert*, and thus adds something important to the Rules.[22]

(2) Reliable methods

The second requirement added in the amendment speaks of "reliable principles and methods," and of course this notion lies at the heart of the *Daubert* standard. This addition to FRE 702 is the one most clearly tied to *Daubert*, and there has never been any doubt that the judge determines these matters, and that they are conditions that must be satisfied if scientific or technical evidence is offered. It is of course this condition that is addressed by the fifteen factors listed above, that come from *Daubert*, from *Downing*, and from the ACN to amended FRE 702, which in turn reflects decisions by many courts.[23]

(3) Reliable application

The question whether the expert has "applied the principles and methods reliably to the facts," now stated in clause (3) of the amended Rule, was essentially new, although the ACN suggests that the requirement was already to be found in the cases.[24]

Reading clause (3) like the other two clauses, as describing questions that the judge resolves under FRE 104(a) because they affect "admissibility," the language actually resolves a conflict in the cases. Prior cases held that the question whether a scientist or technician or expert properly applied the principles and methods was a matter that affected weight rather than admissibility. Under this rubric, some decisions held that issues surrounding laboratory protocol in conducting critical forensic tests were for juries to resolve, but others held that they affect admissibility (not just weight).[25]

---

22. Micro Chemical, Inc. v. Lextron, Inc., 317 F.3d 1387, 1392 (Fed. Cir. 2003) (damage expert had sufficient facts or data despite claim that he relied on statements by others and did not independently investigate feedlot industry or review records; need not evaluate correctness of underlying data).

23. United States v. Mooney, 315 F.3d 54, 62 (1st Cir. 2002) (*Daubert* does not require proponent to prove opinion is correct, only to show it was reached scientifically and follows reliable methods).

24. See ACN to amended FRE 702 (judge "must scrutinize not only the principles and methods," but whether principles and methods "have been properly applied to the facts") linking requirement to *Paoli Railroad* case. See In re Paoli R.R. Yard PCB Litigation, 35 F.3d 717, 745 (3d Cir. 1994).

25. *Compare* United States v. Shea, 211 F.3d 658, 668 (1st Cir. 2000) (flaws in application of methodology go to weight, not admissibility), *with* People v. Castro, 144 Misc. 2d 956, 545 N.Y.S.2d 985, 986 (1989) (committing such matters to judge, applying state version of *Frye* standard).

The amended language reflects the latter view: Under FRE 702(3), judges are to determine whether the principles and methods were reliably applied. Of course it does not follow that judges cannot admit evidence produced by processes and methods that depart from an ideal or standard protocol, nor that *only judges* can consider this matter. It seems, however, that under FRE 702(3) a judge should resolve the question whether the principles and methods were applied reliably enough to justify relying on the evidence.[26] If the judge believes the evidence is reliable and trustworthy (and the other conditions of FRE 702 and *Daubert* are satisfied), she should admit the evidence, but issues relating to application of principles and methods can still be raised at trial itself, and argued and supported or attacked by testimony or other evidence, in the interest of helping the jury weigh the evidence that the trial judge has ruled admissible.

Predictably, courts applying amended FRE 702 stress the breadth of judge's discretion. Still, some reviewing courts have found that the judge erred in applying the new Rule. Occasionally reviewing courts reverse decisions to admit because the requirements of *Daubert* and revised FRE 702 are not satisfied,[27] and sometimes decisions to exclude are reversed on appellate findings that the requirements of *Daubert* and revised FRE 702 are satisfied.[28]

As noted above, on the day *Daubert* was decided there were already questions as to its breadth, as Chief Justice Rehnquist commented in his dissent. *Daubert* itself involved evidence that clearly everyone would classify as "scientific" (reanalysis of epidemiological studies). The decision in *Daubert* is tied to the word "scientific" in FRE 702, and the opinion rests on this basic interpretive move. No doubt engineering and medicine and psychology, for example, rest on science at least in part, and perhaps they should be classified science, but they might also be termed "technical" knowledge, which term also appears in FRE 702. The other term in the Rule ("specialized knowledge") seems better

Daubert applies across the board

---

26. Amorgianos v. National R.R. Passenger Corp., 303 F.3d 256, 264 (2d Cir. 2002) (excluding testimony by industrial hygienist who "failed to apply his own method reliably" because he did not take into account volatility, vapor pressure, temperature, humidity, radiant energy). See also Edward J. Imwinkelried, The Debate in the DNA Cases Over the Foundation for the Admission of Scientific Evidence: The Importance of Human Error as a Cause of Forensic Misanalysis, 69 Wash. U. L. Q. 19 (1991) (matters of lab protocol should affect admissibility, not just weight).

27. Chapman v. Maytag Corp., 297 F.3d 682, 686 (7th Cir. 2002) (error to admit testimony by expert holding degree in mechanical engineering suggesting that failure of insulation in pinched wire let current escape from circuit into chassis without tripping circuit breaker; "resistive short" theory was unsupported by any "study or writing," and witness could not substantiate opinion) (reversing).

28. Sullivan v. U.S. Department of Navy, 365 F.3d 827, 833 (9th Cir. 2004) (in malpractice suit arising out of surgery in naval hospital, error to exclude plaintiff's expert testimony, which reflected generally accepted proposition that duration of surgery bears on likelihood of infection; court abused discretion and "invaded the province of the expert" in requiring underlying texts to state "precise type of harm" that testimony would explain) (reversing, remanding and directing that different judge preside).

than "science" as a description of expertise in such fields as economics, real estate appraisal, and operations of drug traffickers. Adding to the problem of interpreting the case, the criteria spelled out in *Daubert* seem at home with "hard" science, and less congenial to other areas of technical expertise.

Kumho Tire case   The Court addressed this problem in *Kumho Tire* in 1999. The case involved expert testimony that a tire on a minivan failed because it was defective, and the expert announced criteria that he used to decide whether the failure resulted from a defect in design or manufacture, or from improper maintenance. The court excluded this testimony, but the Eleventh Circuit thought *Daubert* did not apply, and reversed. The Supreme Court agreed with the trial judge, and held that *Daubert* applies to all expert testimony, across the board.[29] *Kumho Tire* presented the Court with stark choices, each having its own strengths and drawbacks: One possibility was to limit *Daubert* to a subclass of expert testimony that is "scientific," which would fit the factors that *Daubert* set forth to guide courts in appraising the reliability or validity of testimony, but would also bring the problem of drawing a line between scientific expertise and other kinds, and might require other standards for other branches of expertise. Another possibility was to loosen *Daubert* so it could be applied to evidence as disparate as epidemiology and accounting, at the risk of making the standard vague or general, detracting from any sense of rigor.

Kumho Tire took the second course. To bring home the breadth of *Daubert*, *Kumho Tire* cited the example of a "perfume tester" in making the point that "experience-based" expertise must be examined for reliability. The court commented that a person who can "distinguish among 140 odors at a sniff" may be required at least to show that his preparation is "of a kind that others in the field would recognize as acceptable." After *Kumho Tire*, clearly trial judges have "gatekeeping" responsibilities whenever expert testimony is offered.[30] It is worth noting that a number of states, including some that have adopted the *Daubert* standard, have not followed the lead of *Kumho Tire*, instead imposing the reliability standard only on "scientific" evidence (sometimes only to "novel" science), and not to experiential expertise.[31]

---

29. Kumho Tire Co. v. Carmichael, 526 U.S. 137, 142, 152 (1999) (twice making point that judges have discretion in both choosing among and applying *Daubert* factors).

30. United States v. Lopez-Lopez, 282 F.3d 1, 13-14 (1st Cir. 2002) (applying *Daubert* in admitting testimony by Customs Agent about operations of international drug traffickers), *cert. denied*, 122 S.Ct. 2642; United States v. Langan, 263 F.3d 613, 620-625 (6th Cir. 2001) (*Daubert* applies to expert testimony on accuracy of eyewitness identification).

31. State v. White, 642 S.E.2d 607 (S.C. 2007) (dog handler's evidence based on experience need not satisfy *Daubert* standard because it is not scientific knowledge); Marron v. Stromstad, 123 P.3d 992, 1006 (Alaska 2005) (expert testimony based on "specialized knowledge," experience and intuition, "is not empirically verifiable or objectively testable," and *Daubert* "is useless as a criterion" here) (drawing on work of Professor Stephen Saltzburg).

In *Kumho Tire*, the Court addressed the problem of applying this same standard broadly to experiential expertise by stressing the "flexibility" of the standard and the "discretion" of trial judge. The opinion in *Daubert* had not spoken of discretion, but the *Joiner* decision in 1997 had mentioned discretion in applying *Daubert* not less than 19 times, the Court having been pushed in that direction because *Joiner* involved a review of a peculiar ruling by the Eleventh Circuit that judges were to be reviewed in a more rigorous way if they *excluded* expert testimony under *Daubert*. In effect, the Court in *Joiner* adopted a discretionary rule as a way of rejecting the notion that *Daubert* should be understood as strongly favoring admissibility of expert testimony.[32] *Kumho Tire* used the same term later in the same year at least seven times. The Court wrote in *Kumho Tire* that the *Daubert* factors "do not all necessarily apply" in every case (even if the expertise involves "science" as such), and that *Daubert* is above all a "flexible" standard. Hence a court applying *Daubert* has "broad latitude" not only in deciding whether proffered evidence is reliable, but also in deciding "how to determine reliability."[33]

Writing in 1994 prior to the decision in *Kumho Tire*, the Sixth Circuit cited a good example illustrating the difference between scientific and experience-based expertise in the *Berry* case:

> [I]f one wanted to explain to a jury how a bumblebee is able to fly, an aeronautical engineer might be a helpful witness. Since flight principles have some universality, the expert could apply general principles to the case of the bumblebee. Conceivably, even if he had never seen a bumblebee, he still would be qualified to testify, as long as he was familiar with its component parts.
>
> On the other hand, if one wanted to prove that bumblebees always take off into the wind, a beekeeper with no scientific training at all would be an acceptable expert witness if a proper foundation were laid for his conclusions. The foundation would not relate to his formal training, but to his firsthand observations. In other words, the beekeeper does not know any more about flight principles than the jurors, but he has seen a lot more bumblebees than they have.[34]

A later opinion in Illinois suggested that the hypothetical beekeeper mentioned in *Berry* could testify on the basis of years of experience "that bees always take off into the wind" and that if particular bees "take off heading due west," then one can be sure that "the wind is blowing from the west," and the beekeeper may give those opinions because they rest on "generalized knowledge of bees" coupled with "firsthand

---

32. General Electric Co. v. Joiner, 522 U.S. 136 (1997) (rejecting view that decisions excluding expert testimony are reviewed by a more stringent standard than decisions admitting; in both situations, abuse-of-discretion standard applies).

33. Kumho Tire Co. v. Carmichael, 526 U.S. 137, 142, 152 (1999) (saying twice that judges have discretion in both choosing among and in applying *Daubert* factors).

34. Berry v. City of Detroit, 25 F.3d 1342, 1349-1350 (6th Cir. 1994).

observations," and they help explain his "deductive process" in reaching his conclusions.[35]

Under *Kumho Tire*, a witness who comes to court to give experience-based expert testimony or specialized knowledge must be able to say more than that his opinion rests on his particular experiences in some line of endeavor.[36] He must provide information about the nature of that experience and show how he brought it to bear on the matter at hand. The expert must describe some method of analysis that explains the conclusion he proposes to present, providing some comparable data that can act as a basis for reaching that conclusion.[37] While *Kumho Tire* said courts have discretion *both* in selecting criteria by which to judge the reliability of proffered expertise *and* in deciding whether the criteria are satisfied, *Kumho Tire* clearly did *not* mean that courts can ignore or decide against applying whatever criteria might shed light on reliability. *Kumho Tire* does not mean that courts should give such testimony a free pass. In the words of the 2000 ACN, a witness testifying on the basis of experience "must explain how that experience leads to the conclusion" and "why that experience is a sufficient basis" and "how that experience is reliably applied" to the facts of the case.[38]

On the other hand, *Kumho Tire* did not disapprove experience-based expertise. Witness qualifying as experts on the basis of experience or specialized knowledge need not support their opinions with data that achieves mathematical precision derived from controlled studies, nor with reference to studies or theories developed by others and recognized widely within some recognized field. As the ACN to the amended Rule points out, the amendment does *not* mean that "experience alone—or experience in conjunction with other knowledge, skill, training or education—may not provide a sufficient basis" for expert testimony, and of course the text of amended FRE 702 *continues* to say expert testimony may rest on experience.

Procedure: Often issues relating to the admissibility of scientific or technical
Pretrial Rulings evidence are complicated. Their resolution may require briefs,

---

35. Harris v. Cropmate Co., 706 N.E.2d 55, 60 (Ill. App. 1999). But see Donaldson v. Central Ill. Public Service Co., 767 N.E.2d 314 (Ill. 2002) (disapproving *Harris* as imposing the wrong standard).

36. Mack Trucks, Inc. v. Tamez, 206 S.W.2d 572, 580 (Tex. 2006) (excluding testimony by expert in ignition-caused fuel fires because he "did no more than set out 'factors' and 'facts' which were consistent with his opinion," then suggested that fire began with diesel fuel from tractor; reliability inquiry does not ask whether conclusion is correct, but whether method is reliable); Hoy v. DRM, Inc., 114 P.3d 1268 (Wyo. 2005) (excluding testimony by experts who could not "rule out other causes" for leach field failure, apart from acts by defendant contractor; they "never explained exactly how their experience and knowledge or the texts supported their opinions").

37. United States v. Jones, 107 F.3d 1147, 1160 (6th Cir. 1997) (admitting expert testimony on handwriting; witness "outlined the procedure that he uses" in comparing questioned signature with known one, "then focused on enlargements" and described "in some detail" how he reached his conclusions, so his testimony "enabled the jury to observe firsthand the parts of the various signatures on which he focused").

38. *See* ACN to FRE 702.

affidavits, even live testimony or deposition transcripts. Neither *Daubert* nor *Kumho Tire* mandates any particular form of hearing, nor do they address the question whether the jury should or must be excused when a hearing is held.

Pretty clearly these matters should be taken up in separate hearing, and such hearings should be conducted before trial.[39] Here the court takes testimony and other evidence needed to decide whether the proffered expertise is valid and reliable, considering such things as error rates, acceptance in the relevant community, existence of standards and peer reviewed literature, how closely the testimony fits the case, and whether theory and methods were properly applied.[40]

The burden of satisfying *Daubert* and FRE 702 rests on the proponent, just as it is generally true that the proponent of evidence must show that it is relevant and admissible under whatever Rules of Evidence apply.[41] It follows that ordinarily the proponent of expert testimony should make the pretrial motion, but no rule actually requires a motion. The matter can be brought to the fore by a motion in limine to exclude evidence that the opponent anticipates, which is in effect an advance objection, or by a motion in limine to admit the evidence, which is simply an advance proffer.[42]

Sometimes the matter is not raised by preliminary motion, but arises at trial. The issues are likely to be technical, and often any hearing is

39. Daubert v. Merrell Dow Pharmaceuticals, Inc., 509 U.S. 579 (1993) (court "must determine at the outset" whether science is valid); Clemons v. State, 896 A.2d 1059, 1063 n.6 (Md. 2006) (preferable to rule on admissibility prior to trial; issues are usually "collateral"); In re Air Crash at Little Rock Arkansas, 291 F.3d 503, 514 (8th Cir. 2002) (*Daubert* issues should be "raised prior to trial" and hearing should not be conducted during morning recess in middle of trial; on remand, *Daubert* hearing should be conducted before trial); Alfred v. Caterpillar, Inc., 262 F.3d 1083, 1086 (10th Cir. 2001) (*Daubert* issues should not be deferred to late stage where there has been no motion or concurrent objection; counsel should not sandbag opposing party; *Daubert* contemplates gatekeeping function, not "gotcha" function); Jahn v. Equine Services, PSC, 233 F.3d 382, 393 (6th Cir. 2000) (error to exclude plaintiff's experts in summary judgment motion without hearing, on record that was "insufficient," for *Daubert* requires record that is "complete enough" to asses reliability).

40. United States v. Yousef, 327 F.3d 56, 148 (2d Cir. 2003) (require defense to produce expert for *Daubert* hearing, on pain of excluding testimony if he was not produced); In re Paoli R.R. Yard PCB Litigation, 35 F.3d 717, 738 (3d Cir. 1994) (can authorize opponent to conduct discovery of experts who to testify in hearing; each side to depose other side's experts to critique methodologies); DeLuca by DeLuca v. Merrell Dow Pharmaceuticals, Inc., 911 F.2d 941, 954 (3d Cir. 1990) (to extent that mode of analysis deviates from well-established methods, court must "conduct a hearing and analysis").

41. Zenith Electronics Corp. v. WH-TV Broadcasting Corp., 395 F.3d 416, 419 (7th Cir. 2005) (proponent bears burden of production in showing that *Daubert* standard is satisfied), *cert. denied*, 545 U.S. 1140; United States v. Hicks, 389 F.3d 514, 525 (5th Cir. 2004) (proponent has burden of showing that expert testimony it is reliable under *Daubert*), *cert. denied*, 546 U.S. 1089.

42. Hose v. Chicago Northwestern Transp. Co., 70 F.3d 968, 972 (8th Cir. 1995) (challenges to scientific validity should be addressed prior to trial) (faulting defendant for failing to make pretrial motion to exclude medical testimony based on PET scan and polysomnogram).

lengthy and the substance of the testimony is likely to be beyond the understanding of jurors and of little human interest to a lay audience. Hence it is wiser to excuse the jury. The only clear consideration that cuts in favor of letting the jury observe and listen is that factors affecting admissibility may also affect weight, and letting the jury hear foundation testimony may provide a head start. This consideration does not seem reason enough, however, to subject jurors to these hearings. Their presence is likely to encourage posturing by the witnesses and by the lawyers, and may become problematic because the Rules do not apply to admissibility hearings, and at least some of what is offered in this setting should not be heard by the jury. There is also some risk that allowing a jury to hear the preliminary skirmishes over the validity of the science will lead trial courts to abandon their gatekeeping responsibilities and simply to pass along to the jury the issues presented, which plainly is the wrong approach under *Daubert* and FRE 702 as amended.[43]

Often there is no way to avoid a hearing if the issue is joined, whether by pretrial motion to admit that is met by objection, or by pretrial motion to exclude that is met by a proffer, or in some other way.[44] It may be possible to save time if it turns out that there is some point that is decisive, in which case it is not necessary to range over the whole subject, and the court can decide whether testimony is reliable without considering other factors.[45] In this setting as in others, detailed findings can help explain and make transparent whatever decision on admitting or excluding is ultimately reached, facilitating later review by showing how the judge approached the problem and what factors were behind the decision. Reviewing courts almost never require detailed findings in evidentiary rulings, however, and satisfy themselves on the basis of general indications that trial judge did or did not consider the appropriate criteria. Modern authority includes an important opinion by the late Judge Becker, long a leader in this area, that rejects any requirement that the judge make detailed findings.[46]

43. But see United States v. Mendoza-Paz, 286 F.3d 1104, 1113 (9th Cir. 2002) (rejecting claim that judge should have held *Daubert* hearing outside jury's presence) (expert testimony on value of drugs).

44. United States v. Velarde, 214 F.3d 1204 (10th Cir. 2000) (court did not determine whether *Daubert* was satisfied with expert testimony that victim suffered abuse; court assumed proffered testimony was so "ordinary" that reliability determination was unnecessary, but gave no indication why, or why methods could be taken for granted; reliability determination must be "apparent from the record" and court abused discretion in failing to make it; also error in not holding reliability hearing for testimony by second expert that victim's behavior was consistent with abuse; defense asked for hearings) (reversing).

45. United States v. Cruz, 127 F.3d 791, 800-801 (9th Cir. 1997) (need not require testimony on all *Daubert* factors; these were not intended as definitive checklist but as guide), *cert. denied*, 522 U.S. 1097.

46. United States v. Mitchell, 365 F.3d 215, 233 (3d Cir. 2004) (judge ruled from bench and "elected not to make findings of fact or conclusions of law," but absence of findings does not require plenary review; rulings are reviewed for abuse of discretion), *cert. denied*, 543 U.S. 974.

Often, and indeed perhaps more often than not, it is not necessary to hold a *Daubert* hearing. The pivotal issue presented by proffered expert testimony may already have been resolved in cases that are definitive on the point, or factual issues may have been resolved in other cases in a manner that invites judicial notice. Thus, for example, lie detector evidence is still almost always excluded from trials, and courts generally know (and many cases hold) that such proof does not satisfy either the *Daubert* or the earlier *Frye* standard, and courts may exclude such proof without inquiring anew each time into issues of validity or reliability. This particular shortcut to decision can be explained in terms of *stare decisis* or authoritative precedent, or sometimes in terms of judicial notice (a kind of judicial notice that is not regulated by FRE 201 because it does not involve "adjudicative" facts). In these ways, other cases may provide adequate ground either to resolve issues under *Daubert* and FRE 702 in favor of admissibility,[47] or to resolve them against admitting the proof.[48]

Sometimes other alternatives to a full-fledged hearing are available. The points necessary to decide the issues can sometimes be developed adequately in briefs, or by arguments of counsel, sometimes augmented by affidavits, so that a more elaborate hearing inviting testimony and other proof becomes unnecessary, and courts can rule in more summary fashion on the basis of such material.[49] Sometimes issues of validity or reliability are sufficiently familiar, and the foundational inquiries are simple enough, that a court can avoid a pretrial hearing, as is often true when the validity question turns mostly on the experience of the witness and his degree of familiarity with the relevant facts.[50] Sometimes appropriate findings rest almost entirely on the fact that

Procedure: Scope of review

---

47. United States v. Crisp, 324 F.3d 261, 268 (4th Cir. 2003) ("need not expend scarce judicial resources re-examining" familiar expertise; if theory or technique is firmly established as scientific law, "it need not be examined at all" and may be judicially noticed); United States v. Jokobetz, 955 F.2d 786, 793-794 (2d Cir. 1992) (may take judicial notice of general acceptability of theory and technique), *cert. denied*, 506 U.S. 834; Johnson v. Commonwealth, 12 S.W.3d 258, 261 (Ky. 1999) (courts admit or exclude much evidence without "reinventing the wheel" by requiring "full demonstrations" of validity of methods or techniques that have been scrutinized before; such inquiry not required for comparisons of microscopic samples of human hair) (quoting authors of this Treatise); State v. O'Key, 321 Or. 285, 899 P.2d 663, 673 n.8 (1995) (sometimes validity may be determined by judicial notice) (citing authors of this Treatise).

48. United States v. Prince-Oyibo, 320 F.3d 494, 498 (4th Cir. 2003) (retaining *per se* rule against lie detector evidence).

49. Miller v. Baker Implement Co., 439 F.3d 407, 412 (8th Cir. 2006) (excluding plaintiff's experts without hearing; plaintiff had enough chance to present arguments during motion); United States v. Alatorre, 222 F.3d 1098, 1100 (9th Cir. 2000) (nowhere do *Daubert* or *Kumho Tire* address form or nature of inquiry; hearing outside presence of jury not required; on voir dire, defense could explore qualifications and basis for testimony).

50. United States v. Robertson, 387 F.3d 702, 704 n.2 (8th Cir. 2004) (admitting testimony on modus operandi of drug dealers; *Daubert* hearing is not always required before qualifying expert); United States v. Nichols, 169 F.3d 1255, 1263 (10th Cir. 1999) (declining to hold *Daubert* hearing on testimony by bomb expert; evidence involved no new theory or novel testing methodologies), *cert. denied*, 120 S.Ct. 336.

the proffered evidence has achieved a level of general acceptance that alone suffices to establish reliability,[51] or even unreliability.[52] Sometimes *Daubert* issues can be resolved by consulting journals or treatises, and the experience of regulatory agencies is a pertinent factor to count in appraising official studies, and may suffice as a basis to conclude that the underlying science is valid.[53]

The latitude and discretion accorded to trial judges in applying *Daubert* indicate that the "abuse-of-discretion" standard applies in appellate review of rulings admitting or excluding expert testimony. In its 1997 decision in *Joiner*, the Court affirmed that decisions applying *Daubert* are reviewed under this standard, rejecting an argument that a ruling excluding scientific evidence should satisfy a more stringent standard.[54] It is hard to imagine any debate on this point when it comes to the requirement of "fit" and risks under Rule 403.

Impact of *Daubert* It far less clear, however, that such deference is appropriate for more "substantive" *Daubert* factors relating to validity and reliability, particularly when they obviously transcend considerations peculiar to the case at hand. To be sure, the generality of the *Daubert* factors, and the "flexibility" that trial judges enjoy in selecting and applying them, favor a lenient standard of review. Still, *Daubert* issues lend themselves well to appellate briefing, particularly when reinforced by affidavits or testimony from hearings at the trial level, and appellate courts can reach judgments on issues of reliability that are as good as or better than the ones trial judges can make. Where the issues apply across a wide range of cases, uniformity becomes a higher value, and often credibility issues recede in importance.[55] A casual look at the thousands of appellate opinions raising *Daubert* issues conveys the message that trial judges need help. Questions relating to the validity or reliability of such things as laboratory and statistical methods for gathering and analyzing DNA evidence are more like questions of law than questions of fact. For all these reasons, appellate courts do not always apply a lenient standard on review, nor should they. While many state decisions endorse an abuse-of-discretion standard, a significant minority apply a *de novo* standard to many issues of reliability under *Daubert* or its state equivalent.[56]

51. Daubert v. Merrell Dow Pharmaceuticals, 509 U.S. 579 (1993) (widespread acceptance can be "important factor").

52. United States v. Downing, 753 F.2d 1224, 1237-1242 (3d Cir. 1985) (acceptance "may well be decisive, or nearly so," and known technique that attracts "minimal support" is likely to be unreliable).

53. Ellis v. International Playtex, Inc., 745 F.2d 292, 303-304 (4th Cir. 1984) (government studies are "presumed to reflect methodologies accepted by the scientific community").

54. General Elec. Co. v. Joiner, 520 U.S. 114 (1997) (abuse-of-discretion standard applies to review of rulings applying the *Daubert* standard).

55. *See* Christopher B. Mueller, *Daubert* Asks The Right Questions: Now Appellate Courts Should Help Find the Right Answers, 33 Seton Hall L. Rev. 987 (2003) (developing arguments sketched above); David L. Faigman, Appellate Review of Scientific Evidence Under *Daubert* and *Joiner*, 48 Hastings L. J. 969, 977 (1997) (advocating "hard look" or *de novo* standard for scientific issues).

56. Jennings v. Baxter Healthcare Corp., 14 P.3d 596 (Or. 2000) (decision on scientific validity is reviewed as for "errors of law"); Goeb v. Tharaldson, 615 N.W.2d 800,

Few cases are as influential as *Daubert*. Its impact is roughly indicated by the fact that it was cited in more than three thousand five hundred appellate opinions across the country in the first fifteen years. *Daubert* represented a new departure for federal law, and it applies in federal courts throughout the land. Although not binding in state systems, the opinion has proved influential there as well. A search of reported opinions reveals that 27 states have adopted the *Daubert* standard or take very similar approaches, and that 22 states decline to follow *Daubert* (most following their own versions of the *Frye* standard).[57] Even among the states declining to follow *Daubert*, however, some opinions indicate that the *Daubert* reliability factors count in deciding whether to admit or exclude scientific evidence.

It is hard to say whether *Daubert* tightened or loosened the standard for scientific evidence, but we believe on balance that *Daubert* tightened the standard. *Daubert* came amidst increasing concern over "junk science," and on remand the lower court again excluded the evidence (on a slightly different ground). Also the *Daubert* criteria are more elaborate and specific than the single factor emphasized in *Frye*, inviting closer scrutiny.[58]

814-815 (Minn. 2000) (whether proffered expertise satisfies general acceptance standard "is a question of law that we review de novo," but questions of "foundational reliability" are reviewed for abuse of discretion); Kuhn v. Sandos Pharmaceuticals Corp., 14 P.3d 1170, 1179 (Kan. 2000) (adopting *de novo* standard for review of proof of medical causation); Haddad v. State, 690 S.2d 753, 578 (Fla. 1997) (review of *Frye* issues is *de novo*); Taylor v. State, 889 P.2d 319, 331 (Okla. 1995) (decision to admit novel scientific evidence should be subject to "an independent, thorough review"); State v. Harvey, 699 A.2d 596, 619 (N.J. 1995) (question whether scientific community generally accepts method or test "can transcend a particular dispute," and to extent *Frye* focuses on issues other than credibility or qualifications, "deference to the trial court is less appropriate"); State v. Tankersley, 956 P.2d 486, 464 (Ariz. 1994) (*Frye* issues are subject to *de novo* review); Schultz v. State, 664 A.2d 60, 64 (Md. App. 1994) (question of reliability "does not vary according to the circumstances of each case," so it is inappropriate to review for abuse of discretion); State v. Cauthron, 846 P.2d 502, 505 (Wash. 1993) (court reviews *de novo* a decision to admit or exclude novel scientific evidence); United States v. Porter, 618 A.3d 629, 634 (D.C. Ct. App. 1992) (questions of general acceptance of new scientific techniques invite court "to establish the law of the jurisdiction for future cases," so court would "engage in a broad review").

57. Decisions in 27 states adopt *Daubert* or cite it while taking a similar approach: Alabama, Alaska, Arkansas, Colorado, Connecticut, Delaware, Hawaii, Kentucky, Louisiana, Massachusetts, Michigan (statute covering suits for injury or death), Montana, Nebraska, New Hampshire, New Jersey, New Mexico, North Carolina, Ohio, Oklahoma, Oregon, Rhode Island, South Dakota, Tennessee, Texas, Vermont, West Virginia, and Wyoming. Decisions in 22 other states refrain from following *Daubert*. Among these, most follow something close to *Frye*, but some have abandon *Frye* and still decline to follow *Daubert*: Arizona, California, Florida, Georgia, Idaho, Illinois, Indiana, Iowa, Kansas, Maryland, Maine, Minnesota, Missouri, Mississippi, Nevada, New York, North Dakota, Pennsylvania, South Carolina, Utah, and Washington, and Wisconsin. One state (Virginia) has not decided the issue.

58. *See* Hanson, Fewer post-*Daubert* federal judges allow experts to testify without limitation in civil trials, study finds, 87 A.B.A. J. 28 (2001). *See generally* Huber, Junk Science in the Courtroom, 26 Val. U. L. Rev. 723 (1992); Huber, Galileo's Revenge: Junk Science in the Courtroom (1991). *And see* Daubert v. Merrell Dow Pharmaceuticals, 43 F.3d 1311, 1318-1319 (9th Cir. 1994) (on remand, again excluding the evidence), *cert.*

2. *What Experts May Rely On*

FRE 703

The facts or data in the particular case upon which an expert bases an opinion or inference may be those perceived by or made known to the expert at or before the hearing. If of a type reasonably relied upon by experts in the particular field in forming opinions or inferences upon the subject, the facts or data need not be admissible in evidence in order for the opinion or inference to be admitted. Facts or data that are otherwise inadmissible shall not be disclosed to the jury by the proponent of the opinion or inference unless the court determines that their probative value in assisting the jury to evaluate the expert's opinion substantially outweighs their prejudicial effect.

---

§7.8 Facts Perceived Before Trial—Firsthand Study

Under FRE 703, expert testimony may rest on any of three grounds, including facts or data learned by firsthand observation or study before trial, facts or data learned at trial, and facts or data acquired "secondhand" by reading or talking to others, provided that other experts in the field would rely on such information and that such reliance is reasonable. The first of these three bases is considered here; the other two are taken up in ensuing sections.

Paraphrasing the language of FRE 703, an expert may rely on "facts or data perceived or made known to the expert before the hearing." Essentially this phrase means firsthand observation that would satisfy the personal knowledge standard that FRE 602 sets up for lay witnesses. A treating or examining doctor has such knowledge, as does a fire marshal who inspects a burned building or an accident reconstruction expert who examines the scene and the wreckage. Probably most testifying experts have at least some such knowledge, if only because firsthand information may be critical even if much more is required to formulate a useful opinion, and because an expert who testifies without such knowledge would be a less convincing witness.[1] Usually, however, experts with firsthand knowledge also have secondhand or indirect information in the form of statements, reports, or test results

---

denied, 516 U.S. 869. *See also* Ambrosini v. Labarraque, 966 F.2d 1464, 1467-1470 (D.C. Cir. 1992); Richardson v. Richardson-Merrell, Inc., 857 F.2d 823 (D.C. Cir. 1988), *cert. denied*, 493 U.S. 882 (both indicating skeptical attitude and advocating close scrutiny).

§7.8 1. *See* ACN to FRE 703 (treating physician is expert with firsthand knowledge); Simmons v. Chicago & Northwestern Transp. Co., 993 F.2d 1326, 1327-1328 (8th Cir. 1993) (testimony by patrolman who examined accident scene); United States v. Hill, 655 F.2d 512, 516 (3d Cir. 1981) (testimony by psychologist resting partly on observation); Elgi Holding, Inc. v. Insurance Co. of North America, 511 F.2d 957, 959-960 (2d Cir. 1975) (testimony by fire analyst based partly on inspection of premises).

from others. And many experts have knowledge that is both personal and indirect that comes from inspecting or examining persons or objects or places that share common characteristics with the persons, objects, or places in suit.

§7.9 Facts Learned at Trial—Observing Testimony, Hypothetical Questions

Experts may testify not only on the basis of firsthand knowledge, but on the basis of facts or data made known to them at trial. Paraphrasing FRE 703, an expert may testify on the basis of "facts or data perceived by the expert at the hearing."[1]

Usually experts learn facts or data at trial by watching the proceedings and listening to other witnesses or by hypothetical questions that summarize other testimony. Actually both these approaches involve hypothetical questions: In the first instance, typically the questioner asks the expert whether he has heard the prior testimony, then asks the expert to assume the truth of that testimony (itself a hypothesis) and seeks his opinion. In the second instance, the questioner sums up facts supported by other testimony or evidence and asks the expert to assume the truth of those facts, then seeks his opinion.

Both these approaches remain proper under the Rules. But the mechanism of hypothetical questions is disliked in many quarters and often roundly criticized for reasons taken up below. The Rules reduced the need for hypothetical questions by letting experts testify on the basis of what they learn outside of court by talking to others (subject to a reasonable reliance standard) and by letting them give their opinions first, leaving the bases to be explored on cross as FRE 705 provides. Still, hypothetical questions remain a viable option for presenting expert testimony.[2]

When the expert has watched the proceedings and listened to testimony, hypothetical questions asking the witness to assume the truth of prior testimony may be confusing. The factfinder may have trouble recalling the testimony, and if the trial has been long or the evidence is complicated or convoluted, the questioner may be asked to recite the facts he means to call to the attention of the expert.[3] Where a summary

Assume truth of testimony

---

§7.9 1. Hill v. Reederei F. Laeisz G.M.B.H., Rostock, 435 F.3d 404, 423 (3d Cir. 2006) (relying on trial testimony, expert testifies that it was impossible for lashing rod securing cargo on ships to spring free without being loosened), *cert. denied*, 549 U.S. 820. Air Disaster at Lockerbie, Scotland, 37 F.3d 804, 826 (2d Cir. 1994) (relying on testimony by others, experts say plane was under commercial, not security, priority), *cert. denied*, 513 U.S. 1126.

2. *See* United States v. Hughes, 895 F.2d 1135, 1145 n.14 (6th Cir. 1990); 2 Wigmore, Evidence §686 (3d ed. 1940) (hypothetical question should be optional).

3. Twin City Plaza, Inc. v. Central Surety & Ins. Co., 409 F.2d 1195, 1200 n1 (8th Cir. 1969) (should not ask witness to assume all evidence in exhibits to be true or assume the testimony of other witnesses).

reference is compact, concise, and understandable, a question simply referring to other testimony seems proper.[4]

Assume certain facts

When the expert has not watched and listened, the hypothetical question asks him to assume facts that the questioner spells out. Such questions are proper if there is enough evidence to support a finding that the necessary facts exist, and the facts themselves suffice to support the opinion that the questioner seeks.[5] But unsupported factual hypotheses should be stricken, and the question itself must be disallowed if critical elements drop away.[6] In the setting of many expert opinions, stating literally all the necessary facts, or even all the facts and assumptions that an informed expert would consider in light of the evidence offered at trial, would be cumbersome and perhaps impossible, and hypothetical questions should be allowed even if they are not exhaustive. The important facts must be stated, and there must be enough to enable an expert to give an opinion that he considers responsible in his professional judgment, but questions that satisfy these criteria are sufficient.[7] Pre-Rules tradition sometimes disapproved hypothetical questions inviting an expert to base his opinion on the opinion of others, but this tradition does not comport with FRE 703. An expert may rest his opinion in part on the opinions of others so long as the basis is sufficient and reliance is reasonable.

Even a hypothetical question that embodies enough data to support the opinion being sought may be objectionable under FRE 403 and 611 if it is misleading or too hard to follow, and the court has discretion to reject a question on these grounds.[8]

Hypothetical questions are criticized on essentially two grounds:

Awkward means

First, they are an awkward means to get at the truth because they tend to be long, complicated, and hard for everyone to understand.

---

4. State v. Feliciano, 901 A.2d 631, 643-644 (R.I. 2006) (can present expert testimony by hypothetical questions; must embrace all essential elements as they appear in evidence); People v. Gonzalez, 135 P.3d 649, 657 (Cal. 2006) (expert may testify on basis of hypothetical questions).

5. In re Corryn B, 914 A.2d 978 (R.I. 2007) (expert could rely on hypothetical question even if it did not include entire body of testimony); Carver v. Foster, 928 So. 2d 1017, 1025 (Ala. 2005) (proof of assumptions underlying hypothetical question is essential); Thomas v. Commonwealth, 170 S.W.3d 343, 351 (Ky. 2005) (error to put to toxicologist hypothetical questions that assumed a history of alcohol abuse, which was not supported by evidence) (reversing).

6. Norland v. Washington Gen. Hosp., 461 F.2d 694, 698 (8th Cir. 1972) (reversing because question referred to deposition not introduced); J. Gerber & Co. v. S. S. Sabine Howaldt, 437 F.2d 580, 593-594 (2d Cir. 1971) (questions misstating facts and stating facts not in evidence were unfair) (reversing).

7. Iconco v. Jensen Constr. Co., 622 F.2d 1291, 1301 (8th Cir. 1980) (hypothetical question need assume only basic facts, but should not omit material facts essential to reasonable conclusion); Mears v. Olin, 527 F.2d 1100, 1104 (8th Cir. 1975) (hypothetical questions "assumed all material facts necessary"). *See also* McElhaney, Expert Witnesses and the Federal Rules of Evidence, 28 Mercer L. Rev. 463, 488 (1977) (FRE 705 relaxes detail required in hypothetical questions).

8. Alman Bros. Farms & Feed Mill, Inc. v. Diamond Lab., Inc., 437 F.2d 1295, 1299 (5th Cir. 1971) (court has discretion to limit form and length of hypothetical questions).

Objections to the adequacy of the question muddy the water still further, and objections are so commonplace that courts routinely ask experts to wait before answering, in order to give other parties a chance to state any objections to the question itself. Eventually the conclusion of the witness comes through, but its basis and limits remain obscure, and the opinion may seem anticlimactic because most of what the jury actually hears is lawyers talking.

Second, such questions often have a distorting effect.[9] They tend to stifle detailed or nuanced or qualified responses, and they present assumed facts favorable only to the questioner, while omitting others that may be important and glossing over doubt on the strength of the evidence supporting the various facts. It seems that the expert may properly decline to state an opinion when he believes the basis provided in a question is inadequate.[10]

Distorting effect

§7.10   Secondhand Information—Reasonable Reliance Standard

The second sentence of FRE 703 says expert testimony may rest on facts or data learned before trial regardless whether admissible in evidence, so long as reasonable experts in the field would rely on such material. This reasonable reliance standard points toward broad admissibility of expert testimony, and is an important innovation (pre-Rules practice being far less generous on this score).

The reform accomplished by FRE 703 has two important practical effects: First, it reduces the need for firsthand knowledge on the part of experts.[1] Most experts have at least some such knowledge (the more knowledgeable, the more convincing), but gaps and even complete lack of firsthand knowledge are no longer the barriers they once were. Second, the fact that an expert may testify without firsthand knowledge, when coupled with the principle that usually the basis need not be set out before opinion testimony is given,[2] substantially reduces the need for hypothetical questions, a cumbersome mechanism that is subject to mishandling, abuse, confusion, and the active dislike of experts themselves.

---

9. *See* Diamond & Louisell, The Psychiatrist as an Expert Witness: Some Ruminations and Speculations, 63 Mich. L. Rev. 1335, 1346-1347 (1965) (if inferences depends on considering everything, including psychiatrist's personal and subjective interaction with patient, hypothetical question is dubious).

10. Kaufman v. Edelstein, 539 F.2d 811, 821 (2d Cir. 1976) (expert asked opinion on basis of facts on which he lacks knowledge may decline to answer if question "does not give all the facts required for a full and fair answer").

§7.10   1. Peteet v. Dow Chem. Co., 868 F.2d 1428, 1432 (5th Cir. 1989) (doctor certified in toxicology testified that dioxin caused Hodgkin's disease; objection that he never examined decedent "fails to hit its mark" because FRE 703 reduces need for firsthand knowledge), *cert. denied*, 493 U.S. 935.

2. *See* discussion of FRE 705 in §§7.15-7.16, *infra*.

Adequate?
Right kind?

The focal points of the reasonable reliance standard are the quality and sufficiency of outside information and the manner and reasons for its use. The language of FRE 703 suggests a dual inquiry: Is the underlying information adequate, and is it the kind that similar experts rely on? As a practical matter, the question of adequacy is the harder of the two and gets more attention, but it does matter whether similar experts rely on such information.[3] The judge resolves these issues under FRE 104(a),[4] subject to appellate scrutiny for clear error or perhaps only abuse of discretion.

As framed in FRE 703, the dual standard carries some internal tension since it refers to both adequacy and the practice of experts, and in theory they might rest opinions on inadequate bases. Not surprisingly, some decisions emphasize that courts must decide independently whether the underlying information satisfies the reasonable reliance standard,[5] while others suggest that courts play a deferential role in deciding only whether experts in the field rely on such information.[6]

Judicial decision

Despite the latter decisions, it is inconceivable that courts should defer completely to experts, and it seems clear that courts themselves should appraise the basis of expert testimony. Of course courts should give some weight to testifying experts and the collective judgment of others in the field, and it seems that the degree of deference that is appropriate varies by subject matter and underlying basis. Closer judicial scrutiny is appropriate, for example, where adequacy relates to the credibility of human sources who report conventional factual information.[7] Here the point is not so much that experts can rely only on hearsay that would fit an exception (which FRE 703 clearly does not require), nor even that experts like highway patrol officers and fire marshals are not good at appraising the credibility of human sources. The experience of such people, when coupled with their skill in appraising physical evidence and other factors relating to the problem at hand, probably does help them sort out reliable from unreliable

---

3. Soden v. Freightliner Corp., 714 F.2d 498, 502-505 (5th Cir. 1983) (excluding because statistics were not the sort on which others rely).

4. DeLuca v. Merrell Dow Pharmaceuticals, 911 F.2d 941, 952 (3d Cir. 1990) (court decides whether expert has reasonable basis; epidemiological data provide adequate basis for testimony that drug is teratogenic); Head v. Lithonia Corp., 881 F.2d 941, 943-944 (10th Cir. 1989) (implicit in FRE 703 is that court decides whether underlying data can be reasonably relied on).

5. Soden v. Freightliner Corp., 714 F.2d 498, 502-505 (5th Cir. 1983) (courts must determine reliability of sources on which experts rely; problems affect not merely weight but relevance).

6. United States v. Corey, 207 F.3d 84, 88-91 (1st Cir. 2000) (noting "highly deferential" standard of review); Indian Coffee Corp. v. Procter & Gamble Co., 752 F.2d 891, 895-897 (3d Cir. 1985) (court mistakenly "substituted its own judgment" for that of experts), *cert. denied*, 474 U.S. 863.

7. United States v. Scrima, 819 F.2d 996, 1002 (11th Cir. 1987) (limiting testimony by accountant relying on casual statements by defendant on net worth); Faries v. Atlas Truck Body Mfg. Co., 797 F.2d 619, 623-624 (8th Cir. 1986) (police testimony on cause of accident inadequately supported).

statements. Rather, the point is that courts too are skilled and experienced in the task and should be expected to look closely at reliance issues.

Closer scrutiny seems also appropriate where serious gaps appear in the underlying basis,[8] or the data do not fit closely with the substance of the opinion,[9] or where the expert is a skilled specialist or investigator dealing with conventional factual data that are reasonably accessible and familiar to laypeople.[10] In these and similar situations, courts properly exercise considerable independence in admitting opinions that are well founded and weeding out those that amount to speculation or guesswork because the information is sparse or unpersuasive.[11]

Courts, both trial and appellate, are usually less capable of assessing underlying data in scientific fields that are technical and well established. Here the issue of adequacy usually arises in the context of sophisticated analytic techniques used by highly educated scientists and other experts, and the inquiry required by FRE 703 overlaps with the validity standard that applies to scientific evidence, as indicated by reference in FRE 703 to the practice of experts in the pertinent field.[12] In this setting, courts properly accord more deference to the assurance of experts that the underlying data are indeed adequate in quantity and quality.[13] Even here, however, courts have room to find reliance unreasonable and reject expert testimony.[14]

8. Brown v. Parker-Hannifin Corp., 919 F.2d 308, 311-312 (5th Cir. 1990) (excluding testimony that relied on diagrams in concluding that excessive pressure might have caused oilfield accident; expert did not examine coupling or manufacturing method).

9. Quinones v. Pennsylvania Gen. Ins. Co., 804 F.2d 1167, 1170-1171 (10th Cir. 1986) (in suit by watchmaker, excluding economist's testimony based on statistics for "production workers in jewelry manufacturing").

10. Almonte v. National Union Fire Ins. Co., 787 F.2d 763, 769-770 (1st Cir. 1986) (court should have examined basis of testimony that fire was incendiary, so police officer would not rely on hearsay in identifying person who started fire).

11. Polk v. Ford Motor Co., 529 F.2d 259, 271 (8th Cir. 1976) (there must be enough facts to take testimony out of realm of "guesswork and speculation"), *cert. denied*, 426 U.S. 907.

12. United States v. Carter, 270 F.3d 731, 735 (8th Cir. 2001) (admitting testimony that gun was made in Mira Lona, California, hence traveled in interstate commerce; expert could rely on information stamped on gun, which is reasonably relied on by firearms experts); Re Paoli R.R. Yard PCB Lit., 916 F.2d 829, 853-854 (3d Cir. 1990) (distinction between reasonable reliance on case-specific data under FRE 703 and valid scientific method or technique under FRE 702 "is offtimes subtle if not strained") (using foreign studies of exposure to PCBs raised reliance issue; using "meta-analysis" raised validity issue).

13. Re Paoli R.R. Yard PCB Litig., 916 F.2d 829, 853-854 (3d Cir. 1990) (proper focus is not what court considers reliable, but what experts consider reliable); DeLuca v. Merrell Dow Pharmaceuticals, 911 F.2d 941, 944 (3d Cir. 1990) (similar).

14. Renaud v. Martin Marietta Corp., Inc., 972 F.2d 304, 307-308 (10th Cir. 1992) (court had "independent duty" to decide whether single data point showed exposure to contaminated water, and whether etiological evidence identifying causes of ailment based on tests of nonhumans supported conclusion on causation); Christophersen v. Allied-Signal Corp., 939 F.2d 1106, 1113-1115 (5th Cir. 1991) (summary judgment for defendant in case alleging that toxic fumes caused cancer; doctor relied on facts that were inaccurate and incomplete).

May rest on hearsay

Merely to ask whether outside information would be hearsay or would be admissible is to miss the whole point of FRE 703, nor does it matter that the expert uses such material in important ways in formulating his opinion. Outside information need not play merely a background role.[15]

While expert testimony may rest on hearsay and other excludable evidence, it should not always be allowed to rest on material that is excludable for strong reasons of extrinsic policy serving interests independent of the factfinding process.[16] The purpose of statutes barring use in court of various kinds of required reports, for example, is usually to secure compliance with reporting requirements and encourage candor and completeness, and these purposes would be threatened if such reports could be the basis of expert testimony. Privilege rules serve somewhat similar policies and would be similarly threatened if protected material were freely usable as the basis for expert testimony.

It may be possible at least sometimes to reach an accommodation with such rules of extrinsic policy, and at least sometimes they may be treated as rules creating waivable privileges. In the case of required reports, for example, the reporting party might be allowed to decide whether to open the subject by offering expert testimony that rests in part on such reports. Broader waiver notions could be deployed under which the reporting party loses protection by taking positions on issues that are the subject of such reports, or offering evidence on the same subject, but these approaches would seriously undercut the statutory purpose.

Cannot act as conduit

While an expert may consider remote statements that are not admitted and may be inadmissible, he cannot properly act as a conduit by presenting an opinion that is not his own opinion but that of someone else,[17] and should not testify that others agree with him as a means of

---

15. United States v. Floyd, 281 F.3d 1346, 1349 (11th Cir. 2002) (admitting testimony identifying ammunition maker, for "hearsay testimony" is permitted if reasonably relied on by others in field; expert testified that information from technical advisor satisfied standard; he examined ammunition and consulted maker's catalogue); United States v. Theodoropoulos, 866 F.2d 587, 590 (3d Cir. 1989) (rejecting claim that out-of-court evidence may only be used for noncentral background), *mandamus denied*, 489 U.S. 1009.

16. Robertson v. Union Pac. R. Co., 954 F.2d 1433, 1435 (8th Cir. 1992) (expert should not rely on information compiled by state highway department as required by federal law, where statute makes information inadmissible).

17. Dura Automotive Systems of Indiana, Inc. v. CTS Corporation, 285 F.3d 609, 613-614 (7th Cir. 2002) (expert may base opinion in part on what another expert believes, but problem arises if soundness of underlying expert judgment is questioned; *Daubert* must be applied with "due regard" for specialization of modern science, but scientist is not allowed "to be the mouthpiece of a scientist in a different specialty"); Estate of Arrowwood v. State, 894 P.2d 642, 648 (Alaska 1995) (experts could not rely on ham radio operator relaying calls for sand trucks and observing icy conditions; FRE 703 is not conduit for inadmissible evidence); Ricciardi v. Children's Hosp. Medical Ctr., 811 F.2d 18, 25-26 (1st Cir. 1987) (excluding doctor's opinion that tube came out during surgery, based on statement in hospital chart by neurologist who did not attend and could not recall source).

vouching for or reinforcing any opinion of his own that he presents, at least in relation to central or contested matters.[18] The purpose of FRE 703 is to broaden the basis for expert opinion, but it is not enough that an expert repeats what he read or was told, even if he respects or trusts the people he read or listened to. The distinction between relying on others and repeating what others say can be made clearer as a formal matter by requiring the expert to say "what he thinks," not what "someone else thinks," and insisting on this formality is useful in weeding out cases where the expert has no independent view and being sure that the trier gets the expert's own opinion.

As a matter of substance, the distinction is sometimes hard to draw, especially when remote statements about acts, events, or conditions at the heart of the dispute play an important part in the expert's opinion. Easy rules of thumb are probably wrong: It seems wrong, for instance, to exclude expert testimony merely because remote statements are necessary to the conclusion, or to admit expert testimony only if such statements are merely cumulative or corroborative. There is, after all, nothing about the reasonable reliance standard to suggest that there is anything necessarily amiss in depending on a remote statement for some important point in a conclusion, or to think remote statements can only corroborate something the expert already knows by firsthand knowledge. Perhaps the best that can be said is that the problem calls for a considered judgment that there is enough of the expert's own independent appraisal in what he proposes to say to make his testimony useful and reliable by the force or weight of his own authority.[19]

The point that experts should not act as conduits for remote statements is often made in a slightly different way by pointing out that the expert testimony rule does not obviate hearsay objections to remote statements. Even if experts rely on them, they remain hearsay.[20] That means they are not admissible as proof of what they assert unless they fit some exception, and it means that they may be excluded if admitting them brings too much risk that they will be misused as substantive evidence. In some settings there is perhaps little risk in using an expert as a conduit for remote statements, but courts that allow this tactic are distorting the purpose of FRE 703.

18. United States v. Tran Trong Cuong, 18 F.3d 1132, 1143-1144 (4th Cir. 1994); United States v. Grey Bear, 883 F.2d 1382, 1392-1393 (8th Cir. 1989), *cert. denied*, 493 U.S. 1047.

19. *Compare* Pelster v. Ray, 987 F.2d 514, 524 (8th Cir. 1993) (investigator cannot testify that odometers had been rolled back, which was "especially dangerous" since he relied solely on hearsay) *with* United States v. Affleck, 776 F.2d 1451, 1456-1458 (10th Cir. 1985) (accountant did not simply summarize statements, but presented his own conclusions based on financial records).

20. *See generally* Carlson, Policing the Bases of Modern Expert Testimony, 59 Vand. L. Rev. 577 (1986); Carlson, Collision Course in Expert Testimony: Limitations on Affirmative Introduction of Underlying Data, 36 Fla. L. Rev. 234 (1984). *But see* Rice, Inadmissible Evidence as a Basis for Expert Opinion Testimony: A Response to Professor Carlson, 40 Vand. L. Rev. 583 (1987).

Expert testimony is not supposed to be a conduit for proving inadmissible or easily misused facts such as prior bad acts. Where underlying facts are subject to nonhearsay exclusionary doctrines, the conduit problem is not so much one of ensuring that the expert conveys an opinion that is really his own, but one of accommodating the expert testimony rules with exclusionary policies. It seems that an expert may properly base an opinion on other acts by a party, for instance, but that the calling party should not be able to prove the other acts merely because the expert used them as part of the basis of his testimony.[21] And it should go without saying that litigants cannot properly use the expert testimony conventions to get a witness to prove facts and remote statements while adding no special insights of his own.[22]

Underlying data usually to be kept out

As amended in 2000, FRE 703 blocks _the proponent_ of expert testimony from introducing "otherwise inadmissible" facts or data, upon which the expert relies, in jury trials. The amendment discards prior precedent that allows even the calling party to bring out such material in order to show the basis of expert opinion.[23] In contrast to FRE 403 (where courts admit unless probative worth is "substantially outweighed" by the risk of prejudice), the language of the amendment is cast in favor of exclusion (courts exclude unless probative worth "substantially exceeds" prejudicial effect).[24] Even before the amendment, it was clear that FRE 703 does not discard hearsay and other objections to the underlying material, so exclusion was often appropriate. When _the adverse party_ offers such material, presumably as part of an attack upon the expert and usually through the mechanism of cross-examination, there is nothing in FRE 703 to stand in the way. The party who called the expert might raise objection under FRE 403, but courts customarily allow broad latitude to the cross-examiner and such objections are not likely to succeed.

§7.11   Reasonable Reliance and Defense Confrontation Rights

Expert testimony resting on out-of-court statements invites challenge under the confrontation clause when offered against criminal defendants. Most modern decisions reject this challenge but acknowledge the importance of confrontation issues.

21. Nachtsheim v. Beech Aircraft Corp., 847 F.2d 1261, 1270-1271 (7th Cir. 1988) (expert relied on earlier crash in testifying on cause, and court properly excluded earlier crash).
22. Abernathy v. Superior Hardwoods, Inc., 704 F.2d 963, 970 (7th Cir. 1983) (investigator could not testify that plaintiff's name was not on list of job applicants); United States v. Swaim, 642 F.2d 726, 730 (4th Cir. 1981) (error to admit statements by window clerks entered on daily forms summarizing receipts).
23. _See_ Brennan v. Reinhart Institutional Foods, 211 F.3d 449, 450 (8th Cir. 2000); Hayes v. State, 935 P.2d 700, 703 (Wyo. 1997); United States v. Farley, 992 F.2d 1122, 1125 (10th Cir. 1993); Wilmington Trust Co. v. Manufacturers Life Ins., 749 F.2d 694, 698 (11th Cir. 1985).
24. _See generally_ Doe v. Wal-Mart Stores, Inc., 558 S.E.2d 663, 675 (W.Va. 2001) (adopting standard in amended FRE 703, but reversing for _excluding_ testimony describing basis and remanding for reconsideration under new standard).

The 1985 decision in the *Fensterer* case provides the only Supreme Court pronouncement on expert testimony and confrontation issues, but it did not deal with reliance on hearsay. *Fensterer* was a murder case where an expert testified that two hairs he found on a cat leash (the alleged weapon) had been "forcibly removed." Although he remembered his conclusion and testified that there were three ways to reach it, he could not remember how he actually did reach it, even after consulting his notes. The Court said the confrontation clause guarantees an "opportunity" to cross-examine, adding the rhetorical comment that it does not guarantee cross "that is effective in whatever way, and to whatever extent, the defense might wish" and concluding that it did not matter that the expert could not remember his basis. In failing to recall, he invited the jury "to find that his opinion is as unreliable as his memory," and it was irrelevant that the defense might prefer that he rely on a theory it was "prepared to refute with special vigor."[1] *Fensterer* sends a strong signal that lack of memory and perhaps other uncertainties in expert conclusions do not themselves bring confrontation concerns. Two years later the Court relied on *Fensterer* in rejecting a broad constitutional challenge to the use of prior statements by a testifying witness who could not remember underlying events.[2]

The decision in *Fensterer* does not, however, close the door to defense challenges to expert testimony relying on out-of-court statements. The Court pointedly commented that the state offered no such statements and left room to argue that lack of memory and gaps in the basis of expert testimony might raise insurmountable problems in some cases.[3]

Using experts as a conduit to report the substance of out-of-court statements would violate FRE 703 and would likely constitute a serious violation of confrontation rights,[4] at least if the statements touch directly on substantive issues and are "testimonial" under *Crawford*.[5] Of course much hearsay that experts rely on, including out-of-court source material that provides much of the basic knowledge that enables them to act as experts, is clearly nontestimonial under *Crawford*, and reliance on such material is unproblematic. Even testimonial hearsay,

---

§7.11 1. Delaware v. Fensterer, 474 U.S. 15 (1985) (expert described three methods, but notes did not refresh memory on which method he used).

2. *See* United States v. Owens, 484 U.S. 554 (1988) (required chance for cross is not denied if "past belief" is proved by statement where witness cannot recall basis for it).

3. Delaware v. Fensterer, 474 U.S. 15, 20-23 (1985) (no statement was offered; not deciding whether lapse of memory "may so frustrate any opportunity" for cross as to deny confrontation rights, nor whether opinion "with no basis" could be so unreliable as to deny fair trial).

4. *See* United States v. Lombardozzi, 491 F.3d 61, 72 (2d Cir. 2007) (if expert "communicated out-of-court testimonial statements of cooperating witnesses and confidential informants directly to the jury in the guise of an expert opinion," it would violate *Crawford*) (there were other bases; no plain error); People v. Goldstein, 843 N.E.2d 727, 127 (N.Y. 2005) (reversing murder conviction where psychiatrist retained by prosecutor recited statements about accused; opinion was admissible, but not third-party statements, which were testimonial; speakers understood that psychiatrist was preparing to testify).

5. *See* Crawford v. Washington, 541 U.S. 36, 57 (2004), discussed in §§8.83-8.92, *infra*.

such as statements made to experts that relate to the crime or to the defendant, when given in a setting in which the expert and the person speaking to him share a purpose in investigating a crime or preparing for trial, may not raise serious concerns, at least if such hearsay is not recited as part of the substance of the expert's testimony,[6] and even testimonial hearsay is sometimes admitted for the limiting purpose of showing the basis for the expert's opinion, without violating *Crawford*.[7]

C.   EXPERT TESTIMONY: LIMITS AND TESTING

1.   *Testifying on Ultimate Issues*

> **FRE 704**
>
> (a) Except as provided in subdivision (b), testimony in the form of an opinion or inference otherwise admissible is not objectionable because it embraces an ultimate issue to be decided by the trier of fact.
>
> (b) No expert witness testifying with respect to the mental state or condition of a defendant in a criminal case may state an opinion or inference as to whether the defendant did or did not have the mental state or condition constituting an element of the crime charged or of a defense thereto. Such ultimate issues are matters for the trier of fact alone.

§7.12   Usually Allowed

For both lay and expert testimony, FRE 704 abolished the much disliked "ultimate issue" objection that essentially blocked witnesses from testifying directly to facts that the factfinder must determine. There is little disagreement with the proposition that witnesses, no matter how qualified, informed, or wise, should not testify that "defendant is guilty" or "plaintiff should win," and the ultimate issue objection would block testimony of this sort. But it also stood in the way of much that could be helpful, such as testimony that someone was

---

6. United States v. Law, 528 F.3d 888, 912 (D.C. Cir. 2008) (admitting detective's testimony about operations of drug dealers, based on "thousands of interviews," where he did not relate statements and based his testimony on experience); United States v. Moon, 512 F.3d 359 (7th Cir. 2008) (chemist's testimony that substance was cocaine, based on work done by another chemist; no *Crawford* violation); Veney v. United States, 936 A.2d 809 (D.C. 2007) (expert testifying on DNA analysis based on FBI crime laboratory reports; no *Crawford* violation); State v. O'Maley, 932 A.2d 1 (N.H. 2007) (in DUI case, expert testimony based on blood sample report did not violate *Crawford*); People v. Geier, 161 P.3d 104 (Cal. 2007) (in rape-murder trial, testimony about DNA match based on work done by another in a private laboratory did not violate *Crawford*).

7. See discussion in §8.86, *supra*.

"driving too fast" or that someone "deliberately took aim and fired" because such testimony connected directly and immediately with issues like negligence and criminal intent.

Typically the "ultimate issue" objection was framed in terms of "usurping the function of the jury," and the fear was that lay factfinders would give up their responsibility to look critically at testimony and just take the word of the witness. But the fear was overstated, since juries have the power and authority to reject even decisive and informed testimony and are told as much before deliberating. And the ultimate issue objection did little to help. With lay witnesses, the risk that juries might be "snowed" seems less a function of how closely testimony connects with elements in claims or defenses (ultimate issues) and more a function of the personality, demeanor, and style of witnesses. For experts who testify on technical points, the risk is probably greater, but again it seems less a function of how closely testimony connects with elements or ultimate issues, and here it seems more a function of the subject and nature of the testimony.

To some extent, the ultimate issue objection expressed two other concerns: One is that testimony should be particular rather than general, specific rather than conclusory. For lay witnesses, this preference is expressed directly in FRE 701, and it applies not only to testimony that goes directly to elements or ultimate issues, but to all testimony. The other concern is that witnesses should not ordinarily present legal conclusions as opposed to facts, and this point too continues to be true for both lay and expert witnesses.

Perhaps the most important point is that FRE 704 does not set a standard of admissibility, but merely removes a formal objection that might block expert testimony on such issues as cause, fault, negligence, design defect, and dangerous condition in tort cases.[1] The provision also drains the force from objections that testimony by a "summary witness" who presents an overview based on factual details, should be excluded as invading the province of the jury.[2]

Removes formal objection

In criminal cases, FRE 704 obviates what might have been a barrier against expert testimony describing drug[3] and gambling operations,[4]

---

§7.12   1. Miksis v. Howard, 106 F.3d 754, 762 (7th Cir. 1997) (expert testimony that sleep deprivation caused accident); United States v. Sheffey, 57 F.3d 1419, 1424-1429 (6th Cir. 1995) (lay testimony that defendant drove recklessly in disregard for human life), *cert. denied*, 516 U.S. 1065.

2. *See* United States v. Dotson, 817 F.2d 1127, 1131-1133 (5th Cir. 1987) (tax expert could testify, on basis of increasing net worth, that defendant willfully and intentionally increased income knowing he had not reported taxes due, which is proper summary), *vacated in part*, 821 F.2d 1034 (5th Cir. 1987).

3. United States v. Beaumont, 972 F.2d 553, 565 (5th Cir. 1992) (chemicals, glassware, and other paraphernalia are used in large scale methamphetamine manufacturing); United States v. Lockett, 919 F.2d 585, 590-591 (9th Cir. 1990) (only persons "intimately involved" with cocaine packaging are usually allowed at site).

4. United States v. Angiulo, 897 F.2d 1169, 1189 (1st Cir. 1990) (roles of defendants in poker operation), *cert. denied*, 498 U.S. 845; United States v. Pinelli, 890 F.2d 1461, 1474 (10th Cir. 1989) (similar), *cert. denied*, 495 U.S. 960.

accounting matters in tax cases,[5] and patterns of criminal misconduct.[6] And FRE 704 removes a standard objection to testimony that defendant is pictured in a surveillance photograph showing the crime or scene,[7] and testimony that the voice in a recording belongs to the defendant,[8] or that important trace evidence matches defendant.[9]

Unhelpful testimony

Removing the ultimate issue objection leaves other limits on expert testimony intact. Perhaps the most important one excludes what is unhelpful. The ACN comments that opinions telling the jury "what result to reach" remain excludable and that FRE 704 does not pave the way for all opinion. Thus testimony of the sort quoted in the first paragraph remains excludable,[10] not because it directly touches ultimate issues but because it is not helpful.

The reason FRE 704 does not have these effects is that it does not override other rules. For expert testimony, the criteria in FRE 702 and 703 remain crucial, and expert testimony that does not satisfy the helpfulness requirement[11] or rest on adequate firsthand information or evidence, or on sources that satisfy the reasonable reliance criterion, is not admissible.[12] For lay witnesses, the preference for facts (the concrete or specific) normally prevails under FRE 701, and opinions (the general or conclusory) are admissible only if helpful and rationally based.[13] Nor does FRE 704 require courts to admit testimony that confuses the issues, misleads the jury, wastes time, or introduces unfair prejudice under FRE 403.[14] Finally, lay witnesses must have personal

5. United States v. Duncan, 42 F.3d 97, 101-103 (2d Cir. 1994) (IRS agent's testimony describing transactions and tax system); United States v. Mohney, 949 F.2d 1397, 1406 (6th Cir. 1991) (income was not reported as part of gross receipts).

6. United States v. Webster, 960 F.2d 1301, 1308-1309 (5th Cir. 1992) (unexplained cash receipts showed income from drug sales and gambling).

7. United States v. Langford, 802 F.2d 1176, 1178-1179 (9th Cir. 1986); United States v. Barrett, 703 F.2d 1076, 1084 & n.14 (9th Cir. 1983); United States v. Jackson, 688 F.2d 1121, 1126 (7th Cir. 1982).

8. United States v. Bice-Bey, 701 F.2d 1086, 1090 (4th Cir. 1983) (taped voice was defendant's), *cert. denied*, 464 U.S. 837.

9. United States v. Rose, 731 F.2d 1337, 1345-1347 (8th Cir. 1984) (print on counter matched defendant's shoe), *cert. denied*, 469 U.S. 931.

10. *See* Warren Petroleum Co. v. Thomasson, 268 F.2d 5, 9-10 (5th Cir. 1959) (cannot admit statement by police officer that defendant should "assume liability" for accident).

11. United States v. Cecil, 836 F.2d 1431, 1440-1441 (4th Cir. 1988) (excluding as unhelpful psychiatrist's statement that witness was incapable of telling truth), *cert. denied*, 487 U.S. 1205; Owen v. Kerr-McGee Corp., 698 F.2d 236, 239-240 (5th Cir. 1983) (expert in installing and maintaining gas systems could not say plaintiff was contributorily negligent).

12. Minasian v. Standard Chartered Bank, PLC, 109 F.3d 1212, 1216 (7th Cir. 1997) (opinion of former banker was worthless and inadmissible because he lacked data, did not survey literature or do anything else that experts do).

13. United States v. Forrester, 60 F.3d 52, 62-63 (2d Cir. 1995) (cannot say testimony by G was not inconsistent with what G said before; credibility is for jury; not helpful).

14. *See* Denny v. Hutchinson Sales Corp., 649 F.2d 816, 821-822 (10th Cir. 1981) (cannot say there were "only 42 chances out of a million" that neighborhood composition would exist without discrimination; more prejudicial than probative).

knowledge, for FRE 704 does not pave the way for testimony by uninformed witnesses.

FRE 704 is also limited by the tradition against testimony expressing legal conclusions. That tradition holds generally that courts decide issues on the content of governing law and that expert testimony does not help and may do damage, although some testimony containing mixed legal and factual content is admitted. When expert testimony goes directly to the application of governing law to the facts, it is usually excluded as unhelpful because it amounts to a kind of gratuitous advice telling the jury what to decide,[15] although it is sometimes admitted if the issue presents technicalities that expertise illuminates.[16]

§7.13 Particularity Required on Mental Condition of Accused

Under FRE 704(b) as amended in 1984, expert testimony on sanity and other mental conditions must be stated with particularity. At that time Congress also changed the insanity defense. Federal courts once followed the traditional M'Naghten Rule, but the District of Columbia had adopted the *Durham* "product" standard, and most federal circuits and many states had adopted the ALI "substantial capacity" standard.[1] The 1984 reform is a modern restatement of the M'Naghten Rule, under which defendant is insane if he was "unable to appreciate the nature and quality or the wrongfulness of his acts,"[2] and FRE 704(b) put a formal restriction on expert testimony on sanity and other mental conditions.

Under FRE 704(b) a psychiatrist or other expert should not couch her testimony in terms of the legal elements in the insanity defense. Instead she should stay one step back, explaining the basis for her

---

15. U.S. v. Barile, 286 F.3d 749, 761 (4th Cir. 2002) (testimony on materiality of statements in submission to FDA could not be excluded as embracing ultimate issue; can exclude as legal conclusion).

16. Hangarter v. Provident Life and Acc. Ins. Co., 373 F.3d 998, 1018 (9th Cir. 2004) (admitting testimony that defendants "failed to comport with industry standards," which did not address bad faith or usurp court's role by instructing on law; testimony supported finding of bad faith, but expert did not say defendants were in bad faith). On testimony stating legal conclusions, *see* §7.14, *infra*.

§7.13   1. The M'Naghten Rule held that insanity required a mental disease or defect that kept defendant from understanding the nature and quality or wrongfulness of the act. The *Durham* test asked whether the crime was a "product" of a mental defect. *See* Durham v. United States, 214 F.2d 862 (D.C. Cir. 1954) (abandoned in *Brawner*, *infra*). The ALI standard asks whether defendant lacked "substantial capacity" to appreciate the criminality or wrongfulness of his conduct (cognitive prong) or conform his behavior to the law (volitional prong). *See* Model Penal Code §4.01 (1985); 1 LaFave & Scott, Substantive Criminal Law §§4.2-4.3 (1986); Brawner v. United States, 471 F.2d 969 (D.C. Cir. 1972) (adopting ALI standard).

2. 18 U.S.C. §17 (insanity is an affirmative defense on which defendant has burden of proof by "clear and convincing evidence," and mental disease or defect is not otherwise a defense; insanity means defendant, "as a result of a severe mental disease or defect, was unable to appreciate the nature and quality or the wrongfulness of his acts").

diagnosis,[3] describing defendant's condition by giving the diagnosis itself and the characteristics of the affliction, and saying how such a condition would or might affect the ability of an ordinary person to appreciate the nature and quality or wrongfulness of his acts or conform his conduct to the law (the latter being part of the ALI but not the federal standard),[4] although these last points get so close to the ultimate issue that courts sometimes balk.[5] What FRE 704(b) aims to prevent is expert testimony that goes directly to the legal conclusion. An expert should not testify, for example, that defendant could not appreciate the wrongfulness of his acts or conform his conduct to the requirements of law.[6]

Three related purposes underlie the formal restrictions in FRE 704(b). One is to eliminate the confusing spectacle of diametrically conflicting expert testimony on ultimate issues. The idea is that experts are likely to agree on many aspects of psychiatric diagnoses but to differ on the ultimate question whether defendant was (for example) legally insane, so confining expert testimony to diagnoses and related points reduces conflicts that juries are ill-equipped to resolve. A second purpose is to ensure that juries get details because they need them and because experts who let themselves be used in criminal adjudication have a professional obligation to provide details rather than overarching conclusions. It seems a step in the right direction to require details (something that goes to the substance of the matter), although blocking testimony describing what an affliction actually does to understanding or comprehension or self-control of the defendant seems more questionable. The third purpose is to keep experts from giving testimony beyond their area of competence, since the legal concept and medical understanding of mental conditions overlap but are not identical. This disjunction is but one of many that affects a broad range of scientific evidence.

Reaches all mental conditions   While FRE 704(b) takes aim at the presentation of expert testimony relating to sanity as a defense to criminal charges, the Rule is much broader. It applies to testimony on all mental conditions in the defendant that amount to elements in the charged crimes or defenses. Thus it bars expert testimony that defendant had or did not have criminal intent that is an element in the offense,[7] or had or did not

---

3. United States v. West, 962 F.2d 1243, 1246-1248 (7th Cir. 1992) (can describe "conversations with dead bunnies or with George Washington").

4. United States v. Brown, 32 F.3d 236, 237-238 (7th Cir. 1994) (can testify that depressive episodes do not keep one from appreciating wrongfulness of acts); United States v. Thigpen, 4 F.3d 1573, 1579-1580 (11th Cir. 1993) (can ask whether schizophrenia means one cannot appreciate nature and quality of acts), *cert. denied*, 512 U.S. 1238.

5. United States v. Manley, 893 F.2d 1221, 1222-1224 (11th Cir. 1990) (excluding testimony that one with manic-depressive symptoms can appreciate nature and quality or wrongfulness), *cert. denied*, 498 U.S. 901.

6. United States v. Hiebert, 30 F.3d 1005, 1008 n.2 (8th Cir. 1994), *cert. denied*, 513 U.S. 1029; United States v. West, 962 F.2d 1243, 1246-1248 (7th Cir. 1992).

7. United States v. Ramirez-Velasquez, 322 F.3d 868, 878 (5th Cir. 2003) (in trial of V and R, error to let agent testify in substance that R knew he was carrying drugs in

have the mental state required for defenses like duress, intoxication, extreme emotional disturbance,[8] or entrapment where predisposition is a central issue.[9]

Here too experts may still play a role. They may describe afflictions, including organic problems from drug or alcohol consumption or physical injury or ailment, and should be allowed to say how such afflictions might affect mental processes in someone who suffers them.[10] Probably they should not describe the ways that any such affliction affected the defendant, for such testimony does directly say that he had or lacked such state of mind. Mental states indicating lack of intent are not the same thing as insanity, but insanity is usually understood to conflict with criminal intent, and perhaps foreclose it. Hence testimony that a defendant "could not appreciate the nature or wrongfulness" of his act or "conform his conduct to the law" is essentially testimony that he lacked criminal intent, and is barred by FRE 704(b).[11]

An obvious ploy to avoid FRE 704(b) is to ask an expert to testify "hypothetically on the basis of the following facts," then to frame the facts to mirror the case at hand. If this ploy worked—if an expert could testify to the state of mind one would have if such "hypothetical" facts were so—then the Rule would fail its purpose. This evasion should be seen for what it is, as a violation of the Rule.[12]

"Mirroring" hypotheticals

Where mental state is not linked to serious psychiatric afflictions or psychoses that can be named and described, deciding what to do with expert testimony is harder. Where evidence of an affliction is offered, experts should be allowed to testify that defendant is normal or healthy in mental function or psychological condition, which tends to refute evidence of the affliction and make it more or less likely that he had or did not have a certain mental state.[13]

---

truck) (harmless); United States v. Wood, 207 F.3d 1222, 1236 (10th Cir. 2000) (in trial of doctor for injecting patient with lethal dose of potassium, error to admit expert testimony that death was homicide).

8. United States v. Triplett, 922 F.2d 1174, 1182-1183 (5th Cir. 1991) (excluding testimony that defendant would not set fire as result of "emotional state of rage" induced by drugs); United States v. Lewis, 837 F.2d 415, 418 (9th Cir. 1988) (excluding psychiatric testimony on mental state and motivation), *cert. denied*, 488 U.S. 923.

9. United States v. Newman, 849 F.2d 156, 164-165 (5th Cir. 1988) (cannot say defendant was "induced to commit the crime or lacked predisposition").

10. United States v. Brown, 7 F.3d 648, 651-652 (7th Cir. 1993) (admitting testimony that crack was intended for distribution); United States v. Triplett, 922 F.2d 1174, 1182-1183 (5th Cir. 1991) (may testify "generally about the effect of drugs").

11. United States v. Hillsberg, 812 F.2d 328, 331-332 (7th Cir. 1987), *cert. denied*, 481 U.S. 1014. *But see* United States v. Cox, 826 F.2d 1518, 1524 (6th Cir. 1987) (testimony that defendant knew wrongfulness of act would be impermissible if insanity were issue, but here it was intent to rob), *cert. denied*, 484 U.S. 1028.

12. United States v. Boyd, 55 F.3d 667, 671 (D.C. Cir. 1995) (error to let officer opine, on basis of hypothetical facts that mirrored case, that one would have "intent to distribute" drugs; expert may not say whether such facts prove intent to distribute) (reversing).

13. United States v. Gipson, 862 F.2d 714, 716 (8th Cir. 1988) (defendant did not suffer severe mental disease or defect, offered to prove intent).

If there is no evidence of affliction and an expert proposes to describe some healthy or normal condition, or one that is not so healthy but generally known to the mass of humanity and not considered serious, the answer is less clear. Such testimony may satisfy FRE 704(b) but fail the helpfulness standard of FRE 702: It is doubtful, for example, that an expert should testify that defendant suffered ordinary depression or sleeplessness from financial or personal losses or marital or romantic problems, and that someone in his position could (or could not) readily form an intent to rob or commit an assault.[14] On the other hand, expert "syndrome" evidence describing mental or psychological conditions has become commonplace and is often considered helpful because experts can systematize and explain such conditions better than laypeople. Such testimony is often admitted under FRE 702 and thought consistent with FRE 704(b).[15]

Expert testimony at one remove from such ultimate issues as intent may be admitted even though it indirectly supports a conclusion or suggests an inference on some ultimate issue.[16] Thus testimony describing typical patterns of organized crimes or conspiracies does not violate FRE 704(b) even though it provides evidence that persuades a jury, in light of what defendant and others are shown to have done, that the requisite intent existed.[17] As one court put it, a great deal of expert testimony that directly addresses conventional subjects such as cause of death might well lead to inferences about the mental state of the accused, but FRE 704(b) was not intended either to block such testimony or condemn such inferences, for its only effect is to force the expert to "be silent" in connection with "the last step in the inferential process."[18]

By its terms, FRE 704(b) does not apply in two important situations. First, it restricts expert testimony but not lay testimony, and lay witnesses often do testify about observed behavior that indicates sanity

---

14. United States v. Masat, 896 F.2d 88, 93 (5th Cir. 1990) (excluding testimony that taxpayer's beliefs "were strong and sincerely held" because issue was within ability of ordinary juror).

15. See §7.22, *infra.*

16. United States v. Gonzales, 307 F.3d 906, 911 (9th Cir. 2002) (agent could say drugs in such quantity would be for distribution, not consumption; never testified to mental state); Hannon v. State, 84 P.3d 320, 352 (Wyo. 2004) (reversible error to exclude psychological testimony on susceptibility of defendant to pressure and manipulation, to explain confession) (quoting authors of this Treatise).

17. United States v. Murillo, 255 F.3d 1169, 1176-1178 (9th Cir. 2001) (admitting testimony on travel itineraries of drug curriers, why they use rental cars; no explicit mention of defendant's state of mind), *cert. denied,* 535 U.S. 948. *See also* United States v. Liner, 435 F.3d 920, 924 (8th Cir. 2006) (expert could say scheme was fraudulent; he did not "directly address" intent).

18. United States v. Dunn, 846 F.2d 761, 762-763 (D.C. Cir. 1988). *See* United States v. Watson, 260 F.3d 301, 307 (3d Cir. 2001) (reversing drug convictions where prosecutor "pushed too far" in questioning agents about defendant's intent "by directly referring to defendant's mental state, or mens rea").

or insanity. Of course lay testimony should not speak directly to a technical concept such as insanity because lay witnesses lack the required expertise. However, lay testimony can properly address intent and similar mental conditions directly, and FRE 704(b) does not apply.[19] Second, FRE 704(b) addresses expert testimony on the mental state or condition of defendants, not testimony about third parties.[20]

2. Testifying on Points of Law

§7.14 Expert Testimony on Law

The helpfulness standard, when combined with the abolition of the old "ultimate issue" objection, could be read to mean that experts may freely testify on points of law or directly state legal conclusions. Yet expert testimony on points of law is largely inadmissible because it is not helpful under FRE 702, and abolishing the ultimate issue objection did not create a positive basis for such testimony. In some areas, however, courts admit expert testimony that is largely legal in content, finding the helpfulness standard satisfied.

Perhaps not surprisingly, parties seldom offer expert testimony on what might be termed pure matters of law. When it comes to the content of the law that governs the rights and obligations of the parties in suit, the reason is that courts themselves make this determination, and generally they do so by interpreting primary written sources (mostly cases and statutes) and secondary authorities (like scholarly books and articles, and Restatements). This process involves a kind of judicial notice that is unregulated and does not require formal testimony: Deciding the content of law is itself matter of law.[1]

Pure matters of law

Of course lawyers play critical roles in arguing and briefing points of doctrine. In this setting, conceivably courts could benefit from expert advice given in a special hearing or general discussion in chambers, but it is seldom sought or tendered. Moreover, the dynamics of the profession, and the sense of role and prerogative that most judges bring to their jobs, make it unlikely at best that judges would accept instruction from lawyers or others who might be considered to have expertise in one or another legal field (like professors) on "what the law is." Certainly the Rules of Evidence would not apply if testimony from

---

19. United States v. Rea, 958 F.2d 1206, 1215 (11th Cir. 1992).
20. United States v. Windfelder, 790 F.2d 576, 580-581 (7th Cir. 1986).
§7.14 1. *See* the discussion of FRE 201 in §2.13, *supra.* Questions of nondomestic law may be resolved by taking expert testimony, but this process does not involve jury factfinding, as judges resolve questions on the content of law (foreign or domestic) under FRE 104(a).

such experts were admitted. When parties offer expert testimony on the content of law during ordinary course of trial, it is properly rejected. Courts often say such testimony is not helpful or would interfere with the court's responsibility and cloud or confuse the issue for a jury.[2] Nondomestic law is a different matter.[3]

Mixed questions   More common than expert testimony on points of pure doctrine is expert testimony on what can best be called mixed questions of law and fact, or the application of law to fact. Sometimes such testimony amounts to a thinly disguised attempt to tell the jury what verdict to reach, and it is properly excluded despite the abolition of the ultimate issue objection.[4] And sometimes such testimony is not helpful for more elaborate reasons: Typically it sums up a factual picture also painted by the evidence and characterizes the conduct or responsibility of the parties. Sometimes the opposite is true, and the proffered conclusion seems too thin and not adequately supported by what the witness knows. For either reason generally such testimony is excluded as unhelpful.[5]

Elaborate and carefully supported testimony having mixed legal and factual content, however, is often admissible. Issues of fact and law sometimes overlap so extensively that it is hard or impossible to convey factual information without at the same time suggesting legal conclusions. In such cases experts (and even lay witnesses) properly give testimony using words or concepts that carry both factual and legal meaning. Often it is possible to tell juries that such testimony is admitted as proof of facts it conveys and not as an authoritative pronouncement of the content of governing legal standards.[6] When legal standards embody everyday concepts that are in common usage, and in effect the conventional and the specialized meanings of common language are very similar, testimony that employs the common language and describes those shared concepts can be useful and

---

2. CMI-Trading, Inc. v. Quantum Air, Inc. (6th Cir. 1996) 98 F.3d 887, 890 (excluding testimony by financial consultant on whether parties created loan relationship or joint venture, which involves issues of law within sole competence of court); Marx & Co. v. Diners' Club, Inc., 550 F.2d 505, 509-511 (2d Cir. 1977) (landmark case condemning expert testimony on legal standards), *cert. denied*, 434 U.S. 861.

3. On matters of foreign law, FRCP 44.1 requires notice in pleadings and lets the court seek aid from "any relevant material or source, including testimony, whether or not submitted by a party or admissible under the Federal Rules of Evidence."

4. *See* the discussion of FRE 704 in §7.12, *infra*.

5. Burkhart v. Washington Metro. Area Transit Auth., 112 F.3d 1207, 1212-1213 (D.C. Cir. 1997) (error to admit expert testimony that means of talking with passengers were not "as effective" as communication with others, which involved "erroneous formulation" of applicable law); Estes v. Moore, 993 F.2d 161, 163 (8th Cir. 1993) (excluding expert testimony that there was no probable cause for arrest).

6. Heflin v. Stewart County, Tenn., 958 F.2d 709, 715 (6th Cir. 1992) (admitting testimony that jailers were deliberately indifferent to decedent's need for emergency care); Davis v. Combustion Engg., Inc., 742 F.2d 916, 919 (6th Cir. 1984) (professor of management and marketing testified that plaintiff was terminated because of age).

admissible.[7] Finally, legal standards may exist in multiple levels of detail, from the shortest and most general umbrella concepts (like negligence) to elaborate or specific concepts (driving inattentively is negligence), and in these settings the latter often embody ideas in common understanding to which experts (and sometimes lay witnesses) may testify. To cite the example given in the ACN to FRE 704, a witness should probably not testify that the decedent had "capacity to make a will" but might properly testify that he knew enough about "the nature and extent of his property and the natural objects of his bounty and to formulate a rational scheme of distribution," which means in the end that experts (and even lay witnesses) may sometimes testify that specific legal standards are met because those standards embody evaluative content that is part of the common currency of everyday understanding.[8]

In some suits, complicated legal standards overlap with complicated technical standards in such ways that expert testimony seems almost indispensable, and inevitably such testimony tends to suggest both legal and factual conclusions.[9] This point applies in settings like tax cases where proper accounting and tax treatment of transactions and financial arrangements largely overlap,[10] and in drug cases where testimony of a technical nature may be necessary to identify controlled substances under specific statutory language.[11]

Expertise indispensable

Finally there are many cases where expert testimony describes and characterizes conduct and conditions in the world in ways that point toward obvious legal conclusions ("he was doing countersurveillance to protect the enterprise"). Lay testimony is often similar although usually more particularized ("he was speeding"). Testimony of this sort, which stands at one or two removes from the indicated legal conclusions, cannot properly be faulted for being "too legal" in content.[12]

---

7. United States v. Barbee, 968 F.2d 1026, 1031 (10th Cir. 1992) (admitting DEA Agent's testimony that defendants engaged in drug trafficking); Karns v. Emerson Elec. Co., 817 F.2d 1452, 1459 (10th Cir. 1987) (admitting expert testimony that brushcutter was dangerous beyond expectation of average user).

8. United States v. Just (8th Cir. 1996) 74 F.3d 902, 905 (admitting expert testimony that what defendant sold was a "machinegun" as term is used in statute); United States v. Gold, 743 F.2d 800, 817 (11th Cir. 1984) (in trial for Medicare fraud, expert could say whether claims were eligible for reimbursement).

9. Phillips v. Calhoun, 956 F.2d 949, 952 (10th Cir. 1992) (personnel directors testify to "customary meaning and usage" of terms in manuals and job classification plans); United States v. Buchanan, 787 F.2d 477, 483-484 (10th Cir. 1986) (approving testimony by BATF officer that particular device would have to be registered).

10. United States v. Toushin, 899 F.2d 617, 620 n.3 (7th Cir. 1990) (IRS agent testified that amount in taxpayer's safe at beginning of tax period was not income reportable in earlier years); United States v. Fogg, 652 F.2d 551, 556-557 (5th Cir. 1981) (IRS agent testified that money would be considered constructive dividend).

11. United States v. Buchanan, 787 F.2d 477, 483-484 (10th Cir. 1986) (courts let experts testify that drugs fit a "particular statutory classification").

12. United States v. Theodoropoulos, 866 F.2d 587, 591 (3d Cir. 1989) (FBI agent trained in cryptanalysis and illicit business records testified on basis of transcribed phone conversations on roles played by defendants), *mandamus denied*, 489 U.S. 1009.

3. *Disclosure of Underlying Facts or Data*

FRE 705

Disclosure of Facts or Data Underlying Expert Opinion. The expert may testify in terms of opinion or inference and give reasons therefor without first testifying to the underlying facts or data, unless the court requires otherwise. The expert may in any event be required to disclose the underlying facts or data on cross-examination.

---

§7.15 Disclosing Underlying Data; Ruling on Adequacy of Basis

At least sometimes, the calling party has the option of presenting expert testimony in shorthand form, with the expert stating his conclusion directly and early in the presentation. In a personal injury suit by plaintiff Paula arising out of a car accident, for example, a doctor who qualifies as an expert witness and has examined Paula, may go right to the point: "In my opinion Paula is not likely to regain the use of her legs, and will need mobility assistance for life."[1]

Shorthand-direct model

The shorthand-direct or party choice model, as we might call it, was designed to increase the effectiveness of expert opinion testimony. The idea is to give the proponent more flexibility in presenting such testimony and to allow the main point to be stated early. Authorizing this approach, along with expanding the bases of expert testimony to include reasonable reliance on secondhand facts or data, went far to reduce the need for hypothetical questions and other laborious presentations.

The problem in those more traditional mechanisms is that so much time is spent exploring the bases of the opinion that the opinion itself becomes almost an anticlimax.[2] At least equally important, changes brought by the Rules created a new dynamic that favors generous admissibility of expert testimony and allows the proponent to present

---

§7.15 1. *See* letter of September 27, 1973, William B. Miller to Representative Hungate, enclosing report by Colorado Bar Association, in House Hearings (Supp.) at 355-356 (asked whether he has "an opinion based upon a reasonable degree of medical certainty as to the extent of permanent disability suffered by the plaintiff as a result of this automobile accident," orthopedic surgeon could say yes and then say plaintiff "is totally and permanently disabled"); Bezanson v. Fleet Bank-NH, 29 F.3d 16, 22 (1st Cir. 1994) (admitting statement that better deal "would more likely than not have succeeded" but for misconduct; experts may testify to "bare conclusions"); United States v. Shackelford, 494 F.2d 67, 71 (9th Cir. 1974) (quoting testimony as much to the point as that described above and commenting that "short-handed approach" may have been chosen as matter of strategy), *cert. denied*, 417 U.S. 934.

2. Twin City Plaza, Inc. v. Central Sur. & Ins. Corp., 409 F.2d 1195, 1201 (8th Cir. 1969) (Rules are designed to remove "stereotyped, long, belabored and nonsensical hypothetical questions" from trial).

more of the substance of expert opinion with less attention to under-lying details and bases.

When the calling party takes this shorthand-direct approach, it may already be clear that the expert is qualified and that her testimony is admissible. In the example cited above, it may be clear that the doctor is qualified and that he has treated the person about whom he is to testify, and the question may make it clear that the doctor is the appropriate person to provide the answer, and there is almost no room to argue that the basis for his testimony is inadequate. If any doubt remains or arises on this score, the matter may be further explored and then settled on voir dire.[3] It may be clear as well that the proffered testimony satisfies the helpfulness criterion, which can be resolved by reference to the points to be proved in the setting of the case, and the court can readily make this determination after the preliminaries are explored by the calling party and sometimes tested by others on voir dire.[4]

For these reasons, the calling party can and sometimes does choose the shorthand direct form of presentation, and taking this approach is consistent with the basic message of FRE 705, which can even be said to endorse or encourage parties to proceed in this way.[5]

In fact, however, the shorthand-direct approach is not the most common one, and few lawyers present an expert's somewhat unadorned conclusion and leave it at that. The reasons are not far to seek: To begin with, there is no assurance that unsupported conclu-sions will carry much weight with the jury, and unadorned conclusions may not be sufficient evidence to carry the day. If in fact the expert has done little in the way of preparation or study, or if he has relied on inadequate facts or data or has not applied the critical principles and methods in a reliable fashion, or if his testimony rests on invalid or unreliable theories, then cross-examination can expose these points and the testimony will not carry much weight. The court may end up striking it or finding that it is insufficient. **Path seldom taken**

If on the other hand the expert *is* well prepared and fully informed, and the proponent can satisfy all the requirements that accompany the use of experts, then the calling party would do well to develop the underlying basis during the direct testimony. To be sure, the calling party might take advantage of FRE 705 as the basis for presenting her expert's conclusion in the early going, then return to a lengthier expo-sition of the facts and basis of that conclusion. If the proponent does *not*

3. *See* the discussion of FRE 611 in §6.59, *supra.*
4. *See* the discussion of FRE 702 in §7.5, *supra.*
5. Symbol Technologies, Inc. v. Opticon, Inc., 935 F.2d 1569 (Fed. Cir. 1991) (admit-ting exhibits summarizing expert opinion on infringement without indicating basis; FRE 705 "functions to abbreviate trial by permitting opinion testimony without factual foundation," and cross can show if opinion is wrong); Bulthuis v. Rexall Corp., 789 F.2d 1315, 1316 (9th Cir. 1985) (doctor's affidavit said changes in condition of vaginal tissue "were caused by her mother's ingestion" of DES; court did not require advance dis-closure of facts, but gave opinion no weight because affidavit did not set them out; supporting facts "need not be stated unless requested," so it is unfair to grant summary judgment without opportunity to supply them).

lay out the facts and basis, opposing parties might refrain from doing the spadework for the calling party and leave the conclusion unsupported. This choice is more attractive to opponents than "hanging themselves" by cross-examination that actually helps the proponent by showing that indeed the expert's opinion is well-founded. Of course the proponent might later pursue the factual basis, either on redirect or by calling the witness a second time in rebuttal, but the court has discretion to block belated attempts to do what could easily have been done before.[6]

Admissibility issues must be determined sometime. Where the party-choice model is allowed to operate, and where the proponent takes the shorthand-direct approach, the result may simply be to defer the decision on admissibility. Clearly the mechanism endorsed in FRE 705 does not exempt expert testimony from the requirements of FRE 702 or permit decisions on admissibility to rest on credentials alone.

If expert testimony is admitted before the admissibility issue is resolved, cross-examination by an adverse party may later succeed in showing that the testimony lacks adequate support. The problem may be insufficient personal knowledge where there is no adequate substitute, reliance on facts not established by the evidence where there is no adequate substitute, secondhand reliance on facts or data from sources on which other experts in the field would not reasonably depend, or lack of valid theories that produce reliable results. In such cases, the court should strike the testimony.[7]

If the proponent never lays the foundation, it is often the case that unadorned and unsupported expert conclusions simply do not suffice to take an issue to the jury, and the point can be forced by a motion to strike or a motion seeking judgment as a matter of law. In short, unsupported opinion testimony may be stricken, and the Rule does not exempt experts from this aspect of judicial control.[8]

Requiring basis first   The Rule allows courts to depart from the party-choice model by requiring the basis to be set out first, although the phrasing means that courts should impose this requirement only for special reasons.

Arguably requiring an advance showing of the basis does not actually conflict with the party choice model because the focus of FRE 705 is on *the manner of presenting* expert testimony to the factfinder, not on *any obligation to clear the admissibility hurdle* with the judge, and the 1993 amendment to FRE 705 supports this reading. That amendment abandoned the earlier phrase suggesting that an expert could give evidence "without prior disclosure" of the underlying facts or data, and

---

6. *See generally* the discussion of FRE 611 in §6.54, *supra.*

7. Wilder Enterprises, Inc. v. Allied Artists Pictures Corp., 632 F.2d 1135, 1143 (4th Cir. 1980) (excluding testimony by economist on value of plaintiff's property; he admitted he was not expert in local real estate values; no local realtor furnished facts for calculations; no showing that underlying data about local values was the type that others in field would rely on).

8. Kerr-McGee Corp. v. Helton, 133 S.W.3d 245, 251 (Tex. 2004) (striking testimony on gas well production after cross disclosed that expert had no basis; need not object prior to testimony, so long as objection is raised promptly on discovering lack of basis).

substituted the present language indicating that an expert can give evidence "without first testifying" to the underlying facts or data. The change suggests that disclosure may well be required prior to expert testimony that gives an "opinion or inference," and of course it is disclosure to the court that is necessary in deciding the question whether there is an adequate basis for the expert's testimony. In the same year the Civil Rules were amended to provide for expanded (often automatic) discovery of experts, which means that often adverse parties will already be informed on the underlying bases of expert testimony.[9]

There are at least six situations, somewhat overlapping in nature, in which it makes sense to require the underlying basis to be made known first. As noted above, it is arguable that requiring the proponent to lay out the basis in advance, for purposes of obtaining a ruling on admissibility, does not actually conflict with the party-choice model, and in fact during trial the proponent might still take advantage of the shorthand-direct method of presentation. Here are the six:

(1) Reason to doubt. It seems generally appropriate to take this step where there is reason to doubt that the expert has an adequate basis for his testimony, or to doubt that adverse parties will have an adequate opportunity to test the expert on cross. In such settings, allowing the proponent to take full advantage of the party-choice model would bring undue risk because the testimony would likely have to be stricken and perhaps a mistrial declared, or because the testimony would be unfair to other parties.[10]

(2) Issue presented by pretrial motion. If either party presents the question of admitting expert testimony by pretrial motion, the court can and sometimes must address the gamut of admissibility questions in advance, again requiring the calling party (or proponent) to set out the bases. Ordinarily courts have discretion whether to rule in advance or wait until trial, and if the moving party is the opponent of such testimony the court might prefer to postpone the issue simply to preserve the proponent's flexibility. But regardless who makes the motion, courts are well justified in resolving the issue in a pretrial hearing if the admissibility problem is serious or technical or likely to be time consuming, and may require the proponent to set out the proposed basis of the testimony.[11]

---

9. On discovery of experts in civil cases, *see* FRCP 26(a)(2)(B) (turning over reports by experts who are to testify) and FRCP 26(b)(4)(A) (deposing experts who are to testify).

10. Beaulieu v. The Aube Corp., 796 A.2d 683 (Me. 2002) (in dramshop suit, expert could not testify that patron must have looked intoxicated; no facts supported conclusion; if opponent makes prima facie showing of insufficient basis, must exclude opinion); University of Rhode Island v. A.W. Chesterton Co., 2 F.3d 1200, 1218 (1st Cir. 1993) (excluding testimony by university comptroller estimating damages; bases were hearsay; proponent made "no attempt whatever to assuage" concerns by producing documents).

11. *See* United States v. Sepulveda, 15 F.3d 1161, 1183 (1st Cir. 1993) (government described testimony expected from law officer; defense moved to exclude; court denied motion in light of representation that witness would rely on testimony and experience,

(3) Daubert *issues.* When questions arise under *Daubert* and FRE 702, the issue of admissibility often requires a hearing. Since *Kumho Tire* extends the *Daubert* standard to *all* expert testimony, there is a potential for *Daubert* issues with nearly all expert testimony.[12]

The appearance of *Daubert* issues does not always require lengthy hearings or inquiries, however, and shortcuts are often available. Sometimes pivotal *Daubert* issues have been resolved by authoritative decisions, and sometimes factual issues have been resolved in a manner that invites judicial notice. Sometimes the points necessary to decide *Daubert* issues can be developed in briefs, or by argument, perhaps augmented by affidavits, so a more elaborate hearing is unnecessary, and courts can rule in summary fashion. Sometimes issues of validity or reliability are familiar, and foundational inquiries are simple, so a court can avoid a pretrial hearing, as is often true when the validity question turns mostly on the experience of the witness and his familiarity with the facts. And sometimes appropriate findings rest on the fact that the evidence has achieved a level of general acceptance that alone establishes reliability, or even unreliability. Finally, *Daubert* issues can sometimes be resolved by consulting journals or treatises, and the experience of regulatory agencies is a pertinent factor as well.[13]

It is when such shortcuts are not available that hearings become necessary. In these hearings, clearly the court can and usually must require the proponent to lay out the foundation for the proposed expert testimony, providing information on the theory, the application of the theory, and the factual basis for the testimony, as amended FRE 702 requires.[14] Of course such hearings are best conducted before trial, where the matter can be briefed, argued, and decided without disruption and without taking up the time of jurors who are likely to be kept waiting if such hearings go forward during the trial. Toxic tort cases fit this description: Here the court typically decides questions about the necessity or adequacy of epidemiological evidence, bioassays, animal studies, medical diagnoses, and the technique of "differential diagnosis" in proving causation. In these and similar cases, the proponent must present the basis in advance.[15]

---

but later struck testimony because he relied on "undifferentiated conversations" with "unidentified police officers" and could not "articulate a plausible basis," but it did not follow that court erred in overruling motion) (citing authors of this Treatise).

12. The references are to Daubert v. Merrell Dow Pharmaceuticals, Inc., 509 U.S. 579 (1993), and Kumho Tire Co. v. Carmichael, 526 U.S. 137, 147 (1999), described in §7.7, *supra.*

13. *See* the discussion in §7.7, *supra.*

14. State v. Fortin, 843 A.2d 974, 1000 (N.J. 2004) (error to admit expert testimony on similarity of murder to earlier offense; "uniqueness analysis" was not science, but there are enough "common elements" to apply principles of scientific evidence, which require disclosure of database to strengthen or validate conclusions and allow jury to know if there were flaws in analysis) (reversing).

15. United States v. Brien, 59 F.3d 274, 278 (1st Cir. 1995) (FRE 705 "does not impair—indeed, has nothing to do with—the trial judge's right to insist" on getting "underlying information by proffer" in making preliminary ruling on admissibility) (court applying *Daubert* can require foundation).

(4) Summary judgment motions. In civil cases pretrial motions for summary judgment may require the court to consider and perhaps decide whether expert testimony is admissible. Here it seems that affidavits setting forth conclusory opinions may be discounted simply because the underlying basis is not set forth, although respect for the party choice convention of FRE 705 suggests that courts should give the calling party (proponent) a second chance to provide the underlying support by means of a show-cause order.[16] Some authority suggests that courts should be generous in accepting conclusory presentations as adequate, but this approach would drain the summary judgment mechanism of much of its usefulness.[17]

(5) Mental condition of the accused. Expert testimony on the mental condition of the accused should be presented along with at least some details of the underlying basis. In this setting FRE 704(b) in effect requires experts to keep their testimony at one remove from ultimate issues and to testify more specifically about the existence and nature of any affliction and the ways such affliction might affect the behavior of someone who suffers from it. Giving such details is perhaps not quite the same thing as describing the underlying basis of a diagnosis, but there is considerable overlap. Here at least the party choice convention of FRE 705 should give way to the extent necessary to provide the details that FRE 704(b) requires.[18]

(6) Voir dire. The shorthand-direct approach conflicts in some respects with a longstanding tradition that allows adverse parties to test the qualifications of experts (and even lay witnesses) by voir dire before substantive testimony is given.[19] Indeed, some state provisions expressly protect the old tradition allowing advance disclosure of the basis by voir dire examination. While FRE 705 did not end the practice of voir dire as it relates to expert testimony, preserving the proponent's option to take the shorthand direct approach means that adversaries should not stretch the process of voir dire into a lengthy examination and attack on the expert or on the bases for the proposed testimony.[20]

16. Ambrosini v. Labarraque, 966 F.2d 1464, 1467 (D.C. Cir. 1992) (in suit alleging limb reduction defects, court should not have granted summary judgment because expert testimony on causation did not reveal basis; proponent need not first state facts or data; should not assume expert relied on recalculations from published studies; judge must undertake anew inquiry taken in prior case raising issue).

17. B.F. Goodrich v. Betkoski, 99 F.3d 505, 525 (2d Cir. 1996) (on summary judgment motion, affidavit raised genuine issues; affiant referred to documents supporting opinion, and "need not detail all the facts and data underlying" opinion), *cert. denied*, 524 U.S. 926; Monks v. General Elec. Co., 919 F.2d 1189, 1192 (6th Cir. 1990) (FRE 705 lets expert give opinion without first disclosing data; error to exclude affidavit that "was more than a bare, conclusory allegation" that negligence caused helicopter accident, even though it did not contain extensive detail) (but plaintiff could not prevail even with affidavit).

18. *See* the discussion of FRE 704(b) in §7.13, *supra.*

19. *See* discussion of FRE 611 in §6.59, *supra.*

20. Provisions adopted in Alaska, Delaware, Florida, Maine, and Texas permit voir dire of an expert before he states a conclusion. The Ohio provision requires the basis to be stated first, and Rules in Hawaii and Idaho require disclosure of the data during discovery if the expert is to give conclusions first.

§7.16 Cross-Examining Experts

The second sentence of FRE 705 recognizes the critical importance of cross-examination in connection with expert testimony. Even if the expert has not yet testified to the "facts or data" underlying the opinion that he has provided, he must be prepared to reveal what he has relied on, and what he has ignored or dismissed as insignificant, in reaching the conclusions that he presented in his testimony. On cross-examination, the expert is "required to disclose the underlying facts or data," in the language of the Rule.

Cross-examination is critical even when experts have testified to the underlying facts or data on direct. In cases where the proponent follows the shorthand-direct approach described in the previous section, the task of cross-examination is even more critical. Clearly the Rules place on adverse parties much of the burden of testing the underlying bases of expert testimony.[1]

The second sentence of FRE 705 recognizes the challenge and burden placed on adverse parties, and it is clear that the cross-examiner is entitled to delve into the bases of expert opinion in considerable detail.[2] Since the opinion may rest on hearsay and other inadmissible material, cross-examination rightly and necessarily puts before the fact-finder evidence that would not otherwise be admitted.[3] In a wrongful death suit on behalf of passengers killed in a collision with snowplowing equipment in New Hampshire, for example, the defense was allowed to cross-examine an economist who testified in support of claims for "hedonic damages" (loss of enjoyment of life) and loss of income by

---

§7.16 1. State v. Belken, 633 N.W.2d 786, 800 (Iowa 2001) (DNA profiling expert was not obligated to explain "specific mathematical computations" and defense was responsible to bring out underlying data on cross); State v. Cort, 766 A.2d 260, 266 (N.H. 2000) (admitting testimony on shaken baby syndrome without offering underlying medical literature; defense was free to cross-examine on basis).

2. Wilson By and Through Wilson v. Merrell Dow Pharmaceuticals Inc., 893 F.2d 1149, 1153 (10th Cir. 1990) (drug maker introduced expert testimony based partly on sales charts plotting birth defect rates and number of pills sold, despite objection that data failed to distinguish sales of Bendectin "during the limb development period" from other sales; this failure weakens value but affects weight, not admissibility; on cross, counsel brought out inadequacies). *But see* United States v. Hensel, 699 F.2d 18, 38 (1st Cir. 1983) (after DEA agent testified on habits of drug smugglers and investigation of Turkey Cove, defense sought background material in form of DEA manuals, guidelines, reports, memoranda, and opinions on drug smuggling; court denied production because documents were not involved in investigation or essential to defense; FRE 705 did not require production since agent testified that opinion was based on experience in drug smuggling investigations, not these documents), *cert. denied*, 461 U.S. 958.

3. Carignan v. Wheeler, 898 A.2d 1011, 1016 (N.H. 2006) (motorcycle passenger could cross-examine motorist's expert on statement in deposition on which expert relied); United States v. Whitetail, 956 F.2d 857, 861, (8th Cir. 1992) (defendant in murder trial introduced expert testimony that she suffered from battered woman syndrome; prosecutor could ask about prior fights where she was aggressor; questions about "underlying facts or data" on which experts base conclusions were proper despite FRE 404).

asking him about the impact of the decedent's substance abuse on these matters, including use of "Special K" methamphetamines, LSD, and alcohol, even though such matters suggested bad character and brought obvious risks of unfair prejudice.[4]

Unsavory facts of such description often come out in cross-examining the expert witness, sometimes as a way of suggesting limits to the information that the expert relied on, hence possible flaws in his conclusions, and sometimes by way of suggesting that the opinion must be wrong because it conflicts so sharply with particular information. Of course such questions must themselves reflect facts, or at least creditable information that justify the questions, and they must be relevant to the opinion being tested.[5]

The Rule does not obviate hearsay and other objections to material considered by experts, so the court may exercise its discretion under FRE 403 and FRE 611 to limit or even block cross-examination if the danger is too large that the jury will misuse facts implied by the questions in damaging ways. These concerns make it especially appropriate to restrict direct examination by the calling party,[6] and the cross-examiner should have greater latitude, since presumably the calling party got some benefit from the expert's testimony and adverse parties have a corresponding need to test and challenge it. But proper accommodation of the exclusionary rules may even require some restriction on cross-examination,[7] and of course courts may curtail cross that seems redundant, irrelevant, or only marginally useful.[8]

Cross-examining an expert on the underlying bases of opinion testimony waives objections the adverse party might otherwise make to any mention of these points. The tactic does not, however, foreclose objections to other uses of the material, and he is still entitled to a limiting instruction on request, unless he makes or invites additional use of it. It seems as well that the adverse party is not entitled to make unlimited use of material considered by an expert if the calling party objects and

4. McLaughlin v. Fisher Engineering, 834 A.2d 258, 263 (N.H. 2003) (expert may rely on inadmissible facts or data; cross-examiner may ask about otherwise-inadmissible material, to test knowledge and fairness by asking what changes would affect opinion, and ascertain what he considered).

5. State v. Thornton, 800 A.2d 1016, 1043 (R.I. 2002) (in domestic violence trial, letting prosecutor cross-examine medical expert on violent acts, which conflicted with opinion that defendant's misbehavior resulted from alcohol consumption or drug use) (defense did not contest factual basis).

6. See the discussion in §7.10, *supra*.

7. United States v. Angiulo, 847 F.2d 956, 973 (1st Cir. 1988) (in RICO trial, FBI agent testified on structure and operations of Cosa Nostra and gave opinion on relationships of defendants to organization, relying on informants whose identity he did not disclose, which did not violate FRE 705 or confrontation clause; agent relied on recordings played at trial; defense could cross-examine on factual bases).

8. In re Air Disaster at Lockerbie Scotland on Dec. 21, 1988, 37 F.3d 804, 824 (2d Cir. 1994) (in civil suit arising out of plane crash in Scotland after bomb exploded, limiting defense cross-examination of experts to scenarios that have "evidentiary support" in record, and blocking cross into "other causation theories" in absence of good faith basis to believe theories have evidentiary support) (could draw jury into misleading conjecture).

the material is inadmissible. Calling an expert who relies on hearsay or other evidence that could not be admitted by itself should not be viewed as waiving the calling party's objection to improper use of the underlying data. The entitlement of the adverse party to cross-examine about the data does not extend to using the data in ways other than attacking the credibility of the expert.

Especially with the liberality brought by FRE 703 and FRE 705 in presenting expert testimony, effective cross-examination of expert testimony puts a premium on pretrial preparation and discovery.[9] And the 1993 amendment to FRE 705, and amendments to the civil discovery rules, recognize the importance of discovery in the effective presentation and testing of expert opinion testimony at trial. The amendment to FRE 705 abandoned the original phrase stating that an expert could give evidence "without prior disclosure" of underlying facts or data, and substituted the language presently found in the Rule, indicating that an expert can give evidence "without first testifying" to the underlying facts or data. This change recognizes that in fact disclosure is often expected or required during pretrial discovery, and the main reason is to enable adverse parties to cross-examine experts effectively. Indications that the proponent of expert testimony did not cooperate as expected during pretrial discovery are taken seriously, and in appropriate cases expert testimony should be excluded if adverse parties have been misled or stymied in reasonable attempts to pursue pretrial discovery.[10]

D. COURT-APPOINTED EXPERTS

FRE 706

(a) **Appointment.** The court may on its own motion or on the motion of any party enter an order to show cause why expert witnesses should not be appointed, and may request the parties to submit nominations. The court may appoint any expert witnesses agreed

9. United States v. Lawson, 653 F.2d 299, 301 (7th Cir. 1981) (expert testimony rebutting insanity defense; psychiatrist relied on reports, interviews with physicians, and background supplied by FBI and prosecutor's office; data provided to defense under *Brady* request; opportunity for cross was adequate), *cert. denied*, 454 U.S. 1150.

10. State v. Fortin, 843 A.2d 974, 1000 (N.J. 2004) (error to admit testimony describing similarity of charged offense to other offense committed by defendant, saying that expert never had "seen, heard or read" of such a "combination of behaviors," as state had not produced, when requested, any data supporting conclusion; Rule 705 permits court to require production of such material "to ensure the validity" of expert opinion) (reversing); Smith v. Ford Motor Co., 626 F.2d 784 (10th Cir. 1980) (plaintiff tried to prove internal injuries resulted from seatbelt that malfunctioned, but misled defendant; pretrial submission indicated that doctor would testify on treatment and prognosis, not causation; defendant unable to conduct discovery important for effective cross) (reversing), *cert. denied*, 450 U.S. 918. *But see* State v. Maynard, 88 P.3d 695 (Idaho 2004) (discovery rule did not require advance disclosure to defense of basis for opinion in DUI case; rule 705 and discovery rules are mutually independent; neither required exclusion of testimony for refusing to disclose information).

upon by the parties, and may appoint expert witnesses of its own selection. An expert witness shall not be appointed by the court unless the witness consents to act. A witness so appointed shall be informed of the witness' duties by the court in writing, a copy of which shall be filed with the clerk, or at a conference in which the parties shall have opportunity to participate. A witness so appointed shall advise the parties of the witness' findings, if any; the witness' deposition may be taken by any party; and the witness may be called to testify by the court or any party. The witness shall be subject to cross-examination by each party, including a party calling the witness.

(b) Compensation. Expert witnesses so appointed are entitled to reasonable compensation in whatever sum the court may allow. The compensation thus fixed is payable from funds which may be provided by law in criminal cases and civil actions and proceedings involving just compensation under the fifth amendment. In other civil actions and proceedings the compensation shall be paid by the parties in such proportion and at such time as the court directs, and thereafter charged in like manner as other costs.

(c) Disclosure of appointment. In the exercise of its discretion, the court may authorize disclosure to the jury of the fact that the court appointed the expert witness.

(d) Parties' experts of own selection. Nothing in this rule limits the parties in calling expert witnesses of their own selection.

§7.17 Procedure for Court Appointment

Commentators and decisions generally agree that courts have inherent authority to appoint expert witnesses, and FRE 706 codifies this authority in the federal system, prescribing in detail the procedure to be followed and limits to be observed.

Court appointment of experts is almost entirely discretionary, and it seems most appropriate in two general situations. One is the case where the parties simply fail to produce evidence of clear probity on complicated technical issues that are important.[1] Sometimes the reason is that they cannot find or obtain what they need, and a court might conceivably play a constructive role by appointing an expert who would agree to testify for the court but would hesitate or refuse to act under party sponsorship. The other is the case where the parties call experts who differ sharply on important issues that are again complex and technical, at least where further expertise holds some promise of breaking a deadlock or shedding further useful light on the matter.[2] But conflicts in expert

§7.17 1. Students of California School for Blind v. Honig, 736 F.2d 538, 548-549 (9th Cir. 1984) (approving appointment of expert where court could not decide merits of seismic safety claim after long trial with conflicting expert testimony).

2. Brown v. Ivarans Rederi A/S, 545 F.2d 854, 858 n.6 (3d Cir. 1976) (conflict in medical testimony on future impairment of earnings would present "appropriate circumstances" for court to appoint medical expert), *cert. denied*, 430 U.S. 969.

opinions are routinely encountered in trials, and court appointment of experts holds promise only if significant gaps in coverage appear or conflicts develop on which further perspectives seem useful.[3]

Sparingly exercised   Court authority to appoint expert witnesses should be exercised sparingly. The parties bear the main responsibility to present the case, and they need latitude in selecting and calling witnesses. Courts usually know less about the evidence and issues than the lawyers and are not usually well situated to decide what subjects require more expert information.

Long before trial   The procedure for court-appointed experts works best if set in motion long before trial, but the need for such action may not be apparent early. Careful work at pretrial may help, as may suggestions by parties. Courts may interrupt a trial to appoint an expert, but doing so is usually costly and impracticable, and it seems that courts cannot call experts in mid-trial if doing so would deprive parties of the procedural safeguards established by FRE 706, including the chance to be heard on the propriety of appointment and the scope of the expert's responsibilities, the right to learn the substance of the expected testimony, and the chance to depose the expert if necessary.[4]

Court may act on its own   The procedure established by FRE 706 has five main features:

First, the court may act on its own initiative or on request by a party. In either case the parties should have a chance to be heard on the matter through a show-cause order.[5] While the court is not required to take nominations from the parties, doing so is clearly better practice. If the parties agree on an expert, that fact should weigh very heavily in favor of her selection.[6] Whether or not nominations are submitted, the court may appoint an expert of its own choosing and need not choose someone nominated by a party,[7] and of course the court may solicit outside advice from a suitable professional association on whom to appoint.[8] Actions by the court under FRE 706 do not affect the rights of the parties to call experts of their own. In any case, the trial judge has broad discretion in deciding whether and whom to appoint.

---

3. Walker v. American Home Shield Long Term Disability Plan, 180 F.3d 1065, 1070 (9th Cir. 1999); Oklahoma Natural Gas Co., Div. of Oneok, Inc. v. Mahan & Rowsey, Inc., 786 F.2d 1004, 1007 (10th Cir. 1986), *cert. denied*, 479 U.S. 853.

4. *See* Georgia-Pacific Corp. v. United States, 640 F.2d 328, 334 (Ct. Cl. 1980) (no error to refuse to appoint on request; FRE 706 was not followed); United States v. Weathers, 618 F.2d 663, 664 n.1 (10th Cir. 1980), *cert. denied*, 446 U.S. 956.

5. United States v. Articles Provimi, 425 F. Supp. 228, 231 (D.N.J. 1977) (parties to show cause why court should not appoint designated expert; furnishing curriculum vitae, asking parties to submit directions), supp. op., 74 F.R.D. 126 (D.N.J. 1977) (proposing conference with expert and counsel).

6. *See* 3 Saltzburg, Martin & Capra, Federal Rules of Evidence Manual §706.02[3][b] (2006) ("advantageous" to choose expert agreed on by parties unless there is strong reason to ignore their wishes).

7. Students of California School for Blind v. Honig, 736 F.2d 538, 549 (9th Cir. 1984).

8. *See* Saltzburg, The Unnecessarily Expanding Role of the American Trial Judge, 64 Va. L. Rev. 1, 77-79 (1978) (judge should "play no role" in selecting expert, but should consult a body "able to judge the qualifications of its members" and provide "all possible assurances of independence").

Second, FRE 706 contemplates that an expert may be appointed only if she consents to act, hence that courts should not in effect draft expert witnesses. A court would not likely appoint an expert who did not consent, but parties sometimes succeed in calling involuntary experts and arguably courts can do the same thing.[9] Clearly FRE 706 contemplates otherwise, however, and it appears to be controlling on this question.

Expert must consent

Third, the court-appointed expert is to be advised of her duties in writing, and a copy is to be filed and obviously made available to the parties. Pretty clearly court and parties should consult in advance on the scope of the expert's responsibilities, but it seems that the court has substantial responsibility and authority in this area and may solicit advice and expert assistance in ways and on subjects that the parties do not agree to.

Must be advised of duties

Fourth, FRE 706(a) provides that the expert is to advise the parties of her findings and that any party may take her deposition. This provision represents a departure from prior practice. In criminal cases, the previous rule did not provide for depositions, and general provisions authorize depositions only in limited circumstances.[10] In civil cases, the prior rule sharply restricted depositions of expert witnesses, although discovery of experts was more extensive than the rule suggested, and a change late in 1993 vastly expanded discovery.[11] FRE 706(a) sets no conditions on deposing court-appointed experts, and it seems that the parties have an unqualified right to take such depositions, although probably they may be required to pay expert fees for doing so.

Must advise the parties

Fifth, a court-appointed expert may be called to testify by the court or by any party. Either way, the court and the parties may question the witness, and any party may cross-examine.[12] The fact of court appointment may be disclosed only by court permission, which is discretionary. This provision seeks to ameliorate the oft-repeated objection that a court-appointed expert conveys an aura of impartiality that may well be illusory, and presumably nondisclosure of the fact of court appointment removes or reduces this danger.

May be called by court or any party

---

9. Kaufman v. Edelstein, 539 F.2d 811, 820-821 (2d Cir. 1976) (government properly subpoenaed expert witness to explain services performed and advice given, but not evaluate or conduct studies).

10. *See* former FRCrimP 28 (authorizing court appointment of experts but not providing for depositions). *And see* FRCrimP 15(a) (party may depose his own prospective witness on motion whenever "due to exceptional circumstances" it is in interest of justice that testimony be taken and preserved); 18 U.S.C. §3503 (similar language; if government seeks such testimony, it must certify that proceeding involves organized crime).

11. As amended in 1993, FRCP 26 calls for extensive and automatic discovery of experts, and allows for depositions of experts as well. Former FRCP 26(b)(4)(A)-(B) required a motion and a special showing, in effect discouraging and limiting discovery of experts.

12. *See* Computer Assocs. Intl., Inc. v. Altai, Inc., 982 F.2d 693, 713 (2d Cir. 1992); Johnson Controls, Inc. v. Phoenix Control Sys., Inc., 886 F.2d 1173, 1176 (9th Cir. 1989); Students of California School for Blind v. Honig, 736 F.2d 538, 549 (9th Cir. 1984).

E. SPECIAL AREAS OF TECHNICAL EVIDENCE

§7.18 Statistical Evidence

Using ordinary statistical inference as proof of commonplace events or conditions has had a rocky history in the judicial system. On the civil side, in what are often called "blue bus" cases, courts rebel at arguments that defendant's bus or tire caused the injury simply because defendant is responsible for *most* of the buses or tires that might have caused the injury. And in the landmark criminal decision in the *Collins* case, where eyewitness testimony indicated that a black man and a blond woman mugged a woman in an alley in Los Angeles, the California Supreme Court overturned a conviction after a trial in which the prosecutor argued that various human qualities common to the culprits and the defendants are so rare that statistical probabilities heavily favored the proposition that defendants *were* the culprits.[1]

Different forms, same process   In a sense, statistical inference and ordinary human reasoning are just different forms of the same process. In cases like *Collins*, for example, eyewitness testimony would recall many details shared by the culprits and the defendants, each fairly common in itself, and would depend in part on the proposition that finding them together is less likely than seeing any of them alone. (Other details were that the man had a beard and mustache, the woman had a ponytail, the two comprised an interracial couple, and they drove off in a partly yellow convertible.) If the frequency or scarcity of each quality could be quantified, so could the probability of seeing all these qualities combined. For independent events or qualities, the product rule gives the probability that they will appear together: In flipping a coin, the probability of getting two heads in two flips is $1/4$, which is computed by the product rule $(1/2 \times 1/2)$. In *Collins*, the prosecutor suggested that the probability of finding all the details together was $1/12,000,000$.[2]

Allowing ordinary human inference while rejecting statistical inference cannot be explained by saying only the former is probative. In fact there are at least four other reasons for skepticism—four pitfalls in the use of statistical inference. Some are technical in nature, and some raise larger policy issues.

Pitfalls: No supporting proof   First, statistical inference, whether suggested by testimony or argument, should not be allowed when there is no proof supporting the suggested frequency or probabilities. In *Collins*, for example, there was

---

§7.18 1. People v. Collins, 438 P.2d 33 (Cal. 1968) (reversing second degree robbery conviction because of the misuse of statistics, for many reasons that are explored in this section).

2. For a sampling of the literature generated by *Collins* and probabilistic evidence generally, *see* McCord, A Primer for the Nonmathematically Inclined on Mathematical Evidence in Criminal Cases: People v. Collins and Beyond, 47 Wash. & Lee L. Rev. 741 (1990); Allen, Rationality, Mythology, and the "Acceptability of Verdicts" Thesis, 66 B.U.L. Rev. 541 (1986); Nesson, The Evidence or the Event? On Judicial Proof and the Acceptability of Verdicts, 98 Harv. L. Rev. 1357 (1985); Kaye, The Paradox of the Gatecrasher and Other Stories, 1979 Ariz. St. L.J. 101.

no proof that one car in ten is partly yellow or that one couple in a thousand is "interracial." These were made-up numbers, and the point is not so much that they are too high or too low, but that they purport to add precision to common insights that resist such refinement. The tactic adds a false patina of science to the everyday process of interpretation and evaluation, and suggests that refusing to draw the invited inferences would be unscientific and perhaps unreasonable. Absent proof supporting the quantification, this tactic should be disallowed under FRE 403 as misleading and confusing.

Second, the product rule applies only if each factor is independent. In the case of two coin flips, it is right to multiply one-half times one-half, reaching one-quarter as the probability of getting heads twice in a row. But is would be wrong, for instance, to predict the likelihood of drawing a Queen of Hearts (QH) from a full deck by multiplying the fraction representing queens (1/13) times the fraction representing red cards (1/2) times the fraction representing hearts (1/4), which produces the fraction 1/104, exaggerating the scarcity of the event by making the final fraction smaller than it should be. The probabilities of being a heart and being red are *not* independent (all hearts being red), so multiplying by the fraction for red cards exaggerates the quality of being red. In *Collins*, the court suggested that the fractions for having a beard (1/10) and a moustache (1/4) were overlapping (again exaggerating scarcity by making the final fraction smaller), and obviously the product rule should not be used where the multipliers lack independence.

Pitfalls: Independent factors

Third, the probability generated by the product rule is easily misinterpreted. For those untrained in statistics, the matter is subtle and intuition is a faulty guide. One common error involves the supposition that the result obtained by the product rule *directly yields* the probability that two identical occurrences or observations involve the same person or object, a mistake sometimes made by lawyers and judges, and no doubt by lay people.[3] This fallacy can be illustrated by a thought experiment involving two draws from a hat containing three decks of cards (replacing the first card and mixing before drawing again): Suppose we get a Queen of Hearts (QH) both times, and we want to know the probability that we got the *same* QH both times. The probability of drawing a QH is 1/52, but that figure does *not* represent the probability that the second card is a *different* QH. And the probability that we got the *same* QH both times is *not* 51/52 (which is 1 minus 1/52). In short, the probability of *a discrete outcome* (1/52) in which many quantifiable factors appear together does *not* directly yield the probability of *identity*—the probability

Pitfalls: Easily misinterpreted

3. *See, e.g.*, State v. Garrison, 585 P.2d 563, 565 (Ariz. 1978) (mistakenly construing reported probability of only eight in one million that two sets of teeth would produce identical bite-mark patterns as meaning that there was only an eight in one million probability that teeth marks on victim were not defendant's); United States v. Massey, 594 F.2d 676, 680 (8th Cir. 1978) (reversing, where judge converted probability that only three to five out of 2,500 hair samples would match into probability of mistakenly finding match, and in closing argument prosecutor equated same figure with probability of innocence).

that two identical occurrences or observations involve the same person or object. In *Collins*, the prosecutor committed this error (arguing that there was only one chance in 12,000,000 that defendants were innocent), and the reviewing court was right to be critical.

Of course the scarcity of the combined factors does *bear on* the probability that two identical occurrences or observations involve the same person or object. In that hat-and-card example, the probability that the second card is the same QH is pretty high (it is 1/3, since there are three decks in the hat), and the scarcity of QHs (only 1/52 of all cards) is the reason the probability is that high.[4] *Collins* is harder than the example because we don't know the composition of Los Angeles (which changes with people coming and going every day), and the frequency estimates cannot tell us whether other "magic couples" exist, or how many. The court in *Collins* included an Appendix that only people trained in statistics can easily understand, which purports to demonstrate mathematically that *if* the various estimates were correct (one girl in ten has a ponytail, and so forth), and if the suspect population contains 12,000,000 units (presumably "couples with cars" since one of the estimates was 1/1,000 for interracial couples in a car), *and* if the suspect population were comprised of 12,000,000 units drawn at random from a universe comprised of an infinitely large number of units whose proportions conformed to the suppositions of the prosecutor (one-quarter of the men have beards, and so forth), then there is a 41 percent likelihood of finding one or more *additional* magic couples in the suspect population, given that there is at least one such couple. From this fact one can compute the probability of identity, which comes in at more than 75 percent, meaning a probability of more than 75 percent that the defendants were the culprits.[5] That is an impressive number, but not proof beyond a reasonable doubt, and of course the prosecutor's suggested number was *much* higher than that. Perhaps most importantly, it is both easy and tempting to suppose that the combined scarcity figure directly yields the probability of identity (or guilt, in a case like *Collins*), which is simply wrong.

---

4. If all we knew is that we got a red card on two draws (with replacement after first draw) and we wanted to know how probable it was that we got the same red card both times, the fact that red cards are common (one-half the cards in the hat) would bear on the answer. Given that the hat contains three decks (156 cards, of which 78 are red and 78 are black), the probability that the second red card is the very same one we drew before would be 1/78, a much smaller probability than we found for the QH, which is consistent with the intuition that identical outcomes are more likely to involve the same object if their shared qualities are rare.

5. *See* Cullison, Identification by Probabilities and Trial by Arithmetic (A Lesson for Beginners on How to Be Wrong with Greater Precision), 6 Hous. L. Rev. 471, 485-500 (1969). For an argument that the Appendix in *Collins* is misconceived, *see* Finkelstein & Fairley, a Bayesian Approach to Identification Evidence, 83 Harv. L. Rev. 489, 492-494 (1970) (1/12,000,000 was intended to represent the actual population of Los Angeles, so using it "as the parameter for a 'generational' probability model" is wrong; if we had proof of relative scarcities of the qualities, "it would be possible to state within reasonable margins for error that there was only one" magic couple in the area).

Fourth, there are many larger reasons based in policy for rejecting statistical inferences in conventional cases.

For one thing, jurors may be overwhelmed by the numbers, so much that they neglect their duty to appraise the unquantified evidence. In *Collins*, for example, the jury may have set aside doubts about eyewitness accounts, and yet those accounts might have been mistaken on some or all of the points of detail that were quantified by suggestion at trial: Perhaps the car was not partly yellow, or the man was not black or the woman was not blond. This general argument, however, has been sharply challenged by those who counter that common sense *under-values* the impact of quantified factors that are truly rare.[6]

Another objection is that statistical inference on points relating to identity in criminal cases seems to undermine the requirement of proof beyond reasonable doubt. To the extent the critical inference is statistical, a judgment of conviction quantifies the degree of doubt tolerated by the system, which is likely to reduce respect and confidence.[7] Can we live with convictions based on a statistical inference that there is a 95 percent probability of guilt, or even 99 percent? And to the extent that statistical inferences supplant common sense, the moral function of the beyond-reasonable-doubt standard is diluted, and replaced with false science that eases the way for convictions where reasonable doubt might otherwise exist.

There are yet other reasons to reject statistical inferences of this sort: In civil cases, for instance, allowing such inferences would create counterincentives against seeking more particular proof, conceivably undercut or destroy much of the work of juries, and starkly quantify the risk of error inherent in civil judgments. Consider, for example, the case in which a defective tire explodes in a shop, injuring the worker who is mounting it on a wheel, and the proof shows that defendant makes 80 percent of the tires found in the shop. If this "naked statistical proof" allows the plaintiff to prevail, one who gets this far in preparation need not seek particular proof connecting the tire to the defendant, and might even avoid looking for it (such proof might show the tire was made by someone else). And if proof of 80 percent is enough, what is left for a jury to decide? Denying recovery would be unreasonable, and presumably courts in such cases would enter judgment for plaintiff as a matter of law. Yet judgments resting on such proof would be subject to the criticism of being only 80 percent right, and to the criticism that all similarly situated defendants will lose too, even though only 80 percent should

---

6. *See* Saks and Kidd, Human Information Processing and Adjudication: Trial by Heuristics, 15 Law & Soc. 123 (1980-1981) (humans engage in simplifying techniques to manage complex data, which introduce various kinds of distortion, and undervalue the logical force of statistical proof).

7. *See generally* Tribe, Trial by Mathematics: Precision and Ritual in the Legal Process, 84 Harv. L. Rev. 1329, 1373 (1971) (system should avoid acknowledging a quantitative measure of doubt); Nesson, Reasonable Doubt and Permissive Inferences: The Value of Complexity, 92 Harv. L. Rev. 1187, 1196-1197 (1979) (quantifying reasonable doubt would undercut its function).

suffer this fate. In this and other "blue bus" settings, courts reject statistical inference and arguments.[8]

Bayes' Theorem   The process of inference aided by statistics can be considerably refined by using a theorem originally developed in the nineteenth century by Reverend Thomas Bayes. This theorem describes the degree to which a new item of evidence, when it can be expressed as a datum of known frequency, affects one's prior assessment of an issue on which the new evidence bears. Suppose X stands for the proposition to be proved, E stands for the evidence, and the notation | stands for "given." Then Odds (X | E) stands for the odds of X given evidence E. Bayes' Theorem says these odds are equal to the prior odds of X (without evidence E) multiplied by something called the Likelihood Ratio (LR). In other words, Odds (X | E) = P(X) × LR. The Likelihood Ratio is a fraction in which the numerator is the probability that evidence E would exist if X were so, and the denominator is the probability that Evidence E would exist if X were not so. Hence we have Equation 1:

$$(1)\ \text{Odds}\ (X \mid E) = \frac{P(E \mid X)}{P(E \mid \text{not-}X)} \times \text{Odds}\ (X)$$

Bayes' Theorem may also be case in numeric form to yield probability expressed as a fraction or decimal number, which is easier for some people to grasp, although the equation in this form is more complicated. In Equation 2, P (X | E) stands for the probability of X, given evidence E:

$$(2)\ P(X \mid E) = \frac{P(E \mid X)\ P(X)}{P(E \mid X)\ p(X) + P(E \mid \text{not-}X)} \times P\ (\text{not-}X)$$

We can illustrate the Theorem with a card problem. Suppose we want to know whether a card drawn from a hat containing a full mixed deck is the Queen of Hearts (QH). If asked for an initial estimate, knowing only that the hat contains a full mixed deck, we would say the odds are 1:51 (one chance of drawing that card against 51 chances of drawing some other), and that the probability is 1/52 (or .019). If we were told a red card was drawn and asked how this datum affects the likelihood we

---

8. *See* Guenther v. Armstrong Rubber Co., 406 F.2d 1315, 1318 (3d Cir. 1969) (rejecting plaintiff's claim that proof of the proportion of tires in the store that were made by defendant sufficed to take the case to the jury, since the "probability hypothesis" represented "only a guess"); Smith v. Rapid Transit, 58 N.E.2d 754 (Mass. 1945) (fact that only defendant was allowed to operate buses on street where accident occurred was not enough); Sargent v. Massachusetts Accident Co., 29 N.E.2d 825 (Mass. 1940) (proof that mathematically "the chances somewhat favor a proposition" would not be enough, and proof that "colored" cars outnumber black ones could not justify a conclusion that a particular car fell into the former category); Cohen, The Costs of Acceptability: Blue Buses, Agent Orange, and Aversion to Statistical Evidence, 66 B.U. L. Rev. 563 (1986).

got the QH, we would say the new odds are 1:25 (one chance of getting the QH against 25 chances of getting other red cards), and the probability is 1/26 (or .03846).[9] Bayes' Theorem expresses this reasoning mathematically. For X, substitute QH to mean drawing the QH; for E, substitute R to mean drawing a red card. The equation shows how to modify our original estimate of the odds of drawing the QH, given the datum that the card drawn is red. Using Equation 1, we have:

$$\text{Odds (QH | R)} = \frac{P(R \mid QH)}{P(R \mid \text{not-QH})} \times \text{Odds (QH)}$$

$$= \frac{1}{(25/51)} \times 1{:}51$$

$$= 2.04{:}51$$

$$= 1{:}25$$

The calculations are harder, but we reach the probability of 0.3846 (which is the same as odds 1:25) by applying Equation 1—the Theorem in numeric form.

In paternity cases, Bayes' Theorem provides the underpinning for two numbers that normally support the statistical inference that the defendant is the father. One is the "Paternity Index," which is typically a high number (such as 571), and is derived by carrying out the division in the fraction compromising the Likelihood Ratio that is a central element in Bayes' Theorem.[10] The other number is a so-called probability of paternity, which is typically a high percentage (say 99.82 percent) computed by using Bayes' Theorem.[11] Issues that come with such proof are examined in the next section, but suffice it to say that courts routinely admit such proof in this setting.

Statistical proof in trials

In theory, statistical inferences and Bayes' Theorem could be deployed in cases like *Collins* too. If we solved the problems in the

9. The probability of drawing a QH is 1/52, and odds are 1:51. Probability converts to odds this way: Odds = P/(1 – P). So going to odds, a probability of 1/52 means 1/52 divided by 51/52, or odds of 1:51. And odds convert to probability by taking the number to the left of the colon as numerator in a fraction whose denominator is the sum of the numbers on each side of the colon. Odds of 1:51 means probability of 1/52.

10. The numerator is the probability that the defendant, if he were the father, would pass along certain antigens or genetic markers that the child got from his father (usually a relatively high number, like .4). The denominator is the probability that a "random man" picked from the populace would pass along these antigens or genetic markers (usually a very small number, such as .0007). The result is typically impressive, like 571 (.4 divided by .0007), which means the defendant is 571 times more likely than a "random man" to be the father of the child.

11. Here the Theorem says that the odds of paternity, given the match between the child's paternal antigens or genetic markers and those found in the defendant, is equal to the *prior* odds of paternity (before anything was known about markers) times the likelihood ratio: $O(P \mid M) = LR \times O(P)$, where $O(P \mid M)$ means odds of paternity, given that the child contains paternal markers that the defendant also has; LR means likelihood ratio described in the previous note; $O(P)$ means the prior odds that defendant is the father, meaning the odds of paternity before the genetic markers are considered.

case by offering proof supporting the various reported probabilities (one in four girls has a ponytail, and so forth), and if we knew they were all independent, we could use the LR to report *how much more likely* it is that defendants committed the crime than someone else, and we could use Bayes' Theorem to compute probability of guilt on the assumption that the other evidence in the case could be quantified in some way—as meaning, for instance, that the other evidence gave rise to an estimated probability of guilt lying somewhere between .01 and .99. Assuming all those things, we might say that the defendants are 12,000,000 times more likely than some "random couple" to be the guilty ones, which would raise the probability of guilt to 99.99 percent even if the *prior* estimate of guilt was very low. (In *Collins* itself, there were other indications of guilt, including some false exculpatory statements, the sudden acquisition of money that could have come from the crime, and lack of credible alibi.) Needless to say, however, we do no such thing in cases like *Collins*. In this setting, the objections to statistical inference have prevailed, and the same hold true in civil counterparts to *Collins*, like the exploding tire and blue bus cases.

For various kinds of trace evidence, however, including hair samples and DNA, courts generally admit at least statistics reflecting the scarcity of the sample,[12] and occasionally similar statistics relating to the probability of other natural phenomena.[13] Indeed, in some criminal cases where proof that defendant is the father of a child would itself constitute proof of intercourse, hence guilt of the charged crime, some courts even admit testimony on the paternity index and probability of paternity.[14] In contrast to *Collins* and the blue bus cases, where the facts are personal, social, and economic, most of these cases involve physical and medical facts. Here probability data are less likely to reflect human choice or volition, where we are less comfortable resting specific decisions about particular people on classwide generalizations. These differences may well account for the difference in judicial treatment.

12. *See* Aitken & Robertson, A Contribution to the Discussion of Probabilities and Human Hair Comparisons, 32 J. Forensic Sci. 681 (1987); Bolin v. State, 960 P.2d 784 (Nev. 1998) (only one out of every 26,000 African-Americans would have hair root DNA similar to that found on crime and defense samples), *cert. denied*, 525 U.S. 1179; Duncan v. State, 828 S.W.2d 847, 850 (Ark. App. 1997) (probability of two keys fitting one car). DNA evidence is discussed in §7.19, *infra*.

13. *See* State v. Pankow, 422 N.W.2d 913, 917 (Wis. 1998) (three infants in single household would die of SIDS once every 600,000 years); Rachals v. State, 361 S.E.2d 671, 674 (Ga. App. 1987) (probability of suffering cardiac arrest), *aff'd*, 364 S.E.2d 867 (Ga. 1998); State v. Klindt, 389 N.W.2d 670, 673 (Iowa 1986) (probability exceeds 99 percent that torso was that of a certain person).

14. *See* Griffith v. State, 976 S.W.2d 241 (Tex. Ct. App. 1998) (approving testimony on probability of paternity in criminal case, rejecting defense argument that this evidence infringes presumption of innocence or standard of proof beyond reasonable doubt); State v. Spann, 617 A.2d 247, 262 (N.J. 1993) (noting but not resolving question whether expert testimony on probability of paternity would improperly undermine standard of proof beyond reasonable doubt).

§7.19   DNA Evidence (Criminal and Paternity Cases)

Before the beginning of the twenty-first century, DNA (or genetic profile) evidence had come into its own, and it plays decisive roles in criminal cases, often connecting the defendant to the victim or the crime scene, and often refuting suggestions that someone other than the defendant committed the crime. Of course DNA evidence sometimes exonerates defendants as well. Whether assessed under *Daubert* or the older *Frye* standard, theories underlying DNA evidence and many techniques for analyzing DNA samples, and statistical analyses that come with it, have been approved by courts across the country,[1] and are described in many reference works,[2] and new techniques of analysis have appeared.[3] So well accepted is the underlying science that most of the thousands of modern appellate opinions deal *not* with the scientific technicalities discussed here, but with peripheral issues relating to such things as entitlement to funding or testing, adequacy of legal representation on matters relating to DNA, legality of obtaining samples from defendants, and post-conviction challenges based on DNA evidence pointing to other perpetrators.

Paternity cases are noted further at the end of this section: Here too, DNA and other blood and tissue tests are critical, but some forensic concerns diminish or disappear (like contamination from the crime scene) and the results are reported in different ways.

DNA evidence distinguishes the fluids, bones, hair, tissue, and blood of one person from those of another (for any one person, the same DNA "markers" are found in every biological sample). DNA is the long molecule in the familiar shape of a double helix or twisted ladder that forms the 46 chromosomes each individual inherits from his parents (23 from each). Each rung is comprised of base pairs comprised of nucleotides commonly designated A, C, G, and T, in which A always bonds with C and G with T. Each human has about three billion of these base pairs, and 99.9 percent are arranged the same way in everyone, but the balance (three million pairs) varies among humans.

Genetic individuation

In regions of difference, sometimes called hypervariable loci or alleles (often having no known function), the distinguishing characteristics are that the base pairs are arranged differently on the helix.

§7.19   1. *See* State v. Brochu, 949 A.2d 1035 (Vt. 2008) (mitochondrial DNA); People v. Venegas, 954 P.2d 525 (Cal. 1998) (RFLP); State v. Stills, 957 P.2d 51 (N.M. 1998) (PCR).

2. *See generally* 3 Faigman, Kaye, Saks, & Sanders, Modern Scientific Evidence, Chapter 25 (2002); 2 Gianelli & Imwinkelried, Chapter 18 (3d ed. 1999); National Research Council, The Evaluation of Forensic DNA Evidence (1996) (hereafter cited as "NRC Update"); William C. Thompson & Simon Ford, DNA Typing: Acceptance and Weight of the New Genetic Identification Tests, 75 Va. L. Rev. 45 (1989).

3. *See* State v. Foreman, 954 A.2d 135, 163-164 (Conn. 2008) (accepting testimony on DNA analysis based on computer software that had been subjected to "extensive validation and control processes"); People v. Shreck, 22 P.3d 68 (Colo. 2001) (approving D1S80 test as "hybrid" of RFLP and PCR, and mentioning with approval STR ["short term tandem repeats"] as another form of PCR); State v. Harvey, 699 A.2d 596 (N.J. 1997) (dot intensity analysis).

Identifying these variations (polymorphisms) involves the use of probes comprised of single DNA strands tagged with radioactive components that bond to like strands, and restriction enzymes that cut DNA at specific sites (such as everyplace the sequence GGCC appears). In trials for such crimes as battery or homicide, the forensic use of DNA usually involves proving that a "crime sample," typically comprised of blood found at the scene, matches a "defense sample," typically blood drawn from the defendant. In sexual assault trials, the crime sample is typically semen found in the victim or on her clothing, which is once again compared with blood drawn from the defendant.

RFLP and PCR analysis   The most common genetic profiling technique involves RFLP analysis ("restriction fragment length polymorphism"). In this process, restriction enzymes cut the DNA, producing many fragments of varying length and molecular weight (VNTRs, meaning "variable number tandem repeats"). These fragments are placed in separate lanes in a gel, and an electric current is applied in a process called "electrophoresis," which propels the fragments along the lanes. Being different in weight, they move different distances in the lanes.

The fragments are then "unzipped" (split down the middle) and transferred to a nylon membrane retaining their relative position. They are tagged with probes and X-rayed, which produces a film or "autorad" on which the positions of the fragments appear as blots resembling bar codes, which are then analyzed to see whether one or more match appears—whether the blots in the various lanes appear in the same relative position, indicating that the compared samples have the same molecular weight, hence the same sequence of base pairs (same genetic markers). Sometimes multilocus probes are used, measuring many fragments at once and producing multiple blots on the autorads, in effect making it possible to test for many markers at once.

In a technique called PCR analysis ("polymerase chain reaction"), a substance called DNA polymerase extends or amplifies samples found on the victim or at a crime scene. One advantage is that PCR is simpler and cheaper, and another is that it allows the testing of even tiny samples by producing millions of partial copies that can be probed for specific alleles (typically drawn from larger samples taken from the defendant or the victim). As of this writing, PCR analysis is less discriminating or powerful than RFLP, and sometimes it can only show matches in common alleles, but reportedly advances are being made in PCR that will close the gap significantly between PCR and RFLP.

Legal issue   Both *Daubert* and the older *Frye* standard generally apply to three aspects of DNA profiling: One is the underlying genetic theory; another is the underlying process or technique (most commonly, RFLP and PCR analyses), including laboratory protocol and match criteria; the third is the databases and statistical techniques used to calculate and express matches and the significance of matches. Genetic profiling by DNA analysis passes muster in all three aspects.

Nevertheless, significant issues arise in five areas, in addition to the most commonplace and conventional problem that attends almost all forensic evidence, which is showing "chain of custody" (so one can be sure that the test results actually reflect a sample found at the scene.[4] Here are the five areas:

First are issues relating to gathering, handling, and preparing samples. These issues are factbound (when and where was a particular sample collected?) and technical (did sun or temperature or humidity affect the sample? was it contaminated by some external agent?). Often these points are viewed as going to weight rather than admissibility, and are pursued on cross or supported by experts called by the other side, but the amendment to FRE 703 adopted in 2000 appears to include these issues as matters affecting admissibility.[5]

Gathering, handling, preparation

Second are issues relating to laboratory protocol and proficiency. Courts have approved protocols in major laboratories, including the FBI Crime Laboratory as well as state laboratories and private companies, but the field is fluid and technological changes bring new issues. There exist industry guidelines (known by the acronym TWGAM, which stands for Technical Working Group on DNA Analysis and Methods), as well as recommendations by the National Research Council, but adherence to these is not required as a condition of admissibility, and is normally said to affect weight.[6] Laboratory proficiency studies exist, and can become the subject of cross-examination or testimony countering DNA evidence, and some argue that error rates should be incorporated into the statistical information provided to juries.[7]

Laboratory protocol, proficiency

Perhaps most challenging are issues relating to the handling and testing of particular samples in the laboratory, where once again the issues are factbound and technical. Again these points are often viewed as going to weight rather than admissibility, but again the amendment to FRE 703 adopted in 2000 appears to change this result. In cases in which the judge *admits* the evidence (even if he plays the larger role and determines the points himself), the objecting party can pursue the same points in front of the jury because they still affect weight. But the cases are not always clear, except in saying that actual compliance with protocol is an aspect of the validity standard. Asking judges to play the larger role can be defended on this ground (validity issues under

---

4. State v. McCrary, 183 P.3d 503, 507 (Ariz. 2008) (rejecting tampering claim; state adequately proved chain of custody of DNA sample); Overton v. State, 976 So.2d 536 (Fla. 2007) (storing DNA evidence in home refrigerator did not break chain of custody).

5. *See* the discussion of *Daubert* issues in §7.7, *supra. And see* William Thompson, DNA Evidence in the O.J. Simpson Trial, 67 U. Colo. L. Rev. 827 (1996) (describing defense evidence and theories explaining the matches reported in that trial).

6. Commonwealth v. Sok, 683 N.E.2d 671, 795 (Mass. 1997) (refusing to exclude DNA evidence because crime lab does not comply with TWGDAM).

7. *See* William C. Thompson, Accepting Lower Standards: The National Research Council's Second Report on Forensic DNA Evidence, 37 Jurimetrics 405 (1997); Jonathan J. Koehler, Why DNA Likelihood Ratios Should Account for Error (Even When a National Research Council Report Says They Should Not), 37 Jurimetrics 425 (1997). *But see* Margaret A. Berger, Laboratory Error Seen Through the Lens of Science and Policy, 30 U.C. Davis L. Rev. 1081 (1997).

Daubert and *Frye* are for the judge) and on the ground that the issues are too technical and elaborate for juries.[8]

Match criteria   Third are issues relating to match criteria, which pretty clearly the judge should determine. Suffice it to say that these issues are themselves highly technical, and that different approaches can be defended.[9]

Statistical analysis   Fourth are issues relating to statistical analysis. Cases producing one match often produce many, which leads to use of the product rule to compute a combined probability. But the product rule can properly apply only if each match be independent of others, and two concerns have arisen. One is that certain markers may *not* be independent of others (lacking "linkage equilibrium"). The other is that some markers are more or less common in some racial and ethnic subgroups which, combined with the possibility that mating patterns are *not* random across racial or ethnic lines, would produce some distortion (the combined probabilities will not be in "Hardy-Weinberg" equilibrium). This "population subgroup" problem led to a recommendation to compensate by applying a "ceiling principle" achieved by choosing, from charts relating to the various subgroups, the probability that minimizes the risk of error to the party against whom the evidence is offered (normally that means selecting the highest plausible frequency statistic so that the effect is to *understate the scarcity* of combined matches). These concerns receded as scientists concluded that nonrandom mating patterns do not significantly change the numbers, although it remains common to compare numbers for specific racial or ethnic groups if both the defendant and the culprit are known to belong to a certain group, and to choose the highest plausible frequency (again minimizing the incriminating impact) if the race or ethnicity of the culprit is not known.[10]

Fifth are issues relating to the manner in which the information is imparted to the jury. The prevailing practice is to tell the jury about the probability of the encountering the observed matches in the general population, something like this: "The probability that a randomly chosen person would produce the match observed between the crime sample and the defense sample is one in 16,000," and modern courts approve even testimony indicating that the chance of

8. *Compare* United States v. Martinez, 3 F.3d 1191, 1197 (8th Cir. 1993) (judge must determine whether proper method was followed) *with* State v. Begley, 956 S.W.2d 471, 477 n.13 (Tenn. 1997); Lindsey v. People, 892 P.2d 281, 292 (Colo. 1995) (whether proper method was followed goes to weight). *And see* 2 Imwinkelried & Giannelli, Scientific Evidence §18-5(B) (3d ed. 1999) (judge should decide).

9. *See* People v. Venegas, 954 P.2d 525, 534 (Cal. 1998) (discussing match criteria); David Kaye, The Relevance of "Matching" DNA: Is the Window Half Open or Half Shut? 85 J. Crim. L. & Criminology 676 (1995); William Thompson, Evaluating the Admissibility of New Genetic Tests: Lessons from the "DNA War," 84 J. Crim. L. & Criminology 22, 37-60 (1993).

10. *See* NRC Update, at 53 (product rule can be validly applied; adjustments based on ceiling principle are unnecessary); VNTR Population Data: A Worldwide Study, 2 (FBI 1996) (ethnic and geographical variations do not substantially affect forensic estimates; ceiling principle unnecessary); Commonwealth v. Bly, 862 N.E.2d 341, 355 (Mass. 2007) (DNA database is reliable); Commonwealth v. Blasioli, 713 A.2d 1117 (Pa. 1998) (challenges to product rule have been resolved).

encountering the combined markers in the general populace is so small that a particular profile appears unique.[11] One problem is that this approach presents a temptation to misinterpret the figure as meaning that there is only one chance in 16,000 that someone *else* is the perpetrator (the person responsible for the crime sample), but the statistic does not mean that at all. (This point is discussed in the previous section on statistical evidence.) On the other hand, giving *no* statistical data poses the risk that the jury may interpret "match" to mean too much or too little: It would mean too much if the jury understood that "match" means the defendant *must be* the source of the crime sample, and too little if the jury thought "match" meant the defendant could be the source, but so could a major fraction of the populace (say a quarter or a half). In the end, providing a scarcity statistic seems the wisest course, and some jurisdictions *require* as much, although others permit testimony without statistics.[12]

In a modern development, concerns have arisen in "DNA trawling" or "cold hit" cases in which prosecutors find "sample" DNA taken at a crime scene or found on the victim, which presumably was left by the culprit when he committed the offense, and simply search through databases to see if they find a match. Given a large database now made possible by the Combined DNA Indexing System (CODIS), which is a national database of samples, the argument runs, this method is very likely to come up with a match, and likely to come up with mistaken matches as well. The concern here is that the conventional method of communicating the statistical significance of the match to the jury ("only one in 48 million people would share the characteristics found in the crime scene sample and in the defendant's sample") overstates the significance of the match and should be discounted.[13] Strong arguments have been mounted against this view,[14] however, and modern authorities permit the match data to be presented to the jury in the conventional way, even in the "trawl" cases.[15]

Imparting information to jury

---

11. Gillard v. State, 2008 WL 95767 (Ark. 2008) (crime scene DNA "originated" with defendant "within all scientific certainty") ("one in forty two quadrillion" would have such a profile); State v. Buckner, 941 P.2d 667, 668 (Wash. 1997) (one in 19 billion).

12. *Compare* Sholler v. Commonwealth, 969 S.W.2d 706 (Ky. 1998) (proper to admit testimony describing a match even if no frequency statistics are provided) *with* State v. Williams, 574 N.W.2d 293, 297 (Iowa 1998) (quoting *Yee* decision) *and* United States v. Yee, 134 F.R.D. 161, 181 (N.D. Ohio 1991) (without statistics, jury "does not know whether the patterns are as common as pictures with two eyes, or as unique as the Mona Lisa").

13. National Research Council Committee on DNA Technology in Forensic Science (1992), at 124 (recommending an artificial inflation in random match probability to offset effect of trawling).

14. *See* David H. Kaye, Rounding Up the Usual Suspects: A Logical and Legal Analysis of DNA Trawling Cases, 87 N.C. L. Rev. — (2009); Peter Donnelly and Richard Friedman, DNA Database Searches and the Legal Consumption of Scientific Evidence, 97 Mich. L. Rev. 931 (1999).

15. *See* State v. Bartylla, 755 N.W.2d 8, 19-20 (Minn. 2008) (no hearing required on statistical validity; while there may be "more than one way of expressing" statistical significance in "cold hit" cases, expert could testify to probability of match in general

Paternity cases   In paternity cases, usually DNA evidence consists of a comparison between paternal genetic markers found in the child (derived from testing blood samples of the child and mother) and genetic markers in the blood of the defendant ("putative father"). Often the other types of tests, such as HLA (human leucocyte antigen) can produce similar comparisons.[16] In most cases, the necessary samples can be gathered under clinical conditions, and the sample from the putative father can be analyzed specifically to detect markers that the actual father of the child must have, so great precision in results can be obtained. In cases showing no match for one or more of the relevant markers, the DNA test is virtually conclusive proof of nonpaternity, although sometimes other doctrines like estoppel can render this point moot from a legal perspective.[17]

Paternity index   In cases showing multiple matches, the convention is to report two numbers to a jury—a "Paternity Index" and a "probability of paternity." The Paternity Index is calculated by carrying out the division in a fraction: The numerator is the probability that the defendant, if he were the father, would pass to his child the paternal genetic markers found in the child (typically a high number, like .4). The denominator is the probability that a "random man" picked from the populace would pass to his child the paternal genetic markers found in the child in question (typically a low number, like .0007). The result is typically impressive, like 571 (.4 divided by .0007), which means that the defendant is 571 times more likely than a "random man" to be the father of the child.[18]

Probability of paternity   The "probability of paternity" is typically presented as a very high percentage (say 99.82 percent), which is computed by the use of Bayes'

---

population); People v. Nelson, 185 P.3d 49, 66 (Cal. 2008) ("the rarity statistic is still accurately calculated and appropriately considered in assessing the significance of a cold hit").

16. *See* Peterson, A Few Things You Should Know about Paternity Tests (But Were Afraid to Ask), 22 Santa Clara L. Rev. 667 (1982); Reisner & Bolk, A Layman's Guide to the Use of Blood Group Analysis in Paternity Testing, 20 J. Fam. L. 657 (1982); Ellman & Kaye, Probabilities and Proof: Can HLA and Blood Group Testing Prove Paternity? 54 N.Y.U. L. Rev. 1131 (1979); Koehler, DNA Matches and Statistics, 76 Judicature 222, 224 (1993) (paternity index measures "the strength of the genetic evidence, where higher numbers are more probative of paternity than lower numbers").

17. *See e.g.*, Love v. Love, 1998 WL 255318 (Nev. 1998) (in husband's suit to set aside decree that he was father of wife's child, DNA evidence showing nonpaternity does not compel court to find this point; presumption of paternity arising from fact that defendant was married to the mother conflicts with presumption of nonpaternity arising from negative DNA results; the presumption should prevail that is founded on weightier consideration of policy and logic).

18. *See* Plemel v. Walker, 735 P.2d 1209, 1214 (Or. 1987) (denominator of paternity index is "the same for every putative father," because it represents gene frequency in the population, but numerator varies among different people so the paternity index also varies; any man not excluded by a paternity test could have fathered the child, but they "have different paternity indexes and thus different relative likelihoods" of having fathered the child); Koehler, DNA Matches and Statistics, 76 Judicature 222, 224 (1993) (index measures strength of the genetic evidence, where higher numbers more strongly suggest paternity than lower ones).

Theorem (discussed in the previous section).[19] Bayes' Theorem is a formula that tells how to adjust a prior estimate of the probability of some fact (event or condition) in light of new data shedding further light on the fact. Reduced to simple form in a paternity case, Bayes' Theorem says the odds of paternity, given the match between the child's paternal genetic markers and the markers found in the defendant, is equal to the *prior* odds of paternity (before anything was known about markers) times a likelihood ratio: $O(P \mid M) = LR \times O(P)$. In this notation, $O(P \mid M)$ means odds of paternity, given that the child contains paternal markers that the defendant also has; LR means likelihood ratio, which is the same fraction used in computing the Paternity Index described above; $O(P)$ means the prior odds that defendant is the father, meaning the odds of paternity before the genetic markers are considered.[20]

Hidden behind the probability of paternity is a prior estimate of the odds of paternity, or $O(P)$, which is usually taken to be 1:1 (meaning one chance that defendant is the father as against one chance that he is not). This number is chosen because it is supposedly neutral as between the position of the plaintiff (claiming paternity) and the position of the defendant (resisting). In what seems a constructive step, courts sometimes require that the jury be provided a range of prior probabilities, which should help it appraise the genetic evidence regardless of its view of the strength of the rest of the case.[21] Some have argued that the results should be presented by verbal formula, in which (for instance) a probability of paternity exceeding 99.99 percent could be conveyed to the jury as a "very high probability" that defendant is the father, but this suggestion has generally fallen by the wayside.[22] Defendants can of

---

19. *See* D. N. Beauvais by L. Beauvais v. Luther, 705 A.2d 975 (R.I. 1998) (probability of paternity 99.99 percent); County of El Dorado v. Misura, 38 Cal. Rptr. 2d 908 (Cal. App. 1995) (index 970 yielding percentage 99.69 percent); Commonwealth v. Beausoleil, 490 N.E.2d 788, 795-796 (Mass. 1986) (98.2 percent).

20. Where multiple matches are found, the likelihood ratio is usually very high. The numerator is large (often .2 to .4) and the denominator is small (typically .0001 to .002). The reason is that for any man whose genetic markers produce the observed matches, the probability is high that any child of his will have such markers, but these combined markers are so rare in the general population that any randomly chosen man is unlikely to have them.

21. *See* State v. Spann, 617 A.2d 247, 254 (N.J. 1993) (expert should explain probability of paternity across range of prior probabilities from 1. to .9); Plemel v. Walker, 735 P.2d 1209, 1219 (Or. 1987) (expert to use "more than a single assumption about the strength of the other evidence" so results are shown without overstating probative force).

22. For instance, one might express an impressive number such as 99.44 percent by saying that it puts defendant "in a small group of men who might be the father" or that he is "much more likely to be the father" than a man selected at random, or that the probability exceeds 40 percent that he would pass to his child the genetic markers found in the child in question, and that fewer than "one man in a thousand" would do so. *See* Joint AMA-ABA Guidelines: Present Status of Serologic Testing in Problems of Disputed Parentage, 10 Fam. L.Q. 247, 262 (1976) (suggesting words like "practically proved" to express a high index and "not useful" to express an index lower than 80).

course try to show that other men may have had sexual relations with the plaintiff, hence could be the father, but it is seldom that more than a few such persons can be suggested, which means this kind of defense has little impact on the high paternity index (and high probability of paternity) that nonexcluded males usually have.[23]

One difficulty is that the jury may interpret the probability of paternity to mean the defendant is much more likely to be the actual father than any other man, but in fact every man with the same genetic markers is equally likely to be the father, so far as the DNA evidence goes. The probability of paternity means something different—that the defendant is much more likely than *a man chosen at random* from the population to have the genetic markers that the father has. Sometimes the paternity index is presented to jurors with information on the power of the test to exclude, which may be very high (perhaps in the neighborhood of 95 percent). This figure too can be misunderstood as an estimate of the probability that the defendant is the father, but it is not that.[24]

In practice, many states recognize a "presumption of paternity" if the paternity index is high enough, which effectively puts on the defendant either the burden of production or the burden of persuasion on the issue.[25]

But see County of El Dorado v. Misura, 38 Cal. Rptr. 2d 908, 911 n.1 (Cal. App. 1995); Plemel v. Walker, 735 P.2d 1209, 1219 (Or. 1987) (both disapproving use of these verbal predicates).

23. *See* County of El Dorado v. Misura, 38 Cal. Rptr. 2d 908 (Cal. App. 1995) (making this point and suggesting that a new probability be computed by dividing paternity index of defendant by sum of his index and the indices of untested men, assumed to be one), *cert. denied*, 516 U.S. 1112 (1996). Experimenting with the numbers leads to the conclusion that the paternity index would have to be very low and the number of plausible untested men would have to be high before it would reduce the new calculation significantly. Thus a paternity index of 36 (very low), combined with proof that four other men had relations with the plaintiff, would generate a computation that odds of paternity are 9:1 (probability .9), assuming that there were no *other* reasons for believing or disbelieving the two parties in suit.

24. Suppose the question is whether a card drawn at random from a full deck is the Queen of Hearts (QH). Suppose we have a test that recognizes all red face cards, and the test yields a positive result (red face card). Among the possible "wrong" cards (all that are not QH), this test has the power to exclude 46/51, or 90.2 percent (out of 51 wrong cards, five are red face cards and 46 are something else). The positive result on the test means the drawn card is one out of six red face cards, so the odds are 1:5 that the card is the QH (a probability of 1/6, or 16.7 percent, not 90.2 percent). The percentage of cards that is a QH is 1.9 percent (not 9.8 percent, which is the difference between 90.2 percent and 100 percent). *See* Commonwealth v. Beausoleil, 490 N.E.2d 788, 792 n.5, and 795 (Mass. 1986) (incorrect to equate probability of exclusion with probability that nonexcluded man is father; jury is apt to confuse these, so they should not be presented); Reisner & Bolk, A Layman's Guide to the Use of Blood Group Analysis in Paternity Testing, 20 J. Fam. L. 657, 670-671 (1982).

25. *See* Cal. Family Code §7555 (presumption arises when paternity index is "100 or greater" and may be rebutted by a preponderance of the evidence); N.Y. Family Ct. Act §532 (DNA test indicating at least 95 percent probability raises rebuttable presumption of paternity).

§7.20 Polygraph Evidence

One form of scientific evidence that has generated controversy and judicial skepticism is expert opinion testimony based on the results of a polygraph or "lie detector." In *Frye*, which was for years the leading decision on the standard by which *all* scientific evidence was to be judged, the court excluded polygraph evidence because its accuracy of the polygraph was not accepted by consensus in the scientific community.[1] Although *Frye* was not binding on states, it was followed almost everywhere, and has long come to stand for the proposition that polygraph evidence is inadmissible, even though that machine that goes by that name has undergone many changes in the meantime.

In the early decades of the twenty-first century, polygraph results are excludable from evidence almost everywhere,[2] and most jurisdictions bar comment on any refusal by a criminal defendant to take a polygraph test.[3] A few states (and some federal courts) have adopted more generous rules,[4] and some courts allow such proof in nontrial settings (such as sentencing and parole decisions)[5] or in impeaching witnesses.[6] Statements by defendants, made after taking such tests, are often admitted (of course they fit the admissions doctrine), although concerns arise in this setting about voluntariness.[7] Many courts, both federal and state, admit polygraph evidence on stipulation (at least when

§7.20 1. Frye v. United States, 293 F. 1013 (D.C. App. 1923) (involving primitive form of lie detector without many measurements found in modern instruments).

2. *See* 1 Giannelli & Imwinkelried, Scientific Evidence §§8.01-8.14 (4th ed. 2007) (extended discussion); 5 Faigman, Saks, Sanders, and Cheng, Modern Scientific Evidence §39.19 (2007-2008) (polygraph presents "special challenges" under *Daubert* and under FRE 403 "from invading the province of the jury to overwhelming it," and modern research may have "raised more dust than it has settled"); Wilkins v. State, 190 P.3d 957 (Kan. 2008) (polygraph inadmissible absent stipulation); State v. Jones, 753 N.W.2d 677 (Minn. 2008) (polygraph examinations are inadmissible); People v. Richardson, 183 P.3d 1146 (Cal. 2008) (upholding statute barring use of polygraph evidence).

3. See Cal. Evid. Code §351.1 (barring "reference to an offer to take" polygraph examination, or "failure to take" exam); State v. Gutierrez, 162 P.3d 156, 161 (N.M. 2007) (comment on refusal to take polygraph violates Fifth Amendment privilege) (this state normally admits polygraph evidence).

4. *See, e.g.*, N.M. Rule Evid. §11-707 (making polygraph evidence generally admissible); Commonwealth v. Duguay, 720 N.E.2d 458, 463 (Mass. 1999) (admissibility turns on proof of proficiency of examiner in similar situations); United States v. Cordoba, 104 F.3d 225, 229 (9th Cir. 1997) (under *Daubert*, court must evaluate polygraph with particularity in every case).

5. Compare State v. Hameline, 188 P.3d 1052 (Mont. 2008) (although inadmissible at trial, judge could require defendant to submit to polygraph test as condition of suspended sentence) with In re D.S., 856 N.E.2d 921 (Ohio 2006) (disapproving requirement to take polygraph as condition of probation).

6. State v. Castagna, 901 A.2d 363, 373 (N.J. 2006) (defense should be allowed to ask state witness whether she failed polygraph test).

7. State v. Davis, 751 N.W.2d 332, 341-342 (Wis. 2008) (post-polygraph statements are not per se coerced).

results are also supported as reliable),[8] although others exclude it even in the face of a stipulation on the theory that parties cannot require courts to admit unreliable or misleading evidence.[9]

The *Frye* "consensus" standard for admitting scientific evidence in federal courts was replaced in 1993 by the *Daubert* standard, which rekindled scholarly and judicial interest in the polygraph evidence under FRE 702. Some courts view *Daubert* as an invitation to reexamine and liberalize standards for polygraph evidence, but others have adhere to a rule of per se exclusion.[10]

Scheffer case: Cautionary warning

The Court sent a cautionary warning in the *Scheffer* case in 1998, when it held that criminal defendants have no constitutional right to introduce evidence that they "passed" a polygraph test. *Scheffer* only addressed the question whether courts *must* admit polygraph evidence as a matter of constitutional law, but the decision has broader significance. The opinion holds that a per se ban serves a legitimate governmental interest by ensuring that only reliable evidence is introduced at trial, and the Court said that there is *still* no consensus on the reliability of polygraph evidence (75 years after *Frye*), and the scientific community remains polarized.[11] Although *Daubert* does not actually *require* a consensus of the scientific community, still peer review and scientific acceptance are important factors, as well as error rates. Courts are unlikely to dispense with them casually for a device that has been in existence and available for testing and validation for so long with such debatable results.[12]

FRE 403

Even if polygraphy eventually achieves a status of sufficient reliability to satisfy *Daubert* and FRE 702, it faces even greater hurdles under FRE 403. Two of the three grounds in *Scheffer* relate to FRE 403. First, the Court thought juries would give too much weight to the opinions of a

---

8. *See, e.g.,* United States v. Gordon, 688 F.2d 42, 44 (8th Cir. 1982); McGhee v. State, 253 Ga. 278, 319 S.E.2d 836 (1984); Katz, Dilemmas of Polygraph Stipulations, 14 Seton Hall L. Rev. 285 (1984).

9. *See, e.g.,* Nesbit v. State, 227 S.W.3d 64, 66 n.4 (Tex. Crim. App. 2007) (polygraph inadmissible even if state and defense stipulate).

10. *Compare* United States v. Cordoba, 104 F.3d 225, 228 (9th Cir. 1997), United States v. Posado, 57 F.3d 428, 434 (5th Cir. 1995), *and* United States v. Piccinonna, 885 F.2d 1529, 1536 (11th Cir. 1989) (all abandoning per se ban) *with* United States v. Gilliard, 133 F.3d 809, 815 (11th Cir. 1998), and United States v. Sanchez, 118 F.3d 192 (4th Cir. 1997) (both finding polygraph excludable). *And see generally* McCall, Misconceptions and Reevaluation—Polygraph Admissibility After *Rock* and *Daubert,* 1996 U. Ill. L. Rev. 363.

11. United States v. Scheffer, 523 U.S. 303, 307-313 (1998) (rejecting claims under compulsory process clause; any constitutional claim could not readily be "narrowly contained" as a right solely to introduce exculpatory polygraph evidence; even if technical issues could be resolved, there remain questions about efficacy of countermeasures that might throw off machine and deceive examiner).

12. There are fewer controlled studies than might be expected, and much support comes directly from professional polygraphers. *Compare* Charles R. Honts, David C. Raskin, and John C. Kircher, "The Case For Polygraph Tests," *with* William G. Iacono and David T. Lykken, "The Case Against Polygraph Tests," in 5 Faigman, Saks, Sanders, and Chen, Modern Scientific Evidence §§39.20-39.118 (2007-2008).

polygrapher, and noted again the "aura of infallibility" that comes with the polygraph, which has long concerned courts.[13] Second, *Scheffer* commented that polygraph evidence would raise collateral questions: Did the examiner ask appropriate control questions and test questions? Was the examiner qualified? Could the subject take countermeasures that distort the result, or could other psychological factors (apart from lying or truth-telling) affect the readings? These questions could greatly extend trials and distract juries from their central function, which would justify if not require exclusion under FRE 403 on grounds of confusion, waste of time, or undue delay.

Because polygraph evidence is so rarely admitted without stipulation, other evidentiary objections have not often been examined.[14] One might ask, for example, whether a polygraph test of the accused is relevant if he does not take the stand, or does his performance on a lie detector test indicate consciousness of guilt or innocence that has independent relevance?[15] Does passing or failing a polygraph test amount to character evidence subject to FRE 404 or FRE 608? It seems that neither of these provisions would block opinion testimony by the examiner that defendant was untruthful or truthful when asked certain questions, but such testimony does not appear to be "character" evidence (because it relates particular acts). If such testimony does *not* fit FRE 608, on what basis can it be admitted? Finally, would proof of truthful answers on a polygraph examination amount to improper bolstering? What kind of attack on credibility would overcome such an objection?[16]

Objections rarely tested

With reference to defense efforts to prove truthfulness on a polygraph examination, prosecutors may have a hearsay objection, resting on the ground that such evidence is defendant's out-of-court statement that "I didn't do it" offered for its truth. If defendant testifies and his credibility is attacked, this objection may be overcome by an instruction that the examiner's testimony is not offered to prove the truth of defendant's statements, but as evidence bearing on credibility.[17] If defendant does not testify, a hearsay objection has greater force, but should still be overruled. Under FRE 703 an expert can rely on inadmissible hearsay, and testimony that defendant's performance indicates an innocent frame of mind (no consciousness of guilt) can rest on his

---

13. Bloom v. People, 185 P.3d 797, 807 (Colo. 2008) (polygraph will "prejudice the jury's evaluation" of credibility); State v. Christiansen, 163 P.3d 1175 (Idaho 2007) (polygraph evidence would invade province of jury).

14. *See generally* Imwinkelried & McCall, Issues Once Moot: The *Other* Evidentiary Objections to the Admission of Exculpatory Polygraph Examinations, 32 Wake Forest L. Rev. 1045, 1062-1073 (1997).

15. *See* United States v. Webster, 750 F.2d 307, 330-331 (5th Cir. 1984) (defendant's public statement that he was storing plane at his airport, where it turned out plane was stolen, admissible nonhearsay showing absence of guilty knowledge). *See also* the discussion of consciousness of guilt in §4.4, *supra*.

16. United States v. Castillo, 1997 WL 83746 (E.D. Pa.) (rejecting under FRE 608).

17. Depending on the attack, what was said before might come in as a consistent statement. *See* §§6.49-6.52, *supra*.

responses,[18] although the examiner probably cannot quote them to the jury.[19]

Apart from decisions that courts may finally make, legislatures have become involved: Thus, for example, Congress restricted use of polygraphs in employment.[20] Polygraphs also raise policy concerns relating to the right of privacy, respect for human dignity, and the nature of our judicial system. Even if (or especially if) an infallible polygraph were developed, there would still be concern about the dehumanizing impact of transferring to machine any part of the historic role of juries in deciding questions of credibility and guilt.[21]

§7.21 Evidence on Accuracy of Eyewitness Identification

One branch of psychological expertise that claims much modern attention relates to eyewitness identification testimony.[1] Especially in criminal cases, psychologists are routinely called to provide what has become an almost standard set of insights into the difficulties of human perception and reporting in this area.

Psychological factors
Basing their findings on experiments in which subjects view staged or videotaped scenes and afterwards describe what they saw or answer questions, experts report that the accuracy of eyewitness identification is affected by factors that may not be intuitively obvious and operate in ways that laypeople may not appreciate. It is commonly reported that (1) memory diminishes exponentially rather than arithmetically (nonuniformly, quickly losing its edge, then gradually fading), (2) stress causes inaccuracies in perception and recall (so violent and threatening events are problematic), (3) observers assimilate or incorporate inaccurate information they learn after the event and confuse or conflate with it, (4) conversations afterwards reinforce opinions about identification (feedback factor), (5) accuracy bears little or no relationship with certainty, and (6) cross-racial identifications contain more mistakes than others.[2]

---

18. *See* Imwinkelried & McCall, *supra* note 14 (arguing that defendant's responses during examination are nonhearsay verbal acts or statements offered to prove impact on listener).

19. *See* United States v. Crumby, 895 F. Supp. 1354, 1361 (D. Ariz. 1995) (barring polygraph examiner from quoting defendant's responses to test questions).

20. *See* Employee Polygraph Protection Act, 29 U.S.C. §2001-2009.

21. *See* State v. Lyon, 744 P.2d 231, 240 (Or. 1987) (speaking of fundamental value that parties and witnesses be "treated as persons to be believed or disbelieved by their peers rather than as electrochemical systems to be certified as truthful or mendacious" and asking whether a perfect polygraph increases power to test for truth at cost of diminishing our "common humanity") (Linde, J. concurring).

§7.21 1. *See* Loftus & Doyle, Eyewitness Testimony: Civil and Criminal (4th ed. 2007); 1 Giannelli & Imwinkelried, Scientific Evidence §9.02 (4th ed. 2007); 2 Faigman, Saks, Sanders and Cheng, Modern Scientific Evidence §§16:1-15:47 (2007-1008); Penrod & Cutler, Eyewitness Expert Testimony and Jury Decisionmaking, 52 Law & Contemp. Probs. 43 (1989). For a critical view, *see* McCloskey, Egeth & McKenna, The Experimental Psychologist in Court: The Ethics of Expert Testimony, 10 Law & Hum. Behav. 1 (1986).

2. United States v. Curry, 977 F.2d 1042, 1050-1052 (7th Cir. 1992) (overestimating duration of observation; effect of leading; effect of photo identification, social alcohol, marijuana); United States v. Downing, 753 F.2d 1224 (3d Cir. 1985) (forgetting curve,

Some modern decisions approve such testimony[3] and even reverse judgments because it was excluded or criticize exclusion of such evidence.[4] Others say that closing argument must at least be allowed to explore difficulties in accuracy of eyewitness identification,[5] and there has been some movement toward changing jury instructions that touch on this matter.[6] Still other decisions require courts to consider carefully the utility of such proof and even to hold hearings on the subject,[7] and still others indicate sympathy with such testimony.[8] But some modern courts remain unconvinced, and some decisions disapprove or are highly critical of such evidence.[9] Courts in this camp often comment that cross-examination, arguments by counsel, or cautionary instructions are adequate to control and contain risks, or that juries simply need no help; indeed, courts sometimes say that admitting such testimony would undermine confidence in all eyewitness identifications and lead to a futile "battle of experts" and to still further uses of similar testimony.[10] Some say such evidence lacks scientific validity

Cases split; most favor discretion

stress, assimilation, feedback, noncorrelation of confidence and accuracy); United States v. Smith, 736 F.2d 1103, 1105-1106 (6th Cir. 1984) (viewing lineup and photospread where defendant was only common element; cross-racial identification).

3. United States v. Mathis, 264 F.3d 321, 333-342 (3d Cir. 2001), *cert. denied*, 535 U.S. 908; People v. Enis, 564 N.E.2d 1155 (Ill. 1990); Bloodsworth v. State, 512 A.2d 1056 (Md. 1986); Commonwealth v. Francis, 453 N.E.2d 1204, 1207 (Ma. 1983).

4. State v. Copeland, 226 S.W.3d 287 (Tenn. 2007) (in murder trial, error to exclude testimony on accuracy of cross-racial identifications) (reversing); People v. LeGrand, 867 N.E.2d 374 (N.Y. 2007) (reversing murder conviction for excluding expert testimony on accuracy of eyewitness identification); United States v. Brownlee, 4564 F.3d 131 (3d Cir. 2007) (defendant entitled to offer testimony on (1) show-up procedures and how they affect accuracy, (2) comparison between show-up and other procedures, (3) tendency to focus on weapon, (4) noncorrelation between confidence and accuracy, (5) effect of exposure to multiple witnesses, (6) effect of hair covering, (7) effect of post-event information on confidence, (8) time delay, (9) effect of post-event suggesting, and (10) cross-racial identification) (reversing carjacking conviction). *See also* People v. McDonald, 690 P.2d 709, 726 (Cal. 1984); State v. Chapple, 660 P.2d 1208 (Ariz. 1983).

5. State v. Smith, 880 A.2d 288 (Md. 2005) (error to disallow argument to jury on unreliability cross-racial identification; extended discussion of scientific studies) (reversing).

6. Brodes v. State, 614 S.E.2d 766 (Ga. 2005) (error to tell jury to consider "level of certainty" in eyewitness identification; expert said there is "not a good relationship" between confidence and accuracy).

7. United States v. Smithers, 212 F.3d 306, 314 (6th Cir. 2000); United States v. Downing, 753 F.2d 1224 (3d Cir. 1985) (leading case); United States v. Sebetich, 776 F.2d 412, 418-420 (3d Cir. 1985); Campbell v. People, 814 P.2d 1, 7 (Colo. 1991).

8. *See* Engberg v. Meyer, 820 P.2d 70, 80 (Wyo. 1991); United States v. Moore, 786 F.2d 1308, 1311-1313 (5th Cir. 1986); United States v. Downing, 753 F.2d 1224 (3d Cir. 1985); United States v. Smith, 736 F.2d 1103, 1105-1106 (6th Cir. 1984), *cert. denied*, 469 U.S. 868; People v. McDonald, 690 P.2d 709 (Cal. 1984); State v. Chapple, 660 P.2d 1208 (Ariz. 1983).

9. United States v. Larkin, 978 F.2d 964, 971 (7th Cir. 1992) (issues are "well within the ken of most lay jurors"), *cert. denied*, 507 U.S. 935; United States v. Poole, 794 F.2d 462, 468 (9th Cir. 1986) (questioning scientific basis; cross suffices to reveal deficiencies).

10. United States v. Rincon, 28 F.3d 921, 925-926 (9th Cir. 1994), *cert. denied*, 513 U.S. 1029; United States v. Christophe, 833 F.2d 1296, 1299-1300 (9th Cir. 1987) (both warning that expert testimony may make jurors too skeptical); People v. Enis, 564 N.E.2d 1155, 1165 (Ill. 1990) (could lead to expert testimony on unreliability of other types of testimony, and to using experts to say experts are unreliable).

(others disagree),[11] and some have been reluctant to fund defense requests to hire such experts.[12] By far the bulk of modern authority indicates that trial judges have discretion to admit or exclude such testimony.[13]

Compromise; admit in special cases

There are some indications of a compromise position that would be more favorably inclined toward such testimony when specific factors of need arise.[14] Where identification rests on testimony by someone who knew the defendant well and was in a good position to see the crime, or where identification is well proved by other evidence (like physical evidence connecting defendant to crime), there is little reason to admit such testimony. Where identity is a crucial and closely contested issue, however, and where critical testimony is given by people who did not know the perpetrator, or had only a short time to see him, or were limited or distracted by other factors, expert testimony is more clearly warranted. As in the case of framework and syndrome evidence, here too it seems that experts should not comment directly on reliability of testimony by any particular eyewitness, nor say that she is probably right or wrong in her identification.[15]

§7.22 Syndromes, Social Frameworks, and Profiles

Courts often admit expert testimony describing behavioral syndromes and social frameworks, which are in practice related and overlapping

---

11. *Compare* United States v. Langan, 263 F.3d 613, 620-625 (6th Cir. 2001) (court held *Daubert* hearing and concluded that expert had not shown reliability of transference theory; testimony did not satisfy criterion of "fit") *with* United States v. Rincon, 984 F.2d 1003, 1005 (9th Cir. 1993) (such testimony does not conform to generally accepted theory).

12. Hopkins v. State, 582 N.E.2d 345, 352-354 (Ind. 1991); United States v. Brewer, 783 F.2d 841, 842-843 (9th Cir. 1986); United States v. Purham, 725 F.2d 450, 454 (8th Cir. 1984).

13. United States v. Hicks, 103 F.3d 837, 847 (9th Cir. 1996) (even if testimony satisfies *Daubert*, court has discretion to exclude), *cert. denied*, 520 U.S. 1193; United States v. Brien, 59 F.3d 274, 276-278 (1st Cir. 1995) (avoiding blanket rule), *cert. denied*, 516 U.S. 953. *And see* Engberg v. Meyer, 820 P.2d 70, 79-80 (Wyo. 1991) (collecting cases, approving exclusion by discretion); Campbell v. People, 814 P.2d 1, 7 (Colo. 1991); People v. Sanders, 797 P.2d 561, 579 (Cal. 1990); State v. McCutcheon, 781 P.2d 31, 35 (Ariz. 1989).

14. *See* People v. LeGrand, 867 N.E.2d 374 (N.Y. 2007) (must allow sometimes; case "turned solely on the accuracy of the witnesses' identification" and there was "no corroborating evidence") (reversing murder conviction); State v. McCutcheon, 781 P.2d 31, 35 (Ariz. 1989) (might admit in unusual cases lacking positive identification testimony); People v. Walker, 765 P.2d 70, 81-82 (Cal. 1988) (might admit in unusual case where eyewitness testimony is not substantially corroborated); State v. Moon, 726 P.2d 1263, 1266 (Wash. App. 1986) (expert testimony admissible where identification is principal issue, or defendant presents alibi defense, or little or no other evidence links him to crime).

15. State v. Buell, 489 N.E.2d 785, 804 (Ohio 1986) (absent showing that witness suffers "mental or physical impairment," expert may not testify on identification testimony); Hampton v. State, 385 N.W.2d 868, 872 (Wis. 1979) (generality of testimony favors admitting it; witnesses do not testify on precise questions being tried). On framework testimony, *see* §7.22, *infra*.

phenomena.[1] Both involve patterns of human behavior and mental attitudes typically seen in persons who have experienced psychological stress, usually relating to sexual or physical abuse, but sometimes war, childhood upbringing, or other experiences. Courts generally exclude expert testimony describing what are called profiles of various sorts of criminal offenders, if coupled with attempts to link these directly to the defendant, and this subject is examined briefly at the end of this section.

"Syndrome" aptly describes patterns of behavior and mental attitudes as they appear in particular actors, and syndrome evidence often connects specifically with the persons and events in suit, resting in part on general observations and in part on studies and interviews with those persons. "Framework" aptly describes such patterns and attitudes in their broadest sweep, and framework evidence relates to social or familial settings similar to those in which the events in suit occurred, resting largely on case studies unrelated to those events. Syndrome and framework evidence bring to trials the insight of social science and psychology. These insights help factfinders appraise the attitudes and behavior of the actors, draw inferences from other evidence about what they probably did and thought and intended, and make credibility decisions when they and others testify.

Usually syndrome and framework evidence is offered by prosecutors and it relates to the victim, as in sexual assault and child abuse trials. Sometimes, however, it is offered by the defense and relates to defendants, as in the setting of homicide trials of women charged with killing husbands or intimate companions. And the typical patterns of usage do not always hold true: Defendants sometimes offer evidence that patterns of behavior or attitudes in the alleged victim did not fit patterns or syndromes that are often seen in similar circumstances, and prosecutors sometimes use such evidence to explain the behavior of nonvictim spouses or companions of defendants.

Such evidence raises issues implicating the doctrines on expert testimony and scientific validity, character evidence, impeachment, and support. There are broad areas of consensus but also disagreement and uncertainty.

Expert testimony issues. The most basic issue is scientific validity. In the setting of criminal prosecutions for such crimes as drug trafficking, something close to framework evidence has been admitted for years, based on the experience of law agents and informants, and nobody thinks to treat such evidence as science or to apply the *Daubert* standard. But framework and syndrome testimony comes clothed in the trappings

---

§7.22 1. *See generally* Robert P. Mosteller, Syndromes and Politics in Criminal Trials and Evidence Law, 46 Duke L.J. 461 (1996); Vidmar & Schuller, Juries and Expert Evidence: Social Framework Testimony, 52 Law & Contemp. Probs. 133, 148-155 (1989); Walker & Monahan, Social Facts: Scientific Methodology as Legal Precedent, 76 Calif. L. Rev. 877 (1988); Walker & Monahan, Social Frameworks: A New Use of Social Science in Law, 73 Va. L. Rev. 559 (1987). *And see* 1 Giannelli & Imwinkelried, Scientific Evidence §§9.03-9.07 (4th ed. 2007); 2 Faigman, Saks, Sanders and Cheng, Modern Scientific Evidence §§13:1-15:49 (2007-2008).

of science, and makes special claim for consideration by the factfinder, so the wiser approach is to admit such proof only if it presents valid science, although some states have statutes that exempt some forms of syndrome evidence from the requirement of satisfying a validity standard.[2]

Common syndromes

In keeping with the idea that such evidence is indeed science, it comes with its own jargon and acronyms. Most syndromes reflect aspects of what is broadly known as post-traumatic stress disorder (PTS). In litigation, the most common forms are rape trauma syndrome (RTS), battered woman syndrome (BWS), and two syndromes relating to children that go under the names child sexual abuse accommodation syndrome (CSAAS) and battered child syndrome (BCS).

Despite modern acceptance of such evidence, there remain doubts about scientific validity and conflicts on some points. Briefly, proponents argue that the theories have been examined and tested and there are significant correlations between mental attitudes and behavior patterns on the one hand and previous experience on the other. Critics counter that some forms of syndrome evidence rest on "suppositional science" (hypotheses that are untestable or inadequately tested), that the insights may be useful in formulating legal policy and treatment, but that they are too uncertain for use at trial.[3]

Frameworks and syndromes also raise serious concerns under the pragmatic relevancy requirement set forth in FRE 401-403. Risks of confusing the issues, misleading the jury, and prejudicing the parties count in the balance, along with concerns that the jury may be overwhelmed or overawed by the evidence.

There is also disagreement on the need for syndrome evidence. Proponents argue that experts know more than jurors, who lack experience and insight. Others say these claims are themselves unproved, that the difference between expert and lay understanding is not so great, and that there is a danger that experts can be found on virtually all aspects of human experience, and that trials may become dominated by conflicting expertise on conventional topics.[4] Proponents have persuaded many courts that jurors apply popular stereotypes

2. *See* Cal. Evid. Code §1107 (battered woman syndrome is sometimes provable and is not "a new scientific technique whose reliability is unproven"); State v. Baby, 946 A.2d 463 (Md. 2008) (RTS must be examined in hearing on reliability and validity); State v. Townsend, 897 A.2d 316, 327 (N.J. 2006) (BWS has gained general acceptance as science within professional community; such evidence is reliable regardless whether victim has been diagnosed as suffering BWS); State v. B.H., 870 A.2d 273, 287 (N.J. 2005) (BWS meets requirements of general acceptance and reliability). *And see* §7.6 (testimony on patterns in organized crime) and §7.7 (standard for scientific evidence), *supra.*

3. *See* Faigman, To Have and Have Not: Assessing the Value of Social Science to the Law as Science and Policy, 38 Emory L.J. 1005 (1989); Mosteller, Legal Doctrines Governing the Admissibility of Expert Testimony Concerning Social Framework Evidence, 52 Law & Contemp. Probs. 85 (1989).

4. *See* Commonwealth v. Dunkle, 602 A.2d 830, 836 (Pa. 1992) (reasons why sexually abused children do not come forward immediately "are easily understood by lay people").

or myths,[5] but these claims sometimes merit the criticism that they say less about popular attitudes than about the view of proponents that legal rules and social attitudes are wrong and must be changed by indirection.[6]

Character evidence issues. At a high level of social generality (framework in the strict sense), evidence of behavioral syndromes is purely contextual. As it draws closer to describing qualities personal to the actors or interpreting their attitudes and behavior (syndrome evidence specifically applied), such testimony comes closer to character evidence because it seems to describe specific people and supports backward-looking inferences of likely behavior on the occasion in question.

When viewed as character evidence, expert testimony describing syndromes is highly suspect: Unlike typical character evidence where the testifying witness knew the subject (or his reputation) before the events in suit, experts who give applied syndrome testimony usually rely partly on information provided after the fact (including tests and interviews). Experts are usually looking for attitudes and mental conditions that might reflect events they have already heard about. Thus syndrome evidence is diagnostic, and the purpose is to prepare for trial or other official intervention and provide therapy or treatment.

Highly suspect

Analyzing such evidence as proof of character would bring two sets of Rules into play—those governing proof of character to show conduct and those governing proof of character to show veracity or the lack of it. Insofar as such evidence is offered to support inferences about behavior, it would be subject to FRE 404 and 405: Those provisions require the witness to have an adequate foundation, and they would sharply limit prosecutorial use of syndrome evidence relating to the defendant or victim, since prosecutors generally can offer character evidence only to counter defense character evidence (or in homicide cases to counter evidence that the victim was the first aggressor). Insofar as such evidence is offered to attack or support veracity, it would be subject to FRE 608, which requires the witness to have an adequate foundation on general truthfulness rather than the truth of a particular story, and the evidence cannot be used to show truthfulness unless an attack on veracity has been made.

5. In connection with BWS, *see* State v. B.H., 870 A.2d 273, 287 (N.J. 2005) ("stereotypes and myths"); State v. Koss, 551 N.E.2d 970, 974 (Ohio 1990) (general misconceptions); Commonwealth v. Stonehouse, 555 A.2d 772, 783-784 (Pa. 1989) (blame-victim myths). In connection with RTS, *see* Commonwealth v. King, 834 N.E.2d 1175, 1195 (Mass. 2005) ("prejudicial misconceptions about the nature of rape and rape allegations"); People v. Taylor, 552 N.E.2d 131, 136 (N.Y. 1990) (cultural myths); State v. Bledsoe, 681 P.2d 291, 298 (Cal. 1984) ("widely held misconceptions" and "popular myths"). In connection with child abuse, *see* People v. McAlpin, 812 P.2d 563, 570-571 (Cal. 1991) (myths). In connection with CSAAS, see State v. Schnabel, 952 A.2d 452, 462 (N.J. 2008) (preconceived ideas on child's truthfulness as result of delay); Sanderson v. State, 165 P.3d 83, 90 (Wyo. 2007) (myths about behavior of child who recants).

6. *See, e.g.,* Faigman, To Have and Have Not: Assessing the Value of Social Science to the Law as Science and Policy, 38 Emory L.J. 1005, 1074 (1989) (experts testifying to BWS are saying what they think legal rule ought to be; "ostensibly descriptive testimony is a thinly disguised normative judgment").

Despite the affinity with character evidence, the argument seems powerful that the very qualities that separate expert framework and syndrome testimony from conventional character evidence mean that such evidence, properly handled, need not be classified as proof of character. Instead it can be viewed as evidence of psychological condition or capacity and as a general account of human dynamics. After all, much of the explanatory force comes from models or studies of human behavior rather than appraising personal qualities innate in the subject. The indicated conclusion is that such evidence, properly handled, is dissimilar enough from character evidence to remove it from control of FRE 404-405 and 608.[7] This conclusion reinforces the point that the testifying witness should qualify as an expert and that the testimony is subject to the scientific validity standard.

Proper handling   The key is in proper handling, and two themes appear in the cases. One is that experts giving framework and syndrome testimony are barred from saying whether they think the subject is being truthful, and sometimes even from saying whether she suffered from the syndrome (although such testimony assumes and implies as much). The other is that they cannot talk directly about what they think happened and usually cannot say how the syndrome operated in the case or explains what happened. On the credibility point, courts often explain that "the jury is the judge of credibility" and it needs no help from experts, sometimes alluding to the old notion barring testimony on "ultimate issues."[8]

Not equipped to say   There are two even better reasons: First, while social science might equip an expert to give framework and syndrome evidence, it does not equip her to say what happened or whether a witness is truthful.[9] Second, the expert who offers such conclusions is giving character evidence after all. That means she must have an adequate foundation, and her testimony is limited by FRE 608 when it goes to veracity.[10] Testimony that draws close to commenting directly on what likely happened looks like character evidence, which means that FRE 404-405

7. *See* State v. Haines, 860 N.E.2d 91, 101 (Ohio 2006) (BWS not barred by rule 404(b); "not offered to prove anything about the defendant," but as "background evidence for understanding the victim's behavior"); State v. Petrich, 683 P.2d 173, 179 (Wash. 1984) (rule 608 inapplicable to expert testimony on abused children explaining delay in reporting).

8. State v. Laprade, 958 A.2d 1179 (Vt. 2008) (expert on BWS should not testify about "abusers' reactions when victims attempt to leave" or otherwise "comment on the parties or the specific facts"); State v. Haines, 860 N.E.2d 91, 102 (Ohio 2006) (BWS testimony "crossed the line" when expert said he thought the case was "very consistent with what we see in a battered woman's syndrome scenario") (reversing); United States v. Binder, 769 F.2d 595, 602-603 (9th Cir. 1985) (error to admit testimony that children could distinguish reality from fantasy and truth from falsehood).

9. *See* People v. Beckley, 456 N.W.2d 391, 407-409 (Mich. 1990) (whether child was truthful exceeds scope of expertise); Commonwealth v. Gallagher, 547 A.2d 355, 358 (Pa. 1988) (explaining inability to identify rapist vests opinion with "unwarranted appearance of authority" on credibility).

10. State v. Grecinger, 569 N.W.2d 189, 193 (Minn. 1997) (testimony on BWS is admissible to repair credibility only if it has been attacked). *And see* State v. Rimmasch, 775 P.2d 388, 391-393 (Utah 1989); People v. Snook, 745 P.2d 647 (Colo. 1987); United States v. Azure, 801 F.2d 336, 339-342 (8th Cir. 1986) (all holding that testimony on truthfulness of child abuse victim violated Rule 608).

apply. The traditional sensitivity accorded to defense rights in criminal cases warrants special care when government experts are talking about the defendant even if their testimony stops at one remove from direct comments on what he likely did or thought.[11]

Battered woman syndrome (BWS). The idea of battered woman syndrome is that battering relationships follow patterns or cycles, that a woman in an abusive relationship develops a psychology of learned helplessness that keeps her in the relationship, and that she suffers from a combination of physical and psychological disadvantage that explains why she used deadly force against her abuser even when not under actual or imminent attack.[12] Few seriously argue with these insights as descriptive of human relationships, and most cases accept such evidence as valid science.[13] Yet the theory that these insights are useful as reliable measures of likely behavior on any particular occasion is under strong attack as being unsupported by testing, hence lacking value on the crucial question of self-defense,[14] and a few modern decisions question such evidence.[15]

Many cases approve evidence of battered woman syndrome offered to support claims of self-defense where it sheds some light on defendant's subjective fear and its nature and reasonableness.[16] Use of such evidence is so commonplace that some courts require the woman to

Many cases approve

11. *See* Szymanski v. State, 166 P.3d 879, 888 (Wyo. 2008) (BWS is admissible, but cannot be used to prove defendant's conduct, or it runs afoul of rule against proving character) (quoting authors of this Treatise); Skinner v. State, 33 P.3d 758, 767 (Wyo. 2001) (error to admit testimony on characteristics of battering men, which drew close to commenting directly on what happened and looks like character evidence); *cert. denied*, 122 S. Ct. 1554; State v. Pulizzano, 456 N.W.2d 325, 335-336 (Wis. 1990) (if expert testimony on battering parent syndrome is admissible, ordinarily state cannot offer it during case-in-chief because rule against character evidence precludes strategy). *See also* State v. Hester, 760 P.2d 27, 33 (Idaho 1988); Sanders v. State, 303 S.E.2d 13, 18 (Ga. 1983); State v. Loebach, 310 N.W.2d 58, 63-64 (Minn. 1981); Matter of Cheryl H, 200 Cal. Rptr. 789, 805 (Cal. Ct. App. 1984) (all similar).

12. *See generally* Walker, Terrifying Love: Why Battered Women Kill and How Society Responds (1989); Walker, The Battered Woman Syndrome (1984); Faigman and Wright, The Battered Woman Syndrome in the Age of Science, 39 Ariz. L. Rev. 67 (1997); Raeder, The Double-Edged Sword: Admissibility of Battered Woman Syndrome by and Against Batterers in Cases Implicating Domestic Violence, 67 U. Colo. L. Rev. 789 (1996); Vidmar & Schuller, Juries and Expert Evidence: Social Framework Testimony, 52 Law & Contemp. Probs. 133, 148-155 (1989). *See also* State v. Grecinger, 569 N.W.2d 189, 193 (Minn. 1997); Acoren v. United States, 929 F.2d 1235, 1239-1241 (8th Cir. 1991); State v. Kelly, 478 A.2d 364, 380 (N.J. 1984).

13. *See* Bechtel v. State, 840 P.2d 1, 7 (Okla. Crim. App. 1992); State v. Koss, 551 N.E.2d 970, 974 (Ohio 1990); State v. Hodges, 716 P.2d 563 (Kan. 1986).

14. *See* Morse, The Misbegotten Marriage of Soft Psychology and Bad Law, 14 Law & Hum. Behav. 595 (1990); Note, The Battered Woman Syndrome and Self-Defense: A Legal and Empirical Dissent, 72 Va. L. Rev. 619, 647 (1986) (work by Walker "is unsound and largely irrelevant" in self-defense cases).

15. *See* Hill v. State, 507 S.2d 554, 555 (Ala. Crim. App. 1986); Ibn-Tamas v. United States, 455 A.2d 893 (D.C. 1983). *And see* State v. Hodges, 734 P.2d 1161 (Kan. 1987) (error to exclude evidence questioning validity of BWS).

16. People v. Humphrey, 921 P.2d 1, 15 (Cal. 1996); State v. Koss, 551 N.E.2d 970, 974-975 (Ohio 1990); Commonwealth v. Craig, 783 S.W.2d 387, 389 (Ky. 1990); Commonwealth v. Stonehouse, 555 A.2d 772, 782-783 (Pa. 1989); State v. Hennum, 441 N.W.2d 793, 798 n.2 (Minn. 1989).

submit to an independent examination.[17] Sometimes such evidence is offered to help prosecutors in trials of men rebut claims that the woman's subsequent behavior shows no crime was committed, or why the woman recanted or failed to report.[18]

Limitations   When offered to show self-defense, the expert should not testify that the actions of the defendant were the product of BWS (that the syndrome explains her behavior), that she suffered from BWS, or that BWS shows her story is truthful.[19] Similarly when the purpose is to explain the victim's behavior afterwards, the expert should not testify that BWS shows a crime was committed, that the complaining witness is truthful, or that she suffered from BWS.[20]

Rape trauma syndrome (RTS). Rape trauma syndrome evidence[21] suggests that women go through recognizable phases after being raped, beginning with acute reaction (serious disruption with physical and psychological symptoms characterized by fear of retaliation, men in general, or being alone) followed by longer phases of adjustment and integration (with nightmares and more general phobias and gradual recovery).[22] The main problems with RTS as evidence in sexual assault trials are that most symptoms are not peculiar to rape victims and RTS was developed as a diagnostic tool where the focus was treatment rather than determining the accuracy of an account of rape.[23] The question whether RTS has been adequately tested and studied to qualify as valid science remains subject to dispute.[24] (Parenthetically, it is notable that

17. *See* Smith v. State, 486 S.E.2d 819 (Ga. 1997); State v. Briand, 547 A.2d 235, 240 (N.H. 1988); State v. Myers, 570 A.2d 1260, 1266 (N.J. 1990). *But see* State v. Hennum, 441 N.W.2d 793, 799-800 (Minn. 1989) (exam not required).

18. Earl v. United States, 932 A.2d 1122,1127 (D.C. 2007) (explain why victim "continued to have contact" with defendant after assault); Trujillo v. State, 953 P.2d 1182 (Wyo. 1998); State v. Grecinger, 569 N.W.2d 189 (Minn. 1997); Acoren v. United States, 929 F.2d 1235, 1239-1241 (8th Cir. 1991); State v. Ciskie, 751 P.2d 1165, 1171-1173 (Wash. 1988).

19. Commonwealth v. Craig, 783 S.W.2d 387, 389 (Ky. 1990) (should not say whether shooting was "result" of syndrome); State v. Hennum, 441 N.W.2d 793, 799 (Minn. 1989) (may not say defendant suffers from BWS).

20. State v. Ciskie, 751 P.2d 1165, 1174 (Wash. 1988) (expert could give "final diagnosis" but not say complaining witness was victim or story was true).

21. *See generally* McCord, The Admissibility of Expert Testimony Regarding Rape Trauma Syndrome in Rape Prosecutions, 26 B.C. L. Rev. 1143 (1985); Massaro, Experts, Psychology, Credibility, and Rape: The Rape Trauma Syndrome Issue and Its Implications for Expert Psychological Testimony, 69 Minn. L. Rev. 395 (1985).

22. *See generally* Burgess & Homstrom, Rape Trauma Syndrome, 131 Am. J. Psychiatry 981 (1974); Notman & Natelson, The Rape Victim: Psychodynamic Considerations, 133 Am. J. Psychiatry 408 (1976). *See also* American Psychiatric Association, Diagnostic and Statistical Manual of Mental Disorders 236 (rev. ed. 1987) (criteria of RTS).

23. State v. Bledsoe, 681 P.2d 291, 300-301 (Cal. 1984); State v. Saldana, 324 N.W.2d 227, 230 (Minn. 1982) (both saying RTS is therapeutic tool).

24. For critical views on RTS, *see* Graham, Rape Trauma Syndrome: Is It Probative of Lack of Consent?, 13 Law & Psych. Rev. 25, 41-42 (1989) (research on RTS is not probative on consent, prior trauma, nor cause of current behavior); State v. Black, 745 P.2d 12, 16-18 (Wash. 1987) (RTS lacks scientific reliability); State v. Taylor, 663 S.W.2d 235, 238-240 (Mo. 1984) (RTS not based on sound enough science for use in

at least one case rejects evidence of male sexual victimization as insufficiently validated for use in trial.[25])

When offered to refute a claim of consent, RTS evidence is corroborative of testimony by the victim and represents a response to defense evidence. Courts split on the admissibility question, with some admitting[26] and some excluding it.[27] When used for the more limited purpose of shedding light on the mental condition and behavior of the victim, such evidence has smoother sailing[28] although here too courts sometimes exclude.[29]

Offered on issue of consent

Not surprisingly, RTS testimony is sometimes offered in other contexts: Defendants accused of rape or sexual assault sometimes argue that behavior by the complaining witness that is inconsistent with RTS supports claims of consent or the absence of a criminal act. In this setting, a conclusion that the underlying science is valid enough to support prosecutorial use of RTS also supports defense use,[30] since there is no reason to suppose that the risks of inferential error are greater in the latter case than the former.[31] RTS has also appeared in civil suits by the complaining witness against the perpetrator.[32]

Perhaps the most elaborate and questionable use of RTS is to prove a central element in a charge of rape or sexual assault, using expert testimony describing the syndrome along with proof of the post-event behavior of the victim as proof that an attack (or criminal

Questionable— proof of attack

---

evidence). For positive appraisals, *see* People v. Taylor, 552 N.E.2d 131, 135 (N.Y. 1990) (meets *Frye* standard); State v. Allewalt, 517 A.2d 741, 745-747 (Md. 1986) (widely recognized and commonly accepted).

25. *See* State v. Borchardt, 478 N.W.2d 757, 761 (Minn. 1991) (excluding evidence that defendant was sexually victimized by man he shot) (not valid science).

26. *See* State v. Alberico, 861 P.2d 192, 208-212 (N.M. 1993); State v. Allewalt, 517 A.2d 741, 751 (Md. 1986); State v. Huey, 699 P.2d 1290, 1293-1294 (Ariz. 1985); State v. Liddell, 685 P.2d 918, 923 (Mont. 1984); State v. Marks, 647 P.2d 1292, 1299 (Kan. 1982).

27. *See* State v. Black, 745 P.2d 12, 16-18 (Wash. 1987); State v. Brodniak, 718 P.2d 322, 329 (Mont. 1986) (error to let expert testify on basis of RTS and conversation with complaining witness that she was not "malingering"); State v. Bledsoe, 681 P.2d 291, 300-301 (Cal. 1984).

28. State v. Alberico, 861 P.2d 192, 208-212 (N.M. 1993) (behavior of victim was consistent with rape); State v. Gettier, 438 N.W.2d 1, 5-6 (Iowa 1989) (explain typical reactions); Simmons v. State, 504 N.E.2d 575, 578-579 (Ind. 1987) (explain story that defendant forced victim to tell); Lessard v. State, 719 P.2d 227, 232-233 (Wyo. 1986) (explain why victim asks assailant not to tell).

29. Commonwealth v. Gallagher, 547 A.2d 355, 358 (Pa. 1988) (inadmissible to show why victim could not identify defendant).

30. Henson v. State, 535 N.E.2d 1189, 1192-1193 (Ind. 1989) ("fundamentally unfair" to admit RTS for prosecutor but exclude when offered by defense); State v. McQuillen, 689 P.2d 822, 836-837 (Kan. 1984) (suggesting defense use). *But see* Note, Defense Expert Testimony on Rape Trauma Syndrome: Implications for the Stoic Victim, 42 Hastings L.J. 1143 (1991) (only state should use RTS).

31. Perhaps definitive knowledge will show that RTS appears often among rape victims and seldom among others, but that victims do not exhibit RTS, which would indicate that RTS represents valid science for the prosecution but not the defense. But little is known, and it is incongruous to swallow uncertainties when prosecutors offer the evidence but balk when defendants do.

32. Guttierrez v. Iulo, 591 N.Y.S.2d 711, 713 (N.Y. Sup. Ct. 1992) (admissible to prove after-effects in support of damage claim).

penetration) occurred. Most courts reject this use, which seems the right outcome because this form of expertise does not extend this far.[33]

Defendants in sexual assault prosecutions sometimes seek to compel the complaining witness to undergo an examination by defense psychologists as a means of countering expected RTS testimony, but such requests usually fail because of hardships on the complaining witness and the fear of abuse.[34] It seems that the unavailability of defense examinations makes it all the more crucial to limit prosecution expert testimony to the generalities of RTS.

Precautions   When RTS evidence is admitted, some minimal precautions are important. Clearly the "rape trauma" label is a loaded term that prejudges the case and exaggerates the predictive power of the symptoms, and it should not be used at trial.[35] And to minimize or confine risks of jury overvaluation of expert testimony, courts that admit RTS should insist that experts stop short of testifying directly on central issues. Experts should not say they think the complaining witness was raped or assaulted, or that they believe her story or think she is telling the truth.[36] Pure framework evidence describing patterns of reaction in rape victims has the strongest claim for consideration by the factfinder. If the evidence is accepted as scientifically valid, a somewhat more questionable use of RTS would include expert testimony that symptoms seen in the complaining witness are consistent with symptoms that make up the syndrome.[37]

Abused child syndromes. Various forms of child abuse syndrome are recognized in the cases,[38] including the battered child syndrome (BCS) and child sexual abuse accommodation syndrome (CSAAS).[39]

33. For authority condemning this use, *see* People v. Taylor, 552 N.E.2d 131, 138 (N.Y. 1990) (cannot use to show rape); State v. Gettier, 438 N.W.2d 1, 5-6 (Iowa 1989) (cannot say victim was raped); State v. Bledsoe, 681 P.2d 291, 300-301 (Cal. 1984) (cannot use to show rape). For a case allowing this use, *see* State v. Liddell, 685 P.2d 918, 922 (Mont. 1984).

34. *See* Gilpin v. McCormick, 921 F.2d 928, 932 (9th Cir. 1990) (no due process violation to refuse to order examination of victim); State v. Liddell, 685 P.2d 918, 924 (Mont. 1984); Annot., 45 A.L.R.4th 310 (1986).

35. State v. Gettier, 438 N.W.2d 1, 5-6 (Iowa 1989); State v. Allewalt, 517 A.2d 741, 751 (Md. 1986); State v. Bledsoe, 681 P.2d 291, 301 n.14 (Cal. 1984).

36. *See* State v. Alberico, 861 P.2d 192, 208-212 (N.M. 1993) (may not say victim is truthful, or was abused, or identify perpetrator); State v. McCoy, 366 S.E.2d 731, 737 (W. Va. 1988) (may not say whether woman was raped); People v. Hampton, 746 P.2d 947, 951 (Colo. 1987) (may not say complaining witness was raped); State v. Brodniak, 718 P.2d 322, 329 (Mont. 1986) (RTS expert cannot comment on credibility).

37. *Compare* People v. Hampton, 746 P.2d 947, 951 (Colo. 1987) (expert may describe RTS but may not say complaining witness suffered from it) *with* State v. McQuillen, 689 P.2d 822 (Kan. 1984) (may say complainant exhibits trauma "consistent with" it).

38. *See generally* Myers, Bays, Becker, Berliner, Corwin & Saywitz, Expert Testimony in Child Sexual Abuse Litigation, 68 Neb. L. Rev. 1 (1989); Holmes, Child Sexual Abuse Accommodation Syndrome: Curing the Effects of a Misdiagnosis in the Law of Evidence, 25 Tulsa L.J. 143 (1989); Walker, Handbook on Sexual Abuse of Children, Assessment and Treatment Issues (1988); McCord, Expert Psychological Testimony About Child Complainants in Sexual Abuse Prosecutions: A Foray Into the Admissibility of Novel Psychological Evidence, 77 J. Crim. L. & Criminology 1 (1986).

39. State v. MacLennan, 702 N.W.2d 219 (Minn. 2005) (BCS); Sorensen v. State, 895 P.2d 454, 458 (Wyo. 1995); Commonwealth v. Dunkle, 602 A.2d 830, 835 n.16 (Pa. 1992); State v. J. Q., 617 A.2d 1196, 1207-1209 (N.J. 1993).

It is said that common symptoms are nightmares and new behavioral problems at school. Among very young children symptoms are vomiting, sexualized play, and a regression in toilet training,[40] and among older children disclosure to a friend, withdrawal and daydreaming, and low self-esteem.[41] When testimony rests on interviews with the child and presents psychological analyses or insights, the bulk of opinion in the field considers the theory and science valid as diagnostic tools to detect abuse. But others disagree,[42] and courts reach conflicting conclusions.[43]

Testimony describing these syndromes has been held admissible to shed light on the behavior of sexually abused children,[44] including small children who apparently suffered nonsexual physical abuse,[45] and specifically to explain delay in reporting.[46]

Shed light on behavior

Here too most courts hold that experts should avoid becoming so particular and focused that the testimony in substance says the child seems truthful or her story is true[47] or that she was abused[48] or that

Avoid being too particular

---

40. People v. Fasy, 829 P.2d 1314, 1317 (Colo. 1992) (nightmares, vomiting); Matter of Nicole V., 518 N.E.2d 914, 918 (N.Y. 1987) (age-inappropriate knowledge; enuresis in toilet-trained child; regressive behavior and withdrawal; tantrums or depression).

41. *See* State v. Schnabel, 952 A.2d 452, 462 (N.J. 2008) (secrecy, helplessness, entrapment and accommodation, delayed reporting, recantation); State v. J. Q., 617 A.2d 1196, 1202 (N.J. 1993) (overt or subtle and indirect disclosures to relative, friend, teacher; sexualized play; withdrawal and daydreaming; low self-esteem; shame or guilt; falling grades; pseudomaturity; sexual promiscuity; poor peer relationships; suicide attempt; positive relationship toward offender; phobic attitude toward adults).

42. For arguments favoring validity, *see* Summit, The Child Sexual Abuse Accommodation Syndrome, 7 Child Abuse & Neglect 177 (1983); Myers, Evidence in Child Abuse and Neglect Cases §4.31 (2d ed. 1992). For arguments questioning validity, *see* Freidrich, Psychotherapy of Sexually Abused Children and Their Families 25 (1990) (problems of children are not abuse-specific, and come from lack of nurturance); Hall, The Role of Psychologists as Experts in Cases Involving Allegations of Child Sexual Abuse, 23 Fam. L.Q. 451, 463-464 (1989) (syndromes and profiles "do not exist"); Note, The Unreliability of Expert Testimony on the Typical Characteristics of Sexual Abuse Victims, 74 Geo. L. Rev. 429 (1985); Note, The Unreliability of Expert Testimony in Child Sexual Abuse Prosecutions: A Spectrum of Uses, 68 B.U. L. Rev. 155 (1988).

43. *Compare* State v. MacLennan, 702 N.W.2d 219, 233 (Minn. 2005) (BCS admissible under rule 702, need not satisfy scientific validity standard) *and* United States v. St. Pierre, 812 F.2d 417, 419-420 (8th Cir. 1987) (CSAAS is valid science) *with* Commonwealth v. Dunkle, 602 A.2d 830, 832-835 (Pa. 1992), *and* State v. Black, 537 A.2d 1154, 1157 (Me. 1988) (both finding BCAAS invalid).

44. Copsio v. United States, 927 A.2d 1106, 1135 n.29 (explain child's affection for abuser); United States v. St. Pierre, 812 F.2d 417, 419-420 (8th Cir. 1987) (describe common behavior in victims). *See also* People v. Beckley, 456 N.W.2d 391, 406-407 (Mich. 1990); State v. Spigarolo, 556 A.2d 112, 123 (Conn. 1989); Griego v. State, 761 P.2d 973, 978 (Wyo. 1988).

45. State v. Williams, 451 N.W.2d 866, 891 (Minn. Ct. App. 1990) (malicious punishment of children aged six and eight).

46. State v. Schnabel, 952 A.2d 452, 462 (N.J. 2008); People v. Fasy, 829 P.2d 1314, 1317 (Colo. 1992); People v. McAlpin, 812 P.2d 563, 570 (Cal. 1991); Stewart v. State, 521 N.E.2d 675, 677 (Ind. 1988); Scadden v. State, 732 P.2d 1036, 1037 (Wyo. 1987).

47. Snowden v. Singletary, 135 F.3d 732 (11th Cir. 1998); State v. Keller, 844 P.2d 195, 201 (Or. 1993); State v. J. Q., 617 A.2d 1196, 1211 (N.J. 1993); People v. Fasy, 829 P.2d 1314, 1318 (Colo. 1992); State v. Sims, 608 A.2d 1149, 1153-1154 (Vt. 1991).

48. Robert S. v. Stetson School, Inc., 256 F.3d 159, 169-170 (3d Cir. 2001); Commonwealth v. Federico, 683 N.E.2d 1035, 1039 (Mass. 1997); United States v. Whitted, 11 F.3d 782, 785-786 (8th Cir. 1993); People v. Renfro, 3 Cal. Rptr. 909, 916 (Cal. Ct. App. 1992).

defendant committed the abuse.[49] A few courts, however, allow the expert to draw close to such particulars by saying the child suffers from the syndrome,[50] or that she was abused[51] or that her story is truthful (at least if she has been impeached),[52] and some courts approve testimony that says the child's behavior fits or is consistent with the syndrome.[53] Defense efforts to suggest on cross that the observed symptoms can be caused by trauma other than the crime charged to the defendant invite somewhat more far-ranging testimony by the expert that sexual assault was likely the cause of the observed symptoms.[54] As in the case of RTS, here too it seems that defendants have a good argument that courts should allow use of syndrome evidence to refute charges of abuse since there is no indication that absence of behavioral indicators is less probative of absence of abuse than is the presence of such indicators probative of the fact of abuse. Here too defendants sometimes try to have their own experts examine the child, but courts have been reluctant to grant such requests.[55]

When expert testimony rests on medical diagnoses of physical injuries and accompanying medical history, or on autopsies and medical history, expert opinion that a child suffered a pattern of abuse has smooth sledding.[56] It seems that medical testimony can also sometimes suggest past sexual abuse on the basis of physical conditions that do not amount to injuries in the usual sense.[57]

Where the focus of attention is the parent or guardian rather than the abused child and the testimony presents a psychological rather than physical portrait of an alleged batterer (battering parent syndrome), courts are more skeptical of the science and protective of the

49. State v. Hester, 760 P.2d 27, 34-35 (Idaho 1988); Stephens v. State, 774 P.2d 60, 66-67 (Wyo. 1989); State v. Black, 537 A.2d 1154, 1157 (Me. 1988).

50. State v. Huntington, 575 N.W.2d 268, 279 (Wis. 1998); People v. Fasy, 829 P.2d 1314, 1317 (Colo. 1992); State v. Reser, 767 P.2d 1277, 1283 (Kan. 1989).

51. *See* State v. Edward Charles L, 398 S.E.2d 123, 141 (W. Va. 1990); Shannon v. State, 783 P.2d 942, 945 (Nev. 1989); Glendening v. State, 536 S.2d 212, 220-221 (Fla. 1988), *cert. denied*, 492 U.S. 907.

52. *See* State v. Bachman, 446 N.W.2d 271, 276 (S.D. 1989); State v. Kim, 645 P.2d 1330, 1338-1339 (Haw. 1982).

53. People v. Beckley, 456 N.W.2d 391, 406-407 (Mich. 1990) (may describe syndrome and comment on whether conduct by child fits syndrome); State v. Reser, 767 P.2d 1277, 1282 (Kan. 1989) (expert described syndrome and opined that 14-year-old girl exhibited characteristics of syndrome).

54. People v. Fasy, 829 P.2d 1314, 1318-1319 (Colo. 1992) (defense cross suggested other things could cause symptoms; expert properly replied that sexual incident probably caused them).

55. State v. Goodwin, 813 P.2d 953, 964 (Mont. 1991); Gale v. State, 792 P.2d 570, 576-577 (Wyo. 1990); People v. Lucero, 724 P.2d 1374, 1376 (Colo. App. 1986).

56. *See* Estelle v. McGuire, 502 U.S. 62 (1991) (admitting expert testimony based on rectal tearing, fractured ribs, and other injuries); United States v. Boise, 916 F.2d 497, 503 (9th Cir. 1990) (testimony that six-week-old child died from battered child syndrome).

57. People v. Mendibles, 245 Cal. Rptr. 553, 562-563 (Cal. Ct. App. 1988) (examination of genitalia).

defendant[58] although some decisions approve even testimony of this sort.[59] In this setting, it seems that the doctor can help a jury appraise the question whether observed physical injuries were accidental or the product of a pattern of abuse. Testimony describing parental behavior in reporting abuse has been admitted,[60] and testimony suggesting that abusers can come from many different backgrounds and need not fit narrow images.[61] Some courts allow testimony describing behavioral strategies of pedophiles,[62] but others exclude such evidence.[63]

Profiles. In contrast to syndrome and framework evidence, courts generally exclude testimony describing profiles of typical offenders in settings such as airplane hijackers, drug traffickers, and sometimes abusive spouses or parents, at least where the witness suggests that defendant himself fits such a profile.[64] Generally the term "profile" describes sets of observable behavioral patterns rather than psychological characteristics, and the primary use of profiles is in police and enforcement work, where they are a tool for identifying crime suspects, people engaged in drug trafficking, or people who present high risks in vulnerable areas like airplanes or government facilities. More general descriptions of criminal modus operandi in settings of organized crime, where there is no attempt to link the defendant personally to a "profile" of the typical offender, has smoother sledding.[65]

---

58. State v. Hester, 760 P.2d 27, 33-34 (Idaho 1988) (error to let expert in child sexual abuse testify that defendant had traits consistent with abusers); Sanders v. State, 303 S.E.2d 13, 18 (Ga. 1983) (error to admit testimony describing personality traits and histories of battering parents).

59. People v. Lucero, 724 P.2d 1374, 1375 (Colo. App. 1986) ("typical incest family").

60. People v. McAlpin, 812 P.2d 563, 567-570 (Cal. 1991) (parents often delay reporting known molestation).

61. People v. McAlpin, 812 P.2d 563, 570-571 (Cal. 1991) (no typical profile of child molester).

62. *See* United States v. Cross, 928 F.2d 1030, 1049-1050 (11th Cir. 1991) ("characteristic behaviors of pedophiles"); Shannon v. State, 783 P.2d 942, 945 (Nev. 1989) (similar).

63. *See* United States v. Powers, 59 F.3d 1460, 1471-1472 (4th Cir. 1995) (excluding testimony that defendant lacked profile of pedophile; did not satisfy *Daubert*), *cert. denied*, 516 U.S. 1077.

64. *See* Salcedo v. People, 999 P.2d 833, 837 (Colo. 2000) (excluding evidence of drug currier profile); United States v. Small, 74 F.3d 1276, 1283 (D.C. Cir. 1996); United States v. Lui, 941 F.2d 844 (9th Cir. 1991); United States v. Simpson, 910 F.2d 154, 156-158 (4th Cir. 1990) (all condemning use of drug courier profile on issues of guilt or innocence). *See generally* Mark Kadish, The Drug Courier Profile: In Planes, Trains and Airplanes and Now in the Jury Box, 46 Am. U. L. Rev. 747 (1997).

65. *See* §7.6, *supra.*

CHAPTER 8

Hearsay

A. DOCTRINE AND PURPOSE—AN OVERVIEW

§8.1 What Is Hearsay

Lawyers and judges mostly agree on a one-line definition that runs like this: "Hearsay is an out-of-court statement offered to prove the matter asserted" (or "truth of the matter asserted"). As one-liners go, this definition is not bad, and competent people use it to get the right results most of the time. For example, if the purpose is to prove that Nurse *N* was in the operating room during surgery, a statement by Observer to that effect ("Nurse *N* was in the operating room during the surgery"), made in a conversation with Listener after the event, would be hearsay if offered to prove Nurse *N* was there. In the words of the one-liner, Observer's statement is offered to prove the matter asserted.

It is a hallmark of Anglo-American evidence law, known even to laypeople, that hearsay is ordinarily inadmissible. This principle is of great

Hearsay ordinarily inadmissible

719

importance, finding reinforcement in the confrontation clause of the Sixth Amendment, which says that in criminal cases the defendant is entitled to be "confronted with the witnesses against him." It should be noted, however, that much hearsay is admissible. Roughly 30 exceptions pave the way for various out-of-court statements, and in civil cases most hearsay that seems reliable is likely to be admissible. It is somewhat different in criminal cases, where modern confrontation jurisprudence blocks the use against the accused of "testimonial" hearsay, meaning for the most part actual testimony from other proceedings or earlier stages of the same case, and statements to police investigating crimes.[1] Commentators generally support the hearsay doctrine, but many argue that it should be reshaped by changing the exceptions or the conditions in which they may be invoked. Often the underlying theme is that more hearsay should be admissible, especially in civil cases.[2]

Oral statements   Hearsay statements are often oral, like Observer's remark to Listener about Nurse *N.* Proving an oral statement usually requires testimony by someone who heard it spoken (Listener), and the very term "hearsay" conveys the idea of someone repeating what he heard another say. Sometimes, however, it is possible to prove an oral statement by other evidence, such as a tape recording or testimony by the person who made the statement. Generally speaking, changing the form of proof does not alter the hearsay analysis: With one important qualification,[3] if Observer's comment is offered to show Nurse *N* was in the operating room, the comment is hearsay whether it is proved by a tape recording or by the testimony of Listener or Observer himself.

A person who makes a statement (written or oral) is usually called the "declarant" or the "speaker." The Rules use the term "declarant," which is readily understood to mean someone who makes an oral statement or writes a statement, and this book uses both terms to mean the same thing (one who speaks or writes). In the preceding example, Observer is the speaker or declarant.

Written statements   Of course the hearsay doctrine embraces not just oral statements, but written ones too. If Observer had written a letter with the same statement ("Nurse *N* was in the operating room during the surgery"),

---

§8.1 1. U.S. Const. amend. VI. *See also* Crawford v. Washington, 541 U.S. 36, 57 (2004) and the discussion of the Confrontation Clause and the hearsay doctrine in §§8.83-8.92, *infra.*

2. For examples of modern work, *see* Fenner, Law Professor Reveals Shocking Truth About Hearsay, 62 UMKC L. Rev. 1 (1993); Friedman, Toward a Partial Economic, Game-Theoretic Analysis of Hearsay, 76 Minn. L. Rev. 723 (1992); Millich, Hearsay Antinomies: The Case for Abolishing the Rule and Starting Over, 71 Or. L. Rev. 723 (1992); Park, A Subject Matter Approach to Hearsay Reform, 86 Mich. L. Rev. 51 (1987); Seigel, Rationalizing Hearsay: A Proposal for a Best Evidence Hearsay Rule, 72 B.U. L. Rev. 893 (1992); Swift, A Foundation Fact Approach to Hearsay, 75 U. Cal. L. Rev. 495 (1987); Weinstein, Probative Force of Hearsay, 46 Iowa L. Rev. 331 (1961).

3. The qualification is that there are powerful arguments for admitting out-of-court statements by speakers who also testify, and the Rules make special provision for some such statements. FRE 801(d)(1) defines as "not hearsay" some prior statements by testifying witnesses, even though the statements would be hearsay if this provision were not there. *See* the discussion in §§8.24-8.26, *infra.*

the proponent would still face a hearsay objection if she offered the letter to prove the statement in order to show that Nurse *N* was there. And the same would be true if Observer had written the statement in a diary or on a hospital form, although the latter might fit the business records exception.[4] Nor would the result change if the proponent offered testimony describing the statement by someone who had read the letter, and such testimony would raise not only hearsay issues but problems under the Best Evidence Doctrine, which requires the writing itself if the purpose is to prove what it says (its "content").[5]

§8.2   The Hearsay Risks

At the heart of the hearsay doctrine is the conviction that out-of-court statements are generally an inferior kind of proof. Usually this conviction is explained in terms of the risks that come with relying on the word or say-so of another person, and usually these are grouped in four categories.

One risk is that the speaker may misperceive the act, event, or condition in question. If Observer tells Listener that "Nurse *N* was in the operating room during surgery," it is possible that he mistook someone else for Nurse *N*. He might be nearsighted, or may only have caught a fleeting or partial glimpse of the person he described; he might not hear well or might have heard the voice of the person he identifies against a jumble of background voices; he might be only slightly acquainted with *N*, and her voice and appearance might not yet really have sunk in; he might have been distracted, paying little attention to what he saw or heard, or might have erred because another nurse closely resembles *N* in voice or general appearance.

(1) Misperception

The focal point is the moment of observation, and there are really three concerns. One centers on the sensory capacities of the speaker, meaning mainly what we would call his physical abilities to see and hear (sometimes the other senses of touch, smell, and taste are involved, but less often). Another centers on his mental capacity, which means mostly his judgment and ability to process and make sense of whatever he sees and hears. Both concerns are affected by attitudes, expectations, psychological condition, distractions, and preoccupations that are part of his life at the moment. The third concern is physical circumstances, including lighting conditions, visual obstructions, noises, even weather conditions, that might bear on opportunity to observe. Any or all these factors might prove critical, and being wary does not so much imply a skeptical view of human capabilities as a cautious attitude toward factfinding.

Another risk is that the speaker might err in calling to mind the events or conditions he observed. We commonly think of memory as fading over time. And we think memories of multiple similar events may

(2) Faulty Memory

---

4. *See* the description of FRE 803(6) in §§8.44-8.47, *infra.*
5. *See* the discussion in §§10.1-10.18, *infra.*

become confused or conflated, and that memories are affected by the important things that preoccupy us and absorb the bulk of our energies and attention.

Psychologists report that recollecting does not involve retrieving a datum stored in the mind in static condition (as it might rest in computer memory): It is better understood as creating a new mental image that is affected by—indeed partly comprised of—later memories and today's impressions and ideas.[1] The acuity of memory is affected by factors operating both at the time of observation, such as attentiveness, interest, emotional involvement, and nature of the experience (pleasant information is more easily recalled, unpleasant or traumatic events more readily repressed). It is also affected by factors that come into play when the event is later called to mind, including the type of information (visual perceptions are more easily recalled than verbal descriptions), the attitude of the observer (caution aids in recall), and the suggestivity of the situation.[2]

The focal point is the moment of recollecting, and the stress is on failed or faulty memory. But the real point is broader and less judgmental: The process of formulating ideas about the past introduces changes and distortions, and while we speak of faults or failings (terms that are sometimes quite apt), we might just as well speak in neutral terms of what it means to be human. Once again, being wary implies not so much skepticism as an attitude of caution and care.

(3) Risk of insincerity Another risk is insincerity, meaning that the speaker might shade the truth or blatantly falsify. In everyday experience, the former is more common than the latter, but both happen. And the gathering winds of litigation encourage observers to take sides, sensing the coming dispute and preferring one outcome or one side to the other, thus encouraging conscious, subconscious, or unconscious shadings of the truth.

(4) Narrative ambiguity Finally, we have the risk of narrative ambiguity—the risk that the declarant might misspeak or be misunderstood. There are three concerns: One is that he might say one thing but mean another (a slip of the tongue). The second is that even if he uses words well and chooses the best possible ones to convey his intended meaning, he might still be misinterpreted. Experience differs among people, so the images and meanings that words convey to some people might not be the ones that others take from them. The third is that language, while rich in nuance and variety, may not capture the point of detail, or the qualification or limit, that lies at the heart of a litigated dispute. So even if the speaker chooses the best words and the trier understands them in the same way, the message may be misleading or incomplete.

---

§8.2 1. For a discussion of theories of long-term memory, *see* M. H. Ashcraft, Human Memory and Cognition 56-58 (1989) (information is not really "lost" from memory, but altered, revised, updated, and otherwise modified as new information comes in). *See also* Krist v. Eli Lilly & Co., 897 F.2d 293, 297 (7th Cir. 1990) (summarizing findings of cognitive psychologists on memory).

2. *See* Imwinkelried, The Importance of the Memory Factor in Analyzing the Reliability of Hearsay Testimony: A Lesson Slowly Learnt—And Quickly Forgotten, 41 Fla. L. Rev. 215, 225-226, 251 (1989).

When an out-of-court statement is offered to prove what it asserts (a substantive or hearsay purpose), the hearsay risks are associated with the speaker. Referring to the example, it is the perception, memory, candor, and narrative abilities of *Observer* that are of concern because *his* statement carries the information. In its mission of care and caution, the hearsay doctrine excludes statements unless some special reason appears to suppose that they are trustworthy or reliable, or that they should be admitted on account of some special need (necessity) or for some other reason, and the exceptions define such special cases.

Focus on speaker

Using human statements as evidence of events or conditions in the world actually involves two steps or inferences, although we seldom consciously consider these steps any more than we consciously go step-by-step through the inferential chains that link circumstantial evidence to the point to be proved. With statements, two of the hearsay risks affect one inference, and two affect the other.[3]

Two-step inference

The first inference involves taking the statement as proof of the thoughts or mental state of the speaker: Observer *said* Nurse N was in the operating room, so we infer that he *believes* she was there. This inference is affected by the risks of candor and narrative ambiguity: If he was less than candid or misspoke or was misunderstood, his statement suggests the wrong conclusion about what he thinks. The second involves taking his belief as evidence of the event or condition. If Observer *thinks* Nurse N was in the operating room (and was in a position to know), we infer that she was there. This inference is affected by the risks of misperception and failed memory: If he did not see or hear well, or forgot what he saw, or conflated his memory of the event with his memory of another event, his statement suggests the wrong conclusion about what happened.

§8.3 Safeguards of the Trial Process

Although an out-of-court statement is hearsay if offered to prove what it asserts, the speaker could come into court and say the same thing, testifying as a witness under oath, and the hearsay objection would disappear. Referring again to the example, Observer could take the stand and testify that "Nurse N was in the operating room during the surgery" and there would be no hearsay objection.[1] A moment's

---

3. *See generally* Tribe, Triangulating Hearsay, 87 Harv. L. Rev. 957 (1974) (suggesting, perhaps tongue-in-cheek, triangular diagram in which factfinder takes two-step inferential "journey," beginning at lower left with statement, then traveling up left leg to speaker's mind, then down right leg to the point to be proved, encountering four hearsay risks en route).

§8.3 1. We should be careful here. We imagine that Observer actually testifies to this effect. If instead he testifies that "I told Listener that Nurse N was present," the hearsay objection reappears. Here Observer would be testifying that he made a statement describing the presence of Nurse N. His testimony proves the statement, which in turn proves Nurse N's presence. The statement is still hearsay. Also we assume Observer has knowledge based on firsthand observation that Nurse N was there. If he testifies that

reflection shows that his account is still subject to the risks described in the previous section: Being human, he may have misperceived the event or wrongly remembered it; he might not be candid (shading his testimony or lying outright) or he might misspeak or be misunderstood.

Why, then, does evidence law draw such a sharp distinction between in-court testimony and out-of-court statements? The answer is that the trial process provides three safeguards that reduce the hearsay risks.

(1) Cross-examination
Long considered an indispensable and powerful tool for getting at the truth, cross-examination entails close, pointed, persistent questioning of the witness on the substance of his testimony. If Observer testifies, the adverse party can cross-examine him about his testimonial assertion that "Nurse *N* was in the operating room during the surgery." The right to cross-examine is usually considered the most important safeguard of the trial process.

It is a central tenet in our faith in the adversary system that a trained and skillful lawyer can, by cross-examination, uncover and even correct for problems arising from all four of the hearsay risks.[2] If Observer cannot see or hear well, or his sight or hearing was impeded or fleeting at the critical moment, such facts can be made to appear, and the force of the direct reduced accordingly. Similarly, problems in memory can be brought to light. And if Observer testifies less than candidly, there is hope that cross-examination can make headway, developing tensions or contradictions (inconsistencies) in the account, or shadings or nuances in the words that reveal a conscious or unconscious attempt to color the facts in some way.

Finally, cross-examination can help correct for problems of narrative ambiguity. Observer *said* Nurse *N* was in the operating room. Did he mean she was there the whole time? In an official capacity? Was she participating in the medical procedure or only observing or acting as backup for another nurse?

(2) Oath
Another safeguard of the trial process is that witnesses are asked to swear or solemnly affirm that they will speak the truth. Testifying under oath carries with it the threat of a perjury prosecution for deliberate falsehoods, as the judge or lawyers may remind a witness who seems too casual, evasive, uncooperative, or untruthful in giving evidence. More importantly, the ceremony of the oath brings home to the witness that the time has come to be serious, careful, and honest.

(3) Demeanor
A testifying witness gives her evidence on the stand under the gaze of the trier of fact, and her demeanor provides valuable clues about meaning and credibility. Our assessments of these points are affected by so many qualities and mannerisms that any list is bound to be incomplete,

---

she was there because he guessed or assumed so, his testimony is objectionable for lack of knowledge. *See* §6.5, *supra*. If he testifies that Nurse *N* was there because someone told him so, his testimony conveys hidden or indirect hearsay and is in substance a repetition of what someone told him. Again the usual objection is lack of personal knowledge, but a "hearsay" objection could serve as well. *See* §8.6, *infra*.

2. Cross-examination can bring to light all manner of facts, connections, and interests relating to accuracy or truthfulness, including what is often called "character for truth and veracity." *See* the discussion of impeaching witnesses in §§6.18-6.48, *supra*.

but here are some that all would consider pertinent: Facial expression, bearing, posture and body language, voice pressure and inflection, tone and accent, eye contact and movement, self-possession and presence. And to these may be added various moods, character and personality traits, and attitudes. Taking into account the effect of the setting and the manner of questioning, does the comfort level of the witness vary with the subject of the questioning, and does the apparent level of tension or ease suggest that she is mistaken or untruthful in her testimony? Is the witness generally serious in outlook and attitude, or bemused or supercilious? Is she cooperative and helpful, or resistant and obstructing? How prone is she to rigid preconceptions, how credulous, how objective, how discerning?

When the out-of-court statement of one person is proved by the testimony of another (Observer's comment described by Listener), there is reason to be concerned about the perception, memory, candor, and narrative abilities of the latter. Just as these risks affect the reliability of the statement as proof of the event, so they affect the reliability of the testimony as proof of the statement. The trial safeguards ameliorate these concerns with respect to the testifying witness, helping the factfinder at trial decide whether the statement was made and what was said, but do not ameliorate these concerns with respect to the speaker.

Focus on witness

B. ELEMENTS OF DOCTRINE—A CLOSER LOOK

1. *What Is a Statement?*

> **FRE 801(a)-(b)**
>
> The following definitions apply under this article:
>
> **(a) Statement.** A "statement" is (1) an oral or written assertion or (2) nonverbal conduct of a person, if it is intended by the person as an assertion.
>
> **(b) Declarant.** A "declarant" is a person who makes a statement.

§8.4 Assertive Behavior—Verbal Expressions

The usual one-line definition of "hearsay" (out-of-court statement offered to prove the matter asserted) includes the term "statement." This term generally poses no problem in application. Putting aside nonverbal behavior, "statement" is understood broadly to embrace almost all human verbal expressions, oral and written. (Expressive nonverbal behavior, like shaking the head "no," is also a "statement" for hearsay purposes. This subject is taken up in the next section.)

The Rules are consistent with the one-line definition: FRE 801(c) uses "statement" in defining hearsay, and FRE 801(a) says "statement" includes any oral or written "assertion" that the declarant "intend[s]" as an assertion. The Rule and ACN do not define "assertion" or "intent," but context suggests that the former embraces human verbal behavior in which a person expresses and communicates ideas or information to others and the latter refers to a purpose to express and communicate.[1] Because of the nature of lawsuits, ideas or information usually mean acts (who did what), events (what happened at an accident or crime scene), or conditions (how big the room was)—in other words, "objective facts." But statements expressing the declarant's intent or other mental state, scientific theories, or opinions as to fault (or cause or responsibility) are also embraced by the hearsay doctrine, so it would be a mistake to suppose that it only reaches what we might normally call "factual statements." And while statements almost always express and communicate, it makes no difference whether the declarant actually reached or hoped to reach some other person.[2]

Most words spoken or written by human beings are assertive in all the senses noted above: They express and communicate ideas or information through the conventions of language, and the person who speaks or writes them intends these effects. Apparently the framers of Rule 801 thought that words are not always assertive,[3] but most words are assertive in both senses. Unless otherwise noted, we use "assertive" to describe expressive and communicative effect and purpose, and "statement" and "assertion" to describe human expressions having these qualities.

To belabor the obvious, suppose Bystander sees a man trip on the curb at a street corner. When she says, "that man just tripped on the curb," she makes a verbal statement or assertion, intentionally expressing and communicating information. There is no doubt that if the statement is later offered in court as proof that the man tripped on the curb, it is hearsay. Most verbal behavior intentionally expresses and communicates, so it should be treated as a "statement" for purposes of

---

§8.4 1. *See* Restatement (Second) of Torts §8A (1965) ("intent" means actor "desires to cause the consequences of his act" or believes such consequences are "substantially certain to result").

2. Sometimes we intentionally express ideas without intending to communicate with another: We write notes to ourselves and program computers to issue reminders; we write diaries and poems and hide them from other eyes; to infants and animal companions we speak words whose literal meaning only adults can grasp; we confess misdeeds in audible prayers in the thought that God alone listens; we sing in the shower alone, thinking nobody hears. There is no doubt that such expressions are statements for purposes of the hearsay doctrine even if declarant speaks only to himself and has no communicative purpose in the usual sense. Such instances are rarely encountered in practice, and nothing is gained by treating expressive and communicative purpose independently. Recalling the childhood riddle, the answer that the hearsay doctrine gives to the question whether a tree makes a noise if it falls in the woods and nobody hears is Yes.

3. *See* §8.8, *infra.* Under FRE 801, nonassertive verbal behavior is clearly not hearsay.

the hearsay doctrine, and a party claiming the *absence* of the requisite intent should bear the burden of persuasion on this point.

Grammatically, the example ("that man just tripped on the curb") is a simple declarative sentence. On first glance, it is harder to view expressions cast in other forms as "statements." Suppose, for instance, we have an imperative: The speaker says "Don't trip on the curb!" Or suppose a question: The speaker says "Did that man trip on the curb?" To make the task of interpretation plausible, assume a few contextual facts: The speaker is on a sidewalk near a curb, and in the first example a man is approaching from the street carrying an armload of packages that obscures his forward vision; in the second he is on his hands and knees rising to his feet, gathering up his packages and brushing himself off. Although we may know nothing more about the scene, we would draw on the same common experience we expect juries to bring to trials and seek to understand or interpret what is being said. Literally understood (drawing on dictionary meanings and grammatical rules), the two utterances make no factual claims about acts, events, or conditions in the world, so in a narrow and superficial sense they are not assertions at all.

Queries and imperatives

On closer examination, however, both utterances are "statements" in a larger sense because both seem intentionally to express and communicate ideas or information about the appearance of the scene and the attitude of the speaker. In everyday discourse, these utterances would be understood as imparting factual information. Taking a minimalist view, the first says directly that the speaker wants to prevent the man from tripping on a curb, and the second says directly that she wants to know whether he did trip. Taking a slightly more generous view, the speaker in each case implies additional points, using the word "imply" in the strong sense to mean that her words reasonably suggest this meaning and she intends to convey it: She implies that there is a curb that a person might trip over. In the first instance she implies (again in the strong sense) that someone approaching seems unaware of the curb and the hazard it presents, that she knows the hazard is there, and that he can avoid the peril by watching out; and in the second instance she implies that the appearance of the scene suggests that the man just tripped on the curb, that she did not see the event, and that whoever she addresses is in a position to have seen it.

In short, even questions or commands make claims about events and conditions when subjected to everyday interpretive conventions. And such utterances express and communicate ideas, quite apart from whatever concrete facts they convey. Hence they should be viewed as "statements" for purposes of the hearsay doctrine. It is easy to imagine similar examples—consider, for example, the information and factual content suggested in the simple command "start the car"—and it is actually hard to frame intelligible commands or questions that do *not* have these qualities. Of course it is a very different question whether such statements are hearsay when offered to prove (for example) that there is a curb that a person might trip over, and the answer depends on a closer examination of context and the purpose of the party offering the statement.[4]

Unfortunately courts and commentators sometimes think the term "assertion" has a narrow meaning that does not reach imperatives and questions like the ones described above.[5] Under this view, the term implies a strong claim, based on the literal or plain meaning of words, that certain facts are so. Hence "the man tripped on the curb" would be an assertion but not "did he trip on the curb?" or "don't trip on the curb" since questions and imperatives do not make any strong claim as a matter of literal meaning. And of course it is true that in general usage "assertion" sometimes embodies this narrow idea. Nevertheless this interpretation of FRE 801 is wrong.

"Assertion" has broad meaning

To begin with, the term "assertion," which appears twice in FRE 801(a), came from the vocabulary of common law tradition. There it was interpreted very broadly, and there is no indication that the framers of the Rules intended to narrow its meaning. More likely they chose it for other reasons—to describe behavior that is expressive and communicative and to limit "statement" to *intentional* expressions.[6] Moreover, even general usage fails strongly to support the position that "assertion" excludes questions and commands: Often the term is used to emphasize the link between a proposition (whether strongly or tentatively advanced) and its source, calling attention to the important matter of the reliability of the source, which makes the term especially apt in defining hearsay. Finally and most importantly, the reasons for the hearsay doctrine do not justify excluding utterances framed as questions or commands. Concerns about misperception, failed memory, insincerity, and narrative ambiguity apply just as strongly to such

---

4. On the facts supposed, we would say the question ("did that man trip on the curb?") is hearsay if offered to show the man tripped because the woman implies as much in putting the question (intentionally suggesting this point). *See* §8.14, *infra*. Later we revisit the imperative ("don't trip on the curb"), suggesting that it amounts to mixed act and assertion that may fairly be treated as nonhearsay. *See* §8.22, *infra*.

5. *See* Quartararo v. Hanslmaier, 186 F.3d 91, 98 (2d Cir. 1999) (for purposes of hearsay doctrine, an inquiry is not an assertion), *cert. denied*, 528 U.S. 1170; United States v. Jackson, 88 F.3d 845, 847-848 (10th Cir. 1996) (question "Is this Kenny?" is not an assertion merely because it "conveyed a message" indicating that speaker thought Kenny had a pager and was responding to speaker's message) (preposterous conclusion). The issue arises in drug trials, where arresting officers enter the premises of suspected drug operations and answer incoming phone calls, and a voice at the distant end asks whether drugs are available. Almost always courts admit such conversations, sometimes on the ground that inquiries are not assertions so they cannot be hearsay, sometimes for other reasons. *See generally* §8.22, *infra*. *See also* Wellborn, The Definition of Hearsay in the Federal Rules of Evidence, 61 Tex. L. Rev. 49 (1982) (arguing that only declarative sentences are embraced by the term "statement" in FRE 801 and criticizing Rule as being too narrow). *And see* §8.23, *infra*, discussing whether a statement is hearsay when offered to prove unmentioned points the speaker believes or assumes.

6. The first "assertion" in FRE 801(a) achieves the first purpose (statement is "oral or written assertion"); the next "assertion" achieves the second (nothing is a statement unless "intended as an assertion" by the speaker or actor).

utterances as to declarative sentences.[7] Construing "assertion" to exclude questions and commands wrongly limits its meaning.

The universe of "statements" is vast, and many verbal expressions are neither short nor simple. Language is rich in vocabulary and idiom, and verbal expressions can be long, colorful, rhetorical, complex, slangy, vague, imprecise, figurative, indirect. When viewed from the perspective of litigation, an expression may be inconveniently broad or narrow. It may use common words to express ideas that technical terms capture with more clarity, or special jargon or shorthand to express ideas that can be more fully captured in more formal or technical language. And the rules of grammar are about as useful in appraising such expressions as they are in understanding James Joyce's *Ulysses* (helpful but not enough).

Complex statements and fragments

The hearsay doctrine must be applied in this world, and out-of-court statements cannot be effectively edited to meet the needs of trials.[8] Interpreting the doctrine sensibly outside the context of short and simple declarative sentences is no easy task. Consider, for example, the following string of words:

> Bring in smack? Who are you kidding? In that department the man's practically world class. Find another guy who knows the poppy fields of Pakistan better than his own vegetable garden. Nobody else like Jones. Just about runs the railroad.

Assume Jones is tried on drug charges (importation, possession with intent to sell, sale, and related conspiracies), that these words were spoken out of court by a friend with firsthand knowledge, that we are confident about the terms of reference (the speaker was talking about the same Jones, and so forth), and the words are offered to prove Jones was involved in importing heroin.

Reasonably understood, this string of words makes this claim, and at least to that extent they comprise a statement for purposes of FRE 801. It does not matter that part of the utterance is indirect and rhetorical,

---

7. People v. Reyes, 70 Cal. Rptr. 3d 903, 906-907 (Cal. App. 2008) (some questions "actually are statements," or "conceal statements only thinly," and make claims about events and conditions "when subjected to everyday interpretive conventions" and "express and communicate ideas, quite apart from whatever concrete facts they convey," so co-offender's question asking police if they would have to let them go if police didn't find a gun was an assertion that they had a gun) (quoting this Treatise), *review denied* (2008); United States v. Summers, 414 F.3d 1287, 130 (10th Cir. 2005) (comment to arresting officers, "How did you guys find us so fast?" *was* an assertion; it "intimated both guilt and wonderment" at police ability to apprehend perpetrators so quickly; it was hearsay, not just an inquiry about methods of law enforcement); Stoddard v. State, 887 A.2d 564, 581 (Md. 2005) (in murder trial, child J's question "is Eric going to get me" was hearsay; words "impliedly communicated that [J] had witnessed [defendant] assaulting" another child C; whether utterance is hearsay does not depend on form, and J's question was unreliable as proof that J saw defendant assault C) (citing authors of this Treatise).

8. Sometimes it is possible to admit one part of a statement and exclude another, or require that additional statements be offered when necessary for understanding, but such measures do not solve all the problems. *See* §§1.17-1.18, *supra*.

or that some phrases are vague and apparently not to be taken literally, or that the words include street slang ("smack") rather than a term of broader usage ("heroin"). It makes no difference whether the string is one statement, or two, or ten. Nor does it matter that the words do not all make declarative sentences, that they lack grammatical integrity or include questions, sentence fragments, and imperatives. What counts is that they express and communicate intelligible ideas.

Does not mean statement is hearsay

A word to the wise: Deciding that question, a command, or a string of words is a "statement" does *not* mean it is hearsay. That depends on whether it is offered to prove what it asserts, which in turn depends on the proponent's purpose, the speaker's intent, and often on the broader factual context in which the statement was made.[9]

§8.5   —Action or Conduct (Wordless Statements)

The term "statement" usually found in the one-line definition of hearsay (out-of-court *statement* offered to prove the matter asserted) reaches not only verbal expressions, but nonverbal expressive and communicative behavior when it amounts to a substitute for words. Such wordless statements (like shaking the head no) give rise to the same concerns as ordinary verbal communication. On this point, the Rules are consistent with the one-line definition: When wordless behavior has expressive and communicative intent or purpose, it too is subject to the hearsay doctrine. In the language of FRE 801(a), it too is a "statement," for the term reaches "nonverbal conduct of a person" that is "intended" as an assertion.[1]

Wordless statements

Recalling the example of the Bystander who sees a man approaching the curb carrying bundles, suppose a third person asks her, "Did the man trip on the curb?" and she nods her head. Here the nod incorporates the idea contained in the question and makes a claim about what happened. Bystander becomes the declarant of a statement that the man tripped on the curb, and her statement is hearsay if offered to prove the point.[2]

Most wordless statements are simple nonverbal cues that amount to word substitutes. In our culture, nodding the head means "yes," shaking it means "no," and shrugging the shoulders means "I don't know" or "nothing to be done." Others are readily understood but more context-specific: If a person standing at the base of the Washington

9. The statement about Jones should be viewed as hearsay if offered to prove his involvement in importing heroin. Problems of interpreting statements, in order to apply the hearsay doctrine sensibly, are taken up in §§8.12-8.15, *infra*.

§8.5   1. The Rule and ACN do not define assertion or intent, but context suggests that assertion embraces nonverbal behavior that expresses and communicates ideas or information, and that intent refers to a purpose to express and communicate. *See* §8.4, *supra*.

2. In this case, the query alone should be viewed as a statement but not as hearsay since it is offered for the nonhearsay purpose of giving meaning to Bystander's response.

Monument is asked "which way is north?" and she points toward the White House, her wordless statement means "north is that way" (which is more or less correct). Still others involve gestures that can best be understood in a larger setting of events or prior conversations: A thumbs-up gesture may mean "I got the raise" or "you made a good play," or "we made it" or "let's do it," and conveys a positive, encouraging, or praising message. A hand cupped behind the ear may mean "please say it again," or "turn up the volume," or "I can't hear." All these wordless statements are hearsay when offered to prove what they assert.[3]

Not surprisingly, acts that do not fall within this array of common nonverbal cues usually are *not* "statements" for purposes of FRE 801 because the actor lacks intent to express or communicate.[4] But any conduct *might* have assertive intent, so it *might* be a statement, in which case it would be hearsay if offered to prove whatever the actor sought to express. In this setting, the burden is on the objecting party to prove that the actor had the requisite intent.[5]

§8.6   —Hidden Statements (Hearsay at One Remove)

Ordinary testifying witnesses are expected to report what they know directly, on the basis of firsthand observation. The Rules require as much, and litigators instinctively "lay a foundation" by preliminary questioning. If a party wants to establish, through testimony by Observer, that Nurse *N* was in the operating room during the surgery, typically the first step is to get Observer to say he was there at the time, so he was in a position to know who else was there. In this setting, witnesses may recognize (also instinctively) the difference between passing along what someone told them and saying what they know from firsthand observation.

Sometimes instinct and groundwork are not enough. Asked whether Nurse *N* was in the operating room during surgery, Observer might reply "*X* told me she was there," or "I told *X* that Nurse *N* was present,"

---

3. United States v. Abou-Saada, 785 F.2d 1, 9 (1st Cir. 1986) (pointing out taxi driver was "conduct intended as an assertion," and therefore hearsay), *cert. denied*, 477 U.S. 908; United States v. Ross, 321 F.2d 61, 69 (2d Cir. 1963) (pointing to list, on being asked to identify numbers used by salesman, was "as much a communication as a statement" and was hearsay).

4. It follows that such acts are not hearsay, although this point poses more difficulties than one might suppose. *See* §8.9, *infra*. Acts that seem nonassertive or indecipherable to most observers may carry particular meaning to others, by prearrangement or because of special customs or traditions. Such "coded signals" are hearsay when offered to prove what the actor seeks to convey. *See* in §8.7, *infra*.

5. The ACN says that when evidence of conduct is offered, the court may have to make a "preliminary determination" whether an assertion was intended. The objecting party bears the burden of showing assertive intent, and the ACN says doubtful cases are "resolved against him and in favor of admissibility." *See* United States v. Butler, 763 F.2d 11, 14-15 (1st Cir. 1985); United States v. Hensel, 699 F.2d 18, 30-31 (1st Cir. 1983), *cert. denied*, 461 U.S. 958.

and in these cases of express reference to out-of-court statements, the hearsay problem is transparent.[1] Or Observer might state what appears to be a fact resting on his own knowledge ("Nurse *N* was there"), even though his only information is what *X* told him. Here Observer lacks firsthand knowledge, and in effect his testimony conveys a hidden out-of-court statement, or hearsay at one remove.[2] If later questioning uncovers this point, the adverse party may object and move to strike the testimony for "lack of personal knowledge" or as "hearsay."[3]

Sometimes parties contrive to inject hearsay by indirection to side-step a good hearsay objection. In one prosecution of Police Officer *C* for trafficking in cocaine, for example, the prosecutor sought to prove *C* 's incriminating statements to Informant *J*. The difficulty was that *J* refused to testify. The prosecutor called Detective *S*, who testified to what he himself said to *J*. Thus *S* told *J*, among other things, that *S* "did not intend to front" money to Officer *C*, did not receive the promised sample, and was willing to meet *C* the next day.[4] As the reviewing court recognized, this testimony implicitly described *J*'s half of the conversation too, and it was this hidden half that was most damning to *C*. Taken in the setting of the case, the testimony by Detective *S* put before the factfinder that Informant *J* had said that *C* demanded front money, promised a sample, and wanted to make a sale the next day.[5] In short, a description of half a conversation (what Detective *S* told *J*) is likely to suggest the content of the other half (what *J* must have been telling *S*), even though the exact words in the other half remain hidden from view, and using the hidden half of the conversation to prove what

---

§8.6 1. If an adversary raises a hearsay objection, the court can say to the witness, "tell us only what you know from personal observation; please don't repeat what others told you or what you told others." Sometimes an objection can keep the out-of-court statement from being reiterated. If an objection comes after the answer, the remedy is to strike the answer and tell the jury to disregard. *See* §1.3, *supra*. If the witness lacks knowledge, the proponent must find an exception that applies or prove the point another way.

2. United States v. Reyes, 18 F.3d 65, 67-69 (2d Cir. 1994) (error to let agent say she spoke with two men and concluded that defendant and another were involved in crimes; she conveyed hearsay); United States v. Hall, 989 F.2d 711, 715-716 (4th Cir. 1993) (error to cross-examine defendant, on basis of summary of wife's statement, in manner suggesting he used drugs and that wife said so to prosecutor).

3. If Observer simply assumed Nurse *N* was in the operating room (because she usually is or he saw her headed that way with a surgical mask on), a motion to strike might be appropriate, and again the ground is lack of personal knowledge. Lay witnesses are encouraged to be concrete and specific, but they may state conclusions that rest on observation and help the jury understand their testimony. *See* §7.2, *supra*.

4. Detective *S* could not testify to what Officer *C* said (*S* never talked to *C* in person), and Informant *J*'s statements to *S* would be hearsay if offered to prove what *C* said (*J*'s statements were his assertion that *C* said certain things, offered to prove *C* said them). If a way had been found to prove what *C* said, those statements would be admissible as *C* 's admissions under FRE 801(d)(2)(A). *See* §8.27, *infra*.

5. United States v. Check, 582 F.2d 668 (2d. Cir. 1978) (*S's* testimony "audaciously introduced" *J*'s out-of-court statements, in attempt to provide "information supplied" by *J*, who did not testify) (reversing).

the unheard speaker must have said is hearsay if offered to prove th[e] truth of those unheard comments.

Most of us know much of our own background only because of what we have been told. Our birthdays, parentage, place of birth and early upbringing, and much of the history and backgrounds of our families—even our own names—come to us through the things our parents, childhood guardians, and close relatives say. Yet witnesses routinely testify to such points, and for the most part no one would dream of raising a personal knowledge or hearsay objection.[6] No doubt the approach would differ if such matters were actually contested and somehow directly important to the outcome. Then issues of hearsay and personal knowledge would loom larger. Ordinarily, however, such information is developed as a matter of background, and it is appropriate to be more relaxed.

In one important setting, testimony may rest on hearsay. As FRE 703 makes clear, experts may rely on information learned outside the courtroom, including spoken and written words, so long as other experts in the field would rely on such material. FRE 703 was not intended to create a conduit allowing an expert simply to pass along the conclusions of others, which would amount to either direct hearsay (if an expert openly quoted what others said) or indirect hearsay (if an expert simply adopted as his own, without independent thought or analysis, the conclusions of others). Rather, the intent was to permit experts to rely on the work of others (at least in part), while presenting their own conclusions on the relevant points.[7]

Expert testimony

§8.7 —Coded Signals

Sometimes people express and communicate by code words, symbols, or behavior. Such codes may be set up by agreement or grow out of practice or custom. Drug traffickers, for example, use coded language in written records and spoken conversations—language incomprehensible to outsiders but understood by traders and customers.[1] Commercial transactions lead to practices that give special meaning to contract terms, documents, and actions. And family members develop understandings that give hidden meanings to acts, gestures, or statements, readily understood by spouses, offspring, siblings, and members of the household.

---

6. Several exceptions let witnesses testify directly to statements of "family history." FRE 803(19) paves the way for "reputation" among family members on such matters of "personal or family history," and FRE 804(b)(4) reaches statements by unavailable declarants on such matters. See §§8.61 and 8.77, infra.

7. See the discussion of FRE 703 in §§7.8-7.11, supra.

§8.7 1. Coded entries and conversations are commonly admitted under the admissions doctrine or business records exception. In drug cases, the more common issue is whether an expert should be allowed to interpret such materials, and often expert testimony is admitted. See §7.6, supra.

purposes, such coded expressions should be viewed as ... ch means they are hearsay if offered to prove what they ... lusion follows directly from the definition of statement ... RE 801(a) that embraces all assertions and conduct, ... e declarant or actor has assertive intent.

... coded expressions differ from standard nonverbal ... ng the head) in being essentially obscure (or at least ... rdinary observers. Sometimes the actor is trying to avoid ... d by outsiders. Often there is no room to doubt that ... ssive and communicative purpose, as is usually true ...... written symbols, spoken words, and gestures, and the task is decode what is said.

Sometimes it is hard to know whether the actor intends to express or communicate ideas or information. This difficulty appeared in a prosecution of an accountant for bribing IRS Agent *C*, where the prosecutor showed that *C* made a favorable report on a tax return, and that *after-wards* the accountant gave *C* an envelope containing cash. The accountant claimed he gave the money in appreciation for "expediting the audit" and in sympathy for *C*, who had said he was going off to Marine Corps summer camp, so there was a real question whether the accountant had intended to affect official conduct by the prospect of later payment. To prove he did have this intent, the government offered *C*'s testimony that Agent *L* introduced the accountant to *C*, and that *L* "never introduced me to anyone except someone who was going to pay me off."[2] If, in the office routine observed by the IRS agents or the custom of *C* and *L* in dealing with one another, it was understood that *L* would bring to *C* any taxpayer who indicated his intent to offer inducements, then *L*'s behavior was tantamount to a statement that *C* had given such indications. On this understanding, *L*'s behavior, if offered in proof of this point (as it was), should be viewed as hearsay.[3]

§8.8 Nonassertive Behavior—Verbal Expressions

The framers of FRE 801 apparently thought one can say something while lacking assertive intent—that there is such a thing as verbal

---

2. United States v. Barash, 365 F.2d 395 (2d Cir. 1966) (*L*'s behavior was hearsay because anything "relevant only as implying a statement or opinion of a third person" on a matter is hearsay if a direct statement of the matter would be hearsay). *Barash* is too broad because it construes all human conduct as hearsay if offered to prove the actor's belief in a fact, hence the fact itself. *See* §8.9, *infra.*

3. If there were no understanding between *C* and *L* and no office routine in which such behavior by *L* conveyed this meaning, that behavior would not be a statement and could not be hearsay (nonassertive conduct is *never* hearsay, even when offered to prove the actor's belief in a fact, hence the fact itself). *See* §8.9, *infra.* The behavior might still suggest the accountant did something wrong, if it could be shown that *L* reacted that way when confronted with such people.

behavior in which the speaker (or actor) does not intend to express or communicate ideas or information.

On first blush this category seems odd because writing and speaking are by their very nature expressive and communicative acts. On further reflection, however, it becomes plausible to view *some* verbal expressions as nonassertive in some senses: Perhaps one instance is words that are reflexive, hence more like physical reaction than expression of conscious mental impression. Another candidate is words that embody conventional social pleasantries, since they often have little if any factual content and are in that sense "meaningless." Yet another is words of recitation in which an actor or singer gives voice to the words of another (playwright or lyricist): Here both parties do convey various forms of verbal meaning, since performing and writing are communicative and expressive acts. However, the performer does not necessarily make the words his own (so to speak) and the source may or may not seek to convey the ideas that literal meaning suggests. In fact literary and artistic interpretation involves conventions and purposes far removed from the kinds of inquiry that triers of fact undertake. Finally, courts and commentators sometimes use the notion of nonassertive verbal behavior in specialized senses (usually to avoid hearsay objections that are better analyzed in other ways).

In strict theory, the key element in nonassertive verbal conduct is lack of assertive intent on the part of the speaker. In fact, however, there seems to be at least some assertive intent in most of these areas and the label "nonassertive" usually means such intent plays little or no role in the proposed evidential use. And various exceptions might pave the way to admit such utterances if they are viewed as assertive after all.

Sometimes spoken words are reflexive and unthinking rather than volitional and thoughtful. Consider the word "ouch," spoken in response to sudden pain (a sudden fall or hammer blow to the finger). And think about verbal oaths or expletives that suggest surprise, relief, joy, anger, misery, or frustration—from the blandest "darn it anyway" to pungent swearing and cursing. No doubt such verbal outbursts usually *are* assertive. Whoever says them means to express and communicate such ideas as "that hurts" or "I didn't expect that to happen," or "what am I going to do now?" But sometimes such reactions are so clearly reflexive and unthinking that it becomes plausible to treat them as audible signs of pain, surprise, despair, and frustration, and as nonassertive (and not hearsay) when offered to prove those mental reactions and emotions. **Reflexive verbalizing**

Typically reactive verbalizing is simple in content and meaning, which is not an excuse in itself to ignore hearsay concerns. This fact, however, helps reduce risks of misperception, faulty memory, and narrative ambiguity, and suddenness reduces the risk of lack of candor. At the opposite end of the scale, elaboration and complexity are signs of intent to assert, which moves these reactions into the category of expressions embraced by the hearsay doctrine.

Common social pleasantries such as words of greeting (hi, Sarah; good morning, how are you?), polite response (I'm fine, you're looking **Statements lacking factual content**

good, nice to see you), and leavetaking (well, back to work, I've got to
be on my way) are normally understood in ways that depend very much
on tone of voice, inflection, facial expression, nonverbal cues, setting,
and social custom. In these settings, dictionary meaning offers little or
no help, and the phrases are likely to convey general mood or attitude
rather than the ideas or information a literal reading might suggest.
Such phrases suggest anything from distant and cold politeness, even
disdain, belittlement, or brushoff at one extreme to deep affection or
caring friendship at the opposite extreme.

Social pleasantries of this sort are nonassertive in the limited sense
that they make no positive claim that something is so and do not commit the speaker to any particular viewpoint or action. In this sense,
they are not assertions and thus not hearsay. But even such phrases
may (and usually do) amount to somewhat minimal assertions that
the speaker recognizes and knows the listener from prior contact.[1]
And such phrases can and usually do assert that the speaker wants to
know how the listener is and seeks cordial relations (or formal or distant
ones, as the case may be).[2] Thus understood, the phrases are hearsay,
although the state-of-mind exception paves the way for their use to show
these latter points, and it is essentially immaterial whether such phrases
are admitted as nonhearsay or as hearsay within an exception. Moreover, it is possible to view such phrases as social behavior that fills or acts
out (or gives substance to) the relationship between the declarant and
listener and, in this sense again, nonhearsay when offered to prove
the nature of the relationship and whatever else that might tend to
establish.[3]

Artistic expression   When a Shakespearean actor says on stage in a performance of
Hamlet that the play will prick the conscience of the King, it seems
futile, beside the point, even silly to try to sort out hearsay implications.
And while ordinary people recite lines from plays or poems, and sing
songs written by others, such verbal behavior has no practical importance in the trial of lawsuits, and hearsay issues need not be faced.[4] We
would likely interpret the communicative and expressive intent of poet,
playwright, lyricist, or composer in one way—surely Francis Scott Key
intentionally asserted the flag was still flying over Fort McHenry in
the dawn's early light in 1814, and the famous lyric would be hearsay

---

§8.8   1. Flatly rejecting a hearsay objection, one modern case mistakenly concluded
that greeting someone by name is nonassertive verbal behavior, hence nonhearsay,
when offered to prove the person's identity. *See* United States v. Weeks, 919 F.2d
248, 251-252 (5th Cir. 1990) (admitting proof that inmates called defendant "Gato,"
along with testimony by victims that one abductor answered to that name, as evidence
that defendant was one of the abductors).

2. For purposes of hearsay doctrine, the term "statement" is not limited to expressions that convey objective facts. *See* the discussion in §8.4, *supra.*

3. On mixed act and assertion, *see* §8.22, *infra.*

4. Of course a recitation could be a coded signal, hence hearsay if offered to prove
whatever the signal was intended to assert. *See* §8.7, *supra.* And a speaker might choose
to assert something by quoting a line: The bystander who sees a one-car accident and
says "there's no fool like an old fool" might be understood to claim the driver was
negligent (it would be hearsay if offered for this purpose). *See* §8.14, *infra.*

if offered to prove that point. And we would likely interpret in a different way the expressive and communicative intent of the person who sings the lyrics—one who opens a football game by singing the National Anthem is not making the same point, and her purpose usually has more to do with expressing public spirit than with the specifics of verbal content. It is of course hard to imagine a hearsay use at trial of a performance of the National Anthem.

Some verbal expressions that might appear to fit the instant category probably do not. Sleeptalk and delusional utterances, as well as the statement of a person who is drugged, intoxicated, or hypnotized may be nonvolitional in the sense that the speaker does not exercise normal self-control. But such statements are not so likely to be simple in content or meaning, and the condition of the speaker and effect of the external influence are hard to assess. Risks of misperception, faulty memory, and narrative ambiguity loom large, as do concerns that such proof is unfairly prejudicial or likely to confuse. Courts often treat sleeptalk as hearsay or untrustworthy and exclude it.[5] Similar treatment is warranted in the other instances cited above.

Nonvolitional statements

Courts and commentators sometimes label verbal expressions as nonassertive conduct for four other reasons:

Specialized senses

First, courts sometimes say that questions and imperatives are nonassertive, even though verbal. This position cannot be seriously defended, since such expressions usually assert facts, and almost always they qualify as assertions because they express and communicate ideas and information.[6] If the speaker apparently lacks knowledge of relevant facts and contents herself with asking a question out of ignorance ("what's going on?"), treating such expressions as nonassertive becomes more plausible. But in virtually all settings, questions or commands intentionally express certain minimal points, including the speaker's desire to know or to effect a result, and the hearsay doctrine is implicated.

Second, courts sometimes say words admitted under the verbal act doctrine are nonassertive.[7] It is true enough that words in this category are not hearsay because they are important in themselves without regard to their assertive quality (usually as legally operative utterances). It is not true, however, that people who speak or write words later seen to fit this category lack assertive intent: A borrower who signs a note promising to pay a certain sum every month over a term at a set rate until the loan is paid off normally is asserting that he intends to do what he promises. Also he does mean to assert, when the note recites as much, that the loan has been funded.

---

5. Godfrey v. State, 365 S.E.2d 93 (Ga. 1988) (statutory exception for statements by youthful victims of abuse did not reach victim's sleeptalk, absent proof of reliability, including expert testimony); People v. Knatz, 428 N.Y.S.3d 709 (N.Y. App. Div. 1980) (error to admit girlfriend's testimony describing statements defendant during sleep; being asleep detracted from reliability; utterances were ambiguous and did not unequivocally relate to offense).

6. *See* §8.4, *supra.*

7. *See* §8.16, *infra.*

Third, commentators sometimes use the term "nonassertive verbal conduct" to describe the peculiarly difficult situation in which a statement is offered to prove something that is apparently on the mind of the declarant but is not among the ideas he sought to express or communicate. This aspect of the hearsay doctrine has proved particularly vexing, and is taken up elsewhere.[8]

§8.9 —Action or Conduct

Most human behavior sheds light on the thinking and beliefs of the actor, which in turn suggests conclusions about acts, events, and conditions in the world. Human behavior has this tendency even where the actor has no intent (no thought or purpose) to express or communicate ideas, and such behavior is commonly called "nonassertive conduct." A pedestrian who puts up an umbrella seems to think it is raining, which suggests that it is, and a motorist who halts at a stoplight and then goes forward seems to have thought the light was red and then turned green, which suggests that is exactly what happened.[1]

Two-step inference

Used this way, nonassertive conduct involves the trier of fact in the two-step inference that hearsay always involves.[2] The first step is from conduct to belief (conduct suggests what the person was thinking). The second step is from belief to external realities (what he was thinking suggests something about acts by others, or events or conditions in the world). In short, conduct is offered to prove belief, hence the fact believed.

Nonassertive conduct is not hearsay (FRE 801)

This use of conduct raises some risks that the hearsay doctrine seeks to avoid (misperception and faulty memory). Nevertheless—and this fact is critical in understanding the hearsay doctrine—nonassertive conduct is not hearsay under FRE 801. The framers made this point clear: FRE 801(c) defines hearsay to mean only an out-of-court statement, and FRE 801(a) defines "statement" as verbal expressions and other conduct intended as an assertion. Hence conduct *not* intended as an assertion is not hearsay.

Despite this point of certainty, the question whether nonassertive conduct should be viewed as hearsay when offered in support of the two-step inference (proving belief, hence the fact believed) presents an ongoing challenge to both theory and practice. The reason is that the idea of nonassertive conduct cannot be neatly confined to physical behavior of the sort considered so far. Verbal expressions sometimes blend with physical conduct. And verbal expressions have performative

---

8. *See* §§8.22-8.23, *infra*.

§8.9 1. A warning is in order: *Any* human conduct might be intended as an assertion. If so, it is *not* nonassertive and *is* hearsay if offered to prove the matter asserted. If a person putting up an umbrella had agreed with another that doing so means it is raining (or "the coast is clear"), then proof that he put up the umbrella would be hearsay if offered to show it was raining (or the coast was clear). *See* §8.7, *supra*.

2. *See* §8.2, *supra*.

aspects that make them similar to nonassertive conduct, and these aspects may be critical to understanding. Consider the mugger who points a gun at the victim and says "give me your wallet or I'll shoot." Here physical action and spoken words can only be understood together, for the words add dimension to the acts and vice versa. The words themselves are instrumental in a forced taking and might induce the victim to part with his wallet (even without menacing gestures).[3]

No one argues that conduct should generally be treated as hearsay. It often lies at the heart of legal rights and duties and must be proved to resolve disputes: Did defendant rob the bank? Did plaintiff ingest a toxic substance? Equally important, many uses of human conduct raise no hearsay risks, as is true when it relates directly to rights and obligations. The term "hearsay" suggests a doctrine that applies to what one heard another say, not what one saw another do—a doctrine covering *statements*, not *conduct*—so for the most part nobody even *thinks* to apply it to evidence of ordinary conduct.[4]

> **Nonverbal nonassertive behavior**

Consider a bank robbery case where witnesses testify that the culprits entered wearing masks and brandishing guns, that clerks turned over cash from the drawers and safe, and that the thieves made off in a blue car driven by someone waiting outside. Such conduct is normally intentional and voluntary, and should not be viewed as hearsay because it is nonassertive. We can be confident that this behavior was not an attempt to express or communicate ideas or information, and in this sense much human behavior is nonverbal and nonassertive.[5] We can also be confident that two of the four hearsay risks do not appear. Regardless whether the actor is "an egregious liar or a paragon of veracity," there is no risk of insincerity, and no risk of narrative ambiguity (no worry that he misspoke or used language oddly).[6]

Similar points may be made about behavior that is reactive or reflexive and unthinking, such as grasping the body in a place of sudden pain or injury, raising the arms defensively to shield the head or body from expected impact, or hunching the shoulders and drawing the lapels close to ward off cold or wind, blowing dust or debris, or rain or snow. Such behavior is highly suggestive of the external stimulus that produces it, and the actor might even know that observers can tell what

---

3. Here words are like physical conduct not only in being criminal behavior but in an instrumental sense—they force or achieve a result. Physical behavior (nodding the head) can be a functional substitute for words, and words (the mugger's) can be a functional substitute for physical behavior. In a trial of the mugger, both words and physical behavior could be proved as criminal acts, and the verbal act doctrine would dispose of any hearsay objection. *See* §8.16, *infra.*

4. Falknor, The "Hear-Say" Rule as a "See-Do" Rule: Evidence of Conduct, 33 Rocky Mt. L. Rev. 133, 136 (1961).

5. Thieves are likely to convey by word or gesture that they expect the money and that refusal will lead to dire consequences, and this part of what they do has both assertive and nonassertive elements. But their coming and going, and responses of bank clerks in turning over the money, are nonassertive conduct.

6. *See* Falknor, The "Hear-Say" Rule as a "See-Do" Rule: Evidence of Conduct, 33 Rocky Mt. L. Rev. 133, 136 (1961) (arguing that hearsay rule should not become a "see-do" rule).

is happening. Still his behavior is nonassertive because he has no purpose to express or communicate ideas or information. Hence it is nonhearsay. The same is true of physiological reactions (such as shivering from cold or trembling in fear).[7]

Hearsay risks   As the bank robbery example shows, some uses of nonassertive conduct avoid all four hearsay risks,[8] but those hearsay risks arise whenever conduct is used in support of the two-step inference (belief, hence the fact believed), so refinement and elaboration are required on two fronts.

Analogous difficulty   First, it is true that nonassertive conduct does not raise a risk of narrative ambiguity (which relates to the complexity of language), but it does raise an analogous difficulty. Nonassertive conduct is often ambiguous when offered to prove a particular point.[9] Still it seems wiser not to broaden the hearsay doctrine but to let factfinders rise to the challenge. After all, much evidence is ambiguous: Consider testimony that describes precautions taken by a doctor during treatment, or the relationship of parent to child. Problems of understanding and interpreting such proof are considerable, and doctrine can do little to ease the task. In such settings, the question whether evidence of an act supports a particular conclusion is one of relevancy or sufficiency, not hearsay.

Degree of risk varies   Second, the degree of hearsay risk varies widely when nonassertive conduct is offered in support of the two-step inference. Consider proof that a woman put on an overcoat before leaving home, offered to show it was cold. In the umbrella and stoplight examples, behavior is contemporaneous with the event, mistake is unlikely, and the risk of ambiguity is small. But with the woman putting on her coat, risks of faulty memory, misperception, and ambiguity are bigger. Time has likely passed since she checked or experienced weather conditions; people often put on coats only to take them off on discovering the day is warmer than expected; most important, the suggested inference is

---

7. Cole v. United States, 327 F.2d 360 (9th Cir. 1964) (evidence that bank teller was pale and shaking, offered to prove that robbery involved intimidation, was not hearsay); People v. Gwinn, 314 N.W.2d 562, 572 (Mich. Ct. App. 1981) (behavior of victim of kidnap and sexual assault, who screamed and wept when viewing defendant's picture, was not a statement under MRE 801; it was not "intended as an assertion").

8. Insincerity and narrative ambiguity are not factors, nor misperception and failed memory. Evidence that defendants entered wearing masks and brandishing guns tends to prove an element (the criminal act) without worrying about perception or memory. Most crimes consist of act and intent, and most criminal acts are or may be nonassertive conduct. Regardless how well or poorly robbers perceive or recall, their behavior is the criminal act of bank robbery. But conduct and mental state are not divided by a stone wall: In general intent crimes like bank robbery, act suggests intent, and intent need not be independently proven.

9. The hearsay risk of narrative ambiguity has three facets: The declarant may misspeak or use language oddly; the factfinder may misinterpret; and words may not convey exactly what must be found out in a lawsuit. *See* the discussion in §8.2, *supra*. Nonassertive conduct brings analogous difficulties: The actor may do things that make no sense given his purpose; even if behavior is apt, the factfinder may misunderstand; and behavior may not accurately indicate important points in the suit.

but one of many that are plausible (maybe she put on her coat because she knew she would need it that evening, or just assumed it was cold).

Why doesn't the hearsay doctrine apply to nonassertive conduct offered in support of the two-step inference? If the proponent shows the woman donned a coat on leaving, why isn't it hearsay when offered to prove it was cold?

The Advisory Committee carefully considered the matter, and the ACN to FRE 801 argues three points: First, risks of misperception, faulty memory, and ambiguity are "minimal in the absence of an intent to assert and do not justify the loss of the evidence" as hearsay. Second, any evidence might be made up to create a false impression ("fabricated"), but this possibility is "less likely" with nonassertive ("nonverbal") conduct than with assertions ("assertive verbal conduct"). Third, and perhaps most important: "Motivation, the nature of the conduct, and the presence or absence of reliance will bear heavily upon the weight to be given the evidence." In other words, despite some hearsay risks, this use of nonassertive conduct raises issues that the factfinder can be trusted to resolve by taking into account factors like motivation, nature of the conduct, and reliance.

Where conduct is apparently nonassertive, it is likely to be treated as nonhearsay. The reason is that the party seeking to raise a hearsay objection bears the burden of proving to the satisfaction of the trial judge under FRE 104(a) that the actor intended his conduct to be assertive after all.[10]

In resolving the issue, FRE 801 rejects the broad proposition endorsed by Baron Parke in the famous English case of *Wright v. Tatham.*[11] *Wright* was a will contest involving the attempted use of letters, written to John Marsden, to prove that the writers of the letters *thought* Marsden competent, hence that he probably was. The holding in *Wright* is that the letters were hearsay, and Parke's broad conclusion was that evidence of conduct is *always* hearsay when offered in support of the two-step inference.

FRE 801 rejects this broad conclusion, and only occasional modern decisions treat the subject with care.[12] Nevertheless *Wright* is a

---

10. United States v. Butler, 763 F.2d 11, 14-15 (1st Cir. 1985) (proof of *C*'s driving defendant's car with cocaine in trunk was not hearsay; no evidence that *C* was making an assertion); United States v. Hensel, 699 F.2d 18, 30-31 (1st Cir. 1983) (admitting evidence that glass bearing name "Dink" was found in house, to connect defendant with that nickname to house; defense did not show that placing glass in house was intended as assertion), *cert. denied*, 461 U.S. 958.

11. Wright v. Doe d. Tatham, 7 Ad. & E. 313, 112 Eng. Rep. 488 (1837). For a classical exploration of the case, *see* Maguire, The Hearsay System: Around and Through the Thicket, 14 Vand. L. Rev. 741 (1961). For a modern look at *Wright* concluding that Parke was right, *see* Blakey, You Can Say That If You Want—The Redefinition of Hearsay in Rule 801 of the Proposed Federal Rules of Evidence, 35 Oh. St. L.J. 601, 612-616 (1974) (Vicar may have hoped to convey "lies or half-truths," pretending respect to avoid giving insult to an active but incompetent man or believing another would intercept the letter).

12. *See* Stoddard v. State, 850 A.2d 406 (Md. App. 2004), rev'd 887 A.2d 564 (Md. 2005) (18-month-old cousin of abuse victim asked mother "is Eric going to get me,"

landmark, and Parke's opinion sets out numerous examples, such as the sea captain who inspects a vessel and then embarks with his family, offered to show the vessel was sound. And *Wright* is important for two additional reasons.

"Implied statement" First, the case introduced terminology that has proved durable but misleading. Parke said the letters contained "implied statements" that Marsden was competent and were offered to prove "the truth" of those statements. But in its usual strong sense, "imply" describes meaning the speaker puts into his words. If the writers had "implied" Marsden's competency in this sense, the letters would be hearsay by any reasonable definition, and the case would be easy.[13] Clearly Parke did not use "imply" in the usual strong sense (there was no indication that the writers intended to say anything about Marsden's competency), but in a narrow and weak sense to mean the behavior of the writers suggested they thought Marsden was competent, much in the way that the captain boarding the vessel implied that it was sound.[14]

More unfortunately still, Parke's terminology spread beyond its original context, and today it is sometimes used to describe any unexpressed thought in the mind of any declarant. If Observer says "Nurse *N* was in the operating room during the surgery," some would say those words contain an "implied assertion" that Observer himself was connected with the surgery (present or involved). The term is sometimes used in this sense even if Observer did not try to convey this point and the statement has no important performative aspect—no physical conduct (like emerging from the surgery ward as he speaks) and no attempt to do anything, like referring a concerned doctor or nurse to somebody who could give information about the status of the patient. And here the question whether the hearsay doctrine applies is very difficult.[15]

---

offered to prove that defendant was the one who fatally beat victim) (both opinions citing authors of this Treatise). In *Stoddard*, Judge Moylan's 2004 opinion usefully discusses the two-step inference in concluding that the child's question was not hearsay, but Judge Raker's 2005 opinion concludes that that her question was hearsay. Both opinions consider at length the appropriate scope of the hearsay doctrine.

13. If such was the intent, the letters would be hearsay under FRE 801 when offered to prove this point. *See* §8.14, *infra*. And if the purpose of the woman donning the coat was to express or communicate that it was cold, her act would be hearsay when offered to prove this point. *See* §8.7, *supra*.

14. This fact does not undercut relevancy. It simply means the writers were not trying to express or communicate the point. Behavior suggests many things apparently seen or understood, regardless whether the actor intended to express or communicate. The conduct of the writers surely does suggest they thought Marsden competent—especially the one who wrote in a businesslike way (asking him to arrange a meeting between his lawyer and one for the parish and saying that "a Case should be settled" to avoid disagreeable consequences). They implied that Marsden was of sound mind in the same sense that the woman implied it was cold by putting on a coat. Other explanations are possible, but the suggested inference is not only plausible but likely (the writers thought Marsden competent).

15. Not surprisingly, courts reach conflicting results. On statements lacking performative aspects but offered to prove facts assumed or believed (a form of the two-step inference), *see* discussion in §8.23, *infra*.

Wright is important for a second reason, which is that its facts present a blend of assertive words and nonassertive conduct that is often seen and hard to handle. The difficulty stems from the fact that nonassertive conduct cannot be hearsay but assertive conduct can, from the fact that the elements in the blend usually cannot be separated (each gives meaning to each other), and from the fact that words often have a performative aspect that makes them functionally similar to nonassertive conduct. When the mugger says "give me your wallet or I'll shoot," labeling his words as "assertions" or "statements" is nonsensical. It is nonsensical *not* because he lacks assertive intent, for he surely has it (he does *say* he wants the cash and will harm the victim if he doesn't get it). Rather, the label is nonsensical because it does not begin to capture what he *does* when he speaks, which is to intimidate and force a taking. In less dramatic form, *Wright* itself poses the same question: How should we treat behavior that is partly or wholly verbal and both assertive (expressing, communicating) and performative (doing things, achieving results)? Modern cases split on this question, although it appears that most treat the evidence as nonhearsay.[16]

Often seen; hard to handle

If *Wright* arose today under FRE 801, how should the case be decided? The question is surprisingly hard, and two answers are both defensible.

***Wright* revisited**

Here is an argument against hearsay treatment. The letters did not actually say anything about Marsden's mental condition, and they prove his competence on the theory that the writers treated him normally, which suggests that he was normal. It is the performative aspect of writing those letters that proves the point—the authors wrote to him in the same cordial and respectful manner one would expect in a letter to a competent person, and acting this way suggests their belief on the point without expressing or asserting it.[17] The performative aspect of the business letter is especially clear, for its author tried to start something (bringing lawyers together for a meeting), and if Marsden took him up on it he could not readily beg off by saying he meant only to talk or think about it. The letter committed its author to cooperate with Marsden.

Argument *against* hearsay treatment

Here is an argument for hearsay treatment. Unlike the woman putting on her coat, the authors of the letters expressed ideas. The business letter is probative because its author *said* he wanted to deal with Marsden, and the letter tends to prove Marsden's competence only if we take the author at his word. The performative aspect of the letters is relatively small, the assertive aspect larger. The authors purposefully

Argument *for* hearsay treatment

16. On statements with performative aspects, offered for the two-step inference, *see* §8.22, *infra.*

17. A competent argument for nonhearsay treatment cannot rest on the mere fact that the writers posted the letters, even though posting is physical conduct that is nonassertive by itself. The problem is that one communicates by letter only by posting, and doing so is part of asserting something by letter. Scratching a pen on paper or punching letters on a keyboard are part of asserting something in writing, and expelling air while moving the muscles of the larynx is part of speaking. Hearsay makes no sense if trivial and inevitable behavioral aspects of asserting provide escape from the doctrine.

disclose their intentions, and implicitly their respect for the man. It is very much the attitude expressed by the assertions in the letters that tend to prove what Marsden is like, and hearsay risks are self-evident.

§8.10   —Silence and Noncomplaint; Negative Results of Inquiry

It is often reasonable to suppose that if certain events occurred or conditions existed they would generate comment (maybe complaint or objection) by people who experience them. And it is often reasonable to suppose that if such events occurred or conditions existed, asking questions about them in the right quarters would generate positive responses—"yes, that happened," or "yes, that's how things are." In such situations, if there are no comments or if inquiry generates surprise or lack of knowledge ("I never heard that before"), proof of these points is evidence suggesting the events did not occur or the conditions did not exist.

The hearsay issue is whether such proof conveys statements that assert that the event did not happen or condition did not exist. Usually courts say no, and this result seems right.

Noncomplaint is not hearsay   Proof in the first of these forms (noncomplaint; absence of objection) is easy to analyze: Under FRE 801, silence cannot be hearsay if there is no assertive intent, and in common experience passive behavior is not an attempt to express or communicate. Consider a wrongful death suit brought against a motel by parents of a son who died of carbon monoxide poisoning, alleging that a gas heater in the room was negligently operated and maintained. The owners claimed the death resulted from "unavoidable accident" and testified that no previous occupant of the room complained about the heater. On appeal, the reviewing court affirmed the judgment for the defendants and rejected plaintiffs' claim that the testimony should have been excluded as hearsay.[1] The result on the evidence point seems right: A gas heater displacing oxygen with dangerous amounts of carbon monoxide would likely produce an odor, and occupants would likely notice and complain (if they lived to tell about it). Hence the absence of complaint suggests that the heater was not malfunctioning, which suggests in turn that the owners of the motel had no notice of a problem. Prior guests would not likely have intended their silence as an endorsement of the condition of the room or the heater, so they had no intent to express or communicate this point, and their passivity was not a statement for purposes of the hearsay doctrine.

Reported lack of knowledge   Proof in the second form (negative response to inquiry) is more difficult: When inquiry is directed to those who would likely know about something if it happened or existed, any response is a statement (an assertion intended as such), including responses like "I never

---

§8.10   1. Cain v. George, 411 F.2d 572 (5th Cir. 1969) ("not hearsay").

heard that before" or "I don't know." Even more serious, such statements really are hearsay if we take them as proof that declarant didn't know or hadn't heard of the events. A plausible counterargument proceeds in this vein: When inquiry is directed at people who would know if something existed or happened, we expect that at least some will speak up, making a positive statement that the condition occurred or the event happened. Hence the convincing point is not that they claim knowledge and say they have heard nothing, but rather the absence of a more positive response.[2] In this sense, a negative response to inquiry is like evidence of noncomplaint: It is the silence that speaks volumes, not the claim of ignorance.

It is different if respondents, when asked (for example) whether an accident occurred, reply by saying "there was no accident." And it is different if they are told (for example) to "speak up when it hurts" and, in response to a physician's probing, remain silent. In the first instance, it is hard to argue that respondents were silent where a strong claim was expected, for they made a strong claim (the supposed event did not occur). And in the second, silence can hardly be labeled nonassertive, since a cooperative respondent would be silent in order to convey that he felt no pain. In these settings the hearsay doctrine is implicated.[3]

In these cases of negative response to inquiry, it matters how the evidence is presented. Testimony by a witness who canvassed the relevant populace, asking all or a fair sample whether the event occurred or the condition existed, has a stronger claim to be treated as nonhearsay if the witness says only that he "could find nobody who knew or had heard" of the event or condition. There is no complete escape from the hearsay risks in this setting, but at least such testimony presents relatively little risk of misinterpreting what the respondents said, particularly if the questioner himself is in court and can describe what he asked.

In a few related settings, the Rules in effect resolve (perhaps trump) the hearsay issue by creating exceptions that pave the way for such proof even if it is hearsay. Thus exceptions pave the way to prove the absence of entry in business and public records as evidence that an event did not occur or condition did not exist.[4] And if enough people say something is so, their statements may plausibly be characterized in aggregate as

Resolve or trump hearsay issues

---

2. *See* United States v. Blandina, 895 F.2d 293, 300-301 (7th Cir. 1989) (evidence that survey of coin dealers turned up nobody who bought collection was nonhearsay; it showed diligence in investigating nontaxable income sources). *But see* United States v. Harris, 281 F.3d 667, 671-672 (7th Cir. 2002) (excluding as hearsay evidence that only one of three witnesses selected defendant from lineup as robber).

3. *See* United States v. DeLoach, 654 F.2d 763, 770-771 (D.C. Cir. 1980) (treating as hearsay both a statement that "there was no such address" and a report that "no one heard of Bill's Auto Repair Service").

4. *See* FRE 803(7) (absence of business entry), discussed in §8.48, *infra*, and 803(10) (absence of public entry), discussed in §8.54, *infra.*

reputation in a community or family, and various hearsay exceptions permit proof of such reputation even if it is hearsay.[5]

§8.11   Machine and Animal Statements

On a mechanical level, the question whether information generated by machines or the (sometimes expressive) behavior of animals can be hearsay is easily answered. Under FRE 801(a), a statement is something uttered by "a person," so nothing "said" by a machine or animal is hearsay. But the mechanical answer is only sometimes right.

Machine statements   A watch tells the time of day (and things like date, seconds elapsed between presses of a button, phase of the moon); computer screens tell the price of groceries, stocks, and merchandise as well as the content of libraries and profiles of numerical data; breathalyzers tell blood alcohol content, and radar tells the speed of vehicles. But a moment's thought leads to the conclusion that information produced by machines is, at one remove or many, a reflection of human design, engineering, programming, calibration, and input, all aimed at generating machine output. In a real sense, the latter reflects or interprets human statements, hence raises hearsay concerns.

When information provided by machines is mostly a product of mechanical measurement or manipulation of data by common scientific or mathematical techniques, the hearsay doctrine usually does not apply. Concerns over reliability are addressed instead by requiring the proponent to show the machine and its functions are reliable, that it was correctly adjusted or calibrated, and that basic data put into the machine are accurate.[1] In the case of simple and universal machines (watches, clocks, speedometers, thermometers, and the like), foundation evidence may be more bother than it is worth. Most such machines are accurate enough for ordinary use most of the time, and juries understand their limitations and risks of error (timepieces may be set wrong; cheap thermometers give approximate temperatures and are affected by placement, sun and shade, and so forth). In the case of more sophisticated and less familiar machines, more extensive foundations are usually required.

The output of some machines like tape or digital recorders and computer output of business data that were largely entered into the machine manually by clerks or accountants and similar people are such clear and direct reflections of human statements that ordinary hearsay

---

5. *See* FRE 803(19) (reputation among family members regarding birth, adoption, marriage, divorce, death); FRE 803(20) (reputation in community regarding boundaries or lands or events of general history); FRE 803(21) (reputation concerning character), discussed in §8.61, *infra*.

§8.11   1. The formal term for laying the foundation is "authentication," and FRE 901(b)(9) allows such proof to be authenticated by evidence "describing" the process and showing it "produces an accurate result." *See* §§9.13-9.17, *infra*.

analysis applies.[2] Evidence in such forms is considered hearsay and is admitted (if at all) only if the proponent fits it within an exception, such as the ones for business or public records.[3]

In ordinary experience, most animals do not make assertions relevant to litigation and comprehensible to people. Scientists say many animals, including birds, whales, insects, porpoises, and apes have complex and sophisticated means to communicate with one another, and that they have both intelligence and emotions, but humans cannot reliably understand what they say, and not surprisingly the topics of animal conversation do not often coincide with the concerns of human litigants.

Animal statements

In the case of animals trained to assist humans, such as sniffing or tracking dogs, what they can tell us is sometimes directly useful in litigation. At least the reactions of properly trained and handled dogs support probable cause for arrest and search.[4] Most courts admit dog tracking evidence on the issue of guilt or innocence (to identify defendant as the culprit), although generally insisting that proof of dog tracking can be admitted as only "corroborative evidence" of guilt.[5] Here too, courts generally focus on training and reliability, on foundation facts such as their training and handling, and the nature of the data provided to them rather than on hearsay.[6] Since animals cannot very well be put under oath or cross-examined, and neither judges nor juries are likely to be able to appraise their demeanor, deciding whether to admit what they have to "say" by applying hearsay analysis seems at best fatuous.

2. *Compare* United States v. Hamilton, 413 F.3d 1138, 1142 (10th Cir. 2005) ("header information" on pornographic images was not hearsay; it was "generated instantaneously by the computer without the assistance or input of a person") *with* United States v. Cowley, 720 F.2d 1037, 1044 (9th Cir. 1983) (treating as hearsay a machine-affixed postmark indicating that letter came from Santa Barbara). We think *Hamilton* and *Crowley* should be decided the same way, and that *Hamilton* takes the better approach.

3. *See* FRE 803(6) covering business records, discussed in §§8.44-8.47, *infra*, and FRE 803(8) covering public records, discussed in §§8.49-8.52, *infra*.

4. United States v. Place, 462 U.S. 696 (1983) (dog sniff evidence can establish probable cause); Florida v. Royer, 460 U.S. 491 (1983) (use of trained dogs can support arrest on probable cause); United States v. Brown, 731 F.2d 1491, 1492 n.1 (11th Cir. 1984) (*Place* assumes dog sniff evidence is reliable).

5. *See* United States v. Hubbard, 61 F.3d 1261, 1274 (7th Cir. 1995) (reaction of police dog increased likelihood that defendant had carried narcotics in car); People v. Malgren, 188 Cal. Rptr. 569 (Cal. Ct. App. 1983) (dog tracking provided "corroborative evidence" in burglary prosecution). *But see* Brott v. State, 97 N.W. 593 (Neb. 1903) (reversing burglary conviction; jury cannot know whether dog acted for good reasons or bad, thought scent strong or weak, or could separate one scent from others); State v. Grba, 194 N.W. 250 (Iowa 1923) (rejecting evidence of tracking and dog scent lineup).

6. *See generally* Taslitz, Does the Cold Nose Know? The Unscientific Myth of the Dog Scent Lineup, 42 Hastings L. Rev. 17 (1990) (useful discussion of cases, evidentiary standards, technical problems in dog scent tracking and lineups, and frailties of such evidence).

2. *When Is It Offered to Prove What It Asserts?*

> **FRE 801(c)**
>
> The following definitions apply under this article: . . .
>
>   **(c) Hearsay.** "Hearsay" is a statement, other than one made by the declarant while testifying at the trial or hearing, offered in evidence to prove the truth of the matter asserted.

§8.12   Proponent's Purpose and Declarant's Intent

Under FRE 801(c), a statement is hearsay if "offered to prove the truth of the matter asserted." In other words, it is hearsay if there is a match between what the proponent seeks to prove and what the declarant says.[1] In effect, these elements require the court to look to the proponent's purpose and the declarant's communicative or expressive intent. The first element usually poses little difficulty, but the contrary is true of the second.

Proponent's purpose   Context and unfolding strategy usually make it clear what the proponent seeks to prove. If there is doubt and the adversary raises a hearsay objection, the court can ask the proponent what he is trying to do. If he suggests a hearsay use, the objection should be sustained unless he can fit the statement within an exception.[2] Even if the proponent suggests a nonhearsay use or appropriate exception, the court can still exclude the statement if a jury is likely to misuse it as hearsay— as proof of something it asserts if no exception applies or the only exception would not reach the use to which it will likely be put. Misuse of evidence is a classic instance of "unfair prejudice" under FRE 403.

Speaker's intent   For hearsay purposes, finding the "matter asserted" leads the court to a subjective inquiry because the term refers to the points declarant intended to express or communicate. That a subjective inquiry is required can be seen from the language of the Rule and the ACN[3] and from the logic of the doctrine: Hearsay risks are universal (misperception, failed memory, insincerity, narrative ambiguity), but they always arise in a setting peculiar to the person and her statement. The same is true of the trial

---

§8.12   1. Whether the match exists is for the court to decide. Under FRE 104(a), the issue is one of "admissibility." The judge alone determines what the proponent is trying to prove and what the declarant was trying to say. If a statement is admitted, the trier decides for itself what it shows and what the declarant meant (matters of weight and credibility).

2. *See* Orr v. Bank of America, 285 F.3d 764, 778-779 (9th Cir. 2002) (*B*'s statement that he "saw disparaging documents about [plaintiff] at the FDIC" was hearsay since point was to show documents were submitted there). *See* discussion of FRE 104(a) in §1.12, *supra.*

3. FRE 801(a)(2) says nonverbal conduct is a statement only if "intended" as such by the actor, and the ACN says verbal expressions (anything "oral or written") are statements only if the speaker or writer intends to assert something ("nothing is an assertion unless intended to be one").

safeguards (cross-examination, oath, demeanor) that explain the preference for live testimony over out-of-court statements—they too apply individually to each person and her testimony. In sum, a statement is hearsay only if it is offered to prove what the declarant intended to assert, and the hearsay doctrine would be incoherent if what counted was the plain or literal or objective meaning of words.

Even the simplest statement requires some interpretation if the court is to understand what the speaker meant to say. On an elemental level, most statements contain references that can only be understood in context: When Observer says Nurse N was in the operating room during the surgery, understanding him requires us to figure out which Nurse N, which operating room, which surgery, and so forth. Often (perhaps most of the time) the unfolding case provides enough contextual information to enable the court to be confident on these points, and at this level of interpretation there is usually no controversy.

Beyond such matters of reference, interpretation is harder. It my be hard to say what the declarant intended to assert because the human psyche is complicated, and the same is true of language and communicative intent. Indeed, the very idea of intent is problematic, as experience in substantive areas like contracts and criminal law suggests. After all, the intent underlying expressive and communicative behavior may be the product of long thought or immediate impulse, and common experience suggests that people have many interests, directions, purposes, inclinations, aspirations, ideals, strengths, and weaknesses. These vary in intensity and change over time, and even within a single person they may conflict. All affect expressive and communicative purpose. Implicitly the hearsay doctrine recognizes these realities, for its main purpose is to keep the trier of fact from having to appraise such things in the dark, without benefit of demeanor evidence and contextual information that live questioning develops.

The purposes of the hearsay doctrine are well served if courts apply a somewhat artificial idea of expressive intent that is both broader and narrower than the idea of intent we apply in daily life. Consider the statement "he took the car to work" as a means to explore a broad idea of intent. The main intent of someone who spoke those words may be narrow: He means to say where the car is and who took it. But his statement suggests many other things—there is a car, it works, the person who took it knows how to drive and has a job, and so forth. Even if the speaker's main expressive or communicative intent is narrower, these additional points are so closely connected with what he was trying to say that they should be viewed as part of what he intentionally said for purposes of applying the hearsay doctrine.[4]

Broad idea of intent

---

4. It is hard to say why such a statement tends to prove these additional points unless the speaker sought to express them, even though his main expressive or communicative purpose was narrower. In a novel like *The Golden Bowl*, an author like Henry James might leave no doubt what a speaker intended to communicate. A court applying the hearsay doctrine need not achieve such precision and should construe intent broadly. *See generally* Callen, Hearsay and Informal Reasoning, 47 Vand. L. Rev. 43 (1994).

Narrow idea of intent
Consider Observer's comment ("Nurse *N* was in the operating room during surgery") as a means to explore a narrow idea of intent. The main intent of someone who spoke those words may be broad: Observer meant to express or communicate the more sweeping point that the physician and hospital were negligent because Nurse *N* was not qualified or had been on duty for 24 hours straight, or maybe he meant to say nearly the opposite, that Observer himself did not need to be there because Nurse *N* could perform the tasks he would have performed. If his expressive or communicative intent was to make either of these sweeping points, the statement is hearsay if offered to prove either of them. But even so, a court applying the hearsay doctrine should also interpret intent as reaching the narrow and specific point that Nurse *N* was there (physically present in the surgery). This narrower point is so closely connected with Observer's expressive intent that it should be viewed as part of what he intentionally said for purposes of applying the doctrine.

It has been suggested that a statement that clearly asserts one point should be interpreted as asserting another if the speaker must mean to assert the latter in order to make the former true, and this suggestion carries considerable force.[5] The question is one of subjective intent, even though intent must be assessed by estimating what a person like the speaker would mean in similar circumstances. And assertive intent may include points that the speaker does not need logically to assert in order to make his main point true: In fact no rule of thumb is foolproof.

Should be possible
It should be possible for courts competently to assess declarant's (subjective) intent. For one thing, the same contextual information that answers basic questions of reference is likely to shed light on other aspects of expressive or communicative intent. Knowing more about the hospital, the patient, the nature of the surgery, and so forth provides further assistance in gauging Observer's intent in commenting about Nurse *N*. Finally, the internal logic of the hearsay doctrine makes it self-executing in an important sense. If the logical route from the statement to the point to be proved requires taking the speaker's words as intentional expressions or communications of the point, even if his main expressive or communicative intent was broader or narrower, then the hearsay doctrine applies.

§8.13 Hearsay Uses—Direct Assertions of the Matter to Be Proved

Sometimes people express themselves directly and simply on some point, and literal or plain meaning coincides with intended meaning.

---

5. *See* 2 Saltzburg & Martin, Federal Rules of Evidence Manual 133 (5th ed. 1990) (if one fact "must be being asserted" in order to take as true a statement directly asserting a different fact, the statement is hearsay if offered to prove the former; if the statement may be true when the fact to be proved is not, the statement may still be hearsay if declarant "intended to assert" it).

If the proponent offers such a direct statement to prove that very point, the statement is of course hearsay.

Suppose, for instance, an out-of-court statement says someone did something, or an event occurred or a condition existed, and the proponent offers the statement to prove the act, event, or condition. Consider a statement that "we just got home yesterday after a vacation in Hawaii." Perhaps context makes us confident on the points of reference ("we" means the speaker and his immediate family; "home" means Denver), and confident too that the speaker meant to say what the ordinary meaning of his words suggests. Finally, suppose proponent offers the statement to prove that the speaker and his family got home from Hawaii the day before he made his comment (a regulation requires the speaker's presence at home in order to qualify for some benefit or avoid some penalty). The statement is hearsay.[1]

This simplest of all situations is paradigmatic and well understood in the profession. But read on.

§8.14   —Indirect Assertions (Proving What the Speaker Intended to Say)

Often people express themselves indirectly, so their literal or apparent meaning differs from intended meaning. Suppose the speaker stands at the corner of 4th and Elm at 9 A.M. on Monday, and makes one of the following comments about Smith, who is driving a car toward the intersection: "That man's breaking the sound barrier." "What do you suppose he is in such a hurry for?" "It seems like nobody obeys the speed limit any more." Suppose further that one of these is offered as proof that Smith was speeding, and the other side raises a hearsay objection.

Context might persuade us that all three statements imply Smith was speeding, using "imply" in the strong sense to mean the speaker intended to express or communicate this point. We could interpret the first as figurative speech and exaggeration or hyperbole, the second as a rhetorical question that only pretends to seek explanation, the third as a sardonic comment that generalizes from observed behavior to lament the larger condition of the world. These examples are easily understood as indirect statements because the speaker probably did not mean to say what his formal or literal meaning suggests.

Slightly harder are cases where the speaker intends to assert both the direct and the indirect meaning of his words. After all, a moment's reflection suggests that almost every statement is a direct assertion of something and an indirect assertion of something else, and common experience teaches that people routinely intend to assert both the

---

§8.13   1. United States v. Leo Sure Chief, 438 F.3d 920, 925-926 (9th Cir. 2006) (in abuse trial, excluding school documents offered by defense to show that victim had behavioral problems; documents were hearsay when offered on this point); United States v. Sadler, 234 F.3d 368, 372 (8th Cir. 2000) (defendant's protest of innocence was hearsay if offered to prove that he "was in fact innocent").

direct and the indirect meaning of their words. Suppose the speaker at the intersection comments in reference to Smith, "Somebody ought to give that guy a ticket, the rate he's going." Probably he means what his words say directly (Smith should get a ticket because of his rate of speed) and also what his words suggest indirectly or obliquely (he is driving too fast).

What speaker meant to express

Should such statements, offered as proof that Smith was speeding, escape a hearsay objection because they do not say so in literal meaning? Of course not. FRE 801(c) says a statement is hearsay if it is offered to prove "the matter asserted," and this language must be understood as referring to what the speaker meant to express or communicate. In the examples, if context leads the court to conclude that he meant to say Smith was speeding, and the proponent's purpose is to prove this point, the statement is hearsay. It makes no difference that the literal or formal meaning of the words is different. An indirect assertion is hearsay if the speaker meant to assert the point for which his statement is offered, and the task of the court is to figure out his intended meaning, regardless of so-called plain meaning.[1]

Sentence in ACN misread

Unfortunately the matter has proved slippery. Courts are sometimes confused by the fact that plain meaning differs from intended meaning and proposed use, and fail to recognize statements as hearsay. A sentence in the ACN is sometimes misread, and its importance exaggerated, as a directive to treat out-of-court statements as hearsay only if offered to prove what literal meaning suggests.[2] Approaching the

---

§8.14 1. *See* Krulewitch v. United States, 336 U.S. 440, 441-443 (1949) (in trial for transporting women for prostitution, comment that "it would be better for us two girls to take the blame" than defendant because "he couldn't stand it" was hearsay; speaker "plainly implied" that defendant "was guilty of the crime"); Stoddard v. State, 850 A.2d 406, 418-421 (Md. App. 2004) (if one "sarcastically responds" to question "Is that pure heroin" by saying "Do cops wear blue?" then answer asserts that substance is pure heroin, and statement is hearsay if offered for this purpose; an utterance "need not state directly the thing that the declarant intends to assert," but "may imply it" in the form of "a question, a command, a bit of sarcasm, [or] a statement of something else," which "implied assertion" is "just as assertive as is a direct assertion," the two differing only in "communicative style or rhetorical flourish") (illuminating discussion by Judge Moylan), reversed by Stoddard v. State, 887 A.2d 564 (Md. 2005) (on other grounds). *See also* §8.12, *supra. And see generally* Callen, Hearsay and Informal Reasoning, 47 Vand. L. Rev. 43 (1994).

2. The sentence in the ACN for FRE 801(c) says "verbal conduct which is assertive" should be treated like nonassertive conduct—as nonhearsay if "offered as a basis for inferring something other than the matter asserted." The most plausible interpretation is that verbal utterances with significant performative aspects may be treated as nonhearsay. Reading the comment this way explains use of term "verbal conduct" in lieu of more conventional terms like "assertion" (used elsewhere in the Note) and explains why the Committee likened "verbal conduct" to nonassertive conduct (in each case the performative aspect is primary). *See* §8.22, *infra.* Under a less likely minimalist interpretation, the comment means only that an ordinary statement is not hearsay when offered to prove something other than "the matter asserted" (a truly bland observation). *See* §§8.16-8.21, *infra.* The same sentence says "nonassertive verbal conduct" should also be treated as nonhearsay. *See* the discussion in §8.8, *supra. Compare* Wellborn, The Definition of Hearsay in the Federal Rules of Evidence, 61 Tex. L. Rev. 49, 71 (1982) (ACN mandates nonhearsay treatment for indirect statements or

problem this way makes the hearsay doctrine capricious because the result turns on inconsequential changes in expression, while hearsay risks and intended meaning stay the same. Almost certainly the Advisory Committee did not mean the sentence in the Note to be construed this way, and the ordinary meaning of the words in the sentence does not require this result. Viewed as a whole, the work of the framers discloses a purpose to ensure that "matter asserted" is construed to mean what declarant intended to assert, and the ordinary meaning of the words in the sentence does not cut the other way.

State of mind

Every statement that directly asserts facts also indirectly asserts something about the speaker's state of mind. Such statements intentionally say the speaker has on his mind whatever his statement asserts, and usually such statements intentionally express much more about his feelings, intentions, attitudes, beliefs, and recollection. They are hearsay when offered to prove these points, and they fit the category of indirect assertions.

Consider the statement "that man just tripped on the curb" and the statement "don't trip on the curb."[3] Suppose a party offers the first as proof that the speaker thought the man tripped on the curb, or the second as proof that she thought he was at risk of tripping. Even though the actual words do not include expressions like "I think" or "believe," still they imply (in the strong sense of intentionally expressing) that she entertains these thoughts and beliefs, and they are hearsay when offered for this purpose.[4]

Unfortunately this situation too has proved slippery, largely because lawyers and courts sometimes interpret statements too literally. Such literalism might lead to the conclusion that the statements about the man tripping are "circumstantial evidence" of the woman's state of mind. The first statement suggests *circumstantially* that she thought the man tripped and the second suggests *circumstantially* that she was afraid he would trip and hoped he would not. Viewed as *circumstantial* evidence of what she thought, her words are sometimes considered to be nonhearsay evidence. Now this mistake is inconsequential if the only purpose is actually to prove her mental state, since the state-of-mind exception reaches such statements even if they are viewed as hearsay.[5]

---

statements offered to prove unmentioned points; result is deplorable) *with* Millich, Re-Examining Hearsay Under the Federal Rules: Some Method for the Madness, 39 Kan. L. Rev. 1, 8 (1991) (FRE 801 adopts "intent based definition" making statement hearsay when offered to prove whatever declarant intended to assert). We think Professor Millich has it right.

3. Both these utterances are assertions, hence statements for purposes of FRE 801. *See* §8.4, *supra.*

4. The fact that people sometimes lie does not detract from the point that statements usually and intentionally disclose declarant's state of mind. If they did not, we would stop relying on them, and ordinary discourse would stop or look very different. It is *because* we interpret statements as indicating what the speaker actually thinks that lies sometimes deceive.

5. *See* the discussion of FRE 803(3) in §§8.37-8.41, *infra.*

If, however, the purpose is to prove the underlying events or conditions (the man tripped; he was at risk of tripping), it makes a big difference how the statement is viewed. Viewed as nonhearsay *circumstantial* evidence, the statement can be used ultimately to prove the event or condition. Viewed as hearsay, it cannot because the state-of-mind exception does not allow use of such statements to prove such things.[6] Also courts sometimes hold that the speaker must be competent as a witness if her statement is viewed as hearsay and offered under an exception, but not if the statement is viewed as nonhearsay.[7] The category of nonhearsay circumstantial evidence of state of mind is useful in unusual situations, but not in the everyday situation where a statement simply asserts a fact and is offered to prove the thinking or state of mind of the speaker.[8]

§8.15   —Assertions of Circumstantially Relevant Facts

Sometimes people say things, either directly or indirectly, and the actual point made in the statement counts for little by itself in a later lawsuit, but amounts to circumstantial evidence of something else (a "relevant point") that does count.[1] If the proponent's purpose is to prove the relevant point, the statement is still hearsay if it tends to prove the relevant point only *by first being taken* as proof of the actual point.

Semantic argument   In this circumstance, the proponent might advance a legalistic argument that sounds vaguely plausible but should be rejected. Suppose a medical malpractice suit in which plaintiff tries to prove that a hospital failed to exercise due care during a surgical procedure. Plaintiff might seek to show that a nurse was in attendance, and that she was overworked or unqualified, so using her this way is some indication of negligence. In support of this claim, plaintiff might offer Observer's

---

6. To expand the argument, nonhearsay treatment permits unlimited use. If the statement that the man tripped is nonhearsay circumstantial evidence of the woman's belief, the proponent can urge that her belief shows the man tripped. This logic would slice away a big chunk of hearsay doctrine, since every statement that something happened invites this argument. The outcome would turn on the form of the statement: If the woman said "I think he tripped," nobody would argue that her statement escapes hearsay treatment when offered to prove what she thinks (hence what happened); if she says "the man just tripped on the curb," the argument becomes plausible. Obviously the two statements are substantially identical. Hearsay treatment requires the proponent to invoke the state-of-mind exception to prove what she thought, and this exception does not allow use of a statement to prove events giving rise to state of mind. *See* §8.40, *infra.*

7. *See, e.g.,* Betts v. Betts, 473 P.2d 403 (Wash. Ct. App. 1970) (approving, as nonhearsay circumstantial evidence of fear, emotional outburst of child claiming her mother's new husband killed her brother; since statement was nonhearsay, it made no difference whether child was competent as witness).

8. *See* §§8.20 and 8.22, *infra.*

§8.15   1. Assume we know what the speaker meant to assert. It makes no difference whether he made a simple direct statement in which actual and apparent meaning coincide (*see* §8.13, *supra*) or an indirect or oblique statement in which expressive intent and literal meaning differ (*see* §8.14, *supra*).

statement that "Nurse N was in the operating room during the surgery." Faced with a hearsay objection, plaintiff might argue thus:

> A statement is hearsay only if offered to prove what it asserts. Observer's statement asserts that Nurse N attended the surgery, but that is not what we seek to prove. We seek to prove the hospital was negligent in the way it conducted the surgery, which is a different point altogether.

But the statement *is* being offered to prove the matter asserted. When offered to prove Y (the hospital's negligence) a statement that asserts X (Nurse N's presence in surgery) is being used to prove X if it only tends to prove Y by proving X—if it is only relevant to prove what the proponent is trying to prove when taken as proof of what it actually or literally asserts. Hence the statement is hearsay. To put it another way, the phrase "offered in evidence to prove the truth of the matter asserted" (found in Rule 801(c)) refers to the immediate as well as the ultimate purpose of the proponent. To put it yet another way, a statement is hearsay if it asserts a point that is itself circumstantially relevant as proof of some other point in the case—the point that the proponent is actually trying to prove. Thus in a robbery trial, a statement that defendant was seen leaving the bank carrying bags of money is hearsay even if the ultimate purpose is to prove robbery because the statement tends to prove it only if it is first taken as proof of carrying money bags. Similarly, a statement that a driver was speeding is hearsay if offered to prove the driver's negligence because it only tends to prove negligence by proving that the driver was speeding.

Issues in a lawsuit often differ from the subjects addressed in ordinary discourse, so it is not surprising that litigants proffer out-of-court statements to prove a point that is itself circumstantially relevant in the case. Hearsay objections are routinely made and sustained in this situation.[2]

§8.16 Nonhearsay Uses—Verbal Acts, Parts of Acts

In a wide variety of civil and criminal cases, words carry legal consequences or logical significance independent of their assertive aspect. Threats and demands for cash spoken by a gunman to his victim, for example, are verbal parts of a forced taking that support charges of robbery or theft. And in the case of a bargain struck by two people where one agrees to sell and the other to buy something at a set price, words make a contract that supports a claim for breach if either party does not perform. And consider the statement of a person

---

2. Moore v. United States, 429 U.S. 20 (1976) (proximity to heroin found in apartment was only evidence that defendant possessed it; error to rely on statement by informant that he resided there; it was hearsay); United States v. Jefferson, 925 F.2d 1242, 1252-1254 (10th Cir. 1991) (error to admit phone company bill for pager, as circumstantial evidence of connection to drug ring; whether evidence is circumstantial or direct "has nothing to do with whether it constitutes inadmissible hearsay").

entangled in the wreckage of an automobile, who is heard to say afterwards "I'm alive," where the utterance tends logically (and irrefutably) to show that the speaker lives.

Independent legal significance

In the robbery and contract examples, and countless similar cases, it is usually said that the words themselves are legally significant. When they are offered to prove a transaction, the concerns underlying the hearsay doctrine disappear. The words are "verbal acts" in the sense that they have legal significance independent of their assertive quality, and often they comprise the operative events of the transaction that generates the suit.

Although the assertive aspect is unimportant (the words are not offered to prove the truth of what declarants said), still it matters *what words* were used: If the gunman said only "don't worry, I'm just cleaning my weapon; I won't shoot," his words would not indicate a forced taking, and a conversation about the weather would not make a contract. In short, content still matters. In this setting, however, the focus is not on declarant's subjective intent, but rather on a kind of external meaning found "on the face" of the words or by reference to practice and custom. What counts is the fact that the words were spoken or written, coupled with this external meaning, and in these senses "verbal act" is an apt term.[1]

On the civil side, examples of words used in this way can be found in such areas as contract,[2] fraud, defamation, employment discrimination, hostile workplace, and as proof of innumerable things, including apparent authority and ratification or approval of behavior.[3] On the criminal side, common examples include fraud, perjury, and

---

§8.16 1. Lurking in the robbery and contract examples is the question of intent. Robbery involves intentional taking by force, and contract law protects party expectations. Criminal law also requires an act, and threats and menacing behavior are part of the act. Contract law requires a manifestation of agreement, and words are that manifestation. In short, words are verbal acts because substantive law recognizes and gives effect to them. For a look at this intersection between evidence law and substantive law, *see* Bein, Substantive Influences on the Use of Exceptions to the Hearsay Rule, 23 B.C. L. Rev. 855 (1982).

2. In contract cases, words are verbal acts when offered to prove agreement. *See, e.g.,* Cloverland-Green Spring Dairies, Inc. v. Pennsylvania Milk Marketing Board, 298 F.3d 201, 218 n.20 (3d Cir. 2002). They are also verbal acts when offered to prove such things as breach, waiver, estoppel, conveyance, repudiation, and similar matters. *See* Twin City Fire Ins. Co. v. Country Mutual Ins. Co., 23 F.3d 1175, 1182-1183 (7th Cir. 1994) (in suit for bad faith refusal to settle, demand by claimant against insurer was a "performative utterance").

3. Calmat Co. v. U.S. Dept. of Labor, 364 F.3d 1117, 1124-1125 (9th Cir. 2004) (racially offensive speech in workplace; significance lay in "fact that the statement was made and not in the truth of the matter asserted"); Hunter v. Allis-Chalmers Corp., 797 F.2d 1417, 1423 (7th Cir. 1986) (derogatory remarks were nonhearsay "direct evidence" of attitudes in harassment suit); Lubbock Feed Lots, Inc. v. Iowa Beef Processors, Inc., 630 F.2d 250, 261-262, 264-266 (5th Cir. 1980) (reputation of bankrupt cattle buyer was not hearsay when offered to prove "apparent agency," but was hearsay if offered to prove "actual agency").

conspiracy,[4] and numerous cases where acts having verbal elements are at the heart of the charged crime (like gambling and sales of drugs),[5] as well as many other cases where words amount to threats and force (like extortion, kidnapping, and robbery) or have other operative effect.[6]

In the case of words that have logical significance independent of their assertive quality, once again the term "verbal act" is an apt description. Sometimes it matters what words are said, and sometimes not. In the example of the voice from the wreckage ("I'm alive"), it happens that content does not matter—speaking any words proves life.[7] But suppose the question is which car was involved in the hit-and-run accident, and an eyewitness testifies that "the car that didn't stop was the green Ford with the bumper sticker that said 'No Nukes.'" Here the words on the bumper sticker have logical significance independent of their assertive quality because they help identify the vehicle involved in the accident, and the content of the words does matter (a car with a different bumper sticker would not fit the description).[8]

Independent logical significance

Often human acts and utterances are intertwined in such a way that the utterances give meaning to the acts. If, for example, Smith hands over his car keys to Jones and says "you can have my car for the afternoon, please park it in front when you're done," the words define the transaction. Smith has loaned the car to Jones and has not conveyed title by sale or gift (or tried to do so); the loan is for the afternoon, not a week or a month; apparently nothing is expected in return (no rent or exchange) and no restrictions are placed on use, apart from those implied by the short-term and the reasonable supposition that the car will not be abused, which would be understood by both parties to be implicit in the arrangement. When offered to demonstrate the character or nature of the behavior, such words too are nonhearsay verbal acts.

Verbal parts of acts

Conventional descriptions of the verbal act category, including those offered here, are so loose that it could be construed as an "umbrella" category that reaches essentially all nonhearsay uses of out-of-court statements. But the other nonhearsay categories, explored in the ensuing sections, have more precise definitions, and it is customary to invoke those categories where they apply.

---

4. Commonwealth v. Jordan, 733 N.E.2d 147, 151 (Ct. App. Mass. 2000) (words were nonhearsay evidence of conspiracy), *rev. denied*, 752 N.E.2d 259; United States v. Ballis, 28 F.3d 1399, 1405 (5th Cir. 1994) (what defendant said in meeting generating fraud charge was not hearsay).

5. United States v. Burke, 495 F.2d 1226, 1232 (5th Cir. 1974) (statements were nonhearsay verbal acts showing gambling scheme in operation), *cert. denied*, 419 U.S. 1079.

6. *See* United States v. Rojas, 53 F.3d 1212, 1216 (11th Cir. 1995) (consent to search vessel); United States v. De Vincent, 632 F.2d 147, 151 (1st Cir. 1980) (admitting proof that extortion victim was told defendant had gone to jail for loansharking; to show effect on hearer), *cert. denied*, 449 U.S. 986.

7. The words *happen* to assert the point to be proved (they say "I'm alive" and are offered to prove declarant lives), but the logic supporting the conclusion does not depend on content, nor on declarant's candor, narrative skill, perception, or memory.

8. *See* §8.19, *infra*.

§8.17 —Impeachment

When a witness has made a statement ("the guy in the mask stood guard in front") but later gives inconsistent testimony ("the guy in the mask went to the teller's window"), the prior statement is commonly offered as impeachment.[1]

Conflict; vacillation
When offered in this way, prior statements are universally judged to be nonhearsay. The theory is that the *conflict* between the statement and the testimony shows the witness has vacillated, and such behavior—blowing hot and cold, contradicting himself, saying one thing one day, another thing later—sheds light on credibility without taking the prior statement as proof of what it asserts. On this view, the trier of fact can appraise credibility without making "hearsay use" of the prior statement (taking it as proof of what it asserts).[2]

Somewhat more realistically, a prior inconsistent statement tends to impeach by suggesting that the witness has forgotten the truth, or consciously changed his story on account of bias or influence, or lied. These inferences involve taking the prior statement as truthfully reflecting what the declarant thought, and usually this use of a statement is hearsay because the declarant intends to communicate this point. Still, the custom is to treat the impeaching use of such statements as nonhearsay, and even on the more realistic view suggested here the outcome would be the same because the state-of-mind exception ordinarily allows out-of-court statements to be admitted as proof of declarant's thoughts.

Risk of misuse
It is true that an inconsistent statement might be misused as proof of what it asserts, particularly if it conflicts with live testimony on some important point. The remedy is to seek exclusion under Rule 403 on account of the risk of "unfair prejudice," but the impeaching mechanism is so well established, and this form is considered so important, that an objection on this ground usually fails.[3]

§8.18 —Effect on Listener or Reader

In an astonishing variety of cases, it is important to prove what a person actually knew or understood, what information was provided to her (warning or notice), or what pressures she felt from the urgings or blandishments of others. In such settings, evidence of oral out-of-court statements that she heard, or written statements she read or had a chance to read, is routinely admitted. Such statements can help prove knowledge, notice, encouragement or coercion, and similar

§8.17 1. *See* FRE 613, discussed in §§6.40-6.42, *supra*.

2. Conte v. General Housewares Corp., 215 F.3d 628, 638 (6th Cir. 2000) (statement by *F* that he knew "wires were hot" was not hearsay when offered to impeach his testimony that he did not know).

3. If the *calling party* offers an inconsistent statement, courts may curtail the attack if the purpose is to get the jury to misuse the statement as proof of what it asserts. *See* §6.17, *supra*.

external influences, and this use of such statements is not hearsay because the purpose is not to prove what the statements assert.

Sometimes knowledge or understanding itself counts, as in prosecutions for knowing possession of stolen property.[1] More often the question is whether behavior was reasonable, and the actor's knowledge is an element in a larger picture: In fraud cases, misrepresentations may be actionable only if defendant *knew* he was making false statements; in libel suits, knowledge bears on malice; in many settings "bad faith" is the question, and again knowledge is a critical fact.[2]

Knowledge or understanding

In criminal trials, courts often admit proof of the information that led law enforcement officers to follow or observe the defendant prior to arrest on the theory that without it their behavior would look strange or abusive. Such testimony either conveys the substance of accounts implicating defendants in criminal behavior or at least hints at hidden statements describing such behavior. Nevertheless many cases approve of such evidence on the theory that it is helpful in explaining what might otherwise seem to be overly aggressive or unjustified enforcement efforts, and sometimes the defense itself advances such suggestions.[3]

Investigative background

Granting that the timely presence of arresting officers may seem strange by itself, the "cure" is often worse than the disease—it necessarily conveys the opinions of outsiders that defendants engaged in criminal acts, and detailed revelations may convey stark and dramatic accusations. For the most part these go untested in court, and adequate exploration of such matters would take the trial into collateral inquiries far from the charged offenses. In these cases, clearly the court may exclude such evidence under Rule 403, and it is often wise to do so if the defense does not raise or exploit the issue in some way.[4]

---

§8.18   1. United States v. Kohan, 806 F.2d 18, 22 (2d Cir. 1986); United States v. Norwood, 798 F.2d 1094 (7th Cir. 1986), *cert. denied*, 479 U.S. 1011.

2. Ramirez Rodriguez v. Boehringer Ingelheim, 425 F.3d 67, 76-77 (1st Cir. 2005) (in age discrimination suit, report and statements showed that superiors "had reason, based on a thorough investigation," to think plaintiff engaged in misconduct); Woods v. City of Chicago, 234 F.3d 979, 986-987 (7th Cir. 2000) (in civil rights suit, admitting police reports reflecting outside information, which bore on probable cause to make arrest), *cert. denied*, 122 S. Ct. 354.

3. United States v. Obi, 239 F.3d 662, 668 (4th Cir. 2001) (detective explained that he began investigating defendant because informant said he "knew some dude named Obi"), *cert. denied*, 122 S. Ct. 86; United States v. Aguwa, 123 F.3d 418, 420-421 (6th Cir. 1997) (statements by informant indicating that defendant was not in restaurant, which did not implicate him).

4. United States v. Silva, 380 F.3d 1018 (7th Cir. 2004) (prosecutor made "far too much use" of statements by informant and other hearsay; tips may be relevant if jury would not understand why investigation targeted defendant, but no such argument was made); United States v. Meserve, 271 F.3d 314, 319-320, 330 (1st Cir. 2001) (error to let detective testify that defendant had become suspect because *C* knew him and thought he might be the robber).

§8.19 —Identifying Characteristics; Verbal Objects and Markers

Words in their visible embodiment in written form amount to identifying characteristics of any physical object on which they appear. As such, they are often useful in litigation for descriptive purposes, and can aptly be called "verbal objects." Sometimes words in their audible dimension in spoken form are useful in similar ways as "verbal markers," helping identify a speaker or mark an event or point in time. Words *can be used* for these purposes *without* implicating the hearsay doctrine. Some forms of argument that are tempting in this setting, however, do involve hearsay uses, and making the necessary connection between parties and objects identified in this way can involve hearsay links.

Verbal objects: License tags

Automobile license plates are an obvious example of verbal objects, since their function is to provide an easy and certain way to identify motor vehicles. The insignia and labels that tell the make and model of cars also help, as do bumper stickers, window decals, and special tags hanging from rearview mirrors. So do signs that appear on cars or trucks, often consisting of commercial legends and logos. Written words affixed more or less permanently to any physical object can do the same thing. These include nametags or embossed initials on suitcases or briefcases, slogans and emblems on brochures and matchbooks and similar trinkets that serve an advertising or publicizing function, and brand names and content descriptions on containers (boxes, cans, bottles) or products.

If a witness to a bank robbery testifies to the license number of the car in which the robbers made their escape, or describes other visible qualities of the car, he provides powerful evidence that helps identify the car. If it is known that defendant's car has a certain tag number and there is eyewitness testimony placing a car with that tag at the bank, there is no hearsay issue.

Hearsay issues

To link the getaway car to the defendant, it is usually necessary to prove registration—to show that the relevant agency issued a particular license tag to the defendant for a particular car (itself identified by make, year, VIN). The registration amounts to a hearsay statement that the car is registered to the defendant. This hearsay link is normally not problematic because registration can be proved under the public records exception or special statutes.[1]

In settings like this one, there are often *two* hearsay links. An eyewitness notes the number on the license tag of the vehicle—often at a crime or accident scene—and then makes an oral report or writes the number down. Then whatever he says or writes can be admitted only if it fits an exception, which is one hearsay link. That information

---

§8.19   1. State v. Wurtz, 636 P.2d 246, 252 (Mont. 1981) (in trial for intimidation in which victim reported license tag of car driven by perpetrator, officer's testimony that car was registered to defendant amounted to hearsay; should introduce certified copy of registration record of DMV) (harmless).

must then be paired with proof that a car with that tag number was registered to the defendant, which is the second hearsay link.[2]

As noted above, it is not necessary to prove registration if a witness happens to know that a particular tag is affixed to a car owned by the defendant. And of course there are other ways to identify a car as belonging to the defendant, or to any particular person. The owner of a car sometimes has personalized tags ("GOBUFFS"), and people may come to know that the car with that tag belongs to a particular person. Or the owner may attach other markers or decals or bumper stickers ("Give blood, the gift of life"), and these become known as markers on a car owned by a particular person. In such settings, using these identifying characteristics does not involve the hearsay doctrine, just as other aspects of physical description (like color or dents) do not involve hearsay concerns.

In these cases, the witness essentially authenticates an object. She saw the acts or events in litigation, and saw an object bearing a verbal legend that she describes by referring to it. Then the object itself is connected a party by other competent evidence. The legend helps identify the object, and this use of visible words as identifying characteristics in a physical description does not implicate the hearsay doctrine. The governing principles are not found in the hearsay rules, but in FRE 901, which requires a proponent to show that "the matter in question is what its proponent claims."

Verbal markers: Authenticating function

Using words in their audible form as verbal markers seems harder to grasp, perhaps because spoken words are so obviously assertive and because we know who the declarant is. Still, such words can help mark a point it time, or a place or direction, or almost anything else, and the hearsay doctrine does not stand in the way.

Verbal markers

Suppose *X* sees *J* leave in his car, and at the same moment *X* hears *Y* say "let's go to a movie." Suppose it becomes important to show that *J* left at a certain time, and that *X* remembers what he saw but not what time it was, and that *Y* remembers when she suggested the movie (at 6 P.M. on Saturday), although she did not see what *J* did. On these suppositions, *X* could testify to what he saw *J* do (he drove off in his car), and could describe *Y's* statement ("then Y suggested going to a movie"). *Y* could testify to the time when she said that ("it was about 6 P.M. Saturday that I suggested going to a movie"). *X's* testimony can prove that *J* left in his car, and the testimony of *X* and *Y* together can prove when *J* left. While *X* and *Y* both refer to *Y's* comment, the purpose is to mark the moment in time (6 P.M. Saturday), which is a nonhearsay use.

In a classic case illustrating spoken words as verbal markers, a barmaid discovered that she had been paid with counterfeit bills. She called police and pointed out the men who paid her. At trial, she

The barmaid case

2. United States v. Puente, 826 F.2d 1415 (5th Cir. 1987) (admitting report of border agent recording tags of cars crossing checkpoint); Swart v. United States, 945 F.2d 5 (9th Cir. 1968) (admitting eyewitness notation of license tag on getaway car as past recollection recorded).

described what happened and testified that she pointed out the culprits and that the police took them away, but she could not identify defendants as the ones. Then the officer testified that he arrested the men whom the barmaid identified, and that they were the defendants. Used in this way, what the barmaid did in pointing out the culprits was not hearsay. Pointing out the culprits was an assertion (she was saying "those are the men who passed me this bill"), but she also *testified* that the ones who did that are the ones that she pointed out. She incorporated her own statement identifying the culprits into her testimony as a means of description—similar to saying that the men were six feet tall, that one had red hair and the other wore a baseball cap. The officer's testimony connects her testimony ("the ones I pointed out to the officer passed a counterfeit bill") to the defendants ("they're the ones she pointed out"). In both testimonial accounts, the barmaid's assertion on the scene serves the nonhearsay purpose of marking or identifying the people who passed the counterfeit bills and showing that those people are the defendants.[3]

Assume now the case in which we have firsthand accounts describing verbal objects, using visible written words or legends as part of the description. We have no witness, however, who can link the objects to the parties. Suppose, for example, we have a suitcase with a nametag saying "Frank Burns." Suppose defendant is named Frank Burns, but nobody can testify that defendant carries or owns a suitcase with that nametag.

It is tempting to say that that verbal objects like nametags, license plates or product labels lack assertive quality and therefore lie beyond reach of the hearsay doctrine, as courts sometimes do say.[4] In support of this view, one might say that the person or machine that actually makes a label does not intend to assert anything: That is true of the printing and packing machines in commercial practice (and those who operate them) and true of the people who paint signs or emboss jewelry or luggage or print business cards or advertisements. And of course such things are not complete sentences, and the basic meaning or message is implied rather than express or literal.

Verbal objects are assertions   But however tempting it might be to claim that the hearsay doctrine does not apply, the embarrassing fact—and it is fatal to this view—is that such labels do, after all, express and communicate ideas and information, and not by accident. Some human agency composes them, and anyone who would deny an assertive purpose should be asked to explain the fact that *words* are used (not gibberish) and that we *draw*

---

3. United States v. Barbati, 284 F. Supp 409 (E.D.N.Y. 1968) (pointing out culprits "can be classified as nonhearsay without doing violence to theory by analogizing it to proof of identification of objects").

4. *See* United States v. Alvarez, 972 F.2d 1000, 1004 (9th Cir. 1992) (approving argument, on basis of inscribed words "Garnika, Spain" on firearm, that these showed place of manufacture because inscription is "mechanical trace" that is not hearsay because it is "not a statement"), *cert. denied*, 507 U.S. 977.

meaning from them—even if the only message is that this can contains Jolly Green Giant peas, or this suitcase belongs to Frank Burns.

In many cases the declarant, whose assertive purpose is the one that counts, is not the person who makes or fabricates or attaches the verbal legend, as is true with cans of Jolly Green Giant peas. But it does not follow that there is no declarant: It is realistic to say that whoever composes the label and puts it to use is the declarant, even if the declarant turns out to be a commercial entity (and people behind the corporate form). Sometimes the person who acquires the object to which the legend is attached is the declarant—Frank Burns can be viewed as the declarant if he buys a customized bag with that name on it or receives it as a gift, or makes his own label, and the message is "this bag belongs to Frank Burns."

In the end, using visible words or legends affixed to an object as a means of proving what the object is, or where it came from, or who owns it or who made it, does or at least can involve a hearsay use. Thus, for example, we are right in the middle of the hearsay doctrine if a party trying to prove that a suitcase belongs to Frank Burns argues that "the label on the bag says Frank Burns, so the bag belongs to him." In this setting, it is the assertive quality of the words on the label that counts, and those words are hearsay. They tend to prove that Frank Burns owns the bag because they *say* that he owns the bag.[5]

There are, however, several plausible ways to escape this difficulty.

First, the Rules go far to remove product labels and similar words from the operation of the hearsay doctrine by making labels of the hearsay doctrine. Rule 902(7) provides that "inscriptions, signs, tags, or labels" that were apparently "affixed in the course of business" are self-authenticating to the extent that they indicate "ownership, control, or origin." In effect, FRE 902(7) steps around the hearsay doctrine by saying, "we can believe that a can that says Jolly Green Giant peas really is a can of Jolly Green Giant peas, and if a label saying that is introduced to prove what it says, we will take it at its word."[6] To this extent at least, the hearsay doctrine is no impediment to an argument that a car with a Ford logo is in fact a Ford that was made by the famous company of that name, and a truck with the legend "Acme Cleaners" painted on the door is owned by Acme Cleaners, and a matchbook printed up with the legend "Charlie's Steakhouse, Witchita, Kansas" was made by (and likely came from) that place.

FRE 902(7): Stepping around hearsay doctrine

It should be noted that FRE 902(7) does not apply to handmade or made-to-order labels like the nametag on the suitcase that says Frank Burns. Whether written by pen on a card that slides into a label holder

---

5. Payne v. Janasz, 711 F.2d 1305, 1313-1315 (6th Cir. 1983) (in trial for stealing from sheriff's department pearl-handled automatics seized during raid, testimony by deputy that he saw guns in bag marked with evidence tag bearing inscription "10001 Cedar Avenue" was hearsay; tag was used to show that guns came from raid and belonged to sheriff's office), *cert. denied*, 464 U.S. 1019.

6. FRE 902(7) rejects Keegan v. Green Giant Co., 110 A.2d 599 (Me. 1954) (error to admit can of peas without proof that defendant was its source, even though label said so). *See* discussion in §9.26, *infra*.

tied or attached to a suitcase, or affixed professionally by the seller of the bag by means of some sort of stitched or embossed label, or by an engraving company, a label on a bag is not "affixed in the course of business" for purposes of FRE 902(7). Nor does this provision reach personalized inscriptions on jewelry, sports paraphernalia, mailboxes, or other objects ("All my Love Forever, Jack"). In short, FRE 902(7) provides an escape from hearsay difficulties in some of the cases considered here, but not in all of them.

Second, it is plausible to view at least *some* labels, such as nametags attached to luggage or keys or similar objects, as circumstantial evidence that the object belongs to a person of that name. If the tag on a suitcase says "Frank Burns," it tends to prove a person by that name owns the bag *not just because* whoever made or affixed the tag sought to assert that point (a hearsay use), *but also because* people not named Frank Burns are far less likely to own or carry around a bag with that tag on it than people named Frank Burns. Here the argument is not quite the same as the one described above. The proponent does not say "the label on the bag says Frank Burns, so the bag belongs to him," but instead says something like this: "The bag says Frank Burns where you would expect to find the owner's name, and people who are not called Frank Burns would not likely attach such a label to a bag, and would probably remove it if they found such a label and that was not their name. This bag has that label, so it is probably owned by someone with that name."

Verbal objects: characterizing the thing The latter argument depends not on the assertive quality of the words, but on the fact that they give the bag an identity that makes it more likely that a person named Frank Burns owns it. By analogy, one might say that a person who sells furniture polish is more likely to carry a case containing samples of furniture polish than is a person who sells cosmetics. Both the furniture polish and the name tag are characteristics of the object that tend to connect it to one person more than another.

Similar arguments can be made with respect to things like sports paraphernalia. Owning a "John Elway shirt" was once commonplace in Colorado, where a distinguished football quarterback of that name became a household legend in the closing decades of the twentieth century, so the fact that such a shirt was found in a house in Colorado would not go far in that state to prove that a particular person known to be a Denver Broncos fan had been there. On the other hand, owning such a shirt in Ft. Lauderdale was less commonplace, and finding such a shirt in a house there might well tend to show that a particular Bronco fan living in the area had been at that house. If such an object also bore a nametag on the collar saying, for example, "Albin Stubmite," the argument would be strong that the shirt belonged to a person of that name who is a Bronco fan living in the area. If the name said "Frank," the argument still holds, but probative worth is less because the name is more common.[7]

---

7. United States v. Hensel, 699 F.2d 18, 30-31 (1st Cir. 1983) (admitting glass, found at Turkey Cove and bearing word "Dink," to place Hensel there; glass supported inference that Dink Hensel had glass with name Dink on it, which was "merely circumstantial" inference; label was not hearsay because "no assertion intended by the act of

Suppose we have the barmaid's testimony that "the one I pointed out to the officer passed a counterfeit bill," but nobody testifies that the defendant is the one that the barmaid pointed out. Without *some* additional testimony linking "the one that [she] pointed out" to the defendant, the barmaid's testimony is simply incomplete as a means of identifying the defendant as the culprit.

Often, of course, a crime victim who gets a look at the perpetrator is able to include in her testimony a statement that "the ones who did it are the defendants, sitting right over there," which is nonhearsay present testimony connecting the defendants with the crime. If the victim can describe the crime and say that she pointed out the culprits to the police, but cannot say that defendants are the ones she pointed out, then a police officer can fill in the missing link by testifying "defendants are the ones that she pointed out." And under FRE 801(d)(2)(C), the barmaid's prior statement to the police ("those guys are the ones who passed me the counterfeit bill") would be viewed as *admissible hearsay*. Because of this provision, it is at least sometimes unnecessary to get the link-up testimony by the police officer. If, for example, the crime victim tells police "Chuck Miller passed me this counterfeit bill," and if we can be confident on basic interpretive points (by "Chuck Miller," she meant "defendant" because she knows him), then her statement by itself can be used in a trial of Chuck Miller to identify him as the perpetrator.

Sharply distinguishable from the rationale for nonhearsay treatment described above are notations of names, addresses, phone numbers, and the like written on slips of paper or entered in address books, when offered to connect the person carrying the notation to the person indicated. Here the words are *not* used as identifying characteristics. The nature of the object is of little or no importance, and its origin or ownership is shown by other means (usually by possession). What is important is that the words indicate that whoever wrote them knew the person who is identified by the writing or entry.[8]

Verbal markers as hearsay

Notations are different

§8.20   —Circumstantial Evidence of State of Mind

Usually a statement offered to prove the declarant's state of mind is hearsay. The reason is that when one makes statements that express or communicate ideas, she normally intends to express that she knows or thinks (or feels or hopes or intends) what the statement expresses,[1] and

---

putting the word on the glass" was relevant to chain of inferences and person who put name on glass might work in factory that makes many glasses; glass supports inference that Hensel or someone he knew placed it there, which would be hearsay only if whoever did so had assertive intent, which defendant did not show), *cert. denied*, 461 U.S. 958.

8. *See* discussion in §8.23, *infra*.

§8.20   1. The same point is made at the beginning of the next section, on statements as nonhearsay circumstantial evidence of memory or belief. That category is similar, but the logic differs, and the allowable uses. The category discussed *here* justifies

this assertive aspect is critical in proving her state of mind. This point is easily understood if she expressly says what is on her mind ("I intend to go to Chicago," or in the more usual idiom of the forward-looking present progressive, "I am going to Chicago"). But even bare factual statements ("it is raining") assert what the speaker knows or thinks (she *thinks* it is raining), or feels or hopes or intends (she intends to get to Chicago). These ideas are implicit in almost all statements. They are part of what the speaker or writer intends to convey even if not "put into so many words."[2]

Performative aspect

Usually but not always. Sometimes it is possible to draw inferences about declarant's state of mind by focusing on the behavioral or performative aspect of a statement rather than its assertive aspect. In such cases it becomes reasonable to speak of nonhearsay circumstantial evidence of state of mind. Consider the classic case of *Loetch v. New York City Omnibus Corp.*, where a man sued a bus company for the death of his wife, seeking recovery for financial loss, and the company introduced the woman's will (made four months before she died). It left him one dollar, and said she had been "faithful, dutiful, and loving," but that he "reciprocated my tender affections for him with acts of cruelty and indifference" and "failed to support and maintain me." The question was whether the will was hearsay, and the court held it was not.[3]

One behavioral or performative aspect of the will is obvious: By executing a legal document, the woman determined the disposition of her property on death.[4] But this point does not explain admitting her eloquent protest against kindness met with cruelty, and there is a second and more subtle behavioral aspect that deserves a close look. Spouses seldom tell outsiders their grievances, one with another, because doing so is likely to shape the relationship in decisive ways, straining the trust necessary to intimacy and inflicting injury on the other spouse. Just speaking to others about differences that spouses normally work out in private is an indication of a relationship in trouble, and all the bus company needed to prove its point in *Loetsch* (wife would not likely have

---

nonhearsay use of a statement to prove state of mind and the speaker's later acts; the category discussed in the next section justifies use of a statement to prove these points *and also* acts, events, or conditions in the world. See §8.21, *infra*.

2. *See* the discussion of indirect statements in §8.14, *supra*.

3. Loetsch v. New York City Omnibus Corp., 52 N.E.2d 448 (N.Y. 1943) (will helped show "relations" between husband and wife and her state of mind, which bore on his expectancy of future support; fact that she made it was "compelling evidence" of her feelings).

4. The customary term is "verbal act," but usually it describes words offered to prove only their legal effect. *See* §8.16, *supra. Loetsch* involved another purpose—to show how the woman felt about her husband what she would have done if she had lived. He inherited only one dollar, not so much because she *said* that was all he should get but because she *put it in her will*—she didn't *talk about* it; she left him a dollar.

been generous in supporting husband) was to show such problems in the relationship.[5]

Two further points about *Loetsch* bear emphasis:

First, the argument for nonhearsay treatment of the eloquent protest does not turn on the point that factual claims (I am loving; he is cruel) were offered to prove feelings (I am unhappy and disaffected). The wife conveyed and meant to convey how she felt, and knew her words would be understood in this way. The analysis would be the same even if she had spoken expressly about feelings rather than conduct ("I loathe the man and cannot stand to have him near me"). Her words can *still be characterized as nonhearsay* because they make public what is usually kept private, except where relationships are in trouble.

Does not turn

Second, the content of her words matters to the argument for nonhearsay treatment, but not their truth. Had she spoken words memorializing a happy marriage ("we have loved and prospered in wondrous harmony"), those words could not be characterized as behavior breaching marital trust. But the words she actually spoke tended to prove ill feelings, regardless of their truth: If the husband was cruel and indifferent (or she thought so), her words indicate her disaffection. And if we suppose exactly the opposite (her husband was kind and devoted, and she thought as much), her protest still shows disaffection—perhaps especially so (knowingly false hurtful claims might show disaffection even more strongly).

Content, not truth

It is important to note that the argument justifies treating words as nonhearsay circumstantial evidence of state of mind when the point is only to prove state of mind or future behavior. The argument would not justify admitting words as proof of acts, events, or conditions in the world. It would not justify admitting the wife's protest in *Loetsch*, for example, as evidence that the husband had done bad things or was in fact cruel and indifferent. It should also be noted that in this setting characterization almost does not matter: Viewing the words as nonhearsay paves the way to admit them, but viewing them as hearsay would also pave the way to admit them under the state-of-mind exception, which similarly allows use of her words to prove her feelings but not what the husband did.[6]

Limited use—only to prove state of mind

Compare to hypo 4K. / Nichole

Loetsch provides a clear instance of words properly used as nonhearsay circumstantial evidence of state of mind, and the case is rare but not unique.[7] Another example, virtually an archetype for this category even though it has little importance, is outlandish or nonsensical statements offered to prove the speaker's derangement. If someone goes about saying "I am Napoleon" (or "I am Woody Allen"), such words may be

Words as proof of derangement

---

5. *See* Morgan, Hearsay Dangers and the Application of the Hearsay Concept, 62 Harv. L. Rev. 177, 202 (1948) (statements in will that wife "expects later to be made public" indicate "feeling toward him inconsistent with desire to confer financial benefits," a point that would be "doubly true" if statements were deliberate falsehoods).

6. *See* §8.38, *infra*.

7. For another example, *see* Betts v. Betts, 473 P.2d 403 (Wash. Ct. App. 1970) (in custody dispute between father and mother of five-year-old child, her frightened outburst blaming death of infant brother on mother's boyfriend was nonhearsay circumstantial evidence of her state of mind).

viewed as nonhearsay circumstantial evidence of lack of mental capacity.[8] Many modern cases seize on sharp differences between the surface meaning of words and the state of mind being proved in concluding that the words are nonhearsay circumstantial evidence, even though closer analysis suggests that the truth of the words are crucial to the point to be proved.[9]

Sometimes words *demonstrate* knowledge or familiarity with a subject (speaking French shows knowledge of French) or attitudes about people (angry arguments show hostility). In these settings too the phrase "circumstantial evidence of state of mind" might be used, but the striking performative aspect and directness of such displays distinguishes them from the present topic.[10]

§8.21 —Circumstantial Evidence of Memory or Belief

Again it should be said that usually a statement offered to prove the declarant's state of mind is hearsay. Again the reason is that virtually every statement implies (in the strong sense of intentionally asserting) that declarant knows or thinks (or feels or hopes or intends) what his statement describes even if it makes no express reference to what is on his mind, and the assertive aspects of the statement are usually critical in proving state of mind.[1]

Sometimes, however, there is a striking match between what a statement describes and what independent evidence shows to be true, and the statement becomes persuasive evidence that the speaker had the experience that the statement reflects. If it is unlikely that he would have the knowledge reflected in the statement *without* experiencing what he describes, the assertive aspect of what he says pales in significance and it becomes plausible to treat the statement as nonhearsay circumstantial evidence of memory or belief.

Classic decision   The classic decision in the *Bridges* case provides a useful illustration. *Bridges* involved the trial of a man for taking a child to his room and molesting her. Afterwards she described the room to investigating

8. *See* Betts v. Betts, 473 P.2d 403 (Wash. Ct. App. 1970) ("I am Napoleon Bonaparte" would be nonhearsay circumstantial evidence of insanity).

9. *See* United States v. Reilly, 33 F.3d 1396, 1410 (3d Cir. 1994) (admitting *R*'s instructions to dump ash at sea, as circumstantial evidence of *R*'s state of mind); United States v. Harris, 733 F.2d 994, 1004 (2d Cir. 1984) (statement by defendant that he had encounter with people who could cause him trouble and that *S* brought an agent to him was circumstantial evidence that defendant knew *S* was cooperating with police).

10. *See* next section on circumstantial evidence of knowledge and discussion of mixed act and assertion in §8.22, *infra*.

§8.21   1. The same point is made at the beginning of the previous section, discussing statements treated as nonhearsay circumstantial evidence of *other* states of mind. That category is similar to the one discussed here, but the logic differs, and the allowable uses: The category discussed there justifies nonhearsay use of a statement *only* to prove declarant's state of mind and future behavior. *See* §8.20, *supra*. The category discussed *here* justifies use of a statement to prove these points and also acts, events, or conditions in the world.

police officers, but she was not called to testify. Instead, the prosecutor offered her out-of-court description, along with an officer's testimony describing defendant's room. The Wisconsin Supreme Court approved use of the out-of-court description by the child as "circumstantial evidence" of her knowledge "acquired by reason of her having been in that room and house," even though her account would be "hearsay and, as such, inadmissible" to prove what the room looked like.[2]

In some respects, *Bridges* is an unpersuasive opinion. The child's description would likely fit many rooms, and the opinion offers little elaboration or defense of its conclusion. Yet *Bridges* suggests (almost symbolizes) a sound approach if three conditions are satisfied. First, the statement describes something unique or at least unusual, so accuracy is probably not accidental. Second, the act, event, or condition described in the statement is shown by independent evidence. (The argument is not that the statement is trustworthy evidence of the event or condition, which would be a hearsay use. Rather, the argument is that declarant "got it right," so she must have seen or experienced what she described.) Third, circumstances strongly suggest that declarant would not know of the act, event, or condition unless she had the experience reflected in the statement. Hence the statement is neither a conflation of experiences unrelated to the one in question nor a secondhand repetition of something the declarant was told. When these conditions are satisfied, the conclusion is that the experience reflected in the statement is the only (or the most likely) explanation for the declarant's ability to say what she said, and the evidence need not be treated as hearsay.

In the right setting, the approach outlined here can be useful, but only a few opinions go in this direction,[3] and several decline the invitation.[4] In the nature of things, it is hard to be sure that the third condition is satisfied because it involves an estimation about what the declarant might know or imagine.[5] The problem of child abuse that produced *Bridges* itself has engendered new hearsay exceptions and mechanisms for taking testimony by children, and a striking fact in modern cases is that they often approve hearsay use of statements to

---

2. Bridges v. State, 19 N.W.2d 529, 535 (Wis. 1945).

3. *See* United States v. Muscato, 534 F. Supp. 969 (E.D.N.Y. 1982) (admitting testimony by *G* that he got pistol from *JM*, coupled with evidence that *G* gave detailed description of pistol before learning it was found; statement provides "important confirmation" of testimony and helps link *JM* to conspiracy).

4. State v. Galvan, 297 N.W.2d 344 (Iowa 1980) (apparently defendant took two-year-old daughter along when he beat and stabbed victim; invoking *res gestae* doctrine but refusing to apply *Bridges*, court approves evidence that she took belt from mother's robe, bound her own hands, and "made several gestures as if beating her own chest") (in effect, applying excited utterance exception).

5. In a Swedish case study, a five-year-old victim described a flat like the one occupied by *S*, but interviews suggested that child might have (a) gone to the door of the flat and peered inside while collecting newspapers, (b) seen an identical sink plug in another flat, (c) heard stories about what "dirty old men" do to little boys, and (d) sought to cover up his disobedience (playing with boy his mother had told him to avoid) by inventing a story of assault. *See* Trankell, Case Report: Was Lars Sexually Assaulted? A Study in the Reliability of Witnesses and of Experts (1957).

prove events on the ground that a child could not imagine what she describes without having experienced it.[6] These decisions in effect accept the logic of *Bridges*, but treat the statements as admissible hearsay rather than admissible nonhearsay.

C. BORDERLAND OF THE DOCTRINE

§8.22 Mixed Act and Assertion

In common experience, saying and doing seem separate and distinct, and the ideas seem so different that they hardly touch at all. In more formal terms, "saying" means assertion (or assertive conduct) and "doing" means action (or nonassertive conduct) and a good line can be drawn between these categories: Saying it is cold outside belongs in the former and putting on a coat belongs in the latter. From the standpoint of ease in administering the hearsay doctrine, such clarity is fortunate. We can be sure the statement about the cold is hearsay if offered to prove temperature, but the act of putting on the coat is not.

Saying and doing overlap
But saying and doing overlap, which is not surprising since both involve human behavior, and sometimes behavior that one might describe as assertive is inseparably bound up in behavior that one might equally describe as action.[1] To put it another way, behavior may be important in both its assertive and its performative aspects, so the term "assertion" does not adequately describe what is going on. It becomes wiser to speak of "mixed act and assertion" or "statements having performative aspects" or "actions having assertive aspects," for these cumbersome but broader descriptions capture the reality better.[2] Sometimes the blend is a mix of physical conduct and verbal expression. Perhaps more often the blend is verbal behavior having assertive and performative aspects—expressing and communicating while being instrumental, causing something to happen,

---

6. *See, e.g.*, Nelson v. Farrey, 874 F.2d 1222, 1228-1229 (7th Cir. 1989); Morgan v. Foretich, 846 F.2d 941, 947 (4th Cir. 1988); United States v. Dorian, 803 F.2d 1439 (8th Cir. 1986) (all invoking catchall for statements by children describing sexual abuse, partly because they describe matters children would not know without experience).

§8.22 1. *See generally* McCormick, The Borderland of Hearsay, 39 Yale L.J. 489 (1930) (classic and useful discussion); Mueller, Post-Modern Hearsay Reform: The Importance of Complexity, 76 Minn. L. Rev. 367, 412-422 (1992).

2. Understanding blended cases is made harder by an early decision whose confusing terminology crept into the vocabulary. If offered to show it was cold, donning a coat would be an "implied assertion" in the terminology of that case, because the term was used to describe all conduct offered to prove the actor's belief in a fact, hence the fact itself. But putting on a coat does not normally imply anything in the strong sense (donning a coat normally does not involve assertive intent). Of course the act still implies it is cold in the weak sense of suggesting or indicating as much, as gathering clouds might be said to imply an impending storm. The case introducing this unfortunate terminology is Wright v. Doe d. Tatham, 7 Ad. & E. 313, 112 Eng. Rep. 488 (1837) (described in §8.9, *supra*).

bringing into being or carrying on human relationships, or changing the positions of the declarant or others.

Consider the example of the woman who says "don't trip on the curb," in an attempt to warn a man carrying an armload of packages.[3] Proof of her behavior is offered to show the man was approaching the curb unaware of the hazard or that there was a curb presenting a hazard. Here is a case of mixed act and assertion, a statement having performative and assertive aspects: The woman acts to prevent an accident (performative aspect), and what she does makes the man look down, step carefully, perhaps adjust his armload to get a better view of the pavement.[4] She also expresses and communicates information, directly and by implication in the strong sense of intentionally expressing or communicating (assertive aspect).[5]

A moment's reflection suggests that every statement has some performative aspect that might be important. To prove the speaker is alive, anything he says is important in its performative aspect: If he says "the moon is blue," his statement proves that he is alive in its performative aspect, and the underlying logic and probative force would not change if he said "I'm alive," even though the latter also *asserts the point.* Every statement is performative in this elemental way, and nearly all statements are performative in the sense of creating or constituting an ongoing relationship between speaker and hearer: Whatever a parent says to a child, or one spouse to another, whatever friends say to one another, or rivals or enemies or coworkers, it all goes into making the relationship between them, and words not only say things about relationships, but make them what they are.[6]

"Don't trip on the curb"

---

3. The discussion in §8.4, *supra,* concludes that this utterance is a statement for hearsay purposes.

4. An observer would say the woman did something, not that she said something ("she tried to keep him from tripping," not "she said he shouldn't trip"), and common usage provides a clue. The woman acts. *See generally* J. L. Austin, How to Do Things With Words 13 (2d ed. 1975) (American evidence law treats as nonhearsay a "performative" utterance, which is viewed not so much as something declarant said, "but rather as something he did, an action of his").

5. Directly or by implication, they say that the woman sees a man approaching a curb, that the curb poses imminent risk, that he can avoid the risk by taking care. And they say lots of things about her state of mind—what she thinks, sees, understands, what she hopes will (and won't) happen.

6. *See generally* Mueller, Post-Modern Hearsay Reform: The Importance of Complexity, 76 Minn. L. Rev. 367, 417 n.149 (1992) ("Spouses, for instance, know that words of consideration, criticism, frankness, or evasion are important, not only in what they convey in verbal meaning, but in the way they shape and constitute an ongoing relationship, and in what they reflect about the unseen life of the speaker. Parents know that what they tell children is important, not only in conveying information and fostering understanding, but in expressing expectation, approval and pride, which creates an environment in which the developing selfhood of the child takes shape. Outside family settings, working people watchful of careers and concerned over such matters as advancements and deadends, promotions and layoffs, reassignments and shifting responsibilities, salaries and working conditions know that what they say and what they hear affects them in ways having nothing to do with verbal accuracy. And similar

It does not follow that every statement has a performative aspect that justifies treating it as nonhearsay. If the utterance "I'm alive" were made after a car accident by an injured occupant, its performative aspect would not justify its use to show that the accident was nearly fatal or that declarant was seriously injured. What he said tends to prove those points, but in its assertive rather than its performative aspect (the idea he expressed, not his act of speech).[7]

Statements with performative aspects　　In the end, it is convenient to speak of mixed act and assertion (or statement with a performative aspect) when the performative aspect supports the proposed evidential use. Properly understood, statements with performative aspects can be both hearsay and nonhearsay. Explaining the hearsay aspect is easy: After all, the woman says there is a curb and implies in the strong sense that the man is drawing near and the curb presents danger. Explaining how they are not hearsay is harder, but the key is that nonassertive conduct is not hearsay under FRE 801. Such conduct (putting on a coat) is not hearsay *even* when offered in support of the two-step inference from belief to fact believed (actor thinks it is cold, so it is probably cold).[8] When the woman gives the warning, we need not rely on her words in their assertive aspect in drawing inferences about what she thinks or what the reality is and can rely on what she does. She grabs the man's attention, causing him to look down and watch for the curb, which is best understood and treated as nonassertive conduct.

Hearsay dilemma　　Unfortunately (from the standpoint of ease in application) the hearsay doctrine assumes that evidence is either hearsay or not, at least when offered for a single purpose. Judges and lawyers are adept at understanding that an assertion like "it's cold" is hearsay when offered for one purpose (proving it was cold) but not when offered for another (impeachment, if declarant testifies it was warm). But judges and lawyers are less adept at understanding that mixed acts and assertions like the warning "don't trip on the curb" can be both hearsay and nonhearsay when offered for one purpose (proving there was a hazard). In these marginal cases, we find a lapse in professional understanding and gaps in vocabulary and doctrine.

Singer case　　Courts often reject hearsay objections to mixed act-and-assertion evidence, sensing (if not quite saying) that something more is going on. In the *Singer* case, for example, the Eighth Circuit concluded that an eviction notice sent to "Carlos Almaden" at 600 Wilshire Drive in Minnetonka, Minnesota, was not hearsay when offered to prove that a

---

insights have long been the stock-in-trade of Madison Avenue and political handlers and are the basis of arguments by modern feminists who want to censor pornography or change the character of the workplace.").

7. Some courts might treat this statement as nonhearsay when offered to prove unmentioned ideas in the mind of the declarant (*see* §8.23, *infra*), and statements by accident victims commonly come in as excited utterances to prove what happened (*see* §8.36, *infra*).

8. FRE 801 takes this position even though it is understood that this particular use of such conduct presents risks that are the same as (or similar to) what we call the hearsay risks. *See* §8.9, *supra*.

person known by that name lived there. One can rely on "the landlord's *behavior*" in mailing the letter rather than "the implied truth of its written contents," said the court, noting that the letter was found at that address.[9] *Singer* seems right to recognize there was an assertion—the notice and the address on the envelope say directly or by implication that Almaden takes mail there (hence probably lives there). And the opinion seems right to emphasize what the landlord did. The persuasive point, however, is not that the landlord mailed a letter, but that he was evicting his tenant. Hence the eviction notice (including the address) has both assertive and performative aspects and is really both hearsay and nonhearsay when offered to prove Almaden lived there.

Courts often reach the right outcomes, but few opinions penetrate the problem well. Those that admit such evidence sometimes justify the result by saying the behavior is not an assertion or is not offered to prove what the actor/speaker asserted—positions at odds with reality. Here are some examples:

1. Bets and drug orders. During searches or raids of drug houses or bookmaking establishments, investigating officers often intercept incoming calls from people trying to place bets or buy drugs. Such calls are usually a mix of act and assertion. The voice on the line might commit the caller to a bet or purchase on certain terms, virtually binding him to perform if the terms are accepted. Or the voice simply makes inquiries that convey an interest in doing business, amounting to an attempt to do so or to set something up.

Whether the caller makes a commitment or just tries to make a bet or buy drugs, placing the call is not simply an assertion but action seeking to achieve these ends, and the performative quality of such behavior justifies nonhearsay treatment when it is proved as a means of showing that bets are taken or drugs are sold where the call is received. Courts admit such evidence in both gambling[10] and drug cases,[11] and this result seems sensible. In some settings, one might also avoid the hearsay objection by using the incoming calls as proof of the illegal use to which the premises are put, which is tantamount to saying that placing bets and buying drugs (or attempting to do either one) are themselves elements of an offense relating to the premises.

2. Records showing illegal use of premises. Apparent records of bets and drug transactions are also discovered in raids of gambling

---

9. United States v. Singer, 687 F.2d 1135 (8th Cir. 1982), *modified,* 710 F.2d 431 (1983).

10. United States v. Lewis, 902 F.2d 1176, 1179 (5th Cir. 1990) (bet-placing call).

11. Headley v. Tilghman, 53 F.3d 472, 477 (2d Cir. 1995); Commonwealth v. Washington, 654 N.E.2d 334 (Mass. App. 1995); United States v. Giraldo, 822 F.2d 205, 212-213 (2d Cir. 1987) (all admitting incoming drug calls as nonhearsay). Even inquiries are admitted as nonhearsay, either on the theory that the caller made no assertion, *see* United States v. Oguns, 921 F.2d 442, 448-449 (2d Cir. 1990), *and* United States v. Lewis, 902 F.2d 1176, 1179 (5th Cir. 1990), or on the stronger ground that he assumed rather than asserted that he was calling a drug dealer, *see* United States v. Long, 905 F.2d 1572, 1579-1580 (D.C. Cir. 1990). *And see* Guerra v. State, 897 P.2d 447, 460-461 (Wyo. 1995) (similar treatment for letter).

establishments and drug houses. Courts sometimes admit on the theory that these records are nonhearsay proof of the scope and general nature of activities conducted on the premises—as verbal acts amounting to criminal misconduct.[12] But while it is plausible to argue that verbal behavior seeking to place bets or buy drugs are criminal acts, it is less plausible to suppose that keeping records of bets or sales is criminal misconduct, and such records are better viewed as hearsay evidence of the transactions they record, as several courts have concluded.[13] It does not follow that the records must be excluded, as they may qualify under various exceptions.[14]

3. Lies to mislead police. Lies are an obvious example of mixed act-and-assertion, since the declarant tries to change the course of events by misleading another—perhaps the purpose is to make a purchase or sale, preserve or destroy or reshape a relationship, or change the thinking or behavior of a listener. In such cases it may even be hard to see how lies could be hearsay, since they are usually proved along with evidence of their falsity and are not offered to prove "the truth of the matter asserted."

The most common example is false exculpatory statements, usually spoken by a defendant and offered to show consciousness of guilt, supporting an inference of his guilty involvement. Sometimes such statements are spoken by third persons and they show the speaker's awareness of the involvement of the defendant and try to cover for him. The performative aspect of lying to law enforcement agents or giving false testimony during an investigation[15] justifies treating it as a crime (perjury or obstruction of justice)[16] and provides a strong argument for treating it as nonhearsay evidence.[17] Again it is hard to see such

---

12. United States v. Gonzales, 307 F.3d 906, 909-911 (9th Cir. 2002) ("pay/owe sheets"); United States v. Alosa, 14 F.3d 693, 696 (1st Cir. 1994) (drug records).

13. United States v. Garcia-Duarte, 718 F.2d 42, 46 (2d Cir. 1983) (dealer's customer book is not nonhearsay evidence of drug transactions, in general or with named people); United States v. Ocampo, 650 F.2d 421, 427-428 (2d Cir. 1981) (error to admit testimony based on records of cocaine transactions in order to link codefendants together).

14. *See* discussion of business records exception in §§8.44-8.47, *infra*. Prosecutors may not have access to foundation evidence, but testimony by outsiders confirming bets or orders described in records, along with proof that a co-offender prepared them, go far toward satisfying the foundation requirement.

15. Such falsehoods have obvious performative aspects. The false story may be accepted as true or treated as a tip, and distracting police may help declarant or someone else avoid charges, detection, or even conviction. Of course the declarant asserts something too, but this label captures only part of the picture.

16. On consciousness of guilt, *see* the discussion in §4.4, *supra. And see* United States v. Rodgers, 466 U.S. 475 (1984) (statute making it a felony to falsify or conceal material facts covers lying to FBI).

17. Anderson v. United States, 417 U.S. 211, 219-222 (1974) (false testimony, given after crime in cover-up effort, was not hearsay when offered to prove motive since it was not offered to prove something declarants said was true). *See also* United States v. Simmons, 470 F.3d 1115, 1124-1125 (5th Cir. 2006), *cert. denied*, 127 S.Ct. 3002; Osborne v. Commonwealth, 43 S.W.3d 234, 242 (Ky. 2001) (both admitting false exculpatory statements as nonhearsay).

false statements as hearsay, but again they do assert that the speaker wants the listener to believe what is being said, and they do bring hearsay risks. The key is not that the statement is offered to prove its untruth, but that the performative aspect of the lie gives it probative force independent of its assertive quality even when the speaker is someone other than the defendant.

4. Demonstration and disclosure. Sometimes the important aspect of a statement is that the declarant in effect demonstrates or discloses knowledge, familiarity with, or attitudes toward certain matters.

If the question is whether a person speaks French, evidence that he carried on a literate and spontaneous conversation in the language proves the point. Each spoken word asserts the speaker's knowledge and understanding, but the performative aspect of the display is the dominant fact, and evidence of his conversation is not hearsay if offered to prove fluency and familiarity with the language. Indeed, so persuasive is the performative aspect that this display would likely be admitted as nonhearsay evidence that the speaker had been abroad or spent time among French-speaking people, or at the very least that he had studied French extensively. Similarly a verbal display of insider knowledge of technical subjects is usually treated as nonhearsay evidence when offered to show knowledge or familiarity,[18] prejudice or animosity,[19] and other attitudes.[20]

As proof that involvement in a criminal venture was innocent, statements by the defendant may be admitted as nonhearsay where they disclose his understanding of events or conditions, or his connection with people or transactions, on the theory that if he were guilty he would not advertise what he knows. Here too, the significant point is the act of disclosure rather than the truth of what is said,[21] and the theory closely resembles that for nonhearsay treatment of statements offered as circumstantial evidence of state of mind.[22]

---

18. United States v. Emmons, 24 F.3d 1210, 1216 (10th Cir. 1994) (hand-drawn map, to show knowledge of marijuana cultivation); United States v. Figueroa, 818 F.2d 1020, 1026-1027 (1st Cir. 1987) (discussion of counterfeiting, to show sophistication in counterfeiting).

19. United States v. Hyles, 479 F.3d 958, 970-971 (8th Cir. 2007) (C and T were "arguing about the Pontiac") (not hearsay, to prove hostility); Talley v. Bravo Pitino Restaurant, Ltc., 61 F.3d 1241, 1249-1250 (6th Cir. 1995) (disparaging comments prove racial attitudes); United States v. Mills, 704 F.2d 1553, 1562 (11th Cir. 1983) (angry altercation proves animosity).

20. Israel Travel Advising Serv. v. Israel Identity Tours, 61 F.3d 1250, 1260 (7th Cir. 1995) (customer comments prove confusion); Keisling v. Ser-Jobs for Progress, 19 F.3d 755, 762 (1st Cir. 1994) ("I'm getting too old for this crap," proves defendant spoke of herself this way, lacked discriminatory animus).

21. United States v. Webster, 750 F.2d 307, 330-331 (5th Cir. 1984) (statement by defendant indicating knowledge of stolen airplane on his property was not hearsay when "offered to support an inference of innocence" on theory that "a man with guilty knowledge is not likely to advertise").

22. *See* the discussion in §§8.20-8.21, *supra*. Here too the argument stresses that a statement has performative significance.

5. Omitted complaints. If events have occurred that are of immediate and compelling concern to someone and he knows about them, proof that he speaks of them but omits comment on one or another aspect or detail is another instance of mixed act-and-assertion.[23] Here the manner of speaking seems the significant point, and the words have a performative aspect going beyond what they assert. Here too they reveal the speaker's thoughts, and here too nonhearsay treatment may be warranted.[24]

6. Orders, directives, verbal acts. To borrow a standard classroom illustration, suppose a hospital puts a patient in intensive care, and proof of this point is offered to show the patient was gravely ill. The example makes sense only on the supposition that a doctor gave appropriate orders or made entries in pertinent records (doctors do not usually carry patients to ICU or push gurneys). Even so, it mischaracterizes the case to say that someone *merely said* the patient required such care. In a hospital, orders from a physician set treatment protocols in motion, and words of this sort are quintessentially performative. Similar arguments apply in other settings in which people in authority give directives.[25]

In their performative aspect, words convey title, transfer property, and make contractual commitments.[26] Similarly, words give effect to institutional decisions in countless situations: They commit banks to lend money, admit students to college, set employment conditions, job responsibilities, construction tolerances, and the like. And in their performative aspect, coercive words commit (or help commit) criminal acts like extortion, conspiracy, robbery, or assault.

7. An approach. In applying a hearsay doctrine that demands an either/or decision, what should be done with evidence that fits *both* of

---

23. The argument is similar to the one that silence and noncomplaint are not hearsay. *See* §8.10, *supra.* Here, however, the meaning of silence is in part understood by reference to what is actually said.

24. Such a case split the Second Circuit: The prosecutor showed that gang members held a meeting after *P* was arrested for murdering a witness. The conversation focused on sending *L*, who had accompanied *P*, into hiding. From the fact that nobody criticized *P* for bungling the job or police for arresting him, the prosecutor argued that the conversation showed that everyone knew *P* did the deed. *See* United States v. Pacelli, 491 F.2d 1108 (2d Cir. 1974) (reversing; dissent argues that nobody said anything about *P*'s guilt), *cert. denied*, 419 U.S. 826.

25. Examples include commands by superiors to subordinates in military or quasi-military units (army, police, fire department), directives to employees and parental instructions to children. *See* Bergene v. Salt River Project Agr. Imp. And Power Dist., 272 F.3d 1136, 1141-1142 (9th Cir. 2001) (supervisor's threat); Pastran v. KMart Corp., 210 F.3d 1250, 1260 (10th Cir. 2000) (manager's reprimand); Butters v. Vance International, Inc., 225 F.3d 462, 467 n.1 (4th Cir. 2000) (directive not to promote).

26. If X contracts to sell his 2007 Prius, the contract is a nonhearsay verbal act in a suit for specific performance. *See* §8.16, *supra*. If the question is whether X owns such a car, his agreement to sell it has assertive and performative aspects, for he asserts as much and commits to sell. *See* United States v. Alexander, 48 F.3d 1477, 1486-1487 (9th Cir. 1995) (certificate proves bank federally insured).

the only two categories?[27] It seems foolish to venture an elaborate prescription, but some suggestions may help.

First, a sense of proportion seems important. Sometimes the performative aspect dwarfs the assertive aspect (indicating nonhearsay treatment), sometimes vice versa (indicating hearsay). It is one thing to treat as nonhearsay an eviction notice, offered to prove the addressee lives where the notice was sent, quite another to treat a postcard ("having a nice trip, see you soon") that way. In both examples, the assertive aspect is about the same—reasonably read, the address (an instruction to the postal service) says the recipient takes mail there. But the performative aspect differs: An eviction notice begins legal proceedings, involves a lawyer, forces the tenant out, and carries consequences to owner and tenant if the job is botched. Writing and mailing a postcard are minor gestures, and what counts for more in this setting is the assertive quality of the address, which should be hearsay if offered to prove where the addressee lives.

Sense of proportion

Second, the risks and consequences to the speaker/actor and listener/observer are relevant. If the speaker's behavior puts him at risk, shapes relations with someone of consequence in his life, or commits him to a direction from which he would find it awkward to turn away, such facts suggest that the evidence should be treated as non-assertive conduct. Ordering drugs or betting on horses commits the speaker to come up with money or credit and may put him at risk of retribution, or at least loss of business advantage, if he reneges. In such settings the performative aspect is more than negligible, and nonhearsay treatment may be warranted. Similarly, if the listener/observer is likely only to reflect and reply, or merely to remember the matters conveyed, the assertive aspect seems important. If he is likely to act, to be put in fear, or to abandon one project and take up another, the performative aspect gains importance.

Risks and consequences

Third, the performative aspect of mixed act-and-assertion evidence does not necessarily justify admitting it as proof of everything the words assert. Suppose an intercepted call at a suspected drug house says, "Did Frank get the crack he promised me yet?" In its performative aspect, this call supports an inference that the phone on the receiving end is located in a place used to sell drugs, but the assertive aspect is critical in concluding that Frank is one of the people in the drug business or made a promise to deliver crack. Placing a call in an attempt to buy drugs justifies a conclusion that drugs are sold at the premises, but only the assertions made by the caller would support further inferences on

Not to prove everything

27. We do not mean the criticism of hearsay doctrine to be too severe: Often the hearsay-nonhearsay dichotomy is useful, just as it is useful to describe the earth as made of land and water. For many purposes, behavior is either hearsay or nonhearsay, just as many places *are* either land or water (we know which applies to Half Dome in Yosemite and to the Caribbean). But the land-water dichotomy is troublesome for the trout fisherman knee-deep in the North Platte, and the hearsay-nonhearsay dichotomy is troublesome for the concerned woman ("don't trip on the curb").

the names of the people involved or the terms of agreements already reached.

§8.23 Looking Behind a Statement—Proving Unmentioned Acts, Events, or Conditions

Statements usually shed light on acts, events, or conditions in the world even if the words do not describe them in literal meaning, common usage, or expressive intent. This situation is truly difficult. It is different from cases where the speaker intends to communicate by figurative or nonliteral words. There intended meaning and literal or plain meaning differ but the hearsay doctrine applies where the speaker meant to say what the statement is offered to prove.[1] Here, in contrast, a statement asserting one thing suggests insights into thoughts or beliefs about other things that the speaker did not intend to express or communicate. These may suggest further inferences about unmentioned acts, events, or conditions, typically based partly on the statement and partly on circumstances, and they involve the two classic steps (statement suggests belief, which suggests act, event, or condition).

Consider the statement mentioned in the opening sections of this chapter: Listener testifies that Observer said Nurse *N* was in the operating room during the surgery. Offered to prove Nurse *N* was there then, the statement is hearsay. What if it is offered to show *Observer* was there, or works in surgery? Or that the surgery either followed or departed from routine procedures (inferences that might depend on evidence that Observer often saw Nurse *N* in similar surgeries, or seldom did)? Of course he may have intended to convey or express these points, which makes analysis easy (the statement is hearsay). But what if he did not?

Courts and commentators alike struggle with the hearsay issue in this setting.[2] That the problem is hard can be seen in the fact that neither the terms of FRE 801 nor the logic of the hearsay doctrine yield a clear answer, and strong arguments can be made on both sides of the question.

Arguments *against* hearsay treatment

Arguments *against* hearsay treatment are easily set out: The pivotal concepts of hearsay are assertion and intent, which stress deliberate expression or communication. These play little or no role if someone unconsciously reveals something while deliberately saying something else. Under a focused view of intent, the notion of unconscious

---

§8.23   1. *See* the discussion in §8.14, *supra.*

2. *See generally* Park, "I Didn't Tell Them Anything About You": Implied Assertions as Hearsay Under the Federal Rules of Evidence, 74 Minn. L. Rev. 783, 829 (1990) (decisions accord nonhearsay treatment to statements offered to prove unmentioned points where circumstances "reduce dangers of fabrication by either the declarant or the trial witness"); Bacigal, Implied Hearsay: Defusing the Battle Line Between Pragmatism and Theory, 11 S. Ill. U. L.J. 1127 (1987); Seidelson, Implied Assertions and Federal Rule of Evidence 801: A Quandary for Federal Courts, 24 Duq. L. Rev. 741 (1986) (under intent-based approach of FRE 801, hearsay definition is broader than some think).

disclosure is reasonable because we often draw conclusions about acts, events, or conditions from what another says while believing that he did not intend to say anything about such things (we speak of "revealing" statements). Thus a statement used to prove unmentioned ideas is not hearsay because a key element is missing—proponent's purpose and declarant's expressive or communicative intent do not match. This conclusion finds support in the argument that hearsay risks are reduced if a statement is used to prove an unmentioned point. If the speaker did not intend to express it, he did not intend to mislead. In one sense the risk of verbal ambiguity is also reduced, since the inference comes less from parsing words than appraising the larger situation. And if the point that the statement does assert is established or accepted, using the statement to prove unmentioned points involves some diminution in all the hearsay risks.

This conclusion can be squared with FRE 801. The Rule says something is hearsay if offered to prove what it asserts, which makes expressive or communicative intent critical and means statements used to prove unmentioned points are not hearsay.[3]

Arguments *favoring* hearsay treatment stress that the assertive aspect is paramount whenever a statement lacks the performative aspect found in the mixed act-and-assertion cases. Under a sweeping view of communicative intent, no real line can be drawn between knowledge or beliefs and assertive intent. Such intent is not bounded by a bright line, but fades at the edges because it is humanly hard if not impossible to think with mathematical precision, or to find words that carry such precision, since language is rich but imprecise. At least the line cannot be drawn reliably, and it is possible that the speaker intended, after all, to assert the point for which his statement is offered. He too may have known enough about the circumstances to realize that his words suggest points not expressly mentioned.[4] In the end, it would be surprising if assertive intent were exact or could be exactly understood, and a court looking for intent must make a rough estimate about its scope.

Another reason to prefer hearsay treatment is that using a statement to prove unmentioned points often involves *first* taking it as proving what it asserts. Observer's comment that Nurse *N* was present during surgery might support an inference about Observer's unmentioned

Argument *for* hearsay treatment

---

3. Some argue that the ACN endorses nonhearsay treatment for assertions used in this way. It says "verbal conduct" that is assertive "but offered as a basis for inferring something other than the matter asserted" is excluded from hearsay, but we believe this comment is better read as referring to performative statements. *See* §§8.14 and 8.22, *supra*.

4. Seeking a test to measure assertive intent, one commentator argues that someone seeking to deceive conveys the false message with "enough clarity and credibility" to be understood and believed. He says we can distinguish between a point declarant did *not* seek to express and one that he did by asking whether, if we knew the point to be false, we would conclude that he was "necessarily lying or mistaken." Milich, Re-Examining Hearsay Under the Federal Rules: Some Method for the Madness, 39 Kan. L. Rev. 1 (1991). But the scope of expressive intent eludes a simple test. Do people seeking to deceive speak so clearly that one who knows the truth would conclude they were "lying or mistaken"?

thought that the surgery was (or was not) routine only if the statement is first taken as proof that Nurse *N* was actually in attendance. That suggests that using a statement to prove unmentioned ideas is hearsay because assertive purpose is crucial to the desired inference after all, at least in the absence of significant performative aspects.

Yet another reason to prefer hearsay treatment is that a statement offered in support of the two-step inference brings hearsay risks. All such inferences rely on the perceptions and memory of the speaker. Risks of candor cannot be vanquished despite the fact that the statement is not offered to prove what it says on its face and even if the speaker did not intend to communicate the point that the statement is offered to prove. A lie or mistake on the point asserted could lead to incorrect conclusions on other points, as would be true if Observer were lying or mistaken about Nurse *N*. And risks of verbal ambiguity are possible as well.

The conclusion preferring hearsay treatment can also be squared with FRE 801. The definition of hearsay reaches every statement taken as proof of whatever declarant *intended* to assert, and using this point to support further inferences does not take a statement outside the hearsay category.[5] Under a broad definition of intent, even unmentioned points in the mind of the speaker are within his communicative or expressive intent, and the same is true if the statement is taken to prove what it literally says on the way to drawing further inferences. And arguably the reference in the ACN to nonhearsay treatment for assertions "offered as a basis for inferring something other than the matter asserted" speaks not to ordinary statements, but to "verbal conduct" (to use the term in the ACN) that has important performative aspects (the mixed act-and-assertion cases).

Cases opting for hearsay treatment

Some cases treat statements as hearsay when offered to prove unmentioned points because the truth of what declarant asserts seems crucial. This fact seems salient where one describes her hopes or wishes and the statement supports an inference about unmentioned points *only* insofar as it truthfully describes what she wants.[6]

(1) Sweeping view of intent

Other cases that treat statements as hearsay when offered to prove unmentioned points seem to follow either of two approaches: The first adopts a sweeping view of expressive or interpretive intent, cutting through uncertainties by concluding that assertive intent reaches ideas below the surface. Twice the Supreme Court has taken this approach, in the *Krulewitch* and *Evans* cases.[7] In *Krulewitch*, the government charged two women and a man named Kay with offenses involving

---

5. *See* discussions of indirect assertions in §8.14, and assertions of circumstantially relevant facts in §8.15, *supra*.

6. Lyle v. Koehler, 720 F.2d 426 (6th Cir. 1983) (statements by co-offender asking friends to give false alibi testimony were hearsay; inference to guilty mind was not "severable" from "raw statements"); United States v. Melia, 691 F.2d 672, 675-677 (4th Cir. 1982) (statement by *F* suggesting that he and *M* take stolen jewelry to defendant to "see what price they could get" was hearsay, apparently because it invited an inference that defendant was a fence).

7. Krulewitch v. United States, 336 U.S. 440, 441-443 (1949); Dutton v. Evans, 400 U.S. 74 (1970).

interstate prostitution. The prosecutor showed that one woman asked the other whether she had talked yet, and said "it would be better for us two girls to take the blame than Kay" because "he couldn't stand to take it." The Court held the statement was hearsay when offered to prove Kay's guilt because it "plainly implied" as much. The Court understood the woman as *asserting* what was on her mind as she spoke (Kay was guilty), so she implied Kay's guilt in the strong sense (intentionally communicating it). Similarly in *Evans*, the Court treated as hearsay the statement of an incarcerated coconspirator that "if it hadn't been for that dirty son-of-a-bitch Alex Evans, we wouldn't be in this now," when offered to show Evans's guilt. Thirty five years later the Maryland Supreme Court also took this approach in the *Stoddard* case. There the outcome of an appeal from a murder conviction turned on whether a statement was hearsay. A small child, who had been with defendant Eric Stoddard when he assaulted another child (who later died from the beating), asked her mother whether Eric was "going to get me." The Maryland court concluded that the second child's question was hearsay when offered to prove that Eric had beaten the first child because the words "impliedly" said that the second child had seen Eric beat the victim.[8]

The second approach of courts opting for hearsay treatment accepts a more focused view of expressive or communicative intent, but applies the hearsay doctrine broadly because of the underlying risks. Essentially this approach holds that a statement is hearsay when used to prove unmentioned points through the two-step inference. In the *Reynolds* case, one codefendant told arresting officers in the presence of the other, "I didn't tell them anything about you." The Third Circuit concluded that the statement was hearsay because probative worth depended on "the truth of an assumed fact it implie[d],"[9] accepting the notion that a statement reveals thoughts that the declarant did not intend to assert, but treating them as hearsay anyway.[10]

(2) Focus on risks

Many cases admit statements mentioning names, when offered to prove that the speaker or named people are associated or linked to some place or thing. The cases adopt a focused view of intent by concluding that the point asserted is *not* the connection or association that the statement is offered to prove. A dramatic example is the decision in the *Day* case, where the government charged robbers named Day and Sheffey with murdering Williams (who had been involved with them in a crime spree) and offered testimony by Mason that a few hours before his death Williams gave him a slip of paper that named defendants and set out their phone number ("Beanny, Eric, 635-3135"),

Cases opting for nonhearsay treatment

8. Stoddard v. State, 887 A.2d 564, 581 (Md. 2005) (child J's question "is Eric going to get me" was hearsay; the words "impliedly communicated that [J] had witnessed [defendant] assaulting" C; whether utterance is hearsay does not depend on form; question was unreliable) (citing authors of this Treatise).

9. United States v. Reynolds, 715 F.2d 99, 103 (3d Cir. 1983).

10. *See also* United States v. Day, 591 F.2d 861, 883 (D.C. Cir. 1978) (cannot admit statement by murder victim *W* telling witness to call police if anything happens and giving names; it was a prophecy, which jury would use to infer "prior harmful acts or threats"), *cert. denied*, 455 U.S. 922.

instructing Mason to "call the police" if anything happened and "give them the names on this slip." The reviewing court thought the oral instructions were hearsay, but not the paper because it asserted that defendants "might have a particular telephone number" but was offered only to prove "current association" between them and Williams.[11]

Similar to *Day* are cases approving use of written documents to connect named people with each other[12] or with places or institutions or physical objects, and often the desired link seems confirmed or reinforced by physical facts (where the document is found in relation to the objects or people to be linked together).[13] Hotel registrations present a special challenge that we consider in connection with business records.[14] Items like sales receipts should be viewed as hearsay if offered to prove the address or name or phone number of the purchaser.[15] If documents referring to people are nonhearsay when offered to prove such links or association, arguably the same logic reaches oral statements referring to people by name, and some courts accord nonhearsay treatment in this setting as well.[16]

What is most striking about these cases is that they approve nonhearsay treatment of statements to prove only the most limited point—some link or association connecting people to each other or to something or some place. As explanations of hearsay, the cases are less than satisfying. While the apparent expressive or communicative intent behind the phrases in question was probably not to establish the link or association, most of the statements prove the point most obviously by proving what they assert. In *Day*, the names on the piece of paper amounted to assertions by the victim that he knew the defendants, and in the setting in which he gave the paper to his friend, the message on the paper was part and parcel of the oral message that the court called hearsay (these people might kill me). Title papers and sales receipts prove association between named people and objects because they assert title or purchase,

11. United States v. Day, 591 F.2d 861, 883-885 (D.C. Cir. 1978) (admit statements that are neutral and neither prejudicial nor assertive of complicity "to show association"), *cert. denied*, 455 U.S. 922.

12. United States v. Chavez, 229 F.3d 946, 953 (10th Cir. 2000) (paper with phone number and name); United States v. Cicero, 22 F.3d 1156, 1163 (D.C. Cir. 1994) (business cards); United States v. McIntytre, 997 F.2d 687, 702-704 (receipts), *cert. denied*, 510 U.S. 1063.

13. United States v. Serrano, 434 F.3d 1003, 1004-1005 (7th Cir. 2006) (admitting insurance cards, declarations and related correspondence with defendant's name on them, found in house and trash at 4506 Spatz Avenue, to prove he lived there); United States v. David, 96 F.3d 1477, 1479-1481 (D.C. Cir. 1996) (pager records); United States v. Jackson, 51 F.3d 646, 654 (7th Cir. 1995) (receipts); United States v. Patrick, 959 F.2d 991, 999-1000 (D.C. Cir. 1992) (sales receipt); United States v. Ashby, 864 F.2d 690, 693 (10th Cir. 1988) (title papers).

14. *See* discussion of FRE 803(6) in §8.46, *infra*.

15. *See* Bernadyn v. State, 887 A.2d 602, 607 (Md. 2005) (can't use medical bill at scene addressed to defendant with street number of the place; inadmissible hearsay when offered to prove he lived there).

16. United States v. Perez, 658 F.2d 654, 659-660 (9th Cir. 1981) (approving testimony by one who listened as friend talked to another by phone, describing the latter's "verbal conduct acknowledging that the caller" on the distant end was *R*).

and cases involving such documents would be sounder if they invoked exceptions for public records or business records. Letters prove connections among addressees by asserting that they can be found at the same place; they prove connection between sender and recipient by asserting that the one knows the other. And spoken words addressing others by name prove association by asserting that speaker knows listener.

Given the difficulties, it would be foolhardy to venture a detailed prescription, but a few suggestions may be useful. First, the hearsay doctrine cannot operate coherently if the problem of expressive intent is approached in a mechanical way. Perhaps some statements carry messages about the world that the speaker did not intend to express or communicate, but this possibility does not excuse a narrow or mechanical approach that ignores actual intent. Second, hearsay treatment is warranted when a statement tends to prove an unmentioned idea only if taken first as proof of what it asserts. Third, there is little room for nonhearsay treatment of statements offered for the two-step inference (statement suggests belief, which suggests act, event, or condition) in the absence of significant performative aspects.

Suggestions

Some commentators suggest broadening the definition of hearsay to reach every verbal expression to prove anything in the mind of the declarant.[17] But a broader definition might result in hearsay treatment for statements in the mixed act-and-assertion category, which would claim for the doctrine more than its due and would be inconsistent with the position that nonassertive conduct is not hearsay when offered for the two-step inference. And an amendment would introduce new and unforeseen complications where we already have too many.

D. PRIOR STATEMENTS BY TESTIFYING WITNESSES

FRE 801(d)(1)(A)

(d) **Statements which are not hearsay.** A statement is not hearsay if

(1) **Prior statement by witness.** The declarant testifies at the trial or hearing and is subject to cross-examination concerning the statement, and the statement is (A) inconsistent with the declarant's testimony, and was given under oath subject to the penalty of perjury at a trial, hearing, or other proceeding, or in a deposition. . . .

---

17. _See_ M. Graham, "Stickperson Hearsay": A Simplified Approach to Understanding the Rule Against Hearsay, 1982 U. Ill. L. Rev. 887, 921 (definition should reach statement whose relevance depends on being taken as proof of declarant's belief in "truth or falsity" of matter asserted); Wellborn, The Definition of Hearsay in the Federal Rules of Evidence, 61 Tex. L. Rev. 49, 92 (1982) (statement offered to prove declarant's "belief in a matter"). _But see_ Park, _supra_ note 2, at 829 (could reach verbal expressions whose probative value depends on declarant's credibility, but amending FRE 801 would be unwise).

§8.24 Prior Inconsistent Statements

Under three conditions, FRE 801(d)(1)(A) paves the way for substantive use of a prior inconsistent statement by a testifying witness: The statement must be inconsistent with his later trial testimony, must have been made in a proceeding or deposition where he was under oath subject to the penalty of perjury, and the speaker must be subject to cross-examination on his earlier statement.

This provision is tied to impeachment, for the framers wanted to block general or sweeping substantive use of prior statements. In reaching only some inconsistent statements, FRE 801(d)(1)(A) limits the times when the trial safeguards are called on to help appraise statements given out of court. This limiting notion connects with another purpose, which is to help prosecutors deal with turncoat witnesses. The ACN and congressional reports cite pre-Rules cases dealing with turncoat government witnesses. And government witnesses are the ones most likely to make pretrial statements covered by the Rule: Only they testify in grand jury proceedings, and often only they testify in preliminary hearings. Other factors peculiar to government witnesses—being implicated in crimes, anxious to help themselves by promising to testify, yet faced with the humanly hard task of later helping convict a defendant—make the exception especially useful to prosecutors.

Inconsistency: In general Obviously FRE 801(d)(1)(A) does not authorize substantive use of a statement that is entirely consistent with testimony. Just as clearly, the requirement is satisfied if a statement diametrically opposes or directly contradicts what the witness says at trial.

Far less in the way of inconsistency is enough. The requirement is satisfied if a statement conflicts by implication with testimony, as happens if one is particular and the other general in ways that put the two in tension, or if one includes a point that the other omits, if one is pointed and specific while the other is qualified and general, or if one is categorical and the other uncertain. In such cases the prior statement has impeaching effect because the apparent shift suggests a change in view or a mistake. Assuming the shift matters because it relates to points that count or suggests reasons to doubt the witness, the prior statement should be viewed as inconsistent.[1]

Inconsistency: Claimed lack of memory A prior positive statement should be viewed as inconsistent with a claimed lack of memory at trial. In a sense this result seems strange, since forgetting is a universal experience that does not necessarily suggest dissembling or mistake. There is no literal tension between a positive statement and a later claim of lack of memory, and a factfinder might reasonably believe and fully credit both the statement and the claimed lack of memory. In fact, however, apparent changes in knowledge or memory are likely to mask mistakes or changes of view. In the setting of the turncoat government witness who seems to know

§8.24 1. United States v. Matlock, 109 F.3d 1313, 1319 (8th Cir. 1997) (evasive answers, inability to remember, silence, changes of position).

something and merely to be pretending not to know, it is often plausible to suppose that he seeks to cast doubt on prior positive claims and avoid giving evidence that sends another to jail out of simple reluctance to bring trouble, regret at being the means to convict a friend or acquaintance, or fear of retribution. Other explanations may suggest themselves, including genuine doubt about what happened or recognition that a prior positive statement was false or exaggerated (perhaps because the witness was trying to improve his bargaining position). In the end, courts generally treat prior positive statements as inconsistent with claims at trial of lack of memory.

Sometimes claimed lack of memory seems feigned or dubious, and some discussions suggest that this element is important in finding the prior statement inconsistent.[2] (One pre-Rules decision even took the different tack of treating a false claim of lack of memory as a courtroom performance that verified the prior statement.[3]) But the question whether the inconsistency requirement can be satisfied by a true and credited claim of lack of memory is seldom put,[4] and some decisions refer to lapsed memory as inconsistent without saying whether the lapse must be feigned.[5]

Often prior statement and current testimony have common ground or tendency toward mutual reinforcement despite tension or conflict in meaning, which should not prevent use of the exception. Few witnesses change everything in their accounts, and contextual considerations embedded in the rule of completeness suggest admitting portions of a statement that are consistent with present testimony.[6] Still, it would distort FRE 801(d)(1)(A) to admit prior statements that differ from present testimony only on minor points of detail or wording, or to admit all of what was said before where only a severable part conflicts with present testimony.

To fit FRE 801(d)(1)(A), a statement must be made under oath subject to penalty of perjury at a trial, hearing, other proceeding, or deposition. Grand jury testimony satisfies this requirement.[7]

Made in hearing

---

2. United States v. Mornan, 413 F.3d 372, 379 (3d Cir. 2005) (lack of memory that is "not genuine"); State v. Amos, 658 N.W.2d 201 (Minn. 2003) (witness was "evasive and reluctant," so court could conclude that lack of memory was feigned); United States v. Knox, 124 F.3d 1360, 1363-1364 (10th Cir. 1997) (contrived or purposeful lack of memory).

3. United States v. Insana, 423 F.2d 1165 (2d Cir. 1970), *cert. denied*, 400 U.S. 841.

4. *Compare* United States v. Ragghianti, 560 F.2d 1376, 1380 (9th Cir. 1977) (inconsistent despite apparently genuine lack of memory, but usable only to impeach) *with* United States v. Palumbo, 639 F.2d 123, 128 n.6 (3d Cir. 1981) (excluding because lack of memory genuine), *cert. denied*, 454 U.S. 819.

5. United States v. Russell, 712 F.2d 1256, 1258 (8th Cir. 1983); United States v. Thompson, 708 F.2d 1294, 1301-1303 (8th Cir. 1983).

6. United States v. Distler, 671 F.2d 954, 957-959 (6th Cir. 1981), *cert. denied*, 454 U.S. 827. *See also* §§1.17-1.18, *supra*.

7. *See* State v. Gorman, 854 A.2d 1164, 1173 (Me. 2004), *cert. denied*, 544 U.S. 928; United States v. Jacoby, 955 F.2d 1527, 1539 (11th Cir. 1992); United States v. Orr, 864 F.2d 1505, 1509 (10th Cir. 1988).

So does testimony at a preliminary hearing, prior trial, or deposition.[8]

The terms "hearing" and "other proceeding" reach other contexts as well, and deciding what contexts are included should take into account the two purposes Congress had in mind. The first was to remove doubt that the prior statement was made.[9] Where a statement is made in a formal setting and is reported by shorthand notes (which may be reduced to a typewritten transcript) or recorded by electronic means, there can seldom be any real doubt that it was in fact made. The second purpose was to provide at least the minimal guarantees of truthfulness that an oath and the circumstance of a formalized proceeding tend to assure.[10] (Clearly, however, the prior statement need not have been subject to cross when made, for Congress was satisfied to rely on deferred cross at trial.)

Hence FRE 801(d)(1)(A) is not limited to statements made at some prior step in the proceedings in which they are offered. Statements in separate proceedings involving different parties and transactions seem equally to satisfy the two purposes. And the exception contemplates situations where an official verbatim record is routinely kept, stenographically or by electronic means, under legal authority. Without such a record, and the formalized procedures for making such a record which legal authority tends to assure, the certainty that the statement was made or accurately recorded substantially diminishes.

There is no reason to suppose the exception is limited to judicial proceedings.[11] Where a governmental agency or officer is authorized by law to put witnesses under oath and take their statements on the record, whether for purposes of adjudication, rulemaking, or investigation, it is reasonable to call such activities a "hearing" or "proceeding" for purposes of the exception.

Affidavits   It is uncertain whether the exception reaches a statement in an affidavit filed in a proceeding in a manner and on issues authorized by law. An affidavit too is a sworn statement, and sometimes it too subjects the maker to penalty of perjury. On the other hand, concluding that a statement in an affidavit was "given" at a hearing or proceeding stretches the exception. More importantly, the formalities that surround making an affidavit provide less assurance that a statement was in fact made and sworn to than the formalities that surround a firsthand appearance at an on-the-record proceeding. A possible middle ground is one that would admit an affidavit if the

---

8. United States v. Knox, 124 F.3d 1360, 1363-1364 (10th Cir. 1997) (plea hearing); Pope v. Savings Bank of Puget Sound, 850 F.2d 1345, 1356 (9th Cir. 1988) (deposition in unrelated proceeding); United States v. Smith, 776 F.2d 892, 897 (10th Cir. 1985) (prior trial).

9. *See* State v. Smith, 651 P.2d 207, 210 (Wash. 1982); House Report, at 13 ("there can be no dispute as to whether the prior statement was made").

10. House Report, at 13 (formal proceeding, oath, and opportunity for cross "provide firm additional assurances of the reliability of the prior statement").

11. United States v. Castro-Ayon, 537 F.2d 1055 (9th Cir. 1976) (recorded interrogation under oath at border crossing station), *cert. denied*, 429 U.S. 983.

witness admits in the proceedings where it is offered that he made and swore to it or the party against whom it is offered concedes its authenticity.

A stationhouse or streetside declaration to law enforcement agents, even in the form of a sworn affidavit, should lie outside FRE 801(d)(1)(A) because such statements are not given in "proceedings," but some states disagree on this point and admit such statements.[12] Gathering such a statement during an investigation does not generate a verbatim transcript, and investigations do not require the acquisition of sworn statements, so the process can hardly be classified as part of a "hearing" or "proceeding" under the Rule.

Declaration to enforcement agents

The speaker must be "subject to cross-examination" at trial "concerning" the statement, and the framers relied heavily on this requirement in allowing such a statement have substantive effect. The requirement envisions the situation in which the party offering the statement calls the speaker to the stand, examines her about the statement, and then introduces the statement, whether by offering a written version or getting the speaker to agree to the substance of a statement recited in questioning, and then tenders the witness to the other side for cross-examination. It does *not* envision what amounts to sandbagging tactics in which the party offering the statement calls the speaker but does not put questions on the statement, and introduces it in some other way, which would unfairly force the adverse party to broach the subject of the statement as an original matter.[13]

Cross presupposes a witness under oath, with demeanor observable by the trier of fact, so these additional safeguards are also available. This requirement means the speaker must testify and be cross-examinable, but witnesses who change their stories are often less than fully testable. Sometimes they have forgotten or refuse to answer questions about the acts, events, or conditions they described before, and sometimes they have forgotten the statements themselves. The exception does not require that full testing be possible, and the phrase "subject to cross-examination concerning the statement" seems to set both a sufficiency standard and a minimum.

Cross-examinable

12. United States v. Williams, 272 F.3d 845, 859 (7th Cir. 2001), *cert. denied*, 535 U.S. 947; United States v. Lloyd, 10 F.3d 1197, 1217 (6th Cir. 1993). *Contra* State v. Gorman, 854 A.2d 1164, 1173 (Me. 2004); State v. Smith, 651 P.2d 207 (Wash. 1982); Slavens v. State, 614 S.W.2d 529 (Ark. Ct. App. 1981).

13. Vaska v. State, 135 P.3d 1011, 1106 (Alaska 2006) (error to admit statements by five-year-old abuse victim, who testified only about experiences in fourth grade, age, birthday, and parents, and not about prior statement or abuse; state rule 801(d)(1)(A) requires that witness be "so examined while testifying" as to have a chance "to explain or deny" statement before she is excused; foundational requirements should be met before statement is admitted). *See* ACN (speaker may be cross-examined at trial); Senate Report, at 15-16 (speaker "is on the stand and can explain an earlier position and be cross-examined as to both").

It suffices if the speaker can be questioned about his statement, even if not about the acts, events, or conditions described in it.[14] There are strong reasons in policy to prefer this result. After all, an inability to get anywhere by questioning the speaker about the acts, events, or conditions does not prevent the factfinder from making a judgment about the reliability of a statement. Factors relating to veracity can be explored, including points bearing on the pressures to which he was subject when he spoke. And if the rule were otherwise the speaker could effectively control the use of his own prior statements.[15]

At a minimum, the witness must be testable about the statement, meaning reasonably responsive to questions on the circumstances in which he made it. A witness who stonewalls or remembers nothing about the situation in which he spoke cannot be adequately cross-examined.[16] In short, the cross-examination requirement should not be viewed as an empty formalism that can be satisfied by the mere fact that the witness is present and can be required to sit still long enough for questions to be put. Claims of lack of memory, refusals to answer, and denials of having made prior statements can effectively thwart cross-examination.[17]

Two factors seem most important in deciding whether the speaker is adequately cross-examinable: One is the extent to which the opposing party tries to delve into the circumstances and motives underlying the statement. The other is the extent to which answers shed light on those circumstances and motives. If real efforts to question the speaker prove unsuccessful in exposing those circumstances and motives, the cross-examination requirement has not been satisfied.

14. *See* United States v. Owens, 484 U.S. 554 (1988) (approving substantive use although witness could not remember event; applying exception for statements of identification); United States v. Keeter, 130 F.3d 297, 302 (7th Cir. 1997) (feigned amnesia did not block cross).

15. *See* United States v. Owens, 484 U.S. 554 (1988) (strange if one could avoid inconsistent prior testimony "by simply asserting lack of memory of the facts"); State v. Jaiman, 850 A.2d 984, 989 (R.I. 2004) (in murder trial, admitting co-offender M's statement to police and testimony at prior trial, although M lacked memory about events; cross-examination requirement was satisfied despite malfunctioning memory; cross was "extensive and damaging," bringing out terms of plea agreement, fact that he was the shooter, and "impeaching him extensively on his current inability to recall" basis of previous statements).

16. Farrell v. Wall, 889 A.2d 177, 189 (R.I. 2005) (in challenge to conviction, excluding videotaped recantation of testimony; witness invoked privilege against self-incrimination, so did not testify and was not subject to cross; recantation did not fit exception); United States v. Torrez-Ortega, 184 F.3d 1128, 1132-1134 (10th Cir. 1999) (cannot use grand jury testimony by V, who was not adequately cross-examinable; he did not "respond willingly," and made "obstinate and repeated" privilege claims despite immunity and being told that claims were invalid; he "could hardly have been less forthcoming" as he "refused to acknowledge" grand jury testimony; answers "too elliptical and confusing").

17. *See* United States v. DiCaro, 772 F.2d 1314, 1323-1325 & n.6 (7th Cir. 1985) (one who suffers "total memory lapse" on statement and contents cannot satisfy exception).

> **FRE 801(d)(1)(B)**
>
> **(d) Statements which are not hearsay.** A statement is not hearsay if
>
> **(1) Prior statement by witness.** The declarant testifies at the trial or hearing and is subject to cross-examination concerning the statement, and the statement is ... (B) consistent with the declarant's testimony and is offered to rebut an express or implied charge against the declarant of recent fabrication or improper influence or motive. ...

§8.25 Prior Consistent Statements

FRE 801(d)(1)(B) defines certain prior statements by testifying witnesses as "not hearsay." There are three elements in the definition: First, the statement must be consistent with present testimony by the speaker. Second, it must be admissible to rehabilitate him and must tend to rebut a charge of "recent fabrication or improper influence or motive." Third, he must be subject to cross-examination on the statement.

In one respect, this provision is broad: *Any* consistent statement, sworn or unsworn, oral or written, uttered in or out of court, may fit the exception. And a statement may be proved not merely on redirect examination, but by extrinsic evidence (writing, recording, or testimony by another), provided the speaker testifies and is subject to cross-examination on the statement.[1]

FRE 801(d)(1)(B) is tied to testifying and impeachment. A statement is not consistent with testimony that has not yet been given, so the exception does not apply before the speaker testifies. And testifying by itself is not enough—the exception does not simply enable parties to bolster testimony by piling on prior statements. The exception comes into play only after an impeaching attack, and the exception paves the way only for statements consistent with that part of the testimony that was attacked, although it may do no harm to admit a consistent statement in anticipation of an inevitable attack that later goes forward.[2] These limits express the view that use of remote statements should be limited, and that live testimony is better. Unlimited admissibility would further encourage or press lawyers to collect and offer remote statements. And opposing parties should have some

---

§8.25 1. United States v. Green, 258 F.3d 683, 691-692 (7th Cir. 2001) ("someone other than the declarant"); United States v. Montague, 958 F.2d 1094, 1097-1098 (D.C. Cir. 1992) (third-person).

2. United States v. Kenyon, 397 F.3d 1071, 1080 (8th Cir. 2005) (defense cross suggested that child made up two points in her story, which did not pave the way for testimony recounting child's statements on other points); Wilde v. State, 74 P.3d 699 (Wyo. 2003) (error to admit, during state's case-in-chief, minor's out-of-court accounts; merely testifying does not pave way to use exception) (reversing).

measure of control: The exception lets them choose between opening the door by engaging in impeachment or leaving it shut by refraining.

Consistency The consistency requirement lies at the heart of the exception. No doubt some statements are consistent by any reasonable definition: Trivial variations in wording should not matter, and the exception should reach a statement that repeats important parts of what the witness says at trial even if testimony provides more detail, as successive statements on a single subject inevitably vary.[3]

What seems important is that the exception should not be the means to prove new points not covered in testimony. The exception for inconsistent statements in FRE 801(d)(1)(A) is subject to the limit that they must have been given in proceedings under oath, and it contemplates that statements may prove points not contained in testimony. But FRE 801(d)(1)(B) is much more closely tied to testimony and more limited by the repair function. It seems harmless to admit a statement containing unimportant details not covered by testimony, but the exception should not let a party prove important details lying beyond that testimony merely because statement and testimony are consistent in general tenor.[4]

Attacks charging influence, fabrication A consistent statement fits FRE 801(d)(1)(B) only if it tends to rebut an express or implied charge of "recent fabrication or improper influence or motive." This requirement means there must be an attack raising one of these charges, which involves the court in interpreting what has happened.

Among the usual methods of impeachment, the one that most obviously raises such charges is impeachment for bias. Here the usual purpose is to suggest that the witness has a connection to a party or an interest in the outcome (improper influence or motive). The inference that the attacking party hopes the factfinder will draw is that the testimony is distorted or made up from whole cloth ("recent fabrication"). Sometimes the attacking party asks the witness directly whether he "made it all up" or openly suggests as much (recent fabrication), or openly suggests that the witness is bent on some purpose other than the truth (improper motive), or has succumbed to pressure or temptation by departing from it (improper influence). But sometimes the attack leaves these points below the surface and relies on innuendo or the suggestive force of questions or facts, in which case the charge is implied. When prior consistencies tend to refute such suggestions, they are admissible to repair any damage—it makes no difference whether the attack is express or implied.[5]

---

3. United States v. Vest, 842 F.2d 1319, 1328-1329 (1st Cir. 1988) (consistent statement "need not be identical in every detail"), *cert. denied*, 488 U.S. 965.

4. Lancaster v. State, 43 P.3d 80, 88-92 (Wyo. 2002) (exception should not pave way for statements making points not covered in testimony); United States v. Myers, 972 F.2d 1566, 1575 (11th Cir. 1992) (exclude parts that do not relate to matters on which speaker was impeached).

5. United States v. Londondio, 420 F.3d 777, 784-785 (8th Cir. 2005) (questioning witness about plea agreement suggested motive to lie, paving way for consistent statement); United States v. Montague, 958 F.2d 1094, 1096 (D.C. Cir. 1992) (cross suggested that witness hoped for clemency, which was "at least an implied charge" of motive or fabrication, paving way for consistent statement).

At least three other impeaching attacks sometimes raise similar charges of influence or motive. Impeachment by contradiction suggests the witness was wrong in his direct testimony, and such an attack can raise charges that bring the exception into play.[6] Sometimes impeachment by prior inconsistent statement raises such charges, thus inviting repair by means of prior consistent statement.[7] And attacks suggesting untruthful disposition (bad character for truth and veracity) can similarly suggest these charges, although impeachment showing lack of sensory or mental capacity is not likely to do so.

Other attacks charging influence, fabrication

Regardless which weapon is chosen, any attack might suggest other reasons to doubt the witness, like mistaken perception or judgment. Here prior consistent statements may not rebut or even relate to the attack. Often contradicting the witness suggests simply that he made a mistake in perception or judgment, and consistent statements do not rebut the inference. The same is often true of prior inconsistent statements, where the common observation is that proving prior consistent ones does not remove the doubt raised by the inconsistent statement.[8]

More important than the mechanism of attack is its apparent meaning. If that is in doubt, the judge may ask the attacking party to describe his purpose and require him to conform his closing remarks to that purpose.[9] The question whether an attack by prior inconsistent statements indicates fabrication, influence, or motive turns on the purpose of the attacker, the circumstances, and the interpretation put on them by the court.

Often consistent statements suggest that improper influence or motive does not explain the testimony, and that it is not mere recent fabrication: The witness said before the same thing he says now, and if the prior statement is not a product of the influence or motive suggested by the attack, it is evidence that the later testimony is also free of the taint and may be true after all.

Meeting the attack

Even assuming that an attack suggests influence, motive, or fabrication, however, *some* consistencies do not refute this suggestion, and may even confirm it. This fact accounts for a much-disputed traditional rule that only prior consistencies that came before the motive or influence took effect are admissible to repair credibility. Suppose Witness says on Monday that the blue car had the light in its favor at the time of the accident, that on Tuesday he meets and discusses the matter with Driver (operating blue car), that on Wednesday he repeats the observation, and that at trial he testifies the same way. If he is impeached by suggestions that he testified as he did because Driver bribed or threatened him, the consistent statement on Monday tends to rebut this attack by

6. United States v. Pena, 949 F.2d 751, 757 (5th Cir. 1991); United States v. Cherry, 938 F.2d 748, 755-756 (7th Cir. 1991).

7. United States v. Arias-Sandana, 964 F.2d 1262, 1265 (1st Cir. 1992); United States v. Khan, 821 F.2d 90, 94 (2d Cir. 1987).

8. United States v. Consolidated Packaging Corp., 575 F.2d 117, 130 (7th Cir. 1978).

9. United States v. Feldman, 711 F.2d 758, 766-767 (7th Cir. 1983), *cert. denied*, 464 U.S. 939.

suggesting that Witness did not shape his testimony because of his later talk with Driver (he held the same view before that). But the consistent statement on Wednesday does not have similar effect: It was made after the suggested motive or influence took hold and does not tend to refute the attack. Indeed, it tends to confirm the inference of motive or influence (Witness met Driver, then said he had the light).

Tome and the premotive requirement

In keeping with this tradition, the Supreme Court's decision in the *Tome* case holds that a prior consistent statement fits FRE 801(d)(1)(B) only if uttered before the supposed motive to fabricate arose. The case involved the trial of a man for abusing his four-year-old daughter AT, who was six at the time of trial. Allegedly the abuse occurred while AT was visiting defendant in New Mexico under a joint custody arrangement calling for her to spend part of the time with her mother in Colorado. AT testified, but mostly her testimony consisted of "one- and two-word answers" to leading questions, and cross was slow and difficult. The government adduced testimony by six witnesses describing seven statements in which AT said her father assaulted her, but the Supreme Court concluded that FRE 801(d)(1)(B) "embodies the common-law premotive requirement," and reversed the conviction. The Court commented that extensive use of such statements could shift "the whole emphasis" of trial from what is said in court to what was said before.[10] *Tome* leaves some doubt about the relationship between FRE 801(d)(1)(B) and the broader process of repairing credibility by prior consistent statements. The most likely reading of *Tome* is that consistent statements are only admissible, when the purpose is to refute claims of prior motive or fabrication, if made before the motive came into play, and then they can be used as substantive evidence.[11]

Probably neither *Tome* nor FRE 801(d)(1)(B) deals with consistent statements offered for other rehabilitating purposes. These include refuting a claim that testimony reflects only failed memory or showing

10. United States v. Tome, 513 U.S. 150, 158-160 (1995).

11. *Tome* might be read narrowly, to mean only that a consistent statement offered to refute claims of motive or fabrication cannot be used *as substantive evidence* unless the premotive requirement is satisfied, and some courts take this view. *See* State v. Bujan, 190 P.3d 1255 (Utah 2008) (consistent statements may be admitted, even if made after motive to fabricate arose, "for nonsubstantive purposes" that are rehabilitative). By this reading, *Tome* does not say whether a premotive requirement applies to consistent statements offered solely *to repair credibility*. This reading seems unlikely, since the premotive requirement addresses the repair function more than the hearsay issue. Or *Tome* might be read broadly, to mean prior consistencies *can only be admitted* if they refute claims of motive or fabrication, which would mean such statements could not be used to disprove attacks suggesting lack of memory, or to prove that other statements were not made or were not inconsistent. This reading too seems unlikely, since *Tome* seems to address only FRE 801(d)(1)(B). *See also* Richard Friedman, Prior Statements of a Witness: A Nettlesome Corner of the Hearsay Thicket, 1995 Supreme Court Review 277 (criticizing *Tome*).

that a prior inconsistent statement was not made or that it was not as inconsistent as it otherwise seems.[12]

Unfortunately the premotive rule is hard to apply, and prior to *Tome* many federal decisions had abandoned it.[13] The problem is that it is often hard or impossible to know when a particular motive or influence made itself felt. Unlike the Witness-Driver example, real-world facts are likely to be blurred, as might happen even in the example if Witness and Driver were longstanding acquaintances (it would be harder to know whether motive was rooted in prior acquaintance or sprang up after a particular encounter). And in criminal cases tracing the source of motives is so hard that courts often conclude that faithful application of the traditional rule would lead to blanket exclusion of prior consistencies: Usually government witnesses are implicated in the crime, and their statements are made to enforcement agents when they know they might be prosecuted (as part of bargaining). Defense witnesses too are often pressed to maintain solidarity with the defendant, or are related to or otherwise connected with him. Thus even consistencies uttered immediately after the crime may not qualify under the traditional rule, and yet it seems that such consistencies tend at least somewhat to refute claims that testimony is the product of improper motive or undue influence.[14]

The exception requires the speaker to be cross-examinable at trial on his prior consistent statement. Cross-examinability seems to mean the speaker must be reasonably responsive when questioned on the making of the statement, hence that the requirement is not satisfied if he refuses to answer questions or claims to have forgotten it. The requirement should not be viewed as an empty formalism. If both the testimony and the consistent statement relate to a critical point, and there is a possibility that the statement was given under suggestive circumstances affecting both the statement and the testimony, then responsive answers on cross are important in assessing both statement and testimony. But a statement that is unimportant as substantive evidence, or uttered in the absence of suggestive circumstances, is unlikely to have much damaging effect if it is so consistent with trial testimony that it repeats only the same points. Here cross-examinability may be adequate even without much cooperation.

Cross-examinability

---

12. *See* United States v. Simonelli, 237 F.3d 19, 25-28 (1st Cir. 2001), *cert. denied*, 122 S. Ct. 54; People v. Eppens, 979 P.2d 14, 20 (Colo. 1999). *See also* the discussion in §6.52, *supra*.

13. For a sampling of cases that had abandoned the restriction, *see* United States v. Payne, 944 F.2d 1458, 1471 (9th Cir. 1991); United States v. Farmer, 923 F.2d 1557, 1568 (11th Cir. 1991). For a sampling of cases that retained the restriction, see United States v. Cherry, 938 F.2d 748, 755-746 (7th Cir. 1991); United States v. Wood, 834 F.2d 1382, 1386 n.1 (8th Cir. 1987).

14. On government witnesses, *see* United States v. Ruiz, 249 F.3d 643, 647-648 (7th Cir. 2001); United States v. Montague, 958 F.2d 1094, 1097-1098 (D.C. Cir. 1992) (both approving consistencies by government witnesses). On defense witnesses, *see* United States v. Cherry, 938 F.2d 748, 755-756 (7th Cir. 1991) (admitting consistency by 13-year-old abuse victim, rejecting claim that she had motive to fabricate).

> **FRE 801(d)(1)(C)**
>
>   **(d) Statements which are not hearsay.** A statement is not hearsay if
>
>   **(1) Prior statement by witness.** The declarant testifies at the trial or hearing and is subject to cross-examination concerning the statement, and the statement is . . . (C) one of identification of a person made after perceiving the person. . . .

§8.26   Statements of Identification

A statement of identification of a person after "perceiving" him fits FRE 801(d)(1)(C) if the speaker testifies and is subject to cross-examination on the statement. The exception is important in criminal cases, and pretrial identifications are considered generally more reliable than those made in court. They are likely to come soon after the offense, and in-court identifications are suggestive because the witness knows the defendant is present and where he is. For these very reasons, jurors may discount such identifying testimony unless it is corroborated by prior identification. And the exception seems necessary for the prosecutor, who faces problems from delays in arrest, indictment, and trial. Memories fade, and defendants or others have the chance to try to get the witness to change her mind, sometimes by bribes or threats.

Wide range of circumstances
The exception reaches statements of identification made in a wide range of circumstances. In perhaps the typical case, the speaker saw the subject committing the crime and later sees him again and says "he's the one." Such a statement fits the exception, regardless whether made shortly after the crime or in a chance encounter with the subject much later,[1] or at a showup or lineup arranged by law enforcement agents or a court proceeding like a preliminary hearing.[2] The exception paves the way for a statement based on the speaker's firsthand observation of the subject committing the act followed by examination of a display of photographs[3] and identification made from a sketch, laying the

§8.26 1. United States v. Evans, 438 F.2d 162, 164-165 (D.C. Cir. 1971) (victim's identification of defendant on his arrest after chance encounter on street two weeks after crime), *cert. denied*, 402 U.S. 1010; United States v. Alexander, 430 F.2d 904, 905 (D.C. Cir. 1970) (description to police ten minutes after crime).

2. United States v. Hallman, 439 F.2d 603, 604 (D.C. Cir. 1971) (pretrial lineup identification); Clemons v. United States, 408 F.2d 1230, 1242 (D.C. Cir. 1968) (identification at preliminary hearing), *cert. denied*, 394 U.S. 964.

3. United States v. Simmons, 923 F.2d 934, 950 (2d Cir. 1991) (identification from 13-photo array); United States v. Di Tommaso, 817 F.2d 201, 212-214 (2d Cir. 1987) (statement identifying defendant from photos); United States v. Marchand, 564 F.2d 983, 996 (2d Cir. 1977) (exception does not require perception of subject in person at times of crime and identification), *cert. denied*, 434 U.S. 1015.

groundwork to admit the sketch itself.[4] If the identification is made from mugshots, they should be admitted only if there is a clear need (and not where identity is not seriously at issue), since they inject prejudice by suggesting a criminal record. Care should be taken to avoid drawing attention to the source or implications.[5]

There is no reason to think "perceiving" must be equated with "seeing" or even "direct sensory observation," or to read it as requiring the identifier to be brought into contact with the subject on a second occasion. Hence the following may fit the exception: Evidence that the identifier heard the voice of the culprit while the act was being committed (directly or by electronic means) and, on later hearing defendant's voice, said "he's the one"; evidence that after hearing a recording or seeing a film that captured the voice or features of the culprit, the identifier said on the basis of personal acquaintance "X is the one depicted"; evidence that the identifier, after seeing the act, said on the basis of personal acquaintance "the one who did it is X."[6] Obviously, however, the exception reaches only statements that have some basis in the personal experience of the identifier and not statements that simply repeat or reiterate what other remote sources have said.[7]

"Perceiving"

The exception does not depend on processes of impeachment or rehabilitation. If the identifier consistently points the finger at the defendant, his pretrial statements fit the exception and corroborate his live testimony. They can fit the exception even if they would not fit the one for consistent statements. And if the identifier waffles in court (from corruption, fear, desire not to help prosecutor, lapse of memory, or confusion from change in defendant's appearance), his prior identification can still fit the exception, and it does not matter whether it would fit the provision for inconsistent statements (which must be given under oath in proceedings).[8] Nor does it matter whether the speaker picks out someone else at trial or cannot say one way or another whether the accused is the one.[9]

The exception paves the way not only for testimony by an identifier describing his own pretrial identification, but also for testimony to the same effect by third persons to whom the identifier spoke.[10] Admitting testimony by a third person does not excuse the requirement that the

Third-person testimony

4. United States v. Moskowitz, 581 F.2d 14, 20-22 (2d Cir. 1978), *cert. denied*, 439 U.S. 871; United States v. Marchand, 564 F.2d 983, 996 (2d Cir. 1977), *cert. denied*, 434 U.S. 1015.

5. United States v. Hines, 955 F.2d 1449, 1455-1456 (11th Cir. 1992).

6. Culp v. State, 933 So.2d 264 (Miss. 2006) (victim's statement to police that she "left the Amigo Mart in a car with the same two men with whom he had seen her earlier"); United States v. Lopez, 271 F.3d 472, 484-485 (3d Cir. 2001) (witness statement to police one day after crime), *cert. denied*, 535 U.S. 908.

7. Hallums v. United States, 841 A.2d 1270, 1275 (D.C. Ct. App. 2004) (firsthand knowledge).

8. *See* Commonwealth v. Le, 828 N.E.2d 501, 503 (Mass. 2005) (approving identification even though witness denied making it).

9. United States v. Di Tommaso, 817 F.2d 201, 212-214 & n.15 (2d Cir. 1987) (photo identification; speaker could not identify at trial).

10. United States v. Brink, 39 F.3d 419, 422-424 (3d Cir. 1994).

identifier himself be cross-examinable on his statement. Paraphrasing, the exception requires the identifier to be subject to cross-examination "concerning the prior identifying statement" at trial, and this safeguard is fundamental. In the usual situation, the speaker can be questioned about the identification itself and about the statement. But a careful reading of the exception and a related provision suggest that the identifier need not be cross-examinable on the matter asserted in the statement: FRE 804(a) defines "unavailability as a witness" to include cases where one claims lack of memory or refuses to testify on the "subject matter" of a statement, so the framers had language at hand that would require the witness to be cross-examinable on the matter asserted (the "subject matter" of the statement), and apparently made an intentional choice to stop short of that.

Owens **case**   In the *Owens* case, the Supreme Court confirmed that the cross-examination requirement in FRE 801(d)(1)(C) is satisfied even if the speaker cannot (or will not) provide information about the underlying event.[11] It seems, however, that the cross-examination requirement sets at least a minimum standard requiring that the speaker be reasonably responsive when asked about the statement. *Owens* stops short of saying that mere physical presence of the speaker is enough, acknowledging that privilege claims might fatally "undermine" cross. In that case, the identifier suffered amnesia from a severe blow to the head during the crime, but was not completely unresponsive since he remembered saying Owens was his assailant and recalled knowing "why he had identified" him at the time.[12] Still *Owens* goes to the brink: Not much more than physical presence is required, and challenges to statements of identification based on arguments that the speaker was not forthcoming on cross face tough sledding.

If an identifier (such as the one in *Owens*) cannot remember making a prior statement, or says he never saw his assailant and his prior statement must have rested on something he was told afterwards, cross would be as much stifled as it is when the witness refuses to answer under a claim of privilege. The question whether the requirement is satisfied should turn mainly on two points: One is the extent to which the defense actually tries to delve into the circumstances and motives surrounding the prior statement. The other is the extent to which answers, whether framed as denials of having made the prior statement, claims of lack of memory about it, or refusal to answer questions, shed light on circumstances and motives. If a good-faith effort fails to expose these because of the uncooperative conduct of the witness, the cross-examination requirement should be deemed unsatisfied. But the

11. United States v. Owens, 484 U.S. 554 (1988) (exception designed for case where witness cannot "provide an in-court identification or testify about details of the events" underlying earlier identification).

12. United States v. Owens, 484 U.S. 554 (1988) (in hospital three weeks after assault, guard identified defendant from photo array in talking with FBI; at trial he "could not remember seeing his assailant" or remember hospital visitors other than FBI agent; defense suggested that he also attributed assault to someone else; claimed memory loss does not block required cross).

witness should not be allowed unilaterally to determine by his behavior the admissibility of his own statements.

Somewhat convoluted constitutional doctrines limit use of pretrial identifications obtained by police investigators in two ways: First, they are excludable if obtained in post-indictment lineups or similar proceedings where the defense right to counsel was improperly denied. Second, due process requires exclusion of identification statements gathered in settings that are unnecessarily suggestive unless emergency considerations justify the procedures followed. Sometimes these doctrines require exclusion of courtroom testimony as well.[13] Still, the _Crawford_ doctrine, which has lain at the heart of confrontation jurisprudence since 2004, does not generally impede the use of this exception, since it requires the declarant to be cross-examinable, and generally this face satisfies _Crawford._[14]

Constitutional limits

E. ADMISSIONS BY PARTY OPPONENTS

> **FRE 801(d)(2)(A)**
>
>> **(d) Statements which are not hearsay.** A statement is not hearsay if . . .
>>
>>> **(2) Admission by party opponent.** The statement is offered against a party and is (A) the party's own statement, in either an individual or a representative capacity. . . .

§8.27 Individual Admissions

FRE 801(d)(2)(A) creates what amounts to an exception for statements by a party when offered against him. The principle that the hearsay doctrine does not protect one against use of his own statement is a logical expression of the philosophy of the adversary system and is closely connected with the personal freedom and responsibility that are part of life in a free society: Parties bear the lion's share of responsibility for making or breaking their own cases, and lawsuits are focused inquiries into personal rights and social responsibility. These ideas make it reasonable to say that one cannot claim that his own statement should be excluded because it was not made under oath, or subject to cross-examination, or in view of the trier of fact.[1] Also important is the

---

13. 4 Mueller & Kirkpatrick, Federal Evidence §8:43 (3d ed. 2007); 2 LaFave & Israel, Criminal Procedure §§7.3-7.4 (3d ed. 2007).

14. _See_ Crawford v. Washington, 541 U.S. 36 (2004) (discussed in §8.88, _infra_).

§8.27 1. Many theories have been advanced. _See_ Park, The Rationale of Personal Admissions, 21 Ind. L. Rev. 509 (1988) (admissions bring no problems of surprise or unfettered discretion; concern over government power is answered in criminal cases by constitutional protections); Bein, Parties' Admissions, Agents' Admissions: Hearsay

fact that the party himself is present and can explain, deny, or rebut any such statement. Hence it seems fair to put a party at risk that the trier will accord full evidential force to his own statement unless he comes forward with explanation or counterproof, although in criminal cases this judgment is tempered by constitutional restrictions against using involuntary statements or drawing inferences from the failure of the accused to testify.

Almost infinite breadth

The exception has almost infinite breadth: It makes no difference whether a statement is written or spoken or in the form of nonverbal cues or word substitutes (pointing or nodding), and even an undelivered email can constitute an admission.[2] Statements qualify largely without regard to surrounding circumstances, and the exception reaches statements to police, testimony or pleas from other proceedings, recorded statements, and many others. Admissions include behavior with an assertive aspect, such as handing over an object on request, which in effect says the object is the item requested.[3]

Each statement in a conversation qualifies as an admission by the person who made it. When a speaker agrees with or incorporates remarks by others, the convention is to treat what the speaker said as a reiteration or endorsement of such other remarks, admitting them all under the adoptive admissions provision. Sometimes the situation is simply one in which understanding any one statement requires consideration of comments by others because each speaker seems to have in mind what others have said, and knowing about them helps the trier understand and interpret the various references in statements offered as admissions. In this case such other statements should be admitted as well, not to prove what they say but to aid the interpretive task.[4]

A party who denies making a statement cannot keep it out by objecting on this ground if the proponent presents sufficient proof to support a jury finding that the objecting party made the statement. Such an objection should succeed, however, if there is not sufficient evidence to support that finding. Also words that essentially parrot or repeat the very message that government regulations require or that an outsider forces the party to speak are not admissions by that party. However, requirements to disclose information and more general forms of coercion or pressure to speak or cooperate raise issues that are normally

---

Wolves in Sheep's Clothing, 12 Hofstra L. Rev. 393 (1984) (personal and representative admissions should be treated as hearsay but admitted unless doing so would defeat purposes of rules or interests of justice); Lev, The Law of Vicarious Admissions—An Estoppel, 26 U. Cin. L. Rev. 17 (1957) (estoppel); Strahorn, A Reconsideration of the Hearsay Rule and Admissions, 85 U. Pa. L. Rev. 484 (1937) (admissions as conduct).

2. United States v. Sprick, 233 F.3d 845, 855 (5th Cir. 2000) (undelivered e-mail); United States v. Abou-Saada, 785 F.2d 1, 9 (1st Cir. 1986) ("pointing to the second taxi driver"), *cert. denied*, 477 U.S. 908.

3. United States v. Morgan, 376 F.3d 1002, 1007 (9th Cir. 2004) (sworn statement in bankruptcy petition); United States v. Spiller, 261 F.3d 683, 690 (7th Cir. 2001) (drug ledgers in defendant's handwriting).

4. United States v. Walter, 434 F.3d 30, 3335 (1st Cir. 2006) (admitting recorded conversation between defendant and informant, whose statements provided context for defendant's).

resolved by reference to statutory and constitutional restrictions, and not by interpreting the admissions doctrine as having a protective purpose.[5]

There is no requirement of indicia of reliability. Nor is there any requirement that the statement be against interest when made, and a statement qualifies as an admission even if it exonerates the speaker or states claims or justifications (but are offered against him nonetheless).[6] Courts sometimes say admissions must conflict with the position taken by the speaker at trial, but this point has more to do with avoiding waste of time under FRE 403 than with the admissions doctrine.[7] It is mainly because of these points that admissions are considered "not hearsay" under FRE 801(d)(2) rather than "exceptions." The "true" exceptions defined in FRE 803 and 804 depend in part on various indicia of reliability and are not explainable in terms of the adversary system. **No reliability requirement**

Of course the fact that a statement fits FRE 801(d)(2)(A) does not ensure admissibility. It may still be excludable under exclusionary provisions such as the limits against proving prior bad acts in FRE 404-405 or statutory or constitutional restrictions.[8] Some states limit use of statements by accident victims, largely because of feared abuses by insurance investigators.[9] Admissions are also excludable under FRE 403 if probative worth is outweighed by risks of prejudice, confusion of issues, and so forth.[10] Fitting the exception only removes the hearsay barrier only when the statement is offered against the speaker, not when he offers it himself, although one's own statement may overcome a hearsay objection when offered against an opponent if the latter adopts it.[11]

Personal admissions are not ordinarily excludable on grounds that might apply if the speaker were giving live testimony. An admission is not, for example, excludable for lack of personal knowledge,[12] nor **Personal knowledge not required**

---

5. Lindsay v. Ortho Pharmaceutical Corp., 637 F.2d 87, 94 (2d Cir. 1980) (error to admit labeling changes required by FDA as "admissions" by defendant).

6. United States v. Reed, 227 F.3d 763, 769-770 (7th Cir. 2000); United States v. Barletta, 652 F.2d 218, 219 (1st Cir. 1981).

7. See O'Donnell v. Georgia Osteopathic Hosp., 748 F.2d 1543, 1548 n.6 (11th Cir. 1984) (must be contrary to trial position); Auto-Owners Ins. Co. v. Jensen, 667 F.2d 714, 722 (8th Cir. 1981) (same).

8. See United States v. Manafzadeh, 592 F.2d 81, 89 (2d Cir. 1979) (under FRE 404, should have excluded admission of criminal acts after charged crime). See also Miranda v. Arizona, 384 U.S. 436 (1966) (custodial statements during interrogation without warnings); Mincey v. Arizona, 437 U.S. 385 (1978) (involuntary confessions); 49 U.S.C. §504 (required accident report inadmissible in damage suit).

9. See Minn. Stat. Ann. §602.01 (statement taken from injured person within 30 days is presumed fraudulent in injury or wrongful death suit).

10. United States v. Singleterry, 29 F.3d 733, 739 (1st Cir. 1994), cert. denied, 513 U.S. 1038.

11. United States v. McDaniel, 545-546 (6th Cir. 2005); United States v. Palow, 777 F.2d 52, 56 (1st Cir. 1985), cert. denied, 475 U.S. 1052. See discussion of adoptive admissions in §8.29, infra.

12. United States v. Hernandez, 105 F.3d 1330, 1332 (9th Cir. 1996) (statement about birth despite lack of knowledge), cert. denied, 522 U.S. 890; Mahlandt v. Wild Canid Survival & Research Center, Inc., 588 F.2d 626, 629-630 (8th Cir. 1978) (statement by wolf keeper, although not present during incident).

because it is conclusory even though FRE 701 might require greater particularity by a testifying witness.[13]

Declarant not "bound"

Admitting a statement as a personal admission does not mean the declarant is conclusively "bound" by it. Admissions may be explained, rebutted, or denied in an effort to avoid or reduce their evidential effect.[14]

For purposes of this provision, it makes no difference whether the party spoke in his individual or in some representative capacity,[15] and if a decedent's estate is a party and its interests are represented by an administrator or executor, clearly the latter is a party for purposes of the personal admissions doctrine.[16]

Multiple party problem: Criminal cases

The personal admissions doctrine is sometimes complicated by the fact that multiple parties are involved: In a criminal trial of several defendants, a statement by one implicating himself and another by name or reference would qualify as the speaker's admission. Under the principle of limited admissibility, it might be expected that the statement would be admitted against him with instructions not to consider it against the other codefendant, but as a matter of constitutional law that course of action is impermissible.[17] And in this setting the personal admissions doctrine does not pave the way for statements by a defendant who drops from the case by entering a dispositive plea.[18] However, criminal defendant X cannot object when codefendant Y testifies to codefendant Z's statement (assuming it does not name or refer to X), although at least in theory the government may object.[19]

Multiple party problem: Civil cases

In a civil action against several defendants, one being the actor and others being allegedly responsible as employer or principal, a statement by the actor is admissible against him as his personal admission. If it does not fit the exceptions for authorized admissions or statements by agents or employees (or some other exception), normally it is admissible only against the speaker, subject to the right of others to

---

13. *See* ACN to FRE 801(d)(2) (admissions have long been free from "restrictive influences of the opinion rule"); United States v. Porter, 544 F.2d 936, 938 (8th Cir. 1976) (quoting ACN); Owens v. Atchison, T. & S.F. R. Co., 393 F.2d 77, 79 (5th Cir. 1968) (plaintiff said working conditions were "safe and proper"), *cert. denied*, 393 U.S. 855.

14. Grace United Methodist Church v. Cheyenne, 427 F.3d 775 (10th Cir. 2005) (admissions are only evidence, not conclusive); Murrey v. United States, 73 F.3d 1448, 1455 (7th Cir. 1996).

15. Re Special Federal Grand Jury Empanelled, 819 F.2d 56, 59 (3d Cir. 1987) (statement of defendant in capacity as corporate agent admissible against him); Onujiogu v. United States, 817 F.2d 3, 6 (1st Cir. 1987) (statement by mother who sued in her own right and as next friend of minor son).

16. Estate of Shafer v. Commissioner, 749 F.2d 1216, 1219 (6th Cir. 1984) (executor).

17. Bruton v. United States, 391 U.S. 123 (1968) (discussed in the next section).

18. United States v. Smith, 746 F.2d 1183, 1185 (6th Cir. 1984) (error to admit confession by a co-offender who pled guilty and was severed from case).

19. United States v. Horton, 847 F.2d 313, 324 (6th Cir. 1988) (rejecting argument by one defendant that only government could offer his admission); United States v. Palow, 777 F.2d 52, 56 (1st Cir. 1985) (admission by one defendant may be offered by another), *cert. denied*, 475 U.S. 1052.

800

instructions telling the jury not to consider the statement against them. If such a statement tends to show fault or liability by the speaker, probably it cannot be taken as evidence of these points against other defendants who are substantively responsible for what he has done. Some authority says the liability of the speaker shown by such a statement establishes the liability of his principal or employer "by operation of law,"[20] but other authority seems on better ground in rejecting this approach because each party is entitled to insist that evidence establishing its liability be admissible against it.[21]

§8.28 Spillover Confessions: *Bruton* Issues

In a criminal case where the government offers an admission or confession by one defendant implicating another, the conventional idea behind the doctrine of limited admissibility found in FRE 105 (admit but tell jury to ignore with respect to other parties) came to be seen as inadequate. The landmark case is the Court's 1968 decision in the *Bruton* case, which discarded the endorsement the Court had given to the practice of admitting statements by one codefendant implicating another with limiting instructions. In *Bruton*, one Evans told a postal inspector that he and Bruton committed armed robbery, and the Court concluded that the "basic premise" that a jury could disregard such a confession in assessing the guilt of another had been "repudiated" by a case holding that the judge must determine whether a confession is voluntary before submitting it to the jury, and by the amendment to the Criminal Rules authorizing severance where a defendant might be prejudiced by a joint trial.[1] Even "concededly clear instructions" telling the jury to disregard what Evans said in judging Bruton were not "an adequate substitute" for the constitutional right to cross-examine. *Bruton* means it is constitutional error to use the admissions doctrine to admit statements by one defendant that incriminate others by name or obvious reference.

20. Grayson v. Williams, 256 F.2d 61, 66-67 (10th Cir. 1958) (in suit against company and driver, the latter's statement on fault was admissible; liability imposed on company "by operation of law alone").

21. Branch v. Dempsey, 145 S.E.2d 395 (N.C. 1965) (in suit against truck owner and driver, statement by driver was admissible against him but not competent against owner).

§8.28 1. Bruton v. United States, 391 U.S. 123 (1968) (statement by one defendant that is devastating to another and untested by cross cannot be admitted with instruction; severance can protect rights of defendant). *And see* Jackson v. Denno, 378 U.S. 368 (1964) (defendant entitled to pretrial hearing question whether confession voluntary). *See generally* Bryant Richardson, Casting Light on the *Gray* Area: An Analysis of the Use of Neutral Pronouns in Non-Testifying Codefendant Redacted Confessions Under *Bruton, Richardson*, and *Gray*, 55 U. Miami. L. Rev. 826 (2001) (student note arguing for more complete protection); Christopher Mueller, Tales Out of School—Spillover Confessions and Against-Interest Statements Naming Others, 55 U. Miami. L. Rev. 929 (2001) (author replies and argues for middle ground); Bryant Richardson, Rebuttal, 55 U.Miami L. Rev. 969 (2001) (replying to Mueller).

The *Bruton* doctrine applies even where a statement by one codefendant "interlocks" with a statement by another. Thus a defendant whose own confession is consistent with references to him in statements by others can still object if such statements are admitted. The Court reached this conclusion in *Cruz v. New York*, where the trial court admitted a videotaped confession in which *B* said he along with defendant *E* and two others robbed a gas station, and that *B* killed the attendant after he drew a gun and wounded *E*. *E* too confessed his participation, mentioning that he scuffled with the attendant and that *B* shot him. The majority in *Cruz* rejected the argument that *B*'s videotaped confession was not devastating to *E*, reasoning that a confession by one defendant is "enormously damaging" to another if it "confirms, in all essential respects" the other's own confession.[2]

Does not name or allude   *Bruton* does not mean that individual admissions must be excluded from a criminal trial of several defendants. In the first place, *Bruton* is inapplicable to statements by one defendant that do not name or allude to another.[3] In *Richardson v. Marsh* the Court held that *Bruton* does not apply to a confession by one defendant that makes no reference to another even if it implicates the latter when other evidence links him to events that the statement describes. There Marsh and Williams were tried for assault and murder, and the court admitted a confession by Williams describing his own acts and those of a third participant, Martin, but the confession was edited ("redacted") to omit reference to Marsh or indeed any indication that anyone other than Martin and Williams did the crime. The Court approved, since the confession was not "incriminating on its face" and only became so when "linked with" other evidence in the form of testimony by Marsh herself (she described behavior by Williams and Martin in ways consistent with what Williams had said). When such linkage is necessary, the Court said, "it is a less valid generalization" that the jury will not comply with limiting instructions, and an instruction may well succeed.[4] *Marsh* means an admission by one of several defendants may come in with appropriate instruction even though it proves acts or events that are crucial in the larger case against others. The statement is still inadmissible against them, which suggests that to the extent it is crucial in proving an act that must be proved to convict another defendant, the latter is entitled to be dismissed. Otherwise, however, codefendants must be content with limiting instructions.

The *Bruton* problem   The *Bruton* problem may be accommodated in other ways. For instance, confrontation rights are not infringed by admitting a statement by one of several defendants who takes the stand and is available

---

2. Cruz v. New York, 481 U.S. 186, 192-193 (1987) (interlocking bears "inverse relationship" to devastation; one seeks to avoid confession, so another confession corroborating his harms him), rejecting Parker v. Randolph, 442 U.S. 62 (1979) (*Bruton* inapplicable to interlocking confessions) (plurality).

3. Richardson v. Marsh, 481 U.S. 200 (1987) ("calculus changes" when confessions do not name defendant); United States v. Curry, 977 F.2d 1042, 1056 (7th Cir. 1992) (grand jury testimony "does not directly implicate" another, so *Bruton* does not apply).

4. Richardson v. Marsh, 481 U.S. 200, 208-209 (1987).

for cross-examination by others, regardless whether he admits making the statement[5] or denies making it,[6] and probably where he claims not to remember it.[7] There is some irony in this result because the statement is still inadmissible against others, so their chance to cross-examine amounts to an opportunity to pursue and perhaps seek to discredit or destroy a statement that is inadmissible against them. Other possibilities exist, including use of multiple juries so a statement that implicates a codefendant is not heard by the jury that decides his fate, and this approach occasionally works, but is at best inconvenient because most courtrooms are not built with this use in mind, and keeping the juries separate is logistically complicated.[8]

It follows that the prosecutor may use a statement by one codefendant to impeach him as a witness, since ordinarily the fact that he testifies means other defendants implicated by the statement may cross-examine its maker. And it seems to follow as well that a *Bruton* error is avoided (or obviated) if the government uses a statement by one of several codefendants during its case-in-chief and the speaker later testifies and can be cross-examined.[9]

In unusual cases, it may be possible to avoid *Bruton* problems by editing out references to one defendant in a statement by another ("redaction"). Originally the Supreme Court approved this practice and many cases supported it,[10] but in its 1998 decision in *Gray v. Maryland*, the Court changed course and held that redaction substituting an empty space or blank for an apparent reference to a codefendant was insufficient.[11] *Gray* is realistic in recognizing that redaction may fail to protect other defendants mentioned in the statement, which along

Gray case and redaction

---

5. La France v. Bohlinger, 499 F.2d 29, 32 (1st Cir. 1974) (witness acknowledged statement, denied truth and said he was threatened by officer), *cert. denied*, 419 U.S. 1080.

6. Nelson v. O'Neil, 402 U.S. 622 (1971) (codefendant testified, denied statement and testified "favorably" to defendant).

7. United States v. Insana, 423 F.2d 1165, 1168 (2d Cir. 1970) (admitting grand jury testimony by codefendant who pled guilty even though he could not remember facts), *cert. denied*, 400 U.S. 841.

8. State v. Lakin, 899 A. 2d 777, 788 (Me. 2006) (can try defendants together but exclude their statements, try them together before separate juries, or try them separately), *cert. denied*, 127 S. Ct. 558; State v. Prasertphong, 114 P.3d 828 (Ariz. 2005) (two-jury method), *cert. denied*, 127 S. Ct. 558.

9. Nelson v. O'Neil, 402 U.S. 622 (1971) (admitting statement by one codefendant implicating another; the former testified later and was subject to cross). *But see* United States v. Maddox, 492 F.2d 104, 108 (5th Cir. 1974) (statement should not have been admitted in government's case-in-chief, but became appropriate on cross to impeach), *cert. denied*, 419 U.S. 851.

10. *See* Richardson v. Marsh, 481 U.S. 200 (1987) (*Bruton* can be "complied with by redaction"); Bruton v. United States, 391 U.S. 123 (1968) (approving decisions requiring deletion of references to codefendants where practicable). *See also* United States v. Tapia, 59 F.3d 1137, 1141-1142 (11th Cir. 1995) (redacted confession read as first-person account), *cert. denied*, 516 U.S. 1001.

11. Gray v. Maryland, 523 U.S. 185 (1998) (confession indicating that "Me, [blank] and a few other guys" pursued victim did not comply with *Bruton;* confession still "directly accusatory" of codefendant).

with other testimony may lead jurors to conclude that allusions to others refer to those sitting at the defense table.[12] *Gray* leaves some room for redaction where it is clear that others participated in the crime who are not before the court, and conceivably there may be more effective ways to edit out damaging references to codefendants. But extensive editing would be objectionable to the *speaker* if it changed the basic meaning of his statement (the phrase "Sam and I robbed the bank" could not be "redacted" to say "I robbed the bank"). *Gray* surely means that in most cases whole sentences naming or alluding to other defendants must be removed, or the prosecutor must accommodate *Bruton* in some other way.[13]

Bruton does not require exclusion of statements by co-offenders that fit other exceptions allowing statements to be used against persons other than the speaker.[14] Violations of the *Bruton* rule may be harmless error.[15]

FRE 801(d)(2)(B)

>   **(d) Statements which are not hearsay.** A statement is not hearsay if. . . .
>   **(2) Admission by party opponent.** The statement is offered against a party and is . . . (B) a statement of which the party has manifested an adoption or belief in its truth. . . .

---

§8.29   Adoptive Admissions

A statement is "not hearsay" under FRE 801(d)(2)(B) when offered against a party who "manifested his adoption or belief in its truth." Much of what was said about personal admissions applies here as well: This provision creates a hearsay exception; qualifying does not ensure admissibility if another rule, statute, or constitutional doctrine requires otherwise; a statement that fits the exception may be admitted

---

12. *See* Gray v. Maryland, 523 U.S. 185, 193 (1998) (such redaction "will not likely fool anyone," will encourage jury to speculate); Parker v. Randolph, 442 U.S. 62 (1979) (substituting "blank" or "another person" was ineffective; jurors could have had no doubt on identities); United States v. Hoover, 246 F.3d 1054, 1059 (7th Cir. 2001) (substituting terms "incarcerated leader" and "unincarcerated leader" did not suffice under *Gray*), *cert. denied*, 536 U.S. 958.

13. *See* Posey v. United States, 416 F.2d 545, 551 (5th Cir. 1969) (confession with more than one hundred deletions read to jury, which did not see altered written document), *cert. denied*, 397 U.S. 946.

14. United States v. Saks, 964 F.2d 1514, 1525 (5th Cir. 1992) (deposition fit agent admissions exception; no *Bruton* violation to use against other defendants); United States v. Vazquez, 857 F.2d 857, 864 (1st Cir. 1988) (no *Bruton* obstacle to use of excited utterance by one defendant against another).

15. Parker v. Randolph, 442 U.S. 62 (1979); Brown v. United States, 411 U.S. 223 (1973); Schneble v. Florida, 405 U.S. 427 (1972); Harrington v. California, 395 U.S. 250 (1969).

to prove what it asserts; it does not matter that it is more conclusory than would be allowed in live testimony; the adopted statement is not binding; it may be excluded out of concerns over probative worth versus prejudice.

Adoption is clear if a party agrees to or concurs in an oral statement by another,[1] or hears and repeats it,[2] or reads and signs a statement prepared by another.[3] And if one acts in compliance with a statement by another, such action can indicate adoption and may be a clear indication of adoption.[4] At least here it should make no difference whether the party against whom the statement is offered had personal knowledge of the matter asserted.[5]

Expressly agrees

There is no adoption if a party makes clear his disagreement with a statement spoken in his presence, although later disavowing a statement previously adopted does not remove it from the category of an adoptive admission.[6] Nor does adoption by one party convert a statement into the adoptive admission of others merely because they are on the same side of the suit.

Makes disagreement clear

So-called internal statements, such as one by an agent to his principal or an employee to his employer can be adopted by the principal or employer. Sometimes it is argued that internal statements should not be admissible against principals or employers, but the Advisory Committee rejected this argument, and it should be rejected when conduct indicates adoption.[7] The issue is one of evidence (not agency or respondeat superior) and the question is whether conduct justifies the conclusion that the party has made the statement his own, so it becomes fair to excuse the absence of oath, cross, and demeanor evidence. It is unimportant that the party did not anticipate that someday the statement would be introduced against him.

Where a party has elicited testimony from another in some prior proceeding, the question whether this testimony has been adopted

Eliciting prior testimony

---

§8.29   1. State v. Anderson, 111 P.3d 369, 381 (Ariz. 2005) (admitting statement about crime to which defendant replied "yeah, it was all premeditated"); United States v. Joshi, 896 F.2d 1303, 1311 (11th Cir. 1990) (defendant "nodded" and may have made "uh-hum sound").

2. United States v. Weaver, 565 F.2d 129, 135 (8th Cir. 1977), *cert. denied*, 434 U.S. 1074.

3. McQueeney v. Wilmington Trust Co., 779 F.2d 916, 930 (3d Cir. 1985) (sea service records bearing signature of plaintiff); Pillsbury Co. v. Cleaver-Brooks Div. of Aqua-Chem, Inc., 646 F.2d 1216, 1217-1218 & n.2 (8th Cir. 1981) (admitting accident report prepared by defendant; it contained statements by plaintiff's supervisor and boiler operator; supervisor signed each page).

4. United States v. Beckham, 968 F.2d 47, 50-53 (D.C. Cir. 1992) (actions by defendant endorsed *M*'s statement to officer *D*).

5. Pillsbury Co. v. Cleaver-Brooks Div. of Aqua-Chem, Inc., 646 F.2d 1216, 1218 n.2 (8th Cir. 1981) (fact that initialing supervisor did not know whether statements by plaintiff's boiler operator in report were true did not matter).

6. *See* Wade v. Lane, 189 F. Supp. 661, 665 (D. D.C. 1960), *aff'd*, 290 F.2d 387 (1961).

7. *See* ACN to FRE 801(d)(2)(C) (admissions doctrine embraces internal statements); Pilgrim v. Trustees of Tufts College, 118 F.3d 864, 870 (1st Cir. 1997) (college implemented changes from grievance report, which was adoption).

must be resolved by examining the circumstances. If the testimony is consistent with that of the party herself, or with the general tenor of the case she presented, it seems right to infer adoption.[8] This conclusion expands the admissibility of former testimony, since the proponent need not show the witness is unavailable (as the testimony exception would require). If the party against whom prior testimony is offered sought at the time to dissociate herself from it, introducing contradictory evidence, impeaching the witness or taking similar measures, adoption should not be inferred.[9]

Whether the adoptive admissions doctrine applies against the government admits of question. Some cases say yes and the outcome seems right if the person or institution whose behavior is said to adopt the statement is appropriate,[10] but this result is cast in doubt by a line of cases holding that the admissions doctrine generally does not apply against the government.[11]

Use of written statement In a variety of circumstances the use that a party makes of a written statement prepared by another or her response (or nonresponse) to a written statement prepared by another can indicate her adoption or belief in the truth of the statement. Where, for example, a party obtains the affidavit of another and offers it in a court proceeding in support of a motion or claim, or a request for a warrant, judgment, or court order, such conduct amounts to adoption.[12] Use at trial of an affidavit by a witness may waive any objection that the party offering it might otherwise have to the substantive use of same affidavit by the other side, a result that may be explained in terms of "opening the door," waiving objection, or adopting the substance of the affidavit. Likewise using written statements in various ways, as in efforts to qualify for a status, benefit, or privilege, or in seeking commercial advantage or publicity, where the one is expected to take care in making his presentation, as in applications for credit or loans, may reasonably be viewed as adoption.[13] Mere possession or physical proximity to a written

8. Fox v. Taylor Diving & Salvage Co., 694 F.2d 1349, 1354-1358 (5th Cir. 1983) (attorney did not question economist on status as onshore supervisory employee despite damaging effect; silent adoption).

9. Perricone v. Kansas City S.R. 630 F.2d 317, 321 (5th Cir. 1980) (railroad did not adopt testimony in prior suit arising out of accident at same crossing even though it called witness).

10. United States v. Warren, 42 F.3d 647, 655 (D.C. Cir. 1994) (affidavit attached to criminal complaint); United States v. GAF Corp., 928 F.2d 1253, 1258-1261 (2d Cir. 1991) (bill of particulars).

11. *See* the discussion in §8.32, *infra*.

12. Aluise v. Nationwide Mutual Fire Ins. Co., 625 S.E.2d 260, 267 (W. Va. 2005) (attaching property disclosure statement to complaint meant that plaintiff adopted it). *But see* Powers v. Coccia, 861 A.2d 466, 470 (R.I. 2004) (in tenant's suit for negligence in allowing bird mite infestation, excluding affidavit offered by owner in separate suit for return of deposit, reciting statements by pest control companies) (must show that adversary indicated "approval" of statement, but only showed that he "recounted" it in another suit).

13. Connecticut Mut. Life Ins. Co. v. Hillmon, 188 U.S. 208 (1903) (plaintiff used affidavit to impeach witness; defense could use it for all purposes); Alvord-Polk, Inc. v.

statement is usually *not* enough to show adoption, although these factors can count in finding adoption in some situations.[14]

Sometimes it is argued that failure by a party to reply to a letter from another indicates his adoption of the letter, but the bare facts of receipt and nonresponse do not show adoption. Not surprisingly, usually the author of the letter is the offering party at trial. In this situation the Supreme Court long ago held in no-nonsense language by Justice Holmes that the letter is not an admission by its recipient (one "cannot make evidence for himself by writing a letter containing the statements that he wishes to prove").[15] Nonresponse is insufficient to show that the recipient of a letter or other document adopted its contents.[16] Of course Holmes left open the possibility that "further circumstances" might change the result. And such circumstances are found in a business context if the recipient engaged in a continuing transaction or course of business with the sender, for here it is unlikely that the former would permit a letter to go unanswered if he disagreed on any significant point.[17] By this rationale, a statement of account from a supplier of goods or services to a customer of long standing, or to one who continues to engage in business with the sender, should be admissible as the customer's adoptive admission. The "further circumstances" mentioned by Holmes should also reach the case where a party engages in continuing correspondence with the sender, before and after receiving the letter, where this course of conduct suggests that the recipient would have taken issue with the letter if he had disagreed, and the matter asserted in the letter was within the recipient's personal knowledge.[18]

When faced with an outsider's oral statement offered under what is sometimes called (tongue in cheek) the "Cincinnati exception," judges

Failing to answer letter

Hearing oral statement

F. Schumacher & Co., 37 F.3d 996, 1005 n.6 (3d Cir. 1994) (articles in association publication); Wagstaff v. Protective Apparel Corp., 760 F.2d 1074, 1078 (10th Cir. 1985) (newspaper reprints defendants distributed).

14. *Compare* United States v. Pulido-Jacobo, 377 F.3d 1124, 1132 (10th Cir. 2004) (admitting receipt from wallet for custom car speakers; defendant kept it for two months; speakers were in trunk; possession is not enough, but "possession plus" allows inference of adoption), *cert. denied*, 543 U.S. 1030, *with* United States v. Mouzin, 785 F.2d 682, 692-693 (9th Cir. 1986) (error to admit ledger summarizing drug transactions; fact that it was found in C's residence was insufficient), *cert. denied*, 479 U.S. 985.

15. Leach & Co. v. Peirson, 275 U.S. 120 (1927).

16. Tober v. Graco Children's Products, Inc., 431 F.3d 572, 576 (7th Cir. 2005) (failure of maker of child's swing to reply to letter by insurer saying swing was defective did not adopt letter, which expressed preliminary finding and did not require remedial action or response); Ricciardi v. Children's Hosp. Medical Ctr., 811 F.2d 18, 24 & n.7 (1st Cir. 1987).

17. Megarry Bros., Inc. v. United States, 404 F.2d 479, 488 (8th Cir. 1968) (subcontractor's invoices during transaction involving substantial money, followed by payment and continuing correspondence without objection).

18. Boerner v. United States, 117 F.2d 387, 390-391 (2d Cir. 1941) (official demands in connection with missing items, where plaintiff admitted some charges and expressed hope that he "might find some way to clear himself"; failure to reply to detailed claims justified inference that he "had not found the way to clear himself"), *cert. denied*, 313 U.S. 587.

often ask, "Was the other party there?" This question is perhaps the first one to ask, but not the last, and mere listening presence or active participation in a conversation is not enough to show that one agrees with what someone else says.[19] The philosophy of the adversary system and the underlying notion of personal responsibility do not extend so far as to suggest that parties should be saddled with statements by outsiders to which they have a loose and uncertain connection.

Adoption of an oral statement turns on whether a party replied or otherwise spoke or acted in a manner showing agreement or, if she stood silent, whether circumstances suggest that silence conveys agreement. When a party in her own statements accepts or builds on the assertions of another, it is usually fair to say she adopted them, and in the modern world the advent of e-mail has expanded the possibilities of adopting what another has said.[20] If her own words assert the points to be proved but refer to or embrace ideas or terms in statements by others, it is usually sensible to proceed on a somewhat different theory: What others said is admissible not because she adopted or agreed, but because her own statement (what she herself said and meant) can be best understood in the context of what others said. If a party replies by way of rebuttal or disagreement to some points raised by another but ignores related points she heard the other make, these facts indicate her agreement with the latter points,[21] unless the omission is more readily explainable in some other way, such as familiarity with the points to which she replied as contrasted with lack of knowledge about points she did not address, or tedium or oversight in trying to take exception, or an effort to change the direction of the conversation or turn the occasion toward a more relaxed or respectful mood.[22]

Adoption by silence (tacit admissions)

When, in response to a statement spoken by another, a party does and says nothing indicating reaction, the question whether inaction and silence indicate adoption depends on the situation. At a minimum, it should be made to appear that (a) the party heard the statement, (b) the matter asserted was within his knowledge, and perhaps most importantly, (c) the occasion and nature of the statement were such that he would likely have replied if he did not mean to accept what was said. Even if these conditions be satisfied, the statement should be excluded

19. State v. Carlson, 808 P.2d 1002, 1006 (Or. 1991) (listening presence not enough); National Bank of North America v. Cinco Investors, Inc., 610 F.2d 89, 93-94 (2d Cir. 1979).

20. Sea-Land Service, Inc. v. Lozen International, LLC, 285 F.3d 808, 820-821 (9th Cir. 2002) (internal company e-mail; recipient adopted prior message by exclaiming in reply "Yikes, Pls note the rail screwed us up"); United States v. Robinson, 275 F.3d 371, 383-384 (4th Cir. 2001) (conversations among defendants describing killing), *cert. denied*, 122 S. Ct. 1581; United States v. Allen, 10 F.3d 405, 413 (7th Cir. 1993) (videotaped conversations).

21. United States v. Champion, 813 F.2d 1154, 1172 (11th Cir. 1987) (*G* told *S* not to drink so much, and *S* nudged *G* and told him not to speak about it any further; thus adopted *G*'s statement); United States v. King, 560 F.2d 122, 134-135 (2d Cir. 1977), *cert. denied*, 434 U.S. 925.

22. For express adoption, lack of knowledge should not matter, but lack of knowledge suggests a reason to doubt adoption in cases of silence or incomplete response.

if it appears that (d) the party did not understand the statement or
its significance, (e) some physical or psychological factor explains the
lack of reply, (f) the speaker was someone whom the party would
likely ignore, or (g) the silence came in response to questioning or
comments by a law enforcement officer (or perhaps another) during
custodial interrogation after *Miranda* warnings have been (or should
have been) given (a subject taken up in the next section).[23]

Where a statement relates to one's performance of an obligation or
duty, or suggests obligation or responsibility (or breach), or charges a
criminal act, or indicates some other fact that one would normally deny
or refute if incorrect in order to protect one's interests, the nature of
the statement suggests that silence or nonresponse means adoption,
particularly if the occasion seems to invite a response.[24]

In contrast to such cases is one in which five people were arrested
on drug charges on a moored freighter after being seen dragging
four bales of what turned out to be marijuana along an unlighted
deck. While all five were standing in line after arrest, the one next
to defendant Flecha said in Spanish, apparently to Flecha, "Why
so much excitement? If we are caught, we are caught." On these
facts, the statement was not an adoptive admission by Flecha, for it
was not made under circumstances naturally calling for a reply if he
did not intend to admit it.[25] The circumstances (arrest on a criminal
charge) and nature of the statement (asserting an obvious fait accompli) point to the conclusion that silence lacked meaning, as is often
the case.[26]

23. State v. Gomez, 848 A.2d 221, 236 (R.I. 2004) (consider whether statement was
"incriminating or accusatory," whether it was one to which an innocent would reply,
whether made "within the presence and hearing" of defendant, whether he "understood the meaning" and had "opportunity to deny or reply"); Weston-Smith v. Cooley
Dickinson Hospital, Inc., 282 F.3d 60, 67-68 (1st Cir. 2002) (listing factors bearing on
whether a listening party adopts another's statement).

24. Rogers v. State, 928 So.2d 831 (Miss. 2006) (admitting conversation between
pastors in presence of defendant reciting his admission of committing rape; he "took
no action to deny"); United States v. Alker, 255 F.2d 851, 852-853 (3d Cir. 1958)
(witness described meeting defendant in decedent's office with beneficiaries of will;
defendant removed contents of safe, saying each bundle contained $500, but another
said "No, $5,000"; purpose was to inventory safe in presence of legatees to obviate
dispute; inference of assent arose from "failure to challenge a substantial verbal
correction"), *cert. denied*, 358 U.S. 817.

25. United States v. Flecha, 539 F.2d 874, 876-877 (2d Cir. 1976) (arrested persons
know "silence is usually golden," and it would have been "risible" to deny being caught;
Flecha could have said "speak for yourself," but it was "far more natural to say
nothing").

26. Fuson v. Jago, 773 F.2d 55, 61 (6th Cir. 1985) (noncommittal shrug did not
adopt; defendant not expected to refute statements after being advised of right to
remain silent); Poole v. Perini, 659 F.2d 730, 733 (6th Cir. 1981) (detective played
recording of confessions by *H* and *R* implicating *P*; being silent while others confess
does not adopt), *cert. denied*, 455 U.S. 910.

Judge and jury

The question who should decide whether a party adopted a statement by another (judge or jury) is difficult.[27] Giving full responsibility to the judge means treating adoption as raising questions of "admissibility" under FRE 104(a). If the judge finds adoption, this approach leaves room for the parties to argue the issue to the jury and even offer evidence on the question. Involving the jury initially means treating adoption as a question of "conditional relevancy" under FRE 104(b), although the judge still "screens" the evidence and excludes the statement if a reasonable person could not find adoption.

No one solution seems to work well in all situations. For tacit admissions, the judge alone should decide whether the statement and situation are such that a party would probably dissent or object if he were not in agreement, for this question is one of basic relevancy.[28] Where an outsider's statement implies or openly asserts something harmful to the party against whom it is offered, whether framed as a question ("wasn't it you who robbed the bank?") or a flat claim ("I saw you rob the bank"), and where the statement implies (or circumstances leave room to suppose) the outsider knew something, it is unrealistic to involve the jury in deciding whether a silent party would have replied or an ambiguous reply was an adoption.[29] In theory, the outsider's comment is usable against the party only if he adopted it, but a jury would likely consider it regardless whether the jury thought the silent party agreed or acquiesced.[30] Here the judge should resolve not only these issues but others, such as whether the party heard the statement, or had a chance to reply, or whether some special fact stood in the way of reply.

Sometimes an outsider's statement offered as a tacit admission poses less threat of mischief. If the statement is framed simply as a query that does little or nothing to convey an opinion ("do you know who robbed the bank?"), or is framed as a demand for payment or claim of obligation rather than an assertion of fact, passing the adoption question to the jury poses little risk. Still the judge should decide whether the

---

27. *Compare* McCormick, Evidence §246 (1954) (judge) *with* McCormick, Evidence §269 (2d ed. 1972) (jury) *and* 2 McCormick, Evidence §§261-262 (6th ed. 2006) (most adoption issues are questions of conditional relevancy, such as whether party heard statement and had chance to reply, but "some" are for court; judge decides whether under circumstances innocent person would answer).

28. United States v. Moore, 522 F.2d 1068, 1074-1076 (9th Cir. 1975) (court decides whether innocent defendant would respond), *cert. denied*, 423 U.S. 1049; Arpan v. United States, 260 F.2d 649, 654-656 (8th Cir. 1958) (court decides whether circumstances call for reply) (jury decides whether defendant heard and understood statement).

29. *See* Garland & Schmitz, Of Judges and Juries: A Proposed Revision of Federal Rule of Evidence 104, 23 U.C. Davis L. Rev. 77, 98 (1989); Kaplan, Of Mabrus and Zorgs—An Essay in Honor of David Louisell, 66 Calif. L. Rev. 987, 1003 n.24 (1978) (better for judge to determine preliminary facts before jury could hear evidence); Kaus, All Power to the Jury—California's Democratic Evidence Code, 4 Loy. L.A. L. Rev. 233, 241-242 & n.33 (1971) (deciding admissibility of adoptive admission does not present "only a question of relevance").

30. State v. Carlson, 808 P.2d 1002, 1009 (Or. 1991) (if jury decides, it hears statement and might overlook adoption question or use statement regardless what it decides about adoption).

circumstances are such that the party against whom the statement is offered would probably dissent or object if she were not in agreement (the basic relevancy issue), but the jury can be trusted to decide whether she adopted the statement or whether her silence or ambiguous response is explainable by other factors. In this setting, the jury likely understands that probative force depends on the conduct of the party and is not likely to take the statement as proof of damaging facts unless it thinks she adopted it. In short, these issues fit the conditional relevancy category and should be handled under FRE 104(b).

The decisions are in disarray, and most are written as if one rule should apply across the board. The greater number hold that the judge should play the screening role contemplated in FRE 104(b), passing to the jury the question whether the party adopted the statement.[31] Often cases in this group comment that the judge should require the necessary foundational proof to be offered first to avoid the inevitable risks of jury misuse of the statement if the circumstance does not justify an inference of adoption.[32] A few cases invoke FRE 104(a) and require the judge to decide,[33] and some others confuse the issue by invoking FRE 104(a) but saying the judge plays only a screening function and passes ultimate responsibility to the jury.

§8.30   Silence by the Accused: *Miranda* Issues

The question whether silence or nonresponse by a criminal defendant amounts to a tacit admission is complicated if law enforcement officers are present. The answer comes from an interplay of evidential and constitutional concerns and depends on such factors as whether defendant was in custody, whether he got *Miranda* warnings, whether he replied to some points or stood entirely mute, and whether he was reacting to statements by cohorts or by law enforcement officers.

Where defendant is in custody and questioned by law enforcement officers and he stands mute or claims his privilege against self-incrimination, the Fifth Amendment precludes use of his silence as an adoptive admission. If he has gotten *Miranda* warnings, the result is required by the privilege and arguably due process,[1] and the Court

Custodial statements

---

31. United States v. Joshi, 896 F.2d 1303, 1311 (11th Cir. 1990); United States v. Jenkins, 779 F.2d 606, 612-613 & n.4 (11th Cir. 1986).

32. *See* United States v. Harrison, 296 F.3d 994, 1001 (10th Cir. 2002); United States v. Higgs, 353 F.3d 281, 309-310 (4th Cir. 2003).

33. State v. Carlson, 808 P.2d 1002, 1008 (Or. 1991); Naples v. United States, 344 F.2d 508, 509-511 (D.C. Cir. 1964); Skiskowski v. United States, 158 F.2d 177 (D.C. Cir. 1946), *cert. denied*, 330 U.S. 822.

§8.30   1. *See* Miranda v. Arizona, 384 U.S. 436 (1966) (cannot penalize defendant for exercising 5th Amendment privilege during custodial interrogation; prosecutor may not "use at trial the fact that he stood mute or claimed his privilege in the face of accusation"), citing Griffin v. California, 380 U.S. 609 (1965) (may not comment that defendant did not testify) and Malloy v. Hogan, 378 U.S. 1 (1964) (defendant may be silent and suffer no penalty). A person in custody cannot flee official accusation or questions, so

has said such silence is usually irrelevant.[2] If he did not get warnings, silence or nonresponsive answers in the face of official questions must be excluded unless safety concerns or other emergency justifies what is said to him.[3]

If a defendant in custody waives his rights after being warned, the question of adoption takes a different cast. One who waives his rights may reassert them without losing anything beyond what his statements have already cost him. Still, neither constitutional concerns nor sensible application of the notion of adoption bars evidence that in the midst of voluntary exchanges he failed to reply to incriminating suggestions if, under the circumstances, gaps in his replies suggest agreement with what others say. Of course gaps may signal fatigue, bewilderment, or change in attitude or strategy rather than agreement, but sometimes adoption is the more likely inference.[4]

Noncustodial statements If the defendant is not in custody, his silence in the face of accusatory statements or questions from law enforcement officers is problematic. Warnings are not required, but a defendant who stands mute or gives nonresponsive answers may be protecting himself by selecting the strategy that a warning (and lawyer) would suggest, not signaling agreement with what is said.[5] The constitutional picture is clouded: On the one hand, the privilege does more than create a right to be warned because it also prohibits use of silence in situations that create official

---

there is an obvious sense in which silence is "involuntary." *See* Brown v. Mississippi, 297 U.S. 278 (1936) (due process requires excluding involuntary confession); Mincey v. Arizona, 437 U.S. 385 (1978) (any use of involuntary statement denies due process). *See also* Doyle v. Ohio, 426 U.S. 610 (1976) (unfair to use for impeachment defendant's custodial post-warning silence, which warning makes "insolubly ambiguous").

2. United States v. Hale, 422 U.S. 171 (1975) (circumstances so intimidating that both innocent and guilty may stand mute; suspect may not have heard or understood, or may have felt no need to reply, so silence may indicate fear, unwillingness to incriminate another, or human response to hostile atmosphere).

3. *See* Miranda v. Arizona, 384 U.S. 436 (1966); United States v. Moore, 104 F.3d 377, 386-387 (D.C. Cir. 1997) (may not comment on post-arrest pre-warning silence; defendant did not testify, so impeachment wasn't involved). On the public safety or rescue exception, *see* New York v. Quarles, 467 U.S. 649 (1984) (officer arresting rape suspect asked where gun was; answer admissible despite lack of *Miranda* warning); 1 LaFave & Israel, Criminal Procedure §6.7, pp.506-507 (1984); Pizzi, The Privilege Against Self-Incrimination in a Rescue Situation, 76 J. Crim. L. & Criminology 567 (1985).

4. *See* Anderson v. Charles, 447 U.S. 404 (1980) (where defendant talks to officers after warnings and later testifies, evidence that earlier he did not advance explanation he offers at trial may be admitted to impeach); People v. Combs, 101 P.3d 1007 (Cal. 2004) (using co-offender P's accusatory remarks in presence of detective did not violate confrontation rights; these were adoptive admissions if defendant knew content and indicated adoption or belief in truth and if he was not relying on right of silence; his "direct admissions" confirmed truth of P's statements), *cert. denied*, 545 U.S. 1107.

5. *See* United States v. Flecha, 539 F.2d 874, 877 (2d Cir. 1976) ("many arrested persons know, without benefit of warnings, that silence is usually golden").

pressure to speak.[6] On the other hand, the Court has said the Constitution does not bar use of pre-warning silence to impeach the accused if he testifies.[7] These cases stop short of approving substantive use of silence: Impeachment is a lesser use, and testifying brings special need for leeway in testing credibility.[8] Yet the cases stress the role of warnings in limiting what prosecutors can offer and imply that there are few restrictions in the noncustodial setting. Finally, if the accused replies to some accusations or suggestive questions by officers but not to others, the gaps in his responses may signal agreement, and there is probably no constitutional obstacle to inferring adoption.[9] On balance, these indicators point toward the conclusion that noncustodial silence in the face of statements by law enforcement officers is fully usable.

Silence by the defendant within earshot of officials in the face of accusations or suggestive questions by friends or cohorts is probably admissible if the situation suggests adoption. If defendant is not in custody, such official presence does not block an inference of adoption or raise constitutional concerns, and the inference depends on whether silence suggests agreement under the circumstances.[10] If defendant is in custody, some cases suggest that silence in the face of *nonofficial* statements or questions cannot be admitted, at least if *Miranda* warnings were given.[11] But modern doctrine has tended to focus on active participation and pressure by officials,[12] and it may be that the adoptive

Questions by friends or cohorts

---

6. *See* Griffin v. California, 380 U.S. 609 (1965) (barring prosecutorial comment on fact that accused did not testify); United States v. Davenport, 929 F.2d 1169, 1174 (7th Cir. 1991) (proof of refusal to make statement to police in noncustodial setting violates privilege); United States ex rel. Savory v. Lane, 832 F.2d 1011, 1016-1017 (7th Cir. 1987) (refusal to talk to police; warnings provide "additional reason" to bar evidence, but are not necessary to conclusion).

7. *See* Fletcher v. Weir, 455 U.S. 603 (1982) (post-arrest pre-warning silence); Jenkins v. Anderson, 477 U.S. 231 (1980) (pre-arrest silence), discussed in §6.42, *supra*.

8. Doctrine sometimes turns on which use is made. Most cases involve silence that is probative when paired with positive testimony by the defendant rather than silence that is probative when paired with accusatory statements or questions by officials. *See* Harris v. New York, 401 U.S. 222 (1971) (failure to warn bars substantive use of custodial statements, but impeaching use is proper).

9. United States v. Davenport, 929 F.2d 1169, 1174 (7th Cir. 1991) (proof that defendant refused to talk to police in noncustodial setting violates privilege, but not if she talks and declines to answer followup questions even if agent tells her she does not have to; testifying opens her to cross because privilege does not protect attempts to gain advantage by selective disclosure; agent could testify to what she said, including refusals to answer).

10. United States v. Schaff, 948 F.2d 501, 505 (9th Cir. 1991) (in noncustodial search, officers found notebook and talked to defendant and his sister, who said she prepared them at his direction; her statement coupled with his silence were admissible, and not barred by *Doyle*).

11. United States v. Diaz, 936 F.2d 786, 788-789 (5th Cir. 1991) (government could not say silence after arrest and warning adopted statements by passengers in car telling agents they were there illegally; post-warning silence may not be construed against defendant, or right would be hollow).

12. *See* Illinois v. Perkins, 496 U.S. 292 (1990) (jail cell questioning by undercover agent produced incriminating answers; no warning required because *Miranda* forbids coercion rather than "strategic deception"); Arizona v. Mauro, 481 U.S. 520 (1987)

admissions doctrine *can* apply even here, especially if *Miranda* warnings were not recently given, which would undercut the inference that silence means adoption.[13]

> **FRE 801(d)(2)(C)**
>
>   **(d) Statements which are not hearsay.** A statement is not hearsay if . . .
>
>   **(2) Admission by party opponent.** The statement is offered against a party and is . . . (C) a statement by a person authorized by the party to make a statement concerning the subject . . . The contents of the statement may be considered but are not alone sufficient to establish the declarant's authority under subparagraph (C). . . .

§8.31 Authorized Admissions

FRE 801(d)(2)(C) creates an exception for a statement offered against a party and made by one whom the party authorized to speak for him—sometimes called a "speaking agent." Often such a statement is used as a nonhearsay verbal act that is relevant not as proof of what it asserts, but because the mere fact that it was made is important under circumstances in which substantive law says the statement affects rights or liabilities of the principal. The importance of FRE 801(d)(2)(C) is that it paves the way to use such a statement to prove what it asserts.

Anyone may be authorized   A party may authorize virtually anyone to speak—a spouse, parent, offspring, friend, business partner or associate, employee, attorney, broker, and so forth. The existence and limits of such authority are determined by agency law in light of conduct by the party and the speaker (including words spoken between them) and surrounding circumstances. Sometimes speaking authority exists even though not expressly conferred because the nature of the relationship and the task the speaker is to perform imply this result, as is true of attorneys, brokers, and employees with managerial or supervisory responsibilities,[1] and in other situations

---

(after warnings, defendant declined to talk and demanded counsel; officer openly recorded conversation with wife, where his responses to her desperation incriminated him; no *Miranda* violation because no interrogation).

13. United States v. Monks, 774 F.2d 945, 950-951 (9th Cir. 1985) (in holding cell, co-offender *M* said *H* might have been identified by camera; *H* had been responding to *M's* other questions, and one would expect *H* to respond if innocent; being in cell charged with crime does not mean silence is prudent).

§8.31 1. Grace United Methodist Church v. Cheyenne, 427 F.3d 775 (10th Cir. 2005) (church bishop); Shanklin v. Norfolk Southern Ry. Co., 369 F.3d 978, 990 (6th Cir. 2004) (railroad president); United States v. Amato, 356 F.3d 216, 219-220 (2d Cir. 2003) (defense counsel); Michaels v. Michaels, 767 F.2d 1185, 1201 (7th Cir. 1985) (company's broker).

as well.[2] But sometimes nothing in the relationship or circumstances implies speaking authority, as is true in marriage and other familial connections, friendship, and many kinds of employment, where speaking agency exists only if indicated expressly or by special circumstances.[3]

Typically the authority of a speaking agent is confined to certain subjects or times or settings, and statements outside these limits are beyond the exception, and occasionally other policy reasons cause exclusion of statements, even when made by authorized spkespeople.[4]

As amended in 1997, FRE 801(d)(2) allows a statement offered as an authorized admission to be "considered" as partial proof of the facts on which admissibility depends. But because of the circularity involved in using proffered evidence to prove its own admissibility, and a strong tradition requiring independent proof,[5] the amended Rule also provides that the statement itself is "not alone sufficient" to establish the predicate facts of agency and scope. Of course the judge determines whether these facts have been established (solely for the purpose of applying the exception) and the offering party bears the burden of proof,[6] and the same pattern is followed in connection with admissions by employees and coconspirator statements. A statement that fits another exception, such as the one for excited utterances, may be may be admitted to prove speaking authority, employment, agency, and scope. Other exceptions turn on factual predicates that can be established without depending on the statement itself, so using it to prove agency and scope does not involve bootstrapping.[7]

As the ACN makes clear, FRE 801(d)(2)(C) reaches "internal statements," meaning things said by a person with speaking authority in talking with the party against whom the statement is offered,[8] at

---

2. United States v. McLean-Davis, 785 F.2d 1534, 1536-1537 (11th Cir. 1986) (telex sent by rescuing freighter at request of shrimping vessel on which defendant served as crewman and translator).

3. Reid Bros. Logging Co. v. Ketchikan Pulp Co., 699 F.2d 1292, 1306-1307 (9th Cir. 1983) (company authorized employee of shareholder of parent corporation to do survey of operations), *cert. denied*, 464 U.S. 916; United States v. Shelton, 669 F.2d 446, 457 n.13 (7th Cir. 1982) (statements by salesmen were authorized by defendants and derived from sales pitch book), *cert. denied*, 456 U.S. 934.

4. United States v. Valencia, 826 F.2d 169, 172-174 (2d Cir. 1987) (excluding client's statements to lawyer, offered by prosecutor to prove that client lied; more important to protect lawyer-client relationship) (not deciding privilege issue); United States v. Iaconetti, 540 F.2d 574, 577-578 (2d Cir. 1976) (evidence that person whom defendant contacted told lawyer of solicitation was not authorized admission; cannot assume defendant authorized him to speak to lawyer about bribe), *cert. denied*, 429 U.S. 1041.

5. *See* United States v. Harris, 914 F.2d 927, 932 n.1 (7th Cir. 1990); United States v. Jones, 766 F.2d 412, 415 (9th Cir. 1985); United States v. Portsmouth Paving Corp., 694 F.2d 312, 321 (4th Cir. 1982).

6. American Eagle Ins. Co. v. Thompson, 85 F.3d 327, 333-334 (8th Cir. 1996); United States v. Flores, 679 F.2d 173, 178 (9th Cir. 1982).

7. Murphy Auto Parts Co. v. Ball, 249 F.2d 508, 511-512 (D.C. Cir. 1957) (driver's excited utterance that he was on errand for employer), *cert. denied*, 355 U.S. 932.

8. The ACN says FRE 801(d)(C) is "phrased broadly" to encompass statements "to third persons" and statements "by the agent to the principal." Communication to an outsider "has not generally been thought" essential for an admission.

least so long as the statement relates to matters within the speaker's authority.[9] Under some pre-Rules decisions, it was thought that authorizing a person to speak to outsiders implied no commitment to statements by the person to the party himself, and there is an analogy in the fact that respondeat superior does not apply to transactions between agent and principal.[10] The new approach represents a step forward: In the case of speaking agents, the notion of party responsibility justifies admitting statements and suggests no reason to draw the line at statements to the party himself.

Does not require personal knowledge

There is reason to suppose the authorized admissions doctrine does not require personal knowledge. If an agent is authorized in a specific way to make statements about facts ("the house was built in 1992"), it makes no difference that she has no actual knowledge and relays only what she has been told.

If an agent is authorized more generally to act on a matter ("sell the house") and she makes statements that are part of her task ("the house was built in 1992"), they are admissible in a suit arising out of the transaction when they are "verbal acts" amounting to representations or contract terms. Technically these are nonhearsay uses for which a hearsay exception is unnecessary. Should the authorized admissions doctrine apply to statements of the latter sort offered to prove the facts asserted? If the agent was not told to say what she said ("the house was built in 1992") but she takes it upon herself, and the setting is not a suit over the transaction where the statement is a contract term or representation, it is not so clear that it should be admissible against the principal to prove what it asserts (when house was built). There is broad language in the ACN saying lack of knowledge makes no difference, but the connection between the principal and the agent's statement does not justify admitting it.[11]

Civil pleadings, interrogatory answers

With three caveats noted below, pleadings and answers to interrogatories filed in a civil action on behalf of a party qualify as admissions by

---

9. Bostick Oil Co. v. Michelin Tire Corp., Commercial Div., 702 F.2d 1207, 1221 (4th Cir. 1983) (memorandum by manager for use of superior), *cert. denied,* 464 U.S. 894; Reid Bros. Logging Co. v. Ketchikan Pulp Co., 699 F.2d 1292, 1306-1307 & n.25 (9th Cir. 1983) (report on operations presented to committee and circulated in company), *cert. denied,* 464 U.S. 916.

10. *See* Restatement (Second) of Agency §287 and cmt. a (1958) (statements by agent to principal or another agent "are not admissible against the principal as admissions" but may be admissible under rules of evidence; principal does not intend such statements "to be given to the world or to be considered as his statements" and does not "vouch for their truth"). *See* Standard Oil Co. v. Moore, 251 F.2d 188, 218 (9th Cir. 1958), *cert. denied,* 356 U.S. 975; Nuttall v. Reading Co., 235 F.2d 546, 550 (3d Cir. 1956).

11. The suggestion relates to authorized admissions. Statements by an employee on matters within the scope of his authority are generally admitted against the employer under FRE 801(d)(2)(D). *See* §8.32, *infra. But see* ACN to FRE 801(d)(2) (admissions enjoy freedom from requirements like firsthand knowledge); Baughman v. Cooper-Jarrett, Inc., 530 F.2d 529, 532 (3d Cir. 1976) (admitting evidence that manager told plaintiff he could not be hired because word was out that he was blacklisted; giving reason was statement on subject on which manager was authorized to speak), *cert. denied,* 429 U.S. 825.

the party. Such documents are almost invariably prepared by counsel, and in federal practice counsel signs pleadings (although the client signs interrogatory answers), so it seems appropriate to view such documents as authorized admissions.[12] Of course pleadings and responses to requests for admissions operate as judicial admissions in the action in which they are filed. That means they narrow and define triable issues and are in a strong sense binding on the party. Where these documents operate, it is ordinarily unnecessary to offer or introduce evidence or even make arguments. But it is proper to read from or argue about pleadings filed by another party (with or without offering them) if the latter takes a position or offers evidence inconsistent with them.[13] Interrogatory answers, which are not treated as judicial admissions, may be offered in evidence against the party who made them.[14]

Where a pleading or response to request for admissions has been withdrawn or superseded, it no longer operates as a judicial admission, but this fact does not deprive it of all force as an evidential admission. An earlier pleading is still an ordinary admission.[15] Probably the same holds for responses to requests for admissions,[16] except that where a party is relieved of the effect of failing to respond to a request for admission, it has been suggested that the matter should "pass out of the case entirely."[17]

Prior pleadings in one action do not operate as judicial admissions in another, but they are usable as evidential admissions in other actions whether or not withdrawn or superseded, and interrogatory answers are similarly usable in other suits. Responses to requests for admissions get different treatment, apparently on the theory that they can be especially valuable in the action in which they are filed (they are judicial admissions that bind), and litigants would be discouraged from making them if they could be used in other suits, diminishing the utility of the

12. Oki America, Inc., v. Microtech Intl., Inc., 872 F.2d 312, 313 (9th Cir. 1989).

13. Barnes v. Owens-Corning Fiberglas Corp., 201 F.3d 815, 819 (6th Cir. 2000) (generally complaints are admissible against plaintiff); County of Hennepin v. AFG Indus., Inc., 726 F.2d 149, 153 (8th Cir. 1984) (county's claims against insurer and window maker contained in complaint, where inconsistent with county's position).

14. Wright v. Illinois Dept. of Corrections, 204 F.3d 727, 735 (7th Cir. 2000) (admissible but not binding); FRCP 33(b) (interrogatory answers usable "to the extent permitted by the rules of evidence").

15. Contractor Util. Sales Co. v. Certain-Teed Prods. Corp., 638 F.2d 1061, 1084-1085 (7th Cir. 1981) (can use plaintiff's original complaint, which was superseded by final complaint, offered by defendant); Wiseman v. Reposa, 463 F.2d 226, 227 (1st Cir. 1972) (can explore why original complaint alleged accident on one date and new complaint added another).

16. *See* Nicholson v. Bailey, 182 F. Supp. 509, 512 (S.D. Fla. 1960); United States v. Lemons, 125 F. Supp. 686, 689 (D. Ark. 1954).

17. *See* 8 Wright & Miller, Federal Practice and Procedure (Civil) §2264 (1980). *But see* Pickens v. Equitable Life Assur. Socy., 413 F.2d 1390, 1393-1394 (5th Cir. 1969) (court let withdrawn admission be used as "evidential admission").

device.[18] Limitations placed on voluntary stipulations should also foreclose their use in other suits.[19]

The caveats are as follows:

First, civil litigants are entitled to plead hypothetically, inconsistently, and in the alternative. Where variance between pleadings and interrogatory answers or evidence presented by a party is explainable as an attempt to take advantage of this liberality of modern pleading rules, using the pleading as an evidential admission should be disallowed.[20]

Second, where there is no real inconsistency between the position taken by the party at trial and his prior pleadings, interrogatory answers or admissions, evidence of the latter may be properly excluded under FRE 401-403 as irrelevant, confusing or misleading, or prejudicial.

Third, the party against whom any such document is offered is entitled to show, if he can, that it was filed without his authority. Ordinarily such a showing does not require exclusion, at least if it appears that the attorney who prepared it was in fact retained by the party in connection with the suit.[21]

Opening statements A Second Circuit decision of first impression in the *McKeon* case approved use against the defendant of an opening statement by his counsel in an earlier trial on the same charges, but the court sounded notes of caution.[22] While oral statements and argument by counsel fit the exception,[23] clearly caution is essential as the later decision in the *Valencia* case recognized in rejecting use against the defendant of a pretrial statement by his attorney to a government attorney. The statement had been made in an effort to gain release of the defendant on bail, and it said that his presence with a woman at meetings where she first arranged and then carried out a drug deal was entirely innocent (he simply encountered her the first time and tried to "pick her up," and accidentally met her again at a bus stop and offered her a ride). The government's theory was that the explanation was a false exculpatory

---

18. FRCP 36 says an admission is "for the purpose of the pending action only" and not for "any other purpose" and may not be used "in any other proceeding."

19. Seay v. International Assn. of Machinists, 360 F. Supp. 123, 124 (C.D. Cal. 1973) (voluntary stipulations expressly applicable to particular suit could not be admitted in different and unrelated suit).

20. Svege v. Mercedes-Benz Credit Corp., 329 F. Supp. 2d 285, (D. Conn. 2004) (complaints against defendants based on alternative theories are inadmissible against plaintiffs in view of provisions in FRCP allowing liberal and inconsistent pleadings).

21. *See* Kesmarki v. Kisling, 400 F.2d 97, 102 (6th Cir. 1968) (interrogatory answers may be excluded if party did not supply underlying information); Kunglig Jarnvagsstyrelsen v. Dexter & Carpenter, Inc., 32 F.2d 195, 198 (2d Cir. 1929) (objection that attorney did not have authority for prior pleading was clearly not sustainable), *cert. denied*, 280 U.S. 579.

22. United States v. McKeon, 738 F.2d 26, 31-34 (2d Cir. 1984) (must first decide prior statement is inconsistent; should consider distraction of marginal issues, plausible but prejudicial inferences, deterring counsel from vigorous advocacy, risk that explaining may force party to give up other rights, and risk that prior opening statement might lead to disqualifying lawyer).

23. Williams v. Union Carbide Corp., 790 F.2d 552, 555-556 (6th Cir. 1986) (statements by attorney admissible against client, including opening statements).

version indicating consciousness of guilt. In approving exclusion of this statement, the court stressed that (a) it was oral and made out of court, so it had to be proved by testimony that would generate a dispute on what was said, (b) admitting it would chill prospects of plea negotiations, and (c) the statement was not offered to impeach but for substantive purposes, so the justification was "far less substantial" than that in *McKeon*.[24]

Appellate briefs are also statements by lawyers on behalf of their clients. No doubt they differ from oral argument in court and from private conversations in the sense that they are closely confined in their factual content to the record generated at trial. But argument too is usually limited by the lawyer's perception of plausible interpretations of the evidence, and briefs (appellate and otherwise) advance contentions and positions of the parties, and they too suggest interpretations of evidence. Briefs merit the same sort of caution that the *McKeon* case advised for opening statements.[25]

Appellate briefs

Regardless what form they take, statements by counsel representing a client in proceedings are likely to be surrounded by procedural concerns and calculations that make interpretation problematic. When context suggests that such statements do not represent general concessions, as happens with statements that are in the nature of operating assumptions to be taken as true in resolving collateral issues (like jurisdiction, venue, choice of law, or service of process), those statements should not be admitted in a trial on the merits against the party on whose behalf they were made.[26]

FRE 801(d)(2)(D)

> **(d) Statements which are not hearsay.** A statement is not hearsay if . . .
>
> **(2) Admission by party opponent.** The statement is offered against a party and is . . . (D) a statement by the party's agent or servant concerning a matter within the scope of the agency or employment, made during the existence of the relationship. . . . The contents of the statement may be considered but are not alone sufficient to establish . . . the agency or employment relationship and scope thereof under subparagraph (D). . . .

---

24. United States v. Valencia, 826 F.2d 169, 172-174 (2d Cir. 1987) (judge has broad discretion).

25. Purgess v. Sharrock, 33 F.3d 134, 143-144 (2d Cir. 1994) (should have admitted statement from trial brief in related case).

26. Dartez v. Owens-Illinois, Inc., 910 F.2d 1291, 1294 (5th Cir. 1990) (posttrial briefs describe what record contains rather than facts, and context may indicate that statements should not be excluded).

§8.32 Admissions by Agents and Employees

FRE 801(d)(2)(D) creates an exception for a statement by a servant or agent of a party if made during the agency or employment, relating to a matter within its scope, when offered against the party.

Traditionally being an employee or agent did not make one's statements, even those relating to one's duties, admissible against the employer or principal because such status did not confer speaking authority. The classic case was one in which an employee described an accident, and the injured party sued and offered the statement against the employer. The statement was inadmissible. Traditionally statements by agents or employees to their principal or employer also were excluded because they were seen as "internal statements," meaning that in a sense they were not "statements" at all. Long ago courts started rejecting these limits, or got around them, sometimes finding that the employer had adopted such statements, sometimes admitting statements against the speaker and then using them against the employer "by operation of law" in suits based on respondeat superior, or by applying the excited utterance exception.[1]

"Speaking authority" is unnecessary   FRE 801(d)(2)(D) changed everything: The exception endorses the use against employers or principals of statements by employees or agents if the speaker himself is the tortfeasor. This change does more than add an evidentiary dimension to a principle of agency law, implementing the evidentiary judgment that "speaking authority" should not be necessary when a servant or agent speaks on a matter within the scope of his duties.[2] This judgment is also an expression of the philosophy of the adversary system: Suits assess legal responsibilities of the parties, who are responsible for making or breaking their cases during and before trial, which suggests that employers and principals should answer for statements by their servants and agents. If there *are* answers, employers and principals should have access to the relevant proof.

The notion of necessity also plays a role. Statements covered by FRE 801(d)(2)(D) are necessary because, to put it gently, they may provide the only means to get the actual knowledge of the declarant: With the passage of time, he is likely to come to a growing understanding of his own self-interest; his sympathy for the other side is likely to decrease; he is likely to feel pressure (real or imagined) from his principal or employer to avoid making evidence useful to the other side. Hence he is less likely to be candid and forthcoming in trial testimony.

---

§8.32   1. MCI Communications Corp. v. AT&T, 708 F.2d 1081, 1143 (7th Cir. 1983), *cert. denied*, 464 U.S. 891; Pekelis v. Transcontinental & Western Air, Inc., 187 F.2d 122, 128-129 (2d Cir. 1951), *cert. denied*, 341 U.S. 951.

2. Precision Piping v. E. I. Du Pont de Nemours, 951 F.2d 613, 619 (4th Cir. 1991) (Rule refers to "scope of employment," not specific authority to speak); Crawford v. Garnier, 719 F.2d 1317, 1324 (7th Cir. 1983) (agent "need not be specifically authorized" to speak).

Notions of trustworthiness have little to do with FRE 801(d)(2)(D). The proponent need not show a statement is trustworthy, nor can the adverse party exclude because indications of trustworthiness are missing.[3] Still, most statements admitted under this provision are likely to be trustworthy for reasons that help account for its breadth: First, someone who speaks about his duties during the course of his agency or employment is likely to speak carefully and not loosely, since what he says may put employment at risk (even make him subject to suit by his employer or principal). Second, a speaker describing such matters is likely to be well informed. Third, statements that fit the exception are likely to be against the interest of the speaker.[4]

The exception provides a basis to admit statements against the accused, which is significant when the speaker is an agent of the defendant but not a coconspirator (which would make another exception available).[5] FRE 801(d)(2)(D) is useful in prosecutions under economic or other regulatory statutes. At least where an individual defendant faces possible fine or imprisonment, there is some justification in construing the terms "servant" and "agent" more narrowly than in civil cases.

FRE 801(d)(2)(D) reaches "internal statements" by one agent or employee to another, or to the principal or employer, or to a superior in an organization.[6] Here at least, agency law does not count, and the exception embodies an evidential judgment that such statements should be admitted.

Internal statements

In an age of e-commerce and instant communication, admissions by agents or employees can take the form of e-mail messages. The automatically affixed electronic signature shows the identity of the sender, and of course the admissions doctrine (unlike the business records exception) does not require that statements be made in regular course of business. Hence the admissions doctrine provides a wide avenue for admitting e-mail messages. It makes no difference whether such messages are "internal" (sent by one agent or employee to another, or to the principal or higher-up in the organization), and the main requirement is that the speaker must be an agent whose statement relates to his responsibilities for his principal or employer.[7]

E-mail messages

---

3. United States v. Young, 736 F.2d 565, 568 (10th Cir. 1984) (admissions come in as matter of estoppel, not because reliable), *rev'd on other grounds,* 470 U.S. 1; United States v. Chappell, 698 F.2d 308, 312 (7th Cir. 1983), *cert. denied,* 461 U.S. 931.

4. *See* Nekolny v. Painter, 653 F.2d 1164, 1171-1172 (7th Cir. 1981).

5. United States v. Boling, 869 F.2d 965, 974 (6th Cir. 1989); United States v. Faymore, 736 F.2d 328, 334-335 (6th Cir. 1984), *cert. denied,* 469 U.S. 868.

6. Bostick Oil Co. v. Michelin Tire Corp., 702 F.2d 1207, 1221 (4th Cir. 1983) (memorandum by district manager for corporate superior), *cert. denied,* 464 U.S. 894.

7. Sea-Land Service, Inc. v. Lozen International, LLC, 285 F.3d 808, 820-821 (9th Cir. 2002) (admitting against plaintiff an internal company email containing electronic signature indicating that it was written by plaintiff's service coordinator, dealing with matter within his scope of employment; email was forwarded to defendant by another employee of plaintiff).

Agent or servant

    The exception embraces statements by an agent or servant, and these terms refer to people who would be described that way as a matter of substantive law. Oversimplifying slightly, an agent agrees to act for another in a specific matter, and a servant is an agent who is an employee with ongoing and broader responsibilities. Often a person fits both categories. It seems that the purpose in using the terms "agent" and "servant" was to reach two large groups: One consists of people whose conduct produces liability for their employers or principals, sometimes on the theory of respondeat superior where the conduct looks like a personal tort for which the company is also liable, and sometimes because the people are actors whose conduct contributes significantly to organizational liability.[8] The second category is comprised of people who are passive observers or bystanders rather than actors, but who make statements on matters within the scope of their duties.[9] People of this description are not always authorized spokespeople, and the reason to admit their statements is less compelling than the reasons to admit statements by liability-producing actors.

    In some ways, the terms "agent" and "servant" are puzzling because it is hard to know how much the exception borrows from substantive law.[10] Probably there is at least some borrowing,[11] and probably the framers meant to exclude statements by most independent contractors.[12] An independent contractor is usually not an employee or agent, and the big difference is that a principal or employer exercises less control. Largely for this reason, one who engages an independent contractor is not usually liable in tort for what the independent

---

    8. EEOC v. Watergate at Landmark Condominium, 24 F.3d 635, 638-640 (4th Cir. 1994) (age discrimination suit; statements by members of association and interview committees indicating intent to hire younger person); Mahlandt v. Wild Canid Survival & Research Center, Inc., 588 F.2d 626 (8th Cir. 1978) (statement by keeper of wolf that allegedly bit child).

    9. Yates v. Rexton, Inc., 267 F.3d 793, 2002 (8th Cir. 2001) (declarants were involved in shaping workforce; it didn't matter whether they actually decided to terminate plaintiff); Nekolny v. Painter, 653 F.2d 1164, 1171-1172 (7th Cir. 1981) (statements by liaison saying supervisor planned to fire plaintiffs because they campaigned for opponent); East Troy v. Soo Line R. Co., 653 F.2d 1123, 1133 (7th Cir. 1980) (discussion among railroad employees about excess derailments and placement of empty cars), *cert. denied*, 450 U.S. 922.

    10. Usually agent includes employees or servants as a matter of substantive law, which would make the term "servant" redundant. In substantive law, "agent" embraces independent contractors only sometimes. *See* Restatement (Second) of Agency §2 (1958).

    11. United States v. Wiedyk, 71 F.3d 602, 605-606 (6th Cir. 1995) (traditional master/servant relationship under common law agency doctrine); United States v. Saks, 964 F.2d 1514, 1523-1524 (5th Cir. 1992) (agent refers to "common law principles of agency").

    12. Powers v. Coccia, 861 A.2d 466, 470 (R.I. 2004) (in tenant's suit against landlord, admitting statement by "rooter" hired to remove blockage in pipes; rooter was independent contractor); Daniel v. Ben E. Keith Co., 97 F.3d 1329, 1335 (10th Cir. 1996) (excluding deposition by employee of separate company that assumed defense; even if law imposes liability for company's role in distribution, plaintiff may not circumvent required proof of agency).

contractor does.[13] But there are exceptions where a tort by an independent contractor does produce liability for the person who hired him,[14] and here arguably his statements fit the exception.[15] After all, it seems to have been a purpose of the framers to admit what is said by people whose conduct, if proved, produces liability for the party against whom the statement is offered.

A person who is an agent or employee of an organization may stand in the same relation toward his superiors, such as managers and division or department heads. If one has supervisory or day-to-day authority over other employees, their statements should be admissible against him.[16] But an employee should not be viewed as an agent or servant of everyone who is in some sense his superior in an organizational hierarchy (even if the chain of command runs to such superior). The notion of agency supposes that the person against whom a statement is offered has responsibility and authority actually to supervise or direct, and where a higher-up does not, the exception should not apply to make statements by the lower ranking person against the higher-up.[17]

Statements made before an employment or agency relationship begins, or after it ends, fall outside the exception.[18] And statements by one who is neither servant nor agent of a party cannot fit the exception.[19]

> **Statements before or after relationship**

To fit the exception, a statement must concern "a matter within the scope" of the speaker's agency or employment. This relational phrase is broad. There is no doubt it embraces a statement that describes the speaker's own behavior in performing his duties (whether well or

> **Matter within scope**

---

13. Hornbook law says physical conduct by an independent contractor is not controlled by the principal or subject to his right to control, so physical acts by independent contractor do not make principal liable for "tangible harm." Restatement (Second) of Agency §2 and cmt. b (1958).

14. *See* Richard A. Epstein, Torts §9.11 (1999) (vicarious liability does not apply to torts by independent contractors, but various doctrines, including one turning on "apparent authority" and one turning on "nondelegable duties," reduce the difference between agents and independent contractors and often allow liability to attach); Restatement (Second) of Torts §§409-429.

15. *See* United States v. Rioux (2d Cir. 1996) 97 F.3d 648, 660; Callon Petroleum Co. v. Big Chief Drilling Co., 548 F.2d 1174, 1177 n.3 (5th Cir. 1977).

16. *See* United States v. Agne, 214 F.3d 47, 54-55 (4th Cir. 2000) (in fraud trial admitting against owner *W* the statements of employee *R*; *W* had asked another to "work directly" with *R*, who was "directly responsible" to *W*), *cert. denied*, 531 U.S. 1037; Zaken v. Boerer, 964 F.2d 1319, 1322-1323 (2d Cir. 1992) (admitting against owner B a statement by company vice president *N*, who was "directly responsible" to *B*).

17. Boren v. Sable, 887 F.2d 1032, 1037-1038 (10th Cir. 1989) (excluding statements by shop foreman *B* and employee *R* offered against *S*, who had turned control of plant over to plaintiff; *S* did not control *B* so as to create agency; fact that *R* occupied "subordinate position" did not make him agent of *S*).

18. Blanchard v. Peoples Bank, 844 F.2d 264, 267 n.7 (5th Cir. 1988); United States v. Summers, 598 F.2d 450, 458-459 (5th Cir. 1979); SEC v. Geon Indus., Inc., 531 F.2d 39, 43 n.3 (2d Cir. 1976).

19. Belton v. Washington Metro. Area Transit Auth., 20 F.3d 1197, 1201-1202 (D.C. Cir. 1994) (bystander statement not admissible against bus company, but driver's is); New York v. Pullman, Inc., 662 F.2d 910, 915 n.6 (2d Cir. 1981) (funding did not make federal agency an agent of state agency).

badly).[20] The phrase also reaches (a) an account of activities by another person and appraisals of the work of the other if the speaker is responsible to supervise, oversee, or direct the other,[21] (b) a description of events or conditions that are naturally of concern to the speaker in performing his duties,[22] (c) an account of company practices or policies relating to the speaker's responsibilities,[23] (d) an account of orders the speaker got from someone in authority, and related behavior by the person giving the orders,[24] (e) findings made by the speaker in investigating acts or events on behalf of his employer,[25] and (f) statements relaying messages from the speaker's superior to others.[26]

The speaker need not be engaged in performing his duties or furthering the interests of his employer or principal as he speaks. The basis of the exception is not that the words are acts by the employer or principal or that the speaker is pressed toward accuracy by the atmosphere of workplace. Rather, the basis is the same as the basis for admissions generally: What a party says may be admitted against him, and in the setting of employer-employee or principal-agent relationship what the employee or agent says is a statement by employer or principal. Hence the exception reaches statements made in casual or informal settings far removed from the workplace, including statements to the speaker's spouse or to a friend or fellow

---

20. United States v. Brothers Construction Co., 219 F.3d 300, 310-311 (4th Cir. 2000) (statements in which speaker described his own role), *cert. denied,* 531 U.S. 1037; Rainbow Travel Serv. v. Hilton Hotels Corp., 896 F.2d 1233, 1242 (10th Cir. 1990) (statements by hotel bus driver that his job was "to transport guests who had been bumped" from hotel "and to try to keep them happy").

21. Eliserio v. United Steelworkers of America Local 310, 398 F.3d 1071, 1078 (8th Cir. 2005) (in suit against union alleging hostile environment, admitting statements by board member W and local divisional chair V that "stickers were targeted at" plaintiff).

22. McDonough v. City of Quincy, 452 F.3d 8, 21 (6th Cir. 2006) (in police officer's suit against city alleging retaliation, admitting statements by personnel management officials about decision to put plaintiff on leave); State v. Cornhuskers Motor Lines, Inc., 854 A.2d 189 (Me. 2004) (in trial of carrier for false reports, toll receipts given to inspector by drivers were admissions of carrier); New Plan Realty Trust v. Morgan, 792 So.2d 351, 361 (Ala. 2001) (in tenant's suit against landlord, admitting statement by defendant's "employee-housekeeper" as to what she did with property when plaintiff moved out).

23. Carter v. University of Toledo, 349 F.3d 269, 544 (6th Cir. 2003) (comments by university vice provost responsible for "ensuring compliance with affirmative action requirements"); United States v. Rioux, 97 F.3d 648, 660 (2d Cir. 1996) (statement within scope of duties even if speaker is not decisionmaker, so long as he is advisor or participant in process).

24. Robert R. Jones Assocs., Inc. v. Nino Homes, 858 F.2d 274, 276-277 (6th Cir. 1988) (in infringement action, D could testify that G said L told him to duplicate plans) (G was agent of L).

25. In re Aircrash in Bali, Indonesia, 871 F.2d 812, 816 (9th Cir. 1989) (airline report on safety).

26. United States v. Portsmouth Paving Corp., 694 F.2d 312, 321-322 (4th Cir. 1982) (secretary taking incoming calls for boss and relaying his answers was his agent).

agent or employee, where the speaker is not performing his duties as he talks.[27]

For some other kinds of admissions, it makes no difference whether the speaker had personal knowledge, and the same is true of agent's admissions.[28] The few scraps of legislative history that bear on the question support the conclusion that personal knowledge is not required.[29] There is much to be said for this conclusion as a practical matter. Most importantly, a speaker whose statement fits FRE 801(d)(2)(D) is unlikely to be without useful knowledge: He is probably well informed and has circumstantial knowledge giving him an inside track and making what he has to say worth considering even if he did not personally see or hear what he describes. In the *Mahlandt* case where a man in charge of keeping a wolf at his house said the wolf bit a child, it is likely that he had some insight about the animal even though he did not see the event.[30] Also the adverse party likely has access to relevant information and witnesses.

Personal knowledge

The cases split on the question whether a statement by a superior advising an applicant or employee in his charge about his job prospects or standing in the company should be viewed as admissions if the speaker purports to relay what others told him. If the speaker is charged with making or implementing employment decisions, the better result is to admit his statement regardless whether he purports to speak for himself (hence for the company) or only to pass along what someone else told him to say or do.[31] There are three reasons: First, it is plausible to assume (absent convincing counterproof) that whatever is being relayed comes from someone further up the line with authority to speak for the organization, so each layer of hearsay satisfies the exception. Second, where the speaker has the principal voice on the matter in question and is delivering bad news, it is realistic to suppose that in referring to others he simply hopes to sidestep responsibility and perhaps soften the blow, but that in fact he speaks his own mind and has the requisite authority. Third, the rule that agent's admissions may

Supervisor reports what others say

---

27. Kraus v. Sobel Corrugated Containers, Inc., 915 F.2d 227, 230-231 (6th Cir. 1990) (statement by department manager at holiday dinner in home of plaintiff). *But see* Sorensen v. City of Aurora, 984 F.2d 349, 354 (10th Cir. 1993); Boren v. Sable, 887 F.2d 1032, 1034-1037 (10th Cir. 1989).

28. Hybert v. Hearst Corp., 900 F.2d 1050, 1053 (7th Cir. 1990); Brookover v. Mary Hitchcock Memorial Hosp., 893 F.2d 411, 413-418 (1st Cir. 1990); Mahlandt v. Wild Canid Survival & Research Ctr., Inc., 588 F.2d 626 (8th Cir. 1978).

29. The ACN to FRE 801(d)(2) comments approvingly about "freedom" that admissions enjoy "from the restrictive influences of the opinion rule and the rule requiring firsthand knowledge," and comments on "apparent prevalent satisfaction with the results," concluding that the various admissions doctrines should get "generous treatment" as an "avenue to admissibility."

30. Mahlandt v. Wild Canid Survival & Research Center, Inc., 588 F.2d 626 (8th Cir. 1978) (speaker heard from son that wolf bit child).

31. Green v. Administrators of Tulane Educational Fund, 284 F.3d 642, 659-660 (5th Cir. 2002); Zaben v. Air Prods. & Chems., Inc., 129 F.3d 1453, 1455-1457 (11th Cir. 1997); EEOC v. HBE Corp., 135 F.3d 543, 552 (8th Cir. 1998); Abrams v. Lightolier, 50 F.3d 1204, 1216 (3d Cir. 1995).

come in even where the speaker lacks personal knowledge strongly suggests they should be admitted if the lack of knowledge appears on the face of the statement in the form of a reference to what someone else said. Despite these arguments, a few decisions exclude such statements, invoking a spurious personal knowledge requirement or refusing to make the realistic assumption that what the speaker relays to the listener came from someone with authority.[32]

Government agents   Pre-Rules authority had it that statements by government agents, although admissible to impeach if inconsistent with their testimony, were not admissible substantively against the government.[33] It is said that government agents are uninterested personally in the outcome of trials and are historically unable to bind the sovereign. The validity of this rule is doubtful. Nothing in the language or history of FRE 801(d)(2) suggests the admissions doctrine does not reach statements by government agents. Nor are policy arguments persuasive: While the size of government and protections accorded by civil service may dissociate any agent from success or failure in any one case, similar factors operate in private industry, which is subject to elaborate statutory regulation of employment and sometimes to restrictions in personal contracts and collective bargaining agreements. And the right question is not whether an agent can "bind the sovereign," but whether what he says can be admitted. Some modern cases observe the traditional rule,[34] but the better ones indicate that the admissions doctrine may be invoked against the government.[35] There is considerable doubt that the traditional restriction survived.[36]

Judge decides   Whether the exception applies is for the judge to decide: Whether the speaker is a servant or agent and whether his statement concerns a matter within the scope of his employment or agency are questions of "admissibility" under FRE 104(a). On these matters the preponderance standard should apply, although some courts appear to endorse

---

32. Skillsky v. Lucky Stores, Inc., 893 F.2d 1088, 1090-1092 (9th Cir. 1990); Cedeck v. Hamiltonian Fed. Sav. & Loan Assn., 551 F.2d 1136, 1138 (8th Cir. 1977).

33. *See* United States v. Powers, 467 F.2d 1089, 1095 (7th Cir. 1972) (IRS determination that income was that of co-offender who pled guilty before trial), *cert. denied*, 410 U.S. 983; United States v. Santos, 372 F.2d 177, 179-180 (2d Cir. 1967) (sworn affidavit by narcotics agent).

34. United States v. Yildiz, 355 F.3d 80, 81-82 (2d Cir. 2003) (statements by government agents are not admissions by government) (excluding statement by informant); United States v. Arroyo, 406 F.3d 881, 888 (7th Cir. 2005) (government agents are not party-opponents for purposes of admissions doctrine); United States v. Torres, 901 F.2d 205, 238 (2d Cir. 1990) (complaint by arresting officers).

35. United States v. Branham, 97 F.3d 835, 853 (6th Cir. 1996) (governmental informant); United States v. Van Griffin, 874 F.2d 634, 638 (9th Cir. 1989) (DOT manual); United States v. Kattar, 840 F.2d 118, 130-131 (1st Cir. 1988) (Justice Department).

36. United States v. Anderson, 618 F.2d 487, 491 (8th Cir. 1980); United States v. Morgan, 581 F.2d 933, 938 (D.C. Cir. 1978). For cases admitting adoptive admissions against government, *see* §8.29, *supra*.

a more liberal standard.[37] The preponderance standard is preferable because the judge is supposed to decide the predicate facts, not simply determine that there is enough evidence to let someone else decide.

As amended in 1997, FRE 801(d)(2) allows an utterance offered as a statement by an agent or servant to be "considered" as partial proof of the facts on which admissibility depends. But using proffered evidence to prove its own admissibility involves bootstrapping or circularity, and because a strong tradition required independent proof, the amended Rule also provides that the statement itself is "not alone sufficient" to establish the predicate facts of agency or employment and scope.[38] The same pattern is followed in connection with admissions by employees and coconspirator statements.[39]

FRE 801(d)(2)(E)

   (d) Statements which are not hearsay. A statement is not hearsay if . . .

   (2) Admission by party-opponent. The statement is offered against a party and is . . . (E) a statement by a coconspirator of a party during the course and in furtherance of the conspiracy. The contents of the statement may be considered but are not alone sufficient to establish . . . the existence of the conspiracy and the participation therein of the declarant and the party against whom the statement is offered under subparagraph (E).

§8.33   Coconspirator Statements

The coconspirator exception is one of the most commonly invoked provisions in federal criminal trials, although it appears less often in state trials where conspiracies are less often charged. Much has been written on the subject, and commentators are largely critical of the exception,[1] but the Supreme Court has praised it as paving the way

(margin note: Bootstrapping issue)

---

37. United States v. Jones, 766 F.2d 412, 415 (9th Cir. 1985) (proof must be substantial, but preponderance not necessary); United States v. Flores, 679 F.2d 173, 178 (9th Cir. 1982) (same).

38. Los Angeles News Service v. CBS Broadcasting, Inc., 305 F.3d 924, 934 (9th Cir. 2002) (in infringement suit, plaintiff tried to prove that station KPIX received footage from CBS by testimony that station editor said so; plaintiff offered no evidence of agency; claim that CBS owned station did not suffice; no evidence of scope of editor's relationship to KPIX or CBS "beyond the editor's own hearsay").

39. *See* Bourjaily v. United States, 483 U.S. 171 (1987) (court determining predicate facts of coconspirator exception may consider statement); United States v. Richards, 204 F.3d 177, 202 (5th Cir. 2000) (statement cannot by itself serve as basis to admit), *cert. denied*, 531 U.S. 826.

§8.33   1. *See generally* Humphreys, In Search of the Reliable Conspirator: A Proposed Amendment to Federal Rule of Evidence 801(d)(2)(E), 30 Am. Crim. L. Rev. 337

for evidence that courtroom testimony cannot replicate, adding in the *Crawford* case in 2004 that coconspirator statements are not excludable under the confrontation clause.[2] Application of the exception turns on three predicate facts: The speaker conspired with the person against whom the statement is offered (coventurer requirement); the statement was made during the conspiracy (pendency requirement); it also furthered the conspiracy (furtherance requirement).

Coventurer The exception requires a conspiracy involving the speaker and the party against whom the statement is offered. Proving that the latter participated means at least showing that he knew of the venture and intended to associate with it, and neither knowledge nor association alone is sufficient.[3] The speaker too must have been a member of the venture, but if the statement was made by someone in a conspiracy with the defendant, inability to attribute the statement to a particular person does not prevent resort to the exception.

Conspiracy prosecutions provide the most common setting, but the exception is available in civil cases too. The central idea of the term "conspiracy" does not depend on the substantive definition of a crime or civil wrong, for the exception can apply if people act together by mutual understanding in pursuit of a common purpose ("joint venture" would fit as well as the usual term). The exception can apply even if the proponent does not show the venture is unlawful (or that an element critical substantively is missing).[4]

Defendant's involvement is commonly proved by his own statements or statements by others that he adopts. It used to be that the predicate facts had to be established entirely by evidence independent of the coconspirator statement, which meant the offering party had to prove conspiracy involving defendant by such evidence (the questions of pendency and furtherance being points of detail that could be resolved by analysis). Some independent evidence is still required, and defendant's own statements satisfy this requirement.[5]

(1993) (exception should turn on "amount of reliance placed on the statement by the conspirators"); Mueller, The Federal Coconspirator Exception: Action, Assertion, and Hearsay, 12 Hofstra L. Rev. 323 (1984) (should have reliability requirement); Davenport, The Confrontation Clause and the Co-Conspirator Exception in Criminal Prosecutions: A Functional Analysis, 85 Harv. L. Rev. 1378 (1972) (should be cut back); Levie, Hearsay and Conspiracy, 52 Mich. L. Rev. 1159, 1166 (1954) (relaxes evidential standards out of necessity).

2. Crawford v. Washington, 541 U.S. 36, 55 (2004) ("by their nature" coconspirator statements are not testimonial); United States v. Inadi, 475 U.S. 387, 395 (1986) (coconspirator statements provide evidence of "conspiracy's context that cannot be replicated" if speaker testifies in court).

3. United States v. Hunt, 272 F.3d 488, 495 (7th Cir. 2001).

4. United States v. Gewin, 471 F.3d 197, 201 (D.C. Cir. 2006) ("not limited to unlawful combinations"). *But see* State v. Tonelli, 749 N.W.2d 689 (Iowa 2008) (requires combinations that aim "to accomplish a criminal or unlawful act, or to do a lawful act in an unlawful manner").

5. United States v. Allison, 908 F.2d 1531, 1534 (11th Cir. 1990); United States v. Dworken, 855 F.2d 12, 25-26 (1st Cir. 1988).

The requirement that the party against whom a coconspirator statement is offered be a member of a conspiracy does not mean he must be charged with conspiring. The exception operates even if no conspiracy charges are brought, or if they lead to acquittal, or if the charged conspiracy differs from (or is not as broad as) the one suggested as the basis for admitting coconspirator statements.[6]

To fit the exception, the statement must be uttered during the course of the venture. To some extent, this requirement carries over the agency idea that a conspirator is responsible for acts of another done in the course of the conspiracy. In evidential terms, the requirement can be seen as redundant (furtherance normally includes pendency), or another way of limiting the statements that satisfy the exception. The Supreme Court has held that statements made after the main objective of a conspiracy has been accomplished or thwarted do not fit the exception.[7] But a conspiracy does not end like a football game at a moment that can be fixed with precision, and statements made during what can only be called the last possible minutes in pursuit of the main objective have been held to be during the conspiracy, including those made on apprehension by law enforcement officers but just before actual arrest.[8]

Pendency

Ordinarily statements made during the concealment phase do not satisfy the exception.[9] The Supreme Court once remarked that every criminal endeavor contemplates concealment,[10] and the fear is that the exception would open the door too wide if it embraced statements covering up the main events. But if the government shows the conspirators agreed at the outset to engage in concealment, or that concealment is basic in the sense of being necessary to reap the expected reward, statements in the concealment phase fit the exception.[11]

Concealment phase

If a member of a conspiracy withdraws, later statements by others do not fit the exception when offered against him.[12] But participation is

---

6. United States v. Washington, 434 F.3d 7, 13 (1st Cir. 2006) (applies without conspiracy charges); Commonwealth v. Johnson, 838 A.2d 663, 677 n.7 (Pa. 2003) (applies even if charged conspiracy differs from basis for admitting statements); United States v. Hernandez-Miranda, 78 F.3d 512, 513 (11th Cir. 1996) (can apply even if conspirator is acquitted).

7. Anderson v. United States, 417 U.S. 211 (1974); Dutton v. Evans, 400 U.S. 74 (1970); Wong Sun v. United States, 371 U.S. 471 (1963).

8. United States v. Lyon, 959 F.2d 701, 705 (8th Cir. 1992) (conspiracy ends "after the last overt act, whether charged or not"); United States v. Garate-Vergara, 942 F.2d 1543, 1553 (11th Cir. 1991) (shipboard radio transmission seeking to delay boarding furthered conspiracy).

9. Lutwak v. United States, 344 U.S. 604 (1953) (statements during concealment phase do not fit exception); Krulewitch v. United States, 336 U.S. 440 (1949) (similar).

10. Grunewald v. United States, 353 U.S. 391 (1957) (distinguishing concealment furthering main objectives from similar acts after objectives are attained).

11. United States v. Gajo, 290 F.3d 922, 928 (7th Cir. 2002) (conspiracy ongoing ten months after arson; culprits still trying to collect insurance proceeds); United States v. Mojica-Baez, 229 F.3d 292, 304 (1st Cir. 2000) (conspiracy continued through division of robbery proceeds), *cert. denied*, 532 U.S. 1065.

12. United States v. Nerlinger, 862 F.2d 967, 974 (2d Cir. 1988) (defendant withdrew; should have excluded later statements).

presumed to continue until one takes affirmative steps to get out, which usually requires notifying others or confessing to law enforcement authorities, and in any case ceasing to participate (except by agreement with the government to help detect or thwart the venture). This notion mirrors the idea that a person can avoid guilt of conspiracy by withdrawing, but doing so requires affirmative steps.[13]

If the pendency requirement were to have any force independent of the furtherance requirement, it seems that arrest of a conspirator should be taken as terminating his involvement. It would follow that a statement by an already arrested speaker could not fit the exception if offered against cohorts at large at the time, and that a statement by one at large could not fit the exception if offered against one who was already arrested. Courts generally endorse the first of these propositions, concluding that arrest of the speaker terminates his involvement,[14] although some reach the opposite conclusion on the theory that an arrested participant can say things that further the conspiratorial purpose.[15] The bulk of authority rejects the second conclusion, holding that statements by cohorts at large fit the exception when offered against already-arrested defendants,[16] although a few courts require exclusion.[17]

Furtherance   The furtherance requirement provides some assurance that the statement fits the aims apparently motivating the conspirators, which provides some indication that it can be trusted. The requirement also expresses in evidential terms the agency theory underlying the substantive notion of conspiracy. Perhaps most important, it limits the array of out-of-court statements that fit the exception. Yet the requirement does little in a more positive sense to assure reliability: Courts make wide-ranging suppositions on the purpose of conspirators and the nature of the venture, and decisions finding the requirement satisfied typically make only passing reference to it. Perhaps the real point here is that a statement is likely to seem after the fact to further a scheme merely by being plausible and generally consistent with the aims of the venture, and much that is plausible but mistaken can satisfy the requirement. The Supreme Court has repeatedly endorsed the requirement as important.[18]

Statements generally satisfy the requirement if they try to get transactions started (which often means describing sources of supply and key

13. *See* Model Penal Code §§5.03(6) (affirmative defense that defendant thwarted success of venture under circumstances manifesting complete and voluntary renunciation) and 5.03(7)(c) (one abandons conspiracy if he "advises those with whom he conspired" or informs authorities) (1974); Hyde v. United States, 225 U.S. 347 (1912).

14. Wong Sun v. United States, 371 U.S. 471 (1963); United States v. Zizzo, 120 F.3d 1338, 1348 (7th Cir. 1997).

15. United States v. Howard, 115 F.3d 1151, 1156-1157 (4th Cir. 1997); United States v. Ammar, 714 F.2d 238, 252-253 (3d Cir. 1983), *cert. denied*, 464 U.S. 936.

16. United States v. Robinson, 390 F.3d 853, 882-883 (6th Cir. 2004).

17. United States v. Barnes, 586 F.2d 1052, 1059 (5th Cir. 1978).

18. United States v. Nixon, 418 U.S. 683 (1974); Anderson v. United States, 417 U.S. 211 (1974); Krulewitch v. United States, 336 U.S. 440 (1949).

players and explaining roles in projected projects and transactions),[19] describe past occurrences to other members in order to map out future strategy,[20] or simply to keep them current on the progress and problems of the venture.[21] Keeping members aboard seems a constant problem, and statements further the conspiracy by encouraging trust and cohesiveness among members, or continuing cooperation[22] or membership.[23] More forceful statements or threats further the venture if they seek to enforce discipline or seek compliance with strategies or plans.[24] Statements to outsiders further the conspiracy if they seek to allay their fears in connection with contemplated transactions,[25] often by identifying conspirators to those who seek to buy contraband from the speaker[26] or sell it to him.[27] Statements may satisfy the furtherance requirement where they try to recruit new members[28] or secure cooperation or assistance by outsiders.[29] Also "bookkeeping" statements listing customers or transactions or amounts paid or owing typically satisfy the requirement.[30]

A statement may further a conspiracy even if the speaker talks to a law enforcement agent working under cover without knowing his identity, and even if the speaker knew it but hoped to put him off the scent of an ongoing venture.[31] What counts, it is sometimes said, is the speaker's

---

19. United States v. Cazares, 521 F.3d 991, 999 (8th Cir. 2008) (statements discuss supply source for illegal drugs, identify conspirator's role).

20. United States v. Johnson, 200 F.3d 529, 532-533 (7th Cir. 2000) (statements telling fellow conspirator breadth of venture, geographical divisions, and role); United States v. Christian, 786 F.2d 203, 212 (6th Cir. 1986) (locating drug buy, reporting what another conspirator said about someone in house).

21. United States v. Martinez-Medina, 279 F.3d 105, 116-117 (1st Cir. 2002) (conveying to other conspirators information about operations of drug venture), _cert. denied,_ 537 U.S. 921.

22. United States v. Lee, 374 F.3d 637, 644-645 (8th Cir. 2004) (statements describing murders; purpose was to enlist help of speaker's brother in selling stolen property), _cert. denied,_ 537 U.S. 1000.

23. United States v. Tarantino, 846 F.2d 1384, 1412 (D.C. Cir. 1988) (motivation for continued participation), _cert. denied,_ 488 U.S. 867.

24. United States v. Simmons, 923 F.2d 934, 945 (2d Cir. 1991) ("enforcing discipline").

25. United States v. Thai, 29 F.3d 785, 813-614 (2d Cir. 1994) (instilling confidence), _cert. denied,_ 513 U.S. 977; United States v. Yarbrough, 852 F.2d 1522, 1535-1536 (9th Cir. 1988) (allaying fears), _cert. denied,_ 488 U.S. 866.

26. United States v. Rodriguez, 525 F.3d 85, 101 (1st Cir. 2008) (statement directed potential customer to source of narcotics, steering business toward that person).

27. United States v. Patton, 594 F.2d 444, 447 (5th Cir. 1979).

28. United States v. Kearns, 61 F.3d 1422, 1425-1426 (9th Cir. 1995); United States v. Herrero, 893 F.2d 1512, 1528 (7th Cir. 1990).

29. United States v. Mayberry, 896 F.2d 1117, 1121 (8th Cir. 1990); United States v. Garcia, 893 F.2d 188, 190 (8th Cir. 1990).

30. United States v. Young, 39 F.3d 1561, 1571 (11th Cir. 1994); United States v. Tarantino, 846 F.2d 1384, 1412 (D.C. Cir. 1988), _cert. denied,_ 488 U.S. 867.

31. United States v. Fahey, 769 F.2d 829, 838-839 (1st Cir. 1985); United States v. Diez, 515 F.2d 892, 898-899 (5th Cir. 1975), _cert. denied,_ 423 U.S. 1052.

purpose, and the fact that he miscalculates does not matter.[32] Hence statements to conspirators-turned-informants may satisfy the furtherance requirement.

"Mere narrative" A "mere narrative" does not satisfy the requirement, and the term generally denotes statements relating events or describing responsibilities where the statements serve no conspiratorial purpose. A statement to an outsider such as a spouse or friend or companion is often viewed in this light,[33] and less often statements among coconspirators fail to qualify for this reason.[34]

Statements amounting to confessions to known law enforcement agents fail the furtherance requirement, particularly where the speaker tries to advance his individual interest in avoiding prosecution or getting favorable treatment by helping detect a conspiracy, identify its members, or otherwise build a case for the government.[35]

§8.34 —Procedural Issues

Since enactment of the Rules, the procedure for resolving questions relating to the admissibility of coconspirator statements has been intensely scrutinized. Six points of importance have emerged on which there is almost universal agreement.[1]

Judge determines First, the judge alone determines the predicate facts under FRE 104(a).[2] She considers both the proponent's evidence and the adverse party's counterproof, weighs it, and resolves credibility issues.[3] That is to say, her function is to decide whether the predicate facts exist, not merely determine whether there is "some evidence" of them or whether the proponent has made out a "prima facie case." Of course she performs this function only to decide whether the exception applies. In conspiracy cases, the jury weighs the same evidence and determines the credibility of the same witnesses in deciding whether defendant conspired.

---

32. United States v. Clark, 18 F.3d 1337, 1342-1343 (6th Cir. 1994) (intent to further suffices), *cert. denied*, 513 U.S. 852; United States v. Hamilton, 689 F.2d 1262, 1270 (6th Cir. 1982) (similar).

33. United States v. Johnson, 927 F.2d 999, 1002 (7th Cir. 1991) (statement by owner of school to student); United States v. Urbanik, 801 F.2d 692, 698-699 (4th Cir. 1986) ("casual aside" in discussion of defendant as weight lifter).

34. United States v. Phillips, 664 F.2d 971, 1027 (5th Cir. 1981) ("mere idle conversation"); United States v. Green, 600 F.2d 154, 157-158 (8th Cir. 1979) ("casual comments").

35. United States v. Frazier, 280 F.3d 835, 848 (8th Cir. 2002), *cert. denied*, 122 S. Ct. 2317; United States v. Meacham, 626 F.2d 503, 510-511 n.8 (5th Cir. 1980).

§8.34 1. *See* Mueller, The Federal Coconspirator Exception: Action, Assertion, and Hearsay, 12 Hofstra L. Rev. 323 (1984).

2. Bourjaily v. United States, 483 U.S. 171 (1987) (conspiracy and defendant's involvement are "preliminary questions of fact" that court resolves under FRE 104).

3. United States v. Smith, 46 F.3d 1223, 1235 (1st Cir. 1995) (rulings on coconspirator statements are not findings on sufficiency; may exclude statement and still hold that evidence of conspiracy is sufficient), *cert. denied*, 516 U.S. 864.

Second, the proponent bears the burden of showing by a preponderance that the exception applies (the predicate facts exist). All doubt on the standard was removed by the Court in 1987 in *Bourjaily v. United States*, which agreed that the preponderance standard applies and rejected arguments for a higher standard.[4] Appellate opinions sometimes say the coventurer requirement is satisfied by "slight evidence" (or a "prima facie" showing) that defendant and declarant conspired, but these suggestions make sense only if read to mean the trial judge may provisionally admit coconspirator statements on such a showing, putting off until later the final decision whether predicate facts exist, and then the preponderance standard must be satisfied.

Proponent bears burden; preponderance

Third, the proponent must offer evidence independent of the statement showing conspiracy and defendant's participation with the speaker. *Bourjaily* holds that the statement itself may be considered, but implies that it would not suffice by itself, and the 1997 amendment to FRE 801(d)(2) codifies this result, providing that the statement may be "considered" but is "not alone sufficient" to prove the predicate facts.[5] Requiring independent evidence helps deal with problems of circularity and reliability. Admitting without independent evidence would let a coconspirator statement prove its own provenance or bootstrap itself into admissibility: In its performative or assertive aspect (or both), the statement would be taken to prove the very conspiracy that must be shown to satisfy the exception. But requiring independent evidence reinforces the coventurer requirement, helping it act as a limit or safeguard separate from the evidence under scrutiny. And since coconspirator statements usually indicate conspiracy in some way, independent evidence provides important corroboration, and thus helps deal with the nagging suspicion that coconspirator statements may not be very reliable.

Independent evidence

Fourth, the court should not give a cautionary instruction telling the jury to consider a coconspirator statement as evidence against the defendant only if it first finds that he conspired with the speaker. Such an instruction might make sense if the jury shared responsibility for applying the exception, with the judge only passing on the sufficiency of the evidence to prove the predicate facts under FRE 104(b), but that is not how it works. The judge alone decides under FRE 104(a), and such an instruction is likely to confuse.[6]

No instruction

---

4. Bourjaily v. United States, 483 U.S. 171 (1987).

5. *See* Bourjaily v. United States, 483 U.S. 171 (1987) (court may consider "any evidence it wishes" in appraising coconspirator statements; cumulative force of evidence and statement may be "greater than the constituent parts"; not deciding whether court can rely solely on statements). *See also* United States v. Payne, 437 F.3d 540, 544-546 (6th Cir. 2006) (statement itself can prove that defendant was conspirator, but additional independent corroboration is required) (standard satisfied here), *cert denied*, 547 U.S. 1217.

6. United States v. Hagmann, 950 F.2d 175, 180-181 (5th Cir. 1991); United States v. Swidan, 888 F.2d 1076, 1081 (6th Cir. 1989); United States v. Peters, 791 F.2d 1270, 1285-1286 (7th Cir. 1986), *cert. denied*, 479 U.S. 847.

Admit provisionally

Fifth, coconspirator hearsay may be admitted provisionally, subject to later proof of the predicate facts, but the court has discretion to require the predicate facts to be shown first. In *United States v. James*, the Fifth Circuit suggested a "preferred order of proof" in which the court holds a preliminary hearing outside the jury's presence to decide whether to admit, reasoning that coconspirator statements have great impact and that provisionally admitting them runs the risk of mistrial or an instruction of dubious effect striking what the jury has already heard if the necessary foundation (or connecting) evidence is not offered or proves unpersuasive.[7]

Unfortunately this preferred order of proof raises serious practical problems. Proving conspiracy is a complicated business, and traditionally prosecutors have considerable leeway in the order of proof. Proving the predicate facts is so intertwined with proving the merits that requiring two presentations involves enormous duplication of time and effort. Prudential reasons favor a separate admissibility hearing, but it is time-consuming and fraught with practical difficulties. Hence it is largely settled that a court may admit coconspirator hearsay provisionally.[8]

Clear error standard

Sixth, review of the trial court's decision on these points proceeds under a "clear error" standard.[9] Whether or not the court holds a *James* hearing, reviewing courts generally do not insist on formal on-the-record findings of predicate facts.[10]

F. UNRESTRICTED HEARSAY EXCEPTIONS

> **FRE 803(1)**
>
> **(1) Present sense impression.** A statement describing or explaining an event or condition made while the declarant was perceiving the event or condition, or immediately thereafter.

---

7. United States v. James, 590 F.2d 575, 581-582 (5th Cir. 1979) (if it is not "reasonably practical" to require showing first, may admit statement "subject to being connected up"), *cert. denied*, 442 U.S. 917.

8. *See* United States v. Cates, 251 F.3d 1164, 1167 (8th Cir. 2001); United States v. Blevins, 960 F.2d 1252, 1256 (4th Cir. 1992).

9. United States v. Gessa, 971 F.2d 1257, 1261 (6th Cir. 1992); United States v. Homick, 964 F.2d 899, 905 (9th Cir. 1992); United States v. Page-Bey, 960 F.2d 724, 728 (8th Cir. 1992).

10. United States v. Blevins, 960 F.2d 1252, 1256 (4th Cir. 1992); United States v. Jackson, 757 F.2d 1486, 1490 (4th Cir. 1985), *cert. denied*, 474 U.S. 994. *But see* United States v. Perez, 959 F.2d 264, 268 (10th Cir. 1992) (record findings required).

§8.35 Present Sense Impressions

FRE 803(1) creates an exception for statements describing or explaining an event or condition if made while the speaker was perceiving it "or immediately thereafter." The idea of immediacy lies at the heart of the exception. While the notion of an external event as stimulus is part of the excited utterance exception, immediacy suggests that present sense impressions too are the product of external stimulus. And since the stimulus behind present sense impressions "produces no nervous shock or excitement," it is thought that they are actually more reliable than excited utterances: The speaker is not "distracted by the pull of an emotional upheaval," which might negatively affect powers of speech and perception.[1]

Present sense impressions are considered trustworthy for two reasons, both resting on the time element.[2] First, immediacy removes the risk of lack of memory, or at least reduces it to a negligible possibility. Second, immediacy precludes time for reflection, eliminating or sharply diminishing the possibility of intentional deception. In short, immediacy satisfies two concerns of the hearsay doctrine, leaving only the risks of ambiguity and misperception.

Sometimes a third justification is advanced, tending to reduce even the latter risks: Usually the person who hears the statement perceives the event or condition, and usually he later testifies about the statement and can corroborate what the speaker said. While FRE 803(1) does not require corroboration, courts often emphasize that the statement is corroborated.

The main utility of FRE 803(1) is in cases where the utterance is clearly contemporaneous but nothing startling happened. The exception is useful where the speaker makes an observation immediately before an accident or other exciting event: Spontaneity is assured, and if the speaker does not anticipate what is to come, his statement may be free of the distortion that may result from events as they unfold.[3]

The exception has three requirements. First, the statement must be contemporaneous with the event or condition—made while speaker perceives it or immediately thereafter. The time requirement is strict, for it is the major factor in assuring trustworthiness. In most cases, the

Contemporaneous

§8.35 1. Quoted passages are from Slough, Res Gestae, 2 Kan. L. Rev. 246, 266-267 (1954). *See also* Hutchins & Slesinger, Some Observations on the Law of Evidence, 28 Colum. L. Rev. 432, 439 (1928) (approving statements in immediate response to stimulus that "produces no shock or nervous excitement").

2. Dutton v. Evans, 400 U.S. 74 (1970) (analyzing statement by coconspirator in prison; can think he did not misrepresent defendant's involvement, as statement was spontaneous); Nuttall v. Reading Co., 235 F.2d 546, 551-553 (3d Cir. 1956) (no risk of "lapse of memory," less likelihood of misrepresentation).

3. *See* United States v. Narciso, 446 F. Supp. 252, 285 (E.D. Mich. 1977) (statement comes before speaker knows "something startling" will happen, avoiding distortion caused by excitement).

statement clearly was made during those moments when speaker was perceiving the event or condition.[4] The phrase "immediately thereafter" accommodates human realities: The condition or event may happen so fast that the words do not quite keep pace, and proving a true match of words and events may be impossible for ordinary witnesses. The exception allows enough flexibility to reach statements made a moment after the fact where a small delay or "slight lapse" (to use the phrase in the ACN) is not enough to allow reflection, which would raise doubts about trustworthiness.[5] More significant delays (measured in minutes or hours, especially if the speaker made other statements in the interim) bar resort to FRE 803(1) because they do permit time for reflection and lessen or remove the assurance of trustworthiness.[6] In this respect, the exception for present sense impressions is distinctly narrower than the one for excited utterances.

Perceived event or condition   Second, the speaker must have perceived the event or condition. Perceiving almost always means seeing, but it also reaches hearing and other forms of sensory perception.[7] Absent an indication that the speaker perceived the matter described in his statement, FRE 803(1) does not apply.[8]

Describe event or condition   Third, the statement must describe or explain the event or condition. Contemporaneity would not assure trustworthiness (or even make sense) if the statement did not describe or explain the matter perceived. Most statements admitted under the exception simply assert the existence of the condition or happening of the event, and the term "describe" accurately captures the function of such statements. But some interpret,

4. United States v. Jackson, 124 F.3d 607, 618 (4th Cir. 1997) (mother tells police defendant was threatening to shoot, which was ongoing event), *cert. denied*, 522 U.S. 1066; Bennett v. National Trans. Safety Bd., 66 F.3d 1130, 1137-1138 (10th Cir. 1995) (in license revocation proceeding, admitting statement by another pilot saying "That was pretty close fella," referring to "a near miss").

5. State ex rel. J.A., 949 A.2d 790, 798-799 (N.J. 2008) (statement describing robbery ten minutes later was not "immediately after" it); United States v. Danford, 435 F.3d 682, 687 (7th Cir. 2005) (admitting statement describing just-completed conversation with defendant, as present sense impression); United States v. Parker, 936 F.2d 950, 954-955 (7th Cir. 1991) (redcap's response to defendant at train station in presence of police when she denied owning suitcase, "That's the bag you gave me").

6. United States v. Brewer, 36 F.3d 266, 271-272 (2d Cir. 1994) (statement at lineup linking prior event with present perception did not fit exception); Pau v. Yosemite Park & Curry Co., 928 F.2d 880, 890 (9th Cir. 1991) (excluding statement, on briefly recovering from coma, that bike brakes failed; more than two days passed since accident).

7. *See* Knudson v. Director, 530 N.W.2d 313 (N.D. 1995) (radio call by officer who heard accident, reported it); United States v. Portsmouth Paving Corp., 694 F.2d 312, 322-323 (4th Cir. 1982); Nuttall v. Reading Co., 235 F.2d 546, 551-553 (3d Cir. 1956) (both involving overheard phone conversation).

8. Bemis v. Edwards, 45 F.3d 1369, 1373 (9th Cir. 1995) (excluding 911 call reporting burglary; no showing that caller had personal knowledge; content of call suggested otherwise); McClure v. Price, 300 F.2d 538, 545 (4th Cir. 1962) (excluding statement "the dern fool is going to kill himself" because testimony did not show speaker saw car before collision).

assess, or evaluate what the speaker perceives and are reached by the term "explain."[9]

Modern cases approve use of the exception to admit 911 calls reporting crimes or emergencies.[10] Usually incoming 911 calls are proved by recordings that are routinely made, and these readily satisfy the public records exception. FRE 803(8)(B) seems most applicable, and the fact that a recording is made in a police department should not matter even if it is offered against the accused, since such recordings qualify as "routine and nonadversarial."[11] Insofar as the purpose is to show *what the caller said,* arguably no second exception is required for the *recording* as such, and the problem is to authenticate it as a true depiction of a particular incoming call.[12] Insofar as the purpose is to prove the truth of the caller's statement, FRE 803(1) (or the excited utterance exception) are essential, and the universal use of cellphones increased this use of those exceptions dramatically.

In the *Davis* decision in 2006, the Court made it clear that insofar as the primary purpose of callers is to report ongoing emergencies (which is almost always the case), the confrontation clause does not impede use of such calls against criminal defendants. It is different if such a call reports a criminal act that has ended, with no ongoing emergency, in which case even 911 calls are excludable as testimonial under *Crawford* unless the speaker testifies and can be cross-examined.[13]

911 calls

Confrontation concerns

FRE 803(2)

    (2) Excited utterance. A statement relating to a startling event or condition made while the declarant was under the stress of excitement caused by the event or condition.

---

9. Cargill, Inc. v. Boag Cold Storage Warehouse, Inc., 71 F.3d 545, 555 (6th Cir. 1995) (notes taken while investigating spoiled shipment of turkeys); Makuc v. American Honda Motor Co., 835 F.2d 389, 391-392 (1st Cir. 1987) (statements by mechanic who examined motorcycle "described or explained the condition of the bicycle at the very time the mechanic was engaged in examining it").

10. United States v. Bradley, 145 F.3d 889, 892 (7th Cir. 1998); United States v. Hawkins, 59 F.3d 723, 730-731 (8th Cir. 1995) (admitting 911 call in which wife says husband "just pulled a gun" on her), *vacated on other grounds*, 516 U.S. 1168; United States v. Mejia-Valez, 855 F. Supp. 607, 613-614 (E.D. N.Y. 1994) (911 call by eyewitness after shooting). *But see* Bemis v. Edwards, 45 F.3d 1369, 1373 (9th Cir. 1995) (911 call reporting burglary excluded for failing to show personal knowledge; content of call suggested lack of knowledge). *See also* United States v. Ruiz, 249 F.3d 643 (7th Cir. 2001) (admitting statements on walkie-talkie, made by officer describing defendant's conduct during police stakeout). *See generally* Richard Friedman, Dial-In Testimony, 150 U. Pa. L. Rev. 1171 (2002) (advocating exclusion of such evidence as violating Confrontation Clause).

11. On admitting "routine and nonadversarial" records, *see* §8.51, *infra. See also* Bemis v. Edwards, 45 F.3d 1369, 1373 (9th Cir. 1995) (tape of 911 call fits exceptions for business or public records); United States v. Sallins, 993 F.2d 344, 347-348 (3d Cir. 1993) (911 tape is public record).

12. *See* the discussion of authenticating tapes in §9.13, *infra.*

13. Davis v. Washington, 527 U.S. 813 (2006) (admitting 911 call describing ongoing emergency involving possible danger to caller), discussed in §8.85, *infra.*

§8.36 Excited Utterances

FRE 803(2) creates an exception for a statement by someone speaking under the stress of excitement, expressing his reaction and relating to the causal event or condition. The exception rests on the idea that spontaneous reaction is powerful enough to overcome reflective capacity, and the statement is viewed as the product of the impression made by an external stimulus. Such reactive statements are considered trustworthy for two reasons: The stimulus leaves the speaker momentarily incapable of fabrication, and her memory is fresh because the impression has not yet passed from her mind.[1] In short, risks of insincerity and memory lapse are removed.

Enhances other risks Of course spontaneous reaction enhances other hearsay risks (misstatement and misperception).[2] But this difficulty seems not to be serious enough to discard the exception. One reason is that the exciting event or condition is likely to focus the attention of the speaker, and concentration may be a countervailing force limiting the risk of misperception. And there are other reasons to keep the exception: A startling event is often at the heart of the dispute and is fleeting and hard to prove, so there is a crying need for more rather than less information; a fresh statement by an observer is likely to be as reliable as her later reconstruction after the pressures of litigation have been brought to bear; the parties are likely to know about these statements, so surprise at trial is unlikely. Finally, the startling event is often an accident or violent crime that injures or claims the life of the speaker: Often she was in the best position to see and report, and excluding her statement would mean doing without good evidence and would have the unattractive consequence of shutting out the cries of the victim.

There are three requirements—an external stimulus, an excited reaction, and a statement that relates to the stimulus. In practice, these elements tend to merge. If something seems likely to have startled the speaker, that fact alone suggests that what she said was her reaction; if what she said seems excited, that fact suggests the occasion was exciting.

External stimulus—crime, accident, abuse Usually the external stimulus is an accident or crime. Three situations are worth special note. One is cases of violent criminal assault, where statements by the victim implicating the accused are routinely

---

§8.36 1. *See* Dutton v. Evans, 400 U.S. 74 (1970) (conspirator probably did not misrepresent because statement was "spontaneous"); United States v. Schreane, 331 F.3d 548, 563-564 (6th Cir. 2003) (no possibility of fabrication, coaching, or confabulation). *But see* Ferrier v. Duckworth, 902 F.2d 545, 548 (7th Cir. 1990) ("stress may induce inaccurate, even if sincere, utterances"), *cert. denied*, 498 U.S. 988.

2. Stewart, Perception, Memory, and Hearsay: A Criticism of Present Law and the Proposed Federal Rules of Evidence, 1970 Utah L. Rev. 1, 8-22, 27-29 (excited statements are unreliable); Hutchins & Slesinger, Some Observations on the Law of Evidence, 28 Colum. L. Rev. 432 (1928) (examining empirical data on eyewitness accounts of exciting occurrences).

admitted, as are statements by nonvictim eyewitnesses.[3] The second is accident cases resulting in physical injury, where statements by the injured party describing the event are usually admitted.[4] In both situations, often victims speak while suffering physical and psychological trauma, and often the statement is compelling evidence and apparently the best available account. The third situation is sexual abuse of children, where comments by the child describing acts and identifying the perpetrator are often admitted,[5] and in a decision handed down under the old *Roberts* regime the Supreme Court had approved this use of the exception.[6] Such accounts often seem trustworthy: They display knowledge that a child is not likely to have unless something close to what she describes happened; she speaks in plain age-appropriate language; corroborating evidence and circumstances suggest that she was not making it up.

Here, as with present sense impressions, confrontation concerns arise in criminal cases. These surfaced in the current *Crawford* era, particularly with 911 calls (taken up below). In the *Davis* decision in 2006, however, the Court concluded that insofar as callers are reporting ongoing emergencies and the primary purpose is to resolve them, the confrontation clause does not impede use of such calls against criminal defendants.[7] Not surprisingly, it is often the case that 911 calls comprise excited utterances in which the primary purpose is indeed to resolve such emergencies, but factors other than ongoing emergencies can bring the exception into play, and excited utterances describing crimes that pose no such emergencies, or crimes in which any emergency is over by the time the call is placed, do not satisfy the *Davis* standard and

Confrontation concerns

---

3. United States v. Hadley, 431 F.3d 484, 496 (6th Cir. 2005) (wife's hysterical statements that defendant had gun, held it to her head, was going to kill her), *cert. denied*, 127 S. Ct. 47; United States v. Baptiste, 264 F.3d 578, 590-591 (5th Cir. 2001) (statement by victim dying in pool of blood, identifying defendant as assailant).

4. Insurance Co. v. Mosley, 75 U.S. 397 (1869) (on returning to bed, man says he "had fallen down the back stairs and hurt himself"); McCurdy v. Greyhound Corp., 346 F.2d 224, 225-226 (3d Cir. 1965) (motorist's statement after accident). See also Greene v. B.F. Goodrich Avionics Systems, Inc., 409 F.3d 784, 790-791 (6th Cir. 2005) (in suit against maker of gyroscope, admitting pilot's statement, 19 seconds before crash leading to his death, "I think my gyro just quit").

5. United States v. Jennings, 496 F.3d 344, 349-350 (4th Cir. 2007) (in trial for sexual assault of 13-year-old child on "red-eye" flight, admitting her statements to passengers afterwards describing what happened); United States v. Wilcox, 487 F.3d 1163, 1170-1172 (8th Cir. 2007) (alleged sexual abuse of 14-year-old, who testified; admitting recording of her call to police saying "David" had been on top of her).

6. White v. Illinois, 502 U.S. 736 (1992) (statement by four-year-old victim to mother 30 minutes after event; exception is firmly rooted under *Roberts* doctrine). *But see* Idaho v. Wright, 497 U.S. 805 (1990) (rejecting use of catchall in similar case). Of course the *Roberts* regime defining the standard applied in both *White* and *Wright* has given way to the current *Crawford* regime. See §§8.83-8.92, *infra*.

7. Davis v. Washington, 527 U.S. 813 (2006) (admitting 911 call describing ongoing emergency involving possible danger to caller), discussed in §8.85, *infra*.

cannot be used as evidence against the accused unless the caller testifies and can be cross-examined.[8]

In the three situations described above (cases involving accidents, violent crimes or child abuse), the statements have compelling common elements: The exciting event involves the speaker personally and is likely to be violent and injurious, and in sexual assault cases bewildering and invasive (if not worse), and it lies at the heart of the suit. Yet these elements are not indispensable. The exception is available even if the event was not violent or injurious, and even if the event has no independent significance in the case. It applies even where the speaker participates in events but sustains no injury, and where she is a bystander rather than participant.

911 calls Modern cases approve use of the exception for 911 calls, often placed by crime victims and sometimes by eyewitnesses, usually proved by recordings that satisfy the public records exception.[9] As in the case of 911 calls admitted as present sense impressions, here too concerns may arise if such evidence becomes critical in criminal prosecutions, particularly if the speaker does not testify as a witness and therefore cannot be cross-examined.

As noted above, in 2006 the Court in *Davis* made it clear that insofar as the primary purpose of callers is to report ongoing emergencies (almost always the case), the confrontation clause does not impede use of such calls against criminal defendants. It is another matter altogether, however, if such a call reports a criminal act that has ended, with no ongoing emergency: Here even 911 calls are excludable as testimonial under *Crawford*, unless the speaker testifies and can be cross-examined.[10]

Excitement The speaker must be excited. What counts is that *she* was excited, and the fact that another might not have been does not matter. And in the other direction, the exception does not apply if the speaker was not excited even if another would be. Ordinary observers seeing an accident are likely to be startled and excited even if a police officer would not be. In short, the excitement requirement imposes a subjective

8. *See* Commonwealth v. Lao, 877 N.E.2d 557 (Mass. 2007) (in murder trial, error to admit victim's statements in 911 call describing prior episode where defendant tried to run over her; she had returned from dinner, had spoken to him by phone and called her mother; defendant had left; *Davis* did not apply).

9. State v. Bergevine, 942 A.2d 974 (R.I. 2008) (admitting 911 call by neighbor describing "his friend and neighbor performing an unspeakable act of sexual molestation upon his toddler daughter"); People v. Barrett, 747 N.W.2d 797 (Mich. 2008) (should admit assault victim's 911 call saying defendant kicked door in and beat and tried to strangle her, brandishing hatchet); United States v. Arnold, 486 F.2d 177, 184 (6th Cir. 2007) ("being threatened by a convicted murderer wielding a semi-automatic handgun amounts to a startling event") (admitting 911 call). *See also* United States v. Sallins, 993 F.2d 344 (3d Cir. 1993) (911 tape is public record), and discussion of authenticating recordings in §9.13, *infra*.

10. Davis v. Washington, 527 U.S. 813 (2006) (admitting 911 call describing ongoing emergency involving possible danger to caller), discussed in §8.85, *infra*.

standard.[11] Yet sensible administration requires objective assumptions. Absent evidence showing otherwise, the court assumes the speaker's reactions resemble those that others of similar background would experience in similar circumstances.

The following factors emerge as important: the nature of the event, which may indicate excitement[12] or lack of it;[13] the appearance, behavior, or condition of the speaker, which may suggest excitement[14] or lack of it;[15] the nature or contents of the statement, which may indicate excitement[16] or lack of it.[17] Especially important are surprise or suddenness of the stimulus and physical and psychological distance from events: Something unexpected is more likely to cause excited reaction than something long anticipated; excitement is more probable for one facing injury or death than for one who saw a crime or accident from a safe distance; one is more likely to be startled if a friend or loved one is hurt or potentially at fault than if events involve unknown people. It matters too whether the statement was made in response to questions or came from within as a direct reaction to events or conditions, although a general question does not displace the reactive force of a stimulus that has great impact on the speaker.[18] Sometimes live testimony by the speaker helps resolve the central question.[19]

The exception reaches statements "relating" to an exciting event or condition. Only a loose relationship is required, in contrast to the tight connection required by the terms "describing" and "explaining" in the exception for present sense impressions. In a leading pre-Rules decision in *Murphy Auto Parts Co. v. Ball,* the court rejected a claim that a statement could not be an excited utterance if "it did not illuminate the exciting event." The case involved a car hitting a child, and the critical question was whether the driver was on an errand for his employer. The trial court let plaintiff testify that immediately after the

Statement "relating" to stimulus

11. *See* United States v. Moore, 791 F.2d 566, 570-571 & n.2 (7th Cir. 1986) (startling event need not be one that trier "can objectively perceive," like fall or accident; courts "look primarily to the effect upon the declarant").

12. United States v. Martin, 59 F.3d 767, 769-770 (8th Cir. 1995) (statements after getting phone call that defendant was "gonna' burn the house down"); United States v. Hartman, 958 F.2d 774, 784 (7th Cir. 1992) (hearing one's wife and lover plotting one's own death).

13. United States v. Cain, 587 F.2d 678, 680-681 (5th Cir. 1979) (speaker in CB transmission describing shirtless males leaving truck had no reason to be excited), *cert. denied,* 440 U.S. 975.

14. United States v. Brown, 254 F.3d 454, 459-460 (3d Cir. 2001) (admitting statement describing robbery; appearance, behavior, condition of declarant may show excitement), *cert. denied,* 535 U.S. 935.

15. United States v. Mountain State Fabricating Co., 282 F.2d 263, 265-266 (4th Cir. 1960) (calm and unexcited manner).

16. United States v. Vazquez, 857 F.2d 857, 864 (1st Cir. 1988) (speaker "lashed out" at defendant).

17. United States v. Wolak, 923 F.2d 1193, 1197 (6th Cir. 1991) (comment on arrest scene), *cert. denied,* 501 U.S. 1217.

18. *See* United States v. Glenn, 473 F.2d 191, 194 (D.C. Cir. 1972).

19. *See* United States v. Bailey, 834 F.2d 218, 228 (1st Cir. 1987); United States v. Iron Shell, 633 F.2d 77 (8th Cir. 1980), *cert. denied,* 450 U.S. 1001.

injury the driver said he was sorry and hoped the child was not seriously hurt, and that "he had to call on a customer and was in a bit of a hurry to get home." The court approved this use of the exception, concluding that reliability is not "inflexibly dependent upon the subject matter," but warning that application of the exception becomes more dubious as the subject matter grows more distant from describing the event.[20]

On four points, _Murphy Auto Parts_ is persuasive: First, an excited utterance need not describe or depict the event or condition, and the necessary relation may consist in shedding further light on it.[21] Second, an excited statement can prove the agency or authority of the speaker (or lack of it), at least where he is an actor in the events in issue and the statement sheds light on his purpose or motivation, thus relates closely and naturally to events. Third, such a statement can prove fault or due care by the speaker or another in an accident giving rise to the statement, since judgment calls such as these relate closely and naturally to the event.[22] Finally, the more closely a statement "tracks" an event, the more clearly the required relationship exists, but looser relationships can still satisfy the exception.[23]

During, immediately after   Other things being equal, the more quickly a statement follows the occasion, the more likely it is to be a spontaneous reaction. Statements during or immediately after an exciting occurrence have smooth sledding, but it is the exception for present sense impressions to which immediacy is indispensable, not the excited utterance exception. Resort to the latter is routinely upheld in the face of lapses of minutes between event and utterance, where it is clear that the speaker was still laboring under stress that stilled reflective capacity, as is likely if the event was sudden or violent or frightening or caused injury or pain to the speaker.[24]

Longer lapses   Even much longer lapses, on the order of several hours, may not dissipate the stress resulting from events that cause serious injury or trauma to the speaker. Here the condition of the speaker between the event and the statement is important, and continuing emotional or physical shock, loss of consciousness, persistent pain or unabated fright, isolation, and other factors may prolong the impact of a stressful

20. Murphy Auto Parts Co. v. Ball, 249 F.2d 508, 511-512 (D.C. Cir. 1957), _cert. denied_, 355 U.S. 932.

21. United States v. Moore, 791 F.2d 566, 572 (7th Cir. 1986) (broader than present sense impressions); United States v. Napier, 518 F.2d 316, 317-318 (9th Cir. 1975) (reaction to news photo, where victim identified assailant), _cert. denied_, 423 U.S. 895; Sanitary Grocery Co. v. Snead, 90 F.2d 374, 375-377 (D.C. Cir. 1937) (statement after slip-and-fall that mess "has been on the floor for a couple of hours"), _cert. denied_, 302 U.S. 703.

22. Hilyer v. Howat Concrete Co., 578 F.2d 422, 424 (D.C. Cir. 1978) (truck driver says decedent walked backward into path of truck).

23. United States v. Moore, 791 F.2d 566, 572 (7th Cir. 1986) (going beyond event counts in deciding whether statement is spontaneous).

24. United States v. Sowas, 34 F.3d 447, 452-453 (6th Cir. 1994) (statement by 3-year-old child 20 minutes afterwards identifying assailant), _cert. denied_, 513 U.S. 1117; United States v. Golden, 671 F.2d 369, 371 (10th Cir. 1982) (statement by assault victim 15 minutes after event, following high speed flight in car), _cert. denied_, 456 U.S. 919.

event, particularly one that is long lasting and arduous. Sensible decisions apply the exception despite lapses of this sort when it comes to statements by victims of brutal or terrifying crimes, including assault and kidnap, particularly when they are of tender years.[25]

Events may so traumatize a person that long after stress subsides a chance reminder may have great psychological impact, renewing stress and excitement and producing statements describing the original trauma. While it is not farfetched to apply the exception in this setting, plainly risks of inaccurate memory and suggestivity of later events increase, and the question of admitting such statements turns on close attention to conditions.[26]

Renewed stress or excitement

When lapse of time has dissipated the stress, resort to the exception is improper.[27] There is no mechanical test, and the issue turns on the presence or absence and degree or intensity of the factors that bear on the question whether the speaker was excited at all. With time, it seems increasingly important to know whether or not he talked lucidly on other subjects since the event and whether the statement was or was not elicited by questions. The longer the interval, the more likely the statement does not satisfy the exception and the more likely that reflective thought or other statements have severed the essential connection with the exciting event or condition, indicating that the exception does not apply.[28]

The question whether a statement qualifies as an excited utterance is decided by the trial judge under FRE 104(a). That means, among other things, that the judge must decide whether there was an exciting event. Usually there is no doubt on this score, and the point is proved by evidence apart from the statement offered under the exception. But sometimes the speaker reports an event or condition nobody else saw and no other evidence tends to prove, typically in the situation in which the event was an accident or sudden onset of pain that the speaker endured alone. If he lives to testify, he can prove the event that way, but often the speaker has died and questions surrounding the event are crucial in the suit, sometimes because the central issue is whether an accident happened (which may trigger liability under an insurance policy) or whether an injury was suffered by the speaker at work (which triggers coverage of worker's compensation).

Judge decides

25. State v. Huntington, 575 N.W.2d 268 (Wis. 1998) (admitting statements by 11-year-old two weeks after sexual assault, while crying and hysterical); United States v. Scarpa, 913 F.2d 993, 1017 (2d Cir. 1990) (hospital statement by beating victim identifying assailants five to six hours afterward).

26. Pau v. Yosemite Park & Curry Co., 928 F.2d 880, 890 (9th Cir. 1991) (excluding decedent's statement, on briefly recovering from two-day coma; did not show stress); United States v. Scarpa, 913 F.2d 993, 1017 (2d Cir. 1990) (many factors indicate stress).

27. United States v. Kenyon, 481 F.3d 1054, 1062-1063 (8th Cir. 2007) (statements made "roughly a week after the most recent abuse" and "some three years" after first abuse could not fit exception).

28. United States v. Sherlock, 962 F.2d 1349, 1365 (9th Cir. 1992) (victims had time to think and talk to others), *cert. denied*, 506 U.S. 958; Pfeil v. Rogers, 757 F.2d 850, 860-861 (7th Cir. 1985) (statement that defendants were involved in murder was not excited because made after substantial period), *cert. denied*, 475 U.S. 1107.

The difficulty in using the statement to prove the event is the element of bootstrapping or circularity. Despite this difficulty, better practice permits use of the statement to prove the underlying event. As a matter of construction, FRE 104(a) arguably supports this result because it frees the judge from the constraints of evidence law (privileges apart) in deciding questions of admissibility and there is an obvious need for the proof in these cases. Perhaps most importantly, the problem itself usually dissolves on closer look, since there is almost always independent evidence that strongly suggests an exciting event or condition: The speaker departs from his usual habits in ways that strongly suggest what his words reflect (something startling happened), or his physical condition (temperature, sweating, elevated heart rate or respiration) or demeanor (tension, excitement, surprise) suggest as much. Such collateral indicators are not themselves hearsay, even though they suggest the point, because they are not themselves assertions—they do not intentionally express or communicate it. Hence even a rule that insists on independent evidence of the exciting event or condition can usually be satisfied.[29]

In an early opinion the Supreme Court once approved use of a statement in such a setting without remarking the difficulty, although a dissenting opinion would have excluded the statement for this reason.[30] Some decisions do insist on independent evidence, but others take the opposite (and wiser) approach, and commentators support the proposition that the statement can prove the event.[31]

FRE 803(3)

(3) Then existing, mental, emotional, or physical condition. Statement of the declarant's then existing state of mind, emotion, sensation, or physical condition (such as intent, plan, motive, design, mental feeling, pain, and bodily health), but not including a statement of memory or belief to prove the fact remembered or believed unless it relates to the execution, revocation, identification, or terms of declarant's will.

---

29. *See* United States v. Arnold, 386 F.3d 177 (6th Cir. 2007) (counting as independent evidence the fact that declarant called 911, the fear shown by the "tenor" of her voice, her distraught demeanor, and similar factors); Cole v. United States, 327 F.2d 360, 361 (9th Cir. 1964) (distraught teller). *See also* ACN to FRE 803(2) ("content of the statement" may prove event; cases admitting statements to prove events are "increasing" and represent "prevailing practice").

30. Insurance Co. v. Mosley, 75 U.S. 397 (1869) (widow testified that decedent said he'd fallen down stairs and "almost killed himself"). In *Mosley* there was other proof of accident: The man's voice trembled, and he seemed in pain, and son said he was lying with head on counter.

31. For a case requiring independent evidence, see State v. Post, 901 S.W.2d 231, 234 (Mo. 1995). Cases abandoning this requirement include People v. Barrett, 747 N.W.2d 797 (Mich. 2008); United States v. Moore, 791 F.2d 566, 570-571 & n.2 (7th Cir. 1986); Miller v. Keating, 754 F.2d 507, 511 (3d Cir. 1985); Armour & Co. v. Industrial Com., 243 P. 546, 547 (Colo. 1926). *See also* Morgan, Res Gestae, 12 Wash. L. Rev. 91, 100 (1937) (theory should give way).

§8.37 The "State-of-Mind" Exception—Then-Existing Physical Condition

FRE 803(3) sets forth what is usually called the state-of-mind exception, and it is a provision of extraordinary importance. It covers statements that shed light on present mental attitudes and inclinations of the speaker and his physical condition. In addition, it permits use of statements to prove the speaker's later conduct and facts about his last will and testament.

Notions of trustworthiness and necessity underlie the exception. Statements that fit are considered trustworthy because the risk of misperception is negligible and the risk of faulty memory nonexistent. On the first point, everyone is "the world's foremost authority" on his own state of mind, and much the same may be said about physical feelings.[1] Perhaps sometimes people do not understand their own minds very well, and sometimes they are mistaken about physical feelings, but usually almost everyone understands these points better than others, and human shortcomings in this department are universally understood and can be appraised by juries. Memory problems are minimized not only by the fact that the exception reaches only matters of great personal interest to the speaker, but because (wills cases apart) the exception reaches only statements describing *present* mental conditions and physical feelings.

Trustworthiness and necessity

Of course these points do not ensure sincerity or dispel the risk of ambiguity. There is a kind of immediacy (even "spontaneity") about statements that fit the exception because they reflect thoughts and sensations of the speaker as he talks, but the idea that immediacy deprives him of the chance to fabricate is unrealistic.

Do not ensure sincerity or eliminate risk of ambiguity

A notion of necessity also operates, since contemporaneous statements are likely to be better than the next-best alternative (courtroom testimony by the speaker) despite risks of insincerity or ambiguity. As the Court once put it, if the speaker were called to testify, "his own memory of his state of mind at a former time is no more likely to be clear and true than a bystander's recollection of what he said."[2] The point applies equally to testimony by a witness on what would usually be past physical sensations, compared to reports of contemporaneous out-of-court descriptions. And a live testimonial description of previous sensations is likely to seem artificial and unconvincing (even feigned). If the speaker testifies, cross-examination is likely to be just as effective in exposing falsehood, exaggeration, and self-serving motives in out-of-court statements as in live testimonial descriptions.

The exception reaches statements describing physical condition where the issue is pain and suffering. Clearly the exception lets claimants

Physical condition

---

§8.37 1. Seidelson, The State of Mind Exception to the Hearsay Rule, 13 Duq. L. Rev. 251, 253 (1974); United States v. Ponticelli, 622 F.2d 985, 991 (9th Cir. 1980) (speaker "presumably knows what his thoughts and emotions are"), *cert. denied*, 449 U.S. 1016.

2. Mutual Life Ins. Co. v. Hillmon, 145 U.S. 285, 295 (1892).

introduce their own statements to prove pain and suffering, and in wrong-ful death cases the decedent's statements are usable too.[3] Clearly too, such statements are admissible even though made to spouse or friend (they need not be made to doctors).[4]

When offered to prove physical condition, a statement satisfies the exception only if it sheds light on condition at the time.[5] Depending on circumstances, Monday's statement describing pain ("my back is sore") might bear on how the speaker felt on the previous Sunday and following Tuesday, since many kinds of pain are likely to continue. Other evidence may make it highly probable that Monday's remark applies equally on Sunday and Tuesday, but Monday's statement does not fit the exception if it describes only how the speaker felt the day before. And a statement may fit the exception even though it describes present pain caused by a blow or accident many days earlier, for the statement need not be contemporaneous with the precipitating event.

The exception does not allow statements to show the *cause* of physical feelings.[6] The exception focuses on the subjective and the present and (wills cases apart) does not reach prior acts, events, or conditions in the world at large.

§8.38 —Then-Existing Mental Condition

Where the state of mind of a person is relevant, FRE 803(3) paves the way to prove it by what she said at the time. Problems of memory are negligible, problems of perception minimal, and such statements seem better than the next-best alternative, which is backward-looking testi-mony by the person herself.

Sometimes state of mind itself is an element in a claim or defense. Usually it is the state of mind of a party. Where one party seeks to prove the state of mind of another, the admissions doctrine provides the easiest way to prove the other's statements, but a party wishing to prove *his own* state of mind needs the state-of-mind exception if he wants to offer his own statements. The exception is available to the accused as the basis for introducing his statements to show, for instance,

---

3. Northern P.R. Co. v. Urlin, 158 U.S. 271, 274-275 (1895) (suit for injuries suffered in derailment; admitting statements to doctors describing feelings, aches, and pains in physical exams); Mutual Life Ins. Co. v. Hillmon, 145 U.S. 285, 296 (1892); Insurance Co. v. Mosley, 75 U.S. 397, 404-405 (1869) (expressions of bodily or mental feelings are "natural reflexes" of what might be "impossible to show by other testimony").

4. Northern P.R. Co. v. Urlin, 158 U.S. 271, 274-275 (1895); Insurance Co. v. Mosley, 75 U.S. 397, 404-405 (1869); Casualty Ins. Co. v. Salinas, 333 S.W.2d 109, 116-118 (Tex. 1960).

5. Northern P.R. Co. v. Urlin, 158 U.S. 271, 274-275 (1895) (then-existing feelings); Mabry v. Travelers Ins. Co., 193 F.2d 497, 498 (5th Cir. 1952) ("present pain and suffering").

6. Rock v. Huffco Gas & Oil Co., Inc., 922 F.2d 272, 279 (5th Cir. 1991) (not considering statements by claimant describing accident); Hartford Acc. & Indem. Co. v. Carter, 110 F.2d 355, 356 (5th Cir. 1940) (statements describing blow to head did not fit exception).

good faith, intent, knowledge, or coercion.[1] It is available to a civil plaintiff to show, for instance, mental anguish.[2]

The exception can also be used when a nonparty's state of mind counts. In many criminal trials, the state of mind of the victim is important, and what he said is often admitted to show his purpose or knowledge or attitude.[3] The exception applies in actions for damage to business, where statements by customers can show the effect of conduct or threats.[4]

To fit the exception, a statement must indicate *existing* state of mind. A statement does not fit if it tends only to prove *prior* state of mind. But Monday's statement describing present mental state often sheds light on state of mind on the previous Sunday and the following Tuesday. Where it is reasonable to assume continuity backward[5] or forward[6] from the moment of a statement, the evidentiary effect of the statement may be extended and need not be confined to the moment it was uttered.[7] Sometimes, however, the situation undercuts any assumption of continuity and the exception cannot be used.[8]

Existing **state of mind**

§8.38 1. United States v. Peak, 856 F.2d 825, 832-833 (7th Cir. 1988) (to prove intent to help capture another), *cert. denied,* 488 U.S. 969; United States v. Eisenstein, 731 F.2d 1540, 1544-1545 (11th Cir. 1984) (defendant's statement shows disclosure element in advice-of-counsel defense).

2. Missouri, K.&T.R. Co. v. Linton, 141 S.W. 129, 130 (Tex. Civ. App. 1911) (plaintiff "felt like her heart would burst" and could not live, to prove suffering).

3. United States v. Tokars, 95 F.3d 1520, 1534 (11th Cir. 1996) (statements by victim indicating intent to divorce defendant and turn over incriminating documents, to show his motive for kidnap and murder), *cert. denied,* 520 U.S. 1132; United States v. Donley, 878 F.2d 735, 737-739 (3d Cir. 1989) (similar), *cert. denied,* 494 U.S. 1058.

4. Fun-Damental Too, Ltd. v. Gemmy Indus. Corp., 111 F.3d 993, 1003-1004 (2d Cir. 1997) (statements by customers show confusion); Israel Travel Advising Serv. v. Israel Identity Tours, 61 F.3d 1250, 1260 (7th Cir. 1995) (to show loss of business, proof of customer comments).

5. Mills v. Damson Oil Corp., 691 F.2d 715, 716-717 (5th Cir. 1982) (statements reflected knowledge and state of mind at time and "by inference, prior thereto"); Garford Trucking Corp. v. Mann, 163 F.2d 71, 72-73 (1st Cir. 1947) (hospital statement by truck driver after accident saying he took the route because he "could make better time"), *cert. denied,* 332 U.S. 810.

6. *See* United States v. Green, 680 F.2d 520, 523 (7th Cir. 1982) (statement by kidnap victim that disparaged defendant and said he was bothering her, as proof that later she did not consent to go with him); Raborn v. Hayton, 208 P.2d 133 (Wash. 1949) (statement by murdered wife to lawyer that she would part with deed only for cash, admitted in suit against husband to set aside deed, as proof that deed was not delivered but taken by force when husband killed her days later).

7. Chaffee, The Progress of the Law—Evidence, 1919-1922, 35 Harv. L. Rev. 428, 444 (1922) (mental condition may be proved by prior or later statement; stream of consciousness has enough continuity so same characteristics appear "for some distance up or down the current," but there is point beyond which evidence becomes irrelevant; "Hudson River water at West Twenty-third St. Ferry is no proof of its quality above Fort Edward").

8. United States v. Naiden, 424 F.3d 718, 722 (8th Cir. 2005) (excluding statement that defendant did not think person he met online was fourteen; not "substantially contemporaneous") (also self-serving). United States v. Reyes, 239 F.3d 722, 743 (5th Cir. 2001) (May 4th statement did not fit exception when offered to prove defendant's mental state on February 10), *cert. denied,* 534 U.S. 868.

Fact-laden statements

It is possible to read the exception in a narrow way as reaching only what we might call direct or "pure" state-of-mind statements ("I want another car") that expressly describe some mental aspect. Paraphrasing, the exception refers to a "statement of then existing state of mind" and bars any "statement of memory or belief to prove the fact remembered or believed." In the narrow reading, what we might call a fact-laden statement ("my car's old and spends too much time in the shop") would not fit the exception even though it may be highly probative on state of mind.[9] But the exception is not usually read in that narrow way and should not be. It reaches all statements, including the fact-laden variety, that shed light on state of mind and are offered to prove it.

Applying exception broadly

A moment's reflection explains why the broad reading is right. In the first place, it is in the nature of things that statements shedding light on the speaker's state of mind usually allude to acts, events, or conditions in the world, in the sense of making some claim about them. Humanly speaking, it would be surprising if things were otherwise: Intention and other mental conditions usually spring to life in the midst of beliefs and understandings about acts and events and conditions in the world, and states of mind cannot easily be described without some reference to those external realities. In that sense, mental states are contingent and conditional, and people naturally describe them in those terms. Even the example of a "pure" state-of-mind statement ("I want another car") alludes to conditions in the world—it says the speaker already has a car, and of course it refers to "car," which is itself a reference to a class of things in the world (context would help the trier figure out whether she meant "automobile" or "Pullman" or something else). Statements lacking such allusions are rare: If the question is whether one intended harm to another or knew (or didn't know) what was in a suitcase, virtually any statement that helped answer the question would contain similar allusions.

In the second place, fact-laden statements are usually deliberate expressions of some state of mind. In the example ("my car's old and spends too much time in the shop"), the speaker may knowingly and purposefully express his wish, hope, or intent to get another car by complaining about his present one, and context may make the point clear (he is looking at car ads or talking about seeing a dealer). All statements should be read with reference to the expressive or communicative intent of the speaker. Of course intentionality is hard to assess, but it does not take a rocket scientist (or expert in linguistics or psychology or semiotics) to understand that fact-laden statements are purposeful expressions of some state of mind, or to figure out that ordinary statements in ordinary settings usually carry ordinary meaning. In the end, most fact-laden statements intentionally convey

---

9. No term seems quite right. State of mind is a "fact" too because facts can be psychological realities and abstractions. But "fact-laden" and "factual baggage" seem useful to describe statements that report acts, events, or conditions in the world.

something about state of mind, and if a statement conveys the mental state that the proponent seeks to prove, it fits the exception.[10]

Perhaps because the exception refers to statements of state of mind, and because lawyers are professionally inclined to seek precise meaning in language, courts sometimes find other labels for fact-laden statements offered to prove state of mind. But being fact-laden does not turn a statement into a nonhearsay verbal act.[11] Nor does a fact-laden quality mean a statement should be treated as nonhearsay circumstantial evidence of state of mind. This approach is usually wrong if the speaker intends to express or communicate his state of mind.[12]

Not verbal act; not circumstantial evidence of state of mind

It is true that conclusions about mental state can be drawn from a fact-laden statement without drawing conclusions about acts, events, or conditions described in it—the fact-laden example ("my car's old and spends too much time in the shop") tends to prove the speaker wants another car even if we do not draw conclusions about the condition of his present car. But this point is not a good reason to consider the statement as nonhearsay circumstantial evidence of what the speaker wants if he intends to express this point. Flaws in memory or perception all but disappear if fact-laden statements are not taken as proof of acts, events, or conditions, but these dangers are also minimized in pure state-of-mind statements ("I want another car") and that is why we have the exception.

The question of admissibility is another matter. Where an act, event, or condition described in a statement has no bearing on the case and does not prejudice the objecting party, there is little reason for concern. But mental states proved in trials are affected by the same acts, events, or conditions that are also in issue, and it is those same facts to which statements often refer. Since the exception does not allow use of a statement to prove an act, event, or condition ("a fact remembered or believed"), fact-laden statements introduce more risk of prejudice than pure state-of-mind statements. The question of admissibility turns on weighing probative worth against dangers of jury misuse of a statement as proof of the act, event, or condition it describes.[13]

Extortion cases provide a common example of third-party statements offered to prove mental condition, and it is settled that statements by the victim indicating fear of the defendant are admissible to prove this

Victim statements—admit in extortion trials, not in murder trials

10. *See* State v. Clegg, 31 P.3d 408, 412 (Or. 2001) (all statements shedding light on state of mind fit exception, not just statements expressly describing mental state); United States v. Sayetsitty, 107 F.3d 1405, 1414-1415 (9th Cir. 1997) (in murder trial, invoking exception for fact-laden statements showing intent of defendants).

11. This doctrine is best reserved for statements having operative legal significance. *See* §8.16, *supra.*

12. The approach is appropriate where a statement has an important performative aspect or striking match with reality that only experience explains. *See* §§8.20-8.21, *supra.*

13. *See* Bradley v. State, 937 S.W.2d 628, 631 (Ark. 1997) (admitting testimony that victim said defendant threatened her about talking; this fact-laden statement fit and explained why child delayed in coming forward); United States v. Joe, 8 F.3d 1488, 1493-1495 (10th Cir. 1993) (victim's accusatory statements disclosed memory or belief, did not fit exception), *cert. denied,* 510 U.S. 1184.

point.[14] Here statements that show fear often refer as well to behavior by the defendant (typically threats), sometimes describing that behavior, sometimes alluding to it or suggesting by context that defendant did something to cause the fear. Of course his behavior is also an element in the government's case, and the exception does not authorize use of statements by the victim to prove it. In contrast to extortion trials, statements of fear by the victim are usually excluded in murder trials because they mention or allude to behavior by the defendant that suggests he must be the one who later killed the speaker.[15]

It seems right to be generous in admitting statements by extortion victims for three related reasons: First, fear is an element of extortion, so evidence of fear on the part of the victim is indispensable. The prosecutor's burden (to prove the victim was coerced or afraid and defendant's conduct was the cause) may be described as a dual task, but in practice it is indivisible. Fear tends to be context-specific, and fear of specific behavior is what the prosecutor must prove. Nor is it surprising that statements by the victim talk about what defendant did (or allude to it), and such statements most closely match what the prosecutor must prove. Second, contemporaneous statements by the victim are likely to be the most convincing and reliable proof of fear for the very reasons that justify the exception. By comparison with proof of his contemporaneous reaction, his later courtroom testimony is likely to be artificial and unconvincing. Third, using the exception to prove the nature or direction of the victim's fear is entirely proper. What the exception forbids is use of statements to prove what the defendant did. Thus the exception reaches everything that is directly conveyed in the words "I'm afraid *X* is going to kill me if I don't pay him." Of course the exception does forbid use of those words to prove that defendant made threats or demanded money or did anything else, and of course the speaker may well have been expressing or communicating those points too. But such a statement is useful and probative in the trial of *X* for extortion, and a court might decide to admit it to prove all the things it says directly, with a cautionary instruction (if requested) against using it as proof of anything *X* did.

Self-serving statements   Often state-of-mind statements seem self-serving and give rise to suspicions about candor. They may be accompanied by behavior that reinforces the verbal message. People feeling pain or fear may show it by tone of voice, gesture, posture, visible affect, or behavior like sleeping or taking medication or favoring a limb or steering clear of whoever or whatever is feared. But many statements do not come with added indications of candor, and the exception does not require them. The fact that it is silent about candor means courts should be hesitant to exclude statements that otherwise fit on the basis of suspicion on this score.

---

14. United States v. Collins, 78 F.3d 1021, 1036 (6th Cir. 1996), *cert. denied*, 519 U.S. 872; United States v. Accetturo, 966 F.2d 631, 636-637 & n.12 (11th Cir. 1992), *cert. denied*, 506 U.S. 1082; United States v. Grassi, 783 F.2d 1572, 1577-1578 (11th Cir. 1986), *cert. denied*, 479 U.S. 985.

15. *See* §8.39, *infra.*

The scheme of categorical exceptions reinforces the point (satisfying express requirements is enough). Only a few, like the catchall and the ones for business and public records, include broadbrush references to trustworthiness. Courts split, but the weight of authority holds that doubts on candor do not justify refusing to apply the exception.[16]

It seems that courts should have some leeway, but not a lot. In light of the breadth of the exception, concern over candor can rise to a high level, and accounts of common law tradition indicate that courts could consider this point. Hence the absence of language in the exception may not be determinative, and the framers apparently thought the exception requires a kind of spontaneity that is a good proxy for honesty. It seems wrong to apply a per se rule excluding self-serving statements, but in unusual cases strong indications that a statement is not only self-serving but concocted (never said), contrived (spoken for use in suit), or fabricated (likely false) suggest bases on which courts may act.[17] Also a court should be able to consider candor where a statement brings other concerns: A fact-laden statement brings them if the jury is likely to misuse the statement, as do marginally relevant statements requiring tenuous inferences forward or backward.[18]

§8.39   —Future Conduct

The state-of-mind exception allows use of a statement showing forward-looking intent on the part of the speaker as proof that she later acted accordingly. Subject to limits and reservations, the exception also permits use of such statements to prove what she and another later did together. Both uses are problematic. Statements shedding light on intent and future conduct suggest backward-looking inferences about past acts, events, or conditions in the world, but the exception does not allow this use. Statements suggesting what the speaker and another were going to do together can only prove what both later did by way of other backward-looking inferences (the speaker met and spoke with the other, who indicated his intent to do something with her).

16. United States v. DiMaria, 727 F.2d 265, 271-272 (2d Cir. 1984) (error to exclude defendant's exculpatory statement on arrest; truth or falsity is for jury; self-serving nature affects weight) (reversing). *See also* United States v. DiNome, 954 F.2d 839, 846 (2d Cir. 1992), *cert. denied,* 506 U.S. 830; United States v. Cardascia, 951 F.2d 474, 487-488 (2d Cir. 1991). *But see* United States v Naiden, 424 F.3d 718, 722 (8th Cir. 2005) (excluding statement that defendant did not think person he met online was fourteen, as self-serving) (alternative ground).

17. United States v. Ponticelli, 622 F.2d 985, 991-992 (9th Cir. 1980) (excluding post-arrest statement to lawyer; defendant had "chance for reflection and misrepresentation"), *cert. denied,* 449 U.S. 1016; United States v. Mandel, 437 F. Supp. 262, 265-266 (D. Md. 1977) (judge may consider possible bad faith).

18. Black Hills Jewelry Mfg. Co. v. Gold Rush, Inc., 633 F.2d 746, 752-753 (8th Cir. 1980) (rejecting testimony in other case, describing understanding of witness on meaning of "Black Hills gold," citing "lack of trustworthiness" and saying testimony had "little probative value").

Hillmon case

In endorsing use of statements to prove the speaker's intent, hence future conduct, the exception carries forward a doctrine associated with the famous Supreme Court opinion in *Mutual Life Insurance Co. v. Hillmon.* There three insurance carriers resisted a claim that the insured John Hillmon died of an accidental gunshot at the hands of his traveling companion John Brown at their camp at Crooked Creek, Kansas. The defense theory was that a third man named Frederick Walters was the man who was killed, and that Hillmon and Brown conspired to fake Hillmon's death and collect the proceeds in a suit brought by the beneficiary on policies insuring Hillmon's life. To prove Walters went to Crooked Creek, the carriers offered two letters from him (one to his sister, the other to his fiancée), both saying he intended to leave Wichita and go west toward Colorado. In *Hillmon,* the Court concluded:

> The letters in question were competent, not as narratives of facts communicated to the writer by others, nor yet as proof that [Walters] actually went away from Wichita, but as evidence that, shortly before the time when other evidence tended to show that he went away, he had the intention of going, and of going with Hillmon, which made it more probable both that he did go and that he went with Hillmon than if there had been no proof of such intention.[1]

Prove what
speaker then did

Hillmon was a cause célèbre, and it came to stand for the proposition that a statement indicating the intent of the speaker to do something may be admitted as evidence that he later did it.[2] In keeping with this tradition, many modern cases uphold use of statements of intent to prove later conduct by the speaker,[3] including statements threatening suicide.[4]

---

§8.39 1. Mutual Life Ins. Co. v. Hillmon, 145 U.S. 285, 295-296 (1892). If the carriers had argued only that the body was Walters rather than Hillmon, the letters from Walters would have been important only to show he went west from Wichita. But the carriers tried to place Walters at Crooked Creek *with* Hillmon, which accounts for the controversy over using the exception to prove conduct.

2. *See* Wigmore, Principles of Judicial Proof 856-896 (1913); MacCracken, The Case of the Anonymous Corpse, 19 Am. Heritage 51 (1968). *See also* McFarland, Dead Men Tell Tales: Thirty Times Three Years of the Judicial Process After Hillmon, 30 Vill. L. Rev. 1 (1985); Hinton, States of Mind and the Hearsay Rule, 1 U. Chi. L. Rev. 394, 403-423 (1934); Hutchins & Slesinger, Some Observations on the Law of Evidence—State of Mind to Prove an Act, 38 Yale L.J. 283, 289-298 (1929); Maguire, The Hillmon Case—Thirty-Three Years After, 38 Harv. L. Rev. 709 (1925); Wesson, The Hillmon Case, The Supreme Court, and the McGuffin, in Evidence Law Stories (2006).

3. State v. Yarbrough, 767 N.E.2d 216, 225 (Ohio 2002) (in trial arising out of killing of informant A, admitting D's statement that that he would kill A or have her killed, to prove he did what he said he would) (quoting authors of this Treatise); Phoenix Mutual Life Ins. v. Adams, 30 F.3d 554, 566 (4th Cir. 1994) (admitting statement by insured indicating intent to change beneficiary, to show conduct).

4. United States v. Veltmann, 6 F.3d 1483, 1493 (11th Cir. 1993) (in homicide trial, decedent's statement admissible to prove suicide); Brawner v. Royal Indem. Co., 246 F. 637, 638-640 (5th Cir. 1917) (statements by insured indicating depression and reasons for suicide). Statements inconsistent with such disposition can disprove suicide. *See* United States v. Brown, 490 F.2d 758, 767 (D.C. Cir. 1973).

Statements threatening harm to another also fit the exception. In homicide cases, for example, sometimes the alleged victim has threatened the defendant. Such threats show ill-will or animus toward the defendant, and the threats may be critical evidence on the question who started an affray if defendant claims self-defense. If the threats were communicated to him, they have a nonhearsay use in shedding light on what the defendant thought or feared at the time, hence on the reasonableness of his conduct.[5] Whether or not they were communicated to him, they bear on the intent and behavior of the alleged victim, and using them in this way involves the state-of-mind exception.[6]

Because such statements also bring the risk of prejudice, they may **Risk of prejudice** be excludable on this ground. They cast the alleged victim in a bad light, and are often fact-laden. Hence there may be some sense in excluding marginal statements that only slightly indicate generalized hostility.[7] Some decisions go further, excluding even pointed threats unless, for instance, other evidence suggests that the victim started the affray (there are likely to be ill feelings between victim and defendant, and hostile statements may have little persuasive force), but these cases seem to be a misguided attempt to implement notions of sufficiency.[8] Third-party threats may be admissible as well, as evidence that someone other than the defendant committed the crime.[9]

Of course the hearsay doctrine does not exclude threats by the defendant (they are admissions when offered against him). If communicated to the victim, they seem relevant in assessing the conduct of both at the time of the affray. If not communicated, they would likely be admissible to prove animus or hostility on the part of the defendant, which in turn sheds light on his intent.

Using statements to prove intent, hence later conduct by the speaker, cannot be defended by claims of trustworthiness and necessity so strongly as using them to prove the speaker's state of mind as an end in itself, where immediacy and directness are salient points. When the purpose is to prove conduct, statements of intent lack these qualities, and bring special perils: It is commonplace, for example, to exaggerate or overplay intent, to report wishful thinking as resolve, to speak casually while knowing that such statements are "taken with a grain of salt," to rely on intent as a substitute for doing something, and

5. A threat received by the defendant can show its effect on him, shedding light on the reasonableness of his behavior at the affray. Proving effect on listener is a classic nonhearsay use. *See* §8.18, *supra*.

6. Wiggins v. Utah, 93 U.S. 465, 466-467 (1876) (error to exclude uncommunicated threats by victim showing hostility toward defendant, which indicated that victim tried to kill him at time of encounter).

7. State v. Griffin, 285 S.E.2d 631 (S.C. 1981) (requiring actual threat; excluding decedent's statement that he was not afraid of defendant and had gun).

8. *See* Griffin v. United States, 183 F.2d 990, 992 (D.C. Cir. 1950) (implying that uncommunicated threats by victim are admissible only with evidence that he attacked defendant); State v. Hurdle, 169 S.E.2d 17, 19 (N.C. Ct. App. 1969) (similar).

9. Alexander v. United States, 138 U.S. 353, 356-357 (1891) (error to exclude third-party threats).

even to mistake one's own intent. And it is a familiar fact of life that obstacles, distractions, changes of heart, and weakness intervene between intending and doing, and passage of time may bring to light mistakes or miscalculations that lead one to change course. And when the point is to prove conduct, usually there is nonhearsay evidence that can be tested by courtroom questioning.

Fact-laden statements

For purposes of applying the exception, the form and nature of the statement make no difference. Obviously a direct statement of intent is hearsay when offered to prove intent of the speaker, hence later conduct. Consider the statement "I plan to leave for Chicago tomorrow" or (in the customary idiom of the present progressive) "I'm going to Chicago tomorrow." Just as obviously these statements fit the exception and are likely to be admitted to show the speaker went to Chicago the next day. The same is true of statements that indicate a sense of obligation suggesting intent: "I must (or should, or need to) go to Chicago tomorrow." The inference of intent (hence conduct) may be more attenuated, but the statement still expressly describes state of mind and still suggests the speaker went to Chicago the next day.

Fact-laden statements reporting that events occurred or conditions exist may also indicate intent, and ordinarily these too should be viewed as hearsay that fit the exception when offered to prove intent, hence conduct. Consider these: "My boss asked me to go to Chicago," or "The Art Institute is showing an exhibit of special interest to me." Since the exception does not allow use of a statement to prove acts, events, or conditions of these sorts, the factual baggage presents special difficulties in applying the exception. Putting them aside for a moment, such statements are evidence that the speaker later went to Chicago because they invite one or more of the following interpretations:

First, he is speaking indirectly and means to be understood as disclosing his purpose to go to Chicago, so his statement proves his intent by implication (in the strong sense of purposefully expressing intent), and his intent suggests that he later went. Under this interpretation, these fact-laden statements are truly assertions of intent even though they make no express reference to it, and they fit the exception when offered to prove intent. The point is that all statements should be read to mean whatever the speaker intends to express or communicate. If what he tried to convey is his own intent on some point (like going to Chicago), the statement is hearsay if offered to prove the intent, and it fits the exception.

Second, the statements indicate that the speaker believes the fact reported (his boss asked him to go; the Art Institute has a show), and this belief makes it likely that he later went to Chicago. By this interpretation, the statements are again hearsay. The reason is that a fact-laden statement deliberately expresses and communicates what the speaker believes about the act, event, or condition he describes, so his statement is hearsay when offered to prove this belief. The state-of-mind exception embraces statements offered for just this purpose.

Third, the statements tend to prove the various acts, events, or conditions (what the boss said, what the Art Institute is showing), and these facts themselves make it likely that the speaker later went to Chicago. This interpretation presents greater difficulties. Since the exception does not allow use of statements to prove the reported facts (what the boss said, and so forth), a statement that tends to show intent only by proving them does not fit the exception. Fortunately most cases leave room for the first and second interpretive possibilities, which means that such statements usually fit the exception.

Sometimes courts say that assertions of acts, events, or conditions are nonhearsay circumstantial evidence of state of mind. This approach makes sense for statements with performative aspects that support the desired inference, but the presence of factual baggage is not itself a good reason for this approach. The qualities that make such statements persuasive as evidence of intent invite the interpretations described above, and calling them nonhearsay means missing these qualities.

While fact-laden statements fit the exception, factual content can be crucial in assessing probative worth against prejudice and confusion under FRE 403.

Refer again to the fact-laden statements about going to Chicago (my boss asked me to go; the Art Institute has an exhibit) and suppose the purpose is to show the speaker went to Chicago. If the facts in the statement are inconsequential, unlikely to inject prejudice, or established by overwhelming evidence or general agreement, there is no concern. But if the facts do matter or might inject unfair prejudice or confusion, a court should take special precautions. An instruction limiting use of the statement to prove intent and later behavior by the speaker would be in order. If such an instruction seems futile, a court might exclude the statement under FRE 403.[10] In such cases, the judge can take into account motivational factors that might cast doubt on the candor of the speaker, although ordinarily problems of candor (including the perennial problem of the "self-serving" statement) are for the jury.[11] In sum, fact-laden statements warrant caution, but factual baggage does not mean the exception does not apply.

Behavior by others

Statements of intent often refer to other people and their future behavior. *Hillmon* itself is such a case because Walters said he planned to go west with Hillmon. Recall that plaintiff claimed Hillmon was accidentally shot by his companion John Brown. The carriers claimed the body at Crooked Creek was Walters and that Hillmon murdered Walters and conspired with Brown to collect on policies insuring Hillmon's life. The carriers offered the letters from Walters, and the Court said the letters were competent to prove Walters "had the intention of going, and of going with Hillmon, which made it more probable both that he did go and that he went with Hillmon."

---

10. Shepard v. United States, 290 U.S. 96, 104 (1933) (error to admit statement offered to show speaker wanted to live and refute claim that she killed herself; jury would not distinguish between using it to prove will to live and to prove defendant poisoned her); United States v. Day, 591 F.2d 861, 881-886 (D.C. Cir. 1978); United States v. Brown, 490 F.2d 758 (D.C. Cir. 1973).

11. *See* §8.38, *supra.*

This passage is one of considerable subtlety. It does not say what Walters wrote was competent to prove what Hillmon did, and on this point there was other evidence and no dispute. It says only that what Walters wrote was competent evidence of his conduct with Hillmon, which is different. By analogy, one might say that the statement "I'm taking the Manhattan Limited to New York tomorrow" is competent to prove the speaker took the train but not to prove the train ran that day. By a broad interpretation, however, *Hillmon* can be understood to mean the statement of Walters could prove both what he did and what Hillmon did with him (the speaker was on the train and it actually ran). In the dismal situation in which a homicide victim says he expects to meet the defendant, many cases uphold use of such statements to put the two together at the time of the killing.[12]

The rub   Here is the rub: What someone says can only prove what he and another did if used to support both forward- and backward-looking inferences. The forward-looking inference is that the speaker acted as intended, which is fine. The backward-looking inference is that he had already met the other person when he spoke, that the two had agreed to do something together (the other had spoken words indicating his intent), and that both later acted accordingly. These inferences are *not* fine, and apparently the framers of the exception meant to reject *Hillmon* in its broadest reach. The first clue is the language in the exception barring its use "to prove the fact remembered or believed." The second clue is a one-sentence comment in the ACN that the *Hillmon* rule "allowing evidence of intention as tending to prove the doing of the act intended is, of course, left undisturbed." Since *Hillmon* and the complicating factors are famous and the Committee included scholars who knew them well, this remark is cryptic and cannot carry the weight of approving *Hillmon* in its broadest reach. The third clue is a later comment by the House Judiciary Committee, specific and pointed, rejecting use of a statement by one person to prove conduct by another. The exception should be read "to limit the doctrine of *Hillmon*" so statements of intent can prove only declarant's future conduct, "not the future conduct of another person."[13] This comment should be taken as controlling.

No longer the law: modern compromise   In short, *Hillmon* in its broadest reach is no longer the law. While a Ninth Circuit decision in the *Pheaster* case upheld use of a statement by kidnap victim Larry Adell that he was "going to meet Angelo in the parking lot to get a pound of grass," as proof that he and Angelo did

---

12. *See* State v. McElrath, 366 S.E.2d 442, 452 (N.C. 1988); State v. Santangelo, 534 A.2d 1175, 1184 (Conn. 1987); State v. Terrovona, 716 P.2d 295, 300 (Wash. 1986), *cert. denied*, 499 U.S. 979; People v. Malizia, 460 N.Y.S.2d 23, 27 (N.Y. App. Div. 1983), *aff'd*, 465 N.E.2d 364 (N.Y. 1984), *cert. denied*, 469 U.S. 932; Hunter v. State, 40 N.J.L. 495, 534-540 (1878). *But see* People v. Alcalde, 148 P.2d 627 (Cal. 1944) (*C* told roommate she was going out with *F*, admitted to prove she went out with him) (dissent argues that statement was used to prove *F*'s acts and was incompetent); State v. Vestal, 180 S.E.2d 755, 768-773 (N.C. 1971) (similar), *later app.*, 195 S.E.2d 297 (N.C. 1973), *cert. denied*, 414 U.S. 874.

13. House Report, at 13-14 (1973).

meet (Adell was never seen again), the case may not have intended to say that FRE 803(3) permits this broad use.[14] Yet modern decisions continue to conflict on fact similar to those in *Pheaster*, some holding (correctly in our view) that the exception does not permit use of statements of intent by themselves as proof of what others did, but others continuing to insist that the exception applies when statements are offered to put the speaker together with another and others.[15] A compromise position has also emerged, approving this use of the exception when other evidence confirms what the statement suggests the other did.[16] It is also worth noting that in some cases a victim's statement can put her in proximity with the defendant *without* the need to take what the victim said as proof of a prior arrangement with the defendant.[17]

By one view, even the compromise position cannot be squared with the exception: Independent evidence does not excuse use of a statement in support of the backward-looking inference that is expressly forbidden. By another view, these cases seem right because such statements are competent to prove what the speaker did with another, and the restriction is only violated if they are used to prove what the other did. (To use the earlier analogy, a statement of intent is competent to prove the speaker took the train, and the exception only bars use of the statement to prove the train ran.) If other evidence proves what the other did, the issue can be framed in terms of the risk of jury misuse under FRE 403 rather than violating the limit of the exception. Of course this interpretation requires not merely corroborating evidence of what the other did (which seems to satisfy many courts), but enough such evidence to support an inference that he did what the statement suggests, and it requires too that the court give a limiting instruction if

---

14. United States v. Pheaster, 544 F.2d 353, 374-380 (9th Cir. 1976) (despite "theoretical awkwardness" that Larry's "implicit statement" describing Angelo's intention had nothing to do with Larry's state of mind, *Hillmon* permits this use), *cert. denied*, 429 U.S. 1099 (1977). *Pheaster* may mean that pre-Rules law permitted use of a statement to prove later conduct by the speaker and another but that result would differ under the Rules (not in effect at time of trial). But it is hard to believe the court felt compelled to admit Adell's statement a matter of common law if it thought that FRE 803(3) sets a wise limit.

15. *Compare* Brooks v. State, 787 So.2d 765, 771-772 (Fla. 2001) (cannot use victim's statement of intent to meet defendant as proof that he later killed her); Gual Morales v. Hernandez Vega, 579 F.2d 677, 680 n.2 (1st Cir. 1978) (lawyer's statement of intent to see *A* is not admissible against *A*) *with* Reyes v. State, 819 A.2d 305, 313-314 (Del. 2003); State v. Griffin, 528 S.E.2d 668 (S.C. 2000); Lisle v. State, 941 P.2d 459, 467-468 (Nev. 1997), *cert. denied*, 525 U.S. 830 (1998); State v. Santangelo, 534 A.2d 1175, 1184 (Conn. 1987) (all admitting statements by victim describing anticipated meeting with defendant).

16. United States v. Best, 219 F.3d 192, 197-198 (2d Cir. 2000) (third-party statements of intent relating to defendant require independent proof of defendant's conduct), *cert denied*, 522 U.S. 1007; United States v. Nersesian, 824 F.2d 1294, 1325 (2d Cir. 1987) (statements of intent to meet are admissible against others if there is corroboration), *cert. denied*, 484 U.S. 958; People v. James, 717 N.E.2d 1052, 1060 (N.Y. 1999).

17. State v. Johnson, 131 P.3d 173, 189 (Or. 2006) ("I'm going to Marty's house" admitted to prove that victim went to defendant's house shortly before she was found dead).

requested. Thus understood, this line of cases can be squared with the literal language of the critical passage in *Hillmon* and with the exception as enacted.

Other states of mind

FRE 803(3) paves the way for statements showing other emotional conditions to prove later conduct—affection, fear, jealousy, anger, hate, prejudice, happiness, or despondency may all shed light on behavior. Such statements present two difficulties. One is that these emotions or attitudes are a step or two removed from intent and bear less directly on later conduct. Relevancy is often minimal and risks of prejudice loom larger.[18] The second is that these statements often suggest acts, events, or conditions in the world, even if they make no overt reference to them: Anger or fear, for instance, almost always suggest inferences about the behavior or attitude of another person. And such statements are often fact-laden, describing acts in issue in the suit or otherwise describing acts, events, or conditions that inject prejudice. Statements describing such other emotions or attitudes may be excluded under FRE 403 if these risks are too high,[19] and the danger seems especially great when they speak openly of acts or events.[20]

Victim statements—exclude in murder trials; admit in extortion trials

These issues often arise in homicide cases where statements of fear by the victim are usually excluded because of the risk of jury misuse.[21] They only weakly support proper inferences about what the victim probably did or did not do but strongly suggest improper inferences about what defendant did then or before, making such evidence highly prejudicial. Recall that in extortion cases, usually such statements get in, but the difference is that the victim's state of mind is an element in the prosecutor's case in that setting, so statements by the victim have special relevance.[22] Even in homicide cases, however, the state of mind of the victim sometimes has special relevance: To rebut a claim of self-defense, for example, a statement by the decedent suggesting fear of the defendant is usually admissible to show the former did not start the affray.[23] And if defendant in a homicide case claims the decedent

18. United States v. Brown, 490 F.2d 758, 780 (D.C. Cir. 1973) (in murder trial, error to admit victim's statement indicating fear of defendant, which suffered "overwhelming deficiency in relevance," absent special circumstances, like claim of self-defense) (reversing).

19. United States v. Day, 591 F.2d 861, 881-886 (D.C. Cir. 1978); United States v. Brown, 490 F.2d 758, 778-779 (D.C. Cir. 1973); People v. Ireland, 450 P.2d 580 (Cal. 1969).

20. United States v. Liu, 960 F.2d 449, 452 (5th Cir. 1992) (admitting statements by defendant indicating he feared for life, but not statements that he was afraid government agents would do bad things), *cert. denied,* 506 U.S. 957; United States v. Emmert, 829 F.2d 805, 809-810 (9th Cir. 1987) (excluding statements by defendant that undercover agents made threats).

21. *See* United States v. Joe, 8 F.3d 1488, 1493-1495 (10th Cir. 1993), *cert. denied,* 510 U.S. 1184; United States v. Brown, 490 F.2d 758 (D.C. Cir. 1973). *Contra,* United States v. Baker, 432 F.3d 1189, 1214 (11th Cir. 2005); State v. Dehaney, 803 A.2d 267, 279 (Conn. 2002).

22. *See* the discussion in §8.38, *supra.*

23. United States v. Brown, 490 F.2d 758, 767-769 (D.C. Cir. 1973) (to rebut self-defense, can admit statements of victim that he feared defendant, making it less likely that victim was the aggressor); United States v. Day, 591 F.2d 861, 881-886 (D.C. Cir. 1978) (similar).

committed suicide, statements alluding to acts, events, or conditions that suggest an aversion to dying or determination to live may be admitted to refute the claim of suicide and suggest murder as cause of death.[24] Sometimes such statements are relevant for other reasons too.[25]

There may be other reasons to conclude that statements indicating fear caused by threats or assaults are reliable, but such statements do not generally support an inference of conduct by the speaker of the sort possible in *Hillmon*, and the assurance of reliability that such conduct provides is missing. The situation would be different if the victim announced immediate plans to flee because defendant threatened his life: Such a statement fits the pattern of *Hillmon* and should be admitted if surrounding circumstances indicate reliability.[26]

§8.40   —Facts Remembered or Believed

As noted in the last section, the state-of-mind exception does not allow backward-looking inferences from statements to prove memory, hence the acts, events, or conditions reflected in that memory, including acts by the speaker himself. Apart from wills cases, the exception excludes from coverage "a statement of memory or belief to prove the fact remembered or believed."

If the exception had no such limit, it might devour the hearsay doctrine. Virtually all statements that carry information about acts, events, or conditions can be characterized as statements of memory because they openly disclose the speaker's thoughts: One who says "the light was red" is saying "I know or remember the light was red." If they were admissible to prove everything that memory tends to show, nothing would block inferences about the acts, events, or conditions that

Might devour doctrine

---

24. United States v. Brown, 490 F.2d 758, 767 (D.C. Cir. 1973) (where defense claims decedent committed suicide, statements inconsistent with suicidal bent are admissible). Statements by a victim *supporting* a defense claim that death was suicidal are also admissible. *See* United States v. Veltmann, 6 F.3d 1483, 1493 (11th Cir. 1993). *But see* Shepard v. United States, 290 U.S. 96 (1933) (excluding wife's fact-laden statements accusing husband of poisoning her, to rebut claims that she was suicidal).

25. United States v. Looking Cloud, 419 F.3d 781, 787 (8th Cir. 2005) (admitting proof that people in American Indian Movement accused victim of being informant, and she "spoke of fearing for her life," as nonhearsay proof of motive for killing her); Ex parte Baker, 906 So.2d 277, 283 (Ala. 2004) (victim said she was afraid of defendant, admitted to refute claim that she went willingly with him).

26. Seidelson, The State of Mind Exception to the Hearsay Rule, 13 Duq. L. Rev. 251, 258-261, 266-277 (1974) (in trial of husband for murdering wife, lifelong friend might testify that she answered phone and heard husband ask for her, then watched and listened as she spoke words of fear indicating that he was threatening her life and finally asking to stay the night; admit because statement is contemporaneous and trustworthy; intimacy of marriage gives each spouse "unique capacity" to understand words of the other). *See* critique of Seidelson article in Rice, The State of Mind Exception to the Hearsay Rule: A Response to " 'Secondary' Relevance," 14 Duq. L. Rev. 219 (1976) (arguing that Seidelson distorts exception).

memory reflects, and almost all statements would be admissible to prove them. The hearsay doctrine would nearly vanish.

Shepard case   In a famous opinion by Justice Cardozo, the Supreme Court voiced this fear in reviewing the conviction of an Army doctor for murdering his wife Zenana. The case was *Shepard v. United States*, and the government showed that she asked to have a bottle of liquor tested for poison ("smell and taste were strange") and said "Dr. Shepard has poisoned me." She was speaking two days after she collapsed, and her statements came in as dying declarations. The Court of Appeals approved, but on the narrower ground that they fit the state-of-mind exception if used to show her will to live, rebutting defense arguments that she took her own life.[1] The Supreme Court reversed. The statements were not dying declarations (she did not have a settled expectation of death) nor did they fit the state-of-mind exception. They were not offered for the "strained and narrow purpose" of proving will to live, and had wider impact because they "faced backward" rather than forward in their "most obvious implications" and would likely be taken as proof of "an act committed by some one else" and as evidence that she "was dying of poison given by her husband." After listing cases where the exception may be invoked, the Court concluded:

> [I]n suits upon insurance policies, declarations by an insured that he intends to go upon a journey with another, may be evidence of a state of mind lending probability to the conclusion that the purpose was fulfilled. The ruling in [*Hillmon*] marks the high water line beyond which courts have been unwilling to go. It has developed a substantial body of criticism and commentary. Declarations of intention, casting light upon the future, have been sharply distinguished from declarations of memory, pointing backwards to the past. There would be an end, or nearly that, to the rule against hearsay if the distinction were ignored.[2]

Shepard condemns use of the exception to show the speaker's memory of an act, event, or condition, hence to prove any such point. Wills cases apart, FRE 803(3) takes this position, and for the most part modern courts flatly reject state-of-mind statements when offered to prove memory, hence the past.[3]

Applying the exception turns on the purpose for which a statement is offered and its likely effect on the factfinder. While the form and

---

§8.40   1. Shepard v. United States, 62 F.2d 683 (10th Cir. 1933), *rev'd*, 290 U.S. 96 (1933).

2. Shepard v. United States, 290 U.S. 96 (1933) (it would not do to say jury would use statements for whatever light they might shed about "existence of a vital urge" but reject them to the extent they charged death to someone else, for the "reverberating clang" of the words "would drown all weaker sounds").

3. United States v. Samaniego, 345 F.3d 1280, 1282 (11th Cir. 2003) (thief's apology did not fit exception when offered to prove theft); Firemen's Fund Ins. Co. v. Thien, 63 F.3d 754, 760 (8th Cir. 1995) (statement that speaker was to be laid off did not fit exception when offered to prove he had been laid off); United States v. Tome, 61 F.3d 1446, 1453-1454 (10th Cir. 1995) (statements by child expressing desire to remain with mother could not be used to prove what father did).

substance of a statement count, they are not determinative. Thus statements that report acts, events, or conditions sometimes fit the exception and may be admitted to prove state of mind despite the bar against using "statements of memory or belief to prove the fact remembered or believed." Likewise statements reporting only mental conditions may be excluded if they are offered to prove facts remembered or believed (or likely to be taken that way).

Use counts more than form and substance because fact-laden statements shed light on state of mind, and statements describing mental conditions suggest factual inferences. It is common for people to express themselves purposefully in these cross-over patterns. Consider a statement describing an act ("My boss asked me to go to Chicago"), which tends to prove intent and may be admitted under the exception unless the risk is too great that it will be taken as proof of the act (what the boss said) and the act is important or might cause prejudice. Consider also a statement describing intent ("I have to meet my wife at the train"), which tends to prove acts, events, or conditions, and may be admitted under the exception unless (once again) the risk is too great that it will be taken as proof of the acts, events, or conditions suggested by the state of mind (wife is on train; she and husband agreed to meet) and such inferences would be damaging or prejudicial.

Fact-laden statements

The line-in-the-sand approach taken by *Shepard* and the restrictive language in FRE 803(3) are open to criticism because backward-looking inferences may be safer than forward-looking ones. To speak for a moment of sense and reason, the sharpest criticism of *Shepard* stresses that if we want to know what someone did on Sunday and we can learn what she thinks, then her backward-looking memory on Monday is likely to be at least as reliable as her forward-looking intention on Saturday.[4] Statements reflecting memory and those reflecting intent bring similar risks of candor and narrative ambiguity, and neither brings much risk of misperception or faulty memory when it comes to conclusions about what the speaker thinks. When it comes to conclusions about behavior, it is true that backward-looking statements bring problems of misperception or faulty memory, while forward-looking statements do not. Yet the difference is not entirely persuasive because intent is changeable, hence less reliable to predict the future than memory in recalling the past. (One reason intent is so changeable is that it reflects backward-looking belief, and intent changes when errors in belief are corrected by later information or further thought.)

To speak for a moment of alternate approaches, it is worth noting that FRE 803(3)'s bright line does not always block use of statements to prove facts remembered. Courts sometimes admit words with important performative aspects as nonhearsay circumstantial evidence of memory, which allows them to be used in support of the two-step inference (statement suggests mental state, which suggests acts, events, or

4. Payne, The Hillmon Case—An Old Problem Revisited, 41 Va. L. Rev. 1011, 1023-1024 (1955).

conditions).[5] And courts sometimes allow use of a statement reflecting present state of mind to support inferences about past state of mind where the theory is that present feelings probably began in the past.[6]

In the end, FRE 803(3) and *Shepard* insist on a bright-line distinction that allows inferences looking forward but not those looking back. Despite the difficulties, this approach may be defended in two ways: First, allowing some backward-looking inferences would introduce line-drawing problems and erode the hearsay doctrine in a serious way (Cardozo was right to be concerned). Second, lay factfinders are likely to be appropriately skeptical toward statements suggesting forward-looking inferences because they bring uncertainties that connect with everyday experience, but the risks of backward-looking inferences are more dangerous, more hidden, less familiar.

Some backward-looking inferences — Perhaps after all the state-of-mind exception can be used to support at least some backward-looking inferences. Although the argument has the feel of pulling a rabbit out of a hat, it is theoretically possible to reach this conclusion by combining two conventional notions on which all would agree: The first is that a statement admitted under the exception may prove intent, hence what the speaker later did; the second is that nonassertive conduct may support the standard two-step inference (it shows actor's belief, which in turn shows past acts, events, and conditions). With this combination, a statement can prove what the speaker later did, and what he did (not the statement) can prove prior acts, events, or conditions. It is possible to view *Hillmon* as such a case: The statement proves Walters intended to go west with Hillmon, hence that he did, and the fact that he went west proves he made prior arrangements with another (known to be Hillmon because of the statement).

Annunziato case — A 1961 decision by the Second Circuit in the in *Annunziato* case presents a strong case for using statements of intent as part of a larger circumstantial picture supporting backward-looking inferences about motivating factors. The case is strong because there was lots of independent evidence of the later behavior of the speaker, and he spoke directly about the act that motivated him. There, defendant was a union official charged with taking an illegal payment from a contractor, and the government introduced testimony by Richard Terker that his father Harry (president of contracting company, but dead at time of trial) said he got a call from Annunziato (the defendant) asking for money on a bridge project, and that he (Harry) had agreed to send him some. The comptroller testified that he gave Harry an envelope with $300 in cash. The supervisor at the site testified that Harry gave him an envelope with instructions to give it to Annunziato, and another witness saw the supervisor give an envelope to Annunziato. On appeal, Annunziato argued that Harry's statement should have been excluded as hearsay, but the Second Circuit disagreed. If Harry had dropped the envelope in front of his son and picked it up saying it

5. *See* §8.21, *supra.*
6. *See* §8.38, *supra.*

contained money for Annunziato, the court said, the statement would be admitted to prove plan, hence later acts. The fact that Harry described the plan along with a "natural explanation" of what prompted it in the recent past did not call for different treatment:

> To say that this portion of his statement is sufficiently trustworthy for the jury to consider without confrontation, but that his reference to the telephone call from Annunziato which produced the decision to send the money is not, would truly be swallowing the camel and straining at the gnat. The "vigorous leap" with respect to the hearsay exception for declarations of state of mind was taken when this was extended from cases where "it is material to prove the state of a person's mind, or what was passing in it, and what were his intentions," as to which the declaration may well be the most reliable evidence attainable, to cases where the state of mind is relevant only to prove other action, where it surely is not. True, inclusion of a past event motivating the plan adds the hazards of defective perception and memory to that of prevarication; but this does not demand exclusion or even excision, at least when, as here, the event is recent, is within the personal knowledge of the declarant and is so integrally included in the declaration of design as to make it unlikely in the last degree that the latter would be true and the former false. True also, the statement of the past event would not be admitted if it stood alone, as the *Shepard* case holds; but this would not be the only hearsay exception where the pure metal may carry some alloy along with it.[7]

Annunziato could be dismissed as making the easy mistake of taking form as controlling (echoing a phrase from *Shepard*, *Annunziato* said the statement looked forward), but the outcome seems right. Harry Terker spoke in private to his son on a serious matter with no apparent motive to misrepresent; he described his present intent to do something and gave a reason; he proposed to act immediately, and the events had happened in the recent past and directly explained his plan. And he had died before trial, so better evidence was hard to come by. Risks of ambiguity seem minimal, as do risks of memory and misperception.

Arguably a case like *Annunziato* does not violate the restriction in FRE 803(3), although it pushes the limit. The salient point is that there was ample additional evidence in *Annunziato* that the speaker acted in accord with his stated intent (other proof that Harry Terker got cash, went to the jobsite and gave an envelope to the supervisor who gave it to the defendant). It is reasonable to suggest that an inference of prior fact motivating serious conduct may be drawn when conduct itself is proved by other evidence. The inference of prior fact does not depend on the

---

7. United States v. Annunziato, 293 F.2d 373, 377-378 (2d Cir. 1961) (*Hillmon* approved statement from which jury would infer prior arrangement; in *Shepard*, statement "faced backward and not forward"), *cert. denied*, 368 U.S. 919.

statement itself, and the role of the statement is to define the motivating fact that the later conduct then proves.[8]

§8.41   —Wills Cases

The state-of-mind exception is especially useful in cases involving disputes over wills where the private and personal acts and intentions of an unavailable testator are critical. No special language was needed in FRE 803(3) to pave the way for statements indicating his forward-looking intent, offered to prove his later conduct carrying out that intent. Nor was special language needed for statements indicating his existing state of mind, offered to show his thinking when he spoke and thereafter.

Savings clause   It has long been thought, however, that in wills cases backward-looking statements by testators describing previous acts and conditions should also be admitted, and for this purpose a special clause was added ("unless it relates to the execution, revocation, identification, or terms of declarant's will"). Essentially this provision is a savings clause carving out an exemption from the general proscription against using a "statement of memory or belief to prove the fact remembered or believed." By virtue of this language, backward-looking statements indicating memory are admissible to prove facts about declarant's will. In a sense the clause creates a separate hearsay exception that is combined with the state-of-mind exception because of history and because the important facts about wills are usually bound together with matters of testamentary intent.[1]

Testator's frame of mind   Extending the exception in wills cases is partly motivated by a special sense of need since the testator's frame of mind is important and lurks behind most fact questions, and he cannot give evidence in person. His statements, before and after the fact, are likely to be the best evidence available. There is also some feeling that statements by a testator about his will are peculiarly trustworthy: The subject is important and serious to him, and he is likely to speak with knowledge, serious purpose, and candor.[2] On the other hand, many such statements are made to family members with varied and conflicting stakes. It follows that the witnesses

8. United States v. Ouimette, 753 F.2d 188, 191-192 (1st Cir. 1985) (defendant sought to show he had no gun and none was dropped; can admit testimony that police searched and said they were looking for gun; could show their state of mind; jury could infer that no gun was dropped); Nuttall v. Reading Co., 235 F.2d 546, 551-552 (3d Cir. 1956) (speaker said he had to go to work, which showed railroad required him).

§8.41   1. *See* Throckmorton v. Holt, 180 U.S. 552, 572-579 (1901) (excluding); Sugden v. St. Leonards, 1 P.D. 154, 202 (1876) (approving backward-looking statement by testator); Keen v. Keen, 3 P. & D. 105, 107-108 (1873) (statement by testator can show he changed mind and destroyed will).

2. *See* Timber Access Indus. Co. v. U.S. Plywood-Champion Papers, Inc., 503 P.2d 482, 487 (Or. 1972) (testator "normally has no reason to lie"); Sugden v. St. Leonards, 1 P.D. 154, 202 (1876) (only in "rare instances" does testator mislead). Courts recognize that a testator might be less than candid about intentions (keep good relations, avoid jealousies). *See* Throckmorton v. Holt, 180 U.S. 552, 578 (1901) (no inference "more uncertain or unreliable" than about genuineness of will from what testator says).

most likely to report such statements in court are themselves biased, and that those who make such statements are likely to be driven by the forces that family life generates. No doubt a common human reaction to these forces is to try to avoid giving offense and creating dissention, or to play for advantage by manipulating the prospect of future gain, or perhaps even to use the inevitable uncertainties to sow dissension or play off family members. Despite these risks, it seems likely on balance that most testators are moved in such conversations to be truthful about what they intend to do or have already done, and that cross can deal with the problem of motivation by reporting witnesses.

Even without the savings clause, the exception reaches statements by the testator indicating present frame of mind for the purpose of suggesting (on the basis of assumed continuity) how he felt later.[3] And even without the clause, such statements would be generally admissible for the forward-looking purpose of proving the testator was or was not of sound mind, how he felt toward those whom he was either to mention or not to mention in his will, and that he was or was not under the kind of personal pressure that might later be viewed as "undue influence" providing ground to set aside his will.[4] And again without resort to the clause, statements by the testator may be admitted to show his forward-looking intent to execute, revoke, or modify a will, hence as proof that he did so.[5]

Under the savings clause, there is no doubt that statements indicating frame of mind may prove how the testator felt earlier: The statement, "They got around me and confuddled me" would be admissible to prove that the speaker had felt pressure.[6] And such backward-looking statements may be admitted to prove all kinds of mental conditions that may be relevant to declarant's will.[7]

Earlier feelings

It is unclear whether FRE 803(3) paves the way for statements by the testator describing behavior by others ("They got around me and confuddled me") *when offered to prove that conduct.* What others did may be critical in deciding whether there was undue influence. Statements

---

3. *See* §8.38, *supra.*

4. Malone v. Sheets, 571 S.W.2d 756, 763-764 (Mo. Ct. App. 1978) (statements by testatrix admitted to "susceptibility to influence"); Buchanan v. Davis, 12 S.W.2d 978, 982-983 (Tex. Com. App. 1929) (testatrix said husband was "nagging the life out of her" to sign joint will but she would never do it, as proof of state of mind and effect, but not to prove what others did).

5. Atherton v. Gaslin, 239 S.W. 771 (Ky. 1922) (testator's forward-looking statement to prove holographic will was genuine).

6. Stephenson v. Stephenson, 17 N.W. 456, 457 (Iowa 1883) (approving statement quoted above, "as showing the effect on testator's mind"). *See also* In re Estate of Pouser, 975 P.2d 704 (Az. 1999) (admitting statements by decedent indicating intent to disinherit appellants, to show his prior intent at the time he made his will).

7. Savoy v. Savoy, 220 F.2d 364, 366-367 (D.C. Cir. 1954) (evidence that several months after tearing will testator said he disposed of property in manner provided by torn will, which indicated absence of intent to revoke); Williams v. Bridgeford, 383 S.W.2d 770, 777 (Tenn. Ct. App. 1964) (statements admitted to determine which of two wills was valid).

describing such conduct may also reflect the speaker's mental condition and are admissible to prove this point.[8]

Can they also be used to prove behavior by others that may have generated this reaction? To put it another way, is conduct by others a "fact" that "relates to the execution" of declarant's will for purposes of FRE 803(3). Some pre-Rules state cases disallowed this use of the state-of-mind exception.[9] In wills cases, the importance of the testator's state of mind lends weight to arguments for admitting such statements, and of course FRE 803(3) openly embraces backward-looking statements to prove prior facts or conditions in wills cases, but modern cases have declined to go this far.[10] Of course the main difficulty once again is that most evidence of such statements is testimony by interested witnesses who would describe private conversations with the testator, with little fear of contradiction.

Prior acts   The special clause in FRE 803(3) is critical when the purpose is to use statements to prove prior acts, events, or conditions. Whatever doubt there may be about using the exception to prove conduct by others, clearly it invites use of statements to prove other acts, events, or conditions that are more closely related to execution, revocation, identification, or terms of the speaker's will.[11]

FRE 803(4)

> **(4) Statements for purposes of medical diagnosis or treatment.** Statements made for purposes of medical diagnosis or treatment and describing medical history, or past or present symptoms, pain, or sensations, or the inception or general character of the cause or external source thereof insofar as reasonably pertinent to diagnosis or treatment.

---

8. Primerica Life Insurance Co. v. Watson, 2004 WL 3313613 (Ark. 2004) (in dispute between widow R and ex-wife MJ over life insurance, admitting decedent's statements that R was beneficiary and should receive proceeds); In re Estate of Pouser, 975 P.2d 704 (Ariz. 1999) (admitting statements by decedent, apparently after executing will, indicating intent to disinherit appellants) (citing authors of this Treatise).

9. Buchanan v. Davis, 12 S.W.2d 978, 982-983 (Tex. Com. App. 1929); Stephenson v. Stephenson, 17 N.W. 456, 457 (Iowa 1883).

10. Lasater v. House, 841 N.E.2d 553, 556 (Ind. 2006) (testator's statements cannot prove undue influence brought by others); Bajakian v. Erinakes, 880 A.2d 843, 847 (R.I. 2005) (reading state counterpart as applying only to statements of intention and not to statements of memory).

11. Murphy v. Glenn, 964 P.2d 581, 587 (Colo. App. 1998) (in contest between beneficiaries of will and beneficiaries of inter trust, admitting settlor's statements that she executed mutual wills with husband, to prove she had done so); Plummer v. Waskey, 368 A.2d 478, 485 (Md. Ct. Spec. App. 1977) (statements by testator that will exists, to rebut presumption of revocation); Halamicek v. Halamicek, 542 S.W.2d 246, 249 (Tex. Civ. App. 1976) (statements by decedent that he made later will, to prove execution of lost will).

§8.42   Medical Statements

FRE 803(4) creates an exception for statements made for purposes of getting medical treatment or diagnosis. Common law tradition recognized an exception for statements made for the first of these purposes, but not the second.

The main reason to admit statements made for purposes of getting treatment is that they are trustworthy. Usually they are made by the patient to his physician, and they describe past and present physical sensations relating to his condition, so risks of misperception and faulty memory are minimal. He knows his description helps determine treatment, so he has reason to speak candidly and carefully, and risks of insincerity and ambiguity are minimal.

Statements for purposes of diagnosis offer no similar assurance of candor. The speaker is likely to be trying either to prepare a doctor to testify or aid in litigation, or to get some other personal benefit (job or insurance coverage). He is tempted to maximize or minimize, overstate or understate injuries, pains, symptoms, and disabilities, but the exception reaches those statements anyway.[1]

The original decision to accept this risk is best understood in light of the provisions in FRE 702-703, which let experts testify on the basis of inadmissible evidence, including hearsay. The thought at the time was that if physicians can testify on the basis of statements by patients, and if such statements are going to come out to explain the basis of physician testimony, then we should let juries make general use of them.[2] The amendment of FRE 702 in 2000, however, casts doubt on this logic: As amended, FRE 702 generally *blocks* the calling party from adducing "inadmissible" evidence that experts rely on. Since FRE 803(4), which remained unchanged when FRE 702 was amended, already removes the "hearsay" objection from patient statements, the amendment to FRE 702 does not block the calling party from adducing those statements. But it is odd, to say the least, to find in place a hearsay exception that was broadened on the theory that the statements are going to come out anyway, then to retain the broadened exception after FRE 702 was amended to abandon the practice that was the basis for expanding the exception in the first place!

The rationale of the exception suggests that statements to a diagnosing physician should get in only if she testifies and gives her opinion.

---

§8.42   1. Morgan v. Foretich, 846 F.2d 941, 950 (4th Cir. 1988) (in parental dispute, daughter's statements to psychologist consulted to testify as witness); O'Gee v. Dobbs Houses, Inc., 570 F.2d 1084, 1088-1089 (2d Cir. 1978) (statements by flight attendant to consulting doctor).

2. *See* ACN to FRE 803(4) (experts may describe basis of opinions, and juries are "unlikely" to distinguish between using statements as basis and using them to prove what they say, so exception "rejects the limitation" once observed). Clearly a physician, including one hired only to diagnose and testify, may give conclusions based in part on what the person she diagnosed said, even though FRE 702 and 703 do not authorize use of hearsay for substantive purposes or let experts act as conduits for hearsay. *See generally* the discussion of FRE 702 in §7.10, *supra.*

If the person diagnosed could testify about the nature and cause of his illness or injuries, courts have reason to be cautious in admitting descriptions to a physician consulted only for diagnosis. Experts are not supposed to be mere conduits for hearsay.

Reasonably pertinent

The statement must be "reasonably pertinent" to treatment or diagnosis, and these words set a standard that is objective but broad. Where treatment is sought, the assurance of candor reaches statements pertinent to what the doctor does. In theory the subjective understanding of the speaker determines the extent to which he feels pressed to be truthful. But in practice a court cannot figure out what the speaker was thinking. Hence it is usually reasonable to assume the physician guided the interview so the two come to similar understandings of what is pertinent, and the doctor's opinion on this point deserves considerable weight. Where diagnosis was sought, the idea is to permit substantive use of statements the jury is likely to hear anyway, as part of the basis of testimony the doctor gives. Again what she considers pertinent counts heavily.

Generous construction

Both the range of medical inquiry and the patient's belief in what is important are likely to be broad, so the pertinency standard merits generous construction. In connection with physical injury, statements saying when and how it happened (car accident, slip-and-fall, assault) and mentioning important objects or implements (dashboard, steps, knife or club, fists or feet) are pertinent.[3] In connection with illnesses, the time of onset of symptoms and apparent cause (eating food or ingesting other things, exertion, exposure) are pertinent, as is nature of the symptoms (pain, nausea, fever).[4]

Facts reasonably recited

The pertinency standard should be construed broadly enough to reach facts that a patient would naturally recite in a good-faith effort to provide needed information. If he tells a treating physician he first felt pain while "lifting pipes at work," the fact that diagnosis and treatment would be the same if he said the pain began while "lifting something heavy" should not matter. To exclude details that are natural in a to-the-point description is to erect on the pertinency standard an artificial barrier that does not separate what is trustworthy from what is not. Yet in the recurrent setting in which the question is whether an ailment or injury is "work-related," the cases are split, and some courts exclude statements containing information critical to this

3. Bucci v. Essex Ins. Co., 393 F.3d 285, 298-299 (1st Cir. 2005) (in nightclub patron's suit, medical records could show that assault caused injuries); United States v. Pollard, 790 F.2d 1309, 1312-1313 & n.1 (7th Cir. 1986) (defendant said broken arm was re-injured when "twisted and placed behind his back"); United States v. Iron Thunder, 714 F.2d 765, 772 (8th Cir. 1983) (statement by victim that she was raped).

4. Britt v. Corporacion Peruana de Vapores, 506 F.2d 927, 930 (5th Cir. 1975) (statements describing "general cause" of ailment); Meaney v. United States, 112 F.2d 538, 539 (2d Cir. 1940) (statements describing onset and severity of ailment, as well as past symptoms).

question (in effect narrowly construing the exception)[5] while other courts admit such statements (construing the exception in what we consider the better way).[6]

The pertinency standard does impose a true limit. Blame-casting statements attributing fault or identifying assailants or tortfeasors are not reasonably pertinent.[7] Statements indicating that the injury only happened because someone ran a red light or omitted safety precautions or imposed unreasonable demands at work are immaterial to diagnosis or treatment and fall outside the exception.[8] So do statements suggesting an injury was deliberate or accidental.[9]

Blame-casting statements

Statements may satisfy the pertinency requirement even though they describe prior sensations, symptoms, or events.[10] It is only important that they bear on treatment or diagnosis. In this respect the medical statements exception is broader than FRE 803(3), which reaches only statements describing present sensations or feelings.

Before child victim hearsay provisions appeared in the last decades of the twentieth century (embracing statements by children describing abuse), the medical statements exception was drafted into service in child abuse trials, and the exception has found use in cases of sexual assault as well, when adult victims describe symptoms and the nature of the attack that they suffered. Thes uses have continued. In the *Crawford* era, in which "testimonial statements" are excludable if offered against criminal defendants in trials in which the speaker does not testify and submit to cross-examination, it was initially thought that many such statements would be excluded: Most such statements describe crimes, and doctors are implicated in the investigative process, at least to the point of being required to report instances of abuse and sexual assault, and sometimes child or social services personnel are present when abused children and adult victims are examined (or are at least in

Child abuse cases

5. Rock v. Huffco Gas & Oil Co., Inc., 922 F.2d 272, 277-278 (5th Cir. 1991) (excluding statement that claimant twisted ankle stepping through rusted-out step and slipped in galley); Felice v. Long Island R. Co., 426 F.2d 192, 196-197 (2d Cir. 1970) (excluding statement that plaintiff was "lifting a tank" when he slipped), *cert. denied*, 400 U.S. 820.

6. Lorensen v. Sinclair Refining Co., 271 F.2d 528, 529 (2d Cir. 1959) (admitting statement that claimant slipped on oil on ladder in engine room of tanker); Shell Oil Co. v. Industrial Com., 119 N.E.2d 224, 231 (Ill. 1954) (doctor testified that plaintiff slipped at work "pulling on a pipe, and injured his back").

7. State v. Robinson, 718 N.W.2d 400 (Minn. 2006) (victim's statement to nurse identifying defendant as assailant); United States v. Pollard, 790 F.2d 1309, 1312-1313 & n.1 (7th Cir. 1986) (blaming arresting officer for twisting arm).

8. Brown v. Seaboard Airline R.R. Co., 434 F.2d 1101, 1103-1104 (5th Cir. 1970) (excluding statement by plaintiff that he was walking beside train when struck by projection and knocked under train).

9. Walker v. Prudential Ins. Co., 127 F.2d 938, 940 (5th Cir. 1942) (excluding statement by decedent to doctor about "how he had received his injuries"). *But see* United States v. Cherry, 938 F.2d 748, 757 & n.18 (7th Cir. 1991) (admitting statement by 13-year-old girl that defendant held her arms and told her not to tell anyone).

10. Meaney v. United States, 112 F.2d 538, 539-540 (2d Cir. 1940) (question was whether decedent contracted tuberculosis by January 1919; describing "time of the onset of his disease and its immediate severity" fit exception).

the hospital or readily available).[11] When children and rape victims talk to physicians seeking to provide diagnosis and treatment, however, the *Crawford* doctrine has not stood in the way, although the situation changes when children or other victims talk to child or social service personnel or other officials.[12] Many courts use the exception not only for statements describing abuse, but for statements identifying abusers,[13] although the latter use of the exception is highly questionable and some courts refuse to go that far.[14] Long before *Crawford* was decided, the Court in the decision in the *White* case looked the other way at the somewhat attenuated use of the exception in child victim cases.[15]

Child abuse prosecutions have strained the exception severely. In favor of expansive interpretation, it can be said that children are like adults in being motivated to cooperate with treating physicians in describing symptoms and causes, and natural accounts that stray beyond what is strictly important in diagnosis and treatment are likely to be as trustworthy as statements focused narrowly on clinical symptoms. In a sense, treatment of such victims turns on finding out who harmed them, since caretakers who learn that a parent or member of the household is responsible for the harm will likely take steps to place the child in foster care and arrange to counsel the child.

Expansion is troubling Yet this expansion of the exception is troubling. It builds on the process of providing conventional medical care that requires doctors to learn basic facts from patients. The exception is not grounded in the process of providing larger social remedies aimed at detecting abuse, identifying and punishing abusers, and preventing further mistreatment, which involve skills and social intervention lying beyond the expertise of doctors. Admitting such statements because doctors rely on them in diagnosis is highly questionable. The exception also builds on the notion that patients speak honestly to doctors in the interest of getting good treatment, but the idea that abuse victims speak truthfully to obtain psychological counseling and care is unconvincing. There are

11. *See* Crawford v. Washington, 541 U.S. 36, 57 (2004) discussed in §§8.83-8.92, *infra*.

12. State v. Slater, 939 A.2d 1105, 1118 (Conn. 2008) (admitting statements by rape victim to doctor and nurse administering rape kit, which did not make her statements testimonial); United States v. Peneaux, 432 F.3d 882, 895 (8th Cir. 2005) (statements by 2-year-old to doctor were not testimonial); State v. Vigil, 127 P.3d 916, 925 (Colo. 2006) (similar) (statement by 7-year-old); Commonwealth v. DeOliveira, 849 N.E.2d 218 (Mass. 2006) (similar) (statement by 6-year-old).

13. Goldade v. State, 674 P.2d 721 (Wyo. 1983), *cert. denied*, 467 U.S. 1253; State v. Robinson, 735 P.2d 801, 810 (Ariz. 1987); State v. Nelson, 406 N.W.2d 385, 391 (Wis. 1987).

14. State v. Whipple, 19 P.3d 228, 232 (Mont. 2001) (cannot admit statements by girls 8 and 9 years old identifying defendant) (quoting authors of this Treatise); Commonwealth v. Smith, 681 A.2d 1288 (Pa. 1996) (similar); State v. Veluzat, 578 A.2d 93, 96-97 (R.I. 1990) (similar).

15. White v. Illinois, 502 U.S. 346 (1992) (approving statements by four-year-old child to nurse and doctor describing sexual abuse and identifying defendant, under medical statements exception).

other reasons to be concerned. So high are the stakes in child abuse prosecutions that doctors and social workers who interview children shortly after abuse occurs often act almost as extensions of the offices of prosecutors and police, and in some urban hospitals special areas are set aside to collect statements by abuse victims in order to qualify them under the exception. The risks posed even by natural accounts blaming household members or caretakers are huge.[16]

The exception reaches statements by children of tender years. No rule bars testimony on account of immaturity, and a modern conception of competency developed in the setting of child abuse cases holds that inability to deal with the courtroom justifies special measures that aim not to *exclude* what the child has to say, but to *obtain* it.[17] There is little room to doubt that children who might be unable to testify can make statements that are admissible under the medical statements exception.[18]

The typical statement offered under the exception is made by a patient directly to a doctor, but the exception does not require the speaker to be the patient or the listener to be the doctor. Clearly it reaches statements by family members (parent, sibling, or spouse) who bring the patient to a hospital or doctor's office,[19] and Good Samaritans too.[20] Applying the exception seems appropriate if the patient cannot speak or has trouble making himself understood, so long as the person who speaks for him seems to have useful information. The care implied by the fact that a person has brought the patient for treatment is a factor indicating candor. Obviously the same result is appropriate where parents bring a minor in for treatment, for utmost candor may be assumed and parents are likely to have important information.

Statements by family, Good Samaritans

---

16. *See* Mosteller, The Maturation and Disintegration of the Hearsay Exception for Statements for Medical Examination in Child Sexual Abuse Cases, 65 Law & Contemp. Probs. 47 (2002); Tuerkheimer, Convictions Through Hearsay in Child Sexual Abuse Cases: A Logic Progression Back to Square One, 72 Marq. L. Rev. 47 (1988). *See also* State v. Huntington, 575 N.W.2d 268 (Wis. 1998) (error to admit stepdaughter's statements to counselor and social worker describing abuse).

17. *See* the discussion of competency in §6.3, *supra*. *See also* the discussions of FRE 807 as applied to child victim statements in §8.82, and the discussion of confrontation issues in §8.91, *infra*.

18. *See* White v. Illinois, 502 U.S. 346 (1992) (statements by four-year-old child; no mention of competency); Morgan v. Foretich, 846 F.2d 941, 948-950 (4th Cir. 1988) (statements by four-year-old child to psychologist; exception applies regardless whether she was competent to testify).

19. Bucci v. Essex Ins. Co., 393 F.3d 285, 298-299 (1st Cir. 2005) (admitting medical records to show injuries caused by assault; no requirement that patient be speaker; some statements were made by patient or witness, and purpose was treatment); Miller v. Watts, 436 S.W.2d 515, 519-521 (Ky. 1969) (medical history given by child's mother, including description of incident and later fainting or falling spells).

20. Navarro de Cosme v. Hospital Pavia, 922 F.2d 926, 931-932 (1st Cir. 1991) (notes by social worker on medical record of husband); Leora v. Minneapolis, S.P. & S.S.M. R. Co., 146 N.W. 520, 523-524 (Wis. 1914) (description of railroad accident that injured section hand, who was unconscious and delirious).

Statements to intake people, others

The exception should also reach statements to persons other than the treating or diagnosing physician. Clerical intake people, administrative assistants, nurses and orderlies in hospitals and clinics may be told matters that are later pertinent to diagnosis or treatment, and statements to such people should fit the exception. The same should be true of statements to a doctor for diagnosis or treatment that are passed along to another, and statements by treating physicians to each other.[21] There is little or no diminution in trustworthiness where the person who actually heard the statement testifies to it. It seems, moreover, that the exception is broad enough to pave the way to admit such statements even if the physician testifies to a statement of this sort that has been passed along to him, although his testimony would embrace double or multiple hearsay.[22] Given a serious purpose on the part of each person in the chain to assist the patient, an assurance of trustworthiness continues. The exception is not limited by reference to either speaker or listener, so each such statement in the chain may fit the exception.

Statements to psychiatrists

A psychiatrist is a medical doctor whose services include medical treatment and diagnosis, so there is good reason to suppose statements to psychiatrists for purposes of obtaining these services fit the exception.[23] But psychiatric diagnosis and treatment differ from diagnosis and treatment of physical injuries or ailments, and there is little experience with use of the exception in this context. Caution is warranted, as it is not clear that a patient seeking psychiatric treatment feels pressure to be candid or indeed that candor in the two contexts means the same thing or operates in a similar way to make statements reliable as proof of what they assert. Given the uncertainties and tentativeness of psychiatric diagnoses, virtually any statement would be considered "reasonably pertinent," so the exception would cover almost anything. Hence statements to psychiatrists should be treated with special caution. Ample latitude should be permitted to impeach both the declarant and the testifying witness. A party should not be allowed to

---

21. *See* Wilson v. Zapata Off-Shore Co., 939 F.2d 260, 271-272 (5th Cir. 1991) (statement by plaintiff's sister to social worker in hospital, passed along to treating psychiatrists); O'Gee v. Dobbs Houses, Inc., 570 F.2d 1084, 1088-1089 (2d Cir. 1978) (what patient told doctor, including what patient said other doctors told her).

22. *See* State ex rel. Children, Youth, Families Dept., 955 P.2d 204 (N.M. App. 1998) (statements by social worker to physician brought in for diagnosis); Lovejoy v. United States, 92 F.3d 628, 631-632 (8th Cir. 1996) (statements by common law wife *W* to nurse assisting treatment of child).

23. Swinton v. Potomac Corp., 270 F.3d 794, 807-808 (9th Cir. 2001) (statements to psychologists including account of harassment giving rise to suit), *cert denied*, 535 U.S. 1018; Wilson v. Zapata Off-Shore Co., 939 F.2d 260, 271-272 (5th Cir. 1991) (statements for psychiatric diagnosis; test is whether doctor finds statement pertinent); Ritter v. Coca-Cola Co. (Kenosha-Racine), Inc., 128 N.W.2d 439, 441-443 (Wis. 1964) (symptoms described to psychiatrist after drinking Coke with remains of mouse).

use a psychiatrist as a surrogate witness for purposes of reciting the party's own statements in support of claims or defenses.[24]

> **FRE 803(5)**
>
> **(5) Recorded recollection.** A memorandum or record concerning a matter about which a witness once had knowledge but now has insufficient recollection to enable the witness to testify fully and accurately, shown to have been made or adopted by the witness when the matter was fresh in the witness' memory and to reflect that knowledge correctly. If admitted, the memorandum or record may be read into evidence but may not itself be received as an exhibit unless offered by an adverse party.

§8.43   Past Recollection Recorded

The exception for past recollection recorded set out in FRE 803(5) follows tradition except in providing that the note or writing cannot come in as an exhibit "unless offered by an adverse party," and the offering party must settle for having it "read into evidence."

Notions of necessity and trustworthiness underlie the exception. To the extent the witness has forgotten, admitting his past recorded recollection is the last best chance to get what he once knew. And two requirements suggest that the recollection is trustworthy: The record must have been made or adopted when the matter was freshly in mind (reducing the risk of faulty memory), and must be shown to reflect what the witness once knew (reducing risks of ambiguity and candor). Also the person who made or adopted the statement now testifies and can be questioned. Lack of memory means he is not fully responsive, but his general credibility can be tested and probed, along with the circumstances in which his recollection was recorded. And usually the cross-examiner can get somewhere by asking about the acts, events, or conditions themselves since the witness seldom suffers total memory loss.

The first requirement is that the witness have insufficient present memory to testify "fully or accurately" about the acts, events, or conditions described in his recorded recollection.[1] The reason is to minimize use of partisan statements prepared in anticipation of suit. To show lack

(1) Insufficient memory

---

24. *See* United States v. Matta-Ballesteros, 71 F.3d 754, 767 (9th Cir. 1995) (excluding report by psychologist to prove defendant was illiterate), *cert. denied,* 519 U.S. 1118; Candella v. Subsequent Injury Fund, 353 A.2d 263, 265-267 (Md. 1976) (excluding testimony by psychiatrist whom claimant consulted, resting on case history she provided).

§8.43   1. Vicksburg & Meridian Railroad Co. v. O'Brien, 119 U.S. 99 (1886) (can't use exception where witness has "clear, distinct recollection of every essential fact"); United States v. Dazey, 403 F.3d 1147, 1166-1167 (10th Cir. 2005) (error to admit notes without showing witness lacks memory) (harmless).

of present memory, the party offering a writing as recorded recollection should first use it to try to refresh memory.[2] This strategy is the one preferred in practice if the examiner thinks the witness will endorse the former statement: Usually lawyers would rather have live testimony based on present (albeit refreshed) recollection than recitations of former statements on matters now forgotten. But if the witness takes a position at odds with his statement and the lawyer thinks he will not endorse it or repeat its substance from present memory, he may prefer not to use it to refresh. He may hope instead to make the next-best use, which is to try to discredit the witness, using the statement as a prior inconsistency, which again puts it before the jury.

It is when the effort to refresh memory fails that resort to recorded recollection is appropriate. In practice, it is sometimes hard to know whether a witness is testifying from refreshed recollection or just repeating what he now remembers of the statement he just read or heard, in effect using it to convey the point (which is what the exception is for).[3] Depending on his attitude, the substance of his statement, and the examiner's strategy, a failed effort to refresh memory may lead to use of the statement to repair credibility or impeach it, and the difference is that the latter use does not invite consideration of the statement as substantive evidence.[4]

The exception paves the way for recorded recollection even though the witness remembers the matter in general outline and suffers only an inability to achieve precision or come up with details.[5] Insisting on complete memory failure would be almost perverse: The fact that one remembers the matter recorded in general terms should increase confidence. Assuming other requirements are met, recorded recollection may be used to add precision to points the witness remembers generally (accident happened at 9 A.M.; witness remembers it was morning) and supply details he has forgotten (license number of car; witness cannot remember it).

(2) Correctly reflect   The second requirement is that the recorded recollection correctly reflect prior firsthand knowledge on the part of the witness. If he recalls making the statement and testifies from present memory that he took care to ensure that it correctly reflected what he knew, the requirement is satisfied. But proving correctness usually involves circumstantial

---

2. *See* §§6.66-6.69, *supra.*

3. *See* United States v. Marcantoni, 590 F.2d 1324, 1330 n.6 (5th Cir. 1979) (impossible to say whether detective testified from recollection refreshed or recorded), *cert. denied,* 441 U.S. 937; United States v. Riccardi, 174 F.2d 883, 889 (3d Cir. 1949) (present recollection revived and past recollection recorded are "converging rather than parallel lines"), *cert. denied,* 337 U.S. 941.

4. Inconsistent statements are substantive evidence only if given in proceedings under oath, and if the speaker is presently cross-examinable. *See* FRE 801(d)(1)(A), discussed in §8.24, *supra.*

5. United States v. Cash, 394 F.3d 560, 562-564 (7th Cir. 2005) (witness could read notes of phone conversations; she recalled talking, but couldn't remember words without notes); United States v. Riley, 657 F.2d 1377, 1385-1386 (8th Cir. 1981) (admitting taped and written statements where witness could not remember details), *cert. denied,* 459 U.S. 1111.

evidence: Necessarily the witness has forgotten various aspects of the acts, events, or conditions he described before, and often has little memory about the statement itself. If he does not remember because the statement is one of many entries he routinely makes, he can show accuracy by describing a routine that supports an inference that the statement accurately reflects what he knew.[6]

If the witness cannot recall making the statement despite the fact that the occasion was unique or out of the ordinary, because of the passage of time or for indeterminable reasons rooted in psychology or interest, the question arises whether it is enough if he testifies simply that he would not have signed or prepared it if it were not true. Probably even this tepid endorsement is enough if nothing better may be had, since it provides testimonial support.[7] But it is only a claim of general honesty that sheds faint circumstantial light and is the kind of thing nearly anyone would say almost any time. Accepting such an endorsement reduces the accuracy requirement, and judges should have leeway to exclude statements offered on this basis almost as a matter of instinct if they doubt the substance of the endorsement.[8]

The exception does not expressly say the maker of a statement must attest its accuracy at trial, but a live endorsement seems necessary. Often statements contain truth or accuracy clauses, where the maker says the statement is true and correct and accords with his knowledge. Sometimes he says such things under penalty of perjury, and sometimes the statement is sworn and notarized (affidavit form). But no statement should verify itself, especially by boilerplate language routinely added by police, lawyers, or others experienced in litigation. Some testimonial support of accuracy is necessary. Of course the requirement means a witness may exclude his own statement by refusing to endorse it. But one who takes this position is not necessarily evasive or contemptuous: His refusal may mean his statement is false, and it is not the purpose of the exception to invite trial by affidavits where speakers only testify to lack of memory.

(3) Made or adopted

The third requirement is that the statement be made or adopted by the witness. Where he has written and signed a document in his own hand, there is no question on this point. But the exception requires no particular formality (like signature), and the point is to help assure accuracy and make it reasonable to rely on the testimonial claim of the witness that the record is accurate. Hence it is alright if he signed

6. *See* United States v. Marshall, 532 F.2d 1279, 1285-1286 (9th Cir. 1976) (stressing routine in admitting report by police chemist prepared during tests); Trias-Hernandez v. INS, 528 F.2d 366, 369 (9th Cir. 1975) (stressing routine in INS record).

7. United States v. Patterson, 678 F.2d 774, 779-780 (9th Cir. 1982) (witness "did not think he had lied"), *cert. denied*, 455 U.S. 911; Walker v. Larson, 169 N.W.2d 737, 741-743 (Minn. 1969) (witness would not have signed if statement were not true or without reading it).

8. Maxwell's Exrs. v. Wilkinson, 113 U.S. 656 (1885) (not enough for witness to invoke "habit never to sign a statement unless it was true"); Hodas v. Davis, 196 N.Y.S. 801, 802-803 (App. Div. 1922) (getting "no" on question whether witness ever signed paper that did not contain true facts was not enough).

a document prepared by another or wrote something down without signing it.[9] And the memorandum or record need not be written: If the witness made a recorded statement, that too satisfies the requirement of being made or adopted. If the witness did not participate in making the statement, it may still be used to refresh memory but not as recorded recollection.

(4) Matter fresh in memory

The fourth requirement is that the statement be made when the matter reported was fresh in memory, and many factors count.[10] Gaps or qualifications on the face of a statement reflecting incomplete or uncertain memory suggest it is stale; relative importance of the matters described in the life of the speaker bears on how long memory is fresh; the nature of matters recorded may be such that they would likely be fresh in the mind for a longer time, or be of such complexity or detail that time is likely to wash them away quickly; indications of care and attention in the statement may indicate freshness, particularly if the maker personally and meticulously wrote it out, or (in the case of a writing prepared by another) if he made corrections or changes, while haste and vagueness or uncritical acceptance suggest the matter is stale. Wooden rules of thumb (memory stays fresh about two weeks) are not helpful.

Where one speaks and another writes

If a person sees something and tells another about it, and the latter writes down what he is told, the writing may qualify as recorded recollection. Here it takes two witnesses to satisfy the second requirement: The observer must testify that he once knew the matter and accurately described it to the other while it was fresh in his mind. The latter must testify that he heard what he was told and accurately wrote it down. And the observer must testify that he lacks present recollection. Suppose an eyewitness tells another person the license number of a getaway car at a crime scene or one involved in an accident, and the latter writes it down. If they testify as sketched above, the notation may qualify as recorded recollection to identify the car.[11] Or suppose a witness who testified in a prior proceeding has forgotten the events or conditions, but remembers testifying accurately while the matter was fresh, and the

---

9. *See* United States v. Wimberly, 60 F.3d 281, 285-286 (7th Cir. 1995) (agent wrote down what child said; she read it, made corrections, signed attestation clause, thus made or adopted it), *cert. denied*, 516 U.S. 1063; United States v. Lewis, 954 F.2d 1386, 1394 (7th Cir. 1992) (admitting interview statement that agent wrote up, where witness saw it 15 months later during pretrial and said it was correct).

10. Maxwell's Exrs. v. Wilkinson, 113 U.S. 656 (1885) (20 months is too long); State v. Gorman, 854 A.2d 1164, 1172 (Me. 2004) (admitting grand jury testimony; freshness requirement satisfied; two months between events and testimony), *cert. denied*, 544 U.S. 928; United States v. Green, 258 F.3d 683, 689 (7th Cir. 2001) (admitting trooper's summary of interview with defendant, prepared 11 days later).

11. United States v. Hernandez, 333 F.3d 1168, 1176-1180 (10th Cir. 2003) (T testified that she gave serial number of gun in phone calls with J and R; all three testified, and laid foundation; exception reaches recollections "recorded through the efforts of more than one person," when joint makers testify that facts were observed, reported, transcribed accurately); United States v. Booz, 451 F.2d 719, 724-725 (3d Cir. 1971) (eyewitness K noted license number of truck and B wrote report; if B verifies accuracy of what he wrote and K testifies that he related accurate number, report admissible).

reporter testifies that he accurately transcribed the testimony. Here the transcript can qualify as recollection recorded.[12] Or suppose several people involved in a business transaction participate in producing written notations. Here too they may be able to qualify the notations as recorded recollection.[13] A record prepared by one person of a statement by another cannot be treated simply as joint authorship if the person who made the statement does not testify, and using the record to prove the matter asserted in the statement raises a double hearsay problem.

When a statement is admitted as recorded recollection, the writing may be "read into evidence" but not "received as an exhibit unless offered by an adverse party." The apparent purpose is to prevent the jury from according undue emphasis to the written word, since proper use depends on testimony by the witness.[14] This purpose is achieved if the memorandum is not sent out with the jury during deliberations or made generally available with other exhibits.[15] Obviously a writing offered under the exception is normally lodged with the clerk, and it should be physically included with other exhibits (if admitted) for recordkeeping purposes and review. The right way to introduce recorded recollection is through testimony by the witness reading the writing or by counsel reading it during questioning.[16] If the memorandum is complicated or detailed, it should be proper to use the document itself (or enlargements to help the jury) during trial while the maker is on the stand. The adverse party may offer the document for use during deliberations along with other exhibits.

Read, but not received as exhibit

> **FRE 803(6)**
>
> **(6) Records of regularly conducted activity.** A memorandum, report, record, or data compilation, in any form, of acts, events, or conditions, opinions, or diagnoses made at or near the time by, or from information transmitted by, a person with knowledge, if kept in the course of a regularly conducted business activity, and if it was the regular practice of that business activity to make the memorandum, report, record, or data

12. United States v. Patterson, 678 F.2d 774 (9th Cir. 1982), *cert. denied*, 459 U.S. 911; United States v. Barrow, 363 F.2d 62, 67 (3d Cir. 1966), *cert. denied*, 385 U.S. 1001 (both admitting grand jury testimony).

13. *See* United States v. Civella, 666 F.2d 1122, 1129 (8th Cir. 1981); Curtis v. Bradley, 31 A. 591, 593-596 (Conn. 1894).

14. United States v. Judon, 567 F.2d 1289, 1294 (5th Cir. 1978) (prevent trier from "being overly impressed by the writing").

15. Research Systems Corp. v. IPSOS Publicite, 276 F.3d 914, 923 (7th Cir. 2002) (excluding memoranda because proponent offered them as exhibits), *cert. denied*, 537 U.S. 878; United States v. Ray, 768 F.2d 991, 994-995 (8th Cir. 1985) (reversible error to let transcript go to jury).

16. United States v. Ramsey, 785 F.2d 184, 192 (7th Cir. 1986) (desk calendar could be "read into evidence"), *cert. denied*, 476 U.S. 1186; United States v. Steele, 685 F.2d 793, 809 (3d Cir. 1982) (court let witness read and "interpret" notes), *cert. denied*, 459 U.S. 908.

> compilation, all as shown by the testimony of the custodian or other qualified witness, or by certification that complies with Rule 902(11), Rule 902(12), or a statute permitting certification, unless the source of information or the method or circumstances of preparation indicate lack of trustworthiness. The term "business" as used in this paragraph includes business, institution, association, profession, occupation, and calling of every kind, whether or not conducted for profit.

§8.44 Business Records—Rationale and Requirements

Necessity The business records exception rests in part on necessity. Modern business transactions depend on recorded data, often electronic entries (computer data accessible by means of printouts or screen images) or written documents. No single person is likely to know most of the pertinent facts about even simple transactions. The record is often a composite of information gleaned from many sources, and admitting it obviates the need to take the time for testimony from all who participated in making it, and spares the hours of business and working people who would otherwise spend time in court to give evidence on narrow points. Equally significant from the standpoint of necessity is the fact that people who participate in business transactions are likely to be involved in so many that even if they testify they are often able to do little more than repeat whatever they recall from examining the records themselves.

Trustworthiness The exception rests in part on notions of trustworthiness. The regularity of business and recordmaking, and the routine involvement of the recordmakers in that task provide expertise and reduce the risk of error. Market pressure and individual responsibility for job performance also reduce the risk, as do requirements that the source of information have personal knowledge and that record be made contemporaneously with what it records or reports.

Not all records embraced by the exception are of this sort, however. The exception also reaches investigative findings and professional opinions and diagnoses. It embraces every regularly operated institution and association and every regularly pursued occupation or calling, from the one-person operation to large corporation, regardless whether conducted for profit. In many cases reached by the exception, necessity and trustworthiness apply in ways somewhat different from those described above. Common to all applications, however, is the idea of routine and continuing purpose—of records or entries made again and again, and always for a serious and relatively constant purpose apart from litigation.

Of course self-interest affects most business records. If the pressures described above reduce the risk of mistake in the form of careless error, self-interest raises risks of inaccuracy. Still, self-interest does not disqualify a record, and the exception would be virtually useless if it did—a famous jurist captured the thought in his remark that "there is hardly a grocer's account book which could not be excluded on that basis."[1] Sometimes, however, the obvious risk of distortion or out-and-out falsehood is too great to ignore, and FRE 803(6) authorizes the court to exclude a record if "the source of information or the method or circumstances of preparation indicate lack of trustworthiness."

When materials that might qualify as business records are offered *against* the party who prepared them, ordinarily the admissions doctrine is available and there is no need to satisfy the business records exception.[2] This point is often overlooked, but it is noteworthy in that the requirements of personal knowledge of the source, contemporaneity, and regular preparation in a regular business become unimportant when the material is offered as an admission, as does the trustworthiness clause in the exception.

As framed in FRE 803(6), the business records exception has four elements plus a foundation requirement (separately discussed in the next section). First, the exception reaches records of a "regularly conducted business activity," and the term embraces all kinds of commercial endeavors and nonprofit associations and institutions. The Conference Report says "schools, churches, and hospitals" are included,[3] and the exception reaches charitable and educational institutions as well as political parties, labor and trade associations, private clubs and organizations, provided that their activities are conducted on an organized basis with some degree of formal routine.[4] Clearly the exception reaches illegal enterprises, and illegality by itself is no indication that the requirements of the exception are not met.[5]

Regular business

While business activity usually connotes an enterprise involving, if not many people, at least more than one, it need not be so. One person, even if immediately responsible in his business only to himself, may engage in business for purposes of the exception. The records of a sole proprietorship can qualify, as well as the records of one who hires

---

§8.44   1. Hoffman v. Palmer, 129 F.2d 976, 1002 (2d Cir. 1942) (dissenting opinion by Judge Clark), *aff'd*, Palmer v. Hoffman, 318 U.S. 109 (1943).

2. Abuan v. Level 3 Communications, Inc., 353 F.3d 1158, 1170 (10th Cir. 2003) (admitting oral remarks by employees as admissions; they came in as business records, but oral comments are not business records); United States v. Johnston, 127 F.3d 380, 389 (5th Cir. 1997) (can admit against defendant records of his business regardless whether they fit business records exception), *cert. denied*, 522 U.S. 1152.

3. Conference Report, at 11 ("records of institutions and associations like schools, churches, and hospitals are admissible under this provision").

4. *See* United States v. Sackett, 598 F.2d 739, 742 (2d Cir. 1979) (hospital records); Stone v. Morris, 546 F.2d 730, 738-739 (7th Cir. 1976) (state prison). *See also* Daniel v. Moss, 469 P.2d 50, 51 (Idaho 1970) (decedent's estate); Leach v. State, 189 S.W. 733, 734-735 (Tex. Crim. App. 1916) (Sunday school Bible class attendance record).

5. United States v. Foster, 711 F.2d 871, 882 & n.6 (9th Cir. 1983) (ledger of drug transactions), *cert. denied*, 465 U.S. 1103; United States v. Hedman, 630 F.2d 1184, 1197-1198 (7th Cir. 1980) (notebook or diary kept by lumber company employee reflecting payoffs), *cert. denied*, 450 U.S. 965.

out as an independent contractor. The same is true of records a person makes for himself in illegally exploiting a legitimate business.[6]

Records of a purely personal nature are beyond reach of the exception. Diaries, shopping lists, reminder notes, and household phone messages do not qualify.[7] Nor do personal checking account records maintained by a bank depositor, nor mileage, service, or trip records kept by a car owner or one who owns a plane or machine used for recreational or other personal purposes, nor observations recorded or inventories kept by a hobbyist. The provision approved by the Court would have reached such items, but the congressional insistence to restore the term "business" seems designed to change this result.[8]

Regularly kept   Second, the exception requires that the record be regularly kept. Relating to a regularly conducted business activity is not enough, for the record must be kept as a matter of regular practice.[9] Records made for purposes of pending litigation are usually excluded if they are not routinely made,[10] and unusual records (outside the expertise that business routine helps assure) are excludable for failing this requirement.[11] Frequent repetition (weekly or daily or more often) is not usually required, however, and regularity can be shown by repetition over longer cycles.[12]

6. Munoz v. Strahm Farms, Inc., 69 F.3d 501, 503 (Fed. Cir. 1995) (slides taken by advisor in extension unit, kept in office for use in teaching); United States v. McPartlin, 595 F.2d 1321, 1349 (7th Cir. 1979) (records prepared by someone for his own benefit), *cert. denied*, 444 U.S. 833.

7. Buckley v. Altheimer, 152 F.2d 502, 507 (7th Cir. 1945) (rejecting diary of lawyer who acted as decedent's financial backer; not a money lender, did not keep regular records; not regular entries).

8. The Court-approved draft of FRE 803(6) reached records made in course of "regularly conducted activity," without referring to "business," *see* 56 F.R.D. 183, 300-301 (1969). *See also* Sabatino v. Curtiss Natl. Bank, 415 F.2d 632, 633-636 (5th Cir. 1969) (admitting personal check register), *cert. denied*, 396 U.S. 1057.

9. City of Long Beach v. Standard Oil of California, 46 F.3d 929, 937 (9th Cir. 1995) (excluding handwritten notes; not shown to have been made under company procedures); Wilander v. McDermott Intern., Inc., 887 F.2d 88, 91-92 (5th Cir. 1989) (excluding crewmember's statement taken by barge captain; not shown to be regular business or regularly kept).

10. Palmer v. Hoffman, 318 U.S. 109 (1943) (if exception reached railroad accident reports, "any law office in the land" could record its version of events, leading to "real perversion" of exception); Clark v. Los Angeles, 650 F.2d 1033, 1036-1037 (9th Cir. 1981) (excluding diary prepared by plaintiff describing encounters with police and discussions with street vendors; expressly made for litigation, not in regular course or routine operation), *cert. denied*, 456 U.S. 927.

11. United States v. Casoni, 950 F.2d 893, 912 (3d Cir. 1991) (excluding lawyer's written summary of what client would say, which was advocacy and tool of controversy, not routine record); Broadcast Music, Inc. v. Xanthas, Inc., 855 F.2d 233, 238-239 (5th Cir. 1988) (excluding questionnaires sent to proprietors of places with jukeboxes, offered by copyright holder to prove what was played; no proof proprietors completed forms in course of business; prime utility was litigation).

12. United States v. Jacoby, 955 F.2d 1527, 1537-1538 (11th Cir. 1992) (file memo from bank lawyer describing loan closing; nonroutine records may fit); Kassel v. Gannett Co., Inc., 875 F.2d 935, 944-945 (1st Cir. 1989) (admitting contact forms filled out by VA official; fact that form is not filled out for every phone call does not require exclusion, and some "discontinuity or selectivity" is alright).

Each person who participates in making the record must act in routine of business.[13] There is a "multiple hearsay" aspect to business records involving input from more than one person, and only the fact that all act in course of business justifies admitting such layered hearsay. Records containing information from outsiders are admissible if the purpose is only to prove an outsider made a statement (not to prove the matter asserted) or another exception covers the outsider's statement. Many cases approve records prepared by one business and then integrated into the records of another. Here foundation testimony should show that not only the records of the first business (the source) but also the records of the second (the last entry) fit the exception, but courts often make do with a single knowledgeable witness.[14]

Each participant acts routinely

The third requirement is that the source of information (who along with other participants in the recordmaking process must be acting in course of business) have personal knowledge, which means the kind of firsthand information that FRE 602 requires for testifying witnesses.[15] The source must have personal knowledge, but others in the chain of transmission of information, including the person who physically makes the record, need not have such knowledge.[16]

Source with knowledge

The fourth requirement is that the information be recorded contemporaneously with the event or occurrence.[17] Literal interpretation of this requirement would be foolish, and the purpose is to require the record to be made close in time to the event when the memories of the information source and entrant are fresh. Sometimes the requirement serves the additional purpose of excluding records prepared after self-interest comes into play, although self-interest often affects even contemporaneous records. A delay in preparing a record should not alone suffice to exclude unless it seems likely to give rise to such risks.

Contemporaneous

13. Scheerer v. Hardee's Food Sys., Inc. (8th Cir. 1996) 92 F.3d 702, 706-707 (report describing slip-and-fall in parking lot did not fit exception; it quoted unidentified witness); United States v. Bortnovsky, 879 F.2d 30, 34 (2d Cir. 1989) (excluding report by insurance adjuster that included statement by supplier; no showing he had duty to report).

14. *See generally* the discussion in §8.45, *infra*.

15. Ricciardi v. Children's Hosp. Medical Ctr., 811 F.2d 18, 20-22 (1st Cir. 1987) (excluding record containing entry by neurology resident who lacked knowledge of event reported during surgery). *See* discussion of FRE 602 in §6.5, *supra*.

16. United States v. Ahrens, 530 F.2d 781, 784 n.6 (8th Cir. 1976) (exception does not require maker to have personal knowledge); Lewis v. Baker, 526 F.2d 470, 474 (2d Cir. 1975) (fact that one trainmaster compiled accident report on basis of information supplied by another did not make it inadmissible).

17. Willco Kuwait (Trading) SAK v. De Savary, 843 F.2d 618, 628 (1st Cir. 1988) (telex did not fit; made more than three months after event); United States v. Lemire, 720 F.2d 1327, 1350-1351 (D.C. Cir. 1983) (November memoranda describing prior December-June transaction not timely), *cert. denied*, 467 U.S. 1226. *But see* Wheeler v. Sims, 951 F.2d 796, 804 (7th Cir. 1992) (11-day delay was not excessive), *cert. denied*, 506 U.S. 914.

§8.45 —Foundation Testimony

Alone among the hearsay exceptions, the one for business records refers to the necessary foundation. Ideally the proponent offers foundation testimony by the preparer and original source of the information, and sometimes these are one and the same person. But the exception would be hard to use if the foundation requirement were so strict, and nothing so elaborate is required. Normally the regular custodian can lay the necessary foundation by describing the recordmaking process,[1] and so can one who supervised the making of the record.[2] Others too can provide the necessary information: What is important is that the witness be familiar with the recordmaking practices of the business and with the manner in which records of the particular sort being offered are made and kept, and these points may be shown by anyone with the appropriate knowledge.[3]

Circumstantial knowledge In this setting the usual firsthand knowledge requirement is interpreted loosely. The witness must know enough to say the record was prepared as contemplated by the exception (regularly kept, all participants acting in ordinary course, source with knowledge, timeliness). Thus he needs firsthand knowledge about the normal processes of the business, but he need not be someone who observed any step in creating the record. Nor is it necessary for him to know exactly who participated. His testimony may rely on a kind of circumstantial knowledge, and he may even rely in part on hearsay—what others have told him about recordkeeping processes.[4] It is not fatal, then, that the foundation witness did not prepare the record,[5] or supervise its preparation,[6]

§8.45 1. EEOC v. Alton Packaging Co., 901 F.2d 920, 925-926 (11th Cir. 1990) (custodian who supervised preparation); FDIC v. Staudinger, 797 F.2d 908, 910 (10th Cir. 1986) (custodian testifies that records were the type "normally maintained" in ordinary course).

2. Miller v. Fairchild Indus., Inc., 885 F.2d 498, 514 (9th Cir. 1989) (testimony by chief financial officer who exercised "supervisory authority"), *cert. denied*, 494 U.S. 1056; Theriot v. Bay Drilling Corp., 783 F.2d 527, 533 (5th Cir. 1986) (corporate vice president and operations officer).

3. United States v. Salgado, 250 F.3d 438, 451-452 (6th Cir. 2001) (admitting phone toll records on testimony by security manager; individual knowledge not necessary, just familiarity with recordkeeping practices); United States v. Dixon, 132 F.3d 192, 197 (5th Cir. 1997) (admitting records on testimony by owner, who did not create them or know whether they were accurate), *cert. denied*, 523 U.S. 1096.

4. United States v. Franco, 874 F.2d 1136, 1139 (7th Cir. 1989) (foundation may include "hearsay and other evidence normally inadmissible at trial").

5. FDIC v. Staudinger, 797 F.2d 908, 910 (10th Cir. 1986) (no requirement to "produce the author"); United States v. Bowers, 593 F.2d 376, 380 (10th Cir. 1979) (admitting although records custodian had not prepared it), *cert. denied*, 444 U.S. 852.

6. United States v. Colyer, 571 F.2d 941, 947 (5th Cir. 1978) (not necessary for supervisor to testify), *cert. denied*, 439 U.S. 933.

or observe the process,[7] or have firsthand information about its preparation.[8] And it is not necessary to call the original source (the one with personal knowledge of the matter recorded).[9] Indeed, a witness can lay a proper foundation for a record made before his employment began,[10] and sometimes other circumstantial evidence is so powerful in demonstrating accuracy that foundation testimony can be dispensed with.[11]

But where the foundation witness lacks even circumstantial knowledge, the record should not be admitted under the exception, and minimal acquaintance with "how our records usually look" is not enough to satisfy the foundation requirements.[12]

As amended in 2000, FRE 802(8) and 902 allow the proponent to dispense with foundation testimony, and to offer instead a certificate showing that the proffered records fit the exception. To obviate surprise, the certificate and records must be filed and served in advance, so adverse parties may object to ("challenge") the proffered evidence, and clearly the hope is that the matter can be resolved before trial (although neither the Rule nor the ACN specifies any time limit). It seems that the certificate, and the person signing it, should at least satisfy the somewhat liberal standard described above, in terms of having appropriate understanding of the recordkeeping process and saying the appropriate things to satisfy the exception.[13]

7. United States v. Franks, 939 F.2d 600, 602 (8th Cir. 1991) (witness need not have personal knowledge of preparation); United States v. Ray, 930 F.2d 1368, 1370-1371 (9th Cir. 1991) (need not show "when and by whom" documents were prepared); United States v. Peters, 791 F.2d 1270, 1292 (7th Cir. 1986) (admitting even though witness did not work for company when records were prepared), *cert. denied*, 479 U.S. 847.

8. United States v. Muhammad, 928 F.2d 1461, 1468-1469 (7th Cir. 1991) (need not call someone who participated in making or keeping document); United States v. Moore, 923 F.2d 910, 914-915 (1st Cir. 1991) (foundation witness need not be programmer or one who prepared record).

9. United States v. Duncan, 919 F.2d 981, 985-987 (5th Cir. 1990) (not necessary to call maker of record), *cert. denied*, 500 U.S. 926; United States v. Iredia, 866 F.2d 114, 120 (5th Cir. 1989) (need not personally attest accuracy), *cert. denied*, 492 U.S. 921; United States v. Wables, 731 F.2d 440, 449 (7th Cir. 1984) (witness only needs "knowledge of the procedures").

10. *See* United States v. Sutton, 795 F.2d 1040, 1057 (Temp. Emer. Ct. App. 1986) (need not be employed by business when records made), *cert. denied*, 479 U.S. 1030; United States v. Smith, 609 F.2d 1294, 1301-1302 (9th Cir. 1979) (admitting records on basis of testimony by people not employed at time).

11. United States v. Mendel, 746 F.2d 155, 166-167 (2d Cir. 1984) (records corroborated entries), *cert. denied*, 469 U.S. 1213; United States v. Hines, 564 F.2d 925, 928 (10th Cir. 1977) (owner of stolen car testified to VIN on basis of "invoice or bill of sale" from time of purchase), *cert. denied*, 434 U.S. 1022.

12. United States v. Brika, 416 F.3d 514, 528-529 (6th Cir. 2005) (excluding purported handwritten business record; no foundation; identifying handwriting did not satisfy exception), *cert. denied*, 546 U.S. 1207; United States v. Riley, 236 F.3d 982, 984-985 (8th Cir. 2001) (error to admit state crime lab report on basis of testimony by police officers lacking knowledge about preparation of reports).

13. *See* the discussion of FRE 902(11) and (12) in §9.30, *infra. See also* United States v. Weiland, 420 F.3d 1062, 1072 (9th Cir. 2005) (error to admit penitentiary packet on basis of certificate; government did not provide pretrial notice making record and declaration available) (harmless).

§8.46   —Scope and Standard Applications (Accident Reports; Medical Records; Computerized Data)

FRE 803(6) is a provision of great breadth, reaching records in any form. The idea of business records calls to mind vast arrays of electronic entries (computerized data) that reflect inventories, purchases and sales, services and acquisitions, orders and allocations, and in fact the exception reaches such material and much more besides. Something of the diversity and reach of the exception can best be seen in a sampling of decided cases,[1] and it is worthwhile to consider the exception as it applies in the important areas of accident reports, internal investigations, medical records, computerized data, and Internet websites.

Accident reports   Accident reports sometimes fit the exception and are admitted, although they are more often excluded as untrustworthy, especially when offered by the party that prepared them. In its pre-Rules decision in *Palmer v. Hoffman* (involving a railroad mishap), the Supreme Court once said accident reports could not satisfy the statutory predecessor of FRE 803(6) because they are not related to the main purpose of the enterprise,[2] but *Palmer* has been interpreted not as adopting a per se rule barring such material, but as a cautionary decision to the effect that motivational factors may raise enough suspicion to require exclusion.[3] Hence a blanket rule excluding accident reports does not reflect the philosophy of FRE 803(6), which contains a more flexible proviso authorizing exclusion of untrustworthy records.

Assuming an accident report satisfies the basic requirements of the exception, it should be admissible unless circumstances suggest it is untrustworthy.[4] Despite the obvious concern over liability, it is in the best interest of a business to get an accurate account of an accident in order to cut risks of future losses. And background factors may minimize concerns over trustworthiness: If the report was prepared by people who were not personally involved in or potentially responsible, there is more reason to trust the conclusions. And if a business uses the

---

§8.46   1. *See* Sea-Land Services, Inc. v. Lozen International, LLC, 285 F.3d 1056, 1062 (9th Cir. 2002) (bills of lading); United States v. Salgado, 250 F.3d 438, 451 (6th Cir. 2001) (phone company toll records), *cert. denied*, 122 S. Ct. 306; Countrywide Services Corp. v. SIA Ins. Co., 235 F.3d 390 (8th Cir. 2000) (invoices); Hoselton v. Metz Baking Co., 48 F.3d 1056, 1062 (8th Cir. 1995) (handwritten notes summarizing negotiations).

2. Palmer v. Hoffman, 318 U.S. 109 (1943) (accident report is not "typical of entries made systematically or as a matter of routine").

3. In *Palmer*, the engineer's statement was "dripping with motivations to misrepresent" (as Judge Clark said in dissenting from the Second Circuit opinion). *See* Hoffman v. Palmer, 129 F.2d 976, 1002 (2d Cir. 1942) (exception would be useless if self-interest disqualified a record; "there is hardly a grocer's account book which could not be excluded on that basis") (dissenting opinion), *aff'd*, 318 U.S. 109 (1943).

4. *See* Lewis v. Baker, 526 F.2d 470, 473-474 (2d Cir. 1975) (admitting accident report by trainmasters offered by railroad trustees); Gaussen v. United Fruit Co., 412 F.2d 72, 74 (2d Cir. 1969) (admissibility depends on whether report was made in regular course on information transmitted in regular course by one with knowledge, and on trustworthiness).

report as the basis of changes in design, procedures, or operations, or gathers and regularly uses such reports for that purpose, such facts too suggest the report may be trusted.[5]

Accident reports may be affected by pressures from management and the obvious motivation to resist claims. If reports are prepared by people who were involved in the accident, self-serving motives are likely to make the conclusions and details untrustworthy.[6] The larger picture may suggest that such reports are routinely gathered to defend claims, with litigation on everyone's mind. When such points appear, trustworthiness becomes suspect and exclusion is warranted.[7]

Modern businesses routinely conduct internal investigations of employment practices and conditions, in order to comply with legal obligations to treat employees fairly (avoid discrimination), maintain workplace safety, protect against hostile workplace environment, and insure compliance with laws and regulations. Typically human resource officers or departments are responsible in some of these areas, and there may well be other security or compliance officers or departments as well. Often incidents, or suspicion of incidents, trigger an investigation in which the person in charge must talk to employees to gather information. When such information is compiled in reports, the question may arise whether such reports qualify as business records.

Internal investigations

Not surprisingly, such material is more likely to be admitted against the company. The report itself may be viewed as an admission or business record, and information provided by employees is likely to be viewed as admissions too, since employees who talk to investigators are either speaking on matters within the scope of their duties under FRE 801(d)(2)(D) or are authorized to cooperate with investigators, so their statements fit FRE 801(d)(2)(C). At least in theory, such reports might be admissible when offered by the company too, insofar as such reports otherwise fit the exception—meaning that they are routinely prepared, soon after the event, by people acting in ordinary course. But in fact many such reports are surely prepared with an awareness that dispute or litigation is in the offing, and many people who provide information to company investigators in this setting are doing anything but acting in ordinary course. Hence such material is much less likely to be admitted when offered by the company.[8]

---

5. Pekelis v. Transcontinental & West. Air, Inc., 187 F.2d 122, 129-130 (2d Cir. 1951) (admitting accident report against airline, which changed methods based on report), *cert. denied*, 341 U.S. 951.

6. *See* Hoffman v. Palmer, 129 F.2d 976, 979, 991 (2d Cir. 1942) (exception does not apply where maker knows suit is probable), *aff'd*, 318 U.S. 109.

7. Certain Underwriters at Lloyd's, London v. Sinkovich, 232 F.3d 200, 204-206 (4th Cir. 2000); Sana v. Hawaiian Cruises, Ltd., 181 F.3d 1041, 1044-1045 (9th Cir. 1999).

8. *Compare* Norcon v. Kotowski, 971 P.2d 158 (Alaska, 1999) (in suit alleging sexual harassment in workplace, admitting investigative report, offered by plaintiff) *with* Bean v. Montana Board of Labor Appeals, 965 P.2d 256, 261-262 (Mont. 1998) (in suit by dismissed employee for wrongful termination, excluding employee incident report, offered by defendant).

Hotel registration can prove that someone booked a room at a particular time, which can place the person in that location or put him in proximity with others. In the paradigm case, the question is whether hotel registration can be admitted as proof that someone appeared at the hotel on a particular occasion and booked a room. Suppose a written entry on a hotel registration card showed the signature "Charles Q. Jones." It is fair to view the entry itself as nonhearsay proof that *someone using that name* registered. Registering amounts to a verbal act, because the guest commits to pay for the room and undertakes to follow the rules (not disturbing other guests, not stealing the towels, not using the premises for criminal purposes, leaving by the stated time), and the registration would be admitted as evidence of a contract in any dispute between hotel and guest over the obligations of either.

In other settings the question is slightly different: Is the register admissible to prove that the named person booked the room (hence likely stayed there), or lives where he says he lives or is the person to whom the drivers license or credit card used in the transaction was issued?

The hearsay problem is twofold: First, hotel records are entries in computerized systems in which the clerk keys in critical information when the guest appears. The entry is hearsay when offered to prove that *some* "Charles Q. Jones" appeared and registered, but this hearsay issue is readily resolved: As proof of this point, the entry fits the business records exception. Second, the identifying information is hearsay when offered as proof that the person who registers is the Charles Q. Jones of interest and really lives at the indicated address. In theory, this problem might dissolve into a question of authentication: If someone can identify the person as the Charles Q. Jones of interest, by watching and recognizing the person or fingerprint or handwriting analysis, this second hearsay issue disappears.[9] Short of that, the question is whether the "outside" hearsay can prove the identification and address if the guest produces a drivers license that the clerk glances at, or a credit card that the clerk "runs through the data entry port" to charge the room or make the entry on the register. Since credit cards and drivers licenses are reliable identifiers, it seems wise to accept them and to allow this level of hearsay, which is what the cases do. They admit the registration if the desk clerk requires identification in the form of a driver's license or credit card,[10] but not otherwise when offered for this purpose.[11]

---

9. United States v. Bell, 833 F.2d 272, 276 (11th Cir. 1987) (admitting registration where government showed that signature matched defendant's), *cert. denied*, 486 U.S. 1013.

10. United States v. McIntyre, 997 F.2d 687, 699-701 (10th Cir. 1993) (register proves defendant checked into motel; identity verified by driver's license), *cert. denied*, 510 U.S. 1063; Wilson v. Zapata Off-Shore Co., 939 F.2d 260, 271 (5th Cir. 1991) (similar) (practice to verify by business card or license).

11. United States v. Cestnik, 36 F.3d 904, 910 (10th Cir. 1994) (error to admit motel record; no indication that motel verified identity); United States v. Lieberman, 637 F.2d 95, 99-100 (2d Cir. 1980) (hotel register could not prove co-offender stayed there; no indication that clerk verified identity).

This pattern has proved workable in other contexts in which people enter their names in log books and produce proof of identification, where the entries are admissible to prove that the person in question was at the indicated place at the indicated time.[12] Otherwise they should be excluded when offered for such points.[13]

Medical records kept by hospitals and doctors often fit the exception. **Medical records** Such records may prove the physical condition of the patient on arrival at the hospital or doctor's office, including intoxication or influence of drugs,[14] and routine medical measurements (pulse, temperature, blood pressure), and descriptions of treatment and medication.[15] Such records can show who attended or treated the patient.[16] Medical history is provable by such records,[17] including what the patient says in describing symptoms and cause of injuries, when germane to diagnosis or treatment.[18]

When records kept by a doctor or hospital are offered by the patient, there is a double hearsay issue insofar as they reflect what he or others report to the physician or hospital staff, but usually the problem can be overcome. If the patient offers the record and is the source of the information, the exceptions for business records and medical statements can be combined. If such a record is offered against the patient, the hearsay problem can be overcome by combining the business record exception and the admissions doctrine.[19]

Hospital records that may be admitted to reflect standard or routine diagnoses[20] and also reported results of routine lab tests (analyses of

---

12. United States v. Reyes, 157 F.3d 949, 952-953 (2d Cir. 1998) (admitting prison log to identify people who visited defendant; exception applies if someone has a duty to verify identification).

13. United States v. Vigneau, 187 F.3d 70, 75-78 (1st Cir. 1999) (error to admit "send" orders generating wire transfers; forms named defendant as sender, but Western Union did not verify) (reversing), *cert. denied*, 528 U.S. 1172; United States v. McIntyre, 997 F.2d 687, 701-706 (10th Cir. 1993) (error to admit cellphone application and record of calls placed under name of defendant VH, as proof that she had phone and used it; signature not verified), *cert. denied*, 510 U.S. 1063.

14. Norton v. Colyer, 828 F.2d 384, 386 (6th Cir. 1987) (plaintiff dependent on drugs); United States v. Bohle, 445 F.2d 54, 60-66 (7th Cir. 1971) ("appearance, conduct and reactions").

15. Harris v. Smith, 372 F.2d 806, 816-817 (8th Cir. 1967) ("variations in temperature, pulse, respiration, wound drainage, swelling," and information on drug administration and treatment).

16. Ascher v. Gutierrez, 533 F.2d 1235, 1237 (D.C. Cir. 1976) (defendant was anesthesiologist during birth).

17. United States v. Sackett, 598 F.2d 739, 742-743 (2d Cir. 1979) (patient was kept home with family but was doing worse and family felt she was pre-terminal); Raycraft v. Duluth, M.&I. R.R. Co., 472 F.2d 27, 32 (8th Cir. 1973) (physical condition, prior hospitalization, disability rating).

18. *See* Wilson v. Zapata Off-Shore Co., 939 F.2d 260, 271-272 (5th Cir. 1991) (statement by plaintiff's sister); Higgins v. Martin Marietta Corp., 752 F.2d 492, 497 (10th Cir. 1985) (statement by plaintiff's doctor).

19. FRE 801(d)(2)(A) or FRE 803(4) can be piggybacked with FRE 803(6) to admit records reflecting what the patient said.

20. Bell v. Austin, 607 S.E.2d 569, 573 (Ga. 2005) (in suit for injuries, admitting "narrative medical report" by plaintiff's physician, offered by plaintiff).

blood alcohol content, "positive" tests for routine viral infections, and similar matters).[21] Records reflecting elaborate, difficult, or unusual diagnoses or opinions, including most psychiatric evaluations, are problematic and are seldom admitted. Although the exception makes no reference to the availability of the expert whose diagnosis it is, this factor seems crucial. Where the physician who made the diagnosis testifies, or another with firsthand knowledge testifies, admitting reports reflecting difficult, elaborate, or unusual diagnoses seems easier to justify. Without such testimony, risks of confusing the issues or misleading the jury are likely to justify exclusion under FRE 403.[22]

Records and reports prepared by doctors working outside the hospital setting are equally within reach of the exception.[23] Particularly where a doctor examines someone to prepare for suit or obtain benefits or insurance, motivational factors raise doubts about objectivity, and courts may insist either that the doctor testify or that her report be admissible only against the party who selected her to conduct the examination (the theory being in effect that selection amounts to appointing the doctor or adopting in advance her conclusions).[24]

Although the Rules were adopted more than a decade before computers became universal, the framers anticipated changes in this direction, and the exception applies to computer records (referring to "data compilation[s]" and to records "in any form"). Because computers can analyze, combine, break down, and sort data in many ways, and because the operation of computer programs is technical and complex, evidence issues should be addressed in discovery and pretrial preparation, and these issues transcend hearsay problems and often raise in addition issues of privilege and trade secrets.[25] Such advance cooperation is essential in order to enable adversary testing of such proof, and the proponent of electronic business records bears responsibility for

---

21. Ex parte Department of Health and Environmental Control v. Doe, 565 S.E.2d 293 (S.C. 2002) (HIV test results); Government of Virgin Islands v. St. Ange, 458 F.2d 981, 982 (3d Cir. 1972) (vaginal smear); Kuklis v. Hancock, 428 F.2d 608, 612-613 (5th Cir. 1970) (blood-alcohol).

22. Lovell v. Beavers, 987 S.W.2d 660, 662 (Ark. 1999) (where diagnosing physician testifies, or another with knowledge, it is easier to admit reports reflecting difficult, elaborate, diagnoses; without such testimony, risks of confusion or misleading jury justify exclusion).

23. Mitchell v. American Export Isbrandtsen Lines, Inc., 430 F.2d 1023, 1028-1029 (2d Cir. 1970) (illness report by ship's doctor).

24. *See* Limatta v. Vest, 45 P.3d 310, 318 n.32 (Alaska, 2002) (letter from doctor to government agency); Yates v. Bair Transport, Inc., 249 F. Supp. 681, 688-692 (S.D.N.Y. 1965) (letting plaintiff offer reports by doctors selected by defense, not by doctors selected by plaintiff).

25. See Manual for Complex Litigation §11.446 (4th ed. 2004) (parties should discuss production of computerized data early; allowing access to computer systems could "compromise legally recognized privileges, trade secrets," and personal privacy of employees and customers, and parties should discuss "appropriate applications, file structures, manuals, and other tools" necessary to translate and use data).

explaining underlying processes to insure accuracy and compliance with the exception.[26]

The term "record" in the exception reaches both electronically stored data and retrieved output, and the contemporaneity requirement is satisfied if information was originally entered close in time to the event or transaction, even if the information was only later entered into electronic memory or was rearranged or recombined with other data in electronic memory.[27]

Electronic records

The operations that computers perform on data, from rearranging and reassembling to separating and sorting according to widely variable criteria, both in human-run operations and by means of elaborate programs, can so transfigure the data that a retrieved image or output is not an identifiable counterpart to any preexisting record or input. When such transformations occur in routine of business, that fact in itself provides a basis to conclude that the process does what it purports to do, paving the way to apply the exception.[28] Greater care is warranted if such transformations are done for purposes of litigation, and the proponent should supply more information on what was done. But summaries of complicated information have long been admissible, and even computerized records transformed for purposes of suit may be admissible.[29]

Still the hearsay doctrine, and the underlying concern for accuracy, should not surrender to computer technology. Computerized record-keeping occasionally leads to bungling and misuse, and risks of inaccuracy come from mechanical human input and from programs. Hence the requirements of the exception apply to computerized records, in service of the overall concern over accuracy: Such records must be kept as part of a regularly conducted business; data entry must be done in ordinary course and close in time to events recorded; those who participate must be acting in routine of business; human sources must have personal knowledge; the foundation must show the accuracy

---

26. United States v. Briscoe, 896 F.2d 1476, 1494 (7th Cir. 1990) (phone company record keeper testified that records were compilations of call data entered when subscriber placed call, that computer scanned itself for error every 15 seconds, that records were kept for billing in regular course), *cert. denied*, 498 U.S. 863; United States v. Scholle, 553 F.2d 1109, 1124-1125 n.5 (8th Cir. 1977) (speaking of "adequate opportunity for rebuttal"), *cert. denied*, 434 U.S. 940.

27. United States v. Briscoe, 896 F.2d 1476, 1494 (7th Cir. 1990) (fact that printouts were prepared especially for case didn't matter; data were entered contemporaneously and kept in regular course), *cert. denied*, 498 U.S. 863; United States v. Hernandez, 913 F.2d 1506, 1512 (10th Cir. 1990) (original compilation was prepared under business duty in regular practice; fact that hard copy was printed for purposes of suit made no difference) (INS record), *cert. denied*, 499 U.S. 908.

28. United States v. Salgado, 250 F.3d 438, 451-452 (6th Cir. 2001) (admitting toll records generated by computer itself, rather than being entered by humans), *cert. denied*, 534 U.S. 936; United States v. Croft, 750 F.2d 1354, 1365 (7th Cir. 1984) ("compilations of payroll data").

29. United States v. Loney, 959 F.2d 1332, 1340-1341 (5th Cir. 1992) (compilation of records; exception does not require that summary be routinely kept, but that underlying data be kept that way).

of input procedures and programmed operations.[30] The foundation witness need not be a technical expert in computer programming, but should be able to describe the process, show that it meets the criteria of the exception, and that the processes produce accurate results.[31] Computerized records are often proved in summary form because they are often too elaborate or voluminous for comprehension otherwise.[32]

Internet websites   In the e-commerce era, there is reason to suppose that web postings can satisfy hearsay exceptions such as the one for commercial lists found in FRE 803(17) (which reaches catalogues and market reports). No doubt web postings can fit the business and public records exceptions in FRE 803(6) and (8) as well, even though it is unusual for businesses to make records accessible to the general public. But merchants use websites to track orders placed by customers, and there is reason to suppose that Internet postings of such material fit the exception. Internet service providers are not normally the "declarant" of material that they handle for their customers, and a litigant offering statements drawn from web postings must apply the hearsay doctrine and its exceptions with an eye toward identifying the actual source of such material.[33]

E-mail   E-mail messages as such do not fit the exception. In its most common use, e-mail messages resemble casual notes and recorded phone messages, and these do not amount to permanent or systematic record-keeping, so declining to apply the exception in this setting seems right.[34]

§8.47   —Trustworthiness Factor

FRE 803(6) authorizes courts to exclude business records where the source of information or means of preparation indicate lack of trustworthiness. In *Palmer v. Hoffman*, the Supreme Court grafted an

---

30. Potamkin Cadillac Corp. v. B.R.I. Coverage Corp., 38 F.3d 617, 632-633 (2d Cir. 1994) (excluding accounting history where broker refused to supply underlying records); United States v. Briscoe, 896 F.2d 1476, 1494 (7th Cir. 1990) (phone company compilations of call data entered when subscriber placed call; computer scanned itself for error every 15 seconds; regularly kept for billing; foundation sufficed); United States v. Vela, 673 F.2d 86, 89-90 (5th Cir. 1982) (custodian described process and vouched for reliability).

31. United States v. Miller, 771 F.2d 1219, 1237 (9th Cir. 1985) (can lay foundation even though lacking technical knowledge of computer); United States v. Croft, 750 F.2d 1354, 1364-1365 (7th Cir. 1984) (university payroll director described process).

32. United States v. Loney, 959 F.2d 1332, 1340-1341 (5th Cir. 1992) (admitting 35-page compilation of computer records on 70 frequent flier accounts).

33. United States v. Jackson, 208 F.3d 633, 637-638 (7th Cir. 2000) (web postings claiming responsibility for hate mail; exception might reach such postings, but proponent did not make necessary showing; Internet service providers are "merely conduits"), *cert denied*, 571 U.S. 973.

34. Monotype Corp. PLC v. International Typeface Corp., 43 F.3d 443, 450 (9th Cir. 1994) (e-mail is not so much a systematic business activity and as a "message and retrieval system").

exception on an earlier statute by excluding an accident report prepared by a railroad and offered against a claimant.[1] But *Palmer* was not convincing (it said writing up accidents was not part of railroading and such reports are used in litigating), and the framers of FRE 803(6) were wise to incorporate the concern raised in that decision by including a trustworthiness clause in the exception, rather than suggesting a more particular rule against admitting accident reports.

If the offering party shows a business record that satisfies the basic requirements, the exception applies and the record is considered trustworthy unless the other side shows it is not.[2] The basic requirements (regular business with regularly kept record; source with personal knowledge; record made timely; foundation testimony) are enough in the run of cases to justify the conclusion that the record is trustworthy. The phrasing of the exception points toward this conclusion: It applies *unless* problems of trustworthiness appear.

Trustworthiness factors

Although satisfying the basic requirements brings the exception into play, many more decisions cite trustworthiness as a reason to admit records than untrustworthiness as a reason to exclude. Many factors support a finding of trustworthiness: Foremost among them is the extent to which the matter recorded is important to the business outside the context of litigation,[3] a point that is especially persuasive if the report was acted on in some serious, costly, or elaborate way that tends to verify the point it is offered to prove.[4] In a related vein, absence of motive that might lead to inaccuracy or false statement is important. Thus the fact that a record was prepared with no eye toward litigation counts; it helps too if those who made it would not have seen the point it is offered to prove as important; if the motive of the preparer is apparent and its likely effect on the record is clear, this fact counts toward admitting the record if predictable inaccuracies would aid the objecting party and cuts toward exclusion if they would aid the offering party.

Concern alleviated

Concern over trustworthiness is alleviated if the record was prepared by a third party independent of the litigants,[5] or by people who would not likely be criticized or risk personal liability for what happened.[6] A record that reflects simple facts is more to be trusted than one setting

§8.47   1. *See* Palmer v. Hoffman, 318 U.S. 109 (1943).

2. McKenzie v. Carrol International Corp., 610 S.E.2d 341, 350 (W.Va. 2004); Shelton v. Consumer Products Safety Commission, 277 F.3d 998, 1109 (8th Cir. 2001), *cert. denied*, 537 U.S. 100; Graef v. Chemical Leaman Corp., 106 F.3d 112, 118 (5th Cir. 1997).

3. United States v. Frazier, 53 F.3d 1105, 1110 (10th Cir. 1995); Coates v. Johnson & Johnson, 756 F.2d 524, 549-550 (7th Cir. 1985).

4. Matador Drilling Co. v. Post, 662 F.2d 1190, 1198-1199 (5th Cir. 1981) (oil drilling rig reports, relied on for payroll).

5. Vaccaro v. Alcoa S.S. Co., 405 F.2d 1133, 1135-1137 (2d Cir. 1968) (in seaman's suit, error to exclude Army accident report offered by defendant; Army was not party and entrant was not involved). *But see* Campbell v. Nordco Prods., 629 F.2d 1258, 1264-1265 (7th Cir. 1980) (in suit against maker of lift, excluding airline report that may have tried to state facts favorably to itself).

6. Lewis v. Baker, 526 F.2d 470, 473-474 (2d Cir. 1975) (approving accident report; preparers could not be target of suit).

forth evaluative, conclusory, or speculative material.[7] Also tending to show trustworthiness is the fact that a record was prepared by trained or experienced people or checked for accuracy, or invites legal sanctions for inaccurate reporting. Independent corroborative evidence helps too. Extensive corroboration supports an inference that the record as a whole is trustworthy, and specific corroboration of the point the record is offered to prove also alleviates trustworthiness concerns.[8] If those who played important roles in preparing the record testify and can be cross-examined on the record or the process that produced it, their testimony verifying such points or showing care and prudence also provides ground to conclude that the record is trustworthy.[9]

Required reports   When law requires not only that a record be made but that it be filed with a government agency, filing provides some incentive to be accurate, particularly if mistakes carry penalties, invite investigation or regulatory action, or create embarrassment.[10] But the effect of required filing is complicated by the fact that some statutes either seem to bar all evidential use, or bar their use against the filing party (in effect creating a privilege protecting the filer but not necessarily blocking use against others). And to the extent reports are understood to be working documents aiding in official investigations, they may take on the character of a brief. If so, evaluative material in them may be plausible or arguable, but those qualities do not make them trustworthy.

Showing untrust-   Showing a record to be untrustworthy need not mean disproving
worthiness   what it says, and indeed minor mistakes do not show a record is untrustworthy (minor mistakes and discrepancies are to be expected). But if a record was prepared with an eye toward litigation, this fact is an indication of untrustworthiness,[11] as are motives that incline the preparer toward errors or overstatements that would be detrimental to the objecting party.[12] And serious mistakes revealed by other evidence or

7. United States v. Hyde, 448 F.2d 815, 846 (5th Cir. 1971) (record factual rather than conclusory), *cert. denied*, 404 U.S. 1058; United States v. Peden, 556 F.2d 278, 281 (5th Cir. 1977) (credit card receipts were "purely factual"), *cert. denied*, 434 U.S. 871.

8. United States v. Cincotta, 689 F.2d 238, 243 (1st Cir. 1982) (admitting driver notebook; delivery tickets signed by commercial customers corroborated notebook), *cert. denied*, 459 U.S. 991; United States v. Wigerman, 549 F.2d 1192, 1193-1194 (8th Cir. 1977) (admitting records of motel registrations, car rentals, airline shipments; witnesses corroborated documents).

9. Ferguson v. Snell, 905 So.2d 516, 519 (Miss. 2004) (admitting insurance company records indicating coverage; employee with knowledge of system could be cross-examined on reliability).

10. United States v. Veytia-Bravo, 603 F.2d 1187, 1188-1192 (5th Cir. 1979) (admitting records forwarded as required to BATF, which are trustworthy because seller must show it did not violate sales restrictions), *cert. denied*, 444 U.S. 1024.

11. Lust v. Sealy, Inc., 383 F.3d 580, 588 (7th Cir. 2004) (note suggesting that boss hadn't promoted plaintiff because of "deficiencies in her interpersonal skills" did not qualify; purpose was "to create evidence" for suit); Scheerer v. Hardee's Food Sys., Inc., 92 F.3d 702, 706-707 (8th Cir. 1996) (excluding slip-and-fall report, prepared by restaurant with eye toward litigation).

12. Ledbetter v. Commissioner, 837 F.2d 708, 710-711 (5th Cir. 1988) (in suit challenging deficiency, excluding receipts showing cash contributions to church, as unreliable), *cert. denied*, 488 U.S. 856.

internal contradictions also indicate lack of trustworthiness.[13] And where records reflect important information that comes from sources who cannot be identified or tested, this fact does not necessarily mean the basic requirements of the exception have not been met, but it sometimes suggests strongly that the record should not be trusted.[14] More generally, serious methodological shortcomings undercut the inference of trustworthiness, and these matters must be assessed in the specific context of the proposed use of the records and the nature and complexity of their content.[15]

FRE 803(7)

(7) Absence of entry in records kept in accordance with the provisions of paragraph (6). Evidence that a matter is not included in the memoranda reports, records, or data compilations, in any form, kept in accordance with the provisions of paragraph (6) to prove nonoccurrence or nonexistence of the matter, if the matter was of a kind of which a memorandum, report, record, or data compilation was regularly made and preserved, unless the sources of information or other circumstances indicate lack of trustworthiness.

---

§8.48   Absence of Entries in Business Records

An exception paves the way to prove the absence of business entries, as a means of showing that conditions, events, or acts that would normally be reflected in such entries, if they had existed or occurred, did not exist or occur. It is possible to argue that the evidence is not even hearsay, since inaction by people or entities in not making an entry may not represent any intention to assert anything, but FRE 803(7) removes the need to resolve this question. *(Nonmention proves nonoccurrence)*

The probative worth of such negative evidence is assured by the factors that underlie the business records exception. If records are routinely kept (or entries are routinely made), they are likely to be complete and comprehensive, so nonmention (or nonexistence of a *(Foundation requirement)*

---

13. Meder v. Everest & Jennings, Inc., 637 F.2d 1182, 1186-1187 & n.6 (8th Cir. 1981) (officer's report of wheelchair accident conflicted with eyewitness testimony); Pan-Islamic Trade Corp. v. Exxon Corp., 632 F.2d 539, 560 (5th Cir. 1980) ("glaring inconsistencies"), *cert. denied*, 454 U.S. 927.

14. Ricciardi v. Children's Hosp. Medical Ctr., 811 F.2d 18, 23 (1st Cir. 1987) (excluding medical record indicating that tube came out during surgery; neurology resident made entry, and lacked personal knowledge and did not know where he got information; unknown source is hardly trustworthy); McNeese v. Reading & Bates Drilling Co., 749 F.2d 270, 275 (5th Cir. 1985) (excluding accident report where apparent preparer disowned it and did not know source of information).

15. United States v. Houser, 746 F.2d 55, 61-62 (D.C. Cir. 1984) (BATF "tracer" form was untrustworthy because of possibilities for error in manner of gathering information).

record or entry) is a good indication that act, event, or condition did not occur or exist. The foundation requirements for showing there is no record or entry are similar to those for business records themselves, with some adjustments.[1] In lieu of showing that records were routinely kept by a regular business, the party proving nonmention should show such a business routinely kept records of matters like the one not mentioned; in lieu of showing the matter was recorded contemporaneously by a person with firsthand knowledge acting in regular course, the proponent should show the matter not mentioned would have come to the attention of regular recordkeepers and would have been recorded.

Found no mention   Proof of nonmention under FRE 803(7) is likely to take the form of testimony: The witness says he searched the records and found no mention of the matter.[2] Such testimony should not be rejected as multiple hearsay even if the absence of records indicates that many people did not make entries, but the testifying witness should have firsthand knowledge that there is no record or entry and should not simply relate what others said on searching the records.[3]

FRE 803(8)

  (8) Public records and reports. Records, reports, statements, or data compilations, in any form, of public offices or agencies, setting forth (A) the activities of the office or agency, or (B) matters observed pursuant to duty imposed by law as to which matters there was a duty to report, excluding, however, in criminal cases matters observed by police officers and other law enforcement personnel, or (C) in civil actions and proceedings and against the government in criminal cases, factual findings resulting from an investigation made pursuant to authority granted by law, unless the sources of information or other circumstances indicate lack of trustworthiness.

---

§8.49   Public Records—Rationale and Scope

Extraordinary breadth   The exception for public records and reports is set forth in FRE 803(8). Like the business records exception, this one has extraordinary

---

§8.48 1. United States v. Rich, 580 F.2d 929, 937-939 (9th Cir. 1978), *cert. denied*, 439 U.S. 935; Exxon Corp. v. United States, 45 Fed. Cl. 581, 690 (Ct. Fed. Cl. 1999) (quoting this Treatise), *aff'd in part* and *rev'd in part*, 244 F.3d 1341 (Fed. Cir. 2001).

2. United States v. Rich, 580 F.2d 929, 937-939 (9th Cir. 1978) (checked city directories, credit records, other sources to locate someone), *cert. denied*, 439 U.S. 935; McClanahan v. United States, 292 F.2d 630, 636-637 (5th Cir. 1961) (could find records of no other transactions), *cert. denied*, 368 U.S. 913.

3. United States v. Zeidman, 540 F.2d 314, 319 (7th Cir. 1976) (must be "some firsthand testimony" on records to show absence of entry).

breadth. It embraces records in almost any form,[1] including electronically stored data of all sorts and computer output,[2] and reaches records of any public office or agency, state and local, federal and foreign. And despite restrictions and subject matter limits, the exception paves the way to use public records over a wide range of issues.[3]

The exception contains three clauses that set up overlapping categories. Often it makes no difference whether an item fits clause A rather than B or C, or fits two or even all three. But sometimes it does matter, since the three are subject to different use restrictions and foundation requirements. Ensuing sections treat the clauses separately, although doing so is not wholly satisfying because they do not create watertight compartments. The exception embraces material that reflects multiple layers of hearsay as information is passed among public officials before being finally recorded in what is offered at trial.[4]

Three categories

Public records and reports are considered trustworthy because of the duty that comes with public service. In effect it is presumed that public servants perform their tasks carefully and fairly, without bias or corruption, and this notion finds support in the scrutiny and risk of exposure that surround most government functions. Particularly with investigative reports in clause C, the exception expresses the judgment that officials and agencies have expertise and credibility that make findings trustworthy. All public records that fit the exception are likely to be the product of repetitive practice that adds some protection against mistake and misstatement, although only clause B (records prepared under a duty to report) contains something resembling a routine practice requirement. Otherwise the exception, unlike the one for business records, does not turn on proving routine practice, and foundation requirements are simpler.

Trustworthiness

Necessity also underlies the exception. Many matters reported in public records could not be proved effectively by live testimony because no public official is likely to remember them. And many facts important in lawsuits involve activities of public agencies that are reported in public records, so doing without an exception for the records would lead to calling government officials. That would often be inconvenient and costly as well as less satisfactory than the records themselves.

Necessity

---

§8.49 1. *See* Chandler v. Roudebush, 425 U.S. 840 (1976) (administrative findings); United States v. Pluta, 176 F.3d 43, 49 (2d Cir. 1999) (passports reflecting Polish citizenship), *cert. denied,* 529 U.S. 906; Alexander v. Estepp, 95 F.3d 312, 314 n.2 (4th Cir. 1996) (firefighters applicant register); Culver v. Slater Boat Co., 688 F.2d 280, 309 n45 (5th Cir. 1982) (tables published by Bureau of Labor Statistics), *cert. denied,* 469 U.S. 819.

2. Hughes v. United States, 953 F.2d 531, 540 (9th Cir. 1992); United States v. Orozco, 590 F.2d 789, 793-794 (9th Cir. 1979), *cert. denied,* 442 U.S. 920.

3. *See* Chandler v. Roudebush, 425 U.S. 840 (1976) (discrimination); Complaint of Nautilus Motor Tanker Co., Ltd. 85 F.3d 105, 110-113 (3d Cir. 1996) (Coast Guard accident report); United States v. King, 590 F.2d 253, 255 (8th Cir. 1978) (car ownership), *cert. denied,* 440 U.S. 973; Baker v. Elcona Homes Corp., 588 F.2d 551, 555-556 (6th Cir. 1978) (car ran red light), *cert. denied,* 441 U.S. 933.

4. Matter of Oil Spill by the Amoco Cadiz, 954 F.2d 1279, 1308 (7th Cir. 1992) ("multi-level exception").

Self-authenticating

Foundation requirements are easily satisfied. The public records exception often requires no foundation witness at all: The self-authentication provisions in FRE 902 make it easy to dispense with live testimony to authenticate a public record or show it fits the exception,[5] although the custodian of a public record can of course serve this function.[6]

§8.50 —Varieties of Public Records

Activities of agency

Clause A allows proof of the activities of a public agency by means of its records, whether in the form of old-style hard copy or electronically stored data. An example is records of the Treasury, to prove receipts and disbursements of that department; another is the transcript of a judicial proceeding, to prove that an officer of the court administered an oath to a witness; yet another is the return of a marshal or similar officer, to prove he served papers,[1] and the list could go on.[2]

"Matters observed"

Clause B may be used to introduce records describing an almost endless variety of acts, events, and conditions in the world observed and depicted by public officials. The phrase "matters observed" limits coverage to information that is concrete and simple in nature, however, and clause B contains a use restriction excluding in criminal cases records reflecting "matters observed by police officers and other law enforcement personnel."

The source of the recorded information must have personal knowledge, as the phrase "matters observed" implies.[3] The source must have a legal duty to observe and report as indicated by the two references to "duty" in the clause. The record must be one that the public agency is required by law to prepare, again as implied by the references to "duty." The latter criteria have not proved troublesome. They do not mean a particular statute or regulation must expressly impose duties to observe, report, and keep records, and it suffices if the nature of the responsibilities assigned to the public agency and the person who is the source are such that the record is appropriate to the function of the agency and the work of the source.

---

5. United States v. Hatchett, 245 F.3d 625, 644 (7th Cir. 2001) (exception often requires no foundation witness at all). *See* discussion of FRE 902(1)-(2) in §§9.19-9.20, *infra.*

6. United States v. Central Gulf Lines, Inc., 747 F.2d 315, 319 (5th Cir. 1984).

§8.50 1. Chesapeake & Delaware Canal Co. v. United States, 250 U.S. 123 (1919) (Treasury records); 28 U.S.C. §753(b) (transcript of proceedings); United States v. Union Nacional de Trabajadores, 576 F.2d 388, 390-391 (1st Cir. 1978) (marshal's return).

2. Howard v. Perrin, 200 U.S. 71 (1906) (General Land Office); United States v. Adedoyin, 369 F.3d 337, 343-344 (3d Cir. 2004) (record of conviction based on plea of nolo contendere, to prove fact of conviction), *cert. denied,* 543 U.S. 915; Matter of Oil Spill by the Amoco Cadiz, 954 F.2d 1279, 1308 (7th Cir. 1992) (French government documents proving expenditures).

3. United States v. Chu Kong Yin, 935 F.2d 990, 999 (9th Cir. 1991); United States v. Perlmuter, 693 F.2d 1290, 1292-1293 & n.2 (9th Cir. 1982).

More important than the background criteria is the seemingly innocuous phrase "matters observed." As an original proposition, that term could reach virtually everything, but apparently it was intended to have narrower meaning. When compared with the phrase in clause C ("factual findings resulting from an investigation"), clause B seems designed for material that is more concrete and simple than interpretive or evaluative. Examples include records of weather conditions, Treasury reports of border crossings, and observations in an accident report that describe the scene and equipment and report concrete measurements and easily observable damage or destruction.[4] Like the other clauses in FRE 803(8), clause B reaches records made by one official that embody information provided by another in the course of his duties. To put it another way, a record may fit clause B even if it rests on a chain of internal hearsay within a government agency, or even hearsay passed from one agency or department to another, although it does not reach matters reported to government agencies by outsiders.[5]

Clause C covers "factual findings resulting from an investigation made pursuant to authority granted by law." The animating force is the view that public officials have expertise in their areas that enables them to evaluate information, resolve conflicting indications, and reach factual conclusions that are trustworthy. Examples include investigative findings on official misconduct, everyday police reports on car accidents based on investigating the scene and talking to witnesses and participants, and other accident reports prepared by specialized agencies.[6] Safety studies on products or procedures are sometimes used to show recommended standards,[7] and diagnostic studies relating to issues of public health or toxicity also fit the exception.[8] Many other records may be admitted as investigative findings.[9]

Investigative findings

---

4. *See* Evanston v. Gunn, 99 U.S. 660 (1879) (meteorological observations of Signal Service); United States v. Puente, 826 F.2d 1415, 1417-1418 (5th Cir. 1987) (printouts indicating that car crossed border from Mexico into Texas); Baker v. Elcona Homes Corp., 588 F.2d 551, 554-556 (6th Cir. 1978) (police accident report giving measurements and describing locations of vehicles and physical markings), *cert. denied,* 441 U.S. 933.

5. United States v. De Peri, 778 F.2d 963, 976-977 (3d Cir. 1985), *cert. denied,* 475 U.S. 1110.

6. Beech Aircraft Corp. v. Rainey, 488 U.S. 153 (1988) (Air Force accident report on cause of plane crash in training flight); Carignan v. New Hampshire International Speedway, Inc., 858 A.2d 536 (N.H. 2004) (police accident report) (remand to determine trustworthiness); Complaint of Nautilus Motor Tanker Co., Ltd., 85 F.3d 105, 110-113 (3d Cir. 1996) (Coast Guard accident report).

7. Boerner v. Brown & Williamson Tobacco Co., 394 F.3d 594, 600 (8th Cir. 2005) (Surgeon General reports on health risks of cigarettes); United States v. Midwest Fireworks Mfg. Co., 248 F.3d 563, 566-567 (6th Cir. 2001) (lab reports by Consumer Product Safety Commission), Roth v. Black & Decker, U.S., Inc., 737 F.2d 779, 783 (8th Cir. 1984) (reports on power tool accidents).

8. O'Dell v. Hercules, Inc., 904 F.2d 1194, 1204-1206 (8th Cir. 1990) (CDC report on health risks from exposure to dioxin in soil); Ellis v. International Playtex, Inc., 745 F.2d 292, 299-305 (4th Cir. 1984) (CDC and studies of toxic shock syndrome).

9. Bridgeway Corp. v. Citibank, 201 F.3d 134, 143-144 (2d Cir. 2000) (State Department report on system of justice in Liberia); Staley v. Bridgestone/Firestone, Inc., 106

The trustworthiness clause in the exception may lead to excluding such materials, and sometimes more particular concerns come into play. Statutes may require exclusion, especially with accident reports and safety studies. The purpose is to control and minimize political and other pressures that might make it harder for public agencies to gather information and fix blame or pinpoint cause.[10] Records reflecting staff reports or preliminary findings are sometimes excluded as tentative, untested, and potentially misleading because they seem to carry official imprimatur but do not.[11]

Investigative findings fit the exception even if they rest on outsider statements,[12] but the exception does not permit use of the statements themselves to prove what they assert.[13] In effect, this provision reflects the judgment that public officials have the expertise necessary to resolve conflicts in outside statements and other information. The result parallels the treatment accorded to experts under FRE 702-703, which allows testimony based on information that others in the field would normally credit but does not permit experts merely to report what others think.

Some older cases refused to apply the exception to interpretive or evaluative material. Legislative history provides conflicting signals, and use of the term "factual" in an exception embracing the written product of an investigation was bound to produce interpretive tension. Experience with civil pleading conventions put to rest any notion that one can reliably separate facts from conclusions or interpretations, and clause C's reference to "factual findings" is better understood as requiring that the report have an appropriate basis and some factual meaning. In 1988 the Supreme Court reached this conclusion in *Beech Aircraft Corp. v. Rainey*, which approved use of an accident report by an Air Force Lieutenant suggesting that pilot error caused an airplane crash in a training mission.[14] *Rainey* settles the point that clause C is construed broadly to reach reports that interpret and draw conclusions

---

F.3d 1504, 1513 (10th Cir. 1997) (redacted OSHA investigative report); Moss v. Ole South Real Estate, Inc., 933 F.2d 1300, 1309-1310 (5th Cir. 1991) (Air Force report on housing discrimination).

10. *See* Huber v. United States, 838 F.2d 398, 401-402 (9th Cir. 1988) (regulation makes Coast Guard accident report inadmissible in suit against government).

11. United States v. D'Anjou, 16 F.3d 604, 6210 (4th Cir. 1994) (excluding raw ATF interview transcripts).

12. Moss v. Ole South Real Estate, Inc., 933 F.2d 1300, 1309-1310 (5th Cir. 1991) (testifying experts rely on hearsay; same latitude for officials); Baker v. Elcona Homes Corp., 588 F.2d 551, 556-559 (6th Cir. 1978) (accident report finding car ran red light, based on disputed evidence), *cert. denied*, 441 U.S. 933.

13. United States v. Mackey, 117 F.3d 24, 28-29 (1st Cir. 1997) (defense may not prove third-party statement in FBI report), *cert. denied*, 522 U.S. 975; United States v. Ortiz, 125 F.3d 630, 632-633 (8th Cir. 1997) (excluding DEA report containing statements by informant), *cert. denied*, 522 U.S. 1132.

14. Beech Aircraft Corp. v. Rainey, 488 U.S. 153 (1988) (hard to distinguish facts from conclusions; concern over applying provision too loosely should be answered by examining trustworthiness).

from underlying data, so long as they have factual basis and some factual content.[15]

By its terms, clause C is available in "civil actions" and "against the government" in criminal cases. These words bar use of the clause to admit official investigative findings against criminal defendants, and the restriction is more than a limit on the exception: The purpose was to state a principle that actually requires exclusion of investigative findings.[16] In a landmark case in *United States v. Oates*, the Second Circuit said the restriction barred resort to all other exceptions. *Oates* involved a laboratory report by a Customs Service chemist that white powder was cocaine, and the court thought the report best fit clause C and was inadmissible. The opinion rejected use of the catchall or business records exceptions as alternatives.[17] On the latter points, *Oates* is probably right because the hard-edged restriction in clause C would often be avoided if those exceptions were available.

Oates case: Use restrictions in clause C

But the exclusionary principle in clause C is not absolute,[18] and resort to the recorded recollection exception should be proper despite the broad language in *Oates*: Almost any evaluative report is likely to contain information that does not stay in the mind of its preparer, and producing him in court to lay the necessary foundation for recorded recollection should satisfy the concern to provide a live witness whom the defense can question.[19] Courts have qualified the categorical language of the use restriction in clause B (discussed in the next section) by admitting routine and nonadversarial records prepared by police or law enforcement officers. Arguably the same judge-made qualification applies to evaluative reports, which would make them admissible against the accused if they are routine and nonadversarial.[20] But reports generated in investigating particular crimes or defendants can hardly be nonadversarial, and

Not absolute despite *Oates*

15. Thompson v. Opeiu, 74 F.3d 1492, 1506 (6th Cir. 1966) (public reports are not inadmissible because they contain "facts, conclusions, or evaluations").

16. *See* ACN (evaluative reports are "admissible only in civil cases and against the government in criminal cases in view of the almost certain collision with confrontation rights").

17. United States v. Oates, 560 F.2d 45, 77 (2d Cir. 1977) (clauses B and C make police and evaluative reports inadmissible against the accused, and bar resort to any other exception). *See also* United States v. Pena-Gutierrez, 222 F.3d 1080, 1086 (9th Cir. 2000), *cert. denied*, 531 U.S. 1057. *But see* United States v. Davis, 181 F.3d 147, 149-150 (D.C. Cir. 1999) (admitting "buy report" prepared by officer at scene; *Oates* is "of questionable precedential value" and is "inapposite" because officer testified), *cert. denied*, 528 U.S. 1140.

18. It does not create, for instance, a privilege. *See* United States v. Bent-Santana, 774 F.2d 1545, 1552 (11th Cir. 1985) (clause C did not require exclusion in suppression hearing of Panamanian documents; Rules do not apply, nor use restrictions).

19. United States v. Marshall, 532 F.2d 1279, 1285-1286 (9th Cir. 1976) (admitting police chemist's laboratory analysis as past recollection recorded).

20. *Compare* United States v. Veytia-Bravo, 603 F.2d 1187, 1189-1192 (5th Cir. 1979) (admitting records showing gun sales to defendant, prepared as required), *cert. denied*, 444 U.S. 1024, *with* United States v. Davis, 571 F.2d 1354, 1356-1357 (5th Cir. 1978) (excluding form filled out by arms maker saying gun was shipped interstate; government may not show findings based on investigation).

reports that are extensive or evaluative in the sense of considering and weighing outsider statements are not routine.

Not records prepared by private entities

By its terms, the public records exception does not embrace records prepared by private entities or people who are not public officials, even when filed with public agencies as required.[21] The subject is not touched in legislative history, and the exception could reach such records on the theory that public authority is delegated to private reporters.[22] Blanket application of this logic leads to an exception that seems overbroad. It is one thing to admit reports by hospitals or doctors on births, deaths, or the incidence of disease, or reports by clergymen on such things as marriage or baptism or deaths. Such reports are simple and reliable because they are connected with professional responsibility and the reporting person has little or no financial or other stake in the central points. It is quite another to admit accident reports by motorists or employers, tax returns, or reports by employers on matters like compliance with regulations on employment practices and job safety, which are anything but simple and routine, do not connect with professionalism, and may be self-serving.

Statutory restrictions

Statutes sometimes bar use of such reports as evidence, and usually the purpose is to reduce pressures that might discourage candor or compliance with reporting requirements.[23] Such statutes block use of such reports against the preparer but might not bar their use against others, although presumably the prospect of use both for and against the preparer would create incentives to write reports that tend to exonerate her from liability.[24]

§8.51 —Crime Reports; Recorded 911 Calls; Forensic Lab Reports

We turn to three kinds of material that are vitally important in criminal cases and bring considerable challenge in applying the public records exception. We also consider in some detail the use restrictions in clauses B and C, which complement and dovetail with limits imposed

21. Marsee v. U.S. Tobacco Co., 866 F.2d 319, 324-325 (10th Cir. 1989) (excluding scientific reports not prepared by public office or agency); Lamphere v. Brown Univ., 685 F.2d 743, 748-749 (1st Cir. 1982) (panel of private university investigating discrimination was not public agency).

22. *See* United States v. Lykes Bros. S.S. Co., 432 F.2d 1076, 1079-1080 (5th Cir. 1970) (duty can be delegated to independent agency; report remains official).

23. *See* Huber v. United States, 838 F.2d 398, 401-402 (9th Cir. 1988) (excluding Coast Guard accident report; regulations say reports are not "intended to fix civil or criminal responsibility," and purpose is to promote safety; admitting might make investigators reluctant to be candid); Johnson v. United States, 780 F.2d 902, 908-909 (11th Cir. 1986) (excluding risk management report by insurance adjuster for hospital as required by state statute).

24. *See* Taylor v. Baltimore & Ohio R.R. Co., 344 F.2d 281, 285-287 (2d Cir. 1965) (admitting railroad accident report submitted to Labor Secretary; statute makes report inadmissible, but Congress was not thinking of case where preparer offers report), *cert. denied*, 382 U.S. 831.

by the confrontation clause. First we take up crime reports prepared by police and other law enforcement personnel, which are usually inadmissible against criminal defendants. Second, we consider recordings and transcripts of 911 calls placed by eyewitnesses to crimes and other events, which in the end are sometimes admissible and sometimes inadmissible. Third, we consider forensic lab reports analyzing such things as fingerprints and DNA, an area in which the cases are in deep conflict, but there are promising statutory reforms that states have adopted.

As noted above, crime reports prepared by police and other law enforcement personnel are generally inadmissible against criminal defendants.[1] Language in FRE 803(8) secures this result. Most such material would also be excludable under *Crawford* as violating confrontation rights, because statements in such reports are "testimonial" (generated in investigating and preparing to prosecute crimes).[2] Crime reports do not generally fit clause A of FRE 803(8) because they are not offered to prove activities of an office or agency. Crime reports come closer to fitting clauses B and C, but cannot be admitted under those provisions either: Such reports do reflect, at least in part, things that investigators personally "observe" (such as the position of a body or damage to a door), but they run afoul of special language stating that clause B is unavailable in criminal cases for material reflecting observations of "police officers and other law enforcement personnel." Such reports also look very much like investigative findings described in clause C, but again special language gets in the way, and such findings cannot be offered against the accused (they are admissible *only* in "civil actions and proceedings and against the Government in criminal cases").

Crime reports

Usually the defining language of an exception sets only the extent and limits of the exception. Hence a statement that does not fit one exception may be admitted if it fits another. But the use restrictions in clauses B and C are different: They not only limit resort to the public records exception, but are more broadly designed to block resort to other exceptions that might otherwise be available.[3]

Of course the conclusion, which is that crime reports are inadmissible against defendants in criminal cases, is anything but accidental. The exception was carefully crafted with this result in mind. Nobody thinks prosecutors should be able to use such material in criminal trials. A crime report is generated after a crime was committed, and the main purposes are to investigate, to lay the foundation for criminal charges, and to prepare for trial. Often such reports recite or rest on outsider statements; often these are provided by people who are themselves implicated or involved in various ways and under great pressures

---

§8.51   1. State v. Hammell, 917 A.2d 1267, 1271 (N.H. 2007) (criminal history); State v. Leonard, 818 N.E.2d 229, 258 (Ohio 2004) (crime report); United States v. Campagnuolo, 592 F.2d 852, 863 n.15 (5th Cir. 1979) (FBI report); United States v. Ruffin, 575 F.2d 346, 356 (2d Cir. 1978) (IRS printout).

2. *See* Crawford v. Washington, 541 U.S. 36 (2004), discussed in §§8.83-8.91, *infra*.

3. *See* the discussion of clause C in §8.50, *supra*.

(to talk or not, and to tailor what they say in various ways); often the reports contain evaluative material. So serious are these problems that each seems enough by itself to bar their use against defendants. The point is not that such reports are inaccurate or irresponsible. They may be accurate, and those who prepare them may be doing exactly what they should be doing. Rather, the point is that hearsay concerns are so serious and hard to sort out that judges cannot realistically evaluate such reports, separating trustworthy from untrustworthy material. Nor, if a judge passed preliminarily on trustworthiness and admitted such material, can juries be expected to evaluate it realistically.[4] The framers also recognized that such material is at the heart of the concerns underlying the confrontation clause.

In clause B, the critical reference to "police officers and other law enforcement personnel" reaches most people who prepare law enforcement reports, including officers and agents in the FBI and DEA, the Treasury and Secret Service, the BATF and Customs Service, and counterparts in state criminal investigative departments, highway patrols, and local police. The language reaches undercover agents, and those engaged in surveillance or sting operations.[5]

911 calls   Recordings and transcripts of 911 calls placed by eyewitnesses to crime are quite different from crime reports. Typically such recordings and transcripts are made and kept by public agencies (often police departments). It is worth pausing a moment to reflect that *recordings* are not themselves hearsay when offered as proof of the content of incoming calls (a *recording* is not itself a statement, although the words spoken by the caller are a statement). Hence recordings can prove the content of such calls without worrying about hearsay. A *transcript* of the content of such calls *is* a statement, if made by a human who listens to the call (or recording) and uses a keyboard to produce a verbatim account (it is again different if a transcript is machine-made). In effect, the transcript asserts that the content of the call is accurately set forth in the transcript itself. The transcript likely fits the exception, either because it fits clause A in reflecting the "activities of the office or agency" or, more plausibly, because it fits clause B in reflecting matters "observed"—the 911 call itself. Arguably the person who makes the transcript should *not* be viewed as a "police officer" or "law enforcement personnel" (although this point might not hold up, for the same reasons that lab technicians do not escape this designation), or transcript preparation might be viewed as "routine and nonadversarial" work, which paves the way to admit them even if the transcriber does come within the category of police officer or law enforcement personnel (more on this below).

4. Fischer v. State, 252 S.W.3d 375, 382-383 (Tex. Crim. App. 2008) (we exclude "crime-scene or investigative observations" because they are made while officer engages in competitive enterprise of ferreting out crime; citing "inherently adversarial nature" of on-the-scene or post-hoc investigation).

5. *See* United States v. Puente, 826 F.2d 1415, 1417-1418 (5th Cir. 1987) (Customs Service officials); United States v. Smith, 521 F.2d 957, 968 (D.C. Cir. 1975) (police officer).

Arguably, then, a transcript fits FRE 803(8), which reaches "data compilations in any form," when offered for the limited purpose of proving that a call was made and that the caller spoke.[6]

Of course the important thing about 911 calls is what the *caller* says, and the caller's words cannot themselves fit the exception (callers are not officials). Still, many 911 calls fit the exceptions for excited utterances or present sense impressions. In net effect, then, the recording or transcript can prove the making and content of the call, and exceptions often take care of the hearsay issues with the caller's words. Such calls may *still* be excludable under *Crawford* because reports of criminal acts, made by phone to 911 operators, are often in substance "testimonial" statements by persons seeking to aid police and law enforcement in investigating crimes, and in fact the *Davis* case said that 911 operators can be viewed as police for this purpose. Still, many such calls overcome objections based on *Crawford* because they report ongoing emergencies. They thus fit the *Davis* "emergency" doctrine, which amounts to an exception to *Crawford* (the call is not "testimonial" after all, in cases where the aim is to aid rather than aid in an investigation).[7] It is of course important to note that not *all* 911 calls fit the emergency doctrine even if the caller is acting appropriately in using the 911 "emergency" service. A report describing a bank robbery that has been completed, for example, or an assault that is over when the assailant has fled and there is no fear of his return, may well be appropriate for a 911 call, and the words of the caller may well satisfy the exceptions for excited utterances or present sense impressions, and yet the call cannot overcome a *Crawford* objection because there is no ongoing emergency for purposes of the *Davis* doctrine.[8]

"Emergency" doctrine

We turn now to forensic lab reports that analyze such things as fingerprints, DNA samples, and ballistics evidence. Not surprisingly, prosecutors routinely prove the results of forensic tests, which depend on controlled lab procedures and involve experts, who regularly write up their findings and also testify in court. Questions about the admissibility of the results of such tests involve the *Daubert* standard and the criteria set forth in FRE 702, taken up elsewhere.[9] The question here is whether, assuming that the *Daubert* standard and FRE 702 are satisfied, the reports themselves are admissible. Strong federal authority holds that they are not, once again because of the use restrictions clauses B and C of FRE 803(8), but the matter has proved more complicated than first appears, and the constitutional picture is clouded.

Crime lab reports

The landmark federal decision is the *Oates* case, decided by the Second Circuit in 1977, just two years after the Rules were adopted.

The *Oates* case

6. *See* Bemis v. Edwards, 45 F.3d 1369, 1372 (9th Cir. 1995); United States v. Sallins, 993 F.2d 344, 347-348 (3d Cir. 1993) (both suggesting that tapes of 911 calls fit public records exception).

7. On application of the exceptions for present sense impressions and excited utterances, *see* discussion in §§8.35 and 8.36, *supra*. On the emergency doctrine, see §8.85, *infra*.

8. *See* Commonwealth v. Lao, 877 N.E.2d 557 (Mass. 2007).

9. *See* the discussion in §7.7, *supra*.

In *Oates*, the prosecutor sought to use a Customs Service laboratory report to prove that white powder found in the possession of the defendant was cocaine. The lab technician who had tested the powder called in sick, and the prosecutor called another technician to present the findings. She had not done the tests, so she could only relay what she found by looking at the report. In substance, she became a conduit for the report itself, and *Oates* concluded that the report was inadmissible and reversed the conviction. A Customs Service chemist is within the use restriction in clause B (in substance she is a "police officer" or "law enforcement personnel") because she is aligned with prosecutor and police. Such people are "important participants in the prosecutorial effort" who become government witnesses and "do not mentally disassociate themselves from those who undoubtedly are law enforcement personnel." Even if clause B applies (covering matters "observed"), which is itself a stretch because lab tests do not sound like matters "observed," still such reports are inadmissible. The court in *Oates* thought, reasonably enough, that such a report is better described as an investigative finding, bringing it within clause C, which again leads to the conclusion that it cannot be admitted (the government cannot use clause C in a criminal case; investigative findings are admissible only in civil suits and *against* the government in a criminal case).[10]

Oates is realistic in recognizing that technical people in forensic laboratories have professional and even psychological affinity with on-the-street investigators and prosecutors, which is equally true in both state and federal systems. Everyone in these groups is a player in a team effort to build cases and secure convictions, even though technical people are distant from investigators and attorneys in physical circumstances and job description. This broad reading reaches other investigative or analytical personnel who help the prosecution.[11]

Not business records or catchall exception

If forensic lab reports are inadmissible under the public records exception, does it follow that they are inadmissible under other exceptions? *Oates* addressed this question as well, ruling that other exceptions are not available in such cases, mentioning the catchall and business records exceptions: The "only way" to achieve the "intended effect" of the use restrictions is to block resort to the business records exception "or any of the other exceptions." In short, the use restrictions in clauses B and C really *are* different from language of limitation in other exceptions: They are exclusionary rules, and have more effect than simply setting the parameters of the public records exception. For laboratories operating as public agencies aiding law enforcement, *Oates* seems right to block access to the catchall and business records exception.

---

10. United States v. Oates, 560 F.2d 45, 77 (2d Cir. 1977) (quoting congressional comments) (scholarly opinion by Judge Waterman).

11. *See* United States v. Rosa, 11 F.3d 315, 333 (2d Cir. 1993) (medical examiner); United States v. Oates, 560 F.2d 45, 68 (2d Cir. 1977) (chemist); United States v. Ruffin, 575 F.2d 346, 356 (2d Cir. 1978) (IRS personnel).

Moreover, the answer should stay the same if police or prosecutors hire private laboratories to do tests and make reports because hiring makes them a public agency for this purpose, and enlists them in the prosecutorial effort.

Oates is mostly right in these conclusions. If the business records exception could be used, many laboratory reports would be admitted and the exclusionary purpose of the use restrictions would fail. Typically such reports are contemporaneous with the matters recorded, and they rest largely on firsthand knowledge acquired and transmitted from police to laboratory technicians. At least insofar as they describe physical data, they are routinely made by people acting in ordinary course every step of the way. The business records exception has a trustworthiness clause that might lead to exclusion (material prepared for litigation is often excluded),[12] but the use restriction in clause B is a harder-edged rule. The weight of authority favors the view that the business records exception cannot apply,[13] but some cases reject this view, at least where the preparer actually testifies and can be questioned.[14] *Oates* is also right in rejecting resort to the catchall. Where the officer is available, the congressional purpose to require his testimony points to this conclusion, and the same applies if the officer is unavailable, since Congress considered and rejected an attempt to modify the use restrictions by enacting an exception dedicated to this situation.[15]

Bar resort to *all* other exceptions?

It seems unwise to conclude that *no* other exception can apply to laboratory reports, however, and for that matter to records by police and law enforcement personnel, when offered against the accused. For one thing, we have other narrow exceptions that apply to certain kinds of public records sometimes generated by police or law enforcement personnel, and resort to these should not be affected by the use restrictions.[16] Most particularly, it seems proper to admit, even against criminal defendants, certificates indicating the absence of public record or entry under FRE 803(10). One reason is that Congress probably did not mean to foreclose resort to these narrow exceptions. Another is that materials fitting these exceptions are not nearly so troublesome as police or law enforcement reports because they go to

Can use narrow exceptions

---

12. *See* §8.47, *supra*.

13. *See* United States v. Orellana-Blanco, 294 F.3d 1143, 1149 (9th Cir. 2002); United States v. Blackburn, 992 F.2d 666, 670-672 (7th Cir. 1993); United States v. Nixon, 779 F.2d 126, 134 (2d Cir. 1985); United States v. Cain, 615 F.2d 380, 381-382 (5th Cir. 1980); United States v. Orozco, 590 F.2d 789, 793 (9th Cir. 1979), *cert. denied*, 442 U.S. 920.

14. *See* United States v. Davis, 181 F.3d 147, 149-150 (D.C. Cir. 1999), *cert. denied*, 528 U.S. 1140. United States v. Hayes, 861 F.2d 1225, 1229-1230 (10th Cir. 1988).

15. *See* 5 Mueller & Kirkpatrick, Federal Evidence §8:108 (3d ed. 2007).

16. *See* FRE 803(9) (vital statistics), FRE 803(12) (marriage and other ceremonies), and FRE 803(14) (property records). Court judgments that fit FRE 803(22) or 803(23) should also be admissible against the accused, although the former has a narrow use restriction of its own.

narrow and concrete points and are mostly the product of firsthand observation (not interpretations of eyewitness accounts).[17]

More importantly, the use restrictions in clauses B and C should not bar resort to the exception for past recorded recollection. In the case of crime reports and laboratory tests, live testimony by investigators or technicians is preferable. In effect, the use restrictions require prosecutors to bring them to court to testify to what they know, but investigators and technicians are unlikely to retain in memory every scrap of critical information from their reports. Indeed, technicians running tests are unlikely to recall critical details of any of their tests after a short period of time, and investigators can hardly be expected to retain serial or license numbers, makes of cars, detailed descriptions of objects at crime scenes, or precise details about physical layout. If the preparer testifies to lack of recollection on such points and the report otherwise qualifies as past recorded recollection, admitting it seems wise: The purpose of the use restrictions is satisfied in large measure because an investigator or technician submits to cross, and the report is admissible only insofar as recollection fails. Even with failed recollection, cross can test sources, expose motivational factors, and bring out weaknesses in method.[18]

Perhaps the best solution to the problem of proving results of forensic laboratory testing is the one that many states have adopted by statute. There is considerable variation, but basically there are two kinds. The beginning point is to recognize that the results of forensic laboratory testing should be presented by the testimony of the technician who conducted the tests: Such tests come with risks of error that are not apparent on the face of a report,[19] and producing the technician gives the defense its best (perhaps only) chance to explore methods, execution, and other pitfalls and limitations.[20]

Still, forensic laboratory reports should not be subject to an inflexible exclusionary rule: As noted above, the technician who does the test is likely to have forgotten the details and even the results in any given case. Lack of memory does not make the expert useless, since he can

17. United States v. Metzger, 778 F.2d 1195, 1200-1202 (6th Cir. 1985) (certificates describing searches of BATF records), *cert. denied*, 477 U.S. 906; United States v. Yakobov, 712 F.2d 20, 25 n.5 (2d Cir. 1983) (similar).

18. United States v. Picciandra, 788 F.2d 39, 44 (1st Cir. 1986) (admitting as past recollection DEA undercover agent's report describing drug transaction), *cert. denied*, 479 U.S. 847; United States v. Sawyer, 607 F.2d 1190, 1192-1193 (7th Cir. 1979) (admitting as past recollection officer's report describing phone conversation with defendant); *cert. denied*, 445 U.S. 943.

19. *See generally* Imwinkelried, The Debate in the DNA Cases Over the Foundation for the Admission of Scientific Evidence: The Importance of Human Error as a Cause of Forensic Misanalysis, 69 Wash. U. L.Q. 19 (1991) (surveying empirical studies); Giannelli, The Admissibility of Laboratory Reports in Criminal Trials: The Reliability of Scientific Proof, 49 Ohio St. L.J. 671 (1988) (concluding that most lab reports are trustworthy).

20. United States v. Oates, 560 F.2d 45, 64-65, 81-82 (2d Cir. 1977) (might try to find out whether tests were done right, whether procedures and analyses are reliable, whether equipment was in good order).

still reply to questions about his qualifications, about methods and parameters, even if he cannot say what happened during any given test.

Finally, it is worth noting that some lab tests are routine in the sense of being not only commonplace, but simple and reliable. At least sometimes technicians are so distant, and the questions they must answer are so bland, that it is inconceivable that their work is tainted by the pressures of partisan loyalty. At least sometimes, requiring live testimony may serve little purpose and be more costly than it is worth. One might burden the prosecutor with showing such facts. It might also be possible to require testimony by the technician in any case in which the defense shows a high level of risk, or shows that the test reached a conclusion on which experts may disagree.[21]

As noted, statutes in many states have taken steps in this direction, with variation in detail. Essentially they take one of two approaches. One kind allows the use of reports, but requires the prosecutor to call the technician if the defense requests, then presenting results by live testimony.[22] The other kind allows the use of reports but permits the defense to call the technician.[23]

Because there is a difference between calling the witness and cross-examining one called by the other side, and because the burden of proof rests on prosecutors, we think the former approach is preferable to the latter.[24] In either case, the result should be that the substance of the tests is presented by testimony, and the technician can then be cross-examined, except that in cases in which the defense makes no request or does not call the technician, the results are presented by means of the report. The constitutional question whether proving official laboratory reports against defendant in criminal cases violates the *Crawford* doctrine reached the Supreme Court in 2008.[25]

State should call

Not surprisingly, modern cases conflict on the admissibility of lab reports. In the federal system, authorities conflict in a variety of settings.[26]

Cases conflict

21. *See* Imwinkelried, The Constitutionality of Introducing Evaluative Laboratory Reports Against Criminal Defendants, 30 Hastings L.J. 621, 647 (1979) (court should exclude lab report offered as evidence of essential element on showing that conclusion could be subject to varying opinion).

22. *See* Colo. Rev. Stat §16-3-309(5) (crime lab reports "shall be" admitted, but any party may request preparer to "testify in person" by ten-day notice).

23. *See* Va. Code §19.2-187.1 (certificate of analysis is admissible, reflecting results of analysis in any laboratory; defense can call preparer and cross-examine).

24. *See* Wigglesworth v. Oregon, 49 F.3d 578 (9th Cir. 1995) (state must subpoena technician; leaving the matter to defendant puts him in a "Catch-22 situation," in which choice is to call technician, and "possibly bolster" state's case, or forego cross and lose chance to expose weakness in report).

25. *See* Commonwealth v. Melendez-Diaz, 2007 WL 2189152 (opinion) (Mass. App. 2007) ("drug analysis certificates" indicating that substance seized from defendant was cocaine), *cert. granted*, 128 S. Ct. 1647 (2008) (to decide whether state forensic analyst's lab report is "testimonial" under *Crawford*).

26. On the side of exclusion, *see* United States v. Oates, 560 F.2d 45, 64-65, 81-82 (2d Cir. 1977) (public lab report on cocaine); Stewart v. Cowan, 528 F.2d 79, 85 (6th Cir. 1976) (FBI ballistics report). On the side of admitting reports, *see* United States v. Feliz, 467 F.3d 227 (2d Cir. 2006) (medical examiner's autopsy reports); United States v. Ellis, 460 F.3d 920 (7th Cir. 2006) (hospital lab test showing drug use).

State decisions too are in sharp conflict over a range of different kinds of reports.[27]

Three issues merit further comment.

Other officials   First, the *Oates* approach to the phrase "police officers and other law enforcement personnel" is mostly correct. The term should be broadly construed to reach much further than the badge-wearing armed officer who makes arrests and investigates crime. Nevertheless, many public officials have law enforcement responsibility, but yet remain far removed from police or FBI or similar criminal law enforcement agencies, and from prosecutors. Consider federal and state park rangers, agents who work in motor vehicle licensing departments, fire marshals and building inspectors. Even if such public officials enforce laws in the sense of applying legal standards and making administrative decisions or seeking compliance with regulatory schemes by fines or citations (not indictment and prosecution), such persons are not embraced by the use restriction. The purpose was to exclude reports by public officials who make arrests, investigate crimes, and prepare evidence in aid of prosecution, and the image of the police investigator does underlie the restriction.[28]

Can defendants offer?   Second, the use restriction appears to block *both* the defense *and* the prosecutor from invoking clause B, so *neither* can introduce reports by police or law enforcement personnel. Legislative history indicates, however, that the only concern was to protect defense rights, so arguably defendants should be allowed to offer such material. Cases conflict on this point.[29]

Routine, nonadversarial   Third, the concern behind clause B's use restriction was to bar reports made during a criminal investigation aimed at building a case. But even people who routinely make arrests or investigate crimes also prepare reports in quite different settings. They report abandoned vehicles, note and file identifying information taken from markings on weapons retrieved from crime scenes, report accidents and measure and report the physical layouts of accident scenes. Often these activities are not focused on particular people or schemes or acts. Often they are nonadversarial in the sense that the aim is not to prepare for a specific prosecution. Often they are routine in the sense of being everyday entries reflecting simple factual observations. Excluding such material has seemed unnecessary and overprotective. Hence courts recognize a

---

27. On the side of exclusion, *see* State v. Sandoval-Tena, 71 P.3d 1055 (Idaho 2003) (crime lab report on methamphetamine); State v. Williams, 644 N.W.2d 919, 928-930 (Wis. 2002) (state crime lab report identifying substance as cocaine). On the side of admitting reports, *see* Rollins v. State, 897 A.2d 821, 839 (Md. 2006) (in murder case, admitting state medical examiner's autopsy report).

28. *See* United States v. Riddle, 103 F.3d 423, 430-432 (5th Cir. 1997) (bank examiners are not "police officers" or "other law enforcement personnel").

29. *Compare* United States v. De Peri, 778 F.2d 963, 976-977 (3d Cir. 1985) (defense can offer report under clause B), *cert. denied*, 476 U.S. 1159, *with* United States v. Insaulgarat, 378 F.3d 456, 466-467 (5th Cir. 2004) (defense could not offer report under clause B), *cert. denied*, 543 U.S. 1013.

judge-made exception to the use restriction in clause B, allowing routine and nonadversarial reports to be admitted against the accused even when prepared by police or law enforcement people.[30]

§8.52   —Trustworthiness Factor

Like the business records exception, the one for public records contains a clause authorizing courts to exclude records that are untrustworthy. Although the wording could be read to mean trustworthiness is a separate consideration only for investigative reports offered under clause C, this narrow reading is not compelled and seems unwise. The exception does not set out criteria designed to ensure trustworthiness (instead stating limits and use restrictions), so courts should have authority to exclude untrustworthy records offered under any part of the exception.

   If the proponent satisfies the specific foundation requirements by showing that the material fits any of the three clauses, the burden is on the objecting party to show it is untrustworthy. The wording supports this view (trustworthiness is framed as a qualification at the end), and the result makes sense despite the absence of positive criteria assuring trustworthiness since records that fit the exception are at least likely to be accurate. Where they report the results of scientific investigation, it has been said that the methods and investigation are presumed trustworthy, which makes sense for investigations by a disinterested agency pursuing a subject within the scope of its established expertise.[1]

   Since satisfying the specific requirements brings the exception into play, the proponent need not separately show trustworthiness. Still, positive indications of trustworthiness count as reasons to admit public records. Decisions emphasizing these indications say in effect that the exception is more than satisfied, and they suggest analytic frameworks that can help identify records that are not trustworthy: Serious shortcomings in areas where reported decisions have found reasons to trust other records should count in favor of finding records untrustworthy.

Factors indicating trustworthiness

---

30. United States v. Lopez-Moreno, 420 F.3d 420, 437 (5th Cir. 2005) (A-Files indicating status of deported aliens; preparer made objective evaluations in everyday function, not motivated to do anything else), *cert. denied*, 546 U.S. 1222; United States v. Weiland, 420 F.3d 1062, 1074 (9th Cir. 2005) (penitentiary packet including photograph and fingerprints as nonadversarial document), *cert. denied*, 547 U.S. 1114; United States v. Box, 50 F.3d 345, 356-357 (5th Cir. 1995) (jail cards and logs, arrest reports, bail books), *cert. denied*, 506 U.S. 918; United States v. Smith, 973 F.2d 603, 605 (8th Cir. 1992) (printouts reflecting "matters reported to police" rather than adversarial observations by officers); United States v. Dancy, 861 F.2d 77, 79-80 (5th Cir. 1988) (fingerprint card); United States v. De Water, 846 F.2d 528, 530 (9th Cir. 1988) (intoxilizer test); United States v. Orozco, 590 F.2d 789, 793-794 (9th Cir. 1979) (TECS data cards indicating that defendant's car crossed into Mexico when defendant told officer he was on double date in Los Angeles), *cert. denied*, 442 U.S. 920.

   §8.52   1. Amtrust Inc. v. Larson, 388 F.3d 594, 599 (8th Cir. 2004); Bridgeway Corp. v. Citibank, 201 F.3d 134, 143-144 (2d Cir. 2000).

Many factors support a finding of trustworthiness. Foremost among them are skill or expertise and motivational factors. Skill or expertise seem critical with evaluative material (clause C). And records that reflect matters observed under clause B can include such things as weather or climatic data and market data, where skill or expertise can matter too. Even descriptions of agency action that fit clause A can benefit from skill or expertise, since they may involve such technical matters as accounting.[2]

Motivational factors often count positively. Government agencies sometimes come close to the democratic ideal of being neutral and objective on matters they report, particularly when they have no expectation of eventual litigation. A neutral and objective stance may appear in the setting of routine entries describing transactional details or simple observations. Sometimes similar neutral objectivity appears in evaluative findings setting forth the results of investigations into general issues of serious public interest, and sometimes it can be found in reports on particular accidents or disasters or events.[3] Concerns over motivation diminish where the record or entry became the basis for important and more general agency action indicating its reliance on accuracy.[4]

Sometimes records are trustworthy because the agency held hearings that provided interested parties a chance to present evidence and argument,[5] but failing to hold hearings does not show a record is untrustworthy.[6] Indications of care and sound methodology also suggest that records are trustworthy.[7] Timeliness counts too. Records prepared close to the time of events or conditions they describe are more likely to be trustworthy than records prepared long afterwards.

Other factors count as well in assessing trustworthiness (the four listed in the ACN are not exclusive). It seems worthwhile to consider checking procedures that might catch mistakes and to consider the simplicity of the matter reported and (correlatively) the margin of error within which mistakes would not affect evidential use. Concerns over trustworthiness diminish if the person who prepared the report testifies. Evaluative

---

2. In re Air Disaster at Lockerbie Scotland, 37 F.3d 804, 828 (2d Cir. 1994) (Scottish detective's report that bag came unaccompanied from Frankfurt flight; he was "experienced and skilled"); Bank of Lexington v. Vining-Sparks Secs., 959 F.2d 606, 616-617 (6th Cir. 1992) (citing skill or expertise in NASD letter of caution).

3. Kehm v. Procter & Gamble Mfg. Co., 724 F.2d 613, 618-620 (8th Cir. 1983) (only motive is to "inform the public fairly and accurately").

4. United States v. Hardin, 710 F.2d 1231, 1237 (7th Cir. 1983) (statistical report on price and purity of cocaine; statistics important in performance of duties), *cert. denied*, 464 U.S. 918.

5. Hines v. Brandon Steel Decks, Inc., 886 F.2d 299, 303 (11th Cir. 1989), *cert. denied*, 503 U.S. 971; Perrin v. Anderson, 784 F.2d 1040, 1046-1047 (10th Cir. 1986).

6. Bank of Lexington v. Vining-Sparks Secs., 959 F.2d 606, 616-617 (6th Cir. 1992) (NASD letter of caution); Baker v. Elcona Homes Corp., 588 F.2d 551, 558 (6th Cir. 1978) (accident report), *cert. denied*, 441 U.S. 933.

7. Robbins v. Whelan, 653 F.2d 47, 50-51 (1st Cir. 1981) (agency specifies procedures and conditions, follows strict standard), *cert. denied*, 454 U.S. 1123.

studies attain a measure of trustworthiness if they are subjected to peer review.

The fact that a court disagrees with investigative conclusions does not make a report untrustworthy: What counts is method and care in preparation.[8] Some decisions imply that the trustworthiness clause gives courts authority to assess the credibility of outsiders whose statements form the basis of investigative findings.[9] The better rule is that the credibility of outsiders should be judged in the first instance by those who conduct the investigation and in the second by the factfinder as part of its assessment of the report, rather than by trial judges in deciding whether to admit or exclude.[10]

Where public records are shown to be untrustworthy, they should be excluded even if they satisfy the specific requirements. To carry its burden of showing a record is untrustworthy, the objecting party need not demonstrate that it is wrong or inaccurate. What must be shown is a particular and serious risk that the record is inaccurate. Methodological shortcomings, including serious failures to investigate leads, talk to witnesses, or consider evidence, can show a report is untrustworthy.[11] Failing to show investigative findings were carefully prepared can itself raise sufficient concerns over trustworthiness to justify exclusion, and lack of needed expertise or skill on the part of preparers or agency justifies exclusion if the subject is one on which laypeople might go badly astray.[12] Partiality on the part of an agency or those who prepare a report in favor of one or another side of an issue or toward one or another party suggests untrustworthiness.[13]

Factors indicating untrustworthiness

A public record is excludable as untrustworthy if its conclusions lack reasonable basis, which happens if outsider statements that are indispensable to the conclusion do not suffice to support it or could not be credited by reasonable people.[14] A report may also be untrustworthy if it rests on outsider statements and the person or agency who

---

8. Moss v. Ole South Real Estate, Inc., 933 F.2d 1300, 1306-1308 (5th Cir. 1991) (focus should be preparation and methodology; not credibility but reliability).

9. *See* Miller v. Caterpillar Tractor Co., 697 F.2d 141, 144 (6th Cir. 1983) (criticizing accident report by mining engineer; it rested on "suspect" outsider statements; criticizing police report relying on hearsay).

10. *See* Moss v. Ole South Real Estate, Inc., 933 F.2d 1300, 1306-1308 (5th Cir. 1991); Re Korean Air Lines Disaster, 932 F.2d 1475, 1482-1483 (D.C. Cir. 1991), *cert. denied*, 502 U.S. 994.

11. Moss v. Ole South Real Estate, Inc., 933 F.2d 1300, 1310 (5th Cir. 1991) (excluding HUD report partly because investigator "did not interview a key player"); Jenkins v. Whittaker Corp., 785 F.2d 720, 726 n.15 (9th Cir. 1986) (excluding army reports describing accident with atomic simulators; author arrived more than a week later and "never talked to any of the personnel involved"), *cert. denied*, 479 U.S. 918.

12. Jenkins v. Whittaker Corp., 785 F.2d 720, 726 n.15 (9th Cir. 1986) (author had no competence with atomic simulators), *cert. denied*, 479 U.S. 918; Meder v. Everest & Jennings, Inc., 637 F.2d 1182, 1185-1188 (8th Cir. 1981) (report on wheelchair accident; no showing how information was gathered).

13. Hines v. Brandon Steel Decks, Inc., 886 F.2d 299, 303 (11th Cir. 1989) (citing "investigator's partiality"), *cert. denied*, 503 U.S. 971.

14. *See* Moss v. Ole South Real Estate, Inc., 933 F.2d 1300, 1307 n.5 (5th Cir. 1991) (may exclude report lacking "reasonable basis").

prepared the report lacks experience or expertise in the area of inquiry or the process of factfinding, thus cannot be expected to make sound judgments on the merits or on credibility issues.[15] Hearings are not always required or even useful for public agencies, but failing to hold them or provide adequate safeguards undermines trustworthiness in settings where the question is whether someone has done something wrong and it can be expected that the matter is contested. Untimeliness is itself a serious indication of untrustworthiness if the conclusions depend on testimony or statements by witnesses that are gathered long after the fact.

Partiality and improper motive seem especially large risks when reports or entries are prepared for purpose of litigation and when reports amount to internal investigations in which the agency or those in charge are motivated to favor a particular conclusion.[16] Investigative reports also seem untrustworthy if they are tentative or nonfinal, or if they merely reflect preliminary data or tentative conclusions that are intended for further review and study.[17]

FRE 803(9)

> **(9) Records of vital statistics.** Records or data compilations, in any form, of births, fetal deaths, deaths, or marriages, if the report thereof was made to a public office pursuant to requirements of law.

---

§8.53 Vital Statistics

The exception set forth in FRE 803(9) covers records of vital statistics relating to marriages, births, deaths, and fetal deaths when these are compiled from reports made to a public office as required by law. This exception builds on statutes that require doctors and members of the clergy (and others) to report such matters and provide for the preservation of such information. The language contemplates records based on reports, but the exception reaches both the original reports and transcriptions or compilations made from them.

---

15. *See* Miller v. Caterpillar Tractor Co., 697 F.2d 141, 144 (6th Cir. 1983) (excluding report by engineer who lacked knowledge and was not qualified to give opinion on mechanical failures).

16. United States v. Spano, 421 F.3d 599, 604 (7th Cir. 2005) (excluding minutes of town board meeting indicating that no payments were made; inference of doctoring; trustworthiness clause "tailor-made" for case where defendants control records, not disinterested clerks), *cert. denied*, 546 U.S. 1122.

17. O'Dell v. Hercules, Inc., 904 F.2d 1194, 1204-1206 (8th Cir. 1990) (excluding health assessment recommending further sampling); City of New York v. Pullman, Inc., 662 F.2d 910, 914-915 (2d Cir. 1981) (excluding interim recommendation subject to revision and review), *cert. denied*, 454 U.S. 1164.

There are many reasons to trust such material: Usually the information is gathered by people in the course of public and professional duty and later recorded and preserved by public employees in ordinary course. Usually the information reflects contemporary events and simple facts on which there is little room for dispute: Births, marriages, and deaths mark occasions important to the people who likely supply the information. Ordinarily everyone involved tries to be truthful and accurate; often (although not always) vital statistics are prepared before any thought of litigation, so the forces of dispute usually have no distorting effect. **Reasons to trust**

Birth certificates fit the exception when offered to prove date, time, and place of birth, identity and age of parents, and other facts that are routinely recorded, such as weight and sex of the infant, identity of attending physician, and facts relating to manner of delivery and health of the infant and routine tests or treatments administered at birth if these are customarily recorded.[1] Marriage certificates also fit the exception when offered to prove the fact, date, and place of marriage and other pertinent facts routinely recorded (names of minister or judge and attending witnesses).[2] And of course death certificates also fit when offered to prove the fact, date, time, and place of death.[3] **Birth, marriage, death certificates**

Death certificates are often admissible to prove cause of death, but some care is necessary. It seems reasonable to accept a certificate by a lay coroner listing car accident, gunshot wound, or exposure as cause of death in appropriate settings. Probably, however, lay opinion on such points should not be acceptable where serious medical issues arise or where the question is whether the decedent suffered a fatal heart attack before an accident. When expertise is required to prove medical cause of death, a certificate fits the exception only if prepared by or with aid of an examining physician or the doctor who attended the decedent,[4] not if prepared by a lay coroner.[5] **Proving cause of death**

Sometimes death certificates not only state medical or physical cause but describe the manner of death by stating facts bearing on human fault or criminality—decedent fell in a ditch, for example, or was shot **Proving manner of death**

---

§8.53   1. United States v. Austrew, 202 F. Supp. 816, 822 (D. Md. 1962) (birth certificate to prove birth date of female victim, indicating she was under 18), *aff'd per curiam*, 317 F.2d 926 (4th Cir. 1963).

2. Williams v. Butterfield, 145 F. Supp. 567, 568 (E.D. Mich. 1956) (marriage certificate shows parents married in Britain in 1904), *aff'd*, 250 F.2d 127 (6th Cir. 1957), *cert. denied*, 356 U.S. 946.

3. Aetna Life Ins. Co. v. Mitchell, 180 F. Supp. 674, 678 (M.D. Pa. 1960) (coroner's report saying husband shot wife at 6:50 P.M. and shot himself minutes later, to show who died first).

4. Minyen v. American Home Assurance Co., 443 F.2d 788, 791 (10th Cir. 1971) (death certificate prepared by doctor as proof that decedent died from brain tumor, offered by insurer to disprove accident).

5. Holbrook v. Lykes Bros. S.S. Co., Inc., 80 F.3d 777, 786 (3d Cir. 1996) (excluding part of death certificate, autopsy report and hospital records naming mesothelioma as cause of death); Schulz v. Celotex Corp., 942 F.2d 204, 208 (3d Cir. 1991) (redacting from death certificate notation that asbestosis caused death; cross-examination of physician would be necessary).

by her spouse, or died by accident, suicide, or homicide. Such conclusions are investigative findings that medical training and experience in office may not qualify a coroner or physician to reach, and concerns over trustworthiness increase if the official function is modest in scope and funding and the reporting requirement is essentially uncompensated. Here the exceptions for vital records and public records overlap, and the safeguards in the public records exception should apply, which means they should ordinarily be inadmissible against criminal defendants and that trustworthiness counts heavily in the calculus.[6] Otherwise vital records of this sort should usually be admitted if they seem trustworthy.[7]

The central facts reflected in vital records are usually within the personal knowledge of the public official or the person who reports them directly,[8] but the exception does not require firsthand knowledge of everything reflected in such records and reaches at least some routine facts gleaned from others in the course of preparing the records.[9] Insisting too stringently on direct personal knowledge by the official or reporter would undermine the usefulness of vital records.[10] Doctors reporting on matters of birth and death and celebrants who marry people should be able to rely on statements by those present on such matters as the identity, age, and address of the principals. In many settings, attending physicians or midwives or other medical personnel who deliver a child should be able to rely on statements by the mother identifying the father, but arguably not in the setting of paternity suits where motivation may be problematic at the time of birth. When statements in vital records require expertise, questions on admissibility should be resolved with guidance by the principles that apply to expert testimony.

FRE 803(10)

(10) **Absence of public record or entry.** To prove the absence of a record, report, statement, or data compilation, in any form, or the nonoccurrence or nonexistence of a matter of which a record, report, statement, or data compilation, in any form, was regularly made and preserved by a public office or

---

6. *See* State v. Gould, 704 P.2d 20, 29-30 (Mont. 1985); Bowman v. Redding & Co., 449 F.2d 956, 961 (D.C. Cir. 1971); FRE 803(8)(C), discussed in §8.50, *supra.*

7. *See* Pope v. Travelers Ins. Co., 477 F.2d 557 (5th Cir. 1973) (coroner's certificate; suicide).

8. *See* Charleston Natl. Bank v. Hennessy, 404 F.2d 539, 541 (5th Cir. 1968) (some certificates reflect personal knowledge; court cites notary's acknowledgment, death certificate by treating physician, and certificate of marriage by celebrant).

9. Shell v. Parrish, 448 F.2d 528, 530-531 (6th Cir. 1971) (error to exclude from doctor's death certificate statement that boy fell in ditch; if it came from investigating officers, that affected weight).

10. *See* Charleston Natl. Bank v. Hennessy, 404 F.2d 539, 541 (5th Cir. 1968) (strict requirement of personal knowledge would destroy advantages of vital records); 5 Wigmore, Evidence §1646 (Chadbourn rev. 1974) (similar).

agency, evidence in the form of a certification in accordance with Rule 902, or testimony, that diligent search failed to disclose the record, report, statement, or data compilation, or entry.

§8.54 Absence of Entries in Public Records

An exception allows proof of the absence of public records or entries, as a means of showing that conditions, events, or acts that would normally be reflected there, if they had existed or occurred, did not exist or occur. The exception allows the proponent to offer a certificate by the recordkeeper indicating that a diligent search failed to turn up a record or entry, and clearly live testimony to this effect is also acceptable.[1]

Can prove by certificate, testimony

The probative value of such "negative evidence" turns on factors similar to the ones underlying the exceptions for public records and vital statistics. The public duty that comes with preparing and keeping such records, and the scrutiny and exposure to which government functions are subject offer some assurance of completeness and reliability. This assurance in turn supports an inference that if a matter that would ordinarily be recorded or entered was not, it did not happen or exist; also an inference that if a private submission to the government (a return, report, application, or similar document) would ordinarily be kept or generate an entry of some sort but nothing of this sort can be found, then there was no such submission. The certificate mechanism is justified in similar ways: Again the idea of public duty suggests that the person will make a diligent search and a correct certification, and he can be trusted in this task because he knows the nature of the records and manner of recordkeeping. A notion of necessity supports the certificate mechanism—it is inconvenient to call government officers to testify and unlikely that live testimony would add much to the certificate.

One use of FRE 803(10) is to prove simply that documents were not filed or entries were not made. Thus the exception paves the way to show a tax return[2] or firearms registration[3] or other document was not filed.[4] In a common modern application, the exception paves the way to prove that a defendant charged with re-entering the country without

Proving documents not filed, entries not made

§8.54   1. *See* FRE 803(10) and 902(4); FRCP 44(b); FRCrimP 27 (both authorizing certificate procedure); United States v. Ventura-Melendez, 275 F.3d 9, 14 (1st Cir. 2001) (admitting certificate to show no record authorized defendant to be on island used for military testing).

2. United States v. Spine, 945 F.2d 143, 148-149 (6th Cir. 1991); United States v. Neff, 615 F.2d 1235, 1241-1242 (9th Cir. 1980), *cert. denied*, 447 U.S. 925.

3. United States v. Hale, 978 F.2d 1016, 1020-1021 (8th Cir. 1992), *cert. denied*, 507 U.S. 997; United States v. Rigsby, 943 F.2d 631, 638-639 (6th Cir. 1991), *cert. denied*, 503 U.S. 908.

4. United States v. Herrera-Britto, 739 F.2d 551, 552 (11th Cir. 1984) (registration of vessel); Hunt v. Liberty Lobby, 720 F.2d 631, 651 (11th Cir. 1983) (no CIA memoranda indicating that Hunt was in Dallas when Kennedy was shot).

permission did not in fact have permission, and using a certificate to prove the absence of an order allowing re-entry passes muster under the *Crawford* doctrine.[5] The other use of FRE 803(10) is to prove, from the absence of record or entry, that an event did not happen or condition did not exist if there would ordinarily be an entry or record reflecting such matters. Thus proof of the absence of entry or record can be offered to show that a person was not employed or associated with a particular agency,[6] or that title to property was not conveyed or encumbered in a way that records would normally reflect,[7] or that other events did not occur or other conditions did not exist that would normally be reflected on such records.[8]

The exception is available only if the record or entry in question would normally be made, for otherwise its absence has little or no relevance.[9] The proponent must show a diligent search was made. Where the person whose statement or testimony is offered cannot satisfy even this minimal standard, his testimony or certificate should be excluded.[10] It is hard to imagine an excuse for not using the word "diligent" in any certificate or testimony proffered under FRE 803(10). Still, there is no magic in the term, and failure to use it should not be fatal if the proponent shows a diligent search was made. Conversely, use of the term should not be conclusive if in fact the search was sloppy or half-hearted.

FRE 803(11)

(11) **Records of religious organizations.** Statements of births, marriages, divorces, deaths, legitimacy, ancestry, relationship by blood or marriage, or other similar facts of personal or family history, contained in a regularly kept record of a religious organization.

---

5. United States v. Mendez, 514 F.3d 1035, 1043 (10th Cir. 2008) (testimony describing search of ICE database); United States v. Valdez-Maltos, 443 F.3d 910 (5th Cir. 2006) (certificate). The reference is to Crawford v. Washington, 541 U.S. 36, 57 (2004), discussed in §§8.83-8.92, *infra*.

6. United States v. Wilson, 732 F.2d 404, 413-414 (5th Cir. 1984) (defendant not employed by CIA), *cert. denied*, 469 U.S. 1099.

7. United States v. Jewett, 438 F.2d 495, 497-498 (8th Cir. 1971) (no record of transfer, so Indian title was never extinguished), *cert. denied*, 402 U.S. 947.

8. United States v. Ventura-Melendez, 275 F.3d 9, 14 (1st Cir. 2001) (defendant not authorized to be on island used for military testing); United States v. Rich, 580 F.2d 929, 937-938 (9th Cir. 1978) (no trace of Dale Olson).

9. United States v. McDonald, 905 F.2d 871, 875 (5th Cir. 1990) (exception supposes report would regularly be made), *cert. denied*, 498 U.S. 1002.

10. United States v. Yakobov, 712 F.2d 20, 23-24 (2d Cir. 1983) (certificate misspelled name of person being sought; diligence not shown).

§8.55   Religious Records

The exception for regularly kept records of a religious organization is found in FRE 803(11), and it permits use of such material to prove matters like the fact and date of marriage or baptism, confirmation, or death.[1] Such records may also be admitted to prove facts provided to church officials by outsiders who are in a position to know and likely to speak truthfully.[2] The exception clearly does not reach church records offered to prove, for instance, the amount of contributions made by parishioners when offered in tax disputes (these are not what the term "facts of personal or family history" means), and some authorities display obvious distrust of the exception.[3]

FRE 803(12)-(13)

   (12) Marriage, baptismal, and similar certificates. Statements of fact contained in a certificate that the maker performed a marriage or other ceremony or administered a sacrament, made by a clergyman, public official, or other person authorized by the rules or practices of a religious organization or by law to perform the act certified, and purporting to have been issued at the time of the act or within a reasonable time thereafter.

   (13) Family records. Statements of fact concerning personal or family history contained in family Bibles, genealogies, charts, engravings on rings, inscriptions on family portraits, engravings on urns, crypts, or tombstones, or the like.

---

§8.56   Certificates, Family Records, and Statements

FRE 803(12) covers certificates of marriage, baptism, or other ceremony or sacrament, made by the authorized religious or public official who performed the ceremony or sacrament and issued at the time of the event or shortly thereafter.[1] The notion is that such certificates are

Family certificates

---

§8.55   1. Lewis v. Marshall, 30 U.S. 470, 476 (1831) (burial register extract, proving time of death).

   2. Dailey v. Grand Lodge, B.R.T., 142 N.E. 478, 480 (Ill. 1924) (church record to show date of baptism, hence that subject was born earlier, but not to prove he was born on specific date); Ford v. State, 200 S.W. 841 (Tex. Crim. App. 1918) (register of birth and baptism of Oklahoma church indicating that complainant was born and baptized in late 1901).

   3. Ruberto v. Commissioner, 774 F.2d 61, 63 (2d Cir. 1985) (exception inapplicable to receipts from Universal Life Church offered by taxpayer to prove contributions); Hall v. Commissioner, 729 F.2d 632, 634-635 (9th Cir. 1984) (similar).

§8.56   1. This exception complements and extends ones for vital records discussed in §8.53, *supra*, and the one for religious records discussed in §8.55, *supra*. These cover records in public and religious institutions. FRE 803(12) covers certificates given to people for commemorative purposes.

likely to be trustworthy. They are made on a serious occasion of importance to the participants; they are made by responsible persons unlikely to have an interest or bias in the matter; the recorded information is likely to be simple and routine and to come from sources with firsthand or reliable knowledge on an occasion when truthfulness is expected. The exception reaches certificates of marriage and baptism, and there is reason to think it reaches certificates issued for church confirmation, naturalization, induction into the ministry, and into the bar of state or federal court.[2]

Family records   The family records exception in FRE 803(13) reaches factual statements on "personal or family history" contained in family Bibles, genealogies, charts, engravings on rings and tombstones, inscriptions on family portraits, and the like.[3] The idea is that permanent or enduring statements (written, inscribed, engraved) on objects likely to be heirlooms or symbols of sentimental importance in the life of a family, and relating to matters of personal or family history, are likely to be truthful and carefully made. Usually there is a kind of self-checking mechanism. A false statement in such places as genealogies or Bibles is not likely to go long uncorrected if the person described in or concerned with the statement has access to it. These circumstances excuse the absence of more thorough authentication and proof that the source had personal knowledge.

The exception covers statements on the same subjects as those covered by the exception for church records, meaning that FRE 803(13) embraces statements of "births, marriages, divorces, deaths, legitimacy, ancestry, relationship by blood or marriage, or other similar facts of personal or family history," and it reaches many other events of importance to family history.[4]

FRE 803(14)-(15)

  (14) Records of documents affecting an interest in property. The record of a document purporting to establish or affect an interest in property, as proof of the content of the original recorded document and its execution and delivery by each person by whom it purports to have been executed, if the record is a record of a public office and an applicable statute authorizes the recording of documents of that kind in that office.

---

2. Scott v. McGrath, 104 F. Supp. 267, 270-271 (E.D.N.Y. 1952) (baptismal certificate showing that plaintiff was son of Harry Winfield Scott, who was born in United States); Re St. Clair's Estate, 28 P.2d 894, 896 (Wyo. 1934) (marriage certificate).

3. Here is the infamous exception for engravings on urns and crypts—the one that proves the depths of obscurity and flavor of antiquity that come with the hearsay doctrine, and proves, too, the point that the exceptions go on forever, far into the realm of the trivial. But will your big case turn on this one someday?

4. *See* House Report, at 15 (1973) (family records exception should "include the specific types" of statements covered by FRE 803(11) on church records); Lewis v. Marshall, 30 U.S. 470, 476 (1831) (entry in family Bible proves date of death).

> **(15) Statements in documents affecting an interest in property.** A statement contained in a document purporting to establish or affect an interest in property if the matter stated was relevant to the purpose of the document, unless dealings with the property since the document was made have been inconsistent with the truth of the statement or the purport of the document.

§8.57   Property Records and Documents

Two exceptions cover documents relating to property. One covers dispositive documents like deeds and mortgages and the other covers essentially recorded documents of the same sort.

Statements in documents purporting to establish or affect interests in property fit FRE 803(15) where the matter stated was "relevant to the purpose of the document," unless later dealings with the property are inconsistent with the purport of the document or suggest the statement is wrong. The idea is that statements in dispositive documents are reliable because the matters asserted are important to serious and carefully planned transactions. The conduct of the parties to such a transaction in reliance on the truth of such statements supplies circumstantial indications of reliability. Indeed, the transaction itself (even the verbal part) is nonhearsay evidence of much that the words also assert.[1] In effect, the exception makes careful hearsay analysis unnecessary, since the statement may be treated as hearsay but introduced for its truth anyway.

Dispositive documents

The exception has three requirements: First, the instrument must purport to establish or affect an interest in property. The intent is to cover dispositive documents, and probably it reaches instruments dealing with personal as well as real property. Bills of sale, security agreements, deeds, mortgages, easements, wills, and many others qualify. This coverage insures a proprietary or financial stake, thus minimizing risks of misstatement, misperception, or flawed memory. Second, the statement must be relevant to the purpose of the document. As examples, the ACN suggests a recital in a deed "purporting to have been executed by an attorney in fact" asserting the power of attorney and a recital that the grantors are all the heirs of the last record owner. The proponent must still authenticate the document, but such recitals may be taken as evidence of what they assert.[2] Third, later dealings with the

---

§8.57   1. When X delivers to Y a deed to Greenacre, words in the deed assert and perform the conveyance. When purpose is to prove conveyance, words are called verbal acts. *See* §8.16, *supra*. When purpose is to prove points understood by participants (for instance, that grantor holds title), performative aspects of delivering a deed with those words also justify nonhearsay treatment. *See* §8.22, *supra*.

2. Silverstein v. Chase, 260 F.3d 142, 146 (2d Cir. 2001) (remanding to consider whether statement indicating assignment in cancellation of indebtedness fits

property cannot be inconsistent with the truth of the statement or purport of the document, a requirement that relates directly to the basis of the exception.

Recorded documents
The property records exception in FRE 803(14) covers public records of any document affecting interests in property (if recording is authorized by statute) for the purpose of proving content of the document and its execution and delivery by everyone indicated on its face as its maker. The exception reaches use of recorded documents to prove terms of the original as well as due execution and delivery. The main use of the exception is to prove the essential elements of transactions comprising a chain of title.[3] Technically this exception does contemplate hearsay use of recorded documents, for they can prove terms in original documents that are operative facts of various transactions (verbal acts, or words used in their performative sense). Technically too, the exception does not authorize use of recorded documents for extended purposes like proving facts recited in recorded documents. But FRE 803(15) allows use of the documents themselves for such purposes, and the two exceptions are made to be piggybacked. Thus FRE 803(14) invites use of the recorded document to prove the terms of the original, and FRE 803(15) allows use of original to prove facts it asserts.

A hearsay exception seems a strange way to approach the question whether proof of recording should be taken as evidence of proper "execution" and "delivery" of a document. Recording schemes commonly require deeds and similar documents to be acknowledged before a notary, but the clerk who accepts and records a document knows nothing about execution other than what he sees on the face of the document (including the legend and seal of the notary). It is possible to view recording as an "official statement" that the document was properly acknowledged, hence duly executed (and no doubt FRE 803(14) removes any hearsay objection), but usually recording as proof of execution is handled by presumption rather than hearsay exception. And recording can hardly be an official statement that a document was delivered. The records clerk knows nothing on this point—neither the notary's legend nor a recital in the document is likely to indicate delivery. Again recording often raises a presumption of delivery, since few persons go to the trouble of recording a document that was not delivered.

Apparently the basis of the exception is a formalistic notion: The drafters wanted to pave the way to prove a deed or similar instrument

---

exception); Connecticut Light & Power Co. v. FPC, 557 F.2d 349, 354-356 (2d Cir. 1977) (recorded 1716 deed granting right to pass river as proof it was navigable). Deed recitals of price are unreliable and the exception should not apply. *See* United States v. 478.34 Acres of Land, 578 F.2d 156, 159 (6th Cir. 1978) (excluding survey based on prices in deeds).

3. *See* United States v. Ruffin, 575 F.2d 346, 356-358 (2d Cir. 1978) (recorded mortgage); Amoco Production Co. v. United States, 455 F. Supp. 46, 49-50 (D. Utah 1977) (certified copy of recorded deed), *rev'd on other grounds*, 619 F.2d 1383 (10th Cir. 1980).

by a copy of the recorded document (a copy of the public record) accompanied by a certificate by the custodian. The custodian can certify the authenticity of an official record, but not a private document, so it is formally important to view the recorded instrument as a public document rather than a copy of a private document.[4] Extending the exception to cover "execution" and "delivery" seems to mean that proof of recording is admissible evidence of execution and delivery, leaving open the question whether such evidence is sufficient or raises a presumption. A Supreme Court decision held that, by virtue of the *Erie* doctrine and Texas law, a federal court hearing a Texas case must put the burden of proving equitable title on one "who attacks the legal title and asserts a superior equity."[5] Fairly read, that decision means state law determines whether recording raises a presumption and what its effect might be (at least where state law applies, as it usually does when land title is in issue). By statute or common law tradition in most states, proof of recording raises a presumption that title was affected as the face of the instrument indicates, so recording raises a presumption of execution and delivery.[6]

FRE 803(16)

(16) Statements in ancient documents. Statements in a document in existence twenty years or more the authenticity of which is established.

---

§8.58   Ancient Documents

The ancient documents exception in FRE 803(16) paves the way for statements in documents at least 20 years old where authenticity is established. A special provision in FRE 901 complements the exception by providing that authenticity is shown by evidence that a document has been in existence 20 years or longer, coupled with evidence that its

---

4. That makes the recorded document an official restatement of the original after all, hence hearsay when offered to prove the terms of the original, so an exception is needed. *See* FRE 902(1), (2), and (4), allowing copies of public records on the basis of certificates by the custodian of the original record, the copy and certificate together being self-authenticating. *See also* ACN to FRE 803(14) (use of record to prove execution and delivery raises problem of "lack of firsthand knowledge by the recorder," which is solved by allowing only recording of documents shown by acknowledgment or "form of probate" to have been executed and delivered; the Rules do not violate *Erie* by "endowing the record with an effect independently of local law," because local law does what the exception envisions).

5. Cities Serv. Oil Co. v. Dunlap, 308 U.S. 208, 210-212 (1939) (cited in ACN for exception).

6. *See* Webbe v. McGhie Land Title Co., 549 F.2d 1358, 1360 (10th Cir. 1977) (under Utah law, acknowledged and recorded deed is presumed valid).

condition raises no suspicion and it was found in a place where it would likely be if authentic.[1]

Need is the main justification: The lapse of 20 years since the acts, events, or conditions described almost guarantees a shortage of evidence. Witnesses will have died or disappeared. Written statements that might fit other exceptions (business records, past recollection) are typically thrown out or lost or destroyed. And passage of time lowers the marginal value of live testimony over hearsay: Eyewitness accounts of events 20 years in the past are likely to be less reliable than accounts of recent events, and testimonial descriptions of oral statements made long ago (admissions or excited utterances) are less reliable than descriptions of more recent ones.

Naturally statements in ancient documents are affected by risks of misperception, faulty memory, ambiguity, and lack of candor (they are not intrinsically more reliable than oral statements), and a written statement unreliable when made is unreliable forever. Ancient documents do, however, bring fewer risks of misreporting (because the statement is in writing), and they bring at least some assurance against negative influences: When authenticated, the document leaves little doubt the statement was made; there is little risk of errors in transmission; because of its age, the document is not likely to have suffered from the forces generating the suit, so there is less reason to fear distortion or lack of candor.

The term "document" is not a word of art: The exception reaches written material of all kinds (letters, diaries, newspapers, receipts, maps, and so forth) and can be used to prove virtually anything a statement can prove.[2] It is harder to say whether "document" reaches electronically stored data or sound recordings. The self-authentication provision reaches electronically stored data, and difference in language (the exception refers only to statements "in a document") suggests difference in coverage. Perhaps the ancient documents exception is less necessary for electronically stored material, which often fits the exceptions for business or public records. But the ACN suggests that the ancient documents exception and authentication provision are to be read together, so coverage is probably the same despite different words.

---

§8.58　1. *See* FRE 901(b)(8) (condition must create "no suspicion" on authenticity; document must be found where it "would likely be" if authentic), discussed in §9.12, *infra*.

2. Martha Graham School and Dance Foundation, Inc. v. Martha Graham Center of Contemporary Dance, Inc., 380 F.3d 624, 643 (2d Cir. 2004) (letters written in 1958 and 1971, showing that Martha Graham assigned rights in dances to center), *cert. denied*, 544 U.S. 1060; United States v. Demjanjuk, 367 F.3d 623, 630-631 (6th Cir. 2004) (World War II service pass indicting defendant's presence at prison camp), *cert. denied*, 543 U.S. 970; Threadgill v. Armstrong World Indus., Inc., 928 F.2d 1366, 1375-1376 (3d Cir. 1991) (papers of Sumner Simpson); Bell v. Combined Registry Co., 536 F.2d 164, 166-167 (7th Cir. 1976) (letters and magazine articles), *cert. denied*, 429 U.S. 1001.

(17) **Market reports, commercial publications.** Market quotations, tabulations, lists, directories, or other published compilations, generally used and relied upon by the public or by persons in particular occupations.

§8.59 Market Reports and Commercial Lists

The commercial list exception in FRE 803(17) reaches market quotations, tabulations, lists, directories, and other published compilations "generally used and relied upon" by the public or people in particular occupations. Price catalogues, directories compiling names of people or firms by occupation or specialty, common tabulated information like interest charts and mortality tables, all fit the exception. Sometimes it reaches specialized and elaborate empirical data.

The idea of necessity underlies the exception because it would be hard or impracticable to locate and summon the people whose personal knowledge underlies such material, and even if such people could be found they would not likely recall specific data and could only account for the way they were gathered and assembled. And the material is considered trustworthy because people rely on it: Errors and inaccuracy invite complaint, criticism, and correction; a pattern of unreliability invites users to turn elsewhere, which would make compilers and publishers lose stature and perhaps income. And the kind of information gleaned from such sources is usually concrete and specific, and compiled by people or organizations with experience and expertise.

Clearly the exception reaches price lists,[1] stock market quotations (published in newspapers of general circulation or specialty journals),[2] professional, city, and phone directories,[3] mortality tables,[4] registers of

Price lists, market quotes, directories, tables

§8.59   1. In re Cliquot's Champagne, 70 U.S. 114, 141 (1866) (Parisian wine dealer's wholesale price-current); United States v. Grossman, 614 F.2d 295, 297-298 (1st Cir. 1980) (retail catalogue prepared by maker of cigarette lighters); Fraser-Smith Co. v. Chicago R.I. & P.R. Co., 435 F.2d 1396, 1402 (8th Cir. 1971) (grain pricing index); UCC §2-724 (reports of commodities market in official publications, trade journals, newspapers, or periodicals to show price or value of goods regularly traded).

2. Virginia v. West Virginia, 238 U.S. 202, 212 (1915) (stock market quotes in Richmond Dispatch); United States v. Cassiere, 4 F.3d 1006, 1018-1019 (1st Cir. 1993) (monthly *Country Comps* listing property sales, prices, closing dates); United States v. Anderson, 532 F.2d 1218, 1225 (9th Cir. 1976) (over-the-counter prices in Wall Street Journal), *cert. denied*, 429 U.S. 839.

3. State ex rel. Keefe v. McInerney, 182 P.2d 28, 34 (Wyo. 1947) (city and phone directories); Williams v. Campbell Soup Co., 80 F. Supp. 865, 868 (W.D. Mo. 1948) (city directory).

4. Vicksburg & M.R. Co. v. Putnam, 118 U.S. 545 (1886) (standard life and annuity tables); Kershaw v. Sterling Drug, Inc., 415 F.2d 1009, 1012 (5th Cir. 1969) (mortality tables).

such things as animals and ships,[5] and compilations of estimated value of commonly traded items like used cars, comic books, and postage stamps.[6]

The exception is narrow, and the language in FRE 803(17) defines coverage in terms that clearly do not reach treatises, research papers, or studies that present evaluative conclusions (instead it covers quotations, tabulations, lists, directories, compilations). The limited reach is also emphasized by the requirement that the material be generally used and relied on by the public or by people in specific commercial or professional occupations.[7]

Credit reports   Credit reports present a special challenge. They reflect a reporting agency's appraisal of the financial strength of the subject (sometimes its organization, managerial skills, and business prospects), and pass along information on payment and credit records and relationship with suppliers. Because they are so often used as the basis of credit and investment decisions, some have argued that they should be generally admissible.[8] But often they also reflect rumors and other rank hearsay that may come from people with grudges or in economic competition with the subject.[9] Concerns over accuracy led to reform legislation requiring corrective mechanisms and allowing damage recoveries.[10] In short, credit reports are evaluative in nature and often inaccurate on points of detail. They are generally prepared for a small rather than a general audience (only potential creditors, investors, or insurers), and for the limited purpose of aiding in yes-or-no business judgments. Hence they do not fit the commercial list exception and are often excludable as hearsay.[11]

---

5. United States v. Woods, 321 F.3d 361, 362-363 (3d Cir. 2003) (testimony based on "database compiled by National Insurance Crime Bureau (NICB)" listing vehicles by VIN, to trace manufacture of car to New York; industry and law enforcement accept and rely on database); Slocovich v. Orient Mut. Ins. Co., 14 N.E. 802, 805 (N.Y. 1888) (valuation of ship based on American Lloyds, Green Book, and Record Book).

6. United States v. Johnson, 515 F.2d 730, 732 n.4 (7th Cir. 1975) (Red Book values of Cadillacs).

7. Crane v. Crest Tankers, Inc., 47 F.3d 292, 296 (Future Damages Calculator did not fit exception; plaintiff did not show it is generally used or relied upon).

8. Note, Mercantile Credit Reports as Evidence, 44 Minn. L. Rev. 719 (1960); Note, Commercial Lists, 46 Iowa L. Rev. 455, 459 (1961).

9. Millstone v. O'Hanlon Reports, Inc., 528 F.2d 829 (8th Cir. 1976); Collins v. Retail Credit Co., 410 F. Supp. 924 (E.D. Mich. 1976).

10. *See* Fair Credit Reporting Act, 15 U.S.C. §§1681-1681t (reporting agencies must investigate credit reports if disputed by consumer and delete inaccuracies; providing for damage actions against agencies).

11. *See* United States v. Martin, 167 F. Supp. 301, 302-303 (N.D. Ill. 1958); Phillip Van Heusen, Inc. v. Korn, 460 P.2d 549, 552 (Kan. 1969); Young's Market Co. v. Laue, 141 P.2d 522, 523 (Ariz. 1943).

FRE 803(18)

(18) Learned treatises. To the extent called to the attention of an expert witness upon cross-examination or relied upon by the expert witness in direct examination, statements contained in published treatises, periodicals, or pamphlets on a subject of history, medicine, or other science or art, established as a reliable authority by the testimony or admission of the witness or by other expert testimony or by judicial notice. If admitted, the statements may be read into evidence but may not be received as exhibits.

§8.60   Learned Treatises

The learned treatise exception reaches statements in treatises if called to the attention of an expert witness or he relies on them or they are shown in some other way to be authoritative. The exception reaches published treatises, periodicals, or pamphlets on history, medicine, or other science or art and lets statements in such works be read in evidence but not taken to the jury room.

Trustworthiness, necessity

There is an assurance of trustworthiness in that books and articles are written by people with special training and skills and read by others in the field, so pressures of competition and criticism and the impulse to secure and preserve professional stature provide incentives toward care and accuracy. And there is a need for treatises in litigation because it is impracticable for parties to produce all or even the best experts, and excluding written works by experts whose live testimony is beyond reach deprives the trier of useful information. In professional malpractice cases, difficulties in finding willing experts create special need for treatises as substantive evidence.

Modern media material

In a world where books and articles are published online, material is presented in professional seminars in various electronic forms, and videotapes and interactive computer exercises are routine in educational programs, there is good reason to apply FRE 803(18) to material involving oral presentations and demonstrations, and to various kinds of verbal and illustrative material that never appears in "hard copy."[1] Of course the exception reaches only "published" material, which means at a minimum that it does not reach research papers that have never been read, used, or reviewed by others, and that "published" must mean at least that the material has been read, used, or reviewed by others, and has found its way into broader use by people in

§8.60   1. Costantino v. Herzog, 203 F.3d 164, 170-172 (2d Cir. 2000) (in malpractice suit, admitting videotape "Shoulder Dystocia" prepared by American College of Obstetricians and Gynecologists for educational purposes, disseminated to doctors, maintained by ACOG in video library).

the relevant discipline or profession. If the proponent can show this much, and obtain an endorsement by a qualified expert that the material in question is reliable (as the exception requires), there is no reason to balk at the fact that the material is "published" online, or in the form of videotape, or in some other electronic form that has become a feature of modern life.

Restrictive tradition   Common law tradition was comparatively restrictive, for there was no hearsay exception as such. Theoretically, treatises were kept in the background and could only be used for nonhearsay purposes to support or impeach experts. A variety of technical restrictions were deployed to maintain this separation: During direct examination, some courts barred mention of treatises (keeping reliance hidden), while others allowed limited questioning for the sole purpose of showing basis of opinion. During cross, most courts allowed questions about treatises the expert relied on, and the narrowest rule limited questioning to those alone. The broadest rule let the cross-examiner ask about any learned treatise shown to be authoritative. In-between rules let the cross-examiner ask about a treatise if the expert acknowledged its authority or relied on some treatise.

Practice has not changed as much as one might suppose, but gone are the technical restrictions and the pretense that treatises can only help evaluate expert testimony. What remains is the salient point that treatises must still be offered along with expert testimony.

FRE 803(18) contains two requirements.

Must be reliable   First, the proponent must show the book or article is reliable authority. The most certain way is to offer expert testimony.[2] It suffices if an expert testifies that he knows and respects the author and considers the work reliable, or that experts in the field generally accept author and work as authoritative. Such testimony is enough even if the witness himself disagrees with what the author says. Absent another basis to conclude the material is reliable, expert endorsement of this sort is essential.[3] The first requirement may also be satisfied by stipulation or judicial notice.[4]

Expert must rely   Second, a testifying expert must rely on the book or article on direct, or the proponent must call it to his attention on cross. The purpose is to provide explanation, context, and perspective, and the proponent

---

2. Carroll v. Morgan, 17 F.3d 787, 790 (5th Cir. 1994) (can use medical text in cross-examining one expert where another recognized its authority); Dawson v. Chrysler Corp., 630 F.2d 950, 960-961 (3d Cir. 1980) (expert conceded that DOT studies were reliable; he calculated data from them), *cert. denied*, 450 U.S. 959.

3. United States v. Norman, 415 F.3d 466, 472-474 (5th Cir. 2005) (treatises are exempt from hearsay rule only if used by expert or shown to be established as reliable on cross or by judicial notice), *cert. denied*, 546 U.S. 1117; Commonwealth v. Reese, 781 N.E.2d 1225, 1231 (Mass. 2003) (error to rely on articles not proved authoritative; exception did not apply); Schneider v. Revici, 817 F.2d 987, 990-991 (2d Cir. 1987) (excluding book by defendant who never asked appropriate question of expert).

4. *See* Meschino v. North Am. Drager, Inc., 841 F.2d 429, 434 (1st Cir. 1988) (listing as exhibit does not bar claim that article did not fit exception); Jamison v. Kline, 454 F.2d 1256, 1257-1258 (3d Cir. 1972) (judicial notice of chart).

should ensure that witness and opposing counsel are familiar with the material (giving them a chance to read it if they did not do so before) and elicit the expert's views and reactions.

Often the proponent calls the book or article to the attention of the other side's expert on cross.[5] Since the proponent has the burden of qualifying the material as authoritative, one obvious approach is to ask the expert directly whether he concurs in the relevant points made by the book or article and (if he answers as expected) to explain his disagreements or qualifications. Or the proponent might cross-examine the expert on the material in a way that shows she considers it important and may use it again later. This tactic satisfies the attention-calling requirement, and on redirect or later in the proceedings (case-in-rebuttal or case-in-rejoinder) the adversary can bring to light further reactions or qualifications the expert did not have a chance to express. The thing to prevent is a hide-the-ball approach in which the proponent makes passing reference to the book or article (avoiding any real exchange with the expert) and trots it out later when the expert has left, either in argument or a read-to-the-jury speech or by using a surrogate witness who cannot provide perspective.

Sometimes the proponent satisfies the reliance requirement by showing that her own expert relies on the book or article.[6] Again, if she plans to make substantive use of the material by reading from it and arguing that it proves what it says, she has to ask the expert to explain the passages that relate them to what he conveys in his testimony. Hiding the ball does not satisfy the reliance requirement, and the proponent should not present a book or article as evidence (by reading from it or getting a surrogate to do so) after the expert has left on the basis of casual or passing reference to the material while he testified.

The exception lets passages be read into evidence but not "received as exhibits." Clearly the purpose is to limit and control the jury's exposure to such material. Obviously it is still lodged and made part of the record, and passages of a book or article may be read by counsel or an expert or other appropriate witness during questioning.[7] Also the proponent can make a visual presentation by enlargement projected on a screen or otherwise: Where the material contains charts or diagrams or tables, a visual presentation is the only way to make it intelligible.

Not received as exhibits

Such material should not go to the jury room during deliberations,[8] nor be available for unsupervised use and review, and probably it should not be on permanent display during trial as a continuing claim or suggestion unconnected with current testimony. But juries

5. Tart v. McGann, 697 F.2d 75, 77-78 (2d Cir. 1982); Dawson v. Chrysler Corp., 630 F.2d 950, 960-961 (3d Cir. 1980), *cert. denied*, 450 U.S. 959.

6. Tart v. McGann, 697 F.2d 75, 77-78 (2d Cir. 1982); Johnson v. William C. Ellis & Sons Iron Works, Inc., 609 F.2d 820, 823 (5th Cir. 1980) (plaintiff should have been able to use safety publications established as reliable by his expert).

7. United States v. An Article of Drug, 661 F.2d 742, 745-746 (9th Cir. 1981) (experts read treatise passages).

8. Graham v. Wyeth Labs., 906 F.2d 1399, 1414 (10th Cir. 1990) (error to submit AMA Report to jury), *cert. denied*, 498 U.S. 981.

often ask to rehear passages from testimony presented during trial, and the restriction against books and articles as exhibits does not stop a court in the presence of the parties from letting juries rehear passages along with whatever testimony is important for context.

FRE 803(19)-(21)

    (19) Reputation concerning personal or family history. Reputation among members of a person's family by blood, adoption, or marriage or among a person's associates, or in the community, concerning a person's birth, adoption, marriage, divorce, death, legitimacy, relationship by blood, adoption, or marriage, ancestry, or other similar fact of personal or family history.

    (20) Reputation concerning boundaries or general history. Reputation in a community, arising before the controversy, as to boundaries of or customs affecting lands in the community, and reputation as to events of general history important to the community or State or nation in which located.

    (21) Reputation as to character. Reputation of a person's character among associates or in the community.

---

§8.61   —Reputation on Character and Other Matters

Three exceptions in FRE 803 cover reputation evidence, and all allow evidence of common repute (what people say) to be offered as proof that things are just as people think.

Reputation on character
    The most important is FRE 803(21), which covers reputation relating to character. Such evidence has two common uses where other important regulating rules often generate controversy and disagreement. One involves testimony on reputed character to prove behavior on a particular occasion. Did the person likely do something or likely not do it? If so, how and in what way? And what purpose or mental state was the likely animating force? The other involves testimony by one witness on reputed character of another witness with respect to "truth and veracity." The first of these uses is described as "substantive" (we often see also the larger phrase "character to prove conduct on a particular occasion"), and the second is described in terms of "impeachment" or "support" (sometimes "character to prove credibility").[1]

Character as substantive evidence
    It is understood that one who gives reputation testimony conveys a kind of aggregate community opinion. When used as substantive evidence (proving conduct on a particular occasion) or to impeach or support a witness, such evidence is hearsay because the purpose is

---

§8.61 1. On substantive use of character evidence, *see* discussion of FRE 404-405 in §§4.11-4.20, *supra*. On use to impeach or support credibility, *see* discussion of FRE 608 in §§6.23 and 6.50, *supra*.

to prove the person has the kind of character he is reputed to have. That such proof is hearsay has long been recognized, and it was once thought such proof was the best kind.[2] That view is now largely abandoned, and opinion evidence may be offered as well, but FRE 803(21) continues to pave the way for reputation evidence.

Sometimes character itself is in issue, and evidence of character is not used circumstantially, but as direct proof of an element in a claim or defense, as in libel cases where truth is a defense (claim is defeated if statement accurately described plaintiff) and negligent entrustment cases (tortfeasor is not the sort of person the defendant should have hired). Here too character may be proved by reputation testimony; here too such testimony is hearsay because the witness conveys the aggregate voice of the community to prove what the character actually is; here too the exception applies.

Character itself in issue

Occasionally reputation itself (and not character revealed by reputation) is an element of a claim or defense.[3] Here testimony on reputation is technically nonhearsay because what the witness says he "has heard" is not introduced to prove that character is really what others say it is, but to show what is said about it.

Reputation itself in issue

A second exception for reputation evidence appears in FRE 803(19), which covers reputation among family members, associates, or the community at large on "personal or family history." In some measure, notions of trustworthiness and necessity justify this exception. Family relationships are likely to be known to family members, associates, and the community, sometimes by way of firsthand knowledge, more often by way of discussion and reiteration, or reasonable deduction from observed conduct. Mistakes occur and false information circulates (careless talk, rumor, even determined deception), but usually common repute gets the matter right. The exception embraces one's reputation as it may be found in any of three sources (family member, associates, and community), which is the broadest possible approach and a concession to what the Advisory Committee called "changing times" in which valuable reputation evidence may be found in a family and in "multiple and unrelated worlds of work, religious affiliation, and social activity." In a nonexclusive list, FRE 803(19) makes it clear that the exception embraces reputation offered to prove one's birth or adoption, marriage or divorce, death, legitimacy or relationship by

Reputation among family members

---

2. *See* Michelson v. United States, 335 U.S. 469, 477 (1948) (in proving reputation, witnesses "testify from hearsay" and are not allowed to give their own opinions) (reputation of a person is "the shadow his daily life has cast in his neighborhood"); Badger v. Badger, 88 N.Y. 546, 552 (1882) (reputation paints a picture of "forgotten incidents, passing events, habitual and daily conduct" and "sums up a multitude of trivial details" reflecting "the average intelligence drawing its conclusion") (quoted in *Michelson, supra*).

3. United States v. Certain Real Property, 945 F.2d 1252, 1260 (2d Cir. 1991) (in forfeiture action where woman claimed she did not know son used property for drugs, admitting his reputation for drug use to show her knowledge).

blood, adoption or marriage, ancestry, and any other similar fact of personal or family history.[4]

The third reputation exception is found in FRE 803(20), and it covers two kinds of evidence. One is reputation predating the controversy on boundaries or customs affecting land in the community. The other is reputation on events of general history that were important in the community or surrounding state or nation.

Reputation on boundaries

For precontroversy reputation on boundaries and customs affecting land, there is a kind of necessity: For "ancient" reputation, presumably the sources are dead, and undocumented custom has much to do with land title and usage, and these points cannot be proved in the conventional way by eyewitness testimony and recorded documents. Such evidence is reliable because it is the product of public observation and discussion on matters of some importance and represents a consensus that is probably informed and correct. The exception reaches use of reputation to prove location of boundaries,[5] the use to which property has been put, and the fact of possession or use and identity of the occupant or user.[6]

Reputation on community history

The exception in FRE 803(20) also covers reputation evidence to prove historical events of general interest and notoriety.[7] The term "history" connotes the past and indicates that the exception does not reach reputation on current events.[8] The notions of necessity and trustworthiness are best satisfied if the event happened many years before trial. Only then is there likely to be a true need for reputation, and only then is there reason to think that time and community discourse has sifted out the truth. Sometimes matters that might be shown by reputation evidence are instead established by judicial notice, often aided by book references, so hearsay issues are submerged.[9]

---

4. United States v. Jean-Baptiste, 166 F.3d 102, 110 (2d Cir. 1999) (on basis of exception, father could testify to "his belief" that daughter was born in St. Croix); United States v. Mid-Continent Petroleum Corp., 67 F.2d 37, 44-46 (10th Cir. 1933) (tribal rolls prove "genealogy or pedigree"), *cert. denied*, 290 U.S. 702; Gorden v. Gorden, 119 N.E. 312, 317-318 (Ill. 1918) (marriage). *But see* Blackburn v. United Parcel Service, Inc., 179 F.3d 81, 99 (3d Cir. 1999) (exception reaches reputation in workplace, but can't use exception to prove "allegations regarding relationships" in large company; reputation does not include what one employee tells another about someone else).

5. Nabours v. Whiteley, 466 S.W.2d 62, 65 (Tex. Civ. App. 1971) (reputation of league line as matching fence line).

6. Jackson v. Gallegos, 30 P.2d 719, 727 (N.M. 1934) (in quiet title suit, reputed possession under license).

7. *See* Bow v. Allenstown, 34 N.H. 351, 365 (1857) (incorporation of town may be proved by reputation).

8. *See* Pan American World Airways, Inc. v. Aetna Casualty & Sur. Co., 368 F. Supp. 1098, 1104 n.5 (S.D.N.Y. 1973) (exception eliminates "antiquity" requirement, but term "history" brings requirement of age), *aff'd*, 505 F.2d 989 (2d Cir. 1974).

9. *See* United States v. 1078.27 Acres of Land, 446 F.2d 1030 (5th Cir. 1971) (in land dispute, judge researched historical documents in public library, newspaper morgue, and state library archives), *cert. denied*, 405 U.S. 936.

And sometimes such matters are shown by historical writings that are recognized as hearsay within the learned treatise exception.[10]

FRE 803(22)-(23)

  (22) Judgment of previous conviction. Evidence of a final judgment, entered after a trial or upon a plea of guilty (but not upon a plea of nolo contendere), adjudging a person guilty of a crime punishable by death or imprisonment in excess of one year, to prove any fact essential to sustain the judgment, but not including, when offered by the Government in a criminal prosecution for purposes other than impeachment, judgments against persons other than the accused. The pendency of an appeal may be shown but does not affect admissibility.

  (23) Judgment as to personal, family, or general history, or boundaries. Judgments as proof of matters of personal, family, or general history, or boundaries, essential to the judgment, if the same would be provable by evidence of reputation.

---

§8.62   Court Judgments: Felony Convictions; History and Boundaries

Two exceptions in FRE 803 cover court judgments. The first reaches exception for felony convictions offered to prove the essential underlying facts, which is codified in FRE 803(22). This exception does not reach convictions based on nolo pleas, and in criminal cases the exception does not allow the government to use convictions of persons other than defendant to prove facts in the case, but does allow the government to use such convictions to impeach witnesses. The other exception, which is contained in FRE 803(23), reaches judgments that tend to prove matters of personal or family history, or boundaries.

Evidentiary use of a conviction generates problems peculiar to this kind of hearsay. The trier is likely to be without means to evaluate it. One reason is that it represents a conclusion drawn by a different trier on the basis of evidence presented only to it, and there is no way to assess the credibility of the prior factfinder and tribunal.[1] Another reason is that a conviction represents a commingled conclusion of law and fact handed down in a context likely to differ from the one in which the judgment is offered. Procedural safeguards in the prior proceedings reduce the significance of the first objection, and it is

---

10. Connecticut Light & Power Co. v. FPC, 557 F.2d 349 (2d Cir. 1977) (ALJ consults historical works to determine river navigability).

§8.62   1. *See* ACN to FRE 803(22) (admitting conviction may leave jury "without means to evaluate it" and jury will likely "give it substantial effect"); Note, Judgment of Conviction—Effect in a Civil Case as Res Judicata or as Evidence—New York, 27 Ill. L. Rev. 195, 198 (1932).

surely possible to contest the evidential significance of convictions by offering counterproof and pointing out shortcomings or contextual differences.[2] And in the end, both objections can be handled by excluding a judgment under FRE 403 if probative worth is outweighed by its tendency to mislead or confuse.

Conviction means judgment

FRE 803(22) reaches judgments on pleas of guilty, so it makes no difference whether there was a contest on the merits.[3] The exception covers convictions, not preliminary indicators of guilt, other dispositions, or judgments that have been set aside. Thus it does not reach arrests or charges, which are much weaker indicators of underlying facts. Nor does the exception reach acquittals offered to prove the charged offense was not committed.[4] These too are weaker indicators, which mean the proof did not satisfy the beyond reasonable doubt standard.

In dealing with hearsay use of convictions, the exception has nothing to say about pleas as such or about other uses of convictions. Thus the felony limit does not block use of a guilty plea to a charge when offered against the person who entered the plea.[5] And FRE 803(22) reaches convictions as proof of underlying facts and is not needed for convictions that are important in themselves or as indicators of the official disposition of the convicted person.[6] When offered for such purposes, a judgment readily fits FRE 803(8)(A) (the public records exception) to prove "activities of the office or agency."

Only felonies

The exception reaches only convictions for crimes punishable by "death or imprisonment in excess of one year," which means felonies. What counts is the possible nature and extent of punishment, not punishment actually imposed. Hence a conviction that leads to a suspended or deferred sentence or imprisonment for less than a year may fit the exception.

Finality requirement

As framed in FRE 803(22), the exception contains a finality requirement that seems to turn on formal "entry" of judgment, which suggests that the exception does not apply if defendant in the other case has pled or been found guilty if judgment has not yet been entered. Insisting on entry of judgment, however, seems excessive for three reasons: First, entry adds little to the assurance of trustworthiness surrounding factual determinations underlying pleas and verdicts of guilty. While guilty pleas may be withdrawn even after sentencing (and withdrawn pleas are themselves excludable), still guilty pleas carry considerable weight because they are taken only after the court speaks directly to the defendant, ascertaining that he knows what he is doing. Guilty verdicts are nonfinal (they may be set aside by motion for a judgment of

---

2. Motomura, Using Judgments as Evidence, 70 Minn. L. Rev. 979, 1037-1045 (1986) (juries can adequately appraise judgments; they should be widely admissible).

3. *See* Rozier v. Ford Motor Co., 573 F.2d 1332, 1346-1347 (5th Cir. 1978).

4. United States v. Gricco, 277 F.3d 339, 352-353 (3d Cir. 2002); Borunda v. Richmond, 885 F.2d 1384, 1388 (9th Cir. 1988).

5. Hancock v. Dodson, 958 F.2d 1367, 1371-1372 (6th Cir. 1992).

6. *See* Olsen v. Correiro, 189 F.3d 52, 62-64 (1st Cir. 1999) (to show plaintiff "was legally punished in a way that is relevant to his claim" for damages against police).

acquittal), but judgments too may be set aside on motion or appeal. Yet the exception reaches judgments that are or might be appealed. Second, experience in *res judicata* and collateral estoppel has led away from a mechanical and toward a functional interpretation in which adjudication is final if it is "sufficiently firm to be accorded conclusive effect."[7] This functional approach is at least as appropriate in the present setting when evidential use rather than binding effect is at stake. Third, witnesses probably may be impeached under FRE 609 by verdicts of guilty if judgments based on those verdicts could be used, and there is no apparent reason why the term "final judgment" in the exception should be interpreted more narrowly than the term "conviction" in FRE 609.

The finality requirement can be satisfied and the exception can apply even if an appeal is pending (or possible). Clearly the party against whom a judgment is admitted may show the fact of appeal (and presumably that the time for appeal has not run). She should also be permitted to show that other challenges might be or have been made, and of course the proponent should be allowed to show that no motions were made or appeals taken, or that they were resolved by orders upholding the underlying judgment.

The exception permits use of a conviction only to establish a "fact essential to sustain the judgment," and the idea is that accuracy is assured only for essential findings. Here it seems wise to borrow points from the collateral estoppel doctrine, which similarly applies only to essential facts. Extrinsic evidence should be admissible to help figure out what facts the other judgment determined, and a judgment should not be admitted if this point cannot be resolved,[8] nor to prove facts that do not support or are not essential to it. On issues like these the exception and the collateral estoppel doctrine share common ground and invite a common approach.[9]   **Essential fact requirement**

By its terms, FRE 803(22) does not reach convictions based on nolo pleas. In common application, this restriction makes sense: If one pleads nolo contendere to criminal charges and is later sued for damages arising out of the transaction, the conviction should be excluded. The usual purpose of a nolo plea is to let the accused   **Judgment on nolo plea excluded**

7. Restatement (Second) of Judgments §13 (1982). *See also* Lummus Co. v. Commonwealth Oil Ref. Co., 297 F.2d 80, 89 (2d Cir. 1961) (finality means suit "has reached such a stage that a court sees no really good reason" to allow relitigation), *cert. denied*, 368 U.S. 986.

8. *See* Restatement (Second) of Judgments §27 cmt. f (1982) (can admit extrinsic evidence to show what was decided); Russell v. Place, 94 U.S. 606 (1877) (no collateral estoppel if what was litigated is in doubt).

9. Restatement (Second) of Judgments §27 cmt. h (1982) (nonessential issues may be relitigated); Lloyd v. American Export Lines, Inc., 580 F.2d 1179, 1187-1190 (3d Cir. 1978) (consulting record to determine meaning of judgment, although only conviction is admissible), *cert. denied*, 439 U.S. 969. *See also* 15 U.S.C. §16(a) (some antitrust judgments are "prima facie evidence" against defendant on matters that normally create estoppel); Columbia Plaza Corp. v. Security Natl. Bank, 676 F.2d 780, 789-790 (D.C. Cir. 1982) (excluding verdicts in conspiracy cases; no basis to know which acts jury relied on).

avoid a criminal trial he thinks he cannot win because he is guilty and the government can prove it, without making evidence against himself if he is civilly sued later. The plea itself is excludable under FRE 410, and the policy underlying nolo pleas would be undone if the conviction were freely admissible. Hence the restriction in the exception leaves a hearsay objection intact, and the restriction is actually a rule of exclusion.[10] In other contexts, however, it seems wrong to exclude felony convictions based on nolo pleas because exclusion does not serve the underlying policy. Hence the restriction in FRE 803(22) is too broadly worded. In unrelated cases, for example, a conviction on a nolo plea should be usable to impeach under FRE 609, or to prove other acts under FRE 404(b).[11] It is worth noting too that convictions based on nolo pleas are not excludable under the restrictive language in the exception when they are offered for a nonhearsay purpose because the exception itself is not needed for such uses.[12]

The exception does not reach third-party convictions offered by the government in criminal cases for "purposes other than impeachment." This restriction rests on an old decision in *Kirby v. United States*, which involved a trial on charges for receiving stolen property. There the Court held that the confrontation clause barred use of the convictions of three others for felony theft as proof that the property was stolen.[13] Outside the impeachment context, *Kirby* and the exception bar government use of third-party convictions to show facts essential to the judgment.[14]

Other court judgments

FRE 803(23) covers judgments offered to prove matters essential to them that relate to personal, family or general history, or boundaries, where these would be "provable by reputation evidence." The last phrase provides the key, for the exception rests on a common law anachronism, having grown out of the ancient practice in which the jury was a body of witnesses who reached a conclusion on the basis of information they possessed, whether gleaned from outside sources or

10. *See* Greenberg v. Cutler-Hammer, Inc., 403 F. Supp. 1231, 1234 (E.D. Wis. 1975) (nolo plea judgment may not be used to prove essential facts). *But see* Olsen v. Correiro, 189 F.3d 52, 62-64 (1st Cir. 1999) ("not obvious" that exception bars any evidence; nolo plea judgment might be offered merely to show judgment itself, or to show underlying facts if it fits another exception).

11. *See* discussion of FRE 609 in §6.38, *supra*. *See also* United States v. Wyatt, 762 F.2d 908, 911 (11th Cir. 1985), *cert. denied*, 475 U.S. 1047; United States v. Frederickson, 601 F.2d 1358, 1365 n.10 (8th Cir. 1979) (admitting convictions on nolo pleas to prove acts bearing on intent), *cert. denied*, 444 U.S. 934.

12. Qureshi v. INS, 519 F.2d 1174, 1175-1176 (5th Cir. 1975) (counts for deportation); Sokoloff v. Saxbe, 501 F.2d 571, 574 (2d Cir. 1974) (counts in revoking certificate letting doctor distribute drugs).

13. Neither *Kirby* nor the exception blocks use of a third-party conviction if the fact of conviction is important, as opposed to some act or event it tends to show. *See* Kirby v. United States, 174 U.S. 47, 54 (1899) (if conviction were a condition to trying someone else for receiving the property, it could be proved); 18 U.S.C. §922(d) (crime to sell firearm to person known to be convicted felon).

14. United States v. Diaz, 936 F.2d 786, 788 (5th Cir. 1991) (in trial for transporting illegals, could not prove status by showing their convictions); United States v. Crispin, 757 F.2d 611, 613 & n.1 (5th Cir. 1985) (similar).

from the proceedings. Under that practice, there was some sense in viewing a verdict as evidence of community repute, hence to admit a prior verdict as a kind of proof of community repute, at least on matters on which reputation evidence would be admissible. But this logic does not fit a system in which the jury acts as a factfinding body whose decision must rest in the main on evidence formally adduced in court.

The framers of the Rules were persuaded to keep the exception because (as the ACN reflects) the process of "inquiry, sifting, and scrutiny" on which reputation evidence is based may be found "in perhaps greater measure" in litigation. The exception embraces civil and criminal judgments, and complements the two reputation exceptions, which means that a judgment may be admitted to prove personal milestones (birth, marriage, divorce, and similar points), familial relationships (legitimacy, marriage, ancestry and similar points), and facts of personal or family history. And the exception complements FRE 803(20), so a judgment may be admitted to prove boundaries or customs affecting lands in the community and events of general history important in the community.

G. EXCEPTIONS—DECLARANT UNAVAILABLE

FRE 804(a)

(a) Definition of unavailability. "Unavailability as a witness" includes situations in which the declarant

(1) is exempted by ruling of the court on the ground of privilege from testifying concerning the subject matter of the declarant's statement; or

(2) persists in refusing to testify concerning the subject matter of the declarant's statement despite an order of the court to do so; or

(3) testifies to a lack of memory of the subject matter of the declarant's statement; or

(4) is unable to be present or to testify at the hearing because of death or then existing physical or mental illness or infirmity; or

(5) is absent from the hearing and the proponent of a statement has been unable to procure the declarant's attendance (or in the case of a hearsay exception under subdivision (b)(2), (3), or (4), the declarant's attendance or testimony) by process or other reasonable means.

A declarant is not unavailable as a witness if exemption, refusal, claim of lack of memory, inability, or absence is due to the procurement or wrongdoing of the proponent of a statement for the purpose of preventing the witness from attending or testifying.

§8.63 Unavailability of Declarant—Claim of Privilege; Refusal to Testify

The five exceptions in FRE 804(b) may be invoked only if the declarant is "unavailable as a witness," and this concept is defined in FRE 804(a). Except where behavior by the proponent amounts to "procurement" or "wrongdoing" preventing the declarant from testifying, unavailability is shown by a proper claim of privilege, refusal to testify, lack of memory, death or illness, and unavoidable absence. The unavailability requirement is a rule of preference for live testimony over an out-of-court statement that overcomes a hearsay objection only because it fits an exception in FRE 804(b). In effect, statements covered by these exceptions are considered trustworthy, but less so than those that fit the exceptions in FRE 803, and FRE 804 rests on the philosophy that "less is better than nothing." It is, of course, testimony that is preferred, so FRE 804(a) makes it clear that a declarant may be unavailable even though physically present if his testimony cannot be had.

Unavailability represents a kind of necessity, which is one of the two traditional bases for hearsay exceptions (the other being trustworthiness). Unavailability of the declarant does not show other evidence is also unavailable, and someone who offers a statement under FRE 804(b) need not show other evidence is lacking, although such a showing strengthens claims that the catchall exception should apply. Showing that live testimony by the declarant cannot be had does not itself justify using his statement. Unavailability is a necessary but not sufficient condition for the exceptions in FRE 804(b).[1]

Constitutional dimension

In criminal cases, unavailability has a constitutional dimension. At least where the government offers statements under the former testimony exception, satisfying the unavailability criteria of FRE 804(a) does not necessarily mean it has discharged its constitutional obligation to obtain testimony by the declarant. And where a defendant offers a statement that qualifies under that exception, sometimes failing to satisfy the unavailability requirement cannot constitutionally block him.[2]

Exempt by privilege

One is unavailable under FRE 804(a)(1) if he "is exempted by ruling of the court on the ground of privilege from testifying concerning the subject matter of his statement." Such unavailability is established where a witness properly invokes a common law or statutory privilege or his constitutional privilege against self-incrimination.[3] The criterion is also satisfied if the party against whom a statement is offered claims a privilege that blocks someone from testifying. Thus the offering party

---

§8.63 1. *See* Mattox v. United States, 156 U.S. 237, 248-250 (1895) (unavailability alone does not pave way for hearsay); Rosenfeld v. Basquiat, 78 F.3d 84, 89 (2d Cir. 1996) (similar).

2. On the constitutional dimension of unavailability, see discussion in §8.87, *infra*. On defense rights to introduce hearsay, see discussion in §8.92, *infra*.

3. United States v. Matthews, 20 F.3d 538, 545 (2d Cir. 1994) (Fifth Amendment); United States v. Marchini, 797 F.2d 759, 762-763 (9th Cir. 1986) (testimonial privilege), *cert. denied*, 479 U.S. 1085.

can satisfy the unavailability criterion if the other side invokes a privilege to prevent the speaker from testifying.[4] It seems, however, that the offering party cannot both invoke a privilege to avoid testifying or prevent another from testifying and claim that the unavailability criterion is satisfied. Thus a party claiming a privilege cannot offer his own statement under an exception in FRE 804(b), and one who prevents another from testifying cannot offer her statement under one of those exceptions. Here the proponent's claim of privilege smacks of "procuring" unavailability for "the purpose of preventing" testimony under the last sentence of FRE 804(a).[5]

Since there must be a "ruling of the court" that exempts the witness from testifying or excludes her testimony, a party relying on this kind of unavailability should produce her so a claim of privilege may be made and ruled on. Normally the offering party does not satisfy the unavailability requirement by saying the declarant would have or claim a privilege. If the parties agree that she would properly claim a privilege or this point is clear on the facts, however, sometimes the proponent of a statement is excused from producing the declarant.[6] This principle applies when a party in a criminal case offers statements by a defendant (which may be admissible against the government or other defendants) because defendants have a constitutional right not even to be called to the stand.[7]

A declarant is unavailable under FRE 804(a)(2) if he "persists in refusing to testify concerning the subject matter" of his statement despite a court order. Typically such unavailability appears when the court overrules a privilege claim and tells the witness to answer but he refuses.[8] Sometimes a witness refuses without giving reasons, most often in criminal cases where the prosecutor wants his testimony and the witness is afraid of the defendant, or reluctant to send friends to jail, or to be involved in the effort to punish.[9] If the government can show

Refusal to testify

4. *See* United States v. Lilley, 581 F.2d 182, 187-188 (8th Cir. 1978); United States v. Hayes, 535 F.2d 479, 482 (8th Cir. 1976).

5. *See* United States v. Hughes, 535 F.3d 880, 882 (8th Cir. 2008); United States v. Bolin, 264 F.3d 391, 413 (4th Cir. 2001), *cert denied*, 122 S. Ct. 303; United States v. Kimball, 15 F.3d 54, 55-56 (5th Cir. 1994), *cert. denied*, 513 U.S. 999 (both saying defendant cannot make himself unavailable by claiming privilege, then offer his own statement). *But see* State v. Crawford, 54 P.3d 656 (Wash. 2002) (defendant can both claim privilege that prevents his wife from testifying *and* claim that admitting her statement against him violated confrontation rights), *reversed* by Crawford v. Washington, 541 U.S. 36, 40 n.1 (2004) (noting issue but not resolving it).

6. United States v. Williams, 927 F.2d 95, 98-99 (2d Cir. 1991) (attorneys said witnesses would claim Fifth Amendment), *cert. denied*, 502 U.S. 911; United States v. Brainard, 690 F.2d 1117, 1123-1124 (4th Cir. 1982) (attorney told court he would advise declarant to claim privilege), *cert. denied*, 471 U.S. 1099.

7. United States v. Robbins, 197 F.3d 829, 838 n.5 (7th Cir. 1999); United States v. Gossett, 877 F.2d 901, 907 (11th Cir. 1989), *cert. denied*, 493 U.S. 1082.

8. United States v. Monaco, 702 F.2d 860, 864-867 & n.5 (11th Cir. 1983) (claiming privilege against self-incrimination despite use immunity).

9. United States v. Coachman, 727 F.2d 1293, 1296 (D.C. Cir. 1984) (co-offender refused to answer questions when called by government); United States v. Carlson, 547 F.2d 1346, 1352-1354, 1358-1359 (8th Cir. 1976) (refusal to testify in fear of reprisals), *cert. denied*, 431 U.S. 914.

that its witness is afraid to testify, and that defendant frightened him in order to keep him from testifying, this behavior forfeits defendant's right to exclude as hearsay whatever the witness has already said (and forfeits any constitutional objection), and a special exception paves the way to admit anything the witness said before.[10]

Calling the declarant, obtaining order to testify

Obviously showing this kind of unavailability involves calling the declarant, putting questions that elicit his refusal to answer, and then getting a court order directing him to testify. Representing that he will not testify is usually not enough,[11] although a clear and careful statement refusing to cooperate is sometimes thought sufficient,[12] and a mere claim of privilege is not the same as refusing to testify.[13] Clearly the Rule contemplates a refusal to testify despite judicial pressure. Usually it is appropriate for the judge to tell the witness that continued refusal will put him in contempt and subject him to incarceration or other punishment, since such warnings test the refusal and show an effort to obtain live testimony.[14]

The phrase "concerning the subject matter of his statement" focuses inquiry on the attitude of the witness toward the underlying facts, not his attitude toward the prior statement. One who refuses to testify about something he described before ("I won't say whether defendant dealt drugs") is unavailable even if he replies to questions about having spoken before ("I remember saying to the grand jury that defendant dealt drugs"). Conversely, refusing to answer questions about making a statement ("I won't testify about my grand jury appearance") does not show unavailability if the witness testifies anew about the matters he previously described ("defendant dealt drugs").

§8.64 —Lack of Memory

A declarant is unavailable under FRE 804(a)(3) if he "testifies to a lack of memory of the subject matter of his statement." This provision contemplates calling him, putting questions about the matter asserted or described in his statement, and finding that he no longer remembers

---

10. *See* FRE 804(b)(6), discussed in §8.78, *infra*.

11. United States v. Perez, 963 F.2d 314, 316 (10th Cir. 1992); United States v. Acosta, 769 F.2d 721, 723 (11th Cir. 1985).

12. Jennings v. Maynard, 946 F.2d 1502, 1505 (10th Cir. 1991) (witness testified that he would not obey order to testify); United States v. Boulahanis, 677 F.2d 586, 588 (7th Cir. 1982) (witness refused to testify and said he was afraid of being killed), *cert. denied*, 459 U.S. 1016.

13. United States v. Mathis, 559 F.2d 294, 297-298 (5th Cir. 1977) (wife invoked spousal privilege but said she would testify if she had to; facts did not show unavailability).

14. United States v. MacCloskey, 682 F.2d 468, 478 n.19 (4th Cir. 1982) (best procedure is to order witness to testify, admonish that refusal punishable by contempt); United States v. Zappola, 646 F.2d 48, 54 (2d Cir. 1981) (similar), *cert. denied*, 459 U.S. 866.

the matter.[1] A mere representation to that effect does not suffice. The proponent must make a good-faith effort to bring out what he remembers, and the court could reasonably insist that the proponent try to refresh memory by showing the witness his statement (if written) or reminding him of its substance outside the jury's hearing (if oral).

The Rule speaks of a witness lacking memory about "the subject matter" of her statement, which means the matter described or asserted. Lack of memory on one point does not pave the way for a statement on some other point, nor does testifying to a version of events different from that described before signal lack of memory. Just as clearly, if a witness recalls part of a transaction but not other parts, or one event but not others (memory is fragmented), the proponent should be allowed to introduce her statement giving further information if it fits an exception in FRE 804(b).[2] And the important point is the state of the recollection of the declarant about the underlying realities described or asserted in her statement: The fact that she either does or does not remember *making her statement* does not bear on the question.[3]

Lacking memory on subject matter

Where a statement is offered against a criminal defendant and the speaker is unavailable because he lacks memory about the matter he described, constitutional issues may arise because unavailability undercuts or thwarts defense cross, particularly if the witness has also forgotten that he spoke before. On-the-stand memory lapse is serious when it comes to exceptions that exist largely because trial cross can test what the witness said before,[4] but less serious for statements offered under the exceptions in FRE 804(b) since they are not justified in terms of cross-examining the speaker.

Constitutional issues

§8.65   —Death, Illness, Infirmity

A declarant is unavailable under FRE 804(a)(4) if he cannot be present or testify "because of death or then existing physical or mental illness or

---

§8.64   1. Walden v. Sears, Roebuck & Co., 654 F.2d 443, 446-447 (5th Cir. 1981) (minor injured in bicycle accident was unavailable where he remembered events before and after, but not accident itself).

2. United States v. MacDonald, 688 F.2d 224, 233 n.14 (4th Cir. 1982) (*S* testified but was unavailable because she claimed memory loss on subject of statements offered under against-interest exception), *cert. denied*, 459 U.S. 1103. *But see* North Mississippi Communications, Inc. v. Jones, 792 F.2d 1330, 1336-1337 (5th Cir. 1986) (lack of memory of details was not enough), *cert. denied*, 506 U.S. 863.

3. State v. Varela, 993 P.2d 1280, 1289 (N.M. 1999) (excluding statement offered under against interest exception, where witness forgot making it; important point is "state of the recollection of the declarant about the underlying realities described or asserted in her prior statement," and remembering or not remembering statement does not bear on question) (quoting authors of this Treatise).

4. Inconsistent statements in proceedings, consistent statements, and statements of identification depend on in-court testing, *see* FRE 801(d)(1), but even here the Court has rejected challenges where the witness is forgetful, *see* United States v. Owens, 484 U.S. 554 (1988) (described in §8.88, *infra*).

infirmity." Obviously death makes one unavailable, and this kind of unavailability has long sufficed. The exception for dying statements virtually assumes this kind of unavailability.

Where physical ailment or injury prevents the declarant from testifying and the situation seems likely to persist, he is unavailable,[1] but a temporary or minor illness does not have this effect.[2] Each situation should be assessed on its own facts: Depending on the importance of what the speaker would say, and on his physical condition and psychological relationship to the proceedings, it may be reasonable to obtain his testimony at bedside or continue the proceedings if he is expected soon to be well enough to attend trial.[3] The judge must have wide discretion to decide whether the situation warrants treating such a person as unavailable or selecting among such alternatives in hope of obtaining his live testimony.

Where it is suggested that the witness is unable to testify on account of "mental illness or infirmity," the question is whether he can be brought to court without suffering psychic damage and with a reasonable prospect of being able to give usable evidence. The question is not usually one of competency, since FRE 601 abolishes competency barriers based on mental condition. But a witness who suffers a mental affliction such that exposure to courtroom questioning is likely to cause damage should be viewed as unavailable, as should one whose mental condition is such that he is unlikely to be able to testify at all or give anything that could be used.[4]

A special form of unavailability, based on the expected psychological stress of testifying, has been developed to deal with the plight of minor victims of physical or sexual abuse. This kind of unavailability is not defined in FRE 804(a), but in special statutes that apply in such cases, and the usual result of finding a child to be "psychologically unavailable" is that she can testify from a remote setting or by deposition.[5]

---

§8.65   1. United States v. Donaldson, 978 F.2d 381, 392 (7th Cir. 1992) (delivering child shortly before trial and being ill); Mutuelles Unies v. Kroll & Linstrom, 957 F.2d 707, 712-713 (9th Cir. 1992) (requiring surgery next morning and "indisposed for one to two weeks").

2. Burns v. Clusen, 798 F.2d 931, 938-943 (7th Cir. 1986) (victim not constitutionally unavailable; she suffered mental illness after sexual assault, but condition improved and was temporary).

3. United States v. Faison, 679 F.2d 292, 297 (3d Cir. 1982); United States v. Amaya, 533 F.2d 188, 190-191 (5th Cir. 1976), *cert. denied*, 429 U.S. 1101.

4. *See* United States v. Hughes, 411 F.2d 461, 463-466 (2d Cir. 1969) (schizophrenic witness was incompetent; admitting testimony from prior trial), *cert. denied*, 396 U.S. 867; Haggins v. Warden, Ft. Pillow State Farm, 715 F.2d 1050, 1052, 1055 (6th Cir. 1983) (four-year-old sexual assault victim was constitutionally unavailable where she said she would not tell truth), *cert. denied*, 464 U.S. 1071.

5. *See* the discussion in §8.67, *infra*.

§8.66   —Absent and Out of Reach; Procured Absence

For statements offered as former testimony, a declarant is unavailable if he is absent and the proponent could not, to paraphrase FRE 804(a)(5), "procure his attendance by process or other reasonable means." For statements offered under the exceptions for dying declarations, against-interest statements, or statements of personal or family history, a declarant is unavailable if he is absent and the proponent could not, paraphrasing with attention to the language in parentheses, "procure his attendance *or testimony* by process or other reasonable means."

This form of unavailability turns on three factors, which are in turn qualified by two others. One is the amenability of the declarant to subpoena. Another is the prospect of inducing him to appear. Third is the effort by the proponent to take his deposition, but this factor does not count if the proponent offers testimony in some other form by the declarant—in effect, there is no need to take a deposition if she already testified in *some* forum somewhere and the proponent offers that testimony (provided that there was a suitable opportunity in that other forum to cross-examine the witness). These factors are elements in a burden that is limited by a fourth factor: The proponent is expected to take only such steps as are "reasonable" under the circumstances. And the unavailability criterion cannot be satisfied if a fifth factor appears— the absence of the witness is the result of "procurement or wrongdoing" by the proponent.

Qualified 3-factor test

In civil cases the subpoena power of most state courts of general jurisdiction reaches throughout the state. Federal courts can subpoena anyone in the district and can reach beyond the district as far as 100 miles from the site of the proposed testimony ("bulge" service). When authorized by statute, federal subpoenas may reach even further.[1] There is also a broad statute that authorizes a subpoena requiring any U.S. "national or resident" in a foreign country to return and appear at trial if the court finds her testimony is "necessary in the interest of justice" and cannot be obtained "in admissible form" without her appearance. This provision is seldom used in civil suits because the testimony of such a person can be more easily had in admissible form by deposition taken abroad by commission or letter rogatory.[2]

First factor— amenability to process: civil cases

If the declarant is within geographical reach, a party offering her statement usually cannot satisfy the unavailability requirement without trying to subpoena her. Of course being nearby doesn't mean the

---

§8.66   1. *See* FRE 45(b) (subpoena may be served within district or within 100 miles of place of deposition, hearing, or trial); 15 U.S.C. §23 (service in government antitrust enforcement actions).

2. *See* 28 U.S.C. §1783(a), construed in United States v. Johnson, 735 F.2d 1200 (9th Cir. 1984). *See also* FRCP 32(a)(3) (deposition usable if witness is out of country or more than 100 miles from trial unless absence "procured" by offering party); FRCP 28 (depositions abroad by commission or letter rogatory).

witness can be served. If she evades the process server and frustrates good-faith efforts (designed to obtain her attendance, not prove her unavailability), it is fair to conclude that the proponent could not obtain her attendance. That makes her unavailable (unless the deposition requirement applies), and the same is true if she is served but refuses to appear.[3]

There are three situations in federal civil suits where the declarant is at least potentially unavailable because her presence cannot be obtained by subpoena. She is outside the district and more than 100 miles from court (unless a special statute applies); she is a foreign national living abroad; she cannot be found and served or refuses to appear after being served. "Potentially unavailable" is the right term because a court might require a party offering her statement to make further efforts, but often such efforts are not considered and the declarant is found unavailable.[4]

First factor (again)— amenability to process: criminal cases

In criminal cases the subpoena power of state courts of general jurisdiction usually runs throughout the state. In federal court, the power runs throughout the nation.[5] Both the government and the defense can invoke this power, the defendant's right being secured by the compulsory process clause of the Sixth Amendment. A federal court has statutory authority to secure the release of an incarcerated person to obtain his testimony: The mechanism is a writ of habeas corpus ad testificandum, and it makes no difference whether the person is in state or federal prison.[6] Under the same broad statute that applies in civil cases, a court may subpoena a U.S. "national or resident" in a foreign country to appear in a criminal trial if his testimony is "necessary in the interest of justice," and here the statute is not qualified by a phrase excusing the need to return if a deposition may be had.

In criminal cases too, being within geographical reach does not mean one may be served. Here too the party who wants to offer a statement under FRE 804 must make a good-faith effort to subpoena the declarant, meaning one designed to obtain his attendance (not show his unavailability) and must pay necessary expenses.[7] It is fair to

---

3. Lloyd v. American Export Lines, Inc., 580 F.2d 1179, 1184 (3d Cir. 1978) (unavailability shown where extensive efforts failed), *cert. denied*, 439 U.S. 969.

4. Hangarter v. Provident Life and Acc. Ins. Co., 373 F.3d 998, 1019 (9th Cir. 2004) (in suit tried in California, admitting deposition of Alabama resident; beyond subpoena); United States v. Samaniego, 345 F.3d 1280, 1283 (11th Cir. 2003) (admitting statement under against-interest exception; declarant was citizen of Panama living there, hence beyond subpoena).

5. *See* FRCrimP 17(e)(1) (subpoena for trial or hearing may be served any place in country).

6. *See* 28 U.S.C. §2241 (federal courts may issue writ of habeas corpus, which can reach prisoner if "necessary to bring him to court to testify"); Ballard v. Spradley, 557 F.2d 476, 479-480 (5th Cir. 1977) (authority reaches persons in state custody).

7. United States v. Edwards, 469 F.2d 1362, 1368-1369 (5th Cir. 1972) (refusal to return witness on ground of excessive expense is not due diligence); Government of Virgin Islands v. Aquino, 378 F.2d 540, 549-552 (3d Cir. 1967) (unavailability of rape victim not shown where she might voluntarily return if expenses are paid).

conclude, however, that the proponent cannot obtain his attendance if the declarant evades service by hiding from the marshal.[8]

For statements offered against a criminal defendant, the question whether the prosecutor tried hard enough to subpoena the declarant is complicated by two related factors. One is that the prosecuting authority has resources to help locate and serve someone and the power to arrest (enforce a subpoena) that private parties lack. The other is that there is a constitutional obligation to obtain live testimony, at least when the prosecutor would invoke the former testimony exception. These factors mean more is expected from the prosecutor than from the defense. In some settings it matters whether the source of the duty is the Constitution or FRE 804(a)(5), but they aim at the same end, and for the most part it is not useful to distinguish the duty imposed by one from the duty imposed by the other. The leading cases on the constitutional front are the decisions in *Barber* and *Roberts*. *Barber* means at least that someone is not unavailable for purposes of using her former testimony merely because she is incarcerated outside the district. *Roberts*, largely eclipsed by *Crawford* in its general approach to confrontation, is probably still authoritative in interpreting the unavailability standard for former testimony, but its holding on this matter is harder to interpret: It appears to say that the prosecutor need not follow up stale leads that are distinctly unpromising.[9]

When the prosecutor offers a statement under FRE 804, unavailability is not shown just because the speaker was served with a subpoena, and the prosecutor must also take reasonable steps to secure attendance and to enforce the subpoena.[10] Truly evasive witnesses can be unavailable even to the government, and hypothetical measures that might conceivably succeed are beyond the government's obligation.[11]

If the proponent cannot subpoena the declarant, he might still be available under FRE 804(a)(5) if his presence can be obtained by "other reasonable means." In civil cases, at least in theory a party may be expected to have tried to persuade a person to appear voluntarily. And a court could expect the proponent to offer to pay travel and maintenance expenses. The reality is different if the proponent offers a deposition. In this situation, there is no need to have made such efforts for a witness who cannot be subpoenaed. For other statements offered

Second factor— prospect of inducing declarant to appear

---

8. *See* United States v. Flenoid, 949 F.2d 970, 972-973 (8th Cir. 1991) (defendant tried to serve witness at last known address, made other attempts, exhausted all leads).

9. Barber v. Page, 390 U.S. 719, 723-724 (1968); Ohio v. Roberts, 448 U.S. 56 (1980). *See also* §8.88, *infra*.

10. United States v. Quinn, 901 F.2d 522, 524-529 (6th Cir. 1990) (started too late, did too little).

11. Ewing v. Winans, 749 F.2d 607, 612-613 (10th Cir. 1984) (prosecutor made diligent attempts to subpoena witness who played cat-and-mouse by moving without notice, giving vague instructions on new address, lying about where she was, fleeing efforts to serve her); Ward v. United States, 694 F.2d 654, 666 & n.23 (11th Cir. 1983) (witness escaped from state custody was unavailable).

under FRE 804(b), courts sometime force the proponent to show more than that the declarant is beyond reach of subpoena, but not often.[12]

In criminal cases the phrase "other reasonable means" indicates an obligation to go beyond a subpoena. Again more is expected from a prosecutor than is expected from the defense. A modern examination of the constitutional obligation appears in *Mancusi v. Stubbs,* where the Court decided the confrontation clause did not require a state to try to obtain the presence of a declarant permanently residing in Sweden.[13] *Stubbs* limits the constitutional obligation of state prosecutors but does not directly apply to federal prosecutors (the statute construed in the case now lets federal courts subpoena Americans outside the country). *Stubbs* implies that the prosecuting authority need not try to bring in a declarant who is abroad and beyond subpoena, but there are indications that the duty of the state to bring in witnesses goes further than *Stubbs* suggests. In the usual case where the offense took place in the jurisdiction and the witness was once present and might have been detained or encouraged to remain, the fact that he is abroad and beyond reach of subpoena may not show unavailability. A state must defend its action in letting him go and perhaps show efforts to encourage his return by offering to pay expenses.[14] Arguably, important witnesses should not be viewed as unavailable unless the prosecutor cannot obtain their return by extradition.[15]

The "reasonable means" open to the prosecutor also relates to steps that could be taken early to secure the declarant at trial. The federal government can arrest and detain a material witness until it gets his testimony, although the statute says he must be released if his testimony "can adequately be secured by deposition" and further detention is not "necessary to prevent a failure of justice."[16] And the government may take other steps early to ensure a witness is available for trial.[17]

---

12. Kirk v. Raymark Industries, Inc., 61 F.3d 147, 164-165 (3d Cir. 1995) (in Pennsylvania trial, error to admit testimony in another suit by Nebraska doctor; plaintiff did not offer fee, request attendance).

13. Mancusi v. Stubbs, 408 U.S. 204 (1972). *But see* 28 U.S.C. §1783(a) (amended language suggests that federal court may subpoena someone to appear in state court).

14. *See* United States v. Losada, 674 F.2d 167, 172 (2d Cir. 1982) (government made "reasonable attempt"), *cert. denied,* 457 U.S. 1125; United States v. Mann, 590 F.2d 361, 367 (1st Cir. 1978) (where witness is beyond jurisdiction, government must show diligent effort to secure voluntary return).

15. *See* United States v. Casamento, 887 F.2d 1141, 1169-1170 (2d Cir. 1989), *cert. denied,* 495 U.S. 958; United States v. Squella-Avendano, 478 F.2d 433, 439 (5th Cir. 1973) (both saying witness could not be extradited to this country).

16. *See* 18 U.S.C. §3149 (authorizing detention of material witness who cannot be deposed); FRCrimP 46(g) (court to supervise and eliminate unnecessary detention of witnesses). Arrest and incarceration are possible. *See* United States v. Anfield, 539 F.2d 674, 677 (9th Cir. 1976).

17. United States v. Eufrancio-Torres, 890 F.2d 266, 270-271 (10th Cir. 1989) (government detained aliens for weeks, then deposed and released them, but asked them to return and told them how to get money; government used reasonable means), *cert. denied,* 494 U.S. 1008; United States v. Mann, 590 F.2d 361, 366 (1st Cir. 1978) (government released foreign juvenile co-offender who was principal witness, and she returned to Australia; government should have put her in lesser custody or supplied maintenance and retained passport and ticket).

Where a prosecutor mishandles a witness so he disappears or gets beyond reach of subpoena, arguably she has failed to pursue "reasonable means" to secure his attendance, as some cases conclude as a matter of constitutional law.[18] Reasonableness should be a function of taking ordinary care, considering the foreseeable importance of the testimony of the witness and the nature and degree of risk that he will disappear unless restrained or otherwise kept in view.[19]

Even if the declarant cannot be brought by subpoena or persuaded to appear, she is still not necessarily unavailable under FRE 804(a)(5). For purposes of offering dying statements or those that fit the against-interest or family history exceptions, such a declarant is only unavailable if her "testimony" could not be obtained. The intent is to force the proponent to take her deposition in preference to offering such a statement and (if it was taken) to offer it instead.[20]

Third factor— effort to depose the declarant

The "reasonable means" clause *enlarges* the obligation of the proponent to try to secure live testimony *beyond* simply trying to subpoena the witness. Fairly read, the same clause also *reduces* this obligation, meaning that the proponent need not make efforts that are likely to be unproductive or very costly.[21]

First limiting factor—reasonable means standard

This reasonableness standard implies that the offering party may satisfy the unavailability criteria without trying to serve the declarant if it can be shown that he cannot be found, which suggests that the party should be excused from pursuing other means to secure his testimony, including a deposition.[22] Read in conjunction with the "procurement or wrongdoing" clause at the end of FRE 804(a), the reasonableness clause implies that if the offering party shows his adversary is responsible for the disappearance of the declarant, or for the fact that he cannot be found, less in the way of efforts should be considered sufficient (a point explored further below). Finally, the reasonableness standard suggests that the stakes in suit, the relative resources of the parties, the importance of declarant's statement, the foreseeability of need for the statement, and the relative expense and difficulties that

---

18. United States v. Rothbart, 653 F.2d 462, 464-465 (10th Cir. 1981) (government did not provide notice or proffer expenses); United States v. Mann, 590 F.2d 361, 365-368 (1st Cir. 1978) (government should have supplied maintenance or placed witness in lesser custody while retaining passport and tickets).

19. United States v. Mathis, 550 F.2d 180, 181-182 (4th Cir. 1976) (admitting prior testimony by witness who was inadvertently released and could not be found; prison official did not know she was needed as witness), *cert. denied*, 429 U.S. 1107.

20. Campbell by Campbell v. Coleman Co., 786 F.2d 892, 895-896 (8th Cir. 1986) (error to admit against-interest statements; proponent had taken deposition).

21. *See* United States v. Johnson, 735 F.2d 1200, 1202-1203 (9th Cir. 1984) (admitting deposition of ambassador to Italy; court need not subpoena citizen abroad if deposition would satisfy interests of justice).

22. *See* United States v. Lopez, 777 F.2d 543, 553-554 (10th Cir. 1985) (defendant need not have subpoenaed witness who failed to appear and was indicted for jumping bail).

would be encountered in securing the trial or deposition testimony should all be considered in deciding whether the offering party made enough effort to obtain that testimony.[23]

Second limiting factor— procurement or wrongdoing

Under the last sentence of FRE 804(a), one is not unavailable if his absence or other form of unavailability was caused by "the procurement or wrongdoing" of the party offering his statement, if the purpose of the latter was to keep the witness from "attending or testifying."

Intimidates, kills, kidnaps, hides

Pretty clearly the clause means that the proponent of a statement cannot claim that the declarant is unavailable if the proponent intimidates the declarant so he refuses to testify, or kills him to silence him, or kidnaps or hides him to block process.[24] Indeed, in many of these cases the proponent's behavior benefits *the other side*, as the forfeiture exception in FRE 804(b)(6) allows the other side to offer statements by the declarant.[25] And if one party blocks another's attempt to serve or secure the attendance of a witness, the party thus thwarted has a strong argument that the person is unavailable and should not have to prove efforts to overcome the obstruction.[26]

Mere negligence

Mere negligence or carelessness by a party in letting someone slip away and get beyond reach of process is probably not "procurement or wrongdoing." Those words, coupled with the reference to "purpose," reach only behavior amounting to a purposeful attempt to deprive the factfinder of testimony. But in criminal cases the government is in a special position: The confrontation clause probably imposes a higher standard, and government negligence in letting a witness slip away prevents it from claiming he is unavailable for purposes of FRE 804.[27] Still, government acts that are responsible attempts to achieve other ends, and not purposeful efforts to make the speaker unavailable, are not procurement or wrongdoing.[28]

23. United States v. Pena-Gutierrez, 222 F.3d 1080, 1086 (9th Cir. 2000) (government had no indication that witness deported to Mexico would not willingly return), *cert denied*, 531 U.S. 1057; United States v. Olafson, 213 F.3d 435, 442 (9th Cir. 2000) (prosecutors need not depose witnesses released to return to Mexico), *cert. denied*, 531 U.S. 914; Government of Virgin Islands v. Aquino, 378 F.2d 540, 549-552 (3d Cir. 1967) (balance cost and difficulty in returning witness against significance of her presence).

24. United States v. Pizarro, 717 F.2d 336, 350-351 (7th Cir. 1983) (rejecting claim that defense procured unavailability of witness by making threats), *cert. denied*, 471 U.S. 1139.

25. *See* the discussion in §8.78, *infra*.

26. *See* Motes v. United States, 178 U.S. 458, 468-474 (1900) (if disappearance resulted from "suggestion, procurement, or act" by defendant, government might use preliminary hearing testimony).

27. Motes v. United States, 178 U.S. 458, 467-474 (1900) (cannot admit preliminary hearing testimony by one who escaped due to federal negligence).

28. United States v. Seijo, 595 F.2d 116, 119-120 (2d Cir. 1979) (procurement or wrongdoing requires purpose; government did what it could to hold aliens).

§8.67   —Trauma and Psychological Unavailability; Child Abuse Victims

In child abuse trials, federal and state statutes provide that the victim is unavailable if testifying would likely result in severe trauma or she simply cannot testify in a courtroom. (Typically such statutes apply as well to other children who are eyewitnesses to abuse, but for ease in discussion we refer to victims.) In this setting of "psychological" unavailability or necessity, the statutes generally create hearsay exceptions for statements describing abuse or contemplate resort to a catchall exception, and also provide for remote testimony by the victim using one-way or two-way video monitor systems, and for special videotaped depositions for use at trial.[1] In 1990 Congress enacted a statute authorizing remote testimony and videotaped depositions in federal child abuse prosecutions if the victim is psychologically unavailable.[2]

Any finding of psychological unavailability must rest on a case-specific inquiry. In the *Craig* case in 1990, the Supreme Court approved expert testimony to show a child would be seriously traumatized by testifying and said the finding could be made in a special hearing without calling her. Earlier the Court had condemned blanket policies shielding such witnesses, emphasizing that while face-to-face presence might upset truthful rape victims or abused children, it might also "confound and undo the false accuser, or reveal the child coached by a malevolent adult."[3] But *Craig* held that psychological necessity can justify protecting a child victim by letting her testify from another room by closed-circuit television. The judge must make particularized findings that the child would be "traumatized, not by the courtroom generally, but by the presence of the defendant," and would suffer "serious emotional distress" (hence judges must distinguish between good and bad effects of physical confrontation).[4]

Craig: case-specific inquiry required

Drafted with *Craig* in mind, the federal statute contemplates particularized findings that the child cannot testify because of fear, emotional trauma, mental or other infirmity, or conduct by defendant or defense counsel. To authorize videotaped depositions, the court must make a preliminary finding that the child "is likely to be unable to testify" in

§8.67   1. This section discusses the unavailability that triggers resort to other measures. On remote testimony and use at trial of videotaped depositions, *see* §8.70, *infra*.

2. *See* 18 U.S.C. §3509 (live testimony by two-way closed circuit television; videotaped depositions).

3. Maryland v. Craig, 497 U.S. 836 (1990) (court made specific finding that precaution was necessary to prevent "emotional distress"); Coy v. Iowa, 487 U.S. 1012 (1988) (one-way screen kept 13-year-old girls describing sexual assault from seeing defendant while he could see them).

4. *See* United States v. Bordeaux, 400 F.3d 548, 552 (8th Cir. 2005) (error to let child testify by two-way monitor; *Craig* requires fear of defendant, not fear of courtroom; fear of both is not enough); Price v. Commonwealth, 31 S.W.3d 885, 893 (Ky. 2000) (defendant's 11-year-old stepdaughter not shown to be unavailable by social worker's comment that she would be "more traumatized" than average child); State v. Bray, 535 S.E.2d 636, 640 (N.C. 2000) (failure to make specific findings required reversal and new trial).

the courtroom; there is to be a followup finding at the time of trial that she is still "unable to testify," in which case the deposition may be admitted. To authorize remote testimony by two-way closed-circuit television (court can see and hear child; she can see and hear court), the court must make "findings on the record" and may question the minor on the record in chambers or another "comfortable place" in the presence of counsel for all sides with an adult attendant providing emotional support.[5]

Child need not be questioned

The necessary findings may rest on direct questioning of the child, but neither *Craig* nor the statute requires it. If the prosecutor hopes she can testify in court, there is likely to be a preliminary examination where she does testify in court or in chambers: Such cases often raise "competency" issues, and the federal statute provides for competency hearings if supported by "compelling reasons" (but children are "presumed competent" and "age alone" is not reason for inquiry).[6] For a very young child, one question is whether she can make herself understood and commit herself to speak truthfully. Another is whether the process will be unduly traumatic (making her unavailable despite contrary hopes and assessments), and lurking in the background is the further question whether her testimony could be credited. Preliminary hearings let courts decide these points on the basis of what amounts to a live test, and often the parties stipulate that the child is or is not competent because the demonstration leaves little doubt.[7]

In practice, competency issues overlap issues of psychological trauma because the child may be unable to answer questions, or may be too mortified by the subject or intimidated by the setting to give useful evidence.[8] But there is no thought that incompetency blocks use of an out-of-court statement, deposition, or even remote trial testimony if the only ground of incompetency is that the child cannot behave appropriately or make useful statements in the courtroom itself.[9]

---

5. *See* 18 U.S.C. §3509(b)(1)(B) (testimony by two-way video monitor), (b)(2)(B) (deposition), and (i) (adult attendant).

6. *See* 18 U.S.C. §3509(c) (without jury, court talks to child on basis of questions submitted by both sides; counsel may put questions if she will not suffer trauma; questions to be appropriate to "age and developmental level" on unrelated subjects, focusing on "ability to understand and answer").

7. The unavailability requirement protects the party against whom hearsay is offered (hearsay that cannot be tested). In abuse cases, defendants may prefer depositions or statements over live testimony by a child with appeal. When defendants oppose arguments that she is unavailable, often the position is that she is not credible, that live questioning is critical, or that neither testimony nor statements should be admitted.

8. *See* McGriff v. State, 781 A.2d 534, 543 (Del. 2001) (five-year-old girl with IQ of 55 found unavailable, for purposes of victim hearsay exception; unable to testify about what happened).

9. *See* 18 U.S.C. §3509(c) (deferring to FRE 601 on competency). *And see* People v. District Court (Summit County), 791 P.2d 682 (Colo. 1990) (inability of four-year-old to distinguish truth from falsehood did not make her incompetent); People v. District Court (El Paso County), 776 P.2d 1083, 1087 (Colo. 1989) (incompetency to testify does not require excluding statements).

When a youthful victim would be traumatized by testifying in court, showing psychological unavailability usually involves and probably requires expert testimony.[10] Abuse victims often suffer what amounts to ongoing trauma typified by nightmares, mistrust of adults (or adult men), behavioral difficulties at home and school indicating some regression from prior development, and sometimes other problems (bedwetting and sleep disorders).[11] These symptoms help experts conclude that a testimony from the child would be impossible or damaging—that she simply could not testify or would suffer serious harm if she did.[12]

FRE 804(b)(1)

   (b) Hearsay exceptions. The following are not excluded by the hearsay rule if the declarant is unavailable as a witness:

   (1) Former testimony. Testimony given as a witness at another hearing of the same or a different proceeding, or in a deposition taken in compliance with law in the course of the same or another proceeding, if the party against whom the testimony is now offered, or, in a civil action or proceeding, a predecessor in interest, had an opportunity and similar motive to develop the testimony by direct, cross, or redirect examination.

---

§8.68   Former Testimony—Rationale and Requirements

FRE 804(b)(1) creates an exception for prior testimony by someone who is unavailable at trial where two conditions are satisfied. First, the exception only reaches testimony given in a proceeding. Second, the party against whom that testimony is now offered (or sometimes "a predecessor in interest") must have had an opportunity and similar motive to "develop" the testimony by examining the witness at the earlier time. In criminal cases, use of the former testimony exception

---

10. *See* 18 U.S.C. §3509(b)(1) & (b)(2) (child unavailable if there is "substantial likelihood, established by expert testimony," of emotional trauma); United States v. Moses, 137 F.3d 894, 899 (6th Cir. 1998) (statute requires expert testimony to establish trauma).

11. *See* People v. Fasy, 829 P.2d 1314 (Colo. 1992) (expert describes symptoms of sleeplessness, nightmares, vomiting, stomachaches, and headaches).

12. People v. Newbrough, 803 P.2d 155 (Colo. 1990) (finding six-year-old girl "medically unavailable" where psychologists said testifying would have "lasting effect"; nightmares, schoolwork and behavior problems; she wept and vomited when asked about testifying); Connecticut v. Bonello, 554 A.2d 277 (Conn. 1989) (approving videotaped testimony by five-year-old; social worker said child viewed defendant as authority, would have trouble testifying in front of him, and excluding him would lead to more accurate testimony; child suffered "hyperactivity and anxiety" and would be confused and intimidated by defendant), *cert. denied*, 490 U.S. 1082.

against the accused raises constitutional issues, and these are noted at the end of this section.

The exception may be justified on traditional bases of necessity and trustworthiness. There is necessity because the declarant is unavailable, and testimony that fits the exception is trustworthy because the witness was under oath and could be questioned—usually having been subject to cross-examination by the very party against whom the testimony is now offered. It is the absence of demeanor evidence that most sharply distinguishes former testimony from live testimony.

The exception reaches only testimony given in a "hearing or a proceeding" or a deposition taken "in the course of a proceeding" (using the words of the Rule but compressing for clarity). The term "proceeding" carries broad meaning and embraces any official inquiry conducted in a manner authorized by law, whether judicial, administrative, legislative, investigative, or inquisitorial. The term "testimony" reaches statements that are sworn, subject to penalty of perjury, made in response to questions on the record (transcribed stenographically or electronically), all pursuant to legally authorized routine.

Trial, deposition, hearing, grand jury
Putting aside the question whether the party against whom the testimony is offered (or a predecessor in interest) had opportunity and motive to develop it, the exception embraces testimony taken in a prior trial, deposition, preliminary hearing, grand jury inquest, and other proceedings.[1] The exception does not embrace affidavits, even though prepared for use in proceedings, since affidavits are not testimony that may be developed by examination, nor statements (sworn or not) to law enforcement officers during investigations, which are not "proceedings."[2]

Motive and opportunity
Prior testimony fits the exception only when offered against someone who had "opportunity and similar motive" on the earlier occasion "to develop the testimony by direct, cross, or redirect examination." Clearly an opportunity is enough, and prior testimony need not be excluded merely because the objecting party did not take advantage of it.[3] It does not matter that prior questioning was by direct examination, so long as that was appropriate to the occasion and purpose of the questioner, since a party who calls a witness usually has no need of

---

§8.68   1. *See* Bertrand v. State, 214 S.W.3d 822 (Ark. 2005) (suppression hearing); State v. Finney, 591 S.E.2d 863, 868 (N.C. 2004) (voir dire hearing); Foster-Glocester Regional School Committee v. Board of Review, 854 A.2d 1008, 1017 (R.I. 2004) (arbitration hearing); United States v. Brooks, 966 F.2d 1500, 1505 (D.C. Cir. 1992) (prior trial); Mutuelles Unies v. Kroll & Linstrom, 957 F.2d 707, 713 (9th Cir. 1992) (deposition); United States v. Miller, 904 F.2d 65, 67-68 (D.C. Cir. 1990) (grand jury); King v. State, 780 P.2d 943, 955-956 (Wyo. 1989) (preliminary hearing).

2. *See* United States v. Walker, 557 F.2d 741, 743 n.2 (10th Cir. 1977); NLRB v. McClure Assocs., Inc., 556 F.2d 725, 726 (4th Cir. 1977).

3. United States v. McClellan, 868 F.2d 210, 215 (7th Cir. 1989) (what counts is motive rather than actual challenge); DeLuryea v. Winthrop Labs., 697 F.2d 222, 226-227 (8th Cir. 1983) (what counts is opportunity and motivation).

cross-examination and has enough opportunity fairly to develop the knowledge of the witness without using other questioning techniques.

Where the parties and issues in the prior and present proceedings are identical, testimony from the prior proceeding is likely to fit the exception. Even changes in issues or parties do not necessarily require exclusion.[4] Thus testimony from one tort suit against a railroad arising out of a grade crossing accident may be admitted against the railroad in a later suit by another claimant who had another accident at the same place.[5] And it does not matter that the same lawyer did not represent the party in the prior proceedings or that one of the suits was civil and the other criminal.

Sometimes differences in issues or parties are important enough to mandate exclusion of prior testimony. That happens where the issues are so different that the present party could not or would not have wanted to put the questions it would want to put now.[6]

The exception can be used by both prosecution and defense for testimony taken in a prior trial for the same offense. In other settings, applying the exception is more difficult. Clearly the government cannot invoke it to offer prior grand jury testimony because defendants have no right to attend or question witnesses.[7] The government might make other uses of such testimony, and sometimes can resort to other exceptions, but not the one for former testimony.[8] Can the defense offer grand jury testimony in a criminal case? Putting aside procedural complications of grand jury secrecy and discoverability, the problem is one of motivation: The government has little incentive to press witnesses in grand jury proceedings if they say something helpful to the defense, or to try to catch them if they perjure themselves or say things that conflict with the government's theory. The purpose is to get an indictment, which does not require careful development of its case or pursuit of points that may become crucial at trial. Of course the government's purpose points in the same general direction on both occasions, but on

Criminal cases

---

4. Shanklin v. Norfolk Southern Ry. Co., 369 F.3d 978, 990 (6th Cir. 2004) (deposition by railroad president in another suit arising out of accident at different crossing; president and lawyers had "opportunity and a nearly identical motive" to develop testimony in earlier case); United States v. Reed, 227 F.3d 763, 769-770 (7th Cir. 2000) (admitting prior trial testimony against defendant, although second trial included charges against another defendant).

5. Bailey v. Southern Pac. Transp. Co., 613 F.2d 1385, 1390 (5th Cir. 1980) (prior plaintiff said signal failure caused collision; railroad motivated to oppose this theory; same here), *cert. denied*, 449 U.S. 836.

6. United States v. Fischl, 16 F.3d 927, 928 (8th Cir. 1994) (government did not have similar motive to develop testimony given by codefendant *F* at detention hearing); United States v. North, 910 F.2d 843, 905-906 (D.C. Cir. 1990) (excluding committee testimony; congressional political and legislative goals differ from those of special prosecutor), *cert. denied*, 500 U.S. 941.

7. *See* United States v. Marks, 585 F.2d 164, 166-170 (6th Cir. 1978); Young v. United States, 406 F.2d 960, 961 & n.2 (D.C. Cir. 1968).

8. The government can use grand jury testimony to refresh memory, or as recorded recollection. It might also fit FRE 801(d)(1)(A) if the witness testifies inconsistently or claims lack of memory.

balance the differences between them are too great to support a conclusion that prior questioning adequately tested what the grand jury witness said. The cases are in disarray, with some requiring exclusion of grand jury testimony offered by the defense, some approving its use, some avoiding the question, and some suggesting that in particular cases it might be admissible if government questioning was extensive.[9]

Preliminary hearing testimony
Whether preliminary hearing testimony in a criminal proceeding fits the exception is another hard question. Both the government and the defense have a chance to call and examine witnesses, so it is plausible to suppose the exception might cover such testimony if offered by either side. And in one sense the issue in the preliminary hearing is the same as the issue at trial—did defendant commit the crime? But in another sense the issues are vastly different, since the question in the preliminary hearing is not guilt or innocence but whether defendant should be tried. And the motivation of the parties differs for this very reason.

For defendants, usually the best strategy at a preliminary hearing is not to engage in searching cross-examination or call witnesses because even a persuasive refutation is not likely to block a finding of probable cause. And impeaching government witnesses is usually futile, since credibility is considered a trial issue. Usually the wiser strategy is to hold back, avoid preparing witnesses and government lawyers for what is to come, and only to question witnesses when doing so is useful in discovering information. Despite these realities, the greater number of courts hold that the exception reaches preliminary hearing testimony offered against defendants.[10] In net effect, these cases do not so much reflect the realities of defense motivation as seek to shape them, and the outcome is probably affected by the Supreme Court's stand that admitting such testimony does not violate defense confrontation rights if the witness is unavailable.[11] Some authority prefers a case-by-case approach that pays attention to the actual motivation of the defense on the earlier occasion.[12] Since the Rules (including the hearsay doctrine) do not apply in preliminary hearings, much that might be admitted there is not admissible at trial and may be excluded on defense objection. Some authority excludes preliminary hearing testimony offered against the defendant.[13]

9. *Compare* United States v. Foster, 128 F.3d 949, 954-956 (6th Cir. 1997) (should admit against government, which has same motive to develop testimony during a grand jury proceeding) *with* United States v. Omar, 104 F.3d 519, 522 (1st Cir. 1997) (excluding; government does not attack or vouch for grand jury witnesses, and trials are different).

10. State v. Erickson, 241 N.W.2d 854, 862-863 (N.D. 1976); United States v. Allen, 409 F.2d 611, 613 (10th Cir. 1969); Commonwealth v. Mustone, 233 N.E.2d 1 (Mass. 1968).

11. *See* Ohio v. Roberts, 448 U.S. 56 (1980); California v. Green, 399 U.S. 149 (1970) (both rejecting constitutional challenges to preliminary hearing testimony).

12. King v. State, 780 P.2d 943, 955-956 (Wyo. 1989) (adopting case-by-case analysis of motive).

13. State v. Stuart, 695 N.W.2d 259, 265 (Wis. 2005); People v. Fry, 92 P.3d 970 (Colo. 2004); People v. Elisondo, 757 P.2d 675 (Idaho 1988).

The government too is not strongly motivated to question witnesses at preliminary hearings. It can prevail even if the defense attacks or refutes the witness, and even if he disappoints the government. And the government does not ordinarily want to turn the occasion into a full defense discovery opportunity. Hence arguably preliminary hearing testimony does not fit the exception when offered against the prosecutor, but the cases are few and far between.[14]

Depositions taken in criminal cases and offered by the government present special difficulties. As is true in preliminary hearings, here too lack of defense motive to cross-examine and impeach deserves sympathy. If the requirements of FRCrimP 15 are satisfied (the exception refers to depositions "taken in compliance with law") and the witness is unavailable, the question whether to admit the deposition is decided under the former testimony exception. The unavailability requirement is interpreted strictly against the government. It is said that depositions are taken in criminal cases only in "exceptional circumstances," and the mere fact that the government took a deposition raises suspicion that inadequate efforts were made to bring the deponent to trial.[15] But with these qualifications, courts do sometimes admit against defendants depositions taken in criminal actions,[16] and sometimes prior civil depositions too.[17]

Depositions in criminal cases

In civil cases, depositions present the most common instance of former testimony. When offered in the trial of the suit in which they are taken, depositions are admitted if the deponent is unavailable. When offered in the trial of a later suit, a deposition may be admissible if the deponent is unavailable but subject to some additional criteria.

Civil depositions

By its plain language, FRE 804(b)(1) reaches any deposition. But a provision in the Civil Rules governs the admissibility of a deposition taken in the suit in which it is offered: This provision makes the deposition of a party freely admissible against it, allows use of depositions to impeach deponents who testify at trial, and otherwise allows full use of depositions by witnesses who are unavailable (defining concept in terms differing slightly from definition in FRE 804), provided that notice of the deposition was properly given.[18] A deposition is admissible

---

14. *See* United States. v. Bartelho, 129 F.3d 663, 671-673 (1st Cir. 1997) (excluding), *cert. denied*, 525 U.S. 905; State v. Withers, 337 N.E.2d 780, 781 (Ohio 1975) (excluding), *cert. denied*, 424 U.S. 975.

15. Quoted phrase appears in FRCrimP 15(a) and 18 U.S.C. §3503(a). *See* United States v. Mann, 590 F.2d 361 (1st Cir. 1978); Government of Canal Zone v. P (Pinto), 590 F.2d 1344 (5th Cir. 1979).

16. United States v. Yates, 438 F.3d 1307 (11th Cir. 2007) (deposition to be taken abroad); United States v. Kelly, 892 F.2d 255, 262 (3d Cir. 1989) (depositions taken abroad).

17. United States v. Vecchiarello, 569 F.2d 656, 663-665 (D.C. Cir. 1977).

18. *See* FRCP 32(a) (deposition may be offered "against any party who was present or represented" at deposition or had "reasonable notice," if witness was unavailable as defined in the Rule).

in the civil action in which it was taken if it satisfies the Civil Rule, regardless whether the opposing party had motive to cross-examine.[19] And such a deposition is admissible if the deponent is unavailable as the Civil Rule defines that idea, regardless whether he would be unavailable under FRE 804.[20]

If depositions taken in one action are offered in another, the Civil Rules provide nonexclusive criteria that supplement the former testimony exception. Under FRCP 32(a)(4), a deposition may be offered in another suit "involving the same subject matter" and "the same parties or their representatives or successors in interest," in which case the deposition is treated as if taken in the present suit. Under FRE 804(b)(1), a deposition from another suit can be used if the party against whom it is offered (or his predecessor in interest) had adequate motive and opportunity on the other occasion to develop the testimony. Obviously these criteria overlap: Both Rules are potentially available if the deposition is offered against someone who was a party in the other suit or a predecessor in interest, and a suit involving "the same subject matter" under the Civil Rule is likely to be one in which the party had adequate motive and opportunity to question the witness under FRE 804(b)(1). Hence both provisions are likely to be satisfied, or neither.

In most settings, the theme of the former testimony exception is to admit evidence only if the objecting party had motive and opportunity to examine the witness before. But for depositions, whether in present or prior suits, only Alice in Wonderland could think the condition is satisfied. Sometimes everyone knows the deponent will not be available to testify, typically because she lives beyond reach of an ordinary trial subpoena. In this setting, the purpose uppermost in everyone's mind is to make usable evidence. But far more often everyone expects the deponent to testify at trial, and a party whose cause is injured by that testimony is not strongly motivated to confound the witness by impeaching attacks or extensive questioning. In the setting of depositions, courts applying the former testimony exception seem less intent on understanding and reflecting party motivation than in shaping it. The message is that parties should fully examine witnesses in depositions or assume the risk that the deposition will be later admissible.

Crawford issues   Not surprisingly, almost everything that fits the exception—whether we consider testimony in another trial, testimony in depositions, or testimony in other hearings or proceedings—is "testimonial" for purposes of the *Crawford* doctrine. It does not follow that FRE 804(b)(1) cannot be used against the accused, of course: *Crawford* took pains to say

19. *See* Battle ex rel. Battle v. Memorial Hospital, 228 F.3d 544, 551-552 (5th Cir. 2000) (civil deposition is admissible, in action in which it was taken, against party who took it); Re Complaint of Bankers Trust Co., 752 F.2d 874, 887-888 (3d Cir. 1984) (FRE 804 and FRCP 32 are cumulative; deposition admissible if it fits the latter and not the former).

20. Angelo v. Armstrong World Indus., 11 F.3d 957, 963-964 (10th Cir. 1993) (FRCP creates one exception, FRE 804(b)(1) another; offering party can show deponent unavailable under either).

a prior opportunity to cross-examine could satisfy the confrontation clause, provided that the witness is unavailable at trial, and FRE 804 imposes similar requirements. The point to remember is that the constitutional standard is independent of FRE 804, and both the Rule and the Constitution must be satisfied in this context.[21]

§8.69 "Predecessor in Interest" Problem

If *X* is the party against whom prior testimony is offered and he lacked opportunity or motive to examine the testifying witness in the prior proceeding, the exception can apply only if some "predecessor in interest" to X had such opportunity and motive. A close parsing of the language suggests that the exception can only be invoked in civil proceedings. In criminal cases it can apply only if the very party against whom prior testimony is offered had the requisite opportunity and motive.

The predecessor-in-interest proviso presents two interpretive difficulties. First is to figure out what "predecessor in interest" means. Second is to figure out whether the close reading is right—whether the proviso really does apply only in civil cases.

Congress added the proviso. It was fashioned by the House Judiciary Committee, and there is no legislative history to indicate what "predecessor in interest" means, although the apparent intent was to narrow the exception and reject the functional approach proposed by the Advisory Committee out of concerns over fairness.[1] That approach would have admitted prior testimony against a party who lacked opportunity in the prior proceedings to examine the witness if someone in those proceedings had motive and opportunity to do so. Whether the proviso accomplished this narrowing is open to doubt, since a later Senate committee comment suggests that the proviso means little or nothing.[2]

There are a number of possible approaches:

> "Predecessor in interest"

One equates "predecessor in interest" with the larger notion of a "community of interest," which means at least that a government agency that brings an enforcement action is a predecessor in interest to those it seeks to protect, which may be the public in general or some recognizable subgroup. In *Lloyd v. American Export Lines*, seaman Alvarez claimed that shipowner American Export was liable for injuries

> First approach: "community of interest"

---

21. *See* Crawford v. Washington, 541 U.S. 36, 57 (2004), discussed in §§8.84-8.88, *infra*.

§8.69 1. *See* House Report, at 15 (unfair to impose on one party "the responsibility for the manner in which the witness was previously handled" by another, unless predecessor had motive and opportunity to cross-examine before).

2. *See* Senate Report, at 28 (recognizing "considerable merit" in AC's version but agreeing to "predecessor in interest" because difference between the two versions "is not great"); Lloyd v. American Export Lines, Inc., 580 F.2d 1179, 1185 (3d Cir. 1978) (rejecting view that proviso requires privity or common property interest), *cert. denied*, 439 U.S. 969.

sustained in a fight with seaman Lloyd. Alvarez testified, but Lloyd had disappeared. The court refused to let American Export introduce against Alvarez testimony Lloyd gave in Coast Guard proceedings to revoke his seaman's license for assaulting Alvarez, and this ruling was found to be wrong. Preferring a "realistically generous" interpretation and aiming to present a "complete picture," the reviewing court said the Coast Guard was a predecessor in interest to Alvarez.[3] *Lloyd* suggests that in a private suit against a party previously sued in an enforcement action, the latter may offer testimony from the enforcement action.[4]

The outcome is defensible, but the reasoning seems contrived. The government surely did seek to benefit those most likely to be injured by the conduct at issue, but there was no formal connection of the sort suggested by the phrase "predecessor in interest." One reason to allow (even encourage) private followup suits is that the government may not adequately represent potential claimants and does not act solely in their interests. But *Lloyd* focuses on what ought to be the salient question, which is whether someone before had similar motive and adequate opportunity to question the witness.

Lloyd's interpretation of the proviso could extend well beyond enforcement suits. The notion can embrace parties who bring or defend similar claims in different suits or seek to establish or refute the same legal or factual point, which essentially reads the proviso out of the Rule and leads to an exclusive focus on motive and interest.[5] That was the point of the dissenting judge in *Lloyd*, and this result (even if arguably "right") seems indefensible because it gives the "predecessor-in-interest" proviso no meaning, putting too much weight on the Senate Report and not enough on the ordinary meaning of language in the Rule.

Second approach: "privity"   A second approach holds that the predecessor-in-interest proviso alludes to the law of property, contracts, and procedure and means essentially "privity"—an associative notion that is often advanced in defending the conclusion that one person or party is bound by what another has done.[6] In property law, for instance, talk about privity

---

3. Lloyd v. American Export Lines, Inc., 580 F.2d 1179, 1185-1187 (3d Cir. 1978) (interests are claims or demands or desires that humans seek to satisfy individually or in groups or associations; interest of Alvarez and Coast Guard was to determine culpability and exact penalty), *cert. denied*, 439 U.S. 969.

4. In Re Master Key Antitrust Lit., 72 F.R.D. 108, 109-110 (D. Conn. 1976) (defense in private antitrust suit offers testimony from enforcement action that spawned present suits).

5. *See* Horne v. Owens-Corning Fiberglass Corp., 4 F.3d 276, 283 (4th Cir. 1993) (in asbestos suit, admitting depositions of industrial hygienist; privity is not the key; objecting party must show there were not similar motives to cross-examine in prior suits); United States v. McDonald, 837 F.2d 1287, 1290-1293 (5th Cir. 1988) (mail fraud trial; plaintiff in prior suit might be predecessor to government).

6. *See* Lloyd v. American Export Lines, Inc., 580 F.2d 1179, 1191 (3d Cir. 1978) (dissenting opinion argues that "predecessor in interest" means privity), *cert. denied*, 439 U.S. 969; Metropolitan St. R. Co. v. Gumby, 99 F. 192, 198 (2d Cir. 1900) ("mutual or successive relationships to the same rights of property," like donor and donee, lessor and lessee, and joint tenants).

between grantor and grantee helps express the point that a covenant by the former binds the latter, and in procedure the privity between litigants in two suits helps express the point that a judgment in one suit binds a litigant in another. In the setting of the former testimony exception, it might be said that the grantor who testifies in a suit seeking a judgment invalidating a claimed easement over his land is in "privity" with his later grantee, hence that the grantor's testimony in the action should be admissible against the grantee in a later suit raising anew the question of the easement.

Unfortunately "privity" has the drawbacks of being formalistic, often conclusory, and not helpful as test or explanation. To make sense of the notion, privity would have to mean that the prior and present suits involve the property, transaction, or obligation in which the prior and present party are in privity. And since privity as a substantive notion may justify a burden or benefit on Y because X did something or became bound by a judgment, sensibly using the notion in applying the exception would mean X was Y's predecessor in interest (so testimony in an action involving X might be admissible in an action involving Y) but not vice versa (so testimony in an action involving Y would not be admissible in an action involving X).[7]

The term "predecessor in interest" might better be understood in a less technical sense.[8] At least in cases where testimony from enforcement actions is offered in a private suit brought by parties within contemplation of the enforcement action, the proviso should probably require some formal relationship between a litigant in the prior suit and the one against whom the former testimony is offered, as was true in *Lloyd* itself (where the Coast Guard had such a relationship with Alvarez). The only available explanation for the proviso is that Congress thought it unfair to saddle a litigant with testimony from a former case on the basis that someone had similar motive and opportunity to develop the testimony because one litigant's fortunes should not be tied to those of another who happens to have parallel interests.[9] One might do a better job than the other; if the earlier suit went to judgment and a present litigant is not bound by it, the new suit is supposed to be a whole new ballgame. If the prior and the present litigant had important connections with respect to the property,

Third approach: connection and fairness

---

7. *See* Lilly, Introduction to the Law of Evidence 328 (3d ed. 1996) (decedent is predecessor in interest to personal representative, heirs and legatees; not clear that joint interest satisfies proviso).

8. *See* Supermarket of Marlinton v. Meadow Gold Dairies, 71 F.3d 119, 128 (4th Cir. 1995) (should admit against dairies in price-fixing trial testimony from criminal trial of officials in one dairy; privity is not concern; opponent must show there was no similar motive to cross-examine); 2 McCormick, Evidence §308 (6th ed. 2006) (hard to decide treatment of privity relationships; where party itself was in prior suit, it should be "held responsible for previous strategic or tactical judgments," and otherwise quality of prior cross should be "scrutinized more carefully").

9. *See generally* Weissenberger, The Former Testimony Exception: A Study in Rule-making, Judicial Revisionism, and the Separation of Powers, 67 N.C. L. Rev. 295, 301, 313-315 (1989) (proviso requires "formal, legal nexus," and purpose of proviso was to assure fairness).

transaction, or obligation in issue, then it may be fair to admit testimony from the prior suit. One clear example is a post-merger corporate entity: Testimony in a prior suit involving a corporation *J* later merged into corporation *K* should be admissible in a later action involving corporation *K* if both suits involve claims of liability incurred by corporation *J* that were assumed by corporation *K*, where both fairness and a formal notion of privity point toward admitting the testimony.

Only in civil actions

Read literally, the predecessor-in-interest proviso applies only "in a civil action or proceeding." Hence cross-examination by a predecessor suffices only if prior testimony is offered in a civil case. The exception applies in criminal cases only if the very party against whom former testimony is offered had an opportunity and motive to develop it in the prior proceedings. The indicated conclusion is that the exception does not reach prior testimony offered against the government if it did not appear in the prior proceedings,[10] nor prior testimony offered against a defendant who did not appear before.[11] And it would seem that the exception could never be invoked against the prosecutor to admit in a federal trial testimony given in a prior *state* trial, nor invoked against the prosecutor in a state trial, if the state has adopted FRE 804(b)(1), to admit testimony given in a prior federal trial.[12] Given what is known about the purpose (rejecting a purely functional approach), it is impossible to conclude with confidence that this interpretation is wrong.

Some cases, however, favor the view that the defense in a criminal case should be able to use the exception if there was a party in prior proceedings with opportunity and motive similar to the prosecutor's to cross-examine before.[13] A difficulty in this position is the one that comes with attending more to purpose than terms: Congress may have meant what it seems to have said (judging from reports and debates is problematic), and it is at least arguable that prosecutors (like defendants) should be entitled to exclude prior testimony they did not have a chance to test. If it is unfair to saddle defendants with prior testimony that was only tested by some other party, a similar unfairness arises when the prosecutor faces such testimony. Defending the alternative interpretation requires one to ignore the natural meaning of language and suppose that Congress used overbroad terms where

10. United States v. North, 910 F.2d 843, 905-906 (D.C. Cir. 1990) (in trial of NSC officer prosecuted by independent counsel, excluding congressional testimony by other NSC officer offered by defense; Congress and independent counsel are not same party), *cert. denied*, 500 U.S. 941.

11. *See* State v. Hale, 691 N.W.2d 637, 645 (Wis. 2005) (testimony given in trial of co-offender inadmissible here; fact that co-offender could cross-examine does not satisfy defendant's right); United States v. McDonald, 837 F.2d 1287, 1290-1293 (5th Cir. 1988).

12. United States v. Peterson, 100 F.3d 7, 11-12 (2d Cir. 1996) (state grand jury testimony inadmissible when offered against government, which was not party in state proceedings).

13. United States v. McDonald, 837 F.2d 1287, 1290-1293 (5th Cir. 1988) (in mail fraud trial, plaintiff in prior suit might be predecessor in interest to government).

its only concern in criminal cases was to protect defendants. While that happened elsewhere, nothing supports this interpretation here.[14]

§8.70   —Remote and Deposition Testimony by Child Abuse Victims

In trials for abuse of children, state and federal statutes provide for remote testimony by the victim and use at trial of her videotaped depositions.[1] Typically the statutes authorize these measures on the basis of a case-specific finding that she cannot testify in open court (or doing so would bring serious trauma), so she is "psychologically unavailable." Remote testimony means the child testifies from another room by video monitor systems that relay her image and words to the courtroom. Videotaped depositions are substitutes for trial testimony, and from the beginning it is contemplated that they will be used as evidence.

These special measures are not the only differences that distinguish child victims from other witnesses. Drawings, mannequins, and anatomical dolls are used in clinical interviews, and they may become part of the child's testimony as well.[2] Children in abuse cases are usually patients who get counseling and care, and it is sometimes thought that they cannot tell their story in useful ways without immediate emotional support by one of the treating or caretaking adults, who plays a visible supportive (but theoretically passive) role as the child testifies.[3] Also there is some thought that the interests of a child are not adequately represented by the prosecutor, so a guardian ad litem is sometimes needed to represent the child's separate interests.[4] Finally, obvious privacy issues arise when children tell stories of abuse, and

---

14. FRE 803(8)(B) bars police reports "in criminal cases," but the purpose was only to bar use of such reports against defendants, and some cases permit their use against the government. *See* §8.51, *supra.*

§8.70   1. *See generally* Christiansen, The Testimony of Child Witnesses: Fact, Fantasy, and the Influence of Pretrial Interviews, 62 Wash. L. Rev. 705 (1987); Note, The Testimony of Child Victims in Sex Abuse Prosecutions: Two Legislative Innovations, 98 Harv. L. Rev. 806 (1985).

2. 18 U.S.C. §3509(l) (child may use "anatomical dolls, puppets, drawings, mannequins, or any other demonstrative device" when appropriate).

3. The federal statute says a child has the right to be accompanied by an adult attendant for emotional support, that the court may let this person stay "close" to the child and "hold the child's hand" or let her "sit on the adult attendant's lap" during proceedings. The attendant "shall not provide" answers or "otherwise prompt" child, and image of attendant is to be recorded while child testifies. *See* 18 U.S.C. §3509(i).

4. *See* 18 U.S.C. §3509(h) (appointment of guardian ad litem who may attend depositions and proceedings and have access to reports; guardian may seek order authorizing remote testimony or videotaped deposition) (also guardian plays role in preparing victim impact statement for sentencing, and may seek protective orders to guard privacy). *See also* 18 U.S.C. §3509(g) ("multidisciplinary child abuse team" to assist child victims and witnesses).

Remote testimony: *Coy* and *Craig* cases

special measures are taken to protect the child's privacy, although no similar interest has surfaced to protect the privacy of defendants.[5]

The Supreme Court threw cold water on special testimonial measures in the *Coy* case, but gave substantial approval to their careful use in the later decision in the *Craig* case, and the coming of *Crawford* in 2004 probably did not change the picture.[6] *Craig* is a good illustration of the modern method for taking remote testimony by child abuse victims: The child testifies in another room where she is questioned by prosecutor and defense counsel, and one-way closed-circuit television lets defendant and court (judge and trier of fact) watch and listen by video monitor from the courtroom. The federal statute enacted six months after *Craig* authorizes this mechanism, but provides for a two-way video monitor so the child is seen and heard, and she can also see and hear the courtroom.[7] Bringing to the remote room an image of the defendant may be a nod in the direction of *Coy* (face-to-face confrontation ordinarily required), but it seems a tame substitute. Perhaps seeing the image of the defendant prompts a child to recognize the gravity of the situation, but this measure seems unlikely to help appraise her credibility. Even careful camera work cannot effectively convey to the trier in the courtroom the sense that the child is (or is not) looking at the video image of the defendant or the sense that her reactions and expressions are (or are not) somehow related to his televised presence, and this detail is not constitutionally required.[8]

Direct access to counsel

For remote trial testimony, it is important that defendant have direct and immediate access to counsel as questioning proceeds, since continuous contact may be essential for effectively testing the child's testimony. The two-way monitor scheme itself is not enough, and a separate line allowing defendant and counsel to talk privately back and forth is essential.[9]

---

5. *See* 18 U.S.C. §3509(d)-(e) (all public officials, court employees, defendants and defense counsel, and jurors are not to disclose to outsiders documents, name, or information about child; filed documents to be sealed; court may make protective orders and close courtroom to "all persons, including members of the press," if necessary to prevent harm to child or enable her to communicate effectively).

6. *See* Coy v. Iowa, 487 U.S. 1012 (1988); Maryland v. Craig, 497 U.S. 836 (1990), both discussed in §8.91, *infra*.

7. *See* 18 U.S.C. §3509(b)(1) (remote testimony by two-way closed circuit television, which relays to courtroom the image and voice of the child and relays to deposition room "defendant's image, and the voice of the judge"); Maryland v. Craig, 497 U.S. 836, at nn.3-4 (1990) (37 states authorize one-way video systems and 8 require two-way video). *See also* United States v. Garcia, 7 F.3d 885, 888-889 (9th Cir. 1993) (remote testimony by two-way video monitor); People v. Lofton, 740 N.E.2d 782 (Ill. 2000) (cannot block defendant from observing victim as she testifies).

8. Maryland v. Craig, 497 U.S. 836 (1990) (one-way video prevents child witness from seeing defendant, but does not "impinge upon the truth-seeking or symbolic purposes" of confrontation).

9. *See* 18 U.S.C. §3509(b)(1)(D) (defendant shall have "private, contemporaneous communication" with counsel); Maryland v. Craig, 497 U.S. 836 (1990) (defendant in electronic communication with counsel); Price v. Commonwealth, 31 S.W.3d 885, 893 (Ky. 2000) (cannot block defendant from continuous contact with counsel as victim gives remote testimony).

The videotape deposition differs from remote testimony in that the former happens before trial while the latter is live. Hence depositions may be less immediate and vivid, but modern cases approve their use.[10] Since they are substitutes for live testimony, it seems important that the court be available to rule on objections and difficulties as they arise.[11] Otherwise the parties may be tempted to seek delays or recesses or to press forward quickly, and such tactics may produce distortions if the court cannot resolve disputes quickly.

Videotaped deposition

Typically lawyers question the child during videotaped depositions, as the federal statute envisions, but they can agree to use intermediaries (such as psychologists).[12] Probably the court cannot select questioners to act for defense counsel over objection, since questioning crucial witnesses for the prosecution is central to the role of counsel. It seems unlikely that defense counsel would resort to outrageous behavior because children are appealing witnesses and such tactics are likely to anger juries, but courts can protect children against abusive tactics by defense counsel.[13]

Although tensions between child and defendant are part of the emotional trauma the child suffers, thus reason to order a videotaped deposition, it should not be assumed that defendants should be excluded from the deposition room. The right of face-to-face confrontation emphasized in *Coy* applies to depositions too, since they are substitutes for courtroom testimony. Excluding the defendant is justified only if the court finds specifically that his presence would harm the child or keep her from testifying.[14] Here too, the federal statute apparently seeks to accommodate the interest in face-to-face confrontation by a two-way monitoring scheme that puts the live image of the defendant into the deposition room. If the defendant is excluded, he must have a way to monitor the testimony as the deposition proceeds and to be in immediate contact with the person questioning the child on his

Defendants excluded?

---

10. People v. Thomas, 803 P.2d 144 (Colo. 1990) (videotaped depositions by children aged three and four); Connecticut v. Bonello, 554 A.2d 277 (Conn. 1989) (videotaped testimony by five-year-old victim), *cert. denied*, 490 U.S. 1082.

11. *See* 18 U.S.C. §3509(b)(2) (judge "shall preside" at videotaped deposition and "rule on all questions as if at trial") (statute then lists the "only other" people to be "present," suggesting that presiding means being present too).

12. *See* People v. Thomas, 803 P.2d 144, 151 (Colo. 1990) (by agreement, each party selected therapist to put questions in videotaped depositions); People v. Newbrough, 803 P.2d 155 (Colo. 1990) (approving videotaped deposition where therapist questioned child; defense did not object at time).

13. The federal statute contemplates that conduct by defense counsel might make the child unable to testify, but it also provides (both for remote testimony and depositions) that lawyers for the government and the defense are to be present to question the child. 18 U.S.C. §3509(b)(1) and (2).

14. *See* 18 U.S.C. §3509(b)(2) (court may exclude defendant if reason for deposition is that child cannot testify in his presence; if court excludes defendant from deposition room, it shall provide for televised image of defendant into that room).

behalf (usually his lawyer). Otherwise information essential to effective questioning may be lost at crucial moments.[15]

The videotape medium has some troublesome aspects. Although less vivid than remote trial testimony, videotape presentations are more vivid than transcripts, which are the conventional and most common way of proving former testimony. And videotaped depositions offer a chance for editing: Doing so might remove inadmissible answers, or improper questions or arguments or other behavior that would be objectionable at trial, and in that sense editing might help. But editing invites efforts to clip and rearrange to capture highlights or make a better presentation or otherwise tinker with the raw material for essentially rhetorical purposes. Editing holds some promise but invites misuse and serious dispute.[16]

All videotaped statements comply

The standards for videotaped depositions set by the federal statute are detailed and thoughtful. They could be evaded if prosecutors made their own videotapes of child victims being interviewed by social workers or therapists or others, offering them under other exceptions such as the one for medical statements or the catchall. To give meaning to the statutory standards, it would be wise to insist that all videotaped statements by child victims comply with the statutory requirements.[17]

In addition to the problem of deciding whether a child victim can endure the trauma of testifying, remote testimony and videotaped depositions raise a number of serious difficulties.[18]

Competency issues

One problem involves competency issues. The federal statute contemplates a hearing on competency, and even the possibility of psychological examinations. But the statute defers to FRE 601, which almost never bars a witness from testifying. In extreme cases where a court decides a child cannot make herself understood, or distinguish fact from fantasy or truth from lies, or cannot make an intelligible commitment to speak truthfully, probably the child's testimony should be excluded (including remote testimony and depositions). But the extreme case is rare, and even a finding of incompetency to testify does not mean the child's out-of-court statements cannot be admitted.[19]

---

15. *See* 18 U.S.C. §3509(b)(2) (if defendant is excluded from deposition, shall have "a means of private, contemporaneous communication" with counsel).

16. The federal statute provides for preservation of the videotape, so presumably tampering can be detected. *See* 18 U.S.C. §3509(b)(2)(B) (record of deposition shall be preserved on videotape and stenographically recorded; videotape shall be lodged with clerk and made available for viewing by parties).

17. *See* People v. Newbrough, 803 P.2d 155, 161-162 (Colo. 1990) (cannot admit videotaped interview between therapist and six-year-old; it did not comply with state videotape deposition statute).

18. *See* the discussion of this point in §8.67, *supra*.

19. *See* People v. District Court (Summit County), 791 P.2d 682, 684-685 (Colo. 1990) (four-year-old, who said it would be true to say shirt was red even if it was blue, was competent under statute requiring child to be able to describe events in age-appropriate language); 18 U.S.C. §3509(c) (children are presumed competent; "age alone" does not show not incompetence; question is whether child can "understand and answer simple questions").

Another problem is to figure out how much accommodation is enough. The federal statute contemplates a child holding the hand and sitting on the lap of an emotionally supportive adult. A guardian ad litem may be present too. The child testifies by using dolls, mannequins, and drawings. In the wings are multidisciplinary support teams. Predictably judges have great leeway to decide how much help is enough, but do they know? Does too much help encourage children to exaggerate or prevent defense counsel from exposing overstatements? Does it convey to the jury that the system has already made its judgment, and that putting the defendant away is just an unfinished detail? These concerns are troublesome and not yet fully worked out.[20]

How much accommodation?

Finally there are problems (in addition to clipping and editing) that come with the videotape medium. Lighting and angles, color and sound, cropping and zooming, and the size and quality of the viewing screen and sound system make huge differences.[21] Replaying videotaped testimony repeatedly could also magnify and distort its impact in troubling ways.[22] And taping crews and the quality of the equipment may have their own effect on the impact and meaning of such testimony. Even the elaborate federal statute is silent on these points.

Problems with medium

FRE 804(b)(2)

(b) Hearsay exceptions. The following are not excluded by the hearsay rule if the declarant is unavailable as a witness: . . .

(2) Statement under belief of impending death. In a prosecution for homicide or in a civil action or proceeding, a statement made by a declarant while believing that the declarant's death was imminent, concerning the cause or circumstances of what the declarant believed to be impending death.

---

§8.71 Dying Declarations

The dying declaration exception in FRE 804(b)(2) is among the more colorful and less used provisions. Essentially it reaches dying statements by an unavailable speaker, where these concern the cause

---

20. *See* State v. Rulona, 785 P.2d 615 (Haw. 1990) (error to let eight-year-old testify on lap of counselor, inviting her to violate rule barring support person from communicating with witness); State v. Suka, 777 P.2d 240 (Haw. 1989) (error to let *J* sit with complaining witness, then stand behind her with hand on shoulder, which bolstered testimony by conveying *J*'s belief that witness was truthful).

21. Hochheiser v. Superior Court, 208 Cal. Rptr. 273 (Cal. Ct. App. 1984) (videotaped interviews are more powerful than testimony relating what child said; angles and lighting affect impressions of demeanor; videotape and closed-circuit television enhance credibility by "status-conferral").

22. *See* People v. Talley, 824 P.2d 65 (Colo. Ct. App. 1991) (error to give jury unrestricted and unsupervised access to audiotaped interview).

or circumstances of what he thought to be his imminent death. The exception may be used only in civil actions and homicide prosecutions, and in the latter context the Court in the *Crawford* case signaled strongly that the confrontation clause does not stand as an impediment.[1]

Whether it makes sense to suppose awareness of impending death leads one to be truthful in comments about cause or circumstances may be debated. Some lines in Shakespeare argue that the dying have no need to do mischief by deception and hesitate to deceive before meeting God, but Balzac painted a picture of a wronged woman vicious even in her dying breath, and both viewpoints find echoes in decided cases.[2] In a more secular world the thought persists that psychological forces produce a final truthful impulse, and perhaps memory and perception are not serious risks with dying statements relating to the circumstances of death.

Relate to cause or circumstances

Perhaps more persuasively, death of the speaker creates a kind of necessity in the usual case where the exception applies—a homicide trial where the central question is who did it and the victim's statement gives an answer.[3] Usually the speaker does die, although the exception requires only belief in imminent death.[4]

To fit the exception, a statement must relate to cause or circumstances of impending death. The requirement is satisfied if the statement identifies the person who inflicted what seems to be the mortal wound[5] or describes the accident, assault, or catastrophe that caused what seems to be the fatal injury.[6] But the exception reaches further than such immediate descriptions, which are likely to fit the excited

---

§8.71 1. Crawford v. Washington, 541 U.S. 36, 54 n.6 (2004) (not deciding whether confrontation clause makes exception, but cases admit such statements even if testimonial; any exception is *sui generis* and rests on "historical grounds"). *See also* People v. Monterroso, 101 P.3d 956, 762 (Cal. 2005) (admitting murder victim's statement identifying assailant to police; no confrontation violation).

2. *See* Shakespeare, King John, Act 5, 4, 10-61; Mattox v. United States, 146 U.S. 140, 152 (1892) (expecting death removes temptation to falsehood, ensures truth); United Services Auto. Assn. v. Wharton, 237 F. Supp. 255, 258 (W.D.N.C. 1965) (citing trust in deathbed statements, emphasizing necessity). *But see* Honore de Balzac, Cousine Bette (1847); Carver v. United States, 164 U.S. 694, 697 (1897) (witnesses in agonies of death make false statements "through malice, misapprehension, or weakness of mind").

3. Carver v. United States, 164 U.S. 694, 697 (1897) (dying statements come in by necessity and to prevent failure of justice in homicide cases); Mattox v. United States, 146 U.S. 140, 152 (1892) (necessity).

4. *See* United Services Auto. Assn. v. Wharton, 237 F. Supp. 255, 257-260 (W.D.N.C. 1965) (admitting widow's account of husband's statements just before he drove car into oncoming traffic; his too was dying statement although he lived several years before committing suicide).

5. United States v. Barnes, 464 F.2d 828, 831 (D.C. Cir. 1972) (statement by victim immolated in gasoline fire, apparently naming defendant as assailant), *cert. denied,* 410 U.S. 986. *See also* United States v. Etheridge, 424 F.2d 951, 965-967 (6th Cir. 1970), *cert. denied,* 400 U.S. 1000; Wilson v. State, 468 P.2d 346 (Nev. 1970); Soles v. State, 119 S. 791 (Fla. 1929).

6. United States v. Mobley, 421 F.2d 345, 346-348 (5th Cir. 1970) (hospital statement by bank president shot and beaten, describing assailants and events).

utterance exception in any event.[7] A statement describing a prior threat on the speaker's life, or a prior quarrel or altercation, or past physical pain or sensations, or matters previously inhaled, injected, or ingested fits the exception if the speaker is explaining the predicament that brought him to what seems to be death's door.[8] But a statement describing matters unconnected to the apparent cause or circumstances of imminent death does not fit the exception.[9]

A statement does not fit the exception where declarant could not have had personal knowledge of the matter asserted.[10] If the speaker was shot in the back from a distance in circumstances suggesting that his dying statement represents only his guess or surmise about who shot him, the statement should be excluded.[11] But if it seems likely that the speaker had personal knowledge, that should be enough and the exception can apply since clear and definite proof of knowledge cannot usually be had. Nor should a dying statement be excluded because it conveys an opinion or conclusion, so long as it imparts usable information apparently based on firsthand knowledge. In this respect, the principles that apply to live testimony have been substantially loosened by FRE 701, and even greater liberality is appropriate when the choice is to admit the statement or do without the knowledge of the decedent.

Personal knowledge

The exception requires the speaker to be laboring under the belief that death is imminent. In *Shepard v. United States*, the Supreme Court found this requirement was not satisfied, and reversed the conviction of an Army doctor for murdering his wife Zenana by poisoning her. Two days after she became ill, she asked the nurse to get a bottle of liquor from which she drank just before collapsing, asking whether enough was left to test for poison, saying "the smell and taste were strange" and adding "Dr. Shepard has poisoned me." The nurse testified that Zenana said she was not going to recover and was going to die, but in a Cardozo opinion the Court held that the statement was not a dying declaration. She had been delirious, but things were different

Belief that death is imminent

---

7. *See* United States v. Glenn, 473 F.2d 191, 194-195 (D.C. Cir. 1972) (statement by stabbing victim naming defendant fit excited utterance exception, although she did not think death imminent).

8. United States v. Etheridge, 424 F.2d 951, 959, 966-967 (6th Cir. 1970) (statement names assailant and says speaker was shot for knowing "too much about some bank robbing"), *cert. denied*, 400 U.S. 1000.

9. St. Clair v. Commonwealth, 174 N.W.3d 474, 486 (Ky. 2005) (statement by kidnap/murder victim indicating that daughter was home for weekend and he wanted to go home did not relate to causes of impending death); United States v. Angleton, 269 F. Supp. 2d 878, 885-887 (S.D. Tex. 2003) (excluding suicide notes, prepared by defendant's brother while incarcerated, in part because contents of notes went far beyond describing cause or circumstances of declarant's demise) (citing authors of this Treatise).

10. *See* ACN ("requirement of first-hand knowledge is assured by FRE 602"); Shepard v. United States, 290 U.S. 96, 100-102 (1933) ("inference must be permissible that there was knowledge," and statement stays out if speaker engages in "suspicion or conjecture").

11. *See* State v. Wilks, 213 S.W. 118 (Mo. 1919) (excluding statement that certain people hired assailant; speaker could not know); Jones v. State, 12 S.W. 704 (Ark. 1889) (speaker could not have seen who shot him).

when she spoke. Her mind had cleared, her doctors did not think she was in danger, and her condition had improved. The exception requires a "settled hopeless expectation" of imminent death, and even belief that illness will lead to death is not enough.[12]

The subjective requirement that the speaker thinks death is imminent may be satisfied in many ways. Her own statements may suffice.[13] The requirement may also be satisfied by circumstantial evidence, such as proof of what the declarant has been told,[14] proof of the nature and extent of his injuries or illness,[15] or opinions of a physician or others observing him.[16]

The question whether a statement fits the exception is for the court to decide under FRE 104(a).[17] State practice and occasional pre-Rules federal authority approve sharing this responsibility with the jury by means of an instruction to consider a dying statement only if the jury believes the speaker had a settled expectancy of imminent death.[18] Such an instruction is unwarranted under the Rules, although of course the jury may be told that it decides the weight to be accorded to a dying statement. Of course opposing counsel may argue that such a statement is unworthy of belief and may choose to urge that the victim did not think he was dying and lacked whatever truthful motive such a belief might provide.

At common law, the dying statement exception was available only in homicide cases where the speaker was the victim. FRE 804(b)(2) clearly applies here, and the exception may be invoked not only by the prosecution but by the defense. The provision does not say the speaker must be the victim, but probably it should be read this way, since the exception is not available in other criminal cases and restricting it to homicide cases makes no sense otherwise. That restriction makes little sense in any event, since it means that in trials of other serious offenses the exception does not apply even if a killing occurred during the course of

---

12. Shepard v. United States, 290 U.S. 96, 99-100 (1933) (not until a week after she spoke did she suffer relapse, followed by death; no "ritual of words" is required; despair may exist even if speaker lives longer than expected, but she "must have spoken with the consciousness of a swift and certain doom").

13. United States v. Barnes, 464 F.2d 828, 831 (D.C. Cir. 1972) ("I am not going to make it" and feel "like I am going to die because I am too much in pain"), *cert. denied*, 410 U.S. 986.

14. Carver v. United States, 164 U.S. 694, 695-696 (1897) (victim received extreme unction); Mattox v. United States, 146 U.S. 140, 151-152 (1892) (speaker "was told that the chances were all against him").

15. United States v. Barnes, 464 F.2d 828, 831 (D.C. Cir. 1972) (immolated in gas fire), *cert. denied*, 410 U.S. 986.

16. United States v. Mobley, 421 F.2d 345, 347-348 (5th Cir. 1970) (doctor describes injuries).

17. *See* United States v. Kearney, 420 F.2d 170, 174-175 (D.C. Cir. 1969); Commonwealth v. Cooley, 348 A.2d 103, 108 (Pa. 1975) (question is one of law and not for jury); Commonwealth v. Edwards, 244 A.2d 683, 686-687 (Pa. 1968) (similar); Soles v. State, 119 S. 791, 792 (Fla. 1929) (similar).

18. United States v. Mobley, 421 F.2d 345, 348 (5th Cir. 1970) (jury not to consider statement unless it found speaker knew of impending death); State v. Chaplin, 286 A.2d 325, 332 (Me. 1972).

the criminal venture. The dying statements exception is available in civil litigation, which represents an expansion of common law tradition.

FRE 804(b)(3)

>   **(b) Hearsay exceptions.** The following are not excluded by the hearsay rule if the declarant is unavailable as a witness: . . .
>
>   **(3) Statement against interest.** A statement which was at the time of its making so far contrary to the declarant's pecuniary or proprietary interest, or so far tended to subject the declarant to civil or criminal liability, or to render invalid a claim by the declarant against another, that a reasonable person in the declarant's position would not have made the statement unless believing it to be true. A statement tending to expose the declarant to criminal liability is not admissible unless corroborating circumstances clearly indicate the trustworthiness of the statement.

---

§8.72   Statements Against Interest—Philosophy and General Problems

The exception for statements against interest appears in FRE 804(b)(3). Its common law ancestor reached statements against financial or proprietary interest, but not statements that might subject the speaker to criminal punishment (statements against "penal interest").[1] FRE 804(b)(3) embraces statements in both categories, but not statements against social interest (those that might subject the speaker to ridicule or disgrace).[2] The reasons for the exception are the traditional ones: The speaker must be unavailable (establishing a kind of need) and the against-interest element assures trustworthiness (one does not usually make false statements that hurt one's interests).

A statement fits the exception only if the speaker knew what he said was against his interest.[3] Often this matter must be assessed on circumstantial evidence, so the required understanding is framed in objective terms: Would a reasonable person understand that what he said was

Speaker's knowledge

---

§8.72   1. *See* Donnelly v. United States, 228 U.S. 243 (1913) (in murder trial, excluding third-party confession offered by defense). Wigmore attacked this doctrine, *see* 5 Wigmore, Evidence §§1476-1477 (Chadbourn rev. 1974), and so did Justice Holmes in dissent in *Donnelly*.

2. Congress removed language that would extend the exception to such statements. *See also* United States v. Lemonakis, 485 F.2d 941, 956 n.24 (D.C. Cir. 1973) (suicide note was not sufficiently against interest in avoiding "exposure to hatred, ridicule or disgrace" in eyes of family), *cert. denied*, 415 U.S. 989.

3. Roberts v. Troy, 773 F.2d 720, 725 (6th Cir. 1985) (mother did not know rule required hourly cell checks, so saying she spoke to son less than hour before his suicide was not against her interest); Filesi v. United States, 352 F.2d 339, 343-344 (4th Cir. 1965) (ex-partner said there was dancing, but no proof that he realized "possible serious financial consequences" in cabaret taxes).

against his interest? The aim is to know how the speaker conceived his interests, but absent better evidence the court may attribute to him the knowledge and interests a reasonable person in his situation would have.

A statement disclosing something that would damage the speaker if events unfold as he expects or foresees is against interest even though the consequences have not yet happened and might never happen.[4] The exception reflects the common experience that awareness of self-interest extends beyond recognizing clear and direct threats and reaches as well facts and contingencies at one remove. For statements that pose only remote or fanciful risks, it is implausible to suppose that self-interest led a speaker to be accurate and the against-interest requirement is not satisfied.[5]

Against-interest element

Sometimes the against-interest element poses no difficulty. When one acknowledges owing a debt or committing a crime, such statements have obvious against-interest elements. Absent additional and unlikely facts, they fit the exception. In effect, "interest" means self-regard on matters of money, property, or criminal sanctions.

There are two problems. First, the reality of "interest" is seldom as singular or simple as the examples suggest. Interest is likely to be complicated and many-sided, contextual and individualized, and statements can impair interest in varying degrees. Second, motive and purpose are not always self-regarding: People have purposes and motives that cannot be described this way, and these lead them to say and do things with little or no thought to property, money, or punishment.

For these reasons, applying the against-interest requirement depends on analyzing the statement in the setting of a larger mosaic of facts beyond those suggested by the statement itself, and context and motivation are all-important.[6] An understanding of context and motivation may show that a facially neutral statement is self-serving or against interest,[7] and that a facially self-serving or against-interest statement is neutral or very much the opposite of what it seems.[8] Consider the

---

4. United States v. Annunziato, 293 F.2d 373, 378 (2d Cir. 1961) (contractor tells son that defendant called and asked for money that contractor agreed to send), *cert. denied,* 368 U.S. 919; State v. Parrish, 468 P.2d 143 (Kan. 1970) (speaker says he plans to commit arson).

5. *See* Merritt v. Chonowski, 373 N.E.2d 1060, 1062-1063 (Ill. App. Ct. 1978) (driver coming out of bar said he had six drinks; not against interest because accident had not yet happened) (case seems wrong).

6. *See* Williamson v. United States, 512 U.S. 594, 603 (1994) (whether statement is self-inculpatory "can only be determined by viewing it in context," and facially neutral statements may be against interest); United States v. Candoli, 870 F.2d 496, 509 (9th Cir. 1989) (*K* told agent he "had the only keys" to the place on night of fire; *K* knew agent was investigating arson).

7. Hileman v. Northwest Engg. Co., 346 F.2d 668, 669-670 (6th Cir. 1965) (in suit by worker's compensation carrier against maker of crane, statement by employer that "there was nothing wrong" with it was against interest, subjecting him to higher rates).

8. United States v. Mansaw, 714 F.2d 785, 789-790 (8th Cir. 1983) (excluding post-arrest statement by co-offender that he "only drove the car"; he was being assaulted and threatened and spoke only because he wanted to get to police station), *cert. denied,* 464 U.S. 986.

facially neutral statement "*Q* and I are partners." If the speaker is seeking to avoid a commitment by *Q* that may bind the partnership, the statement is against interest; if he is being pressed to pay off admitted partnership debt, the statement is self-serving in showing there is another source for payment. And consider the facially against-interest statement "*W* and I robbed the bank." Spoken to police as the speaker is being arrested or to a prosecutor during plea bargaining, it looks like an attempt to curry favor by indicating willingness to plead and ability to help get a conviction of *W*.

Conflicting interests on the part of the speaker produce dual-aspect statements that seem both self-serving and disserving. One who admits playing an illegal money-stakes poker game impairs interest by implicating himself in a minor crime, but may advance interest by providing an alibi against charges of a more serious offense that happened somewhere else at the same time. The only workable approach is to figure out which interest preponderated: A statement fits the exception if the speaker was more conscious of giving something up,[9] but not otherwise, and statements that appear to curry favor usually fall in the latter category.[10] Apart from the difficulty of knowing the mindset of the speaker, there is the added difficulty (as the example suggests) of knowing the true facts, which bear on the speaker's mindset.

Dual-aspect statements

Closely related to such dual-aspect statements are those where the speaker has a motive that overrides self-interest. Suppose husband and wife are arrested and get *Miranda* warnings, and the husband confesses and says his wife had "nothing to do with it." The statement seems against interest (husband takes responsibility, forgoes chance for separate deal by helping develop case against wife), but his noble motive undermines arguments that against-interest elements make the statement trustworthy.[11] In the end, it seems that against-interest statements should be excluded when a countervailing motive undermines the inference of trustworthiness.[12]

Overriding motive

9. United States v. Williams, 738 F.2d 172, 178 (7th Cir. 1984) (in fraud trial, defendant denied transferring car to V for resale, said he left it with B for repair; B's statements to V might expose B to theft charges but exonerate him from more serious mail fraud charges) (might not fit exception).

10. Demasi v. Whitney Trust & Sav. Bank, 176 S. 703 (La. Ct. App. 1937) (in depositer's affidavit saying funds were withdrawn by consent, self-interest preponderated; bank required affidavit before releasing balance).

11. 5 Wigmore, Evidence §1464 (Chadbourn rev. 1974) (not required that speaker have no motive to misrepresent; question is whether disserving aspect is counterbalanced by self-serving aspect); 2 McCormick, Evidence §319 (6th ed. 2006) (statement against interest in one respect should be excluded if speaker "had some motive, whether of self-interest or otherwise, which was likely to lead to misrepresentation"); Jefferson, Declarations Against Interest: An Exception to the Hearsay Rule, 58 Harv. L. Rev. 1, 52-57 (1944) (motive to falsify sometimes "overrides pecuniary or proprietary interest").

12. United States v. Mackin, 561 F.2d 958, 962-963 (D.C. Cir. 1977) (statement by prosecution witness recanting testimony was not against interest; no real peril), *cert. denied*, 434 U.S. 959.

Related statements
Where a statement satisfies the against-interest requirement, the exception has been understood to reach related statements that are neutral in character. In its 1994 decision in the *Williamson* case, however, the Supreme Court rejected this view for federal courts applying FRE 804(b)(3).[13] A six-member majority held that the federal exception reaches only statements that are themselves against interest, not those that are "collateral." *Williamson* dealt with third-party statements implicating the accused, which raise special concerns, but the Court's focus on textual interpretation and legislative meaning seems broadly applicable to civil cases too, and to third-party statements exonerating the accused.

Williamson seems right to recognize that the rationale is not that against-interest elements signal a "truthful frame of mind" so everything said at a certain time is trustworthy. Rather, the rationale is that against-interest statements are unlikely to be false or mistaken.[14] To the extent the traditional approach to related statements was mechanical (turning on proximity to "true" against-interest statements or overlapping subject matter), the *Williamson* rejection of this approach seems sound.

The real problem is to determine how much of what a speaker says actually impairs his interest. Often a statement (or series of statements) makes one or more points that are saliently against interest along with related but less salient points. Suppose one signs a purchase contract committing to pay money, describing the item bought, and reciting the time and place of contracting. Or suppose a speaker says "I shot *X*," adding that "I own the gun, and *Y* drove me to *X*'s house." Ordinarily the commitment to pay and the confession ("I shot *X*") would be saliently against interest. What about the balance of what was said?

If it has a close narrative and logical connection to the salient statement, then the balance of what was said may add meaning or dimension to the salient statement (in effect enhancing the against-interest element) or provide more facts that in context further impair the interest of the speaker. To this extent, the balance of what was said seems to satisfy the against-interest requirement. A court following *Williamson*

---

13. *See* Williamson v. United States, 512 U.S. 594 (1994) (exception does not reach neutral collateral statements; in talking to DEA Agent, *H* implicated himself and defendant, but reference to defendant "did little to subject" *H* to liability) (two in majority plus three concurring justices agree to remand to determine whether references to defendant were against *H*'s interest; four disapprove collateral statements and say exception cannot apply). *But see* ACN to FRE 804(b)(3) (exception reaches third-party confessions and "related statements" implicating accused). *See also* United States v. Barrett, 539 F.2d 244, 249-253 (1st Cir. 1976) (in trial of Bucky for stealing stamps, co-offender's statement that "Bucky wasn't involved" because "it was Buzzy" strengthened impression that speaker had inside knowledge and implied his participation).

14. Williamson v. United States, 512 U.S. 594, 600-601 (1994) (exception does not reach statements that are not inculpatory, "even if made within a broader narrative that is generally self-inculpatory"); Jefferson, Declarations Against Interest: An Exception to the Hearsay Rule, 58 Harv. L. Rev. 1, 60 (1944) (basis is not that speaker is in trustworthy frame of mind; trustworthiness comes from asserting disserving facts; should exclude associated self-serving or neutral statements).

could admit the balance for such reasons, and *Williamson* was careful to say that facially neutral statements fit the exception if in context they are against the interest of the speaker. A looser mechanical approach could lead to the same result. In the examples, the description of the item purchased and the recitals of date and place could satisfy the against-interest requirement, and the same is true of the mention of gun ownership and *Y*'s role ("I own the gun, and *Y* drove me to *X*'s house").[15] But in the latter situation where the salient statement confesses to a crime and implicates another, caution is warranted: As the Court said in *Williamson*, implicating others may be self-serving, especially if the speaker himself is arrested and talking with authorities or if he concedes only a minor role and casts major blame on someone else.[16] If someone implicates himself in a crime and expressly exonerates another ("I shot *X*, and *Y* had nothing to do with it"), the balance of the statement may be admitted if it enhances the against-interest aspect of the whole by putting full responsibility on the speaker.[17]

Statements lacking close narrative and logical connection with an against-interest statement should ordinarily be severed and excluded. They might not qualify even under a mechanical approach, and *Williamson* points toward exclusion.[18]

A question noted by commentators lurks behind many of the hard cases described above: Is it the statement that must be against interest, or the matter asserted? Usually an against-interest element appears in both or neither, but not always. If Driver says after an accident, "I was speeding," both the statement and the fact asserted are against interest. The fact shows negligence, and the statement proves the fact. The phrasing of the exception and our usual ways of talking about it suggest that the statement must be against interest. Some commentators argue that the fact asserted must be against interest,[19] although others say the

Statement or fact?

15. Williamson v. United States, 512 U.S. 594, 603 (1994) ("Sam and I went to Joe's house" could be against interest if reasonable speaker knows that being linked to Sam and Joe would implicate him in conspiracy); United States v. Garris, 616 F.2d 626, 629-633 (2d Cir. 1980) (defendant *E*'s sister *P* told FBI agent that *E* said he "had not been photographed" in bank; agent was investigating second robbery where *P* as teller gave thief money; *P* admitted complicity, said she concealed knowing how to reach *E*; statement fit exception; would be probative in trial for second robbery and accessory in first; need not be against interest "standing alone" if "integral to a larger statement" against interest), *cert. denied*, 447 U.S. 926.

16. Williamson v. United States, 512 U.S. 594, 604, 609 (1994) (two Justices say implicating someone else lessens speaker's exposure to liability; four others say arrested person has "strong incentive to shift blame or downplay his own role"); United States v. Lilley, 581 F.2d 182, 187-188 (8th Cir. 1978).

17. United States v. Lopez, 777 F.2d 543, 554 (10th Cir. 1985) (admitting *J*'s statement that he "collaborated alone" with *M* in drug transactions and defendant didn't know anything because *J* "never discussed his activities").

18. United States v. Woolbright, 831 F.2d 1390, 1395 (8th Cir. 1987) (statement by co-offender R that she owned suitcase containing drugs did not justify admitting statement that she and defendant were on honeymoon).

19. *See* 5 Wigmore, Evidence §1462 (Chadbourn rev. 1974); Morgan, Basic Problems of Evidence 291-292 (1963).

exception is broader.[20] Seemingly it can be justified either way, which is to say that one is unlikely to make a statement that impairs interest unless it is true, and unlikely to assert a fact that impairs interest unless the fact is so.

Consider a case where the fact but not the statement seems against interest: After an accident, the driver tells his wife privately "I was speeding." The statement is not likely against interest, nor would the speaker think so. He is likely to think nobody else will learn of it, and he might be able to block discovery and use of it under the spousal confidences privilege (a point he might sense even if he knows nothing about doctrine). Yet the fact of speeding is still against interest and gives reason to suppose the statement is right. Even to people we trust completely, we are not likely to admit serious fault of which we are innocent (and trust adds a reason to be truthful).[21] In this situation, ordinarily the exception can apply.

Consider now a case where the statement but not the fact seems against interest: "*X* brought in the heroin," spoken to a casual acquaintance. The fact asserted (*X* brought in the heroin) does not seem against interest, but is actually hard to characterize. What *X* did might expose the speaker to liability for conspiracy (so even the fact hurts him), but it relieves him of direct responsibility for bringing in heroin (thus advances his interest). Yet the statement may be against interest: It reveals inside knowledge of an illegal scheme, which itself suggests the speaker is involved. Again it seems that the exception applies.[22]

"Curry favor" statement

Suppose an arrested suspect tells police during questioning, or prosecutors during plea bargaining, or a judge at a sentencing hearing, "I brought the heroin in." Or suppose a witness testifies in this vein before a grand jury under a grant of use immunity. Here the fact remains against interest, but the statement seems self-serving because the speaker seeks favorable treatment in return for cooperation (his statement "curries favor"). He may even be able to block use of the statement against him since FRE 410 excludes plea bargaining statements, and the grant of immunity requires exclusion of immunized statements. In such cases, ordinarily the exception does not apply.[23]

---

20. *See* 2 McCormick, Evidence §316 (6th ed. 2006) (either facts must be against interest "or the making of the declaration itself must create evidence that would harm such interests"); Jefferson, Declarations Against Interest: An Exception to the Hearsay Rule, 58 Harv. L. Rev. 1, 8-17 (1944).

21. State v. Pierre, 890 A.2d 474, 490-491 (Conn. 2006) (co-offender's statements to "friend and someone he routinely socialized with"), *cert denied*, 547 U.S. 1197; State v. Yarbrough, 767 N.E.2d 216, 226-228 (Ohio 2002) (statement to wife) (quoting authors of this Treatise).

22. *See* United States v. Nazemian, 948 F.2d 522, 528-532 (9th Cir. 1991) (*K* told *G* he would not sell heroin without advance payment because *N* and another "never paid him for a prior heroin transaction"; implicating *N* was "closely intertwined" with *K*'s admission of drug trafficking), *cert. denied*, 506 U.S. 835.

23. United States v. Albert, 773 F.2d 386, 388-389 (1st Cir. 1985) (excluding statement by co-offender in sentencing hearing, offered by defendant; people speak during sentencing to help themselves).

A useful rule of thumb is that the against-interest exception can apply if either the statement or the fact asserted is against interest, but not if the statement is self-serving regardless of the nature of the underlying fact.

Rule of thumb

§8.73   —Proprietary or Pecuniary Interest

The against-interest exception reaches statements that impair "pecuniary or proprietary interest," subject the speaker to civil liability, or "render invalid" his claim against another if a reasonable person in his position would not have made the statement unless he thought it to be true.

Bearing in mind that context is critical, the exception reaches many statements that directly and immediately impair or qualify the pecuniary or proprietary interest of the speaker. Examples include a statement that he does not own or has no claim to certain property,[1] owes money to another,[2] or that he has been paid by one who owes him money, which might be shown by an entry in books, or a legend on the note indicating payment, or an acknowledgment or receipt given to the obligor.[3] And the exception reaches statements that the speaker received property in trust for another, encumbered or conveyed property to another, holds less than a fee simple interest, or concedes a contractual or other obligation to another.[4] Many other statements conceding a debt or limiting a claim or exposing the speaker to financial or proprietary risk fit the exception.[5]

Doesn't own, owes money, has been paid

The exception reaches statements that impair interests in ways that are indirect and contingent. Thus a statement tending to expose the speaker to tort liability or loss of job or employment opportunity fits the exception, as the District of Columbia Circuit Court held in a landmark decision in *Gichner v. Antonio Troiano Tile & Marble Co.* There, a warehouse owner and insurance carrier sued a building tenant to recover for fire loss, and plaintiffs offered a statement by an employee of defendant named Faulds, which admitted to police officers and a fire inspector some hours after the blaze that he and others had been drinking and

Indirect, contingent

---

§8.73   1. *See* In re Thompson, 205 F. 556, 559-560 (D.N.J. 1913) (statement by bankrupt that he did not own dredge because he had not paid for it).

2. German Ins. Co. v. Bartlett, 58 N.E. 1075 (Ill. 1900) (statement by husband that he was indebted to wife, that property was bought with her money and he held title as trustee).

3. *See* Egbert v. Egbert, 132 N.E.2d 910, 918 (Ind. 1956) (statements by mortgagee that note had been paid). *But see* 5 Wigmore, Evidence §§1460, 1466 (Chadbourn rev. 1974) (if payment revives obligation, receipt is against interest only if entered before statutory period has run; other complications).

4. *See* Martin v. Turner, 218 S.E.2d 789, 791 (Ga. 1975) (in suit on oral contract to make will, statements by decedent that he made agreement with plaintiff fit exception); Monti v. Granite Sav. Bank & Trust Co., 333 A.2d 106, 108-109 (Vt. 1975) (statement by decedent that he got stock to be held in trust).

5. Smith v. Updegraff, 744 F.2d 1354, 1366 n.7 (8th Cir. 1984) (in wrongful discharge suit, statements acknowledging concert of action or being wrong to fire plaintiff); Motorists Mut. Ins. Co. v. Hunt, 549 S.W.2d 845, 847 (Ky. Ct. App. 1977) (statement by motorist that he did not carry insurance).

entered the warehouse at 3 A.M. and smoked cigarettes. A statement fits the exception, the court held, if it "threatens the loss of employment, or reduces the chances for future employment, or entails possible civil liability," and these statements provided "an important link" that suggested that Faulds and others "were responsible for starting the fire."[6] In general, statements that tend to subject the speaker to tort or other civil liability,[7] or to loss of a claim he might have,[8] or to loss of job or employment opportunity[9] fit the exception.

In connection with claims against insurance carriers, statements against penal interest often point to the source or cause of loss or damage. Such statements can bring the claim within coverage[10] or show that it is excluded.[11] Proof of criminal acts is sometimes relevant as the basis for civil liability in other contexts, and can be proved by against-interest statements.[12]

Interest to maximize or minimize

Sometimes circumstances suggest strongly an interest and motivation to overstate or understate, to maximize or minimize something. For example, if someone trying to sell his business speaks of its annual profits, he is likely to set the highest figure he can. He may speak truthfully and may be right, or perhaps not, but it is unlikely that the figure he sets is lower than the right one. And if a taxpayer fills out her return, the figure she sets down for taxable income is likely to be the lowest figure she can reach. Again she may be truthful and she may be right, or maybe not, but it is unlikely that the figure she sets is higher than the right one. Statements of this sort have sometimes been viewed as fitting the exception.[13] If the interest is to maximize, a statement is

6. Gichner v. Antonio Troiano Tile & Marble Co., 410 F.2d 238, 242 (D.C. Cir. 1969) (admitting he was there after hours for personal reasons, and did something that may have destroyed business, might jeopardize standing with employer).

7. Cathey v. Johns-Manville Sales Corp., 776 F.2d 1565, 1574-1575 (6th Cir. 1985) (deposition describing what medical director of asbestos maker knew of relationship between inhaling asbestos fibers and asbestosis), *cert. denied*, 478 U.S. 1021; Pino v. Protection Maritime Ins. Co., Ltd., 599 F.2d 10, 13 (1st Cir. 1979) (statement conceding maritime blacklisting practices), *cert. denied*, 444 U.S. 900.

8. Mills v. Damson Oil Corp., 691 F.2d 715, 716-717 (5th Cir. 1982) (grantee concedes knowing about prior deed conveying property to another).

9. Timber Access Indus. Co. v. U.S. Plywood-Champion Papers, Inc., 503 P.2d 482, 487-488 (Or. 1972) (manager's statement conceding bad deal that would "necessarily reflect adversely" on his ability).

10. Peco Energy Co. v. Boden, 64 F.3d 852, 858-859 (3d Cir. 1995) (statement by employee saying he stole oil from deliveries on orders by company owner).

11. Jamaica Time Petroleum, Inc. v. Federal Ins. Co., 366 F.2d 156, 158-159 (10th Cir. 1966) (suit for loss of plane; admitting statement by one saying he'd been hired to destroy it), *cert. denied*, 385 U.S. 1024.

12. International Distrib. Corp. v. American Dist. Tel. Co., 569 F.2d 136, 138 (D.C. Cir. 1977) (in suit by store against burglar alarm service, admitting statements by employees that they stole merchandise).

13. In a wrongful death case, plaintiff offered a tax return filed by the decedent as proof that she earned at least the amount set forth, but the court said the statement was "self-serving." Veach's Admr. v. Louisville & I.R. Co., 228 S.W. 35 (Ky. 1921). Some would apply the exception. Jefferson, Declarations Against Interest: An Exception to the Hearsay Rule, 58 Harv. L. Rev. 1, 51 (1944); Morgan, Declarations Against Interest, 5 Vand. L. Rev. 451, 471 & n.84 (1952).

"against interest" to the extent it asserts too little, and fits the exception if offered to prove the ceiling (upperbound limit). And if the interest is to minimize, a statement is "against interest" to the extent it asserts too much, and it fits the exception if offered to prove the floor (lower-bound limit).

Trying to fit these plausible arguments into the logic of the exception doesn't quite work because there is no way to figure out whether such statements are actually "against interest"—whether the speaker said "too little" from his point of view, or "too much" from hers. But self-interest suggests such statements are trustworthy for limited uses. Where the interest is to maximize, a statement is trustworthy when offered to prove the ceiling: Whatever may be the truth about the profits of the business, the owner's statement is reliable evidence that the profits are not higher than the figure he gives. And where his interest is to minimize, a statement is trustworthy when offered to prove the floor: Whatever may be the truth about taxable income, the return is reliable evidence that the income is not less than the figure given.

Of course these statements would be admissible against the speaker in a suit against him. But arguably they should be admissible on his behalf too, for the kinds of limited purpose described above, and arguably they should be admissible in cases where he is not a party. FRE 804(b)(3) presents at best an awkward mechanism for such statements. Given the unavailability requirement, it would not usually help someone to offer such a statement on his own behalf.[14]

§8.74   —Penal Interest: Statements Exonerating Defendant

The exception reaches statements against penal interest that exonerate the defendant expressly or by necessary effect. Sometimes a third person admits his involvement in the charged crime, which lessens the likelihood that defendant is guilty.[1] And sometimes the third person implicates himself in a crime in a way that suggests that defendant was fooled or misled, or that supports some other defense.[2]

---

14. *See generally* Re Ollag Constr. Equip. Corp., 665 F.2d 43, 46 (2d Cir. 1981) (in bank's effort to enforce security interest, admitting against bank financial statements prepared by principals, who were likely to overstate assets to obtain refinancing, which would favor bank's position); Plisco v. United States, 306 F.2d 784, 786-789 (D.C. Cir. 1962) (where IRS disallowed gambling losses, admitting taxpayer memoranda to show winnings only; taxpayers "had no incentive to overstate their daily profit figures," so IRS could accept them as minima), *cert. denied,* 371 U.S. 948.

§8.74   1. United States v. Nagib, 56 F.3d 798, 803-804 (7th Cir. 1995), *cert. denied,* 521 U.S. 1127; United States v. Atkins, 558 F.2d 133, 134-136 (3d Cir. 1977), *cert. denied,* 434 U.S. 1071.

2. United States v. Bagley, 537 F.2d 162, 164-165 (5th Cir. 1976) (*S* said he told defendant package contained valium), *cert. denied,* 429 U.S. 1075; People v. Brown, 257 N.E.2d 16 (N.Y. 1970) (on arrest, *S* said he picked up gun, supporting defense claim that homicide victim was armed).

More challenging are statements in which a third party mentions both himself and the defendant. The exception can apply when the speaker implicates himself and the defendant in criminal acts in a way that provides the defendant with an alibi or supports a defense explanation of otherwise damning evidence.[3] Courts disagree about statements in which a third person expressly implicates himself in a crime and says defendant was not involved.[4]

In the setting of a statement *implicating* the accused (where concerns over reliability are at their peak), the Supreme Court held in the *Williamson* case that a reference to the accused should not be admitted if that reference is merely collateral to a statement that fits the exception. Instead the reference to defendant must itself be against the speaker's interest.[5] The logic of the opinion seems broad enough to apply in here too, suggesting that a remark *exonerating* the defendant fits the exception only if it has such close narrative and logical connection to a salient self-implicating statement that it adds meaning or dimension to the latter or provides additional facts that further impair the interest of the speaker. The statement "I killed the victim, and defendant had nothing to do with it" makes fair bid to be admitted as a whole, since the reference to the defendant adds to the against-interest element in the self-inculpatory statement by concentrating responsibility in the speaker.[6] But a statement that exonerates the accused should be severed and excluded if it is not closely connected to a statement against the speaker's interest.[7]

Statements by an arrested suspect to law enforcement officers or prosecutors are affected by a mix of self-serving and against-interest elements. Often *Miranda* warnings are part of the picture, and they tell the speaker he has something to lose in talking, thus making graphic the against-interest element. But the message is also that the arrested person needs to watch out for himself, and to "curry favor,"

---

3. United States v. Toney, 599 F.2d 787, 789-790 (6th Cir. 1979) (defendant said he won bait money in poker game with *K*; should admit *K*'s statement confirming point, which was against interest in revealing illegal gambling).

4. Cases that apply the exception include United States v. Paguio, 114 F.3d 928, 930-933 (9th Cir. 1997) (in trial for false statements to bank, should have admitted statement by father that he negotiated loan and his son, defendant, had little to do with it); United States v. Garcia, 986 F.2d 1135, 1139 (7th Cir. 1993) (co-offender says marijuana was his and defendant knew nothing about it). Cases refusing to apply the exception include United States v. Vegas, 27 F.3d 773, 782 (2d Cir. 1994) (co-offender says *C* was drug source, not defendant), *cert. denied*, 513 U.S. 911; United States v. Marquez, 462 F.2d 893, 895 (2d Cir. 1972) (co-offender says cocaine belonged to him and other guys had nothing to do with it).

5. Williamson v. United States, 512 U.S. 594 (1994) (collateral statements should not be treated differently from other excludable hearsay).

6. United States v. Garcia, 986 F.2d 1135, 1140-1142 (7th Cir. 1993) (error to exclude post-*Miranda* statement to investigator that defendant knew nothing of marijuana in truck; not currying favor) (reversing).

7. United States v. Jimenez, 419 F.3d 34, 43 (1st Cir. 2005) (excluding P's statement describing his relationship to defendant and saying he did not provide him guns for heroin; statement did not incriminate P, but exonerated him), *cert. denied*, 546 U.S. 1189.

and self-serving motives are likely to affect what he says. Even without *Miranda* warnings, this mix of motives is likely. If an arrested person exonerates someone else, his statement may be against interest in shouldering blame and giving up bargaining position. But other motives may be at work: Statements exonerating others may be attempts to suggest personal innocence or lack of awareness, or part of a larger strategy to minimize guilt of all involved. And beyond the immediate pressures that arrest brings, the speaker may know that incriminating others can bring criticism or reprisal or lead to "hard time" in prison, and more noble motives to exonerate cohorts out of friendship or family connection can also operate. These conflicting pressures and motives make it hard to apply the exception sensibly. Some post-arrest statements by third parties are admitted for the defense,[8] and some are excluded.[9]

For third-party statements implicating the speaker and offered to exonerate a criminal defendant, FRE 804(b)(3) requires corroborating circumstances that "clearly indicate trustworthiness." The fear is that third parties will falsely confess, perhaps with the idea of helping the defendant, or that a defense witness will fabricate a plausible confession by one whose unavailability will shield him from perjury charges and impede efforts to impeach or otherwise test the confession. And there is a concern that trials will be prolonged by the need to attack third-party confessions by others not present in court and to explain to the jury why they were not charged.

It is hard to say what is meant by "corroborating circumstances," but without them defendants in criminal cases cannot invoke the exception to admit third-party confessions.[10] The requirement is satisfied by independent evidence that directly or circumstantially tends to prove the same points on which the statement is offered,[11] and the requirement is almost certainly *not met* if the statement is demonstrably false in some important way.[12] But the term seems broader and reaches evidence supporting the veracity of the speaker, including indications that the statement was against interest to an unusual degree or that he repeated the statement or could not be motivated to falsify for the

Corroboration requirement

---

8. United States v. Hilliard, 11 F.3d 618, 619-620 (6th Cir. 1993) (admitting ownership of drugs), *cert. denied*, 510 U.S. 1130; People v. Spriggs, 389 P.2d 377 (Cal. 1964) (similar).

9. United States v. Dean, 59 F.3d 1479, 1492-1494 (5th Cir. 1995) (excluding statements that defendants had not known about drug deal), *cert. denied*, 516 U.S. 1064.

10. State v. Wannamaker, 552 S.E.2d 284, 287 (S.C. 2001) (excluding letter from defendant's friend admitting guilt; no corroboration); United States v. Vega, 221 F.3d 789, 803-804 (5th Cir. 2000) (excluding co-offender's guilty plea colloquy; no corroborating circumstances), *cert. denied*, 531 U.S. 1155.

11. Ingram v. United States, 885 A.2d 257, 266 (D.C. 2005) (error to exclude third-party confession, corroborated by proof that declarant was there smoking marijuana and drinking with victim and defendant).

12. State v. Harrod, 26 P.3d 492, 496-497 (Az. 2001) (excluding defense-proffered confession to murder by inmate, partly because details were "inconsistent with the crime") (inmate described killing victim with one shot; victim was shot five times), *vacated on other grounds*, 536 U.S. 953.

benefit of the accused.[13] The term should embrace other factors suggesting trustworthiness, such as spontaneity.[14] A traditional concern was the risk of false reports of confessions, so it is plausible to suppose the corroboration requirement can be partly satisfied by additional proof that the statement was made.[15] Some opinions mention the credibility of the testifying witness as a factor, but this one does not readily fit into the idea of corroboration, and it seems wiser to leave this matter to the testing process of direct and cross, and to the jury.[16] Simple absence of corroborative evidence means the corroboration requirement is not satisfied.[17]

§8.75   —Penal Interest: Statements Implicating Defendant

The against-interest exception reaches some third-party statements offered against the defendant. Probably the framers anticipated this application: The ACN says a third-party confession may include "statements implicating the accused," at least when made to an acquaintance as opposed to law enforcement officials, and a modern scholar reached the same conclusion.[1]

Statements describing only Declarant's own acts

Ordinarily a statement satisfies the against interest requirement if the speaker describes his own criminal acts without mentioning other persons in any way. Doctrines of accomplice liability, which are embodied in crimes like conspiracy and accessory before or after the fact, mean that the behavior of one person can affect the degree or the way in which the behavior of another is criminal. Even in cases involving no accomplice charges, what one person does can shed light on what another does, or provide context necessary for understanding, and can even suggest what another probably did.

Suppose Abby and Bob are charged with residential burglary, and Abby told a friend she "entered the house and broke into the jewelry box and then fled out the back door." Suppose an eyewitness testifies

13. United States v. Bumpass, 60 F.3d 1099, 1102-1103 (4th Cir. 1995), *cert. denied*, 516 U.S. 1119; United States v. Nagib, 56 F.3d 798, 803-804 (7th Cir. 1995) (both listing circumstantial factors), *cert denied*, 521 U.S. 1127.

14. United States v. Garcia, 986 F.2d 1135, 1139 (7th Cir. 1993) (no close relationship to defendant, no currying favor).

15. United States v. Bagley, 537 F.2d 162, 167 (5th Cir. 1976) (excluding statement on basis of doubt it was made), *cert. denied*, 429 U.S. 1075.

16. *Compare* United States v. Hendrieth, 922 F.2d 748, 750 (11th Cir. 1991) (excluding statement because witness unworthy of belief) *with* United States v. Atkins, 558 F.2d 133, 135 (3d Cir. 1977) (exception directs court to trustworthiness of declarant, not witness), *cert. denied*, 434 U.S. 1071.

17. State v. Staten, 610 S.E.2d 823, 839 (S.C. 2006) (in murder trial, excluding proof of third-party confession, in part for "lack of corroboration"), *vacated in part*, 374 S.C. 9 (2007) (on other grounds).

§8.75   1. Peter Tague, Perils of the Rulemaking Process: The Development, Application and Unconstitutionality of Rule 804(b)(3)'s Penal Interest Exception, 69 Geo. L.J. 851 (1981); United States v. Sarmiento-Perez, 633 F.2d 1092, 1098 (5th Cir. 1981) (legislative history "clearly contemplates" this use), *cert. denied*, 459 U.S. 834.

that Bob was waiting in a car behind the house. In a trial of both for burglary, Abby's statement would be admissible against her as her admission, and it might be admissible against Bob because it fits the exception. It incriminates Bob by connecting his behavior to hers, explaining what he was doing there, even though Abby's statement made no reference to him. Statements such as these, that incriminate defendants in the ways described above, can fit the exception when made in a private setting.[2] Probably the *Crawford* doctrine does not reach such statements because they are nontestimonial.[3]

When similar statements are made in official settings, the picture changes. As a practical matter, statements by co-offenders to law enforcement officers or prosecutors are usually part of an effort to curry favor or enter into plea bargaining. Often as well, co-offenders have been through the preliminaries and negotiated a plea, and they speak in a courtroom in a proceeding in which the responsibility of the judge is to be certain that the plea is proper, meaning that it has a factual basis and is entered without coercion and that the person in question knows what he is giving up, in terms of procedural rights and punishment. Here the *Crawford* doctrine applies, and the statements are testimonial: Although *Crawford* arose in the setting of third-party statements given to police that *directly implicated* the defendant, the decision also disapproved earlier holdings allowing use of one person's guilty plea allocutions against another (even when they made no reference to the defendant, or were redacted to delete such reference). The speaker understands or expects that he is "bearing witness" and what he says may affect a criminal investigation or prosecution, and in some instances these statements are testimonial even if made out of court because they are collected in formal settings in which they are recorded or transcribed in a structured interview in an official setting.[4]

Often persons involved in crime make statements implicating not only themselves, but others, referring to them by name or reference and indicating what role they played. Such a person might say, in substance, "Frank and I robbed the bank," or "Gina brought the drugs in and I sold them," or "Herb went in and held up the teller while I waited outside in the car." Here the reach and application of the exception are far more problematic. There are two main issues, which are to define the reach of the against-interest element and to decide whether the statement is testimonial under *Crawford*, and a third issue that is now at

Statements describing acts by others

2. Padilla v. Terhune, 309 F.3d 614, 618-620 (9th Cir. 2002) (in robbery trial, admitting statement by S or C, co-offenders with defendant P, that they took victim up hill and "jacked him" and that S "shot him one time in the right side of the head") (talking to friend in private; no reason to think police would be involved); United States v. Saccoccia, 58 F.3d 754, 778-779 (1st Cir. 1995) (in money laundering trial of S, admitting statements by D and C implicating themselves and each other in money laundering).

3. Crawford v. Washington, 541 U.S. 36 (2004), discussed in §8.84, *infra.*

4. United States v. Snype, 441 F.3d 119 (2d Cir. 2006) (in bank robbery trial, error to admit co-offender's guilty plea allocution) (harmless), *cert denied,* 127 S. Ct. 285; United States v. Jones, 393 F.3d 107 (2d Cir. 2004) (in drug trial, error to admit guilty plea of co-offender to allowing her apartment to be used to store drugs) (reversing).

least partly eclipsed by the coming of *Crawford*, and has certainly faded in importance, which is to consider whether the speaker was currying favor.

The first challenge is to decide how far the against interest element reaches. The question is often framed in terms of applying the exception to "collateral" or "associated" statements, but the real task is simply to decide whether a statement is against the speaker's interest insofar as it describes what another did or knew. The *Williamson* case dealt with this matter, and approaches to resolving this issue are suggested below. Second is to address the constitutional issue formulated in *Crawford*, which arises whenever statements describing crimes are made to law enforcement officials or in actual testimony, and perhaps in other settings too. The third issue, now eclipsed except in cases where the speaker was also cross-examinable at some point, involves the "curry favor" element. Statements incriminating others are tainted by the motive of the speaker to make a deal for himself if he is talking to police or prosecutors and he incriminates others. Here statements such as "Frank was in on it with me" are often attempts to improve bargaining position, in hope of attaining release, avoiding charges, or winning a reduction in charges. Often the motive to curry favor is overwhelming, having the effect of diminishing to almost nothing any against interest element, meaning that such statements do not fit the exception.

(1) How far does against-interest element reach?   On the question how far the against-interest element reaches, the beginning point is the Court's 1994 opinion in *Williamson*, which held that a statement offered under the exception must *itself* be against interest.[5] That is to say, the against-interest element does not reach other statements, uttered at the same time, that are not themselves against interest. This sound principle is easier to state than to apply. In *Williamson*, the majority thought statements by Reginald Harris implicating Fredel Williamson "did little to subject Harris himself to criminal liability." Harris had been arrested driving a car with cocaine in a suitcase in the trunk, and Williamson had been driving ahead of Harris. In his statements, Harris said the cocaine belonged to Williamson, that Harris had met Williamson in Ft. Lauderdale, that Williamson was traveling with Harris in the other car and had seen Harris being stopped, and that they were taking the cocaine to Atlanta. (In an earlier version, Harris said he got the cocaine from a Cuban who had delivered written instructions in a note, but later Harris admitted that this story was false.) It is true enough that these statements are not *as saliently against interest* as are statements that concede personal blame by describing criminal behavior by the speaker alone. Still, as explored above, even statements referring only to others do affect the criminality of the speaker under ordinary notions of accomplice liability and conspiracy and because the behavior of other people helps understand and illuminate the behavior of the speaker. The point made by the majority is that these statements are not *as seriously incriminating* as statements

5. Williamson v. United States, 512 U.S. 594 (1994).

accepting personal blame, so against-interest elements in less incriminating statements may not be sufficient to satisfy the exception.

The majority in *Williamson* did not mean that literally every word and literally every statement must be against interest if considered in isolation. Concurring in *Williamson*, Justice Scalia gave the example of someone saying he made a legal purchase of a handgun and ammunition and then drove his "1958 blue Edsel" to the bank, parked with the door ajar, and went in and robbed the bank and shot the guard. Scalia argued that this statement could be against interest *in its entirety*, even though talk about buying a gun and driving a certain car to the bank did not confess to "any element of a crime." The *Williamson* majority did not disagree, but cited a less dramatic example: "I hid the gun in Joe's apartment" could be against interest, even though it seems "neutral" on its face, if it helped police find a murder weapon. More generally, the *Williamson* majority said the question whether a statement is against interest "can only be determined by viewing it in context," which is clearly right and very important.

Other things said at the same time are part of the context: A *statement* about buying a gun and driving a particular car to the bank is not, by itself, against interest, but a *statement* about buying a gun and then driving a particular car to the bank and *using the gun in a robbery and killing* is against interest. The combined statement is against interest because *the rest* of the statement confesses to a crime, and because the acts, events or conditions (buying a gun, driving to the place where the driver commits crimes) are themselves parts of the crimes described in the statement.

The *Williamson* majority *also* did not mean to say that mentioning another person takes a statement outside the exception. According to the majority, the statement "Sam and I went to Joe's house" could fit the exception if a reasonable person in the shoes of the speaker would know that "being linked to Joe and Sam" would implicate him in a conspiracy with them. In its 1999 opinion in the *Lilly* case, the Court cited *Williamson* for the proposition that the exception does not reach "non-self-inculpatory" portions of a statement, but *Lilly* involved review of a state conviction, and the focus was constitutional issues. *Lilly* too disapproved use of a statement by one co-offender implicating another: There Mark, brother of defendant, told police after being arrested, "Ben shoots him" and answered "pistol" when asked what Ben used to do the shooting. The decision in *Lilly* split the Court. Four Justices thought that the exception cannot apply to statements of this sort, but three others thought that *in some cases* third-party statements implicating the defendant could be "genuinely self-inculpatory" and two others only agreed on the narrow point that Ben's confrontation rights were violated.[6]

6. Lilly v. Virginia, 527 U.S. 116, 138, 145 (1999) (3-member plurality plus two in concurrence plus three others agree that using Mark's statement incriminating Ben violated Ben's confrontation rights).

The standard endorsed in *Williamson* requires attention to context, including other acts, events, or conditions that the statement describes *and other things the speaker says at the time.* When a statement concedes the speaker's involvement in a crime, or his involvement in acts that constitute part of a crime or connect the speaker with a crime, the question whether the against interest element is satisfied when it comes to references or allusions to others suggesting something about what they knew and did, should be resolved by pursuing the following four lines of inquiry:

(a) Even handed, or blame-shifting?

How evenhanded is the statement? If the speaker is trying to shift blame to another, or if he acknowledges minimal personal responsibility ("Herb went in and held up the teller while I waited outside in the car"), the against-interest element is less likely to be satisfied.[7] If, in contrast, the statement shares responsibility on an equal basis ("Frank and I robbed the bank"), it is more likely to pass muster.[8]

(b) How connected are the speaker and the other?

How connected are the speaker and the other person? As the two are connected more closely, in behavior or knowledge or purposes, it becomes more likely that a reference to the other is itself against interest.[9] When *both* the fact adverse to the defendant *and* the fact adverse to the speaker bear on the speaker's culpability (close logical connection), and where the speaker connects his description of both facts (close narrative connection), the against-interest element is likely present for both facts. Consider a statement that refers to and implicates the speaker and the defendant in transactions that can only move forward by cooperative efforts, or in undertakings that are coordinated and depend on mutual efforts. In this setting, a statement describing a transaction would be artificial—abstract and ungrounded—if it did *not*

---

7. United States v. Monaco, 735 F.2d 1173, 1177 (9th Cir. 1984) (in trial of company president for fraudulently concealing luxury car from creditors of bankrupt brokerage, error to admit statement by comptroller that "minimized his responsibility" and implicated defendant more than himself).

8. State v. Pierre, 890 A.2d 474, 490-491 (Conn. 2006) (admitting co-offender B's statements that he and defendant abducted and beat victim, but B "really jammed the pole down his throat and then twisted the pole" to kill him; B acknowledged responsibility, did not shift blame, spoke to friend on his own); United States v. Franklin, 415 F.3d 537, 544-548 (6th Cir. 2005) (admitting against F statement by codefendant C to longtime friend that F and C were involved in "hitting a truck" and that F came to C and asked for money, saying his "stash" was under surveillance; C "did not minimize his role" and suggested that both "played substantial roles"); United States v. Shea, 211 F.3d 658, 668 (1st Cir. 2000) (admitting statements among friends; there was no blame-shifting), *cert. denied,* 531 U.S. 1154 (2001).

9. State v. Rivera, 844 A.2d 191, 203 (Conn. 2004) (admitting statement by co-offender G to nephew that he and defendant broke into victim's house seeking jewelry, that G stayed in kitchen as lookout while defendant searched, that victim entered kitchen, defendant started choking her and G ran; statement was "squarely" against G's interest, implicating him in burglary and felony murder, exposing G to liability "for the same types of crimes with which the defendant has been charged" and "implicating both"); United States v. Tocco, 200 F.3d 401, 414-415 (6th Cir. 2000) (in RICO trial, admitting statements by now-deceased MP implicating others; MP was talking to son, and "linked himself to others in the conspiracy," and fact that statements implicated others did not make them inadmissible).

refer to others. Usually including such references adds meaning and dimension to the self-inculpatory aspect of the statement (enhancing the against-interest element) simply by making it more realistic and convincing.[10] At the other end of the spectrum, when acts by the speaker have little connection with acts committed by the defendant, or when they differ completely in character, a statement describing the acts of both is less likely to be against interest insofar as it describes what defendant did.[11]

To what degree is the reference to acts or knowledge of another integral to a larger statement describing the declarant's knowledge or acts? The term "statement" in FRE 803(b)(3) contains no temporal boundary, and in theory could reach a series of utterances that begins at noon and ends at five. *Williamson* rejected this idea, stressing that that the exception turns on against-interest elements being present in everything that is offered.[12] Certainly any notion that the exception could reach a five o'clock statement incriminating the defendant because the speaker made self-accusatory comments at noon stretches the exception beyond the breaking point, but the boundaries of the exception expand where the logical connection between asserted facts harmful to the defendant and asserted facts harmful to the speaker is especially close. Still, the exception envisions a close narrative connection. In effect, references to another that are integral to the narrative describing declarant's own acts or knowledge are more likely to satisfy the against-interest requirement,[13] and references that are not closely connected are less likely to satisfy the requirement, so they should be

(c) How integral are references to the other?

10. United States v. Wexler, 522 F.3d 194, 201-203 (2d Cir. 2008) (admitting, in trial of doctor for distributing controlled substances and fraud, statement by deceased addict to friends saying defendant would prescribe anything he wanted, made false claims and gave him kickbacks; not testimonial; unlike *Williamson*, declarant implicated himself as well as defendant). State v. Yarbrough, 767 N.E.2d 216, 226-228 (Ohio 2002) (in trial for killing of informant A, admitting D's statement to wife that he would have A killed or kill her, to show that D hired defendant Y to kill A) (quoting authors of this Treatise).

11. Terry v. Commonwealth, 153 S.W.3d 794, 798 (Ky. 2005) (in murder trial, error to admit co-offender's statement to domestic companion that it was his gun that he retrieved from under mattress, and defendant used gun to kill "Candy Man," as only first part of statement was against interest) (reversing).

12. Williamson v. United States, 512 U.S. 594, 599 (1994) (dictionary definition of "statement" includes "extended declaration" and single remark, but principle points toward "narrower reading" that does not reach parts of statement that do not incriminate declarant).

13. United States v. Garris, 616 F.2d 626, 629-633 (2d Cir. 1980) (defendant E's sister P told agent that E said he had not been photographed in bank robbery; agent was investigating second robbery where P as teller gave thief money; P admitted complicity and said she concealed knowing how to reach E; statement was against P's interest, would be useful in trial of P for second robbery and accessory in first; exception reaches remark "integral to a larger statement" against interest; repeating what E said explained P's motive to help E escape), *cert. denied*, 447 U.S. 926.

severed from parts of the statement that are against interest, and excluded.[14]

(d) How much insider knowledge?

How much insider knowledge does the statement display? A statement can be against interest not only in disclosing (and tending to prove) facts that implicate the speaker—he committed a robbery, for example—but also in *creating evidence*. That is to say, the *statement itself* (and not merely events that the statement discloses) is against interest. Hence a statement can be against interest in suggesting that the speaker must know about the operations of a criminal venture even if the statement itself does not say anything at all about the speaker's own acts or role. This notion has at least some force in proving that *the speaker* is culpable, but it is less satisfactory as proof that someone mentioned in the statement did things that the statement describes because it would be easy to be very wrong on such points and yet display considerable insider knowledge.[15]

(2) Is the statement testimonial?

The second major challenge, whenever a third-party statement implicated the accused by name or obvious reference, is to decide whether the statement is "testimonial" for purposes of the *Crawford* doctrine. Almost certainly such statements are testimonial when made in police interviews or court proceedings, and this general subject is discussed in detail elsewhere.[16] Almost certainly, however, such statements are not testimonial when made in private settings, in which the speaker talks "off the record" so to speak, to friends or acquaintances with no thought to possible investigation or prosecution. Many post-*Crawford* opinions approve the use of such statements, when made in such settings, and the critical factor is to assess the reach of the against-interest element.[17]

The third challenge, now much diminished in importance because so many statements to police are testimonial under *Crawford*, is to decide whether the speaker was trying to curry favor. In *Williamson*, Harris had a powerful motive to curry favor: He'd been caught red-handed transporting cocaine, and uppermost in the mind of someone in that setting would be the possibility of minimizing consequences by making a deal. All nine Justices acknowledged the salience of this fact, which provided an obvious basis to dispose of the case. The majority in *Williamson* focused on whether the exception reaches "associated" or

14. United States v. Innamorati, 996 F.2d 456, 474-475 (1st Cir. 1993) (error to admit grand jury testimony; isolated statements blaming others do not fit exception) (harmless), *cert. denied*, 510 U.S. 955.

15. United States v. Shukri, 207 F.3d 412, 415-418 (7th Cir. 2000) (in trial of S for thefts, admitting statements by K describing what he did with B and S in removing goods and avoiding detection, and conversation between K and B on whether to reimburse S for goods that S bought; K "discussed his intimate knowledge of and involvements" in multiple thefts for which he and S were arrested).

16. See discussion in §8.84, *infra*.

17. United States v. Johnson, 440 F.3d 832, 843 (6th Cir. 2006) (admitting statements by co-offender to informant; not testimonial; declarant was "unaware that his conversations were being recorded" and reasonable person in his position would not anticipate use in investigation or prosecution).

"collateral" statements, rather than on currying favor. But in the passage where the majority said that much of what Harris said was not against interest, the majority also said someone in his position "might even think that implicating someone else would decrease his [own] practical exposure to criminal liability, at least so far as sentencing goes," which refers to the curry favor problem. In *Lilly*, the Court again focused on the motive of co-offenders. Statements like the one that Mark made to police indicating that his brother Ben had done the shooting are "inherently unreliable," quoting its decision in the *Lee* case some thirty years earlier for the proposition that a statement accusing another for crime "under circumstances in which the declarant stands to gain" is "presumptively suspect." The Court added that statements that "shift or spread the blame" to another fall outside the realm of reliable hearsay. Even if Mark's statements were "technically against penal interest" because they implicated Mark too in the killing, and a person in his position will know even without being told that "speaking up" in blaming others "may inure to his advantage."[18]

To make the point in a slightly different way, one cannot assume that a statement by a suspect to arresting officers is true to the extent that it concedes criminal responsibility. Conceding involvement in crime in this situation is not likely to be *against* interest at all: Instead, the concession is *self-serving* under the circumstances because it provides the best chance to avoid or minimize criminal responsibility by offering expressly or implicitly to blame others.

This element often proves to be a "poison pill" requiring exclusion of statements naming or alluding to others *even though* they are in some sense against interest. In today's world, such statements remain excludable even if an objection based on *Crawford* would fail because the speaker was cross-examinable at some earlier time.[19] So powerfully does this motive operate that it sometimes requires exclusion of statements, when offered against others than the speaker himself, even if they make *no reference* to the defendant.[20] Of course such statements are normally admissible against the speaker himself, if he is a defendant,

---

18. Lilly v. Virginia, 527 U.S. 116 (1999) (3-member plurality plus two concurrences plus three others agree that use of Mark's custodial statement incriminating Ben violated Ben's confrontation rights).

19. United States v. Chapman, 345 F.3d 630, 632-636 (8th Cir. 2003) (error to admit statements by co-offender after arrest, describing "regular routine" for delivering marijuana; he spoke "in the course of assisting the authorities with a controlled delivery" and was "casting himself as a mere mule and serving up the repeat buyer," thus "minimizing" liability) (harmless), *cert. denied*, 541 U.S. 955; United States v. Westmoreland, 240 F.3d 618, 625-629 (7th Cir. 2001) (A and J talked to police in custody, and each named defendant M and described things M said and did; use of statements violated confrontation rights; A was in custody; statements by J, made under interrogation by police; J's statements were "essentially an attempt to exonerate" J at expense of A and M, and were blame-shifting) (errors harmless).

20. United States v. Bell, 367 F.3d 452 (5th cir. 2004) (error to admit co-offender's statement, even though it did not mention defendant; speaker talked to police, may have curried favor, shifted blame).

under the admissions doctrine where motive does not count, but the *Bruton* doctrine may still require exclusion.[21]

Despite the risks that come with statements that curry favor, it seems that some are still sufficiently against interest to satisfy the exception,[22] and in the case of statements to informants or undercover agents not known as such by the speaker, arguments that he is currying favor fail.[23] Again *Crawford* requires exclusion of most if not all statements knowingly made to police or law enforcement officers, but they may not be excludable if the declarant testified at some point and was cross-examinable, at an earlier phase of proceedings.[24]

Corroboration While FRE 804(b)(3) requires corroboration for against-interest statements offered to exonerate the accused, the language does not contain a similar requirement for statements that implicate the accused. Congress considered and rejected a provision removing statements in the latter category from the exception, and the silence of the Rule can be chalked up to a congressional decision that the problem is constitutional. Some cases, seeking to alleviate constitutional concerns, have read into the exception a requirement of corroboration for against-interest statements implicating the accused.[25]

Any such requirement should parallel the express corroboration requirement for statements exonerating the accused. In light of the solicitude traditionally accorded to criminal defendants, arguably more in terms of corroboration should be expected in this setting. For any against-interest statements that are admitted *despite* being testimonial (because declarant testifies and can be cross-examined), however, it is arguable that the requirement is less urgent because cross-examination can alleviate concerns. It seems that the corroboration requirement is satisfied by circumstantial evidence indicating that a statement is trustworthy, by independent evidence establishing important points made by the statement itself, and by additional consistent statements by the same declarant (repetition of the same basic story).[26] The point is *not* to bolster the credibility of the witness

---

21. *See* Bruton v. United States, 391 U.S. 123 (1968), discussed in §8.28, *supra*.

22. State v. Cook, 135 P.3d 260, 266 (Or. 2006) (statements to police by co-offenders admitting to murder and implicating defendant satisfied exception; neither shifted blame and both "exposed themselves to the same level of criminal liability," and there were no promises of leniency; but statements were testimonial under *Crawford*) (reversing conviction).

23. United States v. Lang, 589 F.2d 92, 97 (2d Cir. 1978) ("curry favor" argument does not apply; speaker did not know he was with undercover agent).

24. On applying *Crawford* where speaker was cross-examinable on earlier occasion, see §8.87, *infra*.

25. United States v. Shukri, 207 F.3d 412, 415-418 (7th Cir. 2000; United States v. Barone, 114 F.3d 1284, 1300 n.10 (1st Cir. 1997), *cert. denied*, 522 U.S. 1021.

26. United States v. Barone, 114 F.3d 1284, 1300 (1st Cir. 1997) (what is required is not "independent evidence" of matters asserted, but evidence that statements are "worthy of belief, based upon the circumstances"), *cert. denied*, 522 U.S. 1021.

reporting the statement, but to bolster the credibility of the statement itself.[27]

§8.76 —Penal Interest: "Safe" Statements

The fact that a statement was made in a setting that seemed safe because the speaker was among friends does not take his statement outside the exception. Where listeners are casual acquaintances, such a statement carries a risk of disclosure that justifies applying the exception even if he does not think he will be exposed. And where the listeners are longtime friends or even family members, speaking may bring truly minimal risk, but the inference of trustworthiness is supported if the fact asserted is against interest. And in all these settings the trust reposed in the listener suggests a reason for the speaker to be accurate.[1]

It is different if the facts and statement are no longer likely to cause trouble for the speaker. In this setting, the against-interest element is gone or so far diminished that the exception is usually not applied.[2] And if the speaker has been convicted of crimes involving the acts or transactions he describes, against-interest elements are once again too remote to count. There is always a possibility of prevailing on appeal or collateral attack (so facts and statement might count in another trial), but still the against-interest element seems speculative.[3] The speaker may have other concerns, such as hoping for early release or favorable treatment during confinement. If he understands that his chances are better if he helps build a case against another, this fact casts added doubt on statements that incriminate others even if they are self-accusing enough to present against-interest elements.

Other circumstances may lessen or destroy against-interest elements: If the speaker was acquitted of charged crimes arising out of transactions to which his statement relates, he may be constitutionally secure from reprosecution; if the statute of limitations has run, that may block prosecution; if he is beyond reach of extradition, prosecution may be unlikely.[4] Where they appear, such factors may so substantially reduce

27. United States v. Seeley, 892 F.2d 1, 2-4 (1st Cir. 1989) (corroboration requirement does not demand proof of veracity of witness; she testifies and has personal knowledge and can be cross-examined).
§8.76 1. State v. Yarborough, 767 N.E.2d 216, 226 (Ohio 2002) (admitting statement by husband to wife, which fit exception even though he held privilege and could have blocked wife's testimony; he was deceased at time of defendant's trial); United States v. Katsougrakis, 715 F.2d 769, 773-778 (2d Cir. 1983) (admitting hospital confession by arsonist to friend, and statements to wife before job), *cert. denied*, 464 U.S. 1040; United States v. Mock, 640 F.2d 629, 631 (5th Cir. 1981) (statement to ex-wife).
2. United States v. Rhodes, 713 F.2d 463, 472-474 (9th Cir. 1983), *cert. denied*, 465 U.S. 1038; United States v. Love, 592 F.2d 1022, 1025-1026 (8th Cir. 1979).
3. *See* Witham v. Mabry, 596 F.2d 293, 296-298 (8th Cir. 1979); United States v. Satterfield, 572 F.2d 687, 690-693 (9th Cir. 1978), *cert. denied*, 439 U.S. 840.
4. United States v. Fowlie, 24 F.3d 1059, 1068 (9th Cir. 1994) (speaker was in Holland, said he would never return and knew he could not be extradited), *cert. denied*, 513 U.S. 1086.

any risk to the speaker that his statement cannot fit the exception, for neither the statement nor the underlying facts are against interest.[5] However, the number of cases is small, and one could still argue for applying the exception if the speaker did not likely realize how safe he was. In the case of acquittal, most would think they were safe, although a competently advised defendant would likely know that acquittal in state court leaves the possibility of federal charges, and vice versa. In the case of defenses based on the statute of limitations, understanding is less likely. Being beyond reach of extradition is a factor that is hard to assess. The sophistication and circumstances of the speaker count—a fugitive who selects Costa Rica because there is no extradition treaty presumably thinks he is safe, but others might have no such inkling. Yet for all speakers, the question of extradition may never be securely resolved (they may move about, the political climate may change) so against-interest elements may still be in play.

FRE 804(b)(4)

   (b) Hearsay exceptions. The following are not excluded by the hearsay rule if the declarant is unavailable as a witness: . . .

   (4) Statement of personal or family history. (A) A statement concerning the declarant's own birth, adoption, marriage, divorce, legitimacy, relationship by blood, adoption, or marriage, ancestry, or other similar fact of personal or family history, even though declarant had no means of acquiring personal knowledge of the matter stated; or (B) a statement concerning the foregoing matters, and death also, of another person, if the declarant was related to the other by blood, adoption, or marriage or was so intimately associated with the other's family as to be likely to have accurate information concerning the matter declared.

---

§8.77 Personal or Family History

The exception for statements by an unavailable speaker on his own personal or family history, or the personal or family history of relatives or intimate family associates, reaches statements about oneself even though the speaker could not have personal knowledge and statements about another (even without such knowledge) if the speaker was "related" to the person or "so intimately associated" with her family that he likely had "accurate information." The idea is that where live testimony by the speaker cannot be had, such statements are trustworthy enough. The Rule accepts the common experience that such statements are likely to rest on adequate information and to be truthful. The

---

5. United States v. Rogers, 549 F.2d 490, 498 n.8 (8th Cir. 1976), *cert. denied*, 431 U.S. 918.

exception reaches statements relating to birth or adoption,[1] marriage or divorce,[2] legitimacy or relationship by blood, adoption, or marriage,[3] or ancestry[4] or other similar facts relating to the speaker or his family or a family to which he was closely connected.[5] The exception reaches statements describing the death of another.[6]

Sometimes the exception requires independent evidence that the speaker belonged to the family or was intimately associated with it.[7] But such evidence is not required for statements describing the speaker's own role or relationship to a family. Thus a statement in which the speaker says he is or was married to someone, or is the child or parent of someone, requires no such independent proof.[8]

Independent evidence

FRE 804(b)(6)

(b) Hearsay exception. The following are not excluded by the hearsay rule if the declarant is unavailable as a witness: . . .

(6) Forfeiture by wrongdoing. A statement offered against a party who has engaged or acquiesced in wrongdoing that was intended to, and did, procure the unavailability of the declarant as a witness.

---

§8.77 1. Bowden v. Caldron, 554 S.W.2d 25, 28 (Tex. Civ. App. 1977) (husband's affidavit, after death of natural child, that he had no brother or sister); Liacakos v. Kennedy, 195 F. Supp. 630, 633 (D.D.C. 1961) (plaintiff's testimony that mother told him he was born in West Virginia).

2. Lessee of Jewell v. Jewell, 42 U.S. 219, 231 (1843) (statement by decedent that wife's mother was not married to her father); Franzen v. E. I. du Pont De Nemours & Co., 51 F. Supp. 578 (D.N.J. 1943) (statements by decedent that he was not married to plaintiff), aff'd, 146 F.2d 837 (3d Cir. 1944).

3. Re Estate of McClain, 392 A.2d 1371, 1372-1374 (Pa. 1978) (statements by decedent that caveators were his grandnieces and sole heirs-at-law); Will of T, 382 N.Y.S.2d 916, 919 (Sur. Ct. 1976) (statements by decedent that will contestant was her son).

4. Fulkerson v. Holmes, 117 U.S. 389 (1886) (statement in deed that grantor was "only child and heir" of patentee); Strickland v. Humble Oil & Ref. Co., 140 F.2d 83, 86 (5th Cir. 1944) (statement identifying uncle of witness), cert. denied, 323 U.S. 712.

5. United States v. Hernandez, 105 F.3d 1330, 1332 (9th Cir. 1997) (in trial for illegal entry, admitting defendant's statement about his birth), cert. denied, 522 U.S. 890; Pollack v. Metropolitan Life Ins. Co., 138 F.2d 123, 146 (3d Cir. 1943) (statement by decedent indicating age).

6. Cox v. Brice, 159 F. 378 (5th Cir. 1908) (family members said HC was member of command killed in Texas Revolution); Bank of New York v. United States, 174 F. Supp. 911, 915 (S.D.N.Y. 1957) (statement in will that son had disappeared).

7. Fulkerson v. Holmes, 117 U.S. 389 (1886) (relationship of speaker with family must be shown by independent proof); Stein v. Bowman, 38 U.S. 209 (1839) (error to admit statements that plaintiff was brother of S; speakers did not seem to be family).

8. Re Estate of McClain, 392 A.2d 1371, 1372-1374 (Pa. 1978) (on speaker's pedigree, no need for independent evidence); Morgan v. Susino Constr. Co., 33 A.2d 607, 610-611 (N.J. 1943) (admitting statement about parenthood despite lack of independent evidence), aff'd, 36 A.2d 604 (N.J. 1944).

§8.78 Statements Admissible Because of Forfeiture by Wrongdoing

Adopted in 1997, FRE 804(b)(6) paves the way to admit, against a party who has "engaged or acquiesced in wrongdoing that was intended to, and did" make the declarant unavailable as a witness, statements made by such a declarant. This provision was aimed at "organized crime cases," and the paradigm in the mind of the framers was the case in which someone facing criminal charges (or about to be charged) resorts to coercive tactics, personally or though intermediaries, to locate and kill or frighten off witnesses. The idea is to lessen the incentive to behave in this way, in effect saying to criminal defendants "killing or frightening off witnesses may keep them from testifying in person, but the cost to you is that we will admit anything they have already said that may be relevant."

In practice

When the Court adopted a new approach to confrontation in *Crawford* in 2004, it went out of its way to approve the idea of forfeiting confrontation rights, reiterating its approval two years later in *Davis*.[1] Central to the *Crawford* doctrine is the proposition that the only kind of hearsay touched by the confrontation clause is "testimonial" hearsay, meaning mostly actual testimony and statements to police investigating crime. The hearsay forfeiture exception in FRE 804(b)(6) is broader because it covers hearsay of all sorts, including statements in private settings that are mostly *not* testimonial.

In the *Giles* case in 2008, the Court decided that the forfeiture doctrine recognized in *Crawford* and *Davis*, as applied to testimonial statements, requires a showing that defendant engaged in conduct that was designed or intended to prevent the declarant from testifying.[2] Merely "knowing" that a homicidal act will make the witness unavailable is not enough, *Giles* held.

Giles did not answer the question whether the intent standard in the constitutional forfeiture doctrine matches the intent standard in FRE 804(b)(6), which applies to all hearsay ("testimonial" or not), but the two standards are almost certainly the same, as telling language in *Giles* indicates. Hence satisfying the exception means also satisfying the confrontation clause in the typical setting in which a prosecutor offers testimonial hearsay against a defendant on the theory that he acted wrongfully to make the declarant unavailable.[3] *Giles* went far to end debate among commentators, and sharp conflict in decisions, on the

§8.78 1. *See* Crawford v. Washington, 541 U.S. 36, 54 (2004) ("rule of forfeiture by wrongdoing (which we accept) extinguishes confrontation claims on essentially equitable grounds"); Davis v. Washington, 547 U.S. 813, 833 (2006) (FRE 804(b)(6) "codifies the forfeiture doctrine").

2. Giles v. California, 128 S. Ct. 2678 (2008) (homicide victim complained to police about defendant's behavior before he shot and killed her).

3. *See* the discussion of *Giles* in §8.90, *infra*. *See also* People v. Stechly, 870 N.E.2d 333, 351 (Ill. 2007) (hearsay exception and constitutional forfeiture doctrine are "coextensive"); United States v. Emery, 186 F.3d 921, 921 (8th Cir. 1999) (forfeiting confrontation rights means that hearsay rights are similarly forfeited under FRE 804(b)(6)).

matter of intent. It is arguable, in view of the fact that intent is required, that "waiver" is the better term for both the exception and the constitutional doctrine, but forfeiture is the term used in both settings, and we use it in our discussion.[4]

Obviously the exception reaches such things as grand jury testimony (as cases cited in this section indicate). Indeed, FRE 804(b)(6) rests on decisions in the 1970's and 1980's that admitted grand jury testimony by witnesses who had been killed or scared off by defendants before trial.[5] Just as clearly, the exception is not limited to such statements. Modern cases apply the exception to unsworn statements given to law enforcement agents, prosecuting attorneys, and to friends or acquaintances of the declarant, or for that matter to strangers.[6] Some such statements might fit other exceptions (like the one for excited utterances), but many simply report prior criminality and would not fit other exceptions. Equally important, many statements to police (and perhaps others) would be "testimonial" under *Crawford*, hence ordinarily excludable under the confrontation clause, but the constitutional forfeiture doctrine can obviate this objection too.[7]

Reaches all kinds of statements

By its terms, the exception is not limited by concerns over reliability or trustworthiness, or by criteria typical of the categorical exceptions that relate to subject matter or set limits. But hearsay offered under FRE 804(b)(6) should be excluded under FRE 403 when concerns relating to unfair prejudice or confusion of issues become paramount, or when it is likely to be misleading. Concerns over trustworthiness may be a function of factors that a jury would have to consider in appraising statements offered under the exception, and these factors may in turn raise concerns over unfair prejudice, confusion of issues, or tendency to mislead, in which case exclusion may be warranted.[8]

Trustworthiness

The exception turns on three elements: First, there must be a "wrongful act." Second, there must be an "intent" to silence a witness (make him unavailable to testify). Third, the act must *in fact* have made the witness unavailable (must have *caused* the witness to be unavailable). In language that was added at the last minute to the ACN to FRE 804(b)(6), but lost from many published versions of the Rules, the

Elements:
(1) wrongful act,
(2) intent,
(3) cause

---

4. *Compare* Friedman, Confrontation and the Definition of Chutzpa, 31 Israel L. Rev. 506 (1997) (defendant should not be allowed to kill victim, then invoke confrontation rights to exclude her statements) *with* Flanagan, Confrontation, Equity, and the Misnamed Exception for "Forfeiture" by Misconduct, 14 William & Mary Bill of Rights Journal 1193 (2006) (waiver is better term; prosecutors should be required to prove guilt "in a manner consistent with constitutional procedure," as with any guilty defendant who pleads innocent).

5. *See, e.g.*, United States v. Thevis, 665 F.2d 616 (5th Cir. 1982); United States v. Carlson, 547 F.2d 1346 (8th Cir. 1976).

6. *See* United States v. Price, 265 F.3d 1097, 1102-1103 (10th Cir. 2001) (statements to FBI agents), *cert. denied*, 122 S. Ct. 2299; United States v. Johnson, 219 F.3d 349, 356 (4th Cir. 2000) (statements to third parties), *cert denied*, 531 U.S. 1024.

7. See the discussion of "testimonial" hearsay in §8.85, *infra*.

8. *See* United States v. Dhinsa, 243 F.3d 635, 654-656 (2d Cir. 2001) (seemingly suggesting that courts can exclude "facially unreliable" hearsay under FRE 403 even in forfeiture cases).

framers stated their understanding that the exception is triggered by acts committed *"after the event"* (an apparent reference to the charged crime), which would sharply limit the exception to cases that more-or-less fit the paradigm case described above. By its terms, however, the exception does not contain this limit, and many cases apply it when the charged crime and the predicate act are one and the same (a point noted further below).[9]

(1) Wrongful act

The wrongful act requirement is satisfied, in the clearest of all cases, if a defendant who has been charged or is being investigated for some offense or offenses personally kills an informant in order to keep him from testifying. But acts far less extreme suffice,[10] such as threatening a witness where the result is that he flees or hides from the process server and cannot be found, or (if found) refuses to testify in fear of retaliation,[11] and an act can be "wrongful" under the exception even if it is not criminal.[12]

Some cases present serious challenges. Suppose a defendant facing criminal charges talks to a witness who has testified or made statements that incriminate the defendant, and he meets with the witness or contacts him, and argues that his testimony or statements are wrong and asks him to reconsider, to change what he says, or to go into hiding or leave the jurisdiction? Is such conduct necessarily wrongful? If the behavior is coercive, or if the defendant's aim is to get the witness to lie, it does seem wrongful, but it is not so clear that all such conduct is always wrongful, and trying to persuade a witness that his story is mistaken and that he should be saying something else is not wrongful in itself.[13] In *Reynolds*, which is the earliest Supreme Court case to approve the forfeiture principle, all that the defendant was shown to have done was to decline to help a process server locate his other wife (it was a bigamy prosecution; apparently defendant had two wives). *Reynolds*

9. *See* ACN to FRE 804(b)(6) (exception "applies to actions taken after the event to prevent a witness from testifying").

10. Commonwealth v. Edwards, 830 N.E.2d 158, 168-169 (Mass. 2005) (forfeiture doctrine should apply where defendant "murders, threatens, or intimidates a witness in an effort to procure that witness's unavailability," or commits a "criminal act," such as violating a witness tampering statute, to make the witness unavailable; no court has approved "collusion" as a basis for forfeiture, but none has rejected it).

11. *See* United States v. Scott, 284 F.3d 758, 764 (7th Cir. 2002) ("coercion, undue influence or pressure" as well as "threats of harm and suggestions of future retribution"); United States v. Zlatogur, 271 F.3d 1025, 1028 (7th Cir. 2001) (threats), *cert. denied*, 535 U.S. 946; United States v. Aguiar, 975 F.2d 45, 47 (2d Cir. 1992) (letter threatening to expose declarant as murderer, tell other prisoners he was informer).

12. *See* ACN to FRE 804(b)(6) (referring to "aberrant behavior"); United States v. Williams, 443 F.3d 35 (2d Cir. 2006) (wrongdoing "need not consist of a criminal act").

13. *Compare* Commonwealth v. Edwards, 830 N.E.2d 158, 170-171 (Mass. 2005) (series of phonecalls to state's key witness "orchestrating" his departure; forfeiture standard satisfied if defendant "puts forward to a witness the idea to avoid testifying," even by mere "persuasion" or "actively facilitates" intent of witness not to testify, although "merely informing" witness of right to remain silent under 5th Amendment is not enough) *with* United States v. Ochoa, 229 F.3d 631, 639 (7th Cir. 2000) (aiding witness to place calls was not wrongful; not deciding whether doing so would satisfy standard if one knew witness would flee).

serves as the historical basis for recognizing the principle in American law, but the bare facts recited in the case would not justify a finding of forfeiture under FRE 804(b)(6), and actually the former testimony exception could have been applied there without assessing the behavior of the defendant.[14]

Mere actionable misconduct, in the form of negligence for instance, does not trigger the exception: Running over the declarant in an automobile accident is not enough. If the driver knew the identity or potential significance of his victim as a witness, still negligence in killing him is not the same thing as intending to silence him. If the driver did not know his victim's identity or significance as a witness, it is clearer still that the intent requirement is not satisfied.[15]

By its terms, FRE 804(b)(3) says that mere "acquiescence in misconduct" suffices as well. This language apparently reaches situations in which the defendant knows that another is acting in wrongful ways that are likely to frighten off a witness, or to lead to his death or some other form of unavailability, where the defendant has power or influence over the other that he could reasonably bring to bear, but he declines to do so. Mere knowledge coupled with inaction is not enough, and some modern codifications back away from the apparent looseness of the federal language, preferring tighter terminology: Thus the Michigan provision uses the term "encouragement," and the looser term "acquiescence" only makes sense if the defendant's relationship with the actor is one in which inaction really amounts to encouragement. Such situations are riddled with other questions: What "might" the defendant have done that he did not do? What did he know about what another was doing? Could he have stopped the behavior? Trial judges must decide all these matters, often on the basis of circumstantial proof.[16]

Acquiescence in misconduct

A landmark decision by the Tenth Circuit in the *Cherry* case holds that this language reaches conduct that would suffice, under substantive criminal law, to incur criminal liability as an accomplice. It follows that if one person kills a witness to prevent him from testifying, or scares or threatens a witness for this reason, then others who conspire with that person in an undertaking in which killing or suppressing testimony is a necessary and natural consequence, have also forfeited the right to exclude what the witness has said. Obviously a defendant who hires another to kill or threaten a witness to prevent his testimony is covered, as are conspirators who participate in the undertaking for this purpose. This principle, however, does not reach outsiders even if they have knowledge or could do something to prevent the conduct, nor does

Conspirators

14. Reynolds v. United States, 98 U.S. 145 (1878) (defendant told marshal that witness "was not at home," adding when asked where she was, "you will have to find out") (wrongful procurement standard satisfied).

15. *See* United States v. Ochoa, 229 F.3d 631, 639 (7th Cir. 2000) (described in prior note).

16. Steele v. Taylor, 684 F.2d 1193, 1199-1201 (6th Cir. 1982) ("any significant interference" other than by exercising a legal right to object at trial, is a wrongful act, including "force or threats" and a directive to exercise 5th Amendment privilege), *cert denied*, 460 U.S. 1053.

it reach conspirators in a venture in which such acts are not a likely or necessary consequence.[17]

(2) Intent (purpose)

The required element of intent means, at the very least, that the defendant must act wrongfully for the particular purpose of making the witness unavailable.[18] In other words, the purpose of the defendant must be to prevent the witness from appearing or testifying, and the mere fact that a defendant *knows*, for example, that killing a person will prevent her from appearing or testifying is not enough: A defendant in a murder cases has not forfeited his right to exclude hearsay statements by his victim if all that can be said is that the defendant committed the wrongful act of killing the victim and must have known that the result would be that she could not appear or testify.[19]

It seems that intent can lead to forfeiture even if it is not single-minded, and the appearance of additional purposes does not keep the standard from being satisfied.[20] It is not necessary to prove that the defendant anticipated testimony by the victim in the very future proceeding in which her statement is later offered.[21] Also it may not be necessary to prove the expected substance of the testimony that the witness might have given, although its tenor or nature is relevant to the inquiry on intent.[22] And of course statements offered under the exception provide a good clue on this score. Finally, the requisite intent may exist before criminal charges are filed, so long as the person who engages in wrongful conduct has the intent of silencing a potential

---

17. United States v. Cherry, 217 F.2d 811, 818 (10th Cir. 2000) (discussing *Pinkerton* doctrine defining and limiting liability of conspirators). *Accord*, United States v. Thompson, 286 F.3d 950, 963-964 (7th Cir. 2002), United States v. Carson, 455 F.3d 336 (D.C. Cir. 2006), *cert. denied*, 127 S. Ct. 1351 (both following *Cherry*). On accomplice liability, *see* 2 LaFave & Scott, Substantive Criminal Law §6.6 (1986).

18. Giles v. California, 128 S. Ct. 2678 (2008) (quoting authors of this Treatise).

19. State v. Brooks, 249 S.W.3d 323, 329 (Tenn. 2008) (in murder trial of man for beating girlfriend to death, there was no evidence that he threatened harm if victim went to police, no proof he followed her to initiate charges, and no evidence he knew she had spoken with police; after assault, she told police she did not want to press charges and continued to live with him; hours before murder, she told investigator on phone that she "had a warrant" on defendant, but it was unclear whether he overheard) (reversing for error in applying forfeiture doctrine); Commonwealth v. Laich, 777 A.2d 1057, 1062 n.4 (Pa. 2001) (wrongdoing for "another purpose," such as "personal animosity," does not bring forfeiture exception into play).

20. United States v. Dhinsa, 243 F.3d 635, 654 (2d Cir. 2001) (need not show that "sole motivation" was to procure declarant's absence, only motivation in part by desire to silence), *cert. denied*, 534 U.S. 897.

21. Vasquez v. People, 173 P.3d 1099 (Colo. 2007) (in trial for violating restraining order and bail bond, admitting statements by defendant's wife, whom he murdered because "she set [him] up" by contacting police; forfeiture reaches cases where defendant intended to prevent testimony "in one proceeding," then benefitted "perhaps unwittingly" from unavailability in another).

22. United States v. Gray, 405 F.3d 227, 240-243 (4th Cir. 2005) (in fraud trial arising out of wife's attempt to recover insurance on life of husband, admitting his statements to police; she had murdered him, and judge could decide that she was aware of his status as witness on assault charges he had brought against her and boyfriend; exception does not require that declarant would testify at any *particular* trial, nor limit subject of statements to events distinct from events at issue in trial), *cert. denied*, 456 U.S. 912.

witness in a foreseeable criminal or other proceeding.[23] These quali-fiers do not "water down" the intent requirement, which is both real and critical, but rather they are realistic in recognizing that intent is not a unitary or precise concept, that it cannot be assessed with mathemat-ical precision, and that anticipating the future is often an unfocused undertaking.

The exception does *not* apply where the purpose of killing or intim-idating a witness was *not* to silence him on some point, but to take revenge, obtain other personal gain, or give vent to hatred, animus, jealousy, or anger.[24] It is *not* the case that every time a defendant is tried for killing someone or committing some other crime leaving the victim unable or unwilling to testify, everything that the victim said is admis-sible. If this were the outcome, the exception would in effect overturn many decisions that exclude statements by the victim relating to the defendant, which would give the forfeiture exception broader sweep than was intended.[25] In keeping the exception to its proper scope, the key is to apply it only where the purpose of a wrongful act was to silence the witness.

Perhaps not surprisingly, the matter of cause gets little attention, but cause is one of the predicate facts that prosecutors must establish in invoking the exception.[26] If a defendant kills a witness in order to make him unavailable to testify, construing the killing as causing unavailabil-ity actually skips over another question, which is whether the victim *would have testified* if he had lived. Of course this question may be hard to answer, and the same is true if the witness disappears after being threatened or bribed, and even if she simply declines to testify after the defendant has brought pressure to bear. But in most cases, we have at least some help from the defendant himself—*he* thought the witness was ready to testify, or his purposeful and wrongful conduct is hard to explain. And there is the additional fact that the defendant's own behavior causes the dilemma, which adds some justification for drawing the necessary adverse inference on the matter of cause when the facts suggest it.

Hard questions of cause can arise even when the witness is alive and can be brought to court (or when we have her affidavit), but she refuses to testify. In such cases, she may be reticent about saying that her reason

(3) Causation

---

23. State v. Hand, 840 N.E.2d 151, 172 (Ohio 2006) (defendant admitted to cellmate that he killed accomplice to keep him from testifying; it made no difference that there were no pending charges and no evidence that witness intended to testify); United States v. Miller, 116 F.3d 641, 667-669 (2d Cir. 1997) (no requirement of "ongoing proceeding" in which declarant was to testify), *cert. denied*, 524 U.S. 905.

24. Commonwealth v. Laich, 777 A.2d 1057, 1062 n.4 (Pa. 2001) (murder victim's statements were not admissible; wrongdoing based on personal animosity, not intent to make declarant unavailable to testify).

25. In homicide trials, for example, two kinds of statements by the victim are gen-erally excluded (those expressing fear of defendant, and those indicating intent to meet him, when offered to prove what he thereafter did). *See* discussion in §8.39, *supra*.

26. State v. Wright, 726 N.W.2d 464 (Minn. 2007) (remanding assault case so judge could decide whether defendant's conduct caused refusal of victim and her sister to testify).

for not cooperating is that defendant threatened her or did something else to make her afraid. It is to be expected that a witness who refuses to testify because defendant has threatened or frightened her will also refuse *to say* that he has done so. Indeed, defendants who threaten witnesses are likely also to admonish them against *saying* such things. In these cases, the question of cause must be resolved by inference (which is often possible under the preponderance standard, but would be more difficult if clear and convincing evidence were required). Domestic abuse cases fall into this difficult category: Expert testimony may be essential, as well as other statements by the victim, and proof of causation may be circumstantial. Still the requirement must be satisfied.[27] The judge must make a factual determination, subject to review for clear error.[28]

Perhaps not surprisingly, litigants sometimes argue that wrongful behavior can "cause" witnesses to be unavailable, even when it is not coercive. Thus a defendant who escapes confinement and hides from law enforcement might be said to have "caused" the unavailability of a witness who dies or moves away during this period of absence. Even though conduct of this sort may be wrongful in some sense, however, the notion that it caused the witness to be unavailable is too attenuated to satisfy any reasonable concept of causation,[29] and courts have wisely rejected these and like arguments as farfetched.[30]

27. State v. Wright, 726 N.W.2d 464, 482 (Minn. 2007) (must show that conduct "actually did" make witnesses unavailable); State v. Mechling, 633 S.E.2d 311, 324-325 (W.Va. 2006) (reversing domestic battery conviction; no proof that defendant's misconduct kept victim from testifying; court was "painfully aware" of problems in such cases, and dangers to women; still, prosecutors must secure evidence "possibly from third parties" to prove cause); State v. Hansen, 312 N.W.2d 96, 104 (Minn. 1981) (in trial arising out of shooting, error to admit victims' statements; they were afraid to testify, but there was no proof that defendant threatened them).

28. United States v. Montague, 421 F.3d 1099, 1102-1103 (10th Cir. 2005) (admitting grand jury testimony by defendant's wife who refused to testify on basis of privilege; court could find, without asking why she claimed privilege, that defendant procured unavailability on basis of proffered testimony by daughter, history of violence, and behavior in "repeatedly" violating no-contact order); United States v. Scott, 284 F.3d 758, 765 (7th Cir. 2002) (hard to show that defendant's conduct in prison made J unavailable, since J refused to testify to grand jury earlier; task is to assess his refusals, and J "had been thrown from the frying pan into the fire" because he was no longer merely target of investigation, but had been charged; defendant asked another to find out whether government was going to drop contempt charges against J in exchange for testimony; defendant tried to find out whether J was going to testify, and only then, "after which coercion was inferable," did defendant become "happy" that J would not testify; J gave "religious and moral reasons" for not testifying; judge could find that defendant was "real reason").

29. State v. Lopez, 98 P.3d 699, 702 (N.M. 2004) (after indictment, defendant absconded and was missing for seven years; critical witness finished prison sentence and was deported; defendant did not cause absence of witness for purposes of forfeiture) (nor did he intend to make witness unavailable).

30. State v. Warsame, 735 N.W.2d 684, 697 n.7 (Minn. 2007) (cutting phone line so victim could not call 911 would not bring forfeiture doctrine into play); State v. Henderson, 160 P.3d 776, 793 (Kan. 2007) (assaulting child incompetent to testify because of inability to understand duty to tell truth did not forfeit confrontation rights).

Silencing *Y* is likely to involve a criminal act, so a prosecutor who charges *X* for the original misdeeds may tack on additional charges for crimes entailed in the acts that silence *Y*. Indeed, charging *X* with such crimes may be more plausible or attractive than charging *X* with the original misdeeds, so the prosecutor might charge *X only* with crimes entailed in silencing the witness. Here the crimes that bring the exception into play are the very crimes for which the defendant is tried (the focus of trial). This possibility can ordinarily be realized only if the exception embraces *not only* statements by *Y* relating to *X*'s original misdeeds, *but also* statements by *Y* relating to *X*'s conduct toward *Y*. Nothing in the literal terms of FRE 804(b)(6) limits the exception to statements about the original misdeeds, although it is plausible to argue that the *purpose* of the exception is not to enable prosecutors to introduce all manner of hearsay, but rather to deprive wrongdoers of evidence of the very sort that they seek to suppress. The cases read the exception broadly, and do not impose this limit.[31]

Charged crime may be predicate act

In determining the preliminary facts, the judge should hold a hearing outside the presence of the jury, and the burden is on the prosecutor to establish the predicate facts, including wrongful conduct, intent, and cause, by a preponderance of the evidence (some states impose a more exacting standard).[32] One reason for such precautions is that the inquiry always examines misconduct by the defendant, and often such misconduct is not relevant or admissible during the trial itself. Another is that predictably the judge relies on proof that is or may be inadmissible in the trial, including statements by the declarant.[33] The preponderance standard seems appropriate even though most wrongful conduct proved in applying the exception is criminal: After all, the reason for inquiring into such misconduct is not to convict the defendant of a crime for engaging in it, but rather to decide whether to admit statements by the victim, and it is the preponderance standard that applies generally to preliminary issues relating to admissibility. As noted above, it is predictable that proof of all three predicate facts (wrongful conduct, intent, causation) will be largely circumstantial.

Procedural issues

A court can make a tentative decision on the basis of facts uncovered in such a hearing, then admit the statements provisionally, then make a

31. United States v. Dhinsa, 243 F.3d 635, 653 (2d Cir. 2001) (exception puts "no limitation" on "subject matter" of statements that can be offered to prove that defendant murdered declarant), *cert. denied*, 534 U.S. 897.

32. *See* ACN to FRE 804(b)(6) (preponderance standard applies); State v. Moua Her, 750 N.W.2d 258, 274 (Minn. 2008) (resolve issue outside hearing of jury; preponderance); Vasquez v. People, 173 P.3d 1099, 1115 (Colo. 2007) (hearing outside presence of jury; preponderance); State v. Jensen, 727 N.W.2d 518, 536 (Wis. 2007) (preponderance). But see State v. Mason, 162 P.3d 396, 404 (Wash. 2007) ("clear, cogent, and convincing" evidence); People v. Geraci, 625 N.E.2d 817, 822 (N.Y. 1995) ("clear and convincing evidence").

33. *See* §§1.12 and 8.27-8.34, *supra. And see* Davis v. Washington, 547 U.S. 813, 833 (2007) (quoting state decision that judge may rely on hearsay in resolving forfeiture question); People v. Stechly, 870 N.E.2d 333, 371 (Ill. 2007) (court may consider hearsay, including statements by declarant himself).

final decision on admissibility later on. If the court finally decides that statements admitted provisionally do not satisfy the exception, a mistrial may be necessary if an instruction to disregard the statements is likely to be ineffective. As is true in applying the coconspirator exception, making a final decision on the preliminary facts before admitting any such statement would reduce the risk of mistrial. But the reality is that at least *some* evidence of the charged offense will also be relevant in determining the preliminary facts on which the exception depends, and proceeding on the basis of a provisional decision is far more practical.[34]

Like other exceptions, this one obviates hearsay objections but leaves other objections intact, such as those based on relevancy or exclusionary doctrines like the provisions relating to character evidence (the bar against proving bad acts for purposes of showing conduct on a particular occasion) and unfair prejudice.[35]

In the first decade after this new forfeiture exception appeared in the Rules, twelve states adopted similar provisions.[36] Thirteen more states and the District of Columbia recognized the constitutional forfeiture doctrine, as they must because the meaning of the confrontation clause is a matter of federal law on which the Supreme Court is the final authority, but without formally adopting matching hearsay exceptions.[37]

Forfeiture doctrine in the states; trustworthiness issue

This situation presents a stark question that is actually hard to answer: Should forfeiture of confrontation rights also entail forfeiture of the right to exclude hearsay? To add a bit of perspective, we should bear in mind that most states that have spoken to the matter take the view that forfeiting confrontation rights has the effect of also forfeiting hearsay objections, which means that practice in these states closely resembles federal practice.[38] Not all states fit this mold, however. For example, California's forfeiture exception paves the way to admit only statements that comply with criteria aimed at insuring trustworthiness, and some authority elsewhere either assumes or holds that forfeiting confrontation rights leaves hearsay rights intact, so even defendants who wrongfully procure the absence of witnesses can still object to the use of their statements if they do not satisfy an exception that

34. United States v. White, 116 F.3d 903, 915-916 (D.C. Cir. 1997) (approving procedure in which judge admitted statement by murdered declarant on basis of tentative decision that defendant was responsible, then resolved forfeiture issue during trial) (per curiam).

35. United States v. Dhinsa, 243 F.3d 635, 654-656 (2d Cir. 2001) (FRE 403 applies; should also avoid facially unreliable hearsay), *cert. denied*, 534 U.S. 897.

36. States with codified hearsay exceptions based on forfeiture include California, Delaware, Hawaii, Kentucky, Maryland, Michigan, North Dakota, Ohio, Oregon, Pennsylvania, Tennessee, and Vermont.

37. Decisions in the following jurisdictions apply some form of the forfeiture principle: Colorado, Connecticut, District of Columbia, Illinois, Iowa, Kansas, Minnesota, New Jersey, New Mexico, New York, Texas, Washington, and Wisconsin.

38. Citations to state decisions on the question whether forfeiture reaches only confrontation rights or also hearsay rights are collected in §8.90, *infra*.

usually rests in part on notions of trustworthiness.[39] Which approach is preferable?

In favor of the broader approach, in which forfeiting confrontation rights also forfeits hearsay rights, one can say that it goes as far as possible to discourage (remove incentives for) wrongful conduct aimed at frustrating the judicial process. In the most common situation in which a witness has testified in a deposition or before a grand jury, or has made a statement to police describing threats or other misconduct, the broader approach would not only overcome an objection based on *Crawford* that the statement is "testimonial," but also an objection that the statement is hearsay that does not fit an exception. Indeed, the broad approach would pave the way to admit *any and all* relevant statements, which of course includes those made in private settings (which are usually not testimonial under *Crawford*, but which may not fit a standard hearsay exception). In contrast, the narrower approach allows misbehaving defendants to exclude some statements (those fitting no exception), leaving in place *some* incentive for misconduct.

There is, however, something to be said in favor of the narrower approach: Arguably even egregious misbehavior should not lead courts to take more risks of wrongfully convicting someone on the basis of unreliable evidence, and the broad approach would have this effect. One can say also that the narrower approach is adequate to achieve its deterrent purpose, because it paves the way to admit the most common and important statements, and modern hearsay exceptions (such as those covering statements by child victims) are broad enough to make broader forfeiture unnecessary. Finally, one might say that in an analogous setting—that being *civil* cases where litigants misbehave by refusing to do discovery—the Court has approved remedies allowing adverse findings *only if* the misbehavior is logically probative of such findings, and *not* purely as a punitive measure, which points toward the conclusion that drawing adverse factual inferences on the basis of misbehavior as opposed to probative evidence should not be tolerated, which in turn suggests that the more measured response is appropriate in forfeiture cases, and that courts should not abandon standards of reliability purely as punishment.[40]

---

39. See Cal. Ev. Code. §1350 (statement must be recorded or written and notarized "prior to the death or kidnapping" of declarant and made "under circumstances which indicate its trustworthiness" and cannot be made as result of "promise, inducement, threat, or coercion"). See also Vasquez v. People, 173 P.3d 1099 (Colo. 2007) ("more prudent course is to require that the hearsay rules be satisfied separately") (approving statement to police that fit catchall; defendant forfeited confrontation rights by killing witness).

40. *Compare* Hovey v. Elliott, 167 U.S. 409 (1897) (penalizing for failing to obey court order by striking answer denies due process) *with* Hammond Packing Co. v. State of Arkansas, 212 U.S. 322 (1909) (failing to produce "material evidence" justifies striking an answer and entering default where misconduct supports inference of "want of merit in the asserted defense").

H. HEARSAY ON HEARSAY; IMPEACHMENT AND SUPPORT

> **FRE 805**
>
> Hearsay included within hearsay is not excluded under the hearsay rule if each part of the combined statements conforms with an exception to the hearsay rule provided in these rules.

§8.79 Layered or Multiple Hearsay

Under FRE 805, layered (double or multiple) hearsay in which one out-of-court statement incorporates another is not excludable as hearsay if each statement fits an exception.

The concept of layered hearsay is not complicated, but it is awkward to describe, and some illustrations and new terms are useful: Assume *M* learns from *L* that *K* said the light was green. If *M* testifies about *L*'s statement describing what *K* said and the purpose is to prove the light was green, *M*'s testimony involves layered (double) hearsay. What *L* said might be called the final statement since it is the last link in the chain (in this case having two links), and *K*'s is the original statement since it is the first link. Under FRE 805, *M*'s testimony is not barred as hearsay if both the final and original statements fit hearsay exceptions (the same or different ones). This kind of double hearsay is fairly common. Or assume *M* learns from *L* that *K* said that *J* said the light was red. *M*'s testimony describing what *L* said that *K* said that *J* said involves multiple hearsay if the purpose is to prove the light was red. *L*'s statement is again the final one (last in a three-link chain); *K*'s is an intermediate statement (second link) since it does not report that the light was red, but only what *J* said, and *J*'s assertion is the original statement (first link). Under FRE 805, *M*'s testimony is not barred as hearsay if the final, intermediate, and original statements all fit hearsay exceptions (same or different ones). Layered hearsay may involve even more links, although this possibility seldom materializes in practice.[1]

Each link must fit exception To satisfy FRE 805, each statement in the chain must fit "an exception," and this term should be read also to reach statements that qualify as "not hearsay" under FRE 801(d). If defendant in a personal injury suit offers a police report containing plaintiff's description of the cause of the accident, the evidence involves layered hearsay if offered to prove cause, but the report (final statement) should come in if it fits the public records exception since what plaintiff said (original statement) is his admission, hence "not hearsay" under FRE 801(d)(2).

Exceptions embracing layered hearsay Many exceptions embrace layered hearsay and make resort to FRE 805 unnecessary. One obvious example is the one for business records.

---

§8.79 1. United States v. Portsmouth Paving Corp., 694 F.2d 312, 321-323 (4th Cir. 1982) (approving three-link hearsay).

This exception itself reaches final statements that repeat or sum up intermediate statements that in turn repeat or sum up prior statements (so long as each speaker in the chain acts in regular course and the original statement was made by one with firsthand knowledge).[2] Another example is the one for public records. This exception too reaches layered hearsay in the form of records that rest on other statements by government officials, and sometimes on statements by outsiders, as is true of investigative findings that fit FRE 803(8)(C).[3] Less obviously, the same is sometimes true of the doctrine treating statements by agents as admissions by employer or principal, since personal knowledge is not required and the speakers may rely on what others tell them.[4]

The requirements of FRE 805 are satisfied if each link in the chain fits the same exception, as sometimes happens when records of one business incorporate information taken from records of another.[5] The requirements are also satisfied if the various links satisfy different exceptions, as sometimes happens if a medical record that fits the business records exception incorporates a statement that fits the medical statements exception.[6] The requirements of FRE 805 are not satisfied if a statement in the chain does not fit an exception,[7] except that one statement that fits an exception can sometimes be used to prove that another statement was made, where the latter has some valid nonhearsay utility in the case.[8]

FRE 806

When a hearsay statement, or a statement defined in Rule 801(d)(2)(C), (D), or (E), has been admitted in evidence, the credibility of the declarant may be attacked, and if attacked may be supported, by any evidence which would be admissible for those purposes if declarant had testified as a witness. Evidence of a statement or conduct by the declarant at any time,

2. *See* United States v. Plum, 558 F.2d 568, 573-574 (10th Cir. 1977).
3. *See* Fraley v. Rockwell Intl. Corp., 470 F. Supp. 1264, 1266-1267 (S.D. Ohio 1979).
4. Mahlandt v. Wild Canid Survival & Research Center, Inc., 588 F.2d 626, 630-631 (8th Cir. 1978) (admitting statement by corporate agent that wolf attacked child even though based on hearsay). *But see* Cedeck v. Hamiltonian Fed. S&L, 551 F.2d 1136, 1138 (8th Cir. 1977) (excluding statement by defendant's branch manager reciting what he had been told).
5. United States v. Doe, 960 F.2d 221, 223 (1st Cir. 1992) (record of one business including record of another); Yohay v. Alexandria Employees Credit Union, Inc., 827 F.2d 967, 970 (4th Cir. 1987) (admission by one agent including admission by another).
6. Wilson v. Zapata Off-Shore Co., 939 F.2d 260, 271-272 (5th Cir. 1991) (hospital record containing statement fitting medical statements exception); FDIC v. Mmahat, 907 F.2d 546, 551 n.6 (5th Cir. 1990) (public record quoting party admission), *cert. denied*, 499 U.S. 936.
7. Erickson v. Farmland Industries, Inc., 271 F.3d 718, 728 (8th Cir. 2001) (excluding statement by *R*, even if it fit admissions doctrine, *R*'s recital of what *G* said did not fit any exception).
8. United States v. Maddox, 444 F.2d 148, 150-151 (2d Cir. 1971) (admitting medical record containing statement that could only be used to impeach).

> inconsistent with the declarant's hearsay statement, is not subject to any requirement that the declarant may have been afforded an opportunity to deny or explain. If the party against whom a hearsay statement has been admitted calls the declarant as a witness, the party is entitled to examine the declarant on the statement as if under cross-examination.

§8.80 Impeachment and Support of Hearsay Declarants

When an out-of-court statement is admitted to prove the matter asserted, FRE 806 provides that the credibility of the declarant may be attacked (and if attacked may be supported) in accord with the principles governing attack and support of testifying witnesses. The Rule makes one exception to this pattern of equivalency, which is that a party may impeach the out-of-court speaker by evidence of his inconsistent statement regardless whether he gets a chance "to deny or explain" (for testifying witnesses, FRE 613 requires such opportunity).

Impeachment   Where an out-of-court statement is admitted as proof of what it asserts, FRE 806 leaves no doubt that a party who wishes to discredit the speaker may resort to all five of the recognized methods of impeachment. First, the impeaching party may attack the out-of-court speaker by evidence of bias, interest, or motive.[1] Second, the impeaching party may introduce evidence of defects in capacity.[2] Third, the impeaching party may attack the speaker's character for truthfulness,[3] and the attack may take two of the three forms that may be used with testifying witnesses, including reputation or opinion testimony and prior convictions, but it is not clear whether proof of nonconviction misconduct may be offered.[4] Fourth, the attacking party may introduce statements by an out-of-court speaker inconsistent with statements by the speaker that the court admits.[5] Fifth and finally, the attacking party may

---

§8.80   1. United States v. Check, 582 F.2d 668, 684 n.44 (2d Cir. 1978) (whether speaker faced serious charge).

2. United States v. Barrett, 8 F.3d 1296, 1298-1299 (8th Cir. 1993) (after admitting hearsay by three-year-old victim, should admit testimony in hearing indicating she did not know what it meant to tell truth).

3. United States v. Moody, 903 F.2d 321, 327-330 (5th Cir. 1990) (defense may attack character for truth and veracity of speaker whose statements came in under coconspirator exception).

4. *See* United States v. Saada, 212 F.3d 210, 220-222 (3d Cir. 2000); United States v. Burton, 937 F.2d 324, 328-330 (7th Cir. 1991) (convictions). On nonconviction misconduct, see United States v. White, 116 F.3d 903, 920 (D.C. Cir. 1997), *cert. denied*, 522 U.S. 960 (FRE 806 does not modify FRE 608's ban on extrinsic evidence). *But see* State v. Martisco, 566 S.E.2d 274 (W.Va. 2002); United States v. Friedman, 854 F.3d 535, 570 n.8 (2d Cir. 1988) (pointing toward opposite conclusion).

5. Carver v. United States, 164 U.S. 694 (1897) (admitting dying statement by murder victim invites proof of her other contradictory statements); United States v. Myerson, 18 F.3d 153, 160-162 (2d Cir. 1994) (after admitting coconspirator statement, should have admitted speaker's inconsistent statement), *cert. denied*, 513 U.S. 855.

introduce evidence contradicting assertions by the out-of-court speaker that the court admits.[6]

Support or repair

When impeachment proceeds by inconsistent statements, FRE 806 creates an exemption from the usual rule in FRE 613 requiring the witness to have a chance "to explain or deny." There is no need to provide that chance for the out-of-court speaker whose statements have been offered to impeach his credibility.[7] The exemption makes most sense where the impeaching party cannot satisfy the usual condition, as is true if the speaker is unavailable as a witness, but the exemption applies even if he could be called. The impeaching party should be required to observe the other requirement in FRE 613, which is to show or disclose the prior statement to the other side.

When it comes to repairing the credibility, FRE 806 says the governing principles are again those that apply to witnesses. Thus an attack suggesting untruthful disposition may be met with opinion or reputation testimony that the speaker is truthful, and one that suggests an out-of-court statement was fabricated or produced by undue influence or motive may be met by additional out-of-court statements consistent with the first one.[8] But generally such support is proper only after attack, and the supporting evidence must be appropriate to answer the attack.

If one side impeaches an out-of-court speaker, those who wish to support him should be permitted not only to undertake repairs of the sort described above, but also to refute the attack directly. As a practical matter, such a response is likely only when the attacking party has introduced inconsistent statements or evidence of bias or incapacity. Here supporting parties should be allowed to prove that the supposed inconsistent statement was not made or to respond to evidence suggesting bias or incapacity.[9]

I.   THE CATCHALL EXCEPTION

FRE 807

A statement not specifically covered by Rule 803 or 804 but having equivalent circumstantial guarantees of trustworthiness,

---

6. *See* United States v. Serna, 799 F.2d 842, 848-850 (2d Cir. 1986) (defense offered testimony by *C* in his own trial; court told jury that prior jury didn't believe him, which tended to contradict), *cert. denied*, 481 U.S. 1013.

7. United States v. McClain, 934 F.2d 822, 832 (7th Cir. 1991) (FRE 806 paves way for inconsistent statements even if speaker has no chance to deny or explain).

8. United States v. Bernal, 719 F.2d 1475, 1479 (9th Cir. 1983) (coconspirator statement was admitted, then inconsistent statement, then third statement consistent with first, to support credibility).

9. United States v. Graham, 858 F.2d 986, 989-990 (5th Cir. 1988) (defense could call speaker to testify that he never made statement that witness described; can block attempt to get witness to concede that speaker denied making statement), *cert. denied*, 489 U.S. 1020.

is not excluded by the hearsay rule if the court determines that (A) the statement is offered as evidence of a material fact; (B) the statement is more probative on the point for which it is offered than any other evidence that the proponent can procure through reasonable efforts; and (C) the general purposes of these rules and the interests of justice will best be served by admission of the evidence. But a statement may not be admitted under this exception unless its proponent makes known to the adverse party sufficiently in advance of the trial or hearing to provide the adverse party with a fair opportunity to prepare to meet it, the proponent's intention to offer the statement and the particulars of it, including the name and address of the declarant.

§8.81   The Basic Requirements

FRE 807 paves the way for statements having "circumstantial guarantees of trustworthiness" that are "equivalent" to those in the categorical or specific exceptions.

Draws from *Dallas County* opinion

The catchall exception draws from the liberality of the much-admired *Dallas County* opinion, which helped strip away "common law archaisms" and summon the ideas of necessity and trustworthiness out of the reserves and into the front lines. *Dallas County* recognized that the categorical exceptions may not reach all trustworthy hearsay, and there are indications that the catchall gave new life to the *Dallas County* approach as the number of reported cases giving careful attention to untraditional hearsay went up after enactment of the Rules.[1] But the catchall also has behind it the fact that the hearsay doctrine is cast as a rule of exclusion with specific exceptions, that Congress hedged the catchall with conditions designed to make it less accessible, and gave lots of indication that the catchall should be "used very rarely, and only in exceptional circumstances."[2] In short, the message of letting in trustworthy hearsay is tempered with a warning to use the catchall sparingly, and only for statements that are trustworthy and necessary. Here more than elsewhere, precedent has limited value, and attempts to distill much particularity seems futile, but illustrations may help a little.[3]

In criminal cases, the catchall has sometimes had decisive effect as the basis for admitting third-party statements tending to exonerate the

§8.81   1. *See* Dallas County v. Commercial Union Assur. Co., 286 F.2d 388 (5th Cir. 1961) (admitting old newspaper article to prove lightning struck court tower during construction); Raeder, Commentary: A Response to Professor Swift, 76 Minn. L. Rev. 507, 514 (1992) (400 decisions discuss catchall; 54 percent of hearsay offered under catchall is admitted; criminal rate is 61 percent).

2. Senate Report, at 20 (1974).

3. SEC v. First City Fin. Corp., Ltd., 890 F.2d 1215, 1225 (D.C. Cir. 1989) (chronology of events prepared by brokerage); United States v. Simmons, 773 F.2d 1455, 1458-1459 (4th Cir. 1985) (ATF trace forms on place of manufacture of weapons); United States v. Hitsman, 604 F.2d 443, 447 (5th Cir. 1979) (college transcript).

defendant where these could not satisfy the against-interest exception.[4] Courts are rightly reluctant to invoke the catchall to admit statements against the defendant, but it is available even here, as illustrated in modern cases approving use of the exception for statements by child abuse victims.[5]

The central requirement of the catchall is that the statement have "circumstantial guarantees of trustworthiness" that are "equivalent" to those of the categorical exceptions. Circumstantial trustworthiness is a qualitative rather than mechanical standard. Everything that bears on credibility and accuracy counts, including the simplicity or complexity of the statement and matters described, human factors like trust or indifference or animosity toward the people being addressed, motivational factors such as purpose or aim or a stake (or lack of it) in the matters in question.[6] Not surprisingly, the factors that find expression in the categorical exceptions also count in applying the catchall, including spontaneity, careful routine, reliance by the speaker or others, and against-interest elements.[7] And circumstantial indicators that bear directly on the four hearsay risks (misperception, faulty memory, ambiguity, insincerity) also count and point toward admitting statements where these risks seem minimal.[8]

Equivalent guarantees

The fact that a statement nearly fits some categorical exception (but in the end does not) is not a reason to disqualify it under the catchall. There are rare instances where failing to satisfy one exception makes

"Near miss" theory

---

4. State v. Weaver, 554 N.W.2d 240 (Iowa 1996) (in trial of caretaker for murder and child endangerment, should have admitted statements by victim's mother that child suffered injury before being placed in defendant's care) (retrial led to acquittal; mother testified; against-interest exception would not apply). *And compare* United States v. Hall, 165 F.3d 1095, 1110-1111 (7th Cir 1999), *cert. denied*, 527 1029, *with* Demby v. State, 695 A.2d 1152 (Del. 1997) (the former excluding, the latter admitting, third-party confessions under catchall). In *Demby*, defendant was less successful on retrial than defendant in *Weaver*. *See* Demby v. State, 744 A.2d 976 (Del. Supr., 2000) (affirming conviction on retrial; third-party confession apparently did not convince jury).

5. *See* §8.82, *infra*.

6. State v. Hocevar, 7 P.3d 329, 340 (Mont. 2000) (everything bearing on credibility counts) (quoting this Treatise); United States v. Morgan, 385 F.3d 196, 208-209 (2d Cir. 2004) (catchall applies if statement is particularly trustworthy; letter was not written in coercive atmosphere or addressed to law enforcement, but to boyfriend, in privacy of hotel room); King v. Armstrong World Indus., Inc., 906 F.2d 1022, 1025-1026 (5th Cir. 1990) (statement sworn and made by knowledgeable scientist), *cert. denied*, 500 U.S. 941; Brookover v. Mary Hitchcock Memorial Hosp., 893 F.2d 411, 418-421 (1st Cir. 1990) (corroboration).

7. United States v. Valdez-Soto, 31 F.3d 1467, 1472 (9th Cir. 1994) (stationhouse statements; reliable, unhesitating cooperation by speaker who did not know what agents knew; little chance to fabricate), *cert. denied*, 514 U.S. 113; Moffett v. McCauley, 724 F.2d 581, 583-584 (7th Cir. 1984) (report prepared under regular procedure by persons with business duty and public obligation).

8. *See* United States v. Ismoila (5th Cir. 1996 Tex.) 100 F.3d 380, 392 (admitting written statements by credit card holders to bank saying cards were stolen; investigator testified that in 22 years and a thousand investigations, he could not remember cardholders lying about charges), *cert. denied*, 520 U.S. 1219.

resort to another improper or questionable.[9] But almost always a statement that fails to qualify under one exception may be admitted if it qualifies under another, and the so-called near miss theory that would bar resort to the catchall for statements that almost fit some other exception should be rejected.[10] This formalistic notion is not helpful in construing a provision that is designed to admit trustworthy hearsay that fails to pass muster under the categorical exceptions. The most that can usefully be retrieved from the "near miss" theory is that courts should consider the question whether failing to satisfy requirements of a categorical exception indicates a reason to be wary in applying the catchall.

Speaker testifies — Two additional factors count heavily in appraising trustworthiness. One is the presence of the speaker as a testifying witness. If she appears and can be questioned about her statement and the matters reported in it, hearsay concerns substantially diminish.[11]

Corroboration — The other factor is corroboration, which tends to confirm that the statement is correct and thus to confirm trustworthiness (being correct boosts credibility).[12] Operating under the old *Roberts* approach to confrontation rights, the Supreme Court's closely divided 1990 opinion in the *Wright* case held that corroborative evidence does not count for constitutional purposes in assessing trustworthiness of hearsay offered against the accused under the catchall, but this holding has no currency in the *Crawford* era in which the confrontation clause applies only to "testimonial" statements.[13]

Requirements: (1) Material fact — Congress added four additional requirements to the catchall. The first is that the exception applies only if a statement is "offered as evidence of a material fact." In one sense this requirement is unfortunate because all evidence must be material in bearing on a point that matters (making the requirement redundant). Perhaps the purpose was to say the catchall should be invoked only if the point to be proved is important rather than minor. Understood this way, the material fact requirement means that the decision whether to apply the catchall should take special note of the factors set out in FRE

---

9. See §§8.50-8.51, *supra*, discussing the use restrictions in the public records exception.

10. People v. Katt, 662 N.W.2d 12, 18-22 (Mich. 2003) (rejecting "near miss" theory); United States v. Valdez-Soto, 31 F.3d 1467, 1472 (9th Cir. 1994) (almost fitting another exception cuts in favor of admitting).

11. United States v. Grooms, 978 F.2d 425, 427-428 (8th Cir. 1992) (statements to FBI describing sexual abuse; girls testified, were subject to cross); SEC v. First City Fin. Corp., Ltd., 890 F.2d 1215, 1225 (D.C. Cir. 1989) (chronology prepared by brokerage at SEC request; preparers could be cross-examined).

12. United States v. Valdez-Soto, 31 F.3d 1467, 1470 (9th Cir. 1994) (corroborating evidence helps determine trustworthiness), *cert. denied*, 514 U.S. 113; Brookover v. Mary Hitchcock Memorial Hosp., 893 F.2d 411, 418-421 (1st Cir. 1990) (approving statements by hospital patient to mother after slip-and-fall; strong corroboration).

13. Idaho v. Wright, 497 U.S. 805 (1990) (under now-displaced *Roberts* regime, in setting of child describing sexual abuse, corroborating factors do not count for constitutional purposes) (5-4 opinion). See the discussion of the current approach to confrontation under *Crawford* in §§8.83-8.92, *infra*.

403. If the point to be proved is already strongly supported and the proffered hearsay would add little to what is already there, or if it would waste or consume time out of proportion to its apparent value, it does not satisfy the material fact requirement.

The second congressional requirement says the catchall should be used only if the statement is more probative than other evidence the proponent "can procure through reasonable efforts." This language states a dual requirement. In the main, the focus is on the diligence of the proponent: Has she made reasonable efforts to get evidence that would be better? Secondarily the focus is on probative worth: Assuming she has done her best, is the statement more probative than other evidence? The idea of reasonable efforts (diligence) carries a sense of proportion: What is at stake counts, and more effort is expected of proponents on major issues; resources count, and more effort is expected of the government than of the accused; the incremental benefit of better evidence counts, and more effort is expected if other evidence would be superior to a statement offered under the catchall; the possibility of finding better evidence counts, and more is expected if it seems likely that effort would be rewarded.[14] The "more probative" idea is also proportional. Probably the proponent may invoke the catchall only if there is no better evidence in reasonable reach. Showing a statement is the best available clearly helps the proponent, and contrary indications point the other way.

(2) More probative

The third congressional requirement is that a statement offered under the catchall must serve "the general purposes of these rules and the interests of justice." This requirement echoes the directive in FRE 102 to construe the Rules to "secure fairness in administration, elimination of unjustifiable expense and delay, and promotion of growth and development of the law of evidence to the end that the truth may be ascertained and proceedings justly determined." These high aims are important, but are unlikely to provide much guidance in resolving specific problems, and this provision has not proved significant.

(3) Interests of justice

Fourth, Congress added a notice requirement, providing that the catchall cannot be used unless the proponent gives notice of intent to offer the statement "and the particulars of it, including the name and address of the declarant" far enough before trial or hearing to give the other side "a fair opportunity to prepare to meet it." Trial lawyers think they can anticipate hearsay that fits a categorical exception, but that hearsay offered under the catchall could take them by surprise. There is also some fear that judges should not be allowed too much room to "wing it" by admitting hearsay under the catchall. The notice clause seeks to prevent surprise to parties and ensure that they have

(4) Notice

---

14. *Compare* Stokes v. City of Omaha, 23 F.3d 1362, 1366 (8th Cir. 1994) (error to admit affidavit of deceased police officer; his death was expected, and plaintiff could have taken deposition) *with* United States v. Friedman, 593 F.2d 109, 119 (9th Cir. 1979) (approving Chilean travel documents; government "was unable to obtain any other evidence of entrance and exit").

time to prepare to meet and object to evidence offered under the catchall.

By one reading, advance notice is absolutely required. Cases interpreting the notice provision literally and woodenly hold that the proponent who fails to give the notice cannot resort to the catchall even if he reasonably failed to anticipate needing the statement or thought it fit one of the categorical exceptions.[15] By another reading, the notice requirement is more flexible, and adequacy of notice turns more on whether the other side was given enough chance to meet the evidence.[16] Importantly, failing to provide notice is excused if the proponent did not anticipate needing the catchall.[17] In such situations, objections to lack of notice can be accommodated by a continuance to permit the other side to prepare. Objecting while refusing offers of a continuance is rightly understood as insisting on a formality to achieve tactical advantage, a stance that is particularly unattractive and unpromising.[18]

The flexible approach seems preferable. Congressional concern was that the catchall provisions "injected too much uncertainty" into the law, impairing a litigant's ability "to prepare adequately for trial." When failing to give pretrial notice is understandable, offering a continuance to the other side should satisfy concerns over surprise. In this setting, however, an adverse party who seeks a continuance should not be asked to lay out detailed justification or plans of attack. A reasonable request, seasonably advanced, merits respect and should be granted, or the notice requirement and congressional concern to block sandbagging and surprise tactics will dissolve.

§8.82   An Important Use: Child Victim Statements

Modern decisions, both state and federal, invoke the catchall to admit statements by children describing abuse and identifying their abusers. States have enacted special provisions for child victim hearsay, but no comparable provision has been added in the Federal Rules.[1] The special state provisions are essentially rifle-shot catchalls—narrow in

---

15. United States v. Benavente Gomez, 921 F.2d 378, 384-385 (1st Cir. 1990) (error to let government use catchall without advance notice); United States v. Tafollo-Cardenas, 897 F.2d 976, 980 (9th Cir. 1990) (government could not first argue on appeal that statement fit catchall).

16. United States v. Bachsian, 4 F.3d 796, 799 (9th Cir. 1993) (notice requirement excused if proponent had opportunity to attack trustworthiness), *cert. denied*, 510 U.S. 1080; Mutuelles Unies v. Kroll & Linstrom, 957 F.2d 707, 713 (9th Cir. 1992) (notice three days before trial was ample).

17. United States v. Baker, 985 F.2d 1248, 1253 n.3 (4th Cir. 1993) (notice excused in light of government's last-minute need), *cert. denied*, 510 U.S. 1040.

18. *See* United States v. Bailey, 581 F.2d 341, 348 (3d Cir. 1978) (court offered defense time to conduct interviews and research evidence question).

§8.82   1. Three measures are common: A rifle-shot exception for statements by children describing abuse; authorization for depositions for use at trial; a mechanism that lets children give live videotaped testimony from another room. *See* Maryland v. Craig, 497 U.S. 836 (1990).

covering statements by children describing abuse, but broad in requiring case-by-case consideration of trustworthiness.

Typically the child does not testify in abuse trials. Sometimes all parties recognize that she is incompetent. Sometimes an attempt is made to obtain her live testimony, but she is unable to give it. Sometimes it is decided in advance that testifying would be too traumatic. In these settings, she is psychologically unavailable as a witness under special statutory standards and perhaps under FRE 804(a)(4).[2] Sometimes the child does testify. Her statement should still be admitted if it otherwise qualifies, and the mere fact of testifying should not block use of the catchall on the ground that her testimony is more probative.[3]

Child does not testify

On the central question whether such hearsay is trustworthy, the broad notion that children do not make up stories of abuse or seriously err in describing it has not been accepted (and is sharply disputed), although courts cite young age as one indicator that a child is not fabricating. Instead of a rule that children are to be trusted, a vast body of modern case law has appeared, largely in the state systems, and the cases have developed criteria that bear on trustworthiness.

Many factors count, and the Supreme Court itself cited some of these in its decision in the *Wright* case in 1990, although the opinion in that case is no longer authoritative because it addressed only the constitutional issue, and was decided under the now-discarded *Roberts* approach to confrontation jurisprudence, which was displaced by the decision in *Crawford* in 2004.[4] Among the most common are precocious knowledge and age-appropriate language.[5] The former gives new expression to an old idea that a statement may be trusted if it is unlikely that the speaker could say what she said without experiencing something close to what she describes, and this point makes the general experience of the child a relevant factor. The latter means that a statement on difficult or delicate matters, on which children know very little, is more likely to be trustworthy if phrased in terms one would expect of a child, giving it what some courts call a "ring of truth." Behavioral changes are another important factor (fearfulness of men, regression in toilet habits, sleep disturbances, new problems at home or school).[6]

Factors affecting trustworthiness

2. *See* 18 U.S.C. §3509(b) (authorizing remote testimony and videotaped depositions for child victims who would suffer emotional trauma or cannot testify because of fear); FRE 804(a)(4) (unavailability because of physical or mental illness or infirmity), discussed in §§8.67 and 8.70, *supra*.

3. United States v. Grooms, 978 F.2d 425, 427-428 (8th Cir. 1992) (admitting statements to FBI agent by three nine-year-old girls); United States v. St. John, 851 F.2d 1096, 1098 (8th Cir. 1988) (rejecting argument that statements cannot be used as backup).

4. Idaho v. Wright, 497 U.S. 805 (1990) (spontaneity, repetition, mental state or affect, motive, terminology, likelihood of fabrication). The reference is to Crawford v. Washington, 541 U.S. 36, 57 (2004), discussed in §8.84, *infra*.

5. State v. Huntington, 575 N.E.2d 268, 275 (Wis. 1998); United States v. NB, 59 F.3d 771, 776 (8th Cir. 1995); Doe v. United States, 976 F.2d 1071, 1077-1082 (7th Cir. 1992), *cert. denied*, 510 U.S. 812; United States v. Dorian, 803 F.2d 1439, 1444-1445 (8th Cir. 1986).

6. *See* State v. Kuone, 757 P.2d 289, 292-293 (Kan. 1988); State v. Robinson, 735 P.2d 801, 812 (Ariz. 1987); United States v. Dorian, 803 F.2d 1439, 1444-1445 (8th Cir. 1986).

Also counted in the calculus are general demeanor and affect, and particular indications of pain or emotional upset, spontaneity, and sometimes even a matter-of-factness in the telling that reflects a child's way of dealing with events that would outrage older people.[7] Another factor is the presence or absence of bias or other motives on the part of the speaker or the reporting witnesses. This point becomes particularly important if the tale of abuse develops at home in a setting in which parents have domestic problems of their own, or if there are independent signs of tension or disagreement between the child and the person accused of abuse.[8] Another consideration is the training and techniques of people who talk to the child, their experience level, and approach to questioning (whether they led or suggested too much).[9] The number and consistency of repetitions of the basic story make a difference,[10] as does the character of the child.[11]

Corroboration   The decision in *Wright*, which involved a trial for sexual abuse of children, held that the required case-by-case determination of trustworthiness must consider only factors "inherent" in the statement, not independent corroborative evidence. As noted above, however, *Wright* considered only constitutional issues and is no longer authoritative, and in any event this restriction never made sense.[12] Courts applying the catchall to child victim hearsay often cite clinical evidence, eyewitness testimony, and other corroborative proof in assessing the trustworthiness of statements by children offered under the exception, and indeed state provisions often *require* independent corroboration for child victim hearsay and courts view corroborative evidence as providing an assurance of trustworthiness.[13]

---

7. Doe v. United States, 976 F.2d 1071, 1077-1082 (7th Cir. 1992) ("matter-of-fact tone" of three-year-old girl was consistent with reaction of children who describe abuse as part of day's activities without saying it was traumatic or unusual), *cert. denied*, 510 U.S. 812; United States v. Ellis, 935 F.2d 385, 393-395 (1st Cir. 1991) (gestures of child with doll were spontaneous), *cert. denied*, 502 U.S. 869.

8. United States v. George, 960 F.2d 97, 100-102 (9th Cir. 1992) (no motive to lie); State v. Kuone, 757 P.2d 289, 292 (Kan. 1988) (no ill feelings).

9. United States v. Grooms, 978 F.2d 425, 427-428 (8th Cir. 1992) (trained agent asked "open-ended questions" and did not lead); United States v. George, 960 F.2d 97, 100-102 (9th Cir. 1992) (investigator did not lead).

10. United States v. Renville, 779 F.2d 430, 439-440 (8th Cir. 1985) (almost identical statements).

11. *See* People v. District Court (El Paso County), 776 P.2d 1083, 1090 (Colo. 1989) ("general character of the child").

12. Idaho v. Wright, 497 U.S. 805 (1990) (in assessing trustworthiness, cannot consider physical evidence, opportunity to commit offense, other testimony; can consider that young child could not make up statement) (5-4 opinion by Justice O'Connor). A year later the Court approved use of the exceptions for excited utterance and medical statements in a similar setting. *See* White v. Illinois, 502 U.S. 436 (1992).

13. Ex parte C.L.Y., 928 So.2d 1069 (Ala. 2005) (child victim's statements fitting hearsay exception could corroborate other statements admitted under rifle-shot exception requiring corroboration).

Of course constitutional issues under *Crawford* do arise in this setting. Statements by a child victim to police or child services personnel are likely to be testimonial for purposes of the confrontation clause, in which case they are usually excludable from criminal trials unless the child testifies.[14] However, courts reject *Crawford*-based objections when children speak in private settings to friends, parents or guardians, or to doctors or nurses.[15]

Crawford **issues**

Deciding whether a child is psychologically unavailable (she cannot testify in open court or would suffer trauma if she tried) often leads courts to the matter of competence, where the issues are whether the child can communicate or appreciate the importance of being truthful and the difference between truth and falsehood. These issues usually connect more with managerial problems (how to get the child's story) than with any decision to exclude altogether.[16] Even if the court decides a child cannot testify because she cannot communicate (or commit herself to the truth, or distinguish truth from falsehood), her out-of-court statements are not necessarily excludable. They may still fit the catchall or child victim hearsay exceptions.[17] Even out-of-court statements should be excluded, however, if the child is incompetent because she is too young or immature to understand the world around her and form reasonably accurate impressions.[18]

Competence issues

Clearly not all statements by child victims are trustworthy enough to admit, and they should be excluded when circumstantial indications do not support the necessary conclusion. In the setting of abuse at home, disputes between the child's parents or caretakers and indications of coaching that might come from independent proof or the terminology of the statement are strong danger signals that undermine the inference of trustworthiness.[19]

Not all statements

J. HEARSAY AND CONFRONTATION

§8.83 Right of Confrontation—Origins and Basic Meaning

The confrontation clause of the Sixth Amendment says that in criminal cases the accused has the right "to be confronted with the witnesses against him," and it is settled that this provision applies in federal and state courts alike.[1]

---

14. State v. Robinson, 718 N.W.2d 400 (Minn. 2006) (admitting child's statement to nurse identifying defendant as abuser; *Crawford* satisfied; child was cross-examined).

15. United States v. Peneaux, 432 F.3d 882, 896 (8th Cir. 2005) (admitting child's statement to doctor, as nontestimonial under *Crawford*).

16. *See* discussions of psychological unavailability in §8.67, and remote and videotape deposition testimony in §8.70, *supra*.

17. People v. District Court (El Paso County), 776 P.2d 1083, 1087 (Colo. 1989).

18. People v. Bowers, 801 P.2d 511, 518-519 (Colo. 1990).

19. United States v. Barrett, 8 F.3d 1296, 1299-1300 (8th Cir. 1993).

§8.83 1. Pointer v. Texas, 380 U.S. 400 (1965).

Origins: Raleigh case

Discussions of confrontation usually begin by observing that history sheds little light on the subject, and most of what we call the law of confrontation comes from decisions handed down after 1965. Still, most accounts of the origins of the clause cite the notorious prosecution of Sir Walter Raleigh for treason in 1603, and his case dramatically illustrates central modern concerns underlying the right of confrontation.[2]

Raleigh was charged with conspiring against King James (raising money abroad to distribute among malcontents to put Arabella Stuart on the throne). The most damning evidence was what we would call "rank hearsay"—a statement by alleged coconspirator Lord Cobham given during an "examination" (interrogation in the Tower, under pressure if not torture) naming Raleigh as the instigator and claiming that he was raising money for an insurrection. Raleigh denied the charges, offered explanations, and showed that Cobham had recanted. He argued that the statute required two witnesses and urged the court to "call my Accuser" so they might stand "face to face," conceding that a witness need not be called if he "is not to be had conveniently" but pointing out that Cobham was "alive, and in the house." The judges said the statute had been repealed. One said the law allows conviction without witnesses (three may be convicted of conspiracy if "they all confess"). Another told Raleigh that "many horse-stealers may escape, if they may not be condemned without witnesses." Yet another said the law "presumes a man will not accuse himself to accuse another."

"Face to face"

The notion of "face-to-face" confrontation between defendant and his accusers is basic to the Sixth Amendment right. The accused is entitled to be physically present, to see and hear the witnesses against him.[3] In its 1988 decision in *Coy*, the Court held that he is entitled not only to see and hear, but *to be in view of* those witnesses.[4] In a striking development in the 1990s, however, the Court approved protective measures for youthful abuse victims, who can testify from another room by closed circuit video monitor if the state makes a specific showing of need and defendant has adequate substitutes for physical

2. The passages from the Raleigh trial are reported in 2 Howell's State Cases 15-20 (1803). See also Stephen, The Trial of Sir Walter Raleigh, 2 Trans. Royal Hist. Society 172 (4th Series 1919). Raleigh was sentenced to die, but King James sent him to Guyana for gold. The expedition became an embarrassment, and executing Raleigh became convenient (a gesture of good will toward Spain). He was beheaded 15 years after his trial, at age 66. Most historians think he was not plotting with Cobham.

3. Mattox v. United States, 156 U.S. 237, 244 (1895) ("seeing the witness face to face"); Kirby v. United States, 174 U.S. 47, 55 (1899) (witnesses must be people "who confront him at the trial, upon whom he can look while being tried"); Dowdell v. United States, 221 U.S. 325, 330 (1911) (right "to meet the witnesses face to face"); United States v. Benfield, 593 F.2d 815, 821 (8th Cir. 1979) (confrontation "includes a face-to-face meeting at trial").

4. Coy v. Iowa, 487 U.S. 1012 (1988) (condemning translucent screen separating teenage girl from defendant in sexual assault case, permitting defendant to see her but shielding her from seeing him).

confrontation.[5] Moreover, defendant may lose the right to be present by misbehaving, and even the right to exclude hearsay by frightening or killing the declarant.[6]

Beyond these basic points, the right to confront includes the right to cross-examine, with attendant safeguards of oath and demeanor evidence. Most descriptions of the right are functional, and they stress cross-examination as the primary purpose.[7] In various settings, the Court has held that the right to cross-examine brings with it the right to uncover basic information about the witness and raise points relating to bias.[8] At least sometimes, this right to cross-examine entails a defense right to introduce favorable hearsay by the witness.[9]

Right to cross-examine

These elements raise a basic question about confrontation and hearsay: Does the confrontation clause entitle the accused to exclude hearsay? Behind this question are others. Does confrontation block all hearsay? If it blocks some but not all, how do we separate what is allowed from what is not? Does confrontation require contemporaneous cross—a chance to question the witness at trial as he is making the statements being offered? What about prior cross that took place when he testified in other proceedings or earlier stages of the same proceeding? What about deferred cross, where the witness is questioned about what he said before? What if he is unavailable? In criminal cases, do the hearsay doctrine and its exceptions control the meaning of the clause? Or is it the other way around?

Five major themes are discernible in modern confrontation law. Their tone is foreshadowed in early decisions, where the Court seemed to say that the clause preserves common-law protections against hearsay but accommodates evolving doctrine.[10] In one early instance, however,

Five major themes

---

5. Maryland v. Craig, 497 U.S. 836 (1990) (approving remote testimony by one-way video monitor on basis of finding that child victim would be traumatized if forced to testify in court). *See* §8.91, *infra.*

6. Illinois v. Allen, 397 U.S. 337 (1970) (excluding defendant from courtroom during trial for misbehavior). See the discussion of forfeiture in §§8.78, *supra* and 8.90, *infra.*

7. Crawford v. Washington, 541 U.S. 36, 57 (2004) (stressing right to cross-examine); Ohio v. Roberts, 448 U.S. 56 (1980) (right to cross-examine is primary); California v. Green, 399 U.S. 149, 158 (1970) (confrontation insures testimony under oath, cross-examination, and demeanor evidence); Bruton v. United States, 391 U.S. 123 (1968) (right of cross-examination included in right to confront); Barber v. Page, 390 U.S. 719 (1968) (right of confrontation is "basically a trial right" that "includes both the opportunity to cross-examine and the occasion for the jury to weigh the demeanor"); Douglas v. Alabama, 380 U.S. 415, 418 (1965) ("primary interest" is right of cross-examination); Pointer v. Texas, 380 U.S. 400, 406-407 (1965) (major reason to secure give "opportunity to cross-examine").

8. *See* Alford v. United States, 282 U.S. 687 (1931) (address of witness); Smith v. Illinois, 390 U.S. 129 (1968) (name of witness); Davis v. Alaska, 415 U.S. 308 (1974) (right to expose motive).

9. *See* Chambers v. Mississippi, 410 U.S. 284 (1973), discussed in §8.92, *infra.*

10. See the two opinions in Mattox v. United States, 156 U.S. 237 (1895) (testimony from first trial), and Mattox v. United States, 146 U.S. 140 (1892) (dying declarations). See also Snyder v. Massachusetts, 291 U.S. 97 (1934) (dying declarations and

the Court came out dramatically the other way,[11] and several modern opinions condemn use of hearsay in particular settings.[12] It was during the Warren reforms in the 1960s, however, that most of the modern themes took shape.

(1) Prior cross can suffice

First, *prior* cross-examination can suffice. That is to say, defense cross-examination in a prior proceeding can satisfy the confrontation clause, at least with respect to the testimony that the witness gave at that time. On the issue of prior cross, the Court in the *Pointer* case condemned the use in a state trial of testimony from a preliminary hearing, where defendant did not have a lawyer, but Justice Black said the case would be "different" if he had been represented and "given a complete and adequate opportunity to cross-examine."[13] The comment in *Pointer* suggests that prior cross satisfies the clause, and many later opinions indicate that *Pointer* carried the day, except that there is one more requirement: The prosecutor can only offer testimony previously cross-examined if the witness is unavailable at trial. The comment in *Pointer* also implies that a prior *chance* to cross-examine is enough, but this point is sticky and unsettled. Essentially the question is this: Can the prosecutor offer such testimony by a witness who cannot be produced at trial if defendant could have cross-examined before but did not?[14]

(2) Deferred cross suffices

Second, *deferred* cross-examination can suffice. That is to say, cross-examination at trial about something the witness said before can satisfy the confrontation clause. This question reached the Court in *Green* in 1970, and in later cases. Essentially *Green* presented the problem of the turncoat witness who exonerates or fails to incriminate the defendant in trial testimony, but whose prior statements or testimony did incriminate him. In these cases, the Court held or said in passing that trial cross on the prior statement satisfies the clause.[15]

---

documentary evidence are exceptions; these are not static and "may be enlarged from time to time if there is no material departure from the reason of the general rule").

11. See Kirby v. United States, 174 U.S. 47 (1899) (in trial for possessing stolen property, condemning use of conviction to prove it was stolen). *Kirby* is the source of language in FRE 803(22) barring use of third-party felony convictions "to prove any fact essential" to the earlier judgment. See §8.62, *supra.*

12. See Idaho v. Wright, 497 U.S. 805 (1990) (error to admit hearsay under catchall; corroborating evidence cannot be considered); Lee v. Illinois, 476 U.S. 530 (1986) (error to admit statement by codefendant under against-interest exception); Bruton v. United States, 391 U.S. 123 (1968) (error to admit statement by codefendant, even with instructions not to consider it as evidence against defendant).

13. Pointer v. Texas, 380 U.S. 400 (1965) (right of confrontation binds states). Two years earlier, the Court held in Gideon v. Wainwright, 372 U.S. 335 (1963), that an indigent is entitled to appointed counsel in felony trials (previous decisions recognized right in special situations such as capital cases), but *Pointer* was tried before *Gideon* was decided, and *Gideon* was prospective only. Five years after *Pointer*, the Court held that the right applies in preliminary hearings, see Coleman v. Alabama, 399 U.S. 1 (1970) (also applies prospectively), and *Pointer* might better have been decided as a right-to-counsel case.

14. *See* the discussion in §8.87, *infra.*

15. California v. Green, 399 U.S. 149 (1970) (prior statement to police officer properly admitted where witness proved forgetful and evasive at trial). See the discussion in §8.88, *infra.*

Third, even limited uses of out-of-court statements may infringe confrontation rights if the statements cannot be tested by cross-examining
the speaker. In the *Douglas* case, the government sought to "refresh the
recollection" of an already-convicted co-offender named Loyd by reading his confession that implicated the defendant as the trigger man. But
Loyd refused to submit to defense cross-examination, and the Court
held that this use of the confession violated the confrontation clause.[16]
And in *Bruton*, the Court concluded that introducing a confession by
defendant Evans implicating defendant Bruton by name or obvious
reference violated the latter's confrontation rights where Evans could
not be cross-examined because he did not testify, even though the jury
was told that the confession was not evidence against Bruton.[17]

(3) Hearsay without cross may infringe confrontation

Fourth, sometimes the confrontation clause requires the prosecutor to
produce a person in preference to offering his statements. The point of
departure is the 1968 opinion in *Barber*, where the Court held that a state
prosecutor who offered testimony from a preliminary hearing should have
tried to produce the witness, even though he was in a federal penitentiary
in a neighboring state and could not be easily subpoenaed. The former
testimony exception applies when the speaker is unavailable, and *Barber*
added a constitutional dimension to the unavailability requirement.[18] The
decision in *Roberts* in 1980 held that prosecutors *generally* have to produce
witnesses or show that they are unavailable if they wish to introduce hearsay. Even before 2004, when *Roberts* was eclipsed by *Crawford*, the
proposition that the prosecutor could offer hearsay only if the declarant
was unavailable had fallen by the wayside, with the exception of statements
offered as former testimony, but *Crawford* adhered to the idea that former
testimony can be admitted only if the declarant is unavailable.

(4) Prosecutor must produce declarant

Fifth, the confrontation clause sometimes blocks hearsay that would
ordinarily be admissible and sometimes allows hearsay that would ordinarily be excluded. In cases decided in the 1970s, the Court concluded
that the confrontation clause did not block the substantive use of hearsay that would not normally fit hearsay exceptions. In *Green*, the Court
allowed the substantive use of a prior consistent statement by a testifying witness because he could be cross-examined at trial, even though
most evidence codes would *not* permit substantive use. (The code in
California, where *Green* arose, permits substantive use of all prior inconsistent statements. FRE 801(d)(1)(A) permits substantive use of inconsistent statements only if given under oath in proceedings.) In *Dutton*,
the Court rejected a challenge to a statement admitted under a state

(5) Some hearsay excludable

16. Douglas v. Alabama, 380 U.S. 415 (1965) (tactics may have been equivalent of
testimony that Loyd made statement; can confront effectively only if Loyd "affirmed the
statement as his").

17. Bruton v. United States, 391 U.S. 123, 128 n.3 (1968) (statement was "clearly
inadmissible" against Bruton under "traditional rules" because no "recognized exception" made it admissible against him; Court intimates "no view" whether such exceptions raise questions). *See* discussion in §8.28, *supra*.

18. *See* Barber v. Page, 390 U.S. 719 (1968) (authorities made "no effort" to obtain
witness, by federal or state writ or by utilizing cooperative policies of Bureau of Prisons).
See discussion in §8.66, *supra*.

exception for statements by a coconspirator who was already arrested and imprisoned, even though most codes (including the Rules) do not extend the exception to post-arrest statements. And in *Crawford* in 2004 and *Davis* in 2006, the Court concluded that the confrontation clause blocks the use of hearsay that satisfied standard exceptions. *Crawford* required exclusion of a statement found to satisfy the against-interest exception, and *Davis* required exclusion of a statement that satisfied the excited utterance exception.

At least five theories[19] might explain how the confrontation clause operates on hearsay offered against the accused:

(1) Minimalist theory　By one view, the confrontation clause speaks only to live testimony, not out-of-court statements. It entitles defendants to be present and to cross-examine witnesses who testify, but does not stop prosecutors from offering testimonial accounts of what others said or from using prior statements by those who do testify. By this minimalist reading, the term "witnesses" in the Sixth Amendment means people who testify, not makers of out-of-court statements. Long ago Wigmore endorsed this position, and several Supreme Court Justices adopted it, but modern opinions reject it by words and sometimes in holdings.[20]

(2) Production theory　The clause requires the prosecutor to produce an available speaker in preference to his out-of-court statement. *Roberts* adopted this notion, with the major qualification that the prosecutor need not show that the witness is unavailable "if the utility of trial confrontation" is "remote."[21] (As noted above, this "unavailability prong" finds expression where former testimony is offered.) Some have argued that the confrontation clause has *only* this effect, and has nothing to say about statements by people who are unavailable—whose presence or testimony the prosecutor cannot obtain,[22] but this view has not prevailed.[23]

---

19. Many articles advance theories. Among the best are these: Imwinkelried, The Constitutionalization of Hearsay: The Extent to which the Fifth And Sixth Amendments Permit or Require the Liberalization of the Hearsay Rules, 76 Minn. L. Rev. 521 (1992); Lilly, Notes on the Confrontation Clause and Ohio v. Roberts, 36 U. Fla. L. Rev. 207 (1984); Natali, Green, Dutton and Chambers: Three Cases in Search of a Theory, 7 Rutgers-Cam. L.J. 43 (1975); Seidelson, The Confrontation Clause and the Supreme Court: Some Good News and Some Bad News, 17 Hofstra L. Rev. 51 (1988).

20. See 5 Wigmore, Evidence §1397 (Chadbourn rev. ed. 1974). See also White v. Illinois, 502 U.S. 346 (1992) (confrontation clause addresses only live testimony and its equivalent) (concurring opinion by Thomas, joined by Scalia); Dutton v. Evans, 400 U.S. 74 (1970) (concurring opinion by Harlan). But see Idaho v. Wright, 497 U.S. 805 (1990) (condemning use of statement by child victim); Ohio v. Roberts, 448 U.S. 56 (1980) (treating out-of-court speaker as witness for purposes of confrontation clause).

21. Ohio v. Roberts, 448 U.S. 56, 65 n.7 (1980) (showing unavailability "not always required").

22. *See* Peter Westen, Confrontation and Compulsory Process: A Unified Theory of Evidence for Criminal Cases, 91 Harv. L. Rev. 567, 596 (1978) (confrontation and compulsory process clauses protect procedural rights, should be read together; the latter does not force prosecutor to do the impossible by producing unavailable witnesses; the former should not penalize prosecutor by excluding statements by those who cannot be produced).

23. Crawford v. Washington, 541 U.S. 36 (2004) (exclude testimonial statements); Idaho v. Wright, 497 U.S. 805 (1990) (exclude statements by children who could not testify); Ohio v. Roberts, 448 U.S. 56 (1980) (must produce available speakers and exclude unreliable statements).

The clause sets a constitutional standard of reliability for hearsay offered against the defendant that works independently of the hearsay doctrine, although concerns over reliability may be satisfied by circumstances similar to those considered in applying hearsay exceptions, and reliability is unimportant (or less so) if the accused can cross-examine. Until 2004, the Court adhered to this view, which was enshrined in the *Roberts* doctrine, but *Roberts* also qualified this requirement, saying that statements fitting "firmly rooted" hearsay exceptions are reliable enough, which had the effect of requiring a particularized showing of reliability only for statements that do *not* fit firmly rooted exceptions.[24]

(3) Reliability theory

The clause allows use of hearsay on peripheral points or as corroborative or circumstantial proof, but not as direct and critical evidence going to the heart of the prosecutor's case. This view was argued in a 1972 article, and it has textual support in one decision.[25] It also has a kind of common sense appeal because it suggests that the prosecutor should be expected to produce the strongest and most readily testable proof when it is critical to the case, but insisting on this point for all corroborative and circumstantial evidence makes less sense. In a related setting, however, the Court said that such considerations relate to the harmless error doctrine rather than confrontation.[26]

(4) Centrality theory

Even before *Crawford* in 2004, modern scholars argued that the clause does not bar hearsay as such, or set a reliability criterion for hearsay, and that it should be read in a different way. It should be understood as preventing the state from building its case against criminal defendants by gathering out-of-court statements and offering them in lieu of live testimony. What is most troubling about the Raleigh trial, after all, is the abuse of extracting confessions by isolated interrogation and using the results to convict.[27]

(5) Procedural rights theory

In its decision in *Crawford* in 2004, the Court abandoned the *Roberts* approach and adopted in its place a version of the procedural rights

---

24. Ohio v. Roberts, 448 U.S. 56, 66 (1980) (hearsay by nontestifying witnesses must possess "indicia of reliability" to satisfy confrontation clause; reliability "can be inferred without more" where statement fits "firmly rooted" exception; otherwise "particularized guarantees of trustworthiness" are required).

25. K. Graham, The Right of Confrontation and the Hearsay Rule: Sir Walter Raleigh Loses Another One, 8 Crim. L. Bull. 99 (1972) (arguing this view); Dutton v. Evans, 400 U.S. 74 (1970) (stressing that hearsay was neither "crucial" nor "devastating" and was "of peripheral significance at most").

26. Idaho v. Wright, 497 U.S. 805 (1990) (corroborative evidence relates to harmless error, not whether statement satisfies constitutional reliability standard).

27. *See especially* Kirst, The Procedural Dimension of the Confrontation Clause, 66 Neb. L. Rev. 485 (1987); Jonakait, Restoring the Confrontation Clause to the Sixth Amendment, 35 U.C.L.A. L. Rev. 557 (1988); Berger, The Deconstitutionalization of the Confrontation Clause: The Fallacy That Hearsay Rules and the Confrontation Clause Protect Similar Values, 76 Minn. L. Rev. 557 (1992); Haddad, The Future of Confrontation Clause Developments: What will Emerge When the Supreme Court Synthesizes the Diverse Lines of Confrontation Decisions? 81 J. Crim. L. & Criminology 77 (1990).

theory. The confrontation clause bars "testimonial" hearsay from being used against criminal defendants (if there is no chance to cross-examine), meaning at least statements gathered by police from witnesses in interviews and other statements given in formalized judicial settings ("actual testimony"), such as preliminary hearings and grand jury proceedings.[28]

This approach resembles other constitutional exclusionary doctrines descending from the famous decisions in *Mapp, Massiah,* and *Miranda,* which provide counterincentives against police misconduct by requiring exclusion of evidence that might otherwise be admissible.[29] But the focal point of the procedural rights approach to confrontation is not police misconduct on the ground, but a broader idea of misconduct by prosecutors in trying to prove cases by means of statements gathered out of court by police investigators. The Court in *Davis* took pains to say that it was not criticizing police for gathering testimonial statements, and that the confrontation clause "in no way governs police conduct" because it is "the trial *use* of, not the investigatory *collection* of" testimonial statements that offends the clause.[30]

This theory does not restrict the use of statements made *independently* of investigative, prosecutorial, or judicial processes, and offers no protection against unreliable statements. *Crawford* did not actually hold that the *Roberts* reliability criteria no longer apply, but later the Court made it clear in the *Bockting* case that *Roberts* is a dead letter.[31]

In short, prevailing themes in modern opinions chart a twisting course that has stressed the third and fifth theories, adopting mostly the third for a time, and more recently the fifth. Under *Crawford,* testimonial hearsay is excludable (absent an opportunity to cross-examine). The second theory also has currency where former testimony is offered, and then the prosecutor must satisfy a constitutional standard of unavailability.

§8.84 "Testimonial" Hearsay—Reach and Limits of the *Crawford* Doctrine

Beginning with the landmark opinion in *Crawford* in 2004, the confrontation clause requires courts to exclude "testimonial" hearsay, when offered against a defendant in a criminal case.[1] Although *Crawford* represented a fresh start, many older cases would be decided the same way in the new regime. In particular, the Court in *Crawford* took pains to say that the confrontation clause is satisfied if the speaker

---

28. Crawford v. Washington, 541 U.S. 36 (2004) (discussed in §8.84, *infra*).
29. Miranda v. Arizona, 384 U.S. 436 (1966) (doctrine based on right against self-incrimination); Massiah v. United States, 377 U.S. 201 (1964) (doctrine based on right of counsel); Mapp v. Ohio, 367 U.S. 643 (1961) (doctrine based on right against unreasonable searches and seizures).
30. Davis v. Washington, 547 U.S. 813 (2006) (original emphasis).
31. Whorton v. Bockting, 127 S. Ct. 1173 (2007) (*Crawford* "overruled" *Roberts*).
§8.84   1. Crawford v. Washington, 541 U.S. 36 (2004).

testifies at trial and can be cross-examined then about what he said before. In other words, "deferred" or "later" cross satisfies the clause. *Crawford* also said the confrontation clause is satisfied if the speaker is unavailable at trial but was cross-examined at an earlier time. In other words, "prior" cross also satisfies the clause, at least if the speaker is unavailable at trial.[2]

Crawford displaced the approach to confrontation that had coalesced in the *Roberts* case almost twenty five years earlier. *Roberts* had adopted a two-pronged approach turning on unavailability of the declarant and indicia of trustworthiness that would justify dispensing with cross-examination at trial. In theory, the unavailability criterion meant that prosecutors had to call available witnesses, but in practice courts applied this criterion to statements offered under the former testimony exception, and generally not elsewhere. In practice, the indicia of trustworthiness required by *Roberts* was satisfied if a statement fit a "firmly rooted" hearsay exception.[3] This category embraced most major exceptions, but not the against-interest exception (for statements against "penal" interest), nor the catchall, nor child victim hearsay exceptions, and statements offered under these exceptions required particularized guarantees of trustworthiness.

Crawford
displaced *Roberts*

In *Crawford*, a man named Michael Crawford was charged with assault in a stabbing incident in which the victim had allegedly tried to rape defendant's wife Sylvia. Michael and Sylvia were arrested and questioned separately. His account suggested that the victim was armed, but hers could be understood to mean that he was not armed. At trial, Michael Crawford invoked the privilege against adverse spousal testimony, and the state offered Sylvia's statement to police under the against-interest exception. Although it was defendant's claim of privilege that kept Sylvia from testifying, the defense also claimed that using her statement violated his confrontation rights. The Court agreed. The reason was that her statement was "testimonial" in nature: She made it while in custody during formal questioning at the police station, where she had been separated from her husband pursuant to standard investigative strategy, and it is just such statements that are the concern of the confrontation clause.

The *Crawford*
facts

Under *Crawford*, "testimonial" statements include two huge categories of important material—actual testimony in trials or other proceedings, direct substitutes for testimony (like affidavits prepared for court proceedings), and most statements to law enforcement officers investigating crimes.

Actual testimony,
direct substitutes

Beyond these categories, the scope of "testimonial" hearsay is harder to describe. *Crawford* said it was unnecessary to define the concept further because statements "taken by police" during "interrogations" (the very facts of the case) are testimonial under "even a narrow" interpretation. But the Court offered three formulations of "testimonial." One holds that a statement is testimonial if it amounts to "ex parte

2. *See* §§8.87 (prior cross) and 8.88 (later cross), *infra.*
3. Ohio v. Roberts, 448 U.S. 56 (1980).

in-court testimony or its functional equivalent," such as affidavits, custodial examinations, or pretrial statements that the speaker "would reasonably expect to be used" by prosecutors, and prior testimony that defendant could not cross-examine. Another formulation treats as testimonial any out-of-court statement found in "formalized testimonial materials," like affidavits, depositions, prior testimony, or confessions. The third formulation treats as testimonial any statement that would "lead an objective witness reasonably to believe" that the statement "would be available for use at a later trial."[4]

It is this third formulation that has proved problematic.

Troublesome third formulation

One reason is that the third formulation, unlike the first two, reaches some statements made in private settings. Professor Friedman, who went further than anyone else to develop the concept of testimonial hearsay adopted in *Crawford*, argues that such statements are often testimonial. He says, for example, that a statement by one "claiming to the victim of a crime and describing the crime" is "usually" testimonial, whether made to a friend or to authorities, although he also thinks a statement "made before the crime is committed" is not testimonial, at least if the later crime spans "a short period of time."[5]

Emergency exception

A second reason is that the third formulation could qualify the other two, because people speaking to police in exigent situations are sometimes so caught up in the press of the moment that they are unconscious or hardly aware that an investigation might ensue. In such emergency settings, those who talk to police may be seeking aid or trying to solve a pressing problem, and such thoughts might smother any other thoughts or states of mind. In 2006, the Court addressed this matter in the *Davis* case, where it crafted the "emergency exception," finding that testimonial statements are admissible after all, so far as the confrontation clause is concerned (the hearsay doctrine might still pose an obstacle), if the "primary purpose" was "to enable police assistance to meet an ongoing emergency."[6]

Beyond the clear examples of testimonial statements (actual testimony, affidavits and statements to police investigating crimes), it is worth bearing in mind the stress in *Crawford* on the point that statements are testimonial if the speaker is acting as a witness by "bear[ing] testimony" against the accused.

Four factors

This basic idea, and the discussion in *Crawford* and *Davis*, lead to a consideration of four overlapping factors that bear on the question. First is the understanding, expectations, or anticipation of the speaker, Second is the involvement or role of law enforcement or other officials in eliciting or receiving the statement. Third is the effect of privacy—of the impact that being out of official view has on the expectations and understandings of the speaker, which leads to a consideration of the nature of the speaker and the statement (is the speaker a crime victim

---

4. Crawford v. Washington, 541 U.S. 36, 51 (2004).

5. Richard Friedman, Confrontation, The Search for Basic Principles, 86 Geo. L. Rev. 1011, 1040-1043 (1998).

6. *See* Davis v. Washington, 547 U.S. 813 (2006), discussed in §8.85, *infra.*

or an eyewitness? does the statement describe a crime?). Fourth is the presence or absence of formalities. Was the statement taken in a formal setting, such as a courtroom or police interview room, or somewhere else? Was it recorded, or transcribed by a stenographer, or written down, or was it merely an oral utterance, perhaps given spontaneously or off the cuff?

The first and most important factor is the speaker's "expectations" (to use the term found in *Crawford*). Naturally these are very much a function of the nature of the statement, whether describing a crime ("x pulled the trigger") or something entirely innocent in itself ("a blue car pulled out of the parking lot"), and also the circumstances in which the speaker finds himself, whether among friends or relatives, or talking to strangers or police. To the extent that the speaker would understand or expect that what he says will be used in investigating or prosecuting crime, it is likely to be testimonial. To the extent that he would not expect that, the statement is likely not to be testimonial.[7]

(1) Speaker's expectations

What counts is not the stronger or more focused mental state that we call "purpose" or "intent," but a more general notion of expectancy. A statement to police describing a crime can be testimonial even if the speaker was not purposely trying to aid in investigating or preparing for trial, so long as he understood or expected that what he said would be used in this way. This broad standard is appropriate in insuring that the confrontation clause has broad coverage, and it differs from the far narrower standard that applies when the question is whether misbehavior by the defendant forfeits his rights under the clause.[8] The standard is necessarily "objective," meaning that a statement can be testimonial if a reasonable person in the speaker's position would harbor such expectation. A subjective standard would be hard to administer and would likely produce quixotic results. An objective standard serves the underlying values because it amounts to an estimate or approximation that "gets it right" in most cases (most have the expectation that we think a reasonable person would have).[9]

The decision in *Davis* did not modify the expectation standard, but added a qualification. *Davis* stressed the "primary purpose" of the 911 call in dealing with an emergency, apparently referring both to police (acting through the 911 operator) and the caller: In effect, *Davis* said

7. United States v. Larson, 460 F.3d 1200, 1213 (9th Cir. 2006) (speaker's awareness or expectation is determinative); United States v. Hinton, 423 F.3d 355, 360 (3d Cir. 2005) ("where an objective witness reasonably anticipates" that his statement will be used at trial, it is "likely to be testimony in the sense that it is offered to establish or prove a fact"); United States v. Saget, 377 F.3d 223, 228 (2d Cir. 2004) (speaker's awareness or expectation is determinative).

8. *See* discussion of the forfeiture exception in §8.78, *supra*, and discussion of the *Giles* decision in §8.90, *infra*.

9. Crawford v. Washington, 541 U.S. 36, 52 (2004) (referring to circumstances that would lead "an objective witness reasonably to believe" his statement would be available for use at trial); Jensen v. Pliler, 439 F.3d 1086 (9th Cir. 2006) (confession to lawyer implicating defendant was not testimonial; lawyer assured him of privilege, said he would never tell anyone; would not expect statement to be used at trial).

that even if a speaker understands or expects that his statement might be used in investigating or prosecuting crime, it is nontestimonial if his primary purpose is to address an ongoing emergency. In other words, a primary purpose to address an emergency overrides in importance any other expectation of the speaker relating to investigating or prosecuting crime, and in this way removes a statement from the testimonial category.[10] Whether *Davis* can be construed to mean that some other "primary purpose" (such as dealing with injuries) can overcome or displace a testimonial expectation remains to be seen, but some modern authority has moved in this direction.[11]

The second factor is the involvement or lack of involvement of police or law enforcement in taking or eliciting a statement. Such involvement suggests strongly that a statement is testimonial, and the absence of such involvement is often important in deciding that a statement is not testimonial.

When police or law enforcement officers investigate, and when they and prosecutors prepare for trial, their actions count in two ways. First, the fact of official involvement in gathering statements brings into play the concerns underlying the Bill of Rights in protecting citizens against overreaching government. Second, their involvement makes it more likely that the speaker (a reasonable person in his position) would understand that he is participating in an investigation or prosecution. *Crawford* referred to official involvement in mentioning police "interrogations," and *Davis* referred to the same thing in saying that the primary purpose of police was "to investigate a possible crime."[12]

The nature of official conduct also counts: If law enforcement officers *elicit* statements while investigating crimes or preparing for trial, the statements are more likely to be testimonial than *volunteered* statements. The more active official role brings into play the concerns underlying the Bill of Rights, and also makes it even more likely that the speaker expects or understands that he is playing a role in the investigative process. *Crawford* used the term interrogation "in its colloquial" sense, embracing any kind of police questioning during an investigation, including informal interviews on the street or in homes or places of work or crime scenes, again pointing toward a broad view of the testimonial category.[13] *Crawford* contrasted this "colloquial" idea against the "technical legal" notion of interrogation,

---

10. Davis v. Washington, 547 U.S. 813 (2006) ("any reasonable listener" in position of 911 operator would see that caller was facing emergency; caller "was seeking aid").

11. Seely v. State, 2008 WL 963516 (Ark. 2008) (admitting statements by three year old abuse victim, made in hospital to social service worker; "primary purpose" test can be "modified for use" outside context of police interrogations; primary purpose of speaker and listener count; she had duty to report, but primary purpose of social worker was to define scope of examination and insure safety) (nontestimonial).

12. Davis v. Washington, 547 U.S. 813 (2006) (there was no emergency; focus was not "what is happening," but "what happened").

13. Commonwealth v. DeOliveira, 849 N.E.2d 218 (Mass. 2006) (admitting 6-year-old's statements to doctor describing abuse; police were in building, not in room; no indication that they instructed doctor).

which connotes questioning in an interview room in a stationhouse, where police often ask witnesses to write things down or employ stenographers for this purpose, producing signed statements, or record interviews electronically. Of course formalities help insure that statements are testimonial (more on this point below), but the *Crawford* majority did not consider them essential, and were stressing the active role of law enforcement as a relevant factor. Justices Thomas and Alito have taken the opposite view, treating formalities as essential, which would narrow the category substantially.[14]

Still, active official involvement in eliciting statements is neither *necessary* nor *sufficient*. In *Davis*, the Court took pains to say that statements can be testimonial *without* police questioning. A sufficient reason is that a speaker might not only expect, but actually intend to aid in investigating and prosecuting crime even if he comes to police on his own and speaks without being questioned. *Davis* cited the Walter Raleigh case, where the evidence included "a letter from Lord Cobham that was plainly not the result of sustained questioning."[15] On the other side of the coin, the whole idea of the "emergency" exception is that statements elicited by police questioning are *not necessarily* testimonial. *Davis* treated the 911 operator as an agent of police, and she called the woman back (she had hung up and the conversation took place when the operator placed a "reverse" call). The operator questioned the woman, eliciting her statements, and still the emergency doctrine applied and the statements were nontestimonial. We can expect the same outcome if, for example, a woman imperiled by domestic abuse hales an officer seeking help instead of calling 911.[16]

Statements made to police might not be testimonial for other reasons as well. Professor Friedman points out that coconspirator statements to undercover agents are not testimonial, and argues persuasively that the same is true of lies made to police in order to throw them off the scent (often admitted as nonhearsay false exculpatory statements), and incoming calls intercepted by police at places involved in drug selling or illegal betting (usually admitted as nonhearsay). Such statements are not testimonial because they are ongoing criminal behavior, because the speaker is not trying to make evidence or further an investigation, and because police are not trying to make evidence that sheds light on past events.[17]

---

14. See Davis v. Washington, 547 U.S. 813 (2006) (Justice Thomas concurrence) and Giles v. California 128 S. Ct. 2678 (2008) (concurring opinions by Justices Thomas and Alito).

15. Davis v. Washington, 547 U.S. 813 (2006).

16. Davis v. Washington, 547 U.S. 813 (2006).

17. Richard Friedman, Grappling with the Meaning of "Testimonial," 71 Brooklyn L. Rev. 241, 253 (2005). On coconspirator statements made to undercover agents, see the ensuing discussion, and see the discussion of the coconspirator exception in §8.33, *supra*. On incoming drug calls and lies to mislead police, see the discussion in §8.22, *supra*.

(3) The privacy factor

The third factor is the degree of privacy surrounding the statement. Neither *Crawford* nor *Davis* dealt with statements in private settings. The Court has commented, however, that such statements are not testimonial, although it has not yet had to decide the point authoritatively.[18] Scholars disagree on the significance of this factor: One can read *Crawford* and *Davis* as placing so much emphasis on the combination of speaker expectations and official involvement that purely private statements are not testimonial under a kind of per se rule. But it is also possible to read *Crawford* and *Davis* to mean that speaker expectation is the factor overriding importance, in which case some purely private statements may be testimonial.[19]

Consider an account of a crime given by a victim or bystander to a neighbor over the back fence, or to a spouse or friend, which can function very much like testimony if the speaker asks the listener to contact police, and perhaps even if she does not make this request but expects that the listener will do so, and maybe even if the speaker simply assumes that police will uncover what she is saying. A speaker, particularly if she is a crime victim, may anticipate (or intend or hope) that the listener will call the matter to the attention of authorities. Finally, some private statements describing crimes are blatantly "accusatory," purposefully charging another with a criminal act, and this factor counts toward calling the statement testimonial.[20] Such private statements do seem to fit *Crawford*'s conceptual framework if speaker expectations are treated as decisive.

On the other hand, most private statements are not testimonial, and post-*Crawford* decisions have reached this conclusion in overwhelming numbers.[21] A speaker who recounts the story of a crime in a conversation with a friend or spouse usually does not expect that what he says will go any further.[22] Of course most such conversations would not fit hearsay exceptions and would not be admitted, but the point is that admitting them would not likely offend *Crawford*.

---

18. Giles v. California 128 S. Ct. 2678 (2008) (statements about abuse and intimidation, made to "friends and neighbors," as well as statements to doctors in "course of receiving treatment" would be excluded, "if at all, only by the hearsay rules," not as testimonial statements under confrontation clause).

19. *Compare* Richard Friedman, Confrontation: The Search for Basic Principles, 86 Geo. L.J. 1011 (1998) (private statement is testimonial if declarant expects it to be used in prosecuting or investigating crime) *with* Akhil Amar, Confrontation Clause First Principles: A Reply to Professor Friedman, 86 Geo. L.J. 1045 (1998) (limiting testimonial to statements prepared by government to use in court, excluding accusations out of court by one private person to another).

20. State v. Shafer, 128 P.3d 87, 95 (Wash. 2006) (dissent argues that statement to "private individual" may be testimonial, citing parent, teacher, or doctor who suspects abuse and questions child).

21. *See* Robert P. Mosteller, Crawford v. Washington: Encouraging and Ensuring the Confrontation of Witnesses, 39 U. Rich. L. Rev. 511, 540 (2005) (statements to family, friends and acquaintances without intent that they be used at trial are usually found to be nontestimonial, even if they incriminate another).

22. State v. Buda, 949 A.2d 761 (N.J. 2008) (child's statement to mother saying "Daddy beat me" was nontestimonial); Pantano v. State, 138 P.3d 477 (Nev. 2006) (child's statement was not testimonial; parent inquiring about abuse is concerned with "health, safety,

Particularly in connection with private conversations, the nature of the speaker bears on the inquiry, mostly for derivative or secondary reasons: Who the speaker is sheds light on what he likely understood when he spoke, and on the function of his statement in investigating or prosecuting crimes. Contrast the cases in which a victim speaks of a crime, and a bystander speaks of the same crime. If a shop is held up by a gunman, and the owner was on the scene and was victimized by being threatened and by incurring personal losses, her statement recounting the crime is more likely to be testimonial than a similar description by a bystander. The victim, more than a bystander, is likely to anticipate (and hope for and intend) that something be done, and his statement is likely to be the single most important datum on which an investigation will proceed.[23]

Again in private conversations, the nature of the statement bears on the inquiry, mostly for derivative or secondary reasons (it sheds light on the speaker's understanding and the role of the statement in investigating crime or preparing for trial). A statement describing an apparent crime is more likely to be testimonial than one that describes an apparently innocent act. Thus one who tells a friend "it's Jack in there with the gun robbing that shop" is more likely to expect that what he says will be passed along to police than one who says "that guy speeding away from the store is Jack." In terms of the role of such statements in investigating and preparing for trial, either may be critical, but "innocent" statements are less likely to be testimonial because of speaker expectations.[24]

Statements made before crimes are committed, that describe past behavior by the defendant that may be threatening or hostile without being criminal (or not seriously criminal), are sometimes admitted as circumstantial evidence that sheds light on defendant's later conduct. Sometimes such a statement fits the state of mind exception because it bears on what the speaker did or did not do later. By its very nature, such a statement is likely not to be testimonial because it does not describe criminality that the speaker expects will lead to investigation or trial, and because private conversations less often give rise to such expectations.[25]

---

and wellbeing" of child, which is not gathering evidence); State v. Lawson, 619 S.E.2d 410, 413 (N.C. 2005) (victim's statement to friend en route to hospital were nontestimonial; not thinking of "anything outside the scope of their private conversation").

23. In re E.H. v. E.H., 823 N.E.2d 1029, 1035 (Ill. App. 2005) (child's statement to grandmother alleging sexual assault were testimonial), appeal allowed, 833 N.E.2d 295 (2005).

24. State v. Staten, 610 S.E.2d 823 (S.C. 2005), vacated, 374 S.C. 9 (2007) (murder victim's statement to friend that defendant had threatened him with a gun was nontestimonial; objective witness would not think his statement would be available for later use at trial).

25. Griffin v. State, 631 S.E.2d 671 (Ga. 2006) (in murder trial, applying catchall to admit victim's statement to friend indicating that defendant was "not supposed to know where we live").

(4) Testimonial formalities The fourth factor is the presence or absence of testimonial formalities. Few would disagree with the proposition that the *presence* of such formalities can be decisive: Statements in the witness box under oath in court in proceedings are testimonial (they are what everyone means by testimony), as are direct substitutes (depositions and affidavits made to present facts to a court) and statements to police in formal settings (interview rooms, perhaps recorded or written and signed or taken down by a stenographer). Several times *Crawford* alluded to such points: Thus one who "makes a formal statement to government officers bears testimony" in a way that differs from "a casual remark to an acquaintance," and the confrontation clause "reflects an especially acute concern" with such statements. The Court also referred to "formalized testimonial materials, such as affidavits, custodial examinations," and "prior testimony," quoting an earlier concurring opinion in the *White* case.[26] In *Davis*, the Court said most cases applying the confrontation clause involve "formal" testimonial statements, meaning "sworn testimony in prior judicial proceedings or formal depositions under oath."

More problematic is the effect of *absence* of such formalities: Can statements be testimonial even though some or all of the usual formalities are missing? *Davis* indicates that even minimal formalities count on the testimonial side of the calculus: Thus a police interview with the victim on the scene was testimonial, in part because it was "formal enough" to be "conducted in a separate room, away from her husband."[27] Justice Thomas disagreed with the majority in *Davis*, reiterating his view that the confrontation clause applies *only* to formalized statements (he had previously pointed toward this conclusion in *Crawford* and *White*), and in the 2008 opinion in *Giles* on the issue of forfeiting confrontation rights, Justice Thomas again set out this view, and Justice Alito agreed.[28]

Post-*Crawford* decisions usually treat the matter of formalities as a makeweight factor, citing their presence or absence in support of conclusions resting mostly on other grounds, but the factor definitely counts.[29]

---

26. White v. Illinois, 502 U.S. 346, 365 (1992) (Justice Thomas, joined by Justice Scalia, concurring).

27. Davis v. Washington, 547 U.S. 813 (2006) (Justice Thomas, dissenting).

28. Giles v. California 2008 WL 2511298 (2008) (in concurrence, Thomas adheres to view that only "formalized" statements to police are covered; Alito doubts that statement to police was testimonial).

29. State v. Feliciano, 901 A.2d 631 (R.I. 2006) (in murder trial, admitting statement by victim to friend the day before, describing prior assault; casual remark was not a solemn declaration or affirmation); United States v. Danford, 435 F.3d 682, 687 (7th Cir. 2006) (conversation between employee and manager was "more akin to a casual remark" than testimony); United States v. Franklin, 415 F.3d 537, 545 (6th Cir. 2005) (codefendant's statement saying "we hit a truck," referring to defendant and made to friend and confidant "by happenstance," was not testimonial).

§8.85 The _Davis_ "Emergency Exception"

Two years after _Crawford_, the Court revisited the confrontation clause in the _Davis_ case, which was a consolidated review of domestic abuse convictions in Washington and Indiana. The Washington case involved the use of a woman's 911 call reporting abuse, and the Indiana case involved the use of a wife's statements to officers summoned to the scene by a 911 call, in which she described her husband's behavior. In both cases, the statements fit the excited utterance exception, and the complaining witness did not testify. Adopting a "primary purpose" criterion, the Court concluded in the Washington case that the statement was nontestimonial. The reason was that the operator's primary purpose in questioning the caller was "to enable police assistance to meet an ongoing emergency." In the Indiana case, however, the Court concluded that the statement _was_ testimonial because the primary purpose in questioning the wife was to determine "what happened" and "investigate a possible crime," not to determine what was happening _at the time._[1]

As it emerged in _Davis_, the emergency exception was narrowly crafted: With police on the scene in the Indiana case, and the abuser and victim physically separated, the emergency was over, although clearly hostilities might continue that police intervention did not solve. Perhaps the Court anticipated that ongoing assistance would address these risks: The man was arrested and charged, and commonly in such situations police or prosecutors obtain court orders requiring the abuser not to approach the woman as a condition of release from custody. The woman too could probably get assistance. The implicit message is that the emergency exception applies for as long as there is immediate risk of harm, coupled with a need to gather information in order to prevent or mitigate harm.[2]

The Court in _Davis_ rejected a broad argument that only "initial inquiries" are nontestimonial. The line is between accounts describing the present situation in which danger must be assessed, as in the Washington case, and accounts describing what had happened in the past to bring the danger into being, as in the Indiana case. Thus initial contacts with police may be nontestimonial, while later statements may be testimonial, when the focus has shifted from assessing present

---

§8.85 1. Davis v. Washington, 547 U.S. 813 (2006).

2. State v. Boggs, 185 P.3d 111 (Ariz. 2008) (statements by employee of fast food restaurant, after being shot and while dying on ground at rear of restaurant, seeking help and saying bad people might still be there, fit emergency doctrine); United States v. Arnold, 486 F.2d 177, 189-192 (6th Cir. 2007) (911 call by G, threatened by gun carried by convicted murderer A who was G's mother's boyfriend, fit emergency doctrine; G sought "protection" from ongoing emergency because A "remained at large" and was "fixing to shoot her," and fact that G went to car around corner before calling "did not make the emergency less real or less pressing," as G "had no reason to know" whether A had stayed in residence or followed her).

danger and taking steps to end it, and focuses instead on investigating crime.[3]

In *Davis*, the Court took pains to avoid being critical of police (the officer in the Indiana case was doing "precisely what [he] should have done"). Still, both *Crawford* and *Davis* also serve a regulatory or prophylactic purpose. The real message is that investigative material in the form of statements to police, however valuable it might be in deciding whether and how to prosecute and in making strategic decisions about witnesses and investigations and interrogation, is not evidence to be used at trial, and prosecutors in particular, since it is primarily they who plan trial strategy, but also to some extent police and law enforcement officers, must pursue other avenues in preparing cases for trial.

§8.86 Nontestimonial Statements, or Uses of Statements

Crawford mentions three common hearsay exceptions and indicates that statements within them are not testimonial (at least usually)—the exceptions for coconspirator statements, business records, and dying declarations. *Crawford* also indicates that nonhearsay uses of out-of-court statements do not raise confrontation concerns. We take up these matters here. Elsewhere in this work we often note that statements offered under particular exceptions in common situations do or do not pose problems under *Crawford*.

We should also note other situations left untouched by *Crawford*. First, *Crawford* approves the use of statements that fit the former testimony exception, and more generally endorses the proposition that a prior opportunity to cross-examine satisfies the clause. Second, *Crawford* affirms that later cross-examination at trial satisfies the clause, paving the way to use other hearsay exceptions that require declarant be cross-examinable at trial. Third, *Crawford* did not affect admissions in their various forms,[1] and did not change the limit put by the *Bruton* doctrine on using admissions by one defendant implicating others.[2]

(1) Conspirator statements

Coconspirator statements are nontestimonial for purposes of the *Crawford* doctrine. This result makes good sense: These are made during and in furtherance of a conspiracy, and the speaker is not trying to make evidence or bear witness. He has no expectation of advancing an investigation, which places such statements far from the kinds of

---

3. State v. Shea, 2008 WL 3491404 (Vt. 2008) (initial statements by victim of domestic battery fit emergency exception; these described assault and identified perpetrator; later questioning of the victim elicited statements that were testimonial).

§8.86 1. United States v. Sudeen, 434 F.3d 384, 390-391 (5th Cir. 2005) (approving agent's admission but not citing *Crawford*); State v. Adams, 124 P.3d 19 (Kan. 2005) (using confession does not violate confrontation rights by forcing defendant to choose between not testifying and challenging statements).

2. See Bruton v. United States, 391 U.S. 123 (1968), discussed in §8.28, *supra*.

testimonial statements that *Crawford* described.[3] Courts also admit statements by one conspirator to another as nonhearsay, which makes sense when they show the negotiation or planning or setting up of the conspiracy, where they are nonhearsay verbal acts, and *Crawford* does not apply.[4]

There is one situation in which one might argue that coconspirator statements are testimonial after all, and that is where a conspirator unwittingly talks to an undercover agent or informant whose purpose is to further an investigation or bring charges. The coconspirator exception does apply to such statements, on the theory that the subjective purpose of the speaker, if he does not know that the person he speaks to is an informant or undercover agent, is all that counts. Hence such statements can be attempts to further a conspiracy even though they undermine it.[5] For much the same reason, it makes sense to treat even these statements as nontestimonial, as post-*Crawford* decisions do.[6]

Statements made in private settings that shed light on state of mind, and fit the state-of-mind exception in FRE 803(3), are likely to be nontestimonial. Such statements may shed light on knowledge or intent, and they are normally nontestimonial *because* they are made in private settings in which the speaker does not expect what he says to be used in investigating or prosecuting crime, and because they refer to the speaker's own state of mind and are used to prove that point (they are not accusatory statements attributing criminality to another). They may allude to, and support inferences about, prior criminal behavior by another person, but the exception does not allow their use to prove such points, which again lessens the likelihood that such statements could be considered testimonial.[7]

(2) State of mind statements

Crawford identifies business records as nontestimonial. Certainly most records that fit FRE 803(6) are not made for the purpose of aiding an investigation or creating evidence in criminal prosecutions, and certainly the maker of such records does not understand or expect that they will play a role in investigating or prosecuting crimes. Such records are not ordinarily made in response to queries by police or law enforcement.[8] To the extent that they serve a routine business purpose, as the exception requires, they are not testimonial.[9]

(3) Business records

3. United States v. Martinez, 430 F.3d 317, 328-329 (6th Cir. 2005); United States v. Bridgeforth, 441 F.3d 864, 868 (9th Cir. 2006).

4. United States v. Faulkner, 439 F.3d 1221, 1226-1227 (10th Cir. 2006) (coconspirator statements may be "part of the plotting," including statements "directing the conduct of a fellow conspirator or agreeing to follow directions," which are not covered by *Crawford*) (citing author of this Treatise).

5. *See* the discussion of FRE 801(d)(2)(E) in §8.33, *supra*.

6. United States v. Stewart, 433 F.3d 273, 292 (2d Cir. 2006) (not testimonial, even when made to investigating law enforcement officers); United States v. Underwood, 446 F.3d 1340, 1346 (11th Cir. 2006) (coconspirator statement to confidential informant).

7. State v. Johnson, 131 P.3d 173, 189 (Or. 2006) (statement fit exception, was not testimonial).

8. Crawford v. Washington, 541 U.S. 36, 54 (2004) (most hearsay exceptions cover "statements that by their nature" are nontestimonial, including business records).

9. State v. L.R., 890 A.2d 343 (N.J. Superior Ct. 2006) (in trial of juvenile for mischief, damage estimate was nontestimonial business record).

Business records may not be invariably nontestimonial, however. Some are made with the idea of aiding law enforcement. If a store hires security personnel, for example, whose responsibilities include writing up observations of customer theft, the resultant records might include statements about criminal acts and identifying information, and such records seem testimonial if offered in evidence to prove the underlying crime. They are made with the expectation of aiding law enforcement in finding and prosecuting shoplifters.

(4) Dying declarations Another kind of statement identified in *Crawford* as meriting special treatment is dying declarations. The opinion says that dying declarations may be testimonial, but that they enjoy special status under the confrontation clause, a notion that has been challenged by a scholar who argues that dying declarations were not unique as mechanisms to introduce testimonial hearsay.[10] Of course dying declarations often describe criminal acts, and often identify perpetrators to law enforcement officers, which suggests that they do satisfy the central criteria of testimonial hearsay. Even when such statements are made to friends or passers by, a person dying of wounds suffered in a violent encounter is likely to be trying to make evidence or aid an investigative effort. Still, modern authority approves dying declarations, taking seriously the suggestion in *Crawford*.[11]

(5) Forfeiture exception Both *Crawford* and *Davis* approved the principle that a defendant may forfeit his confrontation rights by wrongful conduct that makes a witness unavailable. In the *Giles* case in 2008, the Court resolved the question whether this principle applies only if defendant acts *intentionally* to achieve this outcome (the answer is yes),[12] confirming the status of this principle in confrontation doctrine. It is all but certain that statements that fit the criteria in FRE 804(b)(6) can be admitted without offending the confrontation clause.[13]

(6) Nonhearsay uses *Crawford* commented in passing that nonhearsay uses do not raise confrontation concerns,[14] and many modern decisions hold that the confrontation clause does not block the nonhearsay use of statements offered against the accused, and this idea carries forward

---

10. Michael Polelle, The Death of Dying Declarations in a Post-Crawford World, 71 Mo. L. Rev. 285 (2006) (pointing out that res gestae statements have long been admitted against criminal defendants as well)

11. Crawford v. Washington, 541 U.S. 36, 54 n.6 (2005) (not deciding whether confrontation clause makes special exception, but noting authority admitting even dying declarations that are testimonial; any such exception is sui generis and rests on "historical grounds"). *See also* People v. Monterroso, 101 P.3d 956, 762 (Cal. 2005); State v. Martin, 695 N.W.2d 578, 583 (Minn. 2005); Harkins v. State, 143 P.3d 706 (Nev. 2006) (all admitting dying declarations by murder victim identifying assailant).

12. Crawford v. Washington, 541 U.S. 36 (2004); Davis v. Washington, 547 U.S. 813 (2006); Giles v. California 128 S. Ct. 2678 (2008).

13. *See* the discussion in §8.84, *supra*, and the discussion in §8.90, *infra*.

14. Crawford v. Washington, 541 U.S. 36, 59 n.9 (2004) (confrontation clause "does not bar the use of testimonial statements for purposes other than establishing the truth of the matter asserted").

a longstanding tradition.[15] Thus statements may be admitted to provide context for other statements[16] and the same is true of statements offered as background to explain the acts of law enforcement officers during investigations, which are often admitted as nonhearsay—analytically, as showing what information the officers had.[17]

Similarly, proving that co-offenders or others lied to cover their tracks or mislead police or prosecutors does not offend *Crawford*. Such statements are conduct designed to throw investigators off the scent, and are not hearsay when offered to prove what the actor thought, and for this reason they are also nontestimonial. The result is a little bit odd inasmuch as the speaker/actor certainly does expect (likely intends) that his behavior (words and actions seeking to mislead police) should have an impact. Nevertheless the outcome seems right because the statements are likely to be themselves criminal acts (obstructing an investigation on purpose) and are not generally accusatory.[18]

Under the Rules, one nonhearsay use is restricted by language in FRE 703, which says that a party who adduces expert testimony that rests in whole or in part on outside statements cannot routinely prove those statements (the court can make exception if probative value in evaluating the expert testimony "substantially outweighs" prejudicial effect). Without that provision, parties calling experts might offer such statements to show the basis of the opinion. In fact, there are two checks against this practice: In the first place, FRE 703 says that this practice is normally wrong (unless the statements fit a hearsay exception, and often they do not). In the second place, statements to government experts are likely to be testimonial if they refer to the behavior of the defendant and are made by people who understand that the expert is seeking information in order to testify, and experts cannot properly be used as conduits to get such statements into evidence.[19] In short, overuse and misuse of source material raises confrontation concerns,

---

15. United States v. Inadi, 475 U.S. 387, 398 (1986) (nonhearsay raises no confrontation concerns); Tennessee v. Street, 471 U.S. 409 (1985).

16. Turner v. Commonwealth, 248 S.W.3d 543, 546 (Ky. 2008) (recording of drug transaction included statements by informant who did not testify; all but one "provided context for Turner's portions of the conversations," so did not violate *Crawford*); State v. Roque, 141 P.3d 368 (Ariz. 2006) (videotaped interrogation of defendant referred to wife's statements; what she said was not offered for its truth, was not hearsay, did not violate confrontation rights).

17. United States v. Goosby, 523 F.3d 632, 638 (6th Cir. 2008) (admitting "background information about the investigation" did not violate *Crawford*); Edwards v. State, 200 S.W.3d 500 (Mo. 2006) (statements leading police to discovery of murder weapon were not testimonial; not admitted for truth, but for "limited purpose of explaining" investigation).

18. United States v. Stewart, 433 F.3d 273, 291 (2d Cir. 2006) (in trial for obstructing justice, false statements by co-offender to agents had characteristics of testimonial statements, but *Crawford* does not reach statements offered for purposes other than to establish truth of matter); State v. Newell, 710 N.W.2d 6 (Iowa 2006) (in murder trial, admitting excited utterances by defendant's mother to 911 operator and police, in attempted "cover-up" of murder; not barred by *Crawford*, used for nonhearsay purpose).

19. *See* the discussion in §7.11, *supra*.

although limited use of such material to explain the basis for expert testimony can survive challenge.[20]

Simple reliance on out-of-court hearsay is unlikely to violate the *Crawford* doctrine, even if the statements are testimonial, at least when the expert testimony focuses on broad contextual matters such as the structure and operation of drug trafficking operations or gangs, or on coded expressions common in these cases.[21]

More generally, it seems that a nonhearsay use for a testimonial statement should not overcome an objection under *Crawford* if the statement is likely to be misused as proof of what it asserts. Jury misuse of statements is a familiar problem in implementing the hearsay doctrine, and in the case of testimonial statements in criminal cases, the confrontation clause adds a reason for caution, and may require exclusion even when nonhearsay uses appear.[22]

Elsewhere we argue against a literalistic interpretation of the idea of the term "statement" or "assertion" for hearsay purposes.[23] Sentence fragments, questions, and commands should not be viewed as lying beyond the reach of the hearsay doctrine merely because they do not make a strong claim that some fact is true, at least in which they express or communicate some fact: Thus the question "what time does that clock say?" should be viewed as hearsay if offered to prove, for example, that there is a clock to which the speaker might be referring, or if offered to prove that the speaker wanted to know what time it was (although this use of the statement would likely satisfy the state-of-mind exception). The fact that *Crawford* does not apply to nonhearsay uses of statements creates an incentive for prosecutors to argue that in fact what they are offering is not a statement or an assertion at all, for hearsay purposes. Courts should resist such arguments when statements express or communicate facts relating to acts, events, or conditions in the world and are offered to prove such points.[24]

---

20. Szymanski v. State, 166 P.3d 879 (Wyo. 2007) (in arson trial, admitting officer's testimony on cause, including comments by apartment owner, admissible to show basis) (no *Crawford* violation).

21. United States v. Law, 528 F.3d 888, 912 (D.C. Cir. 2008) (description of typical operations of drug dealers, gleaned from interviews, did not violate *Crawford* doctrine).

22. Thomas v. Hubbard, 273 F.3d 1164, 1170-1174 (9th Cir. 2001) (error to admit testimony by officer F that S said that N said defendant T confronted victim L; this triple hearsay was offered for nonhearsay purpose of rebutting impeachment of F, who had said no when asked whether S told F that L and T argued; even if admissible for limited purpose, this was "precisely the type of statement" jury could not ignore).

23. *See* the discussion in §8.4, *supra*.

24. United States v. Summers, 414 F.3d 1287, 130 (10th Cir. 2005) (comment to arresting officers by codefendant T, "How did you guys find us so fast?" was an assertion; it "intimated both guilt and wonderment at the ability of the police to apprehend the perpetrators of the crime so quickly," and was not just an inquiry about "modern methods of law enforcement") (it was testimonial).

§8.87 Statements Subject to Prior Cross-Examination

The Supreme Court has repeatedly held that a defendant who *previously* cross-examined the declarant about statements that are later offered at trial cannot complain that admitting them violated the confrontation clause if the declarant is unavailable to testify. As early as 1895 in the *Mattox* case, the Court approved the use against the accused of testimony from a prior trial, and in *Crawford* the Court confirmed this point. In earlier landmark decisions, particularly the 1970 opinion in *Green* and the 1980 opinion in *Roberts*, the Court approved the use of preliminary hearing testimony because defendant had cross-examined them and the witnesses were unavailable.[1]

In cases where the principle is stated in passing, the Court says or assumes that the witness is unavailable. In cases where the issue was squarely presented, unavailability to testify at trial was critical. Thus the 1968 decision in *Barber* reversed a conviction for admitting testimony from a preliminary hearing because the state could have taken steps to bring the witness to testify,[2] and in *Motes* in 1900 the Court held that it was wrong to admit testimony from a preliminary hearing where the witness held in custody managed to escape on account of government negligence.[3] In short, the confrontation clause can be satisfied by prior cross, but only if the witness is unavailable at trial without serious fault on the government's part, and a *constitutional* standard of unavailability applies.

Unavailability required

The explanation for this aspect of confrontation law is easy to understand: If the witness cannot testify at trial, the choice is between admitting what she said before and doing without her input. If the missing witness is crucial, doing without means dismissal. While *prior* cross is less than optimal because the trier cannot watch the process and pick up clues from demeanor, still it can accomplish much the same thing as cross-examination at trial—exploring memory, perception, and candor, and (most especially) honing in on the meaning of what the witness says, testing powers of narration and shedding light on ambiguities or uncertainties. In short, prior cross can come close to satisfying central concerns of hearsay doctrine, and close as well to satisfying the ideal that the confrontation clause seeks to preserve—a face-to-face meeting with a chance to cross-examine. While *prior* cross means the main events occur "offstage," so to speak, the face-to-face meeting did happen, and cross-examined testimony can be presented by reading a transcript that replicates what happened word for word, or by playing a

Close to satisfying ideal

---

§8.87 1. Crawford v. Washington, 541 U.S. 36 (2004) (approving principle); Ohio v. Roberts, 448 U.S. 56 (1980) (preliminary hearing testimony); California v. Green, 399 U.S. 149, 165 (1970) (preliminary hearing testimony); Mattox v. United States, 156 U.S. 237 (1895) (trial testimony).

2. Barber v. Page, 390 U.S. 719, 725 (1968).

3. Motes v. United States, 178 U.S. 458 (1900) (prior trial testimony by escaped witness inadmissible).

recording of the prior proceeding capturing audible words and visible images.

Holding in *Green*   In *Green*, the Court adopted the rationale described above. The trial court admitted preliminary hearing testimony by the state's main witness, 16-year-old Melvin Porter. He testified that defendant John Green asked him to sell marijuana (Porter called it "stuff" or "grass") and pick up a shopping bag containing baggies of it in the bushes at the house of Green's parents. Porter did so and sold some to an undercover officer. The defense cross-examined Porter at a preliminary hearing. Porter testified at trial too, but was evasive and uncooperative: He said Green had called and asked him to sell stuff that he would not name, and that later he got baggies of marijuana but didn't know whether Green was his supplier because he was on LSD. He could not remember what happened after Green called and said he could not distinguish fact from fantasy. The prosecutor read excerpts from the preliminary hearing, invoking a statute allowing full use of inconsistent statements. Green was convicted, and the Supreme Court approved: The defense had already cross-examined Porter in a trial-like setting because the earlier hearing proceeded in "circumstances closely approximating those that surround the typical trial." Porter was under oath, and defense counsel had "every opportunity to cross-examine" in proceedings "before a judicial tribunal, equipped to provide a judicial record."[4]

Holding in *Roberts*   Similarly in *Roberts*, which involved a state conviction for forging a check and possessing stolen credit cards belonging to Bernard and Amy Isaacs, the defense questioned the critical witness in a preliminary hearing. The witness was Amy Isaacs, who apparently got the checks and cards from her parents. Anita also let Roberts use her apartment while she was away, and he claimed that she had given the cards to him with the idea of buying a television set, and without telling him she lacked permission to use them. At the preliminary hearing, defense counsel encountered Anita, called her to testify, and tried unsuccessfully to get her to admit that she told Roberts he could use the checks and cards.

Although the defense called Anita, its questioning "partook of" cross-examination as a matter of form (it was "replete" with leading questions) and as a matter of purpose (the defense challenged Anita's sincerity, perception, memory, and meaning). Anita resisted attempts to shift blame away from defendant, but counsel "continued to explore the underlying events in detail" by trying to show that the two were sharing an apartment, which was critical to the claim that she had "ulterior personal reasons" for blaming defendant. Counsel also tried to get her to admit that she authorized Roberts to buy a television, bringing out (when she denied it) that she had an old and cheap one.[5] As in *Green*, the Court in *Roberts* too approved the use at trial of

---

4. California v. Green, 399 U.S. 149, 165 (1970).

5. Ohio v. Roberts, 448 U.S. 56, 70-72 (1980) (immaterial that defendant was not represented by lawyer who conducted defense at preliminary hearing and that questioning was by "direct examination").

testimony from a preliminary hearing. (The *Roberts* approach to confrontation was displaced by *Crawford* in 2004, but *Roberts* remains good law on the efficacy of prior cross.)

Testimony given in prior proceedings is, of course, at the heart of what *Crawford* meant by "testimonial" hearsay, but it may be used against defendants without violating confrontation rights because of prior cross. Such testimony often fits the former testimony exception, which requires unavailability of the declarant and a prior opportunity to cross-examine (see FRE 804(b)(1)).

Legions of cases hold that statements fitting the prior testimony exception also satisfy the confrontation clause. While some decisions predate *Crawford* and apply the *Roberts* standard, nothing in *Crawford* indicates that a different outcome is required today. The decisions approve use of testimony in a prior trial on the same charges,[6] testimony at an earlier phase of the same trial,[7] and testimony in a prior trial on other charges in another system.[8] They accept as well preliminary hearing testimony,[9] as well as testimony in depositions,[10] and testimony in motions and hearings.[11] Again it is worth noting, however, that the second criterion requiring unavailability of the witness is vigorously enforced, and the exception has its own unavailability requirement.[12]

Many cases approve

---

6. Mancusi v. Stubbs, 408 U.S. 204 (1972) (prior trial testimony, despite reversal for incompetent counsel); Mattox v. United States, 156 U.S. 237 (1895) (testimony at first trial; witness had died); United States v. Reed, 227 F.3d 763, 769 (7th Cir. 2000) (in second robbery trial, admitting testimony in first trial; confrontation clause requires necessity and indicia of reliability; criteria were satisfied).

7. State v. Stephenson, 195 S.W.3d 574 (Tenn. 2006) (admitting, in capital resentencing hearing, testimony from guilt phase trial by witness who had become unavailable but was cross-examined at that time); Farmer v. State, 124 P.3d 699, 705 (Wyo. 2005) (admitting testimony from prior trial; rejecting claim that defendant was prevented from exploring inconsistencies before; defense had adequate opportunity to explore recollection, comment on discrepancies in testimony of two brothers).

8. Mancusi v. Stubbs, 408 U.S. 204, 213-214 (1972) (finding "indicia of reliability" sufficient to permit use at second trial of testimony in first trial by man who survived kidnapping leading to murder of wife); United States v. Lombard, 72 F.3d 170, 187-188 (1st Cir. 1995) (testimony in state murder case admitted in later federal firearms trial, exception is firmly rooted).

9. Ohio v. Roberts, 448 U.S. 56 (1980) (cross-examined former testimony rests on solid foundation satisfying confrontation clause); California v. Green, 399 U.S. 149, 165-168 (1970) (preliminary hearing testimony, where witness is absent and unavailable or present and claiming lack of memory).

10. United States v. Salim, 855 F.2d 944, 954-955 (2d Cir. 1988) (rejecting challenge to deposition taken in France under French law); United States v. Kelly, 892 F.2d 255, 260-261 (3d Cir. 1989) (deposition of foreign nationals living abroad fit exception), *cert. denied,* 497 U.S. 1006.

11. Trigones v. Bissonnette, 296 F.3d 1, 5-12 (1st Cir. 2002) (testimony at suppression hearing); People v. Jurado, 131 P.3d 400, 428 (Cal. 2006) (admitting testimony from "conditional examination" of witness, taken by prosecutor because life of witness was in danger); State v. Estrella, 893 A.2d 348, 358 (Conn. 2006) (admitting testimony by accomplice, unavailable at trial, given in probable cause hearing; defense cross-examined then) (no *Crawford* violation).

12. *See* the discussion in §8.68, *supra.*

Three difficulties

There are three issues to consider. One is a great unanswered question: If the defendant has an *opportunity* in some prior proceeding to cross-examine, but declines to take advantage of the opportunity, can he still object under the confrontation clause to use of prior testimony? The second is best understood as a significant difficulty: Prior cross, assuming that it was pursued, may still be *insufficient* to satisfy confrontation rights if it is stymied by rulings or an uncooperative witness. The third is a tricky question that also has yet to be answered: Does prior cross, or a prior opportunity, justify admitting not only prior *testimony* by the witness, but also his prior *statements*, made at other times?

(1) Opportunity not taken

Suppose the critical prosecution witness testifies at a preliminary hearing where he lays out the story of what happened. Suppose he testifies that defendant attacked him at a party in a dispute over a woman, and the witness did nothing to provoke the attack, but sustained injuries because defendant overpowered him and kicked him when he fell to the floor. The defense does not cross-examine, and the witness dies prior to trial for reasons having nothing to do with the crime.

The situation invites arguments that not cross-examining before waives the right to complain about lack of cross at trial. There are, however, two serious objections. First, cross-examination is a *trial right*, as the Court has said, and a defendant who elects *not* to cross-examine in a preliminary hearing or deposition, for example, does not necessarily intend to give up anything.[13] Indeed, in most cases the idea is to *preserve* the opportunity to cross-examine at trial by not giving anything away beforehand, which would allow prosecutor and witness to make adjustments in anticipation of an attack that has already been previewed. Nor can defendant fairly be charged with *knowing* he is giving up anything, in most cases, because there is usually no reason to doubt that the witness will appear at trial.[14]

Second, often defendant is not *motivated* to cross-examine the speaker on the prior occasion. Referring to the common setting of the preliminary hearing, the only question then is the existence of probable cause to believe a crime was committed and that defendant committed it. Defendants seldom get cases knocked out at this stage, so most lawyers faced with the choice between tipping their hand in a long-shot effort to destroy the prosecutor's case at the outset and holding their fire so as to be more effective at trial take the latter course. For this reason, some jurisdictions refuse to admit preliminary hearing testimony, *despite* the fact that the Court has indicated that it is constitutional to do so: These cases stress the requirement in the former

---

13. Barber v. Page, 390 U.S. 719, 725 (1968) (confrontation is "basically a trial right").

14. *Id.* at 725 (defendant could not know witness would be imprisoned at time of trial or that prosecutor would not produce him; not cross-examining could not waive confrontation rights).

testimony exception that paves the way to use such testimony only if there was an "opportunity" or "similar motive" to cross-examine.[15]

The problem under discussion has not escaped the notice of the Court. *Roberts* emphasized that the defense *actually engaged in* "the equivalent" of cross in the preliminary hearing. The Court noted the question whether "a mere opportunity" satisfies the confrontation clause, and quoted an observation of an astute commentator that this question is "difficult to resolve" under "conventional theories" of confrontation.[16]

Until the Court speaks to this issue, it is perilous to predict the answer. In other contexts, however, the Court has gone out of its way to say that it is the "opportunity" that counts, and has rejected claims that the opportunity was inadequate because the witness was unresponsive or cross-examination was stymied. These decisions leave little room to argue that the opportunity was *so* constrained as to be insufficient. If the Court takes a similar attitude in cases where the defense had an opportunity that it did not exercise at all, then it seems likely that the opportunity alone is enough, and that failing to take advantage of it means risking that prior testimony will be admitted. In short, the Court's decisions point toward the conclusion that the defense bears the risk that the witness will disappear, so it must cross-examine on the earlier occasion even if, in the typical case, the witness will testify and can be cross-examined at trial.

(2) Prior cross less than optimal

If the defense cross-examines in a preliminary hearing, but questioning is stifled so that defendant cannot obtain answers that would shed important light on the testimony, can it be said that the opportunity satisfies the confrontation clause? Cross might be stifled for either or both of two general reasons—either the witness does not or cannot cooperate or the court rules questions out of order.

Questions of this kind seem not to have arisen in this setting, but they have come up in the setting of *deferred* cross, when out-of-court statements are offered in evidence at trial and the declarant is *then* subject to cross. (The reason may be that prosecutors almost always offer prior statements where the witness has had a change of heart and does not repeat more incriminating claims he made before. The witness is then confronted with different versions of events that he has provided. It is predictable that he will be uncooperative—he will be evasive or claim privilege or lack of memory, to avoid facing up to having lied or perjured himself.) In the somewhat different situation that is the main concern here, where the witness does *not* testify at trial, but *did* on an earlier occasion when she could be cross-examined, evading or refusing to answer questions is a less likely occurrence.

15. See the discussion of FRE 804(b)(1) in §4.68, *supra*.
16. Ohio v. Roberts, 448 U.S. 56 (1980) (quoting Westen, The Future of Confrontation, 77 Mich. L. Rev. 1185, 1211 (1979)).

Still, it is worth noting that the opportunity to cross-examine is arguably inadequate if any of the following occurs: The witness claims on cross not to remember the acts, events, or conditions to which she testified, or refuses to answer questions trying to get behind what she has said on direct, or the court sustains a privilege claim that entitles her not to answer questions that would shed light on her testimony, or blocks questions on cross that might be important in testing her. In these cases, there are serious arguments that the opportunity for cross provided on the prior occasion does not satisfy the confrontation clause so as to justify the use of prior testimony (or other statements) at trial.

When the problem is an uncooperative witness, the clues given by decisions dealing with *deferred* cross suggest that the defense cannot complain, at least in the absence of extraordinary circumstances in which cross is stymied completely, and claimed lack of memory do not make cross insufficient.[17]

It is harder to say whether rulings that block impeaching attempts on the prior occasion should prevent use at trial of what the witness said. Since the witness does not testify at trial, the defense can hardly cross-examine about prior bad acts not leading to conviction, and FRE 608 might block use of "extrinsic evidence" to prove such acts (requiring questioner to take the answer of the witness). Apart from restrictions on cross on the prior occasion that make sense because the issues are narrower, it still seems that such rulings, even if correct in the earlier setting, can be so restrictive that they cut off the kind of defense cross that should be pursued, and open to pursuit, at trial. This fact can be such a serious impediment that the prior questioning cannot satisfy confrontation rights. When it comes to cross that is deferred until trial, the Court has acknowledged a similar point, and at least potentially prior questioning does not satisfy the confrontation clause.[18]

(3) Prior cross and other statements

Here is the tricky question noted above: Does prior examination, or the opportunity for it, satisfy the confrontation clause so as to justify admitting *yet other statements* on the subject to which the witness/declarant testified before? Suppose an assault victim calls 911, and police are dispatched. They find her boyfriend on the premises, conclude that he is the assailant, and arrest and place him in a squadcar. The victim tells an officer what happened, and her story fits the excited utterance exception because little time has elapsed. Let us assume that the purpose of the victim and the officer are to further a criminal investigation, so what she says is testimonial under *Crawford* and the

17. United States v. Owens, 484 U.S. 554 (1988) (in setting of deferred cross about earlier statement, noting that "assertions of privilege" may "undermine the process to such a degree" as to stifle cross contemplated by FRE 801(d)(1), but rejecting claim that lack of memory has similar effect).

18. United States v. Owens, 484 U.S. 554 (1988) (in the setting of deferred cross-examination at trial about earlier statement, noting that "limitations on the scope of examination" by trial court or assertions of privilege by witness may "undermine the process to such a degree" as to stifle cross contemplated by FRE 801(d)(1), but rejecting claim that lack of memory has similar effect).

"emergency" doctrine does not apply. The boyfriend is charged, and the victim testifies at a preliminary hearing, where she tells her story. At trial, however, she is unavailable for reasons unrelated to the crime or the defendant's behavior. The prosecutor offers her preliminary hearing testimony under FRE 804(b)(1).

Suppose at trial that the prosecutor calls the officer to testify at trial to what the victim told him. Would admitting this testimony comport with the confrontation clause? Putting aside the question whether the defense motive to cross-examine is *ever* enough to justify admitting preliminary hearing testimony, the right answer to this question is probably no.

The prior statement is certain to differ from the preliminary hearing testimony—otherwise why would a prosecutor offer it? If the statement *also was not* offered at the preliminary hearing, the defense had no chance to test *the statement itself*, to probe the details it relates, or to challenge the speaker about it. Whatever headway the defense might make in attacking the witness on her memory or accuracy in describing events is a pale substitute for questioning that challenges the witness on the statement. Even if the defense knew about the statement, there is no reason to burden the defense with raising it, and tactical considerations would incline the defense not to do so.[19] One might even imagine a case in which the statement was made *after* the witness testified in a preliminary hearing, where the defense could not have asked questions about it. In these settings, it stretches beyond the breaking point the idea of an opportunity to cross-examine if one concludes that the defense had an adequate opportunity merely because it could ask the witness about underlying acts, events, or conditions.

§8.88 Statements Subject to Deferred Cross-Examination

Repeatedly since its decision in *Green* in 1970, the Court has said that cross-examination at trial on statements that the witness made before satisfies the confrontation clause. Hence defendants in criminal cases face an uphill battle in advancing a *constitutional* claim of error, at least one based on confrontation, when statements by persons who testify at trial are offered in evidence.

In *Green*, the Court said cross-examination at trial could satisfy the confrontation clause where the main witness told police that the defendant supplied him with marijuana.[1] The very next year in *O'Neil*, the Court concluded that cross at trial on a prior statement sufficed, where a testifying defendant admitted to police his involvement in kidnapping and robbery, and implicated the other defendant in the crime.[2] In *Roberts*, the Court made the same point in passing

---

19. See generally Mueller, Cross-Examination Earlier or Later: When Is It Enough to Satisfy Crawford? 19 Regent U. L. Rev. 319 (2007).
§8.88 1. California v. Green, 399 U.S. 149, 159-160 (1970).
2. Nelson v. O'Neil, 402 U.S. 622, 627 (1971).

(cross-examination at trial could suffice). Again in *Owens* in 1988, the Court approved cross-examination at trial as adequate in testing a statement identifying the defendant as the assailant.[3] Finally in *Crawford*, the Court repeated the point yet again, and here (if not in *Roberts* more than twenty-five years earlier) it achieves the status of definitive principle because *Crawford* speaks comprehensively and puts in place a whole new scheme.[4]

The proposition that deferred cross satisfies the confrontation clause is a salient principle with respect to evidence offered by prosecutors in criminal cases. This principle is often decisive, and operates in many settings.

Full and effective cross In *Green*, the question was whether a prior inconsistent statement could be used to prove what it asserts without violating the confrontation clause. The Court said yes, based on the proposition that cross-examination at trial *can* adequately protect confrontation rights, at least when it is "full and effective." *Green* described in different ways the utility of cross-examination that is delayed to the time of trial, and explained why it suffices. It works because the witness "must now affirm, deny, or qualify" his prior statement under penalty of perjury. If the statement was not under oath, this fact alone might be the "explanation for its inaccuracy." Cross about an inconsistent statement can be "full and effective" at trial because even the most successful *contemporaneous* cross, which focuses on what the witness says *now*, "could hardly hope to accomplish more" than is accomplished by the fact that the witness now tells "a different, inconsistent story." And cross at trial is sufficient because the witness must take a position on the truth of what he said before.

Suppose the witness said before that defendant "shot the teller," but at trial he says someone else shot the teller. The defense cross-examines, and in a way the questioning is friendly because the witness is giving a version of events more favorable to the defense than the version in his prior statement. The witness is associated with the prosecution because the prosecutor called him, and in that sense the prosecutor is responsible for his testimony. Under this somewhat friendly defense cross, the witness answers questions about what happened. He gives additional information about acts, events, and conditions described in the statement and in testimony, and answers questions about the statement itself. Prodded by the defense, he says again that he remembers what happened "like it was yesterday," and it was the *other fellow* who shot the teller, just as he said in his direct testimony. The witness is sure because he was standing next to the defendant, and the other fellow was about ten feet away, and the witness heard the shot and looked at the other fellow and saw him with gun in hand, and he knows the sound didn't come from the defendant's gun. The witness also talks about what he said before. He told police that *defendant* shot the teller partly because he was trying to shield the other fellow (he's afraid of him), and partly

3. United States v. Owens, 484 U.S. 554 (1988) (statement identifying defendant as assailant).

4. Crawford v. Washington, 541 U.S. 36 (2004).

because police and prosecutors were pressing him about the defendant's involvement.

This case is the paradigm, and it seems to be what the Court had in mind in *Green*. The witness denies what he said before and affirms a different version of events, and he answers questions about the statement and about events too. If the jury believes the testimony of the witness (someone else did it), then presumably defendant wins an acquittal, and "full and effective" are words that come readily to mind when appraising cross-examination that succeeds in persuading the jury to *reject* what the witness said before.

On the other hand, if the jury does *not* believe the testimony, and instead believes the prior statement and convicts for that reason, then "full and effective" are not the words that would spring to mind. Whatever happened during defense questioning, apparently it did not persuade the jury to accept what the witness is saying now, and it looks as though cross-examination *failed to* dissuade the jury from crediting the prior statement. Still it is clear that cross *can* be full and effective for constitutional purposes. The Court has said again and again that out-of-court statements can be used against criminal defendants where the speaker testifies and can be cross-examined, so it *must* be the case that cross can be full and effective even if defendants are convicted because juries are persuaded by the out-of-court statements. Post-*Crawford* authority has gotten the message, often commenting or holding that cross at trial satisfies confrontation concerns, sometimes with extended analysis but more often with a simple reference to the fact that the witness testified and was cross-examined.[5]

One problem in achieving "full and effective" cross-examination at trial is that witnesses are forgetful or uncooperative. Sometimes it may be both or, more realistically, it is hard to tell. Does the witness who says he can't remember really suffer failed memory, or is he hiding behind this claim as the best escape from worse choices—incriminating the defendant or defying the tribunal? In this setting, cross does not seem to live up to the idea of being "full and effective." Is the confrontation clause *still* satisfied? Actually the matter is more complicated: When he says he can't remember, the witness could mean he doesn't remember *the statement* or he doesn't remember *the acts, events, or conditions* described in it, or both. He could mean other things, like not remembering who he was talking to, or the circumstances. Does it matter? If he has *forgotten the statement* or details about the situation, but remembers the acts, events, or conditions, is that enough? If he has forgotten *the acts, events, or conditions*, but remembers the statement, is *that* enough? What if he has forgotten both?

Problem: Forgetful or uncooperative

5. United States v. Garcia, 447 F.3d 1327, 1335 (11th Cir. 2006) (*Crawford* did not bar use of statement by declarant who testified at trial); Nolan v. State, 132 P.3d 564, 570 (Nev. 2006) (using victim's statement to police did not violate *Crawford* where victim testified and could be cross-examined); Flonnory v. State, 893 A.3d 507, 520 (Del. 2006) (in murder trial, no confrontation violation where declarant, whose out-of-court statements reporting what defendant said were admitted, testified and were subject to cross).

Consider the witness who remembers the acts, events, or conditions but not his statement (or he refuses to testify about the latter). Here the cross-examiner can probe memory and perceptions, and test the witness on discrepancies between what he recalls and what his statement said. And the questioner can probe veracity and motives on the day of trial, and when the witness spoke before. Still, lack of memory about the statement (or refusal to testify about it) brings a problem, which is that it is hard to discredit or destroy a statement that the witness does not remember making (or refuses to explain), even if it is false or mistaken. It is hard really to test what was going on at the time: If the witness does not remember the statement, he is likely not to remember what might have induced him to make it, or whether he was trying to be truthful.

In the end, if the jury does not believe the testimony (thinking the witness is lying at trial in fear or because he has been bought off), then it might credit the prior statement. Is cross-examination, hampered this way, good enough? Cases on point acknowledge the problem. They accept statements admitted in this situation, but do not dismiss the problem out of hand, seemingly acknowledging its potential to be a severe impediment that might require exclusion.[6]

Now consider the witness who remembers the *statement*, but not the acts, events or conditions described in it. Here the cross-examiner can probe the statement, asking what the witness meant by it and why he spoke as he did, and what was going on. And here too the cross-examiner can examine veracity, and can explore his motives that were in play at the time of the statement and at trial. Still, lack of memory about acts, events, or conditions brings the problem that the cross-examiner will have a hard time getting the witness to admit to any inaccuracy—getting him to concede that what happened is not really what is captured in his statement—even if the statement is false or mistaken and should be disregarded. It is hard to test the statement against reality because the witness does not remember reality.

The decisions in *Green* and *Owens* address this situation.

In *Green*, a young boy named Melvin Porter claimed not to remember the marijuana transaction that generated the charges, and the Court remanded to allow the state court to resolve the "narrow question" whether cross is adequate if witness does not remember acts, events, or conditions reported in his statement. The California Supreme Court said it *could* be adequate: Porter admitted *saying* that Green had agreed to sell him marijuana, and *saying* that Green delivered the marijuana.

---

6. Pantano v. State, 138 P.3d 477 (Nev. 2006) (child was cross-examinable about assault despite not remembering who he talked to in prior statement admitted under child victim exception); State v. Gorman, 854 A.2d 1164 (Me. 2004) (in murder trial, admitting grand jury testimony by defendant's mother and rejecting claim that she was not adequately cross-examinable because of lack of memory, influence of drugs, history of delusions and inability to separate fact from fantasy; impairment does not make witness unavailable for purposes of confrontation; forgetfulness was selective; defense could ask what she did not recall and examine "the reasons for her failure of recollection").

On cross, the defense could then suggest "the usual explanations" for speaking falsely or being wrong, which gave an "opportunity" to test the statement, and the confrontation clause was satisfied.[7]

In *Owens*, the Court concluded that an unremembering witness can be adequately cross-examined. *Owens* involved a trial of an inmate for assaulting correctional counselor Foster, who was beaten with a metal pipe and suffered a skull fracture and memory impairment. Three weeks later an FBI Agent visited Foster in the hospital, and Foster described the attack, naming Owens as his assailant and picking out a picture of Owens from a photo array. At trial Foster again described the attack and recalled identifying Owens, but admitted that he couldn't remember "seeing his assailant" and couldn't remember other hospital visitors or whether they suggested Owens' name. The Court approved the Agent's testimony describing Foster's identification. It relied on its decision in the *Fensterer* case, which approved testimony by an expert who could not remember which of three bases underlay his conclusion.[8] *Owens* concluded that there is no more reason to exclude an out-of-court statement by an unremembering witness than to exclude testimony by one who does not remember all that underlies it.[9]

Decided cases acknowledge the problem, and again accept the use of prior statements, taking their cue from *Green, Fensterer*, and *Owens*. Yet they also recognize problems that could warrant exclusion of prior statements.[10]

Failed memory generally

It seems that a cross-examiner who is stymied in all efforts to test the witness in both these areas has been denied the requisite opportunity, although it sometimes happens that the witness can be tested by questions that probe his credibility generally, and by answers that shift between claims of forgetfulness and revelations that help show that

---

7. People v. Green, 479 P.2d 998, 1004 (Cal. 1971) (tried to a judge, without jury).

8. Delaware v. Fensterer, 474 U.S. 15, 21-22 (1985) (confrontation clause does not guarantee that witness will refrain from giving testimony "marred by forgetfulness, confusion, or evasion," guaranteeing only an "opportunity" for effective questioning, and *not* "cross-examination that is effective in whatever way, and to whatever extent, the defense might wish").

9. United States v. Owens, 484 U.S. 554, 559 (1988) (confrontation guarantees opportunity for effective cross, but not cross that is "effective in whatever way, and to whatever extent, the defense might wish") (opportunity is not denied if witness describes current belief but cannot recall reasons; it suffices that defendant can bring out matters like bias, lack of care and attentiveness, poor eyesight, bad memory).

10. State v. Pierre, 890 A.2d 474, 497 (Conn. 2006) (witness was subject to cross on written statement to police even though claiming he could not remember what he recounted, or reviewing it, and said he signed it "only to stop the police from harassing him," since defense used "plenty of ammunition" to attack credibility and elicited evidence that he signed "to avoid further questioning"); United States v. DiCaro, 772 F.2d 1314, 1325-1328 (7th Cir. 1985) (in trial for robbery, admitting B's grand jury testimony; B claimed amnesia; defendant had "meaningful opportunity" for cross because B did remember testifying to grand jury and was impeached by membership in witness protection program), *cert. denied*, 475 U.S. 1081.

the claimed lack of memory is not true.[11] Sometimes, however, the cases note this point and approve cross-examination anyway.[12] The only counterargument to a blockage of this dimension is that the evasiveness or defiance of the witness is *itself* an adequate indicator of credibility.

Problem: Denying the prior statement

Similar problems arise when the witness denies making a prior statement: The cross-examiner cannot discredit or destroy a statement that the witness denies making, even if the statement is false or mistaken and should be disregarded. And it is hard for the cross-examiner to test what was going on: If the witness denies making the statement, he is likely not to remember what might have induced him to make it, or whether he was trying to be truthful.

This issue surfaced in the *O'Neil* case in 1971. There O'Neil and Runnels were charged with kidnapping, robbery, and car theft. They advanced a common defense (both said they were at O'Neil's place and got the car from a friend). The arresting officer testified that Runnels admitted his involvement and implicated O'Neil, but Runnels testified and denied making the statement. The Court rejected O'Neil's claim of a violation of confrontation rights. O'Neil would have been in "worse straits" if Runnels had "affirmed the statement as his" because counsel would have had to argue that he confessed to a crime he didn't commit or made up the part about O'Neil, and this course would require giving up the joint alibi defense and coming up with a new explanation of O'Neil's presence in the car. If Runnels had admitted the statement but denied its truth (claiming it was "coerced, or made as part of a plea bargain"), cross would be futile because O'Neil could hardly "try to shake that testimony."[13]

Here too, cross-examination is generally found to be adequate, which is, after all, the basic message of *O'Neil*. Yet it is apparent that this stance by the witness blocks the kind of optimal testing that the concept of full and effective cross-examination envisions, and the issue continues to surface occasionally.[14]

11. United States v. Thompson, 708 F.2d 1294, 1302-1304 (8th Cir. 1983) (admitting testimony from prior trial; witness admitted making statement but did not say it was true, and could not recall critical facts; defense had chance to engage in full cross).

12. United States v. Insana, 423 F.2d 1165, 1167-1170 (2d Cir. 1970) (co-offender pled guilty, testified to grand jury, and testified on two points at trial, but then claimed lack of memory and resorted to "mumbling" and "vague and evasive answers," stating his desire not to hurt anyone; prosecutor properly recited grand jury testimony that witness "guessed" at one point he had given, and at other points claimed not to remember; no confrontation violation despite claimed lack of memory), *cert. denied*, 400 U.S. 841.

13. Nelson v. O'Neil, 402 U.S. 622, 627 (1971) (defendants had been arrested after midnight stop led to check revealing that car they were driving was reported stolen; O'Neil did not cross-examine Runnels).

14. *See* United States v. Clark, 989 F.2d 1490, 1497-1499 (7th Cir. 1993) (in bank robbery trial of C and G, admitting against G the statement of C to sister that "we did it," referring to himself and G; C testified and was available for full and effective cross; fact that he denied talking with sister did not matter; nor did it matter that counsel for G chose not to cross-examine C once he denied involvement in robbery).

Similar problems also arise if a court restricts or blocks cross-examination, or the witness claims a privilege with respect to questions about his statement or about the acts, events, or conditions reflected in the statement. The court might limit cross-examination about acts, events or conditions because the questioning seems repetitive or pointless, or to have gone too far afield, and might block cross on the prior statement for similar reasons.

**Problem:
Restrictive rulings**

The Supreme Court acknowledged in *Owens* that cross might be so restricted because the court honors a claim of privilege or simply limits the process so stringently, that the opportunity guaranteed by the confrontation clause is stifled, and exclusion of testimonial statements might be required.[15] Even if such restrictions on cross are correct, and privilege claims should sometimes be upheld, it is possible for such rulings to restrict cross-examination to the point that it simply cannot be full and effective, so prior testimonial statements cannot be admitted without violating confrontation rights.[16]

Cross-examination is sometimes frustrated when a witness is simply unable or unwilling to answer questions naturally suggested by the direct. Sometimes the witness is uncooperative (unwilling to take questions seriously). Other times he is actually *unable* to answer, because of immaturity or for psychological or mental reasons, often because the subject is unpleasant or disturbing and perhaps traumatic. Very young witnesses are sometimes unable to respond to questions about sexual abuse, and the cross-examiner is stuck with monosyllabic responses, nods or shrugs. Here the message carried forward from *Owens* is that courts are to be generous and understanding of the plight of the witness, and the result is that courts approve testimony that is tested only at the margins through answers that add little to the understanding that the trier of fact would achieve by listening to the direct.[17]

**Problem: Witness
uncooperative**

The Court has suggested three general principles that bear on these issues.

**General
principles**

First, in an oft-quoted passage in the *Fensterer* case the Court set the stage for rejecting defense claims that cross-examination could not be

---

15. United States v. Owens, 484 U.S. 554, 561-562 (1988) (privilege claims or limits on scope of cross may "undermine" process contemplated by FRE 801, where speaker is cross-examinable about statement).

16. United States v. Torrez-Ortega, 184 F.3d 1128, 1132-1134 (10th Cir. 1999) (in drug trial, use of V's grand jury testimony violated confrontation rights because V was not adequately subject to cross at trial; V took stand and oath, but "did not respond willingly to questions" because of "obstinate and repeated" claim of privilege against self-incrimination, despite receiving immunity and being told that privilege claims were invalid; V "could hardly have been less forthcoming," since he "refused to acknowledge" that grand jury testimony was his and made clear his refusal to answer questions; his only answers were "too elliptical and confusing" to show adequate cross).

17. United States v. Kappell, 418 F.3d 550, 554 (6th Cir. 2005) (admitting statements by children aged three and six describing sexual abuse, given to psychotherapist and pediatricians, under medical statements exception; children testified, and defense agreed to allow them to testify from remote location by closed-circuit television; sometimes they "unresponsive or inarticulate" on cross).

full and effective. The cross-examiner is not entitled, the Court said in *Fensterer*, to cross-examination "that is effective in whatever way, and to whatever extent, the defense might wish."[18] The context was a challenge to expert testimony by a witness who could not recall the basis for his conclusion. Of course there is a difference between what happened there and the typical case of using testimonial hearsay: In cases like *Fensterer*, the expert can still shed light on the matter to which he testifies, but an unremembering or uncooperative hearsay declarant, or one who denies making the statement, can effectively stonewall so that cross-examination is stifled. But the settings have much in common, because expert testimony often rests on hearsay, and the rules governing expert testimony rely heavily on the proposition that cross-examination can expose flaws in the underlying basis that enables a jury adequately to appraise it.

This principle is in effect a shot over the bows of most defense arguments that cross-examination was so stifled that it could not live up to the ideal of being full and effective. It is also an expression of the notion that in fact hearsay statements may be used to convict defendants under some circumstances, one of which being that the witness testifies and can be cross-examined.

Second, the question is not whether contemporaneous cross-examination would be better than deferred cross-examination, but whether delayed cross is adequate.[19] We could reframe the point by saying that the question is *not* whether we should allow convictions to rest *only* on live trial testimony, but whether we can *tolerate* convictions that rest (at least in part) on out-of-court statements.

Third, questions about adequate cross-examination are usually framed in terms of the adequacy of the *opportunity* to cross-examine, and these in turn lead to issues of waiver, a point discussed in the next section.

§8.89 Waiving Confrontation Rights

Defendants can waive the right to exclude testimonial statements by engaging in various trial tactics, and sometimes by failing to pursue opportunities available at trial. To be distinguished from these forms of waiver are cases in which the accused engages in misconduct that

---

18. Delaware v. Fensterer, 474 U.S. 15, 21-22 (1985) (confrontation clause does not guarantee that witness will refrain from giving testimony "marred by forgetfulness, confusion, or evasion"; confrontation guarantees only "opportunity for effective cross-examination, not cross-examination that is effective in whatever way, and to whatever extent, the defense might wish") (letting expert testify, despite fact that he could not remember which of three grounds was basis of conclusion that hairs had been forcibly removed).

19. California v. Green, 399 U.S. 149, 160-161 (1970) (jury might be "in a better position" if it could watch "gruelling cross-examination" as witness speaks, but question is whether deferred cross provides "satisfactory basis for evaluating the truth of the prior statement").

makes a witness unavailable, where we speak instead of "forfeiture" of confrontation. We take up this subject separately in the next section.

Classic forms of waiver include the tactic of bringing out the very evidence that could be excluded, which can happen when a party pursues a matter on cross-examination or testifies on direct to the matter.[1] In other obvious waiver situations, the defense cross-examines the speaker but fails to pursue or raise some point, in which case defendant cannot complain about lack of opportunity.[2] And if a testifying witness fails or refuses to answer questions but defendant does not seek a court order requiring a response, the confrontation claim is waived.[3]

Some courts go much further in finding waiver. Suppose a witness is available, in the sense of being under subpoena and present and ready to testify, or known to be in the area and servable. If the prosecutor offers her testimonial statement *without calling her to testify*, can it be said the defense could summon the witness and cross-examine, hence that not doing so waives confrontation rights? Does *this* circumstance provide adequate opportunity to cross-examine?

Some courts go much further

Some court have answered these questions in the affirmative. In effect, these cases hold that a defendant who fails to subpoena or call an available witness has waived confrontation claims.[4] Perhaps the reason behind these decisions is not that the prosecutor is excused from calling the witness, but that the defense did not actually want to cross-examine, and the real aim in claiming a violation of confrontation right is *not* to get the witness on the stand to explain or answer questions, but to exclude his statement.

This situation, however, is a far cry from the opportunity to cross-examine that *Roberts* and *Green* described.[5] In the usual case where the burden of proof rests on the prosecutor, it is the prosecutor's burden *actually to produce* the witness, or to show that she cannot be produced. And in the usual case, producing means "calling the witness to the stand." To excuse the prosecutor from actually taking this step is to shift to the defense the burden of producing the witness, which seems wrong if the issue to which the statement relates is an issue on which the prosecutor bears the burden, and arguably wrong regardless who bears

§8.89 1. State v. Harris, 871 A.2d 341, 344 (R.I. 2005) (defense waived *Crawford* objections to use of child's statement to police by cross-examining police on it and using it to impeach police testimony).

2. United States v. Meza-Urtado, 351 F.3d 301, 303-304 (7th Cir. 2003) (admitting co-offender's plea colloquy; statements were inconsistent with testimony and he "could have been cross-examined at length").

3. Fowler v. State, 829 N.E.2d 459, 467 (Ind. 2005) (in trial for domestic battery where wife claimed privilege, defense forfeited confrontation rights by not pressing for ruling requiring her to testify).

4. McKnight v. State, 656 S.E.2d 830, 831 (Ga. 2008) (prosecutor read W's inconsistent statement; W "was not unavailable," but "had already testified and remained subject to recall") (no *Crawford* violation); People v. Cookson, 830 N.E.2d 194 (Ill. 2005) (admitting statements by child victim describing sexual assault; statutory requirement that "child be available to testify at the proceeding" satisfies *Crawford*).

5. *See* Ohio v. Roberts, 448 U.S. 56, 70-72 (1980); California v. Green, 399 U.S. 149, 159-160 (1970) (discussed in §§8.87-8.88, *supra*).

the burden on any particular issue if the prosecutor offers a statement by the witness.

There are many obvious reasons why a *defense opportunity* to call a witness is an inadequate substitute for burdening the prosecutor with *actually calling* her. For one thing, if the defense calls a witness whose statement was offered, cross-examination is separated from presentation of the statement, in contrast with what would occur if the statement were offered while the speaker is on the stand and can be cross-examined moments later. More importantly, an opportunity to call the speaker is distinctly inferior from defendant's viewpoint because the defense almost cannot afford to call such a person and be seen as sponsoring testimony that may be adverse. It isn't an "opportunity" in the usual sense, but an unwelcome burden.[6] Better decisions reject this idea and hold that failing to call a witness does *not* waive confrontation rights.[7]

These issues often arise in child abuse cases, where it sometimes does appear that defendants do not *want* the child to testify, hoping instead *both* that she won't testify and that her statement will be excluded (because there is no chance to cross-examine), giving the defense the best of both worlds.[8] Even here, however, it seems profoundly wrong to make the defense call the witness. The right way to recognize and provide confrontation rights to which defendants are entitled is to require the prosecutor to call the witness, examine her on the issues to which her statement relates, and then allow the defendant to question her.[9]

6. California v. Green, 399 U.S. 149, 159 (1970) (envisioning speaker "present and testifying at trial," and commenting that prior statement "regains most of the lost protections" because he "must now affirm, deny, or qualify the truth of the prior statement under the penalty of perjury").

7. Blanton v. State, 987 So.2d 149 (Fla. 2008) (in trial for capital sexual battery against child, neither availability of discovery deposition nor fact that defense took victim's deposition constituted adequate opportunity for cross; admitting child's statements to police was error) (harmless); State v. Blue, 717 N.W.2d 558 (N.D. 2006) (opportunity to cross-examine required by confrontation clause is not assured by "mere presence" at preliminary hearing; videotaped child victim hearsay is not admissible, but might be if child testifies). See also Myer v. State, 943 A.2d 615 (Md. 2008) (error to admit videotaped interview involving child and social worker after child testified; fact that defense could cross-examine prior to introduction of videotape did not satisfy right of cross secured by confrontation clause) (reversing).

8. In Matter of Pamela A.G., 134 P.3d 746 (N.M. 2006) (in neglect proceedings involving abuse of 4-year-old adoptive child, admitting her statements describing abuse and identifying abuser, and rejecting *Crawford* claim; neither parent called child or asked permission to question her, and instead "simply sought to exclude" her statements; parents "did not indicate below nor have they indicated on appeal" what questions they might put, making it hard to assess value of cross-examining this four-year-old).

9. State v. Snowden, 867 A.2d 314, 331-332 (Md. 2005) (error to admit child's interview with investigator; state bears "threshold burden to produce a prima facie case," and confrontation clause is not satisfied by giving defendant an "opportunity" to call declarant; state bears burden "to produce affirmatively the witnesses needed for its prima facie showing"); Lowery v. Collins, 996 F.2d 770, 771 (5th Cir. 1993) (forcing

Similar issues arise in connection with forensic laboratory reports, where defendants raise confrontation claims in the hope that the result will be that the report stays out *and* that the technician won't testify. Here we think the right solution is that prosecutors should be burdened, on appropriate objection, with calling the preparer, and with presenting the substance of such reports by means of testimony to the extent possible, and to admit the reports as well.[10]

§8.90 The *Giles* Case: Forfeiture of Confrontation Rights

After putting its stamp of approval on the forfeiture doctrine, once in *Crawford* in 2004 and then in *Davis* in 2006, the Supreme Court actually had to come to terms with a critical aspect of the doctrine in the *Giles* case in 2008.[1] *Giles* holds that the accused does not lose confrontation rights simply by committing a wrongful act that makes a witness unavailable—in *Giles*, defendant murdered his ex-girlfriend—and that forfeiture occurs only as a result of wrongful conduct that is "designed" or "intended" to prevent a witness from testifying. In reaching this conclusion, the Court followed the same historical approach it had taken in *Crawford*, and it rejected a broad notion of forfeiture that would have paved the way to admit against a killer any relevant statement by the victim, regardless what motive lay behind the crime.

Crawford had characterized forfeiture as an "equitable" doctrine, and *Davis* used the same term. The California court in *Giles* apparently thought the term meant righting an imbalance, and concluded that a wrongful act depriving a court of evidence should be redressed by admitting the best substitute, meaning statements by the dead witness that are presumably similar to what she would say if she could testify. Perhaps adding to the force of this view, the term is "forfeiture" rather than "waiver," so arguably intent doesn't matter: One waives a right only by purposefully letting it go, but one can lose (forfeit) a right by misconduct. Of course proper behavior cannot be a basis on which a right can forfeited, so the predicate act must be some form of misbehavior, and at this level intent enters the picture again: The California court in *Giles* said a defendant only forfeits his confrontation rights by an "intentional criminal act."

Equitable doctrine

In the view of the California court, the important point was that "intent" does not require a purpose to prevent a witness from testifying or to thwart the judicial process. Particularly if forfeiting confrontation rights *also* entails forfeiting hearsay rights, a point taken up below, this

California view: Intent not required

---

defendant to call child victim unfairly requires him "to choose between his right to cross-examine a complaining witness and his right to rely on the State's burden of proof").

10. *See* the discussion of FRE 803(8) in §8.51, *supra*.

§8.90 1. Crawford v. Washington, 541 U.S. 36, 54 (2004) ("rule of forfeiture by wrongdoing (which we accept) extinguishes confrontation claims on essentially equitable grounds"); Davis v. Washington, 547 U.S. 813, 833 (2006) (FRE 804(b)(6) "codifies the forfeiture doctrine"); Giles v. California, 128 S. Ct. 2678 (2008). this view would result in admitting in homicide cases anything the victim said that is relevant. The notion that doing "equity" means righting an imbalance seems simplistic: Equitable doctrines often turn on the mental state of actors and notions of fairness.[2] As the Colorado Supreme Court commented in a case handed down more than a year before *Giles*, allowing forfeiture without intent would "divorce the forfeiture by wrongdoing doctrine from its very reason for existing," which is to discourage litigants from thwarting the work of courts.[3] Although the Court in *Giles* rejected the California view on the basis of history more than policy, Justices Scalia and Souter both addressed policy, in opinions representing six members of the Court. Both said that taking away trial rights because a judge thinks defendant is guilty of the charged crime undermines the right to a jury trial and seems unfair.[4]

Giles: Historical analysis

In *Giles*, Justice Scalia wrote the opinion of the Court: Although his opinion presents the views of only four members, Justice Souter's concurrence (speaking for himself and one other) agreed with that opinion, except for a small part replying to three dissenters. Scalia approached the forfeiture issue as a kind of historical puzzle. Given that there is ancient precedent, what are the parameters of the forfeiture doctrine today?

Giles begins with the Court's 1879 opinion in *Reynolds* (hitherto remembered mainly for rejecting a religiously based claim of entitlement to enter into bigamous marriage).[5] The matter of forfeiture arose in *Reynolds* because the court admitted testimony given by defendant's second wife in an earlier trial, and defendant challenged the ruling admitting that testimony. The prosecutor had sent a marshal to defendant's house to serve the subpoena, and the defendant himself answered the door. He told the marshal that she was not home and declined to offer any help—"that will be for you to find out," he said when asked where she was, adding that she "does not appear in this case." When the marshal returned with another subpoena, he encountered the first wife, who said the other "was not there, and had not been for three weeks."

2. *See* Precision Instrument Mfg. Co. v. Automotive Maintenance Machinery Co., 324 U.S. 806 (1945) (dismissing patent suit on "equitable maxim" known as clean hands doctrine; plaintiff knew of fraud in patent application, covered up perjury and acted "affirmatively to magnify and increase" its effects).

3. People v. Moreno, 160 P.3d 242, 246 (Colo. 2007) (reversing child abuse conviction for error in admitting victim's statements on forfeiture principle without finding intent). See also People v. Stechly, 870 N.E.2d 333, 350 (Ill. 2007) (assault attempts to undermine judicial process only when "motivated at least in part by an intent to interfere with or impede the process of a trial").

4. Justice Scalia, for four Justices, commented that stripping away trial rights "on the basis of a prior *judicial* assessment" that the defendant is guilty "does not sit well with the right to trial by jury" and is akin to "'dispensing with jury trial because a defendant is obviously guilty'" (quoting *Crawford*). Justice Souter, for himself and Ginsberg, commented that "[e]quity demands something more" than the "near circularity" of admitting against a defendant in a homicide case the statements of his victim because the judge thinks he is guilty. Giles v. California, 128 S. Ct. 2678 (2008).

5. Reynolds v. United States, 98 U.S. 145 (1878).

Giles said that *Reynolds* was addressing the case where defendant's wrongful conduct was "designed to prevent a witness's testimony," but *Giles* went even further back, invoking language from old English precedents—*Lord Morley's* case in 1666, which described witnesses "detained" or "kept away" by "means or procurement," *Harrison's Case* in 1692, which spoke of "procurement" and "one who voluntarily keeps the witnesses away," and *Queen v. Scaife* in 1851, which spoke of a witness "kept away." These phrases, said the majority in *Giles*, make it clear that forfeiture applies "only when the defendant engaged in conduct *designed* to prevent the witness from testifying." That this construction is correct can be seen by examining later practice: If wrongdoing alone forfeited confrontation rights, "one would have expected it to be routinely invoked in murder prosecutions," but it "was never invoked in this way," and the 1997 adoption of FRE 804(b)(6), "which codifies the forfeiture doctrine" according to *Davis*, expressly includes an intent requirement, which means that defendant must have the "particular purpose of making the witness unavailable."

The Court in *Giles* split six to three in favor of the proposition that the constitutional forfeiture principle requires intent on the part of the accused. Among the six who favor an intent standard, however, the four represented by Justice Scalia and the two represented by Justice Souter have different "takes" on what intent means. Also the dissent by Justice Breyer (for three Justices) ventures yet another view. Clearly intent can be defined differently, and it may be useful to consider the extremes: In a weak formulation, intent can mean something close to "knowledge" or even "notice." In a robust formulation, intent comes closer to "purpose" or "design," which are the terms that Justice Scalia uses. In cases like *Giles*, where a defendant kills a girlfriend after previous altercations, the definition of the intent matters a lot. In such a case, an intent standard in a weak formulation could easily be satisfied, and it might not matter that defendant (a) didn't know anything about the possibility of being charged with a crime, (b) didn't know she was in contact with police, or (c) acted for reasons unrelated to past criminality or previous altercations—out of jealousy, for example, or in anger. In such a case, an intent standard in a robust formulation might *not* be satisfied, and it might be critical to establish that defendant (a) thought he was about to be charged with crimes and (b) knew she was talking to police, and (c) acted for these reasons rather than for reasons unrelated to past criminality or previous altercations, such as jealousy or anger.

Which intent standard does *Giles* adopt? As noted, accounts in the three critical opinions vary, and in two troublesome areas—abusive relationships and child abuse—courts have their work cut out for them. We return to them in a moment, but we can be confident that a majority in *Giles* supports a robust definition of the necessary intent.

In his opinion to which six Justices adhere (by signing or concurrence), Justice Scalia adopts a "purpose-based definition." Scalia speaks of acts "done for the purpose of preventing testimony," and of "conduct *designed* to prevent a witness from testifying." Justice Souter

[margin note:] Intent standard: Weak and robust formulations

[margin note:] Giles Adopts robust formulation of intent

stresses "intent to prevent testimony," and speaks as well of "intent to thwart the judicial process." Thus intent for purposes of forfeiture means that defendant has in mind, and is aiming or trying to bring about, the result that the person will not testify in a trial that is already pending (charges have been brought) or expected soon (an investigation is under way; questions are being asked).[6] This *constitutional* standard is apparently the same as the standard found in the hearsay forfeiture exception: Indeed, *Giles* takes note of this standard and quotes a treatise description as shedding light on the constitutional standard.[7] It makes good sense for the standards to match, as it is hard to think of a principled reason for different standards to apply to these different questions: If purposeful misconduct is the basis for forfeiting both a confrontation right and a right to exclude hearsay, the assessment of such conduct should proceed on the same basis in resolving both matters. It is quite another thing whether a forfeiture exception to the hearsay doctrine is a good idea.[8]

Giles firmly *rejected* the proposition that "knowledge is sufficient to show intent," and stressed the purpose of forfeiture as being "aimed at removing the otherwise powerful incentive" to engage in witness tampering because it threatens the "integrity" of judicial proceedings. Only Justice Breyer, speaking in dissent for three members, favored a weak formulation of intent: On the facts of *Giles*, the Breyer opinion stated that defendant "knew that murdering his ex-girlfriend would keep her from testifying," which was "sufficient to show the *intent* that the law ordinarily demands." This view did not prevail, and does not state the law.

Knowledge is not enough

Under *Giles*, a defendant on trial for dealing drugs does not forfeit confrontation rights if he kills a potential witness who was in business with him, in a dispute over authority or territory or in reprisal for some behavior. Even if defendant "knows" that death will prevent the person from testifying, and even if drug charges are pending or contemplated, his act of homicide is not enough *by itself* to bring the forfeiture doctrine into play. The *Giles* rule would require a different outcome if some modern cases were tried today.[9]

In the setting of domestic abuse trials culminating in killing (as in *Giles* itself), or in battery leading to charges, how does a robust intent standard work out? Speaking for four members of the Court, Justice Scalia wrote that domestic violence involves acts that are often "intended to dissuade a victim from resorting to outside help, and

6. Vasquez v. People, 173 P.3d 1099, 1106 (Colo. 2007) (forfeiture requires "intent to deprive the criminal justice system of evidence").

7. Giles v. California, 128 S. Ct. 2678 (2008) (every commentator has concluded that "intent 'means that the exception applies only if the defendant has in mind the particular purpose of making the witness unavailable'") (quoting Mueller & Kirkpatrick, Federal Evidence §8:134 (3d ed. 2007)).

8. *See* the discussion of FRE 804(b)(6) in §8.78, *supra*.

9. State v. Mason, 162 P.3d 396 (Wash. 2007) (admitting statement by murder victim to police; killing forfeited confrontation rights, regardless of intent); State v. Meeks, 88 P.2d 789, 794 (Kan. 2004) (similar).

include conduct designed to prevent testimony to police officers or cooperation" in criminal trials. If abuse "culminates in murder," the Scalia opinion says this fact might support a finding of intent and application of forfeiture doctrine. The Souter concurrence adds that the intent standard "would normally be satisfied" where the abuser engages in conduct "meant to isolate the victim from outside help," including law enforcement, and in such a case it would not matter if defendant acted in a "fit of anger" because it would not show that he "miraculously abandoned the dynamics of abuse" a moment before.

The message of *Giles* is that these cases are not exempt from the requirement to prove intent. Justice Souter's position comes close to recognizing a "presumption" of intent, and Justice Breyer's dissenting opinion for three members uses that term. Justice Scalia stops short of that, however, and we can be sure that there is no per se rule that this situation satisfies the requirement. In short, a defendant who engages in conduct that generates complaints to police or friends, and who later kills the complaining witness, *may* entertain the requisite intent in committing the latter act, even though the testimony that the killing is intended to prevent would have been given in battery trials rather than the homicide trial. Whether intent exists may have to be resolved with the aid of experts, and probably by resort to other statements that the victim has made to friends about her situation. Defendants cannot be forced to testify on such points, although it may be that if they *do* testify in preliminary hearings, what they say cannot be offered against them in a trial on the merits of the homicide charges.[10]

Domestic abuse

In domestic abuse cases that do not lead to homicide, where victims survive but decline to testify, the question of intent remains equally at large. The question of cause also looms large. Here too, expert testimony may be necessary, and resort may be had to other statements by the victim, as victims who are afraid to testify on the pending charges are also likely to be afraid to testify that defendant's conduct made them fearful.[11]

Forfeiture and hearsay

Clearly *Giles* is a constitutional decision that addresses the question when and under what circumstances a defendant forfeits confrontation rights. In the federal system, *Giles* plainly assumed that forfeiting confrontation rights also forfeits rights under the hearsay doctrine,[12] but the Court has not actually faced this question, inasmuch as the three modern decisions that mention forfeiture (*Crawford, Davis,* and *Giles*) involved appeals from state convictions. Still, modern federal decisions affirm that forfeiting confrontation rights also forfeits hearsay objections, and it appears that FRE 804(b)(6) really does "codify" the

---

10. *See* discussion of this subject in 1 Mueller and Kirkpatrick, Federal Evidence §1:33 (3d ed. 2007).

11. State v. Wright, 726 N.W.2d 464, 482 (Minn. 2007); State v. Mechling, 633 S.E.2d 311, 324-325 (W.Va. 2006) (both reversing domestic battery convictions for failure to prove causation).

12. *See* Giles v. California, 128 S. Ct. 2678 (2008) (no case or treatise suggests that a defendant who committed wrongdoing "forfeited his confrontation rights but not his hearsay rights," and any such distinction would be "surprising").

constitutional forfeiture doctrine, meaning that the test or standard for forfeiting confrontation rights is also the test or standard for waiving hearsay objections.[13]

In the state systems, the matter is more complicated. The question whether a defendant forfeits his rights under the confrontation clause by engaging in wrongful behavior purposefully directed at thwarting the judicial process is a federal question, and the Supreme Court's decisions bind the states. But the question whether losing the protection of the confrontation clause entails losing the protection accorded by state hearsay doctrines is one that state courts can resolve by applying their own hearsay law, and sometimes these questions implicate state constitutional counterparts to the confrontation clause, which also raise state law issues. Elsewhere we consider the question whether, as a matter of sound policy, it is preferable to have a forfeiture doctrine that applies both to confrontation rights and to hearsay rights, or whether it is preferable to insist that even a defendant who forfeits his rights under the confrontation clause retains his rights to insist that hearsay be excluded unless it fits an exception.[14]

Suffice it to say here that the issue is very much alive: Only about a dozen states have hearsay exceptions based on the forfeiture principle. Many others have no such provision, and some that do have such provisions have hedged them around with restrictive language. California's, for example, contains a trustworthiness clause, and it is perhaps telling that the trial court in *Giles* did not rely on this provision. In these states it matters considerably whether forfeiting confrontation rights entails forfeiture of hearsay rights.[15] Surely it would make little sense, in states like California that have forfeiture exceptions with trustworthiness clauses, to conclude that forfeiting confrontation rights also forfeits hearsay rights: The result would be to sidestep what was apparently intended to be a limitation, adopted in the positive law of the state, against admitting unreliable hearsay. Despite the comment in *Giles,* and despite the fact that many state decisions indicate that indeed forfeiture of confrontation rights also forfeits any hearsay objection,[16] at least one state does follow the opposite practice, in which loss of confrontation rights does *not* result in forfeiture of the right to exclude hearsay (absent an applicable exception).[17]

13. People v. Stechly, 870 N.E.2d 333, 351 (Ill. 2007) (hearsay exception and constitutional forfeiture doctrine are "coextensive"); United States v. Emery, 186 F.3d 921, 921 (8th Cir. 1999) (forfeiting confrontation rights means hearsay rights are similarly forfeited under FRE 804(b)(6)).

14. *See* the discussion in §8.78, *supra.*

15. States having such exceptions are cited in §8.78, *supra* (also quoting California provision).

16. *See, e.g.,* Pruitt v. State, 191 P.3d 963 (Wyo. 2008); Commonwealth v. Edwards, 830 N.E.2d 158, 170 (Mass. 2005); State v. Meeks, 88 P.2d 789, 794 (Kan. 2004); State v. Hallum, 606 N.W.2d 351, 356 (Iowa 2000); People v. Cotto, 699 N.E.2d 394, 398 (N.Y. 1998); State v. Valencia, 924 P.2d 497, 498 (Ariz. App. 1996).

17. Vasquez v. People, 173 P.3d 1099, 1106 (Colo. 2007) ("the more prudent course is to require that the hearsay rules be satisfied separately").

§8.91 New Hearsay and Protected Witness Testimony

In the closing decades of the last century and the early years of the present one, states across the country adopted new hearsay exceptions, and both state and federal courts found new uses for the against-interest exception and the catchall. In addition, states adopted special provisions allowing children to testify in abuse cases from remote locations, to be spared from some of the frightening aspects of testifying in open court.

Among the important new exceptions are those dealing with child victim hearsay, and typical provisions pave the way to admit out-of-court statements by children describing abuse. Generally these provisions cover both casual accounts, often given to relatives or police or social workers, as well as formalized testimony in pretrial depositions. Some jurisdictions created additional new exceptions which, like those for child victim hearsay, were aimed mostly at specific situations: California, for example, adopted an exception for statements by victims describing physical injuries, which is particularly useful in domestic abuse cases. The against-interest exception, once limited largely to civil cases, found new use as prosecutors offered third-party statements implicating both themselves and the accused. The catchall exception found a new use in cases admitting against defendants grand jury testimony by unavailable witnesses.

New exceptions

Under the old *Roberts* regime, these developments posed unique constitutional challenges: Essentially *Roberts* had paved the way to use against the accused hearsay that fit standard (or "firmly rooted") exceptions. Under *Roberts*, however, hearsay offered against defendants under new exceptions, and hearsay offered under the against-interest or catchall (which was viewed as new), could be admitted only on "particularized indications of trustworthiness," and the Court in *Wright* held that corroborative evidence could not be considered in making the particularized assessment.[1] On the day *Crawford* was decided in 2004, everything changed. There was some thought that the *Roberts* standard still applied to "nontestimonial statements," but the *Bockting* case made it clear that the confrontation clause has nothing to say about non-testimonial hearsay.

In the *Crawford* regime, then, hearsay offered against criminal defendants under new exceptions (and hearsay offered under older exceptions put to new use) is no longer subject to a particularized reliability criterion. But such hearsay is excludable when offered against the accused if it is testimonial, unless the declarant testifies at some point and is subject to cross-examination, or the emergency or forfeiture doctrines apply. Much hearsay offered under child victim hearsay provisions *is* testimonial, such as statements by children describing abuse to police or social workers, as are many statements that were formerly admitted against defendants under the against-interest exception

---

§8.91   1. Idaho v. Wright, 497 U.S. 805 (1990).

(statements by co-offenders implicating themselves and the defendant), and *Crawford* cut back on or eliminated these and other modern innovations.

Impact of *Crawford*

Much hearsay offered under these new exceptions, however, is *not* testimonial—or at least *apparently* not, as some uncertainty remains in marginal areas. Thus, for example, against-interest statements offered against defendants are probably not testimonial if made in private settings, and many statements by children describing abuse are not testimonial, again if made in private settings—or at least that is the strong signal emerging from post-*Crawford* authorities.

Provisions for child victim testimony

In the closing decades of the twentieth century, all states passed statutes authorizing depositions of child victims and allowing their use at trial if the child is psychologically unavailable. Many states also enacted provisions authorizing child victims to give the equivalent of live testimony from outside the courtroom, with voice and image transmitted to court by one-way equipment (people in court can see and hear the child on a monitor) or two-way equipment (the child can also see and hear courtroom people on a monitor). Support personnel are used in these situations as well, to encourage and support children as they convey their stories.

Early efforts: One-way screen and *Coy*

In its 1988 decision in the *Coy* case, the Court had its first encounter with constitutional issues in the setting of special measures to help child victims testify. *Coy* was a sexual assault trial that utilized a screen between the witness stand and the defense table, so the complaining witnesses (two 13-year-old girls) could not see the defendant while testifying, although he could see them. The Court disapproved. It concluded that the confrontation clause guarantees "a face-to-face meeting with witnesses" and thus has an important personal dimension, which creates an appearance of justice because "something deep in human nature" regards face-to-face confrontation as essential (quoting the Bible, Shakespeare, and President Eisenhower's account of life in Abilene). This dimension serves fairness because a witness may feel different when she repeats her story looking at the person she will harm if she distorts or mistakes facts, and it is harder to lie about someone "to his face" than "behind his back." The witness need not look at the defendant, but the trier will "draw its own conclusions" if she "studiously look[s] elsewhere." Some confrontation rights (cross-examination, excluding hearsay) are not absolute, but confrontation has an "irreducible literal meaning" that guarantees a face-to-face encounter. Exceptions must rest on "individualized findings" (not statutory categories). Concurring in *Coy*, Justices O'Connor and White said that modern measures using closed circuit video testimony in child abuse cases remain proper.[2]

---

2. Coy v. Iowa, 487 U.S. 1012 (1988) (girls were assaulted as they camped in tent in backyard next door to defendant's house; assailant wore stocking over head and shined flashlight in their eyes so they could not describe his face; they did not try to identify him; Iowa statute authorized screen, and provided for testimony by closed-circuit television, with parties in same room).

After *Coy*, several courts approved videotaped testimony by child-abuse victims, but a Maryland court thought *Coy* required a face-to-face courtroom encounter between the victim and the defendant before a judge could decide to use one-way closed-circuit television transmitting to the courtroom the sound and image of a child-abuse victim testifying in another room (defendant being in voice contact with his lawyer). The Supreme Court disagreed, deciding in the *Craig* case in 1990 that the state interest in the "physical and psychological well-being" of victims is important enough to outweigh the defense right to face accusers in court. A trial court must make a "case-specific" finding that this procedure is "necessary to protect the welfare of the particular child" and that emotional distress is "more than mere nervousness or excitement or some reluctance to testify." *Craig* avoided specificity on points of detail, but it did say that a finding of "serious emotional distress" keeping the child from reasonably communicating clearly satisfies the constitutional standard. The Court declined, however, to say what "minimum showing of emotional trauma" was required. It rejected the argument that a court had to "observe" the child in the defendant's presence, declined to set "categorical evidentiary prerequisites," and approved findings based on expert testimony.[3]

In net effect, *Coy* set the basic rule, but *Craig* established a critical qualification or exception. These decisions put on trial judges the hard job of distinguishing between the salutary and the unwanted effects of courtroom pressure and psychological trauma—between their value in encouraging honesty and discouraging falsehoods and their drawbacks in causing (further) harm to the victim.[4] Although *Craig* dealt with live remote testimony, not with pretrial depositions, the opinion implies that child victims may testify by pretrial deposition if a court makes a case-specific finding of necessity. There are differences between these techniques, but they do not seem serious enough to warrant a difference in constitutional outcome.[5]

It was only a matter of time before the question arose whether to permit remote videotaped testimony in other exigent situations. A 1999 decision by the Second Circuit in the *Gigante* case answered yes to this question, but seven years later the Sixth Circuit said no in the *Yates* case.

Second encounter: Craig allows remote testimony

Other exigent situations

3. Maryland v. Craig, 497 U.S. 836 (1990) (court need not explore "less restrictive alternatives" and it suffices to employ one-way closed circuit television in which prosecutor and defense counsel could examine child witness in remote room while court and trier of fact watched and listened by video monitor).

4. State v. Boyd, 127 P.3d 998 (Kan. 2006) (error to allow child victim testimony by closed circuit television; court failed to make finding of trauma from testifying in presence of defendant) (harmless).

5. State v. Arroyo, 935 A.2d 975, 986-987 (Conn. 2007) (in child sexual abuse trial, rejecting *Crawford* challenge to videotaped testimony taken before trial, in proceeding in which prosecutor, defense counsel, and judge were present, and defendant could observe by one-way monitor, while in contact with counsel; opportunity to cross-examine satisfied confrontation clause).

Gigante involved a racketeering and murder trial arising out of government moves against "the criminal activity of La Cosa Nostra, also known as the Mafia," where the court admitted remote closed-circuit television testimony (with two-way link) by one Peter Savino, who was at the time "in the final stages of an inoperable, fatal cancer" under medical supervision at an "undisclosed location." District Judge Weinstein concluded that the witness could not appear in court, that the situation satisfied the standards set by FRCrimP 15 for a deposition, but that a deposition was not appropriate and that contemporaneous live televised testimony would better protect confrontation rights. The reviewing court agreed, but stressed that this device "should not be considered a commonplace substitute" for live courtroom testimony because of "intangible elements of the ordeal of testifying in a courtroom that are reduced or even eliminated by remote testimony."[6] *Yates* was a prosecution for crimes arising out of the operation of an internet pharmacy in Alabama, but principal witnesses who were participants in the scheme were located in Australia, and the government told the court that they were unwilling to travel to America. Stressing the possibility of taking their depositions in Australia, where defendants would be entitled to be present, the court in *Yates* said that "confrontation through a video monitor is not the same as physical face-to-face confrontation," and the two are not "constitutionally equivalent."[7]

§8.92 Confrontation Clause and Defense Rights to Introduce Hearsay

In three important cases, the Supreme Court held that excluding hearsay proffered by the defense violates the Constitution, thus establishing an entitlement of uncertain dimension to introduce hearsay that tends to exonerate the accused.[1] But the *Chambers* doctrine, as it is usually called, is narrow and has had little impact, despite its reinforcement in the *Green* case, and most recently in the *Holmes* case in 2006.

Like the situation that provoked the famous dissent arguing that defendants in homicide cases should be able to offer third-party confessions, all three of these cases involved murder trials, and in each case the trial court had excluded a confession by someone who said that he

---

6. United States v. Gigante, 166 F.3d 75, 83 (2d Cir. 1999) (witness satisfied unavailability standard of FRE 804(a)(4), and deposition could have been taken for use at trial; live remote testimony provided a mechanism that better protected confrontation rights).

7. United States v. Yates, 438 F.3d 1307 (11th Cir. 2007) (reversing). See generally C. Olson, Comment, *Accusations from Abroad: Testimony of Unavailable Witnesses Via Live Two-Way Teleconferencing Does Not Violate the Confrontation Clause of the Sixth Amendment*, 41 U.C. Davis L. Rev. 1671 (2008).

§8.92   1. See E.J. Imwinkelried, Exculpatory Evidence: The Accused's Constitutional Right to Introduce Favorable Evidence (1990); The Constitutionalization of Hearsay: The Extent to Which the Fifth and Sixth Amendments Permit or Require the Liberalization of the Hearsay Rules, 76 Minn. L. Rev. 521 (1992).

had done the lethal act. Modern hearsay law is mostly consistent with the constitutional outcomes in these cases, since the against-interest exception paves the way for third-party confessions, but the exception is qualified in requiring that the declarant be unavailable and that the confession be corroborated, and the exception also lets courts exclude some confessions: The exception is satisfied only if a third-party confession "so far tend[ ] to subject the declarant" to criminal sanctions that a reasonable person would not make the statement unless "believing it to be true."[2]

Chambers was a trial for murdering a policeman named Sonny Liberty, as he and others tried to arrest someone in a hostile crowd. Officers testified that, after being shot himself, Liberty shot *Chambers*. One said Chambers shot Liberty first, but others said he did not shoot anybody and that Gable McDonald shot Liberty. McDonald gave a sworn written confession to the lawyer for Chambers, and four other times he said he killed Liberty, but he repudiated his confession at a preliminary hearing. Chambers called him and introduced his confession, but on cross by the state McDonald said he confessed at another's suggestion, thinking he would share a "sizable tort recovery" from the town to be won by Chambers. Invoking the state voucher rule (calling party may not impeach), the court would not let Chambers question McDonald on his oral confessions or introduce testimony describing them.

> **The *Chambers* case**

The Supreme Court reversed. It said that testimony about McDonald's confessions was critical, and its exclusion, in combination with the refusal to let Chambers cross-examine, denied a fair trial and violated due process. The Court carefully said that in other situations excluding statements against penal interest might serve "a valid state purpose" of avoiding "untrustworthy testimony." But excluding the other confessions could not be justified because circumstances provided "considerable assurance of their reliability."[3]

Five years after *Chambers* the Court again held, in a per curiam opinion in the *Green* case, that excluding a third-party confession violated due process. *Green* arose out of separate trials of Moore and Green for raping and murdering Theresa Allen, whom they abducted from a store where she worked and shot two times. Both men were convicted and sentenced to death. During the penalty phase of Green's trial the court

> **The *Green* case**

---

2. *See* discussion in §§8.72-8.76, *supra*. See also Donnelly v. United States, 228 U.S. 243, 277-278 (1913) (Joe Dick said he committed murder charged to Donnelly, prompting Holmes to say "no other statement is so much against interest as a confession of murder") (Dick's confession was circumstantially corroborated).

3. Chambers v. Mississippi, 410 U.S. 284, 300-301 (1973) (each confession was "made spontaneously to a close acquaintance shortly after the murder," and was "corroborated by some other evidence," including sworn confession, eyewitness testimony, proof that McDonald was seen with gun after shooting, and evidence that he had a revolver like the one used and later bought a new gun; "sheer number of independent confessions" corroborated each other, and each was self-incriminating and against interest because McDonald had nothing to gain by confessing to friends and must have known disclosure might lead to prosecution) (also state could have cross-examined McDonald).

excluded testimony that Moore said he killed Allen after sending Green on an errand, and the state argued that the jury could infer that Green fired one of the shots. The Supreme Court reversed, stressing that the excluded testimony was "highly relevant to a critical issue" and that there were "substantial reasons" to think it was reliable—Moore spoke "spontaneously to a close friend," there was "ample" corroborating evidence, the statement was against interest, and there was no reason to think he had "any ulterior motive."[4]

The *Holmes* case   In the *Holmes* case in 2006, defendant was convicted of murder and related offenses, having allegedly sodomized and brutally beaten an 86-year-old woman. The trial court excluded proof that one Jimmy White committed the crime. Witnesses placed him at the scene, and one said he asked White about the murder and that he "put his head down and he raised his head back up and he said, well, you know I like older women," adding that "he did what they say he did" and he had "no regrets about it at all." Another witness, incarcerated with him, said that White admitted the assault, and further that a police officer had asked the witness to "testify falsely." At defendant's preliminary hearing, White denied making the statements and offered an alibi that another witness refuted. Invoking a rule that proof of third-party guilt can be excluded if the proof of defendant's guilt is strong, the trial court excluded the proof pointing to White's involvement. Finding that this rule "does not rationally serve" the end of excluding prejudicial or misleading evidence, or protecting against confusion of issues, the Supreme Court reversed. Citing due process, confrontation, and compulsory process, the Court said the Constitution guarantees defendants what it called "a meaningful opportunity to present a complete defense."[5]

Narrow doctrine   There are many reasons to think *Chambers, Green* and *Holmes* create a narrow doctrine. In *Chambers* and *Green*, the Court wrote highly fact-specific opinions.[6] In all three cases, the question whether to admit defense hearsay was presented in the most dramatic setting—murder trials where the excluded hearsay said the speaker was the killer or assailant, in circumstances indicating that if the excluded statement was right, defendant did not shoot or assault the victim. In *Chambers* and *Green*, the state "got away with" something: *Chambers* involved manipulation of hearsay doctrine to undercut the defense, admitting McDonald's written confession but excluding oral ones, sandbagging

---

4. Green v. Georgia, 442 U.S. 95 (1979) (in "unique circumstances," hearsay rule cannot be applied "mechanistically" to defeat justice) (exception reached statements against pecuniary, not penal, interest).

5. Holmes v. South Carolina, 547 U.S. 319, 324 (2006), quoting Crane v. Kentucky, 476 U.S. 683, 690 (1986).

6. Green v. Georgia, 442 U.S. 95, 97 (1979) (emphasizing facts and "unique circumstances"); Chambers v. Mississippi, 410 U.S. 284, 300 (1973) (excluding oral confessions "coupled with" applying voucher rule to block examination and impeachment of McDonald denied fair trial; establishing "no new principles of constitutional law" and not saying whether excluding against-interest statements in "other circumstances" might serve valid purpose).

the defense by allowing it to try to pin responsibility on McDonald but blocking an attack on his (rather thin) repudiation. *Green* involved a treacherous strategy of keeping one defendant from using the same statement that the state used to convict the other, and inviting a jury to draw the very inference that the statement refuted (prompting the deadpan comment that the state considered the statement "sufficiently reliable to use it against Moore, and to base a sentence of death upon it"). Finally, in *Holmes* the Court invoked the principle that defense evidence cannot be excluded on the basis of "arbitrary" rules, while stressing that states can exclude evidence and citing decisions excluding proof of third-party guilt that is "speculative or remote" or does not tend to "prove or disprove" a material fact.

There are two other reasons, based specifically on *Chambers* as the landmark decision in this line, to think that the doctrine here considered is narrow.

First, *Chambers* laid great stress on the reliability of the excluded confession. The decision seems to apply only if hearsay satisfies a trustworthy-plus standard—surpassing the ordinary standard to the point of being highly trustworthy. Indeed, pretty clearly the against-interest exception was drafted with *Chambers* in mind (requiring "corroborating circumstances"), the justification being that third-party confessions can be fabricated by friendly defense witnesses (and attributed to unavailable speakers) and are hard to rebut even if false.

Second, *Chambers* presented the hearsay issue in a complicated and unlikely procedural and tactical milieu that makes interpretation hard. It is, for example, amazing that McDonald testified rather than claiming his constitutional privilege. Few in his position would testify about what they said or did, and *Chambers* stressed that he did testify: Doing so damaged the defense (he denied shooting Liberty and repudiated his confession), created need for rebuttal, and provided a chance to test his confessions. These facts are salient in *Chambers* and rare in practice (on those facts, McDonald's availability would prevent use of the against-interest exception for his confessions). If he admitted killing Liberty, presumably the defendant would not much need his confessions; if he denied it, presumably the defendant could impeach the denial by asking him about his confessions as inconsistent statements (and maybe prove them by other witnesses); if he claimed lack of memory, that would make him unavailable after all and the confession would fit the exception. Finally, *Chambers* rests on due process, not confrontation or compulsory process (the defense mounted only a due process challenge in state court), but the lawyer who argued the defense case to the Supreme Court has argued that the structure and language of *Chambers* stress ideas central to confrontation and compulsory process, and the reference to all three constitutional clauses in *Holmes* in 2006 indicates that the exact basis of the decision is still somewhat up in the air.[7]

---

7. Westen, Confrontation and Compulsory Process: A Unified Theory of Evidence for Criminal Cases, 91 Harv. L. Rev. 567, 605-610 (1978) (opinion in *Chambers* is

Still, *Chambers* is important. Particularly with the reinforcement provided by *Holmes*, it lends constitutional force to the proposition that the defense can introduce third-party confessions exonerating the accused. It appears to mean that sometimes this right overcomes the requirement in the against-interest exception that the speaker be unavailable as a witness. And *Chambers* seems to say, despite its insistence on the aggregate effect of combined rulings, that each error (blocking cross and excluding the oral confessions) was an independent constitutional mistake. Apart from the availability matter, however, *Chambers* supports the exception as set forth in FRE 804(b)(3), apparently validating the barrier of the trustworthy-plus standard while also supporting at least that much accommodation of defense interests.[8]

While *Chambers* remains a narrow doctrine, *Green* broadened it in two ways, and *Holmes* added reinforcement. First, *Green* emphasized trustworthiness but did not suggest that a third-party confession had to satisfy a trustworthy-plus standard (the crucial comment was not corroborated by eyewitness testimony or repeated often), and the same can be said in *Holmes*. Thus *Green* and *Holmes* suggest that defendants have a constitutional right to admit third-party confessions shown to be reliable under an ordinary standard. This point is strengthened by evolving practice under the against-interest exception, which often admits third-party statements implicating the defendant: They too can be fabricated and are hard to rebut, so imposing a trustworthy-plus standard on third-party confessions offered by the defendant seems unjustified.[9]

Second, *Green* found constitutional error in a single ruling excluding probative hearsay, and *Holmes* implied that the error in excluding exculpatory evidence embraced several different kinds of proof of third-party guilt. *Chambers* had stressed the combination of rulings (cutting off defense impeachment of McDonald and blocking testimony describing his confessions), but *Green* and *Holmes* focused simply on the probativity of excluded proof of third-party guilt. Indeed, *Holmes* affects not only the use of hearsay for the defense, but the use

---

bifurcated; while it relies on due process alone, it relies on confrontation cases in discussing cross, and on confrontation and compulsory process cases in discussing the independent evidence issue) (Westen was on defense brief and argued case in Supreme Court). See also Westen, The Compulsory Process Clause, 30 Mich L. Rev. 71, 151-155 (1974).

8. United States v. MacDonald, 688 F.2d 224, 232 & n.13 (4th Cir. 1982) (exception codified *Chambers* "in large measure" and they "impose the same standard") (exception applies only when declarant is unavailable, but availability in *Chambers* strengthened conclusion that statements were reliable), *cert. denied*, 459 U.S. 1103.

9. Commentators objected to a higher reliability standard for defendants. See Westen, Confrontation and Compulsory Process: A Unified Theory of Evidence for Criminal Cases, 91 Harv. L. Rev. 567, 596-601 (1978) (standard that defense must satisfy should be at least as liberal as standard prosecutor must satisfy); Tague, Perils of the Rulemaking Process: The Development, Application, and Unconstitutionality of Rule 804(b)(3)'s Penal Interest Exception, 69 Geo. L. Rev. 851, 890 (1981) (putting higher standard on defense than prosecutor for third-party confessions is unconstitutional).

of other evidence, including other acts ("reverse 404(b) evidence").[10]

Not surprisingly, *Chambers* is usually invoked as a factor on the scale favoring generous application of the against-interest exception on behalf of criminal defendants. Only a handful of cases, however, invoke the constitutional principle of *Chambers* in granting relief from a conviction. Under *Chambers*, it seems that failing to satisfy the unavailability requirement of FRE 804(a) is sometimes excused, and a statement must be admitted even if the speaker testifies or is not present but not shown to be unavailable.[11] *Chambers* also requires courts to admit trustworthy third-party confessions showing that the speaker, rather than the defendant, shot or killed the victim—those statements that go to the heart of the charged offense and have a clear and direct impact on the question of guilt or penalty.[12] And *Chambers* requires courts to give special consideration to other kinds of defense-sponsored hearsay, and thus affects application of other categorical exceptions,[13] as well as other hearsay that seems to fit no exception or arguably fits the catchalls.[14]

Particularly since the decision in *Holmes*, the defense right to offer exculpatory evidence has been construed more broadly, and this right has spawned at least some decisions relating more generally to exculpatory evidence.[15]

For good reason, cases rejecting arguments based on *Chambers* stress that the statement sought to be introduced lacked circumstantial

Admitting hearsay for defense

10. *See* discussion in §4.15, *supra*.

11. State v. Barts, 362 S.E.2d 235 (N.C. 1987) (in murder trial, error to exclude from penalty phase testimony that defendant's cousin admitted striking fatal blow despite failure to show he was unavailable); Rosario v. Kuhlman, 658 F. Supp. 1408 (S.D.N.Y. 1987) (error under *Chambers* to exclude former testimony offered by defendant who did not satisfy statute in seeking speaker), *aff'd* 839 F.2d 918 (2d Cir.).

12. Apart from *Chambers* and *Green*, *see* State v. Barts, 362 S.E.2d 235 (N.C. 1987); United States v. Benveniste, 564 F.2d 335, 341-342 (9th Cir. 1977).

13. Trussell v. Estelle, 699 F.2d 256, 262 (5th Cir. 1983) (rejecting argument that *Chambers* required court to admit police report saying eyewitness B failed to identify defendant in lineup; court made author available, but defendant declined to call him; B did identify defendant, and report was mistaken) (due process issue would arise if there were proof that B did not identify defendant), *cert. denied*, 464 U.S. 853.

14. People v. Husband, 522 N.Y.S.2d 132 (N.Y. App. 1987) (in trial for attempted robbery where defendant claimed he was trying to collect debt, error under *Chambers* to exclude testimony describing what victim said, which went to "central" issue); Pettijohn v. Hall, 599 F.2d 476, 480-481 (1st Cir. 1979) (constitutional error to exclude evidence that eyewitness identified another), *cert. denied*, 444 U.S. 946.

15. People v. Beaman, 890 N.E.2d 500 (Ill. 2008) (reversing murder conviction for failure to disclose evidence of relationship between female victim and another man) (relying on *Holmes*); State v. Packed, 736 N.W.2d 851 (S.D. 2007) (reversing conviction for sexual assault on 8-year-old girl for error in excluding proof of her relationship with neighbor boy) (relying on *Holmes* and *Chambers*); United States v. Velarde, 485 F.3d 553 (10th Cir. 2007) (granting new trial in sexual assault case for failure to produce evidence that victim had brought prior false charges) (relying on *Holmes*).

guarantees of trustworthiness.[16] Factors that count are those relating to the credibility of the speaker (motives, inconsistencies) and the trustworthiness of the statement (lapse of time, degree of interest impairment), along with those in the category of corroboration or refutation, such as the presence or absence of eyewitness testimony or other evidence tending to confirm or refute the statement and the appearance or absence of evidence tending to contradict the statement. As the Court commented in *Holmes,* in language often paraphrased in later decisions rejecting challenges to rulings excluding defense evidence pointing to third-party guilt, courts can continue to exclude such evidence if it is too "speculative, remote, or immaterial."[17] To satisfy *Holmes,* the defense needs to show that the proffered evidence, alone or in combination with other evidence, demonstrates a connection between the charged crime and proof of third-party behavior.[18] *Chambers* is intended to be more of an anchor to windward, available in extraordinary and unusual cases but not routinely as a check on application of the hearsay doctrine,[19] so real unfairness in the way the trial was conducted is an important element in any *Chambers* argument.[20]

16. Guinn v. Kemna, 489 F.3d 351 (8th Cir. 2007) (excluding third-party confessions; not made close in time to crime; one was not spontaneous; "precious little" corroboration); Sinkfield v. Brigano, 487 F.3d 1013, 1016-1018 (6th Cir. 2007) (excluding third-party confession in which S said he and G murdered victim; statement "did not carry the same indicia of reliability as a truly self-inculpatory statement" and credibility of corroborative evidence was disputed); O'Brien v. Marshall, 453 F.3d 13 (1st Cir. 2006) (excluding third-party confession as unreliable and in suggesting that another was the culprit).

17. United States v. DeCologero, 530 F.3d 36, 73 (1st Cir. 2008) (rejecting claim that cross-examination of state witness was too severely restricted), paraphrasing Holmes v. South Carolina, 547 U.S. 319, at 327 (2006) (quoting secondary source allowing exclusion of defense evidence if it is "speculative or remote, or does not tend to prove or disprove a material fact").

18. United States v. Jordan, 485 F.3d 1214, 1220-1221 (10th Cir. 2007) (rejecting challenge to conviction for prison stabbing; must show nexus between crime charged and alternative perpetrator; no witness placed third party R at scene of stabbing at the time; unidentified DNA sample does not connect crime to R; fact that R had a "similar shank months before" is "suggestive" but "ultimately thin").

19. United States v. North, 910 F.2d 843, 908 (D.C. Cir. 1990) (in trial of Oliver North by independent counsel, excluding congressional testimony by Poindexter, offered by defense; *Chambers* "limited itself to its own facts and circumstances," condemning "extremely strict application of state evidentiary rules" and excluding key pieces of evidence; facts here are "not nearly so extreme"), *cert. denied,* 940 U.S. 104.

20. People v. Frierson, 808 P.2d 1197 (Cal. 1991) (no error under *Chambers;* prosecutor never used statement by friend saying he rather than defendant shot victim) (no reason to think statement was reliable), *cert. denied,* 502 U.S. 1061; United States v. North, 910 F.2d 843, 908 (D.C. Cir. 1990) (record does not "present the hallmarks of procedural arcana, racial prejudice and fundamental unfairness" found in *Chambers*), *cert. denied,* 940 U.S. 104.

CHAPTER 9

Foundational Evidence, Authentication

A. INTRODUCTION
B. TYPES OF FOUNDATIONS
C. SELF-AUTHENTICATION
D. SUBSCRIBING WITNESSES
E. DEMONSTRATIVE EVIDENCE

A. INTRODUCTION

§9.1 Introduction

The requirement of authentication means that unless an exhibit or other form of nontestimonial evidence qualifies as self-authenticating under FRE 902 the trier is not allowed to accept it at face value. Formal proof of identity or authenticity must be offered before the exhibit can be admitted or even shown to the jury. Authentication thus serves to enhance the accuracy of the factfinding process by screening out evidence that might be false or otherwise unreliable, whether as the result of fraud or innocent mistake.[1] Authentication represents a more specific application of the requirement of relevancy. If an exhibit is not supported by evidence sufficient to support a finding that it is "what its proponent claims," it lacks relevance under FRE 401 and is subject to exclusion as confusing and misleading under FRE 403.

---

§9.1   1. *See, e.g.,* Mayer v. Angelica, 790 F.2d 1315, 1338 (7th Cir. 1986) (letters improperly admitted; no proof that purported author wrote them or that defendant received them), *cert. denied,* 479 U.S. 1037.

Although the authentication requirement is most closely associated with exhibits, it applies to evidence in every form except for live testimony.[2] Factfinders may assume that someone who takes the witness stand is a person, that the words he speaks convey the usual meaning they suggest, and so forth, without special proof of all such points. But even live testimony is subject to FRE 901(a) when it describes something such as a writing or telephone conversation that must itself be authenticated.

Rationale for rule   The authentication requirement reflects an "attitude of agnosticism" towards writings and other exhibits that "departs sharply" from people's customs "in ordinary affairs."[3] For this reason, it is sometimes criticized as unnecessarily technical and onerous to litigants, causing increased expense and trial delay, yet not sufficient as a safeguard against fraud in those rare cases where it might actually be attempted.[4] This criticism may be unfair because no rule can provide a guarantee against fabrication, and disputes about the genuineness of evidence must ultimately be resolved though the adversary trial process. Moreover, with some exceptions, existing standards for authentication do not seem overly burdensome, particularly in civil cases where pretrial authentication procedures are available and reciprocal stipulations to admissibility are common.[5] In cases where the genuineness of evidence is uncertain, and especially where it is disputed, requiring the proponent to make a prima facie showing of authenticity provides at least a minimal trial safeguard. The authentication requirement plays an even greater protective role in criminal prosecutions where courts sometimes enforce it more strictly in recognition of the liberty interests at stake.[6]

Until an exhibit has been authenticated, an attorney is not supposed to display it to the jury or reveal its contents, either by reading it or asking a witness to do so. The trial judge has discretion whether to allow exhibits to be taken to the jury room during deliberations. Generally depositions and other written substitutes for testimony are not sent with the jury out of concern that they might be given undue weight in relation to other testimonial evidence.[7]

---

2. Live testimony requires a different type of foundation showing that the witness has personal knowledge of the matter about which she is testifying. *See* FRE 602, discussed in §6.5, *supra.*

3. ACN to FRE 901(a) (quoting early editions of McCormick casebook and hornbook).

4. *See, e.g.,* Broun, Authentication and Contents of Writings, 1969 Law & Soc. Ord. 611; Strong, Liberalizing the Authentication of Private Writings, 52 Cornell L.Q. 284 (1967).

5. *See* §9.2, *infra.*

6. *See, e.g.,* United States v. Wanoskia, 800 F.2d 235, 238 (10th Cir. 1986) (adherence to strict authentication standard for experimental evidence is even more important in criminal trials).

7. *See, e.g.,* United States v. Abbas, 504 F.2d 123, 125 (9th Cir. 1974) (written statement of defendant should not go to jury because of danger "that it would act as a speaking, continuous witness throughout the jury's deliberations"). *Cf.* FRE 803(5) (memorandum of past recollection recorded may be read to jury as exception to hearsay rule, but not admitted as an exhibit unless offered by adverse party).

§9.2   Pretrial Authentication

In civil cases, there are a number of discovery devices that allow parties to resolve questions of authentication in advance of trial. FRCP 26(a)(1)(A)(ii) now requires parties, without awaiting a discovery request, to provide other parties with "a copy of, or a description by category and location, of all documents, electronically stored information, and tangible things that the disclosing party has in its possession, custody, or control and may use to support its claims and defenses, unless the use would be solely for impeachment." Production pursuant to this Rule authenticates the evidence as being what the producing party claims it to be. In addition, the Rule now requires parties at least 30 days prior to trial to provide their opponents with "an appropriate identification of each document or other exhibit, including summaries of other evidence, separately identifying those which the party expects to offer and those which the party may offer if the need arises."[1] Any objections not made within 14 days after such disclosure (unless another time is provided by the court) are deemed waived (unless excused by the court for good cause), except for objections under FRE 402 or 403. These amendments go far toward removing issues of authentication from civil trials.

Another important authentication mechanism is FRCP 36, which authorizes a party to submit a written request for admission of facts, including the genuineness of documents. If the opposing party admits genuineness or fails to deny the request in the time allowed, authenticity is deemed established. Under FRCP 37(c), if the opposing party denies genuineness of the items without having reasonable grounds for doing so, and the requesting party subsequently proves their genuineness, the latter may seek to recover the reasonable expenses incurred in making such proof, including attorneys' fees.

Request for admission

A party can also seek admissions of genuineness from an opponent by interrogatory or deposition.[2] If such admissions are forthcoming, they normally substitute for the formal process of authentication at trial. Authentication matters are often resolved at pretrial conferences under FRCP 16,[3] and a listing of authenticated exhibits (or remaining areas of dispute) is normally included as part of a pretrial order. Authentication issues are also sometimes resolved in pretrial proceedings in criminal cases.[4]

FRCP 10(c) permits a party to attach to his pleading copies of pertinent documents, and as a matter of routine practice the pleader

---

§9.2   1. FRCP 26(a)(3).

2. *See* FRCP 33 (authorizing use of interrogatories to establish genuineness of documents and making interrogatories admissible at trial "to the extent allowed" by FRE); FRCP 30 and 31 (providing for depositions and setting out mechanics for attaching documents).

3. *See* FRCP 16(c)(2)(C) (pretrial conference to cover "admissions and stipulations about facts and documents to avoid unnecessary proof, and ruling in advance on the admissibility of evidence").

4. *See* FRCrimP 17.1 (regulating pretrial proceedings in criminal cases).

alleges that they are true copies of specified material. If the responding party does not deny the allegations, the authenticity of the documents is no longer in dispute.

Where a party produces documents or other matters in response to a subpoena or discovery order, the very act of production is generally thought to authenticate the matter. It constitutes a nonverbal assertion that the items produced are what was requested by the subpoena or order, at least when the responding party is in a position to have the requisite knowledge.[5]

In both civil and criminal cases, the burden of authenticating evidence can be avoided by stipulation of the opponent to authenticity, although such stipulations tend to be more freely given in civil cases than criminal prosecutions.

FRE 901(a)

General provision. The requirement of authentication or identification as a condition precedent to admissibility is satisfied by evidence sufficient to support a finding that the matter in question is what its proponent claims.

---

§9.3 Laying a Foundation

FRE 901(a) provides the standard for authenticating exhibits and other forms of nontestimonial evidence.[1] It establishes an across-the-board rule that something is properly authenticated by "evidence sufficient to support a finding" that it is "what its proponent claims." FRE 901(b) sets forth "[b]y way of illustration only, and not by way of limitation" ten examples of authentication methods that are sufficient as a matter of law.[2]

The preliminary showing required by FRE 901(a) is called "laying the foundation." The kind of foundation necessary depends on the nature of the thing in question, and often a single exhibit can be authenticated in several different ways, including an admission of genuineness by the opposing party.[3] The only bedrock requirement is that

---

5. United States v. Brown, 688 F.2d 1112, 1115-1116 (7th Cir. 1982) (corporate records produced in response to government subpoena were authenticated; "act of production was implicit authentication").

§9.3   1. Surprisingly, the Federal Rules do not explicitly state an authentication requirement. Nonetheless, it is clear that FRE 901(a) adopts by implication the common law requirement that nontestimonial evidence must be authenticated, and the Rule explains how the requirement is satisfied.

2. United States v. Jimenez Lopez, 873 F.2d 769, 772 (5th Cir. 1989) (methods of authentication listed in FRE 901(b) "are not the exclusive means by which the document can be authenticated").

3. *See, e.g.,* Cathey v. Johns-Manville Sales Corp., 776 F.2d 1565, 1574 (6th Cir. 1985) (letters authenticated by admission of party in companion case before same court), *cert. denied,* 478 U.S. 1021.

the proponent introduce sufficient evidence to support a finding by the trier of fact that the matter is what it is claimed to be.[4]

The traditional steps to authenticate and introduce an exhibit are the following: (1) having the exhibit marked for identification by the court reporter or other designated court officer; (2) authenticating the exhibit by the testimony of a witness unless it is self-authenticating; (3) offering the exhibit in evidence; (4) permitting adverse counsel to examine it; (5) allowing adverse counsel an opportunity to object; (6) submitting the exhibit to the court for examination if the court wants; (7) obtaining a ruling by the court; (8) asking permission to have the exhibit, if admitted, presented to the jury by reading it (if it is a writing) or having it displayed or passed among them. These procedures and their sequence vary among jurisdictions and judges and are very much a part of local custom and professional habit.

Steps of process

The process of authentication must be distinguished from a finding of authenticity. Authentication deals only with the foundation required for admitting evidence, and the adequacy of that foundation is determined by the trial judge. Whether the evidence is in fact authentic is ultimately a question for the jury. Moreover, even if the jury finds the evidence to be authentic, this does not establish the truth of hearsay assertions contained within it.[5]

The authentication process is governed by FRE 104(b),[6] under which the court plays only a screening function.[7] The judge is charged not to determine authenticity by a preponderance of evidence but rather to assess whether there is evidence sufficient to support a jury finding of authenticity.[8] If this standard is satisfied, the judge is normally required to admit the exhibit (unless it is excludable on other grounds), even if the judge is not personally persuaded of its authenticity.[9]

Governed by FRE 104(b)

---

4. United States v. Inserra, 34 F.3d 83, 90 (2d Cir. 1994) (probation reports were linked to defendant; all that is needed is "rational basis" on which jury could conclude that "exhibit did, in fact, belong" to him).

5. United States v. Mandycz, 447 F.3d 951, 966 (6th Cir. 2006) (authenticity turns on whether document is what it purports to be, not veracity of content).

6. *See* §§1.13 and 4.3, *supra.* Authentication involves a question of conditional relevancy because probativity depends on a preliminary finding that evidence is authentic. For example, the relevance of an incriminating letter allegedly written by the defendant depends on a finding that he actually wrote it.

7. United States v. Ladd, 885 F.2d 954, 956 (1st Cir. 1989) (on matters of authenticity, trial judge "stands as a sentinel at the gates").

8. Because the jury's ultimate determination of authenticity must be made on the basis of admissible evidence, the evidentiary foundation for the exhibit should normally consist of admissible evidence. Zenith Radio Corp. v. Matushita Elec. Indus. Co., 505 F. Supp. 1190, 1220 (E.D. Pa. 1980) (jury's determination of authenticity to be made on basis of admissible evidence), *modified on other grounds sub nom.* In re Japanese Elec. Prods. Antitrust Litig., 723 F.2d 238 (3d Cir. 1983), *rev'd on other grounds*, 475 U.S. 574 (1986).

9. Ricketts v. City of Hartford, 74 F.3d 1397, 1410-1411 (2d Cir. 1996) (error for to exclude tape because "it was not sure voice on tape was that of Davis"; role of judge is not to determine authenticity but only to determine whether there is sufficient evidence to support a jury finding of authenticity).

The fact that evidence has been sufficiently authenticated to be admitted does not prevent the opponent from introducing counterproof challenging its authenticity.[10] Moreover, satisfying the authentication requirement does not mean the jury is bound to accept the matter or give it the significance in the case that the proponent suggests. The jury remains free to reject the matter as not authentic or accept it as authentic while giving it little or no weight.[11]

At least in civil cases, the jury's usual function may be preempted in cases where the evidence for or against authenticity is so compelling that it permits only one conclusion by a reasonable jury. Where evidence of authenticity is so overwhelming as to be beyond reasonable dispute, the court may instruct the jury to accept the exhibit as authentic, although in criminal cases such an instruction could not be given against the accused.[12] Where counterproof challenging authenticity is compelling, a court may exclude the exhibit.

Under FRE 104(b), the trial judge has discretion to admit evidence subject to later proof of its authenticity,[13] a process sometimes referred to as "connecting up." For example, a letter purportedly written by a party could be admitted, provided the proponent represents to the court that a qualified handwriting expert will later be produced who will testify to the authenticity of the letter. Although this procedure has inherent risks, it is designed to accommodate the uncertainties of trial scheduling and the possibility that an authenticating witness may be unable to appear until later because of travel delays, illness, or other legitimate reasons. If such later proof is not forthcoming, the admitted evidence should be stricken. In a case where admitting the evidence has caused irreparable prejudice, a mistrial may be granted.

B. TYPES OF FOUNDATIONS

> **FRE 901(b)(1)**
>
> **Testimony of witness with knowledge.** Testimony that a matter is what it is claimed to be.

---

10. ACN, FRE 902 ("In no instance is the opposite party foreclosed from disputing authority"). While this observation is made in the context of self-authentication, it is equally true with respect to FRE 901.

11. United States v. Caldwell, 776 F.2d 989, 1002 (11th Cir. 1985) (it remains for the trier of fact "to appraise whether the proffered evidence is in fact what it purports to be").

12. *See* §3.13, *supra.*

13. *See, e.g.,* United States v. Espinoza, 641 F.2d 153, 170 (4th Cir. 1981) (testimony describing telephone conversation between witness and third party "may be conditionally admitted" subject to later introduction of evidence identifying third party), *cert. denied,* 454 U.S. 841.

§9.4 Testimony of Person with Knowledge

Under FRE 901(b)(1), a matter may be authenticated by testimony of a witness with knowledge that it "is what it is claimed to be."[1] This is the most sweeping of the authentication methods listed in FRE 901(b). In some ways it is misleading and overbroad, because most courts do not allow a witness simply to pronounce a matter authentic without explaining how such an identification is made.

In general, a witness's unelaborated statement of identification is sufficient only for relatively distinctive items shown to be personally known to the witness (for example, "This is the rent receipt my landlord gave me."). For a gun, knife, or other tangible object, courts normally require some identification of distinguishing characteristics such as a serial number or initials on the handle. For fungible objects such as drugs, courts normally require showing of a chain of custody.[2]

Basis for identification required

It might seem that the more stringent foundation generally imposed by courts under FRE 901(b)(1) is inconsistent with both the literal wording of the Rule and the lenient standard of authentication in FRE 901(a). But FRE 901(a) requires evidence "sufficient to support a finding" that the item is "what its proponent claims," and courts generally take the view that this standard is not satisfied by a bald assertion of authenticity by a witness who fails to explain how the identification is being made.

To facilitate authentication, most law enforcement officers are trained in proper procedures for handling evidence once it is seized. For example, it is a common practice after seizing a weapon or similar physical evidence for the officer to mark his initials and the date on the item.[3] Officers are taught to store evidence in a secure place prior to trial where access to it is strictly regulated. Where the evidence is to be authenticated by showing its chain of custody, restricting access to it serves the important purpose of limiting the number of links in the chain.

A complete foundation often requires the authenticating witness not only to explain the basis for identification but to say that the object appears to be in the same condition as it was at the time of the events giving rise to the litigation, at least where a change could affect the relevance of the exhibit.[4] If the object is not in the same condition, it may still be admitted if the changes are explained to the jury and its admission will not cause unfair prejudice or confuse or mislead the jury.

In same condition

§9.4 1. *See, e.g.,* United States v. Moore, 936 F.2d 1508, 1519 (7th Cir. 1991) (palm prints were authenticated where officer who took them "unequivocally identified" defendant as person who gave them), *cert. denied,* 502 U.S. 991.

2. *See* §9.5, *infra.*

3. *See, e.g.,* United States v. Sabater, 830 F.2d 7, 10-11 (2d Cir. 1987) (counterfeit bill authenticated in part by officer's "identification based upon markings he had placed on the bill").

4. *See, e.g.,* United States v. Miller, 994 F.2d 441, 443 (8th Cir. 1993) (where physical object is offered, foundation requires showing that condition is substantially unchanged).

It is clear that a witness called to provide authentication testimony must satisfy the personal knowledge requirement of FRE 602.[5] If the witness does not have sufficient knowledge of authenticity, the exhibit may be excluded.[6] However, the authenticating witness need not be absolutely certain of the identification.[7]

Writings   A writing can be authenticated under FRE 901(b)(1) as "what it is claimed to be" by the witness who wrote or executed it,[8] or by others shown to have personal knowledge, such as a person who saw another write or sign it,[9] or one who saw the writing before,[10] or one who is familiar with its contents.[11] A showing of specific authorship is not always necessary to authenticate a writing.[12] Many types of writings are self-authenticating under the various subparts of FRE 902.[13]

Photographs   A photograph can be authenticated under FRE 901(b)(1) by a witness with knowledge who testifies that the photograph accurately represents the scene depicted at the relevant time.[14] The authenticating witness need not be the photographer.[15] Even if the conditions have changed, the photograph may still be admitted at the discretion

---

5. Kassim v. City of Schenectady, 415 F.3d 246, 251 (2d Cir. 2005) (excluding English translation of plaintiff's Arabic store records, for lack of personal knowledge; translator neither spoke nor read Arabic, and admitted transcribing what plaintiff told her to write); United States v. Kayode, 254 F.3d 204 (D.C. Cir. 2001) (seized documents were admitted without foundation; government agent who testified about their location lacked firsthand knowledge).

6. Nolin v. Douglas County, 903 F.2d 1546, 1551-1552 (11th Cir. 1990) (excluding purported copy of county employment guidelines; identifying witness was only "somewhat familiar" with document).

7. United States v. Johnson, 637 F.2d 1224, 1247-1248 (9th Cir. 1980) (admitting ax into evidence, where victim testified that he was "pretty sure" it was the weapon used against him and testified that he was "personally familiar with this particular ax because he had used it in the past").

8. United States v. Helmel, 769 F.2d 1306, 1319 & n.18 (8th Cir. 1985) (approving office lease authenticated by witness who had prepared and signed it).

9. United States v. Gagliardi, 506 F.3d 140, 150 (2d Cir. 2007) (informant and agent posing as 13-year-old girls in Internet chat room testified to accuracy of records of defendant's email and IM exchanges with them, which authenticated transcripts).

10. United States v. Durham, 868 F.2d 1010, 1012 (8th Cir. 1989) (admitting copy of threatening letter to murder victim, on basis of testimony by his mother and sister, both of whom read original letter), *cert. denied*, 493 U.S. 954.

11. Hal Roach Studios, Inc. v. Richard Feiner & Co., 883 F.2d 1429, 1438 (9th Cir. 1989) (corporate registration statement authenticated by testimony of board chairman who had personal knowledge of its contents), *amended*, 896 F.2d 1542 (9th Cir. 1989).

12. United States v. Helmel, 769 F.2d 1306, 1312 (8th Cir. 1985) (proving identity of specific author unnecessary for ledgers of illegal gambling operation to be admitted).

13. *See* §§9.19-9.29, *infra*.

14. United States v. Lawson, 494 F.3d 1046, 1052 (D.C. Cir. 2007) (can authenticate photograph if witness with knowledge of "testifies that it accurately depicts the scene").

15. United States v. Clayton, 643 F.2d 1071, 1074 (5th Cir. 1981) (authenticating witness "need not be the photographer or see the picture taken; it is sufficient if he recognizes and identifies the object depicted and testifies that the photograph fairly and correctly represents it").

of the court if the changes are explained and the jury would not be misled.[16]

Photographs authenticated by a witness familiar with the scene are sometimes described as "pictorial testimony" and are used to explain and illustrate the testimony of the witness. Traditionally, courts have drawn a distinction between photographs introduced as "pictorial testimony" and those introduced under the "silent witness" doctrine. The "silent witness" doctrine applies to photographs, such as bank automated teller machine photographs, where there is no authenticating witness.[17] Photographs in the former category are admitted only as illustrative of testimony,[18] whereas photographs in the latter category are held to constitute independent substantive evidence.[19] However, there has been growing recognition that photographs admitted as an adjunct to testimony can and often should be allowed to do more than merely illustrate that testimony.[20] As one court noted, "[O]ne glimpse at a photograph may provide a more definite and correct idea of a building or a person's features than the most minute and detailed testimony."[21] Thus today it is common for both types of photographs to be sent to the jury without a limiting instruction.

§9.5 Chain of Custody

Authentication by showing the chain of custody is particularly useful for evidence that is fungible, lacking in distinctive means of identification, or likely to deteriorate or change in condition.[1] Such a showing is

16. United States v. Dombrowski, 877 F.2d 520, 524-525 (7th Cir. 1989) (admitting photograph of crime scene on testimony of officer that it was accurate "except that on the night of the crime there was snow on the ground" and photograph was taken from distorted perspective; defense objected that this made alley seem darker than street, but defense could cross-examine on this point and distortion was not sufficient to make photograph irrelevant or unduly prejudicial or misleading), *cert. denied*, 496 U.S. 907.

17. For a discussion of the foundation for admitting photographs under the "silent witness" doctrine, *see* §9.14, *infra*.

18. Gardner, The Camera Goes to Court, 24 N.C.L. Rev. 233, 243 (1946) (cases "which had merely approved the use of photographs to illustrate testimony were unfortunately treated as limiting the use of photographs to illustration").

19. *See, e.g.*, Clarke v. Reiss, 148 F. Supp. 135, 139-140 (D.N.J. 1957) (basing judicial findings on "eloquent though silent" photographic evidence rather than testimony); Fisher v. State, 7 Ark. App. 1, 643 S.W.2d 571, 574-575 (1982) ("silent witness" photographic evidence "speaks for itself and is substantive evidence of what it portrays independent of a sponsoring witness").

20. *See, e.g.*, McCrary-El v. Shaw, 992 F.2d 809, 811, 813 (8th Cir. 1993) (videotape of prisoner being moved from cell treated as substantive evidence providing basis for dismissal of one count and as evidence of prisoner's physical condition on other count).

21. State v. Roberts, 82 P. 100, 103 (Nev. 1905).

§9.5 1. *See, e.g.*, United States v. Anderson, 452 F.3d 66, 80-81 (1st Cir. 2006) (drug evidence lacked readily identifiable feature, making chain of custody important).

normally not necessary for evidence that can be identified by distinctive characteristics or other circumstantial evidence.[2]

Authenticating objects by showing the chain of custody is not expressly mentioned in the Rules, but FRE 901(b)(1), often in combination with FRE 901(b)(4), embraces this technique. Typically chain of custody is established when one or more witnesses first describe the initial recovery or use of the object and others then describe handling the object and passing it along to others.[3] Such testimony depends on firsthand knowledge of the sort envisioned by FRE 901(b)(1)[4] and sometimes also relies on the appearance or characteristics of the object in conjunction with circumstances as envisioned by FRE 901(b)(4).

Establishing chain   Establishing a chain of custody normally requires calling each of the persons who had custody of the item from the time of the relevant event until trial and offering testimony showing (1) when they took custody and from whom, (2) the precautions they took to preserve the item, (3) the item was not changed, substituted, or tampered with while they had it, and (4) when they relinquished custody and to whom.[5] Each witness should also testify that the item offered appears to be in the same condition as when they had custody of it.

Missing links   Each custodian's testimony serves as one link in the chain. Sometimes the testimony of one or more persons in the chain of custody is unavailable. Although serious gaps may raise enough doubt to require exclusion,[6] a break in the chain is not necessarily fatal to admissibility but goes to the weight of the evidence.[7]

---

2. *See, e.g.*, United States v. Derring, 592 F.2d 1003, 1006 (8th Cir. 1979) (car key authenticated by testimony of officer that he found it in defendant's possession; need not show chain of custody).

3. *See, e.g.*, United States v. Carlos Cruz, 352 F.3d 499, 506 (1st Cir. 2003) (in trial for possessing firearm, machine guns were authenticated by agent's testimony that after arrest agents seized pillowcase containing weapons from garbage can, took contents to headquarters, and remained with weapons until transfer to ATF agent, who testified that weapons remained in his possession thereafter).

4. ACN to FRE 901(b)(1) (citing as example "testimony establishing narcotics as taken from an accused and accounting for custody through the period until trial, including laboratory analysis").

5. *See, e.g.*, United States v. Collado, 957 F.2d 38, 39 (1st Cir. 1992) (in drug trial, admitting plastic bag filled with baggies of cocaine; it was seized at time of arrest in early morning hours, described in detail on seizure report, placed in locked safe by means of slot because office was closed; arresting officers described the seizure and identified bag, and custodian of office also identified bag and seizure report as those he found when he opened next morning). *See generally* Giannelli, Chain of Custody and the Handling of Real Evidence, 20 Am. Crim. L. Rev. 527 (1983).

6. *See, e.g.*, State v. Reese, 382 N.E.2d 1193, 1194-1195 (Ohio App. 1978) (error to admit three pills into evidence where six people handled them over period of nine days, and no identifying marks were made on envelope, no continuous chain of custody was shown, and pills were not of unique character).

7. United States v. Clark, 664 F.2d 1174, 1176 (11th Cir. 1981) (a "minor break in the chain of possession" would "affect the weight" of evidence but should not keep it out).

For a successful foundation it is not necessary to eliminate all possibility of alteration or tampering,[8] but normally a showing of reasonable safeguards is required.[9] Some courts hold that there must be a "reasonable probability" that no tampering occurred.[10] Where the item has been in the custody of a government official, the proponent is aided by a presumption that public officers have discharged their responsibilities with due care.[11]

FRE 901(b)(2)

Nonexpert opinion on handwriting. Nonexpert opinion as to the genuineness of handwriting, based upon familiarity not acquired for purposes of the litigation.

---

§9.6 Handwriting—Lay Opinion

Under FRE 901(b)(2), the genuineness of handwriting may be established by nonexpert opinion, provided that the requisite familiarity was "not acquired for purposes of the litigation." A lay witness should not be asked at trial to give an opinion based on a comparison of the questioned document with an exemplar because under FRE 901(b)(3) only an expert witness or the trier of fact may make such a comparison.[1] However, FRE 901(a) does not require familiarity with every page as a condition of admissibility. Therefore, a multipage document may generally be authenticated by identification of the handwriting on the signature page.[2]

8. United States v. Barrow, 448 F.3d 37, 42-43 (1st Cir. 2006) (in drug trial, admitting liquor bottles containing cocaine; officials testified on storage and testing, and chemist testified that bottle broke after testing; defect in chain of custody went to weight); United States v. Mora, 845 F.2d 233, 237 (10th Cir. 1988) (mere possibility of tampering insufficient basis for excluding evidence), *cert. denied*, 488 U.S. 995.

9. Ballou v. Henri Studios, Inc., 656 F.2d 1147, 1155 (5th Cir. 1981) (issue of "alteration, contamination or adulteration of the evidence is a question for the jury once the proponent of the evidence makes a threshold showing that reasonable precautions were taken").

10. United States v. Briley, 319 F.3d 360, 363 (8th Cir. 2003) (can admit physical evidence if there is a reasonable probability that it was not changed or altered; defect in chain of custody goes to weight).

11. United States v. Thomas, 294 F.3d 899, 904-905 (7th Cir. 2002) (if tapes "were in official custody at all times, a presumption arises that [they] were handled properly").

§9.6 1. United States v. Pitts, 569 F.2d 343, 348 (5th Cir. 1978) (excluding opinion testimony as to genuineness of signature on receipt where witness made "one-shot" comparison with genuine signature "for purposes of a pending criminal investigation"), *cert. denied*, 436 U.S. 959. In this respect, FRE 901(b)(3) differs from FRE 901(b)(5), which allows lay opinion testimony on voice identification even when the comparison is made for purposes of trial.

2. United States v. Whittington, 783 F.2d 1210, 1214-1215 (5th Cir. 1986) (rejecting defense objection that authenticating witness could not "identify any of the pages in the document other than the signature page"; if it were "necessary for a witness to a document to identify every page of the document as a condition of admissibility, few documents would be admissible"), *cert. denied*, 479 U.S. 882.

Basis for familiarity   The lay witness need not have been present at the signing[3] and may have acquired the requisite familiarity by having engaged in correspondence with the person,[4] watched the person write on prior occasions,[5] or in various other ways.[6] Family members are likely to have sufficient familiarity with one's handwriting,[7] as are persons in a close business relationship such as employees,[8] employers,[9] or coworkers.[10]

Whether a lay witness knows enough to give a persuasive opinion identifying handwriting is ultimately a question for the jury under FRE 602 and FRE 104(b), although the judge passes on the threshold question whether there is enough indication of knowledge to support a jury finding on the point.[11] If insufficient familiarity is shown, the opinion should be excluded.[12] The issue whether an opinion from the witness would be helpful to the trier of fact is a matter for the court under FRE 701 and FRE 104(a).

The assumption that lay witnesses are able to make accurate handwriting identifications has been questioned,[13] and the scientific basis of handwriting "expertise" is also currently under attack.[14]

---

3. United States v. Whittington, 783 F.2d 1210, 1215 (5th Cir. 1986) (it is "not essential" that witnesses be present when signature is executed), *cert. denied*, 479 U.S. 882.

4. Rogers v. Ritter, 79 U.S. 317, 322 (1870) (witness can identify handwriting of person "if he has personally communicated with him by letter, although he has never seen him write at all").

5. United States v. Mauchlin, 670 F.2d 746, 749 (7th Cir. 1982) (file documents used as exemplars were authenticated by prison official who had "daily contact" with defendant for 16 months and "had seen him write on approximately six occasions").

6. Rogers v. Ritter, 79 U.S. 317, 322 (1870) (in "varied affairs of life" there are many ways in which one may become acquainted with handwriting of another and "no good reason for excluding any of these modes" if court, on preliminary examination of witness, "can see that he has that degree of knowledge of the party's handwriting which will enable him to judge of its genuineness").

7. Throckmorton v. Holt, 180 U.S. 552, 563-564 (1901) (error to exclude testimony of son identifying signature as that of his father).

8. United States v. Dreitzler, 577 F.2d 539, 553 n.24 (9th Cir. 1978) (testimony by former secretary allowed), *cert. denied*, 440 U.S. 921.

9. United States v. Gallagher, 576 F.2d 1028, 1048 (3d Cir. 1978) (proper for vice president to identify signature of branch manager whom he supervised), *cert. denied*, 444 U.S. 1043.

10. United States v. Barker, 735 F.2d 1280, 1283-1284 (11th Cir. 1984) (bank employee's signature properly authenticated by testimony of other bank employees), *cert. denied*, 469 U.S. 933.

11. Hall v. United Ins. Co. of Am., 367 F.3d 1255, 1260-1261 (11th Cir. 2004) (lay authentication of signature based on familiarity must include detailed information on relationship of witness with person signing documents, and must describe documents on which familiarity of witness rests).

12. *Cf.* United States v. Binzel, 907 F.2d 746, 749 (7th Cir. 1990) (affidavit claiming *B*'s signature was forgery insufficient to prevent summary judgment; affiant did not show enough familiarity with *B*'s handwriting).

13. Inbau, Lay Witness Identification of Handwriting (An Experiment), 34 Ill. L. Rev. 433, 440 (1939) (concluding on basis of experiment that "[l]ay witness identifications based upon mental comparisons [of handwriting] are too unreliable to be considered acceptable as legal evidence").

14. *See* §9.7, *infra.*

> **FRE 901(b)(3)**
>
> **Comparison by trier or expert witness.** Comparison by the trier of fact or by expert witnesses with specimens which have been authenticated.

§9.7 Handwriting and Other Specimens—Expert Opinion; Comparison by Trier

Under FRE 901(b)(3), a writing may be authenticated by the testimony of a person qualified as an expert on handwriting who has compared it to an authenticated specimen or exemplar,[1] or even by allowing the trier of fact to do so.[2]

The practice of allowing the jury to make its own comparison of a disputed writing with an exemplar is long established.[3] Before the disputed writing and the exemplar can be submitted to the jury for comparison, however, the trial judge must examine them and find evidence sufficient to support a jury finding that they were written by the same person.[4] If the discrepancies are too great to support an inference of common authorship, the disputed writing is not submitted to the jury.

This method of authentication produces a valid result only if the specimen is itself accurately identified. Wherever possible a stipulation to the authenticity of the exemplars should be obtained. A request can also be made for court-ordered exemplars.[5] In absence of stipulation or court-ordered production, exemplars can be authenticated by the same methods available for any writing.[6] Often handwriting exemplars are obtained from public records, such as tax returns[7] or other writings

Specimen must be authenticated

---

§9.7 1. United States v. Tin Yat Chin, 371 F.3d 31, 38 (2d Cir. 2004) (admitting testimony by handwriting expert identifying defendant's signature).

2. United States v. Papia, 910 F.2d 1357, 1366 (7th Cir. 1990) (since documents in handwriting of defendant were admitted, jury "could compare the note at the bottom of the letter to the writing in those documents" in order to resolve authentication issue).

3. Hickory v. United States, 151 U.S. 303, 305-306 (1894). *See also* 28 U.S.C. §1731 ("admitted or proved handwriting" is admissible "for purposes of comparison, to determine genuineness of other handwriting" attributed to the writer).

4. FRE 104(b).

5. *Cf.* Gilbert v. California, 388 U.S. 263, 266 (1967) (court-compelled taking of handwriting exemplars does not violate privilege against self-incrimination).

6. United States v. Mauchlin, 670 F.2d 746, 749 (7th Cir. 1982) (can admit prison file documents as exemplars where authenticated by testimony of official familiar with defendant's handwriting). *See* §9.4, *supra.*

7. United States v. Mangan, 575 F.2d 32, 41-42 (2d Cir. 1978) (can admit defendant's tax returns as exemplars of his writing; returns were presumptively authentic under statute), *cert. denied,* 439 U.S. 931.

from official files,[8] and such documents may be authenticated on that basis.[9]

Sometimes exemplars are obtained from documents filed in the action itself, such as pleadings. It is improper to select as a handwriting exemplar a document that would inject unfair prejudice into the case when other exemplars are available.[10]

The authenticity of the exemplar, like that of the writing at issue, is ultimately a matter to be determined by the jury under FRE 104(b), and the opposing party may introduce evidence challenging the authenticity of the exemplar. Although some jurisdictions require the authenticity of the exemplar to be "proved to be genuine to the satisfaction of the court,"[11] the Advisory Committee rejected such a requirement under FRE 901(b)(2).[12]

Handwriting expertise   A witness called as a handwriting expert must satisfy the reliability requirement in the *Daubert* standard, as given voice in FRE 702, and modern scholarship has raised serious questions about the reliability and scientific basis of this field of analysis.[13] Although most courts continue to admit testimony by qualified handwriting experts,[14] it faces more serious challenge in modern litigation than it has faced in the past.[15]

FRE 901(b)(4)

Distinctive characteristics and the like. Appearance, contents, substance, internal patters, or other distinctive characteristics, taken in conjunction with circumstances.

---

8. Scharfenberger v. Wingo, 542 F.2d 328, 336-337 (6th Cir. 1976) (can take handwriting exemplars "from documents from the state's official files, which were prepared long before the litigation began").

9. *See* FRE 901(b)(7), discussed in §9.11, *infra.*

10. United States v. Turquitt, 557 F.2d 464, 468-470 (5th Cir. 1977) (improper to use as exemplar a lease application falsified by defendant where other less prejudicial specimens were available).

11. *See, e.g.,* Calif. Evid. Code 1417-1418.

12. ACN, FRE 901(b)(3) ("While explainable as a measure of prudence in the process of breaking with precedent in the handwriting situation, the reservation to the judge of the question of the genuineness of exemplars and the imposition of an unusually high standard of persuasion are at variance with the general treatment of relevancy which depends upon fulfillment of a condition of fact.")

13. *See* Risinger & Saks, Science and Nonscience in the Courts: *Daubert* Meets Handwriting Identification Expertise, 82 Iowa L. Rev. 21 (1996). *See also* discussion of *Daubert* standard in §7.7, *infra.*

14. *See, e.g.,* United States v. Crisp, 324 F.3d 261, 264 (4th Cir. 2003) (expert handwriting analysis satisfies *Daubert* standard).

15. 4 Faigman, Saks, Sanders and Cheng, Modern Scientific Evidence §33:38 (2008) (summing up areas of difficulty and uncertainty).

§9.8 Distinctive Characteristics

Under FRE 901(b)(4), a writing may be authenticated by its "[a]ppearance, contents, substance, internal patterns, or other distinctive characteristics." The characteristics must be sufficiently distinctive so that when considered in conjunction with other circumstances they support a finding of authenticity of the matter in question. This method of authentication comes closest to the principle of self-authentication recognized by FRE 902 because occasionally it allows an exhibit to be authenticated solely on the basis of its contents.[1]

> **Appearance, contents, substance**

The content of a writing may reveal knowledge that is sufficiently distinctive to support a finding that it was authored by a particular individual who had such knowledge. This method of authentication requires matching the apparent knowledge of the writer, as shown by the writing itself, and the knowledge of the person sought to be identified as the writer, as shown by other evidence.[2] Thus writings are sometimes authenticated, at least in part, by their use of code terms likely to be known only by participants in the underlying events,[3] or by other revealing contents, such as correspondence between dates in the document and other dates known only to participants in the events.[4]

Although Wigmore approved this method of authentication only when the revealed knowledge was unique to a particular individual,[5] his view seems unduly restrictive.[6] Certainly the narrower the circle of persons having such knowledge the greater its authenticating force will be. It should be sufficient for the proponent to show that of the small group of persons having such knowledge the person claimed to be the author is the one most likely to have prepared the writing in question.

---

§9.8 1. United States v. Stearns, 550 F.2d 1167, 1171 (9th Cir. 1977) (even where direct foundation testimony is lacking, "the contents of a photograph itself, together with such other circumstances or indirect evidence as bears upon the issue, may serve to explain and authenticate a photograph sufficiently to justify its admission into evidence").

2. United States v. Siddiqui, 325 F.3d 1318, 1321 (11th Cir. 2000) (in trial for submitting fraudulent recommendations for NSF award, emails from defendant were authenticated by fact that they displayed knowledge of actions only he had, apologized for conduct that only he engaged in, came from his email address, were signed with his distinctive nickname, and he referred to them in phone conversations).

3. United States v. Smith, 223 F.3d 554, 570 (7th Cir. 2000) (in drug conspiracy trial, admitting "The List" on basis of recordings of codefendants discussing "The List" and proof that it was found in files of codefendant's girlfriend, labeled as belonging to codefendant, and describing drug distribution scheme).

4. United States v. Mokol, 957 F.2d 1410, 1420 (7th Cir. 1992) (handwritten list of bribe payments properly authenticated by content where dates, initials, and amounts corresponded to payments proven by other evidence), *cert. denied*, 113 S. Ct. 284.

5. *See* 7 Wigmore, Evidence §2148, at 746 (Chadbourn rev. 1978) (only in "special circumstances," where contents "reveal a knowledge or other trait peculiarly referable to a single person," can contents alone suffice).

6. United States v. Mangan, 575 F.2d 32, 41-42 (2d Cir. 1978) (Wigmore's conclusion that contents cannot authenticate unless only author would know details is "contrary to the federal rules and unsound").

A writing cannot be authenticated as being from or connected with a particular person merely because it bears his name,[7] although identity of name is one factor in conjunction with other circumstances that may help authenticate a writing.[8] Use of unusual or distinctive nicknames is a factor often considered by courts in finding the authentication requirement to be satisfied.[9]

Reply doctrine

FRE 901(b)(4) incorporates the common law "reply doctrine," which allows a writing to be authenticated as coming from a particular person by showing that it replies to an earlier communication to that person.[10] Under this doctrine, if it is claimed that *W* wrote a particular letter, the proponent may show that an earlier communication was sent to *W* and that the content of the letter reveals it to be a reply to that earlier communication, justifying an inference that *W* was the author of the letter.[11]

Letterhead doctrine

At common law a writing generally could not be authenticated merely because it appeared on paper containing the printed or embossed letterhead of the person, business, or entity alleged to be the author.[12] The liberalized authentication provisions of FRE 901(b)(4) and FRE 902(7) suggest that a letterhead should suffice to authenticate a writing as from the indicated source, at least in absence of suspicious circumstances relating to the appearance or content of the letterhead itself or the accompanying written material, or of counterproof indicating mistake or fraud.

A writing is more likely to be admitted on the basis of its letterhead in cases where the letterhead is shown not to be generally available to persons other than the purported sender or his agents and where the form, content, and delivery of the writing itself correspond with the usual practices of the purported sender. Modern cases have

7. United States v. Skipper, 74 F.3d 608, 612 (5th Cir. 1996) (similarity in name between criminal defendant and person named in prior conviction does not satisfy FRE 901's authentication requirement).

8. United States v. Gutierrez, 576 F.2d 269, 275-276 (10th Cir. 1978) (fact that check was purchased by Henry A. Gutierrez, which was also defendant's name, "would not be sufficient in itself" to authenticate check, but was "a factor" to be considered in conjunction with others), *cert. denied*, 439 U.S. 954.

9. United States v. Durham, 868 F.2d 1010, 1012 (8th Cir. 1989) (letter authenticated in part by fact that it was signed "Ricky," which was defendant's first name), *cert. denied*, 493 U.S. 954; United States v. Bagaric, 706 F.2d 42, 67 (2d Cir. 1983) (letter authenticated in part by fact that it bore a signature using the alias that *B* "had used in gaining entry into the United States" and reference to one "Crni," which "the proof showed was [alleged co-offender] Ljubas's sobriquet among his confederates"), *cert. denied*, 464 U.S. 917.

10. ACN to FRE 901(b)(4) (letter may be authenticated by "content and circumstances indicating it was in reply to a duly authenticated one").

11. United States v. Weinstein, 762 F.2d 1522, 1533 (11th Cir. 1985) (telexes authenticated under principle that "letters and presumably telegrams are prima facie authentic if their content is responsive to prior properly admitted communications"), *cert. denied*, 475 U.S. 1110.

12. *See* Strong, Liberalizing the Authentication of Private Writings, 52 Cornell L.Q. 284, 296 (1967) (criticizing common law rule and suggesting that unlikelihood of fraud might support recognition of "letterhead doctrine").

admitted writings based on their letterhead in combination with other circumstances,[13] and occasionally even on the basis of the letterhead alone.[14]

A writing may also be authenticated by its internal patterns, such as peculiarities in spelling or misspelling,[15] use of jargon, slang, or vulgarity,[16] punctuation,[17] abbreviation, syntax, or paragraph structure.[18]

Internal patterns

The developing field of psycholinguistics attempts to identify written or spoken expressions on the basis of distinctive word patterns.[19] Use of an expert in psycholinguistics to aid in authentication is compatible with the Rule, provided sufficient expertise is demonstrated under FRE 702. Where such evidence is unduly complex and time-consuming, exclusion may be warranted under FRE 403.[20]

FRE 901(b)(4) contemplates that the distinctive characteristics of a writing be considered in conjunction with other circumstances to determine whether they are sufficiently authenticating. The range of potentially authenticating circumstances is virtually unlimited.[21] One circumstance frequently relied on is that the writing was found in the

Other circumstances

13. United States v. Hoag, 823 F.2d 1123, 1127 (7th Cir. 1987) (letters authenticated in part by fact that all "were written on the Hoag company letterhead"); United States v. Gordon, 634 F.2d 639, 643-644 (1st Cir. 1980) (approving documents on basis of evidence that "on their face" all of them "purported to come from J. John Gordon, the President and Senior Counsel of the International Bank of Commerce, with a residential address at 8 Creswell Road, Worcester, and a telephone numbered 617-754-5000," where address and phone number matched those of defendant).

14. Denison v. Swaco Geolograph Co., 941 F.2d 1416, 1423 (10th Cir. 1991) (document provided during discovery on defendant's company stationery bearing its letterhead had sufficient circumstantial evidence of authenticity).

15. United States v. Larson, 596 F.2d 759, 765 n.5 (8th Cir. 1979) (admitting evidence that defendant misspelled "approach" as "approach" three times in ransom note and "previously did the same in a letter to the Pardon Board"); United States v. Pheaster, 544 F.2d 353, 371-372 (9th Cir. 1976) (manner of spelling is no less an "identifying characteristic" than "the manner of crossing a 't' or looping an 'o' "), *cert. denied*, 429 U.S. 1099.

16. *See generally* Comment, Stylistics Evidence in the Trial of Patricia Hearst, 1977 Ariz. St. L.J. 387, 393-397.

17. Thorndike, The Psychology of Punctuation, 61 Am. J. Psychology 222, 226-227 (1948).

18. United States v. Clifford, 704 F.2d 86, 91 (3d Cir. 1983) (error to exclude letters offered to show stylistic similarities in spelling, abbreviation, syntax, and paragraph structure).

19. *See* Arens & Meadow, Psycholinguistics and the Confession Dilemma, 56 Colum. L. Rev. 19 (1956).

20. *See* United States v. Hearst, 563 F.2d 1331, 1349-1350 (9th Cir. 1977) (excluding testimony by psycholinguistics expert, offered by defense in trial of kidnapped heiress Patty Hearst to prove that she "did not author" statements that she recorded, to avoid delay), *cert. denied*, 435 U.S. 1000.

21. *See, e.g.*, United States v. Paulino, 13 F.3d 20, 23 (1st Cir. 1994) (in drug trial, admitting rent receipt found in apartment, partly because defendant had access, partly because content furnished indicia of authenticity, partly because defendant's name was on it).

possession of the alleged author.[22] In rare cases possession alone may be sufficient to authenticate a writing.[23]

Circumstances surrounding the sending of a communication, such as the date, place, or manner of sending, may also help authenticate it.[24] A writing also can be authenticated under FRE 406 by showing a habit or routine practice of the purported author in preparing writings of this type.[25]

FRE 901(b)(5)

Voice identification. Identification of a voice, whether heard firsthand or through mechanical or electronic transmission or recording, by opinion based upon hearing the voice at any time under circumstances connecting it with the alleged speaker.

---

§9.9   Voice Identification

Perhaps the most common means of authenticating voice communications is by identification of the speaker under FRE 901(b)(5).[1] The witness identifying the voice must have personal knowledge, which may be acquired by hearing the voice at any time either before[2] or after[3] the time in question.[4] Courts have been generous, perhaps overly so, in finding that even casual familiarity supports voice identification

---

22. United States v. Black, 767 F.2d 1334, 1342 (9th Cir. 1985) (in mail fraud trial, fact that documents were in defendant's possession was "strongest support" for claim that government showed adequate connection to satisfy authentication requirement), *cert. denied*, 474 U.S. 1022.

23. Burgess v. Premier Corp., 727 F.2d 826, 835-836 (9th Cir. 1984) (documents authenticated by fact they were found in defendant's warehouse).

24. United States v. Bagaric, 706 F.2d 42, 67 (2d Cir. 1983) (letter authenticated in part by fact that it was addressed to *L* and postmarked Asuncion, Paraguay, where *B* resided), *cert. denied*, 464 U.S. 840; United States v. Gordon, 634 F.2d 639, 643 (1st Cir. 1980) (admitting against defendant documents purporting to come from someone with his name, address, and phone number, having been mailed from states where defendant was, and generating responses with checks which his wife deposited in his account).

25. *See* §§4.21-4.22, *supra*.

§9.9   1. *See, e.g.,* United States v. Orozco-Santillan, 903 F.2d 1262, 1266 (9th Cir. 1990) (phone call authenticated by voice recognition and other factors). On identification of voices of recorded phone conversations, *see* §9.13, *infra*.

2. United States v. Watson, 594 F.2d 1330, 1335 (10th Cir. 1979) (three prior meetings), *cert. denied*, 444 U.S. 840.

3. United States v. Axselle, 604 F.2d 1330, 1338 (10th Cir. 1979) (hearing defendant's voice once during call in question and once 30 days later at hearing was enough to allow voice identification to go to jury). *See also* ACN, FRE 901(b)(5) ("requisite familiarity may be acquired either before or after the particular speaking which is the subject of the identification").

4. United States v. Marin-Cifuentes, 866 F.2d 988, 995 (8th Cir. 1989) (anyone may "identify a speaker's voice if he has heard the voice at any time").

testimony,[5] and it has been permitted where the witness heard the voice on only a few prior occasions[6] or even one other time.[7] But courts may exclude such evidence where the basis of knowledge is so fleeting or remote in time that it cannot reasonably support the identification being made. Voice identification is permitted where the witness relies on voice exemplars[8] or on hearing the voice in question over the phone rather than face-to-face.[9]

Courts are divided about the admissibility of voice identifications made by experts relying on voiceprints or spectrographic analysis, with some admitting such evidence[10] and others disallowing it.[11] Whether to order spectrographic analysis of a party's voice is within the discretion of the trial judge.[12]

Voiceprints

Voice communications can also be authenticated under FRE 901(b)(4) based on their content, such as use of code terms or distinctive names,[13] or by showing that the communication was in response to a communication made to the person in question at an earlier time. Incoming telephone calls can also be authenticated by other types of circumstantial evidence,[14] such as records of the telephone company, as well as by the later admission of a party that he was the person speaking.

Other methods

---

5. United States v. Magna, 118 F.3d 1173, 1207 (7th Cir. 1997) (witness had enough foundation to identify voice on tape based on one encounter with the subject, even though he was drinking at time of prior encounter and speaking Spanish, while voice on tape spoke English; weight is for jury to decide).

6. United States v. DiMuro, 540 F.2d 503, 514 (1st Cir. 1976) (two prior conversations), *cert. denied*, 429 U.S. 1038.

7. United States v. Mansoori, 304 F.3d 635, 665 (7th Cir. 2002) (even though agent "only had one opportunity" to hear defendants speak, that sufficed for voice identification).

8. United States v. Cambindo Valencia, 609 F.2d 603, 640 (2d Cir. 1979) (interpreter could authenticate tapes of defendant's voice by relying on voice exemplars), *cert. denied*, 446 U.S. 940.

9. United States v. Armedo-Sarmiento, 545 F.2d 785, 792 (2d Cir. 1976) ("voice identification may be adequate although the witness and the speaker have never personally met"), *cert. denied*, 430 U.S. 917.

10. United States v. Smith, 869 F.2d 348, 351 (7th Cir. 1989) (expert testimony on spectrographic voice identification admissible on proper foundation). *See generally* Gregory, Voice Spectrography Evidence: Approaches to Admissibility, 20 U. Rich. L. Rev. 357 (1986); Note, Voice Spectrography—Reliability of Voice-Prints Not Established, Therefore Inadmissible, 18 Seton Hall L. Rev. 405 (1988).

11. People v. Jeter, 600 N.E.2d 214 (N.Y. 1992) (voice spectrography is not "generally accepted as reliable based on the case law and existing literature").

12. United States v. Goldstein, 532 F.2d 1305 (9th Cir. 1976) (refusing to order spectrographic analysis; government witness had adequate basis to identify voices on recordings), *cert. denied*, 429 U.S. 960.

13. United States v. Ingraham, 832 F.2d 229, 232-236 (1st Cir. 1987) (phone call authenticated by contents, including using name "MacKeil," shown to be defendant's name at birth), *cert. denied*, 486 U.S. 1009.

14. *See* United States v. Miller, 771 F.2d 1219, 1234 (9th Cir. 1985) (*C* could describe phone call from *B* that was authenticated not merely by self-identification, but by fact that *C* received second call from *L* ten minutes later, during which *L* made reference to *B*'s earlier call).

There is no special provision in the Rules for authentication of incoming telephone calls, although there is one for outgoing calls.[15] An incoming telephone call cannot be authenticated merely on the basis of self-identification by the caller because of the dangers of fabrication and impersonation.[16] The issue of authenticating tape recordings is discussed in a later section.[17]

FRE 901(b)(6)

Telephone conversations. Telephone conversations by evidence that a call was made to the number assigned at the time by the telephone company to a particular person or business, if (A) in the case of a person, circumstances, including self-identification, show the person answering to be the one called, or (B) in the case of a business, the call was made to a place of business and the transaction related to business reasonably transacted over the telephone.

---

§9.10 Outgoing Telephone Calls

In addition to the methods of authentication available for incoming telephone calls, such as voice identification and identification based on contents,[1] FRE 901(b)(6) allows authentication of outgoing telephone calls by a more specific procedure. A call to a person is sufficiently authenticated by a showing that the call was made to the person at the number assigned by the telephone company, and that the person answering identified himself as the person called or by circumstances other than self-authentication that reveal the person to be the one called.[2] A call to a business is sufficiently authenticated by a showing that the call was placed using the number assigned to the business and the conversation related to business that would be reasonably transacted over the telephone.[3]

15. *See* FRE 901(b)(6), discussed in §9.10, *infra*.
16. United States v. Miller, 771 F.2d 1219, 1234 (9th Cir. 1985) (self-identification by caller "does not provide sufficient evidence of identity").
17. *See* §9.13, *infra*.
§9.10 1. *See* §§9.8, 9.9, *supra*.
2. United States v. Smith, 692 F.2d 693, 698 (10th Cir. 1982) (admitting phone conversations in part on basis of testimony by agent that "the number he dialed had been shown by background investigation" to be the residence where defendant lived). *Cf.* First State Bank of Denton v. Maryland Cas. Co., 918 F.2d 38, 40 (5th Cir. 1990) (as proof that JT Mills was not home, admitting proof that dispatcher called number assigned to his residence, asked whether she had reached that residence, received reply that "this is the Millses' residence," and on asking for Mr. Mills was told that "JT Mills is not at home").
3. United States v. Portsmouth Paving Corp., 694 F.2d 312, 322 (4th Cir. 1982) (testimony by R that he called Mr. Saunders' office could authenticate phone call because "one would usually and properly assume upon the dialing of a business office phone number that the person who answers is employed by and has the authority to speak for the business").

In laying the foundation, the calling party should be able to say he dialed the number listed in the telephone directory (a hearsay source that qualifies under FRE 803(17)), or the number given to him by the operator (again a hearsay source, but likely admissible under FRE 807). If the outgoing call is to a number other than the recipient's home or place of business, courts generally require more than self-identification by the answering party to authenticate the conversation as being with that party.[4]

> **FRE 901(b)(7)**
>
> **Public records or reports.** Evidence that a writing authorized by law to be recorded or filed and in fact recorded or filed in a public office, or a purported public record, report, statement, or data compilation, in any form, is from the public office where items of this nature are kept.

§9.11 Public Records or Reports

FRE 901(b)(7) allows certain public documents to be authenticated by showing that they are from the public office where items of that nature are normally kept. This Rule covers two types of documents. The first is writings authorized by law to be recorded or filed, which are in fact recorded or filed in a public office. The second is a purported public record, report, statement, or data compilation in any form. The first category includes documents such as recorded deeds, contracts, security interests, or filed tax returns. The second includes licensing records, property tax assessments, weather bureau records, police reports, court orders or judgments, and similar documents.

The proponent must show only that the document fits one of the two categories and is from the public office where it would normally be kept. It is not necessary to call the custodian or a person from the office, and any person with knowledge can be the authenticating witness. A public writing can also be self-authenticated if it meets the requirements of FRE 902(1), (2), or (3), and a copy of a public writing, if properly certified, is self-authenticating under FRE 902(4).[1]

---

4. United States v. Kingston, 971 F.2d 481, 485 (10th Cir. 1992) (loan default counselor called company owned by defendant and left message; return call indicated that defendant could be reached at a certain number; calling that number produced someone who said he was defendant and was familiar with the property; government properly showed call was placed to defendant).

§9.11 1. *See also* FRCP 44 and FRCrimP 27 (providing alternative ways to authenticate public records).

From any branch of government

The record may be from a "public office" in any of the three branches of government, whether executive, legislative, or judicial,[2] and at any level of government, whether federal, state, or municipal.[3] The Rule also reaches public records of foreign government offices.[4]

If the public document or record is offered for the truth of the matter asserted, proper authentication under FRE 901(b)(7) does not by itself overcome a hearsay objection. However, the document may be admissible under various exceptions to the hearsay rule.[5]

FRE 901(b)(8)

Ancient documents or data compilations. Evidence that a document or data compilation, in any form, (A) is in such condition as to create no suspicion concerning its authenticity, (B) was in a place where it, if authentic, would likely be, and (C) has been in existence 20 years or more at the time it is offered.

---

§9.12   Ancient Documents

Under FRE 901(b)(8), a document or data compilation may be authenticated by evidence that it is at least 20 years old when offered, that it is unsuspicious in appearance, and that it was found in a place where one would expect it to be if authentic. This Rule continues common law practice but reduces the requisite time span from 30 to 20 years.

There is no requirement that the ancient document be a public document or record. The Rule also embraces private writings such as deeds and contracts, personal correspondence, memoranda, newspapers, diaries, and reports,[1] and applies to foreign as well as domestic documents.[2] The Rule expressly reaches computer output and should be interpreted as applying also to recordings.[3]

---

2. *See, e.g.*, United States v. Goichman, 547 F.2d 778, 782-784 (3d Cir. 1976) (documents from state court files entitled "History of Children's Assets" properly authenticated by showing where obtained).

3. *See, e.g.*, United States v. Wilson, 690 F.2d 1267, 1275-1276 (9th Cir. 1982) (receipt for federal prisoner "signed by the director of the West Glenn Center" and "identified by her at trial"), *cert. denied*, 464 U.S. 867.

4. United States v. Chu Kong Yin, 935 F.2d 990, 995 (9th Cir. 1991) (Hong Kong documents authenticated by showing that they were from foreign public office "where items of this nature are kept").

5. *See, e.g.*, FRE 803(8) (exception for officially prepared records and reports but not necessarily writings filed with a public office); FRE 803(9) (records of vital statistics); FRE 803(14) (records of documents affecting an interest in property).

§9.12   1. *See, e.g.*, George v. Celotex Corp., 914 F.2d 26, 30-31 (2d Cir. 1990) (report prepared in 1947 by head engineer in Industrial Hygiene Foundation for Asbestos Textile Institute).

2. United States v. Firishchak, 468 F.3d 1015, 1021-1022 (6th Cir. 2006) (Ukrainian police documents can be proved by their age, appearance and content).

3. The failure to include recordings appears to be an oversight.

The age of the writing may be proved by various methods, including testimony by attesting witnesses or other witnesses with knowledge, as well as by expert testimony, examination of contents, physical appearance, or by analysis of surrounding circumstances indicating execution at a certain date. The date on the face of the writing generally does not alone suffice to qualify the writing as an ancient document.

The Rule requires that the document be free from suspicion, which means that the authenticity of the document is reasonably assured, but not that its contents are necessarily accurate.[4] It should normally be located in the place where it probably would have been kept,[5] be free from deletions, erasures, or discontinuity of writing, and be in apparently proper form. There is no requirement, however, that possession in the case of a title document have been consistent with the document.[6]

Free from suspicion

A document authenticated under this Rule may be admitted to prove the truth of its contents under FRE 803(16), which creates a hearsay exception for "statements in a document in existence twenty years or more the authenticity of which is established."

FRE 901(b)(9)

Process or system. Evidence describing a process or system used to produce a result and showing that the process or system produces an accurate result.

---

§9.13 Process or System—Tape Recordings

Tape recordings are authenticated most commonly under FRE 901(b)(9) by showing the "process" by which the recording was made and that it produced an "accurate result." It is generally sufficient to establish the identities of the speakers and to show that the device was capable of making a true recording and was in good working order, the operator was qualified to operate it and did so properly, no changes were made in the recording (no additions or deletions), and the tape was properly preserved.

Many courts cite the elaborate and overly cautious seven-step foundation set forth in the *McKeever* district court decision in New York[1] and

Foundation required

---

4. United States v. Mandycz, 447 F.3d 951, 966 (6th Cir. 2006) (Soviet interrogation records; FRE 901(b)(8) requires that document be "free of suspicion," which goes to authenticity, not trustworthiness).

5. Chemetall GMBH v. ZR Energy, Inc., 320 F.3d 714, 722-723 (7th Cir. 2003) (excluding documents; court could conclude that they "were not where one would expect to find" authentic copies).

6. *See* ACN, FRE 901(b)(8).

§9.13 1. United States v. McKeever, 169 F. Supp. 426, 430 (S.D.N.Y. 1958) (must show that (1) recording device was capable of taking conversation, (2) operator of device was competent, (3) recording is authentic and correct, (4) no changes, additions

adopted by the Eighth Circuit in the *McMillan* case,[2] but most courts refuse to be bound by this formulation[3] and have developed simpler and more flexible approaches toward authentication of tape recordings.[4]

Alternate foundation

As an alternate foundation, a participant in the conversation, if available, can authenticate the recording by testifying that it fully, fairly, and accurately reflects the conversation.[5] This authentication method fits FRE 901(b)(1), because it involves testimony by a witness with knowledge that "a matter is what it is claimed to be." Sometimes both methods are used in combination to support and reinforce each other.[6]

Under either foundation, an authenticating witness normally must identify the speakers.[7] In some cases, the jury may be allowed to hear the tape and decide for itself whether a particular speaker is the person claimed,[8] although the tape is normally submitted to the jury only after the judge has listened to it and found evidence sufficient to support a jury finding on the point.[9] In some cases, courts have allowed identification of the speakers on the basis of self-identification combined with

---

or deletions were made, (5) recording was preserved in manner shown to court, (6) speakers are identified, and (7) conversation was voluntary and in good faith, without inducement).

2. United States v. McMillan, 508 F.2d 101, 104-105 (8th Cir. 1974), *cert. denied*, 421 U.S. 916.

3. *See, e.g.*, United States v. Lance, 853 F.2d 1177, 1181 (5th Cir. 1988) ("rigid test" in *McMillan* has been "expressly rejected" in this circuit).

4. *See, e.g.*, United States v. Hamilton, 334 F.3d 170 (2d Cir. 2003) (declining to adopt *McKeever* test; recording may be admitted if authenticated by evidence sufficient to support finding that it is what proponent claims); United States v. Green, 324 F.3d 375, 379 (5th Cir. 2003) (to authenticate intercepted wire communications, government must show operator's competency, fidelity of recording equipment, absence of material alterations, and identification of relevant sounds or voices; lesser showing suffices if, on independent examination, court thinks recording "accurately reproduces the auditory experience").

5. United States v. Westmoreland, 312 F.3d 302, 311 (7th Cir. 2002) (despite pretrial death of recorder's operator, agent authenticated tapes by testifying that he was there, tapes of phone calls were made, listened to conversation on headphones, and that tapes were accurate); United States v. Tropeano, 252 F.3d 653 (2d. Cir. 2001) (government need not show chain of custody for audio tapes where participants in the conversation testified that audio tapes were fair and accurate portrayal of conversations).

6. United States v. Biggins, 551 F.2d 64, 66-67 (5th Cir. 1977) (where traditional foundation for tape recording was challenged, court finds adequate authentication because tape "portrayed that conversation precisely as [witnesses] described it").

7. United States v. DeLeon, 247 F.3d 593 (5th Cir. 2001) (government agent authenticated audio tape by testifying to identity of participants in conversation, explaining how recording was made, and vouching for its accuracy).

8. United States v. Sliker, 751 F.2d 477, 500 (2d Cir. 1984) (can let trier of fact compare voice on recording with that of defendant who has testified), *cert. denied*, 471 U.S. 1137.

9. United States v. Sliker, 751 F.2d 477, 497-500 (2d Cir. 1984) (admitting tape where government claimed voice was that of witness, and judge "listened to the tape and determined, based on his own comparison of the voices," that there was "sufficient evidence" that voice was accurately identified; jury made ultimate determination of authenticity), *cert. denied*, 471 U.S. 1137.

other circumstances[10] and sometimes wholly on the basis of circumstantial evidence.[11] A composite tape can be introduced as a summary provided that it is shown to be an accurate and representative condensation of the originals.[12]

The fact that portions of a tape are inaudible or unintelligible does **Inaudibility** not require its rejection, provided such technical difficulties do not make it misleading or untrustworthy.[13] Allegations of tampering generally go to weight rather than admissibility,[14] although if fabrication or material alteration are clearly established the tape should be excluded.

Often transcripts of tape recordings are prepared and distributed to **Transcripts** jurors to aid their understanding when listening to the recording in court.[15] In absence of a stipulation, the accuracy of the transcripts is ultimately an issue for the jury under FRE 901(a) and FRE 104(b).[16] The issues surrounding the use of such transcripts are discussed in a later section.[17]

§9.14 —Photographs, Videotapes, X-rays

Although photographs are most commonly authenticated under FRE 901(b)(1) by testimony of a witness with knowledge,[1] they can also be

---

10. Rush v. Illinois Cent. R.R. Co., 399 F.3d 705, 722 (6th Cir. 2005) (recordings of interviews with railroad accident witnesses, made by railroad risk manager, were authenticated where speakers identified themselves and risk manager testified about time and manner of recording).

11. United States v. Cook, 794 F.2d 561, 567 (10th Cir. 1986) (tape recordings may be authenticated by "circumstantial evidence such as name references during the conversation and pen register records of the numbers called"), *cert. denied*, 479 U.S. 889.

12. United States v. Scarborough, 43 F.3d 1021, 1025 (6th Cir. 1994) (decision to admit composite tape is within sound discretion of trial court, at least where defendant allowed to introduce other portions he deems relevant). *See generally* §10.16, *infra*.

13. United States v. Dawson, 425 F.3d 389, 393 (7th Cir. 2005) (gaps in recorded conversations involving defendant and informants did not make them inadmissible; defendants did not deny that it was their voices, and there was no indication of splicing or other alterations that might change meaning; only complaint was that gaps or erasures might contain exculpatory material, but there was no indication that they did); United States v. Ray, 250 F.3d 596 (8th Cir. 2001) (gaps in audio recording not substantial enough to render entire recording untrustworthy).

14. Smith v. City of Chicago, 242 F.3d 737 (7th Cir. 2001) (conclusory allegations based on mere suspicions insufficient to rebut authentication of audio tapes; authenticity a matter for jury).

15. *But see* United States v. Thompson, 482 F.3d 781, 789 (5th Cir. 2007) (court should not have let jury see videotape of drug transaction, while supplied with transcript of what was said but without audio portion to compare it to).

16. United States v. Gonzalez, 365 F.3d 656, 659-661 (8th Cir. 2004) (parties should try for stipulated transcript; failing that, each should produce its own, and supporting evidence, and should challenge competing version; jury to decide which is accurate).

17. *See* §10.9, *infra*.

§9.14 1. United States v. Goldin, 311 F.3d 191, 197 (3d Cir. 2002) (in trial for offenses during demonstration at Liberty Bell Pavilion, admitting 15-minute edited videotape on testimony by camera operator, and rejecting claim that person who edited

authenticated under FRE 901(b)(9) by showing the process by which they were made. Use of the latter provision is generally required for photographs offered under the "silent witness" doctrine,[2] such as photographs taken by bank surveillance cameras and automatic teller machines[3] where there is no authenticating witness available who saw the scene depicted, or where the witness to the event lacks sufficient memory to authenticate the photograph, as is commonly the case with photographs taken of check cashing transactions.[4] The "silent witness" doctrine is also used in other cases where a camera captures a defendant in the act of committing a crime,[5] sometimes photographed by the defendant himself,[6] or engaging in other activity relevant to the matters at issue.[7]

Required foundation   Although courts do not always agree how photographs should be authenticated under the "silent witness" doctrine,[8] usually the appropriate method is to show the "process" by which the photograph was taken (and of course the time and place) and that it produces an "accurate result."[9] Sometimes courts admit expert testimony by photo analysts (or people who know the person thought to be pictured) to the effect that the person shown in the photograph is indeed that person.[10]

---

tape should authenticate it; FRE 901(b)(1) requires testimony by person with knowledge; camera operator fit this description). For a discussion of admitting photographs under FRE 901(b)(1), *see* §9.4, *supra.*

2. For an engrossing account of the history of photographic evidence, *see* Mnookin, The Image of Truth: Photographic Evidence and the Power of Analogy, 10 Yale J. Law & Hum. 1 (1998).

3. United States v. Rembert, 683 F.2d 1023 (D.C. App. 1988) (photograph taken by automatic teller machine); United States v. Taylor, 530 F.2d 639 (5th Cir. 1976) (bank surveillance camera).

4. *See, e.g.,* United States v. Gray, 531 F.2d 933 (8th Cir. 1976); Sisk v. State, 236 Md. 589, 204 A.2d 684 (1964).

5. Fisher v. State, 643 S.W.2d 571, 574-575 (Ark. App. 1982) (videotape of theft from grocery store); State v. Johnson, 197 S.E.2d 592 (N.C. App. 1973) (videotape of defendant committing larceny).

6. *See, e.g.,* Torres v. State, 442 N.E.2d 1021, 1024 (Ind. 1982) (photographs of defendant sexually molesting child).

7. Barham v. Nowell, 138 So. 2d 493, 496 (Miss. 1962) (defense movie of allegedly physically impaired plaintiff engaging in a variety of activities; film held admissible on issue of damages).

8. *See* United States v. Rembert, 863 F.2d 1023, 1027-1028 (D.C. App. 1988) (photograph of person using kidnap victim's bank card, taken by automatic teller machine, was authenticated by circumstantial evidence, including testimony describing "the loading of the cameras and the security of the film," which sufficed, when combined with "internal indicia of date, place and event depicted in the evidence itself").

9. *See, e.g.,* United States v. Taylor, 530 F.2d 639, 641-642 (5th Cir. 1976) (bank surveillance photographs authenticated by testimony of witnesses "who were not present during the actual robbery" but who testified "as to the manner in which the film was installed in the camera, how the camera was activated, the fact that the film was removed immediately after the robbery, the chain of its possession, and the fact that it was properly developed and contact prints made from it"), *cert. denied,* 429 U.S. 845.

10. *See* discussion of FRE 701 in §§7.2-7.4, *supra.*

In the past, courts sometimes required a more elaborate foundation for videotapes and motion pictures than for photographs.[11] Such a foundation involved showing that the equipment was adequate and in good working order, the operator was qualified and followed proper procedures, the film was developed properly (in the case of motion pictures) and properly preserved, there was no tampering or alteration or editing, and the end product accurately represents what it depicts.[12] Today the trend is toward accepting the simpler foundation allowed for photographs, which is testimony by a witness with knowledge that the videotape or motion picture accurately represents the scene or activity depicted.[13]

The fact that a videotape or motion picture is partially garbled does not make it inadmissible unless it is so unintelligible as to be misleading or untrustworthy.[14] If a videotape or motion picture is objectionable in part, the offending portion can be excluded and the remainder admitted.[15] If the film or videotape has been edited, courts sometime require that the proponent make available the deleted excerpts or outtakes, so the opponent can determine whether the exhibit is a fair and representative portrayal.[16]

Photographic evidence is visually powerful and is subject to exclusion where it is unnecessarily gruesome, inflammatory, or otherwise unfairly prejudicial.[17] It is also excludable where it contains or reveals other inadmissible evidence.[18] With modern technology, it has become easier to manipulate, distort, and fabricate all forms of photographic imagery. Enlargements, filtered lenses, cropping, varied focal length, and changed lighting conditions provide opportunities for manipulation that may be detectable, if at all, only by a sophisticated viewer. For this reason, courts need to exercise caution in admitting such evidence, and in cases of doubt to demand a stricter foundation for photographic

Videotapes, motion pictures

Dangers of photographic evidence

---

11. *See* Hughes & Cantor, Photographs in Civil Litigation ch. VIII, 2 (1973); Annot., Admissibility of Visual Recordings, 41 A.L.R.4th 812; Annot., Admissibility of Videotape Evidence in Criminal Trials, 60 A.L.R.3d 33.

12. *See generally* Ward, Use of Videotape in the Courtroom, 20 De Paul L. Rev. 924 (1971).

13. *See, e.g.,* Louis Vuitton S.A. v. Spencer Handbags Corp., 765 F.2d 966, 973-974 (2d Cir. 1985) (videotape authenticated by testimony that tape "accurately depicted the events in the hotel room").

14. United States v. Nixon, 777 F.2d 958 (5th Cir. 1985).

15. Anderson v. United States, 788 F.2d 517, 520 (8th Cir. 1986) (videotape inadmissible because defendant refused to edit tape to remove expletives; transcript allowed instead).

16. Cisarik v. Palos Community Hosp., 549 N.E.2d 840, 842 (Ill. App. 1989) (film showing "day-in-the-life" of brain-damaged child to be preserved; defendants could view entire film pretrial and use parts of film as their own evidence), *aff'd*, 579 N.E.2d 873 (Ill. 1991).

17. *See, e.g.,* United States v. Hitt, 981 F.2d 422, 424 (9th Cir. 1992) (in prosecution for possession of unregistered machine gun, error to admit photograph of defendant with numerous other "nasty-looking" weapons in background; photo was highly prejudicial and misleading). *See also* §4.10, *supra*.

18. United States v. Torres-Flores, 827 F.2d 1031, 1035-1040 (5th Cir. 1987) (impermissible to introduce photographs of defendant containing police or prison identification numbers; error found here because mug photos suggested prior arrest even though markings were covered by tape).

evidence[19] and sometimes to give the jury cautionary instructions.[20] The authentication requirement nonetheless remains an important safeguard, because a witness who seeks to authenticate an altered photograph through false testimony can do so only at the risk of a perjury prosecution.

X-Rays

The required foundation to authenticate X-rays usually differs from that used for photographs and videotapes because the operator taking the X-ray does not see the matter depicted on the negative and cannot independently confirm its accuracy.[21] For this reason, in absence of a stipulation, X-rays are normally authenticated under FRE 901(b)(9) by showing the "process or system used to produce a result" and that it produces "an accurate result." The acceptance and reliability of the scientific principles underlying X-ray technology can be judicially noticed,[22] but the proponent must still establish that the equipment was correctly operated by a qualified person and identify the X-rays.

The necessary foundation for admission of X-rays is satisfied by a showing of (1) the capability and acceptability of the equipment used, (2) the qualifications of the operator, (3) proper procedures used in operation of the equipment, (4) the time the X-ray was taken, (5) proper development procedures, (6) accuracy and clarity of X-rays, (7) care and custody of negative prior to trial, and (8) identification of the exhibit as the X-ray in question.[23] Often an even more abbreviated foundation is acceptable,[24] and it is not essential that the foundation be established by the technician who took the films.[25]

19. *See* Comment, Truth, Lies and Videotape: Are Current Federal Rules of Evidence Adequate?, 21 Sw. U. L. Rev. 1199 (1992) (discussing dangers of editorial manipulation; proposing "substantially identical" standard for demonstrative videotapes and allowing opponent to pre-screen them and view outtakes); Note, A Picture Is Worth a Thousand Lies: Electronic Imaging and the Future of the Admissibility of Photographs into Evidence, 18 Rutgers Computer & Tech. L.J. 365 (1992) (urging more stringent foundation for photographic evidence).

20. Note, Seeing Can Be Deceiving: Photographic Evidence in a Visual Age—How Much Weight Does It Deserve?, 25 Wm. & Mary L. Rev. 705 (1984) (proposing cautionary instructions).

21. State v. Johnson, 18 N.C. App. 606, 197 S.E.2d 592, 594 (1973) (noting that in case of X-rays, "[t]he eyes of the physician witness did not penetrate the flesh of the patient to see the bones within").

22. ACN, FRE 901(b)(9) (Rule does not "foreclose taking judicial notice of the accuracy of the process or system").

23. *See generally* 3 Scott, Photographic Evidence §1263 (1969); Imwinkelried, Evidentiary Foundations 103 (4th ed. 1998); Hughes & Cantor, Photographs in Civil Litigation, ch. X, §2 at 233 (1973); Siemer, Tangible Evidence: How to Use Exhibits at Trial §5.2 (1984); 38 Am. Jur. P.O.F. 168; 11 Am. Jur. P.O.F. 741.

24. Williams v. Alabama, 451 So. 2d 411, 418 (Ala. 1984) (X-rays were authenticated by radiologist supervisor of hospital who testified that (1) he was custodian of X-ray records, (2) records of victim were under his control, (3) he could identify records, (4) X-rays were taken and preserved in course of business, and (5) X-rays were continuously under his custody); State v. Pulphus, 465 A.2d 153, 161 (R.I. 1983) (an X-ray film "is sufficiently authenticated for admission if there is evidence showing that it was taken by a properly qualified expert, that is, one who is familiar with X-ray techniques and procedures, and that the film is a true representation of what it purports to represent").

25. King v. Williams, 279 S.E.2d 618, 276 S.C. 478 (1981) (X-rays marked with patient's name, the date taken, and the hospital were admitted after chain of custody was established even though technician was unavailable to testify).

§9.15   —Emails, Web Pages

Email is normally introduced by offering written printouts from a computer. The evidentiary hurdles are minimal with respect to authenticating the printout as an accurate copy of the email. A witness who has seen the email in question need only testify that the printout offered as an exhibit is an accurate reproduction.[1] The proponent could also rely on FRE 901(b)(9) to authenticate the process by which a computer sends data to a printer, which prints out emails and establish that this process "produces an accurate result." A court may even take judicial notice of this process. There is no Best Evidence problem with respect to such printouts, because FRE 1001(3) defines "original" to include "any printout or other output readable by sight, shown to reflect the data accurately."

Authenticating the email itself can also be simple depending on the purpose for which the email is offered. A witness can authenticate an email as one sent by that witness merely by identifying it as such.[2] Similarly, a witness can authenticate an email as one received by that witness by so testifying.[3] Such testimony satisfies FRE 901(b)(1) because it is testimony by a witness with knowledge "that the matter in question is what its proponent claims."

The harder task is to establish the authorship of emails where the purported author is unavailable, unable, or unwilling to identify it as one that he sent.[4] Here the proponent must rely on other methods. Certainly testimony by someone who saw the real author write and send the email communication could suffice. If the a particular person owns the computer from which the email was sent, or if the machine was seized from him, such facts may suffice to authenticate the email as coming from him, and there are other circumstances that might convincingly link the computer to that person.

In criminal cases, where establishing defendant's authorship of an email is critical, and where a jury may have to be persuaded of this point beyond a reasonable doubt in order to convict, prosecutors sometimes call technical witnesses who can trace the email in question. Such a witness may rely on the coded Internet Protocol Address appearing in the email header and trace it back to the internet service provider

---

§9.15   1. United States v. Simpson, 152 F.3d 1241,1249-1250 (10th Cir. 1998) (admitting printout of chat room discussion between defendant and undercover officer based on evidence it was what proponent claimed).

2. Fenje v. Feld, 301 F. Supp. 2d 781, 809 (N.D. Ill. 2003) (can authenticate emails by "statements or other communications from the purported author acknowledging" them), *aff'd*, 398 F.3d 620 (7th Cir. 2005).

3. United States v. Gagliardi, 506 F.3d 140, 150 (2d Cir. 2007) (where agent posing as 13-year-old girl in internet chat room testified to accuracy of defendant's email and IM exchanges, court can admit copies).

4. Sometimes, of course, the authenticity of an email can be established in pretrial discovery, including identification at a deposition, in answer to interrogatory, or in response to request for admission. And an admission of authorship can be informal in a pretrial setting, and perhaps even inadvertent, paving the way to authenticate the email at trial by calling someone who heard the admission.

who relayed the message, and sometimes back to a particular computer.[5]

The most common method of authenticating emails is under FRE 901(b)(4), by showing "appearance, contents, substance, internal patterns, or other distinctive characteristics, taken in conjunction with circumstances."[6] The fact that a person's name appears in the header as the "sender" should not necessarily be enough to authenticate the email as being from that person, just as self-identification by a telephone caller is insufficient to authenticate the call as being from that person.[7]

Stronger circumstantial evidence would be a showing that the actual email address, e.g., johndoe@aol.com, matches an account in that person's name with the indicated internet service provider. In most modern cases, courts have relied primarily on the content of the message as a basis for authenticating emails.[8] If an email contains particularized information that only the purported sender is likely to know, this will authenticate the email to the same extent that such knowledge would authenticate a written message. Obviously the more specialized or unique the information, the more such content tends to authenticate the message as being from a particular sender who has such knowledge.[9]

A common type of content used to authenticate is content given in reply to an earlier email message.[10] An email purporting to be a reply to an earlier message sent to a particular person is likely to be authored by that person. Often an email message will include the message to which it is responding as an attachment or even in the body of the message.

Other circumstances that can be used to help authenticate an email include the fact that the purported sender promised to send an email to the recipient and one was later received, the fact that previous messages sent to a particular email address reached the purported sender of the

---

5. Clement v. California Dept. of Corrections, 220 F. Supp. 2d 1098, 1111 (N.D. Cal. 2002) (major email providers include coded IP address in header of every email, which "allows the recipient of an email to identify the sender by contacting the service provider"), *aff'd*, 364 F.3d 1148 (9th Cir. 2004).

6. United States v. Safavian, 435 F. Supp. 2d 36 (D.D.C. 2006), rev'd on other grounds, 528 F.3d 957 (D.C. Cir. 2008) (emails authenticated by distinctive characteristics, including (a) actual email address containing the "@" symbol; (b) name of person connected to address; (c) name of senders and receiver in headers and bodies; (d) content discussing personal and professional matters relating to individuals in question).

7. *See* §9.9, *supra.*

8. United States v. Safavian, 435 F. Supp. 2d 36 (D.D.C. 2006), rev'd on other grounds, 528 F.3d 957 (D.C. Cir. 2008) (emails authenticated in part by content discussing personal and professional matters relating to individuals in question).

9. United States v. Siddiqui, 235 F.3d 1318, 1322 (11th Cir. 2000) (in trial for submitting fraudulent letters of recommendation for NSF award, admitting emails from defendant; they showed knowledge of actions only defendant would likely have, apologized for things defendant himself had done, came from his email address, were signed with his distinctive nickname, and he himself made substantially similar points in conversations thereafter), *cert. denied*, 533 U.S. 940 (2001).

10. *See* discussion of the "reply doctrine" in §9.8, *supra.*

email in question,[11] or the fact that actions were taken by the purported sender in response to emails sent to the purported sender's address,[12] such as the shipping of merchandise. Many other circumstances count as well.[13]

Emails can also be authenticated under FRE 901(b)(3), which authorizes "comparison by the trier of fact or expert witness with specimens which have been authenticated." Thus emails that are not clearly identifiable on their own can be authenticated by allowing the jury to compare them with specimens that have been previously authenticated.[14]

Even if an email is successfully authenticated, it is not admissible to prove the truth of its content unless an additional foundation is laid showing that it fits an exception to the hearsay rule. If the email is shown to be from a party opponent, this will ordinarily suffice to allow its introduction into evidence as an admission.[15] An email forwarding another email may sometimes constitute an adoptive admission of the original email by the person forwarding it.[16] In unusual circumstances, an email statement may qualify as a present sense impression or an excited utterance.[17]

Emails, even if made in the course of business, do not necessarily qualify for admission as business records. While emailed billing statements and similar records may qualify, routine personal and professional email communications, like routine written correspondence, often fail to satisfy the exception because they lack the regularity and systematic checking of information that justifies making business records an exception to the hearsay rule.[18]

11. United States v. Siddiqui, 235 F.3d 138, 1322-1323 (11th Cir 2000) (alleged sender had previously received email at that address).

12. *Id.* at 1322-1323 (11th Cir. 2000) (in a later phone call, alleged sender made same request as was made in the email), *cert. denied*, 533 U.S. 940 (2001).

13. United States v. Simpson, 152 F.3d 1241, 1249-1250 (10th Cir. 1998) (admitting printout of chat room discussion between defendant and undercover police officer where individual using identity "Stavron" identified himself as "B. Simpson" and gave officer his correct street address, and where later exchanges included email address belonging to Simpson, and pages found near computer in home noted name, address, email address and phone number that officer gave to person in chat room).

14. United States v. Safavian, 435 F. Supp. 2d 36 (D.D.C. 2006), rev'd on other grounds, 528 F.3d 957 (D.C. Cir. 2008) (emails may be authenticated by comparing them with other emails that had been authenticated by content and distinctive characteristics).

15. Van Westrienen v. Americontinental Collection Corp., 94 F. Supp. 2d 1087, 1109 (D. Or. 2000) (representations made by defendants on their website are admissible as admissions of a party-opponent).

16. Sea-Land Serv., Inc. v. Lozen Int'l, 285 F.3d 808, 821 (9th Cir. 2002) (employee of plaintiff "incorporated and adopted the contents" of an email message from another of plaintiff's employees when she forwarded it to defendant with a cover note that "manifested an adoption or belief in the truth" of information contained in original email).

17. United States v. Ferber, 966 F. Supp. 90 (D. Mass. 1997) (admitting email as present sense impression).

18. *Id.* at 98 (D. Mass. 1997) (rejecting email offered under business records exception; it may have been employee's practice to make such records, but there was insufficient evidence that employer required them; must show business duty to make and maintain such records).

Web pages. Some early judicial opinions indicated extreme skepticism toward evidence obtained from web pages. One court described the internet as "one large catalyst for rumor, innuendo, and misinformation" and suggested that there is a presumption that information discovered on the internet is "inherently untrustworthy."[19] Recent decisions have been more receptive and approving. There is no reason why evidence from websites should not be admissible for certain purposes, provided it has been adequately authenticated.[20]

Web postings may have particular value when offered against the owner of the website, for example, as an admission by that party or for a nonhearsay purpose such as establishing the price of a product, representations to induce a sale, the terms of a contract, or a warranty.

To authenticate a printout of a web page, the proponent must offer evidence that (1) the printout accurately reflects the computer image of the web page as of a specified date; (2) the website where the posting appears is owned or controlled by a particular person or entity; (3) the authorship of the web posting is reasonably attributable to that person or entity. Evidence that may corroborate these points could include testimony of others who saw the posting on the website, continuation of the posting on the website so that it is available to be seen by the court, or evidence that the party to whom the posting is attributed made similar postings or published the same information elsewhere.[21] If authorship or responsibility for the web posting cannot be sufficiently established, exclusion will normally be required.[22]

If the web posting is offered for the truth of what it asserts, it is necessary to lay an additional foundation to admit it under an exception to the hearsay rule.[23] A distinction must of course be drawn between authenticating a web posting as being from a particular person and offering it to prove the truth of any assertions it contains. In the case of admissions, these issues conflate.[24] If the web posting is

19. St. Clair v. Johns' Oyster & Shrimp, Inc., 76 F. Supp. 2d 773, 774-775 (S.D. Tex. 1999).

20. For an extensive and helpful discussion of the admissibility of a wide variety of electronic evidence, *see* Lorraine v. Markel American Ins. Co., 241 F.R.D. 534 (D. Md. 2007).

21. Perfect 10, Inc. v. Cybernet Ventures, Inc. 213 F. Supp. 2d 1146, 1154 (C.D. Cal. 2002) (in copyright case, declarations that printouts were "true and correct" copies of internet pages, along with "circumstantial indicia of authenticity" like dates and web addresses suffice to enable reasonable juror to find authenticity).

22. Wady v. Provident Life & Accident Ins. Co. of Am., 216 F. Supp. 2d 1060, 1064-1065 (C.D. Cal. 2002) (postings taken from defendant's website were not authenticated; proponent could not establish who maintained website or authorship or accuracy of their contents).

23. Victaulic Co. v. Tieman, 499 F.3d 227, 236 (3d Cir. 2007) (court erred in taking judicial notice of facts about plaintiff's company based on website; anyone may purchase web address; judicial notice permitted only from sources not subject to reasonable dispute).

24. O'Toole v. Northrop Grumman Corp., 499 F.3d 1218, 1224 (10th Cir. 2007) (court should have taken judicial notice of retirement fund earnings posted on defendant's website when offered against defendant; defendant failed to dispute its own information so website met "indisputability" requirement).

adequately authenticated as being from a party opponent, it normally will be admissible as an admission. If the web posting is by a third party and is offered for its truth, an additional foundation is necessary to admit it as an exception to the hearsay rule.[25]

In a criminal prosecution where a defendant is charged with uploading unlawful content to a website, such as child pornography, it is essential for the government properly to establish the linkage between the defendant and the uploaded material.[26]

In the case of government-maintained websites, courts are divided on whether information posted thereon is admissible to prove the matter asserted, with some allowing[27] and some rejecting such evidence.[28] The resolution of this issue should depend on the reasons for the existence of the government website. If its purpose is to function as the equivalent of an official government publication, properly authenticated web postings should be admissible under FRE 902(5).[29]

Foundation

§9.16 —Computer Output

With the dramatic increase in the availability and use of microcomputers has come a corresponding increase in the amount and variety of computer output offered in evidence. The authentication process for computer output is primarily addressed by FRE 901(b)(9), which requires a description of the "process or system used to produce a result" and a showing that it "produces an accurate result."

This standard can generally be satisfied by evidence that (1) the computer equipment is accepted in the field as standard and competent and was in good working order, (2) qualified computer operators were employed, (3) proper procedures were followed in connection with the input and output of information, (4) a reliable software program was utilized, (5) the equipment was programmed and operated correctly, and (6) the exhibit is properly identified as the output in question.[1] If the exhibit contains any unusual or confusing symbols,

---

25. United States v. Jackson, 208 F.3d 633, 637 (7th Cir. 2000) (web postings offered to prove truth of matter asserted must satisfy hearsay exception).

26. United States v. Baker, 538 F.3d 324, 331-333 (5th Cir. 2008) (in trial for distributing child pornography, error to admit images uploaded to website without sufficient evidence that defendant uploaded them).

27. Elliott Assocs., L.P. v. Banco de la Nacion, 194 F.R.D. 116, 121 (S.D.N.Y. 2000) (prime rates published on Federal Reserve Board website satisfy FRE 803(17) as market reports).

28. State v. Davis, 10 P.3d 977, 1009-1010 (Wash. 2000) (printout from state website on population statistics not self-authenticating official publication; also does not fit public records exception).

29. Sannes v. Jeff Wyler Cheverolet, Inc., 1999 WL 33313134, *3 n.3 (S.D. Ohio 1999) (press release of FTC's, posted on its website, was self-authenticating official publication under FRE 902(5)).

§9.16 1. *See* State v. Swinton, 847 A.2d 921, 942 (Conn. 2004) (adopting these standards in approving enhanced photographs of bitemark evidence) (citing this Treatise). *See generally* Joseph, A Simplified Approach to Computer-Generated Evidence and Animations, 156 F.R.D. 327 (1994).

markings, or terminology, the authenticating witness should explain them to the jury.

When the output reflects data specially created or manipulated for purposes of litigation, courts may require a more stringent foundation than for output merely producing routine records. To avoid unfair prejudice, courts sometimes require advance notice by a party of intent to use computerized evidence and an opportunity for pretrial access to the program used to generate the output.[2]

The authenticating witness must be someone generally familiar with the process by which the output was produced, but need not have been personally involved in the particular process generating the data.[3] The witness need not have technical sophistication nor be familiar with every detail of computer operations.[4]

Hearsay concerns   Even if computer output is properly authenticated, it may nonetheless have to surmount a hearsay objection. Whether computer output is hearsay depends on whether it is primarily a reiteration of human statements or an electronic processing, calculation, or tracking of data. A computer printout of business records is hearsay; mathematical calculations by a computer are not. Most computer output is based on statements by persons, which makes it hearsay if offered to prove the truth of the matters asserted.[5] But some computer output involves primarily mechanical or technical processes such as computer-enhanced photographic imaging, automated phone records, and computerized test scoring, and such output generally does not implicate the hearsay rule.[6] Expert testimony may be required to authenticate and explain output that is scientific in nature.

Even where computer output is hearsay, it is often admissible under exceptions such as the ones for business records[7] or public records[8]

---

2. *See, e.g.,* United States v. Weatherspoon, 581 F.2d 595, 598 (7th Cir. 1978) (defense counsel had adequate opportunity to "inquire into the accuracy of the input procedures and the programming used" as well as access to the data for inspection).

3. United States v. Miller, 771 F.2d 1219, 1237 (9th Cir. 1985) (computer records authenticated by testimony of billing supervisor, even though he lacked knowledge of maintenance and technical operation).

4. United States v. Linn, 880 F.2d 209, 216 (9th Cir. 1989) (computer tracking of phone calls authenticated by testimony of hotel communications director, even though he could not distinguish between "menus," "data bases," and computer "code" and could not testify to details of generating computer output).

5. *See* discussion in §§8.11-8.15, *supra.*

6. *See, e.g.,* United States v. Miller, 771 F.2d 1219, 1237 (9th Cir. 1985) (computer generated toll and billing records); People v. Holowko, 486 N.E.2d 877, 878-879 (Ill. 1985) (computerized record of phone calls not hearsay but scientific evidence; foundation need not fit hearsay exception, but must show "method of the recording of the information and the proper functioning of the device").

7. United States v. Hutson, 821 F.2d 1015, 1019-1020 (5th Cir. 1987) (computer records of banking transactions); United States v. Croft, 750 F.2d 1354 (7th Cir. 1984) (payroll records).

8. United States v. Orozco, 590 F.2d 789, 793 (9th Cir. 1979) (admitting computer data from customs officials that listed license plate numbers of automobiles entering United States to prove defendant's car had crossed border on certain night), *cert. denied,* 442 U.S. 920.

(or for proving absence of an entry in business or public records),[9] provided a proper foundation is laid.[10] If the computer output was produced by the opposing party, it may constitute a nonhearsay admission under FRE 801(d)(2). Where the output is essentially a compilation or re-sorting of the input, it usually has the same hearsay status as the input. Therefore, a hearsay objection to the output can normally be overcome by laying a proper foundation qualifying the input under a hearsay exception. Even a special printout made for litigation purposes is admissible, provided the computer process is authenticated as producing accurate output and the underlying data is properly qualified under a hearsay exception.[11] A computerized synopsis of otherwise admissible records may qualify as a summary under FRE 1006.[12]

Computer output rarely poses a problem under the Best Evidence Doctrine because FRE 1001(3) provides that when data are stored in a computer "any printout or other output readable by sight, shown to reflect the data accurately, is an 'original.'" Moreover, where a business or similar organization regularly keeps its records on computer, the computer-stored data is the "original" business record rather than the underlying documents that provided the basis for the data entry.

Authentication of electronic communications via computer, such as emails and web postings, is discussed in an earlier section.[13] The use of computer animations as a form of demonstrative evidence is discussed in a later section.[14]

§9.17 —Polls, Surveys

Survey evidence, whether in the form of an opinion poll or a sampling of statistical or other data, is generally admissible if the proponent establishes that the survey was scientifically conducted and reasonably reliable.[1] Generally, the survey must be authenticated by showing the

---

9. United States v. Neff, 615 F.2d 1235, 1241-1242 (9th Cir. 1980) (allowing testimony that search of IRS computer records showed defendant failed to file tax return), *cert. denied*, 447 U.S. 925.

10. United States v. Scholle, 553 F.2d 1109, 1124-1125 (8th Cir. 1977) (comprehensive foundation required to admit business records in computerized form), *cert. denied*, 434 U.S. 940. *See generally* 2 Bender, Computer Law (1988). *See* discussion in §8.44, *supra*.

11. United States v. Sanders, 749 F.2d 195, 198 (5th Cir. 1984) (provided underlying data qualifies as business records, it is not necessary that printout itself be ordered in ordinary course of business, at least where computer simply "orders it out rather than sorting, compiling or summarizing the information").

12. City of Phoenix v. Com/Sys., Inc., 706 F.2d 1033, 1037-1038 (9th Cir. 1983) (computer summary of work orders and parts requisitions admissible under FRE 1006). *See* §10.15, *infra*.

13. *See* §9.15, *supra*.

14. *See* §9.34, *infra*.

§9.17 1. *See generally* Zeisel, The Uniqueness of Survey Evidence, 45 Cornell L. Q. 322 (1960); Note, Public Opinion Surveys as Evidence: The Pollsters Go to Court, 66 Harv. L. Rev. 498 (1953).

process by which it was conducted and that the process "produces an accurate result."[2] The foundation for an opinion poll should include evidence that (1) the "universe" of persons surveyed or polled was properly defined with reference to the underlying subject, (2) a representative sample of the universe was selected and questioned, (3) the questions were clear, simple, and nonleading, (4) sound interview procedures were followed, (5) the information was carefully gathered and recorded, (6) the data were properly collated and analyzed, and (7) the objectivity of the process was adequately protected by keeping the polling or survey separate from the litigation.[3] Poll results may be excluded if the poll was not scientifically designed or properly conducted.[4]

Expert testimony   Public opinion polls and surveys are generally presented through the testimony of an expert witness, and the expert may be allowed to express an opinion based on the poll even if the poll itself is not admitted into evidence.[5] Under FRE 703, an expert can give an opinion relying on facts or data not admissible in evidence, provided they are "of a type reasonably relied upon by experts in the particular field in forming opinions or inferences upon the subject."[6] However, the survey process must normally be authenticated as described above in order to show that reliance by the expert was reasonable. Courts retain discretion to exclude surveys and polls under FRE 403.[7]

Hearsay concerns   Most surveys and polls, other than statistical samples, involve hearsay because they are compilations of out-of-court statements offered to prove the events or conditions they describe or the beliefs of the speakers on those points. Nonetheless, such responses often fit the state of mind exception[8] or are sufficiently reliable to be admitted under the catchall exception to the hearsay rule.[9]

---

2. FRE 901(b)(9). *See also* Randy's Studebaker Sales, Inc. v. Nissan Motor Corp., 533 F.2d 510, 519-521 (10th Cir. 1976) (customer survey regarding satisfaction with dealer's service); Union Carbide Corp. v. Ever-Ready, Inc., 531 F.2d 366, 381-388 (7th Cir. 1976) (surveys used to establish likelihood of confusion between EVERREADY and Ever-Ready), *cert. denied*, 429 U.S. 830.

3. See Toys "R" Us, Inc. v. Canarsie Kiddie Shop, Inc., 559 F. Supp. 1189, 1205 (E.D.N.Y. 1983).

4. American Footwear Corp. v. General Footwear Co., 609 F.2d 655, 660-661 n.4 (2d Cir. 1979) (survey properly excluded because of methodological defects), *cert. denied*, 445 U.S. 951; Pittsburgh Press Club v. United States, 579 F.2d 751, 755-760 (3d Cir. 1978) (poll excluded; not scientifically designed).

5. Upjohn Co. v. Rachelle Lab., Inc., 661 F.2d 1105, 1111-1112 (6th Cir. 1981) (manager could testify on basis of survey of 40 salesmen, even though survey itself was excluded as hearsay); Baumholser v. Amax Coal Co., 630 F.2d 550, 552-553 (7th Cir. 1980) (admitting expert testimony even though it rested on survey that was hearsay, thus inadmissible).

6. *See* §7.10, *infra*.

7. *See, e.g.*, C. A. May Marine Supply Co. v. Brunswick Corp., 649 F.2d 1049, 1054-1055 (5th Cir. 1981) (excluding survey where relevance was outweighed by prejudice), *cert. denied*, 454 U.S. 1125.

8. *See, e.g.*, Piper Aircraft Corp. v. Wag-Aero, Inc., 741 F.2d 925, 931 (7th Cir. 1984) (survey properly admitted under state-of-mind exception).

9. *See, e.g.*, Brunswick Corp. v. Spinit Reel Co., 832 F.2d 513, 522-523 (10th Cir. 1987) (survey properly admitted under catchall exception as proof of product confusion).

> **FRE 901(b)(10)**
>
> **Methods provided by statute or rule.** Any method of authentication or identification provided by Act of Congress or by other rules prescribed by the Supreme Court pursuant to statutory authority.

§9.18 Other Methods Authorized by Statute or Rule

FRE 901(b)(10) makes clear that the Rules of Evidence do not displace authentication provisions found elsewhere and incorporates by reference authentication methods recognized by federal statutes and by other rules prescribed by the Supreme Court.[1] The Federal Rules of Civil Procedure authorize several methods of authentication.[2] For example, official publications of public documents or copies of public documents may be authenticated by certificates accompanied by seal under FRCP 44.[3]

Various provisions of the Civil Rules permit court reporters to certify transcripts, thus making them essentially self-authenticating at trial. FRCP 30(f)(1) requires the reporter to certify and file the transcript of a deposition (but the judge sometimes dispenses with filing), and such actions make the transcript at least prima facie authentic for whatever use FRCP 32 permits. FRCP 30(f)(1) also permits documents (or copies) to be appended to deposition transcripts, which means that where the deponent identifies the documents in his testimony and where the deposition itself is admissible at trial under FRCP 32, the deposition may be used to authenticate the documents. And FRCP 80(c) provides that when testimony at a trial or hearing is admissible "at a later trial," it may be proved (if "stenographically reported") by means of "the transcript thereof duly certified by the person who reported the testimony," thus again making the transcript at least prima facie authentic.[4]

C. SELF-AUTHENTICATION

§9.19 Self-Authentication Doctrine

FRE 902 provides that various types of writings and other matters are "self-authenticating," which means that their authenticity is taken as

---

§9.18 1. *See, e.g.,* 18 U.S.C. 3505(a) (giving self-authenticating effect in criminal cases to foreign records of regularly conducted activity if certified by custodian in accordance with statute).

2. *See* §9.2, *supra.*

3. This provision is also adopted in criminal cases by FRCrimP 27.

4. *See also* 28 U.S.C. §753(b).

sufficiently established without extrinsic evidence. While authenticating witnesses generally must be called for evidence offered under FRE 901(b),[1] FRE 902 dispenses with that foundation requirement for the categories of evidence specified within the Rule. The principle underlying FRE 902 is that the materials it embraces are unlikely to be anything different from what they appear to be, and that, for the convenience of parties and courts alike, they should be admitted without authenticating evidence.[2]

Like FRE 901, FRE 902 addresses only whether or not an exhibit is sufficiently authenticated to be admissible. At trial, the opponent may introduce evidence contesting authenticity,[3] and the trier makes the ultimate determination. Even though an exhibit is self-authenticating, it may still be excluded under other Rules. Whether a writing is self-authenticating is a question for the trial judge under FRE 104(a), and the judge has discretion to consider the tenor and appearance of proffered matter and decline to treat it as self-authenticating if it is suspicious on its face.[4]

There is uncertainty on the procedural effect of FRE 902 where no counterproof is offered challenging the authenticity of an exhibit. Does FRE 902 merely recognize categories of evidence where the authentication requirement is satisfied as a matter of law or does it go further and create a presumption of authenticity that is binding on the jury in the absence of rebutting evidence?[5] An earlier draft of the Rule provided that evidence falling within the listed categories would be "presumed to be authentic,"[6] but the presumption terminology was eliminated without explanation from the final version.

Cogent and compelling Even though no express presumption is created, exhibits that fit the various categories of FRE 902 usually bear such cogent and compelling indicia of authenticity that the jury should be instructed to find them authentic in the absence of counterproof challenging their authenticity, at least in civil cases and when offered by the accused in

---

§9.19 1. In rare cases under FRE 901(b)(4), "distinctive characteristics" apparent on the face of an exhibit may suffice to authenticate it without need for extrinsic evidence. *See* §9.8, *supra*.

2. ACN, FRE 902 (self-authentication principle based partly on "reasons of policy" but perhaps more on fact that "practical considerations reduce the possibility of unauthenticity to a very small dimension").

3. United States v. Bisbee, 245 F.3d 1001 (8th Cir. 2001) (argument that FRE 902 creates rebuttable presumption rejected as mischaracterization; evidence contradicting facts in self-authenticated documents does not affect admissibility). *See* ACN to FRE 902 (opposing party is not "foreclosed from disputing authenticity").

4. Nolin v. Douglas County, 903 F.2d 1546, 1551-1552 (11th Cir. 1990) (can exclude copy of employment guidelines as untrustworthy; they were "not under seal in accordance with FRE 902" and their authenticity was sufficiently challenged).

5. If FRE 902 creates a presumption of authenticity, the further question arises whether presumption shifts only the burden of production or also the burden of persuasion. Since FRE 301 rejects burden-of-persuasion-shifting presumptions, the latter construction seems implausible. *See* discussion of presumptions in §§3.4-3.8, *supra*.

6. Preliminary Draft of Proposed Rules of Evidence, March 1969, 46 F.R.D. 161, 399 (1969).

a criminal proceeding. As to evidence offered by the government in a criminal prosecution, the special protections afforded the accused preclude a mandatory instruction against him.[7]

When a writing is offered for its truth, the fact that it is properly self-authenticating does not establish its admissibility as an exception to the hearsay rule. But the self-authentication provisions of FRE 902 work together with various hearsay exceptions to facilitate the admission of records under those exceptions.[8]

FRE 902(1)

Domestic public documents under seal. A document bearing a seal purporting to be that of the United States, or of any State, district, Commonwealth, territory, or insular possession thereof, or the Panama Canal Zone, or the Trust Territory of the Pacific Islands, or of a political subdivision, department, officer, or agency thereof, and a signature purporting to be an attestation or execution.

---

§9.20 Domestic Public Documents Under Seal

Under FRE 902(1), extrinsic evidence of authenticity is not required for any document that purports to be a domestic public record bearing what appears to be an official signature of "attestation or execution" and an appropriate official seal. This Rule relates to original public documents and records,[1] while copies of such material are authenticated under FRE 902(4).[2] An affidavit or certificate that complies with FRE 902(1) is admissible to prove the absence or nonexistence of an official record or entry.[3]

The principle underlying this Rule is that forgery of official records, complete with signature and seal, seldom occurs. There are stiff criminal sanctions for forgery and misuse of public records and seals. Most such records are also distinctive enough in appearance to ensure that efforts at forgery would have to be elaborate, and it is hard to forge a seal. Although misuse of public forms and seals may not be difficult

---

7. *See* §3.13, *supra.*

8. *See* FRE 803(8) (public records and reports); FRE 803(9) (records of vital statistics); FRE 803(14) (records of documents affecting an interest in property).

§9.20 1. United States v. Hampton, 464 F.3d 687, 689 (7th Cir. 2006) (in bank robbery trial, photocopies of certificates of FDIC insurance were not self-authenticating; they did not bear original seal, but were copies of sealed documents; admitting such copies would defeat rationale that difficulty of forging seal renders authentication unnecessary, because copies are more easily forged).

2. *See* §9.23, *infra.*

3. *See, e.g.,* United States v. Kimberlin, 805 F.2d 210, 241 (7th Cir. 1986) (certification that diligent search made of National Firearms Register and Transfer Record properly admitted as self-authenticating document), *cert. denied,* 483 U.S. 1023.

for public employees, they would be subject to additional sanctions beyond criminal penalties.

Broad range of documents

FRE 902(1) covers a broad range of public documents from all branches of government—executive, legislative, and judicial, and all levels of government—federal, state, and local,[4] as well as boards, departments, offices, agencies, and other political subdivisions.[5] Foreign public documents are covered by FRE 902(3).[6]

Two requirements

FRE 902(1) has only two express requirements. First, the document must bear "a signature purporting to be an attestation or execution." "Execution" means that the document was written or adopted by the signer, while "attestation" means that the signer examined it after the fact and found it to be a genuine public document or record (as any appropriate form of words accompanying the signature should suffice to convey). No doubt the apparent signature should be that of a person having authority to execute or knowledge to attest the document, and a legend indicating his title would be helpful. But in the absence of suspicious circumstances or appearance, the fact that such a legend is missing should not be fatal. The originals of many official documents bear only stamped or machine-made "facsimile signatures," which should satisfy the requirement in any case in which such facsimile was apparently intended to have the same effect as an original.

Second, the document must bear an appropriate seal.[7] This requirement is plainly satisfied by an embossed impression that includes some sort of legend or symbol indicating origin, traditionally laid out in a circular design. There is no requirement that the seal itself be authenticated, such as by the sealed certificate of another officer. Statutes often provide for judicial notice of various seals. Some public documents are printed with what amounts to "facsimile seals," and these should satisfy the requirement where they were apparently intended to have the same effect as an original and where the elaborateness of the printed image supplies a safeguard against forgery. But it should generally not be sufficient to accept a signed document with the printed, typed, or handwritten word "Seal" as self-authenticating under FRE 902(1).

Other methods

If the document contains no seal, it can be authenticated by testimony of a person with knowledge under FRE 901(b)(1),[8] by showing it

4. *See, e.g.,* Crossley v. Lieberman, 868 F.2d 566, 568 (3d Cir. 1989) ("certified record of the Philadelphia Court of Common Pleas"); Yellow Taxi Co. v. NLRB, 721 F.2d 366, 375 n.29 (D.C. Cir. 1983) (official map of Minnesota bearing state seal).

5. *See, e.g.,* United States v. MacKenzie, 601 F.2d 221, 222-223 (5th Cir. 1979) (order of Texas Board of Medical Examiners canceling appellant's license to practice medicine properly received under FRE 902(1)), *cert. denied,* 444 U.S. 1018.

6. *See* §9.22, *infra.*

7. First Natl. Life Ins. Co. v. California Pac. Life Ins. Co., 876 F.2d 877, 881 (11th Cir. 1989) (copies of pleadings from state suit were not authenticated under FRE 902(1) or (2); they "did not bear the imprint of the New Mexico court's seal").

8. United States v. Jimenez Lopez, 873 F.2d 769, 772-774 (5th Cir. 1989) (record of conviction for illegal entry not admissible under FRE 902 because it lacked seal, but it satisfied FRE 901 on proof that it was what proponent claimed).

was obtained from the appropriate public office under FRE 901(b)(7),[9] or by obtaining the certificate of an officer with a seal under FRE 902(2).[10] A signature alone does not suffice, even for a document from a state having a statute providing that the signature of a proper public official makes the document self-authenticating,[11] because such a statute is not binding on federal courts.[12]

> **FRE 902(2)**
>
> **Domestic public documents not under seal.** A document purporting to bear the signature in the official capacity of an officer or employee or any entity included in paragraph (1) hereof, having no seal, if a public officer having a seal and having official duties in the district or political subdivision of the officer or employee certifies under seal that the signer has the official capacity and that the signature is genuine.

§9.21 Domestic Public Documents Not Under Seal

FRE 902(2) provides for self-authentication of public documents purporting to bear the signature, in an official capacity, of an officer or employee of a designated governmental entity who has no seal, provided that another officer with official duties in that jurisdiction certifies under seal that the signer has official capacity and the signature is genuine.[1] This Rule, like FRE 902(1), authenticates only original public documents and records. Authentication of copies of public records is addressed by FRE 902(4). An affidavit or certificate that complies with FRE 902(2) is also admissible to prove the absence or nonexistence of an official record or entry.[2]

9. *See* §9.11, *supra*.

10. *See* §9.21, *infra*.

11. For a representative example of such a statute, *see* Cal. Evid. Code. §1453 (presuming genuineness of signature of public employee "affixed in his official capacity"). Some federal statutes say that a signature of a particular public officer is alone sufficient to authenticate. Where such statutes apply, they control. *See* FRE 901(b)(10) *and* FRE 902(10).

12. But FRE 901(b)(4) lets the court take into account the appearance and content of a matter in resolving the authentication question, as well as surrounding circumstances, which may justify admitting state public records that were signed but not sealed.

§9.21   1. *See, e.g.*, United States v. Bisbee, 245 F.3d 1001 (8th Cir. 2001) (in tax trial, admitting IRS document titled Certificate of Assessments and Payments with document titled Certificate of Official Record; these were self-authenticated under FRE 902 because the latter was under seal and contained signature of manager of certification unit).

2. Hunt v. Liberty Lobby, 720 F.2d 631, 651 (11th Cir. 1983) (plaintiff in libel suit proved absence of CIA records placing him in Dallas when President Kennedy was shot by affidavits of CIA records custodians stating that on diligent search no such records were found; each affidavit was had certificate by CIA general counsel certifying that each affiant occupied position stated in his affidavit).

The purpose of FRE 902(2) is to accommodate the reality that some public officials or entities, by or for which official documents are executed, lack a seal. In any such case, the approach of this Rule is not to excuse the lack of a seal,[3] but rather to require in lieu of a seal the signed-and-sealed certificate of another public officer in a position to know whether the signature on the document is genuine and whether the signer had the requisite authority. The requirement that the signature of an officer without a seal be certified by an officer with a seal differs from some state laws that presume the genuineness of purported official signatures even in the absence of a seal.[4]

Signature in official capacity

The first major requirement of FRE 902(2) is that the document bear the purported signature of an appropriate public officer "in his official capacity." This modifying phrase is not in FRE 902(1) and compensates for the absence of a seal. If the purported signature appears with a legend indicating the official title of the signer, that should suffice, as should a legend elsewhere on the document indicating that it was executed by or for a named public authority. The necessary inference may also rest on the tenor or appearance of the document if either indicates its official status.

Certificate by official with seal

The second major requirement of FRE 902(2) is a signed-and-sealed certificate. This requirement breaks down into four parts: The certificate must make the appropriate statement; it must be apparently signed; it must be apparently sealed; and the signer must be a public official having official duties in the same "district or political subdivision" from which comes the document in question.

As to what would be an appropriate statement, it seems that the certificate should (1) indicate the official position of its maker and the name and location of his office or authority, (2) state that the signature on the document is genuine or that the certifier knows the signature of the apparent signer and believes the signature is genuine, and (3) state that the signer of the document has authority to execute documents of that sort (if the signature is one of execution) or that the signer is in a position by virtue of his duties to know whether such documents are genuine (if the signature is one of attestation). Of course no particular form of words is required, so long as the certifier supplies information supporting appropriate conclusions on these points.[5]

The signature requirement should be satisfied only by an apparent actual signature, not by a facsimile signature. The certificate requires

---

3. *See* First Natl. Life Ins. Co. v. California Pac. Life Ins. Co., 876 F.2d 877, 881 (11th Cir. 1989) (pleadings from state suit not admissible because they lacked seal).

4. *See, e.g.,* Cal. Evid. Code §1453.

5. United States v. Combs, 762 F.2d 1343, 1347-1348 (9th Cir. 1985) (admitting signed but unsealed reports by ATF agent Davis that defendant had not registered firearm, accompanied by certificate under seal by "Chief of the National Firearms Act Branch" of BATF stating that "Davis had proper custody and control" of relevant records and that affiant "was familiar with her signature," and that signature on report was "true") (rejecting claim that certificate was inadequate because it did not say Davis had "official capacity" as required by FRE 902(2)).

that the certifier actually scrutinize the document, so there is no reason to accept a stamped or machine-made "facsimile" signature. Similarly, the seal requirement should be satisfied only by an apparent actual seal. A certificate attesting the genuineness of another public document is not the kind of official record generated in such numbers and with so little individual care that a facsimile seal should be accepted.

The certifier need not be a superior in terms of rank or authority with respect to the apparent signer. Nor is it necessary that he be employed by the same public agency, or even by the same branch or level of government. A federal officer should be able to certify the signature and authority of a state officer and vice versa, provided they have requisite knowledge. While it may be preferable for the proponent to seek certification from a person up the ladder of official authority in the same agency, this is not required by the Rule. However, the certifying officer must have official duties in the same "district or political subdivision." While a positive statement to this effect should be included, the court may be in a position to take judicial notice that the certifier either has or lacks official duties in the pertinent district or subdivision. If so, notice suffices to establish this fact even if the certificate is silent on this point.

FRE 902(3)

Foreign public documents. A document purporting to be executed or attested in an official capacity by a person authorized by the laws of a foreign country to make the execution or attestation, and accompanied by a final certification as to the genuineness of the signature and official position (A) of the executing or attesting person, or (B) of any foreign official whose certificate of genuineness of signature and official position relates to the execution or attestation or is in a chain of certificates of genuineness of signature and official position relating to the execution or attestation. A final certification may be made by a secretary of embassy or legation, consul general, consul, vice consular, or consular agent of the United States, or a diplomatic or consular official of the foreign country assigned or accredited to the United States. If reasonable opportunity has been given to all parties to investigate the authenticity and accuracy of official documents, the court may, for good cause shown, order that they be treated as presumptively authentic without final certification or permit them to be evidenced by an attested summary with or without final certification.

---

§9.22 Foreign Public Documents

Under FRE 902(3), extrinsic evidence of authenticity is not required for any document purporting to have been executed or attested by a person authorized to do so in his official capacity by the laws of a foreign country, provided that the document is accompanied by a proper certification. FRE 902(3) makes possible the authentication of a wide range of foreign public documents.[1] An affidavit or certificate complying with FRE 902(3) is also admissible to prove the nonexistence of an official foreign record or the absence of a particular entry therein.[2]

FRE 902(3) serves a purpose similar to that of FRCP 44(a)(2), and the Civil Rule was not repealed by the enactment of the Evidence Rules and continues to provide an alternative avenue of admissibility.[3] Authentication of foreign public records is sometimes simpler under FRCP (44)(a)(2) because it dispenses with the requirement of a final certificate provided the records are attested and certified "as provided in a treaty or convention to which the United States and the foreign country in which the official record is located are parties."[4] However, FRE 902(3) is broader than FRCP (44)(a)(2) because it applies to any foreign document purportedly prepared by an authorized representative of a government, while the Civil Rule is limited to "public records." Unlike FRCP 44(a)(2), FRE 902(3) does not allow authentication of foreign public documents by showing they have been officially published, but this method of authentication is covered by FRE 902(5).

Proper certification FRE 902(3) has two major requirements. First, the document must bear the purported signature of an authorized foreign official "in an official capacity."

Signature in official capacity The second requirement is proper certification, which can take either of two forms, both of which require a "final certification" by a

---

§9.22   1. *See, e.g.,* United States v. Deverso, 518 F.3d 1250, 1254-1256 (11th Cir. 2008) (admitting foreign birth certificate under FRE 902(3) to establish that person in pornographic photos in possession of defendant was minor); United States v. Pena-Jessie, 763 F.2d 618, 621 (4th Cir. 1985) (diplomatic note from Panama granting permission to board Panamanian vessel).

2. United States v. Herrera-Britto, 739 F.2d 551, 552 (11th Cir. 1984) (invoking FRE 902(3) and 803(10) to admit "certified document signed by the general commander of the Naval Force of Honduras stating that a search of vessel registration records at the Honduras Naval Command Headquarters revealed no registration for the vessel MISS SHIRLEY").

3. *See* Vatyan v. Mukasey, 508 F.3d 1179, 1184 (9th Cir. 2007) (both FRCP 44 and FRE 901 acknowledge that certification is not exclusive means of authenticating foreign public document; immigration judge erred in requiring asylum applicant to produce official certification to authenticate documents purportedly issued by Armenian government and in failing to weigh applicant's testimony in deciding whether documents were authentic).

4. This language was added by amendment in 1991 and refers to the Hague Convention Abolishing the Requirement of Legalization of Foreign Public Documents, adopted by the Hague Conference on Private International Law on October 26, 1960, T.I.A.S. No. 10,072, 527 U.N.T.S. 189. The Senate ratified this Convention in 1979, and it took effect here on October 15, 1981. *See* Senate Executive Report No. 96-17, 96th Cong., 1st Sess. (1979). Under the Convention, each country designates public officials who may fix a form of certification known as the "apostille" (French for "endorsement"), making the document is admissible. The certification is a single-page form stating that the document was signed by an individual in official capacity and that the seal or stamp is genuine.

diplomatic or consular officer.[5] In the simplest case, the final certificate by the diplomatic or consular officer directly attests the genuineness of the signature on the document and the authority of that person to execute or attest such a document. In what is probably the more usual case, there is a chain of certificates, one by a superior of the original signer attesting his signature and authority, a second by a higher official attesting the signature and authority of the maker of the first certificate, and so on—with a final certificate, again by a diplomatic or consular officer, attesting the signature and authority of the next person down the chain.

For the *final* certificate, FRE 902(3) requires two and perhaps three elements: The certificate must affirm the genuineness of signature and official position of the signer of either the document itself or a preceding certificate, and it must bear an apparent signature by a member of either the diplomatic or consular staff of the United States or the diplomatic or consular staff of that country "assigned or accredited to" the United States. Arguably the certificate should also be sealed, although the Rule does not so require.

Final certificate

Where the parties have had reasonable opportunity to investigate the authenticity and accuracy of foreign official documents, and where good cause is shown, FRE 902(3) permits the court to treat such documents as presumptively authentic without final certification.[6] Resort to this relaxed self-authentication mechanism (in which an apparent signature of execution or attestation is still required) is appropriate in cases in which the cooperation of diplomatic or consular officials cannot be had, and in cases in which peculiarities in foreign law make it impossible to obtain the kind of intermediate certificates that may be essential before a final certificate can be obtained, and in any other necessitous case where closer compliance with the formalities is impossible or impracticable. The proponent should satisfy the court that closer compliance should not be required,[7] and the party opposing the proof must have reasonable opportunity to examine and investigate the authenticity and accuracy of the document in question.

Dispensing with final certification

As an alternative to self-authentication by final certification and even to the relaxed presumption described above, the court may admit as self-authenticating "an attested summary with or without final certification." This approach recognizes the possibility that a foreign government would not permit original records or even copies to be removed from the official depository and would permit responsible officials

Attested summaries

---

5. United States v. Chu Kong Yin, 935 F.2d 990, 995 (9th Cir. 1991) (certificates of trial apparently prepared by Hong Kong officials were not self-authenticating; they lacked "final certification" indicating genuineness of signature and official position of attesting or executing person) (still, documents were authenticated under FRE 901(b)(7)).

6. Raphaely Intl., Inc. v. Waterman Steamship Corp., 972 F.2d 498, 501-502 (2d Cir. 1992) (admitting foreign documents without final certificate where parties had opportunity to investigate and good cause shown), *cert. denied*, 113 S. Ct. 1271.

7. United States v. De Jongh, 937 F.2d 1, 3-7 (1st Cir. 1991) (excluding good conduct certificate apparently issued by government of Bonaire, where final certification was lacking; may relax requirements of FRE 902(3) for good cause) (not shown here).

only to prepare summaries or synopses of official documents. As in the case of documents without final certification, application of the self-authentication principle to attested summaries is appropriate only on a showing of good cause and where the opposing party has had reasonable opportunity to examine and investigate the authenticity and accuracy of the summary. And again, the summary must at least be attested, and the absence of final certification should be excused only if such certification cannot reasonably be had.

> **FRE 902(4)**
>
> **Certified copies of public records.** A copy of any official record or report or entry therein, or of a document authorized by law to be recorded or filed and actually recorded or filed in a public office, including data compilations in any form, certified as correct by the custodian or other person authorized to make the certification, by certificate complying with paragraph (1), (2), or (3) of this rule or complying with any Act of Congress or rule prescribed by the Supreme Court pursuant to statutory authority.

§9.23 Certified Copies of Public Records

FRE 902(4) provides for the self-authentication of copies of official records or reports, or documents recorded or filed pursuant to law in a public office. Its only requirement is that the custodian or other authorized person certify the copy as correct by a certificate complying with either FRE 902(1), (2), or (3), or with a federal statute or rule prescribed by the Supreme Court. FRE 902(4) allows self-authentication of a wide range of federal,[1] state,[2] local,[3] tribal,[4] and foreign public records.[5]

Rationale   The purpose of this Rule is to make it unnecessary to remove original records from official custody when they are needed as evidence in

§9.23   1. *See, e.g.,* United States v. Lechuga, 975 F.2d 397, 399 (7th Cir. 1992) (recording of arraignment and plea before federal magistrate, certified by deputy clerk as "true, accurate and authentic" record of proceedings).

2. *See, e.g.,* United States v. Weiland, 420 F.3d 1062, 1073 (9th Cir. 2005) (admitting penitentiary packet, including record of convictions, fingerprints, and photograph; manager certified he was custodian and records were compared to originals and were correct; Oklahoma Secretary of State certified under seal that manager was authorized to certify documents and signature was genuine).

3. *See, e.g.,* Crossley v. Lieberman, 868 F.2d 566, 568 (3d Cir. 1989) (bankruptcy court properly admitted "certified record of the Philadelphia Court of Common Pleas").

4. United States v. Torres, 733 F.2d 449, 455 n.5 (7th Cir. 1984) (admitting certificates of enrollment certified as accurate representations of material in original Tribal Roll), *cert. denied,* 469 U.S. 864.

5. United States v. Rodriguez Serrate, 534 F.2d 7, 9-10 (1st Cir. 1976) (admitting copies of official documents of Dominican Republic, including identification card, birth certificate, and death certificate).

litigation. The reliability of the copy seems assured by modern copy methods and the integrity of public officials in certifying copies and the unlikelihood of forgery or falsification of a certificate. Normally the certificate must have a seal that gives further indication of reliability. A seal on the certificate is required for a domestic public document by FRE 902(1) and (2) and is usually required for a foreign public document by FRE 902(3).

The limitation to "official" records or reports or lawfully recorded or filed documents is intended to preclude introduction of tentative or preliminary drafts, writings made outside the scope of authority, internal memoranda, or other records or reports that were not intended to have "official" status. The reference in FRE 902(4) to "data compilations in any form" makes it clear that the Rule embraces electronically stored or recorded data and computer output, which are not covered by FRE 902(1)-(3), presumably because it cannot directly be signed or sealed and can better be authenticated by an attached certificate.[6]

The certificate should indicate (1) the official position of its maker and the name and location of his office; (2) that the maker has compared the copy with the original document and that it is true and correct; and (3) compliance with FRE 902(1), (2), (3), or other statute or rule.[7] The certificate should not go beyond these points to make hearsay assertions about the contents of the public records or the manner by which they were prepared. The point of the certificate is to authenticate the copy and the underlying record, not to verify, interpret, or augment its contents.[8]

Contents of certificate

The certificate should bear an apparent actual signature and seal, rather than a facsimile thereof, since the purport of the certificate is that the signer made or supervised the making of the copy and knows that it reproduces the genuine article.[9] While the custodian is the natural person to execute the required certificate, the reference to "authorized" persons makes it clear that others can do so as well. In absence of counterproof or circumstances that raise suspicion, the authority of the certifier should be assumed.[10]

---

6. If the computerized data compilation is only a *summary* of the original documents, its admissibility is also subject to the protections of FRE 1006, which requires that the originals be made available for inspection and copying by the opposing party. *See* §10.16, *infra*.

7. Many statutes make certified copies self-authenticating, and the operative effect of these statutes is preserved by the last clause in FRE 902(4). *See, e.g.,* 28 U.S.C. §1735 (certified copies of court records where originals are lost or destroyed); 28 U.S.C. §1736 (extracts from Journals of Senate and House and from Executive Journal of Senate certified by the Secretary of the Senate or the Clerk of the House admissible "with the same effect as the originals would have").

8. United States v. Johnson, 722 F.2d 407, 410 (8th Cir. 1983) (sentence in certificate by custodian summarizing record "goes beyond the authentication requirements of Rule 902(4)" and appears to have been prepared for purposes of litigation; offending sentence should have been stricken).

9. *See* State v. Stotts, 695 P.2d 1110, 1122 (Ariz. 1985) (copy of certified copy not self-authenticating).

10. United States v. Pent-R-Books, Inc., 538 F.2d 519, 527-528 (2d Cir. 1976) (approving administrative records certified by postal official; court rejects contention that

Even though FRE 902(4) requires a certificate, courts occasionally admit copies of public documents without a certificate where an official seal indicating genuineness is attached.[11] Also where a certificate is lacking, courts sometimes take judicial notice of the authenticity of a public record under FRE 201, provided its genuineness is readily verifiable by indisputable external sources and there is no reasonable dispute regarding the matter.[12]

FRCP 44(a)(1) compared

The most frequently used alternative to FRE 902(4) is FRCP 44(a)(1), which provides for self-authentication of domestic official records. FRE 902(4) is broader than FRCP 44(a) in allowing self-authentication not only of public records, but also documents recorded or filed in a public office as authorized by law. FRCP 44(a)(1) allows only for copies attested by the custodian, whereas FRE 902(4) also recognizes certificates by any "other person authorized to make the certification." Finally, FRE 902(4) requires no second certificate attesting the authority of the first certifier (provided the first certificate is signed and sealed), while FRCP 44(a)(1) always requires a second certificate attesting that the first certifier is indeed the custodian. A copy of a public record may be admitted if it satisfies either FRE 902(4) or FRCP 44(a)(1); it need not satisfy both.[13]

A party may prove the absence or nonexistence of an official record or entry by affidavit or certificate complying with FRE 902(1), (2), or (3), or may introduce properly certified copies of the relevant public records pursuant to this Rule, thereby allowing the nonexistence of a particular record or the absence of an entry to be demonstrated to the trier of fact.

The fact that a certified copy of a public record is self-authenticating does not establish its admissibility. It must comply with other evidentiary requirements, including the hearsay rule (if offered to prove the truth of the matter asserted), although properly authenticated copies of public records may qualify for admission under a hearsay exception.[14] A copy of a public record properly authenticated under FRE 902(4) satisfies the requirements of the Best Evidence Doctrine.[15]

---

certification was improper because not made by custodian; court approves principle that authority of the certifier "should be assumed on the basis of his certification alone"), *cert. denied*, 430 U.S. 906.

11. AMFAC Distrib. Corp. v. Harrelson, 842 F.2d 304, 306-307 (11th Cir. 1988) (copy of state court judgment with official stamp on back was self-authenticating); United States v. Hitsman, 604 F.2d 443, 447 (5th Cir. 1979) (copy of defendant's college transcript bearing university seal was self-authenticating).

12. Kowalski v. Gagne, 914 F.2d 299, 305-306 (1st Cir. 1990) (taking judicial notice of defendant's state conviction for murder; plaintiff failed to produce certified copy).

13. AMFAC Distrib. Corp. v. Harrelson, 842 F.2d 304, 306-307 (11th Cir. 1988) (regardless whether requirements FRCP 44(a) was satisfied, exhibit was authenticated under FRE 902(4)).

14. *See, e.g.*, FRE 803(8) (public records and reports), FRE 803(9) (records of vital statistics), and FRE 803(14) (records of documents affecting an interest in property).

15. *See* FRE 1005, discussed in §10.15, *infra*. FRE 902(4) may be broader than FRE 1005 because it applies to official records, reports, or filed documents, while FRE 1005 covers only official records or filed documents, but it is hard to imagine an official report that would not also be an official record.

A federal statute goes beyond FRE 902(4) and allows self-authentication of foreign records of regularly conducted activity (even if not official in nature) in criminal proceedings,[16] and FRE 902(11) and (12) now allow self-authentication of both domestic and foreign records of regularly conducted activity.[17]

> **FRE 902(5)**
>
>   **Official publications.** Books, pamphlets, or other publications purporting to be issued by public authority.

§9.24   Official Publications

FRE 902(5) provides that books, pamphlets, and other publications purporting to be issued by public authority are self-authenticating.[1] The rationale underlying this Rule is that official publications are likely to be readily identifiable by simple inspection, and forgery or misrepresentation of such material is unlikely. Moreover, government publications seldom contain serious mistakes in reproduction of official pronouncements or other matters warranting official publication. Privately published books are not within this provision and must be independently authenticated,[2] although sometimes the authentication requirement is satisfied by judicial notice.

The official nature of the publication may be shown by any kind of appropriate legend, typically found on a title page, or by a purported facsimile of an official seal or signature. A legend indicating publication by a government printing office or a copyright by an official authority should also suffice.

Although unofficial private publication of official documents is not covered, the Rule reaches publications by a private publisher acting under contract with a public authority to produce official publications. For example, private publishers are often authorized to serve as the

16. 18 U.S.C. §3505 (in criminal cases, a foreign record of regularly conducted activity, or a copy, is not excluded as hearsay if foreign certification by custodian or other qualified person attests, subject to criminal penalty under laws of that country, that record satisfies criteria similar to those of business records and, if it is not the original, that it is a duplicate; also providing for notice and pretrial resolution of issues of authenticity and hearsay). *See* United States v. Garland, 991 F.2d 328, 333 (6th Cir. 1993) (admitting foreign judgment as record of "regularly conducted activity"); United States v. Miller, 830 F.2d 1073, 1077 (9th Cir. 1987) (upholding statute's constitutionality), *cert. denied*, 485 U.S. 1033.

17. *See* discussion in §9.30, *infra.*

§9.24   1. Other publications falling under this Rule include legislative reports, transcripts of hearings, maps and surveys, statistics, studies, and manuals.

2. United States v. Van Wyhe, 965 F.2d 528, 532 (7th Cir. 1992) (excluding photo in privately published book *The Gray Parrot;* it was not authenticated by "witness who had experience in the area of bird breeding or who otherwise had knowledge of the book or photograph").

official publishing authority for government publications such as court reports and statutes.

Hearsay concerns   FRE 902(5) provides only for the authentication, not the admissibility, of official publications. If offered to prove the truth of what it says, the publication must qualify under a hearsay exception.[3] However, statements in official publications may be considered by courts in resolving preliminary questions on the admissibility of other evidence under FRE 104(a), because such usage is not governed by the rules of evidence (except privileges). Also, courts are not bound by the rules of evidence when informing themselves of the law and frequently consider official publications for that purpose.[4]

FRCP 44(a)(1) provides an alternative method of authentication for official publications because it states that an official record "kept within the United States, [or] any state" when admissible for any purpose "may be evidenced by an official publication thereof."[5]

FRE 902(6)

Newspapers and periodicals. Printed materials purporting to be newspapers or periodicals.

---

§9.25   Newspapers and Periodicals

Rule 902(6) provides for self-authentication of printed materials, public or private, purporting to be newspapers or periodicals.[1] The Rule does not require that the publication be generally known or widely circulated, but to qualify as a newspaper or periodical it must appear with some regularity rather than sporadically.

The rationale for self-authentication of newspapers and periodicals is that forgery is unlikely because it is extremely difficult. Most newspapers and periodicals have distinctive layout, typestyle, logo, and other readily discernible characteristics. Effective forgery is hard enough to be unlikely.

FRE 902(6) allows a purported newspaper or periodical offered in evidence to be taken as an actual or true impression of the publication whose identification it carries. The name of the publisher or printer, date, and place of publication, all as indicated by appropriate legends on the face of the document, may be taken at face value as showing that

---

3. *See, e.g.*, FRE 803(6) (records of regularly conducted activity); FRE 803(8) (public records and reports); FRE 803(9) (records of vital statistics); FRE 803(18) (learned treatises).

4. *See* §2.13, *supra*.

5. *See also* FRCrimP 27.

§9.25   1. *See, e.g.*, Stahl v. Novartis Pharm. Corp., 283 F.3d 254, 271 (5th Cir. 2002) (photocopied passages from medical journal articles were authenticated; title and date of journal appeared in photocopy).

the contents were published at the time and place and in the source indicated.

While self-authentication under FRE 902(6) reaches the fact, time, and place of publication, extrinsic evidence may still be necessary to establish authorship of particular articles or letters or responsibility for classified or feature advertisements. The Advisory Committee pointedly noted that "[e]stablishing the authenticity of the publication may, of course, leave still open questions of authority and responsibility for items therein contained."[2] The issues of authorship and responsibility are often critical in particular types of litigation such as defamation, trademark or copyright infringement, invasion of privacy, and breach of contract.

It is preferable to establish authorship or responsibility for particular published items by extrinsic evidence, where such evidence can be easily obtained. Nonetheless, given the improbability that a newspaper or magazine would publish an article under an erroneous byline or run a feature advertisement without authority of its apparent sponsor, FRE 902(6) should be interpreted as permitting self-authentication of such matters. Letters to the editor and classified advertising raise more serious concerns, and the greater danger of mistake or misidentification in publication of such items justifies requiring that their authenticity generally be established by extrinsic evidence.

FRE 902(6) provides only for the self-authentication of newspapers and periodicals. They are not admissible to prove the truth of statements they contain except where such statements fit an exception to the hearsay rule.[3]

FRE 902(7)

Trade inscriptions and the like. Inscriptions, signs, tags, or labels purporting to have been affixed in the course of business and indicating ownership, control, or origin.

---

§9.26   Trade Inscriptions

FRE 902(7) provides that inscriptions, signs, tags, or labels purporting to have been affixed in the course of business and indicating ownership, control, or origin are self-authenticating. The Rule rests on the theory that purported trademarks and tradenames, which are daily and universally relied on in the commercial world and by the public at large, are in fact reliable indicators of the ownership, control, or origin of the matter to which they are affixed. Such marks and names enjoy elaborate

---

2. ACN, FRE 902(6).

3. New England Mut. Life Ins. Co. v. Anderson, 888 F.2d 646, 650 (10th Cir. 1989) (newspaper article inadmissible to prove truth of story alleging that wife admitted conspiracy to kill her husband).

legal protection under both state and federal statutory law, as well as common law tort doctrines. In most instances, they are difficult to forge or falsify.

There are only two requirements under the Rule: First, the inscription must have been affixed in the course of business. Second, it must indicate ownership, control, or origin. There is no requirement that a trademark or tradename be registered. The Rule is broad enough to embrace names of manufacturers, retailers, or distributors, whether doing business nationwide or only regionally or locally. The reference to "business" in the Rule does not exclude inscriptions, insignia, or logos by nonprofit entities such as churches and universities.[1]

The requirement that the inscription be "affixed in the course of business" suggests an appearance that is at least somewhat polished, formal, and elaborate. Normally inscriptions are printed, molded, embossed, cast, etched, or stitched. A hand-scribbled tag should not be sufficient.

The Rule allows self-authentication of a wide range of printed material to which trademarks or trade names are affixed such as records, bills, receipts, forms, catalogues, price lists, instructions for assembly and use, warranties, and so forth.[2] It also applies to inscriptions on chattels[3] as well as videotape footage.[4] Advertisements to which trademarks or tradenames are affixed are also generally self-authenticating, at least where they purport to have been published and circulated by the enterprise whose product or services it promotes or identifies or describes.[5] The issue whether stationery letterhead is sufficient to authenticate a letter as from a particular source is discussed in an earlier section.[6]

FRE 902(7) is useful in product liability actions where it allows the claimant to connect the product to the defendant by means of its identifying name or mark, whether found on the product itself or on its

---

§9.26 1. *Cf.* United States v. Hitsman, 604 F.2d 443, 447 (5th Cir. 1979) (college transcript bearing seal of registrar found self-authenticating).

2. *See, e.g.,* United States v. Hing Shair Chan, 680 F. Supp. 521, 526 (E.D.N.Y. 1988) (admitting Hong Kong hotel because they "bear printed and embossed trade inscriptions indicating their origin").

3. United States v. Alvarez, 972 F.2d 1000, 1004 (9th Cir. 1992) (approving government argument, on basis of inscribed words "Garnika, Spain" found on firearm, that these words indicated where gun was made; court invokes FRE 903(7)).

4. Los Angeles News Serv. v. CBS Broadcast., Inc., 305 F.3d 924, 935-963 (9th Cir. 2002) (videotape obtained by copyright owner from local TV station, which allegedly contained slate identifying defendant's news service as source of owner's copyrighted footage, was authenticated in copyright infringement action; slate was prima facie evidence of its own authenticity; no extrinsic evidence required to authenticate "labels purporting to be affixed in course of business and indicating ownership, control, or origin").

5. In this respect, the Rule appears to change pre-code law. *See* Mancari v. Frank P. Smith, Inc., 114 F.2d 834, 835-836 (D.C. Cir. 1940) (flyer advertising defendant's shoes could not prove that defendant was responsible for its publication).

6. *See* §9.8, *supra.*

container or package, thus rejecting the result of some pre-Rules cases.[7] It is also useful in accident cases where the claimant can connect a vehicle or other instrumentality to the defendant by the names or markings that it bears.[8]

> **FRE 902(8)**
>
> **Acknowledged documents.** Documents accompanied by a certificate of acknowledgment executed in the manner provided by law by a notary public or other officer authorized by law to take acknowledgments.

§9.27   Acknowledged Documents

FRE 902(8) provides for self-authentication of documents acknowledged before a notary public or similar official in a manner provided by applicable state or federal law.[1] The rationale is that a notary is legally obligated to take reasonable steps to ascertain the true identity of the person who appears before him to acknowledge execution of an instrument or swear to a statement, and the notary must truthfully certify such facts. The certificate of the notary is usually sealed, and forgery or false certification is unlikely and subject to stiff penalty.

The Rule does not specify the content of the acknowledgment. Normally the certificate should state that the person has come before a public official authorized to take an acknowledgment, that his identity was known to the official, and that he swore under oath to the official that he executed the document of his own free will. The proponent need not separately prove due execution of the certificate or the commission or authority of the notary. The intent of FRE 902(8) is to permit courts to take at face value a purported notarial certificate of acknowledgment, at least where it appears to be in proper form.[2] A seal is not required, except where made necessary by applicable law

Content of acknowledgment

---

7. *See* Murphy v. Campbell Soup Co., 62 F.2d 564, 565 (1st Cir. 1933) (Campbell's label on can of soup did not "warrant a finding that the can of soup in question was put out by the defendant"); Keegan v. Green Giant Co., 110 A.2d 599, 601 (Me. 1954) (Green Giant label on can of peas did not prove that it produced by Green Giant).

8. *See, e.g.,* Newell v. Harold Shaffer Leasing Co., 489 F.2d 103, 107-109 (5th Cir. 1974) (defendant's name on truck created "rebuttable presumptions" that defendant owned truck and that operator was defendant's employee "engaged in the scope of his employment").

§9.27   1. Under various state and federal statutes, persons other than notaries may acknowledge documents, including justices of the peace, diplomatic and consular officers, and some military personnel. *See, e.g.,* 10 U.S.C. §936 (specified military personnel); 22 U.S.C. §4221 (secretaries of embassy or legation and consular officers); 28 U.S.C. §753 (court reporters).

2. United States v. M'Biye, 655 F.2d 1240, 1242 (D.C. Cir. 1981) (admitting affidavit by personnel administrator in United Nations attesting to absence of records indicating that defendant had been employed by U.N. because it had been "executed and sworn to before a notary public" of New York).

governing acknowledgments. The adverse party may, of course, introduce counterproof that the acknowledgment is false or that the certifier lacks the requisite authority.[3]

Occasionally state statutes provide that an acknowledgment by a notary gives rise to a presumption that the facts stated in the certificate are true. Under FRE 302, state law governs the effect of a presumption concerning a fact that is an element of a claim or defense as to which state law supplies the rule of decision. Therefore, where such a state statute is controlling, an acknowledgment not only makes a document self-authenticating but also gives the assertions contained in the certificate the presumptive effect authorized by state law.

> **FRE 902(9)**
>
> **Commercial paper and related documents.** Commercial paper, signatures thereon, and documents relating thereto to the extent provided by general commercial law.

§9.28 Commercial Paper

Under FRE 902(9), extrinsic evidence of authenticity is not required for commercial paper and related documents to the extent provided by general commercial law. This Rule rests on the proposition that people in the commercial world take at face value many kinds of paper in making important decisions to part with property or otherwise change position and that courts may also safely do so.

The "general commercial law" most likely to be recognized by this provision is the Uniform Commercial Code, which has been adopted by virtually all states.[1] There are at least five provisions of the Code on point: UCC §1-202 provides that bills of lading and certain other documents are "prima facie" authentic; UCC §3-114(3) provides that the date on an instrument is "presumed to be correct"; UCC §3-307(1)(b) provides that a signature on an instrument is "presumed to be genuine or authorized," except in certain cases;[2] UCC §3-510 provides for the

---

3. *See, e.g.,* Langford v. Cameron, 424 N.Y.S.2d 41 (App. Div. 1980) (although acknowledged document constitutes prima facie evidence of authenticity of signature, defendants' affidavit denying execution of note raised triable issue of fact, justifying denial of summary judgment).

§9.28 1. House Report, at 17 ("general commercial law" means "the Uniform Commercial Code, which has been adopted in virtually every state," although "federal commercial law" applies where "federal commercial paper is involved," and in cases where *Erie* requires application of state law, "State law will apply irrespective whether it is the Uniform Commercial Code").

2. *See* United States v. Varner, 13 F.3d 1503 (11th Cir. 1994) (assumption agreements could qualify as self-authenticating under FRE 902(9) even if they did not qualify under UCC §3-307); United States v. Carriger, 592 F.2d 312, 316-317 (6th Cir. 1979) (notes apparently signed by defendant's brother and another were self-authenticating under FRE 902(9) and UCC §3-307 and "no testimony was required").

admissibility of certain documents that "create a presumption of dishonor and of any notice of dishonor therein shown";[3] and UCC §8-105(2)(b) provides that the signature on a security "is presumed to be genuine or authorized."

"Presumption" is defined by the UCC §1-201(31) to mean "that the trier of fact must find the existence of the fact presumed unless and until evidence is introduced which would support a finding of its non-existence." "Prima facie evidence," the term used in the UCC §1-202, is not defined by the UCC, but presumably means that the facial appearance of a document within its terms is sufficient to establish the document's authenticity in absence of counterproof.

Definitions

It is uncertain whether FRE 902(9) addresses only the issue of self-authentication (and hence admissibility) or also compels recognition of a presumption where provided under the UCC or general commercial law (thus controlling the ultimate assessment of authenticity by the trier of fact). At least in diversity cases or other proceedings where state law supplies the rule of decision, FRE 302 requires federal courts to apply state presumptions, including presumptions created under the UCC or other commercial law.

> **FRE 902(10)**
>
> **Presumptions under Acts of Congress.** Any signature, document, or other matter declared by Act of Congress to be presumptively or prima facie genuine or authentic.

§9.29 Statutes Establishing Presumptively Genuine Documents

Under FRE 902(10), extrinsic evidence of authenticity is not required for "[a]ny signature, document, or other matter declared by Act of Congress to be presumptively or prima facie genuine or authentic." This provision along with FRE 901(b)(10) prevents Article IX from displacing provisions found outside the Federal Rules that relate to authentication.[1]

There are numerous federal statutes providing for authentication of various documents, including legislative records and judicial proceedings of any state, territory, or possession,[2] domestic nonjudicial

Federal statutes

---

3. *See* United States v. Hawkins, 905 F.2d 1489, 1493-1494 (11th Cir. 1990) (checks from Federal Redemption Center were self-authenticating under FRE 902(9) and UCC §3-510), *cert. denied,* 498 U.S. 1038.

§9.29   1. *See also* FRE 902(4) (authorizing copies of public records to be certified in manner complying with any applicable federal statute or rules promulgated by the Supreme Court).

2. 28 U.S.C. §1738.

records,[3] specified documents filed with federal agencies,[4] published forms of laws,[5] tax returns,[6] SEC registrations,[7] transcripts of court proceedings,[8] and naturalization records.[9] Many of these statutes provide that various purported official signatures are to be taken as prima facie genuine, and others facilitate authentication by authorizing judicial notice to be taken of various public seals.[10]

Although such statutes continue to operate, it seems clear that if the proponent satisfies the standards of FRE 901 or 902 in authenticating a matter that is also the subject of a statutory authentication provision, the matter in question should be viewed as properly authenticated even if the statute might require some additional proof. Thus, applicable statutes may provide alternative methods of authentication, but they do not limit or constrain the effect of FRE 901 or 902.

FRE 902(11) and (12)

   (11) Certified domestic records of regularly conducted activity. The original or a duplicate of a domestic record of regularly conducted activity that would be admissible under Rule 803(6) if accompanied by a written declaration of its custodian or other qualified person in a manner complying with any Act of Congress or rule prescribed by the Supreme Court pursuant to statutory authority, certifying that the record—

   (A) was made at or near the time of the occurrence of the matters set forth by, or from information transmitted by, a person with knowledge of those matters;

   (B) was kept in the course of the regularly conducted activity; and

   (C) was made by the regularly conducted activity as a regular practice.

   A party intending to offer a record into evidence under this paragraph must provide written notice of that intention to all adverse parties, and must make the record and declaration available for inspection sufficiently in advance of their offer into evidence to provide an adverse party with a fair opportunity to challenge them.

---

3. 28 U.S.C. §1739.

4. *See, e.g.,* 47 U.S.C. §412 (Federal Communications Commission); 28 U.S.C. §1744 (Patent and Trademark Office).

5. *See, e.g.,* 1 U.S.C. §112 (Statutes at Large); 1 U.S.C. §204 (United States Code); 26 U.S.C. §7462 (Tax Court Reports); 44 U.S.C. §1507 (Federal Register); 44 U.S.C. §1510(e) (Code of Federal Regulations).

6. 26 U.S.C. §§6062-6064.

7. 15 U.S.C. §77f.

8. 28 U.S.C. §753(b).

9. 8 U.S.C. §1454(d).

10. *See, e.g.,* 10 U.S.C. §112 (Department of Defense); 15 U.S.C. §1501 (Department of Commerce); 29 U.S.C. §153(b) (National Labor Relations Board); 39 U.S.C. §207 (Postal Service).

(12) Certified foreign records of regularly conducted activity. In a civil case, the original or a duplicate of a foreign record of regularly conducted activity that would be admissible under Rule 803(6) if accompanied by a written declaration by its custodian or other qualified person certifying that the record—

(A) was made at or near the time of the occurrence of the matters set forth by, or from information transmitted by, a person with knowledge of those matters;

(B) was kept in the course of the regularly conducted activity; and

(C) was made by the regularly conducted activity as a regular practice.

The declaration must be signed in a manner that, if falsely made, would subject the maker to criminal penalty under the laws of the country where the declaration is signed. A party intending to offer a record into evidence under this paragraph must provide written notice of that intention to all adverse parties, and must make the record and declaration available for inspection sufficiently in advance of their offer into evidence to provide an adverse party with a fair opportunity to challenge them.

§9.30 Certified Records of Regularly Conducted Activity

FRE 902(11) and (12) allow domestic and foreign records of regularly conducted activity to be authenticated by certificate rather than by testimony as traditionally had been required. They operate in conjunction with amended FRE 803(6), which now allows the foundation for the business records exception to the hearsay rule to be established by certificate.[1] The written declaration must be made by the custodian of the record or by another person sufficiently familiar with the record and the manner in which it was made and kept to certify that it complies with the requirements of the business records exception.[2] The elements that must be set forth in the certificate are the same elements required by FRE 803(6).

FRE 902(11) applies to domestic records in either civil or criminal cases. FRE 902(12) applies to foreign records, but only in civil cases because 18 U.S.C. §3505 already provides a similar means for authenticating foreign records of regularly conducted activity in criminal cases.

---

§9.30 1. _See_ §8.45, _supra._

2. DirecTV, Inc. v. Reyes, 2006 WL 533364 (N.D. Ill. 2006) (conclusory statement that affiant is "custodian" of business records does not necessarily establish that he is a "qualified person" to authenticate records; he must know how record was created and maintained; other facts in affidavit show familiarity).

The two rules differ slightly with respect to the manner of certification required. FRE 902(11) requires that the certificate comply "with any Act of Congress or rule prescribed by the Supreme Court pursuant to its statutory authority." The ACN makes clear that the certification need not be under oath provided it is made under penalty of perjury,[3] nor does it need a seal. FRE 902(12) requires that the declaration must be signed in a manner that if false would subject the maker to criminal penalty under the laws of the country where the declaration is signed.

Both FRE 902(11) and (12) require that advance written notice be given to all adverse parties of an intention to use this method of authentication. The offering party must make the record and declaration available sufficiently in advance of their offer into evidence to provide the adverse party with a fair opportunity to challenge them.

In criminal cases, authentication of business records by certificate rather than testimony has given rise to claims by criminal defendants that their right of confrontation is being denied. Although most federal courts have held such certificates to be nontestimonial under *Crawford v. Washington*,[4] and hence not violative of a defendant's right of confrontation,[5] there is a strong opposing view.[6] Arguably a proper resolution would be to admit business records authenticated by certificate, except where a criminal defendant can show a good faith basis for challenging the foundational statements in the certificate, in which case the government should be required to make the certifier available for cross-examination.

D. SUBSCRIBING WITNESSES

FRE 903

The testimony of a subscribing witness is not necessary to authenticate a writing unless required by the laws of the jurisdiction whose laws govern the validity of the writing.

---

3. The ACN states that compliance with 28 U.S.C. §1746, the statute allowing for unsworn declarations under penalty of perjury, will satisfy the declaration requirement of the Rule.

4. For a discussion of *Crawford, see* §§8.83-8.92, *supra*.

5. *See, e.g.*, United States v. Ellis, 460 F.3d 920, 927 (7th Cir. 2006) (admitting hospital records of blood analysis performed by private hospital that were certified under FRE 902(11); court holds that "the written certification pursuant to Rule 902(11) is nontestimonial just as the underlying business records are"); United States v. Adefehinti, 510 F.3d 319, 327 (D.C. Cir. 2007) (admitting bank records certified under FRE 902(11)).

6. *See* United States v. Wittig, 2005 WL 1227790 (D. Kan. 2005) (excluding business records offered pursuant to certificates, which were testimonial as they were "functional equivalents of ex parte in-court testimony that defendants cannot cross-examine" and certifiers must "reasonably expect" that their certifications "will be used prosecutorially").

§9.31 Testimony of Subscribing Witnesses Unnecessary

FRE 903 provides that a proponent who offers in evidence an attested writing need not call the subscribing witnesses to authenticate it except where the law of the jurisdiction whose law governs the "validity" of the writing requires subscribing witnesses to be called.[1] A subscribing witness is a person who sees a writing executed or hears it acknowledged, and thereupon signs her name as a witness at the request of the party executing or acknowledging the document. FRE 903 repudiates the common law requirement that a party seeking to introduce an attested writing must either call the subscribing witnesses or explain their absence.

It is in diversity litigation that FRE 903 is most likely to lead to a requirement that the proponent of a writing call one or more subscribing witnesses. It is here that the validity of a writing is most likely to be both relevant and determined by state law applied by virtue of the *Erie* doctrine.[2] However, deferral to state law requiring production of attesting witnesses is only required in situations where the "validity" of the writing is at issue, such as where the proponent seeks to prove proper execution or enforce its terms. Where the writing is offered for other purposes, such as proving factual statements made for purposes of impeachment or other reasons unrelated to enforcement of the instrument, the exception contained in the last clause of FRE 903 is inapplicable.

FRE 903 governs only the procedures for authentication of an attested document in a federal court. It does not affect existing laws requiring attestation as a condition of validity. The primary instance in which attestation continues to be required as a condition of validity is wills. In this setting, there is a significant danger of forgery because of the unavailability of the maker. There is also a strong public policy in insuring that only genuine wills are probated. Therefore, it is generally required that wills be attested and that the proponent of an apparent will call one or more of the attesting witnesses or account for their nonproduction.[3] Wills are not probated in federal court, so it is highly unlikely that FRE 903 will ever require deferral to state law in the single instance where production of attesting witnesses is most commonly required.

Attestation of wills

---

§9.31 1. McQueeny v. Wilmington Trust Co., 779 F.2d 916, 928 (3d Cir. 1985) (FRE 903 makes testimony by subscribing witnesses generally unnecessary).

2. Where federal law incorporates state law into the fabric of federal law, which happens in litigation under the Federal Tort Claims Act and in some other cases, the last clause of FRE 903 should not apply. Applying state law on the necessity of calling attesting witnesses should only be required when state law applies of its own force under the *Erie* doctrine.

3. *See, e.g.*, Cal. Prob. Code §8220; Fla. Stat. Ann. §733.201; Mass. Ann. Laws, ch. 192, 2; Minn. Stat. Ann. §524.3-405.

E.   DEMONSTRATIVE EVIDENCE

§9.32   Demonstrative Evidence—Definition and General Principles

Three definitions   There are at least three definitions of demonstrative evidence in current use. One describes demonstrative evidence as anything that "appeals to the senses,"[1] but this definition seems too broad because it reaches essentially everything (even testimony must be heard to be understood). An intermediate definition says that evidence is demonstrative if it conveys a "firsthand sense impression,"[2] thus excluding testimony because it is a secondhand recounting of the witness' perceptions. An even narrower definition equates demonstrative evidence with "illustrative evidence," thus limiting its scope to evidence used to explain or illustrate testimony (or other evidence) but lacking any substantive force of its own.[3] Under such a definition, demonstrative evidence serves merely to add color, clarity, and interest to a party's proof.

The intermediate definition seems the most satisfactory. The narrow definition, which would allow demonstrative evidence only for illustrative purposes, seems too restrictive in excluding exhibits such as photographs or recordings or tangible objects when they have "independent" or "substantive" force, as is often the case. For example, a bank surveillance photograph offered to prove the identity of the perpetrator has a substantive purpose beyond mere illustration.

Real evidence   To the extent demonstrative evidence means anything that conveys a firsthand impression, it encompasses a special subcategory known as "real" evidence. When offered in a homicide prosecution, the gun that caused death is one classic example of real evidence; in a defamation suit, the writing containing the statements complained of is another; in a product liability suit, the contrivance that allegedly caused the injury is another. In such situations it is commonly understood that the thing itself has substantive significance in the case because it is the object that played a pivotal role in the crucial events. Usually such objects are introduced along with testimonial accounts, of course, and the testimony may be essential to give meaning to the object in the suit, as is true of the gun and the product. But sometimes the object itself goes far to

---

§9.32   1. Belli, Demonstrative Evidence: Seeing is Believing, 16 Trial 70 (July 1980).

2. *See* Black's Law Dictionary 432 (6th ed. 1990) (defining demonstrative evidence as "that evidence addressed directly to the senses without intervention of testimony").

3. *See* Brain & Broderick, The Derivative Relevance of Demonstrative Evidence: Charting Its Proper Evidentiary Status, 25 U. Cal. Davis L. Rev. 957, 968-969 (1992) (demonstrative evidence is "any display that is principally used to illustrate or explain" testimony, documentary, or real evidence, or a judicially noticed fact); Mulroy & Rychlak, Use of Real and Demonstrative Evidence at Trial, 33 Trial Law. Guide 550, 555 (1989) (demonstrative evidence is "not the real thing" and "has no probative value in itself, but serves only as an aid to the jury in comprehending testimony"); 2 McCormick, Evidence §214 (6th ed. 2006) (reserving "demonstrative aids" to mean evidence "offered to illustrate or explain" testimony).

prove the case, as is true of the written statement (the words it contains may be libel per se), and in all cases the object can be examined and considered by the trier of fact as having probative force that goes beyond any testimonial account.

At the other end of the spectrum from real evidence is demonstrative evidence that is only illustrative.[4] A witness might make a drawing to clarify her testimony or a party might offer a chart summarizing evidence already admitted. Such a drawing or chart generally has no independent substantive force and serves merely as a visual aid to the jury's understanding of the testimony or other evidence.

Illustrative evidence

Demonstrative evidence must of course satisfy the relevancy standard of FRE 401[5] and can be excluded under FRE 403 where its helpfulness is substantially outweighed by the dangers of unfair prejudice, delay, or confusion. Demonstrative evidence requires particularly careful judicial monitoring because of its capacity to mislead and because of the potent and often inalterable image it leaves in jurors' minds.[6]

With respect to demonstrative evidence that merely illustrates, there seem to be three unresolved procedural issues. What foundation is required to authenticate such evidence? Should it be formally admitted? May it go to the jury room during deliberations?

Clearly, even illustrative evidence requires a foundation,[7] and it should satisfy the FRE 901(a) requirement of evidence sufficient to support a finding that it is "what its proponent claims."[8] For illustrative

Required foundation

---

4. United States v. Howe, 538 F.3d 842 (8th Cir. 2008) (picture of pistol illustrates type of gun used by robber).

5. FRE 401 defines "relevant evidence" as evidence having any tendency to make the existence of a consequential fact more or less probable than it would be otherwise. Technically, no evidence can make the existence of a fact more probable or less probable. Either it is so or it is not. FRE 401 is interpreted to require only that proffered evidence have some tendency to make the apparent existence of a consequential fact more or less probable. *See* §4.2, *supra.* To the extent that demonstrative evidence makes other relevant evidence more clear or comprehensible, it affects the perceived likelihood of consequential facts, thus satisfies the definition of relevancy.

6. Finley v. Marathon Oil Co., 75 F.3d 1225 (7th Cir. 1996) (Posner, J.) (demonstrative evidence is "in some cases too powerful, as we learn in *Julius Caesar* from Antony's masterful demagogic use of Caesar's blood-stained toga and slashed body to arouse the Roman mob").

7. *See, e.g.,* United States v. Wood, 943 F.2d 1048, 1054 (9th Cir. 1991) (summary charts not supported by proof); Handford v. Cole, 402 P.2d 209, 210-211 (Wyo. 1965) (error to let witnesses make and refer to illustrative drawings without foundation or identification of what is portrayed).

8. Because FRE 901(a) speaks of authentication "as a condition precedent to admissibility," it might be argued that the Rule is inapplicable to demonstrative evidence that a party does not offer. But FRE 901(a) should be viewed as coming into play whenever evidence is made known to jurors, even if not offered, and courts have inherent authority (bolstered by FRE 402 and 611(a)) to prevent unauthenticated matter of any kind from being displayed to the jury. Instead of applying the FRE 901(a) authentication standard to illustrative evidence, some courts view illustrative evidence as simply a matter within the discretion of the trial judge. *See, e.g.,* Rogers v. Raymark Indus., 922 F.2d 1426, 1429 (9th Cir. 1991). But there is no reason to allow illustrative evidence to be shown to a jury without a showing "that the matter in question is what its proponent claims."

evidence, the foundation may be easier to lay than for substantive evidence because the proponent need only show that the item is a "fair depiction" or "reasonable facsimile." Thus the prosecutor in a bank robbery prosecution may introduce a handgun to illustrate the approximate size and shape of the gun actually used. The foundation requirement can be satisfied by testimony that the handgun is like the one actually used, and if the point is to help illustrate the fear felt by the teller, it makes little difference that the proffered item is not the actual gun held by the perpetrator.

If a party relies on demonstrative evidence, it should be preserved as part of the record of trial to the extent possible,[9] and this point applies as much to illustrative evidence as any other.[10] For any tangible object like a photograph, writing, or gun, and for a recording that reproduces a conversation or other sound, the item should be marked as an exhibit, assigned a number, and kept with the record so argument about it can be understood by a reviewing court and trial references can be readily connected to a particular exhibit (both during trial and on review later).

May be admitted   Despite the reservations of some courts,[11] it seems clear that demonstrative evidence can properly be admitted,[12] even if it is only illustrative.[13] Where evidence is admitted merely for illustrative purposes, the court should instruct the jury that it is to be used only to help understand testimony.[14] If an exhibit is admitted to demonstrate the type of weapon used by an assailant, the jury should be clearly informed that it is not the actual weapon.[15] If a chart is offered to summarize testimony or other evidence presented earlier in the trial, jurors

---

9. Some forms of demonstrative evidence, such as courtroom demonstrations, are not captured as part of the record, although this is not a basis for disallowing such evidence. *See* United States v. Skinner, 425 F.2d 552, 555 (D.C. Cir. 1970) (it is not an objection that "a demonstration presented as visual evidence" is "practically impossible to transmit to an appellate court" for review; the same is true of much other evidence). Modern technology allows visual demonstrations and displays to be made part of the trial record if the parties so choose.

10. Siemer, Tangible Evidence: How to Use Exhibits at Trial (1984) (even blackboard drawings could be made part of the record by photographing them).

11. *See* United States v. Wood, 943 F.2d 1048, 1053-1054 (9th Cir. 1991) (chart used "only as a testimonial aid" should not be admitted into evidence).

12. The drafters of the Federal Rules apparently contemplated illustrative evidence. *See* ACN, FRE 401 (noting that evidence that is "essentially background in nature" does not usually involve disputed matter, but it is "universally offered and admitted as an aid to understanding," and citing charts, photographs, views of real estate, and murder weapons as examples).

13. Harvey by Harvey v. General Motors Corp., 873 F.2d 1343, 1355 (10th Cir. 1989) (admitting videotape of crash tests); United States v. Lamp, 779 F.2d 1088, 1094 (5th Cir. 1986) (charts and summaries admitted into evidence), *cert. denied*, 476 U.S. 1144.

14. Campbell v. Pitt County Memorial Hosp., Inc., 84 N.C. App. 314, 352 S.E.2d 902, 905-906 (1987) (day-in-life film admissible as "illustrative" of plaintiff's testimony regarding injuries).

15. Carson v. Polley, 689 F.2d 562, 576-579 (5th Cir. 1982) (error to admit knife as illustrative evidence without clearly informing jury that exhibit was not claimed to be actual weapon used).

should be told that in case of conflict between the summary and actual evidence they should decide in accordance with the evidence itself.[16]

Some courts pronounce as a general rule that only substantive evidence, and not illustrative evidence, can go with the jury during deliberations.[17] However, the status of evidence as illustrative or substantive should not be dispositive on whether it can go to the jury room. Even substantive evidence is sometimes kept from the jury when it is too bulky or cumbersome.[18] Also a deposition or other written or taped substitute for testimony normally cannot go to the jury room in order to avoid giving it undue emphasis in relation to other testimony.[19]

It seems clear that courts have discretion to allow illustrative evidence to go to the jury room.[20] For example, photographs often go with the jury whether admitted as substantive or illustrative evidence.[21] Factors that should be considered in determining whether illustrative evidence is sent to the jury room include its importance in clarifying the evidence in the case, whether it represents only a slanted, one-sided version of contested evidence, its transportability, whether special equipment (such as a movie projector or videotape player) is needed,[22] and the danger of the jury misperceiving it as substantive evidence or otherwise misusing it.[23]

May go to jury room

§9.33   Drawings, Charts, Diagrams, Maps, and Models

Drawings, charts, diagrams, maps, and models are among the most common examples of demonstrative evidence.[1] They are particularly

16. Gomez v. Great Lakes Steel Div., Natl. Steel Corp., 803 F.2d 250, 257-258 (6th Cir. 1986) (because chart did not satisfy FRE 1006, exhibit proper only as illustrative evidence or for purposes of argument; limiting instruction required).

17. United States v. Cox, 633 F.2d 871, 874 n.9 (9th Cir. 1980) ("Admission of evidence admitted for illustrative purposes into jury room during deliberations has been discouraged by this Circuit").

18. Annot., Propriety, at Federal Criminal Trial, of Allowing Material, Object, or Model of Object Allegedly Used in Criminal Act to Be Taken into Jury Room During Deliberations, 62 A.L.R. Fed. 950 (1983).

19. *See, e.g.*, United States v. Jonnet, 762 F.2d 16, 20 (3d Cir. 1985) (reversible error to allow jury to take defendant's deposition into jury room). *See also* FRE 803(5) (statement of past recollection recorded can be read to jury but not received as exhibit).

20. United States v. Scaife, 749 F.2d 338, 347 (6th Cir. 1985) (trial court "has broad discretion to permit a jury to take to the jury room any tape recordings that have been admitted as exhibits during trial").

21. 3 Scott, Photographic Evidence §1596 at 412-413 (2d ed. 1969) (sending photographs to jury is essentially a matter for trial judge's discretion).

22. United States v. Bizanowicz, 745 F.2d 120, 123 (1st Cir. 1984) (proper to supply jury with equipment to play audiotape; "An audio exhibit should not be relegated to muteness because it can be perused only through the use of a tape player.").

23. *See* Annot., Propriety of Juror's Tests or Experiments in Jury Room, 31 A.L.R.4th 566 (1984).

§9.33   1. *See, e.g.*, United States v. Espinosa, 771 F.2d 1382, 1406 (10th Cir. 1985) (maps), *cert. denied*, 474 U.S. 1023; United States v. Cox, 633 F.2d 871, 873-874 (9th Cir. 1980) (mock-up of bomb), *cert. denied*, 454 U.S. 844; In re Air Crash Disaster, 635 F.2d 67, 72-73 (2d Cir. 1980) (chart illustrating glide path of aircraft).

useful in helping the jury visualize scenes or follow along with figures or calculations described by a witness. A testifying physician may need a model skeleton to explain a fracture, or a drawing or photograph to clarify a surgical technique.

Foundation   The only foundation necessary to authenticate this type of evidence is testimony that it is an accurate portrayal of the matter in question.[2] Customarily such evidence is authenticated by the person who prepared it or supervised its preparation,[3] and hearsay concerns arise if the preparer is not the person who actually perceived the matter depicted.[4] Sometimes a drawing or diagram is made by a witness while testifying rather than before trial. In such cases, the witness's contemporaneous explanation of what she is drawing serves to authenticate it. Normally the very act of drawing by a witness in response to a question or request ("Please draw the intersection and place an X at the point where you were standing") is sufficient authentication because the drawing represents a communicative response by the witness that is covered by the obligation of the oath. A drawing made by a lawyer is usually not admissible unless authenticated by witnesses (who might verify from firsthand knowledge, for example, that the lawyer's sketch of the layout of a room is right),[5] but courts usually allow lawyer-prepared drawings to be used as a form of argument.[6]

Because drawings and diagrams are primarily used for illustrative purposes, they are sometimes drawn in nonpermanent form such as on a blackboard.[7] But it is better practice to draw on paper (a large sketch pad) that can be marked as an exhibit, referred to by number, and preserved as part of the trial record. Identification and preservation are essential to make trial references to drawings, charts, diagrams, or maps comprehensible during trial and later for a reviewing court.[8]

2. *See* 44 Am. Jur. Proof of Facts 2d 707, Foundation for Admission of Map, Diagram, or Chart.

3. United States v. Jennings, 724 F.2d 436, 442 (5th Cir. 1984) (full cross-examination of witness who prepared summary "served to minimize the risk of prejudice"), *cert. denied*, 467 U.S. 1227.

4. For example, a composite police sketch based on the description of out-of-court witnesses is hearsay, although admissible under FRE 801(d)(2)(C). *See* Note, Hearsay and Relevancy Obstacles to the Admission of Composite Sketches in Criminal Trials, 64 B.U. L. Rev. 1101 (1984).

5. People v. Jones, 205 Cal. App. 2d 460, 23 Cal. Rptr. 418, 423 (1962) (diagram drawn by lawyer not admitted). *But see* State v. Peters, 44 Haw. 1, 352 P.2d 329 (1959) (no prejudice in admitting drawing by lawyer although practice is "irregular").

6. Nelson v. Johnson, 88 So. 2d 358, 362 (Ala. 1956) (diagram by lawyer "was not evidence" but rather a "graphic demonstration" of witness's testimony).

7. *See* Snyder v. State, 393 N.E.2d 802 (Ind. App. 1979) (trial judge let witnesses draw on chalkboard); Annot., Counsel's Use, in Trial of Personal Injury or Wrongful Death Case, of Blackboard, Chart, Diagram, or Placard, Not Introduced in Evidence, Relating to Damages, 86 A.L.R.2d 239.

8. *See* State v. Winston, 520 P.2d 1204, 1209 (Kan. 1974) (review difficult where no attempt was made to reproduce drawing for record on appeal).

A diagram or map need not be drawn to scale, although it should not be such a distortion that it is more misleading than helpful.[9] Any significant discrepancies should be explained to the jury, and trial courts have great discretion to regulate the use of these forms of demonstrative evidence under FRE 611(a) and FRE 403.

A drawing, chart, diagram, map, or model is sometimes admitted as substantive evidence, provided it is properly authenticated, although a more elaborate foundation may be required.[10] While charts summarizing evidence are usually used only for illustrative purposes,[11] summaries admitted under FRE 1006 constitute substantive evidence, at least where they are introduced in lieu of the underlying documents.[12]

§9.34 Displays, Demonstrations

Courts have discretion to allow demonstrative evidence to be displayed to the jury.[1] Courts are particularly likely to allow displays of real evidence such as physical injuries, wounds, scars, tattoos, and other relevant physical attributes,[2] subject to standards of decorum and decency.[3]

A party may make such a display even without taking the stand.[4] A criminal defendant can be required to participate in a display of his person, including compelled wearing of certain clothing or a wig to help a witness or the jury decide the question of identity.[5]

---

9. United States v. Espinosa, 771 F.2d 1382, 1406 (10th Cir. 1985) (handdrawn unscaled map excluded on ground that its probative value was substantially outweighed by danger of misleading jury).

10. United States v. Williams, 657 F.2d 199, 203 (8th Cir. 1981) (employee testified to accuracy of a chart depicting loading of soybean meal).

11. United States v. Howard, 774 F.2d 838, 843-844 (7th Cir. 1985) (chart used as "pedagogical device").

12. *See* §10.16, *infra*.

§9.34 1. *See, e.g.*, Cravens v. County of Wood, 856 F.2d 753, 756 (6th Cir. 1988) (allowing introduction of a replica of a "road closed" sign); Pensivy v. American Metal Works, 8 Mass. App. 945, 398 N.E.2d 727, 728 (1979) (error to bar plaintiff from displaying model of stool involved in accident).

2. *See* Hillman v. Funderburk, 504 A.2d 596, 599-600 (D.C. App. 1986) (plaintiff's exhibition of injuries generally proper, absent overriding policy considerations; here court holds plaintiff should have been allowed to display injuries to her breasts).

3. *See* Bates v. Newman, 264 P.2d 197, 201 (Cal. App. 1954) (court could reject plaintiff's offer to demonstrate to jury his ability to hold an erection).

4. United States v. Bay, 762 F.2d 1314, 1315 (9th Cir. 1984) (even though defendant unwilling to testify, error to refuse to allow defendant to display tattooed hands to jury).

5. United States v. Turner, 472 F.2d 958, 959-960 (4th Cir. 1973) (can require defendant to don dark curly wig and sunglasses to help jury compare appearance with photographs identified of bank robber; no violation of privilege against self-incrimination). *See generally* Annot., Propriety of Requiring Criminal Defendant to Exhibit Self, or Perform Physical Act, or Participate in Demonstration During Trial and in Presence of Jury, 3 A.L.R.4th 374 (1981).

Demonstrations Courts also allow a wide variety of demonstrations[6] such as those that depict mechanical operations or processes[7] or physical limitations resulting from an injury.[8] Whether to allow a demonstration rests within the sound discretion of the trial court.[9] Demonstrations raise somewhat greater evidentiary concerns than displays for several reasons. First, a demonstration may unfairly appeal to the sympathies of the jury, as may happen where an injured plaintiff accompanies the demonstration with painful groans and agonized grimaces, and courts have discretion to bar demonstrations having unfairly prejudicial or emotional impact.[10] Second, a demonstration may exaggerate one party's version of the facts in a manner that would mislead and be unfair.[11] Third, demonstrations present a greater possibility for fabrication or exaggeration, as might happen if a plaintiff feigned the extent of disability caused by a particular injury. Still, a demonstration may present little more danger of fabrication than testimony by the party, at least if he is under oath at the time of the demonstration or subject to cross-examination afterwards.[12]

May involve hearsay Finally, a demonstration may involve hearsay, at least if the actor makes an out-of-court reenactment (as in a videotaped demonstration) and his behavior has strong communicative aspects and amounts essentially to a "statement" within the meaning of FRE 801(a) that is offered for its truth.[13] For example, a type of demonstration particularly likely to raise hearsay dangers is an out-of-court reenactment of a crime or accident where the actor "asserts" his version of how the crime or accident happened. If the actor is a party, such as a criminal defendant,

---

6. United States v. Gregg, 829 F.2d 1430, 1438 (8th Cir. 1987) (can allow demonstration to jury showing how missile system can be assembled from components defendant allegedly exported), *cert. denied*, 486 U.S. 1022.

7. *See, e.g.*, Abernathy v. Superior Hardwoods, Inc., 704 F.2d 963, 968 (7th Cir. 1983) (videotape demonstration of production process);Veliz v. Crown Lift Trucks, 714 F. Supp. 49, 51 (E.D.N.Y. 1989) (in-court demonstration of operation of lift truck).

8. Allen v. Seacoast Products, Inc., 623 F.2d 355, 365 n.23 (5th Cir. 1980) (letting plaintiff demonstrate to jury removal and replacement of artificial eye).

9. United States v. Squella-Avendano, 478 F.2d 433, 439 (5th Cir. 1973) (disallowing demonstration that defendant was unable to lift box weighing 125 pounds, which he said was weight of box he allegedly carried; weight of box was unclear; court had discretion to refuse this "imperfect demonstration").

10. Thomas v. C. G. Tate Constr. Co., Inc., 465 F. Supp. 566, 568 (D.S.C. 1979) (excluding videotape showing plaintiff's physical therapy; it depicted agonized expressions and audible expressions of pain).

11. Espinoza v. Dunn, 38 F.3d 462, 466-467 (9th Cir. 1994) (in suit alleging brutality in arrest, dissimilarity of conditions between demonstration and actual incident, in which plaintiff was kicking and thrashing in back seat, meant demonstration was misleading; court abused discretion in ordering it).

12. United States v. Skinner, 425 F.2d 552, 555 (D.C. Cir. 1970) (demonstrations "should be carefully staged" with "the widest opportunity allowed for cross examination"). Demonstrations are usually not allowed during argument because the time for offering new evidence (even illustrative evidence) has passed and there is no opportunity for cross-examination. *See* Annot., Prejudicial Effect in Civil Trial of Counsel's Use During Summation, of a Litigant for a Physical Demonstration as to How the Accident or Incident Happened, 74 A.L.R.2d 1094 (1960).

13. *See* §8.5, *supra*.

the reenactment may be received against him as an admission, but it may be a hearsay "statement" if offered on his behalf. Demonstrations that show an activity or physical accomplishment carry strong performative aspects that lessen or eliminate hearsay risks,[14] as in the case of a person climbing over a fence to show that one can climb over that fence.[15]

A powerful form of evidence that is gaining increasing acceptance is a day-in-the-life film or videotape showing the effects of injuries upon a plaintiff's daily routine and the nature of the disabilities suffered.[16] Such films must be authenticated as a fair representation of the plaintiff's day and lifestyle and may be excluded if they seem unfairly prejudicial, selective, slanted, or misleading.[17] The fact that some scenes may be unpleasant to view is not a ground for exclusion.[18] Such films often carry strong expressive and communicative aspects that introduce hearsay issues, because the plaintiff may be making nonverbal "assertions" about her condition.[19] A hearsay objection can usually be overcome, however, if the plaintiff testifies and is subject to cross-examination on the film.[20] Conceptually, the film is still hearsay to the extent that it tells the plaintiff's story, but courts often bend the rules by allowing deferred oath and cross-examination (both taking place in court after the film was made).

Day-in-the-life films

§9.35   Computer Animations, Simulations

The rapid advances in computer technology have made possible a dramatic new type of demonstrative evidence in the form of on-screen

14. *See* §8.22, *supra.*

15. Conti v. Ford Motor Co., 578 F. Supp. 1429, 1432 (E.D. Pa. 1983) (no error to admit filmed reenactment of start-up of vehicle), *rev'd on other grounds,* 743 F.2d 195 (3d Cir. 1984), *cert. denied,* 470 U.S. 1028; Jenkins v. Snohomish County Pub. Util. Dist. No. 1, 713 P.2d 79 (Wash. 1986) (allowing videotape of boy climbing over fenced gate of electric utility substation).

16. Arnold v. Burlington N. R.R., 748 P.2d 174, 176 (Or. App. 1988) (admitting videotape of injured plaintiff "doing supposedly representative daily activities"), *rev. denied,* 753 P.2d 1382 (1988).

17. Foster v. Crawford Shipping Co., Ltd., 496 F.2d 788, 791 (3d Cir. 1974) (any value in admitting videotape of plaintiff to show alleged insanity resulting from injury was far outweighed by prejudice in admitting "what amounted to ex parte testimony by the absent incompetent").

18. Trapp v. Cayson, 471 So. 2d 375, 381 (Miss. 1985) (should not exclude tape solely because it contains "emotional overtones," even if the scenes were "unpleasant," because "so too is plaintiff's injury").

19. Grimes v. Employers Mut. Liab. Ins. Co., 73 F.R.D. 607, 611 (D. Alaska 1977) ("day-in-life" film is hearsay but admissible under the residual hearsay exception).

20. Bannister v. Town of Noble, Okla. 812 F.2d 1265, 1269-1270 (10th Cir. 1987) (whether person depicted by film can be cross-examined is important consideration in determining admissibility); Arnold v. Burlington N. Ry., 89 Or. App. 245, 748 P.2d 174, 176 (1988) (rejecting argument that day-in-life film was hearsay where plaintiff "testified to its accuracy, and he was subject to cross-examination"), *rev. denied,* 753 P.2d 1382 (1988).

computer animations or simulations. Animations are visual depictions that serve to illustrate or clarify such things as an eyewitness's recollection of the events at issue,[1] an expert's opinion as to what occurred,[2] or a general phenomenon or principle that served as the basis for an expert's opinion.[3] Animations are usually offered as illustrative evidence.[4]

Simulations, on the other hand, are created by entering known data into a computer program, which analyzes those data according to the rules by which the program operates (e.g., the laws of physics or mathematics) to draw conclusions about what happened and to recreate an event at issue.[5] The program itself, rather than witness testimony, is the source of the visual images depicted and may actually serve as the basis for opinion testimony.[6] Simulations are therefore usually classified as substantive evidence.[7]

A wide variety of computer animations and simulations have been received, including those depicting or recreating accidents, shootings, the operation of machinery, and other events and processes.[8] Animations or simulations are sometimes received to show the results of experiments or tests or to illustrate a litigation theory.[9]

---

§9.35   1. Grosser v. Commonwealth of Kentucky, 31 S.W.3d 897 (Ky. 2000) (approving computer-generated diagram of crime scene based on testimony of witness that it was accurate).

2. Pierce v. State, 718 So. 2d 806, 809-810 (Fla. App. 1997) (admitting computer-generated animation of car accident for demonstrative purposes in criminal trial for vehicular homicide, based on finding that data used by witness were of the kind reasonably relied on by experts in field and animation was fair and accurate depiction of expert's opinion that would help jury understand issues).

3. People v. Cauley, 32 P.3d 602 (Co. Ct. App. 2001) (approving admission of computer animation demonstrating "shaken baby syndrome").

4. Datskow v. Teledyne Continental Motors Aircraft Prods., 826 F. Supp. 677, 686 (W.D.N.Y. 1993) (distinguishing between illustrative presentation of expert's opinion and impermissible recreation; if distinction is made clear, jury has no reason "to credit the illustration more than they credit the underlying opinion.").

5. State v. Farner, 66 S.W.3d 188, 208 (Tenn. 2001) (simulation "is based on scientific or physical principles and data entered into a computer, which is programmed to analyze the data and draw a conclusion from it").

6. Commonwealth v. Serge, 896 A.2d 1170, 1174 n.1 (Pa. 2006) (simulation "creates a result that nobody can testify to with personal knowledge nor is it the representation of an individual's opinion.").

7. State v. Sipin, 123 P.3d 862, 868-869 (Wash. App. 2005) (discussing computer-generated simulations as substantive evidence).

8. See In re Air Crash Disaster, 86 F.3d 498 (6th Cir. 1996) (in action arising from crash of commercial airliner, admitting animation depicting operation of circuit breaker that failed, causing aircraft's warning system to fail); Byrd v. Guess, 137 F.3d 1126, 1134 (9th Cir. 1998) (computer animation of shooting); Datskow v. Teledyne Continental Motors Aircraft Prods., 826 F. Supp. 677, 685-686 (W.D.N.Y. 1993) (video simulation of crash of private airplane).

9. Commonwealth of Pennsylvania v. Serge, 837 A.2d 1255 (Pa. Super. 2003) (approving computer-generated animation illustrating theory of expert on how defendant shot wife and rebutting self-defense theory; experts testified that animation fairly and accurately depicted theory of incident; animation rested on evidence in record and helped jury).

Because animations are typically used to illustrate witness testimony, generally the only foundation necessary is that required of other forms of demonstrative evidence—the testimony of a knowledgeable witness that the animation fairly and accurately depicts what its proponent claims.[10] A limiting instruction should be given telling the jury the purpose for which the animation is admitted and that it is not to be considered as substantive evidence.[11]

A simulation designed to recreate an event at issue is normally offered as substantive evidence and requires a much more rigorous foundation, because the jury is being asked to accept the simulation, which may go beyond anything a witness observed, as evidence of what actually happened. Such simulations are more in the nature of experimental evidence and require a showing of substantial similarity or identity of conditions.[12] If they are based on a mathematical model, the proponent must establish the reliability and trustworthiness of that model. It is essential that the model be based on assumptions and data that are consistent with the evidence in the case rather than on speculation.[13]

A simulation normally must be authenticated by showing: (1) the qualifications of the expert who prepared the simulation; (2) the capability and reliability of the computer hardware and software used; (3) the calculations and processing of data were done on the basis of principles meeting the standards for scientific evidence under FRE 702; (4) the data used to make the calculations were reliable, relevant, complete, and properly inputted; (5) the process produced an accurate result. Simulations that are not properly authenticated are excluded.[14]

Typically, a simulation contains an "assertion" by its creator (often based on input of others) as to how an event occurred, which implicates the hearsay rule. The evidence may qualify under the residual exception, although courts sometimes overlook the hearsay issue entirely

10. State v. Sayles, 662 N.W.2d 1 (Iowa 2003) (admitting computer animation demonstrating shaken baby syndrome, when expert testified that it was accurate depiction; animation did not recreate defendant's handling of baby, where prosecution would have had to prove validity of science and computations underlying conclusion).

11. Wipf v. Kowalski, 519 F.3d 380, 387 (7th Cir. 2008) (admitting videotape of defendant doctor performing normal surgical procedure where judge gave cautionary instruction clarifying limited purpose and dispelling potential impression that video "showed or simulated" actual events of surgery).

12. People v. Cauley, 32 P.3d 602, 606 (Colo. App. 2001) (computer simulations result from data entered in computer "which is programmed to analyze and draw conclusions from it," and "validity of the conclusions drawn depends on proper application of scientific principles") (simulations are subject to standard that applies to other scientific tests).

13. Ramsey County v. Stewart, 643 N.W.2d 281 (Minn. 2002) (error to admit computerized animation to illustrate medical examiner's testimony describing trajectory of shot and wound track; animation based partly on conjecture that went beyond evidence; sequences of defendant's face and eyes at time of shooting were "original evidence" depicting deliberate actions showing intent, a hotly disputed issue).

14. Crispin v. Volkswagenwerk AG, 591 A.2d 966, 974-975 (N.J. App. 1991) (excluding video simulation of high-speed rear-end collision because there were too many variables between simulation and evidence of actual collision).

when the creator or other qualified witness is subject to cross-examination at trial. If there is narration accompanying an animation or simulation, this may also present a hearsay problem unless the narrator or author of the narration takes the stand, adopts the narration, and is subject to cross-examination about any assertions made.[15]

When a party intends to offer an animation or simulation, advance notice should be given to opposing parties so that they can evaluate the evidence and be prepared to challenge or rebut it if necessary.[16] Advance notice and disclosure to the opposing party is sometimes required by court rule.[17]

Economic disparity between parties may affect their ability to produce animations or simulations which can result in an unfairly one-sided presentation of the evidence. Particularly in criminal cases, this factor is occasionally considered by courts in deciding whether to allow a party to introduce an animation or simulation.[18]

Computer-generated video imagery can have a powerful impact on the jury, perhaps overwhelming the jury's fair consideration of other conflicting evidence.[19] Courts often take steps to regulate the potential disproportionate impact of animations or simulations, which can include limiting instructions to the jury, restrictions on repetitive playing of the animation or use of the stop action feature, and barring use of facial features, dramatic colors, narration, or overly emotional content.[20]

---

15. Commonwealth v. Serge, 58 Pa. D. & C. 4th 52, 82 (Pa. Com. Pl. 2001) (computer-generated video exhibits should not "invite hearsay objections by including extra-judicial commentary such as a pre-recorded narration"), *aff'd*, 896 A.2d 1170 (Pa. 2006).

16. Clark v. Cantrell, 529 S.E.2d 528, 536 (S.C. 2000) (whether animation was disclosed to opposing party "within a reasonable period of time before trial" counts in determining admissibility).

17. *See* FRCivP 26(a)(2)(B) (requiring disclosure of exhibits used as "a summary of or support for the opinions" of any expert, which presumably covers animations and simulations, as they are typically offered in connection with expert testimony).

18. Commonwealth v. Serge, 896 A.2d 1170, 1184-1185 (Pa. 2006) (state was under no obligation to provide defendant with funds necessary to create computer animation, but "relative monetary positions" counts in deciding whether to admit animation offered by prosecutor, and inability of defendant to counter with computer generated animation of his own could lead to suppression of one offered by state).

19. *See generally* Note, Are Your Eyes Deceiving You: The Evidentiary Crisis Regarding the Admissibility of Computer-Generated Evidence, 48 N.Y. L. Sch. L. Rev. 295 (2004) (suggesting stricter evidence rules for computer animations and simulations, in light of social science and psychological research showing potential for uncritical acceptance by jurors, hence prejudice); Kassin & Dunn, Computer-Animated Displays and the Jury: Facilitative and Prejudicial Effects, 21 Law & Hum. Behav. 269 (1997) (describing results of an empirical study suggesting that computer animated displays have a greater impact than oral testimony and may lead to judgments contradicting the physical evidence).

20. Commonwealth v. Serge, 896 A.2d 1170, 1183 (2006) (approving computer animation in part because it did not include sounds, facial expressions, evocative or lifelike movements, the suggestion of a "storyline", or any evidence of injury such as blood or wounds; presentation was "devoid of drama" making it less likely that jury would be swayed by emotion).

Because computer-generated imagery gives boundless leeway to its creator and is unconstrained by the laws of gravity or other scientific principles, courts retain broad discretion under FRE 403 to exclude computer animations or simulations, particularly where they are based on questionable assumptions or project such a slanted or distorted view of the evidence as to be unfairly prejudicial or misleading.[21]

Powerful impact

§9.36 Experiments

Experiments, whether conducted in court or out of court, are sometimes used to demonstrate scientific principles,[1] test litigation theories,[2] measure human, animal, or product capabilities,[3] or re-create events at issue.[4] The traditional foundational requirement for experimental evidence is a showing that the experiment was conducted under circumstances substantially similar to the event in question,[5] although this standard has been criticized.[6] The conditions need not be identical but must be close enough to provide a fair comparison.[7] The burden is on the proponent to establish substantial similarity of conditions.[8] If conditions are not sufficiently similar, the experiment is excludable,[9] although insignificant or inevitable dissimilarities go

---

21. State v. Stewart, 643 N.W.2d 281, 296 n.1 (Minn. 2002) (should scrutinize computer-generated evidence to determine whether it is unfairly prejudicial and whether instruction can offset prejudice).

§9.36   1. Brandt v. French, 638 F.2d 209, 212 (10th Cir. 1981) (can admit film of motorcycle passing cars to show how motorcycle leans when it turns).

2. Champeau v. Fruehauf Corp., 814 F.2d 1271, 1278 (8th Cir. 1987) (videotaped experiment of driver of truck traveling 35 miles per hour taking foot off accelerator one-quarter mile from curve to show rig would come to stop short of curve; experiment offered to refute driver's version of accident).

3. United States v. Wanoskia, 800 F.2d 235, 237-239 (10th Cir. 1986) (demonstration that wife could not have used gun to commit suicide by using female model with same arm span).

4. Young v. Illinois Cent. Gulf. R. Co., 618 F.2d 332, 337-338 (5th Cir. 1980) (reversible error to exclude film showing that it was possible for plaintiff's car to have been diverted onto railroad tracks).

5. Four Corners Helicopters, Inc. v. Turbomeca, S.A., 979 F.2d 1434, 1442 (10th Cir. 1992) (experiments purporting to simulate actual events are "admissible if made under conditions which are substantially similar to those which are the subject of litigation").

6. *See* Jonathan M. Hoffman, *If the Glove Don't Fit, Update the Glove: The Unplanned Obsolescence of the Substantial Similarity Standard for Experimental Evidence*, 86 U. Neb. L. Rev. 633 (2008) (criticizing substantial similarity requirement; admissibility of experimental evidence should be determined under Rules 401, 403, 702 and 703).

7. United States v. Gaskell, 985 F.2d 1056, 1060 (11th Cir. 1993) (conditions must be "so nearly the same in substantial particulars as to afford a fair comparison in respect to the particular issue").

8. Jackson v. Fletcher, 647 F.2d 1020, 1027 (10th Cir. 1981) (proponent offering proof of experiment "has a burden of demonstrating substantial similarity of conditions").

9. Finchum v. Ford Motor Co., 57 F.3d 526, 530 (7th Cir. 1990) (excluding videotape of test dummies on sled crashing into barrier to simulate a rear-impact collision; experiment not sufficiently similar to actual event, since dummies were not wearing seatbelts; jury could have been misled and unfairly prejudiced).

to weight rather than admissibility.[10] Some courts dispense with the substantial similarity requirement where the experiment merely illustrates general principles such as those underlying an expert's opinion.[11] Testimony about out-of-court experiments is subject to the usual rules governing expert and scientific evidence.[12]

The trial court has broad discretion to determine whether the substantial similarity requirement has been satisfied[13] and may exclude experiments if they are unfairly prejudicial,[14] misleading,[15] or cumulative of other evidence.[16]

An experiment must relate to the proven facts and cannot rest on mere speculation about what might have happened under different circumstances.[17] Evidence of a successful experiment may be admitted even where other attempts were unsuccessful, provided the opposing party is allowed to explore the experimental process and the failed earlier attempts by questioning suitable witnesses.[18]

Reconstructions   Experimental reconstructions, whether presented by testimony, in-court demonstration, videotape, or other means, raise particular dangers and are subject to stricter scrutiny.[19] If evidence is offered as a reconstruction or recreation of actual events at issue, it arguably should be shown to have been made under "substantially identical" conditions

10. Ramseyer v. General Motors Corp., 417 F.2d 859, 864 (8th Cir. 1969) ("perfect identity" of experimental and actual conditions is "neither attainable nor required").

11. Gilbert v. Cosco, Inc., 989 F.2d 399, 402 (10th Cir. 1993) ("strict adherence" to facts not required where experiment merely illustrates principles underlying expert opinion).

12. *See* FRE 702-703.

13. *See* United States v. Rackley, 742 F.2d 1266, 1272 (11th Cir. 1984).

14. United States v. Gaskell, 985 F.2d 1056, 1061 (11th Cir. 1993) (in manslaughter trial of father for causing death of seven-month-old daughter by shaking, reversible error to allow courtroom demonstration of "shaken baby syndrome" by expert who forcefully shook rubber infant mannequin; conditions were dissimilar because expert acknowledged that neck of doll was stiffer than infant's, thus required more violent shaking; probative value was "overwhelmed by its unfairly prejudicial effects" of seeing an "adult male repeatedly shaking a representation of an infant") (no showing that "either the degree of force or the number of oscillations bore any relationship to the defendant's actions").

15. Gladhill v. General Motors Corp., 743 F.2d 1049, 1051 (4th Cir. 1984) (videotape of car braking on flat surface misleading when accident in question happened on a sloping downhill curve).

16. United States v. Glaze, 643 F.2d 549, 552 (8th Cir. 1981) (results of field test performed on confiscated drugs were cumulative and not essential to case of either party).

17. Ostler v. Albina Transfer Co., Inc., 781 P.2d 445, 448 (Utah App. 1989) (affirming exclusion of videotape because it "did not illustrate the accident, but rather portrayed plaintiff's prediction of events under a different set of facts," so it was "not reconstruction, but speculation"), *cert. denied*, 795 P.2d 1138.

18. Hale v. Firestone Tire & Rubber Co., 820 F.2d 928, 932 (8th Cir. 1987) (approving videotape of experiments, despite objection that tape showed only three successful experiments out of nine attempts to create similar explosion; fact of other unsuccessful experiments was proper subject for cross-examination).

19. Randall v. Warnaco, Inc., 677 F.2d 1226, 1234 n.7 (8th Cir. 1982). *See also* People v. Dabb, 197 P.2d 1, 5 (Cal. 1948) (motion picture of "artificial re-creation of an event" may "unduly accentuate certain phases," and "forceful impression made upon the minds of the jurors" should lead to caution).

to the events at issue.[20] The jury should normally be given a limiting instruction describing differences between the experimental conditions and the real events,[21] and emphasizing that the experiment is only a recreation and not the event itself.[22]

Courts tend to be more reluctant to allow experiments in court than out of court because of the potential for delay or disruption of the proceedings.[23] Also it is often more difficult for an in-court experiment to meet the substantial similarity of conditions requirement.[24] A court may reject an in-court experiment even if it is willing to allow testimony about a similar experiment conducted out of court.[25] If an in-court experiment is approved, it must be conducted during the evidentiary stage of trial rather than during argument so its methodology can be challenged by cross-examination.[26] Judicial hesitancy to permit in-court experiments can sometimes be sidestepped by offering a videotape of an out-of-court experiment, thereby conveying the dramatic impact of that experiment to the jury without the delay and difficulties of conducting the experiment in a courtroom.[27]

Out-of-court experiments

Whether the jury can conduct an experiment on its own during deliberations is a separate issue. Jury initiation of a new experiment is generally improper,[28] but replication of an experiment conducted during trial is sometimes approved.[29]

---

20. *See* Comment, Truth, Lies, and Videotape: Are Current Federal Rules of Evidence Adequate?, 21 Sw. U. L. Rev. 1199 (1992) (advocating "substantially identical" standard for demonstrative videotapes).

21. Champeau v. Fruehauff Corp., 814 F.2d 1271 (8th Cir. 1987) (giving jury list of differences and similarities).

22. Four Corners Helicopters, Inc. v. Turbomeca, S.A., 979 F.2d 1434, 1442 (10th Cir. 1992) (jury should be told that evidence is admitted for "limited purpose only" and experiment does not represent "actual events").

23. United States v. Lasteed, 832 F.2d 1240, 1242 (11th Cir. 1987) (courts "have broad discretion regarding in-court experiments in the presence of the jury"), *cert. denied*, 485 U.S. 1022.

24. United States v. Michelena-Orovio, 702 F.2d 496, 499-500 (5th Cir. 1983) (refusing defense request to let jury smell one of 363 bales of marijuana defendant was accused of possessing; question was whether it could be smelled on vessel at time of boarding; conditions in courtroom were too dissimilar to conditions at sea to justify experiment), *cert. denied*, 465 U.S. 1104).

25. United States v. Lasteed, 832 F.2d 1240, 1243 n.7 (11th Cir. 1987) (refusing to allow in-court experiment; judge permitted experiment out of court and let proponent call witnesses to testify about process and results), *cert. denied*, 485 U.S. 1022.

26. McDonald v. Safeway Stores, Inc., 707 P.2d 416, 420-421 (Idaho 1985) (improper for counsel to conduct experiment involving melting ice cream of type on which plaintiff slipped during closing argument; "experiments are admissible as evidence only during the evidentiary phase of the trial").

27. For a discussion of authenticating and admitting videotapes, *see* §9.14, *supra*.

28. United States v. Beach, 296 F.2d 153, 158 (4th Cir. 1961) (improper for jury to experiment with noise level of adding machines to assess credibility of witness); Wilson v. United States, 116 F. 484, 486 (9th Cir. 1902) (improper for jury to determine whether opium was "prepared for smoking" as charged by prosecution by experiment in jury room involving burning of the opium).

29. Taylor v. Reo Motors, Inc., 275 F.2d 699, 705-706 (10th Cir. 1960) (jury conduct in dismantling and reassembling heat exchanger in jury room not improper where

§9.37 Jury Views

Another form of demonstrative evidence is a view, where jurors are transported to the scene of the event or matter in litigation to examine it for themselves. A view generally raises no authentication difficulties, provided there is a showing that the scene viewed is one relevant to the event in litigation and the jury is informed of any significant changes in condition.

A view is sometimes the most effective way to give a sense for critical facts in a case, but it can result in additional cost and delay and often requires careful control to shield jurors from improper evidence or comment. For these reasons, whether to allow a jury view rests within the sound discretion of the trial judge,[1] and denials of requests for jury views are generally upheld,[2] although in particular cases (like condemnation proceedings) statutes sometimes guarantee a right to a view.[3]

Discretion of court In deciding whether to grant a request for a view, courts consider factors such as the importance of the matter to be viewed, the extent to which personal examination would increase understanding of critical facts, the time, distance, and expense involved, security concerns, whether conditions at the scene have changed, and whether there are adequate substitutes for a view such as maps, photographs, or diagrams. Increasingly courts are finding a videotape of the scene or thing at issue to be a satisfactory and less cumbersome alternative to a jury view.[4] A videotape often has the advantage of capturing the relevant scene at a time closer to the actual event and before conditions change.[5]

Procedures The procedures governing a jury view are generally prescribed by statute or court rule. Usually attendance by the judge is not mandatory, although judicial presence is often advisable in order to regulate the proceedings and prevent improper communication with the jury.[6] When all the dramatis personae attend a view, including judge, parties,

---

same operation had been performed during trial and purpose of experiment was "testing the truth of the statements made concerning the functioning of the heat exchanger").

§9.37 1. United States v. Martinez, 763 F.2d 1297, 1305 (11th Cir. 1985) (whether to take jury view "is within the trial court's sound discretion").

2. United States v. Passos-Paternina, 918 F.2d 979, 986 (1st Cir. 1990) (upholding denial of request for jury view of ship), *cert. denied*, 111 S. Ct. 2809; Bundy v. Dugger, 850 F.2d 1402, 1421 (11th Cir. 1988) (refusal of jury view of crime scene did not violate due process), *cert. denied*, 488 U.S. 1034.

3. *See, e.g.*, 26 Pa. Stat. 1103(1); Camps v. Commonwealth, 50 Pa. 182, 412 A.2d 1112, 1114 (1980).

4. United States v. Willis, 759 F.2d 1486, 1501 (11th Cir. 1985) (admitting videotape showing interior of defendant's in drug smuggling trial; tape showed duffel bags filled with cocaine), *cert. denied*, 474 U.S. 849.

5. *See* State ex rel. Pollution Control Coord. Bd. v. Kerr-McGee Corp., 619 P.2d 858, 863 (Okla. 1980) (admitting movie of dead fish floating in creek allegedly killed by pollution caused by defendant, a scene that could not otherwise be preserved).

6. *See generally* Annot., Necessity for Presence of Judge at View by Jury in Criminal Case, 47 A.L.R.2d 1227 (1956).

counsel, and reporter, there is no reason why testimony should not be taken, or demonstrations and explanations offered for the trier of fact.[7] Generally, however, the practice is otherwise, and a view amounts only to an excursion to the scene.[8]

Usually parties as well as their counsel are permitted to attend. However, at least in civil cases, courts sometimes describe the right to attend as extending only to counsel for the parties.[9] In criminal proceedings, while an accused has a constitutional right to have his counsel attend the view,[10] it is uncertain whether he has a constitutional right to attend himself.[11] Modern authority indicates that the defendant normally should be allowed to attend,[12] and probably is constitutionally entitled to do so in any case where testimony is taken or statements are made to the jury at the view.[13]

Some jurisdictions hold that a view is not itself evidence, but only assists the trier of fact in understanding and evaluating evidence.[14] Such a metaphysical distinction is likely to be lost on jurors, for it is doubtful they can segregate testimonial descriptions of the scene from their personal perceptions and recollections. Modern federal authorities generally reject this semantic quiddity and deem a view to constitute evidence.[15]

7. *See, e.g.*, Rodriques v. Ripley Indus., Inc., 507 F.2d 782, 787 (1st Cir. 1974) (disapproving experiments during view but proper to call attention of jury to relevant measurements).

8. *See, e.g.*, Macon County Comm. v. Sanders, 555 So. 2d 1054, 1057 (Ala. 1990) (disapproving taking of testimony during a view); Cole v. McGhie, 367 P.2d 844, 846 (Wash. 1962) (purpose of view is to enable jury "to better understand the evidence presented at the trial and not to acquire new evidence").

9. Lillie v. United States, 953 F.2d 1188, 1190 (10th Cir. 1992) (in a bench trial, "it is error for a judge to take a view without providing an opportunity for counsel to attend").

10. United States v. Walls, 443 F.2d 1220, 1223 (6th Cir. 1971) (in criminal bench trial, reversible error for judge to base findings on view that neither defendant nor attorney could attend).

11. Snyder v. Massachusetts, 291 U.S. 97, 112 (1934) (no due process violation to exclude defendant from jury view where counsel was present, no testimony was taken, and judge was there; prisoner's presence would not do any good; he could neither ask nor answer questions, nor interfere with acts, observations, or conclusions of jury).

12. In re Application to Take Testimony, 102 F.R.D. 521, 524-526 (E.D.N.Y. 1984) (defendant as well as counsel should be allowed to attend because modern authority deems view to be evidence).

13. Mann v. Dugger, 817 F.2d 1471, 1476 (11th Cir. 1987) (constitutional error to exclude defendant from view where police officer described changes in crime scene to jury) (error was cured, as defense could cross-examine officer at trial), *reh'g en banc*, 844 F.2d 1446 (11th Cir. 1988), *cert. denied*, 489 U.S. 1071.

14. *See, e.g.*, Burns v. Janes, 398 A.2 1125, 1129 (R.I. 1979) (view cannot be used as evidence); Brookhaven Supply Co. v. DeKalb County, 216 S.E.2d 694, 696 (Ga. App. 1975) (jury view os mpt evidence).

15. Snyder v. Massachusetts, 291 U.S. 97, 121 (1934) ("inevitable effect" of a view "is that of evidence, no matter what label the judge may choose to give it"); Lillie v. United States, 953 F.2d 1188, 1190-1192 (10th Cir. 1992) (view "should always be considered evidence").

CHAPTER 10

The Best Evidence
Doctrine

A. SCOPE AND DEFINITIONS
B. THE DOCTRINE IN OPERATION
C. PRODUCTION OF ORIGINAL EXCUSED
D. OTHER EXEMPTIONS

§10.1 Introduction

Early in the history of evidence law, it was frequently stated as fundamental doctrine that a party must produce the best evidence available.[1] How strictly this broad principle was followed even at early common law is questionable,[2] and despite its reiteration in earlier American authorities,[3] it clearly has been rejected today. Under modern authority, litigants are generally allowed freedom of choice among admissible forms of evidence, and they may choose to offer "lesser" forms of proof for reasons of practicality, economy, or tactics. Testimony describing an accident scene may be given instead of taking the jury to the location for a view. A photograph of a tangible object may be received in lieu of the object itself. A hearsay statement may be

---

§10.1 1. Gilbert, The Law of Evidence 3-4 (5th ed. 1791) ("The first, therefore, and most signal rule in relation to evidence is this—that a man must produce the utmost evidence that the nature of the fact is capable of"); 3 Blackstone, Commentaries on the Laws of England 368 (1765) ("[T]he best evidence the nature of the case will admit of shall always be required, if possible to be had; but if not possible then the best evidence that can be had shall be allowed.").

2. *See* Thayer, Preliminary Treatise on Evidence at the Common Law 495-507 (1898).

3. *See, e.g.,* 1 Jones, The Law of Evidence §197 at 439 (1896) ("The best attainable evidence should be adduced to prove every disputed fact.").

admitted in many circumstances instead of calling the declarant as a witness.[4]

Natural incentives to offer best evidence

Parties to litigation have a natural incentive to offer the most direct, reliable, and persuasive evidence available to them to satisfy their allocated proof burdens. Therefore, it is viewed as generally unnecessary for the law of evidence to compel parties to produce the "best" evidence or to bar introduction of secondary evidence.[5] Parties who fail to produce the best evidence available to them take a risk that the jury may infer that such evidence would be adverse to their case.[6] The opposing party may urge the jury to draw such an inference, and sometimes the court instructs the jury that such an inference is proper or that secondary evidence should be viewed with distrust.[7]

Limited to writings, recordings and photographs

The only significant remnant of the rule that the "best evidence" must be produced operates where a litigant seeks to prove the contents of a writing, recording, or photograph. Here, FRE 1002 requires that the original be produced and excludes secondary evidence in lieu thereof, except where the original is shown to be unavailable or secondary evidence is otherwise allowed by rule or statute.[8] This requirement is commonly referred to as the Best Evidence Doctrine although this label is a misnomer because it misleadingly suggests that the doctrine applies to all types of evidence. It is also known as the "original writing" or "original document" rule. By also requiring that the original be produced when the content of recordings and photographs is being proven, FRE 1002 goes beyond the common law, which generally applied the Best Evidence Doctrine only to writings.[9]

---

4. *See* FRE 803 (listing 23 hearsay exceptions that apply regardless of availability of declarant). *Compare* FRE 804 (listing five hearsay exceptions that apply only if unavailability of declarant is established).

5. *See* Territory of Guam v. Ojeda, 758 F.2d 403 (9th Cir. 1985) (pictures of stolen jewelry properly admitted in burglary case; Best Evidence Rule does not require introduction of jewelry itself). *But see* Nance, The Best Evidence Principle, 73 Iowa L. Rev. 227 (1988) (expounding thesis that "there exists, even today, a principle of evidence law that a party should present to the tribunal the best evidence reasonably available on a litigated factual issue").

6. *See* Nation-Wide Check Corp., Inc. v. Forest Hills Distribs., Inc., 692 F.2d 214, 217-218 (1st Cir. 1982) (when contents of a document are relevant, "the trier of fact generally may receive the act of the document's nonproduction or destruction as evidence that the party who has prevented production did so out of the well-founded fear that the contents would harm him"). *See also* Thayer, A Preliminary Treatise on Evidence at the Common Law 507 (1898) ("[T]he fact that a man does not produce the best evidence in his power must always afford strong ground of suspicion.").

7. Cassibo v. Bodwin, 149 Mich. App. 474, 386 N.W.2d 559 (1986) (proper to instruct jury to draw adverse inference for failure to produce relevant, noncumulative evidence in the party's control). *See also* 23 Devitt & Blackmar, Federal Jury Practice and Instructions §72.17 ("If a party fails to produce evidence which is under his control and reasonably available to him and not reasonably available to the adverse party, then you may infer that the evidence is unfavorable to the party who could have produced it and did not.").

8. The Rule does not address the admissibility of secondary evidence when the original is already in evidence, a matter more appropriately regulated by FRE 403 and 611(a). This point is discussed further in §10.6, *infra*.

9. *See, e.g.*, United States v. Conway, 507 F.2d 1047, 1052 (5th Cir. 1975) ("This court has consistently held that the best evidence rule is applicable only to writings.").

At early common law, a dominant concern of the Best Evidence Rule was to protect against the unreliability of copies, which were usually produced manually. With the developments in modern technology that have made trustworthy copying processes widely available, the focus of evidentiary concern has shifted, and duplicates are now generally admissible in lieu of the originals.[10] In its modern form, the exclusionary effect of the Rule is primarily directed against testimony and other forms of secondary evidence offered to prove the content of an original rather than against the use of duplicates.[11]

The continuing existence of the Best Evidence Rule rests upon several considerations. First, writings occupy a central position in the law. The written word has special sanctity, justifying more stringent proof requirements. Second, when the contents of a writing are in issue, any evidence other than the writing itself is distinctly inferior. Language is complex, and the slightest variation in wording can have enormous significance in determining the outcome of a legal dispute.[12] Unless a writing is very short, it is beyond the power of most human memory to summarize the writing with the precision that is often needed in the courtroom. The burden on litigants of requiring them to introduce the writing if available is outweighed by the increased accuracy of the factfinding process. Third, production of the writing, recording, or photograph ensures completeness and prevents any segment from being presented out of context.[13] Finally, the Rule serves as a safeguard against forgery or fraud. Examination of the writing, recording, or photograph itself is sometimes necessary to resolve disputes concerning authenticity or claimed alteration.

Reasons for doctrine

Some of these concerns are addressed in part by expanded discovery procedures that allow parties, at least in civil cases, to examine writings, recordings, and photographs in advance of trial to assess their accuracy and authenticity.[14] However, such procedures are limited in scope and

---

10. *See* FRE 1003; FRE 1001(4). Copies made manually are excluded from the definition of "duplicate." *See* ACN, FRE 1001(4) ("Copies subsequently produced manually, whether handwritten or typed, are not within the definition.").

11. *See* Seiler v. Lucasfilm, Ltd., 808 F.2d 1316, 1319 (9th Cir. 1986) (oral testimony as to terms of writing "is subject to a greater risk of error than oral testimony as to events or other situations" because "human memory is not often capable of reciting the precise terms of a writing, and when the terms are in dispute only the writing itself, or a true copy, provides reliable evidence"), *cert. denied*, 484 U.S. 826.

12. *See* 4 Wigmore, Evidence §1181 (Chadbourn rev. 1972) ("[A] mistake in a few letters of an ordinary deed may represent it as giving to Jones instead of to Jonas or as giving five hundred instead of four hundred acres"); 2 Morgan, Basic Problems of Evidence 332 (1954) ("Slight differences in written words or other symbols may make vast differences in meaning; there is great danger of mistake in observing them, particularly when they are substantially similar to the eye.").

13. Dugan v. R.J. Corman R. Co., 344 F.3d 662, 669 (7th Cir. 2003) (striking affidavit that quoted from Trust Agreement because original text was not attached; meaning of quoted phrases often depends on unquoted text; failure to introduce document violated Best Evidence Doctrine and completeness rule).

14. *See, e.g.*, FRCP 26-37; FRCrimP 15-17.

do not provide a safeguard where the proffered evidence is unanticipated.[15] A leading study concludes:

> Areas remain in which the best evidence rule continues to operate usefully. As the scope of discovery increases, they will diminish correspondingly, but it seems unlikely that they will disappear entirely in the foreseeable future, due to the unlikelihood that any totally comprehensive scheme of discovery will be evolved or can be evolved. A sensibly administered best evidence rule still has a place in a modern system of evidence.[16]

Violations often harmless error

The purpose of the Best Evidence Doctrine is to enhance the accuracy of the factfinding process, not to create an obstacle course for litigants or technical grounds for reversal. If testimony or other secondary evidence is erroneously received in lieu of the original, appellate courts should inquire whether the party claiming error disputes the accuracy of the secondary evidence.[17] If the objection goes only to form, the court should normally find the violation to be harmless error.[18] If testimony or other secondary evidence is erroneously received in addition to the original, it is usually harmless as simply duplicative of admissible evidence. If a court erroneously requires an original when secondary evidence should have been allowed, again the error is normally harmless provided the original was in fact produced.

A. SCOPE AND DEFINITIONS

FRE 1001(1)

Writings and recordings. "Writings" and "recordings" consist of letters, words, or numbers, or their equivalent, set down by

15. *See* ACN to FRE 1001 (enlargement of scope of discovery and related procedures "has measurably reduced the need for the rule," but "important areas of usefulness persist," since discovery of documents outside jurisdiction may require "substantial outlay of time and money," and unanticipated document may not practically be discoverable; in criminal there are "built-in limitations on discovery").

16. Cleary & Strong, The Best Evidence Rule: An Evaluation in Context, 51 Iowa L. Rev. 825, 847-848 (1966). *But see* Broun, Authentication and Contents of Writings, 1969 Law & Soc. Order 611, 616 (disagreeing).

17. *See* FRE 103(a) (cannot claim error on "ruling which admits or excludes evidence unless a substantial right of the party is affected"). To show that error was harmless, the respondent may well be able to prove that the testimony accurately captures the substance of the writing. *See* United States v. Holley, 463 F.2d 634, 637 n.2 (5th Cir. 1972) (error, but harmless, for postal employees to testify to content of regulation; easiest way to show harmless error is to "quote or cite the regulation to this court").

18. *See* §1.7, *supra*. *See also* United States v. Winkle, 587 F.2d 705 (5th Cir. 1979) (finding harmless error despite clear violation of FRE 1002), *cert. denied*, 444 U.S. 827. Older cases tending toward automatic reversal for Best Evidence violations have been largely discredited.

handwriting, typewriting, printing, photostating, photographing, magnetic impulse, mechanical or electronic recording, or other forms of data compilation.

§10.2 Writings, Recordings

FRE 1001(1) defines "writings" and "recordings" in the broadest possible terms to embrace essentially every memorial that preserves written and spoken language.[1] Musical scores, as well as written or recorded communications by code or symbol, are encompassed by the Rule. It is less clear that recorded sounds (other than words or codes) are within the literal wording of the Rule, but the underlying policies justify inclusion.[2] A drawing constitutes a "writing" within the meaning of FRE 1001(1), at least in copyright infringement litigation where a drawing is at the heart of the dispute.[3]

With respect to computer output, FRE 1001(1) must be read in conjunction with FRE 1001(3), which provides that an "original" of such output must be "readable by sight" and "shown to reflect the data accurately." On the larger problem, whether the data itself is reliable, FRE 1001 has nothing to say. Most such material is offered for a hearsay use, however, so the proponent must satisfy a hearsay exception that is likely to contain a trustworthiness requirement in some form, and the authentication rules also help assure reliability.[4]

Generally, the determination of what constitutes a "writing" for purposes of the Best Evidence Doctrine presents little difficulty. The outer limits of the Doctrine are occasionally tested when a party seeks to prove letters, numbers, or other symbols on an inscribed chattel without producing the chattel itself. The issue of whether an inscription constitutes a "writing" may arise when testimony is offered concerning the number on a police officer's badge or a license plate, the words on a tombstone or traffic sign, the odometer reading on an automobile service sticker, the words on a certificate or sales receipt, or the serial number on currency or a manufactured product.[5]

Inscribed chattels

§10.2 1. FRE 1001(1) ("Writings" and "recordings" consist of "letters, words, or numbers, or their equivalent, set down by handwriting, typewriting, printing, photostating, photographing, magnetic impulse, mechanical or electronic recording, or other forms of data compilation.").

2. *See* Cartier v. Jackson, 59 F.3d 1046, 1048 (10th Cir. 1995) (applying Best Evidence Rule to recording of song that consisted of both sounds and words). To resolve any uncertainty, the drafters of URE 1001(1) added "sounds" to its definition of "writings and recordings." *See* URE 1001(1) (1974).

3. *See* Seiler v. Lucasfilm, Ltd., 808 F.2d 1316 (9th Cir. 1986) (barring secondary evidence of drawings by plaintiff that were allegedly used by defendant in making the film "The Empire Strikes Back"), *cert. denied*, 484 U.S. 826.

4. *See* FRE 803(6), discussed in §§8.44-8.47, *supra;* FRE 803(8), discussed in §§8.49-8.52, *supra;* and FRE 901(b)(9), discussed in §9.16, *supra.*

5. *Compare* State v. Powell, 300 S.E.2d 270 (N.C. App. 1983) (Best Evidence Rule does not require state to produce tractors in court to prove their serial numbers), *rev. denied,*

Under a strict interpretation of FRE 1001(1), all such inscriptions would constitute a "writing." However, such an interpretation would go beyond the rationale of the Rule and impose unnecessary burdens upon litigants. Under pre-Rules case law, courts exercised discretion in deciding whether inscribed chattels were to be treated as "writings" for purposes of the Best Evidence Doctrine. The leading case is *United States v. Duffy,*[6] which held that a shirt containing a laundry mark "D-U-F" was not a writing and therefore need not be produced. Testimony was held properly received to prove this laundry mark and hence the possible link between the shirt and the defendant Duffy. The appellate court stated:

> When the disputed evidence [is an inscribed chattel], the trial judge has discretion to treat the evidence as a chattel or as a writing. In reaching his decision, the trial judge should consider the policy considerations behind the "Rule".... Because the writing involved in this case was simple, the inscription "D-U-F," there was little danger that the witness would inaccurately remember the terms of the "writing." Also, the terms of the "writing" were by no means central or critical to the case against Duffy.... Furthermore, it was only one piece of evidence in a substantial case against Duffy.[7]

Under FRE 1001(1), courts continue to have discretion whether to treat an inscribed chattel as a "writing" for Best Evidence purposes, although the definition is so broad that it is often more appropriate to consider whether the inscription is exempt from the requirements of the Best Evidence Doctrine as collateral under FRE 1004(4).[8] In making the determination, the following factors should be considered: (1) the length and complexity of the inscription; (2) the importance of the communicative content of the inscription to the case; (3) the degree of precision necessary in proving the inscription to avoid misleading the trier of fact; (4) the reliability of the proffered secondary evidence; (5) the existence of a dispute as to the content of the inscription; (6) the ease or difficulty of producing the chattel; and (7) the reasons for nonproduction.[9]

FRE 1001(2)

Photographs. "Photographs" include still photographs, X-ray films, videotapes, and motion pictures.

---

301 S.E.2d 101, *with* Davenport v. Ourisman-Mandell Chevrolet, Inc., 195 A.2d 743 (D.C. App. 1963) (Best Evidence Doctrine bars testimony stating mileage on auto service sticker, which should have been produced in court).

6. 454 F.2d 809 (5th Cir. 1972).

7. *Id.* at 812.

8. *See* §10.14, *infra.*

9. *See* United States v. Yamin, 868 F.2d 130, 134 (5th Cir. 1989) (in trial for trafficking in counterfeit designer watches, admitting testimony on counterfeit trademark even though it included writing; "viewing of a simple and recognized trademark is not likely to be inaccurately remembered"), *cert. denied,* 492 U.S. 924.

§10.3 Photographs

FRE 1001(2) defines "photographs" to include "still photographs, X-ray films, videotapes, and motion pictures." The definition is exemplary rather than exclusive and should be interpreted to encompass similar technology and processes currently existing or that may be developed in the future.[1]

Photographs

Photographs rarely raise a Best Evidence problem for several reasons. First, both the negative and any print from the negative qualify as an original under FRE 1001(3). Second, the photograph itself is usually introduced as an exhibit rather than having testimonial evidence of its content be offered as a substitute. Finally, a photograph is commonly offered to illustrate testimony rather than to prove its own content.[2]

However, sometimes the content of a photograph is being proved, for example, to establish its obscene nature or to identify a person in a photograph taken by a bank surveillance camera.[3] In such cases, FRE 1002 bars testimony or other evidence of content in lieu of producing the photograph itself.[4]

X-rays

The definition of "photograph" under FRE 1001(2) includes an X-ray, which means that testimony describing the content of an X-ray is subject to the Best Evidence Doctrine. With respect to X-rays, the Advisory Committee noted that FRE 703 "allows an expert to give an opinion based on matters not in evidence," and therefore FRE 1002 "must be read as being limited accordingly in its application."[5] The Advisory Committee apparently intended that production of an X-ray be excused, even where the expert's opinion is based in part on the X-ray, provided such reliance is authorized by FRE 703.[6]

However, FRE 703 is limited to describing the permissible bases for expert opinion testimony. If the witness testifies specifically about the content of the X-ray or to knowledge derived solely from examination

---

§10.3 1. For example, ultrasound images of which a photographic record is made are within the definition. *See generally* 3 Scott, Photographic Evidence §1260 (1969) (photographic reproductions of fluoroscopic images admissible when properly identified and verified).

2. ACN to FRE 1002 ("usual course is for a witness on the stand to identify the photograph or motion picture as a correct representation of events which he saw or of a scene with which he is familiar," thus adopting the picture as his testimony, or using it "to illustrate his testimony," in which cases "no effort is made to prove the contents of the picture, and the rule is inapplicable").

3. ACN to FRE 1002 (sometimes contents of picture are indeed sought to be proved, as in suits involving copyright, defamation, or invasion of privacy by photograph or motion picture; sometimes as well, the picture is offered "as having independent probative value," as in the case of an "automatic photograph of bank robber"). *See also* United States v. Taylor, 530 F.2d 639, 641-642 (5th Cir. 1976) (bank surveillance camera; admitting photograph even though no teller saw events), *cert. denied*, 429 U.S. 845.

4. United States v. Levine, 546 F.2d 658, 668 (5th Cir. 1977) (in obscenity prosecution, allegedly obscene motion picture must be produced).

5. ACN, FRE 1002.

6. *See* §§7.8-7.11, *supra*.

of the X-ray, the party calling the witness is normally required to produce the X-ray or explain its absence. Such a requirement ensures fairness to the adversary, who may wish to question the witness about the X-ray during cross-examination. A witness may, however, testify to matters observed apart from the X-ray, such as an obvious fracture, even though an X-ray exists that would be "better evidence" of such a fracture.

Production of the X-ray is not necessarily required in cases where an expert's report interpreting the X-ray is offered under 803(6).[7] However, where the content of the X-ray is central to the issues in dispute and there is a genuine question as to its proper interpretation, the trial court has discretion under FRE 611(a) to require its production. If the content of the X-ray is directly at issue, such as where a physician is charged with malpractice for misreading an X-ray, the Best Evidence Doctrine applies.

FRE 1001(3)

Original. An "original" of a writing or recording is the writing or recording itself or any counterpart intended to have the same effect by a person executing or issuing it. An "original" of a photograph includes the negative or any print therefrom. If data are stored in a computer or similar device, any printout or other output readable by sight, shown to reflect the data accurately, is an "original."

---

§10.4 "Original" Defined

"Original" has a technical meaning under the Best Evidence Doctrine that is not defined by chronology. "Original" does not necessarily mean the first writing, recording, or photograph that was made, but rather refers to the writing, recording, or photograph that is at issue in the litigation. The concept of an "original" is entirely relative and depends upon the nature of the claim or defense asserted, the surrounding circumstances, the intention of the parties, and controlling legal principles.[1]

FRE 1001(3) defines the "original" of a writing or recording as "the writing or recording itself," that is, the writing or recording that has the

---

7. ACN to FRE 1002 (hospital records may come in as business records under Rule 803(6) "commonly contain reports interpreting X-rays by the staff radiologist, who qualifies as an expert, and these reports need not be excluded from the records by the instant rule").

§10.4 1. Cartier v. Jackson, 59 F.3d 1046, 1048 (10th Cir. 1995) (copyright infringement action where plaintiff alleged that defendant Jackson used song from demo tape sent to him by plaintiff; demo tape and not first-recorded master tape was "original" because it was only tape heard by defendant).

greatest relevance to the issues in the case.[2] Therefore, a photocopy, carbon copy, or rerecording can qualify as the "original" for purposes of FRE 1001(3) if it is the writing or recording of significance in the litigation. If a copy gave rise to the charge, claim, or defense, production of that copy satisfies FRE 1002 (Best Evidence Rule) and reliance on FRE 1003 is unnecessary. In a fraud case, for example, if the operative document containing the fraudulent statements was a photocopy or carbon copy, such a copy is the "original" for purposes of that litigation.[3]

Whether a writing or recording is an "original" depends upon what it is being offered to prove. As noted by the Advisory Committee:

> [W]hat is an original for some purposes may be a duplicate for others. Thus a bank's microfilm record of checks cleared is the original as a record. However, a print offered as a copy of a check whose contents are in controversy is a duplicate.[4]

Correspondence

With respect to correspondence, if a letter is offered to prove notice or knowledge of the recipient, the delivered writing is the original. If the letter is offered to prove the knowledge or state of mind of the author, the author's retained copy is the original.[5] The retained file copy is a duplicate to prove the content of the letter actually received, and the letter received is a duplicate when proving the content of the file.

Public records

FRE 1005 authorizes proof of public records by certified or compared copies and defines a public record as including "a document authorized to be recorded or filed and actually recorded or filed." The document actually recorded or filed is sometimes a photocopy of an earlier created document. Even if the recorded or filed document is a photocopy, it nonetheless qualifies as an original for purposes of FRE 1001(3).

Photographs

With respect to photographs, not only the negative but any print therefrom qualifies as an "original" under FRE 1001(3).[6] A print made from another print rather than from the original negative is a

---

2. *See* United States v. Tombrello, 666 F.2d 485, 491-492 (11th Cir. 1982) (to prove that defendant was "under indictment," government could offer certified copies of docket entries rather than indictment; docket entries were more relevant because indictment could have been dismissed, and docket entries were not "a substitute for the indictment," but were instead "original documents" showing that on the day in question defendant was "indicted and that the indictment was still pending"), *cert. denied*, 456 U.S. 994.

3. *See* United States v. Rangel, 585 F.2d 344, 346 (8th Cir. 1978) (photocopies of customer's carbon copies of Master Charge receipts were "originals," as they were submitted in support of false claim for government travel expenses).

4. ACN to FRE 1001(4).

5. Hall v. Pierce, 307 P.2d 292, 307 (Or. 1957) (to prove filekeeper's purpose, "original" is not letter in addressee's possession but retained copy on file, which is "paper upon which the filekeeper depends").

6. ACN to FRE 1001(3) ("strictly speaking the original of a photograph might be thought to be only the negative," but "practicality and common usage" require treating any print made from negative as original).

duplicate under FRE 1001(4). Prints are subject to distortion in a wide variety of ways, and distortion and fraud may be detectable only if the negative can be examined. In accepting any print as an original, FRE 1001(3) relegates the problems of potential distortion and fraud to the authentication process and to pretrial discovery. If no print can be authenticated as an accurate representation of the negative, the negative may be required.

Computer output   Any output from a computer that is readable by sight and shown to reflect accurately the data stored in the computer is an "original."[7] But it is an "original" only of the data stored on the computer or diskette. Whether the data stored on the computer constitutes the "original" record in the case depends upon the issues in dispute and the status of the stored information. If the information in the computer constitutes only a summary of the underlying documents, it is admissible only to the extent that a summary is allowed under FRE 1006.[8]

Whether computer output is an original is not affected by the point of time at which it was retrieved; each retrieval is an original provided it reflects the data accurately. The proponent must authenticate both the underlying data and the process used to store or compute the data.[9] In addition, to the extent that the output represents hearsay assertions by a person rather than computations by a computer, the output must satisfy the requirements of the hearsay rule.

Business records   With respect to business records, it is sometimes unclear which record constitutes the "original." Often business records consist of multiple or successive entries or written documents that record the same or similar information. Such records may be generated simultaneously or in a step-by-step process, in which each successive record-maker acts on the basis of one or more prior entries (and perhaps additional information from other sources within the business) and may be used for different purposes within the business. As a general matter, a record that itself satisfies the foundation requirements of the business records exception to the hearsay rule also qualifies as an "original" for purposes of the Best Evidence Doctrine. Thus a regularly made record that is kept in the regular course of business activity can qualify as an "original" even though it was prepared from other documents or is kept in other versions elsewhere in the organization.

If an earlier business record contains significant detail and a later record rests on the earlier one but omits or deletes such detail, it often happens that both satisfy the business records exception to the hearsay rule, and the Best Evidence Doctrine permits the proponent to offer each in proof of its own content.[10] But in some instances this result has

---

7. *See* ACN to FRE 1001(3) (practicality and usage "confer the status of original upon any computer printout").

8. *See* §10.16, *infra*.

9. Computer output is usually authenticated under FRE 901(b)(9). *See* §9.16, *supra*.

10. *See, e.g.*, Brown v. J. C. Penney Co., 688 P.2d 811 (Or. 1984) (no Best Evidence violation in admitting computer printout summary of police reports; plaintiff was seeking to prove content of printout, not reports themselves, so printout was original writing).

seemed so unfair that courts have interpreted the Best Evidence Doctrine as requiring the proponent to produce the more complete record (or show its unavailability).[11] If the proponent seeks specifically to prove the content of the earlier record by evidence in the form of a later record resting upon (and in that sense summarizing) the earlier one, the requirements of FRE 1006 come into play, which means that he must show the later record to be an accurate summary of the earlier one, and the adverse party is entitled to have access to the underlying documents.

Under FRE 1001(3), there can be multiple originals. The definition of an "original" includes "any counterpart intended to have the same effect by a person executing or issuing it." Therefore, when multiple copies of a document are made, each constitutes an original if that is the intent of the person executing or issuing the document.

Multiple originals

Typically, multiple originals are found in the case of preprinted receipts, credit card vouchers, deposit slips, bills of lading, and offers to buy or sell that are included in a formpack where the signature and all fill-in terms are reproduced on succeeding carbon or carbonless copies, along with the pre-printed standard terms.[12] Each copy of a book, magazine, or newspaper run from the same fixed type, plates, or mats also normally qualifies as an "original."

The requisite intent of parties to create multiple "originals" is found when the writing states that it is being executed in duplicate or triplicate (or more). Even where such a statement is lacking, actual execution by the parties of multiple copies should constitute sufficient evidence of their intent that such copies serve as "originals." The Advisory Committee's Note to FRE 1001(3) explicitly states that "[a] carbon copy of a contract executed in duplicate becomes an original."

A counterpart signed by fewer than all the parties may also qualify as an "original" when offered against a signing party, such as the seller's retained copy of a contract containing only the purchaser's signature offered against the purchaser. Normally, an unexecuted file copy will qualify only as a "duplicate" rather than as an "original," except when the file copy is being offered against the author as an admission or as proof of the knowledge or state of mind of the author.[13]

11. *See* Sylvania Elec. Prods., Inc. v. Flanagan, 352 F.2d 1005 (1st Cir. 1965) (plaintiff offered bills and invoices as business records to support claim for unpaid compensation for work performed for defendant; Best Evidence Doctrine requires plaintiff to produce original "tally sheets" recording number of trucks on job and number of hours worked by each truck, or to show their unavailability).

12. *See* ACN to FRE 1001(3) ("sales ticket carbon copy given to a customer" qualifies as original).

13. *See* Hall v. Pierce, 307 P.2d 292, 306-307 (Or. 1957) (admitting retained file copy of letter to show deceased author did not believe he owned property; file copy was equivalent to original memorandum for purpose of establishing author's state of mind).

> **FRE 1001(4)**
>
> **Duplicate.** A "duplicate" is a counterpart produced by the same impression as the original, or from the same matrix, or by means of photography, including enlargements and miniatures, or by mechanical or electronic re-recording, or by chemical reproduction, or by other equivalent technique which accurately reproduces the original.

§10.5   "Duplicate" Defined

The definition of a "duplicate" has considerable importance, because FRE 1003 makes duplicates generally admissible in lieu of originals without showing the unavailability of the original. FRE 1001(4) defines a "duplicate" to mean a counterpart produced by any reliable modern mechanical process—all common copying techniques that do not engage human faculties to comprehend (read or listen to) the original and write it down or repeat it orally.[1] Excluded from this definition are subsequently produced copies prepared by manual methods, such as handwriting or typing. Similarly, a written transcript of a recording is not a duplicate.[2]

Three foundational steps In authenticating a purported duplicate, the proponent shows that it qualifies as the kind of mechanical copy described in FRE 1001(4), that it correctly reflects the content of the source document, and that the source document is itself authentic—that it is an "original" of something that counts in the case such as a contract, a letter, or the like.

Usually there is no question on the first two of these steps, and they may even be overlooked altogether. In the typical case, anyone can see that a proffered document is the product of a modern office copier, and the trial judge accepts the evidence on the basis of personal perception and requires no further proof on this score.[3] (Of course the opponent can, if he has the evidence, try to show the contrary, but such a case is difficult to imagine.) And showing that the duplicate correctly reflects the source document is almost as automatic. In the case of a

---

§10.5   1. FRE 1001(4) (defining "duplicate" as "counterpart produced by the same impression as the original, or from the same matrix, or by means of photography, including enlargements and miniatures, or by mechanical or electronic re-recording, or by chemical reproduction, or by other equivalent technique which accurately reproduces the original"). According to the ACN, such methods of reproduction possess "accuracy which virtually eliminates the possibility of error." Pretty clearly the definition of "duplicate" includes newer technologies, including facsimile communications and copies made by optical scanners.

2. *See* §10.9, *infra.*

3. *But see* Railroad Mgmt. Co., L.L.C. v. CFS Louisiana Midstream Co., 428 F.3d 214, 220 (5th Cir. 2005) (redacted version of assignment agreement was *not* admissible as duplicate; document was not counterpart produced by same impression as original, or from same matrix).

modern office copy, all that would be required is evidence that the original was used in a standard machine to make the copy, perhaps with evidence that the same machine has proved reliable in the routine of office work. The important point is that FRE 1003 does not require the proponent to meet a rigorous standard.[4] In contrast to the requirements of FRE 1005, the proponent need not offer a certificate with a notarial seal that attests to the accuracy of the duplicate nor even testimony to this effect by a witness who has compared the duplicate to the original.[5]

The third point, which is that the source itself is authentic, may be more difficult. Even if the proffered evidence is a mechanical "duplicate" that truly captures the content of the source document, still the opponent may claim there never was an original or (if there was an original) that it did not serve as the source document or did so in an altered form. Even on this point, however, the Rules favor the proponent, who need only offer evidence sufficient to support a jury finding that the source document is genuine.[6] If, for example, plaintiff offers in evidence what he says is a duplicate of a letter he sent to defendant, this proffered item may properly be admitted as a duplicate even if defendant denies ever receiving the original and therefore cannot say whether there ever was an original or whether the proffered duplicate accurately reflects its content.[7]

The judge resolves the first of these three issues. Under FRE 104(a), the question whether a purported copy is a duplicate under FRE 1001(4) is one of "admissibility," and the judge alone determines this point.

Not surprisingly, since most important questions of authentication are for the jury to resolve,[8] the jury decides whether the duplicate accurately captures the source document (a point on which ordinarily no question is raised) and whether the source document was itself authentic—an original of something that matters in the case. FRE 1008 establishes that the jury decides both whether the "asserted" original "ever existed" and whether "other evidence . . . correctly reflects" the content of the original. Thus if the jury decides there was an original, it must also determine whether the purported duplicate was made from the original or from something else. On these jury-determined points, the only burden on the proponent is to offer enough evidence to support the necessary findings.

---

4. *See* United States v. Stewart, 420 F.3d 1007, 1021 (9th Cir. 2005) (in trial for threatening to murder federal judge, admitting duplicate recording of conversation involving defendant; government downloaded to disk data from digital recording; duplicate was not otherwise altered; no unfairness).

5. *See* FRE 1005, discussed in §10.15, *infra*, requiring that a copy of a public record be certified or testified to be correct by a witness who has compared it with the original.

6. *See* FRE 901(a). But even with this foundation, the trial judge still has discretion under FRE 1003 to exclude the duplicate under certain circumstances. *See* the discussion in §10.8, *infra*.

7. *See* Fredericks v. Howell, 426 So. 2d 1200 (Fla. Dist. Ct. App. 1983) (plaintiff's file copy of letter allegedly sent to defendant held admissible to prove content of purported original, even though defendant denied ever receiving original letter).

8. *See* the discussion of FRE 901 in §9.3, *supra*.

Carbon copies   A carbon copy normally qualifies as a "duplicate" despite the possibility that some terms of the original may have been changed by corrections, interlineations, or marginal notes that do not appear legibly or at all on the carbon copy. Such risks should not warrant rejection of the carbon copy, provided it has been authenticated as a duplicate.

Rerecordings   In the case of rerecordings, it is likely that the preparer of the "duplicate" will need to testify regarding the process by which the rerecording was made in order to establish that it faithfully reproduces the original and was not edited or altered. However, testimony by a witness familiar with the original recording that the duplicate is an accurate reproduction is normally sufficient.[9]

An edited or "composite" version of an original recording can be properly received as a "duplicate" when the nature of the editing is known and the relevant portion of the recording has not been altered in any material way. For example, in *United States v. Boley*,[10] the court held an edited version of a tape-recorded conversation admissible as a duplicate when the only deletions were references to a codefendant that were inadmissible, and a copy of the unedited tape had been given to the defense prior to trial. A "composite" tape should generally be viewed as a summary under FRE 1006 and admitted only if the adverse party is given access to the uncut and unaltered originals.[11]

Similarly, an electronically enhanced rerecording designed to eliminate background noise or increase audibility can qualify as a duplicate, provided that such enhancement does not distort the content of the original.[12]

Transcripts   Transcripts of recordings do not qualify as "duplicates" because they are manually prepared copies.[13] Therefore, in absence of a statute authorizing admission of transcripts, a transcript cannot be offered in lieu of the recording itself without a showing of the unavailability of the original recording. However, the overwhelming weight of authority approves the use of transcripts in conjunction with the recording as an aid to understanding, subject to careful regulation by the court.[14]

---

9. United States v. Di Matteo, 716 F.2d 1361, 1368 (11th Cir. 1983) (court found tapes to be "duplicates" under FRE 1001(4) and FRE 1003 based on testimony of informant that tapes were "exact recordings of conversations that were on the original tapes"), *vacated on other grounds*, 469 U.S. 1101.

10. 730 F.2d 1326, 1332-1333 (10th Cir. 1984).

11. United States v. Denton, 556 F.2d 811, 815-816 (6th Cir. 1977) (admitting composite tape where defense counsel had reasonable opportunity to examine originals; accuracy and authenticity were supported by sufficient evidence), *cert. denied*, 434 U.S. 892.

12. United States v. Slade, 627 F.2d 293, 301 (D.C. Cir. 1980) (admitting electronically enhanced copies of recordings as duplicates on testimony that copies "which lowered or deleted background noise, had been compared to the originals for accuracy" by experienced FBI technician and detective, and both originals and copies were admitted), *cert. denied sub nom.* Johnson v. United States, 449 U.S. 1034.

13. Atkins v. State, 523 A.2d 539, 545-546 (Del. 1987) (written transcript does not qualify as duplicate of original tape-recorded statement).

14. *See* further discussion of the admissibility of transcripts in §10.9, *infra*.

Generally, a photographic print is not a duplicate because any print made from the original negative is itself an original under FRE 1001(3). FRE 1001(4) provides that "enlargements and miniatures" are duplicates, which gives the court some discretion to control their admission under FRE 1003. A photocopy of a print or a photograph reproduced in a newspaper is a duplicate, as is a print made from a print rather than from the original negative. A "duplicate" also includes a photograph of a writing, an inscribed chattel, or another photograph. A still image from a videotape made by a bank surveillance camera has been held to be a "duplicate."[15]

FRE 1001(3) defines a computer printout as an "original." However, it is an original only of the data stored on the computer. If the underlying documents constitute the original rather than the stored data, a computer printout may be a "duplicate" of such documents, provided that the data were fed into the computer by a mechanical technique equivalent to those listed in FRE 1001(4), such as an optical scanner.[16] A computer printout would not be a "duplicate" of original data fed into the computer manually, because FRE 1001(4) does not extend to reproduction methods that have a manual component. However, once the underlying documents are manually fed into the computer, the stored information often becomes a business record. Any errors made in entering the underlying data are likely to be caught and corrected when such information is kept and maintained as a business record. A printout of such a record qualifies as an original under FRE 1001(3). A photocopy of a computer printout is a duplicate.

B.   THE DOCTRINE IN OPERATION

FRE 1002

To prove the content of a writing, recording, or photograph, the original writing, recording, or photograph is required, except as otherwise provided in these rules or by Act of Congress.

§10.6   Proving Content

While most of Article X consists of definitions, qualifications, or exceptions to the Best Evidence Rule, the Rule itself is stated in FRE 1002. The Rule requires that the original of a writing, recording, or photograph be produced to prove its content, except as otherwise provided by rule or federal statute. The Best Evidence Rule does not

---

15. United States v. Perry, 925 F.2d 1077, 1082 (8th Cir.), *cert. denied*, 502 U.S. 849.
16. FRE 1001(4).

apply to other physical evidence or impose a generalized requirement that a party produce the best available evidence.[1]

Reading FRE 1001-1003 together, it can be said that the Rules broaden the Best Evidence Doctrine, which now reaches beyond writings to embrace photographs and recordings as well. But it can also be said that the Rules temper the rigor of the doctrine, which no longer insists on "originals" and is instead generous in accepting duplicates made by mechanical means.

Of course there are important exceptions as well, where the proponent need not even offer a duplicate. Rule 1004 allows testimony and other forms of secondary evidence to prove content where the original is shown to be unavailable or where the content relates only to a collateral matter.[2] Rule 1005 allows the use of a certified copy to prove a public record or a document filed or recorded pursuant to law.[3] FRE 1006 allows the use of a chart, summary, or calculation to prove the content of voluminous writings, recordings, or photographs.[4] FRE 1007 dispenses with the requirement of producing an original where the opponent has admitted the content of the original by testimony or writing.[5] Various statutes outside the Federal Rules of Evidence also authorize receipt of duplicates in lieu of originals, and FRE 1002 incorporates such statutory exceptions by reference.[6]

Proof of content The core concept in FRE 1002 is "proof of content." Content may be proved, hence triggering the requirements of FRE 1002, in either of two situations. First, proof of content may be required by the substantive law, such as where the substantive law makes the content of a writing, recording, or photograph controlling on a particular issue[7] or where its content constitutes an element of a charge, claim, or defense.[8]

Second, FRE 1002 applies where a party as a matter of strategy relies on the content of a writing, recording, or photograph to prove a point relevant to the litigation even though proof of such content is not required by the substantive law. A party often has several choices of proof. For example, a party may prove payment by testimony based

---

§10.6 1. *See* §10.1, *supra.*

2. *See* §§10.10-10.14, *infra.*

3. *See* §10.15, *infra.*

4. *See* §10.16, *infra.*

5. *See* §10.17, *infra.*

6. *See, e.g.,* 28 U.S.C. §1732 (copies of business records admissible in lieu of originals); 44 U.S.C. §2116(a) (reproductions of certain National Archives records treated as originals).

7. *See, e.g.,* Shipley v. Commissioner, 572 F.2d 212, 213-214 (9th Cir. 1977) (taxpayer's suit for refund under statute requiring claim to be filed within 90 days of notice of deficiency; IRC §7502(a) provides that "date of the United States postmark stamped on the cover" is the date of "delivery or the date of payment"; court rejects secondary evidence that petition was mailed in time; postmark on envelope indicated that it was mailed one day late and "when a legible postmark appears on an envelope no evidence that the petition was mailed on some other day will be allowed").

8. *See, e.g.,* United States v. Levine, 546 F.2d 658 (5th Cir. 1977) (in obscenity trial, contents of film must be proved as element of crime, and Best Evidence Doctrine applies).

on independent knowledge rather than by offering a receipt.[9] However, if the party chooses to establish payment by proving the content of a receipt, the Best Evidence Rule governs. The party must produce the receipt itself (or account for its nonproduction) rather than merely offering a testimonial account of its content.[10] Similarly, if a party seeks to prove a medical diagnosis by relying on the doctor's report rather than offering testimony by the doctor, then the report itself must be produced or its unavailability demonstrated.[11]

According to the Advisory Committee, proof of absence of content, or nonexistence of an entry, in a writing, recording, or photograph is not governed by FRE 1002.[12] Testimony and other secondary evidence concerning such matters is generally allowed without regard to the Best Evidence Doctrine.[13]

Proof of absence of content

A witness may refer to a writing, recording, or photograph without seeking to prove its content, and such cases are outside the scope of FRE 1002. Testimony about the making, execution, existence, or delivery of a document generally does not offend the Best Evidence Doctrine.[14] The difficulty is that such testimony usually must reveal to some extent the content of the writing, recording, or photograph in order to identify it. As Wigmore noted:

Proof of matters other than content

> Testimony about a document cannot go very far without referring to its terms, and the instances in which some other fact about a document is material, and yet its terms are clearly not, are so few that in the other situations the natural tendency of courts is to lean in favor of requiring production. . . . The line between testifying to terms or contents and testifying to other facts is not only thus difficult to draw in a given case, but its determination tends to become a matter of merely logical subtlety and verbal quibbling.[15]

If the reference to content is minimal and only for purposes of identification, then FRE 1002 should be considered inapplicable, although

---

9. *See* Timmons v. Royal Globe Ins. Co., 653 P.2d 907, 915 (Okla. 1982) (testimony on fact of payment admissible without offering receipt). *See also* ACN to FRE 1002 (payment may be proved "without producing the written receipt," and earnings may be proved "without producing books of account in which they are entered").

10. *See* ACN to FRE 1002 (event may be proved by "nondocumentary evidence" even though written record was made, but if event is to be proved "by the written record," then Best Evidence doctrine applies).

11. United States v. Winkle, 587 F.2d 705, 712 (5th Cir. 1979) (error to admit testimony on treatment based on medical charts, which should themselves have been produced), *cert. denied*, 444 U.S. 827.

12. ACN to FRE 1002 (rule does not apply to "testimony that books or records have been examined and found not to contain any references to a designated matter").

13. United States v. Madera, 574 F.2d 1320, 1323 n.3 (5th Cir. 1978) (can admit testimony that phone directories were examined and did not show existence of particular body shop).

14. *See* Fireman's Fund Ins. Co. v. Stites, 258 F.3d 1016, 1023 (9th Cir. 2001) (best evidence rule inapposite where documents submitted were offered to show transactions between parties had occurred, not to prove their contents).

15. 4 Wigmore, Evidence §1242 at 574 (Chadbourn rev. 1972).

a limiting instruction is appropriate to prevent the jury from considering the evidence for a broader purpose. If the testimony identifying the writing requires revelation of critical content, the concerns underlying the Best Evidence Doctrine come into play and require that the writing be produced or its unavailability shown.

If an expert witness refers to a writing, recording, or photograph not to prove its content but to establish that it served as a basis for the expert's opinion, FRE 1002 is inapplicable.[16] However, to the extent that the expert reveals content, Best Evidence concerns are raised. FRE 703 permits an expert to base an opinion on data not admissible in evidence but does not necessarily authorize the expert to present such inadmissible matter to the jury.[17]

Writing already in evidence

An objection under FRE 1002 should not be confused with the objection "the writing speaks for itself," which is sometimes made when a witness is asked to read or interpret a writing after it has been introduced into evidence. If the writing, recording, or photograph has already been admitted to prove its content, the concerns of FRE 1002 are ended. FRE 701 and FRE 702 control the issue whether opinion or expert testimony should be allowed to assist the jury in understanding the writing, recording, or photograph. Similarly, it is within the discretion of the court under FRE 611(a) whether and when to allow the writing to be read, the recording played, or the photograph shown to the jury.

§10.7 Testimony Based on Independent Knowledge

Many facts of importance in lawsuits happen to be asserted in writings (or captured in recorded statements or depicted in photographs), but under circumstances where the writing, recording or photograph is only one means of proving the point in question. If the witness has independent knowledge of the matter in question, the witness may testify on the basis of such knowledge without producing the writing, recording or photograph.[1]

Thus an oral statement may be proved by a witness who heard the statement even though it was contemporaneously recorded.[2] Former testimony may be proved by a witness who heard the testimony even

16. Jack Jacobs, Inc. v. Allied Sys. Co., 683 P.2d 1011, 1014 (Or. App. 1984) (although projection of future sales was partly based on examination of various records, it does not follow that testimony by witness was proof of "the contents of the records," as witness was describing "the basis for his opinion," not content or accuracy of records), *rev. denied*, 298 Or. 37, 688 P.2d 845 (1984).

17. *See* §§7.8-7.11, *supra*.

§10.7 1. *See, e.g.*, Waterloo Furniture Components v. Haworth, Inc., 467 F.3d 641, 648 (7th Cir. 2006) (Best Evidence Doctrine did not require production of agreement itself, as witness's testimony was based on knowledge of contract negotiations, and not on agreement itself).

2. United States v. Branham, 97 F.3d 835, 853 (6th Cir. 1996) (no Best Evidence violation for informant to describe what was said during inaudible portion of video-taped conversation with defendants; witness was participant and was proving actual conversation rather than content of recording).

though an official transcript was made that would constitute more reliable evidence.[3] However, if the witness acquired knowledge of the out-of-court statement or former testimony solely from hearing a recording or reading a transcript or other written statement, then FRE 1002 would require production of the writing or recording or a showing of its unavailability.

Courts have held that a witness may testify from independent knowl-edge about ownership of property without producing the documents of title,[4] that he has certain employment or income without producing written documentation,[5] that a couple is married without producing the marriage certificate,[6] that goods had a certain cost without produc-ing the purchase contract,[7] and that a partnership had certain earnings without producing the partnership records.[8] Courts have also approved testimony that a dealer is licensed without producing the license[9] and that a bank is federally insured without producing the certificate of insurance,[10] although such cases can also be viewed as instances where the proof is of the existence of a writing rather than its content.

Matters incidentally recorded

A witness generally may not testify to the content of written rules without producing the rules or showing their unavailability,[11] although the result should be different where the writing merely records pre-existing rules known to the witness. Whether a witness may testify to

Testimony about written rules

---

3. Myers v. United States, 171 F.2d 800 (D.C. Cir. 1948) (government witness could recount testimony of defendant's associate at earlier hearing even though transcript was available and ultimately introduced; Best Evidence Doctrine inapplicable because government was proving former testimony, not contents of transcript; dissent argued that Best Evidence Doctrine should bar witness from relating former testimony where transcript is available, citing its greater accuracy), *cert. denied*, 336 U.S. 912.

4. United States v. Hernandez-Fundora, 58 F.3d 802, 808-812 (2d Cir. 1995) (proper for FBI agent to testify that Raybrook Federal Prison was federal property without producing documents).

5. Sayen v. Rydzewski, 387 F.2d 815, 819 (7th Cir. 1967) (negligence action; plaintiff could testify about income; courts do not bar oral proof of matter "merely because it is also provable by a writing" and even though written proof might have been more persuasive, "question is one of admissibility not weight").

6. State v. Neilson, 81 P. 721 (Wash. 1905) (testimony of witness present at wedding ceremony sufficient evidence of marriage).

7. R & R Associates, Inc. v. Visual Scene, Inc., 726 F.2d 36, 38 (1st Cir. 1984) (president of plaintiff corporation could testify on cost of defective sunglasses pur-chased from defendant; production of written contract not required; witness was attempting to prove cost, not contents of writing).

8. Herzig v. Swift & Co., 146 F.2d 444, 445-446 (2d Cir. 1945) (witness can testify to partnership earnings without producing partnership records; court does not decide "closer question" whether percentage share of partner must be proved by the partner-ship agreement).

9. United States v. Beebe, 467 F.2d 222, 225 (10th Cir. 1972) (approving testimony that firearms dealer was "licensed" without requiring license itself), *cert. denied*, 416 U.S. 904.

10. United States v. Sliker, 751 F.2d 477, 483-484 (2d Cir. 1984) (can admit testimony that bank is federally insured; rejecting claim government had to produce "certified copy of the insurance policy itself" because point in issue is fact of insurance, not contents of writing).

11. *See* Conway v. Consolidated Rail Corp., 720 F.2d 221 (1st Cir. 1983) (excluding conductor's testimony that he did not have "authority to stop a passenger from board-ing a train with a footlocker," as written rules would be best evidence).

an organizational policy without producing the writing that adopts or articulates such a policy depends upon several factors, including the extent to which the policy is prescribed by the writing, the specificity of the writing, and the extent to which the actual policy is alleged to be consistent with the writing.[12]

Mixed bases of knowledge

Sometimes it is unclear whether a witness is testifying on the basis of independent knowledge, particularly where the witness has previously reviewed a writing, recording, or photograph of the fact or event being described. In cases involving "mixed" bases of knowledge, the witness's testimony should be excluded only where it is substantially certain that the witness is merely reiterating the content of the writing, recording, or photograph without relating significant, independently acquired knowledge.

FRE 1003

A duplicate is admissible to the same extent as an original unless (1) a genuine question is raised as to the authenticity of the original or (2) in the circumstances it would be unfair to admit the duplicate in lieu of the original.

---

§10.8 Admissibility of Duplicates

The requirement of FRE 1002 that the original writing, recording, or photograph must be produced to prove its contents is qualified by FRE 1003, which provides that duplicates are generally admissible without showing the unavailability of the originals. Although the federal courts had been moving toward increasing acceptance of copies even prior to adoption of the Rules,[1] FRE 1003 nonetheless represents a significant modification of the common law.[2] By elevating duplicates to a new evidentiary status, FRE 1003 conforms the Best Evidence Doctrine to advances of modern technology that have made highly accurate and reliable copying techniques widely available.[3]

---

12. *See* Hood v. Itawamba County, Mississippi, 819 F. Supp. 556, 566 (N.D. Miss. 1993) (admitting testimony properly on policies of sheriff's office in dealing with detainees with mental problems; policies were oral and not written).

§10.8 1. *See, e.g.,* United States v. Wolf, 455 F.2d 984 (9th Cir. 1972) (admitting certified copy of selective service file; if defendant had concerns about accuracy, he could subpoena original).

2. *See, e.g.,* Aircraft Sales & Serv. v. Gantt, 52 So. 2d 388 (Ala. 1951) (photostatic copy inadmissible as secondary evidence, despite "bearing the admitted signature" of adverse party).

3. *See* Equitable Life Assurance Socy. of the United States v. Starr, 489 N.W.2d 857 (Neb. 1992) (common law generally declined to accept subsequent copies since "a Bob Cratchit, fingers numbed by cold in the counting house and fraught with anxiety over the health of Tiny Tim, might distractedly misplace a decimal point, invert a pair of digits or drop a line" while modern copy machines do not "suffer any of the mental lapses that flesh is heir to").

FRE 1003 serves the convenience of the parties and the court by making a duplicate presumptively admissible without a showing of unavailability of the original. Under FRE 1003, the focus of evidentiary concern is shifted from requiring an original instead of a duplicate to requiring either an original or a duplicate instead of oral testimony or other forms of secondary evidence when the content of a writing, recording, or photograph is being proven.

The duplicate is admissible "to the same extent as an original," which means that any objection that could be made to the original can also be made to the duplicate. Thus the foundation for a duplicate requires showing not only that the duplicate was made by a process that accurately reproduces the original, as required by FRE 1001(4),[4] but also that the original is admissible. At a minimum, the original must be authenticated under FRE 901 or FRE 902, and, if offered for a hearsay purpose, a showing must be made that the original satisfies an exception to the hearsay rule.[5]

Admissible to same extent as original

The only "duplicates" admissible under FRE 1003 are those that meet the definition of FRE 1001(4). Manually prepared copies, whether handwritten or typewritten, do not fit the definition. Sometimes a copy qualifies as an original such as where the copy is the writing, recording, or photograph at issue in the case.[6] In such cases, reliance on FRE 1003 is unnecessary.

"Duplicates" include a copy of a copy, or even a copy of a copy of a copy. Such second and third generation (or later) copies qualify as "duplicates," provided they are legible and were produced by a copying method assuring accuracy. Filed or recorded public records are usually copies of the first-created writing, whether it is a deed, mortgage, or similar document. Therefore, a copy of a filed public record is usually a copy of a copy.

The court may reject the duplicate and require production of the original in two situations: first, where "a genuine question is raised as to the authenticity of the original"; and second, where "in the circumstances it would be unfair to admit the duplicate in lieu of the original."

---

4. *See* §10.5, *supra*. It is generally sufficient if by testimony or visual inspection the document is shown to be a legible photocopy or other machine-produced copy. A showing that the duplicate was made by a technique "which accurately reproduces the original" not only satisfies FRE 1001(4), but also serves to authenticate the duplicate as an accurate reflection of the content of the original under FRE 901.

5. The foundation for admitting a duplicate involves a complex interplay between FRE 104(a), FRE 104(b), and FRE 1008. The question whether a duplicate meets the definition of FRE 1001(4) is a question for the court under FRE 104(a). The question whether a duplicate accurately reflects the contents of the original is a question for the jury under FRE 104(b). FRE 1008(c) states that the question "whether other evidence of contents correctly reflects the contents" is also for the trier of fact under FRE 104(b), and of course the question of the authenticity of the original is for the jury under FRE 104(b) as well. If the original is offered as self-authenticating, under FRE 902 the court must decide under FRE 104(a) whether it qualifies. Whether a document satisfies a hearsay exception is a FRE 104(a) question for the court.

6. *See* §10.4, *supra*.

Genuine question concerning authenticity of original

The judge may reject a duplicate under FRE 1003(1) if a genuine question is raised as to the authenticity of the original. The reason for requiring the original is to allow the trier of fact to examine the actual document whose authenticity is questioned. The factors that must be scrutinized to discern forgery or alteration, such as handwriting, typeface, ink color, condition of the paper, interlineations or other markings, are often not reproduced with sufficient clarity or exactitude in a duplicate.[7]

The House Judiciary Committee stated that it approved FRE 1003 "with the expectation that the courts would be liberal in deciding that a 'genuine question is raised as to the authenticity of the original.'"[8] Nonetheless, a party must have some factual basis rather than mere supposition to raise a "genuine question" concerning the authenticity of the original.[9] The opponent of the evidence bears the burden of showing that such a genuine question exists.[10]

The literal wording of FRE 1003 creates a potential anomaly. If the Rule were interpreted to mean that a duplicate must be excluded whenever a genuine question has been raised concerning the authenticity of the original, the trier would be deprived of a category of evidence that could be critical in resolving the question of authenticity.[11] For example, if an opponent claims that the original was altered, a duplicate made before the alleged alteration is likely to be the best available evidence to resolve such a challenge. The objective of the Best Evidence Doctrine is to restrict the introduction of secondary evidence in lieu of the original. That objective is not violated where one party has already offered what it claims to be the "original," and the opposing party offers a "duplicate" to challenge the authenticity of the purported "original." Even if FRE 1003(1) were interpreted to exclude the duplicate in this situation, it could nonetheless qualify for admission under FRE 1004(1) as "other evidence" of content in support of a claim that the original has been "destroyed" through alteration. Moreover, FRE 1008 provides that the question whether "other evidence

---

7. *See* Opals on Ice Lingerie v. Body Lines Inc., 320 F.3d 362, 371-372 (2d Cir. 2003) (in contract suit, version of agreement submitted by plaintiff did not show handwritten addendum that defendant claimed it added when it signed and returned agreement by fax; defendant raised genuine question as to authenticity of original by contending that plaintiff whited out the note added by defendant below its signature; plaintiff's copy was inadmissible under FRE 1003).

8. House Report, at 17.

9. United States v. Leight, 818 F.2d 1297, 1305 (7th Cir. 1987) ("speculation that some relevant differences might exist" between original and copies "is not a sufficient showing of a genuine issue as to authenticity or unfairness"), *cert. denied*, 484 U.S. 958.

10. United States v. Di Matteo, 716 F.2d 1361, 1368 (11th Cir. 1983) (defendant failed to carry burden of "raising a genuine issue as to authenticity of original"), *cert. denied*, 474 U.S. 860.

11. FRE 1008 provides that the questions "whether the asserted [original] writing ever existed" and whether other evidence "correctly reflects the contents" of original are resolved by the jury. FRE 1008 presupposes that "other evidence" of contents, including duplicates, is submitted to the jury when the authenticity of the original is challenged.

of contents correctly reflects the contents" is for the jury, which implies that a party must be allowed to produce its evidence on this point.

If the challenge is only to the authenticity of the duplicate rather than the original, FRE 1003(1) does not by its terms apply, although the duplicate may be subject to exclusion under FRE 1003(2) if its introduction would be unfair, or under FRE 1001(4) if it was not made by a technique that accurately reproduces the original. Courts may refuse admission to a duplicate under FRE 1003 where the nature of the challenge to its authenticity raises a genuine question as to the authenticity of the original.[12]

The fact that the party against whom the duplicate is offered has not seen the original is not a sufficient basis for denying admission of the duplicate under FRE 1003(1),[13] although such a circumstance may be considered in evaluating "unfairness" under FRE 1003(2). Certainly there is potential for forgery or fraud when a duplicate is received under FRE 1003, at least in cases where the opponent has no access to the original and therefore is unable to verify its accuracy. However, FRE 1003 does not significantly expand the opportunity for such mischief. Apart from FRE 1003, duplicates are admissible under FRE 1004 upon a showing of unavailability of the original. A party willing to fabricate a duplicate would also presumably be willing to fabricate a showing of the unavailability of an original, thereby paving the way for admission of a fraudulent duplicate under FRE 1004.[14]

If the party against whom the duplicate is offered introduces sufficient evidence disputing that the original ever existed, the court may find that a genuine question has been raised as to the authenticity of the original.[15] In this circumstance, production of the original or a showing of its unavailability may be required, with the question whether the original ever existed to be determined by the jury under FRE 1008. If unavailability of the original is shown, then the duplicate may be received under FRE 1004 rather than FRE 1003.

Trial courts have considerable leeway to determine when it would be "unfair" to admit a duplicate in lieu of the original under FRE 1003(2).

Unfair to admit duplicate

12. United States v. Haddock, 956 F.2d 1534, 1545 (10th Cir. 1992) (court must be "wary" of admitting duplicates where "circumstances surrounding the execution of the writing" present substantial probability of fraud; here proponent was only person who could recall seeing purported "originals" and documents "did not comport" with similar documents prepared in ordinary course by bank in question).

13. *See, e.g.,* United States v. Moore, 710 F.2d 157, 158-159 (4th Cir. 1983) (photocopy admissible even though original unavailable for purposes of verification of accuracy).

14. *See* Cleary & Strong, The Best Evidence Rule: An Evaluation in Context, 51 Iowa L. Rev. 825, 847 (1966).

15. United States v. Haddock, 956 F.2d 1534, 1545-1546 (10th Cir. 1992) (in trial of bank officer for fraud, excluding defense-proffered photocopies of bank records, where no one from bank was "familiar with the contents of the photocopies" and some witnesses testified that several documents "bore markings and included statements that did not comport with similar documents" prepared in ordinary course; court could exclude photocopies on ground that government raised genuine question on authenticity of originals).

By way of example, the Advisory Committee suggests: "[R]easons for requiring the original may be present when only a part of the original is reproduced and the remainder is needed for cross-examination or may disclose matters qualifying the part offered or otherwise useful to the opposing party."[16]

Duplicates may be excluded not only when they have gaps or omissions[17] but also when they are of poor quality such as when they are partially mutilated, erased, marked, interlined, or illegible. They may also be excluded when they are potentially misleading such as when it is difficult to match the duplicates with the original documents.[18] If substantial questions are raised concerning the accuracy of the copying or rerecording process, because of mechanical failure or other reasons, exclusion of duplicates may also be warranted.[19]

Another instance where it may be found "unfair" to allow use of duplicates arises when the originals have been lost or destroyed by the proponent in bad faith, where such loss or destruction has made it impossible to verify the accuracy of the purported duplicates.[20] If absence of the originals indicates that they are no longer effective or were destroyed with intent to revoke, a court may refuse to admit duplicates.[21] If the proponent has hidden the originals or refused to make them available during discovery, it also may be found unfair to receive the duplicates in lieu of the originals.

Relationship to FRE 1005   With respect to public records, FRE 1003 is qualified by FRE 1005. The latter Rule requires that a copy of a public record be either certified or testified to be correct by a witness who has compared it with the original, whereas FRE 1003 contains no such requirement.[22] If a copy offered under FRE 1005 satisfies the requirements of that Rule, a court lacks the discretion it would otherwise have to exclude it under FRE 1003.

Other statutes authorizing duplicates   By its terms, FRE 1002 defers to statutes that allow duplicates or other forms of proof besides originals. In fact, however, FRE 1003 is generally

---

16. ACN to FRE 1003, citing United States v. Alexander, 326 F.2d 736 (4th Cir. 1964) and Toho Bussan Kaisha, Ltd. v. American President Lines, Ltd., 265 F.2d 418, 76 A.L.R.2d 1344 (2d Cir. 1959).

17. Amoco Prod. Co. v. United States, 619 F.2d 1383, 1391 (10th Cir. 1980) (can exclude file copy of deed because "most critical part," in form of reservation clause, was not completely shown in duplicate).

18. Ruberto v. Commissioner, 774 F.2d 61 (2d Cir. 1985) (photocopies of canceled checks allegedly written to a church excluded where there was difficulty matching photocopies of backs of checks with photocopies of fronts; originals required).

19. Lozano v. Ashcroft, 258 F.3d 1160, 1166 n.5 (10th Cir. 2001) (where date of receipt of letter was at issue and original date-stamped letter was not produced, fairness under FRE 1003 supported court's decision not to give weight to photocopy with partially illegible date stamp).

20. *See* FRE 1004(1).

21. *See* Comment to URE 1003 (1974) (this provision does not "dispense with requirements for explaining the reasons a duplicate is being tendered in lieu of an original" whenever lack of the original might suggest that it "is no longer effective or has been destroyed with an intent to revoke").

22. *See* §10.15, *infra*.

more lenient than the applicable statutes, which consequently have hardly any room left to operate. At most, the statutes tend to confirm, in particular instances, the result that a court would likely reach in applying the Rules.[23]

§10.9 Transcripts

A written transcript of a recording does not qualify as a "duplicate" under FRE 1001(4) because it is prepared manually rather than mechanically.[1] In absence of an authorizing statute,[2] transcripts may not be received to prove the content of an original recording without showing the unavailability of the original.[3] Transcripts may be introduced, however, as an accompaniment to the recording itself to aid the jury's understanding.[4] Whether the jury should have use of transcripts is left to the discretion of the trial judge.[5]

The court should make every effort to obtain a transcript of stipulated accuracy and should require that the recording and proposed transcript be disclosed to the adverse party in advance of trial.[6] If there is a dispute concerning its accuracy, the court may refuse to allow submission of any transcript,[7] allow each party to submit its own transcript,[8] or attempt to resolve the dispute itself before allowing a transcript to be submitted to the jury.[9] The transcript must set forth the exact words used in the taped conversation, not the transcriber's

---

23. *See, e.g.,* 28 U.S.C. §1733(b) (1988) (authenticated copies or transcripts of books, records, papers or documents of federal department or agency "shall be admitted in evidence equally with the originals").

§10.9 1. *See* §10.5, *supra. See also* Wright v. Farmers Co-op of Arkansas and Oklahoma, 681 F.2d 549, 553 n.3 (8th Cir. 1982) (transcript of tape recording is not duplicate).

2. *See* 28 U.S.C. §753(b) (1988) (certified transcript "shall be deemed prima facie a correct statement of the testimony taken and the proceedings had").

3. If unavailability is shown, an authenticated transcript qualifies as "other evidence" of content that is admissible under FRE 1004. *See* United States v. Workinger, 90 F.3d 1409 (9th Cir. 1996) (admitting authenticated transcript to prove content of recorded interview of defendant after showing that tape itself had been destroyed in ordinary course of business).

4. United States v. Calderin-Rodriguez, 244 F.3d 977 (8th Cir. 2001) (use of transcripts of audio tapes permissible where jury only looked at transcripts while tapes played in courtroom, and judge told jury that it should rely on the tapes).

5. United States v. Rena, 971 F.2d 765, 767 (5th Cir. 1993).

6. United States v. Zambrana, 864 F.2d 494, 498 (7th Cir. 1988) (court and parties should try to produce an "official" or "transcript" that "satisfies all sides").

7. United States v. Smith, 537 F.2d 862, 863 (6th Cir. 1976) (error to admit unstipulated transcript).

8. United States v. Rengifo, 789 F.2d 975, 983 (1st Cir. 1986) (if stipulation cannot be obtained, each party can introduce its own transcript, provided that it is properly authenticated).

9. United States v. West, 948 F.2d 1042, 1044 (6th Cir. 1991) (preferred method of determining accuracy is stipulation; when parties dispute accuracy, court should "make a determination of accuracy out of the jury's presence by reading the transcripts while listening to the tapes").

summary or interpretation of the conversation.[10] Moreover, the transcript should not give undue emphasis to any portion.[11]

Authentication of transcript

A transcript must be authenticated by evidence sufficient to support a finding as to its accuracy.[12] Usually the person who listened to the recording and prepared the transcript authenticates it, testifying that he took care to write down what the voices actually said. But the proponent need not call the transcriber as an authenticating witness,[13] and occasionally a transcript is authenticated through testimony by a participant in the conversation, or even an eavesdropper, that the transcript correctly captured what was said.[14]

Not substantive evidence

A transcript of a recording is normally not admissible as substantive evidence unless the parties stipulate to the contrary.[15] Evidentiary use is barred not only by the Best Evidence Doctrine, but also the hearsay rule, in absence of a proper foundation.[16] However, when the preparer qualifies as an expert at interpretation or translation and is subject to cross-examination, some courts admit the transcript as evidence.[17] Usually the transcript is collected from jurors after the recording has been played and does not accompany them to the jury room, at least in absence of a stipulation as to its accuracy,[18] but trial judges have discretion to allow its use during deliberations.[19] The jury should be instructed that if there is a discrepancy between the transcript and

10. United States v. Rena, 981 F.2d 765, 768-769 (5th Cir. 1993) (error to admit transcripts containing "short, one-paragraph synopses" of recorded conversation and comments interpreting key words).

11. United States v. Gonzalez-Maldonado, 115 F.3d 9 (1st Cir. 1997) (transcripts should not emphasize certain portions; error to admit transcript with quote marks around certain words).

12. United States v. Segines, 17 F.3d 847, 855 (6th Cir. 1994) (error to allow jury to use transcript that was not authenticated as accurate).

13. United States v. Green, 40 F.3d 1167, 1173 (11th Cir. 1994) (not necessary for each officer who prepared transcript testify to its accuracy).

14. United States v. Gordon, 688 F.2d 42, 44 (8th Cir. 1982) (jury may review transcripts even though person who prepared them did not testify, where participant in underlying conversation testified that transcripts accurately reflected conversation).

15. United States v. Nunez, 532 F.3d 645, 651 (7th Cir. 2008) (error to tell jury that transcript can be given independent weight).

16. A transcript is the prepare's out-of-court statement that the persons he identifies participated in the conversation and the words he reports are the ones that the participants spoke. With proper foundation, such a transcript can satisfy one of many hearsay exceptions, especially the ones for past recollection recorded in FRE 803(5), the one for business records in FRE 803(6), and the one for public records in FRE 803(8).

17. See United States v. Onori, 535 F.2d 938, 947 (5th Cir. 1976) (use of transcript as jury guide is analogous to "use of expert testimony as a device aiding a jury in understanding other types of real evidence," so it is wrong to think of transcripts as simply aids; they are evidence and may be admitted for limited purposes, such as showing identity of speakers). See also Fishman, Wiretapping and Eavesdropping §36.17 (2004) (transcriber is expert, and transcripts should be accepted as evidence if authenticated).

18. United States v. Scarborough, 43 F.3d 1021, 1025 (6th Cir. 1994) ("preferred practice" is not to submit transcripts to jury unless parties stipulate to accuracy).

19. United States v. Magna, 118 F.3d 1173, 1183 (7th Cir. 1997) (judges have discretion to let transcripts of recordings be sent to jury room).

what they heard on the recording, the recording controls.[20] Similarly, the jury should be told that they are not bound by the transcript's identification of speakers.

C. PRODUCTION OF ORIGINAL EXCUSED

§10.10 Original Unavailable

In a variety of common settings, FRE 1004 exempts the proponent from the requirement to produce an original, paving the way for "other evidence" of content. Under this provision, she need not produce an original if (1) they all are lost or destroyed without bad faith, (2) none can be obtained by court process or procedure, (3) the adverse party has or had the original and was informed that it would be needed at the hearing, or (4) the evidence in question is collateral.

Once the required showing has been made under any subpart of FRE 1004, any form of secondary evidence otherwise admissible may be received to prove the content of the original.[1] No order of preference or "degrees" of secondary evidence are recognized, except that a public record must be proven by a certified copy or a copy that has been compared with the original if either is available.[2] The Advisory Committee's Note states:

> While strict logic might call for extending the principle of preference beyond simply preferring the original, the formulation of a hierarchy of preferences and a procedure for making it effective is believed to involve unwarranted complexities. Most, if not all, that would be accomplished by an extended scheme of preferences will, in any event, be achieved through the normal motivation of a party to present the most convincing evidence possible and the arguments and procedures available to his opponent if he does not.

Thus FRE 1004 is said to follow the English rule and to reject the majority rule of American cases that established an order of preference for secondary evidence.[3] Once unavailability of the original has been

---

20. *See* United States v. McMillan, 508 F.2d 101, 105-106 (8th Cir. 1974) (judge should tell jury that differences in meaning may be caused by various factors, including "inflection in a speaker's voice or inaccuracies in the transcript," so jury should "rely on what they hear rather than on what they read"), *cert. denied*, 421 U.S. 916.

§10.10 1. Burt Rigid Box, Inc. v. Travelers Prop. Cas. Corp., 302 F.3d 83, 92 (2d Cir. 2002) (insured may rely on secondary evidence to prove existence and terms of policy only where he made diligent search for missing policy; diligent search was made; many policies were over 20 years old); United States v. Ross, 33 F.3d 1507, 1513-1514 (11th Cir. 1994) (admitting transcripts of conversations recorded by National Police in Spain where recordings had been destroyed in ordinary course of business; loss or destruction of original justifies "any kind of secondary evidence" to prove content).

2. *See* FRE 1005, discussed in §10.15, *infra*.

3. *See* Doe d. Gilbert v. Ross, 7 M. &. W. 102, 151 Eng. Rep. 696, 697-698 (Exch. 1840).

shown, FRE 1004 allows the proponent to prove its contents by a lesser form of secondary evidence even though a higher form is available.[4]

Showing of duplicate's unavailability not required

Even if a duplicate is available to the proponent, its production is not required. Testimony or other forms of secondary evidence may be received to prove content of the original.[5] However, an incentive to offer a duplicate is created by the fact that a duplicate may be received under FRE 1003 without a showing of unavailability of the original, whereas for any other form of secondary evidence the proponent must first establish the unavailability of the original. Moreover, failure to offer an available duplicate may result in an adverse inference being drawn by the trier of the fact. A trial judge is likely to take a dim view of any attempt to offer other forms of proof if the proponent has a duplicate at the ready. And it seems probable that a proponent who acquires a duplicate during pretrial discovery must offer that duplicate in preference to other evidence.[6]

All forms of secondary evidence

Almost always, the litigant who invokes FRE 1004 hopes to introduce testimony or various kinds of circumstantial evidence in lieu of the document, photograph, or recording. A testimonial account might directly describe the contents of the document. Alternatively, the proponent might offer proof of routine business practice that tends to show, for instance, that a particular provision is always included in certain kinds of contracts, hence that it was included in the document in question.[7] Or, in the case of contracts entered on standard forms, the party might show another counterpart of the form in question to establish at least the content of the "boilerplate" provisions.[8]

Sometimes a party who satisfies FRE 1004 resorts to nontestimonial substitutes for the original, typically a written restatement or summary of the contents of the original, or (in the case of recordings) a transcript of what was said, and such proof may be admitted provided it also satisfies a hearsay exception.[9] Conceivably the proponent might offer a "copy" that does not qualify as a "duplicate" under FRE 1001(4), such as a manually prepared (handwritten) copy or a "compared" copy,

---

4. United States v. Gerhart, 538 F.2d 807, 809 (8th Cir. 1976) (FRE 1004 "recognizes no degrees of secondary evidence," so proponent may prove contents of writing by "any secondary evidence" if FRE 1004 is satisfied "subject to an attack by the opposing party not as to admissibility but to the weight").

5. *Cf.* Neville Const. Co. v. Cook Paint & Varnish Co., 671 F.2d 1107, 1109 (8th Cir. 1982) (admitting testimony on contents of destroyed brochure without requiring production of similar brochure prepared by defendant).

6. *See* §10.12, *infra.*

7. *See* Amoco Prod. Co. v. United States, 619 F.2d 1383, 1389-1390 (10th Cir. 1980) (admitting evidence of routine practice under FRE 406, which included putting a particular clause in a deed, to show that clause was in deed in question).

8. Action Fire Safety Equip., Inc. v. Biscayne Fire Equip. Co., Inc., 383 So. 2d 969, 971 (Fla. App. 1980) (plaintiff established that defendant signed standard contract designed for all employees, which contained noncompetition clause; on showing that contract signed with defendant had been lost, plaintiff could offer copy of contract signed with another ex-employee as secondary evidence).

9. *See* United States v. Workinger, 90 F.3d 1409, 1415 (9th Cir. 1996) (admitting authenticated transcript of deposition tape that had been lost).

on the strength of live testimony that it faithfully reproduces the text of the original.

Before other evidence of content may be received under FRE 1004, not only must there be a showing of unavailability of the original, but the proponent must offer evidence sufficient to support a finding that the original once existed.[10] Secondary evidence of content is admissible only to the same extent as the original. Therefore, the original must itself be authenticated.[11] If its content is being proven for a hearsay purpose, it must be shown to qualify under a hearsay exception. The secondary evidence must also be authenticated as an accurate representation of the original.

FRE 1004(1)

   Originals lost or destroyed. All originals are lost or have been destroyed, unless the proponent lost or destroyed them in bad faith.

---

§10.11   Original Lost or Destroyed

FRE 1004(1) creates an exemption from the requirement of producing originals and allows other evidence of content when the originals have been lost or destroyed.[1] Where there are multiple originals, the showing of loss or destruction must be made with respect to all originals.

Secondary evidence is not admissible to prove the content of the originals when "the proponent lost or destroyed them in bad faith."[2] Voluntary destruction, whether in the ordinary course of business, by mistake, or even by negligence,[3] is not sufficient to establish destruction

---

10. *See, e.g.*, Graybar Elec. Co., Inc. v. Sawyer, 485 A.2d 1384, 1388 (Me. 1985) (plaintiff's file copy of letter was admissible; he testified that he sent original to defendant even though he denied receiving it).

11. *See* United States v. Standing Soldier, 538 F.2d 196, 202-203 (8th Cir. 1978) (rejecting defense claim that testimony about contents of note should have been rejected because original was not authenticated; witness authenticated original by identifying signature on note), *cert. denied*, 429 U.S. 1025.

§10.11   1. *See, e.g.*, Burt Rigid Box, Inc. v. Travelers Prop. Cas. Corp., 302 F.3d 83, 92 (2d Cir. 2002) (insured may rely on secondary evidence to prove existence and terms of policy if he made diligent search for missing policy; insured made diligent search; many policies were over 20 years old).

2. FRE 1004(1). *See* Seiler v. Lucasfilm, Ltd., 797 F.2d 1504, 1509 (9th Cir. 1986) (secondary evidence of drawings rejected; proponent lost or destroyed originals in bad faith), *modified*, 808 F.2d 1316 (9th Cir. 1986).

3. United States v. Workinger, 90 F.3d 1409 (9th Cir. 1996) (authenticated transcript of tape recording admitted on showing that tape was destroyed in ordinary course of business); Estate of Gryder v. Commissioner, 705 F.2d 336, 338 (8th Cir. 1983) (secondary evidence admissible where "documents were destroyed negligently but not in bad faith"), *cert. denied*, 464 U.S. 1008.

in bad faith.[4] Destruction by a proponent includes soliciting or aiding another to lose or destroy the original.[5] Destruction should be interpreted to include deletion, alteration, or other modification of critical terms as well as illegibility and inaudibility, although production of the original may be required to verify such conditions.

Preliminary question for court The issue of whether the originals have been lost or destroyed is a preliminary question for the court under FRE 104(a). In absence of a stipulation by the opposing party, the proponent of the secondary evidence must establish loss or destruction by a preponderance of the evidence.[6] The rules of evidence do not apply to a hearing under FRE 104(a), except for the rules of privilege. Therefore, affidavits, letters, as well as hearsay statements bearing on the issue of loss or destruction may be considered by the court.

The proponent must usually set forth the reasons for believing the original has been lost or destroyed, including the nature of any search undertaken for the original.[7] The trial court has considerable discretion regarding how stringent a showing to require.[8] The intensity of search required depends upon the circumstances, including the importance of the original and whether there is a suspicion of fraud. The proponent is normally required to look in the location where the original is usually kept, where it was last seen, and any other location where it might reasonably be found.[9]

FRE 1004(2)

Original not obtainable. No original can be obtained by any available judicial process or procedure.

---

4. Malkin v. United States, 243 F.3d 120, 123 (2d Cir. 2001) (taxpayer's file had been destroyed by the IRS; no evidence that destruction was anything other than inadvertent; court could admit secondary evidence that taxpayer had submitted a particular form).

5. House Report, at 17 (Committee intends that loss or destruction of original by another person at the instigation of the proponent is "tantamount to loss or destruction in bad faith by the proponent himself").

6. The usual standard of proof for FRE 104(a) issues is preponderance. *See* §§1.10-1.12, *supra*. The proponent may rely on oral or written admissions by the opposing party to establish loss or destruction.

7. Cartier v. Jackson, 59 F.3d 1046, 1048 (10th Cir. 1995) (copyright infringement action; plaintiff alleged that defendant Michael Jackson used song from demo tape that plaintiff sent to him; court excludes secondary evidence of content because plaintiff failed to show diligent search).

8. Wright v. Farmers Co-op, 681 F.2d 549, 553 (8th Cir. 1982) ("troubled by the limited nature of the testimony" on loss or destruction of original, court says that generally "more specific testimony should be adduced" to support finding of loss or destruction of original).

9. Sylvania Elec. Prod., Inc. v. Flanagan, 352 F.2d 1005, 1008 (1st Cir. 1965) ("no universal or fixed rule" determines sufficiency of proof of diligent search; still, proponent "must show that he has used all reasonable means to obtain the original," meaning such search as "the nature of the case would suggest").

§10.12   Original Beyond Reach of Judicial Process

FRE 1004(2) provides that production of the original is not required if a showing is made that "[n]o original can be obtained by any available judicial process or procedure."[1] Whether a writing, recording, or photograph is beyond the reach of judicial process under FRE 1004(2) depends upon what judicial process is available in a given case.[2] Generally, the scope of process is broader in criminal cases than civil cases. States adopting counterparts of FRE 1004(2) have variation in the range of their civil and criminal process statutes.

FRE 1004 does not list the infeasibility of producing an original as a ground of unavailability. However, in some cases, even though the original could be reached by judicial process, the amount in dispute would not justify the expense required. Occasionally inscribed chattels are too heavy or bulky to be brought into the courtroom.[3] The standard of unobtainability under FRE 1004(2) should be tempered by considerations of reasonableness and practicality. FRE 1004(2) should also be construed as satisfied in cases where after reasonable search the person in possession of the original cannot be located to be served, even though it is not clearly established that the person is outside the range of judicial process.

Scope of process

Where a writing, recording, or photograph is in possession of a third person, the procedure commonly used to obtain its production is a subpoena duces tecum.[4] A subpoena for production of documents may be issued under FRCP 45 and FRCrimP 17. FRCP 28 and FRCrimP 17(e) provide for the taking of depositions of witnesses both within and outside the United States. Also a federal statute authorizes district courts to subpoena "a national or resident of the United States who is in a foreign country" under certain circumstances.[5]

Pretrial discovery, however, typically does not provide an "original" for the proponent to offer at trial, but rather a "duplicate" attached to a deposition transcript or provided in response to a request for

---

§10.12   1. *See* United States v. Benedict, 647 F.2d 928, 932-933 (9th Cir. 1981) (testimony by DEA agents as to contents of business documents examined by them in Thailand admissible as other evidence of contents under FRE 1004(2) because originals were beyond reach of process), *cert. denied*, 454 U.S. 1087.

2. FRE 1004(2) has a parallel in FRE 804(a)(5), which defines unavailability of declarant for purposes of certain hearsay exceptions. The standard of unavailability in FRE 804(a)(5) is stricter. It requires that "other reasonable means" to obtain attendance of declarant even where he is beyond the reach of process.

3. *See* People v. Mastin, 171 Cal. Rptr. 780, 783 (Cal. App. 1981) (visualizing situations where best evidence rule should not apply, as in the case of "an inscription on a 30-ton piece of heavy equipment or an item of personal property which should be promptly returned to the owner"). Here a proponent might satisfy Best Evidence requirements by taking a photograph of the chattel and offering the photograph as a "duplicate" under FRE 1001(4) and FRE 1003. See §10.4, *supra* (discussing inscribed chattels).

4. *See* ACN, FRE 1004(2) (judicial procedure includes subpoena duces tecum "as an incident to the taking of a deposition in another jurisdiction").

5. 28 U.S.C. §1782(a) (1988).

production. In this circumstance, a wooden reading of FRE 1004(2) might suggest that the proponent may offer "other evidence" of content because the original was not obtainable, but the better result is to require use of the duplicate produced during discovery, subject, of course, to his own right to claim that the duplicate amounts to a distortion, forgery, or alteration of the original.[6]

Assertion of privilege
The original is not obtainable by judicial process if the party in possession successfully asserts a privilege blocking production either during pretrial proceedings or at trial. Unobtainability should also be found where it is clear that the party in possession of the original could successfully assert a privilege and would be likely to do so.[7]

Issuance of a subpoena should also not be required in cases where a statute precludes production, such as by making a document confidential or prohibiting the removal of a public record. However, if there is reasonable doubt whether a claim of privilege will be asserted, or, if asserted, sustained, the subpoena should be issued and any claim of privilege resolved by judicial ruling.

Enforcement of judicial process
Under FRE 1004(2), the original should normally be viewed as unobtainable if the person in possession defies a subpoena or court order by refusing to produce or make the original available to be copied. The party seeking production of the original is usually not required to initiate contempt proceedings or exhaust all possible enforcement mechanisms to establish the unobtainability of the original.[8] However, a finding of unobtainability should require a showing of reasonable effort in light of all the circumstances.[9] Factors to be considered include the importance of obtaining the original, the nature of available enforcement mechanisms (including their feasibility, expense, and timeliness), the ease of resolution of the disputed issues, the time remaining until trial, and the likelihood of continued defiance by the respondent.

FRE 1004(3)

Original in possession of opponent. At a time when an original was under the control of the party against whom offered, that party

---

6. The very language of FRE 1004(2) can be read to support this result: The original is not beyond reach of "judicial process or procedure" because production can be required for copying and inspection.

7. *See* FRE 804(a), discussed in §8.63, *supra,* which appears to say that the declarant is unavailable for purposes of certain hearsay exceptions only if he actually claims a privilege on the stand. This provision is sometimes viewed as satisfied if he would surely make a successful claim of privilege.

8. United States v. Taylor, 648 F.2d 565, 570 (9th Cir. 1981) (photocopy allowed after government told court that subpoenas requesting original had been served, but original was not produced), *cert. denied,* 454 U.S. 866.

9. United States v. Taylor, 648 F.2d 565, 570 (9th Cir. 1981) (unobtainability requirement satisfied by showing that government subpoenaed original letter from pertinent business entities without success; counsel said he spoke to "everybody involved in this transaction" and no original could be located; FRE 1004(2) "contemplates a relatively lax standard of unavailability"), *cert. denied,* 454 U.S. 866.

> was put on notice, by the pleadings or otherwise, that the contents would be a subject of proof at the hearing, and that party does not produce the original at the hearing.

§10.13 Original in Possession of Opponent

Under FRE 1004(3), production of the original is not required in cases where the adverse party possesses the original and was given proper notice that the contents would be proven at trial. The rationale for this exception is that if notice is given, the party possessing the original can ward off introduction of secondary evidence, or correct any erroneous secondary evidence that is offered, by producing the original. This exception applies only if (1) reasonable notice was given; (2) the adverse party was in possession or control of the original at the time of notice; and (3) the party does not produce the original at the hearing.

Although no particular form of notice is specified by the Rule, the notice given should normally be in writing to avoid dispute about its adequacy. Although notice by letter could suffice, the preferred form of notice is a document denominated a "notice to produce." Such a notice is not the same as a request for production under FRCP 34.[1] Because a notice under FRE 1004(3) has no compulsive force and merely enables the introduction of secondary evidence, a party who truly seeks production of the original from the opponent should use a motion to produce, a subpoena duces tecum, or other available discovery mechanism. Oral notice may be sufficient, although it is disfavored because of the difficulty of proof. Implied notice should also suffice,[2] as occurs where the contents of a writing are obviously central to a litigated dispute, where one of the parties incorporates the terms of a writing in a pleading (or attaches the writing to the pleading), or sometimes where the document has been the object of discovery.

Form of notice

Although no time period for giving notice is specified by the Rule, notice to the adverse party should be sufficiently timely so that the party has an opportunity to bring the original to court. The timeliness of notice depends on how accessible the original is to the party. Notice at the trial itself may be sufficient in cases where the original is located in close proximity to the courthouse and can easily be obtained by the adverse party if desired. In cases where the opposing party has actually brought the original to court, no advance notice should be required.

Timing of notice

---

§10.13 1. *See* ACN to FRE 1004(3) (notice procedure "is not to be confused with orders to produce or other discovery procedures, as the purpose of the procedure under this rule is to afford the opposite party an opportunity to produce the original, not to compel him to do so").

2. *See* United States v. Marcantoni, 590 F.2d 1324, 1330 (5th Cir. 1979) (defendants were "on notice" that serial numbers of counterfeit bills "would be a subject of proof" at trial), *cert. denied*, 441 U.S. 937.

Notice to criminal defendants

Some pre-Rules authority suggested that notice procedures do not apply with respect to criminal defendants because they cannot be required to produce an incriminating document that could be used as part of the prosecutor's proof. However, this view represents a misunderstanding of the purpose of the requirement of notice. The purpose is not to compel production of the original. Rather, notice is required to alert the party possessing the original that proof of its contents will be made at trial so that the party can produce the original if it cares to do so and can use the original to verify the accuracy of the secondary evidence. FRE 1004(3) should be interpreted as applying to criminal defendants as much as to other parties, although special care should be taken to ensure that the jury does not become aware of the notice. A request to produce in the jury's presence or a comment on the defendant's failure to produce could be found to be constitutional error.[3]

FRE 1004(4)

Collateral matters. The writing, recording, or photograph is not closely related to a controlling issue.

---

§10.14   Collateral Matter Exception

FRE 1004(4) contains an "escape clause" that frees the proponent from the general requirement to produce the original where a writing, recording, or photograph is not "closely related to a controlling issue." The Advisory Committee acknowledged that this exception is "difficult to define with precision," offering as guidance only the general suggestion that the exception for "collateral matter," as it is usually called, reaches cases where requiring the original serves "no good purpose."[1]

Purposes other than to prove content

FRE 1004(4) is intended to prevent overly rigid or technical application of the Best Evidence rule. It furthers trial efficiency in situations where the original is so tangential that its production would add little or nothing to the reliability of the factfinding process. Thus incidental references by a witness to road signs, street names, addresses, license plate numbers, billboards, newspaper headlines, names on commercial establishments, brand names, tickets, and similar writings will normally

---

3. *Cf.* Griffin v. California, 380 U.S. 609 (1965).

§10.14   1. Examples cited in the ACN to FRE 1004(4), with citations to decisions, are "the newspaper in an action for the price of publishing defendant's advertisement," and "the streetcar transfer of plaintiff claiming status as a passenger." The court decides under FRE 104(a) whether a writing, recording, or photograph is "collateral." *See also* FRE 1008.

be permitted unless the terms of the writing have particular significance in the litigation.[2]

Reliance on FRE 1004(4) is unnecessary in cases where the writing, recording, or photograph is being offered for purposes other than to prove its content, because FRE 1002 is by its terms inapplicable. In close cases where it is uncertain whether content is being proven, FRE 1004(4) provides the court with another rationale for deciding against requiring production of originals.[3]

There is an overlap between the factors that define evidence as "collateral" and the factors that govern the question whether an "inscribed chattel" is a writing, where a negative answer places the object altogether beyond the reach of the doctrine.[4] In both cases, courts have discretion to make the determination by considering matters such as the centrality and complexity of the writing and the existence or nonexistence of a dispute regarding its content. Even if an inscribed chattel is found to be a "writing" within the meaning of FRE 1001(1), it may nonetheless be excluded from the operation of the Best Evidence Doctrine if found to be collateral under FRE 1004(4).

Inscribed chattels

D. OTHER EXEMPTIONS

FRE 1005

The contents of an official record, or of a document authorized to be recorded or filed and actually recorded or filed, including data compilations in any form, if otherwise admissible, may be proved by copy, certified as correct in accordance with rule 902 or testified to be correct by a witness who has compared it with the original. If a copy which complies with the foregoing cannot be obtained by the exercise of reasonable diligence, then other evidence of the contents may be given.

---

2. *See, e.g.,* Jackson v. Crews, 873 F.2d 1105, 1110 (8th Cir. 1989) (testimony about flyer that described Jackson's arrest and asked for eyewitnesses did not violate FRE 1002; Jackson was trying to show "how the witness learned of the case and came to testify," but even if purpose had been to prove prove content of flyer, the matter was "collateral to the principal issue in the trial").

3. *See, e.g.,* Blachly v. United States, 380 F.2d 665, 674 n.18 (5th Cir. 1967) (in trial for illegal pyramiding scheme, promissory notes by alleged victims were only "collaterally involved," as their existence rather than their content was primary issue; no need for originals).

4. *See, e.g,* United States v. Duffy, 454 F.2d 809, 811-812 (5th Cir. 1972) (pre-Rules case admitting FBI agent's testimony that shirt had laundry marking "D-U-F," linking it with defendant; inscription was not a writing for purposes of Best Evidence Rule, and shirt was "collateral evidence of the crime").

§10.15   Application of Best Evidence Doctrine to Public Records

FRE 1005 exempts public records from the general requirement of FRE 1002 that an original must be produced to prove content. FRE 1005 authorizes proof of the contents of a public record, including data compilations in any form, by a "copy, certified as correct in accordance with rule 902 or testified to be correct by a witness who has compared it with the original." In cases where such a copy cannot be obtained by the exercise of reasonable diligence, other evidence of content may be received.

Production of original public records is not required because "[r]emoving them from their usual place of keeping would be attended by serious inconvenience to the public and to the custodian."[1] If original public records were required in court proceedings, they would be subject to the danger of loss, damage, or destruction, and their absence could impede the functioning of the public agencies or offices that rely on such documents or are entrusted with their safekeeping.

Public records   FRE 1005 encompasses an "official record" of any type. An "official record" under FRE 1005 should be given the same interpretation as an "official record" under FRE 902(4).[2] Such records include official records of governmental entities at all levels—federal, state, and municipal—as well as official records of foreign governments.

FRE 1005 also covers any document "authorized to be recorded or filed and actually recorded or filed." Although the Rule requires authorization for recording or filing as well as actual recording or filing, the latter should be prima facie evidence of the former. Public officials are unlikely to record or file without authority. The Rule covers both permissive and mandatory recording or filing.

Common examples of recorded documents are land sale contracts, deeds, liens, and mortgages. Recorded documents are often copies of the first-prepared document. Therefore, a copy of a recorded public document is often a copy of a copy, but such second generation copies are clearly within the contemplation of the Rule. FRE 1005 covers only proof of the public record; it does not govern proof of the first-prepared private document.[3]

Certified copies   When a public record is proved by a certified copy, the certification must comply with FRE 902(4), which requires that the copy be certified as correct by the custodian or other person authorized to make the certification and that the certificate comply with subsections (1), (2), or (3) of FRE 902, or with other statute or Rule.[4] In most cases, such compliance will require a seal on the certificate.[5]

---

§10.15   1. ACN to FRE 1005.

2. *See* §9.23, *supra.*

3. *See* United States v. Childs, 5 F.3d 1328, 1335 (9th Cir. 1993) (even if document recorded, FRE 1003 rather than FRE 1005 applies if proponent is trying to prove content of original rather than content of public record).

4. *See, e.g.,* FRCP 44(a).

5. United States v. Hampton, 464 F.3d 687, 689-690 (7th Cir. 2006) (in bank robbery trial, photocopies of FDIC certificates of insurance were not admissible under FRE 1005

If the copy is not certified, then a witness generally must testify that **Compared copies**
the copy is accurate based upon a personal comparison of the copy with
the original.[6] The witness need not be the person who made the copy,
but must be a person who has been granted access to both the copy and
the original in order to make such a comparison.

If a certified or compared copy cannot be obtained by the exercise of **Other proof of**
reasonable diligence, then other evidence of contents may be given.[7] **content**
Whether the "reasonable diligence" standard has been satisfied is an
issue for the trial judge.[8] Any search that satisfies the requirements of
FRE 1004(1) and (2) should also be sufficient to satisfy FRE 1005.[9]

For public records, FRE 1005 qualifies the Best Evidence Doctrine in **Interrelationship**
two important respects. First, in what might be called its permissive **between FRE**
aspect, FRE 1005 allows the proponent to prove a public record by **1003 and FRE**
means of a certified or compared "copy" without accounting for the **1005**
absence of the original. Unlike FRE 1003, FRE 1005 does not provide
any grounds for objecting to introduction of a copy in lieu of an
original. Second, in what may be called its preferential aspect, FRE
1005 requires the proponent to prove a public record by means of a
certified or compared copy in preference to "other evidence," including uncertified duplicates. FRE 1005 thus imposes a hierarchy of
secondary evidence in contrast to FRE 1004, which establishes no preference for any particular forms of secondary evidence.[10]

In some instances, public records are themselves duplicates of
other documents, as is true in the case of recorded deeds and
other conveyancing documents affecting real property. Must the proponent offer a copy of the sort preferred by FRE 1005, or can he offer
instead the original or a duplicate of the original, which he himself
might have made privately? If what counts in the suit is the terms of
the original deed, the original should suffice, or a duplicate that
satisfies FRE 1003. If what counts is the content of the public record,
even the original deed may be found an inferior form of proof, and a
duplicate of the original, privately made, cannot be offered as
proof under FRE 1003 because it is neither a certified copy of the
recorded document nor a compared copy within the contemplation
of FRE 1005.

---

despite testimony that they were identical to certificates at bank; testimony failed to
show that certificates were not also copies). For a discussion of authentication under
FRE 902(4), *see* §9.23, *supra.*

6. *See* United States v. Rodriguez, 524 F.2d 485 (5th Cir. 1976) (compared copy is one
that witness testifies to be accurate reproduction of original), *cert. denied*, 424 U.S. 972.

7. *See, e.g.*, Brown v. Bowen, 668 F. Supp. 146, 150 (E.D.N.Y. 1987) (testimonial
account of contents of public record admissible after showing that original record
was destroyed by agency; alternate holding).

8. FRE 104(a); FRE 1008.

9. *See* §10.11, *supra.*

10. *See* §10.10, *supra.* The ACN comments that this preference amounts to "an
appropriate *quid pro quo*" for exempting the proponent from any need to produce
the original.

The term "copy" in FRE 1005 clearly reaches a handmade document and is thus broader than the term "duplicate" in FRE 1003, which reaches only machine-made documents. But office copiers are so common that it is hard to imagine resorting to handmade "copies" in the modern world.

Other grounds for exclusion

A copy of a public record offered under FRE 1005 is admissible only to the same extent as the original, and it is subject to objections on grounds outside the Best Evidence Doctrine.[11] For example, even if a copy of a public record is properly authenticated under FRE 902(4) and admissible under FRE 1005, it may nonetheless be barred by the hearsay rule if it is being offered to prove the truth of what it asserts. FRE 803(8) creates a hearsay exception for many types of public records, but FRE 803(8) has a narrower scope than FRE 1005.[12] Public records that are not admissible under FRE 803(8) may qualify for admission under another hearsay exception.[13]

Statutory alternatives to FRE 1005

Apart from FRE 1005, there are a number of statutes that authorize introduction of certified copies of particular public records.[14] Such statutes overlap rather than conflict with FRE 1005. If a copy of a public record qualifies for admission under either FRE 1005 or the provisions of a specific statute, it should be admitted. In addition, FRCP 44(a) overlaps with and supplements FRE 1005, providing an alternative method of proving official records. Compliance with FRCP 44(a) not only authenticates a public record but establishes its admissibility under the Best Evidence Doctrine.[15] FRCrimP 27 makes the method of proving official records authorized by FRCP 44(a) applicable in criminal cases as well.

FRE 1006

The contents of voluminous writings, recordings, or photographs which cannot conveniently be examined in court may be presented in the form of a chart, summary, or calculation. The originals, or duplicates, shall be made available for examination or copying, or both, by other parties at reasonable time and place. The court may order that they be produced in court.

---

11. FRE 1005 provides that contents of a public record may be proved by certified or compared copy only "if otherwise admissible."

12. For a discussion of the scope of FRE 803(8), *see* §§8.49-8.52, *supra*.

13. *See, e.g.,* FRE 803(6), (9), (14), or (23).

14. *See, e.g.,* 28 U.S.C. §1733(b) (1988) (authenticated copies of records of departments and agencies of United States admissible); 44 U.S.C. §2116(a) (1988) (photographic copies in National Archives to be treated as originals); 44 U.S.C. §3312 (1988) (photographs and microfilms of agency records admissible).

15. FRCP 44 provides that the original record may be sproved by copy, implying that both authentication and Best Evidence requirements are satisfied. Other objections may arise, however, as the copy is admissible only to the extent that the original is "admissible for any purpose."

§10.16   Summaries

Writings, recordings, or photographs are sometimes so voluminous that they cannot conveniently be examined in court. In such cases, FRE 1006 authorizes the admission of written or testimonial summaries, as well as charts and calculations, as an exception to the requirement of producing the originals.[1] The Rule requires that the originals or duplicates be made available for examination and copying by other parties at a reasonable time and place.[2] Although a party may offer the summary, chart, or calculation in lieu of producing the originals, the court retains discretion to require that the originals also be produced.[3]

FRE 1006 applies only where a summary, chart, or calculation is being offered to prove the content of a writing, recording, or photograph. If a summary, chart, or calculation is offered merely for illustrative or pedagogical purposes to organize or aid the presentation of a party's case, FRE 1006 is inapplicable.[4] Such demonstrative use of summaries, charts, and calculations is subject to the discretion of the court pursuant to FRE 611(a) and FRE 403.[5] If a summary is offered of witness testimony, FRE 1006 is by its terms inapplicable.[6] FRE 1006 is also inapplicable when computerized records are offered that constitute the original rather than a summary.[7] FRE 1006 has been relied on to admit summaries to prove absence of contents,[8] although the Best

---

§10.16   1. *See, e.g.*, United States v. Tannehill, 49 F.3d 1049 (5th Cir. 1995) (admitting summary charts illustrating contents of 28,000 documents; such writings were voluminous; in-court examination would have been "more than inconvenient").

2. United States v. Rangel, 350 F.3d 648 (7th Cir. 2003) (purpose in requiring copies of records when offering summaries is to allow opponent adequate opportunity to check accuracy of summary); United States v. Modena, 302 F.3d 626, 632-633 (6th Cir. 2002) (because government did not offer to show underlying documents to the defense, court erred in admitting summaries). If the underlying documents are unavailable for inspection, the adverse party may be able to exclude a summary by objecting to the lack of opportunity to examine or make copies, as FRE 1006 contemplates. If the underlying originals, are lost, destroyed, or beyond reach of process, however, the summary may be admissible as "other evidence" of contents, even where the adverse party had no opportunity to examine them. *See* §§10.10-10.12, *supra*.

3. United States v. Hemphill, 514 F.3d 1350, 1358 (D.C. Cir. 2008) (in embezzlement trial, rejecting argument that government must introduce documents on which it bases summary chart; point of FRE 1006 is to avoid introducing all the documents where foundation has been laid).

4. United States v. Milkiewicz, 70 F.3d 390, 397 (1st Cir. 2006) (summaries can be pedagogical devices to clarify and simplify complex testimony under FRE 611, in which case they must be linked to evidence previously admitted).

5. *See* §§4.9-4.10 *and* §§9.31-9.32, *supra*.

6. United States v. Nguyen, 504 F.3d 561, 571-572 (5th Cir. 2007) (FRE 1006 does not contemplate summarization of live testimony).

7. *See* United States v. Catabran, 836 F.2d 453, 456-457 (9th Cir. 1988) (computer printouts that were company's general ledgers were admissible as business records, not as summaries).

8. *See, e.g.*, United States v. Scales, 594 F.2d 558, 562 (6th Cir. 1979) (government sought to prove union records did not contain certain information, including travel authorization; records themselves could have been admitted to show what contents did not include, wo there was "no reason why Rule 1006 would not apply" to summary of

Evidence Doctrine does not generally apply to proof of the nonexistence of an entry.[9]

Whether the original writings, recordings, or photographs are too voluminous for convenient examination in court is a question for the judge.[10] FRE 1006 does not require that it be literally impossible to examine the originals in court, but only that it would be an inconvenience. In deciding whether the originals can be conveniently examined in court, it is appropriate for the judge to consider not only the number of such originals,[11] but their complexity.[12] Summaries are particularly well suited for financial accounts and for corporate or business records of a detailed or complicated character.[13] The mere fact that the originals have already been admitted into evidence does not establish that they can "conveniently be examined in court," and summaries of admitted exhibits may be received under FRE 1006.[14]

Originals must be made available

A summary will not be admitted under FRE 1006 unless the underlying documents have first been made available for inspection by the opposing party.[15] In many cases, the underlying documents will have already been obtained by the opponent during the normal processes of discovery. In cases where they have not been obtained, the trial judge has discretion to decide what is a "reasonable time and place" for such production by the proponent of the summary. FRE 1006 contemplates that the originals, or duplicates thereof, will be made available for inspection in advance of trial so the opposing party can verify the accuracy of the summary by the time of trial.

---

contents; even though content of records "is negative," that does not "render the fact of omission any less an accurate summary of the content of the records"), *cert. denied*, 441 U.S. 946.

9. *See* §10.6, *supra*.

10. *See* §10.18, *infra*.

11. United States v. Loney, 959 F.2d 1332, 1341 (5th Cir. 1992) (admitting 35-page compilation of computer records of 70 frequent flyer accounts under FRE 1006; underlying records were voluminous and could not be conveniently examined in court). *Compare* Javelin Inv., S.A. v. Municipality of Ponce, 645 F.2d 92, 96 (1st Cir. 1981) (ten short documents not voluminous enough to justify use of FRE 1006).

12. United States v. Carr, 965 F.2d 408, 412 (7th Cir. 1992) (excluding expert testimony by linguist interpreting five taped conversations in English; they were "uncomplicated" and not voluminous, taking fewer than 80 pages of transcript; FRE 702 and 1006 did not justify admitting this interpretive testimony).

13. *See, e.g.,* United States v. Gardner, 611 F.2d 770, 776 (9th Cir. 1980) (alleged income tax evasion; chart admitted summarizing assets, liabilities and expenditures of taxpayer); Colorado Coal Furnace Distrib., Inc. v. Prill Mfg. Co., 605 F.2d 499, 505 (10th Cir. 1979) (admitting testimony and exhibits summarizing complex corporate books and records).

14. *See, e.g.,* United States v. Dorta, 783 F.2d 1179, 1182-1183 (4th Cir. 1986) (summaries admitted of lengthy telephone records already in evidence), *cert. denied*, 477 U.S. 905.

15. Air Safety v. Roman Catholic Archbishop of Boston, 94 F.3d 1, 7-8 (1st Cir. 1996) (excluding summary which had not been designated as such, and underlying documents were not available for examination at trial). In some circumstances, a summary inadmissible under FRE 1006 because of failure to produce underlying documents may be admissible under FRE 1001(3) when summary is the original or when originals are unavailable under FRE 1004.

FRE 1006 requires only that the originals, or duplicates thereof, and not the summary itself, be made available for examination by other parties.[16] But the summary is usually needed for comparison purposes, and pretrial disclosure of summaries is now required by a recent amendment to FRCP 26(a).[17] Courts understandably prefer to have all questions concerning the accuracy and fairness of summaries resolved in advance of trial,[18] and where the summary is not made available, courts may grant the opponent a continuance to obtain additional evidence necessary to challenge the summary.[19]

Before a summary, chart, or calculation may be admitted, the proponent must first lay a foundation establishing the admissibility of the originals unless they have already been received in evidence. A chart, summary, or calculation is normally admissible only to the same extent as the originals.[20] FRE 1006 does not create an exemption from the hearsay rule or other evidentiary requirements.[21]

Originals must be admissible

When the underlying originals constitute hearsay, the admissibility of the summary, chart, or calculation depends on a showing that the originals satisfy an exception to the hearsay rule.[22] FRE 1006 may not be used as a vehicle to bring inadmissible out-of-court witness statements before the jury.[23] If the originals are admissible for only a limited purpose, such as to show the basis of an expert's opinion, the use of a summary, chart, or calculation is similarly restricted.

A challenge to the authenticity or accuracy of the underlying documents does not automatically render a summary, chart, or calculation

16. *See* United States v. Arias-Izquierdo, 449 F.3d 1168, 1184 (11th Cir. 2006) (error to admit typed summary of handwritten business records; proponent did not provide opportunity to examine originals).

17. *See* FRCP 26(a)(3)(A)(iii) (requiring pretrial disclosure of "summaries of other evidence").

18. *See* United States v. Smyth, 556 F.2d 1179, 1184 n.12 (5th Cir. 1977) (framers of FRE 1006 "contemplated a pre-trial resolution of any issues that may be raised concerning the use of summaries" and rule encourages counsel to eliminate objectionable matter and stipulate to form of summary by requiring that the underlying documents be made available to opposing counsel), *cert. denied*, 434 U.S. 862.

19. United States v. Normile, 587 F.2d 784, 787 (5th Cir. 1979) (defense was offered, but declined, continuance to procure documents necessary to challenge summary of his business bank account).

20. United States v. Samaniego, 187 F.3d 1222, 1224 (10th Cir. 1999) (error to admit summaries of subpoenaed phone records to implicate defendant in drug trafficking; government did not lay foundation for records under business records exception); Ford Motor Co. v. Auto Supply Co., 661 F.2d 1171, 1175 (8th Cir. 1981) (summary "drawn from data that is inadmissible" must be excluded).

21. Judson Atkinson Candies v. Latini-Hohberger, 529 F.3d 371 (7th Cir. 2008) (for summaries to be admissible under FRE 1006, foundation must be laid establishing admissibility of underlying documents).

22. State Office Sys. v. Olivetti Corp. of America, 762 F.2d 843, 845-846 (10th Cir. 1985) (testimony in record "satisfied the foundational requirement of proving that the summary of actual damages was based on business records" that fit the business records exception).

23. United States v. Pelullo, 964 F.2d 193, 204 (3d Cir. 1992) (summaries inadmissible when based in part on out-of-court interviews reflecting conclusions of out-of-court speaker; underlying materials must themselves be admissible).

based on those documents inadmissible. If the originals have been sufficiently authenticated under FRE 901(a), a summary of those documents may be received, although the opponent remains free to produce evidence challenging the authenticity of the underlying documents or the accuracy of statements made in them.

Authentication of a summary

The foundation required to introduce a summary includes not only establishing the admissibility of the originals, but also producing sufficient evidence to support a finding that the summary is an accurate representation of the originals.[24] The proponent must usually provide an explanation of how the summary was prepared so the trier of fact can draw the conclusion that it is a reliable condensation. The required foundation depends on the method of preparation and whether the summary is oral, written, recorded, or photographic in nature.[25] In the case of recordings, a composite tape can be introduced as a summary provided that it is shown to be an accurate and representative condensation of the originals.[26]

To establish such a foundation, it is usually necessary to call the person who prepared the summary, and some decisions suggest that the preparer must be available and subject to cross-examination.[27] However, testimony by the preparer is not required by FRE 1006, and sometimes the summary can be sufficiently authenticated by another witness with knowledge, such as a supervisor or coworker.[28]

The summary, chart, or calculation must fairly condense the underlying material[29] and cannot embellish with information not contained in the originals.[30] It cannot be jury argument in disguise,[31] and the rule

---

24. *See* United States v. Taylor, 210 F.3d 311, 314 (5th Cir. 2000) (in drug distribution trial, error to admit chart that did not reflect underlying testimony in significant respects; it showed defendant distributing cocaine to individuals where there was no proof of such distribution, and showed no distribution between others where there was evidence of such distribution).

25. *See, e.g.,* United States v. Smyth, 556 F.2d 1179, 1182-1185 (5th Cir. 1977) (summary presented by computer printout), *cert. denied*, 434 U.S. 862.

26. United States v. Nunez, 658 F. Supp. 828, 838 (D. Colo. 1987) (allowing composite tape summary of 112 tape recordings that were found too numerous to be conveniently examined in court), *aff'd*, 877 F.2d 1470 (10th Cir.), *cert. denied*, 493 U.S. 981.

27. United States v. Radseck, 718 F.2d 233, 237 (7th Cir. 1983) (summary admissible where witness who prepared charts was subject to cross on documents used to prepare it), *cert. denied*, 465 U.S. 1029.

28. United States v. Soulard, 730 F.2d 1292, 1299 (9th Cir. 1984) (admitting summary where expert testified that he performed "substantial review" of other agent's analysis to assure it was correct, based on evidence).

29. Davis & Cox v. Summa Corp., 751 F.2d 1507, 1516 (9th Cir. 1985) (excluding summary that did not "fairly represent the underlying documents").

30. United States v. Drougas, 748 F.2d 8, 25 (1st Cir. 1984) (charts and summaries inadmissible if they contain information "not present" in originals).

31. Gomez v. Great Lakes Steel Div., Natl. Steel Corp., 803 F.2d 250, 257 (6th Cir. 1986) (summary was "more akin to argument than evidence"); United States v. Smyth, 556 F.2d 1179, 1184 n.12 (5th Cir. 1977) ("care must be taken to omit argumentative matter in their preparation lest the jury believe that such matter is itself evidence of the assertion it makes"; here government used headings in computer summary such as "falsified data summarized"), *cert. denied*, 434 U.S. 862. *But see* United States v. Francis,

is not intended to allow a party to repeat its case shortly before jury deliberations.[32] The summary need not be an "encyclopedic" survey of all the evidence.[33] If the summary is likely to confuse or mislead the jury or create unfair prejudice, it may be excluded under FRE 403.[34]

A summary may include expert opinion evidence provided that a sufficient foundation has been laid for the admission of such evidence under FRE 702 and 703.[35] Whether the authenticating witness must qualify as an expert depends upon the nature of the summary or calculation.[36]

A written summary raises hearsay concerns because it constitutes an out-of-court statement by the preparer about the content of the originals.[37] A testimonial summary is not itself hearsay because the witness is subject to cross-examination,[38] but any writings or out-of-court statements summarized by the witness must be shown to satisfy the hearsay doctrine.

The question whether summaries constitute evidence has been made more difficult by a frequent failure of courts to distinguish summaries offered pursuant to FRE 1006 from other types of summaries. Summaries or charts are often used for illustrative or pedagogical purposes to assist juries in understanding or organizing the evidence.[39] Such

FRE 1006 summaries as evidence

---

131 F.3d 1452, 1457-1458 (11th Cir. 1997) (fact that summaries rested on assumptions favorable to government did not make them argumentative or unfair where evidence supported those assumptions).

32. United States v. Nguyen, 504 F.3d 561, 571-572 (5th Cir. 2007) (purpose of rule is not to let government repeat case-in-chief shortly before deliberations).

33. United States v. Bentley, 825 F.2d 1104, 1108 (7th Cir.), *cert. denied*, 484 U.S. 901 (1987).

34. United States v. Drougas, 748 F.2d 8, 25 (1st Cir. 1984) (before admitting summaries or charts, court must find "that possible prejudice or confusion does not outweigh their usefulness in clarifying the evidence"); United States v. Lemire, 720 F.2d 1327, 1347-1348 (D.C. Cir. 1983) (summary may be excluded under FRE 403), *cert. denied*, 467 U.S. 1226.

35. State Office Sys., Inc. v. Olivetti Corp. of America, 762 F.2d 843, 845-846 (10th Cir. 1985) (projections of future lost profits contained in a summary held admissible as expert opinion testimony).

36. United States v. Jennings, 724 F.2d 436, 443 (5th Cir. 1984) (when chart "does not contain complicated calculations requiring the need of an expert for accuracy," no expertise is required in presenting chart), *cert. denied*, 467 U.S. 1227.

37. In this sense, a summary is like a transcript, which is hearsay because it represents assertions of the reporter that the witnesses identified in the transcript gave the testimony that the transcript recites. Like a transcript, a summary may be admissible under a hearsay exception. Where the written summary contains no "statement" or editorial comment by the preparer, but consists only of a series of excerpts from original writings, recordings, or photographs, arguably no additional layer of hearsay is involved. The summary can be verified for accuracy and fairness by comparison with originals or cross-examination of the preparer.

38. United States v. Evans, 572 F.2d 455, 491-492 (5th Cir. 1978) (FBI agent's testimony was summary of evidence admitted at trial, which was before jury in form of exhibits or other testimony), *cert. denied*, 439 U.S. 870.

39. United States v. Buck, 324 F.3d 786, 790 (5th Cir. 2003) (diagram was not admissible under FRE 1006 because it was not introduced to summarize voluminous materials; instruction should have required jury to consider it only as aid in evaluating evidence or as pedagogical device).

summaries or charts are not governed by FRE 1006 but rather by FRE 611(a). Traditionally, summaries used for explanation or illustration during testimony or argument are not received as evidence, and the jury is so informed by a limiting instruction.[40] Such summaries usually do not go to the jury room during deliberations,[41] although the trial judge has discretion to so allow.[42]

Summaries admitted under FRE 1006, on the other hand, are offered to prove the content of the original writings, recordings, or photographs. In cases where the originals are not introduced into evidence, the trier of fact must be allowed to consider the summary as evidence or the objective of FRE 1006 would be denied. FRE 1006 is intended to allow summaries to substitute for the originals, which necessarily requires that they be given evidentiary status.[43]

Even in cases where both the originals and a summary have been admitted, the better view is that a FRE 1006 summary is properly considered to be evidence. The admission of a summary pursuant to FRE 1006 necessarily entails a finding that the originals are too voluminous to be conveniently examined in court.[44] Although some courts hold that a summary of exhibits already admitted is not itself evidence out of apparent concern that the summary not be given equal status with originals in case there are discrepancies,[45] this concern can be more appropriately addressed by a jury instruction than by denying evidentiary status to the summary.[46]

---

40. United States v. Vasilakos, 508 F.3d 401, 412 (6th Cir. 2007) (summary should be accompanied by limiting instruction informing jury of summary's purpose and telling jury that it is not evidence).

41. Pierce v. Ramsey Winch Co., 753 F.2d 416, 431 (5th Cir. 1985) ("visual aids that summarize or organize testimony or documents that have already been admitted in evidence" are "not themselves evidence and, absent the consent of all parties, they should not be sent to the juryroom").

42. United States v. Bray, 139 F.3d 1104, 1112 (6th Cir. 1998) (pedagogical summary may be admitted when it is "so accurate and reliable a summary illustration or extrapolation of testimony or other evidence in the case as to reliably assist the factfinder in understanding the evidence"). *See* §9.31, *supra*.

43. Bristol Steel & Iron Works v. Bethlehem Steel Corp., 41 F.3d 182, 189-190 (4th Cir. 1994) (under FRE 1006, summaries are "introduced as the evidence").

44. *See, e.g.*, United States v. Smyth, 556 F.2d 1179, 1184 (5th Cir. 1977) (FRE 1006 permits summaries to be treated "as evidence under circumstances where, in the court's discretion, examination of the underlying documents in a trial setting cannot be done conveniently"), *cert. denied*, 434 U.S. 862.

45. United States v. Wood, 943 F.2d 1048, 1053 (9th Cir. 1991) (when underlying documents have been admitted, chart "should be used only as a testimonial aid, and should not be admitted into evidence or otherwise used by the jury during deliberations").

46. United States v. Green, 428 F.3d 1131, 1134-1135 (8th Cir. 2005) (charts admitted under FRE 1006 can be treated as evidence and go to jury room during deliberations, but court should issue limiting instructions); United States v. Bishop, 264 F.3d 535, 547-548 (5th Cir. 2001) (summaries may go to jury room along with evidence they summarize; where summaries admitted merely to clarify other admitted evidence, should tell jury that summaries are not evidence).

FRE 1007

> Contents of writings, recordings, or photographs may be proved by the testimony or deposition of the party against whom offered or by that party's written admission, without accounting for the nonproduction of the original.

§10.17   Written or Testimonial Admission of Content

As another exception to the Best Evidence Doctrine, FRE 1007 provides that the content of an original writing, recording, or photograph may be proved by the testimony or written admission of the party against whom it is offered. This form of proof may be used without showing the unavailability of the original. The rationale of FRE 1007 is that production of the original is unnecessary where the opponent has admitted its contents. The testimonial or written admission of the party is deemed to be a reliable alternative form of proof.

A written admission of content may have been made at any time in a memorandum, report, letter, note, or other writing. FRE 1007 admissions include those made in response to written interrogatories or requests for admission. A written admission should be construed to include an admission by an agent or coconspirator under FRE 801(d)(2), at least when the admission is made on the basis of personal knowledge.

Oral admissions, other than those made as part of giving testimony, do not satisfy the requirements of the Rule.[1] The drafters deemed the risk of inaccuracy in oral admissions to be too great, and allowance of oral admissions would conflict with the general policy of the Best Evidence Doctrine to give preference to writings. Thus the English rule of *Slatterie v. Pooley*[2] allowing contents of a document to be proved by an oral admission without accounting for nonproduction of the original is rejected. However, oral admissions may be received as secondary evidence to prove contents under FRE 1004 when the unavailability of the original has been shown.

Oral admissions not sufficient

Testimony admitting content includes testimony by the opponent in the current proceeding as well as at any earlier proceeding or deposition. "Testimony" should be construed to include grand jury testimony and testimony at any other proceeding contemporaneously recorded, regardless whether it was given subject to oath or cross-examination. The testimony need not have been given at a judicial proceeding, and

---

§10.17   1. Even an oral admission that is recorded is not within FRE 1007 unless given in testimony. A recorded oral admission is within the rationale of the Rule, however, because the recording removes doubt about making and content of the utterance in much the same way that a writing does in the case of written admissions.

2. 6 M. & W. 664, 151 Eng. Rep. 579 (Exch. 1840).

the Rule reaches testimony given at administrative and legislative hearings as well.

Nothing in FRE 1007 prevents the party against whom the admission is offered from denying that the admission was made, repudiating the admission, challenging the accuracy of the admission, or offering alternative evidence of contents.[3] FRE 1007 merely provides that the opponent's testimonial or written admission is an acceptable substitute for production of the original writing, recording, or photograph.

> **FRE 1008**
>
> When the admissibility of other evidence of contents or writings, recordings, or photographs under these rules depends upon the fulfillment of a condition of fact, the question whether the condition has been fulfilled is ordinarily for the court to determine in accordance with the provisions of rule 104. However, when an issue is raised (a) whether the asserted writing ever existed, or (b) whether another writing, recording, or (c) whether other evidence of contents correctly reflects the contents, the issue is for the trier of fact to determine as in the case of other issues of fact.

§10.18   Functions of Judge and Jury

In the operation and administration of the Best Evidence Doctrine, a number of preliminary questions arise that require a determination by either the court or the jury. FRE 1008 represents a more particularized statement of the allocation of responsibilities between judge and jury set forth in FRE 104. FRE 1008 provides that preliminary questions or "conditions of fact" arising out of the administration of the Best Evidence Doctrine are "ordinarily for the court to determine in accordance with the provisions of rule 104."[1]

Questions for judge   By way of example, FRE 1008 and FRE 104(a) require the trial judge rather than the jury to determine whether: (1) an item constitutes a "writing," "recording," or "photograph" under FRE 1001(1) and (2); (2) a writing, recording, or photograph is an "original" under FRE 1001(3); (3) a claimed "duplicate" meets the definition of FRE 1001(4); (4) a "genuine question" has been raised about the authenticity of the original under FRE 1003(1); (5) it would be "unfair" to receive a duplicate in lieu of the original under FRE 1003(2); (6) the original has been shown to be "lost" or "destroyed" under FRE 1004(1); (7) the original has been lost or destroyed in "bad faith"

---

3. *See* discussion of FRE 801(d)(2)(A) in §8.27, *supra.*

§10.18   1. ACN to FRE 1008 (most preliminary questions of fact connecting with the rule preferring the original "are for the judge, under the general principles announced in Rule 104").

under FRE 1004(1);[2] (8) the original is unobtainable by judicial process under FRE 1004(2); (9) the original is in possession of the opponent and proper notice was given under FRE 1004(3); (10) the evidence goes to a "collateral" matter under FRE 1004(4); (11) a copy of a public record has been properly certified under FRE 1005; (12) a certified or compared copy of a public record cannot be obtained with "reasonable diligence" under FRE 1005; or (13) writings are too "voluminous" to be examined in court under FRE 1006. In making such determinations, the judge is not bound by the rules of evidence, except those with respect to privileges.[3]

In three major areas, however, issues affecting application of the Best Evidence Doctrine can be so central to a litigated dispute and so close to the merits of the case that the jury should resolve them in the manner that applies generally to authentication issues. Accordingly, FRE 1008 reserves some important questions for juries to decide pursuant to FRE 104(b). The jury decides (1) whether a writing that a party seeks to prove "ever existed"; (2) whether "another" writing produced at trial is the original; and (3) whether "other evidence" of contents "correctly reflects" the original.

Questions for jury

Long ago Professor Morgan saw that the Best Evidence Doctrine might mislead courts into taking over the central issues of trial and warned against this danger in language that directly supports the second sentence of FRE 1008:

> Surely if two documents were produced, the plaintiff claiming one to be the original and the defendant the other, the dispute must be settled by the jury. If the plaintiff has lost his document so that he is unable to produce it, does that make the question of the authenticity of the defendant's document for the judge? If both sides grant that there was an original and one presents a document which the other disputes, by what line of reasoning can either be deprived of the right to have the jury determine whether the presented document is the original?[4]

Of course the issues listed in the second sentence of FRE 1008 do not always go to the jury any more than do other issues allocated to juries under FRE 104(b). All such issues may be taken from the jury, like other issues of fact, if the evidence is such that a reasonable person could decide only one way. In a suit on a contract, for example, a question may arise whether the parties signed a written agreement claimed to constitute that contract. One party might offer "other evidence" of content, claiming the originals are lost, and the other might claim that no "original" was ever signed. The Advisory Committee's Note quite rightly concludes that the second sentence of FRE 1008 applies here, and that the situation presents "jury questions" to which FRE

Not always go to jury

---

2. *See* Seiler v. Lucasfilm, Ltd., 808 F.2d 1316, 1321 (9th Cir. 1986) (bad faith destruction is preliminary question for court), *cert. denied*, 484 U.S. 826.

3. FRE 104(a).

4. Morgan, The Law of Evidence, 1941-1945, 59 Harv. L. Rev. 481, 490 (1946).

104(b) applies.[5] It does not follow, however, that the jury always decides them. The trial court could exclude "other evidence" of content if it concluded that no reasonable person could find from the evidence that there ever was an original, and it could even direct the jury that it must accept the other evidence of content if the evidence is such that no reasonable person could reject it.

5. ACN to FRE 1008 (if judge decides that contract was never executed and excludes secondary evidence, "the case is at an end without ever going to the jury on a central issue," but this rule was "designed to insure treatment of these situations as raising jury questions").

TABLE OF CASES

Table of Cases

Table of Cases

Table of Cases

Table of Cases

Table of Cases

Table of Cases

Table of Cases

Table of Cases

Table of Cases

Table of Cases

Table of Cases

Table of Cases

Table of Cases

Table of Cases

Table of Cases

Table of Cases

Table of Cases

Table of Cases

Table of Cases

Table of Cases

Table of Cases

Table of Cases

Table of Cases

TABLE OF LAW REVIEW ARTICLES

Table of Law Review Articles

Table of Law Review Articles

Table of Law Review Articles

Table of Law Review Articles

Table of Law Review Articles

_____, M., Prior Consistent Statements: Rule 801(d)(1)(B) of the Federal Rules of Evidence, Critique and Proposal, 30 Hastings L.J. 575 (1979), 6.52 n.5

_____, M., The Relationship Among Federal Rules of Evidence 607, 801 (d)(1)(A), and 403: A Reply to Weinstein's Evidence, 55 Tex. L. Rev. 573 (1977), 6.17 n.8

_____, Michael H., Expert Witness Predicament: Determining "Reliable" Under the Gatekeeping Test of Daubert, Kumho, and Proposed Amended Rule 702 of the Federal Rules of Evidence, 54 U. Minn. L. Rev. 317 (2000), 7.7 n.3

Gregory, Voice Spectrography Evidence: Approaches to Admissibility, 20 U. Rich. L. Rev. 357 (1986), 9.9 n.10

Haddad, The Future of Confrontation Clause Developments: What Will Emerge When the Supreme Court Synthesizes the Diverse Lines of Confrontation Decisions?, 81 J. Crim. L. & Criminology 77 (1990), 8.83 n.27

Hall, The Role of Psychologists as Experts in Cases Involving Allegations of Child Sexual Abuse, 23 Fam. L.Q. 451 (1989), 7.22 n.42

Hanson, Fewer Post-Daubert Federal Judges Allow Experts to Testify Without Limitation in Civil Trials, Study Finds, 87 A.B.A. J. 28 (2001), 7.7 n.58

Harris, Constitutional Limits on Criminal Presumptions as an Expression of Changing Concepts of Fundamental Fairness, 77 J. Crim. Law & Criminology 308 (1986), 3.14 n.20

Hay, Bruce, Allocating the Burden of Proof, 72 Ind. L.J. 651 (1997), 3.1 n.16

Hazard, An Historical Perspective on the Attorney-Client Privilege, 66 Cal. L. Rev. 1061 (1978), 5.8 n.6

Heidt, The Conjurer's Circle—The Fifth Amendment Privilege in Civil Cases, 91 Yale L.J. 1062 (1982), 5.4 n.10

Hinton, States of Mind and the Hearsay Rule, 1 U. Chi. L. Rev. 394 (1934), 8.39 n.2

Hoffman, Jonathan M., If the Glove Don't Fit, Update the Glove: The Unplanned Obsolescence of the Substantial Similarity Standard for Experimental Evidence, 86 U. Neb. L. Rev. 633 (2008), 9.36 n.6

Holmes, Child Sexual Abuse Accommodation Syndrome: Curing the Effects of a Misdiagnosis in the Law of Evidence, 25 Tulsa L.J. 143 (1989), 7.22 n.38

Huber, Junk Science in the Courtroom, 26 Val. U. L. Rev. 723 (1992), 7.7 n.58

Humphreys, In Search of the Reliable Conspirator: A Proposed Amendment to Federal Rule of Evidence 801(d)(2)(E), 30 Am. Crim. L. Rev. 337 (1993), 8.33 n.1

Hutchins & Slesinger, Some Observations on the Law of Evidence, 28 Colum. L. Rev. 432 (1928), 8.35 n.1; 8.36 n.2

_____, Some Observations on the Law of Evidence: Family Relations, 13 Minn. L. Rev. 675 (1929), 5.1 n.6

_____, Some Observations on the Law of Evidence—Memory, 41 Harv. L. Rev. 860 (1928), 6.66 n.8

_____, Some Observations on the Law of Evidence—State of Mind to Prove an Act, 38 Yale L.J. 283 (1929), 8.39 n.2

Imwinkelried, The Applicability of the Attorney-Client Privilege to Non-Testifying Experts: Reestablishing the Boundaries Between the Attorney-Client Privilege and the Work Product Protection, 68 Wash. U. L.Q. 19 (1990), 5.10 n.27; 5.30 n.19

_____, The Case for Recognizing a New Constitutional Entitlement: The Right to Present Favorable Evidence in Civil Cases, 1990 Utah L. Rev. 1, 5.5 n.1

_____, The Constitutionality of Introducing Evaluative Laboratory Reports Against Criminal Defendants, 30 Hastings L.J. 621 (1979), 8.51 n.21

_____, The Constitutionalization of Hearsay: The Extent to Which the Fifth and Sixth Amendments Permit or Require the Liberalization of the Hearsay Rules, 76 Minn. L. Rev. 521 (1992), 8.83 n.19; 8.92 n.1

Table of Law Review Articles

Table of Law Review Articles

Table of Law Review Articles

Table of Law Review Articles

Table of Law Review Articles

Table of Law Review Articles

Table of Law Review Articles

Table of Law Review Articles

Table of Law Review Articles

Table of Law Review Articles

Table of Law Review Articles

Abraham, The Judicial Process (6th ed. 1993), 3.11 n.13
Alibrandi & Armani, Privileged Information (1984), 5.21 n.13
American Psychiatric Association, Diagnostic and Statistical Manual of Mental Disorders (rev. ed. 1987), 7.22 n.22
Appleman, Insurance Law and Practice (rev. ed. 1981), 3.1 n.15
Ashcraft, M. H., Human Memory and Cognition, 8.2 n.1
Austin, J.L., How to Do Things With Words (2d ed. 1975), 8.22 n.4

Bacon's Essays, XX, Of Counsel 51 (MacMillan & Co., 1892), 5.8 n.4
Bender, Computer Law (1988), 9.16 n.10
Bentham, A Treatise on Judicial Evidence (M. Dumont ed. 1987), 2.1 n.3; 5.8 n.27
_____, Rationale of Judicial Evidence (Bowring 1843), 6.2 n.3
_____, Rationale of Judicial Evidence (J.S. Mill ed. 1827), 5.8 n.16; 5.31 n.8
Black's Law Dictionary (6th ed. 1990), 5.10 n.2; 9.32 n.2
Blackstone, Commentaries (1765), 5.8 n.26
_____, Commentaries on the Law of England (1768), 5.31 n.4
_____, Commentaries on the Laws of England (1765), 10.1 n.1
BNA Criminal Practice Manual (Feb. 22, 1989), 4.15 n.38
Bok, S., Secrets (Oxford, 1984), 5.1 n.10
Busch, Law Tactics in Jury Trials, 1.16 n.4

Clark, Code Pleading (2d ed. 1947), 3.1 n.20
_____, Law of Domestic Relations in the United States (2d ed. 1987), 3.5 n.17; 3.9 nn.5, 8
Cleary, Foreword to Symposium on Proposed Federal Rules of Evidence, 1969 Law & Soc. Order, 2.3 n.1
Codes of Professional Responsibility, 2d ed. (R. Gorlin ed., BNA 1990), 5.2 n.1
Colorado Jury Instructions 3d (Civil) (1988), 3.6 n.2
Couch on Insurance (Lee R. Russ and Thomas F. Segella, 2000), 3.1 n.15
Cross, The Golden Thread of the English Criminal Law (1976), 3.11 n.13
Cross on Evidence (6th ed. 1985), 5.5 n.37

Davis, Administrative Law Treatise (1958), 2.2 n.1; 2.3 n.2
_____, A System of Judicial Notice Based on Fairness and Convenience, in Perspectives on Law (1964), 2.3 n.23; 2.5 n.3

Table of Books and Treatises

Kalven & Zeisel, The American Jury (1966), 2.4 n.9; 4.11 n.14; 6.29 n.8
Keeton, Trial Tactics and Methods (2d ed. 1973), 1.16 n.4

LaFave, Criminal Law (4th ed. 2003), 3.11 n.14
_____, Substantive Criminal Law (2d ed. 2007), 6.32 n.7
_____,Wayne, Substantive Criminal Law (2d ed. 2003), 6.30 nn.3, 4; 6.32 n.7
LaFave & Israel, Criminal Procedure (3d ed. 2007), 8.26 n.13
LaFave & Israel, Criminal Procedure (1984), 8.30 n.3
LaFave, Israel, King, & Kerr, Criminal Procedure (3d ed. 2007), 6.46 n.10
LaFave, Wayne R., Jerold H. Israel, Nancy J. King, Criminal Procedure (1999), 6.69 nn.5, 8
LaFave & Scott, Criminal Law (2d ed. 1986), 3.12 n.21
_____, Substantive Criminal Law (1986), 3.13 n.1; 7.13 n.1; 8.78 n.17
Lempert, Richard, ed., Evidence Stories (2006), 4.12 n.39; 6.51 n.8
Lilly, Introduction to the Law of Evidence (4th ed. 2006), 6.52 n.2
_____, Introduction to the Law of Evidence (3d ed. 1996), 8.69 n.7
Livingston, Works (1873), 5.8 n.7
Loftus & Doyle, Eyewitness Testimony: Civil and Criminal (2d ed. 1992), 7.21 n.1
Luban, Lawyers and Justice: An Ethical Study (1988), 5.8 nn.8, 21

Maguire, Evidence: Common Sense and Common Law (1947), 6.52 n.12
Manual for Complex Litigation (4th ed. 2004), 8.46 n.25
Mauet, Fundamentals of Trial Techniques (6th ed. 2002), 6.60 n.2
McCormick, Evidence (6th ed. 2006), 1.3 n.12; 3.3 n.6; 3.6 n.2; 3.8 n.14; 6.16 nn.1, 2; 6.19 n.10; 6.40 n.1; 6.47 n.9; 6.56 n.1; 6.63 n.8; 6.65 nn.2, 13; 6.69 nn.10, 11; 8.29 n.27; 8.69 n.8; 8.72 nn.11, 20; 9.32 n.3
_____, Evidence (3d ed. E. Cleary) (1984), 5.8 n.17
_____, Evidence (2d ed. 1972), 6.69 n.10; 8.29 n.27
_____, Evidence (1954), 3.8 n.2; 8.29 n.27
Moenssens, Starrs, Henderson, & Inbau, Scientific Evidence in Civil and Criminal Cases (4th ed. 1995), 7.7 n.2
Moore, Taggart & Wicker, Moore's Federal Practice (2d ed. 1990), 2.13 n.13
Moore's Federal Practice (2d ed. 1985), 2.12 n.4
Morgan, Basic Problems of Evidence (1963), 3.8 n.2; 8.72 n.19
Morgan, Basic Problems of Evidence (1954), 10.1 n.12
_____, Foreword to ALI Model Code of Evidence (1942), 3.8 n.2; 5.34 n.8
_____, Some Problems of Proof (1956), 3.8 n.2
Mueller, C., Of Misshapen Stones and Compromises: *Michelson* and the Modern Law of Character Evidence, in Evidence Stories 75 (Richard Lempert ed., 2006), 4.12 n.39; 6.51 n.8
Mueller & Kirkpatrick, Federal Evidence (3d ed. 2007), 8.51 n.15; 8.90 nn.7, 10
_____, Federal Evidence (2d ed. 1994), 8.26 n.13
Murphy, Ann M., Spin Control and the High-Profile Client—Should the Attorney-Client Privilege Extend to Communications with Public Relations Consultants?, 55 Syracuse L. Rev 545 (2005), 5.10 n.23
Myers, Evidence in Child Abuse and Neglect Cases (2d ed. 1992), 7.22 n.42

National Research Council, The Evaluation of Forensic DNA Evidence (1996), 7.19 n.2

O'Malley, Kevin F., Jay E. Grening, & Hon. William C. Lee, Federal Jury Practice and Instructions (5th ed. 2000), 3.1 n.11; 3.3 n.2

Prosser & Keeton on Torts (5th ed. 1984), 3.2 n.4

Table of Books and Treatises

Table of Books and Treatises

INDEX

References are to chapters (Ch.) and sections.

Index

Index

Index

Index

Index

Index

Index

Index

Index

Index

Index

Index

Index

Inference, 3.4

In-house counsel and attorney-client privilege, 5.10

Insanity. *See* Mental capacity

Inscribed chattels and Best Evidence Doctrine, 10.2, 10.14

Instructions to the jury
criminal trials
Allen charge, 3.14
form of instructions, 3.14
harmless error, 3.14
inference instructions, 3.13, 3.14
presumption of innocence, 3.11
presumptions against accused, 3.13
curative or limiting, 1.7
error, curing, 1.7
explanatory, 1.7
judicial notice, 2.11
limiting instructions, 1.16
court's discretion, 1.16
failure to give as plain error, 1.16
request for, necessity of, 1.16
timing of, 1.16
presumptions, 3.4, 3.7–3.8
criminal cases, 3.14

Insurance, liability, 4.30–4.31
ambiguities in rule, 4.30
collateral source rule, 4.30
direct action statutes, 4.30
exceptions to general exclusion rule, 4.31
admission intertwined with reference to insurance, 4.31
bias of witness, 4.31
prejudice of witness, 4.31
jury misuse of evidence of, 4.30
mistrial upon improper reference to insurance, 4.30
misuse by jury of evidence of, 4.30
subrogation, 4.30

Interpreters, 6.7

Interrogatory answers as admissions, 8.31

Intimidation
of jurors, 6.11
of witnesses, 8.66

Investigative reports
completeness rule and, 1.18

Invited error, 1.4, 1.7

Jencks Act, 6.69

Joinder of issues
evidence admissible on one issue but not others, 1.14

Joinder of parties
evidence admissible against one party but not others, 1.15

Joint defenses and attorney-client privilege, 5.15

Judges, function of
admissibility of evidence, 1.10
prior wrongs and acts, factors, 4.16
relevance, 4.3, 4.9
adoptive admissions, deciding, 8.29
in authentication, 9.3
Best Evidence Doctrine and, 10.18
calling and questioning of witnesses, 6.70

coconspirator statements, hearsay exception for, 8.34
discretion of, 1.7
excited utterance as hearsay exception, deciding, 8.36
"factual" questions, authority to decide, 1.10
"legal" questions, authority to decide, 1.10

Judges as witnesses, competency of, 6.8

Judgments of courts, hearsay exceptions for, 8.62

Judicial notice
adjudicative facts, 2.2
generally known facts, 2.6
indisputability requirement, 2.5
records of prior or related proceedings, 2.7
scientific evidence, 2.7
verifiable facts, 2.7
advanced notice requirement, elimination of, 2.9
at any stage, 2.10
appeals
appealability of, 2.9
use of judicial notice on appeal, 2.1, 2.10
basic facts, 2.4
burden of persuasion or proof, 2.7
civil trials, conclusiveness in, 2.11
common words, idioms, and slang words, 2.4
communicative facts, 2.4
controlling law, 2.13
court's initiative, 2.9
criminal trials
inconclusiveness in, 2.11
posttrial proceedings, 2.10, 2.12
Sixth Amendment issues, 2.12
defined, 2.1
due process, 2.9
evaluative facts, 2.4
general background facts, 2.4
generally known facts, 2.6
hearings on, 2.9
indisputability requirement, 2.5
initiation of, 2.8
introduction, 2.1
jury instructions, 2.11
of law, 2.13
legislative facts, 2.3
indisputability standard, 2.3
process, 2.3
record, matters beyond scope of, 2.3
mandatory feature, 2.8
non-evidence facts, 2.4
nonverbal cues, 2.4
opportunity to be heard, 2.9
party input, 2.9
posttrial proceedings, use in, 2.10
pretrial proceedings, use in, 2.10
records of prior or related proceedings, 2.7
reform of, 2.13
requests for, 2.8, 2.9
rescission of, 2.9

Index

Index

Index

Index

Index

Index

Index

Index

Index